HODDESDON
Broxbourne
Lower Nazeing
HARLOW
TO LONDON STANSTED AIRPORT
Fyfield
A-Z ESSEX COUNTY ATLAS
KU-741-857
A-Z HERTFORDSHIRE COUNTY ATLAS
E S S E X
North Weald Bassett
High Ongar
Thornwood Common
Epping Upland
Chipping Ongar
Any extract from this atlas can be supplied as a custom map in a variety of formats (scale permitting).
For further details please contact us on 01732 781000 or visit our website: www.az.co.uk
CHESHUNT
Waltham Cross
Holyfield
WALTHAM ABBEY
EPPING
Coopersale
Copthall Green
Theydon Bois
Stondon Massey
Doddinghurst
Stapleford Tawney
Kelvedon Hatch
Mountnessing
Enfield Wash
High Beech
Debden Green
Hobbs Cross
Sewardstone
Epping Forest
Debden
Navestock
Navestock Side
Passingford Bridge
Abridge
Pilgrims Hatch
Billericay
LOUGHTON
Stapleford Abbotts
Ponders End
CHINGFORD
Lambourne End
Shenfield
Hutton
South Weald
BRENTWOOD
South Green
CHIGWELL
Chigwell Row
Havering-atte-Bower
Noak Hill
Buckhurst Hill
Wickford
Grange Hill
Hainault
Collier Row
Harold Hill
Brook Street
Warley
Ingrave
Woodford Green
WOODFORD
Great Warley
Herongate
WALTHAMSTOW
Snaresbrook
Barkingside
Gidea Park
Harold Wood
North Benfleet
Chadwell Heath
ROMFORD
Laindon
BASILDON
West Horndon
WANSTEAD
Leytonstone
LEYTON
Goodmayes
ILFORD
Becontree
HORNCHURCH
UPMINSTER
Langdon Hills
Bulphan
Manor Park
OLYMPIC PARK
Elm Park
North Ockendon
HACKNEY
STRATFORD
BARKING
DAGENHAM
BETHNAL GREEN
WEST HAM
EAST HAM
South Hornchurch
Balstonia
Corringham
Horndon on the Hill
STEPNEY
Beckton
Creekmouth
Rainham
South Ockendon
THURROCK
Orsett
Stanford-le-Hope
Coryton
POPLAR
LONDON CITY AIRPORT
River Thames
North Stifford
Thames Haven
Thamesmead
Wennington
Aveley
Blackwall Tunnel
BERMONDSEY
Ferry
Abbey Wood
Belvedere
THURROCK Thurrock Lakeside
Chafford Hundred
Chadwell St. Mary
East Tilbury
WOOLWICH
Purfleet
GRAYS
DEPTFORD
GREENWICH
Charlton
Plumstead
ERITH
West Thurrock
South Stifford
West Tilbury
Cliffe
DARTFORD-THURROCK RIVER CROSSING
TILBURY
Blackheath
Kidbrooke
Welling
Slade Green
Greenhithe
LEWISHAM
ELTHAM
BEXLEYHEATH
Crayford
DARTFORD
Stone
Swanscombe
GRAVESEND
Lee
Blackfen
BEXLEY
Old Bexley
Bluewater
Northfleet
Chalk
CATFORD
New Eltham
Dulwich
Sydenham
Grove Park
Mottingham
SIDCUP
Wilmington
Hawley
Bean
Betsham
Higham
Wainscott
Crystal Palace
North Cray
Hextable
Southfleet
Shorne
Strood
Penge
South Norwood
BECKENHAM
BROMLEY
CHISLEHURST
St. Paul's Cray
Swanley
Sutton at Hone
South Darenth
Horton Kirby
Longfield
New Barn
Istead Rise
Sole Street
Cobham
ROCHESTER
St. Mary Cray
Petts Wood
Hayes
Hartley
Longfield Hill
Meopham Station
Crockenhill
Farningham
Fawkham Green
Cuxton
CHATHAM
Addiscombe
ORPINGTON
Meopham
West Wickham
Eynsford
Shirley
Chelsfield
New Ash Green
Halling
Addington
Keston
Farnborough
Green Street Green
Well Hill
West Kingsdown
New Addington
Stansted
Culverstone Green
Snodland
Sanderstead
Selsdon
Downe
Pratt's Bottom
Badgers Mount
Shoreham
Halstead
Fairseat
Vigo Village
Leaves Green
Farleigh
Biggin Hill
Berry's Green
Cudham
Knockholt
Otford
Kemsing
Wrotham
Aylesford
Chelsham
Larkfield
WARLINGHAM
Chevening
Dunton Green
Seal
Borough Green
Wrotham Heath
West Malling
East Malling
Woldingham
Tatsfield
Chipstead
Ightham
St. Marys Platt
MAIDSTONE
Kings Hill
Barming
Brasted
Sundridge
SEVENOAKS
Ivy Hatch
Plaxtol
CLACKET LANE
Westerham
Limpsfield
Godstone
Oxted
Tandridge
Hurst Green
Crockham Hill
Ide Hill
Shipbourne
K E N T
Loose
Sevenoaks Weald
Hadlow
Coxheath
South Godstone
Four Elms
Marlpit Hill
A-Z KENT COUNTY ATLAS
Hildenborough
Edenbridge
TONBRIDGE
LONDON CK AIRPORT
KEY TO MAP PAGES
Greater London Boundary
SCALE
0 1 2 3 Miles
0 1 2 3 4 Kilometres

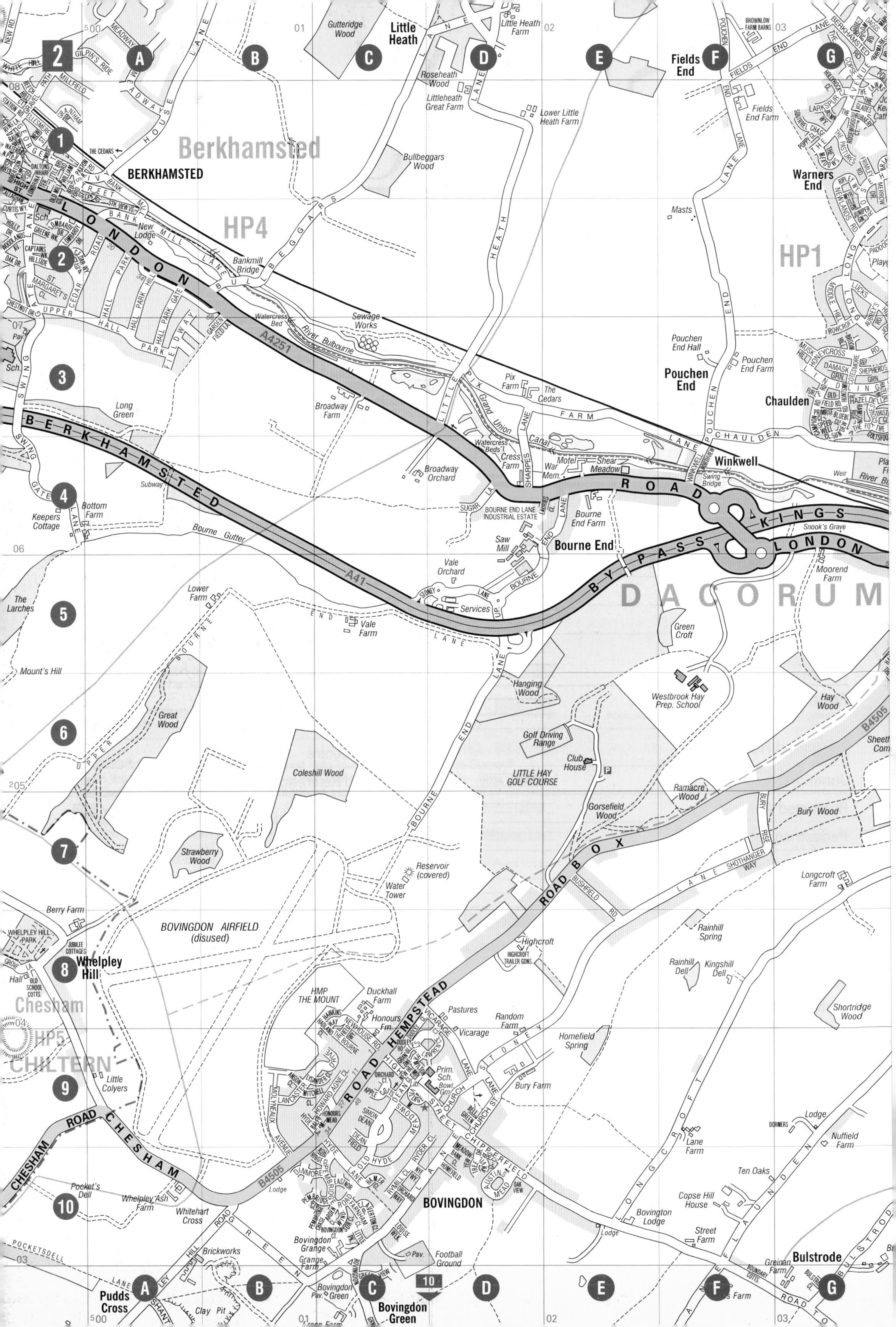

Berkhamsted
BERKHAMSTED
HP4
HP1
HP5
Little Heath
Little Heath Farm
Gutteridge Wood
Roseheath Wood
Littleheath Great Farm
Lower Little Heath Farm
Bullbeggars Wood
Fields End
Fields End Farm
Warners End
Masts
Pouchen End Hall
Pouchen End Farm
Pouchen End
Chaulden
Winkwell
Swing Bridge
River Bulbourne
Sewage Works
Watercress Bed
Bankmill Bridge
New Lodge
Long Green
Broadway Farm
Pix Farm
The Cedars
Grand Union Canal
Watercress Beds
Cress Farm
Broadway Orchard
War Mem.
Motel
Shear Meadow
Bourne End Lane Industrial Estate
Bourne End Farm
Bourne End
Saw Mill
Vale Orchard
Services
Vale Farm
Snook's Grave
Moorend Farm
LONDON ROAD
BERKHAMSTED
A4251
A41
KINGS LANGLEY BY PASS
DACORUM
Keepers Cottage
Bottom Farm
Bourne Gutter
The Larches
Lower Farm
Mount's Hill
Great Wood
Green Croft
Westbrook Hay Prep. School
Hanging Wood
Hay Wood
Golf Driving Range
Club House
LITTLE HAY GOLF COURSE
Coleshill Wood
Ramacre Wood
Bury Wood
Gorsefield Wood
B4505
Strawberry Wood
Reservoir (covered)
Water Tower
Longcroft Farm
BOX ROAD
Berry Farm
BOVINGDON AIRFIELD (disused)
Highcroft
Rainhill Spring
Rainhill Dell
Kingshill Dell
Whelpley Hill
Chesham
CHILTERN
HMP THE MOUNT
Duckhall Farm
Honours Fm.
Pastures
Vicarage
Random Farm
Homefield Spring
Shortridge Wood
Little Colyers
HEMPSTEAD ROAD
Prim. Sch.
Bury Farm
Lodge
Nuffield Farm
CHESHAM ROAD
Lane Farm
Ten Oaks
Pocket's Dell
Whelpley Ash Farm
Whitehart Cross
BOVINGDON
Copse Hill House
Bovingdon Lodge
Street Farm
Brickworks
Bovingdon Grange
Grange Farm
Football Ground
Bulstrode
Pudds Cross
Clay Pit
Bovingdon Green

10

H
J
K
L
M
N
P
Highfield
Gadebridge
Playing Fields
Gadebridge Park
St. Cuthbert Mayne Catholic Sch.
Gade Valley Jun. Mixed & Inf. Sch.
The Cavendish Sch.
The Old Town Hall Arts Cen.
QUEENSWAY
HP2
Adeyfield
Adeyfield School
Broadfield Primary Sch.
Counters End
Hammerfield
Gravelhill Spring
Northridge Park
Shrub Hill Common
Green End
Paradise
HEMEL HEMPSTEAD GENERAL HOSPITAL
ST. ALBANS RD.
A414
A4146
A4251
A41
LEIGHTON BUZZARD ROAD
The Hemel Hempstead School
Heath Park
Boxmoor
St. Rose's Catholic Inf. Sch.
Convent
Rugby Ground
Watercress Beds
STATION ROAD
LONDON ROAD
TWO WATERS WAY
TWO WATERS RD.
Hemel Hempstead
Two Waters
Roughdown Common
Felden
Threefields
Hemel Hempstead
Corner Hall
HEMEL HEMPSTEAD
Frogmore End
Bennetts End
Belswains Playing Field
Dacorum Athletics Grd.
The Snow Centre
Tudor Prim. Sch.
Apsley
Two Waters Primary School
Cock's Head Wood
SHENDISH MANOR GOLF COURSE
Apsley Manor Farm
Shendish Manor
KINGS LANGLEY BY-PASS
Felden Lodge
Hyde Farm Bungalows
HEMEL HEMPSTEAD PRIORY GRANGE
Felden Manor
Felden Orchard
Felden Ash
Felden Ridge
Valley Farm
New Farm
HP3
Old Dean
Great Wood
Phasels Wood
Stony Dene
RUCKLERS LANE
Nash Mills
Shafford Cottages
Kings Langley
High Oak
Rucklers Wood
Merceys Wood
The Hangings
Dark Wood
The Nucket
Barnes Lodge
Barnes Farm
Badgerdell
Badgerdell Wood
Kielder
Fairydell Farm
WD4
Scatterdells Wood
Playing Field
Kings Langley School
Kings Langley Prim. Sch.
Kings Langley Common
KINGS LANGLEY
Hill Farm
The Grove
HEMPSTEAD ROAD
1
2
3
4
5
6
7
8
9
10
11

A
B
C
D
E
F
G
1
2
3
4
5
6
7
8
9
10
07
08
09
10
06
05
04
03
M1 MOTORWAY
Junction 8
M1
M25 MOTORWAY
HP2
HP3
WD4
S T.
THREE RIVERS
DACORUM
Hemel Hempstead
Kings Langley
Abbots
HEMEL HEMPSTEAD
Adeyfield
Leverstock Green
Bennetts End
Nash Mills
Pimlico
BEDMOND
KINGS LANGLEY
MAYLANDS AVENUE
A4147
BREAKSPEAR WAY
A414
ST. ALBANS ROAD
LEVERSTOCK GREEN RD.
LEVERSTOCK GRN. WY.
HEMEL HEMPSTEAD RD.
LONDON RD.
HEMPSTEAD ROAD
A4251
Maylands Wood
Buncefield Terminal
Woodwells Caravan Park
Woodwells Cemetery
Breakspears
Depot
Lucas Aerospace Sports Ground
Esporta Health & Fitness
Hotel
Works
Kentish Wood
The Vistas
Westwick Farm
Football Ground
Westwick Row Farm
Westwick Cottage
Westwick Warren
Westwick House
Corner Farm Cottage
Water Tower
Westwick Hall Cottage
Westwick Hall
Beechtree Cottages
Blackwater Wood
Bunkers Park Open Space
Well Farm
Well Farm Cottages
Bunkers Farm
Great Furzefield Wood
Highwood Hall Farm
High Herts Farm
Pimlico
Potters Crouch Plantations
Longdean House
Long Deans Nature Reserve
Hemel Indoor Tennis Centre
Abbot's Hill School
Tennis Courts
The Lodge
Bedmond Hill
Rose Acre
Mast
Wireless Station
Homefield Farm
Verulam Nursery
Verulam Farm
Heath View
Harthall Farm
Hyde Meadow Farm
Hydelane Spring
Hyde Springs
Hyde Farm
Hyde Lane Farm
Pimlico House
New Plantation
Little Abbots
Hart Hall
White House Farm
Harthall Cottages
Woodlands Poultry Farm
Old Farm
Hilltop Farm
Leewood Farm
Twychells Farm
Deadman Wood
Bedmond Wood
Piecorner Wood
Newlands Park Caravan Site
Moor Wood
Sports Grd.
Primary School
Longspring Wood Nature Reserve
High View Park
Benmore Farm
Denree
Nursery
Great Notley
Ninnings Farm
Poultry Farm
Stowes Wood
Shafford Cottages
Grand Union Canal
Coal Yard
Poultry Fm.
Subway
Playground
Happy Valley Industrial Estate
Kings Langley Prim. Sch.
King's Langley Common
Cricket Grd.
Hobletts Manor Schs.
Council Offs.
Hemel Hempstead Town FC
Adeyfield School
Ed. Support Cen.
Hobbs Hill Wood Prim. School
Longdean School
Chambersbury Prim. Sch.
George Wood
Nash Mills C of E Prim. Sch.
Empire Cin.
Ice Rink
Leis. World
Bowl. Alley
Belswains Prim. Sch.
Mills
Works
Leverstock Green C of E Primary School
Play. Fld.
Lib. & Comm. Cen.
Saracen Industrial Area
Playing Field
Hemel Hempstead Ind. Est.
BREAKSPEAR
HARTHALL LANE
HYDE LANE
TOMS LANE
SHEPPEY'S LANE
CHURCH LANE
BLACKWATER LANE
BUNKERS LANE
HIGH WOOD LANE
CATSDELL BOTTOM
CHAMBERSBURY
3
12

5
Windmillhill Wood
Wildness
Chalk Dell
Garden Cottage
Bruce's Plantation
Gilpins
Gorhambury House
Shepherds Cottages
Cattle Grid
Churchyard Meadow
Townsend
REDBOURN
A5183
River Ver
Rec. Grd.
FOLLY LANE
VERULAM RD.
Old Gorhambury Ho. (remains of)
Oak Wood
Cypress Wood
Gorham Block
The Fosse
Roman Wall (course of)
Roman Theatre
Verulamium Roman Town
Temple Cottage
Temple Wood
AL3
Lord Bacon's Mount
PRAE WOOD
Fish Ponds
Settlement
Mus.
Darrowfield Ho.
Verulamium Pav. Mus.
Vicarage
Tennis Court
Pavilion
Tennis Courts
Playground
Stud Cottages
Prae Wood House
Praewood Farm
BLUEHOUSE HILL
A4147
The Roman Mosaic
ST. ALBANS
VERULAMIUM PARK
The Lake
Square Wood
Cattle Grid
ROAD
HEMEL HEMPSTEAD ROAD
Westminster Lodge Athletic Track
ABBEY VIEW GOLF COURSE
Westminster Lodge Leisure Centre
Club Ho.
Play. Field
St. Columba's College
Hill End Cottage
Hill End Farm
ALBANS
BEECHTREE
BEDMOND LANE
Prim. Sch.
CATHEDRAL CT.
HEMPSTEAD A4147
St. Albans
St. Stephens Recreation Ground
ST. STEPHEN'S HILL
WATLING A5183
A414
M1 MOTORWAY
Longfield Spring
Maidens Crouch Farm
Madam's Wood
Birch Wood
Windridge Farm Cott.
Windridge Farm
Marlborough Sch. Science Coll.
Playing Field
Little Furzefield Wood
Appspond Cottage
Birch Wood
POTTERSCROUCH
Long Spring
Park Wood
Westfield's Farm
Appspond Wood
New Cotts.
RAGGED HALL LANE
Potters Crouch East Farm
Potters Crouch
Potters Crouch Farm
Square Wood
Scrubs Wood
Wimbushes
Cuckman's Farm
B4630
Recreation Ground
St. Julian's Wood
Killigrew Prim. Sch.
Rec. Grd.
CHISWELL GREEN
GREENWOOD PARK
Greenwood Park Leisure Centre
FURZEBUSHES
CHISWELL
Plaistowes Farm
Wellfield Spring
Bone Hill
The Gardens of the Rose
Butterfly World
Daneswick
Little Daneswick
NOKE LANE
AL2
Sergehill
WHITEHOUSE LANE
Serge Hill
Whitehouse Farm
M1
The Conifers
Wayside
Langley
Plaistowes Wood
Noke Farm
NOKE LANE BUSINESS CENTRE
Otium Leisure Club
NORTH ORBITAL RD.
A405
WATFORD ROAD
Burston Manor Fm.
How Wood
HOW WOOD
Hanging Wood
Junction 6a (M1)
Holt Wood
Holt Farm
Moat
Burston Nurseries
Birchwood Farm
Birch Wood
Job's Wood
Millhouse Farm
Searches Farm
SEARCHES LANE
M25
Spielplatz
WD5
Junction 21 (M25)
Tenements Farm
M25 MOTORWAY
Junction 21a
Tenterden House
The Spinney Ten. Cts.
Kettlewell Farm
Winch Hill Wood
13
Bricket Wood Sports & Country Club
Winch Hill Wood
H
J
K
L
M
N
P
1
2
3
4
5
6
7
8
9
10
11
12
13
14
03
04
05
06
07
08

A
B
C
D
E
F
G
1
2
3
4
5
6
7
8
9
10
Townsend
St. Albans City Hospital
Folly Lane
Catherine St.
Verulam Rd.
Fleetville
Verulam School
Museum of St. Albans
St. Albans City FC (Clarence Pk.)
Clarence Park
Hatfield Road
A1057
A4147
A1081
A5183
B691
Victoria Street
St. Albans
Cathedral
St. Albans Sch.
Verulamium Park
Verulamium Mus.
The Lake
Abbey View Golf Course
Westminster Lodge Leisure Centre
St. Columba's College
Holywell Hill
St. Albans Abbey
St. Stephens
St. Julians
Sopwell
Sopwell Ho. Hotel
New Barnes Mill
Verulam Golf Course
Cunningham Hill Playing Fields
The Camp
London Road
Quality Hotel Leisure Club
Nuffield Fitness Cen.
North Orbital Fields
Birklands Meadow
North Orbital Road
A414
A405
B5378
Napsbury La.
Shenley La.
Watling Street
Park Street
Recreation Ground
Park Street C of E Prim. School
Frogmore
How Wood
Birchwood Farm
Birch Wood
Napsbury
South Farm Cottages
South Lodge
Barley-Mo-Farm
Fir Tree Farm
Broad Colney Bridge
All Saints Pastoral Centre (convent)
Hedges Farm
Chalkdell Wood
Flint Cottages
Killigrew Prim. Sch.
Greenwood Park Leisure Centre
St. Julian's Wood
Marlborough Sch. Science Coll.
Mandeville Prim. Sch.
Sopwell Nunnery (rems.)
Cottonmill Bridge
Conolly Ho.
AL1
AL2
AL3
14
15
16
17
08
07
06
05
04
03

5
14

H J K L M N P
18 19 20 21
Oaklands College (Smallford Campus)
Beaumont School
Home Wood
Playing Field
Nursery
St. Davids
Radio Station
Sports Ground
Club House
Boggymead Spring
Garden Centre
Popefield Farm
ST. ALBANS RD. WEST
Ellenbrook
Tennis Ct.
Playground
Rec. Grd.
Nast Hyde
Nast Hyde Farm
Hatfield
AL10
Junction 3
WELWYN HATFIELD
COMET WAY
MOTORWAY
A1(M)
Roehyde
Wilkinsgreen Farm
Wilkins Green
Smallford
Smallford Nurseries
HATFIELD ROAD
A1057
Works
Depot
Factories
Coll.
THE MERLIN CENTRE
Oaklands College
Butterwick Day Centre
Lambourn Gro.
Nicholas Breakspear Catholic Sch.
Highfield Park
Health Club
St. Albans
Sleapshyde
Sleapshyde Farm
Play. Fld.
SMALLFORD WORKS
Smallford Farm
Roehyde Farm
Johnson's Spring
The Bungalow
BARLEY MOW CARAVAN SITE
Little Orchard
Hill End Farm
Colney Heath Rec. Grd.
Sch.
Pav.
Roundhouse Farm
Colney Heath Farm
COLNEY HEATH
Roestock
Play. Fld.
Park Corner
River Colne
Water Works
Colney Heath
Colney Heath Farm
Tyttenhanger
Tyttenhanger Quarry
Winchfield Wood
ST. ALBANS
Highfield Farm
HIGHFIELD HALL
HIGHFIELD MANOR
Knight's Wood
A414 NORTH ORBITAL ROAD
The Mill Ho.
Warren Farm
Playing Field
Frederick's Wood
AL4
Blount Spring
Park Cottage
Tyttenhanger Farm
The Osierb
Wolfsbane
Coppice Wood
Tyttenhanger Ho.
Tyttenhanger Park
Garden Wood
The New Plantation
Coursers Farm
Tanks
NORTH MYMMS PARK
Red Lodge
HERTSMERE
Schs.
Gym
Adventure World
Morris Recreation Ground
Active Workings
Willows Farm Village
Lodge Plantation
LONDON COLNEY
WALSINGHAM WOOD
LONDON COLNEY BY-PASS
A1081
RIVERSIDE IND. EST.
THE BELL ROUNDABOUT
Junction 22
Broad Colney Lakes Nature Reserve
COLNEY FIELDS SHOPPING PARK
Superstore
Depot
M25
M25 MOTORWAY
RIDGE LANE
B556
Cobs As
Round Wood
AL9
Broad Colney
Salisbury Hall Farm
Salisbury Hall
Club
BELL LANE
B5378
1 2 3 4 5 6 7 8 9 10

8
HATFIELD
Ellenbrook
Nast Hyde
Oxlease
University of Hertfordshire (College Lane Campus)
Junction 3
Halls of Residence
South Hatfield
Roehyde
A1(M)
Roehyde Farm
Johnson's Spring
The Bungalow
ST. ALBANS
Bullen's Green
Roundhouse Farm
Roestock
Junction 2
Electricity Sub Station
Tollgate Wood
Tollgate Farm
St. Albans
Park Cottage
AL4
AL10
The Osierbeds
NORTH MYMMS PARK
North Mymms
Vicarage
Church Cottage
Grave Yard
Fish Pond
North Mymms Park
Pumping Tower
WALSINGHAM WOOD
Water Tower
Reservoir (covered)
Cobs Ash
Cangsley Grove
HERTSMERE
Round Wood
Swallow Holes
Oak Lodge
Hawkshead Wood
Teakettle Bri.
Home Fm. Cotts.
Cricket Gd.
The Gables
Red Lodge
East Lodge
War Mem.
Kennels
Pig Farm
Moat
BUSH WOOD
Recreation Grd.
St. Mary's C of E Prim. School
Dellsome Bottom
Angerland Common Playing Fields
Football Grd.
Cemetery
New Barnfield (Herts County Council)
Southfield School
Playing Field
Factory
Warehouse
Nurseries
Marshmoor
Depot
Works
Caravan Park
Welham Green
WELHAM GREEN
WINGATE BUSINESS CENTRE
ALPHA BUS. PK
The Rookery
Skimpans Bridge
Skimpans Farm
Community Cen.
Potterells Farm
Water Splash Cottages
Swallow Hole
Potterells
Water End
Abdale House
Pumping Station
Brick Kiln Wood
Brookmans Park
Primary School
Library
New Cottages
The Royal Veterinary Coll. (Hawkshead Campus)
Blue Bridge
Hawkshead Bridge
Sports Ground
Pilvage Wood
PEPLIN'S WOOD
Nurseries
HATFIELD PARK
COOMBE WOOD
Halfwayoak Pond
MILLWARD'S PARK
Cemetery
Merrows Cottages
Lime Cottages
New Gardens
Home Farm
Orchard Ho.
Dairy Cott.
Dairy Lodges
New Cottages
Bunnyfield House
Buttfield Cottage
Oxleys
Hatfield Leisure Cen
Oak View Prim. sch.
Bishop Hatfield Girls' Sch.
Howe Dell
GREAT NORTH ROAD
A1000
SOUTH WAY
A1001
ROEHYDE WAY
COMET WAY
ORBITAL ROAD
A1(M) MOTORWAY
HAWKSHEAD LANE
DELLSOME LANE
TOLLGATE ROAD
DIXONS HILL ROAD
BRADMORE LANE
WARRENGATE
SWANLAND ROAD
A B C D E F G
1 2 3 4 5 6 7 8 9 10
21 22 23 24
16
7

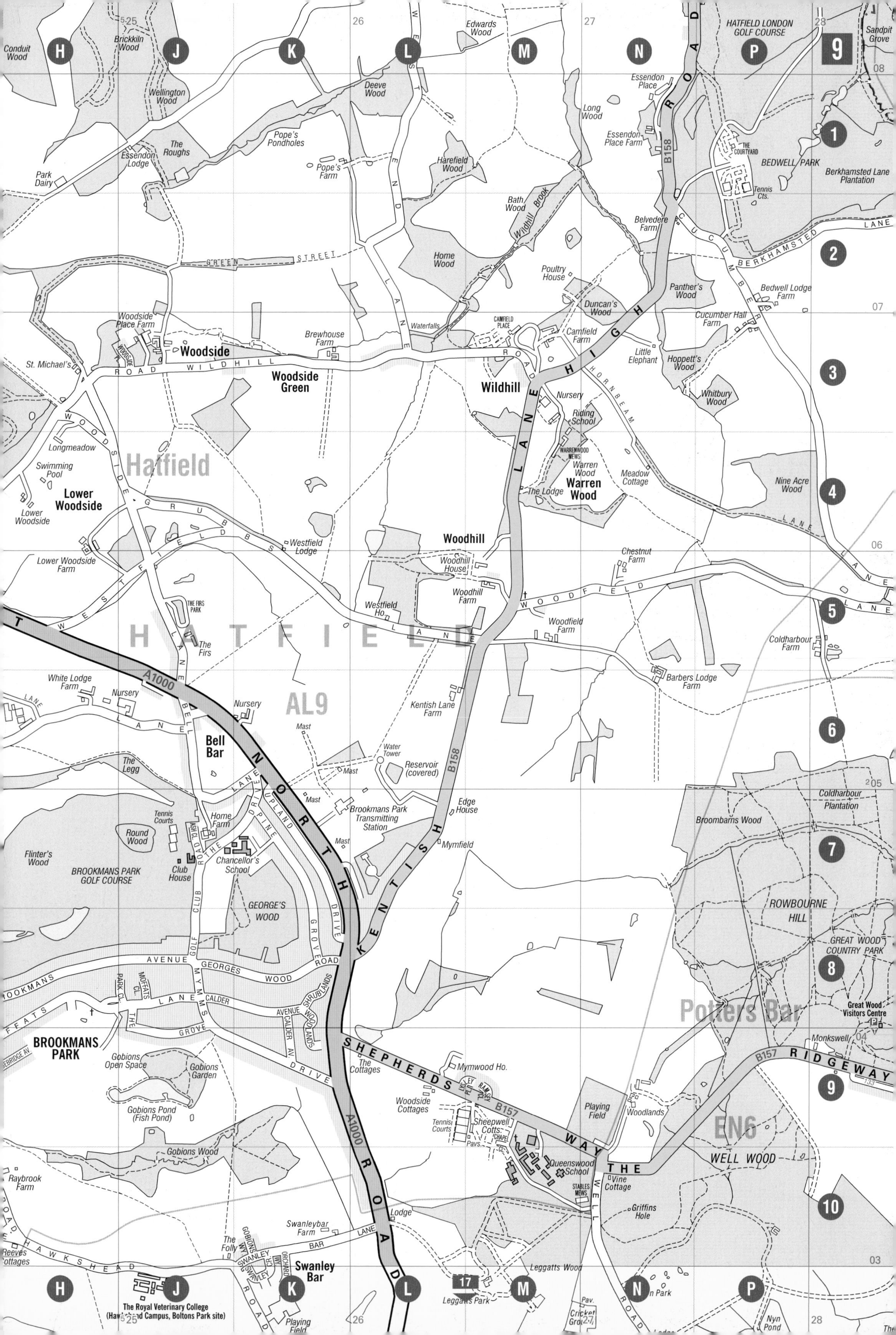

9
Conduit Wood
Brickkiln Wood
Wellington Wood
The Roughs
Essendon Lodge
Park Dairy
Edwards Wood
Deeve Wood
Pope's Pondholes
Pope's Farm
Harefield Wood
Long Wood
Essendon Place
Essendon Place Farm
HATFIELD LONDON GOLF COURSE
Sandpit Grove
THE COURTYARD
BEDWELL PARK
Berkhamsted Lane Plantation
Tennis Cts.
Bath Wood
Wildhill Brook
Home Wood
Belvedere Farm
GREEN STREET
BERKHAMSTED LANE
CUCUMBER
Poultry House
Panther's Wood
Duncan's Wood
Bedwell Lodge Farm
Cucumber Hall Farm
Woodside Place Farm
Brewhouse Farm
Waterfalls
CAMFIELD PLACE
Camfield Farm
Little Elephant
Hoppett's Wood
Woodside
St. Michael's
WILDHILL ROAD
Woodside Green
Wildhill
HIGH LANE
HORNBEAM
Nursery
Riding School
Whitbury Wood
Longmeadow
Swimming Pool
Hatfield
Lower Woodside
WARRENWOOD MEWS
Warren Wood
Meadow Cottage
Nine Acre Wood
The Lodge
Warren Wood
GRUBBS
WESTFIELD
Westfield Lodge
Woodhill
Woodhill House
Woodhill Farm
Chestnut Farm
WOODFIELD LANE
Lower Woodside Farm
THE FIRS PARK
Westfield Ho.
Woodfield Farm
HATFIELD
The Firs
Coldharbour Farm
Barbers Lodge Farm
White Lodge Farm
Nursery
A1000
BELL LANE
Nursery
AL9
Kentish Lane Farm
Mast
Bell Bar
The Legg
Water Tower
Reservoir (covered)
B158
Mast
Mast
Brookmans Park Transmitting Station
Edge House
Coldharbour Plantation
Broombarns Wood
NORTH
Tennis Courts
Home Farm
Round Wood
Flinter's Wood
BROOKMANS PARK GOLF COURSE
Club House
Chancellor's School
Mast
Mymfield
KENTISH LANE
ROWBOURNE HILL
GEORGE'S WOOD
GREAT WOOD COUNTRY PARK
AVENUE
GEORGES WOOD ROAD
Potters Bar
Great Wood Visitors Centre
BROOKMANS PARK
Gobions Open Space
Gobions Garden
SHEPHERDS WAY
The Cottages
Mymwood Ho.
Monkswell
B157 RIDGEWAY
Gobions Pond (Fish Pond)
Woodside Cottages
Tennis Courts
Sheepwell Cotts.
Playing Field
Woodlands
EN6
Gobions Wood
Queenswood School
THE WELL
WELL WOOD
Raybrook Farm
Vine Cottage
STABLES MEWS
Griffins Hole
Lodge
10
A1000 ROAD
Swanleybar Farm
The Folly
Swanley Bar
HAWKSHEAD ROAD
Reeves Cottages
Leggatts Wood
17
Leggatts Park
The Royal Veterinary College (Hawkshead Campus, Boltons Park site)
Playing Field
Cricket Ground
Nyn Pond
H
J
K
L
M
N
P
1
2
3
4
5
6
7
8
25
26
27
28
03
04
05
06
07
08

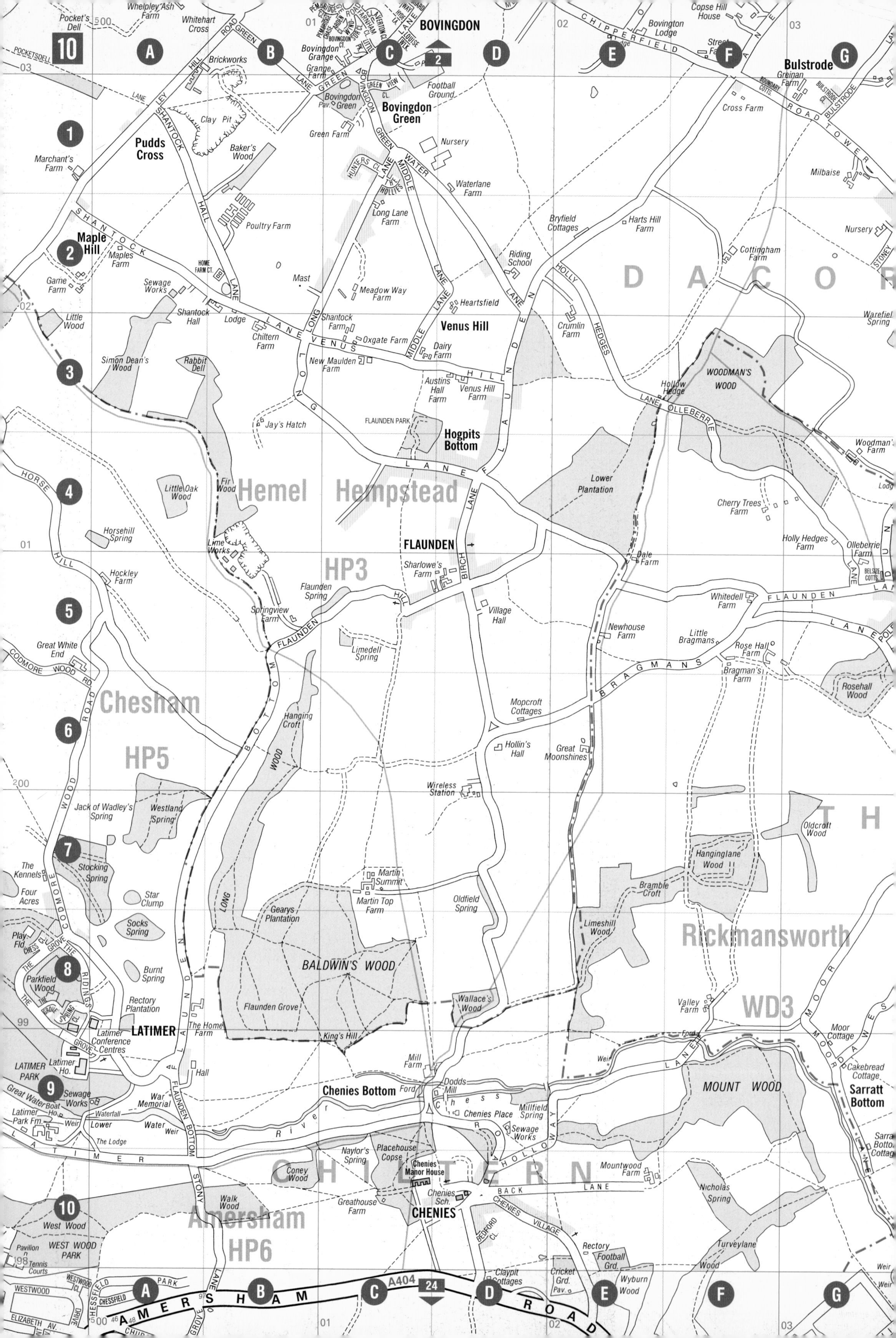
BOVINGDON
Bovingdon Green
Bovingdon Grange Farm
Football Ground
Whelpley Ash Farm
Whitehart Cross
Pocket's Dell
Brickworks
Clay Pit
Baker's Wood
Pudds Cross
Marchant's Farm
Maple Hill
Maples Farm
Game Farm
Poultry Farm
Mast
Sewage Works
Shantock Hall
Lodge
Chiltern Farm
Little Wood
Simon Dean's Wood
Rabbit Dell
Green Farm
Nursery
Waterlane Farm
Long Lane Farm
Meadow Way Farm
Shantock Farm
Oxgate Farm
Heartsfield
Venus Hill
Dairy Farm
New Maulden Farm
Austins Hall Farm
Venus Hill Farm
FLAUNDEN PARK
Hogpits Bottom
Jay's Hatch
Riding School
Bryfield Cottages
Harts Hill Farm
Copse Hill House
Bovington Lodge
Bulstrode
Greinan Farm
Cross Farm
Milbaise
Cottingham Farm
Crumlin Farm
DACOR
Warefield Spring
Woodman's Wood
Hollow Hedge
Woodman's Farm
Lower Plantation
Cherry Trees Farm
Holly Hedges Farm
Olleberrie Farm
Dale Farm
Hemel Hempstead
HP3
Little Oak Wood
Fir Wood
Horsehill Spring
Lime Works
Hockley Farm
FLAUNDEN
Sharlowe's Farm
Flaunden Spring
Springview Farm
Village Hall
Limedell Spring
Whitedell Farm
Newhouse Farm
Little Bragmans
Rose Hall Farm
Bragman's Farm
Rosehall Wood
Great White End
Chesham
HP5
Hanging Croft
Mopcroft Cottages
Hollin's Hall
Great Moonshines
Wireless Station
Jack of Wadley's Spring
Westland Spring
Oldcroft Wood
Hanginglane Wood
Bramble Croft
The Kennels
Stocking Spring
Four Acres
Star Clump
Socks Spring
Martin Summit
Martin Top Farm
Oldfield Spring
Gearys Plantation
Limeshill Wood
Rickmansworth
BALDWIN'S WOOD
Flaunden Grove
Wallace's Wood
King's Hill
Parkfield Wood
Burnt Spring
Rectory Plantation
Valley Farm
WD3
Moor Cottage
LATIMER
The Home Farm
Latimer Conference Centres
Latimer Ho.
LATIMER PARK
Hall
Mill Farm
Dodds Mill
Chenies Bottom
Ford
Chenies Place
Millfield Spring
Sewage Works
Weir
MOUNT WOOD
Cakebread Cottage
Sarratt Bottom
Great Water
Boat Ho.
Latimer Park Fm.
Waterfall
Lower Water
War Memorial
The Lodge
River Chess
Naylor's Spring
Placehouse Copse
Chenies Manor House
Coney Wood
CHILTERN
Mountwood Farm
Greathouse Farm
Chenies Sch.
CHENIES
Nicholas Spring
Walk Wood
Amersham
HP6
West Wood
WEST WOOD PARK
Pavilion
Tennis Courts
Turveylane Wood
Rectory
Football Grd.
Cricket Grd.
Claypit Cottages
Wyburn Wood
A404
24
2
AMERSHAM ROAD
LATIMER ROAD
FLAUNDEN BOTTOM
FLAUNDEN LANE
FLAUNDEN HILL
BIRCH LANE
LONG LANE
VENUS HILL
SHANTOCK LANE
SHANTOCK HALL LANE
LEY HILL ROAD
BOVINGDON GREEN
MIDDLE LANE
HOLLY HEDGES LANE
OLLEBERRIE LANE
BRAGMANS LANE
HOLLOWAY
BACK LANE
CHENIES VILLAGE
BEDFORD CL.
STONY LANE
BOTTOM WOOD
LONG WOOD
HORSE HILL
CODMORE WOOD ROAD
CHIPPERFIELD ROAD
TOWER ROAD
MOOR LANE
WESTWOOD
ELIZABETH AV.
CHESSFIELD PARK
LANE GROVE
POCKETSDELL LANE

Junction 22
LANE RIDGE
7
M25
MOTORWAY
Broad Colney
The Cottage
B5378
B556
LANE BELL
SHENLEY
Superstore
SHOPPING PARK
Depot
Club
Pav.
UCL Sports Ground
Salisbury Hall Farm
Salisbury Hall
De Havilland Aircraft Heritage Centre
Redwell Wood Farm
Ridge Hill
Manor Lodge School
Shenley Lodge Farm
BLACKHORSE LA.
Southridge Animal Centre
PACKHORSE
HILL
Dell Grove
CHESTNUT HOUSE
SHENLEYBURY VILLAS
SHENLEYBURY
SHENLEYBURY COTTS
Shenleybury House
BLACK LION HILL
Combe Wood
Rectory Farm
Shenley Stud Farm
Elliotts Farm
Foxhollows Farm
PINKS FARM
Rabley Park Farm
Rabley Park
Rabley
Bourne
Ford
Catharine
EARLS LANE
DEEVES HALL LANE
St. Catherine's Farm
Ravenscroft Farm
Shenley Hill
RECTORY LANE
MIMMS LANE
Potters Bar
Littleridge Wood
16
RIDGE
Ridge Farm
CROSSOAKS LA.
Goose Farm
SUMMERSWOOD
Bigpursley Wood
EN6
Catherine Bourne
Littlepursley Wood
CROSSOAKS LANE
Crossoaks Farm
Crossoaks Wood
Pursley Farm
LONDON ROAD
SHENLEY
Shenley Park
The Engine Ho.
The Stables
Radlett
Sand Plantation
Cricket Grd.
Pav.
RADLETT ROAD
MERE
WD7
The Gorse
Auriol Farm
WOODHALL LANE
Wood Hall Farm
Wood Hall
Ckt. Grd.
Football Ground
GREEN LANE
Sch.
Spts. Grd.
Kitwells Farm
Lyndhurst
Shenwood Res.
Birch Wood
SILVER HILL ROAD
Silver Hill Cottages
High Canons
Holmshill House
LANE
HIGH CANONS
Bucketts land Farm
BUCKETTSLAND
Wheatsheaf Farm
Well End Farm
WELL END ROAD
Electricity Sub. Station
Well End
Borehamwood
WD6
STREET
COWLEY
B5378
Cowleyhill Farm
The Meadows
Parkside Prim. Sch.
Playing Fields
Organ Hall Farm
Rec. Grd.
29
School
Hertswood School (Lower)
Hertswood Cen.
ROWLEY LANE
Rowley Farm
ALEXANDRA ROAD
Ma
Na
Pa
Qa
Ra
Sa
Ta
1
2
3
4
5
6
7
8
9
10
18
19
520
21
03
02
01
200
99
198
40
50

Round Wood
Swallow Holes
Hawkshead Wood
Oak Lodge
Flint Cottage
Mymmshall Wood
Redwell Wood
The Grange
Woodhill Farm
BLACKHORSE LA.
BLACKHORSE
B556
ST. ALBANS
ROAD
M25
M25 MOTORWAY
Southridge Animal Centre
Town Farm
CECIL
ROAD
B556
A1(M)-MOTORWAY
A1(M)
SWANLAND ROAD
Mymmshall Brook
HAWKSHEAD
LANE
The Royal Veterinary Coll. (Hawkshead Campus)
NORTHUMBERLAND HALL
Pav.
Sports Ground
Pilvage Wood
Hawkshead Bridge
Warrengate Farm
Mimms Hall
Furzefield Wood
King George V Playing Field
Furzefield Centre
Tennis Courts
MUTTON
Windmore Hall
The Wroxham School
Potters Bar
EN6
Dugdale Hill
HERTS
Dame Alice Owen's Sch.
Playing Field
Bridgefoot Farm
Bridgefoot Ho.
BRIDGEFOOT LANE
SOUTH MIMMS
St. Giles' C of E Prim. Sch.
GREYHOUND
Ludlow's Lake
THE MEADOWS
Junction 1 A1(M)
Bignell's Corner
Depot
South Mimms Service Area
BIGNELL'S CORNER
Rabley Park
Catharine Bourne
Ford
EARLS LANE
Earls Farm
DEEVES HALL LANE
THE HAWTHORNS
Church Fm.
Ridge Farm
RIDGE
Imperial Cancer Research Centre
BLANCHE LANE
Blanche Lane Farm
CROSSOAKS LANE
Goose Farm
Crossoaks Farm
SUMMERSWOOD
Summerswood Farm
Borehamwood
WD6
Littleridge Wood
15
Junction 23 (M25)
ST. ALBANS ROAD
A1081
DANCERS
Dancershill Farm
Norfolk Lodge Farm
Laurel House
Laurel Lodge
Dancers Hill
KITTS END
BAKER
BENTLEY
Lower Kitt's End Farm
Kitt's End
EN5
BARNET
BARNET A1 BY-PASS
ROAD
Dyrham Park Farm
DYRHAM LANE
BOTTOM
TROTTERS
DYRHAM PARK GOLF COURSE
Dyrham Park Country Club & Club House
Knightsland Farm
Valentine's Farm
GALLEY LANE
DYRHAM PARK
ARKLEY
Little Dyrham
BRIDGEDOWN GOLF COURSE
OLD FOLD MANOR GOLF COURSE
High Canons
Holmshill House
HOLMSHILL LANE
PACKHORSE LANE
Strangeways Farm
Rowley Farm
Electricity Sub. Stat.
Ua
Va
Wa
Xa
Ya
Za
Ab
8
30
1
2
3
4
5
6
7
8
9
10
21
22
23
24

WELWYN HATFIELD
Swanley Bar
The Royal Veterinary College
(Hawkshead Campus, Boltons Park site)
Playing Field
Osborne House Farm
Little Heath Farm Cottage
LITTLE HEATH
Leggatts Wood
Leggatts Park
Griffins Hole
Nyn Park
Nyn Pond
Cricket Ground
West Lodge
JUDGE'S HILL
NORTHAW RD. WEST
Northaw C of E Prim. Sch.
NORTHAW
Stud Farm
Springfield
Old Owens Sports Ground
POTTERS BAR GOLF COURSE
Mount Grace School
Club House
Fish Pond
HOOK WOOD
Stormont Sch.
THE CAUSEWAY
COOPER'S LANE
Chequers Mead Ho.
Riding Stables
Northaw Park
Oshwal Centre
The Hook
Superstore
Potters Bar
Parkfield
Parkfield Open Space
Bus Garage
Potters Bar FC
Library
Oakmere Park
Oakmere
Five Acre Wood
Fir Wood
Oakmere Prim. Sch.
Youth & Comm. Cen.
Cricket Grd.
Superstore
B556
Pope Paul Catholic Prim. Sch.
HIGH STREET
SOUTHGATE RD.
Pond Wood
BARNET RD.
POTTERS BAR
POTTERS BAR COMM. HOSP.
New Cottage
The Lodge
New Cottage Farm
St. John's Prep. Sch.
M25
Stagg Ridge
Nursery
THE STAGG HILL
Junction 24
M25 MOTORWAY
Elm Farm
Bentleyheath Farm
Works
Chase Farm
Fenny Slade Hill
North Lodge Farm
North Lodge Cottages
THE RIDGEWAY
A1005
Bentley Heath
Ganwick Corner
Chase Wood
Plumridge Hill
Fir Wood
Hornbeam Hills
Plumridge Wood
Wrotham Park
WROTHAM PARK
Ganwick
Three Oak Hill
ENFIELD
Plumridge Farm
Vault Hill Wood
The Cottages
Deadman's Bottom
Spoilbank Wood
Cockshot Hill
Salmon's Brook
Ganwick Farm
Slopers Hill Farm
Park View Cottages
WROTHAM BUSINESS PARK
Barnet
WAGON ROAD
ENFIELD CHASE
Hadley Wood Prim. Sch.
West Lodge Park (Hotel)
Bartram's Quash
Playing Field
Hadley Wood
Lawn Tennis Club
The Beale Arboretum
HADLEY WOOD
Great Broadgates Hill
FERNY HILL
Ferny Hill Farm
Club House
Fernyhill Wood
COCKFOSTERS RD.
GREAT NORTH ROAD
A1000
A111
Bb Cb Db Eb Fb Gb Hb
1 2 3 4 5 6 7 8 9 10
9
18
31

Jb
Kb
Lb
Mb
Nb
Pb
Qb
28
29
30
31
03
02
01
200
99
198
1
2
3
4
5
6
7
8
9
10
Thornton's Farm
High Willows
Vineyard Bridge
The Vineyard
VINEYARD HILL
HEMPS HILL
Northaw C of E Prim. Sch.
VINEYARDS
CHURCH
VICARAGE CL.
Playing Field
NORTHAW
NORTHAW
The Cottage
PARK RD
Park Farm
B156
ROAD
WEST
Fish Pond
Potters Bar
EN6
COLES HILL
Pumping Station
Waterworks Cottages
Hempshill Brook
Wells Farm
Colesdale Farm
Hill View Farm
CATTLEGATE
CATTLEGATE COTTAGES
WELWYN
HATFIELD
Northaw Park
Northaw Valley
Northaw Brook
Oshwal Centre
The Hook
BARVIN PARK
WOODGATE
OAK WELL DR.
COOPERS
LANE
Cattlegate Wood
Robin Hill
Woodhurst
Woodhurst Farm Cottages
Woodhurst Farm
Cattlegate Farm
Cattlegate
BARVIN HILL
HOOKE HILL
Pond Wood
17
Turkey Brook
M25
M25 MOTORWAY
SOUTH HILL
Holly Hill Farm
Sub.
North Lodge Farm
Sch.
ST. NICHOLAS HOUSES
THE DRIVE
Lodge
North Lodge Cottages
South Barvin Farm
THE
A1005
Windrush
RIDGEWAY
Holyhill Brook
LODGE
Vault Hill
Vault Hill Wood
Little Beechhill Wood
Parting Hill
Cricket Ground
Cricket Grd.
Pav.
East Lodge
EAST
BOTANY BAY
Botany Bay Farm
Plumridge Farm
Roundhedge Hill
Salmon's Brook
Barnet
Duncan's Wood
ENFIELD CHASE
EN4
Ash Wood
The Cottage
Parkside House
Park Farm
Park Farm Cottages
Reservoir
Camlet Moat
FERNY HILL
HADLEY
Ferny Hill Cottage
Obelisk
Ferny Hill Farm
Moat Wood
Picnic Area
Camlet Hill
TRENT (COUNTRY PARK)
Ride Wood
32
Fernyhill Wood
Parkside Farm
Pumping Station
Cuckolds Hill
THE RIDGEWAY
B157
EAST RIDGEWAY
THE DRIVEWAY
HILL RISE
KINGSMEAD
PLOUGH HILL
TOLMERS LA.
STARLING LA.
ACORN LA.
OAK LA.
Cuffley Hills Farm
CRANFIELD CRESCENT
BACONS DR.
JAMES' AV.
TOLMERS GS.
LAUREL CL.
KING JAMES' AV.
CHURCH CL.
CUFFLEY
STATION RD.
CUFFLEY
B156
Cuffley
MEADWAY
Brook Farm
Ford
Youth & Comm. Cen.
SOPERS RD.
LAMBS CL.
Works
KINGSWELL RIDE
BURLEIGH WAY
KINGS WAY
COLESDALE
THEOBALDS RD.
THEOBALDS CL.
VALE CL.
SOUTH DR.
GREENFIELDS
Cuffley School
Cuffley Brook
Northaw & Cuffley Lawn Tennis Club
Sports Ground
Bowling Grn.
Soper's Viaduct
Nursery Plantation
Cuffley Brook
Tilekiln Osiers
Owls Hall Farm
Owls Hall
Crews Hill Paddocks
Crews Hill Piggeries
Garden Centre
Crews Hill
(CREWS HILL)
ROAD
Golf Cottages
Club House
Nurseries
CREWS HILL GOLF COURSE
BEECH AV.
ASHRIDE
CYPRESS AV.
GOLF RIDE
TINGEYS TOP
Nurseries
Turkey Brook
ENFIELD
EN2
King's Oak Plain
RECTORY FARM RD.
The Red House
Rectory Farm
Rendlesham Viaduct
KING'S OAK BMI HOSPITAL
CHASE FARM HOSPITAL
OAK AV.
HIGH OAKS
CREST
LAVENDER
THE RIDGEWAY

19
20
33
Rb
Sb
Tb
Ub
Vb
Wb
Xb
1
2
3
4
5
6
7
8
9
10
GOFF'S OAK
GOFF'S LANE
B156
CHURCHGATE
CHESHUNT
BURY GREEN
B R O X B O U R N E
EN7
EN8
EN1
Waltham Cross
M25 MOTORWAY
M25
Junction 25
B198
LIEUTENANT ELLIS WAY
GREAT CAMBRIDGE ROAD
A10
CREWS HILL
WHITEWEBBS WOOD
WHITEWEBBS PARK
WHITEWEBBS GOLF COURSE
WHITEWEBBS ROAD
Whitewebbs Museum of Transport
BULLS CROSS
Enfield
CLAY HILL
HILLY FIELDS PARK
FORTY HILL
Forty Hall Museum
Turkey Street
Enfield Crematorium
Theobalds Pk. Conference Centre
Capel Manor College
Capel Manor Gardens
Lee Valley Park Information Centre
Myddelton House Gardens
St. Ignatius College
Goff's Sports & Arts Cen.
St. Mary's C of E High Sch.
Cheshunt School
Rosedale Sports Ground
Home Wood
Theobalds Manor
Western Cemetery (Jewish)
County Brook Plantation
Caravan & Camping Site
OLD PARK RIDE
THEOBALDS LANE
BULLS CROSS RIDE
BULLSMOOR LA.
HOE LANE
CLAY HILL

CHESHUNT
Cheshunt
Cheshunt Reservoir (South)
Turnford Sch.
Brookland Inf. & Jun. Schs.
Sailing Club
Seventy Acres
Hayes Hill
Hayes Hill Cotts.
Stubbings Cottages
Woodside
Fishers Green
Holyfield Farm
Monkhams Hall
HOLYFIELD RD.
CROOKED MILE
Herts Young Mariners Base
Turnershill Marsh
Hooks Marsh
Cheshunt Lake
Youth Hostel
RIVER LEE NAVIGATION
Timber Yard
Eagle Lodge
ROYAL GUNPOWDER MILLS
Cheshunt Junction
Thistly Marsh
Sand & Gravel Works
Waltham Cross
Powdermill Cut
Hall Marsh
LEE VALLEY REGIONAL PARK
Bowyer's Water
Arboretum
Tree Nursery
Nurseries
Royal Gunpowder Mills
OLD RIVER LEA
HORSEMILL STREAM
Abbey Fish Ponds
Waltham Marsh
Marsh Bridge
Cheshunt Marsh
Lee Valley White Water Centre
Waltham Lock
Harold's Bri.
Waltham Abbey
WALTHAM ABBEY
WALTHAM CROSS
Hazelmere Marina
Town Mead
Holdbrook
Cheshunt School
Playing Field
Grundy Park
Downfield Prim. Sch.
Albury Farm
Rifle Range
Cheshunt FC (The Stadium)
Holy Trinity C of E Prim. Sch.
The Cedars Park
Theobalds Grove
Theobald's Park Farm
Rush Lodge
Sports Ground
BROXBOURNE
EN8
GREAT CAMBRIDGE RD.
A10
B198
B176
A121
WINSTON CHURCHILL WAY
LIEUTENANT ELLIS WAY
THEOBALDS LA.
COLLEGE RD.
TURNER'S HILL
CROSSBROOK ST.
HIGH ST.
ELEANOR CROSS RD.
STATION RD.
HIGHBRIDGE ST.
MERIDIAN WAY
ABBEY VIEW
B194
Junction 25
PARK PLAZA
Gala Bingo
HOLMESDALE TUNNEL
M25 MOTORWAY
M25
A1055
BULLSMOOR LANE
MOLLISON AVENUE
RAMMEY MARSH
Cobbins Brook
Warehouse
MERIDIAN BUSINESS PARK
Meridian Park
GUNPOWDER PARK
Rammey Marsh Flood Relief Channel
Bullsmoor
Lea Valley Sports Centre
FREEZY WATER
Keys Meadow Prim. Sch.
EN3
Oasis Academy Enfield
INNOVA BUSINESS PARK
ENFIELD
Turkey St.
Turkey Street
Turkey Brook
Garden of Remembrance
Enfield Crematorium
Cemy.
Enfield Lock
ENFIELD LOCK
Prince of Wales Prim. Sch.
ENFIELD WASH
Albany Leisure Cen.
Albany Park
Enfield Island Village
Small River Lee or Lea
Cattlegate Flood Relief Channel
WATERWAYS BUSINESS CENTRE
Kingsfield Nurseries
Barnfield Riding Stables
Sewardstone Hall
SEWARDSTONE
SEWARDSTONE RD.
Overflow Channel
Pumping Station
River Station
Hannah Nursery
HERTFORD RD.
A1010
Yb
Zb
Ac
Bc
Cc
Dc
Ec
1
2
3
4
5
6
7
8
9
10
19
34
40

Fc
Gc
Hc
Jc
Kc
Lc
Mc
39
540
41
42
03
02
01
200
99
198
1
2
3
4
5
6
7
8
9
10
HOLYFIELD
North Lodge Farm
Homefield Wood
Stable Lodge
Kennel Wood
Galley Wood House
Aimes Green
Brayshill Spring
Broadgate Springs
CLAVERHAMBURY ROAD
Monkhams Cottage
Aimesgreen Farm
Longcroft Grove
Stocking Grove
Scatterbushes Wood
Maynards Farm
Cobbinsend Farm
COBBINSEND ROAD
Maple Springs
Playground
BREACH BARNS MOBILE HOME PARK
Playing Field
BREACH BARNS LANE
Poultry Farm
Dallance Farm
Nursery
Fernhall Farm
Fernhall Wood
Willows
Brookmeadow Wood
FERNHALL LANE
LONG STREET
Newhouse Farm
Obelisk
Nicholls Farm
Home Farm
Obelisk Farm
Waltham Abbey
EN9
Cobbin's Brook
Oaklands Farm
Nurseries
Cobbin Pond
WARLIES PARK
Warlies Gardens
Warlies Park House
The Temple
Burgess Farm
Copped Hall Green
West Hill
Temple Hill
Nursing Home
Res.
Pickhill Farm
EPPING FOREST
Cricket Ground
Pav.
Warlie's Lodge
UPSHIRE
CROWN HILL
PATERNOSTER HILL
UPSHIRE ROAD
HORSESHOE HILL
Upshire Prim. Sch.
ST. THOMAS'S CL.
Sergeants Green
Warlies Park Farm
SERGEANTS GREEN LANE
UPSHIREBURY GREEN LA.
RUGGED LA.
Oxleys Wood
COPTHALL GREEN
BEULAH PL.
Jun. & Inf. Schs.
King Harold Sch.
Spts. Cen.
Tennis Courts
Playing Field
BROOMSTICK HALL RD.
Hazelwood Children's Cen.
Prim. Sch.
Comm. Cen.
Playground
Recreation Ground
Superstore
Football Ground
Cemetery
Rec. Grd.
The Leverton Infant & Junior Sch.
Honeylands
Waltham Abbey Swim. Pool
King George's Field
ROUNDHILLS
WOODGREEN ROAD
BLIND LA.
GREEN LANE
Woodgreen Farm
Woodgreen Potteries
Potkiln Wood
M25
22
Brambly Shaw
GREEN LANE
Southend Farm
SOUTHEND LANE
Upshire Hall
WOOD GREEN
Woodredon House
Conybury Wood
WOODBINE CLOSE CARAVAN PARK
THE SYCAMORES
Sudbury Farm
Woodredon Farm
Stable Shaw
HONEY LA.
Skillet Hill Farm
Junction 26
M25 MOTORWAY
HONEY LANE
WOODRIDDEN HILL
A121
DOWDING WAY
Quinton Hill Farm
BEECHFIELD WALK
LODGE LA.
Prayer Halls
Cemetery
Honey Lane Plain
Inner Lodge
Lord Padgets Wood
Poplar Shaw
FOREST SIDE
Round Hills
BEECH HILL PARK
Tile Hill Farm
Honey Lane Quarters
Sunshine Plain
CLAYPIT HILL
The Downing Nursery
Beechview Nursery
AVEY LANE
A112
SEWARDSTONE ROAD
Felicia Nursery
Kennels
Portulaca
Providence Nursery
Normandy Nursery
Riding School
BEECH GS.
GREEN
HIGH BEECH GOLF COURSE
The Rookery
Aveylane Farm
Wake Valley Pond
EPPING FOREST
Wake Valley
Great Monk Wood
High Beech Nurseries
Kennels
Piggery
Pynest Green
Avey Cottages
PYNEST GREEN LANE
WELLINGTON HILL
Club House
Riding School
Bowling Green
Youth Hostel
Rushey Plain
WAKE ROAD
A104
EPPING NEW ROAD
Loughton
IG10
Sewardstone Nursery
Chandlers Farm
Thompson's Wood
Mott Street Nursery
E4
Beechside Nursery
Manor Farm
High Beech C of E Primary Sch.
Manor House
HIGH BEECH
Hall
GRAVEL HILL LANE
NURSERY ROAD
Res.
Epping Forest Field Centre
Mount Pleasant
Little Monk Wood
35
MANOR ROAD
MOTT STREET
Oak Farm

Nc
Pc
Qc
Rc
Sc
Tc
Uc
42
43
44
545
03
02
01
200
99
198
1
2
3
4
5
6
7
8
9
10
Gills Plantation
Cobbin's Brook
Bury Farm
BURY LANE
Cobbinsend Farm
COBBINSEND ROAD
Shooting Lodge
Spratt's Hedgerow Wood
Spratt's Hedgerow
Pond Field Plantation
Jenkins's Plantation
B182
BOLT
The Thatch Cottage
Rec. Grd.
Fernhall Farm
LONG STREET
FERNHALL LA.
FERNHALL
Little Rookery Wood
Rookery Wood
Fitches Plantation
Tennis Courts
St. John's C of E Sch.
Cemetery
Sports Ground
Newhouse Farm
Nicholls Farm
Obelisk
Obelisk Farm
Lodge Farm
Copped Hall Gardens
THE HALL BARNS
Copped Hall
Home Farm
Wood House
Paris Hall
New Farm
Griffin's Wood
Epping
CM16
Spts. Grd.
HIGHFIELD PL.
Creeds Farm
Bell Common
B1393
Burgess Farm
Copped Hall Green
The Temple
Temple H.
UPSHIRE
The Selvage
New House Farm
Ladderstile Farm
Millhouse Farm
IVY CHIMNEYS
CROWN HILL
BEULAH PL.
COPTHALL GREEN
Oxleys Wood
Raveners Farm
M25
M25 MOTORWAY
Park Cottages
Bowlands Meadow
Warren Wood
The Warren
Sub.
EPPING
EPPING THICKS
Theydon Towers
Great Gregories Farm
21
Brambly Shaw
Crown Hill Farm
Waltham Abbey
HILL
LODGE ROAD
HIGH ROAD
Ambresbury Banks
Club House
GREEN LANE
GREEN
Little Gregories
Woodredon House
Woodredon Farm
EN9
St. Thomas's Quarters
B1393
Long Running
PIERCING HILL
Piercing Hill
THEYDON BOIS GOLF COURSE
Stable Shaw
Forest Lodge
Riding School
HORSE RIDE
Genesis Slade
WOODRIDDEN
A121
HILL
Jack's Hill
B172
Oak Hill
COPPICE
Theydon Plain
The Coppice
Theydon Bois Prim. Sch.
Wake Arms Roundabout
Oak Hill Farm
COLLEGE PL.
Sunshine Plain
WAKE ROAD
Dulsmead Hollow
Copley Plain
Birch Hall
Birch Hall Farm
Cricket Ground
THEYDON BOIS
Wake Valley Pond
Deershelter Plain
Loughton
NEW ROAD
A104
GOLDINGS
FOREST
Redoak Wood
Birch Wood
Furze Ground
Wake Valley
IG10
Debden House Camp Site
Gaunt's Wood
Great Monk Wood
Broadstrood Plain
DEBDEN GREEN
Ripley Grange
The Boundary
LOUGHTON LANE
GREGSON'S RIDE
Mount Pleasant
Court Hill
Bellringer's Hollow
Golding's Hill Ponds
LOUGHTON GOLF COURSE
Davenant Foundation School
Playing Field
Little Monk Wood
Blackweir Pond
36

23
EPPING
COOPERSALE
COOPERSALE STREET
FIDDLERS HAMLET
Steward's Green
MOUNT END
THEYDON GARNON
HOBBS CROSS
THEYDON MOUNT
Theydon Bois
Ivy Chimneys
Epping
M11 MOTORWAY
M25 MOTORWAY
Junction 27 (M25)
Junction 6 (M11)
F O R E S T
EPPING GOLF COURSE
HOBBS CROSS GOLF COURSE
ABRIDGE GOLF COURSE
Abridge Golf and Country Club
St. Margaret's Hosp.
Coopersale Hall School
Coopersale & Theydon Garnon C of E Prim. Sch.
Gernon Bushes Nature Reserve
Epping Ongar Railway
Roughtalley's Wood
Birching Coppice
Mount Wood
Posternlane Spring
Hawkshill Wood
Redyn's Wood
Forty Acres
Ongar Down
Mount Quarter
Gravelpit Wood
High Warren
Tawney Common
Beachet Wood
Hornes Farm
Searles Hall
Sawkins Farm
North House
Mount Hill Farm
The Rough Patch
Long Plantation
Peakes Farm
Icehouse Plantation
Hill Hall
The Wilderness
Bush Grove Farm
Bush Grove
Bartlemy Grove
Hilly Spring
Barber's Wood
Sewage Works
Garnish Hall
Dawes Bri. Cottages
Fiveponds Wood
Hillair
Theydon Priory
Hobbs Cross Open Farm
Fitzwilliams Cottage
Blunts Farm
Blunts Chase
Parsonage Farm
Thrifts Hall
Thrifts Hall Farm
Council Depot
Springhouse Cottages
Cemetery
Theydon Hall Cottages
Theydon Hall Farm
Hydes
Hobbscross Cottages
Nursery
Brook House
Skinners Farm
Skinners Farm Cottages
Hill Farm
Mossford
River Roding
Romford RM4
Coopersale Cottage
Coopersale Farm
Coopersale House
Coopersale Lodge
Stonards Farm
Ansons Farm
Home Farm
Masons Bridge Farm
Little Thorn Hall Farm
Farm Bungalow
Gardners Farm
Forest Cottage
Timber Yard
The Lake
Epping Plain
Wintry Park Farm
Lindsey Street Fm.
Shaftesbury Farm
Electricity Sub Station
Playing Field
Vc Wc Xc Yc Zc Ad Bd
1 2 3 4 5 6 7 8 9 10
46 47 48 49
37

24
A
B
C
D
E
F
G
500
01
02
03
98
97
96
95
94
93
10
42
CHENIES
Chenies Sch.
Walk Wood
Greathouse Farm
Spring
West Wood
Pavilion
Tennis Courts
WESTWOOD
ELIZABETH AV.
RUSSELL CT.
BEDFORD AV.
CHESSFIELD PARK
AMERSHAM ROAD
A404
CHENIES VILLAGE
Claypit Cottages
Cricket Grd. Pav.
Wyburn Wood
Turveylane Wood
Amersham
HP6
CHURCH GROVE
AMERSHAM WAY
Prim. Sch.
OLD FIELD CL.
OAKINGTON AVENUE
THE RETREAT
LODGE LANE
STONY LANE
VILLAGE WAY
LITTLE CHALFONT
Old Hanging Wood
New Hanging Wood
Netherground Spring
Stonydean Wood
LOUDHAMS WOOD LA.
Depot
Baytree Cottage
Lodge Copse
Homestead
Halsey's Wood
Little Greenstreet Farm
Great Greenstreet Farm
Great Greenstreet Farm Cottages
GREEN STREET
Bullscroft Spring
Chilton's Wood
St. Clement Danes School
CHENIES ROAD
Field Study Centre
MARLINS CL.
NORTH HILL
Pucks Paigles
Loudham's Wood
Lodge Farm
LONG WALK
Whitelands Wood
FARTHINGS
BIRKETT WY.
PARK GRO.
BURTONS LANE
GARDEN REACH
13
NEW RD.
Burton's Farm
Hillas Wood
Carpenter's Wood
WHITELANDS AVENUE
ORCHARD DRIVE
HOMEFIELD RD.
ORCHARD CL.
RICKMANSW
Tennis Ct.
WOODLAND LA.
DARVELLS YD.
COMMON RD.
CHORLEYWOOD COMMON
CHORLEYWOOD GOLF COURSE
Nightingales
Nightingales Farm
Drum Grange
NIGHTINGALES LANE
14
Courtlands
Burton's Wood
CHORLEYWOOD WEST
CARPENTERS WOOD DRIVE
BEECH WOOD AV.
The Russell School
BRUSHWOOD DR.
BADGERS DELL
ST. PETERS WAY
CARPENTERS WOOD DR.
Newhouse Farm
FARM RD.
BLACKETTS WOOD
GROVE WAY
GROVEWOOD CLOSE
MAIN PDE. FLATS
GRENVILLE CT.
NEW PDE. FLATS
LOWER RD.
STATION APPROACH
Chorleywood
GATE COTTS.
COLLEYLAND
Club Ho.
CHORLEYWOOD
Cherry Tree Dell
POLLARDSWOOD GRANGE
THE FLATS
ROUGHWOOD CROFT
Roughwood Croft Farm
Crosslane Wood
CHALFONT LANE
HILLSIDE
SOUTH RD.
HADDON RD.
BERKS
ST. CHRISTOPHERS CT.
Lib.
NORTH RD.
BOTTOM
COMMON GATE RD.
15
BURTON'S LANE
Lodge
CHILTERN
Rose Cottage
Gramesdyke
Roughwood Park
Philipshill Farm
B4442
Elmswell House
SHIRE LANE
BURFIELD RD.
DOVE PARK
QUICKLEY LANE
HUBBARDS RD.
TURNEYS ORCHARD
CLEMENT'S
Clement's Farm
Chorleywood Bottom
Berry Farm
HERONSGATE
RENDLESHAM WAY
FURZE VIEW
WINDERMERE
PENN WAY
Reservoir (covered)
Penn Farm
The Hall Farm
Lewgars
Roughwood Farm
16
Chalfont St. Giles
HP8
The Cottages
Farlands
Welmans
Roughwood Fields
ROUGHWOOD LANE
BULLSLAND LANE
OLD PIGGY LANE
Play. Fld.
The Swillet
Sch.
Hill Farm
RYMAN CT.
EVERARD CL.
WATERFIELD
LONG LANE
Tennis Court
SHEPHERDS LANE
Shortenills Environmental Studies Centre
Grovespring Wood
Bullsland Farm
17
Reservoir Plantation
Kilnpond Wood
PHILIPSHILL WOOD
BRADFORD RD.
NOTTINGHAM ROAD
HALIFAX RD.
STOCKPORT RD.
Heronsgate
The Vache
Dellgarden Plantation
Oak Plantation
Newland Gorse
DEADHEARN LANE
Shortenill's Wood
BARRINGTON
18
CHERRY TREE LA.
Ladywalk
Junction 17
Chiltern Open Air Museum
SHIRE LANE
GORELANDS ROAD
Hentucks Farm
CHERRY RI.
HIGHFIELD
ST. GILES QUAD
ST. GILES COURT
SHRUBS WOOD
Playing Field
BOTTOM WOOD
M25
19
Gorelands
Lodge
Pav.
Swim. Pool
ST. PETERS
Ladywalk Wood
A412
STYLECROFT
VALENTINE WAY
THE BROW
Ashwell's Farm
NEWLAND PARK
Playing Field
CHALFONT LANE
Five Plantation
20
Turner's Wood
Rowan Farm
Rowan Nurseries
Woodoaks Farm
Pollardshill Wood
M25 MOTORWAY
Gerrards Cross
SL9
Turner's Wood Farm
Cricket Field Cottages
AMERSHAM ROAD
CHESHAM LANE
BRAWLINGS LANE
High Trees
DENHAM
Skipping's Farm
Brawlings Farm
Foxdell Wood
Workshops
MAPLE
OAKHILL

H
J
K
L
M
N
P
11
04
05
06
07
98
97
96
95
94
93
Park Cottages
Sarratt Cottages
New Model Farm
Lodge
Great Wood Cottages
Sawpit Spring
Coltyard Spring
Chandler's Cross
Nursery
Scrubbs Wood
Blunts Wood
Willow Wood
Coltspring Riding Stables
Cottage Farm
HARROCKS WOOD
NEW
Sarratmill Bri.
Mead Spring
Fisheries
M25
North Lodge
Lower Lodge
Redhall Farm
Power House
Flint Cottages
WELLING GROVE
Merlin's Wood
Micklefield Hall
New Cotts.
The Bungalow
CHORLEYWOOD HOUSE ESTATE
Dell Cottage
Keepers Cott.
Beechen Hill
Oak Farm
York House School
Round New Spring
Waterdell Spring
BEECHENGROVE WOOD
Long Spring
Round Spring
Model Farm
The Farmhouse
The Hut
Dell Nature Reserve
Cemetery
Trout Farm
Millfield Plantation
Upper Plantation
Cherry Tree Lodge
Thick Spring
Round Spring Farm
Redheath Nursery
LOUDWATER
LITTLE GREEN LA.
M25 MOTORWAY
Riding Stables
Thurlwood House
Croxley House
Killingdown Farm
Christ Church C of E Sch.
Little Lady's Wood
Junction 18
The House
Walden Lodge
Parrot's Dell
Croxley Green
Skate Park
Baldwins La. Play. Fld.
CHORLEYWOOD ROAD
A404
Copthorne Wood
Little Gillions
Home Wood
Loudwater Farm
Rasehill Farm
Playing Fields
Pavilion
Applegarth
Yorke Mead Prim. Sch.
Round Spring
The Fringe
CROXLEY GREEN
Sports Pav.
The Royal Masonic School for Girls
Solomon's Wood
Rickmansworth PNEU School
Nurseries
The Screen
Catlip's Farm
West Herts Riding Sch.
Pheasant's Wood
Tennis Courts
Scotsbridge Mill
Play. Fields
Football Grd.
Sports Ground Pav.
WATFORD ROAD
Harvey Prim.
Rickmansworth
Arnett Hills Sch.
Rickmansworth Sch.
M25
Playing Field
Fortune Common
Croxleyhall Wood
Playing Fields
WD3
Rickmansworth Park
SCOTS HILL
Tudor Pde.
Superstore
St. Joan of Arc Catholic School
Croxleyhall Farm
Rickmansworth
RICKMANSWORTH
Lot Mead Lock
Leisure Centre
Bowling Green
St. John's Catholic Prim. Sch.
Day Cen.
Comm. Cen.
Mill End
Moneyhill
Prim. Sch.
Ebury Pleasure Grd.
Boat Ho.
RIVERSIDE DRIVE
GRAND UNION CANAL
Hampton Hall Farm
Batchworth Lock Canal Cen.
MOOR LANE
A4145
A412
Batchworth Lake
THE AQUADROME
Bury Lake
Boat House
Superstore
Club House
RICKMANSWORTH GOLF COURSE
UXBRIDGE ROAD
Mill Stream Lodge
Colne Valley Trail
The Grove
BATCHWORTH
MOOR PARK
Drayton Ford
Stocker's Lake (Nature Reserve)
Stocker's Lock
St. Mary's C of E Primary Sch.
Depot
Stocker's Farm
Fairfield
Club House
Driving Range
Watercress Beds
Froghall Farm
Garrett Wood
Juniper Hill
Andrews Ley Farm
BATCHWORTH PARK GOLF COURSE
MOOR PARK GOLF COURSE
Watercress Beds
Chalk Pit
High Wood
Juniper Dell
Greenbroom Spring
Cemetery
BATCHWORTH HILL
A404
N. ORBITAL RD.
Springwell Lock
Springwell Lake
Quarry Farm
Sandfield
Pipers
Hertford Place
Maple Cross Ind. Est.
43
HOME FARM RD.
BATCHWORTH HEATH
12
13
14
15
16
17
18
19
20
26

WHIPPENDELL WOOD
Blackets Wood
Leeswood Cotts.
LEES WOOD
Deer Spring
12
Sports Ground
Playing Field
Herts Bowling Club
Cassiobury Infant Sch.
Cassiobury Junior Sch.
WD17
Merlin's Wood
Newland's Spring
Merlin's Spring
JACOTTS HILL
WEST HERTS GOLF COURSE
Iron Bridge Lock
GRAND UNION CANAL
Round Newland's Spring
Dell Wood
Waterdell Spring
The Hut
Watercress Beds
Boating Pond
CASSIOBURY PARK
Long Newland's Spring
Thick Spring
Little Green
Rickmansworth
WATFORD
Watford
Prospect Ho.
College
The Colosseum
Hospice
Croxley House
Little Green Jun. Sch.
Playing Fields
Killingdown Farm
Copthorne Wood
Little Gillions
WD3
Skate Park
Baldwins La. Play. Fld.
Watford Grammar Sch. for Boys
Fish Pond
Cassio Bridge Lock
Marina
RICKMANSWORTH ROAD
WEST WATFORD
Applegarth
Yorke Mead Prim. Sch.
CROXLEY GREEN
Sports
Youth Centre
Inf. Sch.
Tennis Courts
Rec. Grd
Mail Centre
Playing Field
Westfield Community Sports Cen.
St. Anthony's Catholic Prim. Sch.
Westfield Community Tech. Coll.
Harwoods Rec. Grd.
Laurance Haines Prim. Sch.
Croxley
WATFORD ROAD
Harvey Rd. Prim. Sch.
Rickmansworth Sch.
Croxley Centre
HOLYWELL
Long Valley Wood
Weir
Croxleyhall Wood
Playing Fields
Electricity Transmission Station
Croxley Common Moor Local Nature Reserve
Common Moor
King George V Playing Fields
Croxleyhall Wood
Moor Park Crossing
TOLPITS LANE
Brightwells Farm Cotts.
Bowling Green
Sports Grd.
Pavilion
Brightwells Farm
Oxhey Hall
Croxleyhall Farm
Lot Mead Lock
Brightwells Spring
Moat
Tolpits Ho.
RIVER COLNE
THREE RIVERS
Tolpits Plantation
Running Track
Merchant Taylors' School
Pumping Station
Works
HAMPERMILL LANE
MOOR LANE
A4145
The Withey Beds Local Nature Reserve
Northwood Prep. Sch.
Playing Fields
Manor of the Rose
Hampermill Wood
Big Wood
Club House
SANDY LODGE ROAD
Northwood
RICKMANSWORTH GOLF COURSE
Farm Cottage
Moor Park
Club House
Round Spring
Hampermill Spring
MOOR PARK
Club House
Tennis Courts
HA6
SANDY LODGE GOLF COURSE
MOOR PARK
The Roughs
Old Furze Field
LONDON ROAD
BATCHWORTH HILL
MOOR PARK GOLF COURSE
Young Hangings
Home Farm
44
Old Hangings
Oxhey Wood Local Nature Reserve
EASTBURY
SANDY LANE
A4125
A411
A412
A404

Junction 5
BERRYGROVE
WD25
WD23
WD19
M1 MOTORWAY
ELTON WAY A41 (NORTH WESTERN AV.)
OTTERSPOOL WAY
Watford Junction
Watford
Watford High St.
Watford FC (Vicarage Rd. Stadium)
WATFORD GENERAL HOSP.
Bushey
BUSHEY
Bushey Heath
OXHEY
Watford Heath
Merry Hill
Carpenders Park
CARPENDERS PARK
The Rookery
BUSHEY HALL GOLF COURSE
BUSHEY GOLF COURSE
HARTSBOURNE GOLF COURSE
OXHEY PARK GOLF COURSE
South Oxhey Playing Fields
Scotts Wood
Sherwoods Wood
Margeholes Wood
Mutton Wood
David Lloyd Leisure
Bushey Grove Leisure Centre
The Bushey Academy
Bushey Manor Junior School
Queens' School (North Site)
Queens' School (South Site)
Bushey Jewish Cemetery
Carpenders Park Cemetery
Hartsbourne Country Club (Club House)
St. Margaret's Sports Centre
LONDON ROAD
HIGH STREET
STEPHENSON WAY
WATERFIELDS WAY
PINNER ROAD
OXHEY LANE
PRESTWICK ROAD
A4008
A411
A4125
A412
B462
X
Y
Z
Aa
Ba
Ca
Da
11
12
13
14
15
16
17
18
19
20
28
40
45

Ea
Fa
Ga
Ha
Ja
Ka
La
14
15
16
17
98
97
96
95
94
93
Round Bush
Four Want Ways
Delrow
Aldenham Grange
Aldenham Cottage
Holland Farm House
ISKCON Bhaktivedanta Manor
LETCHMORE HEATH
Playing Field
The Farm
Little Kendals Farm
Little Kendals Wood
Hertsmere Jewish Prim. Sch.
Kendal Hall Farm
Radlett Prep. Sch.
WATLING
A5183
Medburn House
Play. Fld.
Winfield Mobile Home Park
Patchetts Equestrian Cen.
Patchetts Green
Watford
Hartspring Cotts.
Delrow Ho.
Holland Farm
WD25
Aldenham School
Playing Field
Boydens Hill
WARDS LANE
Slades Farm
Electricity Transforming Station
Kennels
Gullimore Farm
Sandy La. Caravan Site
Bushey Jewish Cemetery
(NORTH WESTERN AV.)
ELTON
TYLERS WAY
A41
Cemetery
Letchmore Lodge
BUTTERFLY LANE
Moats
Playing Field
The Haberdashers' Aske's Boys' Sch.
Medburn Bri.
Hilfield Farm
ELSTREE AERODROME
Ham Farm
Flying School
Flying Club
ALDENHAM PARK
The Haberdashers' Aske's School for Girls
Tykes Water Lake
M1
Lodge
Hilfield Castle
Boat House
HOGG LANE
Page's Farm
Boathouse
Tyler's Farm
Dam
HILFIELD PARK RESERVOIR
Sewage Works
Home Farm
Bushey Meads School
Meadow Wood Sch.
Kennels
Pumping Station
HERTS
Laboratories
Pumping Station
ALDENHAM COUNTRY PARK
Aldenham Country Pk. Rare Breeds Farm
ALDENHAM RESERVOIR
Aldenham Sailing Club
Sports Ground
Works
Hart's Farm
DAGGER LANE
M1 MOTORWAY
Bushey
Caravan Site
Caldecote Farm
WD23
ROAD WATFORD
A411
Comm. Cen.
Elstree Hill Open Space
LISMIRRANE INDUSTRIAL PARK
THE WATERFRONT
Reservoir
CENTENNIAL PARK
BUSHEY
Tennis Courts
King George Rec. Grd.
Tennis Cts.
Rosary Priory
Immanuel College
ELSTREE ROAD
Caldecote Hill
WATFORD BY-PASS
Heath House
Bushey Spire Hosp.
A409
HEATHBOURNE ROAD
Rec. Grd.
Works
Brockley Hill Farm
Sports Ground
HARROW
Stanmore
BUSHEY HEATH
Belswood Cottage
Royal National Orthopaedic Hospital
Brockley-Hill Ho.
Stanmore Common Local Nature Reserve
HA7
Aspire
Pear Wood Cottages
St. Margaret's Sports Centre
HIGH ROAD
A4140
Hartsbourne Prim. Sch.
Kestrel Grove (Offices)
Club House
Tennis Courts
The Cedars
Tennis Courts
Lodge
Limes House
Wood Farm
Pear Wood
Fish Pond
Cricket Ground
Fish Pond
Grove Field Pavilion
Islamic Centre
Tennis Cts.
Cloisters Wood
HARTSBOURNE GOLF COURSE
Peterborough & St. Margaret's School
Bentley Priory
HA3
COMMON ROAD
Lodge
Heriots
Stanmore Hall
HARROW WEALD COMMON
The Princess Alexandra Home
Deer Park
STANMORE COMMON (Local Nature Reserve)
Levels Wood
Grim's Dyke
Nurseries
Bentley Priory Local Nature Reserve
Heriot's Wood
Grimsdyke Open Space
Harrow Weald Common
Old Barn
STANMORE HILL
BROCKLEY HILL
30
50

14
27
46

29
BOREHAMWOOD
ELSTREE
Well End
Rowley Farm
Hertswood School (Lower)
Hertswood School (Upper)
Meryfield Prim. Sch.
Cowley Hill Prim. Sch.
Aberford Park
Meadow Park
Boreham Wood FC & Enfield FC
Sports Ground
BBC Elstree
Borehamwood Shopping Park
Elstree Studios
Superstore
The Point
Elstree & Borehamwood
Yavneh Coll.
Playing Field
King George's Field
Kenilworth Prim. Sch.
Ripon Park
RADLETT PARK GOLF COURSE
Golf Driving Range
Club House
Parkfields Open Space
South Medburn Farm
Recycling Centre
Cemetery
St. Nicholas Elstree C of E Prim. Sch.
Hill House
Edgwarebury Ho. Farm
Elstree Open Space
The Leys
Elstree Manor
Penniwells Farm
The Dower House
The Chantry
Deacons Hill Open Space
Woodcock Farm
Elstree Tunnel
Scratch Wood
Froghall Wood
Scratchwood Open Space
Boys Hill Wood
Thistle Wood
Scratchwood Open Space
STIRLING CORNER
Hyver Hall
Hyver Manor
Tanglewood
Target Wood
Clump of Trees Wood
MILL HILL GOLF COURSE
NW7
M1 MOTORWAY
Junction 4
BARNET
Edgware
HA8
London Gateway Service Area
Edgware Bury
Bury Farm
Gate Cottages
Nursery Cottage
Edgwarebury Cemetery
Sports Grd.
Broadfields Prim. Sch.
EDGWAREBURY PARK
Playground
Newlands
Driving Range
Stanmore and Edgware Golf Centre
Hemmings Wood
Stoney Wood Lake
Fairway Prim. Sch.
Nut Wood
Mill Hill High Sch.
APEX CORNER
CANONS CORNER
London Academy
WATFORD BY-PASS
BARNET BY-PASS
BARNET LANE
ELSTREE WAY
SHENLEY ROAD
COWLEY HILL
ALLUM LANE
DEACONS HILL
WOODCOCK HILL
EDGWARE WAY
MARSH LANE

30
16
48
DYRHAM PARK
HERTSMERE
Borehamwood
WD6
EN5
NW7
BARNET BY-PASS
A1
A5135
A411
A5109
A1081
B552
ST. ALBANS ROAD
BARNET ROAD
WOOD STREET
TOTTERIDGE COMMON
TOTTERIDGE LANE
HIGHWOOD HILL
MARSH LANE
BARNET WAY
HENDON WOOD LANE
ROWLEY LANE
ARKLEY LANE
GALLEY LANE
MAYS LANE
BARNET GATE LANE
THE RIDGEWAY
Strangeways Farm
Rowley Farm
Saffron Green
Fold Farm
Galley Lane Farm
Poor Clare Monastery
BRIDGEDOWN GOLF COURSE
OLD FOLD MANOR GOLF COURSE
Sports Ground
Shooting Ground
A1 Golf Driving Range
Arkley Lane Open Space
Woodlands Farm
Rowley Green
Rowley Lane Sports Cen.
ROWLEY LANE GOLF COURSE
ARKLEY GOLF COURSE
Rowley Green Common Nature Reserve
Arkley Rise Estate Open Space
Arkley Manor
Rowley Bank Nurseries
Reservoir
Nursing Home
ARKLEY
HIGH BARNET
CHIPPING BARNET
BARNET HOSPITAL
Whalebone Park
Psychiatric Unit
Queen Elizabeth's School
Whitings Hill Prim. Sch.
Whitings Hill Open Space
Ducks Island
Recreation Ground
Windmill
Barnet Gate
STIRLING CORNER
Hyver Hall
Hyver Farm
Hyver Manor
Barnet Gate Wood
Gravel Pit Wood
Tanglewood
(Old Elizabethans) Playing Field
Cottage Farm
Totteridge Park Open Space
Grange Playing Fields
Grange Avenue Open Space
East Barnet Old Grammarians Playing Field
Allendale
Brent Lodge Farm
Dollis Brook
Hendon Wood Lane Open Space
Totteridge Fields Local Nature Reserve
Moat Mount Open Space
Moat Mount Camp Site
Leg of Mutton Pond
Mote End Farm
Mote Mount
Target Wood
The Shrubbery
Nut Wood
White Lodge
Mill Hill High Sch.
Hendon Park
Highwood Park
Highwood Hill
Highwood Hill Cottage
Holcombe Dale
Holcombe Hill
St. Mary's Abbey
Riding School
TOTTERIDGE
Totteridge Park
Totteridge Common
St. Edward's
Abattoir
Oak Lodge
Farmleigh
Boundary House
The Lynch House
Fairlawn
Ellern Mede Centre
Ellern Mede Farm
Montebello
Burnhams
The Warren
Chestnut Cottages
Redings
Hillsdown
Fairlight Cottage
Hillsborough Cottage
Folly Brook & Darland's Lake Nature Reserve
Folly Brook
Folly Farm
Burtonhole Lane Farm Estate
Sports Ground Cricket Club
Cemetery
Nursery
Burtonhole Farm
Fairway Prim. Sch.
APEX CORNER
St. Joseph's College
Lawrence Green
The Mill Field
Belmont Farm
St. Paul's C of E Prim. Sch.
Kenilworth Prim. Sch.
ELSTREE PARK
Hendon Wood
Playing Field
Club House
Ua
Va
Wa
Xa
Ya
Za
Ab
21
22
23
24
98
97
96
95
94
93
11
12
13
14
15
16
17
18
19
20

HADLEY WOOD
The Beale Arboretum
COCKFOSTERS ROAD
BEECH HILL PARK
HADLEY WOOD GOLF COURSE
ENFIELD
MONKEN HADLEY COMMON
MONKEN HADLEY
Hadley Wood Nature Reserve
Barnet
HADLEY
BARNET
EAST BARNET GOLF COURSE
NEW BARNET
COCKFOSTERS
High Barnet
Underhill
Barnet Vale
Lyonsdown
New Barnet
EAST BARNET
Oakleigh Park
SOUTH HERTS GOLF COURSE
OAK HILL PARK
South Barnet
OAKLEIGH PARK
Totteridge and Whetstone
WHETSTONE
BRUNSWICK PARK
NORTH MIDDLESEX GOLF COURSE
N20
N12
A1000
A110
A5109
A109
B550
B1453
A111
B193

17
32
49

TRENT PARK (COUNTRY PARK)
Trent Park
Camlet Moat
Moat Wood
Camlet Hill
Ride Wood
Park Farm Cottages
Reservoir
Picnic Area
Obelisk
Ferny Hill Farm
Fernyhill Wood
Rough Lot
Leeging Beech Gutter
Fish Pond
Icehouse Wood
Seedfield Spinney
Williams Wood
Noddins Well
Middlesex University (Trent Park Campus)
Shaws Wood Cottages
Shaws Wood
College Ho.
The Rookery
Rookery Cotts.
Oak Wood
Reservoir (covered)
Monument
Trent Park Sports Cen.
Hockey Pitches
Sports Ground
Church Wood
TRENT PARK GOLF COURSE
Merryhills Brook
Triangular Wood
Cemetery
Barnet
EN4
Cockfosters
COCKFOSTERS
Depot
Trent Park Stables
Driving Range
Club Ho.
Lodge
Oakwood
Vicarage Farm
Wolverton
Salmon's Brook
Hog Hill
Miniature Rifle Range
Parkside Farm
Pumping Station
CHASE FARM HOSPITAL
EN2
HOSP.
World's End
Moat
Highlands School
Playing Fields
Playing Field
Grange Park Prim. Sch.
Boxer's Lake
Highlands Village
Nursing Home
Superstore
Sports Ground
OAKWOOD PARK
OAKWOOD Yacht Pond
Prim. Sch.
Chicken Shed Theatre
Middlesex Uni. (Cat Hill Campus)
Mus.
Bramley Sports Grd.
De Bohun Prim. Sch.
Saracens Amateur Rugby Football Club
Addison Ho. (PRU)
Oaktree Sch.
East Barnet Sch.
Oak Hill College
Oak Hill Woods Nature Reserve
Bandstand
Playground
OAK HILL PARK
Pavilion
Miniature Golf Course
Monkfrith Prim. Sch.
Tennis Courts
South Barnet
Weirs
OSIDGE
Osidge Prim. Sch.
Brunswick Park Prim. Sch.
BARNET
N14
N11
Superstore
Leisure Cen.
Brunswick Cen.
Southgate
SOUTHGATE
NORTH LONDON PRIORY HOSPITAL
GROVELANDS PARK
Boating Lake
Pitch & Putt Course
Club Ho.
Bowling Green
Ashmole Sch. & Sports Cen.
Playing Fields
Southgate Coll.
Southgate Cricket Club Ground
Cemetery
NEW SOUTHGATE CEMETERY
New Southgate Crematorium
War Mem.
Pymme's Brook
BRUNSWICK PARK
Recreation Grd.
Cricket Ground
Rec. Grd.
PALMERS GREEN
Palmers Green
Bowl. Green
Putting
The Avenue
Sports
Recreation Ground
Club
A111
A110
A1004
A1003
A109
A105
A1005
B1453
ENFIELD ROAD
SLADES ROAD
HADLEY ROAD
COCKFOSTERS ROAD
CAT HILL
BRAMLEY ROAD
CHASE SIDE
THE BOURNE
BOURNE HILL
HIGH STREET
CANNON HILL
ALDERMANS HILL
WATERFALL ROAD
OAKLEIGH ROAD SOUTH
RUSSELL LANE
OSIDGE LANE
FERNY HILL
18
31
50
11
12
13
14
15
16
17
18
19
20
Jb Kb Lb Mb Nb Pb Qb

ENFIELD
ENFIELD TOWN
Enfield Town
Enfield Chase
Gordon Hill
Chase Side
Chase Green
GRANGE PARK
Grange Park
BUSH HILL PARK
Bush Hill Park
WINCHMORE HILL
Winchmore Hill
N21
N13
LOWER EDMONTON
EDMONTON
Edmonton Green
Southbury
ENFIELD GOLF COURSE
BUSH HILL PARK GOLF COURSE
BUSH HILL PARK (Recreation Ground)
JUBILEE PARK
EDMONTON CEMETERY
Firs Farm Playing Fields
PYMMES PARK
Queen Elizabeth Stadium
David Lloyd Leisure
Southbury Leisure Centre
Kingsmead School
Cineworld Cinema
MARTIN DALE INDUSTRIAL ESTATE
ENFIELD RETAIL PK.
HASLEMERE BUSINESS CENTRE
MARTINBRIDGE TRADING ESTATE
GREAT CAMBRIDGE IND. EST.
Playing Fields
Tottenham Park Cemetery
Federation Cemetery (Jewish)
WINDMILL HILL
SOUTHBURY ROAD
GREAT CAMBRIDGE ROAD
HERTFORD ROAD
LONDON ROAD
RIDGE AV.
CHURCH STREET
A10
A110
A105
A1010
B154
A111
Rb
Sb
Tb
Ub
Vb
Wb
Xb
11
12
13
14
15
16
17
18
19
20
19
34
51

34
ENFIELD HIGHWAY
Enfield
PONDERS END
BRIMSDOWN
SEWARDSTONE
CHINGFORD
KING GEORGE'S
RESERVOIR
WILLIAM
GIRLING
RESERVOIR
LEE VALLEY GOLF COURSE
Lee Valley Athletics Centre
Athletics Track
Odeon Cinema
Sewage Works
Refuse Incineration Plant
Power Station
Pumping Station
Overflow Channel
River Lee Navigation
River Lee Diversion
Pickett's Lock
Brimsdown
Ponders End
Southbury
King George's Sailing Club
Chingford Mount Cemetery
Mansfield Park
Ridgeway Park
Durants Park
Montagu Rec. Grd.
Nightingale Academy
Brimsdown Sports & Social Club
Brimsdown Industrial Estate
Ponders End Industrial Estate
Tottenham Cemetery
Federation Cemetery (Jewish)
Yardley Hill
Pole Hill Obelisk
The Hawk Wood
HERTFORD ROAD
NAGS HEAD RD.
LEA VALLEY ROAD
MOLLISON AVENUE
MERIDIAN WAY
SEWARDSTONE ROAD
KINGS HEAD HILL
WALTHAM WAY
OLD CHURCH ROAD
NEW ROAD
A1010
A1055
A110
A112
A1037
A1009
B137
B169
EN3
N9
E4

Mott Street Nursery
Thompson's Wood
Beechside Nursery
Manor Farm
High Beech C of E Primary School
HIGH BEECH
Manor House
Epping Forest Field Centre
Little Monk Wood
Oak Farm
Wallsgrove House
Cricket Ground
Pav.
Aldergrove Wood
Paul's Nursery
Barn Hill
The Vicarage
Dairy Farm
Kate's Cellar
Shelleys Hill
Loughton Camp
Scout Camp Site
Day's Farm
Riding School
Equestrian Centre
EPPING FOREST
Fernhill Wood
Pipers Farm
Field Study Centre
Hill Wood
Debden Slade
Woodbury Hollow
Police Training Camp
Three Horseshoes Farm
Loughton
Springfield Farm
Lippittshill Lodge
Carrolls Farm
Whitehouse Plain
Fairmead Pond
Strawberry Hill Ponds
Round Thicket
Gilwell Park
Club Ho.
WEST ESSEX GOLF COURSE
Ludgate Water
Caravan Site
North Long Hills
Fairmead Bottom
LOUGHTON
Reservoir (covered)
Almshouse Plain
IG10
Bury Wood
Nursery
Long Hills
Tennis Courts
Ludgate Plain
Sewardstonebury
Bury Farm
Peartree Plain
Palmer's Bridge
Superstore
Cuckoo Pits
Woodman's Glade
The Hawk Wood
Bury Wood
Grimston's Oak
Oaklands
Riding School
Buttonseed Corner
Warren Hill
Magpie Hill
Connaught Water
Warren Hill Ho.
ROYAL EPPING FOREST & CHINGFORD GOLF COURSE
Chingford Plain
Recreation Ground
Queen Elizabeth's Hunting Lodge
Powell's Forest
Albany Ho.
Oak Hall
The Warren
Tennis Courts
Warren Pond
Barn Hoppet
Chingford
St. John's C of E Prim. School
Buckhurst Hill
Cricket Ground
Whitehall Plain
CHINGFORD GREEN
Bluehouse Grove
Pimp Hall Nurseries
Pimp Hall Park
Friday Hill
Playing Field
Hatch Forest
Hatch Grove
Reed's Forest
Holly House Hosp.
BUCKHURST HILL
Buckhurst Hill Prim. Sch.
LORD'S BUSHES
Knighton Wood
Woodford Green
IG8
Football Ground
WOODFORD GOLF COURSE
WOODFORD WELLS
Roding Valley
Rugby Football Ground
The Lops
EPPING NEW ROAD
RANGER'S ROAD
A1069
A104
A121
A110
B160
B146
B170
MOTT STREET
HIGH ROAD
WHITEHALL RD.
PALMERSTON RD.
QUEEN'S RD.
RODING LA.
HATCH LA.

DEBDEN GREEN
22
LOUGHTON GOLF COURSE
Mount Pleasant
Court Hill
Bellringer's Hollow
Little Monk Wood
Goldings Hill Ponds
Blackweir Pond
Blackweir Hill
Baldwins Hill
Baldwins Pond
EPPING FOREST
Loughton Camp
Debden Slade
Woodbury Hollow
Loughton Brook
Dryad's Hall
Arewater Green
Ash Green
Davenant Foundation School
Playing Field
Club House
Hillyfields Open Space
Long Shaw
Broadfield Shaw
Deben Park High School
DEBDEN
Viaduct
Sports Field
Loughton Resource Centre
Works
PROSPECT BUSINESS PARK
Debden
LOUGHTON BUSINESS CENTRE
LOUGHTON SEEDBED CENTRE
OAKWOOD HILL IND. EST
WOOLSTON MANOR GOLF COURSE
Golf Driving Range
Woolston Hall
Sports Ground
Club House
Loughton
Corbett Thtre.
Loughton Hall
Epping Forest Coll.
Playing Fields
Library
Traps Hill Cen.
Loughton Leisure Cen.
Cricket Grd.
Roding Valley High Sch.
Superstore
Alderton Inf. & Jun. Schs.
Tennis Courts
LOUGHTON
Loughton
Depot
Loughton Bridge
Sports Ground
Junction 5
M11 MOTORWAY
EPPING
Recreation Ground
Foot Bridge
River Roding
Roding Valley Meadows Nature Reserve
Home Farm
Playing Fields
Grange Farm (Riding for the Disabled)
Rolls Park
Rolls Park Fm.
Grove Cottage
Pettitts Hall
High Wood
Patch Park
Broad Oaks
Cricket Ground
The Grange
Chigwell
Old Farm
Chigwell Prim. Sch.
Sandon Lodge
Wakes Hall
Bramstons
The Rodings
Chigwell Sch.
Chigwell Hall
David Lloyd Leisure
Buckhurst Hill
Rec. Grd.
Sports Grd.
Playing Field
College
IG9
Buckhurst Hill Prim. Sch.
BUCKHURST HILL
Buckhurst Hill
Rose Bridge
IG7
Oaks Farm
Hillside
New Barns Farm
M11
Old Loughtonians Hockey Club
CHIGWELL
Chigwell
Library
Rugby Football Ground
Works
Luxborough
54
The Lodge
35
A121
A1168
A113
A123
B170
RODING LANE
CHIGWELL LANE
ABRIDGE ROAD
RECTORY LANE
CHURCH HILL
HIGH ROAD
LUXBOROUGH LANE
HAINAULT RD.

37
46
47
48
49
Vc
Wc
Xc
Yc
Zc
Ad
Bd
23
Theydon Hall Cottages
ABRIDGE
Theydon Hall Fm.
Epping
CM16
Theydon Hall
Mossford Green Nurseries
B172
Hill Farm
Sewage Works
River Roding
Shalesmere Nursery
98
River Roding
11
Arnolds
M11 MOTORWAY
M11
Hillmans Cottages
A113
ROAD
Arnold's Farm Cottages
Nurseries
WORKS
Piggotts Farm Cottages
Piggotts Farm
Dairy Farm
Bloody Mead
EPPING
ONGAR ROAD
CHURCH LANE
12
STAPLEFORD TAWNEY AIRFIELD
Pryors
Lower Wood
97
Ape's Grove
Lambourne Place
Patch Park
Foxburrow Wood
Theydon Mead
River Roding
Lodge
NEW FARM DRIVE
PANCROFT
THE POPLARS
ORCHID CL.
Cricket Grd.
KNIGHTS WLK.
MIDDLE BOY
ALDERWOOD
MARKET PL.
WHITE HALL
GOULDS COTTS.
LONDON ROAD
ABRIDGE
New Fm.
Alder Wood
13
Chase Meadow
North Lodge
Lambourne Prim. Sch.
ABRIDGE PARK HOMES
Jubilee Plantation
The Chase
Lambourne Hall
Great Wood
14
Maryada Cottage
Sewage Works
Great Downs Farm
Soapley's Wood
Lodge
Church Cotts.
Mutton Corner
Halfmoon Wood
96
Knoll's Wood
Lambourne
Romford
Little London Cottages
GRAVEL
A1112
FEATHERBED LANE
Bishop's Moat
Conduit Wood
15
Turnours Hall
RM4
Marchings
Marchings Farm
Clark's Wood
Dews Hall Farm
38
The Bungalow
Bishop's Hall
Lodge
Farm
HOE LANE
NEW ROAD
LANE
16
F O R E S T
St. John's Farm
Lambourne Park Farm
PARK SQUARE
Gallman's End Farm
Hook Lane Nurseries
Blackbush Farm
HOOK
The Shaws
Isabella Cottages
TUTTLEBY COTTS.
195
Knolls Hill Farm
TAYLORS
Priors
MANOR ROAD
BOURNE BRIDGE LANE
Playing Fields
Blue House Farm
Augusta Cottages
Sports Ground
Pav.
Mansfield Outdoor Centre
17
Taylors Farm
LAMBOURNE END
Crabtree Hill
Thrift House
Hop Pole Farm
LANE
Brownings Farm
The Camelot
MILLER'S LANE
Willow Park Farm
Lambourne Well
Harmes Farm
Cavill's Walk
18
Sewage Works
Three Cornered Plain
PUDDING LANE
Burnt House
Fulham's Farm
LAMBOURNE SQ.
Spurgate Plain
Spurgate
Billingsbourne
Banks Farm
94
Taylor's Plain
Sheepcotes
WEDDRELL'S PLAIN
Lodge
Mile Plantation
Water Works
Reservoir
Camping Site
COOPERS CL.
Cabin Plain
19
Sandhills
Cabin Hill
CHIGWELL ROW
HAVERING
GRAVEL CL.
LAMBOURNE RD.
Sheep Water
Res.
The Chase
20
Lower Sandhills
Miller's Fm.
Roes Well
Grove Cotts.
ROMFORD RD.
REDBRIDGE
Park Farm
B173
30
Tennis Courts
HAINAULT FOREST (COUNTRY PARK)
93
LAMBOURNE
Pav.
Playing Fields
Recreation Ground
LAKESIDE
Tennis Courts
40
55
Visitor Centre
Fox Burrows
FOX BURROW RD.
Foxburrows Rare Breeds Farm & Zoo
Plantation
Play. Field
Park
The

EPPING
MOUNT RD.
Railmead Plantation
Mitchells Farm
River Roding
Shalesmere Nursery
Shalesmere Cottage
Passingford Bridge
Suttons Manor
Suttons
Playing Field
Sutton's Farm
TAWNEY LANE
LONDON RD
M25 MOTORWAY
LONDON RD.
A113
Howle Hall
Arnolds Farm
Little Arnolds
Mill House
ONGAR ROAD
A113
Arnold's Farm Cottages
Warehouse
WORKS
Passingford Bridge Mill
Passingford Bridge
M25
Waters Farm
STAPLEFORD TAWNEY AIRFIELD
ALBYNS LANE
The Lodge
North East Lodge
Lower Wood
burrow Wood
Rookery Wood
Grafton Farm
Green Farm Cotts.
Green Farm
Hammonds
Bons Farm
Church Wood
Albyns Manor
Albyns Hall
B175
Curtismill Green
Curtismill Green
Lady Abdy's Walk
Landend Cottage
Thatched Cottage
Rose Cottages
Willow Cottage
MILL LANE
Woodside Farm
CHURCH TERRACE
Kirton's Fm.
Deerbarn Wood
Bourne Brook
Gordon Cotts.
CHURCH LA.
Church Farm
Bentleyfield Wood
CURTIS
Horsemans Lodge
Old Rectory Farm
EPPING FOREST
The Harrow
Battles Hall
Curtis Mill Cottage
Stapleford Abbotts Prim. Sch.
STAPLEFORD ABBOTTS
CURTIS MILL LANE
Belmont Fm.
STAPLEFORD ROAD
Grove House
Stapleford Hall Fm.
Tyseahill Farm
Spring Farm
Rose Cottage
GUTTERIDGE
High House Farm
Olives Farm
THE PADDOCKS
RM4
Mitchell's Farm
Bourne Brook
Woodlands Fm.
High Willows
NAVESTOCK
Blackbush Farm
Ashwood Farm
Stocks Farm
Tysea Hill
Knolls Hill Farm
Nursery
THE DRIVE
Brook Farm
Stapleford Farm
Twinoaks Farm
Nuper's Farm
Nuper's Hatch
Club House
Skips
BOURNEBRIDGE
Pinchback Bridge
ROAD
OAK
Lyngs Farm
TYSEA HILL
Asheton Fm.
Bournebridge Farm
LANE
Stapleford Common
Crown Park Farm
KENSINGTON PARK
TOWNLEY COTTS.
Bourne Bridge
Butcher's Farm
Boyland's Oak Farm
HILL
Romford
Bournebridge
Nursery
Spencers Farm
Greenacres Farm
Spurgate Brook
Straights Plantation
Lodge
Palace Plantation
Sandpits Plantation
Hilly Park
Home Farm
Osier Bed
Witch Hill Plantation
Horseshoe Farm
Sandhills
Wilderness
Play Fld.
Bower Farm
BOWER FARM
Dame Tipping C of E Prim. School
South Park Plantation
PYRGO PARK
HAVERING
Foreberry Wood North
Lower Sandhills
Pheasant Wood
SAMANTHA M.
ROWLAND WLK.
HAVERING-ATTE-BOWER
St. Francis Hospice
Round House Farm
Park Farm
Avenue Wood
Riding Stables
The Round House
AVENUE
NORTH ROAD
BROXHILL
WELLINGTONIA
ORANGE TREE HILL
ELMER AV.
Ckt. Grd.
Pav.
CLOCKHOUSE
COUNTRY PARK
56
Poultry Farm
Orange Tree Inn
Bower Farm
Foreberry Wood South
Pine Wood
NEWWOOD ROAD
PINEWOOD
Pav.
Field
37
Cd Dd Ed Fd Gd Hd Jd
11 12 13 14 15 16 17 18 19 20
49 550 51 52
98 97 96 195 94 93

Shonks Mill Bri.
Bounce Hill
Hook Wood
Rose Hall Farm
Brook Cottage
Hazle Spring
Wetstaff Ford Bri.
Strawberry Spring
Bois Hall
Twostile Wood
Redgate Wood
Strawberry Wood
Upper Boishall Wood
Lower Boishall Wood
Payne's Shaw
Alder Shaw
Heronland Shaw
Gipsy Bottom
Farm
Yewtree Farm
Randalls Farm
NAVESTOCK
Marleys
Navestock Heath
Chase Cottages
NAVESTOCK SIDE
Sabine's Green
Lashe's Farm
Princes Gate
Loft Hall
Rose House
Sabines Farm
Black Cottage
Tan House
Bower Farm
The Mores
Pentile Hall
COMMON
WEALD
B R E N T W O O D
Navestock Heath Ho.
Brook Farm Bungalow
Horseman Side
New Hall Farm
Honeysuckle Cottage
SOUTH
Oakhurst Farm
Club House
Dychleys
Playing Field
WEALD PARK GOLF COURSE
Coxtie House
Oakhurst Wood
Waterhales Farm
Brentwood
Lee Farm
Waterhales
Gilstead Hall
Gilstead Wood
Lincoln
TAPLEFORD ABBOTTS GOLF COURSE
Moat
Watton Farm
Dycotts
Club House
Weald Side
Weald Brook
CM14
Frieze Hall
Locksmith Wood
Watton's Green
Works
THE PRIORS GOLF COURSE
Weald Bridge
Goldsmith Wood
Curtis Plantation
Wabbing's Plantation
Frieze Hill Cottages
Havering Plain
Lodge
Greyhound Training Track
Sevenacre Plantation
Hou Hatch
St. Vincent's Hamlet
Wright's Bridge
Old MacDonald's Farm Educational & Leisure Park
Rochetts Farm
Wrightsbridge Farm
Tennis Courts
Wealdside
Pentowan Farm
M25
Spice Pits Wood
Sports Ground
Pav.
Spice Pits Farm
Hill Farm
Widdrington Farm
Tench Pond Plantation
Noakhill
Common
NOAK HILL
Carter's Brook
Weald Brook
The Osiers
M25 MOTORWAY
LAKEVIEW PARK
Foxburrow Wood
Manor Farm
Burnt Wood
RM3
DAGNAM PARK
Fir Wood
Tennis Courts
Play. Fld.
Havering College Further & Higher Education Quaries Campus
Cock Wood
Alder Wood
SHONKS MILL ROAD
DUDBROOK RD
CHURCH ROAD
PRINCES ROAD
LANE
MURTHERING LANE
OLD LANE
SABINES ROAD
OLD ROAD
LASHE'S LANE
NAVESTOCK SIDE
SNAKES HILL
TAN HOUSE LANE
HORSEMAN SIDE
DYTCHLEYS RD.
DYTCHLEYS LA.
WHEELERS LANE
COXTIE GREEN ROAD
WARWICK PL.
COLNS LANE
WEALD ROAD
GOATSWOOD LANE
CHURCH LANE
BENSKINS LA.
WRIGHTSBRIDGE RD.
PATERNOSTER ROW
CHEQUERS ROAD
LOWER NOKE CLOSE
NORTH HILL DRIVE
WINCANTON RD
WREXHAM RD
WOODBRIDGE CL
PRIORY ROAD
PRIORY PATH
CASTLE CL
THE MOUNT
KYNANCE CL.
NOAK HILL ROAD
CUMMINGS HALL LA
GREENBANK CL
THE GREEN
TRING WLK.
Kd
Ld
Md
Nd
Pd
Qd
Rd
53
54
55
56
98
97
96
95
94
93
11
12
13
14
15
16
17
18
19
20
40
57

Kelvedon Common
Fox Hatch
Doddinghurst Common
Red House Farm
Dagwood Farm
Cowes Farm
Cow Farm
Park Farm
Moat
Brizes Wood
Alder Shaw
Payne's Shaw
Upper Hall
Playing Field
Kelvedon Hatch Common
Havestock
Club Ho.
Alders Wood
BRENTWOOD CAMPING & CARAVANING SITE
BENTLEY GOLF COURSE
The Green
NAVESTOCK SIDE
BENTLEY
St. Paul's C of E Prim. School
Wishfields Farm
Ashwells Farm
Club
Mores Plantation
Millfield
Days Farm
Crow Green
Clay Hall
The Mores
Nursery
The Oaks
Kennels
COMMON
Green Lane Farm
Pilgrim's Hall
Brick House Wood
Trefusis
Coxtie Green
Oakhurst
Gents Farm
Hullett's Farm
Peniel College of Higher Education
Liby
PILGRIMS HATCH
BRENTWOOD
Coxtie House
Coxtie Green Farm
Playing Field
Pav.
Depot
CM14
Gilstead Wood
39
Bishops Hall Park
Larchwood Prim. Sch.
The Brentwood Centre
Lincolns
Fox Wood
Larch Wood
Shepherds Spinney
Locksmith Wood
Workhouse Wood
Broom Wood
Frieze Hall
Langton's Wood
Goldsmith Wood
High Wood
Larkin's Playing Flds.
Langtons
West Lodge
The Forest
Foxdown Cottage
Sawyer's Hall Farm
Playing Field
Sawyers Hall College
Lodge
WEALD COUNTRY PARK
Cricket Ground
Calcott Hall Farm
Hou Hatch
The Park
Reservoir
The Spinney
Vincent's Hamlet
Rochetts
Weald Country Park Visitors Centre
Sandpit Cottage
Playing Field
Cricket Grd.
Halfway House Farm
Keeper's Cottage
BRENTWOOD
SOUTH WEALD
St. Peter's C of E Prim. Sch.
Colmar
Offices
FRONT PARK
Vicarage
Bennett's Farm
Vicarage Wood
Cemy.
Burnt Wood
M25
M25 MOTORWAY
The Oaks
Warehouse
Depot
Wks.
Cock Wood
Lower Vicarage Wood
Alder Wood
58
Bowl. Grn.
Holly Trees
ONGAR ROAD
A128
A12
BRENTWOOD BY-PASS
A1023
LONDON ROAD
HIGH STREET
KING'S RD.
QUEENS
Sd
Td
Ud
Vd
Wd
Xd
Yd
11
12
13
14
15
16
17
18
19
20
56
57
58
59
93
94
95
96
97
98

MOUNTNESSING
Mountnessing Windmill
HUTTON
SHENFIELD
HUTTON MOUNT
Brentwood
CM15
CM13
Junction 12
MARYLANDS INTERCHANGE
Marylands
MOUNTNESSING BY-PASS
A12
A1023
A129
A128
B1002
B186
CHELMSFORD ROAD
RAYLEIGH ROAD
ROMAN ROAD
THOBY LANE
HALL LANE
SHENFIELD ROAD
INGRAVE ROAD
Shenfield
PARK WOOD
Long Wood
HOME WOOD
Hall Wood
Fox Earth Wood
Icehouse Wood
Arnold's Wood
Arnold's Shaw
Brickley Shaw
Canterbury Tye Spring
River Wid
Pettit's Farm
Bannister Farm
America Farm
Howe's Farm
Blue House
Brick House Farm
Greytoni Farm
Palmer's Farm
Palmer's Farm Cottages
Heard's Farm
Fitzwalter's
Moat
Keepers Cottage
Chainbridge Farm
Master John's Farm
Holbrooks Cottages
Chelmwood Farm
Thoby Farm
Bakers Farm
Drury's Farm
Hillrise Farm
Arnold's Farm
Wynbarns Farm
Shenfield Hall
Shenfield Hall Farm
Shenfield High Sch. & Sports Centre
Long Ridings Prim. Sch.
St. Mary's C of E Prim. Sch.
Willowbrook Prim. Sch.
Fire Brigade HQ
Hutton Rec. Grd.
St. Martin's School
Playing Field
Sports Ground
Brentwood Sch.
BRENTWOOD NUFFIELD HEALTH HOSPITAL
BRENTWOOD COMMUNITY HOSPITAL
Brentwood Prep. Sch.
Brentwood Sch. Track
Hogarth Prim. Sch.
The Endeavour Sch.
Brentwood High Sch.
Shenfield Common
Thriftwood International Scout Activity Centre
Scout Camp
Three Arch Bridge
Seven Arch Bridge
South Hove
Brindles Farm
Hall Wood
Sewage Works
Ingrave Hall
Sutton Shaw
Birches Wood
Ingrave Common
Mountnessing C of E Jun. & Inf. Schs.
St. Helens RC Jun. & Inf. Schs.
Sion Community
Zd
Ae
Be
Ce
De
Ee
Fe
60
61
62
63
98
97
96
94
93
11
12
13
14
15
16
17
18
19
20

59

24
62
A
B
C
D
E
F
G
21
22
23
24
25
26
27
28
29
30
93
92
91
190
89
88
500
01
02
03
CHALFONT COMMON
THE NATIONAL SOCIETY FOR EPILEPSY
QUEEN ELIZABETH MEDICAL CENTRE
Horn Hill
MAPLE CROSS
CHILTERN
THREE
Gravel Hill
WEST HYDE
Gerrards Cross
SL9
CHALFONT ST. PETER
HOGTROUGH WOOD
GERRARDS CROSS GOLF COURSE
AUSTENWOOD
GERRARDS CROSS
SOUTH
BUCKS
NOCKHILL WOOD
JUNIPER WOOD
THE MARISH
OAKEND WOOD
DENHAM AERODROME
DENHAM GOLF COURSE
M25
M25 MOTORWAY
AMERSHAM ROAD
A413
GRAVEL HILL
CHALFONT ST. PETER BY-PASS
AMERSHAM RD
OXFORD RD
A40
WINDSOR RD
PACKHORSE ROAD
B416
KINGSWAY
DENHAM (NORTH ORBITAL ROAD)
A412
CHALFONT LANE
HORNHILL
RICKMANSWORTH LANE
SHIRE LANE
HYDE LANE
TILEHOUSE LANE
OAK LANE
SLADE OAK LANE
MIRRIE LANE
Turner's Wood
Cricket Field Cottages
Playing Field
Skipping's Farm
Workshops
Rowan Nurseries
Brawlings Farm
High Trees
Hornhill Court
Pollardshill Wood
Beechen Wood
Kiln Wood
Tubb's Farm
Village Hall
Springview Farm
Robert's Farm
Robert's Wood
Franklin's Spring
Chalk Cliff
Maple Cross Jun. & Inf. Sch.
Recreation Ground
Lynsters
Round Rocket Plantation
Robertswood School
Beech Ho.
Gravel Pit
Middle Wood
Bloom Wood
Cemetery
Playing Field
Community Centre
Pynesfield Manor
Willow Tree Farm
Warren Farm Cottages
Warren Farm
Winkers Farm
Chalfont Heights Scout Camp
Mopes Farm
Chalfont Lodge
Research Laboratory
Chalfont Park
Cricket Ground
Chiltern Home
St. Mary's Sch.
Square Copse
Round Copse
Coldharbour Farm
Coldharbour Farm Cotts
Meadow Grange
Quarters Wood
Quarters Corner
Boundary Lodge
The Studio
Inwood
Hillery
Lit. Wotton
Tellisford
The Arches
Tirainia
Denham Park Farm
Little Halings Wood
Lesser Halings
Costers Cott
Tile House
Lodge
De Vere Leisure Club
Great Halings Wood
Pumping Ho.
Mid. Halings
Halings House
Marish Farm
The Bungalow
Birch Boughs
Owls Oak
Denham Marsh Wood
Shepherds Holt
The Mirrie
The Little House
Dial Ho.
Lynwood
Pantiles
Isle Of Wight Farm
Little Gordons
Beverley Nursy
Slade Oak
Oakridge
Mill House
Silver Springs
Greenwoods
Greenacre
The Cottage
Flying Training School
White Plains
Sherwood House
Cuckoo Oak
The Lodge
Grove Cott
The Grove
Collsels Wood
Club House
Bailey Hill
Denham Golf Club
River Misbourne
Tennis Cts.
Cricket Grd.
Football Grd.
Pav.
Depot
Comm. Cen.
Recreation Grd.
HOSP
Lib.
Tennis Courts
Austenwood Common
Hollytree Fm.
Gerrards Cross
Superstore
Memorial Cen.
Gerrards Cross Common
The Gerrards Cross C of E School
Mill End
Hotel
Ckt. Grd.
Club House
OVER THE MISBOURNE RD
Weir
Ford

THREE RIVERS
Rickmansworth
WD3
RIVERS
HILLINGDON
Uxbridge
UB9
Batchworth Heath
Woodcock Hill
Hill End
Mount Pleasant
HAREFIELD
HAREFIELD HOSPITAL
SOUTH HAREFIELD
Denham Garden Village
DENHAM GREEN
Newyears Green
BATCHWORTH PARK GOLF COURSE
Driving Range
Garrett Wood
High Wood
Chalk Pit
Springwell Lock
Quarry Farm
Springwell Lake
Maplelodge Farm
Maple Lodge Nature Reserve
Sewage Works
Watercress Beds
Sixteen Acre Spring
Cooks Wood
Cripp's Farm
Weybeards Farm
One Tree Hill
White Heath Farm
Watts Common
Taylors Meadow Sports Ground
Parkwood Farm Kennels
PARK WOOD
Sports Ground
Lynsters Lake
Pynesfield Lake
Nursing Home
Copper Mill Lock
Horse Shoe Bay
Iron Foundry
Colney Farm
Black Jacks Lock
Black Jack's Mill
West Hyde House
Troy Mill Flats
Gravel Pit
El Sub Sta.
BROADWATER
Battlesford Wood
Ranston Covert
Denham Laboratories
Moorhall Cottages
Widewater Lock
Halfway House
Pumping Station
Harefield Moor
Res. (covered)
Green Bridge
Savay Farm
Sand & Gravel Works
Broadwater Farm
War Meml.
Nursery
Park Lodge Farm
Park Lodge Cottage
Dews Farm Sand Pits Nature Reserve
Dewes Farm Cottages
Dewes Farm
Hillingdon Outdoor Activities Centre
Lower Lodge
The Bungalow
Highway Farm
Newyears Green
Braemar Farm
Pylon Farm
High View Farm
BAYHURST WOOD COUNTRY PARK
Warren Farm
Middle Lodge
Breakspear House
Bourne Farm
Langley Farm
Knightscote Farm
Claypits
Kiln Pond
Dell
Scarlet Spring
Ashain Spring
Furzefield
Deadman's Grove
Badminton Shooting Ground
Harefield United FC (Preston Park)
Shepherds Hill House
Shepherds Hill Farm
The Harefield Academy
Play Fld.
The Lodge
Harefield Grove
Waterfall
Pearson's Wood
Woodcock Hill Barns
Bishop's Wood
Poorfield
Lockwell Wood
Reservoir (covered)
Harefield Reservoir (covered)
Slaley
Sikora
Battlers Wells Farm
Battlers Wells Wood
French Grove
Park Wood
Long Spring
Wellingrove House
Woodcock Hill Estate
Pipers Farm
Bush Spring
Sandfield Spring
Greenbroom Spring
Juniper Dell
Andrews Ley Farm
Cemetery
Howard Spring
Whipping Spring
Harefield Jun. & Inf. Schs.
Cricket Grd.
GRAND UNION CANAL
River Colne
DENHAM WAY
(NORTH ORBITAL ROAD)
A412
A404
BATCHWORTH LONDON RD.
BREAKSPEAR ROAD
NORTH
NEW YEARS GREEN LANE
MOORHALL ROAD
HARVIL ROAD
RICKMANSWORTH ROAD
NORTHWOOD ROAD
PARK LANE
HILL END ROAD
SHRUBS RD.
WHITE HILL
WOODCOCK HILL
HAREFIELD RD.
25
63
44

Rickmansworth
Batchworth Heath
MOOR PARK
Moor Park Golf Course
SANDY LODGE GOLF COURSE
THREE RIVERS
EASTBURY
WD3
Bishops Wood BMI Hosp.
Mount Vernon Hospital
Hospice
Esporta Health & Fitness
NORTHWOOD
Northwood
HA6
Northwood College
London Sch. of Theology
St. Helen's School
Northwood Golf Course
NORTHWOOD HILLS
Northwood Hills
Northwood FC
LA Fitness
Haste Hill Golf Course
HILLINGDON
Uxbridge
COPSE WOOD
RUISLIP WOODS (National Nature Reserve)
Poor's Field
Haste Hill
Eleanor's
Ruislip Lido Railway
Lakeside
RUISLIP LIDO
Ruislip Lido Woodlands Centre
Woody Bay
YOUNG WOOD
MAD BESS WOOD
NORTH RIDING WOOD
Mad Bess Wood Cottage
RUISLIP COMMON
Breakspear Crematorium (Ruislip)
PARK WOOD
BAYHURST WOOD COUNTRY PARK
UB9
Ruislip
HA4
Grangewood School
Coteford Junior Sch.
Haydon School
Kings College Playing Fields
Eastcote Hockey & Badminton Club
Hillingdon Athletic Club
Cannons Bridge Farm
Whiteheath Jun. & Inf. Schs.
Winston Churchill Hall
Newyears Green
Highgrove Swim. Pool
A404
A4180
A4125
B469
B472
B466
LONDON ROAD (BATCHWORTH HEATH HILL)
RICKMANSWORTH ROAD
DUCK'S HILL ROAD
GREEN LANE
PINNER ROAD
WATFORD ROAD
SANDY LANE
HIGH STREET
JOEL STREET
BURY STREET
BREAKSPEAR ROAD NORTH
WHITE HILL
KINGS AVENUE
PARK AVENUE
26
43
64

Carpenders Park
GOLF COURSE
St. Joseph's Catholic Primary School
Little Furze Field
X
Y
Z
Aa
Ba
Ca
Da
Mutton Wood
Carpenders Park Cemetery
Beck Mason's Wood
OXHEY WOODS
SOUTH OXHEY
Sandpit Wood
Valley View Farm
GRIM'S DYKE GOLF COURSE
Club House
Weald Wood
Stony Wood
Grimsdyke Open Space
LITTLE OXHEY LANE
B4542
PRESTWICK ROAD
Woodhall Prim. Sch.
Sir James Altham Pool
Nature Reserve
Oxheylane Farm
A4008
OXHEY LANE
Grimswood Lodge
Grimswood House
Highcroft
The Lodge
Harrow
HA3
Nanscot Wood
Birchanger
Reservoir (covered)
Pinnerwood House
Pinnerwood Farm
Pinnerwood Cottage
Saddlers Mead
Hatch End Ten. Club
Playing Fields
The Roger Bannister Sports Centre
Pinner Wood
PINNER HILL GOLF COURSE
Shaftesbury Playing Fields
Hatch End
UXBRIDGE RD.
A410
Harrow Arts Cen.
Hatch End Play. Flds.
HATCH END
Hatch End High Sch.
Cedars Manor Sch.
Pinnerwood Park
Rugby Football Ground
Bedford Coll. Sports Grd.
UXBRIDGE ROAD
A404
ST. THOMAS' DR.
GEORGE V
PINNER
PARK
Headstone Lane
Pinner Park Farm
PINNER GREEN
Montesole Play. Flds.
Pinner Lawn Tennis Club
Headstone Lane Sports Grd.
RICKMANSWORTH RD.
Little Common
Paine's Br.
Cemetery
Harlyn Primary Sch.
CUCKOO HILL
Superstore
Pinner Village Hall
Pinner Memorial Park
Pinner
Nower Hill
Pinner New Cemetery
Headstone Manor Recreation Ground
Harrow Museum & Heritage Cen.
West Lodge First & Middle Sch.
PINNER
Reddiford Sch.
Nower Hill High Sch.
Harrow
HA5
HEADSTONE
B466
ROAD
Pinner Village Gardens
Woodlands Open Space
EASTCOTE VILLAGE
North Harrow
PINNER ROAD
A4090
IMPERIAL DRIVE
The Croft
Feading Brook Open Space
NORTH HARROW
HA2
Cannon Lane First & Mid Schs.
Longfield Schs.
West Harrow
EASTCOTE
Streamside Rec. Grd.
65
VIEW EASTERN
12
13
14

46
GOLF COURSE
Bentley Priory
28
The Princess Alexandra Home
Bentley Priory Local Nature Reserve
STANMORE COUNTRY PARK (Local Nature Reserve)
Levels Wood
HARROW WEALD COMMON
Grim's Ditch
Grim's Dyke
Grimsdyke Open Space
Harrow Weald Common
Nurseries
Weald Wood
REDDING
Stony Wood
Grimswood House
Highcroft
The Old Barn
Priory House
Lower Priory Farm
Heriot's Wood
Deer Park
Heriots
Stanmore Hall
Hertfordshire & Middlesex Country Club
Copse Farm
Nursery
Hermitage Cottages
Hermitage Gate
Bentley Wood High Sch.
Woodland Hall
Harrow Weald Cemetery
Harrow Coll. (Harrow Weald Campus)
Brockhurst Cnr.
STANMORE
Stanmore College
Temple Pond
Club House
STANMORE GOLF COURSE
OXHEY
A4008
Playing Fields
The Roger Bannister Sports Centre
UXBRIDGE
A410
HARROW WEALD
Superstore
Bus Depot
Recreation Ground
Tennis Club
Cedars Manor Sch.
Hatch End High Sch.
First & Mid. Sch.
Headstone Lane
Headstone Lane Sports Grd.
BELMONT
Kenton Lane Farm
Priestmead Rec. Grd.
Belmont Sch.
Salvatorian Coll.
Works
Harrow Crown Court
Harrow & Wealdstone
WEALDSTONE
Byron Recreation Ground
Harrow Leisure Centre
Harrow Driving, Cycling and Road Safety Centre
Cemetery
Headstone Manor
Harrow Museum & Heritage Cen.
Headstone Manor Recreation Ground
Yeading Brook
HEADSTONE
HA1
HA2
HA3
HA7
Civic Centre
Elmgrove First & Middle Schools
Kenton Recreation Ground
KENTON
Old Lyonian Sports Club
Harrow Recreation Ground
GREENHILL
Harrow Cemetery
Rec. Grd.
Superstore
St. Ann's Shopping Cen.
Harrow-on-the-Hill
West Harrow
Northwick Park
Halls of Residence
Univ. of Westminster (Harrow Campus)
Univ. of Westminster Sports Hall
HARROW HILL GOLF COURSE
HARROW
66
Kenton
PINNER
A404
A409
A4005
A4006
A4140
STATION ROAD
KENTON ROAD
CHURCH RD.
THE BROADWAY
STANMORE HILL
HIGH ROAD
BROOKSHILL
COMMON ROAD
SHEEPCOTE ROAD
GREENHILL WAY
LOWLANDS
Ea
Fa
Ga
Ha
Ja
Ka
La
21
22
23
24
25
26
27
28
29
30

47
Golf Centre
Stanmore
Stonegrove
EDGWARE WAY
(WATFORD BY-PASS)
A41
M1
MOTORWAY
APEX CORNER
WATFORD WY.
Edgware
Edgware Bus Sta.
EDGWARE
Mill Hill Broadway
Mill Hill Old Railway Nature Reserve
The Hale
HALE LANE
DEANSBROOK RD.
A5109
STATION RD.
A5100
STONEGROVE
HIGH STREET
BURNT OAK BROADWAY
EDGWARE RD.
A5
CANONS PARK
Canons Park
North London Collegiate School
King George V Memorial Gdns.
WHITCHURCH LANE
B461
LITTLE STANMORE
Chandos Recreation Grd.
Prince Edward Playing Field
BURNT OAK
Burnt Oak
Watling
WATLING
HONEYPOT LANE
A4140
QUEENSBURY
Queensbury
Montrose Recreation Ground
Silkstream Park
Colindale
COLINDALE
COLINDEEP LANE
Roe Green
Roe Green Park
Kingsbury Manor
KINGSBURY RD.
A4006
Kingsbury
KENTON ROAD
FRYENT WAY
FRYENT COUNTRY PARK
KINGSBURY
Kingsbury Green
CHURCH LANE
B454
St. Luke's Hospice
Recreation Ground
FRYENT COUNTRY PARK (Local Nature Reserve)
67
Ma
Na
Pa
Qa
Ra
Sa
Ta
18
19
20
21
22
23
24
25
26
27
28
29
30

48
Ua
Va
Wa
Xa
Ya
Za
Ab
21
22
23
24
25
26
27
28
29
30
Folly Farm
Burtonhole Lane Farm Estate
Playing Field
Riding School
Belmont Farm
Sports Ground
Cricket Club
Cemetery
Nursery
Burtonhole Farm
Sports Ground
St. Mary's Abbey
The Mill Field
Lawrence Green
St. Joseph's College
St. Paul's C of E Prim. Sch.
National Centre for Medical Research
Mill Hill School
Mill Hill Sub. Sta.
MILL HILL CIRCUS
MILL HILL
THE RIDGEWAY
St. Vincent's Catholic Prim. Sch.
Wentworth Hall
Oakfield House
Partingdale Manor
The Mount Sch.
Drivers Hill
NW7
Watch Tower House
M1 MOTORWAY
WATFORD WAY
THE BROADWAY
DAWS LANE
HAMMERS LANE
Featherstone Hill
Arrandene Open Space
Burton Bank
School Park
Ridgeway Ho.
MILL HILL PARK
Cricket Ground
Mill Hill Broadway
Lyndhurst Park
Mill Hill Cemetery
The Hale
SELVAGE LANE
HALE LANE
WATLING AVENUE
(BARNET BY-PASS)
A1
Mill Hill East
Bittacy Hill Park
Depot
BITTACY HILL
Playing Field
Copthall Sch. & Sports Cen.
Chase Lodge Playing Fields
Powerleague Soccer Cen.
Dollis Jun. & Inf. Schs.
METRO PLAYGOLF
Metro Playgolf Driving Range
Copthall Leisure Centre
Shaftesbury Barnet Harriers & Saracens RUFC (Barnet Copthall Stadium)
Club House
Hendon Crematorium
HENDON CEMETERY
Rugby Club
Hasmonean High Sch. for Girls
Junction 2
FIVEWAYS CORNER
BARNET COPTHALL SPORTS CENTRE
HENDON GOLF COURSE
Pavilion
Woodcroft Park
Sports Ground
Grahame Park
High Sch.
RAF Museum London
Battle of Britain Hall
GREAT NORTH WAY
SUNNY HILL PARK
Holders Hill
Windsor Open Space
Colindale
COLINDALE
Peel Centre (Metropolitan Police Training Establishment)
Silkstream Unit East
National Blood Service
Montrose Recreation Ground
Elysian House
Offices
NW9
NW4
THE GARDEN BMI HOSP
COLINDEEP LANE
EDGWARE ROAD
Superstore
WATFORD WAY
The Burroughs
Middlesex University
THE BURROUGHS
CHURCH RD.
FINCHLEY LANE
BRENT STREET
PARSON STREET
HENDON WAY
HENDON
Hendon Central
QUEENS ROAD
Virgin Active
HENDON PARK
Rushgrove Park
Silk Stream
THE HYDE
STATION ROAD
KINGSBURY ROAD
A4006
Kingsbury Green
Malcolm Park
Hendon
WEST HENDON PLAYING FIELDS
Cycle Track
Brent Reservoir
Youth Sailing Base
Cool Oak
Kingsbury Town FC Grd.
BRENT CROSS INTERCHANGE
Brent Cross
Brent Cross
NORTH CIRCULAR RD.
GOLDERS GREEN ROAD
BRENT CROSS FLY-OVER
The Decoy
Monastery
Bowl Grn
47
68
30

49
Bb
Cb
Db
Eb
Fb
Gb
Hb
31
69
50
21
22
23
24
25
26
27
28
29
30
Woodside Park
Woodside Park Club
Sports Ground
North London Hospice
FRIERN BARNET
NORTH MIDDLESEX GOLF COURSE
Friary Park
Bethune Park
Recreation Ground
NORTH FINCHLEY
Wren Academy
Woodhouse College
Tally Ho Corner
Arts Depot
COLNEY HATCH
Coppetts Wood & Glebelands Local Nature Reserve
Compton Sports Cen.
Artificial Pitch
Recycling Centre
Powerleague Soccer Cen.
FINCHLEY GOLF COURSE
West Finchley
David Lloyd Leisure
Wingate & Finchley Rugby FC Grd. Football Ground
Cricket & Football Grounds
Glebe Land Open Space
FINCHLEY MEM. HOSP.
Fallow Corner
Finchley Lido
GREAT NORTH LEISURE PARK
Victoria Park
FINCHLEY
CHURCH END
Finchley Central
Pentland Centre
Islington Crematorium
ST. PANCRAS & ISLINGTON CEM.
Muswell Hill Spts. Grd.
COLDFALL WOOD
Coldfall Prim. Sch.
Martin Prim. Sch.
Avenue House Grounds
Sports Ground
The Sternberg Centre
St. Marylebone Crematorium
Christ's College Finchley
EAST FINCHLEY CEMETERY
Oak Lodge Sch.
EAST FINCHLEY
East Finchley
FORTIS GREEN
Fortismere Sch. (North Wing)
Fortismere Sch. (South Wing)
HENLYS CORNER
Little Wood
Big Wood
HAMPSTEAD GARDEN SUBURB
Cherry Tree Wood
HARINGEY
HIGHGATE GOLF COURSE
HIGHGATE WOOD
HIGHGATE
HIGHGATE HOSPITAL
NW11
N2
N3
N10
N6
N12
N20
N11
Temple Fortune
GOLDERS GREEN
Golders Green Crematorium
Jewish Cemetery
HAMPSTEAD GOLF COURSE
HAMPSTEAD HEATH
Bunkers Hill
HIGH ROAD
A1000
BALLARDS LANE
A598
REGENTS PARK ROAD
FINCHLEY ROAD
NORTH CIRCULAR ROAD
A406
WOODHOUSE ROAD
A1003
FRIERN BARNET LANE
EAST END ROAD
A504
FORTIS GREEN
FALLODEN WAY
A1
LYTTELTON ROAD
AYLMER ROAD
GREAT NORTH ROAD
ARCHWAY RD.
NORTH HILL
COLNEY HATCH LANE
B550
NETHER ST.
NORTH FINCHLEY

50
32
70
69
NEW SOUTHGATE CEMETERY
New Southgate Crematorium
ARNOS PARK
Arnos Grove
PALMERS GREEN
Broomfield Park
Sports Ground
BOWES ROAD
A1110
A406
NORTH CIRCULAR ROAD
New Southgate
NEW SOUTHGATE
FRIERN BARNET
COLNEY HATCH
Coppetts Wood & Glebelands Local Nature Reserve
PINKHAM WAY
BOUNDS GREEN ROAD
Bounds Green
Bowes Park
MUSWELL HILL GOLF COURSE
Alexandra Park School
DURNSFORD RD.
ALEXANDRA PARK RD.
Alexandra Palace
WOOD GREEN
Wood Green
HIGH ROAD
A105
LORDSHIP LA.
Ice Rink
Pitch & Putt Course
ALEXANDRA PARK
Reservoir
Filter Beds
Cricket Ground
Playing Field
MUSWELL HILL
Fortis Green
FORTIS GREEN
N10
N11
N6
N8
PRIORY RD.
HIGH STREET
A504
Hornsey
HORNSEY
TURNPIKE LA.
Turnpike Lane
Cranley Gardens
HIGHGATE WOOD
QUEEN'S WOOD
ARCHWAY RD.
A1
Highgate
HIGHGATE
HIGHGATE HOSP.
CROUCH END
CROUCH END HILL
TOTTENHAM LA.
A103
PARK RD.
A1201
HORNSEY VALE
STROUD GREEN
Harringay
Park Road Leisure Centre
St. Aloysius College Sports Ground
Coolhurst Club
MUSWELL HILL RD.
B550
Jb
Kb
Lb
Mb
Nb
Pb
Qb
21
22
23
24
25
26
27
28
29
30

51
EDMONTON
UPPER EDMONTON
TOTTENHAM
TOTTENHAM HALE
SOUTH TOTTENHAM
WEST GREEN
PYMMES PARK
TOTTENHAM CEMETERY
BRUCE CASTLE PARK
LORDSHIP RECREATION GROUND
DOWNHILLS PARK
LOCKWOOD RESERVOIR
LOW MAYNARD RESERVOIR
WARWICK RESERVOIR (EAST)
WARWICK RESERVOIR (WEST)
RESERVOIR No.1
RESERVOIR No.2
RESERVOIR No.3
NORTH CIRCULAR ROAD
STERLING WAY
SILVER STREET
GREAT CAMBRIDGE ROAD
THE ROUNDWAY
LORDSHIP LANE
WHITE HART LANE
HIGH ROAD
FORE STREET
WEST GREEN ROAD
BROAD LANE
FERRY LANE
MERIDIAN WAY
WATERMEAD WAY
ST. ANN'S ROAD
SEVEN SISTERS RD.
GREEN LANES
CONDUIT LANE
ANGEL RD.
FOREST RD.
Silver Street
White Hart Lane
Northumberland Park
Bruce Grove
Tottenham Hale
Seven Sisters
South Tottenham
Harringay Green Lanes
Stamford Hill
Angel Rd.
NORTH MIDDLESEX UNIVERSITY HOSPITAL
ST. ANN'S HOSPITAL
Tottenham Hotspur FC (White Hart Lane)
Bruce Castle Mus.
Markfield Beam Engine & Museum
Lee Valley Park
River Lee Navigation
Walthamstow Marsh Nature Reserve
Tottenham Marshes
Rb
Sb
Tb
Ub
Vb
Wb
Xb
21
22
23
24
25
26
27
28
29
30
A406
A10
A1010
A109
A503
A504
A1055
A1080
B152
B153
B155
N18
N17
N15
E17
33
71

ENFIELD
N18
Teamsport Karting
Refuse Incineration Plant
Pumping Station
Angel Rd.
ANGEL ROAD
CONDUIT LANE
MERIDIAN WAY
LEA VALLEY VIADUCT
NORTH CIRCULAR ROAD
SOUTHEND ROAD
HALL LANE
NEW ROAD
CHINGFORD MOUNT
SOUTH CHINGFORD
Chase Lane Park
CHINGFORD MOUNT RD.
CHINGFORD RD.
OLD CHURCH RD.
Larkswood
Larks Wood
Larkswood Park
Larkswood Leisure Centre
Suffield Hatch
Greens Health & Fitness
Ainslie Wood Nature Reserve
Rolls Sports Grd.
HIGHAMS PARK
Walthamstow Stadium (Closed)
The Peter May Centre
Playing Field
BANBURY RESERVOIR
HARINGEY
LEE VALLEY PARK
River Lee Navigation
River Lee Diversion
N17
Northumberland Park
Golf Driving Range
Britannia Sports Grd.
CROOKED BILLET
Walthamstow Academy
William Morris Sch.
Chapel End
LLOYD PARK
WALTHAMSTOW
HIGHAM HILL
Waltham Forest Pool & Track
Chestnuts Sports Ground
Town Hall
THORPE COOMBE HOSP.
THE BELL
FOREST ROAD
HOE STREET
LOCKWOOD RESERVOIR
LOW MAYNARD RESERVOIR
HIGH MAYNARD RESERVOIR
Tottenham Hale
Lee Valley Park
FERRY LA.
Blackhorse Rd.
BLACKHORSE ROAD
BLACKHORSE LA.
Douglas Eyre Playing Fields
Douglas Eyre Sports Centre
RESERVOIR No.4
RESERVOIR No.5
WARWICK RESERVOIR (EAST)
Filter Beds
WATER WORKS
Low Hall Sports Ground
Walthamstow Marsh Nature Reserve
St. James St.
ST. JAMES'S PARK
Queens Road Cemetery
Walthamstow Queens Rd.
Walthamstow Central
Kelmscott Leisure Cen.
MARKHOUSE RD.
LEA BRIDGE RD.
HIGH STREET
LEYTON GRN.
Leisure Pool
WALTHAMSTOW

53
Fc
Gc
Hc
Jc
Kc
Lc
Mc
35
73
54
WOODFORD WELLS
WOODFORD GREEN
Woodford Side
Woodford
WOODFORD
SOUTH WOODFORD
South Woodford
SNARESBROOK
Snaresbrook
WANSTEAD
Wanstead
Redbridge
REDBRIDGE
Roding Valley
HIGHAMS PARK
Highams Pk.
HALE END
INGFORD HATCH
UPPER WALTHAMSTOW
Wood St. Walthamstow
Ilford
IG8
IG4
E18
E11
WOODFORD GOLF COURSE
Football Ground
Knighton Wood
Rugby Football Ground
Chigwell Sewage Works
Luxborough
Highams Park
The Highams Park
Boating Lake
The Lops
The Ching
EPPING FOREST
Haven Ho. Foundation
Rugby Football Grd.
Woodford High Sch. for Girls
Woodford Green Prim. Sch.
Bancroft's Sch & Prep. Sch.
James Leal Cen.
Ray Park
Ray Lodge Prim. Sch.
Ashton Playing Fields
Woodford Green Athletic Cen.
Darnalls Playing Field
Playing Field
Winn Bridge
Factory
Works
Cemetery
Sports Ground
Junction 4
CHARLIE BROWN'S ROUNDABOUT
WATERWAYS CORNER
Walthamstow Forest
Reservoir (covered)
Reservoir (cov.)
Gilbert's Slade
Hyland Ho. School
Abbeydale
Boating Pond
Community Hall
Sylvestrian Leisure Cen.
Forest Sch.
Nature Reserve
Round Pond
Eagle Pond
Snaresbrook Crown Court
Hollow Pond (Boating Lake)
WHIPPS CROSS UNIV HOSP.
WOODBURY UNIT
Margaret Centre
Epping Temple Forest
Woodbridge High Sch.
Elmhurst Gdns.
Nightingale Prim. Sch.
Wanstead Youth Cen.
Wanstead High School
Leisure Cen.
Golf Course
Pumping Station
REDBRIDGE ROUNDABOUT
Recreation Grd.
Hatton School
PDSA (Veterinary Centre)
RODING SPIRE HOSPITAL
Warehouse
Beal High Sch.
The Heronry
Lincoln Island
River Roding
M11
M11 MOTORWAY
CHINGFORD LANE
A1009
WOODFORD NEW ROAD
A104
HIGH ROAD WOODFORD GREEN
BROADMEAD ROAD
CHIGWELL ROAD
A113
SOUTHEND ROAD
A406
NORTH CIRCULAR ROAD
FOREST ROAD
A503
NEW ROAD
WOODFORD RD.
LEA BRI. RD.
WHIPPS CROSS ROAD
A114
HOLLYBUSH HILL
A1199
HIGH ROAD SOUTH WOODFORD
HERMON HILL
NEW WANSTEAD
CAMBRIDGE PARK
A106
EASTERN AVENUE
A12
SOUTH WOODFORD TO BARKING RELIEF ROAD
WOODFORD AVENUE
A1400
SNARESBROOK ROAD
GEORGE LA.
THE VIADUCT
BUCKHURST WAY
SNAKES LANE
MONKHAMS AV.
CHURCHFIELDS
GROVE ROAD
CHIGWELL RD.
RODING LANE
HATCH LA.

54
36
53
74
CHIGWELL
Chigwell
EPPING FOREST
M11 MOTORWAY
CHIGWELL ROAD
HIGH ROAD
MANOR ROAD
HAINAULT ROAD
FENCEPIECE ROAD
Chigwell Golf Course
West Hatch High School
Woodford Green Athletic Cen. (Running Track)
Roding Valley Park
Rugby Football Ground
Chigwell Sewage Works
Luxborough
Ashton Playing Fields
WOODFORD BRIDGE
Repton Park
Hospital Hill Wood
Cocked Hat Plantation
Hospital Hill
Egg Clump
Ash Plantation
Grange Hill
GRANGE HILL
Limes Farm Inf. & Jun. Schools
Hainault
New Rush Hall Sch.
Fairlop Prim. Sch.
FAIRLOP
Fairlop
Old Parkonians Association
Redbridge Sports & Leisure Cen.
Oakfield Playing Field
Fairlop Lodge
FAIRLOP WATERS GOLF COURSE
King Solomon High Sch.
FULLWELL CROSS
Ilford High Sch.
CLAYHALL
CLAYHALL PARK
BARKINGSIDE
Barkingside
Redbridge FC (Oakside Stadium)
Ilford Jewish Primary School
Aldborough Ho. Farm
Oaks Park High Sch.
NEWBURY PARK
Newbury Park
GANTS HILL
Gants Hill
Beal High Sch.
PDSA (Veterinary Centre)
WOODFORD AVENUE
WOODFORD AV.
EASTERN AVENUE
CRANBROOK RD.
REDBRIDGE
Redbridge
Valentines High Sch.
Valentines Mansion & Gardens
STH. WOODFORD TO BARKING RELIEF ROAD
IG4
IG5
IG6
IG7
IG8

37
Vc
Wc
Xc
Yc
Zc
Ad
Bd
HAINAULT FOREST (COUNTRY PARK)
Visitor Centre
Fox Burrows
Foxburrows Rare Breeds Farm & Zoo
The Lake
Old Hainault Oak
Dog Kennel Hill
HAINAULT FOREST GOLF COURSE
Nursery
Riding School
Reservoirs (covered)
Cemetery
Forest Park Crematorium
Hainault Lodge Local Nature Reserve
Club Ho.
Golf Driving Range
Hog Hill
Redbridge Cycling Centre
ROMFORD ROAD
A1112
HAINAULT
Recreation Ground
Playing Fields
Tennis Courts
Wood View
Play Field
Fairview
Coppice Prim. Sch.
Res. (covered)
Hainault Forest High Sch.
Elmbridge Sports Ground
Club House
Skate Park
Forest Road Playing Field
Hainault Recreation Ground
Fairlop Oak Recreation Ground
Powerleague Soccer Cen.
Fairlop Sailing Centre
Fairlop Lake
FAIRLOP WATERS COUNTRY PARK
Lagoon
Farm Cottages
Hainault Works
Hainault Farm
Seven Kings Water
Romford
BARKING and DAGENHAM
RM5
RM6
RM7
IG3
WHALEBONE LANE NORTH
ROMFORD ROAD
B174
HOG HILL RD.
Forest Farm Equestrian Centre
Cold Blow Farm
Marks Gate
Football Grd.
City Limits
Whites Farm
Furze Cottage
Furze House Farm
Mill Farm
Chadwell Heath Cemetery
Jun. Sch.
Infant Sch.
Moat
Warren Farm
Red House Farm
Hainault House
Willow Farm
Playing Field
Little Heath Sch.
Sports Ground
PAINTERS ROAD
Aldborough Hall Farm
ALDBOROUGH HATCH
Aldborough Hall Equestrian Centre
EASTERN AVENUE
A12
KING GEORGE HOSPITAL
North Residence
South Residence
GOODMAYES HOSPITAL
LITTLE HEATH
Redbridge College
Newbridge Sch.
Grove Prim. Sch.
Bowling Green
Sports Ground
Club House
Museum
Tennis Courts
Playing Field
Games Court
SEVEN KINGS PARK
Skate Park
Bandstand
Farnham Green Prim. Sch.
Brookside
B177
ST. CHAD'S PARK
Playground
CHADWELL HEATH
A118
HIGH ROAD
MOBY DICK
Driving Range
Warren Park Golf Cen.
Rec. Grd.
Warren Sports Centre
Warren Jun. Sch.
Crown Farm
Crown Cottages
St. Edward's C of E Comp. School
Pavilion
Westlands Playing Fields
West Ham FC Training Grd.
Whalebone Bri.
Mecca Bingo
75
56
Sandhills
Park Farm
Lower Park Farm
Willoughby's Hill
Havering Park
Havering Lodge
Gobions Farm
COLLIER ROW
Works
21
22
23
24
25
26
27
28
29
30
46
47
48
49
88
89
90
91
92
93

56
38
55
76
Havering-Atte-Bower
Havering Park
Havering Country Park
Pine Wood
Kiln Wood
Churchpath Plantation North
Foreberry Wood South
Lower Park Farm
Willoughby's Hill
Bower Farm
Bower House
Bower Wood
Bedfords Park
Larch Wood
Deer Park
Upper Bedfords Farm
Round House Farm
St. Francis Hospice
Riding Stables
Poultry Farm
Orange Tree Inn
Nursery
RM4
RM5
RM7
RM1
RM6
Romford
Chase Cross
Collier Row
Rise Park
Mawney
Crowlands
Heath Park
Havering
Bower Park School
Clockhouse Primary School
Pinewood Prim. Sch.
Crownfield Jun. & Inf. Schs.
Rise Park Jun. & Inf. Schs.
Marshalls Park School
Sunnyside Farm
Club House
Risebridge Golf Course
Gobions Farm
Whites Farm
Crown Farm
Crown Cottages
King Georges Field
Mawney Park
Raphael Park
Lodge Farm Park
Sports Ground
Cottons Park
Romford Stadium (Greyhound)
St. Edward's C of E Comp. School
Westlands Playing Field
West Ham FC Training Grd.
Warren Sports Centre
Queen's Hospital
Havering Mag. Ct.
Romford County Ct.
Town Hall
Esporta Club
Bowl. Alley
The Brewery
Eastern Av. Retail Pk.
Warehouse
Eastern Avenue
London Road
High Rd.
Collier Row Road
Collier Row Lane
Hog Hill Rd.
Chase Cross Road
Havering Road
Orange Tree Hill
Lower Bedfords Road
Havering Lane
North Street
Main Road
Mercury Way
Waterloo Rd.
St. Edwards Way
Thurloe Gs.
Mercury Gardens
South Street
Brentwood Road
Rom Valley Way
Oldchurch Road
Marks Road
Mawney Road
Pettits Lane
Pettits Boulevard
Parkway
Gidea Park
A12
A118
A125
B174
B175
B1459
Cd
Dd
Ed
Fd
Gd
Hd
Jd
21
22
23
24
25
26
27
28
29
30

Kd
Ld
Md
Nd
Pd
Qd
Rd
39
77
58
53
54
55
56
93
92
91
90
89
88
DAGNAM PARK
Fir Wood
Cock Wood
Alder Wood
The Nursery
Play. Fld.
Tennis Courts
BROXHILL CENTRE
THE WHITWORTH CENTRE
Havering College of Further & Higher Education (Quaries Campus)
Hatters Wood
Dycorts Sch.
Ten. Cts.
Moat
King's Wood Sch.
Pyrgo Priory Sch.
MAYLANDS GOLF COURSE
Weald Brook
Putwell Bridge
Club House
Maylands
Maylands Cottage
Maylands Field
Sports Grd.
Central Park
Long Wood
Min. Golf Course
Central Park Leisure Centre
THE DAVID CROMPTON LODGE
Comm. Centre
HAROLD HILL
Sage Wood
Ckt. Grnd.
Day Cen.
RM3
St. Ursula's Catholic Infant School
St. Ursula's Catholic Junior School
Hilldene Prim. Sch.
Mead Prim. Sch.
Prim. Sch.
Football Ground
HAROLD PARK
ELMS INDUSTRIAL ESTATE
Harold Court Prim. Sch.
Paine's Brook
Works
BATES INDUSTRIAL ESTATE
THE OLD BRICKWORKS INDUSTRIAL ESTATE
Ingrebourne River
Sewage Works
Garden Centre
The Chase
Sports Ground
Superstore
HAROLD WOOD
Harold Wood
London South Bank University (Havering)
NHS Walk-in Cen. (Harold Wood)
Gallows Corner
Sports Ground
GALLOWS CORNER
GOLF COURSE
Cissbury Lodge Farm
ST. ETHELBURGA
Cockabourne Bridge
Miniature Golf Course
Pages Farm
Pavilion
Harold Wood Park
Social Cen.
Comm. Cen.
Four Wantz
Emanuel Cottage
PAGES WOOD
Upminster
RM14
Redden Court Sch.
Harold Wood Prim. Sch.
Prospect Farm
Ingrebourne Farm
Cornlands Farm
GIDEA PARK
RM2
David Lloyd Gidea Park
Squirrel's Heath
Gidea Park
ARDLEIGH GREEN
Miniature Golf Course
HAYNES PARK
Drill Roundabout
The Campion School
Playing Field
College
Hotel
Mount Pleasant Farm
The Rosary
Grasslands
Hornchurch
RM11
Lillyputts Equestrian Centre
EMERSON PARK
Goodrington Sch.
HYLANDS PARK
Towers Inf. Sch.
Towers Jun. Sch.
Emerson Pk.
Emerson Park Sch.
Upminster Court
Chapman's Farm
EAST ROAD
COLCHESTER ROAD
A12
SOUTHEND ARTERIAL ROAD
A127
A118
HAROLD COURT ROAD
DAGNAM PARK DRIVE
GOOSHAYS DRIVE
PETERSFIELD AVENUE
HAROLD HILL
SQUIRRELS HEATH
BRENTWOOD ROAD
PARKSTONE AVENUE
SYLVAN AVENUE
NELMES WAY
SHEPHERDS HILL
HILLVIEW
OSBORNE ROAD
21
22
23
24
25
26
27
28
29
30

M25 MOTORWAY
Junction 11 (A12)
Junction 28 (M25)
Junction 29
BRENTWOOD BY-PASS
BROOK STREET
LONDON RD.
A1023
A12
COLCHESTER ROAD
BROOK STREET INTERCHANGE
Alder Wood
Cock Wood
The Oaks
Lower Vicarage Wood
MAYLANDS GOLF COURSE
Weald Brook
Grove Farm
The Grove
Putwell Bridge
Maylands
Maylands Cottage
Maylands Field
Hotel
Works
Wks
Mascalls Cottages
Mascalls
Warley Country Park
Holly Trees Primary School
Bowl. Grn.
Brentwood Mus.
The Duchess of Kent Social Centre
Spts. Grd.
Pav.
Cemy.
WARLEY
Dragons Health Club
Sports Grd.
Warley Woods
Tennis Cts.
Ursuline Prep. Sch.
HARTSWOOD SPIRE HOSP.
Driving Range
Karting Cen.
Brentwood Park Ski & Snowboarding Centre
SpringHealth Leisure Club
Headley Common
Stoney Hall Cottage
Holden's Wood
Tennis Court
Rustlings
Pump Farm
Warley Lea
Warley Lea Farm
Lodge
Pond
Warley Place Nature Reserve
Bachelor's Walk
Lower Belt
CM14
Leverton Hall & House
Boyles Court Farm
Top Plantation
Sewage Disposal Works
River Ingrebourne
ELMS INDUSTRIAL ESTATE
Gibblings Shaw
Tylers Shaw
Wormwalk Shaw
Jermains Wood
Jackson's Wood
Garden Centre
The Chase
Tylers Hall
TYLERS COMMON
GREAT WARLEY
WARLEY ROAD
GREAT WARLEY STREET
B186
Stonyhills Farm
Stonyhills House
Pav. Cricket Ground
The Squirrels Nursing Home
Coombe
Coombe Green
Coombe Wood
Foxburrow Wood
Foxburrows
Barrack Reservoir (disused)
Tooks Farm
Clapgate
Brentwood
Goldings
Fairstead
Warley Elms
Rectory
Ivy Lodge Farm
Ely Cott.
SHEPHERDS HILL
Pages Farm
Montrose
Tomkyns Manor
Riding Stables
Burnside
Great Readings
Tylers Croft
Four Wantz
Four Wantz Cottages
Emanuel Cottage
Greathouse
Chalkfield
Beredens Cotts.
HAVERING
Tyes Cottage
Sutton's Farm
Common Farm
Ashprington
Cornlands Farm
Great Tomkyns Farm
Great Tomkyns
Howard Farm
Emery Farm
Upminster
Upminster Lodge
RM14
Upminster Lodge Farm
Grays Cottages
Hole Farm
Normans
Norman's Cottages
Cricket Ground
Pavilion
Parker's Shaw
Works
Home Meadow
Nursery
Latchet's Shaw
Codham Hall Cottages
Hazle's Pottery Barn
Codham Hall
Hulmers
CODHAM HALL LANE
SOUTHEND ARTERIAL ROAD
A127
Rosary
Grasslands
Chapmans Farm
PANTILE COTTS.
BROOKMANS PARK DR.
Woodcroft Farm Woodlands
Codham Hall Wood
Tabrams Farm
Folkes Farm
FOLKES LANE
Oak Royal Nurseries
Jax Folly
Hobbs Hole
Play. Fld.
Sch.
Ingrebourne
RIVER DRIVE
Emerson Park School
Playing Field
Upminster Court
Tennis Courts
Upminster Hall Playing Fields
CRANHAM
Museum
UPMINSTER
QUEENS GDNS.
FAIRHOLME GDS.
ACACIA GDS.
LABURNHAM
Sd
Td
Ud
Vd
Wd
Xd
Yd
21
22
23
24
25
26
27
28
29
30
57
78
40
56
59
93
92
91
90
89
88
50

Brentwood High Sch. Play. Fld.
Shenfield Common
Three Arch Bridge
Sewage Works
Moat
Ingrave Hall
Zd
Ae
Be
Ce
De
Ee
Fe
41
Seven Arch Bridge
Skate Park
Club House
Min. Golf Course
Bowling Greens
King George's Playing Field
Pav.
INGRAVE
A128
ROAD
BRENTWOOD
Ingrave Common
Birches Wood
Heatleys
Sutton Shaw
Highfield Wood
21
22
23
24
25
26
27
28
29
30
BRENTWOOD GOLF COURSE
Octagon Lodge
Harts Wood
Dairy Farm
Golf Course
Salmond's Farm
Cemetery
Donkey Lane Plantation
INGRAVE
Long Plantation
Thorndon Hall
Kent's Wood
Barrack Wood
THORNDON COUNTRY PARK
Club House
Saw Mill
The Marillac Nursing Home
Lodge
Prim. Sch.
Ingrave Johnstone Play. Fld.
Hillcrest Nursery
Ckt. Grd.
Res. (cov.)
Fouchers Farm
Thorndon Countryside Centre
Chantry Chapel & Mausoleum
Devil's Head Plantation
Little Warley Common
Scrub Hill
Thorndon Country Park North
New Hall Pond
HERONGATE
THORNDON PARK GOLF COURSE
Long Plantation
Heron Ct. Farm
The Green
Brentwood Hard Court Tennis Club
Tennis Courts
Ellen's Wood
Thorndon Corner
Hatch House
Horse Pond
Rushy Piece
Little Warley Lodge
Home Farm
Park Home
Childerditch Wood
Hatch Farm
WARLEY PARK GOLF COURSE
BRENTWOOD
Clapgate Farm
Village Hall
LITTLE WARLEY
Blue House Farm
Club House
Roses Farm
Childerditch Pond
Menagerie Plantation
The Rookery
Thorndon Country Park South
WARLEY PARK GOLF COURSE
Virginia Nursery
The Old Shop
Old Hall Pond
Octagon Plantation
Childerditch
Hill Farm
CM13
Pigeon Mount
Mill Wood
CHILDERDITCH INDUSTRIAL PARK
Childerditch Hall
Jury Hill
Thick Shaw
Mangrove Cottages
St. Peter's Rectory
Barrett's Shaw
Woodlands School (Great Warley)
A127
Woodside Farm
Hollow Bottom Shaw
Straight Path Shaw
EAST HORNDON
Depot
SOUTHEND ARTERIAL ROAD
Round Shaw
Warley Hall Wood
Esporta Health and Fitness
West Horndon Prim. Sch.
West Horndon Playing Fields
Great Warley Hall
Little Warley Hall
Hall Lane Farm
Nuttys Farm
Prettigate Farm
Smallholding
WEST HORNDON
Hall
Engineering Works
HORNDON INDUSTRIAL PARK
Abattoir
Orchard Farm
UPMINSTER TRADING PARK
79
West Horndon
Lower Shaw

62
GERRARDS CROSS
Gerrards Cross Common
Memorial Cen.
The Gerrards Cross C of E School
Mill Wood
Gallows Wood
Woodhill
Gerrards Cross
Little Gallows Wood
M25
OXFORD ROAD
A40
AMERSHAM ROAD
A413
42
Greenacre
Collsels
Club House
Denham Golf Club
Bailey Hill
The Lodge
Grove Cott.
The Grove
Higher Denham
Tom William's Wood
Works
Comm. Cen.
Bradbury's Islands
Moorhouse Farm
El Sub Sta.
Sewage Works
Gasholder Station
Caps Wood
Council Offs.
Baker's Wood
Hedgerows Poultry Farm
Tatling End
Fulmer Corner
The Rancho
Gas Pipeline Station
SL9
St. Huberts
Felbrigg
St. Hubert's Home Farm
Prestwick Place
Little Prestwick
Old Prestwick
Prestwick Cottage
Naboth
Grayleigh
Fulmerfields
The Barn
Alderbourne Manor
Hollybush Cottages
Hollybush Farm
Mount Farm
RED HILL
Redhill Farm
Council Depot
Denham Mount
Maltmas Green
Gladwins Wood
Fish Pond
The Oldhouse Farm
Alderbrook
Hawk's Wood
Hawkswood
Broadspring Wood
Holly Bush
Hay's Wood
M40 MOTORWAY
FULMER
Furzeney
Furzeney Wood
Junction 16 (M25)
Junction 1a (M40)
M25 MOTORWAY
Fulmer House
Fulmer Hall
Fulmer Infant Sch.
Church Farm
Fulmer House Farm
Orchard Cottage
Alderbourne Arches
Rush Green
Gossams Wood
Rush Hill Farm
Durham House
Smallhold
Watersplash Farm
Alder Bourne
Slough
Penn Wood
Fernacres Farm
Brown's Wood
Field End Farm
Ways Farm
Oldhouse Wood
West Hill
Fulmer Rise Manor
The Spinney
Glen Erica
The Thatched Cott.
Home Wood
Parkspring Wood
Alderbourne Farm
Springfield Cottages
Saul's Farm
Home Farm
SOUTH
Cherry Orchard Farm
Blanchards Farm
Caravan Park
Kennels
Belle Farm
Long Coppice
Taidswood
Sevenhills Farm
Dromenagh Playing Field
Dromenagh Farm
Penn Wood
George's Field
Black Firs
Woodland Court
Mount Fidget
Mount Fidget Wood
Upton Ho.
Fulmer Common Ho.
SL3
Oakwood House
Fernacres Cottage
Langley Corner
Convent
Fulmer Common
Langley Common
Strawberry Wood
Heathfield Plantation
Pinewood Film Studios
The Clump
Iver
M25
Blacketts
Upton Plantation
Upton Lake
Upton Farm
Bowlers Plantation
Heatherden Hall
SL0
Broom Warren
Dellfield Fm.
Upton Wood
Spruce Wood
Sycamore Wood
Park Lodge Farm
Brackenwood
Ensbys
Dogkennel Field
Burners Cottage
Cuckoo Pen
Sandhole Wood
BLACK PARK COUNTRY PARK
Heathlands
IVER HEATH
Rowley Wood
Diamond Wood
Park Lodge
Rowleyfield Larches
Rowley Slip
Gallions Wood
Walk Wood
Blackpark Lake
Black Park Countryside Cen.
Warren Lodge
Warren House
Chandlers Hill
Ancoats Lodge
A412
CHURCH ROAD
DENHAM ROAD
SLOUGH ROAD
82
61
Spring Wood
Hollybush Wood
Rowley
Five Points
UXBRIDGE ROAD
South Lodge
A B C D E F G
31 32 33 34 35 36 37 38 39 40
500 01 02 03
88 87 86 185 84 83

63
43
64
83
Denham
DENHAM
NEW DENHAM
Uxbridge
UXBRIDGE
UXBRIDGE MOOR
HILLINGDON
ICKENHAM
Newyears Green
UB9
UB10
UB8
BUCKINGHAMSHIRE GOLF CLUB
DENHAM COUNTRY PARK
UXBRIDGE GOLF COURSE
HILLINGDON GOLF COURSE
HILLINGDON COURT PARK (Recreation Ground)
RAF UXBRIDGE
WILLOWBANK
Frays Valley Local Nature Reserve
Hillingdon Outdoor Activities Centre
Colne Valley Park Cen.
Hillingdon Athletics Stadium
Hillingdon Sports & Leisure Complex
Uxbridge Lido
Uxbridge Coll. (Uxbridge Campus)
West London Community College
Uxbridge Moor Nature Reserve
Junction 1
DENHAM ROUNDABOUT
SWAKELEYS ROUNDABOUT
WESTERN AVENUE
DENHAM AVENUE
OXFORD ROAD
DENHAM ROAD
HAREFIELD ROAD
PARK ROAD
COWLEY ROAD
HILLINGDON ROAD
HILLINGDON HILL
ST. JOHN'S RD.
ROCKINGHAM R.
SWAKELEYS ROAD
BREAKSPEAR ROAD
A40
A412
A4020
A4007
A408
B467
B483
M25
Grand Union Canal
River Colne
Frays River
Shire Ditch
Alder Bourne
Smallholdings
Southlands Manor
Mansfield Farm
Woodlands Park
Denham Place
Court Farm
Harvil Farm
Copthall Farm
Brackenbury Barn
Research Farm
Highway Farm
Dewes Farm
Savay Farm
Weatherlys Covert
Copthall Covert
Newyears Green Covert
Ivy House Farm
Brickfield Farm
Osborne Farm
Field Cottage
Watergate Fm.
Uxbridge Lock
Denham Lock

Newyears Green
Braemar Farm
Pylon Farm
Elm Tree Farm
High View Farm
St. Leonard's Farm
Crows Nest Farm
Old Clack Farm
UB9
The Corner
Tile Kiln
Grays Cottages
Research Farm
Dunster Cottage
Gatemead Farm
Brackenbury Barn
Moat
RUISLIP GOLF COURSE
WEST RUISLIP
Golf Driving Range
Whiteheath Jun. & Inf. Schs
Youth Cen. Wks.
Prim. Sch.
RUISLIP
Winston Churchill Hall
Manor Farm
Church Field Gdns.
BURY ST.
HIGH STREET
EASTCOTE RD.
B466
King's Coll. Play. Flds. Track
Eastcote Hockey & Badminton Club
Warrender Sch.
Highgrove Swim. Pool
Ruislip Manor
Ruislip
West Ruislip
Wealdstone FC (St. George's Stadium)
Sports Grd.
Ruislip Rugby Club
Sacred Heart Catholic Primary School
RUISLIP MANOR
Playing Field
Works
RUISLIP GARDENS
Ruislip Gardens
Ruislip Gardens Primary School
Ruislip High Sch.
WEST END RD.
A4180
Coptha Farm
SWAKELEYS
B467
ICKENHAM
Ickenham
Compass Theatre
Uxbridge
Swakeleys
Sports Ground
The Clump
Vyners School
Adult Learning Centre
Glebe Primary School
Ickenham Manor Play. Flds.
Long Lane Farm
UB10
Ickenham Marsh
Park Wood
WESTERN AVENUE
A40
Hillingdon
HILLINGDON CIRCUS
Motel
RAF NORTHOLT AERODROME
Playing Fields
Playing Field
Freezeland Covert
Yeading Brook
Cutthroat Wood
Gutteridge Wood
HILLINGDON COURT PARK (Recreation Ground)
Bowling Green
Tennis Courts
ACS Hillingdon Intern. Sch.
NORTH HILLINGDON
Ryefield Primary Sch.
Ten Acres
The Gorse
Westways Fm.
Lane Covert
Recreation Ground
Rugby Ground
Hare Plantation
Home Covert
Playing Fld.
Swakeleys School for Girls
Abbotsfield School
Children's Cen.
Comm. Cen.
Charville Prim. Sch.
Hedgewood School
Grosvenor Playing Field
Hayes
Canal Feeder
A437
LONG LANE
UXBRIDGE ROAD
HILLINGDON HILL
Coney Green

65
X
Y
Z
Aa
Ba
Ca
Da
45
85
31
32
33
34
35
36
37
38
39
40
EASTCOTE
Eastcote
Pinner
HA5
Rayners Lane
RAYNERS LANE
Harrow
WEST HARROW
West Harrow
Whitmore High Sch.
Whitmore Sports Cen.
Grange Schs.
ROXETH
South Harrow
SOUTH HARROW
Welldon Park First Sch.
HA2
Ruislip
HA4
SOUTH RUISLIP
South Ruislip
Cavendish Recreation Ground
Bessingby Playing Fields
Pine Gdns.
Bowling Green
Roxborough Rough
Roxbourne Park
Miniature Railway
Roxbourne First & Mid. Schs.
Recreation Ground
Field End Jun. & Inf. Schs.
Newton Farm First & Mid. Sch.
Newton Park West
Newton Ecology Park
Alexandra Sch.
Roxbourne Complex
Heathland Sch.
Rooks Heath Coll.
Cemetery
ALEXANDRA PARK
Harrow Borough FC (Earlsmead Stadium)
Northolt Pk.
Wood End
Deane Park
Deanesfield Prim. Sch.
Queensmead Sch.
Queensmead Sports Cen.
Goals Soccer Centre
Playing Fields
Victoria Retail Park
Warehouses
Solid Waste Transfer Station
Superstore
Depot
Works
ODYSSEY BUSINESS PARK
NORTHOLT PARK
Play Centre
Northolt High Sch.
Lord Halsbury Memorial Playing Flds.
Willow Tree Prim. Sch.
Islip Manor Park
Northolt
NORTHOLT
Bourne Prim. School
Sports Ground
Priors Fm.
POLISH WAR MEMORIAL
C&L GOLF COURSE
LIME TREES PARK GOLF COURSE
Northolt Prim. Sch.
John Chilton Sch.
West London Academy
TARGET ROUNDABOUT
Lime Tree Park
West End
Club House
Downe Barns Fm.
Moat
West London Shooting Grounds
NORTHALA FIELDS
RECTORY PARK (Recreation Ground)
NORTHOLT GOLF COURSE
Gifford Primary Sch.
Belvue Park
Smith's Farm
Ealing Driving Range
Health Club
GREENFORD INDUSTRIAL ESTATE
Greenford
UB6
GREENFORD
Youth & Comm. Cen.
Football Ground
WESTERN AVENUE
A40
A4090
A312
A4180
B455
ALEXANDRA AVENUE
IMPERIAL DRIVE
NORTHOLT ROAD
MANDEVILLE ROAD
CHURCH ROAD
WEST END ROAD
RUISLIP ROAD
VICTORIA ROAD
Yeading Brook
EALING
HILLINGDON
HARROW

HARROW
WEST HARROW
HARROW ON THE HILL
Harrow-on-the-Hill
ROXETH
SOUTH HARROW
South Harrow
NORTH WEMBLEY
SUDBURY
Sudbury Hill
Sudbury Hill Harrow
Sudbury & Harrow Road
Sudbury Town
Northwick Park
NORTHWICK PARK
Kenton
GREENFORD
Greenford
Greenford Green
PERIVALE
Perivale
South Greenford
Northolt
Wood End
UB6
UB5
HA1
HA2
PINNER RD.
LOWLANDS RD.
KENTON RD.
WATFORD ROAD
LOWER RD.
BESSBOROUGH RD.
SUDBURY HILL
SUDBURY COURT DR.
HARROW ROAD
EAST LANE
WHITTON AVENUE WEST
WHITTON AVENUE EAST
GREENFORD ROAD
WESTERN AVENUE
NORTHOLT ROAD
BRIDGEWATER RD.
GREENFORD ROUNDABOUT
NORTHWICK PK. ROUNDABOUT
GRAND UNION CANAL
TEIGNMOUTH GDNS.
University of Westminster (Harrow Campus)
NORTHWICK PARK HOSPITAL
ST. MARK'S HOSP.
Harrow School
Harrow School Playing Fields
HARROW CYGNET HOSPITAL
THE CLEMENTINE CHURCHILL BMI HOSPITAL
Vale Farm Sports Centre
HORSENDEN HILL GOLF COURSE
Horsenden Hill
SUDBURY GOLF COURSE
BERKELEY FIELDS
Perivale Wood Local Nature Reserve
Perivale Park Athletics Track
EALING GOLF COURSE
A404
A312
A4127
A4005
A4088
A4090
A40
B452

KINGSBURY
Kingsbury Green
FRYENT COUNTRY PARK (Local Nature Reserve)
Barn Hill Open Space
Barn Hill
PRESTON
Preston Road
John Billam Playing Fields
Preston Park Recreation Ground
Forty Farm Sports Grd.
Stanmore Junction
Wembley Park
HA9
WEMBLEY PK.
Wembley Arena
Wembley Stadium
Market
North Wembley
Wembley
KING EDWARD VII PARK
WEMBLEY
Wembley Central
TOKYNGTON
Sherrans Farm Open Space
Stonebridge Park
STONEBRIDGE
Brent Junction
Royal Mail Depot
Railway Works
Neasden Depot
NEASDEN JUNCTION
BRENT RESERVOIR
Wembley Sailing Club
Seahorse Sailing Club
CHURCH END
ALPERTON
Alperton
Metropolitan Police Traffic Unit
Alperton Sports Grd.
PARK ROYAL JUNCTION
GRAND UNION CANAL (Paddington Branch)
Lower Place
Harlesden
PARK ROYAL
CENTRAL MIDDLESEX HOSP.
MANHATTAN BUSINESS PARK
Twyford Abbey
FRYENT WAY
SALMON STREET
FORTY LANE
FORTY AVENUE
BLACKBIRD HILL
NEASDEN LA.
WEMBLEY PARK DR.
EMPIRE WAY
BRIDGE RD.
GREAT CENTRAL WAY
SOUTH WAY
HARROW ROAD
HIGH RD.
EALING RD.
HANGER LANE
NORTH CIRCULAR ROAD
BRENTFIELD
HILLSIDE
CRAVEN PK.
CHURCH LANE
ACTON LANE
A4140
A4088
A4089
A479
A404
A406
B4557
B4492
B456
Ma
Na
Pa
Qa
Ra
Sa
Ta
31
32
33
34
35
36
37
38
39
40
47
87

68
Ua
Va
Wa
Xa
Ya
Za
Ab
48
Kingsbury Green
Silver Jubilee Park
WEST HENDON PLAYING FIELDS
Cycle Track
Superstore
Tennis Courts
Pav. Bowling Green
Playground
Kingsbury Town FC Grd.
NW9
Cool Oak Bridge
Youth Sailing Base
WEST HENDON
Old Welsh Harp
Brent Bridge
M1
MOTORWAY
Junc. 1
HENDON
BROADWAY
A5
BRENT CROSS INTERCHANGE
BRENT CROSS SHOPPING CENTRE
Brent Cross
Leisure Cen.
Superstores
A41
A406
Brent Cross
GOLDERS
HENDON WAY
40
31
32
33
34
35
36
37
38
39
40
WOODFIELD PARK
Woodfield Sch.
Sports Ground
Rifle Range
Nursery
BRENT RESERVOIR
Welsh Harp (Brent Reservoir) Nature Reserve
Field Study Cen.
Wembley Sailing Club
Seahorse Sailing Club
Sports Ground
Neasden Recreation Ground
Playground
Youth & Comm. Cen.
JVC BUSINESS PARK
STAPLES CORNER
STAPLES CORNER RETAIL PARK
Cineworld Cinema
CIRCULAR
NORTH CIRCULAR ROAD
EDGWARE ROAD
CLAREMONT WAY INDUSTRIAL ESTATE
Clitterhouse Recreation Ground
Hendon FC (Claremont Rd.)
Brent Sidings
Depot
CRICKLEWOOD
Cricklewood
CRICKLEWOOD BROADWAY
Virgin Active
Bingo Hall
NEASDEN
Braintcroft Prim. Sch.
Academies & 6th Form Cen.
Arts Centre
Dollis Hill House
Tennis Courts
Putting Green
GLADSTONE PARK
DOLLIS HILL
Water Works
Dudding Hill Junction
Reservoir (Covered)
NW2
NEASDEN JUNCTION
DUDDEN HILL
GT. CENTRAL WAY
67
Superstores
Neasden
NEASDEN LANE
Dollis Hill
DUDDEN HILL
Willesden Green
CHURCH END
WILLESDEN
WILLESDEN NEW CEMETERY
Jewish Cemy.
HIGH ROAD
A407
WILLESDEN LANE
A4003
Hindu Temple
Mosque
SHOOT UP HILL
The Hope Cen.
WILLESDEN GREEN
Roundwood Park
Sports Ground
Willesden Cen. for Health & Care
CENTRAL MIDDLESEX HOSP.
Capital City Academy
Willesden Sports Stadium
Willesden Sports Cen.
King Edward VII Recreation Ground
BRONDESBURY PARK
Brondesbury Park
Queens Park Comm. Sch.
City Learning Cen.
HARLESDEN
Harlesden
CRAVEN PK
KENSAL RISE
Kensal Rise
QUEENS PARK
Bandstand
NW10
Power Station
Playing Field
Freightliner Depot
Willesden Junction
HARLESDEN ROAD
TUBBS RD
HARROW RD
KENSAL GREEN
KILBURN
MORTIMER
HARVIST
88
ACTON
21
22
23
24

69
GOLDERS GREEN
Golders Green Crematorium
HAMPSTEAD GOLF COURSE
HIGHGATE GOLF COURSE
HIGHGATE HOSPITAL
HIGHGATE
HARINGEY
N2
N6
NW5
NW3
NW6
NW8
NW1
NW11
HAMPSTEAD HEATH
Golders Green
Kenwood House
Caen Wood
KEN WOOD
GOLDERS HILL PARK
North End
VALE OF HEALTH
Jack Straw's Castle
Leg of Mutton Pond
West Heath
Ladies' Bathing Pond
Highgate Ponds
Men's Bathing Pond
PARLIAMENT HILL
Parliament Hill Fields
CHILD'S HILL
Childs Hill Park
HAMPSTEAD
Hampstead
Hampstead Ponds
Hampstead Heath
Fortune Green
Hampstead Cemetery
Sports Ground
THE ROYAL FREE HOSPITAL
University College School
Camden Arts Cen.
WEST HAMPSTEAD
West Hampstead
West Hampstead Thameslink
Finchley Rd. & Frognal
Finchley Rd.
Belsize Pk.
Gospel Oak
Chalk Farm
Swiss Cottage
South Hampstead
SOUTH HAMPSTEAD
Sigmund Freud Statue
Kilburn
Brondesbury
BRONDESBURY
KILBURN
Kilburn High Road
Kilburn Park
Queens Park
PRIMROSE HILL
Barrow Hill
St. John's Wood
ST. JOHN'S WOOD
Maida Vale
London Zoo
REGENT'S PARK
THE WELLINGTON HOSP.
London Central Mosque
Middlesex CCC (Lord's)
Paddington Cemetery
FINCHLEY ROAD
NORTH END ROAD
HAMPSTEAD LANE
SPANIARDS ROAD
HAVERSTOCK HILL
ABBEY ROAD
MAIDA VALE
PRINCE ALBERT ROAD
WELLINGTON RD.
ADELAIDE ROAD
FITZJOHN'S AV.
ROSSLYN HILL
A41
A502
A598
A407
B519
B509
B510
B511
49
70
89
214
215

70
Jb
Kb
Lb
Mb
Nb
Pb
Qb
50
215
216
217
90
69
31
32
33
34
35
36
37
38
39
40
HIGHGATE
Highgate
CROUCH END
STROUD GREEN
Crouch Hill
HAMPSTEAD LANE
HIGHGATE HIGH ST.
HIGHGATE CEMETERY
WATERLOW PARK
Archway
WHITTINGTON HOSPITAL
Finsbury Park
UPPER HOLLOWAY
Upper Holloway
DARTMOUTH PARK
PARLIAMENT HILL
HOLLOWAY
TUFNELL PARK
Tufnell Pk.
Gospel Oak
GOSPEL OAK
KENTISH TOWN
Kentish Town
Kentish Town W.
Arsenal
Arsenal FC (Emirates Stadium)
Ashburton Grove
Drayton Pk.
Holloway Rd.
LOWER HOLLOWAY
HMP HOLLOWAY
Caledonian Rd.
Caledonian Park
HMP PENTONVILLE
BARNSBURY
Caledonian Rd & Barnsbury
Chalk Farm
PRIMROSE HILL
CAMDEN TOWN
Camden Town
Camden Rd.
Central St. Martins College of Arts and Design
COPENHAGEN
KING'S CROSS
ST. PANCRAS INTERNATIONAL
PENTONVILLE
REGENT'S PARK
Mornington Cres
SOMERS TOWN
British Library
EUSTON
FINSBURY
London Zoo
PRINCE ALBERT ROAD
REGENT'S PARK

Harringay Green Lanes
Manor House
FINSBURY PARK
EAST RESERVOIR
WEST RESERVOIR
West Reservoir Centre
The Castle Climbing Cen.
Sir Thomas Abney Prim. Sch.
Stamford Hill
AMHURST PARK
CLAPTON COMMON
STAMFORD HILL
UPPER CLAPTON
SPRINGFIELD PARK
Walthamstow Marsh Nature Reserve
Coppermill Bridge
Clapton Junction
WARWICK RESERVOIR (WEST)
BROWNSWOOD PARK
CLISSOLD PARK
Abney Park Cemetery (Local Nature Reserve)
STOKE NEWINGTON
Stoke Newington
Rectory Road
North Millfields Recreation Ground
Clapton
South Millfields Rec. Gd.
SHACKLEWELL
LOWER CLAPTON
HACKNEY DOWNS
Mossbourne Community Academy
HIGHBURY
Highbury Pool
Canonbury
CANONBURY
Dalston Kingsland
Hackney Downs
Hackney Cen.
Dalston Junc.
BALLS POND RD.
GRAHAM ROAD
KINGSLAND
DALSTON
HACKNEY
London Fields
LONDON FIELDS
Essex Rd.
ISLINGTON
DE BEAUVOIR TOWN
Haggerston
HAGGERSTON
Hackney City Farm
Cambridge Heath
Britannia Centre
Shoreditch Park
HOXTON
Hoxton
SHORED
Angel
CITY RD.
GOSWELL RD.
Rb
Sb
Tb
Ub
Vb
Wb
Xb
31
32
33
34
35
36
37
38
39
40
51
72
91
218
219

REDBRIDGE
WANSTEAD
EASTERN AVENUE
VALENTINES PARK
Valentines Mansion & Gardens
CRANBROOK
CRANBROOK RD.
WANSTEAD PARK
ILFORD GOLF COURSE
River Roding
CITY OF LONDON CEMETERY
City of London Crematorium
SOUTH WOODFORD TO BARKING RELIEF ROAD
NORTH CIRCULAR ROAD
ALDERSBROOK RD.
FOREST DRIVE
MANOR PARK
Manor Park
ILFORD
Ilford
ILFORD HILL
ILFORD LANE
HIGH ROAD
WINSTON WY.
GREEN LANE
SEVEN KINGS
Seven Kings
Ilford FC (Cricklefield Stadium)
SOUTH PARK
LITTLE ILFORD
LITTLE ILFORD LA.
ROMFORD RD.
HIGH STREET NORTH
LOXFORD
LOXFORD PARK
BARKING PARK
FAIR CROSS
LONGBRIDGE RD.
FANSHAWE AV.
PLASHET
Plashet Jewish Cemetery
PLASHET PARK
EAST AV.
East Ham
BARKING
Barking
NORTHERN RELIEF RD.
Barking Abbey
RIPPLE RD.
ABBEY RD.
LONDON RD.
HIGHBRIDGE RD.
Wallend
Langdon School
Flanders Playing Fields
EAST HAM
CENTRAL PARK
UPTON PARK
BARKING RD.
RON LEIGHTON WAY
CENTRAL PARK RD.
RANCLIFFE RD.
Refuse & Sewage Works
Cuckold's Haven
Showcase Cinema
Hollywood Bowl
ALFRED'S WAY
EAST HAM & BARKING BY-PASS
Nc
Pc
Qc
Rc
Sc
Tc
Uc
54
73
94
IG1
IG2
E12
E6

SEVEN KINGS PARK
SEVEN KINGS
CHADWELL HEATH
Chadwell Heath
Goodmayes
GOODMAYES
GOODMAYES PARK
BEACONTREE HEATH
BECONTREE
VALENCE PARK
Valence Ho. Mus.
PARSLOES PARK
DAGENHAM
Dagenham
Dagenham Heathway
Becontree
Upney
MAYESBROOK PARK
CASTLE GREEN
Rippleside
Dagenham Dock
Romford
RM6
RM8
RM9
IG3
HIGH ROAD
GREEN LANE
LONGBRIDGE ROAD
GOODMAYES ROAD
BARLEY LANE
WOOD LANE
BENNETT'S CASTLE LANE
WHALEBONE LANE NORTH
WHALEBONE LANE SOUTH
HEATHWAY
PORTERS AVENUE
LODGE AVENUE
RIPPLE ROAD
THAMES ROAD
GATEWAY
BECONTREE AVENUE
VALENCE AVENUE
LODGE AVENUE FLYOVER JUNC.
GORESBROOK INTERCHANGE
West Ham FC Training Grd.
Chadwell Heath Industrial Park
Eldenwall Industrial Estate
Mayesbrook Park Arena
Barking & East Ham United FC
Goresbrook Leisure Centre
Scrattons Farm Eco-Park
Ripple Lane Sidings
High Speed 1
BARKING and DAGENHAM
Vc
Wc
Xc
Yc
Zc
Ad
Bd
55
95
31
32
33
34
35
36
37
38
39
40
76
46
47
48
49

78
58
98
Junction 29
M25
M25-MOTORWAY
UPMINSTER
CRANHAM
HAVERING
Upminster
RM14
NORTH OCKENDON
SOUTH OCKENDON
CORBETS TEY
Emerson Park School
Playing Field
UPMINSTER GOLF COURSE
Upminster Court
Upminster Hall Playing Fields
Tennis Courts
Museum
Club House
Bowl. Grn.
Playing Field
Hall Mead School
Hall Lane Miniature Golf Course
Cranham Brickfields Local Nature Reserve
Franks Wood
Franks Farm
Puddle Dock
Westbury Farm
Depot
Upminster
Upminster Windmill
Cranham Court
Club House
CRANHAM GOLF COURSE
The James Oglethorpe Prim. Sch.
Coopers' Company & Coborn Sch.
Playing Field
Clockhouse Gdns.
UPMINSTER PARK
Tennis Courts
Pavilion
Cranham Hall
Cranham Marsh Local Nature Reserve
Thames Chase Forest Centre
Clay Tye Farm
Claynes House
Clay Tye Hill
Hobbs Hole
Spring Wood
Middle Wood
Bonus Wood
Playing Field
Gaynes School Language College
South Essex Crematorium
Upminster Cemetery
Redcrofts Farm
Parklands School
Oakfields Montessori Sch.
The Lodge
Weir Open Space
Great Sunnings
Gay's Cottages
Sullens Farm
Russells Lake
Stubbers Lodge
Stubbers Adventure Centre
Coys Lake
Caravan Site
Manor Farm
Manor Farm Cottages
Bridge Cottages
Cranham Place
Remembrance Cottages
Rectory
Hall Farm
Elec. Sub. Sta.
Kennels
White Post Farm
Groves Farm Cottage
Dennises Cottages
Central Farm
New House
Goresbrook Park
Llantrisant Oaks
Greenacres
Bush Farm
Damyn's Hall
Damyn's Hall Cotts.
Bramble Farm
Sand & Gravel Pit
Freeman's Shaw
Kemps Farm
Moat
Hunt's Hill Cottages
Hunt's Hill Farm
Cockhide
Warwick Wood
White Post Wood
Benyon Prim. Sch.
Ockendon
Jax Folly
Superstore
ST. MARY'S LANE
OCKENDON ROAD
B187
B1421
B186
CLAY TYE ROAD
PIKE LANE
PEA LANE
DENNISES LANE
STUBBERS LANE
SUNNINGS LANE
BRAMBLE LANE
ROMFORD ROAD
DENNIS ROAD
WEST ROAD
CORBETS TEY RD.
HARWOOD HALL LANE
AVELEY ROAD
INGREBOURNE GARDENS
PARK DRIVE
HALL LANE
STATION ROAD
Sd
Td
Ud
Vd
Wd
Xd
Yd
31
32
33
34
35
36
37
38
39
40
56
57
58
59
83
84
85
86
87
88

Smallholding
Abattoir
Orchard Farm
Engineering Works
HORNDON INDUSTRIAL PARK
59
Zd
Ae
Be
Ce
De
Ee
Fe
West Horndon
WEST HORNDON
Lower Shaw
LITTLE WARLEY HALL LANE
WARLEY HALL LA.
CHILDERDITCH LANE
ST. MARY'S LANE
DUNNINGS LANE
B186
STREET
Monks Farm
Old England
Little Tillingham Hall
Brentwood
Moat
Tillingham Hall
Field House
CM13
Clay Tye Wood
Sewage Works
Bury Farm
Grid Sta.
Fairplay Farm
Slough House
CHINA LANE
Hatch Farm
Bullens & Herds
Blankets Farm
Mar Dyke
Caylock's Farm
Home Farm
Stone Hall
FEN LANE
Corner Farm
The Orchard
Club House
TOP MEADOW GOLF COURSE
Fen Farm
HARROW LANE
Judds Farm
Bulphan Fen
The Downes
Redcrofts
THURROCK
Stringcock Fen
Groves Cottages
Groves Farm
Groves Barns
The Wilderness
ROAD
B186 ROAD
South Ockendon
RM15
South Ockendon Hall
HALL LANE
ORSETT FEN
Reservoir
Moat
Bowling Green
Tennis Courts
Rec. Grd.
99
60
61
62
63
88
87
86
85
84
83
31
32
33
34
35
36
37
38
39
40

60
102
FARNHAM ROYAL
BRITWELL
LYNCH HILL
BURNHAM
LENT
LENT RISE
CIPPENHAM
Maidenhead
SL6
SL1
SL4
Slough
Windsor
SOUTH BUCKS
DORNEY
LAKE END
ETON WICK
ETON LITTLE COMMON
ETON GREAT COMMON
DORNEY COMMON
DORNEY LAKE
Dorney Lake Park & Nature Reserve
ROYAL WINDSOR
Junction 6
Junction 7
M4 MOTORWAY
BATH ROAD
A4
A355
A332
B3026
B416
FARNHAM ROAD
TUNS LANE
WINDSOR & ETON RELIEF RD.
Burnham
Cherry Orchard
Recreation Ground
Court Farm
Britwell House
Grenville Court
Cocksherd Wood
Elm Cottages
Deepwood
The Spinney
Kennedy Park Recreation Ground
Reservoirs (covered)
Claycots School
Burnham Grammar Sch.
Burnham Park
Slough Trading Estate
Slough Industrial Estate
Cippenham Green
Mercian Way Rec. Grd.
Maidenhead Huntercombe Hospital
Burnham Abbey
Pondleys Cottage
Lake-end Fm.
Sludge Beds
Filter Beds
Water Pollution Control Works
Pipe Line Station
JUBILEE RIVER
Weir
Roundmoor Ditch
Eton Common Farm
Manor Farm
Saddocks Farm
Long Close
Woodpeckers
Court Farm
Pigeonhouse Farm
Riding School
Elm Farm Bungalow
Stamford
Cress Brook
Boveney Ditch
Eton Wick Rec.Grd.
Crown Farm
The Bungalow
Colenorton Brook
Chalvey Ditch
Montem Primary Sch.
The Westgate Sch.
Farnham Court
St. Anthony's Catholic Prim. Sch.
Beechwood & Arbour Vale Schools
Sports Field
NORTH FIELD
SOUTH FIELD
Masters Field
Water Jump
Athens
A B C D E F G
1 2 3 4 5 6 7 8 9 10

81
61
103
82
SOUTH BUCKS
SL2
SL3
STOKE POGES GOLF COURSE
Spa SPC
Club House
Stoke Park Hotel
Stoke Park Fm.
Manor House
The Clock
Gardens of Remembrance
Gray's Field
Monument
Appletons
Sports Ground
Tennis Courts
Duffield Ho.
Stoke Ho.
STOKE GREEN
Park View
Cricket Grd.
Stoke Place
Nuffield Health Fitness & Wellbeing Cen.
Berry Farm
WEXHAM PARK GOLF COURSE
Grotes Wood
Gallions Wood
Rowleyfield
Rowley
Walk Wood
Spring Wood
Hollybush
Pinewood Nurseries
Green Acres
Bell Fm.
Jubilee Plantation
Rowley Lake
WEXHAM PARK HOSPITAL
John Lister Postgraduate Centre
Wexham
Wexham Sch.
Stone's Wood
Langley Furze
Wexham Court
Wood School
MANOR PARK
Alderbourne
Little Haven
Pinehurst
Oakwood Ho.
Broom Ho.
LANES GOLF COURSE
Driving Range
Club House
Stokeplace Farm
The Park Driving Range
Wexham Park Stadium
Khalsa Prim. Sch.
West Wing Arts Cen.
Slough Crematorium
CEMETERY
Granville Playing Field
Baylis Court Sch.
Godolphin Playing Field
James Elliman Prim. Sch.
Baylis Grds.
GEORGE GREEN
Masons Fm.
Home Farm
The Manor House
Nursery
Grove Fm.
Lavender Farm
Wildcroft
MIDDLE GREEN
The Langley Manor School
Rec. Grd.
Bowyer Play. Fld.
GRAND UNION CANAL
Thomas Gray Cen.
Sports Grd.
Factory
Salt Hill
Salt Hill Pleasure Ground
Absolutely Ten Pin
University of West London
SLOUGH
Slough Superstore
Bus Sta.
Gas Works
THE BUSINESS VILLAGE
Recreation Ground
Burial Gd.
St. Bernard's Prep. Sch.
Superstore
Sorting Office
Empire Cin.
Health Club
Ice Arena
Town Hall
Gala Bingo
Montem Leisure Cen.
County & Mag. Ct.
UPTON HOSP.
CHALVEY
College
Powerleague Soccer Centre
Upton Park
Herschel Park
The Mere
UPTON
Lascelles Playing Fields
Tennis Courts
Long Close Sch.
Upton Court Farm
Spring Cott.
Playing Field
School
Sports Field
Kedermister Park
Agars Plough (Playing Fields)
Cricket Ground
Broadbent House
Beggar's Bri.
ETON
Running Track
Thames Valley Athletics Cen.
Myrke
UPTON COURT PARK
Pumping Station
Hockey Pitch
Recreation Ground
Longmead Bridge
DITTON
Evans Cott.
Gibraltar Bridge
King's Oak
Offices
Fifteen Arch Bri.
Sixpenny or The Field
Fellow's Pond
Cricket Ground
The Playing Fields
Boathouse Cott.
Landing Stage
Reservoir (covered)
Datchet Mead Cottage
Black Potts
THE HOME PARK
Tennis Courts
Eton End School
College Field
WINDSOR and MAIDENHEAD
M4 MOTORWAY
A4
A412
A332
B416
B376
B3022
B3026
LONDON ROAD
UXBRIDGE RD.
WELLINGTON ST.
STOKE ROAD
STOKE POGES LANE
WEXHAM ROAD
DATCHET ROAD
WINDSOR ROAD
SLOUGH ROAD
ETON ROAD
POCOCKS LANE
BAYLIS RD.
FARNHAM ROAD
HIGH STREET
UPTON COURT ROAD
LANGLEY RD.
MIDDLEGREEN ROAD
SUSSEX PLACE

A
B
C
D
E
F
G
62
Rowleyfield
Gallions Wood
Rowley Slip
Walk Wood
Black Park Countryside Cen.
Sawmill Cotts.
BLACK PARK
COUNTRY PARK
Warren Lodge
Warren House
Club
Warren Ho. Fm.
Pav.
CHURCH RD.
SLOUGH ROAD
A412
A4007
Five Points
Fernleigh
Play. Sch. Fld.
IVER HEATH
Ancoats Lodge
South Lodge
Chandlers Hill
Spring Wood
Hollybush Wood
Rowley Farm
Rowley Lake
Jubilee Plantation
Deodar Wood
Column Larches
Temple Grange
Tennis Courts
Sports Ground
Leslie Lodge
Tudors
Homefield
HARDINGS ROW
COOPERS ROW
Home Cottage
Norwood Grange
Bangors Park Farm
Bangors Park
NORWOOD LANE
Clovelly
Nursery
41
42
43
44
45
46
47
48
49
50
WEXHAM PARK LANE
Barry's Plantation
LANGLEY PARK COUNTRY PARK
Roughground Wood
Evreham Adult Learning Cen.
Evreham Sports Centre
Tennis Cts.
Ankerdine
82
Stone's Wood
Langley Furze
UXBRIDGE ROAD
Ashen Cross
BELLSWOOD LANE
Treal Farm
Calves Lane Farm
Riding School
St. John's
Wood Lane Fm.
Heath Lodge
Stables
Love Green
Love Green Farm
Langley Park
Cedar House
The Orchards
SOUTH BUCKS
CORONATION
Play Fld.
HIGH ROAD
B470
SHREDING GREEN
Iver Grove
HOLLYBUSH LANE
Shreding Green Farm
Recreation Ground
Playgrd.
81
Masons Fm.
GEORGE GREEN
Rec. Grd.
Park Stile
Love Hill House Fm.
Slough
Larkfields
Iver
Home Farm
Convent of Our Lady Queen of Apostles
SL3
Devon Ct.
Poultry Farm & Piggery
Warehouses
Nursery
81
The Manor House
St. Paul's House
PARK
Moat Ho.
IVER GOLF COURSE
SL0
Grove Fm.
Wildcroft
MIDDLE GREEN
Southend Farm
ORCHARDS RESIDENTIAL PARK
Moat
Driving Range
Club House
DUDLEY WHARF CARAVANS
Dudley Wharf
Sawyers Green Farm
GRAND UNION CANAL
(SLOUGH ARM)
The Langley Manor School
80
MIDDLEGREEN TRAD. EST.
CHANCERYGATE BUSINESS CEN.
DESERONTO TRADING EST.
MARISH WHARF
LANGLEY PARK
LANGLEY BUSINESS PARK
Works
Langley
MANSION CARAVAN SITE
Works
BATHURST
Chequer Bridge
Withy Bridge
LANGLEY BUS. CEN.
East Berkshire College (Langley Campus)
Hall
Comm. Cen.
STATION RD.
RICHINGS PARK
Play. Fld.
Sports Field
The Langley Academy
Memorial Grd.
School
LANGLEY
Sch.
Play. Fld.
NORTH PARK
79
Kedermister Park
Playground
School
Playing Field
Langley Leisure Cen.
Harvey Pk. (Rec. Grd.)
AXIS PARK
Sutton Court Farm
Home Wood
Club Ho.
Weir
Percy Lodge
RICHINGS PARK GOLF COURSE
LONDON ROAD
A4
Marlborough School
Sch.
Rec. Grd.
Sutton
Mid Sutton
Little Sutton
Oak Plantation
Sports Grd.
Evans Cott.
Mayes Cott.
HIGH ST.
Junction 5
LANGLEY ROUNDABOUT
Sub.
Hotel
M4 MOTORWAY
M4
70
Sutton End Farm
Old Wood
DITTON PARK
78
Creak Cott.
Canal
King's Oak
Offices
Langley Gate
Ditton Fm.
104
LONDON ROAD
500
01
02
03

83
63
84
105
M25
M25-MOTORWAY
M4-MOTORWAY
M4
Junction 15 (M25)
Junction 4b (M4)
Uxbridge UB8
Woodlands Park
Moorwards Cottage
Palmer's Moor Farm
Delaford Manor
Coppins Fm.
Lower Delaford
Iver Lodge
Delaford Park
HUNTSMOOR PARK
Huntsmoor Park Fm.
North Lodge
Yacht Club
Farlows Lake
Sewage Works
Iver Water Treatment Works
Airport Parking
IVER
Iver
THORNEY PARK GOLF COURSE
THORNEY
Mercers Farm
THORNEY COUNTRY PARK
Thorney Pool
Frays Island & Mabey's Meadow Nature Reserve
Old Slade Lake
Iver South SDW
New Wood
Arboretum
Warehouses
Home Farm
Picnic Area
Manor Court
Great Barn
COWLEY
Cowley Lake
Little Britain
Little Britain Lake
Packet Boat Marina
Aqueduct
YIEWSLEY
HILLINGDON
WEST DRAYTON
West Drayton
UB7
Brunel University (Uxbridge Campus)
Halls of Residence
Athletics Centre
Uxbridge High Sch.
Hillingdon Cem.
Uxbridge Cem.
HILLINGDON GOLF COURSE
Bishopshalt School
Brunel Uni. Sports Park
The Grove Nature Reserve
Pield Heath House RC Sch.
PIELD HEATH
COWLEY PEACHEY
HILLINGDON HOSPITAL
COLHAM GREEN
Stockley Academy
STOCKLEY COUNTRY PARK
Uxbridge FC
Recreation Ground
Stockley Park
West Drayton Prim. Sch.
Drayton Hall
St. Georges Meadow
Laurel Lane Prim. Sch.
Cricket Grd.
Playing Field
Cherry La. Prim. Sch.
Heathrow Primary School
Nursery
Hotel
HIGH ST.
A408
A4020
A3044
B470
HARLINGTON RD.
FALLING LANE
STATION ROAD
PIELD ROAD
HOLLOWAY LANE
HARMONDSWORTH
SIPSON RD.
IVER STREET
THORNEY MILL
COLHAM MILL
TROUT LANE
PACKET BOAT LANE
GRAND UNION CANAL
River Colne
River Pinn
Wraysbury River
H J K L M N P
04 05 06 07
83 82 81 80 79 78
40 41 42 43 44 45 46 47 48 49 50

84
64
83
106
HILLINGDON
HILLINGDON HEATH
COLHAM GREEN
HILLINGDON HOSPITAL
HAYES END
WOOD END GREEN
WOOD END
HAYES
HAYES TOWN
Hayes & Harlington
HARLINGTON
Goulds Green
West Drayton
UB10
UB8
UB7
UB4
UB3
UB11
Hayes
Uxbridge
HILLINGDON
Stockley Park
STOCKLEY COUNTRY PARK
STOCKLEY PARK GOLF COURSE
HEATHPARK GOLF COURSE
Bourne Farm Playing Field
Lake Farm Country Park
Cherry Lane Roundabout
Junction 4
M4-MOTORWAY
M4
GRAND UNION CANAL
UXBRIDGE ROAD
HARLINGTON ROAD
STOCKLEY ROAD
WEST DRAYTON ROAD
DAWLEY ROAD
NORTH HYDE ROAD
HIGH STREET
STATION RD
KINGSHILL DRIVE
Yeading Brook Meadows Nature Reserve
Grosvenor Playing Field
Hedgewood School
Hayes Park
Mellow Lane Farm
Rosedale College
Uxbridge FC
Bishopshalt School
Pinkwell Prim. Sch.
Harlington Community Sch.
Heathrow Primary School
Sipson Meadow
Little Harlington Field
CRANFORD PARK
Q
R
S
T
U
V
W
41
42
43
44
45
46
47
48
49
50
07
08
09
510
78
79
80
81
82
83

Northolt
GREENFORD
YEADING
SOUTHALL
Southall
DORMER'S WELLS
NORWOOD GREEN
OSTERLEY PARK
Hounslow
RECTORY PARK (Recreation Ground)
RAVENOR PARK
GREENFORD PARK CEMETERY
King George's Field
Jubilee Park
Public Open Space
Playing Field
Willowtree Marina
Southall Park
WEST MIDDLESEX GOLF COURSE
MINET COUNTRY PARK
AIRLINKS GOLF COURSE
Glade Lane Canalside Park
London Motorcycle Museum
Hillingdon Cycling Circuit
Goals Soccer Centre (Hayes)
Guru Nanak Sikh Prim. & Secondary Schools
Hayes & Yeading Utd. FC (The Warren)
Heston Service Area
Junction 3
M4 MOTORWAY
RUISLIP ROAD
BROADWAY
HIGH ST.
UXBRIDGE ROAD
SOUTH ROAD
MERRICK ROAD
NORWOOD ROAD
TENTELOW LANE
GREENFORD ROAD
THE PARKWAY
GRAND UNION CANAL
GRAND UNION CANAL (PADDINGTON BRANCH)
A312
A4020
A3005
A4127
B455
UB5
UB6
UB1
UB2
TW5
X
Y
Z
Aa
Ba
Ca
Da
41
42
43
44
45
46
47
48
49
50
65
98
107

86
66
85
108
GREENFORD ROUNDABOUT
GREENFORD
Perivale
South Greenford
Perivale Park Athletics Track
PERIVALE PARK
PERIVALE PARK GOLF COURSE
UB6
WESTERN AVENUE
A40
EALING GOLF COURSE
Gurnell Leisure Cen.
Pitshanger Park
RUISLIP ROAD
RUISLIP ROAD EAST
B455
B452
ARGYLE ROAD
SCOTCH COMMON
CASTLEBAR HILL
Castle Bar Pk.
Elthorne Heights
Greenford Bridge
Cardinal Wiseman RC Sch.
Hanwell Community Centre
BRENT VALLEY GOLF COURSE
Brent Lodge Park
Millennium Maze
River Brent
Drayton Green
West Ealing
EALING
WEST EALING
UB1
W7
DORMER'S WELLS
WEST MIDDLESEX GOLF COURSE
GREENFORD ROAD
A4127
UXBRIDGE ROAD
A4020
Hanwell
HANWELL
BROADWAY
City of Westminster Cemetery
Kensington Cemetery
ST. BERNARD'S HOSPITAL
EALING HOSP.
Meadow Ho. Hospice
Hanwell Locks
Southall
Windmill Bridge
WINDMILL LANE
B454
Warren Farm Sports Centre
GRAND UNION CANAL
Osterley Sports Club
Glade Lane Canalside Park
TENTELOW LANE
UB2
OSTERLEY
BOSTON ROAD
A3002
Northfields
NORTHFIELD AVENUE
Blondin Pk. & Nature Area
Boston Manor
BOSTON MANOR ROAD
Boston Manor Park
Boston Manor House
M4
M4 MOTORWAY
HOUNSLOW
Isleworth
TW7
OSTERLEY LANE
Osterley Park House
Osterley Park Farm
PARK
WYKE GREEN GOLF COURSE
Trumpers Wood
Long Wood
Gallows Bridge
Grand Union Canal Warehouse
Clitheroe's Lock
Gunnersbury Catholic Sch.
Walpole Park
LAMMAS PARK
The Questors Theatre
Ealing Abbey
Ealing Coll.
Pitshanger
Ea
Fa
Ga
Ha
Ja
Ka
La
41
42
43
44
45
46
47
48
49
50

Metropolitan Police Traffic Unit
Alperton Sports Grd.
Ma
Na
Pa
Qa
Ra
Sa
Ta
67
Lower Place
GRAND UNION CANAL (Paddington Branch)
Twyford Abbey Prim. Sch.
PARK ROYAL
CENTRAL MIDDLESEX HOSPITAL
Power Station
Grand Union Canal
Freightliner Depot
41
42
43
44
45
46
47
48
49
50
Hanger La.
HANGER LANE
WESTERN AVENUE
Park Royal
Pitch & Putt Course
Hanger Hill
Fox Wood Nature Reserve
NORTH ACTON
North Acton
Tenpin Cinema
West Acton
NORTH ACTON PLAYING FIELDS
GYPSY CORNER
WALES FARM RD.
VICTORIA ROAD
Nth. Ealing
Acton Main Line
EALING CYGNET HOSP.
St. Augustine Priory (Sch.)
Barclays Bank Sports Ground
Cricket Ground
W5
W3
HAVEN GRN.
Ealing Squash & Fitness Club
Ealing Broadway
THE BROADWAY
THE MALL
UXBRIDGE ROAD
EALING COMN.
Ealing Common
GUNNERSBURY LANE
HORN LANE
STEYNE RD.
HIGH ST.
THE VALE
A4020
ACTON
Japanese Sch. London
Sports Ground
EAST ACTON
Acton Central
ACTON PARK
Maples Children's Cen.
88
The Park Club
Thames Valley Uni.
The Falcons Sch. for Girls
Grange Primary School
Popefield Playing Flds.
London Transport Mus. Depot
Reynolds Sports Cen.
Acton Town
SOUTH ACTON
South Acton
ACTON GREEN
SOUTHFIELD RD.
Southfields Rec. Grd.
BEDFORD PARK
GUNNERSBURY PARK
Gunnersbury Park Mus.
Boating Lake
GUNNERSBURY PARK
HOUNSLOW
Miniature Golf Course
International Sch. of London
Kensington Cemetery
Potomac (Fish Pond)
Little Ealing
South Ealing Cemetery
CLAYPONDS HOSP.
POPES LANE
SOUTH EALING ROAD
GUNNERSBURY
Esporta Health Club Chiswick Park
Chiswick Pk.
Acton Sports Club
CHISWICK HIGH ROAD
Gunnersbury
HEATHFIELD TER.
TURNHAM GREEN
Chiswick Common
SOUTH PARADE
M4
M4 MOTORWAY
Junc. 2
Junc. 1
Kew Bridge
WELLESLEY RD.
Brentford Fountain Leis. Cen.
Steam Mus.
The Musical Mus.
Brentford FC (Griffin Pk.)
KEW BRIDGE
HIGH ST.
GT. WEST RD.
CEDARS RD.
ELLESMERE RD.
A4 HOGARTH RD.
109
Kew Pier
Strand on the Green
CHISWICK

88
68
87
110
Ua
Va
Wa
Xa
Ya
Za
Ab
41
42
43
44
45
46
47
48
49
50
NW10
W3
W4
W6
W12
W10
KENSAL RISE
Kensal Rise
KENSAL GREEN
Kensal Green
KENSAL TOWN
HARLESDEN
Willesden Junction
COLLEGE PARK
NORTH ACTON
North Acton
OLD OAK COMMON
North Pole International Depot
WORMWOOD SCRUBS PARK
(Local Nature Reserve)
OLD OAK COMMON
Linford Christie Stadium
HAMMERSMITH HOSP.
QUEEN CHARLOTTE'S &
CHELSEA HOSP.
(Imperial College London)
HMP WORMWOOD SCRUBS
Little Wormwood Scrubs Rec. Grd.
ST. MARY'S RC CEMETERY
KENSAL GREEN CEMETERY
West London Crematorium
Grand Union Canal
Freightliner Depot
NORTH KENSINGTON
ST. CHARLES HOSPITAL
Carmelite Monastery
Athlone Gds.
Ladbroke Gro.
Latimer Rd.
White City
White City
WHITE CITY
Wood La.
BBC Television Centre
QPR FC (Loftus Rd.)
East Acton
EAST ACTON
SAVOY CIRCUS
Acton Cen.
ACTON PARK
Shepherd's Bush Mkt.
SHEPHERD'S BUSH
Shepherd's Bush
Shepherd's Bush Common
HOLLAND PARK
Goldhawk Rd.
Kensington Olympia
Olympia
SOUTHFIELD
BEDFORD PARK
Ravenscourt Park
Ravenscourt Park
Stamford Brook
Turnham Green
CHISWICK
TURNHAM GREEN
Hammersmith
HAMMERSMITH
HAMMERSMITH FLYOVER
Brook Green
WEST KENSINGTON
Barons Court
Barons Court
The Queen's Club
Hammersmith Cemetery
CHARING CROSS HOSP.
Riverside Studios
RIVER THAMES
Hammersmith Pier
Chiswick Eyot
Homefield Recreation Ground
WESTERN AVENUE
WESTWAY
UXBRIDGE ROAD
THE VALE
GOLDHAWK ROAD
KING ST.
GREAT WEST ROAD
TALGARTH RD.
HOLLAND ROAD
WOOD LANE
SCRUBS LANE
HARROW ROAD
LADBROKE GROVE
OLD OAK LANE
VICTORIA ROAD
WEST CROSS ROUTE
SHEPHERD'S BUSH ROAD
FULHAM PALACE RD.
CHISWICK HIGH RD.
SOUTH PARADE
BATH RD.
THE AVENUE
ELLESMERE RD.
HOGARTH

REGENT'S PARK
NW1
Queen Mary's Gardens
Boating Lake
London Central Mosque
Winfield House
MARYLEBONE
Baker St.
Madame Tussaud's
Wallace Collection
St. John's Wood
Middlesex CCC (Lord's)
The Wellington Hosp.
Maida Vale
ST. JOHN'S WOOD
MAIDA VALE
MAIDA HILL
WEST KILBURN
Queens Park
CARLTON VALE
WESTBOURNE GREEN
Westbourne Park
Royal Oak
Warwick Av.
Little Venice
PADDINGTON
Paddington Basin
St. Mary's Hosp.
Edgware Rd.
LISSON GROVE
MARYLEBONE FLYOVER
WESTWAY
HARROW ROAD
EDGWARE RD.
BISHOP'S BRIDGE RD.
BAYSWATER
Bayswater
Queensway
Lancaster Gate
Marble Arch
OXFORD ST.
BAYSWATER RD.
Notting Hill Gate
NOTTING HILL GATE
HOLLAND PARK AVENUE
Holland Park
WESTMINSTER
HYDE PARK
THE SERPENTINE
KENSINGTON GARDENS
Round Pond
Kensington Palace
The Orangery
Peter Pan Statue
Speke's Monument
The Long Water
Serpentine Gallery
Princess of Wales Memorial Fountain
Albert Memorial
Speakers Corner
Reformers Tree
Holocaust Mem. Gdn
Rose Garden
Hyde Park Corner
PARK LANE
KENSINGTON
HOLLAND PARK
KENSINGTON HIGH STREET
High St. Kensington
KENSINGTON GORE
KENSINGTON ROAD
KNIGHTSBRIDGE
Knightsbridge
Royal Albert Hall
Imperial Coll.
Science Museum
Natural History Mus.
Victoria & Albert Museum
Brompton Oratory
Harrods
BROMPTON
CROMWELL ROAD
Gloucester Rd.
Sth. Kensington
SOUTH KENSINGTON
EARL'S COURT
Earl's Court
Earls Court Exhibition Building
West Kensington
West Brompton
BROMPTON ROAD
FULHAM ROAD
KING'S ROAD
CHELSEA
Royal Brompton Hosp.
The Royal Marsden Hosp.
Saatchi Gallery
Sloane Square
SLOANE ST.
Royal Hospital Chelsea
CHELSEA BRIDGE RD.
CHELSEA EMBANKMENT
Bb Cb Db Eb Fb Gb Hb
41 42 43 44 45 46 47 48 49 50

90
Jb
Kb
Lb
Mb
Nb
Pb
Qb
REGENT'S PARK
REGENT'S PARK
HAMPSTEAD RD.
SOMERS TOWN
KING'S CROSS
ST. PANCRAS INTERNATIONAL
PENTONVILLE
PENTONVILLE RD.
FINSBURY
EUSTON
EUSTON RD.
British Library
QUEEN MARY'S GARDENS
MARYLEBONE
ST PANCRAS
CLERKENWELL
BLOOMSBURY
British Museum
Russell Sq.
Warren St.
Goodge St.
Euston Sq.
Regent's Pk.
Gt. Portland St.
Baker St.
MARYLEBONE
HOLBORN
Holborn
Chancery La.
Oxford Circus
Tottenham Ct. R
Bond St.
Marble Arch
SOHO
Covent Gdn.
Leicester Sq.
Piccadilly Circus
Temple
EMBANKMENT
MAYFAIR
HYDE PARK
Green Park
GREEN PARK
ST. JAMES'S PARK
Charing Cross
CHARING CROSS
Embankment
WATERLOO
Waterloo East
Hyde Park Corner
Knightsbridge
Westminster
St. James's Park
Houses of Parliament
Westminster Abbey
Lambeth Nth.
LAMBETH
Victoria
VICTORIA
BELGRAVIA
Sloane Square
WESTMINSTER
PIMLICO
Pimlico
Vauxhall
VAUXHALL CROSS
KENNINGTON
RIVER THAMES
GROSVENOR RD.
41
42
43
44
45
46
47
48
49
50
70
227
228
229
112

91
HOXTON
SHOREDITCH
BETHNAL GREEN
SPITALFIELDS
Old Street
Shoreditch High St.
Barbican
Moorgate
LIVERPOOL ST.
St. Paul's
CITY
Bank
Mansion Ho.
Monument
Aldgate
Aldgate East
WHITECHAPEL
Whitechapel
Shadwell
SHADWELL
Tower Gateway
Tower Hill
The Tower of London
CANNON STREET
BLACKFRIARS
SOUTHWARK
LONDON BRI.
THE BOROUGH
Borough
WAPPING
Wapping
BERMONDSEY
Bermondsey
NEWINGTON
Elephant & Castle
WALWORTH
Kennington
SE5
Rb
Sb
Tb
Ub
Vb
Wb
Xb
41
42
43
44
45
46
47
48
49
50

92
72
114
91
Yb
Zb
Ac
Bc
Cc
Dc
Ec
41
42
43
44
45
46
47
48
49
50
BOW INTERCHANGE
BOW
GLOBE TOWN
Bethnal Grn.
MILE END
MILE END HOSPITAL
Queen Mary University of London
Mile End
Stepney Green
STEPNEY
RATCLIFF
LIMEHOUSE
Limehouse
TOWER HAMLETS CEMETERY PARK
BOW COMMON
Bow Church
Bow Rd.
BROMLEY
Bromley-by-Bow
Devons Rd.
Langdon Pk.
Mile End Park Leisure Centre
Mile End Stadium
Whitechapel
THE ROYAL LONDON HOSP.
Shadwell
SHADWELL
Wapping
Westferry
POPLAR
Poplar
All Saints
West India Quay
Canary Wharf
Canary Wharf Pier
WEST INDIA DOCKS
Heron Quays
South Quay
ISLE OF DOGS
Crossharbour
MILLWALL
CUBITT TOWN
Mudchute
MUDCHUTE PARK
MILLWALL PARK
Island Gds.
Rotherhithe
Canada Water
ROTHERHITHE
Surrey Quays
South Bermondsey
Millwall FC (The Den)
DEPTFORD PARK
DEPTFORD
Cutty Sark for Maritime Greenwich
Greenwich Pier
Greenland Pier
CONVOY'S WHARF
Masthouse Terrace Pier
Hilton Docklands Pier
LIMEHOUSE REACH
RIVER THAMES
GREENWICH REACH
LOWER POOL
COMMERCIAL RD.
EAST INDIA DOCK RD.
THE HIGHWAY
CABLE ST.
MILE END RD.
BURDETT RD.
BOW RD.
BLACKWALL TUNNEL NORTHERN APP.
ROTHERHITHE TUNNEL
LOWER RD.
EVELYN ST.
REDRIFF RD.
SALTER RD.
WESTFERRY RD.
MANCHESTER RD.
PLOUGH WAY
GROVE ST.
JAMAICA RD.
SURREY CANAL RD.
CAMBRIDGE HEATH RD.

Plaistow
West Ham
East London Crematorium
EAST LONDON CEMETERY
Memorial Recreation Ground
PLAISTOW
Newham University Hospital
Cumberland School
Brampton Youth Cen.
Terence McMillan Stadium
Newham Leisure Centre
North Beckton
Star La.
Star Park
BARKING RD.
NEWHAM WAY
A13
CANNING TOWN
Canning Town
Bow Creek Ecology Park
East India
LEAMOUTH
East India Dock Basin Nature Reserve
Blackwall
CUSTOM HOUSE
King George V Park
West Beckton
Newham City Farm
Royal Victoria
Custom House for ExCeL
Prince Regent
ExCeL
ROYAL VICTORIA DOCK
ROYAL ALBERT DOCK
London Regatta Centre
LONDON CITY AIRPORT
Millennium Mill
London's Pleasure Gardens
Pontoon Dock
West Silvertown
Pontoon Dock
SILVERTOWN
Thames Barrier Park
Lyle Park
NORTH WOOLWICH ROAD
SILVERTOWN WAY
LOWER LEA CROSSING
British Music Experience
The O2
Indigo2
North Greenwich
North Greenwich Pier
Emirates Greenwich Peninsula
Emirates Air Line (Opening Summer 2012)
THAMES
WOOLWICH REACH
THAMES BARRIER
Thames Barrier Info. Cen.
Barrier Gardens Pier
Greenwich Yacht Club
Greenwich Peninsula Ecology Park
Greenwich Millennium Village
GREENWICH
SE10
New Charlton
Charlton
Charlton Athletic FC (The Valley)
MARYON WILSON PARK
Maryon Park
Westcombe Park
Maze Hill
WOOLWICH RD.
TRAFALGAR RD.
BLACKWALL TUNNEL SOUTHERN APPROACH
A102
A206
CHARLTON
Charlton School
SE7
Victoria Deep Water Terminal
Delta Wharf
Blackwall Point
Ordnance Wharf
Enderby's Wharf
Primrose Wharf
Morden Wharf
Royal Naval College
Trinity Hospital
Fc Gc Hc Jc Kc Lc Mc
41 42 43 44 45 46 47 48 49 50
73 94 115

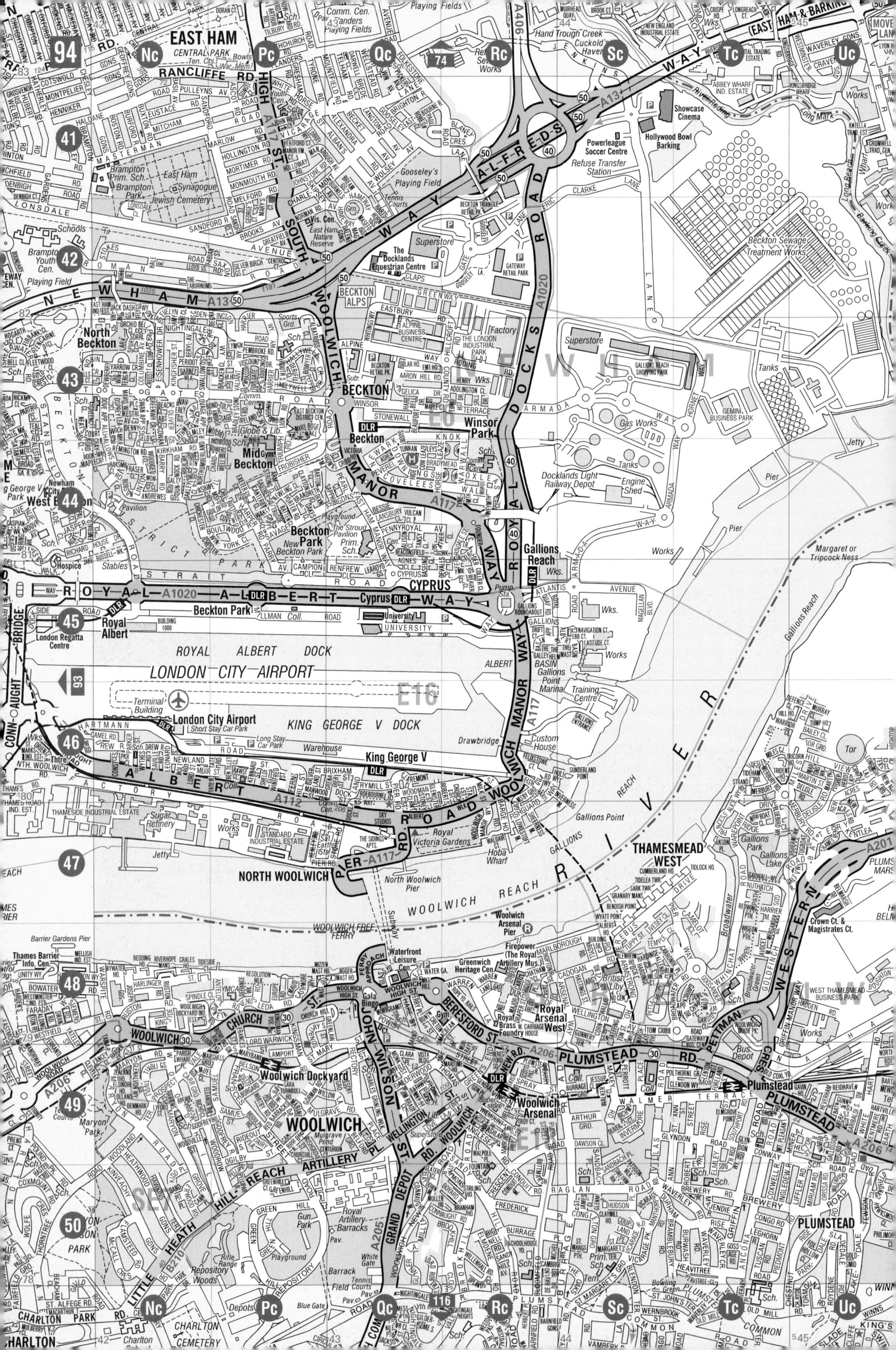
EAST HAM
CENTRAL PARK
RANCLIFFE RD.
HIGH ST. SOUTH
A117
74
Gooseley's Playing Field
East Ham Jewish Cemetery
Brampton Park
Showcase Cinema
Hollywood Bowl Barking
Powerleague Soccer Centre
Refuse Transfer Station
ALFRED'S WAY
A13
NEWHAM WAY
Beckton Sewage Treatment Works
The Docklands Equestrian Centre
BECKTON ALPS
North Beckton
BECKTON
Winsor Park
Mid Beckton
Beckton
Docklands Light Railway Depot
Gas Works
Gallions Reach Shopping Park
ROYAL DOCKS ROAD
A1020
NEWHAM
E6
MANOR WAY
Beckton Park
West Beckton
Gallions Reach
CYPRUS
ROYAL ALBERT WAY
Royal Albert
Beckton Park
University
ROYAL ALBERT DOCK
LONDON CITY AIRPORT
93
E16
London City Airport
KING GEORGE V DOCK
King George V
WOOLWICH MANOR WAY
Custom House
Margaret or Tripcock Ness
Gallions Reach
CONNAUGHT BRIDGE
ALBERT ROAD
A112
Sugar Refinery
Royal Victoria Gardens
NORTH WOOLWICH
North Woolwich Pier
Gallions Point
RIVER
REACH
WOOLWICH REACH
WOOLWICH FREE FERRY
THAMESMEAD WEST
Thames Barrier Info. Cen.
Woolwich Arsenal Pier
Firepower (The Royal Artillery Mus.)
Greenwich Heritage Cen.
Royal Arsenal West
WOOLWICH CHURCH ST.
A206
Woolwich Dockyard
WOOLWICH
Woolwich Arsenal
PLUMSTEAD RD.
Plumstead
PLUMSTEAD
WESTERN WAY
A2016
West Thamesmead Business Park
Crown Ct. & Magistrates Ct.
Gallions Park
Gallions Lake
JOHN WILSON ST.
GRAND DEPOT RD.
A205
Royal Artillery Barracks
Gun Park
Repository Woods
SE18
HEATH RD.
LITTLE HEATH
B210
Maryon Park
CHARLTON PARK
CHARLTON
Charlton Cemetery
116
Nc
Pc
Qc
Rc
Sc
Tc
Uc
41
42
43
44
45
46
47
48
49
50

BARKING and DAGENHAM
Barking
IG11
Dagenham
RM9
CREEKMOUTH
Barking Riverside
The Ripple Nature Reserve
Power Station (disused)
Barking Riverside Recycling Park
Dagenham Sunday Market
Barking Creek Flood Barrier
Barking or False Point
Dagenham Dock
THAMES GATEWAY
A13
High Speed 1
Horse Shoe Corner
Industrial Estate
Oil Storage Depot
Thunderer Jetty
Landing Stage
Pontoon
Power Station
THAMES
BARKING REACH
Cross Ness
Abbey Sluice
Thamesmead North
Driving Range
The Crossness Engines
THAMESVIEW GOLF COURSE
SEWAGE WORKS
Crossness Nature Reserve
SE28
THAMESMEAD CENTRAL
THAMESMEAD
THAMESMEAD SOUTH
THAMESMEAD EAST
Thamesmead South West
Thamesmere Leisure Cen.
Woolwich Polytechnic School
Birchmere Park
Lakeside Centre
Southmere Lake
Erith
BEXLEY
DA18
ERITH MARSHES
The Business Academy, Bexley
EASTERN WAY
CENTRAL WAY
CARLYLE RD.
HARROW MANOR WAY
A2016
A2041
SE2
ABBEY WOOD
Abbey Wood
ABBEY ROAD
B213
Lesnes Abbey
LESNES ABBEY WOODS
Belvedere
DA17
McLEOD RD.
BOSTALL HILL
BOSTALL WOODS
BOSTALL HEATH
Bostall Gdns.
Plumstead Gdns.
Cooperative Woods
Greenwich & Bexley Community Hospice
BELVEDERE PRIVATE HOSP.
St. Luke's Hosp. (Bostall Ho.)
KNEE HILL
WOOLWICH ROAD
A206
WICKHAM LA.
A209
PLUMSTEAD HIGH STREET
WEST HEATH
Clam Field Recreation Ground
Bleak Hill
Southern Outflow Sewers Comm. Cen.
Recreation Ground

96
Dagenham Dock
BARKING and DAGENHAM
Power Station
Motor Works
Dagenham Breach
THAMES GATEWAY PARK
Industrial Estate
Oil Storage Depot
Thunderer Jetty
Landing Stage
Pontoon
Works
Depot
FORD INDUSTRIAL PARK
Dagenham
HORNCHURCH MARSHES
Car Compound
RM9
Beam River
Hornchurch Shoot
Thames Gateway College (CEME)
BASEPOINT BUSINESS CENTRE
SUTTONS BUSINESS PARK
Rainham Steel Mills
BEAM REACH BUSINESS PARK
Sewage Works
Rainham
DOVERS CORNER
Timber Yard
Superstore
Red Bridge
Rainham Hall
ALBRIGHT INDUSTRIAL ESTATE
DENVER INDUSTRIAL ESTATE
FERRY LA. IND. EST.
RM13
FREIGHTMASTER ESTATE
EASTER INDUSTRIAL PARK
Frog Island
Old Man's Head
RIVER THAMES
ERITH REACH
Jenningtree Point
Coldharbour Point
RAINHAM
Warehouse
SEWAGE WORKS
Crossness Nature Reserve
Erith
THAMESMEAD EAST
DA18
EASTERN INDUSTRIAL ESTATE
THAMES INNOVATION CENTRE
EAST THAMESMEAD BUS. PK.
BEXLEY
Belvedere
BELVEDERE
Lighthouse
BELVEDERE IND. EST.
RIVER WHARF BUSINESS PARK
FORDGATE BUSINESS PARK
EURO TRADE CEN.
CALLENDERS COTTS.
BELVEDERE LINK BUS. PK.
Mill
Pier (disused)
CAPITAL INDUSTRIAL ESTATE
Indoor Bowls Club
ELBOURNE TRADING ESTATE
Belvedere Youth Cen.
Belvedere Jun. & Inf. Schs.
Sikh Temple
HILLSIDE
FRANK'S PARK
Bexley College
Trinity Sch. Belvedere
DA17
LESSNESS HEATH
Open Space
Erith DA8
HAMLET INTERNATIONAL IND.EST.
EUROPA TRAD. EST.
ATLAS TRADE PARK
ERITH
Chalk Farm Wharf
Garden Wharf
Sand and Gravel Pit
Lime Wood
Concrete Works
THAMES GATEWAY
A13
A1306
A2016
A206
A220
B213
B253
EASTERN WAY
BRONZE AGE WAY
FRASER ROAD
ERITH ROAD
NEW ROAD
RAINHAM RD.
118
76
95

97
RAINHAM
CHANDLERS CORNER
South Ockendon
RM15
WENNINGTON
AVELEY
PURFLEET
RM19
WENNINGTON MARSHES
AVELEY MARSHES
Rainham Marshes Nature Reserve
Purfleet
KENNINGTON PARK (BELHUS WOODS COUNTRY PARK)
NEW ROAD
A1306
THAMES GATEWAY
A13
LONDON ROAD
WENNINGTON ROAD
SANDY LANE
B1335
ARTERIAL ROAD
PURFLEET BY-PASS
A1090
UPMINSTER ROAD
NORTH WARWICK
Berwick Manor Farm
Jewish Cemetery
Sand & Gravel Pits
Warwick Wood
White Post Wood
The Chafford School
Chafford Sports Complex
East Hall Farm
Wennington Hall
The Willows
Purfleet Industrial Park
Thurrock Commercial Centre
Sports Ground
Purfleet Heritage & Military Centre
Visitor Centre
Crayford Ness
The Saltings
Darent Industrial Park
Thameside Ind. Est.
Flood Barrier
Yacht Club
Mar Dyke
Beacon Hill
Beacon Hill Industrial Estate
Kd
Ld
Md
Nd
Pd
Qd
Rd
77
86
119
41
42
43
44
45
46
47
48
49
50

98
78
97
120
Hunt's Hill Cottages
Hunt's Hill Farm
Cockhide
Upminster
RM14
HAVERING
Warwick Wood
White Post Wood
Common Watercourse
Whitehall Wood
BELHUS WOODS COUNTRY PARK
Visitor Cen.
Romford Lodge
Running Water Wood
Little Brickkiln Wood
Running Water Brook
Brickkiln Wood
Bretts Cottages
Bretts Farm
Moat
Kenningtons
Kennington's Cottages
KENNINGTON PARK (BELHUS WOODS COUNTRY PARK)
Playing Field
BELHUS PARK GOLF COURSE
BELHUS PARK
Belhus Park Leisure Centre
Club House
Golf Driving Range
The Shrubbery
Kenningtons Prim. Sch.
Belhus Chase Specialist Humanities College
Play. Fld.
Pavilion
Sports Ground
Tennis Courts
Recreation Ground
SANDY LA.
Whitehouse Cottage
AVELEY
AVELEY BY-PASS
B1335
Aveley FC (The Mill Field)
Aveley Prim. Sch.
Junction 30
Junction 31
M25
M25 MOTORWAY
South Ockendon
RM15
Ockendon
Factory
Industrial Estate
Store
Tennis Courts
Ockendon Leisure Centre
The Ockendon Sch.
Oak Wood
Ash Plantation
Beacon Hill Sch.
Bonnygate Wood
Bonnygate Prim. Sch.
Dilkes Prim. Sch.
Dilkes Park
Little Dilkes Wood
Shaw Prim. Sch.
The Culver Centre
SOUTH OCKENDON
Holy Cross Catholic Prim. Sch.
Rugby & Football Pitches
School
STIFFORD ROAD
Works
Hangman's Wood
MILLARD'S GARDEN
BRANNETT'S WOOD
THURROCK
Garden Centre
Chestnut Farm
Low Well Wood
Mar Dyke
MARDYKE VALLEY
Davy Down Riverside Park
Davy Down (Information Cen.)
Brickbarn Wood
Combe Wood
A13
Arena Essex
Speedway Circuit
Thurrock Service Area
Motor Sports Complex
Lakeside Karting Raceway
Playing Field
GATEWAY
THAMES
Caravan Site
Sports Ground
Causeway Bri.
Thurrock FC
Mar Dyke Farm
Works
Watt's Wood
Broomhill
ARTERIAL ROAD
A1306
Thurrock Lakeside
Superstore
Vue Cinema
Festival Building
THURROCK LAKESIDE SHOPPING CENTRE
Bus Sta.
Alexandra Lake
LAKESIDE RETAIL PARK
Odeon Cinema
Warehouses
Gala Bingo
TUNNEL ESTATE
THURROCK WAY
Chafford Hundred
Health Club
BURGHLEY ROAD
Warren Prim. Sch.
Chafford Hundred Campus
Purfleet
RM19
QED - QUEEN ELIZABETH DISTRIBUTION PARK
Depot
Warehouse
NEPTUNE BUSINESS PARK
DOLPHIN PARK INDUSTRIAL ESTATE
STONEHOUSE LA.
A1090
PURFLEET BY-PASS
High Speed 1
Depots
BEACON HILL INDUSTRIAL ESTATE
Beacon Hill
Royal Opera Ho. Production Workshop
RM20
Superstore
FROGMORE INDUS. PARK
TUNNEL IND. ESTATE
THE GLADE BUSINESS CEN.
WEST THURROCK
WATERGLADE INDUS. PARK
WEST THURROCK WAY
A126
CANTERBURY WAY
LONDON RD.
Mills
Cemetery
Depot
Rec. Grd.
Bowl.
Pavs.

99
ORSETT FEN
Zd
Ae
Be
Ce
79
De
Ee
Fe
Mar Dyke
Moat
Reservoir
Hobletts
Cemetery
Bowling Green
Rec. Grd.
Tennis Courts
Comm. Cen.
Little Mollands Farm
Lake Alexandria
Great Mollands
Grange Farm
Works
Depot
MOLLANDS LANE
GREEN LANE
Old Rectory
Whitfields
Grangewaters Outdoor Education Centre
BUCKLES LANE
Little Palmer's Shaw
Great Palmer's Shaw
BRIDGE ROAD
Stifford Clays
STIFFORD CLAYS ROAD
Orsett Smock Mill
A13
A1089
Hill Fm.
Club Ho.
MARDYKE VALLEY GOLF COURSE
RM16
Bloomfields Farm
William Edwards Sch. & Sports College
Playing Field
Little Wellhouse Farm
Greygoose Farm Cottage
Greygoose Farm
Hotel
Stifford Bri.
STIFFORD HILL
NORTH STIFFORD
Rec. Grd.
Stifford Clays Jun. & Inf. Schs.
THURROCK COMMUNITY HOSPITAL
100
LONG LANE
A1012
A1306
ARTERIAL ROAD
Caravan Park
Thurrock Rugby Club
Playing Fields
Deneholm Prim. Sch.
Thurrock Athletics Stadium
King George's Field
Civic Hall
Impulse Leisure, Blackshots
DANEHOLES ROUNDABOUT
STANFORD RD.
A1013
Hangmans Wood
ELIZABETH RD.
HOGG LANE
Chafford Gorges Visitor Centre
Warren Gorge
CHAFFORD HUNDRED
Chafford Gorges Nature Park
Grays
FROBISHER GARDENS
The Grays Sch. Media Arts College
GRAYS
LODGE LA.
WOOD VIEW
B149
A126
Oil Depot
Lion Gorge
St. Thomas of Canterbury Catholic Primary Sch.
Quarry Hill Inf. Sch.
Grays Convent High Sch.
Quarry Hill Jun. Sch.
RM17
SOUTHEND ROAD
PALMERS AV.
ORSETT RD.
LITTLE THURROCK
Grays New Cemetery
Palmer's Sports & Fitness Cen
CHADWELL RD.
Stifford Prim. Sch.
Sports Ground
DEVONSHIRE ROAD
TITAN INDUSTRIAL ESTATE
CLARENCE R.
DOCK RD.
Grays STATION
121
560
61
62
63
83
82
81
80
79
78
41
42
43
44
45
46
47
48
49
50

100
ORSETT FEN
Reservoir
Hobletts
Snake Spinney
New Covert
Sticking Hill
Sticking Hill Covert
Long Covert
CONWAYS ROAD
B188
BRENTWOOD ROAD
A128
Home Farm
Fox Holes
Well Wood
ORSETT PARK
Cherry Orchard Farm
Orsett Hall
Linsteads Farm
Cholley's Farm
Poultry Houses
ORSETT ROAD
The Decoy
Old Hall Farm
MALTING LA.
PRINCE CHARLES AVENUE
Orsett Fruit Farm
FEN LANE
GREEN LANE
Poplars Farm
Orsett House
ORSETT
RECTORY RD.
Loft Hall Farm
Old Rectory
ORSETT HOSP.
SCHOOL
Orsett C of E Prim. Sch.
Rec. Grd.
Larch Plantation
Barringtons Farm
Whitfields
CLAYS ROAD
STIFFORD
HIGH
Mill House
Baker Street
BAKER STREET
Orsett Smock Mill
A13
STANFORD ROAD
CRITON INDUSTRIAL ESTATE
WELLING ROAD
Southfields
Foxhound Riding School
Old Kennels Farm
Club Ho.
Mucking Heath
ORSETT GOLF COURSE
Five Chimney Cottages
RM16
THURROCK
A1089
A1013
Whitecroft's
Heath Place
Walnut Tree Cottages
HORNSBY LANE
Brook Farm
Thurrock Rugby Club
Playing Fields
Old House Wood
Rainbow Wood
Ashen Shaw
Thurrock Athletics Stadium
ORSETT HEATH
Grays
King George V Rec. Grd.
Civic Hall
Impulse Leisure, Blackshots
Treetops School
Subway
Recreation Ground
DANEHOLES ROUNDABOUT
Hangmans Wood
Terrels Heath
Woodside Prim. Sch.
High House
Playing Field
Thurrock & Basildon College (Woodview Campus)
Herringham Primary Sch.
CHADWELL ST. MARY
Cemetery
Becksland
CHADWELL RD.
LITTLE THURROCK
Palmer's Sports & Fitness Cen.
Palmer's College
RM17
Cambridge Gds.
Chadwell St. Mary Prim. Sch.
MUCKINGFORD ROAD
Mill House
Works
A126
MARSHFOOT ROAD
APPROACH
Rookery Hill
Bretts Farm
Chadwell Place
CHADWELL BY-PASS
B149
Poultry Farm
Shrove Hill Wood
Holford Farm
Hutts Hill
Hobhill Farm
BLUE ANCHOR LANE
RECTORY RD.
WEST TILBURY
Gateway Academy
122
GUN HILL
Sandy Lane
Manor Farm
West Tilbury Hall
63
64
65
66
83
82
81
80
79
78
A
B
C
D
E
F
G
1
2
3
4
5
6
7
8
9
10
99

HORNDON ON THE HILL
BALSTONIA
THE MANORWAY
A1014
A13
A1013
B1007
ARTERIAL RD.
Abbots Hall Primary Sch.
The Gables
Horndon House
Saffron Garden Cottages
Saffron Gardens
Gas Valve Compound
Hassenbrook School
St. Joseph's Catholic Prim. Sch.
Oak Farm
Great Garlands Farm
The Billet
STANFORD-LE-HOPE
Stanford-le-Hope
Stanford-le-Hope Primary Schs.
Ten. Cts.
Bowl. Grn.
Rec. Grd.
Spts. Grd.
Bowling Green
Tennis Courts
CORRINGHAM ROAD
LONDON ROAD
Club House
Driving Range
St. Clere's School
Cemetery
SS17
STANHOPE INDUSTRIAL PARK
Stanford Le Hope Marshes
Sewage Works
Stanford Warren Nature Reserve
ORSETT INDUSTRIAL PARK
Mayland
ST. CLERE'S HALL GOLF COURSE
Thames Haven Junction
Nursery
MUCKING
The Hall
Bluehouse Farm
Gobians Quarry
Mucking Creek
Illingwood Farm
T H U R R O C K
Active Workings
Jetty
Heronrys Shaw
WALTON HALL CAMPSITE
Sutton's Farm
Turners Farm
MUCKING MARSHES
Works
Linford Woods Local Nature Reserve
LINFORD
Merrie Loots Farm
Pump. Sta.
MUCKINGFORD
Old Counter Wall
Sewage Works
East Tilbury
Pav.
Ten. Cts. Playgrd
Thomas Bata Mem. Pk.
East Tilbury Jun. & Inf. Schs.
THAMES INDUSTRIAL PARK
Sports Ground
Factory
EAST TILBURY MARSHES
EAST TILBURY
Tilbury
RM18
COAL ROAD
LOW STREET
West Cotts.
RIVER THAMES
123
H J K L M N P
1 2 3 4 5 6 7 8 9 10
67 68 69 70
78 79 80 81 82 83

SOUTH BUCKS
DORNEY LAKE
London 2012 Games Venue
Boveney
Boveney Court Farm
Eton College Rowing Centre
RIVER THAMES
Windsor Marina
Bullock's Hatch Bri.
ROYAL WINDSOR RACECOURSE
Racecourse Marina
Grandstand
Stables
Water Jump
Athens
Parade Ring
Cuckoo Weir
Boveney Weir Lock
Mill Stream
Clewer Park
CLEWER VILLAGE
Clewer St. Andrew
Bird Sanctuary
Leisure Cen.
Clewer St. Stephen
The Brocas
Deadwater Ait
ETON
SOUTH MEADOW
Recreation Ground
Masters' Field
College
SOUTH FIELD
Windsor & Eton Central
Alexandra Gds.
WINDSOR ROAD
MAIDENHEAD ROAD
A308
Meadow Lane Farm
GREEN ROAD
B3383
Bishops Farmhouse
THE HAND CLINIC
DEDWORTH ROAD
B3024
OAKLEY GREEN
Fair Acres Farm
Nursery
DEDWORTH
Playing Field
Schools
Superstore
Dedworth Green
Windsor
Clewer Green
Clewer New Town
Clewer Hill
Clewer Within
CLARENCE RD.
GOSLAR WAY
OSBORNE RD.
FRANCES RD.
VALE ROAD
B3025
IMPERIAL ROAD
B3173
Thames Hospicecare
Windsor Girls' Sch.
SL4
ST. LEONARD'S ROAD
B3022
CEMETERY
Windsor FC (Stag Meadow)
Spital
Moat
Queen Mary's Plantation
Alexander First Sch.
Gale House Farm
Tarbay Farm
Nightingale Corner
Reservoirs (covered)
Water Tower
St. Leonardshill
St. Leonard's Farm
LEGOLAND
Main Entrance
Government Lodge
Crown Cotts.
Windsor (Legoland)
Ash Plantation
Withy Cover
Diningroom Close
Spital Meadow
Miniature Rifle Range
Cavalry Exercise Grounds
Paddockhill Copse
Palatine Gate
New Cover
Flemish Farm
Bromley Hill
Star Clump
PRINCE CONSORT'S DRIVE
Flemish Farm
BRACKNELL FOREST
Queen Victoria's Tree
High Standinghill Woods
Forbe's Fields
High Standing Hill
Badgers Bridge
WINDSOR FOREST
School Allotment
Northstreet Bridge
Fish Pond
Forest Park
CRANBOURNE WOOD
Cranbourne Cover
Buck Paddocks
WINDSOR GREAT PARK
CRANBOURNE CHASE
Devil's Gap
Brook's Corner
Pickleherring Pond
CRANBOURNE PARK
Reservoir (covered)
Cranbourne Tower
Ranger's Gate
Ranger's Lodge
Beehive Plantation
Beehive Hill
Sir Andrew Cope's Clump
Sandy Arch
Seymours Plantation
Fiddle Covert
Russel's Pond
Russel's Plantation
SHEET STREET
A332
WINKFIELD
MOUNTS HILL
CRANBOURNE
Cranbourne Hall
NORTH ST.
80
124

Thames Valley Athletics Cen.
Recreation Ground
Fifteen Arch Bri.
Sixpenny or The Pav.
Cricket Ground
The Brook Playing Fields
Fellow's Pond
College Field
Weir
Boathouse Cott.
Boat Ho
Landing Stage
Reservoir (Covered)
Datchet Mead Cottage
Longmead Bridge
DITTON PARK
Gibraltar Bridge
Offices
King's Oak
Langley Gate
Canal
Riding Court Farm
Riding Court House
Slough
Fish Pond
M4 MOTORWAY
COURT ROAD
FARM ROAD
B470
MAJORS
LONDON ROAD
SL3
Cemy.
THE QUEEN MOTHER RESERVOIR
SLOUGH HIGH STREET
B3022
Mus.
Barne's Pool
Mill Race
Cutlers Ait
Romney Lock Cut
Romney Lock
Works
Windsor (Home Pk.)
P+R
Tennis Courts
THE HOME PARK
(Public Recreation Ground)
Lodge
Pav.
Black Potts Weir
Eton End School
DATCHET GOLF COURSE
ETON
SLOUGH ROAD
B3026
B376
KING EDWARD VII AV.
WINDSOR ROAD
Datchet Border
Victoria Bri.
Sumptermead Ait
Churchmead C of E Sch.
Play. Fld.
Cricket Grd.
Datchet Ho.
Club Ho.
Slopes Lodge
Broad Water
Windsor & Eton Riverside
Windsor Bri.
Theatre
St.Georges Chapel
Windsor Castle
CASTLE HILL
Guildhall
East Ter. Gdn.
East Lawn
South Slopes
QUEEN ADELAIDE
VICTORIA
LIME AVENUE
Bathing Pool
DUTCH ELM AV.
Jetties
Jetty
Double Cottages
PRINCE ALBERT'S WALK
HIGH ST.
Datchet
HORTON ROAD
DATCHET
Recreation Ground
Tens. Cts.
THE MONTAGU
THE PADDOCK
THE DRIVE
Datchet Common
MILL PL.
MILL PLACE CARAVAN PARK
The Mill House
Pumping Station
DITTON ROAD
Riding Sch.
Tennis Cts.
Cambridge Gate
ROYAL HOUSEHOLD GOLF COURSE
WINDSOR
Municipal Offs.
Victoria Barracks
SHEET ST.
KING'S ROAD
BROOK ST.
PARK ST.
King's Pavilion
Long Walk Gate
Cricket Ground
Pav.
Adelaide Cottage
Adelaide Lodge
THE WALK
QUEEN ELIZABETH'S WALK
Golf Cottage
HOME PARK
CORONATION
Boat Ho.
Woollacombe
Sandlea Court
Water Intake
Southlea
SOUTHLEA ROAD
B3021
Southlea Farm
MONASTERY
Monastery Cottages
Welly Farm
FRANCES RD.
Hosp.
Frogmore
Frogmore Lodge
Frogmore Cott.
Frogmore House
Royal Mausoleum
Mausoleum
MULBERRY AV.
The Aviary
Prince Consort's Home Farm
Tea Room
Jubilee Mount
Frogmore Lake
FROGMORE BORDER
NEW WINDSOR
OSBORNE RD.
RIVER THAMES
Albert Bridge
Old Windsor Weir
Nickcroft Ait
Sludge Area
HAM FIELDS
Bird Sanctuary
Sewage Works
Lagoons
Sunnymeads
Welley Bri.
Windsor Hall
ROYAL GARDENS
EVERGREEN OAK AV.
AVENUE
Shaw Farm
Shaw Farm
Shawfarm Gate
Lodge
Albert Lodge
Crown Cottages
North Lodge
Crown Cottages
ALBERT ROAD
A308
KING'S ROAD
A332
Queen Anne's Cottage
HOG COMMON
Garrison Sports Ground
Queen Annes Gate Cott.
Park Pale
Kingfisher
Bridge Ho
Fairview
HAM LANE
Ham Island
Ham Bridge
CUT
Sunnymeads Club
Gravel Pit Lake
Moram Lodge
DATCHET RD.
Manor Farm
Bourne
Battle
Albany
MAIDENHEAD
STRAIGHT ROAD
Library
OLD WINDSOR LOCK
The Manor
Remenham House
Remenham Park
Boat Ho.
Wraysbury Lake Sailing Club
Clayhall Farm
CLAYHALL LANE
Moat
CHURCH ROAD
Cemy.
Church Ho.
WHITE HERMITAGE
The Priory
Hunting Lodge
Ground
South Lodge
Tileplace Farm
MILLERS LANE
ST. LUKE'S RD.
OLD WINDSOR
Rec. Grd.
Old Ferry Ho.
Friary Island
Petershill Copse
Peter's Hill
Playgrd
Staines
Manor Farm Estate
WAYLANDS
Coach Ho.
WINDSOR ROAD
WRAYSBURY
Newmeadow Plantation
St. Peter's C of E Mid. Sch.
Play. Fld.
Mount Place
CRIMP HILL
BURFIELD
Sch.
WHARF ROAD
RIVERSIDE
Moat
Crimp Hill Cemetery
Bear's Rails
Bear's Rails Gate
Rush Pond
Bear's Rails Pond
Scout Camp
BEARS RAILS PARK
Woodside Farm
OUSELEY ROAD
TW19
THE EMBANKMENT
Prince of Wales Pond
Old Windsor Wood
PELLING HILL
The Lodge
Dower House
Runnymede House
Pats Croft Eyot
MAGNA CARTA LA.
Withy Bed
Woodside
Beaumont House
Priest Hill House
Playing Field
A328 HILL
PRIEST
Duke of York Plantation
Liddell Plantation
Old Covert
Wild Bd Enclosure
Runnymede
RUNNYMEDE
Magna Carta Island
Marchioness of Hertford Plantation
Sultan Plantation
Prince Consort's Plantation
Equestrian Statue
South Lodge Farm
John F. Kennedy Memorial
THE LONG WALK
H J K L M N P
1 2 3 4 5 6 7 8 9 10
97 98 99 500
78 77 76 75 74 73
81 104 125
M4

Junction 5
LONDON
LANGLEY ROUNDABOUT
Hotel
M4 MOTORWAY
Sports Grd.
Mayes Cott.
Creak Cott.
Evans Cott.
DITTON PARK
Canal
King's Oak
Offices
Langley Gate
Ditton Fm.
Fish Pond
M4
FARM ROAD
B470
RIDING COURT
MAJORS ROAD
Cemy.
A4
COLNBROOK
SLOUGH
Little Sutton
Plantation
Sutton End Farm
Old Wood
SUTTON LANE
Brands Hill
Datchet Watersports Centre
Mildridge Farm
Rec. Grd.
Brook Farm
Camm Cotts.
Colnbrook C of E Primary School
Colnbrook Bridge
Tanhouse Farm
THE QUEEN MOTHER RESERVOIR
Slough
SL3
POYLE
Poyle Manor House
Hotel
Manor Farm
COLNDALE
McKAY TRADING ESTATE
BRITANNIA IND. EST.
BLACKTHORNE
TRIDENT IND. EST.
POYLE TRADING ESTATE
VISCOUNT IND. EST.
POYLE PK.
Poyle Place
HORTON ROAD
Datchet Common
The Mill House
Pumping Station
B376
HORTON ROAD
WINDSOR
Horton Lodge
Rectory
Horton Cedars
Welly Farm
DATCHET ROAD
RAILWAY VIEW
HORTON GARDENS
Brookfield
STANWELL ROAD
HORTON
Play. Fld.
Ashgood Farm
Berkyn Manor Farm
Berkyn Manor
Colne
Arthur Jacob Nature Reserve
Weir
HORTON TRAD. EST.
Depot
Sunnymeads
Works
Welley Bri.
Gravel Pit Lake
and
MAIDENHEAD
Weir
Sunnymeads
Club
Gravel Pit Lake
Airport Parking
Wraysbury Lake Sailing Club
Gravel Pit Lake
Wraysbury Dive Cen.
Whitehall Nurseries
COPPERMILL ROAD
Tithe Fm.
Wraysbury
Rec. Ground
Ford
Coach Ho.
Sch.
Hall
The Green
WINDSOR RD
WRAYSBURY
STAINES ROAD
Gravel Pit
Gravel Pit
Gravel Pit
Observation Platform
WRAYSBURY RESERVOIR
M25 MOTORWAY
M25
Staines
TW19
HERON LAKE
British Disabled Water-Ski Association
Junction 13
MOOR LANE
Cambridge Kennels
The Moor
River Colne
Colne Brook
CARTA LANE
Ankerwycke Farm
Magna Carta Island
Runnymede
Longfield Farm
Hythe End Bridge
Hatts Hill Cottages
126
103
Island
Boat Ho.
Remenham House
Remenham Park
Hunting Lodge
Ferry
Croft Eyot
A B C D E F G
51 52 53 54 55 56 57 58 59 60

Old Slade Lake
Junction 4b (M4)
Junction 15 (M25)
83
Iver South SDW
Lakeside Ind. Est.
Works
Depot
M25 MOTORWAY
Bigley Ditch
New Wood
Wraysbury River
Colne
Arboretum
The Great Barn
Manor Court
Home Farm
Picnic Area
HARMONDSWORTH MOOR WATERSIDE
Scotchlake Farm
Visitor Centre
Comm. Cen.
Harmondsworth Prim. Sch.
Rec. Grd.
Computer Centre
Harmondsworth Immigration Detention Centre
HOLLOWAY LANE
HATCH LANE
A3044
HARMONDSWORTH
West Drayton
UB7
Nursery
Heathrow Primary School
SIPSON
Recreation Ground
COLNBROOK BY-PASS
BATH ROAD
A4
Moor Junction
M25
Argonaut Park
Warehouses
Mad Bridge
Longford Roundabout
Longford Bri.
LONGFORD
Hotel
Depot
NORTHERN PERIMETER ROAD
Longfordmoor
Moor Bri.
Elbow Meadow
Polygon Business Centre
Poyle Industrial Estate
HILLINGDON
LONDON HEATHROW AIRPORT
TERMINAL 5A
Heathrow Terminal 5
TERMINAL 5B
Hounslow
Control Tower
TERMINAL 3
106
Bedfont Court Estate
River Colne
Nurseries
Junction 14
AIRPORT WAY
A3113
Airport Parking
Airside Road Tunnel
Heathrow Express Rail Link
TW6
The Mill
Weir
STANWELL MOOR ROAD
Recreation Ground
Hithermoor Lake
SOUTHERN PERIMETER ROAD
Gravel Pit
Cargo Terminal
Southern Fm.
STANWELL MOOR
Pumping Sta.
PARK ROAD
B378
TOWN LANE
STANWELL
Stanwell Fields C of E Prim. Sch.
WEST BEDFONT
BEDFONT ROAD
Cargo Point
Court Farm Industrial Est.
Cemetery
Recreation Ground
Ashford Town FC
Westview Cotts
Sports Ground
Playing Field
Nurseries
Club
Homers Farm
Ashford Cemetery
ASHFORD HOSP.
LONDON ROAD
A30
SPELTHORNE
KING GEORGE VI RESERVOIR
STAINES RESERVOIRS
127

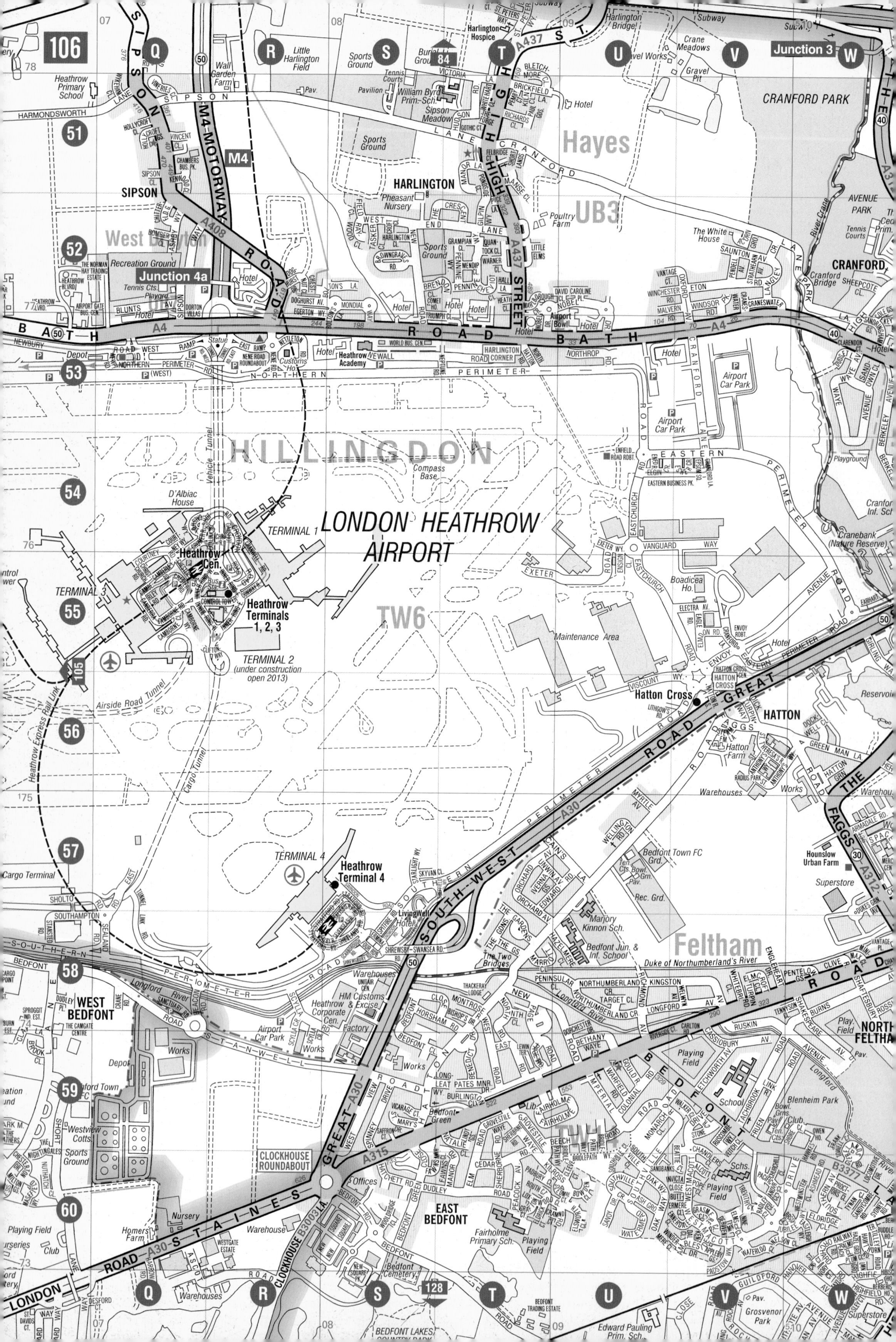
Q
R
S
T
U
V
W
Junction 3
Junction 4a
Heathrow Primary School
Little Harlington Field
Sports Ground
Harlington Hospice
Harlington Bridge
Crane Meadows
Gravel Works
Gravel Pit
CRANFORD PARK
HARMONDSWORTH
SIPSON
SIPSON LANE
M4 MOTORWAY
M4
Wall Garden Farm
William Byrd Prim. Sch.
Sipson Meadow
Hayes
UB3
HARLINGTON
Pheasant Nursery
Sports Ground
Poultry Farm
The White House
AVENUE PARK
Tennis Courts
CRANFORD
Cranford Bridge
West Drayton
Recreation Ground
Tennis Cts.
Playgrd
A4
BATH ROAD
A408
A437
HIGH STREET
Airport Bowl
Depot
NORTHERN PERIMETER RD
Heathrow Academy
Airport Car Park
HILLINGDON
Compass Base
D'Albiac House
LONDON HEATHROW AIRPORT
TERMINAL 1
TERMINAL 3
Heathrow Cen.
Heathrow Terminals 1, 2, 3
TERMINAL 2 (under construction open 2013)
TW6
Maintenance Area
Eastern Business Pk.
Boadicea Ho.
Cranebank (Nature Reserve)
Playground
Hatton Cross
HATTON
Hatton Farm
GREEN MAN LA
Warehouses
Works
Airside Road Tunnel
Heathrow Express Rail Link
Cargo Tunnel
Vehicle Tunnel
TERMINAL 4
Heathrow Terminal 4
Cargo Terminal
GREAT SOUTH-WEST ROAD
A30
Bedfont Town FC Grd.
Rec. Grd.
Marjory Kinnon Sch.
Bedfont Jun. & Inf. School
Feltham
Duke of Northumberland's River
Longford River
THE FAGGS RD
Hounslow Urban Farm
Superstore
STANWELL RD
WEST BEDFONT
HM Customs & Excise
Heathrow Corporate Cen.
Factory
Works
Depot
Westview Cotts.
Sports Ground
Playing Field
Blenheim Park
School
EAST BEDFONT
Bedfont Green
Fairholme Primary Sch.
Playing Field
TW14
CLOCKHOUSE ROUNDABOUT
STAINES ROAD
LONDON ROAD
A315
B3003
Nursery
Homers Farm
Warehouse
Bedfont Cemetery
Warehouses
Grosvenor Park
Edward Pauling Prim. Sch.
BEDFONT TRADING ESTATE
BEDFONT LAKES COUNTRY PARK
NORTH FELTHAM
128
84
105
51
52
53
54
55
56
57
58
59
60

AIRLINKS GOLF COURSE
Heston Service Area
M4 MOTORWAY
M4
OSTERLEY PARK
Cranford Community College Sports Centre
Cranford Community College
Sports Ground
Concorde Centre
PARKWAY TRADING EST.
NORTH HESTON PHOENIX DISTRIBUTION PARK
Thorncliffe House (Hotel)
HESTON PARK
Heston Pool
Berkeley Prim. Sch.
Rectory Farm
CRANFORD
BRABAZON
HESTON
Heston Jun. Sch.
Heston Comm. Sports Hall
Heston Comm. Sch.
Playing Field
Pavilion
TW5
WAGGONERS ROUNDABOUT
HENLYS ROUNDABOUT
PARKWAY
BATH RD.
GREAT WEST ROAD
A4
A312
A30
A3063
A3005
A3006
A315
A314
A244
A316
B361
B358
B3377
Sutton Playing Field
Lampton School
Lampton Sports Cen.
Civic Centre
LAMPTON PARK
SPRING GROVE
LAMPTON RD.
Hounslow East
Hounslow West
Hounslow Central
Cemetery
Beaversfield Park
HOUNSLOW WEST
Cavalry Barracks
Playing Field
Hounslow
Rifle Range
Sports Ground
Reservoir
Warehouse
PROLOGIS PARK
TW4
Central Park Estate
Heath Nurseries
Vis. Cen.
Golf Course
Club House
STAINES ROAD
Baber Bridge
HOUNSLOW HEATH GOLF COURSE
HOUNSLOW HEATH
Hounslow Heath Nature Reserve
The Heathland School
Mosque
WELLINGTON ROAD SOUTH
NELSON ROAD
HANWORTH ROAD
Hounslow Cemy.
HOSPITAL BRIDGE RD.
WHITTON
WHITTON RD.
HOUNSLOW
Maswell Park
Sports Ground
Bridge Farm Nursery
Recreation Grd.
South West Middlesex Crematorium
De Brome Building
Playing Field
Twickenham Cemetery
RICHMOND upon THAMES
Twickenham
TW13
TW2
Feltham Park
Feltham Community College
HARLINGTON ROAD WEST
HARLINGTON RD. EAST
UXBRIDGE RD.
CHERTSEY RD.
FELTHAM
Gala Bingo
Cineworld
Nature Reserve
River Crane
X
Y
Z
Aa
Ba
Ca
Da
85
129
108
51
52
53
54
55
56
57
58
59
60

OSTERLEY PARK
Osterley Park House
OSTERLEY
Osterley
WYKE GREEN GOLF COURSE
86
M4 MOTORWAY
BRENTFORD
Brentford
BRENTFORD END
Syon Lane
SYON PARK
Syon Park
DUKE OF NORTHUMBERLAND ESTATE
The Tropical Forest
Osterley Sports & Athletics Centre
Isleworth Crown Court
West Thames College
SPRING GROVE
LAMPTON
Hounslow East
HOUNSLOW
Hounslow Central
WOODLANDS
ISLEWORTH
Isleworth
Old Isleworth
West Middlesex University Hosp.
King's Observatory
Isleworth Ait Nature Reserve
Old Deer Park Recreation Ground
Richmond Lock
REDLEES PARK
Mogden Sewage Treatment Works
Isleworth Rec. Cen.
Inwood Park
Maswell Park
Hounslow
Twickenham Stadium
World Rugby Museum
Twickenham Trading Estate
Royal Military Sch. of Music (Kneller Hall)
Sports Ground
ST. MARGARETS
St. Margarets
Cole Park
Moor Mead Gd.
Richmond upon Thames College
Harlequins RUFC & Harlequins RLFC Twickenham Stoop
Whitton
WHITTON
Kneller Gdns.
Twickenham Cemetery
Twickenham
TWICKENHAM
Marble Hill Park
Marble Hill House
Orleans Ho. Gallery
Eel Pie Island
RIVER THAMES
Ham House & Garden
Miniature Rifle Range
Playing Field
RICHMOND
130
Ea Fa Ga Ha Ja Ka La
51 52 53 54 55 56 57 58 59 60
107

Junc. 2
Junc. 1
Kew Bridge
WELLESLEY
Gunnersbury
TURNHAM GREEN
CEDARS RD.
ELLESMERE RD.
HOGARTH LA.
CHISWICK
Chiswick House & Gardens
BURLINGTON LA.
Brentford FC (Griffin Pk.)
ST. KEW BRIDGE
Waterman's Arts Centre
Brentford Ait
Strand on the Green
Oliver's Island
Kew Pier
Kew Green
Kew Palace
Orangery
Old Brentford
Princess of Wales Conservatory
KEW
ROYAL BOTANIC GARDENS
KEW GARDENS
Syon Vista
The Lake
King William's Temple
Temple of Bellona
Arboretum
Pagoda Vista
Isleworth Ferry Gate (Closed)
Waterlily Pond
Evolution House
Temperate House
Marianne North Gallery
Conservation Area
Queen Charlotte's Cottage
Pavilion Restaurant
Japanese Gateway & Landscape
Pagoda
DEER
MID-SURREY GOLF COURSE
PARK
The National Archives
Kew Gds.
MORTLAKE
NORTH SHEEN
FULHAM (NORTH SHEEN) CEMETERY
Mortlake Crematorium
Hammersmith Cemetery
CHISWICK BRI.
GROVE PARK
University of Westminster Sports Ground
Riverside Lands
Playing Fields
DUKE'S MEADOWS
Duke's Meadow Golf Course
Driving Range
Chiswick Cemetery
Esporta Health Club Chiswick
Barnes Br.
W4
THAMES
MORTLAKE HIGH ST.
Mortlake
LOWER RICHMOND RD.
RICHMOND
Richmond
Richmond Athletic Ground
London Scottish RUFC
London Welsh RUFC
Pools on the Park
North Sheen
Holy Trinity C of E Prim. Sch.
UPPER RICHMOND ROAD
EAST SHEEN
SW14
Pesthouse Common
East Sheen Cemetery
SHEEN COMMON
Richmond Cemetery
Bog Gate
The Bog
Riding Ring
Sheen Cross Wood
Polo Field
Playing Field
Adam's Pond
Horse Ride
Roehampton Gate
East Sheen Gate
Holly Lodge
Conduit Wood
Barn Wood Pond
RICHMOND
Richmond Gate
(Open during daylight hours only)
THAMES
Saw Pit Plantation
Kidney Wood
Jubilee Plantation
Queen's Ride
Duchess' Wood
Deer Pen
White Lodge Plantation
Queen Mothers Copse
White Lodge Museum
The Royal Ballet Lower School
Victory Plantation
PARK
SIDMOUTH WOOD
King Henry VIII Mound
Pen Ponds
Leg of Mutton Pond
Queen Elizabeth's Plantation
Lawn Plantation
Treebox Wood
SPANKERS HILL WOOD
DEER PARK
Oak Lodge
Pembroke Lodge (Cafeteria)
PETERSHAM
Petersham Meadows
Petersham Farm
Glover's Island
Petersham Gate
Royal Star & Garter Home
The American Int. Uni. in London
Terrace Gardens
Buccleugh Gdns.
The German Sch. London
The Russell Sch. (Juniors)
Strathmore Sch.
Sports Ground
MEADLANDS
131
87
110

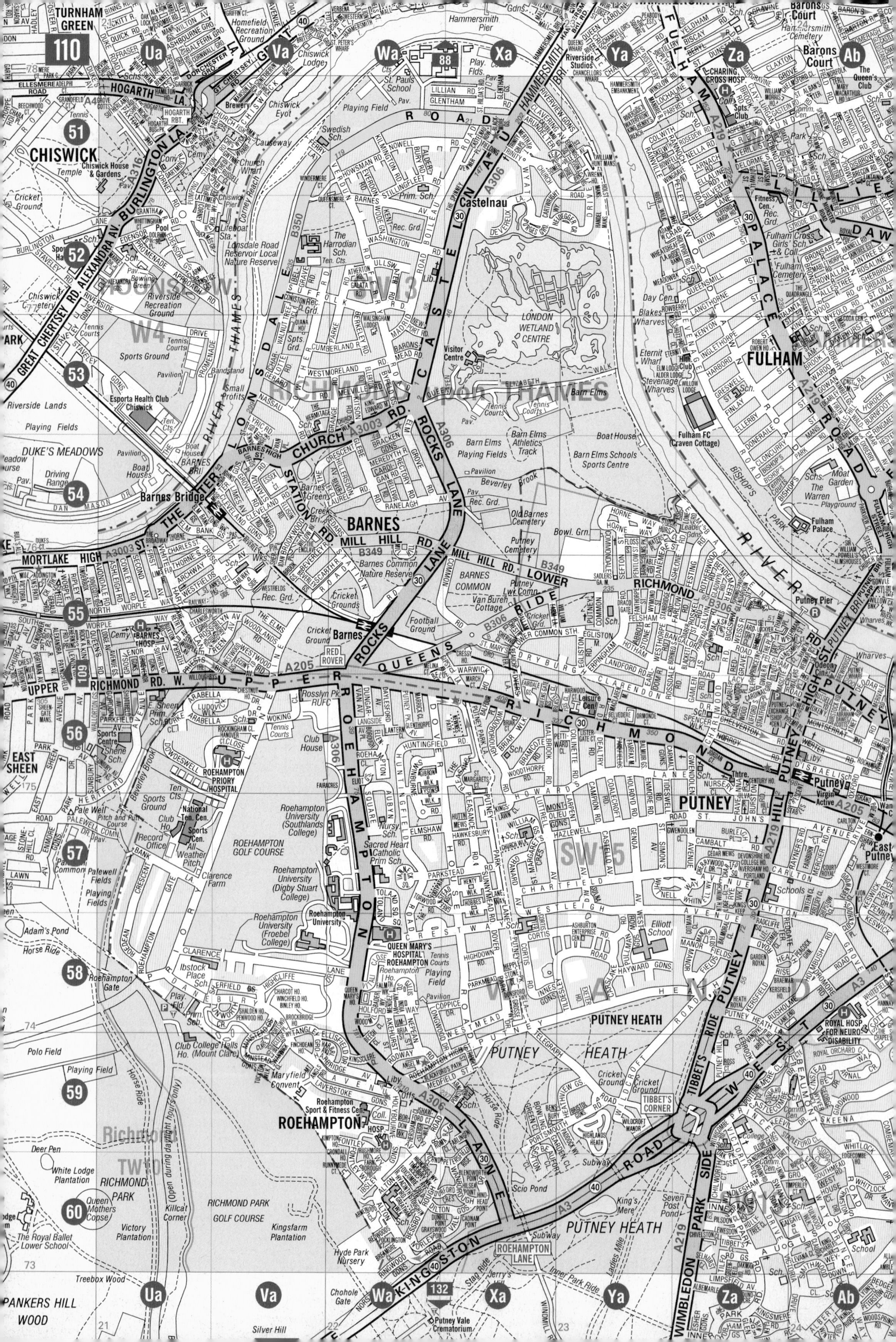
110
88
109
132
Ua
Va
Wa
Xa
Ya
Za
Ab
TURNHAM GREEN
CHISWICK
W4
Chiswick House & Gardens
DUKE'S MEADOWS
Esporta Health Club Chiswick
Riverside Recreation Ground
Barnes Bridge
MORTLAKE HIGH ST.
EAST SHEEN
UPPER RICHMOND RD. W.
BARNES
SW13
RICHMOND upon THAMES
CASTELNAU
LONDON WETLAND CENTRE
Barn Elms
Hammersmith Pier
Riverside Studios
Charing Cross Hosp.
Barons Court
The Queen's Club
FULHAM
Fulham FC (Craven Cottage)
Fulham Palace
Putney Pier
RIVER THAMES
PUTNEY
SW15
East Putney
ROEHAMPTON GOLF COURSE
Roehampton University (Southlands College)
Roehampton University (Digby Stuart College)
Roehampton University (Froebel College)
QUEEN MARY'S HOSPITAL ROEHAMPTON
ROEHAMPTON PRIORY HOSPITAL
National Ten. Cen.
PUTNEY HEATH
TIBBET'S CORNER
ROEHAMPTON
RICHMOND PARK
TW10
RICHMOND PARK GOLF COURSE
Kingsfarm Plantation
Victory Plantation
The Royal Ballet Lower School
Queen Mothers Copse
White Lodge Plantation
PANKERS HILL WOOD
Putney Vale Crematorium
KINGSTON ROAD
WIMBLEDON PARK SIDE
ROYAL HOSP FOR NEURO-DISABILITY
A3
A205
A306
A219
A316
A3003
B349
B306
B350
51
52
53
54
55
56
57
58
59
60
73
74
75
76
77
78
21
22
23
24

CHELSEA
West Brompton
WEST BROMPTON
Brompton Cemetery
Earls Court Exhibition Building
Fulham Broadway
Chelsea FC (Stamford Bridge)
WALHAM GREEN
Parsons Grn
PARSONS GRN
SANDS END
Imperial Wharf
Chelsea Harbour Pier
Cremorne Riverside Centre
Cremorne Gardens
HURLINGHAM PARK
Hurlingham
The Hurlingham Club
SOUTH PARK
THAMES
RIVER
Wandsworth Riverside Quarter Pier
Wandsworth Town
WANDSWORTH
Wandsworth Common
WANDSWORTH COMMON
HMP WANDSWORTH
Wandsworth Cemetery
EARLSFIELD
Earlsfield
SOUTHFIELDS
West Hill
Southfields
BATTERSEA
BATTERSEA PARK
CLAPHAM JUNCTION
Spencer Park
Emanuel School
King George's Park
Lensbury Wharf
THE LONDON HELIPORT
Royal Hospital Chelsea
Chelsea & Westminster Hosp.
KINGS ROAD
FULHAM ROAD
NORTH END ROAD
WANDSWORTH BRIDGE ROAD
BATTERSEA BRIDGE ROAD
ALBERT BRIDGE ROAD
CHELSEA EMBANKMENT
CHEYNE WALK
YORK ROAD
TRINITY ROAD
LAVENDER HILL
ST. JOHN'S HILL
NORTHCOTE ROAD
BOLINGBROKE GROVE
MERTON ROAD
GARRATT LANE
BUCKHOLD RD.
WANDSWORTH HIGH ST.
EARLSFIELD RD.
WINDMILL RD.
THE AVENUE
CLAPHAM COMMON NORTH SIDE
BURNTWOOD
SOUTHSIDE
Bb
Cb
Db
Eb
Fb
Gb
Hb
51
52
53
54
55
56
57
58
59
60
89
112
133

112
RIVER THAMES
CHELSEA EMBANKMENT
GROSVENOR ROAD
Grosvenor Bridge
CHELSEA REACH
BATTERSEA PARK
BATTERSEA
Battersea Power Station (Disused)
NINE ELMS
NINE ELMS LANE
Battersea Park
Queenstown Rd. (Battersea)
QUEENSTOWN RD.
NEW COVENT GARDEN MARKET
Fruit & Vegetable Market
VAUXHALL CROSS
Vauxhall
St. George Wharf
KENNINGTON
Surrey CCC (The Oval)
Oval
VAUXHALL
SOUTH LAMBETH
SOUTH LAMBETH ROAD
Larkhall Park
Stockwell
STOCKWELL
STOCKWELL ROAD
Angell Town
Wandsworth Rd.
WANDSWORTH ROAD
Clapham High St.
Clapham North
LAMBETH HOSPITAL
CLAPHAM
CLAPHAM COMMON NORTH SIDE
Clapham Comm.
CLAPHAM COMMON
CLAPHAM PARK ROAD
ACRE LANE
BRIXTON
Brixton
COLDHARBOUR LANE
LAVENDER HILL
BEDFORD RD.
CLAPHAM PARK
HMP BRIXTON
POYNDERS RD.
ATKINS RD
STREATHAM PL.
CHRISTCHURCH ROAD
BRIXTON HILL
Clapham Sth.
BALHAM HILL
NIGHTINGALE LANE
BALHAM
Balham
STREATHAM HILL
Wandsworth Common
TULSE HILL
Jb
Kb
Lb
Mb
Nb
Pb
Qb
51
52
53
54
55
56
57
58
59
60
90
111
134

Rb
Sb
Tb
Ub
Vb
Wb
Xb
91
135
114
51
52
53
54
55
56
57
58
59
60
CAMBERWELL
PECKHAM
Peckham Rye
EAST DULWICH
East Dulwich
Denmark Hill
Loughborough Junc.
NUNHEAD
Nunhead
PECKHAM RYE COMMON
PECKHAM RYE PARK
HERNE HILL
Herne Hill
North Dulwich
DULWICH VILLAGE
DULWICH PARK
TULSE HILL
Tulse Hill
West Dulwich
BROCKWELL PARK
RUSKIN PARK
Burgess Park
KINGS COLLEGE HOSPITAL
THE MAUDSLEY HOSP
Dulwich Picture Gallery
Horniman Museum
Horniman Gardens
DULWICH & SYDENHAM HILL GOLF COURSE
Camberwell Old Cemetery
Brockwell Park Lido
MYATTS FIELDS
CAMBERWELL GREEN
THE GROVE
SE22
SE21
SE24
SE23
CAMBERWELL NEW ROAD
PECKHAM ROAD
PECKHAM HIGH ST.
QUEEN'S RD.
OLD KENT ROAD
DENMARK HILL
HALF MOON LA.
VILLAGE WAY
DULWICH COMMON
LORDSHIP LANE
EAST DULWICH GROVE
GROVE VALE
DOG KENNEL HILL
RYE LANE
EVELINA RD.
LONDON ROAD
NORWOOD ROAD
CROXTED ROAD
SOUTHAMPTON WAY

114
South Bermondsey
Millwall FC (The Den)
DEPTFORD PARK
92
EVELYN ST.
CONVOY'S WHARF
RIVER THAMES
DEPTFORD
Cutty Sark for Maritime Greenwich
CREEK ROAD
OLD KENT RD.
NEW CROSS RD.
Deptford
Greenwich
New Cross Gate
New Cross
NEW CROSS GATE
NEW CROSS
Goldsmiths College
Queens Rd (Peckham)
Deptford Bridge
BLACKHEATH RD.
ST. JOHNS
St. Johns
Elverson Rd.
Telegraph Hill Park
Nunhead
DRAKEFELL ROAD
LOAMPIT VALE
Lewisham
Lewisham College
Brockley
NUNHEAD CEMETERY
Nunhead Cemetery Nature Reserve
NUNHEAD
SOUTHWARK
HILLY FIELDS
BROCKLEY
LEWISHAM
ADELAIDE RD.
Brockley Cemetery
Crofton Park
Ladywell Cemetery
LADYWELL
Ladywell
PECKHAM RYE PARK
AQUARIUS GOLF COURSE
Newlands
Honor Oak Crematorium
Camberwell Old Cemetery
One Tree Hill Local Nature Reserve
Honor Oak Park
HONOR OAK
HONOR OAK PARK
Lewisham University Hospital
Ladywell Arena (Running Track)
Blythe Hill Fields
Blythe Hill
Catford Bridge
Catford
CATFORD RD.
STANSTEAD ROAD
FOREST HILL
Forest Hill
Horniman Museum
LONDON RD.
CATFORD
136
SE4
SE22
SE23
SE15

GREENWICH
GREENWICH PARK
National Maritime Museum
Royal Observatory Greenwich
Planetarium
Prime Meridian Line
Maze Hill
Westcombe Park
WOOLWICH RD.
TRAFALGAR RD.
VANBRUGH PARK
CHARLTON WY.
CHARLTON RD.
CHARLTON
Charlton Ho.
CHARLTON PARK
MARYON WILSON PARK
QUEEN ELIZABETH HOSPITAL
SE7
SHOOTERS HILL ROAD
OLD DOVER ROAD
SUN-IN-THE-SANDS
Blackheath RUFC (Rectory Fld.)
Hornfair Park
Charlton Lido
Recreation Ground
A2
A102
A207
B210
B211
B212
B220
BLACK HEATH
Blackheath Vale
BLACKHEATH
Blackheath
Morden College (Almshouses)
Blackheath Nursy. & Prep. Sch.
PRINCE OF WALES RD.
KIDBROOKE PARK RD.
KIDBROOKE
Kidbrooke
Kidbrooke School
Sam Montague Boy's Club
Kidbrooke Grn. Nature Res.
Thomas Tallis Sch.
ROCHESTER WAY
ROCHESTER WAY RELIEF ROAD
A2213
BLACKHEATH PARK
Concert Halls
LEE HIGH ROAD
LEE
Lee
ELTHAM RD.
BURNT ASH HILL
BURNT ASH RD.
A2212
A20
A210
A205
Manor House Gdns.
Manor Park
SE13
SE12
SE9
David Lloyd Leis.
Sutcliffe Park Athletics Track
SUTCLIFFE PARK
Horn Park
Colfes Prep. Sch.
Colfes Leisure Cen.
WESTHORNE AVENUE
SIDCUP RD.
ELTHAM
Eltham Green Coll.
Eltham Hill Coll.
Goals Soccer Centre
ELTHAM HILL
Queenscroft Park
HITHER GREEN
Hither Green
Hither Green Sidings
Northbrook Park
Grove Park Nature Reserve
HITHER GREEN CEMETERY
ST. MILDREDS ROAD
BARING ROAD
Horn Park Prim. Sch.
BROMLEY
Mottingham Farm
Mottingham Hall
Hadlow Coll. (Mottingham Campus)
Eltham College Jun. Sch.
Eltham College
MOTTINGHAM
Bannatyne's Health Club
Community Centre
116
137
93

PLUMSTEAD
CHARLTON
CHARLTON PARK
Charlton School
CHARLTON CEMETERY
Cricket Ground
Repository Woods
Royal Artillery Barracks
Gun Park
QUEEN ELIZABETH HOSPITAL
Sports Ground
Hornfair Park
Charlton Lido
WOOLWICH COMMON
ROAD
ACADEMY
A205
Plumstead Common
SHREWSBURY PARK
SE18
Shooters Hill Post 16 Campus
Reservoir (covered)
SHOOTERS HILL GOLF COURSE
SHOOTERS HILL
Eaglesfield Rec. Grd.
Clothworkers Wood
Willow Dene School
SHOOTERS HILL ROAD
A207
HILL
BELLEGROVE
ELTHAM COMMON
MEMORIAL HOSPITAL
Severndroog Castle
CASTLE WOOD
Rose Cottage
JACK WOOD
Jackwood Ho.
Woodlands Farm
Garden Centre
Hillview Cemetery
Council Offices
SE3
Kidbrooke School
Playing Fields
Sam Montague Boy's Club
Sports Ground
CEMETERY
Recreation Ground
G R E E N W I C H
Oxleas Meadows
OXLEAS WOOD
Eastcote Prim. Sch.
ELTHAM PARK
Playing Field
SHEPHERDLEAS WOOD
ELTHAM PARK NORTH
Falconwood Field
Falconwood
FALCONWOOD
Academy Playing Field
WELL HALL ROUNDABOUT
WELL HALL
AVENUE
ROCHESTER WAY
RELIEF ROAD
A2
A205
Eltham
ELTHAM PARK SOUTH
Eltham Cemetery
Eltham Crematorium
ELTHAM WARREN GOLF COURSE
Club House
Nature Study Centre
Crown Woods School
Playing Field
SE9
BEXLEY ROAD
A210
ELTHAM HILL
HIGH STREET
Eltham Green Coll.
Queenscroft Park
Eltham Hill Coll.
Moatbridge Sch.
ELTHAM
Supermarket
Hospice
University of Greenwich (Avery Hill Campus)
AVERY HILL
AVERY HILL PARK
AVERY HILL RD.
B2214
Alderwood Prim. Sch.
Parish Wood
Halls of Residence
Sports Ground
All Weather Pitches
Eltham Palace & Gardens
Bowling Green
Superstore
Club House
ROYAL BLACKHEATH GOLF COURSE
Sparrow's Farm Leisure Centre
Sports Ground
SOUTHEND CRES.
COURT ROAD
A208
A211
GREEN LA.
B263
Community Centre
Bird Sanctuary
The Tarn
Mottingham
SIDCUP ROAD
A20
Fairy Hill
Cricket Ground
New Eltham
Sports Ground
MOTTINGHAM
Eric Liddell Spts. Cen.
Coldharbour Leisure Centre
Dulverton Sch.
Wyncham Stream
HALFWAY ST.
Sports Ground

BOSTALL HILL
BOSTALL HEATH
Greenwich & Bexley Community Hospice
BELVEDERE PRIVATE HOSP.
95
A206 HILL WOOLWICH ROAD
WEST HEATH
BOSTALL WOODS
SE2
Clam Field Recreation Ground
Heathview Day Centre
Bowling Green
Playing Field
Turpins Cave
Woolwich Rockliffe Gds.
Woolwich Cemetery
The William Barefoot Gdn.
PLUMSTEAD CEMETERY
Hill Grove
East Wickham Open Space
EAST WICKHAM
Stevens Park
WICKHAM LANE
A209
UPPER WICKHAM LA.
Welling
WELLING
DA7
DA16
Bexleyheath
BEXLEYHEATH
Bexleyheath Station
Welling Corner
WELLING HIGH ST.
PARK VIEW RD.
A207
CROOK LOG
BROADWAY
Welling United FC (Park View Road)
Bexleyheath Sports Club
Danson House
Danson Park Watersports Centre
DANSON PARK
THE LAKE
Bexley Grammar Sch.
Playing Field
B E X L E Y
Upton
UPTON CENTRE
Red House
DA6
Cemetery
Bexleyheath School
118
56
ALBION ROAD
BEXLEYHEATH GOLF COURSE
Upton Prim. Sch.
Grammar Sch.
A2
ROCHESTER WAY
DANSON INTERCHANGE
DANSON UNDERPASS
A210
ROCHESTER ROAD
Blackfen Sch. for Girls
Sherwood Park Prim. Sch.
Sidcup
BLACKFEN
Hollyoak Wood Park
PENHILL PARK
Blendon
BLENDON RD.
B2210
BRIDGEN RD.
PARKHILL RD.
Bridgen
Bexley Park Wood
Bexley
DA5
DA15
SIDCUP GOLF COURSE
Marlborough Park
Marlborough Sch.
Chatsworth Inf. Sch.
Rose Theatre Lamorbey Park
Rose Bruford College
Lamorbey
A221
PENHILL ROAD
HURST ROAD
A222
Hurtsmere Foundation Sch.
Old Bexley C of E Prim. Sch.
Cricket Ground
Upper College Farm
B2214
STATION ROAD
Sidcup Leisure Centre
Chislehurst & Sidcup Gr. Sch.
139
Albany Park
Vc Wc Xc Yc Zc Ad Bd
46 47 48 49
51 52 53 54 55 56 57 58 59 60

ERITH
Erith
NORTHUMBERLAND HEATH
North End
Slade Green
SLADE GREEN
Barnehurst
BARNEHURST
Bexleyheath
BEXLEYHEATH
CRAYFORD
Crayford
BEXLEY
OLD BEXLEY
Bexley
Coldblow
Maypole
Bowmans
DARTFORD HEATH
DA5
DA6
DA7
DA8
BARNEHURST GOLF COURSE
Hall Place & Gardens
BLACK PRINCE INTERCHANGE
Crayford Stadium (Greyhound)
Perry Street Farm
Erith Stadium
ERITH & DIST. HOSP.
Russell Park
Martens Grove Park
SPORTS FIELD
Churchfield Wood
Sand and Gravel Pit
Lesney Farm Estate
BELMONT ROAD
BEXLEY ROAD
ROCHESTER WAY
DARTFORD RD.
WATLING ST.
LONDON ROAD
BOURNE ROAD
PERRY STREET
NORTHEND ROAD
QUEEN'S ROAD
BROADWAY
GRAVEL HILL
EAST ROCHESTER WAY
OLD BEXLEY LA.
BY-PASS
SHEPHERDS
A2
A206
A207
A220
A221
A222
A223
A2000
A2018
B2174
B2186
B2210
96
117
140
Cd
Dd
Ed
Fd
Gd
Hd
Jd
49
50
51
52
53
54
55
56
57
58
59
60
73
74
75
76
77
78

RIVER THAMES
LONG REACH
PURFLEET
THURROCK
RM16
DARTFORD SALT MARSHES
Dartford Clay Shooting Club
CRAYFORD MARSHES
RIVER DARENT
RIVER CRAY
Erith Yacht Club
The Saltings
Flood Barrier
DARENT INDUSTRIAL PARK
THAMESIDE IND. EST.
RAY LAMB WAY
JOYCE GREEN LANE
Joyce Green Farm
Howbury Farm
Moat
Lower Fm.
Playground
Playing Field
The Grange
Crayford Creek Junction
Crayford Creek
Stanham Farm
Stanham River
BARNES CRAY
Power Station
LITTLEBROOK BUSINESS CENTRE
The Bridge
BOB DUNN WAY
A206
BINNIE ROAD
Dartford
DARTFORD FRESH MARSHES
BURNHAM ROAD
A2026
VICTORIA RD.
RIVERSIDE INDUSTRIAL ESTATE
JOYCE GREEN
Temple Hill
Dartford Creek
Holy Trinity C of E Prim. Sch.
Junction 1a
LITTLEBROOK INTERCHANGE
DARTFORD TUNNEL APPROACH RD.
A282
CROSSWAYS
DA2
Recreation Ground
Dartford Dojo Judo Club
LITTLE BROOK HOSP.
GREENACRES
Bowls & Social Club
A226
WATLING ST.
WEST HILL
EAST HILL
New Town
HOME GDNS
Dartford
Dartford County Ct.
Gala Bingo
LOWFIELD ST.
A225
CENTRAL PARK
Fairfield Pool & Leisure Cen.
Central Park Arena
PRINCES ROAD
Superstore
Brooklands Lake
David Lloyd Leisure
Dartford FC (Princes Pk.)
Goals Soccer Cen.
The Leigh Tech. Academy
Football Pitch
Club House
PRINCES PARK GOLF COURSE
DARTFORD
Dartford Technology College
Dartford Grammar Sch. for Girls
Beckets Sports Cen.
Westgate Prim. Sch.
Playing Fields
DARTFORD GOLF COURSE
Brickhill Wood
Oakfield Prim. Sch.
Junc.1b
PRINCES RD. INTERCHANGE
B2500
THE BRENT
LONDON RD.
LIVINGSTONE HOSP.
Hesketh Park
Sports Ground
Tennis Courts
PARK RD.
A296
B2174
B260
ORBITAL ONE INDUSTRIAL ESTATE
Fleetdown Jun. & Inf. Schs.
Downs Farm
FLEET DOWNS
Kd Ld Md Nd Pd Qd Rd
97
141
51 52 53 54 55 56 57 58 59 60

WEST THURROCK
Purfleet
RM19
RM20
DA1
DA2
PURFLEET BY-PASS
LONDON RD.
A1090
STONEHOUSE LA.
QUEEN ELIZABETH II BRIDGE
DARTFORD TUNNEL
CANTERBURY WAY
A282
OLIVER ROAD
OLIVER CL.
ST. CLEMENTS WY.
STONENESS ROAD
West Thurrock Marshes
Oil Storage Depot
DARTFORD-THURROCK RIVER CROSSING
Tunnel Wharf
Stone Ness
Lighthouse
RIVER
LONG REACH
Power Station
Works
Jetty
Pier
STONE MARSHES
Warehouse
CROSSWAYS
CROSSWAYS BOULEVARD
A206
Dartford
Johnson's Wharf
Ingress Park
Causeway
HIGH ST.
B255
Superstore
Stone Crossing
Greenhithe for Bluewater
COTTON LANE
Junction 1a
LITTLEBROOK INTERCHANGE
B2228
Recreation Ground
Dartford Dojo Judo Club
Bowls & Social Club
LITTLE BROOK HOSP.
STONE
HORNS CROSS
LONDON ROAD
A226
Greenhithe
GREENHITHE
Playing Field
Knockhall Prim. Sch.
Stone Recreation Ground
CHALK PIT (DISUSED)
John's Hole
Stone Prim. Sch.
Coach Park
BLUEWATER PARKWAY
Western Village
Wintergarden
Eastern Village
BLUEWATER SHOPPING CENTRE
Bluewater
Showcase Cinema
Southern Village
Bus Sta.
ST. CLEMENTS WAY
B255
Western Cross
CHALK PIT
PROPOSED EAST DEVELOPMENT
WATLING STREET
A296
PRINCES ROAD
Junc.1b
PRINCES RD. INTERCHANGE
B2500
Blackshole Farm
Helipad
DARENT VALLEY HOSPITAL
Village Green
FLEET DOWNS
Downs Farm
Washmills
Ightham Cotts.
Nursery
Sd Td Ud Vd Wd Xd Yd
51 52 53 54 55 56 57 58 59 60
56 57 58 59
98
119
142

GRAYS
SOUTH STIFFORD
(Proposed)
A126 ROAD
CLARENCE R.
THURROCK RD.
DOCK
Grays
THAMES
NORTHFLEET HOPE
Lighthouse
Broadness Salt Marshes
Swanscombe Marshes
Bell Wharf
Sewage Works
Botany Marshes
Tower Wharf
Thurrock Yacht Club
Grays Beach Riverside Park
Boating Pool
Tilbury North Junction
Rail Container Terminal
Grain Terminal
TILBURY DOCKS
Tilbury
RM18
Northfleet Hope Container Terminal
Rolling Lift Bridge
TILBURY FREE PORT
Tilbury Ness
A1089 DOCK ROAD
ST. ANDREW'S RD.
No. 1 Gate Main Entrance
Warehouse
Works
Jetty
Pier
A226 ROAD GALLEY HILL ROAD
Swanscombe
SWANSCOMBE
Swanscombe Skull Site National Nature Reserve
Swanscombe Heritage Park
Alkerden
Swanscombe DA10
Ebbsfleet United FC
Ebbsfleet International
EBBSFLEET
Gravesend
Northfleet
GRAVESHAM
THAMES WAY
STANHOPE RD.
SOUTHFLEET RD. B259
Recreation Ground
Northfleet Urban Country Park
Weldon PROPOSED
NORTHFLEET WEST DEVELOPMENT SITE
The Observatory
CRESSFIELD
Castle Hill
Wombwell Park
Northfleet Technology College
PERRY STREET
Cygnet Leisure Centre
Superstore
Playgrounds
143
99
122

122
100
121
144
A
B
C
D
E
F
G
1
2
3
4
5
6
7
8
9
10
Grays
RM16
RM17
RM18
DA11
Biggin
Biggin Farm
Hobhill Farm
HOB HILL
Shrove Hill Wood
Poultry Farm
Holford Farm
WEST TILBURY
Manor Farm
West Tilbury Hall
Gunhill Farm
Hallhill Common
Fort Road Common
Parsonage Common
Tilbury
Walton Common
West Tilbury Marshes
TILBURY MARSHES
The Gateway Academy
Tilbury FC Ground
Playing Field
Tilbury Go-Karting Track
Tilbury Manor Jun. Sch. & Manor Inf. Sch.
King George's Field
Tilbury Town
Tilbury Leisure Cen.
TILBURY
TILBURY DOCKS
No. 1 Gate Main Entrance
Warehouse
Warehouses
Works
Bulk Metal Terminal
Cement Terminal
Aggregates Terminal
TILBURY FREE PORT
Riverside Rail Freight Terminal
Fortress Distribution Park
London International Cruise Terminal
Tilbury Landing Stage
Tilbury Fort
Sewage Works
Tilbury Power Station
Bill Meroy Creek
Swing Bridge
Jetty
Pier
Wharf
Quay
Causeway
Foot Ferry
RIVER
DOCK APPROACH RD.
MARSHFOOT ROAD
A126
CHADWELL BY-PASS
ROAD
ST. CHADS ROAD
DOCK A1089 ROAD
ST. ANDREW'S ROAD
FERRY ROAD
A1089
FORT ROAD
COOPERS SHAW ROAD
RECTORY RD.
GUN HILL
CHURCH ROAD
BIGGIN LANE
SANDY LANE
GRAVESEND
Royal Terrace Pier
Lifeboat Sta.
Gravesend Sailing Club
Chantry Heritage Cen.
Northfleet
ROSHERVILLE
Northfleet Nursy. Sch.
MILTON
DENTON
Gravesend
PERRY STREET
Northfleet Urban Country Park
Northfleet Technology College
Wombwell Park
Cygnet Leisure Centre
Cemetery
Sports Ground
St. John's Catholic Comp. Sch.
St. John's Catholic Prim. Sch.
Woodlands Park
LONDON ROAD
OVERCLIFFE
WROTHAM RD.
MILTON RD.
ROCHESTER RD.
A226
B261
B2175
B256
THAMES WAY
DOVER RD.
EAST OLD ROAD
PARROCK ST.
BATH ST.
WEST ST.

101
EAST TILBURY
Sports Ground
Factory
PRINCESS MARGARET ROAD
LOVE LANE
GRASS RD.
COAL ROAD
LOW STREET LANE
STATION ROAD
West Cotts.
Street
Industrial Estate
Goshem's Farm
Barvills Farm
EAST TILBURY MARSHES
Buckland
Bowaters Farm
ROCK
LINLEY CL.
GORDON CL.
Mariner Cotts.
Church Green
Coalhouse Fort & Thameside Aviation Museum
East Tilbury Marshes
Valve Compound
Water Tower
Coalhouse Point
Jetty
THE LOWER HOPE
Wharf
THAMES
GRAVESEND REACH
Higham Saltings
Rochester ME3
Causeway
Shornmead Fort
SHORNE MARSHES
Jetty
London Port Health Authority
North West Kent College
Warehouse
Pav.
Milton Rifle Range
EASTCOURT MARSHES
Sewage Works
Thames & Medway Canal (disused)
LION BUSINESS PARK
Gravesend
Westcourt Marshes
Great Clane Lane Marshes
FILBOROUGH MARSHES
SHAM
NURALITE IND. CEN.
Hoo Junction
Fish Pond
FARM ROAD
Queen's Farm
Queen's Farm Cotts.
DALEFIELD WAY
HOLMES CT.
CULVERS CT.
MAYPOLE RD.
DA12
Coll.
THE MALTINGS ENT. CEN.
Sports Ground
COPPERFIELD CL.
GARGERY CL.
HIGHAM ROAD
Eastcourt Cotts.
Filborough Farm
DARENTH DR.
LAPIS CL.
NICKLEBY RD.
MULLENDER CT.
HAVISHAM RD.
VICARAGE LA.
CHALK
LOWER CHALK
ROMNA
VIA
BROOKE DR.
CASTLE
ORLICK RD.
VILLA CL.
Piggery
LOWER ROAD
QUEEN'S
145
East Court Manor
CHURCH LA.
King's Farm
WESTCOURT
ROAD
Polperro
MILLER RD.
PIRRIP CL.
OSNEY WAY
FORGE LANE
H
J
K
L
M
N
P
1
2
3
4
5
6
7
8
9
10
67
68
69
570
78
77
76
175
74
73

124
102
146
CRANBOURNE
Cranbourne Grange
Kingsmead
Mayfield Farm
MAYFIELD LIGHT IND. EST.
Fernhill Farm
Fernhill Park Gardens
Fernhill Park
The Grove
Cranbourne Court
Springhill
Fernhill Cottages
The Vale
Woodside
Crispin Cotts.
LOVEL LANE
B3034
Lovel Dene
Woodside Ho.
Oak Tree Cott.
Woodend Cotts.
Wood End
WINDSOR ROAD
A332
SHEET STREET ROAD
SUNNINGHILL ROAD
B383
MOUNTS HILL
CRANBOURNE PARK
Pickleherring Pond
Ranger's Lodge
Reservoir (Covered)
Quelmans Head
Forest Farm
Forest Gate Cottages
Forest Gate
Forest Lodge
Isle of Wight Pond
Windsor
Cranbourne Gate
Prince Consort's Workshop
The Village
Rec. Grd.
Bowling Green
Queen Elizabeth II Coronation Grove
SL4
WINDSOR
Poets Lawn
Beehive Hill
Fiddle Covert
Russel's Pond
Russel's Plantation
Russell's Field
Seymours Plantation
Watchoak Plantation
Richardson's Lawn
Timberlodge Hill
Albert Plantation
HOLLY WALK
Sandpit Gate
Duncum Plantation
Dark Wood
BRACKNELL FOREST
South Forest Cottage
SOUTH FOREST
Primrose Hill
Jubilee Statue
Henhouse Covert
Primrosehill Covert
Prince Christian Plantation
Gravel Hill
The Royal Sch.
Queen's Diamond Jubilee Plantation 1897
Woodcock Pen Covert
GREAT WINDSOR and PARK
Hilton's Covert
Mezel Hill
Ivy Bridge
Hawkshill Wood
Square Covert
Shooting Platforms
Great Meadow Pond
Oxshed Covert
Shooting Platform
Slans Hill
Menzies Plantation
Leiper Hill
Mill Covert
Long Wood
North Lodge
Home Farm
Home Farm Cottages
Sunninghill Park
Paddock Wood
Fountainhill Wood
Birch Copse
Fountain Hill
Prince Consort's Gate
Red Cross Grove of Oaks
MAIDENH
Norfolk Plantation
Norfolk Farm
Princess Beatrice Plantation
Rosy Bottom
Otley Cottage
Round Oak
Norfolk Farm Cottages
The Dawrey
Great Pond
The Rookery
The Garden House
Ascot Gate
Horse Shoe Clump
Brewer's Pond
Sunninghill Park
Pond Head
Ash Covert
Ribblesdale Park
Buckhurst Park
Manor Hill
Dark Plantation
Long Plantation
Johnson's Pond
ROYAL ASCOT GOLF COURSE
Lower Farm
Lower Farm Bungalows
Platt's Firs
School
CHEAPSIDE
Buckhurst Hill
Manorhill Cottages
Club House
Ascot Farm
Penslade Bottom
Emmet's Wood
Millhill Plantation
American Clump
Fireball Hill
Heronsbrook Cottage
HILLTOP CLOSE
WATERSPLASH ROAD
Silwood Farm
Nash's Copse
Mill Pond
The Old Mill
RACECOURSE
Course
Straight
Nursery
China Island
New Mile
The New Mile Course (Disused)
Silwood Lake
Virginia Water Lodge
Ascot
Man's Copse
Harewood
Titness House
High Bridge
Tetworth Hall
Larklands
Gunne's Bridge
Halls of Residence
TITNESS PARK
Deer Park
SL5
Lodge
Blacknest Gate
The Cedars
Imperial College London (Silwood Park Campus)
SILWOOD PARK
The Rookery
Science Pk.
Blacknest
Queen's Hill Lodge
St. George's School
Nutfield
ASCOT
LONDON ROAD
A329
Beech Grove
Swan Lake Wild Life Sanctuary
Mount Pleasant
Victory Field
Playgrd.
Tittenhurst
Coworth Park
Coworth Park House
Beggar's Bush
Fish Pond
SUNNINGHILL
The Marist School (Prep. Sch.)
The Marist Schs. (Senior Sch.)
Coombe Meadows
Coworth Park Farm
National School
Government
The Gardens
Market Garden
Cemetery
Bowling Green
Novello Th.
Play. Flds.
SUNNINGDALE
A B C D E F G
1 2 3 4 5 6 7 8 9 10

Withy Bed
Woodside
103
Beaumont House
Runnymede House
Pats Croft Eyot
Magna Carta Island
Liddell Plantation
Old Covert
Wild Boar Enclosure
Playing Field
Cricket Ground
Priest Hill House
Runnymede
RUNNYMEDE
WINDSOR
A308
Duke of York Plantation
Sultan Plantation
Prince Consort's Plantation
Marchioness of ...ord Plantation
Equestrian Statue George III (Copper Horse)
Snow Hill
Spring Hill
The Tilery
Beaumont Farm
St. John's Beaumont School
South Lodge Farm
John F. Kennedy Memorial
Magna Carta Memorial
Priest Hill Farm
Queen Victoria's Plantation
Gore Plantation
Prince of Wales Plantation
Cookes Hill
Beach Hill
Ridgemead House
COOPER'S HILL SLOPES
Oak Lane Cottage
PRIEST HILL
A328
Park Place
RIDGEMEAD
Bishopsgate Cott.
THE DELL
Bishopsgate School
Play. Fld.
Res. (Covered)
Former Brunel University (Runnymede Campus)
COOPER'S HILL
Langham's Pond
Cooper's Hill Coppice
Main Gate Lodges
BISHOPSGATE
Royal Lodge
Chapel Lodge
Dell Park Farm
Bishops Gate
Bishopsgate Ho.
Round Oak
Englefield Green
Air Forces Memorial
Play. Fld.
Sports Ground
Kingswood
COOPERS HILL LANE
Conservatory Covert
Greenbroom Covert
King George VI Coronation Grove
RHODODENDRON RIDE
Castle Hill
Castlehill Farm
DELL PARK
HOLLYCOMBE
KINGSWOOD CL.
KINGSWOOD RISE
CLARENCE DR.
Cow Pond
Cumberland Lodge
Plainfields
Shelley's Cott.
RUNNYMEDE PARK
ENGLEFIELD GREEN
Bulkeley Ho.
ST. JUDES
MIDDLE HILL
Park Close
Egham
PROSPECT LA.
NORTHCROFT
BEAUFORTS
BARLEY MOW ROAD
Inf. School Play. Fld.
HARVEST
LANCASTER
SPENCER GS.
Englefield Lodge
ALDERSIDE
CHILBOLTON
Chapel Wood
Cumberland Gate
Wilderness
KINGS LANE
Town Green Farm
WILLSON RD.
LAUREL AV.
CRESCENT
WILLOW WLK.
BARNWAY
BOND STREET
VICTORIA ST.
THE RETREAT
Shooting Platform
OBELISK
The Savill Garden
Parkside House
TW20
MAGNA ROAD
ALBERT RD.
Jurgen Cen.
EGHAM HILL
A30
Ripley Springs
The Savill Building
Sports Field
ARCHWOOD
ASHWOOD
CHESTNUT CL.
Englefield Green Cemy
St. Jude's C of E Jun. Sch.
Uni.
Royal Holloway (University of London)
126
Halls of Residence
Forest Estate
BEECHTREE AV.
CHERRYWOOD AV.
ILEX CL.
Sch.
BAGSHOT
BAKEHAM LANE
Sports Ground
Sports Centre
Cork Clump
Cumberland Obelisk
Alder Cover
Parkwood
Sandylands
Blays Ho.
BLAYS CL.
Prince Consort's Statue
Harewarren Clump
Fuzzy Clump
Obelisk Pond
Egham Wick
Park House
DAVIDS DR.
PRUNE HILL
Bakeham Ho.
Frank's Plantation
Scarletoak Plantation
Castlewood House
WICK ROAD
ROBERTS WAY
Rushan Crossing
Smith's Lawn (Polo & Equestrian Grounds)
Pavilion
Guards Polo Club
Flying Barn
Cheeseman's Gate
Egham Wick Plantations
Queenswood
RUNNYMEDE
Ulverscroft
Breakheart Hill
Smith's Lawn Cottages
Eton Bridge
Alderhurst
BAKEHAM HILL
Heather Garden
Totem Pole
Larch Bridge
Wick Pond
ACS Egham International School
Glenwood
High Flyer's Hill
Oxshed Clump
CANADIAN MEMORIAL AVENUE
THE VALLEY GARDENS
Broad Ride
Huntersdale
Great Wood
Winter Garden
The Punch Bowl
LONDON ROAD
Virginia Water Plantations
Callow Hill
WOODLEE CL.
The Dell
VIRGINIA WATER
Botany Bay Point
FROSTFARM PLANTATION
VIRGINIA BEECHES
HOLLOW LANE
Merlewood
Stroude Farm
Stroude Crossing
The Clockcase
Kenwolde
BLACKNEST ROAD
A329
"Roman Temple"
Worldsend Gate
Worldsend Cottage
Virginia Lodge
CHRISTCHURCH ROAD
WOODSIDE WAY
WAVERLEY
Christ Church C of E Inf. Sch.
QUENTIN WY.
STUART WY.
VIRGINIA WATER
Virginia Water
GORSE HILL ROAD
PIPER'S END
LAMBLY HILL
CEDAR DRIVE
BELVEDERE WOOD
Cascade Bridge
WENTWORTH
King's Copse
Virginia Wood
General's Copse
Waverley Copse
SPRING WOODS
WELLINGTON AVENUE
B389
WOODLANDS RD.
MORELLA CL.
HEATH CL.
Play. Fld.
TROTSWORTH CT.
Belvedere Fort
CHESTNUT AV.
PINEWOOD
STAYNE END
ABBOTS DRIVE
BROCK WAY
GU25
STATION APP.
MONKS DRIVE
Duke's Copse
147
LAKE RD.
ABBOTS
BADGERS
NUNS WALK
Lido
Virginia Water
Broom Hill
Wentworth Pond
WENTWORTH GOLF COURSE (WEST COURSE)
Wentworth Club
KEEPERS WALK
TRUMPS GRN. CL.
Lodge
MEADOW
PORTNALL DR.
H J K L M N P
1 2 3 4 5 6 7 8 9 10
97 98 99 500
73 72 170 69 68

104
WINDSOR and MAIDENHEAD
RUNNYMEDE
RUNNYMEDE PARK
COOPER'S HILL SLOPES
COOPER'S HILL
Magna Carta Island
Ankerwycke Farm
Longfield Farm
Gravel Pits
Runnymede Pleasure Ground
Warehouse
STAINES ROAD
WRAYSBURY
HYTHE END
Hythe End Bridge
Watts Hill Cottages
Dearsley Island
Wraysbury Hall
Bellweir Lock
Runnymede Bridge
British Disabled Water-Ski Association
Junction 13
M25 MOTORWAY
TW19
The Moor
Moor Farm
Aqueduct
Church Lammas
Queensmead Lake
Hollyhock Island
The Holm
London Stone
Church Island
Water Works
Gas Works
THE CAUSEWAY
A308
A30
B376
STAINES
EGHAM
Strode's Coll.
Egham
Glanty
Pooley Green
Superstore
Pine Trees Business Pk
EGHAM HYTHE
Hythe Prim. Sch.
The Magna Carta Sch.
Egham Leisure Centre
Egham Town FC (Runnymede Stadium)
Glenville Farm
Manorcroft Prim. Sch.
Bowling Club
THORPE LEA
Thorpe Hay Meadow Nature Reserve
TW20
Milton Park
Ripley Springs
Royal Holloway (University of London)
125
Halls of Residence
Sports Centre
Research Laboratories
Rusham Crossing
Milton Park Cottages
Crown Cottages
Whitehall Farm
Great Wood
Luddington House
Stroude
The Dell
Stroude Farm
Stroude Crossing
Great Fosters
Black Lake Farm
Nursery
Nurseries
Crabtree Corner
Thorpe Ind. Park
Egham Bus. Village
Sky Business Park
Cemetery
Spring Farm
Frank Muir Memorial Field
THORPE
Playing Field
Woodcock Farm
Water Gardens
Manor Lake
Eastly End
Thorpe Park
Britannia Arena
St. Ann's Lake
John Battleday Water Ski
Longside Lake
Thorpe Green
Hurst Farm
VIRGINIA WATER
Virginia Water
ST. ANN'S HEATH
GU25
Home Farm
St. Ann's Park
Junction 12 (M25)
148
Junction 2 (M3)
M3 MOTORWAY
THORPE BY-PASS
B388
B389
CHRISTCHURCH ROAD
SANDHILLS
EGHAM HILL
WINDSOR ROAD
R U N N Y M E D E
A B C D E F G
61 62 63 64 65 66 67 68 69 70
500 01 02 03

KING GEORGE VI
RESERVOIR
STAINES
RESERVOIRS
QUEEN MARY
RESERVOIR
105
149
128
H
J
K
L
M
N
P
04
05
06
07
61
62
63
64
65
66
67
68
69
70
71
72
73
170
BYPASS
LONDON ROAD
STAINES BYPASS
KINGSTON ROAD
STANWELL MOOR ROAD
A3044
A30
A308
A320
B376
B377
B378
STAINES
ASHFORD
Ashford
KNOWLE GREEN
Birch Green
Ashford Park
LALEHAM
Laleham Reach
SHEPPERTON GREEN
Shepperton
Chertsey
TW15
TW18
TW17
KT16
SPELTHORNE
CROOKED BILLET ROUNDABOUT
FORDBRIDGE ROUNDABOUT
HMP BRONZEFIELD
ASHFORD MANOR GOLF COURSE
LALEHAM GOLF COURSE
LALEHAM BURWAY
Penton Hook Island
Penton Hook Lock
Penton Hook Marina
Penton Hook Yacht Club
Staines Town FC (Wheatsheaf Pk.)
The Matthew Arnold Sch.
Buckland Primary School
Thomas Knyvett College
St. James Independent Schools (Senior Boys)
Shepperton Film Studios
Laleham C of E Primary School
Ashford Park Primary School
Shortwood Common
Shortwood Farm
Hengrove Farm
Cemetery
Ashford Cemetery
Recreation Ground
Sports Ground
All Weather Pitch
Playing Field
Waterski & Wakeboard Centre
Intake Channel
Pumping Station
Round Copse
Laleham Nurseries
Laleham Park
Abbey Lake
Mountbatten Pavilion
Beomonds Farm
River Ash
River Thames
Sweep's Ditch
Burway Ditch
Abbey River
Works
Reservoir
Lake

EAST BEDFONT
106
TW14
LONDON ROAD
STAINES RD.
A30
Q
R
S
T
U
V
W
Bedfont Cemetery
Fairholme Prim. Sch.
Playing Field
BEDFONT LAKES COUNTRY PARK
Waterski & Wakeboard Centre
Princes Club
Visitor Centre
Bridge Farm
St. James Independent Schools (Senior Boys)
HMYOI FELTHAM
Edward Pauling Prim. Sch.
Vineyard Nurseries
LOWER FELTHAM
Grosvenor Park
ASHFORD
CLOCKHOUSE LANE
B3003
CHATTERN HILL
Piggeries
Recreation Ground
ASHFORD ROAD
B377
FELTHAM ROAD
CHURCH ROAD
B378
FORDBRIDGE
The Echelford Prim. Sch.
CONVENT RD
SCHOOL ROAD
Depot
Spelthorne Prim. Sch.
Laboratories
Sports Ground
Offices
CHERTSEY ROAD
A244
Feltham Hill Jun. & Inf. Schs.
Cemetery
Warehouse
HIGH ST.
Feltham
Rugby Football Ground
FELTHAMHILL
Playing Field
Kenyngton Manor Prim. Sch.
Garden Centre
Croft Farm
ASHFORD MANOR GOLF COURSE
Club House
KINGSTON ROAD
A308
127
STAINES ROAD
Staines Reservoirs Aqueduct
SCHOOL ROAD JUNCTION
Littleton Common
ASHFORD COMMON
SUNBURY COMMON
Club Ho.
Sports Ground
Pumping Station
Filter Beds
Water Works
SUNBURY CROSS
Junc.1
Superstore
Sunbury
Sunbury Manor Sch.
St. Paul's Catholic Coll.
Springfield Prim. Sch.
QUEEN MARY RESERVOIR
CHARLTON
M3 MOTORWAY
M3
WINDMILL ROAD
Upper Halliford
UPPER HALLIFORD ROAD
UPPER HALLIFORD BY-PASS
The Bishop Ward C of E School
Playing Field
Halliford House Rec. Grd.
Caravan Site
Hawkedale Infants School
Driving Range
HAZELWOOD GOLF COURSE
TW16
Sunbury
Manor Farm
Refuse Transfer Station
Driving Range
Club House
UPPER HALLIFORD
SUNBURY GOLF COURSE
Grange Farm
Vicarage Farm
LITTLETON
Shepperton
Shepperton Film Studios
SHEPPERTON GREEN
TW17
LALEHAM
B376
Squire's Bridge
Staines Road Farm
150
River Ash
61
62
63
64
65
66
67
68
69
70

Feltham
HANWORTH
ELTHAM
Middlesex Crematorium
De Brome Building
Heathfield Jun. & Inf. Schs.
Twickenham Cemetery
HOSPITAL BRIDGE ROUNDABOUT
Feltham Community College
Playing Field
UXBRIDGE ROAD
A312
A314
HANWORTH ROAD
CRANE
Twickenham
Nature Reserve
Gala Bingo
Tenpin
Cineworld
LEISURE WEST
FELTHAM BUSINESS COMPLEX
Ordnance Depot
Pav. Sports Ground
Tennis Courts
Feltham Airparcs Leisure Centre
Mount Corner
Hanworth Park House
HANWORTH PARK
HOUNSLOW ROAD
HAMPTON RD. WEST
School
GREAT CHERTSEY ROAD
A316
STAINES RD.
A305
TWICKENHAM RD.
APEX CORNER
Fulwell Park
AMIDA GOLF COURSE
David Lloyd Centre
FULWELL GOLF COURSE
HANWORTH
TW13
Rectory Meadow
SUNBURY WAY
HAMPTON RD. EAST
UXBRIDGE ROAD
PARK ROAD
A313
HAMPTON HILL
Superstore
Playing Field
Hampton Comm. Coll.
Hampton Sports & Fitness Cen.
Hampton School
The Lady Eleanor Holles Sch. (Jun. Dept.)
The Lady Eleanor Holles Sch. (Senior Dept.)
Hampton
Hospice
Marling Hall
Sports Comm. Cen.
COUNTRY WAY
Dairy
Works
Filter Beds
Lindon Bennett Sch.
Kempton Local Nature Reserve
Nature Res.
Play. Fld.
Staines Reservoirs Aqueduct
Depot
Stables
Kempton Park
Reservoir
Half Moon Covert
Sports Ground
Marling Park
Hatherop Park
Upper Thames
TW12
Grandstand
KEMPTON PARK RACECOURSE
Football Ground
Hydes Field
Portlane Bridge
HAMPTON
Hampton & Richmond Borough FC (Beveree Stadium)
Hampton Open Air Pool
Pantile Bridge
Carlisle Park
Clarendon Sch.
A308
UPPER SUNBURY ROAD
A311
HIGH STREET
Adult Educ. Cen.
Sports Grd.
Chennestone Prim. Sch.
Kenton Court Meadow
Stain Hill West Reservoir
Stain Hill East Reservoir
Grand Junction Reservoir
Water Works
Filter Beds
Sunbury Court
Sunbury-on-Thames
Grand Junction Isle
RIVER THAMES
Sunnyside Reservoir
Platt's Eyot
Hurst Park Open Space
HURST PARK
Garrick's Ait
Garrick Lawn
Sunbury Court Island
SUNBURY
Sunbury Park
Sunbury Park Walled Garden
Gallery
Arts Cen.
Rivermead Island
MOLESEY RESERVOIRS
ELMBRIDGE
Thames Lock
Sunbury Locks
Walton-on-Thames
KT12
Apps Court Farm
The Cottage
BESSBOROUGH RESERVOIR
KNIGHTS RESERVOIR
Sports Ground
Football Grd.
Elmbridge Xcel Leisure Complex
Rivernook Farm
HURST ROAD
A3050
WALTON RD.
Grovelands Rec. Grd.
Mole Hall
B369
East & West Molesey Cemy.
Hurst Pool
Molesey Hurst Rec. Grd.
Tennis Courts
The Pav. Sports & Fitness Club
Molesey FC Grd.
Primary Sch.
WEST MOLESEY
MOLESEY HOSP.
Adult Learning Cen.
West Molesey

Ea
Fa
Ga
Ha
Ja
Ka
La
TWICKENHAM
Twickenham
Strawberry Hill
STRAWBERRY HILL GOLF COURSE
St. James's Catholic Primary School
St. Mary's University College
Ham Lands Nature Reserve
Ham Riverside Lands
Thames Young Mariners Base
Ham Fields
Ham House & Garden
HAM
Playing Field
Miniature Rifle Range
Radnor Gardens
Fulwell Park
FULWELL GOLF COURSE
Fulwell
Hampton
HAMPTON HILL
TEDDINGTON
Teddington
Teddington Lock
Teddington Weir
Teddington Studios
Lensbury Club
Sports Ground
National Phy. Lab
Canal Plantation
Upper Lodge
Pantile Bridge
The Brew House
TW12
Hampton Open Air Pool
Round Plantation
Bushy House
B U S H Y
P A R K
Willow Plantation
River Lodge
The Pheasantry Welcome Centre
Broom Clumps
Hawthorn Lodge
Warren Plantation
Deer Pen
Half Moon Plantation
Heron Pond
Oval Plantation
Leg-of-Mutton Pond
Waterhouse Woodland Garden
Waterhouse Pond
Fisher's Pond
Red Brick Bridge
Diana Fountain
The Royal Paddocks
Bushy Lodge
HAMPTON WICK
Hampton Wick Royal Cricket Ground
The King's Field
HAMPTON
Hampton & Richmond Borough FC (Beveree Stad.)
RIVER THAMES
Garrick's Ait
HURST PARK
Hurst Park
Taggs Island
Ash Island
Hampton Court House Sch.
Hampton Court Green
Hampton Court Gardens
Hampton Court Palace
HAMPTON COURT
Privy Garden
Cigarette Island Park
Hampton Court
EAST MOLESEY
East Molesey
ELMBRIDGE
Molesey Hurst Rec. Grd.
Stud House
HAMPTON COURT PARK
The Long Water
Farm Cottages
HAMPTON COURT PALACE
The Rick Pond
CHERTSEY ROAD
STAINES ROAD
HAMPTON ROAD
WELLINGTON RD.
STANLEY ROAD
CHURCH ROAD
WALDEGRAVE ROAD
STRAWBERRY VALE
TWICKENHAM RD.
KINGSTON ROAD
HIGH STREET
BROAD ST.
PARK ROAD
SANDY LANE
UXBRIDGE ROAD
THAMES ST.
HAMPTON COURT ROAD
HURST ROAD
CHESTNUT AVENUE
A316
A305
A311
A309
A310
A313
A308
A3050
B358
B360
B369
B359
61
62
63
64
65
66
67
68
69
70
108
129
152

SIDMOUTH WOOD
PETERSHAM
Petersham Gate
King Henry VIII Mound
Queen Mothers Copse
White Lodge Museum
The Royal Ballet Lower School
Victory
109
Leg of Mutton Pond
Pen Ponds
Lawn Plantation
Treebox Wood
SPANKERS HILL WOOD
Queen Elizabeth's Plantation
Horse Ride
PETERSHAM PARK
Oak Lodge
Pembroke Lodge (Cafeteria)
DEER PARK
King George V Jubilee Plantation
Playing Fields
Beverley Brook
SUDBROOK PARK
Sudbrook Park Club House
The Wilderness
RICHMOND GOLF COURSE
White Ash Lodge
Pond Plantation
R I C H M O N D
Richmond
T H A M E S
(Open during daylight hours only)
Tercentenary Plantation
Pond Slade
(National Nature Reserve)
Prince Charles's Spinney
Robin Hood Gate
Ham Cross Plantation
Isabella Plantation Garden
P A R K
Gibbet Wood
KINGSTON VALE
Ham Bottom
Peg's Pond
Thomson's Pond
Broomfield Hill Wood
Broomfield Hill
HAM GATE AVENUE
HAM COMMON (Nature Reserve)
TW10
Ham Gate
Ham Cross
ISABELLA PLANTATION
Ham Dip
High Wood
Still Pond
Deer Fold
SW15
Walkden Hall
Robin Hood Prim. Sch.
Kingston University (Kingston Hill Campus)
CASSEL HOSP.
UPPER HAM RD.
RICHMOND ROAD
HMP LATCHMERE HOUSE
Coronation Plantation
The Flat
Dann's Pond
KINGSTON HILL
COOMBE PARK
KINGSTON BY-PASS
YMCA Sports Grd.
The Tiffin Girls' Sch.
Tiffins Girls Comm. Spts. Cen.
Fern Hill Prim. Sch.
KT2
Gallows Pond
King's Clump
Ladderstile Gate
Canbury Sch.
Warren House
The Water Gardens
COOMBE HILL GOLF COURSE
Latchmere Sch.
RC Prim. Sch.
Sports Ground
Kingston Gate
COOMBE WOOD GOLF COURSE
COOMBE
WARREN CUTTING
Club House
132
Recreation Ground
Steven's Eyot
Kingston upon Thames
QUEENS ROAD
Holy Cross Preparatory RC Sch.
Rokeby Sch.
Marymount International School
Canbury Gardens
Park Hill Sch.
COOMBE WOOD GOLF COURSE
Tennis Cts.
WEST TRAPS LANE
TEDDINGTON
Fitness Club
KINGSTON HOSPITAL
Coombe Hill Jun. & Inf. Schools
Hampton Wick
Kingston
CROMWELL RD.
The Rotunda Cen.
COOMBE ROAD
Norbiton
Coombe Girls' Sch.
LONDON RD.
CAMBRIDGE RD.
NORBITON
Tiffin Sch.
Leisure Cen.
Islamic Cen.
New Malden
Theatre
The Fairfield Sch.
Recreation Ground
KINGSTON UPON THAMES
Corpus Christi Catholic Prim. School
Kingston Cemetery
Kingston Crematorium
Indoor Bowls Club
AFC Wimbledon & Kingstonian FC (Kingsmeadow)
Athletics Centre
Kingston Univ.
Hogsmill River
Sludge Beds
Retail Park
KT3
Waste Disposal Centre
Sewage Works
SURBITON
Surbiton KT5
Surbiton Cemetery
Berrylands
153
Recreation Ground
PORTSMOUTH RD.
THAMES
Raven's Ait
KINGSTON ROAD
Ma
Na
Pa
Qa
Ra
Sa
Ta
61
62
63
64
65
66
67
68
69
70

PUTNEY HEATH
RICHMOND PARK GOLF COURSE
SPANKERS HILL WOOD
Richmond
TW10
ROEHAMPTON VALE
KINGSTON VALE
PUTNEY VALE
WANDSWORTH
Putney Vale Cemetery
Putney Vale Crematorium
Kingston University (Roehampton Vale Centre)
Wimbledon Windmill Museum
LONDON SCOTTISH GOLF COURSE
WIMBLEDON COMMON
WIMBLEDON COMMON GOLF COURSE
Queen's Mere
Caesar's Camp
ROYAL WIMBLEDON GOLF COURSE
Cannizaro Park
Beverley Meads & Fishpond Woods Nature Reserve
SW15
SW19
SW20
KT3
Wimbledon All England Lawn Tennis & Croquet Club
Museum
PARKSIDE HOSP.
WIMBLEDON
Wimbledon Coll.
King's Coll. Sch.
COPSE HILL
Cottenham Park
COOMBE HILL GOLF COURSE
Kingston upon Thames
NEW VICTORIA HOSPITAL
COOMBE LANE
Raynes Park
Prince George's Playing Field
Bushey Mead
David Lloyd Leisure & Lloyds Lanes Raynes Park
Joseph Hood Recreation Ground
CANNON HILL COMMON (Recreation Ground)
Wimbledon Chase
RAYNES PARK
WEST BARNES
New Malden
NEW MALDEN
SHANNON CORNER
World of Golf Driving Range & Jurassic Encounter
Emanuel School Playing Field
KINGSTON BY-PASS
BEVERLEY WAY
A3
A238
A298
A219
B281
B282
B283
A308
131
154

EARLSFIELD
Earlsfield
SUMMERSTOWN
Wimbledon Stadium (Greyhound)
Lambeth Crematorium
LAMBETH CEMETERY
Wimbledon Cemetery
WANDSWORTH
STREATHAM CEMETERY
UPPER TOOTING
SPRINGFIELD UNIVERSITY HOSPITAL
CENTRAL LONDON GOLF COURSE
Burntwood School
Garratt Green
Tooting Bec
BALHAM
Tooting Broadway
TOOTING
St. George's Uni. of London
ST. GEORGE'S HOSPITAL
TOOTING GRAVENEY
Haydons Road
Wimbledon Park
Wimbledon
SOUTH WIMBLEDON
South Wimbledon
Colliers Wood
COLLIER'S WOOD
Tooting
MERTON
MERTON PARK
Merton Park
Morden Rd.
MORDEN HALL PARK
Morden Hall
Morden Cottage
Morden Lodge
Ravensbury Park
Mitcham
MITCHAM
Lavender Park
Cemetery
Cemy.
Morden
MORDEN
Morden South
South Merton
NELSON HOSP.
Deen City Farm
Canons Leisure Centre
Cricket Green
Phipps Bridge
Belgrave Wlk.
Mostyn Gardens
Kendor Gardens
Ricards Lodge High Sch.
Wimbledon Park Athletics Track
MERTON HIGH STREET
MERANTUN WAY
THE BROADWAY
MORDEN ROAD
LONDON ROAD
GARRATT LANE
BURNTWOOD LANE
DURNSFORD ROAD
PLOUGH LANE
HAYDONS ROAD
GAP ROAD
WESTERN ROAD
MITCHAM ROAD
UPPER TOOTING ROAD
TOOTING HIGH STREET
MORDEN ROAD
CRANMER RD.
COMMONSIDE WEST
Bb
Cb
Db
Eb
Fb
Gb
Hb
61
62
63
64
65
66
67
68
69
70
111
134
155
SW18
SW19
SM4

134
BALHAM
Balham
STREATHAM HILL
Streatham Hill
SW2
SW12
SW16
SW17
Tooting Bec
Tooting Bec Common
TOOTING BEC COMMON
WANDSWORTH
Tooting Graveney Common
Tooting Bec Lido
Tooting Bec Athletic Track
STREATHAM PARK
STREATHAM
Streatham
Streatham Common
STREATHAM COMMON
FURZEDOWN
Furzedown School
Tooting
STREATHAM VALE
Streatham Vale Park
Lonesome
MERTON
Mitcham Eastfields
South London Crematorium
Streatham Park Cemetery
Jewish Cemetery
MITCHAM
MITCHAM COMMON
NORBURY
Norbury
NORBURY PARK
Norwood Grove Recreation Ground
The Rookery
Harris Academy Merton
William Morris Primary Sch.
Sherwood Park
Croydon Athletic FC
MITCHAM GOLF COURSE
BEC ROAD
TOOTING BEC ROAD
STREATHAM HIGH ROAD
MITCHAM LANE
STREATHAM ROAD
LONDON ROAD
STREATHAM COMMON NORTH
CROYDON ROAD
COMMONSIDE WEST
CARSHALTON RD
WINDMILL RD
ROWAN RD
GREYHOUND LA.
GREEN LANE
CHURCH LANE
A23
A24
A214
A216
A217
A236
A237
A239
B221
B242
B272
B273
B241
Jb
Kb
Lb
Mb
Nb
Pb
Qb
112
156
133
61
62
63
64
65
66
67
68
69
70

TULSE HILL
Tulse Hill
DULWICH COMMON
West Dulwich
WEST DULWICH
Dulwich College
DULWICH & SYDENHAM HILL GOLF COURSE
SOUTHWARK
DULWICH
FOREST HILL
Sydenham Hill Wood & Cox's Walk Nature Reserve
Dulwich Wood
SE21
Kingsdale Foundation Sch.
Sydenham Hill
West Norwood Crematorium
West Norwood
WEST NORWOOD
Cemetery
UPPER SYDENHAM
SE26
Sydenham
DARTMOUTH RD.
KIRKDALE
Gipsy Hill
NORWOOD PARK
WESTWOOD HILL
CRYSTAL PALACE PARK
CRYSTAL PALACE PARK RD.
TV Transmitter
Crystal Palace National Sports Centre
CRYSTAL PALACE
Crystal Palace Museum
Crystal Palace Athletics Stadium
Crystal Palace Dinosaurs
Crystal Palace
Penge West
SYDENHAM
Penge East
CROWN DALE
CENTRAL HILL
NORWOOD NEW TOWN
WESTOW HILL
NORWOOD
Westow Park
BEULAH HILL
KNIGHTS HILL
UPPER NORWOOD
The Lawns
CHURCH ROAD
ANERLEY HILL
ANERLEY ROAD
Anerley
ANERLEY
PENGE
The Phil Edwards Cen.
Harris City Academy
Beaulieu Heights
South Norwood Lake
Orchard School Sports Centre
David Livingstone Prim. Sch.
Grangewood Park
Spurgeon's College
SOUTH NORWOOD
Harris Academy
SE25
Crystal Palace FC (Selhurst Park)
WHITEHORSE LANE
Thornton Heath
THORNTON HEATH
SELHURST ROAD
Norwood Junc.
PORTLAND RD.
CROYDON RD.
Birkbeck
Beckenham Crematorium
Blind Corner
Pitch & Putt Course
SOUTH NORWOOD COUNTRY PARK
Croydon Sports Arena
Croydon FC Grd.
St. Chad's Cath. Prim. Sch.
61
62
63
64
65
66
67
68
69
70
113
157
136
Rb
Sb
Tb
Ub
Vb
Wb
Xb

136
114
135
158
CATFORD
FOREST HILL
SE23
SE6
SE26
SE20
SE25
BR3
Beckenham
LOWER SYDENHAM
BELL GREEN
BELLINGHAM
SYDENHAM
NEW BECKENHAM
PENGE
ANERLEY
BECKENHAM
ELMERS END
EDEN PARK
PARK LANGLEY
Forest Hill
Sydenham
Lwr. Sydenham
Bellingham
Beckenham Hill
Penge East
Penge West
New Beckenham
Kent House
Clock Ho.
Beckenham Road
Beckenham Junc.
Birkbeck
Elmers End
Anerley
BECKENHAM PLACE PARK
BECKENHAM PLACE PARK GOLF COURSE
CATOR PARK
Mayow Park
SOUTH NORWOOD COUNTRY PARK
CROYDON
Beckenham Crematorium
KELSEY PARK
STANSTEAD
SYDENHAM
SOUTHEND
BECKENHAM
BROMLEY
HAYES
CROYDON
ELMERS END
HIGH STREET
SOUTHEND ROAD
KIRKDALE
DARTMOUTH RD.
PERRY RISE
PERRY HILL
CATFORD HILL
BROMLEY RD
BECKENHAM HILL ROAD
NEWLANDS PARK
PARISH LANE
ANERLEY RD.
A212
A2218
A2015
A213
A234
A222
A214
A2216
B227
B230
Yb
Zb
Ac
Bc
Cc
Dc
Ec
61
62
63
64
65
66
67
68
69
70

Fc
Gc
Hc
Jc
Kc
Lc
Mc
115
HITHER GREEN CEMETERY
Hither Green Crematorium
Grove Park Nature Reserve
MOTTINGHAM
SE9
SE12
GROVE PARK
CHINBROOK ROAD
FORSTER MEMORIAL PARK
SOUTHEND
DOWNHAM
Downham Health & Leisure Centre
Churchdown Christian Centre
BR1
BR2
BR7
PLAISTOW
SUNDRIDGE
SUNDRIDGE PARK GOLF COURSE
Sundridge Park
ELMSTEAD
ELMSTEAD WOOD
Elmstead Woods
138
Widmore Green
Bromley
BROMLEY
BROMLEY PARK
SHORTLANDS GOLF COURSE
SHORTLANDS
Shortlands
Bromley South
Bromley Nth.
Bromley Civic Centre
WIDMORE
BICKLEY
Virgin Active Health Club
BROMLEY HILL
LONDON ROAD
BURNT ASH LANE
BARING ROAD
TWEEDY RD.
WIDMORE RD.
BICKLEY RD.
CHISLEHURST RD.
MASONS HILL
HAYES ROAD
WESTMORELAND RD.
BROMLEY COMMON
159
61
62
63
64
65
66
67
68
69
70

Mottingham
MOTTINGHAM
Eltham Coll.
Eric Liddell Spts. Cen.
SIDCUP ROAD
COURT ROAD
MOTTINGHAM LA.
GROVE PARK
Sports Ground
Playing Field
Rec. Grd.
Playing Fields
Coldharbour Leisure Centre
Netball Courts
Fairy Hill
116
GREEN LA.
New Eltham
NEW ELTHAM
FIVEWAYS
St. Olave's Prep. School
FOOTS CRAY RD.
Dulverton Sch.
SIDCUP ROAD
MAIN ROAD
HALFWAY
Wyncham Stream
World of Golf at Sidcup
LONGLANDS
Flamingo Park Sports Grd.
Pitch & Putt Course
Kemnal Manor
Ashen Grove
Partridge Shaw
Esporta Health & Fitness
Chislehurst Cemetery
GREENWICH
SE9
Lower Marvels Wood
Marvels Wood
Grove Park Cemetery
Castlecombe Prim. Sch.
Youth Cen.
ELMSTEAD WOOD
Sports Ground
ELMSTEAD
WHITE HORSE HILL
RED HILL
HIGH ST.
Edgebury Prim. Sch.
Foxbury
Chislehurst
Playing Field
Old Elthamians Sports Club
Beaverwood Sch. for Girls
Athletic Ground
Darul Uloom London Islamic Institute
Red Hill Prim. Sch.
CHISLEHURST WEST
Whyte's Woodland
Mead Rd. Inf. Sch.
Selwood
High Grove
Sundridge Park Manor
Botany Bay
Elmstead Woods
Rockpit Wood
Kyd Brook
137
SUNDRIDGE PARK GOLF COURSE
CHISLEHURST
CAMDEN PARK
CHISLEHURST GOLF COURSE
Camden Place Club House
CHISLEHURST COMMON
PERRY LANE
Farringtons School
Icehouse Wood
BROMLEY RD.
ROYAL PDE.
ST. PAUL'S CRAY RD.
Bullers Wood Sch.
The Cedars
Hangman's Cnr.
WATTS LA.
MANOR PARK RD.
B264
Cricket Grd.
Chalkpit Wood
Caves
Bansome Wood
Marjorie McClure Specialist School
Playing Field
Hadresham
The Fantails
Holbrook Wood
Lodge
The Larches
St. Peter & St. Paul RC Prim. Sch.
The Gorse Children's Home
Rifle Range
Hawkwood Nursery
Birch Wood
Butts
Avalon
Gosshill Wood
Chislehurst
SUMMER HILL
OLD HILL
CHISLEHURST RD.
BICKLEY
BICKLEY RD.
BICKLEY PARK
A222
Play. Fld.
Hadlow
Pond Wood
Hawkwood Estate
Hawkwood Farm
Tongs Farm
Walk Wood
Mem.
St. Paul's Cray Common
ORPINGTON RD.
Bickley Junc.
Bickley
Bromley
Virgin Active Health Club
PAGE HEATH
Chislehurst Junction
Great Thrift
Edlmann Memorial Wood
PETTS WOOD
Willett Memorial Wood
St. Mary Cray Junction
BR1
Blackbrook Wood
JUBILEE COUNTRY PARK
Bromley High School
Petts Wood Junction
BR2
Thornet Wood
160
Jubilee Park Nature Res.
Sydney Shaw
SOUTHBOROUGH
PETTS WOOD
Pleasure Ground
Tennis Courts
Rec. Grd.
Nc
Pc
Qc
Rc
Sc
Tc
Uc
61
62
63
64
65
66
67
68
69
70

Berrylands
131
Surbiton
KT5
KT6
KT3
KT4
KT9
KT19
New Malden
BERRYLANDS
SURBITON
SOUTHBOROUGH
TOLWORTH
Tolworth
TOLWORTH JUNCTION
KINGSTON upon THAMES
OLD MALDEN
Malden Manor
Worcester Park
HOOK
Chessington
CHESSINGTON
Chessington North
Chessington South
EPSOM and EWELL
WEST EWELL
KINGSTON BY-PASS
MALDEN (KINGSTON BY-PASS) WY.
A3
A240
A243
B284
B2200
B3364
A3210
KINGSTON ROAD
EWELL ROAD
HOOK ROAD
LEATHERHEAD RD.
BRIGHTON ROAD
DITTON ROAD
RUXLEY LANE
CHESSINGTON RD
SURBITON HILL ROAD
ALEXANDRA DRIVE
Hogsmill River
Recreation Ground
Alexandra Millennium Green
Richard Challoner School
Sports Centre
Tolworth Rec. Cen.
King George's Field Playing Field
Corinthian Casuals FC Grd.
Surbiton Raceway
Linden Bridge School
Riverview C of E Prim. Sch.
Epsom & Ewell High Sch.
Hogsmill Local Nature Reserve
Bonesgate Open Space Local Nature Reserve
Castle Hill Local Nature Reserve
HORTON PARK GOLF COURSE
HORTON COUNTRY PARK
CHESSINGTON GOLF COURSE
Hook Road Arena
St. Ebba's Farm Cottage
173
154
Ma
Na
Pa
Qa
Ra
Sa
Ta
71
72
73
74
75
76
77
78
79
80

MALDEN
KINGSTON RD.
BURLINGTON RD.
SHANNON CORNER
132
WEST BARNES
A3 KINGSTON BY-PASS
MALDEN JUNC.
Coombe Boys Sch.
Motspur Pk.
Raynes Park Playing Fields
St. John Fisher RC Prim. Sch.
Sports Ground
Old Blues Rugby Football Grd.
University of London Athletic Ground
New Malden
North East Surrey Crematorium
MORDEN CEMETERY
MORDEN PARK
TUDOR DRIVE
BBC Sports Ground
MOTSPUR PARK
The Sir Joseph Hood Memorial Playing Fields
Gas Works
KINGSTON upon THAMES
Playing Fields
Merton & Sutton Joint Cemetery
Aragon Prim. Sch.
King George's Field
Green Lane Prim. Sch.
ASM Ten. Cen. MANOR PARK
Malden Manor
Malden Manor Prim. Sch.
Richard Challoner School
OLD MALDEN
Malden Green
Mayflower Park
Refuse Destructor
Worcester Park
Worcester Park
Dorchester Prim. Sch.
St. Anthony's Hosp.
St. Raphael's Hospice
Playing Field
Maori Sports Ground
CENTRAL ROAD
CHEAM COMMON RD.
A2043
WORCESTER PARK
Shadbolt Park
Linden Bridge School
Wandgas Athletics Ground
Cuddington Prim. Sch.
King George's Field
Auriol Park
Cuddington Recreation Ground
Beverley Brook
NORTH CHEAM
Fairlands Pk.
QUEEN VICTORIA
Cheam Leisure Cen.
SM3
Epsom
KT4
KINGSTON RD.
A240
STONELEIGH
Stoneleigh
Meadow Prim. Sch.
Cheam Recreation Ground
Oak Plantation
London Road Plantation
Cheam High Sch.
CHEAM PARK
CHEAM
NONSUCH PARK
Mansion House
EPSOM and EWELL
KT17
KT19
Hogsmill Local Nature Reserve
BEGGAR'S HILL
LONDON RD.
A24
WEST EWELL
David Lloyd Leisure Cen.
Nonsuch High Sch.
Harefield Bri. Playing Field
ORGAN CROSSROADS
EWELL
EWELL BY-PASS
174
Ewell West
Bourne Hall Mus.
Cheam Sports Club
Warren Fm.
EWELL RD.
CHEAM RD.
Ua
Va
Wa
Xa
Ya
Za
Ab
71
72
73
74
75
76
77
78
79
80
153

MORDEN
Morden South
ST. HELIER
ROSEHILL
BENHILTON
SUTTON
West Sutton
Sutton Common
THE WRYTHE
CARSHALTON
Carshalton
Carshalton Beeches
CARSHALTON BEECHES
CARSHALTON ON THE HILL
HACKBRIDGE
Mitcham Junction
St. Helier Open Space
ST. HELIER HOSPITAL
QUEEN MARY'S HOSPITAL FOR CHILDREN
Sutton Arena Leisure Centre
Sutton Cemetery
Rosehill Recreation Ground
Collingwood Road Recreation Ground
Carshalton Athletic FC
Sutton United FC
Tooting & Mitcham United FC (Imperial Fields)
Watermeads
Poulter Park
Bishopsford House
River Wandle
ROSE HILL ROUNDABOUT
Bb
Cb
Db
Eb
Fb
Gb
Hb
133
156
175

MITCHAM COMMON
MERTON
CROYDON ROAD
MITCHAM GOLF COURSE
Mitcham Junction
Playing Fields
Croydon Athletic FC (Keith Tuckey Stadium)
Croydon Crematorium
CROYDON CEMETERY
The Archbishop Lanfranc Sch.
MITCHAM ROAD
Beddington Lane
Traq Motor Racing
Hundred Acre Bridge
Sludge Beds
Mitcham
Sand Plant
CR4
BEDDINGTON CORNER
Irrigation Bridge
Beddington Sewage Treatment Works
Factory
Works
Warehouse
Therapia Lane
LOMBARD ROUNDABOUT
Ampere Way
BEDDINGTON CROSS
Bus Depot
PIONEERS INDUSTRIAL PARK
BEDDINGTON TRADING ESTATE
Superstores
Vue Cinema
Tenpin
Mile Road Bridge
Hackbridge
HACKBRIDGE
FELNEX TRADING ESTATE
SUTTON
Tennis Courts
Sports Ground
Pavilions
BEDDINGTON PARK
Superstore
Warehouse
Waddon Marsh
WADDON
Wilderness Island
Wandle Bri.
River Wandle
Carew Manor & Dovecote
Carew Manor Sch.
The Grange
Boating Lake
Manor Gdn.
Grammar Sch.
Electricity Switching Station
BEDDINGTON
Church Paddock
The Warren
CROYDON ROAD
A232
Waddon Ponds
Waddon
CARSHALTON
Westcroft Leisure Cen.
Council Offices
Studio Thtre.
Wallington
Bandon Hill Cemetery
Bandonhill
Playing Field
FIVEWAYS CORNER
Retail Park
Sports Ground
RUSKIN
The Frying Pan
CARSHALTON PARK
WALLINGTON
SM6
Mellows Park
Bowling Green
STAFFORD ROAD
Wilson's Sch.
Powerleague Soccer Centre (Croydon)
Esporta: The Surrey Health & Racquets Club
Leisure Centre
Kidspace Health Club
SOUTH BEDDINGTON
Foresters Prim. Sch.
Roundshaw
Roundshaw Park (Playing Fields)
Amy Johnson Prim. Sch.
Phoenix Cen.
Roundshaw Park
Roundshaw Downs Local Nature Reserve
Carshalton Beeches
Wallington Cen.
PURLEY WAY
A23
A237
A236
B272
B271
134
155
176
Jb
Kb
Lb
Mb
Nb
Pb
Qb
71
72
73
74
75
76
77
78
79
80

THORNTON HEATH
SELHURST
Selhurst
Norwood Junc.
WOODSIDE
Woodside
Blackhorse La.
Broad Green
CROYDON
West Croydon
East Croydon
George St.
Church St.
Centrale
Wellesley Rd.
Reeves Cnr.
Lebanon Rd.
Sandilands
Addiscombe
ADDISCOMBE
Ashburton Park
SHIRLEY
Shirley Park Golf Course
Oaks Farm
Coombe Farm
COOMBE PARK
LLOYD PARK
Lloyd Park
Coombe Wood
Ballards Plantation
Royal Russell School
Croham Hurst Golf Course
CROHAM HURST
Breakneck Hill
Thrift Wood
Bramley Bank Nature Reserve
SOUTH CROYDON
South Croydon
HALING PARK
Duppas Hill
Sanderstead
Harris Academy Purley
Trinity School Playing Field
Fairfield Halls
Croydon Sports Arena
Croydon Golf Driving Range
SOUTH NORWOOD COUNTRY PARK
Visitors Centre
Heavers Farm Prim. Sch.
Queen's Rd. Cemy.
Ecclesbourne Prim. Sch.
Oasis Academy Shirley Park (Seniors)
Addington Hills
Coombe Lodge Nurseries
Old Ballards Cottage
Geoffrey Harris House
WINDMILL RD.
ST. JAMES'S RD.
WHITEHORSE RD.
WELLESLEY RD.
LOWER ADDISCOMBE RD.
ADDISCOMBE RD.
COOMBE RD.
BRIGHTON RD.
PARK LANE
SELSDON RD.
SHIRLEY RD.
SPRING LA.
LONG LA.
PORTLAND RD.
ROMAN WAY
OLD TOWN
CROYDON FLYOVER
SOUTH END
UPPER SELSDON RD.
WARHAM AV.
BALLARDS WAY
COOMBE LANE
SE25
CR0
CR2
Rb
Sb
Tb
Ub
Vb
Wb
Xb
71
72
73
74
75
76
77
78
79
80
135
158
177

Yb
Zb
Ac
Bc
Cc
Dc
Ec
SOUTH NORWOOD COUNTRY PARK
ELMERS END
EDEN PARK
PARK LANGLEY
136
Croydon Sports Arena Croydon FC Grd.
SE25
Ryelands Prim. Sch.
Arena
Croydon Golf Driving Range
David Lloyd Leisure
Langley Court (Research Labs)
Beckenham
Langley Park Schools
Langley Park Sports Centre
Unicorn Prim. Sch.
Eden Park
UPPER ELMERS END
ELMERS END A214 ROAD
Crouch Oak Wood
BR3
Woodside
Ashburton Park
Monks Orchard Prim. Sch.
MONKS ORCHARD
Edenham High Sch.
Shirley Oaks BMI HOSPITAL
Oasis Academy Shirley Park (Seniors)
Ashburton Playing Fields
Shirley Oaks
BETHLEM ROYAL HOSPITAL
Parkfields Recreation Ground
High Broom Wood
Cold Shaw
Chelsham House
River House
Wickham Park House
Caravan Park
West Wickham
Oak Lodge Prim. Sch.
Blake Recreation Ground
WEST WICKHAM
HIGH STREET
WICKHAM ROAD A232
ADDISCOMBE A232 RD.
A215
Trinity Sch.
SHIRLEY
157
Croydon
CR0
Spring Park Wood
SPRING PARK
Benson Prim. Sch.
Colma Convent Girls' Sch.
Shirley High Sch.
Shirley Windmill
SHIRLEY PARK GOLF COURSE
Foxes Wood
Wychwood
Pinewoods
Lacrosse Pitch
CROYDON
Kennel Wood
UPPER SHIRLEY
THE ADDINGTON GOLF COURSE
The Bungalow
Club House
Addington Hills
Threehalfpenny Wood
Pumping Station
Rugby Ground
Foxhill Shaw
Reservoir (covered)
Coombe Lane
COOMBE LANE
ADDINGTON
ADDINGTON VILLAGE RD.
A2022 WAY
Royal Russell School
Heathfield (Train. Cen.)
Heathfield Farm
Bramley Bank Nature Reserve
ADDINGTON PALACE GOLF COURSE
Addington Palace
ADDINGTON PARK
Addington Village
GRAVEL HILL A212
Gravel Hill
Rowdown Fields
Little David's Sch. (The Time Bridge Centre)
Applegarth Jun. & Inf. Schs.
Castle Hill Prim. Sch.
KENT GATE
South Croydon
Gilbert Scott Primary School & Red Gates School
Monks Hill Sports Cen.
Selsdon High Sch.
John Ruskin College
CR2
SELSDON PARK ROAD A2022
Fieldway
ADDINGTON COURT GOLF COURSE
LITTLEHEATH WOOD
178
Addington Well Pumping Sta.
NEWLANDS WOODS

Bromley
HAYES
Hayes
BR2
BR4
Keston
KESTON
KESTON MARK
CONEY HALL
NASH
NEW ADDINGTON
Wickham
B R O M L E Y
NORMAN PARK
BROMLEY COMMON
HAYES COMMON
PARK
Nuffield Health Fitness & Wellbeing Centre
Bromley FC & Cray Wanderers FC
Norman Park Athletics Track
Bromley College of Further & Higher Education
Bromley PRU at Kingswood
Hayes Prim. Sch.
Hayes Sch.
HAYES GROVE PRIORY HOSP
Hawes Down Jun.& Inf. Schs.
Pickhurst Jun. & Inf. Schs.
Nash College
Ravens Wood Sch.
Keston C of E Prim. Sch.
The Emmaus Centre
Metropolitan Police Dog Training Establishment
Electricity Sub Station
Keston Court Riding School
Keston Windmill
The Temple (Roman Mausoleum)
Scrogginhall Wood
Lord's Wood
Brook Wood
Mazzards Wood
Woodcock Grove
Bolds Wood
Barnet Wood
Padmall Wood
Cooper's Wood
Well Wood
James's Wood
Bradmanshill Wood
Long Shaw
Rushfield Shaw
Broomfieldbank Shaw
Baldwin Shaw
Fuller's Wood
Jackass Shaw
Leafy Grove
Caesars Camp
Holwood
Wilberforce Oak
Keston Court Farm
Westerham Lodge
Rouse Farm
Elm Farm
Nash Farm
North Pole Farm
Five Oaks
Waytes
Wickham Court Farm
Castlehill Ruffs
Sparrow's Den Playing Fields
Coney Hall Rec. Grd.
West Wickham Common
Hayes Court
Baston Manor
Hast Hill
Arlington Orchard
Fox Hill Nursery
Heathfield House
War Bank
Knightons
Forest Lodge
Miry Grove
Ravensbourne
Simpson's Cotts.
Colyers Wood
Gorsewood
Oakley House
Oakley Farm
Hayes Street Farm
Rookery Lake
Fishers Wood
Cupola Wood
Recreation Ground
Sports Ground
Playing Field
CROYDON ROAD
WESTERHAM ROAD
OAKLEY ROAD
COMMON ROAD
HAYES LANE
BASTON ROAD
PICKHURST LANE
WESTMORELAND ROAD
HAYES ROAD
BROMLEY COMMON
HEATHFIELD
LAYHAMS ROAD
BLACKNESS LANE
A232
A233
A21
A2022
B265
B251
B228
B2212
Fc
Gc
Hc
Jc
Kc
Lc
Mc
137
179
160
71
72
73
74
75
76
77
78
79
80
39
40
41
42
63
64
65
66
67
68

138
180
159
SOUTHBOROUGH
PETTS WOOD
Petts Wood
BROMLEY COMMON
Bromley
BR2
BR1
LOCKSBOTTOM
CROFTON
ORPINGTON
KESTON MARK
Keston
FARNBOROUGH
GREEN STREET GREEN
Bromley High School
JUBILEE COUNTRY PARK
Petts Wood Junction
Jubilee Park Local Nature Reserve
Thornet Wood
Sydney Shaw
Southborough Prim. Sch.
St. James' RC Prim. Sch.
Southborough Open Space (Rec. Grd.)
Playing Field
Parkfield Recreation Ground
Youth Cen.
Cemetery
BROMLEY GOLF COURSE
Club Ho.
Driving Range
Bishop Justus C of E School
Princes Plain Prim. Sch.
Prince's Plain
Bromley College of Further & Higher Education
Oakley House
Oakley Farm
Ravens Wood Sch.
Scrubs Farm
Clay Wood
Nobody's Wood
Pokeridden Wood
Knowlehill Wood
Knowlehill Farm
Nursery
Bus Depot
Hollydale Recreation Grounds
Sparrow Wood
Sparrow Common
Roundabout Wood
Crofton Heath
Petts Wood Recreation Ground
Crofton Jun. Sch.
Crofton Inf. Sch.
Gumping Common
Lakeswood Hall
Darrick Wood Swimming Pool
Darrick Wood School
Darrick Wood Sports Cen.
Darrick Wood Jun. & Inf. Schs.
Darrick Wood
Newstead Wood
Newstead Wood Sch. for Girls
Bromley Tennis Centre
Tubbenden Prim. Sch.
PRINCESS ROYAL UNIVERSITY HOSP.
Superstore
Farnborough Recreation Ground
THE FANTAIL
Ninhams Wood
SOUTH PARK
Lake Wood
Caesars Camp
Broom Bank
Woodlands Poultry Farm
The Larches
Holwood Estate
Holwood
Sevenoaks Lodge
Lower Hook Farm
North End Farm
North End Farm Cotts
Blacklands
High Elms Clockhouse
HIGH ELMS GOLF COURSE
HIGH ELMS COUNTRY PARK (Local Nature Reserve)
Bromley Environmental Education Centre at High Elms (BEECHE)
Woodpiece
Whitelands Wood
Cockset Plantation
Cocksett Hill
Ramus Wood
Church Field Plantation
Mill Hill
The Manse
Farnborough Prim. Sch.
Club Sports Ground
Scouts Hall
Westerham Lodge
Holwood Farm
Farthing Street
KESTON COMMON
Keston C of E Prim. Sch.
Forest Lodge
Ravensbourne
COMMON ROAD
HASTINGS ROAD
OAKLEY ROAD
WESTERHAM ROAD
CROYDON ROAD
FARNBOROUGH COMMON
CROFTON ROAD
HIGH STREET FARNBOROUGH
SHIRE LANE
A21
A232
A233
B2158

161
St. Mary Cray
POVEREST
ST. MARY CRAY
BLACKSMITH'S LANE
CROCKENHILL
KEVINGTON
Derry Downs
BR5
Covet Wood
Perry Hall Prim. Sch.
PERRY HALL RD.
Broom Hill
Priory Gardens
RAMSDEN
The Priory School
Hillside Primary School
Grassmeade Recreation Ground
Blenheim Prim. Sch. & Nursery
Burwood School
Orpington
STATION ROAD
SPUR ROAD
A232
A224
COURT ROAD (ORPINGTON BY-PASS)
St. Olave's & St. Saviour's Grammar Sch.
GODDINGTON
Goddington Park
Ontario Centre
BR6
ORPINGTON HOSPITAL
Orpington Sports Club
The Highway Prim. Sch.
CHELSFIELD
Chelsfield
Court Lodge Farm
Chelsfield Village
CHELSFIELD PARK BMI HOSPITAL
Glentrammon Rec. Grd.
High Beeches
Sports Ground
Chelsfield Riding School
Julian Brimstone
CHELSFIELD LAKES GOLF COURSE
Eleven Oaks
Chelsfield Hill Wood
Rounds Wood
Chelsfield Hall
Knockholt
HEWITTS ROUNDABOUT
M25
Maypole
Kynaston Wood
Lilly's Wood
Black Bush Wood
Griff's Wood
Waldens Farm
Walden Manor
Cookham Hill Farm
Cookham Farm
Micklewood Farm
Brown's School
Bucks Cross Farm
Sheepcote Farm
Child's Wood
The Warren
Manor Oak Primary Sch.
Oak View Hospital
Kevington Manor
Little Kevington
Crouch Farm
Lone Barn Farm
Byways Nursery
Sage Wents
Featherc ot
162
181
139
PRATT'S BOTTOM
A21
A223
B258
SEVENOAKS RD.
Vc
Wc
Xc
Yc
Zc
Ad
Bd
46
47
48
49
63
64
65
66
67
68
71
72
73
74
75
76
77
78
79
80

162
140
161
182
Cd
Dd
Ed
Fd
Gd
Hd
Jd
SWANLEY
LONDON
Swanley
BR8
CROCKENHILL
BROMLEY
Orpington
BR6
Sevenoaks
TN14
WELL HILL
Maypole
Hulberry
LULLINGSTONE PARK
LULLINGSTONE PARK GOLF COURSE
LULLINGSTONE COUNTRY PARK
UPPER BEECHEN WOOD
LOWER BEECHEN WOOD
HOME WOOD
M25 MOTORWAY
M25
Junction 4
HEWITTS ROUNDABOUT
SWANLEY BY-PASS
A20
B258
B2173
CROCKENHILL ROAD
CRAY ROAD
EYNSFORD ROAD
GOLDSEL RD.
GREEN COURT RD.
STONES CROSS RD.
BROADWAY
GREEN CT. RD.
CHURCH ROAD
TYLERS GREEN RD.
SKEET HILL LANE
DALTONS ROAD
PARKGATE ROAD
WELL HILL
FIRMINGERS ROAD
REDMANS LANE
COCKERHURST ROAD
ROCK ROAD
WESTED LANE
SHOREHAM ROAD
MAYPOLE LANE
JUBILEE RD.
HOLLYBUSH LA.
CHELSFIELD LA.
HEWITTS RD.
WHEATSHEAF HILL
ORPINGTON RD.
GORSE RD.
HAWSTEAD
HOME FARM
Bourne Wood
Quarry
Tile Kilns Wood
Hook Spring
Marwood Ho. Caravan & Camping Site
Marwood Ho.
Football Ground
Club Ho.
Nursery
Fleetfoot Fm.
Prim. Sch.
Peartrees
Cemetery
Cemy.
Cherry Orchard
Gosenhill Farm
The Mount
Hall
Middle Farm Nursery
Willow Farm
Crouch Farm
Crouch Farm House
Crouch Farm Cottages
Felma House
Waldens Farm
Walden Manor
Sheepcote Farm
Bleak House Farm
East Hall Cottage
Piggery
Orchard View
The Oaks
Lone Barn Farm
Brambles
Byways Nursery
Fairfield
Crown Wood
Crown Wood Fm.
Woodside
Cookham Farm
Feathercot
Micklewood Farm
Davidson House
Playing Field
Skeet Hill Farm
Pollard
Highcroft Hall
Heathfield Shaw
Horncross Shaw
Cacketshill Wood
Football Ground
Wested Farm Cotts.
Wested Meadows
Wested Farm
Little Wested House
Petham Court Cotts.
Petham Court
Industrial Estate
High Firs Prim. Sch.
Rec. Grd.
Baldwins Cottages
Hulberry Farm
Roughet
Snow White Cottages
Park Gate House
Club House
Doctor's Wood
Owen Wood
Driving Range
Reservoir
Westwood Cottage
Goat Hill
Great Cockerhurst
Ridge Farm
Homewood Farm
Westwood Farm
West Wood
Pascalls Wood
Hewitts
Coneyearth Wood
Hollows Wood
Brent Farm
Dalhanna
Longspring Wood
Coombe Hollow
Goss Bushes
Keepers
Bucks Cross Farm
49
550
51
52
68
67
66
165
64
63

163
Junction 3 (M25)
Junction 1 (M20)
M25 MOTORWAY
M20 MOTORWAY
SWANLEY INTERCHANGE
M25
M20
LONDON ROAD
A20
MAIN ROAD
DARTFORD ROAD
A225
GORSE HILL (MAIN ROAD)
EYNSFORD ST.
HIGH ROAD
STATION ROAD
SHOREHAM ROAD
EYNSFORD ROAD
FARNINGHAM WOOD
The Folly
Calfstock Lane
Franks Farm
Franks Hall
Franks Lane
River Darent
Little Franks
Cricket Grd.
Eglantine Villa
Mussenden Cottage
Riseley Hall
Eglantine Farm
Reynolds Pl.
Button Street
Hill Farm
Wildacres
Hill House
Hill Farm House
Farningham Hill Rd
Abington
Old Dartford Rd.
Driving Range
Club House
Reservoir (covered)
Coldharbour Farm
The Beacon
Mill House
The Manor Ho.
Cricket Grd.
Pav.
FARNINGHAM
Pedham Place Farm
Fort Cotts.
PEDHAM PLACE GOLF COURSE
Eglantine Lane
Charton Manor
Charton Farm
Horton Wy.
Hillside
Oliver Cres.
South Hall
Tilmans Mead
Centenary Ct.
White Post Hill
Beesfield Lane
Tabsfield
Polly Shaw
The Little House
Eynsford Hill
Fountain Hoy
Sunfield
Sunhurst
Mount Eagle
Sparepenny Lane
The Anthony Roper Prim. Sch.
Eynsford Castle
Furlongs Farm
Riverside Nursy.
Rec. Grd.
Priory Fields
Tills Cottage
Hall
Beesfield Farm
Cresset Cottage
Donkey Lane
Firpound Shaw
Alchin's Wood
Dartford
DA4
EYNSFORD
Recreation Ground
Glyndel Ho.
Knights Rd.
Eagle Heights Wildlife Park
Viaduct
Home Farm
Riverside
Ford
Walnut Cl.
Saddlers Pk.
Pollyhaugh
Olivers Shaw
Maplescombe Lane
164
Gorse Hill Nursery
SEVENOAKS
Lullingstone Roman Villa
Lullingstone Lane
Newbarn Farm
Lullingstone Park Farm
St. Martins Dr.
Birch Cl.
Station Rd.
Eynsford Rise
Eynsford
Upper Austin Lodge Road
Sandhole Shaw
Lullingstone
World Garden
Lullingstone Castle
Weir
Reservoir
Chalkhurst Wood
Higham
Park House Farm
Black Cottage
Bower Lane
Lower Park Wood
MAPLESCOMBE
Maplescombe Farm
Adder Bank Shaw
Courtfield Shaw
Knatts Lane
Lullingstone Country Park Visitor Centre
The Rookery
Castle Road
Lower Austin Lodge
Bower Park Farm
Hartnips Wood
Maplebank Poultry Farm
Sevenoaks
TN15
The Strikes
The Birches
Coombe Firs
Hog Wood
Upper Austin Lodge
183
Preston Hill Plantation
Kd Ld Md Nd Pd Qd Rd
71 72 73 74 75 76 77 78 79 80
53 54 55 56
63 64 65 66 67 68

56
57
58
59
Sd
Td
Ud
Vd
Wd
Xd
Yd
142
163
184
68
67
66
165
64
63
71
72
73
74
75
76
77
78
79
80
HORTON KIRBY
Horton Kirby Environmental Education Centre
RUSSELL TERRACE
CARLETON
SCHOOL
ASHLEIGH WY.
STREET
LOMBARD
Reynolds Pl.
Reynolds Place Farm
RAYS
HILL
THE
FRANKS
Franks
LANE
Cricket Grd.
Eglantine Villa
SAXON PL.
SAXON PLACE
Riseley Hall
Eglantine Farm
EGLANTINE LANE
MUSSENDEN
Mussenden Cottage
Mussenden Farm
Blue Cottages
SCHOOL LANE
ROAD
CANADA
Beeches Farm
Canada Farm
FARM ROAD
Hill Barn Farm
SCUDDERS HILL
Scudders Farm
Lone Oak Farm
Wickhams
MANOR
The Grange
VALLEY ROAD
Dartford
DA4
M20-MOTORWAY
M20
harton Farm
Hall
MUSSENDEN LANE
HORTON WOOD
GATES
Liberty Farm
THE GROVE CRAFT WORKSHOPS
Grove Farm
THREE LANE
Fawkham
Fawkham C of E Prim. Sch.
Parkfield Wood
FAWKHAM MANOR BMI HOSPITAL
Fawkham Manor Farm
Hopkins Spring Wood
Hatchfield Wood
GORSE
ield Farm
Cresset Cottage
DONKEY LANE
Paygate Cottage
Alchin's Wood
A20
(MAIN ROAD)
60
GABRIEL
SPRING ROAD
Gabrielspring Wood
SCRATCHERS
GABRIEL SPRING ROAD
CAMS COTTS.
Speedgate Farm
Speedgate House
White House Farm
Speedgate
SPEEDGATE HILL
SEVE
Choaks Farm
Choaks Wood
EAST
SUN
Hazlewood
Birchgrove
ST. MICHAELS
HILL ROAD
FAWKHAM GREEN
SMALL GRAINS
WOODMAN VILLAS
FAIRVIEW
Gorse Hill Nursery
Westyc
Greenlands
Cherrywood
The Haven
Springfield
Rowanhurst
HATCH
BRANDS
Brands Hatch Place
BRANDS HATCH RD.
ROGERS
Saxten's Wood
Cage's Wood
BILLET LANE
WOOD LANE
GALLOWS WOOD
Ashen Grove
BRANDS HATCH PK.
Sandhole Shaw
Vineyard Shaw
Shetley Shaws
Stand
Grandstand
CHAPMAN WAY
COLIN
Hotel
Offices
HILL
LONDON
Woodlands
Rogers Wood
Eastwood
Gallows Wood
Little Haven
Billet Wood
Battersea at Brands Hatch
MAPLESCOMBE
Lower Park Wood
Kingsdown Farm
BRANDS HATCH MOTOR RACING CIRCUIT
Cowless Shaw
HEVER AV.
AVENUE
SYMONDS CL.
GILLIES RD.
VIKING WAY
Grove Wood
Maplescombe Farm
Ad64 Bank Shaw
Courtfield Shaw
Maplebank Nursery
BLUE CHALET INDUSTRIAL PARK
PHELPS CL.
STACKLANDS CL.
BRAKES PL.
OAKLANDS CL.
LOVELACE CL.
REGENCY CL.
MILLFIELD RD.
MILLFIELD
BOURNE
PURSE
SHEARS
HEVER
MULTON
NEAL
ROAD
PRIM.
PENSHURST CL.
ASTOR RD.
WOODVIEW CL.
HOWELLS CL.
TURNERS RD.
WHITEGATES AV.
MITCHEM CL.
GAPP
Rec. Grd.
HEVER RD.
WOOD
Westfield Cotts.
FAWKHAM ROAD
CHURCH WOOD
KNATTS
BOTSOM
Maplebank Poultry Farm
To the Woods Caravan & Camping Site
FLORENCE FARM MOBILE HOME PK.
THE BRIARS
CLEARWAYS BUS. EST.
LANE
VALLEY
Sidehilly Wood
CLEARWAYS CARAVAN PK.
RUSHETTS RD.
KAYSLAND PK.
KINGSFISHER CT.
KINGSWOOD CT.
CHURCH
CHANCEL CL.
WEST KINGSDOWN
SOUTHFIELDS
KINGSINGFIELD CL.
KINGSINGFIELD RD.
BIKERS
WINDMILL
GRANGE
Lib.
Sports Ground
Ten. Cts.
WEST KINGSDOWN INDUSTRIAL EST.
ROAD
BLACKTHORN
ASH TREE CL.
WARLAND RD.
VERNON
ST. EDMUNDS
Kingsdown House
Springham's Cotts.
Richardson's Farm
CROWHURST
Crowhurst Farm
Ashen Shaw
THE LONDON GOLF COUR
Broomfield Wood
Mace Wood
Club House
THE LONDON GOLF COURSE
HIGH CASTLE WOOD
Pe
Wo

HARTLEY
Hartley Green
Longfield
LONGFIELD HILL
DA3
GRAVESHAM
NEW ASH GREEN
West Yoke
Hartley Hill
Gravesend
DA13
Sevenoaks
TN15
TONBRIDGE and MALLING
ASH
RIDLEY
New Street
HODSOLL STREET
Pettings
FAWKHAM VALLEY GOLF COURSE
Milestone School
Nine Horse Wood
Redlibbets Wood
Chapel Wood
North Lands Shaw
Foxbrough Wood
Hartley Wood
Hartley Manor
Middleton Cottages
Middleton Farm
Hartley Dell
Redsteadle Wood
Dell Wood
Goldsmiths Shaw
Bridelands Wood
Hartley Bottom Farm
Northdown Farm
Southdown Farm
Idleigh Farm
Idleigh Court
Sunnymead
Larksfield
Court View
Feathercot
Valley's Shaw
Grubb Wood
Middle Wood
White Ash Wood
Bowes Wood
Recreation Ground
Landway Farm
Swan Meadows Farm
Ash Place Farm
Swan Farm
The Old Rectory
Rectory
Hilly Field Shaw
Galsmead
Pease Hill Cottages
Rumney Farm Cottages
Rumney Farm
The Roughets
Goss Wood
Dunmery Grove
Viney Wood
Ridley Wood
Ridley Court Farm
Glebe House
Ridley Farm
Pond Farm
Pilgrim Corner
Newlands Shaw
Jub's Hill Wood
Pettings Wood
Pettings Court Farm
Little Pettings
Piggery
Martin Hill Spring
Haven Wood
Haven Manor
Berry's Maple
Seafield
Woodlands
Baker's Shaw
Baker's Wood
The Old Malt Ho.
Pumping Station
Holywell Park Farm
Holywell Farm
Dairy House Farm
Greenfields
Eldridge Shaw
Eldridge Cottage
Elbows Wood
Ashplat Wood
Eight Acre Wood
Oxens Shaw
Orchard Cottage
New Street Farm
New Street Farm Cottages
Sheeplands Shaw
Long Bottom Wood
Meadow-croft
Carlows Wood
Lion Wood
Selbyfield Shaw
Ten Acre Shaw
Millers Wood
Langley Grove
Shipley Hills Shaw
Millfield Shaw
Rabbit Wood
Broom Wood
Gorse Bottom
Orange Hill
Skinners Hill
Cricket Ground
Manor Farm
Nurstead Hall
Go Bananas Playbarn
Oliver's Farm
Eaglesfield
Football Ground
Sports Club
Pennis Farm
Steephill School
Churchdown Wood
Turner's Oak Shaw
Cuckolds Corner
Delsrop
Hill View
Sunnydale
The Warren
Bazes Shaw
Pumping Station
MAIN ROAD
LONGFIELD ROAD
B260
HARTLEY ROAD
ASH ROAD
MANOR DRIVE
GRANGE ROAD
HARTLEY BOTTOM ROAD
IDLEIGH COURT ROAD
NEW STREET ROAD
SHIPLEY HILLS ROAD
BUNKERS HILL
PEASE HILL
SOUTH ASH ROAD
NORTH ASH ROAD
REDHILL
CHAPEL WOOD ROAD
CASTLE HILL
WEST YOKE
FAIRSEAT LA.
CHAPMAN'S HILL
ROSEMARY
143
185
Zd
Ae
Be
Ce
De
Ee
Fe
71
72
73
74
75
76
77
78
79
80
560
61
62
63
63
64
165
66
67
68

M3 MOTORWAY
M3
Lightwater
GU18
LIGHTWATER
LIGHTWATER BY-PASS
A322
Old House Farm
Broadwaygreen Farm
Lee Lane Farm
Rectory Farm
Manor Farm Wood
Manor Farm Cottages
Sewage Works
Brooklands Farm
Halebourne Copse
Halebourne House
Higher Park Farm
Nurseries
Westcroft Park
Westcroft Farm
White Bridge
Park Wood
Woodlands Farm
Poultry Farm
Shrubb's Farm
Steep Acre Farm
WINDLEMERE GOLF COURSE
Driving Range
Club Ho.
Hookstone Farm
Hookstone Green
A319
Pankhurst Farm
Brook Place
Holly Farm
Playing Field
Turf Hill
B311
BAGSHOT ROAD
GUILDFORD RD.
Gordon's School
WEST END
Streets Heath
The Laurels
SURREY
Holy Trinity C of E Primary School
Penny Pot
New England
Sandpit Hill
Greyspot Hill
Cuckoo Hill
Mortar Range DANGER AREA
Donkey Town
The Oaks
Hatchgate Farm
Beldam Bridge Farm
Beldam Bri.
Lovelands Farm
GU24
Fenns Fm.
Rosedene Farm
Rounce Farm
Dog Hill
Trulley Brook
Lucas Green Manor
Trulleys
New Bridge
Scott's Farm
CHOBHAM GOLF COURSE
Lucas Green
Tennis Courts
Ford Farm
Sports Ground
Pavilion
Hawk Farm
Springfield Fm.
Nursery Cottages
White Cottage Farm
Pine Grove Farm
Rec. Grd.
Bisley Green
Brock Hill
Works
Peatmoor Pond
Lucas Green Farm
BISLEY
Hill Place Farm
Hill Place
The Mews
Bayfield Piggery
Ashgrove Nursery
Furze Farm
Bullhousen Farm
WOKING PRIORY HOSPITAL
Hillview Poultry Farm
BISLEY COMMON
DANGER AREA
Long Siberia Range
HMP COLDINGLEY
Ramsbrook Farm
Miles Green
Stickle Down
High Hoglees
Short Siberia Range
Therapy Centre
Hangmoor Copse
Strawberry Farm
Reldon Hill
Stickledown Range
Bisley Ranges
Polledoak Slade
Chaseley
BISLEY COMMON
Staffordlake Farm
Princess Christian Homes & Training Centre
Wisdom Farm
Staffordlake
Stafford Lake
Century Range
Hog Lees
Wisdom Corner
Clock Tower
Ranges
Grindstone Handle Corner
Knaphill Sch.
Lower Sch.
KNAPHILL
Shrub's Copse
Superstore
BAGSHOT RD
LIMECROFT RD
146
186

167
147
168
187
Burrowhill
Stanners Hill
Stannershill Farm
Mossat Farm
Westways Farm
Little Heath
Paradise Farm
Manx Farm
Burrow Hill Farm
Woods Farm
Henage Corner
Chobham Park House
Chobham Park Farm
Partridge Farm
Stanyards
Greenacres
Stanyards Cottage
Stanyards Farm
Chobham Business Centre
Larkenshaw
Larkenshaw Farm
Fishpool Bridge
Sowmoor Plantation
Sow Moor
Kalima Caravan Site
Copyhold
Riverside Nursery
Emmetts Mill
Brooklands Farm
Burnside Nursery
Sunfield Farm
Little Goldbridge Farm
Wishmore Cross Sch.
Comm. Cen.
Millbourne Bridge
CHOBHAM
Cricket Field
Mill Bourne
WINDSOR ROAD
CHERTSEY ROAD
A319
HIGH ST.
STATION ROAD
A3046
Willow Farm
Highfield
Recreation Ground
Grant's Bridge
Broadford
Broadford Farm
HEATH
Milford Green
Cox Hill
MIMBRIDGE
Milford House
Milford Farm
Coxhill Green
Border Farm
White Lodge Farm
Wapshott Farm
Heather Farm
Horsell Common
Shaw's Farm
Scotchers Farm Cotts.
CASTLE GREEN
Castle Grn.
Sewage Works
Milbrook Animal Centre
Woking
Surrey Rose Farms
Deep Pool Farm
CHOBHAM ROAD
Knaphill Manor Farm
Beetle Cottage
Knaphill Manor
Graylands Farm
Willow View Farm
Parley Brook
Wesbury Farm
Littlewick Common
Lipscombe Farm
Mizens Railway
WOKING
Knapwood House
LITTLEWICK
Knap Hill Nursery
Parley Brook Farm
Horsell Birch
Tracious Copse
Parley Bridge
Goldsworth Park
Recreation Ground
GOLDSWORTH PARK TRADING ESTATE
GOLDSWORTH PARK
Woking High Sch.
HORSELL
St. Andrew's Sch.
Playing Field
Horsell Moor
Waterers Park
Beaufort Prim. Sch.
LOCKFIELD DRIVE
A324
Goldsworth
Surrey History Cen.
Superstore
WOKING
MOUNT HERMON
HERMITAGE ROAD
AMSTEL WY.
Sports Cen.
Woking Crematorium
Woodend Br.
ST. JOHNS
Cricket Ground
GU21
GU22

168
A
B
C
D
E
F
G
Stanners Hill
Hawks Hill
Timber Hill
Ottershaw Park
148
Playing Field
Brox
Southern Wood
Rodwell Nursery
Stanyards
Greenacres
Timber Hill Cotts.
The Mansion
Tennis Courts
Play. Fld.
Ottershaw Park
Hill Crest
Brox Copse
Stanyards Cott.
Stanyards Farm
Long Copse
Miniature Rifle Range
Bramshill
Chertsey
Brox Wood
Bourne Rise Farm
Holly Farm
Rose Park
Beyond
Gable Cottage
Great Wood
Little Blackmole Pond
Sandpit Plantation
Samson's Wood
Berwin Park
CHERTSEY ROAD
A319
Chobham Business Centre
SURREY HEATH
KT16
ANNINGSLEY PARK
Holme Farm
Pleasant View
Beech Hill Clump
Woodlands Cl.
Summerhill
Great Blackmole Pond
The Wey Farm
Anningsley Pk
Halls
The Warren
Birch Wood
Grovers Farm
Copyhold
FAIROAKS AIRPORT
Decoy Plantation
Bridge House
Thatch Cottage
Ware Copse
Anningsley Park
Tennis Court
The Bourne
Riverside Nursery
GU24
Old Farm
Dunford Ho.
Dunford Bridge
Bonsey's Bridge
McClaren Technology Centre
Brooklands Farm
Mill
Burnside Nursery
Sunfield Farm
The Bourne
The Cottage
Hoyt Wood
Grovers Farm Cotts.
The Larches
GUILDFORD ROAD
A320
Tennis Courts
Durnford Farm
Timber Yard
The Hoyte
Hoyte Lodge
B385
Community Recycling Centre
NEW ZEALAND GOLF COURSE
Club House
Young Stroat Farm
Scotchers Farm
Bonseys Cotts.
Pinewood Cotts.
Scotchers Farm Cotts.
Danewell
Anthonys
New Houses
Shaw's Farm
Horsell Common
Danewell Hill
SHEERWATER LANE
A245
Danewell House
Tennis Courts
The Bishop David Brown Sch.
SHEERWATER
Broadmere Prim. Sch.
Sheerwater Recreation Ground
Play. Fld.
Playgrd.
HORSELL COMMON
167
CHOBHAM RD.
SHORES ROAD
WOODHAM
CHERTSEY ROAD
A245
Youth Club
Woodham Hall Estate
Hosp.
Kettlewell
Heathlands Cl.
Sch.
Kingswey Bus. Pk.
Scotswood Park
Works
WEST BYFLEET GOLF COURSE
A3046
GU21
Sheerwater Bus. Cen.
Genesis Business Park
Woking High Sch.
Britannia Wharf
Monument Bridge
Monument Bridge Ind. Est. West
Monument Bus. Cen.
Woking Business Park
Monument Bridge Ind. Est. East
W
O
K
I
N
Ditch
Canal
Playing Field
New Monument School
St. Andrew's Sch.
Horsell
Basingstoke
Chertsey Rd. Bri.
Boundary Bus. Cen.
Lion Retail Park
Mosque
Woking
Playing Field
Pav
Rec. Grd.
War Meml.
Napier Ct.
Horsell Moor
Home
Prim. Sch.
Maybury Est.
MAYBURY
Pyrford Common
Tennis Courts
THE ROUGH
Woking
Spts. Grd.
Club
The Big Apple
Theatres
Civ. Cen.
Sch.
Playing Field
B382
LA Fitness
Goldsworth Ind. Est.
Piggery
Surrey History Cen.
Depot
Goldsworth
Shey Copse
Fox Hill
WOKING
HOEBRIDGE GOLF COURSE
Hockering Estate
Driving Range
Mount Hermon
Play Fld.
Bowl. Grn.
Woking Park
Woking Leisure Cen.
Games Court
Sports Ground
188
White Rose Lane Local Nature Reserve
Monument Hill
Roundbridge Farm
500
01
02
03
63
62
61
160
59
58
81
82
83
84
85
86
87
88
89
90

169
ROW TOWN
NEW HAW
Addlestone
Central Veterinary Laboratory
Grange Farm
WOODHAM
KT15
M25 MOTORWAY
BYFLEET ROAD
A318
Wey Manor Farm
Electricity Switching Station
Rive Ditch
Seven Arches Bridge
The London Bus Museum
Mercedes-Benz World
Brooklands Museum
BROOKLANDS
ELMBRIDGE
Brooklands Industrial Estate
Brooklands Business Park
Superstores
Weybridge
KT13
Byfleet & New Haw
OYSTER LANE
Heathervale Recreation Grd.
Basingstoke Canal
Camphill Industrial Estate
West Byfleet
Dartnell Park
KT14
A245
PARVIS ROAD
West Byfleet
WEST BYFLEET
Woodham & New Cen.
Fullbrook Sch.
Sports Cen.
Woodham Lock
Broadoaks
Tins Wood
Old Wood
The Moat
West Hall Farm
Murray's Bri.
Recreation Ground
Village Hall
St. Mary's C of E Prim. Sch.
BYFLEET
Sanway
Nursery
Common Meadows
River Wey
Bluegates Hole
Plough Bridge Farm
Manor House
The Island
Nuffield Health Fitness & Wellbeing Centre
Byfleet Lawn Tennis Club
Oakfield Sch.
RIDGWAY
TRADITIONS GOLF COURSE
Pyrford C of E Prim. Sch.
PYRFORD
Pyrford Marina
Lock Copse
Peatmoor Wood
Church Farm
The Bungalow
Wisley Bri.
Sewage Works
WISLEY
Sports Ground
Wisley Common
Buxton Wood
GU22
GU23
WISLEY GOLF COURSE
Townslow Meadow
Pyrford Place Farm
PYRFORD GREEN
Elveden Cottages
PYRFORD GOLF COURSE
Home Farm
Pyrford Place
Wren's Nest
Pinetum
WISLEY COMMON
Aberconway House
The Stable Courtyard
Greenhouses
Rock Garden
Garden Cen.
GUILDFORD
RHS Garden Wisley
Battleston Hill
PORTSMOUTH ROAD
A3
Pyrford Stone
Stone Farm
Lady Place
Church Farm
The Hanger
Vicarage
PYRFORD VILLAGE
The Prae
Wheelers Farm
Abbey Stream Bri.
Warren Farm Mobile Home Park
Walsham Lock
Ockham Mill
149
170
189

Q
R
S
T
U
V
W
150
The London Bus Museum
Mercedes-Benz World
Brooklands Museum
BROOKLANDS
Handling Track A
Handling Track B
ST. GEORGE'S HILL
Weybridge
KT13
GOLF COURSE
ST. GEORGE'S HILL GOLF COURSE
Club House
David Lloyd Leisure
Blue Barn Farm
Warren Pond
Recreation Ground
BURHILL GOLF COURSE
Burhill Park
Club House
Walton-on-Thames
KT12
WHITELEY VILLAGE
Dick Turpin's Cottage
Strawberry Hill
Beards Hill
Notre Dame Preparatory & Senior Schools
Burwood Park
Seven Hills Estate
Walton Firs Scout Camp
Manor Pond
Chestnut Lodge Farm
E L M B
BYFLEET ROAD
A245
Plough Bridge
Plough Bridge Farm
Foxholm Covert
Cobham Bus Museum
Silver Mere
Silvermere
SILVERMERE GOLF COURSE
Club House
Driving Range
Home Farm
Thirty Acre Wood
Silvermere Farm Estate
St. George's Nursing Home
Hotel
Lodge
Feltonfleet Sch.
Play. Fld.
PAINSHILL
ESHER ROAD
Superstore
PORTSMOUTH ROAD
Cobham Bridge
Pains Hill
PAINSHILL PARK
Education Cen.
Wood Hill
Gothic Temple
Chinese Bridge
Grotto
The Lake
Heyswood Girl Guide Camp
The Broom
Waterwheel
Wheel Island
Tower Hill
Gothic Tower
Red Hill
Oak Pollard
Long Orchard Farm
Highlands Farm
Bell Wood
A3
The Hangers
Queen Anne's Cottage
Queen Anne's Hills
Nursery
Foxwarren Park
Bluegates Hole
West Byfleet
KT14
BYFLEET
Byfleet Mill
Manor House
The Island
Park Barn Farm
River Wey
Buxton Wood
Clearmount
M25 MOTORWAY
M25
WISLEY INTERCHANGE
Junction 10
Wisley Common
Woolger's Wood
Pond Farm
Cockcrow Hill
Sandpit Hill
Redhill Bottom
Chatley Wood
Chatley Farm
RIVER MOLE
Chatley Cott.
The Bogs
Lodge Cottages
Cobham Court Farm
GUILDFORD
WISLEY COMMON
Woking
GU23
Hut Hill Cottage
Hut Hill
Currie's Clump
OCKHAM COMMON
Chatley Heath
Breach Hill Wood
Telegraph Hill
Chatley Heath Semaphore Tower
Wisley Common, Ockham & Chatley Heath Nature Reserve
Hatchford Wood
Woodside Cottage
Elm Cottage
Bolder Mere
Oakham Village Green
Fellside Cottages
ELM CORNER
Wilderness Farm
Hatchford End
Hatchford Manor
Hatchford Park
Hatchford
Lodge Copse
Little Brickfield Copse
Highfield Farm
Nurseries
Cold Norton Farm
Halfpenny Cross
Wrens Nest Cottage
Bramble Wood
Bramble Cottage
Poynters Farm
Pointers Green
Brickfield Copse
Pondtail Farm
CHILBROOK
PLOUGH LANE
190
169
81
82
83
84
85
86
87
88
89
90
07
08
09
510
63
62
61
160
59
58

NEW ADDINGTON
Electricity Sub Station
Rushfield Shaw
Broomfieldbank Shaw
159
Metropolitan Police Dog Training Establishment
The Temple (Roman Mausoleum)
Keston Court Farm
Wilberforce Oak
Scout Camp
Westerham Lodge
WESTERHAM RD.
DOWNE ROAD
Milchden
CHURCH LANE
BLACKNESS LANE
GLEBE FARM BUSINESS PARK
Pitch & Putt Golf Course
Rowdown Wood
VULCAN BUSINESS CENTRE
ADDINGTON BUSINESS CENTRE
MERIDIAN CENTRE
Addington Vale
Rowdown Primary School
Warehouses
Layham's Farm
Layham's Farm Cottage
Furze Bottom
Longlands Nurseries
Kimberley Poultry Farm
Vale Farm
Keston
BR2
A233
LEAVES GREEN ROAD
Sports Ground
Greyhound Training Kennels
Hoppershatch Shaw
Bowling Green
Milne Park
West Wickham Res. (covered)
Highams Hill
High House Farm
Ashmore Farm
Bradmoor
Greenacres Riding Sch.
The Green
LEAVES GREEN
Milking Lane Farm
Club House
Gushybank Shaw
Fairchildes Prim. Sch.
Addington High Sch.
Tennis Courts
Play. Fld.
Higham's Hill
SHEEPBARN LANE
JEWELS HILL
Jewels Wood
Babington Place
Saltbox Hill Nature Reserve
Terminal
LONDON BIGGIN HILL AIRPORT
Threecorner Grove
Playing Field
Fairchildes Cotts.
SALTBOX HILL
Chapel Hill
Bograms Wood
North Lodge
South Lodge
Fairchildes Farm
Blackmans Cotts.
Coxs Cottages
BLACKMAN'S LA.
OAKLANDS LANE
MAIN ROAD
180
Cudham Lodge Woods
FICKLESHOLE
Fickleshole Farm
Fickleshole Farm Cotts.
B R O M L E Y
South London Aero Club
Greathill Shaw
Skid Hill House
Skid Hill Farm
AIRPORT INDUSTRIAL ESTATE
BIGGIN HILL BUSINESS PARK
Midgley Shaws
Westerham
Jugg Hill
Costains Farm
Honeyoak Wood
RAILPIT
CROWN ASH LANE
CROWN ROAD
TN16
Oaklands Prim. Sch.
Cemetery
Recreation Ground
Biggin Hill Memorial Pool
Church Cotts.
HESIERS ROAD
HESIERS HILL
Norheads Farm
BIGGIN HILL
Lib.
Hall
MOLLARDS WOOD
Norheads Farm Cotts.
Norheads Farm Cotts.
Long Coppice
Jerry Reddins Shaw
Chelsham Court
Chelsham Court Farm
Broom Lodge Farm
CHELSHAM COURT ROAD
Owls Wood
BEDDLESTEAD LANE
Cony Crook
White Bank
Long Coppice
Parsons Shaw
Farley Kennels
Cowyard Shaw
Milbury Cott.
Round Wood
199
Beddlestead House
Kingscote
Isle Shaw
Fc Gc Hc Jc Kc Lc Mc
81 82 83 84 85 86 87 88 89 90
39 40 41 42
58 59 160 61 62 63

180
160
200
179
Nc
Pc
Qc
Rc
Sc
Tc
Uc
81
82
83
84
85
86
87
88
89
90
Keston
BR2
LEAVES GREEN
Milking Lane Farm
LONDON BIGGIN HILL AIRPORT
South London Aero Club
AIRPORT INDUSTRIAL ESTATE
BIGGIN HILL BUSINESS PARK
CONCORDE BUSINESS PK.
BIGGIN HILL
Westerham Lodge
GLEBE FARM BUSINESS PARK
DOWNE ROAD
SHIRE LANE
NEW ROAD HILL
Holwood Farm
PADDOCK MOBILE HOME PARK
Downe Court Riding Centre
LEAVES GREEN RD.
Farthing Street
FARTHING STREET
Farthing Street Farm
FARTHING BARN LA.
Farthings
ORANGE COURT LANE
Orange Court
Green Acres
Meadow Cott.
LOWER HOOK BUSINESS PARK
BOGEY LANE
North End Farm
North End Farm Cotts.
NORTH END LANE
CROWHILL
Little Crowhill
Hazels
ROOKERY
ROOKERY VILLAS
Rookery Cotts.
Long Acre
ROOKERY ROAD
MILL
STANDARD R.
HIGH VW. R.
Gorringes
LANE
Play Fld.
Rec. Grd.
Cemy.
Sch.
BUTCHERS YD.
WELLER PL.
DOWNE
HIGH ST.
Petleys Farm
Petleys
CUDHAM ROAD
Downe Hall
Downe Hall Farm
Christmas Tree Farm
Thompson Wood
Downe Lodge
LUXTED
The Vicarage
Green Hill
HILL
Club House
MILKING LANE GREEN HILL WEST
Down House
Downe Court
Buckston Browne Research Farm
WEST KENT GOLF COURSE
Cricket Grd.
Pav.
SOW WOOD
Snotsdale Wood
Cudham Lodge Woods
Spencers Grove
Luxted
LANE
Ladies Wood
Luxted Fm.
Downe Camp
Clock Twr.
Leasons Wood
Bird House Wood
BIRDHOUSE
Great Southfield Shaw
Bromley Croft
Single Street
SINGLE STREET
Strakes Shaw
St. Julians Farm
Playing Fld.
Darwin Sports Centre
Charles Darwin School
Barn Farm
Costains Farm
JAIL LANE
MAGNOLIA DRIVE
ACER
SPRUCE RD.
Cemetery
Recreation Ground
Biggin Hill Memorial Pool
MAPLE LEAF CL.
Biggin Hill Prim. Sch.
Grubb Grounds Farm
OLD TYE AVENUE
Westerham
Primrose Farm
Golden Acres
Littlewood Farm
Brickyard Farm
Parkfield Fm.
Cudham C of E Prim. Sch.
LANE
Bertrey Cotts.
BERRYS
Homeleigh Farm
CHERRY LODGE GOLF COURSE
Club House
Oak Farm
Warren Farm
Foal Farm Animal Rescue Centre
Laurel Farm
Pimlico Wood
TN16
Aperfield
APERFIELD
JUNIPER CL.
NELSON CL.
VILLAGE GREEN AVENUE
HAIG RD.
DOUGLAS CT.
TUDOR CT.
Hall
ALLENBY
CHURCH RIDINGS
SUTHERLAND
A233
MAIN ROAD
GROVE
MOSELLE RD.
FOXEARTH CL.
ST. WINIFRED'S
BELVEDERE
WOODBURY CL.
CLARENCE RD.
EDWARD RD.
Farley Kennels
Baverstock Farm
Withins Wood
Sunnymede
Park Farm
Saunderstead
Kennels
Silver Beech Fm.
Buckhurst Farm
BUCKHURST
HARROW LANE
NEW ROAD
Valley View
New Barn Farm
BERRY'S GREEN
RESTAVON CARAVAN SITE
Blackbush Shaw
Underhill Farm
Rosehaugh Farm
Corkers Fm.
Piggeries
Bottom Barn Farm
CHURCH HILL
Cudham Ct. Farm
Rec. Grd.
Pav.
CUDHAM
CHURCH APP.
Cudham Hall
LORD DARBY MEWS
Hall
Vicarage
Parsonage Fm.
Westbrook Farm
Maple Farm
Nurseries
The Grove
Thrift Farm
THRIFT LA.
Cedar Cott.
HORNS GREEN
Portlan
CUDHAM FRITH
Cudham Frith
Cackets Cotts.
The Lodge
CACKET'S
Angas Home (Site)
Hook Wood
Foxburrow Wood
Church Hill Farm
Holmleigh
Granada Ho.
Fairways
Hostye Fm.
Hostye Bungalow
Hostye Lodge
Overshaws
The Shaws (Girl Guides' Camp)
Mace Farm
Mace Farm Cotts.
MACE LANE
Lordfield Shaw
Downe Bank Nature Reserve
HANGROVE HILL
Hang Grove
Beechwood
The Boundary
Shaws Cott.
DOWNE
Flora Cottage
Brownsea Hut (Boy Scouts)
Greenacres
Twenty Acre Shaw
Square Shaw
Avondale Farm
Hang Grove Farm
Hazel Wood
Oak Lodge
HAZELWOOD
HAZELWOOD ROAD
DOWNE AV.
SPINNEY WY.
Spinney Way Nurseries
Endsleigh
Southfields
Rose Cott.
The Oaks
Snag Lane Fm.
Millfield Wood
SNAG LANE
Snag Farm
White Earth
The Shack
CUDHAM PK. RD.
Burnt Gorse
BROMLEY
Great Molloms Wood
Cuckoo Lodge
CUCKOO WOOD
HIGH ELMS GOLF COURSE
High Elms Clockhouse
HIGH ELMS ROAD
Blacklands
The Rookery
Club House
HIGH ELMS COUNTRY PARK (Local Nature Reserve)
Whitelands Wood
Rec. Grd.
Playgrd.
NORTH

SEVENOAKS ROAD
A21
Pratt's Bottom
Pratt's Bottom
Chelsfield Lakes Golf Course
Knockholt
Hewitts Roundabout
M25
A224
Orpington By-Pass Rd.
Court Rd.
Chelsfield Hill
Church Hill
Eleven Oaks
Chelsfield Hill Wood
Rounds Wood
Yew Tree Cottage
The Hillside
Roseneath Cl.
Broke Farm Drive
Turnpike Dr.
Orchard Road
Stonehouse Road
Stonehouse Farm
Broke Lodge
Club House
Broke Hill Golf Course
Old London Road
Watercrofts
Watercroft Road
Cadlocks Station Road
Charmwood Farm
Charmwood Lane
Little Mollom's Wood
Orpington
BR6
Charm Wood
Norsted Lane
The Green
Lambardes Cl.
Foxwood Gro.
Rock-Field Shaw
Pratt's Grove
Prim. Sch.
Pratts Bottom Wood
Hook Wood
Hookwood Cotts
Rushmore Hill Wood
Birthday Wood
Stud Farm
Church Lane
Widmore Farm
Gardeners Cottages
Halstead Pl.
Homefield Spring
Norsted Manor Farm
Sumachs
Port Hill
Budgin's Hill
Fairtrough Farm
Fairtrough Rd
Hillside Farm
Works
Beech Cott.
Lattice Coppice
Rec. Grd.
Pav.
Yew Tree Cotts
Clarks La.
Shoreham Road
Beldam Haw
Halstead
Halstead Primary Sch.
Otford Road
The Meadows
Southdene
Parkside
Meadway
Chalkhurst Wood
Broom Wood
High Wood
Lower Brooms Wood
Upper Brooms Wood
Garden Cen.
Rushmore Road
Deerleap La.
Deerleap Wood
Warren Court Farm
Kilnwood
Lower Randle's Wood
Perrys La.
Stubbs Hill
The Washneys
Perry Wood
Kangles Wood
Closeheath Wood
Park Farm
Hunters Walk
Knockholt Road
Woodvale Cott.
Tangles Farm
Newyears Wood
Washneys Lane
Hayman's Wood
Piece Wood
New Stables Farm
Nursery
Curry Wood Farm
Curry Farm
Broomfield Cottage
Newlands Wood
Singles Cross La.
Randles Lane
Hawfield Wood
Singles Cross
Park Cnr.
Halstead Hill
Waylands Cl.
Long Bottoms Shaw
Birches Croft
Pound La.
Bond St.
Bond Cl.
Chapel Croft
Old Harrow Rd
London Road
Aldwyn Lodge
Knockholt Pound
Birchwood Lane
Sevenoaks
Jockey's Wood
Blueberry Farm
The Spinney Nurseries
Main Road
Ivy Farm
Tennis Cts.
Mast
Knockholt Village Centre
Play. Fields
Garden Centre
Chine Farm Place
Chevening Lane
Lees Wood
Star Hill
Lett's Green
Cophall Wood
Shelleys
Shelleys Lane
New Years Lane
Homefield
Blueberry Lane
TN14
Lodge
Burlings
Baston Wood
Knockholt
Sundridge Lane
St. Katharine's Knockholt C of E Prim. Sch.
Cooper's Wood
The Keyhole
Ashfield Wood
Wood Farm
Ash Platt
Lord Chatham's Ride
Minny Wood
Crittleshaw
Mount Road
WT Sta.
Masts
Knockholt Beeches
Knockholt Lodge
Park House
Knockholt Wood
Bowman's Orchard
Highfield House
Sand Banks
High Land
Burwood
Mountross Farm
Keepers Cottage
Summerhouse Wood
Poultry Hos.
Royal Oak
Main Hill
The Mount
Minquintin
Park Wood
Coalhearth Cottage
The Spinney
Sundridge Hill Farm
Pilgrims' Way (course of)
Hazlet Wood
Hazlet Farm
Roughfields Wood
Stonings Lane
Pilgrims Ho.
Brasted Hill
Hagbush Wood
Chevening
Chevening House
Stoneing Cottage
Scott's
NORTH DOWNS

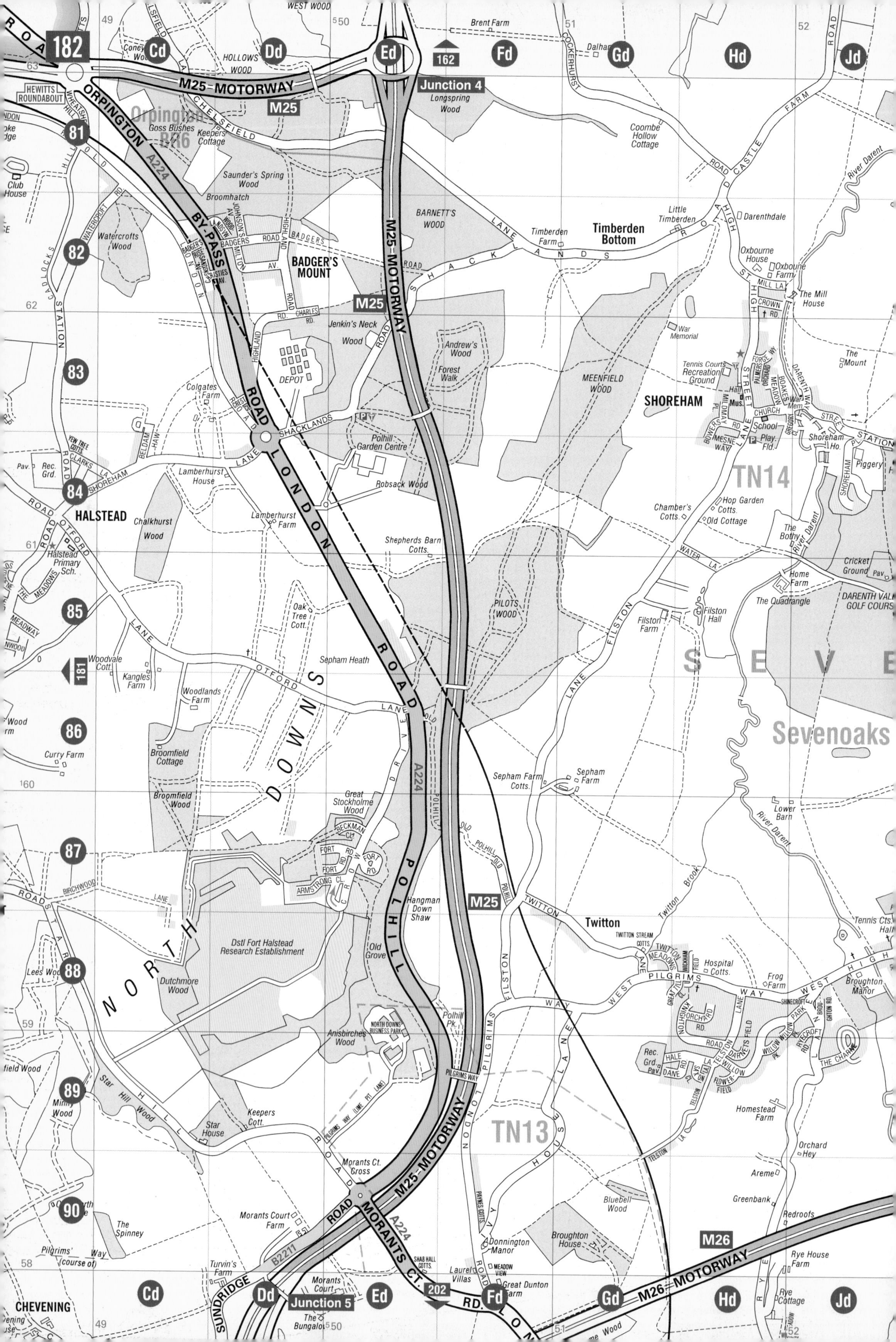
162
181
202
Junction 4
Junction 5
M25 MOTORWAY
M25
M26 MOTORWAY
M26
A224
B2211
ORPINGTON BY-PASS
LONDON ROAD
POLHILL
MORANTS CT. RD.
HEWITTS ROUNDABOUT
WHEATSHEAF HILL
OLD HILL
CHELSFIELD LANE
COCKERHURST
CASTLE FARM ROAD
SHACKLANDS ROAD
OTFORD LANE
SHOREHAM LANE
STATION ROAD
CADLOCKS
WATERCROFT RD.
HIGHLAND ROAD
CHARLES RD.
BADGERS ROAD
JOHNSONS AV.
MILTON AV.
CRISTIES AV.
BADGERS RISE
CREST RD.
BELDAM HAW
CLARKS LA.
YEW TREE COTTS.
THE MEADOWS
MEADWAY
STAR HILL ROAD
BIRCHWOOD LANE
FORT RD.
BECKMAN CL.
ARMSTRONG CL.
CROW DRIVE
OLD POLHILL
PILGRIMS WAY
PILGRIMS WAY (LIME PIT LANE)
PAYNES COTTS.
TWITTON LANE
FILSTON LANE
HOUSE LANE
TELSTON LA.
WATER LA.
WEST PILGRIMS WAY
HIGH STREET
MILL LA.
CROWN RD.
CHURCH ST.
BOWERS RD.
MESNE WAY
MILDMAY PL.
STATION RD.
DARENTH WAY
GREGORY CL.
BOAKES MEADOW
PALMERS ORCHARD
FORGE WY.
SHOREHAM PL.
DARNETS FIELD
FLOWERFIELD
WILLOW PK.
HALE
DANE
ORCHARD RD.
CHARNE
SUNDRIDGE
Orpington BR6
TN13
TN14
Sevenoaks
SEVE
NORTH DOWNS
BADGER'S MOUNT
HALSTEAD
SHOREHAM
CHEVENING
Timberden Bottom
Twitton
WEST WOOD
Brent Farm
Coney Wood
HOLLOWS WOOD
Longspring Wood
Dalham
Coombe Hollow Cottage
Goss Bushes
Keepers Cottage
Saunder's Spring Wood
Broomhatch
Watercrofts Wood
Club House
BARNETT'S WOOD
Timberden Farm
Little Timberden
Darenthdale
Oxbourne House
Oxbourne Farm
The Mill House
Jenkin's Neck Wood
DEPOT
Andrew's Wood
Forest Walk
MEENFIELD WOOD
War Memorial
Tennis Courts
Recreation Ground
Hall
Mus.
School
Play. Fld.
War Mem.
Shoreham Ho.
The Mount
Piggery
Colgates Farm
Polhill Garden Centre
Robsack Wood
Pav.
Rec. Grd.
Lamberhurst House
Chalkhurst Wood
Lamberhurst Farm
Halstead Primary Sch.
Chamber's Cotts.
Hop Garden Cotts.
Old Cottage
The Bothy
River Darent
Cricket Ground
Home Farm
The Quadrangle
DARENTH VALLEY GOLF COURSE
Shepherds Barn Cotts.
PILOTS WOOD
Oak Tree Cott.
Filston Farm
Filston Hall
Woodvale Cott.
Kangles Farm
Sepham Heath
Woodlands Farm
Wood
Curry Farm
Broomfield Cottage
Broomfield Wood
Sepham Farm Cotts.
Sepham Farm
Great Stockholme Wood
Lower Barn
Twitton Brook
Hangman Down Shaw
Old Grove
Dstl Fort Halstead Research Establishment
TWITTON STREAM COTTS.
TWITTON MEADOWS
WICKHAM FIELD
Hospital Cotts.
Frog Farm
Broughton Manor
Tennis Cts.
Lees Wood
Dutchmore Wood
Polhill Pk.
NORTH DOWNS BUSINESS PARK
Anisbirches Wood
Rec. Grd.
field Wood
Minny Wood
Star House
Keepers Cott.
Homestead Farm
Morants Ct. Cross
Orchard Hey
Areme
Greenbank
Redroofs
Bluebell Wood
Morants Court Farm
The Spinney
Pilgrims' Way (course of)
Donnington Manor
Broughton House
Rye House Farm
SHAB HALL COTTS.
Laurel Villas
MEADOW VIEW
Great Dunton Farm
Turvin's Farm
Morants Court
The Bungalow
Rye Cottage
Wood
49
50
51
52
63
62
61
160
59
58
81
82
83
84
85
86
87
88
89
90
Cd
Dd
Ed
Fd
Gd
Hd
Jd

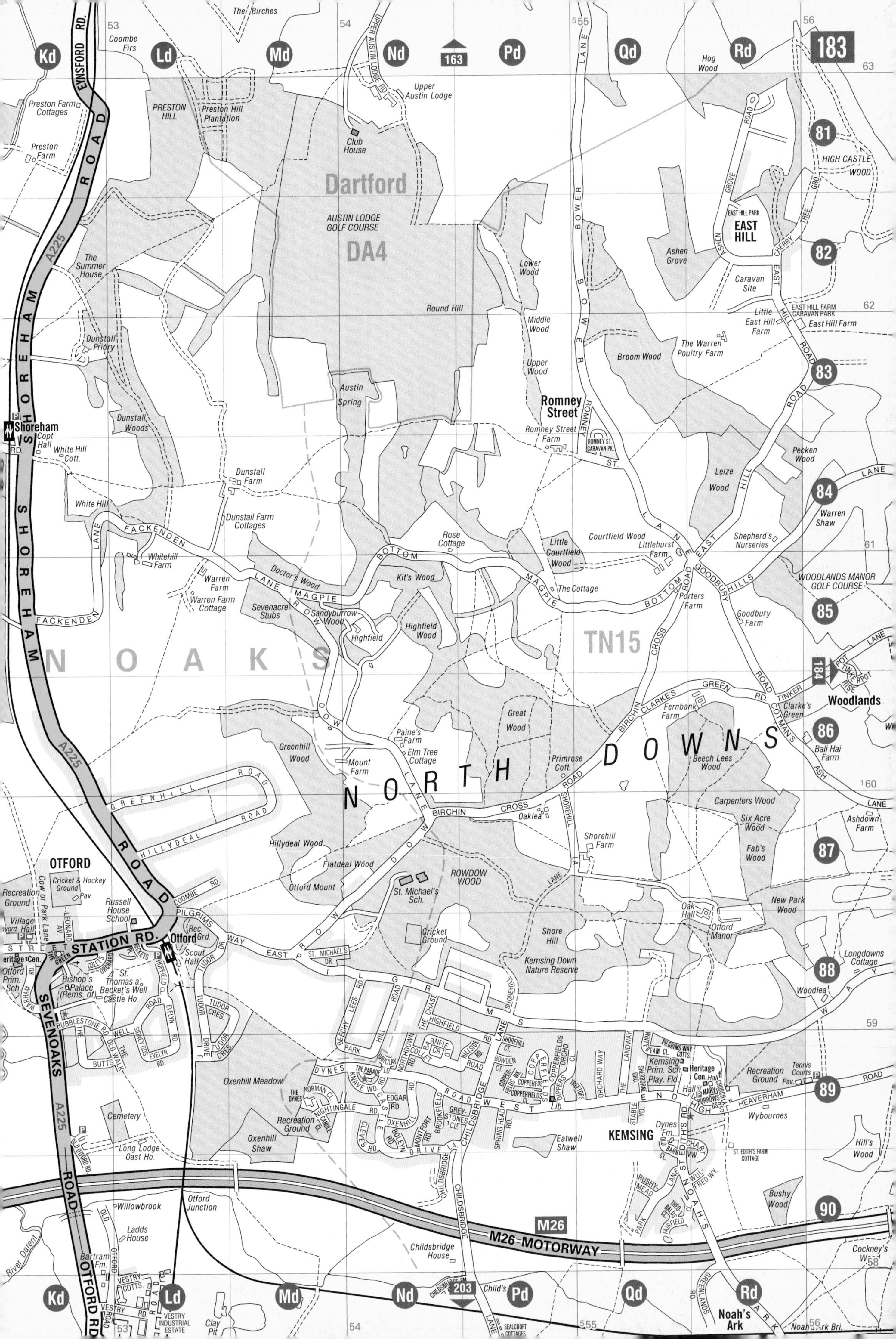
163
203
184
Kd
Ld
Md
Nd
Pd
Qd
Rd
53
54
55
56
63
62
61
60
59
58
The Birches
Coombe Firs
EYNSFORD RD.
Upper Austin Lodge
UPPER AUSTIN LODGE RD.
Club House
Hog Wood
Preston Farm Cottages
PRESTON HILL
Preston Hill Plantation
Preston Farm
Dartford
AUSTIN LODGE GOLF COURSE
DA4
HIGH CASTLE WOOD
EAST HILL PARK
EAST HILL
Ashen Grove
Caravan Site
EAST HILL FARM CARAVAN PARK
East Hill Farm
Little East Hill Farm
The Warren Poultry Farm
Broom Wood
Round Hill
Lower Wood
Middle Wood
Upper Wood
The Summer House
Dunstall Priory
Dunstall Woods
Austin Spring
Romney Street
Romney Street Farm
ROMNEY ST. CARAVAN PK.
BOWER LANE
Shoreham
Copt Hall
White Hill Cott.
Dunstall Farm
Dunstall Farm Cottages
White Hill
Pecken Wood
Leize Wood
Warren Shaw
FACKENDEN LANE
Whitehill Farm
Warren Farm
Warren Farm Cottage
Doctor's Wood
Rose Cottage
Kit's Wood
BOTTOM
MAGPIE LANE
Little Courtfield Wood
Courtfield Wood
Littlehurst Farm
The Cottage
Shepherd's Nurseries
WOODLANDS MANOR GOLF COURSE
Sevenacre Stubs
Sandyburrow Wood
Highfield
Highfield Wood
MAGPIE BOTTOM
Porters Farm
Goodbury Farm
SHOREHAM ROAD
SEVENOAKS
TN15
Great Wood
CLARKE'S GREEN RD
Fernbank Farm
TINKER POT LANE
Clarke's Green
Woodlands
Bali Hai Farm
Greenhill Wood
Paine's Farm
Elm Tree Cottage
Mount Farm
Primrose Cott.
NORTH DOWNS
Beech Lees Wood
Carpenters Wood
Six Acre Wood
Ashdown Farm
GREENHILL ROAD
HILLYDEAL ROAD
Hillydeal Wood
Flatdeal Wood
BIRCHIN CROSS
Oaklea
Shorehill Farm
Fab's Wood
ROWDOW
OTFORD
Cricket & Hockey Ground
Recreation Ground
Otford Mount
ROWDOW WOOD
St. Michael's Sch.
New Park Wood
Russell House School
Village Hall
Cow or Park Lane
COOMBE RD.
PILGRIMS WAY EAST
Rec. Grd.
Otford
Cricket Ground
Shore Hill
Oak Hall
Otford Manor
Longdowns Cottage
Heritage Cen.
Otford Prim. Sch.
STATION RD.
Scout Hall
ST. MICHAEL'S DR.
Kemsing Down Nature Reserve
Bishop's Palace (Rems. of)
St. Thomas a' Becket's Well
Castle Ho.
TUDOR DR.
TUDOR CRES.
PILGRIMS WAY
Woodlea
BUBBLESTONE RD.
BEECHY LEES RD.
HILL ROAD
THE CHASE
HIGHFIELD RD.
SHOREHILL LANE
NORTHDOWN RD.
COLLET RD.
BANFIELD CT.
HILLSIDE RD.
COPPERFIELDS
ORCHARD WAY
THE LANDWAY
Kemsing Prim. Sch.
Play. Fld.
Heritage Cen.
Recreation Ground
Tennis Courts
Pav.
HEAVERHAM ROAD
Oxenhill Meadow
DYNES RD.
THE PARADE
KNAVE WD.
NORMAN CL.
NIGHTINGALE RD.
EDGAR RD.
Recreation Ground
CASTLE RD.
OXENHILL RD.
BOLEYN RD.
MONTFORT RD.
BROOKFIELD RD.
GREYSTONES CL.
CHILDSBRIDGE LA.
WEST END
SPRING HEAD RD.
Lib.
STABLE YD.
Wybournes
Cemetery
Oxenhill Shaw
Eatwell Shaw
KEMSING
Dynes Fm.
ST. EDITH'S RD.
ST. EDITH'S FARM COTTAGE
Hill's Wood
Long Lodge Oast Ho.
CLEVES RD.
CHILDSBRIDGE WAY
Bushy Wood
M26
M26 MOTORWAY
Willowbrook
Otford Junction
RUSHYMEAD
NOAH'S ARK
Ladds House
Childsbridge House
River Darent
Bartram Fm.
OTFORD RD
VESTRY COTTS.
VESTRY RD.
VESTRY INDUSTRIAL ESTATE
Clay Pit
Child's Pd
SEALCROFT COTTAGES
Cockney's Wood
Noah's Ark
Noah's Ark Bri.
GREENLANDS RD.

West Kingsdown
Knatts Valley
East Hill
Woodlands
Knockmill
Cotman's Ash
Crowdleham
Heaverham
Kemsing
Exedown
SEVENOAKS
N O R T H
High Castle Wood
Blooming Wood
Kingsingfield Shaw
Sports Ground
West Kingsdown Industrial Est.
West Kingsdown C of E Prim. Sch.
Richardson's Farm
Ashen Shaw
Southfield Shaw
Inges Shaw
The London Golf Course
Little Boutshole Shaw
Hatch Wood
Bouts Corner
Springham's Cotts.
Crowhurst Farm
West Kingsdown Smockmill
Mill Farm
Caravan Site
Little East Hill Farm
East Hill Farm
East Hill Farm Caravan Park
East Hill Park
Shalom Place
Piggery
Knatts Farm
Stacklands Wood
Stacklands Retreat House
Pells Farm
Noah's Rough
Rose Cottage
Abbott's Wood
Subway
Woodlands Garden Cen.
Peckham Wood Corner
Peckham Wood
Water Wood
Gravelpit Wood
Knockmill Wood
Tinkerpot Shaw
Barn Gate
Pecken Wood
Warren Shaw
Shepherd's Nurseries
Woodlands Manor Golf Course
Goodbury Farm
Club House
Leize Wood
Terry's Lodge Farm
Drane Farm
Birches Wood
Arboretum
Whitehill Wood
Clarke's Green
Bali Hai Farm
WT Station
Ashdown Farm
Carpenters Wood
Six Acre Wood
Fab's Wood
Summeryards Wood
Shoulder of Mutton
Chalk Pit Wood
White Hill
Kester
Cotmans Ash
New Park Wood
Downlands
Longdowns Cottage
Woodlea Farm
The Bothy
The Wilderness
St. Clere
Coney Shaw
St. Edith Cotts.
Recreation Ground
Tennis Courts
Crowdleham House
Manor House
Chequers
Lower St. Clere
West Yaldham Farm
Yaldham Manor
Wybournes
St. Edith's Farm Cottage
Hill's Wood
Martin Spring Wood
Broughton Cottages
Bushy Wood
Cockney's Wood
Spindles
Chaucer Business Park
Hook Wood
Rumley Wood
Fen Pond Cotts.
Noah's Ark
Noah's Ark Bri.
London Road
A20
M20 Motorway
M26 Motorway
Knatts Valley Road
East Hill Road
School Lane
Manor Road
Hollywood La.
The Grove
Stansted Lane
Pells Lane
Crowhurst Lane
Tinker Pot Lane
Knock Mill Lane
Terry's Lodge Road
Exedown Road
Pilgrims' Way
Kemsing Road
Heaverham Road
Watery Lane
Fen Pond Road
Cotman's Ash Lane
Woodlands Lane
Sd
Td
Ud
Vd
Wd
Xd
Yd
164
183
204
81
82
83
84
85
86
87
88
89
90
56
57
58
59
63
62
61
60
59
58

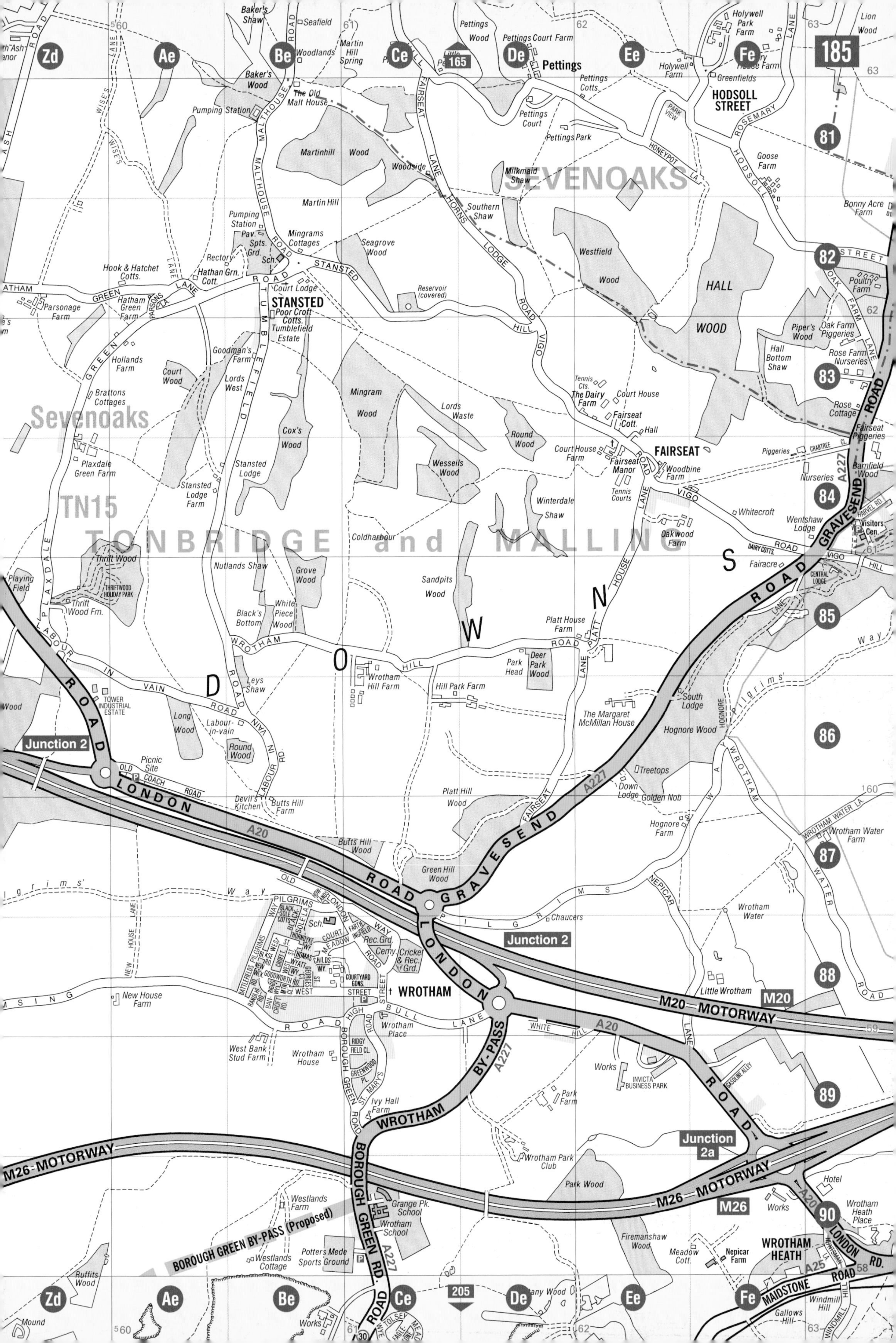
Zd
Ae
Be
Ce
De
Ee
Fe
Baker's Shaw
Seafield
Martin Hill Spring
Pettings Wood
Pettings Court Farm
Holywell Park Farm
Lion Wood
Woodlands
165
Pettings
Holywell Farm
Greenfields
HODSOLL STREET
Baker's Wood
The Old Malt House
Pettings Cotts.
Pumping Station
Pettings Court
Pettings Park
81
Martinhill Wood
Woodside
Milkmaid Shaw
SEVENOAKS
Goose Farm
Martin Hill
Southern Shaw
Bonny Acre Farm
Pumping Station
Pav.
Spts. Grd.
Sch.
Mingrams Cottages
Seagrove Wood
Westfield Wood
82
Hook & Hatchet Cotts.
Rectory
Hathan Grn. Cott.
Court Lodge
Reservoir (covered)
HALL WOOD
Poultry Farm
Parsonage Farm
Hatham Green Farm
STANSTED
Poor Croft Cotts.
Tumblefield Estate
Piper's Wood
Oak Farm Piggeries
Hall Bottom Shaw
Rose Farm Nurseries
83
Hollands Farm
Goodman's Farm
Court Wood
Lords West
Mingram Wood
Tennis Cts.
The Dairy Farm
Court House
Brattons Cottages
Sevenoaks
Lords Waste
Fairseat Cott.
Hall
Rose Cottage
Cox's Wood
Round Wood
Fairseat Piggeries
Plaxdale Green Farm
Stansted Lodge
Wesseils Wood
Court House Farm
Fairseat Manor
FAIRSEAT
Woodbine Farm
Piggeries
Nurseries
Barnfield Wood
Stansted Lodge Farm
Tennis Courts
Winterdale Shaw
Whitecroft
84
TN15
Wentshaw Lodge
Visitors Cen.
TONBRIDGE and MALLING
Coldharbour
Oakwood Farm
Thrift Wood
Nutlands Shaw
Grove Wood
Sandpits Wood
DAIRY COTTS.
Fairacre
CENTRAL LODGE
Playing Field
THRIFTWOOD HOLIDAY PARK
Thrift Wood Fm.
White Piece Wood
Black's Bottom
85
Platt House Farm
DOWNS
Park Head
Deer Park Wood
Wrotham Hill Farm
Hill Park Farm
Leys Shaw
South Lodge
TOWER INDUSTRIAL ESTATE
Wood
The Margaret McMillan House
Hognore Wood
86
Long Wood
Labour-in-vain
Junction 2
Round Wood
Picnic Site
Treetops
Platt Hill Wood
Down Lodge
Golden Nob
Devil's Kitchen
Butts Hill Farm
Hognore Farm
Wrotham Water Farm
Butts Hill Wood
87
Green Hill Wood
Pilgrims' Way
Chaucers
Sch.
Rec.Grd.
Cemy.
Cricket & Rec. Grd.
Junction 2
Wrotham Water
88
WROTHAM
Little Wrotham
M20 MOTORWAY
New House Farm
Wrotham Place
West Bank Stud Farm
Wrotham House
Works
INVICTA BUSINESS PARK
89
Ivy Hall Farm
Park Farm
Junction 2a
M26 MOTORWAY
Wrotham Park Club
Park Wood
Hotel
Westlands Farm
Grange Pk. School
Wrotham School
Works
Wrotham Heath Place
90
BOROUGH GREEN BY-PASS (Proposed)
Firemanshaw Wood
Meadow Cott.
Nepicar Farm
WROTHAM HEATH
Ruffits Wood
Westlands Cottage
Potters Mede Sports Ground
205
Mound
Works
Windmill Hill
Gallows Hill
A20
A227
A25
LONDON ROAD
GRAVESEND ROAD
WROTHAM BY-PASS
BOROUGH GREEN RD.
MAIDSTONE ROAD

A
B
C
D
E
F
G
1
2
3
4
5
6
7
8
9
10
93
94
95
96
58
57
56
155
54
53
166
Hog Lees
Century Range
Wisdom Farm
Wisdom Corner
Princess Christian Homes & Training Centre
Staffordlake
Stafford Lake
Nursery
Grindstone Handle Corner
Lower Sch.
Superstore
KNAPHILL
BROOKWOOD COUNTRY PARK
Clock Tower
Shorts Range
Bisley Camp
Cow Moor
BISLEY CAMP (National Rifle Association)
No 4 Range
Shrubb's Copse
Nursery
Sheet's Heath
Recreation Ground
Lord Roberts Centre
Cowshot Common
Running Track
Sports Ground
Pirbright Camp
Sports Ground
Ten. Cts.
BROOKWOOD
Prim. Sch.
Cowshot Hill
Victoria Farm
Basingstoke Canal
Hall
Club House
Parade Gd.
PIRBRIGHT CAMP
Alexander Barracks
Pirbright Bridge
The Slade
Brookwood
Cowshot Manor Bri.
Memorial
Military Cemetery
Woking
WEST H
PIRBRIGHT COMMON
The Cottage
Works
Basingstoke Canal
New Pond
Club Ho.
PIRBRIGHT GOLF COURSE
Dawney's Hill
GAPEMOUTH RD.
GOLE ROAD
B3012
Stanley Pool
Manyuema
MODEL COTTS.
THE CEDARS
Causeway Farm
BROOKWOOD CEMETERY
Aruwimi Wood
Furzehill Place
Furze Hill
Mazamboni Farm
Holy Island
Ruwenzori Hill
Cook's Green
Wickham's Farm
Pirbright Village Prim. School
Sch.
Pav.
West Heath
Burrow Hill
PIRBRIGHT
Hall
GU24
West Hall Farm
Grove Farm Nurseries
No. 1 Range
The Manor House
Mill Ho.
Cove Bri.
Manor Farm
Vines Farm
Hazelacre Hill
Pirbright Lodge
Crammond House
Nursery
White's Farm
Hogleys Farm
PIRBRIGHT COMMON
No. 2 Range
Piggery
Burner's Heath
Rowe Lane Farm
Bowling Hill
Furzefield Copse
Admiral's Walk
Heatherwood
Gorselands
GUILDFORD
Ardeley
Chair Hill
Bush Bottom
Track End
Bullswater Common
BULLSWATER COMMON
Bullswater Bridge
Fox Corner
Kiln Hill
Berrylands Farm
Upper Stanford Bridge
Bakersgate
Fox Corner Community Wildlife Area
The Bungalow
Rails Farm
Stream Farm
Stanford Farm
Sludge Lagoons
Filter Beds
Sewage Disposal Works
Oldfield Wood
Stanford Common
Lower Stanford Bridge
PIRBRIGHT COMMON
Peat Moor
STANFORD COMMON
The Animal Virus Research Institute
Sludge Beds
Westwind
Peatmoor Pond
Henley Park Ranges
Henleypark Lake
COBBETTHILL COMMON
MERRIST WOOD
Standinghill Wood
Wireless Station (Disused)
COBBETT HILL
Guildford College of Further & Higher Education (Merrist Wood Campus)
GU3
Slyfield Wood
Leapingbar Copse
Mercury Lodge
Deyrolles
Park Farm
MERRIST WOOD GOLF COURSE
Guildford College of Further & Higher Education (Merrist Wood Campus-Equine Centre)
Club House
The Glen
Engineering Works
Henley Pk. Fm.
Finavon
Clasford Bridge
Island Copse
Clasford Common
FAIROAKS CARAVAN PARK
Littlefield Common
Littlefield Cottages
CONNAUGHT ROAD
BROOKWOOD ROAD
A324
A322
BAGSHOT ROAD
DAWNEY HILL
PIRBRIGHT GRN.
GUILDFORD RD.
GUILDFORD ROAD
ALDERSHOT ROAD
PIRBRIGHT ROAD
ASH ROAD
B380
B3032
B3405
GRANGE ROAD
SCHOOL LANE
STANLEY HILL
CEMETERY PALES
CHAPEL LANE
CHURCH LANE
MILL LANE
MALTHOUSE LANE
HENLEY GATE
COBBETT HILL
A323

187
188
WOKING
MOUNT HERMON
ST. JOHNS
HOOK HEATH
HERMITAGE ROAD
HERMITAGE RD.
A324
30
AMSTEL WY.
Woking Crematorium
Cricket Ground
St. John's Lye
Football Ground
Club House
Basingstoke
Canal
WOKING GOLF COURSE
HOOK HEATH
GOLF COURSE
The Old Gardens
Nursery
Brook Farm
Fisher's Hill House
Fisher's Hill
GU22
SAUNDERS ROAD
HOOK HEATH ROAD
WORPLESDON HILL HOUSE
Pinewood House
Club House
W O K I N G
WORPLESDON GOLF COURSE
Crastock Farm
Crastock Br.
Crastock Manor
Berryhill Nursery
SMART'S HEATH LANE
ROAD
B380
Smart's Heath
Recreation Ground
Nurseries
Mayford Green
MAYFORD GREEN
MAYFORD
The Oaks Centre
Churchill Ho.
EGLEY
GUILDFORD RD.
WESTFIELD
Barnsbury Primary School
Westfield Prim. Sch.
Westfield Common
Mayford Meadows Local Nature Reserve
Loampits Farm
Club House
Elm Trees Farm
Green Lane Farm
Prey Heath
Beech Hill
SUTTON GREEN GOLF COURSE
Hoe Stream
Prey Heath or Pray Heath
PREY HEATH ROAD
Worplesdon
Kemishford Bridge
KEMISHFORD
Bridley Manor Farm
Bridley Manor
Bonnieshott Wood Farm
Burdenshott Hill
BURDENSHOTT ROAD
Havering Farm
PYLE HILL
Wingstone
Bridley Copse
Box Corner
Blanketmill Farm
Rye Farm
White Lodge
Hockley Lands
Nursery
Whitmoor Pond
Rickford Mill
Brook Farm
Gooserye
Guildford
Whitmoor Common
Frog Lane Farm
Sunridge House
Whitmoor House
Elm Nursery
Whitmoor Wood
Whitmoor Farm
Rickford Common
Perryhill Cottage
Norton Farm
Upper Jordan
Gooserye Cottage
Whitmoor Hatch
JORDAN HILL
Woodcorner Farm
Heather Court
Poor Jack's Wood
WORPLESDON
Whitmoor & Rickford Commons
Local Nature Reserve
Cox's Farm
Perry Hill
The Old Cottage
Sports Ground
Vine House
Perry Hill Farm
WHITMOOR COMMON
GU4
WOKING ROAD
GUILDFORD ROAD
A320
Maryland
Mount Pleasant
Hurst View
Willow Grange
Rectory
Greenacre
Sudpre
Nursery
Britten's Pond
A322
WORPLESDON ROAD
Pitmore Farm
Driving Range
Rifle & Pistol Range
PITCH PLACE
Field Research Sta.
Tangley Place Farm
SALT BOX ROAD
Stringer's Common
Stringers Common
JACOBS WELL
H
J
K
L
M
N
P
1
2
3
4
5
6
7
8
9
10
97
98
99
500
57
56
155
54
53

188
168
187
A
B
C
D
E
F
G
91
92
93
94
95
96
97
98
99
100
WOKING
MOUNT HERMON
KINGFIELD
OLD WOKING
WESTFIELD
MAYFORD
CARTBRIDGE
SEND
SUTTON GREEN
PYLE HILL
JACOBS WELL
GU22
GU4
Guildford
W O K I N G
Crickets Hill
Sutton Park
SUTTON PARK
SUTTON GREEN GOLF COURSE
HOEBRIDGE GOLF COURSE
Woking Leisure Cen.
Pool in the Park
WOKING PARK
Woking FC (Kingfield Stadium)
David Lloyd Leisure
Kingfield Green
St. John the Baptist School
Woking College
Barnsbury Primary School
Westfield Prim. Sch.
Westfield Common
White Rose Lane Local Nature Reserve
Hoe Bridge Sch. (Pre-Preparatory)
Monument Hill
Club House
Roundbridge Farm
Hoebridge Farm
Sewage Works
Site of Woking Palace
Wokingpark Farm
Oldhall Copse
Grave Yard
Riverdale Farm
Broad Mead
Broadmead Cut
River Wey Navigation
Prews Farm
Lancaster Hall
Send Hill
St. Bede's C of E Jun. Sch.
Send C of E First Sch.
Sendbarns
Hilland
Woodhill Cottage
Woodhill Farm Cottage
Woodhill House Farm
Old Woodhill Cottage
Sendhurst Grange
Old Timbers
Old Timbers Cottage
Nutbourne Fruit Farm
Three Fords
Ford Cottage
Whitehouse Farm
Nuthill Farm
Broadoak Br.
Bower's Lock
Burpham Court Farm
Sutton Place
Statue
The Pavilion
Sutton Boxes
Sutton Park House
Stables Cottage
Ladygrove Farm
St. Edward's Well
Vine Cottage
Oak House
Cox's Farm
Whitmoor Farm
Whitmoor House
Whitmoor Wood
Elm Nursery
Sunridge House
Tadpole House
Sutton Green House
Manor House
The Bungalow
Frog Lane Farm
Wareham's Farm
Triggs Lock
Triggs Lock Bridge
Runtleywood Farm
Lower Westfield Farm
Runtley Wood
Fisher's Farm
Ashburton House
Worsfold Gates
Depot
Cricketshill Farm
Sendholme
Cemetery
Send Hill Riding Stables
Sendcourt Farm
Send Grove
Fell Hill
Hillside Farm
Little Moorlane Farm
Loampits Farm
Elm Trees Farm
Green Lane Farm
Beech Hill
Wingstone
Mill Moor
Sports Ground
Cartbridge House
HIGH STREET
KINGFIELD ROAD
BROADMEAD ROAD
SEND ROAD
SEND BARNS
GUILDFORD ROAD
WESTFIELD ROAD
LONDON ROAD
OLD WOKING RD.
A247
A320
A3
B380
B381
B382
B368
B2215
FRITHYS

PYRFORD VILLAGE
Vicarage
Hanger
The Prae
Wheelers Farm
The Bourne
Abbey Stream Bri.
Abbey Stream
WARREN FARM MOBILE HOME PARK
Sludge Bed
Walsham Lock
Walsham Plantation
Newark Priory (Remains of)
Newark New Bri.
R. Wey Navigation
Newark Lock
Irish Hole
RIVER WEY
Walsham Meadow
Mill House
Mill Stream
Ockham Mill Stream
Sewage Works
BARATARIA PK. CARAVAN SITE
Homewood Farm
Lodge
Ripley Green
HALF MOON COTTS.
Cricket Grd.
Dunsborough Park
Dunsborough Farm
Bridgefoot Farm
RIPLEY
Mus.
Sch.
Chapel Farm
Ripley Ct. Sch.
Tennis Court
Hurst Farm
Devonia Farm
Papercourt Farm
Works
Papercourt Sailing Club
Industrial Estate
Woking
GUILDFORD
Willow Farm
Grove Heath Farm
Grove Heath
GU23
SEND MARSH
Garlick's Arch Copse
Garlick's Arch
Hangover Ho.
Three Bridges
The Paddocks
Nursery
BURNTCOMMON
Oldlands
Oldlands Copse
Depot
Tithe Barns
Tythebarns Farm
Cedarwood
Oak Ride Farm
Hazelhurst Cottage
Sussex Farm
Holride Farm
Blendon
Highcotts Wood
The Oaks
Southernwood
HMP SEND
Guildford
GU4
Dedswell Manor Farm House
Dedswell Manor Farm
Nursery
WEST CLANDON
Clandon
Birch Farm
Buttinham Copse
Fish Pond
Humphreys Copse
Martin Furze
Gason Wood
Roam Wells
Furze Copse
August Hill
Sheppardsgrove Copse
Brambleride Copse
Brambleride
Jury Farm
Lower Hammond's Farm
Hungry Hill Cottage
Hungry Hill
Ryde Farm
Loveland's Copse
Roborow
Roborow Wood
Guileshill Farm
Guileshill Lodge
OCKHAM PARK
Park Wood
Ockham Park
Chimneys
Tankards
Buckingham Lodge
Old Rectory Farm
Church End
Chestnut Farm
Romer Cottage
The Old Cottage
Bachelor's Copse
Russets
Works
Wisley Airfield (Disused)
El. Sub. Sta.
Stratford Bridge
Ockham Mill
Ockham Mill Farm
Nursery
Rock Garden
Garden Cen.
RHS Garden Wisley
Battleston Hill
Ockham Village
A3 PORTSMOUTH RD.
RIPLEY BY PASS
B2215
B367
B2039
A247
OCKHAM ROAD NORTH
HIGH STREET
PORTSMOUTH ROAD
CLANDON ROAD
THE STREET
169
190

190
PORTSMOUTH
A3
ROAD
Q
R
S
T
U
V
W
07
08
09
510
Oakham
Village Green
Cottages
ELM CORNER
Wilderness Farm
Hunt's Copse
THE GARDENS
Hatchford End
Hatchford Wood
Woodside Cott.
Elm Cottage
Nurseries
170
HATCHFORD MANOR
Hatchford Park
Hatchford
Poynters Farm
Pointers Green
Brickfield Copse
Little Birchfield Copse
Pondtail Farm
Highfield Farm
Nurseries
NORTON LA
M25
50
Cold Norton Farm
Tennis Courts
Orchard Farm
Hazeldene Farm
Norton Wood
91
Wisley Airfield (disused)
El. Sub Sta.
92
Bridge End Farm
HYDE LA
HATCH LA
Little Upton Cottages
MARTYR'S GREEN
Pound Farm
May's Green
The Lodge
Upton Farm
Tanner's Copse
Old Oak Common
Cobham
The New Preserve
57
Old Rectory Farm
Bridge End
Chestnut Farm
Appstree Farm
Trulliber Copse
Roundabout
Chaffers Copse
KT11
Hurst Hill
93
Pavilion
Recreation Ground
Hall
OCKHAM
Church End
Alms Heath
SCHOOL LA
Hook Wood
Brick Kiln Copse
Woking
Stumps Grove Farm
Stumps Grove
Stumpsgrove Cottages
Barns Thorns
Clamp Rough
94
Guileshill Lodge
Tennis Court
B2039
Blackmoor Farm
GU23
Effingham Junction
Gallows Grove
56
LONG
REACH
Slade Farm
Bramble Cottage
Slade Cottage
Ridings Copse
95
DRIFT GOLF COURSE
Romer Cottage
The Old Cottage
RIDINGS LA
Rydings Farm
BARNSTHORNS WOOD
Bachelor's Copse
189
Russets
Blue Ride
Club House
EFFINGHAM COMMON
BACHELORS
Even Wood
GREEN LANE
The Drift
96
Works
Old Brickyard
Waterloo Farm
HORSLEY CAMPING & CARAVANNING CLUB SITE
The Forest Nature Reserve
North Forest Lodge
Effingham Common
ORCHARD CL.
Lee Brook
G U I L D F O
55
Broom House
NIGHTINGALE
NORTHCOTE CRES
OCKHAM DR.
CRESCENT
AVENUE
The Forest
HIGHLANDS
FALCONWOOD
HEATHWAY
WILDWOOD CL.
Hook Farm
97
WEST
GREEN LANE
Gas Pumping Station
Football Ground
Pav.
Tennis Courts
The Raleigh School
EDWIN
EDWIN CL.
HEATHERDENE
Sch.
Playing Field
PARKSIDE
Horsley
FOREST CL.
NIGHTINGALE RD.
Depot
Manor Farm
Jury Farm
SILKMORE
FARLEYS CL.
WOODSIDE
Lollesworth Wood
COBHAM
THE RISE
THE CHASE
KT24
RIDE
98
GREEN BANK
Hall
GLENDENE AV.
THE BIRCHES
Lib.
Little Ridings
Leewood Field Plantation
54
Furze Copse
Roundtree Farm
Lollesworth Wood
Kingston Meadows Rec. Grd.
LOLLESWORTH LA
WEST HORSLEY
WOODLAND
The Wallep
99
Parkrow Copse
OAKWOOD DR.
PENNYMEAD
Play. Fld.
Ridings Wood
Orestan Plantation
Cricket Ground
Pav.
Lollesworth Wood
Tennis Courts
Gravel Hill Pond
Garden Grove
Frenchlands Copse
Pennymead Lake
Lower-Hammond's Farm
RICKSONS LA
TINTELLS LA
KENYONS
PARK CORNER DR.
LYNX
EAST HORSLEY
100
Wells
LOWER PERYERS
HIGHFIELDS
House Pond
Barcombe Farm
53
Dene Place
Pincott Farm
West Horsley Place
Place Farm
Nomad Theatre
Horsley Towers
Hammonds Farm
SCHOOL LA
ST. MARTIN'S CT.
Dancing Pit
Busbridge Rew
SOUTH
ROAD

ELMBRIDGE
Downside
Downside Common
Downside Farm
Downside Farm Cottage
Downside Saw Mill
Sports Ground
171
M25
M25 MOTORWAY
50
Cobham Service Area
Due open Mid 2012
Muggeridge Wood
Wrens Hill Wood
Thornets Wood
Down Wood
Spring Meadow Wood
Chasemore Wood
Chasemoor Farm
Yehudi Menuhin Hall
Yehudi Menuhin School
Bookham Lodge Stud
Bookham Lodge
Gardeners Cottage
Gate Lodge
Little Slyfield
Slyfield House
Slyfield Farm
Slyfield Cotts.
Little Wood
Sheepbell Farm
Bushy Copse
Cattle Grid
Stoke D'Abernon Bri.
Weir
Heathfield
Barracks Farm
Monksgreen Farm
Nursery
Godstone Ho.
Ashspring Copse
Rye Salters
Bull Riding Farm
Withy Bed
Peaked Rough
New Barn Wood
Newmarsh Farm
North Surrey Gun Club
Hundred Pound Bridge Wood
Hundred Pound Bridge
Hill Farm
The Birches
Bank's Common
Bank's Farm
Little Bookham Common
GREAT BOOKHAM COMMON
The Common
Merritt's Farm
Oak Tree Cottage
Manor Cottage
The White House
Bushy Thicket
Thicket Copse
Little Mornshill Wood
Banks Way House
Mornshill Farm
GREAT MORNSHILL WOOD
Sewage Works
Beehive Farm
KT22
KT23
Leatherhead
Slater's Oak
Norwood Farm
Long Maddox Farm
Bookham
Merrylands Farm
Pikes Pool
Herons Reach
Mallards Mere
Lower Farm
Little Bookham
OAKEN WOOD
MOLE VALLEY
Indian Farm
Moat
Upper Leewood Farm
THORNET WOOD
GREATLEE WOOD
Littlelee Wood
Great Ridings Plantation
Cook's Coppice
Effingham Lodge Farm
Preston Farm
The Vineries
Preston Cross
The Grange (Training Centre)
Manor Farm
Sports Centre
Manor House Sch.
Howard of Effingham School
King George's Field
EFFINGHAM
Rolls Farm
Nursery
Orestan Farm
Parrott's Coppice
Home Farm
The Nook Farm
Works
The Short Wood
Floriana Farm
Club House
Tennis Courts
EFFINGHAM GOLF COURSE
Goldstone Farm
GREAT BOOKHAM
Jun. Sch.
Inf. Sch.
Keswick
The Dawnay Sch.
Rec. Grd.
Bowling Green
Polesden Lacey Infant Sch.
Kenilworth Riding Stables
Phoenice Park Cottage
Connicut Wood
North Lodge
GUILDFORD ROAD
LEATHERHEAD ROAD
A246
192
X
Y
Z
Aa
Ba
Ca
Da
91
92
93
94
95
96
97
98
99
100

Ea
Fa
Ga
Ha
Ja
Ka
La
172
PACHESHAM PARK GOLF COURSE
Heathfield Copse
West Orchard
Brook Willow Farm
Pachesham Farm
The Mounts
Research Laboratories
LEATHERHEAD COMMON
West Hill Sch.
Sewage Works
Refuse Composting Plant
Household Waste Recycling Site
River Mole Local Nature Reserve
Slyfield Farm
Bushy Copse
Gutter's Bri.
Bushy Platt
RANDALLS ROAD
A245
M25 MOTORWAY
M25
Junc. 9
BY-PASS RD.
Barnett Wood
LOWER ASHTEAD
Play. Field
St. Peter's Prim. Sch.
Randalls Park Crematorium (Leatherhead)
Randalls Park Lawn Cemetery
Therfield Sch.
Randalls Research Park
Leatherhead
Barracks Farm
Monksgreen Farm
Nursery
Ashspring Copse
COBHAM ROAD
Nurseries
Sports Field
Leatherhead Trinity Prim. School
Fairfield
Play. Fld
KNOLL R'BOUT
EPSOM ROAD
LERET WY.
STATION R.
KT22
Nature Reserve
LEATHERHEAD COMMUNITY HOSP.
Woodlands Sch.
LEATHERHEAD
Leatherhead FC (Fetcham Grove)
Spts. Grd.
Thorncroft Manor
Leatherhead Leisure Centre
Boating Lake
Rifle Range
HIGHLANDS RD.
B2033
Fetcham Village Inf. Sch.
Oakfield Jun. Sch.
FETCHAM
Leatherhead
Hall
Cherry Orchard Farm
Elmer Water Works
Hawk's Hill House
Hawk's Hill
M O L E
River Mole Local Nature Reserve
Vale Lodge
Downside Farm
Reservoir (covered)
Downside
Naomi Acres
GUILDFORD ROAD
YOUNG STREET
A246
Bocketts Farm Park
B2122
B2450
DORKING ROAD
BY-PASS
A24
Oakwood Court
Seven Gables
Givons Grove
Sunpatch
GREAT BOOKHAM
LEATHERHEAD ROAD
The Junipers
The Hazels
The Crown of the Hill
Pressforward Cotts.
Lilac Cottage
Icehouse Combe
Norbury Park Farm
The Priory
Nursery
Roaringhouse Farm
Denshire Hill
Updown Wood
Walnut Tree Clump
Fetcham Downs
Norbury Park
Dorking
The Scrubs
Polesden Lacey Infant Sch.
Kenilworth Riding Stables
KT23
Saw Mill
Norbury Park
Mole Cott.
Box Hill Sch.
St.Michael C of E First Sch.
MICKLEHAM
NORBURY PARK
Bookham Wood
Druids Grove
Swanworth Farm
RH5
Mickleham Hall
Charley Mount
MICKLEHAM BY-PASS
LONDON ROAD
Phoenice Park Cottage
Phoenice Farm
Lodge Farm
Cowslip Fm.
Junipehill
JUNIPERHILL WOOD
Connicut Wood
North Lodge
Beechy Wood
Cowslip Cottage
B2209
91
92
93
94
95
96
97
98
99
100
191
14
515
16
17
58
57
56
55
54
53

193
EPSOM DOWNS
Langley Vale
ASHTEAD PARK
173
ASHTEAD
Ashtead
KT21
RAC GOLF COURSE
Langley Bottom
Langley Bottom Wood
Langley Bottom Farm
EPSOM and EWELL
Epsom
KT18
City of London Freemen's Sch.
William III Gate
Playing Field
Sports Hall
Pitch
ASHTEAD HOSP.
Prim. Sch.
Larch Field
Tudor Croft
Ermyn Lodge
Chase Farm Stud
Thirty Acres Barn
Gillette Cottages
Nohome Farm
Trial Course
Addlestead Wood
Addlestead Farm
North Lodge
Loretta Lodge
Fourfield Close
Little Hurst Wood
The Hurst
Walton Hurst Farm
Highdale
Highlands Farm
Reservoir (covered)
Hambleton Wood
Play. Fld.
Headley Court Rehabilitation Cen.
Lee Green
Headley Park Farm
Headley Park
Hook Wood
GREAT HURST WOOD
Edes Barn Cottages
M25
M25 MOTORWAY
Tyrrell's Wood
Club House
Round Wood
Pignut Wood
Court Farm
Oyster Hill
Great Hurst Wood
TYRRELLS WOOD GOLF COURSE
Shepherds Close
VALLEY
REIGATE ROAD
B2033
MILL WAY
LEECH LA.
NOWER WOOD
Golf Course
Paddock Cottage
Radio Bungalow
Leatherhead Downs
The Garden Ho.
Wellbottom Cottage
Cherkley Court
Stane Street
CHERKLEY WOOD
Costal Wood
Subway
Tumber House
Tunbarr
Tot Hill
Hayes Cotts.
HEADLEY
Rectory
WALTON
Kingsbarns
Manor House
Heath Farm
Goodman's Furze
Great Hayes
Mickleham Downs
Garden Cottage
Dean Wood
Cricket Ground
White Lodge
Cockshoot Wood
LODGEBOTTOM LANE
MICKLEHAM DOWNS
Cockshot Cottage
White Hill
TYE LANE
Herring Grove
Warren Farm
Warren Farm Cottages
High Ashurst (Camping Site)
HEADLEY HEATH
HEADLEY COMMON
Headley Grove Farm
Headley Grove
Junipers
Whitehill Cottage
Middlehill Wood
Bullen Wood
Headley Reservoir
Pebble Coombe
Sch.
Ma
Na
Pa
Qa
Ra
Sa
Ta
91
92
93
94
95
96
97
98
99
100
194
18
19
20
21
53
54
55
56
57
58

EPSOM DOWNS
THE HILL
EPSOM DOWNS RACECOURSE
Tattenham Corner
Tattenham Cnr.
174
TATTENHAM CORNER
Playing Field
Superstore
REIGATE RD.
A240
Lonesome Ponds
BURGH HEATH
Downs House
Racing Stables
EPSOM DOWNS
Langley Vale
Langley Bottom
The Warren
Trial Course
EPSOM and EWELL
WALTON DOWNS
Epsom Downs Prim. Sch. & Children's Cen.
Banstead Athletic FC Grd. & Epsom & Ewell FC
The Phoenix Centre
Banstead Sports Cen.
Marbles Pond
Pit Wood
South Tadworth Farm
EPSOM DOWNS METRO CEN.
PITWOOD PK. IND. EST.
Tadworth
KT20
Tadworth Park
Garden Farm
Millennia Ho.
St. Margaret's Sch.
THE CHILDREN'S TRUST
Tadworth Prim. Sch.
TADWORTH
BRIGHTON
A217
BONSOR
B2032
B2220
B290
Nohome Farm
Epsom
Downs View Wood
Downs View
KT18
Round Wood
Little Hurst Wood
The Hurst
Wingfield Stud Farm
Wildwoods Riding Centre
Wildwoods
Twistwood
Police Training School
Edes Barn Cottages
Chinthurst Sch.
Priests Mere Pond
Hedge Corner
Workhouse Pond
Sports Ground
Hockey Ground
Mere Pond
193
GREAT HURST WOOD
SANDHILL WOOD
Ebbisham Farm
M25
Walton Manor
Walton Manor Farm
Bramley Sch.
WALTON ON THE HILL
Prim. Sch.
Comm. Cen.
Heath Farm
Subway
Great Hurst Wood
REIGATE and
Castle House
Dowding Lodge
BANSTEAD
Stables
Recreation Ground
Club House
The Gallops
HEATH
Red Lodge Mobile Home Park
WALTON PARK WOOD
M25 MOTORWAY
Rectory
Manor House
Heath Farm
Great Hayes
PRIORY GRANGE STURT HOUSE
Recreation Ground
Works
Pav.
WALTON HEATH GOLF COURSE
WALTON HEATH
Chussex Plain
Frith Park
Frith Park Farm
Hedgecroft
Walton Heath
White Lodge
Herring Grove
Headley Grove Farm
Headley Grove
Queen's Wood
LITTLE HEATH
Walton Oaks
The Hermitage
Little Heath Cottages
Rookery Cottages
Natural Gas Pressure Reducing Station
Mogador Cottages
MOGADOR
Wayside Farm
HEADLEY COMMON
B2033
DORKING ROAD
Pebble Coombe
Sch.
206
Round Wood
Ua
Va
Wa
Xa
Ya
Za
Ab
91
92
93
94
95
96
97
98
99
100

Minquintin
The Mount
Hazlet Wood Farm
Stoneings Lane
Roughfields Wood
Sundridge Hill Farm
181
Park Wood
Pilgrims' Way (course of)
Laurel Cottage
Scott's Lodge
Hitherfield
Pilgrims Ho.
Stoneings Cottage
Stoneings
Brasted Lane
Hagbush Wood
CHEVENING
Chevening House
Shootfield
Shootfield Cottage
West Lodge
Home Farm
Brasted Hill
Brasted Hill Farm
Shootfield Wood
CHEVENING PARK
Home Wood
The Nower
Hogtrough Hill
Oveny Green Cottages
Oveny Green Farm
Combe Bank Farm
Grove House
Homewood
Sundridge Lodge
Ovenden Lodge
Ovenden Road
Combe Bank Cottages
North Lodge
Woodlands
Combebank Wood
Hogtrough Cott.
Court Lodge Farm
Combe Bank Wood
M25 Motorway
M25
Watercress Beds
Court Lodge Cottages
COMBE WOOD
Sevenoaks
B2211
Combe Wood
Ashwood
SEVENOAKS
Holywell Shaw
Park Wood
Pumping Station
The Cottage
Glebe Cotts.
St. Martins Meadow
Thorns Meadow
Combe Bank Sch.
Recreation Ground
Little Combe Bank
R. Darent
Chevening Road
Station Rd.
Coles La.
Tanners
Rectory
Rectory Lane
Church Road
Mill Cottage
Mill Farm
The Old Rectory
BRASTED
Depot
Lodge
Weirs
Market Gdns.
Bowl. Grn.
Pav.
War Mem.
SUNDRIDGE
A25
202
Warren Farm
Piggeries
Main Road
High Street
Manor Rd.
Chapmans Road
Woodside Rd.
Maple T.
TN14
The Old Rectory
Park Farm
Charmans Farm
Tennis Courts
Rec. Grd.
Hall
Watermill Cl.
Alms Row
Elliotts La.
Orchard Farm
The Carriageway
Brasted Place
The Rookeries
Playing Fld.
Oast Hill Farm
Meadlands
Sundridge & Brasted C of E Prim. Sch.
Applecroft
St. Mary's Church Rd.
The Warren
Park Fm. Cott.
River Darent
Training Centre
Heverswood Lodge
Westend
Camrie
Quarry Cott.
The Quarry
Brasted Place Farm
Netherdowns
Birchwood
Sundridge Place Farm
Valence Lodge
Lodge Wood
The Red Ho.
The White House
Oast Cottages
Westerham Road
A233
Fountain Cotts.
Twin Cedars
Slaney
Old Merralls
Long Barn
Birchfield Farm
Greystone Park
Little Mead
Mullion
Twelve Acre Cott.
Cricket Grd.
Club House
The Gardens
Heverswood Farm
Colinette Cotts.
Little Cacketts
Greenacre
Spring Shaw
Valence Sch.
Neptune Pond
Foxwold Lodge
Cacketts Cotts.
Overdale Meadow
Cacketts Lodge
Cobs Lea
Colinette
Birchfield Wood
Birchfield Cottage
Manor Farm
Lodge Barn Farm
Dunsdale Cott.
Colinette Farm
Vines Gate Shaw
Park Shaw
Old Bartholmy Brooms
Cacketts
Kennels
VALENCE WOOD
WESTERHAM GOLF COURSE
Pipers Lane
GREAT WOOD
Les Etoiles
Gowanbank
Hill Water Bottom Wood
Vines Gate
Greenhills
Birchfield
Willow
Foxwold
Wayside Cott.
Ivy Cott.
Mile End
The Chantry
Vale Cott.
Piper's Farm
Piper's Green
Brasted Chart
Bracken House
Chapman's Wood
Gillhams
Cricket Grd.
Fieldway
Rec. Grd.
Turtle House
Thatches
QUORNDEN WOOD
Plateau
Penn Farm
Manning's Wood
Piper's Green Rd
Phillipines Shaw
Newmans Rise
Brook Place Cotts
Little Norman St.
Manning's Wood
Chartside Cottage
The Shaw
Ebor Wood
Stanhope Wood
Little Redwood
Round Wood
Quornden
Starvecrowl
Ide Hill Road
Penn Lane
Little Lane
The Bungalow
Brook Place
Norman Street
French Street
Cleeve
Pilgroves
Saltwood
Parson's Marsh
Phillippines Shaw
Emmetts Lane
Pigeon Croft
North Lodge
Newman's Hill
Valence End
Quakers
Willowcroft

CHEVENING
Chevening House
The Spinney
Coalhearth Cottage
Morants Court Farm
Morants Court
Turvin's Farm
Bungalow
Edward Shaw
Alder Shaw
Rakefield Wood
Laurel Villas
Great Dunton Farm
Broughton House
Rye House Farm
Rye Cottage
Redroofs
Wickens Caravan Site
Boat Ho.
Home Wood
CHEVENING ROAD
SUNDRIDGE ROAD
Chevening Cross
Grove House
Claypit Shaw
Homewood
M25 MOTORWAY
M25-MOTORWAY
M26 MOTORWAY
M26
M25
Junction 5 (M25)
MORANTS CT. RD.
LONDON ROAD
A224
B2211
182
DUNTON GREEN
Dunton Green
Rye Wood
Rye Lane Pottery
Ryewood Cottages
River Darent
Subway
Donnington Hall
Prim. Sch.
Days Cotts.
STATION RD.
Longford
Sevenoaks Wildlife Reserve
Jeffery Harrison Visitor Centre
Works
Knole Academy (West)
Windmill Farm
Froghole
Chevening (St. Botolph's) C of E Prim. Sch.
Froghall Farm
Brickfield Cott.
Willow Fm.
Rec. Grd.
Chipstead Sailing Club
Chipstead Lake Cheshire Home
Superstore
Hardy's Yard
CHIPSTEAD
RIVERHEAD
BRADBOURNE
Bradbourne Riding Cen.
Bradbourne Lakes
Children's Play Area
The Square
Moat Farm
The Rectory
Chipstead Ho.
Chipstead Comn.
Tennis Courts
Amherst Sch.
Holmesdale Sports Grd.
Riverhead Infants' School
The Stone Ho.
Riverhead Mews
Sevenoaks Mag. Ct.
Morewood Cl. Ind. Est.
Council Refuse Transfer Cen.
Council Yard
Garden Centre
Offices
MAIN ROAD
WESTERHAM ROAD
A25
201
Piggeries
Warren Farm
SUNDRIDGE
Old Rectory
WORSHIPS HILL
AMHERST HILL
LONDON ROAD
Ant Wood
MONTREAL PARK
Bessels Green
Byways
COLD ARBOR RD.
Dryhill Local Nature Reserve
Cold Arbor Wood
Wellers Farm
Dryhill
Dryhill Farm
Ash Platt Wood
Obelisk Wood
Sevenoaks
Brittains Farm
Sevenoaks
TN13
TN14
The Warren
Sundridge Place Farm
Oast Cottages
Salters Heath
Cods Corner
Little Britain's Wood
Middlings Wood
Kippington
Kippington House
SEVENOAKS BY PASS
A21
B2042
Red Grove
Greenlane Farm
Greenlane Farm Cotts.
Manor Farm
Lodge Barn Farm
Hill Water Bottom Wood
Greenlane Wood
Furzefield Wood
Shrubs Corner
Pollard's Barn
Dibden
Dibden Farm
Great Britain's Wood
Playing Field
The New Beacon Sch.
Cross Keys
WILLOW WOOD
Nursery
Hawks Wood
Whitley
Mildridge Wood
Mill Bank Wood
Fig Street Farm
Fig Street
White Lodge
Longspring Wood
Tennis Courts
Greystones
Knapp
Brook Place Cotts.
Brook Place
Little Norman Street Farm
The Bungalow
NORMAN STREET
Mackerels Plain
Nightingale Cott.
Whitley Forest
Seven Wents
The Woodman
Whitley Row
Rustwood
Goldsmith's Bottom
SEVENOAKS BY-PASS
91
92
93
94
95
96
97
98
99
100
Cd
Dd
Ed
Fd
Gd
Hd
Jd
49
50
51
52
53
54
55
56
57
58

GATTON
Kingswood Knoll
Grove Shaw
Gatlands Shaw
Gatton East Field Shaw
North Lodge
195
MARGERY
KT20
REIGATE HILL INTERCHANGE
M25 MOTORWAY
M25
Junction 8
Catsbrain Shaw
Jubilee Plantations
High Beeches
Royal Alexandra & Albert School
GATTON PARK
East Lodge Farm
Margery Ho.
Reservoir (covered)
Margery Hall Nursery
Margery Hall Pig Farm
Margery Farm
Little Buck Wood
Halfmoon Clump
Hop Garden Pond
Engine Pond
The Burpit
The Serpentine
THE LAKE
Boat Ho.
Water Tower
Pilgrims Holt
Two Acre Wood
Margery Hall
Blackhorse Wood
Great Buck Wood
Wingate Hill
Gatton
Serpentine Wood
Temple Wood
Temple Lodge
Nut Wood
Greenclump Hill
Four Acre Upper Woods
Rock Farm
Fort (dismantled)
Queen's Park
The Beeches
Reigate Hill
Piggeries
Pilgrims' Way
Broadleas
Reigate
RH2
Colley Wood
St. Bede's Sch.
COLES MEADS
Redhill
Redhill Tennis Club
REDHILL
Wray Common
Brooklands Sch.
Fire Brigade East Division HQ
Wray Common Prim. Sch.
Indoor Bowls Club
TA Centre
Donyngs Rec. Cen.
STATION
Reigate
Superstore
Castle Grds.
Reigate Coll.
Town Hall
Law Cts.
REIGATE
Reigate Gram. Sch.
Cemetery
Reigate Parish Church Sch.
Priory Museum
Reigate Priory Playing Fields
Priory Pond
REIGATE PARK
Park Hill
Monument
REDHILL COMMON
Jubilee Plantation
St. John's
Dunottar Day Sch. for Girls
MEAD VALE
EARLSWOOD
Earlswood
Sports Ground
YMCA Sports Centre
SOUTH PARK
King George's Field
Playing Field
Woodhatch
WOODHATCH
Reigate Sch.
REDHILL & REIGATE GOLF COURSE
EARLSWOOD COMMON (Local Nature Reserve)
Boat Houses
Boating Lake
Earlswood Lakes
New Pond
Household Waste Recycling Centre
Redhill Football Club
Sewage Works
Petridge Wood Common
New Pond Farm
Community Centre
Rushetts Farm
Dovers Green Sch.
Recreation Ground
DOVERSGREEN
Felland Copse
Slipshatch Cotts.
Withy Wood
Slipshatch Wood
Hartswood Farm Cotts.
Hartswood Farm
Playing Fields
Dovers Farm
Turner's Shaw
A217
A242
A25
A23
A2044
B2034
208
REIGATE and BANSTEAD

208
GATTON
MERSTHAM
Junction 7 (M25)
Junction 8 (M23)
Reigate
RH2
GATTON PARK
THE LAKE
Boat Ho.
Jetty
Gatton Point
Temple Wood
Temple Lodge
Middle Lodge
The Bushetts
East Lodge Farm
Club House
REIGATE HILL GOLF COURSE
Alexandra & ert School
LONDON ROAD
A23
SOUTH
GATTON PARK RD.
A242
Merstham
Rec. Grd.
Furzefield Wood
Playing Field
The Oakley Youth Club
Playing Field
The Grove
Crossways Rest Gdn.
SOUTH MERSTHAM
Woodfield Sch.
St. Nicholas Sch.
Works
Poultry Houses
Coppice Lea
Warwick Wold Farm
Yew Tree Cottage
WARWICK WOLD
North Lodge
Residential Caravan Park
M23
M23 MOTORWAY
Redhill
Sewage Works
Mercers Country Park
Mercers Farm
East Surrey Coll. (Gatton Point North)
East Surrey Coll. (Gatton Point S.)
Pupil Referral Unit
HOLMETHORPE
The Moors
Ford Bri.
Nutfield Marsh
Ckt. Grd.
Marsh Cotts
Glebe Lake
Redhill
Redhill Tennis Club
Chilmead Farm
REIGATE and BANSTEAD
RH1
REDHILL
Play. Fld.
The Warwick Sch.
Sandpit
Park Wood
Pimlico Hill
NUTFIELD
Sports Grd.
Robert Denholm House
Capenor Nursery
Kennedys Wood
Works
Patteson Court
A25
ROAD HIGH ST. BLETCHINGLEY
Adlington Cotts.
Fox Hole
North Park
Nutfield Priory Hotel
Playing Field
Furze Hill
Kingfisher House
Nursery Cottage
NUTFIELD
HILL
Redstone Hall
Nutfield Lodge
Byes Wood
Hillsbrow
Stockers Hill
Priory Farm
Steners Hill
Redstone Hill
Little Cormongers Farm
Nutfield Priory Lake
Bowerhill Wood
Bower Hill
High Beech
Cemetery
RNIB Redhill College
Bower Hill Farm
Bray's Farm
Rec. Grd.
Nutfield Church C of E Primary School
Lyttel Hall
Ckt. Grd.
EARLSWOOD
Playing Field
Sports Ground
Jun. Sch.
Nutfield
SOUTH NUTFIELD
Cricket Grd.
Old Gladstone's House
Maple Farm
King's Mill
Thepps Shaw
YMCA Sports Centre
Old Garston's House
Garston's Wood
Works
Nutfield Park
Ketwin's Wood
Crab Hill House
Theppswood Hse.
Ridge Green
REDHILL GOLF COURSE
Driving Range
Club Ho.
Redhill Football Club
EAST SURREY HOSPITAL
Robin Cooks Farm
Depot
Warehouse
Staplehurst Farm
Hale Farm
Crab Hill Farm
Crab Hill
Nutfield Nurseries
M23 MOTORWAY
White Bushes
Hazelhurst Farm
The Rookery
Helicopter Landing Square
REDHILL AERODROME AND HELIPORT
Tennis Courts
Eugene Bann Indoor Tennis Centre
Perimeter Cotts.
HORLEY ROAD
A B C D E F G
1 2 3 4 5 6 7 8 9 10
28 29 30 31
53 52 51 50 49 48
196
207

H
J
K
L
M
N
P
197
Quarry Hall Farm
Little Park Hill
War Coppice House
Freer Farm
Castle View
GODSTONE INTERCHANGE
Black Bushes
Subway
Conduit Shaw
Rose Farm
Green Croft
ROUGHETS LANE
The Yews
The Roughets
Roughets House
Dinmore
Surrey Crest
L'Etac
NORTH
White Hill House
Whitehill Roughets
M25
M25 - MOTORWAY
Junc. 6
Tyler's Green
Redhill Brook
Black Bushes
Conduit Shaw
Kitchen Copse
The Orpheus Centre
Big Pickle
Pendell Farm Cotts.
Pendell Farm
GODSTONE
East Reservoir
Nature Reserve
OXTED RD.
Place Farm
PLACE FARM ROAD
Orchard Cotts.
Elm Platt
The Hawthorns School Sports Centre
The Hawthorns Sch.
Brewerstreet Farm
The Old Rectory
BREWER
DAIRY BUSINESS PARK
North Park Cotts.
Little Place Fm.
Bay Pond
BLETCHINGLEY RD.
A25
Godstone Green
Old Garston Farmhouse
TANDRIDGE
Cockley Plantation
Dormers Farm
BLETCHINGLEY GOLF COURSE
Garden Centre
Stangrave Hall
Ivy Mill Farm
WATERHOUSE
Water House Farm
Dell Cotts.
Eden Brook
Stratton
Godstone Inn & Playbarn
BLETCHINGLEY
Club House
Court Lodge Farm
Cemetery
Godstone
RH9
CASTLE STREET
HIGH ST.
GODSTONE ROAD
Bletchingley Comm. Learning Cen.
Play. Fld.
Spts. Grd.
School
Play. Flds.
CONEYBURY
White Post
Castle Place
Castle Hill
Coombes Coppice
Stanley's Wood
Bletchingley Castle
Harlings Shaw
Garston Park
Roman Road
210
Pound Farm
Poor Man's Shaw
Castlehill Farm
M23
Subway
Snatts Hill
HEATH ROAD
Tilburstowhill or Tilbusterhill Plantation
Tilburstow or Tilbuster Hill
Mitchener's Bank
Gravelhill Wood
Coldharbour House
Coldharbour Farm
Penduck Shaw
Eleven Acre Shaw
Sandhills
Oakbarn Cotts.
Springfield Shaw
Moors Wood
Long Shaw
Tilburstowhill Farm
Sandhills Farm
Crookedfield Shaw
Wychcroft
Prickloves Farm
Blackvent Wood
Nash's F
Nutfield
OUTWOOD LANE
SOUTH PARK
Tye Copse
Hawksnest Ghyll
CUCKSEYS LANE
Fountains Cotts.
Brook
South Park
Cuckseys Farm
South Park Farm
Norbryghts Hole
Furze Wood
Bletchingley Tunnel
Maple Wood
Kennels Farm
The Park
Henhaw Farm
Cinderhill Wood
Four Acre Wood
TERRACOTTA RD.
LAMBS BUSINESS PARK
Bransland Wood
Poundhill Wood
Prickle Shaw
Temple Wood
Birchen Coppice
Salfords Stream
32
33
34
35
53
52
51
50
49
48

Junction 6
M25 MOTORWAY
GODSTONE INTERCHANGE
198
209
Godstone Vineyards
Kennel Shaw
Castle View
Generals Grove
Flint Hall Farm
Nixon's Pit
Hanging Wood
Primrose Bank
Tandridge Hill Farm
Robins Grove Wood
Barrow Green Court
Barrow Green Farm
Barrow Green Farm Cotts.
North Model Farm
THE ABBEYS
Priory Shaw
The Firs
Greenacres
Duckpit Wood
Coney Hill Sand Pit
Tandridge Priory Farm
Kennels
Oxted Sand Pit
Buttersgreen Shaw
Palmer's Wood
Palmers Wood Oilfield
Flower Wood
Flower Farm
Club House
Rooks Nest
GODSTONE GOLF COURSE
School Plantation
Tyler's Green
GODSTONE HILL
OXTED ROAD
GODSTONE ROAD
A22
A25
B2235
B2236
GODSTONE
Bay Pond
Little Place Fm.
Garden Centre
Nags Hall
Furzefield Plantation
TANDRIDGE GOLF COURSE
Bushey Croft Rec. Grd.
East Reservoir Nature Reserve
BLETCHINGLEY RD.
Godstone Green
Old Garston Farmhouse
Church Town
The Rectory
Moore's Shaw
Glebe Water
A22 BY-PASS
Windmillstadle Wood
The Birches
Oxted Place
Little Court Farm
Flowergarden Plantation
Beechwood Hill
New Bustons Wood
The Mount
The Glebe House
The Old Pack House
Stratton
Godstone Farm & Playbarn
Castlehill Wood
The Lodge
Tandridge Court
Bustons Wood
Stonepit Shaw
Leigh Place
Leigh Place Pond
Castlehill Wood
Oldpark Wood
Tandridge Court Fm.
Round Wood
Maizenhill Shaw
ST. EASTBOURNE
Stratton Brook
Leigh Mill House
TANDRIDGE
TANDRIDGE PARK
Southlands
Taylors Hill Depot
Refuse Tips
Dean Shaw Cottages
Dean Shaw
St. Peter's C of E Inf. Sch.
Reddings Wood
Roman Road
Tilburstowhill or Tilbursterhill Common
Smokey Hollow
Mereland Wood
GODSTONE BY-PASS
Sewage Works
Gibbs Brook
Tandridge Hall
Southlands Shaws
Tilburstowhill or Tilbusterhill Plantation
Hopgarden Wood
Southlands Lodge
Godstone
Beechwood Plantation
Tilburstow or Tilbuster Hill
HEATH ROAD
RABIES
RH1
RH9
Southlands Wood
Garston Park
Eleven Acre Shaw
Brakey Hill
WONHAM PL.
Stow Coppice
Long Shaw
Slurry Lagoons
Tilburstowhill Farm
Orme House
Newhouse Farm
EASTBOURNE ROAD
NEW ROAD
Brook Farm
Blackvent Wood
HARTS LANE
MILES LANE
Steadmanshill Wood
Paygate Wood
Piper's Wood
New Zealand Cottages
Nash's Farm
Barnfield Shaw
Park Pale
Postern Gate Farm
Hawksnest Ghyll
Gibbs Brook
Lagham Wood
Furze Wood
St. Stephen's C of E Prim.Sch.
SOUTH GODSTONE
Chathill
Chathill Park Farm
TERRACOTTA
LAMBS BUSINESS PARK
BROOKSIDE
RUSHTON AV.
STATION RD.
Godstone
Old Hall Farm
Playing Field
Lagham Park Farm
Prickle Shaw
Oakhurst Court
RSPCA Animal Cen.
Lagham Manor
Kings Farm
WATER LANE
Moat
Works
Birchen Coppice
Crowhurst Lane End
CROWHURST LANE END
Depot
Drewsherne Farm
Brickmakers' Wood
Lingfield
A B C D E F G
1 2 3 4 5 6 7 8 9 10
35 36 37 38
48 49 50 51 52 53

OXTED
Oxted
MASTER PARK
OLD OXTED
LIMPSFIELD
Hookwood Park
Wymondley
Grubbe Wood
Sunridge
The Rips
Kentish Border
Hookwood Bungalows
Swimming Pool
Oxted Sch.
Theatre
Laverock Sch.
Kennels
Cemetery
The Bogs
Ten. Cts.
Liby.
Tandridge DC Offs.
Leisure Cen.
Superstore
Playing Field
De Tillens
Scout Hall
Pebble Hill
Pebble Hill Ho.
Ckt. Gd.
Sch.
Club Ho.
The Gate House
Watts Hill
Court Langley
Ballards Shaw
Ridlands Fm.
LIMPSFIELD CHART
Andrew's Wood
Oakshaw Cott
LIMPSFIELD COMMON
LIMPSFIELD CHART GOLF COURSE
Briars Cross
Wildshaw
West Heath
West Heath
Pollards Wood
Greenflags
Broadway
The Red House
Woodhurst Bridge
Limpsfield Tunnel
Court Hayes
Hazelwood School
Pains Hill
Chartfield Ho.
Little Heath
Tenchleys Park
Tenchleys Wood
Reservoir (covered)
Mill Barn
Oxted Mill
Viewlands
Stonehall Farm
Stone Hall
Broadham House
Playing Field
The Alders
Boulthurst Fm.
Chart Edge
Hurst Green
Weir
Tanhouse Fm.
HURST GREEN
Broadham Green
Hall
Comm. Cen.
Hurst Green Inf. Sch.
Moor House Sch.
Loampit Wood
Whitegates Farm
Grants Cottage
Oxted
RH8
Ten. Cts.
Pav.
Mill Lane Playing Field
Grants Paddock
Itchingwood Common
Crabbett Wood
Crabbett Wood Farm
Tenchleys Manor
Doghurst
HOLLAND
Perrysfield Fm.
Redlane Cotts
Mill Pond
FAIRVIEW INDUSTRIAL ESTATE
ITCHINGWOOD COMMON
Coltsford House
Red Lane Farm
Parishcroft Wood
Crooked River
King George's Field
Holland Junior Sch.
Stockett's Manor
Caperway Cottages
Depot
Sewage Treatment Works
Dunks Pond
Parishcroft Wood Farm
Rose Farm
Stockett's Manor Farm
Connerton Farm
Stockenden Fm.
Pav.
Playing Fld.
Collesters Wood
Honesland Wood
Gincox Farm
Finch's Cross
Mollstones Wood
River Eden
Holly Bush Farm
Gincox Tolt
Playing Field
Hall
Coudens Farm
Brills Farm
Bushey Croft
River
Merle Common
Kitchengarden Shaw
Tennis Court
High Ridge Farm
Little Earls Wood
Comforts Cottage
Foyle Tolt
Foyle Fm.
Sunt Wood
Monks Fm.
Great Earls Wood
Caper's Farm
Foyle Tolt
Five Acre Wood
Staffhurst Wood Nature Reserve
Edenbridge
Sunt Farm
Kiln Coppice
Pound Wood
White House Farm
TN8
Black Robin's Farm
Kent Brook
Grubbs Farm
Butcherswood Bank
Partridge Fm.
Playing Field
Hall
RH7
St. George's Cottages
Pound Farm
Caterfield Bridge
Whitehouse Wood
Batchelor's Wood
A25
B2025
B269
199
WEST HILL
EAST HILL
WESTERHAM ROAD
DETILLENS LA.
HIGH STREET
KENT HATCH ROAD
RIDLANDS LANE
CHAPEL ROAD
PASTENS ROAD
ITCHINGWOOD COMMON ROAD
PAINS HILL
GRANTS LANE
POLLARDS WOOD ROAD
WOLFS ROAD
WOLFS WOOD
HURST GREEN ROAD
HOLLAND ROAD
SHORT LANE
RED LANE
MERLE COMMON ROAD
POPES LANE
BROADHAM GREEN ROAD
TANHOUSE ROAD
SPRING LANE
WOODHURST LANE
GIBBS BROOK LANE
STAFFHURST WOOD ROAD
MONKS LANE
CATERFIELD LANE
ICEHOUSE WOOD
OAST ROAD
CHURCH WAY
HURST LANE
WARREN LANE
MEADOWLANDS
ROSEACRE
H
J
K
L
M
N
P
1
2
3
4
5
6
7
8
9
10
39
40
41
42
48
49
50
51
52
53

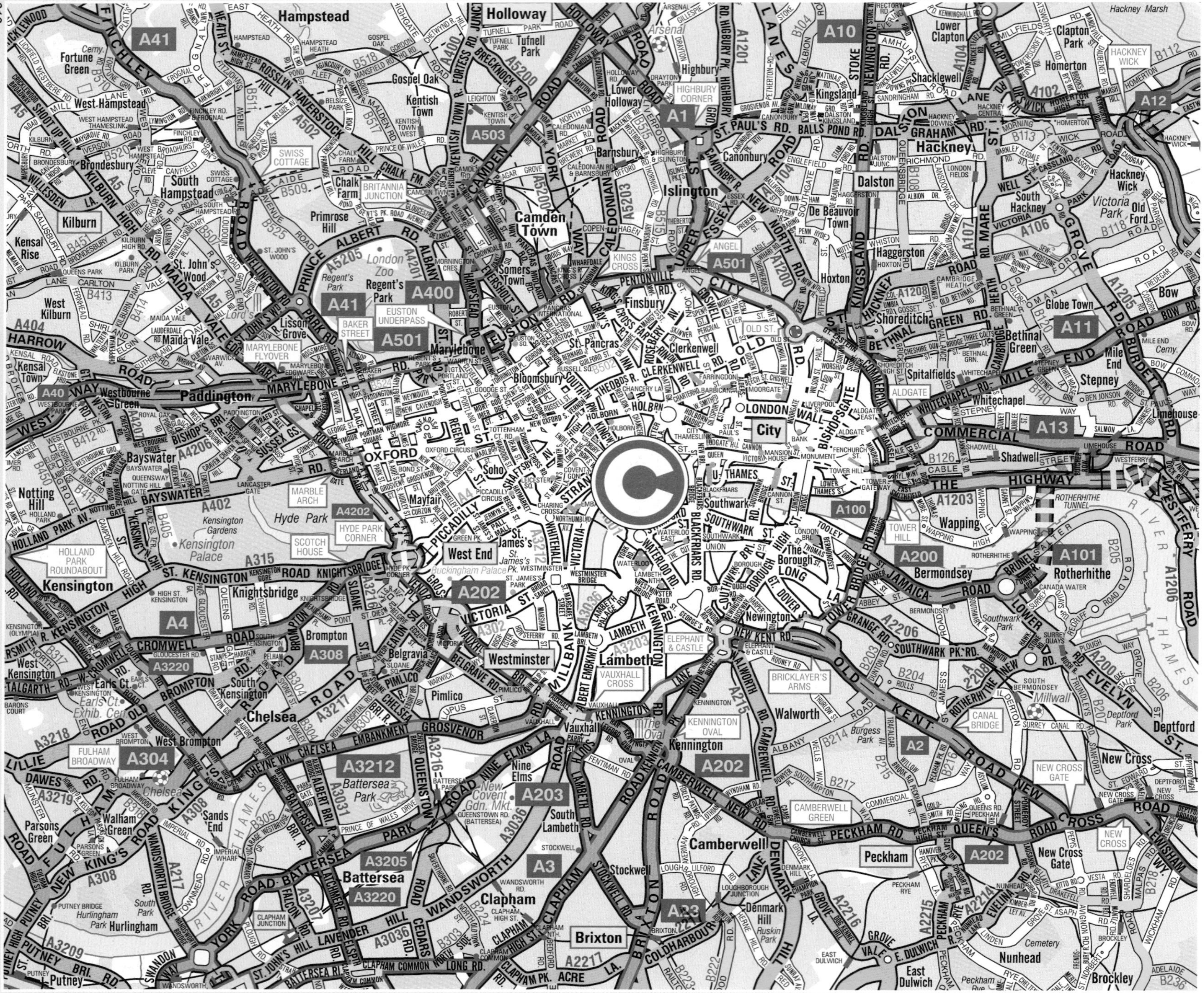
Hampstead
Holloway
Highbury
Lower Holloway
Islington
Barnsbury
Camden Town
Kentish Town
Gospel Oak
South Hampstead
Primrose Hill
Chalk Farm
Kilburn
West Hampstead
Brondesbury
Kensal Rise
West Kilburn
St. John's Wood
Maida Vale
Lisson Grove
Regent's Park
London Zoo
Marylebone
Paddington
Bayswater
Notting Hill
Kensington
Kensington Palace
Kensington Gardens
Hyde Park
Knightsbridge
Mayfair
Soho
West End
St. James's
Westminster
Belgravia
Pimlico
Chelsea
Brompton
South Kensington
West Brompton
West Kensington
Earls Ct.
Fulham
Walham Green
Parsons Green
Sands End
Hurlingham
Putney
Battersea
Battersea Park
Nine Elms
Vauxhall
Lambeth
South Lambeth
Kennington
The Oval
Stockwell
Clapham
Brixton
Camberwell
Denmark Hill
Walworth
Newington
The Borough
Southwark
Bermondsey
Rotherhithe
Wapping
Shadwell
Stepney
Whitechapel
Spitalfields
Shoreditch
Hoxton
Haggerston
Dalston
De Beauvoir Town
Canonbury
Kingsland
Shacklewell
Lower Clapton
Clapton Park
Homerton
Hackney
South Hackney
Hackney Wick
Hackney Marsh
Victoria Park
Old Ford
Bow
Mile End
Globe Town
Bethnal Green
Limehouse
Millwall
Deptford
New Cross
New Cross Gate
Peckham
Nunhead
Brockley
East Dulwich
City
Clerkenwell
Finsbury
St. Pancras
Bloomsbury
Somers Town
Holborn
Burgess Park
Southwark Park
Deptford Park
RIVER THAMES

Congestion Charging Zone

- The daily charge applies Mon.-Fri. 7-00am to 6-00pm excluding English bank and public holidays and designated non-charging days.
- Payment of the daily charge allows you to drive in, around, leave and re-enter the charging zone as many times as required.
- Payment must be made before or on the day of travel by midnight. Drivers who forget to pay the charge for the previous day's journey can pay a late payment charge the next day up until midnight by telephone or online and avoid a Penalty Charge.
- You can pay using Congestion Charging Auto Pay (registration required), online (www.cclondon.com), by telephone (0845 900 1234), by SMS text message (registration required) or at selected petrol stations and retail outlets.
- Exemptions include motorcycles, mopeds and bicycles.
  Registration for discount schemes, including Congestion Charging Auto Pay, Fleet Auto Pay, Blue Badge holders, residents, greener and electric vehicles, is available from Transport for London.
- Penalty charge for non-payment of the daily charge by midnight on the day after the day of travel.

This information is correct at the time of publication.

For further information www.tfl.gov.uk

LARGE SCALE SECTION

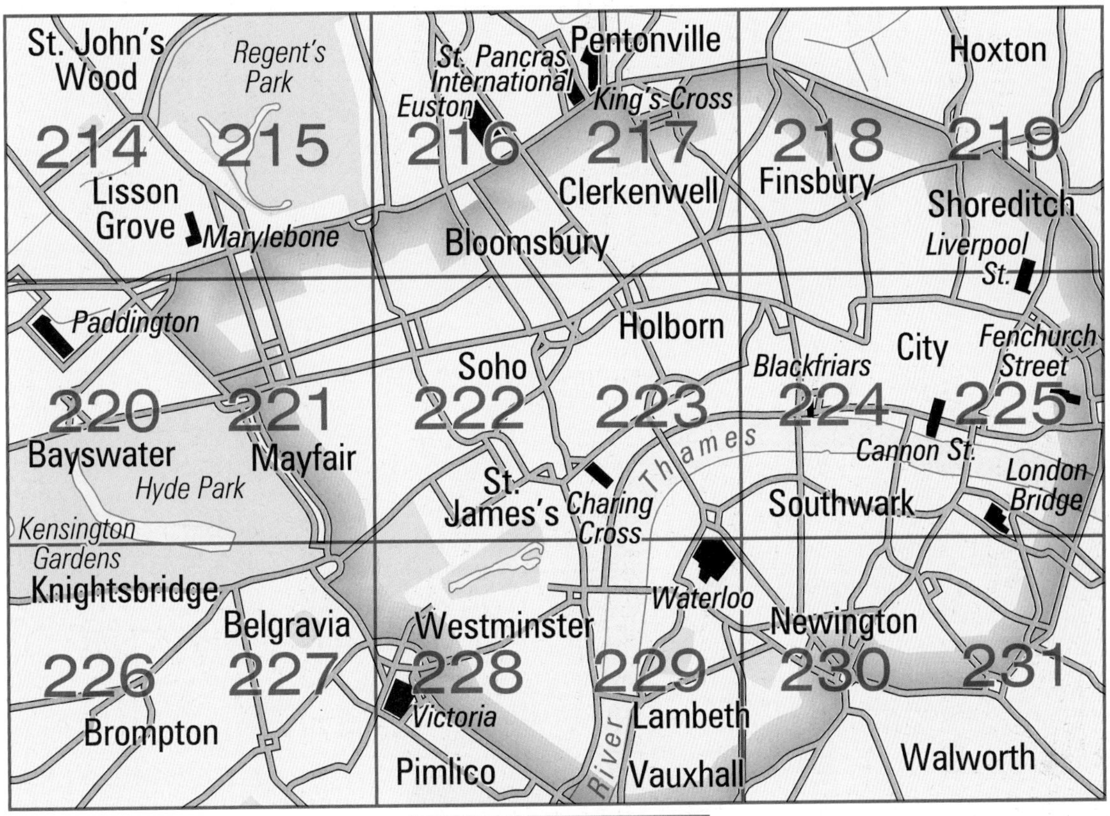
St. John's Wood
Regent's Park
214
215
Lisson Grove
Marylebone
St. Pancras International
Pentonville
Euston
King's Cross
216
217
Clerkenwell
Bloomsbury
218
Finsbury
Hoxton
219
Shoreditch
Liverpool St.
Paddington
Holborn
Soho
Blackfriars
City
Fenchurch Street
220
221
222
223
224
225
Bayswater
Mayfair
Hyde Park
Thames
Cannon St.
London Bridge
Kensington Gardens
St. James's
Charing Cross
Southwark
Knightsbridge
Waterloo
Belgravia
Westminster
Newington
226
227
228
229
230
231
Victoria
Lambeth
Brompton
Pimlico
River
Vauxhall
Walworth

REFERENCE

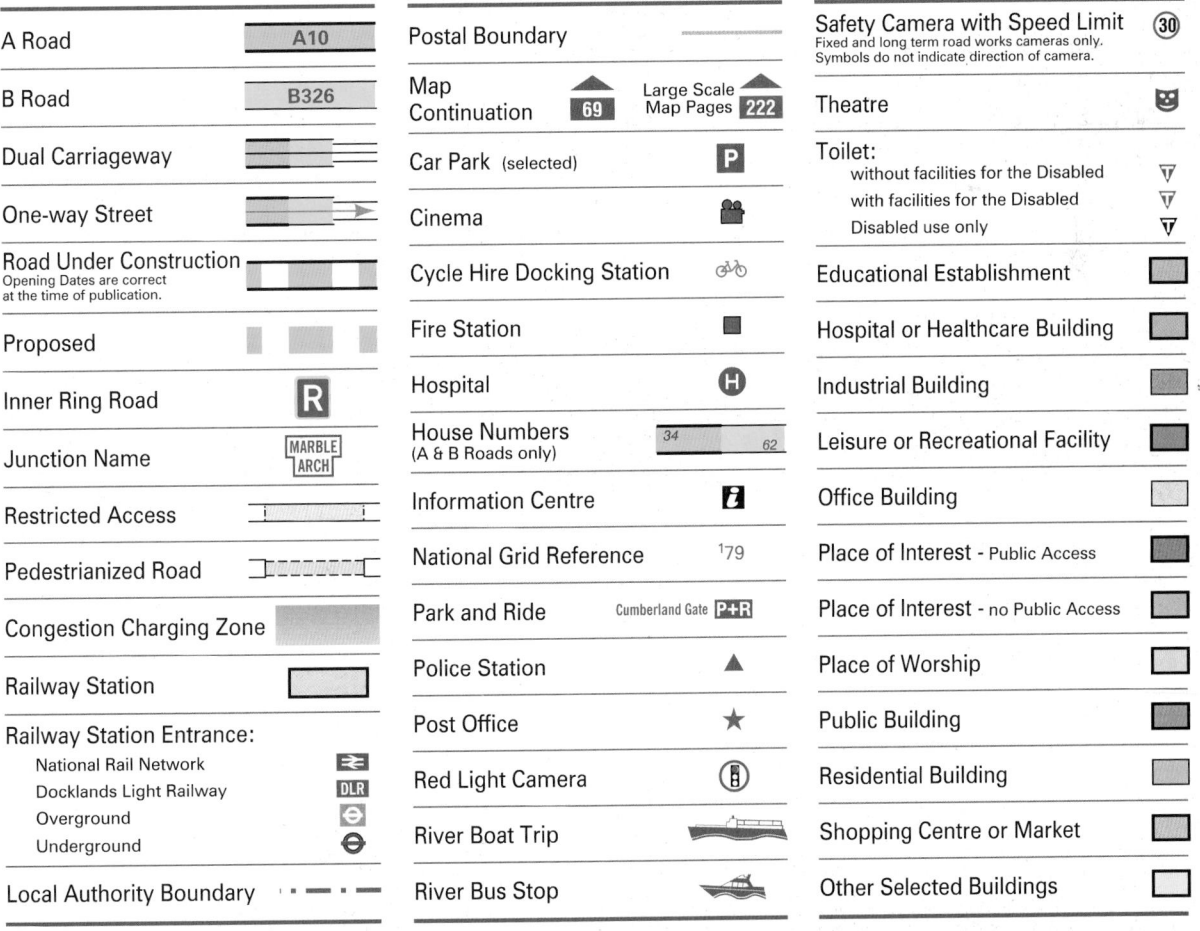

A Road — A10
B Road — B326
Dual Carriageway
One-way Street
Road Under Construction
Opening Dates are correct at the time of publication.
Proposed
Inner Ring Road — R
Junction Name — MARBLE ARCH
Restricted Access
Pedestrianized Road
Congestion Charging Zone
Railway Station
Railway Station Entrance:
- National Rail Network
- Docklands Light Railway — DLR
- Overground
- Underground

Local Authority Boundary

Postal Boundary
Map Continuation — 69 — Large Scale Map Pages — 222
Car Park (selected) — P
Cinema
Cycle Hire Docking Station
Fire Station
Hospital — H
House Numbers (A & B Roads only) — 34 — 62
Information Centre — i
National Grid Reference — ¹79
Park and Ride — Cumberland Gate P+R
Police Station
Post Office
Red Light Camera
River Boat Trip
River Bus Stop

Safety Camera with Speed Limit — 30
Fixed and long term road works cameras only.
Symbols do not indicate direction of camera.
Theatre
Toilet:
- without facilities for the Disabled
- with facilities for the Disabled
- Disabled use only

Educational Establishment
Hospital or Healthcare Building
Industrial Building
Leisure or Recreational Facility
Office Building
Place of Interest - Public Access
Place of Interest - no Public Access
Place of Worship
Public Building
Residential Building
Shopping Centre or Market
Other Selected Buildings

SCALE

0 50 100 200 300 Yards ¼ ½ Mile

0 50 100 200 300 400 500 750 Metres

Pages 214-231
1:7,040
9 inches
(22.7cm) to 1 mile
14.2cm to 1km

214
69
ST. JOHN'S WOOD
MAIDA VALE
NW8
W9
W2
LISSON GROVE
WESTMINSTER
Middlesex County Cricket Club & Marylebone CC
Lord's Cricket Ground
MCC Cricket Museum & Tours
Media Cen.
The American School in London
Quintin Kynaston Sch.
St. John's Wood Barracks
Robinsfield Inf. Sch.
New London Synagogue
Arnold House Sch.
St. John's Wood Syn.
Hospital of St John & St. Elizabeth
St. John's Hospice
Convent of Mercy
The Wellington Hosp.
The Wellington Hospital
Abercorn Sch.
Recording Studio
St. Mark's Ch.
Barrow Hill Jun. Sch.
Pol. Sta.
St. John's Wood Church Gardens
St. John the Baptist's Ch. & Sch.
London Central Mosque
REGENT'S CANAL
CLOSED Midnight - 7am
The Liberal Jewish Synagogue
Church of Our Lady
Electricity Transformer Station
St. Joseph's R.C. Prim. Sch.
Gateway Prim. Sch.
Lisson Green
Cockpit
Paddington Green Prim. Sch.
Catholic Apostolic Ch.
Little Venice Sports Cen.
St. Mary's Gardens
City of Westminster College
St. David's Ch.
St. Mary's Ch.
City of Westminster Coll.
King Solomon Academy
St. Edward's RC Prim. Sch. & Convent
Nightingale Capio Hosp.
Police Sta.
Fire Sta.
St. Saviour's Ch.
WARWICK AVENUE
Little Venice
Warwick Gdns.
EDGWARE ROAD
MARYLEBONE FLYOVER
St. Dunstan's
Swedish Ch.
Surgery
ST. JOHN'S WOOD
WELLINGTON RD.
FINCHLEY RD.
A41
B507
A5
A5205
A40
A501
B525
B413
220
ST. JOHN'S WOOD ROAD
GROVE END ROAD
MAIDA VALE
EDGWARE ROAD
LISSON GROVE
PRINCE ALBERT ROAD
ABBEY ROAD
BOUNDARY ROAD
CLIFTON GARDENS
CLIFTON ROAD
HALL ROAD
ELM TREE ROAD
CIRCUS ROAD
CAVENDISH AVENUE
WELLINGTON PLACE
PARK ROAD
HARROW ROAD
MARYLEBONE ROAD
BLOMFIELD ROAD
HAMILTON TERRACE
LODGE ROAD
GROVE END
CHURCH STREET
BELL STREET
TOWNSHEND ROAD
ACACIA ROAD
ORDNANCE HILL
ST. JOHN'S WOOD HIGH STREET
A B C D E
1 2 3 4 5 6 7

215
REGENT'S PARK
NW1
CAMDEN
W1
MARYLEBONE
Primrose Hill
Playground
Cumberland Basin
PRINCE ALBERT ROAD
PARKWAY
DELANCEY STREET
Car & Coach Park
Snowdon Aviary
Main Entrance
London Zoo
REGENT'S CANAL
Primrose Hill Bri.
Running Track
Macclesfield Bridge
St. Edmund's Ct.
Danes Ct.
Ormonde Ct.
Kings Ct.
Consort Ct.
Prince Albert Ct.
St. James's Ter. M.
Nth. Bri. Ho. Prep. Sch.
Holyrood Ct.
A5205
OUTER CIRCLE
CLOSED Midnight - 7am
GLOUCESTER GATE
GLOUCESTER GATE M.
PARK VILLAGE WEST
Nash Ho.
Danish Ch.
ST. KATHARINE'S PRECINCT
CUMBERLAND TERRACE
ALBANY STREET
A4201
Regent's Park Barracks
Silsoe Ho.
Richmond Ho.
Camberley Ho.
Swinley Ho.
Bagshot Ho.
Christ Ch. C of E Prim. Sch.
Ascot Ho.
Cath.
REDHILL ST.
Rothay
Windsor
Thirlmere
Windermere
Wasdale
Grasmere
ROBERT STREET
Libr.
Troutbeck
Tilehurst
Swallowfield
Pol. Sta.
Esther Randall Ct.
Walton Ho.
LONGFORD
The White Ho.
Royal College of Physicians
ST. ANDREWS PL.
OSNABURGH TERRACE
Holy Trinity Ch.
Albany Ter.
Cricket Ground
The Hub
Refreshments
Cumberland Gate
CHESTER TERRACE
CHESTER RD.
CHESTER GATE
Chester Walk Gate
Avenue Gdns.
English Gdns.
Playground
CAMBRIDGE GATE
St. John's Lodge
Frazer Lodge
Parks Department
Lodge
Nursery
Regent's Park Open Air
Chester Road Gates
QUEEN MARY'S GARDENS
INNER CIRCLE
The Holme
Refreshments
Jubilee Gates
New Lodge
Tennis Courts
Regent's College
YORK BRIDGE
Bandstand
Boating Lake
Children's Boating Pond
Clarence Gate
Park Square Gardens
PARK SQUARE EAST
PARK SQUARE WEST
ULSTER PL.
International Comm. Sch.
Harley House
REGENT'S PARK
Crescent Gardens
Central London Co. Ct.
Central London Civil Justice Centre
GT. PORTLAND ST.
Ryl. Nat. Orthopaedic Hosp.
The Portland Hosp.
PARK CRESCENT
A501
MARYLEBONE ROAD
Ryl. Academy of Music Mus.
Madame Tussaud's
Nottingham Ter.
YORK TERRACE WEST
YORK TERRACE EAST
St. Marylebone Ch.
The London Clinic
DEVONSHIRE PLACE
University of Westminster (Marylebone Campus)
The Princess Grace Hosp.
The St. Marylebone Sch.
BAKER STREET
Lost Property Off.
Chiltern Ct.
Berkeley Court
Dorset Ho.
LA Fitness
Marathon Ho.
Regis Ct.
Melcombe Ct.
Portman Mans.
York Pl. Mans.
Bickenhall Mansions
Town Hall
Lib.
The Sherlock Holmes Mus.
Chalfont Ct.
Royal Coll. of Obstetricians & Gynaecologists
London Business Sch.
Francis Holland Sch.
St. Cyprian's Ch.
Radley Ho.
Ivor Ct.
Rossmore Ct.
GLOUCESTER PLACE
DORSET SQ.
A41
MARYLEBONE
Meth. Ch.
York Mans.
Luxborough Tower
Newcastle Ho.
Luxborough Ho.
Tenby Mans.
PADDINGTON STREET
B524
Paddington Street Gdns.
Screen on Baker St.
St. Andrews Mans.
Wendover Ho.
West London Coll.
Hosp. (Outpatients)
King Edward VII's Hosp.
BBC Offs.
Macintosh Ho.
Beaumont Ct.
Basildon Ct.
Copperfield Ho.
The Heart Hospital
Hlth. Cen.
The Harley St. Clinic
Portland Pl. Sch.
Central Synagogue
RIBA
BBC Broadcasting House
Goodwood Ct.
Hallam Ct.
Bryanston Mans.
St. Mary's Prim. Sch.
St. Mary's Ch.
York St. Cham.
B506

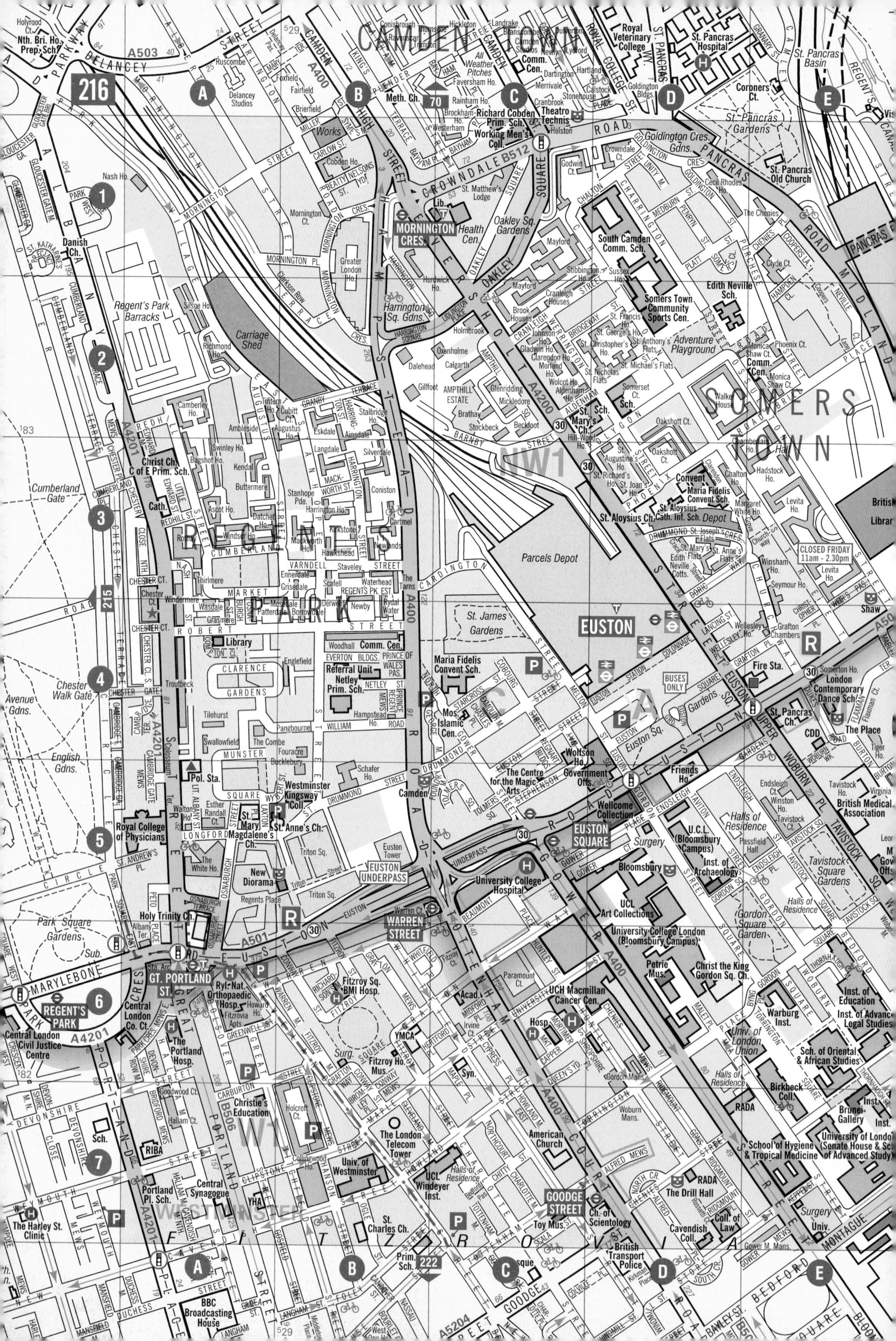

216
CAMDEN TOWN
SOMERS TOWN
REGENT'S PARK
NW1
W1
FITZROVIA
215
222
70
A
B
C
D
E
1
2
3
4
5
6
7
Royal Veterinary College
St. Pancras Hospital
St. Pancras Basin
St. Pancras Gardens
St. Pancras Old Church
Coroners' Ct.
Delancey Studios
All Weather Pitches
Comm. Cen.
Meth. Ch.
Richard Cobden Prim. Sch.
Working Men's Coll.
Theatro Technis
Works
MORNINGTON CRES.
Health Cen.
Oakley Sq. Gardens
Lib.
Greater London Ho.
Harrington Sq. Gdns.
Regent's Park Barracks
Carriage Shed
South Camden Comm. Sch.
Somers Town Community Sports Cen.
Edith Neville Sch.
Adventure Playground
AMPTHILL ESTATE
Walker House
Chamberlain Ho.
Hall
Convent Maria Fidelis Convent Sch.
St. Aloysius Cath. Inf. Sch.
St. Aloysius Ch.
Depot
Parcels Depot
CLOSED FRIDAY 11am - 2.30pm
British Library
EUSTON
St. James Gardens
Maria Fidelis Convent Sch.
Mos. Islamic Cen.
Christ Ch. C of E Prim. Sch.
Cath.
Library
Comm. Cen.
Referral Unit
Netley Prim. Sch.
Cumberland Gate
Chester Walk Gate
Avenue Gdns.
English Gdns.
Pol. Sta.
Westminster Kingsway Coll.
St. Mary Magdalene's Ch.
St. Anne's Ch.
Royal College of Physicians
The White Ho.
New Diorama
EUSTON UNDERPASS
Euston Tower
Regents Place
Holy Trinity Ch.
Park Square Gardens
WARREN STREET
GT. PORTLAND ST.
REGENT'S PARK
Central London Co. Ct.
Central London Civil Justice Centre
Ryl. Nat. Orthopaedic Hosp.
The Portland Hosp.
Fitzroy Sq. BMI Hosp.
YMCA
Fitzroy Ho. Mus.
Syn.
The London Telecom Tower
Christie's Education
RIBA
Central Synagogue
Portland Pl. Sch.
The Harley St. Clinic
Univ. of Westminster
UCL Windeyer Inst.
Halls of Residence
St. Charles Ch.
Prim. Sch.
BBC Broadcasting House
University College Hospital
EUSTON SQUARE
Wellcome Collection
Wolfson Ho.
Government Offs.
The Centre for the Magic Arts
Fire Sta.
Friends Ho.
Euston Sq. Gardens
St. Pancras Ch.
London Contemporary Dance Sch.
The Place
CDD
U.C.L. (Bloomsbury Campus)
Inst. of Archaeology
Bloomsbury
UCL Art Collections
University College London (Bloomsbury Campus)
Petrie Mus.
Christ the King Gordon Sq. Ch.
Gordon Square Garden
Tavistock Square Gardens
British Medical Association
UCH Macmillan Cancer Cen.
Hosp.
Acad.
Paramount Ct.
American Church
Woburn Mans.
Warburg Inst.
Inst. of Education
Inst. of Advanced Legal Studies
Univ. of London Union
Sch. of Oriental & African Studies
Birkbeck Coll.
RADA
Brunei Gallery
School of Hygiene & Tropical Medicine
University of London (Senate House & Sch. of Advanced Study)
The Drill Hall
Coll. of Law
Cavendish Coll.
GOODGE STREET
Ch. of Scientology
Toy Mus.
British Transport Police
Surgery
Univ.
Halls of Residence
EUSTON ROAD
MARYLEBONE ROAD
TOTTENHAM COURT ROAD
HAMPSTEAD ROAD
GOWER STREET
GREAT PORTLAND STREET
PORTLAND PLACE
ALBANY STREET
CAMDEN HIGH STREET
EVERSHOLT STREET
PANCRAS ROAD
MIDLAND ROAD
CROWNDALE ROAD
DRUMMOND STREET
OAKLEY SQUARE
MORNINGTON CRESCENT
GOODGE STREET
NEW CAVENDISH STREET
WOBURN PLACE
MONTAGUE PLACE
BEDFORD WAY
A400
A4200
A4201
A501
A503
B512
A5204
B506

217
218
223
KING'S CROSS
PENTONVILLE
ISLINGTON
ST. PANCRAS
CLERKENWELL
BLOOMSBURY
HOLBORN
ST. PANCRAS INTERNATIONAL
KING'S CROSS ST. PANCRAS
CHANCERY LANE
RUSSELL SQ.
Central St. Martins College of Art and Design
Handyside Canopies & Goods Shed
GRANARY SQUARE
PANCRAS SQUARE
Kings Place
London Canal Mus.
Regents Canal
Thornhill Bridge
Blessed Sacrament Cath. Prim. Sch.
Copenhagen Prim. Sch.
Young Actors Theatre Sch.
Vittoria Prim. Sch.
Police Sta.
Superstore
Tunnel
NHS Surgery
Priory Green Estate
Elizabeth Garrett Anderson Language Coll.
Winton Prim. Sch.
Joseph Grimaldi Park
The Gower Sch.
White Lion Cen.
Utd. Reformed Ch.
Crafts Council
The Angel Centre
Reservoir
London Studio Cen.
King's Cross Mission Ch.
Sch. of Oriental & African Studies
Peel Cen.
Baptist Ch.
St. Mark's Ch.
Royal National Throat, Nose & Ear Hosp.
Nuffield Cen.
Clerkenwell Magistrates Court
Clerkenwell Parochial C of E Prim. Sch.
Town Hall
Argyle Prim. Sch.
RNIB
St. Mary's German Ch.
Holy Cross Ch.
Halls of Residence
Westminster Kingsway Coll. (Kings Cross Cen.)
Lumen Utd. Ref. Ch.
Eastman Dental Hosp. & Institute
St. Andrews Gdns.
Mount Pleasant Sorting Office
The British Postal Mus.
Ch. of Our Most Holy Redeemer
London Metropolitan Archives
The Urdang
Thomas Coram Early Childhood Cen.
The Foundling Mus.
Sch. of Pharmacy
Mecklenburgh Square Gardens
The Wolfson Assessment Cen.
Coram's Fields
Brunswick Centre
Renoir
Nuffield Fitness Cen.
The Charles Dickens Mus.
Independent Television News
Fitness First
The National Hospital for Neurology and Neurosurgery
Gt. Ormond Street Hospital for Children
The Royal London Homoeopathic Hosp.
St. George the Martyr C of E Prim. Sch.
Buddhist Cen. London
Library
Russell Square Gardens
St. Giles Coll. London Central
St. George the Martyr Ch.
Mary Ward Cen.
LA Fitness
Pol. Sta.
Gray's Inn Gardens
Gray's Inn
St. Alban's C of E Prim. Sch.
Conway Hall
British Museum
Bloomsbury Square Gdns.
Cochrane
Islamic Cen.
St. Martins Coll.
St. Peter's Ch.
Fire Sta.
Gov. Offs.
Depot
PENTONVILLE ROAD
CALEDONIAN ROAD
GRAY'S INN ROAD
KING'S CROSS ROAD
FARRINGDON ROAD
CLERKENWELL ROAD
THEOBALD'S ROAD
GUILFORD STREET
SOUTHAMPTON ROW
RUSSELL SQUARE
ST. JOHN STREET
ROSEBERY AVENUE
EUSTON ROAD

218
70
71
224
A
B
C
D
E
1
2
3
4
5
6
7
ISLINGTON
FINSBURY
CLERKENWELL
CAMDEN
CITY OF LONDON
BARBICAN
N1
EC1
Young Actors Theatre Sch.
Business Design Centre
City of London Academy-Islington
Richard Cloudesley Sch.
Police Sta.
N1 Shop. Centre
Vue Cin.
Superstore
Islington Tunnel
Surgery
NHS
Polish Catholic Ch.
Convent
St. John's Ch.
St. John Prim. Sch.
ANGEL
Angel Sq.
Utd. Reformed Ch.
Crafts Council
White Lion Cen.
Duncan Ter. Gardens
Hanover Prim. Sch.
City Road Lock
Fitness First
Old Red Lion
Virgin Active
RNIB
Sixth Form College
Alice Owen Tech. Cen.
The Angel Centre
Reservoir
St. Mark's Ch.
Baptist Chap.
Sadler's Wells
The Nautilus Bldg.
New River Head
Clerkenwell Parochial Prim. Sch.
Hugh Myddelton Prim. Sch.
City University London (Northampton Sq. Campus)
Univ.
Lib. & Mus.
The Urdang
RC Ch.
Ch. of Our Most Holy Redeemer
Spa Fields Open Space
London Metropolitan Archives
Fire Sta.
Woodbridge Chapel
St. James's Church
Church of St. John
Mus. St. John's Gate
St. John's Gdns.
City Pavilion
FARRINGDON
Queen Mary University of London (Charterhouse Square)
Charterhouse
The Italia Conti
School
BARBICAN
Smithfield
Central Markets
St. Bartholomew the Great Ch.
Moreland Prim. Sch.
St. Clement with St. Barnabas & St. Matthew Ch.
King Square Gardens
CITY FORUM
Holy Trinity Ch.
Ironmonger Row Baths
Finsbury Leisure Cen.
Dance Square
Halls of Residence
Saddlers Sports Cen.
County Court
St. Peter & St. Paul RC Sch.
Dallington Sch.
LSO St. Lukes
London Coll. of Fashion
Richard Cloudesley Sch.
Leisure Cen.
Tennis Courts
Fortune St. Pk.
Schools
GOLDEN LA. CAMPUS
Barbican Trade Cen.
Jewin Ch.
YMCA
Barbican Arts Cen.
Lib.
City of London Sch. for Girls
Guildhall Sch. of Music &
Ironmongers Hall
Barber Surgeon's Hall
Museum of London
Haberdashers
St. Etheldreda's Ch.
Islamic Cen.
St. Alban's C of E Prim. Sch.
Cen. St. Martins Coll.
St. Peter's Ch.
Works
Canal Building
Comm. Cen.
Shepherdess Walk
Wenlock Basin
City Road Basin
Warehouses
Packington St. Bri.
PENTONVILLE ROAD
CITY ROAD
GOSWELL ROAD
ST. JOHN STREET
ALDERSGATE STREET
CLERKENWELL ROAD
FARRINGDON ROAD
OLD STREET
ROSEBERY AVENUE
ISLINGTON HIGH ST.
UPPER STREET
A1
A401
A501
A5201
B502
B501
B515
B144
B500
B521
A104
A201
A5200

219
71
HAGGERSTON
HOXTON
SHOREDITCH
SPITALFIELDS
EC2
E1
E2
SHOREDITCH PARK
Play Park
Tennis Courts
Britannia Leisure Centre
Whitmore Prim. Sch.
Burbage Prim. Sch.
St. Annes with St. Columba Ch.
Bridge Academy
Mosque
Randal Cremer Prim. Sch.
St. Mary's Community Garden
Haggerston Sch.
Geffrye Mus.
Geffrye's Gdns.
Trust HQ & Hlth. Cen.
Hoxton Hall
Hoxton Comm. Garden
St. Chad's Ch.
Mecca Bingo
St. John the Baptist C of E Prim. Sch.
St. John the Baptist Ch.
True Jesus Ch.
Hackney Comm. Coll. (Shoreditch Campus)
Lib.
Ravenscroft Park
Columbia Mkt. Nursy. Sch.
Regent's Vocational Coll.
Moorfields Eye Hosp.
City Coll.
St. Monica's RC Prim. Sch.
St. Monica's RC Church
Asko Gdns.
Courtyard
The Energy Centre
Shoreditch Town Hall
St. Leonard's Ch.
Mildmay Hosp.
Boundary Gds.
ARNOLD CIRCUS
Tech. College
Sports Cen.
Fire Sta.
OLD STREET
Central Foundation Boys' Sch.
AOP Gallery
Wesley's Chapel & Mus.
Wesley's Ho.
Bunhill Fields Burial Ground
Virgin Active
TA Centre
Holywell Cen.
London Coll. of Fashion
The Lyceum Sch.
Government Offices
HAC Ground
The College of Law
Fitness First
SHOREDITCH HIGH STREET
Broadgate Tower
Exchange House
Exchange Square
Chapel of the Open Book
LIVERPOOL STREET
225
St. Mary Moorfields Ch.
Broadgate Circle
Broadgate Ice Rink
Broadgate Arena
Walk-in Cen.
Institute & Libs.
SPAB
Old Spitalfields Market
Christ Ch.
Christ Church Prim. Sch.
Ch. & Hall
Mosque
Pol. Sta.
Guildhall Sch.
MOORGATE
Citypoint
Bandstand
Bowling Green
London
A10
A1200
A1202
A1208
A1209
A5201
A501
B100
B101
B118
B122
B134
B135
B144
30

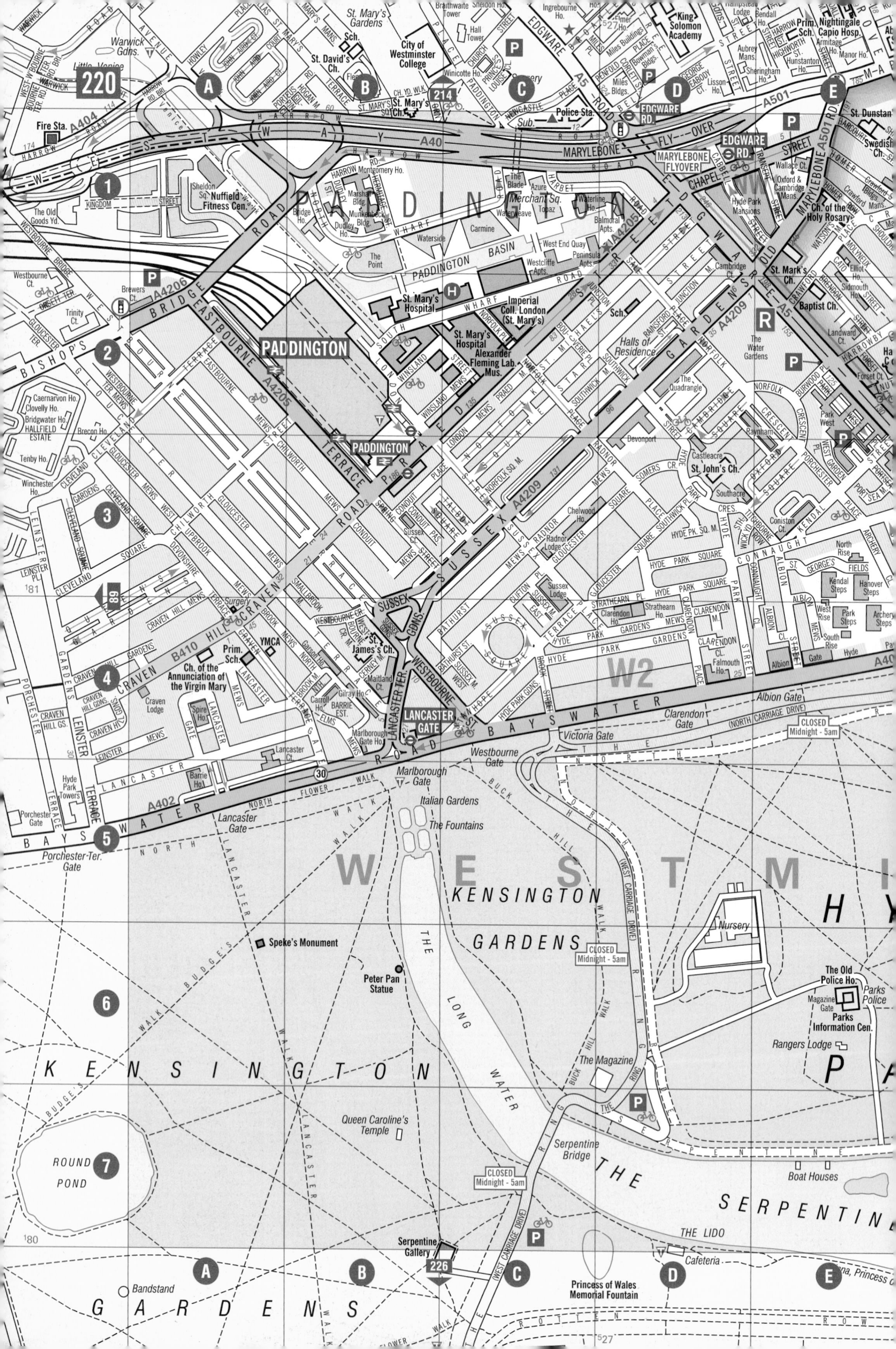
220
214
226
68
A
B
C
D
E
1
2
3
4
5
6
7
Little Venice
Warwick Gdns.
WARWICK
St. Mary's Gardens
Sch.
St. David's Ch.
City of Westminster College
Hall Tower
Braithwaite Tower
Winicotte Ho.
St. Mary's Ch.
King Solomon Academy
Miles Bldgs.
Lisson Ho.
Aubrey Mans.
Sheringham Ho.
Prim. Sch.
Nightingale Capio Hosp.
Manor Ho.
Fire Sta.
Police Sta.
EDGWARE RD.
MARYLEBONE FLYOVER
St. Dunstan
Swedish Ch.
HARROW ROAD
WESTWAY
A40
A404
A5
A501
MARYLEBONE FLY-OVER
Sheldon Sq.
Nuffield Fitness Cen.
The Old Goods Yd.
KINGDOM STREET
PADDINGTON
Harrow Montgomery Ho.
Marshall Bldg.
Munkenbeck Bldg.
Dudley Ho.
Bridge Ho.
The Blade
Azure
Merchant Sq.
Waterline Ho.
Topaz
Waterweave
Balmoral Apts.
Waterside
Carmine
The Point
PADDINGTON BASIN
West End Quay
Peninsula Apts.
Westcliffe Apts.
St. Mary's Hospital
Imperial Coll. London (St. Mary's)
St. Mary's Hospital Alexander Fleming Lab. Mus.
Wallace Ct.
Oxford & Cambridge Mans.
Hyde Park Mansions
Ch. of the Holy Rosary
St. Mark's Ch.
Baptist Ch.
Cambridge Ct.
Sch.
Halls of Residence
Westbourne Ct.
Brewers Ct.
Trinity Ct.
BISHOP'S BRIDGE ROAD
A4206
A4205
A4209
PRAED STREET
EASTBOURNE TERRACE
Caernarvon Ho.
Clovelly Ho.
Bridgwater Ho.
HALLFIELD ESTATE
Brecon Ho.
Tenby Ho.
Winchester Ho.
The Water Gardens
The Quadrangle
Devonport
Castleacre
St. John's Ch.
Southacre
Raynham
Park West
Landward Ct.
Coniston Ct.
North Rise
Kendal Steps
Hanover Steps
West Rise
Park Steps
Archery Steps
South Rise
Albion
Hyde
Chelwood Ho.
Radnor Lodge
Sussex Lodge
Clarendon Ho.
Strathearn Ho.
Falmouth Ho.
SUSSEX GARDENS
SUSSEX SQUARE
HYDE PARK SQUARE
HYDE PARK GARDENS
CONNAUGHT STREET
W2
Surgery
CRAVEN HILL
B410
Prim. Sch.
YMCA
Ch. of the Annunciation of the Virgin Mary
Craven Lodge
Spire Ho.
St. James's Ch.
Maitland Ct.
Gilray Ho.
Carroll Ho.
BARRIE EST.
Marlborough Gate Ho.
Lancaster Ct.
Barrie Ho.
LANCASTER GATE
Hyde Park Towers
Porchester Gate
BAYSWATER ROAD
A402
30
Albion Gate
Clarendon Gate
Victoria Gate
Westbourne Gate
Marlborough Gate
Lancaster Gate
Porchester Ter. Gate
CLOSED Midnight - 5am
Italian Gardens
The Fountains
WESTMINSTER
KENSINGTON GARDENS
HYDE PARK
Nursery
Speke's Monument
Peter Pan Statue
THE LONG WATER
The Old Police Ho.
Parks Police
Magazine Gate
Parks Information Cen.
Rangers Lodge
The Magazine
Queen Caroline's Temple
Serpentine Bridge
THE SERPENTINE
Boat Houses
THE LIDO
Cafeteria
Serpentine Gallery
Princess of Wales Memorial Fountain
ROUND POND
Bandstand
KENSINGTON GARDENS
181
180
527

221
222
227
MAYFAIR
W1
GREEN PARK
Town Hall
Lib.
Bickenhall Mansions
Screen on Baker St.
Paddington Street Gdns.
West London Coll.
St. Vincent's Cath. Sch.
Fitness First
Meth. Ch.
Hosp. (Outpatients)
King Edward VII's Hosp.
The Heart Hospital
Hlth. Cen.
London Welbeck Hospital
Queen's Coll.
BBC Broadcasting House
Central Synagogue
RIBA
St. Mary's Prim. Sch.
St. Mary's Ch.
St. James's Ch. in Spanish Pl.
Wallace Collection
St. Paul's Ch.
College
Chapel Convent
Wigmore Hall
Univ. of Westminster (Regent Campus)
Entrance to Underground Car Park
London Coll. of Fashion
St. Peter's Ch.
Buses & Taxis only Mon. - Sat. 7am- 7pm
Selfridges
Bond St.
West One Shop. Cen.
Kings Weigh Ho. Ch.
TA Cen.
Hanover Square Gdns.
Sylvia Young Theatre Sch.
West London Synagogue
Syns.
Police Sta.
Ch. of the Annunciation
Marble Arch
Odeon
Connaught Ho. School
Tyburn Tree (Site of)
Park House
Virgin Active
Montessori Centre International
Roosevelt Mem.
American Embassy
Speakers' Corner
Stanhope Place Gate
Entrance to Underground Car Park
Cumberland Gate Park & Ride
Animals in War Memorial
Refreshment Kiosk
Parade Ground
Reformers Tree
The Lookout Education Cen.
Reservoir
Diana, Princess of Wales Memorial Walk
Joy of Life Fountain
Library
St. George's Gdns.
Grosvenor Chapel
St. George's (Hanover Sq.) Prim. Sch.
Ch. of the Immaculate Conception
Third Ch. of Christ Scientist
Curzon
London Bombing Memorial
Achilles Statue
Queen Elizabeth Gate
Wellington Museum
Apsley Ho.
Hyde Park Corner
New Zealand War Meml.
Bandstand
Restaurant
Boating Lake
Nannies Lawn
Fishermans Keep
The Dell
The Holocaust Memorial Garden
Rose Garden
Pier
Serpentine
A41
A5204
A40
A4202
B524
A4201
B406
A4
A5
OXFORD STREET
WIGMORE STREET
PORTMAN SQUARE
GROSVENOR SQUARE
BERKELEY SQUARE
CAVENDISH SQ.
PARK LANE
PICCADILLY
BAKER STREET
MARYLEBONE HIGH ST.
EDGWARE ROAD

222
221
216
228
A
B
C
D
E
1
2
3
4
5
6
7
RIBA
The Harley St. Clinic
Queen's Coll.
BBC Broadcasting House
All Souls' Ch.
Univ. of Westminster
UCL Windeyer Inst.
Halls of Residence
St. Charles Ch.
Prim. Sch.
GOODGE STREET
Ch. of Scientology
Toy Mus.
Mosque
British Transport Police
School of Hygiene & Tropical Medicine
Senate House & Sch. of Advanced Stud
RADA
The Drill Hall
Coll. of Law
Davendish Coll.
Surgery
Architectural Association
Odeon
Central YMCA
Dominion
TOTTENHAM COURT ROAD
Centrepoint
Sorting Office
Academy
Chapel
Convent
Coll.
Wigmore Hall
Harcourt Ho.
Univ. of Westminster (Regent Campus)
ENTRANCE TO UNDERGROUND CAR PARK
London Coll. of Fashion
OXFORD CIRCUS
Buses & Taxis only Mon. - Sat. 7am - 7pm
All Saints Ch.
Welsh Baptist Chapel
The Plaza Shop. Cen.
French Protestant Ch.
St. Peter's Ch.
Regent Hall
Hanover Square Gdns.
Photographers' Gallery
Youth Hostel
Fitness First
London Palladium
College of Beauty Therapy
Marshall St. Leisure Cen.
St. Patrick's Ch.
Soho
NHS Cen.
Phoenix
Caxton Walk
Prince Edward
Adult Ed. Cen.
SOHO
W1
Palace
Ambassadors
Curzon
Fire Sta.
St. Anne's Ch.
Westminster Kingsway Coll.
St. James Residences
Sch.
Queen's
Gielgud
Apollo
Lyric
Piccadilly
St. George's Ch.
Pol. Sta.
Ch.
Chap
Prince Charles
Leicester Sq.
Empire
Vue
Trocadero Cen.
Cineworld
London Pav.
Prince of Wales
Leicester Fields
Odeon
PICCADILLY CIRCUS
Eros
Criterion
Comedy Store
Comedy
Royal Institution Faraday Mus.
Royal Academy of Arts (Burlington Ho.)
Ch. of the Immaculate Conception
Jermyn St.
Apollo W. End
St. James's Ch.
Britain & London Visitor Centre
Cineworld
LA Fitness
Haymarket
Her Majesty's
Odeon Cen. Ref. Lib.
National Portrait Gallery
National Gallery (Sainsbury Wing)
Canada Ho.
Rosebery Ct.
Third Ch. of Christ Scientist
London Library
SW1
ST. JAMES'S
Waterloo Gdns.
HQ of the Inst. of Directors
Admiralty Arch
Mall Galleries
ICA
Duke of York Column
Old Admiralty Offices
RAC
Marlborough House (Commonwealth Conference Centre)
King George VI Memorial
CLOSED SUNDAY
Guards Mem.
Curzon
GREEN PARK
Arlington Ho.
Spencer Ho.
Queen's Chapel
Chapel Royal
St. James's Palace
Clarence Ho.
Lancaster Ho.
Stable Yard Gate
GREEN PARK
ST. JAMES'S PARK
Refreshments
Duck Island
Canada Memorial
Park Towers
OXFORD STREET
REGENT STREET
PICCADILLY
PALL MALL
THE MALL
SHAFTESBURY AVENUE
CHARING CROSS ROAD
TOTTENHAM COURT ROAD
NEW OXFORD STREET
GREAT PORTLAND STREET
PORTLAND PLACE
NEW BOND STREET
CONDUIT STREET
WARDOUR STREET
BERWICK STREET
DEAN STREET
GREEK STREET
FRITH STREET
SOHO SQUARE
GOLDEN SQUARE
BERKELEY SQUARE
HANOVER SQUARE
CAVENDISH SQUARE
ST. JAMES'S SQUARE
BEDFORD SQUARE
JERMYN STREET
ST. JAMES'S STREET
HAYMARKET
COVENTRY STREET
WIGMORE ST.
MORTIMER STREET
GOODGE STREET
CAVENDISH PL.
LANGHAM PL.
A4201
A5204
A40
A4
A401
A400
B506
B406

223
224
229
HOLBORN
COVENT GARDEN
WC1
WC2
EC4
SE1
LAMBETH
RIVER THAMES
EMBANKMENT
CHANCERY LANE
HOLBORN
COVENT GARDEN
TEMPLE
EMBANKMENT
CHARING CROSS
LEICESTER SQ.
WATERLOO
WATERLOO EAST
Lincoln's Inn Fields
Gray's Inn Gardens
Royal Courts of Justice
Royal Opera House
Somerset House
King's Coll. (Strand Campus)
London School of Economics
Bush Ho.
Australia Ho.
India Ho.
St. Clement Danes Ch.
St. Mary-le-Strand Ch.
Temple Bar
Inner Temple
Middle Temple
Victoria Embankment Gardens
Cleopatra's Needle
Savoy Pier
Festival Pier
Embankment Pier
Hungerford Bridge
The Golden Jubilee Bridges
Jubilee Gardens
London Eye
London Eye Millennium Pier
Royal Festival Hall
Queen Elizabeth Hall
Purcell Room
Hayward Gallery
Southbank Centre
National Theatre
BFI Southbank
IMAX
The London Television Centre
HQS Wellington
HMS President
Lifeboat Station
Old War Office
Ministry of Defence
Banqueting House
Whitehall Ct.
Trafalgar Studios
Playhouse
New Players
Charing Cross Pol. Sta.
St. Martin-in-the-Fields Ch.
Coliseum
Garrick
Wyndham's
Noel Coward
Donmar
Cambridge
Adelphi
Vaudeville
Savoy
Lyceum
Duchess
Novello
Aldwych
Fortune
Drury Lane
Peacock
Shaftesbury
Cochrane
Freemasons' Hall
Connaught Rooms
City Lit
Sir John Soane's Museum
Lincoln's Inn Hall
Land Registry Office
Royal Coll. of Surgeons
The Hunterian Mus.
Old Curiosity Shop
London Transport Mus.
The Market
St. Paul's Ch.
Courtauld Galleries
Embankment Galleries
Temple Ch.
King's College Maughan Lib.
St. Dunstan-in-the-West Ch.
Gray's Inn
Islamic Cen.
Holborn Bars
Waterloo Bridge
A40
A4
A4200
A3211
A3212
A301
A3200
A5200
B400
B402
B401
B308

224
FARRINGDON
BARBICAN
CHANCERY LA.
CITY THAMESLINK
ST. PAUL'S
MANSION HO.
BLACKFRIARS
SOUTHWARK
WATERLOO EAST
WATERLOO
EC1
EC4
SE1
LAMBETH
SOUTHWARK
RIVER
Central Markets
(Smithfield)
St. Bartholomew the Great Ch.
St. Bartholomew's Hospital
Museum of London
Barbican Arts Cen.
Guildhall School of Music
City of London Sch. for Girls
Ironmongers Hall
Barber Surgeons' Hall
Haberdashers' Hall
Postmans Park
British Telecom Centre
Central Criminal Ct.
Old Bailey
London Stock Exchange
St. Paul's Cathedral
St. Paul's Cathedral Sch.
Chapter Ho.
Temple Bar Gate
Youth Hostel
Festival Gdns.
Goldsmiths Hall
Wax Chandlers Hall
ONE NEW CHANGE
St. Mary-le-Bow Ch.
St. Vedast's Ch.
Fleet Building
St. Bride's Ch.
St. Bride Foundation
Fleetbank Ho.
The Patent Off.
King's College Maughan Lib.
St. Dunstan-in-the-West Ch.
Temple Ch.
Inner Temple Hall
Mid. Temple Hall
Inner Temple Garden
Temple Bar
St. Etheldreda's Ch.
City Temple
St. Andrew's Ch.
Dr Johnson's Ho.
Islamic Cen.
St. Alban's C of E Prim. Sch.
Holborn Bars
Coll. of Arms
St. Andrew-by-the-Wardrobe
St. Benet's Guild Ch.
Salvation Army HQ
St. Nicholas Cole Abbey
City of London Sch.
Painters Hall
Vintners Hall
Millennium Bridge
Bankside Pier
Blackfriars Millennium Pier
HMS President
HQS Wellington
Stamford Wharf
OXO TOWER WHARF
The Sea Containers Ho.
Bankside Gallery
Shakespeare's Globe & Exhibition
Tate Modern
Falcon Point
Express Newspapers
The London Television Centre
The London Nautical Sch.
Christ Church
Sports & Comm. Cen.
PEABODY ESTATE
Bankside Mix
Great Guildford Business Square
Menier Chocolate Factory
Precious Blood Ch.
Fire Brigade HQ
Jerwood Space Art Gallery
London Fire Brigade Museum
Blackfriars Crown Court
The Young Vic
Southwark Coll. (Waterloo Cen.)
King's College London
St. John's Ch.
The Cathedral Sch. of St. Saviour & St. Mary Overy
St. Joseph's Cath. Prim. Sch.
Nelson Sq. Gdn.
HOLBORN
HOLBORN VIADUCT
NEWGATE STREET
FLEET STREET
LUDGATE HILL
QUEEN VICTORIA ST.
UPPER THAMES STREET
VICTORIA EMBANKMENT
BLACKFRIARS BRIDGE
SOUTHWARK BRIDGE
SOUTHWARK STREET
STAMFORD STREET
UNION STREET
ALDERSGATE
LONDON WALL
CHEAPSIDE
CANNON STREET
FARRINGDON ROAD
NEW BRIDGE STREET
A40
A201
A4208
A3211
A3200
A300
B300
218
223
230

225
219
231
F
G
H
J
K
1
2
3
4
5
6
7
SPITALFIELDS
WHITECHAPEL
EC2
EC3
E1
CITY
BERMONDSEY
THAMES
THE POOL
UPPER POOL
Upper Pool
LIVERPOOL STREET
MOORGATE
BANK
MONUMENT
CANNON ST.
FENCHURCH ST.
TOWER HILL
TOWER GATEWAY
ALDGATE
ALDGATE EAST
LONDON BRIDGE
Guildhall Sch.
Citypoint
Finsbury Sq.
Finsbury Pavement
St. Mary Moorfields Ch.
Broadgate Circle
Broadgate Ice Rink
Broadgate Arena
Exchange Square
Exchange House
Chapel of the Open Book
Old Spitalfields Market
Christ Ch. & All Saints Hall
Mosque
Christ Church Prim. Sch.
London Fruit Exchange
Bishopsgate Institute & Libraries
Walk-in Cen.
Pol. Sta.
Hlth. Cen.
London Metropolitan Univ.
Salisbury House
London Wall Buildings
Bandstand
Bowling Green
Broad Street Place
Finsbury Circus
Girdlers' Hall
LA Fitness
All Hallows Ch.
St. Botolph Ch.
Heron Tower
Liby.
St. Ethelburga's Ch.
St. Helen's Ch.
Tower 42
Dutch Ch.
"The Gherkin"
St. Andrew Undershaft Ch.
Police Sta.
Tapestry Bldg.
Western Courtyard
Central Courtyard
Cutlers Gardens
Wentworth Dwellings
Petticoat Tower
St. Botolphs
Toynbee Hall
Toynbee Studios
Canon Barnett Prim. Sch.
Women's Library
Arcadia Ct.
Evershed Ho.
Whitechapel High St.
Aldgate High St.
Braham St. Park
Bus Station
Comm. Cen.
English Martyrs Cath. Prim. Sch.
Guinness Ct.
Iveagh Ct.
Prospero Ho.
Fitness First
Bank of England
Mus.
Royal Exchange
Grocers' Hall
Temple of Mithras (Rems.)
Ch. of St. Stephen Walbrook
Mansion Ho.
Lloyd's Building
Leadenhall Mkt.
Plantation Place
Clothworkers Hall
St. Olave's Ch.
Port of London Authority Building
Trinity Ho.
Trinity Square Gdns.
St. Margaret Pattens Ch.
London Underwriting Centre
St. Mary at Hill Ch.
St. Dunstan in the East
The Monument
St. Clement's Ch.
Fishmongers Hall
St. Magnus the Martyr's Ch.
Old Billingsgate Mkt.
Custom House
All Hallows by the Tower
Tower Place
Welcome Cen.
The Ditch
Royal Chapel of St. Peter
The Tower of London
Traitors' Gate
Tower Beach
Tower Gdns.
Tower Millennium Pier
London Bridge City Pier
HMS Belfast
St. Katharine Docks
St. Katharine's Pier
Tower Hotel
Ivory House
International Ho.
Royal Mint Court
Commodity Quay
East Smithfield
Tower Bridge Exhibition
Tower Bridge
Tower Bridge Approach
Butlers Wharf Pier
Nuffield Health Club
Fire Sta.
Swan La. Pier
Grants Quay Wharf
Sugar Quay
Three Quays
Horseshoe Wharf
St. Mary Overie's Dock
Golden Hinde
Glaziers Hall
Southwark Cath.
Borough Market
London Bridge Hosp.
Cottons Centre
Hay's Galleria
Southwark Crown Ct.
More London Place
More London Riverside
The Scoop
City Hall
London Bridge City Park
Potters Fields
London Dungeon
Britain at War Experience
Southwark Playhouse
The Shard
Old Operating Theatre Mus.
Chapel
Guy's Hospital
Guy's Hosp. Extension
Guy's Nuffield Ho.
Greenwood
City Banking Coll.
Unicorn
St. John's Churchyard
Police Sta.
Design Mus.
Anchor Brewhouse
Butlers Wharf West
Spice Quay Heights
Cardamom Building
Tamarind Ct.
London Bridge
Tooley Street
Borough High St.
St. Thomas St.
Bermondsey St.
Crucifix La.
Snowsfields
Gracechurch St.
Bishopsgate
Houndsditch
Minories
Mansell St.
Leman St.
Commercial St.
Lower Thames St.
Upper Thames St.
Cannon St.
King William St.
Eastcheap
Fenchurch St.
Leadenhall St.
Cornhill
Threadneedle St.
Lombard St.
Old Broad St.
London Wall
Wormwood St.
Camomile St.
Bevis Marks
Duke's Pl.
Moorgate
Coleman St.
Liverpool St.
Byward St.
Tower Hill
A10
A11
A100
A1211
A1202
A3211
A200
A3
A1203
A2205
A2207
A501
B100
B134
B126

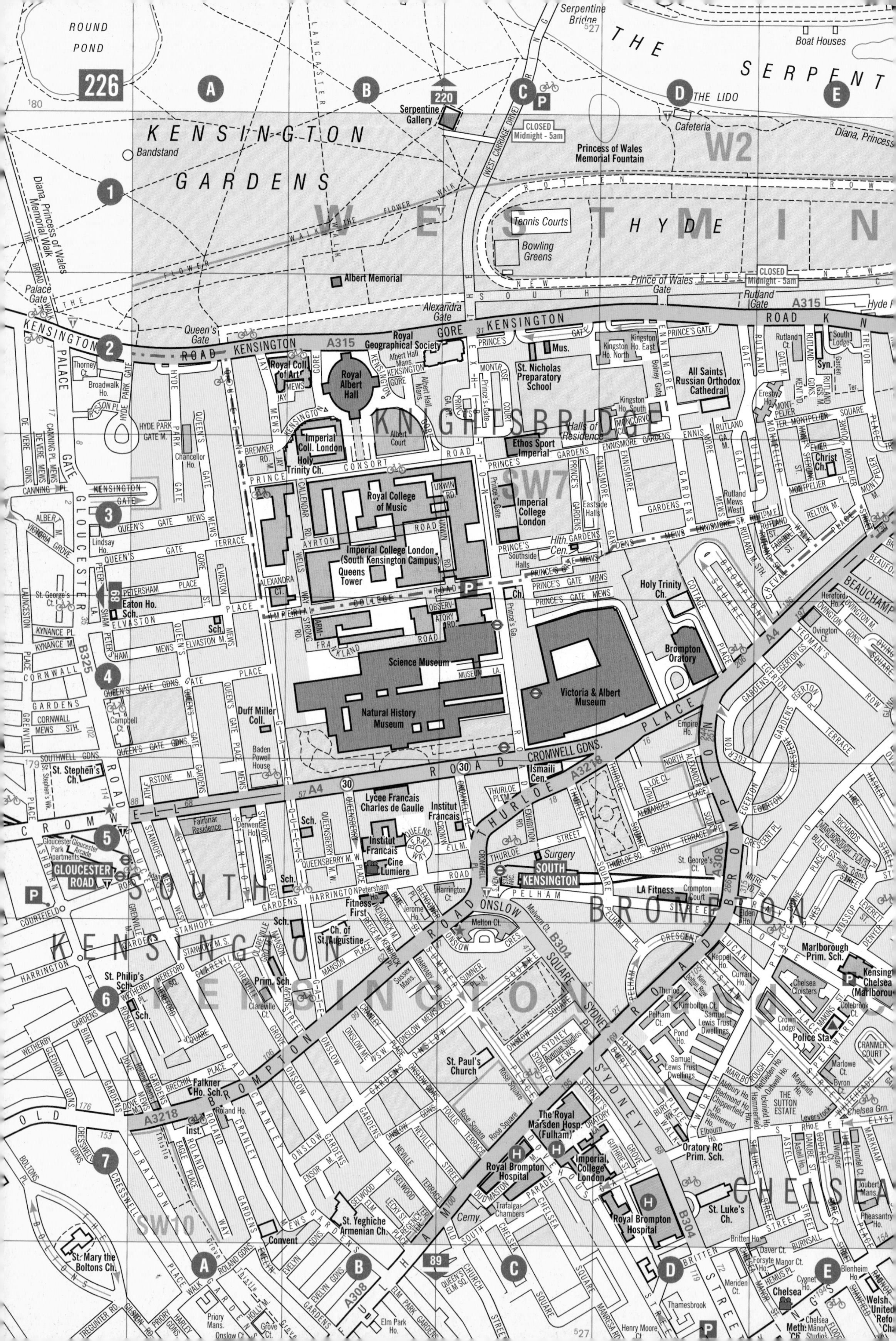

226
220
ROUND POND
KENSINGTON GARDENS
Bandstand
Diana, Princess of Wales Memorial Walk
Serpentine Bridge
THE SERPENTINE
Boat Houses
Serpentine Gallery
THE LIDO
Cafeteria
CLOSED Midnight - 5am
Princess of Wales Memorial Fountain
W2
WESTMINSTER
HYDE PARK
ROTTEN ROW
Tennis Courts
Bowling Greens
Albert Memorial
Prince of Wales Gate
Alexandra Gate
Rutland Gate
Queen's Gate
Palace Gate
A315
KENSINGTON ROAD
KENSINGTON GORE
Royal Geographical Society
Royal Coll. of Art
Royal Albert Hall
St. Nicholas Preparatory School
All Saints Russian Orthodox Cathedral
KNIGHTSBRIDGE
Halls of Residence
Ethos Sport Imperial
Imperial Coll. London
Holy Trinity Ch.
Royal College of Music
SW7
Imperial College London
Imperial College London (South Kensington Campus)
Queens Tower
Holy Trinity Ch.
Brompton Oratory
Science Museum
Natural History Museum
Victoria & Albert Museum
Duff Miller Coll.
Baden Powell House
St. Stephen's Ch.
Eaton Ho. Sch.
B325
CROMWELL ROAD
A4
CROMWELL GDNS.
Ismaili Cen.
THURLOE PLACE
A3218
Lycee Francais Charles de Gaulle
Institut Francais
Cine Lumiere
SOUTH KENSINGTON
GLOUCESTER ROAD
SOUTH KENSINGTON
BROMPTON
LA Fitness
Fitness First
Ch. of St. Augustine
St. Philip's Sch.
Falkner Ho. Sch.
St. Paul's Church
The Royal Marsden Hosp. (Fulham)
Royal Brompton Hospital
Imperial College London
Oratory RC Prim. Sch.
St. Luke's Ch.
CHELSEA
Marlborough Prim. Sch.
Police Sta.
THE SUTTON ESTATE
St. Yeghiche Armenian Ch.
Convent
St. Mary the Boltons Ch.
SW10
FULHAM ROAD
A308
89
B304
SYDNEY STREET
ONSLOW SQUARE
OLD BROMPTON ROAD
BROMPTON ROAD
EGERTON GARDENS
BEAUCHAMP PL.
ENNISMORE GARDENS
PRINCE'S GATE
QUEEN'S GATE
GLOUCESTER ROAD

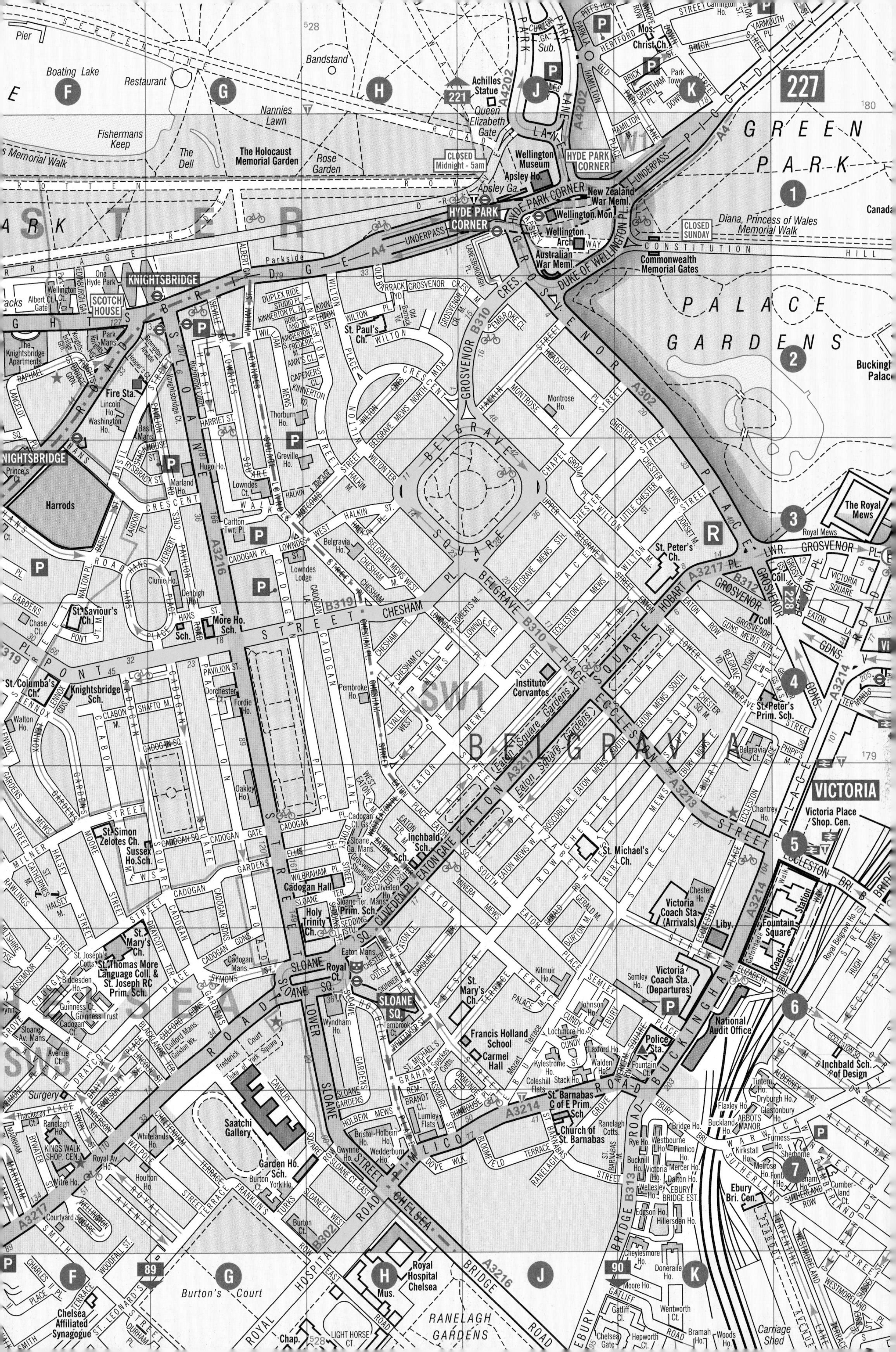
227
Pier
Boating Lake
Restaurant
Bandstand
Fishermans Keep
Nannies Lawn
The Dell
The Holocaust Memorial Garden
Rose Garden
Memorial Walk
SERPENTINE
ROTTEN ROW
CARRIAGE DRIVE
Achilles Statue
Queen Elizabeth Gate
CLOSED Midnight - 5am
221
Wellington Museum
Apsley Ho.
Apsley Ga.
HYDE PARK CORNER
New Zealand War Meml.
Wellington Mon.
Wellington Arch
Australian War Meml.
CLOSED SUNDAY
Diana, Princess of Wales Memorial Walk
CONSTITUTION HILL
Commonwealth Memorial Gates
GREEN PARK
PALACE GARDENS
Buckingham Palace
The Royal Mews
Royal Mews
Canada
PARK LANE
HAMILTON PLACE
PICCADILLY
A4
A4202
UNDERPASS
DUKE OF WELLINGTON PL.
Christ Ch.
Park Towers
KNIGHTSBRIDGE
One Hyde Park
Parkside
SCOTCH HOUSE
Albert Gate
Wellington Ct.
The Knightsbridge Apartments
Park Mans.
Fire Sta.
Lincoln Ho.
Washington Ho.
Basil Mans.
Marland Ho.
Hugo Ho.
Harrods
Prince's Ct.
Thorburn Ho.
Greville Ho.
Lowndes Ct.
Carlton Twr. Pl.
St. Paul's Ch.
Lowndes Lodge
Belgravia Ho.
Clunie Ho.
Denbigh Ho.
St. Saviour's Ch.
Chase Ct.
Sch.
More Ho. Sch.
St. Columba's Ch.
Knightsbridge Sch.
Walton Ho.
Dorchester Ct.
Fordie Ho.
Oakley Ho.
Pembroke Ct.
Montrose Ho.
St. Peter's Ch.
Instituto Cervantes
SW1
BELGRAVIA
BELGRAVE SQUARE
GROSVENOR CRES.
GROSVENOR PLACE
EATON SQUARE
Eaton Square Gardens
CHESHAM PL.
CHESHAM STREET
PONT STREET
SLOANE STREET
CADOGAN PLACE
LOWNDES SQUARE
A3216
A302
A3217
A3214
A3213
B310
B319
B312
B313
B302
HOBART PL.
ECCLESTON STREET
LWR. GROSVENOR PL.
Coll.
228
VICTORIA SQUARE
St. Peter's Prim. Sch.
Belgravia Ct.
Chantrey Ho.
VICTORIA
Victoria Place Shop. Cen.
Fountain Square
Coach Sta.
St. Michael's Ch.
Inchbald Sch.
Cadogan Hall
Holy Trinity Ch.
Prim. Sch.
St. Simon Zelotes Ch.
Sussex Ho. Sch.
St. Mary's Ch.
St. Thomas More Language Coll. & St. Joseph RC Prim. Sch.
Guinness Trust
Sloane Av. Mans
Avenue Ct.
Surgery
Cadogan Mans.
Royal Ct.
SLOANE SQ.
Eaton Mans.
Wyndham Ho.
Tambrook Ct.
St. Mary's Ch.
Francis Holland School
Carmel Hall
Kilmuir Ho.
Victoria Coach Sta. (Arrivals)
Liby.
Chester Ho.
Victoria Coach Sta. (Departures)
Semley Ho.
Johnson Ho.
Lochmore Ho.
Police Sta.
Fountain Ct.
Laxford Ho.
Walden Ho.
Kylestrome Ho.
Stack Ho.
Coleshill Flats
St. Barnabas C of E Prim. Sch.
Church of St. Barnabas
Ranelagh Cotts.
National Audit Office
Inchbald Sch. of Design
Tintern Ho.
Dryburgh Ho.
Glastonbury Ho.
Flaxley Ho.
Buckland Ho.
ABBOTS MANOR
Kirkstall Ho.
Furness Ho.
Sherborne Ho.
Melrose Ho.
Fontana Ho.
Cumberland Ct.
Ebury Bri. Cen.
Bridge Ho.
Westbourne Ho.
Pimlico Ho.
Rye Ho.
Bucknill Ho.
Victoria Ho.
Mercer Ho.
Wellesley Ho.
Dalton Ho.
EBURY BRIDGE EST.
Edgson Ho.
Hillersden Ho.
Cheylesmore Ho.
Doneraile Ho.
Moore Ho.
Wentworth Ct.
Gatliff Ct.
Chelsea Gate
Hepworth Ct.
Bramah Ho.
Woods Ho.
Carriage Shed
Saatchi Gallery
Duke of York Square
Frederick Court
Garden Ho. Sch.
Burton Ct.
York Ho.
Sloane Ct.
Bristol Ho.
Holbein Ho.
Wedderburn Ho.
Lumley Flats
Sloane Gardens
Spakes Cotts.
Whitelands Ho.
Houlton Ho.
Royal Av. Ho.
Ranelagh Ho.
KINGS WALK SHOP. CEN.
Mitre Ho.
Courtyard Square
Thackeray Place
KINGS ROAD
SW3
CHELSEA
Royal Hospital Chelsea
Mus.
Burton's Court
RANELAGH GARDENS
Chap.
LIGHT HORSE CT.
CHELSEA BRIDGE ROAD
ROYAL HOSPITAL ROAD
PIMLICO ROAD
EBURY BRIDGE ROAD
BUCKINGHAM PALACE ROAD
ROYAL AVENUE
Chelsea Affiliated Synagogue
89
90
F G H J K
R
1 2 3 4 5 6 7

228
222
227
90
GREEN PARK
ST. JAMES'S PARK
PALACE GARDENS
WESTMINSTER
PIMLICO
SW1
Canada Memorial
Diana, Princess of Wales Memorial Walk
CLOSED SUNDAY
CONSTITUTION HILL
Commonwealth Memorial Gates
Queen Victoria Memorial
The Forecourt
The Quadrangle
Buckingham Palace
Ambassadors' Court
Queen's Gallery
The Royal Mews
Royal Mews
Spencer Ho.
Marlborough House (Commonwealth Conference Centre)
King George VI Memorial
Queen's Chapel
Chapel Royal
St. James's Palace
Clarence Ho.
Lancaster Ho.
Stable Yard Gate
Refreshments
Duck Island
St. James's Park Lake
Clive Steps
Parks Police
Playground
Cockpit Steps
Queen Anne's Gate
Buckingham Gate
BIRDCAGE WALK
Wellington Barracks
Guards' Chapel
Guards' Mus.
Caxton Ho. (Dept. for Work & Pensions)
Methodist Central Hall
Queen Elizabeth II Conference Cen.
ST. JAMES'S PARK
BROADWAY SHOP. MALL
Caxton Hall
New Scotland Yard
Dept. for Business Innovation & Skills
Westminster Abbey Choir Sch.
Dept. for Educ.
Westminster Chapel
Westminster Kingsway College
Westminster City Sch.
Westminster City Hall
Dept. for Communities
SW1 Gall.
LA Fitness
CARDINAL PLACE
Victoria Palace
VICTORIA
Victoria Place Shop. Cen.
Apollo Victoria
Ashdown Ho.
Fire Sta.
Westminster RC Cathedral
Westminster Prim. Sch.
Westminster Cath. Choir Sch.
Convent
The Grey Coat Hosp. Sch.
Channel 4 TV
Home Office
RHS Lawrence Hall & Conf. Cen.
St. Stephen's Ch. Prim. Sch.
Westminster Coll.
RHS Lindley Hall
Health Cen.
Coroner's Ct.
Dept. for Transport
Pavilion
Westminster School Playing Field
Passport Office
The Queen Mother Sports Cen.
Superstore
Victoria Coach Sta. (Arrivals)
Victoria Coach Sta. (Departures)
Fountain Square
Coach Station
Liby.
National Audit Office
St. Peter's Ch.
St. Peter's Prim. Sch.
Eccleston Sch.
The Buddhist Society UK
Inchbald Sch. of Design
Gordon Hospital
Millbank Prim. Sch.
Millbank Nurs. Sch.
The Grey Coat Hosp. (St. Michael Bldg.)
St. James the Less Ch.
Fairley Ho. Sch.
PIMLICO
St. Gabriel's Ch.
Church of the Holy Apostles
St. Saviour's Ch.
Young England Kindergarten
Pimlico Academy
Prim. Sch.
Churchill Gdns. Prim. Sch.
Toy Lib.
Ebury Bri. Cen.
Carriage Shed
VICTORIA STREET
BUCKINGHAM PALACE ROAD
VAUXHALL BRIDGE ROAD
BELGRAVE ROAD
GROSVENOR PLACE
GREYCOAT PL.
HORSEFERRY RD.
MARSHAM STREET
JOHN ISLIP ST.
BESSBOROUGH GDNS.
LUPUS ST.
ST. GEORGE'S SQ.
WARWICK WAY
ECCLESTON STREET
ROCHESTER ROW
ARTILLERY RW.
A302
A3213
A3214
A202
B323
B324
B326
B312
A3217

229
WATERLOO EAST
230
WATERLOO
LAMBETH
SE1
SE11
VAUXHALL
RIVER THAMES
ARCHBISHOP'S PARK
Westminster Bridge
Lambeth Bridge
Houses of Parliament
Big Ben
Westminster Hall
Westminster Abbey
St. Margaret's Ch.
Supreme Court
New Palace Yard
Victoria Tower Gardens
Black Rod Garden
Jewel Tower
Abbey Garden
Westminster Sch.
The Cloisters
Little Cloisters
Westminster Abbey Mus.
Poets' Corner
The Close
Dean's Yd.
Parliament Square
Parliament St.
Whitehall
Banqueting Ho.
Scotland Office
Wales Office
Ministry of Defence
Cenotaph
Former New Scotland Yard
Treasury
Northern Ireland Office
Old War Office
Horse Guards Avenue
Richmond Terrace
Downing St.
Derby Gate
Canon Row
Portcullis Ho.
WESTMINSTER
RAF Memorial
Whitehall Stairs
Victoria Embankment
A3211
A3212
A302
A3203
A3200
A3036
A23
A301
A3204
A202
B300
London Eye
London Eye Millennium Pier
Westminster Millennium Pier
Millbank Millennium Pier
Jubilee Gardens
Jubilee Bridges
London Film Mus.
Sea Life London Aquarium
County Hall (Former)
London's Death Trap
Shell Centre
Belvedere Road
Chicheley St.
North Block
East Block
West Block
South Block
Forum Magnum Sq.
County Hall Apartments
Concert Hall Approach
IMAX
Waterloo Road
Tenison Way
Mepham St.
Sandell St.
Alaska St.
King's College London
St. John's Ch.
The Old Vic
Waterloo Millennium Green
Leake St.
Lower Marsh
The Old Vic Tunnels
Addington St.
Westminster Bridge Road
Florence Nightingale Mus.
St. Thomas' Hospital
Evelina Children's Hosp.
King's College London
King's College London (St. Thomas' Campus)
Albert Embankment
Lambeth Palace Road
Lambeth Palace
The Garden Museum
Lambeth Pier
Kagyu Samye Dzong London
Marine Institute
College of the Sea
St. Thomas' Youth Cen.
Fairley Ho. Sch.
Police Support Headquarters
Lambeth Road
Lambeth Walk
Lambeth Walk Open Space
Walnut Tree Walk Prim. Sch.
Imperial War Museum
Lambeth Towers Surgery
Wedgwood Ho.
Morley Coll.
Christ Ch. & Upton Chapel
Police Sta.
LAMBETH NORTH
Kennington Road
Baylis Road
Johanna Prim. Sch.
Liby.
Stangate
Canterbury Ho.
Royal St.
Carlisle Lane
Hercules Road
Centaur St.
Cosser St.
Morton St.
Old Paradise St.
Black Prince Road
Parliament View
Recreation Ground
Fire Sta.
Whitgift St.
Works
Salamanca Square
Pedlers Park
Vauxhall Meth. Ch.
Vauxhall Prim. Sch.
All Nations Cen.
Vauxhall City Farm
Spring Gardens
Vauxhall Walk
Leopold Walk
Tinworth St.
Glasshouse Walk
Jonathan St.
Kennington Lane
Sancroft St.
Ethelred Nursery Sch.
St. Anselm's Ch.
Kennington Palace Ct.
Lambeth County Ct.
Archbishop Sumner C of E Prim. Sch.
The OLIVE Sch.
Walcot Sq.
St. Mary's Gdns.
Brook Dr.
Millbank
Tate Britain
Millbank Tower
Northern Ireland Office (Thames Ho.)
Dept. for Environment
Ryl. Coll. of Vet. Surgeons
St. John's Concert Hall
Smith Square
St. John's Gdns.
Horseferry Road
Albert Embankment Gdns.
Peninsula Heights
Riverside Gardens
Riverwalk Ho.
Camelford Ho.
Government Offices
Vauxhall Bridge

230
229
90
91
A
B
C
D
E
1
2
3
4
5
6
7
SOUTHWARK
BOROUGH
NEWINGTON
LAMBETH
KENNINGTON
WALWORTH
SE11
King's College London
St. John's Ch.
WATERLOO EAST
WATERLOO
Waterloo East
The Young Vic
Southwark Coll. (Waterloo Cen.)
The Old Vic
Waterloo Millennium Green
Union
Grand Vitesse Ind. Cen.
Great Guildford Business Square
Menier Chocolate Factory
Precious Blood Ch.
Fire Brigade HQ
Jerwood Space Art Gallery
Blackfriars Crown Court
London Fire Brigade Museum
Fire Sta.
Sports Ground
Nelson Sq. Gdn.
Youth & Community Cen.
Friars Primary Foundation Sch.
Teacher Training Cen.
Peabody Square
Rec. Grnd.
St. Andrews Ch.
The Cathedral of St. Saviour & St. Mary Overie
St. Joseph Cath. Prim. Sch.
Lit. Dorrit Park
Charles Dickens Prim. Sch.
BOROUGH
Police Sta.
Court Annexe
The Henry Wood Hall
Inner London Crown Court (Sessions House)
Newington Gardens
Mosque
Surgery
Deeper Life Bible Ch.
London South Bank University
London Sth. Bank Univ.
London South Bank Univ. Technopark
Perry Lib.
LAMBETH NORTH
Christ Ch. & Upton Chapel
Morley Coll.
Police Sta.
St. George's RC Cathedral
Prim. Sch.
Notre Dame School
Siobhan Davis Dance Studios
Geraldine Mary Harmsworth Park
Imperial War Museum
Charlotte Sharman Foundation Prim. Sch.
West Sq. Gdn.
Imperial War Mus. (All Saints Annexe)
ELEPHANT & CASTLE
Coronet Theatre
Elephant & Castle Shopping Centre
Palace Bingo Superbowl
London College of Communication
Metropolitan Tabernacle
Elephant & Castle Leisure Cen.
St. Mary's Churchyard
Strata Tower
Comm. Cen.
St. Matthews Ch.
Halls of Residence
Brotherhood of the Cross & Star Church
Crossway Ch.
Castle Ind. Est.
Comm. Care Cen.
The OLIVE Sch.
Archbishop Sumner C of E Prim. Sch.
Jamyang Buddhist Centre
Cuming Museum
Municipal Offices
Lib.
St. John's Ch.
St. John's Prim. Sch.
Police Station
Crampton Prim. Sch.
Pedlars Acre
St. Mary's Ch.
KENNINGTON
Lambeth County Ct.
Tibetan Buddhist Cen.
Depot
Ethelred Nursery Sch.
St. Anselm's Ch.
London Art Sch.
Tel. Ex.
TA Cen.
Walworth Gdn. Farm
Keyworth Prim. Sch.
Pasley Park
Kennington Palace Ct.
Imperial Court
Johanna Prim. Sch.
A3202
A3203
A3204
A3
A300
A201
A301
A302
A215
A3201
B300
B240
WESTMINSTER BRIDGE ROAD
ST. GEORGE'S ROAD
LAMBETH ROAD
KENNINGTON ROAD
KENNINGTON LANE
KENNINGTON PARK ROAD
NEWINGTON BUTTS
BOROUGH ROAD
BOROUGH HIGH STREET
LONDON ROAD
BLACKFRIARS ROAD
SOUTHWARK BRIDGE ROAD
NEWINGTON CAUSEWAY
WALWORTH ROAD
NEW KENT ROAD
HARPER ROAD
THE CUT
UNION STREET
ST. GEORGE'S CIRCUS

LONDON BRI.
231
225
London Bridge City Park
Butlers Wharf Pier
UPPERPOOL
Southwark Playhouse
Britain at War Experience
More London Riverside
Unicorn
Potters Fields
Guy's Hospital
Guy's Hosp. Extension
Guy's Nuffield Ho.
Chapel
F
G
H
J
K
1
2
3
4
5
6
7
A200
A2207
A2198
A2205
A2206
A100
A2
A201
A3
B202
B203
B204
B214
B215
20
30
ST. THOMAS ST.
BERMONDSEY STREET
TOOLEY STREET
TOWER BRIDGE ROAD
JAMAICA RD.
CRUCIFIX LA.
DRUID ST.
TANNER ST.
LONG LANE
ABBEY STREET
GRANGE RD.
GREAT DOVER STREET
OLD KENT ROAD
NEW KENT ROAD
ROLLS RD.
SOUTHWARK PK. RD.
MANDELA WAY
DUNTON ROAD
HUMPHREY ST.
EAST STREET
SURREY SQUARE
ALBANY ROAD
TOWER BRIDGE ROAD
SNOWSFIELDS
Greenwood
Coll.
Lib.
Leathermarket Gdns.
Community Park
Guy St. Park
Bermondsey Pgrd.
Fashion & Textile Mus.
Design Mus.
St. John's Churchyard
London City Mission HQ
Tower Bri. Prim. Sch.
Police Sta.
St. Mary Magdalen Ch.
Churchyard
Shortwave
Grange Prim. Sch.
Haddon Hall Baptist Ch.
BRICKLAYER'S ARMS
The Green
Tabard Gardens
Mayflower Gdns.
St. Saviour's & St. Olave's Sch.
Globe Academy Prim. Sch.
Globe Academy Sec. Sch.
Bermondsey Spa Gardens (Recreation Ground)
Municipal Offs.
Kagyu Samye Dzong London
Harris Academy Bermondsey
Kintore Wy. Children's Cen.
Boutcher C of E Prim. Sch.
Depots
Depot
Warehouse
Superstore
BRICKLAYERS ARMS DISTRIBUTION CENTRE
RICH INDUSTRIAL ESTATE
SOUTHERNWOOD RETAIL PARK
Paragon Gdns.
Townsend Prim. Sch.
Lady Margaret's Ch.
SE17
English Martyrs Ch.
English Martyrs RC Prim. Sch.
Nursery Row Park
St. Christopher's Ch.
Surrey Sq. Jun. & Inf. Schs.
All Saint's Ch.
Surrey Square Park
Walworth Acad.
Walworth Academy (Upper Sch.)
Surgery
Faraday Gdns.
St. Peter's C of E Prim. Sch.
Michael Faraday House
Methodist Ch.
Fire Sta.
Mos.
91
Victory Community Park

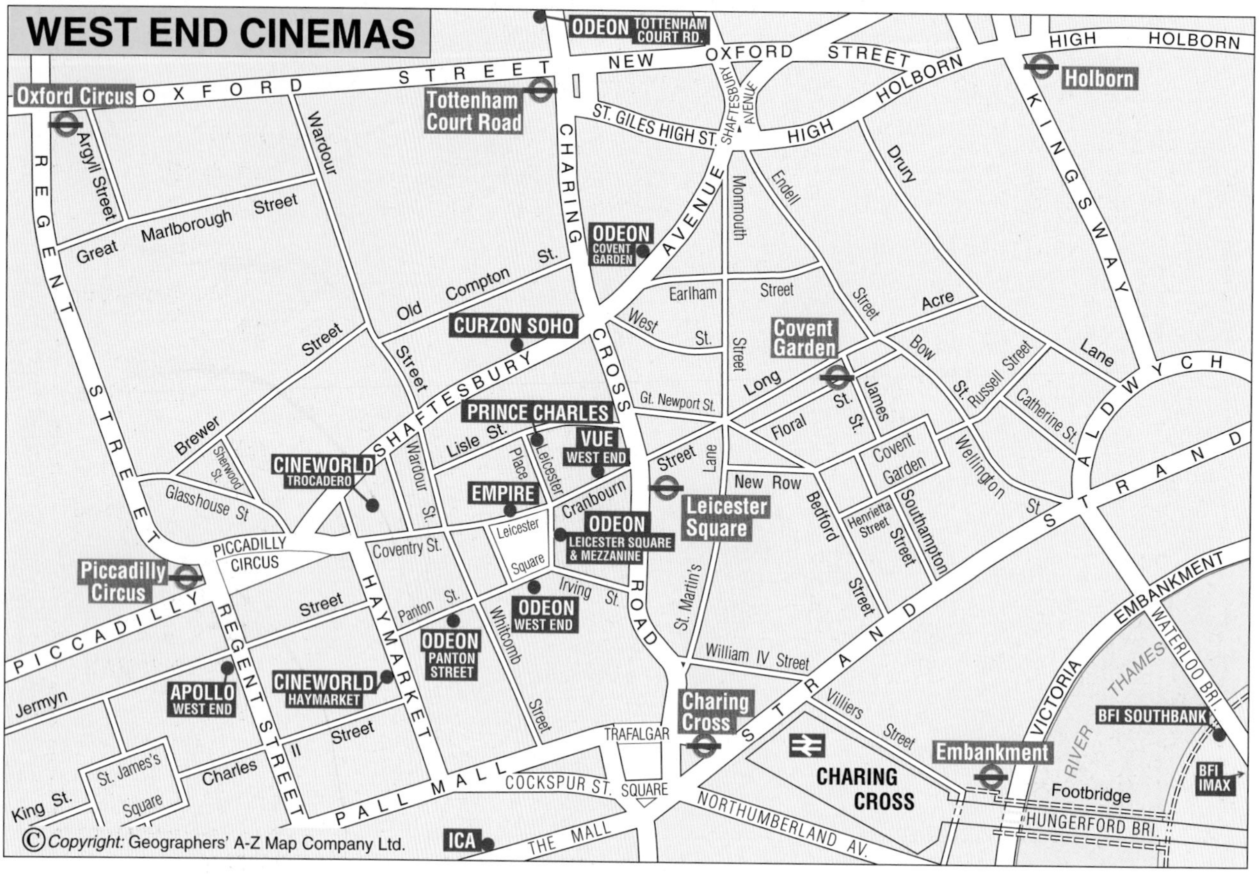
WEST END CINEMAS
ODEON TOTTENHAM COURT RD.
Oxford Circus
Tottenham Court Road
Holborn
OXFORD STREET
NEW OXFORD STREET
HIGH HOLBORN
ST. GILES HIGH ST.
SHAFTESBURY AVENUE
Argyll Street
Wardour
CHARING CROSS ROAD
KINGSWAY
Great Marlborough Street
Old Compton St.
ODEON COVENT GARDEN
Monmouth
Endell
Drury
Earlham Street
CURZON SOHO
West St.
Covent Garden
Long Acre
Bow St.
Russell Street
Lane
ALDWYCH
Catherine St.
Brewer Street
Sherwood St.
PRINCE CHARLES
Lisle St.
Wardour St.
Leicester Place
VUE WEST END
Gt. Newport St.
Floral St.
James St.
Covent Garden
Wellington St.
CINEWORLD TROCADERO
EMPIRE
Cranbourn Street
Leicester Square
New Row
Bedford Street
Henrietta Street
Southampton Street
STRAND
Glasshouse St
PICCADILLY CIRCUS
Coventry St.
ODEON LEICESTER SQUARE & MEZZANINE
Piccadilly Circus
Panton St.
Irving St.
ODEON WEST END
St. Martin's Lane
PICCADILLY
REGENT STREET
HAYMARKET
Whitcomb Street
ODEON PANTON STREET
William IV Street
EMBANKMENT
VICTORIA EMBANKMENT
WATERLOO BRI.
RIVER THAMES
Jermyn Street
APOLLO WEST END
CINEWORLD HAYMARKET
Charles II Street
Charing Cross
Villiers Street
BFI SOUTHBANK
St. James's Square
King St.
TRAFALGAR SQUARE
PALL MALL
COCKSPUR ST.
CHARING CROSS
Embankment
BFI IMAX
Footbridge
HUNGERFORD BRI.
NORTHUMBERLAND AV.
ICA
THE MALL
© Copyright: Geographers' A-Z Map Company Ltd.

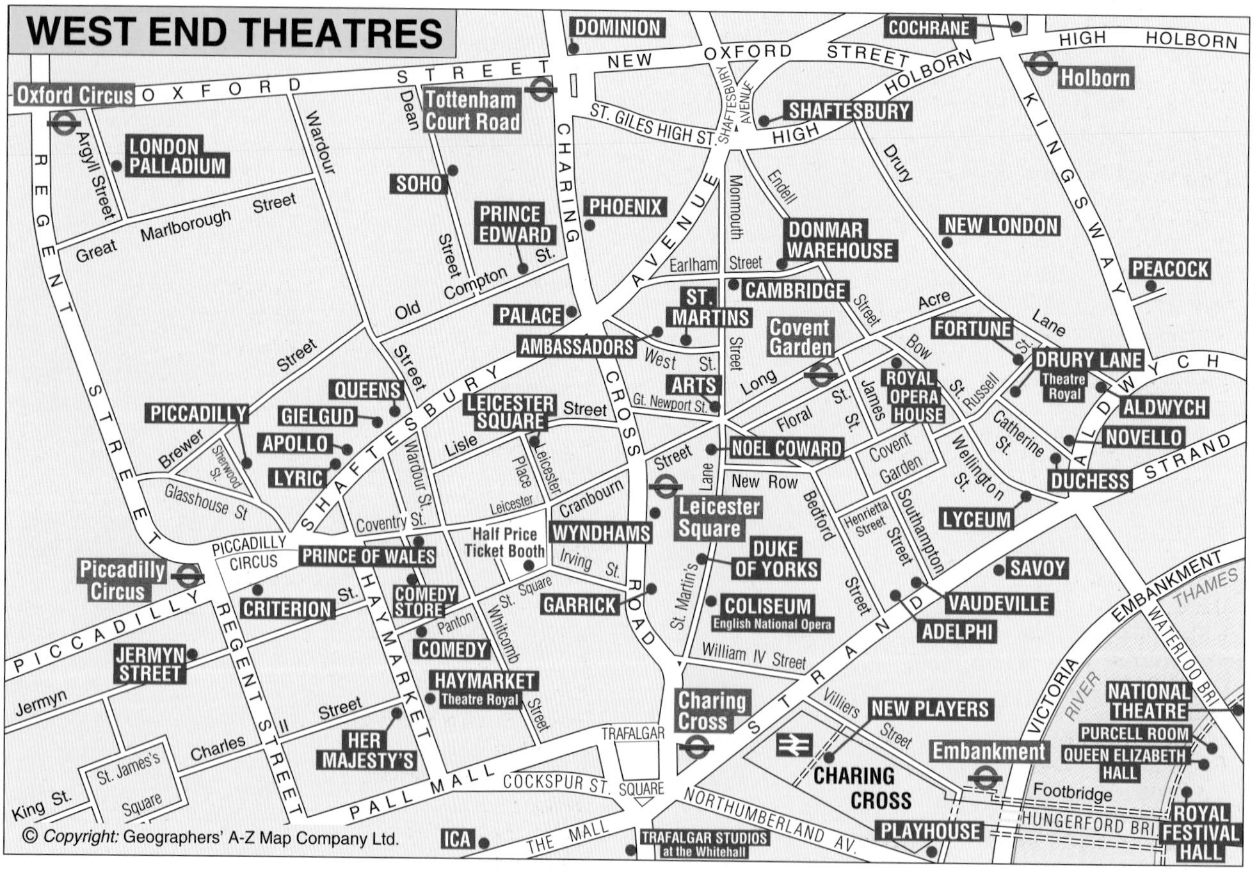
WEST END THEATRES
DOMINION
COCHRANE
Oxford Circus
Tottenham Court Road
Holborn
OXFORD STREET
NEW OXFORD STREET
HIGH HOLBORN
ST. GILES HIGH ST.
SHAFTESBURY
LONDON PALLADIUM
SOHO
Dean Street
PRINCE EDWARD
PHOENIX
DONMAR WAREHOUSE
NEW LONDON
PEACOCK
Great Marlborough Street
Old Compton St.
CAMBRIDGE
PALACE
ST. MARTINS
AMBASSADORS
Covent Garden
FORTUNE
DRURY LANE Theatre Royal
ARTS
ROYAL OPERA HOUSE
ALDWYCH
QUEENS
PICCADILLY
GIELGUD
LEICESTER SQUARE
APOLLO
LYRIC
NOVELLO
NOEL COWARD
DUCHESS
Leicester Square
LYCEUM
Half Price Ticket Booth
WYNDHAMS
PRINCE OF WALES
Piccadilly Circus
DUKE OF YORKS
SAVOY
CRITERION
COMEDY STORE
GARRICK
COLISEUM English National Opera
VAUDEVILLE
ADELPHI
COMEDY
JERMYN STREET
HAYMARKET Theatre Royal
Charing Cross
NEW PLAYERS
NATIONAL THEATRE
PURCELL ROOM
QUEEN ELIZABETH HALL
HER MAJESTY'S
Embankment
CHARING CROSS
Footbridge
HUNGERFORD BRI.
ROYAL FESTIVAL HALL
PLAYHOUSE
TRAFALGAR STUDIOS at the Whitehall
ICA
THE MALL
PALL MALL
COCKSPUR ST.
TRAFALGAR SQUARE
NORTHUMBERLAND AV.
© Copyright: Geographers' A-Z Map Company Ltd.

ROAD MAPS

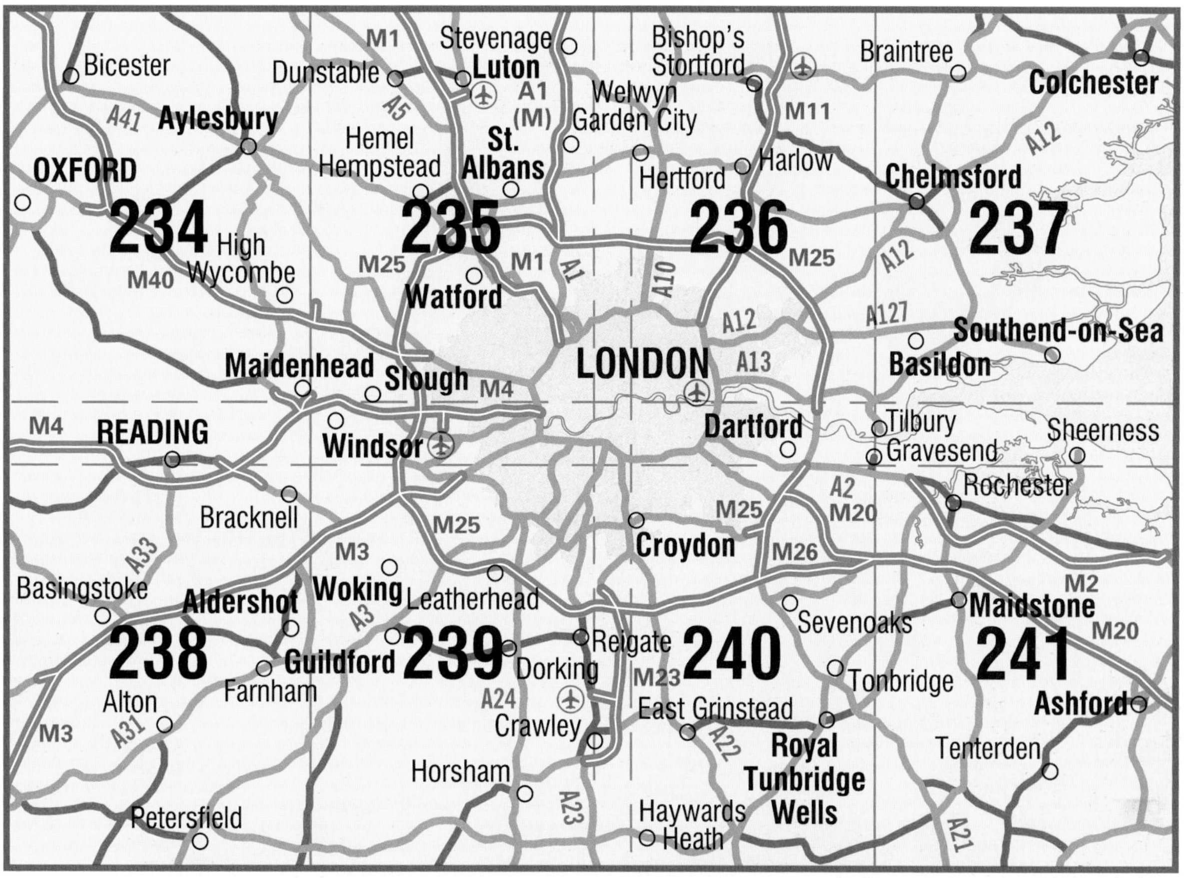

Bicester
A41
Aylesbury
OXFORD
234
High Wycombe
M40
Dunstable
M1
A5
Stevenage
Luton
A1 (M)
Hemel Hempstead
St. Albans
235
M25
M1
Watford
Bishop's Stortford
Welwyn Garden City
Hertford
Harlow
M11
236
M25
A10
A1
Braintree
Colchester
A12
Chelmsford
237
A12
A127
Southend-on-Sea
Basildon
Maidenhead
Slough
M4
LONDON
A12
A13
M4
READING
Windsor
Dartford
Tilbury
Gravesend
Sheerness
Rochester
A2
M20
Bracknell
A33
M25
M3
Croydon
M25
M26
Basingstoke
Aldershot
Woking
A3
Leatherhead
M2
Maidstone
M20
238
Guildford
239
Dorking
Reigate
240
Sevenoaks
Tonbridge
241
Alton
Farnham
A24
M23
East Grinstead
Ashford
M3
A31
Crawley
A22
Royal Tunbridge Wells
Tenterden
Horsham
A23
Haywards Heath
Petersfield
A21

REFERENCE AND TOURIST INFORMATION

Motorway — M1
Motorway Junctions with Numbers
- Unlimited interchange 4
- Limited interchange 5

Motorway Service Area — HESTON
Major Road Service Areas with 24 hour Facilities — A23 PEASE POTTAGE
Primary Route (with junction number) — A12 4
Primary Route Destination — LUTON
Dual Carriageways (A & B Roads)
Class A Road — A129
Class B Road — B177
Major Roads Under Construction
Major Roads Proposed
Safety Cameras with Speed Limits
- Single Camera — 30
- Multiple Cameras located along road — 50
- Single & Multiple Variable Speed Cameras — V

Toll — TOLL
Gradient 1:5 (20%) & steeper (Ascent in direction of arrow)
Mileage between markers — 8
Railway and Station
Level Crossing and Tunnel
River or Canal
County or Unitary Authority Boundary
Built-Up Area
Village or Hamlet
Wooded Area
Spot Height in Feet — .813

Height above Sea Level
- 400' - 1,000' — 122m - 305m
- 1,000' - 1,400' — 305m - 427m
- 1,400' - 2,000' — 427m - 610m
- 2,000'+ — 610m +

National Grid Reference (Kilometres) — 100
Page Continuation — 234

Airport
Airfield
Heliport
Battle Site and Date — 1066
Castle (Open to Public)
Castle with Garden (Open to Public)
Cathedral, Church, Abbey, Friary, Priory
Country Park
Ferry (Vehicular) (Foot only)
Garden (Open to Public)
Golf Course 9 Hole 18 Hole
Historic Building (Open to Public)
Historic Building with Garden (Open to Public)
Horse Racecourse
Lighthouse
Motor Racing Circuit

Museum, Art Gallery
National Park
National Trust Property (Open) (Restricted Opening) — NT
Nature Reserve or Bird Sanctuary
Nature Trail or Forest Walk
Place of Interest — Monument
Picnic Site
Railway, Steam or Narrow Gauge
Theme Park
Tourist Information Centre
Viewpoint
Visitor Information Centre
Wildlife Park
Windmill
Zoo or Safari Park

SCALE 1: 200,000

0 1 2 3 4 5 10 Miles

0 1 2 3 4 5 10 15 Kilometres

3.156 Miles to 1 inch
2 Kms to 1 cm

234
Fritwell
Baynard's Green
A43
Hardwick
Hethe
Stoke Lyne
Fringford
Fewcott
Ardley
CHERWELL VALLEY
Upper Heyford
Bainton
Bucknell
Caversfield
Bicester
Woodfield
B4030
Caulcott
M40
Middleton Stoney
Chesterton
A41
Weston-on-the-Green
Kirtlington
Wendlebury
Ambrosden
Bletchingdon
Merton
Lower Arncott
Upper Arncott
Charlton-on-Otmoor
Fencott
Murcott
Hampton Poyle
Kidlington
Oddington
Islip
DANGER AREA
OT MOOR
Noke
Gosford
A34
Horton-cum-Studley
Woodeaton
Beckley
OXFORD PEAR TREE
Elsfield
Sunnymead
OXFORD
Stanton St. John
Marston
Barton
Sandhills
Forest Hill
Headington
A40
A4142
Holton
Wheatley
Horspath
Grandpont
South Hinksey
Cowley
Iffley
Littlemore
Kennington
Blenheim
Denton
Garsington
Cuddesdon
Bayworth
Sandford-on-Thames
Toot Baldon
Radley
Nuneham Courtenay
Marsh Baldon
Chislehampton
Stadhampton
ABINGDON
Northcourt
Berinsfield
Clifton Hampden
Burcot
Drayton St. Leonard
Culham
Long Wittenham
Dorchester on Thames
Appleford
Little Wittenham
Shillingford
Sutton Courtenay
Didcot
Brightwell-cum-Sotwell
Slade End
Wallingford
North Moreton
East Hagbourne
Northbourne
Coscote
West Hagbourne
South Moreton
Aston Upthorpe
Cholsey
Upton
Aston Tirrold
Blewbury
Moulsford
North Stoke
South Stoke
Streatley
Compton
Aldworth
Goring
Cleeve
Woodcote
Lower Basildon
Basildon Park
Upper Basildon
Ashampstead
Hampstead Norreys
Bothampstead
Quick's Green
Eling
Yattendon
Burnt Hill
Frilsham
Oare
Hermitage
Bradfield
M4
Chetwode
Preston Bissett
Hillesden
Steeple Claydon
Stratton Audley
Twyford
Poundon
Grebe Lake
Charndon
Calvert
Marsh Gibbon
Launton
Edgcott
Grendon Underwood
Blackthorn
Ludgershall
Piddington
Wotton House
Wotton Underwood
Boarstall Decoy
Boarstall
Brill
Dorton
Little London
Oakley
Chilton
Easington
Long Crendon
Worminghall
Ickford
Shabbington
Waterperry
Waterstock
Draycot
North Weston
Thame
Tiddington
Moreton
Milton Common
Great Milton
Great Haseley
Latchford
Little Milton
Little Haseley
Tetsworth
Stoke Talmage
Adwell
South Weston
Chalgrove
Newington
Easington
Lewknor
Brightwell Baldwin
Cuxham
Pyrton
Shirburn
Warborough
Berrick Salome
Rokemarsh
Roke
Watlington
Britwell Salome
Benson
Ewelme
Crowmarsh Gifford
Winterbrook
Nuffield
Cookley Green
Russell's Water
Maidensgrove
Park Corner
Nettlebed
Crocker End
Ipsden
Highmoor
Witheridge Hill
Highmoor Cross
Checkendon
Stoke Row
Satwell
Exlade Street
Wyfold Grange
Sonning Common
Rotherfield Greys
Rotherfield Peppard
Cray's Pond
Gallowstree Common
Whitchurch Hill
Cane End
Goring Heath
Whitchurch-on-Thames
Kidmore End
Tokers Green
Pangbourne
Mapledurham
Purley on Thames
Caversham Heights
Caversham
Tidmarsh
Sulham
Tilehurst
READING
238
Adstock
Addington
Winslow
Middle Claydon
East Claydon
Botolph Claydon
BUCKINGHAMSHIRE
Granborough
North Marston
Quainton
Pitchcott
Oving
Kingswood
Westcott
Waddesdon
Waddesdon Manor
Upper Winchendon
Ashendon
Pollicott
Lower Winchendon
Nether Winchendon House
Cuddington
Chearsley
Haddenham
Aston Sandford
Kingsey
Towersey
Ilmer
Owlswick
Longwick
Emmington
Henton
Sydenham
Kingston Blount
Postcombe
Aston Rowant
Chinnor
Bledlow
Stokenchurch
The City
Radnage
Beacon's Bottom
Piddington
Ibstone
Christmas Common
Northend
Greenfield
Turville Heath
Turville
Pishill
Stonor
Fingest
Skirmett
Cadmore End
Frieth
Parmoor
Fawley
Hambleden
Middle Assendon
Lower Assendon
Bix
Aston
Remenham
Medmenham
Mill End
HENLEY-ON-THAMES
Harpsden
Binfield Heath
Lower Shiplake
Shiplake
Wargrave
Dunsden Green
Emmer Green
Play Hatch
Sonning Eye
Charvil
Sonning
Twyford
Woodley
Hurst
Drayton Parslow
Mursley
Shipton
Swanbourne
Hollingdon
Soulbury
Stewkley Dean
Stewkley
Hoggeston
Dunton
Littlecote
Burcott
Whitchurch
Cublington
Wing
Aston Abbotts
Hardwick
Weedon
Rowsham
Wingrave
Crafton
Hulcott
Watermead
Quarrendon
Bierton
Puttenham
AYLESBURY
Stone
Upton
Dinton
Westlington
Southcourt
Stoke Mandeville
Weston Turville
Aston Clinton
Halton
Buckland
Bishopstone
Ford
Marsh
Kimble Wick
Nash Lee
North Lee
Terrick
Wendover
Little Kimble
Ellesborough
Meadle
Great Kimble
Askett
Monks Risborough
Princes Risborough
Horsenden
Saunderton
Loosley Row
Lacey Green
Speen
Prestwood
Great Hampden
Little Hampden
Dunsmore
Kingsash
Great Missenden
Saunderton Lee
Rout's Green
Bledlow Ridge
Upper North Dean
Bradenham
Naphill
Hughenden Valley
Walter's Ash
Cryers Hill
Widmer End
Hazlemere
Downley
West Wycombe
HIGH WYCOMBE
Booker
Wycombe Marsh
Loudwater
Lane End
Handy Cross
Flackwell Heath
Chisbridge Cross
Rockwell End
Marlow Bottom
Lower Woodend
Bovingdon Green
Marlow Common
MARLOW
Little Marlow
Bourne End
Bisham
Cookham Dean
Cookham Rise
Hurley
Pinkneys Green
Remenham Hill
Cockpole Green
Burchett's Green
MAIDENHEAD
Crazies Hill
Warren Row
Knowl Hill
Littlewick Green
Kiln Green
Hare Hatch
White Waltham
Woodlands Park
Waltham St. Lawrence
Ruscombe
Shurlock Row
West End
Paley Street
Moneyrow Green
Touchen-end
Hawthorn Hill
Warfield
Bray Wick
A404(M)
A4010
A418
A413
A4146

235
CENTRAL BEDS
HERTFORDSHIRE
Toddington
TODDINGTON
Barton-le-Clay
Pegsdon
HITCHIN
Great Wymondley
Little Wymondley
Weston
Hall's Green
Graveley
Potsgrove
Battlesden
Heath and Reach
Upper Sundon
Streatley
Fancott
Chalton
Tebworth
Wingfield
Hockliffe
Leighton Buzzard
Eggington
Tilsworth
Stanbridge
Houghton Regis
Lower Sundon
Sundon Park
Limbury
Lilley
Great Offley
Offley Hoo
Charlton
Gosmore
St. Ippolyts
Walkern
STEVENAGE
Shephall
Aston
Knebworth
Datchworth
Watton at Stone
Luton
LUTON
LONDON LUTON
Leagrave
Stopsley
Cockernhoe
Ley Green
Preston
King's Walden
Breachwood Green
St. Paul's Walden
Langley
Bendish
Whitwell
Rush Green
Old Knebworth
Knebworth House
Rableyheath
Codicote
Woolmer Green
Bull's Green
Burnham Green
Digswell
Tewin
Welwyn
Harmer Green
Stapleford
Bramfield
Waterford
DUNSTABLE
Sewell
Totternhoe
Eaton Bray
Edlesborough
Northall
Honeywick
Church End
Chaul End
New Town
Caddington
Slip End
Aley Green
Kensworth
Kensworth Common
Whipsnade
Studham
Dagnall
Ivinghoe
Ivinghoe Aston
Pitstone
Markyate
FLAMSTEAD
Flamstead
Kinsbourne Green
Chiltern Green
Peter's Green
Kimpton
East Hyde
Blackmore End
Ayot St. Lawrence
Mackerye End
The Folly
Ayot St. Peter
Ayot Green
HARPENDEN
Wheathampstead
Amwell
Hatching Green
Coleman Green
Lemsford
WELWYN GARDEN CITY
Cole Green
Hatfield Hyde
Letty Green
Ringshall
Little Gaddesden
Jockey End
Trowley Bottom
Bulbourne
New Mill
Upper Dunsley
Aldbury
Tring
St. Margaret's
Great Gaddesden
Water End
Holtsmere End
Redbourn
Childwick Green
Sandridge
Stanborough
Hatfield Garden Village
HATFIELD
Wigginton
Hastoe
Nettleden
Frithsden
Potten End
Piccotts End
New Greens
Townsend
Marshalswick
Fleetville
Ellenbrook
Essendon
West End
Little Berkhamsted
Bayford
Woodside
Epping Green
Northchurch
Cholesbury
St. Leonards
BERKHAMSTED
Buckland Common
Bellingdon
Warners End
Chaulden
Bourne End
Boxmoor
HEMEL HEMPSTEAD
ST. ALBANS
Colney Heath
London Colney
Welham Green
Brookmans Park
Ashley Green
Whelpley Hill
Lye Green
Felden
Bovingdon
Rucklers Lane
Kings Langley
Bedmond
Potters Crouch
Chiswell Green
Park Street
Frogmore
Water End
POTTERS BAR
South Mimms
SOUTH MIMMS
Northaw
Lee Clump
Chartridge
Botley
Ley Hill
Chipperfield
Abbots Langley
Bricket Wood
Colney Street
Shenleybury
Shenley
RADLETT
Ridge
Bentley Heath
Crews Hill
Botany Bay
236
CHESHAM
South Heath
Waterside
Hyde Heath
Flaunden
Belsize
Bucks Hill
Hunton Bridge
Langleybury
Chesham Bois
Sarratt
Latimer
Chenies
Micklefield Green
Chandler's Cross
Aldenham
Letchmore Heath
Green Street
BOREHAMWOOD
Patchetts Green
Elstree
Monken Hadley
Hadley Wood
Cockfosters
High Barnet
BARNET
Arkley
Totteridge
EAST BARNET
Little Missenden
AMERSHAM
Penn Street
Coleshill
Winchmore Hill
Penn
Knotty Green
Forty Green
BEACONSFIELD
Chalfont St. Giles
Seer Green
Jordans
Heronsgate
Little Chalfont
CHORLEYWOOD
WATFORD
Croxley Green
RICKMANSWORTH
Batchworth
BUSHEY
Oxhey
Bushey Heath
South Oxhey
Eastbury
LONDON GATEWAY
Whetstone
FRIERN BARNET
Chalfont Common
Chalfont St. Peter
Layter's Green
Maple Cross
West Hyde
NORTHWOOD
Hatch End
STANMORE
Harrow Weald
EDGWARE
Mill Hill
FINCHLEY
WOOD GREEN
Muswell Hill
HORNSEY
Harefield
Ruislip Common
Denham Green
Wealdstone
Kingsbury
HENDON
Golders Green
Highgate
BEACONSFIELD
Gerrards Cross
Hedgerley
Wooburn
Newyears Green
Denham
Ickenham
PINNER
HARROW
KENTON
Eastcote
RUISLIP
Harrow on the Hill
Neasden
Cricklewood
HAMPSTEAD
CAMDEN TOWN
Farnham Common
Egypt
Fulmer
Stoke Poges
Tatling End
New Denham
UXBRIDGE
Rayners Lane
NORTHOLT
WEMBLEY
WILLESDEN
Kilburn
East Burnham
Burnham
Farnham Royal
Wexham Street
Taplow
SLOUGH
Iver Heath
Hillingdon
Shreding Green
George Green
Cowley
Yeading
GREENFORD
HAYES
MARYLEBONE
PADDINGTON
WEST END
Richings Park
West Drayton
Yiewsley
SOUTHALL
Hanwell
EALING
ACTON
Shepherd's Bush
KENSINGTON
WESTMINSTER
Cippenham
Dorney
Upton
Langley
Sutton
HESTON
CHISWICK
HAMMERSMITH
CHELSEA
Eton Wick
Boveney
Eton
Oakley Green
WINDSOR
Datchet
Colnbrook
Harmondsworth
Sipson
Harlington
Heston
Osterley
Brentford
Kew
North Sheen
BARNES
FULHAM
BATTERSEA
Horton
Poyle
Longford
Cranford
LONDON HEATHROW
ISLEWORTH
PUTNEY
Old Windsor
Wraysbury
Stanwell Moor
Stanwell
239
HOUNSLOW
RICHMOND
Roehampton
WANDSWORTH
CLAPHAM
Hythe End
East Bedfont
TWICKENHAM
Cranbourne
WINDSOR GREAT PARK
Legoland
M1
M25
M4
M40
A1(M)
A5
A6
A41
A40
A4
A30
A3
A413
A355
A414
A602
A505
A312
A316
A406

236
235
240
HERTFORDSHIRE
STEVENAGE
WELWYN GARDEN CITY
HERTFORD
WARE
HODDESDON
Broxbourne
CHESHUNT
Waltham Cross
WALTHAM ABBEY
HARLOW
Sawbridgeworth
BISHOP'S STORTFORD
Stansted Mountfitchet
LONDON-STANSTED
EPPING
Theydon Bois
LOUGHTON
CHIGWELL
Chipping Ongar
North Weald Bassett
BRENTWOOD
ENFIELD
CHINGFORD
EAST BARNET
SOUTHGATE
EDMONTON
WALTHAMSTOW
WOODFORD
TOTTENHAM
HORNSEY
WANSTEAD
ILFORD
ROMFORD
UPMINSTER
HORNCHURCH
LONDON
STRATFORD
BARKING
DAGENHAM
Rainham
HACKNEY
ISLINGTON
CAMDEN TOWN
WESTMINSTER
CITY
POPLAR
WOOLWICH
GREENWICH
LEWISHAM
CATFORD
ELTHAM
ERITH
Bexleyheath
Bexley
DARTFORD
GRAYS
TILBURY
Northfleet
THURROCK
Dartford-Thurrock River Crossing
Great Dunmow
Takeley
Buntingford
M11
M25
A10
A120
A414
A12
A13
A602

237
241
COLCHESTER
CHELMSFORD
BRAINTREE
WITHAM
MALDON
BASILDON
BILLERICAY
RAYLEIGH
SOUTHEND-ON-SEA
CANVEY ISLAND
GRAVESEND
SHEERNESS
Halstead
Coggeshall
Kelvedon
Tiptree
Wivenhoe
West Mersea
MERSEA ISLAND
Tollesbury
Heybridge
Danbury
South Woodham Ferrers
Burnham-on-Crouch
Southminster
Bradwell-on-Sea
Tillingham
Wickford
Hockley
Rochford
Hadleigh
Thundersley
South Benfleet
Corringham
Stanford-le-Hope
Shoeburyness
Great Wakering
FOULNESS ISLAND
Wallasea Island
Potton Island
Osea Island
Northey Island
Hullbridge
Great Baddow
Galleywood
Laindon
Minster
Thamesport
Isle of Grain
River Thames
River Crouch
RIVER BLACKWATER
Maplin Sands
Virley Channel
SHOEBURY NESS
Sales Point
Holliwell Point
Foulness Point
Warden Point
A12
A120
A130
A13
A127
A131
A414
A228
A249

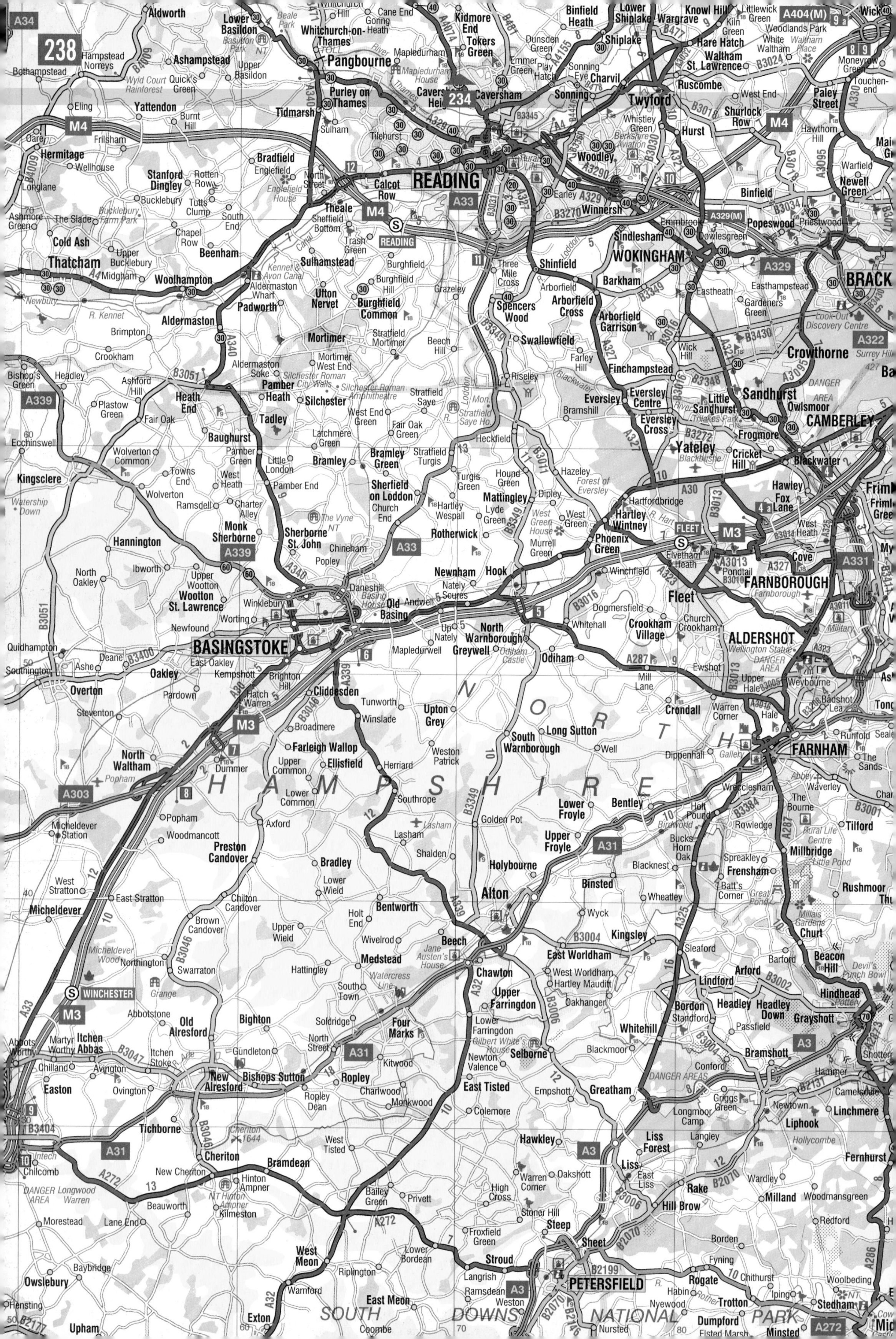

A34
238
Aldworth
Lower Basildon
Beale Park
Basildon Park
Whitchurch-on-Thames
Whitchurch Hill
Cane End
Goring Heath
Kidmore End
Tokers Green
Binfield Heath
Lower Shiplake
Wargrave
Knowl Hill
Littlewick Green
A404(M)
Wick
Hampstead Norreys
Ashampstead
Upper Basildon
Pangbourne
Mapledurham
Mapledurham House
Dunsden Green
Shiplake
Kiln Green
Woodlands Park
White Waltham
Waltham Place
Hare Hatch
Waltham St. Lawrence
Moneyrow Green
Touchen-end
Bothampstead
Wyld Court Rainforest
Quick's Green
Purley on Thames
Caversham Heights
234
Caversham
Emmer Green
Play Hatch
Sonning Eye
Charvil
Sonning
Twyford
Ruscombe
West End
Paley Street
Eling
Yattendon
Burnt Hill
Tidmarsh
Sulham
Tilehurst
Whistley Green
Berkshire Aviation
Hurst
Shurlock Row
M4
Hawthorn Hill
Oare
Frilsham
Hermitage
Wellhouse
Longlane
Bradfield
Englefield
Englefield House
Stanford Dingley
Rotten Row
Bucklebury
Tutts Clump
North Street
Calcot Row
READING
A33
Woodley
Winnersh
Earley
Rural Life
Warfield
Newell Green
Binfield
Ashmore Green
The Slade
Bucklebury Farm Park
South End
Chapel Row
Beenham
Theale
Sheffield Bottom
Trash Green
READING
Sindlesham
Emmbrook
Dowlesgreen
Popeswood
Priestwood
A329(M)
Cold Ash
Upper Bucklebury
Thatcham
Midgham
Newbury
Woolhampton
Kennet & Avon Canal
Aldermaston Wharf
Sulhamstead
Burghfield
Burghfield Hill
Three Mile Cross
Shinfield
Arborfield
WOKINGHAM
Barkham
A329
Easthampstead
Eastheath
BRACK
Padworth
Ufton Nervet
Burghfield Common
Grazeley
Spencers Wood
Arborfield Cross
Arborfield Garrison
Gardeners Green
Look-Out Discovery Centre
R. Kennet
Aldermaston
Brimpton
Crookham
Mortimer
Stratfield Mortimer
Mortimer West End
Beech Hill
Swallowfield
Farley Hill
Finchampstead
Wick Hill
Crowthorne
A322
Surrey Hill
Bishop's Green
Headley
Ashford Hill
Aldermaston Soke
Silchester Roman City Walls
Silchester Roman Amphitheatre
Pamber Heath
Silchester
Stratfield Saye
Stratfield Saye Ho.
Riseley
Blackwater
Eversley
Eversley Centre
Eversley Cross
Bramshill
Little Sandhurst
Sandhurst
Owlsmoor
Trilakes Park
A339
Plastow Green
Heath End
Fair Oak
Tadley
West End Green
Fair Oak Green
Heckfield
CAMBERLEY
Ecchinswell
Baughurst
Latchmere Green
Yateley
Blackbushe
Frogmore
Cricket Hill
Blackwater
Wolverton Common
Pamber Green
Little London
Bramley
Bramley Green
Stratfield Turgis
Hound Green
Hazeley
Forest of Eversley
Kingsclere
Towns End
West Heath
Pamber End
Sherfield on Loddon
Turgis Green
Mattingley
Dipley
Hawley
Fox Lane
Frimley
Watership Down
Wolverton
Ramsdell
Charter Alley
Church End
Hartley Wespall
Lyde Green
West Green
West Green House
Hartfordbridge
Hartley Wintney
FLEET
M3
West Heath
Monk Sherborne
The Vyne
Sherborne St. John
Rotherwick
Phoenix Green
Murrell Green
Elvetham Heath
Cove
A331
Hannington
A339
Chineham
Popley
A33
A3013
Pondtail
A327
North Oakley
Ibworth
Upper Wootton
Wootton St. Lawrence
Newnham
Hook
Winchfield
FARNBOROUGH
Farnborough
Winklebury
Daneshill
Basing House
Old Basing
Andwell
Nately Scures
Dogmersfield
Fleet
B3051
Worting
Newfound
Up Nately
North Warnborough
Whitehall
Crookham Village
Church Crookham
ALDERSHOT
Wellington Statue
Military
Quidhampton
BASINGSTOKE
Deane
Ashe
B3400
Mapledurwell
Greywell
Odiham Castle
Odiham
A287
Ewshot
DANGER AREA
Southington
East Oakley
Oakley
Kempshott
Brighton Hill
Mill Lane
Upper Hale
Weybourne
Overton
Pardown
Hatch Warren
Cliddesden
Tunworth
Badshot Lea
Steventon
Winslade
Upton Grey
Crondall
Warren Corner
Hale
Broadmere
M3
NORTH
Long Sutton
South Warnborough
Runfold
Farleigh Wallop
Weston Patrick
Well
Dippenhall
Gallery
FARNHAM
North Waltham
Dummer
Upper Common
Ellisfield
Herriard
The Sands
Popham
HAMPSHIRE
A303
Lower Common
Southrope
Wrecclesham
Waverley
Abbey
Lasham
Golden Pot
Lower Froyle
Bentley
Holt Pound
The Bourne
Micheldever Station
Popham
Woodmancott
Axford
Lasham
Upper Froyle
Birdworld
Rowledge
Rural Life Centre
Tilford
Preston Candover
Shalden
A31
Bucks Horn Oak
Spreakley
Millbridge
Little Pond
Bradley
Holybourne
Blacknest
Frensham
West Stratton
Lower Wield
Binsted
Wheatley
Batt's Corner
Great Pond
Rushmoor
East Stratton
Chilton Candover
Alton
Micheldever
Bentworth
Wyck
Millais Gardens
Holt End
Brown Candover
Upper Wield
Wivelrod
Beech
B3004
Kingsley
Churt
Jane Austen's House
Micheldever Wood
Northington
Medstead
East Worldham
Sleaford
Barford
Beacon Hill
Devil's Punch Bowl
Swarraton
Hattingley
Watercress Line
Chawton
West Worldham
Hartley Mauditt
Arford
Grange
South Town
Upper Farringdon
Oakhanger
Lindford
WINCHESTER
Abbotstone
Hindhead
M3
Old Alresford
Bighton
Soldridge
Four Marks
Lower Farringdon
Gilbert White's House
Bordon
Standford
Headley
Headley Down
Grayshott
Abbots Worthy
Martyr Worthy
Itchen Abbas
Itchen Stoke
North Street
Whitehill
Passfield
A3
B3047
Gundleton
A31
Selborne
Blackmoor
Bramshott
Shottermill
Chilland
Avington
New Alresford
Kitwood
Newton Valence
Conford
Hammer
Easton
Ovington
Bishops Sutton
Ropley
Charlwood
East Tisted
Empshott
Greatham
DANGER AREAS
Griggs Green
B2131
Camelsdale
Ropley Dean
Monkwood
Longmoor Camp
Newtown
Linchmere
B3404
Tichborne
Cheriton 1644
Colemore
Liphook
Langley
Hollycombe
West Tisted
Hawkley
Liss Forest
A31
A3
Fernhurst
Chilcomb
Cheriton
New Cheriton
Bramdean
Oakshott
Liss
East Liss
Hinton Ampner
NT Hinton Ampner
Warren Corner
Rake
Wardley
DANGER Longwood Warren AREA
Beauworth
A272
Kilmeston
Bailey Green
Privett
High Cross
Hill Brow
B3006
B2070
Milland
Woodmansgreen
Morestead
Lane End
Stoner Hill
Steep
Redford
A272
Froxfield Green
Sheet
Borden
Owslebury
Baybridge
West Meon
Lower Bordean
Stroud
Langrish
Fyning
Rogate
Chithurst
A286
Riplington
PETERSFIELD
B2199
Woolbeding
Hensting
Warnford
Ramsdean
A3
Habin
Iping
Stedham
East Meon
Weston
Nyewood
Trotton
Rother
B2177
Upham
Exton
SOUTH
Coombe
DOWNS
Nursted
NATIONAL
Dumpford
PARK
Elsted Marsh
A272
Minsted

239
235
240
Dorney
Eton Wick
Eton
Boveney
Oakley Green
WINDSOR
Datchet
Colnbrook
Poyle
Horton
Wraysbury
Drayton
Upton
Langley
Sutton
Harmondsworth
Sipson
Harlington
Longford
Cranford
HESTON
LONDON HEATHROW
Hatton
Stanwell
Stanwell Moor
East Bedfont
Brentford
Osterley
Heston
CHISWICK
HAMMERSMITH
BARNES
FULHAM
Kew
North Sheen
Syon Park
ISLEWORTH
HOUNSLOW
RICHMOND
PUTNEY
BATTERSEA
CHELSEA
CLAPHAM
WANDSWORTH
Roehampton
Upper Tooting
WIMBLEDON
STREATHAM
Old Windsor
WINDSOR GREAT PARK
Legoland
Cranbourne
Hythe End
ASHFORD
FELTHAM
Feltham hill
TWICKENHAM
Ham
Richmond Park
Hanworth
Hampton
TEDDINGTON
Hampton Wick
Hampton Court
Woodside
Englefield Green
Runnymede
Savill
Egham Hythe
STAINES
Cheapside
Ascot
EGHAM
Thorpe
Virginia Water
Sunningdale
South Ascot
Sunninghill
Laleham
Littleton
Queen Mary Resr.
SUNBURY
Upper Halliford
West Molesey
East Molesey
Thames Ditton
Shepperton
CHERTSEY
WALTON-ON-THAMES
SURBITON
Long Ditton
Tolworth
KINGSTON UPON THAMES
NEW MALDEN
MERTON
MORDEN
MITCHAM
Worcester Park
CARSHALTON
Beddington
SUTTON
WALLINGTON
Cheam
Broomhall
Trumps Green
Lyne
Longcross
Windlesham
WEYBRIDGE
Addlestone
New Haw
Ottershaw
Row Town
St. George's Hill
Hersham
Whiteley Village
ESHER
Claygate
Claremont
Hook
Chessington
Chessington World of Adventures
Bourne Hall
Valley End
Burrowhill
Lightwater
Chobham
Mimbridge
Fairoaks
Woodham
Donkey Town
West End
Castle Green
Sheerwater
Horsell
Byfleet
West Byfleet
Brooklands
Cobham
Fairmile
Oxshott
Malden Rushett
EPSOM
EWELL
Ashtead
Pachesham
Stoke D'Abernon
Painshill Park
Wisley
Pyrford
Pyrford Village
Downside
Bisley
Knaphill
WOKING
Old Woking
Ripley
Martyr's Green
Ockham
Semaphore Tower
COBHAM
LEATHERHEAD
Woodmansterne
BANSTEAD
Burgh Heath
Chipstead
COULSDON
Epsom Downs
Tadworth
Walton on the Hill
Kingswood
Hooley
Chaldon
Deepcut
Brookwood
Mayford
Send Marsh
Send
Effingham Common
Little Bookham
Fetcham
Headley
Mugswell
Pirbright
Fox Corner
Pyle Hill
Cartbridge
Burntcommon
Sutton Green
Worplesdon
Pitch Place
Jacobswell
West Horsley
East Horsley
Great Bookham
Mickleham
Lower Kingswood
Margery
Gatton
Merstham
Normandy
Fairlands
Willey Green
Wood Street Village
Stoughton
Burpham
Merrow
West Clandon
East Clandon
Clandon Park
Hatchlands Park
Newlands Corner
Effingham
Polesden Lacey
Westhumble
Box Hill
Ranmore Common
Denbies Wine Estate
Buckland
REDHILL
Wyke
Flexford
Onslow Village
Wanborough
GUILDFORD
Silent Pool
Sherbourne Farm
Westcott
DORKING
Betchworth
Brockham
REIGATE
Nutfield
South Nutfield
Artington
Littleton
Shalford
Chilworth
Albury
Shere
Gomshall
Wotton
Abinger Hammer
Puttenham
Compton
Loseley Park
Peasmarsh
Hog's Back
Shackleford
Farncombe
Wonersh
Blackheath
Brook
Sutton Abinger
Friday Street
Abinger Common
North Holmwood
South Holmwood
Strood Green
Stonebridge
Blackbrook
Gadbrook
Dawesgreen
Leigh
Doversgreen
Sidlow
Salfords
Redhill
Nalderswood
Peper Harow
Hurtmore
Eashing
Bramley
Catteshall
GODALMING
Shamley Green
Farley Green
Peaslake
Holmbury St. Mary
Hurtwood Common
Coldharbour
Leith Hill
Leith Hill Tower
Beare Green
Newdigate
Cudworth
Parkgate
Norwood Hill
Meath Green
HORLEY
Hookwood
LONDON-GATWICK
Elstead
Milford
Busbridge
Busbridge Lakes
Thorncombe Street
Winkworth Arboretum
Tuesley
Hydestile
Grafham
Rowly
Ewhurst
Forest Green
Capel
Ockley
Clark's Green
Charlwood
Lowfield Heath
Russ Hill
Tinsley Green
Langley Green
Fernhill
Wheelerstreet
Witley
Hascombe
Ewhurst Green
Mayes Green
Cranleigh
Walliswood
Hannah Peschar Sculpture
Ifieldwood
Ifield
CRAWLEY
Three Bridges
Pound Hill
Bowlhead Green
Wormley
Hambledon
Oakhurst Cottage
Loxhill
Vachery Pond
Oakwoodhill
Rusper
Lambs Green
Gossops Green
Maidenbower
Worth
Brook
Sandhills
Dunsfold
Alfold Crossways
Ellen's Green
Kingsfold
Faygate
Broadfield
Chiddingfold
Highstreet Green
Cox Green
Rowhook
Rudgwick
Warnham
Holmbush Farm World
Pease Pottage
PEASE POTTAGE
Haslemere
Ramster
Ramsnest Common
Alfold
Alfold Bars
Bucks Green
Strood Green
Broadbridge Heath
Roffey
Colgate
Tilgate Forest Row
ST. LEONARDS FOREST
Anstead brook
Fisherstreet
The Lake
Plaistow
Ifold
Loxwood
Tisman's Common
Park Street
The Haven
Slinfold
HORSHAM
Doomsday Green
High Beeches
Handcross
Balcombe
Roundhurst
Black Down
Northchapel
Ebernoe
Roundstreet Common
Five Oaks
Itchingfield
Tower Hill
Denne Park
Mannings Heath
Plummers Plain
Ashfold Crossways
Nymans
Staplefield
Slaugham
Lurgashall Winery
Dial Green
Lurgashall
Kirdford
Newpound Common
Barns Green
Southwater Street
Monk's Gate
Lower Beeding
Nuthurst
Brook Street
Slough Green
Lickfold
Bexleyhill
Balls Cross
Fishers Farm Park
Wisborough Green
Billingshurst
Southwater
Warninglid
Cuckfield
Crabtree
Strood Green
Parbrook
Brooks Green
Copsale
Maplehurst
WEST SUSSEX
Petworth House & Park
Lodsworth
River
Upperton
Adversane
Coneyhurst Common
Dragons Green
Bolney
Ansty
Petworth
Byworth
Tillington
Bedham
North Heath
Gay Street
Coolham
Broadford Bridge
Broomer's Corner
Shipley
Whitehall
Belloc's Mill
Knepp Castle
Cowfold
Kent Street
South Ambersham
Selham
SURREY
DOWNS
M25
M4
M3
M23
A4
A30
A3
A24
A25
A29
A31
A217
A232
A240
A243
A246
A264
A272
A281
A308
A316
A205
A214
A23

240
236
239
BERMONDSEY
LAMBETH
DEPTFORD
GREENWICH
WOOLWICH
ERITH
Purfleet
GRAYS
TILBURY
CAMBERWELL
BATTERSEA
BRIXTON
Charlton
Plumstead
Dartford-Thurrock River Crossing
West Thurrock
South Stifford
Blackheath
Kidbrooke
Welling
Bexleyheath
Slade Green
PUTNEY
CLAPHAM
LEWISHAM
ELTHAM
DARTFORD
Crayford
Greenhithe
Northfleet
Stone
Swanscombe
Ebbsfleet
WANDSWORTH
Lee
Blackfen
Bexley
Bluewater
CATFORD
Grove Park
Mottingham
New Eltham
SIDCUP
Old Bexley
Wilmington
Bean
Perry Street
Upper Tooting
Dulwich
West Norwood
Foots Cray
North Cray
Hextable
Hawley
Darenth
South Darenth
Betsham
Southfleet
Hook Green
Istead Rise
STREATHAM
Crystal Palace
Sydenham
Penge
South Norwood
CHISLEHURST
St. Paul's Cray
Swanley
Sutton at Hone
Longfield
New Barn
MERTON
MITCHAM
Thornton Heath
BECKENHAM
Petts Wood
St. Mary Cray
Horton Kirby
MORDEN
BROMLEY
Hayes
ORPINGTON
Crockenhill
Farningham
Hartley
Longfield Hill
Meopham Station
Addiscombe
Beddington
West Wickham
CROYDON
Keston
Eagle Heights
Roman Villa
Eynsford
Fawkham Green
New Ash Green
Meopham
CARSHALTON
Addington
Farnborough
Chelsfield
Well Hill
Maplescombe
Lullingstone Castle
Brands Hatch
Ash
SUTTON
WALLINGTON
New Addington
Green Street Green
Pratt's Bottom
West Kingsdown
Ridley
Selsdon
Leaves Green
Down House
Downe
Badgers Mount
Halstead
Shoreham
Knatts Valley
Stansted
Hodsoll Street
Fairseat
PURLEY
Sanderstead
Selsdon Wood
London Biggin Hill
Farleigh
Woodlands
Woodmansterne
Hamsey Green
Berry's Green
Cudham
Knockholt
Knockholt Pound
Otford
Kemsing
Heaverham
Wrotham
BANSTEAD
Kenley
Whyteleafe
Old Coulsdon
Chelsham
Biggin Hill
Chevening
COULSDON
Chipstead
Beaver Water World
Tatsfield
Dunton Green
Borough Green
Platt
WARLINGHAM
Chipstead
Riverhead
Seal
Ightham
Kingswood
Hooley
Chaldon
Woldingham
Clacket Lane
Brasted
Sundridge
SEVENOAKS
Claygate Cross
Crouch
Mugswell
CATERHAM
Godstone Vineyards
Titsey
Westerham
Knole
Ivy Hatch
Stone Street
Mereworth Woods
Plaxtol
Old Soar Manor
Limpsfield
Brasted Chart
Ightham Mote
Dunk's Green
Gatton
Merstham
Oxted
Moorhouse
Squerryes
Quebec Ho
French Street
The Chart
Emmetts
Ide Hill
Goathurst Common
Riverhill
Shipbourne
Warwick Wold
Godstone
Brewer Street
Limpsfield Chart
Hurst Green
Tandridge
Crockham Hill
Chartwell
Toy's Hill
Underriver
Sevenoaks Weald
REDHILL
Bletchingley
Nuffield
Coldharbour
Fletcher's Green
Pootings
Cooper's Corner
Pittswood
Hildenborough
SURREY
South Nutfield
Redhill
South Godstone
Marlpit Hill
Four Elms
Bough Beech Reservoir
Higham Wood
Golden Green
Crowhurst Lane End
Crowhurst
Chiddingstone Causeway
TONBRIDGE
Sidlow
Salfords
Outwood
Blindley Heath
Edenbridge
Bough Beech
How Green
Eden Valley
Haxted Mill
Leigh
Haysden
Tudeley
Five Oak Green
Wasp Green
Hever
Hever Castle
Chiddingstone
Chiddingstone Castle
Penshurst Place
Meath Green
HORLEY
Horne
British Wildlife Centre
Lingfield
Marsh Green
Penshurst
Bidborough
Crockhurst Street
Chiddingstone Hoath
Hookwood
Smallfield
Newchapel
Lingfield Park
Dormansland
Markbeech
Southborough
Salomons
High Brooms
LONDON-GATWICK
Burstow
Felcourt
Smart's Hill
Speldhurst
Charlwood
Lowfield Heath
Fernhill
Shipley Bridge
Tinsley Green
Copthorne
Dormans Park
Cowden
Langton Green
Rusthall
ROYAL TUNBRIDGE WELLS
Kipping's Cross
Langley Green
Felbridge
Hammerwood
EAST GRINSTEAD
Hammerwood Park
Holtye
Blackham
Fordcombe
Ashurst
Stone Cross
The Pantiles
Ifield
Three Bridges
Pound Hill
Crawley Down
Sunnyside
Ashurst Wood
Ball's Green
Groombridge
Groombridge Place
High Rocks
Spa Valley Railway
Worth
Maidenbower
Saint Hill
Standen
Forest Row
Upper Hartfield
Hartfield
Withyham
Harrison's Rocks
Park Corner
Eridge Green
Eridge Park
Frant
Bells Yew Green
Broadfield
Turners Hill
Weir Wood Resr.
Mott's Mill
The Platt
Wood's Green
Pease Pottage
Selsfield Common
Priest House
Coleman's Hatch
Pooh Bridge
Lye Green
Friar's Gate
Chuck Hatch
Wych Cross
Tilgate Forest Row
Balcombe Lane
West Hoathly
Sharpthorne
Boarshead
Durgates
Ashdown Forest
Llama Park
ASHDOWN FOREST
Steel Cross
Wakehurst Place
CROWBOROUGH
Poundfield
Mark Cross
Best Beech Hill
Handcross
Nymans
High Beeches
West Hill
Balcombe
South of England Centre
Ardingly Resr.
Highbrook
Ardingly
Chelwood Gate
Nutley Marlpits
Poundgate
Town Row
Jarvis Brook
Rotherfield
Riseden
Tidebrook
Staplefield
WEST SUSSEX
Horsted Keynes
Chelwood Common
Duddleswell
Slaugham
Viaduct
Danehill
Bluebell Railway
Nutley
Heron's Ghyll
Coggins Mill
EAST
Brook Street
Slough Green
Borde Hill
HAYWARDS HEATH
Whitemans Green
Heaven Farm
Furner's Green
Fairwarp
High Hurstwood
Mayfield
River Rother
Cuckfield
Lindfield
Sheffield Green
Sheffield Park
Butcher's Cross
Hadlow Down
Five Ashes
Maresfield
Five Ash Down
Pound Green
Wilderness Wood
Paine's Corner
Bolney
Ansty
Scayne's Hill
Fletching
Piltdown
Buxted
Uckfield
Grisling Common
North Common
North Chailey
Newick
Shortbridge
Pounsley
Blackboys
Rosers Cross
Cross in Hand
Heathfield
Cade Street
Broad Oak
M25
M20
M26
M23
A20
A21
A22
A23
A25
A26
A264
A272

Blythe Sands
Linford
East Tilbury
Coalhouse Fort
The Lower Hope
Cliffe Marshes
Halstow Marshes
St. Mary's Marshes
Allhallows-on-Sea
Allhallows
St. Mary Hoo
Grain
Cliffe
Cooling
High Halstow
Fenn Street
Lower Stoke
237
A228
B2001
Stoke
Wallend
Isle of Grain
Heritage Cen.
SHEERNESS
GRAVESEND
Chantry
DANGER AREA
Chalk
Church Street
Cooling Street
Lower Higham
Cliffe Woods
Sharnal Street
Hoo St. Werburgh
North Street
Thamesport
A249
Mile Town
Marine Town
Halfway Houses
Minster
East End
Warden Point
Higham
Chattenden
B2000
Shorne
Shorne Ridgeway
Thong
Wainscott
Lower Upnor
Upper Upnor
Kingsnorth
RIVER MEDWAY
B2007
Queenborough
Chetney Marshes
Rushenden
A250
B2008
Eastchurch
Brambledown
B2231
Warden
Leysdown-on-Sea
Owletts NT
Cobham
Frindsbury
STROOD
Brompton
Borstal
Cath.
ROCHESTER
GILLINGHAM
B2004
Lower Rainham
Upchurch
Otterham Quay
Ham Green
Lower Halstow
Iwade
ISLE OF SHEPPEY
Elmley Island
Isle of Harty
The Swale
Henley Street
Cuxton
Green
Luddesdown
North Halling
Upper Halling
Halling
Wouldham
M2
MEDWAY TOWNS
CHATHAM
Rainham
Hempstead
Wigmore
Walderslade
Rochester
A228
A229
A2045
A278
Hartlip
Newington
A2
Howt Green
Bobbing
Milton Regis
Kemsley
Sittingbourne & Kemsley Light Railway
Key Street
SITTINGBOURNE
Conyer
Teynham Street
Uplees
Oare
Graveney
Burham
Blue Bell Hill
Kit's Coty House
Eccles
MEDWAY
Yelsted
Bredhurst
Stockbury
Danaway
Oad Street
Borden
Tunstall
Bapchild
Rodmersham
Highsted
Rodmersham Green
Lynsted
Teynham
Luddenham
FAVERSHAM
Lewson Street
Ospringe
Preston
A299
Snodland
Birling
Ham Hill
New Hythe
Lunsford
The Friars
Aylesford
Leybourne
Larkfield
West Malling
East Malling
Ditton
Allington
Sandling
Boxley
Detling
Thurnham
Kent County Showground
South Green
Hucking
Bicknor
Swanton Street
Bredgar
Bredgar & Wormshill Light Railway
Wormshill
Milstead
Frinsted
Dungate
Erriottwood
M2
Newnham
Bluetown
Doddington
Doddington Place
Painter's Forstal
Brogdale
North Street
Eastling
Belmont
Sheldwich
Sheldwich Lees
Hogben's Hill
Selling
A251
A2
Offham
MAIDSTONE
B2246
Broad Street
MAIDSTONE
M20
Hollingbourne
Eyhorne Street
Ringlestone
Wichling
West Street
Throwley
Perrywood
Badlesmere
Throwley Forstal
Leaveland
Shottenden
Kings Hill
Kent Street
Barming Heath
Barming
B2010
Bearsted
Stoneacre NT
Teston
Shepway
Otham
Leeds
Wateringbury
West Farleigh
East Farleigh
Loose
A274
A26
Nettlestead
B2163
Boughton Green
Langley
Chart Corner
Leeds
Broomfield
Langley Heath
Harrietsham
Lenham
Warren Street
Stalisfield Green
A20
Leadingcross Green
Sandway
Platt's Heath
Lenham Heath
Charing Hill
Stocker's Head
A252
Challock
Molash
Nettlestead Green
B2015
Coxheath
Yalding
Linton
Boughton Monchelsea
Chart Sutton
Kingswood
Fairbourne Heath
Charing Heath
Charing
Paddock
The Lees
Beech Court
Bilting
Boughton Aluph
Hale Street
Laddingford
Benover
Hunton
A229
Sutton Valence
Ulcombe
Grafty Green
Boughton Malherbe
Westwell Leacon
Wye
East Peckham
Hop Farm Family Park
Beltring
B2162
Chainhurst
Beult
Egerton
Egerton Forstal
Westwell
Boughton Lees
Kempe's Corner
Queen Street
Collier Street
Milebush
Wanshurst Green
Cross-at-Hand
Hawkenbury
Southernden
Pluckley
Little Chart
Ram Lane
Goat Lees
M20
A2042
Bybrook
Paddock Wood
LOW WEALD
Claygate
Marden
Headcorn
Lashenden Air Warfare
Hothfield
Godinton House
Kennington
ASHFORD
Willesborough Lees
Hinxhill
Marden Beech
Marden Thorn
Staplehurst
Smarden Bell
Lashenden (Headcorn)
Biddenden Green
Maltman's Hill
B2160
Castle Hill
Brenchley
Iden Croft Herbs
Sinkhurst Green
Smarden
Great Chart
B2229
Willesborough
Matfield
Winchet Hill
Curtisden Green
Frittenden
Lashenden
Haffenden Quarter
Wissenden
Daniel's Water
Singleton
Chilmington Green
Sevington
Pembury
Petteridge
Horsmonden
Sprivers NT
Standen
Bethersden
A21
Marle Place
Hazel Street
A229
Three Chimneys
Hareplain
Kingsnorth
To CHANNEL TUNNEL 8 Miles
Lamberhurst Quarter
Cranbrook Common
Sissinghurst Castle NT
Brissenden Green
Stubb's Cross
Cheeseman's Green
Goudhurst
Flishinghurst
Biddenden
Shadoxhurst
Bromley Green
Aldington Frith
A262
Iden Green
Glassenbury
Wilsley Green
Sissinghurst
Durrant Green
High Halden
A2070
Lamberhurst
Finchcocks
Goddard's Green
Union
Hemsted Forest
Biddenden Vineyards
Shirkoak
Bonnington
Scotney Castle
Riseden
B2085
Cranbrook
East End
St. Michaels
Woodchurch
Orlestone
Bilsington
Vineyard
Kilndown
Hartley
Goddard's Green
Railway
Tenterden
South of England Rare Breeds Centre
Hamstreet
Ruckinge
Monument
B2100
B2079
B2086
Benenden
B2067
Brook Street
Cousley Wood
Wadhurst
Bewl Water
Bedgebury National Pinetum
Bedgebury Forest
Hole Park
Strood
Leigh Green
Kenardington
Warehorne
Three Leg Cross
Union Street
Gill's Green
Iden Green
Gun Green
Dingleden
Rolvenden
B2082
B2080
Home's Place Chapel
Royal Military Canal
Newchurch
Flimwell
Hawkhurst
A268
Vehicles
Rolvenden Layne
Vineyard
Small Hythe
Smallhythe Place NT
Reading Street
Appledore Heath
Snave
ROMNEY MARSH
Ticehurst
B2099
B2087
Horns Corner
The Moor
Four Throws
Standen Street
Sandhurst
A28
Peening Quarter
Isle of Oxney
Appledore
Snargate
Pashley Manor
King John's Lodge
Swiftsden
Merriments
Vineyard
Wittersham
Stone in Oxney
B2080
Ivychurch
A229
Hurst Green
Sandhurst Cross
Newenden
Kent & East Sussex Railway
Moon's Green
The Stocks
Brenzett
Aeronautical
SUSSEX
A21
Rother
Stocks
Rother Levels
Fairfield
Etchingham
Bodiam
NT
Great Dixter
R. Rother
Witherenden Hill
A268
Brookland
Old Romney
Burwash
A265
R. Dudwell
Bateman's
Salehurst
B2244
Northiam
Beckley
Four Oaks
A259
Ewhurst Green
Mill Corner
Peasmarsh
Iden
Clayhill
Rye Foreign
B2082
Houghton Green
WALLAND MARSH
Burwash Weald
Robertsbridge
Staplecross
B2165
A259
B2075
Oxley's Green
Playden
Brightling
Hollingrove
Darwell
John's Cross
Vinehall
Cripp's Corner
B2089
Chitcombe
A28
Rye
East Guldeford
Lydd
A20
Selling
Broad Street

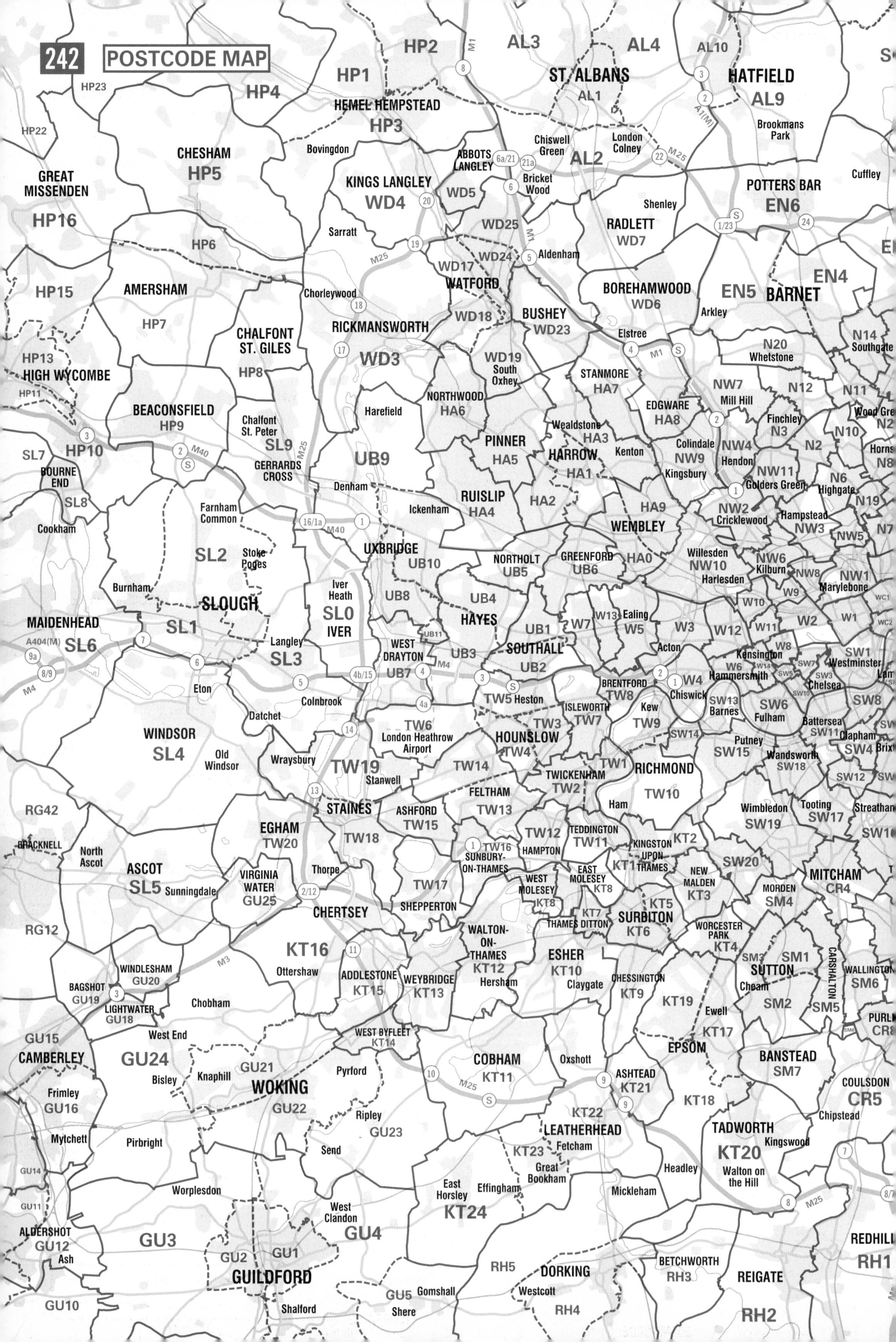
HP2
AL3
AL4
AL10
HP1
HP4
ST. ALBANS
AL1
HATFIELD
AL9
HP23
HEMEL HEMPSTEAD
HP3
Brookmans Park
HP22
Bovingdon
Chiswell Green
London Colney
AL2
CHESHAM
HP5
ABBOTS LANGLEY
Bricket Wood
Cuffley
GREAT MISSENDEN
KINGS LANGLEY
WD4
WD5
POTTERS BAR
EN6
HP16
Shenley
Sarratt
WD25
RADLETT
WD7
HP6
WD24
Aldenham
WD17
WATFORD
EN4
HP15
AMERSHAM
Chorleywood
BOREHAMWOOD
WD6
EN5
BARNET
Arkley
HP7
RICKMANSWORTH
BUSHEY
WD23
WD18
CHALFONT ST. GILES
Elstree
N14
Southgate
HP13
WD3
WD19
South Oxhey
N20
Whetstone
HIGH WYCOMBE
HP8
STANMORE
HA7
NW7
Mill Hill
N12
N11
HP11
NORTHWOOD
HA6
Harefield
EDGWARE
HA8
BEACONSFIELD
HP9
Chalfont St. Peter
SL9
Wealdstone
HA3
Finchley
N3
N10
Wood Green
N22
SL7
HP10
PINNER
HA5
Kenton
Colindale
NW4
NW9
N2
Hornsey
N8
BOURNE END
GERRARDS CROSS
UB9
HARROW
HA1
Hendon
Kingsbury
NW11
Golders Green
N6
Highgate
SL8
Farnham Common
Denham
RUISLIP
HA4
HA2
HA9
N19
Cookham
Ickenham
NW2
Cricklewood
Hampstead
NW3
WEMBLEY
N7
NW5
SL2
Stoke Poges
UXBRIDGE
UB10
NORTHOLT
UB5
GREENFORD
UB6
HA0
Willesden
NW10
NW6
Kilburn
NW8
NW1
Marylebone
Burnham
SLOUGH
Iver Heath
UB8
UB4
Harlesden
W9
W10
WC1
MAIDENHEAD
SL1
SL0
IVER
HAYES
UB1
W7
W13
Ealing
W5
W3
W12
W11
W2
W1
WC2
SL6
Langley
SL3
WEST DRAYTON
UB11
UB3
SOUTHALL
UB2
Acton
W8
Kensington
W14
SW7
SW1
Westminster
UB7
W6
Hammersmith
SW5
SW3
Chelsea
SW10
A404(M)
M4
Eton
Colnbrook
TW5
Heston
BRENTFORD
TW8
W4
Chiswick
SW13
Barnes
SW6
Fulham
SW8
Datchet
ISLEWORTH
TW7
Kew
TW9
Battersea
SW11
Clapham
WINDSOR
SL4
Old Windsor
TW6
London Heathrow Airport
TW3
HOUNSLOW
TW4
SW14
Putney
SW15
Wandsworth
SW18
SW4
Brixton
Wraysbury
TW19
Stanwell
TW14
TW1
RICHMOND
TWICKENHAM
TW2
SW12
SW9
RG42
STAINES
ASHFORD
TW15
FELTHAM
TW13
Ham
TW10
Wimbledon
SW19
Tooting
SW17
Streatham
SW16
BRACKNELL
North Ascot
EGHAM
TW20
TW18
TW12
HAMPTON
TW16
SUNBURY-ON-THAMES
TEDDINGTON
TW11
KINGSTON UPON THAMES
KT2
KT1
SW20
ASCOT
SL5
Sunningdale
VIRGINIA WATER
GU25
Thorpe
TW17
WEST MOLESEY
KT8
EAST MOLESEY
NEW MALDEN
KT3
MITCHAM
CR4
MORDEN
SM4
CHERTSEY
SHEPPERTON
KT7
THAMES DITTON
SURBITON
KT5
KT6
WORCESTER PARK
KT4
RG12
KT16
WALTON-ON-THAMES
KT12
Hersham
ESHER
KT10
Claygate
SM3
SM1
SUTTON
Cheam
SM2
CARSHALTON
SM5
WALLINGTON
SM6
WINDLESHAM
GU20
M3
Ottershaw
ADDLESTONE
KT15
WEYBRIDGE
KT13
CHESSINGTON
KT9
KT19
Ewell
BAGSHOT
GU19
LIGHTWATER
GU18
Chobham
PURLEY
CR8
GU15
West End
WEST BYFLEET
KT14
KT17
EPSOM
BANSTEAD
SM7
CAMBERLEY
GU24
Knaphill
GU21
Pyrford
COBHAM
KT11
Oxshott
ASHTEAD
KT21
Bisley
WOKING
M25
Frimley
GU16
GU22
Ripley
GU23
KT22
KT18
TADWORTH
COULSDON
CR5
Chipstead
Mytchett
Pirbright
Send
LEATHERHEAD
Fetcham
KT23
Great Bookham
KT20
Kingswood
GU14
East Horsley
Effingham
Headley
Walton on the Hill
Worplesdon
KT24
Mickleham
GU11
West Clandon
GU4
ALDERSHOT
GU12
Ash
GU3
GU2
GU1
GUILDFORD
RH5
DORKING
BETCHWORTH
RH3
REIGATE
REDHILL
RH1
GU5
Gomshall
Westcott
RH4
GU10
Shalford
Shere
RH2

HODDESDON
EN11
CM19
HARLOW
CM18
CM17
CM1
CHELMSFORD
BROXBOURNE
EN10
Writtle
North Weald
Bassett
ONGAR
CM5
CM2
EN7
Cheshunt
WALTHAM CROSS
EN8
WALTHAM
ABBEY
EN9
EPPING
CM16
Galleywood
INGATESTONE
CM4
Stock
Theydon
Bois
ENFIELD
EN1
EN3
Ponders
End
LOUGHTON
IG10
CM15
CM3
Abridge
RM4
Stapleford
Abbotts
CM14
SS11
N9
Edmonton
Chingford
E4
BUCKHURST
HILL
IG9
CHIGWELL
IG7
Shenfield
BRENTWOOD
BILLERICAY
CM12
CM11
SS12
N18
WOODFORD GREEN
IG8
Hainault
Harold Hill
RM3
Tottenham
N17
RM5
RM1
Ingrave
CM13
E17
Walthamstow
E18
IG5
IG6
ROMFORD
RM2
SS15
SS14
Laindon
BASILDON
SS13
N15
IG4
ILFORD
RM6
E11
Wanstead
IG2
RM7
RM11
West
Horndon
Stoke
Newington
N16
E10
Leyton
IG1
IG3
HORNCHURCH
UPMINSTER
SS16
E5
E12
RM8
RM10
RM12
Elm Park
RM14
E8
Hackney
E9
E20
Stratford
E15
E7
DAGENHAM
Corringham
E3
Bow
E13
East Ham
E6
BARKING
IG11
RM9
SOUTH
OCKENDON
SS17
STANFORD-LE-HOPE
E2
LONDON
E1
RAINHAM
RM13
RM15
RM16
EC2
EC3
Poplar
E14
E16
City
Airport
Thamesmead
SE28
Aveley
Chadwell
St. Mary
Southwark
SE1
SE16
DA18
BELVEDERE
PURFLEET
RM19
GRAYS
RM17
SE17
SE8
SE7
Charlton
Woolwich
SE18
SE2
DA17
ERITH
DA8
West
Thurrock
RM20
Camberwell
SE5
Greenwich
SE10
SE14
Peckham
SE15
SE3
Blackheath
WELLING
DA16
DA7
BEXLEYHEATH
TILBURY RM18
SE4
SE13
Lewisham
DA6
Crayford
ME3
SE22
SE12
Eltham
DA1
GREENHITHE
DA9
Northfleet
SWANSCOMBE
DA10
SE21
Dulwich
SE23
Catford
SE6
SE9
DA15
BEXLEY
DA5
DARTFORD
DA11
GRAVESEND
Mottingham
SIDCUP
Wilmington
DA2
Higham
SE27
SE26
Grove Park
DA14
DA12
Norwood
SE19
CHISLEHURST
BR7
BR1
Shorne
SE20
Hextable
ROCHESTER
BECKENHAM
BR3
BROMLEY
St. Paul's Cray
BR5
SWANLEY
DA4
LONGFIELD
Cobham
SE25
St. Mary Cray
BR8
DA3
ME2
BR2
Hayes
Farningham
M20
Meopham
CROYDON
CR0
WEST
WICKHAM
BR4
ORPINGTON
BR6
M25
New Ash
Green
DA13
ME1
Chelsfield
Eynsford
Halling
Farnborough
SOUTH CROYDON
CR2
Sanderstead
KESTON
BR2
New
Addington
West
Kingsdown
ME5
SNODLAND
ME6
Downe
Halstead
Otford
KENLEY
CR8
WARLINGHAM
CR6
WHYTELEAFE
CR3
Biggin
Hill
Kemsing
M26
Wrotham
AYLESFORD
ME20
Larkfield
Ditton
TN14
Borough
Green
TN15
WEST MALLING
ME19
Seal
CATERHAM
CR3
Woldingham
TN16
SEVENOAKS
Ightham
Kings Hill
MAIDSTONE
ME16
WESTERHAM
TN13
Mereworth
Limpsfield
OXTED
RH8
GODSTONE
ME18
ME15
RH9
South
Godstone
TN11
ME17
Hildenborough
TN10
Posttown Boundary
Postcode Boundary
RH7
EDENBRIDGE
TN8
TONBRIDGE
TN9
TN12
M11
M2

Bovingdon
Chesham
AMERSHAM
Kings Langley
Abbots Langley
Chiswell Green
London Colney
Bricket Wood
Radlett
Brookmans Park
South Mimms
SOUTH MIMMS
Potters Bar
Borehamwood
Cockfosters
BARNET
WATFORD
Chorleywood
Rickmansworth
Bushey
Elstree
LONDON GATEWAY
Mill Hill
Southgate
South Oxhey
Chalfont St. Giles
Chalfont St. Peter
Northwood
Stanmore
Edgware
Finchley
BEACONSFIELD
Harefield
Pinner
Wealdstone
HARROW
Hendon
Gerrards Cross
Denham
Ruislip
Highgate
Cricklewood
Neasden
Hampstead
Holloway
Sudbury
Wembley
Uxbridge
Northolt
Willesden
Harlesden
Kilburn
Camden Town
Stoke Poges
Hillingdon
Greenford
Burnham
Iver
Yiewsley
Hayes
EALING
Acton
Paddington
Marylebone
SLOUGH
Langley
West Drayton
Southall
Hanwell
Shepherds Bush
Kensington
West End
Westminster
Eton
Windsor
Datchet
Colnbrook
Harmondsworth
Harlington
HESTON
Brentford
Kew
Chiswick
Hammersmith
Chelsea
Fulham
Battersea
Poyle
LONDON HEATHROW AIRPORT
HOUNSLOW
Isleworth
Barnes
Clapham
RICHMOND
Putney
Wandsworth
Wraysbury
Stanwell
Feltham
Twickenham
Englefield Green
Egham
STAINES
Ashford
Teddington
Tooting
Wimbledon
Hampton
Sunbury
KINGSTON UPON THAMES
New Malden
Merton
Morden
Mitcham
Ascot
Virginia Water
Sunningdale
West Molesey
East Molesey
Chertsey
Shepperton
Surbiton
Worcester Park
Walton-on-Thames
Esher
SUTTON
Wallington
Windlesham
Weybridge
Addlestone
Chessington
Carshalton
Cheam
Ewell
Chobham
Lightwater
West End
West Byfleet
Byfleet
Oxshott
EPSOM
Cobham
Banstead
Bisley
Ashtead
WOKING
COBHAM
Due Open Late 2012
Chipstead
Ripley
LEATHERHEAD
Tadworth
Pirbright
Fetcham
Kingswood
Walton on the Hill
East Horsley
Great Bookham
DORKING
Redhill
GUILDFORD
REIGATE
M1
M3
M4
M25
M40
A1(M)
SCALE

ZONE GREATER LONDON LOW EMISSION ZONE

Cheshunt
Cuffley
Waltham Cross
Waltham Abbey
Epping
Chipping Ongar
Theydon Bois
Margaretting
Ingatestone
Kelvedon Hatch
Abridge
Stapleford Abbotts
ENFIELD
Loughton
BILLERICAY
BRENTWOOD
Chingford
Edmonton
Chigwell
Buckhurst Hill
Woodford
Hainault
Collier Row
Harold Hill
Wood Green
Tottenham
Walthamstow
Redbridge
ROMFORD
Laindon
Harringay
Chadwell Heath
Hornchurch
Wanstead
Leyton
Stoke Newington
Ilford
Upminster
Elm Park
Dagenham
Stratford
Islington
Hackney
BARKING
North Ockendon
West Ham
East Ham
Shoreditch
Bethnal Green
Bow
Rainham
City
Stepney
Canning Town
Docklands
South Ockendon
Aveley
Southwark
Bermondsey
Thamesmead
THURROCK
Lambeth
Woolwich
Erith
Purfleet
West Thurrock
Grays
Chadwell St. Mary
Deptford
Charlton
Greenwich
Camberwell
Peckham
Welling
Tilbury
Lewisham
Blackheath
Brixton
Swanscombe
Eltham
Bexleyheath
Crayford
Northfleet
Catford
Bexley
DARTFORD
GRAVESEND
Sidcup
Wilmington
Sydenham
Penge
Chislehurst
BROMLEY
Beckenham
Longfield
St. Mary Cray
Swanley
West Wickham
Crockenhill
Meopham
ORPINGTON
CROYDON
New Ash Green
Keston
Farnborough
Chelsfield
West Kingsdown
New Addington
Downe
Halstead
Sanderstead
Cudham
Kenley
Whyteleafe
Biggin Hill
Knockholt
Coulsdon
Warlingham
West Malling
Borough Green
Tatsfield
Caterham
SEVENOAKS
Kings Hill
CLACKET LANE
Westerham
Oxted
Godstone

LOW EMISSION ZONE

The Low Emission Zone is a specified area of Greater London within which the most polluting diesel-engined vehicles are required to meet specific emissions standards. If they do not they will need to pay a daily charge.

From 3rd January 2012 any lorry, bus, coach or other heavy diesel vehicle (more than 3.5 tonnes) must meet Euro IV emission standard for particulate matter (PM) - at present this is Euro III.

From 3rd January 2012 any larger van (1.205 tonnes), minibus or specialist diesel vehicle

INDEX

Including Streets, Places & Areas, Industrial Estates,
Selected Flats & Walkways, Junction Names & Service Areas and Selected Places of Interest.

HOW TO USE THIS INDEX

1. Each street name is followed by its Postcode District (or, if outside the London Postcodes, by its Locality Abbreviation(s)) and then by its map reference; e.g. **Abbey Av.** HA0: Wemb . . . . 40Na **67** is in the HA0 Postcode District and the Wembley Locality and is to be found in square 40Na on page **67**. The page number being shown in bold type.

2. A strict alphabetical order is followed in which Av., Rd., St., etc. (though abbreviated) are read in full and as part of the street name; e.g. **Alder M.** appears after **Aldermary Rd.** but before **Aldermoor Rd.**

3. Streets and a selection of flats and walkways that cannot be shown on the mapping, appear in the index with the thoroughfare to which they are connected shown in brackets; e.g. **Abbey Pde.** *SW19 . . . .66Eb* ***133*** *(off Merton High St.)*

4. Addresses that are in more than one part are referred to as not continuous.

5. Places and areas are shown in the index in **BLUE TYPE** and the map reference is to the actual map square in which the town centre or area is located and not to the place name shown on the map; e.g. **ABBEY WOOD 49Yc 95**

6. An example of a selected place of interest is **Barnet Mus. 14Ab 30**

7. Park & Ride are shown in the index in **Blue Type**; e.g. **Bromley (Park & Ride) 72Kc 159**

8. Junction names and Service Areas are shown in the index in **BOLD CAPITAL TYPE**; e.g. **ANGEL EDMONTON JUNC. 22Wb 51**

9. Map references for entries that appear on large scale pages **214-231** are shown first, with small scale map references shown in brackets; e.g. **Abbey St.** SE1 . . . .3J **231** (48Ub **91**)

GENERAL ABBREVIATIONS

All. : Alley
App. : Approach
Arc. : Arcade
Av. : Avenue
Bk. : Back
Blvd. : Boulevard
Bri. : Bridge
B'way. : Broadway
Bldg. : Building
Bldgs. : Buildings
Bungs. : Bungalows
Bus. : Business
C'way. : Causeway
Cen. : Centre
Chu. : Church
Chyd. : Churchyard
Circ. : Circle
Cir. : Circus
Cl. : Close
Coll. : College
Comn. : Common
Cnr. : Corner
Cott. : Cottage
Cotts. : Cottages
Ct. : Court
Cres. : Crescent
Cft. : Croft
Dpt. : Depot
Dr. : Drive
E. : East
Emb. : Embankment
Ent. : Enterprise
Est. : Estate
Fld. : Field
Flds. : Fields
Gdn. : Garden
Gdns. : Gardens
Gth. : Garth
Ga. : Gate
Gt. : Great
Grn. : Green
Gro. : Grove
Hgts. : Heights
Ho. : House
Ho's. : Houses
Ind. : Industrial
Info. : Information
Intl. : International
Junc. : Junction
La. : Lane
Lit. : Little
Lwr. : Lower
Mnr. : Manor
Mans. : Mansions
Mkt. : Market
Mdw. : Meadow
Mdws. : Meadows
M. : Mews
Mt. : Mount
Mus. : Museum
Nth. : North
No. : Number
Pal. : Palace
Pde. : Parade
Pk. : Park
Pas. : Passage
Pav. : Pavilion
Pl. : Place
Pct. : Precinct
Prom. : Promenade
Quad. : Quadrant
Res. : Residential
Ri. : Rise
Rd. : Road
Rdbt. : Roundabout
Shop. : Shopping
Sth. : South
Sq. : Square
Sta. : Station
St. : Street
Ter. : Terrace
Twr. : Tower
Trad. : Trading
Up. : Upper
Va. : Vale
Vw. : View
Vs. : Villas
Vis. : Visitors
Wlk. : Walk
W. : West
Yd. : Yard

LOCALITY ABBREVIATIONS

Ab L : **Abbots Langley**
Abr : **Abridge**
Addtn : **Addington**
Add : **Addlestone**
A'ham : **Aldenham**
Ark : **Arkley**
Asc : **Ascot**
Ash : **Ash**
Ashf : **Ashford**
Asht : **Ashtead**
Avel : **Aveley**
Bad M : **Badger's Mount**
Bans : **Banstead**
Bark : **Barking**
Barn : **Barnet**
Beac : **Beaconsfield**
Bean : **Bean**
Beck : **Beckenham**
Bedd : **Beddington**
Bedf : **Bedfont**
Bedm : **Bedmond**
Belv : **Belvedere**
Berk : **Berkhamsted**
Bes G : **Bessels Green**
Bet : **Betchworth**
Bexl : **Bexley**
Bex : **Bexleyheath**
Big H : **Biggin Hill**
Bisl : **Bisley**
Blet : **Bletchingley**
Bluew : **Bluewater**
Bookh : **Bookham**
Bore : **Borehamwood**
Bor G : **Borough Green**
Bov : **Bovingdon**
Box H : **Box Hill**
Bras : **Brasted**
B Char : **Brasted Chart**
Bford : **Brentford**
B'wood : **Brentwood**
Brick W : **Bricket Wood**
Brim : **Brimsdown**
Brom : **Bromley**
Brk P : **Brookmans Park**
Brkwd : **Brookwood**
Buck H : **Buckhurst Hill**
Bkld : **Buckland**
Bucks : **Bucks Hill**
Bulp : **Bulphan**
Burn : **Burnham**
Burp : **Burpham**
Bush : **Bushey**
B Hea : **Bushy Heath**
Byfl : **Byfleet**
Cars : **Carshalton**
Cat'm : **Caterham**
Chad H : **Chadwell Heath**
Chaf H : **Chafford Hundred**
Chal G : **Chalfont St Giles**
Chal P : **Chalfont St Peter**
Chan C : **Chandler's Cross**
Cheam : **Cheam**
Chels : **Chelsfield**
Chen : **Chenies**
Chert : **Chertsey**
Chesh : **Cheshunt**
Chess : **Chessington**
Chev : **Chevening**
Chig : **Chigwell**
Chfd : **Chipperfield**
Chip : **Chipstead**
Chst : **Chislehurst**
Chis G : **Chiswell Green**
Chob : **Chobham**
Chor : **Chorleywood**
Clay : **Claygate**
Cobh : **Cobham**
Cockf : **Cockfosters**
Col R : **Collier Row**
Coln : **Colnbrook**
Col H : **Colney Heath**
Col S : **Colney Street**
Coop : **Coopersale**
Corr : **Corringham**
Coul : **Coulsdon**
Cowl : **Cowley**
Cran : **Cranford**
Cray : **Crayford**
Crew H : **Crews Hill**
Crock : **Crockenhill**
Crou : **Crouch**
C'rst : **Crowhurst**
Crox G : **Croxley Green**
C'don : **Croydon**
Cud : **Cudham**
Cuff : **Cuffley**
Dag : **Dagenham**
Daren : **Darenth**
Dart : **Dartford**
Dat : **Datchet**
Den : **Denham**
Dodd : **Doddinghurst**
Dor : **Dorney**
Dor R : **Dorney Reach**
Downe : **Downe**
D'side : **Downside**
D Grn : **Dunk's Green**
Dun G : **Dunton Green**
E Barn : **East Barnet**
E Clan : **East Clandon**
E Hor : **East Horsley**
E Mos : **East Molesey**
E Til : **East Tilbury**
Eastc : **Eastcote**
Ebbs : **Ebbsfleet**
Eden : **Edenbridge**
Edg : **Edgware**
Eff : **Effingham**
Eff J : **Effingham Junction**
Egh : **Egham**
E'tree : **Elstree**
Enf : **Enfield**
Enf H : **Enfield Highway**
Enf L : **Enfield Lock**
Enf W : **Enfield Wash**
Eng G : **Englefield Green**
Epp : **Epping**
Eps : **Epsom**
Eps D : **Epsom Downs**
Erith : **Erith**
Esh : **Esher**
Ess : **Essendon**
Eton : **Eton**
Eton W : **Eton Wick**
Ewe : **Ewell**
Eyns : **Eynsford**
Fair : **Fairseat**
Farnb : **Farnborough**
Farn C : **Farnham Common**
Farn R : **Farnham Royal**
Farni : **Farningham**
Fawk : **Fawkham**
Felt : **Feltham**
Fet : **Fetcham**
Fidd H : **Fiddlers Hamlet**
Flau : **Flaunden**
F'mre : **Frogmore**
Ful : **Fulmer**
G Grn : **George Green**
Ger X : **Gerrards Cross**
God G : **Godden Green**
G'stone : **Godstone**
G Oak : **Goff's Oak**
Grav'nd : **Gravesend**
Grays : **Grays**
Gt War : **Great Warley**
G'frd : **Greenford**
Ghithe : **Greenhithe**
Grn St : **Green Street Green**
Guild : **Guildford**
Had W : **Hadley Wood**
Hals : **Halstead**
Ham : **Ham**
Hamp : **Hampton**
Hamp H : **Hampton Hill**
Hamp W : **Hampton Wick**
Hanw : **Hanworth**
Hare : **Harefield**
Harl : **Harlington**
Harm : **Harmondsworth**
Hrld W : **Harold Wood**
Harr : **Harrow**
Hrw W : **Harrow Weald**
Hartl : **Hartley**
Hat E : **Hatch End**
Hat : **Hatfield**
Have B : **Havering-Atte-Bower**
Hawl : **Hawley**
Hayes : **Hayes**
Head : **Headley**
Hedg : **Hedgerley**
Hem H : **Hemel Hempstead**
Heron : **Herongate**
Herons : **Heronsgate**
Hers : **Hersham**
Hest : **Heston**
Hext : **Hextable**
High'm : **Higham**
H Beech : **High Beech**
Hil : **Hillingdon**
Hin W : **Hinchley Wood**
Hod S : **Hodsoll Street**
Horn : **Hornchurch**
Horn H : **Horndon-on-the-Hill**
Hort : **Horton**
Hort K : **Horton Kirby**
Houn : **Hounslow**
Hunt C : **Hunton Cross**
Hut : **Hutton**
Ick : **Ickenham**
Ide H : **Ide Hill**
Igh : **Ightham**
Ilf : **Ilford**
Inga : **Ingatestone**
Ingve : **Ingrave**
Isle : **Isleworth**
Ist R : **Istead Rise**
Iver : **Iver**
Iver H : **Iver Heath**
Ivy H : **Ivy Hatch**
Jac W : **Jacobs Well**
Kel C : **Kelvedon Common**
Kel H : **Kelvedon Hatch**
Kems'g : **Kemsing**
Kenley : **Kenley**
Kenton : **Kenton**
Kes : **Keston**
Kew : **Kew**
K Lan : **Kings Langley**
King T : **Kingston upon Thames**
Kgswd : **Kingswood**
Knap : **Knaphill**
Knat : **Knatts Valley**
Knock : **Knockholt**
Lale : **Laleham**
L'ly : **Langley**
Lang : **Langleybury**
Lat : **Latimer**
Lea : **Leatherhead**
Leigh : **Leigh**
Let H : **Letchmore Heath**
Ley H : **Ley Hill**
Light : **Lightwater**
Limp : **Limpsfield**
Linf : **Linford**
L Chal : **Little Chalfont**
L War : **Little Warley**
Lon C : **London Colney**
H'row A : **London Heathrow Airport**
Longc : **Longcross**
Lfield : **Longfield**
Long H : **Longfield Hill**
Lford : **Longford**
Loud : **Loudwater**
Lough : **Loughton**
Lwr K : **Lower Kingswood**
Lyne : **Lyne**
Map C : **Maple Cross**
Mawney : **Mawney**
Meop : **Meopham**
Mers : **Merstham**
Mick : **Mickleham**
Mitc : **Mitcham**
Mord : **Morden**
Mount : **Mountnessing**
Nave : **Navestock**
N'side : **Navestockside**
New Ad : **New Addington**
New A : **New Ash Green**
New Bar : **New Barnet**
New S : **Newgate Street**
New H : **New Haw**
N Mald : **New Malden**
Noak H : **Noak Hill**
Norm : **Normandy**
N'thaw : **Northaw**
Nflt : **Northfleet**
Nflt G : **Northfleet Green**
N Mym : **North Mymms**
N Ock : **North Ockendon**
N'olt : **Northolt**
N Stif : **North Stifford**
N Weald : **North Weald**
Nwood : **Northwood**
Nutf : **Nutfield**
Oak G : **Oakley Green**
Ock : **Ockham**
Old Win : **Old Windsor**
Orp : **Orpington**
Ors : **Orsett**
Otf : **Otford**
Ott : **Ottershaw**
Oxs : **Oxshott**
Oxt : **Oxted**
Park : **Park Street**
Pet W : **Petts Wood**
Pil H : **Pilgrims Hatch**
Pinn : **Pinner**
Pirb : **Pirbright**
Plat : **Platt**
Plax : **Plaxtol**
Pond E : **Ponders End**
Pott E : **Potten End**
Pot B : **Potters Bar**
Pot C : **Potters Crouch**
Poyle : **Poyle**
Prat B : **Pratts Bottom**
Purf : **Purfleet**
Purl : **Purley**
Pyr : **Pyrford**
R'lett : **Radlett**
Rain : **Rainham**
Ran C : **Ranmore Common**
Redh : **Redhill**
Reig : **Reigate**
Rich P : **Richings Park**
Rich : **Richmond**
Rick : **Rickmansworth**
Ridge : **Ridge**
Rip : **Ripley**
Riv : **Riverhead**
Rom : **Romford**
Roug : **Roughway**
Ruis : **Ruislip**
Rush G : **Rush Green**
St A : **St Albans**
St M Cry : **St Mary Cray**
St P : **St Pauls Cray**
Sande : **Sanderstead**
Sarr : **Sarratt**
Seal : **Seal**
Sels : **Selsdon**
Send : **Send**
S'oaks : **Sevenoaks**
Shenf : **Shenfield**
Shenl : **Shenley**
Shep : **Shepperton**
S'brne : **Shipbourne**
S'ham : **Shoreham**
Shorne : **Shorne**
Sidc : **Sidcup**
Sip : **Sipson**
Slou : **Slough**
S'ford : **Smallford**
Sole S : **Sole Street**
S'hall : **Southall**
S Croy : **South Croydon**
S Dar : **South Darenth**
Sflt : **Southfleet**
S God : **South Godstone**
S Mim : **South Mimms**
S Nut : **South Nutfield**
S Ock : **South Ockendon**
S Weald : **South Weald**
Staines : **Staines**
Stan H : **Stanford-le-Hope**
Stan : **Stanmore**
Stans : **Stansted**
Stanw : **Stanwell**
Stanw M : **Stanwell Moor**
Stap A : **Stapleford Abbotts**
Stap T : **Stapleford Tawney**
Stock P : **Stockley Park**
Stoke D : **Stoke D'Abernon**
Stoke P : **Stoke Poges**
Strood : **Strood**
Sun : **Sunbury**
Sund : **Sundridge**
S'dale : **Sunningdale**
S'hill : **Sunninghill**
Surb : **Surbiton**
Sutt : **Sutton**
Sut H : **Sutton at Hone**
Sut G : **Sutton Green**
Swan : **Swanley**
Swans : **Swanscombe**
Tad : **Tadworth**
Tand : **Tandridge**
Tap : **Taplow**
Tats : **Tatsfield**
Tatt C : **Tattenham Corner**
Tedd : **Teddington**
T Ditt : **Thames Ditton**
They B : **Theydon Bois**
They G : **Theydon Garnon**
They M : **Theydon Mount**
Thorn : **Thorney**
Thor H : **Thornton Heath**
Thorpe : **Thorpe**
Tilb : **Tilbury**
T'sey : **Titsey**
Tros : **Trottiscliffe**
Twick : **Twickenham**
Under : **Underriver**
Upm : **Upminster**
Uxb : **Uxbridge**
Vir W : **Virginia Water**
Wadd : **Waddon**
Wall : **Wallington**
Walt A : **Waltham Abbey**
Walt C : **Waltham Cross**
Walt T : **Walton-on-Thames**
Walt H : **Walton on the Hill**
W'ley : **Warley**
W'ham : **Warlingham**
Wat O : **Water Oakley**
Wat : **Watford**
W'stone : **Wealdstone**
Wel G : **Welham Green**
Well H : **Well Hill**
Well : **Welling**
Wemb : **Wembley**
Wenn : **Wennington**
W Byf : **West Byfleet**
W Cla : **West Clandon**
W Dray : **West Drayton**
W End : **West End**
W H'dn : **West Horndon**
W Hor : **West Horsley**
W Hyd : **West Hyde**
W King : **West Kingsdown**
W Mole : **West Molesey**
W Thur : **West Thurrock**
W Til : **West Tilbury**
W W'ck : **West Wickham**
Westrm : **Westerham**
Westh : **Westhumble**
Wex : **Wexham**
Weyb : **Weybridge**
Whel : **Whelpley Hill**
W Vill : **Whiteley Village**
Whitt : **Whitton**
Whyt : **Whyteleafe**
Wilm : **Wilmington**
W'sham : **Windlesham**
Wind : **Windsor**
Wink : **Winkfield**
Wis : **Wisley**
Wok : **Woking**
Wold : **Woldingham**
Wbrn G : **Wooburn Green**
Wfd G : **Woodford Green**
Wdhm : **Woodham**
Wor Pk : **Worcester Park**
Worp : **Worplesdon**
Wray : **Wraysbury**
Wro : **Wrotham**
Wro H : **Wrotham Heath**
Yead : **Yeading**
Yiew : **Yiewsley**

1st Bowl 55Ec 114
2 Willow Road 35Gb 69
60 St Martins La. WC2 4F 223
198 Contemporary Arts and Learning 58Rb 113 (off Railton Rd.)
201 Bishopsgate EC2 7J 219

A

A1 Golf Driving Range 13Ua 30
Aaron Hill Rd. E6 43Qc 94
Aashiana Ct. WD18: Wat 16W 26
Abady Ho. SW1 5E 228
Abberley M. SW4 55Kb 112
Abberton Wlk. RM13: Rain 39Hd 76
Abbess Cl. E6 43Nc 94
SW2 60Rb 113
Abbess Ter. IG10: Lough 13Qc 36
Abbeville M. SW4 56Mb 112
Abbeville Rd. N8 29Mb 50
SW4 58Lb 112
Abbey Av. AL3: St A 5N 5
HA0: Wemb 40Na 67
Abbey Bus. Cen. SW8 53Lb 112
Abbey Chase KT16: Chert 73K 149
Abbey Cl. BR6: Chels 77Xc 161
E5 35Wb 71
GU22: Pyr 88G 168
HA5: Pinn 27X 45
RM1: Rom 30Jd 56
SL1: Slou 5C 80
SW8 53Mb 112
UB3: Hayes 46X 85
UB5: N'olt 41Ba 85
Abbey Ct. AL1: St A 3B 6 (off Holywell Hill)
EN9: Walt A 6Dc 20
KT16: Chert 73K 149
NW8 1A 214
SE17 50Sb 91 (off Macleod St.)
TW12: Hamp 66Ca 129
TW18: Lale 70L 127
Abbey Cres. DA17: Belv 49Cd 96
Abbeydale Rd. HA0: Wemb 39Pa 67
Abbey Dr. DA2: Wilm 61Gd 140
SW17 64Jb 134
TW18: Lale 69L 127
WD5: Ab L 4W 12
Abbey Est. NW8 39Db 69
Abbeyfield Cl. CR4: Mitc 68Gb 133
Abbeyfield Est. SE16 49Yb 92
Abbeyfield Rd. SE16 49Yb 92 (not continuous)
Abbeyfields Cl. NW10 41Qa 87
Abbey Gdns. BR7: Chst 67Qc 138
KT16: Chert 72J 149
NW8 2A 214 (40Eb 69)
SE16 49Wb 91
TW15: Ashf 64R 128
W6 51Ab 110
Abbey Gateway AL3: St A 2A 6
Abbey Grn. KT16: Chert 72J 149
Abbey Gro. SE2 49Xc 95
Abbeyhill Rd. DA15: Sidc 61Yc 139
Abbey Ho. E15 40Gc 73 (off Baker's Row)
NW8 3A 214
Abbey Ind. Est. CR4: Mitc 71Hb 155
HA0: Wemb 39Pa 67
Abbey La. BR3: Beck 66Cc 136
E15 40Ec 72 (not continuous)
Abbey La. Commercial Est. E15 40Gc 73
Abbey Life Ct. E16 43Kc 93
Abbey Lodge NW8 4E 214
Abbey Mead Ind. Est. EN9: Walt A 7Ec 20
Abbey Mead Ind. Pk. EN9: Walt A 6Dc 20
Abbey Mdws. KT16: Chert 73L 149
Abbey M. AL1: St A 3B 6 (off Holywell Hill)
E17 29Cc 52
TW7: Isle 53Ka 108
TW18: Lale 70L 127
Abbey Mill End AL3: St A 3A 6
Abbey Mill La. AL3: St A 3A 6
Abbey Mills EN9: Walt A 5Dc 20
Abbey Moor Golf Course 76J 149
Abbey Mt. DA17: Belv 50Bd 95
Abbey Orchard St. SW1 3D 228 (48Mb 90)
Abbey Orchard St. Est. SW1 3E 228 (48Mb 90) (not continuous)
Abbey Pde. SW19 66Eb 133 (off Merton High St.)
W5 41Pa 87
Abbey Pk. BR3: Beck 66Cc 136
Abbey Pk. Ind. Est. IG11: Bark 40Sc 74
Abbey Pk. La. SL1: Burn 3C 60
Abbey Pl. DA1: Dart 57Md 119
KT16: Chert 69J 127
Abbey Retail Pk. IG11: Bark 38Rc 74
Abbey Rd. CR0: C'don 76Rb 157
CR2: Sels 82Zb 178
DA7: Bex 56Ad 117
DA9: Ghithe 57Yd 120
DA12: Grav'nd 10G 122
DA17: Belv 49Zc 95
E15 40Fc 73
EN1: Enf 15Ub 33
EN8: Walt C 6Ac 20
GU21: Wok 9N 167
GU25: Vir W 1P 147
IG2: Ilf 29Tc 54
IG11: Bark 39Rc 74
KT16: Chert 73K 149
NW6 38Db 69
NW8 1A 214 (38Db 69)
NW10 39Ra 67
SE2 49Zc 95
SW19 66Eb 133
TW17: Shep 74Q 150
Abbey Rd. Apartments NW8 2A 214
Abbey Sports Cen. 39Sc 74
Abbey St. E13 42Jc 93
SE1 3J 231 (48Ub 91)
Abbey Ter. SE2 49Yc 95
Abbey Theatre 3A 6
Abbey Trad. Est. SE26 64Bc 136
Abbey Vw. AL1: St A 4B 6
EN9: Walt A 5Dc 20
NW7 20Va 30
WD7: R'lett 7Ha 14
WD25: Wat 8Z 13
Abbey View Golf Course 3P 5
Abbey Vw. Rd. AL3: St A 2A 6
Abbey Wlk. KT8: W Mole 69Da 129
Abbey Wharf Ind. Est. IG11: Bark 41Tc 94
ABBEY WOOD 49Yc 95
Abbey Wood SL5: S'dale 3E 146
Abbey Wood Caravan Club Site SE2 49Yc 95
Abbey Wood La. RM13: Rain 40Md 77
Abbey Wood Rd. SE2 49Xc 95
Abbot Cl. HA4: Ruis 34Z 65
KT14: Byfl 82M 169
TW18: Staines 66M 127
Abbot Ct. SW8 52Nb 112 (off Hartington Rd.)
Abbot Ho. E14 45Dc 92 (off Smythe St.)
Abbots Av. AL1: St A 5C 6
KT19: Eps 83Qa 173
Abbots Av. W. AL1: St A 5B 6
Abbotsbury NW1 38Mb 70 (off Camley St.)
Abbotsbury Cl. E15 40Ec 72
W14 47Ab 88
Abbotsbury Ct. WD25: Wat 4X 13
Abbotsbury Gdns. HA5: Eastc 31Y 65
Abbotsbury Ho. W14 47Ab 88
Abbotsbury M. SE15 55Yb 114
Abbotsbury Rd. BR2: Hayes 75Hc 159
SM4: Mord 71Db 155
W14 47Ab 88
Abbots Bus. Pk. WD4: K Lan 10A 4
Abbots Cl. BR5: Farnb 74Sc 160
CM15: Shenf 18Ce 41
RM13: Rain 40Ld 77
Abbots Ct. RM3: Hrld W 25Pd 57 (off Queen's Pk. Rd.)
W8 47Db 89 (off Thackeray St.)
Abbots Dr. GU25: Vir W 1M 147
HA2: Harr 33Ca 65
Abbots Fld. DA12: Grav'nd 5E 144
Abbotsford Av. N15 28Sb 51
Abbotsford Cl. GU22: Wok 89C 168
Abbotsford Gdns. IG8: Wfd G 24Jc 53
Abbotsford Rd. IG3: Ilf 33Wc 75
Abbots Gdns. N2 28Fb 49
Abbots Grn. CR0: Addtn 79Zb 158
Abbotshade Rd. SE16 46Zb 92
Abbotshall Av. N14 20Lb 32
Abbotshall Rd. SE6 60Fc 115
Abbots Hill HP3: Hem H 7A 4
Abbot's Ho. W14 48Bb 89 (off St Mary Abbots Ter.)
Abbots La. CR8: Kenley 88Sb 177
ABBOTS LANGLEY 3U 12
Abbotsleigh Cl. SM2: Sutt 80Db 155
Abbotsleigh Rd. SW16 63Lb 134
Abbots Mnr. SW1 7K 227 (49Kb 90) (not continuous)
Abbotsmede Cl. TW1: Twick 61Ha 130
Abbots Pk. AL1: St A 4E 6
SW2 60Qb 112
Abbots Pl. NW6 39Db 69
WD6: Bore 9Ra 15
Abbots Ri. RH1: Redh 4A 208
WD4: K Lan 8P 3
Abbots Rd. E6 39Mc 73
HA8: Edg 24Sa 47
WD5: Ab L 3S 12
Abbots Ter. N8 30Nb 50
Abbotstone Rd. SW15 55Ya 110
Abbot St. E8 37Vb 71
Abbots Vw. WD4: K Lan 9P 3
Abbots Wlk. SL4: Wind 4C 102
W8 48Db 89
Abbots Way BR3: Beck 71Ac 158
KT16: Chert 73H 149
Abbotswell Rd. SE4 57Bc 114
Abbotswood KT13: Weyb 76V 150
Abbotswood Cl. DA17: Belv 48Ad 95
Abbotswood Dr. KT13: Weyb 82T 170
Abbotswood Gdns. IG5: Ilf 27Pc 54
Abbotswood Rd. SE22 56Ub 113
SW16 62Mb 134
Abbotswood Way UB3: Hayes 46X 85
Abbott Av. SW20 67Za 132
Abbott Cl. TW12: Hamp 65Aa 129
UB5: N'olt 37Ba 65
Abbott Rd. E14 43Ec 92 (not continuous)
TN15: Bor G 92Be 205
Abbotts Cl. BR8: Swan 70Jd 140
N1 37Sb 71
RM7: Mawney 27Dd 56
SE28 45Yc 95
UB8: Cowl 43M 83
Abbotts Cres. E4 21Fc 53
EN2: Enf 12Rb 33
Abbotts Dr. EN9: Walt A 5Jc 21
HA0: Wemb 33Ka 66
SS17: Stan H 1M 101
Abbotts Hall Chase SS17: Stan H 1N 101
Abbotts Ho. SW1 7D 228
Abbotts Mead TW10: Ham 63Ma 131
Abbotts Pk. Rd. E10 31Ec 72
Abbotts Rd. CR4: Mitc 70Lb 134
EN5: New Bar 14Db 31
SM3: Cheam 77Ab 154
UB1: S'hall 46Aa 85
Abbott's Tilt KT12: Hers 76Aa 151
Abbotts Wlk. CR3: Cat'm 94Xb 197
DA7: Bex 52Zc 117
Abbotts Way SL1: Slou 6B 80
Abbott's Wharf E14 44Cc 92 (off Stainsby Pl.)
Abbotts Wharf Moorings E14 44Cc 92 (off Stainsby Rd.)
Abbs Cross RM12: Horn 32Ld 77
Abbs Cross Gdns. RM12: Horn 32Ld 77
Abbs Cross Health & Fitness Club 34Ld 77
Abbs Cross La. RM12: Horn 34Ld 77
Abchurch La. EC4 4G 225 (45Tb 91) (not continuous)
Abchurch Yd. EC4 4F 225 (45Tb 91)
Abdale La. AL9: N Mym 9D 8
Abdale Rd. W12 46Xa 88
Abel Cl. HP2: Hem H 2A 4
Abel Ho. SE11 51Qb 112 (off Kennington Rd.)
Abelia Cl. GU24: W End 5C 166
Abell Ct. KT15: Add 78K 149
Abenberg Way CM13: Hut 19De 41
Abenglen Ind. Est. UB3: Hayes 47T 84
Aberavon Rd. E3 41Ac 92
Abercairn Rd. SW16 66Lb 134
Aberconway Rd. SM4: Mord 70Db 133
Abercorn Cl. CR2: Sels 85Zb 178
NW7 24Ab 48
NW8 2A 214 (41Eb 89)
Abercorn Commercial Cen. HA0: Wemb 39Ma 67
Abercorn Cotts. NW8 3A 214
Abercorn Cres. HA2: Harr 32Da 65
Abercorn Dell WD23: B Hea 19Ea 28
Abercorn Gdns. HA3: Kenton 31Ma 67
RM6: Chad H 30Xc 55
Abercorn Gro. HA4: Ruis 28T 44
Abercorn Mans. NW8 2A 214
Abercorn M. TW10: Rich 56Pa 109
Abercorn Pl. NW8 3A 214 (41Eb 89)
Abercorn Rd. HA7: Stan 24La 46
NW7 24Ab 48
Abercorn Wlk. NW8 3A 214 (41Eb 89)
Abercorn Way GU21: Wok 10L 167
SE1 50Wb 91
Abercrombie Dr. EN1: Enf 11Wb 33
Abercrombie St. SW11 54Gb 111
Aberdale Ct. SE16 47Zb 92 (off Garter Way)
Aberdale Gdns. EN6: Pot B 4Bb 17
Aberdare Cl. BR4: W W'ck 75Ec 158
Aberdare Gdns. NW6 38Db 69
NW7 24Za 48
Aberdare Rd. EN3: Pond E 14Yb 34
Aberdeen Av. SL1: Slou 5E 80
Aberdeen Cotts. HA7: Stan 24La 46
Aberdeen Ct. W9 6B 214
Aberdeen La. N5 36Sb 71
Aberdeen Mans. WC1 5F 217
Aberdeen Pde. N18 22Xb 51 (off Aberdeen Rd.)
Aberdeen Pk. N5 36Sb 71
Aberdeen Pl. NW8 6B 214 (42Fb 89)
Aberdeen Rd. CR0: C'don 77Sb 157
HA3: W'stone 26Ha 46
N5 35Sb 71
N18 22Wb 51 (not continuous)
NW10 36Va 68
Aberdeen Sq. E14 46Bc 92
Aberdeen Ter. SE3 54Fc 115
Aberdeen Wharf E1 46Xb 91 (off Wapping High St.)
Aberdour Rd. IG3: Ilf 34Xc 75
Aberdour St. SE1 4H 231 (49Ub 91)
Aberfeldy Ho. SE5 52Rb 113 (not continuous)
Aberfeldy St. E14 43Ec 92 (not continuous)
Aberford Gdns. SE18 53Nc 116
Aberford Rd. WD6: Bore 12Qa 29
Aberfoyle Rd. SW16 65Mb 134 (not continuous)
Abergeldie Rd. SE12 58Kc 115
Abernethy Rd. SE13 56Gc 115
Abersham Rd. E8 36Vb 71
Abery St. SE18 49Uc 94
Abigail M. RM3: Hrld W 26Pd 57
Ability Pl. E14 47Dc 92
Ability Towers EC1 3D 218
Abingdon W14 49Bb 89 (off Kensington Village)
Abingdon Cl. GU21: Wok 10N 167
KT4: Wor Pk 76Xa 154
NW1 37Mb 70
SE1 49Vb 91 (off Bushwood Dr.)
SW19 65Eb 133
UB10: Hil 39P 63
Abingdon Ct. EN8: Walt C 5Ac 20 (off High St.)
GU22: Wok 90B 168
W8 48Cb 89 (off Abingdon Vs.)
Abingdon Gdns. W8 48Cb 89
Abingdon Ho. BR1: Brom 66Kc 137
E2 5K 219
Abingdon Lodge BR2: Brom 68Hc 137 (off Beckenham La.)
W8 48Cb 89
Abingdon Mans. W8 48Cb 89 (off Pater St.)
Abingdon Pl. EN6: Pot B 4Db 17
Abingdon Rd. N3 26Eb 49
SW16 68Nb 134
W8 48Cb 89
Abingdon St. SW1 3F 229 (48Nb 90)
Abingdon Vs. W8 48Cb 89
Abingdon Way BR6: Chels 77Xc 161
Abinger Av. SM2: Cheam 81Ya 174
Abinger Cl. BR1: Brom 69Nc 138
CR0: New Ad 79Ec 158
IG11: Bark 35Wc 75
SM6: Wall 78Nb 156
Abinger Ct. SM6: Wall 78Nb 156 (off Abinger Cl.)
W5 45La 86
Abinger Dr. RH1: Redh 8N 207
Abinger Gdns. TW7: Isle 55Ga 108
Abinger Gro. SE8 51Bc 114
Abinger Ho. SE1 2F 231
Abinger M. W9 42Cb 89
Abinger Rd. W4 48Ua 88
Abington Ct. RM14: Upm 32Sd 78
Ablett St. SE16 50Yb 92
Abney Gdns. N16 33Vb 71
Abney Pk. Cemetery (Local Nature Reserve) 33Ub 71
Abney Pk. Ter. N16 33Vb 71 (off Cazenov Rd.)
Aborfield NW5 36Lb 70
Aboyne Dr. SW20 68Wa 132
Aboyne Rd. NW10 34Ua 68
SW17 62Fb 133
Abraham Cl. WD19: Wat 21X 45
Abraham Ct. RM14: Upm 33Qd 77
Abraham Fisher Ho. E12 36Qc 74
ABRIDGE 13Xc 37
Abridge Cl. EN8: Walt C 7Zb 20
Abridge Gdns. RM5: Col R 23Cd 56
Abridge Golf Course 9Bd 23
Abridge Pk. Homes RM4: Abr 14Wc 37
Abridge Rd. CM16: Abr, Lough, They B 9Vc 23
IG7: Abr, Chig 16Tc 36
RM4: Abr 11Wc 37
Abridge Way IG11: Bark 40Xc 75
Absolutely Ten Pin 6H 81
Abyssinia Cl. SW11 56Gb 111
Abyssinia Ct. N8 29Pb 50
Abyssinia Rd. SW11 56Gb 111
Acacia Av. GU22: Wok 2P 187
HA4: Ruis 32W 64
HA9: Wemb 36Na 67
N17 24Tb 51
RM12: Horn 33Hd 76
TW8: Bford 52Ka 108
TW17: Shep 71Q 150
TW19: Wray 56A 104
UB3: Hayes 44V 84
UB7: Yiew 45P 83
Acacia Bus. Cen. E11 34Gc 73
Acacia Cl. BR5: Pet W 71Tc 160
HA7: Stan 23Ga 46
KT15: Wdhm 82H 169
SE8 49Ac 92
SE20 68Wb 135
Acacia Ct. DA11: Grav'nd 9C 122
EN9: Walt A 6Jc 21 (off Lamplighters Cl.)
HA1: Harr 29Da 45
Acacia Dr. KT15: Wdhm 82H 169
RM14: Upm 35Qd 77
SM3: Sutt 74Bb 155
SM7: Bans 86Za 174
Acacia Gdns. BR4: W W'ck 75Ec 158
NW8 1C 214 (40Fb 69)
RM14: Upm 31Td 78
Acacia Gro. KT3: N Mald 69Ta 131
SE21 61Tb 135
Acacia Hall 59Nd 119
Acacia Ho. N22 25Qb 50 (off Douglas Rd.)
SL9: Chal P 25A 42
Acacia M. UB7: Harm 51M 105
Acacia Pl. NW8 1C 214 (40Fb 69)
Acacia Rd. BR3: Beck 69Bc 136
CR4: Mitc 68Jb 134
DA1: Dart 60Md 119
DA9: Ghithe 58Ud 120
E11 33Gc 73
E17 30Ac 52
EN2: Enf 11Tb 33
N22 25Qb 50
NW8 1C 214 (40Fb 69)
SW16 67Nb 134
TW12: Hamp 65Ca 129
TW18: Staines 64K 127
W3 45Sa 87
Acacias, The EN4: E Barn 15Fb 31
Acacia St. AL10: Hat 3C 8
Acacia Wlk. BR8: Swan 68Fd 140
SW10 52Eb 111 (off Tadema Rd.)
Acacia Way DA15: Sidc 60Vc 117
Academia Way N17 23Ub 51
Academy, The SW8 51Pb 112
Academy Apartments E8 36Xb 71 (off Institute Pl.)
Academy Bldgs. N1 3H 219
Academy Ct. AL2: Lon C 8F 6
DA5: Bexl 61Gd 140 (off Beaconsfield Rd.)
E2 41Yb 92 (off Kirkwall Pl.)
NW6 39Cb 69
WD6: Bore 14Qa 29
Academy Flds. Cl. RM2: Rom 29Jd 56
Academy Flds. Rd. RM2: Rom 29Kd 57
Academy Gdns. CR0: C'don 74Vb 157
UB5: N'olt 40Z 65
W8 47Cb 89
Academy Ho. E3 43Dc 92 (off Violet Rd.)
WD6: Bore 14Qa 29 (off Station Rd.)
Academy Pl. SE18 53Pc 116
TW7: Isle 53Ga 108
Academy Rd. SE18 53Pc 116
Academy Way E17 25Cc 52
RM8: Dag 35Xc 75
Acanthus Dr. SE1 50Wb 91
Acanthus Rd. SW11 55Jb 112
Accommodation La. UB7: Harm 51L 105
UB7: Lford 53J 105
Accommodation Rd. E4 20Fc 35 (off Ashwood Rd.)
KT16: Longc 6P 147
KT17: Ewe 78Wa 154
NW11 32Bb 69
AC Court KT7: T Ditt 72Ja 152
Accrington Ho. RM3: Rom 22Md 57 (off Montgomery Cres.)
Ace Pde. KT9: Chess 76Na 153
Acer Av. RM13: Rain 41Md 97
UB4: Yead 43Aa 85
Acer Ct. EN3: Enf H 13Ac 34 (off Enstone Rd.)
Acer Dr. GU24: W End 5D 166
Acer Rd. E8 38Vb 71
TN16: Big H 88Mc 179
Acers AL2: Park 10A 6
BR7: Chst 66Nc 138
Acfold Rd. SW6 53Db 111
Achilles Cl. HP2: Hem H 1P 3
SE1 50Wb 91
Achilles Ho. E2 40Xb 71 (off Old Bethnal Grn. Rd.)
Achilles Pl. GU21: Wok 9N 167
Achilles Rd. NW6 36Cb 69
Achilles Statue 7J 221 (46Jb 90)
Achilles St. SE14 52Ac 114
Achilles Way W1 7J 221 (46Jb 90)
Acklam Rd. W10 43Ab 88 (not continuous)
Acklington Dr. NW9 25Ua 48
Ackmar Rd. SW6 53Cb 111
Ackroyd Dr. E3 43Bc 92
Ackroyd Rd. SE23 59Zb 114
Acland Cl. SE18 52Tc 116
Acland Cres. SE5 55Tb 113
Acland Ho. SW9 53Pb 112
Acland Rd. NW2 37Xa 68
Acle Cl. IG6: Ilf 24Rc 54
Acme Rd. WD24: Wat 10W 12
Acme Studios E14 43Ec 92 (Gillender St.)
E14 43Ec 92 (off Leven Rd.)
Acock Gro. UB5: N'olt 35Da 65
Acol Ct. NW6 38Cb 69
Acol Cres. HA4: Ruis 36X 65
Acol Rd. NW6 38Cb 69
Aconbury Rd. RM9: Dag 39Xc 75
Acorn Cen., The IG6: Ilf 23Xc 55
Acorn Cl. BR7: Chst 64Sc 138
E4 22Dc 52
EN2: Enf 11Rb 33
HA7: Stan 24Ka 46
RM1: Rom 26Gd 56
SL3: L'ly 50D 82
TW12: Hamp 65Da 129
Acorn Ct. AL2: Lon C 9F 6
E3 40Cc 72 (off Morville St.)
E6 38Nc 74
EN8: Walt C 5Zb 20
IG2: Ilf 30Uc 54
Acorn Gdns. SE19 67Vb 135
W3 43Ta 87
Acorn Gro. GU22: Wok 93A 188
HA4: Ruis 35V 64
KT20: Kgswd 96Bb 195
UB3: Harl 52V 106
Acorn Ho. BR8: Swan 68Hd 140 (off Squirrels Cl.)
Acorn Ind. Pk. DA1: Cray 57Jd 118
Acorn La. EN6: Cuff 1Nb 18
Acorn Pde. SE15 52Xb 113
Acorn Pl. WD24: Wat 9W 12
Acorn Production Cen. N7 38Nb 70
Acorn Rd. DA1: Cray 57Hd 118
HP3: Hem H 3A 4
Acorns, The AL4: St A 2H 7
IG7: Chig 21Uc 54
TN13: S'oaks 95Jd 202
Acorns Way KT10: Esh 78Ea 152
Acorn Trad. Est. RM20: Grays 51Zd 121
Acorn Wlk. SE16 46Ac 92
Acorn Way BR3: Beck 71Ec 158
BR6: Farnb 77Rc 160
SE23 62Zb 136
Acqua Ho. TW9: Kew 52Ra 109
Acre Dr. SE22 56Wb 113
Acrefield Ho. NW4 28Za 48 (off Belle Vue Est.)
Acrefield Rd. SL9: Chal P 27A 42
Acre La. SM5: Cars 77Jb 156
SM6: Wall 77Kb 156
SW2 56Nb 112
Acre Pas. SL4: Wind 3H 103
Acre Path UB5: N'olt 37Aa 65 (off Arnold Rd.)
Acre Rd. KT2: King T 67Na 131
RM10: Dag 38Dd 76
SW19 65Fb 133
Acres, The SS17: Stan H 1P 101
Acres Gdns. KT20: Tad 91Za 194
Acre Vw. RM11: Horn 28Nd 57
Acre Way HA6: Nwood 25V 44
Acrewood HP2: Hem H 3N 3
Acrewood Way AL4: St A 2K 7
Acris St. SW18 57Eb 111
Acropolis Ho. KT1: King T 69Pa 131 (off Winery La.)
Active Sports and Fitness Cen. 24Vb 51
ACTON 46Sa 87
Acton Central Ind. Est. W3 46Ra 87
Acton Cl. EN8: Chesh 3Ac 20
N9 19Wb 33
ACTON GREEN 48Sa 87
Acton Hill M. W3 46Ra 87
Acton Ho. E8 39Vb 71 (off Lee St.)
W3 44Sa 87
Acton La. NW10 41Sa 87
W3 47Sa 87
W4 49Sa 87 (not continuous)
Acton M. E8 39Vb 71
Acton Pk. Est. W3 47Ta 87
Acton Sports Club 49Qa 87
Acton St. WC1 4H 217 (41Pb 90)
Acton Swimming Baths 46Sa 87 (off Salisbury St.)
Acton Va. Ind. Pk. W3 47Va 88
Acuba Rd. SW18 61Db 133
Acworth Cl. N9 17Yb 34
Acworth Ho. SE18 51Rc 116 (off Barnfield Rd.)
Acworth Pl. DA1: Dart 58Ld 119
Ada Cl. N11 20Hb 31
Ada Ct. N1 39Sb 71 (off Packington St.)
W9 4A 214 (41Eb 89)
Ada Gdns. E14 44Fc 93
E15 39Hc 73
Adagio Point SE8 51Dc 114 (off Copperas St.)
Ada Ho. E2 39Wb 71 (off Ada Pl.)
Adair Cl. SE25 69Xb 135
Adair Gdns. CR3: Cat'm 93Sb 197
Adair Ho. SW3 51Gb 111 (off Oakley St.)
Adair Rd. W10 42Ab 88
Adair Twr. W10 42Ab 88 (off Appleford Rd.)
Adair Wlk. GU24: Brkwd 3A 186
Ada Kennedy Ct. SE10 52Ec 114 (off Greenwich Sth. St.)
Ada Lewis Ho. HA9: Wemb 35Pa 67
Adam & Eve Ct. W1 2C 222
Adam & Eve M. W8 48Cb 89
Ada Maria Ct. E1 44Xb 91 (off James Voller Way)
Adam Cl. SE6 63Bc 136
SL1: Slou 6E 80
Adam Ct. SE11 6B 230
SW7 5A 226
Adam Rd. E4 23Bc 52
Adams Bri. Bus. Cen. HA9: Wemb 36Ra 67
Adams Cl. KT5: Surb 72Pa 153
N3 24Cb 49
NW9 33Ra 67
Adams Ct. E17 30Ac 52
EC2 2G 225 (44Ub 91)
WD25: Wat 8Z 13
Adams Cft. GU24: Brkwd 2A 186
Adams Gdns. Est. SE16 47Yb 92
Adams Ho. E14 44Fc 93 (off Aberfeldy St.)
Adams M. N22 24Pb 50
SW17 61Hb 133
Adamson Ct. N2 27Gb 49
Adamson Rd. E16 44Jc 93
NW3 38Fb 69
Adamson Way BR3: Beck 71Ec 158

Adams Pl. E14 ... 46Dc 92
(off The Nth. Colonnade)
N7 ... 36Pb 70
Adams Quarter TW8: Bford ... 52La 108
Adamsrill Cl. EN1: Enf ... 16Tb 33
Adamsrill Rd. SE26 ... 63Zb 136
Adams Rd. BR3: Beck ... 71Ac 158
N17 ... 26Tb 51
SS17: Stan H ... 2N 101
Adam's Row W1 ... 5J 221 (45Jb 90)
Adams Sq. DA6: Bex ... 55Ad 117
Adams Ter. E3 ... 41Cc 92
(off Rainhill Way)
Adam St. WC2 ... 5G 223 (45Nb 90)
Adams Wlk. KT1: King T ... 68Na 131
Adams Way CR0: C'don ... 72Vb 157
SE25 ... 71Xb 157
Adam Wlk. SW6 ... 52Ya 110
Adana SE13 ... 54Ec 114
Ada Pl. E2 ... 39Wb 71
Adare Wlk. SW16 ... 62Pb 134
Ada Rd. HA0: Wemb ... 34Ma 67
SE5 ... 52Ub 113
Adastral Ho. WC1 ... 7H 217
Adastra Way SM6: Wall ... 79Nb 156
Ada St. E8 ... 39Xb 71
Ada Workshops E8 ... 39Xb 71
Adcock Wlk. BR6: Orp ... 77Vc 161
Adderley Gdns. SE9 ... 63Qc 138
Adderley Gro. SW11 ... 57Jb 112
Adderley Rd. HA3: W'stone ... 25Ha 46
Adderley St. E14 ... 44Ec 92
Addey Ho. SE8 ... 52Bc 114
ADDINGTON ... 78Cc 158
Addington Bus. Cen. CR0: New Ad ... 82Gc 179
Addington Cl. SL4: Wind ... 5E 102
Addington Ct. SW14 ... 55Ta 109
Addington Court Golf Course ... 81Cc 178
Addington Dr. N12 ... 23Fb 49
Addington Golf Course, The ... 77Bc 158
Addington Gro. SE26 ... 63Ac 136
Addington Hgts. CR0: New Ad ... 83Ec 178
Addington Ho. SW9 ... 54Pb 112
(off Stockwell Rd.)
Addington Lofts SE5 ... 52Sb 113
(off Wyndham Est.)
Addington Place Golf Course ... 79Ac 158
Addington Rd. BR4: W W'ck ... 77Ec 158
CR0: C'don ... 74Qb 156
CR2: Sande, Sels ... 83Wb 177
E3 ... 41Cc 92
E16 ... 42Gc 93
N4 ... 30Qb 50
Addington Sq. SE5 ... 51Tb 113
Addington St. SE1 ... 2J 229 (47Pb 90)
Addington Village Rd.
CR0: Addtn ... 79Bc 158
(not continuous)
Addis Cl. EN3: Enf H ... 11Zb 34
ADDISCOMBE ... 74Wb 157
Addiscombe Av. CR0: C'don ... 74Wb 157
Addiscombe Cl. HA3: Kenton ... 29La 46
Addiscombe Ct. Rd. CR0: C'don ... 74Ub 157
Addiscombe Gro. CR0: C'don ... 75Ub 157
Addiscombe Rd. CR0: C'don ... 75Tb 157
(not continuous)
WD18: Wat ... 14X 27
Addis Ho. E1 ... 43Yb 92
(off Lindley St.)
Addisland Ct. W14 ... 47Ab 88
(off Holland Vs. Rd.)
Addison Av. N14 ... 16Kb 32
TW3: Houn ... 53Ea 108
W11 ... 46Ab 88
Addison Bri. Pl. W14 ... 49Bb 89
Addison Cl. BR5: Pet W ... 72Sc 160
CR3: Cat'm ... 94Tb 197
HA6: Nwood ... 25W 44
SL0: Iver ... 45G 82
Addison Ct. CM16: Epp ... 3Wc 23
NW6 ... 39Cb 69
(off Brondesbury Rd.)
Addison Cres. W14 ... 48Ab 88
(not continuous)
Addison Dr. SE12 ... 57Kc 115
Addison Gdns. KT5: Surb ... 70Pa 131
RM17: Grays ... 49Ee 99
W14 ... 48Za 88
Addison Gro. W4 ... 48Ua 88
Addison Ho. NW8 ... 3B 214
Addison Pk. Mans. W14 ... 48Za 88
(off Richmond Way)
Addison Pl. SE25 ... 70Wb 135
UB1: S'hall ... 45Ca 85
W11 ... 46Ab 88
Addison Rd. BR2: Brom ... 71Lc 159
CR3: Cat'm ... 93Tb 197
E11 ... 30Jc 53
E17 ... 29Dc 52
EN3: Enf H ... 11Yb 34
GU21: Wok ... 89B 168
IG6: Ilf ... 25Sc 54
SE25 ... 70Wb 135
TW11: Tedd ... 65Ka 130
W14 ... 47Ab 88
Addisons Cl. CR0: C'don ... 75Bc 158
Addison Ter. W4 ... 49Sa 87
(off Chiswick Rd.)
Addison Way HA6: Nwood ... 25V 44
NW11 ... 28Bb 49
UB3: Hayes ... 44W 84
Addle Hill EC4 ... 3C 224 (44Rb 91)
ADDLESTONE ... 77K 149
Addlestone Ho. KT15: Add ... 76K 149
W10 ... 43Ya 88
(off Sutton Way)
Addlestone Leisure Cen. ... 77J 149
ADDLESTONE MOOR ... 75K 149
Addlestone Moor KT15: Add ... 75L 149
Addlestone Pk. KT15: Add ... 78K 149
Addlestone Rd. KT13: Weyb ... 77N 149
KT15: Add ... 77N 149
Addle St. EC2 ... 1E 224 (44Sb 91)
Addy Ho. SE16 ... 49Yb 92
Adecroft Way KT8: W Mole ... 69Ea 130
Adela Av. KT3: N Mald ... 71Xa 154
Adela Ho. W6 ... 50Ya 88
(off Queen Caroline St.)
Adelaide Av. SE4 ... 56Bc 114
Adelaide Cl. EN1: Enf ... 10Ub 19
HA7: Stan ... 21Ja 46
SL1: Slou ... 7E 80
SW9 ... 56Qb 112
Adelaide Ct. BR3: Beck ... 66Cc 136
E9 ... 36Ac 72
(off Kenworthy Rd.)
Adelaide Ct. NW8 ... 2A 214
W7 ... 47Ha 86
Adelaide Gdns. RM6: Chad H ... 29Ad 55
Adelaide Gro. W12 ... 46Wa 88
Adelaide Ho. E15 ... 40Hc 73
E17 ... 26Bc 52
SE5 ... 54Ub 113
W11 ... 44Bb 89
(off Portobello Rd.)
Adelaide Pl. KT13: Weyb ... 77T 150
Adelaide Rd. BR7: Chst ... 64Rc 138
E10 ... 34Dc 72
IG1: Ilf ... 33Rc 74
KT6: Surb ... 71Na 153
KT12: Walt T ... 76W 150
NW3 ... 38Fb 69
RM18: Tilb ... 3B 122
SL4: Wind ... 3K 103
SW18 ... 57Cb 111
TW5: Hest ... 53Aa 107
TW9: Rich ... 56Pa 109
TW11: Tedd ... 65Ha 130
TW15: Ashf ... 64M 127
UB2: S'hall ... 49Aa 85
W13 ... 46Ja 86
Adelaide Sq. SL4: Wind ... 4H 103
Adelaide St. AL3: St A ... 1B 6
WC2 ... 5F 223 (45Nb 90)
(not continuous)
Adelaide Ter. TW8: Bford ... 50Ma 87
Adela St. W10 ... 42Ab 88
Adelina Gro. E1 ... 43Yb 92
Adelina M. SW12 ... 60Mb 112
Adelina Yd. E1 ... 43Yb 92
(off Adelina Gro.)
Adeline Pl. WC1 ... 1E 222 (43Mb 90)
Adeliza Cl. IG11: Bark ... 38Sc 74
Adelphi Ct. E8 ... 38Vb 71
(off Celandine Dr.)
SE16 ... 47Zb 92
(off Garter Way)
W4 ... 51Ta 109
Adelphi Cres. RM12: Horn ... 33Jd 76
UB4: Hayes ... 41U 84
Adelphi Gdns. SL1: Slou ... 7J 81
Adelphi Rd. KT17: Eps ... 85Ta 173
Adelphi Ter. WC2 ... 5G 223 (45Nb 90)
Adelphi Theatre ... 5G 223
Adelphi Way UB4: Hayes ... 41V 84
Adeney Cl. W6 ... 51Za 110
Aden Gro. N16 ... 35Tb 71
Adenmore Rd. SE6 ... 59Cc 114
Aden Rd. EN3: Brim ... 14Ac 34
IG1: Ilf ... 31Sc 74
Aden Ter. N16 ... 35Tb 71
ADEYFIELD ... 2A 4
Adeyfield Gdns. HP2: Hem H ... 1P 3
Adeyfield Ho. EC1 ... 4G 219
Adeyfield Rd. HP2: Hem H ... 2N 3
Adhara Rd. HA6: Nwood ... 22W 44
Adie Rd. W6 ... 48Ya 88
Adine Rd. E13 ... 42Kc 93
Adler Ind. Est. UB3: Hayes ... 47T 84
Adler St. E1 ... 44Wb 91
Adley St. E5 ... 36Ac 72
Adlington Cl. N18 ... 22Tb 51
Admark Ho. KT18: Eps ... 87Ra 173
Admaston Rd. SE18 ... 52Sc 116
Admiral Cl. BR5: St P ... 70Zc 139
KT13: Weyb ... 75U 150
Admiral Ct. IG11: Bark ... 40Xc 75
SE5 ... 53Ub 113
(off Havil St.)
SM5: Cars ... 74Gb 155
SW10 ... 53Eb 111
(off Admiral Sq.)
W1 ... 1H 221
Admiral Hood Ho. SL9: Chal P ... 21A 42
Admiral Ho. SW1 ... 5C 228
TW11: Tedd ... 63Ja 130
Admiral Hyson Ind. Est. SE16 ... 50Xb 91
Admiral M. SW19 ... 66Eb 133
W10 ... 42Za 88
Admiral Pl. N8 ... 28Rb 51
SE16 ... 46Ac 92
Admirals Cl. AL4: Col H ... 5A 8
E18 ... 28Kc 53
Admirals Ct. E6 ... 44Rc 94
(off Trader Rd.)
HA6: Nwood ... 22V 44
SE1 ... 7K 225
Admiral Seymour Rd. SE9 ... 56Pc 116
Admiral's Ga. SE10 ... 53Dc 114
Admirals Lodge RM1: Rom ... 28Hd 56
Admiral Sq. SW10 ... 53Eb 111
Admirals Rd. GU24: Pirb ... 7A 186
KT22: Fet ... 98Fa 192
KT23: Bookh ... 100Ea 192
Admiral Stirling Ct. KT13: Weyb ... 77P 149
Admiral St. SE8 ... 54Cc 114
Admirals Wlk. AL1: St A ... 4E 6
CR5: Coul ... 92Pb 196
DA9: Ghithe ... 57Xd 120
NW3 ... 34Eb 69
Admirals Way DA12: Grav'nd ... 8F 122
E14 ... 47Cc 92
Admiralty Arch ... 6E 222 (46Mb 90)
Admiralty Cl. SE8 ... 52Cc 114
UB7: W Dray ... 47N 83
Admiralty Rd. TW11: Tedd ... 65Ha 130
Admiralty Way TW11: Tedd ... 65Ha 130
Admiral Wlk. W9 ... 43Cb 89
Adnams Wlk. RM13: Rain ... 37Jd 76
Adolf St. SE6 ... 63Dc 136
Adolphus Rd. N4 ... 33Rb 71
Adolphus St. SE8 ... 52Bc 114
Adomar Rd. RM8: Dag ... 34Zc 75
Adpar St. W2 ... 7B 214 (43Fb 89)
Adrian Av. NW2 ... 32Xa 68
Adrian Boult Ho. E2 ... 41Xb 91
(off Mansford St.)
Adrian Cl. EN5: Barn ... 16Za 30
HP1: Hem H ... 3K 3
UB9: Hare ... 25M 43
Adrian Ho. E15 ... 38Fc 73
(off Jupp Rd.)
N1 ... 1J 217
SW8 ... 52Nb 112
(off Wyvil Rd.)
Adrian M. SW10 ... 51Db 111
Adrian Rd. WD5: Ab L ... 3U 12
Adrians Wlk. SL2: Slou ... 6K 81
Adriatic Apartments E16 ... 45Jc 93
(off Western Gateway)
Adriatic Bldg. E14 ... 45Ac 92
(off Horseferry Rd.)
Adriatic Ho. E1 ... 42Zb 92
(off Ernest St.)
Adrienne Av. UB1: S'hall ... 42Ba 85
Adron Ho. SE16 ... 49Yb 92
(off Millender Wlk.)
Adstock Ho. N1 ... 38Rb 71
(off The Sutton Est.)
Adstock M. SL9: Chal P ... 25A 42
Adstock Way RM17: Grays ... 49Be 99
Advance Rd. SE27 ... 63Sb 135
Adventure Kingdom ... 68Kc 137
(off Stockwell Cl.)
Adventurers Ct. E14 ... 45Fc 93
(off Newport Av.)
Adventure World ... 8H 7
Advent Way N18 ... 22Yb 52
Advice Av. RM16: Grays ... 47Ce 99
Adys Lawn NW2 ... 37Xa 68
Ady's Rd. SE15 ... 55Vb 113
Aegean Apartments E16 ... 45Jc 93
(off Western Gateway)
Aegon Ho. E14 ... 48Dc 92
(off Lanark Sq.)
Aerodrome Rd. NW4 ... 27Wa 48
NW9 ... 26Va 48
Aerodrome Way TW5: Hest ... 51Y 107
WD25: Wat ... 6V 12
Aeroville NW9 ... 26Ua 48
AFC Hornchurch ... 33Qd 77
AFC Wimbledon ... 69Ra 131
Affleck St. N1 ... 2J 217 (40Pb 70)
Afghan Rd. SW11 ... 54Gb 111
Afsil Ho. EC1 ... 1A 224
Aftab Ter. E1 ... 42Xb 91
(off Tent St.)
Afton Dr. RM15: S Ock ... 44Xd 98
Agamemnon Rd. NW6 ... 35Bb 69
Agar Cl. KT6: Surb ... 75Pa 153
Agar Gro. NW1 ... 38Lb 70
Agar Gro. Est. NW1 ... 38Mb 70
Agar Ho. KT1: King T ... 69Na 131
(off Denmark Rd.)
Agar Pl. NW1 ... 38Lb 70
Agars Pl. SL3: Dat ... 1L 103
Agar St. WC2 ... 5F 223 (45Nb 90)
Agate Cl. E16 ... 44Mc 93
NW10 ... 41Qa 87
Agate Rd. W6 ... 48Ya 88
Agates La. KT21: Asht ... 90Ma 173
Agatha Cl. E1 ... 46Xb 91
Agaton Path SE9 ... 61Sc 138
Agaton Rd. SE9 ... 61Sc 138
Agave Rd. NW2 ... 35Ya 68
Agdon St. EC1 ... 5B 218 (42Rb 91)
Age Exchange Reminiscence Cen.
... 55Hc 115
Ager Av. RM8: Dag ... 32Zc 75
Agincourt SL5: Asc ... 9A 124
Agincourt Rd. NW3 ... 35Hb 69
Agister Rd. IG7: Chig ... 22Wc 55
Agnes Av. IG1: Ilf ... 35Qc 74
Agnes Cl. E6 ... 45Qc 94
Agnesfield Cl. N12 ... 23Gb 49
Agnes Gdns. RM8: Dag ... 35Zc 75
Agnes George Wlk. E16 ... 46Mc 93
Agnes Ho. W11 ... 45Za 88
(off St Ann's Rd.)
Agnes Rd. W3 ... 46Va 88
Agnes Scott Ct. KT13: Weyb ... 76R 150
(off Palace Dr.)
Agnes St. E14 ... 44Bc 92
Agnew Rd. SE23 ... 59Zb 114
Agricola Ct. E3 ... 39Bc 72
(off Parnell Rd.)
Agricola Pl. EN1: Enf ... 15Vb 33
Agua Ho. KT16: Chert ... 73L 149
Ahoy Sailing Cen. ... 50Cc 92
(off Stretton Mans.)
Aidan Cl. RM8: Dag ... 35Ad 75
Aigburth Mans. SW9 ... 52Qb 112
(off Mowll St.)
Ailantus Ct. HA8: Edg ... 22Pa 47
Aileen Wlk. E15 ... 38Hc 73
Ailsa Av. TW1: Twick ... 57Ja 108
Ailsa Ho. E16 ... 45Qc 94
(off University Way)
Ailsa Rd. TW1: Twick ... 57Ka 108
Ailsa St. E14 ... 43Ec 92
Ailsa Wlk. E14 ... 47Cc 92
(off Alpha Gro.)
AIMES GREEN ... 1Hc 21
Ainger M. NW3 ... 38Hb 69
(off Ainger Rd., not continuous)
Ainger Rd. NW3 ... 38Hb 69
Ainsdale NW1 ... 2B 216
Ainsdale Cl. BR6: Orp ... 74Tc 160
Ainsdale Cres. HA5: Pinn ... 27Ca 45
Ainsdale Dr. SE1 ... 50Wb 91
Ainsdale Rd. W5 ... 42Ma 87
WD19: Wat ... 20Y 27
Ainsley Av. RM7: Rom ... 30Dd 56
Ainsley Cl. N9 ... 18Ub 33
Ainsley St. E2 ... 41Xb 91
Ainslie Ct. HA0: Wemb ... 40Na 67
Ainslie Wlk. SW12 ... 59Kb 112
Ainslie Wood Cres. E4 ... 22Dc 52
Ainslie Wood Gdns. E4 ... 21Dc 52
Ainslie Wood Nature Reserve ... 22Dc 52
Ainslie Wood Rd. E4 ... 22Cc 52
Ainsty Est. SE16 ... 47Zb 92
Ainsty St. SE16 ... 47Yb 92
Ainsworth Cl. NW2 ... 34Wa 68
SE15 ... 54Ub 113
Ainsworth Ct. NW10 ... 41Xa 88
(off Plough Cl.)
Ainsworth Ho. NW8 ... 39Db 69
(off Ainsworth Way)
W10 ... 41Ab 88
(off Kilburn La.)
Ainsworth Rd. CR0: C'don ... 74Rb 157
E9 ... 38Yb 72
Ainsworth Way NW8 ... 39Eb 69
Aintree Av. E6 ... 39Nc 74
Aintree Cl. DA12: Grav'nd ... 2D 144
SL3: Poyle ... 53G 104
UB8: Hil ... 44R 84
Aintree Cres. IG6: Ilf ... 26Sc 54
Aintree Est. SW6 ... 52Ab 110
(off Aintree St.)
Aintree Gro. RM14: Upm ... 34Pd 77
Aintree Rd. UB6: G'frd ... 40Ka 66
Aintree St. SW6 ... 52Ab 110
Airbourne Ho. SM6: Wall ... 77Lb 156
(off Maldon Rd.)
Air Call Bus. Cen. NW9 ... 27Ta 47
Airco Cl. NW9 ... 27Ta 47
Aird Ho. SE1 ... 4D 230
Airdrie Cl. N1 ... 38Pb 70
UB4: Yead ... 43Aa 85
Airedale Av. W4 ... 49Va 88
Airedale Av. Sth. W4 ... 50Va 88
Airedale Cl. DA2: Dart ... 60Sd 120
Airedale Rd. SW12 ... 59Hb 111
W5 ... 48La 86
Airedale Wlk. E15 ... 38Gc 73
(off Maiden Rd.)
Aire Dr. RM15: S Ock ... 42Xd 98
Airey Neave Ct.
RM17: Grays ... 47Ce 99
Airfield Pathway RM12: Horn ... 38Ld 77
Airfield Way RM12: Horn ... 37Kd 77
Air Forces Memorial ... 3P 125
Airlie Gdns. IG1: Ilf ... 32Rc 74
W8 ... 46Cb 89
Airlinks Golf Course ... 50Y 85
Air Links Ind. Est.
TW13: Hanw ... 62Aa 129
Airlinks Ind. Est. TW5: Cran ... 50Y 85
Air Pk. Way TW13: Felt ... 61X 129
Airport Bowl ... 53U 106
Airport Gate Bus. Cen.
UB7: Sip ... 52P 105
Airport Ind. Est. TN16: Big H ... 87Mc 179
Airport Way TW19: Stanw M ... 56H 105
Air St. W1 ... 5C 222 (45Lb 90)
Airthrie Rd. IG3: Ilf ... 33Xc 75
Aisgill Av. W14 ... 50Bb 89
(not continuous)
Aisher Rd. SE28 ... 45Yc 95
Aisher Way TN13: Riv ... 93Gd 202
Aislibie Rd. SE12 ... 56Gc 115
Aiten Pl. W6 ... 49Wa 88
Aithan Ho. E14 ... 44Bc 92
(off Copenhagen Pl.)
Aitken Cl. CR4: Mitc ... 73Hb 155
E8 ... 39Wb 71
Aitken Rd. EN5: Barn ... 15Ya 30
SE6 ... 61Dc 136
Aitman Dr. TW8 ... 50Qa 87
Aits Vw. KT8: W Mole ... 69Da 129
Ajax Av. NW9 ... 27Ua 48
SL1: Slou ... 5F 80
Ajax Ho. E2 ... 40Xb 71
(off Old Bethnal Grn. Rd.)
Ajax Rd. NW6 ... 35Bb 69
Akabusi Cl. CR0: C'don ... 72Wb 157
Akbar Ho. E14 ... 49Dc 92
(off Cahir St.)
Akehurst La. TN13: S'oaks ... 97Ld 203
Akehurst St. SW15 ... 58Wa 110
Akeman Cl. AL3: St A ... 4M 5
Akenside Rd. NW3 ... 36Fb 69
Akerman Rd. KT6: Surb ... 72La 152
SW9 ... 54Rb 113
Akers Cl. EN8: Walt C ... 4Ac 20
Akers La. WD3: Chor ... 16F 24
Akintaro Ho. SE8 ... 51Bc 114
(off Alverton St.)
Alabama St. SE18 ... 52Tc 116
Alacross Rd. W5 ... 47La 86
Alamaro Lodge SE10 ... 48Hc 93
(off Teal St.)
Alamein Gdns. DA2: Dart ... 59Td 120
Alamein Rd. DA10: Swans ... 58Zd 121
Alana Hgts. E4 ... 17Dc 34
Alanbrooke DA12: Grav'nd ... 9E 122
Alanbrooke Cl. GU21: Knap ... 10G 166
Alan Cl. DA1: Dart ... 56Ld 119
Alandale Dr. HA5: Pinn ... 25X 45
Aland Ct. SE16 ... 48Ac 92
Alander M. E17 ... 28Ec 52
Alan Dr. EN5: Barn ... 16Ab 30
Alan Gdns. RM7: Rush G ... 31Cd 76
Alan Hilton Ct. KT16: Ott ... 79F 148
(off Cheshire Cl.)
Alan Hocken Way E15 ... 40Gc 73
Alan Preece Ct. NW6 ... 38Za 68
Alan Rd. SW19 ... 64Ab 132
Alanthus Cl. SE12 ... 58Jc 115
Alan Way SL3: G Grn ... 44A 82
Alaska Apartments E16 ... 45Jc 93
(off Western Gateway)
Alaska Bldg. SE10 ... 53Dc 114
(off Deal's Gateway)
Alaska Bldgs. SE1 ... 4K 231 (48Ub 91)
Alaska St. SE1 ... 7K 223 (46Qb 90)
Alastor Ho. E14 ... 48Ec 92
(off Strattondale Ho.)
Alba Cl. UB4: Yead ... 42Z 85
Albacore Cres. SE13 ... 58Dc 114
Albacore Way UB3: Hayes ... 45V 84
Alba Gdns. NW11 ... 30Ab 48
Albain Cres. TW15: Ashf ... 61N 127
Alba M. SW18 ... 61Cb 133
Alban Arena (Theatre & Cinema) ... 2B 6
Alban Av. AL3: St A ... 1B 6
Alban Ct. AL1: St A ... 2F 6
(off Burleigh Rd.)
Alban Cres. DA4: Farni ... 74Qd 163
WD6: Bore ... 11Ra 29
Alban Highwalk EC2 ... 1E 224
(not continuous)
Alban Ho. WD6: Bore ... 11Ra 29
Albanian Ct. AL1: St A ... 3E 6
Alban Pk. AL4: St A ... 2K 7
Albans Vw. WD25: Wat ... 5X 13
Albanwood WD25: Wat ... 5X 13
Albany, The ... 52Cc 114
Albany N12 ... 23Db 49
W1 ... 5B 222 (45Lb 90)
Albany, The IG8: Wfd G ... 21Hc 53
Albany Cl. DA5: Bexl ... 59Yc 117
KT10: Esh ... 81Ca 171
N15 ... 28Rb 51
RH2: Reig ... 3J 207
SW14 ... 56Ra 109
UB10: Ick ... 36Q 64
WD23: Bush ... 16Fa 28
Albany Ct. CM16: Epp ... 2Vc 23
E1 ... 44Wb 91
(off Plumber's Row)
E4 ... 16Cc 34
(Chelwood Cl.)
E4 ... 22Bc 52
(Westward Rd.)
E10 ... 31Cc 72
HA8: Edg ... 25Ta 47
KT13: Weyb ... 77R 150
(Hillcrest)
KT13: Weyb ... 75U 150
(Oakhill Gdns.)
Albany Ct. NW8 ... 2B 214
NW10 ... 41Xa 88
(off Trenmar Gdns.)
TW15: Ashf ... 66S 128
TW20: Egh ... 64D 126
Albany Courtyard W1 ... 5C 222 (45Lb 90)
Albany Cres. HA8: Edg ... 24Qa 47
KT10: Clay ... 79Ga 152
Albany Ga. AL1: St A ... 3B 6
Albany Hgts. RM17: Grays ... 50Ce 99
(off Hogg La.)
Albany Leisure Cen. ... 10Zb 20
Albany Mans. SW11 ... 52Gb 111
Albany M. AL2: Chis G ... 9N 5
(off Nth. Orbital Rd.)
BR1: Brom ... 65Jc 137
KT2: King T ... 65Ma 131
N1 ... 38Qb 70
SE5 ... 51Sb 113
SM1: Sutt ... 78Db 155
Albany Pde. TW8: Bford ... 51Na 109
Albany Pk. SL3: Coln ... 53F 104
Albany Pk. Av. EN3: Enf W ... 11Yb 34
Albany Pk. Rd. KT2: King T ... 65Ma 131
KT22: Lea ... 91Ja 192
Albany Pas. TW10: Rich ... 57Na 109
Albany Pl. TW8: Bford ... 51Ma 109
TW20: Egh ... 63D 126
Albany Reach KT7: T Ditt ... 71Ha 152
Albany Rd. BR7: Chst ... 64Rc 138
CM15: Pil H ... 16Xd 40
DA5: Bexl ... 59Yc 117
DA17: Belv ... 51Bd 117
E10 ... 31Cc 72
E12 ... 35Mc 73
E17 ... 30Ac 52
EN3: Enf W ... 9Zb 20
KT3: N Mald ... 70Ta 131
KT12: Hers ... 77Z 151
N4 ... 30Qb 50
N18 ... 22Yb 52
RM6: Chad H ... 30Bd 55
RM12: Horn ... 32Jd 76
RM18: Tilb ... 3C 122
SE5 ... 7J 231 (51Tb 113)
SL4: Old Win ... 7L 103
SL4: Wind ... 4H 103
SW19 ... 64Db 133
TW8: Bford ... 51Ma 109
TW10: Rich ... 57Pa 109
W13 ... 45Ka 86
Albany St. NW1 ... 1K 215 (40Kb 70)
Albany Ter. NW1 ... 6A 216
TW10: Rich ... 57Pa 109
(off Albany Pas.)
Albany Vw. IG9: Buck H ... 18Jc 35
Albany Way TW18: Staines ... 65M 127
Albany Works E3 ... 39Ac 72
(off Gunmakers La.)
Alba Pl. W11 ... 44Bb 89
Albatross NW9 ... 26Va 48
Albatross Cl. E6 ... 43Pc 94
Albatross Gdns. CR2: Sels ... 83Zb 178
Albatross St. SE18 ... 52Uc 116
Albatross Way SE16 ... 47Zb 92
Albemarle SW19 ... 61Za 132
Albemarle App. IG2: Ilf ... 30Rc 54
Albemarle Av. EN6: Pot B ... 5Db 17
TW2: Whitt ... 60Ba 107
Albemarle Cl. RM17: Grays ... 47Ce 99
Albemarle Gdns. IG2: Ilf ... 30Rc 54
KT3: N Mald ... 70Ta 131
Albemarle Ho. SE8 ... 49Bc 92
(off Foreshore)
SW9 ... 55Qb 112
Albemarle Pk. BR3: Beck ... 67Dc 136
HA7: Stan ... 22La 46
Albemarle Rd. BR3: Beck ... 67Dc 136
EN4: E Barn ... 17Gb 31
Albemarle St. W1 ... 5A 222 (45Kb 90)
Albemarle Way EC1 ... 6B 218 (42Rb 91)
Alberon Gdns. NW11 ... 28Bb 49
Alberta Av. SM1: Sutt ... 77Ab 154
Alberta Est. SE17 ... 7C 230
Alberta Rd. DA8: Erith ... 53Ed 118
EN1: Enf ... 16Vb 33
Alberta St. SE17 ... 7B 230 (50Rb 91)
Albert Av. E4 ... 21Cc 52
KT16: Chert ... 69J 127
SW8 ... 52Pb 112
Albert Barnes Ho. SE1 ... 4D 230
Albert Basin Way E16 ... 45Tc 94
Albert Bigg Point E15 ... 40Ec 72
(off Godfrey St.)
Albert Bri. SW3 ... 51Gb 111
Albert Bri. Rd. SW11 ... 52Gb 111
Albert Carr Gdns. SW16 ... 64Nb 134
Albert Cl. E9 ... 39Xb 71
N22 ... 25Mb 50
RM16: Grays ... 48Ee 99
SL1: Slou ... 8K 81
Albert Cotts. E1 ... 43Wb 91
(off Deal St.)
Albert Ct. E7 ... 35Jc 73
EN8: Walt C ... 6Bc 20
(off Holdbrook Sth.)
SW7 ... 2B 226 (48Fb 89)
Albert Ct. Ga. SW1 ... 2F 227
Albert Cres. E4 ... 21Cc 52
Albert Dane Cen. UB2: S'hall ... 48Aa 85
Albert Dr. GU21: Wok ... 87E 168
SW19 ... 61Ab 132
TW18: Staines ... 64H 127
Albert Emb. SE1 ... 4H 229 (48Pb 90)
(Lambeth Pal. Rd.)
SE1 ... 7G 229 (50Nb 90)
(Vauxhall Bri.)
Albert Gdns. E1 ... 44Zb 92
Albert Ga. SW1 ... 1G 227 (47Hb 89)
Albert Gray Ho. SW10 ... 52Fb 111
(off Worlds End Est.)
Albert Gro. SW20 ... 67Za 132
Albert Hall Mans. SW7 ... 2B 226 (47Fb 89)
Albert Ho. E18 ... 27Kc 53
(off Albert Rd.)
SE28 ... 48Sc 94
Albertine Cl. KT17: Eps D ... 88Xa 174
Albert Mans. CR0: C'don ... 74Tb 157
(off Lansdowne Rd.)
SW11 ... 53Hb 111
(off Albert Bri. Rd.)
Albert Memorial
Knightsbridge ... 2B 226 (47Fb 89)
Albert M. E14 ... 45Ac 92
(off Northey St.)
N4 ... 32Pb 70

Albert M. RH1: Redh 9A 208
SE4 .... 56Ac 114
UB9: Den 30H 43
(off Patrons Way W.)
W8 .... 3A 226 (48Eb 89)
Albert Murray Cl. DA12: Grav'nd 9E 122
Albert Pal. Mans. SW11 .... 53Kb 112
(off Lurline Gdns.)
Albert Pl. N3 .... 25Cb 49
N17 .... 27Vb 51
SL4: Eton W 10E 80
W8 .... 48Db 89
Albert Rd. BR2: Brom 71Mc 159
BR5: St M Cry 72Xc 161
BR6: Chels 78Wc 161
CR4: Mitc 69Hb 133
CR6: W'ham 89Bc 178
DA2: Wilm 62Ld 141
DA5: Bexl 58Cd 118
DA10: Swans 58Be 121
DA17: Belv 50Bd 95
E10 .... 33Ec 72
E16 .... 46Nc 94
E17 .... 29Cc 52
E18 .... 27Kc 53
EN4: E Barn 14Eb 31
HA2: Harr 27Ea 46
IG1: Ilf 34Rc 74
IG9: Buck H 19Mc 35
KT1: King T 68Pa 131
KT3: N Mald 70Va 132
KT15: Add 76M 149
KT17: Eps 85Va 174
KT21: Asht 90Pa 173
N4 .... 32Pb 70
N15 .... 30Ub 51
N22 .... 25Lb 50
NW4 .... 28Za 48
NW6 .... 40Bb 69
NW7 .... 22Va 48
RH1: Mers 1C 208
RM1: Rom 29Hd 56
RM8: Dag 32Ad 76
SE9 .... 62Nc 138
SE20 .... 65Zb 136
SE25 .... 70Wb 135
SL4: Old Win, Wind 5H 103
SM1: Sutt 78Fb 155
TW1: Twick 60Ha 108
TW3: Houn 56Ca 107
TW10: Rich 57Na 109
TW11: Tedd 65Ha 130
TW12: Hamp H 64Ea 130
TW15: Ashf 64P 127
TW20: Eng G 5P 125
UB2: S'hall 48Z 85
UB3: Hayes 48U 84
UB7: Yiew 46N 83
W5 .... 42Ka 86
Albert Rd. Cen. NW6 .... 40Bb 69
(off Albert Rd.)
Albert Rd. Est. DA17: Belv 50Bd 95
Albert Rd. Nth. RH2: Reig 5H 207
WD17: Wat 13X 27
Albert Rd. Sth. WD17: Wat 13X 27
Alberts Ct. NW1 .... 5E 214
Albert Sleet Ct. N9 .... 20Xb 33
(off Colthurst Dr.)
Albert Sq. E15 .... 36Gc 73
SW8 .... 52Pb 112
Albert Starr Ho. SE8 .... 49Zb 92
(off Haddonfield)
Albert St. AL1: St A 3B 6
CM14: W'ley 22Yd 58
N12 .... 22Eb 49
NW1 .... 1A 216 (39Kb 70)
SL1: Slou 8K 81
(not continuous)
SL4: Wind 3F 102
Albert Studios SW11 .... 53Hb 111
Albert Ter. IG9: Buck H 19Nc 36
NW1 .... 39Jb 70
NW10 .... 39Sa 67
W5 .... 42Ka 86
W6 .... 50Wa 88
(off Beavor La.)
Albert Ter. M. NW1 .... 39Jb 70
Albert Victoria Ho. N22 .... 25Qb 50
Albert Wlk. E16 .... 47Qc 94
Albert Way SE15 .... 52Xb 113
Albert Westcott Ho.
SE17 .... 7C 230 (50Rb 91)
Albert Whicher Ho. E17 .... 28Ec 52
Albert Yd. SE19 .... 65Vb 135
Albery Ct. E8 .... 38Vb 71
(off Middleton Rd.)
Albion Av. N10 .... 25Jb 50
SW8 .... 54Mb 112
Albion Bldgs. N1 .... 2G 217
Albion Cl. RM7: Rom 30Fd 56
SL2: Slou 6L 81
W2 .... 4E 220 (45Gb 89)
Albion Ct. SE10 .... 49Gc 93
(off Azof St.)
SM2: Sutt 80Fb 155
W6 .... 49Xa 88
(off Albion Pl.)
Albion Dr. E8 .... 38Vb 71
Albion Est. SE16 .... 47Zb 92
Albion Gdns. W6 .... 49Xa 88
Albion Ga. W2 .... 4E 220
(not continuous)
Albion Gro. N16 .... 35Ub 71
Albion Hill HP2: Hem H 3M 3
IG10: Lough 15Lc 35
Albion Ho. E16 .... 46Rc 94
(off Church St.)
GU21: Wok 89B 168
SE8 .... 52Cc 114
(off Watsons St.)
Albion M. N1 .... 39Qb 70
NW6 .... 38Bb 69
W2 .... 3E 220 (45Gb 89)
W6 .... 49Xa 88
Albion Pde. DA12: Grav'nd 8F 122
N16 .... 35Tb 71
Albion Pk. IG10: Lough 15Mc 35
Albion Pl. EC1 .... 7B 218 (43Rb 91)
EC2 .... 1G 225 (43Tb 91)
SL4: Wind 4E 102
W6 .... 49Xa 88
Albion Riverside Bldg. SW11 .... 52Gb 111
Albion Rd. AL1: St A 2D 6
DA6: Bex 56Bd 117
DA12: Grav'nd 9E 122
E17 .... 27Ec 52
Albion Rd. KT2: King T 67Sa 131
N16 .... 35Tb 71
N17 .... 26Wb 51
RH2: Reig 7L 207
SM2: Sutt 79Fb 155
TW2: Twick 60Ga 108
TW3: Houn 56Ca 107
UB3: Hayes 44U 84
Albion Sq. E8 .... 38Vb 71
(not continuous)
Albion St. CR0: C'don 74Rb 157
SE16 .... 47Yb 92
W2 .... 3E 220 (44Gb 89)
Albion Ter. DA12: Grav'nd 8E 122
E4 .... 14Dc 34
E8 .... 38Vb 71
Albion Vs. Rd. SE26 .... 62Yb 136
Albion Wlk. N1 .... 2G 217
Albion Way EC1 .... 1D 224 (43Sb 91)
HA9: Wemb 34Qa 67
SE13 .... 56Ec 114
Albion Yd. E1 .... 43Xb 91
N1 .... 2G 217 (40Nb 70)
Albon Ho. SW18 .... 58Db 111
(off Neville Gill Cl.)
Albright Ind. Est. RM13: Rain 42Hd 96
Albrighton Rd. SE22 .... 55Ub 113
Albuhera Cl. EN2: Enf 11Qb 32
Albury Av. DA7: Bex 54Ad 117
SM2: Cheam 81Ya 174
TW7: Isle 52Ha 108
Albury Cl. KT16: Longc 6L 147
KT19: Eps 81Ra 173
TW12: Hamp 65Da 129
Albury Ct. CR0: C'don 77Sb 157
(off Tanfield Rd.)
CR4: Mitc 68Fb 133
SE8 .... 51Cc 114
(off Albury St.)
SM1: Sutt 77Eb 155
UB5: N'olt 41Y 85
(off Canberra Dr.)
Albury Dr. HA5: Pinn 25Y 45
Albury Gro. Rd. EN8: Chesh 2Zb 20
Albury Ho. SE1 .... 2C 230
Albury M. E12 .... 33Lc 73
Albury Pl. RH1: Mers 1C 208
Albury Ride EN8: Chesh 3Zb 20
Albury Rd. KT9: Chess 78Na 153
KT12: Hers 79U 150
RH1: Mers 1C 208
Albury St. SE8 .... 51Cc 114
Albury Wlk. EN8: Chesh 2Yb 20
(not continuous)
Albyfield BR1: Brom 70Pc 138
Albyn Ho. HP2: Hem H 2M 3
Albyn Rd. SE8 .... 53Cc 114
Albyns Cl. RM13: Rain 38Jd 76
Albyns La. RM4: Stap T 12Ed 38
Alcester Ct. SM6: Wall 77Kb 156
Alcester Cres. E5 .... 33Xb 71
Alcester Ho. RM3: Rom 22Md 57
(off Northallerton Way)
Alcester Rd. SM6: Wall 77Kb 156
Alcock Cl. SM6: Wall 80Mb 156
Alcock Rd. TW5: Hest 52Z 107
Alcocks Cl. KT20: Tad 92Ab 194
Alcocks La. KT20: Kgswd, Tad 93Ab 194
Alconbury DA6: Bex 57Dd 118
Alconbury Cl. WD6: Bore 11Pa 29
Alconbury Rd. E5 .... 33Wb 71
Alcorn Cl. SM3: Sutt 75Cb 155
Alcott Cl. TW14: Felt 60V 106
W7 .... 43Ha 86
Alcuin Ct. HA7: Stan 24La 46
Aldam Pl. N16 .... 33Vb 71
Aldborough Ct. IG2: Ilf 29Vc 55
(off Aldborough Rd. Nth.)
ALDBOROUGH HATCH 28Vc 55
Aldborough Rd. RM10: Dag 37Ed 76
RM14: Upm 33Pd 77
Aldborough Rd. Nth. IG2: Ilf 29Vc 55
Aldborough Rd. Sth. IG3: Ilf 32Uc 74
Aldborough Spur SL1: Slou 4J 81
Aldbourne Rd. SL1: Burn 3A 80
W12 .... 46Va 88
Aldbridge St. SE17 .... 7J 231 (50Ub 91)
Aldburgh M. W1 .... 2J 221 (44Jb 90)
Aldbury Av. HA9: Wemb 38Ra 67
Aldbury Cl. WD25: Wat 8Z 13
Aldbury Ho. SW3 .... 6D 226
Aldbury M. N9 .... 17Tb 33
Aldbury Rd. WD3: Rick 17H 25
Aldebert Ter. SW8 .... 52Nb 112
Aldeburgh Cl. E5 .... 33Xb 71
Aldeburgh Pl. IG8: Wfd G 21Jc 53
SE10 .... 49Jc 93
(off Aldeburgh St.)
Aldeburgh St. SE10 .... 50Jc 93
Alden Av. E15 .... 41Hc 93
Alden Ct. CR0: C'don 76Ub 157
ALDENHAM 10Da 13
Aldenham Av. WD7: R'lett 8Ja 14
Aldenham Cl. SL3: L'ly 8P 81
Aldenham Country Pk. 15Ka 28
Aldenham Country Pk. Rare Breeds Farm
.... 15Ka 28
Aldenham Dr. UB8: Hil 42R 84
Aldenham Golf Course 10Da 13
Aldenham Gro. WD7: R'lett 7Ja 14
Aldenham Ho. NW1 .... 2C 216
Aldenham Pk. 13La 28
Aldenham Rd. WD6: E'tree 13Ja 28
WD7: R'lett 7Ja 14
WD19: Wat 16Aa 27
WD23: Bush 16Aa 27
WD25: Let H 11Ga 28
Aldenham Sailing Club 15La 28
Aldenham St. NW1 .... 2C 216 (40Lb 70)
Aldenholme KT13: Weyb 79U 150
Alden Ho. E8 .... 39Xb 71
(off Duncan Rd.)
Alden Mead HA5: Hat E 23Ca 45
(off The Avenue)
Aldensley Rd. W6 .... 48Xa 88
Alden Vw. SL4: Wind 3B 102
Alder Av. RM14: Upm 35Pd 77
Alderbourne La. SL0: Iver H 5P 61
SL3: Ful 5P 61
Alderbrook Rd. SW12 .... 58Kb 112
Alderbury Rd. SL3: L'ly 47B 82
SW13 .... 51Wa 110
Alderbury Rd. W. SL3: L'ly 47B 82
Alder Cl. AL2: Park 10P 5
DA18: Erith 47Bd 95
SE15 .... 51Vb 113
Alder Cl. SL1: Slou 6D 80
TW20: Eng G 64A 126
Aldercombe La. CR3: Cat'm 99Ub 197
Alder Ct. E7 .... 36Jc 73
N11 .... 23Lb 50
Alder Cft. CR5: Coul 88Pb 176
Alder Dr. RM15: S Ock 42Yd 98
Alderglade Nature Reserve, The 36M 63
Alder Gro. NW2 .... 33Wa 68
Aldergrove Gdns. TW3: Houn 54Aa 107
Aldergrove Wlk. RM12: Horn 37Ld 77
Alder Ho. E3 .... 39Bc 72
(off Hornbeam Sq.)
NW3 .... 37Hb 69
SE4 .... 55Cc 114
SE15 .... 51Vb 113
(off Alder Cl.)
Alder Lodge SW6 .... 53Ya 110
Alderman Av. IG11: Bark 41Wc 95
Aldermanbury EC2 .... 2E 224 (44Sb 91)
Aldermanbury Sq. EC2 .... 1E 224 (43Sb 91)
Alderman Cl. AL9: Wel G 6E 8
DA1: Cray 59Gd 118
Alderman Judge Mall
KT1: King T 68Na 131
(off Eden St.)
Aldermans Hill N13 .... 21Nb 50
Aldermans Wlk. EC2 .... 1H 225 (43Ub 91)
Aldermary Rd. BR1: Brom 67Jc 137
Alder M. N19 .... 33Lb 70
Aldermoor Rd. SE6 .... 62Bc 136
Alderney Av. TW5: Hest, Isle 52Da 107
Alderney Ct. SE10 .... 51Fc 115
(off Trafalgar Rd.)
Alderney Gdns. UB5: N'olt 38Ba 65
Alderney Ho. EN3: Enf W 10Zb 20
N1 .... 37Sb 71
(off Arran Wlk.)
WD18: Wat 16V 26
Alderney M. SE1 .... 3F 231 (48Tb 91)
Alderney Rd. DA8: Erith 52Jd 118
E1 .... 42Zb 92
Alderney St. SW1 .... 6A 228 (49Kb 90)
Alder Rd. DA14: Sidc 62Vc 139
SL0: Iver H 40F 62
SW14 .... 55Ta 109
UB9: Den 37L 63
Alders, The BR4: W W'ck 74Dc 158
KT14: W Byf 84L 169
N21 .... 16Qb 32
SW16 .... 63Lb 134
TW5: Hest 51Ba 107
TW13: Hanw 63Aa 129
UB9: Den 37L 63
Alders Av. IG8: Wfd G 23Gc 53
ALDERSBROOK 33Kc 73
Aldersbrook Av. EN1: Enf 12Ub 33
Aldersbrook Dr. KT2: King T 65Pa 131
Aldersbrook La. E12 .... 34Pc 74
Aldersbrook Rd. E11 .... 33Kc 73
E12 .... 33Kc 73
Alders Cl. E11 .... 33Kc 73
HA8: Edg 22Sa 47
W5 .... 48Ma 87
Aldersey Gdns. IG11: Bark 37Tc 74
Aldersford Cl. SE4 .... 57Zb 114
Aldersgate Ct. EC1 .... 1D 224
Aldersgate St. EC1 .... 7D 218 (43Sb 91)
Alders Gro. KT8: E Mos 71Fa 152
Aldersgrove EN9: Walt A 6Gc 21
Aldersgrove Av. SE9 .... 62Mc 137
Aldershot Rd. GU24: Pirb 9B 186
NW6 .... 39Bb 69
Aldershot Ter. SE18 .... 52Qc 116
Alderside Wlk. TW20: Eng G 64A 126
Aldersmead Av. CR0: C'don 72Zb 158
Aldersmead Rd. BR3: Beck 66Ac 136
Alderson Pl. UB2: S'hall 46Ea 86
Alderson St. W10 .... 42Ab 88
Alders Rd. HA8: Edg 22Sa 47
RH2: Reig 4K 207
ALDERSTEAD HEATH 97Mb 196
Alderstead Heath Caravan Site
RH1: Mers 96Mb 196
Alderstead La. RH1: Mers 97Mb 196
Alderton Cl. CM15: Pil H 15Xd 40
IG10: Lough 14Qc 36
NW10 .... 34Ta 67
Alderton Ct. KT8: W Mole 70Ba 129
(off Walton Rd.)
Alderton Cres. NW4 .... 29Xa 48
Alderton Hall La. IG10: Lough 14Qc 36
Alderton Hill IG10: Lough 15Nc 36
Alderton M. IG10: Lough 14Qc 36
Alderton Ri. IG10: Lough 14Qc 36
Alderton Rd. CR0: C'don 73Vb 157
RM16: Ors 4G 100
SE24 .... 55Sb 113
Alderton Way IG10: Lough 15Pc 36
NW4 .... 29Xa 48
Alderville Rd. SW6 .... 54Bb 111
Alder Wlk. IG1: Ilf 36Sc 74
WD25: Wat 7X 13
Alder Way BR8: Swan 68Fd 140
Alderwick Ct. N7 .... 37Pb 70
(off Cornelia St.)
Alderwick Dr. TW3: Houn 55Fa 108
Alderwood Cl. CR3: Cat'm 97Ub 197
RM4: Abr 13Xc 37
Alderwood Dr. RM4: Abr 13Xc 37
Alderwood Ho. WD19: Wat 20Y 27
Alderwood M. EN4: Had W 10Eb 17
Alderwood Rd. SE9 .... 58Tc 116
Aldford Ho. W1 .... 6H 221
Aldford St. W1 .... 6H 221 (46Jb 90)
ALDGATE 3K 225 (44Vb 91)
Aldgate E1 .... 44Vb 91
(off Whitechapel High St.)
EC3 .... 3K 225 (44Ub 91)
Aldgate Av. E1 .... 2K 225 (44Vb 91)
Aldgate Barrs E1 .... 2K 225
Aldgate High St. EC3 .... 3K 225 (44Vb 91)
Aldgate Twr. E1 .... 2K 225 (44Vb 91)
Aldham Dr. RM15: S Ock 43Yd 98
Aldham Ho. SE4 .... 54Bc 114
(off Malpas Rd.)
Aldin Av. Nth. SL1: Slou 7L 81
Aldin Av. Sth. SL1: Slou 7L 81
Aldine Ct. W12 .... 47Ya 88
(off Aldine St.)
Aldine Pl. W12 .... 47Ya 88
Aldine St. W12 .... 47Ya 88
Aldingham Ct. RM12: Horn 36Kd 77
(off Easedale Dr.)
Aldingham Gdns. RM12: Horn 36Jd 76
Aldington Cl. RM8: Dag 32Yc 75
Aldington Ct. E8 .... 38Wb 71
(off London Flds. W. Side)
Aldington Rd. SE18 .... 48Mc 93
Aldis M. EN3: Enf L 9Cc 20
SW17 .... 64Gb 133
Aldis St. SW17 .... 64Gb 133
Aldred Rd. NW6 .... 36Cb 69
Aldren Rd. SW17 .... 62Eb 133
Aldrich Cres. CR0: New Ad 81Ec 178
Aldriche Way E4 .... 23Ec 52
Aldrich Gdns. SM3: Cheam 76Bb 155
Aldrich Ter. SW18 .... 61Eb 133
Aldrick Ho. N1 .... 1J 217
Aldridge Av. EN3: Enf L 10Cc 20
HA4: Ruis 33Y 65
HA7: Stan 25Na 47
HA8: Edg 20Ra 29
Aldridge Ct. W11 .... 43Bb 89
(off Aldridge Rd. Vs.)
Aldridge Ri. KT3: N Mald 73Ua 154
Aldridge Rd. SL2: Slou 2E 80
Aldridge Rd. Vs. W11 .... 43Bb 89
Aldridge Wlk. N14 .... 17Nb 32
Aldrin Cl. SS17: Stan H 1N 101
Aldrington Rd. SW16 .... 64Lb 134
Aldsworth Cl. W9 .... 42Db 89
Aldwick AL1: St A 4F 6
Aldwick Cl. SE9 .... 62Tc 138
Aldwick Ct. AL1: St A 4F 6
Aldwick Rd. CR0: Bedd 76Pb 156
Aldworth Gro. SE13 .... 58Ec 114
Aldworth Rd. E15 .... 38Gc 73
Aldwych WC2 .... 4H 223 (44Pb 90)
Aldwych Av. IG6: Ilf 28Sc 54
Aldwych Bldgs. WC2 .... 2G 223
Aldwych Cl. RM12: Horn 33Jd 76
Aldwych Ct. E8 .... 38Vb 71
(off Middleton Rd.)
Aldwych Theatre 3H 223
Aldwyck Ct. HP1: Hem H 1L 3
Aldwyn Ho. SW8 .... 52Nb 112
(off Davidson Gdns.)
Aldwyn Pl. TW20: Eng G 5M 125
Aldykes AL10: Hat 1B 8
Alers Rd. DA6: Bex 57Zc 117
Alesia Cl. N22 .... 24Nb 50
Alestan Beck Rd. E16 .... 44Mc 93
Alexa Ct. SM2: Sutt 79Cb 155
W8 .... 49Cb 89
Alexander Av. NW10 .... 38Xa 68
Alexander Cl. BR2: Hayes 74Jc 159
DA15: Sidc 58Uc 116
EN4: E Barn 14Fb 31
TW2: Twick 61Ga 130
UB2: S'hall 46Ea 86
Alexander Ct. BR3: Beck 67Fc 137
EN8: Chesh 2Zb 20
HA7: Stan 27Pa 47
Alexander Cres. CR3: Cat'm 93Sb 197
Alexander Evans M. SE23 .... 61Zb 136
Alexander Fleming Laboratory Mus.
.... 2C 220 (44Fb 89)
Alexander Godley Cl. KT21: Asht 91Pa 193
Alexander Ho. E14 .... 48Cc 92
(off Tiller Rd.)
KT2: King T 67Na 131
(off Seven Kings Way)
RM14: Upm 30Ud 58
SE15 .... 54Xb 113
(off Godman Rd.)
Alexander La. CM13: Hut 16De 41
CM15: Shenf 15Ce 41
Alexander M. SW16 .... 64Lb 134
W2 .... 44Db 89
Alexander Pl. RH8: Oxt 100Gc 199
SW7 .... 5D 226 (49Gb 89)
Alexander Raby Mill KT15: Add 78N 149
(off Bourneside Rd.)
Alexander Rd. AL2: Lon C 7G 6
BR7: Chst 65Rc 138
CR5: Coul 87Kb 176
DA7: Bex 54Zc 117
DA9: Ghithe 57Yd 120
N19 .... 34Nb 70
RH2: Reig 9J 207
TW20: Egh 64E 126
Alexander Sq. SW3 .... 5D 226 (49Gb 89)
Alexander St. W2 .... 44Cb 89
Alexander Studios SW11 .... 56Fb 111
(off Haydon Way)
Alexanders Wlk. CR3: Cat'm 98Vb 197
Alexander Ter. SE2 .... 50Xc 95
Alexandra Av. CR6: W'ham 89Bc 178
HA2: Harr 32Ba 65
N22 .... 25Mb 50
SM1: Sutt 76Cb 155
SW11 .... 53Jb 112
UB1: S'hall 45Ba 85
W4 .... 52Ta 109
Alexandra Cl. BR8: Swan 68Gd 140
HA2: Harr 34Ca 65
KT12: Walt T 75W 150
RM16: Grays 7D 100
SE8 .... 51Bc 114
TW15: Ashf 66T 128
TW18: Staines 65M 127
Alexandra Cotts. SE14 .... 53Bc 114
Alexandra Ct. HA9: Wemb 35Pa 67
N14 .... 15Lb 32
SE5 .... 51Sb 113
(off Urlwin St.)
SL4: Wind 4H 103
(off Alexandra Rd.)
SW7 .... 3A 226
TW3: Houn 54Da 107
TW15: Ashf 65T 128
UB6: G'frd 40Da 65
W2 .... 45Db 89
(off Moscow Rd.)
W9 .... 5A 214
WD24: Wat 12Y 27
Alexandra Cres. BR1: Brom 65Hc 137
Alexandra Dr. KT5: Surb 73Qa 153
SE19 .... 64Ub 135
Alexandra Gdns. GU21: Knap 10G 166
N10 .... 28Kb 50
SM5: Cars 80Jb 156
TW3: Houn 54Da 107
W4 .... 52Ua 110
Alexandra Gro. N4 .... 32Rb 71
N12 .... 22Db 49
Alexandra Ho. E16 .... 46Kc 93
(off Wesley Av.)
IG8: Wfd G 24Qc 54
W6 .... 50Ya 88
(off Queen Caroline St.)
Alexandra Lodge KT13: Weyb 77R 150
(off Monument Hill)
Alexandra Mans. KT17: Eps 85Va 174
(off Alexandra Rd.)
SW3 .... 51Fb 111
(off King's Rd.)
W12 .... 46Ya 88
(off Stanlake Rd.)
Alexandra M. N2 .... 27Hb 49
SW19 .... 65Bb 133
WD17: Wat 12W 26
Alexandra National Ho. N4 .... 32Rb 71
Alexandra Palace 26Mb 50
Alexandra Pal. Way N22 .... 28Lb 50
Alexandra Pde. HA2: Harr 35Da 65
Alexandra Pk. Rd. N10 .... 26Kb 50
N22 .... 25Lb 50
Alexandra Pk. Sports Cen. 25Lb 50
Alexandra Pl. CR0: C'don 74Ub 157
NW8 .... 39Eb 69
SE25 .... 71Tb 157
Alexandra Rd. AL1: St A 2C 6
(not continuous)
CM14: B'wood 20Yd 40
CR0: C'don 74Ub 157
CR4: Mitc 66Gb 133
CR6: W'ham 89Bc 178
DA8: Erith 51Hd 118
DA12: Grav'nd 9G 122
E6 .... 41Qc 94
E10 .... 34Ec 72
E17 .... 30Bc 52
E18 .... 27Kc 53
EN3: Pond E 14Zb 34
HP2: Hem H 1M 3
KT2: King T 66Qa 131
KT7: T Ditt 71Ha 152
KT15: Add 77M 149
(not continuous)
KT17: Eps 85Va 174
N8 .... 27Qb 50
N9 .... 17Xb 33
N10 .... 24Kb 50
N15 .... 29Tb 51
NW4 .... 28Za 48
NW8 .... 39Eb 69
RM1: Rom 30Hd 56
RM6: Chad H 30Ad 55
RM13: Rain 39Hd 76
RM18: Tilb 4B 122
SE26 .... 65Zb 136
SL1: Slou 8H 81
SL4: Wind 4H 103
SW14 .... 55Ta 109
SW19 .... 65Bb 133
TN16: Big H 91Kc 199
TW1: Twick 58La 108
TW3: Houn 54Da 107
TW8: Bford 51Ma 109
TW9: Kew 54Pa 109
TW15: Ashf 66T 128
TW20: Eng G 5N 125
UB8: Uxb 40M 63
W4 .... 47Ta 87
WD3: Sarr 8J 11
WD4: Chfd 2J 11
WD4: K Lan 1Q 12
WD6: Bore 10Ta 15
WD17: Wat 12W 26
Alexandra Rd. Ind. Est.
EN3: Pond E 14Zb 34
Alexandra Sq. SM4: Mord 71Cb 155
Alexandra St. E16 .... 43Jc 93
SE14 .... 52Ac 114
Alexandra Ter. DA1: Dart 58Md 119
E14 .... 50Dc 92
(off Westferry Rd.)
Alexandra Wlk. DA4: S Dar 68Qd 142
SE19 .... 64Ub 135
Alexandra Way EN8: Walt C 6Bc 20
KT19: Eps 83Qa 173
RM18: E Til 9K 101
Alexandra Wharf E2 .... 39Xb 71
(off Darwen Pl.)
Alexandra Yd. E9 .... 39Zb 72
Alexandria Apartments SE17 .... 5H 231
Alexandria Rd. W13 .... 45Ja 86
Alex Ct. HP2: Hem H 1M 3
Alexia Sq. E14 .... 48Dc 92
Alexis St. SE16 .... 49Wb 91
Alfan La. DA2: Wilm 64Fd 140
Alfearn Rd. E5 .... 35Yb 72
Alford Ct. N1 .... 2E 218
Alford Grn. CR0: New Ad 79Fc 159
Alford Ho. N6 .... 30Lb 50
Alford Pl. N1 .... 2E 218 (40Sb 71)
Alford Rd. DA8: Erith 50Ed 96
Alfoxton Av. N15 .... 28Rb 51
Alfreda St. SW11 .... 53Kb 112
Alfred Cl. W4 .... 49Ta 87
Alfred Ct. SE16 .... 49Xb 91
(off Bombay St.)
Alfred Dickens Ho. E16 .... 44Hc 93
(off Hallsville Rd.)
Alfred Finlay Ho. N22 .... 26Rb 51
Alfred Gdns. UB1: S'hall 45Aa 85
Alfred Ho. DA11: Nflt 10B 122
E9 .... 36Ac 72
(off Homerton Rd.)
E12 .... 38Nc 74
(off Tennyson Av.)
Alfred M. W1 .... 7D 216 (43Mb 90)
Alfred Nunn Ho. NW10 .... 39Va 68
Alfred Pl. DA11: Nflt 10B 122
WC1 .... 7D 216 (43Mb 90)
Alfred Prior Ho. E12 .... 35Qc 74
Alfred Rd. CM14: B'wood 19Zd 41
DA2: Hawl 63Nd 141
DA11: Grav'nd 1D 144
DA17: Belv 50Bd 95
E15 .... 36Hc 73
IG9: Buck H 19Mc 35
KT1: King T 69Na 131
RM15: Avel 46Sd 98
SE25 .... 71Wb 157
SM1: Sutt 78Eb 155
TW13: Felt 61Y 129
W2 .... 43Cb 89
W3 .... 46Sa 87
Alfred Salter Ho. SE1 .... 6K 231
Alfred's Gdns. IG11: Bark 40Uc 74
Alfred St. E3 .... 41Bc 92
RM17: Grays 51Ee 121
Alfreds Way IG11: Bark 41Rc 94
Alfreds Way Ind. Est. IG11: Bark 40Wc 75
Alfred Vs. E17 .... 28Ec 52

Alfreton Cl. SW19 .62Za 132
Alfriston KT5: Surb .72Pa 153
Alfriston Av. CR0: C'don .73Nb 156
HA2: Harr .30Ca 45
Alfriston Cl. DA1: Cray .58Gd 118
KT5: Surb .71Pa 153
Alfriston Rd. SW11 .57Hb 111
Algar Cl. HA7: Stan .22Ha 46
TW7: Isle .55Ja 108
Algar Ho. SE1 .2B 230
Algar Rd. TW7: Isle .55Ja 108
Algarve Rd. SW18 .60Db 111
Algernon Rd. NW4 .30Wa 48
NW6 .39Cb 69
SE13 .56Dc 114
Algers Cl. IG10: Lough .15Mc 35
Algers Mead IG10: Lough .15Mc 35
Algers Rd. IG10: Lough .15Mc 35
Algiers Rd. SE13 .56Cc 114
Alibon Gdns. RM10: Dag .36Cd 76
Alibon Rd. RM9: Dag .36Bd 75
RM10: Dag .36Bd 75
Alice Cl. *EN5: New Bar .14Eb 31*
(off Station App.)
Alice Gilliatt Ct. *W14 .51Bb 111*
(off Star Rd.)
Alice La. E3 .39Bc 72
Alice M. TW11: Tedd .64Ha 130
Alice Owen Technology Cen. EC1 .3B 218
Alice Ruston Pl. GU22: Wok .1N 187
Alice Shepherd Ho. *E14 .47Ec 92*
(off Manchester Rd.)
Alice St. SE1 .4H 231 (48Ub 91)
(not continuous)
Alice Thompson Cl. SE12 .61Lc 137
Alice Walker Cl. SE24 .56Rb 113
Alice Way TW3: Houn .56Da 107
Alicia Av. HA3: Kenton .28Ka 46
Alicia Cl. HA3: Kenton .28La 46
Alicia Gdns. HA3: Kenton .28Ka 46
Alicia Ho. DA16: Well .53Xc 117
Alie St. E1 .3K 225 (44Vb 91)
Alington Cres. NW9 .31Sa 67
Alington Gro. SM6: Wall .81Lb 176
Alison Cl. CR0: C'don .74Zb 158
E6 .44Qc 94
GU21: Wok .87A 168
HA5: Eastc .30X 45
Alison Ct. HP2: Hem H .1C 4
Aliwal M. SW11 .56Gb 111
Aliwal Rd. SW11 .56Gb 111
ALKERDEN .59Zd 121
Alkerden La. DA9: Ghithe .58Yd 120
DA10: Swans .58Yd 120
Alkerden Rd. W4 .50Ua 88
Alkham Rd. N16 .33Vb 71
Alkham Twr. *BR5: St M Cry .70Yc 139*
(off Bapchild Pl.)
Allan Barclay Cl. N15 .30Vb 51
Allan Cl. KT3: N Mald .71Ta 153
Allandale AL3: St A .5P 5
HP2: Hem H .1M 3
Allandale Av. N3 .27Ab 48
Allandale Cres. EN6: Pot B .4Ab 16
Allandale Pl. BR6: Chels .76Zc 161
Allandale Rd. EN3: Enf W .8Zb 20
RM11: Horn .31Hd 76
Allanson Ct. *E10 .33Cc 72*
(off Leyton Grange Est.)
Allan Way W3 .43Sa 87
Allard Cl. BR5: Orp .73Yc 161
Allard Cres. WD23: B Hea .18Ea 28
Allard Gdns. SW4 .57Mb 112
Allard Ho. *NW9 .26Va 48*
(off Boulevard Dr.)
Allardyce St. SW4 .56Pb 112
Allbrook Cl. TW11: Tedd .64Ga 130
Allcroft Rd. NW5 .36Jb 70
Allder Way CR2: S Croy .80Rb 157
Alldicks Rd. HP3: Hem H .4P 3
Allenby Av. CR2: S Croy .81Sb 177
Allenby Cl. UB6: G'frd .41Ca 85
Allenby Cres. RM17: Grays .50De 99
Allenby Dr. RM11: Horn .32Nd 77
Allenby Rd. SE23 .62Ac 136
SE28 .48Sc 94
TN16: Big H .89Nc 180
UB1: S'hall .41Ca 85
Allen Cl. CR4: Mitc .67Kb 134
TW16: Sun .67X 129
WD7: Shenl .4Na 15
Allen Ct. AL10: Hat .2D 8
E17 .30Cc 52
(off Yunus Khan Cl.)
UB6: G'frd .36Ha 66
Allendale Av. UB1: S'hall .44Ca 85
Allendale Cl. DA2: Dart .60Td 120
SE5 .54Tb 113
SE26 .64Zb 136
Allendale Rd. HA0: Wemb .37Ka 66
UB6: G'frd .37Ka 66
Allen Edwards Dr. SW8 .53Nb 112
Allenford Ho. *SW15 .58Va 110*
(off Tunworth Cres.)
Allen Ho. *W8 .48Cb 89*
(off Allen St.)
Allen Ho. Pk. GU22: Wok .2N 187
Allen Mans. *W8 .48Cb 89*
(off Allen St.)
Allen Rd. BR3: Beck .68Zb 136
CR0: C'don .74Qb 156
E3 .40Bc 72
KT23: Bookh .98Da 191
N16 .35Ub 71
RM13: Rain .40Ld 77
TW16: Sun .67X 129
Allensbury Pl. NW1 .38Mb 70
Allens La. TN15: Plax .100Ce 205
Allens Mead DA12: Grav'nd .10H 123
Allens Rd. EN3: Pond E .15Yb 34
Allen St. W8 .48Cb 89
Allensway SS17: Stan H .1P 101
Allenswood SW19 .60Ab 110
Allenswood Rd. SE9 .55Nc 116
Allen Way SL3: Dat .3N 103
Allerds Rd. SL2: Farn R .9D 60
Allerford Ct. HA2: Harr .29Ea 46
Allerford Rd. SE6 .62Dc 136
Allerton Cl. WD6: Bore .10Pa 15
Allerton Ho. N1 .3F 219
Allerton Rd. N16 .33Sb 71
WD6: Bore .10Na 15
Allerton St. N1 .3G 219 (41Tb 91)
Allerton Wlk. N7 .33Pb 70
Allestree Rd. SW6 .52Ab 110
Alleyn Cres. SE21 .61Tb 135
Alleyndale Rd. RM8: Dag .33Yc 75
Alleyn Ho. SE1 .4G 231
Alleyn Pk. SE21 .61Tb 135
UB2: S'hall .50Ca 85
Alleyn Rd. SE21 .62Tb 135
Alleys, The HP2: Hem H .1M 3
Alley Way UB8: Uxb .38M 63
Allfarthing La. SW18 .58Db 111
Allgood Cl. SM4: Mord .72Za 154
Allgood St. E2 .40Vb 71
Allhallows La. EC4 .5F 225 (45Tb 91)
All Hallows Rd. N17 .25Ub 51
Allhallows Rd. E6 .43Nc 94
Allhusen Gdns. SL3: Ful .35A 62
Alliance Cl. HA0: Wemb .35Ma 67
TW4: Houn .57Ba 107
Alliance Ct. TW15: Ashf .63S 128
W3 .43Ra 87
Alliance Rd. E13 .43Lc 94
SE18 .51Wc 117
W3 .42Ra 87
Allied Ct. *N1 .38Ub 71*
(off Enfield Rd.)
Allied Ind. Est. W3 .47Ua 88
Allied Way W3 .47Ua 88
Allingham Cl. W7 .45Ha 86
Allingham Ct. BR2: Brom .70Hc 137
Allingham M. N1 .1D 218
Allingham Rd. RH2: Reig .9J 207
Allingham St. N1 .1D 218 (40Sb 71)
Allington Av. N17 .23Ub 51
TW17: Shep .69U 128
Allington Cl. DA12: Grav'nd .10H 123
SW19 .64Za 132
UB6: G'frd .38Ea 66
Allington Ct. *CR0: C'don .72Yb 158*
(off Chart Cl.)
EN3: Pond E .15Zb 34
SL2: Slou .4K 81
SW1 .4A 228
SW8 .54Lb 112
Allington Rd. BR6: Orp .75Tc 160
HA2: Harr .29Ea 46
NW4 .29Xa 48
W10 .41Ab 88
Allingtons RH2: Reig .3J 207
Allington St. SW1 .4A 228 (48Kb 90)
Allison Cl. EN9: Walt A .4Jc 21
SE10 .53Ec 114
Allison Gro. SE21 .60Ub 113
Allison Rd. N8 .29Qb 50
W3 .44Sa 87
Alliston Ho. *E2 .41Vb 91*
(off Gibraltar Wlk.)
Allistonway SS17: Stan H .1P 101
Allitsen Rd. NW8 .2D 214 (40Gb 69)
(not continuous)
Allkins Ct. SL4: Wind .4H 103
All Nations Ho. *E8 .38Xb 71*
(off Martello St.)
Allnutts Rd. CM16: Epp .5Wc 23
Allnutt Way SW4 .57Mb 112
Alloa Rd. IG3: Ilf .33Wc 75
SE8 .50Zb 92
Allom Ho. *W11 .45Ab 88*
(off Clarendon Rd.)
Allonby Dr. HA4: Ruis .31R 64
Allonby Gdns. HA9: Wemb .32La 66
Allonby Ho. *E14 .43Ac 92*
(off Aston St.)
Allotment La.
TN13: S'oaks .94Ld 203
Allotment Way NW2 .34Za 68
Alloway Cl. GU21: Wok .10M 167
Alloway Rd. E3 .41Ac 92
Allport Ho. *SE5 .55Tb 113*
(off Champion Pk.)
Allport M. *E1 .42Yb 92*
(off Hayfield Pas.)
All Saints Cl. DA10: Swans .57Be 121
IG7: Chig .20Xc 37
N9 .19Wb 33
SW8 .53Nb 112
All Saints Ct. *E1 .45Yb 92*
(off Johnson St.)
SW11 .52Kb 112
(off Prince of Wales Dr.)
TW5: Hest .53Z 107
(off Springwell Rd.)
All Saints Cres. WD25: Wat .5Z 13
All Saints Dr. CR2: Sande .84Vb 177
SE3 .54Gc 115
(not continuous)
All Saints Ho. *W11 .43Bb 89*
(off All Saints Rd.)
All Saints La. WD3: Crox G .16Q 26
All Saints M. HA3: Hrw W .23Ga 46
All Saints Pas. SW18 .57Cb 111
All Saints Rd. DA11: Nflt .10B 122
GU18: Light .2A 166
SM1: Sutt .76Db 155
SW19 .66Eb 133
(not continuous)
W3 .48Sa 87
W11 .43Bb 89
All Saints St. N1 .1H 217 (40Pb 70)
All Saints Twr. E10 .31Dc 72
Allsop Pl. NW1 .6G 215 (42Hb 89)
All Souls Av. NW10 .40Xa 68
All Souls' Pl. W1 .1A 222 (43Kb 90)
Allum Gro. KT20: Tad .93Xa 194
Allum La. WD6: E'tree .15Ma 29
Allum Way N20 .18Eb 31
Alluvium Ct. *SE1 .3H 231*
(off Long La.)
Allwood Cl. SE26 .63Zb 136
Allyn Cl. TW18: Staines .65H 127
Alma, The DA12: Grav'nd .4H 145
Alma Av. E4 .24Ec 52
RM12: Horn .35Nd 77
Alma Barn M. BR6: Orp .75Zc 161
Alma Birk Ho. NW6 .38Ab 68
Almack Rd. E5 .35Yb 72
Alma Cl. GU21: Knap .9J 167
N10 .25Kb 50
Alma Ct. *CR3: Cat'm .93Sb 197*
(off Coulsdon Rd.)
EN6: Pot B .2Eb 17
HA2: Harr .33Fa 66
SL1: Burn .1A 80
WD6: Bore .10Pa 15
Alma Cres. SM1: Sutt .78Ab 154
Alma Cut AL1: St A .3C 6
Alma Gro. SE1 .49Vb 91
Alma Ho. N9 .21Wb 51
TW8: Bford .51Na 109
Alma Pl. CR7: Thor H .71Qb 156
NW10 .41Xa 88
SE19 .66Vb 135
WD25: Wat .8Aa 13
Alma Rd. AL1: St A .3C 6
BR5: Orp .75Zc 161
DA10: Swans .57Be 121
DA14: Sidc .62Wc 139
EN3: Enf H, Pond E .15Ac 34
KT10: Esh .74Ga 152
N10 .24Kb 50
RH2: Reig .5K 207
SL4: Eton W .9D 80
SL4: Wind .4G 102
SM5: Cars .78Gb 155
SW18 .56Eb 111
UB1: S'hall .45Aa 85
Alma Rd. Ind. Est. EN3: Pond E .14Zb 34
Alma Row HA3: Hrw W .25Fa 46
Alma Sq. NW8 .2A 214 (40Eb 69)
Alma St. E15 .37Ec 73
NW5 .37Kb 70
Alma Ter. *E3 .39Bc 72*
(off Beale Rd.)
SW18 .59Fb 111
W8 .48Cb 89
Almeida St. N1 .39Rb 71
Almeida Theatre .39Rb 71
(off Almeida St.)
Almeric Rd. SW11 .56Hb 111
Almer Rd. SW20 .66Wa 132
Almington St. N4 .32Pb 70
Almners Rd. KT16: Lyne .74C 148
(not continuous)
Almond Av. GU22: Wok .3P 187
SM5: Cars .75Hb 155
UB7: W Dray .48Q 84
UB10: Ick .34R 64
W5 .48Ma 87
Almond Cl. BR2: Brom .73Qc 160
HA4: Ruis .34V 64
RM16: Grays .8C 100
SE15 .54Wb 113
SL4: Wind .4F 102
TW13: Felt .60W 106
TW17: Shep .68S 128
TW20: Eng G .5M 125
UB3: Hayes .45U 84
Almond Dr. BR8: Swan .68Fd 140
Almond Gro. TW8: Bford .52Ka 108
Almond Ho. *E15 .41Gc 93*
(off Teasel Way)
Almond Rd. DA2: Dart .59Sd 120
KT19: Eps .83Ta 173
N17 .24Wb 51
SE16 .49Xb 91
SL1: Burn .1A 80
Almonds, The AL1: St A .6F 6
Almonds Av. IG9: Buck H .19Jc 35
Almond Wlk. AL10: Hat .3C 8
Almond Way BR2: Brom .73Qc 160
CR4: Mitc .71Mb 156
HA2: Harr .26Da 45
WD6: Bore .14Ra 29
Almons Way SL2: Slou .3M 81
Almorah Rd. N1 .38Tb 71
TW5: Hest .53Z 107
Alms Heath GU23: Ock .93R 190
Almshouse La. EN1: Enf .6Xb 19
KT9: Chess .81La 172
Alms Houses, The IG11: Bark .37Sc 74
Almshouses IG10: Lough .11Pc 36
KT16: Chert .73J 149
Almshouses, The *EN8: Chesh .2Zb 20*
(off Turner's Hill)
Alms Row TN16: Bras .96Xc 201
Alnmouth Ct. *UB1: S'hall .44Ea 86*
(off Fleming Rd.)
Alnwick N17 .24Xb 51
Alnwick Ct. *DA2: Dart .58Rd 119*
(off Osbourne Rd.)
Alnwick Gro. SM4: Mord .70Db 133
Alnwick Rd. E16 .44Lc 93
SE12 .58Kc 115
ALPERTON .40Na 67
Alperton La. HA0: Wemb .41La 86
UB6: G'frd .41La 86
Alperton St. W10 .42Bb 89
Alphabet Gdns. SM5: Cars .72Fb 155
Alphabet Sq. E3 .43Cc 92
Alpha Bus. Cen. E17 .29Bc 52
Alpha Bus. Pk. AL9: Wel G .5E 8
Alpha Cl. NW1 .4E 214 (42Gb 89)
Alpha Ct. CR3: Whyt .90Wb 177
WD17: Wat .13Y 27
(off Grosvenor Rd.)
Alpha Est. UB3: Hayes .47U 84
Alpha Gro. E14 .47Cc 92
Alpha Ho. NW6 .40Cb 69
NW8 .6D 214
SW4 .56Pb 112
Alpha Pl. NW6 .40Cb 69
SM4: Mord .74Za 154
SW3 .51Gb 111
Alpha Rd. CM13: Hut .16Fe 41
CR0: C'don .74Ub 157
E4 .20Cc 34
EN3: Pond E .14Ac 34
GU22: Wok .88D 168
GU24: Chob .2K 167
KT5: Surb .72Pa 153
N18 .23Wb 51
SE14 .53Bc 114
TW11: Tedd .64Fa 130
UB10: Hil .42R 84
Alpha St. SE15 .54Wb 113
Alpha St. Nth. SL1: Slou .7L 81
Alpha St. Sth. SL1: Slou .8K 81
Alpha Way TW20: Thorpe .67E 126
Alphea Cl. SW19 .66Gb 133
Alpine Av. KT5: Surb .75Sa 153
Alpine Bus. Cen. E6 .43Qc 94
Alpine Cl. CR0: C'don .76Ub 157
SL5: S'hill .2B 146
Alpine Copse BR1: Brom .68Qc 138
Alpine Gro. E9 .38Yb 72
Alpine Rd. E10 .33Dc 72
KT12: Walt T .73W 150
RH1: Redh .3A 208
SE16 .50Zb 92
Alpine Vw. SM5: Cars .78Gb 155
Alpine Wlk. HA7: Stan .19Ga 28
Alpine Way E6 .43Qc 94
Alric Av. KT3: N Mald .69Ua 132
NW10 .38Ta 67
Alroy Rd. N4 .31Qb 70
Alsace Rd. SE17 .7H 231
Alsager *KT22: Lea .91Ja 192*
(off Clements Mead)
Alscot Rd. SE1 .5K 231 (49Vb 91)
Alscot Rd. Ind. Est. SE1 .4K 231 (48Vb 91)
Alscot Way SE1 .5K 231 (49Vb 91)
Alsike Rd. DA18: Erith .48Zc 95
SE2 .48Zc 95
Alsom Av. KT4: Wor Pk .77Wa 154
Alsop Cl. AL2: Lon C .9J 7
Alston Cl. KT6: Surb .73Ka 152
Alstonfield KT10: Esh .78Ea 152
Alston Rd. EN5: Barn .13Ab 30
HP1: Hem H .3J 3
N18 .22Xb 51
SW17 .63Fb 133
Alston Works EN5: Barn .13Ab 30
Altair Cl. N17 .23Vb 51
Altair Way HA6: Nwood .21V 44
Altamont CR6: W'ham .91Xb 197
Altash Way SE9 .61Pc 138
Altenburg Av. W13 .48Ka 86
Altenburg Gdns. SW11 .56Hb 111
Alterton Cl. GU21: Wok .9L 167
Alt Gro. SW19 .66Bb 133
Altham Ct. HA2: Harr .25Da 45
Altham Gdns. WD19: Wat .21Z 45
Altham Rd. HA5: Pinn .24Aa 45
Altham Way WD19: Wat .22Aa 45
Althea St. SW6 .54Db 111
Althorne Gdns. E18 .28Hc 53
Althorne Rd. RH1: Redh .8A 208
Althorne Way RM10: Dag .33Cd 76
Althorp Cl. EN5: Ark .17Wa 30
Althorpe M. SW11 .53Fb 111
Althorpe Rd. HA1: Harr .29Ea 46
Althorp Rd. AL1: St A .1D 6
SW17 .60Hb 111
Altima Ct. *SE22 .56Wb 113*
(off E. Dulwich Rd.)
Altior Ct. N6 .30Lb 50
Altitude Apartments *CR0: C'don .76Tb 157*
(off Altyre Rd.)
Altius Apartments *E3 .40Cc 72*
(off Wick La.)
Altmore Av. E6 .38Pc 74
Alton Av. HA7: Stan .24Ha 46
Altona Way SL1: Slou .4F 80
Alton Cl. DA5: Bexl .60Ad 117
TW7: Isle .54Ha 108
Alton Cotts. DA4: Eyns .74Nd 163
Alton Ct. TW18: Staines .67G 126
Alton Gdns. BR3: Beck .66Cc 136
TW2: Whitt .59Fa 108
Alton Ho. *E3 .41Dc 92*
(off Bromley High St.)
RH1: Redh .4A 208
Alton Rd. CR0: Wadd .76Qb 156
N17 .27Tb 51
SW15 .60Wa 110
TW9: Rich .56Na 109
Alton St. E14 .43Dc 92
Altura Twr. SW11 .54Fb 111
Altwood Cl. SL1: Slou .3C 80
Altyre Cl. BR3: Beck .71Bc 158
Altyre Rd. CR0: C'don .75Tb 157
Altyre Way BR3: Beck .71Bc 158
Aluna Ct. SE15 .55Yb 114
Aluric Cl. RM16: Grays .9D 100
Alvanley Gdns. NW6 .36Db 69
Alva Way WD19: Wat .19Z 27
Alverstoke Rd. RM3: Rom .24Nd 57
Alverstone Av. EN4: E Barn .17Gb 31
SW19 .61Cb 133
Alverstone Gdns. SE9 .60Sc 116
Alverstone Ho. SE11 .51Qb 112
Alverstone Rd. E12 .35Qc 74
HA9: Wemb .32Pa 67
KT3: N Mald .70Va 132
NW2 .38Ya 68
Alverston Gdns. SE25 .71Ub 157
Alverton St. SE8 .50Bc 92
(not continuous)
Alveston Av. HA3: Kenton .27Ka 46
Alveston Sq. E18 .26Jc 53
Alvey St. SE17 .7H 231 (50Ub 91)
Alvia Gdns. SM1: Sutt .77Eb 155
Alvington Cres. E8 .36Vb 71
Alvista Av. SL6: Tap .4A 80
Alway Av. KT19: Ewe .78Ta 153
Always Rd. RM15: S Ock .43Xd 98
Alwin Pl. WD18: Wat .14U 26
Alwold Cres. SE12 .58Kc 115
Alwyn Av. W4 .50Ta 87
Alwyn Cl. CR0: New Ad .80Dc 158
WD6: E'tree .16Pa 29
Alwyne Av. CM15: Shenf .16Ce 41
Alwyne Ct. GU21: Wok .88A 168
Alwyne La. N1 .38Rb 71
Alwyne Pl. N1 .37Sb 71
Alwyne Rd. N1 .38Sb 71
SW19 .65Bb 133
W7 .45Ga 86
Alwyne Sq. N1 .37Sb 71
Alwyne Vs. N1 .38Rb 71
Alwyn Gdns. NW4 .28Wa 48
W3 .44Ra 87
Alwyns Cl. KT16: Chert .72J 149
Alwyns La. KT16: Chert .72H 149
Alyth Gdns. NW11 .30Cb 49
Alzette Ho. *E2 .40Zb 72*
(off Mace St.)
Amadeus Ho. *BR1: Brom .69Kc 137*
(off Elmfield Rd.)
Amalgamated Dr. TW8: Bford .51Ka 108
Amanda Cl. IG7: Chig .23Tc 54
Amanda Ct. SL3: L'ly .8P 81
TW15: Ashf .61P 127
(off Edward Way)
Amanda M. RM7: Rom .29Ed 56
Amar Ct. SE18 .49Vc 95
Amar Deep Ct. SE18 .50Vc 95
Amazon Bldg. N8 .28Pb 50
Amazon St. E1 .44Wb 91
Ambassador, The SL5: S'dale .3F 146
Ambassador Cl. TW3: Houn .54Aa 107
Ambassador Gdns. E6 .43Pc 94
Ambassador Ho. NW8 .1A 214 (39Eb 69)
Ambassadors Cinema
Woking .89A 168
(off Victoria Way)
Ambassadors Ct. *E8 .38Vb 71*
(off Holly St.)
SW1 .7C 222
Ambassador Sq. E14 .49Dc 92
Ambassadors Theatre .3E 222
Amber Av. E17 .25Ac 52
Amber Cl. EN5: New Bar .16Db 31
Amber Ct. CR0: C'don .74Ub 157
E15 .39Ec 72
(off Warton Rd.)
KT5: Surb .73Pa 153
N7 .37Qb 70
(off Bride St.)
TW18: Staines .64H 127
(off Laleham Rd.)
Ambercroft Way CR5: Coul .91Rb 197
Amberden Av. N3 .27Cb 49
Ambergate St. SE17 .7C 230 (50Rb 91)
Amber Gro. NW2 .32Za 68
Amber Ho. *E1 .44Zb 92*
(off Aylward St.)
Amber La. IG6: Ilf .24Rc 54
Amberley Cl. BR6: Chels .78Vc 161
GU23: Send .97H 189
HA5: Pinn .27Ba 45
Amberley Ct. BR3: Beck .66Bc 136
DA14: Sidc .64Yc 139
Amberley Dr. KT15: Wdhm .82H 169
Amberley Gdns. EN1: Enf .17Ub 33
KT19: Ewe .77Va 154
Amberley Gro. CR0: C'don .73Vb 157
SE26 .64Xb 135
Amberley Pl. *SL4: Wind .3H 103*
(off Peascod St.)
Amberley Rd. E10 .31Cc 72
EN1: Enf .17Vb 33
IG9: Buck H .18Lc 35
N13 .19Pb 32
SE2 .51Zc 117
SL2: Slou .3C 80
W9 .43Cb 89
Amberley Ter. *WD19: Wat .16Aa 27*
(off Villiers Rd.)
Amberley Way RM7: Mawney .28Dd 56
SM4: Mord .73Bb 155
TW4: Houn .57Y 107
UB10: Uxb .40N 63
Amber M. *N22 .27Qb 50*
(off High Rd.)
Amberside Cl. TW7: Isle .58Fa 108
Amberside Ct. HP3: Hem H .5K 3
Amber Way W3 .47Ua 88
Amber Wharf E2 .1K 219
Amberwood Cl. SM6: Wall .78Nb 156
Amberwood Ri. KT3: N Mald .72Ua 154
Amblecote KT11: Cobh .83Aa 171
Amblecote Cl. SE12 .62Kc 137
Amblecote Mdws. SE12 .62Kc 137
Amblecote Rd. SE12 .62Kc 137
Ambler Rd. N4 .34Rb 71
Ambleside BR1: Brom .65Fc 137
CM16: Epp .3Wc 23
NW1 .2A 216
RM19: Purf .50Sd 98
SW19 .60Ab 110
Ambleside Av. BR3: Beck .71Ac 158
KT12: Walt T .74Y 151
RM12: Horn .36Kd 77
SW16 .63Mb 134
Ambleside Cl. E9 .36Yb 72
E10 .31Dc 72
N17 .27Vb 51
RH1: Redh .10B 208
Ambleside Cres. EN3: Enf H .13Zb 34
Ambleside Dr. TW14: Felt .60V 106
Ambleside Gdns. CR2: Sels .81Zb 178
HA9: Wemb .32Ma 67
IG4: Ilf .28Nc 54
SM2: Sutt .79Eb 155
SW16 .64Mb 134
Ambleside Point *SE15 .52Yb 114*
(off Tustin Est.)
Ambleside Rd. DA7: Bex .54Cd 118
GU18: Light .3A 166
NW10 .38Va 68
Ambleside Wlk. UB8: Uxb .39M 63
Ambleside Way TW20: Egh .66D 126
Ambrey Way SM6: Wall .81Mb 176
Ambrooke Rd. DA17: Belv .48Cd 96
Ambrosden Av. SW1 .4C 228 (48Lb 90)
Ambrose Av. NW11 .31Ab 68
Ambrose Cl. BR6: Orp .76Vc 161
DA1: Cray .56Hd 118
E6 .43Pc 94
Ambrose Ho. *E14 .43Cc 92*
(off Selsey St.)
Ambrose M. SW11 .54Hb 111
Ambrose St. SE16 .49Xb 91
Ambrose Wlk. E3 .40Cc 72
Ambulance Rd. E11 .29Fc 53
AMC Bus. Cen. NW10 .41Ra 87
Amelia Cl. W3 .46Ra 87
Amelia Ho. *NW9 .26Va 48*
(off Boulevard Dr.)
TW9: Kew .52Ra 109
W6 .50Ya 88
(off Queen Caroline St.)
Amelia St. SE17 .7C 230 (50Sb 91)
Amelle Gdns. RM3: Hrld W .23Rd 57
Amen Cnr. EC4 .3C 224 (44Rb 91)
SW17 .65Hb 133
Amen Ct. EC4 .3C 224 (44Rb 91)
Amenity Way SM4: Mord .73Ya 154
Amerden Way SL1: Slou .7E 80
American International University in London, The
Kensington Campus -
Ansdell Street .48Db 89
St Albans Grove .48Db 89
Young Street .47Db 89
Richmond Hill Campus .58Na 109
American University of London, The .34Pb 70
America Sq. EC3 .4K 225 (45Vb 91)
America St. SE1 .7D 224 (46Sb 91)
Amerland Rd. SW18 .57Bb 111
Amersham Av. N18 .23Tb 51
Amersham Cl. RM3: Rom .23Pd 57
Amersham Dr. RM3: Rom .23Nd 57
Amersham Gro. SE14 .52Bc 114
Amersham Ho. *WD18: Wat .17U 26*
(off Chenies Way)
Amersham Rd. CR0: C'don .72Sb 157
HP6: L Chal .11A 24
RM3: Rom .23Nd 57
SE14 .53Bc 114
SL9: Chal P .21A 42
SL9: Ger X .28B 42
(not continuous)
UB9: Den .30C 42
WD3: Chen .11A 24

Amersham Va. SE14 52Bc 114
Amersham Wlk. RM3: Rom 23Pd 57
Amersham Way HP6: L Chal 11A 24
Amery Gdns. NW10 39Ya 68
RM2: Rom 27Md 57
Amery Ho. SE17 7J 231
Amery Rd. HA1: Harr 33Ja 66
Amesbury EN9: Walt A 4Jc 21
Amesbury Av. SW2 61Nb 134
Amesbury Cl. CM16: Epp 3Vc 23
KT4: Wor Pk 74Ya 154
Amesbury Ct. EN2: Enf 12Qb 32
Amesbury Dr. E4 16Dc 34
Amesbury Rd. BR1: Brom 69Mc 137
CM16: Epp 3Vc 23
RM9: Dag 38Zc 75
SL1: Slou 7D 80
TW13: Felt 61Z 129
Amesbury Twr. SW8 54Lb 112
Ames Cotts. *E14* 43Ac 92
(off Maroon St.)
Ames Ho. *E2* 40Zb 72
(off Mace St.)
Ames Rd. DA10: Swans 58Ae 121
Amethyst Cl. N11 24Mb 50
Amethyst Ct. *BR6: Chels* 78Uc 160
(off Farnborough Hill)
EN3: Enf H 13Ac 34
(off Enstone Rd.)
Amethyst Rd. E15 35Fc 73
Amey Dr. KT23: Bookh 96Ea 192
AMF Bowling
Gravesend 8C 122
Amherst Av. W13 44La 86
Amherst Cl. BR5: St M Cry 70Xc 139
Amherst Dr. BR5: St M Cry 70Vc 139
Amherst Gdns. *W13* 44La 86
(off Amherst Rd.)
Amherst Hill TN13: Riv 95Hd 202
Amherst Ho. *SE16* 47Zb 92
(off Wolfe Cres.)
Amherst Pl. TN13: Riv 94Hd 202
Amherst Rd. TN13: S'oaks 94Kd 203
W13 44La 86
Amhurst Cl. EN3: Enf W 9Zb 20
Amhurst Gdns. TW7: Isle 54Ja 108
Amhurst Pde. *N16* 31Vb 71
(off Amhurst Pk.)
Amhurst Pk. N16 31Tb 71
Amhurst Pas. E8 35Wb 71
Amhurst Rd. E8 36Xb 71
N16 35Vb 71
Amhurst Ter. E8 35Wb 71
Amhurst Wlk. SE28 46Wc 95
Amias Dr. HA8: Edg 21Na 47
Amias Ho. EC1 5D 218
Amicia Gdns. SL2: Stoke P 9K 61
Amida Golf Course 62Ca 129
Amidas Gdns. RM8: Dag 35Xc 75
Amiel St. E1 42Yb 92
Amies St. SW11 55Hb 111
Amigo Ho. SE1 3A 230
Amina Way SE16 48Wb 91
Amiot Ho. *NW9* 26Va 48
(off Heritage Av.)
Amis Av. KT15: New H 82J 169
KT19: Ewe 79Ra 153
Amisha Ct. SE1 4K 231
Amis Rd. GU21: Wok 1J 187
Amity Ct. DA9: Ghithe 56Wd 120
Amity Gro. SW20 67Xa 132
Amity Rd. E15 38Hc 73
Ammanford Grn. NW9 30Ua 48
Ammonite Ho. E15 38Hc 73
Amner Rd. SW11 58Jb 112
Amor Rd. W6 48Ya 88
Amory Ho. N1 1J 217
Amott Rd. SE15 55Wb 113
Amoy Pl. E14 45Cc 92
(not continuous)
Ampere Way CR0: Wadd 73Nb 156
Ampleforth Cl. BR6: Chels 77Yc 161
Ampleforth Rd. SE2 47Xc 95
Amport Pl. NW7 23Ab 48
Ampthill Est. NW1 2C 216 (40Lb 70)
Ampthill Ho. *RM3: Rom* 22Md 57
(off Montgomery Cres.)
Ampthill Sq. NW1 2C 216 (40Lb 70)
Ampton Pl. WC1 4H 217 (41Pb 90)
Ampton St. WC1 4H 217 (41Pb 90)
Amroth Cl. SE23 60Xb 113
Amroth Grn. NW9 30Ua 48
Amstel Ct. SE15 52Vb 113
Amstel Way GU21: Wok 10K 167
Amsterdam Rd. E14 48Ec 92
Amundsen Ct. *E14* 50Cc 92
(off Napier Av.)
Amundsen Ho. *NW10* 38Ta 67
(off Stonebridge Pk.)
Amwell Cl. EN2: Enf 15Tb 33
WD25: Wat 7Aa 13
Amwell Ct. EN9: Walt A 5Hc 21
Amwell Ct. Est. N4 33Sb 71
Amwell St. EC1 3K 217 (41Qb 90)
Amwell Vw. IG6: Chig, Ilf 22Xc 55
Amyand Cotts. TW1: Twick 58Ka 108
Amyand La. TW1: Twick 59Ka 108
Amyand Pk. Gdns.
TW1: Twick 59Ka 108
Amyand Pk. Rd. TW1: Twick 59Ja 108
Amy Cl. SM6: Wall 80Nb 156
Amy Johnson Ct. HA8: Edg 26Ra 47
Amy Rd. RH8: Oxt 1J 211
Amyruth Rd. SE4 57Cc 114
Amy Warne Cl. E6 42Nc 94
Anarth Ct. KT13: Weyb 74U 150
Anatola Rd. N19 33Lb 70
Ancaster Cres. KT3: N Mald 72Wa 154
Ancaster M. BR3: Beck 69Zb 136
Ancaster Rd. BR3: Beck 69Zb 136
Ancaster St. SE18 52Uc 116
Anchor SW18 56Db 111
Anchorage Cl. SW19 64Cb 133
Anchorage Ho. *E14* 45Fc 93
(off Clove Cres.)
Anchorage Point *E14* 47Bc 92
(off Cuba St.)
Anchorage Point Ind. Est.
SE7 48Lc 93
Anchor & Hope La. SE7 48Kc 93
Anchor Bay Ind. Est. DA8: Erith 51Jd 118
Anchor Blvd. DA2: Dart 56Sd 120
Anchor Brewhouse
SE1 7K 225 (46Vb 91)
Anchor Bus. Cen. CR0: Bedd 76Nb 156
Anchor Cl. IG11: Bark 41Xc 95
Anchor Ct. DA8: Erith 52Hd 118
EN1: Enf 15Ub 33
RM17: Grays 52De 121
SW1 6D 228
Anchor Cres. GU21: Knap 9H 167
Anchor Dr. RM13: Rain 41Kd 97
Anchor Hill GU21: Knap 9H 167
Anchor Ho. *E16* 43Hc 93
(off Barking Rd.)
E16 44Lc 93
(off Prince Regent La.)
EC1 5D 218
SW10 51Fb 111
(off Cremorne Est.)
Anchor La. HP1: Hem H 4K 3
(not continuous)
Anchor M. N1 37Ub 71
SW12 58Kb 112
Anchor Retail Pk. E1 42Yb 92
Anchor St. SE16 49Xb 91
Anchor Ter. E1 42Yb 92
SE1 6E 224
Anchor Wharf *E3* 43Dc 92
(off Yeo St.)
Anchor Yd. EC1 5E 218 (42Sb 91)
Ancient Almshouses *EN8: Chesh* 2Zb 20
(off Turner's Hill)
Ancill Cl. W6 51Ab 110
Ancona Rd. NW10 40Wa 68
SE18 50Tc 94
Andace Pk. Gdns. BR1: Brom 68Lc 137
Andalus Rd. SW9 55Nb 112
Ander Cl. HA0: Wemb 35Ma 67
Andermans SL4: Wind 3B 102
Anderson Cl. KT19: Eps 84Ra 173
N21 15Pb 32
SM3: Sutt 74Cb 155
UB9: Hare 25J 43
W3 44Ta 87
Anderson Ct. NW2 32Ya 68
RH1: Redh 9A 208
Anderson Dr. TW15: Ashf 63S 128
Anderson Hgts. SW16 68Pb 134
Anderson Ho. AL4: St A 3H 7
E14 45Ec 92
(off Woolmore St.)
IG11: Bark 39Tc 74
SW17 64Fb 133
Anderson Pl. TW3: Houn 56Da 107
Anderson Rd. E9 37Zb 72
IG8: Wfd G 27Mc 53
KT13: Weyb 76T 150
WD7: Shenl 5Qa 15
Andersons SS17: Stan H 1P 101
Anderson Sq. *N1* 39Rb 71
(off Gaskin St.)
Anderson St. SW3 7F 227 (50Hb 89)
Anderson Way DA17: Belv 47Dd 96
Anderton Cl. SE5 55Tb 113
Anderton Ct. N22 26Mb 50
Andora Ct. *NW6* 38Ab 68
(off Brondesbury Pk.)
Andorra Ct. BR1: Brom 67Lc 137
Andover Av. E16 44Mc 93
Andover Cl. KT19: Eps 83Ta 173
TW14: Felt 60V 106
UB6: G'frd 42Da 85
UB8: Uxb 40K 63
Andover Ct. TW19: Stanw 59M 105
Andover Pl. NW6 40Db 69
Andover Rd. BR6: Orp 74Tc 160
N7 33Pb 70
TW2: Twick 60Fa 108
Andoversford Ct. *SE15* 51Ub 113
(off Bibury Cl.)
Andover Ter. *W6* 49Xa 88
(off Raynham Rd.)
Andrea Av. RM16: Grays 47Ce 99
Andreck Ct. *BR3: Beck* 68Ec 136
(off Crescent Rd.)
Andre St. E8 36Wb 71
Andrew Cl. DA1: Cray 57Fd 118
IG6: Ilf 23Tc 54
WD7: Shenl 5Pa 15
Andrew Ct. SE23 61Zb 136
Andrewes Gdns. E6 44Nc 94
Andrewes Highwalk EC2 1E 224
Andrewes Ho. EC2 1E 224
SM1: Sutt 77Cb 155
Andrew Gibb Memorial, The 53Hc 115
Andrew Hill La. SL2: Hedg 3G 60
Andrew Pl. SW8 52Mb 112
Andrew Reed Ct. *WD24: Wat* 12Y 27
(off Keele Cl.)
Andrew Reed Ho. *SW18* 59Ab 110
(off Linstead Way)
Andrews Cl. BR5: St P 68Zc 139
HA1: Harr 31Fa 66
HP2: Hem H 1M 3
IG9: Buck H 19Lc 35
KT4: Wor Pk 75Ya 154
KT17: Eps 86Va 174
Andrews Crosse WC2 3K 223
Andrews Ho. CR2: S Croy 79Sb 157
NW3 38Hb 69
(off Fellows Rd.)
Andrew's La. EN7: Chesh, G Oak 1Vb 19
Andrews Pl. DA2: Wilm 61Gd 140
SE9 58Rc 116
Andrew's Rd. E8 39Xb 71
Andrew St. E14 44Ec 92
Andrews Wlk. SE17 51Rb 113
Andringham Lodge *BR1: Brom* 67Kc 137
(off Palace Gro.)
Andromeda Ct. RM3: Rom 24Ld 57
Andrula Ct. N22 25Rb 51
Andwell Cl. SE2 47Xc 95
ANERLEY 67Xb 135
Anerley Gro. SE19 66Vb 135
Anerley Hill SE19 65Vb 135
Anerley Pk. SE20 66Wb 135
Anerley Pk. Rd. SE20 66Xb 135
Anerley Rd. SE19 66Wb 135
SE20 66Wb 135
Anerley Sta. Rd. SE20 67Xb 135
Anerley Va. SE19 66Vb 135
Aneurin Bevan Ct. NW2 33Xa 68
Aneurin Bevan Ho. N11 24Mb 50
Anfield Cl. SW12 59Lb 112
Angas Ct. KT13: Weyb 78S 150
ANGEL 2A 218 (40Qb 70)
Angela Carter Cl. SW9 55Qb 112
Angela Davies Ind. Est. SE24 56Rb 113
Angel All. *E1* 44Vb 91
(off Whitechapel High St.)
Angel Centre, The N1 2A 218
Angel Cl. N18 22Vb 51
TW12: Hamp H 64Ea 130
Angel Cnr. Pde. N18 21Wb 51
Angel Ct. EC2 2G 225 (44Tb 91)
SW1 7C 222 (46Lb 90)
ANGEL EDMONTON JUNC. 22Wb 51
Angelfield TW3: Houn 56Da 107
Angel Ga. EC1 3C 218 (41Rb 91)
(not continuous)
Angel Hill SM1: Sutt 76Db 155
Angel Hill Dr. SM1: Sutt 76Db 155
Angelica Cl. UB7: Yiew 44N 83
Angelica Dr. E6 43Qc 94
Angelica Gdns. CR0: C'don 74Zb 158
Angelica Ho. *E3* 39Bc 72
(off Sycamore Av.)
Angelica Rd. GU24: Bisl 7E 166
Angelina Ho. *SE15* 53Wb 113
(off Goldsmith Rd.)
Angelis Apartments N1 2C 218
Angel La. E15 37Fc 73
EC4 5F 225 (45Tb 91)
UB3: Hayes 43T 84
Angell Pk. Gdns. SW9 55Qb 112
Angell Rd. SW9 55Qb 112
ANGELL TOWN 53Qb 112
Angell Town Est. SW9 54Qb 112
Angel M. E1 45Xb 91
N1 2A 218 (40Qb 70)
SW15 59Wa 110
Angelo M. SW16 69Pb 134
Angelo's *SL4: Eton* 10H 81
(off Common La.)
Angel Pl. N18 21Wb 51
RH2: Reig 9K 207
SE1 1F 231 (47Tb 91)
Angel Rd. HA1: Harr 30Ga 46
KT7: T Ditt 73Ja 152
N18 22Wb 51
Angel Rd. Works N18 22Yb 52
Angel Sq. EC1 2B 218 (40Rb 71)
Angel St. EC1 2D 224 (44Sb 91)
Angel Wlk. W6 49Ya 88
Angel Way RM1: Rom 29Gd 56
Angel Wharf N1 1E 218 (40Sb 71)
Angel Yd. N6 32Jb 70
Angerstein Bus. Pk. SE10 49Jc 93
Angerstein La. SE3 53Hc 115
Anglais M. *NW9* 28Ua 48
(off Colin Cl.)
Anglebury *W2* 44Cb 89
(off Talbot Rd.)
Angle Cl. UB10: Hil 39Q 64
Angle Grn. RM8: Dag 32Yc 75
Angle Rd. RM20: Grays 51Zd 121
Anglers, The *KT1: King T* 69Ma 131
(off High St.)
Anglers Cl. TW10: Ham 63La 130
Angler's La. NW5 37Kb 70
Anglers Reach KT6: Surb 71Ma 153
Anglesea Av. SE18 49Rc 94
Anglesea Ho. *KT1: King T* 70Ma 131
(off Anglesea Rd.)
Anglesea M. SE18 49Rc 94
Anglesea Pl. *DA11: Grav'nd* 8D 122
(off New Rd.)
Anglesea Rd. BR5: St M Cry 72Yc 161
KT1: King T 70Ma 131
SE18 49Rc 94
Anglesea Ter. W6 48Xa 88
Anglesey Cl. TW15: Ashf 62Q 128
Anglesey Ct. W7 42Ha 86
Anglesey Ct. Rd. SM5: Cars 79Jb 156
Anglesey Dr. RM13: Rain 42Jd 96
Anglesey Gdns. SM5: Cars 79Jb 156
Anglesey Ho. *E14* 44Cc 92
(off Lindfield St.)
Anglesey Rd. EN3: Pond E 14Xb 33
WD19: Wat 22Y 45
Anglesmede Cres. HA5: Pinn 27Ca 45
Anglesmede Way HA5: Pinn 27Ca 45
Angles Rd. SW16 63Nb 134
Anglia Cl. N17 24Xb 51
Anglia Ct. *RM8: Dag* 32Zc 75
(off Spring Cl.)
Anglia Ho. *E14* 44Ac 92
(off Salmon La.)
Anglian Cl. WD24: Wat 12Y 27
Anglian Ind. Est. IG11: Bark 42Vc 95
Anglian Rd. E11 34Fc 73
Anglia Wlk. *E6* 39Qc 74
(off Napier Rd.)
Anglo Rd. E3 40Bc 72
Angrave Ct. *E8* 39Vb 71
(off Scriven St.)
Angrave Pas. E8 39Vb 71
Angus Cl. KT9: Chess 78Qa 153
Angus Dr. HA4: Ruis 35Y 65
Angus Gdns. NW9 25Ta 47
Angus Ho. SW2 59Mb 112
Angus Rd. E13 41Lc 93
Angus St. SE14 52Ac 114
Anhalt Rd. SW11 52Gb 111
Ankerdine Cres. SE18 52Rc 116
Anlaby Rd. TW11: Tedd 64Ga 130
Anley Rd. W14 47Za 88
Anmersh Gro. HA7: Stan 25Ma 47
Annabel Cl. E14 44Dc 92
Annabell Av. RM16: Ors 4F 100
Annabels M. W5 42Ma 87
Annables Ct. *AL1: St A* 2C 6
(off Victoria St.)
Anna Cl. E8 39Vb 71
Annadale Ct. *RH1: Redh* 5P 207
(off Warwick Rd.)
Annalee Gdns. RM15: S Ock 43Xd 98
Annalee Rd. RM15: S Ock 43Xd 98
Annaleigh Pl. KT12: Hers 77Z 151
Annandale Gro. UB10: Ick 34S 64
Annandale Rd. CR0: C'don 75Wb 157
DA15: Sidc 59Uc 116
SE10 51Hc 115
W4 50Ua 88
Annan Dr. SM5: Cars 81Jb 176
Anna Neagle Cl. E7 35Jc 73
Annan Way RM1: Rom 25Gd 56
Anne Boleyn Ct. SE9 58Sc 116
Anne Boleyn's Wlk. KT2: King T 66Na 131
SM3: Cheam 80Za 154
Anne Case M. KT3: N Mald 69Ta 131
Anne Compton M. SE12 59Hc 115
Anne Goodman Ho. *E1* 44Yb 92
(off Jubilee St.)
Anne Heart Cl. RM16: Chaf H 49Zd 99
Anne M. IG11: Bark 38Sc 74
Anne Nastri Ct. *RM2: Rom* 29Kd 57
(off Heath Pk. Rd.)
Anne of Cleeves Ct. SE9 58Tc 116
Anne of Cleves Rd. DA1: Dart 57Md 119
Anners Cl. TW20: Thorpe 69E 126
Annes Ct. NW1 5E 214
Annesley Av. NW9 27Ta 47
Annesley Cl. NW10 34Ua 68
Annesley Dr. CR0: C'don 76Bc 158
Annesley Ho. SW9 53Qb 112
Annesley Rd. SE3 53Kc 115
Annesley Wlk. N19 33Lb 70
Annesmere Gdns. SE3 55Mc 115
Anne St. E13 42Jc 93
Anne Sutherland Ho. BR3: Beck 66Ac 136
Anne's Wlk. CR3: Cat'm 92Ub 197
Annett Cl. TW17: Shep 70U 128
Annette Cl. HA3: W'stone 26Ga 46
Annette Cres. N1 38Sb 71
Annette Rd. N7 34Pb 70
(not continuous)
Annett Rd. KT12: Walt T 73W 150
Annetts Hall TN15: Bor G 91Ce 205
Anne Way IG6: Ilf 23Sc 54
KT8: W Mole 70Da 129
Annexe Mkt. E1 7K 219
Annie Besant Cl. E3 39Bc 72
Annie Brookes Cl. TW18: Staines 62F 126
Annie Taylor Ho. *E12* 35Qc 74
(off Walton Rd.)
Annifer Way RM15: S Ock 43Xd 98
ANNINGSLEY PARK 82E 168
Anningsley Pk. KT16: Ott 82D 168
Anning St. EC2 5J 219 (42Ub 91)
Annington Rd. N2 27Hb 49
Annis Rd. E9 37Ac 72
Ann La. SW10 51Fb 111
Ann Moss Way SE16 48Yb 92
Ann's Cl. SW1 2G 227
Ann's Pl. E1 1K 225
Ann St. SE18 50Sc 94
(not continuous)
Ann Stroud Ct. SE12 57Jc 115
Anns Wlk. RH1: Blet 5K 209
Answorthy Av. CR7: Thor H 69Tb 135
Answorthy Cres. SE25 68Tb 135
Ansar Gdns. E17 29Bc 52
Ansculf Rd. SL2: Slou 1E 80
Ansdell Rd. SE15 54Yb 114
Ansdell St. W8 48Db 89
Ansdell Ter. W8 48Db 89
Ansell Gro. SM5: Cars 74Jb 156
Ansell Ho. *E1* 43Yb 92
(off Mile End Rd.)
Ansell Rd. SW17 62Gb 133
Anselm Cl. CR0: C'don 76Vb 157
Anselm Rd. HA5: Hat E 24Ba 45
SW6 51Cb 111
Ansford Rd. BR1: Brom 64Ec 136
Ansleigh Pl. W11 45Za 88
Ansley Cl. CR2: Sande 86Xb 177
Anslow Gdns. SL0: Iver H 40F 62
Anslow Pl. SL1: Slou 3A 80
Anson Cl. AL1: St A 4F 6
HP3: Bov 9B 2
RM7: Mawney 26Dd 56
Anson Ho. *E1* 42Ac 92
(off Shandy St.)
SW1 51Lb 112
(off Churchill Gdns.)
Anson Pl. SE28 47Tc 94
Anson Rd. N7 35Lb 70
NW2 35Xa 68
Anson Ter. UB5: N'olt 37Da 65
Anson Wlk. HA6: Nwood 21S 44
Anstead Dr. RM13: Rain 40Jd 76
Anstey Ct. W3 47Ra 87
Anstey Ho. *E9* 39Yb 72
(off Templecombe Rd.)
Anstey Rd. SE15 55Wb 113
Anstey Wlk. N15 28Rb 51
Anstice Cl. W4 52Ua 110
Anstridge Path SE9 58Tc 116
Anstridge Rd. SE9 58Tc 116
Antelope Av. RM16: Grays 48Ce 99
Antelope Rd. SE18 48Pc 94
Antelope Wlk. KT6: Surb 71Ma 153
Antenor Ho. *E2* 40Xb 71
(off Old Bethnal Grn. Rd.)
Anthony Cl. NW7 21Ua 48
TN13: Dun G 92Gd 202
WD19: Wat 18Y 27
Anthony Cope Ct. N1 3G 219
Anthony Ct. W3 47Ua 88
Anthony Ho. CR5: Coul 94Mb 196
NW8 6D 214
Anthony La. BR8: Swan 67Jd 140
Anthony Rd. DA16: Well 53Wc 117
SE25 72Wb 157
UB6: G'frd 41Ga 86
WD6: Bore 12Pa 29
ANTHONYS 84C 168
Anthony St. E1 44Xb 91
Anthony Way N18 23Zb 52
SL1: Slou 5B 80
Anthorne Cl. EN6: Pot B 3Db 17
Anthus M. HA6: Nwood 24U 44
Antigua M. E13 41Kc 93
Antigua Wlk. SE19 64Tb 135
Antilles Bay E14 47Ec 92
Antill Rd. E3 41Ac 92
N15 28Wb 51
Antill Ter. E1 44Zb 92
Antlers Hill E4 15Dc 34
Antoinette Ct. WD5: Ab L 1V 12
Antoinette M. NW2 37Wa 68
Anton Cres. SM1: Sutt 76Cb 155
Antoneys Cl. HA5: Pinn 26Z 45
Antonine Ga. AL3: St A 3N 5
Antonine Hgts. SE1 2H 231
Anton Pl. HA9: Wemb 34Ra 67
Anton Rd. RM15: S Ock 43Xd 98
Anton St. E8 36Wb 71
Antony Ho. *SE16* 49Yb 92
(off Raymouth Rd.)
Antrim Gro. NW3 37Hb 69
Antrim Ho. *E3* 39Bc 72
(off Birdsfield La.)
Antrim Rd. NW3 37Hb 69
Antrobus Cl. SM1: Sutt 78Bb 155
Antrobus Rd. W4 49Sa 87
Anvil Cl. HP3: Bov 10D 2
SW16 66Lb 134
Anvil Ct. SL3: L'ly 49C 82
Anvil La. KT11: Cobh 86W 170
Anvil Pl. AL2: Chis G 8N 5
Anvil Rd. TW16: Sun 69W 128
Anvil Ter. DA2: Wilm 61Gd 140
Anworth Cl. IG8: Wfd G 23Kc 53
Anyards Rd. KT11: Cobh 85X 171
Anzio Gdns. CR3: Cat'm 93Sb 197
AOP Gallery 5H 219
Apeldoorn Dr. SM6: Wall 81Nb 176
Aperdele Rd. KT22: Lea 90Ja 172
APERFIELD 89Nc 180
Aperfield Rd. DA8: Erith 51Hd 118
TN16: Big H 89Nc 180
Aperfields TN16: Big H 89Nc 180
Apers Av. GU22: Wok 93B 188
Apex Cl. BR3: Beck 67Dc 136
APEX CORNER
Feltham 62Ba 129
Mill Hill 21Ua 48
Apex Ct. KT14: W Byf 84K 169
W13 45Ja 86
Apex Ho. E1 5K 219
Apex Ind. Est. NW10 42Va 88
Apex Pde. *NW7* 21Ta 47
(off Selvage La.)
Apex Point AL9: Wel G 4E 8
Apex Retail Pk. TW13: Hanw 62Ba 129
Aphrodite Ct. *E14* 49Cc 92
(off Homer Dr.)
E15 39Ec 72
(off Warton Rd.)
Apley Rd. RH2: Reig 9J 207
Aplin Way TW7: Isle 53Ga 108
Apollo Av. BR1: Brom 67Kc 137
HA6: Nwood 22W 44
Apollo Bldg. E14 49Cc 92
Apollo Bus. Cen. SE8 50Zb 92
Apollo Cinema
Brentwood 19Yd 40
Apollo Cl. RM12: Horn 33Kd 77
Apollo Ct. *E1* 45Wb 91
(off Thomas More St.)
E15 39Ec 72
(off High St.)
SW9 53Qb 112
(off Southey Rd.)
Apollo Ho. *E2* 40Xb 71
(off St Jude's Rd.)
E3 40Cc 72
(off Garrison Rd.)
N6 31Hb 69
SW10 52Fb 111
(off Milman's St.)
Apollo Pl. E11 34Gc 73
GU21: Wok 1L 187
SW10 52Fb 111
Apollo Theatre
Soho 4D 222
Apollo Victoria Theatre 4B 228
Apollo Way DA8: Erith 49Fd 96
SE28 48Tc 94
Apollo West End Cinema 5D 222
Apostles, The *SE23* 61Zb 136
(off Church Ri.)
Apostle Way CR7: Thor H 68Rb 135
Apothecary St. EC4 3B 224 (44Rb 91)
Appach Rd. SW2 57Qb 112
Appian Ct. *E3* 40Bc 72
(off Parnell Rd.)
Apple Barn Ct. TN15: Crou 94Ee 205
Apple Blossom Ct. *SW8* 52Mb 112
(off Pascal St.)
Appleby Cl. BR5: Pet W 73Uc 160
E4 23Ec 52
N15 29Tb 51
TW2: Twick 61Fa 130
UB8: Hil 44S 84
Appleby Ct. *W3* 47Sa 87
(off Newport Rd.)
Appleby Dr. RM3: Rom 22Ld 57
WD3: Crox G 14R 26
Appleby Gdns. TW14: Felt 60V 106
Appleby Grn. RM3: Rom 22Ld 57
Appleby Ho. KT19: Eps 83Ta 173
Appleby Rd. E8 38Wb 71
E16 44Hc 93
Appleby St. E2 1K 219 (40Vb 71)
Apple Cotts. HP3: Bov 9C 2
Applecroft AL2: Park 10P 5
Appledore Av. DA7: Bex 53Ed 118
HA4: Ruis 34X 65
Appledore Cl. BR2: Brom 71Hc 159
HA8: Edg 25Qa 47
RM3: Rom 25Ld 57
SW17 61Hb 133
Appledore Cres. DA14: Sidc 62Uc 138
Appledore Way NW7 24Za 48
Appledown Ri. CR5: Coul 87Lb 176
Appleford Ho. *W10* 42Ab 88
(off Bosworth Rd.)
Appleford Rd. W10 42Ab 88
Apple Gth. TW8: Bford 49Ma 87
Applegarth CR0: New Ad 80Dc 158
(not continuous)
KT10: Clay 78Ha 152
Applegarth Dr. DA1: Dart 61Nd 141
IG2: Ilf 28Vc 55
Applegarth Ho. DA8: Erith 54Hd 118
SE1 1C 230
SE15 52Wb 113
(off Bird in Bush Rd.)
Applegarth Rd. SE28 46Xc 95
W14 48Za 88
Apple Ga. CM14: Pil H 15Vd 40
Apple Gro. EN1: Enf 13Ub 33
HA2: Harr 32Ca 65
KT9: Chess 77Na 153
Apple Mkt. *KT1: King T* 68Ma 131
(off Market Pl.)
Apple Orchard BR8: Swan 70Fd 140
Apple Rd. E11 34Gc 73
Appleshaw Cl. DA11: Grav'nd 4C 144
Appleshaw Ho. SE5 55Ub 113
Appleton Cl. DA7: Bex 54Ed 118
Appleton Dr. DA2: Wilm 62Kd 141
Appleton Gdns. KT3: N Mald 72Wa 154
Appleton Rd. IG10: Lough 13Rc 36
SE9 55Nc 116
Appleton Sq. CR4: Mitc 67Gb 133
Appleton Way RM12: Horn 32Md 77
Apple Tree Av. UB7: Yiew 43P 83
UB8: Hil 43P 83
Apple Tree Cl. KT22: Fet 96Ea 192
Appletree Cl. SE20 67Xb 135
Appletree Gdns. EN4: E Barn 14Gb 31
Appletree La. SL3: L'ly 8N 81
Apple Tree Rdbt. UB7: Yiew 44P 83
Apple Trees Pl. GU22: Wok 1N 187

Appletree Wlk. WD25: Wat 6X 13
Apple Tree Yd. E1 41Zb 92
(off Longnor Rd.)
SW1 6C 222 (46Lb 90)
Applewood Cl. N20 18Gb 31
NW2 34Xa 68
UB10: Ick 35N 63
Applewood Dr. E13 42Kc 93
Appleyard Ter. EN3: Enf W 9Yb 20
Appold St. DA8: Erith 51Hd 118
EC2 7H 219 (43Ub 91)
Apprentice Gdns. UB5: N'olt 41Ba 85
Apprentice Way E5 35Xb 71
Approach, The BR6: Orp 75Vc 161
EN1: Enf 12Xb 33
EN6: Pot B 4Bb 17
KT23: Bookh 95Aa 191
NW4 29Za 48
RM14: Upm 34Rd 77
W3 44Ta 87
Approach Cl. N16 35Ub 71
Approach Rd. AL1: St A 3C 6
CR8: Purl 84Qb 176
E2 40Yb 72
EN4: E Barn 14Fb 31
HA8: Edg 23Qa 47
KT8: W Mole 71Ca 151
SW20 68Ya 132
TW15: Ashf 65S 128
Apps Mdw. Cl. KT8: W Mole 70Ba 129
Appspond La. AL2: Pot C 5H 5
HP3: Hem H 5H 5
Aprey Gdns. NW4 28Ya 48
April Cl. BR6: Chels 78Vc 161
KT21: Asht 90Pa 173
TW13: Felt 62W 128
W7 45Ga 86
April Ct. E2 40Wb 71
(off Teale St.)
April Glen SE23 62Zb 136
April St. E8 35Vb 71
Aprilwood Cl. KT15: Wdhm 83H 169
Apsledene DA12: Grav'nd 5F 144
APSLEY 6N 3
Apsley Centre, The NW2 33Wa 68
Apsley Cl. HA2: Harr 29Ea 46
Apsley Ct. BR5: St M Cry 72Xc 161
Apsley Grange HP3: Hem H 7N 3
Apsley House 1J 227 (47Jb 90)
Apsley Ho. E1 43Yb 92
(off Stepney Way)
NW8 1B 214
SL1: Slou 7L 81
TW4: Houn 56Ba 107
Apsley Ind. Est. HP3: Hem H 6M 3
Apsley Lock HP3: Hem H 7N 3
Apsley Mills Retail Pk.
HP3: Hem H 6N 3
Apsley Rd. KT3: N Mald 69Sa 131
SE25 70Xb 135
Apsley Way NW2 33Wa 68
W1 1J 227 (47Jb 90)
(not continuous)
Aquadrome, The 19L 25
Aqua Ho. NW10 41Qa 87
Aquarelle Ho. EC1 3D 218 (41Sb 91)
Aquarius TW1: Twick 60Ka 108
Aquarius Bus. Pk. NW2 32Wa 68
(off Priestley Way)
Aquarius Golf Course 58Yb 114
Aquarius Way HA6: Nwood 22W 44
Aquasplash 3P 3
Aquila Cl. KT22: Lea 93Na 193
Aquila St. NW8 1C 214 (40Fb 69)
Aquinas St. SE1 7A 224 (46Qb 90)
Arabella Ct. NW8 1A 214
Arabella Dr. SW15 56Ua 110
Arabia Cl. E4 17Fc 35
Arabian Ho. E1 42Ac 92
(off Ernest St.)
Arabin Rd. SE4 56Ac 114
Arado Ho. NW9 26Va 48
(off Boulevard Dr.)
Araglen Av. RM15: S Ock 43Xd 98
Aragon Av. KT7: T Ditt 71Ha 152
KT17: Ewe 82Xa 174
Aragon Cl. BR2: Brom 74Pc 160
CR0: New Ad 82Gc 179
EN2: Enf 10Pb 18
IG10: Lough 16Nc 36
RM5: Col R 23Dd 56
TW16: Sun 65V 128
Aragon Ct. GU21: Knap 9H 167
IG6: Ilf 24Sc 54
KT8: E Mos 70Ea 130
SE11 7K 229
Aragon Dr. HA4: Ruis 32Z 65
IG6: Ilf 24Sc 54
Aragon Ho. E16 46Jc 93
(off Capulet M.)
Aragon M. CM16: Epp 1Yc 23
Aragon Pl. SM4: Mord 73Ab 154
Aragon Rd. KT2: King T 64Na 131
SM4: Mord 72Za 154
Aragon Twr. SE8 49Bc 92
Aragon Wlk. KT14: Byfl 85P 169
Aral Ho. E1 42Zb 92
(off Ernest St.)
Aram Ct. GU22: Wok 87E 168
Aran Ct. KT13: Weyb 75T 150
Arandora Cres. RM6: Chad H 31Xc 75
Aran Dr. HA7: Stan 21La 46
Aran Lodge NW6 38Cb 69
(off Woodchurch Rd.)
Aran M. N7 38Qb 70
(off St Clements St.)
Arapiles Ho. E14 44Fc 93
(off Blair St.)
Arbery Rd. E3 41Ac 92
Arbon Ct. N1 39Sb 71
(off Linton St.)
Arbor Cl. BR3: Beck 68Dc 136
Arbor Ct. N16 33Tb 71
Arboretum Ct. N1 37Tb 71
(off Dove Rd.)
Arboretum Pl. IG11: Bark 38Sc 74
(off Clockhouse Av.)
Arborfield Cl. SL1: Slou 8J 81
SW2 60Pb 112
Arborfield Ho. E14 45Cc 92
(off E. India Dock Rd.)
Arbor Ho. BR6: Orp 75Wc 161
(off Orchard Gro.)
Arbor Rd. E4 20Fc 35
Arbour Cl. CM14: W'ley 22Yd 58
KT22: Fet 95Ha 192
Arbour Ho. E1 44Zb 92
(off Arbour Sq.)
Arbour Rd. EN3: Pond E 13Zb 34
Arbour Sq. E1 44Zb 92
Arbour Way RM12: Horn 36Kd 77
Arbroath Grn. WD19: Wat 20W 26
Arbroath Rd. SE9 55Nc 116
Arbrook Chase KT10: Esh 79Ea 152
Arbrook Cl. BR5: St P 69Wc 139
Arbrook Hall KT10: Clay 79Ha 152
Arbrook La. KT10: Esh 79Ea 152
Arbury Ter. SE26 62Wb 135
Arbuthnot La. DA5: Bexl 58Ad 117
Arbuthnot Rd. SE14 54Zb 114
Arbutus Cl. RH1: Redh 8L 207
Arbutus Rd. RH1: Redh 9L 207
Arbutus St. E8 39Vb 71
Arc, The 94Sb 197
Arcade CR0: C'don 75Sb 157
Arcade, The CR0: C'don 76Sb 157
(off High St.)
E17 28Cc 52
E20 37Ec 72
(within Westfield Stratford City Shop. Cen.)
EC2 1H 225
IG11: Bark 38Sc 74
N7 35Nb 70
(off Macready Pl.)
RH1: Redh 5P 207
(off Station Rd.)
RM3: Rom 22Md 57
(off Farnham Rd.)
SE9 58Qc 116
(off High St.)
Arcade Chambers SE9 58Qc 116
Arcade Ct. N11 21Kb 50
Arcade Pde. KT9: Chess 78Ma 153
Arcade Pl. RM1: Rom 29Gd 56
Arcadia Av. N3 26Cb 49
Arcadia Centre, The W5 45Ma 87
Arcadia Cl. SM5: Cars 77Jb 156
Arcadia Ct. E1 2K 225
Arcadia M. KT3: N Mald 69Ua 132
Arcadian Av. DA5: Bexl 58Ad 117
Arcadian Cl. DA5: Bexl 58Ad 117
Arcadian Gdns. N22 24Pb 50
Arcadian Pl. SW18 59Bb 111
Arcadian Rd. DA5: Bexl 58Ad 117
Arcadia Rd. DA13: Ist R 7B 144
Arcadia St. E14 44Cc 92
Arcany Rd. RM15: S Ock 42Xd 98
Archangel St. SE16 47Zb 92
Archates Av. RM16: Grays 48Ce 99
Archbishop Lanfranc School Sports Cen.
72Nb 156
Archbishop's Pl. SW2 59Pb 112
Archdale Bus. Cen. HA2: Harr 33Ea 66
Archdale Ct. W12 46Xa 88
Archdale Ho. SE1 3H 231
Archdale Pl. KT3: N Mald 69Ra 131
Archdale Rd. SE22 57Vb 113
Archel Rd. W14 51Bb 111
Archer Apartments N1 1H 219
Archer Cl. EN5: Barn 16Bb 31
KT2: King T 66Na 131
WD4: K Lan 1P 11
Archer Ho. N1 1J 219
SE14 53Ac 114
SW11 53Fb 111
W11 45Bb 89
(off Westbourne Gro.)
W13 46Ka 86
(off Sherwood Cl.)
Archer M. SW9 55Nb 112
TW12: Hamp H 65Ea 130
Archer Rd. BR5: St M Cry 71Wc 161
SE25 70Xb 135
Archers Ct. BR2: Brom 70Kc 137
CR2: S Croy 78Sb 157
(off Nottingham Rd.)
RH1: Redh 7P 207
(off Brighton Rd.)
RM15: S Ock 43Xd 98
Archers Dr. EN3: Enf H 12Yb 34
Archers Lodge SE16 50Wb 91
(off Culloden Cl.)
Archer Sq. SE14 51Ac 114
Archer St. W1 4D 222 (45Mb 90)
Archer Ter. UB7: Yiew 45N 83
Archer Way BR8: Swan 68Hd 140
Archery Cl. HA3: W'stone 27Ha 46
W2 3E 220 (44Gb 89)
Archery Flds. Ho. WC1 3J 217
Archery La. BR2: Brom 72Mc 159
Archery Rd. SE9 57Pc 116
Archery Steps W2 4E 220
Arches SW8 51Nb 112
Arches, The E16 42Gc 93
HA2: Harr 33Da 65
NW1 38Kb 70
SE8 51Ac 114
SL4: Wind 3G 102
(off Alma Rd.)
SW8 52Mb 112
WC2 6G 223
Arches Bus. Cen., The UB2: S'hall 47Ba 85
(off Merrick Rd.)
Arches Leisure Cen. 51Gc 115
Archgate Bus. Cen. N12 22Eb 49
Archibald Cl. EN3: Enf W 8Zb 20
Archibald M. W1 5J 221 (45Kb 90)
Archibald Rd. N7 35Mb 70
RM3: Hrld W 25Qd 57
Archibald St. E3 41Cc 92
Archie Cl. UB7: W Dray 47Q 84
Archie St. SE1 2J 231 (47Ub 91)
Archington Ct. AL1: St A 3C 6
(off Oswald Rd.)
Arch Rd. KT12: Hers 76Z 151
Arch St. SE1 4D 230 (48Sb 91)
ARCHWAY 33Lb 70
Archway RM3: Rom 23Kd 57
Archway Bus. Cen. N19 34Mb 70
Archway Cl. N19 33Lb 70
SM6: Bedd 76Mb 156
SW19 62Db 133
W10 43Za 88
Archway Ct. HP1: Hem H 1M 3
(off Chapel St.)
Archway Leisure Cen. 33Lb 70
Archway Mall N19 33Lb 70
Archway M. SW15 56Ab 110
(off Putney Bri. Rd.)
Archway Rd. N6 30Jb 50
N19 30Jb 50
Archway St. SW13 55Ua 110
Arcola St. E8 36Vb 71
Arcola Theatre 36Vb 71
Arcon Dr. UB5: N'olt 42Aa 85
Arcon Ter. N9 17Wb 33
Arctic Ho. NW9 26Va 48
(off Heritage Av.)
Arctic St. NW5 36Kb 70
Arcus Rd. BR1: Brom 65Gc 137
Ardbeg Rd. SE24 57Tb 113
Arden Cl. HA1: Harr 34Fa 66
HP3: Bov 10C 2
RH2: Reig 10K 207
SE28 44Zc 95
TW4: Houn 59Ba 107
WD23: B Hea 17Ha 28
Arden Ct. WD3: Rick 19J 25
WD17: Wat 11W 26
(off Lockhart Rd.)
Arden Ct. Gdns. N2 30Fb 49
Arden Cres. E14 49Cc 92
RM9: Dag 38Yc 75
Arden Est. N1 2H 219 (40Ub 71)
Arden Grange N12 21Eb 49
Arden Gro. BR6: Farnb 77Rc 160
Arden Ho. N1 2H 219
SE11 6H 229
SW9 54Nb 112
(off Grantham Rd.)
Arden M. E17 29Dc 52
Arden Mhor HA5: Eastc 28X 45
Arden Rd. N3 27Bb 49
W13 45La 86
Ardent Cl. SE25 69Ub 135
Ardent Ho. E3 40Ac 72
(off Roman Rd.)
Ardentinny AL1: St A 3C 6
(off Grosvenor Rd.)
Ardesley Wood KT13: Weyb 77U 150
Ardfern Av. SW16 69Qb 134
Ardfillan Rd. SE6 60Fc 115
Ardgowan Rd. SE6 59Gc 115
Ardilaun Rd. N5 35Sb 71
Ardingly Cl. CR0: C'don 76Zb 158
Ardingly Ct. KT18: Eps 86Ta 173
Ardleigh Cl. RM11: Horn 27Md 57
Ardleigh Ct. BR1: Brom 66Hc 137
(off London Rd.)
CM15: Shenf 17Be 41
Ardleigh Gdns. CM13: Hut 16Fe 41
SM3: Sutt 73Cb 155
ARDLEIGH GREEN 28Ld 57
Ardleigh Grn. Rd. RM11: Horn 29Md 57
Ardleigh Ho. IG11: Bark 39Sc 74
Ardleigh M. IG1: Ilf 34Rc 74
Ardleigh Rd. E17 25Bc 52
N1 37Ub 71
Ardleigh Ter. E17 25Bc 52
Ardley Cl. HA4: Ruis 31S 64
NW10 34Ua 68
SE6 62Ac 136
Ardlui Rd. SE27 61Sb 135
Ardmay Gdns. KT6: Surb 71Na 153
Ardmere Rd. SE13 58Fc 115
Ardmore La. IG9: Buck H 17Kc 35
Ardmore Pl. IG9: Buck H 17Kc 35
Ardmore Rd. RM15: S Ock 42Xd 98
Ardoch Rd. SE6 61Fc 137
Ardra Rd. N9 20Zb 34
Ardrossan Cl. SL2: Slou 2G 80
Ardrossan Gdns. KT4: Wor Pk 76Wa 154
Ardross Av. HA6: Nwood 22U 44
Ardshiel Cl. SW15 55Za 110
Ardshiel Dr. RH1: Redh 8N 207
Ardwell Av. IG6: Ilf 29Sc 54
Ardwell Rd. SW2 61Nb 134
Ardwick Rd. NW2 35Cb 69
Arena, The EN3: Enf L 10Bc 20
Arena Bus. Cen. N4 30Sb 51
Arena Essex 47Xd 98
Arena Ho. E3 40Cc 72
(off Lefevre Wlk.)
Arena Shop. Pk. N4 30Rb 51
Arena Sq. HA9: Wemb 35Qa 67
Ares Ct. E14 49Cc 92
(off Homer Dr.)
Arethusa Ho. E14 49Cc 92
(off Cahir St.)
Arethusa Pl. DA9: Ghithe 56Xd 120
Arethusa Way GU24: Bisl 8D 166
AREWATER GREEN 12Qc 36
Argali Ho. DA18: Erith 48Ad 95
(off Kale Rd.)
Argall Av. E10 31Zb 72
Argall Way E10 32Zb 72
Argan Cl. EN5: Barn 13Bb 31
Argenta Way HA9: Wemb 37Qa 67
NW10 38Ra 67
Argent Cen., The UB3: Hayes 47W 84
Argent Cl. TW20: Egh 65E 126
Argent Ct. E14 43Cc 92
(off Thomas Rd.)
EN5: New Bar 14Eb 31
(off Leicester Rd.)
KT6: Surb 76Qa 153
RM17: Grays 52Ce 121
Argenton Twr. SW18 58Db 111
(off Mapleton Cres.)
Argent St. RM17: Grays 51Ae 121
Argles Cl. DA9: Ghithe 57Wd 120
Argo Bus. Cen. NW6 41Cb 89
Argonaut Pk. SL3: Poyle 53H 105
Argon M. SW6 52Cb 111
Argon Rd. N18 22Yb 52
Argos Ct. SW9 53Qb 112
(off Caldwell St.)
Argos Ho. E2 40Xb 71
(off Old Bethnal Grn. Rd.)
Argosy Gdns. TW18: Staines 65H 127
Argosy Ho. SE8 49Ac 92
Argosy La. TW19: Stanw 59M 105
Argus Cl. RM7: Mawney 25Dd 56
Argus Way UB5: N'olt 41Aa 85
Argyle Av. TW3: Houn 58Ca 107
Argyle Cl. W13 42Ja 86
Argyle Ct. WD18: Wat 14V 26
Argyle Gdns. RM14: Upm 33Td 78
Argyle Ho. E14 48Ec 92
Argyle Pas. N17 25Vb 51
Argyle Pl. W6 49Xa 88
Argyle Rd. E1 42Zb 92
E15 35Gc 73
E16 44Kc 93
EN5: Barn 14Ya 30
HA2: Harr 30Da 45
IG1: Ilf 33Qc 74
N12 22Db 49
Argyle Rd. N17 25Wb 51
N18 21Wb 51
TN13: S'oaks 97Kd 203
TW3: Houn 57Da 107
UB6: G'frd 41Ha 86
W13 43Ja 86
Argyle Sq. WC1 3G 217 (41Nb 90)
(not continuous)
Argyle St. WC1 3F 217 (41Nb 90)
Argyle Wlk. WC1 4F 217 (41Nb 90)
Argyle Way SE16 50Wb 91
Argyll Av. SL1: Slou 5E 80
UB1: S'hall 46Da 85
Argyll Cl. SW9 55Pb 112
Argyll Ct. SW2 59Nb 112
(off New Pk. Rd.)
Argyll Gdns. HA8: Edg 26Ra 47
Argyll Mans. SW3 51Fb 111
W14 49Ab 88
(off Hammersmith Rd.)
Argyll Rd. RM17: Grays 50Ce 99
SE18 48Sc 94
W8 47Cb 89
Argyll St. W1 3B 222 (44Lb 90)
Aria Ct. IG2: Ilf 30Sc 54
Arica Ho. SE16 48Xb 91
(off Slippers Pl.)
Arica Rd. SE4 56Ac 114
Ariel Apartments E16 44Jc 93
Ariel Cl. DA12: Grav'nd 3H 145
Ariel Ct. SE11 6B 230 (49Rb 91)
Ariel Rd. NW6 37Cb 69
Ariel Way TW4: Houn 55X 107
W12 46Ya 88
Arisdale Av. RM15: S Ock 43Xd 98
Arista Ct. TW20: Eng G 4P 125
Aristotle Rd. SW4 55Mb 112
Arizona Bldg. SE10 53Dc 114
(off Deal's Gateway)
Ark, The W6 50Za 88
(off Talgarth Rd.)
Ark Av. RM16: Grays 48Ce 99
Arkell Gro. SE19 66Rb 135
Arkindale Rd. SE6 62Ec 136
Arklay Cl. UB8: Hil 42P 83
ARKLEY 15Wa 30
Arkley Cres. E17 29Bc 52
Arkley Dr. EN5: Ark 14Wa 30
Arkley Golf Course 15Va 30
Arkley La. EN5: Ark 10Va 16
Arkley Pk. EN5: Ark 17Ta 29
Arkley Rd. E17 29Bc 52
Arkley Vw. EN5: Ark 14Xa 30
Arklow Ct. WD3: Chor 14F 24
Arklow Ho. SE17 51Tb 113
Arklow M. KT6: Surb 75Na 153
Arklow Rd. SE14 51Bc 114
Arklow Rd. Trad. Est. SE14 51Ac 114
Arkwright Rd. CR2: Sande 82Vb 177
NW3 36Eb 69
RM18: Tilb 4C 122
SL3: Poyle 54G 104
Arlesey Cl. SW15 57Ab 110
Arlesford Rd. SW9 55Nb 112
Arlidge Ho. EC1 7A 218
Arlingford Rd. SW2 57Qb 112
Arlingham M. EN9: Walt A 5Ec 20
(off Sun St.)
Arlington N12 20Cb 31
Arlington Av. N1 1E 218 (39Sb 71)
(not continuous)
Arlington Bldg. E3 40Cc 72
Arlington Cl. DA15: Sidc 59Uc 116
SE13 57Fc 115
SM1: Sutt 75Cb 155
TW1: Twick 58La 108
Arlington Ct. RH2: Reig 4K 207
W3 47Ra 87
(off Mill Hill Rd.)
Arlington Cres. EN8: Walt C 6Ac 20
Arlington Dr. HA4: Ruis 30T 44
SM5: Cars 75Hb 155
Arlington Gdns. IG1: Ilf 32Qc 74
RM3: Hrld W 25Nd 57
W4 50Sa 87
Arlington Grn. NW7 24Za 48
Arlington Ho. EC1 3A 218
SE8 51Bc 114
(off Evelyn St.)
SW1 6B 222 (46Lb 90)
TW9: Kew 52Ra 109
UB7: W Dray 47P 83
W12 46Xa 88
(off Tunis Rd.)
Arlington Lodge KT13: Weyb 77R 150
SW2 56Pb 112
Arlington Pk. Mans. W4 50Sa 87
(off Sutton La. Nth.)
Arlington Pas. TW11: Tedd 63Ha 130
Arlington Pl. SE10 52Ec 114
Arlington Rd. IG8: Wfd G 25Jc 53
KT6: Surb 72Ma 153
N14 19Kb 32
NW1 1A 216 (39Kb 70)
TW1: Twick 58La 108
TW10: Ham 61Ma 131
TW11: Tedd 63Ha 130
TW15: Ashf 64P 127
W13 44Ka 86
Arlington Sq. N1 1E 218 (39Sb 71)
Arlington St. SW1 6B 222 (46Lb 90)
Arlington Way EC1 3A 218 (41Qb 90)
Arliss Ho. HA1: Harr 29Ha 46
Arliss Way UB5: N'olt 39Y 65
Arlow Rd. N21 18Qb 32
Armada Ct. RM16: Grays 49Ce 99
SE8 51Cc 114
Armadale Cl. N17 28Xb 51
Armadale Rd. GU21: Wok 9L 167
SW6 52Cb 111
TW14: Felt 57W 106
Armada St. SE8 51Cc 114
Armada Way E6 43Rc 94
Armagh Rd. E3 39Bc 72
Armand Cl. WD17: Wat 10V 12
Armfield Cl. KT8: W Mole 71Ba 151
Armfield Cres. CR4: Mitc 68Hb 133
Armfield Rd. EN2: Enf 11Tb 33
Arminger Rd. W12 46Xa 88
Armistice Gdns. SE25 69Wb 135
Armitage Cl. WD3: Loud 14M 25
Armitage Ct. SL5: S'hill 2A 146
Armitage Ho. NW1 7E 214
Armitage Rd. NW11 32Ab 68
SE10 50Hc 93
Armor Rd. RM19: Purf 49Td 98
Armour Cl. N7 37Pb 70
Armoury Dr. DA12: Grav'nd 9E 122
Armoury Ho. E3 39Ac 72
(off Gunmakers La.)
Armoury Rd. SE8 54Dc 114
Armoury Way SW18 57Cb 111
Armsby Ho. E1 43Yb 92
(off Stepney Way)
Armstead Wlk. RM10: Dag 38Cd 76
Armstrong Av. IG8: Wfd G 23Gc 53
Armstrong Cl. AL2: Lon C 9J 7
BR1: Brom 69Nc 138
E6 44Pc 94
HA5: Eastc 30W 44
KT12: Walt T 72W 150
RM8: Dag 31Zc 75
SS17: Stan H 1N 101
TN14: Hals 87Dd 182
WD6: Bore 13Sa 29
Armstrong Cres. EN4: Cockf 13Fb 31
Armstrong Gdns. WD7: Shenl 4Na 15
Armstrong Ho. UB8: Uxb 38L 63
(off High St.)
Armstrong Pl. HP1: Hem H 1M 3
(off High St.)
Armstrong Rd. NW10 38Ua 68
SE18 48Sc 94
SW7 4B 226 (48Fb 89)
TW13: Hanw 64Aa 129
TW20: Eng G 5N 125
W3 46Va 88
Armstrong Way UB2: S'hall 47Da 85
Armytage Rd. TW5: Hest 52Z 107
Arnal Cres. SW18 59Ab 110
Arncliffe NW6 40Db 69
Arncliffe Cl. N11 23Jb 50
Arncroft Ct. IG11: Bark 41Xc 95
Arndale Wlk. SW18 57Db 111
Arndale Way TW20: Egh 64C 126
Arne Cl. SS17: Stan H 1M 101
Arne Gro. BR6: Orp 76Vc 161
Arne Ho. SE11 7H 229
Arne St. WC2 3G 223 (44Nb 90)
Arnett Cl. WD3: Rick 16J 25
Arnett Sq. E4 23Bc 52
Arnett Way WD3: Rick 16J 25
Arne Wlk. SE3 56Hc 115
Arneways Av. RM6: Chad H 27Zc 55
Arneway St. SW1 4E 228 (48Mb 90)
Arnewood Cl. KT22: Oxs 86Da 171
SW15 60Wa 110
Arneys La. CR4: Mitc 72Jb 156
Arngask Rd. SE6 59Fc 115
Arnhem Av. RM15: Avel 46Sd 98
Arnhem Dr. CR0: New Ad 83Fc 179
Arnhem Pl. E14 48Cc 92
Arnhem Way SE22 57Ub 113
Arnhem Wharf E14 48Bc 92
Arnison Rd. KT8: E Mos 70Fa 130
Arnold Av. E. EN3: Enf L 10Cc 20
Arnold Av. W. EN3: Enf L 10Bc 20
Arnold Bennett Way N8 27Qb 50
Arnold Cir. E2 4K 219 (41Vb 91)
Arnold Cl. HA3: Kenton 31Pa 67
Arnold Ct. N22 24Nb 50
Arnold Cres. TW7: Isle 57Fa 108
Arnold Dr. KT9: Chess 79Ma 153
Arnold Est. SE1 2K 231 (47Vb 91)
(not continuous)
Arnold Gdns. N13 22Rb 51
Arnold Ho. SE3 52Lc 115
(off Shooters Hill Rd.)
SE17 7C 230
Arnold Mans. W14 51Bb 111
(off Queen's Club Gdns.)
Arnold Pl. RM18: Tilb 3E 122
Arnold Rd. DA12: Grav'nd 1F 144
E3 41Cc 92
EN9: Walt A 7Ec 20
GU21: Wok 87D 168
N15 27Vb 51
RM9: Dag 38Bd 75
RM10: Dag 38Bd 75
SW17 66Hb 133
TW18: Staines 66L 127
UB5: N'olt 37Z 65
Arnolds Av. CM13: Hut 15Ee 41
Arnolds Cl. CM13: Hut 15Ee 41
Arnolds Farm La. CM13: Mount 14Fe 41
Arnold's La. DA4: Sut H 65Pd 141
Arnold Ter. HA7: Stan 22Ha 46
Arnold Way KT19: Eps 84Pa 173
Arnos Gro. N14 21Mb 50
Arnos Gro. Ct. N11 22Lb 50
(off Palmer's Rd.)
Arnos Rd. N11 22Lb 50
Arnos Swimming Pool 22Mb 50
Arnot Ho. SE5 52Sb 113
(off Comber Gro.)
Arnott Cl. SE28 46Yc 95
W4 49Ta 87
Arnould Av. SE5 56Tb 113
Arnsberg Way DA6: Bex 56Cd 118
DA7: Bex 56Cd 118
Arnside Gdns. HA9: Wemb 32Ma 67
Arnside Ho. SE17 51Tb 113
(off Arnside St.)
Arnside Rd. DA7: Bex 53Cd 118
Arnside St. SE17 51Tb 113
Arnulf St. SE6 63Dc 136
Arnulls Rd. SW16 65Rb 135
Arodene Rd. SW2 58Pb 112
Arona Ho. BR3: Beck 68Ec 136
Arosa Rd. TW1: Twick 58Ma 109
Arpley Sq. SE20 66Yb 136
(off High St.)
Arragon Gdns. BR4: W W'ck 76Dc 158
SW16 66Nb 134
Arragon Rd. E6 39Mc 73
SW18 60Cb 111
TW1: Twick 59Ja 108
Arran Cl. DA8: Erith 51Fd 118
HP3: Hem H 4C 4
SM6: Wall 77Kb 156
Arran Ct. NW9 26Va 48
NW10 34Ta 67
Arran Dr. E12 32Mc 73
Arran Grn. WD19: Wat 21Z 45
Arran Ho. E14 46Ec 92
(off Raleana Rd.)
WD18: Wat 16W 26
Arran M. W5 46Pa 87
Arranmore Ct. WD23: Bush 14Aa 27
Arran Rd. SE6 61Dc 136
Arran Wlk. N1 38Sb 71
Arran Way KT10: Esh 75Da 151

Arras Av. SM4: Mord 71Eb 155
Arretine Cl. AL3: St A 4M 5
Arreton Mead GU21: Wok 86B 168
Arrol Ho. SE1 4E 230 (48Sb 91)
Arrol Rd. BR3: Beck 69Yb 136
Arrow Ct. SW5 49Cb 89
(off W. Cromwell Rd.)
Arrow Ho. N1 1J 219
Arrow Rd. E3 41Dc 92
Arrowscout Wlk. UB5: N'olt 41Aa 85
(off Argus Way)
Arrows Ho. SE15 52Yb 114
(off Clifton Way)
Arrowsmith Cl. IG7: Chig 22Vc 55
Arrowsmith Ho. SE11 7H 229
Arrowsmith Path IG7: Chig 22Vc 55
Arrowsmith Rd. IG7: Chig 22Uc 54
Arsenal FC 35Qb 70
Arsenal Rd. SE9 54Pc 116
Arsenal Way SE18 48Sc 94
Arta Ho. E1 44Yb 92
(off Devonport St.)
Artbrand Ho. SE1 2H 231
Artemis SW11 54Hb 111
Artemis Cl. DA12: Grav'nd 9G 122
Artemis Ct. E14 49Cc 92
(off Homer Dr.)
Artemis Pl. SW18 59Bb 111
Arterberry Rd. SW20 66Ya 132
Arterial Av. RM13: Rain 42Kd 97
Arterial Rd. RM16: N Stif 48Vd 98
RM19: Purf, W Thur 49Rd 97
RM20: W Thur 48Vd 98
SS17: Stan H 1L 101
Artesian Cl. NW10 38Ta 67
RM11: Horn, Rom 30Hd 56
Artesian Gro. EN5: New Bar 14Eb 31
Artesian Ho. SE1 4K 231
Artesian Rd. W2 44Cb 89
Artesian Wlk. E11 34Gc 73
Arthingworth St. E15 39Gc 73
Arthur Barnes Ct. RM16: Grays 8E 100
Arthur Ct. CR0: C'don 76Ub 157
(off Fairfield Path)
SW11 53Jb 112
W2 44Db 89
(off Queensway)
W10 44Za 88
(off Silchester Rd.)
Arthur Deakin Ho. E1 43Wb 91
(off Hunton St.)
Arthurdon Rd. SE4 57Cc 114
Arthur Gro. SE18 49Sc 94
Arthur Henderson Ho. SW6 54Bb 111
(off Fulham Rd.)
Arthur Horsley Wlk. E7 36Hc 73
(off Tower Hamlets Rd.)
Arthur Ho. N1 39Ub 71
(off New Era Est.)
Arthur Jacob Nature Reserve 55E 104
Arthur Newton Ho. SW11 55Fb 111
(off Winstanley Est.)
Arthur Rd. AL1: St A 2F 6
E6 40Pc 74
KT2: King T 66Qa 131
KT3: N Mald 71Xa 154
N7 35Pb 70
N9 19Vb 33
RM6: Chad H 30Yc 55
SL1: Slou 7H 81
SL4: Wind 3G 102
SW19 64Bb 133
TN16: Big H 87Lc 179
Arthur's Bri. Rd. GU21: Wok 9N 167
Arthur's Bri. Wharf GU21: Wok 9P 167
Arthur St. DA8: Erith 52Hd 118
DA11: Grav'nd 9C 122
EC4 4G 225 (45Tb 91)
RM17: Grays 51Ee 121
WD23: Bush 14Z 27
Arthur St. W. DA11: Grav'nd 9C 122
Arthur Toft Ho. RM17: Grays 51De 121
(off New Rd.)
Arthur Wade Ho. E2 3K 219
Arthur Wallis Ho. E12 34Qc 74
(off Grantham Rd.)
Artichoke Dell WD3: Chor 14G 24
Artichoke Hill E1 45Xb 91
Artichoke M. SE5 53Tb 113
(off Artichoke Pl.)
Artichoke Pl. SE5 53Tb 113
Artillery Building, The E1 1J 225
(off Artillery La.)
Artillery Cl. IG2: Ilf 30Sc 54
Artillery Ho. E3 39Ac 72
(off Barge La.)
E15 37Gc 73
SE18 50Qc 94
(off Connaught M.)
Artillery La. E1 1J 225 (43Ub 91)
W12 44Wa 88
Artillery Mans. SW1 4D 228
Artillery Pas. E1 1J 225
Artillery Pl. HA3: Hrw W 24Ea 46
SE18 49Pc 94
SW1 4D 228 (48Mb 90)
Artillery Row DA12: Grav'nd 9E 122
SW1 4D 228 (48Lb 90)
Artillery Sq. SE18 48Rc 94
(off No 1 St.)
Artington Cl. BR6: Farnb 77Sc 160
Artisan Cl. E6 44Rc 94
Artisan Ct. E8 37Wb 71
Artisan Cres. AL3: St A 1A 6
(not continuous)
Artisan M. NW10 41Za 88
(off Warfield Rd.)
Artisan Quarter NW10 41Za 88
(off Wellington Rd.)
Artizan St. E1 2J 225
Art School Yd. AL1: St A 2B 6
(off Victoria St.)
Arts Depot 22Eb 49
Arts Theatre 4F 223
Arun RM18: E Til 9L 101
Arun Ct. SE25 71Wb 157
Arundale KT1: King T 70Ma 131
(off Anglesea Rd.)
Arundel Av. CR2: Sande 82Wb 177
KT17: Ewe 82Xa 174
SM4: Mord 70Bb 133
Arundel Bldgs. SE1 4J 231
Arundel Cl. CR0: Wadd 76Rb 157
DA5: Bexl 58Bd 117
E15 35Gc 73
EN8: Chesh 1Yb 20
Arundel Cl. HP2: Hem H 1B 4
SW11 57Gb 111
TW12: Hamp H 64Da 129
Arundel Ct. BR2: Brom 68Gc 137
HA2: Harr 35Ca 65
N12 23Gb 49
N17 25Wb 51
SE16 50Xb 91
(off Verney Rd.)
SL3: L'ly 9P 81
SW3 7E 226
SW13 51Xa 110
(off Arundel Ter.)
W11 45Bb 89
(off Arundel Gdns.)
Arundel Dr. BR6: Chels 78Xc 161
HA2: Harr 35Ba 65
IG8: Wfd G 24Jc 53
WD6: Bore 14Sa 29
Arundel Gdns. HA8: Edg 24Ta 47
IG3: Ilf 33Wc 75
N21 18Qb 32
W11 45Bb 89
Arundel Gt. Ct. WC2 4J 223 (45Pb 90)
Arundel Gro. N16 36Ub 71
Arundel Ho. CR0: C'don 78Tb 157
(off Heathfield Rd.)
UB8: Cowl 42L 83
W3 47Ra 87
(off Park Rd. Nth.)
WD6: Bore 14Sa 29
(off Arundel Dr.)
Arundel Mans. SW6 53Bb 111
(off Kelvedon Rd.)
Arundel Pl. N1 37Qb 70
Arundel Rd. CR0: C'don 72Tb 157
DA1: Dart 56Ld 119
EN4: Cockf 13Gb 31
KT1: King T 68Ra 131
RM3: Hrld W 24Pd 57
SM2: Cheam, Sutt 80Bb 155
TW4: Houn 55Y 107
UB8: Uxb 40K 63
WD5: Ab L 4W 12
Arundel Sq. N7 37Qb 70
Arundel St. WC2 4J 223 (45Pb 90)
Arundel Ter. SW13 51Xa 110
Arun Ho. KT2: King T 67Ma 131
Arvon Rd. N5 36Qb 70
(not continuous)
Asa Ct. UB3: Harl 48V 84
Asbaston Ter. IG1: Ilf 37Sc 74
IG11: Bark 37Sc 74
Asbridge Ct. W6 48Xa 88
(off Dalling Rd.)
Asbury Ct. N21 15Nb 32
(off Pennington Dr.)
Ascalon Ho. SW8 52Lb 112
(off Thessaly Rd.)
Ascalon St. SW8 52Lb 112
Ascension Rd. RM5: Col R 23Ed 56
Ascensis Twr. SW18 56Eb 111
Ascent Ho. KT13: Weyb 78U 150
(off Ellesmere Rd.)
NW9 26Wa 48
(off Boulevard Dr.)
Ascham Dr. E4 24Dc 52
Ascham End E17 25Ac 52
Ascham St. NW5 36Lb 70
Aschurch Rd. CR0: C'don 73Vb 157
ASCOT 9A 124
Ascot Cl. IG6: Ilf 23Uc 54
TN15: Bor G 92De 205
UB5: N'olt 36Ca 65
WD6: E'tree 15Qa 29
Ascot Ct. DA5: Bexl 59Bd 117
NW8 4B 214
WD3: Crox G 16R 26
Ascot Gdns. EN3: Enf W 9Yb 20
RM12: Horn 35Nd 77
UB1: S'hall 42Ba 85
Ascot Ho. NW1 3A 216
SL4: Wind 3D 102
(off Paddock Cl.)
W9 42Cb 89
(off Harrow Rd.)
Ascot Lodge NW6 39Db 69
Ascot M. SM6: Wall 81Lb 176
Ascot Pl. HA7: Stan 22La 46
Ascot Rd. BR5: St M Cry 70Vc 139
DA12: Grav'nd 2D 144
E6 41Pc 94
N15 29Tb 51
N18 21Wb 51
SW17 65Jb 134
TW14: Bedf 60Q 106
WD18: Wat 15U 26
Ascott Av. W5 47Na 87
Ascott Cl. HA5: Eastc 28W 44
ASH 78Ae 165
Ashanti M. E8 36Yb 72
Ashbeam Cl. CM13: Gt War 23Yd 58
Ashbee Ho. E2 41Yb 92
(off Portman Pl.)
Ashbourne Av. DA7: Bex 52Ad 117
E18 28Kc 53
HA2: Harr 33Fa 66
N20 19Hb 31
NW11 29Bb 49
Ashbourne Cl. CR5: Coul 90Lb 176
N12 21Db 49
W5 43Qa 87
Ashbourne Ct. AL4: St A 5G 6
E5 35Ac 72
N12 21Db 49
(off Ashbourne Cl.)
Ashbourne Gro. NW7 22Ta 47
SE22 56Vb 113
W4 50Ua 88
Ashbourne Ho. SL1: Slou 7J 81
Ashbourne Pde. NW11 28Bb 49
W5 42Pa 87
Ashbourne Ri. BR6: Orp 77Uc 160
Ashbourne Rd. CR4: Mitc 66Jb 134
RM3: Rom 21Ld 57
W5 42Pa 87
Ashbourne Sq. HA6: Nwood 23U 44
Ashbourne Ter. SW19 66Bb 133
Ashbourne Way NW11 28Bb 49
Ashbridge Rd. E11 31Gc 73
Ashbridge St. NW8 6D 214 (42Gb 89)
Ashbrook HA8: Edg 23Pa 47
Ashbrook Rd. N19 32Mb 70
RM10: Dag 34Dd 76
SL4: Old Win 9M 103
Ashburn Gdns. SW7 49Eb 89
Ashburnham Av. HA1: Harr 30Ha 46
Ashburnham Cl. N2 27Fb 49
TN13: S'oaks 99Ld 203
WD19: Wat 20W 26
Ashburnham Ct. BR3: Beck 68Ec 136
Ashburnham Dr. WD19: Wat 20W 26
Ashburnham Gdns. HA1: Harr 30Ha 46
RM14: Upm 32Rd 77
Ashburnham Gro. SE10 52Dc 114
Ashburnham Mans. SW10 52Eb 111
(off Ashburnham Rd.)
Ashburnham Pk. KT10: Esh 77Ea 152
Ashburnham Pl. SE10 52Dc 114
Ashburnham Retreat SE10 52Dc 114
Ashburnham Rd. DA17: Belv 49Ed 96
NW10 41Ya 88
SW10 52Eb 111
TW10: Ham 62Ka 130
Ashburnham Twr. SW10 52Fb 111
(off Worlds End Est.)
Ashburn Pl. SW7 5A 226 (49Eb 89)
Ashburton Av. CR0: C'don 74Xb 157
IG3: Ilf 36Uc 74
Ashburton Cl. CR0: C'don 74Wb 157
Ashburton Ent. Cen. SW15 58Ya 110
Ashburton Gdns. CR0: C'don 75Wb 157
ASHBURTON GROVE 35Qb 70
Ashburton Ho. W9 42Bb 89
(off Fernhead Rd.)
Ashburton Memorial Homes
CR0: C'don 73Xb 157
Ashburton Rd. CR0: C'don 75Wb 157
E16 44Jc 93
HA4: Ruis 33W 64
Ashburton Ter. E13 40Jc 73
Ashburton Triangle N7 35Qb 70
Ashbury Cl. AL10: Hat 1A 8
Ashbury Dr. UB10: Ick 34R 64
Ashbury Gdns. RM6: Chad H 29Zc 55
Ashbury Pl. SW19 65Eb 133
Ashbury Rd. SW11 55Hb 111
Ashby Av. KT9: Chess 79Qa 153
Ashby Cl. BR4: W W'ck 76Fc 159
RM11: Horn 32Qd 77
RM16: Ors 4G 100
Ashby Ct. NW8 5C 214
Ashby Gdns. AL1: St A 6B 6
Ashby Gro. N1 38Sb 71
(not continuous)
Ashby Ho. N1 38Sb 71
(off Essex Rd.)
SW9 54Rb 113
UB5: N'olt 42Ba 85
Ashby M. SE4 54Bc 114
SW2 57Nb 112
(off Prague Pl.)
Ashby Rd. N15 29Wb 51
SE4 54Bc 114
WD24: Wat 10W 12
Ashbys Ct. E3 40Bc 72
(off Centurion La.)
Ashby St. EC1 4C 218 (41Rb 91)
Ashby Wlk. CR0: C'don 72Sb 157
Ashby Way UB7: Sip 52Q 106
Ashchurch Gro. W12 48Wa 88
Ashchurch Pk. Vs. W12 48Wa 88
Ashchurch Ter. W12 48Wa 88
Ash Cl. AL9: Brk P 7J 9
BR5: Pet W 71Tc 160
BR8: Swan 68Ed 140
CM15: Pil H 15Vd 40
DA14: Sidc 62Xc 139
GU22: Pyr 87J 169
GU22: Wok 92A 188
HA7: Stan 23Ja 46
HA8: Edg 21Sa 47
KT3: N Mald 68Ta 131
RH1: Mers 2C 208
RM5: Col R 24Dd 56
SE20 68Yb 136
SL3: L'ly 48D 82
SM5: Cars 75Hb 155
UB9: Hare 25M 43
WD5: Ab L 4T 12
WD25: Wat 7X 13
Ashcombe Av. KT6: Surb 73Ma 153
Ashcombe Cl. TW15: Ashf 62N 127
Ashcombe Ct. TW15: Ashf 61P 127
Ashcombe Gdns. HA8: Edg 21Qa 47
Ashcombe Ho. E3 41Dc 92
(off Bruce Rd.)
EN3: Pond E 13Zb 34
Ashcombe Pde. GU22: Wok 92C 188
(off Kingfield Rd.)
Ashcombe Pk. NW2 34Ua 68
Ashcombe Rd. RH1: Mers 99Lb 196
SM5: Cars 79Jb 156
SW19 64Cb 133
Ashcombe Sq. KT3: N Mald 69Sa 131
Ashcombe St. SW6 54Db 111
Ashcombe Ter. KT20: Tad 92Xa 194
Ash Copse AL2: Brick W 3Ba 13
Ash Ct. KT15: Add 78K 149
KT19: Ewe 77Sa 153
KT22: Lea 92Ha 192
N11 23Lb 50
SW19 66Ab 132
Ashcroft HA5: Hat E 23Ca 45
N14 19Mb 32
Ashcroft Av. DA15: Sidc 58Wc 117
Ash Cft. Ct. DA3: New A 76Ae 165
Ashcroft Ct. DA1: Dart 59Qd 119
N20 19Fb 31
SL1: Burn 10A 60
Ashcroft Cres. DA15: Sidc 58Wc 117
Ashcroft Dr. UB9: Den 30H 43
Ashcroft Ho. SW8 53Lb 112
(off Wadhurst Rd.)
Ashcroft Pk. KT11: Cobh 84Aa 171
Ashcroft Pl. KT22: Lea 93La 192
Ashcroft Ri. CR5: Coul 88Nb 176
Ashcroft Rd. KT9: Chess 76Pa 153
E3 41Ac 92
Ashcroft Sq. W6 49Ya 88
Ashcroft Theatre 76Tb 157
(in Fairfield Halls)
Ashdale KT23: Bookh 98Ea 192
Ashdale Cl. TW2: Whitt 59Ea 108
TW19: Stanw 61N 127
Ashdale Gro. HA7: Stan 23Ha 46
Ashdale Ho. N4 31Tb 71
Ashdale Rd. SE12 60Kc 115
Ashdales AL1: St A 6B 6
Ashdale Way TW2: Whitt 59Da 107
Ashdene HA5: Pinn 27Y 45
SE15 52Xb 113
Ashdene Cl. TW15: Ashf 66S 128
Ashdene Ho. TW20: Eng G 5N 125
Ashdon Cl. CM13: Hut 16Ee 41
IG8: Wfd G 23Kc 53
RM15: S Ock 44Xd 98
Ashdon Rd. NW10 39Va 68
WD23: Bush 13Z 27
Ashdown W13 43Ka 86
(off Clivedon Ct.)
Ashdown Cl. BR3: Beck 68Dc 136
DA5: Bexl 59Ed 118
GU22: Wok 90A 168
RH2: Reig 10K 207
Ashdown Ct. E17 26Ec 52
IG11: Bark 37Rc 74
SM2: Sutt 79Eb 155
Ashdown Cres. EN8: Chesh 1Ac 20
NW5 36Jb 70
Ashdown Dr. WD6: Bore 12Pa 29
Ashdowne Ct. N17 25Wb 51
Ashdown Gdns. CR2: Sande 87Xb 177
Ashdown Ho. SW1 4C 228
Ashdown Pl. KT7: T Ditt 73Ja 152
KT17: Ewe 80Va 154
Ashdown Rd. EN3: Enf H 12Yb 34
KT1: King T 68Na 131
KT17: Eps 85Va 174
RH2: Reig 10K 207
UB10: Hil 40Q 64
Ashdown Wlk. E14 49Cc 92
RM7: Mawney 25Dd 56
Ashdown Way SW17 61Jb 134
Ash Dr. AL10: Hat 3C 8
RH1: Redh 8A 208
Ashe Ho. TW1: Twick 58Ma 109
Ashen E6 44Qc 94
Ashenbank Wood (Ancient Woodland)
8J 145
Ashenden SE17 5D 230
Ashenden Rd. E5 36Ac 72
Ashenden Wlk. SL2: Farn C 5H 61
Ashen Dr. DA1: Dart 58Jd 118
Ashen Gro. SW19 62Cb 133
Ashen Gro. Rd. TN15: Knat 82Rd 183
Ashentree Ct. EC4 3A 224
Ashen Va. CR2: Sels 81Zb 178
Asher Loftus Way N11 23Hb 49
Asher Way E1 45Wb 91
Ashfield Av. TW13: Felt 60X 107
WD23: Bush 16Da 27
Ashfield Cl. BR3: Beck 66Cc 136
KT21: Asht 91Na 193
TW10: Ham 60Na 109
Ashfield Ct. SW9 54Nb 112
(off Clapham Rd.)
Ashfield Ho. W14 50Bb 89
(off W. Cromwell Rd.)
Ashfield La. BR7: Chst 65Rc 138
(not continuous)
Ashfield Pde. N14 18Mb 32
Ashfield Rd. N4 30Sb 51
N14 20Lb 32
W3 46Va 88
Ashfields IG10: Lough 12Pc 36
WD25: Wat 7V 12
Ashfields Ct. RH2: Reig 4K 207
Ashfield St. E1 43Xb 91
(not continuous)
Ashfield Yd. E1 43Yb 92
ASHFORD 63P 127
Ashford Av. CM14: B'wood 20Xd 40
N8 28Nb 50
TW15: Ashf 65R 128
UB4: Yead 44Z 85
Ashford Bus. Complex
TW15: Ashf 64S 128
Ashford Cl. E17 30Bc 52
TW15: Ashf 63N 127
ASHFORD COMMON 66T 128
Ashford Ct. HA8: Edg 20Ra 29
NW2 35Za 68
RM17: Grays 50Fe 99
Ashford Cres. EN3: Enf H 12Yb 34
TW15: Ashf 62N 127
Ashford Gdns. KT11: Cobh 88Z 171
Ashford Grn. WD19: Wat 22Z 45
Ashford Ho. SE8 51Bc 114
SW9 56Rb 113
Ashford Ind. Est. TW15: Ashf 63S 128
Ashford La. SL4: Dor 7A 80
Ashford Manor Golf Course 65P 127
Ashford M. N17 25Wb 51
ASHFORD PARK 63M 127
Ashford Pas. NW2 35Za 68
Ashford Rd. E6 38Qc 74
E18 26Kc 53
NW2 35Za 68
SL0: Iver H 39E 62
TW13: Felt 63T 128
TW15: Ashf 66S 128
TW18: Lale, Staines 68L 127
Ashford St. N1 3H 219 (41Ub 91)
Ashford Tennis Club 63M 127
Ash Grn. UB9: Den 37K 63
Ash Gro. BR4: W W'ck 75Ec 158
E8 39Xb 71
(not continuous)
EN1: Enf 17Ub 33
HA0: Wemb 35Ja 66
HP3: Hem H 6P 3
N10 28Kb 50
N13 20Sb 33
NW2 35Za 68
SE12 60Jc 115
SE20 68Yb 136
SL2: Stoke P 8K 61
TW5: Hest 53Z 107
TW14: Felt 60U 106
TW18: Staines 65L 127
UB1: S'hall 43Ca 85
UB3: Hayes 45T 84
UB7: Yiew 45P 83
UB9: Hare 25M 43
W5 47Na 87
Ashgrove Ct. W9 43Cb 89
(off Elmfield Way)
Ashgrove Ho. SW1 7E 228
Ashgrove Rd. BR1: Brom 65Fc 137
IG3: Ilf 32Vc 75
TN13: S'oaks 99Jd 202
TW15: Ashf 64S 128
Ash Hill Cl. WD23: Bush 18Da 27
Ash Hill Dr. HA5: Pinn 27Y 45
Ash Ho. DA3: New A 75Ae 165
E14 47Ec 92
(off E. Ferry Rd.)
SE1 6K 231
Ash Ho. TW15: Ashf 63P 127
(off Station Rd.)
W10 42Ab 88
(off Heather Wlk.)
Ashingdon Cl. E4 20Ec 34
Ashington Ho. E1 42Xb 91
(off Barnsley St.)
Ashington Rd. SW6 54Bb 111
Ash Island KT8: E Mos 69Fa 130
Ashlake Rd. SW16 63Nb 134
Ashland Pl. W1 7H 215 (43Jb 90)
Ashlands Ct. RM18: E Til 8L 101
Ash La. RM1: Rom 23Jd 56
RM11: Horn 28Qd 57
SL4: Wind 4B 102
TN15: Ash, W King 84Yd 184
Ashlar Pl. SE18 49Rc 94
Ashlea Ct. CR6: W'ham 90Wb 177
Ashlea Rd. SL9: Chal P 26A 42
Ashleigh Av. TW20: Egh 66E 126
Ashleigh Commercial Est. SE7 48Lc 93
Ashleigh Ct. EN9: Walt A 6Jc 21
N14 17Lb 32
W5 49Ma 87
(off Murray Rd.)
WD3: Rick 17M 25
WD17: Wat 13Y 27
(off Loates La.)
Ashleigh Gdns. RM14: Upm 34Td 78
SM1: Sutt 75Db 155
Ashleigh M. SE15 55Vb 113
(off Oglander Rd.)
Ashleigh Point SE23 62Zb 136
Ashleigh Rd. SE20 69Xb 135
SW14 55Ua 110
Ashley Av. IG6: Ilf 26Rc 54
KT18: Eps 85Ta 173
SM4: Mord 71Cb 155
Ashley Cen. KT18: Eps 85Ta 173
Ashley Cl. HA5: Pinn 26X 45
HP3: Hem H 1P 3
KT12: Walt T 74V 150
KT23: Bookh 97Ba 191
NW4 26Ya 48
TN13: S'oaks 96Kd 203
Ashley Ct. EN5: New Bar 15Eb 31
GU21: Wok 10K 167
KT18: Eps 85Ta 173
NW4 26Ya 48
NW9 26Ya 48
(off Guilfoyle)
SW1 4B 228
UB5: N'olt 39Aa 65
Ashley Cres. N22 26Qb 50
SW11 55Jb 112
Ashley Dr. KT12: Walt T 76W 150
SM7: Bans 86Cb 175
TW2: Whitt 59Da 107
TW7: Isle 51Ga 108
WD6: Bore 15Qa 29
Ashley Gdns. BR6: Orp 78Uc 160
HA9: Wemb 33Na 67
N13 21Sb 51
RM16: Grays 46Ee 99
SW1 4C 228 (48Lb 90)
(not continuous)
TW10: Ham 61Ma 131
Ashley Gro. IG10: Lough 13Nc 36
Ashley La. CR0: Wadd 77Rb 157
NW4 25Ya 48
ASHLEY PARK 76W 150
Ashley Pk. Av. KT12: Walt T 75V 150
Ashley Pk. Cres.
KT12: Walt T 74W 150
Ashley Pk. Rd. KT12: Walt T 75W 150
Ashley Pl. KT12: Walt T 75W 150
(off Ashley Rd.)
SW1 4B 228 (48Lb 90)
(not continuous)
Ashley Ri. KT12: Walt T 77W 150
Ashley Rd. AL1: St A 2G 6
CR7: Thor H 70Pb 134
E4 23Cc 52
E7 38Lc 73
EN3: Enf H 12Yb 34
GU21: Wok 10K 167
KT7: T Ditt 72Ha 152
KT12: Walt T 77V 150
KT18: Eps, Eps D 85Ta 173
N17 27Wb 51
N19 32Nb 70
SW19 65Db 133
TN13: S'oaks 96Kd 203
TW9: Rich 55Na 109
TW12: Hamp 67Ca 129
UB8: Uxb 40K 63
Ashleys WD3: Rick 17H 25
Ashley Sq. KT18: Eps 85Ta 173
(off South St.)
Ashley Wlk. NW7 24Za 48
Ashley Way GU24: W End 5B 166
Ashling Rd. CR0: C'don 74Wb 157
Ashlin Rd. E15 35Fc 73
Ash Lodge TW16: Sun 66V 128
(off Forest Dr.)
Ashlone Rd. SW15 55Ya 110
Ashlyn Cl. WD23: Bush 14Aa 27
Ashlyn Ct. WD23: Bush 14Aa 27
Ashlyn Gro. RM11: Horn 27Md 57
Ashlyns Pk. KT11: Cobh 85Aa 171
Ashlyns Rd. CM16: Epp 2Vc 23
Ashlyns Way KT9: Chess 79Ma 153
Ashmead N14 15Lb 32
Ashmead Bus. Cen. E16 42Fc 93
Ashmead Dr. UB9: Den 33J 63
Ashmead Ga. BR1: Brom 67Lc 137
Ashmead Ho. E9 36Ac 72
(off Homerton Rd.)
Ashmead La. UB9: Den 33J 63
Ashmead M. SE8 54Cc 114
Ashmead Rd. SE8 54Cc 114
TW14: Felt 60W 106
Ashmeads IG10: Lough 13Pc 36
Ashmeads Ct. WD7: Shenl 5Ma 15
Ashmere Av. BR3: Beck 68Fc 137
Ashmere Cl. SM3: Cheam 78Za 154
Ashmere Gro. SW2 56Nb 112
Ash M. KT18: Eps 85Ua 174
NW5 36Lb 70
Ashmill St. NW1 7D 214 (43Gb 89)
Ashmole Pl. SW8 51Pb 112
Ashmole St. SW8 51Pb 112
Ashmoor Rd. SE18 52Pc 116
Ashmore NW1 38Mb 70
(off Agar Gro.)
Ashmore Cl. SE15 52Vb 113

Ashmore Ct. N11 . . . . . 23Hb 49
TW5: Hest 51Ca 107
Ashmore Gdns. DA11: Nflt 62Fe 143
HP3: Hem H 3B 4
Ashmore Gro. DA16: Well 55Tc 116
Ashmore Ho. *W14* *48Ab 88*
(off Russell Rd.)
Ashmore La. BR2: Kes 83Lc 179
Ashmore Rd. W9 . . . . . 40Bb 69
Ashmount Cres. SL1: Slou 7E 80
Ashmount Est. N19 . . . . . 31Mb 70
Ashmount Rd. N15 . . . . . 29Vb 51
N19 . . . . . 31Lb 70
Ashmount Ter. W5 . . . . . 49Ma 87
Ashmour Gdns. RM1: Rom 26Fd 56
Ashneal Gdns. HA1: Harr 34Fa 66
Ashness Gdns. UB6: G'frd 37Ka 66
Ashness Rd. SW11 . . . . . 57Hb 111
Ashpark Ho. *E14* *44Bc 92*
(off Norbiton Rd.)
Ash Platt, The TN15: Seal 92Nd 203
Ash Platt Rd. TN15: Seal 93Nd 203
Ash Ride EN2: Crew H 7Qb 18
Ashridge Cl. HA3: Kenton 30La 46
HP3: Bov 10B 2
Ashridge Ct. N14 . . . . . 15Lb 32
UB1: S'hall *44Ea 86*
(off Redcroft Rd.)
Ashridge Cres. SE18 . . . . . 52Sc 116
Ashridge Dr. AL2: Brick W 2Aa 13
WD19: Wat 22Y 45
Ashridge Gdns. HA5: Pinn 28Aa 45
N13 . . . . . 22Mb 50
Ashridge Ho. *WD18: Wat* *17U 26*
(off Chenies Way)
Ashridge Way SM4: Mord 69Bb 133
TW16: Sun 65W 128
Ash Rd. BR6: Chels 80Vc 161
CR0: C'don 75Cc 158
DA1: Dart 60Md 119
DA2: Hawl 63Pd 141
DA3: Hartl, Lfield, New A 69Ae 143
DA12: Grav'nd 3E 144
E15 . . . . . 36Gc 73
GU22: Wok 2P 187
GU24: Pirb 8D 186
SM3: Sutt 73Ab 154
TN15: Ash, New A 77Zd 165
TN16: Westrm 97Tc 200
TW17: Shep 70Q 128
Ash Row BR2: Brom 73Qc 160
ASHTEAD 90Pa 173
Ashtead Common (National Nature Reserve)
. . . . . 87La 172
Ashtead Gap KT22: Lea 88Ka 172
ASHTEAD PARK 90Qa 173
Ashtead Pk. (Local Nature Reserve)
. . . . . 89Qa 173
Ashtead Rd. E5 . . . . . 31Wb 71
Ashtead Woods Rd. KT21: Asht 89La 172
Ashton Cl. KT12: Hers 79X 151
SM1: Sutt 77Cb 155
Ashton Ct. E4 . . . . . 20Gc 35
HA1: Harr 34Ha 66
Ashton Gdns. RM6: Chad H 30Ad 55
TW4: Houn 56Ba 107
Ashton Ga. RM3: Rom 24Md 57
Ashton Hgts. SE23 . . . . . 60Yb 114
Ashton Ho. SE11 . . . . . 7B 230
SW9 . . . . . 52Qb 112
Ashton Pl. KT10: Clay 80Ha 152
Ashton Rd. E15 . . . . . 36Fc 73
EN3: Enf W 8Ac 20
GU21: Wok 9K 167
RM3: Rom 24Md 57
Ashton St. E14 . . . . . 45Ec 92
Ashtree Av. CR4: Mitc 68Fb 133
Ash Tree Cl. CR0: C'don 72Ac 158
KT6: Surb 75Na 153
RM18: Tilb *4C 122*
(off Montreal Rd.)
TN15: W King 81Vd 184
Ashtree Cl. BR6: Farnb 77Rc 160
Ash Tree Ct. TN15: W King 81Vd 184
TW15: Ashf *64R 128*
(off Feltham Hill Rd.)
Ashtree Ct. AL1: St A 2D 6
EN9: Walt A *6Jc 21*
(off Horseshoe Cl.)
Ash Tree Dell NW9 . . . . . 29Sa 47
Ash Tree Dr. TN15: W King 80Vd 164
Ash Tree Ho. *SE5* *52Sb 113*
(off Pitman St.)
Ash Tree Rd. WD24: Wat 8X 13
Ash Tree Way CR0: C'don 71Zb 158
Ashtree Way HP1: Hem H 3J 3
Ashurst KT18: Eps 86Ta 173
Ashurst Cl. CR8: Kenley 87Tb 177
DA1: Cray 55Hd 118
HA6: Nwood 24U 44
KT22: Lea 93Ja 192
SE20 . . . . . 67Xb 135
Ashurst Dr. IG2: Ilf 30Rc 54
IG6: Ilf 29Sc 54
(Aldwych Av.)
IG6: Ilf 28Sc 54
(Walnut Cl.)
TW17: Shep 71N 149
Ashurst Gdns. SW2 . . . . . 60Qb 112
Ashurst Pk. SL5: S'hill 9C 124
Ashurst Rd. EN4: Cockf 15Hb 31
KT20: Tad 93Xa 194
N12 . . . . . 22Gb 49
Ashurst Wlk. CR0: C'don 75Xb 157
Ash Va. WD3: Map C 22F 42
Ashvale Ct. *E3* *40Cc 72*
(off Matilda Gdns.)
Ashvale Dr. RM14: Upm 33Ud 78
Ashvale Gdns. RM5: Col R 22Fd 56
RM14: Upm 33Ud 78
Ashvale Rd. SW17 . . . . . 64Hb 133
Ashview Cl. TW15: Ashf 64N 127
Ashview Gdns. TW15: Ashf 64N 127
Ashville Rd. E11 . . . . . 33Fc 73
Ash Wlk. HA0: Wemb 35La 66
RM15: S Ock 41Zd 99
Ashwater Rd. SE12 . . . . . 60Jc 115
Ashway Centre, The KT2: King T 67Na 131
Ashwell Cl. E6 . . . . . 44Nc 94
Ashwell Ct. TW15: Ashf 61N 127
Ashwell Pl. WD24: Wat 9W 12
Ashwells Rd. CM15: Pil H 13Td 40
Ashwell St. AL3: St A 1B 6
Ashwick Cl. CR3: Cat'm 96Wb 197
Ashwindham Ct. GU21: Wok 10K 167
Ashwin St. E8 . . . . . 37Vb 71
Ashwood CR6: W'ham 92Yb 198
Ashwood Av. RM13: Rain 42Kd 97
UB8: Hil 44Q 84
Ashwood Gdns. CR0: New Ad 79Ec 158
UB3: Harl 49V 84
Ashwood Ho. *HA5: Hat E* *23Ca 45*
(off The Avenue)
NW4 . . . . . *28Ya 48*
(off Harmony Way)
Ashwood M. AL1: St A 4B 6
Ashwood Pk. GU22: Wok 90C 168
KT22: Fet 95Ea 192
Ashwood Pl. DA2: Bean 62Xd 142
GU22: Wok 90C 168
SL5: S'dale 3C 146
Ashwood Rd. E4 . . . . . 20Fc 35
EN6: Pot B 5Db 17
GU22: Wok 90B 168
TW20: Eng G 5M 125
Ashworth Av. *TN15: W King* *80Td 164*
(off London Rd.)
Ashworth Cl. SE5 . . . . . 54Tb 113
Ashworth Est. CR0: Bedd 74Nb 156
Ashworth Mans. *W9* *41Db 89*
(off Elgin Av.)
Ashworth Rd. W9 . . . . . 41Db 89
Aske Ho. N1 . . . . . 3H 219
Asker Ho. N7 . . . . . 35Nb 70
Askern Cl. DA6: Bex 56Zc 117
Aske St. N1 . . . . . 3H 219 (41Ub 91)
Askew Cres. W12 . . . . . 47Va 88
Askew Est. *W12* *46Va 88*
(off Uxbridge Rd.)
Askew Rd. HA6: Nwood 19T 26
W12 . . . . . 47Va 88
Askews Farm La. RM17: Grays 50Ae 99
Askham Ct. W12 . . . . . 46Wa 88
Askham Rd. W12 . . . . . 46Wa 88
Askill Dr. SW15 . . . . . 57Ab 110
Askwith Rd. RM13: Rain 41Fd 96
Asland Rd. E15 . . . . . 39Gc 73
Aslett St. SW18 . . . . . 59Db 111
Aslin Ct. *AL1: St A* *2C 6*
(off Hatfield Rd.)
Asman Ho. N1 . . . . . 1B 218
Asmara Rd. NW2 . . . . . 36Ab 68
Asmar Cl. CR5: Coul 87Nb 176
Asmuns Hill NW11 . . . . . 29Cb 49
Asmuns Pl. NW11 . . . . . 29Bb 49
Asolando Dr. SE17 . . . . . 6E 230 (49Sb 91)
Aspasia Cl. AL1: St A 3D 6
Aspdin Rd. DA11: Nflt 62Fe 143
Aspect Ct. *E14* *47Ec 92*
(off Manchester Rd.)
SW6 . . . . . 54Eb 111
Aspects SM1: Sutt 78Db 155
Aspects Ct. SL1: Slou 7J 81
Aspen Cl. AL2: Brick W 2Aa 13
BR6: Chels 78Wc 161
BR8: Swan 67Fd 140
KT11: Stoke D 88Aa 171
KT19: Eps 81Ta 173
N19 . . . . . 33Lb 70
SL2: Slou 3F 80
TW18: Staines 62H 127
UB7: Yiew 46P 83
W5 . . . . . 47Pa 87
Aspen Copse BR1: Brom 68Pc 138
Aspen Ct. CM13: B'wood 20Ce 41
DA1: Dart 58Qd 119
GU25: Vir W 70A 126
NW4 . . . . . 26Ab 48
Aspen Dr. HA0: Wemb 34Ja 66
Aspen Gdns. CR4: Mitc 71Jb 156
TW15: Ashf 64S 128
W6 . . . . . 50Xa 88
Aspen Grn. DA18: Erith 48Bd 95
Aspen Gro. HA5: Eastc 27V 44
RM14: Upm 35Qd 77
Aspen Ho. CR6: W'ham 87Dc 178
DA15: Sidc 61Wc 139
E15 . . . . . *41Gc 93*
(off Teasel Way)
SE15 . . . . . *51Yb 114*
(off Sharratt St.)
Aspen La. UB5: N'olt 41Aa 85
Aspenlea Rd. W6 . . . . . 51Za 110
Aspen Lodge *W8* *48Db 89*
(off Abbots Wlk.)
Aspen Pk. Dr. WD25: Wat 7X 13
Aspens, The *EN9: Walt A* *7Lc 21*
(in Woodbine Cl. Caravan Pk.)
Aspens Pl. HP1: Hem H 5H 3
Aspen Sq. KT13: Weyb 76T 150
Aspen Va. CR3: Whyt 89Vb 177
Aspen Way E14 . . . . . 45Dc 92
EN3: Enf W 7Zb 20
RM15: S Ock 41Zd 99
SM7: Bans 86Za 174
TW13: Felt 62X 129
Aspern Gro. NW3 . . . . . 36Gb 69
Aspinall Rd. SE4 . . . . . 55Zb 114
(not continuous)
Aspinden Rd. SE16 . . . . . 49Xb 91
ASPIRE National Training Cen. 19Ka 28
Aspley Rd. SW18 . . . . . 57Db 111
Asplins Rd. N17 . . . . . 25Wb 51
Asprey Gro. CR3: Cat'm 96Wb 197
Asprey M. BR3: Beck 71Bc 158
Asprey Pl. BR1: Brom 68Nc 138
Asquith Cl. RM8: Dag 32Yc 75
Asquith Ho. *SM7: Bans* *87Bb 175*
(off Dunnymans Rd.)
SW1 . . . . . 4E 228
Assam St. *E1* *44Wb 91*
(off White Church La.)
Assata M. N1 . . . . . 37Rb 71
Assembly Apartments *SE15* *53Yb 114*
(off York Gro.)
Assembly Pas. E1 . . . . . 43Yb 92
Assembly Wlk. SM5: Cars 73Gb 155
Assher Rd. KT12: Hers 76Aa 151
Ass Ho. La. HA3: Hrw W 21Da 45
Astall Cl. HA3: Hrw W 25Ga 46
Astbury Bus. Pk. SE15 . . . . . 53Yb 114
Astbury Ho. SE11 . . . . . 4K 229
Astbury Rd. SE15 . . . . . 53Yb 114
Astede Pl. KT21: Asht 90Pa 173
Astell Ho. SW3 . . . . . 7E 226
Astell St. SW3 . . . . . 7E 226 (50Gb 89)
Aster Ct. *E5* *33Yb 72*
(off Woodmill Rd.)
Asters, The EN7: G Oak 1Tb 19
Aste St. E14 . . . . . 47Ec 92
Astey's Row N1 . . . . . 38Sb 71
Asthall Gdns. IG6: Ilf 28Sc 54
Astins Ho. E17 . . . . . 28Dc 52
Astleham Rd. TW17: Shep 69N 127
Astle St. SW11 . . . . . 54Jb 112
Astley RM17: Grays 51Be 121
Astley Av. NW2 . . . . . 36Ya 68
Astley Ho. SE1 . . . . . 7K 231
SW13 . . . . . *51Xa 110*
(off Wyatt Dr.)
W2 . . . . . *43Cb 89*
(off Alfred Rd.)
Astley Rd. HP1: Hem H 2L 3
Aston Av. HA3: Kenton 31La 66
Aston Cl. DA14: Sidc 62Wc 139
KT21: Asht 90La 172
WD23: Bush 16Ea 28
WD24: Wat 12Y 27
Aston Ct. IG8: Wfd G 23Jc 53
Aston Grn. TW4: Cran 54Y 107
Aston Ho. SW8 . . . . . 53Mb 112
W11 . . . . . *45Bb 89*
(off Westbourne Gro.)
Aston Mead SL4: Wind 3C 102
Aston M. RM6: Chad H 31Yc 75
W10 . . . . . 41Za 88
Aston Pl. SW16 . . . . . 65Rb 135
Aston Rd. KT10: Clay 78Ga 152
SW20 . . . . . 68Ya 132
W5 . . . . . 44Ma 87
Astons Rd. HA6: Nwood 20S 26
Aston St. E14 . . . . . 43Ac 92
Aston Ter. SW12 . . . . . 58Kb 112
Astonville St. SW18 . . . . . 60Cb 111
Aston Way EN6: Pot B 4Fb 17
KT18: Eps 87Va 174
Aston Webb Ho. SE1 . . . . . 7H 225
Astor Av. RM7: Rom 30Ed 56
Astor Cl. KT2: King T 65Ra 131
KT15: Add 77M 149
Astor Ct. *E16* *44Lc 93*
(off Ripley Rd.)
SW6 . . . . . *52Eb 111*
(off Maynard Cl.)
Astoria Ct. *CR8: Purl* *83Rb 177*
(off High St.)
E8 . . . . . *38Vb 71*
(off Queensbridge Rd.)
Astoria Ho. *NW9* *26Va 48*
(off Boulevard Dr.)
Astoria Mans. SW16 . . . . . 62Nb 134
Astoria Wlk. SW9 . . . . . 55Qb 112
Astor Rd. TN15: W King 79Ud 164
Astra Cl. RM12: Horn 37Kd 77
Astra Ct. WD18: Wat 15V 26
Astra Dr. DA12: Grav'nd 4G 144
Astra Ho. *E3* *41Bc 92*
(off Alfred St.)
SE14 . . . . . *51Bc 114*
(off Arklow Rd.)
Astral Ho. E1 . . . . . 1J 225
Astrid Ho. TW13: Felt 61Y 129
Astrop M. W6 . . . . . 48Ya 88
Astrop Ter. W6 . . . . . 47Ya 88
Astwood M. SW7 . . . . . 49Eb 89
Asylum Arch Rd. RH1: Redh 9P 207
Asylum Rd. SE15 . . . . . 52Xb 113
Atalanta Cl. CR8: Purl 82Qb 176
Atalanta St. SW6 . . . . . 52Za 110
Atbara Rd. TW11: Tedd 65Ka 130
Atcham Rd. TW3: Houn 56Ea 108
Atcost Rd. IG11: Bark 43Wc 95
Atcraft Cen. HA0: Wemb 39Na 67
Atelier Ct. Central *E14* *43Ec 92*
(off Leven Rd.)
Atelier Ct. Nth. *E14* *43Ec 92*
(off Leven Rd.)
Atelier Ct. Sth. *E14* *43Ec 92*
(off Leven Rd.)
Atfield Gro. GU20: W'sham 9B 146
Atheldene Rd. SW18 . . . . . 60Db 111
Athelney St. SE6 . . . . . 62Cc 136
Athelstan Cl. RM3: Hrld W 26Pd 57
Athelstane Gro. E3 . . . . . 40Bc 72
Athelstane M. N4 . . . . . 32Qb 70
Athelstan Gdns. NW6 . . . . . 38Ab 68
Athelstan Ho. *E9* *36Bc 72*
(off Homerton Rd.)
KT1: King T *70Pa 131*
(off Athelstan Rd.)
Athelstan Rd. HP3: Hem H 5P 3
KT1: King T 70Pa 131
RM3: Hrld W 25Pd 57
Athelstan Way BR5: St P 67Wc 139
Athelstone Rd. HA3: W'stone 26Fa 46
Athena Bldgs. E15 . . . . . 39Ec 72
Athena Cl. HA2: Harr 33Fa 66
KT1: King T 69Pa 131
Athena Ct. SE1 . . . . . 2H 231
Athenaeum Ct. N5 . . . . . 35Sb 71
Athenaeum Pl. N10 . . . . . 27Kb 50
Athenaeum Rd. N20 . . . . . 18Eb 31
Athena Pl. HA6: Nwood 25V 44
Athene Pl. EC4 . . . . . 2A 224
Athenia Cl. EN7: G Oak 1Rb 19
Athenia Ho. *E14* *44Fc 93*
(off Blair St.)
Athenlay Rd. SE15 . . . . . 57Zb 114
Athens Gdns. *W9* *42Cb 89*
(off Harrow Rd.)
Atherden Rd. E5 . . . . . 35Yb 72
Atherfield Ho. *RH2: Reig* *9L 207*
(off Atherfield Rd.)
Atherfield Rd. RH2: Reig 9L 207
Atherfold Rd. SW9 . . . . . 55Nb 112
Atherley Way TW4: Houn 59Ba 107
Atherstone Ct. *W2* *43Db 89*
(off Delamere Ter.)
Atherstone M. SW7 . . . . . 5A 226 (49Eb 89)
Atherton Cl. TW19: Stanw 58M 105
Atherton Ct. SL4: Eton 2H 103
Atherton Dr. SW19 . . . . . 63Za 132
Atherton Gdns. RM16: Grays 9E 100
Atherton Hgts. HA0: Wemb 38La 66
Atherton Ho. *RM3: Rom* *24Nd 57*
(off Leyburn Cres.)
Atherton Leisure Cen. 37Hc 73
Atherton M. E7 . . . . . 37Hc 73
Atherton Pl. HA2: Harr 27Fa 46
UB1: S'hall 45Ca 85
Atherton Rd. E7 . . . . . 37Hc 73
IG5: Ilf 26Nc 54
SW13 . . . . . 52Wa 110
Atherton St. SW11 . . . . . 54Gb 111
Athill Ct. TN13: S'oaks 94Ld 203
Athlone KT10: Clay 79Ga 152
Athlone Cl. E5 . . . . . 36Xb 71
WD7: R'lett 8Ja 14
Athlone Ct. E17 . . . . . 27Fc 53
Athlone Ho. *E1* *44Yb 92*
(off Sidney St.)
Athlone Rd. SW2 . . . . . 59Pb 112
Athlone Sq. SL4: Wind 3G 102
Athlone St. NW5 . . . . . 37Jb 70
Athlon Ind. Est. HA0: Wemb 39Ma 67
Athlon Rd. HA0: Wemb 40Ma 67
Athol Cl. HA5: Pinn 25X 45
Athole Gdns. EN1: Enf 15Ub 33
Athol Gdns. HA5: Pinn 25X 45
Atholl Ho. W9 . . . . . 4A 214
Atholl Rd. IG3: Ilf 31Wc 75
Athol Rd. DA8: Erith 50Ed 96
Athol Sq. E14 . . . . . 44Ec 92
Athol Way UB10: Hil 41Q 84
Atkin Bldg. WC1 . . . . . 7J 217
Atkins Cl. GU21: Wok 10L 167
TN16: Big H 84Lc 179
Atkins Ct. *E3* *39Bc 72*
(off Willow Tree Cl.)
Atkins Dr. BR4: W W'ck 75Fc 159
Atkins Lodge *W8* *47Cb 89*
(off Thornwood Gdns.)
Atkinson Cl. BR6: Chels 78Wc 161
WD23: Bush 17Ga 28
Atkinson Ct. *E10* *31Dc 72*
(off Kings Cl.)
Atkinson Ho. *E2* *40Wb 71*
(off Pritchards Rd.)
E13 . . . . . *42Hc 93*
(off Sutton Rd.)
SE17 . . . . . 6G 231
SW11 . . . . . *53Jb 112*
(off Austin Rd.)
Atkinson Morley Av. SW17 . . . . . 62Fb 133
Atkinson Rd. E16 . . . . . 43Lc 93
Atkins Rd. E10 . . . . . 30Dc 52
SW12 . . . . . 59Lb 112
Atlanta Blvd. RM1: Rom 30Gd 56
Atlanta Bldg. *SE10* *53Dc 114*
(off Deal's Gateway)
Atlanta Ct. CR7: Thor H 69Sb 135
Atlanta Ho. *SE16* *48Ac 92*
(off Brunswick Quay)
Atlantic Apartments *E16* *45Jc 93*
(off Seagull La.)
Atlantic Cl. DA10: Swans 57Ae 121
Atlantic Ct. *E14* *45Fc 93*
(off Jamestown Way)
Atlantic Rd. SW9 . . . . . 56Qb 112
Atlantic Wharf E1 . . . . . 45Zb 92
Atlantis Av. E16 . . . . . 45Rc 94
Atlantis Cl. IG11: Bark 41Xc 95
Atlas Bus. Cen. NW2 . . . . . 32Xa 68
Atlas Cres. HA8: Edg 19Ra 29
Atlas Gdns. SE7 . . . . . 49Lc 93
Atlas M. E8 . . . . . 37Vb 71
N7 . . . . . 37Pb 70
Atlas Rd. DA1: Dart 55Pd 119
E13 . . . . . 40Jc 73
HA9: Wemb 35Sa 67
N11 . . . . . 24Jb 50
NW10 . . . . . 41Ua 88
Atlas Trade Pk. DA8: Erith 50Fd 96
Atlas Wharf E9 . . . . . 37Cc 72
Atlip Rd. HA0: Wemb 39Na 67
Atney Rd. SW15 . . . . . 56Ab 110
Atria Rd. HA6: Nwood 22W 44
Atrium, The IG9: Buck H 19Mc 35
Atrium Apartments *N1* *39Tb 71*
(off Felton St.)
Atrium Ho. SE8 . . . . . 52Bc 114
Attenborough Cl. WD19: Wat 20Aa 27
Atterbury Cl. TN16: Westrm 98Tc 200
Atterbury Rd. N4 . . . . . 30Qb 50
Atterbury St. SW1 . . . . . 6F 229 (49Nb 90)
Attewood Av. NW10 . . . . . 34Ua 68
Attewood Rd. UB5: N'olt 37Aa 65
Attfield Cl. N20 . . . . . 19Fb 31
Attfield Ct. *KT1: King T* *68Pa 131*
(off Albert Rd.)
Attilburgh Ho. SE1 . . . . . 3K 231
Attleborough Ct. SE23 . . . . . 61Wb 135
Attle Cl. UB10: Hil 40Q 64
Attlee Cl. CR7: Thor H 71Sb 157
UB4: Yead 41X 85
UB5: N'olt 41X 85
Attlee Ct. RM17: Grays 48Ce 99
Attlee Dr. DA1: Dart 57Qd 119
Attlee Rd. SE28 . . . . . 45Xc 95
UB4: Yead 41W 84
Attlee Ter. E17 . . . . . 28Dc 52
Attneave St. WC1 . . . . . 4K 217 (41Qb 90)
Attwood Cl. CR2: Sande 86Xb 177
Atunbi Ct. *NW1* *38Lb 70*
(off Farrier St.)
Atwater Cl. SW2 . . . . . 60Qb 112
Atwell Cl. E10 . . . . . 30Dc 52
Atwell Pl. KT7: T Ditt 74Ha 152
Atwell Rd. SE15 . . . . . 54Wb 113
Atwood KT23: Bookh 96Aa 191
Atwood Av. TW9: Kew 54Qa 109
Atwood Ho. *W14* *49Bb 89*
(off Beckford Cl.)
Atwood Rd. W6 . . . . . 49Xa 88
Atwoods All. TW9: Kew 53Qa 109
Aubert Ct. N5 . . . . . 35Rb 71
Aubert Pk. N5 . . . . . 35Rb 71
Aubert Rd. N5 . . . . . 35Rb 71
Aubretia Cl. RM3: Hrld W 25Nd 57
Aubrey Av. AL2: Lon C 8G 6
Aubrey Beardsley Ho. SW1 . . . . . 6C 228
Aubrey Mans. NW1 . . . . . 7D 214
Aubrey Moore Point *E15* *40Ec 72*
(off Abbey La.)
Aubrey Pl. NW8 . . . . . 2A 214 (40Eb 69)
Aubrey Rd. E17 . . . . . 27Cc 52
N8 . . . . . 29Nb 50
W8 . . . . . 46Bb 89
Aubrey's Rd. HP1: Hem H 3G 2
Aubrey Wlk. W8 . . . . . 46Bb 89
Auburn Cl. SE14 . . . . . 52Ac 114
Aubyn Hill SE27 . . . . . 63Sb 135
Aubyn Sq. SW15 . . . . . 57Wa 110
Auckland Av. RM13: Rain 41Hd 96
Auckland Cl. EN1: Enf 9Xb 19
RM18: Tilb 4C 122
SE19 . . . . . 67Vb 135
Auckland Ct. UB4: Yead 42Y 85
Auckland Gdns. SE19 . . . . . 67Ub 135
Auckland Hill SE27 . . . . . 63Sb 135
Auckland Ho. KT12: Walt T 74W 150
W12 . . . . . *45Xa 88*
(off White City Est.)
Auckland Ri. SE19 . . . . . 67Ub 135
Auckland Rd. CR3: Cat'm 94Ub 197
E10 . . . . . 34Dc 72
EN6: Pot B 4Ab 16
IG1: Ilf 32Rc 74
KT1: King T 70Pa 131
SE19 . . . . . 67Vb 135
SW11 . . . . . 56Gb 111
Auckland St. SE11 . . . . . 50Pb 90
Audax NW9 . . . . . 26Va 48
Auden Dr. WD6: Bore 15Qa 29
Auden Pl. NW1 . . . . . 39Jb 70
SM3: Cheam 77Ya 154
Audleigh Pl. IG7: Chig 23Qc 54
Audley Cl. KT15: Add 78K 149
N10 . . . . . 24Kb 50
SW11 . . . . . 55Jb 112
WD6: Bore 13Qa 29
Audley Ct. E18 . . . . . 28Hc 53
HA5: Pinn 26Y 45
TW2: Twick 62Fa 130
UB5: N'olt 41Y 85
Audley Dr. CR6: W'ham 87Yb 178
E16 . . . . . 46Kc 93
Audley Firs KT12: Hers 77Y 151
Audley Gdns. EN9: Walt A 6Ec 20
IG3: Ilf 33Vc 75
IG10: Lough 12Sc 36
(not continuous)
Audley Ho. KT15: Add 78K 149
Audley Pl. SM2: Sutt 80Db 155
Audley Rd. EN2: Enf 12Rb 33
NW4 . . . . . 29Wa 48
TW10: Rich 57Pa 109
W5 . . . . . 43Pa 87
Audley Sq. W1 . . . . . 6J 221 (46Jb 90)
Audley Wlk. BR5: St M Cry 72Yc 161
Audrey Cl. BR3: Beck 72Dc 158
Audrey Gdns. HA0: Wemb 33Ka 66
Audrey Rd. IG1: Ilf 34Rc 74
Audrey St. E2 . . . . . 40Wb 71
Audric Cl. KT2: King T 67Qa 131
Audwick Cl. EN8: Chesh 1Ac 20
Augur Cl. TW18: Staines 64H 127
Augurs La. E13 . . . . . 41Kc 93
Augusta Cl. KT8: W Mole 69Ba 129
Augusta Rd. TW2: Twick 61Ea 130
Augustas La. N1 . . . . . 38Qb 70
Augusta St. E14 . . . . . 44Dc 92
August End SL3: G Grn 44A 82
Augustine Bell Twr. *E3* *40Cc 72*
(off Pancras Way)
Augustine Cl. SL3: Poyle 55G 104
Augustine Ct. EN9: Walt A 5Dc 20
Augustine Rd. BR5: St P 69Zc 139
DA12: Grav'nd 9E 122
(not continuous)
HA3: Hrw W 25Da 45
W14 . . . . . 48Za 88
Augustus Bldg. *E1* *44Xb 91*
(off Tarling St.)
Augustus Cl. AL3: St A 4N 5
HA7: Stan 20Ma 29
TW8: Bford 52La 108
W12 . . . . . 47Xa 88
Augustus Ct. SE1 . . . . . 5H 231
SW16 . . . . . 61Mb 134
TW13: Hanw 63Ba 129
Augustus Ho. NW1 . . . . . 2B 216
Augustus La. BR6: Orp 75Wc 161
Augustus Rd. SW19 . . . . . 60Za 110
Augustus St. NW1 . . . . . 2A 216 (40Kb 70)
Aulay Ho. SE16 . . . . . 48Vb 91
Aultone Way SM1: Sutt 75Db 155
SM5: Cars 76Hb 155
Aultone Yd. Ind. Est. SM5: Cars 76Hb 155
Aulton Pl. SE11 . . . . . 50Qb 90
Aura Ct. SE15 . . . . . 56Xb 113
Aura Ho. TW9: Kew 53Ra 109
Aurelia Gdns. CR0: C'don 71Pb 156
Aurelia Rd. CR0: C'don 72Nb 156
Auriel Av. RM10: Dag 37Fd 76
Auriga M. N1 . . . . . 36Tb 71
Auriol Cl. KT4: Wor Pk 76Ua 154
Auriol Dr. UB6: G'frd 38Fa 66
UB10: Hil 37Q 64
Auriol Ho. *W12* *46Xa 88*
(off Ellerslie Rd.)
Auriol Mans. *W14* *49Ab 88*
(off Edith Rd.)
Auriol Pk. Rd. KT4: Wor Pk 76Ua 154
Auriol Rd. W14 . . . . . 49Ab 88
Aurora Bldg. *E14* *46Ec 92*
(off Blackwall Way)
Aurora Ct. *DA12: Grav'nd* *8E 122*
(off Romulus Rd.)
Aurora Ho. *E14* *44Dc 92*
(off Kerbey St.)
Ausden Pl. *WD17: Wat* *15Y 27*
(off Pumphouse Cl.)
Austell Gdns. NW7 . . . . . 20Ua 30
Austell Hgts. *NW7* *20Ua 30*
(off Austell Gdns.)
Austen Apartments SE20 . . . . . 68Xb 135
Austen Cl. DA9: Ghithe 58Yd 120
IG10: Lough 13Tc 36
RM18: Tilb 4E 122
SE28 . . . . . 46Xc 95
Austen Ct. *KT22: Lea* *93Ja 192*
(off Highbury Dr.)
Austen Gdns. DA1: Dart 56Pd 119
Austen Ho. *NW6* *41Cb 89*
(off Cambridge Rd.)
SW17 . . . . . *62Fb 133*
(off St George's Gro.)
Austen Rd. DA8: Erith 52Dd 118
HA2: Harr 33Da 65
Austen Vw. SL3: L'ly 51B 104
Austen Way SL3: L'ly 51B 104
Austenway SL9: Chal P 27A 42
AUSTENWOOD 28A 42
Austenwood La.
SL9: Chal P . . . . . 26A 42 & 27A 42
Austin Av. BR2: Brom 71Nc 160
Austin Cl. CR5: Coul 90Rb 177
SE23 . . . . . 59Ac 114
TW1: Twick 57La 108
Austin Ct. E6 . . . . . 39Lc 73
EN1: Enf 15Ub 33
SE15 . . . . . *55Wb 113*
(off Peckham Rye)
Austin Friars EC2 . . . . . 2G 225 (44Tb 91)
Austin Friars Pas. EC2 . . . . . 2G 225
Austin Friars Sq. EC2 . . . . . 2G 225
Austin Ho. *SE14* *52Bc 114*
(off Achilles St.)
Austin Lodge Golf Course 81Nd 183

Austin Rd. BR5: St M Cry . . . 72Wc 161
DA11: Nflt . . . 10B 122
SW11 . . . 53Jb 112
UB3: Hayes . . . 47V 84
Austin's La. HA4: Ruis . . . 34S 64
UB10: Ick . . . 34S 64
Austins Mead HP3: Bov . . . 10D 2
Austins Pl. HP2: Hem H . . . 1M 3
Austin St. E2 . . . 4K 219 (41Vb 91)
Austin Ter. SE1 . . . 3A 230
Austin Waye UB8: Uxb . . . 39L 63
Austral Cl. DA15: Sidc . . . 62Vc 139
Austral Dr. RM11: Horn . . . 31Md 77
Australia Ho. WC2 . . . 3J 223
Australian War Memorial . . . 1J 227
Australia Rd. SL1: Slou . . . 7M 81
W12 . . . 45Xa 88
Austral St. SE11 . . . 5B 230 (49Rb 91)
Austyn Gdns. KT5: Surb . . . 74Ra 153
Austyns Pl. KT17: Ewe . . . 81Wa 174
Autumn Cl. EN1: Enf . . . 11Wb 33
SL1: Slou . . . 6D 80
SW19 . . . 65Eb 133
Autumn Dr. SM2: Sutt . . . 81Db 175
Autumn Glades HP3: Hem H . . . 4C 4
Autumn Gro. BR1: Brom . . . 65Kc 137
Autumn Lodge *CR2: S Croy . . . 77Ub 157*
(off South Pk. Hill Rd.)
Autumn St. E3 . . . 39Cc 72
Avalon Cl. BR6: Chels . . . 76Zc 161
EN2: Enf . . . 12Qb 32
SW20 . . . 68Ab 132
W13 . . . 43Ja 86
WD25: Wat . . . 4Aa 13
Avalon Ct. WD25: A'ham . . . 11Ca 27
Avalon Rd. BR6: Chels . . . 75Yc 161
SW6 . . . 53Db 111
W13 . . . 42Ja 86
Avante KT1: King T . . . 69Ma 131
Avard Gdns. BR6: Farnb . . . 77Sc 160
Avarn Rd. SW17 . . . 65Hb 133
Avebury SL1: Slou . . . 5E 80
Avebury Ct. *N1 . . . 39Tb 71*
(off Imber St.)
Avebury Pk. KT6: Surb . . . 73Ma 153
Avebury Rd. BR6: Orp . . . 76Tc 160
E11 . . . 32Fc 73
SW19 . . . 67Bb 133
Avebury St. N1 . . . 39Tb 71
AVELEY . . . 46Td 98
Aveley By-Pass RM15: Avel . . . 45Sd 98
Aveley Cl. DA8: Erith . . . 51Hd 118
RM15: Avel . . . 46Td 98
Aveley FC . . . 45Sd 98
Aveley Mans. *IG11: Bark . . . 38Rc 74*
(off Whiting Av.)
Aveley Rd. RM1: Rom . . . 28Fd 56
RM14: Avel, Upm . . . 37Rd 77
Aveline St. SE11 . . . 7K 229 (50Qb 90)
Aveling Cl. CR8: Purl . . . 85Pb 176
Aveling Pk. Rd. E17 . . . 26Cc 52
Avelon Rd. RM5: Col R . . . 23Fd 56
RM13: Rain . . . 39Jd 76
Ave Maria La. EC4 . . . 3C 224 (44Rb 91)
Avenell Mans. N5 . . . 35Rb 71
Avenell Rd. N5 . . . 34Rb 71
Avenfield Ho. W1 . . . 4G 221
Avening Rd. SW18 . . . 59Cb 111
Avening Ter. SW18 . . . 59Cb 111
Avenons Rd. E13 . . . 42Jc 93
Aventine Ct. *AL1: St A . . . 3B 6*
(off Holywell Hill)
Avenue, The BR1: Brom . . . 69Mc 137
BR2: Kes . . . 77Mc 159
BR3: Beck . . . 67Dc 136
BR4: W W'ck . . . 73Ec 158
BR5: St P . . . 66Xc 139
BR6: Orp . . . 75Vc 161
CM13: B'wood . . . 23Ae 59
CM15: Kel H . . . 11Ud 40
CR0: C'don . . . 76Ub 157
CR3: Whyt . . . 91Wb 197
CR5: Coul . . . 87Mb 176
DA5: Bexl . . . 59Zc 117
DA9: Ghithe . . . 56Xd 120
DA11: Grav'nd . . . 10C 122
DA12: Cobh . . . 10K 145
E4 . . . 23Fc 53
E11 . . . 30Kc 53
EC2 . . . 2J 225 (44Ub 91)
EN5: Barn . . . 13Ab 30
EN6: Pot B . . . 2Bb 17
GU3: Worp . . . 9J 187
GU24: Chob . . . 1L 167
HA3: Hrw W . . . 25Ha 46
HA5: Hat E . . . 23Ba 45
HA5: Pinn . . . 30Ba 45
HA6: Nwood . . . 23S 44
HA9: Wemb . . . 32Na 67
HP1: Hem H . . . 1G 2
IG9: Buck H . . . 19Lc 35
IG10: Lough . . . 16Mc 35
KT4: Wor Pk . . . 75Va 154
KT5: Surb . . . 72Pa 153
KT10: Clay . . . 79Ga 152
KT15: New H . . . 82J 169
KT17: Ewe . . . 80Xa 154
KT20: Tad . . . 94Xa 194
KT22: Oxs . . . 83Ha 172
N3 . . . 26Cb 49
N8 . . . 27Qb 50
N10 . . . 26Lb 50
N11 . . . 22Kb 50
N17 . . . 27Tb 51
NW6 . . . 39Za 68
RH1: S Nut . . . 9E 208
RM1: Rom . . . 28Fd 56
RM12: Horn . . . 33Ld 77
SE10 . . . 52Fc 115
SL2: Farn C . . . 5F 60
SL3: Dat . . . 3M 103
SL4: Old Win . . . 7M 103
SM2: Cheam . . . 81Bb 175
SM3: Cheam . . . 80Ya 154
SM5: Cars . . . 80Jb 156
SW4 . . . 56Jb 112
SW18 . . . 59Gb 111
TN15: Bor G . . . 91Ce 205
TN16: Tats, Westrm . . . 94Pc 200
TW1: Twick . . . 57Ka 108
TW3: Houn . . . 57Da 107
TW5: Cran . . . 52W 106
TW9: Kew . . . 54Pa 109
TW12: Hamp . . . 65Ba 129
TW16: Sun . . . 67X 129
TW18: Staines . . . 67K 127
Avenue, The TW19: Wray . . . 5P 103
TW20: Egh . . . 63D 126
UB8: Cowl . . . 42M 83
UB10: Ick . . . 35Q 64
W4 . . . 48Ua 88
W13 . . . 44Ka 86
WD7: R'lett . . . 5Ja 14
WD17: Wat . . . 12W 26
WD23: Bush . . . 14Ba 27
Avenue App. WD4: K Lan . . . 2Q 12
Avenue C KT15: Add . . . 76N 149
Avenue Cl. KT20: Tad . . . 94Xa 194
N14 . . . 16Lb 32
NW8 . . . 1E 214 (39Gb 69)
(not continuous)
RM3: Hrld W . . . 24Pd 57
TW5: Cran . . . 53X 107
UB7: W Dray . . . 48M 83
Avenue Ct. IG5: Ilf . . . 27Nc 54
KT20: Tad . . . 95Xa 194
N14 . . . 16Lb 32
NW2 . . . 34Bb 69
SW3 . . . 6F 227
Avenue Cres. TW5: Cran . . . 53X 107
W3 . . . 47Ra 87
Avenue de Cagny GU24: Pirb . . . 4D 186
Avenue Elmers KT6: Surb . . . 71Na 153
Avenue Gdns. SE25 . . . 68Wb 135
SW14 . . . 55Ua 110
TW5: Cran . . . 52X 107
TW11: Tedd . . . 66Ha 130
W3 . . . 47Ra 87
Avenue Ga. IG10: Lough . . . 16Lc 35
Avenue Ho. *NW6 . . . 38Ab 68*
(off The Avenue)
NW8 . . . 2D 214
NW10 . . . 40Xa 68
(off All Souls Av.)
Avenue Ind. Est. E4 . . . 23Cc 52
RM3: Hrld W . . . 26Md 57
Avenue Lodge *NW8 . . . 38Fb 69*
(off Avenue Rd.)
RM17: Grays . . . 50Ee 99
Avenue Mans. *NW3 . . . 36Db 69*
(off Finchley Rd.)
Avenue M. N10 . . . 27Kb 50
Avenue One KT15: Add . . . 77N 149
Avenue Pde. N21 . . . 17Tb 33
TW16: Sun . . . 69X 129
Avenue Pk. Rd. SE27 . . . 61Rb 135
Avenue Ri. WD23: Bush . . . 15Ca 27
Avenue Rd. AL1: St A . . . 1C 6
BR3: Beck . . . 68Zb 136
CM14: W'ley . . . 21Yd 58
CM16: They B . . . 9Tc 22
CR3: Cat'm . . . 94Tb 197
DA7: Bex . . . 55Ad 117
DA8: Erith . . . 52Ed 118
DA17: Belv, Erith . . . 49Ed 96
E7 . . . 35Kc 73
HA5: Pinn . . . 27Aa 45
IG8: Wfd G . . . 23Lc 53
KT1: King T . . . 69Na 131
KT3: N Mald . . . 70Ua 132
KT11: Cobh . . . 88Z 171
KT18: Eps . . . 86Ta 173
N6 . . . 31Lb 70
N12 . . . 21Eb 49
N14 . . . 17Lb 32
N15 . . . 29Tb 51
NW3 . . . 38Fb 69
NW8 . . . 1D 214 (38Fb 69)
NW10 . . . 40Va 68
RM3: Hrld W . . . 24Pd 57
RM6: Chad H . . . 31Xc 75
SE20: Beck . . . 67Yb 136
SE25 . . . 68Vb 135
SM2: Sutt . . . 82Cb 175
SM6: Wall . . . 80Lb 156
SM7: Bans . . . 87Db 175
SW16 . . . 68Mb 134
SW20 . . . 68Xa 132
TN13: S'oaks . . . 96Ld 203
TN16: Tats . . . 92Nc 200
TW7: Isle . . . 53Ha 108
TW8: Bford . . . 50La 86
TW11: Tedd . . . 66Ja 130
TW12: Hamp . . . 67Da 129
TW13: Felt . . . 62V 128
TW18: Staines . . . 64F 126
UB1: S'hall . . . 46Ba 85
W3 . . . 47Ra 87
Avenue Sth. KT5: Surb . . . 73Qa 153
Avenue Studios SW3 . . . 6C 226
Avenue Ter. KT3: N Mald . . . 69Sa 131
WD19: Wat . . . 16Aa 27
Avenue Three KT15: Add . . . 76N 149
Avenue Two KT15: Add . . . 77N 149
Avenue Vs. RH1: Mers . . . 1C 208
Averil Ct. SL6: Tap . . . 4A 80
Averil Gro. SW16 . . . 65Rb 135
Averill St. W6 . . . 51Za 110
Avern Gdns. KT8: W Mole . . . 70Da 129
Avern Rd. KT8: W Mole . . . 70Da 129
Avershaw Ho. SW15 . . . 57Za 110
Avery Farm Row SW1 . . . 6K 227 (49Jb 90)
Avery Gdns. IG2: Ilf . . . 29Pc 54
AVERY HILL . . . 58Tc 116
Avery Hill Rd. SE9 . . . 58Tc 116
Avery Row W1 . . . 4K 221 (45Kb 90)
Avery Way DA1: Dart . . . 61Pd 141
Avey La. EN9: Lough, Walt A . . . 8Fc 21
IG10: H Beech, Lough . . . 10Hc 21
Avia Cl. HP3: Hem H . . . 6M 3
Avian Av. AL2: F'mre . . . 10C 6
Aviary Cl. E16 . . . 43Hc 93
Aviary Rd. GU22: Pyr . . . 88J 169
Aviation Dr. NW9 . . . 26Wa 48
Aviator Pk. KT15: Add . . . 76M 149
Aviemore Cl. BR3: Beck . . . 71Bc 158
Aviemore Way BR3: Beck . . . 71Ac 158
Avigdor M. N16 . . . 33Tb 71
Avignon Rd. SE4 . . . 55Zb 114
Avingdor Ct. *W3 . . . 46Sa 87*
(off Horn La.)
Avington Ct. SE1 . . . 6J 231
Avington Gro. SE20 . . . 66Yb 136
Avion Cres. NW9 . . . 25Wa 48
Avior Dr. HA6: Nwood . . . 21V 44
Avis Sq. E1 . . . 44Zb 92
Avoca Rd. SW17 . . . 63Jb 134
Avocet Cl. SE1 . . . 50Wb 91
Avocet M. SE28 . . . 48Tc 94
Avon Cl. DA12: Grav'nd . . . 1F 144
KT4: Wor Pk . . . 75Wa 154
KT15: Add . . . 79J 149
Avon Cl. SL1: Slou . . . 5C 80
SM1: Sutt . . . 77Eb 155
UB4: Yead . . . 42Y 85
WD25: Wat . . . 6Y 13
Avon Ct. E4 . . . 18Ec 34
HA5: Hat E . . . 24Ca 45
(off The Avenue)
IG9: Buck H . . . 18Kc 35
N12 . . . 22Db 49
SW15 . . . 57Ab 110
UB6: G'frd . . . 42Da 85
W9 . . . 43Cb 89
(off Elmfield Way)
Avondale Av. EN4: E Barn . . . 18Hb 31
KT4: Wor Pk . . . 74Va 154
KT10: Hin W . . . 76Ja 152
N12 . . . 22Db 49
NW2 . . . 34Ua 68
TW18: Staines . . . 66H 127
Avondale Cl. IG10: Lough . . . 17Pc 36
KT12: Hers . . . 78Y 151
Avondale Ct. AL1: St A . . . 2C 6
E11 . . . 32Gc 73
E16 . . . 43Gc 93
E18 . . . 25Kc 53
SM2: Sutt . . . 80Eb 155
(off Brighton Rd.)
Avondale Cres. EN3: Enf H . . . 13Ac 34
IG4: Ilf . . . 29Mc 53
Avondale Dr. IG10: Lough . . . 17Pc 36
UB3: Hayes . . . 46W 84
Avondale Gdns. TW4: Houn . . . 57Ba 107
Avondale High CR3: Cat'm . . . 93Xb 197
Avondale Ho. *SE1 . . . 50Wb 91*
(off Avondale Sq.)
Avondale Mans. *SW6 . . . 53Bb 111*
(off Rostrevor Rd.)
Avondale Pk. Gdns. W11 . . . 45Ab 88
Avondale Pk. Rd. W11 . . . 45Ab 88
Avondale Pavement SE1 . . . 50Wb 91
Avondale Ri. SE15 . . . 55Vb 113
Avondale Rd. BR1: Brom . . . 65Gc 137
CR2: S Croy . . . 79Sb 157
DA16: Well . . . 54Yc 117
E16 . . . 43Gc 93
E17 . . . 31Cc 72
HA3: W'stone . . . 27Ha 46
N3 . . . 25Eb 49
N13 . . . 19Qb 32
N15 . . . 29Rb 51
SE9 . . . 61Nc 138
SW14 . . . 55Ua 110
SW19 . . . 64Db 133
TW15: Ashf . . . 62M 127
Avondale Sq. SE1 . . . 50Wb 91
Avonfield Ct. E17 . . . 27Fc 53
Avon Grn. RM15: S Ock . . . 44Xd 98
Avon Ho. KT2: King T . . . 67Ma 131
RM14: Upm . . . 31Ud 78
W8 . . . 48Cb 89
(off Allen St.)
W14 . . . 49Bb 89
(off Kensington Village)
Avonhurst Ho. NW2 . . . 38Ab 68
Avonley Rd. SE14 . . . 52Yb 114
Avonmead GU21: Wok . . . 10N 167
Avon M. HA5: Hat E . . . 24Ba 45
Avonmore Gdns. W14 . . . 49Bb 89
Avonmore Mans. *W14 . . . 49Ab 88*
(off Avonmore Rd.)
Avonmore Pl. W14 . . . 49Ab 88
Avonmore Rd. W14 . . . 49Ab 88
Avonmor M. GU23: Rip . . . 94K 189
Avonmouth Rd. DA1: Dart . . . 57Md 119
Avonmouth St. SE1 . . . 3D 230 (48Sb 91)
Avon Path CR2: S Croy . . . 79Sb 157
Avon Pl. SE1 . . . 2E 230 (47Sb 91)
Avon Rd. E17 . . . 27Fc 53
RM14: Upm . . . 30Td 58
SE4 . . . 55Cc 114
TW16: Sun . . . 66V 128
UB6: G'frd . . . 42Ca 85
Avonstowe Cl. BR6: Farnb . . . 76Sc 160
Avontar Rd. RM15: S Ock . . . 42Xd 98
Avon Way E18 . . . 27Jc 53
Avonwick Rd. TW3: Houn . . . 54Da 107
Avril Way E4 . . . 22Ec 52
Avro Ct. *E9 . . . 36Ac 72*
(off Mabley St.)
Avro Ho. *NW9 . . . 26Va 48*
(off Boulevard Dr.)
SW8 . . . 52Kb 112
(off Havelock Ter.)
Avro Way KT13: Weyb . . . 82N 169
SM6: Wall . . . 80Nb 156
Awberry Ct. WD18: Wat . . . 16T 26
Awlfield Av. N17 . . . 25Tb 51
Awliscombe Rd. DA16: Well . . . 54Vc 117
Axe St. IG11: Bark . . . 39Sc 74
(not continuous)
Axholme Av. HA8: Edg . . . 25Qa 47
Axiom Apartments *BR2: Brom . . . 70Kc 137*
(off Masons Hill)
RM1: Rom . . . 28Hd 56
(off Mercury Gdns.)
Axis Ct. *SE10 . . . 51Gc 115*
(off Woodland Cres.)
SE16 . . . 47Wb 91
(off East La.)
Axis Ho. *SE13 . . . 56Ec 114*
(off Lewisham High St.)
Axis Pk. SL3: L'ly . . . 50D 82
Axminster Cres. DA16: Well . . . 53Yc 117
Axminster Rd. N7 . . . 34Nb 70
Axon Pl. IG1: Ilf . . . 33Sc 74
Axtaine Rd. BR5: St M Cry . . . 73Zc 161
Axtane DA13: Sflt . . . 66Be 143
Axtane Cl. DA4: S Dar . . . 68Sd 142
Axwood KT18: Eps . . . 87Sa 173
Aybrook St. W1 . . . 1H 221 (43Jb 90)
Aycliffe Cl. BR1: Brom . . . 70Pc 138
Aycliffe Ho. *SE17 . . . 51Tb 113*
(off Portland St.)
Aycliffe Rd. W12 . . . 46Wa 88
WD6: Bore . . . 11Na 29
Ayebridges Av. TW20: Egh . . . 66E 126
Ayelands DA3: New A . . . 75Ae 165
Ayelands La. DA3: New A . . . 76Ae 165
Ayerst Ct. E10 . . . 31Ec 72
Aylands Cl. HA9: Wemb . . . 33Na 67
Aylands Rd. EN3: Enf W . . . 8Yb 20
Aylesbury Cl. E7 . . . 37Hc 73
Aylesbury Ct. SM1: Sutt . . . 76Eb 155
Aylesbury Cres. SL1: Slou . . . 4H 81
Aylesbury Ho. *SE15 . . . 51Wb 113*
(off Friary Est.)
Aylesbury Rd. BR2: Brom . . . 69Jc 137
SE17 . . . 7G 231 (50Tb 91)
Aylesbury St. EC1 . . . 6B 218 (42Rb 91)
NW10 . . . 34Ta 67
Aylesford Av. BR3: Beck . . . 71Ac 158
Aylesford Ho. SE1 . . . 2G 231
Aylesford St. SW1 . . . 7D 228 (50Mb 90)
Aylesham Cen. SE15 . . . 53Wb 113
Aylesham Cl. NW7 . . . 24Wa 48
Aylesham Rd. BR6: Orp . . . 73Vc 161
Ayles Rd. UB4: Yead . . . 41X 85
Aylestone Av. NW6 . . . 38Za 68
Aylesworth Av. SL2: Slou . . . 1E 80
Aylesworth Spur SL4: Old Win . . . 9M 103
Aylett Rd. RM14: Upm . . . 33Sd 78
SE25 . . . 70Xb 135
TW7: Isle . . . 54Ga 108
Ayley Cft. EN1: Enf . . . 15Wb 33
Ayliffe Cl. KT1: King T . . . 68Qa 131
Aylmer Cl. HA7: Stan . . . 21Ja 46
Aylmer Ct. N2 . . . 29Hb 49
Aylmer Dr. HA7: Stan . . . 21Ja 46
Aylmer Ho. SE10 . . . 50Fc 93
Aylmer Pde. N2 . . . 29Hb 49
Aylmer Rd. E11 . . . 32Hc 73
N2 . . . 29Gb 49
RM8: Dag . . . 34Ad 75
W12 . . . 47Va 88
Ayloffe Rd. RM9: Dag . . . 37Bd 75
Ayloffs Cl. RM11: Horn . . . 28Md 57
Ayloffs Wlk. RM11: Horn . . . 29Md 57
Aylsham Dr. UB10: Ick . . . 33S 64
Aylsham La. RM3: Rom . . . 21Ld 57
Aylton Est. SE16 . . . 47Yb 92
Aylward Rd. SE23 . . . 61Zb 136
SW20 . . . 68Bb 133
Aylwards Ri. HA7: Stan . . . 21Ja 46
Aylward St. E1 . . . 44Yb 92
(Jamaica St.)
E1 . . . 44Yb 92
(Jubilee St.)
Aylwin Est. SE1 . . . 3J 231 (48Ub 91)
Aymer Cl. TW18: Staines . . . 67G 126
Aymer Dr. TW18: Staines . . . 67G 126
Aynhoe Mans. *W14 . . . 49Za 88*
(off Aynhoe Rd.)
Aynhoe Rd. W14 . . . 49Za 88
Aynho St. WD18: Wat . . . 15X 27
Aynscombe Angle BR6: Orp . . . 73Wc 161
Aynscombe Path SW14 . . . 54Sa 109
Ayot Path WD6: Bore . . . 9Qa 15
Ayr Ct. W3 . . . 43Pa 87
Ayres Cl. E13 . . . 41Jc 93
Ayres St. SE1 . . . 1E 230 (47Sb 91)
Ayr Grn. RM1: Rom . . . 25Gd 56
Ayron Rd. RM15: S Ock . . . 42Xd 98
Ayrsome Rd. N16 . . . 34Ub 71
Ayrton Gould Ho. *E2 . . . 41Zb 92*
(off Roman Rd.)
Ayrton Rd. SW7 . . . 3B 226 (48Fb 89)
Ayr Way RM1: Rom . . . 25Gd 56
Aysgarth Ct. SM1: Sutt . . . 76Db 155
Aysgarth Pl. SL0: Iver H . . . 39F 62
Aysgarth Rd. SE21 . . . 59Ub 113
Ayston Ho. *SE16 . . . 49Zb 92*
(off Plough Way)
Aytoun Pl. SW9 . . . 54Pb 112
Aytoun Rd. SW9 . . . 54Pb 112
Azalea Cl. AL2: Lon C . . . 9F 6
IG1: Ilf . . . 36Rc 74
W7 . . . 46Ha 86
Azalea Ct. GU22: Wok . . . 1P 187
IG8: Wfd G . . . 23Gc 53
W7 . . . 46Ha 86
Azalea Dr. BR8: Swan . . . 70Fd 140
Azalea Ho. *SE14 . . . 52Bc 114*
(off Achilles St.)
TW13: Felt . . . 60X 107
Azalea Wlk. HA5: Eastc . . . 29X 45
Azalea Way SL3: G Grn . . . 44A 82
Azania M. NW5 . . . 37Kb 70
Azenby Rd. SE15 . . . 54Vb 113
Azof St. SE10 . . . 49Gc 93
Azov Ho. *E1 . . . 42Ac 92*
(off Commodore St.)
Aztec Ho. IG1: Ilf . . . 33Tc 74
IG6: Ilf . . . 25Sc 54
Azura Ct. *E15 . . . 39Ec 72*
(off Warton Rd.)
Azure W2 . . . 1C 220
Azure Ct. *NW9 . . . 29Qa 47*
(off Kingsbury Cir.)
Azure Ho. *E2 . . . 41Wb 91*
(off Buckfast St.)
Azure Pl. TW3: Houn . . . 56Da 107

B

Baalbec Rd. N5 . . . 36Rb 71
Babbacombe Cl. KT9: Chess . . . 78Ma 153
Babbacombe Gdns. IG4: Ilf . . . 28Nc 54
Babbacombe Rd. BR1: Brom . . . 67Jc 137
Baber Bri. Caravan Site TW14: Felt . . . 57Y 107
Baber Dr. TW14: Felt . . . 58Y 107
Babington Ct. WC1 . . . 7H 217
Babington Ho. SE1 . . . 1E 230
Babington Ri. HA9: Wemb . . . 37Qa 67
Babington Rd. NW4 . . . 28Xa 48
RM8: Dag . . . 36Yc 75
RM12: Horn . . . 32Kd 77
SW16 . . . 64Mb 134
Babmaes St. SW1 . . . 5D 222 (45Mb 90)
Babylon La. KT20: Lwr K . . . 99Cb 195
Bacchus Wlk. N1 . . . 2H 219
Bachelors Acre SL4: Wind . . . 3H 103
Bachelors La. GU23: Ock . . . 96P 189
Bache's St. N1 . . . 4G 219 (41Tb 91)
Back All. EC3 . . . 3J 225
Bk. Church La. E1 . . . 44Wb 91
Back Grn. KT12: Hers . . . 79Y 151
Back Hill EC1 . . . 6A 218 (42Qb 90)
Backhouse Pl. SE17 . . . 6J 231 (49Ub 91)
Back La. DA5: Bexl . . . 59Cd 118
HA8: Edg . . . 25Sa 47
IG9: Buck H . . . 19Mc 35
N8 . . . 29Nb 50
NW3 . . . 35Eb 69
RH2: Reig . . . 1M 207
RM6: Chad H . . . 31Zc 75
RM16: N Stif . . . 47Yd 98
RM19: Purf . . . 48Ud 98
RM20: W Thur . . . 48Xd 98
TN13: Bes G . . . 100Dd 202
TN14: Ide H . . . 100Dd 202
TN15: God G . . . 96Qd 203
Back La. TN15: Igh . . . 96Yd 204
TW8: Bford . . . 51Ma 109
TW10: Ham . . . 62La 130
WD3: Chen . . . 10D 10
WD25: Let H . . . 11Ga 28
Backley Gdns. SE25 . . . 72Wb 157
Back of High St. GU24: Chob . . . 3J 167
Back Pas. EC1 . . . 7C 218
Back Path RH1: Blet . . . 5J 209
Back Rd. DA14: Sidc . . . 63Wc 139
TW11: Tedd . . . 66Ga 130
Bacon Gro. SE1 . . . 4K 231 (48Vb 91)
Bacon La. HA8: Edg . . . 25Qa 47
NW9 . . . 28Ra 47
(not continuous)
Bacon Link RM5: Col R . . . 23Dd 56
Bacon's College Sports Cen. . . . 46Ac 92
Bacons Dr. EN6: Cuff . . . 1Nb 18
Bacons La. N6 . . . 32Jb 70
Baconsmead UB9: Den . . . 33J 63
Bacon St. E1 . . . 5K 219 (42Vb 91)
E2 . . . 5K 219 (42Vb 91)
Bacon Ter. RM8: Dag . . . 36Xc 75
Bacton NW5 . . . 36Jb 70
Bacton St. E2 . . . 41Yb 92
Badburgham Ct. EN9: Walt A . . . 5Hc 21
Baddeley Cl. EN3: Enf L . . . 9Cc 20
Baddeley Ho. *KT8: W Mole . . . 71Ca 151*
(off Down St.)
Baddesley Ho. SE11 . . . 7J 229
Baddow Cl. IG8: Wfd G . . . 23Lc 53
RM10: Dag . . . 39Cd 76
Baddow Wlk. *N1 . . . 39Sb 71*
(off New North Rd.)
Baden Cl. TW18: Staines . . . 66K 127
Baden Pl. SE1 . . . 1F 231 (47Tb 91)
Baden Powell Cl. KT6: Surb . . . 75Pa 153
RM9: Dag . . . 39Ad 75
Baden Powell Ho. *DA17: Belv . . . 48Cd 96*
(off Ambrooke Rd.)
SW7 . . . 4A 226
Baden Powell Rd. TN13: Riv . . . 93Gd 202
Baden Rd. IG1: Ilf . . . 36Rc 74
N8 . . . 28Mb 50
Bader Cl. CR8: Kenley . . . 87Tb 177
Bader Ct. *NW9 . . . 26Va 48*
(off Runway Cl.)
Bader Gdns. SL1: Slou . . . 7E 80
Bader Wlk. DA11: Nflt . . . 2B 144
Bader Way RM13: Rain . . . 37Jd 76
SW15 . . . 58Wa 110
Badger Cl. IG2: Ilf . . . 30Sc 54
TW4: Houn . . . 55Y 107
TW13: Felt . . . 62X 129
Badger Ct. NW2 . . . 34Ya 68
Badgersbridge Ride SL4: Wink . . . 9A 102
Badgers Cl. EN2: Enf . . . 13Rb 33
GU21: Wok . . . 10N 167
HA1: Harr . . . 30Fa 46
TW15: Ashf . . . 64P 127
UB3: Hayes . . . 45U 84
WD6: Bore . . . 12Pa 29
Badgers Copse BR6: Orp . . . 75Vc 161
KT4: Wor Pk . . . 75Va 154
Badgers Ct. KT17: Eps . . . 85Ua 174
WD25: Wat . . . 6V 12
Badgers Cft. HP2: Hem H . . . 3D 4
N20 . . . 17Ab 30
SE9 . . . 62Qc 138
Badgers Dell WD3: Chor . . . 14D 24
Badgers Hill GU25: Vir W . . . 1N 147
Badgers Hole CR0: C'don . . . 77Zb 158
Badgers La. CR6: W'ham . . . 92Yb 198
Badger's Lodge KT17: Eps . . . 85Ua 174
BADGER'S MOUNT . . . 82Dd 182
Badgers Mt. RM16: Ors . . . 1C 100
Badger's Ri. TN14: Bad M . . . 82Cd 182
Badgers Rd.
TN14: Bad M, S'ham . . . 82Dd 182
Badgers Wlk. CR3: Whyt . . . 90Vb 177
CR8: Purl . . . 83Lb 176
KT3: N Mald . . . 68Ua 132
WD3: Chor . . . 14H 25
Badgers Wood CR3: Cat'm . . . 97Tb 197
SL2: Farn C . . . 6G 60
Badger Wlk. GU3: Norm . . . 10A 186
Badger Way AL10: Hat . . . 2D 8
Badingham Dr. KT22: Fet . . . 95Ga 192
Badlis Rd. E17 . . . 27Cc 52
Badlow Cl. DA8: Erith . . . 52Gd 118
Badma Cl. N9 . . . 20Yb 34
Badminton Cl. HA1: Harr . . . 28Ga 46
UB5: N'olt . . . 37Ca 65
WD6: Bore . . . 12Qa 29
Badminton Ho. *WD24: Wat . . . 12Y 27*
(off Anglian Cl.)
Badminton M. E16 . . . 46Jc 93
Badminton Rd. SW12 . . . 58Jb 112
Badric Ct. SW11 . . . 54Fb 111
Badsworth Rd. SE5 . . . 53Sb 113
Baffin Way E14 . . . 46Ec 92
Bafton Ga. BR2: Hayes . . . 74Kc 159
Bagenal Ho. WD5: Ab L . . . 4V 12
Bagley Cl. UB7: W Dray . . . 47N 83
Bagley's La. SW6 . . . 53Db 111
Bagleys Spring RM6: Chad H . . . 28Ad 55
Bagnigge Ho. WC1 . . . 4K 217
Bagot Cl. KT21: Asht . . . 88Pa 173
Bagshot Ct. SE18 . . . 53Qc 116
Bagshot Ho. NW1 . . . 3A 216
Bagshot Rd. EN1: Enf . . . 17Vb 33
GU3: Worp . . . 10F 166
GU21: Knap . . . 10F 166
GU22: Wok . . . 10F 166
GU24: Brkwd, Wok . . . 10F 166
GU24: Chob, W End . . . 4C 166
SL5: Asc, S'hill . . . 4A 146
TW20: Eng G . . . 6N 125
Bagshot St. SE17 . . . 7J 231 (50Ub 91)
Bahram Rd. KT19: Eps . . . 82Ta 173
Baigents La. GU20: W'sham . . . 9B 146
Baildon *E2 . . . 40Yb 72*
(off Cyprus St.)
Baildon St. SE8 . . . 52Bc 114
Bailey Cl. E4 . . . 21Ec 52
N11 . . . 24Mb 50
RM19: Purf . . . 49Td 98
SE28 . . . 46Uc 94
SL4: Wind . . . 4E 102
Bailey Cotts. *E14 . . . 43Ac 92*
(off Maroon St.)
Bailey Cres. KT9: Chess . . . 80Ma 153
Bailey Ho. *E3 . . . 41Dc 92*
(off Talwin St.)
SW10 . . . 52Db 111
(off Coleridge Gdns.)

Bailey M. SW2 57Qb 112
W4 *51Ra 109*
(off Hervert Gdns.)
Bailey Pl. N16 36Ub 71
SE26 65Zb 136
Baileys M. *HP1: Hem H* *1M 3*
(off High St.)
Baillie Cl. RM13: Rain 42Kd 97
Baillie M. KT16: Ott 79F 148
Baillies Wlk. W5 47Ma 87
Bainbridge Cl. TW10: Ham 64Na 131
Bainbridge Rd. RM9: Dag 35Bd 75
Bainbridge St. WC1 2E 222 (44Mb 90)
Baines Cl. CR2: S Croy 78Tb 157
Bainton Mead GU21: Wok 9L 167
Baird Av. UB1: S'hall 45Da 85
Baird Cl. E10 32Cc 72
NW9 30Sa 47
SL1: Slou 7F 80
WD23: Bush 16Da 27
Baird Gdns. SE19 63Ub 135
Baird Ho. *W12* *45Xa 88*
(off White City Est.)
Baird Memorial Cotts. *N14* *19Mb 32*
(off Balaams La.)
Baird Rd. EN1: Enf 13Xb 33
Baird St. EC1 5E 218 (42Sb 91)
Bairny Wood App. IG8: Wfd G 23Kc 53
Bairstow Cl. WD6: Bore 11Na 29
Baizdon Rd. SE3 54Gc 115
Bakeham La. TW20: Eng G 6P 125
Bakehouse M. TW12: Hamp 66Ca 129
Baker Beal Ct. DA7: Bex 55Dd 118
Baker Boy La. CR0: Sels 85Ac 178
Baker Ct. WD6: Bore 12Ra 29
Baker Cres. DA1: Dart 59Ld 119
Baker Hill Cl. DA11: Nflt 3B 144
Baker Ho. *E3* *41Dc 92*
(off Bromley High St.)
W7 46Ha 86
WC1 6G 217
Baker La. CR4: Mitc 68Jb 134
Baker Pas. NW10 39Ua 68
Baker Pl. KT19: Ewe 79Sa 153
Baker Rd. NW10 39Ua 68
SE18 52Nc 116
Bakers Av. E17 30Dc 52
TN15: W King 80Ud 164
Bakers Cl. AL1: St A 3E 6
CR8: Kenley 86Sb 177
Bakers Ct. CM14: B'wood 20Yd 40
RH1: Redh 7P 207
SE25 69Ub 135
UB8: Uxb 38M 63
Bakers End SW20 68Ab 132
Baker's Fld. N7 35Nb 70
Bakers Gdns. SM5: Cars 75Gb 155
Bakersgate Courtyard GU24: Pirb 8E 186
Bakersgate Gdns. GU24: Pirb 7E 186
Bakers Hall Ct. EC3 5J 225
Bakers Hill E5 32Yb 72
EN5: New Bar 12Db 31
Bakers Ho. *W5* *45Ma 87*
(off The Grove)
Bakers La. CM16: Epp 2Vc 23
N6 30Hb 49
Bakers Mead RH9: G'stone 2A 210
Bakers M. BR6: Chels 79Vc 161
W1 2H 221 (44Jb 90)
Bakers Pas. *NW3* *35Eb 69*
(off Heath St.)
Baker's Rents E2 4K 219 (41Vb 91)
Bakers Rd. EN7: Chesh 2Xb 19
UB8: Uxb 38M 63
Baker's Row E15 40Gc 73
EC1 6K 217 (42Qb 90)
BAKER STREET 4A 100
BAKER STREET 7G 215 (43Hb 89)
Baker St. EN1: Enf 13Tb 33
EN6: Pot B 7Ab 16
KT13: Weyb 77Q 150
NW1 6G 215 (42Hb 89)
RM16: Ors 4A 100
W1 6G 215 (43Hb 89)
Bakers Villas, The CM16: Epp 2Vc 23
BAKERS WOOD 32F 62
Bakers Wood UB9: Den 33F 62
Bakers Yd. EC1 6K 217
UB8: Uxb 38M 63
Bakery Cl. SW9 52Pb 112
Bakery M. KT6: Surb 74Qa 153
Bakery Path *HA8: Edg* *23Ra 47*
(off St Margaret's Rd.)
Bakery Pl. SW11 56Hb 111
Bakewell Way KT3: N Mald 68Ua 132
Balaam Ho. SM1: Sutt 77Cb 155
Balaam Leisure Cen. 42Jc 93
Balaams La. N14 19Mb 32
Balaam St. E13 42Jc 93
Balaclava Rd. KT6: Surb 73La 152
SE1 6K 231 (49Vb 91)
Bala Grn. *NW9* *30Ua 48*
(off Ruthin Cl.)
Balcaskie Rd. SE9 57Pc 116
Balchen Rd. SE3 54Mc 115
Balchier Rd. SE22 58Xb 113
Balcombe Cl. DA6: Bex 56Zc 117
Balcombe Ho. NW1 5E 214
Balcombe St. NW1 5F 215 (42Hb 89)
Balcon Ct. W5 44Pa 87
Balcon Way WD6: Bore 11Sa 29
Balcorne St. E9 38Yb 72
Balder Ri. SE12 61Kc 137
Balderton Flats W1 3J 221
Balderton St. W1 3J 221 (44Jb 90)
Baldewyne Ct. N17 25Wb 51
Baldocks Rd. CM16: They B 7Uc 22
Baldock St. E3 40Dc 72
Baldock Way WD6: Bore 14Pa 29
Baldrey Ho. *SE10* *50Hc 93*
(off Blackwall La.)
Baldry Gdns. SW16 65Nb 134
Baldwin Cres. SE5 53Sb 113
Baldwin Gdns. TW3: Houn 53Ea 108
Baldwin Ho. SW2 60Qb 112
Baldwin Rd. SL1: Burn 1A 80
SW11 58Jb 112
Baldwin's Bec *SL4: Eton* *1H 103*
(off Baldwin's Shore)
Baldwins Gdns. EC1 7K 217 (43Qb 90)
Baldwins Hill IG10: Lough 12Pc 36
Baldwin's La. WD3: Crox G 14Q 26
Baldwins Shore SL4: Eton 1H 103
Baldwin St. EC1 4F 219 (41Tb 91)
Baldwin Ter. N1 1D 218 (40Sb 71)
Baldwyn Gdns. W3 45Ta 87
Baldwyn's Pk. DA5: Bexl 61Fd 140
Baldwyn's Rd. DA5: Bexl 61Fd 140
Balearic Apartments *E16* *45Jc 93*
(off Western Gateway)
Bale Rd. E1 43Ac 92
Bales Ter. N9 20Vb 33
Balfern Gro. W4 50Ua 88
Balfern St. SW11 54Gb 111
Balfe St. N1 1G 217 (40Nb 70)
Balfont Cl. CR2: Sande 85Wb 177
Balfour Av. GU22: Wok 94A 188
W7 46Ha 86
Balfour Bus. Cen. UB2: S'hall 48Y 85
Balfour Ct. RM17: Grays 49Fe 99
Balfour Gro. N20 20Hb 31
Balfour Ho. KT13: Weyb 77Q 150
SW11 *53Jb 112*
(off Forfar Rd.)
W10 *43Za 88*
(off St Charles Sq.)
Balfour M. HP3: Bov 9C 2
N9 20Wb 33
W1 6J 221 (46Jb 90)
Balfour Pl. SW15 56Xa 110
W1 5J 221 (45Jb 90)
Balfour Rd. BR2: Brom 71Mc 159
HA1: Harr 29Fa 46
IG1: Ilf 33Rc 74
KT13: Weyb 77Q 150
N5 35Sb 71
RM17: Grays 49Ee 99
SE25 71Wb 157
SM5: Cars 80Hb 155
SW19 66Db 133
TW3: Houn 55Da 107
UB2: S'hall 48Z 85
W3 43Sa 87
W13 47Ja 86
Balfour St. SE17 5F 231 (49Tb 91)
Balfour Ter. N3 26Db 49
Balfron Twr. E14 44Ec 92
Balgonie Rd. E4 18Fc 35
Balgores Cres. RM2: Rom 27Kd 57
Balgores La. RM2: Rom 27Kd 57
Balgores Sq. RM2: Rom 28Kd 57
Balgove Ct. *NW10* *37Xa 68*
(off Eden Gro.)
Balgowan Cl. KT3: N Mald 71Ua 154
Balgowan Rd. BR3: Beck 69Ac 136
Balgowan St. SE18 49Vc 95
BALHAM 60Jb 112
Balham Continental Mkt. *SW12* *60Kb 112*
(off Shipka Rd.)
Balham Gro. SW12 59Jb 112
Balham High Rd. SW12 62Jb 134
SW17 62Jb 134
Balham Hill SW12 59Kb 112
Balham Leisure Cen. 61Kb 134
Balham New Rd. SW12 59Kb 112
Balham Pk. Rd. SW12 60Hb 111
Balham Rd. N9 19Wb 33
Balham Sta. Rd. SW12 60Kb 112
Balin Ho. SE1 1F 231
Balkan Wlk. E1 45Xb 91
Balladier Wlk. E14 43Dc 92
Ballamore Rd. BR1: Brom 62Jc 137
Ballance Rd. E9 37Zb 72
Ballands North, The KT22: Fet 94Ga 192
Ballands South, The KT22: Fet 95Ga 192
Ballantine St. SW18 56Eb 111
Ballantrae Ho. NW2 35Bb 69
Ballantyne Cl. SE9 63Nc 138
Ballantyne Dr. KT20: Kgswd 93Bb 195
Ballard Cl. KT2: King T 66Ta 131
Ballard Grn. SL4: Wind 2C 102
Ballard Ho. *SE10* *51Dc 114*
(off Thames St.)
Ballards Cl. RM10: Dag 39Dd 76
Ballards Farm Rd. CR0: C'don 79Xb 157
CR2: C'don, S Croy 79Wb 157
Ballards Grn. KT20: Tad 91Ab 194
Ballards La. N3 25Cb 49
N12 25Cb 49
RH8: Limp 1N 211
Ballards M. HA8: Edg 23Qa 47
Ballards Ri. CR2: Sels 79Wb 157
Ballards Rd. NW2 33Wa 68
RM10: Dag 40Dd 76
Ballards Way CR0: C'don 79Wb 157
CR2: Sels 79Wb 157
Ballast Quay SE10 50Fc 93
Ballater Cl. WD19: Wat 21Y 45
Ballater Rd. CR2: S Croy 78Vb 157
SW2 56Nb 112
Ball Ct. EC3 3G 225
Ballencrieff Rd. SL5: S'dale 3D 146
Balletica Apartments WC2 3G 223
Ball Ho. *NW9* *27Va 48*
(off Aerodrome Rd.)
Ballina St. SE23 59Zb 114
Ballin Ct. *E14* *47Ec 92*
(off Stewart St.)
Ballingdon Rd. SW11 58Jb 112
Ballinger Ct. WD18: Wat 13X 27
Ballinger Point *E3* *41Dc 92*
(off Bromley High St.)
Ballinger Way UB5: N'olt 42Aa 85
Balliol Av. E4 21Gc 53
Balliol Rd. DA16: Well 54Xc 117
N17 25Ub 51
W10 44Ya 88
Balloch Rd. SE6 60Fc 115
Ballogie Av. NW10 35Ua 68
Balloon Cnr. AL9: Wel G 5D 8
Ballow Cl. SE5 52Ub 113
Balls Pond Pl. N1 37Tb 71
Balls Pond Rd. N1 37Tb 71
Balmain Cl. W5 46Ma 87
Balmain Ct. TW3: Houn 53Da 107
Balmain Lodge *KT5: Surb* *70Na 131*
(off Cranes Pk. Av.)
Balman Ho. *SE16* *49Zb 92*
(off Rotherhithe New Rd.)
Balmer Rd. E3 40Bc 72
Balmes Rd. N1 39Tb 71
Balmoral Apartments W2 1D 220
Balmoral Av. BR3: Beck 70Ac 136
N11 23Jb 50
Balmoral Cl. AL2: Park 10A 6
SL1: Slou 4C 80
SW15 58Za 110
Balmoral Ct. *BR3: Beck* *67Ec 136*
(off The Avenue)
HA9: Wemb 34Pa 67
KT4: Wor Pk 75Xa 154
NW8 1B 214
Balmoral Ct. SE12 63Kc 137
SE16 *46Zb 92*
(off King & Queen Wharf)
SE17 *50Tb 91*
(off Lytham St.)
SE27 63Sb 135
SM2: Sutt 80Cb 155
Balmoral Cres. KT8: W Mole 69Ca 129
Balmoral Dr. GU22: Wok 88E 168
UB1: S'hall 43Ba 85
UB4: Hayes 42U 84
WD6: Bore 15Ta 29
Balmoral Gdns. CR2: Sande 82Tb 177
DA5: Bexl 59Bd 117
IG3: Ilf 32Vc 75
SL4: Wind 5H 103
W13 48Ja 86
Balmoral Gro. N7 37Pb 70
Balmoral Ho. *E14* *48Dc 92*
(off Lanark Sq.)
E16 *46Kc 93*
(off Keats Av.)
W14 *49Ab 88*
(off Windsor Way)
Balmoral M. W12 48Va 88
Balmoral Rd. CM15: Pil H 16Xd 40
DA4: Sut H 66Rd 141
E7 35Lc 73
E10 33Dc 72
EN3: Enf W 8Zb 20
HA2: Harr 35Ca 65
KT1: King T 70Pa 131
KT4: Wor Pk 76Xa 154
NW2 37Xa 68
RM2: Rom 29Kd 57
RM12: Horn 34Md 77
WD5: Ab L 4W 12
WD24: Wat 10Y 13
Balmoral Trad. Est. IG11: Bark 43Vc 95
Balmoral Way SM2: Sutt 82Cb 175
Balmore Cl. E14 44Ec 92
Balmore Cres. EN4: Cockf 15Jb 32
Balmore St. N19 33Kb 70
Balmuir Gdns. SW15 56Ya 110
Balnacraig Av. NW10 35Ua 68
Balniel Ga. SW1 7E 228 (50Mb 90)
Balquhain Cl. KT21: Asht 89Ma 173
Balsam Ho. *E14* *45Dc 92*
(off E. India Dock Rd.)
BALSTONIA 1N 101
Baltic Apartments *E16* *45Jc 93*
(off Western Gateway)
Baltic Centre, The TW8: Bford 50Ma 87
Baltic Cl. SW19 66Fb 133
Baltic Ct. *E1* *46Yb 92*
(off Clave St.)
SE16 47Zb 92
Baltic Ho. SE5 54Sb 113
Baltic Pl. N1 39Ub 71
Baltic St. E. EC1 6D 218 (42Sb 91)
Baltic St. W. EC1 6D 218 (42Sb 91)
Baltimore Cl. DA17: Belv 47Dd 96
Baltimore Ct. SW1 6D 228
Baltimore Ho. SE11 6K 229
SW18 55Eb 111
Baltimore Pl. DA16: Well 54Vc 117
Baltimore Wharf E14 48Dc 92
Balvaird Pl. SW1 7E 228 (50Mb 90)
Balvernie Gro. SW18 59Bb 111
Balvernie M. SW18 59Cb 111
Bamber Ho. IG11: Bark 39Sc 74
Bamber Rd. SE15 53Vb 113
Bamborough Gdns. W12 47Ya 88
Bamburgh N17 24Xb 51
Bamford Av. HA0: Wemb 39Pa 67
Bamford Ct. E15 36Dc 72
Bamford Rd. BR1: Brom 64Ec 136
IG11: Bark 37Sc 74
Bamford Way RM5: Col R 22Dd 56
Bampfylde Cl. SM6: Wall 76Lb 156
Bampton Ct. W5 44Ma 87
Bampton Dr. NW7 24Wa 48
Bampton Rd. RM3: Rom 24Nd 57
SE23 62Zb 136
Bampton Way GU21: Wok 10L 167
Banavie Gdns. BR3: Beck 67Ec 136
Banbury Av. SL1: Slou 3D 80
Banbury Cl. EN2: Enf 11Rb 33
Banbury Ct. SM2: Sutt 80Cb 155
WC2 4F 223
Banbury Ho. E9 38Zb 72
Banbury Rd. E9 38Zb 72
E17 24Zb 52
Banbury St. SW11 54Gb 111
WD18: Wat 15W 26
Banbury Vs. DA13: Sflt 65Be 143
Banbury Wlk. *UB5: N'olt* *40Ca 65*
(off Brabazon Rd.)
Banchory Rd. SE3 52Kc 115
Banckside DA3: Hartl 70Ae 143
Bancroft Av. IG9: Buck H 19Jc 35
N2 29Gb 49
Bancroft Chase RM12: Horn 33Hd 76
Bancroft Cl. TW15: Ashf 64Q 128
Bancroft Ct. RH2: Reig 6K 207
SW8 *52Nb 112*
(off Allen Edwards Dr.)
UB5: N'olt 39Y 65
Bancroft Gdns. BR6: Orp 74Vc 161
HA3: Hrw W 25Ea 46
Bancroft Ho. *E1* *42Yb 92*
(off Cephas St.)
Bancroft Rd. E1 41Yb 92
HA3: Hrw W 26Ea 46
RH2: Reig 6J 207
TN15: Wro 88Be 185
Band La. TW20: Egh 64B 126
Bandon Cl. UB10: Uxb 40P 63
BANDONHILL 78Mb 156
Bandon Ri. SM6: Wall 78Mb 156
Banfield Rd. SE15 55Xb 113
Banfor Ct. SM6: Wall 78Lb 156
Bangalore St. SW15 55Ya 110
Bangla Ho. *E8* *39Vb 71*
(off Clarissa St.)
Bangor Cl. UB5: N'olt 36Da 65
Bangors Cl. SL0: Iver 44G 82
Bangors Pk. 42G 82
Bangors Rd. Nth. SL0: Iver H 39F 62
Bangors Rd. Sth. SL0: Iver, Iver H 41G 82
Banim St. W6 49Xa 88
Banister Ho. E9 36Zb 72
SW8 *53Lb 112*
(off Wadhurst Rd.)
W10 *41Ab 88*
(off Bruckner St.)
Banister M. NW6 38Db 69
Banister Rd. W10 41Za 88
Bank, The N6 32Kb 70
Bank Av. CR4: Mitc 68Fb 133
Bank Bldgs. *E4* *23Fc 53*
(off The Avenue)
Bank Ct. DA1: Dart 58Nd 119
HP1: Hem H 3L 3
Bank End SE1 6E 224 (46Sb 91)
Bankfoot RM17: Grays 50Be 99
Bankfoot Rd. BR1: Brom 63Gc 137
Bank Ho. KT15: Add 77K 149
Bankhurst Rd. SE6 59Bc 114
Bank La. KT2: King T 66Na 131
SW15 57Ua 110
Bank M. SM1: Sutt 79Eb 155
Bank Mill HP4: Berk 1A 2
Bank Mill La. HP4: Berk 2A 2
Bank of England 3F 225 (44Tb 91)
Bank of England Mus. 3G 225
Bank of England Sports Cen. 57Ua 110
Bank Pl. CM14: B'wood 19Yd 40
Banks Ho. SE1 4D 230
Banksian Wlk. TW7: Isle 53Ga 108
Banksia Rd. N18 22Zb 52
Bankside CR2: S Croy 79Vb 157
DA11: Nflt 58Ee 121
EN2: Enf 11Rb 33
GU21: Wok 10M 167
(not continuous)
KT17: Eps D 88Ya 174
SE1 5D 224 (45Sb 91)
(not continuous)
TN13: Dun G 93Fd 202
UB1: S'hall 46Z 85
Bankside Av. SE13 55Ec 114
UB5: N'olt 40W 64
Bankside Cl. DA5: Bexl 63Fd 140
SM5: Cars 79Gb 155
TN16: Big H 90Lc 179
TW7: Isle 56Ha 108
UB9: Hare 23J 43
Bankside Down WD3: Rick 16L 25
Bankside Dr. KT7: T Ditt 74Ka 152
Bankside Gallery 5C 224 (45Rb 91)
Bankside Lofts SE1 6C 224
Bankside Mix SE1 6D 224 (46Sb 91)
Bankside Pk. IG11: Bark 41Wc 95
Bankside Pl. N4 30Sb 51
Bankside Rd. IG1: Ilf 36Sc 74
Bankside Way SE19 65Ub 135
Banks La. CM16: Fidd H, They M 5Ad 23
DA6: Bex 56Bd 117
KT24: Eff J 95W 190
Bank Spur SL1: Slou 7F 80
Banks Rd. WD6: Bore 12Sa 29
Bank St. DA12: Grav'nd 8D 122
E14 46Dc 92
TN13: S'oaks 97Ld 203
Banks Way E12 35Qc 74
Banks Yd. TW5: Hest 51Ba 107
Bankton Rd. SW2 56Qb 112
Bankwell Rd. SE13 56Gc 115
Bannatyne's Health Club
Chafford Hundred 48Yd 98
Chingford 23Cc 52
Grove Park 61Kc 137
Bann Cl. RM15: S Ock 45Xd 98
Banner Cl. RM19: Purf 49Td 98
Banner Ct. *SE16* *49Yb 92*
(off Rotherhithe New Rd.)
Banner Ho. EC1 6E 218
Bannerman Ho. SW8 51Pb 112
Banner St. EC1 6E 218 (42Sb 91)
Banning St. SE10 50Gc 93
Bannister Cl. SL3: L'ly 47A 82
SW2 60Qb 112
UB6: G'frd 36Fa 66
Bannister Dr. CM13: Hut 16Ee 41
Bannister Gdns. BR5: St P 69Yc 139
Bannister Ho. *HA3: W'stone* *27Ga 46*
(off Headstone Dr.)
SE14 *51Zb 114*
(off John Williams Cl.)
Bannockburn Rd. SE18 49Uc 94
Bannon Ct. *SW6* *53Db 111*
(off Michael Rd.)
Bannow Cl. KT19: Ewe 77Ua 154
Banqueting House 7F 223 (46Nb 90)
BANSTEAD 87Db 175
Banstead Ct. W12 45Va 88
Banstead Downs Golf Course 83Cb 175
Banstead Gdns. N9 20Ub 33
Banstead Rd. CR3: Cat'm 93Tb 197
CR8: Purl 83Qb 176
KT17: Ewe 82Xa 174
SM5: Cars 81Fb 175
SM7: Bans 82Xa 174
Banstead Rd. Sth. SM2: Sutt 83Eb 175
Banstead Sports Cen. 92Ya 194
Banstead St. SE15 55Yb 114
Banstead Way SM6: Wall 78Nb 156
Banstead Wood SM7: Bans 90Eb 175
Banstock Rd. HA8: Edg 23Ra 47
Bantam Ho. *NW9* *26Va 48*
(off Heritage Av.)
Banting Dr. N21 15Pb 32
Banting Ho. NW2 34Wa 68
Bantock Ho. *W10* *41Ab 88*
(off Third Av.)
Banton Cl. EN1: Enf 12Xb 33
Bantry Ho. *E1* *42Zb 92*
(off Ernest St.)
Bantry Rd. SL1: Slou 7D 80
Bantry St. SE5 52Tb 113
Banwell Rd. DA5: Bexl 58Zc 117
Banyard Rd. SE16 48Xb 91
Banyards RM11: Horn 28Nd 57
Bapchild Pl. BR5: St M Cry 70Yc 139
Baptist Gdns. NW5 37Jb 70
Baquba SE13 54Dc 114
Barandon Rd. *W11* *45Za 88*
(off Grenfell Rd.)
Barandon Wlk. W11 45Za 88
Barataria Pk. Caravan Site
GU23: Rip 92H 189
Barbanel Ho. *E1* *42Yb 92*
(off Cephas St.)
Barbara Brosnan Ct. NW8 2B 214 (40Fb 69)
Barbara Castle Cl. SW6 51Bb 111
Barbara Cl. TW17: Shep 71R 150
Barbara Hucklesby Cl. N22 26Rb 51
Barbauld Rd. N16 34Ub 71
Barbel Cl. EN8: Walt C 6Cc 20
Barber Beaumont Ho. *E1* *41Zb 92*
(off Bancroft Rd.)
Barber Cl. N21 17Qb 32
Barberry Cl. RM3: Rom 24Ld 57
Barberry Ct. E15 37Gc 73
Barberry Rd. HP1: Hem H 2J 3
Barbers All. E13 41Kc 93
Barbers Rd. E15 40Dc 72
Barbican *EC2* *43Sb 91*
(off Silk St.)
Barbican Arts Cen. 7E 218 (43Sb 91)
Barbican Cinema 7E 218
Barbican Rd. UB6: G'frd 44Da 85
Barbican Theatre 7E 218
Barbican Trade Cen. EC1 7E 218
Barb M. W6 48Ya 88
Barbon All. EC2 2J 225
Barbon Cl. WC1 7G 217 (43Pb 90)
Barbot Cl. N9 20Wb 33
Barchard St. SW18 57Db 111
Barchester Cl. UB8: Cowl 42L 83
W7 46Ha 86
Barchester Rd. HA3: Hrw W 26Fa 46
SL3: L'ly 47B 82
Barchester St. E14 43Dc 92
Barclay Cl. KT22: Fet 95Da 191
SW6 52Cb 111
WD18: Wat 16W 26
Barclay Fld. TN15: Kems'g 89Nd 183
Barclay Ho. *E9* *38Yb 72*
(off Well St.)
Barclay Oval IG8: Wfd G 21Jc 53
Barclay Path E17 29Ec 52
Barclay Rd. CR0: C'don 76Tb 157
E11 32Hc 73
E13 42Lc 93
E17 29Ec 52
N18 23Tb 51
SW6 52Cb 111
Barclay Way RM20: W Thur 50Vd 98
Barcombe Av. SW2 61Nb 134
Barcombe Cl. BR5: St P 69Vc 139
Bardell Ho. *SE1* *47Wb 91*
(off Parkers Row)
Barden Cl. UB9: Hare 24L 43
Barden St. SE18 52Uc 116
Bardeswell Cl. CM14: B'wood 19Yd 40
Bardfield Av. RM6: Chad H 27Zc 55
Bardney Rd. SM4: Mord 70Db 133
Bardolph Av. CR0: Sels 81Ac 178
Bardolph Rd. N7 35Nb 70
TW9: Rich 55Pa 109
Bardon Wlk. GU21: Wok 9M 167
Bard Rd. W10 45Za 88
Bards Cnr. HP1: Hem H 1K 3
Bards Ct. RM3: Rom 24Kd 57
Bardsey Pl. E1 42Yb 92
Bardsey Wlk. *N1* *37Sb 71*
(off Douglas Rd. Nth.)
Bardsley Cl. CR0: C'don 76Vb 157
Bardsley Ho. *SE10* *51Ec 114*
(off Bardsley La.)
Bardsley La. SE10 51Ec 114
Bardwell Ct. *AL1: St A* *3B 6*
(off Bardwell Rd.)
Bardwell Rd. AL1: St A 3B 6
Barents Ho. *E1* *42Zb 92*
(off White Horse La.)
Barfett St. W10 42Bb 89
Barfield DA4: Sut H 67Rd 141
Barfield Av. N20 19Hb 31
Barfield Ct. RH1: Redh 4A 208
Barfield Rd. BR1: Brom 69Qc 138
E11 32Hc 73
Barfields IG10: Lough 14Qc 36
RH1: Blet 5H 209
Barfields Gdns. IG10: Lough 14Qc 36
Barfields Path IG10: Lough 14Qc 36
Barfleur La. SE8 49Bc 92
Barfolds AL9: Wel G 5E 8
Barford Cl. NW4 26Wa 48
Barford Ho. *E3* *40Bc 72*
(off Tredegar Rd.)
Barford St. N1 1A 218 (39Qb 70)
Barforth Rd. SE15 55Xb 113
Barfreston Way SE20 67Xb 135
Bargate Cl. KT3: N Mald 73Wa 154
SE18 50Vc 95
Barge Ct. DA9: Ghithe 56Yd 120
Barge Ho. HP3: Hem H 6P 3
Barge Ho. Rd. E16 47Rc 94
Barge Ho. St. SE1 6A 224 (46Qb 90)
Barge La. E3 39Ac 72
Bargery Rd. SE6 60Dc 114
Barge Wlk. KT1: Hamp W 69Ma 131
KT1: King T 67Ma 131
KT8: E Mos 71Ja 152
(Boyle Farm Island)
KT8: E Mos 69Fa 130
(Hampton Ct. Cres.)
SE10 48Hc 93
Bargrove Av. HP1: Hem H 3J 3
Bargrove Cl. SE20 66Wb 135
Bargrove Cres. SE6 61Bc 136
Barham Av. WD6: E'tree 13Pa 29
Barham Cl. BR2: Brom 74Nc 160
BR7: Chst 64Rc 138
DA12: Grav'nd 10H 123
HA0: Wemb 37Ka 66
KT13: Weyb 77S 150
RM7: Mawney 26Dd 56
Barham Ct. *CR2: S Croy* *77Sb 157*
(off Barham Rd.)
Barham Ho. SE17 7J 231
Barham Rd. BR7: Chst 64Rc 138
CR2: S Croy 77Sb 157
DA1: Dart 59Qd 119
SW20 66Wa 132
Baring Cl. SE12 61Jc 137
Baring Ct. *N1* *39Tb 71*
(off Baring St.)
Baring Ho. *E14* *44Cc 92*
(off Canton St.)
Baring Rd. CR0: C'don 74Wb 157
EN4: Cockf 14Fb 31
SE12 59Jc 115
Baring St. N1 39Tb 71
Baritone Ct. *E15* *39Hc 73*
(off Church St.)
Bark Burr Rd. RM16: Chaf H 47Be 99
Barker Cl. HA6: Nwood 24V 44
KT3: N Mald 70Ra 131
KT16: Chert 73G 148
TW9: Kew 54Ra 109
Barker Dr. NW1 38Lb 70
Barker Ho. SE17 6H 231
Barker M. SW4 56Kb 112
Barker Rd. KT16: Chert 73G 148
Barkers Arc. W8 47Db 89

Berebinder Ho. E3 . . . 40Bc 72
(off Tredegar Rd.)
Bere Cl. DA9: Ghithe . . . 57Yd 120
Beredens La. CM13: Gt War . . . 27Vd 58
Beregaria Ct. SE11 . . . 51Qb 112
(off Kennington Pk. Rd.)
Berengers Ct. RM6: Chad H . . . 31Bd 75
(off Whalebone La. Sth.)
Berengers Pl. RM9: Dag . . . 37Xc 75
Berenger Twr. SW10 . . . 52Fb 111
(off Worlds End Est.)
Berenger Wlk. SW10 . . . 52Fb 111
(off Worlds End Est.)
Berens Ct. DA14: Sidc . . . 63Vc 139
Berens Rd. BR5: St M Cry . . . 71Zc 161
NW10 . . . 41Za 88
Berens Way BR7: Chst . . . 69Vc 139
Beresford Av. HA0: Wemb . . . 39Pa 67
KT5: Surb . . . 74Ra 153
N20 . . . 19Hb 31
SL2: Slou . . . 5N 81
TW1: Twick . . . 58La 108
W7 . . . 43Fa 86
Beresford Ct. E9 . . . 36Ac 72
(off Mabley St.)
Beresford Dr. BR1: Brom . . . 69Nc 138
IG8: Wfd G . . . 21Lc 53
Beresford Gdns. EN1: Enf . . . 14Ub 33
RM6: Chad H . . . 29Ad 55
TW4: Houn . . . 57Ba 107
Beresford Rd. AL1: St A . . . 3F 6
DA11: Nflt . . . 9A 122
E4 . . . 18Gc 35
E17 . . . 25Dc 52
HA1: Harr . . . 29Fa 46
KT2: King T . . . 67Pa 131
KT3: N Mald . . . 70Sa 131
N2 . . . 27Gb 49
N5 . . . 36Tb 71
N8 . . . 29Qb 50
SM2: Sutt . . . 80Bb 155
UB1: S'hall . . . 46Z 85
WD3: Rick . . . 18H 25
Beresford Sq. SE18 . . . 49Rc 94
Beresford St. SE18 . . . 48Rc 94
Beresford Ter. N5 . . . 36Sb 71
Berestede Rd. W6 . . . 50Va 88
Bere St. E1 . . . 45Zb 92
Bergen Ho. SE5 . . . 54Sb 113
(off Carew St.)
Bergenia Ct. GU24: W End . . . 5C 166
Bergenia Ho. TW13: Felt . . . 60W 106
Bergen Sq. SE16 . . . 48Ac 92
Berger Cl. BR5: Pet W . . . 72Tc 160
Berger Rd. E9 . . . 37Zb 72
Berghem M. W14 . . . 48Za 88
Bergholt Av. IG4: Ilf . . . 29Nc 54
Bergholt Cres. N16 . . . 31Ub 71
Bergholt M. NW1 . . . 38Mb 70
Berglen Ct. E14 . . . 44Ac 92
Bering Sq. E14 . . . 50Cc 92
Bering Wlk. E16 . . . 44Mc 93
Berisford M. SW18 . . . 58Eb 111
Berkeley Av. DA7: Bex . . . 53Zc 117
IG5: Ilf . . . 26Qc 54
RM5: Col R . . . 24Ed 56
TW4: Cran . . . 53W 106
UB6: G'frd . . . 37Fa 66
(not continuous)
Berkeley Cl. BR5: Pet W . . . 73Uc 160
EN6: Pot B . . . 4Ab 16
HA4: Ruis . . . 34W 64
KT2: King T . . . 66Na 131
RM11: Horn . . . 33Rd 77
TW19: Staines . . . 61F 126
WD5: Ab L . . . 4V 12
WD6: E'tree . . . 15Qa 29
Berkeley Ct. BR8: Swan . . . 69Gd 140
CR0: C'don . . . 77Tb 157
(off Coombe Rd.)
KT6: Surb . . . 73Ma 153
KT13: Weyb . . . 75T 150
KT21: Asht . . . 90Pa 173
N3 . . . 25Db 49
N14 . . . 16Lb 32
NW1 . . . 6G 215
NW10 . . . 35Ua 68
NW11 . . . 31Bb 69
(off Ravenscroft Av.)
SM6: Wall . . . 76Lb 156
W5 . . . 45La 86
WD3: Crox G . . . 15T 26
Berkeley Cres. DA1: Dart . . . 60Pd 119
EN4: E Barn . . . 15Fb 31
Berkeley Dr. KT8: W Mole . . . 69Ba 129
RM11: Horn . . . 32Qd 77
SL4: Wink . . . 10A 102
Berkeley Gdns. KT10: Clay . . . 79Ja 152
KT12: Walt T . . . 73V 150
KT14: W Byf . . . 86H 169
N21 . . . 17Tb 33
W8 . . . 46Cb 89
Berkeley Ho. E3 . . . 41Cc 92
(off Wellington Way)
SE8 . . . 50Bc 92
(off Grove St.)
TW8: Bford . . . 51Ma 109
(off Albany Rd.)
Berkeley M. AL1: St A . . . 3F 6
SL1: Slou . . . 4B 80
TW16: Sun . . . 69Y 129
W1 . . . 3G 221 (44Hb 89)
Berkeley Pl. KT18: Eps . . . 87Ta 173
SW19 . . . 65Za 132
Berkeley Rd. E12 . . . 36Nc 74
N8 . . . 29Mb 50
N15 . . . 30Tb 51
NW9 . . . 28Qa 47
SW13 . . . 53Wa 110
UB10: Hil . . . 38S 64
Berkeleys, The KT22: Fet . . . 96Ga 192
SE25 . . . 70Wb 135
Berkeley Sq. W1 . . . 5K 221 (45Kb 90)
Berkeley St. W1 . . . 5A 222 (45Kb 90)
Berkeley Ter. RM18: Tilb . . . 2C 122
Berkeley Twr. E14 . . . 46Bc 92
(off Westferry Cir.)
Berkeley Wlk. N7 . . . 33Pb 70
(off Durham Rd.)
Berkeley Waye TW5: Hest . . . 51Z 107
Berkhampstead Rd. DA17: Belv . . . 50Cd 96
BERKHAMSTED . . . 1A 2
Berkhamsted Av. HA9: Wemb . . . 37Pa 67
Berkhamsted By-Pass HP1: Hem H . . . 3A 2
HP4: Berk . . . 3A 2
Berkhamsted La. AL9: Ess . . . 3P 9
Berkhamsted Rd. HP1: Hem H . . . 1G 2
(not continuous)
Berkley Av. EN8: Walt C . . . 6Zb 20
Berkley Cl. TW2: Twick . . . 62Ga 130
(off Wellesley Rd.)
Berkley Cres. DA12: Grav'nd . . . 8E 122
Berkley Gro. NW1 . . . 38Jb 70
Berkley Pl. EN8: Walt C . . . 6Zb 20
Berkley Rd. DA12: Grav'nd . . . 8D 122
NW1 . . . 38Hb 69
Berks Hill WD3: Chor . . . 15E 24
Berkshire Av. SL1: Slou . . . 4F 80
Berkshire Cl. CR3: Cat'm . . . 94Tb 197
Berkshire Ct. W7 . . . 42Ha 86
(off Copley Cl.)
Berkshire Gdns. N13 . . . 23Qb 50
N18 . . . 22Xb 51
Berkshire Ho. SE6 . . . 63Cc 136
Berkshire Rd. E9 . . . 37Bc 72
Berkshire Way CR4: Mitc . . . 70Nb 134
RM11: Horn . . . 29Qd 57
Berkshire Yeomanry Mus. . . . 6H 103
Berman's Cl. CM13: Hut . . . 19De 41
Bermans Way NW10 . . . 35Ua 68
Bermer Rd. WD24: Wat . . . 11Y 27
BERMONDSEY . . . 7J 225 (47Wb 91)
Bermondsey Exchange SE1 . . . 2J 231
Bermondsey Sq. SE1 . . . 3J 231 (48Ub 91)
Bermondsey St. SE1 . . . 7H 225 (46Ub 91)
Bermondsey Trad. Est. SE16 . . . 50Yb 92
Bermondsey Wall E. SE16 . . . 47Wb 91
Bermondsey Wall W. SE16 . . . 47Wb 91
Bermuda Rd. RM18: Tilb . . . 4C 122
Bernal Cl. SE28 . . . 45Zc 95
Bernard Angell Ho. SE10 . . . 51Fc 115
(off Trafalgar Rd.)
Bernard Ashley Dr. SE7 . . . 50Kc 93
Bernard Av. W13 . . . 48Ka 86
Bernard Cassidy St. E16 . . . 43Hc 93
Bernard Gdns. SW19 . . . 64Bb 133
Bernard Gro. EN9: Walt A . . . 5Dc 20
Bernard Hegarty Lodge E8 . . . 38Wb 71
(off Lansdowne Dr.)
Bernard Ho. E1 . . . 1K 225
Bernard Mans. WC1 . . . 6F 217
Bernard Myers Ho. SE5 . . . 52Ub 113
(off Harris St.)
Bernard Pl. KT17: Ewe . . . 82Ya 174
Bernard Rd. N15 . . . 29Vb 51
RM7: Rush G . . . 31Ed 76
SM6: Wall . . . 77Kb 156
Bernards Cl. IG6: Ilf . . . 24Tc 54
Bernard Shaw Ct. NW1 . . . 38Lb 70
(off St Pancras Way)
Bernard Shaw Ho. NW10 . . . 39Ta 67
(off Knatchbull Rd.)
Bernard St. AL3: St A . . . 1B 6
DA12: Grav'nd . . . 8D 122
WC1 . . . 6F 217 (42Nb 90)
Bernard Sunley Ho. SW9 . . . 52Qb 112
(off Sth. Island Pl.)
Bernays Cl. HA7: Stan . . . 23La 46
Bernays Gro. SW9 . . . 56Pb 112
Bernel Dr. CR0: C'don . . . 76Bc 158
Berne Rd. CR7: Thor H . . . 71Sb 157
Berners Cl. SL1: Slou . . . 5C 80
Berners Dr. AL1: St A . . . 5C 6
W13 . . . 45Ja 86
Berners Ho. N1 . . . 1K 217
Berners M. W1 . . . 1C 222 (43Lb 90)
Berners Pl. W1 . . . 2C 222 (44Lb 90)
Berners Rd. N1 . . . 1B 218 (39Rb 71)
N22 . . . 25Qb 50
Berners St. W1 . . . 1C 222 (43Lb 90)
Berner Ter. E1 . . . 44Wb 91
(off Fairclough St.)
Berney Ho. BR3: Beck . . . 71Ac 158
Berney Rd. CR0: C'don . . . 73Tb 157
Bernhard Baron Ho. E1 . . . 44Wb 91
(off Henriques St.)
Bernhardt Cres. NW8 . . . 5D 214 (42Gb 89)
Bernhart Cl. HA8: Edg . . . 24Sa 47
Bernice Cl. RM13: Rain . . . 42Ld 97
Bernie Grant Arts Cen. . . . 28Vb 51
Berniville Way HA3: Kenton . . . 29Pa 47
Bernwell Rd. E4 . . . 20Gc 35
Berridge Grn. HA8: Edg . . . 24Qa 47
Berridge M. NW6 . . . 36Cb 69
Berridge Rd. SE19 . . . 64Tb 135
Berriman Rd. N7 . . . 34Pb 70
Berrington Dr. KT24: E Hor . . . 96V 190
Berrington Ho. W2 . . . 45Cb 89
(off Herrington Rd.)
Berrington M. SL1: Slou . . . 6D 80
Berriton Rd. HA2: Harr . . . 32Ba 65
Berry Av. WD24: Wat . . . 8X 13
Berrybank Cl. E4 . . . 19Ec 34
Berry Cl. N21 . . . 18Rb 33
RM10: Dag . . . 36Cd 76
RM12: Horn . . . 36Ld 77
WD3: Rick . . . 17K 25
Berry Cotts. E14 . . . 44Ac 92
(off Maroon St.)
Berry Ct. TW4: Houn . . . 57Ba 107
Berrydale Rd. UB4: Yead . . . 42Aa 85
Berryfield SL2: Slou . . . 4N 81
Berryfield Cl. BR1: Brom . . . 67Nc 138
E17 . . . 28Dc 52
Berryfield Rd. SE17 . . . 7C 230 (50Rb 91)
BERRYGROVE . . . 10Ba 13
Berry Gro. La. WD25: A'ham . . . 10Ba 13
(Otterspool La.)
WD25: A'ham . . . 11Ca 27
(Otterspool Way)
Berry Hill HA7: Stan . . . 21Ma 47
Berryhill SE9 . . . 56Rc 116
Berryhill Gdns. SE9 . . . 56Rc 116
Berry Ho. E1 . . . 42Xb 91
(off Headlam St.)
SW11 . . . 54Hb 111
(off Culvert Rd.)
BERRYLANDS . . . 72Qa 153
Berrylands BR6: Chels . . . 76Yc 161
DA3: Hartl . . . 72Ce 165
KT5: Surb . . . 72Pa 153
SW20 . . . 69Ya 132
Berrylands Rd. KT5: Surb . . . 72Pa 153
Berry La. GU3: Worp . . . 7G 186
(not continuous)
GU22: Wok . . . 6H 187
KT12: Hers . . . 78Z 151
(off New Berry La.)
SE21 . . . 63Tb 135
WD3: Chor, Rick . . . 16F 24
Berryman Cl. RM8: Dag . . . 34Yc 75
Berryman's La. SE26 . . . 63Zb 136
Berrymead HP2: Hem H . . . 1P 3
Berry Meade KT21: Asht . . . 89Pa 173
Berry Meade Cl. KT21: Asht . . . 89Pa 173
Berrymead Gdns. W3 . . . 46Sa 87
Berrymede Rd. W4 . . . 48Ta 87
Berry Pl. EC1 . . . 4C 218 (41Rb 91)
Berrys Ct. KT14: Byfl . . . 83M 169
Berryscroft Ct. TW18: Staines . . . 66L 127
Berryscroft Rd. TW18: Staines . . . 66L 127
BERRY'S GREEN . . . 88Rc 180
Berry's Grn. Rd. TN16: Big H . . . 88Rc 180
Berry's Hill TN16: Big H . . . 88Rc 180
Berry's La. KT14: Byfl . . . 83M 169
Berry St. EC1 . . . 5C 218 (42Rb 91)
Berry Wlk. KT21: Asht . . . 91Pa 193
Berry Way W5 . . . 48Na 87
WD3: Rick . . . 17K 25
Bersham La. RM17: Grays . . . 49Be 99
Bertal Rd. SW17 . . . 63Fb 133
Bertelli Pl. TW13: Felt . . . 60X 107
Bertha Hollamby Ct. DA14: Sidc . . . 64Yc 139
(off Sidcup Hill)
Bertha James Ct. BR2: Brom . . . 70Kc 137
Berther Rd. RM11: Horn . . . 31Md 77
Berthold M. EN9: Walt A . . . 5Dc 20
Berthons Gdns. E17 . . . 29Fc 53
(off Wood St.)
Berthon St. SE8 . . . 52Cc 114
Bertie Rd. NW10 . . . 37Wa 68
SE26 . . . 65Zb 136
Bertram Cotts. SW19 . . . 66Cb 133
Bertram Rd. EN1: Enf . . . 14Wb 33
KT2: King T . . . 66Qa 131
NW4 . . . 30Wa 48
Bertram St. N19 . . . 33Kb 70
Bertrand Ho. E16 . . . 44Kc 93
(off Russell Rd.)
SW16 . . . 62Nb 134
(off Leigham Av.)
Bertrand St. SE13 . . . 55Dc 114
Bertrand Way SE28 . . . 45Xc 95
Bert Rd. CR7: Thor H . . . 71Sb 157
Bert Way EN1: Enf . . . 14Vb 33
Berwick Av. SL1: Slou . . . 5F 80
UB4: Yead . . . 44Z 85
Berwick Cl. EN8: Walt C . . . 6Cc 20
HA7: Stan . . . 23Ha 46
TW2: Whitt . . . 60Ca 107
Berwick Ct. SE1 . . . 2E 230
Berwick Cres. DA15: Sidc . . . 59Uc 116
Berwick Gdns. SM1: Sutt . . . 76Eb 155
Berwick Ho. N2 . . . 26Fb 49
Berwick Pond Cl. RM13: Rain . . . 40Md 77
Berwick Pond Rd. RM13: Rain . . . 40Nd 77
RM14: Rain, Upm . . . 38Pd 77
Berwick Rd. DA16: Well . . . 53Xc 117
E16 . . . 44Kc 93
N22 . . . 25Rb 51
RM13: Rain . . . 40Md 77
WD6: Bore . . . 10Pa 15
Berwick St. W1 . . . 2C 222 (44Lb 90)
Berwick Way BR6: Orp . . . 74Wc 161
TN14: S'oaks . . . 92Kd 203
Berwyn Av. TW3: Houn . . . 53Da 107
Berwyn Rd. SE24 . . . 60Rb 113
TW10: Rich . . . 56Ra 109
Beryl Av. E6 . . . 43Nc 94
Beryl Ho. SE18 . . . 50Vc 95
(off Spinel Cl.)
Beryl Rd. W6 . . . 50Za 88
Berystede KT2: King T . . . 66Ra 131
Besant Cl. NW2 . . . 34Ab 68
Besant Ct. N1 . . . 36Tb 71
SE28 . . . 46Xc 95
(off Titmuss Av.)
Besant Ho. NW8 . . . 39Eb 69
(off Boundary Rd.)
WD24: Wat . . . 12Z 27
Besant Pl. SE22 . . . 56Vb 113
Besant Rd. NW2 . . . 35Ab 68
Besant Wlk. N7 . . . 33Pb 70
Besant Way NW10 . . . 36Sa 67
Besford Ho. E2 . . . 40Wb 71
(off Pritchard's Rd.)
Besley St. SW16 . . . 65Lb 134
Bessant Dr. TW9: Kew . . . 53Ra 109
Bessborough Gdns. SW1 . . . 7E 228 (50Mb 90)
Bessborough Ho. DA9: Ghithe . . . 56Yd 120
(off Carmichael Av.)
Bessborough Pl. SW1 . . . 7D 228 (50Mb 90)
Bessborough Rd. HA1: Harr . . . 32Fa 66
SW15 . . . 60Wa 110
Bessborough St. SW1 . . . 7D 228 (50Mb 90)
BESSELS GREEN . . . 96Fd 202
Bessels Grn. Rd. TN13: Bes G . . . 95Fd 202
Bessels Mdw. TN13: Bes G . . . 96Fd 202
Bessels Way TN13: Bes G . . . 96Fd 202
Bessemer Cl. SL3: L'ly . . . 50B 82
Bessemer Ct. NW1 . . . 38Lb 70
(off Rochester Sq.)
Bessemer Pk. Ind. Est. SE24 . . . 56Rb 113
Bessemer Pl. SE10 . . . 48Hc 93
Bessemer Rd. SE5 . . . 54Sb 113
Bessie Lansbury Cl. E6 . . . 44Qc 94
Bessingby Rd. HA4: Ruis . . . 33X 65
Bessingham Wlk. SE4 . . . 56Zb 114
(off Aldersford Cl.)
Besson St. SE14 . . . 53Yb 114
Bessy St. E2 . . . 41Yb 92
Bestobell Rd. SL1: Slou . . . 4G 80
Best Ter. BR8: Crock . . . 72Ed 162
Bestwood St. SE8 . . . 49Zb 92
Beswick M. NW6 . . . 37Db 69
Beta Ct. CR0: C'don . . . 74Tb 157
(off Sydenham Rd.)
Betam Rd. UB3: Hayes . . . 47T 84
Beta Pl. SW4 . . . 56Pb 112
Beta Rd. GU22: Wok . . . 88D 168
GU24: Chob . . . 2K 167
Beta Way TW20: Thorpe . . . 67E 126
BETCHWORTH . . . 6A 206
Betchworth Cl. SM1: Sutt . . . 78Fb 155
Betchworth Rd. IG3: Ilf . . . 33Uc 74
Betchworth Way CR0: New Ad . . . 81Ec 178
Betenson Av. TN13: S'oaks . . . 94Hd 202
Betham Rd. UB6: G'frd . . . 41Fa 86
Bethany Cl. RM12: Horn . . . 34Ld 77
Bethany Pl. GU21: Wok . . . 10P 167
Bethany Waye TW14: Bedf . . . 59U 106
Bethecar Rd. HA1: Harr . . . 29Ga 46
Bethel Cl. NW4 . . . 29Za 48
Bethell Av. E16 . . . 42Hc 93
IG1: Ilf . . . 31Qc 74
Bethel Rd. DA16: Well . . . 55Yc 117
TN13: S'oaks . . . 95Ld 203
Bethersden Cl. BR3: Beck . . . 66Bc 136
Bethersden Ho. SE17 . . . 7J 231
Bethlehem Ho. E14 . . . 45Bc 92
(off Limehouse C'way.)
BETHNAL GREEN . . . 41Xb 91
Bethnal Green Cen. for Sports & Performing Arts . . . 4K 219 (41Vb 91)
Bethnal Grn. Rd. E1 . . . 5K 219 (42Vb 91)
E2 . . . 5K 219 (42Vb 91)
Bethune Av. N11 . . . 21Hb 49
Bethune Cl. N16 . . . 32Ub 71
Bethune Rd. N16 . . . 31Tb 71
NW10 . . . 42Ta 87
Bethwin Rd. SE5 . . . 52Rb 113
Betjeman Cl. CR5: Coul . . . 89Pb 176
HA5: Pinn . . . 28Ca 45
Betjeman Ct. UB7: Yiew . . . 46M 83
Betjeman Gdns. WD3: Chor . . . 14F 24
Betjeman Way HP1: Hem H . . . 1K 3
Betley Ct. KT12: Walt T . . . 76X 151
Betony Cl. CR0: C'don . . . 74Zb 158
Betony Rd. RM3: Rom . . . 23Ld 57
Betoyne Av. E4 . . . 21Gc 53
BETSHAM . . . 63Be 143
Betsham Ho. SE1 . . . 1F 231
Betsham Rd. DA8: Erith . . . 52Hd 118
DA10: Swans . . . 59Ae 121
DA13: Sflt . . . 64Zd 143
Betstyle Cir. N11 . . . 21Kb 50
Betstyle Ho. N10 . . . 24Jb 50
Betstyle Rd. N11 . . . 21Kb 50
Bettenson Cl. BR7: Chst . . . 64Pc 138
Betterton Dr. DA14: Sidc . . . 61Ad 139
Betterton Ho. WC2 . . . 3G 223
Betterton Rd. RM13: Rain . . . 41Gd 96
Betterton St. WC2 . . . 3F 223 (44Nb 90)
Bettles Cl. UB8: Uxb . . . 40L 63
Bettons Pk. E15 . . . 39Gc 73
Bettridge Rd. SW6 . . . 54Bb 111
Betts Cl. BR3: Beck . . . 68Ac 136
Betts Ho. E1 . . . 45Xb 91
(off Betts St.)
Betts M. E17 . . . 30Bc 52
Betts Rd. E16 . . . 45Kc 93
Betts St. E1 . . . 45Xb 91
Betts Way KT6: Surb . . . 74Ka 152
SE20 . . . 67Xb 135
Betty Brooks Ho. E11 . . . 34Fc 73
Betty Entwistle Ho. AL1: St A . . . 5B 6
Betty May Gray Ho. E14 . . . 49Ec 92
(off Pier St.)
Betty Paterson Ho. HP1: Hem H . . . 2L 3
(off Astley Rd.)
Betula Cl. CR8: Kenley . . . 87Tb 177
Betula Wlk. RM13: Rain . . . 41Md 97
Between Streets KT11: Cobh . . . 86W 170
Beulah Av. CR7: Thor H . . . 68Sb 135
Beulah Cl. HA8: Edg . . . 20Ra 29
Beulah Cres. CR7: Thor H . . . 68Sb 135
Beulah Gro. CR0: C'don . . . 72Sb 157
Beulah Hill SE19 . . . 65Rb 135
Beulah Path E17 . . . 29Ec 52
Beulah Pl. EN9: Walt A . . . 5Nc 22
Beulah Rd. CM16: Epp . . . 1Wc 23
CR7: Thor H . . . 69Sb 135
E17 . . . 29Dc 52
RM12: Horn . . . 34Md 77
SM1: Sutt . . . 77Cb 155
SW19 . . . 66Bb 133
Beulah Wlk. CR3: Wold . . . 92Ac 198
Beult Rd. DA1: Cray . . . 56Jd 118
Bevan Av. IG11: Bark . . . 38Wc 75
Bevan Cl. HP3: Hem H . . . 4M 3
Bevan Ct. CR0: Wadd . . . 78Qb 156
E3 . . . 40Cc 72
(off Tredegar Rd.)
Bevan Ho. IG11: Bark . . . 38Xc 75
N1 . . . 1H 219
(off New Era Est.)
RM16: Grays . . . 47Fe 99
TW1: Twick . . . 58Ma 109
WC1 . . . 7G 217
WD24: Wat . . . 12Z 27
Bevan M. W12 . . . 47Wa 88
Bevan Pk. KT17: Ewe . . . 82Va 174
Bevan Pl. BR8: Swan . . . 70Hd 140
Bevan Rd. EN4: Cockf . . . 14Hb 31
SE2 . . . 50Xc 95
Bevans Cl. DA9: Ghithe . . . 58Yd 120
Bevan St. N1 . . . 1E 218 (39Sb 71)
Bevan Way RM12: Horn . . . 35Pd 77
Bev Callender Cl. SW8 . . . 55Kb 112
Bevenden St. N1 . . . 3G 219 (41Tb 91)
Bevercote Wlk.
DA17: Belv . . . 51Bd 117
(off Osborne Rd.)
Beveree Stadium . . . 67Da 129
Beveridge Ct. N21 . . . 15Nb 32
(off Pennington Dr.)
SE28 . . . 45Xc 95
(off Saunders Way)
Beveridge Rd. NW10 . . . 38Ua 68
Beverley Av. DA15: Sidc . . . 59Vc 117
SW20 . . . 67Va 132
TW4: Houn . . . 56Ba 107
Beverley Cl. EN1: Enf . . . 14Ub 33
KT9: Chess . . . 77La 152
KT13: Weyb . . . 75U 150
KT15: Add . . . 78M 149
KT17: Ewe . . . 83Ya 174
N21 . . . 18Sb 33
RM11: Horn . . . 31Pd 77
RM16: Ors . . . 4F 100
SW11 . . . 56Fb 111
SW13 . . . 54Wa 110
Beverley Cotts. SW15 . . . 62Ua 132
Beverley Ct. HA2: Harr . . . 27Fa 46
HA3: Kenton . . . 28La 46
N2 . . . 28Hb 49
(off Western Rd.)
N14 . . . 17Lb 32
NW6 . . . 38Eb 69
(off Fairfax Rd.)
SE4 . . . 55Bc 114
(not continuous)
SL1: Slou . . . 7M 81
TW4: Houn . . . 56Ba 107
W4 . . . 50Sa 87
Beverley Cres. IG8: Wfd G . . . 25Kc 53
Beverley Dr. HA8: Edg . . . 27Qa 47
Beverley Gdns. EN7: Chesh . . . 2Wb 19
HA7: Stan . . . 25Ja 46
HA9: Wemb . . . 32Pa 67
KT4: Wor Pk . . . 74Wa 154
NW11 . . . 31Ab 68
RM11: Horn . . . 31Pd 77
SW13 . . . 55Va 110
Beverley Hgts. RH2: Reig . . . 4K 207
Beverley Ho. BR1: Brom . . . 64Fc 137
(off Brangbourne Rd.)
Beverley Hyrst CR0: C'don . . . 75Vb 157
Beverley La. KT2: King T . . . 66Ua 132
SW15 . . . 62Va 132
Beverley Meads & Fishpond Woods Nature Reserve . . . 65Va 132
Beverley M. E4 . . . 23Fc 53
Beverley Path SW13 . . . 54Va 110
Beverley Rd. BR2: Brom . . . 75Nc 160
CR3: Whyt . . . 88Ub 177
CR4: Mitc . . . 70Mb 134
DA7: Bex . . . 54Ed 118
E4 . . . 23Fc 53
E6 . . . 41Mc 93
HA4: Ruis . . . 33W 64
KT1: Hamp W . . . 67La 130
KT3: N Mald . . . 70Wa 132
KT4: Wor Pk . . . 75Ya 154
RM9: Dag . . . 35Ad 75
SE20 . . . 68Xb 135
SW13 . . . 55Va 110
TW16: Sun . . . 67V 128
UB2: S'hall . . . 49Aa 85
W4 . . . 50Va 88
Beverley Trad. Est. SM4: Mord . . . 73Za 154
Beverley Way KT3: N Mald . . . 67Va 132
SW20 . . . 67Va 132
Beversbrook Rd. N19 . . . 34Mb 70
Beverstone Rd. CR7: Thor H . . . 70Qb 134
SW2 . . . 57Pb 112
Beverston M. W1 . . . 1F 221
Bevile Ho. RM17: Grays . . . 52De 121
Bevill Allen Cl. SW17 . . . 64Hb 133
Bevill Cl. SE25 . . . 69Wb 135
Bevin Cl. SE16 . . . 46Ac 92
Bevin Ct. WC1 . . . 3J 217 (41Pb 90)
Bevington Path SE1 . . . 2K 231
Bevington Rd. BR3: Beck . . . 68Dc 136
W10 . . . 43Ab 88
Bevington St. SE16 . . . 47Wb 91
Bevin Ho. E2 . . . 41Yb 92
(off Butler St.)
E3 . . . 41Cc 92
(off Alfred St.)
Bevin Rd. UB4: Yead . . . 41W 84
Bevin Sq. SW17 . . . 62Hb 133
Bevin Wlk. SS17: Stan H . . . 1M 101
Bevin Way WC1 . . . 3K 217 (40Qb 70)
Bevis Cl. DA2: Dart . . . 59Sd 120
Bevis Marks EC3 . . . 2J 225 (44Ub 91)
Bewcastle Gdns. EN2: Enf . . . 14Nb 32
Bew Ct. SE22 . . . 59Wb 113
Bewdley St. N1 . . . 38Qb 70
Bewick M. SE15 . . . 52Xb 113
Bewick St. SW8 . . . 54Kb 112
Bewley Cl. EN8: Chesh . . . 3Zb 20
Bewley Ho. E1 . . . 45Xb 91
(off Bewley St.)
Bewley La. TN15: Bor G, Plax . . . 97Yd 204
Bewley St. E1 . . . 45Yb 92
SW19 . . . 65Eb 133
Bewlys Rd. SE27 . . . 64Rb 135
Bexhill Cl. TW13: Felt . . . 61Aa 129
Bexhill Dr. RM17: Grays . . . 51Ae 121
Bexhill Rd. N11 . . . 22Mb 50
SE4 . . . 58Bc 114
SW14 . . . 55Sa 109
Bexhill Wlk. E15 . . . 39Gc 73
BEXLEY . . . 59Cd 118
Bexley Cl. DA1: Cray . . . 57Gd 118
Bexley Cotts. DA4: Hort K . . . 70Rd 141
Bexley Gdns. N9 . . . 20Tb 33
RM6: Chad H . . . 29Xc 55
BEXLEYHEATH . . . 56Cd 118
Bexleyheath Golf Course . . . 57Ad 117
Bexleyheath Sports Club . . . 56Yc 117
Bexley High St. DA5: Bexl . . . 59Cd 118
Bexley Ho. SE4 . . . 56Ac 114
Bexley La. DA1: Cray . . . 57Gd 118
DA14: Sidc . . . 63Yc 139
Bexley Mus. Collection, The . . . 58Ed 118
Bexley Music & Dance Cen. . . . 63Wc 139
(off Station Rd.)
Bexley Rd. DA8: Erith . . . 52Ed 118
SE9 . . . 57Rc 116
Bexley St. SL4: Wind . . . 3G 102
Beynon Rd. SM5: Cars . . . 78Hb 155
Bezier Apartments EC2 . . . 5G 219 (42Tb 91)
BFI Southbank . . . 6J 223
Bianca Ho. N1 . . . 2H 219
Bianca Rd. SE15 . . . 51Wb 113
Bibsworth Rd. N3 . . . 26Bb 49
Bibury Cl. SE15 . . . 51Ub 113
(not continuous)
Bicester Rd. TW9: Rich . . . 55Qa 109
Bickels Yd. SE1 . . . 2J 231 (47Ub 91)
Bickenhall Mans. W1 . . . 7G 215
(not continuous)
Bickenhall St. W1 . . . 7G 215 (43Hb 89)
Bickersteth Rd. SW17 . . . 65Hb 133
Bickerton Ho. WD17: Wat . . . 14Y 27
(off Pumphouse Cres.)
Bickerton Rd. N19 . . . 33Lb 70
BICKLEY . . . 69Nc 138
Bickley Cres. BR1: Brom . . . 70Nc 138
Bickley Pk. Rd. BR1: Brom . . . 69Nc 138
Bickley Rd. BR1: Brom . . . 68Mc 137
E10 . . . 31Dc 72
Bickley St. SW17 . . . 64Gb 133
Bicknell Ho. E1 . . . 44Wb 91
(off Ellen St.)
Bicknell Rd. SE5 . . . 55Sb 113
Bickney Way KT22: Fet . . . 94Ea 192
Bicknoller Cl. SM2: Sutt . . . 82Db 175
Bicknoller Rd. EN1: Enf . . . 11Ub 33
Bicknor Rd. BR6: Orp . . . 73Uc 160
Bicycle M. SW4 . . . 55Mb 112
Bidborough Cl. BR2: Brom . . . 71Hc 159
Bidborough St. WC1 . . . 4F 217 (41Nb 90)
Biddenden Way DA13: Ist R . . . 6A 144
SE9 . . . 63Qc 138
Biddenham Ho. SE16 . . . 49Zb 92
(off Plough Way)
Biddenham Turn WD25: Wat . . . 7Y 13
Bidder St. E16 . . . 43Gc 93
(not continuous)
Biddesden Ho. SW3 . . . 6F 227
Biddestone Rd. N7 . . . 35Pb 70
Biddles Cl. SL1: Slou . . . 6C 80
Biddulph Ho. SE18 . . . 49Pc 94
Biddulph Mans. W9 . . . 41Db 89
(off Elgin Av.)
Biddulph Rd. CR2: S Croy . . . 82Sb 177
W9 . . . 41Db 89

Bideford Av. UB6: G'frd 40Ka 66
Bideford Cl. HA8: Edg 25Qa 47
RM3: Rom 25Ld 57
TW13: Hanw 62Ba 129
Bideford Gdns. EN1: Enf 17Ub 33
Bideford Rd. BR1: Brom 62Hc 137
DA16: Well 52Xc 117
EN3: Enf L 10Bc 20
HA4: Ruis 34X 65
Bideford Spur SL2: Slou 1F 80
Bidhams Cres. KT20: Tad 93Ya 194
Bidwell Gdns. N11 24Lb 50
Bidwell St. SE15 53Xb 113
Bield, The RH2: Reig 8J 207
Big Apple, The 89B 168
Big Ben 2G 229 (47Nb 90)
Bigbury Cl. N17 24Tb 51
Big Comn. La. RH1: Blet 5H 209
Biggerstaff Rd. E15 39Ec 72
Biggerstaff St. N4 33Qb 70
BIGGIN 1D 122
Biggin Av. CR4: Mitc 67Hb 133
BIGGIN HILL 89Mc 179
Biggin Hill SE19 67Rb 135
BIGGIN HILL AIRPORT 84Mc 179
Biggin Hill Bus. Pk. TN16: Big H 87Mc 179
Biggin Hill Cl. KT2: King T 64La 130
Biggin Hill Memorial Pool 88Mc 179
Biggin La. RM16: Grays 1D 122
Biggin Way SE19 66Rb 135
Bigginwood Rd. SW16 66Rb 135
Biggs Row SW15 55Za 110
Biggs Sq. E9 37Bc 72
Big Hill E5 32Xb 71
Bigland St. E1 44Xb 91
Bignell Rd. SE18 50Rc 94
BIGNELL'S CORNER 5Xa 16
BIGNELL'S CORNER 6Wa 16
Bignells Cnr. EN6: S Mim 6Xa 16
Bignold Rd. E7 35Jc 73
Bigwood Ct. NW11 29Db 49
Bigwood Rd. NW11 29Db 49
Bike Shed, The *IG11: Bark* 38Sc 74
(off Ripple Rd.)
Biko Cl. UB8: Cowl 44L 83
Bilberry Ho. *E3* 43Cc 92
(off Watts Gro.)
Billericay Rd. CM13: Heron 24Fe 59
BILLET, THE 2P 101
Billet Cl. RM6: Chad H 27Zc 55
Billet Hill TN15: Ash 77Yd 164
Billet La. RM11: Horn 32Md 77
SL0: Iver H 41D 82
SL3: L'ly 45D 82
SS17: Stan H 2M 101
Billet Rd. E17 25Zb 52
RM6: Chad H 27Xc 55
TW18: Staines 62J 127
Billets Hart Cl. W7 47Ga 86
Bill Everett Community Cen. 8W 12
Bill Hamling Cl. SE9 61Pc 138
Billing Cl. RM9: Dag 38Yc 75
Billingford Cl. SE4 56Zb 114
Billing Ho. *E1* 44Zb 92
(off Bower St.)
Billingley *NW1* 39Lb 70
(off Pratt St.)
Billing Pl. SW10 52Db 111
Billing Rd. SW10 52Db 111
Billingsgate Market 46Dc 92
Billings Hill Shaw DA3: Hartl 72Be 165
Billing St. SW10 52Db 111
Billington M. *W3* 46Ra 87
(off High St.)
Billington Rd. SE14 52Zb 114
Billinton Hill CR0: C'don 75Tb 157
Billiter Sq. EC3 3J 225
Billiter St. EC3 3J 225 (44Ub 91)
Bill Nicholson Way *N17* 24Vb 51
(off High Rd.)
Billockby Cl. KT9: Chess 79Pa 153
Billson St. E14 49Ec 92
Billy Lows La. EN6: Pot B 3Cb 17
Bilsby Gro. SE9 63Mc 137
Bilsby Lodge *HA9: Wemb* 34Sa 67
(off Chalklands)
Bilton Cen. KT22: Lea 91Ha 192
Bilton Cen., The UB6: G'frd 39Ka 66
Bilton Cl. SL3: Poyle 54G 104
Bilton Rd. DA8: Erith 52Jd 118
UB6: G'frd 39Ja 66
Bilton Towers W1 3G 221
Bilton Way EN3: Enf L 11Ac 34
UB3: Hayes 47Y 84
Bina Gdns. SW5 6A 226 (49Eb 89)
Binbrook Ho. *W10* 43Ya 88
(off Sutton Way)
Bincote Rd. EN2: Enf 13Pb 32
Binden Rd. W12 48Va 88
Bindon Grn. SM4: Mord 70Db 133
Binfield Rd. CR2: S Croy 78Vb 157
KT14: Byfl 84N 169
SW4 53Nb 112
Bingfield St. N1 39Nb 70
(not continuous)
Bingham Cl. RM15: S Ock 44Yd 98
Bingham Ct. *N1* 38Rb 71
(off Halton Rd.)
Bingham Dr. GU21: Wok 10K 167
TW18: Staines 66M 127
Bingham Pl. W1 7H 215 (43Jb 90)
Bingham Point *SE18* 49Rc 94
(off Wilmount St.)
Bingham Rd. CR0: C'don 74Wb 157
Bingham St. N1 37Tb 71
Bingley Rd. E16 44Lc 93
TW16: Sun 66W 128
UB6: G'frd 42Ea 86
Binley Ho. SW15 58Va 110
Binney St. W1 3J 221 (44Jb 90)
Binnie Ct. *SE10* 52Dc 114
(off Greenwich High Rd.)
Binnie Ho. SE1 4D 230
Binnie Rd. DA1: Dart 54Nd 119
Binnington Twr. BR2: Brom 72Nc 160
Binns Rd. W4 50Ua 88
Binns Ter. W4 50Ua 88
Binsey Wlk. SE2 47Yc 95
(not continuous)
Binstead Cl. UB4: Yead 43Aa 85
Binyon Cres. HA7: Stan 22Ha 46
Biraj Ho. E6 39Pc 74
Birbetts Rd. SE9 61Pc 138
Bircham Path *SE4* 56Zb 114
(off Aldersford Cl.)
Birchanger Rd. SE25 71Wb 157
Birch Av. CR3: Cat'm 96Tb 197
KT22: Lea 92Ha 192
N13 20Sb 33
UB7: View 44P 83
Birch Cl. DA3: Lfield 68Ee 143
DA4: Eyns 76Md 163
E16 43Gc 93
GU21: Wok 1N 187
GU23: Send 97H 189
IG9: Buck H 20Mc 35
KT15: New H 81M 169
N19 33Lb 70
RM7: Mawney 27Dd 56
RM15: S Ock 42Zd 99
SE15 54Wb 113
SL0: Iver H 40F 62
SM7: Bans 86Ab 174
TN13: S'oaks 95Kd 203
TW3: Houn 54Fa 108
TW8: Bford 52Ka 108
TW11: Tedd 64Ja 130
TW17: Shep 68U 128
Birch Copse AL2: Brick W 2Aa 13
Birch Ct. HA6: Nwood 23S 44
KT22: Lea 92Ha 192
N12 21Db 49
RM6: Chad H 30Yc 55
SM1: Sutt 77Eb 155
SM6: Wall 77Kb 156
Birch Cres. RM11: Horn 28Nd 57
RM15: S Ock 41Zd 99
UB10: Uxb 39P 63
Birchcroft Cl. CR3: Cat'm 97Sb 197
Birchdale SL9: Ger X 2P 61
Birchdale Cl. KT14: W Byf 83L 169
Birchdale Gdns. RM6: Chad H 31Zc 75
Birchdale Rd. E7 36Lc 73
Birchdene Dr. SE28 46Wc 95
Birchdown Ho. *E3* 41Dc 92
(off Rainhill Way)
Birch Dr. AL10: Hat 1C 8
WD3: Map C 22F 42
Birchen Cl. NW9 33Ta 67
Birchend Cl. CR2: S Croy 79Tb 157
Birchen Gro. NW9 33Ta 67
Birches, The AL2: Lon C 9G 6
BR2: Brom 70Hc 137
(off Durham Rd.)
BR6: Farnb 77Qc 160
BR8: Swan 68Gd 140
CM13: B'wood 20Ae 41
E12 35Nc 74
EN9: Walt A 6Hc 21
GU22: Wok 90B 168
HP3: Hem H 5H 3
KT24: E Hor 98U 190
N21 16Pb 32
SE5 54Ub 113
SE7 51Kc 115
TW4: Houn 59Ba 107
WD23: Bush 15Ea 28
Birches Cl. CR4: Mitc 69Hb 133
HA5: Pinn 29Aa 45
KT18: Eps 87Ua 174
Birchfield RM16: N Stif 46Zd 99
TN14: Sund 99Ad 201
Birchfield Cl. CR5: Coul 88Pb 176
KT15: Add 77K 149
Birchfield Ct. *KT12: Walt T* 73X 151
(off Grove Cres.)
Birchfield Gro. KT17: Ewe 82Ya 174
Birchfield Ho. *E14* 45Cc 92
(off Birchfield St.)
Birchfield Rd. EN8: Chesh 1Xb 19
Birchfield St. E14 45Cc 92
Birch Gdns. RM10: Dag 34Ed 76
BIRCH GREEN 63J 127
Birch Grn. HP1: Hem H 1H 3
NW9 24Ua 48
TW18: Staines 63H 127
Birch Gro. DA16: Well 56Wc 117
E11 35Gc 73
EN6: Pot B 4Cb 17
GU22: Pyr 87F 168
KT11: Cobh 86Y 171
KT20: Kgswd 96Ab 194
SE12 59Hc 115
SL2: Slou 3F 80
SL4: Wind 3B 102
TW17: Shep 68U 128
W3 46Qa 87
Birchgrove Ho. TW9: Kew 52Ra 109
Birch Hill CR0: C'don 78Zb 158
Birch Ho. *N22* 25Qb 50
(off Acacia Rd.)
SE14 53Bc 114
SW2 58Qb 112
UB7: W Dray 47P 83
(off Park Lodge Av.)
W10 42Ab 88
(off Droop St.)
Birchin Cross Rd. TN15: Knat 87Nd 183
Birchington Cl. BR5: Orp 74Yc 161
DA7: Bex 53Dd 118
Birchington Ct. *NW6* 39Db 69
(off West End La.)
Birchington Ho. E5 36Xb 71
Birchington Rd. KT5: Surb 73Pa 153
N8 30Mb 50
NW6 39Cb 69
SL4: Wind 4E 102
Birchin La. EC3 3G 225 (44Tb 91)
Birchlands Av. SW12 59Hb 111
Birch La. CR8: Purl 83Nb 176
GU24: W End 4B 166
HP3: Flau 5D 10
Birchmead BR6: Farnb 75Qc 160
WD17: Wat 10V 12
Birchmead Av. HA5: Pinn 28Y 45
Birchmere Bus. Pk. SE28 47Wc 95
Birchmere Lodge *SE16* 50Xb 91
(off Sherwood Gdns.)
Birchmere Row SE3 54Hc 115
Birchmore Hall N5 34Sb 71
Birchmore Wlk. N5 34Sb 71
(not continuous)
Birch Pk. HA3: Hrw W 24Ea 46
Birch Pl. DA9: Ghithe 58Ud 120
TN13: S'oaks 96Jd 202
Birch Platt GU24: W End 5B 166
Birch Rd. GU20: W'sham 9C 146
RM7: Mawney 27Dd 56
TW13: Hanw 64Z 129
Birch Row BR2: Brom 73Qc 160
Birch Tree Av. BR4: W W'ck 78Hc 159
Birch Tree Wlk. WD17: Wat 9V 12
Birch Tree Way CR0: C'don 75Xb 157
Birch Va. KT11: Cobh 84Ca 171
Birch Va. Ct. NW8 5C 214
Birch Vw. CM16: Epp 1Xc 23
Birchville Ct. WD23: B Hea 18Ga 28
Birch Wlk. CR4: Mitc 67Kb 134
DA8: Erith 51Ed 118
IG3: Ilf 35Uc 74
(off Loxford La.)
KT14: W Byf 84J 169
(not continuous)
WD6: Bore 11Qa 29
Birch Way AL2: Lon C 9H 7
CR6: W'ham 90Ac 178
RH1: Redh 8B 208
Birchway TN15: W King 81Vd 184
UB3: Hayes 46W 84
Birchwood EN9: Walt A 6Gc 21
WD7: Shenl 6Qa 15
Birchwood Av. BR3: Beck 70Bc 136
DA14: Sidc 61Xc 139
N10 27Jb 50
SM6: Wall 76Jb 156
Birchwood Cl. CM13: Gt War 23Yd 58
SM4: Mord 70Db 133
Birchwood Ct. HA8: Edg 26Sa 47
KT13: Weyb 78S 150
N13 22Rb 51
Birchwood Dr. DA2: Wilm 63Gd 140
GU18: Light 2A 166
KT14: W Byf 84J 169
NW3 34Db 69
Birchwood Gro. TW12: Hamp 65Ca 129
Birchwood La. CR3: Cat'm 97Rb 197
KT10: Esh 81Fa 172
KT22: Oxs 81Fa 172
TN14: Dun G 87Bd 181
Birchwood Pde. DA2: Wilm 63Gd 140
Birchwood Pk. Av. BR8: Swan 69Gd 140
Birchwood Pk. Golf Course 66Ed 140
Birchwood Rd. BR5: Pet W 70Tc 138
BR8: Swan 67Ed 140
DA2: Wilm 64Gd 140
KT14: W Byf 84J 169
SW17 64Kb 134
Birchwood Way AL2: Park 10P 5
Birdbrook Cl. CM13: Hut 16De 41
RM10: Dag 38Ed 76
Birdbrook Ho. *N1* 38Sb 71
(off Popham Rd.)
Birdbrook Rd. SE3 56Lc 115
Birdcage Wlk. SW1 2B 228 (47Lb 90)
Birdham Cl. BR1: Brom 71Nc 160
Birdhouse La. BR6: Downe 87Qc 180
Birdhurst Av. CR2: S Croy 77Tb 157
Birdhurst Ct. *SM6: Wall* 80Lb 156
(off Woodcote Av.)
Birdhurst Gdns. CR2: S Croy 77Tb 157
Birdhurst Ri. CR2: S Croy 78Ub 157
Birdhurst Rd. CR2: S Croy 78Ub 157
SW18 57Eb 111
SW19 65Gb 133
Bird in Bush BMX Track 52Xb 113
(off Bird in Bush Rd.)
Bird in Bush Rd. SE15 52Wb 113
Bird in Hand La. BR1: Brom 68Mc 137
Bird-in-Hand M. *SE23* 61Yb 136
(off Bird-in-Hand Pas.)
Bird-in-Hand Pas. SE23 61Yb 136
Bird in Hand Path *CR0: C'don* 73Tb 157
(off Sydenham Rd.)
Bird in Hand Yd. NW3 35Eb 69
Bird La. CM13: Gt War, L War 27Yd 58
RM14: Upm 29Td 58
UB9: Hare 26L 43
Birdsall Ho. SE5 55Ub 113
Birds Farm Av. RM5: Col R 24Dd 56
Birdsfield La. E3 39Bc 72
Birds Gro. GU21: Knap 10F 166
Birds Hill Dr. KT22: Oxs 85Fa 172
Birds Hill Ri. KT22: Oxs 85Fa 172
Birds Hill Rd. KT22: Oxs 85Fa 172
Bird St. W1 3J 221 (44Jb 90)
Birdswood Dr. GU21: Wok 1J 187
Bird Wlk. TW2: Whitt 60Ba 107
Birdwood Av. DA1: Dart 54Pd 119
SE13 58Fc 115
Birdwood Cl. CR2: Sels 83Yb 178
TW11: Tedd 63Ga 130
Birdwood Sq. DA1: Dart 54Qd 119
Birkbeck Av. UB6: G'frd 39Ea 66
W3 45Sa 87
Birkbeck Ct. W3 46Ta 87
Birkbeck Gdns. IG8: Wfd G 19Jc 35
Birkbeck Gro. W3 47Ta 87
Birkbeck Hill SE21 60Rb 113
Birkbeck M. E8 36Vb 71
W3 46Ta 87
Birkbeck Pl. SE21 61Sb 135
Birkbeck Rd. BR3: Beck 68Yb 136
CM13: Hut 16Fe 41
DA14: Sidc 62Wc 139
E8 36Vb 71
EN2: Enf 11Tb 33
IG2: Ilf 29Tc 54
N8 28Nb 50
N12 22Eb 49
N17 25Vb 51
NW7 22Va 48
RM7: Rush G 32Fd 76
SW19 64Db 133
W3 46Ta 87
W5 49La 86
Birkbeck St. E2 41Xb 91
Birkbeck Way UB6: G'frd 39Fa 66
Birkdale Av. HA5: Pinn 27Ca 45
RM3: Hrld W 24Pd 57
Birkdale Cl. BR6: Orp 73Tc 160
SE16 50Xb 91
SE28 44Zc 95
Birkdale Ct. *UB1: S'hall* 44Ea 86
(off Redcroft Rd.)
Birkdale Gdns. CR0: C'don 77Zb 158
WD19: Wat 20Z 27
Birkdale Rd. SE2 49Wc 95
W5 42Na 87
Birkenhead Av. KT2: King T 68Pa 131
Birkenhead St. WC1 3G 217 (41Nb 90)
Birken M. HA6: Nwood 22R 44
Birkett Way HP8: Chal G 13A 24
Birkhall Rd. SE6 60Fc 115
Birkheads Rd. RH2: Reig 5J 207
Birkin Ct. KT14: Byfl 83M 169
Birklands La. AL1: St A 6F 6
Birklands Pk. AL1: St A 6F 6
Birkwood Cl. SW12 59Mb 112
Birley Lodge NW8 1C 214
Birley Rd. N20 19Eb 31
SL1: Slou 4H 81
Birley St. SW11 54Jb 112
Birling Rd. DA8: Erith 52Fd 118
Birnam Cl. GU23: Rip 96J 189
Birnam Rd. N4 33Pb 70
Birnbeck Ct. EN5: Barn 14Za 30
NW11 29Bb 49
Birrell Ho. *SW9* 54Pb 112
(off Stockwell Rd.)
Birse Cres. NW10 34Ua 68
Birstal Grn. WD19: Wat 21Z 45
Birstall Rd. N15 29Ub 51
Birtrick Dr. DA13: Meop 10B 144
(not continuous)
Birtwhistle Ho. *E3* 39Bc 72
(off Parnell Rd.)
Biscay Ho. *E1* 42Zb 92
(off Mile End Rd.)
Biscayne Av. E14 46Fc 93
Biscay Rd. W6 50Za 88
Biscoe Cl. TW5: Hest 51Ca 107
Biscoe Way SE13 55Fc 115
Biscott Ho. E3 42Dc 92
Bisenden Rd. CR0: C'don 75Ub 157
Bisham Cl. SM5: Cars 74Hb 155
Bisham Ct. *SL1: Slou* 7K 81
(off Park St.)
Bisham Gdns. N6 32Jb 70
Bishams Ct. CR3: Cat'm 96Vb 197
Bishop Butt Cl. BR6: Orp 76Vc 161
Bishop Ct. TW9: Rich 55Na 109
Bishop Duppas Pk. TW17: Shep 73U 150
Bishop Fox Way KT8: W Mole 70Ba 129
Bishop Ken Rd. HA3: W'stone 26He 46
Bishop King's Rd. W14 49Ab 88
Bishop Ramsey Cl. HA4: Ruis 31V 64
Bishop Rd. N14 17Kb 32
Bishops Av. BR1: Brom 68Lc 137
E13 39Kc 73
HA6: Nwood 21U 44
RM6: Chad H 30Yc 55
SW6 54Za 110
WD6: E'tree 15Pa 29
Bishops Avenue, The N2 31Fb 69
Bishop's Bri. Rd. W2 2A 220 (44Db 89)
Bishops Cl. AL10: Hat 1B 8
CR5: Coul 90Qb 176
E17 28Dc 52
EN1: Enf 12Xb 33
EN5: Barn 16Za 30
N19 34Lb 70
SE9 61Sc 138
SM1: Sutt 76Cb 155
TW10: Ham 62Ma 131
UB10: Hil 40Q 64
W4 50Sa 87
Bishops Ct. CR0: C'don 75Vb 157
DA9: Ghithe 57Vd 120
EC4 2B 224
EN8: Chesh 2Yb 20
HA0: Wemb 35Ka 66
RM16: Ors 3C 100
W2 44Db 89
(off Bishop's Bri. Rd.)
WC2 2K 223
WD5: Ab L 3V 12
Bishopsdale Ho. *NW6* 39Cb 69
(off Kilburn Vale)
Bishops Dr. TW14: Bedf 58T 106
UB5: N'olt 39Aa 65
Bishops Farm Cl. SL4: Oak G 4A 102
Bishopsford Rd. SM4: Mord 73Eb 155
BISHOPS GATE 2L 125
Bishopsgate EC2 3H 225 (44Ub 91)
Bishopsgate Arc. EC2 1J 225
Bishopsgate Churchyard
EC2 2H 225 (43Ub 91)
Bishopsgate Institute & Libraries 1J 225
Bishopsgate Rd. TW20: Eng G 2K 125
Bishopsgate Twr. EC3 3H 225
Bishops Grn. BR1: Brom 67Lc 137
Bishops Gro. GU20: W'sham 9A 146
N2 30Gb 49
TW12: Hamp 63Ba 129
Bishops Grove Caravan Site
TW12: Hamp, Hamp H 63Ca 129
Bishop's Hall KT1: King T 68Ma 131
Bishop's Hall Rd. CM15: Pil H 16Xd 40
Bishops Hill KT12: Walt T 73W 150
Bishops Ho. *SW8* 52Nb 112
(off Sth. Lambeth Rd.)
Bishop's Mans. SW6 54Za 110
Bishops Mead HP1: Hem H 4K 3
SE5 52Sb 113
(off Camberwell Rd.)
Bishopsmead Cl. KT19: Ewe 82Ta 173
KT24: E Hor 100U 190
Bishopsmead Ct. KT19: Ewe 82Ua 174
Bishopsmead Dr. KT24: E Hor 100U 190
Bishopsmead Pde. KT24: E Hor 100U 190
Bishops Orchard SL2: Farn R 1F 80
Bishops Pk. Rd. SW6 54Za 110
SW16 67Nb 134
Bishops Pl. SM1: Sutt 78Eb 155
Bishops Ri. AL10: Hat 1B 8
Bishops Rd. CR0: C'don 73Rb 157
N6 30Jb 50
SL1: Slou 7L 81
SS17: Stan H 1P 101
SW6 53Ab 110
SW11 52Gb 111
UB3: Hayes 44S 84
W7 47Ga 86
Bishops Sq. E1 7J 219 (43Ub 91)
Bishop's Ter. SE11 5A 230 (49Qb 90)
Bishopsthorpe Rd. SE26 63Zb 136
Bishop St. N1 39Sb 71
Bishops Vw. Ct. N10 28Kb 50
Bishops Wlk. BR7: Chst 67Sc 138
CR0: Addtn 78Zb 158
CR0: Addtn 78Zb 158
HA5: Pinn 27Aa 45
Bishops Way E2 40Xb 71
TW20: Egh 65E 126
Bishops Wharf Ho. *SW11* 52Gb 111
(off Parkgate Rd.)
Bishops Wood GU21: Wok 9K 167
Bishops Wood Almshouses *E5* 35Xb 71
(off Lwr. Clapton Rd.)
Bishopswood Rd. N6 31Hb 69
Bishop Wlk. CM15: Shenf 19Be 41
Bishop Wilfred Wood Cl. SE15 54Wb 113
Bishop Wilfred Wood Ct. *E13* 40Lc 73
(off Pragel St.)
Biskra WD17: Wat 11W 26
BISLEY 7E 166
BISLEY CAMP 1B 186
Bisley Cl. EN8: Walt C 5Zb 20
KT4: Wor Pk 74Ya 154
Bisley Ct. GU24: Bisl 8D 166
Bison Ct. TW14: Felt 59X 107
Bispham Rd. NW10 41Pa 87
Bissextile Ho. SE13 54Dc 114
Bisson Rd. E15 40Ec 72
Bisterne Av. E17 27Fc 53
BITCHET GREEN 98Td 204
Bittacy Bus. Cen. NW7 24Ab 48
Bittacy Cl. NW7 23Za 48
Bittacy Ct. NW7 24Ab 48
Bittacy Hill NW7 23Za 48
Bittacy Pk. Av. NW7 22Za 48
Bittacy Ri. NW7 23Ya 48
Bittacy Rd. NW7 23Za 48
Bittams La. KT16: Chert 77F 148
Bittern Cl. HP3: Hem H 7P 3
UB4: Yead 43Z 85
Bittern Ct. NW9 26Ua 48
SE8 51Cc 114
Bitterne Dr. GU21: Wok 9K 167
Bittern Ho. SE1 2D 230
Bittern Pl. N22 26Pb 50
Bittern St. SE1 2D 230 (47Sb 91)
Bittoms, The KT1: King T 69Ma 131
(not continuous)
Bittoms Ct. KT1: King T 69Ma 131
Bixley Cl. UB2: S'hall 49Ba 85
Blackacre Rd. CM16: They B 9Uc 22
Blackall St. EC2 5H 219 (42Ub 91)
Blackberry Cl. TW17: Shep 70U 128
Blackberry Ct. HA9: Wemb 31Na 67
Blackberry Farm Cl. TW5: Hest 52Aa 107
Blackberry Fld. BR5: St P 67Wc 139
Blackbird Ct. NW9 34Ta 67
Blackbird Hill NW9 33Sa 67
Blackbirds La. WD25: A'ham 6Ea 14
Blackbird Yd. E2 41Vb 91
Blackborne Rd. RM10: Dag 37Cd 76
Blackborough Cl. RH2: Reig 6L 207
Blackborough Ho. *IG9: Buck H* 19Mc 35
(off Beatrice Ct.)
Blackborough Rd. RH2: Reig 7L 207
Black Boy La. N15 29Sb 51
Black Boy Wood AL2: Brick W 2Ca 13
Blackbridge Rd. GU22: Wok 1P 187
Blackbrook La. BR1: Brom 71Pc 160
BR2: Brom 71Qc 160
Black Bull Yd. EC1 7K 217
Blackburn NW9 26Va 48
Blackburn, The KT23: Bookh 96Ba 191
Blackburne's M. W1 4H 221 (45Jb 90)
Blackburn Rd. NW6 37Db 69
Blackburn Trad. Est. TW19: Stanw 58P 105
Blackburn Way TW4: Houn 57Aa 107
Blackbury Cl. EN6: Pot B 3Eb 17
Blackbush Av. RM6: Chad H 29Zc 55
Blackbush Cl. SM2: Sutt 80Db 155
Black Bush La. SS17: Horn H 1F 100
Black Cut AL1: St A 3C 6
Blackdown Av. GU22: Pyr 87G 168
Blackdown Cl. GU22: Pyr 88E 168
N2 26Eb 49
Blackdown Ter. SE18 53Pc 116
Black Eagle Cl. TN16: Westrm 99Sc 200
Black Eagle Dr. DA11: Nflt 57Ce 121
Black Eagle Sq. TN16: Westrm 99Sc 200
Blackett Cl. TW18: Staines 68G 126
Blackett St. SW15 55Za 110
Blacketts Wood Dr. WD3: Chor 15D 24
Black Fan Cl. EN2: Enf 11Sb 33
BLACKFEN 58Wc 117
Blackfen Pde. DA15: Sidc 58Wc 117
Blackfen Rd. DA15: Sidc 57Uc 116
Blackford Cl. CR2: S Croy 81Rb 177
Blackford Rd. WD19: Wat 22Z 45
Blackford's Path SW15 59Wa 110
Blackfriars Bri. EC4 4B 224 (45Rb 91)
Blackfriars Ct. *AL1: St A* 1C 6
(off Newsom Pl.)
EC4 4B 224
Black Friars La. EC4 4B 224 (44Rb 91)
(not continuous)
Blackfriars Pas. EC4 4B 224 (45Rb 91)
Blackfriars Rd. SE1 6B 224 (47Rb 91)
Blackfriars Underpass
EC4 4B 224 (45Qb 90)
Black Gates HA5: Pinn 27Ba 45
Black Grn. Wood Cl. AL2: Park 1Da 13
Blackhall La.
TN15: God G, S'oaks 95Md 203
BLACKHEATH 54Hc 115
Blackheath Av. SE10 52Fc 115
Blackheath Bus. Est. *SE10* 53Ec 114
(off Blackheath Hill)
Blackheath Concert Halls 55Hc 115
Blackheath Gro. SE3 54Hc 115
Blackheath Hill SE10 53Ec 114
BLACKHEATH PARK 55Jc 115
Blackheath Pk. SE3 55Hc 115
Blackheath Ri. SE13 54Ec 114
(not continuous)
Blackheath Rd. SE10 53Dc 114
Blackheath RUFC 52Kc 115
BLACKHEATH VALE 54Hc 115
Blackheath Va. SE3 54Gc 115
Blackheath Village SE3 55Hc 115
Blackhills KT10: Esh 81Ba 171
Black Horse Cl. SL4: Wind 4B 102
Black Horse Ct. SE1 3G 231 (48Tb 91)
Blackhorse La. CR0: C'don 73Wb 157
E17 26Zb 52
EN6: S Mim 2Ua 16
KT20: Lwr K 1K 207
Blackhorse M. TN15: Bor G 92Ce 205
Blackhorse M. E17 27Zb 52
Black Horse Pde. HA5: Eastc 29X 45
Black Horse Pl. UB8: Uxb 39K 63
BLACKHORSE ROAD 28Zb 52
Blackhorse Rd. DA14: Sidc 63Wc 139
E17 28Zb 52
GU22: Wok 2H 187
SE8 51Ac 114
Black House Yd. SL4: Wind 3H 103
UB8: Uxb 39K 63
Black Lake Cl. TW20: Egh 67C 126
Blacklands Dr. UB4: Hayes 42S 84
Blacklands Mdw. RH1: Nutf 5E 208
Blacklands Rd. SE6 63Ec 136
Blacklands Ter. SW3 6F 227 (49Hb 89)
Blackley Cl. WD17: Wat 9V 12
Black Lion Hill WD7: Shenl 4Na 15
Black Lion La. W6 49Wa 88

Black Lion M. W6 49Wa 88
Blackmans Cl. DA1: Dart 60Ld 119
Blackman's La. CR6: W'ham 86Gc 179
Blackmans Yd. E2 42Wb 91
Blackmead TN13: Riv 93Gd 202
Blackmoor La. WD18: Wat 15T 26
Blackmore Av. UB1: S'hall 46Fa 86
Blackmore Cl. RM17: Grays 50De 99
Blackmore Ct. EN9: Walt A 5Jc 21
Blackmore Cres. GU21: Wok 87E 168
Blackmore Dr. NW10 38Ra 67
Blackmore Gdns. SW13 51Xa 110
Blackmore Ho. N1 1J 217
Blackmore Rd. IG9: Buck H 17Nc 36
Blackmore's Gro. TW11: Tedd 65Ja 130
Blackmore Twr. W3 48Sa 87
(off Stanley Rd.)
Blackmore Way UB8: Uxb 37M 63
Blackness La. BR2: Kes 81Mc 179
GU22: Wok 91A 188
BLACKNEST 9F 124
Blacknest Ga. Rd. SL5: S'hill 9F 124
Blacknest Rd. GU25: Vir W 9H 125
SL5: S'hill 9H 125
Black Pk. Country Pk. 39C 62
Black Pk. Countryside Cen. 40B 62
Black Pk. Rd. SL3: Ful, Wex 40A 62
Black Path E10 31Ac 72
Blackpond La. SL2: Farn C, Farn R 7F 60
Blackpool Gdns. UB4: Hayes 42U 84
Blackpool Rd. SE15 54Xb 113
Black Prince Cl. KT14: Byfl 86P 169
BLACK PRINCE INTERCHANGE 58Dd 118
Black Prince Rd. SE1 6H 229 (49Pb 90)
SE11 6H 229 (49Pb 90)
Black Rd. E11 30Gc 53
Black Rod Cl. UB3: Hayes 48V 84
Blackshaw Rd. SW17 63Eb 133
Blackshots La. RM16: Grays 45Ee 99
Blacksmith Cl. KT21: Asht 91Pa 193
Blacksmith Row HP3: Hem H 3C 4
SL3: L'ly 49C 82
Blacksmiths Cl. RM6: Chad H 30Yc 55
Blacksmiths Hill CR2: Sande 85Wb 177
Blacksmiths Ho. E17 28Cc 52
(off Gillards M.)
Blacksmiths La. AL3: St A 2P 5
BR5: St M Cry 71Yc 161
KT16: Chert 73J 149
RM13: Rain 39Hd 76
TW18: Lale 69K 127
UB9: Den 33E 62
Blacksole Cotts. TN15: Wro 87Be 185
Blacksole La. TN15: Wro 88Be 185
Blacksole Rd. TN15: Wro 88Be 185
Blacks Rd. W6 50Ya 88
Blackstock M. N4 33Rb 71
Blackstock Rd. N4 33Rb 71
N5 33Rb 71
Blackstone Cl. RH1: Redh 7N 207
Blackstone Est. E8 38Wb 71
Blackstone Hill RH1: Redh 7M 207
Blackstone Ho. SW1 50Lb 90
(off Churchill Gdns.)
Blackstone Rd. NW2 36Ya 68
Blackstroud La. E. GU18: Light 3B 166
Blackstroud La. W. GU18: Light 3B 166
Black Swan Yd. SE1 1H 231 (47Ub 91)
Black's Yd. TN13: S'oaks 97Ld 203
(off Bank St.)
Blackthorn Av. N7 37Qb 70
UB7: W Dray 49Q 84
Blackthorn Cl. RH2: Reig 8L 207
TN15: W King 81Vd 184
WD25: Wat 4X 13
Blackthorn Ct. E15 35Fc 73
(off Hall Rd.)
TW5: Hest 52Aa 107
Blackthorne Av. CR0: C'don 74Yb 158
Blackthorne Cl. AL10: Hat 3B 8
Blackthorne Ct. SE15 52Vb 113
(off Cator St.)
TW15: Ashf 66S 128
UB1: S'hall 46Da 85
(off Dormer's Wells La.)
Blackthorne Cres. SL3: Poyle 54G 104
Blackthorne Dell SL3: L'ly 8N 81
Blackthorne Dr. E4 21Fc 53
Blackthorne Ind. Est. SL3: Poyle 55G 104
Blackthorne Rd. KT23: Bookh 98Ea 192
SL3: Poyle 55G 104
Blackthorn Gro. DA7: Bex 55Ad 117
Blackthorn Rd. IG1: Ilf 36Tc 74
RH2: Reig 8L 207
RM16: Grays 46De 99
TN16: Big H 88Mc 179
Blackthorn St. E3 42Cc 92
Blackthorn Way CM14: W'ley 22Zd 59
Blacktree M. SW9 55Qb 112
BLACKWALL 46Ec 92
Blackwall La. SE10 50Gc 93
Blackwall Trad. Est. E14 43Fc 93
Blackwall Tunnel E14 46Fc 93
(not continuous)
Blackwall Tunnel App. E14 45Ec 92
Blackwall Tunnel Northern App.
E3 41Ec 92
E14 42Ec 92
Blackwall Tunnel Southern App.
SE10 48Gc 93
Blackwall Way E14 46Ec 92
Blackwater CM14: B'wood 18Xd 40
Blackwater Cl. E7 35Hc 73
RM13: Rain 43Fd 96
Blackwater Ho. NW8 7C 214
Blackwater La. HP3: Hem H 6E 4
Blackwater St. SE22 57Vb 113
Blackwell Cl. E5 35Zb 72
HA3: Hrw W 24Fa 46
N21 15Nb 32
Blackwell Dr. WD19: Wat 16Y 27
Blackwell Gdns. HA8: Edg 21Qa 47
Blackwell Ho. SW4 58Mb 112
Blackwell Rd. WD4: K Lan 1Q 12
Blackwood Av. N18 22Zb 52
Blackwood Cl. KT14: W Byf 84L 169
Blackwood Ho. E1 42Xb 91
(off Collingwood St.)
Blackwood St. SE17 7F 231 (50Tb 91)
Blade, The W2 1C 220
Blade Ct. RM7: Rush G 30Gd 56
Blade M. SW15 56Bb 111
Bladen Cl. KT13: Weyb 79T 150
Bladen Ho. E1 44Zb 92
(off Dunelm St.)
Blades Cl. KT22: Lea 92Ma 193
Blades Ct. SW15 56Bb 111
W6 50Xa 88
(off Lower Mall)
Blades Ho. SE11 51Qb 112
(off Kennington Oval)
Bladindon Dr. DA5: Bexl 59Yc 117
Bladon Ct. SW16 65Nb 134
Bladon Gdns. HA2: Harr 30Da 45
Blagdens Cl. N14 19Mb 32
Blagdens La. N14 19Lb 32
Blagdon Ct. W7 45Ga 86
Blagdon Rd. KT3: N Mald 70Va 132
SE13 58Dc 114
Blagdon Wlk. TW11: Tedd 65La 130
Blagrove Rd. W10 43Ab 88
Blair Av. KT10: Esh 75Ea 152
NW9 31Ua 68
Blair Cl. DA15: Sidc 57Uc 116
N1 37Sb 71
UB3: Harl 49W 84
Blair Ct. BR3: Beck 67Dc 136
NW8 39Fb 69
SE6 60Hc 115
Blairderry Rd. SW2 61Nb 134
Blair Dr. TN13: S'oaks 95Kd 203
Blairgowrie Ct. E14 44Fc 93
(off Blair St.)
Blairhead Dr. WD19: Wat 20X 27
Blair Ho. SW9 54Pb 112
Blair Rd. SL1: Slou 6J 81
Blair St. E14 44Ec 92
Blake Av. IG11: Bark 39Uc 74
Blakeborough Dr. RM3: Hrld W 26Nd 57
Blake Bldg. N8 27Pb 50
Blake Cl. AL1: St A 5E 6
DA16: Well 53Uc 116
RM13: Rain 39Hd 76
SM5: Cars 74Gb 155
UB4: Hayes 40T 64
W10 43Ya 88
Blake Ct. KT19: Eps 84Pa 173
N21 15Pb 32
NW6 41Cb 89
(off Malvern Rd.)
SE16 50Xb 91
(off Stubbs Dr.)
Blakeden Dr. KT10: Clay 79Ha 152
Blakefield Gdns. CR5: Coul 90Pb 176
Blake Gdns. DA1: Dart 56Pd 119
SW6 53Db 111
Blake Hall Cres. E11 32Jc 73
Blake Hall Rd. E11 31Jc 73
Blakehall Rd. SM5: Cars 79Hb 155
Blake Ho. E14 47Cc 92
(off Admirals Way)
SE1 3K 229 (48Qb 90)
SE8 51Cc 114
(off New King St.)
Blake M. TW9: Kew 53Qa 109
Blakemore Rd. CR7: Thor H 71Pb 156
SW16 62Nb 134
Blakemore Way DA17: Belv 48Ad 95
Blakeney Av. BR3: Beck 67Bc 136
Blakeney Cl. E8 36Wb 71
KT19: Eps 83Ta 173
N20 18Eb 31
NW1 38Mb 70
Blakeney Rd. BR3: Beck 66Bc 136
Blakenham Rd. SW17 63Hb 133
Blaker Ct. SE7 52Lc 115
(not continuous)
Blake Rd. CR0: C'don 75Ub 157
CR4: Mitc 69Gb 133
E16 42Hc 93
N11 24Lb 50
Blaker Rd. E15 40Ec 72
Blakes Av. KT3: N Mald 71Va 154
Blakes Ct. KT16: Chert 74J 149
BLAKES GREEN 97Td 204
Blake's Grn. BR4: W W'ck 74Ec 158
Blakes La. KT3: N Mald 71Va 154
Blakesley Av. W5 44La 86
Blakesley Ho. E12 34Qc 74
(off Grantham Rd.)
Blakesley Wlk. SW20 68Bb 133
Blake's Rd. SE15 52Ub 113
Blakes Ter. KT3: N Mald 71Wa 154
Blakesware Gdns. N9 17Tb 33
Blake Way RM18: Tilb 4E 122
(off Coleridge Rd.)
Blakewood Cl. TW13: Hanw 63Y 129
Blakewood Ct. SE20 66Xb 135
(off Anerley Pk.)
Blanchard Cl. SE9 62Nc 138
Blanchard Dr. WD18: Wat 14U 26
Blanchard Gro. EN3: Enf L 10Dc 20
Blanchard Ho. TW1: Twick 58Ma 109
(off Clevedon Rd.)
Blanchard M. RM3: Hrld W 24Pd 57
Blanchards Hill
GU4: Jac W, Sut G 100A 188
Blanchard Way E8 37Wb 71
Blanch Cl. SE15 52Yb 114
Blanchedowne SE5 56Tb 113
Blanche La. EN6: S Mim 4Wa 16
Blanche St. E16 42Hc 93
Blanchland Rd. SM4: Mord 71Db 155
Blanchman's Rd. CR6: W'ham 90Ac 178
Blandfield Rd. SW12 59Jb 112
Blandford Av. BR3: Beck 68Ac 136
TW2: Whitt 60Da 107
Blandford Cl. CR0: Bedd 76Nb 156
GU22: Wok 89D 168
N2 28Eb 49
RM7: Mawney 28Dd 56
SL3: L'ly 8P 81
Blandford Ct. N1 38Ub 71
(off St Peter's Way)
NW6 38Za 68
SL3: L'ly 8P 81
Blandford Cres. E4 17Ec 34
Blandford Ho. SW8 52Pb 112
(off Richborne Ter.)
Blandford Rd. AL1: St A 2E 6
BR3: Beck 68Yb 136
TW11: Tedd 64Fa 130
UB2: S'hall 49Ca 85
W4 48Ua 88
W5 47Ma 87
Blandford Rd. Nth. SL3: L'ly 8P 81
Blandford Rd. Sth. SL3: L'ly 8P 81
Blandford Sq. NW1 6E 214 (42Gb 89)
Blandford St. W1 2G 221 (44Hb 89)
Blandford Waye UB4: Yead 44Y 85
Bland Ho. SE11 7J 229
Bland St. SE9 56Mc 115
Blaney Cres. E6 41Rc 94
Blanford M. RH2: Reig 6M 207
Blanford Rd. RH2: Reig 7L 207
Blanmerle Rd. SE9 60Rc 116
Blann Cl. SE9 58Mc 115
Blantyre St. SW10 52Fb 111
Blantyre Twr. SW10 52Fb 111
(off Blantyre St.)
Blantyre Wlk. SW10 52Fb 111
(off Worlds End Est.)
Blashford NW3 38Hb 69
(off Adelaide Rd.)
Blashford St. SE13 59Fc 115
Blasker Wlk. E14 50Dc 92
Blatchford Ct. KT12: Walt T 75W 150
Blattner Cl. WD6: E'tree 14Na 29
Blawith Rd. HA1: Harr 28Ga 46
Blaxland Ho. W12 45Xa 88
(off White City Est.)
Blaydon Cl. HA4: Ruis 31U 64
N17 24Xb 51
Blaydon Ct. UB5: N'olt 37Ca 65
Blaydon Wlk. N17 24Xb 51
Blays Cl. TW20: Eng G 5N 125
Blay's La. TW20: Eng G 6M 125
Blazer Ct. NW8 4C 214
Bleak Hill La. SE18 51Vc 117
Blean Gro. SE20 66Yb 136
Bleasdale Av. UB6: G'frd 40Ja 66
Blechynden Ho. W10 44Za 88
(off Kingsdown Cl.)
Blechynden St. W10 45Za 88
Bledlow Cl. NW8 6C 214 (42Fb 89)
SE28 45Yc 95
Bledlow Ri. UB6: G'frd 40Ea 66
Bleeding Heart Yd. EC1 1A 224
Blegborough Rd. SW16 65Lb 134
Blemundsbury WC1 7H 217
Blencarn Cl. GU21: Wok 8K 167
BLENDON 58Zc 117
Blendon Dr. DA5: Bexl 58Zc 117
Blendon Path BR1: Brom 66Hc 137
Blendon Rd. DA5: Bexl 58Zc 117
Blendon Row SE17 6F 231
Blendon Ter. SE18 50Sc 94
Blendworth Point SW15 60Xa 110
Blenheim Av. IG2: Ilf 30Qc 54
Blenheim Bus. Cen. CR4: Mitc 68Hb 133
(off London Rd.)
Blenheim Cen., The TW3: Houn 55Da 107
Blenheim Cl. DA1: Dart 58Ld 119
KT14: W Byf 85H 169
N21 18Sb 33
RM7: Mawney 28Ed 56
RM14: Upm 32Ud 78
SE12 60Kc 115
SL3: L'ly 46B 82
SM6: Wall 80Lb 156
SW20 69Ya 132
UB6: G'frd 40Fa 66
WD19: Wat 17Y 27
Blenheim Ct. BR2: Brom 70Hc 137
DA14: Sidc 62Tc 138
HA3: Kenton 30Ja 46
IG8: Wfd G 24Kc 53
N7 37Nb 70
N19 33Nb 70
RM12: Horn 36Ld 77
SE10 50Jc 93
(off Denham St.)
SE16 46Zb 92
(off King & Queen Wharf)
SM2: Sutt 79Eb 155
TW18: Staines 63F 126
Blenheim Cres. CR2: S Croy 80Sb 157
HA4: Ruis 33T 64
W11 45Ab 88
Blenheim Dr. DA16: Well 53Vc 117
Blenheim Gdns. CR2: Sande 84Wb 177
GU22: Wok 1M 187
HA9: Wemb 34Na 67
KT2: King T 66Ra 131
NW2 37Ya 68
RM15: Avel 46Rd 97
SM6: Wall 79Lb 156
SW2 58Pb 112
Blenheim Gro. DA12: Grav'nd 9E 122
SE15 54Wb 113
Blenheim Ho. E16 46Kc 93
(off Constable Av.)
SE18 48Sc 94
SW3 7E 226
TW3: Houn 55Ca 107
Blenheim M. WD7: Shenl 5Na 15
Blenheim Pde. UB10: Hil 42R 84
Blenheim Pk. Rd. CR2: S Croy 81Sb 177
Blenheim Pas. NW8 1A 214 (40Eb 69)
Blenheim Pl. TW11: Tedd 64Ha 130
Blenheim Ri. N15 28Vb 51
Blenheim Rd. AL1: St A 1D 6
BR1: Brom 70Nc 138
BR6: Orp 75Yc 161
CM15: Pil H 16Wd 40
DA1: Dart 58Ld 119
DA15: Sidc 60Yc 117
E6 41Mc 93
E15 35Gc 73
E17 27Zb 52
EN5: Barn 13Za 30
HA2: Harr 30Da 45
KT19: Eps 83Ta 173
NW8 1A 214 (40Eb 69)
SE20 66Yb 136
SL3: L'ly 9P 81
SM1: Sutt 76Cb 155
SW20 69Ya 132
UB5: N'olt 37Da 65
W4 48Ua 88
WD5: Ab L 4W 12
Blenheim Shop. Cen. SE20 66Yb 136
Blenheim St. W1 3K 221 (44Kb 90)
Blenheim Ter. NW8 1A 214 (40Eb 69)
Blenheim Way TW7: Isle 53Ja 108
Blenkarne Rd. SW11 58Hb 111
Bleriot NW9 26Va 48
(off Belvedere Strand)
Bleriot Av. KT15: Add 80J 149
Bleriot Rd. TW5: Hest 52Y 107
Blessbury Rd. HA8: Edg 25Sa 47
Blessington Cl. SE13 55Fc 115
Blessington Rd. SE13 55Fc 115
Blessing Way IG11: Bark 41Yc 95
BLETCHINGLEY 5J 209
Bletchingley Cl. CR7: Thor H 70Rb 135
RH1: Mers 1C 208
Bletchingley Golf Course 5K 209
Bletchingley Rd. RH1: Mers 1C 208
RH1: Nutf 2F 208
RH9: G'stone 3N 209
Bletchley Ct. N1 2F 219
Bletchley St. N1 2E 218 (40Tb 71)
Bletchmore Cl. UB3: Harl 50T 84
Bletsoe Wlk. N1 1E 218 (40Sb 71)
Blewbury Ho. SE2 47Yc 95
(not continuous)
Blewitts Cotts. RM13: Rain 41Hd 96
(off Dunedin Rd.)
Blick Ho. SE16 48Yb 92
(off Neptune St.)
Bligh Rd. DA11: Grav'nd 8C 122
Bligh's Ct. TN13: S'oaks 97Ld 203
(off Bligh's Rd.)
Bligh's Mdw. TN13: S'oaks 97Ld 203
(off High St.)
Bligh's Rd. TN13: S'oaks 97Ld 203
Bligh's Wlk. TN13: S'oaks 97Kd 203
(off Bligh's Rd.)
Blincoe Cl. SW19 61Za 132
Blinco La. SL3: G Grn 44A 82
Blind La. EN9: Walt A 5Lc 21
GU24: Chob 2D 166
IG10: Lough 12Gc 35
RH8: Oxt 2J 211
SM7: Bans 87Gb 175
Blindman's La. EN8: Chesh 2Zb 20
Bliss Cres. SE13 54Dc 114
Blissett St. SE10 53Ec 114
Bliss Ho. EN1: Enf 10Wb 19
Bliss M. W10 41Ab 88
Blisworth Cl. UB4: Yead 42Aa 85
Blisworth Ho. E2 39Wb 71
(off Whiston Rd.)
Blithbury Rd. RM9: Dag 37Xc 75
Blithdale Rd. SE2 49Wc 95
Blithehale Ct. E2 41Xb 91
(off Witham St.)
Blithfield St. W8 48Db 89
Blockhouse Rd. RM17: Grays 51Ee 121
Blockley Rd. HA0: Wemb 33Ka 66
Block Wharf E14 47Cc 92
(off Cuba St.)
Bloemfontein Av. W12 46Xa 88
Bloemfontein Rd. W12 45Xa 88
Bloemfontein Way W12 46Xa 88
Blomfield Ct. W9 5A 214
Blomfield Mans. W12 46Ya 88
(off Stanlake Rd.)
Blomfield Rd. W9 7A 214 (43Db 89)
Blomfield St. EC2 1G 225 (43Tb 91)
Blomfield Vs. W2 43Db 89
Blomville Rd. RM8: Dag 34Ad 75
Blondell Cl. UB7: Harm 51M 105
Blondel St. SW11 54Jb 112
Blondin Av. W5 49La 86
Blondin Park & Nature Area 49Ka 86
Blondin St. E3 40Cc 72
Bloomberg Ct. SW1 6D 228
Bloomburg St. SW1 6C 228 (49Mb 90)
Bloomfield Cl. GU21: Knap 9J 167
Bloomfield Ct. E10 34Dc 72
(off Brisbane Rd.)
N6 30Jb 50
Bloomfield Cres. IG2: Ilf 30Rc 54
Bloomfield Ho. E1 43Wb 91
(off Old Montague St.)
Bloomfield Pl. W1 4A 222
Bloomfield Rd. BR2: Brom 71Mc 159
KT1: King T 70Na 131
N6 30Jb 50
SE18 51Rc 116
Bloomfield Ter. SW1 7J 227 (50Jb 90)
TN16: Westrm 97Tc 200
Bloomfield Wlk. RM16: Ors 3C 100
Bloom Gro. SE27 62Rb 135
Bloomhall Rd. SE19 64Tb 135
Bloom Pk. Rd. SW6 52Bb 111
BLOOMSBURY 7G 217 (43Nb 90)
Bloomsbury Cl. KT19: Eps 82Ta 173
NW7 24Wa 48
W5 45Pa 87
Bloomsbury Ct. HA5: Pinn 27Ba 45
TW5: Cran 53X 107
WC1 1G 223
Bloomsbury Ho. SW4 58Mb 112
Bloomsbury Mans. BR1: Brom 67Kc 137
(off Widmore Rd.)
Bloomsbury M. IG8: Wfd G 23Nc 54
Bloomsbury Pl. SW18 57Eb 111
WC1 7G 217 (43Nb 90)
Bloomsbury Sq. WC1 1G 223 (43Nb 90)
Bloomsbury St. WC1 1E 222 (43Mb 90)
Bloomsbury Theatre 5D 216
Bloomsbury Way WC1 2F 223 (43Nb 90)
Blore Cl. SW8 53Mb 112
Blore Ct. W1 4D 222
Blore Ho. SW10 52Db 111
(off Coleridge Gdns.)
Blossom Cl. CR2: S Croy 78Vb 157
RM9: Dag 39Bd 75
W5 47Na 87
Blossom Dr. BR6: Orp 75Vc 161
Blossom La. EN2: Enf 11Sb 33
Blossom Pl. SE28 48Sc 94
Blossom St. E1 6J 219 (42Ub 91)
Blossom Way UB7: W Dray 49Q 84
UB10: Hil 38P 63
Blossom Waye TW5: Hest 51Aa 107
Blount St. E14 44Ac 92
Bloxam Gdns. SE9 57Nc 116
Bloxhall Rd. E10 32Bc 72
Bloxham Cres. TW12: Hamp 66Ba 129
Bloxworth Cl. SM6: Wall 76Lb 156
Blucher Rd. SE5 52Sb 113
Blue Anchor All. TW9: Rich 56Na 109
Blue Anchor La. RM18: W Til 9G 100
SE16 49Wb 91
Blue Anchor Yd. E1 45Wb 91
Blue Ball La. TW20: Egh 64B 126
Blue Ball Yd. SW1 7B 222 (46Lb 90)
Blue Barn La. KT13: Weyb 83Q 170
Bluebell Av. E12 36Mc 73
Bluebell Cl. AL2: Park 9A 6
BR6: Farnb 75Sc 160
E9 39Yb 72
HP1: Hem H 3G 2
RM7: Rush G 33Gd 76
SE26 63Vb 135
SM6: Wall 74Kb 156
UB5: N'olt 37Ba 65
Bluebell Ct. GU22: Wok 1P 187
Bluebell Dr. EN7: G Oak 1Tb 19
WD5: Bedm 9F 4
Blue Bell La. KT11: Stoke D 89Ca 171
Bluebell La. KT24: E Hor 100U 190
Bluebell M. RM17: Grays 50De 99
Bluebell Way IG1: Ilf 37Rc 74
Blueberry Cl. IG8: Wfd G 23Jc 53
Blueberry Gdns. CR5: Coul 88Pb 176
Blueberry La. TN14: Knock 88Yc 181
Bluebird La. RM10: Dag 38Cd 76
Bluebird Way AL2: Brick W 2Ba 13
SE28 47Tc 94
Bluebridge Av. AL9: Brk P 9H 9
Bluebridge Rd. AL9: Brk P 8G 8
Blue Bldg. SE10 50Hc 93
(off Glenforth St.)
Blue Cedars SM7: Bans 86Za 174
Blue Cedars Pl. KT11: Cobh 84Z 171
Blue Chalet Ind. Pk.
TN15: W King 78Td 164
Blue Ct. N1 39Tb 71
(off Sherborne St.)
Blue Elephant Theatre 52Sb 113
(off Bethwin Rd.)
Bluefield Cl. TW12: Hamp 64Ca 129
Blue Fin Bldg. SE1 6C 224
Bluegate M. E1 45Xb 91
Bluegate Pk. CM14: B'wood 20Xd 40
Bluegates KT17: Ewe 80Wa 154
Blue Ho. Cotts. DA2: Bean 62Zd 143
Bluehouse Gdns. RH8: Oxt 100Jc 199
Bluehouse Hill AL3: St A 3N 5
Bluehouse La. RH8: Limp, Oxt 100Gc 199
Bluehouse Rd. E4 19Gc 35
Blue Leaves Av. CR5: Coul 93Mb 196
Blue Lion Pl. SE1 3H 231 (48Ub 91)
Blueprint Apartments SW12 59Kb 112
(off Balham Gro.)
Blue Riband Ind. Est. CR0: C'don 75Rb 157
Blues St. E8 37Vb 71
Bluett Rd. AL2: Lon C 9H 7
BLUEWATER 60Vd 120
Blue Water SW18 56Db 111
Bluewater Parkway
DA9: Bluew, Ghithe 59Vd 120
Bluewater Shop. Cen.
DA9: Bluew 59Vd 120
Blumfield Ct. SL1: Slou 2B 80
Blumfield Cres. SL1: Slou 2B 80
Blundel La. KT11: Stoke D 88Ba 171
Blundell Cl. E8 36Wb 71
Blundell Rd. HA8: Edg 25Ta 47
Blundell St. N7 38Nb 70
Blunden Cl. RM8: Dag 32Yc 75
Blunden Ct. SW6 52Cb 111
(off Farm La.)
Blunden Dr. SL3: L'ly 49D 82
Blunesfield EN6: Pot B 3Fb 17
Blunt Rd. CR2: S Croy 78Tb 157
Blunts Av. UB7: Sip 52Q 106
Blunts La. AL2: Pot C 6K 5
WD5: Bedm 9K 5
Blunts Rd. SE9 57Qc 116
Blurton Rd. E5 35Yb 72
Blydon Ct. N21 15Pb 32
(off Chaseville Pk. Rd.)
Blyth Cl. E14 49Fc 93
TW1: Twick 58Ha 108
WD6: Bore 11Pa 29
Blyth Ct. BR1: Brom 67Hc 137
(off Blyth Rd.)
Blythe Cl. SE6 59Bc 114
SL0: Iver 44H 83
BLYTHE HILL 59Bc 114
Blythe Hill BR5: St P 67Vc 139
SE6 59Bc 114
Blythe Hill La. SE6 59Bc 114
Blythe Hill Pl. SE23 59Ac 114
Blythe Ho. SE11 51Qb 112
SL1: Slou 6B 80
Blythe M. W14 48Za 88
Blythendale Ho. E2 40Wb 71
(off Mansford St.)
Blythe Rd. W14 48Za 88
Blythe St. E2 41Xb 91
Blytheswood Pl. SW16 63Pb 134
Blythe Va. SE6 60Bc 114
Blyth Hill Pl. SE23 59Ac 114
(off Brockley Pk.)
Blyth Ho. DA8: Erith 50Gd 96
Blyth Rd. BR1: Brom 67Hc 137
E17 31Bc 72
SE28 45Yc 95
UB3: Hayes 47U 84
Blyth's Wharf E14 45Ac 92
Blythswood Rd. IG3: Ilf 32Wc 75
Blyth Wlk. RM14: Upm 30Ud 58
Blyth Wood Pk. BR1: Brom 67Hc 137
Blythwood Rd. HA5: Pinn 25Z 45
N4 31Nb 70
Boades M. NW3 35Fb 69
Boadicea Cl. SL1: Slou 6C 80
Boadicea St. N1 39Pb 70
Boakes Cl. NW9 28Sa 47
Boakes Mdw. TN14: S'ham 83Hd 182
Boar Cl. IG7: Chig 22Wc 55
Boardman Av. E4 15Dc 34
Boardman Cl. EN5: Barn 15Ab 30
Boardman Pl. CM14: B'wood 20Xd 40
Board School Rd. GU21: Wok 88B 168
Boardwalk Pl. E14 46Ec 92
Boarhound NW9 26Va 48
(off Further Acre)
Boarlands Cl. SL1: Slou 5D 80
Boarlands Path SL1: Slou 5D 80
Boarley Ho. SE17 6H 231
Boars Head Yd. TW8: Bford 52Ma 109
Boatemah Wlk. SW9 54Qb 112
(off Peckford Pl.)
Boathouse Centre, The W10 42Za 88
(off Canal Cl.)
Boathouse Wlk. SE15 52Vb 113
(not continuous)
Boat Lifter Way SE16 49Ac 92
Boat Quay E16 45Lc 93
Boatyard Apartments E14 50Dc 92
Bob Anker Cl. E13 41Jc 93
Bobbin Cl. SW4 55Lb 112
Bobby Moore Way N10 24Hb 49
Bob Dunn Way DA1: Dart 56Ld 119
Bob Hope Theatre, The 58Pc 116
Bob Marley Way SE24 56Qb 112
Bobs La. RM1: Rom 24Jd 56
Bocketts Farm Pk. 97Ha 192
Bocketts La. KT22: Fet 96Ha 192
Bockhampton Rd. KT2: King T 66Pa 131
Bocking St. E8 39Xb 71
Boddicott Cl. SW19 61Ab 132

Boddington Gdns. W3 47Qa 87
Boddington Ho. SE14 53Yb 114
(off Pomeroy St.)
SW13 51Xa 110
(off Wyatt Dr.)
Bodell Cl. RM16: Grays 48De 99
Bodeney Ho. SE5 53Ub 113
(off Peckham Rd.)
Boden Ho. E1 43Wb 91
(off Woodseer St.)
Bodiam Cl. EN1: Enf 12Ub 33
Bodiam Rd. SW16 66Mb 134
Bodiam Way NW10 41Pa 87
Bodicea M. TW4: Houn 58Ba 107
Bodington Ct. W12 47Za 88
Bodle Av. DA10: Swans 59Ae 121
Bodleian Ho. SE20 67Wb 135
Bodley Cl. CM16: Epp 2Vc 23
KT3: N Mald 71Ua 154
Bodley Ho. SL0: Iver H 40F 62
Bodley Mnr. Way SW2 59Qb 112
Bodley Rd. KT3: N Mald 72Ta 153
Bodmin NW9 26Va 48
(off Further Acre)
Bodmin Av. SL2: Slou 3E 80
Bodmin Cl. BR5: Orp 74Yc 161
HA2: Harr 34Ba 65
Bodmin Ct. RM3: Rom 25Md 57
Bodmin Gro. SM4: Mord 71Db 155
Bodmin St. SW18 60Cb 111
Bodnant Gdns. SW20 69Wa 132
Bodney Rd. E8 36Xb 71
Bodwell Cl. HP1: Hem H 1J 3
Boeing Way UB2: S'hall 48X 85
Boevey Path DA17: Belv 50Bd 95
Bogart Ct. E14 45Cc 92
(off Premiere Pl.)
Bogey La. BR6: Downe 80Qc 160
Bognor Gdns. WD19: Wat 22Y 45
Bognor Rd. DA16: Well 53Zc 117
Bohemia HP2: Hem H 1N 3
Bohemia Pl. E8 37Yb 72
Bohn Rd. E1 43Ac 92
Bohun Gro. EN4: E Barn 16Gb 31
Boileau Pde. W5 44Pa 87
(off Boileau Rd.)
Boileau Rd. SW13 52Wa 110
W5 44Pa 87
Bois Hall Rd. KT15: Add 78M 149
Boisseau Ho. E1 43Yb 92
(off Stepney Way)
Boissy Cl. AL4: St A 3J 7
Bolanachi Bldg. SE16 48Vb 91
Bolberry Rd. RM5: Col R 22Fd 56
Bolden St. SE8 54Dc 114
Boldero Pl. NW8 6D 214
Bolderwood Way BR4: W W'ck 75Dc 158
Bolding Ho. La. GU24: W End 5D 166
Boldmere Rd. HA5: Eastc 31Y 65
Bold's Ct. SL2: Stoke P 8L 61
Boleyn Av. EN1: Enf 11Xb 33
KT17: Ewe 82Xa 174
Boleyn Cl. E17 28Cc 52
IG10: Lough 16Nc 36
RM16: Chaf H 48Be 99
TW18: Staines 64G 126
Boleyn Ct. GU21: Knap 10G 166
(off Tudor Way)
IG9: Buck H 18Jc 35
KT8: E Mos 70Fa 130
(off Bridge Rd.)
RH1: Redh 5A 208
(off St Anne's Ri.)
Boleyn Dr. AL1: St A 4B 6
HA4: Ruis 33Z 65
KT8: W Mole 69Ba 129
Boleyn Gdns. BR4: W W'ck 75Dc 158
CM13: B'wood 20Ce 41
RM10: Dag 38Ed 76
Boleyn Ground / Upton Pk. 40Lc 73
Boleyn Gro. BR4: W W'ck 75Ec 158
Boleyn Ho. E16 46Jc 93
(off Southey M.)
Boleyn Rd. E6 40Mc 73
E7 38Jc 73
N16 36Ub 71
TN15: Kems'g 89Nd 183
Boleyn Row CM16: Epp 1Yc 23
Boleyn Wlk. KT22: Lea 92Ha 192
Boleyn Way DA10: Swans 59Ae 121
EN5: New Bar 13Eb 31
IG6: Ilf 23Sc 54
Bolina Rd. SE16 50Yb 92
Bolingbroke Gro. SW11 56Gb 111
Bolingbroke Rd. W14 48Za 88
Bolingbroke Wlk. SW11 53Fb 111
Bolingbroke Way UB3: Hayes 46T 84
Bolliger Ct. NW10 42Sa 87
Bollo Bri. Rd. W3 48Ra 87
Bollo Ct. W3 48Sa 87
(off Bollo Bri. Rd.)
Bollo La. W3 47Ra 87
W4 49Sa 87
Bolney Ga. SW7 2D 226 (47Gb 89)
Bolney St. SW8 52Pb 112
Bolney Way TW13: Hanw 62Aa 129
Bolsover Gro. RH1: Mers 1E 208
Bolsover St. W1 6A 216 (42Kb 90)
Bolstead Rd. CR4: Mitc 67Kb 134
Bolster Gro. N22 24Mb 50
Bolt Cellar La. CM16: Epp 2Uc 22
Bolt Ct. EC4 3A 224 (44Qb 90)
Bolters La. SM7: Bans 86Bb 175
Bolt Ho. N1 1J 219
Boltmore Cl. NW4 27Za 48
Bolton Av. SL4: Wind 5G 102
Bolton Cl. KT9: Chess 79Ma 153
SE20 68Wb 135
Bolton Cres. SE5 52Rb 113
SL4: Wind 5G 102
Bolton Dr. SM4: Mord 73Eb 155
Bolton Gdns. BR1: Brom 65Hc 137
NW10 40Za 68
SW5 50Db 89
TW11: Tedd 65Ja 130
Bolton Gdns. M. SW10 50Eb 89
Bolton Ho. SE10 50Gc 93
(off Trafalgar Rd.)
SE11 5B 230
Bolton Pl. NW8 39Db 69
(off Bolton Rd.)
Bolton Rd. E15 37Hc 73
HA1: Harr 28Ea 46
KT9: Chess 79Ma 153
N18 22Vb 51
NW8 39Db 69
Bolton Rd. NW10 39Ua 68
SL4: Wind 5G 102
W4 52Sa 109
Boltons, The HA0: Wemb 35Ha 66
IG8: Wfd G 21Jc 53
SW10 7A 226 (50Eb 89)
Boltons Cl. GU22: Pyr 88J 169
Boltons Ct. SW5 50Db 89
(off Old Brompton Rd.)
Boltons La. GU22: Pyr 88J 169
UB3: Harl 53S 106
(not continuous)
Boltons Pl. SW5 7A 226 (50Eb 89)
Bolton St. W1 6A 222 (46Kb 90)
Bolton Studios SW10 50Eb 89
Bolton Wlk. N7 33Pb 70
(off Durham Rd.)
Bombay Ct. SE16 47Yb 92
(off St Marychurch St.)
Bombay St. SE16 49Xb 91
Bombers La. TN16: Westrm 91Tc 200
Bomer Cl. UB7: Sip 52Q 106
Bomore Rd. W11 45Ab 88
Bonaly Ho. RH8: Oxt 3G 210
Bonar Pl. BR7: Chst 66Nc 138
Bonar Rd. SE15 52Wb 113
Bonaventure Ct. DA12: Grav'nd 3H 145
Bonchester Cl. BR7: Chst 66Qc 138
Bonchurch Cl. SM2: Sutt 80Db 155
Bonchurch Ct. RM19: Purf 50Sd 98
Bonchurch Rd. W10 43Ab 88
W13 46Ka 86
Bond Cl. SL0: Iver H 38D 62
TN14: Knock 87Zc 181
UB7: Yiew 45M 83
Bond Ct. EC4 3F 225 (45Tb 91)
Bondfield Av. UB4: Yead 41W 84
Bondfield Rd. E6 43Pc 94
Bondfield Wlk. DA1: Dart 56Pd 119
Bond Gdns. SM6: Wall 77Lb 156
Bond Ho. NW6 40Bb 69
(off Rupert Rd.)
SE14 52Ac 114
(off Goodwood Rd.)
Bonding Yd. Wlk. SE16 48Ac 92
Bond Rd. CR4: Mitc 68Gb 133
CR6: W'ham 90Zb 178
KT6: Surb 75Pa 153
Bond St. E15 36Gc 73
RM17: Grays 51Ee 121
TN14: Knock 87Ad 181
TW20: Eng G 4M 125
W4 49Ta 87
W5 45Ma 87
Bondway SW8 51Nb 112
Boneashe La. TN15: Plat 93Fe 205
Bone Mill La. RH9: G'stone 6C 210
Bonesgate Open Space Local Nature Reserve
79Qa 153
Boneta Rd. SE18 48Pc 94
Bonfield Rd. SE13 56Ec 114
Bonham Cl. DA17: Belv 50Bd 95
Bonham Dr. RM16: Ors 3C 100
Bonham Gdns. RM8: Dag 33Zc 75
Bonham Ga. KT12: Walt T 74V 150
(off New Zealand Av.)
Bonham Ho. W11 46Bb 89
(off Boyne Ter. M.)
Bonham Rd. RM8: Dag 33Zc 75
SW2 57Pb 112
Bonham Way DA11: Nflt 60Ee 121
Bonheur Rd. W4 47Ta 87
Bonhill St. EC2 6G 219 (42Tb 91)
Boniface Gdns. HA3: Hrw W 24Da 45
Boniface Rd. UB10: Ick 34R 64
Boniface Wlk. HA3: Hrw W 24Da 45
Bonington Ho. EN1: Enf 15Wb 33
Bonington Rd. RM12: Horn 36Md 77
Bonita M. SE4 55Zb 114
Bon Marche Ter. M. SE27 63Ub 135
(off Gypsy Rd.)
Bonner Hill Rd. KT1: King T 68Pa 131
Bonner Rd. E2 40Yb 72
Bonners Cl. GU22: Wok 94B 188
Bonnersfield Cl. HA1: Harr 30Ha 46
Bonnersfield La. HA1: Harr 30Ha 46
(not continuous)
Bonner St. E2 40Yb 72
Bonner Wlk. RM16: Chaf H 48Be 99
Bonnett M. RM11: Horn 32Nd 77
Bonneville Gdns. SW4 58Lb 112
Bonney Gro. EN7: Chesh 2Wb 19
Bonney Way BR8: Swan 68Gd 140
Bonnington Ct. UB5: N'olt 40Z 65
(off Gallery Gdns.)
Bonnington Ho. N1 2H 217 (40Pb 70)
Bonningtons CM13: B'wood 20De 41
Bonnington Sq. SW8 51Pb 112
Bonnys Rd. RH2: Reig 7F 206
Bonny St. NW1 38Lb 70
Bonser Rd. TW1: Twick 61Ha 130
Bonsey Cl. GU22: Wok 93A 188
Bonsey La. GU22: Wok 93A 188
Bonseys La. GU24: Chob 81B 168
Bonsey's Yd. UB8: Uxb 38M 63
Bonsor Dr. KT20: Kgswd 94Ab 194
Bonsor Ho. SW8 53Lb 112
Bonsor St. SE5 52Ub 113
Bonville Gdns. NW4 28Xa 48
Bonville Rd. BR1: Brom 64Hc 137
Bookbinders Cott. Homes N20 20Hb 31
Bookbinders Ct. E1 42Xb 91
(off Cudworth St.)
Booker Cl. E14 43Bc 92
Booker Rd. N18 22Wb 51
Bookham Comn. Rd.
KT23: Bookh 93Aa 191
Bookham Ct. CR4: Mitc 69Fb 133
KT23: Bookh 95Ba 191
Bookham Gro. KT23: Bookh 98Da 191
Bookham Ind. Est. KT23: Bookh 95Ba 191
Bookham Rd. KT11: D'side 91Y 191
Boomes Ind. Est. RM13: Rain 42Hd 96
Boone Ct. N9 20Yb 34
Boones Rd. SE13 56Gc 115
Boone St. SE13 56Gc 115
Boord St. SE10 48Gc 93
Boot All. AL3: St A 2B 6
(off Chequer St.)
Boothby Ct. E4 20Ec 34
Boothby Rd. N19 33Mb 70
Booth Cl. E9 39Xb 71
SE28 46Xc 95
Booth Dr. TW18: Staines 65M 127
Booth Ho. TW8: Bford 52La 108
(off High St.)
Booth La. EC4 4D 224
Boothman Ho. HA3: Kenton 27Ma 47
Booth Rd. CR0: C'don 75Rb 157
E16 47Lc 93
NW9 26Ta 47
Booths Cl. AL9: Wel G 6F 8
Booth's Ct. CM13: Hut 16Ee 41
Booth's Pl. W1 1C 222 (43Lb 90)
Boot Pde. HA8: Edg 23Qa 47
(off High St.)
Boot St. N1 4H 219 (41Ub 91)
Bordars Rd. W7 43Ga 86
Bordars Wlk. W7 43Ga 86
Bordeaux Ho. E15 36Gc 73
(off Luxembourg M.)
Borden Av. EN1: Enf 16Tb 33
Border Cres. SE26 64Xb 135
Border Gdns. CR0: C'don 77Dc 158
Bordergate CR4: Mitc 67Hb 133
Border Rd. SE26 64Xb 135
Borders Cres. IG10: Lough 14Rc 36
(off Border's La.)
Borderside SL2: Slou 4L 81
Border's La. IG10: Lough 14Qc 36
Borders Wlk. IG10: Lough 14Qc 36
(off Border's La.)
Bordesley Rd. SM4: Mord 71Db 155
Bordeston Ct. TW8: Bford 52La 108
(off The Ham)
Bordon Wlk. SW15 59Wa 110
Boreas Wlk. N1 2C 218
Boreham Av. E16 44Jc 93
Boreham Cl. E11 32Ec 72
Boreham Holt WD6: E'tree 14Pa 29
Boreham Rd. N22 26Sb 51
BOREHAMWOOD 13Qa 29
Borehamwood Ent. Cen.
WD6: Bore 13Pa 29
Borehamwood Ind. Pk.
WD6: Bore 12Ta 29
Borehamwood Shop. Pk.
WD6: Bore 13Qa 29
Boreman Ho. SE10 51Ec 114
(off Thames St.)
Borgard Rd. SE18 49Pc 94
Borkwood Pk. BR6: Orp 77Vc 161
Borkwood Way BR6: Orp 77Uc 160
Borland Cl. DA9: Ghithe 57Wd 120
Borland Rd. SE15 56Yb 114
TW11: Tedd 66Ka 130
Borley Ct. RM16: Ors 4F 100
TW19: Stanw 60N 105
Bornedene EN6: Pot B 3Ab 16
Borneo St. SW15 55Ya 110
BOROUGH, THE 2E 230 (47Tb 91)
Borough Grange CR2: Sande 84Wb 177
BOROUGH GREEN 92Be 205
Borough Grn. Rd.
TN15: Bor G, Igh 93Zd 205
(not continuous)
TN15: Wro 89Ce 185
Borough High St. SE1 2E 230 (47Sb 91)
Borough Hill CR0: Wadd 76Rb 157
Borough Mkt. SE1 7F 225
Borough Rd. CR4: Mitc 68Gb 133
KT2: King T 67Qa 131
SE1 3B 230 (48Rb 91)
TN16: Tats 93Mc 199
TW7: Isle 53Ga 108
Borough Sq. SE1 2D 230
Borough Way EN6: Pot B 4Ab 16
Borrett Cl. SE17 7D 230 (50Sb 91)
Borrodaile Rd. SW18 58Db 111
Borromeo Way CM14: B'wood 18Xd 40
Borrowdale NW1 4B 216
Borrowdale Av. HA3: W'stone 26Ja 46
Borrowdale Cl. CR2: Sande 85Vb 177
IG4: Ilf 28Nc 54
N2 26Eb 49
TW20: Egh 66D 126
Borrowdale Ct. EN2: Enf 11Sb 33
Borrowdale Dr. CR2: Sande 84Vb 177
Borthwick M. E15 35Gc 73
Borthwick Rd. E15 35Gc 73
NW9 30Va 48
Borthwick St. SE8 50Cc 92
Borwick Av. E17 27Bc 52
Bosanquet Cl. UB8: Cowl 42M 83
Bosbury Rd. SE6 62Ec 136
Boscastle Rd. NW5 34Kb 70
Boscobel Cl. BR1: Brom 68Pc 138
Boscobel Ho. E8 37Xb 71
Boscobel Pl. SW1 5J 227 (49Jb 90)
Boscobel St. NW8 6C 214 (42Fb 89)
Bosco Cl. BR6: Orp 77Uc 161
Boscombe Av. E10 31Fc 73
RM11: Horn 31Md 77
RM17: Grays 49Fe 99
Boscombe Cir. NW9 25Ta 47
Boscombe Cl. E5 36Ac 72
TW20: Egh 67E 126
Boscombe Gdns. SW16 65Nb 134
Boscombe Ho. CR0: C'don 74Tb 157
(off Sydenham Rd.)
Boscombe Rd. KT4: Wor Pk 74Ya 154
SW17 65Jb 134
SW19 67Db 133
W12 46Wa 88
Bose Cl. N3 25Ab 48
Bosgrove E4 19Ec 34
Boshers Gdns. TW20: Egh 65B 126
Bosman Dr. GU20: W'sham 7A 146
Boss Ho. SE1 1K 231
Boss St. SE1 1K 231 (47Vb 91)
Bostall Hill SE2 50Wc 95
Bostall La. SE2 49Xc 95
Bostall Mnr. Way SE2 49Xc 95
Bostall Pk. Av. DA7: Bex 52Ad 117
Bostall Rd. BR5: St P 66Xc 139
Bostock Ho. TW5: Hest 51Ca 107
Boston Bus. Pk. W7 48Ga 86
Boston Ct. SE25 70Vb 135
SM2: Sutt 80Eb 155
Boston Gdns. TW8: Bford 49Ja 86
W4 51Ua 110
W7 49Ja 86
Boston Gro. HA4: Ruis 30S 44
SL1: Slou 4G 80
Boston Ho. SW5 49Db 89
(off Collingham Rd.)
BOSTON MANOR 49Ja 86
Boston Manor House 50Ka 86
Boston Mnr. Rd. TW8: Bford 49Ka 86
Boston Pde. W7 48Ja 86
Boston Pk. Rd. TW8: Bford 50La 86
Boston Pl. NW1 6F 215 (42Hb 89)
Boston Rd. CR0: C'don 72Pb 156
E6 41Nc 94
E17 30Cc 52
HA8: Edg 24Sa 47
W7 46Ga 86
Bostonthorpe Rd. W7 47Ga 86
Boston Va. W7 49Ja 86
Bosun Cl. E14 47Cc 92
Bosville Av. TN13: S'oaks 95Jd 202
Bosville Dr. TN13: S'oaks 95Jd 202
Bosville Rd. TN13: S'oaks 95Jd 202
Boswell Cl. BR5: Orp 72Yc 161
WD7: Shenl 4Na 15
Boswell Ct. KT2: King T 67Pa 131
(off Clifton Rd.)
W14 48Za 88
(off Blythe Rd.)
WC1 7G 217 (43Nb 90)
Boswell Ho. WC1 7G 217
Boswell Path UB3: Harl 49V 84
Boswell Rd. CR7: Thor H 70Sb 135
Boswell Row CR3: Cat'm 94Wb 197
Boswell St. WC1 7G 217 (43Nb 90)
Boswood Ct. TW3: Houn 55Ba 107
Bosworth Cl. E17 25Bc 52
Bosworth Ct. SL1: Slou 5A 80
Bosworth Cres. RM3: Rom 23Ld 57
Bosworth Ho. DA8: Erith 50Gd 96
(off Saltford Cl.)
W10 42Ab 88
(off Bosworth Rd.)
Bosworth Rd. EN5: New Bar 13Cb 31
N11 23Mb 50
RM10: Dag 34Cd 76
W10 42Ab 88
BOTANY BAY 8Mb 18
Botany Bay La. BR7: Chst 69Sc 138
Botany Cl. EN4: E Barn 14Gb 31
Botany Cotts. RM19: Purf 50Qd 97
Botany Rd. DA11: Nflt 56Ce 121
Botany Way RM19: Purf 49Rd 97
Boteley Cl. E4 19Fc 35
Botery's Cross RH1: Blet 5H 209
Botham Cl. HA8: Edg 24Sa 47
Botham Dr. SL1: Slou 8J 81
Botha Rd. E13 43Kc 93
Bothwell Cl. E16 43Hc 93
Bothwell Rd. CR0: New Ad 82Ec 178
Bothwell St. W6 51Za 110
Bothy, The GU22: Pyr 89H 169
SM7: Bans 90Eb 175
Botolph All. EC3 4H 225
Botolph La. EC3 5H 225 (45Ub 91)
Botsford Rd. SW20 68Ab 132
Botsom La. TN15: W King 79Sd 164
Bottle Cotts. TN13: S'oaks 94Jd 202
Bottom La. WD3: Bucks 7K 11
WD4: Bucks 7K 11
Bottom Waltons Caravan Site
SL2: Farn R 10C 60
Bott Rd. DA2: Hawl 63Pd 141
Botts M. W2 44Cb 89
Botwell Comn. Rd.
UB3: Hayes 45T 84
Botwell Cres. UB3: Hayes 44U 84
Botwell Green Sports & Leisure Cen.
46V 84
Botwell La. UB3: Hayes 45U 84
Boucher Cl. TW11: Tedd 64Ha 130
Boucher Dr. DA11: Nflt 2B 144
Bouchier Ho. N2 26Fb 49
Bouchier Wlk. RM13: Rain 37Jd 76
Bough Beech Ct. EN3: Enf W 9Zb 20
Boughton Av. BR2: Hayes 73Hc 159
Boughton Hall Av. GU23: Send 96H 189
Boughton Ho. SE1 1F 231
Boughton Rd. SE28 48Uc 94
Boulcott St. E1 44Zb 92
Boulevard, The DA9: Ghithe 56Yd 120
IG8: Wfd G 23Qc 54
SW6 53Eb 111
SW17 61Jb 134
SW18 56Db 111
WD18: Wat 15T 26
Boulevard 25 WD6: Bore 13Qa 29
Boulevard Dr. NW9 26Va 48
Boulmer Rd. UB8: Cowl 41L 83
Boulogne Ho. SE1 3K 231
Boulogne Rd. CR0: C'don 72Sb 157
Boulter Cl. BR1: Brom 69Qc 138
Boulter Gdns. RM13: Rain 37Jd 76
Boulter Ho. SE14 53Yb 114
(off Kender St.)
Boulters Cl. SL1: Slou 6E 80
Boulthurst Way RH8: Oxt 4M 211
Boulton Ho. TW8: Bford 50Na 87
Boulton Rd. RM8: Dag 33Ad 75
Boultwood Rd. E6 44Pc 94
Bounce, The HP2: Hem H 1M 3
BOUNCE HILL 11Kd 39
Bounces La. N9 19Xb 33
Bounces Rd. N9 19Xb 33
Boundaries Rd. SW12 61Hb 133
TW13: Felt 60Y 107
Boundary Av. E17 31Bc 72
Boundary Bus. Cen.
GU21: Wok 87C 168
Boundary Bus. Ct. CR4: Mitc 69Fb 133
Boundary Cl. EN5: Barn 11Bb 31
IG3: Ilf 35Uc 74
KT1: King T 69Ra 131
SE20 68Wb 135
UB2: S'hall 50Ca 85
Boundary Cotts. HP3: Bov 1F 10
Boundary Ct. CM16: Epp 4Tc 22
N18 23Vb 51
(off Snells Pk.)
Boundary Dr. CM13: Hut 17Fe 41
Boundary Ho. DA11: Nflt 10B 122
(off Victoria Rd.)
EN8: Chesh 4Zb 20
SE5 52Sb 113
W11 46Za 88
(off Queensdale Cres.)
Boundary La. E13 41Mc 93
SE17 51Sb 113
Boundary Pk. HP2: Hem H 1C 4
KT13: Weyb 76U 150
Boundary Pas. E2 5K 219 (42Vb 91)
Boundary Rd. AL1: St A 1C 6
DA15: Sidc 57Uc 116
E13 40Lc 73
E17 31Bc 72
GU21: Wok 88C 168
HA5: Eastc 31Z 65
HA9: Wemb 34Na 67
Boundary Rd. IG11: Bark 39Tc 74
(King Edwards Rd.)
IG11: Bark 40Sc 74
(The Clarksons)
N9 16Yb 34
N22 27Rb 51
NW8 39Db 69
RM1: Rom 30Jd 56
RM14: Upm 34Qd 77
SM5: Cars 79Kb 156
SM6: Wall 79Kb 156
SW19 65Fb 133
TW15: Ashf 64L 127
Boundary Row SE1 1B 230 (47Rb 91)
Boundary St. DA8: Erith 52Hd 118
E2 4K 219 (41Vb 91)
Boundary Way CR0: Addtn 78Cc 158
GU21: Wok 87C 168
HP2: Hem H 1C 4
WD25: Wat 4X 13
Boundfield Rd. SE6 62Gc 137
BOUNDS GREEN 23Mb 50
Bounds Grn. Ct. N11 23Mb 50
(off Bounds Grn. Rd.)
Bounds Grn. Ind. Est. N11 23Lb 50
Bounds Grn. Rd. N11 23Lb 50
N22 23Lb 50
Bourbon Ho. SE6 64Ec 136
Bourbon La. W12 46Za 88
Bourchier Cl. TN13: S'oaks 98Kd 203
Bourchier St. W1 4D 222 (45Mb 90)
Bourdon Pl. W1 4A 222
Bourdon Rd. SE20 68Yb 136
Bourdon St. W1 4A 222 (45Kb 90)
Bourke Cl. NW10 37Ua 68
SW4 58Nb 112
Bourke Hill CR5: Chip 90Hb 175
Bourlet Cl. W1 1B 222 (43Lb 90)
Bourn Av. EN4: E Barn 15Fb 31
N15 28Tb 51
UB8: Hil 42Q 84
Bournbrook Rd. SE3 55Mc 115
Bourne, The HP3: Bov 9C 2
N14 18Mb 32
Bourne Av. HA4: Ruis 36Y 65
KT16: Chert 69J 127
N14 19Nb 32
SL4: Wind 5G 102
UB3: Harl 48S 84
BOURNEBRIDGE 18Dd 38
Bournebridge Cl. CM13: Hut 17Fe 41
Bournebridge La. RM4: Stap A 17Bd 37
Bourne Bus. Pk. KT15: Add 77N 149
Bourne Cir. UB3: Harl 48S 84
Bourne Cl. KT7: T Ditt 75Ha 152
KT14: W Byf 85K 169
TW7: Isle 55Ga 108
Bourne Ct. CR3: Cat'm 95Wb 197
HA4: Ruis 36X 65
IG8: Wfd G 27Mc 53
W4 51Sa 109
Bourne Dr. CR4: Mitc 68Fb 133
BOURNE END 4E 2
Bourne End RM11: Horn 31Qd 77
Bourne End La. HP1: Hem H 7C 2
Bourne End La. Ind. Est. HP1: Hem H 4D 2
Bourne End Rd. HA6: Nwood 21U 44
Bourne Ent. Cen. TN15: Bor G 91Ce 205
Bourne Est. EC1 7K 217 (43Qb 90)
Bournefield Rd. CR3: Whyt 90Wb 177
Bourne Gdns. E4 21Dc 52
Bourne Gro. KT21: Asht 91Ma 193
Bournehall WD23: Bush 16Ca 27
Bournehall Av. WD23: Bush 15Ca 27
Bournehall La. WD23: Bush 16Ca 27
Bourne Hall Mus. 81Va 174
Bournehall Rd. WD23: Bush 16Ca 27
Bourne Hill N13 19Nb 32
Bourne Hill Cl. N13 19Pb 32
Bourne Ho. IG9: Buck H 20Mc 35
TW15: Ashf 64Q 128
Bourne Ind. Pk. DA1: Cray 57Gd 118
Bourne La. CR3: Cat'm 93Tb 197
TN15: Plax 98Be 205
Bourne Mead DA5: Bexl 57Fd 118
Bournemead WD23: Bush 16Da 27
Bournemead Av. UB5: N'olt 40W 64
Bournemead Cl. UB5: N'olt 40W 64
Bourne Mdw. TW20: Thorpe 70D 126
Bournemead Way UB5: N'olt 40X 65
Bourne M. RH9: G'stone 2A 210
W1 2J 221 (44Jb 90)
Bournemouth Cl. SE15 54Wb 113
Bournemouth Rd. SE15 54Wb 113
SW19 67Cb 133
Bourne Pde. DA5: Bexl 59Dd 118
Bourne Pk. Cl. CR8: Kenley 88Ub 177
Bourne Pl. KT16: Chert 74K 149
W4 50Ta 87
Bourne Rd. BR2: Brom 70Mc 137
DA1: Cray 58Ed 118
DA5: Bexl, Dart 59Dd 118
DA12: Grav'nd 1H 145
E7 34Hc 73
GU25: Vir W 1P 147
N8 30Nb 50
RH1: Mers 2C 208
SL1: Slou 7G 80
WD23: Bush 15Ca 27
Bournes Ho. N15 30Ub 51
(off Chisley Rd.)
Bourneside GU25: Vir W 3L 147
Bourneside Cres. N14 18Mb 32
Bourneside Gdns. SE6 64Ec 136
Bourneside Rd. KT15: Add 77M 149
Bourne St. CR0: C'don 75Rb 157
SW1 6H 227 (49Jb 90)
Bourne Ter. W2 43Db 89
Bourne Va. BR2: Hayes 74Hc 159
TN15: Plax 99Ce 205
Bournevale Rd. SW16 63Nb 134
Bourne Vw. CR8: Kenley 87Tb 177
UB6: G'frd 37Ha 66
Bourneville Rd. SE6 59Cc 114
Bourne Way BR2: Hayes 75Hc 159
BR8: Swan 69Ed 140
GU22: Wok 4P 187
KT15: Add 78L 149
KT19: Ewe 77Sa 153
SM1: Sutt 78Bb 155
Bournewood Rd. BR5: Orp 73Yc 161
SE18 52Wc 117
Bournwell Cl. EN4: Cockf 13Hb 31
Bourton Cl. UB3: Hayes 46W 84
Bousfield Rd. SE14 54Zb 114
Bousley Ri. KT16: Ott 79F 148

Boutflower Rd. SW11 56Gb 111
Boutique Hall SE13 56Ec 114
Bouton Pl. *N1* *38Rb 71*
(off Waterloo Ter.)
Bouverie Gdns. CR8: Purl 86Pb 176
HA3: Kenton 30Ma 47
Bouverie M. N16 33Ub 71
Bouverie Pl. W2 2C 220 (44Fb 89)
Bouverie Rd. CR5: Chip 90Jb 176
HA1: Harr 30Ea 46
N16 33Ub 71
Bouverie St. EC4 3A 224 (44Qb 90)
Bouverie Way SL3: L'ly 50A 82
Bouvier Rd. EN3: Enf W 10Yb 20
BOVENEY 1B 102
Boveney Cl. SL1: Slou 7E 80
Boveney New Rd. SL4: Eton W 9C 80
Boveney Rd. SE23 59Zb 114
SL4: Dor 9A 80
Boveney Wood La. SL1: Burn 4B 60
Bovey Way RM15: S Ock 43Xd 98
Bovill Rd. SE23 59Zb 114
BOVINGDON 9C 2
Bovingdon Av. HA9: Wemb 37Qa 67
Bovingdon Cl. N19 33Lb 70
Bovingdon Ct. HP3: Bov 10C 2
WD23: Bush *15Da 27*
(off Farrington Av.)
Bovingdon Cres. WD25: Wat 6Z 13
BOVINGDON GREEN 1C 10
Bovingdon Grn. HP3: Bov 1C 10
Bovingdon La. NW9 25Ua 48
Bovingdon Rd. SW6 53Db 111
Bovril Ct. *SW6* *52Db 111*
(off Fulham Rd.)
BOW 41Bc 92
Bow Arrow La. DA1: Dart 58Qd 119
DA2: Dart 58Qd 119
Bowater Cl. NW9 29Ta 47
SW2 58Nb 112
Bowater Gdns. TW16: Sun 68Y 129
Bowater Ho. EC1 6D 218
Bowater Pl. SE3 52Kc 115
Bowater Ridge KT13: Weyb 82T 170
Bowater Rd. HA9: Wemb 34Ra 67
SE18 48Mc 93
Bow Bell Twr. *E3* *39Cc 72*
(off Pancras Way)
Bow Bri. Est. E3 41Dc 92
Bow Brook, The *E2* *40Zb 72*
(off Mace St.)
Bow Central Sports Cen. *41Bc 92*
(off Harley Gro.)
Bow Chyd. EC4 3E 224
BOW COMMON 43Cc 92
Bow Comn. La. E3 42Bc 92
Bow Creek Ecology Pk. 44Gc 93
Bowden Cl. TW14: Bedf 60U 106
Bowden Ct. TN15: Kems'g 89Pd 183
Bowden Dr. RM11: Horn 32Nd 77
Bowden Ho. *E3* *41Dc 92*
(off Rainhill Way)
Bowden Rd. SL5: S'hill 1A 146
Bowden St. SE11 7A 230 (50Qb 90)
Bowditch SE8 49Bc 92
Bowdon Rd. E17 31Cc 72
Bowen Dr. SE21 62Ub 135
Bowen Rd. HA1: Harr 31Ea 66
Bowen St. E14 44Dc 92
Bowens Wood CR0: Sels 81Bc 178
Bowen Way CR5: Coul 94Mb 196
Bower Av. SE10 53Gc 115
Bower Cl. RM5: Col R 24Fd 56
UB5: N'olt 40Y 65
Bower Ct. CM16: Epp 4Wc 23
E4 *18Ec 34*
(off The Ridgeway)
GU22: Wok 88D 168
SL1: Slou 5D 80
Bowerdean St. SW6 53Db 111
Bowerden Ct. NW10 40Xa 68
Bower Farm Rd. RM4: Have B 20Ed 38
Bower Hill CM16: Epp 3Wc 23
Bower Hill Cl. RH1: S Nut 9E 208
Bower Hill Ind. Est.
CM16: Epp 4Wc 23
Bower Hill La. RH1: S Nut 7D 208
Bower La. DA4: Eyns 75Nd 163
TN15: Knat 82Qd 183
Bowerman Av. SE14 51Ac 114
Bowerman Ct. *N19* *33Mb 70*
(off St John's Way)
Bowerman Rd. RM16: Grays 9C 100
Bower Rd. BR8: Hext 66Jd 140
Bowers RM11: Horn 29Md 57
Bowers Av. DA11: Nflt 3B 144
Bowers Rd. TN14: S'ham 83Hd 182
Bower St. E1 44Zb 92
Bowers Wlk. E6 44Pc 94
Bower Ter. CM16: Epp 4Wc 23
Bower Va. CM16: Epp 4Wc 23
Bower Way SL1: Slou 5C 80
Bowery Ct. RM10: Dag 37Dd 76
Bowes Cl. DA15: Sidc 58Xc 117
Bowes Ct. *DA2: Dart* *58Rd 119*
(off Osbourne Rd.)
Bowesden La.
DA12: Shorne, Strood 6N 145
Bowe's Ho. IG11: Bark 38Rc 74
Bowes Lyon Cl. *SL4: Wind* *3G 102*
(off Mountbatten Sq.)
Bowes-Lyon Hall *E16* *46Jc 93*
(off Wesley Av.)
Bowes Lyon M. AL3: St A 2B 6
BOWES PARK 23Nb 50
Bowes Rd. KT12: Walt T 75X 151
N11 22Lb 50
N13 22Lb 50
RM8: Dag 35Yc 75
TW18: Staines 64G 126
W3 45Ua 88
Bowes Wood DA3: New A 76Be 165
Bow Exchange *E3* *43Dc 92*
(off Yeo St.)
Bow Fair *E3* *40Cc 72*
(off Fairfield Rd.)
Bowfell Rd. W6 51Ya 110
Bowford Av. DA7: Bex 53Ad 117
Bowgate AL1: St A 1C 6
Bowhay CM13: Hut 19Ce 41
Bowhill Cl. SW9 52Qb 112
Bow Ho. *E3* *41Cc 92*
(off Bow Rd.)
N1 1H 219
Bowie Cl. SW4 59Mb 112
BOW INTERCHANGE 40Dc 72
Bowland Rd. IG8: Wfd G 23Lc 53
SW4 56Mb 112
Bowland Yd. SW1 2G 227
Bow La. EC4 3E 224 (44Sb 91)
N12 24Eb 49
SM4: Mord 72Ab 154
Bowlby Ho. *SE4* *56Zb 114*
(off Frendsbury Rd.)
Bowl Ct. EC2 6J 219 (42Ub 91)
Bowlers Grn. WD7: Shenl 2La 14
Bowles Cl. KT7: T Ditt 73Ka 152
Bowles Ct. N12 24Gb 49
Bowles Grn. EN1: Enf 8Xb 19
Bowles Rd. SE1 51Wb 113
Bowley Cl. SE19 65Vb 135
Bowley Ho. SE16 48Wb 91
Bowley La. SE19 64Vb 135
Bowling, The KT12: Walt T 73W 150
Bowling Cl. UB10: Uxb 39P 63
Bowling Ct. WD18: Wat 14W 26
Bowling Grn. Cl. SW15 59Xa 110
Bowling Grn. Ct. HA9: Wemb 33Pa 67
Bowling Grn. Ho. *SW10* *52Fb 111*
(off Riley St.)
Bowling Grn. La. EC1 5A 218 (42Qb 90)
Bowling Grn. Pl. SE1 1F 231 (47Tb 91)
Bowling Grn. Rd. GU24: Chob 1J 167
Bowling Grn. Row SE18 48Pc 94
Bowling Grn. St. SE11 51Qb 112
Bowling Grn. Wlk. N1 3H 219 (41Ub 91)
Bow Locks E3 42Ec 92
Bowls, The IG7: Chig 20Uc 36
Bowls Cl. HA7: Stan 22Ka 46
Bowman Av. E16 45Hc 93
Bowman Ho. N1 1J 219
Bowman M. SW18 60Bb 111
BOWMANS 59Hd 118
Bowman's Bldgs. NW1 7D 214
Bowmans Cl. EN6: Pot B 4Fb 17
SL1: Burn 9A 60
W13 46Ka 86
Bowmans Grn. WD25: Wat 8Aa 13
Bowmans Lea SE23 59Yb 114
Bowmans Mdw. SM6: Wall 76Kb 156
Bowman's M. E1 44Wb 91
N7 34Nb 70
Bowman's Pl. N7 34Nb 70
Bowman's Rd. DA1: Dart 59Hd 118
Bowman Trad. Est. NW9 27Qa 47
Bowmead SE9 61Pc 138
Bowmont Cl. CM13: Hut 16De 41
Bowmore Wlk. NW1 38Mb 70
Bown Cl. RM18: Tilb 5D 122
Bowness Cl. *E8* *37Vb 71*
(off Beechwood Rd.)
Bowness Cres. SW15 64Ua 132
Bowness Dr. TW4: Houn 56Aa 107
Bowness Ho. *SE15* *52Yb 114*
(off Hillbeck Cl.)
Bowness Rd. DA7: Bex 54Dd 118
SE6 59Dc 114
Bowness Way RM12: Horn 36Jd 76
Bowood Rd. EN3: Enf H 12Zb 34
SW11 57Jb 112
Bowring Grn. WD19: Wat 22Y 45
Bow Rd. E3 41Bc 92
Bowrons Av. HA0: Wemb 38Ma 67
Bowry Dr. TW19: Wray 58B 104
Bowry Ho. *E14* *43Bc 92*
(off Wallwood St.)
Bowsley Ct. TW13: Felt 61W 128
Bowsprit, The KT11: Cobh 87Y 171
Bowsprit Point *E14* *48Cc 92*
(off Westferry Rd.)
Bow St. E15 36Gc 73
WC2 3G 223 (44Nb 90)
Bow Triangle Bus. Cen. E3 42Cc 92
(not continuous)
Bowyer Cl. E6 43Pc 94
Bowyer Ct. EN8: Walt C 5Bc 20
Bowyer Cres. UB9: Den 30H 43
Bowyer Dr. SL1: Slou 6C 80
Bowyer Ho. N1 1J 219
Bowyer Pl. SE5 52Sb 113
BOWYERS 1M 3
Bowyers HP2: Hem H 1M 3
Bowyers Cl. KT21: Asht 90Pa 173
Bowyers Ct. TW1: Isle 56Ka 108
Bowyer St. SE5 52Sb 113
Boxall Rd. SE21 58Ub 113
Boxelder Cl. HA8: Edg 22Sa 47
Boxford Cl. CR2: Sels 84Zb 178
Boxgrove Rd. SE2 48Yc 95
Boxhill Rd.
KT20: Box H 2A 206 & 100Ta 193
Box La. HP3: Hem H 7E 2
IG11: Bark 40Xc 75
Boxley Rd. SM4: Mord 70Eb 133
Boxley St. E16 46Kc 93
BOXMOOR 4K 3
Boxmoor Ho. *E2* *39Wb 71*
(off Whiston Rd.)
W11 *46Za 88*
(off Queensdale Cres.)
Boxmoor Playhouse Theatre 4L 3
Boxmoor Rd. HA3: Kenton 28Ka 46
RM5: Col R 22Ed 56
Boxoll Rd. RM9: Dag 35Bd 75
Box Ridge Av. CR8: Purl 84Pb 176
Boxted Cl. IG9: Buck H 18Nc 36
Boxted Rd. HP1: Hem H 1H 3
Box Tree Ho. SE8 51Ac 114
Boxtree La. HA3: Hrw W 25Ea 46
Boxtree Rd. HA3: Hrw W 24Fa 46
Box Tree Wlk. BR5: Orp 74Zc 161
RH1: Redh 9L 207
Boxwood Cl. UB7: W Dray 47P 83
Boxwood Way CR6: W'ham 89Zb 178
Boxworth Cl. N12 22Fb 49
Boxworth Gro. N1 39Pb 70
Boyard Rd. SE18 50Rc 94
Boyce Cl. WD6: Bore 11Na 29
Boyce Ct. *WD17: Wat* *11W 26*
(off Lockhart Rd.)
Boyce Ho. SW16 64Lb 134
W10 *41Bb 89*
(off Bruckner St.)
Boyce Rd. SS17: Stan H 1L 101
Boyce Way E13 42Jc 93
Boycroft Av. NW9 30Sa 47
Boyd Av. UB1: S'hall 46Ba 85
Boyd Carpenter Ho. SL9: Chal P 22B 42
Boyd Cl. KT2: King T 66Qa 131
Boydell Ct. NW8 38Fb 69
(not continuous)
Boyden Ho. E17 27Ec 52
Boyd Rd. SW19 65Fb 133
Boyd St. E1 44Wb 91
Boyes Cres. AL2: Lon C 8F 6
Boyfield St. SE1 2C 230 (47Rb 91)
Boyland Rd. BR1: Brom 64Hc 137
Boyle Av. HA7: Stan 23Ja 46
Boyle Cl. UB10: Uxb 40P 63
Boyle Farm Island KT7: T Ditt 72Ja 152
Boyle Farm Rd. KT7: T Ditt 72Ja 152
Boyle St. W1 4B 222 (45Lb 90)
Boyne Av. NW4 28Za 48
Boyne Rd. RM10: Dag 34Cd 76
SE13 55Ec 114
Boyne Ter. M. W11 46Bb 89
Boyseland Ct. HA8: Edg 19Sa 29
Boyson Rd. SE17 51Sb 113
(not continuous)
Boyson Wlk. SE17 51Tb 113
Boyton Cl. E1 42Yb 92
N8 27Nb 50
Boyton Ho. NW8 1C 214
Boyton Rd. N8 27Nb 50
Brabant Ct. EC3 4H 225
Brabant Rd. N22 26Pb 50
Brabazon Av. SM6: Wall 80Nb 156
Brabazon Ct. SW1 7D 228
Brabazon Rd. TW5: Hest 52Y 107
UB5: N'olt 40Ca 65
Brabazon St. E14 44Dc 92
Brabiner Gdns. CR0: New Ad 82Fc 179
Brabner Ho. *E2* *41Wb 91*
(off Wellington Row)
Brabourne Cl. SE19 64Ub 135
Brabourne Cres. DA7: Bex 51Bd 117
Brabourne Hgts. NW7 20Ua 30
Brabourne Ri. BR3: Beck 71Ec 158
Brabourn Gro. SE15 54Yb 114
Brabrook Ct. SM6: Wall 77Kb 156
Brabstone Ho. UB6: G'frd 40Ha 66
Bracer Ho. N1 1J 219
Bracewell Av. UB6: G'frd 36Ha 66
Bracewell Rd. W10 43Ya 88
Bracewood Gdns. CR0: C'don 76Vb 157
Bracey M. N4 33Nb 70
Bracey St. N4 33Nb 70
Bracken, The E4 19Ec 34
Bracken Av. CR0: C'don 76Dc 158
SW12 58Jb 112
Brackenbridge Dr. HA4: Ruis 34Z 65
Brackenbury *N4* *32Qb 70*
(off Osborne Rd.)
Brackenbury Gdns. W6 48Xa 88
Brackenbury Rd. N2 27Eb 49
W6 48Xa 88
Bracken Cl. E6 43Pc 94
GU22: Wok 90B 168
IG10: Lough 11Rc 36
KT23: Bookh 96Ba 191
SL2: Farn C 5H 61
TW2: Whitt 59Ca 107
TW16: Sun 65V 128
WD6: Bore 11Ra 29
Bracken Ct. IG6: Ilf 23Vc 55
Brackendale EN6: Pot B 5Cb 17
N21 19Pb 32
Brackendale Cl. TW3: Houn 53Da 107
TW20: Eng G 5N 125
Brackendale Gdns. RM14: Upm 35Sd 78
Brackendene AL2: Brick W 2Ba 13
DA2: Wilm 63Gd 140
Brackendene Cl. GU21: Wok 87C 168
Bracken Dr. IG7: Chig 23Rc 54
Bracken End TW7: Isle 57Fa 108
Brackenfield Cl. E5 34Xb 71
Brackenforde SL3: L'ly 7N 81
Bracken Gdns. SW13 54Wa 110
Brackenhill HA4: Ruis 35Aa 65
KT11: Cobh 84Da 171
Bracken Hill Cl. BR1: Brom 67Hc 137
Bracken Hill La. BR1: Brom 67Hc 137
Bracken Ho. *E3* *43Cc 92*
(off Devons Rd.)
Bracken Ind. Est. IG6: Ilf 24Uc 54
Bracken M. E4 18Ec 34
RM7: Rom 30Dd 56
Bracken Path KT18: Eps 85Ra 173
Brackens BR3: Beck 66Cc 136
Brackens, The BR6: Chels 78Wc 161
EN1: Enf 17Ub 33
HP2: Hem H 1Ld 3
TN13: S'oaks 95Ld 203
Brackens Dr. CM14: W'ley 22Yd 58
Bracken Way GU24: Chob 2K 167
Brackenwood TW16: Sun 67W 128
Brackenwood Lodge *EN5: New Bar* *14Cb 31*
(off Prospect Rd.)
Brackenwood Rd. GU21: Wok 1H 187
Brackley KT13: Weyb 78T 150
Brackley Av. SE15 55Yb 114
Brackley Cl. SM6: Wall 80Nb 156
Brackley Ct. NW8 5B 214
Brackley Rd. BR3: Beck 66Bc 136
W4 50Ua 88
Brackley Sq. IG8: Wfd G 24Mc 53
Brackley St. EC1 7E 218 (42Sb 91)
Brackley Ter. W4 50Ua 88
Bracklyn Ct. N1 1F 219 (40Tb 71)
(not continuous)
Bracklyn St. N1 1F 219 (40Tb 71)
Bracknell Cl. N22 25Qb 50
Bracknell Gdns. NW3 35Db 69
Bracknell Ga. NW3 36Db 69
Bracknell Way NW3 35Db 69
Bracondale KT10: Esh 78Ea 152
Bracondale Av. DA13: Ist R 7B 144
Bracondale Rd. SE2 49Wc 95
Bracton La. DA2: Wilm 61Hd 140
Bradbeer Ho. *E2* *41Yb 92*
(off Cornwall Av.)
Bradbery WD3: Map C 22F 42
Bradbourne Ct. TN13: S'oaks 94Kd 203
Bradbourne Pk. Rd.
TN13: S'oaks 95Jd 202
Bradbourne Rd. DA5: Bexl 59Cd 118
RM17: Grays 51De 121
TN13: S'oaks 94Kd 203
Bradbourne St. SW6 54Cb 111
Bradbourne Va. Rd.
TN13: S'oaks 94Hd 202
Bradbury Cl. UB2: S'hall 49Ba 85
WD6: Bore 11Ra 29
Bradbury Ct. DA11: Nflt 10B 122
Bradbury Gdns. SL3: Ful 5P 61
Bradbury M. N16 36Ub 71
Bradbury St. N16 36Ub 71
Bradby Ho. *NW8* *40Db 69*
(off Hamilton Ter.)
Bradby's *HA1: Harr* *32Ga 66*
(off High St.)
Bradcaster Gro. KT22: Lea 93Na 193
Bradd Cl. RM15: S Ock 41Yd 98
Braddock Cl. RM5: Col R 25Dd 56
TW7: Isle 54Ha 108
Braddon Ct. EN5: Barn 13Ab 30
Braddon Rd. TW9: Rich 55Pa 109
Braddyll St. SE10 50Gc 93
Bradenham *SE17* *51Tb 113*
(off Bradenham Cl.)
Bradenham Av. DA16: Well 56Wc 117
Bradenham Cl. SE17 51Tb 113
Bradenham Rd.
HA3: Kenton 28Ka 46
UB4: Hayes 41U 84
Bradenhurst Cl. CR3: Cat'm 98Vb 197
Braden St. W9 42Db 89
Bradfield Cl. GU22: Wok 90A 168
Bradfield Ct. *NW1* *38Kb 70*
(off Hawley Rd.)
RM19: Purf *50Rd 97*
(off Linnet Way)
Bradfield Dr. IG11: Bark 36Wc 75
Bradfield Ho. IG8: Wfd G 23Qc 54
Bradfield Rd. E16 47Jc 93
HA4: Ruis 36Aa 65
Bradford Cl. BR2: Brom 74Pc 160
N17 23Vb 51
SE26 63Xb 135
Bradford Dr. KT19: Ewe 79Va 154
Bradford Ho. *W14* *48Za 88*
(off Spring Va. Ter.)
Bradford Rd. IG1: Ilf 32Tc 74
SL1: Slou 4E 80
W3 47Ua 88
WD3: Herons 17E 24
Bradfords Cl. IG9: Buck H 21Mc 53
Bradgate Rd. SE6 58Dc 114
Brading Cres. E11 33Kc 73
Brading Rd. CR0: C'don 72Pb 156
SW2 59Pb 112
Brading Ter. W12 48Wa 88
Bradiston Rd. W9 41Bb 89
Bradleigh Av. RM17: Grays 50Ee 99
Bradley Cl. N7 37Nb 70
SM2: Sutt 82Cb 175
Bradley Ct. *EN3: Enf L* *10Ac 20*
(off Bradley Rd.)
Bradley Gdns. W13 44Ka 86
Bradley Ho. *E3* *41Dc 92*
(off Bromley High St.)
IG8: Wfd G 24Jc 53
SE16 *49Yb 92*
(off Raymouth Rd.)
Bradley M. SW17 60Hb 111
Bradley Rd. EN3: Enf L 10Ac 20
EN9: Walt A 7Ec 20
N22 26Pb 50
SE19 65Sb 135
SL1: Slou 5H 81
Bradley's Cl. N1 1A 218 (40Qb 70)
Bradley Stone Rd. E6 43Pc 94
Bradman Ho. *NW8* *41Eb 89*
(off Abercorn Pl.)
Bradman Row HA8: Edg 24Sa 47
Bradmead SW8 52Kb 112
Bradmore Ct. *EN3: Enf H* *13Ac 34*
(off Enstone Rd.)
Bradmore Grn. AL9: Brk P 8G 8
Bradmore La. AL9: N Mym 9E 8
Bradmore Pk. Rd. W6 49Xa 88
Bradmore Way AL9: Brk P 8G 8
CR5: Coul 89Nb 176
Bradon *NW9* *26Va 48*
(off Further Acre)
Brad Rd. NW7 23Za 48
Bradshaw Cl. SL4: Wind 3C 102
SW19 65Cb 133
Bradshaw Cotts. *E14* *44Ac 92*
(off Repton St.)
Bradshaw Dr. NW7 24Za 48
Bradshawe Rd.
RM16: Grays 46Ce 99
Bradshawe Waye UB8: Hil 43P 83
Bradshaw Rd. WD24: Wat 11Y 27
Bradshaws AL10: Hat 4B 8
Bradshaws Cl. SE25 69Wb 135
Bradstock Ho. E9 38Zb 72
Bradstock Rd. E9 37Zb 72
KT17: Ewe 78Wa 154
Brad St. SE1 7A 224 (46Qb 90)
Bradwell Av. RM10: Dag 33Cd 76
Bradwell Cl. E18 28Hc 53
RM12: Horn 37Kd 77
Bradwell Ct. *CM13: Hut* *16Ee 41*
(off Bradwell Grn.)
CR3: Whyt *91Wb 197*
(off Godstone Rd.)
Bradwell Grn. CM13: Hut 16Ee 41
Bradwell Ho. *NW6* *39Db 69*
(off Mortimer Cres.)
Bradwell M. N18 21Wb 51
Bradwell Rd. IG9: Buck H 17Nc 36
Brady Av. IG10: Lough 12Sc 36
Brady Ct. RM8: Dag 32Zc 75
Brady Dr. BR1: Brom 69Qc 138
Brady Ho. *SW8* *53Lb 112*
(off Corunna Rd.)
Bradymead E6 44Qc 94
Brady St. E1 42Xb 91
Braeburn Ct. *BR6: Orp* *75Vc 161*
(off Blossom Dr.)
EN4: E Barn 14Fb 31
Brae Ct. KT2: King T 67Qa 131
Braemar SW15 58Za 110
Braemar Av. CR2: S Croy 82Sb 177
CR7: Thor H 69Qb 134
DA7: Bex 56Ed 118
HA0: Wemb 38Ma 67
N22 25Nb 50
NW10 34Ta 67
SW19 61Cb 133
Braemar Cl. *SE16* *50Xb 91*
(off Masters Dr.)
Braemar Ct. *SE6* *60Hc 115*
(off Cumberland Pl.)
WD23: Bush 16Ca 27
Braemar Gdns. BR4: W W'ck 74Ec 158
DA15: Sidc 62Tc 138
NW9 25Ta 47
RM11: Horn 30Qd 57
SL1: Slou 7E 80
Braemar Ho. W9 4A 214
Braemar Mans. *SW7* *48Db 89*
(off Cornwall Gdns.)
Braemar Rd. E13 42Hc 93
KT4: Wor Pk 76Xa 154
N15 29Ub 51
TW8: Bford 51Ma 109
Braeside BR3: Beck 64Cc 136
KT15: New H 83K 169
Braeside Av. SW19 67Ab 132
TN13: S'oaks 96Hd 202
Braeside Cl. HA5: Hat E 24Ca 45
TN13: S'oaks 95Hd 202
Braeside Cres. DA7: Bex 56Ed 118
Braeside Rd. SW16 66Lb 134
Braes Mead RH1: S Nut 7E 208
Braes St. N1 38Rb 71
Braesyde Cl. DA17: Belv 49Bd 95
Brafferton Rd. CR0: C'don 77Sb 157
Braganza St. SE17 7B 230 (50Rb 91)
Bragg Cl. RM8: Dag 37Xc 75
Bragg Rd. TW11: Tedd 65Ga 130
Bragmans La. WD3: Sarr 6E 10
Braham Ho. SE11 7J 229 (50Pb 90)
Braham St. E1 44Vb 91
Braid Av. W3 44Ua 88
Braid Cl. TW13: Hanw 61Ba 129
Braid Ho. *SE10* *53Ec 114*
(off Blackheath Hill)
Braidwood Pas. EC1 7D 218
Braidwood Rd. SE6 60Fc 115
Braidwood St. SE1 7H 225 (46Ub 91)
Brailsford Cl. CR4: Mitc 66Gb 133
Brailsford Rd. SW2 57Qb 112
Brainton Av. TW14: Felt 59X 107
Braintree Av. IG4: Ilf 28Nc 54
Braintree Ho. *E1* *42Yb 92*
(off Malcolm Rd.)
Braintree Rd. HA4: Ruis 35X 65
RM10: Dag 34Cd 76
Braintree St. E2 41Yb 92
Braithwaite Av. RM7: Rush G 31Cd 76
Braithwaite Gdns. HA7: Stan 25La 46
Braithwaite Ho. EC1 5F 219
Braithwaite Rd. EN3: Brim 13Bc 34
Braithwaite St. E1 6K 219 (42Vb 91)
Braithwaite Twr. W2 7B 214
Brakefield Rd. DA13: Sflt 65De 143
Brakes Pl. TN15: W King 79Ud 164
Brakey Hill RH1: Blet 6L 209
Bramah Grn. SW9 53Qb 112
Bramah Ho. SW1 7K 227 (50Kb 90)
Bramalea Cl. N6 30Jb 50
Bramall Cl. E15 36Hc 73
Bramall Ct. *N7* *36Pb 70*
(off George's Rd.)
Bramber WC1 4F 217
Bramber Ct. *DA2: Dart* *58Rd 119*
(off Bow Arrow La.)
SL1: Slou 6E 80
TW8: Bford 49Na 87
W14 *51Bb 111*
(off North End Rd.)
Bramber Ho. *KT2: King T* *67Na 131*
(off Seven Kings Way)
Bramber Rd. N12 22Gb 49
W14 51Bb 111
Bramber Way CR6: W'ham 88Bc 178
Brambleacres Cl. SM2: Sutt 80Cb 155
Bramble Av. DA2: Bean 62Yd 142
Bramble Banks SM5: Cars 81Jb 176
Bramblebury Rd. SE18 50Sc 94
Bramble Cl. BR3: Beck 71Ec 158
CR0: C'don 77Cc 158
HA7: Stan 24Ma 47
IG7: Chig 18Sc 36
N15 28Wb 51
RH1: Redh 8A 208
RH8: Oxt 5M 211
SE19 67Tb 135
SL9: Chal P 23A 42
TW17: Shep 69T 128
UB8: Hil 44P 83
WD25: Wat 6W 12
Bramble Ct. IG6: Ilf 23Vc 55
Bramble Cft. DA8: Erith 49Ed 96
Brambledene Cl. GU21: Wok 10N 167
Brambledown DA3: Hartl 70Be 143
TW18: Staines 67K 127
Brambledown Cl. BR4: W W'ck 71Gc 159
Brambledown Rd. CR2: Sande 80Ub 157
SM5: Cars 80Jb 156
SM6: Wall 80Jb 156
Bramblefield Cl. DA3: Lfield 69Zd 143
Bramble Gdns. W12 45Va 88
Bramble Ho. *E3* *43Cc 92*
(off Devons Rd.)
Bramble La. RM14: Upm 39Sd 78
TN13: S'oaks 100Kd 203
TW12: Hamp 65Ba 129
Bramble M. DA12: Grav'nd 3F 144
Bramble Ri. KT11: Cobh 87Y 171
Bramble Rd. AL10: Hat 1P 7
Brambles, The AL1: St A 4B 6
EN8: Chesh 3Zb 20
IG7: Chig 23Sc 54
SM1: Sutt 75Fb 155
SW19 *64Bb 133*
(off Woodside)
UB7: W Dray 49M 83
Brambles Cl. CR3: Cat'm 94Ub 197
TW7: Isle 52Ka 108
Brambles Farm Dr. UB10: Hil 41Q 84
Brambletye Pk. Rd. RH1: Redh 8P 207
Bramble Wlk. KT18: Eps 86Ra 173
RH1: Redh 8A 208
Bramble Way GU23: Rip 96H 189
Bramblewood RH1: Mers 1B 208
Bramblewood Cl. SM5: Cars 74Gb 155
Brambling Cl. DA9: Ghithe 58Wd 120
WD23: Bush 14Aa 27
Brambling Ct. *SE8* *51Bc 114*
(off Abinger Gro.)
Bramblings, The E4 21Fc 53
Bramcote Av. CR4: Mitc 70Hb 133
Bramcote Ct. *CR4: Mitc* *70Hb 133*
(off Bramcote Av.)
Bramcote Gro. SE16 50Yb 92
Bramcote Ho. KT13: Weyb 77S 150
Bramcote Rd. SW15 56Xa 110
Bramdean Cres. SE12 60Jc 115
Bramdean Gdns. SE12 60Jc 115
Bramerton *NW6* *38Za 68*
(off Willesden La.)
Bramerton Rd. BR3: Beck 69Bc 136
Bramerton St. SW3 51Gb 111
Bramfield WD25: Wat 6Aa 13
Bramfield Ct. *N4* *33Sb 71*
(off Queens Dr.)

Bramfield Rd. SW11 58Gb 111
Bramford Ct. N14 19Mb 32
Bramford Rd. SW18 56Eb 111
Bramham Ct. HA6: Nwood 22U 44
Bramham Gdns. KT9: Chess 77Ma 153
SW5 50Db 89
Bramhope La. SE7 51Kc 115
Bramlands Cl. SW11 55Gb 111
Bramleas WD18: Wat 15V 26
Bramley Av. CR5: Coul 87Lb 176
TW17: Shep 69U 128
Bramley Bank Nature Reserve 79Yb 158
Bramley Cl. BR6: Farnb 74Rc 160
BR8: Swan 70Gd 140
CR2: S Croy 78Sb 157
DA13: Ist R 6B 144
E17 26Ac 52
HA5: Eastc 27V 44
IG8: Wfd G 24Lc 53
KT16: Chert 74K 149
N14 15Kb 32
NW7 20Ua 30
RH1: Redh 8N 207
TW2: Whitt 58Ea 108
TW18: Staines 65L 127
UB3: Hayes 45W 84
Bramley Ct. *BR6: Orp* *75Vc 161*
(off Blossom Dr.)
CR4: Mitc 68Fb 133
DA16: Well 53Xc 117
E4 *18Ec 34*
(off The Ridgeway)
EN4: E Barn 14Gb 31
RH1: Redh 4N 207
UB1: S'hall *45Ea 86*
(off Haldane Rd.)
WD25: Wat 4X 13
Bramley Cres. IG2: Ilf 30Qc 54
SW8 52Mb 112
Bramley Gdns. WD19: Wat 23Y 45
Bramley Gro. KT21: Asht 91Na 193
Bramley Hill CR2: S Croy 78Rb 157
Bramley Ho. RH1: Redh 7A 208
SW15 *58Va 110*
(off Tunworth Cres.)
TW4: Houn 56Ba 107
W10 44Za 88
Bramley Ho. Ct. EN2: Enf 9Tb 19
Bramley Hyrst CR2: S Croy 78Sb 157
Bramley Lodge HA0: Wemb 35Ma 67
Bramley Pde. N14 14Mb 32
Bramley Pl. DA1: Cray 56Jd 118
Bramley Rd. N14 15Kb 32
SM1: Sutt 78Fb 155
SM2: Cheam 81Za 174
W5 48La 86
W10 44Za 88
Bramleys SS17: Stan H 1M 101
Bramley Shaw EN9: Walt A 5Hc 21
Bramley Sports Ground 15Jb 32
Bramley Way AL4: St A 3G 6
BR4: W W'ck 75Dc 158
KT21: Asht 89Pa 173
TW4: Houn 57Ba 107
Brammas Cl. SL1: Slou 8G 80
Brampton WC1 1H 223
Brampton Cl. E5 33Xb 71
EN7: Chesh 1Wb 19
Brampton Ct. NW4 28Xa 48
RM7: Rush G *30Fd 56*
(off Union Rd.)
Brampton Gdns. KT12: Hers 78Y 151
N15 29Sb 51
Brampton Gro. HA3: Kenton 28Ja 46
HA9: Wemb 32Qa 67
NW4 28Xa 48
Brampton La. NW4 28Ya 48
Brampton Pk. Rd. N22 27Qb 50
Brampton Rd. AL1: St A 1E 6
CR0: C'don 73Vb 157
DA7: Bex 55Zc 117
E6 41Mc 93
N15 29Sb 51
NW9 28Qa 47
SE2 51Yc 117
UB10: Hil 40R 64
WD19: Wat 20W 26
Brampton Ter. *WD6: Bore* *10Qa 15*
(off Stapleton Rd.)
Bramshaw Gdns. WD19: Wat 22Z 45
Bramshaw Ri. KT3: N Mald 72Ua 154
Bramshaw Rd. E9 37Zb 72
Bramshill Cl. IG7: Chig 22Uc 54
Bramshill Gdns. NW5 34Kb 70
Bramshill Rd. NW10 40Va 68
Bramshot Av. SE7 51Jc 115
Bramshot Way WD19: Wat 19W 26
Bramshurst *NW8* *39Db 69*
(off Abbey Rd.)
Bramston Cl. IG6: Ilf 23Vc 55
Bramston Rd. NW10 40Wa 68
SW17 62Eb 133
Bramwell Cl. TW16: Sun 68Z 129
Bramwell Ho. SE1 4E 230 (48Sb 91)
SW1 *50Lb 90*
(off Churchill Gdns.)
Bramwell M. N1 39Pb 70
Bramwell Way E16 46Lc 93
Brancaster Dr. NW7 24Wa 48
Brancaster Ho. *E1* *41Zb 92*
(off Moody St.)
Brancaster La. CR8: Purl 82Sb 177
Brancaster Pl. IG10: Lough 13Pc 36
Brancaster Rd. E12 35Pc 74
IG2: Ilf 30Uc 54
SW16 62Nb 134
Brancepeth Gdns. IG9: Buck H 19Jc 35
Branch Hill NW3 34Eb 69
Branch Hill Ho. NW3 34Db 69
Branch Pl. N1 39Tb 71
Branch Rd. AL2: Park 9B 6
AL3: St A 1P 5
E14 45Ac 92
IG6: Ilf 22Xc 55
Branch St. SE15 52Ub 113
Brancker Rd. HA3: Kenton 27Ma 47
Brancroft Way EN3: Brim 11Ac 34
Brand Cl. N4 32Rb 71
Brandesbury Sq. IG8: Wfd G 24Qc 54
Brandlehow Rd. SW15 56Bb 111
Brandon Cl. RM16: Chaf H 47Be 99
Brandon Est. SE17 51Rb 113
Brandon Groves Av.
RM15: S Ock 41Yd 98
Brandon Ho. *BR3: Beck* *64Dc 136*
(off Beckenham Hill Rd.)
Brandon Mans. *W14* *51Ab 110*
(off Queen's Club Gdns.)
Brandon M. EC2 1F 225
SE17 6E 230
Brandon Mobile Home Pk. AL4: St A 2H 7
Brandon Rd. DA1: Dart 59Qd 119
E17 28Ec 52
N7 38Nb 70
SM1: Sutt 77Db 155
UB2: S'hall 50Ba 85
Brandon St. DA11: Grav'nd 9D 122
SE17 6E 230 (49Sb 91)
(not continuous)
Brandram M. *SE13* *56Gc 115*
(off Brandram Rd.)
Brandram Rd. SE13 55Gc 115
Brandrams Wharf SE16 47Yb 92
Brandreth Ct. HA1: Harr 30Ha 46
Brandreth Rd. E6 44Pc 94
SW17 61Kb 134
Brandries, The SM6: Bedd 76Mb 156
Brands Hatch Motor Racing Circuit
78Ud 164
Brands Hatch Pk. DA3: Fawk 76Vd 164
Brands Hatch Rd. DA3: Fawk 76Wd 164
BRANDS HILL 51D 104
Brands Ho. *NW6* *39Bb 69*
(off Lincoln M.)
Brandsland RH2: Reig 10K 207
Brands Rd. SL3: L'ly 51D 104
Brand St. SE10 52Ec 114
Brandville Gdns. IG6: Ilf 28Rc 54
Brandville Rd. UB7: W Dray 47N 83
Brandy Way SM2: Sutt 80Cb 155
Branfill Rd. RM14: Upm 33Rd 77
Brangbourne Rd. BR1: Brom 64Ec 136
Brangton Rd. SE11 7J 229 (50Pb 90)
Brangwyn Ct. *W14* *48Ab 88*
(off Blythe Rd.)
Brangwyn Cres. SW19 67Eb 133
Branham Ho. SE18 50Rc 94
Branksea St. SW6 52Ab 110
Branksome *KT13: Weyb* *79T 150*
(off Gower Rd.)
Branksome Av. N18 23Vb 51
Branksome Cl. HP2: Hem H 1A 4
KT12: Walt T 75Z 151
TW11: Tedd 63Fa 130
Branksome Ho. *SW8* *52Pb 112*
(off Meadow Rd.)
Branksome Rd. SW2 57Nb 112
SW19 67Cb 133
Branksome Way HA3: Kenton 30Pa 47
KT3: N Mald 67Sa 131
Branksone Ct. N2 27Eb 49
Bransby Rd. KT9: Chess 79Na 153
Branscombe NW1 1C 216
Branscombe Ct. BR2: Brom 71Hc 159
Branscombe Gdns. N21 17Qb 32
Branscombe Ho. WD24: Wat 9W 12
Branscombe St. SE13 55Dc 114
Bransdale Cl. NW6 39Cb 69
Bransell Cl. BR8: Crock 72Ed 162
Bransgrove Rd. HA8: Edg 25Pa 47
Branston Cres. BR5: Pet W 74Tc 160
Branstone Ct. RM19: Purf 50Rd 97
Branstone Rd. TW9: Kew 53Pa 109
Branton Rd. DA9: Ghithe 58Vd 120
Brants Wlk. W7 42Ga 86
Brantwood Av. DA8: Erith 52Ed 118
TW7: Isle 56Ja 108
Brantwood Cl. E17 27Dc 52
KT14: W Byf 85J 169
Brantwood Ct. *KT14: W Byf* *85H 169*
(off Brantwood Dr.)
Brantwood Dr. KT14: W Byf 85H 169
Brantwood Gdns. EN2: Enf 14Nb 32
IG4: Ilf 28Nc 54
KT14: W Byf 85H 169
Brantwood Ho. *SE5* *52Sb 113*
(off Wyndam Est.)
Brantwood Rd. CR2: S Croy 81Sb 177
DA7: Bex 54Dd 118
N17 23Wb 51
SE24 57Sb 113
Brantwood Way BR5: St P 69Yc 139
Branxholme Ct. *BR1: Brom* *67Hc 137*
(off Highland Rd.)
Brasenose Dr. SW13 51Ya 110
Brasher Cl. UB6: G'frd 36Fa 66
Brassett Point *E15* *39Gc 73*
(off Abbey Rd.)
Brassey Cl. RH8: Oxt 1L 211
TW14: Felt 60W 106
Brassey Hill RH8: Oxt 2L 211
Brassey Ho. *E14* *49Dc 92*
(off Cahir St.)
Brassey Rd. NW6 37Bb 69
RH8: Oxt 2K 211
Brassey Sq. SW11 55Jb 112
Brassie Av. W3 44Ua 88
Brass Talley All. SE16 47Zb 92
BRASTED 96Yc 201
BRASTED CHART 100Xc 201
Brasted Cl. BR6: Orp 75Wc 161
DA6: Bex 57Zc 117
SE26 63Yb 136
SM2: Sutt 82Cb 175
Brasted Hill TN14: Knock, Sund 91Wc 201
Brasted Hill Rd. TN16: Bras 93Xc 201
Brasted La. TN14: Knock 91Wc 201
Brasted Lodge BR3: Beck 66Cc 136
Brasted Rd. DA8: Erith 52Gd 118
TN16: Westrm 98Uc 200
Brathay NW1 2C 216
Brathway Rd. SW18 59Cb 111
Bratley St. E1 42Wb 91
Bratten Ct. CR0: C'don 72Tb 157
Brattle Wood TN13: S'oaks 100Ld 203
Braund Av. UB6: G'frd 42Da 85
Braundton Av. DA15: Sidc 60Vc 117
Braunston Dr. UB4: Yead 42Aa 85
Bravington Cl. TW17: Shep 71P 149
Bravington Pl. W9 42Bb 89
Bravington Rd. W9 40Bb 69
Bravingtons Wlk. N1 2G 217
Brawlings La. SL9: Chal P 21C 42
Brawne Ho. *SE17* *51Rb 113*
(off Brandon Est.)
Braxfield Rd. SE4 56Ac 114
Braxted Pk. SW16 65Pb 134
Bray NW3 38Gb 69
Brayards Rd. SE15 54Xb 113
Brayards Rd. Est. *SE15* *54Xb 113*
(off Caulfield Rd.)
Braybourne Cl. UB8: Uxb 37L 63
Braybourne Dr. TW7: Isle 52Ha 108
Braybrooke Gdns. SE19 66Ub 135
Braybrook St. W12 43Va 88
Brayburne Av. SW4 54Lb 112
Bray Cl. WD6: Bore 11Sa 29
Bray Ct. *E2* *41Zb 92*
(off Meath Cres.)
SW16 64Nb 134
Braycourt Av. KT12: Walt T 73X 151
Bray Cres. SE16 47Zb 92
Braydon Rd. N16 32Wb 71
Bray Dr. E16 45Hc 93
Brayfield Ter. N1 38Qb 70
Brayford Sq. E1 44Yb 92
Bray Gdns. GU22: Pyr 88G 168
Bray Pas. E16 45Jc 93
Bray Pl. SW3 6F 227 (49Hb 89)
Bray Rd. KT11: Stoke D 88Aa 171
NW7 23Za 48
Bray Springs EN9: Walt A 6Gc 21
Brayton Gdns. EN2: Enf 14Mb 32
Braywood Av. TW20: Egh 65B 126
Braywood Rd. SE9 56Tc 116
Brazier Cres. UB5: N'olt 42Ba 85
Brazil Cl. CR0: Bedd 73Nb 156
Breach Barns La. EN9: Walt A 2Hc 21
Breach Barns Mobile Home Pk.
EN9: Walt A 2Kc 21
Breach La. RM9: Dag 41Cd 96
Breach Rd. RM20: W Thur 51Vd 120
Bread St. EC4 4E 224 (44Sb 91)
(not continuous)
Breakfield CR5: Coul 88Nb 176
Breakneck Hill DA9: Ghithe 57Xd 120
Breakspear Av. AL1: St A 3D 6
Breakspear Ct. WD5: Ab L 2V 12
Breakspear Crematorium (Ruislip)
HA4: Ruis 29S 44
Breakspeare Cl. WD24: Wat 10X 13
Breakspeare Rd. WD5: Ab L 3U 12
Breakspear M. UB9: Hare 27M 43
Breakspear Path UB9: Hare 27M 43
Breakspear Pl. WD5: Ab L 2V 12
Breakspear Rd. HA4: Ruis 31R 64
Breakspear Rd. Nth. UB9: Hare 25L 43
Breakspear Rd. Sth. UB9: Hare 34P 63
UB10: Ick 34P 63
Breakspears Dr. BR5: St P 67Wc 139
Breakspears M. SE4 54Bc 114
Breakspears Rd. SE4 56Bc 114
(not continuous)
Breakspear Way HP2: Hem H 2C 4
Breakwell Ct. *W10* *42Ab 88*
(off Wornington Rd.)
Bream Cl. N17 28Xb 51
Bream Gdns. E6 41Qc 94
Breamore Cl. SW15 60Wa 110
Breamore Ct. IG3: Ilf 33Wc 75
Breamore Ho. *SE15* *52Wb 113*
(off Friary Est.)
Breamore Rd. IG3: Ilf 33Vc 75
Bream's Bldgs. EC4 2K 223 (44Qb 90)
Bream St. E3 38Cc 72
Breamwater Gdns. TW10: Ham 62Ka 130
Brearley Cl. HA8: Edg 24Sa 47
UB8: Uxb 37N 63
Breasley Cl. SW15 56Xa 110
Breasy Pl. *NW4* *28Xa 48*
(off Burroughs Gdns.)
Brechin Pl. SW7 7A 226 (49Eb 89)
Brecknock Rd. N7 36Mb 70
N19 35Lb 70
Brecknock Rd. Est. N19 35Lb 70
Breckonmead BR1: Brom 68Lc 137
Brecon Cl. CR4: Mitc 69Nb 134
KT4: Wor Pk 75Ya 154
Brecon Ct. SL1: Slou 7G 80
Brecon Grn. NW9 30Ua 48
Brecon Ho. *E3* *40Bc 72*
(off Ordell Rd.)
W2 2A 220
Brecon M. N7 36Mb 70
Brecon Rd. EN3: Pond E 14Yb 34
W6 51Ab 110
Brecons, The KT13: Weyb 77T 150
Brede Cl. E6 41Qc 94
Bredel Ho. *E14* *43Cc 92*
(off St Paul's Way)
Bredgar SE13 57Dc 114
Bredgar Rd. N19 33Lb 70
Bredhurst Cl. SE20 65Yb 136
Bredinghurst SE22 59Wb 113
Bredin Ho. *SW10* *52Db 111*
(off Coleridge Gdns.)
Bredo Ho. IG11: Bark 41Xc 95
Bredon Rd. CR0: C'don 73Vb 157
Bredune CR8: Kenley 87Tb 177
Breech La. KT20: Walt H 96Wa 194
Breer St. SW6 55Db 111
Breezers Ct. *E1* *45Wb 91*
(off The Highway)
Breezer's Hill E1 45Wb 91
Breeze Ter. EN8: Chesh 1Zb 20
Brember Rd. HA2: Harr 33Ea 66
Bremer M. E17 28Dc 52
Bremer Rd. TW18: Staines 62J 127
Bremner Cl. BR8: Swan 70Jd 140
Bremner Rd. SW7 3A 226 (48Eb 89)
Brenchley Av. DA11: Grav'nd 4D 144
Brenchley Cl. BR2: Brom 72Hc 159
BR7: Chst 67Qc 138
Brenchley Gdns. SE23 58Yb 114
Brenchley Rd. BR5: St P 68Vc 139
Bren Ct. *EN3: Enf L* *9Cc 20*
(off Colgate Pl.)
Brendans Cl. RM11: Horn 32Nd 77
Brenda Rd. SW17 61Hb 133
Brenda Ter. DA10: Swans 59Ae 121
Brende Gdns. KT8: W Mole 70Da 129
Brendon Av. NW10 35Ua 68
Brendon Cl. DA8: Erith 53Gd 118
KT10: Esh 79Ea 152
UB3: Harl 52S 106
Brendon Ct. UB2: S'hall 49Da 85
WD7: R'lett 6Ka 14
Brendon Dr. KT10: Esh 79Ea 152
Brendon Gdns. HA2: Harr 35Da 65
IG2: Ilf 29Uc 54
Brendon Gro. N2 26Eb 49
Brendon Rd. RM8: Dag 32Bd 75
SE9 61Tc 138
Brendon St. W1 2E 220 (44Gb 89)
Brendon Vs. N21 18Sb 33
Brendon Way EN1: Enf 17Ub 33
Brenley Cl. CR4: Mitc 69Jb 134
Brenley Gdns. SE9 56Mc 115
Brenley Ho. SE1 1F 231
Brennand Ct. N19 34Lb 70
Brennan Rd. RM18: Tilb 4D 122
Brent, The DA1: Dart 59Qd 119
DA2: Dart 59Qd 119
Brent Cl. DA2: Dart 58Rd 119
DA5: Bexl 60Ad 117
Brentcot Cl. W13 42Ka 86
Brent Ct. NW11 31Za 68
W7 45Fa 86
Brent Cres. NW10 40Pa 67
BRENT CROSS 31Ya 68
Brent Cross Fly-Over NW2 31Za 68
NW4 31Za 68
Brent Cross Gdns. NW4 30Za 48
BRENT CROSS INTERCHANGE 30Ya 48
Brent Cross Shop. Cen. NW4 31Ya 68
Brentfield NW10 38Ra 67
Brentfield Cl. NW10 37Ta 67
Brentfield Gdns. NW2 31Za 68
Brentfield Ho. NW10 38Ta 67
Brentfield Rd. DA1: Dart 58Qd 119
NW10 37Ta 67
BRENTFORD 51Ma 109
Brentford Bus. Cen. TW8: Bford 52La 108
Brentford Cl. UB4: Yead 42Z 85
BRENTFORD END 52Ka 108
Brentford FC 51Ma 109
Brentford Fountain Leisure Cen. 50Qa 87
Brentford Ho. TW1: Twick 59Ka 108
Brentford Karting Raceway 24Yd 58
Brent Grn. NW4 29Ya 48
Brent Grn. Wlk. HA9: Wemb 34Sa 67
Brentham Club 41La 86
Brentham Way W5 42Ma 87
Brent Ho. *E9* *37Yb 72*
(off Brenthouse Rd.)
Brenthouse Rd. E9 38Yb 72
Brenthurst Rd. NW10 37Va 68
Brentlands Dr. DA1: Dart 60Qd 119
Brent La. DA1: Dart 59Pd 119
Brent Lea TW8: Bford 52La 108
Brentleigh Ct. CM14: B'wood 20Wd 40
Brentmead Cl. W7 45Ga 86
Brentmead Gdns. NW10 40Pa 67
Brentmead Pl. NW11 30Za 48
Brentmoor Rd. GU24: W End 5A 166
Brent Mus. *37Xa 68*
(off High Rd.)
Brent New Ent. Cen. NW10 37Va 68
Brenton Ct. *E9* *36Ac 72*
(off Mabley St.)
Brenton St. E14 44Ac 92
Brent Pk. Ind. Est. UB2: S'hall 48X 85
Brent Pk. Rd. NW4 31Xa 68
NW9 31Xa 68
Brent Pl. EN5: Barn 15Bb 31
Brent Rd. CR2: Sels 81Xb 177
E16 44Jc 93
SE18 52Rc 116
TW8: Bford 51La 108
UB2: S'hall 48Y 85
Brent Side TW8: Bford 51La 108
Brentside Cl. W13 42Ja 86
Brentside Executive Cen.
TW8: Bford 51Ka 108
Brent St. NW4 28Ya 48
Brent Ter. NW2 32Ya 68
(not continuous)
Brent Trad. Cen. NW10 36Ua 68
Brentvale Av. HA0: Wemb 39Pa 67
UB1: S'hall 46Fa 86
Brent Valley Golf Course 45Ga 86
Brent Vw. Rd. NW9 30Wa 48
Brentwaters Bus. Pk. TW8: Bford 52La 108
Brent Way DA2: Dart 58Rd 119
HA9: Wemb 37Ra 67
N3 23Cb 49
TW8: Bford 52Ma 109
Brentwick Gdns. TW8: Bford 49Na 87
BRENTWOOD 19Zd 41
Brentwood By-Pass
CM14: B'wood, Pil H, S Weald 21Td 58
CM15: B'wood, Pil H, Shenf 16Yd 40
Brentwood Camping & Caravanning Site
CM15: Dodd 12Vd 40
Brentwood Cathedral 19Zd 41
Brentwood Centre, The 16Yd 40
Brentwood Cl. SE9 60Sc 116
Brentwood Ct. KT15: Add 77K 149
Brentwood Golf Course 21Ae 59
Brentwood Ho. *SE18* *52Mc 115*
(off Portway Gdns.)
Brentwood Lodge *NW4* *29Za 48*
(off Holmdale Gdns.)
Brentwood Mus. 21Yd 58
Brentwood Pk. Ski & Snowboarding Cen.
24Xd 58
Brentwood Pl. CM15: B'wood 18Zd 41
Brentwood Rd.
CM13: Heron, Ingve, W H'dn 21Ce 59
RM1: Rom 30Hd 56
RM2: Rom 30Hd 56
RM14: Bulp 1E 100
RM16: Grays, Ors 9D 100
Brentwood School Sports Cen. 19Zd 41
Brentwood Theatre 18Zd 41
Brereton Ct. HP3: Hem H 4N 3
Brereton Rd. N17 24Vb 51
Bressay Dr. NW7 24Wa 48
Bressenden Pl. SW1 3A 228 (48Kb 90)
Bressey Av. EN1: Enf 11Wb 33
Bressey Gro. E18 26Hc 53
Bretlands Rd. KT16: Chert 75G 148
Breton Highwalk EC2 7E 218
Breton Ho. EC2 7E 218
SE1 3K 231
Bretons Outdoor Recreation Cen. 37Hd 76
Brett Cl. N16 33Ub 71
UB5: N'olt 41Z 85
Brett Ct. N9 19Yb 34
Brett Cres. NW10 39Ta 67
Brettell St. SE17 7G 231 (50Tb 91)
Brettenham Av. E17 25Cc 52
Brettenham Rd. E17 26Cc 52
N18 21Wb 51
Brett Gdns. RM9: Dag 38Ad 75
Brettgrave KT19: Eps 82Sa 173
Brett Ho. EN8: Chesh 1Zb 20
Brett Ho. Cl. SW15 59Za 110
Brettinghurst *SE1* *50Wb 91*
(off Avondale Sq.)
Brett Pas. E8 36Xb 71
Brett Pl. WD24: Wat 9W 12
Brett Rd. E8 36Xb 71
EN5: Barn 15Ya 30
Brevet Cl. RM19: Purf 49Td 98
Brewers Bldgs. EC1 3B 218
Brewers Ct. W2 2A 220 (43Eb 89)
Brewer's Fld. DA2: Wilm 63Ld 141
Brewer's Grn. SW1 3D 228
Brewer's Hall Gdn. EC2 1E 224
Brewers La. TW9: Rich 57Ma 109
Brewers Rd. DA12: Shorne 7L 145
Brewer St. RH1: Blet 3J 209
W1 5C 222 (45Lb 90)
Brewery, The EC2 7F 219 (43Sb 91)
RM1: Rom 29Gd 56
Brewery Cl. HA0: Wemb 36Ja 66
Brewery Ind. Estate, The N1 2E 218
Brewery La. KT14: Byfl 85N 169
TN13: S'oaks 97Kd 203
TW1: Twick 59Ha 108
Brewery M. Cen. TW7: Isle 55Ja 108
Brewery Rd. BR2: Brom 74Nc 160
GU21: Wok 9P 167
N7 38Nb 70
SE18 50Tc 94
Brewery Sq. EC1 5C 218 (42Rb 91)
SE1 7K 225
Brewery Wlk. RM1: Rom 29Gd 56
Brewhouse La. E1 46Xb 91
SW15 55Ab 110
Brewhouse Rd. SE18 49Pc 94
Brewhouse Wlk. SE16 46Ac 92
Brewhouse Yd. DA12: Grav'nd 8D 122
EC1 5B 218 (42Rb 91)
Brewin Ter. UB4: Yead 43Y 85
Brewood Rd. RM8: Dag 37Xc 75
Brewster Ct. CM14: W'ley 22Xd 58
Brewster Gdns. W10 43Ya 88
Brewster Ho. *E14* *45Bc 92*
(off Three Colt St.)
SE1 5K 231
Brewster Pl. KT1: King T 68Sa 131
Brewster Rd. E10 32Dc 72
Brian Av. CR2: Sande 84Ub 177
Brian Cl. RM12: Horn 35Kd 77
Briane Rd. KT19: Eps 82Sa 173
Brian Rd. RM6: Chad H 29Yc 55
Briant Ho. SE1 4K 229
Briants Cl. HA5: Pinn 26Ba 45
Briant St. SE14 53Zb 114
Briar Av. SW16 66Pb 134
Briarbank Rd. W13 44Ja 86
Briar Banks SM5: Cars 81Jb 176
Briarcliff HP1: Hem H 1G 2
Briar Cl. CR6: W'ham 88Cc 178
EN8: Chesh 1Yb 20
IG9: Buck H 19Mc 35
KT14: W Byf 83K 169
N2 27Db 49
N13 20Sb 33
SL6: Tap 4A 80
TW7: Isle 57Ha 108
TW12: Hamp 64Ba 129
Briar Ct. *E3* *40Cc 72*
(off Morville St.)
SM3: Cheam 77Ya 154
SW15 56Xa 110
Briar Cres. UB5: N'olt 37Da 65
Briardale HA8: Edg 21Ta 47
Briardale Gdns. NW3 34Cb 69
Briarfield Av. N3 27Db 49
(not continuous)
Briarfield Cl. DA7: Bex 54Cd 118
Briar Gdns. BR2: Hayes 74Hc 159
Briar Gro. CR2: Sande 85Wb 177
Briar Hill CR8: Purl 83Nb 176
Briaris Cl. N17 24Xb 51
Briar La. BR4: Addtn 77Dc 158
SM5: Cars 81Jb 176
Briarleas Gdns. RM14: Upm 31Ud 78
Briar Rd. DA5: Bexl 62Fd 140
GU23: Send 96D 188
HA3: Kenton 29La 46
NW2 35Ya 68
RM3: Rom 24Ld 57
SW16 69Nb 134
TW2: Twick 60Ga 108
TW17: Shep 71P 149
WD25: Wat 6W 12
Briars, The CM15: Kel H 11Ud 40
EN8: Chesh 3Ac 20
SL3: L'ly 50B 82
TN15: W King 79Td 164
TW19: Stanw M 57J 105
WD3: Sarr 8J 11
WD23: B Hea 17Ga 28
Briars Ct. KT22: Oxs 86Fa 172
Briars La. AL10: Hat 1C 8
Briars Wlk. RM3: Hrld W 26Pd 57
Briars Way DA3: Hartl 71Ce 165
Briarswood EN7: G Oak 1Tb 19
Briarswood Way BR6: Chels 78Vc 161
Briar Wlk. HA8: Edg 24Sa 47
KT14: W Byf 84J 169
SW15 56Xa 110
W10 42Ab 88
Briar Way SL2: Slou 3F 80
UB7: W Dray 47Q 84
Briar Wood Cl. BR2: Brom 75Nc 160
Briarwood Cl. NW9 30Sa 47
TW13: Felt 63U 128
Briarwood Ct. *KT4: Wor Pk* *74Wa 154*
(off The Avenue)
Briarwood Dr. HA6: Nwood 26W 44
Briarwood Rd. GU21: Wok 1H 187
KT17: Ewe 79Wa 154
SW4 57Mb 112
Briary Cl. NW3 38Gb 69
Briary Ct. DA14: Sidc 64Xc 139
E16 44Hc 93
Briary Gdns. BR1: Brom 64Kc 137
Briary Gro. HA8: Edg 26Ra 47
Briary La. N9 20Vb 33
Briary Lodge BR3: Beck 67Ec 136
Briavels Ct. KT18: Eps 87Ua 174
Brickbarn Cl. *SW10* *52Eb 111*
(off King's Barn)
Brickbat All. KT22: Lea 93Ka 192
Brick Ct. EC4 3K 223 (44Qb 90)
RM17: Grays *51Ce 121*
(off Columbia Wharf Rd.)
Brickenden Ct. EN9: Walt A 5Hc 21
Bricket Rd. AL1: St A 2B 6
Brickett Cl. HA4: Ruis 29S 44
BRICKET WOOD 2Ba 13
Bricket Wood Common 4Ca 13
Bricket Wood Sports & Country Club
1Ca 13
Brick Farm Cl. TW9: Kew 53Ra 109

Brickfield AL10: Hat 3C 8
Brickfield Av. HP3: Hem H 3B 4
Brickfield Cl. E9 37Yb 72
TW8: Bford 52La 108
Brickfield Cotts. BR7: Chst 64Qc 138
SE18 51Vc 117
Brickfield Ct. AL10: Hat 3D 8
Brickfield Farm DA3: Lfield 69Ce 143
Brickfield Farm Cl. DA3: Lfield 69Be 143
Brickfield Farm Gdns. BR6: Farnb 77Sc 160
Brickfield La. EN5: Ark 16Va 30
UB3: Harl 51T 106
Brickfield Rd. CM16: Coop 1Zc 23
CR7: Thor H 67Rb 135
SW19 63Db 133
Brickfields HA2: Harr 33Fa 66
(not continuous)
Brickfields Cotts. WD6: Bore 13Pa 29
Brickfields Way UB7: W Dray 48P 83
BRICK HILL 7G 146
Brick Kiln Cl. WD19: Wat 16Aa 27
Brick Kiln La. RH8: Limp 2N 211
Brick Knoll Pk. AL1: St A 3G 6
Brick La. E1 5K 219 (42Vb 91)
E2 4K 219 (41Vb 91)
EN1: Enf 12Xb 33
EN3: Enf H 12Xb 33
HA7: Stan 24Ma 47
UB5: N'olt 41Ba 85
Brick Lane Music Hall 46Mc 93
BRICKLAYER'S ARMS 4G 231 (49Tb 91)
Bricklayers Arms Distribution Cen.
SE1 5J 231 (49Ub 91)
(not continuous)
Brickmakers La. HP3: Hem H 3B 4
Brickmakers Mdws. TN15: Plat 92Ee 205
Brickstock Furze CM15: Shenf 16Ce 41
Brick St. W1 7K 221 (46Kb 90)
Brickwall La. HA4: Ruis 32U 64
Brickwood Cl. SE26 62Xb 135
Brickwood Rd. CR0: C'don 75Ub 157
Brickworks Cotts. TN14: S'oaks 92Md 203
Brideale Cl. SE15 51Vb 113
Bride Ct. EC4 3B 224
Bride La. EC4 3B 224 (44Rb 91)
Bridel M. N1 1B 218
Brides M. N7 37Pb 70
Brides Pl. N1 38Ub 71
Bride St. N7 37Pb 70
Bridewain St. SE1 3K 231 (48Vb 91)
Bridewell Pl. E1 46Xb 92
EC4 3B 224 (44Rb 91)
Bridford M. W1 7A 216 (43Kb 90)
BRIDGE, THE 55Qd 119
Bridge, The HA3: W'stone 28Ha 46
SW8 52Kb 112
WD4: K Lan 1R 12
Bridge Academy 1K 219
Bridge App. NW1 38Jb 70
Bridge Av. RM14: Upm 34Qd 77
W6 49Ya 88
W7 43Fa 86
Bridge Av. Mans. *W6* 50Ya 88
(off Bridge Av.)
Bridge Barn La. GU21: Wok 10P 167
Bridge Bus. Cen., The
UB2: S'hall 47Ca 85
Bridge Cl. CM13: B'wood 20Ae 41
DA2: Dart 55Td 120
EN1: Enf 12Xb 33
GU21: Wok 9N 167
KT12: Walt T 73V 150
KT14: Byfl 84P 169
RM7: Rush G 30Gd 56
SL1: Slou 5D 80
TW11: Tedd 63Ha 130
TW18: Staines 63G 126
W10 44Za 88
Bridge Ct. E10 32Bc 72
E14 45Fc 93
(off Newport Av.)
GU21: Wok 9P 167
KT12: Walt T 74V 150
(off Bridge St.)
KT13: Weyb 77R 150
KT22: Lea 94Ja 192
RM17: Grays 51De 121
(off Bridge Rd.)
WD7: R'lett 7Ka 14
Bridgedown Golf Course 11Za 30
Bridge Dr. N13 21Pb 50
BRIDGE END 92R 190
Bridge End E17 25Ec 52
Bridge End Cl. KT2: King T 67Qa 131
Bridgefield Cl. SM7: Bans 87Ya 174
Bridgefield Ho. *W2* 44Db 89
(off Queensway)
Bridgefield Rd. SM1: Sutt 79Cb 155
Bridgefoot SE1 50Nb 90
TW16: Sun 67V 128
Bridgefoot Ho. WD7: R'lett 3Ha 14
Bridgefoot La. EN6: Pot B 5Ya 16
Bridgeford Ho. WD18: Wat 13X 27
Bridge Gdns. KT8: E Mos 70Fa 130
N16 35Tb 71
TW15: Ashf 66S 128
Bridge Ga. N21 17Sb 33
Bridgeham Cl. KT13: Weyb 78Q 150
Bridge Hill CM16: Epp 5Vc 23
Bridgehill Cl. HA0: Wemb 39Ma 67
Bridge Ho. *CR0: C'don* 76Sb 157
(off Surrey St.)
DA1: Dart 59Nd 119
E9 37Zb 72
(off Shepherds La.)
KT16: Chert 73L 149
NW3 38Jb 70
(off Adelaide Rd.)
NW10 40Za 68
(off Chamberlayne Rd.)
SE4 56Bc 114
SM2: Sutt 79Db 155
(off Bridge Rd.)
SW1 7K 227
UB7: W Dray 46M 83
W2 1B 220
Bridgehouse Ct. SE1 1B 230
Bridge Ho. Quay E14 46Ec 92
Bridgeland Rd. E16 45Jc 93
Bridgelands Cl. BR3: Beck 66Bc 136
Bridge La. GU25: Vir W 71A 148
NW11 28Ab 48
SW11 53Gb 111
Bridge Leisure Centre, The 63Bc 136
Bridgeman Ct. SL4: Wind 4E 102
Bridgeman Dr. SL4: Wind 4E 102
Bridgeman Ho. *E9* 38Yb 72
(off Frampton Pk. Rd.)
Bridgeman Rd. N1 38Pb 70
TW11: Tedd 65Ja 130
Bridgeman St. NW8 2D 214 (40Gb 69)
Bridge Mead GU24: Pirb 8D 186
Bridge Mdws. SE14 51Zb 114
Bridge M. GU21: Wok 9P 167
BRIDGEN 59Ad 117
Bridgend Rd. EN1: Enf 7Yb 20
SW18 56Eb 111
Bridgenhall Rd. EN1: Enf 11Vb 33
Bridgen Ho. *E1* 44Xb 91
(off Nelson St.)
Bridgen Rd. DA5: Bexl 59Ad 117
Bridge Pde. *N21* 17Sb 33
(off Ridge Av.)
Bridge Pk. 38Ra 67
Bridgepark SW18 57Cb 111
Bridge Pl. CR0: C'don 74Tb 157
SW1 5A 228 (49Kb 90)
WD17: Wat 15Z 27
Bridge Point RM11: Horn 27Nd 57
Bridgepoint Ct. *AL2: Brick W* 2Aa 13
(off Old Watford Rd.)
Bridgepoint Lofts E7 38Lc 73
Bridgepoint Pl. *N6* 32Lb 70
(off Hornsey La.)
Bridgeport Pl. E1 46Wb 91
Bridger Cl. WD25: Wat 5Z 13
Bridge Rd. BR3: Beck 66Bc 136
BR5: St M Cry 72Xc 161
DA7: Bex 54Ad 117
DA8: Erith 54Hd 118
E6 38Pc 74
E11 30Fc 53
E15 38Fc 73
E17 31Bc 72
HA9: Wemb 34Qa 67
KT8: E Mos 70Fa 130
KT9: Chess 78Na 153
KT13: Weyb 77P 149
KT16: Chert 73K 149
KT17: Eps 84Va 174
N9 20Wb 33
N22 25Nb 50
NW10 37Ua 68
RM13: Rain 42Jd 96
RM17: Grays 51De 121
SL5: S'hill 1B 146
SM2: Sutt 79Db 155
SM6: Wall 78Kb 156
TW1: Twick 58Ka 108
TW3: Houn, Isle 55Fa 108
TW7: Isle 55Fa 108
UB2: S'hall 47Ba 85
UB8: Uxb 40L 63
WD4: Hunt C 5S 12
Bridge Rd. Depot E15 39Gc 73
Bridge Row CR0: C'don 74Tb 157
Bridges Ct. SW11 55Fb 111
(not continuous)
Bridges Dr. DA1: Dart 57Rd 119
Bridges Ho. *SE5* 52Tb 113
(off Elmington Est.)
Bridgeside Lodge N1 1D 218
Bridges La. CR0: Bedd 77Nb 156
Bridges Pl. SW6 53Bb 111
Bridges Rd. HA7: Stan 22Ha 46
SW19 65Db 133
Bridges Rd. M. SW19 65Db 133
Bridge St. HA5: Pinn 27Aa 45
HP1: Hem H 3M 3
KT12: Walt T 74U 150
KT22: Lea 94Ja 192
SL3: Coln 52F 104
SW1 2F 229 (47Nb 90)
TW9: Rich 57Ma 109
TW18: Staines 63G 126
W4 49Ta 87
Bridges Wharf SW11 55Fb 111
Bridge Ter. E15 38Fc 73
Bridgetown Cl. SE19 64Ub 135
Bridge Vw. DA9: Ghithe 56Xd 120
SL5: S'dale 3F 146
W6 50Ya 88
Bridge Vw. Ct. SE1 4J 231
Bridgeview Ct. IG6: Ilf 23Tc 54
Bridge Vw. Ind. Est.
RM20: W Thur 51Wd 120
Bridge Wlk. *IG1: Ilf* 33Rc 74
(in The Exchange)
SE8 51Dc 114
(off Copperas St.)
Bridgewalk Hgts. SE1 1G 231
Bridgewater GU21: Wok 88B 168
Bridgewater Cl. BR7: Chst 69Uc 138
Bridgewater Ct. SL3: L'ly 49C 82
Bridgewater Gdns. HA8: Edg 26Pa 47
Bridgewater Highwalk EC2 7D 218
Bridgewater Rd. HA0: Wemb 37La 66
KT13: Weyb 79T 150
Bridgewater Sq. EC2 7D 218 (43Sb 91)
Bridgewater St. EC2 7D 218 (43Sb 91)
Bridgewater Ter. SL4: Wind 3H 103
Bridgewater Way SL4: Wind 3H 103
WD23: Bush 16Da 27
Bridge Way CR5: Chip 91Gb 195
KT11: Cobh 85V 170
N11 20Lb 32
NW11 29Bb 49
TW2: Whitt 59Ea 108
UB10: Ick 36R 64
Bridgeway HA0: Wemb 38Na 67
IG11: Bark 38Vc 75
Bridgeway St. NW1 2C 216 (40Lb 70)
Bridge Wharf E2 40Zb 72
KT16: Chert 73L 149
N1 1H 217
Bridge Wharf Rd. TW7: Isle 55Ka 108
Bridgewood Cl. SE20 66Xb 135
Bridgewood Rd.
KT4: Wor Pk 77Wa 154
SW16 66Mb 134
Bridge Works UB8: Cowl 42L 83
Bridge Yd. SE1 6G 225 (46Tb 91)
Bridgford St. SW18 62Eb 133
Bridgland Rd. RM19: Purf 50Sd 98
Bridgman Rd. W4 48Sa 87
Bridgnorth Ho. *SE15* 51Wb 113
(off Friary Est.)
Bridgwater Cl. RM3: Rom 22Md 57
Bridgwater Ho. W2 2A 220
Bridgwater Rd. HA4: Ruis 35W 64
RM3: Rom 22Ld 57
Bridgwater Wlk. RM3: Rom 22Md 57
Bridle Cl. EN3: Enf L 9Bc 20
KT1: King T 70Ma 131
KT19: Ewe 78Ta 153
TW16: Sun 69W 128
Bridle End KT17: Eps 85Va 174
Bridle La. KT11: Stoke D 87Da 171
KT22: Oxs 87Da 171
TW1: Twick 58Ka 108
W1 4C 222 (45Lb 90)
WD3: Loud 13L 25
Bridle M. EN5: Barn 14Bb 31
Bridle Path CR0: Bedd 76Nb 156
WD17: Wat 12X 27
Bridle Path, The IG8: Wfd G 24Gc 53
KT17: Ewe 82Ya 174
Bridlepath Way TW14: Bedf 59U 106
Bridle Rd. CR0: C'don 76Cc 158
CR2: Sande 81Wb 177
HA5: Eastc 30X 45
KT10: Clay 79Ka 152
KT17: Eps 85Va 174
Bridle Road, The CR8: Purl 82Nb 176
Bridle Way BR6: Farnb 77Sc 160
CR0: C'don 78Cc 158
Bridle Way, The CR0: Sels 82Ac 178
SM6: Wall 78Lb 156
Bridleway, The CR5: Coul 86Kb 176
Bridleway Cl. KT17: Ewe 82Ya 174
Bridlington Cl. TN16: Big H 91Kc 199
Bridlington Rd. N9 17Xb 33
WD19: Wat 20Z 27
Bridlington Spur SL1: Slou 8F 80
Bridport SE17 7F 231
Bridport Av. RM7: Rom 30Dd 56
Bridport Ho. *N1* 39Tb 71
(off Bridport Pl.)
N18 22Vb 51
(off College Gdns.)
Bridport Pl. N1 1G 219 (39Tb 71)
(not continuous)
Bridport Rd. CR7: Thor H 69Qb 134
N18 22Ub 51
UB6: G'frd 39Da 65
Bridport Way SL2: Slou 2F 80
Bridstow Pl. W2 44Cb 89
Brief St. SE5 53Rb 113
Brierfield NW1 1B 216
Brier Lea KT20: Lwr K 98Bb 195
Brierley CR0: New Ad 79Dc 158
(not continuous)
Brierley Av. N9 18Yb 34
Brierley Cl. RM11: Horn 30Ld 57
SE25 70Wb 135
Brierley Ct. W7 45Ga 86
Brierley Rd. E11 35Fc 73
SW12 61Lb 134
Brierly Gdns. E2 40Yb 72
Brier Rd. KT20: Tad 91Xa 194
Briers, The EN6: Pot B 4Db 17
Briery Ct. WD3: Chor 14J 25
Briery Fld. WD3: Chor 14J 25
Briery Way HP2: Hem H 1A 4
Brigade Cl. HA2: Harr 33Fa 66
Brigade Pl. CR3: Cat'm 94Sb 197
Brigade St. *SE3* 54Hc 115
(off Tranquil Va.)
Brigadier Av. EN2: Enf 10Sb 19
Brigadier Hill EN2: Enf 10Sb 19
Brigadier Ho. *NW9* 26Va 48
(off Heritage Av.)
Briggeford Cl. E5 33Wb 71
Briggs Cl. CR4: Mitc 67Kb 134
Briggs Ho. E2 3K 219
Brighstone Ct. RM19: Purf 50Rd 97
Bright Cl. DA17: Belv 49Zc 95
Brightfield Rd. SE12 57Gc 115
Brightlands DA11: Nflt 3A 144
Brightlands Rd. RH2: Reig 4L 207
Brightling Rd. SE4 58Bc 114
Brightlingsea Pl. E14 45Bc 92
Brightman Rd. SW18 60Fb 111
Brighton Av. E17 29Bc 52
Brighton Bldgs. SE1 4H 231
Brighton Cl. KT15: Add 78L 149
UB10: Hil 38R 64
Brighton Dr. UB5: N'olt 37Ca 65
Brighton Gro. SE14 53Ac 114
Brighton Ho. *SE5* 53Tb 113
(off Camberwell Grn.)
Brighton Rd. CR2: S Croy 78Sb 157
CR5: Coul 95Kb 196
CR8: Purl 83Qb 176
E6 41Qc 94
(not continuous)
KT6: Surb 72La 152
KT15: Add 78L 149
KT20: Kgswd, Lwr K, Tad 93Ab 194
N2 26Eb 49
N16 35Ub 71
RH1: Mers 95Kb 196
RH1: Redh 7P 207
SM2: Bans, Sutt 83Cb 175
SM7: Bans 93Ab 194
WD24: Wat 10W 12
Brighton Spur SL2: Slou 2F 80
Brighton Ter. RH1: Redh 7P 207
SW9 56Pb 112
Brights Av. RM13: Rain 42Kd 97
Brightside, The EN3: Enf H 11Zb 34
Brightside Av. TW18: Staines 66L 127
Brightside Rd. SE13 58Fc 115
Bright St. E14 43Dc 92
Brightview Cl. AL2: Brick W 1Aa 13
Brightwell Cl. CR0: C'don 74Qb 156
Brightwell Ct. *N7* 36Pb 70
(off Mackenzie Rd.)
Brightwell Cres. SW17 64Hb 133
Brightwell Rd. WD18: Wat 15W 26
Brightwen Gro. HA7: Stan 19Ja 28
Brig M. SE8 51Cc 114
Brigstock Ho. SE5 54Sb 113
Brigstock Rd. CR5: Coul 87Kb 176
CR7: Thor H 71Qb 156
DA17: Belv 49Dd 96
Brill Pl. NW1 2E 216 (40Mb 70)
Brimfield Rd. RM19: Purf 49Td 98
Brim Hill N2 28Eb 49
Brimpsfield Cl. SE2 48Xc 95
(not continuous)
BRIMSDOWN 12Bc 34
Brimsdown Av. EN3: Enf H 12Ac 34
Brimsdown Ho. E3 42Dc 92
Brimsdown Ind. Est. EN3: Brim 11Bc 34
(Lockfield Av.)
EN3: Brim 12Bc 34
(Stockingswater La.)
Brimshot La. GU24: Chob 1J 167
Brimstone Cl. BR6: Chels 80Yc 161
Brimstone Ho. *E15* 38Gc 73
(off Victoria St.)
Brind Cotts. GU24: Chob 2K 167
Brindle Ga. DA15: Sidc 60Uc 116
Brindles RM11: Horn 28Nd 57
Brindles, The SM7: Bans 89Bb 175
Brindles Cl. CM13: Hut 19Ee 41
SS17: Linf 9J 101
Brindley Cl. DA7: Bex 55Dd 118
HA0: Wemb 39Ma 67
Brindley Ho. *W2* 43Cb 89
(off Alfred Rd.)
Brindley St. SE14 53Bc 114
Brindley Way BR1: Brom 64Jc 137
HP3: Hem H 7P 3
UB1: S'hall 45Da 85
Brindwood Rd. E4 20Bc 34
Brine Ho. *E3* 40Ac 72
(off St Stephen's Rd.)
Brinkburn Cl. HA8: Edg 27Ra 47
SE2 49Wc 95
Brinkburn Gdns. HA8: Edg 27Qa 47
Brinkley KT1: King T 68Qa 131
Brinkley Rd. KT4: Wor Pk 75Xa 154
Brinklow Ct. AL3: St A 5P 5
Brinklow Cres. SE18 52Rc 116
Brinklow Ho. *W2* 43Cb 89
(off Torquay St.)
Brinkworth Pl. SL4: Old Win 9M 103
Brinkworth Rd. IG5: Ilf 27Nc 54
Brinkworth Way E9 37Bc 72
Brinley Cl. EN8: Chesh 3Zb 20
Brinsdale Rd. NW4 27Za 48
Brinsley Ho. *E1* 44Yb 92
(off Tarling St.)
Brinsley Rd. HA3: Hrw W 26Fa 46
Brinsmead AL2: F'mre 9C 6
Brinsmead Rd. RM3: Hrld W 26Qd 57
Brinsworth Cl. TW2: Twick 60Fa 108
Brinsworth Ho. TW2: Twick 61Fa 130
Brinton Wlk. SE1 7B 224
Brion Pl. E14 43Ec 92
Brisbane Av. SW19 67Db 133
Brisbane Ho. RM18: Tilb 3C 122
W12 45Xa 88
(off White City Est.)
Brisbane Rd. E10 33Dc 72
IG1: Ilf 31Rc 74
W13 47Ja 86
Brisbane Road Stadium 34Dc 72
Brisbane St. SE5 52Tb 113
Briscoe Cl. E11 33Hc 73
Briscoe Rd. RM13: Rain 40Ld 77
SW19 65Fb 133
Briset Rd. SE9 55Mc 115
Briset St. EC1 7B 218 (43Rb 91)
Briset Way N7 33Pb 70
Brisson Cl. KT10: Esh 78Ba 151
Bristol Cl. SM6: Wall 80Nb 156
TW4: Houn 59Ca 107
TW19: Stanw 58N 105
Bristol Ct. TW19: Stanw 58N 105
Bristol Gdns. SW15 59Ya 110
W9 42Db 89
Bristol Ho. *IG11: Bark* 38Wc 75
(off Margaret Bondfield Av.)
SE11 4K 229
SW1 7H 227
WC1 1G 223
WD6: Bore 12Qa 29
(off Eldon Av.)
Bristol M. W9 42Db 89
Bristol Pk. Rd. E17 28Ac 52
Bristol Rd. DA12: Grav'nd 2F 144
E7 37Lc 73
SM4: Mord 71Eb 155
UB6: G'frd 39Da 65
Bristol Way SL1: Slou 6K 81
Briston Gro. N8 30Nb 50
Briston M. NW7 24Wa 48
Bristow Ct. *E8* 39Xb 71
(off Triangle Rd.)
Bristowe Cl. SW2 58Qb 112
Bristowe Dr. RM16: Ors 4F 100
Bristow Rd. CR0: Bedd 77Nb 156
DA7: Bex 53Ad 117
SE19 64Ub 135
TW3: Houn 55Ea 108
Britain & London Vis. Cen. 6D 222
Britannia Bldg. N1 3F 219
Britannia Bus. Cen. NW2 35Za 68
Britannia Bus. Pk. EN8: Walt C 6Bc 20
Britannia Cen., The
IG10: Lough 14Tc 36
Britannia Cl. DA8: Erith 51Hd 118
SW4 56Mb 112
UB5: N'olt 41Z 85
Britannia Ct. *EN8: Walt C* 6Bc 20
(off Eleanor Cross Rd.)
KT2: King T 67Ma 131
(off Skerne Wlk.)
UB7: W Dray 48M 83
Britannia Dr. DA12: Grav'nd 4H 145
Britannia Ga. E16 46Jc 93
Britannia Ind. Est. SL3: Poyle 54G 104
BRITANNIA JUNC. 39Kb 70
Britannia La. TW2: Whitt 59Ea 108
Britannia Leisure Cen. 1G 219 (39Tb 71)
Britannia Rd. CM14: W'ley 22Yd 58
E14 49Cc 92
EN8: Walt C 6Bc 20
IG1: Ilf 34Rc 74
KT5: Surb 73Pa 153
N12 20Eb 31
SW6 52Db 111
Britannia Row N1 39Rb 71
Britannia St. WC1 3H 217 (41Pb 90)
Britannia Wlk. N1 2F 219 (40Tb 71)
(not continuous)
Britannia Way NW10 42Ra 87
SW6 52Db 111
(off Britannia Rd.)
TW19: Stanw 59M 105
Britannic Highwalk EC2 1F 225
British Disabled Water-Ski Association
60E 104
British Genius Site 52Jb 112
British Gro. W4 50Va 88
British Gro. Pas. W4 50Va 88
British Gro. Sth. W4 50Va 88
British Legion Rd. E4 19Hc 35
British Library 3E 216 (41Mb 90)
British Mus. 7F 217 (43Nb 90)
British Music Experience 46Gc 93
British Postal Mus. and Archive, The
5K 217 (42Qb 90)
British St. E3 41Bc 92
British Telecom Cen. EC1 2D 224
British Wharf Ind. Est. SE14 50Zb 92
Britley Ho. *E14* 44Bc 92
(off Copenhagen Pl.)
Briton Cl. CR2: Sande 83Ub 177
Briton Cres. CR2: Sande 83Ub 177
Briton Hill Rd. CR2: Sande 82Ub 177
Brittain Ct. SE9 60Nc 116
Brittain Rd. KT12: Hers 78Z 151
RM8: Dag 34Ad 75
Brittains La. TN13: S'oaks 96Hd 202
Brittany Ho. EN2: Enf 10Sb 19
Brittany Point SE11 6K 229 (49Qb 90)
Britten Cl. NW11 32Db 69
WD6: E'tree 16Ma 29
Britten Ct. E15 40Fc 73
Brittenden Cl. BR6: Chels 79Vc 161
Brittenden Pde. BR6: Chels 79Vc 161
Britten Dr. UB1: S'hall 44Ca 85
Britten Ho. SW3 7D 226
Brittens Cl. GU2: Guild 10L 187
Britten St. SW3 7D 226 (50Gb 89)
Brittidge Rd. NW10 38Ua 68
Britton Av. AL3: St A 2B 6
Britton Cl. SE6 59Fc 115
Britton St. EC1 6B 218 (42Rb 91)
BRITWELL 1E 80
Britwell Gdns. SL1: Burn 1B 80
Britwell Rd. SL1: Burn 1A 80
Brixham Cres. HA4: Ruis 32W 64
Brixham Gdns. IG3: Ilf 36Uc 74
Brixham Rd. DA16: Well 53Zc 117
Brixham St. E16 46Qc 94
BRIXTON 56Pb 112
Brixton Hill SW2 59Nb 112
Brixton Hill Ct. SW2 57Pb 112
Brixton Hill Pl. SW2 59Nb 112
Brixton Oval SW2 56Qb 112
Brixton Recreation Cen. *55Qb 112*
(off Brixton Sta. Rd.)
Brixton Rd. SE11 51Qb 112
SW9 56Qb 112
WD24: Wat 11X 27
Brixton Sta. Rd. SW9 55Qb 112
Brixton Water La. SW2 57Pb 112
Broad Acre AL2: Brick W 2Aa 13
Broadacre TW18: Staines 64J 127
Broadacre Cl. UB10: Ick 34R 64
Broadbent Cl. N6 32Kb 70
Broadbent St. W1 4K 221 (45Kb 90)
Broadberry Ct. N18 23Xb 51
Broadbridge Cl. SE3 52Jc 115
Broad Cl. KT12: Hers 76Z 151
BROAD COLNEY 1Ma 15
Broad Colney Lakes Nature Reserve 10H 7
Broad Comn. Est. *N16* 32Wb 71
(off Osbaldeston Rd.)
Broadcoombe CR2: Sels 80Yb 158
Broad Ct. WC2 3G 223 (44Nb 90)
Broadcroft Av. HA7: Stan 26Ma 47
Broadcroft Rd. BR5: Pet W 73Tc 160
Broad Ditch Rd.
DA13: Ist R, Nflt G 66Ee 143
Broadeaves Cl. CR2: S Croy 78Ub 157
Broadfield NW6 37Db 69
Broadfield Cl. CR0: Wadd 75Pb 156
KT20: Tad 92Ya 194
NW2 34Ya 68
RM1: Rom 29Hd 56
Broadfield Ct. *HA2: Harr* 25Da 45
(off Broadfields)
WD23: B Hea 19Ga 28
Broadfield La. NW1 38Nb 70
Broadfield Pde. *HA8: Edg* 20Ra 29
(off Glengall Rd.)
Broadfield Rd. HP2: Hem H 2P 3
SE6 59Gc 115
Broadfields EN7: G Oak 1Rb 19
HA2: Harr 26Da 45
KT8: E Mos 72Ga 152
Broadfields Av. HA8: Edg 21Ra 47
N21 16Qb 32
Broadfields Hgts. HA8: Edg 21Ra 47
Broadfields La. WD19: Wat 18X 27
Broadfield Sq. EN1: Enf 12Xb 33
Broadfields Way NW10 36Va 68
Broadfield Way IG9: Buck H 20Lc 35
WD25: A'ham 8Da 13
Broadford Ho. *E1* 42Ac 92
(off Commodore St.)
Broadford La. GU24: Chob 4J 167
Broadgate EC2 1H 225
EN9: Walt A 5Hc 21
Broadgate Arena 1H 225 (43Ub 91)
Broadgate Circ. EC2 7H 219 (43Ub 91)
Broadgate Ice Rink 1H 225
Broadgate Plaza EC2 7J 219 (43Ub 91)
Broadgate Rd. E16 44Mc 93
Broadgates Av. EN4: Had W 11Db 31
Broadgates Ct. SE11 7A 230
Broadgates Rd. SW18 60Fb 111
Broadgate Twr. EC2 6J 219 (42Ub 91)
BROAD GREEN 73Rb 157
Broad Grn. Av. CR0: C'don 73Rb 157
Broad Hall *AL10: Hat* 2B 8
(off Bishops Ri.)
BROADHAM GREEN 4H 211
Broadham Grn. Rd. RH8: Oxt 4H 211
Broadham Pl. RH8: Oxt 3H 211
Broadhead Strand NW9 25Va 48
Broadheath Dr. BR7: Chst 64Pc 138
Broad Highway KT11: Cobh 86Z 171
Broadhinton Rd. SW4 55Kb 112
Broadhoath TN15: Ivy H 98Ud 204
Broadhope Av. SS17: Stan H 3L 101
Broadhurst KT21: Asht 88Na 173
Broadhurst Av. HA8: Edg 21Ra 47
IG3: Ilf 35Vc 75
Broadhurst Cl. NW6 37Eb 69
TW10: Rich 57Pa 109
Broadhurst Gdns. HA4: Ruis 33Y 65
IG7: Chig 21Sc 54
(not continuous)
NW6 37Db 69
RH2: Reig 9K 207
Broadhurst Wlk. RM13: Rain 37Jd 76
Broadlake Cl. AL2: Lon C 9H 7
Broadlands E17 27Ac 52
RM17: Grays 50Be 99
TW13: Hanw 62Ca 129
Broadlands Av. EN3: Enf H 13Xb 33
SW16 61Nb 134
TW17: Shep 72S 150

Broadlands Cl. EN3: Enf H 13Yb 34
EN8: Walt C 6Yb 20
N6 . . . . 31Jb 70
SW16 . . . . 61Nb 134
Broadlands Ct. TW9: Kew 52Qa 109
(off Kew Gdns. Rd.)
Broadlands Dr. CR6: W'ham 91Yb 198
SL5: Asc, S'hill 3A 146
Broadlands Lodge N6 . . . . 31Hb 69
Broadlands Rd. BR1: Brom 63Kc 137
N6 . . . . 31Hb 69
Broadlands Way KT3: N Mald 72Va 154
Broad La. DA2: Wilm 63Kd 140
EC2 . . . . 7H 219 (43Ub 91)
N8 . . . . 29Pb 50
N15 . . . . 28Vb 51
TW12: Hamp 66Ba 129
Broad Lawn SE9 . . . . 61Qc 138
Broadlawns Ct. HA3: Hrw W 25Ha 46
Broadley Gdns. WD7: Shenl 4Na 15
Broadley Grn. GU20: W'sham 10B 146
Broadleys SL4: Wind 5D 102
Broadley St. NW8 . . . . 7C 214 (43Fb 89)
Broadley Ter. NW1 . . . . 6E 214 (42Gb 89)
Broadmark Rd. SL2: Slou 5M 81
Broadmayne SE17 . . . . 7F 231
Broadmead KT21: Asht 89Pa 173
RH1: Mers 100Lb 196
(off Station Rd.)
SE6 . . . . 62Cc 136
W14 . . . . 49Ab 88
Broadmead Av. KT4: Wor Pk 73Wa 154
Broadmead Cen. IG8: Wfd G 24Lc 53
(off Navestock Cres.)
Broadmead Cl. HA5: Hat E 24Aa 45
TW12: Hamp 65Ca 129
Broadmead Ct. IG8: Wfd G 23Jc 53
Broadmead Rd. GU22: Wok 94D 188
GU23: Send 94D 188
IG8: Wfd G 23Jc 53
(not continuous)
UB4: Yead 42Aa 85
UB5: N'olt 42Aa 85
Broadmeads GU23: Send 94D 188
Broad Oak IG8: Wfd G 22Kc 53
SL2: Slou 2G 80
TW16: Sun 65V 128
Broadoak Av. EN3: Enf W 7Zb 20
Broad Oak Cl. BR5: St P 68Wc 139
E4 . . . . 22Cc 52
Broadoak Cl. DA4: Sut H 65Qd 141
Broad Oak Ct. SL2: Slou 2G 80
Broadoak Ct. SW9 . . . . 55Qb 112
(off Gresham Rd.)
Broadoak Ho. NW6 . . . . 39Db 69
(off Mortimer Cres.)
Broadoak Rd. DA8: Erith 52Fd 118
Broadoaks CM16: Epp 3Vc 23
KT6: Surb 75Ra 153
Broadoaks Cres. KT14: W Byf 85K 169
Broadoaks Way BR2: Brom 71Hc 159
Broad Platts SL3: L'ly 8P 81
Broad Rd. DA10: Swans 58Ae 121
Broad Sanctuary SW1 . . . . 2E 228 (47Mb 90)
Broadstone NW1 . . . . 38Mb 70
(off Agar Gro.)
Broadstone Ho. SW8 . . . . 52Pb 112
(off Dorset Rd.)
Broadstone Pl. W1 . . . . 1H 221 (43Jb 90)
Broadstone Rd. RM12: Horn 33Jd 78
Broad St. GU24: W End 5B 166
HP2: Hem H 1M 3
RM10: Dag 38Cd 76
TW11: Tedd 65Ha 130
Broad St. Av. EC2 . . . . 1H 225 (43Ub 91)
Broad St. Mkt. RM10: Dag 38Cd 76
Broad St. Pl. EC2 . . . . 1G 225
Broadstrood IG10: Lough 10Qc 22
Broadview NW9 . . . . 30Qa 47
Broadview Av. RM16: Grays 47Fe 99
Broadview Rd. SW16 . . . . 66Mb 134
Broad Wlk. BR6: Chels 76Zc 161
CR3: Cat'm 94Vb 197
CR5: Coul 95Jb 196
KT18: Tatt C 91Za 194
N21 . . . . 19Pb 32
NW1 . . . . 1J 215 (39Jb 70)
SE3 . . . . 54Lc 115
TN15: S'oaks 100Nd 203
TW5: Hest 53Z 107
TW9: Kew 52Pa 109
W1 . . . . 5G 221 (45Hb 89)
Broad Walk, The KT8: E Mos 70Ha 130
W8 . . . . 1A 226 (46Db 89)
Broadwalk E18 . . . . 27Hc 53
HA2: Harr 29Ca 45
Broadwalk, The HA6: Nwood 26S 44
Broadwalk Ct. W8 . . . . 46Cb 89
(off Palace Gdns. Ter.)
Broadwalk Ho. EC2 . . . . 7H 219
SW7 . . . . 2A 226
Broad Wlk. La. NW11 . . . . 31Bb 69
Broadwalk Nth., The
CM13: B'wood 20Ce 41
(not continuous)
Broadwalk Shop. Cen. HA8: Edg 23Ra 47
Broadwalk Sth., The
CM13: B'wood 21Ce 59
Broadwall SE1 . . . . 6A 224 (46Qb 90)
Broadwater EN6: Pot B 2Db 17
Broadwater Cl. GU21: Wok 84F 168
KT12: Hers 78W 150
TW19: Wray 59B 104
Broadwater Farm Est. N17 . . . . 26Tb 51
Broadwater Gdns. BR6: Farnb 77Rc 160
UB9: Hare 28L 43
Broadwater La. UB9: Hare 28K 43
Broadwater Pk. UB9: Den 30J 43
Broadwater Pl. KT13: Weyb 75U 150
Broadwater Rd. N17 . . . . 25Ub 51
SE28 . . . . 48Tc 94
SW17 . . . . 63Gb 133
Broadwater Rd. Nth. KT12: Hers 78V 150
Broadwater Rd. Sth. KT12: Hers 78V 150
Broadway BR8: Crock 72Ed 162
DA6: Bex 56Ad 117
(not continuous)
E13 . . . . 40Kc 73
E15 . . . . 38Fc 73
GU21: Knap 10F 166
IG11: Bark 39Sc 74
RM2: Rom 26Jd 56
RM13: Rain 42Jd 96
RM17: Grays 51Ee 121
RM18: Tilb 4E 122
SL4: Wink 10A 102
Broadway SW1 . . . . 2D 228 (48Mb 90)
TW18: Staines 64K 127
W7 . . . . 46Ga 86
W13 . . . . 46Ja 86
Broadway, The AL1: St A 2B 6
CR0: Bedd 77Nb 156
E4 . . . . 23Fc 53
EN6: Pot B 4Bb 17
(not continuous)
GU21: Wok 89B 168
HA3: W'stone 26Ga 46
HA6: Nwood 26W 44
HA7: Stan 22La 46
HA9: Wemb 34Na 67
IG8: Wfd G 23Kc 53
IG10: Lough 14Sc 36
KT7: T Ditt 74Ga 152
KT15: New H 82J 169
N8 . . . . 30Nb 50
N9 . . . . 20Wb 33
N11 . . . . 22Hb 49
N14 . . . . 18Mb 32
(off The Bourne)
N22 . . . . 26Qb 50
NW7 . . . . 22Ua 48
RM8: Dag 32Bd 75
RM12: Horn 35Kd 77
SL2: Farn C 7G 60
SL9: Chal P 25A 42
(off Market Pl.)
SM1: Sutt 78Eb 155
SM3: Cheam 79Ab 154
SW13 . . . . 54Ua 110
SW19 . . . . 65Bb 133
TW18: Lale 69L 127
UB1: S'hall 45Z 85
UB6: G'frd 42Ea 86
W3 . . . . 47Qa 87
(off Ridgeway Dr.)
W5 . . . . 45Ma 87
WD17: Wat 13Y 27
Broadway Arc. W6 . . . . 49Ya 88
(off Hammersmith B'way.)
Broadway Av. CR0: C'don 71Tb 157
TW1: Twick 58Ka 108
Broadway Centre, The W6 . . . . 49Ya 88
Broadway Chambers W6 . . . . 49Ya 88
(off Hammersmith B'way.)
Broadway Cl. CR2: Sande 86Xb 177
IG8: Wfd G 23Kc 53
Broadway Ct. BR3: Beck 69Ec 136
GU21: Knap 9G 166
SW19 . . . . 65Cb 133
Broadway E. UB9: Den 30J 43
Broadway Gdns. CR4: Mitc 70Gb 133
IG8: Wfd G 23Kc 53
Broadway Ho. BR1: Brom 64Fc 137
(off Bromley Rd.)
E8 . . . . 39Xb 71
(off Ada St.)
GU21: Knap 10G 166
Broadway Mans. SW6 . . . . 52Cb 111
(off Fulham Rd.)
Broadway Mkt. E8 . . . . 39Xb 71
(not continuous)
IG6: Ilf 25Tc 54
(not continuous)
SW17 . . . . 63Hb 133
Broadway Mkt. M. E8 . . . . 39Wb 71
Broadway M. E5 . . . . 31Vb 71
N13 . . . . 22Pb 50
N21 . . . . 18Rb 33
Broadway Pde. E4 . . . . 23Ec 52
HA2: Harr 29Da 45
N8 . . . . 30Nb 50
RM12: Horn 35Kd 77
(off The Broadway)
UB3: Hayes 46W 84
Broadway Pl. SW19 . . . . 65Bb 133
Broadway Retail Pk. NW2 . . . . 35Za 68
Broadway Rd. GU18: Light 2A 166
GU20: W'sham 2A 166
Broadway Shop. Cen. DA6: Bex 56Cd 118
Broadway Shop. Mall
SW1 . . . . 3D 228 (48Mb 90)
Broadway Sq. DA6: Bex 56Cd 118
Broadway Theatre, The
Barking 39Sc 74
Catford 59Dc 114
Broadway Wlk. E14 . . . . 47Cc 92
Broadwell Ct. TW5: Hest 53Z 107
(off Springwell Rd.)
Broadwell Pde. NW6 . . . . 37Db 69
(off Broadhurst Gdns.)
Broadwick St. W1 . . . . 4C 222 (45Lb 90)
Broadwood DA11: Grav'nd 4D 144
Broadwood Av. HA4: Ruis 30T 44
Broadwood Rd. CR5: Coul 93Mb 196
Broadwood Ter. W8 . . . . 49Bb 89
Broad Yd. EC1 . . . . 6B 218 (42Rb 91)
Brocas Cl. NW3 . . . . 38Gb 69
Brocas St. SL4: Eton 2H 103
Brocas Ter. SL4: Eton 2H 103
Brockbridge Ho. SW15 . . . . 58Va 110
Brockdene Dr. BR2: Kes 77Mc 159
Brockdish Av. IG11: Bark 36Vc 75
Brockenhurst KT8: W Mole 71Ba 151
Brockenhurst Av. KT4: Wor Pk 74Ua 154
Brockenhurst Cl. GU21: Wok 86B 168
Brockenhurst Dr. SS17: Stan H 3L 101
Brockenhurst Gdns. IG1: Ilf 36Sc 74
NW7 . . . . 22Ua 48
Brockenhurst M. N18 . . . . 21Wb 51
Brockenhurst Rd. CR0: C'don 73Xb 157
SL5: Asc 1A 146
Brockenhurst Way SW16 . . . . 68Mb 134
Brocket Cl. IG7: Chig 21Vc 55
Brocket Ho. SW8 . . . . 54Mb 112
Brocket Rd. RM16: Grays 8C 100
Brocket Way IG7: Chig 22Uc 54
Brock Grn. RM15: S Ock 44Xd 98
Brockham Cl. SW19 . . . . 64Bb 133
Brockham Ct. CR2: S Croy 78Sb 157
RH1: Redh 4B 208
(off Goodworth Rd.)
Brockham Cres. CR0: New Ad 80Fc 159
Brockham Dr. IG2: Ilf 30Rc 54
SW2 . . . . 59Pb 112
Brockham Ho. NW1 . . . . 1C 216
SW2 . . . . 59Pb 112
(off Brockham Dr.)
Brockham St. SE1 . . . . 3E 230 (48Sb 91)
Brockhill GU21: Wok 9L 167
Brockhurst Cl. HA7: Stan 23Ha 46
Brockill Cres. SE4 . . . . 56Ac 114
Brocklebank Ct. CR3: Whyt 90Wb 177
Brocklebank Ho. E16 . . . . 46Qc 94
(off Glenister St.)
Brocklebank Ind. Est. SE7 . . . . 49Jc 93
Brocklebank Rd. SE7 . . . . 49Kc 93
SW18 . . . . 59Eb 111
Brocklehurst St. SE14 . . . . 52Zb 114
Brocklesbury Cl. WD24: Wat 13Z 27
Brocklesby Rd. SE25 . . . . 70Xb 135
BROCKLEY 56Zb 114
Brockley Av. HA7: Stan 20Na 29
Brockley Cl. HA7: Stan 21Na 47
Brockley Combe KT13: Weyb 77T 150
Brockley Cres. RM5: Col R 24Ed 56
Brockley Cross SE4 . . . . 55Ac 114
Brockley Cross Bus. Cen. SE4 . . . . . 55Ac 114
Brockley Footpath SE4 . . . . 57Ac 114
(not continuous)
SE15 . . . . 55Yb 114
Brockley Gdns. SE4 . . . . 54Bc 114
Brockley Gro. CM13: Hut 18Ce 41
SE4 . . . . 57Bc 114
Brockley Hall Rd. SE4 . . . . 57Ac 114
Brockley Hill HA7: Stan 18La 28
Brockley Jack Theatre 57Ac 114
Brockley M. SE4 . . . . 57Ac 114
Brockley Pk. SE23 . . . . 59Ac 114
Brockley Ri. SE23 . . . . 60Ac 114
Brockley Rd. SE4 . . . . 55Bc 114
Brockleyside HA7: Stan 21Na 47
Brockley Vw. SE23 . . . . 59Ac 114
Brockley Way SE4 . . . . 57Zb 114
Brockman Ri. BR1: Brom 63Fc 137
Brockmer Ho. E1 . . . . 45Xb 91
(off Crowder St.)
Brock Pl. E3 . . . . 42Dc 92
Brock Rd. E13 . . . . 43Kc 93
Brocks Dr. SM3: Cheam 76Ab 154
Brockshot Cl. TW8: Bford 50Ma 87
Brocksparkwood CM13: B'wood 20De 41
Brock St. SE15 . . . . 55Yb 114
Brockton Cl. RM1: Rom 28Hd 56
Brock Way GU25: Vir W 1N 147
Brockway TN15: Bor G 92Ce 205
Brockway Cl. E11 . . . . 33Gc 73
Brockweir E2 . . . . 40Yb 72
(off Cyprus St.)
Brockwell Av. BR3: Beck 71Dc 158
Brockwell Cl. BR5: St M Cry 71Vc 161
Brockwell Ct. SW2 . . . . 57Qb 112
Brockwell Ho. SE11 . . . . 51Pb 112
(off Vauxhall St.)
Brockwell Pk. 58Rb 113
Brockwell Pk. Gdns. SE24 . . . . 59Qb 112
Brockwell Pk. Lido 58Rb 113
Brockwell Pk. Row SW2 . . . . 59Qb 112
Brockwell Pas. SE24 . . . . 58Rb 113
Broderick Gro. KT23: Bookh 98Ca 191
Brodewater Rd. WD6: Bore 12Ra 29
Brodia Rd. N16 . . . . 34Ub 71
Brodick Ho. E3 . . . . 40Bc 72
(off Saxon Rd.)
Brodie Ho. SE1 . . . . 7K 231
Brodie Rd. E4 . . . . 18Ec 34
EN2: Enf 10Sb 19
Brodie St. SE1 . . . . 7K 231 (50Vb 91)
Brodlove La. E1 . . . . 45Zb 92
Brodrick Gro. SE2 . . . . 49Xc 95
Brodrick Rd. SW17 . . . . 61Gb 133
Brody Ho. E1 . . . . 1K 225
Brograve Gdns. BR3: Beck 68Dc 136
Broke Farm Dr. BR6: Prat B 81Yc 181
Broke Hill Golf Course 81Bd 181
Broken Furlong SL4: Eton 10F 80
Brokengate La. UB9: Den 32E 62
Broken Wharf EC4 . . . . 4D 224 (45Sb 91)
Brokes Cres. RH2: Reig 4J 207
Brokesley St. E3 . . . . 41Bc 92
Brokes Rd. RH2: Reig 4J 207
Broke Wlk. E8 . . . . 39Vb 71
Bromar Rd. SE5 . . . . 55Ub 113
Bromborough Grn. WD19: Wat 22Y 45
Bromefield HA7: Stan 25La 46
Bromefield Ct. EN9: Walt A 5Jc 21
Bromehead St. E1 . . . . 44Yb 92
Bromell's Rd. SW4 . . . . 56Lb 112
Brome Rd. SE9 . . . . 55Pc 116
Bromet Cl. WD17: Wat 10V 12
(not continuous)
Bromfelde Rd. SW4 . . . . 55Mb 112
Bromfelde Wlk. SW4 . . . . 54Mb 112
Bromfield Ct. SE16 . . . . 48Wb 91
(off Ben Smith Way)
Bromfield St. N1 . . . . 1A 218 (39Qb 70)
Bromford Cl. RH8: Oxt 5L 211
Bromhall Rd. RM8: Dag 37Xc 75
RM9: Dag 37Xc 75
Bromhead Rd. E1 . . . . 44Yb 92
(off Jubilee St.)
Bromhedge SE9 . . . . 62Pc 138
Bromholm Rd. SE2 . . . . 48Xc 95
Bromleigh Ct. SE23 . . . . 61Wb 135
Bromleigh Ho. SE1 . . . . 3K 231
BROMLEY
BR1 . . . . 68Jc 137
E3 . . . . 41Dc 92
Bromley (Park & Ride) 72Kc 159
Bromley RM17: Grays 51Ce 121
Bromley Av. BR1: Brom 66Gc 137
Bromley Coll. BR1: Brom 67Jc 137
BROMLEY COMMON 73Nc 160
Bromley Comn. BR2: Brom 70Lc 137
Bromley Cres. BR2: Brom 69Hc 137
HA4: Ruis 35V 64
Bromley Environmental Education Cen.
at High Elms (BEECHE) 79Tc 160
Bromley FC 71Kc 159
Bromley Gdns. BR2: Brom 69Hc 137
Bromley Golf Course 73Nc 160
Bromley Gro. BR2: Brom 68Fc 137
Bromley Hall Rd. E14 . . . . 43Ec 92
Bromley High St. E3 . . . . 41Dc 92
Bromley Hill BR1: Brom 65Gc 137
Bromley Ho. BR1: Brom 67Jc 137
(off North St.)
Bromley Indoor Bowls Cen. 74Yc 161
Bromley Ind. Cen. BR1: Brom 69Mc 137
Bromley La. BR7: Chst 66Sc 138
Bromley Little Theatre 67Jc 137
Bromley Mus. 73Xc 161
BROMLEY PARK 67Gc 137
Bromley Pk. BR1: Brom 67Hc 137
Bromley Pl. W1 . . . . 7B 216 (43Lb 90)
Bromley Rd. BR1: Brom 60Dc 114
BR2: Brom 68Dc 136
BR3: Beck 68Dc 136
BR7: Chst 67Rc 138
Bromley Rd. E10 . . . . 30Dc 52
E17 . . . . 27Cc 52
N17 . . . . 25Vb 51
N18 . . . . 20Tb 33
SE6 . . . . 60Dc 114
Bromley Ski Cen. 67Ad 139
Bromley St. E1 . . . . 43Zb 92
Bromley Tennis Cen. 76Tc 160
Bromley Valley Gymnastics Cen.
. . . . 68Wc 139
BROMPTON 4E 226 (48Gb 89)
Brompton Arc. SW3 . . . . 2G 227
Brompton Cl. SE20 . . . . 68Wb 135
TW4: Houn 57Ba 107
Brompton Cotts. SW10 . . . . 51Eb 111
(off Hollywood Rd.)
Brompton Ct. BR1: Brom 67Jc 137
(off Tweedy Rd.)
Brompton Dr. DA8: Erith 52Kd 119
Brompton Gro. N2 . . . . 28Gb 49
Brompton Oratory 4D 226 (48Gb 89)
Brompton Pk. Cres. SW6 . . . . 51Db 111
Brompton Pl. SW3 . . . . 3E 226 (48Gb 89)
Brompton Rd. SW1 . . . . 5D 226 (49Gb 89)
SW3 . . . . 5D 226 (49Gb 89)
Brompton Sq. SW3 . . . . 3D 226 (48Gb 89)
Brompton Ter. SE18 . . . . 53Pc 116
Brompton Vs. SW6 . . . . 51Cb 111
(off Lillie Rd.)
Bromwich Av. N6 . . . . 33Jb 70
Bromyard Av. W3 . . . . 45Ua 88
Bromyard Ho. SE15 . . . . 52Xb 113
(off Commercial Way)
Bromycroft Rd. SL2: Slou 1E 80
Bron Ct. NW6 . . . . 39Cb 69
BRONDESBURY 38Bb 69
Brondesbury Ct. NW2 . . . . 37Za 68
Brondesbury M. NW6 . . . . 38Cb 69
BRONDESBURY PARK 39Ya 68
Brondesbury Pk. NW2 . . . . 37Ya 68
NW6 . . . . 37Ya 68
Brondesbury Pk. Mans. NW6 . . . . . . 39Ab 68
(off Salusbury Rd.)
Brondesbury Rd. NW6 . . . . 40Bb 69
Brondesbury Vs. NW6 . . . . 40Bb 69
Bronhill Ter. N17 . . . . 25Wb 51
Bronsart Rd. SW6 . . . . 52Ab 110
Bronsdon Way UB9: Den 33H 63
Bronson Rd. SW20 . . . . 68Za 132
Bronte Cl. DA8: Erith 52Dd 118
E7 . . . . 35Jc 73
IG2: Ilf 28Qc 54
RM18: Tilb 4E 122
SL1: Slou 7J 81
Bronte Ct. RH1: Redh 5A 208
W3 . . . . 47Qa 87
W14 . . . . 48Za 88
(off Girdler's Rd.)
Bronte Gro. DA1: Dart 56Pd 119
Bronte Ho. N16 . . . . 36Ub 71
NW6 . . . . 41Cb 89
SW4 . . . . 59Lb 112
SW17 . . . . 62Fb 133
(off Grosvenor Way)
Bronte Vw. DA12: Grav'nd 10E 122
Bronti Cl. SE17 . . . . 7E 230 (50Sb 91)
Bronwen Ct. NW8 . . . . 4B 214
Bronze Age Way DA8: Erith 47Dd 96
DA17: Belv 47Dd 96
Bronze St. SE8 . . . . 52Cc 114
Brook Av. HA8: Edg 23Ra 47
HA9: Wemb 33Pa 67
RM10: Dag 38Dd 76
Brook Bank EN1: Enf 9Xb 19
Brookbank Av. W7 . . . . 43Fa 86
Brookbank Rd. SE13 . . . . 55Cc 114
Brook Bus. Cen. UB8: Uxb 40K 63
Brook Cl. HA4: Ruis 31U 64
KT19: Ewe 81Ua 174
NW7 . . . . 24Ab 48
RM2: Rom 25Hd 56
SW17 . . . . 61Jb 134
SW20 . . . . 69Xa 132
TW19: Stanw 59P 105
W3 . . . . 46Qa 87
WD6: Bore 12Ra 29
Brook Ct. BR3: Beck 67Bc 136
E11 . . . . 34Gc 73
E17 . . . . 27Ac 52
HA8: Edg 22Ra 47
IG11: Bark 39Vc 75
(Sebastian Ct.)
IG11: Bark 40Sc 74
(Spring Pl.)
SE12 . . . . 62Lc 137
WD7: R'lett 5Ja 14
Brook Cres. E4 . . . . 21Cc 52
N9 . . . . 21Xb 51
SL1: Slou 4C 80
Brookdale N11 . . . . 21Lb 50
Brookdale Av. RM14: Upm 34Qd 77
Brookdale Cl. RM14: Upm 34Rd 77
Brookdale Rd. DA5: Bexl 58Ad 117
E17 . . . . 27Cc 52
SE6 . . . . 59Dc 114
(Catford B'way.)
SE6 . . . . 58Dc 114
(Medusa Rd.)
Brookdales NW11 . . . . 28Ab 48
Brookdene Av. WD19: Wat 17X 27
Brookdene Dr. HA6: Nwood 24V 44
Brookdene Rd. SE18 . . . . 49Uc 94
Brook Dr. HA1: Harr 28Ea 46
HA4: Ruis 31U 64
SE11 . . . . 4A 230 (48Qb 90)
WD7: R'lett 5Ha 14
Brooke Av. HA2: Harr 34Ea 66
Brooke Cl. WD23: Bush 17Ea 28
Brooke Ct. W10 . . . . 40Ab 68
(off Kilburn La.)
Brooke Dr. DA12: Grav'nd 10K 123
Brooke Ho. SE14 . . . . 53Ac 114
WD23: Bush 17Ea 28
Brookehowse Rd. SE6 . . . . 61Cc 136
Brookend Rd. DA15: Sidc 60Uc 116
Brooke Rd. E5 . . . . 34Wb 71
E17 . . . . 28Ec 52
N16 . . . . 34Vb 71
RM17: Grays 50Ce 99
Brooker Rd. EN9: Walt A 6Ec 20
(not continuous)
Brookers Cl. KT21: Asht 89La 172
Brooke's Ct. EC1 . . . . 1K 223 (43Qb 90)
Brooke's Mkt. EC1 . . . . 7K 217
Brooke St. EC1 . . . . 1K 223 (43Qb 90)
Brooke Trad. Est. RM1: Rom 31Hd 76
Brooke Way WD23: Bush 17Ea 28
Brook Farm Rd. KT11: Cobh 87Z 171
Brookfield GU21: Wok 8M 167
N6 . . . . 34Jb 70
TN15: Kems'g 89Nd 183
Brookfield Av. E17 . . . . 28Ec 52
NW7 . . . . 23Xa 48
SM1: Sutt 77Fb 155
W5 . . . . 42Ma 87
Brookfield Cl. CM13: Hut 16Ee 41
KT16: Ott 79F 148
KT21: Asht 92Na 193
NW7 . . . . 23Xa 48
Brookfield Ct. N12 . . . . 21Db 49
UB6: G'frd 41Ea 86
Brookfield Cres. HA3: Kenton 29Na 47
NW7 . . . . 23Xa 48
Brookfield Gdns. KT10: Clay 79Ha 152
Brookfield Ho. HP2: Hem H 3M 3
(off Selden Hill)
Brookfield Pk. NW5 . . . . 34Kb 70
Brookfield Path IG8: Wfd G 23Gc 53
Brookfield Pl. KT11: Cobh 87Aa 171
Brookfield Rd. E9 . . . . 37Ac 72
N9 . . . . 20Wb 33
W4 . . . . 47Ta 87
Brookfields EN3: Pond E 14Zb 34
Brookfields Av. CR4: Mitc 71Gb 155
Brook Gdns. E4 . . . . 21Dc 52
KT2: King T 67Sa 131
SW13 . . . . 55Va 110
Brook Ga. W1 . . . . 5G 221 (45Hb 89)
BROOK GREEN 49Za 88
Brook Grn. GU24: Chob 2K 167
(off Chertsey Rd.)
W6 . . . . 48Za 88
Brook Grn. Flats W14 . . . . 48Za 88
(off Dunsany Rd.)
Brook Hill RH8: Oxt 2G 210
Brookhill Cl. EN4: E Barn 15Gb 31
SE18 . . . . 50Rc 94
Brookhill Rd. EN4: E Barn 15Gb 31
SE18 . . . . 51Rc 116
Brook Ho. E1 . . . . 45Wb 91
(off Fletcher St.)
SL1: Slou 8H 81
W6 . . . . 49Ya 88
(off Shepherd's Bush Rd.)
Brookhouse Gdns. E4 . . . . 21Gc 53
Brook Ho's. NW1 . . . . 2C 216
Brookhurst Rd. KT15: Add 79K 149
Brook Ind. Est. UB4: Yead 46Z 85
Brook Ind. Pk. BR5: St M Cry 70Yc 139
Brooking CM14: B'wood 20Xd 40
Brooking Cl. RM8: Dag 34Yc 75
Brooking Rd. E7 . . . . 36Jc 73
Brookland Cl. NW11 . . . . 28Cb 49
Brookland Ct. RH2: Reig 4K 207
Brookland Gth. NW11 . . . . 28Db 49
Brookland Hill NW11 . . . . 28Db 49
Brookland Ri. NW11 . . . . 28Cb 49
BROOKLANDS 82P 169
Brooklands DA1: Dart 60Nd 119
Brooklands, The TW7: Isle 53Fa 108
Brooklands App. RM1: Rom 28Fd 56
Brooklands Av. DA15: Sidc 61Tc 138
SW19 . . . . 61Db 133
Brooklands Bus. Pk. KT13: Weyb . . . 83N 169
Brooklands Cl. KT11: Cobh 87Aa 171
RM7: Rom 28Fd 56
TW16: Sun 67U 128
Brooklands Ct. AL1: St A 2C 6
CR4: Mitc 68Fb 133
KT1: King T 70Ma 131
(off Surbiton Rd.)
KT15: New H 82M 169
N21 . . . . 15Tb 33
NW6 . . . . 38Bb 69
Brooklands Dr. KT13: Weyb 82P 169
UB6: G'frd 39La 66
Brooklands Gdns. EN6: Pot B 4Ab 16
RM11: Horn 30Ld 57
Brooklands Ind. Est. KT13: Weyb . . . 82N 169
Brooklands La. KT13: Weyb 79P 149
RM7: Rom 28Fd 56
(not continuous)
Brooklands Mus. 81Q 170
Brooklands Pk. SE3 . . . . 55Jc 115
Brooklands Pas. SW8 . . . . 53Mb 112
Brooklands Pl. TW12: Hamp H 64Da 129
Brooklands Rd. KT7: T Ditt 74Ha 152
KT13: Weyb 84Q 170
RM7: Rom 28Fd 56
Brooklands Way RH1: Redh 4N 207
Brook La. BR1: Brom 65Jc 137
DA5: Bexl, Bex 58Zc 117
GU23: Send 94G 188
GU24: Chob 3H 167
SE3 . . . . 54Kc 115
TN15: Plax 99Ce 205
Brook La. Bus. Cen. TW8: Bford 50Ma 87
Brook La. Nth. TW8: Bford 50Ma 87
(not continuous)
Brooklea Cl. NW9 . . . . 25Ua 48
Brookleys GU24: Chob 2K 167
Brook Lodge NW11 . . . . 29Za 48
(off Nth. Circular Rd.)
RM7: Rom 28Fd 56
(off Brooklands Rd.)
Brooklyn SE20 . . . . 66Wb 135
Brooklyn Av. IG10: Lough 14Nc 36
SE25 . . . . 70Xb 135
Brooklyn Cl. GU22: Wok 91A 188
SM5: Cars 75Gb 155
Brooklyn Ct. GU22: Wok 91A 188
IG10: Lough 14Nc 36
W12 . . . . 46Ya 88
(off Frithville Gdns.)
Brooklyn Gro. SE25 . . . . 70Xb 135
Brooklyn Pas. W12 . . . . 47Ya 88
(off Lime Gro.)
Brooklyn Rd. BR2: Brom 71Mc 159
GU22: Wok 90A 168
SE25 . . . . 70Xb 135
Brooklyn Way UB7: W Dray 48M 83
Brookman Ho. E3 . . . . 40Bc 72
(off Mostyn Gro.)
Brookmans Av. AL9: Brk P 8H 9
RM16: Grays 46Ee 99
Brookmans Cl. RM14: Upm 31Ud 78
BROOKMANS PARK 8G 8
Brookmans Pk. Dr. RM14: Upm 29Ud 58
Brookmans Pk. Golf Course 7J 9
Brookmarsh Ind. Est. SE10 . . . . 52Dc 114
Brook Mead KT19: Ewe 79Ua 154
Brookmead CR0: Bedd 72Lb 156

Brookmead Av. BR1: Brom 71Pc 160
Brookmead Cl. BR5: St M Cry 73Xc 161
Brookmead Ind. Est. CR0: Bedd 72Lb 156
Brook Mdw. N12 20Db 31
Brook Mdw. Cl. IG8: Wfd G 23Gc 53
Brookmeadow Way EN9: Walt A 2Kc 21
Brookmead Rd. CR0: C'don 72Lb 156
Brookmead Way BR5: St M Cry 72Xc 161
Brook M. IG7: Chig 20Rc 36
N13 22Qb 50
WC2 3E 222
Brook M. Nth. W2 4A 220 (45Eb 89)
Brookmill Cl. WD19: Wat 17X 27
Brookmill Rd. SE8 53Cc 114
Brook Pde. IG7: Chig 20Rc 36
Brook Pk. DA1: Dart 61Qd 141
Brook Pk. Cl. N21 15Rb 33
Brook Path IG10: Lough 14Nc 36
SL1: Slou 5D 80
(not continuous)
Brook Pl. EN5: Barn 15Cb 31
Brook Ri. IG7: Chig 20Qc 36
Brook Rd. BR8: Swan 69Fd 140
CM14: B'wood 20Vd 40
CM16: Epp 5Wc 23
CR7: Thor H 70Sb 135
DA11: Nflt 10A 122
EN8: Walt C 6Bc 20
IG2: Ilf 30Uc 54
IG9: Buck H, Wfd G 19Jc 35
IG10: Lough 14Nc 36
KT6: Surb 75Na 153
N8 28Nb 50
N22 27Pb 50
NW2 33Va 68
RH1: Mers 1C 208
RH1: Redh 7P 207
RM2: Rom 26Hd 56
TW1: Twick 58Ja 108
WD6: Bore 11Qa 29
Brook Rd. Sth. TW8: Bford 51Ma 109
Brooks Av. E6 42Pc 94
Brooksbank Ho. E9 37Yb 72
(off Retreat Pl.)
Brooksbank St. E9 37Yb 72
Brooksby Ho. N1 38Qb 70
(off Liverpool Rd.)
Brooksby M. N1 38Qb 70
Brooksby St. N1 38Qb 70
Brooksby's Wlk. E9 36Zb 72
Brooks Cl. KT13: Weyb 82Q 170
SE9 61Qc 138
Brooks Ct. SW8 52Lb 112
Brookscroft CR0: Sels 82Bc 178
E17 27Dc 52
Brookscroft Rd. E17 25Dc 52
(not continuous)
Brooks Farm 31Dc 72
Brookshill HA3: Hrw W 22Fa 46
Brookshill Av. HA3: Hrw W 22Fa 46
Brookshill Dr. HA3: Hrw W 22Fa 46
Brookshill Ga. HA3: Hrw W 22Fa 46
Brooks Ho. CM14: B'wood 18Yd 40
Brookside AL10: Hat 1P 7
BR6: Orp 73Vc 161
EN4: E Barn 16Gb 31
EN6: S Mim 4Wa 16
EN9: Walt A 4Gc 21
GU4: Jac W 10P 187
IG6: Ilf 23Sc 54
KT16: Chert 73G 148
N21 16Pb 32
RH9: S God 10B 210
RM11: Horn 29Nd 57
SL3: Coln 52E 104
SM5: Cars 78Jb 156
UB10: Uxb 38P 63
WD24: Wat 9Z 13
Brookside Av. TW15: Ashf 64L 127
TW19: Wray 55A 104
Brookside Caravans WD19: Wat 17X 27
Brookside Cl. EN5: Barn 16Ab 30
HA2: Harr 35Aa 65
HA3: Kenton 29Ma 47
TW13: Felt 62W 128
Brookside Cotts. WD4: Hunt C 6S 12
Brookside Cres. KT4: Wor Pk 74Wa 154
Brookside Gdns. EN1: Enf 9Yb 20
Brookside Rd. DA13: Ist R 6B 144
N9 21Xb 51
(not continuous)
N19 33Lb 70
NW11 30Ab 48
UB4: Yead 45Y 85
WD19: Wat 17X 27
Brookside Sth. EN4: E Barn 17Jb 32
Brookside Wlk. N12 23Cb 49
NW11 28Ab 48
Brookside Way CR0: C'don 72Zb 158
Brooks La. W4 51Qa 109
Brooks Lodge N1 1J 219
Brook's M. W1 4K 221 (45Kb 90)
Brook Sq. SE18 53Nc 116
Brooks Rd. E13 39Jc 73
W4 50Qa 87
BROOK STREET 21Vd 58
Brook St. CM14: B'wood 22Td 58
DA8: Erith 50Dd 96
DA17: Belv, Erith 50Dd 96
KT1: King T 68Na 131
N17 26Vb 51
SL4: Wind 4H 103
W1 4J 221 (45Kb 90)
W2 4C 220 (45Fb 89)
BROOK STREET INTERCHANGE 22Td 58
Brooksville Av. NW6 39Ab 68
Brooks Wlk. N3 27Ab 48
Brooks Way BR5: St P 68Yc 139
Brook Va. DA8: Erith 53Dd 118
Brookview Ct. EN1: Enf 15Ub 33
Brookview Rd. SW16 64Lb 134
Brookville Rd. SW6 52Bb 111
Brook Wlk. HA8: Edg 23Ta 47
N2 25Fb 49
Brook Way IG7: Chig 20Qc 36
KT22: Lea 90Ja 172
RM13: Rain 43Kd 97
Brookway SE3 55Jc 115
BROOKWOOD 2E 186
Brookwood Av. SW13 54Va 110
Brookwood Cl. BR2: Brom 70Hc 137
Brookwood Country Pk. 1G 186
Brookwood Ho. SE1 2C 230
Brookwood Lye Rd. GU24: Brkwd 2F 186
Brookwood Rd. SW18 60Bb 111
TW3: Houn 54Da 107
Broom Av. BR5: St P 68Xc 139
Broom Cl. AL10: Hat 3B 8
BR2: Brom 72Nc 160
KT10: Esh 78Da 151
TW11: Tedd 66Ma 131
Broomcroft Av. UB5: N'olt 41Y 85
Broomcroft Cl. GU22: Pyr 88F 168
Broomcroft Dr. GU22: Pyr 87F 168
Broome Cl. KT18: Head 98Sa 193
Broome Ct. KT20: Tad 91Ab 194
Broome Lodge TW18: Staines 64J 127
(off Kingston Rd.)
Broome Pl. RM15: Avel 46Td 98
Broome Rd. TW12: Hamp 66Ba 129
Broomer Pl. EN8: Chesh 1Yb 20
Broome Way SE5 52Tb 113
Broom Farm Est. SL4: Wind 4A 102
Broomfield AL2: Park 9A 6
E17 31Bc 72
NW1 38Jb 70
(off Ferdinand St.)
TW16: Sun 67W 128
TW18: Staines 65J 127
Broomfield Av. IG10: Lough 16Pc 36
N13 22Pb 50
Broomfield Cl. RM5: Col R 24Fd 56
SL5: S'dale 3F 146
Broomfield Ct. KT13: Weyb 79R 150
Broomfield Ga. SL2: Slou 2F 80
Broomfield Ho. HA7: Stan 20Ja 28
(off Stanmore Hill)
SE17 6H 231
Broomfield La. N13 21Nb 50
Broomfield Pk. SL5: S'dale 2F 146
Broomfield Pl. W13 46Ka 86
Broomfield Ride KT22: Oxs 84Fa 172
Broomfield Ri. WD5: Ab L 4T 12
Broomfield Rd. BR3: Beck 69Ac 136
DA6: Bex 57Cd 118
DA10: Swans 57Ae 121
KT5: Surb 74Pa 153
KT15: New H 83K 169
N13 22Nb 50
RM6: Chad H 31Zc 75
TN13: S'oaks 94Hd 202
TW9: Kew 53Pa 109
TW11: Tedd 65La 130
W13 46Ka 86
Broomfields DA3: Hartl 71Ae 165
KT10: Esh 78Ea 152
Broomfield St. E14 43Cc 92
Broom Gdns. CR0: C'don 76Cc 158
Broom Gro. WD17: Wat 10W 12
Broomgrove Gdns. HA8: Edg 25Qa 47
Broomgrove Rd. SW9 54Pb 112
BROOMHALL 2E 146
Broom Hall KT22: Oxs 86Fa 172
Broomhall End GU21: Wok 88A 168
(off Broomhall La.)
Broomhall La. GU21: Wok 88A 168
SL5: S'dale 2E 146
Broomhall Rd. CR2: Sande 81Tb 177
GU21: Wok 88A 168
BROOM HILL 73Vc 161
Broom Hill HP1: Hem H 3G 2
SL2: Stoke P 8L 61
Broomhill Ct. IG8: Wfd G 23Jc 53
Broomhill Ri. DA6: Bex 57Cd 118
Broomhill Rd. BR6: Orp 73Wc 161
DA1: Dart 58Kd 119
IG3: Ilf 33Wc 75
IG8: Wfd G 23Jc 53
(not continuous)
SW18 57Cb 111
Broomhills DA13: Sflt 63Ae 143
Broomhill Wlk. IG8: Wfd G 23Hc 53
Broom Ho. SL3: L'ly 49B 82
Broomhouse La. SW6 54Cb 111
Broomhouse Rd. SW6 54Cb 111
Broomlands La.
RH8: Limp, T'sey 98Mc 199
Broom La. GU24: Chob 1J 167
Broomloan La. SM1: Sutt 75Cb 155
Broom Lock TW11: Tedd 65La 130
Broom Mead DA6: Bex 58Cd 118
Broom Pk. TW11: Tedd 66Ma 131
Broom Rd. CR0: C'don 76Cc 158
TW11: Tedd 64Ka 130
Broomsleigh Bus. Pk. SE26 64Bc 136
Broomsleigh St. NW6 36Bb 69
Broomstick Hall Rd.
EN9: Walt A 5Gc 21
Broom Water TW11: Tedd 65La 130
Broom Water W. TW11: Tedd 64La 130
Broom Way KT13: Weyb 77U 150
Broomwood Cl. CR0: C'don 71Zb 158
DA5: Bexl 61Fd 140
Broomwood Gdns. CM15: Pil H 16Wd 40
Broomwood Rd. BR5: St P 68Xc 139
SW11 58Hb 111
Broseley Gdns. RM3: Rom 21Nd 57
Broseley Gro. SE26 64Ac 136
Broseley Rd. RM3: Rom 21Nd 57
Brosse Way BR2: Brom 72Nc 160
Broster Gdns. SE25 69Vb 135
Brougham Ct. DA2: Dart 58Rd 119
(off Hardwick Cres.)
Brougham Rd. E8 39Wb 71
W3 44Sa 87
Brougham St. SW11 54Hb 111
Brough Cl. KT2: King T 64Ma 131
SW8 52Nb 112
Broughinge Rd. WD6: Bore 12Ra 29
Broughton Av. N3 27Ab 48
TW10: Ham 62Ka 130
Broughton Ct. W13 45Ka 86
Broughton Dr. SW9 56Qb 112
Broughton Gdns. N6 30Lb 50
Broughton Rd. BR6: Orp 75Tc 160
CR7: Thor H 72Qb 156
SW6 54Db 111
TN14: Otf 88Jd 182
W13 45Ka 86
Broughton Rd. App. SW6 54Db 111
Broughton St. SW8 54Jb 112
Broughton St. Ind. Est. SW11 54Jb 112
Broughton Way WD3: Rick 17J 25
Brouncker Rd. W3 47Sa 87
Brow, The HP8: Chal G 20A 24
WD25: Wat 5X 13
Brow Cl. BR5: Orp 73Zc 161
Brow Cres. BR5: Orp 74Yc 161
Browells La. TW13: Felt 61X 129
(not continuous)
Brown Bear Ct. TW13: Hanw 63Z 129
Brown Cl. SM6: Wall 80Nb 156
Browne Cl. CM14: B'wood 18Xd 40
GU22: Wok 92D 188
RM5: Col R 22Dd 56
Browne Ho. SE8 52Cc 114
(off Deptford Chu. St.)
Brownfield Area E14 44Dc 92
Brownfield St. E14 44Dc 92
Browngraves Rd. UB3: Harl 52S 106
Brown Hart Gdns.
W1 4J 221 (45Jb 90)
Brownhill Rd. SE6 59Dc 114
Browning Av. KT4: Wor Pk 74Xa 154
SM1: Sutt 77Gb 155
W7 44Ha 86
Browning Cl. DA16: Well 53Uc 116
E17 28Ec 52
RM5: Col R 24Bd 55
TW12: Hamp 63Ba 129
W9 6A 214 (42Eb 89)
Browning Ct. W14 51Bb 111
(off Turneville Rd.)
Browning Ho. N16 35Ub 71
(off Shakspeare Wlk.)
SE14 53Ac 114
(off Loring Rd.)
W12 44Ya 88
(off Wood La.)
Browning M. W1 1J 221 (43Kb 90)
Browning Rd. DA1: Dart 56Pd 119
E11 31Hc 73
E12 36Pc 74
EN2: Enf 9Tb 19
KT22: Fet 97Fa 192
Brownings, The AL2: Lon C 9F 6
Browning St. SE17 7E 230 (50Sb 91)
Browning Wlk. RM18: Tilb 4E 122
(off Coleridge Rd.)
Browning Way TW5: Hest 53Z 107
Brownlea Gdns. IG3: Ilf 33Wc 75
Brownlow Cl. EN4: E Barn 15Fb 31
Brownlow Ct. N2 29Eb 49
N11 23Nb 50
(off Brownlow Rd.)
Brownlow Farm Barns
HP1: Hem H 1F 2
Brownlow Ho. SE16 47Wb 91
(off George Row)
Brownlow M. WC1 5J 217 (42Pb 90)
Brownlow Rd. CR0: C'don 77Ub 157
E7 35Jc 73
E8 39Vb 71
N3 24Db 49
N11 23Nb 50
NW10 38Ua 68
RH1: Redh 6N 207
W13 46Ja 86
WD6: Bore 14Qa 29
Brownlow St. WC1 1J 223 (43Pb 90)
Brownrigg Rd. TW15: Ashf 63Q 128
Brown Rd. DA12: Grav'nd 10G 122
Brown's Bldgs. EC3 3J 225 (44Ub 91)
Browns Ct. SL1: Slou 5C 80
Brownsea Wlk. NW7 23Za 48
Browns La. KT24: Eff 99Z 191
NW5 36Kb 70
Brownspring Dr. SE9 63Rc 138
Browns Rd. E17 27Cc 52
KT5: Surb 73Pa 153
Brown St. W1 2F 221 (44Hb 89)
Brownswell Rd. N2 26Fb 49
BROWNSWOOD PARK 33Rb 71
Brownswood Rd. N4 34Rb 71
BROX 80E 148
Broxash Rd. SW11 58Jb 112
Broxbourne Av. E18 28Kc 53
Broxbourne Gdns. BR6: Orp 74Vc 161
(off Broxbourne Rd.)
Broxbourne Ho. E3 42Dc 92
(off Empson St.)
Broxbourne Rd. BR6: Orp 74Vc 161
E7 34Jc 73
Broxburn Dr. RM15: S Ock 45Wd 98
Broxburn Pde. RM15: S Ock 45Wd 98
Broxhill Cen. RM4: Have B 21Kd 57
Broxhill Rd. RM4: Have B 20Gd 38
Broxholme Cl. SE25 70Tb 135
Broxholme Ho. SW6 53Db 111
(off Harwood Rd.)
Broxholm Rd. SE27 62Qb 134
Brox La. KT15: Add 80E 148
KT16: Ott 80E 148
Brox M. KT16: Ott 79E 148
Brox Rd. KT16: Ott 79E 148
Broxted M. CM13: Hut 16Ee 41
Broxted Rd. SE6 61Bc 136
Broxwood Way NW8 1E 214 (39Gb 69)
Bruce Av. RM12: Horn 33Ld 77
TW17: Shep 72S 150
Bruce Castle Ct. N17 25Vb 51
(off Lordship La.)
Bruce Castle Mus. 25Ub 51
Bruce Castle Rd. N17 25Vb 51
Bruce Cl. DA16: Well 53Xc 117
KT14: Byfl 85M 169
SL1: Slou 6E 80
W10 43Za 88
Bruce Ct. DA15: Sidc 63Vc 139
Bruce Dr. CR2: Sels 81Zb 178
Bruce Gdns. N20 20Hb 31
Bruce Gro. BR6: Orp 74Wc 161
N17 25Ub 51
WD24: Wat 10Y 13
Bruce Hall M. SW17 63Jb 134
Bruce Ho. W10 43Za 88
Bruce Rd. CR4: Mitc 66Jb 134
E3 41Dc 92
EN5: Barn 13Ab 30
HA3: W'stone 26Ga 46
NW10 38Ta 67
SE25 70Tb 135
Bruces Wharf Rd.
RM17: Grays 51Ce 121
Bruce Wlk. SL4: Wind 4B 102
Bruce Way EN8: Walt C 5Zb 20
Bruckner St. W10 41Ab 88
Brudenell SL4: Wind 5D 102
Brudenell Rd. SW17 62Hb 133
Bruffs Mdw. UB5: N'olt 37Aa 65
Bruford Ct. SE8 51Cc 114
Bruges Pl. NW1 38Lb 70
(off Randolph St.)
Brumana Cl. KT13: Weyb 79R 150
Brumfield Rd. KT19: Ewe 78Sa 153
Brummel Cl. DA7: Bex 55Ed 118
Brune Ho. E1 1K 225
Brunei Gallery 7E 216 (43Mb 90)
Brunel Cl. RM1: Rom 28Gd 56
RM18: Tilb 5D 122
SE19 65Vb 135
TW5: Cran 52X 107
UB5: N'olt 41Ba 85
Brunel Ct. AL1: St A 1C 6
(off Newsom Pl.)
HP3: Hem H 4M 3
SE16 47Yb 92
(off Canon Beck Rd.)
SW13 54Va 110
(off Westfields Av.)
Brunel Est. W2 43Cb 89
Brunel Ho. CM14: B'wood 20Yd 40
E14 50Dc 92
(off Ship Yd.)
Brunel M. W10 41Za 88
(off Kilburn La.)
Brunel Mus. 47Yb 92
Brunel Pl. UB1: S'hall 44Da 85
Brunel Rd. E17 30Ac 52
IG8: Wfd G 22Pc 54
SE16 47Yb 92
W3 43Ua 88
Brunel Science Pk. UB8: Cowl 41N 83
Brunel St. E16 44Hc 93
Brunel University
Uxbridge Campus 41M 83
Brunel University Indoor Athletics Cen.
41N 83
Brunel University Sports Pk. 42P 83
Brunel Wlk. N15 29Ub 51
SW10 52Fb 111
(off Cheyne Rd.)
TW2: Whitt 59Ca 107
Brunel Way DA1: Dart 55Pd 119
SL1: Slou 6K 81
Brune St. E1 1K 225 (43Vb 91)
Brunlees Ho. SE1 4D 230
Brunner Cl. NW11 29Db 49
Brunner Ct. KT16: Ott 78E 148
Brunner Ho. SE6 63Ec 136
Brunner Rd. E17 29Ac 52
W5 42Ma 87
Bruno Pl. NW9 33Sa 67
Brunswick Av. N11 20Jb 32
RM14: Upm 31Ud 78
Brunswick Cen. WC1 5F 217 (42Nb 90)
Brunswick Cl. DA6: Bex 56Zc 117
HA5: Pinn 30Aa 45
KT7: T Ditt 74Ha 152
KT12: Walt T 75Y 151
TW2: Twick 62Fa 130
Brunswick Cl. Est. EC1 4B 218 (41Rb 91)
Brunswick Ct. CM14: W'ley 22Xd 58
EC1 4B 218
EN4: E Barn 15Fb 31
RM14: Upm 31Vd 78
SE1 2J 231 (47Ub 91)
SM1: Sutt 77Db 155
SW1 6E 228
Brunswick Cres. N11 20Jb 32
Brunswick Dr. GU24: Brkwd 2B 186
Brunswick Fitness Cen. 18Mb 32
Brunswick Flats W11 44Cb 89
(off Westbourne Gro.)
Brunswick Gdns. IG6: Ilf 24Sc 54
W5 42Na 87
W8 46Cb 89
Brunswick Gro. KT11: Cobh 85Y 171
N11 20Jb 32
Brunswick Ho. E2 1K 219
N3 25Bb 49
SE16 48Ac 92
(off Brunswick Quay)
Brunswick Ind. Pk. N11 21Kb 50
Brunswick Mans. WC1 5G 217
Brunswick M. SW16 65Mb 134
W1 2G 221 (44Hb 89)
BRUNSWICK PARK 20Hb 31
Brunswick Pk. SE5 53Ub 113
Brunswick Pk. Gdns. N11 19Jb 32
Brunswick Pk. Rd. N11 19Jb 32
Brunswick Pl. N1 4G 219 (41Tb 91)
NW1 6J 215 (42Jb 90)
(not continuous)
SE19 66Wb 135
Brunswick Quay SE16 48Zb 92
Brunswick Rd. DA6: Bex 56Zc 117
E10 32Ec 72
E14 44Ec 92
EN3: Enf L 10Cc 20
GU24: Brkwd 3A 186
(not continuous)
KT2: King T 67Qa 131
N15 28Ub 51
(not continuous)
SM1: Sutt 77Db 155
W5 42Ma 87
Brunswick Sq. N17 23Vb 51
WC1 5G 217 (42Nb 90)
Brunswick St. E17 29Ec 52
Brunswick Ter. BR3: Beck 67Dc 136
Brunswick Vs. SE5 53Ub 113
Brunswick Wlk. DA12: Grav'nd 9F 122
(not continuous)
Brunswick Way N11 21Kb 50
Brunton Pl. E14 44Ac 92
Brushfield St. E1 7J 219 (43Ub 91)
Brushfield Way GU21: Knap 1G 186
Brushrise WD24: Wat 8X 13
Brushwood Cl. E14 43Dc 92
Brushwood Dr. WD3: Chor 14E 24
Brussels Rd. SW11 56Fb 111
Bruton Cl. BR7: Chst 66Pc 138
Bruton La. W1 5A 222 (45Kb 90)
Bruton Pl. W1 5A 222 (45Kb 90)
Bruton Rd. SM4: Mord 70Eb 133
Bruton St. W1 5A 222 (45Kb 90)
Bruton Way W13 43Ja 86
Brutus Ct. SE11 6B 230
Bryan Av. NW10 38Xa 68
Bryan Cl. TW16: Sun 66W 128
Bryan Ho. NW10 38Xa 68
SE16 47Bc 92
Bryan Rd. SE16 47Bc 92
Bryan's All. SW6 54Db 111
Bryanston Av. TW2: Whitt 60Da 107
Bryanston Cl. UB2: S'hall 49Ba 85
Bryanston Ct. HP2: Hem H 3M 3
W1 2F 221
(not continuous)
Bryanstone Ct. SM1: Sutt 76Eb 155
Bryanstone Rd. EN8: Walt C 6Bc 20
N8 29Mb 50
Bryanston Mans. W1 7F 215
Bryanston M. E. W1 1F 221 (43Hb 89)
Bryanston M. W. W1 1F 221 (43Hb 89)
Bryanston Pl. W1 1F 221 (43Hb 89)
Bryanston Rd. RM18: Tilb 4E 122
Bryanston Sq. W1 1F 221 (43Hb 89)
Bryanston St. W1 3F 221 (44Hb 89)
Bryant Av. RM3: Hrld W 25Md 57
SL2: Slou 3H 81
Bryant Cl. EN5: Barn 15Bb 31
Bryant Ct. E2 1K 219
(not continuous)
W3 46Ta 87
Bryant Ho. E3 40Cc 72
(off Thomas Fyre Dr.)
Bryant Rd. UB5: N'olt 41Y 85
Bryant Row RM3: Rom 19Ld 39
Bryant St. E15 38Fc 73
Bryantwood Rd. N7 36Qb 70
Brycedale Cres. N14 21Mb 50
Bryce Ho. SE14 51Zb 114
(off John Williams Cl.)
Bryce Rd. RM8: Dag 35Yc 75
Brydale Ho. SE16 49Zb 92
(off Rotherhithe New Rd.)
Bryden Cl. SE26 64Ac 136
Brydges Pl. WC2 5F 223 (45Nb 90)
Brydges Rd. E15 36Fc 73
Brydon Wlk. N1 39Nb 70
Bryer Ct. EC2 7D 218
Bryer Pl. SL4: Wind 5B 102
Bryett Rd. N7 34Nb 70
Bryher Ct. SE11 7K 229
Brymay Cl. E3 40Cc 72
Brynford Cl. GU21: Wok 87A 168
Brynmaer Rd. SW11 53Hb 111
Bryn-y-mawr Rd. EN1: Enf 14Vb 33
Bryony Cl. IG10: Lough 14Rc 36
UB8: Hil 43P 83
Bryony Rd. W12 45Wa 88
Bryony Way TW16: Sun 65W 128
Bubblestone Rd. TN14: Otf 88Kd 183
Buccleuch Rd. SL3: Dat 2L 103
Buccleugh Ho. E5 31Wb 71
Buchanan Cl. N21 15Pb 32
RM15: Avel 46Sd 98
Buchanan Ct. SE16 49Zb 92
(off Worgan St.)
WD6: Bore 12Sa 29
Buchanan Gdns. NW10 40Xa 68
Buchan Cl. UB8: Cowl 41L 83
Buchan Ho. W3 47Ra 87
(off Hanbury Rd.)
Buchan Rd. SE15 55Yb 114
Bucharest Rd. SW18 59Eb 111
Buckbean Path RM3: Rom 24Ld 57
Buckden Cl. N2 28Hb 49
SE12 58Jc 115
Bucketsland La. WD6: Bore 10Ta 15
Buckfast Ct. W13 45Ja 86
(off Romsey Rd.)
Buckfast Ho. N14 15Lb 32
Buckfast Rd. SM4: Mord 70Db 133
Buckfast St. E2 41Wb 91
Buckfield Ct. SL0: Rich P 47H 83
Buckham Thorns Rd.
TN16: Westrm 98Sc 200
Buck Hill Wlk. W2 5C 220 (45Fb 89)
Buckhold Rd. SW18 58Cb 111
Buckhurst Av. SM5: Cars 74Gb 155
TN13: S'oaks 97Ld 203
Buckhurst Ct. RH1: Redh 4N 207
Buckhurst Ct. IG9: Buck H 18Mc 35
BUCKHURST HILL
IG9 19Mc 35
SL5 7D 124
Buckhurst Hill Ho. IG9: Buck H 19Kc 35
Buckhurst Ho. N7 36Mb 70
Buckhurst La. SL5: S'hill 9D 124
TN13: S'oaks 97Ld 203
Buckhurst Rd. SL5: Asc, S'hill 7D 124
TN16: Westrm 93Qc 200
Buckhurst St. E1 42Xb 91
Buckhurst Way IG9: Buck H 21Mc 53
Buckingham Arc. WC2 5G 223
Buckingham Av. CR7: Thor H 67Qb 134
DA16: Well 56Uc 116
KT8: W Mole 68Da 129
N20 17Eb 31
SL1: Slou 4C 80
TW14: Felt 58X 107
UB6: G'frd 39Ja 66
Buckingham Av. E. SL1: Slou 4G 80
Buckingham Chambers SW1 5C 228
Buckingham Cl. BR5: Pet W 73Uc 160
EN1: Enf 12Ub 33
RM11: Horn 30Md 57
TW12: Hamp 64Ba 129
W5 43La 86
Buckingham Ct. AL1: St A 1D 6
(off Lemsford Rd.)
NW4 27Wa 48
SM2: Sutt 81Cb 175
TW18: Staines 63J 127
(off Kingston Rd.)
UB5: N'olt 40Aa 65
W7 42Ha 86
(off Copley Cl.)
W11 45Cb 89
(off Kensington Pk.)
Buckingham Dr. BR7: Chst 63Sc 138
Buckingham Gdns. CR7: Thor H 68Qb 134
HA8: Edg 24Na 47
KT8: W Mole 68Da 129
SL1: Slou 7K 81
Buckingham Ga. SW1 3B 228 (48Lb 90)
Buckingham Gro. UB10: Hil 40Q 64
WD6: Bore 14Ta 29
Buckingham Hill Rd.
SS17: Ors, Stan H 6H 101
Buckingham La. SE23 59Ac 114
Buckingham Mans. NW6 36Db 69
(off West End La.)
Buckingham M. N1 37Ub 71
NW10 40Va 68
SW1 3B 228
Buckingham Palace 2A 228 (47Kb 90)
Buckingham Pal. Rd.
SW1 6K 227 (49Kb 90)
Buckingham Pde. HA7: Stan 22La 46
SL9: Chal P 25A 42
(off Market Pl.)
Buckingham Pl. SW1 3B 228 (48Lb 90)
Buckingham Rd. CR4: Mitc 70Nb 134
DA11: Nflt 59Fe 121
E10 34Dc 72
E11 29Lc 53

Buckingham Rd. E15 .36Hc 73
E18 .25Hc 53
HA1: Harr .29Fa 46
HA8: Edg .24Pa 47
IG1: Ilf .33Tc 74
KT1: King T .70Pa 131
N1 .37Ub 71
N22 .25Nb 50
NW10 .40Va 68
TW10: Ham .61Ma 131
TW12: Hamp .63Ba 129
WD6: Bore .14Ta 29
WD24: Wat .9Y 13
Buckinghamshire Golf Course .33L 63
Buckinghamshire New University
Uxbridge Campus .37L 63
Buckingham St. WC2 .5G 223 (45Nb 90)
Buckingham Way SM6: Wall .81Lb 176
BUCKLAND .5C 206
Buckland WD19: Wat .20Z 27
Buckland Av. SL3: Slou .9M 81
Buckland Cl. NW7 .21Wa 48
Buckland Ct. N1 .1H 219
RH1: Redh .4B 208
UB10: Ick .33S 64
Buckland Ct. Gdns. RH3: Bkld .5C 206
Buckland Cres. NW3 .38Fb 69
SL4: Wind .3D 102
Buckland Ga. SL3: Wex .1M 81
Buckland Ho. SW1 .7K 227
Buckland La. KT20: Walt H .100Wa 194
RH3: Bkld .2C 206
Buckland Ri. HA5: Pinn .25Y 45
Buckland Rd. BR6: Orp .77Uc 160
E10 .33Ec 72
KT9: Chess .78Pa 153
KT20: Lwr K .1H 207
RH2: Reig .5F 206
SM2: Cheam .82Ya 174
Bucklands, The WD3: Rick .17J 25
Bucklands Rd. TW11: Tedd .65La 130
Buckland St. N1 .2G 219 (40Tb 71)
Buckland's Wharf KT1: King T .68Ma 131
Buckland Wlk. SM4: Mord .70Eb 133
W3 .47Sa 87
Buckland Way KT4: Wor Pk .74Ya 154
Buck La. NW9 .29Ta 47
Bucklebury NW1 .5B 216
Buckleigh Av. SW20 .69Ab 132
Buckleigh Rd. SW16 .65Mb 134
Buckleigh Way SE19 .66Vb 135
Buckler Ct. N7 .36Pb 70
Buckler Gdns. SE9 .62Pc 138
Bucklers All. SW6 .51Bb 111
(not continuous)
Bucklersbury EC4 .3F 225 (44Tb 91)
Bucklersbury Pas. EC4 .3F 225 (44Tb 91)
Bucklers Ct. CM14: W'ley .22Yd 58
Buckler's Way SM5: Cars .76Hb 155
Buckles Ct. DA17: Belv .49Zc 95
Buckles La. RM15: S Ock .43Yd 98
Buckle St. E1 .44Vb 91
Buckles Way SM7: Bans .88Ab 174
Buckley Cl. DA1: Cray .54Hd 118
SE23 .59Xb 113
Buckley Ct. NW6 .38Bb 69
Buckley Ho. W14 .47Ab 88
(off Holland Pk. Av.)
Buckley Rd. NW6 .38Bb 69
Buckmaster Cl. SW9 .55Qb 112
(off Stockwell Pk. Rd.)
Buckmaster Ho. N7 .35Pb 70
Buckmaster Rd. SW11 .56Gb 111
Bucknalls Cl. WD25: Wat .4Aa 13
Bucknalls Dr. AL2: Brick W .3Ba 13
Bucknalls La. WD25: Wat .4Z 13
Bucknall St. WC2 .2E 222 (44Nb 90)
Bucknall Way BR3: Beck .70Dc 136
Bucknell Cl. SW2 .56Pb 112
Buckner Rd. SW2 .56Pb 112
Bucknill Ho. SW1 .7K 227
Bucknills Cl. KT18: Eps .86Sa 173
Buckrell Rd. E4 .19Fc 35
Buckridge Ho. EC1 .7K 217
Buck's Av. WD19: Wat .17Aa 27
Bucks Cl. KT14: W Byf .86K 169
Bucks Cross Rd. BR6: Chels .78Ad 161
DA11: Nflt .2B 144
Buckshead Ho. W2 .43Cb 89
(off Gt. Western Rd.)
BUCKS HILL .7M 11
Bucks Hill WD4: Bucks .5L 11
Buckstone Cl. SE23 .58Yb 114
Buckstone Rd. N18 .22Wb 51
Buck St. NW1 .38Kb 70
Buckters Rents SE16 .46Ac 92
Buckthorne Rd. SE4 .57Ac 114
Buckthorn Ho. DA15: Sidc .62Vc 139
(off Longlands Rd.)
E15 .41Gc 93
(off Manor Rd.)
Buckton Rd. WD6: Bore .10Pa 15
Buck Wlk. E17 .28Fc 53
Buckwell Pl. TN13: S'oaks .100Ld 203
Buckwheat Ct. DA18: Erith .48Zc 95
Budd Cl. N12 .21Db 49
Buddings Circ. HA9: Wemb .34Sa 67
Buddleia Ho. TW13: Felt .60W 106
Budd's All. TW1: Twick .57La 108
Budebury Rd. TW18: Staines .64J 127
Bude Cl. E17 .29Bc 52
Budge La. CR4: Mitc .73Hb 155
Budgen Dr. RH1: Redh .3A 208
Budge Row EC4 .3E 224 (45Tb 91)
Budge's Wlk. W2 .7A 220
Budgin's Hill BR6: Prat B .84Yc 181
Budleigh Cres. DA16: Well .53Yc 117
Budleigh Ho. SE15 .52Wb 113
(off Bird in Bush Rd.)
Budoch Ct. IG3: Ilf .33Wc 75
Budoch Dr. IG3: Ilf .33Wc 75
Buer Rd. SW6 .54Ab 110
Buff Av. SM7: Bans .86Db 175
Buffers La. KT22: Lea .91Ja 192
Bug Hill CR3: Wold .92Zb 198
CR6: W'ham, Wold .92Zb 198
Bugsby's Way SE7 .49Hc 93
SE10 .49Hc 93
Buick Ho. E3 .42Cc 92
(off Wellington Way)
KT1: King T .68Qa 131
Building 50 SE18 .48Sc 94
Building 1000 E16 .45Nc 94
Bulbarrow NW8 .39Db 69
(off Abbey Rd.)
Bulbeggars La. RH9: G'stone .4A 210
Bulbourne Cl. HP1: Hem H .3J 3
Bulbourne Ho. HP1: Hem H .4L 3
(off Cotterells)
Bulganak Rd. CR7: Thor H .70Sb 135
Bulinga St. SW1 .6F 229
Bulkeley Av. SL4: Wind .5F 102
Bulkeley Cl. TW20: Eng G .4N 125
Bullace Cl. HP1: Hem H .1J 3
Bullace La. DA1: Dart .58Nd 119
Bullace Row SE5 .53Tb 113
Bull All. DA16: Well .55Xc 117
Bullard Rd. TW11: Tedd .65Ga 130
Bullard's Pl. E2 .41Zb 92
Bullbanks Rd. DA17: Belv .49Ed 96
Bullbeggars La. GU21: Wok .8M 167
HP4: Berk, Pott E .2B 2
Bull Cl. RM16: Chaf H .47Be 99
Bulleid Way SW1 .6A 228 (49Kb 90)
Bullen Ho. E1 .42Xb 91
(off Collingwood St.)
BULLEN'S GREEN .4B 8
Bullens Grn. La. AL4: Col H .4A 8
Bullen St. SW11 .54Gb 111
Buller Cl. SE15 .52Wb 113
Buller Rd. CR7: Thor H .68Tb 135
IG11: Bark .38Uc 74
N17 .26Wb 51
N22 .26Qb 50
NW10 .41Za 88
Bullers Cl. DA14: Sidc .64Ad 139
Bullers Wood Dr. BR7: Chst .66Pc 138
Bullescroft Rd. HA8: Edg .20Qa 29
Bullfinch Cl. TN13: Riv .94Fd 202
Bullfinch Dene TN13: Riv .94Fd 202
Bullfinch La. TN13: Riv .94Fd 202
Bullfinch Rd. CR2: Sels .82Zb 178
Bullhead Rd. WD6: Bore .13Sa 29
Bull Hill DA4: Hort K .70Sd 142
KT22: Lea .93Ja 192
Bullingham Mans. W8 .47Cb 89
(off Pitt St.)
Bull Inn Ct. WC2 .5G 223
Bullivant Cl. DA9: Ghithe .57Wd 120
Bullivant St. E14 .45Ec 92
Bull La. BR7: Chst .66Tc 138
N18 .22Ub 51
RM10: Dag .34Dd 76
SL9: Chal P, Ger X .27A 42
TN15: Wro .88Ce 185
Bull Rd. E15 .40Hc 73
Bullrush Cl. AL10: Hat .1D 8
CR0: C'don .72Ub 157
SM5: Cars .75Gb 155
Bullrush Gro. UB8: Cowl .42L 83
Bull's All. SW14 .54Ta 109
Bulls Bri. Cen. UB3: Hayes .48W 84
Bullsbridge Ind. Est. UB2: S'hall .49Y 85
Bulls Bri. Rd. UB2: S'hall .49Y 85
UB3: Hayes .48X 85
Bullsbrook Rd. UB4: Yead .46Y 85
BULLS CROSS .7Wb 19
Bulls Cross EN2: Enf .7Wb 19
Bulls Cross Ride EN7: Enf, Walt C .5Wb 19
Bulls Gdns. SW3 .5E 226 (49Gb 89)
Bulls Head Pas. EC3 .3H 225
Bulls Head Row RH9: G'stone .3P 209
Bulls Head Yd. DA1: Dart .58Nd 119
(off High St.)
Bullsland Gdns. WD3: Chor .16D 24
Bullsland La. WD3: Chor .18D 24
(not continuous)
Bulls La. AL9: Brk P, Wel G .6F 8
BULLSMOOR .7Yb 20
Bullsmoor Cl. EN8: Walt C .7Yb 20
Bullsmoor Gdns. EN8: Walt C .7Xb 19
Bullsmoor La. EN1: Enf .7Wb 19
EN3: Enf W .7Xb 19
EN7: Walt C .7Wb 19
Bullsmoor Ride EN8: Walt C .7Yb 20
Bullsmoor Way EN8: Walt C .7Yb 20
BULLSWATER COMMON .8E 186
Bullswater Comn. Rd. GU24: Pirb .8E 186
Bullswater La. GU24: Pirb .7E 186
Bull Theatre, The .14Bb 31
Bullwell Cres. EN8: Chesh .1Ac 20
Bull Yd. SE15 .53Wb 113
Bulmer Gdns. HA3: Kenton .31Ma 67
Bulmer M. W11 .45Cb 89
Bulmer Pl. W11 .46Cb 89
Bulmer Wlk. RM13: Rain .40Ld 77
Bulow Est. SW6 .53Db 111
(off Pearscroft Rd.)
Bulrington Cnr. NW1 .38Lb 70
(off Camden Rd.)
BULSTRODE .1G 10
Bulstrode Av. TW3: Houn .54Ba 107
Bulstrode Ct. WD4: Chfd .1G 10
Bulstrode Ct. SL9: Ger X .30A 42
Bulstrode Gdns. TW3: Houn .55Ca 107
Bulstrode La. HP3: Hem H .7J 3
WD4: Chfd, K Lan .1G 10
Bulstrode Pl. SL1: Slou .8K 81
W1 .1J 221 (43Jb 90)
Bulstrode Rd. TW3: Houn .55Ca 107
Bulstrode St. W1 .2J 221 (44Jb 90)
Bulstrode Way SL9: Ger X .29A 42
Bulwer Ct. E11 .32Fc 73
Bulwer Ct. Rd. E11 .32Fc 73
Bulwer Gdns. EN5: New Bar .14Eb 31
Bulwer Rd. E11 .31Fc 73
EN5: New Bar .14Db 31
N18 .21Ub 51
Bulwer St. W12 .46Ya 88
Bunbury Ho. SE15 .52Wb 113
(off Fenham Rd.)
Bunbury Way KT17: Eps D .88Xa 174
Bunby Rd. SL2: Stoke P .8K 61
Bunce Dr. CR3: Cat'm .95Tb 197
Buncefield La. HP2: Hem H .1C 4
(not continuous)
Buncefield Terminal HP2: Hem H .1D 4
Bunce's Cl. SL4: Eton W .10F 80
Bunce's La. IG8: Wfd G .24Hc 53
Bundy's Way TW18: Staines .65H 127
Bungalow Rd. SE25 .70Ub 135
Bungalows, The E10 .30Ec 52
HA2: Harr .35Ba 65
IG6: Ilf .25Uc 54
SM6: Wall .78Kb 156
SW16 .66Kb 134
Bunhill Row EC1 .5F 219 (42Tb 91)
Bunhouse Pl. SW1 .7H 227 (50Jb 90)
Bunkers Hill DA14: Sidc .62Bd 139
DA17: Belv .49Cd 96
NW11 .31Eb 69
TN15: Ash .79De 165
Bunkers La. HP3: Hem H .7A 4
Bunning Way N7 .38Nb 70
Bunns La. NW7 .23Ua 48
(not continuous)
Bunny Hill DA12: Shorne .5N 145
Bunsen Ho. E3 .40Ac 72
(off Grove Rd.)
Bunsen St. E3 .40Ac 72
Bunten Meade SL1: Slou .6F 80
Buntingbridge Rd. IG2: Ilf .29Tc 54
Bunting Cl. CR4: Mitc .71Hb 155
N9 .18Zb 34
Bunting Ct. NW9 .26Ua 48
Bunton St. SE18 .48Qc 94
Bunwell Ho. E3 .42Bc 92
Bunyan Ct. EC2 .7D 218
Bunyan Rd. E17 .27Ac 52
Bunyan's La. GU24: Chob .6G 166
Bunyard Dr. GU21: Wok .86E 168
Buonaparte M.
SW1 .7D 228 (50Mb 90)
Burbage Cl. EN8: Chesh .3Bc 20
SE1 .4F 231 (48Tb 91)
UB3: Hayes .44T 84
Burbage Ho. N1 .1G 219
SE14 .51Zb 114
(off Samuel Cl.)
Burbage Rd. SE21 .58Sb 113
SE24 .58Sb 113
Burberry Cl. KT3: N Mald .68Ua 132
Burbery Cl. UB9: Hare .26M 43
Burbidge Rd. TW17: Shep .70Q 128
Burbridge Way N17 .26Wb 51
Burcham St. E14 .44Dc 92
Burcharbro Rd. SE2 .51Zc 117
Burchell Ct. WD23: Bush .17Ea 28
Burchell Ho. SE11 .7J 229
Burchell Rd. E10 .32Dc 72
SE15 .53Xb 113
Burcher Gale Gro. SE15 .52Vb 113
Burchetts Way TW17: Shep .72R 150
Burchett Way RM6: Chad H .30Bd 55
Burch Rd. DA11: Nflt .8B 122
Burchwall Cl. RM5: Col R .24Ed 56
Burcote KT13: Weyb .79T 150
Burcote Rd. SW18 .59Fb 111
Burcott Gdns. KT15: Add .79L 149
Burcott Rd. CR8: Purl .86Qb 176
Burden Cl. TW8: Bford .50La 86
Burden Ho. SW8 .52Nb 112
(off Thorncroft St.)
Burdenshot Hill GU3: Worp .7L 187
Burdenshott Av. TW10: Rich .56Ra 109
Burdenshott Rd. GU3: Worp .7L 187
Burden Way E11 .33Kc 73
Burder Cl. N1 .37Ub 71
Burder Rd. N1 .37Ub 71
Burdett Av. DA12: Shorne .3N 145
SW20 .67Wa 132
Burdett Cl. DA14: Sidc .64Ad 139
W7 .46Ha 86
Burdett M. NW3 .37Fb 69
W2 .44Db 89
Burdett Rd. CR0: C'don .72Tb 157
E3 .42Ac 92
E14 .42Ac 92
TW9: Rich .54Pa 109
Burdetts Rd. RM9: Dag .39Bd 75
Burdock Cl. CR0: C'don .74Zb 158
GU18: Light .3A 166
Burdock Rd. N17 .27Wb 51
Burdon La. SM2: Cheam .80Ab 154
Burdon Pk. SM2: Cheam .81Bb 175
Bure RM18: E Til .8L 101
Bure Ct. EN5: New Bar .15Db 31
Burfield Cl. SW17 .63Fb 133
Burfield Dr. CR6: W'ham .91Yb 198
Burfield Rd. SL4: Old Win .8L 103
WD3: Chor .15E 24
Burford Cl. IG6: Ilf .28Sc 54
RM8: Dag .34Yc 75
UB10: Ick .35N 63
Burford Gdns. N13 .20Pb 32
SL1: Slou .3A 80
Burford Ho. KT17: Ewe .83Ya 174
TW8: Bford .50Ma 87
Burford La. KT17: Ewe .83Ya 174
Burford Rd. BR1: Brom .70Nc 138
E6 .41Nc 94
E15 .39Fc 73
KT4: Wor Pk .73Va 154
SE6 .61Bc 136
SM1: Sutt .75Cb 155
TW8: Bford .50Na 87
Burford Wlk. SW6 .52Eb 111
Burford Way CR0: New Ad .79Ec 158
Burford Wharf Apartments E15 .39Fc 73
(off Cam Rd.)
Burgate Cl. DA1: Cray .55Hd 118
Burges Cl. RM11: Horn .30Pd 57
Burges Gro. SW13 .52Xa 110
Burges Rd. E6 .38Nc 74
Burgess Av. NW9 .30Ta 47
SS17: Stan H .2N 101
Burgess Bus. Pk. SE5 .52Tb 113
Burgess Cl. TW13: Hanw .63Aa 129
Burgess Ct. CM15: B'wood .18Zd 41
E6 .38Qc 74
UB1: S'hall .44Da 85
(off Fleming Rd.)
WD6: Bore .10Pa 15
(off Aycliffe Rd.)
Burgess Hill NW2 .35Cb 69
Burgess Ho. SE5 .52Sb 113
(off Bethwin Rd.)
Burgess Lofts SE5 .52Sb 113
(off Wyndham Est.)
Burgess M. SW19 .65Db 133
Burgess Pk. .51Tb 113
(off Albany Rd.)
Burgess Pk. Kart Track .51Tb 113
Burgess Rd. E6 .38Qc 74
E15 .35Gc 73
SM1: Sutt .77Db 155
Burgess St. E14 .43Cc 92
Burge St. SE1 .4G 231 (48Tb 91)
Burgess Way TW18: Staines .64J 127
Burgett Rd. SL1: Slou .8F 80
Burgh Cft. KT17: Eps .87Va 174
Burghfield KT17: Eps .87Va 174
Burghfield Rd. DA13: Ist R .6B 144
BURGH HEATH .91Ab 194
Burgh Heath Rd.
KT17: Eps, Eps D .86Va 174
Burgh House .35Fb 69
Burghill Rd. SE26 .63Ac 136
Burghley Av. KT3: N Mald .67Ta 131
WD6: Bore .15Sa 29
Burghley Hall Cl. SW19 .60Ab 110
Burghley Ho. SW19 .62Ab 132
Burghley Pas. E11 .32Gc 73
(off Burghley Rd.)
Burghley Pl. CR4: Mitc .71Hb 155
Burghley Rd. E11 .32Gc 73
N8 .27Qb 50
NW5 .35Kb 70
RM16: Chaf H .48Yd 98
SW19 .63Za 132
Burghley Twr. W3 .45Va 88
Burgh Mt. SM7: Bans .87Bb 175
Burgh St. N1 .1C 218 (40Rb 71)
Burgh Wood SM7: Bans .87Ab 174
Burgoine Quay KT1: Hamp W .67Ma 131
Burgon St. EC4 .3C 224 (44Rb 91)
Burgos Cl. CR0: Wadd .79Qb 156
Burgos Gro. SE10 .53Dc 114
Burgoyne Rd. N4 .30Rb 51
SE25 .70Vb 135
SW9 .55Pb 112
TW16: Sun .65V 128
Burgundy Ho. EN2: Enf .10Sb 19
(off Bedale Rd.)
Burgundy Pl. W12 .46Za 88
Burham Cl. SE20 .66Yb 136
BURHILL .81X 171
Burhill Golf Course .81W 170
Burhill Gro. HA5: Pinn .26Aa 45
Burhill Rd. KT12: Hers .81X 171
Burke Cl. SW15 .56Ua 110
Burke Lodge E13 .41Kc 93
Burke St. E16 .43Hc 93
(not continuous)
Burket Cl. UB2: S'hall .49Aa 85
Burland Rd. CM15: B'wood .18Zd 41
RM5: Col R .23Ed 56
SW11 .57Hb 111
Burlea Cl. KT12: Hers .78X 151
Burleigh Av. DA15: Sidc .57Vc 117
SM6: Wall .76Jb 156
Burleigh Cl. KT15: Add .78K 149
RM7: Mawney .28Dd 56
Burleigh Ct. KT22: Lea .94Ja 192
Burleigh Gdns. GU21: Wok .89B 168
N14 .18Lb 32
TW15: Ashf .64S 128
Burleigh Ho. SW3 .51Fb 111
(off Beaufort St.)
W10 .43Ab 88
(off St Charles Sq.)
Burleigh Pde. N14 .18Mb 32
Burleigh Pk. KT11: Cobh .84Aa 171
Burleigh Pl. SW15 .57Za 110
Burleigh Rd. AL1: St A .2F 6
EN1: Enf .14Ub 33
EN8: Chesh .4Ac 20
HP2: Hem H .3C 4
KT15: Add .78K 149
SM3: Sutt .74Ab 154
UB10: Hil .39R 64
Burleigh St. WC2 .4G 223 (45Pb 90)
Burleigh Wlk. SE6 .60Ec 114
Burleigh Way EN2: Enf .13Tb 33
EN6: Cuff .2Nb 18
Burlescombe Ho. RH1: Redh .4A 208
(off Burrage Rd.)
Burley Cl. E4 .22Cc 52
SW16 .68Mb 134
Burley Ho. E1 .44Zb 92
(off Chudleigh St.)
WD5: Ab L .4V 12
Burley Orchard KT16: Chert .72J 149
Burley Rd. E16 .44Lc 93
BURLINGS .89Vc 181
Burlings La. TN14: Knock .89Vc 181
Burlington Arc. W1 .5B 222 (45Lb 90)
Burlington Av. RM7: Rom .30Dd 56
SL1: Slou .7J 81
TW9: Kew .53Qa 109
Burlington Cl. BR6: Farnb .75Rc 160
E6 .44Nc 94
HA5: Eastc .27X 45
TW14: Bedf .59T 106
W9 .42Cb 89
Burlington Ct. RH1: Redh .5P 207
(off Station Rd.)
SL1: Slou .7J 81
Burlington Gdns. RM6: Chad H .31Ad 75
SW6 .54Ab 110
W1 .5B 222 (45Lb 90)
W3 .46Sa 87
W4 .50Sa 87
Burlington Ho. N15 .30Tb 51
(off Tewkesbury Rd.)
UB7: W Dray .47P 83
(off Park Lodge Av.)
Burlington La. W4 .52Sa 109
Burlington M. SW15 .57Bb 111
W3 .46Sa 87
Burlington Pl. IG8: Wfd G .20Kc 35
RH2: Reig .5J 207
SW6 .54Ab 110
TN13: S'oaks .95Jd 202
Burlington Ri. EN4: E Barn .18Gb 31
Burlington Rd. CR7: Thor H .68Sb 135
EN2: Enf .11Tb 33
KT3: N Mald .70Va 132
N10 .27Jb 50
N17 .25Wb 51
SL1: Burn .2A 80
SL1: Slou .7J 81
SW6 .54Ab 110
TW7: Isle .53Fa 108
W4 .50Sa 87
Burma M. N16 .35Tb 71
Burman Cl. DA2: Dart .59Sd 120
Burma Rd. GU24: Chob .6K 147
N16 .35Tb 71
Burmarsh NW5 .37Jb 70
Burmarsh Ct. SE20 .67Yb 136
Burma Ter. SE19 .64Ub 135
Burmester Rd. SW17 .62Eb 133
Burnaby Cres. W4 .51Sa 109
Burnaby Gdns. W4 .51Ra 109
Burnaby Rd. DA11: Nflt .9A 122
Burnaby St. SW10 .52Eb 111
Burnand Ho. W14 .48Za 88
(off Redan St.)
Burnbrae Cl. N12 .23Db 49
Burnbury Rd. SW12 .60Lb 112
Burn Cl. KT15: Add .77M 149
KT22: Oxs .87Fa 172
WD25: A'ham .13Fa 28
Burncroft Av. EN3: Enf H .12Yb 34
Burndell Way UB4: Yead .43Z 85
Burne Jones Ho. W14 .49Ab 88
Burnell Av. DA16: Well .54Wc 117
TW10: Ham .64La 130
Burnell Gdns. HA7: Stan .26Ma 47
Burnelli Bldg. SW8 .52Kb 112
(off Sopwith Way)
Burnell Rd. SM1: Sutt .77Db 155
Burnell Wlk. CM13: Gt War .23Yd 58
SE1 .50Vb 91
(off Cadet Dr.)
Burnels Av. E6 .41Qc 94
Burness Cl. N7 .37Pb 70
UB8: Uxb .40M 63
Burne St. NW1 .7D 214 (43Gb 89)
Burnet Cl. GU24: W End .5C 166
HP3: Hem H .3N 3
Burnet Gro. KT19: Eps .85Sa 173
Burnett Cl. E9 .36Yb 72
Burnett Ho. SE13 .54Ec 114
(off Lewisham Hill)
Burnett Rd. DA8: Erith .51Md 119
IG6: Ilf .24Rc 54
Burnetts Rd. SL4: Wind .3C 102
Burney Av. KT5: Surb .71Pa 153
Burney Cl. KT22: Fet .97Ea 192
Burney Dr. IG10: Lough .12Rc 36
(not continuous)
Burney Ho. KT22: Lea .93Ja 192
(off Highbury Dr.)
Burney St. SE10 .52Ec 114
Burnfoot Av. SW6 .53Ab 110
BURNHAM .1A 80
Burnham NW3 .38Gb 69
Burnham Av. UB10: Ick .35S 64
BURNHAM BEECHES .6F 60
Burnham Beeches Golf Course .9B 60
Burnham Beeches National Nature Reserve
.7D 60
Burnham Cl. EN1: Enf .10Ub 19
GU21: Knap .10H 167
HA3: W'stone .28Ja 46
NW7 .24Wa 48
SE1 .6K 231 (49Vb 91)
SL4: Wind .4B 102
Burnham Ct. NW4 .28Ya 48
(off Brent St.)
NW6 .38Eb 69
(off Fairhazel Gdns.)
W2 .45Db 89
(off Moscow Rd.)
Burnham Cres. DA1: Dart .56Ld 119
E11 .28Lc 53
Burnham Dr. KT4: Wor Pk .75Za 154
RH2: Reig .5J 207
Burnham Est. E2 .41Yb 92
(off Burnham St.)
Burnham Gdns. CR0: C'don .73Vb 157
TW4: Cran .53X 107
UB3: Harl .48T 84
Burnham Hgts. SL1: Slou .4A 80
Burnham La. SL1: Slou .3B 80
Burnham Rd. AL1: St A .2E 6
DA1: Dart .56Ld 119
DA14: Sidc .61Ad 139
E4 .22Bc 52
GU21: Knap .10H 167
RM7: Rom .27Fd 56
RM9: Dag .38Xc 75
SM4: Mord .70Db 133
Burnhams Gro. KT19: Eps .83Ra 173
Burnhams Rd. KT23: Bookh .96Aa 191
Burnham St. E2 .41Yb 92
KT2: King T .67Qa 131
Burnham Ter. DA1: Dart .57Md 119
Burnham Trad. Est. DA1: Dart .56Md 119
Burnham Way SE26 .64Bc 136
W13 .49Ka 86
Burnhill Cl. SE15 .52Xb 113
Burnhill Ho. EC1 .4D 218
Burnhill Rd. BR3: Beck .68Cc 136
Burnley Cl. WD19: Wat .22Y 45
Burnley Rd. NW10 .36Va 68
RM20: W Thur .53Vd 120
SW9 .54Pb 112
Burnsall St. SW3 .7E 226 (50Gb 89)
Burns Av. DA15: Sidc .58Xc 117
RM6: Chad H .31Yc 75
TW14: Felt .58W 106
UB1: S'hall .45Ca 85
Burns Cl. DA8: Erith .53Hd 118
DA16: Well .53Vc 117
E17 .28Ec 52
SM5: Cars .81Jb 176
SW19 .65Fb 133
UB4: Hayes .43V 84
Burns Dr. SM7: Bans .86Ab 174
Burns Ho. E2 .41Yb 92
(off Cornwall Av.)
SE17 .50Rb 91
(off Doddington Gro.)
Burnside AL1: St A .4F 6
KT21: Asht .90Pa 173
Burnside Av. E4 .23Bc 52
Burnside Cl. EN5: New Bar .13Cb 31
SE16 .46Zb 92
TW1: Twick .58Ja 108
Burnside Ct. SM5: Cars .76Jb 156
Burnside Cres. HA0: Wemb .39Ma 67
Burnside Ind. Est. IG6: Ilf .22Xc 55
Burnside Rd. RM8: Dag .33Yc 75
Burns Pl. RM18: Tilb .3D 122
Burns Rd. HA0: Wemb .40Na 67
NW10 .39Va 68
SW11 .54Hb 111
W13 .47Ka 86
Burns Way CM13: Hut .16Fe 41
TW5: Hest .54Z 107
Burnt Ash Hgts. BR1: Brom .64Kc 137
Burnt Ash Hill SE12 .58Hc 115
Burnt Ash La. BR1: Brom .66Jc 137
Burnt Ash Rd. SE12 .57Hc 115
BURNTCOMMON .97H 189
Burnt Comn. Cl. GU23: Rip .97H 189
Burnt Comn. La. GU23: Rip .97J 189
Burntfarm Ride EN2: Crew H .6Qb 18
EN7: Walt C .5Rb 19
Burnt Ho. La. DA1: Dart .62Nd 141
DA2: Hawl .63Nd 141
Burnthwaite Rd. SW6 .52Bb 111
BURNT OAK .25Ra 47
Burnt Oak Apartments E16 .44Jc 93
(off Pacific Rd.)
Burnt Oak B'way. HA8: Edg .24Qa 47
Burnt Oak Flds. HA8: Edg .25Sa 47

Burnt Oak La. DA15: Sidc 58Wc 117
Burnt Pollard La. GU18: Light 2C 166
Burntwood CM14: B'wood 20Yd 40
Burntwood Av. RM11: Horn 30Md 57
Burntwood Cl. CM13: W H'dn 30Fe 59
CR3: Cat'm 93Wb 197
SW18 ....60Gb 111
Burntwood Grange Rd. SW18 ......60Fb 111
Burntwood Gro. TN13: S'oaks 99Kd 203
Burntwood La. CR3: Cat'm 94Ub 197
SW17 ....62Eb 133
Burntwood Rd. TN13: S'oaks 100Kd 203
Burntwood Vw. SE19 ....64Vb 135
Burn Wlk. SL1: Burn 1A 80
Burnway RM11: Horn 31Nd 77
Buross St. E1 ....44Xb 91
Burpham Cl. UB4: Yead 43Z 85
Burrage Ct. SE16 ....49Zb 92
(off Worgan St.)
Burrage Gro. SE18 ....49Sc 94
Burrage Pl. SE18 ....50Rc 94
Burrage Rd. RH1: Redh 4B 208
SE18 ....50Sc 94
Burrard Ho. E2 ....40Yb 72
(off Bishop's Way)
Burrard Rd. E16 ....44Kc 93
NW6 ....36Cb 69
Burr Bank Ter. DA2: Wilm 63Ld 141
Burr Cl. AL2: Lon C 9J 7
DA7: Bex 55Bd 117
E1 ....46Wb 91
Burrell Cl. CR0: C'don 72Ac 158
HA8: Edg 19Ra 29
Burrell Row BR3: Beck 68Cc 136
Burrells, The KT16: Chert 74K 149
Burrell St. SE1 ....6B 224 (46Rb 91)
Burrells Wharf Sq. E14 ....50Dc 92
Burrell Towers E10 ....31Cc 72
Burrfield Dr. BR5: St M Cry 71Zc 161
Burrhill Ct. SE16 ....48Zb 92
(off Worgan St.)
Burr Hill La. GU24: Chob 1K 167
Burritt Rd. KT1: King T 68Qa 131
Burroughs, The NW4 ....28Xa 48
Burroughs Club, The 28Xa 48
Burroughs Cotts. E14 ....43Ac 92
(off Halley St.)
Burroughs Gdns. NW4 ....28Xa 48
Burroughs Pde. NW4 ....28Xa 48
Burroway Rd. SL3: L'ly 48D 82
Burrow Cl. IG7: Chig 22Vc 55
Burrow Grn. IG7: Chig 22Vc 55
BURROW HILL 4C 186
BURROWHILL 1J 167
Burrow Hill Grn. GU24: Chob 1H 167
Burrow Ho. SW9 ....54Qb 112
(off Stockwell Pk. Rd.)
Burrow Rd. IG7: Chig 22Vc 55
SE22 ....56Ub 113
Burrows Chase EN9: Walt A 7Fc 21
Burrows Cl. KT23: Bookh 96Ba 191
Burrows M. SE1 ....1B 230 (47Rb 91)
Burrows Rd. NW10 ....41Ya 88
Burrow Wlk. SE21 ....59Sb 113
Burr Rd. SW18 ....60Cb 111
Bursar St. SE1 ....7H 225 (46Ub 91)
Bursdon Cl. DA15: Sidc 61Vc 139
Burses Way CM13: Hut 17De 41
Bursland Rd. EN3: Pond E 14Zb 34
Burslem Av. IG6: Ilf 23Wc 55
Burslem St. E1 ....44Wb 91
Burstead Cl. KT11: Cobh 84Z 171
Burstock Rd. SW15 ....56Ab 110
Burston Dr. AL2: Park 10A 6
Burston Rd. SW15 ....57Za 110
Burston Vs. SW15 ....57Za 110
(off St John's Av.)
Burstow Rd. SW20 ....67Ab 132
Burtenshaw Rd. KT7: T Ditt 73Ja 152
Burtley Cl. N4 ....32Sb 71
Burton Av. WD18: Wat 14W 26
Burton Bank N1 ....38Tb 71
(off Yeate St.)
Burton Cl. CR7: Thor H 69Tb 135
GU20: W'sham 9B 146
KT9: Chess 80Ma 153
Burton Ct. KT7: T Ditt 72Ja 152
SE20 ....68Yb 136
SW3 ....7G 227
(not continuous)
Burton Dr. EN3: Enf L 9Cc 20
Burton Gdns. TW5: Hest 53Ba 107
Burton Gro. SE17 ....7F 231 (50Tb 91)
Burtonhole Cl. NW7 ....21Za 48
Burtonhole La. N12 ....21Ab 48
NW7 ....22Ya 48
Burton Ho. SE16 ....47Xb 91
(off Cherry Gdn. St.)
Burton La. EN7: G Oak 1Ub 19
SW9 ....54Qb 112
(not continuous)
Burton M. SW1 ....6J 227 (49Jb 90)
Burton Pl. WC1 ....5E 216 (41Mb 90)
Burton Rd. E18 ....27Kc 53
IG10: Lough 14Sc 36
KT2: King T 66Na 131
NW6 ....38Bb 69
SW9 ....54Rb 113
(Akerman Rd.)
SW9 ....54Qb 112
(Evesham Wlk.)
Burtons Ct. E15 ....38Fc 73
Burton's La. HP8: Chal G 13A 24
WD3: Chor 15B 24
Burton's Rd. TW12: Hamp H 63Da 129
Burton St. WC1 ....4E 216 (41Mb 90)
Burton Way SL4: Wind 5C 102
Burtonwood Ho. N4 ....31Tb 71
Burtop Rd. Est. SW17 ....62Eb 133
Burt Rd. E16 ....46Lc 93
Burts Wharf DA17: Belv 45Ed 96
Burtt Ho. N1 ....3H 219
Burtwell La. SE27 ....63Tb 135
Burvale Ct. WD18: Wat 13X 27
Burwash Ct. BR5: St M Cry 71Yc 161
Burwash Ho. SE1 ....2G 231
Burwash Rd. SE18 ....50Tc 94
Burway Cl. CR2: S Croy 79Ub 157
Burway Cres. KT16: Chert 70J 127
Burwell KT1: King T 68Qa 131
(off Excelsior Rd.)
Burwell Av. UB6: G'frd 37Ga 66
Burwell Cl. E1 ....44Xb 91
Burwell Rd. E10 ....32Ac 72
Burwell Rd. Ind. Est. E10 ....32Ac 72
Burwell Wlk. E3 ....42Cc 92
Burwood Av. BR2: Hayes 75Kc 159
CR8: Kenley 86Rb 177
HA5: Eastc 29X 45
Burwood Cl. KT6: Surb 74Qa 153
KT12: Hers 79Y 151
RH2: Reig 6M 207
Burwood Gdns. RM13: Rain 41Hd 96
Burwood Ho. SW9 ....56Rb 113
Burwood Pde. KT16: Chert 73J 149
(off Guildford St.)
BURWOOD PARK
KT11 ....84W 170
KT12 ....78W 150
Burwood Pk. Rd. KT12: Hers 77X 151
Burwood Pl. EN4: Had W 11Eb 31
W2 ....2E 220 (44Gb 89)
Burwood Rd. KT12: Hers 80U 150
Bury, The HP1: Hem H 1L 3
WD3: Rick 18M 25
Bury Av. HA4: Ruis 30S 44
UB4: Hayes 40U 64
Bury Cl. GU21: Wok 8P 167
SE16 ....46Zb 92
Bury Ct. EC3 ....2J 225 (44Ub 91)
HP1: Hem H 2L 3
Burydell La. AL2: Park 9B 6
Buryfield Ct. SE8 ....49Zb 92
(off Lower Rd.)
BURY GREEN 3Wb 19
Bury Grn. HP1: Hem H 1L 3
Bury Grn. Rd. EN7: Chesh, Walt C 3Wb 19
(not continuous)
Bury Gro. SM4: Mord 71Db 155
Bury Hall Vs. N9 ....17Vb 33
Bury Hill HP1: Hem H 1K 3
Bury Hill Cl. HP1: Hem H 1L 3
Bury La. CM16: Epp 1Tc 22
GU21: Wok 8N 167
WD3: Rick 18M 25
Bury Mdws. WD3: Rick 18M 25
Bury M. RM1: Rom 30Hd 56
WD3: Rick 18M 25
(off Bury La.)
Bury Pl. WC1 ....1F 223 (43Nb 90)
Bury Ri. HP3: Hem H 7F 2
Bury Rd. CM16: Epp 3Uc 22
E4 ....13Fc 35
HP1: Hem H 1L 3
N22 ....26Qb 50
RM10: Dag 36Dd 76
Buryside Cl. IG2: Ilf 28Vc 55
Bury St. EC3 ....3J 225 (44Ub 91)
HA4: Ruis 29S 44
N9 ....17Vb 33
SW1 ....6B 222 (46Lb 90)
Bury St. W. N9 ....17Tb 33
Bury Wlk. SW3 ....6D 226 (49Gb 89)
Busbridge Ho. E14 ....43Cc 92
(off Brabazon St.)
Busby Ho. SW16 ....63Lb 134
Busby M. NW5 ....37Mb 70
Busby Pl. NW5 ....37Mb 70
Busch Cl. TW7: Isle 53Ka 108
Bushbaby Cl. SE1 ....4H 231 (48Ub 91)
Bushberns EN7: Chesh 1Wb 19
Bushberry Rd. E9 ....37Ac 72
Bush Cl. IG2: Ilf 29Tc 54
KT15: Add 78L 149
Bush Cotts. SW18 ....57Cb 111
Bush Ct. N14 ....18Mb 32
W12 ....47Za 88
Bushell Cl. SW2 ....61Pb 134
Bushell Grn. WD23: B Hea 19Fa 28
Bushell St. E1 ....46Wb 91
Bushell Way BR7: Chst 64Qc 138
Bush Elms Rd. RM11: Horn 31Jd 76
Bushetts Gro. RH1: Mers 1B 208
BUSHEY 16Ca 27
Bushey Av. BR5: Pet W 73Tc 160
E18 ....27Hc 53
Bushey Cl. CR8: Kenley 88Vb 177
E4 ....20Ec 34
UB10: Ick 33Q 64
Bushey Ct. DA8: Erith 53Jd 118
SW20 ....69Xa 132
Bushey Cft. RH8: Oxt 2G 210
Bushey Down SW12 ....61Kb 134
Bushey Golf Course 16Ca 27
Bushey Grove Leisure Cen. 13Ba 27
Bushey Gro. Rd. WD23: Bush 14Z 27
Bushey Hall Dr. WD23: Bush 14Aa 27
Bushey Hall Golf Course 14Aa 27
Bushey Hall Pk. WD23: Bush 13Aa 27
Bushey Hall Rd. WD23: Bush 14Z 27
BUSHEY HEATH 18Fa 28
Bushey Hill Rd. SE5 ....53Ub 113
Bushey La. SM1: Sutt 77Cb 155
Bushey Lees DA15: Sidc 58Vc 117
BUSHEY MEAD 68Za 132
Bushey Mill Cres. WD24: Wat 9Y 13
Bushey Mill La. WD24: Bush, Wat 9Y 13
(not continuous)
Bushey Mill Rd. WD23: Bush 10Z 13
Bushey Mus. & Art Gallery 16Ca 27
Bushey Pk. WD23: Bush 16Ca 27
Bushey Rd. CR0: C'don 75Cc 158
E13 ....40Lc 73
N15 ....30Ub 51
SM1: Sutt 77Cb 155
SW20 ....69Xa 132
UB3: Harl 49U 84
UB10: Ick 33Q 64
Bushey Shaw KT21: Asht 89Ka 172
Bushey Vw. Wlk. WD24: Wat 12Z 27
Bushey Way BR3: Beck 72Fc 159
Bush Fair Ct. N14 ....16Kb 32
Bushfield Cl. HA8: Edg 19Ra 29
Bushfield Cres. HA8: Edg 19Ra 29
Bushfield Dr. RH1: Redh 10A 208
Bushfield Rd. HP3: Bov 7E 2
Bushfields IG10: Lough 15Qc 36
Bushfield Wlk. DA10: Swans 58Ae 121
Bush Gro. HA7: Stan 25Ma 47
NW9 ....31Sa 67
Bushgrove Rd. RM8: Dag 35Zc 75
Bush Hill N21 ....17Sb 33
Bush Hill Pde. EN1: Enf 17Tb 33
N9 ....17Tb 33
BUSH HILL PARK 16Vb 33
Bush Hill Pk. Golf Course 15Sb 33
Bush Hill Rd. HA3: Kenton 30Pa 47
N21 ....16Tb 33
Bush Ind. Est. N19 ....34Lb 70
NW10 ....42Ta 87
Bush La. EC4 ....4F 225 (45Tb 91)
GU23: Send 96F 188
Bushmead Cl. N15 ....28Vb 51
Bushmoor Cres. SE18 ....52Rc 116
Bushnell Rd. SW17 ....61Kb 134
Bush Rd. E8 ....39Xb 71
E11 ....31Hc 73
IG9: Buck H 21Mc 53
SE8 ....49Zb 92
(off Rotherhithe New Rd.)
TW9: Kew 51Pa 109
TW17: Shep 71P 149
Bush Theatre 47Ya 88
Bushway RM8: Dag 35Zc 75
Bushwood E11 ....31Hc 73
Bushwood Cl. AL9: Wel G 5D 8
Bushwood Dr. SE1 ....6K 231 (49Vb 91)
Bushwood Rd. TW9: Kew 51Qa 109
Bushy Cl. RM1: Rom 23Fd 56
Bushy Ct. KT1: Hamp W 67La 130
(off Beverley Rd.)
Bushy Pk. 66Fa 130
Bushy Pk. Gdns. TW11: Tedd 64Fa 130
Bushy Pk. Rd. TW11: Tedd 66Ka 130
(not continuous)
Bushy Rd. KT22: Fet 94Da 191
TW11: Tedd 65Ha 130
Business Centre, The RM3: Rom 24Md 57
Business Design Cen. N1 ....1A 218
Business Innovation Cen., The
EN3: Enf L 8Bc 20
(off Innova Bus. Pk.)
Business Pk. 5 KT22: Lea 92Ha 192
Business Pk. 8 KT22: Lea 91Ka 192
Business Pk. 25 RH1: Redh 4B 208
Business Village, The SL2: Slou 6M 81
SW18 ....57Cb 111
Buspace Studios W10 ....42Ab 88
(off Conlan St.)
Busty La. TN15: Igh 93Zd 205
Butcher Row E14 ....45Zb 92
Butchers Hill DA12: Shorne 4N 145
Butcher's La. TN15: Ash, Hartl 75Zd 165
Butchers M. UB3: Hayes 45V 84
(off Hemmen La.)
Butchers Rd. E16 ....44Jc 93
Butchers Yd. BR6: Downe 83Qc 180
Butcher Wlk. DA10: Swans 59Ae 121
Bute Av. TW10: Ham 61Na 131
Bute Ct. SM6: Wall 78Lb 156
Bute Gdns. SM6: Wall 78Lb 156
TW10: Ham 60Na 109
W6 ....49Za 88
Bute Gdns. W. SM6: Wall 78Lb 156
Bute M. NW11 ....29Eb 49
Bute Rd. CR0: C'don 74Qb 156
IG6: Ilf 29Rc 54
SM6: Wall 77Lb 156
Bute St. SW7 ....5B 226 (49Fb 89)
Bute Wlk. N1 ....37Tb 71
Butfield Ho. E9 ....37Yb 72
(off Stevens Av.)
Butler Av. HA1: Harr 31Fa 66
Butler Cl. HA8: Edg 26Ra 47
Butler Ct. HA0: Wemb 35Ja 66
RM8: Dag 33Cd 76
(off Gosfield Rd.)
Butler Farm Cl. TW10: Ham 63Ma 131
Butler Hall AL10: Hat 2B 8
(off Bishops Ri.)
Butler Ho. E2 ....41Yb 92
(off Bacton St.)
E3 ....43Bc 92
(off Geoffrey Chaucer Way)
E14 ....44Bc 92
(off Burdett St.)
RM17: Grays 51De 121
(off Argent St.)
SW9 ....53Rb 113
(off Lothian Rd.)
Butler Pl. SW1 ....3D 228 (48Mb 90)
Butler Rd. HA1: Harr 31Ea 66
NW10 ....38Va 68
RM8: Dag 35Xc 75
Butlers & Colonial Wharf SE1 ....1K 231
Butlers Cl. SL4: Wind 3B 102
TW4: Houn 55Ba 107
Butlers Ct. EN8: Walt C 4Ac 20
Butlers Dene Rd. CR3: Wold 92Bc 198
Butlers Dr. E4 ....10Ec 20
Butler's Pl. TN15: Ash 76Ae 165
Butler St. E2 ....41Yb 92
UB10: Hil 42R 84
Butlers Wharf SE1 ....7K 225 (46Vb 91)
Butlers Wharf W. SE1 ....7K 225
Butler Wlk. RM17: Grays 49Fe 99
Butley Ct. E3 ....40Ac 72
(off Ford St.)
Buttell Cl. RM17: Grays 50Fe 99
Buttercross La. CM16: Epp 2Wc 23
Buttercup Cl. RM3: Hrld W 25Md 57
UB5: N'olt 37Ba 65
Buttercup Sq. TW19: Stanw 60M 105
Butterfield Cl. N17 ....23Sb 51
SE16 ....47Xb 91
TW1: Twick 58Ha 108
Butterfield La. AL1: St A 6C 6
Butterfields E17 ....29Ec 52
Butterfield Sq. E6 ....44Pc 94
Butterfly Ct. NW9 ....25Ua 48
Butterfly La. SE9 ....58Rc 116
WD6: E'tree 13Ja 28
Butterfly Wlk. CR6: W'ham, Wold 92Yb 198
SE5 ....53Tb 113
(off Denmark Hill)
Butterfly World
St Albans 8M 5
Butter Hill SM5: Cars 76Jb 156
SM6: Wall 76Jb 156
Butteridges Cl. RM9: Dag 39Bd 75
Butterly Av. DA1: Dart 61Pd 141
Buttermere NW1 ....3A 216
Buttermere Av. SL1: Slou 3A 80
Buttermere Cl. AL1: St A 3F 6
E15 ....35Fc 73
SE1 ....6K 231 (49Vb 91)
SM4: Mord 72Za 154
TW14: Felt 60V 106
Buttermere Ct. NW8 ....39Fb 69
(off Boundary Rd.)
Buttermere Dr. SW15 ....57Ab 110
Buttermere Gdns. CR8: Purl 85Tb 177
Buttermere Ho. E3 ....41Bc 92
(off Mile End Rd.)
Buttermere Pl. WD25: Wat 5W 12
Buttermere Rd. BR5: St P 70Zc 139
Buttermere Wlk. E8 ....37Vb 71
Buttermere Way TW20: Egh 66D 126
Butterscotch Row WD5: Ab L 4T 12
Butterwick W6 ....49Za 88
WD25: Wat 8Aa 13
Butterworth Gdns. IG8: Wfd G 23Jc 53
Butterworth Ter. SE17 ....7E 230
Buttery M. N14 ....20Nb 32
Buttesland St. N1 ....3G 219 (41Tb 91)
Buttfield Cl. RM10: Dag 37Dd 76
Butt Fld. Vw. AL1: St A 6A 6
Buttlehide WD3: Map C 22F 42
Buttmarsh Cl. SE18 ....50Rc 94
Button Rd. RM17: Grays 49Be 99
Buttonscroft Cl. CR7: Thor H 69Sb 135
Button St. BR8: Swan 68Ld 141
Button St. Bus. Cen. BR8: Swan 68Ld 141
Butts, The TN14: Otf 88Kd 183
TW8: Bford 51La 108
TW16: Sun 69Y 129
Buttsbury Rd. IG1: Ilf 36Sc 74
Butts Cotts TW13: Hanw 62Aa 129
Butts Cres. TW13: Hanw 62Ca 129
Butts End HP1: Hem H 1J 3
Butts Grn. Rd. RM11: Horn 30Md 57
Butts La. SS17: Stan H 2K 101
Buttsmead HA6: Nwood 24S 44
Butts Piece UB5: N'olt 40X 65
Butts Rd. BR1: Brom 64Gc 137
GU21: Wok 89A 168
SS17: Stan H 2L 101
Buxhall Cres. E9 ....37Bc 72
Buxted Rd. E8 ....38Vb 71
N12 ....22Gb 49
SE22 ....56Ub 113
Buxton Av. CR3: Cat'm 93Ub 197
Buxton Cl. IG8: Wfd G 23Mc 53
KT19: Eps 83Ra 173
N9 ....19Yb 34
Buxton Ct. E11 ....31Hc 73
N1 ....3E 218
(not continuous)
Buxton Cres. SM3: Cheam 77Ab 154
Buxton Dr. E11 ....28Gc 53
KT3: N Mald 68Ta 131
Buxton Gdns. W3 ....45Ra 87
Buxton Ho. E11 ....28Gc 53
Buxton La. CR3: Cat'm 92Tb 197
Buxton M. SW4 ....54Mb 112
Buxton Path WD19: Wat 20Y 27
Buxton Pl. CR3: Cat'm 92Tb 197
Buxton Rd. CM16: They B 8Uc 22
CR7: Thor H 71Rb 157
DA8: Erith 52Fd 118
E4 ....17Fc 35
E6 ....41Nc 94
E15 ....36Gc 73
E17 ....28Ac 52
(not continuous)
EN9: Walt A 4Jc 21
IG2: Ilf 30Uc 54
N19 ....32Mb 70
NW2 ....37Xa 68
RM16: Grays 7A 100
SW14 ....55Ua 110
TW15: Ashf 64M 127
Buxton St. E1 ....6K 219 (42Vb 91)
Buzzard Creek Ind. Est.
IG11: Bark 43Wc 95
Byam St. SW6 ....54Eb 111
Byards Ct. SE16 ....49Zb 92
(off Worgan St.)
Byards Cft. SW16 ....67Mb 134
Byas Ho. E3 ....41Bc 92
(off Benworth St.)
Byatt Wlk. TW12: Hamp 65Aa 129
Bybend Cl. SL2: Farn R 9F 60
Bychurch End TW11: Tedd 64Ha 130
Bycliffe Ter. DA11: Grav'nd 9B 122
Bycroft Rd. UB1: S'hall 42Ca 85
Bycroft St. SE20 ....66Zb 136
Bycullah Av. EN2: Enf 13Rb 33
Bycullah Rd. EN2: Enf 12Rb 33
Bye, The W3 ....44Ua 88
Byegrove Rd. SW19 ....65Fb 133
Byelands Cl. SE16 ....46Zb 92
Byers Cl. EN6: Pot B 6Eb 17
(not continuous)
Byewaters WD18: Wat 16S 26
Bye Way, The HA3: W'stone 25Ga 46
Byeway, The SW14 ....55Sa 109
WD3: Rick 19N 25
Byeways TW2: Twick 62Da 129
Byeways, The KT5: Surb 71Qa 153
Byfeld Gdns. SW13 ....53Wa 110
Byfield Cl. SE16 ....47Bc 92
Byfield Ct. CM13: W H'dn 30Ee 59
Byfield Rd. TW7: Isle 55Ja 108
BYFLEET 84N 169
Byfleet Ind. Est. KT14: Byfl 82M 169
WD18: Wat 18S 26
Byfleet Rd. KT11: Cobh 84Q 170
KT14: Byfl 84Q 170
KT15: New H 80M 149
Byfleet Technical Cen. KT14: Byfl 83M 169
Byford Cl. E15 ....38Gc 73
Byford Ho. EN5: Barn 14Za 30
Bygrove CR0: New Ad 79Dc 158
Bygrove St. E14 ....44Dc 92
(not continuous)
Byland Cl. N21 ....17Pb 32
SM4: Mord 73Eb 155
Bylands GU22: Wok 91C 188
Bylands Cl. SE2 ....48Xc 95
Byne Rd. SE26 ....65Yb 136
SM5: Cars 75Gb 155
Bynes Rd. CR2: S Croy 80Tb 157
Byng Dr. EN6: Pot B 3Cb 17
Byng Pl. WC1 ....6E 216 (42Mb 90)
Byng Rd. EN5: Barn 12Za 30
Byng St. E14 ....47Cc 92
Bynon Av. DA7: Bex 55Bd 117
By-Pass Rd. KT22: Lea 92Ka 192
SS17: Horn H 1L 101
Byrd Way SS17: Stan H 1L 101
Byre Rd. N14 ....16Kb 32
Byrne Cl. CR0: C'don 72Sb 157
Byrne Rd. SW12 ....60Kb 112
Byron SL3: L'ly 50D 82
Byron Av. CR5: Coul 87Nb 176
E12 ....37Nc 74
E18 ....27Hc 53
KT3: N Mald 71Wa 154
NW9 ....28Ra 47
SM1: Sutt 77Fb 155
TW4: Cran 54W 106
WD6: Bore 15Qa 29
WD24: Wat 11Z 27
Byron Av. E. SM1: Sutt 77Fb 155
Byron Cl. E8 ....39Wb 71
GU21: Knap 9J 167
KT12: Walt T 74Aa 151
KT23: Bookh 96Ca 191
SE20 ....69Xb 135
SE26 ....63Ac 136
SE28 ....46Yc 95
SW16 ....65Nb 134
TW12: Hamp 63Ba 129
Byron Ct. E11 ....28Kc 53
(off Makepeace Rd.)
EN2: Enf 12Rb 33
HA1: Harr 30Ga 46
NW6 ....38Eb 69
(off Fairfax Rd.)
SE22 ....60Wb 113
SL4: Wind 5E 102
SW3 ....6E 226
W7 ....49Ja 86
(off Boston Rd.)
W9 ....42Cb 89
(off Lanhill Rd.)
WC1 ....5H 217
Byron Dr. DA8: Erith 52Dd 118
N2 ....30Fb 49
Byron Gdns. RM18: Tilb 3E 122
SM1: Sutt 77Fb 155
Byron Hill Rd. HA2: Harr 32Fa 66
Byron Ho. DA1: Cray 57Gd 118
Byron Mans. RM14: Upm 34Sd 78
Byron M. NW3 ....35Gb 69
W9 ....42Cb 89
Byron Pde. UB10: Hil 42S 84
Byron Pl. KT22: Lea 94Ka 192
Byron Rd. CM13: Hut 17Fe 41
CR2: Sels 82Xb 177
DA1: Dart 56Rd 119
E10 ....32Dc 72
E17 ....27Cc 52
HA0: Wemb 33La 66
HA1: Harr 30Ga 46
HA3: W'stone 26Ha 46
KT15: Add 77N 149
NW2 ....33Xa 68
NW7 ....22Wa 48
W5 ....46Pa 87
Byron St. E14 ....44Ec 92
Byron Ter. N9 ....16Yb 34
SE7 ....52Lc 115
Byron Way RM3: Rom 25Ld 57
UB4: Hayes 42V 84
UB5: N'olt 41Aa 85
UB7: W Dray 49P 83
Bysouth Cl. IG5: Ilf 25Rc 54
N15 ....28Tb 51
By the Wood WD19: Wat 19Z 27
Bythorn St. SW9 ....55Pb 112
Byton Rd. SW17 ....65Hb 133
Byttom Hill RH5: Mick 98La 192
Byward Av. TW14: Felt 58Y 107
Byward St. EC3 ....5J 225 (45Ub 91)
Bywater Ho. SE18 ....48Nc 94
Bywater Pl. SE16 ....46Ac 92
Bywater St. SW3 ....7F 227 (50Hb 89)
Byway E11 ....29Lc 53
Byway, The EN6: Pot B 5Cb 17
KT19: Ewe 77Va 154
SM2: Sutt 81Fb 175
Byways, The KT21: Asht 90Ma 173
Bywell Pl. W1 ....1B 222
Bywood Av. CR0: C'don 72Yb 158
Bywood Cl. CR8: Kenley 87Rb 177
SM7: Bans 89Bb 175
By-Wood End SL9: Chal P 22C 42
Byworth Wlk. N19 ....32Nb 70

C

Cabbell Pl. KT15: Add 77L 149
Cabbell St. NW1 ....1D 220 (43Gb 89)
Cabborns Cres.
SS17: Stan H 3M 101
Caberfeigh Cl. RH1: Redh 6M 207
Cabinet Way E4 ....23Bc 52
Cable Ct. SE16 ....49Ac 92
(off Rope St.)
Cable Ho. WC1 ....3K 217
Cable Ho. Ct. GU21: Wok 87A 168
Cable Pl. SE10 ....53Ec 114
Cable St. E1 ....45Wb 91
Cable Trade Pk. SE7 ....49Lc 93
Cabot Cl. CR0: Wadd 76Qb 156
Cabot Ct. SE16 ....49Zb 92
(off Worgan St.)
Cabot Sq. E14 ....46Cc 92
Cabot Way E6 ....39Mc 73
Cabrera Av. GU25: Vir W 2N 147
Cabrera Cl. GU25: Vir W 2P 147
Cab Rd. SE1 ....7K 223
Cabul Rd. SW11 ....54Gb 111
Caci Ho. W14 ....49Bb 89
(off Kensington Village)
Cacket's La. TN14: Cud 87Tc 180
Cacketts Cotts. TN16: B Char 98Yc 201
Cactus Cl. SE15 ....54Ub 113
Cactus Wlk. W12 ....44Va 88
Cadbury Cl. TW7: Isle 53Ja 108
TW16: Sun 66U 128
Cadbury Rd. TW16: Sun 66U 128
Cadbury Way SE16 ....48Vb 91
Caddington Cl. EN4: E Barn 15Gb 31
Caddington Rd. NW2 ....34Ab 68
Caddis Cl. HA7: Stan 24Ha 46
Caddy Cl. TW20: Egh 64C 126
Cade La. TN13: S'oaks 100Ld 203
Cadell Cl. E2 ....2K 219 (40Vb 71)
Cade Rd. SE10 ....53Fc 115
Cader Rd. SW18 ....58Eb 111
Cadet Dr. SE1 ....49Vb 91
Cadet Pl. SE10 ....50Gc 93
Cadiz Ct. RM10: Dag 38Fd 76
Cadiz Rd. RM10: Dag 38Fd 76
Cadiz St. SE17 ....7E 230 (50Sb 91)
Cadley Ter. SE23 ....61Yb 136
Cadlocks Hill TN14: Hals 82Bd 181
Cadman Cl. SW9 ....52Rb 113
Cadman Ct. SE16 ....50Ra 87
(off Chaseley Dr.)
Cadmer Cl. KT3: N Mald 70Ua 132
Cadmore Ct. EN8: Chesh 1Zb 20
Cadmore Ho. N1 ....38Rb 71
(off The Sutton Est.)
Cadmore La. EN8: Chesh 1Zb 20
Cadmus Cl. SW4 ....55Mb 112

Cadmus Ct. SW9 53Qb 112
(off Southey Rd.)
Cadnam Lodge E14 48Ec 92
(off Schooner Cl.)
Cadnam Point SW15 60Xa 110
Cadogan Av. CM13: W H'dn 30Fe 59
DA2: Dart 59Td 120
Cadogan Cl. BR3: Beck 67Fc 137
E9 38Bc 72
HA2: Harr 35Da 65
TW11: Tedd 64Ga 130
Cadogan Ct. E9 38Bc 72
(off Cadogan Ter.)
SM2: Sutt 79Db 155
SW3 6F 227
Cadogan Ct. Gdns. SW1 5H 227
Cadogan Gdns. E18 27Kc 53
N3 25Db 49
N21 15Qb 32
SW3 5G 227 (49Hb 89)
Cadogan Ga. SW1 5G 227 (49Hb 89)
Cadogan Hall 5G 227
Cadogan Ho. IG8: Wfd G 24Rc 54
SW3 51Fb 111
(off Beaufort St.)
Cadogan La. SW1 3H 227 (48Jb 90)
Cadogan Mans. SW3 6G 227
Cadogan Pl. CR8: Kenley 89Sb 177
SW1 3G 227 (48Hb 89)
Cadogan Rd. KT6: Surb 71Ma 153
SE18 48Sc 94
Cadogan Sq. SW1 4F 227 (48Hb 89)
Cadogan St. SW3 6F 227 (49Hb 89)
Cadogan Ter. E9 37Bc 72
Cadoxton Av. N15 30Vb 51
Cadwallon Rd. SE9 61Rc 138
Caedmon Rd. N7 35Pb 70
Caenshill Ho. KT13: Weyb 80Q 150
Caenshill Pl. KT13: Weyb 80Q 150
Caenshill Rd. KT13: Weyb 80Q 150
Caenwood Hill KT13: Weyb 82Q 170
Caenwood Cl. KT13: Weyb 79Q 150
Caen Wood Rd. KT21: Asht 90La 172
Caerleon Cl. DA14: Sidc 64Yc 139
KT10: Clay 80Ka 152
Caerleon Ter. SE2 49Xc 95
Caernafon Ho. HA7: Stan 22Ja 46
Caernarvon Cl. CR4: Mitc 69Nb 134
HP2: Hem H 2M 3
RM11: Horn 32Qd 77
Caernarvon Ct. HP2: Hem H 2M 3
Caernarvon Dr. IG5: Ilf 25Qc 54
Caernarvon Ho. E16 46Kc 93
(off Audley Dr.)
W2 2A 220
Caesar Ct. E2 40Zb 72
(off Palmer's Rd.)
Caesars Ct. AL3: St A 2B 6
(off Verulam Rd.)
Caesars Wlk. CR4: Mitc 71Hb 155
Caesars Way TW17: Shep 72T 150
Café Gallery 48Yb 92
Cage Pond Rd. WD7: Shenl 5Pa 15
Cages Wood Dr. SL2: Farn C 5F 60
Cage Yd. RH2: Reig 6J 207
Cahill St. EC1 6E 218 (42Sb 91)
Cahir St. E14 49Dc 92
Caillard Rd. KT14: Byfl 83N 169
Cain Cl. AL1: St A 4D 6
Cain Ct. EN8: Chesh 1Zb 20
(off Wycliffe Cl.)
W5 43La 86
(off Castlebar M.)
Caine Ho. W3 47Ra 87
(off Hanbury Rd.)
Cain's La. TW14: Felt 57U 106
Caird St. W10 41Ab 88
Cairn Av. W5 46Ma 87
Cairn Ct. KT17: Ewe 82Va 174
Cairncross M. N8 30Nb 50
(off Felix Av.)
Cairndale Cl. BR1: Brom 66Hc 137
Cairnfield Av. NW2 34Ua 68
Cairngorm Cl. TW11: Tedd 64Ja 130
Cairngorm Pl. SL2: Slou 2H 81
Cairns Av. IG8: Wfd G 23Nc 54
Cairns Cl. AL4: St A 3H 7
DA1: Dart 57Md 119
Cairns M. SE18 53Nc 116
Cairns Rd. SW11 57Gb 111
Cairn Way HA7: Stan 23Ha 46
Cairo New Rd. CR0: C'don 75Rb 157
Cairo Rd. E17 28Cc 52
Caishowe Rd. WD6: Bore 11Ra 29
Caister Cl. HP2: Hem H 3N 3
Caister Ho. N7 37Pb 70
Caistor Ho. E15 39Hc 73
(off Caistor Pk. Rd.)
Caistor M. SW12 59Kb 112
Caistor Pk. Rd. E15 39Hc 73
Caistor Rd. SW12 59Kb 112
Caithness Dr. KT18: Eps 86Ta 173
Caithness Gdns. DA15: Sidc 58Vc 117
Caithness Ho. N1 39Pb 70
(off Twyford St.)
Caithness Rd. CR4: Mitc 66Kb 134
W14 48Za 88
Calabria Rd. N5 37Rb 71
Calais Cotts. DA3: Fawk 75Wd 164
Calais Ga. SE5 53Rb 113
Calais St. SE5 53Rb 113
Calbourne Av. RM12: Horn 36Kd 77
Calbourne Rd. SW12 59Hb 111
Calbroke Rd. SL2: Slou 2D 80
Calcott Cl. CM14: B'wood 18Xd 40
Calcott Ct. W14 48Ab 88
(off Blythe Rd.)
Calcott Wlk. SE9 63Nc 138
Calcraft Ho. E2 40Yb 72
(off Bonner Rd.)
Calcroft Av. DA9: Ghithe 57Yd 120
Calcutta Rd. RM18: Tilb 4B 122
Caldbeck EN9: Walt A 6Fc 21
(not continuous)
Caldbeck Av. KT4: Wor Pk 75Wa 154
Caldecot Av. EN7: Chesh 1Vb 19
Caldecote KT1: King T 68Qa 131
(off Excelsior Cl.)
Caldecote Gdns. WD23: Bush 17Ga 28
CALDECOTE HILL 17Ha 28
Caldecote La. WD23: Bush 16Ha 28
Caldecot Rd. SE5 54Sb 113
Caldecott Way E5 34Zb 72
Calder RM18: E Til 9L 101
Calder Av. AL9: Brk P 8J 9
UB6: G'frd 40Ha 66
Calder Cl. EN1: Enf 13Ub 33
Calder Ct. SE16 46Bc 92
SL3: L'ly 50B 82
Calder Gdns. HA8: Edg 27Qa 47
Calderon Ho. NW8 1D 214
Calderon Pl. W10 43Ya 88
Calderon Rd. E11 35Ec 72
Calder Rd. SM4: Mord 71Eb 155
Caldervale Rd. SW4 57Mb 112
Calder Way SL3: Poyle 55G 104
Calderwood DA12: Grav'nd 4G 144
Calderwood Pl. EN4: Had W 11Db 31
Calderwood St. SE18 49Qc 94
Caldew Ct. NW7 24Wa 48
Caldew St. SE5 52Tb 113
Caldicote Grn. NW9 30Ua 48
Caldon Ho. UB5: N'olt 42Ba 85
Caldwell Ho. SW13 52Ya 110
(off Trinity Chu. Rd.)
Caldwell Rd. GU20: W'sham 8B 146
SS17: Stan H 2K 101
WD19: Wat 21Z 45
Caldwell St. SW9 52Pb 112
Caldy Rd. DA17: Belv 48Dd 96
Caldy Wlk. N1 38Sb 71
Caleb St. SE1 1E 230 (47Sb 91)
Caledonia Ct. IG11: Bark 40Yc 75
(off Keel Cl.)
Caledonia Ho. E14 44Ac 92
(off Salmon La.)
Caledonian Cl. IG3: Ilf 32Xc 75
Caledonian Ct. UB5: N'olt 42Aa 85
WD17: Wat 12X 27
Caledonian Rd. N1 2G 217 (40Nb 70)
N7 35Pb 70
Caledonian Sq. NW1 37Mb 70
Caledonian Wharf E14 49Fc 93
Caledonia Rd. TW19: Stanw 60N 105
Caledonia St. N1 2G 217 (40Nb 70)
Caledon Rd. AL2: Lon C 8G 6
E6 39Pc 74
SM6: Wall 77Jb 156
Calendar M. KT6: Surb 72Ma 153
Cale St. SW3 7D 226 (50Gb 89)
Caletock Way SE10 50Hc 93
Calfstock La. DA4: Farni 70Pd 141
Calgarth NW1 2C 216
Calgary Ct. RM7: Mawney 28Dd 56
SE16 47Yb 92
(off Canada Est.)
Caliban Twr. N1 2H 219
Calico Ho. EC4 3E 224
Calico Row SW11 55Eb 111
Calidore Cl. SW2 58Pb 112
California Bldg. SE10 53Dc 114
(off Deal's Gateway)
California Cl. SM2: Sutt 82Cb 175
California La. WD23: B Hea 18Fa 28
California Pl. WD23: B Hea 18Fa 28
(off High Rd.)
California Rd. KT3: N Mald 70Ra 131
Caling Cft. DA3: New A 74Be 165
Caliph Cl. DA12: Grav'nd 2H 145
Callaby Ter. N1 37Tb 71
Callaghan Cl. SE13 56Gc 115
Callaghan Cl. HP4: Berk 1A 2
Callahan Cotts. E1 43Yb 92
(off Lindley St.)
Callander Rd. SE6 61Dc 136
Callanders, The WD23: B Hea 18Ga 28
Callan Gro. RM15: S Ock 45Xd 98
Callard Av. N13 21Rb 51
Callcott Ct. NW6 38Bb 69
Callcott Rd. NW6 38Bb 69
Callcott St. W8 46Cb 89
Callendar Rd. SW7 3B 226 (48Fb 89)
Callender Ct. CR0: C'don 72Sb 157
(off Harry Cl.)
Callenders Cotts. DA17: Belv 47Fd 96
Calley Down Cres. CR0: New Ad 82Fc 179
Callingham Cl. E14 43Bc 92
Callis Farm Cl. TW19: Stanw 58N 105
Callisons Pl. SE10 50Gc 93
Callis Rd. E17 30Bc 52
Calliston Ct. E16 43Jc 93
(off Hammersley Rd.)
Callonfield E17 28Zb 52
Callow Fld. CR8: Purl 85Qb 176
Callow Hill GU25: Vir W 9N 125
Callowland Cl. WD24: Wat 10X 13
Callowlands WD24: Wat 11X 27
(off Leavesden Rd.)
Callow St. SW3 51Fb 111
Calluna Ct. GU22: Wok 90B 168
Cally Swimming Pool 39Pb 70
Calmington Rd. SE5 51Ub 113
Calmont Rd. BR1: Brom 65Fc 137
Calmore Cl. RM12: Horn 36Ld 77
Calne Av. IG5: Ilf 25Rc 54
Calonne Rd. SW19 63Za 132
Calshot Av. RM16: Chaf H 47Be 99
Calshot Ct. DA2: Dart 58Rd 119
(off Osbourne Rd.)
Calshot Ho. N1 1H 217
Calshot Rd. TW6: H'row A 54Q 106
Calshot St. N1 1H 217 (40Pb 70)
Calshot Way EN2: Enf 13Rb 33
TW6: H'row A 54Q 106
Calstock NW1 1D 216
Calstock Ho. SE11 7A 230
Calthorpe Gdns. HA8: Edg 22Na 47
(not continuous)
SM1: Sutt 76Eb 155
Calthorpe St. WC1 5J 217 (42Pb 90)
Calton Av. SE21 58Ub 113
Calton Rd. EN5: New Bar 16Eb 31
Calverley Cl. BR3: Beck 65Dc 136
Calverley Ct. KT19: Ewe 77Ta 153
Calverley Cres. RM10: Dag 33Cd 76
Calverley Gdns. HA3: Kenton 31Ma 67
Calverley Gro. N19 32Mb 70
Calverley Rd. KT17: Ewe 79Wa 154
Calvert Av. E2 4J 219 (41Ub 91)
Calvert Cl. DA14: Sidc 65Ad 139
DA17: Belv 49Cd 96
KT19: Eps 82Ra 173
Calvert Ct. TW9: Rich 56Pa 109
Calvert Dr. DA2: Wilm 61Fd 140
Calvert Ho. W12 45Xa 88
(off White City Est.)
Calverton SE5 51Ub 113
(off Albany Rd.)
Calverton Rd. E6 39Qc 74
Calvert Rd. EN5: Barn 12Za 30
KT24: Eff 100X 191
SE10 50Hc 93
Calvert's Bldgs. SE1 7F 225 (46Tb 91)
Calvert St. NW1 39Jb 70
Calvin Cl. BR5: St P 69Zc 139
Calvin St. E1 6K 219 (42Vb 91)
Calydon Rd. SE7 50Kc 93
Calypso Cres. SE15 52Vb 113
Calypso Way SE16 48Bc 92
Camac Rd. TW2: Twick 60Fa 108
Camarthen Grn. NW9 29Ua 48
Cambalt Rd. SW15 57Za 110
Cambay Ho. E1 42Ac 92
(off Harford St.)
Camber Ho. SE15 51Yb 114
Camberley Av. EN1: Enf 14Ub 33
SW20 68Xa 132
Camberley Cl. SM3: Cheam 76Za 154
Camberley Ho. NW1 2A 216
Camberley Rd. TW6: H'row A 55Q 106
Cambert Way SE3 56Kc 115
CAMBERWELL 53Tb 113
Camberwell Bus. Cen. SE5 52Tb 113
Camberwell Chu. St. SE5 53Tb 113
Camberwell Glebe SE5 53Tb 113
CAMBERWELL GREEN 53Sb 113
Camberwell Grn. SE5 53Tb 113
Camberwell Gro. SE5 53Tb 113
Camberwell Leisure Cen. 53Tb 113
Camberwell New Rd. SE5 51Qb 112
Camberwell Pl. SE5 53Sb 113
Camberwell Rd. SE5 51Sb 113
Camberwell Sta. Rd. SE5 53Sb 113
Camberwell Trad. Est. SE5 53Rb 113
Cambeys Rd. RM10: Dag 36Dd 76
Camborne Av. RM3: Rom 24Nd 57
W13 47Ka 86
Camborne Cl. TW6: H'row A 55Q 106
Camborne Cres. TW6: H'row A 55Q 106
Camborne M. SW18 59Cb 111
W11 44Ab 88
Camborne Rd. CR0: C'don 73Wb 157
DA14: Sidc 62Yc 139
DA16: Well 54Vc 117
SM2: Sutt 80Cb 155
SM4: Mord 71Za 154
SW18 59Cb 111
TW6: H'row A 55Q 106
Camborne Way RM3: Rom 24Nd 57
TW5: Hest 53Ca 107
TW6: H'row A 55Q 106
Cambourne Av. N9 17Zb 34
Cambourne Wlk. TW10: Rich 58Ma 109
Cambrai Ct. N13 20Nb 32
Cambray Rd. BR6: Orp 73Vc 161
SW12 60Lb 112
Cambria Cl. DA15: Sidc 60Tc 116
TW3: Houn 56Ca 107
Cambria Ct. DA9: Ghithe 56Wd 120
SL3: L'ly 7N 81
TW14: Felt 59X 107
TW18: Staines 63G 126
Cambria Cres. DA12: Grav'nd 3G 144
Cambria Gdns. TW19: Stanw 59N 105
(not continuous)
Cambria Ho. DA8: Erith 52Gd 118
(off Larner Rd.)
E14 44Ac 92
(off Salmon La.)
SE26 63Wb 135
(off High Level Dr.)
Cambrian Av. IG2: Ilf 29Uc 54
Cambrian Cl. SE27 62Rb 135
Cambrian Grn. NW9 29Ua 48
(off Snowden Dr.)
Cambrian Gro. DA11: Grav'nd 9C 122
Cambrian Rd. E10 31Cc 72
TW10: Rich 58Pa 109
Cambria Rd. SE5 55Sb 113
Cambria St. SW6 52Db 111
Cambridge Arc. E9 38Yb 72
(off Elsdale St.)
Cambridge Av. DA16: Well 56Vc 117
KT3: N Mald 69Ua 132
(not continuous)
NW6 40Cb 69
RM2: Rom 27Ld 57
SL1: Burn 10A 60
SL1: Slou 4E 80
UB6: G'frd 36Ha 66
Cambridge Barracks Rd. SE18 49Pc 94
Cambridge Cir. WC2 3E 222 (44Mb 90)
Cambridge Cl. E17 30Bc 52
EN4: E Barn 16Hb 31
EN8: Chesh 1Yb 20
GU21: Wok 10K 167
N22 25Qb 50
NW10 34Sa 67
SW20 67Xa 132
TW4: Houn 56Aa 107
UB7: Harm 51M 105
Cambridge Cotts. TW9: Kew 51Qa 109
Cambridge Ct. E2 40Xb 71
(off Cambridge Heath Rd.)
N16 31Ub 71
(off Amhurst Pk.)
NW6 40Cb 69
(not continuous)
W2 1D 220
W6 49Ya 88
(off Shepherd's Bush Rd.)
Cambridge Cres. E2 40Xb 71
TW11: Tedd 64Ja 130
Cambridge Dr. EN6: Pot B 3Za 16
HA4: Ruis 33Y 65
SE12 57Jc 115
Cambridge Gdns. EN1: Enf 12Wb 33
KT1: King T 68Qa 131
N10 25Jb 50
N17 24Tb 51
N21 17Tb 33
NW6 40Cb 69
RM16: Grays 9C 100
W10 44Za 88
Cambridge Ga. NW1 5K 215 (42Kb 90)
Cambridge Ga. M. NW1 5A 216 (42Kb 90)
Cambridge Grn. SE9 60Rc 116
Cambridge Gro. SE20 67Xb 135
W6 49Xa 88
Cambridge Gro. Rd. KT1: King T 69Qa 131
(not continuous)
Cambridge Heath Rd. E1 43Xb 91
E2 43Xb 91
Cambridge Ho. SL4: Wind 3G 102
W6 49Xa 88
(off Cambridge Gro.)
W13 44Ja 86
Cambridge Pde. EN1: Enf 11Wb 33
Cambridge Pk. E11 30Jc 53
TW1: Twick 58La 108
Cambridge Pk. Ct. TW1: Twick 59Ma 109
Cambridge Pk. Rd. E11 31Jc 73
(off Lonsdale Rd.)
Cambridge Pl. W8 47Db 89
Cambridge Rd. AL1: St A 3E 6
BR1: Brom 66Jc 137
CR4: Mitc 69Lb 134
DA14: Sidc 63Uc 138
E4 18Fc 35
E11 30Hc 53
HA2: Harr 29Ca 45
IG3: Ilf 32Uc 74
IG11: Bark 38Sc 74
KT1: King T 68Pa 131
KT2: King T 68Pa 131
KT3: N Mald 70Ta 131
KT8: W Mole 70Ba 129
KT12: Walt T 72X 151
NW6 40Cb 69
(not continuous)
SE20 69Xb 135
SM5: Cars 79Gb 155
SW11 53Hb 111
SW13 54Va 110
SW20 67Wa 132
TW1: Twick 58Ma 109
TW4: Houn 56Aa 107
TW9: Kew 52Qa 109
TW11: Tedd 63Ha 130
TW12: Hamp 66Ba 129
TW15: Ashf 66S 128
UB1: S'hall 46Ba 85
UB8: Uxb 37M 63
W7 47Ha 86
WD18: Wat 14Y 27
Cambridge Rd. Nth. W4 50Ra 87
Cambridge Rd. Sth. W4 50Ra 87
Cambridge Row SE18 50Rc 94
Cambridge Sq. RH1: Redh 9A 208
W2 2D 220 (44Gb 89)
Cambridge St. SW1 6A 228 (49Kb 90)
Cambridge Ter. HP4: Berk 1A 2
N9 17Ub 33
NW1 4K 215 (41Kb 90)
Cambridge Ter. M. NW1 4A 216 (41Kb 90)
Cambridge Theatre 3F 223
Cambridge Yd. W7 47Ha 86
Cambstone Cl. N11 19Jb 32
Cambus Cl. UB4: Yead 43Aa 85
Cambus Rd. E16 43Jc 93
Cam Ct. SE15 51Vb 113
Camdale Rd. SE18 52Vc 117
Camden Arts Cen. 36Db 69
Camden Av. TW13: Felt 60Y 107
UB4: Yead 45Z 85
Camden Cl. BR7: Chst 67Sc 138
DA11: Nflt 60Ee 121
RM16: Grays 9D 100
Camden Cotts. KT13: Weyb 76Q 150
Camden Ct. DA17: Belv 50Cd 96
NW1 38Lb 70
(off Rousden St.)
Camden Gdns. CR7: Thor H 69Rb 135
NW1 38Kb 70
SM1: Sutt 78Db 155
Camden Gro. BR7: Chst 65Rc 138
Camden High St. NW1 1B 216 (38Kb 70)
Camden Hill Rd. SE19 65Ub 135
Camden Ho. HP1: Hem H 3M 3
SE8 50Bc 92
Camdenhurst St. E14 44Ac 92
Camden La. N7 36Mb 70
Camden Lock Market 38Kb 70
(off Camden Lock Pl.)
Camden Lock Pl. NW1 38Kb 70
Camden Markets 38Kb 70
(off Camden Lock Pl.)
Camden M. NW1 38Lb 70
Camden Pk. Rd. BR7: Chst 66Pc 138
NW1 37Mb 70
Camden Pas. N1 1B 218 (40Rb 71)
Camden Peoples Theatre 5B 216
Camden Rd. DA5: Bexl 60Ad 117
E11 30Kc 53
E17 30Bc 52
N7 35Nb 70
NW1 38Lb 70
RM16: Chaf H 48Ae 99
SM1: Sutt 78Db 155
SM5: Cars 77Hb 155
TN13: S'oaks 94Kd 203
Camden Row HA5: Pinn 27Y 45
SE3 54Gc 115
Camden Sq. NW1 38Mb 70
(not continuous)
SE15 53Vb 113
Camden St. NW1 1C 216 (38Lb 70)
Camden Studios NW1 1C 216
Camden Ter. NW1 37Mb 70
TN15: Seal 93Pd 203
CAMDEN TOWN 1C 216 (39Kb 70)
Camden Wlk. N1 1B 218 (39Rb 71)
Camden Way BR7: Chst 66Pc 138
CR7: Thor H 69Rb 135
Cameford Ct. SW2 59Nb 112
Camelford NW1 39Lb 70
(off Royal Coll. St.)
Camelford Ct. W11 44Ab 88
Camelford Ho. RM3: Rom 21Nd 57
(off Chudleigh Rd.)
SE1 7G 229 (50Nb 90)
Camelford Wlk. W11 44Ab 88
Camel Gro. KT2: King T 64Ma 131
Camellia Cl. CM13: W H'dn 30Ee 59
E10 33Cc 72
RM3: Hrld W 25Nd 57
Camellia Ct. GU24: W End 5D 166
Camellia Ho. SE8 52Bc 114
(off Idonia St.)
TW13: Felt 60W 106
(off Tilley Rd.)
Camellia La. KT5: Surb 70Ra 131
Camellia M. TW20: Eng G 6N 125
Camellia Pl. TW2: Whitt 59Da 107
Camellia St. SW8 52Nb 112
(not continuous)
Camelot Cl. SE28 47Tc 94
SW19 63Bb 133
TN16: Big H 88Lc 179
Camelot Ho. NW1 37Mb 70
Camel Rd. E16 46Nc 94
Camera Pl. SW10 51Fb 111
Camera Press Gallery, The 1K 231
(off Queen Elizabeth St.)
Cameret Ct. W11 47Za 88
(off Holland Rd.)
Cameron Cl. CM14: W'ley 21Zd 59
DA5: Bexl 62Gd 140
N18 21Xb 51
N20 19Fb 31
N22 24Pb 50
Cameron Cres. HA8: Edg 25Ra 47
Cameron Dr. DA1: Dart 54Qd 119
EN8: Walt C 6Zb 20
Cameron Ho. BR1: Brom 67Hc 137
NW8 1D 214
SE5 52Sb 113
Cameron Pl. E1 44Xb 91
SW16 61Qb 134
Cameron Rd. BR2: Brom 71Jc 159
CR0: C'don 72Rb 157
IG3: Ilf 32Uc 74
SE6 61Bc 136
Cameron Sq. CR4: Mitc 67Gb 133
Cameron Ter. SE12 62Kc 137
Camerton Cl. E8 37Vb 71
Camfield Pl. AL9: Ess 3M 9
Camgate Cen., The TW19: Stanw 58P 105
Camgate Mans. SE5 51Sb 113
(off Camberwell Rd.)
Cam Grn. RM15: S Ock 44Xd 98
Camilla Cl. KT23: Bookh 97Da 191
TW16: Sun 65V 128
Camilla Rd. SE16 49Xb 91
Camille Cl. SE25 69Wb 135
Camlan Rd. BR1: Brom 63Hc 137
Camlet St. E2 5K 219 (42Vb 91)
Camlet Way AL3: St A 1P 5
EN4: Barn, Had W 12Cb 31
Camley St. N1 1E 216 (38Mb 70)
Camley Street Natural Pk. Vis. Cen.
1E 216 (40Mb 70)
Camm Av. SL4: Wind 5C 102
Camm Gdns. KT1: King T 68Pa 131
KT7: T Ditt 73Ha 152
Camomile Av. CR4: Mitc 67Hb 133
Camomile Rd. RM7: Rush G 33Fd 76
Camomile St. EC3 2H 225 (44Ub 91)
Camomile Way UB7: Yiew 44N 83
CAMP, THE 4F 6
Campaign Ct. W9 42Bb 89
(off Chantry Cl.)
Campana Rd. SW6 53Cb 111
Campania Bldg. E1 45Zb 92
(off Jardine Rd.)
Campaspe Bus. Pk. TW16: Sun 71V 150
Campbell Av. GU22: Wok 93B 188
IG6: Ilf 28Rc 54
Campbell Cir. KT13: Weyb 82P 169
Campbell Cl. HA4: Ruis 30W 44
KT14: Byfl 84M 169
RM1: Rom 23Gd 56
SE18 53Qc 116
SW16 63Mb 134
TW2: Twick 60Fa 108
Campbell Ct. N17 25Vb 51
NW9 30Sa 47
SE22 60Wb 113
SW7 4A 226
Campbell Cft. HA8: Edg 22Qa 47
Campbell Gordon Way NW2 35Xa 68
Campbell Ho. SW1 7B 228
W2 7B 214
W12 45Xa 88
(off White City Est.)
Campbell Rd. CR0: C'don 73Rb 157
CR3: Cat'm 93Tb 197
DA11: Grav'nd 10B 122
E3 41Cc 92
E6 39Nc 74
E15 35Hc 73
E17 28Bc 52
KT8: E Mos 69Ga 130
KT13: Weyb 80Q 150
N17 25Vb 51
TW2: Twick 61Fa 130
W7 45Ga 86
Campbell Wlk. N1 39Nb 70
(off Outram Pl.)
Campdale Rd. N7 34Mb 70
Campden Cres. HA0: Wemb 34Ka 66
RM8: Dag 35Xc 75
Campden Gro. W8 47Cb 89
Campden Hill W8 47Cb 89
Campden Hill Ct. W8 47Cb 89
Campden Hill Gdns. W8 46Cb 89
Campden Hill Ga. W8 47Cb 89
Campden Hill Mans. W8 46Cb 89
(off Edge St.)
Campden Hill Pl. W11 46Bb 89
Campden Hill Rd. W8 46Cb 89
Campden Hill Sq. W8 46Bb 89
Campden Hill Towers W11 46Cb 89
Campden Ho. NW6 38Fb 69
(off Harben Rd.)
W8 46Cb 89
(off Sheffield Ter.)
Campden Ho. Cl. W8 47Cb 89
Campden Houses W8 46Cb 89
Campden Ho. Ter. W8 46Cb 89
(off Kensington Chu. St.)
Campden Mans. W8 46Cb 89
(off Kensington Chu. St.)
Campden Rd. CR2: S Croy 78Ub 157
UB10: Ick 34P 63
Campden St. W8 46Cb 89
Campden Way RM8: Dag 35Xc 75
Campe Ho. N10 24Jb 50
Campen Cl. SW19 61Ab 132
Camp End Rd. KT13: Weyb 84S 170
Camperdown Ho. SL4: Wind 4G 102
Camperdown St. E1 3K 225 (44Vb 91)
Campfield Rd. AL1: St A 3E 6
SE9 59Mc 115
Camphill Ct. KT14: W Byf 84J 169
Camphill Ind. Est.
KT14: W Byf 83K 169
Camphill Rd. KT14: W Byf 84J 169
Campion Cl. CR0: C'don 77Ub 157
DA11: Nflt 3A 144
E6 45Pc 94
HA3: Kenton 30Pa 47
RM7: Rush G 33Fd 76
UB8: Hil 43P 83
UB9: Den 34J 63
WD25: Wat 5W 12
Campion Ct. HA0: Wemb 40Na 67
RM17: Grays 51Fe 121
Campion Dr. KT20: Tad 92Xa 194
Campion Gdns. IG8: Wfd G 22Jc 53

Campion Ho. E14 44Bc 92
(off Frances Wharf)
RH1: Redh 3P 207
Campion Pl. SE28 46Wc 95
Campion Rd. E10 31Dc 72
HP1: Hem H 3G 2
SW15 56Ya 110
TW7: Isle 53Ha 108
Campions IG10: Lough 10Qc 22
Campions, The WD6: Bore 10Pa 15
Campions Cl. WD6: Bore 9Ra 15
Campion Ter. NW2 34Za 68
Campion Way HA8: Edg 21Sa 47
Cample La. RM15: S Ock 45Wd 98
Camplin Rd. HA3: Kenton 29Na 47
Camplin St. SE14 52Zb 114
Camp Rd. AL1: St A 2D 6
CR3: Wold 92Ac 198
SL9: Ger X 1N 61
SW19 64Xa 132
(not continuous)
Campsbourne, The N8 28Nb 50
Campsbourne Ho. N8 28Nb 50
(off Pembroke Rd.)
Campsbourne Pde. N8 28Nb 50
(off High St.)
Campsbourne Rd. N8 27Nb 50
(not continuous)
Campsey Gdns. RM9: Dag 38Xc 75
Campsey Rd. RM9: Dag 38Xc 75
Campsfield Ho. N8 27Nb 50
(off Campsfield Rd.)
Campsfield Rd. N8 27Nb 50
Campshill Pl. SE13 57Ec 114
Campshill Rd. SE13 57Ec 114
Campus, The HP2: Hem H 1B 4
IG10: Lough 14Rc 36
Campus Ct. IG10: Lough 14Qc 36
Campus Ho. TW7: Isle 52Ga 108
Campus Rd. E17 30Bc 52
Campus Way NW4 27Xa 48
Camp Vw. SW19 64Xa 132
Camp Vw. Rd. AL1: St A 3F 6
Cam Rd. E15 39Fc 73
Camrose Av. DA8: Erith 51Dd 118
HA8: Edg 26Pa 47
TW13: Felt 63Y 129
Camrose Cl. CR0: C'don 73Ac 158
SM4: Mord 70Cb 133
Camrose St. SE2 50Wc 95
Canada Av. N18 23Sb 51
RH1: Redh 10A 208
Canada Cres. W3 43Sa 87
Canada Dr. RH1: Redh 10A 208
Canada Est. SE16 48Yb 92
Canada Farm Rd. DA2: Grn St 68Xd 142
DA3: Fawk 70Wd 142
DA4: S Dar 70Wd 142
Canada Gdns. SE13 57Ec 114
Canada Heights Motorcycle Circuit 69Md 141
Canada House 6E 222
Canada Ho. SE16 48Ac 92
(off Brunswick Quay)
SW1 46Mb 90
(off Trafalgar Sq.)
Canada Memorial 1A 228
Canada Pl. E14 46Dc 92
(off Up. Bank St.)
Canada Rd. DA8: Erith 52Kd 119
KT11: Cobh 85Y 171
KT14: Byfl 83M 169
SL1: Slou 7M 81
W3 43Sa 87
Canada Sq. E14 46Dc 92
Canada St. SE16 47Zb 92
Canada Way W12 45Xa 88
Canada Wharf SE16 46Bc 92
Canadian Av. SE6 60Dc 114
Canadian Memorial Av.
TW20: Eng G 8K 125
Canal App. SE8 50Ac 92
Canal Bank KT15: Add 79M 149
Canal Bank M. GU21: Wok 89A 168
Canal Basin DA12: Grav'nd 8F 122
Canal Blvd. NW1 37Mb 70
CANAL BRIDGE 51Wb 113
Canal Bri. KT15: Add 80M 149
Canal Bldg. N1 1D 218 (40Sb 71)
Canal Cl. E1 42Ac 92
W10 42Za 88
Canal Cotts. E3 39Bc 72
(off Parnell Rd.)
Canal Ct. HP4: Berk 1A 2
Canal Gro. SE15 51Xb 113
Canal Ind. Est. SL3: L'ly 47C 82
Canal Ind. Pk. DA12: Grav'nd 8F 122
Canal Market 38Kb 70
(off Castlehaven Rd.)
Canal Path E2 39Vb 71
Canal Rd. DA12: Grav'nd 8E 122
Canal Side UB9: Hare 24J 43
Canalside RH1: Mers, Redh 3B 208
SE28 45Zc 95
Canalside Activity Cen. 42Za 88
Canalside Gdns. UB2: S'hall 49Aa 85
Canalside Sq. N1 1E 218
Canal Side Studios NW1 39Mb 70
(off St Pancras Way)
Canalside Studios N1 39Ub 71
(off Orsman Rd.)
Canal St. SE5 51Tb 113
Canal Wlk. CR0: C'don 72Ub 157
N1 39Tb 71
NW10 38Sa 67
(off Westend Cl.)
SE26 64Yb 136
Canal Way UB9: Hare 23J 43
W10 42Za 88
Canal Wharf SL3: L'ly 47C 82
UB6: G'frd 39Ja 66
Canberra Cl. NW4 27Wa 48
RM10: Dag 39Fd 76
RM12: Horn 35Ld 77
Canberra Cres. RM10: Dag 38Fd 76
Canberra Dr. UB4: N'olt 41Z 85
UB5: N'olt 41Y 85
Canberra Ho. AL1: St A 2B 6
(off London Rd.)
Canberra Rd. DA7: Bex 51Zc 117
E6 39Pc 74
SE7 51Lc 115
TW6: H'row A 55Q 106
W13 46Ja 86
Canberra Sq. RM18: Tilb 4C 122
Canbury Av. KT2: King T 67Pa 131
Canbury Bus. Cen. KT2: King T 67Na 131
Canbury Bus. Pk. KT2: King T 67Na 131
(off Canbury Pk. Rd.)
Canbury Ct. KT2: King T 66Ma 131
Canbury M. SE26 62Wb 135
Canbury Pk. Rd. KT2: King T 67Na 131
Canbury Pas. KT2: King T 67Ma 131
Canbury Path BR5: St M Cry 70Wc 139
Cancell Rd. SW9 53Qb 112
Candahar Rd. SW11 54Gb 111
Cander Way RM15: S Ock 45Xd 98
Candida Ct. NW1 38Kb 70
Candid Ho. NW10 41Xa 88
(off Trenmar Gdns.)
Candlefield Cl. HP3: Hem H 5A 4
Candlefield Rd. HP3: Hem H 5A 4
Candlefield Wlk. HP3: Hem H 5A 4
Candle Gro. SE15 55Xb 113
Candlelight Ct. E15 37Hc 73
(off Romford Rd.)
Candler M. TW1: Twick 59Ja 108
Candler St. N15 30Tb 51
Candlerush Cl. GU22: Wok 89D 168
Candle St. E1 43Ac 92
C & L Golf Course 38X 65
Candover Cl. UB7: Harm 52M 105
Candover Rd. RM12: Horn 32Kd 77
Candover St. W1 1B 222 (43Lb 90)
Candy Cft. KT23: Bookh 98Da 191
Candy St. E3 39Bc 72
Candy Wharf E3 42Ac 92
Cane Hill RM3: Hrld W 26Md 57
Caneland Ct. EN9: Walt A 6Hc 21
Canewdon Cl. GU22: Wok 91A 188
Caney M. NW2 33Za 68
Canfield Dr. HA4: Ruis 36X 65
Canfield Gdns. NW6 38Db 69
Canfield Ho. N15 30Ub 51
(off Albert Rd.)
Canfield Pl. NW6 37Eb 69
Canfield Rd. IG8: Wfd G 24Nc 54
RM13: Rain 39Hd 76
Canford Av. UB5: N'olt 39Ba 65
Canford Cl. EN2: Enf 12Qb 32
Canford Dr. KT15: Add 75K 149
Canford Gdns. KT3: N Mald 72Ua 154
Canford Pl. TW11: Tedd 65La 130
Canford Rd. SW11 57Jb 112
Cangels Cl. HP1: Hem H 4J 3
Canham Rd. SE25 69Ub 135
W3 47Ua 88
Can Hatch KT20: Tad 90Ab 174
Canmore Gdns. SW16 66Lb 134
CANN HALL 35Gc 73
Cann Hall Rd. E11 35Gc 73
Cann Ho. W14 48Ab 88
(off Russell Rd.)
Canning Cres. N22 25Pb 50
Canning Cross SE5 54Ub 113
Canning Ho. W12 45Xa 88
(off Australia Rd.)
Canning Pas. W8 48Eb 89
Canning Pl. W8 3A 226 (48Eb 89)
Canning Pl. M. W8 3A 226
Canning Rd. CR0: C'don 75Vb 157
E15 40Gc 73
E17 28Ac 52
HA3: W'stone 27Ga 46
N5 34Rb 71
Cannington Rd. RM9: Dag 37Yc 75
CANNING TOWN 44Hc 93
CANNING TOWN 43Gc 93
Cannizaro Rd. SW19 65Ya 132
Cannock Ct. E17 26Ec 52
Cannock Ho. N4 31Sb 71
Cannonbury Av. HA5: Pinn 30Z 45
Cannon Cl. SS17: Stan H 1P 101
SW20 69Ya 132
TW12: Hamp 65Da 129
Cannon Ct. EC1 5C 218
Cannon Cres. GU24: Chob 3J 167
Cannon Dr. E14 45Cc 92
Cannon Ga. SL2: Slou 5N 81
Cannon Gro. KT22: Fet 94Ga 192
Cannon Hill N14 20Nb 32
NW6 36Cb 69
Cannon Hill La. SW20 71Za 154
Cannon Hill M. N14 20Nb 32
Cannon Ho. SE11 6J 229
Cannon La. HA5: Pinn 29Aa 45
NW3 34Fb 69
Cannon M. EN9: Walt A 5Dc 20
Cannon Pl. NW3 34Fb 69
SE7 50Nc 94
Cannon Retail Pk. SE28 45Wc 95
Cannon Rd. DA7: Bex 53Ad 117
N14 20Nb 32
WD18: Wat 15Y 27
Cannonside KT22: Fet 94Ga 192
Cannon St. AL3: St A 1B 6
EC4 3D 224 (44Sb 91)
Cannon St. Rd. E1 44Xb 91
Cannon Trad. Est. HA9: Wemb 35Ra 67
Cannon Wlk. DA12: Grav'nd 9E 122
(off Albert Murray Cl.)
Cannon Way KT8: W Mole 70Ca 129
KT22: Fet 93Ga 192
Cannon Wharf Bus. Cen.
SE8 49Ac 92
Cannon Workshops E14 45Cc 92
(off Cannon Dr.)
Canon All. EC4 3D 224
Canon Av. RM6: Chad H 29Xc 55
Canon Beck Rd. SE16 47Yb 92
Canonbie Rd. SE23 59Yb 114
CANONBURY 37Sb 71
Canonbury Bus. Cen. N1 39Sb 71
Canonbury Cotts. EN1: Enf 11Ub 33
Canonbury Ct. N1 38Rb 71
(off Hawes St.)
Canonbury Cres. N1 38Sb 71
Canonbury Gro. N1 38Sb 71
Canonbury Hgts. N1 37Tb 71
(off Dove Rd.)
Canonbury La. N1 38Rb 71
Canonbury Pk. Nth. N1 37Sb 71
Canonbury Pk. Sth. N1 37Sb 71
Canonbury Pl. N1 37Rb 71
(not continuous)
Canonbury Rd. EN1: Enf 11Ub 33
N1 37Rb 71
Canonbury Sq. N1 38Rb 71
Canonbury St. N1 38Sb 71
Canonbury Vs. N1 38Rb 71
Canon Mohan Cl. N14 16Jb 32
Canon Rd. BR1: Brom 69Lc 137
Canon Row SW1 2F 229 (47Nb 90)
(not continuous)
Canons Cl. HA8: Edg 23Pa 47
N2 31Fb 69
RH2: Reig 5H 207
WD7: R'lett 7Ka 14
Canons Cnr. HA8: Edg 21Na 47
Canons Ct. E15 35Gc 73
HA8: Edg 23Pa 47
Canons Dr. HA8: Edg 23Na 47
Canon's Hill CR5: Coul, Purl 89Rb 177
Canons La. KT20: Tad 90Ab 174
Canonsleigh Rd. RM9: Dag 38Xc 75
Canons Leisure Cen.
Mitcham 70Hb 133
CANONS PARK 24Ma 47
Canons Pk. HA7: Stan 23Ma 47
Canons Pk. Cl. HA8: Edg 24Na 47
Canon St. N1 39Sb 71
Canon's Wlk. CR0: C'don 76Zb 158
Canons Yd. RH2: Reig 9K 207
Canopus Way HA6: Nwood 21W 44
TW19: Stanw 59N 105
Canrobert St. E2 40Xb 71
Cantelowes Rd. NW1 37Mb 70
Canterbury Av. DA15: Sidc 61Xc 139
IG1: Ilf 31Nc 74
RM14: Upm 32Vd 78
SL2: Slou 2G 80
Canterbury Cl. BR3: Beck 67Dc 136
DA1: Dart 59Qd 119
E6 44Pc 94
HA6: Nwood 23V 44
IG7: Chig 20Vc 37
KT4: Wor Pk 75Za 154
SE5 54Sb 113
(off Lilford Rd.)
UB6: G'frd 43Da 85
Canterbury Ct. AL1: St A 1D 6
(off Battlefield Rd.)
CM15: Pil H 15Vd 40
CR2: S Croy 80Sb 157
(off St Augustines Av.)
NW6 40Cb 69
(off Canterbury Rd.)
NW9 26Ua 48
SE5 52Rb 113
SE12 62Kc 137
TW15: Ashf 63P 127
Canterbury Cres. SW9 55Qb 112
Canterbury Gro. SE27 63Qb 134
Canterbury Hall KT4: Wor Pk 73Xa 154
Canterbury Ho. CR0: C'don 74Tb 157
(off Sydenham Rd.)
DA8: Erith 52Hd 118
E3 41Dc 92
(off Bow Rd.)
IG11: Bark 38Wc 75
(off Margaret Bondfield Av.)
KT19: Eps 83Qa 173
(off Queen Alexandra's Way)
SE1 3J 229 (48Pb 90)
WD6: Bore 12Qa 29
(off Stratfield Rd.)
WD24: Wat 12Y 27
(off Anglian Cl.)
Canterbury Ind. Pk. SE15 51Yb 114
Canterbury M. KT22: Oxs 85Ea 172
SL4: Wind 4E 102
Canterbury Pde. RM15: S Ock 41Yd 98
Canterbury Pl. RM17: Grays 50Fe 99
SE17 6C 230 (50Rb 91)
Canterbury Rd. CR0: C'don 73Pb 156
DA12: Grav'nd 1E 144
E10 31Ec 72
HA1: Harr 29Da 45
HA2: Harr 29Da 45
NW6 40Bb 69
(Carlton Va.)
NW6 40Cb 69
(Princess Rd.)
SM4: Mord 73Db 155
TW13: Hanw 61Aa 129
WD6: Bore 12Qa 29
WD17: Wat 13X 27
Canterbury Ter. NW6 40Cb 69
Canterbury Way CM13: Gt War 23Yd 58
RM19: Purf 50Ud 98
RM20: W Thur 52Ud 120
WD3: Crox G 13S 26
Cantium Retail Pk. SE1 51Wb 113
Cantley Gdns. IG2: Ilf 30Sc 54
SE19 67Vb 135
Cantley Rd. W7 48Ja 86
Canto Ct. EC1 5E 218
Canton St. E14 44Cc 92
Cantrell Rd. E3 42Bc 92
Cantwell Rd. SE18 52Rc 116
Canute Gdns. SE16 49Zb 92
Canvey St. SE1 6D 224 (46Sb 91)
Capability Way DA9: Ghithe 56Yd 120
Cape Cl. IG11: Bark 38Rc 74
Cape Henry Ct. E14 45Fc 93
(off Jamestown Way)
Cape Ho. E8 37Vb 71
(off Dalston La.)
Capelands DA3: New A 75Ce 165
Capel Av. SM6: Wall 78Pb 156
Capel Cl. BR2: Brom 74Nc 160
N20 20Eb 31
SS17: Stan H 1N 101
Capel Ct. EC2 3G 225
SE20 67Yb 136
Capel Cres. HA7: Stan 19Ja 28
Capel Gdns. HA5: Pinn 28Ba 45
IG3: Bark, Ilf 35Vc 75
Capel Ho. E9 38Yb 72
(off Loddiges Rd.)
WD19: Wat 21Z 45
Capella Rd. HA6: Nwood 21V 44
Capell Av. WD3: Chor 15E 24
Capell Rd. WD3: Chor 15F 24
Capell Way WD3: Chor 15F 24
Capel Manor Gdns. 7Wb 19
Capel Pl. DA2: Wilm 63Ld 141
Capel Rd. E7 35Kc 73
E12 35Kc 73
EN1: Enf 8Xb 19
EN4: E Barn 16Gb 31
WD19: Wat 16Aa 27
Capelvere Wlk. WD17: Wat 11U 26
Capener's Cl. SW1 2G 227
Capern Rd. SW18 60Eb 111
Cape Rd. AL1: St A 2F 6
N17 27Wb 51
Cape Yd. E1 46Wb 91
Capital Bus. Cen. CR2: S Croy 80Tb 157
HA0: Wemb 40Ma 67
WD24: Wat 8Z 13
Capital Bus. Pk. WD6: Bore 13Sa 29
Capital E. Apartments E16 45Jc 93
(off Western Gateway)
Capital Ind. Est. CR4: Mitc 71Hb 155
DA17: Belv 48Dd 96
Capital Interchange Way
TW8: Bford 50Qa 87
Capital Pk. GU22: Wok 93D 188
Capital Trad. Est. IG11: Bark 40Tc 74
Capital Wharf E1 46Wb 91
Capitol Ind. Pk. NW9 27Sa 47
Capitol Sq. KT17: Eps 85Ua 174
Capitol Way NW9 27Sa 47
Capland Ho. NW8 5C 214
Capland St. NW8 5C 214 (42Fb 89)
Caple Ho. SW10 52Eb 111
(off King's Rd.)
Caple Rd. NW10 40Va 68
Capon Cl. CM14: B'wood 18Xd 40
Capper St. WC1 6C 216 (42Lb 90)
Caprea Cl. UB4: Yead 43Z 85
Capricorn Cen. RM8: Dag 31Bd 75
Capri Ho. E17 26Bc 52
Capri Rd. CR0: C'don 74Vb 157
Capstan Cen. RM18: Tilb 52Fe 121
Capstan Cl. RM6: Chad H 30Xc 55
Capstan Ct. DA2: Dart 56Sd 120
E1 45Yb 92
(off Wapping Wall)
Capstan Dr. RM13: Rain 42Jd 96
Capstan Ho. E14 45Fc 93
(off Clove Cres.)
E14 49Ec 92
(off Stebondale St.)
Capstan M. DA11: Nflt 9A 122
Capstan Ride EN2: Enf 12Qb 32
Capstan Rd. SE8 49Bc 92
Capstan Sq. E14 47Ec 92
Capstans Wharf GU21: Wok 10K 167
Capstan Way SE16 46Ac 92
Capstone Rd. BR1: Brom 63Hc 137
Capswood Bus. Cen. UB9: Den 32E 62
Captains Wlk. HP4: Berk 2A 2
Capthorne Av. HA2: Harr 32Aa 65
Capuchin Cl. HA7: Stan 23Ka 46
Capulet M. E16 46Jc 93
Capulet Sq. E3 41Dc 92
(off Talwin St.)
Capworth St. E10 32Cc 72
Caractacus Cott. Vw. WD18: Wat 17W 26
Caractacus Grn. WD18: Wat 16V 26
Caradoc Cl. W2 44Cb 89
Caradoc Evans Cl. N11 22Kb 50
(off Springfield Rd.)
Caradoc St. SE10 50Gc 93
Caradon Cl. E11 32Gc 73
GU21: Wok 10M 167
Caradon Way N15 28Tb 51
Cara Ho. N1 38Qb 70
(off Liverpool Rd.)
Caramel Ct. E3 40Dc 72
(off Taylor Pl.)
Caranday Vs. W11 46Za 88
(off Norland Rd.)
Carat Ho. E14 43Cc 92
(off Ursula Gould Way)
Caravan La. WD3: Rick 17N 25
Caravel Cl. E14 48Cc 92
RM16: Chaf H 48Be 99
Caravelle Gdns. UB5: N'olt 41Z 85
Caravel M. SE8 51Cc 114
Caraway Apartments SE1 1K 231
Caraway Cl. E13 43Kc 93
Caraway Hgts. E14 45Ec 92
(off Poplar High St.)
Caraway Pl. SM6: Wall 76Kb 156
Carberry Rd. SE19 65Ub 135
Carbery Av. W3 47Pa 87
Carbery La. SL5: Asc 9A 124
Carbis Cl. E4 18Fc 35
Carbis Rd. E14 44Bc 92
Carbrooke Ho. E9 39Yb 72
(off Templecombe Rd.)
Carbuncle Pas. N17 26Wb 51
Carburton St. W1 7A 216 (43Kb 90)
Carbury Cl. RM12: Horn 37Ld 77
Cardale St. E14 47Ec 92
Cardamon Bldg. SE1 7K 225
Carden Rd. SE15 55Xb 113
Cardiff Cl. RM5: Col R 24Fd 56
Cardiff Ho. SE15 51Wb 113
(off Friary Est.)
Cardiff Rd. EN3: Pond E 14Xb 33
W7 48Ja 86
WD18: Wat 16X 27
Cardiff Rd. Ind. Est. WD18: Wat 16X 27
Cardiff St. SE18 52Uc 116
Cardiff Way WD5: Ab L 4W 12
Cardigan Cl. GU21: Wok 10J 167
SL1: Slou 5D 80
Cardigan Ct. W7 42Ha 86
(off Copley Cl.)
Cardigan Gdns. IG3: Ilf 33Wc 75
Cardigan Ho. RM3: Rom 22Md 57
(off Bridgwater Wlk.)
Cardigan Pl. SE3 54Fc 115
Cardigan Rd. E3 40Bc 72
SW13 54Wa 110
SW19 65Eb 133
TW10: Rich 58Na 109
Cardigan St. SE11 7K 229 (50Qb 90)
Cardigan Wlk. N1 38Sb 71
(off Ashby Gro.)
Cardinal Av. KT2: King T 64Na 131
SM4: Mord 72Ab 154
WD6: Bore 13Ra 29
Cardinal Bourne St.
SE1 4G 231 (48Tb 91)
Cardinal Cap All. SE1 5D 224 (46Sb 91)
Cardinal Cl. BR7: Chst 77Wc 161
CR2: Sande 85Wb 177
HA8: Edg 24Sa 47
KT4: Wor Pk 77Wa 154
SM4: Mord 72Ab 154
Cardinal Ct. E1 45Wb 91
(off Thomas More St.)
WD6: Bore 13Qa 29
Cardinal Cres. KT3: N Mald 68Sa 131
Cardinal Dr. IG6: Ilf 23Sc 54
KT12: Walt T 74Z 151
Cardinal Gro. AL3: St A 4P 5
Cardinal Hinsley Cl. NW10 40Wa 68
Cardinal Mans. SW1 5B 228
Cardinal Pl. SW1 3B 228 (48Lb 90)
(not continuous)
SW15 56Za 110
Cardinal Rd. HA4: Ruis 32Z 65
RM16: Chaf H 48Ae 99
TW13: Felt 60X 107
Cardinals Wlk. SL6: Tap 4A 80
TW12: Hamp 66Ea 130
TW16: Sun 65U 128
Cardinals Way N19 32Mb 70
Cardinal Wlk. SW1 4B 228
Cardinal Way HA3: W'stone 27Ga 46
RM13: Rain 40Md 77
Cardine M. SE15 52Xb 113
Cardingham GU21: Wok 9L 167
Cardington Sq. TW4: Houn 56Z 107
Cardington St. NW1 3C 216 (41Lb 90)
Cardinham Rd. BR6: Chels 77Vc 161
Cardozo Rd. N7 36Nb 70
Cardrew Av. N12 22Fb 49
Cardrew Cl. N12 22Gb 49
Cardrew Ct. N12 22Fb 49
Cardross Ho. W6 48Xa 88
(off Cardross St.)
Cardross St. W6 48Xa 88
Cardwell Cres. SL5: S'hill 1A 146
Cardwell Rd. N7 35Nb 70
Cardwell Ter. N7 35Nb 70
(off Cardwell Rd.)
Cardy Rd. HP1: Hem H 3K 3
Career Ct. SE16 47Zb 92
(off Christopher Cl.)
Carew Cl. CR5: Coul 91Rb 197
N7 33Pb 70
RM16: Chaf H 48Ae 99
Carew Ct. RM6: Chad H 30Xc 55
(off Quarles Pk. Rd.)
SE14 51Zb 114
(off Samuel Cl.)
SM2: Sutt 81Db 175
Carew Manor & Dovecote 76Lb 156
Carew Mnr. Cotts. SM6: Bedd 76Mb 156
Carew Rd. CR4: Mitc 68Jb 134
CR7: Thor H 70Rb 135
HA6: Nwood 23U 44
N17 26Wb 51
SM6: Wall 79Lb 156
TW15: Ashf 65S 128
W13 47La 86
Carew St. SE5 54Sb 113
Carew Way BR5: Orp 74Yc 161
WD19: Wat 20Ba 27
Carey Cl. SL4: Wind 5F 102
Carey Ct. DA6: Bex 57Dd 118
SE5 52Sb 113
Carey Gdns. SW8 53Lb 112
Carey La. EC2 2D 224 (44Sb 91)
Carey Mans. SW1 5D 228
Carey Pl. SW1 6D 228 (49Mb 90)
WD17: Wat 14Y 27
Carey Rd. RM9: Dag 35Ad 75
Carey's Fld. TN13: Dun G 92Gd 202
Carey St. WC2 3J 223 (44Pb 90)
Carey Way HA9: Wemb 35Ra 67
Carfax Ho. SE20 67Wb 135
Carfax Pl. SW4 56Mb 112
Carfax Rd. RM12: Horn 35Hd 76
UB3: Harl 50V 84
Carfree Cl. N1 38Qb 70
Cargill Rd. SW18 60Db 111
Cargo Point TW19: Stanw 58P 105
Cargreen Pl. SE25 70Vb 135
Cargreen Rd. SE25 70Vb 135
Cargrey Ho. HA7: Stan 22La 46
Carholme Rd. SE23 60Bc 114
Carillon Ct. E1 43Wb 91
(off Greatorex St.)
W5 45Ma 87
Carinthia Ct. SE16 49Ac 92
(off Plough Way)
Carisbrook N10 26Kb 50
Carisbrook Cl. CM16: Epp 3Wc 23
EN1: Enf 11Vb 33
Carisbrooke Av. DA5: Bexl 60Zc 117
WD24: Wat 11Z 27
Carisbrooke Cl. HA7: Stan 26Ma 47
RM11: Horn 32Qd 77
TW4: Houn 59Aa 107
Carisbrooke Ct. DA2: Dart 58Rd 119
(off Osbourne Rd.)
SL1: Slou 5K 81
SM2: Cheam 80Bb 155
UB5: N'olt 39Ba 65
(off Eskdale Av.)
W1 1J 221
W3 47Sa 87
(off Brouncker Rd.)
Carisbrooke Gdns. SE15 52Vb 113
Carisbrooke Ho. HA6: Nwood 22V 44
KT2: King T 67Na 131
(off Seven Kings Way)
TW10: Rich 57Qa 109
UB7: W Dray 47P 83
(off Park Lodge Av.)
Carisbrooke Rd. BR2: Brom 70Lc 137
CM15: Pil H 16Xd 40
CR4: Mitc 70Mb 134
E17 28Ac 52
Carisbrook Rd. AL2: Chis G 8P 5
Carker's La. NW5 36Kb 70
Carlbury Cl. AL1: St A 3F 6
Carl Ekman Ho. DA11: Nflt 59Fe 121
Carleton Av. SM6: Wall 81Mb 176
Carleton Cl. KT10: Esh 74Fa 152
Carleton Gdns. N19 36Lb 70
Carleton Pl. DA4: Hort K 70Sd 142
Carleton Rd. DA1: Dart 59Qd 119
N7 36Mb 70
Carleton Vs. NW5 36Lb 70
Carlile Cl. E3 40Bc 72
Carlile Ho. SE1 4G 231
Carlina Gdns. IG8: Wfd G 22Kc 53
Carlingford Gdns. CR4: Mitc 66Hb 133
Carlingford Rd. N15 27Rb 51
NW3 35Fb 69
SM4: Mord 72Za 154
Carlisle Av. AL1: St A 1B 6
AL3: St A 1B 6
EC3 3J 225 (44Vb 91)
W3 44Ua 88
Carlisle Cl. HA5: Pinn 31Aa 65
KT2: King T 67Qa 131
Carlisle Gdns. HA3: Kenton 31Ma 67
IG1: Ilf 30Nc 54
Carlisle Ho. IG1: Ilf 30Nc 54
WD6: Bore 12Qa 29

Carlisle La. SE1 4J 229 (48Pb 90)
Carlisle Mans. SW1 5B 228
Carlisle M. KT2: King T 67Qa 131
Carlisle Pl. N11 21Kb 50
SW1 4B 228 (48Lb 90)
TW10: Rich 58Pa 109
Carlisle Rd. DA1: Dart 58Qd 119
E10 32Cc 72
N4 31Qb 70
NW6 39Ab 68
NW9 27Sa 47
RM1: Rom 29Jd 56
SL1: Slou 5H 81
SM1: Sutt 79Bb 155
TW12: Hamp 66Da 129
Carlisle St. W1 3D 222 (44Mb 90)
Carlisle Wlk. E8 37Vb 71
Carlisle Way SW17 64Jb 134
Carlos Pl. W1 5J 221 (45Jb 90)
Carlow St. NW1 1B 216 (40Lb 70)
Carlson Ct. SW15 56Bb 111
Carlton Av. CR2: S Croy 80Ub 157
DA9: Ghithe 58Ud 120
HA3: Kenton 29Ka 46
N14 15Mb 32
TW14: Felt 58Y 107
UB3: Harl 49U 84
Carlton Av. E. HA9: Wemb 33Ma 67
Carlton Av. W. HA0: Wemb 33Ka 66
Carlton Cl. GU21: Wok 86B 168
HA8: Edg 22Qa 47
KT9: Chess 79Ma 153
NW3 33Cb 69
RM14: Upm 33Rd 77
UB5: N'olt 36Ea 66
WD6: Bore 14Ta 29
Carlton Ct. IG6: Ilf 27Tc 54
N3 24Cb 49
SE20 67Xb 135
SW9 53Rb 113
TW18: Staines 64J 127
UB8: Cowl 43M 83
W9 40Db 69
(off Maida Va.)
WD19: Wat 16Y 27
Carlton Cres. SM3: Cheam 77Ab 154
Carlton Dr. IG6: Ilf 27Tc 54
SW15 57Za 110
Carlton Gdns. SW1 6D 222 (46Mb 90)
W5 44La 86
Carlton Grn. DA14: Sidc 63Vc 139
RH1: Redh 3N 207
Carlton Gro. SE15 53Xb 113
Carlton Hill NW8 1A 214 (40Db 69)
Carlton Ho. IG10: Lough 15Mc 35
NW6 40Cb 69
(off Canterbury Ter., not continuous)
SE16 47Zb 92
(off Wolfe Cres.)
TW3: Houn 58Ca 107
TW14: Felt 58V 106
Carlton Ho. Ter. SW1 7D 222 (46Mb 90)
Carlton Lodge N4 31Qb 70
(off Carlton Rd.)
Carlton Mans. N16 32Vb 71
NW6 39Cb 69
(off West End La.)
W9 41Db 69
W14 47Ab 88
(off Holland Pk. Gdns.)
Carlton M. NW6 36Cb 69
(off West Cotts.)
Carlton Pde. BR6: St M Cry 73Xc 161
HA9: Wemb 33Na 67
TN13: S'oaks 94Ld 203
Carlton Pk. Av. SW20 68Za 132
Carlton Pl. HA6: Nwood 22R 44
KT13: Weyb 77R 150
(off Castle Vw. Rd.)
Carlton Rd. CR2: S Croy 79Tb 157
DA8: Erith 51Dd 118
DA14: Sidc 64Vc 139
DA16: Well 55Xc 117
E11 32Hc 73
E12 35Mc 73
E17 25Ac 52
GU21: Wok 86C 168
KT3: N Mald 68Ua 132
KT12: Walt T 73X 151
N4 31Qb 70
N11 22Jb 50
RH1: Redh 4M 207
RH2: Reig 4M 207
RM2: Rom 29Hd 56
RM16: Grays 7B 100
SL2: Slou 5M 81
SW14 55Sa 109
TW16: Sun 66V 128
W4 47Ta 87
W5 45La 86
Carlton Sq. E1 42Zb 92
(not continuous)
Carlton St. SW1 5D 222 (45Mb 90)
Carlton Ter. E7 38Lc 73
E11 29Kc 53
(not continuous)
N18 20Tb 33
SE26 62Yb 136
Carlton Twr. Pl. SW1 3G 227 (48Hb 89)
Carlton Towers SM5: Cars 76Hb 155
Carlton Vale NW6 40Bb 69
Carlton Vs. SW15 57Ab 110
Carlton Works, The SE15 52Xb 113
(off Asylum Rd.)
Carlwell St. SW17 64Gb 133
Carlyle Av. BR1: Brom 69Mc 137
UB1: S'hall 45Ba 85
Carlyle Cl. KT8: W Mole 68Da 129
N2 30Eb 49
Carlyle Ct. SW6 53Db 111
(off Imperial Rd.)
SW10 53Eb 111
(off Chelsea Harbour Dr.)
Carlyle Gdns. UB1: S'hall 45Ba 85
Carlyle Ho. KT8: W Mole 71Ca 151
(off Down St.)
N16 34Ub 71
SE5 52Sb 113
(off Bethwin Rd.)
SW3 51Fb 111
(off Old Church St.)
Carlyle Mans. SW3 51Gb 111
(off Cheyne Wlk.)
W8 46Cb 89
(off Kensington Mall)
Carlyle M. E1 42Zb 92
Carlyle Pl. SW15 56Za 110
Carlyle Rd. CR0: C'don 75Wb 157
E12 35Nc 74
NW10 39Ta 67
SE28 45Xc 95
TW18: Staines 66J 127
W5 49La 86
Carlyle's House 51Gb 111
(off Cheyne Row)
Carlyle Sq. SW3 50Fb 89
Carly M. E2 41Wb 91
(off Barnet Gro.)
Carlyon Av. HA2: Harr 35Ba 65
Carlyon Cl. HA0: Wemb 39Na 67
Carlyon Rd. HA0: Wemb 40Na 67
UB4: Yead 43Y 85
(not continuous)
Carlys Cl. BR3: Beck 68Zb 136
Carmalt Gdns. KT12: Hers 78Y 151
SW15 56Ya 110
Carmarthen Ct. W7 42Ha 86
(off Copley Cl.)
Carmarthen Pl. SE1 1H 231 (47Ub 91)
Carmarthen Rd. SL1: Slou 5J 81
Carmel Cl. GU22: Wok 90A 168
Carmel Ct. HA9: Wemb 33Ra 67
W8 47Db 89
(off Holland St.)
Carmelite Cl. HA3: Hrw W 25Ea 46
Carmelite Rd. HA3: Hrw W 25Ea 46
Carmelite St. EC4 4A 224 (45Qb 90)
Carmelite Wlk. HA3: Hrw W 25Ea 46
Carmelite Way DA3: Hartl 71Be 165
HA3: Hrw W 26Ea 46
Carmel Lodge SW6 51Cb 111
(off Lillie Rd.)
Carmel Way TW9: Rich 54Ra 109
Carmen Ct. WD6: Bore 11Pa 29
(off Aycliffe Rd.)
Carmen St. E14 44Dc 92
Carmichael Av. DA9: Ghithe 56Yd 120
Carmichael Cl. HA4: Ruis 35W 64
SW11 55Fb 111
Carmichael Ct. SW13 54Va 110
(off Grove Rd.)
Carmichael Ho. E14 45Ec 92
(off Poplar High St.)
Carmichael M. SW18 59Fb 111
Carmichael Rd. SE25 71Vb 157
Carmine W2 1C 220
Carmine Ct. BR1: Brom 66Hc 137
Carmine Wharf E14 44Bc 92
Carminia Rd. SW17 61Kb 134
Carnaby St. W1 3B 222 (44Lb 90)
Carnach Grn. RM15: S Ock 45Wd 98
Carnac St. SE27 63Tb 135
Carnanton Rd. E17 25Fc 53
Carnarvon Av. EN1: Enf 13Vb 33
Carnarvon Dr. UB3: Harl 48S 84
Carnarvon Rd. E10 29Ec 52
E15 37Hc 73
E18 25Hc 53
EN5: Barn 13Ab 30
Carnation Cl. RM7: Rush G 33Gd 76
Carnation St. SE2 50Xc 95
Carnbrook M. SE3 55Mc 115
Carnbrook Rd. SE3 55Mc 115
Carnecke Gdns. SE9 57Nc 116
Carnegie Cl. EN3: Enf L 10Dc 20
KT6: Surb 75Pa 153
Carnegie Ct. SL2: Farn C 7F 60
Carnegie Pl. SW19 62Za 132
Carnegie Rd. HA1: Harr 31Ha 66
Carnegie St. N1 1J 217 (39Pb 70)
Carnell Apartments E14 43Bc 92
(off St Anne's Row)
Carnet Cl. DA1: Cray 59Gd 118
Carnforth Cl. KT19: Ewe 79Ra 153
Carnforth Gdns. RM12: Horn 36Hd 76
Carnforth Rd. SW16 66Mb 134
(not continuous)
Carnie Lodge SW17 62Kb 134
Carnival Ho. SE1 1K 231
Carnoustie Cl. SE28 44Zc 95
Carnoustie Dr. N1 38Pb 70
(not continuous)
Carnwath Rd. SW6 55Cb 111
Caroe Ct. N9 18Xb 33
Caro La. HP3: Hem H 4B 4
Carol Cl. NW4 28Za 48
Carole Ho. NW1 39Hb 69
(off Regent's Pk. Rd.)
Carolina Cl. E15 36Gc 73
Carolina Rd. CR7: Thor H 68Rb 135
Caroline Cl. CR0: C'don 77Ub 157
N10 26Kb 50
SW16 62Pb 134
TW7: Isle 52Fa 108
UB7: W Dray 47M 83
W2 45Db 89
Caroline Ct. HA7: Stan 23Ja 46
SE6 63Fc 137
TW15: Ashf 65R 128
Caroline Gdns. E2 3J 219 (41Ub 91)
SE15 52Xb 113
(not continuous)
Caroline Ho. W2 45Db 89
(off Bayswater Rd.)
W6 50Ya 88
(off Queen Caroline St.)
Caroline Pl. SW11 54Jb 112
UB3: Harl 52U 106
W2 45Db 89
WD19: Wat 16Aa 27
Caroline Pl. M. W2 45Db 89
Caroline Rd. SW19 66Bb 133
Caroline St. E1 44Zb 92
Caroline Ter. SW1 6H 227 (49Jb 90)
Caroline Wlk. W6 51Ab 110
(off Lillie Rd.)
Carol St. NW1 39Lb 70
Carolyn Cl. GU21: Wok 1K 187
Carolyn Dr. BR6: Chels 76Wc 161
Caronia Ct. SE16 49Ac 92
(off Plough Way)
Caroon Dr. WD3: Sarr 8K 11
Carpenders Av. WD19: Wat 20Aa 27
CARPENDERS PARK 20Z 27
Carpenter Cl. KT17: Ewe 81Va 174
Carpenter Gdns. N21 19Rb 33
Carpenter Ho. E14 43Cc 92
(off Burgess St.)
NW11 30Eb 49
Carpenter Path CM13: Hut 15Fe 41
Carpenters Arms Path SE9 56Pc 116
(off Eltham High St.)
Carpenters Cl. EN5: New Bar 16Db 31
Carpenters Ct. NW1 39Lb 70
(off Pratt St.)
TW2: Twick 61Ga 130
Carpenters M. N7 36Nb 70
Carpenters Pl. SW4 56Mb 112
Carpenters Rd. E15 38Ec 72
EN1: Enf 8Yb 20
Carpenter St. W1 5K 221 (45Kb 90)
Carpenters Wood Dr. WD3: Chor 14D 24
Carpenter Way EN6: Pot B 5Eb 17
Carp Ho. E3 39Bc 72
(off Old Ford Rd.)
Carrack Ho. DA8: Erith 50Gd 96
(off Saltford Cl.)
Carradale Ho. E14 44Ec 92
(off St Leonard's Rd.)
Carrara Cl. SE24 56Qb 113
SW9 56Rb 113
Carrara M. E8 37Wb 71
(off Dalston La.)
Carrara Wharf SW6 55Ab 110
Carr Cl. HA7: Stan 23Ja 46
Carre M. SE5 53Rb 113
(off Calais St.)
Carr Gro. SE18 49Nc 94
Carr Ho. DA1: Cray 57Gd 118
Carriage Dr. E. SW11 52Jb 112
Carriage Dr. Nth. SW11 51Jb 112
(Carriage Dr. E.)
SW11 52Hb 111
(The Parade)
Carriage Dr. Sth. SW11 53Hb 111
(not continuous)
Carriage Dr. W. SW11 52Hb 111
Carriage M. IG1: Ilf 33Sc 74
Carriage Pl. N16 34Tb 71
SW16 64Lb 134
Carriage St. SE18 48Rc 94
Carriageway, The TN16: Bras 96Zc 201
Carrick Cl. TW7: Isle 55Ja 108
Carrick Dr. IG6: Ilf 25Sc 54
TN13: S'oaks 95Kd 203
Carrick Gdns. N17 24Ub 51
Carrick Gate KT10: Esh 76Ea 152
Carrick Ho. N7 37Pb 70
(off Caledonian Rd.)
SE11 7B 230 (50Qb 90)
Carrick M. SE8 51Cc 114
Carrigshaun KT13: Weyb 78T 150
Carrill Way DA17: Belv 48Zc 95
Carrington Av. TW3: Houn 57Da 107
WD6: Bore 15Ra 29
Carrington Cl. CR0: C'don 73Ac 158
EN5: Ark 15Wa 30
KT2: King T 64Sa 131
RH1: Redh 5P 207
WD6: Bore 15Sa 29
Carrington Ct. SW11 56Gb 111
(off Barnard Rd.)
Carrington Gdns. E7 35Jc 73
Carrington Ho. W1 7K 221
Carrington Pl. KT10: Esh 77Da 151
Carrington Rd. DA1: Dart 58Pd 119
SL1: Slou 5J 81
TW10: Rich 56Qa 109
Carrington Sq. HA3: Hrw W 23Ea 46
Carrington St. W1 7K 221 (46Kb 90)
Carrock Ct. RM7: Rush G 30Gd 56
(off Union Rd.)
Carrol Cl. NW5 35Kb 70
Carroll Cl. E15 36Hc 73
Carroll Ct. W3 48Ra 87
(off Osborne Rd.)
Carroll Hill IG10: Lough 13Pc 36
Carroll Ho. W2 4B 220
Carronade Ct. N7 36Pb 70
Carronade Pl. SE28 48Sc 94
Carron Cl. E14 44Dc 92
Carroun Rd. SW8 52Pb 112
Carroway La. UB6: G'frd 41Fa 86
Carrow Rd. KT12: Walt T 76Z 151
RM9: Dag 38Xc 75
Carr Rd. E17 26Bc 52
UB5: N'olt 37Ca 65
Carrs La. N21 15Sb 33
Carr St. E14 43Ac 92
CARSHALTON 77Jb 156
Carshalton Athletic FC 76Gb 155
CARSHALTON BEECHES 81Gb 175
Carshalton Gro. SM1: Sutt 77Fb 155
Carshalton Lodge KT13: Weyb 76T 150
(off Oatlands Dr.)
CARSHALTON ON THE HILL 80Jb 156
Carshalton Pk. Rd. SM5: Cars 78Hb 155
Carshalton Pl. SM5: Cars 78Jb 156
Carshalton Rd. CR4: Mitc 70Jb 134
SM1: Sutt 78Eb 155
SM5: Cars 78Eb 155
SM7: Bans 86Hb 175
Carsington Gdns. DA1: Dart 61Md 141
Carslake Rd. SW15 58Ya 110
Carson Rd. E16 42Jc 93
EN4: Cockf 14Hb 31
SE21 61Tb 135
Carson Ter. W11 46Ab 88
(off Princes Pl.)
Carstairs Rd. SE6 62Ec 136
Carston Cl. SE12 57Hc 115
Carswell Cl. CM13: Hut 16Fe 41
IG4: Ilf 28Mc 53
Carswell Rd. SE6 59Ec 114
CARTBRIDGE 94D 188
Cartbridge Cl. GU23: Send 95D 188
Cartel Cl. RM19: Purf 49Td 98
Carter Av. TN15: W King 80Ud 184
Carter Cl. NW9 30Ta 47
RM5: Col R 24Cd 56
SL4: Wind 4E 102
Carter Ct. EC4 3C 224
Carter Dr. RM5: Col R 22Dd 56
Carteret Ho. W12 45Xa 88
(off White City Est.)
Carteret St. SW1 2D 228 (47Mb 90)
Carteret Way SE8 49Ac 92
Carterhatch La. EN1: Enf 10Vb 19
Carterhatch Rd. EN3: Enf H 11Yb 34
Carter Ho. E1 1K 225
Carter La. EC4 3C 224 (44Rb 91)
Carter Pl. SE17 7E 230 (50Sb 91)
Carter Rd. E13 39Kc 73
SW19 65Fb 133
Carters Cl. KT4: Wor Pk 75Za 154
NW5 36Mb 70
(off Torriano Av.)
Carter's Cotts. RH1: Redh 8N 207
Cartersfield Rd. EN9: Walt A 6Ec 20
CARTER'S HILL 100Rd 203
Carter's Hill TN15: Under 100Rd 203
Carters Hill Cl. SE9 60Lc 115
Carters La. GU22: Wok 92E 188
SE23 61Ac 136
Carters Rd. KT17: Eps 87Va 174
Carters Row DA11: Nflt 10B 122
Carter St. SE17 51Sb 113
Carter's Yd. SW18 57Cb 111
Carthew Rd. W6 48Xa 88
Carthew Vs. W6 48Xa 88
Carthouse La. GU21: Wok 6J 167
Carthusian St. EC1 7D 218 (43Sb 91)
Cartier Circ. E14 46Dc 92
Carting La. WC2 5G 223 (45Nb 90)
Cart La. E4 18Gc 35
RM17: Grays 50De 99
Cartmel NW1 3B 216
Cartmel Cl. N17 24Xb 51
RH2: Reig 4N 207
Cartmel Ct. UB5: N'olt 37Aa 65
Cartmel Gdns. SM4: Mord 71Eb 155
Cartmel Rd. DA7: Bex 53Cd 118
Carton Ho. W11 45Za 88
(off St Ann's Rd.)
Cartoon Mus. 1F 223
Cart Path WD25: Wat 5Y 13
Cartridge Pl. SE18 48Rc 94
Cart Track, The HP3: Hem H 7P 3
Cartwright Gdns. WC1 4F 217 (41Nb 90)
Cartwright Ho. SE1 4E 230
Cartwright Rd. RM9: Dag 38Bd 75
Cartwright St. E1 45Vb 91
Cartwright Way SW13 52Xa 110
Carvel Ho. E14 50Ec 92
(off Manchester Rd.)
Carver Cl. W4 48Sa 87
Carver Rd. SE24 58Sb 113
Carville Cres. TW8: Bford 49Na 87
Carville St. N4 33Qb 70
Cary Rd. E11 35Gc 73
Carysfort Rd. N8 29Mb 50
N16 34Tb 71
Cary Wlk. WD7: R'lett 6Ka 14
Casby Ho. SE16 48Wb 91
(off Marine St.)
Cascade Av. N10 28Lb 50
Cascade Cl. BR5: St P 69Yc 139
IG9: Buck H 19Mc 35
Cascade Rd. IG9: Buck H 19Mc 35
Cascades CR0: Sels 82Bc 178
Cascades Ct. SW19 66Bb 133
Cascades Leisure Cen. 3J 145
Cascades Twr. E14 46Bc 92
Casel Ct. HA7: Stan 19Ja 28
(off Brightwen Gro.)
Caselden Cl. KT15: Add 78L 149
Casella Rd. SE14 52Zb 114
Casewick Rd. SE27 64Qb 134
Casey Cl. NW8 4D 214 (41Gb 89)
Casey Ct. SE14 53Zb 114
(off Besson St.)
Casimir Rd. E5 33Yb 72
Casino Av. SE24 57Sb 113
Caspian Cl. RM19: Purf 49Qd 97
Caspian St. SE5 52Tb 113
Caspian Wlk. E16 44Mc 93
Caspian Way DA10: Swans 57Ae 121
RM19: Purf 50Qd 97
Caspian Wharf E3 43Dc 92
(off Violet Rd.)
Cassander Pl. HA5: Pinn 25Aa 45
(off Holly Gro.)
Cassandra Cl. RM13: Rain 39Hd 76
UB5: N'olt 35Fa 66
Casselden Rd. NW10 38Ta 67
Cassell Cl. RM16: Ors 3C 100
Cassell Ho. SW9 54Pb 112
(off Stockwell Gdns. Est.)
Cass Ho. E9 37Zb 72
(off Harrowgate Rd.)
Cassidy Rd. SW6 52Cb 111
(not continuous)
Cassilda Rd. SE2 49Wc 95
Cassilis Rd. E14 47Cc 92
TW1: Twick 57Ka 108
Cassini Apartments E16 44Jc 93
Cassio Apartments WD17: Wat 12X 27
(off Malden Rd.)
Cassiobridge Rd. WD18: Wat 14U 26
Cassiobury Av. TW14: Felt 59V 106
Cassiobury Ct. WD17: Wat 12U 26
Cassiobury Dr. WD17: Wat 10U 12
Cassiobury Pk. 13U 26
Cassiobury Pk. Av. WD18: Wat 13U 26
Cassiobury Rd. E17 29Ac 52
Cassio Ho. WD18: Wat 14V 26
(off Manhattan Av.)
Cassio Metro Leisure Cen. 14V 26
Cassio Pl. WD18: Wat 14U 26
Cassio Rd. WD18: Wat 13X 27
Cassio Wharf WD18: Wat 15T 26
Cassis Ct. IG10: Lough 14Sc 36
Cassland Rd. CR7: Thor H 70Tb 135
E9 38Zb 72
Casslee Rd. SE6 59Bc 114
Cassocks Sq. TW17: Shep 73T 150
Casson Ho. E1 43Wb 91
(off Hanbury St.)
Casson St. E1 43Wb 91
Casstine Cl. BR8: Hext 66Hd 140
Castalia Ct. DA1: Dart 55Pd 119
Castalia Sq. E14 47Ec 92
Castano Ct. WD5: Ab L 3U 12
Castellain Mans. W9 42Db 89
(off Castellain Rd., not continuous)
Castellain Rd. W9 42Db 89
Castellan Av. RM2: Rom 27Kd 57
Castellane Cl. HA7: Stan 24Ha 46
Castell Ho. SE8 52Cc 114
Castello Av. SW15 57Ya 110
Castell Rd. IG10: Lough 11Sc 36
CASTELNAU 51Xa 110
Castelnau SW13 53Wa 110
Castelnau Gdns. SW13 51Xa 110
Castelnau Mans. SW13 51Xa 110
(off Castelnau, not continuous)
Castelnau Row SW13 51Xa 110
Casterbridge NW6 39Db 69
(off Abbey Rd.)
W11 44Bb 89
(off Dartmouth Cl.)
Casterbridge Rd. SE3 55Jc 115
Casterton St. E8 37Xb 71
Castile Ct. EN8: Walt C 6Cc 20
Castile Gdns. WD4: K Lan 1P 11
Castile Rd. SE18 49Qc 94
Castillon Rd. SE6 61Gc 137
Castlands Rd. SE6 61Bc 136
Castleacre W2 3D 220
Castle Av. E4 22Fc 53
KT17: Ewe 81Wa 174
RM13: Rain 38Gd 76
SL3: Dat 1L 103
UB7: Yiew 45N 83
Castlebar Ct. W5 43La 86
Castlebar Hill W5 43La 86
Castlebar M. W5 43La 86
Castlebar Pk. W5 43Ka 86
Castlebar Rd. W5 43La 86
Castle Baynard St. EC4 4C 224 (45Rb 91)
Castlebrook Cl. SE11 5B 230 (49Rb 91)
Castle Bus. Cen. TW12: Hamp 67Da 129
(off Castle M.)
Castle Climbing Centre, The 33Sb 71
Castle Cl. BR2: Brom 69Gc 137
E9 36Ac 72
RH1: Blet 5J 209
RH2: Reig 10K 207
RM3: Rom 20Ld 39
SW19 62Ya 132
TW16: Sun 66U 128
W3 47Ra 87
WD23: Bush 16Da 27
Castlecombe Dr. SW19 59Ya 110
Castlecombe Rd. SE9 63Nc 138
Castle Ct. EC3 3G 225
SE26 63Ac 136
Castleden Ho. NW3 38Fb 69
(off Hilgrove Rd.)
Castledine Rd. SE20 66Xb 135
Castle Dr. IG4: Ilf 30Nc 54
RH2: Reig 10J 207
TN15: Kems'g 89Nd 183
Castle Farm Caravan Site
SL4: Wind 4B 102
Castle Farm Rd.
TN14: S'ham 81Hd 182
Castlefield Ct. RH2: Reig 6K 207
Castlefield Rd. RH2: Reig 6J 207
Castlefields DA13: Ist R 7B 144
Castleford Av. SE9 60Rc 116
Castleford Cl. N17 23Vb 51
WD6: Bore 10Pa 15
Castleford Ct. NW8 5C 214
Castlegate TW9: Rich 55Pa 109
CASTLE GREEN 5H 167
Castle Grn. KT13: Weyb 76U 150
Castle Gro. Rd. GU24: Chob 5H 167
Castlehaven Rd. NW1 38Kb 70
Castle Hgts. RM9: Dag 39Xc 75
CASTLE HILL 61Ae 143
Castle Hill DA3: Fawk, Hartl 70Zd 143
SL4: Wind 3H 103
Castle Hill Av. CR0: New Ad 81Dc 178
Castle Hill Local Nature Reserve 79Qa 153
Castle Hill Pde. W13 45Ka 86
(off The Avenue)
Castle Hill Rd. TW20: Eng G 3M 125
Castle Ho. SE1 5D 230
SM2: Sutt 79Cb 155
SW8 52Nb 112
(off Sth. Lambeth Rd.)
Castle Ind. Est. SE17 5D 230 (49Sb 91)
Castle La. DA12: Grav'nd 1K 145
SW1 3B 228 (48Lb 90)
Castleleigh Ct. EN2: Enf 15Tb 33
Castlemaine Av. CR2: S Croy 78Vb 157
KT17: Ewe 81Xa 174
Castlemain St. E1 43Xb 91
Castle Mead HP1: Hem H 4K 3
SE5 52Sb 113
Castle M. KT13: Weyb 76U 150
N12 22Eb 49
NW1 37Kb 70
SW17 63Gb 133
TW12: Hamp 67Da 129
(not continuous)
Castle Pde. KT17: Ewe 80Wa 154
Castle Pl. NW1 37Kb 70
W4 49Ua 88
Castle Point E13 40Lc 73
(off Boundary Rd.)
Castlereagh Ho. HA7: Stan 23Ka 46
Castlereagh St. W1 2F 221 (44Hb 89)
Castle Rd. AL1: St A 2F 6
CR5: Chip 92Gb 195
DA4: Eyns 79Kd 163
DA10: Swans 58Be 121
EN3: Enf H 11Ac 34
GU21: Wok 86B 168
KT13: Weyb 76T 150
KT18: Eps 87Ra 173
N12 22Eb 49
NW1 37Kb 70
RM9: Dag 39Xc 75
RM17: Grays 51Be 121
TW7: Isle 54Ha 108
UB2: S'hall 48Ba 85
UB5: N'olt 37Da 65
Castle Row W4 50Ta 87
Castle Sq. RH1: Blet 5J 209
Castle St. DA9: Ghithe 57Wd 120
DA10: Swans 58Be 121
E6 40Lc 73
KT1: King T 68Na 131
RH1: Blet 5H 209
SL1: Slou 8K 81
Castleton Av. DA7: Bex 53Fd 118
HA9: Wemb 35Na 67
Castleton Cl. CR0: C'don 72Ac 158
SM7: Bans 87Cb 175
Castleton Dr. SM7: Bans 87Cb 175
Castleton Gdns. HA9: Wemb 34Na 67
Castleton Ho. E14 49Ec 92
(off Pier St.)
Castleton Rd. CR4: Mitc 70Mb 134
E17 26Fc 53
HA4: Ruis 32Z 65
IG3: Ilf 32Wc 75
SE9 63Mc 137
Castletown Rd. W14 50Ab 88
Castle Vw. KT18: Eps 86Ra 173
Castleview Cl. N4 33Sb 71
Castleview Gdns. IG1: Ilf 30Nc 54
Castleview Pde. SL3: L'ly 9P 81
Castle Vw. Rd. KT13: Weyb 77R 150
Castleview Rd. SL3: L'ly 9N 81
Castle Wlk. RH2: Reig 6J 207
TW16: Sun 69Y 129

Castle Way KT17: Ewe .82Wa 174
SW19 .62Za 132
TW13: Hanw .63Y 129
Castle Wharf *E14* .45Gc 93
(off Orchard Pl.)
Castlewood Dr. SE9 .54Pc 116
Castlewood Rd. EN4: Cockf .13Fb 31
N15 .30Wb 51
N16 .30Wb 51
Castle Yd. N6 .31Jb 70
SE1 .6C 224 (46Rb 91)
TW10: Rich .57Ma 109
Castor La. E14 .45Dc 92
Catalina Av. RM16: Chaf H .47Be 99
Catalina Ct. *AL1: St A* .2C 6
(off Beaconsfield Rd.)
Catalina Rd. TW6: H'row A .54R 106
Catalin Ct. *EN9: Walt A* .5Fc 21
(off Howard Cl.)
Catalonia Apartments *WD18: Wat* .14V 26
(off Metropolitan Sta. App.)
Catalpa Ct. SE13 .58Fc 115
Caterfield La. RH8: Oxt .10L 211
CATERHAM .95Ub 197
Caterham Av. IG5: Ilf .26Pc 54
Caterham By-Pass CR3: Cat'm .92Xb 197
Caterham Cl. GU24: Pirb .3C 186
Caterham Ct. EN9: Walt A .6Hc 21
Caterham Dr. CR5: Coul .90Rb 177
CATERHAM-ON-THE-HILL .94Ub 197
Caterham Rd. SE13 .55Fc 115
Catesby Ho. *E9* .38Yb 72
(off Frampton Pk. Rd.)
Catesby St. SE17 .6G 231 (49Tb 91)
CATFORD .59Dc 114
Catford B'way. SE6 .59Dc 114
CATFORD GYRATORY .59Dc 114
Catford Hill SE6 .60Bc 114
Catford Island SE6 .59Dc 114
Catford M. SE6 .59Dc 114
Catford Rd. SE6 .59Cc 114
Catford Trad. Est. SE6 .61Dc 114
Cathall Leisure Cen. .33Gc 73
Cathall Rd. E11 .33Fc 73
Catham Cl. AL1: St A .4F 6
Catharine Cl. RM16: Chaf H .47Be 99
Catharine Ho. WD19: Wat .20X 27
Cathay Ho. SE16 .47Xb 91
Cathay St. SE16 .47Xb 91
Cathay Wlk. *UB5: N'olt* .40Ca 65
(off Brabazon Rd.)
Cathcart Dr. BR6: Orp .75Uc 160
Cathcart Hill N19 .34Lb 70
Cathcart Ho. *SW10* .50Eb 89
(off Cathcart Rd.)
Cathcart Rd. SW10 .51Db 111
Cathcart St. NW5 .37Kb 70
Cathedral Ct. AL3: St A .4P 5
Cathedral Lodge EC1 .7D 218
Cathedral Mans. SW1 .5B 228
Cathedral Piazza SW1 .4B 228 (48Lb 90)
Cathedral Pl. CM14: B'wood .19Zd 41
Cathedral St. SE1 .6F 225 (46Tb 91)
Cathedral Vw. *AL3: St A* .2B 6
(off High St.)
Cathedral Wlk. SW1 .3B 228
Catherall Rd. N5 .34Sb 71
Catherine Cl. CM15: Pil H .15Wd 40
IG10: Lough .16Pc 36
KT14: Byfl .86N 169
NW4 .28Xa 48
Catherine Ct. IG2: Ilf .29Sc 54
N14 .15Lb 32
SW3 .51Fb 111
(off Callow St.)
SW19 .64Bb 133
Catherine Dr. TW9: Rich .56Na 109
TW16: Sun .65V 128
Catherine Gdns. TW3: Houn .56Fa 108
Catherine Griffiths Ct. EC1 .5A 218
Catherine Gro. SE10 .53Dc 114
Catherine Ho. *E3* .40Cc 72
(off Thomas Fyre Dr.)
N1 .1J 219
Catherine Howard Ct. *KT13: Weyb* .76R 150
(off Old Palace Rd.)
SE9 .58Tc 116
Catherine of Aragon Ct. SE9 .58Sc 116
Catherine Parr Ct. SE9 .58Tc 116
Catherine Pl. HA1: Harr .29Ha 46
SW1 .3B 228 (48Lb 90)
Catherine Rd. EN3: Enf W .9Ac 20
KT6: Surb .71Ma 153
RM2: Rom .29Kd 57
Catherines Cl. UB7: W Dray .47M 83
Catherine St. AL3: St A .1B 6
WC2 .4H 223 (45Pb 90)
Catherine Wheel All. E1 .1J 225 (43Ub 91)
Catherine Wheel Rd. TW8: Bford .52Ma 109
Catherine Wheel Yd. SW1 .7B 222
Catherwood Ct. N1 .2F 219
Cat Hill EN4: E Barn .16Gb 31
Cathles Rd. SW12 .58Kb 112
Cathnor Rd. W12 .47Xa 88
Catisfield Rd. EN3: Enf W .9Ac 20
Catkin Cl. HP1: Hem H .1K 3
Catlin Cres. TW17: Shep .71T 150
Catlin Gdns. RH9: G'stone .2P 209
Catling Cl. SE23 .62Yb 136
Catlin's La. HA5: Eastc .27X 45
Catlin St. HP3: Hem H .5K 3
SE16 .50Wb 91
Cator Cl. CR0: New Ad .83Gc 179
Cator Cres. CR0: New Ad .83Gc 179
Cator La. BR3: Beck .67Bc 136
Cato Rd. SW4 .55Mb 112
Cator Pk. Sports Cen. .65Ac 136
Cator Rd. SE26 .65Zb 136
SM5: Cars .78Hb 155
Cator St. SE15 .52Vb 113
(Commercial Way)
SE15 .51Vb 113
(Ebley Cl.)
Cato's Hill KT10: Esh .77Da 151
Cato St. W1 .1E 220 (43Gb 89)
Catsdell Bottom HP3: Hem H .5B 4
Catsey La. WD23: Bush .17Ea 28
Catsey Woods WD23: Bush .17Ea 28
Catterick Cl. N11 .23Jb 50
Catterick Way WD6: Bore .11Pa 29
Cattistock Rd. SE9 .64Nc 138
CATTLEGATE .5Nb 18
Cattlegate Cotts. EN6: N'thaw .3Mb 18
Cattlegate Hill EN6: Cuff, N'thaw .4Mb 18
Cattlegate Rd. EN2: Crew H .6Nb 18
EN6: Cuff, N'thaw .3Mb 18
Cattley Cl. EN5: Barn .14Ab 30
Cattlins Cl. EN7: Chesh .1Ub 19
Catton St. WC1 .1H 223 (43Pb 90)
Cattsdell HP2: Hem H .1N 3
Caudwell Ter. SW18 .58Fb 111
Caughley Ho. SE11 .4K 229
Caulfield Ct. *NW1* .38Lb 70
(off Baynes St.)
Caulfield Rd. E6 .39Nc 74
SE15 .54Xb 113
W3 .48Sa 87
Causeway, The EN6: Pot B .3Eb 17
(not continuous)
KT9: Chess .77Na 153
KT10: Clay .80Ha 152
N2 .28Gb 49
SM2: Sutt .81Eb 175
SM5: Cars .76Jb 156
SW18 .57Db 111
SW19 .64Ya 132
TW4: Houn .56W 106
TW11: Tedd .65Ha 130
TW14: Felt, Houn .56W 106
TW18: Staines .63E 126
Causeway Cl. EN6: Pot B .3Fb 17
Causeway Corporate Cen.
TW18: Staines .63E 126
Causeway Ct. GU21: Wok .10K 167
Causeway Ho. BR6: Orp .74Wc 161
WD5: Ab L .3U 12
Causeyware Rd. N9 .17Yb 34
Causton Cotts. *E14* .44Ac 92
(off Galsworthy Av.)
Causton Ho. SE5 .51Sb 113
SW9 .53Pb 112
Causton Rd. N6 .31Kb 70
Causton Sq. RM10: Dag .37Cd 76
Causton St. SW1 .6E 228 (49Mb 90)
Cautley Av. SW4 .57Lb 112
Cavalier Cl. RM6: Chad H .28Zc 55
Cavalier Ct. KT5: Surb .72Pa 153
Cavalier Gdns. UB3: Hayes .44T 84
Cavalli Apartments *WD18: Wat* .14U 26
(off Moderna M.)
Cavalry Cres. SL4: Wind .5G 102
TW4: Houn .56Z 107
Cavalry Gdns. SW15 .57Bb 111
Cavalry Sq. SW3 .6G 227 (50Hb 89)
Cavan Ct. AL10: Hat .1C 8
Cavan Pl. HA5: Hat E .25Ba 45
Cavania Point *SE8* .51Dc 114
(off Copperas St.)
Cavaye Ho. *SW10* .51Eb 111
(off Cavaye Pl.)
Cavaye Pl. SW10 .50Eb 89
Cavell Cres. DA1: Dart .56Qd 119
RM3: Hrld W .26Nd 57
Cavell Dr. EN2: Enf .12Qb 32
Cavell Ho. *N1* .39Ub 71
(off Colville Est.)
Cavell Rd. N17 .24Tb 51
Cavell St. E1 .43Xb 91
Cavell Way GU21: Knap .1G 186
KT19: Eps .83Qa 173
Cavendish Av. DA8: Erith .51Ed 118
DA15: Sidc .59Wc 117
DA16: Well .55Vc 117
HA1: Harr .35Fa 66
HA4: Ruis .36X 65
IG8: Wfd G .25Kc 53
KT3: N Mald .71Wa 154
N3 .26Cb 49
NW8 .2C 214 (40Fb 69)
RM12: Horn .37Kd 77
TN13: S'oaks .94Jd 202
W13 .43Ja 86
Cavendish Cl. N18 .22Xb 51
NW6 .37Bb 69
NW8 .3C 214 (41Fb 89)
TW16: Sun .65V 128
UB4: Hayes .43U 84
Cavendish Ct. EC3 .2J 225
KT13: Weyb .79S 150
KT16: Chert .74J 149
(off Victory Rd.)
SE6 .60Dc 114
(off Bromley Rd.)
SL3: Poyle .53G 104
SM6: Wall .79Kb 156
TW16: Sun .65V 128
WD3: Crox G .15T 26
Cavendish Cres. RM12: Horn .37Kd 77
WD6: E'tree .14Qa 29
Cavendish Dr. E11 .32Fc 73
HA8: Edg .23Pa 47
KT10: Clay .78Ga 152
Cavendish Gdns. IG1: Ilf .32Qc 74
IG11: Bark .36Uc 74
RH1: Redh .5A 208
RM6: Chad H .29Ad 55
RM15: Avel .47Sd 98
SW4 .58Lb 112
Cavendish Ho. *CR0: C'don* .74Tb 157
(off Tavistock Rd.)
NW8 .2C 214
SW1 .4E 228
UB7: W Dray .47P 83
(off Park Lodge Av.)
W1 .1B 222
Cavendish Mans. EC1 .6K 217
NW6 .36Cb 69
Cavendish Meads SL5: S'hill .2B 146
Cavendish M. Nth. W1 .7A 216 (43Kb 90)
Cavendish M. Sth. W1 .1A 222 (43Kb 90)
Cavendish Pde. *SW4* .58Kb 112
(off Clapham Comn. Sth. Side)
TW4: Houn .54Aa 107
Cavendish Pl. *AL10: Hat* .1B 8
(off Aldykes)
BR1: Brom .70Pc 138
NW2 .37Za 68
SW4 .57Mb 112
W1 .2A 222 (44Kb 90)
Cavendish Rd. AL1: St A .2D 6
CR0: C'don .74Rb 157
E4 .23Ec 52
EN5: Barn .13Ya 30
GU22: Wok .1P 187
KT3: N Mald .70Va 132
KT13: Weyb .81R 170
N4 .30Rb 51
N18 .22Xb 51
NW6 .38Ab 68
RH1: Redh .6A 208
SM2: Sutt .80Eb 155
SW12 .58Kb 112
Cavendish Rd. SW19 .66Fb 133
TW16: Sun .65V 128
W4 .53Sa 109
Cavendish Sq. DA3: Lfield .69Zd 143
W1 .2A 222 (44Kb 90)
Cavendish St. N1 .2F 219 (40Tb 71)
Cavendish Ter. E3 .41Bc 92
TW13: Felt .61W 128
Cavendish Wlk. KT19: Eps .83Ra 173
Cavendish Way AL10: Hat .1B 8
BR4: W W'ck .74Dc 158
Cavenham Cl. GU22: Wok .91A 188
Cavenham Gdns. IG1: Ilf .34Tc 74
RM11: Horn .29Ld 57
Caverleigh Pl. BR1: Brom .68Lc 137
Caverleigh Way KT4: Wor Pk .74Wa 154
Cave Rd. E13 .41Kc 93
TW10: Ham .63La 130
Caversham Av. N13 .20Qb 32
SM3: Cheam .75Ab 154
Caversham Ct. *N11* .20Jb 32
(off Brunswick Pk. Rd.)
Caversham Ho. *KT1: King T* .68Na 131
(off Lady Booth Rd.)
N15 .28Sb 51
(off Caversham Rd.)
SE15 .51Wb 113
(off Haymerle Rd.)
Caversham M. *SW3* .51Hb 111
(off Caversham St.)
Caversham Rd. KT1: King T .68Pa 131
N15 .28Sb 51
NW5 .37Lb 70
Caversham St. SW3 .51Hb 111
Caverswall St. W12 .44Ya 88
Caveside Cl. BR7: Chst .67Qc 138
Cavour Ho. SE17 .7C 230
Cawcott Dr. SL4: Wind .3C 102
Cawdor Av. RM15: S Ock .45Wd 98
Cawdor Cres. W7 .49Ja 86
Cawdor Ho. CM14: W'ley .21Zd 59
Cawnpore St. SE19 .64Ub 135
Cawsey Way GU21: Wok .89A 168
Cawston Ct. BR1: Brom .66Hc 137
Caxton Av. KT15: Add .79J 149
Caxton Cl. DA3: Hartl .69Be 143
Caxton Ct. EN8: Walt C .7Ac 20
SW11 .54Gb 111
Caxton Dr. UB8: Uxb .40M 63
Caxton Gro. E3 .41Cc 92
Caxton Hall SW1 .3D 228
Caxton La. RH8: Limp .3P 211
Caxton M. TW8: Bford .51Ma 109
Caxton Pl. IG1: Ilf .34Qc 74
Caxton Ri. RH1: Redh .5A 208
Caxton Rd. N22 .26Pb 50
SW19 .64Eb 133
UB2: S'hall .48Z 85
W12 .47Za 88
Caxtons, The *SW9* .52Rb 113
(off Langton Rd.)
Caxton St. SW1 .3C 228 (48Lb 90)
Caxton St. Nth. E16 .44Hc 93
Caxton Trad. Est. UB3: Hayes .47U 84
Caxton Wlk. WC2 .3E 222 (44Mb 90)
Caxton Way RM1: Rom .28Gd 56
WD18: Wat .17T 26
Cayenne Ct. SE1 .7K 225 (47Vb 91)
Caygill Cl. BR2: Brom .70Hc 137
Cayley Rd. UB2: S'hall .48Da 85
Cayton Pl. EC1 .4F 219
Cayton Rd. CR5: Coul .94Lb 196
UB6: G'frd .40Ga 66
Cayton St. EC1 .4F 219 (41Tb 91)
Cazenove Rd. E17 .25Cc 52
N16 .33Vb 71
Cearns Ho. E6 .39Mc 73
Cearn Way CR5: Coul .87Pb 176
Cecil Av. EN1: Enf .14Vb 33
HA9: Wemb .36Pa 67
IG11: Bark .38Tc 74
RM11: Horn .27Nd 57
RM16: Chaf H .47Be 99
Cecil Cl. KT9: Chess .77Ma 153
TW15: Ashf .66S 128
W5 .43Ma 87
Cecil Ct. CR0: C'don .75Vb 157
EN2: Enf .14Tb 33
EN5: Barn .13Za 30
EN8: Chesh .4Ac 20
NW6 .38Db 69
SW10 .51Eb 111
(off Fawcett St.)
WC2 .4F 223 (45Nb 90)
Cecile Pk. N8 .30Nb 50
Cecil Ho. E17 .25Cc 52
Cecilia Cl. N2 .27Eb 49
Cecilia Rd. E8 .36Vb 71
Cecil Manning Cl. UB6: G'frd .39Ja 66
Cecil Mans. SW17 .61Jb 134
Cecil Pk. HA5: Pinn .28Aa 45
Cecil Pl. CR4: Mitc .71Hb 155
Cecil Rhodes Ho. NW1 .1D 216
Cecil Rd. AL1: St A .2D 6
CR0: C'don .72Nb 156
DA11: Grav'nd .10B 122
E11 .34Hc 73
E13 .39Jc 73
E17 .25Cc 52
EN2: Enf .13Sb 33
EN6: S Mim .4Wa 16
EN8: Chesh .4Ac 20
HA3: W'stone .27Ga 46
IG1: Ilf .35Rc 74
N10 .26Kb 50
N14 .18Lb 32
NW9 .27Ua 48
NW10 .39Ua 68
RM6: Chad H .31Zc 75
SL0: Iver .44G 82
SM1: Sutt .79Bb 155
SW19 .66Db 133
TW3: Houn .54Ea 108
TW15: Ashf .66S 128
W3 .43Sa 87
Cecil Rosen Ct. HA0: Wemb .34Ka 66
Cecil Sharp House .39Jb 70
(off Gloucester Av.)
Cecil St. WD24: Wat .10X 13
Cecil Way BR2: Hayes .74Jc 159
SL2: Slou .2D 80
Cedar Av. DA12: Grav'nd .3E 144
DA15: Sidc .59Wc 117
EN3: Enf H .12Yb 34
EN4: E Barn .17Gb 31
EN8: Walt C .5Zb 20
Cedar Av. HA4: Ruis .36Y 65
KT11: Cobh .87Y 171
RM6: Chad H .29Ad 55
RM14: Upm .35Qd 77
TW2: Whitt .58Da 107
UB3: Hayes .44W 84
UB7: Yiew .45P 83
Cedar Cl. BR2: Brom .76Nc 160
BR8: Swan .68Ed 140
CM13: Hut .17Fe 41
CR6: W'ham .91Ac 198
E3 .39Bc 72
EN6: Pot B .2Cb 17
IG1: Ilf .36Tc 74
IG9: Buck H .19Mc 35
KT8: E Mos .70Ga 130
KT10: Esh .79Ba 151
KT17: Eps .86Va 174
RH2: Reig .8L 207
RM7: Rom .28Ed 56
SE21 .60Sb 113
SL0: Iver H .39E 62
SL1: Burn .2A 80
SM5: Cars .79Hb 155
SW15 .63Ta 131
TW18: Lale .69L 127
Cedar Copse BR1: Brom .68Pc 138
Cedar Ct. AL4: St A .2H 7
CM16: Epp .3Wc 23
E18 .25Jc 53
KT15: Add .77L 149
KT16: Ott .78E 148
KT22: Fet .94Ja 192
N1 .38Sb 71
N10 .26Jb 50
N11 .22Lb 50
N20 .18Fb 31
SE1 .2J 231
SE7 .51Lc 115
SE13 .56Fc 115
SL4: Wind .4E 102
SM2: Sutt .80Db 155
SW19 .62Za 132
TW8: Bford .51La 108
TW20: Egh .63C 126
WD25: Wat .5Z 13
(off Lych Ga.)
Cedar Cres. BR2: Brom .76Nc 160
Cedarcroft Rd. KT9: Chess .77Pa 153
Cedar Dr. DA4: Sut H .68Rd 141
HA5: Hat E .23Ca 45
IG10: Lough .13Rc 36
KT22: Fet .95Ga 192
N2 .28Gb 49
SL5: S'dale .3E 146
SL5: S'hill .10H 125
Cedar Gdns. GU21: Wok .10M 167
GU24: Chob .2K 167
RM14: Upm .34Sd 78
SM2: Sutt .79Eb 155
Cedar Grange EN1: Enf .15Ub 33
Cedar Gro. DA5: Bexl .58Zc 117
GU24: Bisl .7E 166
KT13: Weyb .77S 150
UB1: S'hall .43Ca 85
W5 .48Na 87
Cedar Hgts. NW2 .37Bb 69
TW10: Ham .60Na 109
Cedar Hill KT18: Eps .88Sa 173
Cedar Ho. *E2* .40Xb 71
(off Mowlem St.)
E14 .47Ec 92
(off Manchester Rd.)
KT22: Lea .91Ha 192
N22 .25Qb 50
(off Acacia Rd.)
SE14 .53Zb 114
SE16 .47Zb 92
(off Woodland Cres.)
SW6 .54Eb 111
TW9: Kew .53Ra 109
TW16: Sun .66V 128
(off Spelthorne Gro.)
UB4: Yead .42Y 85
W8 .48Db 89
(off Marloes Rd.)
Cedarhurst BR1: Brom .66Gc 137
Cedarhurst Cotts. DA5: Bexl .59Cd 118
Cedarhurst Dr. SE9 .57Lc 115
Cedarland Ter. SW20 .66Xa 132
Cedar Lawn Av. EN5: Barn .15Ab 30
Cedar M. SW15 .57Za 110
Cedar Mt. SE9 .60Mc 115
Cedarne Rd. SW6 .52Db 111
Cedar Pk. CR3: Cat'm .93Ub 197
Cedar Pk. Gdns. RM6: Chad H .31Zc 75
SW19 .64Xa 132
Cedar Pk. Rd. EN2: Enf .10Sb 19
Cedar Pl. HA6: Nwood .23S 44
SE7 .50Lc 93
Cedar Ri. N14 .17Jb 32
RM15: S Ock .42Yd 98
Cedar Rd. AL10: Hat .1C 8
BR1: Brom .68Lc 137
CM13: Hut .16Fe 41
CR0: C'don .75Tb 157
DA1: Dart .60Md 119
DA8: Erith .53Jd 118
EN2: Enf .10Rb 19
GU22: Wok .2M 187
HP4: Berk .2A 2
KT8: E Mos .70Ga 130
KT11: Cobh .86X 171
KT13: Weyb .77Q 150
N17 .25Vb 51
NW2 .35Ya 68
RM7: Rom .28Ed 56
RM12: Horn .34Ld 77
RM16: Grays .8C 100
SM2: Sutt .79Eb 155
TW4: Cran .54Y 107
TW11: Tedd .64Ja 130
TW14: Bedf .60T 106
WD19: Wat .16Y 27
Cedars SM7: Bans .86Hb 175
SS17: Stan H .1N 101
Cedars, The AL3: St A .1A 6
E9 .38Zb 72
(off Banbury Rd.)
E15 .38Hc 73
EN9: Walt A .7Lc 21
(in Woodbine Cl. Caravan Pk.)
GU24: Pirb .4B 186
HP4: Berk .1A 2
IG9: Buck H .18Jc 35
KT14: Byfl .84P 169
Cedars, The KT22: Lea .93Ma 193
KT23: Bookh .98Ea 192
RH2: Reig .6M 207
SL2: Slou .1D 80
SL3: Dat .3N 103
SM6: Wall .77Lb 156
TW11: Tedd .65Ha 130
W13 .44La 86
WD3: Rick .17M 25
Cedars Av. CR4: Mitc .70Jb 134
E17 .29Cc 52
WD3: Rick .18L 25
Cedars Cl. NW4 .27Za 48
SE13 .55Fc 115
SL9: Chal P .22A 42
WD6: Bore .14Ra 29
Cedars Ct. N9 .19Ub 33
Cedars Dr. UB10: Hil .40P 63
Cedars Ho. E17 .27Dc 52
WD3: Chor .14H 25
Cedars M. SW4 .56Kb 112
(not continuous)
Cedars Rd. BR3: Beck .68Ac 136
CR0: Bedd .76Nb 156
E15 .37Gc 73
KT1: Hamp W .67La 130
N9 .19Wb 33
N21 .19Rb 33
SM4: Mord .70Cb 133
SW4 .55Kb 112
SW13 .54Wa 110
W4 .50Sa 87
Cedars Wlk. WD3: Chor .14H 25
Cedar Ter. TW9: Rich .56Na 109
Cedar Ter. Rd.
TN13: S'oaks .95Ld 203
Cedar Tree Gro. SE27 .65Rb 135
Cedar Vw. *KT1: King T* .69Ma 131
(off Milner Rd.)
Cedarville Gdns. SW16 .65Pb 134
Cedar Wlk. CR8: Kenley .88Sb 177
EN9: Walt A .6Fc 21
HP3: Hem H .4M 3
KT10: Clay .79Ha 152
KT20: Tad .92Ab 194
Cedar Way HP4: Berk .2A 2
N1 .38Mb 70
SL3: L'ly .50A 82
TW16: Sun .66U 128
Cedar Way Ind. Est. N1 .38Mb 70
Cedar Wood Dr. WD25: Wat .7X 13
Cedarwood Dr. AL4: St A .2H 7
Cedra Ct. N16 .32Wb 71
Cedric Av. RM1: Rom .27Gd 56
Cedric Chambers NW8 .5B 214
Cedric Rd. SE9 .62Sc 138
Celadon Cl. EN3: Enf H .13Ac 34
Celandine Cl. E14 .43Cc 92
RM15: S Ock .42Yd 98
Celandine Ct. E4 .20Dc 34
Celandine Dr. E8 .38Vb 71
SE28 .46Xc 95
Celandine Gro. N14 .15Lb 32
Celandine Rd. KT12: Hers .77Aa 151
Celandine Way E15 .41Gc 93
Celbridge M. W2 .43Db 89
Celedon Cl. RM16: Chaf H .48Ae 99
Celestial Gdns. SE13 .56Fc 115
Celia Av. *TN15: W King* .80Ud 164
(off London Rd.)
Celia Cres. TW15: Ashf .65M 127
Celia Ho. N1 .2H 219
Celia Johnson Ho.
WD6: Bore .11Sa 29
Celia Rd. N19 .35Lb 70
Cell Barnes Cl. AL1: St A .4F 6
Cell Barnes La. AL1: St A .3E 6
(not continuous)
Cell Farm Av. SL4: Old Win .7M 103
Celtic Av. BR2: Brom .69Gc 137
Celtic Rd. KT14: Byfl .86N 169
Celtic St. E14 .43Dc 92
Cement Block Cotts.
RM17: Grays .51Ee 121
Cemetery Hill HP1: Hem H .3L 3
Cemetery La. SE7 .51Nc 116
TW17: Shep .73R 150
Cemetery Pales GU24: Brkwd .4D 186
Cemetery Rd. E7 .36Hc 73
N17 .24Ub 51
SE2 .52Xc 117
Cemmaes Ct. Rd. HP1: Hem H .2L 3
Cemmaes Mdw. HP1: Hem H .2L 3
Cenacle Cl. NW3 .34Cb 69
Cenotaph .1F 229 (47Nb 90)
Centaur Ct. TW8: Bford .50Na 87
Centaurs Bus. Pk. TW7: Isle .51Ja 108
Centaur St. SE1 .3J 229 (48Pb 90)
Centaurus Sq. AL2: F'mre .9C 6
Centenary Cl. TN13: Dun G .92Gd 202
Centenary Ct. DA4: Farni .73Qd 163
RH1: Redh .5P 207
(off Warwick Rd.)
Centenary Rd. EN3: Brim .14Bc 34
Centenary Trad. Est. EN3: Brim .13Bc 34
Centennial Av. WD6: E'tree .17Ka 28
Centennial Ct. WD6: E'tree .17La 28
Centennial Pk. WD6: E'tree .17La 28
Central Apartments HA9: Wemb .36Na 67
Central Av. DA12: Grav'nd .1D 144
DA16: Well .54Vc 117
E11 .33Fc 73
EN1: Enf .12Xb 33
EN8: Walt C .5Ac 20
HA5: Pinn .30Ba 45
KT8: W Mole .70Ba 129
N2 .26Fb 49
N9 .20Ub 33
RM15: Avel .47Sd 98
RM18: Tilb .3C 122
RM20: W Thur .50Vd 98
SM6: Wall .78Nb 156
SW11 .52Hb 111
TW3: Houn .56Ea 108
UB3: Hayes .46V 84
Central Bus. Cen. NW10 .36Ua 68
Central Cir. NW4 .29Xa 48
Central Cl. KT15: Add .77L 149
Central Courtyard EC2 .1J 225
Central Criminal Court
Old Bailey .2C 224 (44Rb 91)
Central Dr. AL4: St A .1G 6
RM12: Horn .34Nd 77
SL1: Slou .5D 80
Centrale Shop. Cen.
CR0: C'don .75Sb 157

Central Gallery IG1: Ilf 33Rc 74
(in The Exchange)
Central Gdns. SM4: Mord 71Db 155
Central Hgts. WD18: Wat 14V 26
(off Manhattan Av.)
Central Hill SE19 ....64Tb 135
Central Ho. E15 ....40Dc 72
IG11: Bark 38Sc 74
Central Lodge TN15: Wro 85Fe 185
Central London Civil Justice Cen. 6K 215
Central London Golf Course 61Fb 133
Central Mall SW18 ....58Db 111
(off Southside Shop. Cen.)
Central Mans. NW4 ....29Xa 48
(off Watford Way)
Central Markets (Smithfield) 1B 224
Central Pde. CR0: New Ad 82Ec 178
DA15: Sidc 62Wc 139
E17 ....28Cc 52
EN3: Enf H 12Yb 34
HA1: Harr 29Ha 46
IG2: Ilf 30Tc 54
KT6: Surb 72Na 153
KT8: W Mole 70Ba 129
RH1: Redh 5P 207
SE20 ....66Zb 136
(off High St.)
TW5: Hest 52Ba 107
TW14: Felt 59Y 107
UB6: G'frd 41Ja 86
W3 ....47Ra 87
Central Pk. Arena 60Nd 119
Central Pk. Av. RM10: Dag 34Dd 76
Central Pk. Est. TW4: Houn 57Z 107
Central Pk. Leisure Cen. 22Nd 57
Central Pk. Rd. E6 ....40Mc 73
Central Pl. SE25 ....71Wb 157
Central Rd. DA1: Dart 57Nd 119
HA0: Wemb 36Ka 66
KT4: Wor Pk 74Wa 154
SM4: Mord 72Cb 155
SS17: Stan H 2M 101
Central St Martins College of Art & Design
Back Hill Campus 6A 218 (42Qb 90)
Byam Shaw Campus 33Mb 70
King's Cross Campus
....1F 217 (39Nb 70)
Central School Path SW14 ....55Sa 109
Central Sq. HA9: Wemb 36Na 67
(off Sevenex Pde.)
NW11 ....30Db 49
Central St. EC1 ....3D 218 (41Sb 91)
Central Ter. BR3: Beck 69Zb 136
Central Wlk. KT19: Eps 85Ta 173
Central Walkway N19 ....35Mb 70
(off Pleshey Rd.)
Central Way HA6: Nwood 24U 44
NW10 ....41Sa 87
RH8: Oxt 99Fc 199
SE28 ....46Wc 95
SM5: Cars 80Gb 155
TW14: Felt 57W 106
Central Wharf E14 ....44Cc 92
(off Thomas Rd.)
Centre, The
Slough 5G 80
Watford 20Y 27
Centre, The KT12: Walt T 74W 150
TW3: Houn 55Da 107
TW13: Felt 60X 107
Centre Av. CM16: Epp 4Vc 23
W3 ....46Ta 87
Centre Cl. CM16: Epp 4Vc 23
Centre Comn. Rd. BR7: Chst 65Sc 138
Centre Ct. Shop. Cen. SW19 ....65Bb 133
Centre Dr. CM16: Epp 4Vc 23
Centre for the Magic Arts, The 5C 216
Centre for Wildlife Gardening Vis. Cen.
....55Vb 113
Centre Grn. CM16: Epp 4Vc 23
Centre Hgts. NW3 ....38Fb 69
(off Finchley Rd.)
Centre of Cell 43Xb 91
(off Newark St.)
Centre Point SE1 ....50Wb 91
Centrepoint WC2 ....2E 222
Centre Point Ho. WC2 ....2E 222
Centre Rd. DA3: New A 76Ae 165
E7 ....33Jc 73
E11 ....33Jc 73
RM10: Dag 40Dd 76
SL4: Wind 2A 102
Centre Sq. SW18 ....57Cb 111
(off Buckhold Rd.)
Centre St. E2 ....40Xb 71
Centre Vw. Apartments
CR0: C'don 76Sb 157
(off Whitgift St.)
Centre Way E17 ....24Ec 52
N9 ....19Yb 34
Centreway IG1: Ilf 33Sc 74
(off High Rd.)
Centreway Apartments IG1: Ilf 33Sc 74
(off Axon Pl.)
Centric Cl. NW1 ....39Jb 70
Centrillion Point CR0: C'don 77Sb 157
(off Mason's Av.)
Centrium AL1: St A 4A 6
GU22: Wok 89B 168
Centro Ct. E6 ....42Pc 94
Centurion Bldg. SW8 ....51Kb 112
Centurion Cl. N7 ....38Pb 70
Centurion Ct. AL1: St A 3E 6
(off Camp Rd.)
SE18 ....49Qc 94
SM6: Wall 75Kb 156
Centurion La. E3 ....39Bc 72
Centurion Sq. SE18 ....53Nc 116
Centurion Way DA18: Erith 48Bd 95
RM19: Purf 49Pd 97
Centuryan Pl. DA1: Cray 56Kd 119
Century Cl. AL3: St A 1A 6
NW4 ....29Za 48
Century Ct. GU21: Wok 88B 168
NW8 ....4C 214
WD18: Wat 17S 26
Century Gdns. CR2: Sande 85Wb 177
Century Ho. HA9: Wemb 33Pa 67
SM7: Bans 87Db 175
SW15 ....56Za 110
Century M. E5 ....35Yb 72
N5 ....34Rb 71
(off Conewood St.)
Century Pk. WD17: Wat 15Y 27
Century Plaza HA8: Edg 23Qa 47
(off Station Rd.)
Century Rd. E17 ....27Ac 52
TW18: Staines 64E 126
Century Way GU24: Brkwd 1B 186
Century Yd. SE23 ....61Yb 136
(not continuous)
Cephas Av. E1 ....42Yb 92
Cephas Ho. E1 ....42Yb 92
(off Doveton St.)
Cephas St. E1 ....42Yb 92
Ceres Rd. SE18 ....49Vc 95
Cerise Rd. SE15 ....53Wb 113
Cerne Cl. UB4: Yead 45Y 85
Cerne Rd. DA12: Grav'nd 3G 144
SM4: Mord 72Eb 155
Cerney M. W2 ....4B 220 (45Fb 89)
Cerotus Pl. KT16: Chert 73H 149
Cervantes Ct. HA6: Nwood 24V 44
W2 ....44Db 89
Cervia Way DA12: Grav'nd 2H 145
Cester St. E2 ....39Wb 71
Ceylon Rd. W14 ....48Za 88
Ceylon Wharf Apartments SE16 ....47Yb 92
(off St Marychurch St.)
Cezanne Rd. WD25: Wat 8Z 13
Chabot Dr. SE15 ....55Xb 113
Chace Av. EN6: Pot B 4Fb 17
Chadacre Av. IG5: Ilf 27Pc 54
Chadacre Ct. E15 ....39Jc 73
(off Vicars Cl.)
Chadacre Ho. SW9 ....56Rb 113
(off Loughborough Pk.)
Chadacre Rd. KT17: Ewe 79Xa 154
Chadbourn St. E14 ....43Dc 92
Chadbury Ct. NW7 ....25Wa 48
Chad Cres. N9 ....20Yb 34
Chadd Dr. BR1: Brom 69Nc 138
Chadd Grn. E13 ....39Jc 73
(not continuous)
Chadfields RM18: Tilb 2C 122
Chadston Ho. N1 ....38Rb 71
(off Halton Rd.)
Chadswell WC1 ....4G 217
Chadview Ct. RM6: Chad H 31Zc 75
Chadville Gdns. RM6: Chad H 29Zc 55
Chadway RM8: Dag 32Yc 75
Chadwell Av. EN8: Chesh 1Yb 20
RM6: Chad H 31Xc 75
Chadwell By-Pass RM16: Grays 10B 100
CHADWELL HEATH 31Zc 75
Chadwell Heath Ind. Pk.
RM8: Dag 32Ad 75
Chadwell Heath La. RM6: Chad H 28Xc 55
Chadwell Hill RM16: Grays 10D 100
Chadwell Ho. SE17 ....7G 231
Chadwell La. N8 ....27Pb 50
Chadwell Rd. RM17: Grays 49Ee 99
CHADWELL ST MARY 8D 100
Chadwell St. EC1 ....3A 218 (41Qb 90)
Chadwick Av. E4 ....21Fc 53
N21 ....15Pb 32
SW19 ....65Cb 133
Chadwick Cl. DA11: Nflt 1A 144
SW15 ....59Va 110
TW11: Tedd 65Ja 130
W7 ....43Ha 86
Chadwick Dr. RM3: Hrld W 26Md 57
Chadwick Gdns. UB8: Uxb 38N 63
Chadwick M. W4 ....51Ra 109
Chadwick Pl. KT6: Surb 73La 152
Chadwick Rd. E11 ....30Gc 53
IG1: Ilf 33Rc 74
NW10 ....39Va 68
SE15 ....54Vb 113
Chadwick St. SW1 ....4E 228 (48Mb 90)
Chadwick Way SE28 ....45Zc 95
Chadwin Rd. E13 ....43Kc 93
Chadworth Ho. EC1 ....4D 218
N4 ....32Sb 71
Chadworth Way KT10: Clay 78Fa 152
Chaffers Mead KT21: Asht 88Pa 173
Chaffinch Av. CR0: C'don 72Zb 158
Chaffinch Bus. Pk. BR3: Beck 70Zb 136
Chaffinch Cl. CR0: C'don 71Zb 158
KT6: Surb 76Qa 153
N9 ....18Zb 34
Chaffinches Grn. HP3: Hem H 6A 4
Chaffinch La. WD18: Wat 17V 26
Chaffinch Rd. BR3: Beck 67Ac 136
Chafford CM14: B'wood 18Xd 40
Chafford Gdns. CM13: W H'dn 30Fe 59
Chafford Gorges Nature Reserve 48Zd 99
Chafford Gorges Vis. Cen. 48Zd 99
CHAFFORD HUNDRED 48Be 99
Chafford Sports Complex 43Ld 97
Chafford Wlk. RM13: Rain 40Ld 77
Chafford Way RM6: Chad H 28Yc 55
RM16: Grays 46Ce 99
Chagford Ho. E3 ....41Dc 92
(off Talwin St.)
Chagford St. NW1 ....6F 215 (42Hb 89)
Chailey Av. EN1: Enf 12Vb 33
Chailey Cl. TW5: Hest 53Z 107
Chailey Ind. Est. UB3: Hayes 47W 84
Chailey Pl. KT12: Hers 77Aa 151
Chailey St. E5 ....34Yb 72
Chairman's Wlk. UB9: Den 29H 43
Chalbury Wlk. N1 ....1J 217 (40Pb 70)
Chalcombe Rd. SE2 ....48Xc 95
Chalcot Cl. SM2: Sutt 80Cb 155
Chalcot Cres. NW1 ....39Hb 69
Chalcot Gdns. NW3 ....37Hb 69
Chalcot M. SW16 ....62Nb 134
Chalcot Rd. NW1 ....38Jb 70
Chalcot Sq. NW1 ....38Jb 70
(not continuous)
Chalcott SL1: Slou 8J 81
Chalcott Gdns. KT6: Surb 74La 152
Chalcroft Rd. SE13 ....57Gc 115
CHALDON 96Qb 196
Chaldon Cl. RH1: Redh 8N 207
Chaldon Comn. Rd.
CR3: Cat'm 96Sb 197
Chaldon Ct. SE19 ....67Tb 135
Chaldon Path CR7: Thor H 70Rb 135
Chaldon Rd. CR3: Cat'm 96Tb 197
SW6 ....52Ab 110
Chaldon Way CR5: Coul 89Nb 176
Chale Ct. SS17: Stan H 3L 101
Chale Rd. SW2 ....58Nb 112
Chalet Cl. DA5: Bexl 63Fd 140
TW15: Ashf 65T 128
Chalet Ct. CR7: Thor H 71Sb 157
Chalet Est. NW7 ....21Wa 48
Chale Wlk. SM2: Sutt 81Db 175
Chalfont Av. HA9: Wemb 37Ra 67
HP6: L Chal 11A 24
Chalfont Cen. for Epilepsy
SL9: Chal P 22B 42
CHALFONT COMMON 22B 42
Chalfont Ct. HA1: Harr 30Ha 46
(off Northwick Pk. Rd.)
NW1 ....6G 215
NW9 ....27Va 48
Chalfont Grn. N9 ....20Ub 33
Chalfont Ho. SE16 ....48Xb 91
(off Keetons Rd.)
WD18: Wat 16U 26
Chalfont La. WD3: Chor 15D 24
WD3: W Hyd 23E 42
Chalfont M. UB10: Hil 38R 64
Chalfont Pk. 27B 42
Chalfont Pl. AL1: St A 2C 6
Chalfont Rd. HP8: Chal G, Map C 19D 24
N9 ....20Ub 33
SE25 ....69Vb 135
UB3: Hayes 47W 84
WD3: Map C 19D 24
CHALFONT ST PETER 25A 42
Chalfont St Peter By-Pass
SL9: Chal P, Ger X 25A 42
Chalfont Sta. Rd. HP7: L Chal 11A 24
Chalfont Wlk. HA5: Pinn 26Y 45
Chalfont Way W13 ....48Ka 86
Chalford NW6 ....37Eb 69
(off Finchley Rd.)
Chalford Cl. KT8: W Mole 70Ca 129
Chalforde Gdns. RM2: Rom 28Kd 57
Chalford Rd. SE21 ....63Tb 135
Chalford Wlk. IG8: Wfd G 25Mc 53
Chalgrove Av. SM4: Mord 71Cb 155
Chalgrove Cres. IG5: Ilf 26Nc 54
Chalgrove Gdns. N3 ....27Ab 48
Chalgrove Rd. N17 ....25Xb 51
SM2: Sutt 80Fb 155
Chalice Cl. SM6: Wall 79Mb 156
Chalice Ct. N2 ....28Gb 49
Chalice Way DA9: Ghithe 57Ud 120
CHALK 10J 123
Chalk Ct. RM17: Grays 51Ce 121
(off Argent St.)
Chalkdell Hill HP2: Hem H 2N 3
Chalkdell Ho. WD25: Wat 5Y 13
Chalkenden Cl. SE20 ....66Xb 135
CHALKER'S CORNER 55Ra 109
CHALK FARM 38Jb 70
Chalk Farm Pde. NW3 ....38Jb 70
(off Adelaide Rd.)
Chalk Farm Rd. NW1 ....38Jb 70
Chalk Hill WD19: Wat 16Aa 27
Chalk Hill Rd. W6 ....49Za 88
Chalkhill Rd. HA9: Wemb 34Ra 67
Chalklands HA9: Wemb 34Sa 67
Chalk La. EN4: Cockf 13Hb 31
KT18: Eps, Eps D 87Ta 173
KT21: Asht 91Pa 193
Chalkley Cl. CR4: Mitc 68Hb 133
Chalkmead RH1: Mers 2C 208
Chalkmill Dr. EN1: Enf 13Xb 33
Chalk Paddock KT18: Eps 87Ta 173
Chalk Pit Av. BR5: St P 69Yc 139
Chalk Pit La. SL1: Burn 8A 60
Chalkpit La. CR3: Wold 97Ec 198
KT23: Bookh 99Ba 191
RH8: Oxt 97Ec 198
Chalk Pit Rd. KT18: Eps D 91Sa 193
SM7: Bans 89Cb 175
Chalk Pit Way SM1: Sutt 78Eb 155
Chalkpit Wood RH8: Oxt 99Fc 199
Chalk Rd. DA12: Grav'nd 10J 123
E13 ....43Kc 93
Chalkstone Cl. DA16: Well 53Wc 117
Chalkwell Ho. E1 ....44Zb 92
(off Pitsea St.)
Chalkwell Pk. Av. EN1: Enf 14Ub 33
Chalky Bank DA11: Grav'nd 3C 144
Chalky La. KT9: Chess 82Ma 173
Challacombe Cl. CM13: Hut 18De 41
Challenge Cl. DA12: Grav'nd 3H 145
NW10 ....39Ua 68
Challenge Ct. KT22: Lea 91Ka 192
TW2: Twick 59Ga 108
Challenger Ho. E14 ....45Ac 92
(off Victory Pl.)
Challenge Rd. TW15: Ashf 62T 128
Challice Way SW2 ....60Pb 112
Challin St. SE20 ....67Yb 136
Challis Rd. TW8: Bford 50Ma 87
Challock Cl. TN16: Big H 88Lc 179
Challoner Cl. N2 ....26Fb 49
Challoner Ct. BR2: Brom 68Fc 137
W14 ....50Bb 89
(off Challoner St.)
Challoner Cres. W14 ....50Bb 89
Challoner Mans. W14 ....50Bb 89
(off Challoner St.)
Challoners Cl. KT8: E Mos 70Fa 130
Challoner St. W14 ....50Bb 89
Chalmers Ct. WD3: Crox G 16P 25
Chalmers Ho. E17 ....29Dc 52
Chalmers Rd. SM7: Bans 87Fb 175
TW15: Ashf 64R 128
Chalmers Rd. E. TW15: Ashf 63R 128
Chalmers Wlk. SE17 ....51Rb 113
(off Hillingdon St.)
Chalmers Way TW1: Isle 56Ka 108
TW14: Felt 57X 107
Chaloner Ct. SE1 ....1F 231
Chalsey Rd. SE4 ....56Bc 114
Chalton Dr. N2 ....30Fb 49
Chalton Ho. NW1 ....4D 216
Chalton St. NW1 ....1C 216 (40Lb 70)
(not continuous)
CHALVEY 8H 81
Chalvey Gdns. SL1: Slou 7J 81
Chalvey Gro. SL1: Slou 8F 80
Chalvey Pk. SL1: Slou 7J 81
Chalvey Rd. E. SL1: Slou 7J 81
Chalvey Rd. W. SL1: Slou 7H 81
Chamberlain Cl. IG1: Ilf 34Sc 74
SE28 ....48Tc 94
UB3: Hayes 45V 84
Chamberlain Cotts. SE5 ....53Tb 113
Chamberlain Cres. BR4: W W'ck 74Dc 158
Chamberlain Gdns. TW3: Houn 53Ea 108
Chamberlain Ho. E1 ....45Yb 92
(off Cable St.)
NW1 ....2D 216
SE1 ....2K 229
Chamberlain La. HA5: Eastc 27W 44
Chamberlain Pl. E17 ....27Ac 52
Chamberlain Rd. N2 ....26Eb 49
W13 ....47Ja 86
Chamberlain St. NW1 ....38Hb 69
Chamberlain Wlk. TW13: Hanw 63Aa 129
Chamberlain Way HA5: Eastc 27X 45
KT6: Surb 73Na 153
Chamberlayne Av. HA9: Wemb 34Na 67
Chamberlayne Mans. NW10 ....41Za 88
(off Chamberlayne Rd.)
Chamberlayne Rd. NW10 ....39Ya 68
Chamberlens Garages W6 ....49Xa 88
(off Dalling Rd.)
Chambers, The SW10 ....53Eb 111
(off Chelsea Harbour Dr.)
Chambers Av. DA14: Sidc 65Ad 139
Chambersbury La. HP3: Hem H 7A 4
(not continuous)
Chambers Bus. Pk. UB7: Sip 51Q 106
Chambers Cl. DA9: Ghithe 57Wd 120
Chambers Gdns. N2 ....25Fb 49
Chambers La. NW10 ....38Xa 68
Chambers Pl. CR2: S Croy 80Tb 157
Chambers Rd. N7 ....35Nb 70
Chambers St. SE16 ....47Wb 91
Chamber St. E1 ....4K 225 (45Vb 91)
Chambers Wlk. HA7: Stan 22Ka 46
Chambers Wharf SE16 ....47Wb 91
Chambon Pl. W6 ....49Wa 88
Chambord Ho. E2 ....4K 219
Chambord St. E2 ....3K 219 (41Vb 91)
Chamomile Ct. E17 ....30Cc 52
(off Yunus Khan Cl.)
Champa Cl. N17 ....26Vb 51
Champion Cres. SE26 ....63Ac 136
Champion Down KT24: Eff 100Aa 191
Champion Gro. SE5 ....55Tb 113
Champion Hill SE5 ....55Tb 113
Champion Hill Est. SE5 ....55Ub 113
Champion Ho. SE7 ....51Lc 115
(off Charlton Rd.)
Champion Pk. SE5 ....54Tb 113
Champion Rd. RM14: Upm 33Rd 77
SE26 ....63Ac 136
Champions Way NW4 ....25Xa 48
NW7 ....25Xa 48
Champlain Ho. W12 ....45Xa 88
(off White City Est.)
Champness Cl. SE27 ....63Tb 135
Champness Rd. IG11: Bark 37Vc 75
Champney Cl. SL3: Hort 55C 104
Champneys WD19: Wat 19Aa 27
Champneys Cl. SM2: Cheam 80Bb 155
Chance Cl. RM16: Chaf H 48Be 99
Chancel Cl. TN15: W King 80Ud 164
Chancel Ct. W1 ....4D 222
Chancel Ind. Est. NW10 ....36Va 68
Chancellor Gdns. CR2: S Croy 81Rb 177
Chancellor Gro. SE21 ....61Sb 135
Chancellor Ho. E1 ....46Xb 91
(off Green Bank)
SW7 ....3A 226
Chancellor Pas. E14 ....46Cc 92
Chancellor Pl. NW9 ....26Va 48
Chancellors Ct. WC1 ....7H 217
Chancellor's Rd. W6 ....50Ya 88
Chancellors St. W6 ....50Ya 88
Chancellors Wharf W6 ....50Ya 88
Chancellor Way TN13: S'oaks 94Jd 202
Chancelot Rd. SE2 ....49Xc 95
Chancel St. SE1 ....7B 224 (46Rb 91)
Chancery Bldgs. E1 ....45Xb 91
(off Lowood St.)
Chancery Ct. DA1: Dart 59Qd 119
Chancerygate UB7: Yiew 46Q 84
Chancerygate Bus. Cen. HA4: Ruis 35Aa 65
SL3: L'ly 47A 82
UB2: S'hall 48Y 85
Chancery La. BR3: Beck 68Dc 136
WC2 ....1J 223 (44Qb 90)
Chancery M. SW17 ....61Gb 133
Chance St. E1 ....5K 219 (42Vb 91)
E2 ....5K 219 (42Vb 91)
Chanctonbury Chase RH1: Redh 6A 208
Chanctonbury Cl. SE9 ....62Rc 138
Chanctonbury Dr. SL5: S'dale 3C 146
Chanctonbury Gdns. SM2: Sutt 80Db 155
Chanctonbury Way N12 ....21Bb 49
Chandaria Ct. CR0: C'don 76Sb 157
(off Church Rd.)
Chandler Av. E16 ....43Jc 93
Chandler Cl. TW12: Hamp 67Ca 129
Chandler Ct. TW14: Felt 58W 106
Chandler Ho. NW6 ....39Bb 69
(off Willesden La.)
WC1 ....6G 217
Chandler Rd. IG10: Lough 11Rc 36
Chandlers Av. SE10 ....48Hc 93
Chandlers Cl. KT8: W Mole 71Da 151
TW14: Felt 59V 106
CHANDLERS CORNER 41Ld 97
Chandlers Cnr. RM13: Rain 41Ld 97
Chandlers Ct. SE12 ....60Kc 115
CHANDLER'S CROSS 10P 11
Chandlers Dr. DA8: Erith 49Fd 96
Chandler's La. WD3: Chan C 8N 11
Chandlers M. DA9: Ghithe 56Yd 120
E14 ....47Cc 92
Chandler St. E1 ....46Xb 91
Chandlers Way RM1: Rom 29Gd 56
SW2 ....59Qb 112
Chandler Way SE15 ....51Ub 113
Chandlery, The SE1 ....3A 230
Chandlery Ho. E1 ....44Wb 91
(off Gower's Wlk.)
Chandon Lodge SM2: Sutt 80Eb 155
Chandos Av. E17 ....26Cc 52
N14 ....20Lb 32
N20 ....18Eb 31
W5 ....49La 86
Chandos Cl. IG9: Buck H 19Kc 35
Chandos Ct. HA7: Stan 23Ka 46
HA8: Edg 24Pa 47
N14 ....19Mb 32
Chandos Cres. HA8: Edg 24Pa 47
Chandos Gdns. CR5: Coul 91Rb 197
Chandos Mall SL1: Slou 7K 81
(within Queensmere Shop. Cen.)
Chandos Pde. HA8: Edg 24Pa 47
Chandos Pl. WC2 ....5F 223 (45Nb 90)
Chandos Rd. E15 ....36Fc 73
HA1: Harr 29Ea 46
HA5: Eastc 31Z 65
N2 ....26Fb 49
N17 ....26Ub 51
NW2 ....36Ya 68
NW10 ....42Ua 88
TW18: Staines 64F 126
WD6: Bore 12Pa 29
Chandos St. W1 ....1A 222 (43Kb 90)
Chandos Way NW11 ....32Db 69
Change All. EC3 ....3G 225 (44Tb 91)
Chanin M. NW2 ....36Ya 68
Chanlock Path
RM15: S Ock 45Xd 98
Channel 4 TV 4D 228
Channel Cl. TW5: Hest 53Ca 107
Channel Ga. Rd. NW10 ....41Ua 88
Channel Ho. E14 ....43Ac 92
(off Aston St.)
SE16 ....47Zb 92
(off Water Gdns. Sq.)
Channel Islands Est. N1 ....37Sb 71
Channelsea Bus. Cen. E15 ....40Fc 73
Channelsea Path E15 ....39Fc 73
Channelsea Rd. E15 ....39Fc 73
Channing Cl. RM11: Horn 31Pd 77
Channings GU21: Wok 87A 168
Channon Ct. KT6: Surb 71Na 153
(off Maple Rd)
Chantilly Way KT19: Eps 82Ra 173
Chanton Dr. KT17: Cheam 82Ya 174
SM2: Cheam, Ewe 82Ya 174
Chantress Cl. RM10: Dag 39Ed 76
Chantrey Ho. SW1 ....5K 227
Chantrey Rd. SW9 ....55Pb 112
Chantreywood
CM13: B'wood 20Ce 41
Chantry, The E4 ....18Ec 34
UB8: Hil 41P 83
Chantry Av. DA3: Hartl 72Ae 165
Chantry Cl. DA14: Sidc 64Ad 139
EN2: Enf 10Sb 19
HA3: Kenton 29Pa 47
KT21: Asht 91La 192
NW7 ....16Va 30
SE2 ....48Yc 95
SL4: Wind 3E 102
TW16: Sun 66W 128
W9 ....42Cb 89
WD4: K Lan 1Q 12
Chantry Ct. AL10: Hat 1C 8
DA12: Grav'nd 8E 122
SM5: Cars 76Gb 155
Chantry Cres. NW10 ....37Va 68
SS17: Stan H 2L 101
Chantry Heritage Cen. 8E 122
Chantry Ho. KT1: King T 70Na 131
RM13: Rain 40Fd 76
Chantry Hurst KT18: Eps 87Ta 173
Chantry La. AL2: Lon C 8H 7
AL10: Hat 1B 8
(not continuous)
BR2: Brom 71Mc 159
Chantry Pl. HA3: Hrw W 25Da 45
Chantry Rd. HA3: Hrw W 25Da 45
KT9: Chess 78Pa 153
KT16: Chert 73L 149
Chantry Sq. W8 ....48Db 89
Chantry St. N1 ....1C 218 (39Rb 71)
Chantry Way CR4: Mitc 69Fb 133
RM13: Rain 40Fd 76
Chant Sq. E15 ....38Fc 73
Chant St. E15 ....38Fc 73
(not continuous)
Chapel, The CM14: W'ley 22Xd 58
(off The Galleries)
SW15 ....58Ab 110
Chapel Av. KT15: Add 77K 149
Chapel Cl. AL9: Brk P 9M 9
DA1: Cray 57Gd 118
NW10 ....36Va 68
RM20: W Thur 51Xd 120
WD25: Wat 6V 12
Chapel Cotts. HP2: Hem H 1M 3
Chapel Ct. DA10: Swans 58Ae 121
E10 ....33Dc 72
(off Rosedene Ter.)
N2 ....27Gb 49
SE1 ....1F 231 (47Tb 91)
SE18 ....51Wc 117
UB3: Hayes 45V 84
CHAPEL CROFT 3J 11
Chapel Cft. WD4: Chfd 3J 11
CHAPEL END 25Dc 52
Chapel Farm Rd. SE9 ....62Pc 138
Chapel Grn. CR8: Purl 85Qb 176
Chapel Gro. KT15: Add 77K 149
KT18: Tatt C 91Ya 194
Chapel High CM14: B'wood 19Yd 40
(off High St.)
Chapel Hill DA1: Cray 57Gd 118
KT24: Eff 99Z 191
Chapel Ho. St. E14 ....50Dc 92
Chapelier Ho. SW18 ....56Cb 111
Chapel La. GU24: Pirb 4E 186
HA5: Pinn 27Z 45
IG7: Chig 20Vc 37
KT23: Bookh, Westh 100Ea 192
RM6: Chad H 31Zc 75
SL2: Stoke P 8M 61
UB8: Hil 44Q 84
Chapel Lodge RM13: Rain 41Jd 96
Chapel Mkt. N1 ....1K 217 (40Qb 70)
Chapel M. IG8: Wfd G 23Qc 54
Chapel Mill Rd. KT1: King T 69Pa 131
Chapelmount Rd. IG8: Wfd G 23Pc 54
Chapel of St John the Evangelist 5K 225
(in The Tower of London)
Chapel of St Peter & St Paul 51Fc 115
Chapel Pk. Rd. KT15: Add 77K 149
Chapel Path E11 ....30Kc 53
(off Woodbine Pl.)
Chapel Pl. AL1: St A 5B 6
EC2 ....4H 219 (41Ub 91)
N1 ....1A 218 (40Qb 70)
N17 ....24Vb 51
W1 ....3K 221 (44Kb 90)
Chapel Rd. CM16: Epp 2Vc 23
CR6: W'ham 90Zb 178
DA7: Bex 56Cd 118
IG1: Ilf 34Qc 74
KT20: Tad 95Ya 194
RH1: Redh 6P 207
RH8: Limp 2N 211
SE27 ....63Rb 135
TW1: Twick 59Ka 108
TW3: Houn 55Da 107
W13 ....46Ka 86
Chapel Row TN15: Igh 93Yd 204
UB9: Hare 25L 43
Chapels Cl. SL1: Slou 6C 80
Chapel Side W2 ....45Db 89
Chapel Sq. GU25: Vir W 70A 126
Chapel Stones N17 ....25Vb 51

Chapel St. EN2: Enf 13Sb 33
GU21: Wok 89B 168
HP2: Hem H 1M 3
NW1 . . . . . 1D 220 (43Gb 69)
SL1: Slou 7K 81
SW1 . . . . . 3J 227 (48Jb 90)
UB8: Uxb 39L 63
Chapel Ter. IG10: Lough 14Nc 36
Chapel Vw. CR2: Sels 79Yb 158
TN15: Igh 93Yd 204
Chapel Wlk. CR0: C'don 75Sb 157
CR5: Coul 94Mb 196
DA5: Bexl 61Gd 140
(off Pinewood Pl.)
NW4 . . . . . 28Xa 48
(not continuous)
Chapel Way KT18: Tatt C 91Ya 194
N7 . . . . . 34Pb 70
WD5: Bedm 9F 4
Chapel Wood DA3: New A 74Ae 165
(not continuous)
Chapelwood Pl. DA13: Sole S 10E 144
Chapel Wood Rd. DA3: Hartl 76Ae 165
TN15: Ash 76Ae 165
Chapel Yd. SW18 . . . . . 57Db 111
(off Wandsworth High St.)
Chaplaincy Gdns. RM11: Horn 32Nd 77
Chaplin Cl. HA0: Wemb 37Ma 67
SE1 . . . . . 1A 230 (47Qb 90)
Chaplin Ct. DA4: Sut H 65Qd 141
Chaplin Cres. TW16: Sun 65U 128
Chaplin Ho. DA14: Sidc 63Wc 139
(off Sidcup High St.)
N1 . . . . . 39Tb 71
Chaplin M. SL3: L'ly 50B 82
Chaplin Rd. E15 . . . . . 40Hc 73
HA0: Wemb 37La 66
N17 . . . . . 27Vb 51
NW2 . . . . . 37Wa 68
RM9: Dag 38Ad 75
Chaplin Sq. N12 . . . . . 24Fb 49
Chapman Cl. UB7: W Dray 48P 83
Chapman Ct. DA1: Dart 54Qd 119
EN8: Chesh 2Zb 20
Chapman Cres. HA3: Kenton 30Na 47
Chapman Grn. N22 . . . . . 25Qb 50
Chapman Hall AL10: Hat 2B 8
(off Bishops Ri.)
Chapman Ho. E1 . . . . . 44Xb 91
(off Bigland St.)
Chapman Pl. N4 . . . . . 33Rb 71
Chapman Rd. CR0: C'don 74Qb 156
DA17: Belv 50Cd 96
E9 . . . . . 37Bc 72
Chapmans Cl. TN14: Sund 96Ad 201
Chapman's Hill DA13: Meop 79Fe 165
Chapman's La. BR5: St P, Swan 68Zc 139
SE2: Belv 49Yc 95
Chapmans Pk. Ind. Est. NW10 . . . . . 37Va 68
Chapman Sq. SW19 . . . . . 61Za 132
Chapmans Rd. TN14: Sund 96Ad 201
Chapman's Ter. N22 . . . . . 25Rb 51
Chapman St. E1 . . . . . 45Xb 91
Chapone Pl. W1 . . . . . 3D 222 (44Mb 90)
Chapter Chambers SW1 . . . . . 6D 228
Chapter Cl. UB10: Hil 38P 63
W4 . . . . . 48Sa 87
Chapter House 3D 224
Chapter Ho. E2 . . . . . 42Wb 91
(off Dunbridge St.)
Chapter M. SL4: Wind 2H 103
Chapter Rd. NW2 . . . . . 36Wa 68
SE17 . . . . . 50Rb 91
Chapter St. SW1 . . . . . 6D 228 (49Mb 90)
Chapter Way SW19 . . . . . 67Fb 133
TW12: Hamp 63Ca 129
Chara Pl. W4 . . . . . 51Ta 109
Charcot Ho. SW15 . . . . . 58Va 110
Charcroft Ct. W14 . . . . . 47Za 88
(off Minford Gdns.)
Charcroft Gdns. EN3: Pond E 14Zb 34
Chardin Ho. SW9 . . . . . 53Qb 112
(off Gosling Way)
Chardin Rd. W4 . . . . . 49Ua 88
Chardins Cl. HP1: Hem H 1H 3
Chardmore Rd. N16 . . . . . 32Wb 71
Chard Rd. TW6: H'row A 54R 106
Chardwell Cl. E6 . . . . . 44Pc 94
Charecroft Way W12 . . . . . 47Za 88
W14 . . . . . 47Za 88
Charfield Ct. W9 . . . . . 42Db 89
(off Shirland Rd.)
Charford Rd. E16 . . . . . 43Jc 93
Chargate Cl. KT12: Hers 79V 150
Chargeable La. E13 . . . . . 42Hc 93
Chargeable St. E16 . . . . . 42Hc 93
Chargrove Cl. SE16 . . . . . 47Zb 92
Charing Cl. BR6: Orp 77Vc 161
Charing Ct. BR2: Brom 68Gc 137
Charing Cross SW1 . . . . . 6F 223
Charing Cross Rd. WC2 . . . . . 3E 222 (44Mb 90)
Charing Cross Sports Club 51Za 110
Charing Cross Underground Shop. Cen.
WC2 . . . . . 5F 223
Charing Ho. SE1 . . . . . 1A 230
Chariot Cl. E3 . . . . . 39Cc 72
Chariotts Pl. SL4: Wind 3H 103
Charis Ho. E3 . . . . . 41Dc 92
(off Grace St.)
Charkham M. AL9: Wel G 6E 8
Charlbert Ct. NW8 . . . . . 1D 214
Charlbert St. NW8 . . . . . 1D 214 (40Gb 69)
Charlbury Av. HA7: Stan 22Ma 47
Charlbury Cl. RM3: Rom 23Ld 57
Charlbury Cres. RM3: Rom 23Ld 57
Charlbury Gdns. IG3: Ilf 33Vc 75
Charlbury Gro. W5 . . . . . 44La 86
Charlbury Rd. UB10: Ick 34P 63
Charldane Rd. SE9 . . . . . 62Rc 138
Charlecombe Ct. TW18: Staines 64K 127
Charlecote Gro. SE26 . . . . . 62Xb 135
Charlecote Rd. RM8: Dag 34Ad 75
Charlemont Rd. E6 . . . . . 42Pc 94
Charles II Pl. SW3 . . . . . 7E 226 (50Hb 89)
Charles II St. SW1 . . . . . 6D 222 (46Mb 90)
Charles Auffray Ho. E1 . . . . . 43Yb 92
(off Smithy St.)
Charles Babbage Cl. KT9: Chess 80La 152
Charles Barry Cl. SW4 . . . . . 55Lb 112
Charles Bradlaugh Ho. N17 . . . . . 24Xb 51
(off Haynes Cl.)
Charles Burton Ct. E5 . . . . . 36Ac 72
(off Homerton Rd.)
Charles Chu. Wlk. IG1: Ilf 30Pc 54
Charles Cl. DA14: Sidc 63Xc 139
Charles Cobb Gdns. CR0: Wadd 78Qb 156
Charles Ct. DA8: Erith 51Gd 118
Charles Coveney Rd. SE15 . . . . . 53Vb 113
Charles Cres. HA1: Harr 31Fa 66
(not continuous)
Charles Curran Ho. UB10: Ick 34R 64
Charles Darwin Ho. E2 . . . . . 41Xb 91
(off Canrobert St.)
Charles Dickens Ho. E2 . . . . . 41Wb 91
(off Mansford St.)
Charles Dickens Museum, The 6J 217
Charle Sevright Dr. NW7 . . . . . 22Za 48
Charlesfield SE9 . . . . . 62Lc 137
Charles Flemwell M. E16 . . . . . 46Jc 93
Charles Gdns. SL2: Slou 4M 81
Charles Gardner Ct. N1 . . . . . 3G 219
Charles Grinling Wlk. SE18 . . . . . 49Qc 94
Charles Gro. N14 . . . . . 18Lb 32
Charles Haller St. SW2 . . . . . 59Qb 112
Charles Harrod Ct. SW13 . . . . . 51Ya 110
(off Somerville Av.)
Charles Hocking Ho. W3 . . . . . 47Sa 87
(off Bollo Bri. Rd.)
Charles House 49Bb 89
(off Kensington High St.)
Charles Ho. KT16: Chert 74H 149
(off Sth. Guildford St.)
N17 . . . . . 24Vb 51
(off Love La.)
SL4: Wind 3G 102
UB2: S'hall 47Ca 85
Charles Lamb Ct. N1 . . . . . 1C 218
Charles La. NW8 . . . . . 2C 214 (40Gb 69)
Charles Lesser Ho. KT9: Chess 78Ma 153
Charles Mackenzie Ho. SE16 . . . . . 49Wb 91
(off Linsey St.)
Charlesmere Gdns. SE28 . . . . . 47Uc 94
(off Thames Reach)
Charles Nex M. SE21 . . . . . 61Sb 135
Charles Pl. E4 . . . . . 17Fc 35
NW1 . . . . . 4C 216 (41Lb 90)
Charles Rd. E7 . . . . . 38Lc 73
RM6: Chad H 30Zc 55
RM10: Dag 37Fd 76
SW19 . . . . . 67Cb 133
TN14: Bad M 82Dd 182
TW18: Staines 65M 127
W13 . . . . . 44Ja 86
Charles Rowan Ho. WC1 . . . . . 4K 217
Charles Simmons Ho. WC1 . . . . . 4J 217
Charles Sq. N1 . . . . . 4G 219 (41Tb 91)
Charles Sq. Est. N1 . . . . . 4G 219
Charles St. CM16: Epp 4Wc 23
CR0: C'don 76Sb 157
DA9: Ghithe 57Ud 120
(not continuous)
E16 . . . . . 46Lc 93
EN1: Enf 15Vb 33
HP1: Hem H 3L 3
KT16: Chert 74H 149
RM17: Grays 51De 121
SL4: Wind 3G 102
SW13 . . . . . 54Ua 110
TW3: Houn 54Ba 107
UB10: Hil 42R 84
W1 . . . . . 6K 221 (46Kb 90)
Charleston Cl. TW13: Felt 62W 128
Charleston St. SE17 . . . . . 6E 230 (49Sb 91)
Charles Townsend Ho. EC1 . . . . . 4B 218
Charles Uton Ct. E8 . . . . . 35Wb 71
Charles Whincup Rd. E16 . . . . . 46Kc 93
Charlesworth Cl. HP3: Hem H 4M 3
Charlesworth Ho. E14 . . . . . 44Cc 92
(off Dod St.)
Charlesworth Pl. SW13 . . . . . 55Ua 110
Charleville Cir. SE26 . . . . . 64Wb 135
Charleville Ct. W14 . . . . . 50Bb 89
(off Charleville Rd.)
Charleville Mans. W14 . . . . . 50Ab 88
(off Charleville Rd., not continuous)
Charleville M. TW7: Isle 56Ka 108
Charleville Rd. W14 . . . . . 50Ab 88
CHARLIE BROWN'S RDBT. 26Lc 53
Charlie Chaplin Wlk. SE1 . . . . . 7J 223 (46Pb 90)
Charlieville Rd. DA8: Erith 52Ed 118
Charlmont Rd. SW17 . . . . . 65Gb 133
Charlock Way WD18: Wat 16V 26
Charlotte Av. SL2: Slou 5K 81
Charlotte Cl. AL4: St A 2J 7
DA6: Bex 57Ad 117
IG6: Ilf 25Sc 54
KT21: Asht 90Na 173
WD19: Wat 17Y 27
Charlotte Ct. IG2: Ilf 30Qc 54
KT10: Esh 78Ea 152
N8 . . . . . 30Mb 50
RM11: Horn 31Md 77
SE1 . . . . . 5H 231
W6 . . . . . 49Wa 88
(off Invermead Cl.)
Charlotte Despard Av. SW11 . . . . . 53Jb 112
Charlotte Gdns. RM5: Col R 23Dd 56
Charlotte Ho. E16 . . . . . 46Kc 93
(off Fairfax M.)
W6 . . . . . 50Ya 88
(off Queen Caroline St.)
Charlotte M. KT10: Esh 77Da 151
(off Heather Pl.)
RM13: Rain 40Md 77
W1 . . . . . 7C 216 (43Lb 90)
W10 . . . . . 44Za 88
W14 . . . . . 49Ab 88
Charlotte Pk. Av. BR1: Brom 69Nc 138
Charlotte Pl. NW9 . . . . . 29Sa 47
RM20: W Thur 51Xd 120
SW1 . . . . . 6B 228 (49Lb 90)
W1 . . . . . 1C 222 (43Lb 90)
Charlotte Rd. EC2 . . . . . 4H 219 (41Ub 91)
RM10: Dag 37Dd 76
SM6: Wall 79Lb 156
SW13 . . . . . 53Va 110
Charlotte Row SW4 . . . . . 55Lb 112
Charlotte Sq. TW10: Rich 58Pa 109
Charlotte St. W1 . . . . . 7C 216 (43Lb 90)
Charlotte Ter. KT10: Esh 79Ea 152
(off Princess Sq.)
N1 . . . . . 1J 217 (39Pb 70)
Charlow Cl. SW6 . . . . . 54Eb 111
CHARLTON
SE7 . . . . . 52Mc 115
TW17 . . . . . 69S 128
Charlton SL4: Wind 4A 102
Charlton Athletic FC 50Lc 93
Charlton Av. KT12: Hers 77X 151
Charlton Chu. La. SE7 . . . . . 50Lc 93
Charlton Cl. SL1: Slou 7F 80
UB10: Ick 33R 64
Charlton Ct. E2 . . . . . 1K 219 (39Vb 71)
NW5 . . . . . 36Mb 70
Charlton Cres. IG11: Bark 40Vc 75
Charlton Dene SE7 . . . . . 52Lc 115
Charlton Dr. TN16: Big H 89Mc 179
Charlton Gdns. CR5: Coul 90Lb 176
Charlton Ga. Bus. Pk. SE7 . . . . . 49Lc 93
Charlton Ho. TW8: Bford 51Na 109
Charlton Kings KT13: Weyb 76U 150
Charlton King's Rd. NW5 . . . . . 36Mb 70
Charlton La. SE7 . . . . . 49Mc 93
TW17: Shep 69S 128
(not continuous)
Charlton Lido 52Mc 115
Charlton Pk. La. SE7 . . . . . 52Mc 115
Charlton Pk. Rd. SE7 . . . . . 51Mc 115
Charlton Pl. N1 . . . . . 1B 218 (40Rb 71)
SL4: Wind 4A 102
(off Charlton)
Charlton Rd. HA3: Kenton 28Ma 47
HA9: Wemb 32Pa 67
N9 . . . . . 18Zb 34
NW10 . . . . . 39Ua 68
SE3 . . . . . 52Jc 115
SE7 . . . . . 52Jc 115
TW17: Shep 69S 128
Charlton Row SL4: Wind 4A 102
Charlton Sq. SL4: Wind 4A 102
(off Charlton)
Charlton St. RM20: Grays 51Zd 121
Charlton Wlk. SL4: Wind 4A 102
Charlton Way SE3 . . . . . 53Gc 115
SL4: Wind 4A 102
Charlwood CR0: Sels 81Bc 178
Charlwood Cl. HA3: Hrw W 23Ga 46
KT23: Bookh 96Da 191
Charlwood Dr. KT22: Oxs 87Fa 172
Charlwood Ho. SW1 . . . . . 6D 228
TW9: Kew 52Ra 109
Charlwood Ho's. WC1 . . . . . 4G 217
(off Midhope St.)
Charlwood Pl. RH2: Reig 6K 207
SW1 . . . . . 6C 228 (49Lb 90)
Charlwood Rd. SW15 . . . . . 56Za 110
Charlwood St. SW1 . . . . . 7B 228 (50Lb 90)
(not continuous)
Charlwood Ter. SW15 . . . . . 56Za 110
Charman Rd. RH1: Redh 6N 207
Charmans Ho. SW8 . . . . . 52Nb 112
(off Wandsworth Rd.)
Charmeuse Ct. E2 . . . . . 40Xb 71
(off Silk Weaver Way)
Charmian Av. HA7: Stan 27Ma 47
Charmian Ho. N1 . . . . . 2H 219
Charminster Av. SW19 . . . . . 68Cb 133
Charminster Ct. KT6: Surb 73Ma 153
Charminster Rd. KT4: Wor Pk 74Za 154
SE9 . . . . . 63Mc 137
Charmouth Ct. TW10: Rich 57Pa 109
Charmouth Ho. SW8 . . . . . 52Pb 112
Charmouth Rd. AL1: St A 1E 6
DA16: Well 53Yc 117
Charmwood La. BR6: Prat B 81Xc 181
Charne, The TN14: Otf 89Jd 182
Charnock BR8: Swan 70Gd 140
Charnock Ho. W12 . . . . . 45Xa 88
(off White City Est.)
Charnock Rd. E5 . . . . . 34Xb 71
Charnwood SL5: S'dale 2D 146
Charnwood Av. SW19 . . . . . 68Cb 133
Charnwood Cl. KT3: N Mald 70Ua 132
Charnwood Dr. E18 . . . . . 27Kc 53
Charnwood Gdns. E14 . . . . . 49Cc 92
Charnwood Pl. N20 . . . . . 20Eb 31
Charnwood Rd. EN1: Enf 8Xb 19
SE25 . . . . . 71Tb 157
UB10: Hil 40Q 64
Charnwood St. E5 . . . . . 33Xb 71
Charrington Bowl 75Ra 153
Charrington Ct. RM1: Rush G 30Gd 56
Charrington Pl. AL1: St A 3D 6
Charrington Rd. CR0: C'don 75Sb 157
Charrington St. NW1 . . . . . 1D 216 (40Mb 70)
(not continuous)
Charsley Rd. SE6 . . . . . 61Dc 136
Charta Rd. TW20: Egh 64E 126
Chart Cl. BR2: Brom 67Gc 137
CR0: C'don 72Yb 158
CR4: Mitc 70Hb 133
Charter Av. IG2: Ilf 32Tc 74
Charter Bldgs. SE10 . . . . . 53Dc 114
(off Catherine Gro.)
Charter Cl. AL1: St A 2B 6
SL1: Slou 8K 81
Charter Ct. HP2: Hem H 2M 3
KT3: N Mald 69Ua 132
N4 . . . . . 32Qb 70
N22 . . . . . 25Mb 50
UB1: S'hall 46Ca 85
Charter Cres. TW4: Houn 56Aa 107
Charter Dr. DA5: Bexl 59Ad 117
Charterhouse 6C 218
Charter Ho. SM2: Sutt 79Db 155
(off Mulgrave Rd.)
WC2 . . . . . 3G 223
Charterhouse Apartments SW18 . . . . . 56Eb 111
Charterhouse Av. HA0: Wemb 35La 66
Charterhouse Bldgs. EC1 . . . . . 6D 218 (42Sb 91)
Charterhouse Dr. TN13: S'oaks 95Jd 202
Charterhouse M. EC1 . . . . . 7C 218 (43Rb 91)
Charterhouse Rd. BR6: Chels 76Wc 161
E8 . . . . . 35Wb 71
Charterhouse Sq. EC1 . . . . . 7C 218 (43Rb 91)
Charterhouse St. EC1 . . . . . 1A 224 (43Qb 90)
Charteris Community Sports Cen. 39Cb 69
Charteris Rd. IG8: Wfd G 24Kc 53
N4 . . . . . 32Qb 70
NW6 . . . . . 39Bb 69
Charter Pl. TW18: Staines 65J 127
UB8: Uxb 38M 63
WD17: Wat 14Y 27
Charter Quay KT1: King T 68Ma 131
(off Wadbrook St.)
Charter Rd. KT1: King T 69Ra 131
SL1: Slou 5C 80
Charter Road, The IG8: Wfd G 23Gc 53
Charters SL5: S'hill 2C 146
Charters Cl. SE19 . . . . . 64Ub 135
SL5: S'hill 1B 146
Charters Ct. SL5: S'hill 2B 146
Charters Gdn. Ho. SL5: S'hill 2C 146
Charters Health Club 3G 6
Charters La. SL5: S'hill 1B 146
Charters Leisure Cen. 3B 146
Charter Sq. KT1: King T 68Ra 131
Charters Rd. SL5: S'dale 3B 146
Charters Way SL5: S'dale 3D 146
Charter Way N3 . . . . . 28Bb 49
N14 . . . . . 16Lb 32
Chartes Ho. SE1 . . . . . 3J 231
Chartfield Av. SW15 . . . . . 57Xa 110
Chartfield Pl. KT13: Weyb 78R 150
Chartfield Rd. RH2: Reig 7L 207
Chartfield Sq. SW15 . . . . . 57Za 110
Chartham Ct. SW9 . . . . . 55Qb 112
(off Canterbury Cres.)
Chartham Gro. SE27 . . . . . 62Rb 135
Chartham Ho. SE1 . . . . . 3G 231
Chartham Rd. SE25 . . . . . 69Xb 135
Chart Hills Cl. SE28 . . . . . 44Ad 95
Chart Ho. CR4: Mitc 68Hb 133
E14 . . . . . 50Dc 92
(off Burrells Wharf Sq.)
Chart La. RH2: Reig 7N 207
TN16: Bras, B Char 100Xc 201
Chartley Av. HA7: Stan 23Ha 46
NW2 . . . . . 34Ua 68
Charton Cl. DA17: Belv 51Bd 117
Chartres Ct. UB6: G'frd 40Fa 66
Chartridge SE17 . . . . . 51Tb 113
(off Westmoreland Rd.)
WD19: Wat 19Z 27
Chartridge Cl. EN5: Ark 15Wa 30
WD23: Bush 16Ea 28
Chartridge Way HP2: Hem H 2C 4
Chart St. N1 . . . . . 3G 219 (41Tb 91)
Chart Vw. TN15: Kems'g 89Rd 183
Chartway RH2: Reig 5K 207
TN13: S'oaks 96Ld 203
Chartwell GU22: Wok 90A 168
(off Mt. Hermon Rd.)
Chartwell Bus. Cen. BR1: Brom 69Mc 137
Chartwell Cl. CR0: C'don 74Tb 157
EN9: Walt A 5Gc 21
SE9 . . . . . 61Tc 138
UB6: G'frd 39Da 65
Chartwell Ct. EN5: Barn 14Ab 30
IG8: Wfd G 24Hc 53
UB3: Hayes 45V 84
Chartwell Dr. BR6: Farnb 78Tc 160
Chartwell Gdns. SM3: Cheam 77Ab 154
Chartwell Ho. W11 . . . . . 46Bb 89
(off Ladbroke Rd.)
Chartwell Lodge BR3: Beck 66Cc 136
Chartwell Pl. HA2: Harr 33Fa 66
KT18: Eps 86Ua 174
SM3: Cheam 77Ab 154
Chartwell Rd. HA6: Nwood 23V 44
Chartwell Way SE20 . . . . . 67Xb 135
Charville Ct. HA1: Harr 30Ha 46
SE10 . . . . . 51Fc 115
(off Trafalgar Gro.)
Charville La. UB4: Hayes 41S 84
Charville La. W. UB10: Hil 41R 84
(not continuous)
Charwood SW16 . . . . . 63Qb 134
Charwood Cl. WD7: Shenl 5Na 15
Chase, The BR1: Brom 69Kc 137
BR6: Prat B 84Wc 181
CM13: Ingve 22Ee 59
CM14: B'wood 20Zd 41
CM14: W'ley 21Xd 58
(Cromwell Rd.)
CM14: W'ley 22Zd 59
(Nelson Cl.)
CR5: Coul 86Lb 176
DA7: Bex 55Dd 118
E12 . . . . . 35Mc 73
EN7: G Oak 1Rb 19
HA5: Eastc 30Y 45
HA5: Pinn 28Ba 45
HA7: Stan 23Ja 46
HA8: Edg 25Ra 47
HP2: Hem H 3N 3
IG7: Chig 21Sc 54
IG10: Lough 17Mc 35
KT20: Kgswd 94Cb 195
KT21: Asht 90La 172
KT22: Oxs 87Ea 172
KT24: E Hor 98V 190
RH2: Reig 7M 207
RM1: Rom 27Gd 56
RM6: Chad H 30Ad 55
RM7: Rush G 34Fd 76
(not continuous)
RM13: Rain 39Kd 77
RM14: Upm 34Ud 78
RM20: Grays 51Zd 121
SM6: Wall 78Nb 156
SW4 . . . . . 55Kb 112
SW16 . . . . . 66Pb 134
SW20 . . . . . 67Ab 132
TN15: Kems'g 88Nd 183
TW16: Sun 67X 129
UB10: Ick 36Q 64
WD7: R'lett 7Ha 14
WD18: Wat 14U 26
Chase Bank Ct. N14 . . . . . 16Lb 32
(off Avenue Rd.)
Chase Centre, The NW10 . . . . . 41Ta 87
Chase Ct. SW3 . . . . . 4F 227
SW20 . . . . . 68Ab 132
TW7: Isle 54Ja 108
Chase Ct. Gdns. EN2: Enf 13Sb 33
CHASE CROSS 23Gd 56
Chase Cross Rd. RM5: Col R 24Ed 56
Chase End KT19: Eps 84Ta 173
Chasefield Rd. SW17 . . . . . 63Hb 133
Chase Gdns. E4 . . . . . 21Cc 52
TW2: Whitt 59Fa 108
Chase Grn. EN2: Enf 13Sb 33
Chase Grn. Av. EN2: Enf 12Rb 33
Chase Hill EN2: Enf 13Sb 33
Chase Ho. Gdns. RM11: Horn 29Pd 57
Chase La. IG2: Ilf 29Tc 54
IG6: Ilf 29Tc 54
IG7: Chig 20Vc 37
Chaseley Ct. KT13: Weyb 74U 150
Chaseley Dr. CR2: Sande 82Tb 177
W4 . . . . . 50Ra 87
Chaseley St. E14 . . . . . 44Ac 92
Chasemore Cl. CR4: Mitc 73Hb 155
Chasemore Gdns. CR0: Wadd 78Qb 156
Chasemore Ho. SW6 . . . . . 52Ab 110
(off Williams Cl.)
Chase Nature Reserve, The 34Hd 76
Chase Ridings EN2: Enf 12Qb 32
Chase Rd. CM14: B'wood 20Yd 40
KT19: Eps 84Ta 173
N14 . . . . . 15Lb 32
NW10 . . . . . 42Ta 87
Chase Rd. Trad. Est. NW10 . . . . . 42Ta 87
CHASE SIDE 11Tb 33
Chase Side EN2: Enf 13Sb 33
N14 . . . . . 16Jb 32
Chase Side Av. EN2: Enf 12Sb 33
SW20 . . . . . 67Ab 132
Chaseside Cl. RM1: Rom 23Gd 56
Chase Side Cres. EN2: Enf 11Sb 33
Chaseside Gdns. KT16: Chert 73K 149
Chase Side Ind. Est. N14 . . . . . 17Mb 32
Chase Side Pl. EN2: Enf 12Sb 33
Chase Sq. DA11: Grav'nd 8D 122
Chaseville Pde. N21 . . . . . 15Pb 32
Chaseville Pk. Rd. N21 . . . . . 15Nb 32
Chase Way N14 . . . . . 19Kb 32
Chaseway Lodge E16 . . . . . 44Jc 93
(off Butchers Rd.)
Chaseways Vs. RM5: Col R 25Bd 55
Chasewood Av. EN2: Enf 12Rb 33
Chasewood Ct. NW7 . . . . . 22Ta 47
Chasewood Pk. HA1: Harr 34Ha 66
Chastilian Rd. DA1: Dart 59Hd 118
Chaston Pl. NW5 . . . . . 36Jb 70
(off Grafton Ter.)
Chater Ho. E2 . . . . . 41Zb 92
(off Roman Rd.)
Chatfield SL2: Slou 3E 80
Chatfield Ct. CR3: Cat'm 94Tb 197
Chatfield Rd. CR0: C'don 74Rb 157
SW11 . . . . . 55Eb 111
Chatham Av. BR2: Hayes 73Hc 159
Chatham Cl. NW11 . . . . . 29Cb 49
SE18 . . . . . 48Rc 94
SM3: Sutt 73Bb 155
Chatham Ct. SL1: Slou 8L 81
(off Grove Cl.)
Chatham Hill Rd. TN14: S'oaks 93Ld 203
Chatham Ho. SM6: Wall 78Kb 156
(off Melbourne Rd.)
Chatham Pl. E9 . . . . . 37Yb 72
Chatham Rd. E17 . . . . . 27Ac 52
E18 . . . . . 26Hc 53
KT1: King T 68Qa 131
SW11 . . . . . 58Hb 111
Chatham St. SE17 . . . . . 5F 231 (49Tb 91)
Chatham Way CM14: B'wood 19Yd 40
CHATHILL 9F 210
Chatley Heath Semaphore Tower . . . 89T 170
Chatsfield KT17: Ewe 82Wa 174
Chatsfield Pl. W5 . . . . . 44Na 87
Chats Palace Arts Cen. 36Zb 72
Chatsworth Av. BR1: Brom 63Kc 137
DA15: Sidc 60Wc 117
HA9: Wemb 36Pa 67
NW4 . . . . . 26Ya 48
SW20 . . . . . 67Ab 132
Chatsworth Cl. BR4: W W'ck 75Hc 159
NW4 . . . . . 26Ya 48
W4 . . . . . 51Sa 109
WD6: Bore 13Qa 29
Chatsworth Ct. AL1: St A 2D 6
(off Granville Rd.)
HA7: Stan 22La 46
SW16 . . . . . 69Pb 134
W8 . . . . . 49Bb 89
(off Pembroke Rd.)
Chatsworth Cres. TW3: Houn 56Fa 108
Chatsworth Dr. EN1: Enf 17Wb 33
Chatsworth Est. E5 . . . . . 35Zb 72
Chatsworth Gdns. HA2: Harr 32Da 65
KT3: N Mald 71Va 154
W3 . . . . . 46Ra 87
Chatsworth Ho. BR2: Brom 70Jc 137
(off Westmoreland Rd.)
E16 . . . . . 46Kc 93
(off Wesley Av.)
Chatsworth Lodge W4 . . . . . 50Ta 87
(off Bourne Pl.)
Chatsworth M. WD24: Wat 10W 12
Chatsworth Pde. BR5: Pet W 71Sc 160
Chatsworth Pk. SM7: Bans 89Db 175
Chatsworth Pl. CR4: Mitc 69Hb 133
KT22: Oxs 85Fa 172
TW11: Tedd 63Ja 130
Chatsworth Ri. W5 . . . . . 42Pa 87
Chatsworth Rd. CR0: C'don 77Tb 157
DA1: Dart 57Ld 119
E5 . . . . . 34Yb 72
E15 . . . . . 36Hc 73
NW2 . . . . . 37Ya 68
SM3: Cheam 78Za 154
UB4: Yead 42X 85
W4 . . . . . 51Sa 109
W5 . . . . . 42Pa 87
Chatsworth Way SE27 . . . . . 62Rb 135
Chatteris Av. RM3: Rom 23Ld 57
CHATTERN HILL 63R 128
Chattern Hill TW15: Ashf 63R 128
Chattern Rd. TW15: Ashf 63S 128
Chatterton Ct. TW9: Kew 54Pa 109
Chatterton M. N4 . . . . . 34Rb 71
(off Chatterton Rd.)
Chatterton Rd. BR2: Brom 70Mc 137
N4 . . . . . 34Rb 71
Chatton Row GU24: Bisl 9E 166
Chatto Rd. SW11 . . . . . 57Hb 111
Chaucer Av. KT13: Weyb 80Q 150
TW4: Cran 54X 107
TW9: Rich 55Qa 109
UB4: Hayes 43W 84
Chaucer Bus. Pk. TN15: Kems'g 90Td 184
Chaucer Cl. N11 . . . . . 22Lb 50
RM18: Tilb 4E 122
SL4: Wind 5H 103
SM7: Bans 86Ab 174
Chaucer Ct. EN5: New Bar 15Db 31
N16 . . . . . 35Ub 71
RH1: Redh 3A 208
SW17 . . . . . 62Fb 133
(off Lanesborough Way)
Chaucer Dr. SE1 . . . . . 6K 231 (49Vb 91)
Chaucer Gdns. SM1: Sutt 76Cb 155
Chaucer Grn. CR0: C'don 73Xb 157
Chaucer Gro. WD6: Bore 14Qa 29
Chaucer Ho. EN5: Barn 14Za 30
SM1: Sutt 76Cb 155
(off Chaucer Gdns.)
SW1 . . . . . 50Lb 90
(off Churchill Gdns.)
Chaucer Mans. W14 . . . . . 51Ab 110
(off Queen's Club Gdns.)
Chaucer Pk. DA1: Dart 59Pd 119
Chaucer Rd. DA11: Nflt 62Fe 143
DA15: Sidc 60Yc 117
DA16: Well 53Uc 116
E7 . . . . . 37Jc 73
E11 . . . . . 30Jc 53

Chaucer Rd. E17 .26Ec 52
RM3: Rom .24Kd 57
SE24 .57Qb 112
SM1: Sutt .77Cb 155
TW15: Ashf .63N 127
W3 .46Sa 87
Chaucer Way DA1: Dart .56Qd 119
(not continuous)
KT15: Add .79J 149
SL1: Slou .6K 81
SW19 .65Fb 133
CHAULDEN .3H 3
Chaulden Ho. EC1 .4G 219
Chaulden Ho. Gdns. HP1: Hem H .4H 3
Chaulden La. HP1: Hem H .4F 2
Chaulden Ter. HP1: Hem H .3H 3
Chauncey Cl. N9 .20Wb 33
Chauncey Ho. WD18: Wat .16U 26
Chauncy Av. EN6: Pot B .5Eb 17
Chaundrye Cl. SE9 .58Pc 116
Chauntler Cl. E16 .44Kc 93
Chave Cft. KT18: Tatt C .91Ya 194
Chavecroft Ter. KT18: Tatt C .91Ya 194
Chave Rd. DA2: Wilm .62Nd 141
Chaville Ct. N11 .21Jb 50
Chaville Way N3 .25Cb 49
Chaworth Cl. KT16: Ott .79E 148
Chaworth Rd. KT16: Ott .79E 148
Cheadle Ct. NW8 .5C 214
Cheadle Ho. *E14* .44Bc 92
(off Copenhagen Pl.)
CHEAM .79Ab 154
Cheam Cl. KT20: Tad .93Xa 194
Cheam Comn. Rd. KT4: Wor Pk .75Xa 154
Cheam Leisure Cen. .77Za 154
Cheam Mans. SM3: Cheam .80Ab 154
Cheam Pk. Way SM3: Cheam .79Ab 154
Cheam Rd. KT17: Ewe .82Wa 174
SM1: Sutt .79Bb 155
SM2: Cheam .82Xa 174
Cheam Sports Club .80Za 154
Cheam St. SE15 .55Yb 114
CHEAM VILLAGE .79Ab 154
CHEAPSIDE .7C 124
Cheapside EC2 .3D 224 (44Sb 91)
GU21: Wok .6P 167
N13 .21Tb 51
N22 .27Qb 50
Cheapside La. UB9: Den .33H 63
Cheapside Pas. EC2 .3D 224
Cheapside Rd. SL5: Asc .9A 124
Chearsley SE17 .5E 230
Cheddar Cl. N11 .23Hb 49
Cheddar Waye UB4: Yead .44X 85
Cheddington Ho. *E2* .39Wb 71
(off Whiston Rd.)
Cheddington Rd. N18 .20Ub 33
Chedworth Cl. *E16* .44Hc 93
(off Wouldham Rd.)
Chedworth Ho. *N15* .28Tb 51
(off West Grn. Rd.)
Cheelson Rd. RM15: S Ock .40Yd 78
Cheena Ho. SL9: Chal P .24B 42
Cheeseman Cl. TW12: Hamp .65Aa 129
Cheesemans Ter. W14 .50Bb 89
(not continuous)
Cheffery Ct. TW15: Ashf .65R 128
Cheldon Av. NW7 .24Za 48
Chelford Rd. BR1: Brom .64Fc 137
Chelmer Cres. IG11: Bark .40Xc 75
Chelmer Dr. CM13: Hut .16Fe 41
RM15: S Ock .45Yd 98
Chelmer Ho. *RM16: Grays* .10C 100
(off River Vw.)
Chelmer Rd. E9 .36Zb 72
RM14: Upm .30Td 58
RM16: Grays .10C 100
Chelmsford Av. RM5: Col R .24Fd 56
Chelmsford Cl. E6 .44Pc 94
SM2: Sutt .81Cb 175
W6 .51Za 110
Chelmsford Ct. *N14* .17Mb 32
(off Chelmsford Rd.)
Chelmsford Dr. RM14: Upm .34Pd 77
Chelmsford Gdns. IG1: Ilf .31Nc 74
Chelmsford Ho. *N7* .35Pb 70
(off Holloway Rd.)
Chelmsford Rd. CM15: Shenf .16Be 41
E11 .32Fc 73
E17 .30Cc 52
E18 .25Hc 53
N14 .17Lb 32
Chelmsford Sq. NW10 .39Ya 68
Chelmsine Ct. HA4: Ruis .29S 44
CHELSEA .7E 226 (50Gb 89)
Chelsea Bri. SW1 .51Kb 112
Chelsea Bri. Rd. SW1 .7H 227 (50Jb 90)
Chelsea Bri. Wharf SW8 .51Kb 112
Chelsea Cinema .7E 226 (50Gb 89)
Chelsea Cloisters SW3 .6E 226 (49Gb 89)
Chelsea Cl. HA8: Edg .26Qa 47
KT4: Wor Pk .73Wa 154
NW10 .39Ta 67
TW12: Hamp H .64Ea 130
Chelsea Ct. *BR1: Brom* .69Nc 138
(off Holmdene Ct.)
KT18: Eps .85Ta 173
(off Ashley Rd.)
SW3 .51Hb 111
(off Embankment Gdns.)
Chelsea Cres. NW2 .37Bb 69
SW10 .53Eb 111
Chelsea Emb. SW3 .51Gb 111
Chelsea Farm Ho. Studios *SW10* .51Fb 111
(off Cremorne Est.)
Chelsea FC .52Db 111
Chelsea Flds. SW19 .67Fb 133
Chelsea Gdns. SM3: Cheam .77Ab 154
SW1 .50Jb 90
W13 .43Ha 86
Chelsea Ga. SW1 .7J 227
Chelsea Harbour SW10 .53Eb 111
Chelsea Harbour Design Cen.
SW10 .53Eb 111
(off Chelsea Harbour Dr.)
Chelsea Harbour Dr. SW10 .53Eb 111
Chelsea Lodge *SW3* .51Hb 111
(off Tite St.)
Chelsea Mnr. Ct. SW3 .51Gb 111
Chelsea Mnr. Gdns. SW3 .50Gb 89
Chelsea Mnr. St.
SW3 .7D 226 (50Gb 89)
Chelsea Mnr. Studios SW3 .7E 226
Chelsea M. RM11: Horn .32Kd 77
Chelsea Pk. Gdns. SW3 .51Fb 111
Chelsea Physic Garden .51Hb 111
Chelsea Reach Twr. *SW10* .52Fb 111
(off Worlds End Est.)
Chelsea Sports Cen. .50Gb 89
Chelsea Sq. SW3 .7C 226 (50Fb 89)
Chelsea Studios *SW6* .52Db 111
(off Fulham Rd.)
Chelsea Theatre, The .52Eb 111
Chelsea Towers *SW3* .51Gb 111
(off Chelsea Mnr. Gdns.)
Chelsea Village *SW6* .52Db 111
(off Fulham Rd.)
Chelsea Vista SW6 .53Eb 111
Chelsea Wharf *SW10* .52Fb 111
(off Lots Rd.)
CHELSFIELD .78Xc 161
Chelsfield Av. N9 .17Zb 34
Chelsfield Gdns. SE26 .62Yb 136
Chelsfield Grn. N9 .17Zb 34
(not continuous)
Chelsfield Hill BR6: Chels .81Yc 181
Chelsfield Ho. SE17 .6H 231
Chelsfield Lakes Golf Course .80Ad 161
Chelsfield La. BR5: Orp .73Zc 161
BR6: Chels, Orp .75Zc 161
BR6: Well H .80Cd 162
TN14: S'ham .80Cd 162
Chelsfield Point *E9* .38Zb 72
(off Penshurst Rd.)
Chelsfield Rd. BR5: St M Cry .72Yc 161
CHELSFIELD VILLAGE .78Ad 161
CHELSHAM .89Cc 178
Chelsham Cl. CR6: W'ham .90Ac 178
CHELSHAM COMMON .88Cc 178
Chelsham Comn. Rd.
CR6: W'ham .89Cc 178
Chelsham Ct. Rd. CR6: W'ham .90Fc 179
Chelsham Rd. CR2: S Croy .80Tb 157
CR6: W'ham .90Bc 178
SW4 .55Mb 112
Chelsing Ri. HP2: Hem H .3C 4
Chelsiter Ct. DA14: Sidc .63Vc 139
Chelston App. HA4: Ruis .33W 64
Chelston Rd. HA4: Ruis .32W 64
Chelsworth Cl. RM3: Hrld W .24Pd 57
Chelsworth Dr. RM3: Hrld W .25Nd 57
SE18 .51Tc 116
Cheltenham Av. TW1: Twick .59Ja 108
Cheltenham Cl. DA12: Grav'nd .4E 144
KT3: N Mald .69Sa 131
UB5: N'olt .37Da 65
Cheltenham Ct. *AL1: St A* .3E 6
(off Dexter Cl.)
HA7: Stan .22La 46
(off Marsh La.)
Cheltenham Gdns. E6 .40Nc 74
IG10: Lough .16Nc 36
Cheltenham Ho. IG8: Wfd G .23Qc 54
UB3: Harl .48S 84
(off Skipton Dr.)
WD24: Wat .12Y 27
(off Exeter Cl.)
Cheltenham Pl. HA3: Kenton .28Na 47
W3 .46Ra 87
Cheltenham Rd. BR6: Chels .76Wc 161
E10 .30Ec 52
SE15 .56Yb 114
Cheltenham Ter. SW3 .7G 227 (50Hb 89)
Cheltenham Vs. TW19: Stanw M .58H 105
Chelverton Rd. SW15 .56Za 110
Chelwood N20 .19Fb 31
Chelwood Cl. CR5: Coul .91Lb 196
E4 .16Dc 34
HA6: Nwood .24S 44
KT17: Eps .84Va 174
Chelwood Ct. CR2: S Croy .78Sb 157
SW11 .53Fb 111
(off Westbridge Rd.)
Chelwood Gdns. TW9: Kew .54Qa 109
Chelwood Gdns. Pas. TW9: Kew .54Qa 109
Chelwood Ho. W2 .3C 220
Chelwood Wlk. SE4 .56Ac 114
Chenappa Cl. E13 .41Jc 93
Chenduit Way HA7: Stan .22Ha 46
Chene Dr. AL3: St A .1B 6
Chene M. AL3: St A .1B 6
Cheney Ct. SE23 .60Zb 114
Cheney Row E17 .25Bc 52
Cheneys Rd. E11 .34Gc 73
Cheney St. HA5: Eastc .28Y 45
CHENIES .10D 10
Chenies HA6: Nwood .22V 44
Chenies, The BR6: Pet W .72Uc 160
DA2: Wilm .63Gd 140
NW1 .1E 216
CHENIES BOTTOM .9C 10
Chenies Ho. *W2* .45Db 89
(off Moscow Rd.)
W4 .52Va 110
(off Corney Reach Way)
Chenies Manor House .10C 10
Chenies M. WC1 .6D 216 (42Mb 90)
Chenies Pl. EN5: Ark .15Wa 30
NW1 .1E 216 (40Mb 70)
Chenies Rd. WD3: Chen, Chor .12F 24
Chenies St. WC1 .7D 216 (43Mb 90)
Chenies Village WD3: Chen .10D 10
Chenies Way WD18: Wat .17U 26
Cheniston Cl. KT14: W Byf .85J 169
Cheniston Ct. SL5: S'dale .3E 146
Cheniston Gdns. W8 .48Db 89
Chenla SE13 .54Dc 114
Chennells AL10: Hat .1B 8
Chepstow Av. RM12: Horn .34Nd 77
Chepstow Cl. SW15 .57Ab 110
Chepstow Cnr. *W2* .44Cb 89
(off Chepstow Pl.)
Chepstow Ct. *W11* .45Cb 89
(off Chepstow Vs.)
Chepstow Cres. IG3: Ilf .30Uc 54
W11 .45Cb 89
Chepstow Gdns. UB1: S'hall .44Ba 85
Chepstow Ho. *RM3: Rom* .22Qd 57
(off Leamington Rd.)
Chepstow Pl. W2 .44Cb 89
Chepstow Ri. CR0: C'don .76Ub 157
Chepstow Rd. CR0: C'don .76Ub 157
W2 .44Cb 89
W7 .48Ja 86
Chepstow Vs. W11 .45Bb 89
Chequers IG9: Buck H .18Kc 35
Chequers, The HA5: Pinn .27Z 45
Chequers Cl. BR5: St P .70Vc 139
DA13: Ist R .8A 144
KT20: Walt H .97Wa 194
NW9 .27Ua 48
Chequers Ct. EC1 .6F 219
Chequers Ho. NW8 .5D 214
Chequers La. KT20: Walt H .97Wa 194
RM9: Dag .42Bd 95
(not continuous)
WD25: Wat .2X 13
Chequers Orchard SL0: Iver .44H 83
Chequers Pde. N13 .22Sb 51
RM9: Dag .39Bd 75
SE9 .58Pc 116
(off Eltham High St.)
Chequers Rd. CM14: N'side, Rom .19Nd 39
IG10: Lough .15Qc 36
RM3: Rom .19Nd 39
Chequers Sq. UB8: Uxb .38L 63
Chequer St. AL1: St A .2B 6
EC1 .6E 218 (42Sb 91)
(not continuous)
Chequers Wlk. EN9: Walt A .5Hc 21
Chequers Way N13 .22Rb 51
Chequer Tree Cl. GU21: Knap .8J 167
Cherbury Cl. SE28 .44Zc 95
Cherbury Ct. N1 .2G 219
Cherbury St. N1 .2G 219 (40Tb 71)
Cherchefelle M. HA7: Stan .22Ka 46
Cherimoya Gdns. KT8: W Mole .69Da 129
Cherington Rd. W7 .46Ga 86
Cheriton Av. BR2: Brom .71Hc 159
Cheriton Cl. EN4: Cockf .13Hb 31
W5 .43La 86
Cheriton Ct. KT12: Walt T .74Y 151
SE12 .59Jc 115
Cheriton Dr. SE18 .52Tc 116
Cheriton Lodge HA4: Ruis .32V 64
Cheriton Sq. SW17 .61Jb 134
Cherkley Hill KT22: Lea .98La 192
Cherries, The SL2: Slou .4M 81
Cherry Acre SL9: Chal P .21A 42
Cherry Av. BR8: Swan .70Fd 140
CM13: B'wood .20Be 41
SL3: L'ly .7P 81
UB1: S'hall .46Z 85
Cherry Bank *HP2: Hem H* .1M 3
(off Chapel St.)
Cherry Blossom Cl. N13 .22Rb 51
Cherry Bounce HP1: Hem H .1M 3
Cherry Cl. E17 .29Dc 52
HA0: Wemb .34Ma 67
HA4: Ruis .34V 64
NW9 .26Ua 48
SL0: Iver .45H 83
SM4: Mord .70Ab 132
SM5: Cars .75Hb 155
SM7: Bans .86Za 174
SW2 .59Qb 112
W5 .48Ma 87
Cherrycot Hill BR6: Farnb .77Sc 160
Cherrycot Ri. BR6: Farnb .77Sc 160
Cherry Cotts. KT20: Walt H .96Xa 194
Cherry Ct. HA5: Pinn .26Z 45
IG6: Ilf .27Rc 54
W3 .46Ua 88
Cherry Cres. TW8: Bford .52Ka 108
Cherry Cft. WD3: Crox G .16R 26
Cherrycroft Gdns. HA5: Hat E .24Ba 45
Cherrydale WD18: Wat .14V 26
Cherrydown RM16: Grays .46Fe 99
Cherrydown Av. E4 .20Bc 34
Cherrydown Cl. E4 .20Cc 34
Cherrydown Rd. DA14: Sidc .61Zc 139
Cherrydown Wlk. RM7: Mawney .26Dd 56
Cherry Gdn. Ho. *SE16* .47Xb 91
(off Cherry Gdn. St.)
Cherry Gdns. RM9: Dag .36Bd 75
UB5: N'olt .38Da 65
Cherry Gdn. St. SE16 .47Xb 91
Cherry Gth. TW8: Bford .50Ma 87
Cherry Grn. Cl. RH1: Redh .8B 208
Cherry Gro. UB3: Hayes .46X 85
UB8: Hil .43R 84
Cherry Hill AL2: Chis G .7N 5
EN5: New Bar .16Db 31
HA3: Hrw W .23Ha 46
WD3: Loud .13K 25
(not continuous)
Cherry Hill Gdns. CR0: Wadd .77Pb 156
Cherry Hills WD19: Wat .22Aa 45
Cherry Hollow WD5: Ab L .3V 12
Cherrylands Cl. NW9 .33Sa 67
Cherry La. UB7: W Dray .49P 83
Cherry Laurel Wlk. SW2 .58Pb 112
Cherry Lodge Golf Course .89Qc 180
Cherry Orchard KT21: Asht .90Ra 173
SE7 .51Lc 115
SL2: Stoke P .8M 61
TW18: Staines .64J 127
UB7: W Dray .47N 83
Cherry Orchard Cl.
BR5: St M Cry .71Yc 161
Cherry Orchard Gdns. CR0: C'don .74Tb 157
KT8: W Mole .69Ba 129
Cherry Orchard Rd. BR2: Brom .75Nc 160
CR0: C'don .75Tb 157
KT8: W Mole .69Ca 129
Cherry Ri. HP8: Chal G .19A 24
Cherry Rd. EN3: Enf W .10Yb 20
Cherry St. GU21: Wok .90A 168
RM7: Rom .29Fd 56
Cherry Tree Av. AL2: Lon C .8H 7
TW18: Staines .65K 127
UB7: Yiew .44P 83
Cherry Tree Cl. E9 .39Yb 72
HA0: Wemb .35Ja 66
RM13: Rain .40Jd 76
RM17: Grays .51Fe 121
Cherry Tree Ct. CR5: Coul .90Pb 176
KT22: Lea .92Ha 192
(off Park Vw. Rd.)
NW1 .38Lb 70
(off Camden Rd.)
NW9 .28Sa 47
SE7 .51Lc 115
Cherry Tree Dr. RM15: S Ock .42Qd 99
SW16 .62Nb 134
Cherry Tree Grn. CR2: Sande .86Xb 177
Cherry Tree Gro. TN15: Knat .82Rd 183
Cherry Tree Hill N2 .29Gb 49
Cherry Tree Ho. N22 .24Nb 50
Cherry Tree La. DA2: Wilm .62Hd 140
EN6: Pot B .6Db 17
RM13: Rain .41Gd 96
SL0: Iver H .39J 63
SL3: Ful .37B 62
WD3: Herons .18E 24
Cherrytree La. SL9: Chal P .26A 42
Cherry Tree Ri. IG9: Buck H .21Lc 53
Cherry Tree Rd. E15 .36Gc 73
N2 .28Hb 49
SL2: Farn R .8G 60
WD24: Wat .8X 13
Cherry Trees DA3: Hartl .71Be 165
Cherrytrees CR5: Coul .93Mb 196
Cherry Tree Ter. SE1 .2J 231
Cherry Tree Wlk. BR3: Beck .70Bc 136
BR4: W W'ck .77Hc 159
EC1 .6E 218 (42Sb 91)
Cherry Tree Way E13 .42Mc 93
HA7: Stan .23Ka 46
Cherry Wlk. BR2: Hayes .74Jc 159
RM13: Rain .40Jd 76
RM16: Grays .8C 100
WD3: Sarr .12L 25
Cherry Way AL10: Hat .3C 8
KT19: Ewe .79Ta 153
SL3: Hort .55E 104
TW17: Shep .70T 128
Cherrywood Av. TW20: Eng G .6M 125
Cherrywood Cl. E3 .41Ac 92
KT2: King T .66Qa 131
Cherrywood Ct. TW11: Tedd .64Ja 130
Cherrywood Dr. DA11: Nflt .3A 144
SW15 .57Za 110
Cherrywood La. SM4: Mord .70Ab 132
Cherrywood Lodge *SE13* .58Fc 115
(off Birdwood Av.)
Cherry Wood Way W5 .43Qa 87
Cherston Gdns. IG10: Lough .14Qc 36
Cherston Rd. IG10: Lough .14Qc 36
CHERTSEY .73J 149
Chertsey Abbey (remains) .72J 149
Chertsey Bri. Rd. KT16: Chert .73M 149
Chertsey Camping & Caravanning Club
KT16: Chert .73L 149
Chertsey Cl. CR8: Kenley .87Rb 177
Chertsey Ct. SW14 .55Ra 109
Chertsey Cres. CR0: New Ad .82Ec 178
Chertsey Dr. SM3: Cheam .75Ab 154
Chertsey Ho. *E2* .4K 219
(off Arnold Cir.)
KT16: Chert .74L 149
Chertsey La. KT19: Eps .84Qa 173
TW18: Staines .64G 126
CHERTSEY LOCK .73L 149
CHERTSEY MEADS .74N 149
Chertsey Meads KT16: Chert .74M 149
Chertsey Meads Local Nature Reserve
.74N 149
Chertsey Mus. .72J 149
Chertsey Rd. E11 .33Fc 73
GU20: W'sham .9B 146
GU21: Wok .89B 168
GU24: Chob .2K 167
(Alpha Rd.)
GU24: Chob .7H 147
(Windsor Rd.)
IG1: Ilf .35Tc 74
KT14: Byfl .83M 169
KT15: Add .75K 149
TW1: Twick .58Ha 108
TW2: Twick .61Da 129
TW13: Felt .62U 128
TW15: Ashf .66T 128
TW16: Sun .66T 128
TW17: Shep .73N 149
CHERTSEY SOUTH .76G 148
Chertsey St. SW17 .64Jb 134
Chertsey Wlk. KT16: Chert .73J 149
Chervil Cl. TW13: Felt .62W 128
Chervil M. SE28 .46Xc 95
Cherwell Cl. SL3: L'ly .51D 104
WD3: Crox G .15Q 26
Cherwell Ct. KT19: Ewe .77Sa 153
Cherwell Gro. RM15: S Ock .45Xd 98
Cherwell Ho. NW8 .6C 214
Cherwell Way HA4: Ruis .30S 44
Cheryls Cl. SW6 .53Db 111
Cheseman St. SE26 .62Xb 135
Chesfield Rd. KT2: King T .66Na 131
Chesham Av. BR5: Pet W .72Rc 160
Chesham Cl. RM7: Rom .28Fd 56
SM2: Cheam .82Ab 174
SW1 .4H 227
Chesham Ct. HA6: Nwood .23V 44
Chesham Cres. SE20 .67Yb 136
Chesham Flats W1 .4J 221
Chesham Ho. *RM3: Rom* .23Nd 57
(off Leyburn Cres.)
SE8 .53Cc 114
(off Brookmill Rd.)
Chesham La. HP8: Chal G .21A 42
SL9: Chal P .21A 42
Chesham M. SW1 .3H 227
Chesham Pl. SW1 .4H 227 (48Jb 90)
(not continuous)
Chesham Rd. HP3: Bov .10A 2
HP5: Bov, Whel .10A 2
KT1: King T .68Qa 131
SE20 .68Yb 136
SW19 .64Fb 133
Chesham St. NW10 .34Ta 67
SW1 .4H 227 (48Jb 90)
Chesham Ter. W13 .47Ka 86
Chesham Way WD18: Wat .16U 26
Cheshire Cl. CR4: Mitc .69Nb 134
E17 .25Dc 52
KT16: Ott .79F 148
RM11: Horn .29Qd 57
SE4 .54Bc 114
Cheshire Ct. EC4 .3A 224
SL1: Slou .7M 81
Cheshire Dr. WD25: Wat .6V 12
Cheshire Gdns. KT9: Chess .79Ma 153
Cheshire Ho. *KT16: Ott* .79F 148
(off Crawshaw Rd.)
N18 .21Xb 51
SM4: Mord .73Db 155
Cheshire Rd. N22 .24Pb 50
Cheshire St. E2 .5K 219 (42Vb 91)
Cheshir Ho. NW4 .28Ya 48
Chesholm Rd. N16 .34Ub 71
CHESHUNT .1Zb 20
Cheshunt EN8: Chesh .1Zb 20
Cheshunt FC .3Ac 20
Cheshunt Ho. *NW6* .39Db 69
(off Mortimer Cres.)
Cheshunt Rd. DA17: Belv .50Cd 96
E7 .37Kc 73
Chesil Ct. E2 .40Yb 72
SW3 .51Gb 111
Chesilton Rd. SW6 .53Bb 111
Chesil Way UB4: Hayes .41V 84
Chesley Gdns. E6 .40Mc 73
Cheslyn Gdns. .9V 12
Chesney Ct. *W9* .42Cb 89
(off Shirland Rd.)
Chesney Cres. CR0: New Ad .80Ec 158
Chesney Ho. *SE13* .56Fc 115
(off Mercator Rd.)
Chesney St. SW11 .53Jb 112
Chesnut Gro. N17 .27Vb 51
Chesnut Rd. N17 .27Vb 51
Chesnut Row *N3* .24Cb 49
(off Nether St.)
Chess Cl. HP5: Lat .8A 10
WD3: Loud .14M 25
Chessell Cl. CR7: Thor H .70Rb 135
Chessfield Pk. HP6: L Chal .11A 24
Chess Hill WD3: Loud .14M 25
Chessholme Ct. *TW16: Sun* .66W 128
(off Scotts Av.)
Chessholme Rd. TW15: Ashf .65S 128
Chessing Ct. *N2* .27Hb 49
(off Fortis Grn.)
CHESSINGTON .78Na 153
Chessington Av. DA7: Bex .52Ad 117
N3 .27Ab 48
Chessington Cl. KT19: Ewe .79Sa 153
Chessington Ct. HA5: Pinn .28Ba 45
N3 .27Bb 49
(off Charter Way)
Chessington Golf Course .80Ma 153
Chessington Hall Gdns.
KT9: Chess .80Ma 153
Chessington Hill Pk. KT9: Chess .78Qa 153
Chessington Ho. *KT17: Ewe* .81Va 174
(off Spring St.)
SW8 .54Mb 112
Chessington Lodge N3 .27Bb 49
Chessington Mans. E10 .31Cc 72
E11 .31Gc 73
Chessington Pde. KT9: Chess .79Ma 153
Chessington Pk. KT9: Chess .77Qa 153
Chessington Rd. KT17: Ewe .79Ra 153
KT19: Ewe .79Qa 153
Chessington Sports Cen. .80Ma 153
Chessington Trade Pk.
KT9: Chess .77Qa 153
Chessington Way BR4: W W'ck .75Dc 158
Chessington World of Adventures
.82La 172
Chess La. WD3: Loud .14M 25
Chesson Rd. W14 .51Bb 111
Chess Va. Ri. WD3: Crox G .16P 25
Chess Way WD3: Chor .13J 25
Chesswood Ct. WD3: Rick .18M 25
Chesswood Way HA5: Pinn .26Z 45
Chestbrook Ct. *EN1: Enf* .15Ub 33
(off Forsyth Pl.)
Chester Av. RM14: Upm .33Ud 78
TW2: Whitt .60Ba 107
TW10: Rich .58Pa 109
Chester Cl. EN6: Pot B .1Db 17
IG10: Lough .11Sc 36
RM16: Chaf H .47Ae 99
SM1: Sutt .75Cb 155
SW1 .2K 227 (47Kb 90)
SW13 .55Xa 110
TW10: Rich .58Pa 109
TW15: Ashf .64T 128
UB8: Hil .44R 84
Chester Cl. Nth. NW1 .3A 216 (41Kb 90)
Chester Cl. Sth. NW1 .4A 216 (41Kb 90)
Chester Cotts. SW1 .6H 227
Chester Ct. *BR2: Brom* .70Hc 137
(off Durham Rd.)
NW1 .3A 216 (41Kb 90)
(not continuous)
SE5 .52Tb 113
(off Lomond Gro.)
SE8 .50Zb 92
W6 .49Za 88
(off Wolverton Gdns.)
Chester Cres. E8 .36Vb 71
Chester Dr. HA2: Harr .30Ba 45
Chesterfield Cl. BR5: St M Cry .70Ad 139
SE13 .54Fc 115
Chesterfield Ct. *KT5: Surb* .71Na 153
(off Cranes Pk.)
Chesterfield Dr. DA1: Dart .57Kd 119
KT10: Hin W .75Ja 152
TN13: Riv .93Fd 202
Chesterfield Flats *EN5: Barn* .15Za 30
(off Bells Hill)
Chesterfield Gdns. N4 .29Rb 51
SE10 .53Fc 115
W1 .6K 221 (46Kb 90)
Chesterfield Gro. SE22 .57Vb 113
Chesterfield Hill W1 .6K 221 (46Kb 90)
Chesterfield Ho. W1 .6J 221
Chesterfield Lodge *N21* .17Pb 32
(off Church Hill)
Chesterfield M. N4 .29Rb 51
TW15: Ashf .63N 127
Chesterfield Rd. E10 .30Ec 52
EN3: Enf W .9Ac 20
EN5: Barn .15Za 30
KT19: Ewe .80Ta 153
N3 .23Cb 49
TW15: Ashf .63N 127
W4 .51Sa 109
Chesterfield St. W1 .6K 221 (46Kb 90)
Chesterfield Wlk. SE10 .53Fc 115
Chesterfield Way SE15 .52Yb 114
UB3: Hayes .47W 84
Chesterford Gdns. NW3 .35Db 69
Chesterford Ho. *SE18* .53Mc 115
(off Tellson Av.)
Chesterford Rd. E12 .36Pc 74
Chester Gdns. EN3: Pond E .16Xb 33
SM4: Mord .72Eb 155
W13 .44Ka 86
Chester Ga. NW1 .4K 215 (41Kb 90)
Chester Gibbons Grn. AL2: Lon C .8H 7
Chester Grn. IG10: Lough .11Sc 36
Chester Ho. N10 .26Kb 50
SE8 .51Bc 114
SW1 .5K 227
SW9 .52Qb 112
(off Cranmer Rd.)
UB8: Cowl .42L 83
Chesterman Ct. *W4* .52Ua 110
(off Corney Reach Way)
Chester M. E17 .26Cc 52
SW1 .3K 227 (48Kb 90)
Chester Path IG10: Lough .11Sc 36
Chester Pl. *HA6: Nwood* .24U 44
(off Green La.)
NW1 .3K 215 (41Kb 90)

Chester Rd. DA15: Sidc .57Uc 116
E7 .38Mc 73
E11 .30Kc 53
E16 .42Gc 93
E17 .29Zb 52
HA6: Nwood .24U 44
IG3: Ilf .32Vc 75
IG7: Chig .20Qc 36
IG10: Lough .12Rc 36
KT24: Eff .100X 191
N9 .18Xb 33
N17 .27Tb 51
N19 .33Kb 70
NW1 .4J 215 (41Jb 90)
SL1: Slou .4H 81
SW19 .65Ya 132
TW4: Houn .55X 107
TW6: H'row A .55Q 106
WD6: Bore .13Sa 29
WD18: Wat .15W 26
Chester Row SW1 .6H 227 (49Jb 90)
Chesters, The KT3: N Mald .67Ua 132
Chester Sq.
SW1 .5J 227 (49Jb 90)
Chester Sq. M. SW1 .4K 227
Chester St. E2 .42Wb 91
SW1 .3J 227 (48Jb 90)
Chester Ter. IG11: Bark .37Tc 74
NW1 .3K 215 (41Kb 90)
(not continuous)
Chesterton Cl. SW18 .57Cb 111
UB6: G'frd .40Da 65
Chesterton Ct. W3 .48Ra 87
(off Bollo Bri. Rd.)
W5 .43Ma 87
Chesterton Dr. RH1: Mers .100Nb 196
TW19: Stanw .60P 105
Chesterton Ho. CR0: C'don .77Tb 157
(off Heathfield Rd.)
SW11 .55Fb 111
(off Ingrave St.)
W10 .43Ab 88
(off Portobello Rd.)
Chesterton Rd. E13 .41Jc 93
W10 .43Za 88
Chesterton Sq. W8 .49Cb 89
Chesterton Ter. E13 .41Jc 93
KT1: King T .68Qa 131
Chesterton Way RM18: Tilb .4E 122
(off Brennan Rd.)
Chester Way SE11 .6A 230 (49Qb 90)
Chesthunte Rd. N17 .25Sb 51
Chestlands Ct. UB10: Hil .37Q 64
Chestnut All. SW6 .51Bb 111
Chestnut Av. BR4: W W'ck .78Gc 159
CM14: S Weald .17Ud 40
DA9: Bluew .59Vd 120
E7 .35Kc 73
GU25: Vir W .10K 125
HA0: Wemb .36Ka 66
HA6: Nwood .26V 44
HA8: Edg .23Na 47
IG9: Buck H .20Mc 35
KT8: E Mos .69Ha 130
KT10: Esh .73Fa 152
KT12: W Vill .81U 170
KT13: Weyb .80S 150
KT19: Ewe .77Ua 154
N8 .29Nb 50
RM12: Horn .33Hd 76
RM16: Grays .47De 99
SL3: L'ly .47A 82
SW14 .55Ta 109
TN16: Westrm .94Mc 199
TW8: Bford .49Ma 87
TW11: Tedd .68Ha 130
TW12: Hamp .66Ca 129
UB7: Yiew .45P 83
WD3: Rick .15J 25
Chestnut Av. Nth. E17 .28Fc 53
Chestnut Av. Sth. E17 .29Ec 52
Chestnut Cen., The
EN8: Chesh .1Zb 20
Chestnut Cl. BR6: Chels .78Wc 161
DA11: Nflt .8B 122
DA15: Sidc .60Wc 117
GU23: Rip .97H 189
IG9: Buck H .20Mc 35
KT15: Add .78M 149
KT20: Kgswd .95Cb 195
N14 .15Lb 32
N16 .33Tb 71
RH1: Redh .8B 208
RM12: Horn .35Ld 77
SE6 .64Ec 136
SE14 .53Bc 114
SL9: Chal P .25B 42
SM5: Cars .74Hb 155
SW16 .63Qb 134
TW15: Ashf .63R 128
TW16: Sun .65V 128
TW20: Eng G .5M 125
UB3: Hayes .45U 84
UB7: Harl, Sip .52R 106
Chestnut Copse RH8: Oxt .4M 211
Chestnut Ct. CR2: S Croy .77Sb 157
(off Bramley Hill)
KT22: Lea .92Ha 192
N8 .29Nb 50
RH1: Redh .8P 207
SW6 .51Bb 111
TW13: Hanw .64Z 129
W8 .48Db 89
(off Abbots Wlk.)
WD18: Wat .14U 26
Chestnut Cres. KT12: W Vill .81U 170
Chestnut Dr. AL4: St A .1F 6
DA7: Bex .55Zc 117
E11 .30Jc 53
HA3: Hrw W .24Ha 46
HA5: Pinn .30Z 45
HP4: Berk .2A 2
SL4: Wind .6C 102
TW20: Egh .5P 125
Chestnut Glen RM12: Horn .33Hd 76
Chestnut Gro.
CM14: B'wood .19Yd 40
CR2: Sels .80Xb 157
CR4: Mitc .71Mb 156
DA2: Wilm .63Fd 140
EN4: E Barn .15Hb 31
GU22: Wok .92A 188
HA0: Wemb .36Ka 66
IG6: Ilf .23Uc 54
KT3: N Mald .69Ta 131
SE20 .66Xb 135
Chestnut Gro. SW12 .59Jb 112
TW7: Isle .56Ja 108
TW18: Staines .65L 127
W5 .48Ma 87
Chestnut Ho. E3 .39Bc 72
(off Sycamore Av.)
SW15 .56Va 110
W4 .49Ua 88
(off The Orchard)
WD7: Shenl .2Na 15
Chestnut La. GU24: Chob .8G 146
KT13: Weyb .78R 150
N20 .18Ab 30
TN13: S'oaks .96Kd 203
Chestnut Mnr. Cl. TW18: Staines .64K 127
Chestnut Mead RH1: Redh .5N 207
Chestnut Pl. KT13: Weyb .78R 150
(off Pine Gro.)
KT17: Ewe .83Wa 174
KT21: Asht .91Na 193
SE26 .63Vb 135
Chestnut Plaza E20 .37Ec 72
(within Westfield Stratford City Shop. Cen.)
Chestnut Ri. SE18 .51Tc 116
WD23: Bush .17Da 27
Chestnut Rd. DA1: Dart .60Md 119
EN3: Enf W .8Ac 20
KT2: King T .66Na 131
SE27 .62Rb 135
SW20 .68Za 132
TW2: Twick .61Ga 130
TW15: Ashf .63R 128
Chestnuts CM13: Hut .18De 41
Chestnuts, The HA5: Hat E .24Ba 45
HP3: Hem H .6H 3
IG10: Lough .15Mc 35
KT12: Walt T .75W 150
N5 .35Sb 71
(off Highbury Grange)
RM4: Abr .13Xc 37
UB10: Uxb .38N 63
Chestnut Ter. SM1: Sutt .77Db 155
Chestnut Wlk. IG8: Wfd G .22Jc 53
KT12: W Vill .81U 170
KT14: Byfl .84N 169
SL9: Chal P .24A 42
TN15: S'oaks .100Nd 203
TW17: Shep .70U 128
WD24: Wat .9W 12
Chestnut Way TW13: Felt .62X 129
Cheston Av. CR0: C'don .75Ac 158
Chestwood Gro. UB10: Hil .38P 63
Cheswick Cl. DA1: Cray .56Hd 118
Chesworth Cl. DA8: Erith .54Gd 118
Chettle Cl. SE1 .3F 231
Chettle Ct. N8 .30Qb 50
Chetwode Dr. KT18: Tatt C .90Za 174
Chetwode Ho. NW8 .5D 214
Chetwode Rd. KT20: Tad .91Ya 194
SW17 .62Hb 133
Chetwood Wlk. E6 .43Nc 94
(off Greenwich Cres.)
Chetwynd Av. EN4: E Barn .18Hb 31
Chetwynd Dr. UB10: Hil .40P 63
Chetwynd Rd. NW5 .35Kb 70
Chetwynd Vs. NW5 .35Kb 70
(off Chetwynd Rd.)
Chevalier Cl. HA7: Stan .21Na 47
Cheval Pl. SW7 .3E 226 (48Gb 89)
Cheval St. E14 .48Cc 92
Cheveley Cl. RM3: Hrld W .25Nd 57
Cheveley Gdns. SL1: Burn .10A 60
Chevely Cl. CM16: Coop .1Zc 23
Cheveney Wlk. BR2: Brom .69Jc 137
CHEVENING .91Bd 201
Chevening Cross TN14: Chev .92Cd 202
Chevening La. TN14: Knock .87Ad 181
Chevening Rd. NW6 .40Za 68
SE10 .50Hc 93
SE19 .65Tb 135
TN13: Chip .91Bd 201
TN14: Chev .91Bd 201
TN14: Sund .95Ad 201
Chevenings, The DA14: Sidc .62Yc 139
Cheverell Ho. E2 .40Wb 71
(off Pritchard's Rd.)
CHEVERELLS .94Gc 199
Cheverton Rd. N19 .32Mb 70
Chevet St. E9 .36Ac 72
Chevington NW2 .37Bb 69
Chevington Pl. RM12: Horn .36Md 77
Chevington Vs. RH1: Blet .4L 209
Chevington Way RM12: Horn .35Md 77
Cheviot N17 .24Xb 51
(off Northumberland Gro.)
Cheviot Cl. DA7: Bex .54Gd 118
EN1: Enf .12Tb 33
SM2: Sutt .81Fb 175
SM7: Bans .87Db 175
UB3: Harl .52T 106
WD23: Bush .16Ea 28
Cheviot Ct. SE14 .51Yb 114
(off Avonley Rd.)
UB2: S'hall .49Da 85
Cheviot Gdns. NW2 .33Za 68
SE27 .63Rb 135
Cheviot Ga. NW2 .33Ab 68
Cheviot Ho. DA11: Nflt .58Fe 121
(off Laburnum Gro.)
E1 .44Xb 91
(off Commercial Rd.)
Cheviot Rd. RM11: Horn .31Jd 76
SE27 .64Qb 134
SL3: L'ly .50C 82
Cheviots AL10: Hat .3C 8
Cheviot Way IG2: Ilf .28Uc 54
Chevron Cl. E16 .44Jc 93
Chevron Ho. RM17: Grays .52De 121
Chevy Rd. UB2: S'hall .47Ea 86
Chewter La. GU20: W'sham .7A 146
Chewton Rd. E17 .28Ac 52
Cheyham Gdns. SM2: Cheam .82Za 174
Cheyham Way SM2: Cheam .82Ab 174
Cheylesmore Ho. SW1 .7K 227
Cheyne Av. E18 .27Hc 53
TW2: Whitt .60Ba 107
Cheyne Cl. BR2: Brom .76Nc 160
NW4 .29Ya 48
SL9: Ger X .32A 62
Cheyne Ct. SM7: Bans .87Db 175
SW3 .51Hb 111
WD23: Bush .14Aa 27
Cheyne Gdns. SW3 .51Gb 111
Cheyne Hill KT5: Surb .70Pa 131
Cheyne Ho. SW3 .51Hb 111
(off Chelsea Emb.)
Cheyne M. SW3 .51Gb 111
Cheyne Pk. Dr. BR4: W W'ck .76Ec 158
Cheyne Path W7 .43Ha 86
Cheyne Pl. SW3 .51Hb 111
Cheyne Rd. TW15: Ashf .66T 128
Cheyne Row SW3 .51Gb 111
Cheyne Wlk. CR0: C'don .75Wb 157
DA3: Lfield .69Zd 143
N21 .15Rb 33
NW4 .30Ya 48
SW3 .52Fb 111
(not continuous)
SW10 .52Fb 111
Cheyneys Av. HA8: Edg .23Ma 47
Chichele Gdns. CR0: C'don .77Ub 157
Chichele Ho. HA8: Edg .21Pa 47
Chichele Rd. NW2 .36Za 68
RH8: Oxt .100Gc 199
Chicheley Gdns. HA3: Hrw W .24Ea 46
(not continuous)
Chicheley Rd. HA3: Hrw W .24Ea 46
Chicheley St. SE1 .1J 229 (47Pb 90)
Chichester Av. HA4: Ruis .33T 64
Chichester Cl. E6 .44Nc 94
RM15: Avel .46Td 98
RM16: Chaf H .49Zd 99
SE3 .52Lc 115
TW12: Hamp .65Ba 129
Chichester Ct. HA7: Stan .27Na 47
HA8: Edg .23Qa 47
(off Whitchurch La.)
KT17: Ewe .81Va 174
NW1 .38Lb 70
(off Royal Coll. St.)
SL1: Slou .8M 81
TW19: Stanw .60N 105
UB5: N'olt .39Ba 65
Chichester Dr. CR8: Purl .84Pb 176
TN13: S'oaks .97Hd 202
Chichester Gdns. IG1: Ilf .31Nc 74
Chichester Ho. CM14: B'wood .19Yd 40
(off Sir Francis Way)
KT19: Eps .84Qa 173
NW6 .40Cb 69
SW9 .52Qb 112
(off Cranmer Rd.)
Chichester M. SE27 .63Qb 134
Chichester Rents WC2 .2K 223
Chichester Ri. DA12: Grav'nd .3F 144
Chichester Rd. CR0: C'don .76Ub 157
DA9: Ghithe .58Vd 120
E11 .34Gc 73
N9 .18Wb 33
NW6 .40Cb 69
W2 .43Db 89
Chichester St. SW1 .7C 228 (50Lb 90)
Chichester Way E14 .49Fc 93
TW14: Felt .59Y 107
WD25: Wat .5Aa 13
Chichester Wharf DA8: Erith .50Gd 96
Chicken La. AL2: Lon C .9H 7
Chicken Shed Theatre .15Jb 32
Chicksand Ho. E1 .43Wb 91
(off Chicksand St.)
Chicksand St. E1 .43Vb 91
(not continuous)
Chidbrook Ho. WD18: Wat .16U 26
Chiddingfold N12 .20Cb 31
Chiddingstone SE13 .57Ec 114
Chiddingstone Av. DA7: Bex .52Bd 117
Chiddingstone Cl. SM2: Sutt .82Cb 175
Chiddingstone St. SW6 .54Cb 111
Chieftan Dr. RM19: Purf .49Qd 97
Chieveley Pde. DA7: Bex .55Dd 118
Chieveley Rd. DA7: Bex .56Dd 118
Chiffinch Gdns. DA11: Nflt .2A 144
Chignell Pl. W13 .46Ja 86
CHIGWELL .20Rc 36
Chigwell Ct. E9 .37Ac 72
(off Ballance Rd.)
Chigwell Golf Course .22Qc 54
Chigwell Grange IG7: Chig .17Sc 36
Chigwell Hill E1 .45Xb 91
Chigwell Hurst Ct. HA5: Pinn .27Z 45
Chigwell La. IG7: Chig, Lough .15Sc 36
IG10: Lough .15Sc 36
Chigwell Pk. IG7: Chig .21Rc 54
Chigwell Pk. Dr. IG7: Chig .21Qc 54
Chigwell Ri. IG7: Chig .19Qc 36
Chigwell Rd. E18 .27Kc 53
IG8: Wfd G .25Lc 53
CHIGWELL ROW .20Xc 37
Chigwell Vw. RM5: Col R .23Cd 56
Chilberton Dr. RH1: Mers .2C 208
Chilbolton TW20: Egh .64A 126
Chilbrook Rd. KT11: D'side .90W 170
Chilcombe Ho. SW15 .59Wa 110
(off Fontley Way)
Chilcot Cl. E14 .44Dc 92
Chilcott Cl. HA0: Wemb .35La 66
Chilcott Rd. WD24: Wat .8U 12
Childebert Rd. SW17 .61Kb 134
CHILDERDITCH .27Ce 59
Childerditch Hall Dr. CM13: L War .27Ce 59
Childerditch Ind. Pk. CM13: L War .27Be 59
Childerditch La.
CM13: B'wood, L War, W H'dn
.24Ae 59
Childerditch St. CM13: L War .26Ce 59
Childeric Rd. SE14 .52Ac 114
Childerley KT1: King T .69Qa 131
(off Burritt Rd.)
Childerley St. SW6 .53Ab 110
Childers, The IG8: Wfd G .22Pc 54
Childers St. SE8 .51Ac 114
Child La. SE10 .48Hc 93
Childs Av. UB9: Hare .26L 43
Childsbridge Farm Pl.
TN15: Seal .91Nd 203
Childsbridge La.
TN15: Kems'g, Seal .89Pd 183
Childsbridge Way TN15: Seal .92Pd 203
Childs Cl. RM11: Horn .30Ld 57
Childs Ct. UB3: Hayes .45W 84
Childs Cres. DA10: Swans .58Zd 121
Childs Hall Cl. KT23: Bookh .97Ba 191
Childs Hall Dr. KT23: Bookh .97Ba 191
Childs Hall Rd. KT23: Bookh .97Ba 191
CHILD'S HILL .34Bb 69
Childs Hill Wlk. NW2 .34Bb 69
(off Cricklewood La.)
Child's La. SE19 .65Ub 135
Child's M. SW5 .49Cb 89
(off Child's Pl.)
Child's Pl. SW5 .49Cb 89
Child's St. SW5 .49Cb 89
Child's Wlk. SW5 .49Cb 89
(off Child's St.)
Childs Way NW11 .29Bb 49
TN15: Wro .88Be 185
Childwick Ct. HP3: Hem H .5B 4
Chilham Cl. DA5: Bexl .59Bd 117
HP2: Hem H .3N 3
UB6: G'frd .40Ja 66
Chilham Ho. SE1 .3G 231 (48Tb 91)
SE15 .51Yb 114
Chilham Rd. SE9 .63Nc 138
Chilham Way BR2: Hayes .73Jc 159
Chilianwalla Memorial .51Jb 112
Chillerton Rd. SW17 .64Jb 134
Chillingford Ho. SW17 .63Eb 133
Chillington Dr. SW11 .56Fb 111
Chillingworth Gdns. TW1: Twick .62Ha 130
Chillingworth Rd. N7 .36Qb 70
Chilmans Dr. KT23: Bookh .97Da 191
Chilmark Gdns. KT3: N Mald .72Wa 154
RH1: Mers .1E 208
Chilmark Rd. SW16 .68Mb 134
Chilmead RH1: Redh .5P 207
Chilmead La. RH1: Nutf .4D 208
Chilsey Grn. Rd. KT16: Chert .72G 148
Chiltern Av. TW2: Whitt .60Ca 107
WD23: Bush .16Ea 28
Chiltern Bus. Village UB8: Uxb .40K 63
Chiltern Cl. CR0: C'don .76Ub 157
DA7: Bex .53Gd 118
GU22: Wok .4N 187
KT4: Wor Pk .74Ya 154
TW18: Staines .64J 127
UB10: Ick .33Q 64
WD6: Bore .12Pa 29
WD18: Wat .14V 26
WD23: Bush .16Da 27
Chiltern Ct. BR2: Brom .75Nc 160
(off Gravel Rd.)
EN5: New Bar .15Eb 31
HA1: Harr .29Fa 46
N10 .26Jb 50
NW1 .6G 215
SE14 .52Yb 114
(off Avonley Rd.)
SL4: Wind .3F 102
(off Fawcett Rd.)
UB8: Hil .42R 84
Chiltern Ct. M. SL4: Wind .3F 102
(off Fawcett Rd.)
Chiltern Dene EN2: Enf .14Pb 32
Chiltern Dr. KT5: Surb .72Qa 153
WD3: Rick .17H 25
Chiltern Gdns. BR2: Brom .70Hc 137
NW2 .34Za 68
RM12: Horn .34Ld 77
Chiltern Hill SL9: Chal P .25A 42
Chiltern Ho. N9 .20Wb 33
SE17 .51Tb 113
(off Portland St.)
W5 .43Na 87
W10 .43Ab 88
(off Telford Rd.)
Chiltern Open Air Mus. .18B 24
Chiltern Rd. DA11: Nflt .2A 144
E3 .42Cc 92
HA5: Eastc .29Y 45
IG2: Ilf .29Uc 54
SL1: Burn .3A 80
SM2: Sutt .81Db 175
Chilterns AL10: Hat .3C 8
Chilterns, The BR1: Brom .68Kc 137
(off Murray Av.)
SM2: Sutt .81Db 175
Chiltern St. W1 .7H 215 (43Jb 90)
Chiltern Vw. Rd. UB8: Uxb .40L 63
Chiltern Way IG8: Wfd G .20Jc 35
Chilthorne Cl. SE6 .59Bc 114
Chilton Av. W5 .49Ma 87
Chilton Ct. KT12: Walt T .77W 150
N22 .24Nb 50
(off Truro Rd.)
SL6: Tap .4A 80
Chilton Gro. SE8 .49Zb 92
CHILTON HILLS .3P 145
Chiltonian Ind. Est. SE12 .58Hc 115
Chilton Rd. HA8: Edg .23Qa 47
RM16: Grays .8C 100
TW9: Rich .55Qa 109
Chiltons, The E18 .26Jc 53
Chiltons Cl. SM7: Bans .87Db 175
Chilton St. E2 .42Vb 91
Chilvers Cl. TW2: Twick .61Ga 130
Chilver St. SE10 .50Hc 93
Chilwell Gdns. WD19: Wat .21Y 45
Chilwick Rd. SL2: Slou .2D 80
Chilworth Ct. SW19 .60Za 110
Chilworth Gdns. SM1: Sutt .76Eb 155
Chilworth M. W2 .3A 220 (44Fb 89)
Chilworth St. W2 .3A 220 (44Eb 89)
Chimes Av. N13 .22Qb 50
Chimes Ho. BR3: Beck .67Ac 136
Chime Sq. AL3: St A .1C 6
Chimes Shop. Cen., The UB8: Uxb .38M 63
Chimney Ct. E1 .46Xb 91
(off Brewhouse La.)
Chimneys, The WD23: Bush .15Ba 27
China Ct. E1 .46Xb 91
(off Asher Way)
China Hall M. SE16 .48Yb 92
China La. RM14: Bulp .34Fe 79
China M. SW2 .59Pb 112
China Town .4E 222
China Wlk. SE11 .4J 229 (49Pb 90)
China Wharf SE1 .47Wb 91
Chinbrook Cres. SE12 .62Kc 137
Chinbrook Rd. SE12 .62Kc 137
Chinchilla Dr. TW4: Houn .54Y 107
Chindits La. CM14: W'ley .22Yd 58
Chine, The HA0: Wemb .36Ka 66
N10 .28Lb 50
N21 .16Rb 33
Chine Farm Pl. TN14: Knock .88Zc 181
Ching Ct. WC2 .3F 223
Chingdale Rd. E4 .20Gc 35
CHINGFORD .18Ec 34
Chingford Av. E4 .20Cc 34
CHINGFORD GREEN .18Fc 35
CHINGFORD HATCH .21Fc 53
Chingford Ind. Cen. E4 .22Ac 52
Chingford La. IG8: Wfd G .21Gc 53
CHINGFORD MOUNT .21Cc 52
Chingford Mt. Rd. E4 .21Cc 52
Chingford Rd. E4 .23Cc 52
E17 .25Dc 52
Chingley Cl. BR1: Brom .65Gc 137
Ching Way E4 .23Bc 52
(not continuous)
Chinnery Cl. EN1: Enf .11Vb 33
Chinnock's Wharf E14 .45Ac 92
(off Narrow St.)
Chinnor Cres. UB6: G'frd .40Da 65
Chinthurst M. CR5: Coul .88Jb 176
Chipka St. E14 .47Ec 92
(not continuous)
Chipley St. SE14 .51Ac 114
Chipmunk Gro. UB5: N'olt .41Aa 85
Chippendale All. UB8: Uxb .38M 63
Chippendale Ho. SW1 .50Kb 90
(off Churchill Gdns.)
Chippendale St. E5 .34Zb 72
Chippendale Waye UB8: Uxb .38M 63
Chippenham KT1: King T .68Pa 131
(off Excelsior Cl.)
Chippenham Av. HA9: Wemb .36Ra 67
Chippenham Cl. HA5: Eastc .28V 44
RM3: Rom .22Md 57
Chippenham Gdns. NW6 .41Cb 89
RM3: Rom .22Md 57
Chippenham M. W9 .42Cb 89
Chippenham Rd. RM3: Rom .23Md 57
W9 .42Cb 89
Chippenham Wlk. RM3: Rom .23Md 57
CHIPPERFIELD .3J 11
Chipperfield Cl. RM14: Upm .32Ud 78
CHIPPERFIELD COMMON .4K 11
Chipperfield Ho. SW3 .7D 226
Chipperfield Rd. BR5: St P .67Wc 139
(not continuous)
HP3: Bov .9D 2
HP3: Hem H .6L 3
WD4: Chfd .9D 2
WD4: K Lan .2L 11
CHIPPING BARNET .14Ab 30
Chipping Cl. EN5: Barn .13Ab 30
CHIPSTEAD
CR5 .90Hb 175
TN13 .94Ed 202
Chipstead Av. CR7: Thor H .70Rb 135
CHIPSTEAD BOTTOM .93Fb 195
Chipstead Cl. CR5: Coul .88Jb 176
RH1: Redh .7P 207
SE19 .66Vb 135
SM2: Sutt .81Db 175
Chipstead Ct. GU21: Knap .9J 167
Chipstead Gdns. NW2 .33Xa 68
Chipstead Golf Course .90Hb 175
Chipstead La. CR5: Chip, Coul .96Eb 195
KT20: Kgswd .97Bb 195
TN13: Chip, Riv .94Ed 202
Chipstead Pk. TN13: Chip .94Fd 202
Chipstead Pk. Cl. TN13: Chip .94Ed 202
Chipstead Pl. Gdns. TN13: Chip .94Ed 202
Chipstead Rd. DA8: Erith .52Gd 118
SM7: Bans .89Bb 175
Chipstead Sailing Club .94Ed 202
Chipstead Sq. TN13: Chip .94Ed 202
Chipstead Sta. Pde. CR5: Chip .90Hb 175
Chipstead St. SW6 .53Cb 111
Chipstead Valley Rd. CR5: Coul .88Jb 176
Chipstead Way SM7: Bans .88Hb 175
Chip St. SW4 .55Mb 112
Chirdland Ho. WD18: Wat .16U 26
Chirk Cl. UB4: Yead .42Aa 85
Chirton Wlk. GU21: Wok .10L 167
Chisenhale Rd. E3 .40Ac 72
Chisholm Ct. W6 .50Wa 88
Chisholm Rd. CR0: C'don .75Ub 157
TW10: Rich .58Pa 109
Chisledon Wlk. E9 .37Bc 72
(off Osborne Rd.)
CHISLEHURST .65Rc 138
Chislehurst Av. N12 .24Eb 49
Chislehurst Caves .67Qc 138
Chislehurst Golf Course .66Rc 138
Chislehurst Rd. BR1: Brom .68Mc 137
BR5: Pet W .70Uc 138
BR6: Orp, Pet W, St M Cry .70Uc 138
BR7: Chst .68Mc 137
DA14: Sidc .64Wc 139
TW10: Rich .57Na 109
CHISLEHURST WEST .65Qc 138
Chislet Cl. BR3: Beck .66Cc 136
Chisley Rd. N15 .30Ub 51
Chiswell Ct. WD24: Wat .10Y 13
CHISWELL GREEN .7N 5
Chiswell Grn. La. AL2: Chis G, Pot C .7K 5
Chiswell Sq. SE3 .54Kc 115
Chiswell St. EC1 .7E 218 (43Sb 91)
SE5 .52Tb 113
(off Edmund St.)
CHISWICK .50Ta 87
Chiswick Bri. SW14 .54Sa 109
Chiswick Cl. CR0: Bedd .76Pb 156
Chiswick Comn. Rd. W4 .49Ta 87
Chiswick Community Sports Hall .52Ta 109
Chiswick Ct. HA5: Pinn .27Ba 45
W4 .49Ra 87
Chiswick High Rd.
TW8: Bford .50Qa 87
W4 .50Ra 87
Chiswick House & Gardens .51Ta 109
Chiswick La. W4 .50Ua 88
Chiswick La. Sth. W4 .51Va 110
Chiswick Mall W4 .51Va 110
W6 .50Wa 88
Chiswick Pk. W4 .49Ra 87
Chiswick Plaza W4 .51Sa 109
Chiswick Quay W4 .53Sa 109
Chiswick Rd. N9 .19Wb 33
W4 .49Sa 87
CHISWICK RDBT. .50Qa 87
Chiswick Sq. W4 .51Ua 110
Chiswick Staithe W4 .53Sa 109
Chiswick Ter. W4 .49Sa 87
(off Chiswick High Rd.)
Chiswick Village W4 .51Qa 109
Chiswick Wharf W4 .51Va 110
Chittenden Cotts. GU23: Wis .88N 169
Chitterfield Ga. UB7: Sip .52Q 106
Chitty's La. RM8: Dag .33Zc 75
Chitty St. W1 .7C 216 (43Lb 90)
Chivalry Rd. SW11 .57Gb 111
Chivelston SW19 .60Za 110
Chivenor Gro. KT2: King T .64Ma 131
Chivenor Pl. AL4: St A .4G 6
Chivers Rd. E4 .20Dc 34
Choats Mnr. Way RM9: Dag .40Ad 75
Choats Rd. IG11: Bark .40Yc 75
RM9: Bark, Dag .40Yc 75
CHOBHAM .3J 167
Chobham Bus. Cen. GU24: Chob .2P 167

Chobham Cl. KT16: Ott 79D 148
Chobham Common Memorial Cross 5H 147
Chobham Common National Nature Reserve 6H 147
Chobham Gdns. SW19 61Za 132
Chobham Golf Course 7H 167
Chobham La. KT16: Longc 6K 147
Chobham Mus. 3J 167
Chobham Pk. La. GU24: Chob 2L 167
Chobham Rd. E15 36Fc 73
GU21: Knap, Wok 10F 166
GU21: Wok 5N 167
(Horsell Comn. Rd.)
GU21: Wok 89B 168
(The Broadway)
GU21: Wok 88A 168
(Wheatsheaf Cl.)
GU24: Chob 3F 146
KT16: Ott 80C 148
SL5: S'dale 3F 146
Chocolate Studios N1 3F 219
Choice Vw. *IG1: Ilf 33Sc 74*
(off Axon Pl.)
Choir Grn. GU21: Knap 9J 167
Cholesbury WD19: Wat 19Aa 27
Cholmeley Cl. N6 31Kb 70
Cholmeley Cres. N6 31Kb 70
Cholmeley Lodge N6 32Kb 70
Cholmeley Pk. N6 32Kb 70
Cholmley Gdns. NW6 36Cb 69
Cholmley Rd. KT7: T Ditt 72Ka 152
Cholmley Ter. *KT7: T Ditt 73Ka 152*
(off Portsmouth Rd.)
Cholmley Vs. *KT7: T Ditt 72Ka 152*
(off Portsmouth Rd.)
Cholmondeley Av. NW10 40Wa 68
Cholmondeley Wlk. TW9: Rich 57La 108
Choppin's Ct. E1 46Xb 91
Chopwell Cl. E15 38Fc 73
CHORLEYWOOD 14F 24
CHORLEYWOOD BOTTOM 15F 24
Chorleywood Bottom WD3: Chor 15F 24
Chorleywood Cl. WD3: Rick 17M 25
Chorleywood Coll. Est. WD3: Chor 14H 25
Chorleywood Cres. BR5: St P 68Vc 139
Chorleywood Golf Course 14F 24
Chorleywood Ho. WD3: Chor 13G 24
Chorleywood Ho. Dr. WD3: Chor 13G 24
Chorleywood House Estate 12H 25
Chorleywood Lodge La. WD3: Chor 13H 25
Chorleywood Rd. WD3: Rick 14J 25
CHORLEYWOOD WEST 14D 24
Choudhury Mans. *N1 38Nb 70*
(off Pembroke St.)
Choumert Gro. SE15 54Wb 113
Choumert M. SE15 54Wb 113
Choumert Rd. SE15 55Vb 113
Choumert Sq. SE15 54Wb 113
Chow Sq. E8 36Vb 71
Chrislaine Cl. TW19: Stanw 58M 105
Chrisp Ho. *SE10 51Gc 115*
(off Maze Hill)
Chrisp St. E14 43Dc 92
(not continuous)
Christabel Cl. TW7: Isle 55Ga 108
Christabel Pankhurst Ct. *SE5 52Tb 113*
(off Brisbane St.)
Christchurch Av. DA8: Erith 51Fd 118
HA0: Wemb 37Na 67
HA3: Kenton, W'stone 28Ha 46
N12 23Eb 49
NW6 39Za 68
RM13: Rain 40Hd 76
TW11: Tedd 64Ja 130
Christchurch Cl. AL3: St A 1A 6
EN2: Enf 12Sb 33
N12 24Fb 49
SW19 66Fb 133
Christ Church Ct. NW10 39Ua 68
Christchurch Ct. EC4 2C 224
NW6 38Ab 68
(off Willesden La.)
UB4: Yead 42Y 85
(off Dunedin Way)
Christchurch Cres. DA12: Grav'nd 9E 122
WD7: R'lett 8Ja 14
Christchurch Flats TW9: Rich 55Na 109
Christchurch Gdns. HA3: W'stone 28Ja 46
KT19: Eps 83Ra 173
Christchurch Grn. HA0: Wemb 37Na 67
Christchurch Hill NW3 34Fb 69
Christchurch Ho. RM8: Dag 36Xc 75
SW2 60Pb 112
(off Christchurch Rd.)
Christchurch La. EN5: Barn 12Ab 30
Christchurch Lodge EN4: Cockf 14Hb 31
Christ Chu. Mt. KT19: Eps 84Ra 173
(not continuous)
Christchurch Pk. SM2: Sutt 80Eb 155
Christchurch Pas. EN5: Barn 12Ab 30
NW3 34Eb 69
Christchurch Path UB3: Harl 48S 84
Christchurch Pl. KT19: Eps 83Ra 173
SW8 54Mb 112
Christ Chu. Rd. BR3: Beck 68Cc 136
KT5: Surb 72Pa 153
KT19: Eps 84Na 173
Christchurch Rd. CR8: Purl 83Rb 177
DA1: Dart 59Ld 119
DA12: Grav'nd 10E 122
DA15: Sidc 63Vc 139
GU25: Vir W 9L 125
HP2: Hem H 1M 3
IG1: Ilf 32Rc 74
N8 30Nb 50
RM18: Tilb 3C 122
SW2 60Pb 112
SW14 57Ra 109
SW19 66Fb 133
TW6: H'row A 55Q 106
Christchurch Sq. E9 39Yb 72
Christchurch St. SW3 51Hb 111
Christchurch Ter. *SW3 51Hb 111*
(off Christchurch St.)
Christchurch Way GU21: Wok 89B 168
SE10 50Gc 93
Christian Ct. SE16 46Bc 92
CHRISTIAN FIELDS 3F 144
Christian Flds. SW16 66Qb 134
Christian Flds. Av.
DA12: Grav'nd 3E 144
Christian Pl. *E1 44Wb 91*
(off Burslem St.)
Christian Sq. SL4: Wind 3G 102
Christian St. E1 44Wb 91
Christie Cl. GU18: Light 2A 166
KT23: Bookh 97Ba 191
Christie Ct. CM14: B'wood 20Yd 40
N19 33Nb 70
WD18: Wat 15W 26
Christie Dr. CR0: C'don 71Wb 157
Christie Gdns.
RM6: Chad H 30Xc 55
Christie Ho. *SE10 50Hc 93*
(off Blackwall La.)
W12 44Xa 88
(off Du Cane Rd.)
Christie Rd. E9 37Ac 72
EN9: Walt A 7Dc 20
Christies Av. TN14: Bad M 82Cd 182
Christie Wlk. CR3: Cat'm 94Tb 197
Christina Sq. N4 32Rb 71
Christina St. EC2 5H 219 (42Ub 91)
Christine Ct. RM13: Rain 43Jd 96
Christine Worsley Cl.
N21 18Rb 33
Christmas La. SL2: Farn C 4G 60
Christmas Tree Farm 84Qc 180
Christopher Av. W7 48Ja 86
Christopher Bell Twr. *E3 40Cc 72*
(off Pancras Way)
Christopher Cl. DA15: Sidc 57Vc 117
RM12: Horn 35Md 77
SE16 47Zb 92
Christopher Ct. *E1 44Wb 91*
(off Leman St.)
HP3: Hem H 5M 3
KT20: Tad 95Ya 194
TW15: Ashf 64N 127
Christopher Gdns. RM9: Dag 36Zc 75
Christopher Ho. *DA15: Sidc 61Wc 139*
(off Station Rd.)
Christopher Pl. *AL3: St A 2B 6*
(off Verulam Rd.)
N22 24Nb 50
(off Myddleton Rd.)
NW1 4E 216 (41Mb 90)
Christopher Rd. UB2: S'hall 49X 85
Christophers M. W11 46Ab 88
Christopher St. EC2 6G 219 (42Tb 91)
Christy Rd. TN16: Big H 87Lc 179
Chrstnut Ho. *BR8: Swan 69Hd 140*
(off Squirrels Cl.)
Chryssell Rd. SW9 52Qb 112
Chrystie La. KT23: Bookh 98Da 191
Chubworthy St. SE14 51Ac 114
Chucks La. KT20: Walt H 96Ya 194
Chudleigh DA14: Sidc 63Xc 139
Chudleigh Cres. IG3: Ilf 35Uc 74
Chudleigh Gdns. SM1: Sutt 76Eb 155
Chudleigh Rd. NW6 38Za 68
RM3: Rom 21Nd 57
SE4 57Bc 114
TW2: Twick 58Ga 108
Chudleigh St. E1 44Zb 92
Chudleigh Way HA4: Ruis 32W 64
Chulsa Rd. SE26 64Xb 135
Chumleigh Gdns. *SE5 51Ub 113*
(off Chumleigh St.)
Chumleigh St. SE5 51Ub 113
Chumleigh Wlk. KT5: Surb 70Pa 131
Church All. CR0: C'don 74Qb 156
DA11: Grav'nd 8D 122
(off High St.)
WD25: A'ham 10Ea 14
Church App. SE21 62Tb 135
TN14: Cud 87Sc 180
TW19: Stanw 58M 105
TW20: Thorpe 69E 126
Church Av. BR3: Beck 67Cc 136
DA14: Sidc 64Wc 139
E4 23Fc 53
(not continuous)
HA4: Ruis 32T 64
HA5: Pinn 30Aa 45
NW1 37Kb 70
SW14 55Ta 109
UB2: S'hall 48Aa 85
UB5: N'olt 38Ba 65
Churchbank *E17 28Cc 52*
(off Eastfield Rd.)
Churchbury Cl. EN1: Enf 12Ub 33
Churchbury Ho. *EN8: Walt C 4Zb 20*
(off High St.)
Churchbury La. EN1: Enf 13Tb 33
Churchbury Rd. EN1: Enf 12Ub 33
SE9 59Mc 115
Church Cloisters EC3 5H 225
Church Cl. CM15: Mount 11Fe 41
EN6: Cuff 1Nb 18
GU21: Wok 8P 167
GU24: Brkwd 3D 186
HA6: Nwood 24V 44
HA8: Edg 22Sa 47
IG10: Lough 12Pc 36
KT15: Add 77K 149
KT17: Eps 85Ua 174
KT20: Lwr K 99Bb 195
KT22: Fet 96Fa 192
N20 20Gb 31
SL4: Eton 1H 103
SS17: Horn H 1H 101
TW3: Houn 54Aa 107
TW18: Lale 69L 127
UB4: Hayes 43T 84
UB7: W Dray 48N 83
UB8: Uxb 40K 63
W8 47Db 89
WD7: R'lett 8Ja 14
Church Cotts. KT15: Add 76N 149
Church Ct. EC4 3K 223 (44Qb 90)
KT10: Esh 79Ea 152
(off Princess Sq.)
RH2: Reig 6K 207
SE16 47Bc 92
(off Rotherhithe St.)
TW9: Rich 57Ma 109
Church Cres. AL3: St A 1A 6
CM15: Mount 11Fe 41
E9 38Zb 72
N3 25Bb 49
N10 28Kb 50
N20 20Gb 31
RM15: S Ock 41Yd 98
Church Cft. AL4: St A 4G 6
Churchcroft Cl. SW12 59Jb 112
Churchdown BR1: Brom 63Gc 137
Church Dr. BR4: W W'ck 76Gc 159
HA2: Harr 30Ca 45
NW9 32Ta 67
Church Elm La. RM10: Dag 37Cd 76
CHURCH END
GU23 93P 189
N3 25Bb 49
NW10 38Ua 68
WD3 10H 11
Church End E17 28Dc 52
NW4 27Xa 48
Church Entry EC4 3C 224
Church Est. Almshouses
TW9: Rich 56Pa 109
(off Sheen Rd.)
Church Farm Cl. BR8: Crock 72Ed 162
Church Farm House Mus. 27Xa 48
Church Farm La. SM3: Cheam 79Ab 154
Church Farm Pool 17Hb 31
Church Farm Way WD25: A'ham 10Da 13
Church Fld. CM16: Epp 1Wc 23
DA2: Wilm 61Md 141
TN13: Riv 94Hd 202
Churchfield Av. N12 23Fb 49
Churchfield Cl. HA2: Harr 28Ea 46
UB3: Hayes 45V 84
Church Fld. Cotts. TN15: Seal 92Pd 203
Churchfield Ct. RH2: Reig 6K 207
Churchfield Ho. *KT11: Cobh 86X 171*
(off Lushington Dr.)
W2 6B 214
Churchfield Mans. *SW6 54Bb 111*
(off New Kings Rd.)
Churchfield M. SL2: Slou 4L 81
Churchfield Path EN8: Chesh 1Yb 20
(not continuous)
Churchfield Pl. KT13: Weyb 77Q 150
TW17: Shep 73R 150
Churchfield Rd. DA16: Well 55Wc 117
KT12: Walt T 74W 150
KT13: Weyb 77Q 150
RH2: Reig 5H 207
SL9: Chal P 25A 42
W3 46Sa 87
W7 47Ga 86
W13 46Ka 86
Churchfields E18 25Jc 53
GU21: Wok 88A 168
IG10: Lough 14Nc 36
KT8: W Mole 69Ca 129
SE10 51Ec 114
Churchfields Av. KT13: Weyb 77R 150
TW13: Hanw 62Ba 129
Churchfields Rd. BR3: Beck 68Zb 136
WD24: Wat 8V 12
Churchfield Way N12 23Eb 49
Church Gdns. HA0: Wemb 35Ja 66
KT22: Lea 92Ka 192
W5 47Ma 87
Church Gth. *N19 33Mb 70*
(off St John's Gro.)
CHURCHGATE 1Xb 19
Church Ga. SW6 55Ab 110
Churchgate EN8: Chesh 1Xb 19
Churchgate Rd. EN8: Chesh 1Xb 19
Church Grn. KT12: Hers 79Y 151
KT20: Walt H 96Wa 194
SW9 53Qb 112
UB3: Hayes 44V 84
Church Gro. HP6: L Chal 11A 24
KT1: Hamp W 67La 130
SE13 57Dc 114
SL3: Wex 3N 81
Church Hill BR6: Orp 73Wc 161
CM16: Epp 1Wc 23
CR3: Cat'm 96Vb 197
CR8: Purl 82Nb 176
DA1: Cray 56Gd 118
DA2: Wilm 61Md 141
DA9: Ghithe 57Ud 120
E17 28Cc 52
GU21: Wok 8P 167
GU22: Pyr 89H 169
HA1: Harr 32Ga 66
IG10: Lough 13Nc 36
N21 17Pb 32
RH1: Mers 98Kb 196
RH1: Nutf 5F 208
SE18 48Pc 94
SM5: Cars 78Hb 155
SS17: Stan H 2L 101
SW19 64Bb 133
TN14: Cud 87Sc 180
TN15: Plax 99Ae 205
TN16: Tats 94Mc 199
UB9: Hare 27L 43
WD5: Bedm 7F 4
Church Hill Rd. E17 28Dc 52
EN4: E Barn 16Gb 31
KT6: Surb 71Na 153
SM3: Cheam 76Za 154
Church Hill Wood BR5: St M Cry 71Vc 161
Church Hollow RM19: Purf 50Qd 97
Church Ho. EC1 5C 218
SW1 3E 228
Church Hyde SE18 51Uc 116
Churchill Av. HA3: Kenton 30Ka 46
UB10: Hil 41R 84
Churchill Bus. Pk.
TN16: Westrm 98Uc 200
Churchill Cl. CR6: W'ham 89Yb 178
DA1: Dart 60Rd 119
KT22: Fet 95Ga 192
TW14: Felt 60V 106
UB10: Hil 41R 84
Churchill Ct. BR6: Farnb 78Sc 160
HA2: Harr 33Da 65
(Eastcote Av.)
HA2: Harr 29Da 45
(Montrose Ct.)
HA5: Hat E 25Aa 45
HA6: Nwood 23T 44
N4 31Qb 70
N9 18Ub 33
SE18 49Pc 94
TN16: Westrm 98Tc 200
TW18: Staines 65K 127
UB5: N'olt 36Ca 65
(off Newmarket Av.)
W5 42Pa 87
Churchill Cres. AL9: Wel G 6E 8
Churchill Dr. KT13: Weyb 77S 150
Churchill Gdns. *SW1 50Lb 90*
(off Churchill Gdns. Rd., not continuous)
W3 44Qa 87
Churchill Gdns. Rd. SW1 50Kb 90
Churchill Ho. *SM7: Bans 86Bb 175*
(off Dunnymans Rd.)
Churchill Lodge IG6: Ilf 28Sc 54
Churchill Pk. DA1: Dart 57Qd 119
Churchill Pl. E14 46Dc 92
HA1: Harr 28Ga 46
Churchill Rd. AL1: St A 1E 6
CR2: S Croy 81Sb 177
DA4: Hort K 70Sd 142
DA11: Grav'nd 10B 122
E16 44Lc 93
HA8: Edg 23Pa 47
KT19: Eps 83Qa 173
NW2 37Xa 68
NW5 35Kb 70
RM17: Grays 51Fe 121
SL3: L'ly 49B 82
Churchills M. IG8: Wfd G 23Hc 53
Churchill Ter. E4 21Cc 52
Churchill Theatre 68Jc 137
Churchill Wlk. E9 36Yb 72
Churchill War Rooms 1E 228 (47Mb 90)
Churchill Way BR1: Brom 68Jc 137
TN16: Big H 87Mc 179
TW16: Sun 64W 128
Church Island 63F 126
CHURCH LAMMAS 63G 126
Churchlands Way KT4: Wor Pk 75Za 154
Church La. AL4: Col H 4M 7
BR2: Brom 74Nc 160
BR7: Chst 67Sc 138
CM13: Gt War 30Zd 59
CR3: Cat'm 96Qb 196
CR5: Coul 94Jb 196
CR6: W'ham 89Zb 178
(Church Rd.)
CR6: W'ham 88Dc 178
(Ledgers Rd.)
DA12: Grav'nd 2L 145
E11 32Gc 73
E17 28Dc 52
EN1: Enf 13Tb 33
EN6: N'thaw 2Jb 18
EN8: Chesh 1Xb 19
GU3: Worp 9J 187
GU23: Send 98D 188
GU24: Bisl 7E 166
GU24: Pirb 4B 186
HA3: W'stone 25Ha 46
HA5: Pinn 27Aa 45
HP3: Bov 9D 2
IG10: Lough 13Pc 36
KT7: T Ditt 72Ha 152
KT9: Chess 79Pa 153
KT13: Weyb 77Q 150
KT18: Head 96Sa 193
KT18: Tad 89Za 174
N2 27Fb 49
N8 28Pb 50
N9 19Wb 33
N17 25Ub 51
NW9 30Sa 47
RH1: Blet 5K 209
RH8: Oxt 2H 211
RH9: G'stone 4B 210
RM1: Rom 28Gd 56
RM4: Abr 12Ad 37
RM4: Stap A 14Ed 38
RM10: Dag 38Ed 76
RM13: Wenn 44Md 97
RM14: N Ock 36Xd 78
RM19: Purf 50Qd 97
SL2: Stoke P 2K 81
SL3: Wex 2M 81
SL4: Wind 3H 103
SL5: S'dale 1F 146
SL5: S'hill 10B 124
SL9: Chal P 25A 42
SM6: Bedd 76Mb 156
(not continuous)
SW17 64Hb 133
SW19 67Bb 133
TN15: Kems'g 89Rd 183
TW1: Twick 60Ja 108
TW10: Ham 60Na 109
TW11: Tedd 64Ha 130
UB3: Hayes 44U 84
UB8: Uxb 40K 63
W5 47La 86
WD3: Rick 18J 25
WD3: Sarr 10H 11
WD4: K Lan 1Q 12
WD25: A'ham 10Da 13
Church La. Av. CR5: Coul 94Kb 196
Church La. Dr. CR5: Coul 94Kb 196
Churchley Rd. SE26 63Xb 135
Church Manorway DA8: Erith 49Fd 96
SE2 50Wc 95
Church Mead *SE5 52Sb 113*
(off Camberwell Rd.)
Churchmead Cl. EN4: E Barn 16Gb 31
Church Mdw. KT6: Surb 75La 152
Churchmead Rd. NW10 37Wa 68
Church M. KT15: Add 77L 149
Churchmore Rd. SW16 67Lb 134
Church Mt. N2 29Fb 49
Church Paddock Ct. SM6: Bedd 76Mb 156
Church Pde. TW15: Ashf 63P 127
Church Pas. *EC2 2E 224*
(off Gresham St.)
EN5: Barn 13Ab 30
KT6: Surb 71Na 153
TW1: Twick 60Ka 108
Church Path BR8: Swan 67Kd 141
CR0: C'don 75Sb 157
CR4: Mitc 69Gb 133
(not continuous)
CR5: Coul 90Qb 176
DA9: Ghithe 57Vd 120
DA11: Nflt 58Ee 121
E11 29Jc 53
E17 28Dc 52
GU21: Wok 89B 168
KT11: Cobh 86X 171
N5 36Rb 71
N8 29Pb 50
(off Tottenham La.)
N12 20Eb 31
(Woodside La.)
N12 21Eb 49
(Woodside Pk. Rd.)
N17 24Ub 51
NW10 38Ua 68
RH1: Mers 99Kb 196
RM1: Rom 29Gd 56
(off Market Pl.)
RM17: Grays 51Ce 121
SL5: Asc, S'hill 9C 124
SW14 55Ta 109
(not continuous)
Church Path SW19 68Bb 133
UB1: S'hall 46Ca 85
UB2: S'hall 48Ba 85
(not continuous)
W3 47Sa 87
(not continuous)
W4 48Sa 87
Church Pl. CR4: Mitc 69Gb 133
SW1 5C 222 (45Lb 90)
UB10: Ick 34S 64
W5 47Ma 87
Church Ri. KT9: Chess 79Pa 153
SE23 61Zb 136
Church Rd. BR2: Brom 68Jc 137
(Edison Rd.)
BR2: Brom 69Gc 137
(Hazelwood Ho's.)
BR2: Kes 80Mc 159
BR6: Chels 80Yc 161
BR6: Farnb 78Sc 160
BR8: Crock 73Fd 162
BR8: Swan 67Md 141
CM15: Mount 11Fe 41
CR0: C'don 76Sb 157
(not continuous)
CR3: Cat'm 95Vb 197
CR3: Whyt 90Vb 177
CR3: Wold 94Zb 198
CR4: Mitc 67Fb 133
CR6: W'ham 89Zb 178
CR8: Kenley 87Tb 177
CR8: Purl 82Nb 176
DA3: Hartl, New A 71Be 165
DA4: Sut H 65Pd 141
DA7: Bex 54Bd 117
DA8: Erith 50Fd 96
DA9: Ghithe 57Vd 120
DA10: Swans 58Be 121
DA12: Grav'nd 5E 144
DA13: Cobh 8E 144
DA13: Ist R, Cobh 6C 144
DA14: Sidc 63Wc 139
DA16: Well 54Xc 117
E10 32Cc 72
E12 36Nc 74
E17 26Ac 52
EN3: Pond E 16Yb 34
EN6: Pot B 2Cb 17
GU20: W'sham 9A 146
GU21: Wok 87A 168
(Beech Gdns.)
GU21: Wok 1L 187
(St John's Hill Rd.)
GU24: W End 4D 166
HA6: Nwood 24V 44
HA7: Stan 22Ka 46
HP3: Hem H 4C 4
IG2: Ilf 30Uc 54
IG9: Buck H 18Kc 35
IG10: H Beech, Lough 13Jc 35
IG11: Bark 37Sc 74
KT1: King T 68Pa 131
KT4: Wor Pk 74Ua 154
KT6: Surb 74La 152
KT8: E Mos 70Fa 130
KT10: Clay 79Ha 152
KT14: Byfl 86N 169
KT15: Add 78J 149
KT17: Eps 84Ua 174
KT19: Ewe 80Ta 153
KT21: Asht 90Ma 173
KT22: Lea 94Ka 192
KT23: Bookh 95Ba 191
N1 37Sb 71
N6 30Jb 50
N17 25Ub 51
(not continuous)
NW4 28Xa 48
NW10 38Ua 68
RH1: Redh 8N 207
RH2: Reig 8J 207
RM3: Hrld W 25Qd 57
RM4: Nave 12Md 39
RM4: Noak H 18Ld 39
RM18: Tilb 3B 122
RM18: W Til 1G 122
SE19 67Ub 135
SL0: Iver H 41E 82
SL2: Farn R 1G 80
SL4: Old Win 7M 103
SL5: S'dale 2E 146
SM3: Cheam 79Ab 154
SM6: Bedd 76Mb 156
SW13 54Va 110
SW19 64Ab 132
(Courthope Rd.)
SW19 67Fb 133
(Reynolds Cl.)
TN14: Hals 83Ad 181
TN14: Sund 99Ad 201
TN15: Ash 78Ae 165
TN15: Ivy H, Seal 95Ud 204
TN15: Seal 93Pd 203
TN15: W King 80Ud 164
TN16: Big H 89Mc 179
TN16: Bras 96Xc 201
TW5: Cran 50X 85
TW5: Hest 52Ca 107
TW7: Isle 53Fa 108
TW9: Rich 56Na 109
TW10: Ham 63Ma 131
TW10: Rich 57Na 109
TW11: Tedd 63Ga 130
TW13: Hanw 64Z 129
TW15: Ashf 62P 127
TW17: Shep 73R 150
TW20: Egh 64B 126
UB2: S'hall 48Ba 85
UB3: Hayes 46V 84
UB5: N'olt 40Z 65
UB7: W Dray 48M 83
UB8: Cowl 42M 83
UB9: Hare 27L 43
W3 46Sa 87
W7 45Fa 86
WD17: Wat 11W 26
Church Rd. Almshouses *E10 33Dc 72*
(off Church Rd.)
Church Rd. Ind. Est. E10 32Cc 72
Church Row BR7: Chst 67Sc 138
NW3 35Eb 69
RM16: Ors 2C 100
(off Malting La.)
SW6 52Db 111
(off Park Rd.)
Church Row M. BR7: Chst 66Sc 138

Church Side KT18: Eps ... 85Ra 173
Churchside Cl. TN16: Big H ... 89Lc 179
Church Sq. TW17: Shep ... 73R 150
Church St. AL3: St A ... 1B 6
CR0: C'don ... 76Rb 157
DA11: Grav'nd ... 8D 122
DA13: Sflt ... 64Ce 143
E15 ... 39Gc 73
E16 ... 46Rc 94
EN2: Enf ... 13Sb 33
EN9: Walt A ... 5Ec 20
GU22: Wok ... 93E 188
HP2: Hem H ... 1M 3
HP3: Bov ... 9D 2
KT1: King T ... 68Ma 131
KT10: Esh ... 77Da 151
KT11: Cobh ... 87X 171
KT12: Walt T ... 74W 150
KT13: Weyb ... 77Q 150
KT17: Eps ... 85Ua 174
KT17: Ewe ... 81Wa 174
KT22: Lea ... 94Ka 192
KT24: Eff ... 99Z 191
N9 ... 17Tb 33
NW8 ... 7C 214 (43Fb 89)
(not continuous)
RH2: Reig ... 6J 207
RH3: Bet ... 7A 206
RM10: Dag ... 37Dd 76
RM17: Grays ... 51Ee 121
SL1: Burn ... 2A 80
SL1: Slou ... 7G 80
(Damson Gro.)
SL1: Slou ... 7K 81
(Osborne St.)
SL4: Wind ... 3H 103
SM1: Sutt ... 78Db 155
TN14: S'ham ... 83Hd 182
TN15: Seal ... 93Qd 203
TW1: Twick ... 60Ja 108
TW7: Isle ... 55Ka 108
TW12: Hamp ... 67Ea 130
TW16: Sun ... 69X 129
TW18: Staines ... 63F 126
W2 ... 7C 214 (43Fb 89)
(not continuous)
W4 ... 51Va 110
WD3: Rick ... 18N 25
WD18: Wat ... 14Y 27
Church St. E. GU21: Wok ... 89B 168
Church St. Est. NW8 ... 6C 214 (42Fb 89)
Church St. Nth. E15 ... 39Gc 73
Church St. Pas. *E15* ... *39Gc 73*
(off Church St.)
Church St. W. GU21: Wok ... 89A 168
Church Stretton Rd. TW3: Houn ... 57Ea 108
Church Ter. NW4 ... 27Xa 48
RM4: Stap A ... 14Ed 38
SE13 ... 55Gc 115
SL4: Wind ... 4C 102
TW10: Rich ... 57Ma 109
CHURCH TOWN ... 4B 210
Church Trad. Est. DA8: Erith ... 52Hd 118
Church Va. N2 ... 27Hb 49
SE23 ... 61Zb 136
Church Vw. BR8: Swan ... 69Fd 140
RM14: Upm ... 33Rd 77
RM15: Avel ... 47Sd 98
TW10: Rich ... 57Na 109
Churchview Cl. CR3: Cat'm ... 96Wb 197
Church Vw. Gro. SE26 ... 65Zb 136
Churchview Rd. TW2: Twick ... 60Fa 108
Church Vs. TN13: Riv ... 94Gd 202
Church Wlk. CM15: B'wood ... 17Xd 40
CR3: Cat'm ... 96Wb 197
DA2: Wilm ... 62Md 141
DA4: Eyns ... 76Nd 163
DA12: Grav'nd ... 10F 122
EN2: Enf ... 13Tb 33
KT7: T Ditt ... 72Ha 152
KT12: Walt T ... 74W 150
(not continuous)
KT13: Weyb ... 76Q 150
KT16: Chert ... 72J 149
KT22: Lea ... 94Ka 192
N6 ... 34Jb 70
N16 ... 34Tb 71
(not continuous)
NW2 ... 34Bb 69
NW4 ... 27Ya 48
NW9 ... 33Ta 67
RH1: Blet ... 5K 209
(not continuous)
RH2: Reig ... 6K 207
(not continuous)
SL1: Burn ... 2A 80
(not continuous)
SW13 ... 53Wa 110
SW15 ... 57Xa 110
SW16 ... 68Lb 134
SW20 ... 69Ya 132
TW8: Bford ... 51La 108
(not continuous)
TW9: Rich ... 57Ma 109
UB3: Hayes ... 44U 84
WD23: Bush ... 16Ca 27
Churchward Ho. *SE17* ... *51Rb 113*
(off Lorrimore Sq.)
W14 ... *50Bb 89*
(off Ivatt Pl.)
Church Way CR2: Sande ... 82Vb 177
EN4: Cockf ... 14Hb 31
HA8: Edg ... 23Qa 47
N20 ... 20Gb 31
RH8: Oxt ... 4K 211
Churchway NW1 ... 3E 216 (41Mb 90)
(not continuous)
Churchwell Path E9 ... 36Yb 72
Churchwood Gdns. IG8: Wfd G ... 21Jc 53
Church Wood Reserve ... 2K 61
Churchyard Pas. SE5 ... 54Tb 113
Churchyard Row SE11 ... 5C 230 (49Rb 91)
Church Yd. Wlk. W2 ... 7B 214
Churston Av. E13 ... 39Kc 73
Churston Cl. SW2 ... 60Qb 112
Churston Dr. SM4: Mord ... 71Za 154
Churston Gdns. N11 ... 23Lb 50
Churston Mans. WC1 ... 6J 217
Churton Pl. SW1 ... 6C 228 (49Lb 90)
Churton St. SW1 ... 6C 228 (49Lb 90)
Chusan Pl. E14 ... 44Bc 92
Chute Ho. *SW9* ... *54Qb 112*
(off Stockwell Pk. Rd.)
Chuter Ede Ho. *SW6* ... *51Bb 111*
(off North End Rd.)
Chuters Cl. KT14: Byfl ... 84N 169
Chuters Gro. KT17: Eps ... 84Va 174
Chyne, The SL9: Ger X ... 29B 42
Chyngton Cl. DA15: Sidc ... 62Vc 139
Cibber Rd. SE23 ... 61Zb 136
Cicada Rd. SW18 ... 58Eb 111
Cicely Ho. NW8 ... 2C 214
Cicely Rd. SE15 ... 53Wb 113
Cimba Wood DA12: Grav'nd ... 3G 144
Cinderella Path NW11 ... 32Db 69
Cinderford Way BR1: Brom ... 63Gc 137
Cinder Path GU22: Wok ... 1N 187
Cine Lumiere ... 5B 226
Cineworld Cinema
Bexleyheath ... 56Dd 118
Chelsea, Fulham Rd. ... 50Eb 89
Chelsea, King's Rd. ... 51Fb 111
Ealing ... *45Ma 87*
(off New Broadway)
Enfield ... 14Wb 33
Feltham ... 61X 129
Hammersmith ... 49Xa 88
Haymarket ... 5D 222
Ilford ... *34Rc 74*
(off Clements Rd.)
Shaftesbury Av. ... 5D 222
Staples Corner ... 32Xa 68
Wandsworth ... 57Db 111
West India Quay ... 45Cc 92
Wood Green ... *26Qb 50*
(in Wood Green Shop. City)
Cinnabar Wharf Central *E1* ... *46Wb 91*
(off Wapping High St.)
Cinnabar Wharf E. *E1* ... *46Wb 91*
(off Wapping High St.)
Cinnabar Wharf W. *E1* ... *46Wb 91*
(off Wapping High St.)
Cinnamon Cl. CR0: C'don ... 73Nb 156
SE15 ... 52Vb 113
SL4: Wind ... 3D 102
Cinnamon M. N13 ... 19Qb 32
Cinnamon Row SW11 ... 55Eb 111
Cinnamon St. E1 ... 46Xb 91
Cinnamon Wharf *SE1* ... *47Vb 91*
(off Shad Thames)
Cintra Pk. SE19 ... 66Vb 135
CIPPENHAM ... 5C 80
Cippenham Cl. SL1: Slou ... 5D 80
Cippenham La. SL1: Slou ... 5D 80
Circa Apartments NW1 ... 38Jb 70
Circle, The NW2 ... 34Ua 68
NW7 ... 23Ta 47
RM18: Tilb ... 3C 122
SE1 ... 1K 231
Circle Gdns. KT14: Byfl ... 85P 169
SW19 ... 68Cb 133
Circle Rd. KT12: W Vill ... 81U 170
Circuit Cen. KT13: Weyb ... 83N 169
Circuits, The HA5: Pinn ... 28Y 45
Circular Rd. N17 ... 27Vb 51
Circular Way SE18 ... 51Pc 116
(not continuous)
Circus, The *KT22: Lea* ... *92Ka 192*
(off By-Pass Rd.)
Circus Lodge NW8 ... 3B 214
Circus M. W1 ... 7F 215
Circus Pl. EC2 ... 1G 225 (43Tb 91)
Circus Rd. NW8 ... 3B 214 (41Fb 89)
Circus St. SE10 ... 52Ec 114
Cirencester St. W2 ... 43Db 89
Cirrus Cl. SM6: Wall ... 80Nb 156
Cirrus Cres. DA12: Grav'nd ... 3G 144
Cissbury Ho. SE26 ... 62Wb 135
Cissbury Ring Nth. N12 ... 22Bb 49
Cissbury Ring Sth. N12 ... 22Bb 49
Cissbury Rd. N15 ... 29Tb 51
Citadel Pl. SE11 ... 7H 229 (50Pb 90)
Citius Apartments *E3* ... *40Cc 72*
(off Tredegar La.)
Citizen Ho. N7 ... 35Qb 70
Citizen Rd. N7 ... 35Qb 70
Citrus Ho. *SE8* ... *50Bc 92*
(off Alverton St.)
City Apartments *E1* ... *44Wb 91*
(off White Church La.)
City Bus. Cen. SE16 ... 48Yb 92
City Ct. CR0: C'don ... 73Rb 157
City Cross Bus. Pk. SE10 ... 49Gc 93
City E. Bldg. *E1* ... *45Xb 91*
(off Cable St.)
City Forum EC1 ... 3D 218 (41Sb 91)
City Gdn. Row N1 ... 2C 218 (40Rb 71)
City Ga. Ho. *IG2: Ilf* ... *30Qc 54*
(off Eastern Av.)
City Hall ... 7J 225 (46Ub 91)
City Harbour *E14* ... *48Dc 92*
(off Selsdon Way)
City Hgts. *E8* ... *39Vb 71*
(off Kingsland Rd.)
City Lights Ct. SE11 ... 7A 230
City Limits
Collier Row ... 26Bd 55
City Mill River Path E15 ... 39Ec 72
CITY OF LONDON ... 2G 225 (44Tb 91)
City of London Almshouses SW9 ... 56Pb 112
City of London Crematorium E12 ... 34Nc 74
City of London Point *N7* ... *37Mb 70*
(off York Way)
City of Westminster College
Paddington Green Campus ... 7B 214
City Pav. EC1 ... 7B 218
City Pl. Ho. EC2 ... 1E 224
Citypoint EC2 ... 7F 219
City Rd. EC1 ... 2B 218 (40Rb 71)
City Tower EC2 ... 1F 225
City University London
Goswell Pl. ... 4C 218 (41Rb 91)
Northampton Square Campus
... 4B 218 (41Rb 91)
Whitechapel ... 43Xb 91
City University Saddlers Sports Centre, The
... 5C 218 (42Rb 91)
City Vw. *IG1: Ilf* ... *33Sc 74*
(off Axon Pl.)
Cityview SE7 ... 51Lc 115
City Vw. Apartments *N1* ... *38Sb 71*
(off Essex Rd.)
City Vw. Ct. SE22 ... 59Wb 113
City Wlk. SE1 ... 3H 231 (47Ub 91)
City Wlk. Apartments EC1 ... 4C 218
City Wharf Ho. KT7: T Ditt ... 72Ka 152
Civic Cl. AL1: St A ... 2B 6
Civic Sq. RM18: Tilb ... 4C 122
Civic Way HA4: Ruis ... 36Z 65
IG6: Ilf ... 28Sc 54
Civil and Family Courts
Barnet ... 25Cb 49
Clabon M. SW1 ... 4F 227 (48Hb 89)
Clacket La. TN16: Westrm ... 96Nc 200
CLACKET LANE SERVICE AREA ... 98Nc 200
Clack La. HA4: Ruis ... 32S 64
Clack St. SE16 ... 47Yb 92
Clacton Rd. E6 ... 41Mc 93
E17 ... 30Ac 52
N17 ... 26Vb 51
Claigmar Gdns. N3 ... 25Db 49
Claire C'way. DA2: Dart ... 56Ud 120
Claire Cl. CM13: B'wood ... 21Be 59
Claire Ct. EN8: Chesh ... 4Zb 20
HA5: Hat E ... 24Ba 45
N12 ... 21Eb 31
NW2 ... 37Ab 68
WD23: B Hea ... 18Fa 28
Claire Gdns. HA7: Stan ... 22La 46
Claire Ho. IG1: Ilf ... 35Rc 74
Claire Pl. E14 ... 48Cc 92
Claireville Ct. RH2: Reig ... 6M 207
Clairvale RM11: Horn ... 31Nd 77
Clairvale Rd. TW5: Hest ... 53Z 107
Clairview Rd. SW16 ... 64Kb 134
Clairville Gdns. W7 ... 46Ga 86
Clairville Point *SE23* ... *62Zb 136*
(off Dacres Rd.)
Clammas Way UB8: Cowl ... 43L 83
Clamp Hill HA7: Stan ... 21Fa 46
Clancarty Rd. SW6 ... 54Cb 111
Clandon Av. TW20: Egh ... 66E 126
Clandon Cl. KT17: Ewe ... 79Va 154
W3 ... 47Ra 87
Clandon Gdns. N3 ... 27Cb 49
Clandon Ho. SE1 ... 2C 230
Clandon Rd. GU4: W Cla ... 97H 189
GU23: Send ... 97H 189
IG3: Ilf ... 33Uc 74
Clandon St. SE8 ... 54Cc 114
Clandon Ter. SW20 ... 68Za 132
Clanricarde Gdns. W2 ... 45Cb 89
Clapgate Rd. WD23: Bush ... 16Da 27
CLAPHAM ... 56Lb 112
CLAPHAM COMMON ... 56Mb 112
Clapham Comn. Nth. Side SW4 ... 56Hb 111
Clapham Comn. Sth. Side SW4 ... 58Kb 112
Clapham Comn. W. Side SW4 ... 56Hb 111
(not continuous)
Clapham Cres. SW4 ... 56Mb 112
Clapham High St. SW4 ... 56Mb 112
CLAPHAM JUNCTION ... 55Gb 111
Clapham Junc. App.
SW11 ... 55Gb 111
Clapham Leisure Cen. ... 55Mb 112
Clapham Mnr. Ct. SW4 ... 55Lb 112
Clapham Mnr. St. SW4 ... 55Lb 112
CLAPHAM PARK ... 59Mb 112
Clapham Pk. Est. SW4 ... 58Mb 112
Clapham Pk. Rd. SW4 ... 56Lb 112
Clapham Pk. Ter. *SW2* ... *57Nb 112*
(off Lyham Rd.)
Clapham Picturehouse ... 56Lb 112
Clapham Rd. SW9 ... 55Nb 112
Clapham Rd. Est. SW4 ... 55Nb 112
Clap La. RM10: Dag, Rush G ... 33Dd 76
Clappers La. GU24: Chob ... 3G 166
Clags Ga. La. E6 ... 42Qc 94
Clapton Comn. E5 ... 31Vb 71
(not continuous)
CLAPTON PARK ... 35Zb 72
Clapton Pk. Est. E5 ... 35Zb 72
Clapton Pas. E5 ... 36Yb 72
Clapton Sq. E5 ... 36Yb 72
Clapton Ter. E5 ... 32Wb 71
Clapton Way E5 ... 35Wb 71
Clara Grant Ho. *E14* ... *48Cc 92*
(off Mellish St.)
Clara Nehab Ho. *NW11* ... *29Bb 49*
(off Leeside Cres.)
Clara Pl. SE18 ... 49Qc 94
Clare Cl. KT14: W Byf ... 85J 169
N2 ... 27Eb 49
WD6: E'tree ... 16Pa 29
Clare Cnr. SE9 ... 59Rc 116
Clare Cotts. RH1: Blet ... 5H 209
Clare Ct. AL1: St A ... 3D 6
CR3: Wold ... 95Cc 198
EN3: Enf W ... 7Ac 20
HA6: Nwood ... 22S 44
RM15: Avel ... 47Sd 98
W11 ... *45Ab 88*
(off Clarendon Rd.)
WC1 ... 4G 217
Clare Cres. KT22: Lea ... 90Ja 172
Claredale GU22: Wok ... 91A 188
Claredale Ho. *E2* ... *40Xb 71*
(off Claredale St.)
Claredale St. E2 ... 40Wb 71
Clare Dr. SL2: Farn C ... 5F 60
Clarefield Ct. SL5: S'dale ... 3E 146
Clare Gdns. E7 ... 35Jc 73
IG11: Bark ... 37Vc 75
TW20: Egh ... 64C 126
W11 ... 44Ab 88
Claregate EN6: Pot B ... 2Eb 17
Clare Hill KT10: Esh ... 78Da 151
Clare Ho. E3 ... 39Bc 72
E16 ... *45Qc 94*
(off University Way)
HA8: Edg ... *26Sa 47*
(off Burnt Oak B'way.)
SE1 ... 7K 231
Clare La. N1 ... 38Sb 71
Clare Lawn Av. SW14 ... 57Ta 109
Clare Mkt. WC2 ... 3J 223 (44Pb 90)
Clare M. SW6 ... 52Db 111
Claremont AL2: Brick W ... 3Ca 13
EN7: Chesh ... 1Vb 19
TW17: Shep ... *72R 150*
(off Laleham Rd.)
Claremont Av. GU22: Wok ... 91A 188
HA3: Kenton ... 29Na 47
KT3: N Mald ... 71Wa 154
KT10: Esh ... 79Ba 151
KT12: Hers ... 77Z 151
TW16: Sun ... 67X 129
Claremont Cl. BR6: Farnb ... 77Pc 160
CR2: Sande ... 87Xb 177
E16 ... 46Qc 94
KT12: Hers ... 78Y 151
N1 ... 2A 218 (40Qb 70)
RM16: Grays ... 48Ee 99
SW2 ... 60Nb 112
Claremont Ct. *E2* ... *40Xb 71*
(off Cambridge Heath Rd.)
E2 ... *40Wb 71*
(off Claredale St.)
Claremont Ct. *W2* ... *44Db 89*
(off Queensway)
W9 ... *40Bb 69*
(off Claremont Rd.)
Claremont Cres. DA1: Cray ... 56Gd 118
WD3: Crox G ... 15S 26
Claremont Dr. GU22: Wok ... 91A 188
KT10: Esh ... 81Ca 171
TW17: Shep ... 72R 150
Claremont End KT10: Esh ... 79Da 151
Claremont Gdns. IG3: Ilf ... 33Uc 74
KT6: Surb ... 71Na 153
RM14: Upm ... 32Td 78
Claremont Gro. IG8: Wfd G ... 23Lc 53
W4 ... 52Ua 110
Claremont Ho. SM2: Sutt ... 80Db 155
WD18: Wat ... 16T 26
Claremont Landscape Garden ... 80Ba 151
Claremont La. KT10: Esh ... 78Da 151
CLAREMONT PARK ... 80Da 151
Claremont Pk. N3 ... 25Ab 48
Claremont Pk. Rd. KT10: Esh ... 79Da 151
Claremont Pl. *DA11: Grav'nd* ... *9D 122*
(off Arthur St.)
IG7: Chig ... 20Rc 36
KT10: Clay ... 79Ha 152
Claremont Road ... 33Za 68
Claremont Rd. BR1: Brom ... 70Nc 138
BR8: Hext ... 66Gd 140
CR0: C'don ... 74Wb 157
E7 ... 36Kc 73
E11 ... 34Fc 73
E17 ... 26Ac 52
EN4: Had W ... 10Eb 17
HA3: W'stone ... 26Ga 46
KT6: Surb ... 71Na 153
KT10: Clay ... 80Ga 152
KT14: W Byf ... 84J 169
N6 ... 31Lb 70
NW2 ... 31Za 68
RH1: Redh ... 3A 208
RM11: Horn ... 30Jd 56
SL4: Wind ... 4G 102
TW1: Twick ... 58Ka 108
TW11: Tedd ... 64Ha 130
TW18: Staines ... 64F 126
W9 ... 40Ab 68
W13 ... 43Ja 86
Claremont Sq. N1 ... 2K 217 (40Qb 70)
Claremont St. E16 ... 47Qc 94
N18 ... 23Wb 51
SE10 ... 51Dc 114
Claremont Ter. KT7: T Ditt ... 73Ka 152
Claremont Vs. *SE5* ... *52Tb 113*
(off Southampton Way)
Claremont Way NW2 ... 32Ya 68
(not continuous)
Claremont Way Ind. Est. NW2 ... 32Ya 68
Claremount Cl. KT18: Tatt C ... 89Ya 174
Claremount Gdns. KT18: Tatt C ... 89Ya 174
Clarence Av. BR1: Brom ... 70Nc 138
IG2: Ilf ... 30Qc 54
KT3: N Mald ... 68Sa 131
RM14: Upm ... 32Qd 77
SW4 ... 59Mb 112
Clarence Cl. EN4: E Barn ... 15Fb 31
KT12: Hers ... 77X 151
WD23: B Hea ... 17Ha 28
Clarence Ct. NW7 ... 22Ua 48
RM17: Grays ... *51De 121*
(off Clarence Rd.)
SL4: Wind ... 3F 102
TW20: Egh ... *64B 126*
(off Clarence St.)
W6 ... *49Xa 88*
(off Cambridge Gro.)
Clarence Cres. DA14: Sidc ... 62Xc 139
SL4: Wind ... 3G 102
SW4 ... 58Mb 112
Clarence Dr. TW20: Eng G ... 3N 125
Clarence Gdns. NW1 ... 4A 216 (41Kb 90)
Clarence Ga. IG8: Ilf, Wfd G ... 23Qc 54
Clarence Ga. Gdns. NW1 ... 6G 215
Clarence House ... 1C 228
Clarence Ho. *KT12: Hers* ... *78X 151*
(off Queens Rd.)
SE17 ... *51Tb 113*
(off Merrow St.)
Clarence La. SW15 ... 58Ua 110
Clarence M. E5 ... 36Xb 71
SE16 ... 46Zb 92
SW12 ... 59Kb 112
Clarence Pk. ... 2D 6
Clarence Pk. M. AL1: St A ... 2D 6
Clarence Pl. DA12: Grav'nd ... 9D 122
E5 ... 36Xb 71
Clarence Rd. AL1: St A ... 2D 6
BR1: Brom ... 69Mc 137
CM15: Pil H ... 16Xd 40
CR0: C'don ... 73Tb 157
DA6: Bex ... 56Ad 117
DA14: Sidc ... 62Xc 139
E5 ... 35Xb 71
E12 ... 35Lc 73
E16 ... 42Gc 93
E17 ... 26Zb 52
EN3: Pond E ... 15Xb 33
KT12: Hers ... 77X 151
N15 ... 29Sb 51
N22 ... 24Nb 50
NW6 ... 38Bb 69
RH1: Redh ... 9M 207
RM17: Grays ... 51Ce 121
SE8 ... 51Dc 114
SE9 ... 61Nc 138
SL4: Wind ... 3E 102
SM1: Sutt ... 78Db 155
SM6: Wall ... 78Kb 156
SW19 ... 65Db 133
TN16: Big H ... 90Pc 180
TW9: Kew ... 53Pa 109
TW11: Tedd ... 65Ha 130
W4 ... 50Qa 87
Clarence Row DA12: Grav'nd ... 9D 122
Clarence St. KT1: King T ... 68Ma 131
TW9: Rich ... 56Na 109
TW18: Staines ... 63G 126
TW20: Egh ... 65B 126
UB2: S'hall ... 48Z 85
Clarence Ter. NW1 ... 5G 215 (42Hb 89)
TW3: Houn ... 56Da 107
Clarence Wlk. RH1: Redh ... 9M 207
SW4 ... 54Nb 112
Clarence Way NW1 ... 38Kb 70
RM15: S Ock ... 44Zd 99
Clarenden Pl. DA2: Wilm ... 64Gd 140
Clarendon Cl. BR5: St P ... 69Wc 139
E9 ... 38Yb 72
HP2: Hem H ... 1M 3
W2 ... 4D 220 (45Gb 89)
Clarendon Ct. *BR3: Beck* ... *67Dc 136*
(off Blair Ct.)
HA6: Nwood ... 22V 44
NW2 ... 38Ya 68
NW11 ... 28Bb 49
SL2: Slou ... 5M 81
SL4: Wind ... 3F 102
TW5: Cran ... 53W 106
TW9: Kew ... 53Pa 109
W9 ... 5A 214
Clarendon Cres. TW2: Twick ... 62Fa 130
Clarendon Cross W11 ... 45Ab 88
Clarendon Dr. SW15 ... 56Ya 110
Clarendon Flds. WD3: Chan C ... 10P 11
Clarendon Flats W1 ... 3J 221
Clarendon Gdns. DA2: Dart ... 59Td 120
HA9: Wemb ... 34Ma 67
IG1: Ilf ... 31Pc 74
NW4 ... 27Wa 48
W9 ... 6A 214 (42Eb 89)
Clarendon Ga. KT16: Ott ... 79F 148
Clarendon Grn. BR5: St P ... 70Wc 139
Clarendon Gro. BR5: St P ... 70Wc 139
CR4: Mitc ... 69Hb 133
NW1 ... 3D 216 (41Mb 90)
Clarendon Ho. *KT2: King T* ... *67Na 131*
(off Cowleaze Rd.)
NW1 ... 2C 216
W2 ... 4D 220
Clarendon Lodge *W11* ... *45Ab 88*
(off Clarendon Rd.)
Clarendon Lofts *WD17: Wat* ... *13X 27*
(off Clarendon Rd.)
Clarendon M. DA5: Bexl ... 60Dd 118
KT21: Asht ... *91Pa 193*
(off Rectory La.)
W2 ... 4D 220 (45Gb 89)
WD6: Bore ... 13Qa 29
Clarendon Pde. EN8: Chesh ... 1Zb 20
Clarendon Path BR5: St P ... 70Wc 139
(not continuous)
Clarendon Pl. TN13: S'oaks ... 97Jd 202
W2 ... 4D 220 (45Gb 89)
Clarendon Ri. SE13 ... 56Ec 114
Clarendon Rd. CR0: C'don ... 75Rb 157
DA12: Grav'nd ... 8E 122
E11 ... 32Fc 73
E17 ... 30Dc 52
E18 ... 27Jc 53
EN8: Chesh ... 1Zb 20
HA1: Harr ... 30Ga 46
N8 ... 27Pb 50
N15 ... 28Sb 51
N18 ... 23Wb 51
N22 ... 26Pb 50
RH1: Redh ... 5P 207
SM6: Wall ... 79Lb 156
SW19 ... 66Gb 133
TN13: S'oaks ... 96Jd 202
TW15: Ashf ... 63P 127
UB3: Hayes ... 47V 84
W5 ... 41Na 87
W11 ... 45Ab 88
WD6: Bore ... 13Qa 29
WD17: Wat ... 12X 27
Clarendon St. SW1 ... 7A 228 (50Kb 90)
Clarendon Ter. W9 ... 5A 214 (42Eb 89)
Clarendon Wlk. W11 ... 44Ab 88
Clarendon Way BR5: St P ... 69Vc 139
BR7: Chst ... 69Vc 139
N21 ... 16Sb 33
Clarens St. SE6 ... 61Bc 136
Clare Pl. SW15 ... 59Va 110
Clare Point *NW2* ... *32Za 68*
(off Whitefield Av.)
Clare Rd. E11 ... 30Fc 53
NW10 ... 38Wa 68
SE14 ... 53Bc 114
SL6: Tap ... 4A 80
TW4: Houn ... 55Ba 107
TW19: Stanw ... 60M 105
UB6: G'frd ... 37Fa 66
Clares, The CR3: Cat'm ... 96Wb 197
Clare St. E2 ... 40Xb 71
Claret Gdns. SE25 ... 69Ub 135
Claret Ho. WD17: Wat ... 12X 27
Clareville Ct. SW7 ... 6A 226
Clareville Gro. SW7 ... 6A 226 (49Eb 89)
Clareville Gro. M. SW7 ... 6A 226 (49Eb 89)
Clareville Rd. BR5: Farnb ... 75Sc 160
CR3: Cat'm ... 96Wb 197
Clareville St. SW7 ... 6A 226 (49Eb 89)
Clare Way DA7: Bex ... 53Ad 117
TN13: S'oaks ... 100Ld 203
Clare Wood KT22: Lea ... 90Ka 172
Clarewood Ct. W1 ... 1F 221
Clarewood Wlk. SW9 ... 56Qb 112
Clarges M. W1 ... 6K 221 (46Kb 90)
Clarges St. W1 ... 6A 222 (46Kb 90)
Claribel Rd. SW9 ... 54Rb 113
Clarice Way SM6: Wall ... 81Nb 176
Claridge Ct. SW6 ... 54Bb 111
Claridge Rd. RM8: Dag ... 32Zc 75
Clarinda Ho. *DA9: Ghithe* ... *56Yd 120*
(off Clovelly Pl.)
Clarinet Ct. HA8: Edg ... 24Ra 47
Clarion Ho. *E3* ... *40Ac 72*
(off Roman Rd.)
SW1 ... 7C 228
W1 ... 3D 222
Clarissa Ho. *E14* ... *44Dc 92*
(off Cordelia St.)
Clarissa Rd. RM6: Chad H ... 31Zc 75
Clarissa St. E8 ... 39Vb 71
Clark Cl. DA8: Erith ... 53Jd 118
Clarkebourne Dr. RM17: Grays ... 51Fe 121
Clarke Cl. CR0: C'don ... 72Sb 157
Clarke Grn. WD25: Wat ... 7W 12
Clarke Mans. *IG11: Bark* ... *38Vc 75*
(off Upney La.)
Clarke M. N9 ... 20Xb 33
Clarke Path N16 ... 32Wb 71
Clarkes Av. KT4: Wor Pk ... 74Za 154
Clarkes Dr. UB8: Hil ... 43N 83
Clarke's Grn. Rd.
TN15: Knat ... 86Qd 183
Clarke's M. W1 ... 7J 215 (43Jb 90)
Clarke Way WD25: Wat ... 7W 12
Clarkfield WD3: Rick ... 18K 25
Clark Gro. IG3: Ilf ... 35Uc 74
Clark Ho. *SW10* ... *52Eb 111*
(off Coleridge Gdns.)

Clarks La. CM16: Epp 3Vc 23
RH8: T'sey 95Jc 199
TN14: Hals 84Bd 181
TN16: Tats, Westrm 95Jc 199
Clarks Mead WD23: Bush 17Ea 28
Clarkson Rd. E16 44Hc 93
Clarkson Row NW1 2B 216
Clarksons, The IG11: Bark 40Sc 74
Clarkson St. E2 41Xb 91
Clarks Rd. IG1: Ilf 33Tc 74
Clark St. E1 43Xb 91
(not continuous)
Clark Way TW5: Hest 52Z 107
Classic Mans. E9 38Xb 71
(off Wells St.)
Classon Cl. UB7: W Dray 47N 83
Claston Cl. DA1: Cray 56Gd 118
Claude Rd. E10 33Ec 72
E13 39Kc 73
SE15 54Xb 113
Claude St. E14 49Cc 92
Claudia Jones Ho. N17 25Sb 51
Claudia Jones Way SW2 58Nb 112
Claudian Pl. AL3: St A 3N 5
Claudian Way RM16: Grays 8D 100
Claudia Pl. SW19 60Ab 110
Claudius Cl. HA7: Stan 20Ma 29
Claughton Ct. AL4: St A 3G 6
Claughton Rd. E13 40Lc 73
Claughton Way CM13: Hut 16Fe 41
Clauson Av. UB5: N'olt 36Da 65
Clavell St. SE10 51Ec 114
Claverdale Rd. SW2 59Pb 112
Claver Dr. SL5: S'hill 10B 124
Claverhambury Rd. EN9: Walt A 1Jc 21
Clavering Av. SW13 51Xa 110
Clavering Cl. TW1: Twick 63Ja 130
Clavering Gdns. CM13: W H'dn 30Fe 59
Clavering Ho. SE13 56Fc 115
(off Blessington Rd.)
Clavering Pl. SW12 58Jb 112
Clavering Rd. E12 32Mc 73
Claverings Ind. Est. N9 19Yb 34
(off Centre Way)
Clavering Way CM13: Hut 16Ee 41
Claverley Gro. N3 25Db 49
Claverley Vs. N3 24Db 49
Claverton KT21: Asht 89Na 173
Claverton Cl. HP3: Bov 10C 2
Claverton St. SW1 7C 228 (50Lb 90)
Clave St. E1 46Yb 92
Claxton Gro. W6 50Za 88
Claxton Path SE4 56Zb 114
(off Coston Wlk.)
Clay Av. CR4: Mitc 68Kb 134
Claybank Gro. SE13 55Dc 114
Claybourne M. SE19 66Ub 135
Claybridge Rd. SE12 63Lc 137
Claybrook Cl. N2 27Fb 49
Claybrook Rd. W6 51Za 110
Clayburn Gdns. RM15: S Ock 45Xd 98
Claybury WD23: Bush 17Da 27
Claybury B'way. IG5: Ilf 27Nc 54
Claybury Hall IG8: Wfd G 24Pc 54
Claybury Rd. IG8: Wfd G 24Nc 54
Clay Cl. KT15: Add 78K 149
(off Monks Cres.)
Claycorn Ct. KT10: Clay 79Ga 152
Clay Cnr. KT16: Chert 74K 149
Clay Ct. E17 27Fc 53
SE1 3H 231
(off Long La.)
Claydon SE17 5D 230
Claydon Ct. TW18: Staines 63J 127
(off Kingston Rd.)
Claydon Dr. CR0: Bedd 77Nb 156
Claydon End SL9: Chal P 27A 42
Claydon Ho. NW4 26Za 48
(off Holders Hill Rd.)
Claydon La. SL9: Chal P 27A 42
Claydon Rd. GU21: Wok 8L 167
Claydown M. SE18 50Qc 94
Clayfarm Rd. SE9 61Sc 138
CLAYGATE 79Ha 152
Claygate Cl. RM12: Horn 35Jd 76
Claygate Common (Local Nature Reserve) 80Ha 152
Claygate Cres. CR0: New Ad 79Ec 158
CLAYGATE CROSS 96Ce 205
Claygate La. EN9: Walt A 2Ec 20
KT7: T Ditt 74Ja 152
KT10: Clay, Hin W 75Ja 152
Claygate Lodge Cl. KT10: Clay 80Ga 152
Claygate Rd. W13 48Ka 86
CLAYHALL 27Nc 54
Clayhall Av. IG5: Ilf 27Nc 54
Clayhall Ct. E3 40Bc 72
(off St Stephen's Rd.)
Clayhall Ho. RH2: Reig 5J 207
(off Somers Cl.)
Clayhall La. RH2: Reig 10F 206
SL4: Old Win 7K 103
CLAY HILL 9Sb 19
Clay Hill EN2: Enf 9Sb 19
Clayhill KT5: Surb 71Qa 153
Clayhill Cres. SE9 63Mc 137
Claylands Pl. SW8 52Qb 112
Claylands Rd. SW8 51Pb 112
Clay La. GU4: Burp, Jac W 10P 187
HA3: Kenton 28Ma 47
HA8: Edg 19Qa 29
KT18: Head 96Ra 193
RH1: S Nut 7C 208
TW19: Stanw 59P 105
WD23: B Hea 17Ga 28
Claymill Ho. SE18 50Sc 94
Claymills M. HP3: Hem H 5A 4
Claymore Cl. SM4: Mord 73Cb 155
Clay Path E17 26Cc 52
Claypit Hill
EN9: H Beech, Lough, Walt A 8Lc 21
Claypole Ct. E17 29Cc 52
(off Yunus Khan Cl.)
Claypole Dr. TW5: Hest 53Aa 107
Claypole Rd. E15 40Ec 72
Clayponds Av. TW8: Bford 49Ma 87
Clayponds Gdns. W5 49Ma 87
(not continuous)
Clayponds La. TW8: Bford 50Na 87
(not continuous)
Clay Ride IG10: Lough 11Mc 35
Clayside IG7: Chig 22Sc 54
Clay's La. IG10: Lough 11Qc 36
Clay St. W1 1G 221 (43Hb 89)
Clayton Av. HA0: Wemb 38Na 67
RM14: Upm 36Rd 77
Clayton Bus. Cen. UB3: Hayes 47U 84
Clayton Cl. E6 44Pc 94
Clayton Ct. SL3: L'ly 48C 82
Clayton Cres. N1 39Nb 70
TW8: Bford 50Ma 87
Clayton Cft. Rd. DA2: Wilm 61Jd 140
Clayton Dr. HP3: Hem H 4D 4
SE8 50Ac 92
Clayton Fld. NW9 24Ua 48
Clayton Ho. E9 38Yb 72
(off Frampton Pk. Rd.)
KT7: T Ditt 74Ka 152
SW13 52Ya 110
(off Trinity Church Rd.)
Clayton Mead RH9: G'stone 2P 209
Clayton M. SE10 53Fc 115
Clayton Pde. EN8: Chesh 2Zb 20
Clayton Rd. KT9: Chess 77La 152
KT17: Eps 84Ua 174
RM7: Rush G 32Ed 76
SE15 53Wb 113
TW7: Isle 55Ga 108
UB3: Hayes 47U 84
Clayton St. SE11 51Qb 112
Clayton Ter. UB4: Yead 43Aa 85
Claytonville Ter. DA17: Belv 47Ed 96
Clayton Way UB8: Cowl 42M 83
Clay Tye Rd. RM14: Upm 33Yd 78
Clay Wood Cl. BR6: Orp 73Uc 160
Claywood La. DA2: Bean 62Zd 143
Clayworth Cl. DA15: Sidc 58Xc 117
Cleall Av. EN9: Walt A 6Ec 20
Cleanthus Cl. SE18 53Rc 116
Cleanthus Rd. SE18 54Rc 116
(not continuous)
Clearbrook Way E1 44Yb 92
Cleardown GU22: Wok 90D 168
Cleares Pasture SL1: Burn 1A 80
Clears, The RH2: Reig 4G 206
Clears Cotts. RH2: Reig 4G 206
Clearwater Pl. KT6: Surb 72La 152
Clearwater Ter. W11 47Za 88
Clearwater Yd. NW1 39Kb 70
(off Inverness St.)
Clearway Ct. CR3: Cat'm 94Wb 197
Clearways Bus. Est.
TN15: W King 80Ud 164
Clearways Caravan Pk.
TN15: W King 80Td 164
Clearwell Dr. W9 42Db 89
Cleave Av. BR6: Chels 79Uc 160
UB3: Harl 49U 84
Cleaveland Rd. KT6: Surb 71Ma 153
Cleave Prior CR5: Chip 91Gb 195
Cleaverholme Cl. SE25 72Xb 157
Cleaver Ho. NW3 38Hb 69
(off Adelaide Rd.)
Cleaver Sq. SE11 7A 230 (50Qb 90)
Cleaver St. SE11 7A 230 (50Qb 90)
Cleaves Almshouses KT2: King T 68Na 131
(off London Rd.)
Cleeve Ct. TW14: Bedf 60U 106
Cleeve Hill SE23 60Xb 113
Cleeve Ho. E2 4J 219
Cleeve Pk. Gdns. DA14: Sidc 61Xc 139
Cleeve Rd. KT22: Lea 92Ha 192
Cleeves Ct. RH1: Redh 5A 208
(off St Anne's Mt.)
Cleeves Vw. DA1: Dart 58Md 119
(off Priory Pl.)
Cleeve Way SM1: Sutt 74Db 155
SW15 59Va 110
Cleeve Workshops E2 4J 219
Clegg Ho. SE3 56Kc 115
SE16 48Yb 92
(off Moodkee St.)
Clegg St. E1 46Xb 91
E13 40Jc 73
Cleland Ho. E2 40Yb 72
(off Sewardstone Rd.)
Cleland Path IG10: Lough 11Rc 36
Cleland Rd. SL9: Chal P 26A 42
Clematis Apartments E3 41Bc 92
(off Merchant St.)
Clematis Cl. RM3: Rom 24Ld 57
Clematis Gdns. IG8: Wfd G 22Jc 53
Clematis St. W12 45Wa 88
Clem Attlee Ct. SW6 51Bb 111
Clem Attlee Pde. SW6 51Bb 111
(off North End Rd.)
Clemence Rd. RM10: Dag 39Ed 76
Clemence St. E14 43Bc 92
Clement Av. SW4 56Mb 112
Clement Cl. CR8: Purl 88Rb 177
NW6 38Ya 68
W4 49Ta 87
Clement Danes Ho. W12 44Xa 88
Clement Gdns. UB3: Harl 49U 84
Clementhorpe Rd. RM9: Dag 37Yc 75
Clement Ho. SE8 49Ac 92
W10 43Ya 88
(off Dalgarno Gdns.)
Clementina Ct. E3 42Ac 92
(off Copperfield Rd.)
Clementina Rd. E10 32Bc 72
Clementine Cl. W13 47Ka 86
Clementine Wlk. IG8: Wfd G 24Jc 53
Clementine Way HP1: Hem H 4K 3
Clement Rd. BR3: Beck 68Zb 136
SW19 64Ab 132
Clement's Av. E16 45Jc 93
Clements Cl. N12 21Db 49
SL1: Slou 7M 81
Clements Ct. IG1: Ilf 34Rc 74
TW4: Houn 56Z 107
WD25: Wat 6Y 13
Clements Ho. KT22: Lea 91Ja 192
Clement's Inn WC2 3J 223 (44Pb 90)
Clement's Inn Pas. WC2 3J 223
Clements La. EC4 4G 225 (45Tb 91)
IG1: Ilf 34Rc 74
Clements Mead KT22: Lea 91Ja 192
Clements Pl. TW8: Bford 50Ma 87
Clements Rd. E6 38Nc 74
IG1: Ilf 34Rc 74
KT12: Walt T 75X 151
SE16 48Wb 91
WD3: Chor 15F 24
CLEMENT STREET 65Md 141
Clement St. BR8: Swan 65Md 141
DA4: Swan 65Md 141
Clement Way RM14: Upm 34Pd 77
Clemson Ho. E8 39Vb 71
Clemson M. KT17: Eps 84Va 174
Clenches Farm TN13: S'oaks 99Jd 202
Clenches Farm La. TN13: S'oaks 98Jd 202
Clenches Farm Rd.
TN13: S'oaks 98Jd 202
Clendon Way SE18 49Tc 94
Clennam St. SE1 1E 230 (47Sb 91)
Clensham Ct. SM1: Sutt 75Cb 155
Clensham La. SM1: Sutt 75Cb 155
Cleopatra Cl. HA7: Stan 20Ma 29
Cleopatra's Needle 6H 223 (46Nb 90)
Clephane Rd. N1 37Sb 71
Clephane Rd. Nth. N1 37Sb 71
Clephane Rd. Sth. N1 37Tb 71
Clere Pl. EC2 5G 219 (42Tb 91)
Clere St. EC2 5G 219 (42Tb 91)
Clerics Wlk. TW17: Shep 73T 150
CLERKENWELL 6A 218 (42Qb 90)
Clerkenwell Cl. EC1 5A 218 (42Qb 90)
(not continuous)
Clerkenwell Grn. EC1 6A 218 (42Qb 90)
Clerkenwell Rd. EC1 7K 217 (42Qb 90)
Clerks Cft. RH1: Blet 5K 209
Clerk's Piece IG10: Lough 13Pc 36
Clerk's Pl. EC2 2H 225 (44Ub 91)
Clermont Rd. E9 39Yb 72
Clevedon KT13: Weyb 78T 150
Clevedon Cl. N16 34Vb 71
Clevedon Ct. CR2: S Croy 78Ub 157
SW11 53Gb 111
(off Bolingbroke Wlk.)
Clevedon Gdns. TW5: Cran 53X 107
UB3: Harl 48T 84
Clevedon Ho. SM1: Sutt 77Eb 155
Clevedon Mans. NW5 35Jb 70
Clevedon Pas. N16 33Vb 71
Clevedon Rd. KT1: King T 68Qa 131
SE20 67Zb 136
TW1: Twick 58Ma 109
Cleve Ho. NW6 38Db 69
Clevehurst Cl. SL2: Stoke P 7L 61
Cleveland Av. SW20 68Bb 133
TW12: Hamp 66Ba 129
W4 49Va 88
Cleveland Cl. KT12: Walt T 76X 151
Cleveland Ct. W13 43Ka 86
Cleveland Cres. WD6: Bore 15Sa 29
Cleveland Dr. TW18: Staines 68K 127
Cleveland Gdns. KT4: Wor Pk 75Ua 154
N4 29Sb 51
NW2 33Za 68
SW13 54Va 110
W2 3A 220 (44Eb 89)
Cleveland Gro. E1 42Yb 92
Cleveland Ho. DA11: Nflt 58Fe 121
N2 26Fb 49
(off The Grange)
Cleveland Mans. NW6 38Bb 69
(off Willesden La.)
SW9 52Qb 112
(off Mowll St.)
W9 42Cb 89
Cleveland M. W1 7B 216 (43Lb 90)
Cleveland Pk. TW19: Stanw 58N 105
Cleveland Pk. Av. E17 28Cc 52
Cleveland Pk. Cres. E17 28Cc 52
Cleveland Pl. SW1 6C 222 (46Lb 90)
Cleveland Ri. SM4: Mord 73Za 154
Cleveland Rd. DA16: Well 54Vc 117
E18 27Jc 53
HP2: Hem H 1B 4
IG1: Ilf 34Rc 74
KT3: N Mald 70Ua 132
KT4: Wor Pk 75Ua 154
N1 38Tb 71
N9 17Xb 33
SW13 54Va 110
TW7: Isle 56Ja 108
UB8: Cowl, Uxb 42M 83
W4 48Sa 87
W13 43Ja 86
Cleveland Row SW1 7B 222 (46Lb 90)
Cleveland Sq. W2 3A 220 (44Eb 89)
Cleveland St. W1 6A 216 (42Kb 90)
Cleveland Ter. W2 3A 220 (44Eb 89)
Cleveland Way E1 42Yb 92
HP2: Hem H 1B 4
Cleveley Cl. SE7 49Mc 93
Cleveley Cres. W5 40Na 67
Cleveleys Rd. E5 34Xb 71
Cleve Pl. KT13: Weyb 78T 150
Cleverly Est. W12 46Wa 88
Cleve Rd. DA14: Sidc 62Zc 139
NW6 38Cb 69
Cleves Av. CM14: B'wood 18Xd 40
KT17: Ewe 81Xa 174
Cleves Cl. IG10: Lough 16Nc 36
KT11: Cobh 86X 171
Cleves Ct. DA1: Dart 59Nd 119
KT17: Eps 84Va 174
SL4: Wind 5D 102
Cleves Cres. CR0: New Ad 83Ec 178
Cleves Ho. E16 46Jc 93
(off Southey M.)
Cleves Rd. E6 39Mc 73
TN15: Kems'g 89Nd 183
TW10: Ham 62La 130
Cleves Wlk. IG6: Ilf 24Sc 54
Cleves Way HA4: Ruis 32Z 65
TW12: Hamp 66Ba 129
TW16: Sun 65V 128
Cleves Wood KT13: Weyb 77U 150
Clewer Av. SL4: Wind 4E 102
Clewer Ct. E10 32Cc 72
(off Leyton Grange Est.)
Clewer Ct. Rd. SL4: Wind 2F 102
Clewer Cres. HA3: Hrw W 25Fa 46
Clewer Flds. SL4: Wind 3G 102
CLEWER GREEN 4D 102
CLEWER HILL 5C 102
Clewer Hill Rd. SL4: Wind 4C 102
Clewer Ho. SE2 47Zc 95
(off Wolvercote Rd.)
CLEWER NEW TOWN 4E 102
Clewer New Town SL4: Wind 4E 102
Clewer Pk. SL4: Wind 2E 102
CLEWER ST ANDREW 2F 102
CLEWER ST STEPHEN 2F 102
CLEWER VILLAGE 2E 102
CLEWER WITHIN 3G 102
Clew's La. GU24: Bisl 8E 166
Cley Ho. SE4 56Zb 114
Clichy Est. E1 43Yb 92
Clichy Ho. E1 43Yb 92
(off Stepney Way)
Clifden M. E5 35Zb 72
Clifden Rd. E5 36Yb 72
TW1: Twick 60Ha 108
TW8: Bford 51Ma 109
Cliffe Ho. SE10 50Hc 93
(off Blackwall La.)
Cliff End CR8: Purl 84Rb 177
Cliffe Rd. CR2: S Croy 78Tb 157
Cliffe Wlk. SM1: Sutt 78Eb 155
(off Greyhound Rd.)
Clifford Av. BR7: Chst 65Pc 138
IG5: Ilf 25Rc 54
SM6: Wall 77Lb 156
SW14 55Ra 109
Clifford Cl. UB5: N'olt 39Aa 65
Clifford Ct. W2 43Db 89
(off Westbourne Pk. Vs.)
Clifford Dr. SW9 56Rb 113
Clifford Gdns. NW10 40Ya 68
UB3: Harl 49U 84
Clifford Gro. TW15: Ashf 63Q 128
Clifford Haigh Ho. SW6 52Za 110
Clifford Ho. BR3: Beck 65Dc 136
(off Calverley Cl.)
W14 49Bb 89
(off Edith Vs.)
Clifford Rd. E16 42Hc 93
E17 26Ec 52
EN5: New Bar 13Db 31
HA0: Wemb 38Ma 67
N1 39Ub 71
N9 16Yb 34
RM16: Chaf H 47Be 99
SE25 70Wb 135
TW4: Houn 55Z 107
TW10: Ham 61Ma 131
Clifford's Inn Pas. EC4 3K 223 (44Qb 90)
Clifford St. W1 5B 222 (45Lb 90)
Clifford Way NW10 35Va 68
Cliff Pl. RM15: S Ock 41Zd 99
Cliff Reach DA9: Bluew 58Vd 120
Cliff Rd. NW1 37Mb 70
Cliffsend Ho. SW9 53Qb 112
(off Cowley Rd.)
Cliff Ter. SE8 54Cc 114
Cliffview Rd. SE13 55Cc 114
Cliff Vs. NW1 37Mb 70
Cliff Wlk. E16 43Hc 93
Clifton Av. E17 27Zb 52
HA7: Stan 26Ka 46
HA9: Wemb 37Pa 67
N3 25Bb 49
SM2: Sutt 83Db 175
TW13: Felt 62Y 129
W12 46Va 88
Clifton Cl. BR6: Farnb 78Sc 160
CR3: Cat'm 95Tb 197
EN8: Chesh 1Ac 20
KT15: Add 75K 149
Clifton Ct. BR3: Beck 67Dc 136
HP3: Hem H 4M 3
IG8: Wfd G 23Jc 53
KT5: Surb 73Pa 153
KT19: Eps 84Pa 173
N4 33Qb 70
NW8 5B 214
SE15 52Xb 113
TW19: Stanw 58N 105
Clifton Cres. SE15 52Xb 113
Clifton Est. SE15 53Xb 113
Clifton Gdns. EN2: Enf 14Nb 32
N15 30Vb 51
NW11 30Bb 49
UB10: Hil 40R 64
W4 49Ta 87
(not continuous)
W9 6A 214 (42Eb 89)
Clifton Ga. SW10 51Eb 111
Clifton Gro. DA11: Grav'nd 9D 122
E8 37Wb 71
Clifton Hill NW8 1A 214 (40Db 69)
Clifton Hill Studios NW8 40Eb 69
Clifton Ho. E2 5K 219
E11 33Gc 73
Clifton Lodge SL4: Eton W 10E 80
Clifton Marine Pde.
DA11: Nflt, Grav'nd 8B 122
Clifton M. SE25 70Ub 135
Clifton Pde. TW13: Felt 62Y 129
Clifton Pk. Av. SW20 68Ya 132
Clifton Pl. SE16 47Yb 92
SM7: Bans 87Cb 175
SW10 51Eb 111
(off Hollywood Rd.)
W2 3C 220 (44Fb 89)
Clifton Ri. SE14 52Ac 114
(not continuous)
SL4: Wind 3B 102
Clifton Rd. CR5: Coul 87Kb 176
DA11: Grav'nd 8C 122
DA14: Sidc 63Uc 138
DA16: Well 55Yc 117
E7 37Mc 73
E16 43Gc 93
HA3: Kenton 28Pa 47
IG2: Ilf 30Tc 54
IG10: Lough 14Nc 36
KT2: King T 66Pa 131
N1 37Sb 71
N3 25Eb 49
N8 30Mb 50
N22 25Lb 50
NW10 40Wa 68
RM11: Horn 30Jd 56
SE25 70Ub 135
SL1: Slou 7M 81
SM6: Wall 78Kb 156
SW19 65Za 132
TW7: Isle 54Ga 108
TW11: Tedd 63Ga 130
UB2: S'hall 49Aa 85
UB6: G'frd 42Ea 86
W9 5A 214 (42Eb 89)
WD18: Wat 15X 27
Clifton's La. RH2: Reig 4F 206
Clifton St. AL1: St A 1C 6
EC2 6H 219 (42Ub 91)
Clifton Ter. N4 33Qb 70
Clifton Vs. W9 43Eb 89
Cliftonville Ct. SE12 60Jc 115
Clifton Wlk. DA2: Dart 58Rd 119
W6 49Xa 88
(off King St.)
Clifton Way CM13: Hut 18Fe 41
GU21: Wok 9K 167
HA0: Wemb 39Na 67
SE15 52Xb 113
TW6: H'row A 55Q 106
WD6: Bore 11Qa 29
Climb, The WD3: Rick 16K 25
Climsland Ho. SE1 6A 224 (46Qb 90)
Cline Rd. N11 23Lb 50
Clinger Ct. N1 1H 219
Clink Prison Mus. 6F 225
Clink St. SE1 6E 224 (46Tb 91)
Clink Wharf SE1 6F 225
Clinton Av. DA16: Well 56Wc 117
KT8: E Mos 70Ea 130
Clinton Cl. GU21: Knap 10H 167
KT13: Weyb 75R 150
Clinton Cres. IG6: Ilf 23Uc 54
Clinton End HP2: Hem H 2C 4
Clinton Ho. KT6: Surb 73Ma 153
(off Lovelace Gdns)
Clinton Rd. E3 41Ac 92
E7 35Jc 73
KT22: Lea 95La 192
N15 28Tb 51
Clinton Ter. SE8 51Cc 114
(off Watergate St.)
Clipper Apartments SE10 51Ec 114
(off Welland St.)
Clipper Blvd. DA2: Dart 55Ud 120
Clipper Blvd. W. DA2: Dart 55Td 120
Clipper Cl. SE16 47Zb 92
Clipper Cres. DA12: Grav'nd 3H 145
Clipper Ho. E14 50Ec 92
(off Manchester Rd.)
Clipper Pk. RM18: Tilb 52Fe 121
Clipper Way SE13 56Ec 114
Clippesby Cl. KT9: Chess 79Pa 153
Clipstone M. W1 7B 216 (43Lb 90)
Clipstone Rd. TW3: Houn 55Ca 107
Clipstone St. W1 7A 216 (43Kb 90)
Clissold Cl. N2 27Hb 49
Clissold Ct. N4 33Sb 71
Clissold Cres. N16 34Tb 71
Clissold Leisure Cen. 34Tb 71
Clissold Rd. N16 34Tb 71
Clitheroe Av. HA2: Harr 32Ca 65
Clitheroe Gdns. WD19: Wat 20Z 27
Clitheroe Rd. RM5: Col R 22Ed 56
SW9 54Nb 112
Clitherow Av. W7 48Ja 86
Clitherow Ct. TW8: Bford 50La 86
Clitherow Pas. TW8: Bford 50La 86
Clitherow Rd. TW8: Bford 50Ka 86
Clitterhouse Cres. NW2 32Ya 68
Clitterhouse Rd. NW2 32Ya 68
Clive Av. DA1: Cray 58Hd 118
N18 23Wb 51
Clive Cl. EN6: Pot B 3Bb 17
Clive Ct. SL1: Slou 7H 81
W9 5A 214 (42Eb 89)
Cliveden Cl. CM15: Shenf 17Be 41
N12 21Eb 49
Cliveden Ho. E16 46Jc 93
(off Fitzwilliam M.)
SW1 5H 227
Cliveden Pl. SW1 5H 227 (49Jb 90)
TW17: Shep 72S 150
Cliveden Rd. SW19 67Bb 133
Clivedon Ct. W13 43Ka 86
Clivedon Rd. E4 22Gc 53
Clive Ho. SE10 51Ec 114
(off Haddo St.)
Clive Lloyd Ho. N15 29Sb 51
(off Woodlands Pk. Rd.)
Clive Lodge NW4 30Za 48
Clive Pde. HA6: Nwood 24U 44
Clive Pas. SE21 62Tb 135
Clive Rd. CM13: Gt War 24Yd 58
DA11: Grav'nd 8D 122
DA17: Belv 49Cd 96
EN1: Enf 14Wb 33
KT10: Esh 77Da 151
RM2: Rom 29Kd 57
SE21 62Tb 135
SW19 65Gb 133
TW1: Twick 63Ha 130
TW14: Felt 58W 106
Clivesdale Dr. UB3: Hayes 46X 85
Clive Way EN1: Enf 14Wb 33
WD24: Wat 11Y 27
Cloak La. EC4 4E 224 (45Sb 91)
Clochar Ct. NW10 39Va 68
Clock Ct. E11 28Kc 53
CLOCK HOUSE 86Kb 176
Clock Ho. E3 41Ec 92
E17 28Fc 53
(off Wood St.)
Clockhouse, The SW19 62Ya 132
Clockhouse Av. IG11: Bark 39Sc 74
Clock Ho. Cl. KT14: Byfl 84P 169
Clockhouse Cl. SW19 61Ya 132
Clockhouse Ct. BR3: Beck 68Ac 136
CLOCKHOUSE JUNC. 22Pb 50
Clock Ho. La. TN13: S'oaks 95Jd 202
(not continuous)
Clockhouse La. RM4: Have B 21Dd 56
RM5: Col R 24Dd 56
RM16: Chaf H, N Stif 46Zd 99
(not continuous)
TW14: Bedf 63Q 128
TW15: Ashf 63Q 128
Clockhouse La. E. TW20: Egh 66D 126
Clockhouse La. W. TW20: Egh 66C 126
Clock Ho. Mead KT22: Oxs 86Da 171
Clockhouse M. WD3: Chor 13G 24
Clock Ho. Pde. E11 30Kc 53
Clockhouse Pde. N13 22Qb 50
Clockhouse Pl. SW15 58Ab 110
Clock Ho. Rd. BR3: Beck 69Ac 136
CLOCKHOUSE RDBT. 60R 106
Clockhouse Stables DA2: Grn St 65Wd 142
Clock Museum, The 2E 224
Clock Pde. EN2: Enf 15Tb 33
Clock Pl. SE1 5C 230
Clock Twr. CM14: W'ley 22Xd 58
Clock Tower, The AL2: Lon C 9F 6
Clock Twr. Ind. Est. TW7: Isle 55Ha 108
Clock Twr. M. N1 1E 218 (39Sb 71)
SE28 45Xc 95
W7 46Ga 86
Clock Twr. Pl. N7 37Nb 70
(off Market Est.)
Clock Twr. Rd. TW7: Isle 55Ha 108
Clock Vw. Cres. N7 37Nb 70
Clodhouse Hill GU22: Wok 4H 187
Cloister Cl. RM13: Rain 42Kd 97
TW11: Tedd 64Ka 130
Cloister Gdns. HA8: Edg 22Sa 47
SE25 72Xb 157
Cloister Gth. AL1: St A 6C 6
Cloister Rd. NW2 34Bb 69
W3 43Sa 87

Cloisters, The ... 3F 229
Cloisters SS17: Stan H ... 1N 101
Cloisters, The *DA1: Dart* ... *58Nd 119*
(off Orchard St.)
E1 ... 7K 219
GU22: Wok ... 93D 188
HP3: Hem H ... 5A 4
SL1: Slou ... *7H 81*
(off Henry Rd.)
SL4: Wind ... 4E 102
SW9 ... 53Qb 112
TW7: Isle ... *55Ja 108*
(off Pulteney Cl.)
WD3: Rick ... 17N 25
WD4: K Lan ... 1Q 12
WD18: Wat ... 14Y 27
WD23: Bush ... 16Da 27
Cloisters Av. BR2: Brom ... 71Pc 160
Cloisters Bus. Cen. *SW8* ... *52Kb 112*
(off Battersea Pk. Rd.)
Cloisters Ct. DA7: Bex ... 55Dd 118
WD3: Rick ... 17N 25
Cloisters Mall KT1: King T ... 68Na 131
Clonard Way HA5: Hat E ... 23Ca 45
Clonbrock Rd. N16 ... 35Ub 71
Cloncurry St. SW6 ... 54Za 110
Clonmel Cl. HA2: Harr ... 33Fa 65
Clonmell Rd. N17 ... 27Tb 51
Clonmel Rd. SW6 ... 52Bb 111
TW11: Tedd ... 63Fa 130
Clonmel Way SL1: Burn ... 1A 80
Clonmore St. SW18 ... 60Bb 111
Cloonmore Av. BR6: Chels ... 77Vc 161
Clorane Gdns. NW3 ... 34Cb 69
Close, The AL1: St A ... 5A 6
AL9: Brk P ... 8G 8
BR3: Beck ... 70Ac 136
BR5: Pet W ... 72Uc 160
CM14: B'wood ... 20Zd 41
CR4: Mitc ... 70Hb 133
CR8: Purl ... 82Pb 176
(Russell Hill)
CR8: Purl ... 82Rb 177
(Wyvern Rd.)
DA2: Wilm ... 62Ld 141
DA3: Lfield ... 68De 143
DA5: Bexl ... 58Cd 118
DA14: Sidc ... 63Xc 139
E4 ... 24Ec 52
EN4: E Barn ... 16Hb 31
EN6: Pot B ... 4Cb 17
GU25: Vir W ... 1P 147
HA0: Wemb ... 37Na 67
HA2: Harr ... 26Ea 46
HA5: Eastc ... 31Y 65
HA5: Pinn ... 31Ba 65
HA9: Wemb ... 34Sa 67
IG2: Ilf ... 30Uc 54
KT3: N Mald ... 68Sa 131
KT6: Surb ... 72Na 153
KT10: Esh ... 79Da 151
KT12: Hers ... 78W 150
KT14: W Byf ... 85J 169
N10 ... 26Kb 50
N14 ... 19Mb 32
N20 ... 19Bb 31
RH2: Reig ... 7K 207
RM6: Chad H ... 30Ad 55
RM16: Grays ... 47Ee 99
SE3 ... 54Fc 115
SE25 ... 72Wb 157
SL0: Iver H ... 41E 82
SL1: Slou ... 5B 80
SM3: Sutt ... 73Bb 155
SM5: Cars ... 81Gb 175
TN13: S'oaks ... 96Gd 202
TN15: Bor G ... 91Ce 205
TN15: Igh ... 93Zd 205
TN16: Big H ... 88Rc 180
TW7: Isle ... 54Fa 108
TW9: Rich ... 55Ra 109
UB10: Hil ... 39Q 64
WD3: Rick ... 18K 25
WD7: R'lett ... 5Ha 14
WD23: Bush ... 16Da 27
Closemead Cl. HA6: Nwood ... 23S 44
Cloth Ct. EC1 ... 1C 224
Cloth Fair EC1 ... 1C 224 (43Rb 91)
Clothier St. E1 ... 2J 225 (44Ub 91)
Cloth St. EC1 ... 7D 218 (43Sb 91)
Clothworkers Rd. SE18 ... 52Tc 116
Cloudberry Rd. RM3: Rom ... 23Md 57
Cloudesdale Rd. SW17 ... 61Kb 134
Cloudesley Cl. DA14: Sidc ... 63Vc 139
Cloudesley Mans. N1 ... 1K 217
Cloudesley Pl. N1 ... 1K 217 (39Qb 70)
Cloudesley Rd. DA7: Bex ... 53Bd 117
DA8: Erith ... 53Hd 118
N1 ... 1K 217 (39Qb 70)
(not continuous)
Cloudesley Sq. N1 ... 39Qb 70
Cloudesley St. N1 ... 1A 218 (39Qb 70)
Clouston Cl. SM6: Wall ... 78Nb 156
Clova Rd. E7 ... 37Hc 73
Clove Cres. E14 ... 45Ec 92
Clove Hitch Quay SW11 ... 55Eb 111
Clovelly Av. CR6: W'ham ... 91Xb 197
NW9 ... 28Va 48
UB10: Ick ... 35S 64
Clovelly Cl. HA5: Eastc ... 27X 45
UB10: Ick ... 35S 64
Clovelly Ct. *KT17: Eps* ... *85Va 174*
(off Alexandra Rd.)
NW2 ... 36Ya 68
RM11: Horn ... 33Qd 77
Clovelly Gdns. EN1: Enf ... 17Ub 33
RM7: Mawney ... 25Dd 56
SE19 ... 67Vb 135
Clovelly Ho. W2 ... 2A 220
Clovelly Pl. DA9: Ghithe ... 56Yd 120
Clovelly Rd. DA7: Bex ... 51Ad 117
N8 ... 28Mb 50
TW3: Houn ... 54Ca 107
W4 ... 47Ta 87
W5 ... 47La 86
Clovelly Way BR6: St M Cry ... 72Vc 161
E1 ... 44Yb 92
HA2: Harr ... 33Ba 65
Clover Cl. E11 ... 33Fc 73
Clover Ct. GU22: Wok ... 10P 167
RM17: Grays ... 51Fe 121
Cloverdale Ct. SM6: Wall ... 79Kb 156
Cloverdale Gdns. DA15: Sidc ... 58Vc 117
Clover Field, The WD23: Bush ... 16Ba 27
Clover Hill CR5: Coul ... 93Kb 196
Cloverland AL10: Hat ... 3B 8
Clover Leas CM16: Epp ... 1Vc 23
Cloverleys IG10: Lough ... 15Mc 35
Clover M. SW3 ... 51Hb 111
Clovers, The DA11: Nflt ... 3A 144
Clover Way HP1: Hem H ... 1K 3
SM6: Wall ... 74Jb 156
Clove St. E13 ... 42Jc 93
Clowders Rd. SE6 ... 62Bc 136
Clowser Cl. SM1: Sutt ... 78Eb 155
Cloysters Grn. E1 ... 46Wb 91
Cloyster Wood HA8: Edg ... 24Ma 47
Club Gdns. Rd. BR2: Hayes ... 73Jc 159
Club Row E1 ... 5K 219 (42Vb 91)
E2 ... 5K 219 (42Vb 91)
GU24: Brkwd ... 1B 186
Cluff Ct. CM14: W'ley ... 21Yd 58
Clump, The WD3: Rick ... 15J 25
Clumps, The TW15: Ashf ... 63T 128
Clunas Gdns. RM2: Rom ... 27Md 57
Clunbury Av. UB2: S'hall ... 50Ba 85
Clunbury St. N1 ... 2G 219 (40Tb 71)
Clune Ct. CM15: Shenf ... 17Ce 41
Clunie Ho. SW1 ... 3G 227
Cluny Est. SE1 ... 3H 231 (48Ub 91)
Cluny M. SW5 ... 49Cb 89
Cluny Pl. SE1 ... 3H 231 (48Ub 91)
Cluse Ct. N1 ... 1D 218
(not continuous)
Clutterbucks WD3: Sarr ... 8J 11
Clutton St. E14 ... 43Dc 92
Clydach Rd. EN1: Enf ... 14Vb 33
Clyde RM18: E Til ... 9L 101
Clyde Av. CR2: Sande ... 87Xb 177
Clyde Cir. N15 ... 28Ub 51
Clyde Cl. RH1: Redh ... 5A 208
Clyde Ct. NW1 ... 1E 216
Clyde Cres. RM14: Upm ... 30Ud 58
Clyde Flats *SW6* ... *52Bb 111*
(off Rhylston Rd.)
Clyde Ho. KT2: King T ... 67Ma 131
Clyde Pl. E10 ... 31Dc 72
Clyde Rd. CR0: C'don ... 75Vb 157
N15 ... 28Ub 51
N22 ... 25Mb 50
SM1: Sutt ... 78Cb 155
SM6: Wall ... 79Lb 156
TW19: Stanw ... 60M 105
Clydesdale EN3: Pond E ... 14Zb 34
Clydesdale Av. HA7: Stan ... 27Ma 47
Clydesdale Cl. TW7: Isle ... 55Ha 108
WD6: Bore ... 15Ta 29
Clydesdale Ct. N20 ... 18Fb 31
Clydesdale Gdns. TW10: Rich ... 56Ra 109
Clydesdale Ho. *DA18: Erith* ... *47Ad 95*
(off Kale Rd.)
W11 ... *44Bb 89*
(off Clydesdale Rd.)
Clydesdale Path *WD6: Bore* ... *15Ta 29*
(off Clydesdale Cl.)
Clydesdale Rd. RM11: Horn ... 31Hd 76
W11 ... 44Bb 89
Clyde St. SE8 ... 51Bc 114
Clyde Ter. SE23 ... 61Yb 136
Clyde Va. SE23 ... 61Yb 136
Clyde Way RM1: Rom ... 24Gd 56
Clyde Wharf E16 ... 46Jc 93
Clydon Cl. DA8: Erith ... 51Gd 118
Clyfford Rd. HA4: Ruis ... 35V 64
Clymping Dene TW14: Felt ... 59X 107
Clynes Ho. *E2* ... *41Zb 92*
(off Knottisford St.)
RM10: Dag ... *34Cd 76*
(off Uvedale Rd.)
Clyston Rd. WD18: Wat ... 16V 26
Clyston St. SW8 ... 54Lb 112
Clyve Way TW18: Staines ... 67G 126
Coach & Horses Yd. W1 ... 4A 222 (45Lb 90)
Coach Ho. La. N5 ... 35Rb 71
SW19 ... 63Za 132
Coach Ho. M. KT12: W Vill ... 81U 170
RH1: Redh ... 7P 207
SE1 ... 3H 231
SE23 ... 58Zb 114
SM2: Sutt ... 79Db 155
Coachhouse M. SE20 ... 66Xb 135
Coach Ho. Yd. *NW3* ... *35Eb 69*
(off Heath St.)
SW18 ... 56Db 111
Coachmaker M. *SW4* ... *55Nb 112*
(off Bedford Rd.)
W4 ... *48Ta 87*
(off Berrymede Rd.)
Coachmans Lodge *SL4: Wind* ... *4H 103*
(off Frances Rd.)
Coach M. AL1: St A ... 2F 6
Coach Rd. KT16: Ott ... 79E 148
TN15: Igh, Ivy H ... 96Wd 204
Coach Yd. M. N19 ... 32Nb 70
Coal Ct. RM17: Grays ... 52Ce 121
Coaldale Wlk. SE21 ... 59Sb 113
Coalecroft Rd. SW15 ... 56Ya 110
Coales Hall *AL10: Hat* ... *2B 8*
(off Bishops Ri.)
Coalhouse Fort ... 3M 123
Coalport Ho. SE11 ... 5K 229
Coal Post Cl. BR6: Chels ... 79Vc 161
Coal Rd. RM18: E Til, W Til ... 9H 101
Coalstore Ct. E1 ... 43Ac 92
Coatbridge Ho. *N1* ... *38Pb 70*
(off Carnoustie Dr.)
Coates Av. SW18 ... 58Gb 111
Coates Cl. CR7: Thor H ... 69Sb 135
Coates Dell WD25: Wat ... 5Aa 13
Coates Hill Rd. BR1: Brom ... 68Qc 138
Coates Rd. WD6: E'tree ... 17Ma 29
Coate St. E2 ... 40Wb 71
Coates Wlk. TW8: Bford ... 51Na 109
Coates Way WD25: Wat ... 4Z 13
Cobalt SE28 ... 47Wc 95
Cobalt Building, The EC2 ... 6D 218
Cobalt Cl. BR3: Beck ... 70Zb 136
Cobalt Sq. *SW8* ... *51Pb 112*
(off Sth. Lambeth Rd.)
Cobb Cl. SL3: Dat ... 3P 103
WD6: Bore ... 15Ta 29
Cobbett Cl. EN3: Enf W ... 8Yb 20
Cobbett Hill Rd. GU3: Norm ... 10C 186
Cobbett Rd. SE9 ... 55Nc 116
TW2: Whitt ... 60Ca 107
Cobbetts Av. IG4: Ilf ... 29Mc 53
Cobbetts Cl. GU3: Norm ... 10D 186
GU21: Wok ... 9M 167
Cobbetts Hill KT13: Weyb ... 79R 150
Cobbett St. SW8 ... 52Pb 112
Cobbetts Wlk. GU24: Bisl ... 7E 166
Cobb Grn. WD25: Wat ... 4X 13
Cobbins, The EN9: Walt A ... 5Gc 21
Cobbinsbank EN9: Walt A ... 5Fc 21
Cobbinsend Rd. EN9: Walt A ... 1Mc 21
Cobble La. N1 ... 38Rb 71
Cobble M. N5 ... 34Sb 71
N6 ... *32Jb 70*
(off Highgate W. Hill)
Cobblers Cl. SL2: Farn R ... 10F 60
Cobblers Wlk. KT1: Hamp W ... 67Ja 130
KT8: E Mos ... 67Ja 130
TW11: Tedd ... 67Ja 130
TW12: Hamp ... 67Ea 130
Cobbles, The CM15: B'wood ... 19Ae 41
RM14: Upm ... 31Vd 78
Cobblestone Pl. CR0: C'don ... 74Sb 157
Cobbold Ct. SW1 ... 5D 228
Cobbold Ind. Est. NW10 ... 37Va 68
Cobbold M. W12 ... 47Va 88
Cobbold Rd. E11 ... 34Hc 73
NW10 ... 37Va 68
W12 ... 47Ua 88
Cobb's Ct. EC4 ... 3C 224
Cobb's Hall *SW6* ... *51Za 110*
(off Fulham Pal. Rd.)
Cobb's Rd. TW4: Houn ... 56Ba 107
Cobbsthorpe Vs. SE26 ... 63Zb 136
Cobb St. E1 ... 1K 225 (43Vb 91)
Cobden Bldgs. WC1 ... 3H 217
Cobden Cl. UB8: Uxb ... 39L 63
Cobden Ct. BR2: Brom ... 70Lc 137
Cobden Hill WD7: R'lett ... 8Ka 14
Cobden Ho. *E2* ... *41Wb 91*
(off Nelson Gdns.)
NW1 ... 1B 216
Cobden M. SE26 ... 64Xb 135
Cobden Rd. BR6: Farnb ... 77Tc 160
E11 ... 34Gc 73
SE25 ... 71Wb 157
TN13: S'oaks ... 95Ld 203
Cobdens IG7: Chig ... 23Tc 54
Cob Dr. DA12: Shorne ... 4N 145
COBHAM
DA12 ... 10J 145
KT11 ... 86X 171
Cobham RM16: Grays ... 47De 99
Cobham Av. KT3: N Mald ... 71Wa 154
Cobhambury Rd. DA12: Cobh ... 10J 145
Cobham Bus Mus. ... 84S 170
Cobham Cl. BR2: Brom ... 73Nc 160
DA9: Ghithe ... 58Xd 120
DA15: Sidc ... 58Xc 117
EN1: Enf ... 13Wb 33
HA8: Edg ... 26Ra 47
SL1: Slou ... 7D 80
SM6: Wall ... 79Nb 156
SW11 ... 58Gb 111
Cobham Ct. CR4: Mitc ... 68Fb 133
Cobham Ga. KT11: Cobh ... 86X 171
Cobham Grange *KT11: Cobh* ... *86X 171*
(off Between Streets)
Cobham Ho. DA8: Erith ... 52Hd 118
IG11: Bark ... 39Sc 74
Cobham M. NW1 ... 38Mb 70
Cobham Mill ... 87Y 171
Cobham Pk. KT11: D'side ... 88X 171
Cobham Pk. Rd. KT11: D'side ... 89X 171
Cobham Pl. DA6: Bex ... 57Ad 117
Cobham Rd. E17 ... 25Ec 52
IG3: Ilf ... 33Uc 74
KT1: King T ... 68Qa 131
KT11: Stoke D ... 90Ca 171
KT22: Fet ... 90Ca 171
N22 ... 27Rb 51
TW5: Hest ... 52Y 107
Cobham St. DA11: Grav'nd ... 9C 122
Cobham Ter. DA9: Ghithe ... 57Xd 120
DA11: Nflt ... *10B 122*
(off Southfleet Rd.)
Cobham Way KT24: E Hor ... 98U 190
Cobill Cl. RM11: Horn ... 28Ld 57
Cobland Rd. SE12 ... 63Lc 137
Coborn M. *E3* ... *41Bc 92*
(off Coborn St.)
Coborn Rd. E3 ... 40Bc 72
Coborn St. E3 ... 41Bc 92
Cobourg Rd. SE5 ... 7K 231 (51Vb 113)
Cobourg St. NW1 ... 4C 216 (41Lb 90)
Cobs Cl. TN15: Igh ... 93Yd 204
Cobsdene DA12: Grav'nd ... 5F 144
Cobs Way KT15: New H ... 82L 169
Coburg Cl. SW1 ... 5C 228 (49Lb 90)
Coburg Cres. SW2 ... 60Pb 112
Coburg Dwellings *E1* ... *44Yb 92*
(off Hardinge St.)
Coburg Gdns. IG5: Ilf ... 26Mc 53
Coburg Rd. N22 ... 27Pb 50
Cochrane Cl. NW8 ... 2C 214
Cochrane Ct. *E10* ... *32Cc 72*
(off Leyton Grange Est.)
Cochrane Dr. DA1: Dart ... 58Md 119
Cochrane Ho. *E14* ... *47Cc 92*
(off Admirals Way)
UB8: Uxb ... 39L 63
Cochrane M. NW8 ... 2C 214 (40Fb 69)
Cochrane Pl. GU20: W'sham ... 8B 146
Cochrane Rd. SW19 ... 66Ab 132
Cochrane St. NW8 ... 2C 214 (40Fb 69)
Cochrane Theatre ... 1G 223
Cockabourne Ct. *RM3: Hrld W* ... *26Qd 57*
(off Archibald Rd.)
Cockburn Ho. *SW1* ... *50Mb 90*
(off Aylesford St.)
COCKCROW HILL ... 74Ma 153
Cockerell Rd. E17 ... 31Ac 72
Cockerhurst Rd. TN14: S'ham ... 79Fd 162
Cocker Rd. EN1: Enf ... 8Xb 19
Cockett Rd. SL3: L'ly ... 48A 82
COCKFOSTERS ... 14Hb 31
Cockfosters Pde. EN4: Cockf ... 14Jb 32
Cockfosters Rd.
EN4: Cockf, Had W ... 10Gb 17
Cock Hill E1 ... 1J 225 (43Ub 91)
Cock La. EC1 ... 1B 224 (43Rb 91)
KT22: Fet ... 94Ea 192
Cockle Way WD7: Shenl ... 5Na 15
Cockmannings La. BR5: St M Cry ... 74Zc 161
Cockmannings Rd. BR5: St M Cry ... 73Zc 161
Cockpit Steps SW1 ... 2E 228
Cockpit Theatre ... 6D 214
Cockpit Yd. WC1 ... 7J 217 (43Pb 90)
Cocks Cres. KT3: N Mald ... 70Va 132
Cocksett Av. BR6: Chels ... 79Uc 160
Cockshot Hill RH2: Reig ... 7K 207
Cockshot Rd. RH2: Reig ... 7K 207
Cockspur Ct. SW1 ... 6E 222 (46Mb 90)
Cockspur St. SW1 ... 6E 222 (46Mb 90)
Cocksure La. DA14: Sidc ... 62Cd 140
Cock's Yd. *UB8: Uxb* ... *38M 63*
(off High St.)
Coda Centre, The SW6 ... 52Ab 110
Code St. E1 ... 42Vb 91
Codham Hall La. CM13: Gt War ... 29Xd 58
Codicote Dr. WD25: Wat ... 6Z 13
Codicote Ho. *SE8* ... *49Zb 92*
(off Chilton Gro.)
Codicote Ter. N4 ... 33Sb 71
Codling Cl. E1 ... 46Wb 91
Codling Way HA0: Wemb ... 35Ma 67
Codmore Wood Rd. HP5: Lat ... 5A 10
Codrington Ct. E1 ... 42Xb 91
GU21: Wok ... 10K 167
SE16 ... 45Ac 92
Codrington Cres. DA12: Grav'nd ... 4E 144
Codrington Gdns. DA12: Grav'nd ... 4F 144
(not continuous)
Codrington Hill SE23 ... 59Ac 114
Codrington M. W11 ... 44Ab 88
Cody Cl. HA3: Kenton ... 27Ma 47
SM6: Wall ... 80Mb 156
Cody Rd. E16 ... 42Fc 93
Coe Av. SE25 ... 72Wb 157
Coe's All. EN5: Barn ... 14Ab 30
Coe Spur SL1: Slou ... 7F 80
Coffey St. SE8 ... 52Cc 114
Coftards SL2: Slou ... 4N 81
Cogan Av. E17 ... 25Ac 52
Cohen Cl. EN8: Chesh ... 3Ac 20
Coin St. SE1 ... 6K 223 (46Qb 90)
(not continuous)
Coity Rd. NW5 ... 37Jb 70
Cokers La. SE21 ... 60Tb 113
Coke St. E1 ... 44Wb 91
Colas M. NW6 ... 39Cb 69
Colbeck M. SW7 ... 49Db 89
Colbeck Rd. HA1: Harr ... 31Ea 66
Colberg Pl. N16 ... 31Vb 71
Colbert *SE5* ... *53Ub 113*
(off Sceaux Gdns.)
Colborne Ho. *E14* ... *45Cc 92*
(off E. India Dock Rd.)
WD18: Wat ... 16U 26
Colborne Way KT4: Wor Pk ... 76Ya 154
Colbrook Av. UB3: Harl ... 48T 84
Colbrook Cl. UB3: Harl ... 48T 84
Colburn Av. CR3: Cat'm ... 96Vb 197
HA5: Hat E ... 23Aa 45
Colburn Way SM1: Sutt ... 76Fb 155
Colby M. SE19 ... 64Ub 135
Colby Rd. KT12: Walt T ... 74W 150
SE19 ... 64Ub 135
Colchester Av. E12 ... 35Pc 74
Colchester Dr. HA5: Pinn ... 29Z 45
Colchester Ho. *E3* ... *39Bc 72*
(off Parnell Rd.)
Colchester Rd. CM14: B'wood ... 25Md 57
E10 ... 31Ec 72
E17 ... 30Cc 52
HA6: Nwood ... 26W 44
HA8: Edg ... 24Sa 47
RM3: Hrld W, Rom ... 25Md 57
Colclough Ct. *CR0: C'don* ... *72Sb 157*
(off Simpson Cl.)
Colcokes Rd. SM7: Bans ... 88Cb 175
Cold Arbor Rd. TN13: Bes G ... 96Fd 202
Coldart Bus. Cen. DA1: Dart ... 58Md 119
Coldbath Sq. EC1 ... 5K 217 (42Qb 90)
Coldbath St. SE13 ... 53Dc 114
COLDBLOW ... 60Ed 118
Cold Blow Cres. DA5: Bexl ... 60Fd 118
Cold Blow La. SE14 ... 52Zb 114
(not continuous)
Cold Blows CR4: Mitc ... 69Hb 133
Coldershaw Rd. W13 ... 46Ja 86
Coldfall Av. N10 ... 26Jb 50
Coldham Ct. N22 ... 25Rb 51
Coldham Gro. EN3: Enf W ... 9Ac 20
Coldharbour E14 ... 47Ec 92
Coldharbour Cl. TW20: Thorpe ... 69E 126
Coldharbour Crest SE9 ... 62Qc 138
Coldharbour Ho. WD25: Wat ... 8Aa 13
Coldharbour Ind. Est. SE5 ... 54Sb 113
Coldharbour La. CR8: Purl ... 83Qb 176
GU22: Pyr ... 87H 169
GU24: W End ... 3D 166
RH1: Blet ... 6M 209
RM13: Rain ... 44Gd 96
RM19: Purf ... 49Kd 97
SE5 ... 55Sb 113
SW9 ... 56Qb 112
TW20: Thorpe ... 69E 126
UB3: Hayes ... 46W 84
WD23: Bush ... 16Da 27
Coldharbour Leisure Cen. ... 61Pc 138
Coldharbour Pl. SE5 ... 54Sb 113
Coldharbour Rd. CR0: Wadd ... 78Qb 156
DA11: Nflt ... 1A 144
GU22: Pyr ... 87H 169
KT14: W Byf ... 86H 169
Coldharbour Way CR0: Wadd ... 78Qb 156
Coldshott RH8: Oxt ... 5L 211
Coldstream Gdns. SW18 ... 58Bb 111
Coldstream Rd. CR3: Cat'm ... 93Sb 197
Cold War Bunker Gravesend ... 1C 144
Cole Av. RM16: Grays ... 9E 100
Colebeck M. N1 ... 37Rb 71
Colebert Av. E1 ... 42Yb 92
Colebert Ho. *E1* ... *42Yb 92*
(off Colebert Av.)
Colebrook KT16: Ott ... 79F 148
Colebrook Cl. NW7 ... 23Za 48
SW15 ... 59Za 110
Colebrook Ct. SW3 ... 6E 226
Colebrooke Av. W13 ... 44Ka 86
Colebrooke Ct. DA14: Sidc ... 62Xc 139
Colebrooke Dr. E11 ... 31Lc 73
Colebrooke Pl. N1 ... 1C 218 (39Rb 71)
Colebrooke Ri. BR2: Brom ... 68Gc 137
Colebrooke Rd. RH1: Redh ... 4N 207
Colebrooke Row N1 ... 2B 218 (40Rb 71)
Colebrook Gdns. IG10: Lough ... 12Rc 36
Colebrook Ho. *E14* ... *44Dc 92*
(off Ellesmere St.)
SE18 ... 52Qc 116
Colebrook La. IG10: Lough ... 12Rc 36
Colebrook Path IG10: Lough ... 12Rc 36
Colebrook Pl. KT16: Ott ... 80D 148
Colebrook Rd. SW16 ... 67Nb 134
Cole Brook St. DA8: Erith ... 51Hd 118
Colebrook Way N11 ... 22Kb 50
Coleby Path SE5 ... 52Tb 113
Colechurch Ho. *SE1* ... *50Wb 91*
(off Avondale Sq.)
Cole Cl. SE28 ... 46Xc 95
Cole Ct. RM3: Rom ... 22Nd 57
TW1: Twick ... 59Ja 108
Coledale Dr. HA7: Stan ... 25La 46
Coleford Ho. *RM3: Rom* ... *23Nd 57*
(off Kingsbridge Rd.)
Coleford Rd. SW18 ... 57Eb 111
Cole Gdns. TW5: Cran ... 52W 106
Colegrave Rd. E15 ... 36Fc 73
Colegrove Rd. SE15 ... 51Vb 113
Coleherne Ct. SW5 ... 50Db 89
Coleherne Mans. *SW5* ... *50Db 89*
(off Old Brompton Rd.)
Coleherne M. SW10 ... 50Db 89
Coleherne Rd. SW10 ... 50Db 89
Colehill Gdns. SW6 ... 54Ab 110
Colehill La. SW6 ... 53Ab 110
Cole Ho. SE1 ... 2A 230
Coleman Cl. SE25 ... 68Wb 135
Coleman Ct. SW18 ... 59Cb 111
Coleman Flds. N1 ... 39Sb 71
Coleman Mans. N8 ... 31Nb 70
Coleman Rd. DA17: Belv ... 49Cd 96
RM9: Dag ... 37Ad 75
SE5 ... 52Ub 113
Colemans Heath SE9 ... 62Qc 138
Coleman St. EC2 ... 2F 225 (44Tb 91)
Coleman St. Bldgs. EC2 ... 2F 225
Colenorton Cres. SL4: Eton W ... 9C 80
Colenso Dr. NW7 ... 24Wa 48
Colenso Rd. E5 ... 35Yb 72
IG2: Ilf ... 32Uc 74
COLE PARK ... 58Ja 108
Cole Pk. Gdns. TW1: Twick ... 57Ja 108
Cole Pk. Rd. TW1: Twick ... 58Ja 108
Cole Pk. Vw. TW1: Twick ... 58Ja 108
Colepits Wood Rd. SE9 ... 57Tc 116
Coleraine Rd. N8 ... 27Qb 50
SE3 ... 51Hc 115
Coleridge Av. E12 ... 37Nc 74
SM1: Sutt ... 77Gb 155
Coleridge Cl. SW8 ... 54Kb 112
Coleridge Ct. *EN5: New Bar* ... *15Db 31*
(off Station Rd.)
N1 ... *39Sb 71*
(off Popham Rd.)
SW1 ... 5D 228
W14 ... *48Za 88*
(off Blythe Rd.)
Coleridge Cres. SL3: Poyle ... 53G 104
Coleridge Dr. HA4: Ruis ... 30X 45
Coleridge Gdns. NW6 ... 38Eb 69
SW10 ... 52Db 111
Coleridge Ho. SE17 ... 7E 230
SW1 ... *50Lb 90*
(off Churchill Gdns.)
Coleridge La. N8 ... 30Nb 50
Coleridge Rd. CR0: C'don ... 73Yb 158
DA1: Dart ... 56Rd 119
E17 ... 28Bc 52
N4 ... 33Qb 70
N8 ... 30Mb 50
N12 ... 22Eb 49
RM3: Rom ... 24Kd 57
RM18: Tilb ... 4E 122
TW15: Ashf ... 63N 127
Coleridge Sq. *SW10* ... *52Eb 111*
(off Coleridge Gdns.)
W13 ... 44Ja 86
Coleridge Wlk. CM13: Hut ... 17Ee 41
NW11 ... 28Cb 49
Coleridge Way BR6: St M Cry ... 72Wc 161
UB4: Hayes ... 44W 84
UB7: W Dray ... 49N 83
WD6: Bore ... 14Qa 29
Cole Rd. TW1: Twick ... 58Ja 108
WD17: Wat ... 11X 27
Colesburg Rd. BR3: Beck ... 69Bc 136
Coles Cres. HA2: Harr ... 33Da 65
Colescroft Hill CR8: Purl ... 87Qb 176
Colesdale EN6: Cuff ... 2Nb 18
Coles Grn. IG10: Lough ... 11Qc 36
WD23: B Hea ... 18Ea 28
Coles Grn. Ct. NW2 ... 33Wa 68
Coles Grn. Rd. NW2 ... 32Wa 68
Coles Hill HP1: Hem H ... 1J 3
Coleshill Flats SW1 ... 6J 227
Coleshill Rd. TW11: Tedd ... 65Ga 130
Coles La. TN16: Bras ... 95Yc 201
Colesmead Rd. RH1: Redh ... 3P 207
COLES MEADS ... 3P 207
Colestown St. SW11 ... 54Gb 111
Cole St. SE1 ... 2E 230 (47Sb 91)
Colesworth Ho. *HA8: Edg* ... *26Sa 47*
(off Burnt Oak B'way.)
Colet Cl. N13 ... 23Rb 51
Colet Ct. *W6* ... *49Za 88*
(off Hammersmith Rd.)
Colet Flats *E1* ... *44Xc 92*
(off Troon St.)
Colet Gdns. W14 ... 49Za 88
Colet Ho. *SE17* ... *50Rb 91*
(off Doddington Gro.)
Colet Rd. CM13: Hut ... 15Ee 41
Colets Orchard TN14: Off ... 88Kd 183
Colette Ct. *SE16* ... *47Zb 92*
(off Eleanor Cl.)
Coley Av. GU22: Wok ... 90C 168
Coley St. WC1 ... 6J 217 (42Pb 90)
Colfe & Hatcliffe Glebe *SE13* ... *57Dc 114*
(off Lewisham High St.)
Colfe Rd. SE23 ... 60Ac 114
Colfes Leisure Cen. ... 58Jc 115
Colgate Pl. EN3: Enf L ... 9Cc 20
Colham Av. UB7: Yiew ... 46N 83
COLHAM GREEN ... 43Q 84
Colham Grn. Rd. UB8: Hil ... 43Q 84
Colham Mill Rd. UB7: W Dray ... 47M 83
Colham Rd. UB8: Hil ... 42P 83
Colham Rdbt. UB8: Hil ... 44Q 84
Colina M. N15 ... 28Rb 51
Colina Rd. N15 ... 29Rb 51
Colin Chapman Way
DA3: Fawk ... 77Ud 164
Colin Cl. BR4: W W'ck ... 76Hc 159
CR0: C'don ... 76Bc 158
DA2: Dart ... 58Rd 119
NW9 ... 28Ua 48
Colin Ct. SE6 ... 59Bc 114
Colin Cres. NW9 ... 28Va 48
COLINDALE ... 27Ta 47
Colindale Av. AL1: St A ... 4D 6
NW9 ... 27Ta 47
Colindale Bus. Pk. NW9 ... 27Sa 47
Colindale Retail Pk. NW9 ... 28Ta 47
Colindeep Gdns. NW4 ... 28Wa 48

Colindeep La. NW4 .27Ua 48
NW9 .27Ua 48
Colin Dr. NW9 .29Va 48
Colinette Rd. SW15 .56Ya 110
Colin Gdns. NW9 .28Va 48
Colin Pde. NW9 .28Ua 48
Colin Pk. Rd. NW9 .28Ua 48
Colin Pond Ct. RM6: Chad H .28Zc 55
Colin Rd. CR3: Cat'm .95Wb 197
NW10 .37Wa 68
Colinsdale N1 .1B 218
Colinswood SL2: Farn C .4G 60
Colinton Rd. IG3: Ilf .33Xc 75
Colin Way SL1: Slou .8F 80
Colin Winter Ho. *E1* .42Yb 92
(off Nicholas Rd.)
Coliseum Theatre .5F 223
Coliston Pas. *SW18* .59Cb 111
(off Coliston Rd.)
Coliston Rd. SW18 .59Cb 111
Collamore Av. SW18 .60Gb 111
Collapit Cl. HA1: Harr .30Da 45
Collard Av. IG10: Lough .12Sc 36
Collard Cl. CR8: Kenley .92Tb 197
Collard Grn. IG10: Lough .12Sc 36
Collard Pl. NW1 .38Kb 70
Collards Almshouses *E17* .29Ec 52
(off Maynard Rd.)
Collection Pl. *NW8* .39Db 69
(off Bolton Pl.)
College *SL4: Eton* .1H 103
(off Westons Yd.)
College App. SE10 .51Ec 114
College Av. HA3: Hrw W .25Ga 46
KT17: Eps .86Va 174
RM17: Grays .49De 99
SL1: Slou .8J 81
TW20: Egh .65D 126
College Cl. AL9: N Mym .10F 8
E9 .36Yb 72
HA3: Hrw W .24Ga 46
IG10: Lough .14Rc 36
N18 .22Vb 51
RM17: Grays .49Ee 99
TW2: Twick .60Fa 108
College Ct. EN3: Pond E .15Yb 34
EN8: Chesh .2Yb 20
NW3 .37Fb 69
(off College Cres.)
RM2: Rom .29Kd 57
(off Scholars Way)
SW3 .50Hb 89
(off West Rd.)
W5 .45Na 87
W6 .50Ya 88
(off Queen Caroline St.)
College Cres. NW3 .37Eb 69
RH1: Redh .3A 208
SL4: Wind .4F 102
College Cross N1 .38Qb 70
College Dr. HA4: Ruis .31W 64
KT7: T Ditt .73Ga 152
College East E1 .1K 225 (43Vb 91)
College Flds. Bus. Cen.
SW19 .67Gb 133
College Gdns. E4 .17Dc 34
EN2: Enf .11Tb 33
IG4: Ilf .29Nc 54
KT3: N Mald .71Va 154
N18 .22Wb 51
SE21 .60Ub 113
SW17 .61Gb 133
(not continuous)
College Grn. SE19 .66Ub 135
College Gro. NW1 .39Lb 70
College Hill EC4 .4E 224 (45Sb 91)
College Hill Rd.
HA3: Hrw W .24Ga 46
College Ho. SW15 .57Za 110
TW7: Isle .52Ga 108
College La. AL10: Hat .2A 8
(not continuous)
GU22: Wok .1N 187
NW5 .35Kb 70
College Mans. *NW6* .39Ab 68
(off Salusbury Rd.)
College M. *N1* .38Qb 70
(off College Cross, not continuous)
SW1 .3F 229
SW18 .57Db 111
College of Arms .4D 224
College Pde. *NW6* .39Ab 68
(off Salusbury Rd.)
COLLEGE PARK .41Xa 88
College Pk. Cl. SE13 .56Fc 115
College Pk. Rd. N17 .23Vb 51
College Pl. AL3: St A .2A 6
CM16: They B .8Sc 22
DA9: Ghithe .56Yd 120
E17 .28Gc 53
NW1 .1C 216 (39Lb 70)
SW10 .52Eb 111
College Point E15 .37Hc 73
College Rd. AL1: St A .3F 6
BR1: Brom .67Jc 137
BR8: Hext .67Gd 140
CR0: C'don .75Tb 157
DA11: Nflt .57De 121
E17 .29Ec 52
EN2: Enf .12Tb 33
EN8: Chesh .2Yb 20
GU22: Wok .88D 168
HA1: Harr .30Ga 46
HA3: Hrw W .25Ga 46
HA9: Wemb .32Ma 67
KT17: Eps .86Va 174
N17 .23Vb 51
N21 .19Qb 32
NW10 .40Ya 68
RM17: Grays .49Ee 99
SE19 .59Ub 113
SE21 .59Ub 113
SL1: Slou .6D 80
SW19 .65Fb 133
TW7: Isle .53Ha 108
W13 .44Ka 86
WD5: Ab L .3V 12
College Rdbt. KT1: King T .69Na 131
College Row E9 .36Zb 72
College Slip BR1: Brom .67Jc 137
College St. AL3: St A .2B 6
EC4 .4E 224 (45Sb 91)
College Ter. E3 .41Bc 92
N3 .26Bb 49
College Vw. SE9 .60Mc 115
College Wlk. KT1: King T .69Na 131
College Way HA6: Nwood .23T 44
TW15: Ashf .63P 127
UB3: Hayes .45W 84
College Yd. *AL3: St A* .2B 6
(off Lwr. Dagnall St.)
NW5 .35Kb 70
NW6 .39Ab 68
WD24: Wat .10X 13
Collens Fld. GU24: Pirb .6D 186
Collent St. E9 .37Yb 72
Coller Cres. DA2: Daren .64Ud 142
Collerston Ho. *SE10* .50Hc 93
(off Armitage Rd.)
Colless Rd. N15 .29Vb 51
Collet Rd. TN15: Kems'g .89Nd 183
Collett Rd. HP1: Hem H .2L 3
SE16 .48Wb 91
Collett Way UB2: S'hall .47Da 85
Colley Hill La. SL2: Hedg .4K 61
Colley Ho. UB8: Uxb .39M 63
Colleyland WD3: Chor .14F 24
Colley La. RH2: Reig .5G 206
Colley Mnr. Dr. RH2: Reig .5F 206
Colley Way RH2: Reig .3G 206
Collier Cl. E6 .45Rc 94
KT19: Ewe .79Qa 153
Collier Ct. RM16: Grays .46De 99
Collier Dr. HA8: Edg .26Qa 47
COLLIER ROW .24Dd 56
Collier Row La. RM5: Col R .24Dd 56
Collier Row Rd. RM5: Col R .25Bd 55
Colliers CR3: Cat'm .97Wb 197
Colliers Cl. GU21: Wok .9M 167
Colliers Ct. *CR0: C'don* .77Tb 157
(off St Peter's Rd.)
Colliers Shaw BR2: Kes .77Mc 159
Collier St. N1 .2H 217 (40Pb 70)
Colliers Water La. CR7: Thor H .71Qb 156
COLLIERS WOOD .66Fb 133
COLLIERS WOOD .66Fb 133
Collindale Av. DA8: Erith .52Dd 118
DA15: Sidc .60Wc 117
Collingbourne Rd. W12 .46Xa 88
Collingham Gdns. SW5 .49Db 89
Collingham Pl. SW5 .49Db 89
Collingham Rd. SW5 .49Db 89
Collingsbourne *KT15: Add* .77L 149
(off High St.)
Collings Cl. N22 .23Pb 50
Collington Cl. DA11: Nflt .9A 122
Collington St. SE10 .50Fc 93
Collingtree Rd. SE26 .63Yb 136
Collingwood Av. KT5: Surb .74Sa 153
N10 .27Jb 50
Collingwood Cl. SE20 .67Xb 135
TW2: Whitt .59Ca 107
Collingwood Ct. EN5: New Bar .15Db 31
W5 .43Pa 87
Collingwood Dr. AL2: Lon C .7H 7
Collingwood Ho. DA9: Ghithe .57Yd 120
E1 .42Xb 91
(off Darling Row)
SE16 .47Xb 91
(off Cherry Gdn. St.)
SW1 .50Mb 90
(off Dolphin Sq.)
W1 .7B 216
Collingwood Pl. KT12: Walt T .76W 150
Collingwood Rd. CR4: Mitc .69Gb 133
E17 .30Cc 52
N15 .28Ub 51
RM13: Rain .40Hd 76
SM1: Sutt .76Cb 155
UB8: Hil .42R 84
Collingwood St. E1 .42Xb 91
Collins Av. HA7: Stan .26Na 47
Collins Cl. SS17: Stan H .1N 101
Collins Ct. E8 .37Wb 71
WD23: Bush .15Da 27
(off Lea Cl.)
Collins Dr. HA4: Ruis .33Y 65
Collins Ho. *E14* .45Ec 92
(off Newby Pl.)
SE10 .50Hc 93
(off Armitage Rd.)
Collinson Ct. SE1 .2D 230
Collinson Ho. *SE15* .52Wb 113
(off Peckham Pk. Rd.)
Collinson St. SE1 .2D 230 (47Sb 91)
Collinson Wlk. SE1 .2D 230 (47Sb 91)
Collins Path TW12: Hamp .65Ba 129
Collins Rd. N5 .35Sb 71
Collins Sq. SE3 .54Hc 115
Collins St. SE3 .54Gc 115
(not continuous)
Collinswood Rd. SL2: Farn C .2E 60
Collin's Yd. N1 .39Rb 71
Collinwood Av. EN3: Enf H .13Yb 34
Collinwood Gdns. IG5: Ilf .29Pc 54
Collis All. TW2: Twick .60Ga 108
Collison Pl. N16 .32Ub 71
Coll's Rd. SE15 .53Yb 114
Collum Grn. Rd.
SL2: Farn C, Hedg, Stoke P .4H 61
Collyer Av. CR0: Bedd .77Nb 156
Collyer Pl. SE15 .53Wb 113
Collyer Rd. AL2: Lon C .9H 7
CR0: Bedd .77Nb 156
Colman Cl. KT18: Tatt C .89Ya 174
SS17: Stan H .1M 101
Colman Ct. HA7: Stan .23Ka 46
N12 .23Eb 49
Colman Ho. RH1: Redh .4P 207
Colman Pde. EN1: Enf .13Ub 33
Colman Rd. E16 .43Lc 93
Colmans Wharf *E14* .43Dc 92
(off Morris Rd.)
Colman Way RH1: Redh .4N 207
Colmar Cl. E1 .42Zb 92
Colmer Pl. HA3: Hrw W .24Fa 46
Colmer Rd. SW16 .67Nb 134
Colmore M. SE15 .53Xb 113
Colmore Rd. EN3: Pond E .14Yb 34
COLNBROOK .52F 104
Colnbrook By-Pass SL3: Coln, L'ly .51E 104
UB7: Harm .52K 105
Colnbrook Cl. AL2: Lon C .9J 7
Colnbrook Ct. SL3: Poyle .53H 105
Colnbrook St. SE1 .4B 230 (48Rb 91)
Colndale Rd. SL3: Poyle .54G 104
Colne RM18: E Til .8L 101
Colne Av. UB7: W Dray .47L 83
WD3: Rick .19J 25
WD19: Wat .16X 27
Colne Bank SL3: Hort .55E 104
Colnebridge Cl. TW18: Staines .63G 126
Colne Bri. Retail Pk. WD17: Wat .16Z 27
Colne Cl. RM15: S Ock .45Yd 98
Colne Ct. KT19: Ewe .77Sa 153
RM18: E Til .8L 101
W7 .44Fa 86
(off High La.)
Colnedale Rd. UB8: Uxb .36M 63
Colne Dr. KT12: Walt T .76Z 151
RM3: Rom .23Pd 57
Colne Gdns. AL2: Lon C .9J 7
Colne Ho. IG11: Bark .38Rc 74
NW8 .6C 214
Colne Lodge WD3: Rick .18J 25
Colne Mead WD3: Rick .19J 25
Colne Orchard SL0: Iver .44H 83
Colne Pk. Caravan Site
UB7: W Dray .49L 83
Colne Reach TW19: Stanw M .57H 105
Colne Rd. E5 .35Ac 72
N21 .17Tb 33
TW1: Twick .60Ga 108
TW2: Twick .60Ga 108
Colne St. E13 .41Jc 93
Colne Valley RM14: Upm .30Ud 58
Colne Valley Pk. Cen. .34K 63
Colne Valley Retail Pk.
WD17: Wat .15Z 27
Colne Way TW19: Staines .61D 126
WD24: Wat .8Y 13
WD25: Wat .8Y 13
Colne Way Ct. WD24: Wat .9Z 13
Colne Way Ind. Pk. WD25: Wat .8Z 13
Colney Flds. Shop. Pk.
AL2: Lon C .10K 7
COLNEY HATCH .23Hb 49
Colney Hatch La. N10 .24Jb 50
N11 .23Hb 49
COLNEY HEATH .5P 7
Colney Heath La. AL4: St A .2H 7
Colney Rd. DA1: Dart .58Pd 119
COLNEY STREET .2Ga 14
Colnmore Ct. *E2* .41Zb 92
(off Meath Cres.)
Coln Trad. Est. SL3: Poyle .53H 105
Cologne Rd. SW11 .56Fb 111
Coloma Ct. BR4: W W'ck .77Gc 159
Colombo Rd. IG1: Ilf .32Sc 74
Colombo St. SE1 .7B 224 (46Rb 91)
Colombo Street Sports & Community Cen.
.7B 224
Colomb St. SE10 .50Gc 93
Colonel's La. KT16: Chert .72J 149
Colonel's Wlk. EN2: Enf .13Rb 33
Colonial Av. TW2: Whitt .58Ea 108
Colonial Bus. Pk. WD24: Wat .11Y 27
Colonial Ct. N7 .34Pb 70
Colonial Dr. W4 .49Sa 87
Colonial Rd. SL1: Slou .7L 81
TW14: Felt .59U 106
Colonial Way WD24: Wat .11Y 27
Colonnade WC1 .6F 217 (42Nb 90)
Colonnade, The *AL3: St A* .2B 6
(off Verulam Rd.)
SE8 .49Bc 92
Colonnades, The W2 .44Db 89
Colonnades Leisure Centre, The .79Qb 156
Colonnade Wlk. SW1 .6K 227 (49Kb 90)
Colonsay HP3: Hem H .4C 4
Colony Mans. *SW5* .50Db 89
(off Earl's Ct. Rd.)
Colony M. *N1* .36Tb 71
(off Mildmay Gro. Nth.)
Colorado Apartments *N8* .27Pb 50
(off Gt. Amwell La.)
Colorado Bldg. *SE10* .53Dc 114
(off Deal's Gateway)
Colosseum, The .13W 26
Colosseum Apartments *E2* .40Zb 72
(off Palmers Rd.)
Colosseum Ter. NW1 .4A 216
Colour Ct. SW1 .7C 222
Colour Ho. SE1 .2J 231
Colour House Theatre .67Eb 133
Colroy Ct. NW11 .29Ab 48
Colson Gdns. IG10: Lough .14Rc 36
Colson Grn. IG10: Lough .15Rc 36
Colson Path IG10: Lough .14Qc 36
Colson Rd. CR0: C'don .75Ub 157
IG10: Lough .14Qc 36
Colson Way SW16 .63Lb 134
Colstead Ho. *E1* .44Xb 91
(off Watney Mkt.)
Colsterworth Rd. N15 .28Vb 51
(not continuous)
Colston Av. SM5: Cars .77Gb 155
Colston Ct. SM5: Cars .77Hb 155
Colston Rd. E7 .37Mc 73
SW14 .56Sa 109
Coltash Ct. EC1 .5E 218
Colthurst Cres. N4 .33Rb 71
Colthurst Dr. N9 .20Xb 33
Coltishall Rd. RM12: Horn .37Ld 77
Coltman Ho. *SE10* .51Ec 114
(off Welland St.)
Coltman St. E14 .43Ac 92
Colt M. EN3: Enf L .9Cc 20
Coltness Cres. SE2 .50Xc 95
Colton Gdns. N17 .27Sb 51
Colton Rd. HA1: Harr .29Ga 46
Coltsfoot, The HP1: Hem H .3G 2
Coltsfoot Ct. RM17: Grays .51Fe 121
Coltsfoot Dr. UB7: Yiew .44N 83
Coltsfoot La. RH8: Oxt .5K 211
Coltsfoot Path RM3: Rom .24Ld 57
Coltstead DA3: New A .75Ae 165
Columbas Dr. NW3 .32Fb 69
Columbia Av. HA4: Ruis .32X 65
HA8: Edg .25Ra 47
KT4: Wor Pk .73Va 154
Columbia Ho. *E3* .42Bc 92
(off Hamlets Way)
Columbia Point *SE16* .48Yb 92
(off Canada Est.)
Columbia Rd. E2 .3K 219 (41Vb 91)
E13 .42Hc 93
Columbia Road Flower Market .3K 219
(off Columbia Rd.)
Columbia Sq. SW14 .56Sa 109
Columbia Wharf EN3: Pond E .16Ac 34
Columbia Wharf Rd.
RM17: Grays .51Ce 121
Columbine Av. CR2: S Croy .80Rb 157
E6 .43Nc 94
Columbine Way RM3: Hrld W .25Nd 57
SE13 .54Ec 114
Columbus Ct. DA8: Erith .52Hd 118
SE16 .46Yb 92
(off Rotherhithe St.)
Columbus Courtyard E14 .46Cc 92
Columbus Gdns. HA6: Nwood .25W 44
Columbus Sq. DA8: Erith .51Hd 118
Colva Wlk. N19 .33Kb 70
Colvern Ho. RM7: Rom .29Ed 56
Colverson Ho. *E1* .43Yb 92
(off Lindley St.)
Colvestone Cres. E8 .36Vb 71
Colview Ct. SE9 .60Mc 115
Colville Est. N1 .39Ub 71
Colville Est. W. *E2* .41Vb 91
(off Turin St.)
Colville Gdns. GU18: Light .3A 166
W11 .44Bb 89
(not continuous)
Colville Ho. *E2* .40Yb 72
(off Waterloo Gdns.)
Colville Ho's. W11 .44Bb 89
Colville M. W11 .44Bb 89
Colville Pl. W1 .1C 222 (43Lb 90)
Colville Rd. E11 .34Ec 72
E17 .26Ac 52
N9 .18Xb 33
W3 .48Ra 87
W11 .44Bb 89
Colville Sq. W11 .44Bb 89
Colville Ter. W11 .44Bb 89
Colvin Cl. SE26 .64Yb 136
Colvin Gdns. E4 .20Ec 34
E11 .28Kc 53
EN8: Walt C .7Zb 20
IG6: Ilf .25Sc 54
Colvin Ho. *W10* .44Za 88
(off Kingsdown Cl.)
Colvin Rd. CR7: Thor H .71Qb 156
E6 .38Nc 74
Colwall Gdns. IG8: Wfd G .22Jc 53
Colwell Rd. SE22 .57Vb 113
Colwick Cl. N6 .31Mb 70
Colwith Rd. W6 .51Ya 110
Colwood Gdns. SW19 .66Fb 133
Colworth Gro. SE17 .6E 230 (49Sb 91)
Colworth Rd. CR0: C'don .74Wb 157
E11 .30Gc 53
Colwyn Av. UB6: G'frd .40Ha 66
Colwyn Cl. SW16 .64Lb 134
Colwyn Cres. TW3: Houn .53Ea 108
Colwyn Grn. *NW9* .30Ua 48
(off Snowdon Dr.)
Colwyn Ho. SE1 .4K 229 (48Qb 90)
Colwyn Rd. NW2 .34Xa 68
Colyer Cl. SE9 .61Rc 138
Colyer Rd. DA11: Nflt .61Ee 143
Colyers Cl. DA8: Erith .53Fd 118
Colyers La. DA8: Erith .53Ed 118
Colyers Wlk. DA8: Erith .53Gd 118
Colyton Cl. DA16: Well .53Zc 117
GU21: Wok .10N 167
HA0: Wemb .37La 66
Colyton La. SW16 .64Qb 134
Colyton Rd. SE22 .57Xb 113
Colyton Way N18 .22Wb 51
Combe, The NW1 .4A 216 (41Kb 90)
Combe Av. SE3 .52Hc 115
Combe Bank Dr. TN14: Sund .94Ad 201
Combedale Rd. SE10 .50Jc 93
Combe Ho. *W2* .43Cb 89
(off Gt. Western Rd.)
WD18: Wat .16U 26
Combemartin Rd. SW18 .59Ab 110
Combe M. SE3 .52Hc 115
Comber Cl. NW2 .34Xa 68
Comber Gro. SE5 .52Sb 113
Comber Ho. SE5 .52Sb 113
Combermere Cl. SL4: Wind .4F 102
Combermere Rd. SM4: Mord .72Db 155
SW9 .55Pb 112
Combe Rd. WD18: Wat .16V 26
Comberton *KT1: King T* .68Qa 131
(off Eureka Rd.)
Comberton Rd. E5 .33Xb 71
Combeside SE18 .52Vc 117
Combe St. HP1: Hem H .2L 3
Combewood WD25: Wat .4Y 13
Combwell Cres. SE2 .48Wc 95
Comedy Store .5D 222
Comedy Theatre .5D 222
Comely Bank Rd. E17 .29Ec 52
Comeragh Cl. GU22: Wok .2L 187
Comeragh M. W14 .50Ab 88
Comeragh Rd. W14 .50Ab 88
Comer Cres. *UB2: S'hall* .47Ea 86
(off Windmill Av.)
Comerell Pl. SE10 .50Hc 93
Comerford Rd. SE4 .56Ac 114
Comer Ho. EN5: New Bar .14Eb 31
Comet Cl. E12 .35Mc 73
RM19: Purf .49Qd 97
WD25: Wat .6V 12
Comet Ho. UB3: Harl .52S 106
Comet Pl. SE8 .52Cc 114
(not continuous)
Comet Rd. TW19: Stanw .59M 105
Comet St. SE8 .52Cc 114
Comet Way AL10: Hat .1A 8
Comforts Farm Av. RH8: Oxt .5K 211
Comfort St. SE15 .51Ub 113
Comfrey Ct. RM17: Grays .51Fe 121
Commerce Pk. CR0: Wadd .75Pb 156
Commerce Rd. N22 .25Pb 50
TW8: Bford .51La 108
Commerce Way CR0: Wadd .75Pb 156
Commercial Dock Path *SE16* .48Bc 92
(off Gulliver St.)
Commercial Pl. DA12: Grav'nd .8E 122
Commercial Rd. E1 .44Wb 91
E14 .44Yb 92
N18 .22Ub 51
TW18: Staines .65J 127
Commercial Rd. Ind. Est. N18 .23Vb 51
Commercial St. E1 .6K 219 (42Vb 91)
Commercial Way GU21: Wok .89A 168
NW10 .40Ra 67
SE10 .49Hc 93
SE15 .52Vb 113
Commerell St. SE10 .50Gc 93
Commersville Way CR0: Wadd .76Qb 156
Commodity Quay E1 .5K 225 (45Vb 91)
Commodore Ct. *SE8* .53Cc 114
(off Albyn Rd.)
Commodore Ho. *E14* .45Ec 92
(off Poplar High St.)
SW18 .55Eb 111
Commodore Sq. SW10 .53Eb 111
Commodore St. E1 .42Ac 92
COMMON, THE .94Ba 191
Common, The E15 .37Gc 73
HA7: Stan .19Ga 28
KT21: Asht .88Ma 173
UB2: S'hall .49Y 85
UB7: W Dray .49L 83
W5 .45Na 87
(not continuous)
WD4: Chfd .4J 11
WD4: K Lan .10A 4
WD7: Shenl .3Ka 14
Common Cl. GU21: Wok .6P 167
Commondale SW15 .54Ya 110
Commonfield La. SW17 .64Gb 133
Commonfield Rd. SM7: Bans .86Cb 175
Commonfields GU24: W End .4E 166
Common Ga. Rd. WD3: Chor .15F 24
Common La. DA2: Wilm .61Jd 140
KT10: Clay .80Ja 152
KT15: New H .81L 169
SL1: Burn .4B 60
SL4: Eton .10H 81
WD4: K Lan .10P 3
WD7: R'lett .11Ga 28
WD25: Let H .11Ga 28
Common La. Ho. *SL4: Eton* .10H 81
(off Common La.)
Commonmeadow La. WD25: A'ham .6Da 13
Common Mile Cl. SW4 .57Mb 112
Common Rd. CM13: Ingve .22Ee 59
HA7: Stan .21Fa 46
KT10: Clay .79Ja 152
RH1: Redh .8P 207
SL3: L'ly .49C 82
SL4: Dor, Eton W .9A 80
SL4: Eton W .9D 80
SW13 .55Xa 110
TN15: Igh .95Xd 204
WD3: Chor .14F 24
Common Side KT18: Eps .87Qa 173
Commonside BR2: Kes .77Lc 159
KT23: Bookh .94Ca 191
(not continuous)
Commonside Cl. CR5: Coul .92Rb 197
SM2: Sutt .83Db 175
Commonside E. CR4: Mitc .69Jb 134
(not continuous)
Commonside W. CR4: Mitc .69Hb 133
Commons La. HP2: Hem H .1N 3
Commonwealth Av. UB3: Hayes .44T 84
W12 .45Xa 88
(not continuous)
Commonwealth Conference Cen. .7C 222
Commonwealth Rd. CR3: Cat'm .95Wb 197
N17 .24Wb 51
Commonwealth Way SE2 .50Xc 95
COMMONWOOD .6K 11
Common Wood SL2: Farn C .5G 60
Community Cl. TW5: Cran .53X 107
UB10: Ick .34R 64
Community La. N7 .36Mb 70
Community Rd. E15 .36Fc 73
UB6: G'frd .39Ea 66
Community Wlk. KT10: Esh .77Ea 152
Community Way WD3: Crox G .15Q 26
Como Rd. SE23 .61Ac 136
Como St. RM7: Rom .29Fd 56
COMP .93Fe 205
Compass Cl. HA8: Edg .21Pa 47
TW15: Ashf .66S 128
Compass Ct. SE1 .7K 225
Compass Hill TW10: Rich .58Ma 109
Compass Ho. SW18 .56Db 111
Compass La. *BR1: Brom* .67Jc 137
(off North St.)
Compass Point *E14* .45Bc 92
(off Grenade St.)
Compass Theatre .34S 64
Compayne Gdns. NW6 .38Db 69
Compayne Mans. *NW6* .37Db 69
(off Fairhazel Gdns.)
Comp La. TN15: Plat .93Ee 205
Comport Grn. CR0: New Ad .84Gc 179
Compter Pas. EC2 .3E 224
Compton Av. CM13: Hut .18Ee 41
E6 .40Mc 73
HA0: Wemb .35La 66
N1 .37Rb 71
N6 .31Gb 69
RM2: Rom .27Ld 57
Compton Cl. E3 .43Cc 92
HA8: Edg .24Sa 47
KT10: Esh .79Fa 152
NW1 .4A 216
NW11 .34Za 68
SE15 .52Wb 113
W13 .44Ja 86
Compton Ct. SE19 .65Ub 135
SL1: Slou .4C 80
SM1: Sutt .77Eb 155
Compton Cres. KT9: Chess .78Na 153
N17 .24Sb 51
UB5: N'olt .39Z 65
W4 .51Sa 109
Compton Gdns. AL2: Chis G .8P 5
KT15: Add .78K 149
(off Monks Cres.)
Compton Ho. SW11 .53Gb 111
Compton Pas. EC1 .5C 218 (42Rb 91)
Compton Pl. DA8: Erith .51Hd 118
WC1 .5F 217 (42Nb 90)
WD19: Wat .20Aa 27
Compton Ri. HA5: Pinn .29Aa 45
Compton Rd. CR0: C'don .74Xb 157
N1 .37Rb 71
N21 .18Qb 32
NW10 .41Za 88
SW19 .65Bb 133
UB3: Hayes .45U 84
Compton Sports Cen. .23Gb 49
Compton St. EC1 .5B 218 (42Rb 91)
Compton Ter. N1 .37Rb 71
N21 .18Qb 32
Comreddy Cl. EN2: Enf .11Rb 33
Comus Ho. SE17 .6H 231
Comus Pl. SE17 .6H 231 (49Ub 91)
Comyne Rd. WD24: Wat .9U 12
Comyn Rd. SW11 .56Gb 111
Comyns, The WD23: B Hea .18Ea 28
Comyns Cl. E16 .43Hc 93
Comyns Rd. RM9: Dag .38Cd 76
Conant Ho. *SE11* .51Rb 113
(off St Agnes Pl.)
Conant M. E1 .45Wb 91

Conaways Cl. KT17: Ewe 82Wa 174
Conanicon Rd. SW2 . . . . 56Pb 112
Concert Hall App. SE1 . . . . 7J 223 (46Pb 90)
Concord Bus. Cen. W3 . . . . 42Ra 87
Concord Cl. UB5: N'olt 41Z 85
Concord Ct. KT1: King T 69Pa 131
(off Winery La.)
Concorde Bus. Pk. TN16: Big H 87Mc 179
Concorde Cl. TW3: Houn 54Da 107
UB10: Uxb 40N 63
Concorde Ct. SL4: Wind 4E 102
Concorde Dr. E6 . . . . 43Pc 94
HP2: Hem H 2M 3
Concorde Ho. RM12: Horn 37Kd 77
(off Cavendish Av.)
Concorde Way SE16 . . . . 49Zb 92
SL1: Slou 7G 80
Concord Ho. KT3: N Mald 69Ua 132
N17 . . . . 24Vb 51
(off Park La.)
Concordia Wharf E14 . . . . 46Ec 92
(off Coldharbour)
Concord Rd. EN3: Pond E 15Xb 33
W3 . . . . 42Ra 87
Concord Ter. HA2: Harr 33Da 65
(off Coles Cres.)
Concourse, The N9 . . . . 19Wb 33
(within Edmonton Grn. Shop. Cen.)
NW9 . . . . 25Ua 48
Condell Rd. SW8 . . . . 53Lb 112
Conder St. E14 . . . . 44Ac 92
Condor Ct. WD24: Wat 10X 13
Condor Path UB5: N'olt 40Ca 65
(off Union Rd.)
Condor Rd. TW18: Lale 69L 127
Condor Wlk. RM12: Horn 38Kd 77
Condover Cres. SE18 . . . . 52Rc 116
Condray Pl. SW11 . . . . 52Gb 111
Conduit, The RH1: Blet 1K 209
Conduit Av. SE10 . . . . 53Fc 115
Conduit Ct. WC2 . . . . 4F 223
Conduit La. CR0: C'don 78Wb 157
CR2: S Croy 78Wb 157
EN3: Pond E 16Ac 34
N18 . . . . 22Yb 52
SL3: L'ly 51A 104
Conduit M. SE18 . . . . 50Rc 94
W2 . . . . 3B 220 (44Fb 89)
Conduit Pas. W2 . . . . 3B 220
Conduit Pl. W2 . . . . 3B 220 (44Fb 89)
Conduit Rd. SE18 . . . . 50Rc 94
Conduit St. W1 . . . . 4A 222 (45Kb 90)
Conduit Way NW10 . . . . 38Sa 67
Conegar Ct. SL1: Slou 6J 81
Conewood St. N5 . . . . 34Rb 71
Coney Acre SE21 . . . . 60Sb 113
Coneyberry RH2: Reig 10L 207
Coney Burrows E4 . . . . 19Gc 35
Coneybury RH1: Blet 6L 209
Coneybury Cl. CR6: W'ham 91Xb 197
Coney Cl. AL10: Hat 2D 8
Coney Gro. UB8: Hil 41Q 84
Coneygrove Path UB5: N'olt 37Aa 65
(off Arnold Rd.)
CONEY HALL 76Gc 159
Coney Hall Pde.
BR4: W W'ck 76Gc 159
Coney Hill Rd. BR4: W W'ck 75Gc 159
Coney Way SW8 . . . . 51Pb 112
Conference Cl. E4 . . . . 19Ec 34
Conference Rd. SE2 . . . . 49Yc 95
Congers Ho. SE8 . . . . 52Cc 114
Congleton Gro. SE18 . . . . 50Sc 94
Congo Dr. N9 . . . . 20Yb 34
Congo Rd. SE18 . . . . 50Tc 94
Congress Rd. SE2 . . . . 49Yc 95
Congreve Ho. N16 . . . . 36Ub 71
Congreve Rd. EN9: Walt A 5Gc 21
SE9 . . . . 55Pc 116
Congreve St. SE17 . . . . 5H 231 (49Ub 91)
Congreve Wlk. E16 . . . . 43Mc 93
(off Fulmer Rd.)
Conical Cnr. EN2: Enf 12Sb 33
Conifer Av. DA3: Hartl 72Ae 165
RM5: Col R 22Dd 56
Conifer Cl. BR6: Orp 77Tc 160
EN7: Chesh 1Vb 19
RH2: Reig 4J 207
Conifer Ct. TW15: Ashf 64P 127
(off The Crescent)
Conifer Dr. CM14: W'ley 22Zd 59
Conifer Gdns. EN1: Enf 16Ub 33
SM1: Sutt 75Db 155
SW16 . . . . 62Pb 134
Conifer Ho. SE4 . . . . 56Bc 114
(off Brockley Rd.)
Conifer La. TW20: Egh 64E 126
Conifer Pk. KT17: Eps 83Ua 174
Conifers KT13: Weyb 77U 150
Conifers, The HP3: Hem H 5H 3
WD25: Wat 7Y 13
Conifers Cl. TW11: Tedd 66Ka 130
Conifer Wlk. SL4: Wind 2A 102
Conifer Way BR8: Swan 67Ed 140
HA0: Wemb 34La 66
UB3: Hayes 45W 84
Coniger Rd. SW6 . . . . 54Cb 111
Coningesby Dr. WD17: Wat 11U 26
Coningham Ct. SW10 . . . . 52Eb 111
(off King's Rd.)
Coningham M. W12 . . . . 46Wa 88
Coningham Rd. W12 . . . . 47Xa 88
Coningsby Av. NW9 . . . . 26Ua 48
Coningsby Bank AL1: St A 6B 6
Coningsby Cl. AL9: Wel G 6F 8
Coningsby Cotts. W5 . . . . 47Ma 87
Coningsby Ct. CR4: Mitc 68Jb 134
WD7: R'lett 8Ha 14
Coningsby Dr. EN6: Pot B 5Fb 17
Coningsby Gdns. E4 . . . . 23Dc 52
Coningsby Rd. CR2: S Croy 81Sb 177
N4 . . . . 31Rb 71
W5 . . . . 47Ma 87
Conington Rd. SE13 . . . . 54Dc 114
Conisbee Ct. N14 . . . . 15Lb 32
Conisborough Ct. DA2: Dart 58Rd 119
(off Osbourne Rd.)
Conisborough Cres. SE6 . . . . 62Ec 136
Conisbrough NW1 . . . . 1B 216
Consicliffe Cl. BR7: Chst 67Qc 138
Conisciffe Rd. N13 . . . . 20Sb 33
Conista Ct. GU21: Wok 8K 167
Coniston NW1 . . . . 3B 216
Coniston Av. DA16: Well 55Uc 116
IG11: Bark 38Uc 74
RM14: Upm 35Sd 78
Coniston Av. RM19: Purf 50Sd 98
UB6: G'frd 41Ka 86
Coniston Cl. DA1: Dart 60Kd 119
DA7: Bex 53Ed 118
DA8: Erith 52Gd 118
HP3: Hem H 3C 4
IG11: Bark 38Uc 74
N20 . . . . 20Eb 31
SW13 . . . . 52Va 110
SW20 . . . . 72Za 154
W4 . . . . 52Sa 109
Coniston Ct. CM16: Epp 3Wc 23
GU18: Light 2A 166
KT13: Weyb 79R 150
NW7 . . . . 24Ab 48
(off Langstone Way)
SE16 . . . . 47Zb 92
(off Eleanor Cl.)
SM6: Wall 77Kb 156
TW15: Ashf 62M 127
W2 . . . . 3E 220
Coniston Cres. SL1: Slou 3A 80
Conistone Way N7 . . . . 38Nb 70
Coniston Gdns. HA5: Eastc 28W 44
HA9: Wemb 32La 66
IG4: Ilf 28Nc 54
N9 . . . . 18Yb 34
NW9 . . . . 29Ta 47
SM2: Sutt 79Fb 155
Coniston Ho. E3 . . . . 42Bc 92
(off Southern Gro.)
SE5 . . . . 52Sb 113
(off Wyndham Rd.)
Coniston Lodge WD17: Wat 12W 26
Coniston Rd. BR1: Brom 65Gc 137
CR0: C'don 73Wb 157
CR5: Coul 88Lb 176
DA7: Bex 53Ed 118
GU22: Wok 92D 188
N10 . . . . 26Kb 50
N17 . . . . 23Wb 51
TW2: Whitt 58Da 107
WD4: K Lan 10P 3
Coniston Wlk. E9 . . . . 36Yb 72
Coniston Way KT9: Chess 76Na 153
RH2: Reig 5N 207
RM12: Horn 36Jd 76
TW20: Egh 66D 126
Conlan St. W10 . . . . 42Ab 88
Conley Rd. NW10 . . . . 37Ua 68
Conley St. SE10 . . . . 50Gc 93
Connaught Av. E4 . . . . 17Fc 35
EN1: Enf 12Ub 33
EN4: E Barn 18Hb 31
IG10: Lough 14Mc 35
RM16: Grays 47De 99
SW14 . . . . 55Sa 109
TW4: Houn 56Aa 107
TW15: Ashf 63N 127
Connaught Bri. E16 . . . . 46Mc 93
Connaught Bus. Cen. CR0: Wadd . . . 79Pb 156
CR4: Mitc 71Hb 155
NW9 . . . . 29Va 48
Connaught Cl. E10 . . . . 33Ac 72
EN1: Enf 12Ub 33
HP2: Hem H 1A 4
SM1: Sutt 75Fb 155
UB8: Hil 42S 84
W2 . . . . 3E 220 (44Gb 89)
Connaught Ct. E17 . . . . 28Dc 52
(off Orford Rd.)
W2 . . . . 3F 221
Connaught Cres. GU24: Brkwd 2D 186
Connaught Dr. KT13: Weyb 83Q 170
NW11 . . . . 28Cb 49
Connaught Gdns. N10 . . . . 29Kb 50
N13 . . . . 21Rb 51
SM4: Mord 70Eb 133
Connaught Hgts. E16 . . . . 46Mc 93
(off Agnes George Wlk.)
UB10: Hil 42S 84
(off Uxbridge Rd.)
Connaught Hill IG10: Lough 14Mc 35
Connaught Ho. NW10 . . . . 41Xa 88
(off Trenmar Gdns.)
W1 . . . . 5K 221
Connaught La. IG1: Ilf 33Sc 74
Connaught Lodge N4 . . . . 31Qb 70
(off Connaught Rd.)
Connaught M. NW3 . . . . 35Gb 69
SE18 . . . . 50Qc 94
SW6 . . . . 53Ab 110
Connaught Pl. IG10: Lough 14Nc 36
W2 . . . . 4F 221 (45Hb 89)
Connaught Rd. E4 . . . . 17Gc 35
E11 . . . . 32Fc 73
E16 . . . . 46Mc 93
E17 . . . . 29Cc 52
EN5: Barn 16Za 30
GU24: Brkwd 3C 186
HA3: W'stone 25Ha 46
IG1: Ilf 33Tc 74
KT3: N Mald 70Ua 132
N4 . . . . 31Qb 70
NW10 . . . . 39Ua 68
RM12: Horn 34Md 77
SE18 . . . . 50Qc 94
SL1: Slou 7M 81
SM1: Sutt 75Fb 155
TW10: Rich 57Pa 109
TW11: Tedd 64Fa 130
W13 . . . . 45Ka 86
Connaught Rdbt. E16 . . . . 45Mc 93
(off Victoria Dock Rd.)
Connaught Sq. W2 . . . . . . 3F 221 (44Hb 89)
Connaught St. W2 . . . . 3D 220 (44Gb 89)
Connaught Way N13 . . . . 21Rb 51
Connaught Works E3 . . . . 39Ac 72
(off Old Ford Rd.)
Connections Bus. Pk.
TN14: S'oaks 91Ld 203
Connect La. IG6: Ilf 26Sc 54
Connell Ct. SE14 . . . . 51Zb 114
(off Myers La.)
Connell Cres. W5 . . . . 42Pa 87
Connemara Cl. WD6: Bore 16Ta 29
Connicut La. KT23: Bookh 100Da 191
Conniffe Ct. SE9 . . . . 57Rc 116
Connington Cres. E4 . . . . 20Fc 35
Connolly Ct. GU25: Vir W 70A 126
RM7: Rush G 30Gd 56
(off Union Rd.)
Connop Rd. EN3: Enf W 10Zb 20
Connor Cl. E11 . . . . 31Gc 73
IG6: Ilf 25Sc 54
Connor Ct. SW11 . . . . 53Kb 112
Connor Rd. RM9: Dag 35Bd 75
Connor St. E9 . . . . 39Zb 72
Conolly Dell W7 . . . . 46Ga 86
(off Conolly Rd.)
Conolly Rd. W7 . . . . 46Ga 86
Conqueror Ct. RM3: Rom 24Md 57
Conquest Rd. KT15: Add 78J 149
Conrad Cl. RM16: Grays 47De 99
Conrad Ct. SS17: Stan H 2L 101
Conrad Dr. KT4: Wor Pk 74Ya 154
Conrad Gdns. RM16: Grays 47Ce 99
Conrad Ho. E8 . . . . 37Wb 71
E14 . . . . 45Ac 92
(off Victory Pl.)
E16 . . . . 46Kc 93
(off Wesley Av.)
N16 . . . . 36Ub 71
(off Matthias Rd.)
SW8 . . . . 52Nb 112
(off Wyvil Rd.)
Conrad Rd. SS17: Stan H 1N 101
Conrad Twr. W3 . . . . 48Ra 87
Consfield Av. KT3: N Mald 70Wa 132
Consort Cl. CM14: W'ley 22Yd 58
Consort Ct. GU22: Wok 90A 168
(off York Rd.)
W8 . . . . 48Db 89
(off Wright's La.)
Consort Ho. E14 . . . . 50Dc 92
(off St Davids Sq.)
SW6 . . . . 54Eb 111
(off Lensbury Av.)
W2 . . . . 45Db 89
(off Queensway)
Consort Lodge NW8 . . . . 1F 215
Consort M. TW7: Isle 57Fa 108
Consort Rd. SE15 . . . . 53Xb 113
Cons St. SE1 . . . . 1A 230 (47Qb 90)
Constable Av. E16 . . . . 46Kc 93
Constable Cl. N11 . . . . 22Hb 49
NW11 . . . . 30Db 49
UB4: Hayes 40S 64
Constable Ct. SE16 . . . . 50Xb 91
(off Stubbs Dr.)
W4 . . . . 50Ra 87
(off Chaseley Dr.)
Constable Cres. N15 . . . . 29Wb 51
Constable Gdns. HA8: Edg 25Qa 47
TW7: Isle 57Fa 108
Constable Ho. NW3 . . . . 38Hb 69
UB5: N'olt 40Z 65
(off Gallery Gdns.)
Constable Ho's. E14 . . . . 47Cc 92
(off Cassilis Rd.)
Constable M. BR1: Brom 68Kc 137
RM8: Dag 35Xc 75
Constable Rd. DA11: Nflt 2A 144
Constable Wlk. SE21 . . . . 62Ub 135
Constance Allen Ho. W10 . . . . 44Za 88
(off Bridge Cl.)
Constance Cl. SW15 . . . . 63Ta 131
Constance Cres. BR2: Hayes 73Hc 159
Constance Gro. DA1: Dart 58Md 119
Constance Rd. CR0: C'don 73Rb 157
EN1: Enf 16Ub 33
SM1: Sutt 77Eb 155
TW2: Whitt 59Da 107
Constance St. E16 . . . . 46Nc 94
Constant Ho. E14 . . . . 45Dc 92
(off Harrow La.)
Constantine Ct. E1 . . . . 44Wb 91
(off Fairclough St.)
Constantine Ho. UB3: Hayes 44T 84
Constantine Pl. UB10: Hil 39P 63
Constantine Rd. NW3 . . . . 35Gb 69
Constant Mdw. TN13: S'oaks 97Ld 203
Constitution Cres. DA12: Grav'nd . . . 10E 122
(off Constitution Hill)
Constitution Hill DA12: Grav'nd 10E 122
GU22: Wok 91A 188
SW1 . . . . 1K 227 (47Kb 90)
Constitution Ri. SE18 . . . . 53Qc 116
Consul Av. RM9: Dag, Rain 41Ed 96
RM13: Rain 41Ed 96
Consul Gdns. BR8: Hext 66Hd 140
Consul Ho. E3 . . . . 42Cc 92
(off Wellington Way)
Content St. SE17 . . . . 6F 231 (49Tb 91)
Contessa Cl. BR6: Farnb 78Uc 160
Continuity Ct. DA9: Ghithe 56Wd 120
Control Twr. Rd. TW6: H'row A 55Q 106
Convair Wlk. UB5: N'olt 41Z 85
Convent Cl. BR3: Beck 66Ec 136
EN5: Barn 12Bb 31
GU22: Wok 89D 168
Convent Gdns. W5 . . . . 49La 86
W11 . . . . 44Ab 88
Convent Hill SE19 . . . . 65Sb 135
Convent La. KT11: Cobh 83U 170
Convent Rd. SL4: Wind 4D 102
TW15: Ashf 64R 128
Convent Way UB2: S'hall 49Y 85
Conway Cl. BR3: Beck 67Ac 136
HA7: Stan 23Ja 46
RM13: Rain 38Jd 76
Conway Ct. SL9: Ger X 32D 62
Conway Cres. RM6: Chad H 30Yc 55
UB6: G'frd 40Ga 66
Conway Dr. SM2: Sutt 79Db 155
TW15: Ashf 65S 128
UB3: Harl 48S 84
Conway Gdns. CR4: Mitc 70Nb 134
EN2: Enf 10Ub 19
HA9: Wemb 31La 66
RM17: Grays 52De 121
Conway Gro. W3 . . . . 43Ta 87
Conway Ho. E14 . . . . 49Cc 92
(off Cahir St.)
SW3 . . . . 50Hb 89
(off Ormonde Ga.)
WD6: Bore 14Sa 29
Conway M. W1 . . . . 6B 216
Conway Rd. N14 . . . . 20Nb 32
N15 . . . . 29Rb 51
NW2 . . . . 33Ya 68
SE18 . . . . 49Tc 94
SL6: Tap 4A 80
SW20 . . . . 67Ya 132
TW4: Houn 59Ba 107
TW6: H'row A 55R 106
TW13: Hanw 64Z 129
Conways Rd. RM16: Ors 1C 100
Conway St. W1 . . . . 6B 216 (42Lb 90)
(not continuous)
Conway Wlk. TW12: Hamp 65Ba 129
Conybeare NW3 . . . . 38Gb 69
Conybury Cl. EN9: Walt A 4Jc 21
Conyerd Rd. TN15: Bor G 92Be 205
Conyers Cl. IG8: Wfd G 23Gc 53
KT12: Hers 78Z 151
Conyer's Rd. SW16 . . . . 64Mb 134
Conyer St. E3 . . . . 40Ac 72
Conyers Way IG10: Lough 13Rc 36
Cooden Cl. BR1: Brom 66Kc 137
Cook Ct. DA8: Erith 52Hd 118
SE8 . . . . 50Ac 92
(off Evelyn St.)
SE16 . . . . 46Yb 92
(off Rotherhithe St.)
Cooke Cl. RM16: Chaf H 48Ae 99
Cookes Cl. E11 . . . . 33Hc 73
Cookes La. SM3: Cheam 79Ab 154
Cooke St. IG11: Bark 39Sc 74
Cookham Cl. UB2: S'hall 48Da 85
Cookham Cres. SE16 . . . . 47Zb 92
Cookham Dene Cl.
BR7: Chst 67Tc 138
Cookham Hill BR5: Orp 76Cd 162
Cookham Ho. E2 . . . . 5K 219
Cookham Rd. BR8: Swan 67Cd 140
Cookhill Rd. SE2 . . . . 47Xc 95
Cook Rd. RM9: Dag 39Ad 75
Cooks Cl. E14 . . . . 46Cc 92
(off Cabot Sq.)
RM5: Col R 25Ed 56
SL9: Chal P 23A 42
Cooks Hole Rd. EN2: Enf 10Rb 19
Cooks Mead WD23: Bush 16Da 27
Cookson Gro. DA8: Erith 52Dd 118
Cook Sq. DA8: Erith 52Hd 118
Cooks Rd. E15 . . . . 40Dc 72
SE17 . . . . 51Rb 113
Cooks Way AL10: Hat 2D 8
Coolfin Rd. E16 . . . . 44Jc 93
Coolgardie Av. E4 . . . . 22Fc 53
IG7: Chig 20Qc 36
Coolgardie Rd. TW15: Ashf 64S 128
Coolhurst Tennis & Squash Club . . . 30Mb 50
Coolhurst Rd. N8 . . . . 30Mb 50
Cool Oak La. NW9 . . . . 31Ua 68
Coomassie Rd. W9 . . . . 42Bb 89
COOMBE 66Sa 131
Coombe, The RH3: Bet 3A 206
Coombe Av. CR0: C'don 77Ub 157
TN14: S'oaks 92Kd 203
Coombe Bank KT2: King T 67Ua 132
Coombe Cl. HA8: Edg 26Pa 47
TW3: Houn 56Ca 107
Coombe Cnr. N21 . . . . 18Rb 33
Coombe Ct. CR0: C'don 77Tb 157
(off Coombe Rd.)
TN14: S'oaks 92Kd 203
Coombe Cres. TW12: Hamp 66Ba 129
Coombe Dene BR2: Brom 70Hc 137
(off Cumberland Rd.)
Coombe Dr. HA4: Ruis 32X 65
KT15: Add 79H 149
Coombe End KT2: King T 66Ta 131
Coombefield Cl. KT3: N Mald 71Ua 154
Coombe Gdns. KT3: N Mald 70Va 132
SW20 . . . . 68Wa 132
Coombe Hill Ct. SL4: Wind 6B 102
Coombe Hill Glade KT2: King T 66Ua 132
Coombe Hill Golf Course 66Ta 131
Coombe Hill Rd. KT2: King T 66Ua 132
WD3: Rick 17J 25
Coombe Ho. E4 . . . . 23Bc 52
N7 . . . . 36Mb 70
Coombe Ho. Chase KT3: N Mald 67Ta 131
Coombehurst Cl. EN4: Cockf 12Hb 31
Coombelands La. KT15: Add 79J 149
COOMBE LANE 67Ua 132
Coombe La. CR0: C'don 78Xb 157
GU3: Worp 10G 186
(not continuous)
KT12: W Vill 81V 170
SL5: S'hill 10A 124
SW20 . . . . 67Va 132
Coombe La. Flyover SW20 . . . . 67Va 132
Coombe La. W. KT2: King T 67Ra 131
Coombe Lea BR1: Brom 69Nc 138
Coombe Lodge SE7 . . . . 51Lc 115
Coombe Mnr. GU24: Bisl 7E 166
Coombe Neville KT2: King T 66Ta 131
Coombe Pk. KT2: King T 64Sa 131
Coombe Pl. KT2: King T 64Sa 131
Coomber Ho. SW6 . . . . 55Db 111
(off Wandsworth Bri. Rd.)
Coombe Ridings KT2: King T 64Sa 131
Coombe Ri. CM15: Shenf 18Ee 41
KT2: King T 67Sa 131
SS17: Stan H 1N 101
Coombe Rd. CR0: C'don 77Tb 157
DA12: Grav'nd 1E 144
KT2: King T 67Qa 131
KT3: N Mald 68Ua 132
N22 . . . . 26Qb 50
NW10 . . . . 34Ta 67
RM3: Hrld W 27Pd 57
SE26 . . . . 63Xb 135
TN14: Otf 87Ld 183
TW12: Hamp 65Ba 129
W4 . . . . 50Ua 88
W13 . . . . 48Ka 86
WD23: Bush 17Fa 28
Coomber Way CR0: Bedd 73Mb 156
Coombes Rd. AL2: Lon C 8G 6
RM9: Dag 39Bd 75
Coombe Va. SL9: Ger X 32A 62
Coombe Wlk. SM1: Sutt 76Db 155
Coombe Way KT14: Byfl 84P 169
Coombewood Dr. RM6: Chad H 30Bd 55
Coombe Wood Golf Course 66Ra 131
Coombe Wood Hill CR8: Purl 85Sb 177
Coombe Wood Local Nature Reserve
. . . . 66Va 132
Coombe Wood Rd. KT2: King T 64Sa 131
Coombfield Dr. DA2: Daren 63Td 142
Coombrook Ct. SE16 . . . . 47Ac 92
(off Elgar St.)
Coombs St. N1 . . . . 2C 218 (40Rb 71)
Coomer M. SW6 . . . . 51Bb 111
Coomer Pl. SW6 . . . . 51Bb 111
Coomer Rd. SW6 . . . . 51Bb 111
Cooms Wlk. HA8: Edg 25Sa 47
Coope Ct. RM7: Rush G 30Gd 56
(off Union Rd.)
Cooperage, The SE1 . . . . 7K 225
SW8 . . . . 52Pb 112
(off Regent's Bri. Gdns.)
Cooperage Cl. N17 . . . . 23Vb 51
Co-operative Ho. SE15 . . . . 55Wb 113
Cooper Av. E17 . . . . 25Ac 52
Cooper Cl. DA9: Ghithe 57Vd 120
SE1 . . . . 2A 230 (47Qb 90)
Cooper Ct. SE18 . . . . 51Rc 116
Cooper Cres. SM5: Cars 76Hb 155
Cooper Ho. NW8 . . . . 6B 214
SE4 . . . . 57Zb 114
(off St Norbert Rd.)
TW4: Houn 55Ba 107
Cooper Rd. CR0: Wadd 77Rb 157
GU20: W'sham 9B 146
NW4 . . . . 30Za 48
NW10 . . . . 36Wa 68
COOPERSALE 1Zc 23
Coopersale Cl. IG8: Wfd G 24Lc 53
Coopersale Comn.
CM16: Coop, Epp, N Weald 1Zc 23
Coopersale La.
CM16: They B, They G 9Wc 23
Coopersale Rd. E9 . . . . 36Zb 72
COOPERSALE STREET 3Yc 23
Coopersale St. CM16: Epp, Fidd H . . . 4Yc 23
Coopers Cl. DA4: S Dar 67Td 142
E1 . . . . 42Yb 92
IG7: Chig 19Xc 37
RM10: Dag 37Dd 76
TW18: Staines 64G 126
Coopers Ct. E3 . . . . 42Bc 92
(off Eric St.)
TW7: Isle 54Ha 108
(off Woodlands Rd.)
W3 . . . . 46Sa 87
(off Church Rd.)
Coopers Cres. WD6: Bore 11Sa 29
Coopers Dr. DA2: Wilm 61Gd 140
Coopers Ga. AL4: Col H 4M 7
Coopers Hill Dr. GU24: Brkwd 2A 186
Coopers Hill La. TW20: Egh, Eng G . . 2N 125
Cooper's Hill Rd. RH1: Nutf, S Nut . . . 6G 208
Coopers La. E10 . . . . 32Dc 72
EN6: N'thaw, Pot B 3Fb 17
NW1 . . . . 1E 216 (40Mb 70)
(not continuous)
RM18: W Til 1G 122
SE12 . . . . 61Kc 137
TW18: Staines 63J 127
Coopers La. Rd. EN6: N'thaw, Pot B . . 3Fb 17
Coopers Lodge SE1 . . . . 1K 231
Coopers M. BR3: Beck 68Cc 136
WD25: Wat 3Y 13
Coopers Rd. DA10: Swans 59Be 121
DA11: Nflt 10B 122
EN6: Pot B 2Eb 17
SE1 . . . . 7K 231 (50Vb 91)
Coopers Row EC3 . . . . 4K 225 (45Vb 91)
SL0: Iver H 42E 82
Coopers Shaw Rd. RM18: W Til 2F 122
Cooper St. E16 . . . . 43Hc 93
Coopers Wlk. E15 . . . . 36Gc 73
EN8: Chesh 1Zb 20
Coopers Yd. N1 . . . . 38Rb 71
(off Upper St.)
SE19 . . . . 65Ub 135
Cooper Way HP4: Berk 1A 2
SL1: Slou 8F 80
Coote Gdns. RM8: Dag 34Bd 75
Coote Rd. DA7: Bex 53Bd 117
RM8: Dag 34Bd 75
Cope Ho. EC1 . . . . 4E 218
Copeland Dr. E14 . . . . 49Cc 92
Copeland Ho. SE11 . . . . 4J 229
SW17 . . . . 63Fb 133
Copeland Rd. E17 . . . . 30Dc 52
SE15 . . . . 54Wb 113
Copeman Cl. SE26 . . . . 64Yb 136
Copeman Rd. CM13: Hut 17Fe 41
Copenhagen Gdns. W4 . . . . 47Ta 87
Copenhagen Ho. N1 . . . . 1J 217
Copenhagen Pl. E14 . . . . 44Bc 92
(not continuous)
Copenhagen St. N1 . . . . . . 1K 217 (39Nb 70)
Copenhagen Way KT12: Walt T 76X 151
Cope Pl. W8 . . . . 48Cb 89
Copers Cope Rd. BR3: Beck 66Bc 136
Cope St. SE16 . . . . 49Zb 92
Copford Cl. IG8: Wfd G 23Nc 54
Copford Wlk. N1 . . . . 39Sb 71
(off Popham St.)
Copgate Path SW16 . . . . 65Pb 134
Copinger Wlk. HA8: Edg 25Ra 47
Copland Av. HA0: Wemb 36Ma 67
Copland Cl. HA0: Wemb 36La 66
Copland Ho. UB1: S'hall 47Ba 85
Copland M. HA0: Wemb 37Na 67
Copland Rd. HA0: Wemb 37Na 67
SS17: Stan H 2M 101
Copleigh Dr. KT20: Tad 92Ab 194
Copleston M. SE15 . . . . 54Vb 113
Copleston Pas. SE5 . . . . 54Vb 113
Copleston Rd. SE15 . . . . 55Vb 113
Copley Cl. GU21: Wok 1J 187
RH1: Redh 4N 207
SE17 . . . . 51Sb 113
W7 . . . . 42Ha 86
Copley Dene BR1: Brom 67Mc 137
Copley Pk. SW16 . . . . 65Pb 134
Copley Rd. HA7: Stan 22La 46
Copley St. E1 . . . . 43Zb 92
Copley Way KT20: Tad 92Za 194
Copmans Wick WD3: Chor 15F 24
Coppard Gdns. KT9: Chess 79La 152
Coppelia Rd. SE3 . . . . 56Hc 115
Coppen Rd. RM8: Dag 31Bd 75
Copperas St. SE8 . . . . 51Dc 114
Copper Beech Cl. BR5: St M Cry 71Yc 161
DA12: Grav'nd 9F 122
GU22: Wok 3M 187
HP3: Hem H 5H 3
IG5: Ilf 25Qc 54
SL4: Wind 3B 102
Copperbeech Cl. NW3 . . . . 36Fb 69
Copper Beech Ct. IG10: Lough 11Qc 36
Copper Beeches TW7: Isle 53Fa 108
Copper Beech Ho. GU22: Wok 89B 168
Copper Beech Rd. RM15: S Ock 41Yd 98
Copper Cl. N17 . . . . 24Xb 51
SE19 . . . . 66Vb 135
Copperdale Cl. WD18: Wat 15U 26
Copperdale Rd. UB3: Hayes 47W 84
Copperfield IG7: Chig 22Tc 54
Copperfield Av. UB8: Hil 43Q 84
Copperfield Cl. CR2: Sande 83Sb 177
DA12: Grav'nd 10J 123
Copperfield Ct. KT22: Lea 93Ja 192
Copperfield Dr. N15 . . . . 28Vb 51
Copperfield Gdns. CM14: B'wood . . . 18Xd 40

Copperfield Ho. *SE1* *47Wb* **91**
(off Wolseley St.)
W1 . . . . . 7J **215**
W11 . . . . . *46Za* **88**
(off St Ann's Rd.)
Copperfield M. *E2* *40Wb* **71**
(off Claredale St.)
N18 . . . . . 21Ub **51**
Copperfield Ri. KT15: Add 78H **149**
Copperfield Rd. E3 . . . . . 42Ac **92**
SE28 . . . . . 44Yc **95**
Copperfields BR3: Beck 67Ec **136**
HA1: Harr 31Ga **66**
KT22: Fet 94Ea **192**
TN15: Kems'g 89Pd **183**
Copperfields Cl. TN15: Kems'g 89Pd **183**
Copperfields Ct. W3 . . . . . 47Qa **87**
Copperfields Orchard
TN15: Kems'g 89Pd **183**
Copperfields Shop. Cen.
DA1: Dart *58Nd* **119**
(off Spital St.)
Copperfield St. SE1 . . . . . 1C **230** (47Rb **91**)
Copperfields Wlk. TN15: Kems'g . . . 89Pd **183**
Copperfields Way RM3: Hrld W 25Md **57**
Copperfield Ter. *SL2: Slou* *5M* **81**
(off Mirador Cres.)
Copperfield Way BR7: Chst 65Sc **138**
HA5: Pinn 28Ba **45**
Coppergate Cl. BR1: Brom 67Kc **137**
Coppergate Ct. *EN9: Walt A* *6Jc* **21**
(off Farthingale La.)
Copper Horse Ct. SL4: Wind 4E **102**
Coppermead Cl. NW2 . . . . . 34Ya **68**
Copper M. W4 . . . . . 48Sa **87**
Coppermill Ct. WD3: W Hyd 24H **43**
Copper Mill Dr. TW7: Isle 54Ha **108**
Copper Mill La. SW17 . . . . . 63Eb **133**
Coppermill La. E17 . . . . . 30Yb **52**
UB9: Hare 24G **42**
WD3: Hare, W Hyd 24G **42**
Coppermill Rd. TW19: Wray 58C **104**
Copper Ridge SL9: Chal P 22B **42**
Copper Row SE1 . . . . . 7K **225**
Copperworks, The N1 . . . . . 2G **217**
Coppetts Cen. N12 . . . . . 24Hb **49**
Coppetts Cl. N12 . . . . . 24Gb **49**
Coppetts Rd. N10 . . . . . 24Hb **49**
Coppetts Wood &
Glebelands Local Nature Reserve
. . . . . 23Hb **49**
Coppice, The DA5: Bexl 62Fd **140**
EN2: Enf 14Rb **33**
EN5: New Bar *16Db* **31**
(off Great Nth. Rd.)
HP2: Hem H 1B **4**
TW15: Ashf 65R **128**
UB7: Yiew 44N **83**
WD19: Wat 16Y **27**
Coppice Cl. AL10: Hat 3B **8**
BR3: Beck 70Dc **136**
HA4: Ruis 30T **44**
HA7: Stan 23Ha **46**
SW20 . . . . . 69Ya **132**
Coppice Dr. SW15 . . . . . 58Xa **110**
TW19: Wray 9P **103**
Coppice End GU22: Pyr 88G **168**
Coppice La. RH2: Reig 4H **207**
Coppice Path IG7: Chig 21Xc **55**
Coppice Rd. RH2: Reig 5G **206**
Coppice Row CM16: They B 8Sc **22**
Coppice Wlk. N20 . . . . . 20Cb **31**
Coppice Way E18 . . . . . 28Hc **53**
SL2: Hedg 3H **61**
Coppies Gro. N11 . . . . . 21Kb **50**
Copping Cl. CR0: C'don 77Ub **157**
Coppins, The CR0: New Ad 79Dc **158**
HA3: Hrw W 23Ga **46**
Coppins La. SL0: Iver 43H **83**
Coppock Cl. SW11 . . . . . 54Gb **111**
Coppsfield KT8: W Mole 69Ca **129**
Copse, The CR3: Cat'm 98Wb **197**
CR6: W'ham 89Ac **178**
E4 . . . . . 18Hc **35**
GU23: Send 96H **189**
HP1: Hem H 1G **2**
KT22: Fet 95Da **191**
N2 . . . . . 27Hb **49**
RH1: S Nut 8E **208**
TN16: Tats 92Lc **199**
WD23: Bush 13Z **27**
Copse Av. BR4: W W'ck 75Dc **158**
Copse Bank TN15: Seal 92Pd **203**
Copse Cl. HA6: Nwood 26S **44**
SE7 . . . . . 51Kc **115**
SL1: Slou 6D **80**
UB7: W Dray 48M **83**
Copse Edge Av. KT17: Eps 85Va **174**
Copse Glade KT6: Surb 73Ma **153**
COPSE HILL 66Wa **132**
Copse Hill CR8: Purl 85Nb **176**
SM2: Sutt 80Db **155**
SW20 . . . . . 67Wa **132**
Copsem Dr. KT10: Esh 79Da **151**
Copsem La. KT10: Esh, Oxs 79Ea **152**
KT22: Oxs 79Ea **152**
Copsem Way KT10: Esh 79Ea **152**
Copsen Wood KT22: Oxs 83Ea **172**
Copse Rd. GU21: Wok 10K **167**
KT11: Cobh 85X **171**
RH1: Redh 8L **207**
Copse Side DA3: Hartl 69Ae **143**
Copse Vw. CR2: Sels 81Zb **178**
Copse Wood SL0: Iver H 39F **62**
Copsewood Cl. DA15: Sidc 58Uc **116**
Copse Wood Ct. RH2: Reig 4N **207**
Copsewood Rd. WD24: Wat 11X **27**
Copse Wood Way HA6: Nwood 25R **44**
Coptain Ho. SW18 . . . . . 56Cb **111**
Coptefield Dr. DA17: Belv 48Zc **95**
Coptfold Rd. CM14: B'wood 19Yd **40**
Copthall Av. EC2 . . . . . 2G **225** (44Tb **91**)
(not continuous)
Copthall Bldgs. EC2 . . . . . 2F **225**
Copthall Cl. EC2 . . . . . 2F **225** (44Tb **91**)
SL9: Chal P 24B **42**
Copthall Cnr. SL9: Chal P 24A **42**
Copthall Dr. NW7 . . . . . 24Wa **48**
Copthall Gdns. NW7 . . . . . 24Wa **48**
TW1: Twick 60Ha **108**
COPTHALL GREEN 5Nc **22**
Copthall La. SL9: Chal P 24A **42**
Copthall Leisure Cen. 24Xa **48**
Copt Hall Rd. TN15: Igh 95Wd **204**
Copthall Rd. DA13: Meop, Sole S . . . 10D **144**
Copthall Rd. E. UB10: Ick 33Q **64**
Copthall Rd. W. UB10: Ick 33Q **64**
Copthall Way KT15: New H 82H **169**
Copt Hill La. KT20: Tad 92Ab **194**
Copthorne Av. BR2: Brom 75Pc **160**
IG6: Ilf 23Rc **54**
SW12 . . . . . 59Mb **112**
Copthorne Chase TW15: Ashf 63P **127**
Copthorne Cl. TW17: Shep 72S **150**
WD3: Crox G 15P **25**
Copthorne Ct. KT22: Lea 94Ja **192**
Copthorne Dr. GU18: Light 2A **166**
Copthorne Gdns. RM11: Horn 29Qd **57**
Copthorne M. UB3: Harl 49U **84**
Copthorne Ri. CR2: Sande 85Tb **177**
Copthorne Rd. KT22: Lea 92Ka **192**
WD3: Crox G 16P **25**
Coptic St. WC1 . . . . . 1F **223** (43Nb **90**)
Copwood Cl. N12 . . . . . 21Fb **49**
Coral Apartments *E16* *45Jc* **93**
(off Western Gateway)
Coral Cl. RM6: Chad H 27Zc **55**
Coral Gdns. HP2: Hem H 1P **3**
Coral Ho. *E1* *42Ac* **92**
(off Harford St.)
NW10 . . . . . 41Qa **87**
Coraline Cl. UB1: S'hall 41Ba **85**
Coralline Wlk. SE2 . . . . . 48Yc **95**
Coral Mans. *NW6* *39Cb* **69**
(off Kilburn High Rd.)
Coral Row SW11 . . . . . 55Eb **111**
Coral St. SE1 . . . . . 2A **230** (47Qb **90**)
Coram Grn. CM13: Hut 16Fe **41**
Coram Ho. *W4* *50Ua* **88**
(off Wood St.)
WC1 . . . . . 5F **217**
Coram Mans. *WC1* *6H* **217**
(off Millman St.)
Coram St. WC1 . . . . . 6F **217** (42Nb **90**)
Coran Cl. N9 . . . . . 17Zb **34**
Corban Rd. TW3: Houn 55Ca **107**
Corbar Cl. EN4: Had W 11Fb **31**
Corbden Cl. SE15 . . . . . 53Vb **113**
Corben M. SW8 . . . . . 54Lb **112**
Corbet Cl. SM6: Wall 74Jb **156**
Corbet Ct. EC3 . . . . . 3G **225** (44Tb **91**)
Corbet Ho. N1 . . . . . 1K **217**
SE5 . . . . . *52Sb* **113**
(off Wyndham Rd.)
Corbet Pl. E1 . . . . . 7K **219** (43Vb **91**)
Corbet Rd. KT17: Ewe 82Ua **174**
Corbets Av. RM14: Upm 36Rd **77**
CORBETS TEY 36Sd **78**
Corbets Tey Rd. RM14: Upm 35Rd **77**
Corbett Cl. CR0: New Ad 84Fc **179**
Corbett Ct. SE26 . . . . . 63Bc **136**
Corbett Gro. N22 . . . . . 24Nb **50**
Corbett Ho. *SW10* *51Eb* **111**
(off Cathcart Rd.)
Corbett Rd. E11 . . . . . 30Lc **53**
E17 . . . . . 27Ec **52**
Corbetts La. SE16 . . . . . 49Yb **92**
(not continuous)
Corbetts Pas. *SE16* *49Yb* **92**
(off Corbetts La.)
Corbetts Wharf *SE16* *47Xb* **91**
(off Bermondsey Wall E.)
Corbett Theatre 13Rc **36**
Corbicum E11 . . . . . 31Gc **73**
Corbidge Ct. SE8 . . . . . 51Dc **114**
Corbiere Ct. SW19 . . . . . 65Za **132**
Corbiere Ho. *N1* *39Tb* **71**
(off De Beauvoir Est.)
Corbin Ho. *E3* *41Dc* **92**
(off Bromley High St.)
Corbins La. HA2: Harr 34Da **65**
Corbridge N17 . . . . . 24Xb **51**
Corbridge Cres. E2 . . . . . 40Xb **71**
Corbridge M. RM1: Rom 29Hd **56**
Corby Cl. AL2: Chis G 7N **5**
TW20: Eng G 5N **125**
Corby Cres. EN2: Enf 14Nb **32**
Corby Dr. TW20: Eng G 5M **125**
Corbylands Rd. DA15: Sidc 59Uc **116**
Corbyn St. N4 . . . . . 32Nb **70**
Corby Rd. NW10 . . . . . 40Ta **67**
Corby Way E3 . . . . . 42Cc **92**
Corcorans CM15: Pil H 16Xd **40**
Cordelia Cl. SE24 . . . . . 56Rb **113**
Cordelia Gdns. TW19: Stanw 59N **105**
Cordelia Ho. N1 . . . . . 1J **219**
Cordelia Rd. TW19: Stanw 59N **105**
Cordelia St. E14 . . . . . 44Dc **92**
Cordell Ho. *N15* *29Vb* **51**
(off Newton Rd.)
Corder Cl. AL3: St A 5N **5**
Corderoy Pl. KT16: Chert 72G **148**
Cordingley Rd. HA4: Ruis 33T **64**
Cording St. E14 . . . . . 43Dc **92**
Cordons Cl. SL9: Chal P 25A **42**
Cordrey Gdns. CR5: Coul 87Nb **176**
(not continuous)
Cordrey Ho. KT15: Add 75J **149**
Cordwainers Ct. *E9* *38Yb* **72**
(off St Thomas's Sq.)
Cordwainers Wlk. E13 . . . . . 40Jc **73**
Cord Way E14 . . . . . 48Cc **92**
Cordwell Rd. SE13 . . . . . 57Gc **115**
Corefield Cl. N11 . . . . . 19Jb **32**
Corelli Ct. SE1 . . . . . 49Xb **91**
SW5 . . . . . *49Cb* **89**
(off W. Cromwell Rd.)
Corelli Rd. SE3 . . . . . 54Nc **116**
Coresbrook Way GU21: Knap 10E **166**
Corfe Av. HA2: Harr 35Ca **65**
Corfe Cl. HP2: Hem H 3N **3**
KT21: Asht 90La **172**
TW4: Houn 60Aa **107**
UB4: Yead 44Y **85**
WD6: Bore 13Ta **29**
Corfe Gdns. SL1: Slou 5E **80**
Corfe Ho. *SW8* *52Pb* **112**
(off Dorset Rd.)
Corfe Twr. W3 . . . . . 47Ra **87**
Corfield Rd. N21 . . . . . 15Pb **32**
Corfield St. E2 . . . . . 41Xb **91**
Corfton Lodge W5 . . . . . 43Na **87**
Corfton Rd. W5 . . . . . 44Na **87**
Corhaven Ho. DA8: Erith 52Gd **118**
Coriander Av. E14 . . . . . 44Fc **93**
Coriander Ct. SE1 . . . . . 1K **231**
Cories Cl. RM8: Dag 33Zc **75**
Corinium Cl. HA9: Wemb 35Pa **67**
Corinium Ga. AL3: St A 4N **5**
Corinne Rd. N19 . . . . . 35Lb **70**
Corinthian Manorway DA8: Erith 49Fd **96**
Corinthian Rd. DA8: Erith 49Fd **96**
Corinthian Way TW19: Stanw 59M **105**
Corkers Path IG1: Ilf 33Sc **74**
Corker Wlk. N7 . . . . . 33Pb **70**
Cork Ho. SW19 . . . . . 63Db **133**
Corkran Rd. KT6: Surb 73Ma **153**
Corkscrew Hill BR4: W W'ck 75Ec **158**
Cork Sq. E1 . . . . . 46Xb **91**
Cork St. W1 . . . . . 5B **222** (45Lb **90**)
Cork St. M. W1 . . . . . 5B **222**
Cork Tree Ho. *SE27* *64Rb* **135**
(off Lakeview Rd.)
Cork Tree Retail Pk. E4 . . . . . 22Ac **52**
Cork Tree Way E4 . . . . . 22Ac **52**
Corlett St. NW1 . . . . . 7D **214** (43Gb **89**)
Cormongers La. RH1: Nutf 3D **208**
Cormont Rd. SE5 . . . . . 53Rb **113**
Cormorant Cl. E17 . . . . . 24Ac **52**
Cormorant Ct. *SE8* *51Bc* **114**
(off Pilot Cl.)
Cormorant Ho. EN3: Pond E 15Zb **34**
Cormorant Lodge *E1* *46Wb* **91**
(off Thomas More St.)
Cormorant Pl. SM1: Sutt 78Bb **155**
Cormorant Rd. E7 . . . . . 36Hc **73**
Cormorant Wlk. RM12: Horn 37Kd **77**
Cornbury Ho. *SE8* *51Bc* **114**
(off Evelyn St.)
Cornbury Rd. HA8: Edg 24Ma **47**
Cornel Ho. DA15: Sidc 62Wc **139**
SL4: Wind 5H **103**
Cornelia Dr. UB4: Yead 42Y **85**
Cornelia Ho. *TW1: Twick* *58Ma* **109**
(off Denton Rd.)
Cornelia Pl. DA8: Erith 51Gd **118**
Cornelia St. N7 . . . . . 37Pb **70**
Cornelius Ho. *WD18: Wat* *14V* **26**
(off Chiltern Cl.)
Cornell Bldg. *E1* *44Wb* **91**
(off Coke St.)
Cornell Cl. DA14: Sidc 65Ad **139**
Cornell Ct. EN3: Enf H 13Ac **34**
Cornell Ho. HA2: Harr 34Ba **65**
Cornell Sq. SW8 . . . . . 53Mb **112**
Cornell Way RM5: Col R 22Cd **56**
Corner, The KT14: W Byf 85J **169**
W5 . . . . . 46Na **87**
Corner Ct. *E2* *42Xb* **91**
(off Three Colts La.)
Cornercroft *SM3: Cheam* *78Za* **154**
(off Wickham Av.)
Corner Farm Cl. KT20: Tad 94Ya **194**
Corner Fielde SW2 . . . . . 60Pb **112**
Corner Grn. SE3 . . . . . 54Jc **115**
CORNER HALL 4M **3**
Corner Hall HP3: Hem H 4L **3**
(not continuous)
Corner Hall Av. HP3: Hem H 4M **3**
Corner Ho. St. WC2 . . . . . 6F **223**
Corner Mead NW9 . . . . . 24Va **48**
Cornerside TW15: Ashf 66S **128**
Cornerstone Ho. CR0: C'don 73Sb **157**
Corner Vw. AL9: Wel G 6E **8**
Corney Reach Way W4 . . . . . 52Ua **110**
Corney Rd. W4 . . . . . 51Ua **110**
Cornfield Cl. UB8: Uxb 40M **63**
Cornfield Rd. RH2: Reig 7L **207**
WD23: Bush 14Da **27**
Cornfields, The HP1: Hem H 3K **3**
Cornflower La. CR0: C'don 74Zb **158**
Cornflower Ter. SE22 . . . . . 58Xb **113**
Cornflower Way RM3: Hrld W 25Nd **57**
Cornford Cl. BR2: Brom 71Jc **159**
Cornford Gro. SW12 . . . . . 61Kb **134**
Cornhill EC3 . . . . . 3G **225** (44Tb **91**)
Cornhill Cl. KT15: Add 75K **149**
Cornhill Dr. EN3: Enf W 9Ac **20**
Cornick Ho. *SE16* *48Xb* **91**
(off Slippers Pl.)
Cornish Ct. N9 . . . . . 17Xb **33**
Cornish Gro. SE20 . . . . . 67Xb **135**
Cornish Ho. *SE17* *51Rb* **113**
(off Brandon Est.)
TW8: Bford 50Pa **87**
Cornmill EN9: Walt A 5Dc **20**
Corn Mill Dr. BR6: Orp 73Wc **161**
Cornmill La. SE13 . . . . . 55Ec **114**
Cornmow Dr. NW10 . . . . . 36Va **68**
Cornshaw Rd. RM8: Dag 32Zc **75**
Cornsland CM14: B'wood 20Zd **41**
Cornsland Cl. RM14: Upm 27Sd **58**
Cornsland Ct. CM14: B'wood 20Yd **40**
Cornthwaite Rd. E5 . . . . . 34Yb **72**
Cornwall Av. DA16: Well 55Uc **116**
E2 . . . . . 41Yb **92**
KT10: Clay 80Ha **152**
KT14: Byfl 86P **169**
N3 . . . . . 24Cb **49**
N22 . . . . . 25Nb **50**
SL2: Slou 2G **80**
UB1: S'hall 43Ba **85**
Cornwall Cl. EN8: Walt C 5Ac **20**
IG11: Bark 37Vc **75**
RM11: Horn 28Qd **57**
SL4: Eton W 10C **80**
Cornwall Ct. HA5: Hat E 24Ba **45**
TW18: Staines *65G* **126**
(off Cornwall Way)
W7 . . . . . *42Ha* **86**
(off Copley Cl.)
Cornwall Cres. W11 . . . . . 44Ab **88**
Cornwall Dr. BR5: St P 66Yc **139**
Cornwall Gdns. NW10 . . . . . 37Xa **68**
SE25 . . . . . 70Vb **135**
SW7 . . . . . 4A **226** (48Db **89**)
Cornwall Gdns. Wlk. SW7 . . . . . 48Db **89**
Cornwall Ga. RM19: Purf 49Qd **97**
Cornwall Gro. W4 . . . . . 50Ua **88**
Cornwall Ho. *SW7* *48Db* **89**
(off Cornwall Gdns.)
Cornwallis Av. N9 . . . . . 19Xb **33**
SE9 . . . . . 61Tc **138**
Cornwallis Cl. CR3: Cat'm 94Sb **197**
DA8: Erith 51Hd **118**
Cornwallis Ct. *SW8* *53Nb* **112**
(off Lansdowne Grn.)
Cornwallis Gro. N9 . . . . . 19Xb **33**
Cornwallis Ho. *SE16* *47Xb* **91**
(off Cherry Gdn. St.)
W12 . . . . . *45Xa* **88**
(off India Way)
Cornwallis Rd. E17 . . . . . 28Zb **52**
N9 . . . . . 19Xb **33**
N19 . . . . . 33Nb **70**
RM9: Dag 35Zc **75**
SE18 . . . . . 48Sc **94**
Cornwallis Sq. N19 . . . . . 33Nb **70**
Cornwallis Wlk. SE9 . . . . . 55Pc **116**
Cornwall Mans. *SW10* *52Eb* **111**
(off Cremorne Rd.)
W8 . . . . . *47Db* **89**
(off Kensington Ct.)
W14 . . . . . *48Za* **88**
(off Blythe Rd.)
Cornwall M. Sth. SW7 . . . . . 4A **226** (48Eb **89**)
Cornwall M. W. SW7 . . . . . 48Db **89**
Cornwall Rd. AL1: St A 4C **6**
CM15: Pil H 15Xd **40**
CR0: C'don 75Rb **157**
DA1: Dart 55Pd **119**
HA1: Harr 30Ea **46**
HA4: Ruis 34V **64**
HA5: Hat E 24Ba **45**
N4 . . . . . 31Qb **70**
N15 . . . . . 29Tb **51**
N18 . . . . . 22Wb **51**
SE1 . . . . . 6K **223** (46Qb **90**)
SM2: Sutt 80Bb **155**
TW1: Twick 59Ja **108**
UB8: Uxb 37M **63**
Cornwall Sq. SE11 . . . . . 7B **230**
Cornwall St. E1 . . . . . 45Xb **91**
Cornwall Ter. NW1 . . . . . 6G **215** (42Hb **89**)
Cornwall Ter. M. NW1 . . . . . 6G **215**
Cornwall Way TW18: Staines 65G **126**
Corn Way E11 . . . . . 34Fc **73**
Cornwell Av. DA12: Grav'nd 2E **144**
Cornwell Cres. SS17: Stan H 1N **101**
Cornwell Rd. SL4: Old Win 8L **103**
Cornwood Cl. N2 . . . . . 29Fb **49**
Cornwood Dr. E1 . . . . . 44Yb **92**
Cornworthy Rd. RM8: Dag 36Yc **75**
Corona Bldg. *E14* *46Ec* **92**
(off Blackwall Way)
Corona Rd. SE12 . . . . . 59Jc **115**
Coronation Av. N16 . . . . . 35Vb **71**
RM18: E Til 9K **101**
SL3: G Grn 43A **82**
SL4: Wind 4L **103**
Coronation Cl. DA5: Bexl 58Zc **117**
IG6: Ilf 28Sc **54**
Coronation Ct. DA8: Erith 52Fd **118**
E15 . . . . . 37Hc **73**
KT1: King T *70Na* **131**
(off Surbiton Rd.)
RM18: E Til *9L* **101**
(off Coronation Av.)
W10 . . . . . *43Ya* **88**
(off Brewster Gdns.)
Coronation Dr. RM12: Horn 36Kd **77**
Coronation Hill CM16: Epp 2Vc **23**
Coronation Rd. E13 . . . . . 41Lc **93**
NW10 . . . . . 41Qa **87**
UB3: Harl 49V **84**
Coronation Vs. NW10 . . . . . 42Ra **87**
Coronation Wlk. TW2: Whitt 60Ca **107**
Coroners Court
City of London 4F **225** (45Tb **91**)
North London 14Bb **31**
Poplar *45Dc* **92**
(off Poplar High St.)
St Pancras 1E **216** (39Mb **70**)
Southwark 1F **231** (47Tb **91**)
West London 55Eb **111**
Westminster 5E **228** (49Mb **90**)
Coronet Cinema *46Cb* **89**
(off Notting Hill Ga.)
Coronet Pde. HA0: Wemb 37Na **67**
Coronet St. N1 . . . . . 4H **219** (41Ub **91**)
Coronet Theatre 4D **230**
Corporate Dr. TW13: Felt 62X **129**
Corporate Ho. HA3: Hrw W 25Fa **46**
Corporation Av. TW4: Houn 56Aa **107**
Corporation Row EC1 . . . . . 5A **218** (42Qb **90**)
Corporation St. E15 . . . . . 40Gc **73**
N7 . . . . . 36Nb **70**
Corrance Rd. SW2 . . . . . 56Nb **112**
Corran Way RM15: S Ock 45Xd **98**
Corri Av. N14 . . . . . 21Mb **50**
Corrib Ct. N13 . . . . . 20Pb **32**
Corrib Dr. SM1: Sutt 78Gb **155**
Corrie Gdns. GU25: Vir W 3N **147**
Corrie Rd. GU22: Wok 92D **188**
KT15: Add 77M **149**
Corrigan Av. CR5: Coul 87Jb **176**
Corrigan Cl. NW4 . . . . . 27Ya **48**
Corringham Ct. AL1: St A 1D **6**
NW11 . . . . . 31Cb **69**
Corringham Ho. *E1* *44Zb* **92**
(off Pitsea St.)
Corringham Rd. HA9: Wemb 33Qa **67**
NW11 . . . . . 31Cb **69**
SS17: Stan H 2M **101**
Corringway NW11 . . . . . 31Db **69**
W5 . . . . . 42Qa **87**
Corris Grn. NW9 . . . . . 29Ua **48**
Corry Dr. SW9 . . . . . 56Rb **113**
Corry Ho. *E14* *45Dc* **92**
(off Wade's Pl.)
Corry's End AL4: Col H 4A **8**
Corsair Cl. TW19: Stanw 59M **105**
Corsair Rd. TW19: Stanw 59N **105**
Corscombe Cl. KT2: King T 64Sa **131**
Corsehill St. SW16 . . . . . 65Lb **134**
Corsellis Sq. *TW1: Isle* *56Ka* **108**
(off Varley Dr.)
Corsham St. N1 . . . . . 4G **219** (41Tb **91**)
Corsica St. N5 . . . . . 37Rb **71**
Corsley Way E9 . . . . . 37Bc **72**
Corston Hollow *RH1: Redh* *7P* **207**
(off Woodlands Rd.)
Cortayne Ct. TW2: Twick 61Ga **130**
Cortayne Rd. SW6 . . . . . 54Bb **111**
Cortis Rd. SW15 . . . . . 58Xa **110**
Cortis Ter. SW15 . . . . . 58Xa **110**
Cortland Cl. DA1: Cray 58Gd **118**
IG8: Wfd G 25Lc **53**
Corunna Rd. SW8 . . . . . 53Lb **112**
Corunna Ter. SW8 . . . . . 53Lb **112**
Corve La. RM15: S Ock 45Xd **98**
Corvette Sq. SE10 . . . . . 51Fc **115**
Corwell Gdns. UB8: Hil 44S **84**
Corwell La. UB8: Hil 44S **84**
Cory Dr. CM13: Hut 17De **41**
Coryton Path *W9* *42Bb* **89**
(off Ashmore Rd.)
Cosbycote Av. SE24 . . . . . 57Sb **113**
Cosdach Av. SM6: Wall 80Mb **156**
Cosedge Cres. CR0: Wadd 78Qb **156**
Cosgrove Cl. N21 . . . . . 19Sb **33**
UB4: Yead 42Aa **85**
Cosgrove Ho. *E2* *39Wb* **71**
(off Whiston Rd.)
Cosmia Ct. *WD23: Bush* *15Aa* **27**
(off Vale Rd.)
Cosmo Pl. WC1 . . . . . 7G **217** (43Nb **90**)
Cosmur Cl. W12 . . . . . 48Va **88**
Cossall Wlk. SE15 . . . . . 54Xb **113**
Cossar M. SW2 . . . . . 57Qb **112**
Cosser St. SE1 . . . . . 3K **229** (48Qb **90**)
Costa St. SE15 . . . . . 54Wb **113**
Costead Mnr. Rd. CM14: B'wood . . . 18Xd **40**
Costells Mdw. TN16: Westrm 98Tc **200**
Costins Wlk. *HP4: Berk* *1A* **2**
(off Robertson Rd.)
Costons Av. UB6: G'frd 41Fa **86**
Costons La. UB6: G'frd 41Fa **86**
(not continuous)
Coston Wlk. SE4 . . . . . 56Zb **114**
Cosway Mans. NW1 . . . . . 7E **214**
Cosway St. NW1 . . . . . 7E **214** (43Gb **89**)
Cotall St. E14 . . . . . 43Cc **92**
Coteford Cl. HA5: Eastc 29W **44**
IG10: Lough 12Rc **36**
Coteford St. SW17 . . . . . 63Hb **133**
Cotelands CR0: C'don 76Ub **157**
Cotesbach Rd. E5 . . . . . 34Yb **72**
Cotes Ho. NW8 . . . . . 6D **214**
Cotesmore Gdns. RM8: Dag 35Yc **75**
Cotesmore Rd. HP1: Hem H 3G **2**
Cotford Rd. CR7: Thor H 70Sb **135**
Cotham St. SE17 . . . . . 6E **230** (49Sb **91**)
Cotherstone KT19: Ewe 82Ta **173**
Cotherstone Rd. SW2 . . . . . 60Pb **112**
Cotland Acres RH1: Redh 8M **207**
Cotlandswick AL2: Lon C 7G **6**
Cotleigh Av. DA5: Bexl 61Zc **139**
Cotleigh Rd. NW6 . . . . . 38Cb **69**
RM7: Rom 30Fd **56**
Cotman Cl. NW11 . . . . . 30Eb **49**
SW15 . . . . . 58Za **110**
Cotmandene Cres. BR5: St P 68Wc **139**
Cotman Gdns. HA8: Edg 26Qa **47**
Cotman Ho. NW8 . . . . . 1D **214**
UB5: N'olt *40Z* **65**
(off Academy Gdns.)
Cotman M. *RM8: Dag* *36Yc* **75**
(off Highgrove Rd.)
COTMAN'S ASH 87Sd **184**
Cotman's Ash La. TN15: Kems'g 86Rd **183**
Cotmans Cl. UB3: Hayes 46W **84**
Coton Rd. DA16: Well 55Wc **117**
Cotsford Av. KT3: N Mald 71Sa **153**
Cotsmoor *AL1: St A* *2D* **6**
(off Granville Rd.)
Cotswold Av. WD23: Bush 16Ea **28**
Cotswold Cl. DA7: Bex 54Gd **118**
KT2: King T 65Sa **131**
KT10: Hin W 75Ha **152**
N11 . . . . . 21Jb **50**
SL1: Slou 8G **80**
TW18: Staines 64J **127**
UB8: Uxb 39L **63**
Cotswold Ct. EC1 . . . . . 5D **218**
UB6: G'frd *40Ha* **66**
(off Hodder Dr.)
Cotswold Gdns. CM13: Hut 17Fe **41**
E6 . . . . . 41Mc **93**
IG2: Ilf 31Tc **74**
NW2 . . . . . 33Za **68**
Cotswold Ga. NW2 . . . . . 32Ab **68**
Cotswold Grn. EN2: Enf 14Pb **32**
Cotswold M. SW11 . . . . . 53Fb **111**
Cotswold Ri. BR6: St M Cry 72Vc **161**
Cotswold Rd. DA11: Nflt 2A **144**
RM3: Hrld W 26Pd **57**
SM2: Sutt 82Db **175**
TW12: Hamp 64Ca **129**
Cotswolds AL10: Hat 2C **8**
Cotswold St. SE27 . . . . . 63Rb **135**
Cotswold Way EN2: Enf 13Pb **32**
KT4: Wor Pk 75Ya **154**
Cottage Av. BR2: Brom 74Nc **160**
Cottage Cl. *E1* *42Yb* **92**
(off Mile End Rd.)
HA2: Harr 33Fa **66**
HA4: Ruis 32T **64**
KT16: Ott 79E **148**
WD3: Crox G 16P **25**
WD17: Wat 12V **26**
Cottage Farm Way TW20: Thorpe 69E **126**
Cottage Fld. Cl. DA14: Sidc 60Yc **117**
Cottage Gdns. EN8: Chesh 1Zb **20**
Cottage Grn. SE5 . . . . . 52Tb **113**
Cottage Gro. KT6: Surb 72Ma **153**
SW9 . . . . . 55Nb **112**
Cottage M. RM11: Horn 28Ld **57**
Cottage Pk. Rd. SL2: Hedg 3H **61**
Cottage Pl. SW3 . . . . . 3D **226** (48Gb **89**)
Cottage Rd. KT19: Ewe 80Ta **153**
N7 . . . . . 36Pb **70**
(not continuous)
Cottages, The UB10: Ick 33N **63**
Cottage St. E14 . . . . . 45Dc **92**
Cottage Wlk. N16 . . . . . 34Vb **71**
Cottenham Dr. NW9 . . . . . 27Va **48**
SW20 . . . . . 66Xa **132**
Cottenham Pde. SW20 . . . . . 68Xa **132**
COTTENHAM PARK 67Xa **132**
Cottenham Pk. Rd. SW20 . . . . . 67Wa **132**
(not continuous)
Cottenham Pl. SW20 . . . . . 66Xa **132**
Cottenham Rd. E17 . . . . . 28Bc **52**
Cotterells HP1: Hem H 2L **3**
Cotterells Hill HP1: Hem H 2L **3**
Cotterill Rd. KT6: Surb 75Na **153**
Cottesbrooke Cl. SL3: Coln 53F **104**
Cottesbrook St. SE14 . . . . . 52Ac **114**
Cottesloe Cl. GU24: Bisl 8D **166**
Cottesloe Ho. NW8 . . . . . 5D **214**
Cottesloe M. SE1 . . . . . 3A **230**
Cottesloe Theatre *6K* **223**
(in National Theatre)
Cottesmore Av. IG5: Ilf 26Qc **54**
Cottesmore Ct. *W8* *48Db* **89**
(off Stanford Rd.)
Cottesmore Gdns. W8 . . . . . 48Db **89**
Cottimore Av. KT12: Walt T 74X **151**
Cottimore Cres. KT12: Walt T 73X **151**
Cottimore La. KT12: Walt T 73X **151**
Cottimore Ter. KT12: Walt T 73X **151**
Cottingham Chase HA4: Ruis 34W **64**
Cottingham Rd. SE20 . . . . . 66Zb **136**
SW8 . . . . . 52Pb **112**
Cottington Rd. TW13: Hanw 63Z **129**
Cottington St. SE11 . . . . . 7A **230** (50Qb **90**)
Cottis La. CM16: Epp 2Vc **23**
Cottle Way *SE16* *47Xb* **91**
(off Paradise St.)

Cotton Av. W3 . . . 44Ta 87
Cotton Cl. E11 . . . 33Gc 73
RM9: Dag . . . 38Yc 75
Cottongrass Cl. CR0: C'don . . . 74Zb 158
Cotton Hall Ho. *SL4: Eton* . . . *1G 102*
(off Eton Wick Rd.)
Cottonham Cl. N12 . . . 22Fb 49
Cotton Hill BR1: Brom . . . 63Ec 136
Cotton Ho. SW2 . . . 59Nb 112
Cotton La. DA2: Dart, Ghithe . . . 57Sd 120
DA9: Ghithe . . . 57Sd 120
Cottonmill Cres. AL1: St A . . . 3B 6
Cottonmill La. AL1: St A . . . 4B 6
Cotton Rd. EN6: Pot B . . . 3Eb 17
Cotton Row SW11 . . . 55Eb 111
Cottons App. RM7: Rom . . . 29Fd 56
Cottons Cen. SE1 . . . 6H 225 (46Ub 91)
Cottons Ct. RM7: Rom . . . 29Fd 56
Cotton's Gdns. E2 . . . 3J 219 (41Ub 91)
Cottons La. SE1 . . . 6G 225 (46Tb 91)
Cotton St. E14 . . . 45Ec 92
Cottrell Ct. *SE10* . . . *49Hc 93*
(off Hop St.)
Cottrill Gdns. E8 . . . 37Xb 71
Cotts Cl. W7 . . . 43Ha 86
Couchmore Av. IG5: Ilf . . . 26Pc 54
KT10: Hin W . . . 75Ga 152
Coulgate St. SE4 . . . 55Ac 114
COULSDON . . . 88Mb 176
Coulsdon Common . . . 93Sb 197
Coulsdon Court Golf Course . . . 88Pb 176
Coulsdon Ct. Rd. CR5: Coul . . . 88Pb 176
Coulsdon La. CR5: Chip . . . 91Hb 195
Coulsdon Nth. Ind. Est.
CR5: Coul . . . 88Mb 176
Coulsdon Pl. CR3: Cat'm . . . 94Tb 197
Coulsdon Ri. CR5: Coul . . . 89Nb 176
Coulsdon Rd. CR3: Cat'm . . . 94Tb 197
CR5: Coul . . . 87Pb 176
Coulson Cl. RM8: Dag . . . 32Yc 75
Coulson Ct. AL2: Lon C . . . 9H 7
Coulson St. SW3 . . . 7F 227 (50Hb 89)
Coulson Way SL1: Burn . . . 3A 80
Coulter Cl. UB4: Yead . . . 42Aa 85
Coulter Ho. DA9: Ghithe . . . 57Yd 120
Coulter Rd. W6 . . . 48Xa 88
Coulthurst Ct. *SW16* . . . *66Nb 134*
(off Heybridge Av.)
Coulton Av. DA11: Nflt . . . 9A 122
Council Av. DA11: Nflt . . . 58Ee 121
Council Cotts. GU23: Wis . . . 87M 169
GU24: W End . . . 4D 166
Councillor St. SE5 . . . 52Sb 113
Counter Ct. SE1 . . . 7F 225
Counters Cl. HP1: Hem H . . . 2J 3
Counters Ct. *W14* . . . *48Ab 88*
(off Holland Rd.)
COUNTERS END . . . 2J 3
Counter St. SE1 . . . 7H 225 (46Ub 91)
Countess Cl. UB9: Hare . . . 26L 43
Countess Rd. NW5 . . . 36Lb 70
Countisbury Av. EN1: Enf . . . 17Vb 33
Countisbury Gdns. KT15: Add . . . 78K 149
Country Way TW13: Hanw . . . 65X 129
County Court
Bow . . . *37Hc 73*
(off Romford Rd.)
Brentford . . . 51Ma 109
Bromley . . . 67Jc 137
Central London . . . 6K 215
Clerkenwell and Shoreditch
. . . 5D 218 (42Sb 91)
Croydon . . . 75Tb 157
Dartford . . . 58Nd 119
Edmonton . . . 23Wb 51
Kingston upon Thames . . . 68Ma 131
Lambeth . . . 7A 230 (50Qb 90)
Reigate . . . 6M 207
Romford . . . 28Hd 56
St Albans . . . 2C 6
Slough . . . 7J 81
Staines . . . 64J 127
Uxbridge . . . 43V 84
Wandsworth . . . 57Ab 110
Watford . . . 12X 27
West London . . . *50Za 88*
(off Talgarth Rd.)
Willesden . . . 40Va 68
Woolwich . . . 48Qc 94
County Ga. EN5: New Bar . . . 16Db 31
SE9 . . . 62Sc 138
County Gro. SE5 . . . 53Sb 113
County Hall Apartments SE1 . . . 1H 229
County Hall (Former) . . . 1H 229 (47Pb 90)
County Ho. *SW9* . . . *53Qb 112*
(off Brixton Rd.)
County Pde. TW8: Bford . . . 52Ma 109
County Rd. CR7: Thor H . . . 68Rb 135
E6 . . . 43Rc 94
County St. SE1 . . . 4E 230 (48Sb 91)
Couper Ho. WD18: Wat . . . 16U 26
Coupland Pl. SE18 . . . 50Sc 94
Courage Cl. RM11: Horn . . . 30Ld 57
Courage Ct. CM13: Hut . . . 16Ee 41
Courage Wlk. CM13: Hut . . . 16Fe 41
Courcy Rd. N8 . . . 27Qb 50
Courier Rd. RM9: Dag . . . 42Ed 96
Courland Gro. SW8 . . . 53Mb 112
Courland Rd. KT15: Add . . . 76K 149
Courland St. SW8 . . . 53Mb 112
Course, The SE9 . . . 62Qc 138
Coursers Rd. AL4: Col H . . . 9L 7
Court, The CR6: W'ham . . . 90Ac 178
HA4: Ruis . . . 35Aa 65
Court Annexe . . . 2E 230 (47Sb 91)
Courtauld Cl. SE28 . . . 46Wc 95
Courtauld Ho. *E2* . . . *39Wb 71*
(off Goldsmiths Row)
Courtauld Institute of Art Gallery . . . 4H 223
Courtauld Rd. N19 . . . 32Nb 70
Courtaulds WD4: Chfd . . . 2K 11
Court Av. CR5: Coul . . . 90Qb 176
DA17: Belv . . . 50Bd 95
RM3: Hrld W . . . 24Qd 57
Court Bushes Rd.
CR3: W'ham . . . 91Wb 197
Court Cl. HA3: Kenton . . . 27Na 47
NW8 . . . *38Fb 69*
(off Boydell Ct., not continuous)
SM6: Wall . . . 80Mb 156
TW2: Twick . . . 62Da 129
Court Cl. Av. TW2: Twick . . . 62Da 129
Court Cres. BR8: Swan . . . 69Hd 140
KT9: Chess . . . 78Ma 153
SL1: Slou . . . 4H 81
Court Downs Rd. BR3: Beck . . . 68Dc 136
Court Dr. CR0: Wadd . . . 77Pb 156
HA7: Stan . . . 21Na 47
SM1: Sutt . . . 77Gb 155
UB10: Hil . . . 39P 63
Courtenay Av. HA3: Hrw W . . . 24Ea 46
N6 . . . 31Gb 69
SM2: Sutt . . . 81Cb 175
Courtenay Dr. BR3: Beck . . . 68Fc 137
RM16: Chaf H . . . 48Be 99
Courtenay Gdns. HA3: Hrw W . . . 26Ea 46
RM14: Upm . . . 32Sd 78
Courtenay M. E17 . . . 29Ac 52
GU21: Wok . . . 88C 168
Courtenay Pl. E17 . . . 29Ac 52
Courtenay Rd. E11 . . . 34Hc 73
E17 . . . 28Zb 52
GU21: Wok . . . 88C 168
HA9: Wemb . . . 34Ma 67
KT4: Wor Pk . . . 76Ya 154
SE20 . . . 65Zb 136
Courtenay Sq. SE11 . . . 7K 229 (50Qb 90)
Courtenay St. SE11 . . . 7J 229 (50Qb 90)
Courtens M. HA7: Stan . . . 24La 46
Court Farm Av. KT19: Ewe . . . 78Ta 153
Court Farm Cl. SL1: Slou . . . 6F 80
Court Farm Gdns. KT19: Eps . . . 83Sa 173
Court Farm Ind. Est.
TW19: Stanw . . . 58P 105
Court Farm La. UB5: N'olt . . . 38Ca 65
Court Farm Pk. CR6: W'ham . . . 88Wb 177
Court Farm Rd. CR6: W'ham . . . 90Wb 177
SE9 . . . 61Mc 137
UB5: N'olt . . . 38Ca 65
Courtfield W5 . . . 43La 86
Courtfield Av. HA1: Harr . . . 29Ha 46
Courtfield Cres. HA1: Harr . . . 29Ha 46
Courtfield Gdns. HA4: Ruis . . . 33V 64
SW5 . . . 49Db 89
UB9: Den . . . 34J 63
W13 . . . 44Ja 86
Courtfield Ho. EC1 . . . 7K 217
UB8: Uxb . . . *37M 63*
(off Fairfield Rd.)
Courtfield M. SW5 . . . 49Eb 89
Courtfield Ri. BR4: W W'ck . . . 76Fc 159
Courtfield Rd. SW7 . . . 6A 226 (49Eb 89)
TW15: Ashf . . . 65R 128
Court Gdns. N1 . . . 37Qb 70
N7 . . . 37Qb 70
RM3: Hrld W . . . 23Qd 57
Courtgate Cl. NW7 . . . 23Va 48
Court Grn. Hgts.
GU22: Wok . . . 2N 187
Court Haw SM7: Bans . . . 87Gb 175
Court Hill CR2: Sande . . . 84Ub 177
CR5: Chip . . . 90Gb 175
Courthill Rd. SE13 . . . 56Ec 114
Courthope Ho. *SE16* . . . *48Yb 92*
(off Lower Rd.)
SW8 . . . *52Nb 112*
(off Hartington Rd.)
Courthope Rd. NW3 . . . 35Hb 69
SW19 . . . 64Ab 132
UB6: G'frd . . . 40Fa 66
Courthope Vs. SW19 . . . 66Ab 132
Courthouse Gdns. N3 . . . 23Cb 49
Courthouse La. N16 . . . 35Vb 71
Court Ho. Mans. KT19: Eps . . . 84Ta 173
Courthouse Rd. N12 . . . 23Db 49
Courtland Av. E4 . . . 19Hc 35
IG1: Ilf . . . 33Pc 74
NW7 . . . 20Ta 29
SW16 . . . 66Pb 134
Courtland Dr. IG7: Chig . . . 20Rc 36
Courtland Gro. SE28 . . . 44Zc 95
Courtland Rd. E6 . . . 39Nc 74
Courtlands KT12: Walt T . . . 73W 150
TW10: Rich . . . 57Qa 109
Courtlands Av. BR2: Hayes . . . 74Gc 159
KT10: Esh . . . 79Ba 151
SE12 . . . 57Kc 115
SL3: L'ly . . . 9P 81
TW9: Kew . . . 54Ra 109
TW12: Hamp . . . 65Ba 129
Courtlands Cl. CR2: Sande . . . 82Vb 177
HA4: Ruis . . . 31V 64
WD24: Wat . . . 7U 12
Courtlands Cres.
SM7: Bans . . . 87Cb 175
Courtlands Dr. KT19: Ewe . . . 79Ua 154
WD17: Wat . . . 9U 12
WD24: Wat . . . 9U 12
Courtlands Rd. KT5: Surb . . . 73Qa 153
Court La. KT19: Eps . . . 85Sa 173
SE21 . . . 58Ub 113
SL0: Iver . . . 46H 83
(not continuous)
SL1: Burn . . . 1B 80
SL4: Dor . . . 8A 80
Court La. Gdns. SE21 . . . 59Ub 113
Courtleas KT11: Cobh . . . 85Ca 171
Courtleet Dr. DA8: Erith . . . 53Dd 118
Courtleigh NW11 . . . 29Bb 49
Courtleigh Av. EN4: Had W . . . 10Fb 17
Courtleigh Gdns. NW11 . . . 28Ab 48
Court Lodge DA12: Shorne . . . 5N 145
DA17: Belv . . . 50Cd 96
SW1 . . . *6H 227*
(off Sloane Sq.)
Courtman Rd. N17 . . . 24Sb 51
Court Mead UB5: N'olt . . . 41Ba 85
Courtmead Cl. SE24 . . . 58Sb 113
Court Mdw. TN15: Wro . . . 88Be 185
Courtnell St. W2 . . . 44Cb 89
Courtney Cl. SE19 . . . 65Ub 135
Courtney Ct. N7 . . . 36Qb 70
Courtney Cres. SM5: Cars . . . 80Hb 155
Courtney Ho. *NW4* . . . *27Ya 48*
(off Mulberry Cl.)
W14 . . . *48Ab 88*
(off Russell Rd.)
Courtney Pl. CR0: Wadd . . . 76Qb 156
KT11: Cobh . . . 84Ba 171
Courtney Rd. CR0: Wadd . . . 76Qb 156
N7 . . . 36Qb 70
RM16: Grays . . . 7E 100
SW19 . . . 66Gb 133
TW6: H'row A . . . 55Q 106
Courtney Way TW6: H'row A . . . 54Q 106
Court Pde. HA0: Wemb . . . 34Ka 66
Courtrai Rd. SE23 . . . 58Ac 114
Court Rd. BR6: Chels, Orp . . . 73Xc 161
CR3: Cat'm . . . 95Tb 197
DA2: Daren . . . 64Ud 142
RH9: G'stone . . . 3A 210
SE9 . . . 58Pc 116
Court Rd. SE25 . . . 68Vb 135
SM7: Bans . . . 88Cb 175
UB2: S'hall . . . 49Ba 85
UB10: Ick . . . 36R 64
Court Royal SW15 . . . 57Ab 110
Courtside AL3: St A . . . 1B 6
N8 . . . 30Mb 50
SE26 . . . 62Xb 135
Court St. BR1: Brom . . . 68Jc 137
E1 . . . 43Xb 91
Courtville Ho. *W10* . . . *41Ab 88*
(off Third Av.)
Court Way NW9 . . . 28Ua 48
RM3: Hrld W . . . 26Nd 57
TW2: Twick . . . 59Ha 108
W3 . . . 43Sa 87
Courtway IG6: Ilf . . . 27Sc 54
IG8: Wfd G . . . 22Lc 53
Courtway, The WD19: Wat . . . 19Aa 27
Courtwood Dr. TN13: S'oaks . . . 96Jd 202
Courtwood La. CR0: Sels . . . 83Bc 178
Court Yd. SE9 . . . 58Pc 116
Courtyard SW3 . . . 7F 227
Courtyard, The AL4: St A . . . 2K 7
AL9: Ess . . . 1P 9
BR2: Kes . . . 79Nc 160
CM15: B'wood . . . 17Xd 40
CR3: Whyt . . . 90Vb 177
E2 . . . *41Vb 91*
(off Ezra St.)
EC3 . . . *3G 225*
(in Royal Exchange)
HP3: Hem H . . . 8M 3
KT14: W Byf . . . 84J 169
KT20: Kgswd . . . 95Eb 195
N1 . . . 38Pb 70
NW1 . . . 38Jb 70
SE14 . . . *53Zb 114*
(off Besson St.)
SL3: L'ly . . . 47C 82
SW3 . . . *51Fb 111*
(off Waldron M.)
TN16: Westrm . . . 99Tc 200
Courtyard Gdns. TN15: Wro . . . 88Ce 185
Courtyard Ho. SW6 . . . 54Eb 111
Courtyard M. BR5: St P . . . 66Wc 139
DA9: Ghithe . . . 58Wd 120
RM13: Rain . . . 39Hd 76
Courtyards, The WD18: Wat . . . 17T 26
Courtyard Theatre
Chipstead . . . 92Hb 195
Shoreditch . . . 4H 219 (41Ub 91)
Cousin La. EC4 . . . 5F 225 (45Tb 91)
Cousins Cl. UB7: Yiew . . . 45N 83
Couthurst Rd. SE3 . . . 51Kc 115
Coutts Av. DA12: Shorne . . . 3N 145
KT9: Chess . . . 78Na 153
Coutt's Cres. NW5 . . . 34Jb 70
Couzens Ho. *E3* . . . *43Bc 92*
(off Weatherley Cl.)
Couzins Wlk. DA1: Dart . . . 54Qd 119
Coval Gdns. SW14 . . . 56Ra 109
Coval La. SW14 . . . 56Ra 109
Coval Pas. SW14 . . . 56Sa 109
Coval Rd. SW14 . . . 56Ra 109
Coveham Cres. KT11: Cobh . . . 85W 170
Covelees Wall E6 . . . 44Qc 94
Covell Ct. *EN2: Enf* . . . *10Pb 18*
(off The Ridgeway)
SE8 . . . 52Cc 114
Covell Ho. KT19: Eps . . . 82Ra 173
Covenbrook CM13: B'wood . . . 20Ee 41
COVENT GARDEN . . . 4G 223 (45Nb 90)
Covent Garden . . . 4G 223 (45Nb 90)
Covent Gdn. WC2 . . . 4G 223 (45Nb 90)
Coventry Cl. E6 . . . 44Pc 94
NW6 . . . 40Cb 69
Coventry Hall SW16 . . . 64Nb 134
Coventry Rd. E1 . . . 42Xb 91
E2 . . . 42Xb 91
IG1: Ilf . . . 33Rc 74
SE25 . . . 70Wb 135
Coventry St. W1 . . . 5D 222 (45Mb 90)
Coverack Cl. CR0: C'don . . . 73Ac 158
N14 . . . 16Lb 32
Coverdale Cl. HA7: Stan . . . 22Ka 46
Coverdale Ct. EN3: Enf W . . . 9Ac 20
Coverdale Gdns. CR0: C'don . . . 76Vb 157
Coverdale Rd. N11 . . . 23Jb 50
NW2 . . . 38Za 68
W12 . . . 47Xa 88
Coverdales, The IG11: Bark . . . 40Tc 74
Coverdale Way SL2: Slou . . . 2E 80
Coverham Ho. *SE4* . . . *56Zb 114*
(off Billingford Cl.)
Coverley Cl. CM13: Gt War . . . 23Yd 58
E1 . . . 43Wb 91
Coverley Point SE11 . . . 6H 229
Covert, The BR6: Pet W . . . 72Uc 160
HA6: Nwood . . . 25S 44
SE19 . . . *66Vb 135*
(off Fox Hill)
SL5: Asc . . . 3A 146
Coverton Rd. SW17 . . . 64Gb 133
Covert Rd. IG6: Ilf . . . 22Vc 55
Coverts, The CM13: Hut . . . 18Ce 41
Coverts Rd. KT10: Clay . . . 80Ha 152
Covert Way EN4: Had W . . . 12Eb 31
Covesfield DA11: Grav'nd . . . 9B 122
Covet Wood Cl. BR5: St M Cry . . . 72Vc 161
Covey Cl. SW19 . . . 68Db 133
Covey Rd. KT4: Wor Pk . . . 75Za 154
Covington Gdns. SW16 . . . 66Rb 135
Covington Way SW16 . . . 65Pb 134
(not continuous)
Cowan Cl. E6 . . . 43Nc 94
Cowan Ct. NW10 . . . 38Ta 67
Coward Ind. Est. RM16: Grays . . . 10D 100
Cowbridge La. IG11: Bark . . . 38Rc 74
Cowbridge Mdw. GU24: Pirb . . . 5D 186
Cowbridge Rd. HA3: Kenton . . . 28Pa 47
Cowcross St. EC1 . . . 7B 218 (43Rb 91)
Cowdenbeath Path N1 . . . 39Pb 70
Cowden Rd. BR6: Orp . . . 73Vc 161
Cowden St. SE6 . . . 63Cc 136
Cowdray Rd. UB10: Hil . . . 39S 64
Cowdray Way RM12: Horn . . . 35Jd 76
WD3: Crox G . . . 14R 26
Cowdrey Cl. EN1: Enf . . . 12Ub 33
Cowdrey Ct. DA1: Dart . . . 59Kd 119
Cowdrey Rd. SW19 . . . 64Db 133
Cowen Av. HA2: Harr . . . 33Fa 66
Cowgate Rd. UB6: G'frd . . . 41Fa 86
Cowick Rd. SW17 . . . 63Hb 133
Cowings Mead UB5: N'olt . . . 37Aa 65
Cowland Av. EN3: Pond E . . . 14Yb 34
Cow La. UB6: G'frd . . . 40Fa 66
WD23: Bush . . . 16Ca 27
WD25: Wat . . . 8Y 13
Cow Leaze E6 . . . 44Qc 94
Cowleaze Rd. KT2: King T . . . 67Na 131
COWLEY . . . 42M 83
Cowley Av. DA9: Ghithe . . . 57Vd 120
KT16: Chert . . . 73H 149
Cowley Bus. Pk. UB8: Cowl . . . 41L 83
Cowley Cl. CR2: Sels . . . 81Yb 178
Cowley Cres. KT12: Hers . . . 77Y 151
UB8: Cowl . . . 43L 83
Cowley Hill WD6: Bore . . . 9Qa 15
(not continuous)
Cowley La. E11 . . . 34Gc 73
KT16: Chert . . . 73H 149
Cowley Lodge KT16: Chert . . . 73H 149
Cowley Mill Rd. UB8: Uxb . . . 40K 63
Cowley Mill Trad. Est. UB8: Uxb . . . 40K 63
COWLEY PEACHEY . . . 44M 83
Cowley Pl. NW4 . . . 29Ya 48
Cowley Retail Pk. UB8: Cowl . . . 45M 83
Cowley Rd. E11 . . . 29Kc 53
IG1: Ilf . . . 31Pc 74
RM3: Rom . . . 24Kd 57
SW9 . . . 53Qb 112
(not continuous)
SW14 . . . 55Ua 110
UB8: Uxb . . . 40L 63
W3 . . . 46Va 88
Cowley St. SW1 . . . 4F 229 (48Nb 90)
Cowling Cl. W11 . . . 46Ab 88
Coworth Cl. SL5: S'dale . . . 1F 146
Coworth Pk. . . . 10G 124
Coworth Rd. SL5: S'dale . . . 1E 146
Cowper Av. E6 . . . 38Nc 74
RM18: Tilb . . . 3D 122
SM1: Sutt . . . 77Fb 155
Cowper Cl. BR2: Brom . . . 70Mc 137
DA16: Well . . . 57Wc 117
KT16: Chert . . . 72H 149
Cowper Ct. WD24: Wat . . . 9W 12
Cowper Gdns. N14 . . . 16Kb 32
SM6: Wall . . . 79Lb 156
Cowper Ho. SE17 . . . 7E 230
SW1 . . . 7E 228
Cowper Rd. BR2: Brom . . . 70Mc 137
DA17: Belv . . . 49Cd 96
HP1: Hem H . . . 4K 3
KT2: King T . . . 64Pa 131
N14 . . . 18Kb 32
N16 . . . 36Ub 71
N18 . . . 22Wb 51
RM13: Rain . . . 42Jd 96
SL2: Slou . . . 2E 80
SW19 . . . 65Eb 133
W3 . . . 46Ta 87
W7 . . . 45Ha 86
Cowper's Ct. EC3 . . . 3G 225
Cowper St. EC2 . . . 5G 219 (42Tb 91)
Cowper Ter. W10 . . . 43Za 88
COWSHOT COMMON . . . 2C 186
Cowshot Cres. GU24: Brkwd . . . 2B 186
Cowslip Cl. UB10: Uxb . . . 38N 63
Cowslip La. GU21: Wok . . . 7M 167
RH5: Mick . . . 100Ja 192
(not continuous)
Cowslip Rd. E18 . . . 26Kc 53
Cowthorpe Rd. SW8 . . . 53Mb 112
Cox Cl. WD7: Shenl . . . 4Pa 15
Cox Ct. EN4: E Barn . . . 14Gb 31
Coxdean KT18: Tatt C . . . 91Ya 194
Coxe Pl. HA3: W'stone . . . 28Ja 46
Coxfield Cl. HP2: Hem H . . . 3N 3
Cox Ho. *W6* . . . *51Ab 110*
(off Field Rd.)
Cox La. KT9: Chess . . . 77Pa 153
KT19: Ewe . . . 78Ra 153
(not continuous)
Coxley Ri. CR8: Purl . . . 85Sb 177
Coxmount Rd. SE7 . . . 50Mc 93
Coxon Dr. RM16: Chaf H . . . 48Ae 99
Coxs Av. TW17: Shep . . . 69U 128
Coxson Way SE1 . . . 2K 231 (47Vb 91)
Cox's Wlk. SE21 . . . 60Wb 113
COXTIE GREEN . . . 15Sd 40
Coxtie Grn. Rd.
CM14: N'side, Pil H, S Weald . . . 14Qd 39
Coxwell Rd. SE18 . . . 50Tc 94
SE19 . . . 66Ub 135
Coxwold Path KT9: Chess . . . 80Na 153
Crabbs Cft. Cl. BR6: Farnb . . . 78Sc 160
Crab Hill BR3: Beck . . . 66Fc 137
Crab Hill La. RH1: S Nut . . . 10F 208
Crab La. WD25: A'ham . . . 7Da 13
Crabtree Av. HA0: Wemb . . . 40Na 67
RM6: Chad H . . . 28Zc 55
Crabtree Cl. E2 . . . 2K 219 (40Vb 71)
HP3: Hem H . . . 4M 3
KT23: Bookh . . . 98Ea 192
TN15: Fair . . . 84Fe 185
WD23: Bush . . . 15Da 27
Crabtree Ct. EN5: New Bar . . . 14Db 31
HP3: Hem H . . . 4N 3
Crabtree Dr. KT22: Lea . . . 96La 192
Crabtree Hall *SW6* . . . *52Ya 110*
(off Crabtree La.)
CRABTREE HILL . . . 17Bd 37
Crabtree La. HP3: Hem H . . . 4M 3
KT18: Head . . . 98Sa 193
KT23: Bookh . . . 98Ea 192
SW6 . . . 52Ya 110
(not continuous)
Crabtree Manorway Nth.
DA17: Belv, Erith . . . 47Ed 96
Crabtree Manorway Sth.
DA17: Belv . . . 48Ed 96
Crabtree Office Village
TW20: Thorpe . . . 68E 126
Crabtree Rd. TW20: Thorpe . . . 68E 126
Crabtree Wlk. CR0: C'don . . . 74Wb 157
Crabwood RH8: Oxt . . . 100Gc 199
Crace St. NW1 . . . 3D 216 (41Mb 90)
Cracknell Cl. EN1: Enf . . . 8Xb 19
Craddock Rd. EN1: Enf . . . 13Vb 33
Craddocks Av. KT21: Asht . . . 89Na 173
Craddocks Cl. KT21: Asht . . . 88Qa 173
Craddocks Pde. KT21: Asht . . . 89Na 173
Craddock St. NW5 . . . 37Jb 70
Cradley Rd. SE9 . . . 60Tc 116
Crafts Council & Gallery . . . 2A 218 (40Qb 70)
Cragg Av. WD7: R'lett . . . 8Ha 14
Cragie Ho. *SE1* . . . *49Vb 91*
(off Balaclava Rd.)
Craigdale Rd. RM11: Horn . . . 30Hd 56
Craig Dr. UB8: Hil . . . 44R 84
Craigen Av. CR0: C'don . . . 74Xb 157
Craigen Gdns. IG3: Ilf . . . 35Uc 74
Craigerne Rd. SE3 . . . 52Kc 115
Craig Gdns. E18 . . . 26Hc 53
Craigholm SE18 . . . 54Qc 116
Craigie Ct. DA1: Dart . . . 59Qd 119
Craigmore Ct. HA6: Nwood . . . 24U 44
Craigmore Twr. *GU22: Wok* . . . *91A 188*
(off Constitution Hill)
Craig Mt. WD7: R'lett . . . 7Ka 14
Craigmuir Pk. HA0: Wemb . . . 39Pa 67
Craignair Rd. SW2 . . . 59Qb 112
Craignish Av. SW16 . . . 68Pb 134
Craig Pk. Rd. N18 . . . 21Xb 51
Craig Rd. TW10: Ham . . . 63La 130
Craig's Ct. SW1 . . . 6F 223 (46Nb 90)
Craigton Rd. SE9 . . . 56Pc 116
Craigweil Av. WD7: R'lett . . . 7Ka 14
Craigweil Cl. HA7: Stan . . . 22Ma 47
Craigweil Dr. HA7: Stan . . . 22Ma 47
Craigwell Av. TW13: Felt . . . 62W 128
Craigwell Cl. TW18: Staines . . . 67G 126
Craik Ct. *NW6* . . . *40Bb 69*
(off Carlton Vale)
Crail Row SE17 . . . 6G 231 (49Tb 91)
Crakell Rd. RH2: Reig . . . 7L 207
Crakers Mead WD18: Wat . . . 13X 27
Crales Ho. SE18 . . . 48Nc 94
Cramer St. W1 . . . 1J 221 (43Jb 90)
Crammavill St. RM16: Grays . . . 45Ce 99
Crammerville Wlk. RM13: Rain . . . 42Kd 97
Crammond Cl. W6 . . . 51Ab 110
Cramond Ct. TW14: Bedf . . . 60U 106
Cramonde Ct. DA16: Well . . . 54Wc 117
Crampshaw La. KT21: Asht . . . 91Pa 193
Crampton Ho. SW8 . . . 53Lb 112
Crampton Rd. SE20 . . . 65Yb 136
Cramptons Rd. TN14: S'oaks . . . 92Kd 203
Crampton St. SE17 . . . 6D 230 (49Sb 91)
Cranberra Pl. TW9: Rich . . . 55Qa 109
Cranberry Cl. UB5: N'olt . . . 40Z 65
Cranberry Ent. Pk. *N17* . . . *24Vb 51*
(off White Hart La.)
Cranberry La. E16 . . . 42Gc 93
Cranborne Av. EN6: Pot B . . . 2Ab 16
KT6: Surb . . . 76Qa 153
UB2: S'hall . . . 49Ca 85
Cranborne Cl. EN6: Pot B . . . 3Ab 16
Cranborne Ct. EN3: Enf W . . . 8Zb 20
Cranborne Cres. EN6: Pot B . . . 3Ab 16
Cranborne Gdns. RM14: Upm . . . 33Rd 77
Cranborne Ind. Est. EN6: Pot B . . . 2Ab 16
(not continuous)
Cranborne Pde. EN6: Pot B . . . 3Za 16
Cranborne Rd. EN6: Pot B . . . 2Ab 16
EN8: Chesh . . . 4Zb 20
IG11: Bark . . . 39Tc 74
Cranborne Waye UB4: Yead . . . 44X 85
(not continuous)
Cranbourn All. WC2 . . . 4E 222
CRANBOURNE . . . 10A 102
Cranbourne *NW1* . . . *38Mb 70*
(off Agar Gro.)
Cranbourne Av. E11 . . . 28Kc 53
SL4: Wind . . . 4D 102
Cranbourne Cl. KT12: Hers . . . 79Y 151
SL1: Slou . . . 6G 80
SW16 . . . 69Nb 134
Cranbourne Cotts. SL4: Wink . . . 2A 124
Cranbourne Ct. *SW11* . . . *52Gb 111*
(off Albert Bri. Rd.)
Cranbourne Dr. HA5: Pinn . . . 29Z 45
Cranbourne Gdns. IG6: Ilf . . . 27Sc 54
NW11 . . . 29Ab 48
Cranbourne Hall Cotts. *SL4: Wink* . . . *10A 102*
(off Squirrel La.)
Cranbourne Pas. SE16 . . . 47Xb 91
Cranbourne Rd. E12 . . . 36Nc 74
E15 . . . 35Ec 72
HA6: Nwood . . . 27V 44
N10 . . . 26Kb 50
SL1: Slou . . . 6G 80
Cranbourn Ho. *SE16* . . . *47Xb 91*
(off Marigold St.)
Cranbourn St. WC2 . . . 4E 222 (45Mb 90)
CRANBROOK . . . 32Pc 74
Cranbrook NW1 . . . 1C 216
Cranbrook Cl. BR2: Hayes . . . 72Jc 159
Cranbrook Ct. CR2: S Croy . . . 78Ub 157
TW8: Bford . . . 51La 108
Cranbrook Dr. AL4: St A . . . 2J 7
KT10: Esh . . . 74Ea 152
RM2: Rom . . . 28Ld 57
TW2: Whitt . . . 60Da 107
Cranbrook Est. E2 . . . 40Zb 72
Cranbrook Ho. *DA8: Erith* . . . *52Hd 118*
(off Boundary St.)
Cranbrook La. N11 . . . 21Kb 50
Cranbrook M. E17 . . . 29Bc 52
Cranbrook Pk. N22 . . . 25Qb 50
Cranbrook Ri. IG1: Ilf . . . 30Pc 54
Cranbrook Rd. CR7: Thor H . . . 68Sb 135
DA7: Bex . . . 53Bd 117
EN4: E Barn . . . 16Fb 31
IG1: Ilf . . . 31Qc 74
IG2: Ilf . . . 29Qc 54
IG6: Ilf . . . 29Qc 54
SE8 . . . 53Cc 114
SW19 . . . 66Ab 132
TW4: Houn . . . 56Ba 107
W4 . . . 50Ua 88
Cranbrook St. E2 . . . 40Zb 72
Cranbury Rd. SW6 . . . 54Db 111
Crandley Ct. SE8 . . . 49Ac 92
(not continuous)
Crandon Wlk. DA4: S Dar . . . 68Ud 142
Crane Av. TW7: Isle . . . 57Ja 108
W3 . . . 45Sa 87
Cranebank M. TW1: Twick . . . 56Ja 108
Cranebank (Nature Reserve) . . . 54W 106
Cranebrook TW2: Twick . . . 61Ea 130
Crane Cl. HA2: Harr . . . 34Ea 66
RM10: Dag . . . 37Cd 76
Crane Ct. EC4 . . . 3A 224 (44Qb 90)
KT19: Ewe . . . 77Sa 153
Cranefield Dr. WD25: Wat . . . 4Aa 13
Craneford Cl. TW2: Twick . . . 59Ha 108
Craneford Way TW2: Twick . . . 59Ga 108
Crane Gdns. UB3: Harl . . . 49V 84
Crane Gro. N7 . . . 37Qb 70
Crane Ho. *E3* . . . *40Ac 72*
(off Roman Rd.)
SE15 . . . 53Vb 113
TW13: Hanw . . . 62Ca 129
Cranell Grn. RM15: S Ock . . . 46Xd 98
Crane Lodge Rd. TW5: Cran . . . 51X 107

Crane Mead SE16 . . . . . 50Yb 92
Crane Mead Ct. TW1: Twick 59Ha 108
Crane Pk. Island Nature Reserve
. . . . . 61Ba 129
Crane Pk. Rd. TW2: Whitt 61Da 129
Crane Rd. TW2: Twick 60Ga 108
TW19: Stanw 58Q 106
Cranesbill Cl. NW9 . . . . . 27Ta 47
SW16 . . . . . 68Mb 134
Cranes Dr. KT5: Surb 70Na 131
Cranes Pk. KT5: Surb 70Na 131
Cranes Pk. Av. KT5: Surb 70Na 131
Cranes Pk. Cres. KT5: Surb 70Pa 131
Crane St. SE10 . . . . . 50Fc 93
SE15 . . . . . 53Vb 113
Craneswater UB3: Harl 52V 106
Craneswater Pk. UB2: S'hall 50Ba 85
Cranes Way WD6: Bore 15Sa 29
Crane Way TW2: Whitt 59Ea 108
Cranfield Cl. SE27 . . . . . 62Sb 135
Cranfield Ct. GU21: Wok 10L 167
W1 . . . . . 1E 220
Cranfield Cres. EN6: Cuff 1Nb 18
Cranfield Dr. NW9 . . . . . 24Ua 48
Cranfield Ho. WC1 . . . . . 7F 217
Cranfield Rd. SE4 . . . . . 55Bc 114
Cranfield Rd. E. SM5: Cars 81Jb 176
Cranfield Rd. W.
SM5: Cars 81Hb 175
Cranfield Row SE1 . . . . . 3A 230
CRANFORD 52W 106
Cranford Av. N13 . . . . . 22Nb 50
TW19: Stanw 59N 105
Cranford Cl. CR8: Purl 85Sb 177
SW20 . . . . . 66Xa 132
TW19: Stanw 59N 105
Cranford Community College Sports Cen.
. . . . . 51X 107
Cranford Cotts. *E1* *45Zb 92*
(off Cranford St.)
Cranford Dr. UB3: Harl 49V 84
Cranford La. TW5: Cran, Hest 52X 107
TW6: H'row A 53V 106
(Bath Rd.)
TW6: H'row A 55V 106
(Envoy Av.)
UB3: Cran, Harl 51T 106
Cranford M. BR2: Brom 71Nc 160
Cranford Pk. Rd. UB3: Harl 49V 84
Cranford Ri. KT10: Esh 78Ea 152
Cranford Rd. DA1: Dart 60Nd 119
Cranford St. E1 . . . . . 45Zb 92
Cranford Way N8 . . . . . 28Pb 50
CRANHAM 31Ud 78
Cranham Brickfields Local Nature Reserve
. . . . . 31Vd 78
Cranham Gdns. RM14: Upm 32Ud 78
Cranham Golf Course 33Wd 78
Cranham Hall M. RM14: Upm 34Ud 78
Cranham Marsh Local Nature Reserve
. . . . . 35Ud 78
Cranham Rd. RM11: Horn 30Kd 57
Cranhurst Rd. NW2 . . . . . 36Ya 68
Cranleigh *W11* *46Bb 89*
(off Ladbroke Rd.)
Cranleigh Cl. BR6: Chels 76Wc 161
CR2: Sande 84Wb 177
DA5: Bexl 58Dd 118
EN7: Chesh 1Wb 19
SE20 . . . . . 68Xb 135
Cranleigh Ct. CR4: Mitc 69Fb 133
TW9: Rich 55Qa 109
UB1: S'hall 44Ba 85
Cranleigh Dr. BR8: Swan 70Gd 140
Cranleigh Gdns.
CR2: Sande 84Wb 177
HA3: Kenton 29Na 47
IG10: Lough 16Pc 36
IG11: Bark 38Tc 74
KT2: King T 65Pa 131
N21 . . . . . 15Qb 32
SE25 . . . . . 69Ub 135
SM1: Sutt 75Db 155
UB1: S'hall 44Ba 85
Cranleigh Gdns. Ind. Est.
UB1: S'hall 44Ba 85
Cranleigh Ho's. NW1 . . . . . 2C 216
Cranleigh M. SW11 . . . . . 54Gb 111
Cranleigh Rd. KT10: Esh 74Ea 152
N15 . . . . . 29Sb 51
SW19 . . . . . 69Cb 133
TW13: Felt 63V 128
Cranleigh St. NW1 . . . . . 2C 216 (40Lb 70)
Cranley Dene Ct. N10 . . . . . 28Kb 50
Cranley Dr. HA4: Ruis 33V 64
IG2: Ilf 31Sc 74
CRANLEY GARDENS 28Kb 50
Cranley Gdns. N10 . . . . . 28Kb 50
N13 . . . . . 20Pb 32
SM6: Wall 80Lb 156
SW7 . . . . . 7A 226 (50Eb 89)
Cranley M. SW7 . . . . . 7A 226 (50Eb 89)
Cranley Pde. *SE9* *63Nc 138*
(off Beaconsfield Rd.)
Cranley Pl. GU21: Knap 10H 167
SW7 . . . . . 6B 226 (49Fb 89)
Cranley Rd. E13 . . . . . 43Kc 93
IG2: Ilf 30Sc 54
KT12: Hers 78V 150
Cranmer Av. W13 . . . . . 48Ka 86
Cranmer Cl. CR6: W'ham 89Ac 178
EN6: Pot B 2Eb 17
HA4: Ruis 32Z 65
HA7: Stan 24La 46
KT13: Weyb 80Q 150
SM4: Mord 72Za 154
Cranmer Ct. *GU21: Knap* *10G 166*
(off Hampton Cl.)
N3 . . . . . 26Ab 48
SW3 . . . . . 6E 226 (49Gb 89)
SW4 . . . . . 55Mb 112
TW12: Hamp H 64Da 129
Cranmere Ct. EN2: Enf 12Qb 32
Cranmer Farm Cl. CR4: Mitc 70Hb 133
Cranmer Gdns. CR6: W'ham 89Ac 178
RM10: Dag 35Ed 76
Cranmer Ho. *SW9* *52Qb 112*
(off Cranmer Rd.)
SW11 . . . . . *53Gb 111*
(off Surrey La. Est.)
Cranmer Rd. CR0: C'don 76Rb 157
CR4: Mitc 70Hb 133
E7 . . . . . 35Kc 73
HA8: Edg 20Ra 29
KT2: King T 64Na 131
SW9 . . . . . 52Qb 112
Cranmer Rd. TN13: Riv 95Gd 202
TW12: Hamp H 64Da 129
UB3: Hayes 44T 84
Cranmer Ter. SW17 . . . . . 64Fb 133
Cranmore Av. TW7: Isle 52Ea 108
Cranmore Ct. *AL1: St A* *1D 6*
(off Avenue Rd.)
Cranmore La.
KT24: W Hor . . . . 100R 190 & 100S 190
Cranmore Rd. BR1: Brom 62Hc 137
BR7: Chst 64Pc 138
Cranmore Way N10 . . . . . 28Lb 50
Cranston Cl. RH2: Reig 7K 207
TW3: Houn 54Aa 107
UB10: Ick 33T 64
Cranstone Lodge *HP1: Hem H* *4L 3*
(off Cotterells)
Cranston Est. N1 . . . . . 1G 219 (40Tb 71)
Cranston Gdns. E4 . . . . . 23Dc 52
Cranston Pk. Av.
RM14: Upm 35Rd 77
Cranston Rd. SE23 . . . . . 60Ac 114
Cranswick Rd. SE16 . . . . . 50Xb 91
Crantock Rd. SE6 . . . . . 61Dc 136
Cranwell Cl. AL4: St A 4G 6
E3 . . . . . 42Dc 92
Cranwell Gro. TW17: Shep 70P 127
Cranwell Rd. TW6: H'row A 54R 106
Cranwells La. SL2: Farn C 4G 60
Cranwich Av. N21 . . . . . 17Tb 33
Cranwich Rd. N16 . . . . . 31Tb 71
Cranwood Ct. EC1 . . . . . 4G 219
Cranwood St. EC1 . . . . . 4G 219 (41Tb 91)
Cranworth Cres. E4 . . . . . 18Fc 35
Cranworth Gdns. SW9 . . . . . 53Qb 112
Craster Rd. SW2 . . . . . 59Pb 112
Crathie Rd. SE12 . . . . . 58Kc 115
Cravan Av. TW13: Felt 61W 128
Craven Av. UB1: S'hall 43Ba 85
W5 . . . . . 45La 86
Craven Cl. N16 . . . . . 31Wb 71
UB4: Hayes 44W 84
Craven Cottage 54Za 110
Craven Ct. NW10 . . . . . 39Ua 68
RM6: Chad H 30Ad 55
Craven Gdns. IG6: Ilf 26Tc 54
IG11: Bark 40Uc 74
RM3: Hrld W 23Sd 58
RM5: Col R 22Cd 56
SW19 . . . . . 64Db 133
Craven Hill W2 . . . . . 4A 220 (45Eb 89)
Craven Hill Gdns. W2 . . . . . 4A 220 (45Eb 89)
(not continuous)
Craven Hill M. W2 . . . . . 4A 220 (45Eb 89)
Craven Ho. *N2* *26Fb 49*
(off High Rd. E. Finchley)
Craven Lodge *SW6* *53Za 110*
(off Harbord St.)
W2 . . . . . 4A 220
Craven M. SW11 . . . . . 55Jb 112
Craven Pk. NW10 . . . . . 39Ta 67
Craven Pk. M. NW10 . . . . . 38Ua 68
Craven Pk. Rd. N15 . . . . . 30Vb 51
NW10 . . . . . 39Ua 68
Craven Pas. WC2 . . . . . 6F 223
Craven Rd. BR6: Chels 76Zc 161
CR0: C'don 74Xb 157
KT2: King T 67Pa 131
NW10 . . . . . 39Ta 67
W2 . . . . . 4A 220 (45Eb 89)
W5 . . . . . 45La 86
Craven St. WC2 . . . . . 6F 223 (46Nb 90)
Craven Ter. W2 . . . . . 4A 220 (45Eb 89)
Craven Wlk. N16 . . . . . 31Wb 71
Crawford Av. DA1: Dart 58Md 119
HA0: Wemb 36Ma 67
RM16: Grays 46De 99
Crawford Bldgs. W1 . . . . . 1E 220
Crawford Cl. TW7: Isle 54Ga 108
Crawford Compton Cl. RM12: Horn . . . 37Ld 77
Crawford Est. SE5 . . . . . 54Sb 113
Crawford Gdns. N13 . . . . . 20Rb 33
UB5: N'olt 41Ba 85
Crawford Mans. W1 . . . . . 1E 220
Crawford M. W1 . . . . . 1F 221 (43Hb 89)
Crawford Pas. EC1 . . . . . 6K 217 (42Qb 90)
Crawford Pl. W1 . . . . . 2E 220 (44Gb 89)
Crawford Rd. SE5 . . . . . 53Sb 113
Crawfords BR8: Hext 66Gd 140
Crawford St. NW10 . . . . . 38Ta 67
W1 . . . . . 1E 220 (43Gb 89)
Crawley Ct. DA11: Grav'nd 8C 122
Crawley Rd. E10 . . . . . 32Dc 72
EN1: Enf 17Ub 33
N22 . . . . . 26Sb 51
Crawshaw Rd. KT16: Ott 79F 148
Crawshay Cl. TN13: S'oaks 95Jd 202
Crawshay Ct. SW9 . . . . . 53Qb 112
Crawthew Gro. SE22 . . . . . 56Vb 113
Cray Av. BR5: St M Cry 72Xc 161
KT21: Asht 88Na 173
Craybrooke Rd. DA14: Sidc 63Xc 139
Crayburne DA13: Sflt 64Be 143
Craybury End SE9 . . . . . 61Sc 138
Cray Cl. DA1: Cray 56Jd 118
Craydene Rd. DA8: Erith 53Hd 118
Crayfields Bus. Pk. BR5: St P 67Yc 139
Crayfields Ind. Pk. BR5: St P 68Yc 139
CRAYFORD 57Hd 118
Crayford Cl. E6 . . . . . 44Nc 94
Crayford High St. DA1: Cray 57Gd 118
Crayford Ho. SE1 . . . . . 2G 231
Crayford Ind. Est. DA1: Cray 57Hd 118
Crayford Rd. DA1: Cray 57Hd 118
N7 . . . . . 35Mb 70
Crayford Stadium (Greyhound) 58Gd 118
Crayford Way DA1: Cray 57Hd 118
Cray Ho. NW8 . . . . . 7C 214
Crayke Hill KT9: Chess 80Na 153
Craylands BR5: St P 69Yc 139
Craylands La.
DA10: Ghithe, Swans 57Zd 121
Craylands Sq. DA10: Swans 57Zd 121
Crayle Ho. EC1 . . . . . 5B 218
Crayleigh Ter. DA14: Sidc 65Yc 139
Crayle St. SL2: Slou 1E 80
Craymill Sq. DA1: Cray 54Hd 118
Crayonne Cl. TW16: Sun 67U 128
Cray Rd. BR8: Crock 72Ed 162
DA14: Sidc 65Yc 139
DA17: Belv 51Cd 118
Crayside Ind. Est. DA1: Cray 56Kd 119
Crayside Leisure Cen. 58Gd 118
Cray's Pde. BR5: St P 68Yc 139
Cray Valley Golf Course 68Ad 139
Cray Valley Rd. BR5: St M Cry 71Wc 161
Cray Vw. Cl. *BR5: St M Cry* *70Yc 139*
(off Market Mdw.)
Cray Wanderers FC 71Kc 159
Crealock Gro. IG8: Wfd G 22Hc 53
Crealock St. SW18 . . . . . 58Db 111
Creasey Cl. RM11: Horn 33Kd 77
Creasy Cl. WD5: Ab L 3V 12
Creasy Ct. EN8: Walt C 6Zb 20
Creasy Est. SE1 . . . . . 4H 231 (48Ub 91)
Creative Ho. *SW8* *52Kb 112*
(off Prince of Wales Dr.)
Crebor St. SE22 . . . . . 58Wb 113
Crecy Ct. SE11 . . . . . 7K 229
Credenhall Dr. BR2: Brom 74Pc 160
Credenhill Ho. SE15 . . . . . 52Xb 113
Credenhill St. SW16 . . . . . 65Lb 134
Crediton Hgts. *NW10* *39Za 68*
(off Okehampton Rd.)
Crediton Hill NW6 . . . . . 36Db 69
Crediton Rd. E16 . . . . . 44Jc 93
NW10 . . . . . 39Za 68
Crediton Way KT10: Clay 78Ja 152
Credon Rd. E13 . . . . . 40Lc 73
SE16 . . . . . 50Xb 91
Credo Way RM20: W Thur 51Xd 120
Creechurch La. EC3 . . . . . 3J 225 (44Ub 91)
(not continuous)
Creechurch Pl. EC3 . . . . . 3J 225
Creed Ct. E1 . . . . . 41Ac 92
EC4 . . . . . 3C 224
Creed La. EC4 . . . . . 3C 224 (44Rb 91)
Creeds Cotts. CM16: Epp 4Uc 22
Creek, The DA11: Nflt 57De 121
TW16: Sun 71W 150
Creek Cotts. *KT8: E Mos* *70Ga 130*
(off Creek Rd.)
Creek Ho. *W14* *48Ab 88*
(off Russell Rd.)
CREEKMOUTH 42Vc 95
Creekmouth Ind. Pk.
IG11: Bark 42Vc 95
Creek Rd. IG11: Bark 41Vc 95
KT8: E Mos 70Ga 130
SE8 . . . . . 51Cc 114
SE10 . . . . . 51Cc 114
Creekside RM13: Rain 42Gd 96
SE8 . . . . . 52Dc 114
Creekside Foyer *SE8* *51Dc 114*
(off Stowage)
Creek Way RM13: Rain 43Gd 96
Creeland Gro. SE6 . . . . . 60Bc 114
Cree's Mdw. GU20: W'sham 9A 146
Cree Way RM1: Rom 24Gd 56
Crefeld Cl. W6 . . . . . 51Ab 110
Creffield Rd. W3 . . . . . 45Pa 87
W5 . . . . . 45Pa 87
Creighton Av. AL1: St A 6B 6
E6 . . . . . 40Mc 73
N2 . . . . . 27Gb 49
N10 . . . . . 27Gb 49
Creighton Cl. W12 . . . . . 45Wa 88
Creighton Rd. N17 . . . . . 24Ub 51
NW6 . . . . . 40Za 68
W5 . . . . . 48Ma 87
Cremer Bus. Cen. E2 . . . . . 2K 219
Cremer Ho. *SE8* *52Cc 114*
(off Deptford Chu. St.)
Cremer St. E2 . . . . . 2K 219 (40Vb 71)
Cremorne Est. SW10 . . . . . 51Fb 111
(not continuous)
Cremorne Gdns. KT19: Ewe 82Ta 173
Cremorne Riverside Cen. 52Fb 111
Cremorne Rd. DA11: Nflt 9B 122
SW10 . . . . . 52Eb 111
Creon Ct. *SW9* *52Qb 112*
(off Caldwell St.)
Crescent EC3 . . . . . 4K 225 (45Vb 91)
Crescent, The AL2: Brick W 2Ca 13
BR3: Beck 67Cc 136
BR4: W W'ck 72Gc 159
CM14: B'wood 20Xd 40
CM16: Epp 4Vc 23
CR0: C'don 71Tb 157
CR3: Wold 95Cc 198
DA3: Lfield 69Ae 143
DA5: Bexl 59Yc 117
DA9: Ghithe 57Yd 120
DA11: Nflt 1B 144
DA14: Sidc 63Vc 139
E17 . . . . . 30Ac 52
EN5: New Bar 12Db 31
HA0: Wemb 33Ka 66
HA2: Harr 32Ea 66
IG2: Ilf 30Qc 54
IG10: Lough 15Mc 35
KT3: N Mald 69Sa 131
KT6: Surb 71Na 153
KT8: W Mole 70Ca 129
KT13: Weyb 76Q 150
KT16: Chert 70J 127
KT18: Eps 86Qa 173
(not continuous)
KT22: Lea 94Ka 192
N9 . . . . . 19Xb 33
N11 . . . . . 21Hb 49
NW2 . . . . . 34Xa 68
RH1: Redh 9M 207
RH2: Reig 6K 207
RM14: Upm 31Ud 78
SL1: Slou 7J 81
(not continuous)
SM1: Sutt 78Fb 155
SM2: Sutt 83Cb 175
SW13 . . . . . 54Va 110
SW19 . . . . . 62Cb 133
TN13: S'oaks 93Md 203
TN15: Bor G 91Ce 205
TW15: Ashf 64P 127
TW17: Shep 73V 150
TW20: Egh 65A 126
UB1: S'hall 47Ba 85
UB3: Harl 52S 106
W3 . . . . . 44Ua 88
WD3: Crox G 16R 26
WD5: Ab L 2V 12
WD18: Wat 14Y 27
WD25: A'ham 10Da 13
Crescent Arc. *SE10* *51Ec 114*
(off Creek Rd.)
Crescent Av. RM12: Horn 33Hd 76
RM17: Grays 50Fe 99
(not continuous)
Crescent Cotts. TN13: Dun G 92Gd 202
Crescent Ct. KT6: Surb 71Ma 153
RH1: Redh *4A 208*
(off Foxboro Rd.)
Crescent Ct. RM17: Grays 50Fe 99
SW4 . . . . . *57Mb 112*
(off Park Hill)
Crescent Ct. Bus. Cen. E16 . . . . . 42Fc 93
Crescent Dr. BR5: Pet W 71Rc 160
CM15: Shenf 18Ae 41
Crescent E. EN4: Had W 10Eb 17
Crescent Gdns. BR8: Swan 68Ed 140
HA4: Ruis 31X 65
SW19 . . . . . 62Cb 133
Crescent Gro. CR4: Mitc 70Gb 133
SW4 . . . . . 56Lb 112
Crescent Ho. EC1 . . . . . 6D 218
SE13 . . . . . 54Dc 114
Crescent La. SW4 . . . . . 56Lb 112
Crescent Mans. *W11* *45Ab 88*
(off Elgin Cres.)
Crescent M. N22 . . . . . 25Nb 50
Crescent Pde. UB10: Hil 41Q 84
Crescent Pl. SW3 . . . . . 5E 226 (49Gb 89)
Crescent Ri. EN4: E Barn 15Gb 31
N3 . . . . . 25Bb 49
N22 . . . . . 25Mb 50
Crescent Rd. BR1: Brom 66Jc 137
BR3: Beck 68Dc 136
CM14: W'ley 21Xd 58
CR3: Cat'm 96Wb 197
DA8: Erith 51Hd 118
DA15: Sidc 62Vc 139
E4 . . . . . 17Gc 35
E6 . . . . . 39Lc 73
E10 . . . . . 33Dc 72
E13 . . . . . 39Jc 73
E18 . . . . . 25Lc 53
EN2: Enf 14Rb 33
EN4: E Barn 14Fb 31
HP2: Hem H 2M 3
KT2: King T 66Qa 131
N3 . . . . . 25Bb 49
N8 . . . . . 30Mb 50
N9 . . . . . 18Wb 33
N11 . . . . . 21Hb 49
N15 . . . . . 27Rb 51
N22 . . . . . 25Mb 50
RH1: Blet 5J 209
RH2: Reig 8J 207
RM10: Dag 34Dd 76
RM15: Avel 47Sd 98
SE18 . . . . . 50Rc 94
SW20 . . . . . 67Za 132
TW17: Shep 71S 150
Crescent Row EC1 . . . . . 6D 218 (42Sb 91)
Crescent Stables SW15 . . . . . 57Ab 110
Crescent St. N1 . . . . . 38Pb 70
Crescent Vw. IG10: Lough 16Mc 35
Crescent Wlk. RM15: Avel 47Sd 98
Crescent Way BR6: Orp 78Uc 160
N12 . . . . . 23Gb 49
RM15: Avel 46Td 98
SE4 . . . . . 55Cc 114
SW16 . . . . . 65Pb 134
Crescent West EN4: Had W 11Eb 31
Crescent Wharf E16 . . . . . 47Kc 93
(not continuous)
Crescent Wood Rd. SE26 . . . . . 62Wb 135
Cresford Rd. SW6 . . . . . 53Db 111
Crespigny Rd. NW4 . . . . . 30Xa 48
Cressage Cl. UB1: S'hall 42Ca 85
Cressage Ho. *TW8: Bford* *51Na 109*
(off Ealing Rd.)
Cressal Ho. *E14* *48Cc 92*
(off Tiller Rd.)
Cressall Cl. KT22: Lea 92Ka 192
Cressall Mead KT22: Lea 92Ka 192
Cress End WD3: Rick 18J 25
Cresset Ho. E9 . . . . . 37Yb 72
Cresset Rd. E9 . . . . . 37Yb 72
Cresset St. SW4 . . . . . 55Mb 112
CRESSFIELD 61Ce 143
Cressfield Cl. NW5 . . . . . 36Jb 70
Cressida Rd. N19 . . . . . 32Lb 70
Cressingham Gro. SM1: Sutt 77Eb 155
Cressingham Rd. HA8: Edg 23Ta 47
SE13 . . . . . 55Ec 114
Cressinghams, The KT18: Eps 85Ta 173
Cressington Cl. N16 . . . . . 36Ub 71
Cress M. BR1: Brom 64Fc 137
Cress Rd. SL1: Slou 7F 80
Cresswell NW9 . . . . . 26Va 48
Cresswell Gdns. SW5 . . . . . 7A 226 (50Eb 89)
Cresswell Ho. HA9: Wemb 34Na 67
TW19: Stanw *58N 105*
(off Douglas Rd.)
Cresswell Pk. SE3 . . . . . 55Hc 115
Cresswell Pl. SW10 . . . . . 7A 226 (50Eb 89)
Cresswell Rd. SE25 . . . . . 70Wb 135
TW1: Twick 58Ma 109
TW13: Hanw 62Aa 129
Cresswell Way N21 . . . . . 17Qb 32
Cressy Ct. E1 . . . . . 43Yb 92
W6 . . . . . 48Xa 88
Cressy Ho. SW15 . . . . . 55Xa 110
Cressy Ho's. *E1* *43Yb 92*
(off Hannibal Rd.)
Cressy Pl. E1 . . . . . 43Yb 92
Cressy Rd. NW3 . . . . . 36Hb 69
Crest, The KT5: Surb 71Qa 153
N13 . . . . . 21Qb 50
NW4 . . . . . 29Ya 48
Cresta Ct. W5 . . . . . 42Pa 87
Cresta Dr. KT15: Wdhm 82H 169
Cresta Ho. *E3* *42Cc 92*
(off Dimson Cres.)
NW3 . . . . . *38Fb 69*
(off Finchley Rd.)
Crest Av. RM17: Grays 52De 121
Crestbrook Av. N13 . . . . . 20Rb 33
Crestbrook Pl. *N13* *20Rb 33*
(off Green Lanes)
Crest Cl. TN14: Bad M 83Dd 182
Crest Ct. NW4 . . . . . 29Ya 48
Crest Dr. EN3: Enf W 10Yb 20
Crestfield St. WC1 . . . . . 3G 217 (41Nb 90)
Crest Gdns. HA4: Ruis 34Y 65
Cresthill Av. RM17: Grays 49Ee 99
Creston Av. GU21: Knap 9J 167
Creston Way KT4: Wor Pk 74Za 154
Crest Pk. HP2: Hem H 1C 4
Crest Rd. BR2: Hayes 73Hc 159
CR2: Sels 80Xb 157
NW2 . . . . . 33Va 68
Crest Vw. DA9: Ghithe 56Wd 120
HA5: Pinn 28Z 45
Crest Vw. Dr. BR5: Pet W 71Rc 160
Crestway SW15 . . . . . 58Wa 110
Crestwood Way TW4: Houn 57Aa 107
Creswell GU21: Knap 9H 167
Creswell Cnr. GU21: Knap 9H 167
Creswell Dr. BR3: Beck 71Dc 158
Creswick Ct. W3 . . . . . 45Ra 87
Creswick Rd. W3 . . . . . 45Ra 87
Creswick Wlk. E3 . . . . . 41Cc 92
NW11 . . . . . 28Bb 49
Crete Hall Rd. DA11: Nflt 58Fe 121
Creton St. SE18 . . . . . 48Qc 94
Creukhorne Rd. NW10 . . . . . 38Ua 68
Crewdson Rd. SW9 . . . . . 52Qb 112
Crewe Ct. KT20: Tad 94Ya 194
Crewe Pl. NW10 . . . . . 41Va 88
Crewe's Av. CR6: W'ham 88Yb 178
Crewe's Cl. CR6: W'ham 89Yb 178
Crewe's Farm La. CR6: W'ham 88Zb 178
Crewe's La. CR6: W'ham 88Yb 178
Crewkerne Ct. *SW11* *53Fb 111*
(off Bolingbroke Wlk.)
CREWS HILL 7Rb 19
Crews Hill EN2: Crew H 6Pb 18
Crews Hill Golf Course 7Pb 18
Crews St. E14 . . . . . 49Cc 92
Crewys Rd. NW2 . . . . . 33Bb 69
SE15 . . . . . 54Xb 113
Crichton Av. SM6: Bedd 78Mb 156
Crichton Ho. DA14: Sidc 65Zc 139
Crichton Rd. SM5: Cars 79Hb 155
Crichton St. SW8 . . . . . 54Lb 112
Crick Ct. *IG11: Bark* *40Sc 74*
(off Spring Pl.)
Cricketers Arms Rd. EN2: Enf 12Sb 33
Cricketers Cl. AL3: St A 1C 6
DA8: Erith 50Gd 96
KT9: Chess 77Ma 153
N14 . . . . . 17Lb 32
Cricketers Ct. SE11 . . . . . 6B 230
Cricketers La. CM13: Heron 23Fe 59
GU20: W'sham 8B 146
Cricketers M. SW18 . . . . . 57Db 111
Cricketers Row CM13: Heron 24Fe 59
Cricketers Ter. SM5: Cars 76Gb 155
Cricketers Wlk. SE26 . . . . . 64Yb 136
Cricket Fld. Rd. UB8: Uxb 39M 63
Cricketfield Rd. E5 . . . . . 35Xb 71
UB7: W Dray 49L 83
Cricket Grn. CR4: Mitc 69Hb 133
Cricket Ground Rd. BR7: Chst 67Rc 138
Cricket Hill RH1: S Nut 8F 208
Cricket La. BR3: Beck 65Ac 136
CRICKETS HILL 97D 188
Cricket Vw. KT13: Weyb 78R 150
Cricket Way KT13: Weyb 75U 150
Cricklade Av. RM3: Rom 23Md 57
SW2 . . . . . 61Nb 134
Cricklefield Stadium 33Uc 74
CRICKLEWOOD 35Za 68
Cricklewood B'way. NW2 . . . . . 34Ya 68
Cricklewood La. NW2 . . . . . 35Za 68
Cridland St. E15 . . . . . 39Hc 73
Crieff Ct. TW11: Tedd 66La 130
Crieff Rd. SW18 . . . . . 58Eb 111
Criffel Av. SW2 . . . . . 61Mb 134
Crimp Hill SL4: Old Win 9K 103
TW20: Eng G 2L 125
Crimscott St. SE1 . . . . . 4J 231 (48Ub 91)
Crimsworth Rd. SW8 . . . . . 53Mb 112
Crinan St. N1 . . . . . 1G 217 (40Nb 70)
Cringle Ct. EN6: Pot B 2Eb 17
Cringle St. SW8 . . . . . 52Lb 112
Cripplegate St. EC2 . . . . . 7E 218 (43Sb 91)
Cripps Grn. UB4: Yead 42X 85
Crispe Ho. IG11: Bark 40Tc 74
N1 . . . . . 1J 217
Crispen Rd. TW13: Hanw 63Aa 129
Crispian Cl. NW10 . . . . . 35Ua 68
Crispin Cl. CR0: Bedd 75Nb 156
KT21: Asht 90Pa 173
Crispin Ct. SE17 . . . . . 6J 231
Crispin Cres. CR0: Bedd 76Mb 156
Crispin Ind. Cen. N18 . . . . . 22Yb 52
Crispin Lodge N11 . . . . . 22Hb 49
Crispin M. NW11 . . . . . 29Bb 49
Crispin Pl. E1 . . . . . 7K 219 (43Vb 91)
Crispin Rd. HA8: Edg 23Sa 47
Crispin St. E1 . . . . . 1K 225 (43Vb 91)
Crispin Way SL2: Farn C 5H 61
UB8: Hil 42P 83
Crisp Rd. W6 . . . . . 50Ya 88
Cristowe Rd. SW6 . . . . . 54Bb 111
Critchley Av. DA1: Dart 58Md 119
Criterion Bldgs. *KT7: T Ditt* *73Ka 152*
(off Portsmouth Rd.)
Criterion Ct. *E8* *38Vb 71*
(off Middleton Rd.)
Criterion M. N19 . . . . . 33Mb 70
SE24 . . . . . *57Rb 113*
(off Shakespeare Rd.)
Criterion Theatre 5D 222
Criton Ind. Est. RM16: Ors 46G 100
CRITTALLS CORNER 66Yc 139
Crockenhall Way DA13: Ist R 6A 144
CROCKENHILL 72Fd 162
Crockenhill La.
BR8: Crock, Eyns, Farni 73Jd 162
DA4: Eyns, Farni 73Jd 162
Crockenhill Rd. BR5: St M Cry 71Zc 161
BR8: Crock 71Zc 161
Crockerton Rd. SW17 . . . . . 61Hb 133
Crockery La. GU4: E Clan 100N 189
Crockford Cl. KT15: Add 77L 149
Crockford Pk. Rd. KT15: Add 78L 149
Crockham Way SE9 . . . . . 63Qc 138
Crocus Cl. CR0: C'don 74Zb 158
Crocus Fld. EN5: Barn 16Bb 31
Croffets KT20: Tad 93Za 194
Croft, The AL2: Chis G 7N 5
BR8: Swan 69Ed 140
CR0: C'don 76Vb 157
E4 . . . . . 19Gc 35
EN5: Barn 14Ab 30
HA0: Wemb 36La 66
HA4: Ruis 35Y 65
HA5: Pinn 31Ba 65
HA8: Edg 24Ra 47
IG10: Lough 12Qc 36
KT17: Eps 86Va 174
KT22: Fet 95Ga 192
NW10 . . . . . 40Va 68
TW5: Hest 51Aa 107
W5 . . . . . 43Na 87
Croft Av. BR4: W W'ck 74Ec 158
Croft Cl. BR7: Chst 64Pc 138
DA17: Belv 50Bd 95
NW7 . . . . . 20Ua 30
SL9: Chal P 26A 42

Croft Cl. UB3: Harl 52S **106**
UB10: Hil 38Q **64**
WD4: Chfd 2J **11**
Croft Cnr. SL4: Old Win 7M **103**
Croft Ct. HA4: Ruis 32V **64**
SE13 .... 58Ec **114**
SM1: Sutt 75Fb **155**
WD6: Bore 13Ta **29**
Croftdown Rd. NW5 .... 34Jb **70**
Croft End Cl. KT9: Chess 76Pa **153**
Croft End Rd. WD4: Chfd 2J **11**
Crofters SL4: Old Win 8L **103**
Crofters Cl. RH1: Redh 8B **208**
TW7: Isle 57Fa **108**
TW19: Stanw 58L **105**
Crofters Ct. *SE8 .... 49Ac 92*
(off Croft St.)
Crofters Mead CR0: Sels 81Bc **178**
Crofters Rd. HA6: Nwood 21U **44**
Crofters Way NW1 .... 39Mb **70**
Croft Fld. WD4: Chfd 2J **11**
Croft Gdns. HA4: Ruis 32V **64**
W7 .... 47Ja **86**
Crofthill Rd. SL2: Slou 2F **80**
Croft Ho. E17 .... 28Dc **52**
W10 .... 41Ab 88
(off Third Av.)
Croft La. WD4: Chfd 2J **11**
Croftleigh Av. CR8: Purl 88Qb **176**
Croft Lodge Cl. IG8: Wfd G 23Kc **53**
Croft Mdw. WD4: Chfd 2J **11**
Croft M. N12 .... 20Eb **31**
CROFTON 75Sc **160**
Crofton KT21: Asht 90Na **173**
Crofton Av. BR6: Farnb 75Sc **160**
DA5: Bexl 59Zc **117**
KT12: Walt T 76Y **151**
W4 .... 52Sa **109**
Crofton Cl. KT16: Ott 80E **148**
Croftongate Way SE4 .... 57Ac **114**
Crofton Gro. E4 .... 21Fc **53**
Crofton Ho. *SW3 .... 51Gb 111*
(off Old Church St.)
Crofton La.
BR5: Farnb, Orp, Pet W 75Tc **160**
BR6: Pet W 73Tc **160**
CROFTON PARK 57Bc **114**
Crofton Pk. Rd. SE4 .... 58Bc **114**
Crofton Rd. BR6: Farnb, Orp 76Qc **160**
E13 .... 42Kc **93**
RM16: Grays 7A **100**
SE5 .... 53Ub **113**
Crofton Roman Villa 75Uc **160**
Crofton Ter. E5 .... 36Ac **72**
TW9: Rich 56Pa **109**
Crofton Way EN2: Enf 12Qb **32**
EN5: New Bar 16Db **31**
Croft Rd. BR1: Brom 65Jc **137**
CR3: Wold 94Cc **198**
EN3: Enf H 11Ac **34**
SL9: Chal P 26A **42**
SM1: Sutt 78Gb **155**
SW16 .... 67Qb **134**
SW19 .... 66Eb **133**
TN16: Westrm 98Rc **200**
Crofts, The HP3: Hem H 3B **4**
TW17: Shep 70U **128**
Crofts Ho. *E2 .... 40Wb 71*
(off Teale St.)
Croftside, The SE25 .... 69Wb **135**
Crofts La. N22 .... 24Qb **50**
Crofts Path HP3: Hem H 4A **4**
Crofts Rd. HA1: Harr 30Ja **46**
Crofts St. E1 .... 45Wb **91**
Croft St. SE8 .... 49Ac **92**
Crofts Vs. HA1: Harr 30Ja **46**
Croft Way DA15: Sidc 62Uc **138**
TN13: S'oaks 97Hd **202**
Croftway NW3 .... 35Cb **69**
TW10: Ham 62Ka **130**
Crogsland Rd. NW1 .... 38Jb **70**
Croham Cl. CR2: S Croy 80Ub **157**
Croham Hurst Golf Course 79Vb **157**
Croham Mnr. Rd. CR2: S Croy 80Ub **157**
Croham Mt. CR2: S Croy 80Ub **157**
Croham Pk. Av. CR2: S Croy 78Ub **157**
Croham Rd. CR2: S Croy 78Tb **157**
Croham Valley Rd.
CR2: Sels 79Wb **157**
Croindene Rd. SW16 .... 67Nb **134**
Crokesley Ho. *HA8: Edg 26Sa 47*
(off Burnt Oak B'way.)
Cromar Ct. GU21: Wok 8N **167**
Cromartie Rd. N19 .... 31Mb **70**
Cromarty Ct. SW2 .... 57Pb **112**
Cromarty Ho. *E1 .... 43Ac 92*
(off Ben Jonson Rd.)
Cromarty Rd. HA8: Edg 19Ra **29**
Cromberdale Ct. *N17 .... 25Wb 51*
(off Spencer Rd.)
Crombie Cl. IG4: Ilf 29Pc **54**
Crombie M. SW11 .... 54Gb **111**
Crombie Rd. DA15: Sidc 60Tc **116**
Crome Ho. *UB5: N'olt 40Aa 65*
(off Parkfield Dr.)
Cromer Cl. UB8: Hil 44S **84**
Cromer Ct. SL1: Slou 4J **81**
Cromer Hyde SM4: Mord 71Db **155**
Crome Rd. NW10 .... 37Ua **68**
Cromer Pl. BR6: Orp 74Uc **160**
Cromer Rd. E10 .... 31Fc **73**
EN5: New Bar 14Eb **31**
IG8: Wfd G 21Jc **53**
N17 .... 26Wb **51**
RM6: Chad H 30Ad **55**
RM7: Rom 30Ed **56**
RM11: Horn 31Md **77**
SE25 .... 69Xb **135**
SW17 .... 65Jb **134**
TW6: H'row A 54Q **106**
WD24: Wat 10Y **13**
Cromer St. WC1 .... 4F **217** (41Nb **90**)
Cromer Ter. E8 .... 36Wb **71**
RM6: Chad H 29Xc **55**
Cromer Vs. Rd. SW18 .... 58Bb **111**
Cromford Cl. BR6: Orp 76Uc **160**
Cromford Path E5 .... 35Zb **72**
Cromford Rd. SW18 .... 57Cb **111**
Cromford Way KT3: N Mald 67Ta **131**
Cromlix Cl. BR7: Chst 68Rc **138**
Crompton Ct. SW3 .... 5D **226** (49Gb **89**)
Crompton Hall SL9: Ger X 29B **42**
Crompton Ho. SE1 .... 4E **230**
W2 .... 6B **214**
Crompton Pl. EN3: Enf L 10Cc **20**
Crompton St. W2 .... 6B **214** (42Fb **89**)
Cromwell Av. BR2: Brom 70Kc **137**
EN7: Chesh 2Xb **19**
KT3: N Mald 71Va **154**
N6 .... 32Kb **70**
W6 .... 50Xa **88**
Cromwell Cen. IG6: Ilf 22Xc **55**
IG11: Bark 41Wc **95**
NW10 .... 41Ta **87**
Cromwell Cen., The *RM8: Dag 31Bd 75*
(off Coppen Rd.)
Cromwell Cl. BR2: Brom 70Kc **137**
E1 .... 46Wb **91**
KT12: Walt T 74X **151**
N2 .... 28Fb **49**
TW18: Staines 65L **127**
W3 .... 46Sa **87**
(not continuous)
W4 .... 50Ra 87
(off Harvard Rd.)
Cromwell Ct. EN3: Pond E 15Zb **34**
GU21: Knap 1G 186
(off Tudor Way)
Cromwell Cres. SW5 .... 49Cb **89**
Cromwell Dr. SL1: Slou 4J **81**
Cromwell Gdns. SW7 .... 4C **226** (48Fb **89**)
Cromwell Gro. CR3: Cat'm 93Sb **197**
W6 .... 48Ya **88**
Cromwell Highwalk EC2 .... 7E **218**
Cromwell Ho. CR0: C'don 76Rb **157**
SW11 .... 53Jb 112
(off Charlotte Despard Av.)
Cromwell Ind. Est. E10 .... 32Ac **72**
Cromwell Lodge DA6: Bex 57Ad **117**
E1 .... 42Yb 92
(off Cleveland Gro.)
IG11: Bark 36Uc **74**
Cromwell Mans. *SW5 .... 49Cb 89*
(off Cromwell Rd.)
Cromwell M. SW7 .... 5C **226** (49Fb **89**)
Cromwell Pl. EC2 .... 7E **218**
N6 .... 32Kb **70**
SW7 .... 5C **226** (49Fb **89**)
SW14 .... 55Sa **109**
Cromwell Rd. BR3: Beck 68Ac **136**
CM14: W'ley 21Xd **58**
CR0: C'don 73Tb **157**
CR3: Cat'm 93Sb **197**
E7 .... 38Lc **73**
E17 .... 29Ec **52**
HA0: Wemb 40Na **67**
KT2: King T 67Na **131**
KT4: Wor Pk 76Ta **153**
KT12: Walt T 74X **151**
N3 .... 25Eb **49**
N10 .... 24Jb **50**
(not continuous)
RH1: Redh 6P **207**
RM17: Grays 49Ce **99**
SW5 .... 49Cb **89**
SW7 .... 5A **226** (49Cb **89**)
SW9 .... 53Rb **113**
SW19 .... 64Cb **133**
TW3: Houn 56Ca **107**
TW11: Tedd 65Ja **130**
TW13: Felt 60X **107**
UB3: Hayes 44T **84**
WD6: Bore 11Na **29**
Cromwells Ct. SL3: L'ly 46B **82**
Cromwells Mere RM1: Rom 23Fd **56**
Cromwell St. TW3: Houn 56Ca **107**
Cromwell Twr. EC2 .... 7E **218**
Cromwell Trad. Cen. IG11: Bark 41Uc **94**
Cromwell Wlk. RH1: Redh 5P **207**
Crondace Rd. SW6 .... 53Cb **111**
Crondall Ct. N1 .... 2H **219**
Crondall Ho. SW15 .... 59Wa **110**
Crondall St. N1 .... 2G **219** (40Tb **71**)
Crone Ct. *NW6 .... 40Bb 69*
(off Denmark Rd.)
Cronin St. SE15 .... 52Vb **113**
Cronks Hill RH1: Redh 8L **207**
RH2: Reig 8L **207**
Cronks Hill Cl. RH1: Redh 8M **207**
Cronks Hill Rd. RH1: Redh 8M **207**
CROOKED BILLET 24Cc **52**
Crooked Billet SW19 .... 65Ya **132**
CROOKED BILLET RDBT. 63J **127**
Crooked Billet Yd. E2 .... 3J **219**
Crooked La. DA12: Grav'nd 8D **122**
Crooked Mile EN9: Walt A 1Ec **20**
Crooked Usage N3 .... 27Ab **48**
Crooke Rd. SE8 .... 50Ac **92**
Crookham Rd. SW6 .... 53Bb **111**
Crook Log DA6: Bex 55Zc **117**
Crook Log Sports Cen. 55Zc **117**
Crookston Rd. SE9 .... 55Qc **116**
Croombs Rd. E16 .... 43Lc **93**
Croom's Hill SE10 .... 52Ec **114**
Croom's Hill Gro. SE10 .... 52Ec **114**
Cropley Ct. N1 .... 1F **219**
(not continuous)
Cropley St. N1 .... 1F **219** (40Tb **71**)
Croppath Rd. RM10: Dag 35Cd **76**
Cropthorne Ct. W9 .... 4A **214** (41Eb **89**)
Crosbie NW9 .... 26Va **48**
Crosbie Ho. *E17 .... 27Ec 52*
(off Prospect Hill)
Crosby Cl. AL4: St A 5G **6**
TW13: Hanw 62Aa **129**
Crosby Ct. IG7: Chig 22Uc **55**
SE1 .... 1F **231** (47Tb **91**)
Crosby Ho. E7 .... 37Jc **73**
E14 .... 48Ec 92
(off Manchester Rd.)
Crosby Rd. E7 .... 37Jc **73**
RM10: Dag 40Dd **76**
Crosby Row SE1 .... 2F **231** (47Tb **91**)
Crosby Sq. EC3 .... 2H **225** (44Ub **91**)
Crosby Wlk. E8 .... 37Vb **71**
SW2 .... 59Qb **112**
Crosby Way SW2 .... 59Qb **112**
Crosfield Ct. *WD18: Wat 15Y 27*
(off Lwr. High St.)
Crosier Cl. SE3 .... 53Nc **116**
Crosier Rd. UB10: Ick 35S **64**
Crosier Way HA4: Ruis 34U **64**
Crosland Pl. SW11 .... 55Jb **112**
Crossacres GU22: Pyr 88G **168**
Cross Av. SE10 .... 51Fc **115**
Crossbow Ho. N1 .... 1H **219**
W13 .... 46Ka 86
(off Sherwood Cl.)
Crossbow Rd. IG7: Chig 22Vc **55**
Crossbrook AL10: Hat 1A **8**
Crossbrook Ct. EN8: Chesh 3Zb **20**
Crossbrook Rd. SE3 .... 54Nc **116**
Crossbrook St. EN8: Chesh 3Zb **20**
Crossby Cl. CM15: Mount 11Fe **41**
Cross Cl. SE15 .... 54Xb **113**
Cross Ct. *SE28 .... 45Xc 95*
(off Titmuss Av.)
Cross Deep TW1: Twick 61Ha **130**
Cross Deep Gdns. TW1: Twick 61Ha **130**
Crossett Grn. HP3: Hem H 4C **4**
Crossfell Rd. HP3: Hem H 3C **4**
Crossfield Ct. *W10 .... 44Za 88*
(off Cambridge Gdns.)
Crossfield Ho. SL9: Ger X 28A **42**
W11 .... 45Ab 88
(off Mary Pl.)
Crossfield Pl. KT13: Weyb 80R **150**
Crossfield Rd. N17 .... 27Sb **51**
NW3 .... 37Fb **69**
Crossfields AL3: St A 5P **5**
IG10: Lough 15Rc **36**
Crossfield St. SE8 .... 52Cc **114**
(not continuous)
Crossford St. SW9 .... 54Pb **112**
Cross Ga. HA8: Edg 20Qa **29**
Crossgate UB6: G'frd 37Ka **66**
Crossing Rd. CM16: Epp 4Wc **23**
CROSS KEYS 99Jd **202**
Cross Keys Cl. N9 .... 19Wb **33**
TN13: S'oaks 99Jd **202**
W1 .... 1J **221** (43Jb **90**)
Cross Keys Sq. EC1 .... 1D **224**
Cross Lances Rd. TW3: Houn 56Da **107**
Crossland Ho. *GU25: Vir W 70A 126*
(off Holloway Dr.)
Crossland Rd. CR7: Thor H 72Rb **157**
RH1: Redh 6A **208**
Crosslands KT16: Chert 77G **148**
WD3: Map C 22G **42**
Crosslands Av. UB2: S'hall 50Ba **85**
W5 .... 46Pa **87**
Crosslands Rd. KT19: Ewe 79Ta **153**
Cross La. DA5: Bexl 59Bd **117**
EC3 .... 5H **225** (45Ub **91**)
(not continuous)
KT16: Ott 79D **148**
N8 .... 27Pb **50**
(not continuous)
Cross La. E. DA12: Grav'nd 1D **144**
Cross Lanes SL9: Chal P 22A **42**
Cross Lanes Cl. SL9: Chal P 22B **42**
Cross La. W. DA11: Grav'nd 1D **144**
Crossleigh Ct. *SE14 .... 52Bc 114*
(off New Cross Rd.)
Crosslet St. SE17 .... 5G **231** (49Tb **91**)
Crosslet Va. SE10 .... 53Dc **114**
Crossley Cl. TN16: Big H 87Mc **179**
Crossley St. N7 .... 37Qb **70**
Crossmead SE9 .... 60Pc **116**
WD19: Wat 16X **27**
Crossmead Av. UB6: G'frd 41Ca **85**
Crossmount Ho. *SE5 .... 52Sb 113*
(off Bowyer St.)
Crossness Engines, The 44Bd **95**
Crossness Footpath DA18: Erith 46Bd **95**
Crossness La. SE2 .... 45Ad **95**
Crossness Nature Reserve 46Cd **96**
Crossness Rd. IG11: Bark 41Vc **95**
Cross Oak SL4: Wind 4E **102**
Crossoaks La. EN6: Ridge, S Mim 6Ua **16**
WD6: Bore 7Ta **15**
Crosspath, The WD7: R'lett 7Ja **14**
Cross Rd. BR2: Brom 75Nc **160**
BR5: St M Cry 71Xc **161**
CR0: C'don 74Tb **157**
CR8: Purl 85Rb **177**
DA1: Dart 58Ld **119**
DA2: Hawl 63Pd **141**
DA11: Nflt 8B **122**
DA14: Sidc 63Xc **139**
E4 .... 18Fc **35**
EN1: Enf 14Ub **33**
EN8: Walt C 5Ac **20**
HA1: Harr 28Fa **46**
HA2: Harr 34Da **65**
HA3: W'stone 26Ja **46**
IG8: Wfd G 23Pc **54**
KT2: King T 66Pa **131**
KT13: Weyb 76T **150**
KT20: Tad 94Ya **194**
N11 .... 22Kb **50**
N22 .... 24Qb **50**
RM6: Chad H 31Yc **75**
RM7: Mawney 28Cd **56**
SE5 .... 54Ub **113**
SL5: S'dale 4D **146**
SM1: Sutt 78Fb **155**
SM2: Sutt 82Cb **175**
SW19 .... 66Cb **133**
TW13: Hanw 63Aa **129**
UB8: Uxb 38L **63**
WD19: Wat 16Aa **27**
Cross Roads IG10: H Beech 12Kc **35**
Crossroads, The KT24: Eff 100Z **191**
Cross St. AL3: St A 2B **6**
DA8: Erith 51Gd **118**
DA12: Grav'nd 8D 122
(off Terrace St.)
N1 .... 39Rb **71**
N18 .... 22Wb **51**
SE5 .... 55Tb **113**
SW13 .... 54Ua **110**
TW12: Hamp H 64Ea **130**
UB8: Uxb 38L **63**
WD17: Wat 13Y **27**
Cross Ter. *EN9: Walt A 6Gc 21*
(off Stonyshotts)
Crossthwaite Av. SE5 .... 56Tb **113**
Crosstrees Ho. *E14 .... 48Cc 92*
(off Cassilis Rd.)
Crosswall EC3 .... 4K **225** (45Vb **91**)
Cross Way NW10 .... 38Wa **68**
Cross Way, The HA3: W'stone 26Ga **46**
Crossway BR5: Pet W 70Tc **138**
EN1: Enf 17Ub **33**
HA4: Ruis 35Y **65**
HA5: Pinn 26X **45**
IG8: Wfd G 21Lc **53**
KT12: Walt T 75X **151**
N12 .... 23Fb **49**
N16 .... 36Ub **71**
NW9 .... 28Va **48**
RM8: Dag 34Yc **75**
SE28 .... 44Xc **95**
SS17: Stan H 1P **101**
SW20 .... 70Ya **132**
UB3: Hayes 46W **84**
W13 .... 42Ja **86**
Crossway, The N22 .... 24Rb **51**
SE9 .... 61Mc **137**
UB10: Hil 40P **63**
Crossway Ct. SE4 .... 54Ac **114**
Crossway Pde. *N22 .... 24Rb 51*
(off The Crossway)
Crossways CM15: Shenf 16Ce **41**
CR2: Sels 80Ac **158**
DA2: Dart 56Sd **120**
HP3: Hem H 2B **4**
IG10: Lough 15Qc **36**
KT24: Eff 99Z **191**
N21 .... 16Sb **33**
RM2: Rom 27Kd **57**
SM2: Sutt 81Fb **175**
TN16: Tats 91Lc **199**
TW16: Sun 66V **128**
TW20: Egh 65F **126**
Crossways, The CR5: Coul 91Pb **196**
HA9: Wemb 33Qa **67**
KT5: Surb 74Ra **153**
RH1: Mers 1C **208**
TW5: Hest 52Ba **107**
Crossways 25 Bus. Pk. DA2: Dart 56Sd **120**
Crossways Blvd. DA2: Dart 56Sd **120**
DA9: Ghithe 56Ud **120**
Crossways Ct. *SL4: Wind 4G 102*
(off Osbourne Rd.)
Crossways La. RH2: Reig 100Eb **195**
(not continuous)
Crossways Rd. BR3: Beck 70Cc **136**
CR4: Mitc 69Kb **134**
Crossways Ter. E5 .... 35Yb **72**
Crosthwaite Way SL1: Slou 3B **80**
Croston St. E8 .... 39Wb **71**
Crothall Cl. N13 .... 20Pb **32**
CROUCH 95De **205**
Crouch Av. IG11: Bark 40Xc **75**
Crouch Cl. BR3: Beck 65Cc **136**
Crouch Cft. SE9 .... 62Qc **138**
CROUCH END 31Mb **70**
Crouch End Hill N8 .... 31Mb **70**
Crouchfield HP1: Hem H 3K **3**
Crouch Hall Ct. N19 .... 32Nb **70**
Crouch Hall Rd. N8 .... 30Mb **50**
Crouch Hill N4 .... 30Nb **50**
N8 .... 30Nb **50**
Crouch Ind. Est. KT22: Lea 91Ka **192**
Crouch La. TN15: Bor G 92Ce **205**
Crouchman Cl. RM16: Grays 47Ee **99**
Crouchman's Cl. SE26 .... 62Vb **135**
Crouch Oak La. KT15: Add 77L **149**
Crouch Rd. NW10 .... 38Ta **67**
RM16: Grays 10C **100**
Crouch Valley RM14: Upm 31Ud **78**
Crowborough Cl. CR6: W'ham 90Ac **178**
Crowborough Dr. CR6: W'ham 90Ac **178**
Crowborough Path WD19: Wat 21Z **45**
Crowborough Rd. SW17 .... 65Jb **134**
Crowden Way SE28 .... 45Yc **95**
Crowder Cl. N12 .... 25Eb **49**
Crowder St. E1 .... 45Xb **91**
CROWDLEHAM 89Td **184**
Crow Dr. TN14: Hals 87Ed **182**
Crowfield Ho. N5 .... 35Sb **71**
Crowfoot Cl. E9 .... 36Bc **72**
SE28 .... 46Uc **94**
CROW GREEN 13Vd **40**
Crow Grn. La. CM15: Pil H 15Wd **40**
Crow Grn. Rd. CM15: Pil H 15Vd **40**
Crow Hill TN15: Bor G 92Ce **205**
Crowhill BR6: Downe 82Qc **180**
Crow Hill Rd. TN15: Bor G 92Ce **205**
Crowhurst Cl. SW9 .... 54Qb **112**
Crowhurst Ho. *SW9 .... 54Pb 112*
(off Aytoun Rd.)
Crowhurst La. RH7: C'rst 10F **210**
RH8: Oxt 10G **210**
TN15: Ash, W King 81Wd **184**
TN15: Bor G 96Zd **205**
CROWHURST LANE END 10F **210**
Crowhurst La. End RH7: C'rst 10G **210**
RH8: C'rst, Tand 10F **210**
Crowhurst Mead RH9: G'stone 2A **210**
Crowhurst Rd. TN15: Bor G 93Be **205**
Crowhurst Way BR5: St M Cry 71Yc **161**
Crowland Av. UB3: Harl 49U **84**
Crowland Gdns. N14 .... 17Nb **32**
Crowland Ho. *NW8 .... 39Eb 69*
(off Springfield Rd.)
Crowland Rd. CR7: Thor H 70Tb **135**
N15 .... 29Vb **51**
CROWLANDS 31Dd **76**
Crowlands Av. RM7: Rom 30Dd **56**
Crowlands Heath Golf Course 32Dd **76**
Crowland Ter. N1 .... 38Tb **71**
Crowland Wlk. SM4: Mord 72Db **155**
Crow La. RM7: Rush G 31Bd **75**
Crowley Cres. CR0: Wadd 78Qb **156**
Crowline Wlk. N1 .... 37Sb **71**
Crowmarsh Gdns. SE23 .... 59Yb **114**
Crown, The TN16: Westrm 98Tc **200**
Crown All. *SE9 .... 58Pc 116*
(off Court Yd.)
Crown Arc. KT1: King T 68Ma **131**
Crown Ash Hill TN16: Big H 86Kc **179**
Crown Ash La. CR6: W'ham 88Jc **179**
Crownbourne Ct. *SM1: Sutt 77Db 155*
(off St Nicholas Way)
Crown Bldgs. E4 .... 18Ec **34**
Crown Cl. BR6: Chels 78Wc **161**
E3 .... 39Cc **72**
IG9: Buck H 18Kc **35**
KT12: Walt T 73Y **151**
N22 .... 25Qb **50**
NW6 .... 37Db **69**
NW7 .... 19Va **30**
SL3: Coln 52E **104**
UB3: Hayes 47V **84**
Crown Cl. Bus. Cen. *E3 .... 39Cc 72*
(off Crown Cl.)
Crown Cotts. RM5: Col R 25Cd **56**
SL4: Wind 6H **103**
Crown Court
Blackfriars 1C **230** (47Rb **91**)
Croydon 75Tb **157**
Harrow 27Fa **46**
Inner London 3D **230** (48Sb **91**)
Isleworth 53Ga **108**
Kingston upon Thames 69Ma **131**
St Albans 2C **6**
Snaresbrook 29Hc **53**
Southwark 6H **225** (46Ub **91**)
Wood Green 25Qb **50**
Woolwich 47Uc **94**
Crown Ct. EC2 .... 3E **224**
N10 .... 24Jb **50**
NW8 .... 4E **214**
RM18: Tilb 4C **122**
SE12 .... 58Kc **115**
WC2 .... 3G **223** (44Nb **90**)
Crown Crest Ct. *TN13: S'oaks 93Ld 203*
(off Seal Rd.)
Crown Dale SE19 .... 65Rb **135**
(not continuous)
Crowndale Ct. NW1 .... 1D **216**
Crowndale Rd. NW1 .... 1C **216** (40Lb **70**)
Crownfield Av. IG2: Ilf 30Uc **54**
Crownfield Rd. E15 .... 35Fc **73**
Crownfields TN13: S'oaks 97Kd **203**
Crowngate Ho. *E3 .... 40Bc 72*
(off Hereford Rd.)
Crown Grn. DA12: Shorne 4N **145**
Crown Grn. M. HA9: Wemb 33Na **67**
Crown Hill CR0: C'don 75Sb **157**
EN9: Walt A 5Nc **22**
Crownhill Rd. IG8: Wfd G 24Nc **54**
NW10 .... 39Va **68**
Crown Ho. KT3: N Mald 69Sa **131**
NW10 .... 41Ta **87**
Crown La. BR2: Brom 71Mc **159**
BR7: Chst 67Sc **138**
DA12: Shorne 4N **145**
GU25: Vir W 2P **147**
N14 .... 18Lb **32**
SL2: Farn R 10E **60**
SM4: Mord 70Cb **133**
SW16 .... 64Qb **134**
Crown La. Gdns. SW16 .... 64Qb **134**
Crown La. Spur BR2: Brom 72Mc **159**
Crown Lodge SW3 .... 6E **226**
Crown Mdw. SL3: Coln 52D **104**
Crown Mdw. Ct. BR2: Brom 72Nc **160**
Crownmead Way RM7: Mawney 28Dd **56**
Crown M. *E1 .... 43Zb 92*
(off White Horse La.)
E13 .... 39Lc **73**
W6 .... 49Wa **88**
Crown Office Row EC4 .... 4K **223** (45Qb **90**)
Crown Pde. N14 .... 18Lb **32**
SM4: Mord 69Cb **133**
Crown Pas. *KT1: King T 68Ma 131*
(off Church St.)
SW1 .... 7C **222** (46Lb **90**)
WD18: Wat 14Y **27**
Crown Pl. EC2 .... 7H **219** (43Ub **91**)
NW5 .... 37Kb **70**
SE16 .... 50Xb **91**
Crown Point SE19 .... 65Rb **135**
Crown Point Pde. *SE19 .... 65Rb 135*
(off Crown Dale)
Crown Reach SW1 .... 7E **228** (50Mb **90**)
Crown Ri. KT16: Chert 74H **149**
WD25: Wat 6Y **13**
Crown Rd. BR6: Chels 78Wc **161**
CM14: Kel H 11Td **40**
EN1: Enf 13Wb **33**
GU25: Vir W 2N **147**
HA4: Ruis 36Z **65**
IG6: Ilf 28Tc **54**
KT3: N Mald 67Sa **131**
N10 .... 24Jb **50**
RM17: Grays 51Ce **121**
SM1: Sutt 77Db **155**
SM4: Mord 70Db **133**
TN14: S'ham 82Hd **182**
TW1: Twick 58Ka **108**
WD6: Bore 11Qa **29**
Crown Sq. *GU21: Wok 89B 168*
(off Chertsey Rd.)
Crownstone Ct. SW2 .... 57Qb **112**
Crownstone Rd. SW2 .... 57Qb **112**
Crown St. CM14: B'wood 19Yd **40**
HA2: Harr 32Fa **66**
RM10: Dag 37Ed **76**
(not continuous)
SE5 .... 52Sb **113**
TW20: Egh 63C **126**
W3 .... 46Ra **87**
Crown Ter. *N14 .... 18Mb 32*
(off Crown La.)
TW9: Rich 56Pa **109**
Crown Trad. Cen. UB3: Hayes 47U **84**
Crowntree Cl. TW7: Isle 51Ha **108**
Crown Wlk. HA9: Wemb 34Pa **67**
HP3: Hem H 6N **3**
UB8: Uxb 38L **63**
Crown Way UB7: Yiew 46P **83**
Crown Wharf *E14 .... 46Ec 92*
(off Coldharbour)
SE8 .... 50Bc 92
(off Grove St.)
Crown Woods SE18 .... 54Rc **116**
Crown Woods Way SE9 .... 57Tc **116**
Crown Yd. SW6 .... 54Cb **111**
TW3: Houn 55Ea **108**
Crow Piece La. SL2: Farn R 8D **60**
Crowshott Av. HA7: Stan 26La **46**
Crows Rd. CM16: Epp 2Vc **23**
E3 .... 41Fc **93**
E15 .... 41Fc **93**
IG11: Bark 37Rc **74**
Crowstone Rd. RM16: Grays 47Ee **99**
Crowther Av. TW8: Bford 49Na **87**
Crowther Cl. *SW6 .... 51Bb 111*
(off Bucklers All.)
Crowther Rd. SE25 .... 71Wb **157**
Crowthorne Cl. SW18 .... 59Bb **111**
Crowthorne Rd. W10 .... 44Za **88**
Croxall Ho. KT12: Walt T 72Y **151**
Croxdale Rd. WD6: Bore 12Pa **29**
Croxden Cl. HA8: Edg 27Qa **47**
Croxden Wlk. SM4: Mord 72Eb **155**
Croxford Gdns. N22 .... 24Rb **51**
Croxford Way RM7: Rush G 32Fd **76**
CROXLEY CENTRE 16T **26**
Croxley Cl. BR5: St P 68Xc **139**
Croxley Common Moor Local Nature Reserve 17S **26**
CROXLEY GREEN 14Q **26**
Croxley Grn. BR5: St P 67Xc **139**
Croxley Green Skate Pk. 14Q **26**
Croxley Rd. W9 .... 41Bb **89**
Croxley Vw. WD18: Wat 16U **26**
Croxted Cl. SE21 .... 59Sb **113**
Croxted M. SE24 .... 58Sb **113**
Croxted Rd. SE21 .... 59Sb **113**
SE24 .... 59Sb **113**
Croxteth Ho. SW8 .... 54Mb **112**
Croyde Av. UB3: Harl 49U **84**
UB6: G'frd 41Ea **86**

Croyde Cl. DA15: Sidc 59Tc 116
CROYDON 76Sb 157
Croydon N17 26Tb 51
(off Gloucester Rd.)
Croydon Airport Ind. Est.
CR0: Wadd 79Pb 156
Croydon Airport Vis. Cen. 79Qb 156
Croydon Athletic FC 71Nb 156
Croydon Clocktower 76Sb 157
(off Katherine St.)
Croydon Crematorium
CR0: C'don 71Pb 156
Croydon Flyover, The CR0: C'don 77Rb 157
Croydon Golf Driving Range 71Yb 158
Croydon Gro. CR0: C'don 74Rb 157
Croydon High Sports Club 83Yb 178
Croydon Ho. SE1 1A 230
Croydon La. SM7: Bans 86Eb 175
Croydon La. Sth. SM7: Bans 86Eb 175
Croydon Rd. BR2: Hayes, Kes 76Lc 159
BR3: Beck 71Zb 158
BR4: Hayes, W W'ck 76Gc 159
CR0: Bedd, Wadd 77Kb 156
CR0: C'don 70Jb 134
CR3: Cat'm 95Wb 197
CR4: Mitc 70Jb 134
E13 42Hc 93
RH2: Reig 6K 207
SE20 68Xb 135
SM6: Bedd, Wall 77Kb 156
TN16: Westrm 95Pc 200
TW6: H'row A 54R 106
Croydon Rd. Ind. Est. BR3: Beck 70Zb 136
Croydon Sports Arena 71Yb 158
Croydon Valley Trade Pk.
CR0: Bedd 73Nb 156
(off Therapia La.)
Croyland Rd. N9 18Wb 33
Croylands Dr. KT6: Surb 73Na 153
Croysdale Av. TW16: Sun 69W 128
Crozier Dr. CR2: Sels 82Xb 177
Crozier Ho. SE3 55Kc 115
SW8 52Pb 112
(off Wilkinson St.)
Crozier Ter. E9 36Zb 72
(not continuous)
Crucible Cl. RM6: Chad H 30Xc 55
Crucifix La. SE1 1H 231 (47Ub 91)
Cruden Ho. E3 40Bc 72
(off Vernon Rd.)
SE17 51Rb 113
(off Brandon Est.)
Cruden Rd. DA12: Grav'nd 2H 145
Cruden St. N1 1C 218 (39Rb 71)
Cruick Av. RM15: S Ock 44Yd 98
Cruikshank Ho. NW8 1D 214
Cruikshank Rd. E15 35Gc 73
Cruikshank St. WC1 3K 217 (41Qb 90)
Crummock Cl. SL1: Slou 4A 80
Crummock Gdns. NW9 29Ua 48
Crumpsall St. SE2 49Yc 95
Crundale Av. NW9 29Qa 47
Crundale Twr. BR5: Orp 74Yc 161
(off Tintagel Rd.)
Crunden Rd. CR2: S Croy 80Tb 157
Crusader Cl. RM19: Purf 49Qd 97
Crusader Ct. DA1: Dart 57Pd 119
Crusader Gdns. CR0: C'don 76Ub 157
Crusader Ind. Est. N4 30Sb 51
Crusader Way WD18: Wat 16V 26
Crushes Cl. CM13: Hut 16Fe 41
Crusoe M. N16 33Tb 71
Crusoe Rd. CR4: Mitc 66Hb 133
DA8: Erith 50Fd 96
Crutched Friars EC3 4J 225 (45Ub 91)
Crutchfield La. KT12: Walt T 75X 151
Crutchley Rd. SE6 61Gc 137
Crystal Av. RM12: Horn 35Nd 77
Crystal Ct. SE19 64Vb 135
(off College Rd.)
Crystal Ho. SE18 50Vc 95
CRYSTAL PALACE 65Vb 135
Crystal Palace Athletics Stadium
65Wb 135
Crystal Palace Dinosaurs 65Wb 135
Crystal Palace FC 70Ub 135
Crystal Palace Indoor Bowling Club
67Xb 135
Crystal Palace Mus. 65Vb 135
Crystal Palace National Sports Cen.
65Wb 135
Crystal Pal. Pde. SE19 65Vb 135
Crystal Palace Pk. 64Wb 135
Crystal Palace Pk. Farm 65Wb 135
Crystal Pal. Pk. Rd. SE26 64Wb 135
Crystal Pal. Rd. SE22 58Vb 113
Crystal Pal. Sta. Rd. SE19 65Wb 135
Crystal Pl. KT4: Wor Pk 75Xa 154
Crystal Ter. SE19 65Tb 135
Crystal Vw. Ct. BR1: Brom 63Fc 137
Crystal Way HA1: Harr 29Ha 46
RM8: Dag 32Yc 75
Crystal Wharf N1 2C 218 (40Rb 71)
Cuba Dr. EN3: Enf H 12Yb 34
Cuba St. E14 47Cc 92
Cube Ho. SE16 4K 231 (48Vb 91)
Cubitt Bldg. SW1 50Kb 90
Cubitt Ct. NW1 2B 216
Cubitt Ho. SW4 58Lb 112
Cubitt Sq. UB2: S'hall 46Ea 86
Cubitt Steps E14 46Cc 92
Cubitt St. WC1 4J 217 (41Pb 90)
Cubitt's Yd. WC2 4G 223
Cubitt Ter. SW4 55Lb 112
CUBITT TOWN 49Ec 92
Cubitt Way GU21: Knap 10H 167
Cuckmans Dr. AL2: Chis G 7N 5
Cuckmere Way BR5: Orp 74Zc 161
Cuckoo Av. W7 42Ga 86
Cuckoo Dene W7 43Fa 86
Cuckoo Hall La. N9 17Yb 34
Cuckoo Hall Rd. N9 17Yb 34
Cuckoo Hill HA5: Eastc, Pinn 27Y 45
Cuckoo Hill Dr. HA5: Pinn 27Y 45
Cuckoo Hill Rd. HA5: Pinn 28Y 45
Cuckoo La. GU24: W End 5B 166
RM16: N Stif 46Be 99
(not continuous)
W7 45Ga 86
Cuckoo Pound TW17: Shep 71U 150
Cuckoo Va. GU24: W End 5B 166
Cuckseys La. RH1: Blet 8K 209
Cucumber La. AL9: Ess 2N 9
SG13: New S 2N 9
Cudas Cl. KT19: Ewe 77Va 154
Cuddington SE17 5D 230
Cuddington Av. KT4: Wor Pk 76Va 154
Cuddington Cl. KT20: Tad 92Ya 194
Cuddington Ct. SM2: Cheam 81Za 174
Cuddington Glade KT19: Eps 84Qa 173
Cuddington Golf Course 85Ab 174
Cuddington Pk. Cl. SM7: Bans 85Bb 175
Cuddington Way SM2: Cheam 84Za 174
CUDHAM 87Tc 180
Cudham Cl. SM2: Sutt 82Cb 175
Cudham Dr. CR0: New Ad 82Ec 178
Cudham La. Nth. BR6: Downe 86Sc 180
TN14: Cud 86Sc 180
Cudham La. Sth.
TN14: Cud, Knock 87Sc 180
Cudham Pk. Rd. TN14: Cud 82Uc 180
Cudham Rd. BR6: Downe 83Qc 180
TN16: Tats 91Nc 200
Cudham St. SE6 59Ec 114
Cudworth Ho. SW8 53Lb 112
Cudworth St. E1 42Xb 91
Cuff Cres. SE9 58Mc 115
CUFFLEY 1Nb 18
Cuffley Av. WD25: Wat 6Z 13
Cuffley Hill EN7: Cuff, G Oak 1Pb 18
Cuffley Ho. W10 43Ya 88
(off Sutton Way)
Cuff Point E2 3K 219
Cugley Rd. DA2: Dart 59Sd 120
Culand Ho. SE17 6H 231
Culcroft DA3: Hartl 69Be 143
Culford Gdns. SW3 6G 227 (49Hb 89)
Culford Gro. N1 37Ub 71
Culford Mans. SW3 6G 227
Culford M. N1 37Ub 71
Culford Rd. N1 38Ub 71
RM16: Grays 47Ee 99
Culford Ter. N1 37Ub 71
(off Balls Pond Rd.)
Culgaith Gdns. EN2: Enf 14Nb 32
Culham Ho. E2 4K 219
W2 43Cb 89
(off Gt. Western Rd.)
Cullen Sq. RM15: S Ock 46Yd 98
Cullen Way NW10 42Sa 87
Cullera Cl. HA6: Nwood 23V 44
Cullerne Cl. KT17: Ewe 82Va 174
Cullesden Rd. CR8: Kenley 87Rb 177
Culling Rd. SE16 48Yb 92
Cullings Ct. EN9: Walt A 5Hc 21
Cullington Cl. HA3: W'stone 28Ja 46
Cullingworth Rd. NW10 36Wa 68
Culloden Cl. SE7 51Kc 115
SE16 50Wb 91
Culloden Rd. EN2: Enf 12Rb 33
Cullum St. EC3 4H 225 (45Ub 91)
Cullum Welch Ct. N1 3G 219
Cullum Welch Ho. EC1 6D 218
Culmington Pde. W13 46La 86
(off Uxbridge Rd.)
Culmington Rd. CR2: S Croy 81Sb 177
W13 46La 86
Culmore Rd. SE15 52Xb 113
Culmstock Rd. SW11 57Jb 112
Culpeper Cl. IG6: Ilf 23Rc 54
Culpepper Cl. N18 22Xb 51
Culpepper Ct. SE11 5K 229
Culross Cl. N15 28Sb 51
Culross Ho. W10 44Za 88
(off Bridge Cl.)
Culross St. W1 5H 221 (45Jb 90)
Culsac Rd. KT6: Surb 75Na 153
Culverden Ct. KT13: Weyb 76T 150
(off Oatlands Dr.)
Culverden Rd. SW12 61Lb 134
WD19: Wat 20X 27
Culverden Ter. KT13: Weyb 76T 150
Culver Dr. RH8: Oxt 2J 211
Culver Gro. HA7: Stan 26La 46
Culverhay KT21: Asht 88Na 173
Culverhouse WC1 1H 223
Culverhouse Gdns. SW16 62Pb 134
Culverlands Cl. HA7: Stan 21Ka 46
Culverley Rd. SE6 60Dc 114
Culver Rd. AL1: St A 1C 6
Culvers Av. SM5: Cars 75Hb 155
Culvers Ct. DA12: Grav'nd 10H 123
Culvers Retreat SM5: Cars 74Hb 155
Culverstone Cl. BR2: Brom 72Hc 159
Culvers Way SM5: Cars 75Hb 155
Culvert La. UB8: Uxb 40K 63
Culvert Pl. SW11 54Jb 112
Culvert Rd. N15 29Ub 51
(not continuous)
SW11 54Hb 111
Culvey Cl. DA3: Hartl 71Ae 165
Culworth Ho. NW8 1D 214
Culworth St. NW8 2D 214 (40Gb 69)
Culzean Cl. SE27 62Rb 135
Cumberland Av. DA12: Grav'nd 9E 122
DA16: Well 55Uc 116
GU2: Guild 10L 187
NW10 41Ra 87
RM12: Horn 34Nd 77
SL2: Slou 2G 80
Cumberland Bus. Pk. NW10 41Ra 87
Cumberland Cl. E8 37Vb 71
HP3: Hem H 6E 4
IG6: Ilf 25Sc 54
KT19: Ewe 82Ua 174
RM12: Horn 34Nd 77
SW20 66Za 132
TW1: Twick 58Ka 108
Cumberland Ct. AL3: St A 1C 6
CR0: C'don 74Tb 157
DA16: Well 54Uc 116
HA1: Harr 27Ga 46
(off Princes Dr.)
SW1 7A 228
TN13: Dun G 92Fd 202
W1 3G 221
Cumberland Cres. W14 49Ab 88
(not continuous)
Cumberland Dr. DA1: Dart 59Pd 119
DA7: Bex 52Ad 117
KT9: Chess 76Na 153
KT10: Hin W 75Ja 152
Cumberland Gdns. NW4 26Ab 48
WC1 3K 217 (41Qb 90)
Cumberland Gate (Park & Ride)
4F 221 (45Hb 89)
Cumberland Ga. W1 4F 221 (45Hb 89)
Cumberland Ho. E16 46Jc 93
(off Wesley Av.)
KT2: King T 66Ra 131
N9 18Yb 34
(off Cumberland Rd.)
Cumberland Ho. SE28 47Sc 94
W8 47Db 89
(off Kensington Ct.)
Cumberland Mans. W1 2F 221
Cumberland Mkt. NW1 3A 216 (41Kb 90)
Cumberland M. SE11 7A 230 (50Qb 90)
Cumberland Mills Sq. E14 50Fc 93
Cumberland Obelisk 6K 125
Cumberland Pk. W3 45Sa 87
Cumberland Pk. Ind. Est. NW10 41Wa 88
Cumberland Pl. NW1 3K 215 (41Kb 90)
SE6 60Hc 115
TW16: Sun 70W 128
Cumberland Rd. BR2: Brom 70Gc 137
E12 35Mc 73
E13 43Kc 93
E17 26Ac 52
HA1: Harr 29Da 45
HA7: Stan 27Pa 47
N9 18Yb 34
N22 26Pb 50
RM16: Chaf H 47Ae 99
SE25 72Xb 157
SW13 53Va 110
TW9: Kew 52Qa 109
TW15: Ashf 62M 127
W3 45Sa 87
W7 47Ha 86
Cumberlands CR8: Kenley 87Tb 177
Cumberland St. SW1 7A 228 (50Kb 90)
TW18: Staines 64F 126
Cumberland Ter. NW1 2K 215 (40Kb 70)
Cumberland Ter. M. NW1 2K 215
(not continuous)
Cumberland Vs. W3 45Sa 87
(off Cumberland Rd.)
Cumberland Wharf SE16 47Yb 92
(off Rotherhithe St.)
Cumberlow Av. SE25 69Vb 135
Cumberlow Pl. HP2: Hem H 3C 4
Cumbernauld Gdns. TW16: Sun 64V 128
Cumberton Rd. N17 25Tb 51
Cumbrae Cl. SL2: Slou 6L 81
Cumbrae Gdns. KT6: Surb 75Ma 153
Cumbria Ct. RH2: Reig 5M 207
Cumbrian Av. DA7: Bex 54Gd 118
Cumbrian Gdns. NW2 33Za 68
Cumbrian Way UB8: Uxb 38M 63
Cuming Mus. 6D 230
Cummings Hall La.
RM3: Rom 20Ld 39
Cumming St. N1 2J 217 (40Pb 70)
Cumnor Cl. SW9 54Pb 112
(off Robsart St.)
Cumnor Gdns. KT17: Ewe 79Wa 154
Cumnor Ri. CR8: Kenley 89Sb 177
Cumnor Rd. SM2: Sutt 79Eb 155
Cunard Ct. HA7: Stan 19Ja 28
(off Brightwen Gro.)
Cunard Cres. N21 16Tb 33
Cunard Pl. EC3 3J 225 (44Ub 91)
Cunard Rd. NW10 41Ta 87
Cunard Wlk. SE16 49Zb 92
Cundy Rd. E16 44Lc 93
Cundy St. SW1 6J 227 (49Jb 90)
Cunliffe Cl. KT18: Head 96Ra 193
Cunliffe Pde. KT19: Ewe 77Va 154
Cunliffe Rd. KT19: Ewe 77Va 154
Cunliffe St. SW16 65Lb 134
Cunningham Av. AL1: St A 4D 6
EN3: Enf W 8Ac 20
Cunningham Cl. BR4: W W'ck 75Dc 158
RM6: Chad H 29Yc 55
Cunningham Ct. E10 34Dc 72
(off Oliver Rd.)
W9 6A 214
Cunningham Hill Rd. AL1: St A 5D 6
Cunningham Ho. SE5 52Tb 113
(off Elmington Est.)
Cunningham Pk. HA1: Harr 29Ea 46
Cunningham Pl.
NW8 5B 214 (42Fb 89)
Cunningham Rd. N15 28Wb 51
SM7: Bans 87Fb 175
Cunnington St. W4 48Sa 87
Cupar Rd. SW11 53Jb 112
Cupola Cl. BR1: Brom 64Kc 137
Curates Wlk. DA2: Wilm 62Md 141
Curchin Cl. TN16: Big H 84Lc 179
Cureton St. SW1 6E 228 (49Mb 90)
Curfew Bell Rd.
KT16: Chert 73H 149
Curfew Ho. IG11: Bark 39Sc 74
Curfew Yd. SL4: Wind 2H 103
Curie Ct. HA1: Harr 31Ka 66
Curie Gdns. NW9 26Ua 48
Curlew Cl. CR2: Sels 83Zb 178
SE28 45Zc 95
Curlew Ct. KT6: Surb 76Qa 153
W13 42Ha 86
Curlew Ho. EN3: Pond E 15Zb 34
SE4 56Ac 114
(off St Norbert Rd.)
SE15 53Vb 113
Curlews, The DA12: Grav'nd 1F 144
Curlew St. SE1 1K 231 (47Vb 91)
Curlew Way UB4: Yead 43Z 85
Curling Cl. CR5: Coul 92Pb 196
Curling La. RM17: Grays 50Be 99
Curness St. SE13 56Ec 114
Curnick's La. SE27 63Sb 135
Curo Pk. AL2: F'mre 9C 6
Curran Av. DA15: Sidc 57Vc 117
SM6: Wall 76Jb 156
Curran Cl. UB8: Cowl 42L 83
Curran Ho. SW3 6D 226
Currey Rd. UB6: G'frd 37Fa 66
Curricle St. W3 46Ua 88
Currie Hill Cl. SW19 63Bb 133
Curriers La. SL1: Burn 6B 60
Curry Ri. NW7 23Za 48
Cursitor St. EC4 2K 223 (44Qb 90)
Curtain Pl. EC2 5J 219 (41Ub 91)
Curtain Rd. EC2 4J 219 (42Ub 91)
Curthwaite Gdns. EN2: Enf 14Mb 32
Curtis Cl. WD3: Rick 18J 25
Curtis Dr. W3 44Ta 87
Curtis Fld. Rd. SW16 63Pb 134
Curtis Ho. N11 22Lb 50
(off Ladderswood Way)
SE17 7F 231
Curtis La. HA0: Wemb 37Na 67
Curtismill Cl. BR5: St P 69Xc 139
CURTISMILL GREEN 14Hd 38
Curtis Mill La. RM4: Nave 14Gd 38
Curtismill Way BR5: St P 69Xc 139
Curtis Rd. HP3: Hem H 3D 4
KT19: Ewe 77Sa 153
RM11: Horn 32Pd 77
TW4: Houn 59Ba 107
Curtiss Dr. WD25: Wat 6V 12
Curtis St. SE1 5K 231 (49Vb 91)
Curtis Way HP4: Berk 2A 2
SE1 5K 231 (49Vb 91)
SE28 45Xc 95
Curtlington Ho. HA8: Edg 26Sa 47
(off Burnt Oak B'way.)
Curvan Cl. KT17: Ewe 82Va 174
Curve, The W12 45Wa 88
Curwen Av. E7 35Kc 73
Curwen Rd. W12 47Wa 88
Curzon Av. EN3: Pond E 15Zb 34
HA7: Stan 25Ja 46
Curzon Cinema
Mayfair 7K 221
Richmond 57Ma 109
Soho 4E 222
Curzon Cl. BR6: Orp 77Tc 160
KT13: Weyb 77Q 150
Curzon Ct. SW6 53Eb 111
(off Imperial Rd.)
Curzon Cres. IG11: Bark 40Vc 75
NW10 38Ua 68
Curzon Dr. RM17: Grays 52Ee 121
Curzon Ga. W1 7J 221 (46Jb 90)
Curzon Ga. Ct. WD17: Wat 11W 26
Curzon Mall SL1: Slou 7K 81
(within Queensmere Shop. Cen.)
Curzon Pl. HA5: Eastc 29Y 45
Curzon Rd. CR7: Thor H 72Qb 156
KT13: Weyb 78Q 150
N10 26Kb 50
W5 42Ka 86
Curzon Sq. W1 7J 221 (46Jb 90)
Curzon St. W1 7J 221 (46Jb 90)
Cusack Cl. TW1: Twick 63Ha 130
Cussans Ho. WD18: Wat 16U 26
Cussons Cl. EN7: Chesh 1Wb 19
Custance Ho. N1 2F 219
Custance St. N1 3F 219 (41Tb 91)
CUSTOM HOUSE 44Lc 93
Custom Ho. EC3 5H 225 (45Ub 91)
Custom Ho. Reach SE16 47Bc 92
Custom Ho. Wlk. EC3 5H 225 (45Ub 91)
Cut, The SE1 1A 230 (47Qb 90)
SL2: Slou 2E 80
Cutbush Ho. N7 36Mb 70
Cutcombe Rd. SE5 54Sb 113
Cuthberga Cl. IG11: Bark 38Sc 74
Cuthbert Bell Twr. E3 40Cc 72
(off Pancras Way)
Cuthbert Ct. CR3: W'ham 91Wb 197
(off Godstone Rd.)
Cuthbert Gdns. SE25 69Ub 135
Cuthbert Harrowing Ho. EC1 6D 218
Cuthbert Ho. W2 7B 214
Cuthbert Rd. CR0: C'don 75Rb 157
E17 27Ec 52
N18 22Wb 51
Cuthberts Cl. EN7: Chesh 1Vb 19
Cuthbert St. W2 6B 214 (43Fb 89)
Cuthill Wlk. SE5 53Tb 113
Cutlers Gdns. EC2 1J 225 (43Ub 91)
Cutlers Gdns. Arc. EC2 2J 225
Cutlers Sq. E14 49Cc 92
Cutlers Ter. N1 37Ub 71
(off Balls Pond Rd.)
Cutler St. E1 2J 225 (44Ub 91)
Cutmore Dr. AL4: Col H 4M 7
Cutmore St. DA11: Grav'nd 9D 122
Cutter Ho. DA8: Erith 49Gd 96
Cutter La. SE10 47Gc 93
Cutthroat All. TW10: Ham 61La 130
Cutting, The RH1: Redh 8P 207
Cuttsfield Ter. HP1: Hem H 3H 3
Cutty Sark 51Ec 114
Cutty Sark Gdns. SE10 51Ec 114
(off King William Wlk.)
Cuxton BR5: Pet W 71Sc 160
Cuxton Cl. DA6: Bex 57Ad 117
Cuxton Ho. SE17 7J 231
Cyclamen Cl. TW12: Hamp 65Ca 129
Cyclamen Rd. BR8: Swan 70Fd 140
Cyclamen Way KT19: Ewe 78Sa 153
Cyclopark 3B 144
Cyclops M. E14 49Cc 92
Cygmus Ct. CR8: Purl 83Rb 177
(off Brighton Rd.)
Cygnet Av. TW14: Felt 59Y 107
Cygnet Cl. GU21: Wok 8M 167
HA6: Nwood 23S 44
NW10 36Ta 67
WD6: Bore 11Sa 29
Cygnet Gdns. DA11: Nflt 1B 144
Cygnet Ho. SW3 7E 226
Cygnet Ho. Nth. E14 44Dc 92
(off Chrisp St.)
Cygnet Ho. Sth. E14 44Dc 92
(off Chrisp St.)
Cygnet Leisure Cen. 1A 144
Cygnets, The TW13: Hanw 63Aa 129
TW18: Staines 64H 127
Cygnets Cl. RH1: Redh 4A 208
Cygnet St. E1 5K 219 (42Vb 91)
Cygnet Vw. RM20: W Thur 49Vd 98
Cygnet Way UB4: Yead 43Z 85
Cygnus Bus. Cen. NW10 36Va 68
Cymbeline Ct. AL3: St A 1A 6
(off The Lawns)
HA1: Harr 30Ha 46
(off Gayton Rd.)
Cynthia St. N1 2J 217 (40Pb 70)
Cyntra Pl. E8 38Xb 71
Cypress Av. EN2: Crew H 7Qb 18
TW2: Whitt 59Ea 108
Cypress Cl. E5 33Wb 71
EN9: Walt A 6Fc 21
Cypress Ct. E15 35Fc 73
(off Langthorne Rd.)
GU25: Vir W 70A 126
SM1: Sutt 78Cb 155
Cypress Gdns. SE4 57Ac 114
Cypress Gro. IG6: Ilf 23Uc 54
Cypress Ho. SE14 53Zb 114
SE16 47Zb 92
(off Woodland Cres.)
SL3: L'ly 50D 82
Cypress Path RM3: Rom 24Md 57
Cypress Pl. W1 6C 216 (42Lb 90)
Cypress Rd. HA3: Hrw W 26Fa 46
SE25 68Ub 135
Cypress Tree Cl. DA15: Sidc 60Vc 117
Cypress Wlk. TW20: Eng G 5M 125
WD25: Wat 7X 13
Cypress Way SM7: Bans 86Za 174
CYPRUS 45Qc 94
Cyprus Av. N3 26Ab 48
Cyprus Cl. N4 30Rb 51
Cyprus Gdns. N3 26Ab 48
Cyprus Pl. E2 40Yb 72
E6 45Qc 94
Cyprus Rd. N3 26Bb 49
N9 19Vb 33
Cyprus St. E2 40Yb 72
(not continuous)
Cyrena Rd. SE22 58Vb 113
Cyril Dumpleton Ho. AL2: Lon C 8H 7
Cyril Lodge DA14: Sidc 63Wc 139
Cyril Mans. SW11 53Hb 111
Cyril Rd. BR6: Orp 73Wc 161
DA7: Bex 54Ad 117
Cyrils Way AL1: St A 5B 6
Cyrus Ho. EC1 5C 218
Cyrus St. EC1 5C 218
Czar St. SE8 51Cc 114

D

Dabbling Cl. DA8: Erith 52Kd 119
Dabbs Hill La. UB5: N'olt 37Ba 65
(not continuous)
Dabbs La. EC1 6A 218
Dabbs Pl. DA13: Cobh 8F 144
D'Abernon Chase KT22: Oxs 86Ja 172
D'Abernon Cl. KT10: Esh 77Ca 151
D'Abernon Dr. KT11: Stoke D 88Aa 171
Dabin Cres. SE10 53Ec 114
Dacca St. SE8 51Bc 114
Dace Rd. E3 39Cc 72
Dacorum District Sports Cen. 4L 3
Dacorum Way HP1: Hem H 2L 3
(not continuous)
Dacre Av. IG5: Ilf 26Qc 54
RM15: Avel 46Td 98
Dacre Cl. IG7: Chig 21Sc 54
UB6: G'frd 40Da 65
Dacre Cres. RM15: Avel 46Td 98
Dacre Gdns. IG7: Chig 21Sc 54
SE13 56Gc 115
WD6: Bore 15Ta 29
Dacre Ho. SW3 51Fb 111
(off Beaufort St.)
Dacre Ind. Est. EN8: Chesh 1Bc 20
Dacre Pk. SE13 55Gc 115
Dacre Pl. SE13 55Gc 115
Dacre Rd. CR0: C'don 73Nb 156
E11 32Hc 73
E13 39Kc 73
Dacres Est. SE23 62Zb 136
Dacres Ho. SW4 55Kb 112
Dacres Rd. SE23 61Zb 136
Dacre St. SW1 3D 228 (48Mb 90)
Dade Way UB2: S'hall 50Ba 85
Daerwood Cl. BR2: Brom 74Pc 160
Daffodil Av. CM15: Pil H 15Xd 40
Daffodil Cl. CR0: C'don 74Zb 158
Daffodil Dr. GU24: Bisl 8E 166
Daffodil Gdns. IG1: Ilf 36Rc 74
Daffodil Pl. TW12: Hamp 65Ca 129
Daffodil St. W12 45Va 88
Dafforne Rd. SW17 62Jb 134
Da Gama Pl. E14 50Cc 92
DAGENHAM 37Cd 76
Dagenham & Redbridge FC 36Dd 76
Dagenham Av. RM9: Dag 39Ad 75
(not continuous)
Dagenham Bowl 39Ad 75
Dagenham Leisure Pk. RM9: Dag 39Ad 75
Dagenham Pk. Leisure Cen. 38Cd 76
Dagenham Rd. E10 32Bc 72
RM7: Rush G 31Fd 76
RM10: Dag, Rush G 35Ed 76
RM13: Rain 38Fd 76
Dagenham Swimming Pool 33Cd 76
Dagger La. WD6: E'tree 16Ja 28
Daggsdell Rd. HP1: Hem H 1G 2
Dagmar Av. HA9: Wemb 35Pa 67
Dagmar Ct. E14 48Ec 92
Dagmar Gdns. NW10 40Za 68
Dagmar M. UB2: S'hall 48Aa 85
(off Dagmar Rd.)
Dagmar Pas. N1 39Rb 71
(off Cross St.)
Dagmar Rd. KT2: King T 67Pa 131
N4 31Qb 70
N15 28Tb 51
N22 25Mb 50
RM10: Dag 38Ed 76
SE5 53Ub 113
SE25 71Ub 157
SL4: Wind 4H 103
UB2: S'hall 48Aa 85
Dagmar Ter. N1 39Rb 71
Dagnall Cres. UB8: Cowl 43L 83
Dagnall Pk. SE25 72Ub 157
Dagnall Rd. SE25 71Ub 157
Dagnall St. SW11 54Hb 111
Dagnam Pk. Cl. RM3: Rom 22Qd 57
Dagnam Pk. Dr. RM3: Rom 22Nd 57
Dagnam Pk. Gdns. RM3: Rom 23Qd 57
Dagnam Pk. Sq. RM3: Rom 23Rd 57
Dagnan Rd. SW12 59Kb 112
Dagobert Ho. E1 43Yb 92
(off Smithy St.)
Dagonet Gdns. BR1: Brom 62Jc 137
Dagonet Rd. BR1: Brom 62Jc 137
Dahlia Dr. BR8: Swan 68Hd 140
Dahlia Gdns. CR4: Mitc 70Mb 134
IG1: Ilf 37Rc 74
Dahlia Rd. SE2 49Xc 95
Dahomey Rd. SW16 65Lb 134
Daiglen Dr. RM15: S Ock 42Xd 98
Daimler Ho. E3 42Cc 92
(off Wellington Way)
Daimler Way SM6: Wall 80Nb 156
Dain Ct. W8 49Cb 89
(off Lexham Gdns.)
Daines Cl. E12 34Pc 74
RM15: S Ock 42Wd 98
Dainford Cl. BR1: Brom 64Fc 137
Dainton Cl. BR1: Brom 67Kc 137
Dainton Ho. W2 43Cb 89
(off Gt. Western Rd.)
Daintry Cl. HA3: W'stone 28Ja 46
Daintry Lodge HA6: Nwood 23V 44
Daintry Way E9 37Bc 72
Dairsie Ct. BR1: Brom 67Lc 137

Dairsie Rd. SE9 55Qc 116
Dairy Bus. Pk. RH1: Blet 3J 209
Dairy Cl. BR1: Brom 66Kc 137
CR7: Thor H 68Sb 135
DA4: Sut H 66Rd 141
NW10 39Wa 68
SW6 53Cb 111
UB6: G'frd 40Fa 66
Dairy Cotts. TN15: Fair 84Fe 185
Dairy Farm La. UB9: Hare 26L 43
Dairyglen Av. EN8: Chesh 3Ac 20
Dairy La. SE18 49Pc 94
Dairyman Cl. NW2 34Za 68
Dairyman's Wlk. GU4: Burp 100D 188
Dairy M. N2 28Gb 49
RM6: Chad H 31Zc 75
SW9 55Nb 112
WD18: Wat 15W 26
Dairy Wlk. SW19 63Ab 132
Dairy Way WD5: Ab L 1V 12
Daisy Cl. CR0: C'don 74Zb 158
NW9 33Sa 67
Daisy Dobbings Wlk. N19 31Nb 70
(off Jessie Blythe La.)
Daisy La. SW6 55Cb 111
Daisy Mdw. TW20: Egh 64C 126
Daisy Rd. E16 42Gc 93
E18 26Kc 53
Dakin Pl. E1 43Ac 92
Dakota Bldg. SE10 53Dc 114
(off Deal's Gateway)
Dakota Cl. SM6: Wall 80Pb 156
Dakota Gdns. E6 42Nc 94
UB5: N'olt 41Aa 85
Dakota Ho. CR7: Thor H 72Rb 157
Dalberg Rd. SW2 56Qb 112
(not continuous)
Dalberg Way SE2 48Zc 95
Dalby Rd. SW18 56Eb 111
Dalbys Cres. N17 23Ub 51
Dalby St. NW5 37Kb 70
Dalcross Rd. TW4: Houn 54Aa 107
Dale, The BR2: Kes 77Mc 159
EN9: Walt A 6Gc 21
Dale Av. HA8: Edg 25Pa 47
TW4: Houn 55Aa 107
Dalebury Rd. SW17 61Hb 133
Dale Cl. DA1: Cray 58Hd 118
EN5: New Bar 16Db 31
HA5: Pinn 25X 45
KT15: Add 78K 149
KT23: Bookh 97Ea 192
RM15: S Ock 44Wd 98
SE3 55Jc 115
SL5: S'dale 1E 146
Dale Ct. EN2: Enf 11Sb 33
KT2: King T 66Pa 131
(off York Rd.)
SL1: Slou 7G 80
WD25: Wat 5W 12
Dale Dr. UB4: Hayes 42V 84
Dale End DA1: Cray 58Hd 118
Dalefield IG9: Buck H 18Lc 35
(off Roebuck La.)
Dalefield Way DA12: Grav'nd 9H 123
Dale Gdns. IG8: Wfd G 21Kc 53
Dalegarth Gdns. CR8: Purl 85Tb 177
Dale Grn. Rd. N11 20Kb 32
Dale Gro. N12 22Eb 49
Daleham Av. TW20: Egh 65C 126
Daleham Dr. UB8: Hil 44R 84
Daleham Gdns. NW3 36Fb 69
Daleham M. NW3 37Fb 69
Dalehead NW1 2B 216
Dale Ho. N1 39Ub 71
(off New Era Est.)
NW8 39Eb 69
(off Boundary Rd.)
SE4 56Ac 114
Dale Lodge N6 30Lb 50
Dale Lodge Rd. SL5: S'dale 1E 146
Dalemain M. E16 46Jc 93
Dale Pk. Av. SM5: Cars 75Hb 155
Dale Pk. Rd. SE19 67Sb 135
Dale Rd. BR8: Swan 68Ed 140
CR8: Purl 84Qb 176
DA1: Cray 58Hd 118
DA13: Sflt 63Ce 143
KT12: Walt T 73V 150
NW5 36Jb 70
SE17 51Rb 113
SM1: Sutt 77Bb 155
TW16: Sun 66V 128
UB6: G'frd 43Da 85
Dale Row W11 44Ab 88
Dale Side SL9: Ger X 32A 62
Daleside BR6: Chels 78Wc 161
Daleside Cl. BR6: Chels 79Wc 161
Daleside Dr. EN6: Pot B 5Bb 17
Daleside Gdns. IG7: Chig 20Sc 36
Daleside Rd. KT19: Ewe 79Ta 153
SW16 64Kb 134
Dales Path WD6: Bore 15Ta 29
Dales Rd. WD6: Bore 15Ta 29
Dalestone M. RM3: Rom 23Kd 57
Dale St. W4 50Ua 88
Dale Vw. DA8: Erith 54Hd 118
GU21: Wok 10M 167
KT18: Head 95Ra 193
Dale Vw. Av. E4 19Ec 34
Dale Vw. Cres. E4 19Ec 34
Dale Vw. Gdns. E4 20Fc 35
Daleview Rd. N15 30Ub 51
Dale Wlk. DA2: Dart 60Sd 120
Dalewood Cl. RM11: Horn 31Pd 77
Dalewood Gdns. KT4: Wor Pk 75Xa 154
Dale Wood Rd. BR6: Orp 73Uc 160
Daley Ho. W12 44Xa 88
Daley St. E9 37Zb 72
Daley Thompson Way SW8 54Kb 112
Dalgarno Gdns. W10 43Ya 88
Dalgarno Way W10 42Ya 88
Dalgleish St. E14 44Ac 92
Daling Way E3 39Ac 72
Dalkeith Ct. SW1 6E 228
Dalkeith Gro. HA7: Stan 22Ma 47
Dalkeith Ho. SW9 53Rb 113
(off Lothian Rd.)
Dalkeith Rd. IG1: Ilf 34Sc 74
SE21 60Sb 113
Dallas Rd. NW4 31Wa 68
SE26 62Xb 135
SM3: Cheam 79Ab 154
W5 43Pa 87
Dallas Ter. UB3: Harl 48V 84
Dallega Cl. UB3: Hayes 45T 84
Dallinger Rd. SE12 58Hc 115
Dalling Rd. W6 49Xa 88
Dallington Cl. KT12: Hers 79Y 151
Dallington Sq. EC1 5C 218
(off Dallington St.)
Dallington St. EC1 5C 218 (42Rb 91)
Dallin Rd. DA6: Bex 56Zc 117
SE18 52Rc 116
Dalmain Rd. SE23 60Zb 114
Dalmally Rd. CR0: C'don 73Vb 157
Dalmany Pas. CR0: C'don 73Vb 157
Dalmeny Av. N7 35Mb 70
SW16 68Qb 134
Dalmeny Cl. HA0: Wemb 37La 66
Dalmeny Cres. TW3: Houn 56Fa 108
Dalmeny Rd. DA8: Erith 53Dd 118
EN5: New Bar 16Eb 31
KT4: Wor Pk 76Xa 154
N7 34Mb 70
(not continuous)
SM5: Cars 80Jb 156
Dalmeny Way KT18: Eps 86Sa 173
Dalmeyer Rd. NW10 37Va 68
Dalmore Av. KT10: Clay 79Ha 152
Dalmore Rd. SE21 61Sb 135
Dalo Lodge E3 43Cc 92
(off Gale St.)
Dalroy Cl. RM15: S Ock 44Wd 98
Dalrymple Cl. N14 17Mb 32
Dalrymple Rd. SE4 56Ac 114
DALSTON 37Vb 71
Dalston Gdns. HA7: Stan 25Na 47
Dalston La. E8 37Vb 71
Dalston Sq. E8 37Vb 71
(not continuous)
Dalton Av. CR4: Mitc 68Gb 133
Dalton Cl. BR6: Orp 76Uc 160
CR8: Purl 84Sb 177
UB4: Hayes 42T 84
Dalton Grn. SL3: L'ly 51B 104
Dalton Ho. E3 40Ac 72
(off Ford St.)
HA7: Stan 22Ja 46
SE14 51Zb 114
(off John Williams Cl.)
SW1 7K 227
Dalton Rd. HA3: W'stone 26Fa 46
Daltons Rd. BR6: Well H 76Dd 162
BR8: Crock 76Dd 162
Daltons Shaw RM16: Ors 3C 100
Dalton St. AL3: St A 1B 6
SE27 62Rb 135
Daltons Wharf HP4: Berk 1A 2
Dalton Way WD17: Wat 15Z 27
Dalwood St. SE5 53Ub 113
Daly Dr. BR1: Brom 69Qc 138
Dalyell Rd. SW9 55Pb 112
Damascene Wlk. SE21 60Sb 113
Damask Cl. GU24: W End 5C 166
Damask Ct. SM1: Sutt 74Db 155
Damask Cres. E16 42Gc 93
Damask Grn. HP1: Hem H 3G 2
Damer Ter. SW10 52Eb 111
Dames Rd. E7 34Jc 73
Dame St. N1 1D 218 (40Sb 71)
Damien Ct. E1 44Xb 91
(off Damien St.)
Damien St. E1 44Xb 91
Damigos Rd. DA12: Grav'nd 10H 123
Damon Cl. DA14: Sidc 62Xc 139
Damory Ho. SE16 49Xb 91
(off Abbeyfield Est.)
Damson Ct. BR8: Swan 70Fd 140
Damson Dr. UB3: Hayes 45W 84
Damson Gro. SL1: Slou 7G 80
Damson Way AL4: St A 1G 6
SM5: Cars 81Hb 175
Damsonwood Rd. UB2: S'hall 48Ca 85
Danbrook Rd. SW16 67Nb 134
Danbury Cl. CM15: Pil H 15Vd 40
RM6: Chad H 27Zc 55
Danbury Cres. RM15: S Ock 44Xd 98
Danbury Mans. IG11: Bark 38Rc 74
(off Whiting Av.)
Danbury M. SM6: Wall 77Kb 156
Danbury Rd. IG10: Lough 17Nc 36
RM13: Rain 39Hd 76
Danbury St. N1 1C 218 (40Rb 71)
Danbury Way IG8: Wfd G 23Lc 53
Danby Ct. EN2: Enf 13Sb 33
Danby Ho. E9 38Yb 72
(off Frampton Pk. Rd.)
W10 41Ab 88
(off Bruckner St.)
Danby St. SE15 55Vb 113
Dance Ho. SE4 57Zb 114
(off St Norbert Rd.)
Dancer Rd. SW6 53Bb 111
TW9: Rich 55Qa 109
DANCERS HILL 8Za 16
Dancers Hill Rd. EN5: Barn 8Ya 16
Dancers La. EN5: Barn 7Ya 16
Dance Sq. EC1 4D 218 (41Sb 91)
Dandelion Cl. RM7: Rush G 33Gd 76
Dando Cres. SE3 55Kc 115
Dandridge Cl. SE10 50Hc 93
SL3: L'ly 9P 81
Dandridge Ho. E1 7K 219
Danebury CR0: New Ad 79Ec 158
Danebury Av. SW15 58Ua 110
Daneby Rd. SE6 62Dc 136
Dane Cl. BR6: Farnb 78Tc 160
DA5: Bexl 59Cd 118
Dane Ct. GU22: Pyr 87H 169
Danecourt Gdns. CR0: C'don 76Vb 157
Danecroft Rd. SE24 57Sb 113
Danehill Wlk. DA14: Sidc 62Wc 139
Daneholes Rdbt. RM16: Grays 48Fe 99
Danehurst TW8: Bford 52La 108
Danehurst Cl. TW20: Egh 65A 126
Danehurst Ct. KT17: Eps 85Va 174
Danehurst Gdns. IG4: Ilf 29Nc 54
Danehurst St. SW6 53Ab 110
Daneland EN4: E Barn 16Hb 31
Danemead Gro. UB5: N'olt 36Da 65
Danemere St. SW15 55Ya 110
Dane Pl. E3 40Ac 72
Dane Rd. CR6: W'ham 89Zb 178
IG1: Ilf 36Sc 74
N18 20Yb 34
SW19 67Eb 133
TN14: Otf 89Hd 182
TW15: Ashf 65S 128
UB1: S'hall 45Aa 85
W13 46La 86
Danes, The AL2: Park 10A 6
Danesbury Rd. TW13: Felt 60X 107
Danes Cl. DA11: Nflt 62Ee 143
KT22: Oxs 86Ea 172
Danescombe SE12 60Jc 115
Danes Ct. HA9: Wemb 34Ra 67
NW8 1F 215
Danescourt Cres. SM1: Sutt 75Eb 155
Danescroft NW4 29Za 48
Danescroft Av. NW4 29Za 48
Danescroft Gdns. NW4 29Za 48
Danesdale Rd. E9 37Ac 72
Danesfield GU23: Rip, Send 95H 189
SE5 51Ub 113
(off Albany Rd.)
Danesfield Cl. KT12: Walt T 76X 151
Danes Ga. HA1: Harr 27Ga 46
Danes Hill GU22: Wok 90C 168
Daneshill RH1: Redh 5N 207
Daneshill Cl. RH1: Redh 5N 207
Danes Hill School Dr. KT22: Oxs 86Ea 172
Danes Ho. W10 43Ya 88
(off Sutton Way)
Danesmead KT11: Cobh 83Ca 171
Danes Rd. RM7: Rush G 31Ed 76
Dane St. WC1 1H 223 (43Pb 90)
Danes Way CM15: Pil H 15Wd 40
KT22: Oxs 86Fa 172
Daneswood Av. SE6 62Ec 136
Daneswood Cl. KT13: Weyb 78R 150
Danethorpe Rd. HA0: Wemb 37Ma 67
Danetree Cl. KT19: Ewe 80Sa 153
Danetree Rd. KT19: Ewe 80Sa 153
Danette Gdns. RM10: Dag 33Cd 76
Daneville Rd. SE5 53Tb 113
Dangan Rd. E11 30Jc 53
Daniel Bolt Cl. E14 43Dc 92
Daniel Cl. N18 21Yb 52
RM16: Chaf H 47Ae 99
RM16: Grays 8D 100
SW17 65Gb 133
TW4: Houn 59Ba 107
Daniel Ct. NW9 25Ua 48
Daniel Gdns. SE15 52Vb 113
Daniel Lambert Mill KT15: Add 78N 149
(off Bourneside Rd.)
Daniell Ho. N1 1G 219
Daniell Way CR0: Wadd 74Nb 156
Daniel Pl. NW4 31Xa 68
Daniel Rd. W5 45Pa 87
Daniels La. CR6: W'ham 88Bc 178
Daniels Rd. SE15 55Yb 114
Daniel Way SM7: Bans 86Db 175
Danleigh Ct. N14 17Mb 32
Dan Leno Wlk. SW6 52Db 111
Dan Mason Dr. W4 54Sa 109
Danny Fiszman Bri. N5 35Qb 70
N7 35Qb 70
Dansey Pl. W1 4D 222
Dansington Rd. DA16: Well 56Wc 117
Danson Cres. DA16: Well 55Xc 117
Danson House 56Yc 117
DANSON INTERCHANGE 57Zc 117
Danson La. DA16: Well 56Xc 117
Danson Mead DA16: Well 55Yc 117
Danson Pk. 57Yc 117
Danson Pk. Watersports Cen. 56Yc 117
Danson Rd. DA5: Bexl, Bex 58Yc 117
DA6: Bex 57Zc 117
SE17 7C 230 (50Rb 91)
Danson Underpass DA15: Sidc 58Yc 117
Dante Pl. SE11 6C 230 (49Rb 91)
Dante Rd. SE11 5B 230 (49Rb 91)
Danube Apartments N8 27Pb 50
(off Gt. Amwell La.)
Danube Cl. N9 20Yb 34
Danube Ct. SE15 52Vb 113
(off Daniel Gdns.)
Danube St. SW3 7E 226 (50Gb 89)
Danvers Ho. E1 44Wb 91
(off Christian St.)
Danvers Rd. N8 28Mb 50
Danvers St. SW3 51Fb 111
Danvers Way CR3: Cat'm 95Sb 197
Danyon Cl. RM13: Rain 40Ld 77
Danziger Way WD6: Bore 11Sa 29
Dao Ct. E13 39Kc 73
Da Palma Ct. SW6 51Cb 111
(off Anselm Rd.)
Daphne Ct. KT4: Wor Pk 75Ua 154
Daphne Gdns. E4 20Ec 34
Daphne Ho. N22 25Qb 50
(off Acacia Rd.)
Daphne St. SW18 58Eb 111
Daplyn St. E1 43Wb 91
D'Arblay St. W1 3C 222 (44Lb 90)
Darby Cl. CR3: Cat'm 94Sb 197
RM19: Purf 49Sd 98
Darby Cres. TW16: Sun 68Y 129
Darby Dr. EN9: Walt A 5Ec 20
Darby Gdns. TW16: Sun 68Y 129
Darcy Av. SM6: Wall 77Lb 156
Darcy Cl. CM13: Hut 17De 41
CR5: Coul 91Rb 197
EN8: Chesh 3Ac 20
N20 19Fb 31
D'Arcy Dr. HA3: Kenton 28Ma 47
Darcy Gdns. HA3: Kenton 28Ma 47
RM9: Dag 39Bd 75
Darcy Ho. E8 39Xb 71
(off London Flds. E. Side)
D'Arcy Pl. BR2: Brom 70Jc 137
KT21: Asht 89Pa 173
Darcy Rd. KT21: Asht 89Pa 173
SM3: Cheam 77Za 154
SW16 68Nb 134
TW7: Isle 53Ja 108
Dare Gdns. RM8: Dag 34Ad 75
Darell Rd. TW9: Rich 55Qa 109
Darent Cl. TN13: Chip 94Ed 202
DARENTH 64Sd 142
Darenth Country Pk. 61Td 142
Darenth Dr. DA12: Grav'nd 10K 123
Darenth Gdns. TN16: Westrm 98Tc 200
Darenth Hill DA2: Daren 64Sd 142
Darenth Hill Trad. Est.
DA2: Daren 64Rd 141
DARENTH INTERCHANGE 62Rd 141
Darenth La. RM15: S Ock 44Wd 98
TN13: Dun G 93Gd 202
Darent Ho. BR1: Brom 64Fc 137
NW8 7C 214
Darenth Pk. Av. DA2: Dart 61Td 142
Darenth Pl. DA2: Daren 64Td 142
Darenth Rd. DA1: Dart 59Pd 119
DA16: Well 53Wc 117
N16 31Vb 71
Darenth Rd. Sth. DA2: Daren 63Rd 141
Darenth Valley Golf Course 84Jd 182
Darenth Way TN14: S'ham 83Jd 182
Darenth Wood Rd. DA2: Dart 63Ud 142
(not continuous)
Darent Ind. Pk. DA8: Erith 51Md 119
Darent Mead DA4: Sut H 67Rd 141
Darfield NW1 39Lb 70
(off Bayham St.)
Darfield Rd. SE4 57Bc 114
Darfield Way W10 44Za 88
Darfur St. SW15 55Za 110
Dargate Cl. SE19 66Vb 135
Dariel Cl. SL1: Slou 7D 80
Darien Rd. SW11 55Fb 111
Daring Ho. E3 40Ac 72
(off Roman Rd.)
Darkes La. EN6: Pot B 4Cb 17
Darkhole Ride SL4: Wink 7A 102
Dark Ho. Wlk. EC3 5G 225 (45Tb 91)
Dark La. CM14: Gt War 23Vd 58
EN7: Chesh 2Wb 19
GU20: W'sham 8A 146
Darlands Dr. EN5: Barn 15Za 30
Darlan Rd. SW6 52Bb 111
Darlaston Rd. SW19 66Za 132
Darley Cl. CR0: C'don 72Ac 158
KT15: Add 78L 149
Darley Cft. AL2: Park 10P 5
Darley Dene Ct. KT15: Add 77L 149
Darley Dr. KT3: N Mald 68Ta 131
Darley Gdns. SM4: Mord 72Eb 155
Darley Ho. SE11 7H 229
Darley Rd. N9 18Vb 33
SW11 58Hb 111
Darling Ho. TW1: Twick 58Ma 109
Darling Rd. SE4 55Cc 114
Darling Row E1 42Xb 91
Darlington Ct. CM15: Pil H 16Wd 40
SE6 60Hc 115
Darlington Gdns. RM3: Rom 22Md 57
Darlington Ho. SW8 52Mb 112
(off Hemans St.)
Darlington Path RM3: Rom 22Md 57
Darlington Rd. SE27 64Rb 135
Darlton Cl. DA1: Cray 55Hd 118
Darmaine Cl. CR2: S Croy 80Sb 157
Darnall Ho. SE10 53Ec 114
(off Royal Hill)
Darnaway Pl. E14 43Ec 92
(off Aberfeldy St.)
Darnay Apartments E15 37Fc 73
Darndale Cl. E17 26Bc 52
Darnets Fld. TN14: Otf 89Hd 182
Darnhills WD7: R'lett 7Ha 14
Darnley Ct. DA11: Grav'nd 9C 122
(off Darnley Rd.)
Darnley Ho. E14 44Ac 92
(off Camdenhurst St.)
Darnley Mausoleum 10N 145
Darnley Pk. KT13: Weyb 76R 150
Darnley Rd. DA11: Grav'nd 10C 122
(not continuous)
E9 37Yb 72
IG8: Wfd G 25Jc 53
RM17: Grays 51De 121
Darnley St. DA11: Grav'nd 9C 122
Darnley Ter. W11 46Za 88
Darns Hill BR8: Crock 73Ed 162
Darrell Charles Ct. UB8: Uxb 38N 63
Darrell Cl. SL3: L'ly 49B 82
Darrell Rd. SE22 57Wb 113
Darren Cl. N4 31Pb 70
Darren Ct. N7 35Nb 70
Darrick Wood Rd. BR6: Orp 75Tc 160
Darrick Wood Sports Cen. 76Sc 160
Darrick Wood Swimming Pool 76Sc 160
Darrington Rd. WD6: Bore 11Na 29
Darris Cl. UB4: Yead 42Aa 85
Darsley Dr. SW8 53Mb 112
Dart Cl. RM14: Upm 30Td 58
SL3: L'ly 50D 82
Dartfields RM3: Rom 23Md 57
DARTFORD 58Nd 119
Dartford Av. N9 16Yb 34
Dartford Borough Mus. 59Nd 119
Dartford By-Pass DA1: Bexl, Dart 60Gd 118
DA2: Bean, Daren, Dart, Hawl
63Pd 141
DA5: Bexl, Dart 60Gd 118
Dartford Clay Shooting Club 52Nd 119
Dartford Ct. KT19: Eps 84Na 173
Dartford Dojo Judo Club 58Sd 120
Dartford FC 60Qd 119
Dartford Gdns. RM6: Chad H 29Xc 55
Dartford Golf Course 61Kd 141
DARTFORD HEATH 60Hd 118
Dartford Heath Retail Pk.
DA1: Dart 60Ld 119
Dartford Ho. SE1 6K 231
Dartford Rd. DA1: Dart 58Jd 118
DA4: Farni, Hort K, Knock, S Dar
72Pd 163
DA5: Bexl 60Ed 118
TN13: S'oaks 96Ld 203
Dartford St. SE17 51Sb 113
Dartford-Thurrock River Crossing
RM20: W Thur 54Ud 120
Dartford Trade Pk. DA1: Dart 61Nd 141
Dartford Tunnel DA1: Dart 55Td 120
Dartford Tunnel App. Rd.
DA1: Dart 59Rd 119
Dart Grn. RM15: S Ock 43Xd 98
Dartington NW1 1C 216
Dartington Ho. SW8 54Mb 112
(off Union Gro.)
W2 43Db 89
(off Senior St.)
Dartle Ct. SE16 47Wb 91
(off Scott Lidgett Cres.)
Dartmoor Wlk. E14 49Cc 92
(off Severnake Cl.)
Dartmouth Av. GU21: Wok 86E 168
Dartmouth Cl. W11 44Bb 89
Dartmouth Ct. SE10 53Ec 114
Dartmouth Grn. GU21: Wok 86F 168
Dartmouth Gro. SE10 53Ec 114
Dartmouth Hill SE10 53Ec 114
Dartmouth Ho. KT2: King T 67Na 131
(off Seven Kings Way)
SE10 53Dc 114
(off Catherine Gro.)
DARTMOUTH PARK 34Kb 70
Dartmouth Pk. Av. NW5 34Kb 70
Dartmouth Pk. Hill N19 32Kb 70
NW5 32Kb 70
Dartmouth Pk. Rd. NW5 35Kb 70
Dartmouth Path GU21: Wok 86F 168
Dartmouth Pl. SE23 61Yb 136
W4 51Ua 110
Dartmouth Rd. BR2: Hayes 73Jc 159
HA4: Ruis 34W 64
NW2 37Za 68
NW4 30Wa 48
SE23 62Xb 135
SE26 62Xb 135
Dartmouth Row SE10 54Ec 114
Dartmouth St. SW1 2D 228 (47Mb 90)
Dartmouth Ter. SE10 53Fc 115
Dartnell Av. KT14: W Byf 84K 169
Dartnell Cl. KT14: W Byf 84K 169
Dartnell Ct. KT14: W Byf 84L 169
Dartnell Cres. KT14: W Byf 84K 169
DARTNELL PARK 84K 169
Dartnell Pk. Rd. KT14: W Byf 84K 169
Dartnell Pl. KT14: W Byf 84K 169
Dartnell Rd. CR0: C'don 73Vb 157
Darton Ct. W3 46Sa 87
Dartrey Twr. SW10 52Eb 111
(off Worlds End Est.)
Dartrey Wlk. SW10 52Eb 111
Dart St. W10 41Ab 88
Dartview Cl. RM17: Grays 9A 100
Darvel Cl. GU21: Wok 8L 167
Darvell Ho. SE17 7G 231
Darvells Yd. WD3: Chor 14F 24
Darville Rd. N16 34Vb 71
Darvill's La. SL1: Slou 7H 81
Darwell Cl. E6 40Qc 74
Darwen Pl. E2 40Xb 71
Darwin Cl. BR6: Farnb 78Tc 160
N11 20Kb 32
Darwin Ct. CR2: S Croy 78Rb 157
(off Warham Rd.)
E13 41Kc 93
NW1 39Kb 70
(not continuous)
SE17 6G 231
Darwin Dr. UB1: S'hall 44Da 85
Darwin Gdns. WD19: Wat 22Y 45
Darwin Ho. SW1 51Lb 112
(off Grosvenor Rd.)
Darwin Ri. DA11: Nflt 60De 121
Darwin Rd. DA16: Well 55Vc 117
N22 25Rb 51
RM18: Tilb 3B 122
SL3: L'ly 47B 82
W5 50La 86
Darwin Sports Cen. 87Pc 180
Darwin St. SE17 5G 231 (49Tb 91)
(not continuous)
Darwood Ct. NW6 38Eb 69
(off Belsize Rd.)
Daryngton Dr. UB6: G'frd 40Fa 66
Daryngton Ho. SE1 2F 231
SW8 52Nb 112
(off Hartington Rd.)
Dashwood Cl. DA6: Bex 57Cd 118
KT14: W Byf 84L 169
SL3: L'ly 9N 81
Dashwood Lang Rd.
KT15: Add 77M 149
Dashwood Rd. DA11: Grav'nd 10C 122
N8 30Pb 50
Dassett Rd. SE27 64Rb 135
Data Point Bus. Cen. E16 42Fc 93
Datchelor Pl. SE5 53Tb 113
DATCHET 3M 103
DATCHET COMMON 3P 103
Datchet Golf Course 2L 103
Datchet Ho. E2 4K 219
NW1 3A 216
Datchet Pl. SL3: Dat 3M 103
Datchet Rd. SE6 61Bc 136
SL3: Hort 5B 104
SL3: Slou 9K 81
SL4: Old Win 6L 103
SL4: Wind 2H 103
Datchet Watersports Cen. 52D 104
Datchworth Ct. EN1: Enf 15Ub 33
Datchworth Ho. N1 38Rb 71
(off The Sutton Est.)
Datchworth Turn HP2: Hem H 2C 4
Date St. SE17 7E 230 (50Tb 91)
Daubeney Gdns. N17 24Sb 51
Daubeney Pl. TW12: Hamp 67Ea 130
(off High St.)
Daubeney Rd. E5 35Ac 72
N17 24Sb 51
Daubeney Twr. SE8 50Bc 92
(off Bowditch)
Dault Rd. SW18 58Eb 111
Dauncey Ho. SE1 2B 230
Davall Ho. RM17: Grays 51De 121
(off Argent St.)
Dave Adams Ho. E3 40Bc 72
(off Norman Gro.)
Davema Cl. BR7: Chst 67Qc 138
Davenant Ho. E1 43Wb 91
(off Old Montague St.)
Davenant Rd. CR0: C'don 77Rb 157
N19 33Mb 70
Davenant St. E1 43Wb 91
Davenham Av. HA6: Nwood 22V 44
Davenham Pl. HA6: Nwood 22V 44
Davenport Cen. IG11: Bark 39Xc 75
Davenport Cl. TW11: Tedd 65Ja 130
Davenport Ct. CR0: C'don 73Rb 157
Davenport Ho. SE11 4K 229
UB7: W Dray 47P 83
Davenport Lodge TW5: Hest 52Aa 107
Davenport Rd. DA14: Sidc 61Ad 139
SE6 58Dc 114
Daventer Dr. HA7: Stan 24Ha 46
Daventry Av. E17 30Cc 52
Daventry Cl. SL3: Poyle 53H 105
Daventry Gdns. RM3: Rom 22Ld 57
Daventry Grn. RM3: Rom 22Ld 57
Daventry Rd. RM3: Rom 22Ld 57
Daventry St. NW1 7D 214 (43Gb 89)
Daver Ct. SW3 7E 226 (50Gb 89)
W5 42Ma 87
Davern Cl. SE10 49Hc 93
Davey Cl. N7 37Pb 70
N13 22Pb 50
Davey Rd. E9 38Cc 72
Davey's Ct. WC2 4F 223
Davey St. SE15 51Vb 113
David Av. UB6: G'frd 41Ga 86
David Cl. UB3: Harl 52U 106
David Coffer Ct. DA17: Belv 49Dd 96
David Ct. N20 20Eb 31

David Crompton Lodge, The
RM3: Rom . . . 22Nd 57
David Dr. RM3: Hrld W . . . 23Qd 57
Davidge Ho. SE1 . . . 2A 230
Davidge St. SE1 . . . 2B 230 (47Rb 91)
David Hewitt Ho. E3 . . . 43Dc 92
(off Watts Gro.)
David Ho. DA15: Sidc . . . 62Wc 139
SW8 . . . 52Nb 112
(off Wyvil Rd.)
David Lean Cinema . . . 76Sb 157
(off Katharine St.)
David Lean Ct. UB9: Den . . . 29H 43
(off Patrons Way W.)
David Lee Point E15 . . . 39Gc 73
(off Leather Gdns.)
David Lloyd Leisure
Barnet . . . 24Fb 49
Beckenham . . . 70Bc 136
Buckhurst Hill . . . 18Pc 36
Bushey . . . 12Ca 27
Cheam . . . 80Za 154
Dartford . . . 60Pd 119
Ealing . . . 36Fa 66
Enfield . . . 12Wb 33
Epsom . . . 82Qa 173
Fulham . . . 52Cb 111
(within Fulham Broadway Shop. Cen.)
Hampton . . . 62Ca 129
Hornchurch . . . 27Md 57
Hounslow . . . 50Y 85
Kidbrooke . . . 56Kc 115
Kingston upon Thames . . . 68Na 131
(in The Rotunda Cen.)
Merton . . . 69Za 132
Sidcup . . . 64Yc 139
South Kensington . . . 49Db 89
(off Point West)
Weybridge . . . 82Q 170
Woking . . . 92B 188
David M. W1 . . . 7H 215 (43Hb 89)
David Rd. RM8: Dag . . . 33Ad 75
SL3: Poyle . . . 54H 105
David's Ct. UB1: S'hall . . . 44Ea 86
(off Whitecote Rd.)
Davidson Gdns. SW8 . . . 52Nb 112
Davidson Ho. HP2: Hem H . . . 1M 3
Davidson La. HA1: Harr . . . 31Ha 66
Davidson Rd. CR0: C'don . . . 74Ub 157
Davidson Terraces E7 . . . 36Kc 73
(off Claremont Rd.)
Davidson Way RM7: Rush G . . . 31Gd 76
David's Rd. SE23 . . . 60Yb 114
David St. E15 . . . 37Fc 73
David's Way IG6: Ilf . . . 24Uc 54
David Ter. RM3: Hrld W . . . 24Qd 57
David Twigg Cl. KT2: King T . . . 67Na 131
Davies Cl. CR0: C'don . . . 72Wb 157
RM13: Rain . . . 41Ld 97
Davies La. E11 . . . 33Gc 73
Davies M. W1 . . . 4K 221 (45Kb 90)
Davies St. W1 . . . 3K 221 (44Kb 90)
Davies Wlk. TW7: Isle . . . 53Fa 108
Da Vinci Ct. SE16 . . . 50Xb 91
(off Rossetti Rd.)
WD25: Wat . . . 8Z 13
Da Vinci Lodge SE10 . . . 48Hc 93
(off West Parkside)
Davington Gdns. RM8: Dag . . . 36Xc 75
Davington Rd. RM8: Dag . . . 37Xc 75
Davinia Cl. IG8: Wfd G . . . 23Pc 54
Davis Av. DA11: Nflt . . . 10A 122
Davis Cl. TN13: S'oaks . . . 94Ld 203
Davis Ct. AL1: St A . . . 2C 6
Davis Ho. W12 . . . 45Xa 88
(off White City Est.)
Davison Cl. KT19: Eps . . . 83Ra 173
Davison Dr. EN8: Chesh . . . 1Zb 20
Davison Rd. SL3: L'ly . . . 50B 82
Davis Rd. KT9: Chess . . . 77Qa 153
KT13: Weyb . . . 82P 169
RM15: Avel . . . 46Td 98
RM16: Chaf H . . . 48Be 99
W3 . . . 46Va 88
Davis Road Ind. Pk.
KT9: Chess . . . 77Qa 153
Davis St. E13 . . . 40Kc 73
Davisville Rd. W12 . . . 47Wa 88
Davis Way DA14: Sidc . . . 65Ad 139
Davmor Ct. TW8: Bford . . . 50La 86
Davos Cl. GU22: Wok . . . 91A 188
Davy Down (Information Cen.) . . . 46Yd 98
Davy Down Riverside Pk. . . . 46Yd 98
Davy Ho. AL1: St A . . . 3D 6
Davy's Pl. DA12: Grav'nd . . . 5G 144
Dawell Dr. TN16: Big H . . . 89Lc 179
Dawes Av. RM12: Horn . . . 34Md 77
TW7: Isle . . . 57Ja 108
Dawes Cl. DA9: Ghithe . . . 57Vd 120
Dawes Ct. KT10: Esh . . . 77Da 151
Dawes East Rd. SL1: Burn . . . 2A 80
Dawes Ho. SE17 . . . 6F 231
Dawes La. WD3: Sarr . . . 9G 10
Dawes Moor Cl. SL2: Slou . . . 4N 81
Dawes Rd. SW6 . . . 52Ab 110
UB10: Uxb . . . 40N 63
Dawes St. SE17 . . . 7G 231 (50Tb 91)
Dawley Av. UB8: Hil . . . 43S 84
Dawley Grn. RM15: S Ock . . . 44Wd 98
Dawley Pde. UB3: Hayes . . . 45S 84
Dawley Pk. UB3: Hayes . . . 47T 84
Dawley Ride SL3: Poyle . . . 53G 104
Dawley Rd. UB3: Harl, Hayes . . . 45S 84
Dawlish Av. N13 . . . 21Nb 50
SW18 . . . 61Db 133
UB6: G'frd . . . 40Ja 66
Dawlish Dr. HA4: Ruis . . . 33W 64
HA5: Pinn . . . 29Aa 45
IG3: Ilf . . . 35Uc 74
Dawlish Rd. E10 . . . 32Ec 72
N17 . . . 27Wb 51
NW2 . . . 37Za 68
Dawlish Wlk. RM3: Rom . . . 25Ld 57
Dawnay Gdns. SW18 . . . 61Fb 133
Dawnay Rd. KT23: Bookh . . . 98Da 191
SW18 . . . 61Eb 133
Dawn Cl. TW4: Houn . . . 55Aa 107
Dawn Ct. AL1: St A . . . 3E 6
Dawn Cres. E15 . . . 39Fc 73
Dawney Hill GU24: Pirb . . . 3C 186
Dawneys Rd. GU24: Pirb . . . 4C 186
Dawn Redwood Cl. SL3: Hort . . . 55C 104
Dawpool Rd. NW2 . . . 33Va 68
Daws Ct. SL0: Iver . . . 44H 83
Daws Hill E4 . . . 12Ec 34
Daws La. NW7 . . . 22Va 48
Dawson Av. BR5: St P . . . 68Xc 139
IG11: Bark . . . 38Uc 74
Dawson Cl. SE18 . . . 49Sc 94
SL4: Wind . . . 4E 102
UB3: Hayes . . . 43T 84
Dawson Dr. BR8: Hext . . . 66Gd 140
RM13: Rain . . . 38Kd 77
Dawson Gdns. IG11: Bark . . . 38Vc 75
Dawson Ho. E2 . . . 41Yb 92
(off Sceptre Rd.)
Dawson Pl. W2 . . . 45Cb 89
Dawson Rd. KT1: King T . . . 69Pa 131
KT14: Byfl . . . 83M 169
NW2 . . . 36Ya 68
Dawson St. E2 . . . 2K 219 (40Vb 71)
Dawson Ter. N9 . . . 17Yb 34
Daws Pl. RH1: Mers . . . 3C 208
Dax Ct. TW16: Sun . . . 69Y 129
Daybrook Rd. SW19 . . . 68Db 133
Day Ho. SE5 . . . 52Sb 113
(off Bethwin Rd.)
Daylesford Av. SW15 . . . 56Wa 110
Daylesford Gro. SL1: Slou . . . 7D 80
Daylop Dr. IG7: Chig . . . 20Xc 37
Daymer Gdns. HA5: Eastc . . . 28X 45
Daymerslea Ridge KT22: Lea . . . 93La 192
Daynor Ho. NW6 . . . 39Cb 69
(off Quex Ho.)
Days Acre CR2: Sande . . . 82Vb 177
Daysbrook Rd. SW2 . . . 60Pb 112
Days La. CM15: Dodd, Pil H . . . 14Wd 40
DA15: Sidc . . . 59Uc 116
Daytona Sandown Pk. . . . 76Ea 152
Dayton Dr. DA8: Erith . . . 50Md 97
Dayton Gro. SE15 . . . 53Yb 114
Deacon Cl. AL1: St A . . . 6B 6
CR8: Purl . . . 81Nb 176
KT11: D'side . . . 91X 191
Deacon Ct. SL4: Wind . . . 4B 102
Deaconess Ct. N15 . . . 28Vb 51
(off Tottenham Grn. E.)
Deacon Est., The E4 . . . 23Bc 52
Deacon Ho. SE11 . . . 6J 229
Deacon M. N1 . . . 38Tb 71
Deacon Pl. CR3: Cat'm . . . 95Sb 197
Deacon Rd. KT2: King T . . . 67Pa 131
NW2 . . . 36Wa 68
Deacons Cl. HA5: Pinn . . . 26X 45
WD6: E'tree . . . 14Qa 29
Deacons Ct. TW1: Twick . . . 61Ha 130
Deaconsfield Rd. HP3: Hem H . . . 5M 3
Deacons Hgts. WD6: E'tree . . . 16Qa 29
Deacons Hill WD6: E'tree . . . 16Pa 29
WD19: Wat . . . 16Y 27
Deacon's Hill Rd. WD6: E'tree . . . 14Pa 29
Deacons Leas BR6: Orp . . . 77Tc 160
Deacon's Ri. N2 . . . 29Fb 49
Deacons Ter. N1 . . . 37Sb 71
(off Harecourt Rd.)
Deacons Wlk. TW12: Hamp . . . 63Ca 129
Deacon Way IG8: Wfd G . . . 24Pc 54
SE17 . . . 5D 230 (49Sb 91)
Deadhearn La. HP8: Chal G . . . 18A 24
Deadman's Ash La. WD3: Sarr . . . 8K 11
Deakin Cl. WD18: Wat . . . 17U 26
Deakins Ter. BR6: Orp . . . 73Wc 161
Deal Av. SL1: Slou . . . 4D 80
Deal Ct. NW9 . . . 26Va 48
(off Hazel Cl.)
UB1: S'hall . . . 44Ea 86
(off Haldane Rd.)
Deal Ho. SE15 . . . 51Zb 114
(off Lovelinch La.)
SE17 . . . 7J 231
Deal M. W5 . . . 49Ma 87
Deal Porters Wlk. SE16 . . . 47Zb 92
Deal Porters Way SE16 . . . 48Yb 92
Deal Rd. SW17 . . . 65Jb 134
Deal's Gateway SE10 . . . 53Cc 114
Deal St. E1 . . . 43Wb 91
Dealtry Rd. SW15 . . . 56Ya 110
Deal Wlk. SW9 . . . 52Qb 112
Dean Abbott Ho. SW1 . . . 5D 228
Deanacre Cl. SL9: Chal P . . . 23A 42
DEAN BOTTOM . . . 69Xd 142
Dean Bradley St. SW1 . . . 4F 229 (48Nb 90)
Dean Cl. E9 . . . 36Yb 72
GU22: Pyr . . . 87G 168
SE16 . . . 46Zb 92
SL4: Wind . . . 5B 102
UB10: Hil . . . 38P 63
Dean Ct. HA0: Wemb . . . 34Ka 66
HA8: Edg . . . 23Ra 47
RM7: Rom . . . 29Fd 56
SW8 . . . 52Nb 112
(off Thorncroft St.)
W3 . . . 44Ta 87
WD25: Wat . . . 5Z 13
Deancroft Rd. SL9: Chal P . . . 23A 42
Deancross St. E1 . . . 44Yb 92
Dean Dr. HA7: Stan . . . 26Na 47
Deane Av. HA4: Ruis . . . 36Y 65
Deane Ct. HA6: Nwood . . . 25U 44
Deane Cft. Rd. HA5: Eastc . . . 30Y 45
Deanery Cl. N2 . . . 28Gb 49
Deanery M. W1 . . . 6J 221
Deanery Rd. E15 . . . 37Gc 73
Deanery St. W1 . . . 6J 221 (46Jb 90)
Deane Way HA4: Ruis . . . 30X 45
Dean Farrar St. SW1 . . . 3E 228 (48Mb 90)
Dean Fld. HP3: Bov . . . 9C 2
Deanfield Gdns. CR0: C'don . . . 77Tb 157
Dean Gdns. E17 . . . 28Fc 53
Deanhill Ct. SW14 . . . 56Ra 109
Deanhill Rd. SW14 . . . 56Ra 109
Dean Ho. E1 . . . 44Yb 92
(off Tarling St.)
SE14 . . . 52Ac 114
(off New Cross Rd.)
Dean La. RH1: Mers . . . 95Kb 196
Dean Moore Cl. AL1: St A . . . 3A 6
Dean Rd. CR0: C'don . . . 77Tb 157
NW2 . . . 37Ya 68
SE28 . . . 46Wc 95
TW3: Houn . . . 57Da 107
TW12: Hamp . . . 64Ca 129
Dean Ryle St. SW1 . . . 5F 229 (49Nb 90)
Deansbrook Cl. HA8: Edg . . . 24Sa 47
Deansbrook Rd. HA8: Edg . . . 24Ra 47
Dean's Bldgs. SE17 . . . 6F 231 (49Tb 91)
Deans Cl. CR0: C'don . . . 76Vb 157
HA8: Edg . . . 23Sa 47
KT20: Walt H . . . 96Xa 194
SL2: Stoke P . . . 9M 61
W4 . . . 51Ra 109
WD5: Ab L . . . 4T 12
Deans Ct. EC4 . . . 3C 224 (44Rb 91)
GU20: W'sham . . . 10B 146
Deanscroft Av. NW9 . . . 32Sa 67
Deans Dr. HA8: Edg . . . 22Ta 47
N13 . . . 23Rb 51
Deans Factory Est. RM13: Rain . . . 42Ld 97
Deansfield CR3: Cat'm . . . 97Vb 197
Deans Ga. Cl. SE23 . . . 62Zb 136
Deanshanger Ho. SE8 . . . 49Zb 92
(off Chilton Gro.)
Deans La. HA8: Edg . . . 23Sa 47
KT20: Walt H . . . 96Xa 194
RH1: Nutf . . . 5G 208
W4 . . . 51Ra 109
(off Deans Cl.)
Dean's M. W1 . . . 2A 222 (44Kb 90)
Deans Rd. CM14: W'ley . . . 21Xd 58
RH1: Mers . . . 2C 208
SM1: Sutt . . . 76Db 155
W7 . . . 46Ha 86
Dean Stanley St. SW1 . . . 4F 229 (48Nb 90)
Deanston Wharf E16 . . . 47Kc 93
(not continuous)
Dean St. E7 . . . 36Jc 73
W1 . . . 2D 222 (44Mb 90)
Dean's Wlk. CR5: Coul . . . 90Qb 176
Deans Way HA8: Edg . . . 22Sa 47
Deansway HP3: Hem H . . . 5P 3
N2 . . . 28Fb 49
N9 . . . 20Ub 33
Deanswood N11 . . . 23Mb 50
Dean's Yd. SW1 . . . 3E 228 (48Mb 90)
Dean Trench St. SW1 . . . 4F 229 (48Nb 90)
Dean Wlk. HA8: Edg . . . 23Sa 47
KT23: Bookh . . . 98Da 191
Dean Way UB2: S'hall . . . 47Da 85
Dearmer Ho. SL9: Chal P . . . 22A 42
(off Micholls Av.)
Dearne Cl. HA7: Stan . . . 22Ja 46
De'Arn Gdns. CR4: Mitc . . . 69Gb 133
Dearsley Ho. RM13: Rain . . . 40Fd 76
Dearsley Rd. EN1: Enf . . . 13Wb 33
Death Trap, London's . . . 2H 229
Deauville Ct. SE16 . . . 47Zb 92
(off Eleanor Cl.)
SW4 . . . 58Lb 112
De Barowe M. N5 . . . 35Rb 71
Debdale Ho. E2 . . . 39Wb 71
(off Whiston Rd.)
DEBDEN . . . 14Sc 36
Debden N17 . . . 26Tb 51
(off Gloucester Rd.)
Debden Cl. IG8: Wfd G . . . 24Mc 53
KT2: King T . . . 64Ma 131
NW9 . . . 25Ua 48
DEBDEN GREEN . . . 10Rc 22
Debden Ho. IG10: Lough . . . 10Rc 22
Debden La. IG10: Lough . . . 10Sc 22
Debden Rd. IG10: Lough . . . 10Rc 22
Debden Wlk. RM12: Horn . . . 37Kd 77
De Beauvoir Ct. N1 . . . 38Tb 71
(off Northchurch Rd.)
De Beauvoir Cres. N1 . . . 39Ub 71
De Beauvoir Est. N1 . . . 39Ub 71
De Beauvoir Pl. N1 . . . 37Ub 71
De Beauvoir Rd. N1 . . . 39Ub 71
De Beauvoir Sq. N1 . . . 38Ub 71
DE BEAUVOIR TOWN . . . 39Ub 71
Deben RM18: E Til . . . 8L 101
Debenham Ct. E8 . . . 39Wb 71
(off Pownall Rd.)
EN5: Barn . . . 15Ya 30
Debham Ct. NW2 . . . 34Ya 68
Debnams Rd. SE16 . . . 49Yb 92
De Bohun Av. N14 . . . 16Kb 32
Deborah Cl. TW7: Isle . . . 53Ga 108
Deborah Ct. E18 . . . 27Kc 53
(off Victoria Rd.)
Deborah Cres. HA4: Ruis . . . 31T 64
Deborah Lodge HA8: Edg . . . 25Ra 47
Debrabant Cl. DA8: Erith . . . 51Fd 118
De Brome Rd. TW13: Felt . . . 60Y 107
De Bruin Ct. E14 . . . 50Ec 92
(off Ferry St.)
De Burgh Gdns. KT20: Tad . . . 91Za 194
De Burgh Pk. SM7: Bans . . . 87Db 175
Deburgh Rd. SW19 . . . 66Eb 133
Debussy NW9 . . . 26Va 48
Decies Way SL2: Stoke P . . . 9L 61
Decima St. SE1 . . . 3H 231 (48Ub 91)
Decima Studios SE1 . . . 3H 231
Decimus Cl. CR7: Thor H . . . 70Tb 135
Deck Cl. SE16 . . . 46Zb 92
Decoy Av. NW11 . . . 29Ab 48
De Crespigny Pk. SE5 . . . 54Tb 113
Dedswell Dr. GU4: W Cla . . . 100J 189
DEDWORTH . . . 3C 102
Dedworth Dr. SL4: Wind . . . 3D 102
DEDWORTH GREEN . . . 4C 102
Dedworth Mnr. SL4: Wind . . . 3D 102
Dedworth Rd. SL4: Wind . . . 4A 102
Dee Cl. RM14: Upm . . . 30Ud 58
Dee Ct. W7 . . . 44Fa 86
(off Hobbayne Rd.)
Dee Ho. KT2: King T . . . 67Ma 131
(off May Bate Av.)
Deeley Rd. SW8 . . . 53Mb 112
Deena Cl. SL1: Slou . . . 5C 80
W3 . . . 44Pa 87
Deen City Farm . . . 68Eb 133
Deepdale SW19 . . . 63Za 132
Deepdale Av. BR2: Brom . . . 70Hc 137
Deepdale Cl. N11 . . . 23Jb 50
Deepdale Ct. CR2: S Croy . . . 77Tb 157
(off Birdhurst Av.)
Deep Dene W5 . . . 42Pa 87
Deepdene EN6: Pot B . . . 3Za 16
Deepdene Av. CR0: C'don . . . 76Vb 157
Deepdene Cl. E11 . . . 28Jc 53
Deepdene Ct. BR2: Brom . . . 69Gc 137
N21 . . . 16Rb 33
Deepdene Gdns. SW2 . . . 59Pb 112
Deepdene Mans. SW6 . . . 53Bb 111
(off Rostrevor Rd.)
Deepdene Path IG10: Lough . . . 14Qc 36
(not continuous)
Deepdene Point SE23 . . . 62Zb 136
Deepdene Rd. DA16: Well . . . 55Wc 117
IG10: Lough . . . 14Qc 36
SE5 . . . 56Tb 113
Deep Fld. SL3: Dat . . . 2M 103
Deepfield Way CR5: Coul . . . 88Nb 176
Deep Pool La. GU24: Wok . . . 6M 167
Deepwell Cl. TW7: Isle . . . 53Ja 108
Deepwood La. UB6: G'frd . . . 41Fa 86
Deerbrook Rd. SE24 . . . 60Rb 113
Deercote Ct. EN8: Chesh . . . 2Zb 20
Deerdale Rd. SE24 . . . 56Sb 113
Deere Av. RM13: Rain . . . 37Jd 76
Deerfield Cl. NW9 . . . 29Va 48
Deerfield Cotts. NW9 . . . 29Va 48
Deerhurst Cl. DA3: Lfield . . . 69Ee 143
TW13: Felt . . . 63X 129
Deerhurst Ct. CR0: C'don . . . 74Rb 157
(off Parson's Mead)
Deerhurst Cres. TW12: Hamp H . . . 64Ea 130
Deerhurst Ho. SE15 . . . 51Wb 113
(off Haymerle Rd.)
Deerhurst Rd. NW2 . . . 37Za 68
SW16 . . . 64Pb 134
Deerings Dr. HA5: Eastc . . . 29W 44
Deerings Rd. RH2: Reig . . . 6K 207
Deerleap Gro. E4 . . . 15Dc 34
Deerleap La. TN14: Knock . . . 85Ad 181
Deer Mead Ct. RM1: Rom . . . 29Hd 56
Dee Rd. SL4: Wind . . . 2A 102
TW9: Rich . . . 56Pa 109
Deer Pk. Cl. KT2: King T . . . 66Ra 131
Deer Pk. Gdns. CR4: Mitc . . . 70Fb 133
Deer Pk. Rd. SW19 . . . 68Db 133
Deer Pk. Way BR4: W W'ck . . . 75Hc 159
EN9: Walt A . . . 8Dc 20
Deers Farm Cl. GU23: Wis . . . 88N 169
Deerswood Av. AL10: Hat . . . 2D 8
Deerswood Cl. CR3: Cat'm . . . 96Wb 197
Deeside Rd. SW17 . . . 62Fb 133
Dee St. E14 . . . 44Ec 92
Deeves Hall La. EN6: Ridge . . . 5Ua 16
Dee Way KT19: Ewe . . . 82Ua 174
RM1: Rom . . . 24Gd 56
Defence Cl. SE28 . . . 46Uc 94
Defiance Wlk. SE18 . . . 48Pc 94
Defiant NW9 . . . 26Va 48
(off Further Acre)
Defiant Way SM6: Wall . . . 80Nb 156
Defoe Av. TW9: Kew . . . 52Qa 109
Defoe Cl. DA8: Erith . . . 53Gd 118
SE16 . . . 47Bc 92
SW17 . . . 65Gb 133
Defoe Ho. EC2 . . . 7D 218
Defoe Pde. RM16: Grays . . . 8D 100
Defoe Pl. EC2 . . . 7D 218
SW17 . . . 63Hb 133
Defoe Rd. N16 . . . 34Ub 71
Defoe Way RM5: Col R . . . 23Cd 56
De Frene Rd. SE26 . . . 63Zb 136
Degema Rd. BR7: Chst . . . 64Rc 138
Dehar Cres. NW9 . . . 31Va 68
De Havilland Aircraft Heritage Cen.
. . . 1Ra 15
Dehavilland Cl. UB5: N'olt . . . 41Z 85
De Havilland Ct. N17 . . . 27Xb 51
WD7: Shenl . . . 4Na 15
De Havilland Dr. KT13: Weyb . . . 83N 169
SE18 . . . 51Rc 116
De Havilland Rd. HA8: Edg . . . 26Qa 47
TW5: Hest . . . 52Y 107
Dehavilland Studios E5 . . . 33Yb 72
(off Theydon Rd.)
De Havilland Way TW19: Stanw . . . 58M 105
WD5: Ab L . . . 4V 12
Deirdre Chapman Ho.
DA10: Swans . . . 58Ae 121
(off Craylands La.)
Dekker Ho. SE5 . . . 52Tb 113
(off Elmington Est.)
Dekker Rd. SE21 . . . 58Ub 113
Delabole Rd. RH1: Mers . . . 1E 208
Delacourt Rd. SE3 . . . 52Kc 115
Delacy Ct. SM2: Sutt . . . 83Cb 175
Delafield Ho. E1 . . . 44Wb 91
(off Christian St.)
Delafield Rd. RM17: Grays . . . 50Fe 99
SE7 . . . 50Kc 93
Delaford Cl. SL0: Iver . . . 44J 83
Delaford Rd. SE16 . . . 50Xb 91
Delaford St. SW6 . . . 52Ab 110
Delagarde Rd. TN16: Westrm . . . 98Sc 200
Delahay Ho. SW3 . . . 51Hb 111
(off Chelsea Emb.)
Delamare Ct. SE6 . . . 62Dc 136
Delamare Cres. CR0: C'don . . . 72Yb 158
Delamare Rd. EN8: Chesh . . . 2Ac 20
Delamere Ct. E17 . . . 26Ec 52
Delamere Gdns. NW7 . . . 23Ta 47
Delamere Rd. RH2: Reig . . . 10K 207
SW20 . . . 67Za 132
UB4: Yead . . . 45Z 85
W5 . . . 47Na 87
WD6: Bore . . . 11Ra 29
Delamere St. W2 . . . 43Db 89
Delamere Ter. W2 . . . 43Db 89
Delancey Pas. NW1 . . . 1A 216
Delancey St. NW1 . . . 1K 215 (39Kb 70)
Delancey Studios NW1 . . . 1A 216 (39Kb 70)
Delany Ho. SE10 . . . 51Ec 114
(off Thames St.)
Delaporte Cl. KT17: Eps . . . 84Ua 174
De Lapre Cl. BR5: St M Cry . . . 73Zc 161
De Lara Way GU21: Wok . . . 10P 167
Delarch Ho. SE1 . . . 2B 230
Delargy Cl. RM16: Grays . . . 8D 100
De Laune St. SE17 . . . 7B 230 (50Rb 91)
Delaware Mans. W9 . . . 42Db 89
(off Delaware Rd.)
Delaware Rd. W9 . . . 42Db 89
Delawyk Cres. SE24 . . . 58Sb 113
Delcombe Av. KT4: Wor Pk . . . 74Ya 154
Delderfield KT22: Lea . . . 92Ma 193
Delderfield Ho. RM1: Rom . . . 26Fd 56
(off Portnoi Cl.)
Delft Ho. KT2: King T . . . 66Pa 131
(off Acre Rd.)
Delft Way SE22 . . . 57Ub 113
Delhi Rd. EN1: Enf . . . 17Vb 33
Delhi St. N1 . . . 39Nb 70
Delia St. SW18 . . . 59Db 111
Delisle Rd. SE28 . . . 47Uc 94
(not continuous)
Delius Cl. WD6: E'tree . . . 16La 28
Delius Gro. E15 . . . 40Fc 73
Delius Way SS17: Stan H . . . 1L 101
Dell, The AL1: St A . . . 1E 6
CM13: Gt War . . . 23Xd 58
DA5: Bexl . . . 60Gd 118
DA9: Ghithe . . . 57Xd 120
EN9: Walt A . . . 8Ec 20
GU21: Wok . . . 1N 187
HA0: Wemb . . . 36Ka 66
HA5: Pinn . . . 26Z 45
HA6: Nwood . . . 19U 26
IG8: Wfd G . . . 20Kc 35
Dell, The KT13: Weyb . . . 80P 149
KT20: Tad . . . 93Ya 194
RH2: Reig . . . 5J 207
SE2 . . . 50Wc 95
SE19 . . . 67Vb 135
SL9: Chal P . . . 23A 42
TW8: Bford . . . 51La 108
TW14: Felt . . . 59X 107
TW20: Eng G . . . 2L 125
WD7: R'lett . . . 8Ja 14
Della Path E5 . . . 34Wb 71
Dellbow Rd. TW14: Felt . . . 57X 107
Dell Cl. E15 . . . 39Fc 73
IG8: Wfd G . . . 20Kc 35
KT22: Fet . . . 95Fa 192
RH5: Mick . . . 99La 192
SL2: Farn C . . . 6G 60
SM6: Wall . . . 77Lb 156
Dell Ct. HA6: Nwood . . . 24T 44
RM12: Horn . . . 33Nd 77
Dell Farm Rd. HA4: Ruis . . . 29T 44
Dellfield AL1: St A . . . 3D 6
Dellfield Cl. BR3: Beck . . . 67Ec 136
WD7: R'lett . . . 7Ha 14
WD17: Wat . . . 12W 26
Dellfield Ct. WD17: Wat . . . 12W 26
Dellfield Cres. UB8: Cowl . . . 42M 83
Dellfield Pde. UB8: Cowl . . . 42L 83
Dell La. KT17: Ewe . . . 78Wa 154
Dell Mdw. HP3: Hem H . . . 6N 3
Dellmeadow WD5: Ab L . . . 2U 12
Dell Nature Reserve . . . 12H 25
Dellors Cl. EN5: Barn . . . 15Za 30
Dellow Cl. IG2: Ilf . . . 31Tc 74
Dellow Ho. E1 . . . 45Xb 91
(off Dellow St.)
Dellow St. E1 . . . 45Xb 91
Dell Ri. AL2: Park . . . 8P 5
Dell Rd. EN3: Enf W . . . 10Yb 20
KT17: Ewe . . . 79Wa 154
RM17: Grays . . . 49De 99
UB7: W Dray . . . 49P 83
WD24: Wat . . . 9W 12
Dells, The HP3: Hem H . . . 3B 4
Dells Cl. E4 . . . 17Dc 34
TW11: Tedd . . . 65Ha 130
Dell Side WD24: Wat . . . 9W 12
Dellside UB9: Hare . . . 29L 43
Dell's M. SW1 . . . 6C 228
Dellsome La. AL4: Col H . . . 5A 8
AL9: Wel G . . . 5B 8
Dell Wlk. KT3: N Mald . . . 68Ua 132
Dell Way W13 . . . 44La 86
Dellwood WD3: Rick . . . 18K 25
Dellwood Gdns. IG5: Ilf . . . 27Qc 54
Delmar Av. HP2: Hem H . . . 3D 4
Delmare Cl. SW9 . . . 56Pb 112
Delme Cres. SE3 . . . 54Kc 115
Delmer Ct. WD6: Bore . . . 10Pa 15
(off Aycliffe Rd.)
Delmerend Ho. SW3 . . . 7D 226
Delmey Cl. CR0: C'don . . . 76Vb 157
Deloraine Ho. SE8 . . . 53Cc 114
Delorme St. W6 . . . 51Za 110
Delphina Ho. CM14: B'wood . . . 19Zd 41
DELROW . . . 11Ea 28
Delroy Ct. N20 . . . 17Eb 31
Delta Bldg. E14 . . . 44Ec 92
(off Ashton St.)
Delta Cen. HA0: Wemb . . . 39Pa 67
Delta Cl. GU24: Chob . . . 2K 167
KT4: Wor Pk . . . 76Va 154
Delta Ct. NW2 . . . 33Wa 68
SE8 . . . 51Ac 114
(off Trundleys Rd.)
Delta Gain WD19: Wat . . . 19Z 27
Delta Gro. UB5: N'olt . . . 41Z 85
Delta Ho. KT16: Chert . . . 73L 149
N1 . . . 3F 219
Delta Pk. SW18 . . . 56Db 111
Delta Pk. Ind. Est. EN3: Brim . . . 13Bc 34
Delta Point CR0: C'don . . . 74Sb 157
(off Wellesley Rd.)
E2 . . . 41Wb 91
(off Delta St.)
Delta Rd. CM13: Hut . . . 16Fe 41
GU21: Wok . . . 88C 168
GU24: Chob . . . 2K 167
KT4: Wor Pk . . . 76Ua 154
Delta St. E2 . . . 41Wb 91
Delta Way TW20: Thorpe . . . 67E 126
De Luci Rd. DA8: Erith . . . 50Ed 96
De Lucy St. SE2 . . . 49Xc 95
Delvan Cl. SE18 . . . 52Qc 116
Delvers Mead RM10: Dag . . . 35Ed 76
Delverton Ho. SE17 . . . 7C 230
Delverton Rd. SE17 . . . 7C 230 (50Rb 91)
Delves KT20: Tad . . . 93Za 194
Delvino Rd. SW6 . . . 53Cb 111
De Mel Cl. KT19: Eps . . . 84Ra 173
Demesne Rd. SM6: Wall . . . 77Mb 156
Demeta Cl. HA9: Wemb . . . 34Sa 67
De Montfort Pde. SW16 . . . 62Nb 134
De Montfort Rd. SW16 . . . 62Nb 134
De Morgan Rd. SW6 . . . 55Db 111
Dempster Cl. KT6: Surb . . . 74La 152
Dempster Rd. SW18 . . . 57Eb 111
Den, The . . . 50Yb 92
Denbar Pde. RM7: Rom . . . 28Ed 56
Denberry Dr. DA14: Sidc . . . 62Xc 139
Denbigh Cl. BR7: Chst . . . 65Pc 138
HA4: Ruis . . . 33V 64
HP2: Hem H . . . 3N 3
RM11: Horn . . . 28Qd 57
SM1: Sutt . . . 78Bb 155
UB1: S'hall . . . 44Ba 85
W11 . . . 45Bb 89
Denbigh Ct. E6 . . . 41Mc 93
W7 . . . 43Ha 86
(off Copley Cl.)
Denbigh Dr. UB3: Harl . . . 47S 84
Denbigh Gdns. TW10: Rich . . . 57Pa 109
Denbigh Ho. RM3: Rom . . . 23Nd 57
(off Kingsbridge Cir.)
SW1 . . . 3G 227
W11 . . . 45Bb 89
(off Westbourne Gro.)
Denbigh M. SW1 . . . 6B 228
Denbigh Pl. SW1 . . . 7B 228 (50Lb 90)
Denbigh Rd. E6 . . . 41Mc 93
TW3: Houn . . . 54Da 107
UB1: S'hall . . . 44Ba 85
W11 . . . 45Bb 89
W13 . . . 45Ka 86
Denbigh St. SW1 . . . 6B 228 (49Lb 90)
(not continuous)

Denbigh Ter. W11 45Bb 89
Denbridge Rd. BR1: Brom 68Pc 138
Denbury Ho. E3 41Dc 92
(off Talwin St.)
Denby Ct. SE11 5J 229
Denby Rd. KT11: Cobh 84Y 171
Dence Ho. E2 41Wb 91
(off Turin St.)
Denchworth Ho. SW9 54Qb 112
Dencliffe TW15: Ashf 64Q 128
Den Cl. BR3: Beck 69Fc 137
Dencora Cen., The AL1: St A 2E 6
EN3: Brim 13Ac 34
Dendridge Cl. EN1: Enf 9Xb 19
Dene, The CR0: C'don 77Zb 158
HA9: Wemb 35Na 67
KT8: W Mole 71Ba 151
SM2: Cheam 83Bb 175
TN13: S'oaks 98Kd 203
W13 43Ka 86
Dene Av. DA15: Sidc 59Xc 117
TW3: Houn 55Ba 107
Dene Cl. BR2: Hayes 74Hc 159
CR5: Chip 91Gb 195
DA2: Wilm 63Gd 140
E10 33Dc 72
KT4: Wor Pk 75Va 154
SE4 55Ac 114
Dene Ct. CR2: S Croy 78Sb 157
(off Warham Rd.)
W5 43La 86
Denecroft Cres. UB10: Hil 39R 64
Denecroft Gdns.
RM17: Grays 48Fe 99
Dene Dr. BR6: Chels 76Xc 161
DA3: Lfield 68De 143
Denefield Dr. CR8: Kenley 87Tb 177
Dene Gdns. HA7: Stan 22La 46
KT7: T Ditt 75Ja 152
Dene Holm Rd. DA11: Nflt 62Fe 143
Dene Ho. N14 17Mb 32
Denehurst Gdns. IG8: Wfd G 21Kc 53
NW4 30Ya 48
TW2: Twick 59Fa 108
TW10: Rich 56Qa 109
W3 46Ra 87
Dene Lodge Cl. TN15: Bor G 92Be 205
Dene Path RM15: S Ock 44Wd 98
Dene Pl. GU21: Wok 10N 167
Dene Rd. DA1: Dart 59Pd 119
HA6: Nwood 23S 44
IG9: Buck H 18Mc 35
KT21: Asht 91Pa 193
N11 18Hb 31
Denes, The HP3: Hem H 6P 3
Denesfield Ct. TN13: Chip 95Dd 202
Denesmead SE24 57Sb 113
Dene Wlk. DA3: Lfield 69Ae 143
Denewood EN5: New Bar 15Eb 31
KT17: Eps 85Ua 174
Denewood Cl. WD17: Wat 9V 12
Denewood M. WD17: Wat 9V 12
Denewood Rd. N6 30Hb 49
Denford St. SE10 50Hc 93
(off Glenforth St.)
Dengie Wlk. N1 39Sb 71
(off Basire St.)
DENHAM 34H 63
Denham Aerodrome 29G 42
Denham Av. UB9: Den 33H 63
Denham Cl. DA16: Well 55Yc 117
UB9: Den 34J 63
Denham Country Pk. 32K 63
Denham Ct. NW6 38Eb 69
(off Fairfax Rd.)
SE26 62Xb 135
(off Kirkdale)
UB1: S'hall 45Ea 86
(off Baird Av.)
Denham Ct. Dr. UB9: Den 35J 63
Denham Cres. CR4: Mitc 70Hb 133
Denham Dr. IG2: Ilf 30Sc 54
DENHAM GARDEN VILLAGE 29H 43
Denham Golf Course 30F 42
DENHAM GREEN 30H 43
Denham Grn. Cl. UB9: Den 31J 63
Denham Grn. La. UB9: Den 29G 42
Denham Ho. UB7: W Dray 47P 83
(off Park Lodge Av.)
W12 45Xa 88
(off White City Est.)
Denham La. SL9: Chal P 23B 42
Denham Lodge UB9: Den 37L 63
Denham Pde. UB9: Den 34H 63
(off Oxford Rd.)
Denham Rd. KT17: Eps 84Va 174
N20 20Hb 31
SL0: Iver H 39F 62
TW14: Felt 59Y 107
TW20: Egh 63C 126
UB9: Den 36H 63
DENHAM RDBT. 35J 63
Denham St. SE10 50Jc 93
Denham Wlk. SL9: Chal P 23B 42
Denham Way IG11: Bark 39Uc 74
UB9: Den 34J 63
(Old Mill Rd.)
UB9: Den 27H 43
(Wyatt's Covert)
WD3: Map C, W Hyd 23G 42
WD6: Bore 11Sa 29
Denholme Rd. W9 41Bb 89
Denholme Wlk. RM13: Rain 37Hd 76
Denison Cl. N2 27Eb 49
Denison Ho. E14 48Dc 92
Denison Rd. SW19 65Fb 133
TW13: Felt 63V 128
W5 42La 86
Deniston Av. DA5: Bexl 62Ad 117
Denis Way SW4 55Mb 112
Denland Ho. SW8 52Pb 112
(off Dorset Rd.)
Denleigh Gdns. KT7: T Ditt 72Ga 152
N21 18Qb 32
Denley Sq. UB8: Uxb 38M 63
Denly Way GU18: Light 2A 166
Denman Dr. KT10: Clay 78Ja 152
NW11 29Cb 49
TW15: Ashf 65R 128
Denman Dr. Nth. NW11 29Cb 49
Denman Dr. Sth. NW11 29Cb 49
Denman Ho. N16 33Ub 71
Denman Pl. W1 4D 222
Denman Rd. SE15 53Vb 113
Denman St. W1 5D 222 (45Mb 90)
Denmark Av. SW19 66Ab 132
Denmark Ct. KT13: Weyb 76R 150
(off Grotto Rd.)
SM4: Mord 72Cb 155
Denmark Gdns. SM5: Cars 76Hb 155
Denmark Gro. N1 1K 217 (40Qb 70)
DENMARK HILL 55Sb 113
Denmark Hill SE5 53Tb 113
Denmark Hill Dr. NW9 27Wa 48
Denmark Hill Est. SE5 56Tb 113
Denmark Ho. SE7 49Nc 94
Denmark Mans. SE5 54Sb 113
(off Coldharbour La.)
Denmark Path SE25 71Xb 157
Denmark Pl. E3 41Cc 92
WC2 2E 222 (44Mb 90)
Denmark Rd. BR1: Brom 67Kc 137
KT1: King T 69Na 131
N8 28Qb 50
NW6 40Bb 69
SE5 53Sb 113
SE25 71Wb 157
SM5: Cars 76Hb 155
SW19 65Za 132
TW2: Twick 62Fa 130
W13 45Ka 86
Denmark St. E11 34Gc 73
E13 43Kc 93
N17 25Xb 51
WC2 3E 222 (44Mb 90)
WD17: Wat 12X 27
Denmark Ter. N2 27Hb 49
Denmark Wlk. SE27 63Sb 135
Denmead Cl. SL9: Ger X 31A 62
Denmead Ho. SW15 58Va 110
(off Highcliffe Dr.)
Denmead Rd. CR0: C'don 74Rb 157
Denmore Ct. SM6: Wall 78Kb 156
Dennan Rd. KT6: Surb 74Pa 153
Dennard Way BR6: Farnb 77Rc 160
Denner Rd. E4 19Cc 34
Denne Ter. E8 39Vb 71
Dennett Rd. CR0: C'don 74Qb 156
Dennett's Gro. SE14 54Zb 114
Dennett's Rd. SE14 53Yb 114
Denning Av. CR0: Wadd 77Qb 156
Denning Cl. NW8 3A 214 (41Eb 89)
TW12: Hamp 64Ba 129
Denning M. SW12 58Jb 112
Denning Point E1 2K 225
Denning Rd. NW3 35Fb 69
Dennington Cl. E5 33Yb 72
Dennington Pk. Rd. NW6 37Cb 69
Denningtons, The KT4: Wor Pk 75Ua 154
Dennis Av. HA9: Wemb 36Pa 67
Dennis Cl. RH1: Redh 4N 207
TW15: Ashf 66T 128
Dennises La. RM14: Upm 39Ud 78
Dennis Gdns. HA7: Stan 22La 46
Dennis Ho. E3 40Bc 72
(off Roman Rd.)
SM1: Sutt 77Db 155
Dennis La. HA7: Stan 20Ka 28
Dennison Point E15 38Ec 72
Dennis Pde. N14 18Mb 32
Dennis Pk. Cres. SW20 67Ab 132
Dennis Reeve Cl. CR4: Mitc 67Hb 133
Dennis Rd. DA11: Grav'nd 2C 144
KT8: E Mos 70Ea 130
RM15: S Ock 38Wd 78
Dennis Way SL1: Slou 5B 80
SW4 55Mb 112
Denny Av. EN9: Walt A 6Fc 21
Denny Cl. E6 43Nc 94
Denny Ct. DA2: Dart 58Rd 119
(off Bow Arrow La.)
Denny Cres. SE11 7A 230 (50Qb 90)
Denny Gdns. RM9: Dag 38Xc 75
Denny Rd. N9 18Xb 33
SL3: L'ly 48Y 85
Denny St. SE11 7A 230 (50Qb 90)
De Novo Pl. AL1: St A 2D 6
(off Stanhope Rd.)
Den Rd. BR2: Brom 69Fc 137
Densham Dr. CR8: Purl 86Qb 176
Densham Ho. NW8 2C 214
Densham Rd. E15 39Gc 73
Densole Cl. BR3: Beck 67Ac 136
Denstone Ho. SE15 51Wb 113
(off Haymerle Rd.)
Densworth Gro. N9 19Yb 34
Dent Cl. RM15: S Ock 44Wd 98
Dent Ho. SE17 6H 231
DENTON 9G 122
Denton NW1 37Jb 70
Denton Cl. EN5: Barn 15Ya 30
RH1: Redh 10A 208
Denton Ct. BR2: Brom 73Qc 160
Denton Ct. Rd. DA12: Grav'nd 9G 122
Denton Gro. KT12: Walt T 75Aa 151
Denton Ho. N1 38Rb 71
(off Halton Rd.)
WD19: Wat 20Y 27
Denton Rd. DA1: Dart 59Gd 118
DA5: Bexl 61Gd 140
DA16: Well 52Yc 117
N8 29Pb 50
N18 21Ub 51
TW1: Twick 58Ma 109
Denton St. DA12: Grav'nd 9G 122
SW18 58Db 111
Denton Ter. DA5: Bexl 61Gd 140
Denton Way E5 34Zb 72
GU21: Wok 9K 167
Denton Wharf DA12: Grav'nd 8G 122
Dents Gro. KT20: Lwr K 100Bb 195
Dents Rd. SW11 58Hb 111
Denvale Wlk. GU21: Wok 10L 167
Denver Cl. BR6: Pet W 72Uc 160
Denver Ind. Est. RM13: Rain 43Hd 96
Denver Rd. DA1: Dart 59Jd 118
N16 31Ub 71
Denwood SE23 62Zb 136
Denyer St. SW3 6E 226 (49Gb 89)
Denys Ho. EC1 7K 217
Denziloe Av. UB10: Hil 41R 84
Denzil Rd. NW10 36Va 68
Deodar Rd. SW15 56Ab 110
Deodora Cl. N20 20Gb 31
Department for Communities 3B 228
De Paul Way CM14: B'wood 18Xd 40
Depot App. NW2 35Za 68
Depot Rd. KT17: Eps 85Ua 174
TW3: Houn 55Fa 108
W12 45Ya 88
Depot St. SE5 51Tb 113
DEPTFORD 52Cc 114
Deptford Bri. SE8 53Cc 114
Deptford B'way. SE8 53Cc 114
Deptford Bus. Pk. SE15 51Yb 114
Deptford Chu. St. SE8 51Cc 114
Deptford Creek Bri. SE8 51Dc 114
(off Creek Rd.)
Deptford Ferry Rd. E14 49Cc 92
Deptford Grn. SE8 51Cc 114
Deptford High St. SE8 51Cc 114
Deptford Pk. Bus. Cen. SE8 50Ac 92
Deptford Strand SE8 49Bc 92
Deptford Trad. Est. SE8 50Ac 92
Deptford Wharf SE8 49Bc 92
De Quincey Ho. SW1 7B 228
De Quincey M. E16 46Jc 93
De Quincey Rd. N17 25Tb 51
Derby Arms Rd. KT18: Eps D 89Va 174
Derby Av. HA3: Hrw W 25Fa 46
N12 22Eb 49
RM7: Rom 30Ed 56
RM14: Upm 34Pd 77
Derby Cl. KT18: Tatt C 91Xa 194
Derby Ga. SW1 1F 229 (47Nb 90)
(not continuous)
Derby Hill SE23 61Yb 136
Derby Hill Cres. SE23 61Yb 136
Derby Ho. HA5: Pinn 26Z 45
SE11 5K 229
Derby Lodge N3 26Bb 49
WC1 3H 217
Derby Rd. CR0: C'don 74Rb 157
E7 38Mc 73
E9 39Zb 72
E18 25Hc 53
EN3: Pond E 15Xb 33
KT5: Surb 74Qa 153
N18 22Yb 52
RM17: Grays 50De 99
SM1: Sutt 79Bb 155
SW14 56Ra 109
SW19 66Db 133
TW3: Houn 56Da 107
UB6: G'frd 39Da 65
UB8: Uxb 40L 63
WD17: Wat 13Y 27
(not continuous)
Derby Rd. Bri. RM17: Grays 51De 121
Derby Rd. Ind. Est.
TW3: Houn 56Da 107
Derbyshire St. E2 41Wb 91
(not continuous)
Derby Sq., The KT19: Eps 85Ta 173
(off High St.)
Derby Stables Rd.
KT18: Eps D 89Va 174
Derby St. W1 7J 221 (46Jb 90)
Dereham Ho. SE4 56Zb 114
(off Frendsbury Rd.)
Dereham Pl. EC2 4J 219 (41Ub 91)
RM5: Col R 23Dd 56
Dereham Rd. IG11: Bark 36Vc 75
Derek Av. HA9: Wemb 38Ra 67
KT19: Ewe 79Qa 153
SM6: Wall 77Kb 156
Derek Cl. KT19: Ewe 78Ra 153
Derek Walcott Cl. SE24 57Rb 113
Derham Gdns. RM14: Upm 34Sd 78
Deri Av. RM13: Rain 42Kd 97
Dericote St. E8 39Xb 71
Deri Dene Cl. TW19: Stanw 58N 105
Derifall Cl. E6 43Pc 94
Dering Pl. CR0: C'don 77Sb 157
Dering Rd. CR0: C'don 77Sb 157
Dering St. W1 3K 221 (44Kb 90)
Dering Way DA12: Grav'nd 10H 123
Dering Yd. W1 3A 222 (44Kb 90)
Derinton Rd. SW17 63Hb 133
Derisley Cl. KT14: Byfl 84M 169
Derley Rd. UB2: S'hall 48Y 85
Dermody Gdns. SE13 57Fc 115
Dermody Rd. SE13 57Fc 115
Deronda Rd. SE24 60Rb 113
De Ros Pl. TW20: Egh 65C 126
Deroy Cl. SM5: Cars 79Hb 155
Derrick Av. CR2: Sande 82Sb 177
Derrick Gdns. SE7 48Lc 93
Derrick Rd. BR3: Beck 69Bc 136
Derry Av. RM15: S Ock 44Wd 98
Derrycombe Ho. W2 43Cb 89
(off Gt. Western Rd.)
Derrydown GU22: Wok 3N 187
DERRY DOWNS 72Yc 161
Derry Downs BR5: St M Cry 72Yc 161
Derry Ho. NW8 6C 214
Derry M. N19 33Nb 70
Derry Rd. CR0: Bedd 76Nb 156
Derry St. W8 47Db 89
Dersingham Av. E12 35Pc 74
Dersingham Rd. NW2 34Ab 68
Derwent NW1 4B 216
Derwent Av. EN4: E Barn 18Hb 31
HA5: Hat E 23Aa 45
N18 22Tb 51
NW7 23Ta 47
NW9 29Ua 48
SW15 63Ua 132
UB10: Ick 33Q 64
Derwent Cl. DA1: Dart 60Kd 119
KT10: Clay 79Ga 152
KT15: Add 78M 149
TW14: Felt 60V 106
WD25: Wat 6Y 13
Derwent Ct. SE16 47Zb 92
(off Eleanor Cl.)
Derwent Cres. DA7: Bex 54Cd 118
HA7: Stan 26La 46
N20 20Eb 31
Derwent Dr. BR5: Pet W 73Tc 160
CR8: Purl 85Tb 177
SL1: Slou 3A 80
UB4: Hayes 43U 84
Derwent Gdns. HA9: Wemb 31La 66
IG4: Ilf 28Nc 54
Derwent Gro. SE22 56Vb 113
Derwent Ho. E3 42Bc 92
(off Southern Gro.)
KT2: King T 67Ma 131
(off May Bate Av.)
SW7 5A 226
Derwent Lodge KT4: Wor Pk 75Xa 154
TW7: Isle 54Fa 108
Derwent Pde. RM15: S Ock 44Wd 98
Derwent Point EC1 3B 218
(off Goswell Rd.)
Derwent Ri. NW9 30Ua 48
Derwent Rd. GU18: Light 3A 166
HP3: Hem H 3C 4
N13 21Pb 50
SE20 68Wb 135
SW20 72Za 154
TW2: Whitt 58Da 107
TW20: Egh 66D 126
UB1: S'hall 44Ba 85
W5 48La 86
Derwent St. SE10 50Gc 93
Derwent Wlk. SM6: Wall 80Kb 156
Derwentwater Rd. W3 46Sa 87
Derwent Way RM12: Horn 36Kd 77
Derwent Yd. W5 48La 86
(off Derwent Rd.)
De Salis Rd. UB10: Hil 42S 84
Desborough Cl. TW17: Shep 73Q 150
W2 43Db 89
Desborough Ho. W14 51Bb 111
(off North End Rd.)
Desborough Sailing Club 73R 150
Desborough St. W2 43Db 89
(off Cirencester St.)
Desenfans Rd. SE21 58Ub 113
Deseronto Trad. Est. SL3: L'ly 47A 82
Desford Ct. TW15: Ashf 61Q 128
Desford Rd. E16 42Gc 93
Desford Way TW15: Ashf 61P 127
Design Mus. 47Vb 91
Desmond Ho. EN4: E Barn 16Gb 31
Desmond Rd. WD24: Wat 8V 12
Desmond St. SE14 51Ac 114
Desmond Tutu Dr. SE23 60Bc 114
Despard Rd. N19 32Lb 70
De Stafford Sports Cen. 93Vb 197
Desvignes Dr. SE13 58Fc 115
De Tany Ct. AL1: St A 3B 6
Dethick Ct. E3 39Ac 72
Detillens La. RH8: Limp 1L 211
Detling Cl. RM12: Horn 36Ld 77
Detling Ho. SE17 6H 231
Detling Rd. BR1: Brom 64Jc 137
DA8: Erith 52Fd 118
DA11: Nflt 60Fe 121
Detmold Rd. E5 33Yb 72
Deva Cl. AL3: St A 4N 5
Devalls Cl. E6 45Rc 94
Devana End SM5: Cars 76Hb 155
Devane Way SE27 62Rb 135
Devas Rd. SW20 67Ya 132
Devas St. E3 42Dc 92
Devenay Rd. E15 38Hc 73
Devenish La. SL5: S'dale 4C 146
Devenish Rd. SE2 47Wc 95
SL5: S'dale, S'hill 2A 146
Deventer Cres. SE22 57Ub 113
Deveraux Cl. BR3: Beck 71Ec 158
De Vere Cl. SM6: Wall 80Nb 156
De Vere Cotts. W8 48Eb 89
(off De Vere Gdns.)
De Vere Gdns. IG1: Ilf 33Pc 74
W8 3A 226 (47Eb 89)
De Vere Leisure Club 27G 42
Deverell St. SE1 4F 231 (48Tb 91)
De Vere M. W8 3A 226
Devereux Ct. WC2 3K 223
Devereux Dr. WD17: Wat 10U 12
Devereux La. SW13 52Xa 110
Devereux Rd. RM16: Chaf H 48Be 99
SL4: Wind 4H 103
SW11 58Hb 111
De Vere Wlk. WD17: Wat 12U 26
Deverills Way SL3: L'ly 49E 82
Deveron Gdns. RM15: S Ock 44Wd 98
Deveron Way RM1: Rom 25Gd 56
Devey Cl. KT2: King T 66Va 132
Devil's La. TW18: Staines 66F 126
TW20: Egh 65E 126
Devitt Cl. KT21: Asht 88Qa 173
Devitt Ho. E14 45Dc 92
(off Wade's Pl.)
Devizes Ho. RM3: Rom 22Md 57
(off Montgomery Cres.)
Devizes St. N1 39Tb 71
Devoke Way KT12: Walt T 75Z 151
Devon Av. SL1: Slou 4G 80
TW2: Twick 60Ea 108
Devon Cl. CR8: Kenley 88Vb 177
IG9: Buck H 19Kc 35
N17 27Vb 51
UB6: G'frd 39La 66
Devon Ct. AL1: St A 3C 6
DA4: Sut H 67Rd 141
TW12: Hamp 66Ca 129
W7 43Ha 86
(off Copley Cl.)
Devon Cres. RH1: Redh 6M 207
Devoncroft Gdns. TW1: Twick 59Ja 108
Devon Gdns. N4 30Rb 51
Devon Ho. CR3: Cat'm 96Vb 197
E17 26Bc 52
N1 1B 218
Devonhurst Pl. W4 50Ta 87
Devonia Gdns. N18 23Sb 51
Devonia Rd. N1 1C 218 (40Rb 71)
Devon Mans. HA3: Kenton 29La 46
(off Woodcock Hill)
SE1 2K 231
Devon Pde. HA3: Kenton 29La 46
HA5: Eastc 31Y 65
Devonport W2 3D 220 (44Gb 89)
Devonport Gdns. IG1: Ilf 30Pc 54
Devonport Ho. W2 43Cb 89
(off Gt. Western Rd.)
Devonport M. W12 47Xa 88
Devonport Rd. W12 46Xa 88
(not continuous)
Devonport St. E1 44Yb 92
Devon Ri. N2 28Fb 49
Devon Rd. DA4: S Dar, Sut H 67Rd 141
IG11: Bark 39Uc 74
KT12: Hers 77Y 151
RH1: Mers 2C 208
SM2: Cheam 81Ab 174
WD24: Wat 11Z 27
Devons Est. E3 41Dc 92
Devonshire Av. DA1: Dart 58Kd 119
GU21: Wok 86E 168
SM2: Sutt 80Eb 155
Devonshire Bus. Cen.
EN6: Pot B 2Ab 16
Devonshire Bus. Pk. WD6: Bore 13Ta 29
Devonshire Cl. E15 35Gc 73
N13 20Qb 32
SL2: Farn R 10F 60
W1 7K 215 (43Kb 90)
Devonshire Ct. E1 41Yb 92
(off Bancroft Rd.)
HA5: Hat E 25Ba 45
(off Devonshire Rd.)
N17 23Sb 51
TW13: Felt 61X 129
WC1 7G 217
Devonshire Cres. NW7 24Za 48
Devonshire Dr. KT6: Surb 74Ma 153
SE10 52Dc 114
Devonshire Gdns. N17 23Sb 51
N21 17Sb 33
SS17: Linf 8J 101
W4 52Sa 109
Devonshire Grn. SL2: Farn R 10F 60
Devonshire Gro. SE15 51Xb 113
Devonshire Hall E9 37Yb 72
(off Frampton Pk. Rd.)
Devonshire Hill La. N17 23Rb 51
(not continuous)
Devonshire Ho. E14 49Cc 92
(off Westferry Rd.)
IG8: Wfd G 24Rc 54
NW6 37Bb 69
(off Kilburn High Rd.)
SE1 3D 230
SM2: Sutt 80Eb 155
SW1 7E 228
SW15 57Za 110
W2 7C 214
WD23: Bush 14Ba 27
Devonshire Ho. Bus. Cen.
BR2: Brom 70Kc 137
(off Devonshire Sq.)
Devonshire M. N13 21Qb 50
SW10 51Fb 111
(off Park Wlk.)
W4 50Ua 88
Devonshire M. Nth. W1 7K 215 (43Kb 90)
Devonshire M. Sth. W1 7K 215 (43Kb 90)
Devonshire M. W. W1 6J 215 (42Jb 90)
Devonshire Pas. W4 50Ua 88
Devonshire Pl. NW2 34Cb 69
W1 6J 215 (42Jb 90)
W8 48Db 89
Devonshire Pl. M. W1 6J 215 (43Jb 90)
Devonshire Point TW15: Ashf 62S 128
Devonshire Rd. BR6: Orp 73Wc 161
CR0: C'don 73Tb 157
DA6: Bex 56Ad 117
DA12: Grav'nd 10D 122
E16 44Kc 93
E17 30Cc 52
HA1: Harr 30Fa 46
HA5: Eastc 30Y 45
HA5: Hat E 25Ba 45
IG2: Ilf 31Tc 74
KT13: Weyb 77Q 150
N9 18Yb 34
N13 21Pb 50
N17 23Sb 51
NW7 24Za 48
RM12: Horn 33Ld 77
RM16: Chaf H, Grays 50Ae 99
SE9 61Nc 138
SE23 60Yb 114
SM2: Sutt 80Eb 155
SM5: Cars 77Jb 156
SW19 66Gb 133
TW13: Hanw 62Aa 129
UB1: S'hall 43Ca 85
W4 50Ua 88
W5 48La 86
Devonshire Road Nature Reserve
59Zb 114
Devonshire Road Nature Reserve Vis. Cen.
59Zb 114
Devonshire Row EC2 1J 225 (43Ub 91)
Devonshire Row M. W1 6A 216
Devonshires, The KT18: Eps 86Va 174
Devonshire Sq. BR2: Brom 70Kc 137
EC2 2J 225 (44Ub 91)
Devonshire St. W1 7J 215 (43Jb 90)
W4 50Ua 88
Devonshire Ter. W2 3A 220 (44Eb 89)
Devonshire Way CR0: C'don 75Ac 158
UB4: Yead 44X 85
Devons Rd. E3 41Dc 92
Devon St. SE15 51Xb 113
Devon Way KT9: Chess 78La 152
KT19: Ewe 78Ra 153
UB10: Hil 40P 63
Devon Waye TW5: Hest 52Ba 107
Devon Wharf E14 43Fc 93
De Walden Ho. NW8 1D 214
De Walden St. W1 1J 221 (43Jb 90)
Dewar Spur SL3: L'ly 51B 104
Dewar St. SE15 55Wb 113
Dewberry Gdns. E6 43Nc 94
Dewberry St. E14 43Ec 92
Dewey La. SW2 58Qb 112
(off Tulse Hill)
Dewey Path RM12: Horn 37Ld 77
Dewey Rd. N1 1K 217 (40Qb 70)
RM10: Dag 37Dd 76
Dewey St. SW17 64Hb 133
Dewgrass Gro. EN8: Walt C 7Zb 20
Dewhurst Rd. EN8: Chesh 1Xb 19
W14 48Za 88
Dewlands RH9: G'stone 3A 210
(not continuous)
Dewlands Av. DA2: Dart 59Rd 119
Dewlands Rd. RH9: G'stone 3A 210
Dewsbury Cl. HA5: Pinn 30Aa 45
RM3: Rom 23Nd 57
Dewsbury Ct. W4 49Sa 87
Dewsbury Gdns. KT4: Wor Pk 76Wa 154
RM3: Rom 23Md 57
Dewsbury Rd. NW10 36Wa 68
RM3: Rom 23Md 57
Dewsbury Ter. NW1 39Kb 70
Dews Farm Sand Pits Nature Reserve
30M 43
Dexter Apartments SE15 53Xb 113
(off Queen's Rd.)
Dexter Cl. AL1: St A 3E 6
RM17: Grays 48Ce 99
Dexter Ho. DA18: Erith 48Ad 95
(off Kale Rd.)
Dexter Rd. EN5: Barn 16Za 30
UB9: Hare 26L 43
Deyncourt Gdns. RM14: Upm 33Sd 78
Deyncourt Rd. N17 25Sb 51
Deynecourt Gdns. E11 28Lc 53
D'Eynsford Rd. SE5 53Tb 113
Dharam Marg WD25: A'ham, Let H 12Ea 28

Dhonau Ho. SE1 5K 231
Diadem Ct. W1 3D 222
Dial Cl. DA9: Ghithe 57Yd 120
Dialmead EN6: Ridge 6Va 16
Dial Stone Ct. KT13: Weyb 78S 150
Dial Walk, The W8 47Db 89
Diamedes Av. TW19: Stanw 59M 105
Diameter Rd. BR5: Pet W 73Rc 160
Diamond Cl. RM8: Dag 32Yc 75
RM16: Chaf H 48Be 99
Diamond Ct. BR5: St P 67Xc 139
RH1: Redh 5A 208
(off St Anne's Mt.)
RM11: Horn 32Jd 76
Diamond Est. SW17 62Gb 133
Diamond Ho. *E3* 40Ac 72
(off Roman Rd.)
Diamond Pl. RH2: Reig 5K 207
Diamond Rd. HA4: Ruis 35Z 65
SL1: Slou 7L 81
WD24: Wat 10W 12
Diamond St. NW10 38Ta 67
SE15 52Ub 113
Diamond Ter. SE10 53Ec 114
Diamond Way SE8 51Cc 114
Diana Cl. DA14: Sidc 61Ad 139
E18 25Kc 53
RM16: Chaf H 48Be 99
SE8 51Bc 114
SL3: G Grn 44A 82
Diana Ct. DA8: Erith 51Gd 118
Diana Gdns. KT6: Surb 75Pa 153
Diana Ho. SW13 53Va 110
Diana, Princess of Wales Memorial Playground 46Db 89
Diana, Princess of Wales Memorial Walk 46Eb 89
(in Kensington Gdns.)
Diana Rd. E17 27Bc 52
Dianne Ct. SE12 60Jc 115
Dianne Way EN4: E Barn 14Gb 31
Dianthus Cl. KT16: Chert 73G 148
SE2 50Xc 95
Dianthus Ct. GU22: Wok 10P 167
Diban Av. RM12: Horn 35Kd 77
Diban Ct. *RM12: Horn* 35Kd 77
(off The Broadway)
DIBDEN 99Gd 202
Dibden Ho. SE5 52Ub 113
Dibden La. TN14: Ide H, S'oaks 98Gd 202
Dibden St. N1 39Sb 71
Dibdin Cl. SM1: Sutt 76Cb 155
Dibdin Ho. W9 40Db 69
Dibdin Rd. SM1: Sutt 76Cb 155
Dibdin Row SE1 3A 230 (48Qb 90)
Diceland Lodge *SM7: Bans* 88Bb 175
(off Diceland Rd.)
Diceland Rd. SM7: Bans 88Bb 175
Dicey Av. NW2 35Ya 68
Dickens Av. DA1: Dart 56Qd 119
N3 25Eb 49
RM18: Tilb 3D 122
UB8: Hil 44R 84
Dickens Cl. AL3: St A 1B 6
DA3: Hartl 71Be 165
DA8: Erith 52Dd 118
TW10: Ham 61Na 131
UB3: Harl 49U 84
Dickens Ct. *E11* 28Jc 53
(off Makepeace Rd.)
SW17 62Fb 133
(off Grosvenor Way)
Dickens Dr. BR7: Chst 65Sc 138
KT15: Add 79H 149
Dickens Est. SE1 47Wb 91
SE16 48Wb 91
Dickens Ho. *NW6* 41Cb 89
(off Malvern Rd.)
NW8 5C 214
SE17 50Rb 91
(off Doddington Gro.)
WC1 5F 217
Dickens La. N18 22Ub 51
Dickens M. EC1 7B 218
Dickenson Cl. N9 18Wb 33
Dickenson Rd. N8 31Nb 70
TW13: Hanw 64Y 129
Dickensons La. SE25 71Wb 157
(not continuous)
Dickensons Pl. SE25 72Wb 157
Dickens Pl. SL3: Poyle 53G 104
Dickens Ri. IG7: Chig 20Rc 36
Dickens Rd. DA12: Grav'nd 10G 122
E6 40Mc 73
Dickens Sq. SE1 3E 230 (48Sb 91)
Dickens St. SW8 54Kb 112
Dickens Way RM1: Rom 28Gd 56
Dickenswood Cl. SE19 66Rb 135
Dickerage La. KT3: N Mald 69Sa 131
Dickerage Rd. KT1: King T 67Sa 131
KT3: N Mald 67Sa 131
Dickinson Av. WD3: Crox G 16Q 26
Dickinson Ct. EC1 6C 218
Dickinson Quay HP3: Hem H 7N 3
Dickinson Sq. WD3: Crox G 16R 26
Dicksee Ho. NW8 6B 214
Dickson Fold HA5: Pinn 28Z 45
Dickson Ho. *E1* 44Xb 91
(off Philpot St.)
N1 38Qb 70
(off Drummond Way)
Dickson Rd. SE9 55Nc 116
Dick Turpin Way TW14: Felt 56V 106
Didsbury Cl. E6 39Pc 74
Dieppe Cl. W14 50Bb 89
Digby Bus. Cen. *E9* 37Zb 72
(off Digby Rd.)
Digby Cres. N4 33Sb 71
Digby Gdns. RM10: Dag 39Cd 76
Digby Mans. *W6* 50Xa 88
(off Hammersmith Bri. Rd.)
Digby Pl. CR0: C'don 76Vb 157
Digby Rd. E9 37Zb 72
IG11: Bark 38Vc 75
Digby St. E2 41Yb 92
Digby Wlk. RM12: Horn 37Ld 77
Digby Way KT14: Byfl 84P 169
Digdens Ri. KT18: Eps 87Sa 173
Diggens Ct. IG10: Lough 13Nc 36
Diggon St. E1 43Zb 92
Dighton Ct. SE5 51Sb 113
Dighton Rd. SW18 57Eb 111
Dignum St. N1 1K 217 (40Qb 70)
Digswell Cl. WD6: Bore 10Qa 15
Digswell St. N7 37Qb 70
Dilhorne Cl. SE12 62Kc 137
Dilke St. SW3 51Hb 111
Dillon Cl. KT19: Eps 84Pa 173
Dilloway La. UB2: S'hall 47Aa 85
Dillwyn Cl. SE26 63Ac 136
Dilston Cl. UB5: N'olt 41Y 85
Dilston Gro. SE16 49Yb 92
Dilston Rd. KT22: Lea 91Ja 192
Dilton Gdns. SW15 60Wa 110
Dilwyn Ct. E17 26Ac 52
Dimes Pl. W6 49Xa 88
Dimmock Dr. UB6: G'frd 36Fa 66
Dimmocks La. WD3: Sarr 8K 11
Dimond Cl. E7 35Jc 73
Dimsdale Dr. EN1: Enf 17Wb 33
NW9 32Sa 67
SL2: Farn C 6C 60
Dimsdale Hgts. *E1* 44Xb 91
(off Spencer Way)
Dimsdale Wlk. E13 40Jc 73
Dimson Cres. E3 41Cc 92
Dinerman Ct. NW8 39Eb 69
Dingle, The UB10: Hil 41R 84
Dingle Cl. EN5: Ark 16Va 30
Dingle Gdns. E14 45Cc 92
Dingle Rd. TW15: Ashf 64R 128
Dingles Ct. HA5: Pinn 25Z 45
Dingley La. SW16 61Mb 134
Dingley Pl. EC1 4E 218 (41Sb 91)
Dingley Rd. EC1 3E 218 (41Sb 91)
Dingwall Av. CR0: C'don 75Sb 157
Dingwall Gdns. NW11 30Cb 49
Dingwall Rd. CR0: C'don 74Tb 157
SM5: Cars 81Hb 175
SW18 59Eb 111
Dinmont Est. E2 40Wb 71
Dinmont Ho. *E2* 40Wb 71
(off Pritchard's Rd.)
Dinmont St. E2 40Xb 71
Dinmore HP3: Bov 10B 2
Dinmore Ho. *E9* 39Yb 72
(off Templecombe Rd.)
Dinnington Ho. *E1* 42Xb 91
(off Coventry Rd.)
Dinsdale Cl. GU22: Wok 90C 168
Dinsdale Gdns. EN5: New Bar 15Db 31
SE25 71Ub 157
Dinsdale Rd. SE3 51Hc 115
Dinsmore Rd. SW12 59Kb 112
Dinton Ho. NW8 5D 214
Dinton Rd. KT2: King T 66Pa 131
SW19 65Fb 133
Diploma Av. N2 28Gb 49
Diploma Ct. N2 28Gb 49
Dippers Cl. TN15: Kems'g 89Pd 183
Diprose Lodge SW17 63Fb 133
Dirdene Cl. KT17: Eps 84Va 174
Dirdene Gdns. KT17: Eps 84Va 174
Dirdene Gro. KT17: Eps 84Ua 174
Dirleton Rd. E15 39Hc 73
Dirtham La. KT24: Eff 100X 191
Disbrowe Rd. W6 51Ab 110
Discover 38Fc 73
Discover Greenwich Vis. Cen. 51Ec 114
Discovery Bus. Pk. *SE16* 48Wb 91
(off St James's Rd.)
Discovery Dock Apartments E.
E14 47Dc 92
(off Sth. Quay Sq.)
Discovery Dock Apartments W.
E14 47Dc 92
(off Sth. Quay Sq.)
Discovery Ho. *E14* 45Ec 92
(off Newby Pl.)
Discovery Wlk. E1 46Xb 91
Dishforth La. NW9 24Ua 48
Disley Ct. *UB1: S'hall* 44Da 85
(off Howard Rd.)
Disney Pl. SE1 1E 230 (47Sb 91)
Disney St. SE1 1E 230 (47Sb 91)
Dison Cl. EN3: Enf H 11Zb 34
Disraeli Cl. SE28 46Yc 95
W4 48Ta 87
Disraeli Ct. SL3: L'ly 51D 104
Disraeli Gdns. SW15 56Bb 111
Disraeli Rd. E7 37Jc 73
NW10 40Ta 67
SW15 56Ab 110
W5 46Ma 87
Diss St. E2 2K 219 (41Vb 91)
Distaff La. EC4 4D 224 (45Sb 91)
Distillery, The SE8 53Cc 114
Distillery La. W6 50Ya 88
Distillery Rd. W6 50Ya 88
Distillery Wlk. TW8: Bford 51Na 109
Distin St. SE11 6K 229 (49Qb 90)
District Rd. HA0: Wemb 36Ka 66
Ditch All. SE13 53Dc 114
Ditchburn St. E14 45Ec 92
Ditches La. CR3: Cat'm, Coul 92Nb 196
CR5: Coul 92Nb 196
Ditches Ride, The
CM16: Lough, They B 10Qc 22
IG10: Lough 10Qc 22
Ditchfield Rd. UB4: Yead 42Aa 85
Ditchley Ct. *W7* 43Ha 86
(off Templeman Rd.)
Ditchling Ct. *AL1: St A* 2C 6
(off Bricket Rd.)
Dittisham Rd. SE9 63Nc 138
Ditton Cl. KT7: T Ditt 73Ja 152
Dittoncroft Cl. CR0: C'don 77Ub 157
Ditton Grange Cl. KT6: Surb 74Ma 153
Ditton Grange Dr. KT6: Surb 74Ma 153
Ditton Hill KT6: Surb 74La 152
Ditton Hill Rd. KT6: Surb 74La 152
Ditton Lawn KT7: T Ditt 74Ja 152
Ditton Pk. 10P 81
Ditton Pk. Rd. SL3: L'ly 51A 104
Ditton Pl. SE20 67Xb 135
Ditton Reach KT7: T Ditt 72Ka 152
Ditton Rd. DA6: Bex 57Zc 117
KT6: Surb 75Ma 153
SL3: Dat 3P 103
SL3: L'ly 50B 82
UB2: S'hall 50Ba 85
Divis Way *SW15* 58Xa 110
(off Dover Pk. Dr.)
Dixon Clark Ct. N1 37Rb 71
Dixon Cl. E6 44Pc 94
Dixon Dr. KT13: Weyb 82P 169
Dixon Ho. *W10* 44Za 88
(off Darfield Way)
Dixon Pl. BR4: W W'ck 74Dc 158
Dixon Rd. SE14 53Ac 114
SE25 69Ub 135
Dixon's All. SE16 47Xb 91
Dixons Hill Cl. AL9: N Mym 7D 8
Dixons Hill Rd. AL9: N Mym, Wel G 7D 8
Dixon Way NW10 38Ua 68
Dobbin Cl. HA3: Kenton 26Ja 46
Dobell Rd. SE9 57Pc 116
Doble Ct. CR2: Sande 84Wb 177
Dobree Av. NW10 38Xa 68
Dobson Cl. NW6 38Fb 69
Dobson Ho. *SE14* 51Zb 114
(off John Williams Cl.)
Dobson Rd. DA12: Grav'nd 4G 144
Doby Ct. EC4 4E 224
Dock App. Rd. RM16: Grays 1A 122
RM17: Grays 1A 122
Dock Cotts. *E1* 45Yb 92
(off The Highway)
Dockers Tanner Rd. E14 48Cc 92
Dockett Eddy KT16: Chert 74N 149
Dockett Eddy La. TW17: Shep 74P 149
Dockett Moorings KT16: Chert 74N 149
Dockhead SE1 2K 231 (47Vb 91)
Dockhead Wharf SE1 1K 231
Dock Hill Av. SE16 46Zb 92
Docklands Ct. *E14* 44Bc 92
(off Wharf La.)
Docklands Equestrian Centre, The 42Qc 94
Docklands Sailing Cen. 48Cc 92
Dockland St. E16 46Qc 94
(not continuous)
Dockley Rd. SE16 48Wb 91
Dockley Rd. Ind. Est. *SE16* 48Wb 91
(off Dockley Rd.)
Dock Offices *SE16* 48Yb 92
(off Surrey Quays Rd.)
Dock Rd. E16 45Hc 93
IG11: Bark 40Sc 74
RM17: Grays 51Fe 121
(Broadway)
RM17: Grays 1A 122
(Dock App. Rd.)
RM18: Tilb 3A 122
TW8: Bford 52Ma 109
Dockside Ct. E5 33Yb 72
Dockside Rd. E16 45Mc 93
Dock St. E1 45Wb 91
Dockwell Cl. TW14: Felt 56W 106
Dockwell's Ind. Est. TW14: Felt 57X 107
Doctor Johnson Av. SW17 62Kb 134
Dr Johnson's House 2A 224
Doctors Cl. SE26 64Yb 136
Doctors La. CR3: Cat'm 95Qb 196
Docura Ho. N7 33Pb 70
Docwra's Bldgs. N1 37Ub 71
Dodbrooke Rd. SE27 62Qb 134
Dodd Ho. *SE16* 49Xb 91
(off Rennie Est.)
Doddinghurst Rd.
CM15: B'wood, Dodd, Pil H 11Zd 41
Doddington Gro. SE17 7C 230 (51Rb 113)
Doddington Pl. SE17 51Rb 113
Dodds Cres. KT14: W Byf 86K 169
Doddsfield Rd. SL2: Slou 1E 80
Dodd's La. GU22: Pyr 86J 169
Dodsley Pl. N9 20Yb 34
Dodson St. SE1 2A 230 (47Qb 90)
Dod St. E14 44Bc 92
Doebury Wlk. *SE18* 52Wc 117
(off Prestwood Cl.)
Doel Cl. SW19 66Eb 133
Dog & Duck Yd. WC1 7H 217
Doggett Rd. SE6 59Cc 114
Doggetts Cl. EN4: E Barn 15Gb 31
Doggett's Cnr. RM11: Horn 33Pd 77
Doggetts Farm Rd. UB9: Den 31E 62
Doggetts Way AL1: St A 4B 6
Doghurst Av. UB3: Harl 52R 106
Doghurst Dr. UB7: Sip 52R 106
Doghurst La. CR5: Chip 92Hb 195
Dog Kennel Hill SE22 55Ub 113
Dog Kennel Hill Est. *SE22* 55Ub 113
(off Albrighton Rd.)
Dog Kennel La. WD3: Chor 14H 25
Dog La. NW10 35Ua 68
Dogwood Cl. DA11: Nflt 3B 144
Doherty Rd. E13 42Jc 93
Dokal Ind. Est. UB2: S'hall 47Aa 85
Dolben Ct. SW1 6E 228
Dolben St. SE1 7B 224 (46Rb 91)
(not continuous)
Dolby Rd. SW6 54Bb 111
Dolland Ho. SE11 7J 229
Dolland St. SE11 7J 229 (50Pb 90)
Dollar Bay Ct. *E14* 47Ec 92
(off Lawn Ho. Cl.)
Dollary Pde. *KT1: King T* 69Ra 131
(off Kingston Rd.)
Dolliffe Cl. CR4: Mitc 68Gb 133
Dollis Av. N3 25Bb 49
Dollis Brook Wlk. EN5: Barn 16Ab 30
Dollis Cres. HA4: Ruis 32Y 65
Dolliscroft NW7 24Ab 48
DOLLIS HILL 33Xa 68
Dollis Hill Av. NW2 34Xa 68
Dollis Hill La. NW2 35Va 68
Dollis M. N3 25Cb 49
Dollis Pk. N3 25Bb 49
Dollis Rd. N3 24Ab 48
NW7 24Ab 48
Dollis Valley Dr. EN5: Barn 16Bb 31
Dollis Valley Way EN5: Barn 16Bb 31
Dollypers Hill Nature Reserve 90Rb 177
Dolman Cl. N3 26Eb 49
Dolman Rd. W4 49Ta 87
Dolman St. SW4 56Pb 112
Dolphin App. RM1: Rom 28Hd 56
Dolphin Cl. KT6: Surb 71Ma 153
SE16 47Zb 92
SE28 44Zc 95
Dolphin Ct. IG7: Chig 20Rc 36
NW11 30Ab 48
SL1: Slou 7M 81
TW18: Staines 62J 127
Dolphin Ct. Nth. TW18: Staines 62J 127
Dolphin Est. TW16: Sun 67U 128
Dolphin Ho. *SW6* 54Eb 111
(off Lensbury Av.)
SW18 56Db 111
Dolphin La. E14 45Dc 92
Dolphin Pk. Ind. Est. RM19: Purf 50Ud 98
Dolphin Point RM19: Purf 50Ud 98
Dolphin Rd. SL1: Slou 7M 81
TW16: Sun 67U 128
UB5: N'olt 40Ba 65
Dolphin Rd. Nth. TW16: Sun 67U 128
Dolphin Rd. Sth. TW16: Sun 67U 128
Dolphin Rd. W. TW16: Sun 67U 128
Dolphin Sq. SW1 50Lb 90
W4 52Ua 110
Dolphin St. KT1: King T 68Na 131
Dolphin Twr. *SE8* 51Bc 114
(off Abinger Gro.)
Dolphin Way RM19: Purf 49Ud 98
Dolphin Yd. *AL1: St A* 3B 6
(off Holywell Hill)
Dolphin Yd., The *DA12: Grav'nd* 8D 122
(off Queen St.)
Dombey Ho. *SE1* 47Wb 91
(off Wolseley St.)
W11 46Za 88
(off St Ann's Rd.)
Dombey St. WC1 7H 217 (43Pb 90)
(not continuous)
DOME, THE 8Y 13
Dome, The RH1: Redh 5P 207
Domecq Ho. EC1 5C 218
Dome Hill CR3: Cat'm 99Ub 197
Dome Hill Pk. SE26 63Vb 135
Dome Hill Peak CR3: Cat'm 98Ub 197
Domelton Ho. *SW18* 58Db 111
(off Iron Mill Rd.)
Domett Cl. SE5 56Tb 113
Dome Way RH1: Redh 5P 207
Domfe Pl. E5 35Yb 72
Domingo St. EC1 5D 218 (42Sb 91)
Dominica Cl. E13 40Mc 73
Dominic Ct. EN9: Walt A 5Dc 20
Dominion Bus. Pk. N9 19Zb 34
Dominion Cen., The UB2: S'hall 47Aa 85
Dominion Cl. TW3: Houn 54Fa 108
Dominion Ct. *E8* 38Vb 71
(off Middleton Rd.)
Dominion Dr. RM5: Col R 23Dd 56
Dominion Ho. *E14* 50Dc 92
(off St Davids Sq.)
Dominion Ind. Est. *UB2: S'hall* 47Aa 85
(off Feather Rd.)
Dominion Pde. HA1: Harr 29Ha 46
Dominion Rd. CR0: C'don 73Vb 157
UB2: S'hall 47Aa 85
Dominion St. EC2 7G 219 (43Tb 91)
Dominion Theatre 2E 222
Dominion Way RM13: Rain 41Jd 96
Domonic Dr. SE9 63Rc 138
Domville Cl. N20 19Fb 31
Domville Ct. *SE17* 50Ub 91
(off Bagshott St.)
Donald Biggs Dr. DA12: Grav'nd 10E 122
Donald Dr. RM6: Chad H 29Yc 55
Donald Hunter Ho. *E7* 36Kc 73
(off Woodgrange Rd.)
Donald Rd. CR0: C'don 73Qb 156
E13 39Kc 73
Donaldson Rd. NW6 39Bb 69
SE18 53Qc 116
Donald Woods Gdns. KT5: Surb 75Ra 153
Donato Dr. SE15 51Ub 113
Doncaster Dr. UB5: N'olt 36Ba 65
Doncaster Gdns. N4 30Sb 51
UB5: N'olt 36Ba 65
Doncaster Grn. WD19: Wat 22Y 45
Doncaster Rd. N9 17Xb 33
Doncaster Way RM14: Upm 34Pd 77
Doncel Ct. E4 17Cc 35
Doncella Cl. RM16: Chaf H 48Zd 99
Donegal Ho. *E1* 42Xb 91
(off Cambridge Heath Rd.)
Donegal St. N1 2J 217 (40Pb 70)
Doneraile Ho. SW1 7K 227
Doneraile St. SW6 54Za 110
Dongola Rd. E1 43Ac 92
E13 41Kc 93
N17 27Ub 51
Dongola Rd. W. E13 41Kc 93
Don Gratton Ho. *E1* 43Wb 91
(off Old Montague St.)
Donington Av. IG2: Ilf 29Sc 54
IG6: Ilf 29Sc 54
Donkey All. SE22 59Wb 113
Donkey La. DA4: Farni 75Rd 163
EN1: Enf 12Wb 33
UB7: W Dray 49L 83
DONKEY TOWN 5B 166
Donkin Ho. *SE16* 49Xb 91
(off Rennie Est.)
Donmar Warehouse Theatre 3F 223
Donnafields GU24: Bisl 8E 166
Donnatt's Rd. SE14 53Bc 114
Donne Ct. SE24 58Sb 113
Donnefield Av. HA8: Edg 24Na 47
Donne Gdns. GU22: Pyr 87G 168
Donne Ho. *E14* 44Cc 92
(off Dod St.)
SE14 51Zb 114
(off Samuel Cl.)
Donnelly Ct. *SW6* 52Ab 110
(off Dawes Rd.)
Donnelly Ho. SE1 3K 229
Donne Pl. CR4: Mitc 70Kb 134
SW3 5E 226 (49Gb 89)
Donne Rd. RM8: Dag 33Yc 75
Donnington Ct. *DA2: Dart* 58Rd 119
(off Osbourne Rd.)
NW1 38Kb 70
(off Castlehaven Rd.)
NW10 38Xa 68
(off Donnington Rd.)
Donnington Mans. *NW10* 39Ya 68
(off Donnington Rd.)
Donnington Rd. HA3: Kenton 29Ma 47
KT4: Wor Pk 75Wa 154
NW10 38Xa 68
TN13: Dun G 92Fd 202
Donnybrook Ct. *E3* 39Bc 72
(off Old Ford Rd.)
Donnybrook Rd. SW16 66Lb 134
Donoghue Bus. Pk. NW2 34Za 68
Donoghue Cotts. *E14* 43Ac 92
(off Galsworthy Av.)
Donovan Av. N10 26Kb 50
Donovan Cl. KT19: Eps 82Ta 173
Donovan Ct. *SW10* 50Fb 89
(off Drayton Gdns.)
Donovan Ho. *E1* 45Yb 92
(off Cable St.)
Donovan Pl. N21 15Pb 32
Donovan's Gdn. CM13: Heron 24Fe 59
Don Phelan Cl. SE5 53Tb 113
Don Way RM1: Rom 24Gd 56
Donyngs Recreation Cen. 5N 207
Doods Pk. Rd. RH2: Reig 5L 207
Doods Pl. RH2: Reig 5M 207
Doods Rd. RH2: Reig 5L 207
Doods Way RH2: Reig 5M 207
Doolittle Mdws. HP3: Hem H 7N 3
Doone Cl. TW11: Tedd 65Ja 130
Doon St. SE1 7K 223 (46Qb 90)
Dorado Gdns. BR6: Chels 76Zc 161
Dora Ho. *E14* 44Bc 92
(off Rhodeswell Rd.)
W11 45Za 88
(off St Ann's Rd.)
Doral Way SM5: Cars 78Hb 155
Doran Ct. E6 40Pc 74
RH1: Redh 6M 207
RH2: Reig 6M 207
Dorando Cl. W12 45Xa 88
Doran Dr. RH1: Redh 6M 207
Doran Gdns. RH1: Redh 6M 207
Doran Gro. SE18 52Uc 116
Doran Mnr. *N2* 29Hb 49
(off Great Nth. Rd.)
Doran Wlk. E15 38Ec 72
Dora Rd. SW19 64Cb 133
Dora St. E14 44Bc 92
Dora Way SW9 54Qb 112
Dorchester Av. DA5: Bexl 60Zc 117
HA2: Harr 30Ea 46
N13 21Sb 51
Dorchester Cl. BR5: St P 66Xc 139
DA1: Dart 59Pd 119
KT10: Hin W 75Ha 152
UB5: N'olt 36Da 65
Dorchester Ct. *AL1: St A* 3E 6
(off Dexter Cl.)
E18 25Hc 53
(off Buckingham Rd.)
GU22: Wok 88C 168
N1 38Ub 71
(off Englefield Rd.)
N10 27Kb 50
N14 17Kb 32
NW2 34Za 68
RH2: Reig 5M 207
SE24 57Sb 113
SW1 4G 227
TW18: Staines 63J 127
WD3: Crox G 15S 26
WD19: Wat 16Aa 27
(off Chalk Hill)
Dorchester Dr. SE24 57Sb 113
TW14: Bedf 58U 106
Dorchester Gdns. E4 21Cc 52
NW11 28Cb 49
Dorchester Gro. W4 50Ua 88
Dorchester Ho. TW9: Kew 52Ra 109
Dorchester M. KT3: N Mald 70Ta 131
TW1: Twick 58La 108
Dorchester Rd. DA12: Grav'nd 2F 144
KT4: Wor Pk 74Ya 154
KT13: Weyb 76R 150
SM4: Mord 73Db 155
UB5: N'olt 36Da 65
Dorchester Ter. *NW2* 34Za 68
(off Needham Ter.)
Dorchester Way HA3: Kenton 30Pa 47
Dorchester Waye UB4: Yead 44X 85
(not continuous)
Dorcis Av. DA7: Bex 54Ad 117
Dordrecht Rd. W3 46Ua 88
Dore Av. E12 36Qc 74
Doreen Av. NW9 32Ta 67
Doreen Capstan Ho. *E11* 34Gc 73
(off Apollo Pl.)
Dore Gdns. SM4: Mord 73Db 155
Dorell Cl. UB1: S'hall 43Ba 85
Doresa Cl. KT15: Add 78J 149
Dorey Ho. *TW8: Bford* 52La 108
(off High St.)
Doria Dr. DA12: Grav'nd 2G 144
Dorian Dr. SL5: Asc 7C 124
Dorian Rd. RM12: Horn 32Jd 76
Doria Rd. SW6 54Bb 111
Doric Dr. KT20: Tad 92Bb 195
Doric Ho. *E2* 40Zb 72
(off Mace St.)
Doric Way NW1 3D 216 (41Mb 90)
Dorie M. N12 21Db 49
Dorien Rd. SW20 68Za 132
Dorin Ct. CR6: W'ham 92Xb 197
GU22: Pyr 87G 168
Doris Ashby Cl. UB6: G'frd 39Ja 66
Doris Av. DA8: Erith 53Ed 118
Doris Emmerton Ct. SW11 56Eb 111
Doris Rd. E7 38Jc 73
TW15: Ashf 65T 128
Dorking Cl. KT4: Wor Pk 75Za 154
SE8 51Bc 114
Dorking Ct. *N17* 25Wb 51
(off Hampden La.)
Dorking Gdns. RM3: Rom 22Md 57
Dorking Ho. SE1 3G 231 (48Tb 91)
Dorking Ri. RM3: Rom 21Md 57
Dorking Rd. KT18: Eps 88Qa 173
KT20: Tad, Walt H 1A 206
KT22: Lea 94Ka 192
KT23: Bookh 98Da 191
RM3: Rom 22Md 57
Dorking Vs. GU21: Knap 9H 167
Dorking Wlk. RM3: Rom 21Md 57
Dorking Way RM14: Upm 31Ud 78
Dorlcote Rd. SW18 59Gb 111
Dorling Dr. KT17: Eps 84Va 174
Dorly Cl. TW17: Shep 71U 150
Dorman Pl. N9 19Wb 33
Dormans Cl. HA6: Nwood 24T 44
Dorman Wlk. NW10 36Ta 67
Dorman Way NW8 39Fb 69
Dorma Trad. Pk. E10 32Zb 72
Dormay St. SW18 57Db 111
Dormer Cl. E15 37Hc 73
EN5: Barn 15Za 30
Dormers HP3: Bov 9G 2
Dormer's Av. UB1: S'hall 44Ca 85
Dormers Ri. UB1: S'hall 44Da 85
DORMER'S WELLS 44Ca 85
Dormer's Wells La. UB1: S'hall 44Ca 85
Dormers Wells Leisure Cen. 44Da 85
Dormstone Ho. SE17 6H 231
Dormywood HA4: Ruis 29V 44
Dornberg Cl. SE3 52Jc 115
Dornberg Rd. SE3 52Kc 115
Dorncliffe Rd. SW6 54Ab 110
Dornels SL2: Slou 4N 81
DORNEY 8A 80
Dorney NW3 38Gb 69
Dorney Gro. KT13: Weyb 75R 150
Dorney Hill Sth. HP9: Beac 1E 60

Dorney Lake 1A 102
Dorney Lake Park & Nature Reserve 10A 80
Dorney Ri. BR5: St M Cry 70Vc 139
Dorney Way TW4: Houn 57Aa 107
Dorney Wood Rd. SL1: Burn 4A 60
Dornfell St. NW6 . . . . 36Bb 69
Dornford Gdns. CR5: Coul 91Sb 197
Dornoch Ho. E3 . . . . 40Bc 72
(off Anglo Rd.)
Dornton Rd. CR2: S Croy 78Tb 157
SW12 . . . . 61Kb 134
Dorothy Av. HA0: Wemb 38Na 67
Dorothy Evans Cl. DA7: Bex 56Dd 118
Dorothy Gdns. RM8: Dag 35Xc 75
Dorothy Pettingell Ho. SM1: Sutt . . . 76Db 155
(off Angel Hill)
Dorothy Rd. SW11 . . . . 55Hb 111
Dorothy Smith La. N17 . . . . 24Tb 51
Dorrell Pl. SW9 . . . . 55Qb 112
Dorrien Wlk. SW16 . . . . 61Mb 134
Dorrington Ct. SE25 . . . . 68Ub 135
Dorrington Gdns. RM12: Horn 32Md 77
Dorrington Point E3 . . . . 41Dc 92
(off Bromley High St.)
Dorrington St. EC1 . . . . 7K 217 (43Qb 90)
Dorrington Way BR3: Beck 71Ec 158
Dorrit Ho. W11 . . . . 46Za 88
(off St Ann's Rd.)
Dorrit M. N18 . . . . 22Ub 51
Dorrit St. SE1 . . . . 1E 230 (47Sb 91)
Dorrit Way BR7: Chst 65Sc 138
Dorrofield Cl. WD3: Crox G 15S 26
Dorryn Ct. SE26 . . . . 64Zb 136
Dors Cl. NW9 . . . . 32Ta 67
Dorset Av. DA16: Well 56Vc 117
RM1: Rom 28Fd 56
UB2: S'hall 49Ca 85
UB4: Hayes 41U 84
Dorset Bldgs. EC4 . . . . 3B 224 (44Rb 91)
Dorset Cl. NW1 . . . . 7F 215 (43Hb 89)
UB4: Hayes 41U 84
Dorset Ct. HA6: Nwood 25V 44
KT17: Eps 84Ua 174
N1 . . . . 38Ub 71
(off Hertford Rd.)
UB5: N'olt 41Aa 85
W7 . . . . 43Ha 86
(off Copley Cl.)
Dorset Cres. DA12: Grav'nd 3G 144
Dorset Dr. GU22: Wok 89D 168
HA8: Edg 23Pa 47
Dorset Gdns. CR4: Mitc 70Pb 134
HA0: Wemb 36La 66
SS17: Linf 7J 101
Dorset Ho. NW1 . . . . 6G 215
Dorset Mans. SW6 . . . . 51Za 110
(off Lille Rd.)
Dorset M. N3 . . . . 25Cb 49
SW1 . . . . 3K 227 (48Kb 90)
Dorset Ri. EC4 . . . . 3B 224 (44Rb 91)
Dorset Rd. BR3: Beck 69Zb 136
CR4: Mitc 68Gb 133
E7 . . . . 38Lc 73
HA1: Harr 30Ea 46
N15 . . . . 28Tb 51
N22 . . . . 25Nb 50
SE9 . . . . 61Nc 138
SL4: Wind 3G 102
SM2: Sutt 82Cb 175
SW8 . . . . 52Nb 112
SW19 . . . . 67Cb 133
TW15: Ashf 62M 127
W5 . . . . 48La 86
Dorset Sq. KT19: Ewe 82Ta 173
NW1 . . . . 6F 215 (42Hb 89)
Dorset St. TN13: S'oaks 97Ld 203
W1 . . . . 1G 221 (43Hb 89)
Dorset Way KT14: Byfl 82M 169
TW2: Twick 60Fa 108
UB10: Hil 40P 63
Dorset Waye TW5: Hest 52Ba 107
Dorset Wharf W6 . . . . 52Ya 110
(off Rainville Rd.)
Dorton Cl. SE15 . . . . 52Ub 113
Dorton Dr. TN15: Seal 94Pd 203
(not continuous)
Dorton Vs. UB7: Sip 52Q 106
Dorton Way GU23: Rip 93K 189
Dorville Cres. W6 . . . . 48Xa 88
Dorville Rd. SE12 . . . . 57Hc 115
Dothill Rd. SE18 . . . . 52Sc 116
Douai Gro. TW12: Hamp 67Ea 130
Doubleday Rd. IG10: Lough 13Sc 36
Doughty Ct. E1 . . . . 46Xb 91
(off Prusom St.)
Doughty Ho. SW10 . . . . 51Eb 111
(off Netherton Gro.)
Doughty M. WC1 . . . . 6H 217 (42Pb 90)
Doughty St. WC1 . . . . 5H 217 (42Pb 90)
Douglas Av. E17 . . . . 25Bc 52
HA0: Wemb 38Na 67
KT3: N Mald 70Xa 132
RM3: Hrld W 26Nd 57
WD24: Wat 9Z 13
Douglas Bader Ho. TW7: Isle 55Fa 108
Douglas Cl. EN4: Had W 10Fb 17
GU4: Jac W 10P 187
HA7: Stan 22Ja 46
IG6: Ilf 24Rc 54
RM16: Chaf H 48Ae 99
SM6: Wall 79Nb 156
Douglas Ct. CR3: Cat'm 94Sb 197
KT1: King T 70Na 131
(off Geneva Rd.)
N3 . . . . 26Db 49
NW6 . . . . 38Cb 69
(off Quex Rd.)
TN16: Big H 89Nc 180
Douglas Cres. UB4: Yead 42Y 85
Douglas Dr. CR0: C'don 76Cc 158
Douglas Est. N1 . . . . 37Sb 71
(off Oransay Rd.)
Douglas Eyre Sports Cen. 29Zb 52
Douglas Ho. EN8: Chesh 1Zb 20
(off Davison Dr.)
KT6: Surb 74Pa 153
RH2: Reig 5J 207
Douglas Ho's. KT23: Bookh 96Ca 191
Douglas Johnstone Ho.
SW6 . . . . 51Bb 111
(off Clem Attlee Ct.)
Douglas La. TW19: Wray 57B 104
Douglas Mans. TW3: Houn 55Da 107
Douglas M. NW2 . . . . 34Ab 68
SM7: Bans 88Bb 175
Douglas Path E14 . . . . 50Ec 92
(off Manchester Rd.)
Douglas Rd. DA16: Well 53Xc 117
E4 . . . . 17Gc 35
E16 . . . . 43Jc 93
IG3: Ilf 31Wc 75
KT1: King T 68Ra 131
KT6: Surb 75Pa 153
KT10: Esh 75Da 151
KT15: Add 76K 149
N1 . . . . 38Sb 71
N22 . . . . 25Qb 50
NW6 . . . . 39Bb 69
RH2: Reig 5J 207
RM11: Horn 30Hd 56
SL2: Slou 3H 81
TW3: Houn 55Da 107
TW19: Stanw 58M 105
Douglas Rd. Nth. N1 . . . . 37Sb 71
Douglas Rd. Sth. N1 . . . . 37Sb 71
Douglas Robinson Ct. SW16 . . . . 66Nb 134
(off Streatham High Rd.)
Douglas Sq. SM4: Mord 72Cb 155
Douglas St. SW1 . . . . 6D 228 (49Mb 90)
Douglas Ter. E17 . . . . 25Bc 52
Douglas Waite Ho. NW6 . . . . 38Cb 69
Douglas Way SE8 . . . . 52Bc 114
(Stanley St.)
SE8 . . . . 52Cc 114
(Watsons St.)
Doug Siddons Ct. RM17: Grays 51De 121
Doulton Ho. SE11 . . . . 4J 229
Doulton M. NW6 . . . . 37Db 69
Doultons, The TW18: Staines 66J 127
Dounesforth Gdns. SW18 . . . . 60Db 111
Dounsell Ct. CM15: Pil H 16Wd 40
Douro Pl. W8 . . . . 48Db 89
Douro St. E3 . . . . 40Cc 72
Douthwaite Sq. E1 . . . . 46Wb 91
Dove App. E6 . . . . 43Nc 94
Dove Cl. CR2: Sels 83Zb 178
NW7 . . . . 24Va 48
RM16: Chaf H 48Ae 99
SM6: Wall 80Pb 156
UB5: N'olt 42Z 85
Dove Commercial Cen. NW5 . . . . 36Lb 70
Dovecot Cl. HA5: Eastc 29Y 45
Dovecote Av. N22 . . . . 27Qb 50
Dovecote Cl. KT13: Weyb 76R 150
Dovecote Gdns. SW14 . . . . 55Ta 109
Dovecote Ho. SE16 . . . . 47Zb 92
(off Water Gdns. Sq.)
Dove Ct. AL10: Hat 1C 8
Dovedale Av. HA3: Kenton 30La 46
IG5: Ilf 26Qc 54
Dovedale Bus. Est. SE15 . . . . 54Wb 113
(off Blenheim Gro.)
Dovedale Cl. DA16: Well 54Wc 117
UB9: Hare 26L 43
Dovedale Ri. CR4: Mitc 66Hb 133
Dovedale Rd. DA2: Dart 60Sd 120
SE22 . . . . 57Xb 113
Dovedon Cl. N14 . . . . 19Nb 32
Dovehouse Ct. UB5: N'olt 41Z 85
(off Delta Gro.)
Dove Ho. Cres. SL2: Slou 1C 80
Dove Ho. Gdns. E4 . . . . 19Cc 34
Dovehouse Grn. KT13: Weyb 76T 150
Dovehouse Mead IG11: Bark 40Tc 74
Dovehouse St. SW3 . . . . 7C 226 (50Fb 89)
Dove La. EN6: Pot B 6Eb 17
Dove M. SW5 . . . . 6A 226 (49Eb 89)
Doveney Cl. BR5: St P 69Yc 139
Dove Pk. HA5: Hat E 24Ca 45
WD3: Chor 16D 24
Dover Cl. NW2 . . . . 33Za 68
RM5: Col R 26Ed 56
Dover Ct. EC1 . . . . 5B 218
N1 . . . . 38Tb 71
(off Southgate Rd.)
Dovercourt Av. CR7: Thor H 71Qb 156
Dovercourt Est. N1 . . . . 37Tb 71
Dovercourt Gdns. HA7: Stan 22Na 47
Dovercourt La. SM1: Sutt 76Eb 155
Dovercourt Rd. SE22 . . . . 58Ub 113
Doverfield EN7: G Oak 1Sb 19
Doverfield Rd. SW2 . . . . 59Nb 112
Dover Flats SE1 . . . . 6J 231 (49Ub 91)
Dover Gdns. SM5: Cars 76Hb 155
Dover Ho. N18 . . . . 22Vb 51
SE15 . . . . 51Yb 114
Dover Ho. Rd. SW15 . . . . 56Wa 110
Doveridge Gdns. N13 . . . . 21Rb 51
Dove Rd. N1 . . . . 37Tb 71
Dove Row E2 . . . . 39Wb 71
Dover Pk. Dr. SW15 . . . . 58Xa 110
Dover Patrol SE3 . . . . 54Kc 115
Dover Rd. DA11: Nflt 59Fe 121
E12 . . . . 33Lc 73
N9 . . . . 19Yb 34
RM6: Chad H 30Ad 55
SE19 . . . . 65Tb 135
SL1: Slou 4D 80
Dover Rd. E. DA11: Grav'nd 9A 122
DOVERS CORNER 41Jd 96
Dovers Cnr. RM13: Rain 41Jd 96
Dovers Cnr. Ind. Est. RM13: Rain 41Hd 96
DOVERSGREEN 10K 207
Dovers Grn. Rd. RH2: Reig 10K 207
Doversmead GU21: Knap 8J 167
Dover St. W1 . . . . 5A 222 (45Kb 90)
Dovers W. RH2: Reig 10K 207
Dover Ter. TW9: Rich 54Pa 109
(off Sandycombe Rd.)
Dover Way WD3: Crox G 15R 26
Dover Yd. W1 . . . . 6B 222
Doves Cl. BR2: Brom 75Nc 160
Doves Cotts. IG7: Chig 20Wc 37
Doves Yd. N1 . . . . 1A 218 (39Qb 70)
Dovet Ct. SW9 . . . . 53Pb 112
Doveton Ho. E1 . . . . 42Yb 92
(off Doveton St.)
Doveton Rd. CR2: S Croy 78Tb 157
Doveton St. E1 . . . . 42Yb 92
Dovetree Ct. RM3: Rom 21Md 57
(off North Hill Dr.)
Dove Wlk. RM12: Horn 36Kd 77
SW1 . . . . 7H 227 (50Jb 90)
Dovey Lodge N1 . . . . 38Qb 70
(off Bewdley St.)
Dovoll Ct. SE16 . . . . 48Wb 91
(off Marine St.)
Dowanhill Rd. SE6 . . . . 60Fc 115
Dowd Cl. N11 . . . . 19Jb 32
Dowdeswell Cl. SW15 . . . . 56Ua 110
Dowding Dr. SE9 . . . . 57Lc 115
Dowding Ho. N6 . . . . 31Jb 70
(off Hillcrest)
Dowding Pl. HA7: Stan 23Ja 46
Dowding Rd. TN16: Big H 87Mc 179
UB10: Uxb 38P 63
Dowding Wlk. DA11: Nflt 2A 144
Dowding Way EN9: Walt A 8Fc 21
RM12: Horn 38Kd 77
WD25: Wat 6V 12
Dowdney Cl. NW5 . . . . 36Lb 70
Dowe Ho. SE3 . . . . 55Gc 115
Dower Av. SM6: Wall 81Kb 176
Dower Pk. SL4: Wind 6C 102
Dowes Ho. SW16 . . . . 62Nb 134
Dowgate Hill EC4 . . . . 4F 225 (45Tb 91)
Dowgate Ho. KT13: Weyb 76Q 150
Dowland Cl. SS17: Stan H 1L 101
Dowland St. W10 . . . . 41Ab 88
Dowlans Cl. KT23: Bookh 99Ca 191
Dowlans Rd. KT23: Bookh 99Da 191
Dowlas St. SE5 . . . . 52Ub 113
Dowler Ct. KT2: King T 67Na 131
Dowler Ho. E1 . . . . 44Wb 91
(off Burslem St.)
Dowlerville Rd. BR6: Chels 79Vc 161
Dowling Ct. HP3: Hem H 5M 3
Dowling Ho. DA17: Belv 48Bd 95
Dowman Cl. SW19 . . . . 66Db 133
Downage NW4 . . . . 27Ya 48
(not continuous)
Downage, The DA11: Grav'nd 1C 144
Downalong WD23: B Hea 18Fa 28
Downbank Av. DA7: Bex 53Fd 118
Down Barns Rd. HA4: Ruis 34Z 65
Downbarton Ho. SW9 . . . . 53Qb 112
(off Gosling Way)
Downbury M. SW18 . . . . 57Cb 111
Down Cl. UB5: N'olt 40X 65
Downderry Rd. BR1: Brom 62Fc 137
DOWNE 83Qc 180
Downe Av. TN14: Cud 84Tc 180
Downe Bank Nature Reserve 85Rc 180
Downe Cl. DA16: Well 52Yc 117
Downedge AL3: St A 1P 5
Downend SE18 . . . . 52Rc 116
Downend Ct. SE15 . . . . 51Ub 113
(off Bibury Cl.)
Downer Dr. WD3: Sarr 8J 11
Downe Rd. BR2: Kes 81Nc 180
CR4: Mitc 68Hb 133
TN14: Cud 85Sc 180
Downer's Cott. SW4 . . . . 56Lb 112
Downesbury NW3 . . . . 37Hb 69
(off Steele's Rd.)
Downes Cl. TW1: Twick 58Ka 108
Downes Ct. N21 . . . . 18Qb 32
Downes Ho. CR0: Wadd 77Rb 157
(off Violet La.)
Downe Ter. TW10: Rich 58Na 109
Downey Ho. E1 . . . . 42Zb 92
(off Globe Rd.)
Downfield KT4: Wor Pk 74Va 154
Downfield Cl. W9 . . . . 42Db 89
Downfield Rd. EN8: Chesh 3Ac 20
Down Hall Rd. KT2: King T 67Ma 131
DOWNHAM 64Fc 137
Downham Cl. RM5: Col R 24Cd 56
Downham Ct. KT12: Walt T 76Y 151
(off Long Lodge Dr.)
N1 . . . . 38Tb 71
(off Downham Rd.)
Downham Ent. Cen. SE6 . . . . 61Hc 137
Downham Health & Leisure Cen. 63Hc 137
Downham La. BR1: Brom 64Fc 137
Downham Rd. N1 . . . . 38Tb 71
Downham Way BR1: Brom 64Fc 137
Downhills Av. N17 . . . . 27Tb 51
Downhills Pk. Rd. N17 . . . . 27Sb 51
Downhills Way N17 . . . . 27Sb 51
Down House 84Qc 180
Downhurst Av. NW7 . . . . 22Ta 47
Downhurst Ct. NW4 . . . . 27Ya 48
Downing Cl. HA2: Harr 27Ea 46
Downing Ct. WC1 . . . . 6G 217
WD6: Bore 11Pa 29
(off Bennington Dr.)
Downing Dr. UB6: G'frd 39Fa 66
Downing Ho. W10 . . . . 44Za 88
(off Cambridge Gdns.)
Downing Path SL2: Slou 2C 80
Downing Rd. RM9: Dag 38Bd 75
Downings E6 . . . . 44Qc 94
Downing St. SW1 . . . . 1F 229 (47Nb 90)
Downings Wood WD3: Map C 22F 42
Downland Cl. KT18: Tatt C 90Xa 174
N20 . . . . 18Eb 31
Downland Ct. E11 . . . . 33Gc 73
Downland Gdns. KT18: Tatt C 90Xa 174
Downlands EN9: Walt A 6Gc 21
Downlands Cl. CR5: Coul 86Kb 176
Downlands Rd. CR8: Purl 85Nb 176
Downland Way KT18: Tatt C 90Xa 174
Downleys Cl. SE9 . . . . 61Nc 138
Downman Rd. SE9 . . . . 55Nc 116
Down Pl. W6 . . . . 49Xa 88
Down Rd. TW11: Tedd 65Ka 130
Downs, The AL10: Hat 2C 8
KT22: Lea 97La 192
SW20 . . . . 66Za 132
Downs Av. BR7: Chst 64Pc 138
DA1: Dart 59Od 119
HA5: Pinn 30Aa 45
KT18: Eps 86Ua 174
Downs Bri. Rd. BR3: Beck 67Fc 137
Downs Ct. RH1: Redh 3A 208
UB6: G'frd 41Ja 86
Downs Ct. Pde. E8 . . . . 36Xb 71
(off Amhurst Rd.)
Downs Ct. Rd. CR8: Purl 84Rb 177
Downsell Rd. E15 . . . . 35Ec 72
Downsfield AL10: Hat 3D 8
Downsfield Rd. E17 . . . . 30Ac 52
Downshall Av. IG3: Ilf 30Uc 54
Downs Hill BR3: Beck 66Fc 137
DA13: Nflt G 66Ee 143
Downs Hill Rd. KT18: Eps 86Ua 174
Downshire Hill NW3 . . . . 35Fb 69
Downs Ho. TN13: S'oaks 94Ld 203
Downs Ho. Rd. KT18: Eps D 90Ua 174
DOWNSIDE 90X 171
Downside HP2: Hem H 1N 3
KT16: Chert 74H 149
KT18: Eps 86Ua 174
TW1: Twick 62Ha 130
TW16: Sun 67W 128
Downside Bri. Rd. KT11: Cobh 86X 171
Downside Cl. SW19 . . . . 65Eb 133
Downside Comn. KT11: D'side 90X 171
Downside Comn. Rd. KT11: D'side . . . 90X 171
Downside Ct. RH1: Mers 1C 208
Downside Cres. NW3 . . . . 36Gb 69
W13 . . . . 42Ja 86
Downside Orchard GU22: Wok 89C 168
Downside Rd. KT11: D'side 88X 171
SM2: Sutt 79Fb 155
Downside Wlk. TW8: Bford 51Ma 109
(off Windmill Rd.)
UB5: N'olt 41Ba 85
Downsland Dr. CM14: B'wood 20Yd 40
Downs La. AL10: Hat 2C 8
E5 . . . . 35Xb 71
KT22: Lea 95Ka 192
Downs Lodge Ct. KT17: Eps 86Ua 174
Downs Pk. Rd. E5 . . . . 36Vb 71
E8 . . . . 36Vb 71
Downs Res. Site, The
CR3: Cat'm 99Xb 197
Downs Rd. BR3: Beck 68Dc 136
CR5: Coul 90Mb 176
CR7: Thor H 67Sb 135
CR8: Purl 83Rb 177
DA13: Nflt G, Ist R 63Fe 143
E5 . . . . 35Wb 71
EN1: Enf 14Ub 33
KT18: Eps D 92Sa 193
KT18: Eps, Eps D 87Ua 174
RH5: Mick 100La 192
SL3: L'ly 7P 81
SM2: Sutt 82Db 175
Downs Side SM2: Cheam 83Bb 175
Down St. KT8: W Mole 71Ca 151
W1 . . . . 7K 221 (46Kb 90)
Down St. M. W1 . . . . 7K 221 (46Kb 90)
Downs Valley DA3: Hartl 70Ae 143
Downs Vw. KT20: Tad 93Xa 194
TW7: Isle 53Ha 108
Downsview Av. GU22: Wok 93B 188
Downs Vw. Cl. BR6: Prat B 82Yc 181
Downsview Cl. BR8: Swan 69Hd 140
KT11: D'side 91X 191
Downsview Gdns. SE19 . . . . 66Rb 135
Downs Vw. Rd. KT23: Bookh 99Ea 192
Downsview Rd. SE19 . . . . 66Sb 135
TN13: S'oaks 97Hd 202
Downs Way KT18: Eps 88Va 174
KT20: Tad 93Xa 194
KT23: Bookh 98Ea 192
RH8: Oxt 99Gc 199
Downsway BR6: Orp 78Uc 160
CR2: Sande 83Ub 177
CR3: Whyt 88Vb 177
Downsway, The SM2: Sutt 81Eb 175
Downsway Cl. KT20: Tad 93Wa 194
Downs Wood KT18: Tatt C 89Xa 174
Downswood RH2: Reig 3M 207
Downton Av. SW2 . . . . 61Nb 134
Downtown Rd. SE16 . . . . 47Ac 92
Down Way UB5: N'olt 41X 85
Dowrey St. N1 . . . . 39Qb 70
Dowry Wlk. WD17: Wat 10V 12
Dowsett Rd. N17 . . . . 26Vb 51
Dowson Cl. SE5 . . . . 56Tb 113
Dowson Ho. E1 . . . . 44Zb 92
(off Bower St.)
Doyce St. SE1 . . . . 1D 230 (47Sb 91)
Doyle Cl. DA8: Erith 53Gd 118
Doyle Gdns. NW10 . . . . 39Wa 68
Doyle Ho. SW13 . . . . 52Ya 110
(off Trinity Chu. Rd.)
Doyle Rd. SE25 . . . . 70Wb 135
Doyle Way RM18: Tilb 4E 122
(off Coleridge Rd.)
D'Oyley St. SW1 . . . . 5H 227 (49Jb 90)
D'Oyly Carte Island KT13: Weyb 74R 150
Doynton St. N19 . . . . 33Kb 70
Draco Ga. SW15 . . . . 55Ya 110
Draco St. SE17 . . . . 51Sb 113
Dragmore St. SW4 . . . . 58Mb 112
Dragonfly Cl. E13 . . . . 41Kc 93
Dragon La. KT13: Weyb 83Q 170
Dragon Rd. SE15 . . . . 51Ub 113
Dragons Health Club
Brentwood 22Yd 58
Northolt 39Ca 65
Dragon Yd. WC1 . . . . 2G 223 (44Nb 90)
Dragor Rd. NW10 . . . . 42Sa 87
Drake Av. CR3: Cat'm 94Sb 197
SL3: L'ly 9P 81
TW18: Staines 64H 127
Drake Cl. CM14: W'ley 22Ae 59
SE16 . . . . 47Zb 92
Drake Ct. DA8: Erith 52Hd 118
(off Frobisher Rd.)
KT5: Surb 70Na 131
(off Cranes Pk. Av.)
SE1 . . . . 2E 230
SE19 . . . . 64Vb 135
W12 . . . . 47Ya 88
(off Scott's Rd.)
Drake Cres. SE28 . . . . 44Yc 95
Drakefell Rd. SE4 . . . . 54Zb 114
SE14 . . . . 54Zb 114
Drakefield Rd. SW17 . . . . 62Jb 134
Drake Hall E16 . . . . 46Kc 93
(off Wesley Av.)
Drake Ho. E1 . . . . 43Yb 92
(off Stepney Way)
E14 . . . . 45Ac 92
(off Victory Pl.)
SW1 . . . . 51Mb 112
(off Dolphin Sq.)
Drakeland Ho. W9 . . . . 42Bb 89
(off Fernhead Rd.)
Drakeley Ct. N5 . . . . 35Rb 71
Drake M. BR2: Brom 70Lc 137
DA12: Grav'nd 3F 144
RM12: Horn 37Jd 76
Drake Point DA8: Erith 50Gd 96
Drake Rd. CR0: C'don 73Pb 156
CR4: Mitc 72Jb 156
HA2: Harr 33Ba 65
KT9: Chess 78Qa 153
RM16: Chaf H 48Ae 99
SE4 . . . . 55Cc 114
Drakes, The SE8 . . . . 51Cc 114
Drake's Cl. KT10: Esh 77Ca 151
Drakes Ct. SE23 . . . . 60Yb 114
Drakes Courtyard NW6 . . . . 38Bb 69
Drakes Dr. AL1: St A 5F 6
HA6: Nwood 25R 44
Drake St. EN2: Enf 11Tb 33
WC1 . . . . 1H 223 (43Pb 90)
Drakes Wlk. E6 . . . . 39Pc 74
Drakes Way AL10: Hat 2D 8
GU22: Wok 4P 187
Drakewood Rd. SW16 . . . . 66Mb 134
Draper Cl. DA17: Belv 49Bd 95
TW7: Isle 54Fa 108
Draper Ct. BR1: Brom 70Nc 138
Draper Ho. SE1 . . . . 5C 230
Draper Pl. N1 . . . . 39Rb 71
(off Dagmar Ter.)
Drapers Almshouses E3 . . . . 41Dc 92
(off Rainhill Way)
Drapers Cott. Homes NW7 . . . . 21Va 48
(not continuous)
Drapers Ct. RM12: Horn 33Nd 77
SW11 . . . . 53Jb 112
(off Battersea Pk. Rd.)
Drapers Cres. KT12: W Vill 82V 170
Drapers Gdns. EC2 . . . . 2G 225 (44Tb 91)
Drapers Rd. E15 . . . . 35Fc 73
EN2: Enf 12Rb 33
N17 . . . . 27Vb 51
Drappers Way SE16 . . . . 49Wb 91
Draven Cl. BR2: Hayes 73Hc 159
Drawdock Rd. SE10 . . . . 47Fc 93
Drawell Cl. SE18 . . . . 50Uc 94
Drax Av. SW20 . . . . 66Wa 132
Draxmont SW19 . . . . 65Ab 132
Draycot Rd. E11 . . . . 30Kc 53
KT6: Surb 74Qa 153
Draycott Av. HA3: Kenton 30Ka 46
SW3 . . . . 5E 226 (49Gb 89)
Draycott Cl. HA3: Kenton 30Ka 46
NW2 . . . . 34Za 68
SE5 . . . . 52Tb 113
(not continuous)
Draycott Ct. SW11 . . . . 53Gb 111
(off Westbridge Rd.)
Draycott M. SW6 . . . . 54Bb 111
(off Laurel Bank Gdns.)
Draycott Pl. SW3 . . . . 6F 227 (49Hb 89)
Draycott Ter. SW3 . . . . 6G 227 (49Hb 89)
Dray Ct. HA0: Wemb 36Ja 66
(off Brewery Cl.)
Drayford Cl. W9 . . . . 42Bb 89
Dray Gdns. SW2 . . . . 57Pb 112
Draymans M. SE15 . . . . 54Vb 113
Draymans Way TW7: Isle 55Ha 108
Drayside M. UB2: S'hall 47Ba 85
Drayson Cl. EN9: Walt A 4Gc 21
Drayson M. W8 . . . . 47Cb 89
Drayton Av. BR6: Farnb 74Rc 160
EN6: Pot B 4Ab 16
IG10: Lough 17Pc 36
W13 . . . . 45Ja 86
Drayton Bri. Rd. W7 . . . . 45Ha 86
W13 . . . . 45Ha 86
Drayton Cl. IG1: Ilf 32Tc 74
KT22: Fet 96Ga 192
TW4: Houn 57Ba 107
Drayton Ct. UB7: W Dray 49P 83
Drayton Ford WD3: Rick 19J 25
Drayton Gdns. N21 . . . . 17Rb 33
SW10 . . . . 7A 226 (50Eb 89)
UB7: W Dray 47N 83
W13 . . . . 45Ja 86
Drayton Grn. W13 . . . . 45Ja 86
Drayton Grn. Rd. W13 . . . . 45Ka 86
Drayton Gro. W13 . . . . 45Ja 86
Drayton Ho. E11 . . . . 32Fc 73
SE5 . . . . 52Tb 113
(off Elmington Rd.)
Drayton Pk. N5 . . . . 35Qb 70
Drayton Pk. M. N5 . . . . 36Qb 70
Drayton Rd. CR0: C'don 75Rb 157
E11 . . . . 32Fc 73
N17 . . . . 26Ub 51
NW10 . . . . 39Va 68
W13 . . . . 45Ja 86
WD6: Bore 14Qa 29
Drayton Waye HA3: Kenton 30Ka 46
Dray Wlk. E1 . . . . 6K 219 (42Vb 91)
Dreadnought Cl. SW19 . . . . 68Fb 133
Dreadnought St. SE10 . . . . 48Gc 93
Drenon Sq. UB3: Hayes 45V 84
Dresden Cl. NW6 . . . . 37Db 69
Dresden Ho. SE11 . . . . 5J 229
SW11 . . . . 54Jb 112
(off Dagnall St.)
Dresden Rd. N19 . . . . 32Lb 70
Dresden Way KT13: Weyb 78S 150
Dressington Av. SE4 . . . . 58Cc 114
Drew Av. NW7 . . . . 23Ab 48
Drewery Ct. SE3 . . . . 55Gc 115
Drewett Ho. E1 . . . . 44Wb 91
(off Christian St.)
Drew Gdns. UB6: G'frd 37Ha 66
Drew Ho. SW16 . . . . 62Nb 134
Drew Mdw. SL2: Farn C 5G 60
Drew Pl. CR3: Cat'm 95Tb 197
Drew Rd. E16 . . . . 46Mc 93
(not continuous)
Drewstead La. SW16 . . . . 61Mb 134
Drewstead Rd. SW16 . . . . 61Mb 134
Drey, The SL9: Chal P 22A 42
Drey Ct. KT4: Wor Pk 74Va 154
Driffield Ct. NW9 . . . . 25Ua 48
(off Pageant Av.)
Driffield Rd. E3 . . . . 40Ac 72
Drift, The BR2: Brom 76Mc 159
DRIFT BRIDGE 86Ya 174
Drift Ct. E16 . . . . 45Rc 94
Drift Golf Course 95V 190
Drift La. KT11: Stoke D 88Ba 171
Drift Rd. KT24: E Hor, Eff J 96T 190
SL4: Wink 10A 102
Drift Way SL3: Coln 53E 104
Driftway, The CR4: Mitc 67Jb 134
HP2: Hem H 2P 3
KT22: Lea 95Ka 192
(not continuous)
SM7: Bans 87Ya 174
Driftway Ho. E3 . . . . 40Bc 72
(off Stafford Rd.)
Driftwood Av. AL2: Chis G 8N 5
Driftwood Dr. CR8: Kenley 89Rb 177
Drill Hall Arts 7D 216
Drill Hall Rd. KT16: Chert 73J 149
Drinkwater Ho. SE5 . . . . 52Tb 113
(off Picton St.)
Drinkwater Rd. HA2: Harr 33Da 65
Drive, The AL2: Lon C 7E 6
AL9: Brk P 7J 9
BR3: Beck 68Cc 136

Drive, The BR4: W W'ck 73Fc 159
BR6: Orp 75Vc 161
BR7: Chst 69Vc 139
CM13: Gt War 22Yd 58
CR5: Coul 86Nb 176
CR7: Thor H 70Tb 135
DA3: Lfield 69De 143
DA5: Bexl 58Yc 117
DA8: Erith 52Dd 118
DA12: Grav'nd 3F 144
DA14: Sidc 62Xc 139
E4 17Fc 35
E17 27Dc 52
E18 28Jc 53
EN2: Enf 11Tb 33
(Farr Rd.)
EN2: Enf 7Jb 18
(St Nicholas Ho's.)
EN5: Barn 13Ab 30
EN5: New Bar 16Eb 31
EN6: Pot B 5Bb 17
EN7: G Oak 1Rb 19
GU22: Wok 2M 187
GU25: Vir W 71B 148
HA2: Harr 31Ca 65
HA6: Nwood 26U 44
HA8: Edg 22Qa 47
HA9: Wemb 33Sa 67
IG1: Ilf 30Nc 54
IG9: Buck H 17Lc 35
IG10: Lough 13Nc 36
IG11: Bark 38Vc 75
KT2: King T 66Sa 131
KT6: Surb 73Na 153
KT10: Esh 74Ea 152
KT11: Cobh 86Aa 171
KT18: Head 95Na 193
KT19: Ewe 79Va 154
KT20: Lwr K 98Bb 195
KT22: Fet 94Ga 192
KT22: Lea 95Na 193
N3 24Cb 49
N6 29Hb 49
N7 37Pb 70
(not continuous)
N11 23Lb 50
NW10 39Va 68
NW11 31Ab 68
RM3: Hrld W 25Nd 57
RM4: Stap A 17Ed 38
RM5: Col R 24Fd 56
SL3: Dat 3M 103
SL3: L'ly 47A 82
SL9: Chal P 24A 42
SM2: Cheam 84Bb 175
SM4: Mord 71Eb 155
SM5: Cars 81Hb 175
SM6: Wall 82Lb 176
SM7: Bans 89Ab 174
SW6 54Ab 110
SW20 66Ya 132
TN13: S'oaks 96Kd 203
TW3: Houn 54Fa 108
TW7: Isle 54Fa 108
TW14: Felt 59Y 107
TW15: Ashf 66T 128
TW19: Wray 7P 103
UB10: Ick 35N 63
W3 44Sa 87
WD3: Rick 15K 25
WD5: R'lett 6Ja 14
WD17: Wat 9T 12
Drive Ct. HA8: Edg 22Qa 47
Drive Mans. SW6 54Ab 110
(off Fulham Rd.)
Drive Mead CR5: Coul 86Nb 176
Drive Rd. CR5: Coul 92Mb 196
(not continuous)
Drive Spur KT20: Kgswd 93Db 195
Driveway, The E17 30Dc 52
(off Hoe St.)
EN6: Cuff 1Nb 18
HP1: Hem H 3K 3
Droitwich Cl. SE26 62Wb 135
Dromey Gdns. HA3: Hrw W 24Ha 46
Dromore Rd. SW15 58Ab 110
Dronfield Gdns. RM8: Dag 36Yc 75
Dron Ho. E1 43Yb 92
(off Adelina Gro.)
Droop St. W10 41Za 88
Drop La. AL2: Brick W 2Da 13
Dropmore Ho. SL1: Burn 4A 60
Dropmore Rd. SL1: Burn 5A 60
Drovers Ct. KT1: King T 68Na 131
(off Fairfield E.)
Drovers Mead CM14: W'ley 21Xd 58
Drovers Pl. SE15 52Yb 114
Drovers Rd. CR2: S Croy 78Tb 157
Drovers Way AL3: St A 2B 6
N7 37Nb 70
Drove Way, The DA13: Ist R 6A 144
Droveway IG10: Lough 12Rc 36
Druce Rd. SE21 58Ub 113
Drudgeon Way DA2: Bean 62Xd 142
Druids Cl. KT21: Asht 92Pa 193
Druid St. SE1 1J 231 (47Ub 91)
(not continuous)
Druids Way BR2: Brom 70Fc 137
Drumaline Ridge KT4: Wor Pk 75Ua 154
Drummond Av. RM7: Rom 28Fd 56
Drummond Cl. DA8: Erith 53Gd 118
Drummond Ct. CM15: B'wood 17Yd 40
KT19: Eps 84Pa 173
N12 24Gb 49
Drummond Cres. NW1 3D 216 (41Mb 90)
Drummond Dr. HA7: Stan 24Ha 46
Drummond Gdns. KT19: Eps 83Sa 173
Drummond Ga. SW1 7E 228 (50Mb 90)
Drummond Ho. E2 40Wb 71
(off Goldsmiths Row)
N2 26Eb 49
(off Font Hills)
SL4: Wind 5H 103
(off Balmoral Gdns.)
Drummond Pl. TW1: Twick 59Ka 108
Drummond Rd. CR0: C'don 75Sb 157
E11 30Lc 53
RM7: Rom 28Fd 56
SE16 48Xb 91
Drummonds, The CM16: Epp 2Wc 23
IG9: Buck H 19Kc 35
Drummonds Pl. TW9: Rich 56Na 109
Drummond St. NW1 5B 216 (42Lb 90)
Drummond Way N1 38Qb 70
Druries HA1: Harr 32Ga 66
(off High St.)
Drury Cres. CR0: Wadd 75Qb 156
Drury Ho. SW8 53Lb 112
Drury La. WC2 2G 223 (44Nb 90)
Drury Lane Theatre Royal 3H 223
Drury Rd. HA1: Harr 31Ea 66
Drury Way NW10 36Ta 67
Drury Way Ind. Est. NW10 36Sa 67
Dryad St. SW15 55Za 110
Dry Arch Rd. SL5: S'dale 2D 146
Dryburgh Gdns. NW9 27Qa 47
Dryburgh Ho. SW1 7K 227
Dryburgh Rd. SW15 55Xa 110
Dryden Av. W7 44Ha 86
Dryden Bldg. E1 44Wb 91
(off Commercial Rd.)
Dryden Cl. IG6: Ilf 23Vc 55
SW4 57Mb 112
Dryden Ct. SE11 6A 230 (49Rb 91)
Dryden Mans. W14 51Ab 110
(off Queen's Club Gdns.)
Dryden Pl. RM18: Tilb 3C 122
Dryden Rd. DA16: Well 53Vc 117
EN1: Enf 16Ub 33
HA3: W'stone 25Ha 46
SW19 65Eb 133
Dryden St. WC2 3G 223 (44Nb 90)
Dryden Towers RM3: Rom 24Kd 57
Dryden Way BR6: Orp 74Wc 161
Dryfield Cl. NW10 37Sa 67
Dryfield Rd. HA8: Edg 22Sa 47
Dryfield Wlk. SE8 51Cc 114
DRYHILL 96Dd 202
Dryhill La. TN14: Sund 95Dd 202
Dryhill Local Nature Reserve 96Dd 202
Dryhill Rd. DA17: Belv 51Bd 117
Dryland Av. BR6: Orp 77Vc 161
Dryland Rd. TN15: Bor G 93Be 205
Drylands Rd. N8 30Nb 50
Drynham Pk. KT13: Weyb 76U 150
Drysdale Av. E4 17Dc 34
Drysdale Cl. HA6: Nwood 24U 44
Drysdale Dwellings E8 36Vb 71
(off Dunn St.)
Drysdale Pl. N1 3J 219 (41Ub 91)
Drysdale St. N1 3J 219 (41Ub 91)
Duarte Pl. RM16: Chaf H 48Be 99
Dublin Av. E8 39Wb 71
Dublin Ct. HA2: Harr 33Fa 66
(off Northolt Rd.)
Dubrae Cl. AL3: St A 4N 5
Du Burstow Ter. W7 47Ga 86
Ducaine Apartments E3 41Bc 92
(off Merchant St.)
Ducal St. E2 4K 219 (41Vb 91)
Du Cane Cl. W12 44Ya 88
Du Cane Ct. SW17 60Jb 112
Du Cane Rd. W12 44Va 88
Ducavel Ho. SW2 60Pb 112
Duchess Cl. N11 22Kb 50
SM1: Sutt 77Eb 155
Duchess Ct. KT13: Weyb 76T 150
Duchess Gro. IG9: Buck H 19Kc 35
Duchess M. W1 1A 222 (43Kb 90)
Duchess of Bedford Ho. W8 47Cb 89
(off Duchess of Bedford's Wlk.)
Duchess of Bedford's Wlk. W8 47Cb 89
Duchess St. SL1: Slou 6C 80
W1 1A 222 (43Kb 90)
Duchess Theatre 4H 223
Duchess' Wlk. TN15: S'oaks 98Nd 203
Duchy Rd. EN4: Had W 10Fb 17
Duchy St. SE1 6A 224 (46Qb 90)
(not continuous)
Ducie St. SW4 56Pb 112
Duckett M. N4 30Rb 51
Duckett Rd. N4 30Rb 51
Duckett's Apartments E3 38Bc 72
(off Wick La.)
Ducketts Rd. DA1: Cray 57Hd 118
Duckett St. E1 42Zb 92
Ducking Stool Ct. RM1: Rom 28Gd 56
Duck La. W1 3D 222
Duck Lees La. EN3: Pond E 14Ac 34
Duck's Hill Rd. HA4: Ruis 25R 44
HA6: Nwood 25R 44
DUCKS ISLAND 16Za 30
Ducks Wlk. TW1: Twick 57La 108
Duckworth Dr. KT21: Asht 92Ma 193
Du Cros Dr. HA7: Stan 23Ma 47
Du Cros Rd. W3 46Ua 88
Dudbrook Rd. CM14: Kel C, Nave 11Sd 40
DUDDEN HILL 36Xa 68
Dudden Hill La. NW10 35Va 68
Dudden Hill Pde. NW10 35Va 68
Duddington Cl. SE9 63Mc 137
Dudley Av. EN8: Walt C 4Zb 20
HA3: Kenton 27La 46
Dudley Cl. HP3: Bov 9C 2
KT15: Add 76L 149
RM16: Chaf H 47Ae 99
Dudley Ct. NW11 28Bb 49
SL1: Slou 8L 81
W1 3F 221
WC2 2F 223 (44Nb 90)
Dudley Dr. HA4: Ruis 36X 65
SM4: Mord 74Ab 154
Dudley Gdns. HA2: Harr 32Fa 66
RM3: Rom 23Md 57
W13 47Ka 86
Dudley Gro. KT18: Eps 86Sa 173
Dudley Ho. HP3: Bov 9C 2
W2 1B 220
Dudley M. SW2 58Qb 112
Dudley Pl. TW19: Stanw 58P 105
UB3: Harl 49T 84
Dudley Rd. DA11: Nflt 9A 122
E17 26Cc 52
HA2: Harr 33Ea 66
IG1: Ilf 35Rc 74
KT1: King T 69Pa 131
KT12: Walt T 72W 150
N3 26Db 49
NW6 40Ab 68
RM3: Rom 23Md 57
SW19 65Cb 133
TW9: Rich 54Pa 109
TW14: Bedf 60S 106
TW15: Ashf 64P 127
UB2: S'hall 47Z 85
Dudley St. W2 1B 220 (43Fb 89)
Dudley Wharf Caravans SL0: Iver 46D 82
Dudlington Rd. E5 33Yb 72
Dudmaston M. SW3 7C 226
Dudrich Cl. N11 23Hb 49
Dudrich M. EN2: Enf 11Qb 32
SE22 57Vb 113
Dudsbury Rd. DA1: Dart 58Kd 119
DA14: Sidc 65Xc 139
Dudset La. TW5: Cran 53W 106
Duett Ct. TW5: Hest 52Aa 107
Duffell Ho. SE11 7J 229
Dufferin Av. EC1 6F 219
Dufferin Ct. EC1 6F 219
Dufferin St. EC1 6E 218 (42Sb 91)
Duffield Cl. HA1: Harr 29Ha 46
RM16: Chaf H 48Be 99
Duffield Dr. N15 28Vb 51
Duffield La. SL2: Stoke P 7K 61
Duffield Pk. SL2: Stoke P 1L 81
Duffield Rd. KT20: Walt H 96Xa 194
Duffins Orchard KT16: Ott 80E 148
Duffins Orchard Mobile Homes
KT16: Ott 80E 148
Duff St. E14 44Dc 92
Dufour's Pl. W1 3C 222 (44Lb 90)
Dufton Dwellings E15 35Gc 73
(off High Rd. Leyton)
Dugard Way SE11 5B 230 (49Rb 91)
Dugdale Ct. NW10 41Xa 88
(off Harrow Rd.)
DUGDALE HILL 5Ab 16
Dugdale Hill La. EN6: Pot B 5Ab 16
Dugdale Ho. TW20: Egh 64E 126
(off Rowan Av.)
Dugdales WD3: Crox G 14Q 26
Duggan Dr. BR7: Chst 65Nc 138
Dugolly Av. HA9: Wemb 34Ra 67
Duke Gdns. IG6: Ilf 28Tc 54
Duke Humphrey Rd. SE3 53Gc 115
Duke of Cambridge Cl.
TW2: Whitt 58Fa 108
Duke of Clarence Ct. SE17 7D 230
Duke of Edinburgh Rd. SM1: Sutt 75Fb 155
Duke of Wellington Av. SE18 48Rc 94
Duke of Wellington Pl.
SW1 2J 227 (47Jb 90)
Duke of York Column (Memorial) 7D 222
Duke of York Sq. SW3 6G 227 (50Hb 89)
Duke of York's Theatre 5F 223
Duke of York St. SW1 6C 222 (46Lb 90)
Duke Pl. SL1: Slou 5K 81
(off Montague Rd.)
Duke Rd. IG6: Ilf 28Tc 54
W4 50Ta 87
Dukes Av. CM16: They B 7Uc 22
HA1: Harr 28Ga 46
HA2: Harr 30Ba 45
HA8: Edg 23Pa 47
KT2: King T 63La 130
KT3: N Mald 69Ua 132
N3 25Db 49
N10 27Kb 50
RM17: Grays 48Ce 99
TW4: Houn 56Aa 107
TW10: Ham 63La 130
UB5: N'olt 38Aa 65
W4 50Ta 87
Dukes Cl. SL9: Ger X 2P 61
TW12: Hamp 64Ba 129
TW15: Ashf 63S 128
Dukes Ct. E6 39Qc 74
(not continuous)
GU21: Wok 89B 168
KT15: Add 77L 149
KT19: Ewe 81Ua 174
SE13 54Ec 114
SW14 54Ta 109
W2 45Db 89
(off Moscow Rd.)
Dukes Dr. SL2: Farn C 6D 60
Dukes Ga. W4 49Sa 87
Dukes Grn. Av. TW14: Felt 57W 106
Dukes Head Pas. TW12: Hamp 66Ea 130
Duke's Head Yd. N6 32Kb 70
Dukes Hill CR3: Wold 92Ac 198
Duke Shore Wharf E14 45Bc 92
Duke's Ho. SW1 5E 228
Dukes Kiln Dr. SL9: Ger X 2N 61
Dukes La. SL4: Wind 6E 124
SL5: Asc 6E 124
SL9: Ger X 31A 62
W8 47Db 89
Duke's La. Chambers W8 47Db 89
(off Dukes La.)
Duke's La. Mans. W8 47Db 89
(off Dukes La.)
Dukes Lodge W8 46Bb 89
(off Holland Wlk.)
Dukes M. N10 27Kb 50
W1 2J 221
Dukes Orchard DA5: Bexl 60Ed 118
Duke's Pas. E17 28Ec 52
Duke's Pl. CM14: B'wood 18Yd 40
EC3 3J 225 (44Ub 91)
Dukes Point N6 32Kb 70
(off Dukes Head Yd.)
Dukes Ride SL9: Ger X 32A 62
UB10: Ick 35N 63
Dukes Rd. E6 39Qc 74
KT12: Hers 78Z 151
W3 42Qa 87
WC1 4E 216 (41Mb 90)
Dukesthorpe Rd. SE26 63Zb 136
Duke St. GU21: Wok 89B 168
SL4: Wind 4G 102
SM1: Sutt 77Fb 155
TW9: Rich 56Ma 109
W1 2J 221 (44Jb 90)
WD17: Wat 13Y 27
Duke St. Hill SE1 6G 225 (46Tb 91)
Duke St. Mans. W1 3J 221
Duke St St James's SW1 6C 222 (46Lb 90)
Dukes Valley SL9: Ger X 3M 61
Dukes Way BR4: W W'ck 76Gc 159
HA9: Wemb 36Na 67
UB8: Uxb 39K 63
Dukes Wood Av. SL9: Ger X 31A 62
Dukes Wood Dr. SL9: Ger X 2N 61
Dukes Yd. W1 4J 221 (45Jb 90)
WD24: Wat 10W 12
Dulas St. N4 32Pb 70
Dulcie Cl. DA9: Ghithe 58Ud 120
Dulford St. W11 45Ab 88
Dulka Rd. SW11 57Hb 111
Dullshot Grn. KT17: Eps 85Ua 174
Dulverton NW1 1C 216
Dulverton Mans. WC1 6J 217
Dulverton Rd. CR2: Sels 82Yb 178
HA4: Ruis 32W 64
RM3: Rom 23Md 57
SE9 61Sc 138
DULWICH 61Ub 135
Dulwich & Sydenham Hill Golf Course
61Vb 135
Dulwich Bus. Cen. SE23 60Zb 114
Dulwich Comn. SE21 60Ub 113
SE22 60Ub 113
Dulwich Lawn Cl. SE22 57Vb 113
Dulwich Leisure Cen. 56Wb 113
Dulwich Oaks, The SE21 62Vb 135
Dulwich Picture Gallery 59Tb 113
Dulwich Ri. Gdns. SE22 57Vb 113
Dulwich Rd. SE24 57Qb 112
Dulwich Upper Wood Nature Pk. 64Vb 135
DULWICH VILLAGE 59Ub 113
Dulwich Village SE21 58Tb 113
Dulwich Way WD3: Crox G 15Q 26
Dulwich Wood Av. SE19 63Ub 135
Dulwich Wood Pk. SE19 63Ub 135
Dumain Ct. SE11 6B 230
Dumas Way WD18: Wat 14U 26
Dumbarton Av. EN8: Walt C 6Zb 20
Dumbarton Ct. SW2 58Nb 112
Dumbarton Rd. SW2 58Nb 112
Dumbleton Cl. KT1: King T 67Ra 131
Dumbletons, The WD3: Map C 21G 42
Dumbreck Rd. SE9 56Pc 116
Dumfries Cl. WD19: Wat 20V 26
Dumont Rd. N16 34Ub 71
Dumpton Pl. NW1 38Jb 70
Dumsey Eyot KT16: Chert 73N 149
Dumville Dr. RH9: G'stone 3P 209
Dunally Pk. TW17: Shep 73T 150
Dunbar Av. BR3: Beck 70Ac 136
RM10: Dag 34Cd 76
SW16 68Qb 134
Dunbar Cl. SL2: Slou 5L 81
UB4: Hayes 43X 85
Dunbar Ct. BR2: Brom 69Hc 137
(off Durham Rd.)
KT12: Walt T 74Y 151
SM1: Sutt 78Fb 155
Dunbar Gdns. RM10: Dag 36Cd 76
Dunbar Rd. E7 37Jc 73
KT3: N Mald 70Sa 131
N22 25Qb 50
Dunbar St. SE27 62Sb 135
Dunbar Twr. E8 37Vb 71
(off Dalston Sq.)
Dunbar Wharf E14 45Bc 92
(off Narrow St.)
Dunblane Cl. HA8: Edg 19Ra 29
Dunblane Rd. SE9 55Nc 116
Dunboe Pl. TW17: Shep 73S 150
Dunboyne Pl. SL4: Old Win 6L 103
Dunboyne Rd. NW3 36Hb 69
Dunbridge Ho. SW15 58Va 110
(off Highcliffe Dr.)
Dunbridge St. E2 42Wb 91
Duncan Cl. EN5: New Bar 14Eb 31
Duncan Ct. AL1: St A 4D 6
E14 43Ec 92
(off Teviot St.)
N21 18Rb 33
Duncan Gdns. TW18: Staines 65J 127
Duncan Gro. W3 44Ua 88
Duncan Ho. NW3 38Hb 69
(off Fellows Rd.)
SW1 50Lb 90
(off Dolphin Sq.)
Duncannon Cres. SL4: Wind 5B 102
Duncannon Ho. SW1 7E 228
Duncannon Pl. DA9: Ghithe 56Yd 120
Duncannon St. WC2 5F 223 (45Nb 90)
Duncan Rd. E8 39Xb 71
KT20: Tad 91Ab 194
TW9: Rich 56Na 109
Duncan St. N1 1B 218 (40Rb 71)
Duncans Yd. TN16: Westrm 98Tc 200
Duncan Ter. N1 2B 218 (40Rb 71)
(not continuous)
Duncan Way WD23: Bush 12Ba 27
Dunch St. E1 44Xb 91
Dunchurch Ho. RM10: Dag 38Cd 76
Duncombe Ct. RM19: Purf 50Rd 97
(off Wingrove Dr.)
TW18: Staines 66H 127
Duncombe Hill SE23 59Ac 114
Duncombe Rd. N19 32Mb 70
Duncrievie Rd. SE13 58Fc 115
Duncroft SE18 52Uc 116
SL4: Wind 5D 102
Duncroft Cl. RH2: Reig 6H 207
Duncroft Mnr. TW18: Staines 63G 126
Dundalk Ho. E1 44Yb 92
(off Clark St.)
Dundalk Rd. SE4 55Ac 114
Dundas Gdns. KT8: W Mole 69Da 129
Dundas Ho. E2 40Yb 72
(off Bishop's Way)
Dundas M. EN3: Enf L 9Cc 20
Dundas Rd. SE15 54Yb 114
Dundee Ct. E1 46Xb 91
(off Wapping High St.)
SE1 3H 231
(off Long La.)
Dundee Ho. W9 3A 214
Dundee Rd. E13 40Kc 73
SE25 71Xb 157
SL1: Slou 4D 80
Dundee St. E1 46Xb 91
Dundee Way EN3: Brim 13Ac 34
Dundee Wharf E14 45Bc 92
Dundela Gdns. KT4: Wor Pk 77Xa 154
Dundonald Cl. E6 44Nc 94
Dundonald Rd. NW10 39Za 68
SW19 66Ab 132
Dundrey Cres. RH1: Mers 1E 208
Dundry Ho. SE26 62Wb 135
Dunedin Dr. CR3: Cat'm 97Ub 197
Dunedin Ho. E16 46Pc 94
(off Manwood St.)
Dunedin M. SW2 60Nb 112
Dunedin Rd. E10 34Dc 72
IG1: Ilf 32Sc 74
RM13: Rain 41Hd 96
Dunedin Way UB4: Yead 42Y 85
Dunelm Gro. SE27 62Sb 135
Dunelm St. E1 44Zb 92
Dunfee Way KT14: Byfl 84N 169
Dunfermline Ho. WD19: Wat 20Y 27
Dunfield Gdns. SE6 64Dc 136
Dunfield Rd. SE6 64Dc 136
(not continuous)
Dunford Ct. HA5: Hat E 24Ba 45
Dunford Rd. N7 35Pb 70
Dungarvan Av. SW15 56Wa 110
Dungates La. RH3: Bkld 5C 206
Dunheved Cl. CR7: Thor H 72Qb 156
Dunheved Rd. Nth. CR7: Thor H 72Qb 156
Dunheved Rd. Sth. CR7: Thor H 72Qb 156
Dunheved Rd. W. CR7: Thor H 72Qb 156
Dunhill Point SW15 60Wa 110
Dunholme Grn. N9 20Vb 33
Dunholme La. N9 20Vb 33
Dunholme Rd. N9 20Vb 33
Dunkeld Rd. RM8: Dag 33Xc 75
SE25 70Tb 135
Dunkellin Gro. RM15: S Ock 44Wd 98
Dunkellin Way RM15: S Ock 44Wd 98
Dunkery Rd. SE9 63Mc 137
Dunkin Rd. DA1: Dart 56Qd 119
Dunkirk Cl. DA12: Grav'nd 4E 144
Dunkirk Ho. SE1 2G 231
Dunkirk St. SE27 63Sb 135
DUNK'S GREEN 100Ce 205
Dunlace Rd. E5 35Yb 72
Dunleary Cl. TW4: Houn 59Ba 107
Dunley Dr. CR0: New Ad 80Dc 158
Dunlin Ho. SE16 49Zb 92
(off Tawny Way)
Dunloe Av. N17 27Tb 51
Dunloe Ct. E2 2K 219 (40Vb 71)
Dunloe Pas. E2 40Vb 71
(off Dunloe Ct.)
Dunloe St. E2 2K 219 (40Vb 71)
Dunlop Cl. DA1: Dart 55Nd 119
RM18: Tilb 4B 122
Dunlop Pl. SE16 48Vb 91
Dunlop Rd. RM18: Tilb 3B 122
Dunmail Dr. CR8: Purl 86Ub 177
Dunmore Point E2 4K 219
Dunmore Rd. NW6 39Ab 68
SW20 67Ya 132
Dunmow Cl. IG10: Lough 16Nc 36
RM6: Chad H 29Yc 55
TW13: Hanw 62Aa 129
Dunmow Dr. RM13: Rain 39Hd 76
Dunmow Gdns. CM13: W H'dn 30Fe 59
Dunmow Ho. KT14: Byfl 85N 169
RM9: Dag 39Xc 75
SE11 7J 229
Dunmow Rd. E15 35Fc 73
Dunmow Wlk. N1 39Sb 71
(off Popham St.)
Dunnage Cres. SE16 49Ac 92
(not continuous)
Dunnell Cl. TW16: Sun 67W 128
Dunnets GU21: Knap 9J 167
Dunnett Ho. E3 40Bc 72
(off Vernon Rd.)
Dunnico Ho. SE17 7H 231
Dunning Cl. RM15: S Ock 44Wd 98
Dunningford Cl. RM12: Horn 36Hd 76
Dunnings La. CM13: Bulp, W H'dn 31De 79
RM14: Bulp 31De 79
Dunn Mead NW9 24Va 48
Dunnock Cl. N9 18Zb 34
WD6: Bore 14Qa 29
Dunnock Rd. E6 44Nc 94
Dunnose Ct. RM19: Purf 50Rd 97
Dunn's Pas. WC1 2G 223
Dunn St. E8 36Vb 71
Dunny La. WD4: Chfd 5G 10
Dunnymans Rd. SM7: Bans 87Bb 175
Dunollie Pl. NW5 36Lb 70
Dunollie Rd. NW5 36Lb 70
Dunoon Gdns. SE23 59Zb 114
Dunoon Ho. N1 39Pb 70
(off Bemerton Est.)
Dunoon Rd. SE23 59Yb 114
Dunoran Home BR1: Brom 67Nc 138
Dunottar Cl. RH1: Redh 8M 207
Dunraven Dr. EN2: Enf 12Qb 32
Dunraven Rd. W12 46Wa 88
Dunraven St. W1 4G 221 (45Hb 89)
Dunsany Rd. W14 48Za 88
DUNSBOROUGH PARK 93L 189
Dunsbury Cl. SM2: Sutt 81Db 175
Dunsfold Ct. SM2: Sutt 80Db 155
(off Blackbush Cl.)
Dunsfold Ri. CR5: Coul 85Mb 176
Dunsfold Way CR0: New Ad 81Dc 178
Dunsford Way SW15 58Xa 110
Dunsmore WD19: Wat 18Z 27
Dunsmore Cl. UB4: Yead 42Aa 85
WD23: Bush 16Fa 28
Dunsmore Rd. KT12: Walt T 72X 151
Dunsmore Way WD23: Bush 16Fa 28
Dunsmure Rd. N16 32Ub 71
Dunspring La. IG5: Ilf 26Rc 54
Dunstable Cl. RM3: Rom 23Md 57
Dunstable M. W1 7J 215 (43Jb 90)
Dunstable Rd. KT8: W Mole 70Ba 129
RM3: Rom 23Md 57
SS17: Stan H 1L 101
TW9: Rich 56Na 109
Dunstall Grn. GU24: Chob 1N 167
Dunstall Rd. SW20 65Xa 132
Dunstall Way KT8: W Mole 69Da 129
Dunstall Welling Est. DA16: Well 54Xc 117
Dunstan Cl. N2 27Eb 49
Dunstan Glade BR5: Pet W 72Tc 160
Dunstan Ho's. E1 43Yb 92
(off Stepney Grn.)
Dunstan Rd. CR5: Coul 89Mb 176
NW11 32Bb 69
Dunstan's Gro. SE22 58Xb 113
Dunstan's Rd. SE22 59Wb 113
Dunster Av. SM4: Mord 74Za 154
Dunster Cl. EN5: Barn 14Za 30
RM5: Col R 26Ed 56
UB9: Hare 25K 43
Dunster Ct. EC3 4J 225 (45Ub 91)
WD6: Bore 13Ta 29
Dunster Cres. RM11: Horn 33Qd 77
Dunster Dr. NW9 32Sa 67
Dunster Gdns. NW6 38Bb 69
SL1: Slou 5E 80
Dunster Ho. SE6 62Ec 136
Dunsterville Way SE1 2G 231 (47Tb 91)
Dunster Way HA2: Harr 34Aa 65
SM6: Wall 74Jb 156
Dunston Ct. TW18: Staines 63J 127
Dunston Rd. E8 39Vb 71
(not continuous)
SW11 54Jb 112
Dunston St. E8 39Ub 71
Dunton Cl. KT6: Surb 74Na 153
Dunton Ct. SE23 61Xb 135
DUNTON GREEN 92Gd 202
Dunton Rd. E10 31Dc 72
RM1: Rom 28Gd 56
SE1 7K 231 (50Vb 91)

Duntshill Rd. SW18 60Db **111**
Dunvegan Cl. KT8: W Mole 70Da **129**
Dunvegan Ho. RH1: Redh 6P **207**
Dunvegan Rd. SE9 56Pc **116**
Dunwich Ct. *RM6: Chad H* *29Xc* **55**
(off Glandford Way)
Dunwich Rd. DA7: Bex 53Bd **117**
Dunworth M. W11 44Bb **89**
Duplex Ride SW1 2G **227** (47Hb **89**)
Dupont Rd. SW20 68Za **132**
Duppas Av. CR0: Wadd 77Rb **157**
Duppas Cl. TW17: Shep 71T **150**
Duppas Ct. *CR0: C'don* *76Rb* **157**
(off Duppas Hill Ter.)
Duppas Hill La. CR0: C'don 77Rb **157**
Duppas Hill Rd. CR0: Wadd 77Qb **156**
Duppas Hill Ter. CR0: C'don 76Rb **157**
Duppas Rd. CR0: Wadd 76Qb **156**
Dupre Cl. RM16: Chaf H 48Ae **99**
SL1: Slou 7C **80**
Dupree Rd. SE7 50Kc **93**
Dura Den Cl. BR3: Beck 66Dc **136**
Durand Cl. SM5: Cars 74Hb **155**
Durand Gdns. SW9 53Pb **112**
Durands Wlk. SE16 47Bc **92**
Durand Way NW10 38Sa **67**
Durant Rd. BR8: Hext 65Jd **140**
Durants Pk. Av. EN3: Pond E 14Zb **34**
Durants Rd. EN3: Pond E 14Yb **34**
Durant St. E2 40Wb **71**
Durban Ct. E7 38Mc **73**
Durban Gdns. RM10: Dag 38Ed **76**
Durban Ho. *W12* *45Xa* **88**
(off White City Est.)
Durban Rd. BR3: Beck 68Bc **136**
E15 41Gc **93**
E17 25Bc **52**
IG2: Ilf 32Uc **74**
N17 23Ub **51**
SE27 63Sb **135**
Durban Rd. E. WD18: Wat 14W **26**
Durban Rd. W. WD18: Wat 14W **26**
Durbin Rd. KT9: Chess 77Na **153**
Durdan Cotts. *UB1: S'hall* *44Ba* **85**
(off Denbigh Rd.)
Durdans Ho. *NW1* *38Kb* **70**
(off Farrier St.)
Durdans Rd. UB1: S'hall 44Ba **85**
Durell Gdns. RM9: Dag 36Zc **75**
Durell Ho. *SE16* *47Zb* **92**
(off Wolfe Cres.)
Durell Rd. RM9: Dag 36Zc **75**
Durfey Pl. SE5 52Tb **113**
Durfold Dr. RH2: Reig 6L **207**
Durford Cres. SW15 60Xa **110**
Durham Av. BR2: Brom 70Hc **137**
IG8: Buck H, Wfd G 22Mc **53**
RM2: Rom 28Ld **57**
SL1: Slou 4E **80**
TW5: Hest 50Ba **85**
Durham Cl. SW20 68Xa **132**
Durham Ct. KT22: Lea 94Ja **192**
NW6 *40Cb* **69**
(off Kilburn Pk. Rd.)
TW11: Tedd 63Ga **130**
Durham Hill BR1: Brom 63Hc **137**
Durham Ho. BR2: Brom 70Gc **137**
IG11: Bark *38Wc* **75**
(off Margaret Bondfield Av.)
NW8 4D **214**
RM10: Dag 36Ed **76**
WD6: Bore *12Qa* **29**
(off Canterbury Rd.)
Durham Ho. St. WC2 5G **223**
Durham Pl. IG1: Ilf 35Sc **74**
SW3 7F **227** (50Hb **89**)
Durham Ri. SE18 50Sc **94**
Durham Rd. BR2: Brom 69Hc **137**
DA14: Sidc 64Xc **139**
E12 35Mc **73**
E16 42Gc **93**
HA1: Harr 29Da **45**
N2 27Gb **49**
N7 33Pb **70**
N9 19Wb **33**
RM10: Dag 36Ed **76**
SW20 67Xa **132**
TW14: Felt 59Y **107**
W5 48Ma **87**
WD6: Bore 13Sa **29**
Durham Row E1 43Ac **92**
Durham St. SE11 50Pb **90**
Durham Ter. W2 44Db **89**
Durham Wharf Dr. TW8: Bford 52La **108**
Durham Yd. E2 41Xb **91**
Duriun Way DA8: Erith 52Kd **119**
Durleston Pk. Dr. KT23: Bookh 97Ea **192**
Durley Av. HA5: Pinn 31Aa **65**
Durley Gdns. BR6: Chels 76Xc **161**
Durley Rd. N16 31Ub **71**
Durlings Orchard TN15: Igh 93Zd **205**
Durlston Rd. E5 33Wb **71**
KT2: King T 65Na **131**
Durndale La. DA11: Nflt 3A **144**
Durnell Way IG10: Lough 13Qc **36**
Durnford Ho. SE6 62Ec **136**
SL4: Eton *1H* **103**
(off Slough Rd.)
Durnford St. N15 29Ub **51**
SE10 51Ec **114**
Durninge Wlk. RM16: Grays 45De **99**
Durning Pl. SL5: Asc 9A **124**
Durning Rd. SE19 64Tb **135**
Durnsford Av. SW19 61Cb **133**
Durnsford Ct. *EN3: Enf H* *13Ac* **34**
(off Enstone Rd.)
Durnsford Rd. N11 25Mb **50**
SW19 61Cb **133**
Durrant Ct. HA3: Hrw W 26Ga **46**
Durrant Ho. EC1 7G **219**
Durrants Cl. RM13: Rain 40Ld **77**
Durrants Dr. WD3: Crox G 13S **26**
Durrants Hill Rd. HP3: Hem H 5M **3**
Durrants Ho. WD3: Crox G 13R **26**
Durrant Way BR6: Farnb 78Tc **160**
DA10: Swans 59Ae **121**
Durrell Rd. SW6 53Bb **111**
Durrell Way TW17: Shep 72T **150**
Durrels Ho. *W14* *49Bb* **89**
(off Warwick Gdns.)
Durrington Av. SW20 66Ya **132**
Durrington Pk. Rd. SW20 67Ya **132**
Durrington Rd. E5 35Ac **72**
Durrington Twr. SW8 54Lb **112**
Durrisdeer Ho. *NW2* *35Bb* **69**
(off Lyndale)
Dursley Cl. SE3 54Lc **115**
Dursley Gdns. SE3 53Mc **115**
Dursley Rd. SE3 54Lc **115**
Durward Ho. *W8* *47Db* **89**
(off Kensington Ct.)
Durward St. E1 43Xb **91**
Durweston M. W1 7G **215**
Durweston St. W1 1G **221** (43Hb **89**)
Duty Falls Cl. RM11: Horn 32Qd **77**
Dury Falls Cl. RM5: Col R 26Ed **56**
Dury Rd. EN5: Barn 11Bb **31**
Dutch Barn Cl. TW19: Stanw 58M **105**
Dutch Elm Av. SL4: Wind 2K **103**
Dutch Gdns. KT2: King T 65Ra **131**
Dutch Yd. SW18 57Cb **111**
Dutton St. SE10 53Ec **114**
Dutton Way SL0: Iver 44G **82**
Duval Ho. *N19* *33Mb* **70**
(off Ashbrook Rd.)
Duxberry Av. TW13: Felt 62Y **129**
Duxberry Cl. BR2: Brom 71Nc **160**
Duxford Cl. RM12: Horn 37Ld **77**
Duxford Ho. *SE2* *47Zc* **95**
(off Wolvercote Rd.)
Dux Hill TN15: Plax 98Be **205**
Dux La. TN15: Plax 98Be **205**
Duxons Turn HP2: Hem H 1B **4**
Dwelly La. TN8: Eden 9M **211**
Dwight Rd. WD18: Wat 17T **26**
Dye Ho. La. E3 39Cc **72**
Dyer Ho. TW12: Hamp 67Da **129**
Dyer's Bldgs. EC1 1K **223** (43Qb **90**)
Dyers Hall Rd. E11 32Gc **73**
Dyers Hill Rd. E11 33Fc **73**
Dyers La. SW15 56Xa **110**
Dyers Way RM3: Rom 24Kd **57**
Dyke Dr. BR5: Orp 73Yc **161**
Dykes Path GU21: Wok 87E **168**
Dykes Way BR2: Brom 69Hc **137**
Dykewood Cl. DA5: Bexl 62Fd **140**
Dylan Cl. WD6: E'tree 17Ma **29**
Dylan Rd. DA17: Belv 48Cd **96**
SE24 56Rb **113**
Dylways SE5 56Tb **113**
Dymchurch Cl. BR6: Orp 77Uc **160**
IG5: Ilf 26Qc **54**
Dymes Path SW19 61Za **132**
Dymock St. SW6 55Db **111**
Dymoke Rd. RM11: Horn 31Hd **76**
Dyneley Rd. SE12 62Lc **137**
Dyne Rd. NW6 38Ab **68**
Dynes, The TN15: Kems'g 89Md **183**
Dynes Rd. TN15: Kems'g 89Md **183**
Dynevor Rd. N16 34Ub **71**
TW10: Rich 57Na **109**
Dynham Rd. NW6 38Cb **69**
Dyott St. WC1 2E **222** (44Mb **90**)
Dyrham La. EN5: Barn 8Wa **16**
Dyrham Pk. 10Wa **16**
Dyrham Pk. Country Club & Golf Course 9Xa **16**
Dysart Av. KT2: King T 64La **130**
Dysart St. EC2 6H **219** (42Tb **91**)
Dyson Cl. SL4: Wind 5F **102**
Dyson Ct. HA0: Wemb 35Ja **66**
NW2 32Ya **68**
WD17: Wat 14Y **27**
Dyson Ho. *SE10* *50Hc* **93**
(off Blackwall La.)
Dyson Rd. E11 30Gc **53**
E15 37Hc **73**
Dysons Cl. EN8: Walt C 5Zb **20**
Dysons Rd. N18 22Xb **51**
Dytchleys La. CM14: N'side 14Qd **39**
Dytchleys Rd. CM14: N'side 14Pd **39**

E

Eade Rd. N4 31Sb **71**
Eagans Cl. N2 27Fb **49**
Eagle Av. RM6: Chad H 30Ad **55**
Eagle Cl. EN3: Pond E 14Yb **34**
EN9: Walt A 6Jc **21**
RM12: Horn 37Kd **77**
SE16 50Yb **92**
SM6: Wall 79Nb **156**
Eagle Ct. E11 28Jc **53**
EC1 7B **218** (43Rb **91**)
Eagle Dr. NW9 26Ua **48**
Eagle Dwellings EC1 3E **218**
Eagle Hgts. SW11 55Gb **111**
Eagle Heights Wildlife Pk. 75Kd **163**
Eagle Hill SE19 65Tb **135**
Eagle Ho. *E1* *42Xb* **91**
(off Headlam St.)
N1 1F **219**
RM17: Grays 51Be **121**
Eagle Ho. M. SW4 57Lb **112**
Eagle La. E11 28Jc **53**
Eagle Lodge NW11 31Bb **69**
Eagle Mans. *N16* *36Vb* **71**
(off Salcombe Rd.)
Eagle M. N1 37Ub **71**
Eagle Pl. SW1 5C **222**
SW7 7A **226** (50Eb **89**)
Eagle Rd. HA0: Wemb 38Ma **67**
SL1: Slou 5D **80**
TW6: H'row A 55V **106**
Eagles Dr. TN16: Tats 90Mc **179**
Eaglesfield Equestrian Cen. 76Zd **165**
Eaglesfield Rd. SE18 53Rc **116**
Eagles Rd. DA9: Ghithe 56Xd **120**
Eaglestone Ct. TN15: Bor G 91Ce **205**
Eagle St. WC1 1H **223** (43Pb **90**)
Eagle Ter. IG8: Wfd G 24Kc **53**
Eagle Trad. Est. CR4: Mitc 72Hb **155**
Eagle Way AL10: Hat 2C **8**
CM13: Gt War 23Xd **58**
DA11: Nflt 57Ce **121**
Eagle Wharf Ct. SE1 7K **225**
Eagle Wharf E. *E14* *45Ac* **92**
(off Narrow St.)
Eagle Wharf Rd. N1 1E **218** (40Sb **71**)
Eagle Wharf W. *E14* *45Ac* **92**
(off Narrow St.)
Eagle Works E. E1 6K **219**
Eagle Works W. E1 6K **219**
Eagling Cl. E3 41Cc **92**
Ealdham Sq. SE9 56Lc **115**
EALING 45Ma **87**
Ealing B'way. Cen. W5 45Ma **87**
Ealing Cl. WD6: Bore 11Ta **29**
EALING COMMON 45Pa **87**
Ealing Driving Range 39Ca **65**
Ealing Golf Course 41Ka **86**
Ealing Grn. W5 46Ma **87**
Ealing Pk. Gdns. W5 49La **86**
Ealing Pk. Mans. *W5* *48Ma* **87**
(off Sth. Ealing Rd.)
Ealing Rd. HA0: Wemb 37Na **67**
TW8: Bford 49Ma **87**
UB5: N'olt 39Ca **65**
Ealing Squash & Fitness Club 44Na **87**
Ealing Studios 46Ma **87**
Ealing Village W5 44Na **87**
Eamont Cl. HA4: Ruis 31R **64**
Eamont Ct. NW8 1E **214**
Eamont St. NW8 1D **214** (40Gb **69**)
Eardemont Cl. DA1: Cray 56Hd **118**
Eardley Cres. SW5 50Cb **89**
Eardley Point *SE18* *49Rc* **94**
(off Wilmount St.)
Eardley Rd. DA17: Belv 50Cd **96**
SW16 64Lb **134**
TN13: S'oaks 96Kd **203**
Earhart Way TW6: Cran, H'row A 55W **106**
Earl Cl. N11 22Kb **50**
Earldom Rd. SW15 56Ya **110**
Earle Gdns. KT2: King T 66Na **131**
Earle Ho. SW1 6E **228**
Earleswood KT11: Cobh 84Aa **171**
Earleswood Ct. HP3: Hem H 6M **3**
Earleydene SL5: Asc 4A **146**
Earlham Ct. E11 31Hc **73**
Earlham Gro. E7 36Hc **73**
N22 24Pb **50**
Earlham St. WC2 3E **222** (44Nb **90**)
Earl Ho. NW1 6E **214**
Earlom Ho. WC1 4K **217**
Earl Ri. SE18 50Tc **94**
Earl Rd. DA11: Nflt 1A **144**
SW14 56Sa **109**
Earlsbrook Rd. RH1: Redh 8P **207**
(not continuous)
Earlsbury Gdns. HA8: Edg 21Qa **47**
Earls Cnr. EN6: S Mim 5Wa **16**
EARL'S COURT 49Db **89**
Earls Court Exhibition Building 50Cb **89**
Earl's Ct. Gdns. SW5 49Db **89**
Earls Ct. Rd. SW5 48Cb **89**
W8 48Cb **89**
Earl's Ct. Sq. SW5 50Db **89**
Earls Cres. HA1: Harr 28Ga **46**
Earlsdown Ho. IG11: Bark 40Tc **74**
Earlsferry Way N1 38Nb **70**
(not continuous)
EARLSFIELD 60Eb **111**
Earlsfield Ho. *KT2: King T* *67Ma* **131**
(off Skerne Rd.)
Earlsfield Rd. SW18 60Eb **111**
Earlshall Rd. SE9 56Pc **116**
Earls Ho. TW9: Kew 52Ra **109**
Earls La. EN6: Ridge, S Mim 4Ua **16**
SL1: Slou 6D **80**
Earlsmead HA2: Harr 35Ca **65**
Earlsmead Rd. N15 29Vb **51**
NW10 41Ya **88**
Earlsmead Stadium 35Ba **65**
Earl's Path IG10: Lough 12Lc **35**
Earls Ter. W8 48Bb **89**
Earlsthorpe M. SW12 58Jb **112**
Earlsthorpe Rd. SE26 63Zb **136**
Earlstoke St. EC1 3B **218** (41Rb **91**)
Earlston Gro. E9 39Xb **71**
Earl St. EC2 7G **219** (43Tb **91**)
WD17: Wat 13Y **27**
Earls Wlk. RM8: Dag 35Xc **75**
W8 48Cb **89**
EARLSWOOD 8P **207**
Earlswood Av. CR7: Thor H 71Qb **156**
Earlswood Cl. SE10 51Gc **115**
Earlswood Common (Local Nature Reserve) 9M **207**
Earlswood Ct. RH1: Redh 8P **207**
Earlswood Gdns. IG5: Ilf 27Qc **54**
Earlswood Rd. RH1: Redh 7P **207**
Earlswood St. SE10 50Gc **93**
Early M. NW1 39Kb **70**
Earnshaw Ho. EC1 4C **218**
Earnshaw St. WC2 2E **222** (44Mb **90**)
Earsby St. W14 49Ab **88**
(not continuous)
Easby Cres. SM4: Mord 72Db **155**
Easebourne Rd. RM8: Dag 36Yc **75**
Easedale Dr. RM12: Horn 36Jd **76**
Easedale Ho. TW7: Isle 57Ha **108**
Eashing Point *SW15* *60Xa* **110**
(off Wanborough Dr.)
Easington Way RM15: S Ock 43Wd **98**
Easleys M. W1 2J **221** (44Jb **90**)
East 10 Ent. Pk. E10 32Ac **72**
EAST ACTON 45Va **88**
E. Acton Arc. W3 44Ua **88**
E. Acton Ct. W3 45Ua **88**
E. Acton La. W3 46Ua **88**
E. Arbour St. E1 44Zb **92**
East Av. E12 38Nc **74**
E17 28Dc **52**
KT12: W Vill 82V **170**
SM6: Wall 78Pb **156**
UB1: S'hall 45Ba **85**
UB3: Hayes 46V **84**
East Bank N16 31Ub **71**
E. Bank Cl. E17 29Dc **52**
Eastbank Rd. TW12: Hamp H 64Ea **130**
EAST BARNET 16Gb **31**
East Barnet Golf Course 13Db **31**
E. Barnet Rd. EN4: E Barn 14Fb **31**
E. Beckton District Cen. E6 45Pc **94**
EAST BEDFONT 59U **106**
East Block SE1 1J **229**
Eastbourne Av. W3 44Ta **87**
Eastbourne Gdns. SW14 55Sa **109**
Eastbourne M. W2 2A **220** (44Eb **89**)
Eastbourne Rd. E6 41Qc **94**
(not continuous)
E15 39Gc **73**
N15 30Ub **51**
RH9: G'stone, S God 4A **210**
SL1: Slou 4E **80**
SW17 65Jb **134**
TW8: Bford 50La **86**
TW13: Felt 61Z **129**
W4 51Sa **109**
Eastbourne Ter. W2 2A **220** (44Eb **89**)
Eastbournia Av. N9 20Xb **33**
Eastbridge SL2: Slou 7M **81**
Eastbrook Av. N9 17Yb **34**
RM10: Dag 35Ed **76**
Eastbrook Cl. GU21: Wok 88C **168**
RM10: Dag 35Ed **76**
Eastbrook Dr. RM7: Rush G 34Gd **76**
Eastbrookend Country Pk. 35Gd **76**
Eastbrook Rd. EN9: Walt A 5Gc **21**
SE3 53Kc **115**
Eastbrook Way HP2: Hem H 2N **3**
EAST BURNHAM 8E **60**
E. Burnham La. SL2: Farn R 9E **60**
EASTBURY 21V **44**
Eastbury Av. EN1: Enf 11Vb **33**
HA6: Nwood 22U **44**
IG11: Bark 39Uc **74**
Eastbury Ct. AL1: St A 1D **6**
EN5: New Bar *15Eb* **31**
(off Lyonsdown Rd.)
IG11: Bark 39Uc **74**
WD19: Wat 17Y **27**
Eastbury Farm Cl. HA6: Nwood 21U **44**
Eastbury Gro. W4 50Ua **88**
Eastbury Manor House 39Vc **75**
Eastbury Pl. HA6: Nwood 22V **44**
Eastbury Rd. BR5: Pet W 72Tc **160**
E6 42Qc **94**
HA6: Nwood 23U **44**
KT2: King T 66Na **131**
RM7: Rom 30Fd **56**
WD19: Wat 17X **27**
Eastbury Sq. IG11: Bark 39Vc **75**
Eastbury Ter. E1 42Zb **92**
Eastcastle St. W1 2B **222** (44Lb **90**)
Eastcheap EC3 4G **225** (45Ub **91**)
E. Churchfield Rd. W3 46Ta **87**
Eastchurch Rd. TW6: H'row A 54U **106**
East Cl. AL2: Chis G 7P **5**
EN4: Cockf 14Jb **32**
RM13: Rain 42Kd **97**
UB6: G'frd 40Ea **66**
W5 42Qa **87**
Eastcombe Av. SE7 51Kc **115**
East Comn. SL9: Ger X 30A **42**
EASTCOTE 31X **65**
Eastcote BR6: Orp 74Vc **161**
Eastcote Av. HA2: Harr 33Da **65**
KT8: W Mole 71Ba **151**
UB6: G'frd 36Ja **66**
Eastcote Hockey & Badminton Club 30V **44**
Eastcote Ho. KT17: Eps 84Ua **174**
Eastcote Ind. Est. HA4: Ruis 31Y **65**
Eastcote La. HA2: Harr 35Aa **65**
UB5: N'olt 36Ba **65**
(not continuous)
Eastcote La. Nth. UB5: N'olt 37Ba **65**
Eastcote Pl. HA5: Eastc 30X **45**
Eastcote Rd. DA16: Well 54Tc **116**
HA2: Harr 34Ea **66**
HA4: Ruis 31U **64**
HA5: Pinn 29Z **45**
Eastcote St. SW9 54Pb **112**
Eastcote Vw. HA5: Pinn 28Y **45**
EASTCOTE VILLAGE 29X **45**
Eastcott Cl. KT2: King T 64Sa **131**
East Ct. HA0: Wemb 33La **66**
East Cres. EN1: Enf 15Vb **33**
N11 21Hb **49**
SL4: Wind 3D **102**
East Cres. Rd. DA12: Grav'nd 8E **122**
Eastcroft SL2: Slou 2F **80**
Eastcroft Rd. KT19: Ewe 80Ua **154**
E. Cross Route E3 38Bc **72**
E9 36Bc **72**
(Crowfoot Cl.)
E9 38Bc **72**
(Wansbeck Rd.)
E10 36Bc **72**
Eastdean Av. KT18: Eps 85Ra **173**
E. Dene Dr. RM3: Rom 22Md **57**
Eastdown Ct. SE13 56Fc **115**
Eastdown Ho. E8 35Wb **71**
Eastdown Pk. SE13 56Fc **115**
East Dr. AL4: St A 1J **7**
BR5: St M Cry 72Xc **161**
GU25: Vir W 3L **147**
HA6: Nwood 19U **26**
SL2: Stoke P 1J **81**
SM5: Cars 81Gb **175**
WD25: Wat 8X **13**
E. Duck Lees La. EN3: Pond E 14Ac **34**
EAST DULWICH 56Vb **113**
E. Dulwich Gro. SE22 57Ub **113**
E. Dulwich Rd. SE15 56Vb **113**
SE22 56Vb **113**
(not continuous)
East End Farm HA5: Pinn 27Ba **45**
East End Rd. N2 27Db **49**
N3 26Cb **49**
East End Way HA5: Pinn 27Aa **45**
East Entrance RM10: Dag 40Dd **76**
Easter Ind. Pk. RM13: Rain 45Gd **96**
Eastern App. IG11: Bark 39Wc **75**
Eastern Av. E11 30Kc **53**
EN8: Walt C 5Bc **20**
HA5: Pinn 31Z **65**
IG2: Ilf 30Rc **54**
IG4: Ilf 30Kc **53**
KT16: Chert 69J **127**
RM6: Chad H 28Xc **55**
RM15: Avel 46Sd **98**
RM20: W Thur 50Vd **98**
Eastern Av. E. RM1: Rom 27Fd **56**
RM2: Rom 27Fd **56**
RM3: Rom 27Fd **56**
Eastern Av. Retail Pk. RM7: Rom 28Ed **56**
Eastern Av. W. RM1: Rom 28Ad **55**
RM5: Rom 28Ad **55**
RM7: Chad H, Mawney, Rom 28Ad **55**
Eastern Bus. Pk. TW6: H'row A 54U **106**
Eastern Ct. *E15* *37Gc* **73**
(off Gt. Eastern Rd.)
Eastern Gateway E16 45Lc **93**
Eastern Ho. *E2* *41Xb* **91**
(off Bethnal Grn. Rd.)
Eastern Ind. Est. DA18: Erith 47Cd **96**
Eastern Path RM12: Horn 38Md **77**
RM13: Horn, Rain 39Ld **77**
Eastern Perimeter Rd.
TW6: H'row A 54V **106**
Eastern Quay Apartments *E16* *46Kc* **93**
(off Portsmouth M.)
Eastern Rd. E13 40Kc **73**
E17 29Ec **52**
N2 27Hb **49**
N22 25Nb **50**
RM1: Rom 29Gd **56**
(not continuous)
RM17: Grays 49Fe **99**
SE4 56Cc **114**
Eastern Rdbt. IG1: Ilf 33Sc **74**
Eastern Vw. TN16: Big H 89Lc **179**
Easternville Gdns. IG2: Ilf 30Sc **54**
Eastern Way DA17: Belv 47Wc **95**
DA18: Erith 47Wc **95**
RM17: Grays 51Ce **121**
SE2: Belv, Erith 47Wc **95**
SE28 47Wc **95**
Easter Way RH9: S God 9C **210**
EAST EWELL 82Ya **174**
E. Ferry Rd. E14 49Dc **92**
Eastfield Av. WD24: Wat 11Z **27**
Eastfield Cl. SL1: Slou 8L **81**
Eastfield Gdns. RM10: Dag 35Cd **76**
Eastfield Rd. CM14: B'wood 19Zd **41**
E17 28Cc **52**
EN3: Enf W 10Zb **20**
EN8: Walt C 3Bc **20**
N8 27Nb **50**
RH1: Redh 7C **208**
RM9: Dag 35Bd **75**
RM10: Dag 35Bd **75**
Eastfields HA5: Eastc 29Y **45**
Eastfields Av. SW18 56Cb **111**
Eastfields Rd. CR4: Mitc 68Jb **134**
W3 43Sa **87**
Eastfield St. E14 43Ac **92**
EAST FINCHLEY 28Gb **49**
East Flint HP1: Hem H 1H **3**
(not continuous)
East Gdns. GU22: Wok 89E **168**
SW17 65Gb **133**
Eastgate SM7: Bans 86Bb **175**
Eastgate Bus. Pk. E10 32Ac **72**
Eastgate Cl. SE28 44Zc **95**
Eastglade HA5: Pinn 27Ba **45**
HA6: Nwood 22V **44**
East Grn. HP3: Hem H 7P **3**
E. Hall La. RM13: Wenn 44Md **97**
E. Hall Rd. BR5: St M Cry 73Ad **161**
EAST HAM 40Pc **74**
E. Ham & Barking By-Pass
IG11: Bark 40Tc **74**
Eastham Cl. EN5: Barn 15Ab **30**
Eastham Cres. CM13: B'wood 21Ce **59**
E. Ham Ind. Est. E6 42Nc **94**
East Ham Leisure Cen. 39Pc **74**
E. Ham Mnr. Way E6 44Qc **94**
East Ham Nature Reserve 42Pc **94**
East Ham Nature Reserve Vis. Cen. 42Pc **94**
E. Harding St. EC4 2A **224** (44Qb **90**)
E. Heath Rd. NW3 34Eb **69**
EAST HILL 82Rd **183**
East Hill CR2: Sande 82Ub **177**
DA1: Dart 59Pd **119**
DA4: S Dar 67Sd **142**
GU22: Wok 88E **168**
HA9: Wemb 33Qa **67**
RH8: Oxt 1J **211**
SW18 57Db **111**
TN16: Big H 90Kc **179**
East Hill Ct. RH8: Oxt 2J **211**
East Hill Dr. DA1: Dart 59Pd **119**
East Hill Farm Caravan Pk.
TN15: Knat 82Rd **183**
East Hill Pk. TN15: Knat 82Rd **183**
East Hill Rd. RH8: Oxt 1J **211**
TN15: Knat 82Rd **183**
Eastholm NW11 28Db **49**
East Holme DA8: Erith 53Fd **118**
Eastholme UB3: Hayes 46W **84**
EAST HORNDON 28Fe **59**
EAST HORSLEY 100V **190**
E. India Bldgs. *E14* *45Cc* **92**
(off Saltwell St.)
E. India Ct. *SE16* *47Yb* **92**
(off St Marychurch St.)
East India Dock Basin Nature Reserve 45Gc **93**
E. India Dock Ho. E14 44Ec **92**
E. India Dock Rd. E14 44Cc **92**
E. India Way CR0: C'don 74Vb **157**
E. Kent Av. DA11: Nflt 58Ee **121**
Eastlake Ho. NW8 6C **214**
Eastlake Rd. SE5 54Sb **113**
Eastlands Cl. RH8: Oxt 99Fc **199**
Eastlands Cres. SE21 58Vb **113**
Eastlands Way RH8: Oxt 99Fc **199**
East La. DA4: S Dar 68Td **142**
HA0: Wemb 34Ka **66**
HA9: Wemb 34Ka **66**
KT1: King T 69Ma **131**
KT24: W Hor 98S **190**
SE16 47Wb **91**
(Chambers St.)
SE16 47Wb **91**
(Scott Lidgett Cres.)
WD5: Ab L, Bedm 10F **4**
WD25: Wat 1W **12**
East La. Bus. Pk. HA9: Wemb 33Ma **67**
Eastlea Av. WD25: Wat 9Aa **13**
Eastlea M. E16 42Gc **93**
Eastleigh Av. HA2: Harr 33Da **65**
Eastleigh Cl. NW2 34Ua **68**
SM2: Sutt 80Db **155**
Eastleigh Rd. DA7: Bex 55Ed **118**
E17 26Bc **52**
Eastleigh Wlk. SW15 59Wa **110**
Eastleigh Way TW14: Felt 60W **106**
East Lodge *E16* *46Jc* **93**
(off Wesley Av.)
E. Lodge La. EN2: Crew H, Enf 8Mb **18**
E. London Crematorium
E13 41Hc **93**
East London Gymnastic Cen. 44Pc **94**
EASTLY END 69G **126**
East Mall *RM17: Grays* *51De* **121**
(off Grays Shop. Cen.)
TW18: Staines *63H* **127**
(in The Elmsleigh Cen.)
Eastman Ho. SW4 58Lb **112**
Eastman Rd. W3 47Ta **87**
Eastman Way KT19: Eps 82Ra **173**
East Mead HA4: Ruis 34Z **65**
Eastmead GU21: Wok 9M **167**
Eastmead Av. UB6: G'frd 41Da **85**
Eastmead Cl. BR1: Brom 68Nc **138**
Eastmearn Rd. SE21 61Sb **135**
East Mill DA11: Grav'nd 8B **122**
E. Milton Rd. DA12: Grav'nd 9F **122**
East Mimms HP2: Hem H 1N **3**
EAST MOLESEY 70Fa **130**
Eastmont Rd. KT10: Hin W 75Ga **152**
Eastmoor Pl. SE7 48Mc **93**
Eastmoor St. SE7 48Mc **93**

East Mt. St. E1 43Xb 91
(not continuous)
Eastney Rd. CR0: C'don 74Rb 157
Eastney St. SE10 50Fc 93
Eastnor HP3: Bov 10C 2
Eastnor Cl. RH2: Reig 8H 207
Eastnor Pl. RH2: Reig 8J 207
Eastnor Rd. RH2: Reig 9J 207
SE9 60Sc 116
Eastone Apartments *E1* 43Vb 91
(off Lolesworth Cl.)
Easton Gdns. WD6: Bore 14Ua 30
Easton St. WC1 5K 217 (42Qb 90)
East Pk. Cl. RM6: Chad H 29Zc 55
East Parkside CR6: W'ham 88Cc 178
SE10 47Gc 93
East Pas. EC1 7C 218
East Pl. SE27 63Sb 135
East Point SE1 50Wb 91
E. Pole Cotts. N14 14Mb 32
E. Poultry Av. EC1 1B 224 (43Rb 91)
East Ramp TW6: H'row A 53R 106
East Ridgeway EN6: Cuff 1Nb 18
East Rd. DA16: Well 54Xc 117
E15 39Jc 73
EN3: Enf W 10Yb 20
EN4: E Barn 18Jb 32
HA1: Harr 31Ka 66
HA8: Edg 25Ra 47
KT2: King T 67Na 131
KT13: Weyb 80T 150
N1 4F 219 (41Tb 91)
RH2: Reig 5H 207
RM6: Chad H 29Ad 55
RM7: Rush G 31Fd 76
SW3 7H 227 (50Jb 90)
SW19 65Eb 133
TW14: Bedf 59T 106
UB7: W Dray 49P 83
E. Rochester Way DA5: Bexl 57Uc 116
DA15: Bexl, Sidc 57Uc 116
East Row E11 30Jc 53
W10 42Ab 88
Eastry Av. BR2: Hayes 72Hc 159
Eastry Ho. *SW8* 52Nb 112
(off Hartington Rd.)
Eastry Rd. DA8: Erith 52Cd 118
EAST SHEEN 56Sa 109
E. Sheen Av. SW14 57Ta 109
East Side *W12* 47Ya 88
(off Shepherd's Bush Mkt.)
Eastside Halls SW7 3C 226
Eastside M. *E3* 40Cc 72
(off Morville St.)
Eastside Rd. NW11 28Bb 49
East Smithfield E1 5K 225 (45Vb 91)
East Sq. E10 31Dc 72
East Stand N5 34Rb 71
East St. BR1: Brom 68Jc 137
DA7: Bex 56Cd 118
HP2: Hem H 2M 3
IG11: Bark 39Sc 74
KT17: Eps 85Ua 174
KT23: Bookh 97Da 191
RM17: Grays 51Ee 121
RM20: Grays 51Ae 121
SE17 7E 230 (50Sb 91)
(not continuous)
TW8: Bford 52La 108
E. Surrey Gro. SE15 52Vb 113
East Surrey Mus. 96Vb 197
E. Tenter St. E1 44Vb 91
East Ter. DA12: Grav'nd 8E 122
DA15: Sidc 60Uc 116
SL4: Wind 3J 103
E. Thamesmead Bus. Pk.
DA18: Erith 47Bd 95
E. Thurrock Rd. RM17: Grays 51Ee 121
EAST TILBURY 9K 101
E. Tilbury Rd. SS17: Linf 7J 101
East Twr. *E14* 47Dc 92
(off Pan Peninsula Sq.)
East Towers HA5: Pinn 29Z 45
East Va. W3 46Va 88
East Vw. E4 22Ec 52
EN5: Barn 12Bb 31
Eastview Av. SE18 52Uc 116
Eastville Av. NW11 30Bb 49
East Wlk. EN4: E Barn 17Jb 32
RH2: Reig 6K 207
UB3: Hayes 46W 84
East Way BR2: Hayes 73Jc 159
CR0: C'don 75Ac 158
E11 29Kc 53
HA4: Ruis 32W 64
UB3: Hayes 46W 84
Eastway E9 37Bc 72
(not continuous)
KT19: Eps 83Ta 173
SM4: Mord 71Za 154
SM6: Wall 77Lb 156
Eastway Cres. HA2: Harr 33Da 65
Eastwell Cl. BR3: Beck 66Ac 136
Eastwell Ho. SE1 3G 231
Eastwick Cres. WD3: Rick 19H 25
Eastwick Dr. KT23: Bookh 95Ca 191
EAST WICKHAM 53Yc 117
Eastwick Pk. Av.
KT23: Bookh 96Da 191
Eastwick Rd. KT12: Hers 79X 151
KT23: Bookh 97Da 191
Eastwick Row HP2: Hem H 3A 4
East Wintergarden 46Dc 92
(off Bank St.)
East Wood WD25: A'ham 8Da 13
Eastwood *KT13: Weyb* 79T 150
(off Bridgewater Rd.)
Eastwood Cl. E18 26Jc 53
N7 36Qb 70
N17 24Xb 51
Eastwood Ct. HP2: Hem H 1A 4
Eastwood Dr. RM13: Rain 44Kd 97
Eastwood Rd. E18 26Jc 53
IG3: Ilf 32Wc 75
N10 26Jb 50
UB7: W Dray 47Q 84
East Woodside DA5: Bexl 59Ad 117
Eastwood St. SW16 65Lb 134
EASTWORTH 74K 149
Eastworth Rd. KT16: Chert 74J 149
Eatington Rd. E10 29Fc 53
Eaton Av. SL1: Slou 5A 80
Eaton Cl. HA7: Stan 21Ka 46
SW1 6H 227 (49Jb 90)
Eaton Ct. E18 26Jc 53
HA8: Edg 21Qa 47
Eaton Dr. KT2: King T 66Qa 131
RM5: Col R 24Dd 56
SW9 56Rb 113
Eaton Gdns. RM9: Dag 38Ad 75
Eaton Ga. HA6: Nwood 23S 44
SW1 5H 227 (49Jb 90)
Eaton Ho. *E14* 45Bc 92
(off Westferry Cir.)
SW11 53Fb 111
Eaton La. SW1 4A 228 (48Kb 90)
Eaton Mans. SW1 6H 227
Eaton M. Nth. SW1 5H 227 (49Jb 90)
Eaton M. Sth. SW1 5J 227 (49Jb 90)
Eaton M. W. SW1 5J 227 (49Jb 90)
Eaton Pk. KT11: Cobh 86Aa 171
Eaton Pk. Rd. KT11: Cobh 86Aa 171
N13 19Qb 32
Eaton Pl. CR3: Cat'm 94Tb 197
SW1 4H 227 (49Jb 90)
Eaton Ri. E11 29Lc 54
W5 43Ma 87
Eaton Rd. AL1: St A 2F 6
DA14: Sidc 61Zc 139
EN1: Enf 14Ub 33
NW4 29Ya 48
RM14: Upm 33Ud 78
SM2: Sutt 79Fb 155
TW3: Houn 56Fa 108
Eaton Row SW1 4K 227 (48Kb 90)
Eatons Mead E4 19Cc 34
Eaton Sq. DA3: Lfield 69Zd 143
SW1 5H 227 (49Jb 90)
Eaton Ter. E3 41Ac 92
SW1 5H 227 (49Jb 90)
Eaton Ter. M. SW1 5H 227
Eatonville Rd. SW17 61Hb 133
Eatonville Vs. SW17 61Hb 133
Eaton Way WD6: Bore 11Pa 29
Eaves Cl. KT15: Add 79L 149
Ebbage Ct. GU22: Wok 90A 168
Ebbas Way KT18: Eps 87Ra 173
Ebb Ct. E16 45Sc 94
Ebberns Rd. HP3: Hem H 5M 3
Ebbett Ct. W3 43Ta 87
Ebbisham Cen., The KT19: Eps 85Ta 173
Ebbisham Dr. SW8 51Pb 112
Ebbisham La.
KT20: Eps D, Tad, Walt H 93Va 194
Ebbisham Rd. KT4: Wor Pk 75Ya 154
KT18: Eps 86Ra 173
Ebbisham Sports Club 83Sa 173
EBBSFLEET 59Ce 121
Ebbsfleet Gateway DA10: Ebbs 60Ce 121
Ebbsfleet Ind. Est. DA11: Nflt 57Ce 121
Ebbsfleet Rd. NW2 36Ab 68
Ebbsfleet United FC 57Ce 121
Ebbsfleet Wlk. DA11: Nflt 58De 121
Ebdon Way SE3 55Kc 115
Ebenezer Ho. SE11 6A 230 (49Rb 91)
Ebenezer Mussel Ho. *E2* 40Yb 72
(off Patriot Sq.)
Ebenezer St. N1 3F 219 (41Tb 91)
Ebenezer Wlk. SW16 67Lb 134
Ebley Cl. SE15 51Vb 113
Ebner St. SW18 57Db 111
Ebony Ho. *E2* 41Wb 91
(off Buckfast St.)
Ebor Cotts. SW15 62Ua 132
Ebor St. E1 5K 219 (42Vb 91)
Ebrington Rd. HA3: Kenton 30Ma 47
Ebsworth St. SE23 59Zb 114
Eburne Rd. N7 34Nb 70
Ebury App. WD3: Rick 18M 25
Ebury Bri. SW1 7K 227 (50Kb 90)
Ebury Bri. Est. SW1 7K 227 (50Kb 90)
Ebury Bri. Rd. SW1 7J 227 (50Jb 90)
Ebury Cl. BR2: Kes 76Nc 160
HA6: Nwood 22S 44
Ebury M. N5 34Sb 71
SE27 62Rb 135
SW1 5J 227 (49Kb 90)
Ebury M. E. SW1 5K 227 (48Kb 90)
Ebury Rd. WD3: Rick 18M 25
WD17: Wat 13Y 27
Ebury Rdbt. WD3: Rick 18M 25
Ebury Sq. SW1 6J 227 (49Jb 90)
Ebury St. SW1 6J 227 (49Jb 90)
Ecclesbourne Apartments *N1* 38Tb 71
(off Ecclesbourne Rd.)
Ecclesbourne Cl. N13 22Qb 50
Ecclesbourne Gdns. N13 22Qb 50
Ecclesbourne Rd. CR7: Thor H 71Sb 157
N1 38Sb 71
Eccleshill *BR2: Brom* 70Hc 137
(off Durham Rd.)
Eccles Rd. SW11 56Hb 111
Eccleston Bri. SW1 5A 228 (49Kb 90)
Eccleston Cl. BR6: Orp 74Tc 160
EN4: Cockf 14Hb 31
Eccleston Cres. RM6: Chad H 31Xc 75
Ecclestone Ct. HA9: Wemb 36Na 67
Ecclestone M. HA9: Wemb 36Na 67
Ecclestone Pl. HA9: Wemb 36Pa 67
Eccleston Ho. SW2 58Qb 112
Eccleston M. SW1 4J 227 (48Jb 90)
Eccleston Pl. SW1 6K 227 (49Kb 90)
Eccleston Rd. W13 45Ja 86
Eccleston Sq. SW1 6A 228 (49Kb 90)
(not continuous)
Eccleston Sq. M. SW1 6A 228 (49Kb 90)
Eccleston St. SW1 4J 227 (48Kb 90)
Echelforde Dr. TW15: Ashf 63Q 128
Echo Ct. DA12: Grav'nd 1E 144
Echo Hgts. E4 18Dc 34
Echo Sq. DA12: Grav'nd 1E 144
Eckford St. N1 1K 217 (40Qb 70)
Eckington Ho. *N15* 30Tb 51
(off Fladbury Rd.)
Eckstein Rd. SW11 56Gb 111
Eclipse, The KT10: Esh 75Da 151
Eclipse Bldg. *N1* 37Qb 70
(off Laycock St.)
Eclipse Ho. *N22* 26Pb 50
(off Station Rd.)
Eclipse Ind. Est. KT19: Eps 85Sa 173
Eclipse Rd. E13 43Kc 93
Ecology Centre and Arts Pavilion 41Ac 92
Ecton Rd. KT15: Add 77K 149
Ector Rd. SE6 61Gc 137
Edam Ct. DA15: Sidc 62Wc 139
Edans Ct. W12 47Va 88
Edar Ho. CR0: New Ad 79Dc 158
Edbrooke Rd. W9 42Bb 89
Eddinton Cl. CR0: New Ad 79Ec 158
Eddisbury Ho. SE26 62Wb 135
Eddiscombe Rd. SW6 54Bb 111
Eddy Cl. RM7: Rom 30Dd 56
Eddystone Rd. SE4 57Ac 114
Eddystone Twr. SE8 50Ac 92
Eddystone Wlk. TW19: Stanw 59N 105
Ede Cl. TW3: Houn 55Ba 107
Ede Ct. *KT17: Eps* 84Va 174
(off East St.)
Edenbridge Cl. BR5: St M Cry 70Zc 139
SE16 50Xb 91
(off Masters Dr.)
Edenbridge Rd. E9 38Zb 72
EN1: Enf 16Ub 33
Eden Cl. DA5: Bexl 63Fd 140
EN3: Enf L 10Cc 20
HA0: Wemb 39Ma 67
KT15: New H 82K 169
NW3 33Cb 69
SL3: L'ly 50C 82
W8 48Cb 89
Eden Ct. IG6: Ilf 24Tc 54
Edencourt Rd. SW16 65Kb 134
Edendale W3 45Ra 87
Edendale Rd. DA7: Bex 53Fd 118
Edenfield Gdns. KT4: Wor Pk 76Va 154
Eden Grn. RM15: S Ock 43Xd 98
Eden Gro. E17 29Dc 52
N7 36Pb 70
NW10 37Xa 68
Eden Gro. Rd. KT14: Byfl 85N 169
Edenhall Cl. HP2: Hem H 3D 4
RM3: Rom 22Ld 57
Edenhall Glen RM3: Rom 22Ld 57
Edenhall Rd. RM3: Rom 22Ld 57
Edenham Way W10 42Bb 89
Eden Ho. NW8 6D 214
SE8 52Cc 114
(off Deptford High St.)
SE16 47Zb 92
(off Water Gdns. Sq.)
Edenhurst TN13: S'oaks 97Jd 202
Edenhurst Av. SW6 55Bb 111
Eden Lodge NW6 38Za 68
Eden M. SW17 62Eb 133
EDEN PARK 71Cc 158
Eden Pk. Av. BR3: Beck 70Ac 136
Eden Pl. DA12: Grav'nd 9D 122
SL5: S'dale 3E 146
Eden Rd. BR3: Beck 70Ac 136
CR0: C'don 77Tb 157
DA5: Bexl 63Ed 140
E17 29Dc 52
SE27 63Rb 135
Edenside Rd. KT23: Bookh 96Ba 191
Edensor Gdns. W4 52Ua 110
Edensor Rd. W4 52Ua 110
Eden St. KT1: King T 68Ma 131
Edenvale EN7: G Oak 1Xb 19
Edenvale Cl. CR4: Mitc 66Jb 134
Edenvale Rd. CR4: Mitc 66Jb 134
Edenvale St. SW6 54Eb 111
Eden Wlk. KT1: King T 68Na 131
Eden Way BR3: Beck 71Bc 158
CR6: W'ham 90Ac 178
E3 39Bc 72
Ederline Av. SW16 69Pb 134
Edes Flds. RH2: Reig 8G 206
Edgar Cl. BR8: Swan 69Hd 140
Edgar Ct. KT3: N Mald 68Ua 132
Edgar Ho. *E9* 36Ac 72
(off Homerton Rd.)
E11 31Jc 73
SW8 52Nb 112
(off Wyvil Rd.)
Edgar Kail Way SE22 56Ub 113
Edgarley Ter. SW6 53Ab 110
Edgar Myles Ho. *E16* 43Hc 93
(off Ordnance Rd.)
Edgar Rd. CR2: Sande 81Tb 177
E3 41Dc 92
RM6: Chad H 31Zc 75
TN15: Kems'g 89Nd 183
TN16: Tats 93Mc 199
TW4: Houn 59Ba 107
UB7: Yiew 45N 83
Edgar Wallace Cl. SE15 52Ub 113
Edgar Wright Ct. *SW6* 52Bb 111
(off Dawes Rd.)
Edgbaston Dr. WD7: Shenl 4Na 15
Edgbaston Rd. WD19: Wat 20X 27
Edgcott Ho. *W10* 43Ya 88
(off Sutton Way)
Edge, The *SE8* 52Bc 114
(off Glenville Gro.)
Edge Apartments E15 38Fc 73
Edgeborough Way BR1: Brom 66Mc 137
Edgebury BR7: Chst 63Rc 138
Edgebury Wlk. BR7: Chst 63Sc 138
Edge Bus. Centre, The NW2 33Xa 68
Edge Cl. KT13: Weyb 80Q 150
Edgecombe Ho. SE5 54Ub 113
SW19 60Ab 110
Edgecoombe CR2: Sels 80Yb 158
Edgecoombe Cl. KT2: King T 66Ta 131
Edgecote Cl. W3 46Sa 87
Edgecot Gro. N15 29Ub 51
Edgefield Av. IG11: Bark 38Vc 75
Edgefield Cl. DA1: Dart 60Rd 119
RH1: Redh 10A 208
Edgefield Ct. *IG11: Bark* 38Vc 75
(off Edgefield Av.)
Edge Hill SE18 51Rc 116
SW19 66Za 132
Edge Hill Av. N3 28Cb 49
Edge Hill Ct. DA14: Sidc 63Vc 139
SW19 66Za 132
Edgehill Ct. KT12: Walt T 74Y 151
Edgehill Gdns. DA13: Ist R 7B 144
RM10: Dag 35Cd 76
Edgehill Ho. SW9 54Rb 113
Edgehill Rd. BR7: Chst 62Sc 138
CR4: Mitc 67Kb 134
CR8: Purl 82Qb 176
W13 43La 86
Edgeley KT23: Bookh 96Aa 191
Edgeley La. SW4 55Mb 112
Edgeley Rd. SW4 55Mb 112
Edgell Cl. GU25: Vir W 69B 126
Edgell Rd. TW18: Staines 64H 127
Edgel St. SW18 56Db 111
Edge Point Cl. SE27 64Rb 135
Edge St. W8 46Cb 89
Edgewood Dr. BR6: Chels 79Vc 161
Edgewood Grn. CR0: C'don 74Zb 158
Edgeworth Av. NW4 29Wa 48
Edgeworth Cl. CR3: Whyt 90Wb 177
NW4 29Wa 48
Edgeworth Ct. *EN4: Cockf* 14Gb 31
(off Fordham Rd.)
Edgeworth Cres. NW4 29Wa 48
Edgeworth Ho. *NW8* 39Eb 69
(off Boundary Rd.)
Edgeworth Rd. EN4: Cockf 14Gb 31
SE9 56Lc 115
Edgington Rd. SW16 65Mb 134
Edgington Way DA14: Sidc 66Yc 139
Edgson Ho. SW1 7K 227
EDGWARE 23Qa 47
EDGWARE BURY 18Pa 29
Edgwarebury Gdns. HA8: Edg 22Qa 47
Edgwarebury La. HA8: Edg 18Pa 29
WD6: E'tree 17Na 29
Edgware Ct. HA8: Edg 23Qa 47
Edgware Rd. NW2 32Xa 68
NW9 26Sa 47
W2 6B 214 (42Fb 89)
Edgware Way HA8: Edg 21Pa 47
NW7 21Pa 47
WD6: E'tree 18Ma 29
Edinburgh Av. SL1: Slou 3E 80
WD3: Rick 16J 25
Edinburgh Cl. E2 40Yb 72
HA5: Pinn 31Z 65
UB10: Ick 35R 64
Edinburgh Ct. DA8: Erith 52Fd 118
KT1: King T 69Na 131
(off Watersplash Cl.)
SE16 46Zb 92
(off Rotherhithe St.)
SW20 71Za 154
Edinburgh Cres. EN8: Walt C 5Ac 20
Edinburgh Dr. TW18: Staines 65M 127
UB10: Ick 35R 64
WD5: Ab L 4W 12
Edinburgh Gdns. SL4: Wind 5H 103
Edinburgh Ga. SW1 1F 227 (47Hb 89)
UB9: Den 30H 43
Edinburgh Ho. NW4 27Ya 48
RM2: Rom 27Ld 57
W9 41Db 89
(off Maida Va.)
Edinburgh M. RM18: Tilb 4D 122
Edinburgh Rd. E13 40Kc 73
E17 29Cc 52
(not continuous)
N18 22Wb 51
SM1: Sutt 75Eb 155
W7 47Ha 86
Edington NW5 37Jb 70
Edington Rd. EN3: Enf H 12Yb 34
SE2 48Xc 95
Edison Av. RM12: Horn 32Hd 76
Edison Bldg. E14 47Cc 92
Edison Cl. AL4: St A 3G 6
E17 29Cc 52
RM12: Horn 32Gd 76
UB7: W Dray 47P 83
Edison Ct. *CR0: C'don* 73Rb 157
(off Campbell Rd.)
SE10 48Hc 93
(off Schoolbank Rd.)
W3 47Ua 88
WD18: Wat 16W 26
Edison Dr. HA9: Wemb 34Na 67
UB1: S'hall 44Da 85
Edison Gro. SE18 52Vc 117
Edison Ho. *HA9: Wemb* 34Sa 67
(off Barnhill Rd.)
SE1 5F 231
Edison Rd. BR2: Brom 68Jc 137
DA16: Well 53Vc 117
EN3: Brim 12Bc 34
N8 30Mb 50
Edison's Pk. DA2: Dart 55Td 120
Edis St. NW1 39Jb 70
Editha Mans. *SW10* 51Eb 111
(off Edith Gro.)
Edith Bell Ho. SL9: Chal P 23A 42
Edith Brinson Ho. *E14* 44Fc 93
(off Oban St.)
Edith Cavell Cl. N19 31Nb 70
Edith Cavell Ho. *E14* 44Dc 92
(off Sturry St.)
Edith Cavell Way SE18 53Nc 116
Edith Gdns. KT5: Surb 73Ra 153
Edith Gro. SW10 51Eb 111
Edith Ho. EN9: Walt A 5Dc 20
W6 50Ya 88
(off Queen Caroline St.)
Edithna St. SW9 55Nb 112
Edith Nesbit Wlk. SE9 57Pc 116
Edith Neville Cotts. NW1 3D 216
Edith Ramsay Ho. *E1* 43Ac 92
(off Duckett St.)
Edith Rd. BR6: Chels 78Wc 161
E6 38Mc 73
E15 36Fc 73
N11 24Mb 50
RM6: Chad H 31Zc 75
SE25 71Tb 157
SW19 65Db 133
W14 49Ab 88
Edith Row SW6 53Db 111
Edith St. E2 40Wb 71
Edith Summerskill Ho. *SW6* 52Bb 111
(off Clem Attlee Est.)
Edith Ter. SW10 52Eb 111
Edith Vs. W14 49Bb 89
Edith Yd. SW10 52Eb 111
Ediva Rd. DA13: Meop 10C 144
Edmansons Cl. N17 25Vb 51
Edmeston Cl. E9 37Ac 72
Edmond Beaufort Dr. AL3: St A 1B 6
Edmond Ct. SE14 53Yb 114
Edmonscote W13 43Ja 86
EDMONTON 20Wb 33
Edmonton Ct. *SE16* 48Yb 92
(off Canada Est.)
Edmonton Grn. Shop. Cen. N9 19Wb 33
Edmonton Leisure Cen. 20Wb 33
Edmund Ct. DA13: Meop 10C 144
Edmund Gro. TW13: Hanw 61Ba 129
Edmund Halley Way SE10 47Gc 93
Edmund Ho. SE17 51Rb 113
Edmund Hurst Dr. E6 43Rc 94
Edmund M. WD4: K Lan 1Q 12
Edmund Rd. BR5: St M Cry 72Yc 161
CR4: Mitc 69Gb 133
DA16: Well 55Wc 117
RM13: Rain 40Gd 76
RM16: Chaf H 47Zd 99
Edmunds Av. BR5: St P 69Zc 139
Edmundsbury Ct. Est. SW9 56Pb 112
Edmunds Cl. UB4: Yead 43Y 85
Edmund St. SE5 52Tb 113
Edmunds Wlk. N2 28Gb 49
Edmunds Way SL2: Slou 3M 81
Ednam Ho. *SE15* 51Wb 113
(off Haymerle Rd.)
Edna Rd. SW20 68Za 132
Edna St. SW11 53Gb 111
Edred Ho. *E9* 35Ac 72
(off Lindisfarne Way)
Edrich Ho. SW4 53Nb 112
Edric Ho. SW1 5E 228
Edrick Rd. HA8: Edg 23Sa 47
Edrick Wlk. HA8: Edg 23Sa 47
Edric Rd. SE14 52Zb 114
Edridge Cl. RM12: Horn 36Md 77
WD23: Bush 15Ea 28
Edridge Rd. CR0: C'don 76Sb 157
Edson Cl. WD25: Wat 5V 12
Edulf Rd. WD6: Bore 11Ra 29
Edward II Av. KT14: Byfl 86P 169
Edward VII Mans. *NW10* 41Za 88
(off Chamberlayne Rd.)
Edward Alderton Theatre 55Zc 117
Edward Amey Cl. WD25: Wat 8Y 13
Edward Av. E4 23Dc 52
SM4: Mord 71Fb 155
Edward Bond Ho. *WC1* 4G 217
(off Cromer St.)
Edward Clifford Ho. *SE17* 6G 231
(off Elsted St.)
Edward Cl. AL1: St A 3D 6
N9 17Vb 33
NW2 35Za 68
RM2: Rom 27Ld 57
RM16: Chaf H 47Zd 99
TW12: Hamp H 64Ea 130
WD5: Ab L 4V 12
Edward Ct. E16 43Jc 93
EN9: Walt A 5Hc 21
HP3: Hem H 6M 3
TW18: Staines 65L 127
Edward Dodd Ct. N1 3G 219
Edward Edward's Ho. SE1 7B 224
Edwardes Pl. W8 48Bb 89
Edwardes Sq. W8 48Bb 89
Edward Gro. EN4: E Barn 15Fb 31
Edward Heylin Ct. *E15* 40Dc 72
(off High St.)
Edward Heylyn Ho. *E3* 40Cc 72
(off Thomas Fyre Dr.)
Edward Ho. RH1: Redh 9A 208
SE11 7J 229
W2 6B 214
Edward Kennedy Ho. *W10* 42Ab 88
(off Wornington Rd.)
Edward Mann Cl. *E1* 44Zb 92
(off Pitsea St.)
Edward M. NW1 2A 216 (41Kb 90)
Edward Pl. SE8 51Bc 114
Edward Rd. BR1: Brom 66Kc 137
BR7: Chst 64Rc 138
CR0: C'don 73Ub 157
CR5: Coul 87Mb 176
E17 28Zb 52
EN4: E Barn 15Fb 31
GU20: W'sham 9B 146
HA2: Harr 27Ea 46
RM6: Chad H 30Ad 55
SE20 66Zb 136
TN16: Big H 90Nc 180
TW12: Hamp H 64Ea 130
TW14: Felt 57T 106
UB5: N'olt 40Y 65
Edward's Av. HA4: Ruis 37X 65
Edwards Cl. CM13: Hut 16Fe 41
KT4: Wor Pk 75Za 154
Edward's Cotts. N1 37Rb 71
Edwards Ct. *CR0: C'don* 77Ub 157
(off South Pk. Hill Rd.)
DA4: Eyns 76Nd 163
EN8: Chesh 2Ac 20
SL1: Slou 7J 81
Edwards Dr. N11 24Mb 50
Edwards Gdns. BR8: Swan 70Fd 140
Edward's La. N16 33Ub 71
Edwards Mans. *IG11: Bark* 38Vc 75
(off Upney La.)
Edwards M. N1 38Rb 71
W1 3H 221 (44Jb 90)
Edward Sq. N1 1H 217 (39Pb 70)
SE16 46Ac 92
Edwards Rd. DA17: Belv 49Cd 96
Edward St. E16 42Jc 93
(not continuous)
SE8 51Bc 114
SE14 52Ac 114
Edwards Way CM13: Hut 16Fe 41
Edwards Yd. HA0: Wemb 39Na 67
Edward Temme Av. E15 38Hc 73
Edward Tyler Rd. SE12 61Lc 137
Edward Way TW15: Ashf 61P 127
Edwick Ct. EN8: Chesh 1Zb 20
Edwina Gdns. IG4: Ilf 29Nc 54
Edwin Arnold Ct. DA14: Sidc 63Vc 139
Edwin Av. E6 40Qc 74
(not continuous)
Edwin Cl. DA7: Bex 51Bd 117
KT24: W Hor 97T 190
RM13: Rain 41Hd 96
Edwin Hall Pl. SE13 58Fc 115
Edwin Ho. SE15 52Wb 113
Edwin Petty Pl. DA2: Dart 59Sd 120
Edwin Pl. *CR0: C'don* 74Ub 157
(off Leslie Gro.)
Edwin Rd. DA2: Wilm 62Kd 141
HA8: Edg 23Ta 47
KT24: W Hor 97S 190
TW1: Twick 60Ha 108
TW2: Twick 60Ga 108
Edwin's Mead E9 35Ac 72
Edwin Stray Ho. TW13: Hanw 61Ca 129
Edwin St. DA12: Grav'nd 9D 122
E1 42Yb 92
E16 43Jc 93
Edwin Ware Ct. HA5: Pinn 26Y 45
Edwy Ho. *E9* 35Bc 72
(off Homerton Rd.)
Edwyn Cl. EN5: Barn 16Ya 30
Edwyn Ho. *SW18* 58Db 111
(off Neville Gill Cl.)
Eel Brook Cl. SW6 53Db 111
Eel Pie Island TW1: Twick 60Ja 108
Effie Pl. SW6 52Cb 111
Effie Rd. SW6 52Cb 111
EFFINGHAM 99Z 191

Effingham Cl. SM2: Sutt 80Db 155
EFFINGHAM COMMON 96V 190
Effingham Comn. Rd.
KT24: Eff, Eff J 95W 190
Effingham Community Sports Cen. 99Aa 191
Effingham Ct. GU22: Wok 91A 188
(off Constitution Hill)
Effingham Golf Course 100Z 191
EFFINGHAM JUNCTION 95W 190
Effingham Lodge KT1: King T 70Ma 131
Effingham Pl. KT24: Eff 99Z 191
Effingham Rd. CR0: C'don 73Pb 156
KT6: Surb 73Ka 152
N8 .... 29Qb 50
RH2: Reig 7K 207
SE12 .... 57Gc 115
Effort St. SW17 .... 64Gb 133
Effra Cl. SW19 .... 65Db 133
Effra Ct. SW2 .... 57Pb 112
(off Brixton Hill)
Effra Pde. SW2 .... 57Qb 112
Effra Rd. SW2 .... 56Qb 112
SW19 .... 65Db 133
Effra Rd. Retail Pk. SW2 .... 57Qb 112
Egan Cl. CR8: Kenley 92Tb 197
Egan Way UB3: Hayes 45U 84
Egbert Ho. E9 .... 36Ac 72
(off Homerton Rd.)
Egbert St. NW1 .... 39Jb 70
Egbury Ho. SW15 .... 58Va 110
(off Tangley Gro.)
Egdean Wlk. TN13: S'oaks 95Ld 203
Egeremont Rd. SE13 .... 54Dc 114
Egerton Av. BR8: Hext 66Hd 140
Egerton Cl. DA1: Dart 60Kd 119
HA5: Eastc 28W 44
Egerton Ct. E11 .... 31Fc 73
Egerton Cres. SW3 .... 5E 226 (49Gb 89)
Egerton Dr. SE10 .... 53Dc 114
Egerton Gdns. IG3: Ilf 34Vc 75
NW4 .... 28Xa 48
NW10 .... 39Ya 68
SW3 .... 4D 226 (49Gb 89)
W13 .... 44Ka 86
Egerton Gdns. M. SW3 .... 4E 226 (48Gb 89)
Egerton Pl. KT13: Weyb 79S 150
SW3 .... 4E 226 (48Gb 89)
Egerton Rd. HA0: Wemb 38Pa 67
KT3: N Mald 70Va 132
KT13: Weyb 79S 150
N16 .... 31Vb 71
SE25 .... 69Ub 135
SL2: Slou 2C 80
TW2: Twick 59Ga 108
Egerton Ter. SW3 .... 4E 226 (48Gb 89)
Egerton Way UB3: Harl 52R 106
Eggardon Ct. UB5: N'olt 37Da 65
Egg Farm La. WD4: K Lan 2R 12
WD5: Ab L 2R 12
Egg Hall CM16: Epp 1Wc 23
EGHAM 64C 126
Egham Bus. Village TW20: Thorpe 68E 126
Egham By-Pass TW20: Egh 64B 126
Egham Cl. SM3: Cheam 75Ab 154
SW19 .... 61Ab 132
Egham Cres. SM3: Cheam 76Ab 154
Egham Hill TW20: Egh, Eng G 5P 125
EGHAM HYTHE 64G 126
Egham Leisure Cen. 65D 126
Egham Mus. 64C 126
Egham Rd. E13 .... 43Kc 93
Egham Rdbt. TW18: Staines 64G 126
EGHAM WICK 6L 125
Eglantine La. DA4: Farni, Hort K 73Qd 163
Eglantine Rd. SW18 .... 57Eb 111
Egleston Rd. SM4: Mord 72Db 155
Egley Dr. GU22: Wok 4P 187
Egley Rd. GU22: Wok 4P 187
Eglington Ct. SE17 .... 51Sb 113
Eglington Rd. E4 .... 17Fc 35
Eglinton Hill SE18 .... 51Rc 116
Eglinton Rd. DA10: Swans 58Be 121
SE18 .... 51Qc 116
Eglise Rd. CR6: W'ham 89Ac 178
Egliston M. SW15 .... 55Ya 110
Egliston Rd. SW15 .... 55Ya 110
Eglon M. NW1 .... 38Hb 69
Egmont Av. KT6: Surb 74Pa 153
Egmont Ct. KT12: Walt T 73X 151
(off Egmont Rd.)
Egmont M. KT19: Ewe 77Ta 153
Egmont Pk. Rd. KT20: Walt H 97Wa 194
Egmont Rd. KT3: N Mald 70Va 132
KT6: Surb 74Pa 153
KT12: Walt T 73X 151
SM2: Sutt 80Eb 155
Egmont St. SE14 .... 52Zb 114
Egmont Way KT20: Tad 91Ab 194
Egremont Gdns. SL1: Slou 6E 80
Egremont Ho. SE13 .... 54Dc 114
(off Russett Way)
Egremont Rd. SE27 .... 62Qb 134
Egret Ho. SE16 .... 49Zb 92
(off Tawny Way)
Egret Way UB4: Yead 43Z 85
EGYPT 5F 60
Egypt La. SL2: Farn C 3F 60
Eider Cl. E7 .... 36Hc 73
UB4: Yead 43Z 85
Eider Ct. SE8 .... 51Bc 114
(off Pilot Cl.)
Eight Acres SL1: Burn 2A 80
Eighteenth Rd. CR4: Mitc 70Nb 134
Eighth Av. E12 .... 35Pc 74
KT20: Lwr K 98Ab 194
UB3: Hayes 46W 84
Eileen Rd. SE25 .... 71Tb 157
Eindhoven Cl. SM5: Cars 74Jb 156
Einstein Ho. HA9: Wemb 34Sa 67
Eisenhower Dr. E6 .... 43Nc 94
Ekarro Ho. SW8 .... 53Nb 112
(off Guildford Rd.)
Elaine Gro. NW5 .... 36Jb 70
Elam Cl. SE5 .... 54Rb 113
Elam St. SE5 .... 54Rb 113
Elan Ct. E1 .... 43Xb 91
Eland Pl. CR0: Wadd 76Rb 157
Eland Rd. CR0: Wadd 76Rb 157
SW11 .... 55Hb 111
Elan Rd. RM15: S Ock 43Wd 98
Elba Pl. SE17 .... 5E 230 (49Sb 91)
Elberon Av. CR0: Bedd 72Lb 156
Elbe St. SW6 .... 54Eb 111
Elborough Rd. SE25 .... 71Wb 157
Elborough St. SW18 .... 60Cb 111
Elbourne Ct. SE16 .... 48Zb 92
(off Worgan St.)
Elbourne Trad. Est. DA17: Belv 48Dd 96
Elbourn Ho. SW3 .... 7D 226
Elbow Mdw. SL3: Poyle 53H 105
Elbury Dr. E16 .... 44Jc 93
Elcho Rd. GU24: Brkwd 1A 186
Elcho St. SW11 .... 52Gb 111
Elcot Av. SE15 .... 52Xb 113
Elden Ho. SW3 .... 5D 226
Eldenwall Ind. Est. RM8: Dag 32Ad 75
Elder Av. N8 .... 29Nb 50
Elderbek Cl. EN7: Chesh 1Wb 19
Elderberry Cl. IG6: Ilf 24Rc 54
Elderberry Gro. SE27 .... 63Sb 135
Elderberry Rd. W5 .... 47Na 87
Elderberry Way E6 .... 41Pc 94
WD25: Wat 7X 13
Elder Cl. DA15: Sidc 60Vc 117
N20 .... 19Db 31
UB7: Yiew 45N 83
Elder Ct. WD23: B Hea 19Ga 28
Elderfield Ho. E14 .... 45Cc 92
(off Pennyfields)
Elderfield Pl. SW17 .... 63Kb 134
Elderfield Rd. E5 .... 35Zb 72
SL2: Stoke P 7K 61
Elderfield Wlk. E11 .... 29Kc 53
Elderflower Way E15 .... 38Gc 73
Elder Gdns. SE27 .... 64Sb 135
Elder Ho. E15 .... 41Gc 93
(off Manor Rd.)
Elder Oak Cl. SE20 .... 67Xb 135
Elder Oak Ct. SE20 .... 67Xb 135
(off Anerley Ct.)
Elder Rd. GU24: Bisl 7E 166
SE27 .... 64Sb 135
Eldersley Cl. RH1: Redh 4P 207
Eldersley Gdns. RH1: Redh 4P 207
Elderslie Cl. BR3: Beck 71Cc 158
Elderslie Rd. SE9 .... 57Qc 116
Elder St. E1 .... 7K 219 (42Vb 91)
(not continuous)
Elderton Rd. SE26 .... 63Ac 136
Eldertree Pl. CR4: Mitc 67Lb 134
Eldertree Way CR4: Mitc 67Lb 134
Elder Wlk. N1 .... 39Rb 71
(off Popham St.)
SE13 .... 55Ec 114
Elder Way RM13: Rain 41Md 97
SL3: L'ly 47B 82
Elderwood Pl. SE27 .... 64Sb 135
Eldon Av. CR0: C'don 75Yb 158
TW5: Hest 52Ca 107
WD6: Bore 12Qa 29
Eldon Ct. KT13: Weyb 78S 150
NW6 .... 39Cb 69
Eldon Gro. NW3 .... 36Fb 69
Eldon Pk. SE25 .... 70Xb 135
Eldon Rd. CR3: Cat'm 93Tb 197
E17 .... 28Bc 52
N9 .... 18Yb 34
N22 .... 25Rb 51
W8 .... 48Db 89
Eldon St. EC2 .... 1G 225 (43Tb 91)
Eldon Way NW10 .... 41Ra 87
Eldred Dr. BR5: Orp 74Yc 161
Eldred Gdns. RM14: Upm 31Ud 78
Eldred Rd. IG11: Bark 39Uc 74
Eldrick Ct. TW14: Bedf 60T 106
Eldridge Cl. TW14: Felt 60W 106
Eldridge Ct. RM10: Dag 37Dd 76
SE16 .... 48Wb 91
Eleanor Av. KT19: Ewe 82Ta 173
Eleanor Cl. N15 .... 27Vb 51
SE16 .... 47Zb 92
Eleanor Ct. E2 .... 39Wb 71
(off Whiston Rd.)
Eleanor Cres. NW7 .... 22Za 48
Eleanor Cross Rd. EN8: Walt C 6Ac 20
Eleanor Gdns. EN5: Barn 15Za 30
RM8: Dag 33Bd 75
Eleanor Gro. SW13 .... 55Ua 110
UB10: Ick 34R 64
Eleanor Ho. SL9: Chal P 22A 42
(off Micholls Av.)
W6 .... 50Ya 88
(off Queen Caroline St.)
Eleanor Rathbone Ho. N6 .... 31Mb 70
(off Avenue Rd.)
Eleanor Rd. E8 .... 37Xb 71
E15 .... 37Hc 73
EN8: Walt C 5Ac 20
N11 .... 23Nb 50
Eleanor St. E3 .... 41Cc 92
Eleanor Wlk. DA9: Ghithe 56Yd 120
SE18 .... 49Nc 94
Eleanor Way CM14: W'ley 22Zd 59
EN8: Walt C 6Bc 20
Electra Av. TW6: H'row A 55V 106
Electra Bus. Pk. E16 .... 43Fc 93
Electric Av. EN3: Enf L 8Bc 20
SW9 .... 56Qb 112
Electric Cinema 44Bb 89
Electric Empire, The SE14 .... 53Zb 114
(off New Cross Rd.)
Electric Ho. E3 .... 41Cc 92
(off Bow Rd.)
Electric La. SW9 .... 56Qb 112
(not continuous)
Electric Pde. E18 .... 26Jc 53
(off George La.)
IG3: Ilf 33Uc 74
KT6: Surb 72Ma 153
Electron Trade Cen.
BR5: St M Cry 70Xc 139
Elektron Twr. E14 .... 45Fc 93
ELEPHANT & CASTLE 4C 230 (48Rb 91)
Elephant & Castle SE1 .... 5C 230 (49Rb 91)
Elephant & Castle Leisure Cen. 5C 230 (49Rb 91)
Elephant & Castle Shop. Cen.
SE1 .... 5D 230 (49Sb 91)
Elephant La. SE16 .... 47Yb 92
Elephant Rd. SE17 .... 5D 230 (49Sb 91)
Elers Rd. UB3: Harl 49T 84
W13 .... 47La 86
Eleven Acre Ri. IG10: Lough 13Pc 36
Eleventh Av. KT20: Lwr K 98Bb 195
Eley Rd. N18 .... 21Zb 52
Eley Rd. Retail Pk. N18 .... 22Yb 52
Eleys Est. N18 .... 20Zb 34
(not continuous)
Elfindale Rd. SE24 .... 57Sb 113
Elfin Gro. TW11: Tedd 64Ha 130
Elford Cl. SE3 .... 56Kc 115
Elford M. SW4 .... 57Lb 112
Elfort Rd. N5 .... 35Qb 70
Elfrida Cres. SE6 .... 63Cc 136
Elfrida Rd. WD18: Wat 15Y 27
Elf Row E1 .... 45Yb 92
Elfwine Rd. W7 .... 43Ga 86
Elgal Cl. BR6: Farnb 78Rc 160
Elgar N8 .... 27Nb 50
(off Boyton Cl.)
Elgar Av. KT5: Surb 74Qa 153
NW10 .... 37Ta 67
(not continuous)
SW16 .... 69Nb 134
W5 .... 47Na 87
Elgar Cl. E13 .... 40Lc 73
IG9: Buck H 19Mc 35
SE8 .... 52Cc 114
UB10: Ick 33Q 64
WD6: E'tree 17Ma 29
Elgar Ct. NW6 .... 41Cb 89
W14 .... 48Ab 88
(off Blythe Rd.)
Elgar Gdns. RM18: Tilb 3C 122
Elgar Ho. NW6 .... 38Eb 69
(off Fairfax Rd.)
SW1 .... 50Kb 90
(off Churchill Gdns.)
Elgar St. SE16 .... 48Ac 92
Elgin Av. HA3: Kenton 26Ja 46
RM3: Hrld W 24Rd 57
TW15: Ashf 65S 128
W9 .... 42Bb 89
W12 .... 47Wa 88
Elgin Cl. W12 .... 47Xa 88
Elgin Ct. CR2: S Croy 77Sb 157
(off Bramley Hill)
W9 .... 42Db 89
Elgin Cres. CR3: Cat'm 94Wb 197
TW6: H'row A 54U 106
W11 .... 45Ab 88
Elgin Dr. HA6: Nwood 24U 44
Elgin Est. W9 .... 42Cb 89
(off Elgin Av.)
Elgin Ho. CM14: W'ley 21Zd 59
E14 .... 44Dc 92
(off Ricardo St.)
RM6: Chad H 30Bd 55
(off High Rd.)
Elgin Mans. W9 .... 41Db 89
Elgin M. W11 .... 44Ab 88
Elgin M. Nth. W9 .... 41Db 89
Elgin M. Sth. W9 .... 41Db 89
Elgin Pl. KT13: Weyb 79S 150
Elgin Rd. CR0: C'don 75Vb 157
EN8: Chesh 2Yb 20
IG3: Ilf 32Uc 74
KT13: Weyb 78Q 150
N22 .... 26Lb 50
SM1: Sutt 76Eb 155
SM6: Wall 79Lb 156
Elgood Av. HA6: Nwood 23V 44
Elgood Cl. W11 .... 45Ab 88
Elgood Ho. NW8 .... 2C 214
SE1 .... 2F 231
Elham Cl. BR1: Brom 66Mc 137
Elham Ho. E5 .... 36Xb 71
Elia M. N1 .... 2B 218 (40Rb 71)
Elias Ho. CM14: B'wood 19Zd 41
Elias Pl. SW8 .... 51Qb 112
Elia St. N1 .... 2B 218 (40Rb 71)
Elibank Rd. SE9 .... 56Pc 116
Elim Est. SE1 .... 3H 231 (48Ub 91)
Elim St. SE1 .... 3G 231 (48Tb 91)
(not continuous)
Elim Way E13 .... 41Hc 93
Eliot Bank SE23 .... 61Xb 135
Eliot Cotts. SE3 .... 54Gc 115
Eliot Ct. SW18 .... 58Db 111
Eliot Dr. HA2: Harr 33Da 65
Eliot Gdns. SW15 .... 56Wa 110
Eliot Hill SE13 .... 54Ec 114
Eliot M. NW8 .... 2A 214 (40Eb 69)
Eliot Pk. SE13 .... 54Ec 114
Eliot Pl. SE3 .... 54Gc 115
Eliot Rd. DA1: Dart 57Rd 119
RM9: Dag 35Zc 75
Eliot Va. SE3 .... 54Fc 115
Elis David Almshouses
CR0: C'don 76Rb 157
Elizabethan Cl. TW19: Stanw 59M 105
Elizabethan Way
TW19: Stanw 59M 105
Elizabeth Av. EN2: Enf 13Rb 33
HP6: L Chal 11A 24
IG1: Ilf 33Tc 74
N1 .... 39Sb 71
TW18: Staines 65L 127
Elizabeth Barnes Ct. SW6 .... 54Db 111
(off Marinefield Rd.)
Elizabeth Blackwell Ho. N22 .... 25Qb 50
(off Progress Way)
Elizabeth Blount Ct. E14 .... 44Ac 92
(off Carr St.)
Elizabeth Bri. SW1 .... 6K 227 (49Kb 90)
Elizabeth Cl. E14 .... 44Dc 92
EN5: Barn 13Za 30
RM7: Mawney 25Dd 56
RM18: Tilb 4D 122
SM1: Sutt 77Bb 155
W9 .... 6A 214 (42Eb 89)
Elizabeth Clyde Cl. N15 .... 28Ub 51
Elizabeth Cotts. TW9: Kew 53Pa 109
Elizabeth Ct. BR1: Brom 67Hc 137
(off Highland Rd.)
CR0: C'don 76Ub 157
(off The Avenue)
CR3: Cat'm 94Sb 197
CR3: Whyt 90Vb 177
DA11: Grav'nd 8C 122
E4 .... 22Bc 52
E10 .... 31Dc 72
IG8: Wfd G 24Lc 53
KT2: King T 67Na 131
KT13: Weyb 77T 150
NW1 .... 5E 214
SL1: Slou 7L 81
SL4: Wind 4G 102
(off Beaumont Rd.)
SW1 .... 4E 228
SW10 .... 51Fb 111
(off Milman's St.)
TW11: Tedd 64Ga 130
TW16: Sun 69Y 129
(off Elizabeth Gdns.)
WD17: Wat 10V 12
Elizabeth Croll Ho. WC1 .... 3J 217
Elizabeth Dr. CM16: They B 8Uc 22
SM7: Bans 90Eb 175
Elizabeth Fry Ho. UB3: Harl 49V 84
Elizabeth Fry M. E8 .... 38Xb 71
Elizabeth Fry Pl. SE18 .... 53Nc 116
Elizabeth Gdns. HA7: Stan 23La 46
SL5: Asc 1A 146
TW7: Isle 56Ja 108
TW16: Sun 69Y 129
W3 .... 46Va 88
Elizabeth Garrett Anderson Ho.
DA17: Belv 48Cd 96
(off Ambrook Rd.)
Elizabeth Hart Ct. KT13: Weyb 78P 149
Elizabeth Ho. CR3: Cat'm 96Wb 197
E3 .... 41Dc 92
(off St Leonard's St.)
HP2: Hem H 1M 3
(off Chapel St.)
RM2: Rom 28Ld 57
RM16: Grays 46De 99
SE11 .... 6A 230
SM3: Cheam 79Ab 154
(off Park La.)
SM7: Bans 90Eb 175
W6 .... 50Ya 88
(off Queen Caroline St.)
WD24: Wat 12Y 27
Elizabeth Huggins Cotts.
DA11: Grav'nd 1D 144
Elizabeth Ind. Est. SE14 .... 51Zb 114
Elizabeth M. E2 .... 40Wb 71
(off Kay St.)
HA1: Harr 30Ga 46
NW3 .... 37Gb 69
Elizabeth Newcomen Ho. SE1 .... 1F 231
Elizabeth Pl. DA4: Farni 72Pd 163
N15 .... 28Tb 51
Elizabeth Ride N9 .... 17Xb 33
Elizabeth Rd. CM15: Pil H 16Xd 40
E6 .... 39Mc 73
N15 .... 29Ub 51
RM13: Rain 43Kd 97
RM16: Grays 47Be 99
Elizabeth Sq. SE16 .... 45Ac 92
(off Sovereign Cres.)
Elizabeth St. DA9: Ghithe 57Ud 120
SW1 .... 5J 227 (49Jb 90)
Elizabeth Ter. SE9 .... 58Pc 116
Elizabeth Way BR5: St M Cry 71Yc 161
SE19 .... 66Tb 135
SL2: Stoke P 9K 61
TW13: Hanw 63Y 129
Eliza Cook Cl. DA9: Ghithe 56Xd 120
Elkanette M. N20 .... 19Eb 31
Elkington Point SE11 .... 6K 229
Elkington Rd. E13 .... 42Kc 93
Elkins, The RM1: Rom 26Gd 56
Elkins Rd. SL2: Hedg 3J 61
Elkstone Rd. W10 .... 43Bb 89
Ella Cl. BR3: Beck 68Cc 136
Ellacott M. SW16 .... 61Mb 134
Ellaline Rd. W6 .... 51Za 110
Ella M. NW3 .... 35Hb 69
Ellanby Cres. N18 .... 21Xb 51
Elland Cl. EN5: New Bar 15Fb 31
Elland Ho. E14 .... 44Bc 92
(off Copenhagen Pl.)
Elland Rd. KT12: Walt T 75Z 151
SE15 .... 56Yb 114
Ella Rd. N8 .... 31Nb 70
Ellement Cl. HA5: Pinn 29Z 45
Ellena Ct. N14 .... 20Nb 32
(off Conway Rd.)
Ellenborough Ho. W12 .... 45Xa 88
(off White City Est.)
Ellenborough Pl. SW15 .... 56Wa 110
Ellenborough Rd. DA14: Sidc 64Zc 139
N22 .... 25Sb 51
Ellenbridge Way CR2: Sande 81Ub 177
ELLENBROOK 1P 7
Ellenbrook Cl. WD24: Wat 11Y 27
Ellenbrook Cres. AL10: Hat 1P 7
Ellenbrook La. AL10: Hat 1P 7
Ellen Cl. BR1: Brom 69Mc 137
HP2: Hem H 1P 3
Ellen Ct. E4 .... 18Ec 34
(off The Ridgeway)
N9 .... 19Yb 34
Ellen Julia Ct. E1 .... 44Yb 92
(off James Voller Way)
Ellen M. HP2: Hem H 1P 3
Ellen St. E1 .... 44Wb 91
Ellen Terry Ct. NW1 .... 38Kb 70
(off Farrier St.)
Ellen Webb Dr. HA3: W'stone 27Ga 46
Ellen Wilkinson Ho. E2 .... 41Zb 92
(off Usk St.)
RM10: Dag 34Cd 76
SW6 .... 51Bb 111
(off Clem Attlee Ct.)
Elleray Rd. TW11: Tedd 65Ha 130
Ellerby St. SW6 .... 53Za 110
Ellerdale Cl. NW3 .... 35Eb 69
Ellerdale Rd. NW3 .... 36Eb 69
Ellerdale St. SE13 .... 56Dc 114
Ellerdine Rd. TW3: Houn 56Ea 108
Ellerker Gdns. TW10: Rich 58Na 109
Ellerman Av. TW2: Whitt 60Ba 107
Ellerman Rd. RM18: Tilb 3B 122
Ellerslie Ct. DA12: Grav'nd 9F 122
(off Copper Beech Cl.)
Ellerslie Gdns. NW10 .... 39Wa 68
Ellerslie Rd. W12 .... 46Xa 88
Ellerslie Sq. Ind. Est. SW2 .... 57Nb 112
Ellerton Gdns. RM9: Dag 38Yc 75
Ellerton Lodge N3 .... 26Cb 49
Ellerton Rd. KT6: Surb 75Pa 153
RM9: Dag 38Yc 75
SW13 .... 53Wa 110
SW18 .... 60Fb 111
SW20 .... 66Wa 132
Ellery Ho. SE17 .... 6G 231 (49Tb 91)
Ellery Rd. SE19 .... 66Tb 135
Ellery St. SE15 .... 54Xb 113
Ellesborough Cl. WD19: Wat 22Y 45
Ellesmere Av. BR3: Beck 68Ec 136
NW7 .... 20Ta 29
Ellesmere Cl. E11 .... 29Hc 53
HA4: Ruis 31S 64
SL3: Dat 1L 103
Ellesmere Ct. KT13: Weyb 79U 150
SE12 .... 60Jc 115
W4 .... 50Ta 87
Ellesmere Dr. CR2: Sande 86Xb 177
Ellesmere Gdns. IG4: Ilf 29Nc 54
Ellesmere Gro. EN5: Barn 15Bb 31
Ellesmere Ho. SW10 .... 51Eb 111
(off Fulham Rd.)
Ellesmere Mans. NW6 .... 37Eb 69
(off Canfield Gdns.)
Ellesmere Pl. KT12: Hers 78U 150
Ellesmere Rd. E3 .... 40Ac 72
HP4: Berk 1A 2
KT13: Weyb 80U 150
NW10 .... 36Wa 68
TW1: Twick 58La 108
UB6: G'frd 42Ea 86
W4 .... 51Ta 109
Ellesmere St. E14 .... 44Dc 92
Ellice Rd. RH8: Oxt 1K 211
Ellie Cl. SS17: Stan H 1L 101
Ellies M. TW15: Ashf 61N 127
Elliman Av. SL2: Slou 5J 81
Elliman Sq. SL1: Slou 7K 81
(within Queensmere Shop. Cen.)
Ellingfort Rd. E8 .... 38Xb 71
Ellingham GU22: Wok 91A 188
Ellingham Cl. HP2: Hem H 1A 4
Ellingham Rd. E15 .... 35Fc 73
HP2: Hem H 1P 3
KT9: Chess 79Ma 153
W12 .... 47Wa 88
Ellington Ct. N14 .... 19Mb 32
Ellington Ho. SE1 .... 4E 230 (48Sb 91)
SE18 .... 52Qc 116
Ellington Rd. N10 .... 28Kb 50
TW3: Houn 54Da 107
TW13: Felt 63V 128
Ellington St. N7 .... 37Qb 70
Ellington Way KT18: Tatt C 89Xa 174
Elliot Cl. E15 .... 38Gc 73
HA9: Wemb 34Pa 67
Elliot Ct. IG8: Wfd G 23Mc 53
Elliot Ho. SW17 .... 62Fb 133
(off Grosvenor Way)
W1 .... 1E 220
Elliot Rd. NW4 .... 30Xa 48
Elliott Av. HA4: Ruis 33X 65
Elliott Gdns. RM3: Rom 25Kd 57
TW17: Shep 70Q 128
Elliott Rd. BR2: Brom 70Mc 137
CR7: Thor H 70Rb 135
HA7: Stan 23Ja 46
SW9 .... 53Rb 113
W4 .... 49Ua 88
Elliotts Cl. UB8: Cowl 43L 83
Elliotts La. TN16: Bras 96Yc 201
Elliott's Pl. N1 .... 39Rb 71
Elliott Sq. NW3 .... 38Gb 69
Elliotts Row SE11 .... 5C 230 (49Rb 91)
Elliott St. DA12: Grav'nd 9F 122
Ellis Av. RM13: Rain 43Jd 96
SL1: Slou 7J 81
SL9: Chal P 25B 42
Ellis Cl. BR8: Swan 70Fd 140
CR5: Coul 92Pb 196
HA8: Edg 23Ua 48
NW10 .... 37Xa 68
RM16: Ors 4D 100
SE9 .... 61Sc 138
Elliscombe Mt. SE7 .... 51Lc 115
Elliscombe Rd. SE7 .... 51Lc 115
Ellis Ct. E1 .... 44Yb 92
(off James Voller Way)
W7 .... 43Ha 86
Ellis Farm Cl. GU22: Wok 4P 187
Ellisfield Dr. SW15 .... 59Wa 110
Ellis Franklin Ct. NW8 .... 1A 214
Ellis Ho. AL1: St A 3D 6
SE17 .... 7F 231
Ellison Apartments E3 .... 41Cc 92
(off Merchant St.)
Ellison Cl. SL4: Wind 5D 102
Ellison Gdns. UB2: S'hall 49Ba 85
Ellison Ho. SE13 .... 54Dc 114
(off Lewisham Rd.)
SL4: Wind 3H 103
(off Victoria St.)
Ellison Rd. DA15: Sidc 60Tc 116
SW13 .... 55Va 110
SW16 .... 66Mb 134
Ellis Rd. CR4: Mitc 72Hb 155
CR5: Coul 92Pb 196
UB2: S'hall 46Ea 86
Ellis St. SW1 .... 5G 227 (49Jb 90)
Elliston Ho. SE18 .... 49Qc 94
(off Wellington St.)
Elliston Way KT21: Asht 91Na 193
Ellis Way DA1: Dart 61Pd 141
Ellmore Cl. RM3: Rom 25Kd 57
Ellora Rd. SW16 .... 64Mb 134
Ellswood Ct. KT6: Surb 73Ma 153
Ellsworth St. E2 .... 41Xb 91
Ellwood Ct. W9 .... 42Db 89
(off Clearwell Dr.)
WD25: Wat 6X 13
Ellwood Gdns. WD25: Wat 6Y 13
Ellwood Ho. SL9: Chal P 25A 42
Elmar Grn. SL2: Slou 1E 80
Elmar Rd. N15 .... 28Tb 51
Elm Av. HA4: Ruis 32W 64
RM14: Upm 34Rd 77
TW19: Stanw 61N 127
W5 .... 46Na 87
WD19: Wat 17Aa 27
Elmbank N14 .... 17Nb 32
Elmbank Av. EN5: Barn 14Ya 30
TW20: Eng G 5M 125
Elm Bank Dr. BR1: Brom 68Mc 137
Elm Bank Gdns. SW13 .... 54Ua 110
Elmbank Way W7 .... 43Fa 86
Elmbourne Dr. DA17: Belv 49Dd 96
Elmbourne Rd. SW17 .... 62Kb 134
Elmbridge Av. KT5: Surb 71Ra 153
Elmbridge Cl. HA4: Ruis 30W 44
Elmbridge Dr. HA4: Ruis 29V 44
Elmbridge Est. GU22: Wok 91B 188
Elmbridge La. GU22: Wok 91B 188
Elmbridge Mus. 77Q 150
Elmbridge Rd. IG6: Ilf 23Wc 55
Elmbridge Wlk. E8 .... 38Wb 71
Elmbridge Xcel Leisure Complex 71X 151
Elmbrook Cl. TW16: Sun 67X 129
Elmbrook Gdns. SE9 .... 56Nc 116
Elmbrook Rd. SM1: Sutt 77Bb 155
Elm Cl. CR2: S Croy 79Ub 157
CR6: W'ham 89Zb 178
DA1: Dart 60Ld 119
E11 .... 30Kc 53
EN9: Walt A 6Fc 21
GU21: Wok 7P 167

Elm Cl. GU23: Rip 96J 189
HA2: Harr 30Da 45
IG9: Buck H 19Mc 35
KT5: Surb 73Sa 153
KT22: Lea 94Ka 192
N19 33Lb 70
NW4 29Za 48
RM7: Mawney 25Dd 56
SL2: Farn C 7G 60
SM5: Cars 74Hb 155
SW20 70Ya 132
TW2: Twick 61Da 129
TW19: Stanw 60M 105
UB3: Hayes 44W 84
ELM CORNER 90Q 170
Elmcote HA5: Pinn 26Z 45
Elmcote Way WD3: Crox G 16P 25
Elm Cotts. CR4: Mitc 68Hb 133
Elm Ct. CR4: Mitc 68Hb 133
EC4 3K 223
EN4: E Barn 17Gb 31
GU21: Knap 9H 167
KT8: W Mole 70Da 129
SE1 2H 231
SE13 55Fc 115
SW9 53Qb 112
(off Cranworth Gdns.)
TW16: Sun 66V 128
(off Grangewood Dr.)
W9 43Cb 89
(off Admiral Wlk.)
WD17: Wat 13X 27
Elmcourt Rd. SE27 61Rb 135
Elm Cres. KT2: King T 67Na 131
W5 46Na 87
Elm Cft. SL3: Dat 3N 103
Elmcroft *GU22: Wok* 90B 168
(off Fairview Av.)
KT23: Bookh 96Ca 191
N6 31Lb 70
N8 29Pb 50
Elmcroft Av. DA15: Sidc 59Vc 117
E11 29Kc 53
N9 16Xb 33
NW11 31Bb 69
Elmcroft Cl. E11 28Kc 53
KT9: Chess 76Na 153
TW14: Felt 58V 106
W5 44Ma 87
Elmcroft Cres. HA2: Harr 27Ca 45
NW11 31Ab 68
Elmcroft Dr. KT9: Chess 76Na 153
TW15: Ashf 64Q 128
Elmcroft Gdns. NW9 28Qa 47
Elmcroft Rd. BR6: Orp 73Wc 161
Elmcroft St. E5 35Yb 72
Elmcroft Ter. UB8: Hil 44Q 84
Elmdale Rd. N13 22Pb 50
Elmdene KT5: Surb 74Sa 153
Elmdene Av. RM11: Horn 29Pd 57
Elmdene Cl. BR3: Beck 72Bc 158
Elmdene Ct. *GU22: Wok* 91A 188
(off Constitution Hill)
Elmdene Rd. SE18 50Rc 94
Elmdon Rd. RM15: S Ock 43Wd 98
TW4: Houn 54Z 107
TW6: H'row A 55V 106
Elm Dr. AL4: St A 2G 6
AL10: Hat 1C 8
BR8: Swan 68Fd 140
EN8: Chesh 1Ac 20
GU24: Chob 2K 167
HA2: Harr 30Da 45
KT22: Lea 95Ka 192
SL4: Wink 10A 102
TW16: Sun 68Y 129
Elmer Av. RM4: Have B 20Gd 38
Elmer Cl. EN2: Enf 13Pb 32
RM13: Rain 38Jd 76
Elmer Cotts. KT22: Fet 95Ja 192
Elmer Gdns. HA8: Edg 24Ra 47
RM13: Rain 38Jd 76
TW7: Isle 55Fa 108
Elmer Ho. NW8 7D 214
Elmer M. KT22: Fet 94Ja 192
Elmer Rd. SE6 59Ec 114
Elmers Dr. TW11: Tedd 65Ka 130
ELMERS END 70Ac 136
Elmers End Rd. BR3: Beck 68Yb 136
SE20 68Yb 136
Elmerside Rd. BR3: Beck 70Ac 136
Elmers Lodge BR3: Beck 70Zb 136
Elmers Rd. SE25 73Wb 157
Elm Farm Caravan Pk. KT16: Lyne 73D 148
Elmfield HA1: Harr 31Ha 66
KT23: Bookh 95Ca 191
Elmfield Av. CR4: Mitc 67Jb 134
N8 29Nb 50
TW11: Tedd 64Ha 130
Elmfield Cl. DA11: Grav'nd 10D 122
EN6: Pot B 5Ab 16
HA1: Harr 33Ga 66
Elmfield Ct. DA16: Well 53Xc 117
Elmfield Ho. *N2* 26Fb 49
(off The Grange)
NW8 40Db 69
(off Carlton Hill)
W9 42Cb 89
(off Goldney Rd.)
Elmfield Pk. BR1: Brom 69Jc 137
Elmfield Rd. BR1: Brom 68Jc 137
E4 19Ec 34
E17 30Zb 52
EN6: Pot B 4Ab 16
N2 27Fb 49
SW17 61Jb 134
UB2: S'hall 48Aa 85
Elmfield Way CR2: Sande 81Vb 177
W9 43Cb 89
Elm Friars Wlk. NW1 38Mb 70
Elm Gdns. CR4: Mitc 70Mb 134
EN2: Enf 10Tb 19
KT10: Clay 79Ha 152
KT18: Tatt C 91Ya 194
N2 27Eb 49
Elmgate Av. TW13: Felt 62X 129
Elmgate Gdns. HA8: Edg 22Sa 47
Elm Grn. W3 44Ua 88
Elmgreen Cl. E15 39Gc 73
Elm Gro. BR6: Orp 74Vc 161
CR3: Cat'm 94Ub 197
DA8: Erith 52Fd 118
GU24: Bisl 8E 166
HA2: Harr 31Ca 65
IG8: Wfd G 22Hc 53
KT2: King T 67Na 131
Elm Gro. KT12: Walt T 74W 150
KT18: Eps 86Sa 173
N8 30Nb 50
NW2 35Za 68
RM11: Horn 30Nd 57
SE15 54Vb 113
SM1: Sutt 77Db 155
SW19 66Ab 132
UB7: Yiew 45P 83
WD24: Wat 9W 12
Elmgrove Cl. GU21: Wok 1H 187
Elmgrove Cres. HA1: Harr 29Ha 46
Elmgrove Gdns. HA1: Harr 29Ja 46
Elmgrove M. KT13: Weyb 76R 150
Elm Gro. Pde. SM6: Wall 76Jb 156
Elmgrove Point SE18 49Tc 94
Elm Gro. Rd. KT11: Cobh 88Z 171
SW13 53Wa 110
W5 47Na 87
Elmgrove Rd. CR0: C'don 73Xb 157
HA1: Harr 29Ha 46
HA3: W'stone 29Ja 46
KT13: Weyb 77Q 150
Elm Hall Gdns. E11 29Kc 53
(not continuous)
Elm Hatch HA5: Hat E 24Ba 45
Elm Ho. *E3* 39Bc 72
(off Sycamore Av.)
E14 47Ec 92
(off E. Ferry Rd.)
KT2: King T 66Pa 131
(off Elm Rd.)
W10 42Ab 88
(off Briar Wlk.)
Elmhurst DA9: Ghithe 58Xd 120
DA17: Belv 51Ad 117
Elmhurst Av. CR4: Mitc 66Kb 134
N2 27Fb 49
Elmhurst Cl. WD23: Bush 14Aa 27
Elmhurst Ct. CR0: C'don 77Tb 157
Elmhurst Dr. E18 26Jc 53
RM11: Horn 32Ld 77
Elmhurst Lodge SM2: Sutt 80Eb 155
Elmhurst Mans. SW4 55Mb 112
Elmhurst Rd. E7 38Kc 73
EN3: Enf W 9Yb 20
N17 26Vb 51
SE9 61Nc 138
SL3: L'ly 48C 82
Elmhurst St. SW4 55Mb 112
Elmhurst Way IG10: Lough 17Pc 36
Elmington Cl. DA5: Bexl 58Dd 118
Elmington Est. SE5 52Tb 113
Elmington Rd. SE5 52Tb 113
Elmira St. SE13 55Dc 114
Elm La. GU23: Ock 91Q 190
KT11: Cobh 91Q 190
SE6 61Bc 136
Elm Lawn Cl. UB8: Uxb 38N 63
Elm Lawns Cl. AL1: St A 1C 6
Elmlea Dr. UB3: Hayes 43U 84
Elm Lea Trad. Est. N17 23Xb 51
Elmlee Cl. BR7: Chst 65Pc 138
Elmley Cl. E6 43Nc 94
Elmley St. SE18 50Tc 94
(not continuous)
Elm Lodge SW6 53Ya 110
Elmore Cl. HA0: Wemb 40Na 67
Elmore Ho. *N1* 38Tb 71
(off Elmore St.)
SW9 54Rb 113
Elmore Rd. CR5: Chip, Coul 93Hb 195
E11 34Ec 72
EN3: Enf W 10Zb 20
Elmores IG10: Lough 13Qc 36
Elmore St. N1 38Sb 71
Elm Pde. DA14: Sidc 63Wc 139
RM12: Horn 35Kd 77
ELM PARK 35Kd 77
Elm Pk. HA7: Stan 22Ka 46
SL5: S'dale 4C 146
SW2 58Pb 112
Elm Pk. Av. N15 29Vb 51
RM12: Horn 35Jd 76
Elm Pk. Chambers *SW10* 50Fb 89
(off Fulham Rd.)
Elm Pk. Ct. HA5: Pinn 26Y 45
Elm Pk. Gdns. CR2: Sels 82Yb 178
NW4 29Za 48
SW10 7B 226 (50Fb 89)
Elm Pk. Ho. SW10 7B 226 (50Fb 89)
Elm Pk. La. SW3 50Fb 89
Elm Pk. Mans. *SW10* 51Eb 111
(off Park Wlk.)
Elm Pk. Rd. E10 32Ac 72
HA5: Pinn 25Y 45
N3 24Bb 49
N21 17Sb 33
SE25 69Vb 135
SW3 51Fb 111
Elm Pas. EN5: Barn 14Bb 31
Elm Pl. SW7 7B 226 (50Fb 89)
TW15: Ashf 64Q 128
Elm Quay Ct. SW8 51Mb 112
Elm Rd. BR3: Beck 68Bc 136
BR6: Chels 80Wc 161
CR6: W'ham 89Zb 178
CR7: Thor H 70Tb 135
CR8: Purl 85Rb 177
DA1: Dart 60Md 119
DA8: Erith 53Jd 118
DA9: Ghithe 58Ud 120
DA12: Grav'nd 2E 144
DA14: Sidc 63Wc 139
E7 37Hc 73
E11 33Fc 73
E17 29Ec 52
EN5: Barn 14Bb 31
GU21: Wok 87B 168
(Heath Rd.)
GU21: Wok 10P 167
(The Mount)
HA9: Wemb 36Na 67
KT2: King T 67Pa 131
KT3: N Mald 68Ta 131
KT9: Chess 77Na 153
KT10: Clay 79Ha 152
KT17: Ewe 79Va 154
KT22: Lea 94Ka 192
N22 25Rb 51
RH1: Redh 6N 207
RM7: Mawney 26Dd 56
RM15: Avel 46Td 98
RM17: Grays 51Ee 121
SL4: Wind 5F 102
SM6: Wall 74Jb 156
Elm Rd. SW14 55Sa 109
TN16: Westrm 97Uc 200
TW14: Bedf 60T 106
Elm Rd. W. SM3: Sutt 73Bb 155
Elm Row NW3 34Eb 69
Elmroyd Av. EN6: Pot B 5Bb 17
Elmroyd Cl. EN6: Pot B 5Bb 17
Elms, The *CR0: C'don* 74Sb 157
(off Tavistock Rd.)
CR6: W'ham 87Yb 178
E12 37Mc 73
EN9: Walt A 7Lc 21
(in Woodbine Cl. Caravan Pk.)
IG10: Lough 12Hc 35
KT10: Clay 80Ha 152
SW13 55Va 110
TW15: Ashf 64Q 128
Elms Av. N10 27Kb 50
NW4 29Za 48
Elms Cl. RM11: Horn 31Kd 77
Elmscott Gdns. N21 16Sb 33
Elmscott Rd. BR1: Brom 64Gc 137
Elms Ct. HA0: Wemb 35Ja 66
Elms Cres. SW4 58Lb 112
Elmscroft Gdns. EN6: Pot B 4Bb 17
Elmsdale Rd. E17 28Bc 52
Elmsdene M. HA6: Nwood 23S 44
Elms Farm Rd. RM12: Horn 36Ld 77
Elms Gdns. HA0: Wemb 35Ja 66
RM9: Dag 35Bd 75
Elmshaw Rd. SW15 57Wa 110
Elmshorn KT17: Eps D 88Ya 174
Elmshott La. SL1: Slou 5C 80
Elmshurst Cres. N2 28Fb 49
Elmside CR0: New Ad 79Dc 158
Elmside Rd. HA9: Wemb 34Qa 67
Elms Ind. Est. RM3: Hrld W 24Rd 57
Elms La. HA0: Wemb 34Ja 66
Elmsleigh Av. HA3: Kenton 28Ka 46
Elmsleigh Cen., The
TW18: Staines 63H 127
Elmsleigh Ct. SM1: Sutt 76Db 155
Elmsleigh Ho. *TW2: Twick* 61Fa 130
(off Staines Rd.)
Elmsleigh Rd. TW2: Twick 61Fa 130
TW18: Staines 64H 127
Elmslie Cl. IG8: Wfd G 23Pc 54
KT18: Eps 86Sa 173
Elmslie Point *E3* 43Bc 92
(off Leopold St.)
Elms M. W2 4B 220 (45Fb 89)
Elms Pk. Av. HA0: Wemb 35Ja 66
Elms Rd. HA3: Hrw W 24Ga 46
SL9: Chal P 24A 42
SW4 57Lb 112
ELMSTEAD 65Pc 138
Elmstead Av. BR7: Chst 64Pc 138
HA9: Wemb 32Na 67
Elmstead Cl. KT19: Ewe 78Ua 154
N20 19Cb 31
TN13: Riv 94Gd 202
Elmstead Gdns. KT4: Wor Pk 76Wa 154
Elmstead Glade BR7: Chst 65Pc 138
Elmstead La. BR7: Chst 66Nc 138
Elmstead Rd. DA8: Erith 53Gd 118
IG3: Ilf 33Uc 74
KT14: W Byf 85J 169
Elmsted Cres. DA16: Well 51Yc 117
Elmstone Rd. SW6 53Cb 111
Elmstone Ter. BR5: St M Cry 70Yc 139
Elm St. WC1 6J 217 (42Pb 90)
Elmsway TW15: Ashf 64Q 128
Elmswood IG7: Chig 23Tc 54
KT23: Bookh 96Ba 191
Elmsworth Av. TW3: Houn 54Da 107
Elm Ter. HA3: Hrw W 25Fa 46
NW2 34Cb 69
NW3 35Gb 69
RM20: W Thur 51Xd 120
SE9 58Qc 116
Elm Terrace Fitness Cen. 58Qc 116
Elmton Ct. NW8 5B 214
Elm Tree Av. KT10: Esh 73Fa 152
Elm Tree Cl. KT16: Chert 75G 148
NW8 3B 214 (41Fb 89)
TW15: Ashf 64R 128
UB5: N'olt 40Ba 65
Elmtree Cl. KT14: Byfl 85N 169
Elm Tree Ct. NW8 3B 214
SE7 51Lc 115
Elm Tree Rd. NW8 3B 214 (41Fb 89)
Elmtree Rd. TW11: Tedd 63Ga 130
Elm Tree Wlk. WD3: Chor 13H 25
Elm Vw. Ct. UB2: S'hall 49Ca 85
Elm Vw. Ho. UB3: Harl 49T 84
Elm Wlk. BR6: Farnb 76Pc 160
NW3 33Cb 69
RM2: Rom 27Jd 56
SW20 70Ya 132
WD7: R'lett 8Ha 14
Elm Way CM14: B'wood 21Wd 58
KT4: Wor Pk 76Ya 154
KT19: Ewe 78Ta 153
N11 23Jb 50
NW10 35Ua 68
WD3: Rick 18K 25
Elmway RM16: Grays 45Ee 99
Elmwood Av. HA3: Kenton 29Ja 46
N13 22Nb 50
TW13: Felt, Hanw 61W 128
WD6: Bore 14Ra 29
Elmwood Cl. KT17: Ewe 81Wa 174
KT21: Asht 89Ma 173
SM6: Wall 75Kb 156
Elmwood Ct. *E10* 32Cc 72
(off Goldsmith Rd.)
HA0: Wemb 34Ja 66
KT21: Asht 89Ma 173
SW11 53Kb 112
(off Candy St.)
Elmwood Cres. NW9 28Sa 47
Elmwood Dr. DA5: Bexl 59Ad 117
KT17: Ewe 79Wa 154
Elmwood Gdns. W7 44Ga 86
Elmwood Gro. HP3: Hem H 5P 3
Elmwood Ho. *NW10* 40Xa 68
(off All Souls Av.)
Elmwood Pk. SL9: Ger X 32A 62
Elmwood Rd. CR0: C'don 73Rb 157
CR4: Mitc 69Hb 133
GU21: Wok 1H 187
RH1: Redh 2A 208
SE24 57Tb 113
SL2: Slou 5M 81
W4 51Sa 109
Elmworth Gro. SE21 61Tb 135
Elnathan M. W9 42Db 89
Elphinstone Cl. GU24: Brkwd 3D 186
Elphinstone Ct. SW16 65Nb 134
Elphinstone Rd. E17 26Bc 52
Elphinstone St. N5 35Rb 71
Elrick Cl. DA8: Erith 51Gd 118
Elrington Rd. E8 37Wb 71
IG8: Wfd G 22Jc 53
Elruge Cl. UB7: W Dray 48M 83
Elsa Cotts. *E14* 43Ac 92
(off Halley St.)
Elsa Ct. BR3: Beck 67Bc 136
Elsa Rd. DA16: Well 54Xc 117
Elsa St. E1 43Ac 92
Elsdale St. E9 37Yb 72
Elsden M. E2 40Yb 72
Elsden Rd. N17 25Vb 51
Elsdon Rd. GU21: Wok 10L 167
Elsenham Rd. E12 36Qc 74
Elsenham St. SW18 60Bb 111
Elsham Rd. E11 34Gc 73
W14 47Ab 88
Elsham Ter. *W14* 48Ab 88
(off Elsham Rd.)
Elsiedene Rd. N21 17Sb 33
Elsie La. Ct. *W2* 43Cb 89
(off Westbourne Pk. Vs.)
Elsiemaud Rd. SE4 57Bc 114
Elsie Rd. SE22 56Vb 113
Elsinge Rd. EN1: Enf 8Xb 19
Elsinore Av. TW19: Stanw 59N 105
Elsinore Gdns. NW2 34Ab 68
Elsinore Ho. N1 1K 217
SE5 54Sb 113
(off Denmark Rd.)
SE7 49Nc 94
W6 50Za 88
(off Fulham Pal. Rd.)
Elsinore Rd. SE23 60Ac 114
Elsinore Way TW9: Rich 55Ra 109
Elsley Ct. HA9: Wemb 37Ra 67
Elsley Rd. SW11 55Hb 111
Elspeth Rd. HA0: Wemb 36Na 67
SW11 56Hb 111
Elsrick Av. SM4: Mord 71Cb 155
Elstan Way CR0: C'don 73Ac 158
Elstead Ct. SM3: Sutt 74Ab 154
Elstead Ho. *SW2* 59Pb 112
(off Redlands Way)
Elsted St. SE17 6G 231 (49Tb 91)
Elstow Cl. HA4: Ruis 31Z 65
SE9 57Pc 116
(not continuous)
Elstow Gdns. RM9: Dag 39Ad 75
Elstow Grange NW6 38Za 68
Elstow Rd. RM9: Dag 39Ad 75
ELSTREE 16Ma 29
Elstree Aerodrome 13Ha 28
Elstree & Borehamwood Mus. 14Qa 29
Elstree Cl. RM12: Horn 38Kd 77
Elstree Distribution Pk. WD6: Bore 13Ta 29
Elstree Gdns. DA17: Belv 49Ad 95
IG1: Ilf 36Sc 74
N9 18Xb 33
Elstree Ga. WD6: Bore 12Ta 29
Elstree Hill BR1: Brom 66Gc 137
Elstree Hill Nth. WD6: E'tree 15Ma 29
Elstree Hill Sth. WD6: E'tree 17La 28
Elstree Ho. *WD6: Bore* 12Ta 29
(off Elstree Way)
Elstree Pk. WD6: Bore 16Ta 29
Elstree Rd. WD6: E'tree 17Ha 28
WD23: B Hea 17Fa 28
Elstree Studios WD6: Bore 13Ra 29
Elstree Twr. *WD6: Bore* 12Ta 29
(off Elstree Way)
Elstree Way WD6: Bore 13Ra 29
Elswick Rd. SE13 54Dc 114
Elswick St. SW6 54Eb 111
Elsworth Cl. TW14: Bedf 60U 106
Elsworthy KT7: T Ditt 72Ga 152
Elsworthy Ct. *NW3* 38Hb 69
(off Primrose Hill Rd.)
Elsworthy Ri. NW3 38Gb 69
Elsworthy Rd. NW3 39Gb 69
Elsworthy Ter. NW3 38Gb 69
Elsynge Rd. SW18 57Fb 111
ELTHAM 58Pc 116
Eltham Av. SL1: Slou 6C 80
Eltham Cen. 57Qc 116
Eltham Crematorium SE9 56Tc 116
Eltham Grn. SE9 57Mc 115
Eltham Grn. Rd. SE9 56Lc 115
Eltham High St. SE9 58Pc 116
Eltham Hill SE9 57Mc 115
Eltham Palace & Gardens 59Nc 116
Eltham Pal. Rd. SE9 58Lc 115
ELTHAM PARK 56Qc 116
Eltham Pk. Gdns. SE9 56Qc 116
Eltham Rd. SE9 57Hc 115
SE12 57Hc 115
Eltham Warren Golf Course 57Rc 116
Elthiron Rd. SW6 53Cb 111
Elthorne Av. W7 47Ha 86
Elthorne Ct. TW13: Felt 60Y 107
ELTHORNE HEIGHTS 43Ga 86
Elthorne Pk. Rd. W7 47Ha 86
Elthorne Rd. N19 33Mb 70
NW9 31Ta 67
UB8: Uxb 40M 63
Elthorne Sports Cen. 48Ha 86
Elthorne Way NW9 30Ta 47
Elthruda Rd. SE13 58Fc 115
Eltisley Rd. IG1: Ilf 35Rc 74
Elton Av. EN5: Barn 15Bb 31
HA0: Wemb 36Ka 66
UB6: G'frd 37Ga 66
Elton Cl. KT1: Hamp W 66La 130
Elton Ho. *E3* 39Bc 72
(off Candy St.)
Elton Pk. WD17: Wat 12W 26
Elton Pl. N16 36Ub 71
Elton Rd. CR8: Purl 84Lb 176
KT2: King T 67Pa 131
Elton Way WD25: A'ham 11Ca 27
Eltringham St. SW18 56Eb 111
Eluna Apartments *E1* 45Xb 91
(off Wapping La.)
Elvaston M. SW7 3A 226 (48Eb 89)
Elvaston Pl. SW7 4A 226 (48Eb 89)
Elveden Cl. GU22: Pyr 89K 169
Elveden Ho. SE24 57Rb 113
Elveden Pl. GU22: Pyr 89K 169
NW10 40Qa 67
Elveden Rd. NW10 40Qa 67
Elvedon Rd. KT11: Cobh 83X 171
TW13: Felt 62V 128
Elvendon Rd. N13 23Nb 50
Elven M. SE15 53Yb 114
Elver Gdns. E2 41Wb 91
Elverson Rd. SE8 54Dc 114
Elverton St. SW1 5D 228 (49Mb 90)
Elvet Av. RM2: Rom 28Ld 77
Elvin Dr. RM16: N Stif 46Zd 99
Elvington Grn. BR2: Brom 71Hc 159
Elvington La. NW9 25Ua 48
Elvino Rd. SE26 64Ac 136
Elvis Rd. NW2 37Ya 68
Elwell Cl. TW20: Egh 65C 126
Elwick Ct. DA1: Cray 56Kd 119
Elwick Rd. RM15: S Ock 44Yd 98
Elwill Way BR3: Beck 70Ec 136
DA13: Ist R 7B 144
Elwin St. E2 41Wb 91
Elwood Cl. EN5: New Bar 14Eb 31
Elwood St. N5 34Rb 71
Elworth Ho. *SW8* 52Pb 112
(off Oval Pl.)
Elwyn Gdns. SE12 59Jc 115
Ely Av. SL1: Slou 3G 80
Ely Cl. DA8: Erith 54Hd 118
KT3: N Mald 68Va 132
Ely Cotts. SW8 52Pb 112
Ely Ct. EC1 1A 224
KT1: King T 68Qa 131
NW6 40Cb 69
(off Chichester Rd.)
Ely Gdns. IG1: Ilf 31Nc 74
RM10: Dag 34Ed 76
WD6: Bore 15Ta 29
Ely Ho. *SE15* 52Wb 113
(off Friary Est.)
Elyne Rd. N4 30Qb 50
Ely Pl. EC1 1A 224 (43Qb 90)
IG8: Wfd G 23Qc 54
Ely Rd. AL1: St A 3F 6
CR0: C'don 71Tb 157
E10 30Ec 52
TW4: Houn 55Y 107
TW6: H'row A 54V 106
(off Esher Cl.)
Elysian Av. BR5: St M Cry 72Vc 161
Elysian Pl. CR2: S Croy 80Sb 157
Elysium Pl. *SW6* 54Bb 111
(off Elysium St.)
Elysium St. SW6 54Bb 111
Elystan Bus. Cen. UB4: Yead 45Y 85
Elystan Cl. SM6: Wall 81Lb 176
Elystan Pl. SW3 7E 226 (50Gb 89)
Elystan St. SW3 6D 226 (49Gb 89)
Elystan Wlk. N1 1K 217 (39Qb 70)
Ely's Yd. E1 7K 219 (43Vb 91)
Emanuel Av. W3 44Sa 87
Emanuel Dr. TW12: Hamp 64Ba 129
Emanuel Ho. SW1 4D 228 (48Mb 90)
Embankment SW15 54Za 110
Embankment, The TW1: Twick 60Ja 108
TW19: Wray 9N 103
Embankment Galleries 5H 223
Embankment Gdns. SW3 51Hb 111
Embankment Ho. KT16: Chert 74L 149
Embankment Pl. WC2 6G 223 (46Nb 90)
Embassy Apartments *SE5* 54Sb 113
(off Coldharbour La.)
Embassy Ct. DA14: Sidc 62Xc 139
DA16: Well 55Xc 117
E2 42Xb 91
(off Brady St.)
N11 23Mb 50
(off Bounds Grn. Rd.)
NW8 2C 214
SM6: Wall 79Kb 156
W5 45Pa 87
Embassy Gdns. BR3: Beck 67Bc 136
Embassy Ho. NW6 38Db 69
Embassy Lodge *N3* 26Bb 49
(off Cyprus Rd.)
Embassy Theatre
Central School of Speech & Drama
38Fb 69
(off College Cres.)
Emba St. SE16 47Wb 91
Ember Cen. KT12: Walt T 75Aa 151
Ember Cl. BR5: Pet W 73Sc 160
KT15: Add 78N 149
Ember Ct. NW9 26Va 48
Embercourt Rd. KT7: T Ditt 72Ga 152
Ember Farm Av. KT8: E Mos 72Fa 152
Ember Farm Way KT8: E Mos 72Fa 152
Ember Gdns. KT7: T Ditt 73Ga 152
Ember La. KT8: E Mos 73Fa 152
KT10: Esh 73Fa 152
Ember Rd. SL3: L'ly 48D 82
Emberton *SE5* 51Ub 113
(off Albany Rd.)
Emberton Ct. EC1 4B 218
Embleton Rd. SE13 56Dc 114
WD19: Wat 20W 26
Embleton Wlk. TW12: Hamp 64Ba 129
Embroidery World Bus. Cen.
IG8: Wfd G 26Mc 53
Embry Cl. HA7: Stan 21Ja 46
Embry Dr. HA7: Stan 23Ja 46
Embry Rd. SE9 57Lc 115
Embry Way HA7: Stan 22Ja 46
Emden Cl. UB7: W Dray 47Q 84
Emden St. SW6 53Db 111
Emerald Cl. E16 44Mc 93
Emerald Ct. CR5: Coul 87Mb 176
SL1: Slou 7J 81
WD6: Bore 11Pa 29
(off Aycliffe Rd.)
Emerald Gdns. RM8: Dag 32Cd 76
Emerald Rd. NW10 39Ta 67
(not continuous)
Emerald Sq. UB2: S'hall 48Z 85
Emerald St. WC1 7H 217 (43Pb 90)
Emerson Apartments N8 27Pb 50
Emerson Dr. RM11: Horn 31Md 77
Emerson Gdns. HA3: Kenton 30Pa 47
Emerson Ho. RM11: Horn 30Md 57
EMERSON PARK 31Nd 77
Emerson Pk. Ct. RM11: Horn 31Md 77
Emerson Rd. IG1: Ilf 31Pc 74
Emersons Av. BR8: Hext 66Hd 140
Emerson St. SE1 6D 224 (46Sb 91)
Emerton Cl. DA6: Bex 56Ad 117
Emerton Rd. KT22: Fet 93Fa 192
Emery Hill St. SW1 4C 228 (48Lb 90)
Emery St. SE1 3A 230 (48Qb 90)
Emery Theatre 44Dc 92
(off Annabel Cl.)
Emery Walker Trust 50Wa 88

Emes Rd. DA8: Erith 52Ed 118
Emilia Cl. EN3: Pond E 15Xb 33
Emily Bowes Ct. N17 . . . . . 27Xb 51
Emily Ct. DA2: Wilm 63Ld 141
SE1 . . . . . 2D 230
Emily Davison Dr. KT18: Tatt C 90Xa 174
Emily Duncan Pl. E7 . . . . . 35Kc 73
Emily Ho. *W10* *42Ab 88*
(off Kensal Rd.)
Emily Jackson Cl. TN13: S'oaks 96Kd 203
Emily St. *E16* *44Hc 93*
(off Jude St.)
Emirates Air Line 47Hc 93
Emirates Stadium 35Qb 70
Emley Rd. KT15: Add 76J 149
Emlyn Bldgs. SL4: Eton 2G 102
Emlyn Gdns. W12 . . . . . 47Ua 88
Emlyn La. KT22: Lea 94Ja 192
Emlyn Rd. RH1: Redh 8A 208
W12 . . . . . 47Ua 88
Emma Ho. RM1: Rom 28Gd 56
Emmanuel Ct. E10 . . . . . 31Dc 72
Emmanuel Ho. SE11 . . . . . 6K 229 (49Qb 90)
Emmanuel Lodge EN8: Chesh 2Yb 20
Emmanuel Rd. HA6: Nwood 24V 44
SW12 . . . . . 60Lb 112
Emma Rd. E13 . . . . . 40Hc 73
Emma St. E2 . . . . . 40Xb 71
Emmaus Way IG7: Chig 22Qc 54
Emmeline Ct. KT12: Walt T 73Y 151
Emmett Cl. WD7: Shenl 5Na 15
Emmetts Cl. GU21: Wok 9P 167
Emmetts La. TN14: Ide H 100Zc 201
Emminster *NW6* *39Db 69*
(off Abbey Rd.)
Emmott Av. IG6: Ilf 29Sc 54
Emmott Cl. E1 . . . . . 42Ac 92
NW11 . . . . . 30Eb 49
Emms Pas. KT1: King T 68Ma 131
Emperor's Ga. SW7 . . . . . 48Eb 89
Empingham Ho. *SE8* *49Zb 92*
(off Chilton Gro.)
Empire Av. N18 . . . . . 22Sb 51
Empire Cen. WD24: Wat 11Y 27
Empire Cinema
Bromley *68Jc 137*
(off High St.)
Hemel Hempstead 3P 3
Leicester Sq. 4E 222
Slough 7K 81
Sutton 78Db 155
Empire Cl. SE7 . . . . . 51Kc 115
Empire Ct. HA9: Wemb 34Ra 67
Empire Ho. SW7 . . . . . 4D 226
Empire M. SW16 . . . . . 64Nb 134
Empire Pde. HA9: Wemb 34Qa 67
N18 . . . . . 23Tb 51
Empire Rd. UB6: G'frd 39Ka 66
Empire Sq. N7 . . . . . 34Nb 70
SE1 . . . . . 2F 231
SE20 . . . . . *66Zb 136*
(off High St.)
Empire Sq. E. SE1 . . . . . 2F 231
Empire Sq. Sth. SE1 . . . . . 2F 231
Empire Sq. W. SE1 . . . . . 2F 231
Empire Wlk. DA9: Ghithe 56Yd 120
Empire Way HA9: Wemb 35Pa 67
Empire Wharf *E3* *39Ac 72*
(off Old Ford Rd.)
Empire Wharf Rd. E14 . . . . . 49Fc 93
Empress App. SW6 . . . . . 50Cb 89
Empress Av. E4 . . . . . 24Dc 52
E12 . . . . . 33Lc 73
IG1: Ilf 33Pc 74
IG8: Wfd G 24Hc 53
Empress Dr. BR7: Chst 65Rc 138
Empress M. SE5 . . . . . 54Sb 113
Empress Pde. E4 . . . . . 24Cc 52
Empress Pl. SW6 . . . . . 50Cb 89
Empress Rd. DA12: Grav'nd 9G 122
Empress State Bldg. SW6 . . . . . 50Cb 89
Empress St. SE17 . . . . . 51Sb 113
Empson St. E3 . . . . . 42Dc 92
Emsworth Cl. N9 . . . . . 18Yb 34
Emsworth Ct. SW16 . . . . . 62Nb 134
Emsworth Rd. IG6: Ilf 26Rc 54
Emsworth St. SW2 . . . . . 61Pb 134
EMT House E6 . . . . . 43Qc 94
Emu Rd. SW8 . . . . . 54Kb 112
Enard Ho. *E3* *40Bc 72*
(off Cardigan Rd.)
Ena Rd. SW16 . . . . . 69Nb 134
Enborne Grn. RM15: S Ock 43Wd 98
Enbrook St. W10 . . . . . 41Ab 88
Enclave, The SW13 . . . . . 54Va 110
Enclave Ct. EC1 . . . . . 5C 218
Endale Cl. SM5: Cars 75Hb 155
Endeavour Ho. *E14* *47Cc 92*
(off Cuba St.)
Endeavour Way CR0: Bedd 73Nb 156
IG11: Bark 40Wc 75
SW19 . . . . . 63Db 133
Endell St. WC2 . . . . . 2F 223 (44Nb 90)
Enderby St. SE10 . . . . . 50Fc 93
Enderley Cl. HA3: Hrw W 26Ga 46
Enderley Rd. HA3: Hrw W 25Ga 46
Endersby Rd. EN5: Barn 15Ya 30
Enders Cl. EN2: Enf 10Qb 18
Endersleigh Gdns. NW4 . . . . . 28Wa 48
Endlebury Rd. E4 . . . . . 19Ec 34
Endlesham Rd. SW12 . . . . . 59Jb 112
Endsleigh Cl. CR2: Sels 82Yb 178
Endsleigh Ct. WC1 . . . . . 5E 216
Endsleigh Gdns. IG1: Ilf 33Pc 74
KT6: Surb 72La 152
KT12: Hers 78Y 151
WC1 . . . . . 5D 216 (42Mb 90)
Endsleigh Ind. Est. UB2: S'hall 49Aa 85
Endsleigh Pl. WC1 . . . . . 5E 216 (42Mb 90)
Endsleigh Rd. RH1: Mers 1C 208
UB2: S'hall 49Aa 85
W13 . . . . . 45Ja 86
Endsleigh St. WC1 . . . . . 5D 216 (42Mb 90)
Endway KT5: Surb 73Ra 153
Endwell Rd. SE4 . . . . . 54Ac 114
Endymion Rd. N4 . . . . . 31Qb 70
SW2 . . . . . 58Pb 112
Energen Cl. NW10 . . . . . 37Ua 68
Energize Fitness Club *50Ab 88*
(in Hammersmith & West London College)
Energy Centre, The N1 . . . . . 4H 219
ENFIELD 13Tb 33
Enfield Bus. Cen. EN3: Enf H 12Yb 34
Enfield Cloisters N1 . . . . . 3H 219
Enfield Cl. UB8: Uxb 40M 63
Enfield College Sports Cen. 13Yb 34
Enfield Crematorium EN1: Enf 9Xb 19
Enfield Golf Course 14Rb 33
ENFIELD HIGHWAY 13Yb 34
Enfield Ho. *RM3: Rom* *24Nd 57*
(off Leyburn Cres.)
SW9 . . . . . *54Nb 112*
(off Stockwell Rd.)
ENFIELD ISLAND VILLAGE 9Cc 20
ENFIELD LOCK 9Bc 20
Enfield Lock EN3: Enf L 10Cc 20
Enfield Retail Pk. EN1: Enf 13Wb 33
Enfield Rd. EN2: Enf 14Mb 32
N1 . . . . . 38Ub 71
TW6: H'row A 54U 106
TW8: Bford 50Ma 87
W3 . . . . . 47Ra 87
Enfield Rd. Rdbt. TW6: H'row A 54U 106
ENFIELD TOWN 13Tb 33
Enfield Wlk. TW8: Bford 50Ma 87
ENFIELD WASH 9Zb 20
Enford St. W1 . . . . . 7F 215 (43Hb 89)
Engadine Cl. CR0: C'don 76Vb 157
Engadine St. SW18 . . . . . 60Bb 111
Engate St. SE13 . . . . . 56Ec 114
Engayne Gdns. RM14: Upm 32Rd 77
Engel Pk. NW7 . . . . . 23Ya 48
Engine Ct. SW1 . . . . . 7C 222
Engineer Cl. SE18 . . . . . 51Qc 116
Engineers Way HA9: Wemb 35Qa 67
Englands La. IG10: Lough 12Qc 36
NW3 . . . . . 37Hb 69
England Way KT3: N Mald 70Ra 131
Englefield NW1 . . . . . 4B 216
Englefield Cl. BR5: St M Cry 71Vc 161
CR0: C'don 72Sb 157
EN2: Enf 12Qb 32
TW20: Eng G 5N 125
Englefield Cres. BR5: St M Cry 70Vc 139
ENGLEFIELD GREEN 4N 125
Englefield Path BR5: St M Cry 70Wc 139
Englefield Rd. GU21: Knap 9G 166
N1 . . . . . 38Tb 71
Engleheart Dr. TW14: Felt 58V 106
Engleheart Rd. SE6 . . . . . 59Dc 114
Englehurst TW20: Eng G 5N 125
Englemere Pk. KT22: Oxs 85Da 171
Englewood Rd. SW12 . . . . . 58Kb 112
Engliff La. GU22: Pyr 88J 169
English Gdns. TW19: Wray 6P 103
English Grounds SE1 . . . . . 7H 225 (46Ub 91)
English St. E3 . . . . . 42Bc 92
Enid Cl. AL2: Brick W 3Ba 13
Enid St. SE16 . . . . . 3K 231 (48Vb 91)
Enmore Av. SE25 . . . . . 71Wb 157
Enmore Gdns. SW14 . . . . . 57Ta 109
Enmore Rd. SE25 . . . . . 71Wb 157
SW15 . . . . . 56Ya 110
UB1: S'hall 42Ca 85
Ennerdale NW1 . . . . . 3B 216
Ennerdale Av. HA7: Stan 27La 46
RM12: Horn 36Jd 76
Ennerdale Cl. AL1: St A 4F 6
SM1: Sutt 77Bb 155
TW14: Felt 60V 106
Ennerdale Ct. *E11* *31Jc 73*
(off Cambridge Rd.)
Ennerdale Cres. SL1: Slou 3A 80
Ennerdale Dr. NW9 . . . . . 29Ua 48
WD25: Wat 7Y 13
Ennerdale Gdns. HA9: Wemb 32La 66
Ennerdale Ho. E3 . . . . . 42Bc 92
Ennerdale Rd. DA7: Bex 53Cd 118
TW9: Kew, Rich 54Pa 109
Ennersdale Rd. SE13 . . . . . 57Fc 115
Ennis Ho. *E14* *44Dc 92*
(off Vesey Path)
Ennismore Av. UB6: G'frd 37Ga 66
W4 . . . . . 49Va 88
Ennismore Gdns. KT7: T Ditt 72Ga 152
SW7 . . . . . 2D 226 (47Gb 89)
Ennismore Gdns. M.
SW7 . . . . . 3D 226 (48Gb 89)
Ennismore M. SW7 . . . . . 2D 226 (48Gb 89)
Ennismore St. SW7 . . . . . 3D 226 (48Gb 89)
Ennis Rd. N4 . . . . . 32Qb 70
SE18 . . . . . 51Sc 116
Ennor Ct. SM3: Cheam 77Ya 154
Ensbury Ho. *SW8* *52Pb 112*
(off Carroun Rd.)
Ensign Cl. CR8: Purl 82Qb 176
TW6: H'row A 55U 106
TW19: Stanw 60M 105
Ensign Dr. N13 . . . . . 20Sb 33
Ensign Est. RM19: Purf 49Rd 97
Ensign Ho. *E14* *47Cc 92*
(off Admirals Way)
RM17: Grays 51Be 121
SW18 . . . . . 55Eb 111
Ensign Ind. Cen. *E1* *45Wb 91*
(off Ensign St.)
Ensign St. E1 . . . . . 45Wb 91
Ensign Way SM6: Wall 80Nb 156
TW19: Stanw 60M 105
Enslin Rd. SE9 . . . . . 58Qc 116
Ensor M. SW7 . . . . . 7B 226 (50Fb 89)
Enstone Rd. EN3: Enf H 13Ac 34
UB10: Ick 34P 63
Enterdent, The RH9: G'stone 5B 210
Enterdent Cotts. RH9: G'stone 5B 210
Enterdent Rd. RH9: G'stone 6A 210
Enterprise Bus. Pk. E14 . . . . . 47Dc 92
Enterprise Centre, The *BR3: Beck* *64Ac 136*
(off Cricket La.)
EN6: Pot B 2Ab 16
Enterprise Cl. CR0: C'don 74Qb 156
Enterprise Ct. *RH1: Redh* *7P 207*
(off Mill St.)
Enterprise Ho. E4 . . . . . 17Ec 34
E9 . . . . . *38Yb 72*
(off Tudor Gro.)
E14 . . . . . *50Dc 92*
(off St Davids Sq.)
IG11: Bark 41Vc 95
KT12: Walt T 73X 151
Enterprise Ind. Est. SE16 . . . . . 50Yb 92
Enterprise Row N15 . . . . . 29Vb 51
Enterprise Trad. Est. UB2: S'hall 47Da 85
Enterprise Way NW10 . . . . . 41Va 88
SW18 . . . . . 56Cb 111
TW11: Tedd 65Ha 130
Enterprize Way SE8 . . . . . 49Bc 92
Entertainment Av. SE10 . . . . . 46Gc 93
Enville Ho. WD19: Wat 20Y 27
Envoy Av. TW6: H'row A 55V 106
Envoy Rdbt. TW6: H'row A 55V 106
Eothen Cl. CR3: Cat'm 96Wb 197
Epcot M. NW10 . . . . . 41Za 88
Epirus M. SW6 . . . . . 52Cb 111
Epirus Rd. SW6 . . . . . 52Bb 111
EPPING 2Wc 23
Epping Cl. E14 . . . . . 49Cc 92
RM7: Mawney 27Dd 56
Epping Forest District Mus. 5Ec 20
Epping Glade E4 . . . . . 16Ec 34
Epping Golf Course 5Xc 23
Epping La.
RM4: Abr, Stap T . . . . 12Xc 37 & 11Cd 38
Epping New Rd. IG9: Buck H 19Kc 35
IG10: Buck H, H Beech, Lough . . . 12Lc 35
Epping Pl. N1 . . . . . 37Qb 70
Epping Rd. CM16: Epp, N Weald 1Yc 23
CM16: Epp, They B 8Pc 22
Epping Sports Cen. 3Vc 23
Epping Way E4 . . . . . 16Dc 34
Epple Rd. SW6 . . . . . 53Bb 111
EPSOM 85Ta 173
Epsom Bus. Pk. KT17: Eps 83Ua 174
Epsom Cl. DA7: Bex 55Dd 118
DA12: Grav'nd 5E 144
UB5: N'olt 36Ba 65
Epsom College Fitness Cen. 87Wa 174
Epsom Common Local Nature Reserve
. . . . . 85Pa 173
Epsom Ct. WD3: Rick 18K 25
EPSOM DOWNS 90Ua 174
Epsom Downs Metro Cen.
KT20: Tad 92Xa 194
Epsom Downs Racecourse 90Va 174
Epsom Gap KT9: Lea 87Ka 172
Epsom Golf Course 87Wa 174
Epsom Ho. *RM3: Rom* *22Nd 57*
(off Dagnam Pk. Dr.)
SL4: Wind *3D 102*
(off Paddock Cl.)
Epsom La. Nth. KT18: Tad, Tatt C . . . 90Xa 174
KT20: Tad 90Xa 174
Epsom La. Sth. KT20: Tad 93Ya 194
Epsom Playhouse 85Ta 173
Epsom Rd. CR0: Wadd 77Qb 156
E10 . . . . . 30Ec 52
IG3: Ilf 30Vc 55
KT17: Ewe 83Va 174
KT21: Asht 90Pa 173
KT22: Lea 93Ka 192
SM3: Sutt 73Bb 155
SM4: Mord 73Bb 155
Epsom Sports Club 87Ta 173
Epsom Sq. TW6: H'row A 54V 106
Epsom Trade Pk. KT19: Eps 83Ta 173
Epsom Way RM12: Horn 35Pd 77
Epstein Rd. SE28 . . . . . 46Wc 95
Epworth Rd. TW7: Isle 52Ka 108
Epworth St. EC2 . . . . . 6G 219 (42Tb 91)
Equana Apartments *SE8* *50Ac 92*
(off Evelyn St.)
Equestrian Statue George III (Copper Horse)
. . . . . 1H 125
Equiano Ho. *SW9* *53Pb 112*
(off Lett Rd.)
Equinox Ct. IG2: Ilf 29Rc 54
Equinox Ho. IG11: Bark 37Sc 74
Equity M. W5 . . . . . 46Ma 87
Equity Sq. E2 . . . . . 4K 219
Equus Cl. SL9: Ger X 2N 61
Equus Equestrian Cen. 82Pa 173
Erasmus St. SW1 . . . . . 6E 228 (49Mb 90)
Erconwald St. W12 . . . . . 44Va 88
Erebus Dr. SE28 . . . . . 48Sc 94
Eresby Dr. BR3: Beck 74Cc 158
Eresby Ho. SW7 . . . . . 2E 226
Eresby Pl. NW6 . . . . . 38Cb 69
Erica Cl. GU24: W End 5C 166
SL1: Slou 5C 80
Erica Ct. BR8: Swan 70Gd 140
GU22: Wok 10P 167
Erica Gdns. CR0: C'don 76Dc 158
Erica Ho. *N22* *25Qb 50*
(off Acacia Rd.)
SE4 . . . . . 55Bc 114
Erica St. W12 . . . . . 45Wa 88
Eric Clarke La. IG11: Bark 42Rc 94
Eric Cl. E7 . . . . . 35Jc 73
Ericcson Cl. SW18 . . . . . 57Cb 111
Eric Fletcher Ct. *N1* *38Sb 71*
(off Essex Rd.)
Eric Liddell Sports Cen. 61Mc 137
Eric Rd. E7 . . . . . 35Jc 73
NW10 . . . . . 37Va 68
RM6: Chad H 31Zc 75
Eric Shipman Ter. *E13* *42Jc 93*
(off Balaam St.)
Ericson Ho. *SE13* *56Fc 115*
(off Blessington Rd.)
Eric Steele Ho. AL2: Park 9P 5
Eric St. E3 . . . . . 42Bc 92
(not continuous)
Eric Wilkins Ho. *SE1* *50Wb 91*
(off Old Kent Rd.)
Eridge Grn. Cl. BR5: Orp 74Yc 161
Eridge Rd. W4 . . . . . 48Ta 87
Erin Cl. BR1: Brom 66Gc 137
IG3: Ilf 30Wc 55
SW6 . . . . . 52Cb 111
Erindale SE18 . . . . . 51Tc 116
Erindale Ter. SE18 . . . . . 51Tc 116
Erin M. N22 . . . . . 25Rb 51
Eriswell Cres. KT12: Hers 79U 150
Eriswell Rd. KT12: Hers 77V 150
ERITH 50Hd 96
Erith Ct. RM19: Purf 49Qd 97
Erith Cres. RM5: Col R 25Ed 56
Erith High St. DA8: Erith 50Gd 96
(not continuous)
Erith Leisure Cen. 51Gd 118
Erith Playhouse *50Hd 96*
(off Wharfside Cl.)
Erith Rd. DA7: Bex 56Dd 118
DA8: Erith 50Cd 96
(Picardy Rd.)
DA8: Erith 56Dd 118
(Watling St.)
DA17: Belv, Erith 50Cd 96
ERITH RDBT. 50Gd 96
Erith School Community Sports Cen.
. . . . . 52Ed 118
Erith Stadium 51Gd 118
Erith Yacht Club 51Kd 119
Erkenwald Cl. KT16: Chert 73G 148
Erlanger Rd. SE14 . . . . . 53Zb 114
Erlesmere Gdns. W13 . . . . . 48Ja 86
Erlich Cotts. *E1* *43Yb 92*
(off Sidney St.)
Ermine Cl. AL3: St A 3N 5
EN7: Chesh 3Xb 19
TW4: Houn 54Y 107
Ermine Ho. *E3* *39Bc 72*
(off Parnell Rd.)
N17 . . . . . *24Vb 51*
(off Moselle St.)
Ermine M. E2 . . . . . 1K 219 (39Vb 71)
Ermine Rd. N15 . . . . . 30Vb 51
SE13 . . . . . 56Dc 114
Ermine Side EN1: Enf 15Wb 33
Ermington Rd. SE9 . . . . . 61Sc 138
Ermyn Cl. KT22: Lea 93Ma 193
Ermyn Way KT22: Lea 93Ma 193
Ernald Av. E6 . . . . . 40Nc 74
Ernan Cl. RM15: S Ock 43Wd 98
Ernan Rd. RM15: S Ock 43Wd 98
Erncroft Way TW1: Twick 58Ha 108
Ernest Av. SE27 . . . . . 63Rb 135
Ernest Cl. BR3: Beck 71Cc 158
Ernest Cotts. KT17: Ewe 80Va 154
Ernest Gdns. W4 . . . . . 51Ra 109
Ernest Gro. BR3: Beck 71Bc 158
Ernest Harriss Ho. *W9* *42Cb 89*
(off Elgin Av.)
Ernest Rd. KT1: King T 68Ra 131
RM11: Horn 30Nd 57
Ernest Shackleton Lodge *SE10* *49Gc 93*
(off Christchurch Way)
Ernest Sq. KT1: King T 68Ra 131
Ernest St. E1 . . . . . 42Zb 92
Ernle Rd. SW20 . . . . . 66Xa 132
Ernshaw Pl. SW15 . . . . . 57Ab 110
Eros 5D 222 (45Mb 90)
Eros Ho. Shops *SE6* *59Dc 114*
(off Brownhill Rd.)
Erpingham Rd. SW15 . . . . . 55Ya 110
Erridge Rd. SW19 . . . . . 68Cb 133
Erriff Dr. RM15: S Ock 43Vd 98
Errington Cl. RM16: Grays 8D 100
Errington Dr. SL4: Wind 3E 102
Errington Rd. W9 . . . . . 42Bb 89
Errol Gdns. KT3: N Mald 70Wa 132
UB4: Yead 42X 85
Erroll Rd. RM1: Rom 28Hd 56
Errol St. EC1 . . . . . 6E 218 (42Sb 91)
Erskine Cl. SM1: Sutt 76Gb 155
Erskine Cres. N17 . . . . . 28Xb 51
Erskine Hill NW11 . . . . . 28Cb 49
Erskine Ho. *SW1* *50Lb 90*
(off Churchill Gdns.)
TN13: S'oaks 97Jd 202
WD19: Wat 20Z 27
Erskine M. *NW3* *38Hb 69*
(off Erskine Rd.)
Erskine Rd. E17 . . . . . 28Bc 52
NW3 . . . . . 38Hb 69
SM1: Sutt 77Fb 155
Erwood Rd. SE7 . . . . . 50Nc 94
Esam Way SW16 . . . . . 64Qb 134
Escombe Ct. *CR3: Whyt* *91Wb 197*
(off Godstone Rd.)
Escombe Dr. GU2: Guild 10M 187
Escot Rd. TW16: Sun 66U 128
Escott Gdns. SE9 . . . . . 63Nc 138
Escott Pl. KT16: Ott 79E 148
Escot Way EN5: Barn 15Ya 30
Escreet Gro. SE18 . . . . . 49Qc 94
Esdaile Gdns. RM14: Upm 31Td 78
ESHER 77Da 151
Esher Av. KT12: Walt T 73W 150
RM7: Rom 30Ed 56
SM3: Cheam 76Za 154
Esher By-Pass KT9: Chess 82Ea 172
KT10: Clay 82Ea 172
KT10: Esh 82Ca 171
KT11: Cobh 85V 170
KT22: Oxs 82Ea 172
Esher Cl. DA5: Bexl 60Ad 117
KT10: Esh 78Da 151
ESHER COMMON 82Ea 172
Esher Common (Local Nature Reserve)
. . . . . 82Ca 171
Esher Cres. TW6: H'row A 54V 106
Esher Gdns. SW19 . . . . . 61Za 132
Esher Grn. KT10: Esh 77Da 151
Esher Grn. Dr. KT10: Esh 76Ca 151
Esher M. CR4: Mitc 69Jb 134
Esher Pk. Av. KT10: Esh 77Da 151
Esher Pl. Av. KT10: Esh 77Ca 151
Esher Rd. IG3: Ilf 34Uc 74
KT8: E Mos 72Fa 152
KT12: Hers 78Z 151
Esher RUFC 75Aa 151
Eskdale AL2: Lon C 9K 7
NW1 . . . . . 2B 216
Eskdale Av. UB5: N'olt 39Ba 65
Eskdale Cl. DA2: Dart 61Sd 142
HA9: Wemb 33Ma 67
Eskdale Gdns. CR8: Purl 86Tb 177
Eskdale Rd. DA7: Bex 54Cd 118
UB8: Uxb 40K 63
Eskdale Rd. Ind. Est. UB8: Uxb 40K 63
Esk Ho. *E3* *42Bc 92*
(off British St.)
Eskley Gdns. RM15: S Ock 43Xd 98
(not continuous)
Eskmont Ridge SE19 . . . . . 66Tb 135
Esk Rd. E13 . . . . . 42Jc 93
Esk Way RM1: Rom 24Fd 56
Esmar Cres. NW9 . . . . . 31Wa 68
Esmeralda Rd. SE1 . . . . . 49Wb 91
Esmond Cl. RM13: Rain 38Kd 77
Esmond Ct. *W8* *48Db 89*
(off Thackeray St.)
Esmond Gdns. W4 . . . . . 49Ta 87
Esmond Rd. NW6 . . . . . 39Bb 69
W4 . . . . . 49Ta 87
Esmond St. SW15 . . . . . 56Ab 110
Esparto St. SW18 . . . . . 59Db 111
Esparto Way DA4: S Dar 67Sd 142
Esporta Health & Fitness
Chislehurst 64Uc 138
Chiswick 53Ua 110
Chiswick Pk. 49Ra 87
Enfield 14Tb 33
Finchley Rd. *37Fb 69*
(in O2 Cen.)
Hemel Hempstead 1C 4
Ilford *34Rc 74*
(off Clements Rd.)
Islington 39Rb 71
Kingston upon Thames 67Na 131
Little Warley 29Be 59
New Southgate 22Jb 50
Northwood 24R 44
Esporta Health & Fitness
Repton Park 24Qc 54
Romford 29Gd 56
Wandsworth 56Db 111
Wimbledon 65Bb 133
Esporta: The Surrey Health & Racquets Club
. . . . . 79Pb 156
Esprit Ct. E1 . . . . . 1K 225
Essan Ho. W5 . . . . . 43Ka 86
Essence Ct. HA9: Wemb 33Pa 67
Essendene Cl. CR3: Cat'm 95Ub 197
Essendene Rd. CR3: Cat'm 95Ub 197
Essenden Rd. CR2: S Croy 80Ub 157
DA17: Belv 50Cd 96
Essendine Mans. W9 . . . . . 41Cb 89
Essendine Rd. W9 . . . . . 41Cb 89
Essex Av. SL2: Slou 3G 80
TW7: Isle 55Ga 108
Essex Cl. E17 . . . . . 28Ac 52
HA4: Ruis 32Z 65
KT15: Add 77L 149
RM7: Mawney 28Dd 56
SM4: Mord 73Za 154
Essex Ct. EC4 . . . . . 3K 223
SW13 . . . . . 54Va 110
W6 . . . . . *48Ya 88*
(off Hammersmith Gro.)
Essex Gdns. N4 . . . . . 30Rb 51
RM11: Horn 29Qd 57
SS17: Linf 7J 101
Essex Gro. SE19 . . . . . 65Tb 135
Essex Hall E17 . . . . . 25Zb 52
Essex Ho. *E14* *44Dc 92*
(off Giraud St.)
Essex La. WD4: Hunt C 5T 12
Essex Mans. E11 . . . . . 31Fc 73
Essex Pk. N3 . . . . . 23Db 49
Essex Pk. M. W3 . . . . . 46Ua 88
Essex Pl. W4 . . . . . 49Sa 87
(not continuous)
Essex Pl. Sq. W4 . . . . . 49Ta 87
Essex Rd. DA1: Dart 58Md 119
(not continuous)
DA3: Lfield 68Zd 143
DA11: Grav'nd 10C 122
E4 . . . . . 18Gc 35
E10 . . . . . 30Ec 52
E12 . . . . . 36Nc 74
E17 . . . . . 30Ac 52
E18 . . . . . 26Kc 53
EN2: Enf 14Tb 33
IG11: Bark 38Tc 74
N1 . . . . . 1B 218 (39Rb 71)
NW10 . . . . . 38Ua 68
RM6: Chad H 31Yc 75
RM7: Mawney 28Dd 56
RM10: Dag 36Ed 76
RM20: W Thur 51Wd 120
W3 . . . . . 45Sa 87
W4 . . . . . 49Ta 87
WD6: Bore 13Qa 29
WD17: Wat 12W 26
Essex Rd. Sth. E11 . . . . . 31Fc 73
Essex St. AL1: St A 1C 6
E7 . . . . . 36Jc 73
WC2 . . . . . 3K 223 (44Qb 90)
Essex Twr. *SE20* *67Xb 135*
(off Jasmine Gro.)
Essex Vs. W8 . . . . . 47Cb 89
Essex Way CM13: Gt War 23Yd 58
Essex Wharf E5 . . . . . 33Zb 72
Essian St. E1 . . . . . 43Ac 92
Essoldo Way HA8: Edg 27Pa 47
Estate Cotts. RH5: Mick 99Ma 193
Estate Way E10 . . . . . 32Bc 72
Estcourt Rd. SE25 . . . . . 72Xb 157
SW6 . . . . . 52Bb 111
WD17: Wat 13Y 27
Estella Apartments *E15* *37Fc 73*
(off Grove Cres. Rd.)
Estella Av. KT3: N Mald 70Xa 132
Estella Ho. *W11* *45Za 88*
(off St Ann's Rd.)
Estelle Rd. NW3 . . . . . 35Hb 69
Esterbrooke St. SW1 . . . . . 6D 228 (49Mb 90)
Este Rd. SW11 . . . . . 55Gb 111
Esther Cl. N21 . . . . . 17Qb 32
Esther Randall Ct. NW1 . . . . . 5A 216
Esther Rd. E11 . . . . . 31Gc 73
Estoria Cl. SW2 . . . . . 59Qb 112
Estorick Collection of Modern Italian Art
. . . . . 37Rb 71
Estreham Rd. SW16 . . . . . 65Mb 134
Estridge Cl. TW3: Houn 56Ca 107
Estuary Cl. IG11: Bark 41Xc 95
Estuary Ho. *E16* *46Mc 93*
(off Agnes George Wlk.)
Eswarah Ho. *KT17: Eps* *83Va 174*
(off Epsom Cl.)
Eswyn Rd. SW17 . . . . . 63Hb 133
Etal Ho. *N1* *38Rb 71*
(off The Sutton Est.)
Etcetera Theatre *38Kb 70*
(off Camden High St.)
Etchingham Ct. N3 . . . . . 24Db 49
Etchingham Pk. Rd. N3 . . . . . 24Db 49
Etchingham Rd. E15 . . . . . 35Ec 72
Eternit Wlk. SW6 . . . . . 53Ya 110
Etfield Gro. DA14: Sidc 64Xc 139
Ethel Bailey Cl. KT19: Eps 84Qa 173
Ethelbert Cl. BR1: Brom 68Jc 137
Ethelbert Ct. *BR1: Brom* *69Jc 137*
(off Ethelbert Rd.)
Ethelbert Gdns. IG2: Ilf 29Pc 54
Ethelbert Ho. *E9* *35Ac 72*
(off Homerton Rd.)
Ethelbert Rd. BR1: Brom 69Jc 137
BR5: St P 69Zc 139
DA2: Hawl 63Nd 141
DA8: Erith 52Ed 118
SW20 . . . . . 67Za 132
Ethelbert St. SW12 . . . . . 60Kb 112
Ethel Brooks Ho. SE18 . . . . . 51Rc 116
Ethelburga Rd. RM3: Hrld W 25Pd 57
Ethelburga St. SW11 . . . . . 53Gb 111
Ethelburga Twr. *SW11* *53Gb 111*
(off Maskelyne Cl.)
Etheldene Av. N10 . . . . . 28Lb 50
Ethelden Rd. W12 . . . . . 46Xa 88
Ethelred Ct. *CR3: Whyt* *91Wb 197*
(off Godstone Rd.)
Ethel Rd. E16 . . . . . 44Kc 93
TW15: Ashf 64N 127
Ethel St. SE17 . . . . . 6E 230 (49Sb 91)
Ethel Ter. BR6: Prat B 81Yc 181
Ethelwine Pl. WD5: Ab L 2V 12

Etheridge Grn. IG10: Lough 13Sc 36
Etheridge Rd. IG10: Lough 12Rc 36
NW4 31Ya 68
(not continuous)
Etherley Rd. N15 29Sb 51
Etherow St. SE22 59Wb 113
Etherstone Grn. SW16 63Qb 134
Etherstone Rd. SW16 63Qb 134
Ethnard Rd. SE15 51Xb 113
Ethorpe Cl. SL9: Ger X 29A 42
Ethorpe Cres. SL9: Ger X 29A 42
Ethorpe Ho. SL9: Ger X 29A 42
Ethos Sport Imperial 3C 226 (47Fb 89)
Ethronvi Rd. DA7: Bex 55Ad 117
Etloe Ho. E10 32Cc 72
Etloe Rd. E10 33Cc 72
Etna Rd. AL3: St A 1B 6
ETON 1H 103
Eton Av. EN4: E Barn 16Gb 31
HA0: Wemb 35Ka 66
KT3: N Mald 71Ta 153
N12 24Eb 49
NW3 38Fb 69
TW5: Hest 51Ba 107
Eton Cl. SL3: Dat 1L 103
SW18 59Db 111
Eton College 10G 80
Eton Coll. Rd. NW3 37Hb 69
Eton College Rowing Cen. 2B 102
Eton Ct. HA0: Wemb 35La 66
NW3 38Fb 69
SL4: Eton 2H 103
TW18: Staines 64H 127
Eton Garages NW3 37Gb 69
Eton Gro. NW9 27Qa 47
SE13 55Gc 115
Eton Hall NW3 37Hb 69
Eton Ho. *KT18: Eps* 85Sa 173
(off Dalmeny Way)
N5 35Rb 71
(off Leigh Rd.)
UB7: W Dray 47P 83
WD24: Wat 12Y 27
(off Anglian Cl.)
Eton Mnr. Ct. *E10* 33Cc 72
(off Leyton Grange Est.)
Eton Pl. NW3 38Jb 70
Eton Ri. NW3 37Hb 69
Eton Riverside SL4: Eton 2H 103
Eton Rd. BR6: Chels 77Xc 161
IG1: Ilf 35Sc 74
NW3 38Hb 69
SL3: Dat 10K 81
UB3: Harl 52V 106
Eton Sq. SL4: Eton 2H 103
Eton St. TW9: Rich 57Na 109
Eton Vs. NW3 37Hb 69
Eton Wlk. *SL1: Slou* 8J 81
(off Upton Pk.)
Eton Way DA1: Dart 56Ld 119
ETON WICK 9D 80
Eton Wick Rd. SL4: Eton, Eton W 9C 80
Etta St. SE8 51Ac 114
Etton Cl. RM12: Horn 33Nd 77
Ettrick St. E14 44Ec 92
(not continuous)
Etwell Pl. KT5: Surb 72Pa 153
Eucalyptus M. SW16 65Mb 134
Euclid Way RM20: W Thur 50Vd 98
Euesden Cl. N9 20Xb 33
Eugene Bann Indoor Tennis Cen. 10F 208
Eugene Cl. RM2: Rom 28Ld 57
Eugene Cotter Ho. SE17 6G 231
Eugenia Rd. SE16 49Yb 92
Eugenie M. BR7: Chst 67Rc 138
Eureka Rd. KT1: King T 68Qa 131
Eurobet Ho. *GU21: Wok* 89A 168
(off Church St. W.)
Euro Cl. NW10 37Wa 68
Eurolink Bus. Cen. SW2 57Qb 112
Europa Ho. *E16* 44Hc 93
(off Shirley St.)
Europa Pk. RM20: Grays 50Yd 98
Europa Pl. EC1 4D 218 (41Sb 91)
Europa Trade Pk. E16 42Gc 93
Europa Trad. Est. DA8: Erith 50Fd 96
European Bus. Cen. NW9 27Sa 47
(not continuous)
European Design Cen. NW9 27Ta 47
Europe Rd. SE18 48Pc 94
Euro Trade Cen. DA17: Belv 47Ed 96
Eustace Bldg. SW8 51Kb 112
Eustace Ho. SE11 5H 229
Eustace Pl. SE18 49Pc 94
Eustace Rd. E6 41Nc 94
RM6: Chad H 31Zc 75
SW6 52Cb 111
Euston Av. WD18: Wat 15V 26
Euston Gro. NW1 4D 216
Euston Rd. CR0: C'don 74Qb 156
NW1 6A 216 (42Kb 90)
Euston Sq. NW1 4D 216 (41Mb 90)
(not continuous)
Euston Sta. Colonnade
NW1 4D 216 (41Mb 90)
Euston St. NW1 5C 216 (41Lb 90)
Euston Twr. NW1 5B 216 (42Lb 90)
EUSTON UNDERPASS 5C 216 (42Lb 90)
Eva Ct. CR2: S Croy 79Ub 157
Evan Cook Cl. SE15 53Yb 114
Evandale Rd. SW9 54Qb 112
Evangelist Ho. *EC4* 3B 224
(off Black Friars La.)
Evangelist Rd. NW5 35Kb 70
Evans Av. WD25: Wat 7V 12
Evans Bus. Cen. NW2 34Wa 68
Evans Cl. DA9: Ghithe 57Wd 120
E8 37Vb 71
WD3: Crox G 15Q 26
Evansdale RM13: Rain 41Hd 96
Evans Gro. TW13: Hanw 61Ca 129
Evans Ho. *SW8* 52Mb 112
(off Wandsworth Rd.)
TW13: Hanw 61Ca 129
W12 45Xa 88
(off White City Est.)
Evans Rd. SE6 61Gc 137
Evanston Av. E4 24Ec 52
Evanston Gdns. IG4: Ilf 30Nc 54
Evans Wharf HP3: Hem H 6N 3
Eva Rd. RM6: Chad H 31Yc 75
Evedon Ho. *N1* 1H 219
(off New Era Est.)
Evelina Mans. SE5 52Tb 113
Evelina Rd. SE15 55Yb 114
SE20 66Yb 136
Eveline Lowe Est. SE16 48Wb 91
Eveline Rd. CR4: Mitc 67Hb 133
Evelyn Av. HA4: Ruis 31U 64
NW9 28Ta 47
RH8: T'sey 96Lc 199
Evelyn Cl. GU22: Wok 92B 188
TW2: Whitt 59Da 107
Evelyn Cotts. RH9: S God 9C 210
Evelyn Ct. E8 35Wb 71
N1 2F 219
Evelyn Cres. TW16: Sun 67V 128
Evelyn Denington Ct. *N1* 38Rb 71
(off The Sutton Est.)
Evelyn Denington Rd. E6 42Nc 94
Evelyn Dr. HA5: Pinn 24Z 45
Evelyn Fox Ct. W10 43Ya 88
Evelyn Gdns. RH9: G'stone 2A 210
SW7 7A 226 (50Eb 89)
TW9: Rich 56Na 109
Evelyn Gro. UB1: S'hall 44Ba 85
W5 46Pa 87
Evelyn Ho. *SE14* 53Ac 114
(off Loring Rd.)
W8 47Db 89
(off Hornton Pl.)
W12 47Va 88
(off Cobbold Rd.)
Evelyn Mans. SW1 4B 228
W14 51Ab 110
(off Queen's Club Gdns.)
Evelyn Rd. E16 46Jc 93
E17 28Ec 52
EN4: Cockf 14Hb 31
SW19 64Db 133
TW14: Otf 88Ld 183
TW9: Rich 55Na 109
TW10: Ham 62La 130
W4 48Ta 87
Evelyns Cl. UB8: Hil 44Q 84
Evelyn Sharp Cl. RM2: Rom 27Md 57
Evelyn Sharp Ho. HP2: Hem H 3B 4
RM2: Rom 27Md 57
Evelyn's Sq. SE8 49Ac 92
Evelyn Ter. TW9: Rich 55Na 109
Evelyn Wlk. CM13: Gt War 23Yd 58
DA9: Ghithe 56Wd 120
N1 2F 219 (40Tb 71)
Evelyn Way KT11: Stoke D 88Ba 171
KT19: Eps 83Qa 173
SM6: Bedd 77Mb 156
TW16: Sun 67V 128
Evelyn Yd. W1 2D 222 (44Mb 90)
Evening Hill BR3: Beck 66Ec 136
Evenlode Ho. SE2 47Yc 95
Evensyde WD18: Wat 16S 26
Evenwood Cl. SW15 57Ab 110
Everall Cl. HP1: Hem H 2L 3
Everard Av. BR2: Hayes 74Jc 159
SL1: Slou 7J 81
Everard Cl. AL1: St A 4B 6
Everard Ct. N13 20Pb 32
Everard Ho. *E1* 44Wb 91
(off Boyd St.)
Everard La. CR3: Cat'm 94Xb 197
Everard Way HA9: Wemb 34Na 67
Everatt Cl. SW18 58Bb 111
Everdon Rd. SW13 51Wa 110
Everest Cl. DA11: Nflt 2A 144
Everest Ct. GU21: Wok 8J 167
Everest Pl. BR8: Swan 70Fd 140
E14 43Ec 92
Everest Rd. SE9 57Pc 116
TW19: Stanw 59M 105
Everest Way HP2: Hem H 1A 4
Everett Cl. HA5: Eastc 27V 44
WD23: B Hea 18Ga 28
Everett Ct. WD7: R'lett 6Ja 14
Everett Ho. SE17 7G 231
Everett Wlk. *DA17: Belv* 50Bd 95
(off Osborne Rd.)
Everglade TN16: Big H 90Mc 179
Everglade Cl. DA3: Hartl 70Ae 143
Everglade Ho. E17 26Bc 52
Everglade Strand NW9 25Va 48
Evergreen Apartments *IG8: Wfd G* 25Hc 53
(off High Rd. Woodford Grn.)
Evergreen Cl. SE20 66Yb 136
Evergreen Ct. TW19: Stanw 59M 105
Evergreen Oak Av. SL4: Wind 5L 103
Evergreen Sq. E8 38Vb 71
Evergreen Wlk. HP3: Hem H 4N 3
Evergreen Way TW19: Stanw 59M 105
UB3: Hayes 45V 84
Everilda St. N1 39Pb 70
Evering Rd. E5 34Vb 71
N16 34Vb 71
Everington Rd. N10 26Hb 49
Everington St. W6 51Za 110
(not continuous)
Everitt Rd. NW10 41Ta 87
Everlands Cl. GU22: Wok 90A 168
Everlasting La. AL3: St A 1A 6
(not continuous)
Everleigh St. N4 32Pb 70
Eve Rd. E11 35Gc 73
E15 40Gc 73
GU21: Wok 87D 168
N17 27Ub 51
TW7: Isle 56Ja 108
Eversfield Gdns. NW7 23Ua 48
Eversfield Rd. RH2: Reig 6K 207
TW9: Kew 54Pa 109
Evershed Ho. E1 2K 225
Evershed Wlk. W4 48Sa 87
Eversholt Ct. EN5: New Bar 15Eb 31
Eversholt St. NW1 1C 216 (40Lb 70)
Evershot Rd. N4 32Pb 70
Eversleigh Ct. N3 24Bb 49
Eversleigh Gdns. RM14: Upm 32Td 78
Eversleigh Rd. E6 39Mc 73
EN5: New Bar 15Eb 31
N3 24Bb 49
SW11 55Hb 111
Eversley Av. DA7: Bex 54Fd 118
HA9: Wemb 33Qa 67
Eversley Cl. IG10: Lough 13Sc 36
N21 16Pb 32
Eversley Cres. HA4: Ruis 33U 64
N21 16Qb 32
TW7: Isle 53Fa 108
Eversley Cross DA7: Bex 54Gd 118
Eversley Ho. *E2* 41Wb 91
(off Gosset St.)
Eversley Mt. N21 16Pb 32
Eversley Pk. SW19 65Xa 132
Eversley Pk. Rd. N21 16Pb 32
Eversley Rd. KT5: Surb 70Pa 131
SE7 51Kc 115
SE19 66Tb 135
Eversley Way CR0: C'don 76Cc 158
TW20: Thorpe 68E 126
Everthorpe Rd. SE15 55Vb 113
Everton Bldgs. NW1 4B 216 (41Lb 90)
Everton Ct. *HA7: Stan* 27Na 47
(off Honeypot La.)
Everton Dr. HA7: Stan 27Na 47
Everton Rd. CR0: C'don 74Wb 157
Everyman Cinema
Oxted 1J 211
Reigate 6J 207
Evesham Av. E17 26Cc 52
Evesham Cl. RH2: Reig 5H 207
SM2: Sutt 80Cb 155
UB6: G'frd 40Da 65
Evesham Ct. TW10: Rich 58Pa 109
W13 46Ja 86
(off Tewkesbury Rd.)
Evesham Grn. SM4: Mord 72Db 155
Evesham Ho. *E2* 40Yb 72
(off Old Ford Rd.)
NW8 39Eb 69
(off Abbey Rd.)
SW1 7A 228
Evesham Rd. DA12: Grav'nd 1F 144
E15 38Hc 73
N11 22Lb 50
RH2: Reig 5H 207
SM4: Mord 72Db 155
Evesham Rd. Nth. RH2: Reig 5H 207
Evesham St. W11 45Za 88
Evesham Ter. KT6: Surb 72Ma 153
Evesham Wlk. SE5 54Tb 113
SW9 54Qb 112
Evesham Way IG5: Ilf 27Qc 54
SW11 55Jb 112
Evette M. IG5: Ilf 25Qc 54
Evolution WD25: Wat 6Z 13
Evreham Rd. SL0: Iver 44G 82
Evreham Sports Cen. 43F 82
Evry Rd. DA14: Sidc 65Yc 139
Ewald Rd. SW6 54Bb 111
Ewanrigg Ter. IG8: Wfd G 22Lc 53
Ewan Rd. RM3: Hrld W 26Md 57
Ewart Gro. N22 25Pb 50
Ewart Pl. E3 40Bc 72
Ewart Rd. SE23 59Zb 114
Ewe Cl. N7 37Nb 70
EWELL 81Va 174
Ewell By-Pass KT17: Ewe 80Wa 154
Ewell Ct. Av. KT19: Ewe 78Ua 154
Ewell Downs Rd. KT17: Ewe 83Wa 174
Ewell Gro. Ct. *KT17: Ewe* 81Va 174
(off West St.)
Ewell Ho. *KT17: Ewe* 82Va 174
(off Ewell Ho. Gro.)
Ewell Ho. Gro. KT17: Ewe 82Va 174
Ewell Ho. Pde. *KT17: Ewe* 82Va 174
(off Epsom Rd.)
Ewellhurst Rd. IG5: Ilf 26Nc 54
Ewell Pk. Gdns. KT17: Ewe 80Wa 154
Ewell Pk. Way KT17: Ewe 79Wa 154
Ewell Rd. KT6: Surb 73Ka 152
(Effingham Rd.)
KT6: Surb 72Na 153
(South Ter.)
SM3: Cheam 79Za 154
Ewelme Rd. SE23 60Yb 114
Ewen Cres. SW2 59Qb 112
Ewen Henderson Ct. *SE14* 52Ac 114
(off Goodwood Rd.)
Ewen Ho. N1 1H 217
Ewer St. SE1 7D 224 (46Sb 91)
Ewhurst Av. CR2: Sande 81Vb 177
Ewhurst Cl. E1 43Yb 92
SM2: Cheam 81Ya 174
Ewhurst Ct. CR4: Mitc 69Fb 133
Ewhurst Rd. SE4 58Bc 114
Exbury Ho. E9 38Yb 72
SW1 7D 228
Exbury Rd. SE6 61Cc 136
ExCeL 45Kc 93
Excel Ct. WC2 5E 222
Excel Marina E16 45Jc 93
Excelsior Cl. KT1: King T 68Qa 131
Excelsior Gdns. SE13 54Ec 114
Excelsior Ind. Est. SE15 51Yb 114
Excel Waterfront E16 45Kc 93
Exchange, The *CR0: C'don* 76Sb 157
(off Surrey St.)
IG1: Ilf 33Rc 74
Exchange Apartments
BR2: Brom 70Kc 137
(off Sparkes Cl.)
Exchange Arc. EC2 7J 219 (43Ub 91)
Exchange Bldg. E1 6K 219
Exchange Cl. N11 19Jb 32
Exchange Ct. WC2 5G 223 (45Nb 90)
Exchange Ho. EC2 7J 219
NW10 38Xa 68
SW1 6D 228
Exchange Mans. NW11 31Bb 69
Exchange Pl. EC2 7H 219 (43Ub 91)
Exchange Rd. SL5: S'hill 1A 146
(not continuous)
WD18: Wat 13X 27
Exchange Sq. EC2 7H 219 (43Ub 91)
Exchange St. EC1 4D 218 (41Sb 91)
RM1: Rom 29Gd 56
Exchange Wlk. HA5: Pinn 31Aa 65
Executive Pk. AL1: St A 2H 7
Exedown Rd. TN15: Wro 86Xd 184
Exeforde Av. TW15: Ashf 63Q 128
Exeter Cl. E6 44Pc 94
WD24: Wat 12Y 27
Exeter Ct. *KT6: Surb* 71Na 153
(off Maple Rd.)
NW6 40Cb 69
(off Cambridge Rd.)
Exeter Gdns. IG1: Ilf 32Nc 74
Exeter Ho. *IG11: Bark* 38Wc 75
(off Margaret Bondfield Av.)
N1 1H 219
(off New Era Est.)
SE15 51Wb 113
(off Friary Est.)
SW15 58Ya 110
TW13: Hanw 61Ba 129
(off Watermill Way)
W2 44Eb 89
(off Hallfield Est.)
WD6: Bore 12Qa 29
Exeter Mans. NW2 37Ab 68
Exeter M. NW6 37Db 69
SW6 52Cb 111
Exeter Rd. CR0: C'don 73Ub 157
DA12: Grav'nd 2F 144
DA16: Well 54Vc 117
E16 43Jc 93
E17 29Cc 52
EN3: Pond E 13Zb 34
HA2: Harr 33Aa 65
N9 19Yb 34
N14 18Kb 32
NW2 36Ab 68
RM10: Dag 37Dd 76
TW6: H'row A 55T 106
TW13: Hanw 62Ba 129
Exeter St. WC2 4G 223 (45Nb 90)
Exeter Way SE14 52Bc 114
TW6: H'row A 54U 106
Exford Ct. *SW11* 53Fb 111
(off Bolingbroke Wlk.)
Exford Gdns. SE12 60Kc 115
Exford Rd. SE12 61Kc 137
Exhibition Cl. W12 45Ya 88
Exhibition Grounds HA9: Wemb 35Ra 67
Exhibition Rd. SW7 2C 226 (47Fb 89)
Exit Rd. N2 26Fb 49
Exmoor Cl. IG6: Ilf 25Sc 54
Exmoor Ho. *E3* 40Ac 72
(off Gernon Rd.)
Exmoor St. W10 42Za 88
Exmouth Ho. *E14* 49Dc 92
(off Cahir St.)
EC1 5A 218
Exmouth Mkt. EC1 5K 217 (42Qb 90)
Exmouth M. NW1 4C 216 (41Lb 90)
Exmouth Pl. E8 38Xb 71
Exmouth Rd. DA16: Well 53Yc 117
E17 29Bc 52
HA4: Ruis 34Y 65
RM17: Grays 51De 121
UB4: Hayes 41U 84
Exmouth St. E1 44Yb 92
Exning Rd. E16 42Gc 93
Exon Apartments *RM1: Rom* 28Hd 56
(off Mercury Gdns.)
Exonbury *NW8* 39Db 69
(off Abbey Rd.)
Exon St. SE17 6H 231 (50Ub 91)
Explorer Av. TW19: Stanw 60N 105
Explorer Dr. WD18: Wat 16V 26
Explorers Ct. *E14* 45Fc 93
(off Newport Av.)
Export Ho. SE1 2J 231
Express Dr. IG3: Ilf 32Xc 75
Express Newspapers SE1 6B 224
Express Wharf *E14* 47Cc 92
(off Hutchings St.)
Exton Gdns. RM8: Dag 36Yc 75
Exton Rd. NW10 38Sa 67
Exton St. SE1 7K 223 (46Qb 90)
Eyebright Cl. CR0: C'don 74Zb 158
Eyhurst Av. RM12: Horn 34Jd 76
Eyhurst Cl. KT20: Kgswd 95Bb 195
NW2 33Wa 68
Eyhurst Pk. KT20: Kgswd 95Eb 195
Eyhurst Spur KT20: Kgswd 96Bb 195
Eylewood Rd. SE27 64Sb 135
Eynella Rd. SE22 59Vb 113
Eynham Rd. W12 44Ya 88
EYNSFORD 75Nd 163
Eynsford Castle 75Nd 163
Eynsford Cl. BR5: Pet W 73Sc 160
Eynsford Cres. DA5: Bexl 60Yc 117
Eynsford Ho. SE1 2F 231
SE15 51Yb 114
SE17 6H 231
Eynsford Ri. DA4: Eyns 77Md 163
Eynsford Rd. BR8: Crock 72Fd 162
DA4: Eyns, Farni 74Pd 163
DA9: Ghithe 57Yd 120
IG3: Ilf 33Uc 74
TN14: Eyns, S'ham 80Kd 163
Eynsford Ter. UB7: Yiew 44P 83
Eynsham Dr. SE2 49Wc 95
Eynswood Dr. DA14: Sidc 64Xc 139
Eyot Gdns. W6 50Va 88
Eyot Grn. W4 50Va 88
Eyot Ho. *SE16* 48Wb 91
(off Frean St.)
Eyre Cl. RM2: Rom 28Kd 57
Eyre Ct. NW8 1B 214 (40Fb 69)
Eyre Grn. SL2: Slou 1E 80
Eyre St. Hill EC1 6K 217 (42Qb 90)
Eysham Ct. EN5: New Bar 15Db 31
Eyston Dr. KT13: Weyb 82Q 170
Eythorne Rd. SW9 53Qb 112
Ezra St. E2 41Vb 91

F

Faber Gdns. NW4 29Wa 48
Fabian Bell Twr. *E3* 40Cc 72
(off Pancras Way)
Fabian Rd. SW6 52Bb 111
Fabian St. E6 42Pc 94
Facade, The RH2: Reig 5J 207
SE23 61Yb 136
Fackenden La. TN14: S'ham 85Kd 183
Factory La. CR0: C'don 74Qb 156
N17 26Vb 51
Factory Rd. DA11: Nflt 58Ee 121
E16 46Mc 93
Factory Yd. W7 46Ga 86
Faesten Way DA5: Bexl 62Gd 140
Faggots Cl. WD7: R'lett 7La 14
Faggs Rd. TW14: Felt 56V 106
Fagus Av. RM13: Rain 41Md 97
Faints Cl. EN7: Chesh 1Vb 19
Fairacre HA5: Eastc 28W 44
HP3: Hem H 6P 3
KT3: N Mald 69Ua 132
Fairacre Ct. HA6: Nwood 24U 44
Fairacre Pl. DA3: Hartl 69Ae 143
Fair Acres BR2: Brom 71Jc 159
CR0: Sels 81Bc 178
Fairacres HA4: Ruis 31V 64
KT11: Cobh 84Z 171
KT20: Tad 93Ya 194
SW15 56Va 110
Fairacres Cl. EN6: Pot B 5Bb 17
Fairacres Ind. Est. SL4: Wind 4B 102
Fairbairn Cl. CR8: Purl 85Qb 176
Fairbairn Grn. SW9 53Rb 113
Fairbank Av. BR6: Farnb 75Rc 160
Fairbank Est. N1 2G 219 (40Tb 71)
Fairbanks Ct. HA0: Wemb 39Na 67
Fairbanks Lodge WD6: Bore 14Qa 29
Fairbanks Rd. N17 27Vb 51
Fairbourne KT11: Cobh 85Z 171
Fairbourne Cl. GU21: Wok 10L 167
Fairbourne Ho. UB3: Harl 48S 84
Fairbourne La. CR3: Cat'm 94Sb 197
Fairbourne Rd. N17 27Ub 51
SW4 58Mb 112
Fairbriar Ct. *KT18: Eps* 85Ua 174
(off Hereford Cl.)
Fairbriar Residence SW7 5A 226
Fairbridge Rd. N19 33Mb 70
Fairbrook Cl. N13 22Qb 50
Fairbrook Rd. N13 23Qb 50
Fairburn Cl. WD6: Bore 11Qa 29
Fairburn Ct. SW15 57Ab 110
Fairburn Ho. *W14* 50Bb 89
(off Ivatt Pl.)
Fairby Grange DA3: Hartl 72Ae 165
Fairby Ho. SE1 5K 231
Fairby La. DA3: Hartl 72Ae 165
Fairby Rd. SE12 57Kc 115
Faircharm Trad. Est. SE8 52Dc 114
Fairchild Cl. SW11 54Fb 111
Fairchildes Av. CR0: New Ad 84Fc 179
Fairchildes Rd. CR6: W'ham 86Fc 179
Fairchild Ho. *E2* 40Xb 71
(off Cambridge Cres.)
E9 38Yb 72
(off Frampton Pk. Rd.)
N1 3H 219
N3 25Cb 49
Fairchild Pl. EC2 6J 219
Fairchild St. EC2 6J 219 (42Ub 91)
Fair Cl. WD23: Bush 17Da 27
Fairclough Cl. UB5: N'olt 42Ba 85
Fairclough St. E1 44Wb 91
Faircroft SL2: Slou 2F 80
Faircroft Ct. TW11: Tedd 65Ja 130
FAIR CROSS 36Uc 74
Faircross Av. IG11: Bark 37Sc 74
RM5: Col R 24Fd 56
Faircross Ho. *WD17: Wat* 13X 27
(off High St.)
Faircross Pde. IG11: Bark 36Uc 74
Faircross Way AL1: St A 1E 6
Fairdale Gdns. SW15 56Xa 110
UB3: Hayes 47W 84
Fairdene Rd. CR5: Coul 90Mb 176
Fairey Av. UB3: Harl 49V 84
Fairfax Av. KT17: Ewe 81Xa 174
RH1: Redh 5N 207
Fairfax Cl. KT12: Walt T 74X 151
RH8: Oxt 2H 211
Fairfax Ct. DA1: Dart 58Qd 119
NW6 38Eb 69
(off Fairfax Rd.)
Fairfax Gdns. SE3 53Lc 115
Fairfax Ho. *KT1: King T* 69Pa 131
(off Livesey Cl.)
Fairfax Mans. *NW6* 38Eb 69
(off Finchley Rd.)
Fairfax M. E16 46Kc 93
N8 28Rb 51
SW15 56Ya 110
Fairfax Pl. NW6 38Eb 69
W14 48Ab 88
Fairfax Rd. GU22: Wok 92D 188
N8 28Qb 50
NW6 38Eb 69
RM17: Grays 50De 99
RM18: Tilb 3B 122
TW11: Tedd 65Ja 130
W4 48Ua 88
Fairfax Way N10 24Jb 50
FAIRFIELD 93Ka 192
Fairfield *E1* 43Yb 92
(off Redman's Rd.)
KT1: King T 68Pa 131
N20 17Fb 31
NW1 1B 216
Fairfield App. TW19: Wray 8P 103
Fairfield Av. HA4: Ruis 31S 64
HA8: Edg 23Ra 47
NW4 30Xa 48
RM14: Upm 34Sd 78
RM16: Grays 45Ee 99
SL3: Dat 2N 103
TW2: Whitt 60Da 107
TW18: Staines 63H 127
WD19: Wat 20Y 27
Fairfield Cl. CR4: Mitc 66Gb 133
DA15: Sidc 58Vc 117
EN3: Pond E 14Zb 34
HA6: Nwood 22S 44
KT19: Ewe 78Ua 154
N12 21Eb 49
RM12: Horn 32Jd 76
SL3: Dat 2P 103
TN15: Kems'g 90Qd 183
WD7: R'lett 9Ga 14
Fairfield Cotts. KT23: Bookh 97Da 191
Fairfield Ct. HA4: Ruis 32T 64
HA6: Nwood 26W 44
KT22: Lea 93Ka 192
(off Leret Way)
NW10 39Wa 68
Fairfield Cres. HA8: Edg 23Ra 47
Fairfield Dr. HA2: Harr 27Ea 46
SW18 57Db 111
UB6: G'frd 39La 66
Fairfield East KT1: King T 68Na 131
Fairfield Gdns. N8 29Nb 50
Fairfield Gro. SE7 51Mc 115
Fairfield Halls 76Tb 157
Fairfield La. GU24: W End 4E 166
SL2: Farn R 10F 60
Fairfield Nth. KT1: King T 68Na 131
Fairfield Pk. KT11: Cobh 86Z 171
Fairfield Path CR0: C'don 76Tb 157
Fairfield Pl. KT1: King T 69Na 131
Fairfield Pool & Leisure Cen. 59Nd 119
Fairfield Rd. BR1: Brom 66Jc 137
BR3: Beck 68Cc 136
BR5: Pet W 72Tc 160
CM14: B'wood 20Yd 40
CM16: Epp 1Xc 23
CR0: C'don 76Tb 157
DA7: Bex 54Bd 117
E3 40Cc 72
E17 26Ac 52
IG1: Ilf 37Rc 74
IG8: Wfd G 23Jc 53
KT1: King T 68Na 131
KT22: Lea 93Ka 192

Fairfield Rd. N8 29Nb 50
N18 21Wb 51
SL1: Burn 1A 80
TN15: Bor G 91Be 205
TW19: Wray 8P 103
UB1: S'hall 44Ba 85
UB7: Yiew 45N 83
UB8: Uxb 37M 63
Fairfields DA12: Grav'nd 4G 144
KT16: Chert 74J 149
Fairfields Cl. NW9 29Sa 47
Fairfields Cres. NW9 28Sa 47
Fairfield Sth. KT1: King T 68Na 131
Fairfield Sq. DA11: Grav'nd 8C 122
Fairfields Rd. TW3: Houn 55Ea 108
Fairfield St. SW18 57Db 111
Fairfield Trade Pk. KT1: King T 69Pa 131
Fairfield Wlk. EN8: Chesh 1Ac 20
KT22: Lea 93Ka 192
(off Fairfield Rd.)
Fairfield Way CR5: Coul 86Mb 176
EN5: Barn 15Cb 31
KT19: Ewe 78Ua 154
Fairfield West KT1: King T 68Na 131
Fairfolds WD25: Wat 8Aa 13
Fairfoot Rd. E3 42Cc 92
Fairford SE6 60Cc 114
Fairford Av. CR0: C'don 71Zb 158
DA7: Bex 53Fd 118
Fairford Cl. CR0: C'don 71Ac 158
KT14: W Byf 86H 169
RH2: Reig 4L 207
RM3: Rom 23Rd 57
Fairford Ct. SM2: Sutt 80Db 155
Fairford Gdns. KT4: Wor Pk 75Va 154
Fairford Ho. SE11 6A 230 (49Qb 90)
Fairford Way RM3: Rom 23Rd 57
Fairgreen EN4: Cockf 13Hb 31
Fairgreen Ct. EN4: Cockf 13Hb 31
Fairgreen E. EN4: Cockf 13Hb 31
Fairgreen Rd. CR7: Thor H 71Rb 157
Fairhall Ct. KT5: Surb 73Pa 153
Fairham Av. RM15: S Ock 45Wd 98
Fairhaven AL2: Park 9B 6
TW20: Egh 64B 126
Fairhaven Av. CR0: C'don 72Zb 158
Fairhaven Ct. *CR2: S Croy 78Sb 157*
(off Warham Rd.)
TW18: Staines 65G 126
(off Bowes Rd.)
TW20: Egh 64B 126
Fairhaven Cres. WD19: Wat 20W 26
Fairhaven Rd. RH1: Redh 2A 208
Fairhazel Gdns. NW6 37Db 69
Fairhazel Mans. *NW6 38Eb 69*
(off Fairhazel Gdns.)
Fairhill HP3: Hem H 6P 3
Fairholme TW14: Bedf 59T 106
Fairholme Av. RM2: Rom 29Jd 56
Fairholme Cl. N3 28Ab 48
Fairholme Ct. HA5: Hat E 23Ba 45
Fairholme Cres. KT21: Asht 89La 172
UB4: Hayes 42V 84
Fairholme Gdns. N3 27Ab 48
RM14: Upm 31Vd 78
Fairholme Rd. CR0: C'don 73Qb 156
HA1: Harr 29Ha 46
IG1: Ilf 31Pc 74
SM1: Sutt 79Bb 155
TW15: Ashf 64N 127
W14 50Ab 88
Fairholt Cl. N16 32Ub 71
Fairholt Rd. N16 32Tb 71
Fairholt St. SW7 3E 226 (48Gb 89)
Fairkytes Av. RM11: Horn 32Md 77
Fairland Ho. BR2: Brom 70Kc 137
Fairland Rd. E15 37Hc 73
Fairlands Av. CR7: Thor H 70Pb 134
IG9: Buck H 19Jc 35
SM1: Sutt 75Cb 155
Fairlands Ct. SE9 58Qc 116
Fair La. CR5: Coul 97Eb 195
Fairlawn KT13: Weyb 78U 150
KT23: Bookh 96Ba 191
SE7 52Lc 115
Fairlawn Av. DA7: Bex 54Zc 117
N2 28Gb 49
W4 49Sa 87
Fairlawn Cl. KT2: King T 65Sa 131
KT10: Clay 79Ha 152
N14 16Lb 32
TW13: Hanw 63Ba 129
Fairlawn Ct. SE7 52Lc 115
(not continuous)
W4 49Sa 87
Fairlawn Dr. IG8: Wfd G 24Jc 53
RH1: Redh 8N 207
Fairlawnes SM6: Wall 78Kb 156
Fairlawn Gdns. UB1: S'hall 45Ba 85
Fairlawn Gro. SM7: Bans 85Fb 175
W4 49Sa 87
Fairlawn Mans. SE14 53Zb 114
Fairlawn Pk. GU21: Wok 86A 168
SE26 64Ac 136
SL4: Wind 6C 102
Fairlawn Rd. SM5: Cars 83Eb 175
SM7: Bans 84Fb 175
SW19 66Bb 133
Fairlawns CM14: B'wood 20Wd 40
CM16: Epp 1Xc 23
HA5: Pinn 26Z 45
KT15: Add 78K 149
KT15: Wdhm 83H 169
TW1: Twick 58La 108
TW16: Sun 69W 128
WD17: Wat 10V 12
Fairlawns Cl. RM11: Horn 31Pd 77
TW18: Staines 65K 127
Fairlead Ho. *E14 48Cc 92*
(off Alpha Gro.)
Fairlea Pl. W5 42La 86
Fairley Way EN7: Chesh 1Xb 19
Fairlie Ct. *E3 41Dc 92*
(off Stroudley Wlk.)
Fairlie Gdns. SE23 59Yb 114
Fairlie Rd. SL1: Slou 4E 80
Fairlight TW12: Hamp H 64Da 129
Fairlight Av. E4 19Fc 35
IG8: Wfd G 23Jc 53
NW10 40Ua 68
SL4: Wind 4H 103
Fairlight Cl. E4 19Fc 35
KT4: Wor Pk 77Ya 154
Fairlight Ct. NW10 40Ua 68
UB6: G'frd 40Ea 66
Fairlight Cross DA3: Lfield 69De 143
Fairlight Dr. UB8: Uxb 37M 63
Fairlight Rd. SW17 63Fb 133
Fairline Ct. BR3: Beck 68Ec 136
FAIRLOP 25Uc 54
Fairlop Cl. RM12: Horn 37Kd 77
Fairlop Ct. E11 32Fc 73
Fairlop Gdns. IG6: Ilf 24Sc 54
Fairlop Rd. E11 31Fc 73
IG6: Ilf 26Sc 54
Fairlop Sailing Cen. 25Vc 55
Fairlop Waters Country Pk. 26Vc 55
Fairlop Waters Golf Course 26Uc 54
Fairmark Dr. UB10: Hil 37Q 64
Fairmead BR1: Brom 70Pc 138
GU21: Wok 10N 167
KT5: Surb 74Ra 153
Fairmead Cl. BR1: Brom 70Pc 138
KT3: N Mald 69Ta 131
TW5: Hest 52Z 107
Fairmead Ct. TW9: Rich 54Ra 109
Fairmead Cres. HA8: Edg 20Sa 29
Fairmead Gdns. IG4: Ilf 29Nc 54
Fairmead Ho. E9 35Ac 72
Fairmead Rd. CR0: C'don 73Pb 156
IG10: H Beech, Lough 15Kc 35
N19 34Mb 70
Fairmeads IG10: Lough 12Rc 36
KT11: Cobh 85Ba 171
Fairmeadside IG10: Lough 15Lc 35
FAIRMILE 84Ba 171
Fairmile Av. KT11: Cobh 86Aa 171
SW16 64Mb 134
Fairmile Ct. KT11: Cobh 84Aa 171
Fairmile Golf Range 83Y 171
Fairmile Ho. TW11: Tedd 63Ja 130
Fairmile La. KT11: Cobh 84Z 171
Fairmile Pk. Copse KT11: Cobh 85Ba 171
Fairmile Pk. Rd. KT11: Cobh 85Ba 171
Fairmont Av. E14 46Fc 93
Fairmont Cl. DA17: Belv 50Bd 95
Fairmont Ho. *E3 42Cc 92*
(off Wellington Way)
Fairmount Rd. SW2 58Pb 112
Fairoak Cl. BR5: Pet W 73Rc 160
CR8: Kenley 87Rb 177
KT22: Oxs 84Fa 172
Fairoak Dr. SE9 57Tc 116
Fairoak Gdns. RM1: Rom 26Gd 56
Fair Oak La. KT9: Chess 84Ea 172
KT22: Oxs 84Ea 172
Fair Oak Pl. IG6: Ilf 26Sc 54
Fairoaks Caravan Pk. GU3: Worp 10E 186
Fairoaks Ct. *KT15: Add 78K 149*
(off Liberty La.)
Fairoaks Gro. EN3: Enf W 9Zb 20
FAIRSEAT 84Ee 185
Fairseat Cl. WD23: B Hea 19Ga 28
Fairseat La. TN15: Stans 81Ce 185
TN15: Wro 87De 185
Fairs Rd. KT22: Lea 91Ja 192
Fairstead Lodge *IG8: Wfd G 23Jc 53*
(off Snakes La.)
Fairstead Wlk. *N1 39Sb 71*
(off Popham St.)
Fair St. SE1 1J 231 (47Ub 91)
TW3: Houn 55Ea 108
Fairthorne Vs. *SE7 50Jc 93*
(off Felltram Way)
Fairthorn Rd. SE7 50Jc 93
Fairtrough Rd. BR6: Prat B 84Xc 181
Fairview DA3: Fawk 76Xd 164
DA8: Erith 52Hd 118
EN6: Pot B 1Db 17
HA4: Ruis 35Y 65
KT17: Ewe 83Ya 174
Fairview Av. CM13: Hut 17Fe 41
GU22: Wok 90A 168
HA0: Wemb 37Ma 67
RM13: Rain 40Md 77
SS17: Stan H 2L 101
Fairview Chase SS17: Stan H 3L 101
Fairview Cl. E17 25Ac 52
GU22: Wok 90B 168
IG7: Chig 21Uc 54
SE26 64Ac 136
Fairview Ct. NW4 26Za 48
TW15: Ashf 64Q 128
Fairview Cres. HA2: Harr 32Ca 65
Fairview Dr. BR6: Orp 77Tc 160
IG7: Chig 21Uc 54
TW17: Shep 71P 149
WD17: Wat 8U 12
Fairview Est. NW10 41Sa 87
Fairview Gdns. IG8: Wfd G 25Kc 53
Fairview Ho. SW2 59Pb 112
Fairview Ind. Est. RH8: Oxt 5L 211
Fairview Ind. Pk. RM13: Rain 43Fd 96
Fairview Pl. SW2 59Pb 112
Fairview Rd. DA13: Ist R, Nflt G 66Fe 143
EN2: Enf 11Qb 32
IG7: Chig 21Uc 54
KT17: Ewe 83Va 174
N15 29Vb 51
SL2: Slou 2D 80
SM1: Sutt 78Fb 155
SW16 67Pb 134
Fairviews RH8: Oxt 5L 211
Fairview Vs. E4 24Dc 52
Fairview Way HA8: Edg 21Qa 47
Fairwall Ho. SE5 53Ub 113
Fairwater Av. DA16: Well 56Wc 117
Fairwater Dr. KT15: New H 81M 169
TW17: Shep 71S 150
Fairwater Ho. TW11: Tedd 63Ja 130
Fairway BR5: Pet W 71Tc 160
DA6: Bex 57Ad 117
GU25: Vir W 2N 147
HP3: Hem H 6P 3
IG8: Wfd G 22Lc 53
KT16: Chert 74K 149
RM16: Grays 46De 99
SM5: Cars 83Eb 175
SW20 69Ya 132
Fairway, The BR1: Brom 71Pc 160
DA11: Grav'nd 1C 144
EN5: New Bar 16Db 31
GU3: Worp 6G 186
HA0: Wemb 34Ka 66
HA4: Ruis 35Y 65
HA6: Nwood 21U 44
KT3: N Mald 67Ta 131
KT8: W Mole 69Da 129
KT13: Weyb 83Q 170
KT22: Lea 90Ja 172
N13 20Sb 33
N14 16Kb 32
Fairway, The NW7 20Ta 29
RM14: Upm 31Sd 78
SL1: Burn 10A 60
UB5: N'olt 37Ea 66
UB10: Hil 41P 83
W3 44Ua 88
WD5: Ab L 4T 12
Fairway Av. NW9 27Ra 47
UB7: W Dray 46L 83
WD6: Bore 12Ra 29
Fair Way Cl. KT10: Surb 76Ka 152
Fairway Cl. AL2: Park 9A 6
CR0: C'don 71Ac 158
GU22: Wok 1M 187
KT19: Ewe 77Sa 153
NW11 31Eb 69
TW4: Houn 57Y 107
(Amberley Way)
TW4: Houn 57Z 107
(Islay Gdns.)
UB7: W Dray 46M 83
Fairway Ct. EN5: New Bar 16Db 31
HP3: Hem H 6P 3
NW7 20Ta 29
SE16 47Zb 92
(off Christopher Cl.)
Fairway Dr. DA2: Dart 59Rd 119
SE28 44Zc 95
UB6: G'frd 38Da 65
Fairway Gdns. BR3: Beck 72Fc 159
IG1: Ilf 36Sc 74
Fairway Ho. *WD6: Bore 13Ra 29*
(off Eldon Av.)
Fairways CR8: Kenley 89Sb 177
E17 28Ec 52
EN9: Walt A 6Gc 21
HA7: Stan 26Na 47
KT24: Eff J 95V 190
TW7: Isle 53Fa 108
TW11: Tedd 66Ma 131
TW15: Ashf 65R 128
Fairways, The RH1: Redh 9M 207
Fairways Bus. Pk. E10 33Ac 72
Fairway Trad. Est. TW4: Houn 57Y 107
Fairweather Cl. N15 28Ub 51
Fairweather Ct. N13 20Pb 32
Fairweather Ho. N7 35Nb 70
Fairweather Rd. N16 30Wb 51
Fairwell La. KT24: W Hor 100R 190
Fairwyn Rd. SE26 63Ac 136
Faith Ct. *E3 40Cc 72*
(off Lefevre Wlk.)
SE1 50Vb 91
(off Cooper's Rd.)
Faithfield WD23: Bush 16Aa 27
Fakenham Cl. NW7 24Wa 48
UB5: N'olt 37Ba 65
Fakruddin St. E1 42Wb 91
Falaise TW20: Egh 64A 126
Falcon WC1 7G 217
Falcon Av. BR1: Brom 70Nc 138
RM17: Grays 52De 121
Falconberg M. W1 2D 222 (44Mb 90)
Falcon Bus. Cen. RM3: Rom 24Nd 57
Falcon Cl. AL10: Hat 2C 8
DA1: Dart 57Pd 119
EN9: Walt A 6Jc 21
HA6: Nwood 24U 44
W4 51Sa 109
Falcon Ct. *E18 27Kc 53*
(off Albert Rd.)
EC4 3K 223 (44Qb 90)
EN5: New Bar 14Eb 31
GU21: Wok 85E 168
HA4: Ruis 33U 64
N1 2C 218
Falcon Cres. EN3: Pond E 15Zb 34
Falcon Dr. TW19: Stanw 58M 105
Falconer Ct. *N17 24Sb 51*
(off Compton Cres.)
Falconer Rd. IG6: Ilf 22Xc 55
WD23: Bush 16Ba 27
Falconer Wlk. N7 33Pb 70
Falconet Ct. *E1 46Xb 91*
(off Wapping High St.)
Falcon Gro. SW11 55Gb 111
Falcon Highwalk EC2 1D 224
Falcon Ho. BR1: Brom 67Hc 137
E14 50Dc 92
(off St Davids Sq.)
NW6 39Db 69
(off Springfield Wlk.)
SW5 50Db 89
(off Old Brompton Rd.)
Falconhurst KT22: Oxs 87Fa 172
Falcon La. SW11 55Gb 111
Falcon Lodge *W9 43Cb 89*
(off Admiral Wlk.)
Falcon M. DA11: Nflt 10A 122
Falcon Pk. Ind. Est. NW10 35Ua 68
Falcon Point SE1 5C 224 (45Rb 91)
Falcon Rd. EN3: Pond E 15Zb 34
SW11 54Gb 111
TW12: Hamp 66Ba 129
Falconry Ct. CM16: Epp 2Vc 23
KT1: King T 69Na 131
(off Fairfield Sth.)
Falcons Cl. TN16: Big H 89Mc 179
Falcon St. E13 42Jc 93
Falcon Ter. SW11 55Gb 111
Falcon Way E11 28Jc 53
E14 49Dc 92
HA3: Kenton 29Na 47
NW9 26Ua 48
RM12: Horn 38Jd 76
TW14: Felt 57X 107
TW16: Sun 68U 128
WD25: Wat 6Aa 13
Falcon Wharf SW11 54Fb 111
FALCONWOOD 56Vc 117
FALCONWOOD 56Tc 116
Falcon Wood KT22: Lea 92Ha 192
Falconwood KT24: E Hor 96V 190
TW20: Egh 64A 126
Falconwood Av.
DA16: Well 54Tc 116
Falconwood Ct. *SE3 54Hc 115*
(off Montpelier Row)
Falconwood Pde. DA16: Well 56Uc 116
Falconwood Rd. CR0: Sels 81Bc 178
Falcourt Cl. SM1: Sutt 78Db 155
Faldo Ct. CM14: B'wood 20Xd 40
Falkirk Cl. RM11: Horn 32Qd 77
Falkirk Ct. *SE16 46Zb 92*
(off Rotherhithe St.)
Falkirk Gdns. WD19: Wat 22Z 45
Falkirk Ho. *W9 40Db 69*
(off Maida Va.)
Falkirk St. N1 2J 219 (40Ub 71)
Falkland Av. N3 24Cb 49
N11 21Kb 50
Falkland Ho. SE6 63Ec 136
W8 48Db 89
W14 50Bb 89
(off Edith Vs.)
Falkland Pk. Av. SE25 69Ub 135
Falkland Pl. NW5 36Lb 70
Falkland Rd. EN5: Barn 12Ab 30
N8 28Qb 50
NW5 36Lb 70
Fallaize Av. IG1: Ilf 35Rc 74
Falling La. UB7: Yiew 45N 83
Falloden Way NW11 28Cb 49
Fallodon Ho. *W11 43Bb 89*
(off Tavistock Cres.)
Fallow Cl. IG7: Chig 22Vc 55
FALLOW CORNER 24Eb 49
Fallow Ct. *SE16 50Wb 91*
(off Argyle Way)
Fallow Ct. Av. N12 24Eb 49
Fallowfield DA2: Bean 62Xd 142
HA7: Stan 21Ja 46
Fallowfield Cl. UB9: Hare 25L 43
Fallowfield Ct. HA7: Stan 20Ja 28
Fallow Flds. IG10: Lough 16Lc 35
Fallowfields Dr. N12 23Gb 49
Fallowhurst Path N3 24Eb 49
Fallows Cl. N2 26Fb 49
Fallsbrook Rd. SW16 65Kb 134
Falman Cl. N9 18Wb 33
Falmer Rd. E17 27Dc 52
EN1: Enf 14Ub 33
N15 29Sb 51
Falmouth Av. E4 22Fc 53
Falmouth Cl. N22 24Pb 50
SE12 57Hc 115
Falmouth Ct. AL3: St A 1A 6
Falmouth Gdns. IG4: Ilf 28Mc 53
Falmouth Ho. HA5: Hat E 24Ba 45
KT2: King T 67Ma 131
(off Skerne Rd.)
SE11 7A 230
W2 4D 220
Falmouth Rd. KT12: Hers 77Y 151
SE1 4E 230 (48Sb 91)
SL1: Slou 4E 80
Falmouth St. E15 36Fc 73
Falmouth Wlk. SW15 58Wa 110
Falmouth Way E17 29Bc 52
Falstaff Bldg. *E1 45Xb 91*
(off Cannon St. Rd.)
Falstaff Cl. DA1: Cray 59Gd 118
Falstaff Ct. SE11 6B 230
Falstaff Gdns. AL1: St A 5P 5
Falstaff Ho. N1 2H 219
Falstaff M. *TW12: Hamp H 64Fa 130*
(off High St.)
Falstone GU21: Wok 10M 167
Fambridge Cl. SE26 63Bc 136
Fambridge Ct. *RM7: Rom 29Fd 56*
(off Marks Rd.)
Fambridge Rd. RM8: Dag 32Cd 76
Famet Av. CR8: Purl 85Sb 177
Famet Cl. CR8: Purl 85Sb 177
Famet Gdns. CR8: Kenley 85Sb 177
Famet Wlk. CR8: Purl 85Sb 177
Fancourt M. BR1: Brom 69Qc 138
Fane St. W14 51Bb 111
Fangrove Pk. KT16: Lyne 74C 148
Fan Museum, The 52Ec 114
Fanns Ri. RM19: Purf 49Qd 97
Fann St. EC1 6D 218 (42Sb 91)
EC2 6D 218 (42Sb 91)
(not continuous)
Fanshawe Av. IG11: Bark 37Sc 74
Fanshawe Cres. RM9: Dag 36Ad 75
RM11: Horn 30Md 57
Fanshawe Rd. RM16: Grays 8C 100
TW10: Ham 63La 130
Fanshaw St. N1 3H 219 (41Ub 91)
FANTAIL, THE 76Pc 160
Fantail Cl. SE28 44Yc 95
Fantasia Ct. CM14: W'ley 22Xd 58
Fanthorpe St. SW15 55Ya 110
Faraday Av. DA14: Sidc 61Wc 139
Faraday Cl. N7 37Pb 70
SL2: Slou 3F 80
WD18: Wat 16T 26
Faraday Ct. WD18: Wat 16W 26
Faraday Ho. *E14 45Bc 92*
(off Brightlingsea Pl.)
EN3: Enf L 9Bc 20
(off Velocity Way)
HA9: Wemb 34Sa 67
SE1 2F 231
W10 43Ab 88
(off Wornington Rd.)
WD18: Wat 16T 26
Faraday Lodge SE10 48Hc 93
Faraday Mans. *W14 51Ab 110*
(off Queen's Club Gdns.)
Faraday Pl. KT8: W Mole 70Ca 129
Faraday Rd. DA16: Well 55Wc 117
E15 37Hc 73
KT8: W Mole 70Ca 129
SL2: Slou 3F 80
SW19 65Cb 133
UB1: S'hall 45Da 85
W3 45Sa 87
W10 43Ab 88
Faraday Way BR5: St M Cry 70Xc 139
CR0: Wadd 74Pb 156
SE18 48Mc 93
Fardell Ct. *AL1: St A 2D 6*
(off Newsom Pl.)
Fareham Ho. HP1: Hem H 3M 3
Fareham Rd. TW14: Felt 59Y 107
Far End AL10: Hat 3D 8
Farewell Pl. CR4: Mitc 67Gb 133
Fari Ct. *E17 28Cc 52*
(off Tower M.)
Faringdon Av. BR2: Brom 73Qc 160
RM3: Rom 25Ld 57
Faringford Cl. EN6: Pot B 3Fb 17
Faringford Rd. E15 38Gc 73
Farington Acres KT13: Weyb 76T 150
Faris Barn Dr. KT15: Wdhm 84H 169
Faris La. KT15: Wdhm 83H 169
Farjeon Ho. *NW6 38Fb 69*
(off Hilgrove Rd.)
Farjeon Rd. SE3 53Mc 115
Farland Rd. HP2: Hem H 2B 4
FARLEIGH 86Bc 178
Farleigh Av. BR2: Hayes 73Hc 159
FARLEIGH COMMON 86Ac 178
Farleigh Ct. CR2: S Croy 78Sb 157
Farleigh Court Golf Course 84Cc 178
Farleigh Ct. Rd. CR6: W'ham 86Bc 178
Farleigh Dean Cres.
CR0: Sels 83Dc 178
Farleigh Ho. *N1 38Rb 71*
(off Halton Rd.)
Farleigh Pl. N16 35Vb 71
Farleigh Rd. CR6: W'ham 90Zb 178
KT15: New H 83J 169
N16 35Vb 71
Farleton Cl. KT13: Weyb 79T 150
Farley Ct. NW1 6H 215
W14 48Bb 89
Farleycroft TN16: Westrm 98Sc 200
Farley Dr. IG3: Ilf 32Uc 74
Farley Ho. SE26 62Xb 135
Farley La. TN16: Westrm 98Rc 200
Farley M. SE6 59Ec 114
Farley Nursery TN16: Westrm 99Sc 200
Farley Pk. RH8: Oxt 2H 211
Farley Pl. SE25 70Wb 135
Farley Rd. CR2: Sels 80Xb 157
DA12: Grav'nd 10H 123
SE6 59Dc 114
Farleys Cl. KT24: W Hor 98S 190
Farlington Pl. SW15 59Xa 110
Farlow Cl. DA11: Nflt 2B 144
Farlow Rd. SW15 55Za 110
Farlton Rd. SW18 60Db 111
Farman Gro. UB5: N'olt 41Z 85
Farman Ter. HA3: Kenton 28Ma 47
Farm Av. BR8: Swan 69Ed 140
HA0: Wemb 37La 66
HA2: Harr 31Ba 65
NW2 34Ab 68
SW16 63Nb 134
Farmborough Cl. HA1: Harr 31Fa 66
Farm Cl. BR4: W W'ck 76Hc 159
CM13: Hut 17Ee 41
CR5: Chip 92Hb 195
EN5: Barn 15Ya 30
EN8: Chesh 2Yb 20
GU3: Worp 10G 186
IG9: Buck H 20Lc 35
KT14: Byfl 84P 169
KT16: Lyne 72C 148
KT22: Fet 96Fa 192
KT24: E Hor 100V 190
RM10: Dag 38Ed 76
SL5: S'hill 1A 146
SM2: Sutt 80Fb 155
SM6: Wall 82Lb 176
SW6 52Cb 111
TW17: Shep 73Q 150
TW18: Staines 64G 126
UB1: S'hall 45Da 85
UB10: Ick 33R 64
WD6: Bore 10Ma 15
WD7: Shenl 2Na 15
Farmcote Rd. SE12 60Jc 115
Farm Ct. NW4 27Wa 48
Farm Cres. AL2: Lon C 8E 6
SL2: Slou 3M 81
Farmcroft DA11: Grav'nd 1C 144
Farmdale Rd. SE10 50Jc 93
SM5: Cars 80Gb 155
Farm Dr. CR0: C'don 75Bc 158
CR8: Purl 84Mb 176
RM16: Grays 45Ee 99
SL4: Old Win 8M 103
Farm End E4 15Gc 35
HA6: Nwood 25R 44
Farmer Rd. E10 32Dc 72
Farmers Cl. WD25: Wat 5X 13
Farmers Ct. EN9: Walt A 5Jc 21
Farmers Rd. SE5 52Rb 113
TW18: Staines 64G 126
Farmer St. W8 46Cb 89
Farm Fld. WD17: Wat 10U 12
Farmfield Rd. BR1: Brom 64Gc 137
Farm Flds. CR2: Sande 83Ub 177
Farm Hill Rd. EN9: Walt A 5Fc 21
Farm Holt DA3: New A 74Be 165
Farmhouse Cl. GU22: Pyr 87F 168
Farm Ho. Ct. NW7 24Wa 48
Farmhouse Rd. SW16 66Lb 134
Farmilo Rd. E17 31Bc 72
Farmington Av. SM1: Sutt 76Fb 155
Farmlands EN2: Enf 11Qb 32
HA5: Eastc 28W 44
Farmlands, The UB5: N'olt 37Ba 65
Farmland Wlk. BR7: Chst 64Rc 138
Farm La. CR0: C'don 75Bc 158
CR8: Purl 82Lb 176
GU23: Send 96E 188
KT15: Add 80J 149
KT18: Eps D 89Qa 173
KT21: Asht 89Qa 173
KT24: E Hor 100V 190
N14 17Kb 32
SL1: Slou 5H 81
SM5: Cars 82Hb 175
SW6 51Cb 111
WD3: Loud 13L 25
Farm La. Trad. Est. SW6 51Cb 111
Farmleigh N14 17Lb 32
Farmleigh Gro. KT12: Hers 78V 150
Farmleigh Ho. SW9 57Rb 113
Farm M. CR4: Mitc 68Kb 134
Farm Pl. DA1: Cray 56Jd 118
W8 46Cb 89
Farm Rd. AL1: St A 1F 6
CR6: W'ham 91Ac 198
GU22: Wok 92D 188
HA6: Nwood 22R 44
HA8: Edg 23Ra 47
KT10: Esh 74Da 151
N21 18Sb 33
NW10 39Ta 67
RM13: Rain 41Ld 97
RM16: Ors 7B 100
RM18: E Til 9L 101
SM2: Sutt 80Fb 155
SM4: Mord 71Db 155
TN14: S'oaks 92Ld 203
TW4: Houn 60Aa 107
TW18: Staines 65K 127
WD3: Chor 14C 24
Farmside Pl. KT19: Eps 84Pa 173
Farmstead KT19: Eps 81Qa 173
Farmstead Ct. *SM6: Wall 78Kb 156*
(off Melbourne Rd.)

Farmstead Rd. HA3: Hrw W ... 25Fa 46
SE6 ... 63Dc 136
Farm St. W1 ... 5K 221 (45Kb 90)
Farm Va. DA5: Bexl ... 58Dd 118
Farm Vw. KT11: Cobh ... 88Z 171
KT20: Lwr K ... 99Bb 195
Farm Wlk. NW11 ... 29Bb 49
Farm Way HA6: Nwood ... 21U 44
HP2: Hem H ... 1P 3
IG9: Buck H ... 21Lc 53
KT4: Wor Pk ... 76Ya 154
RM12: Horn ... 35Ld 77
TW19: Stanw M ... 58H 105
WD23: Bush ... 14Da 27
Farmway RM8: Dag ... 34Yc 75
Farm Yd. SL4: Wind ... 2H 103
Farmyard Funworld ... 13Ba 27
Farnaby Dr. TN13: S'oaks ... 98Hd 202
Farnaby Ho. W10 ... 41Bb 89
(off Bruckner St.)
Farnaby Rd. BR1: Brom ... 66Fc 137
BR2: Brom ... 66Fc 137
SE9 ... 56Lc 115
Farnaby Way SS17: Stan H ... 1L 101
Farnan Av. E17 ... 26Cc 52
Farnan Lodge SW16 ... 64Nb 134
Farnan Rd. SW16 ... 64Nb 134
FARNBOROUGH ... 78Sc 160
Farnborough Av. CR2: Sels ... 81Zb 178
E17 ... 27Ac 52
Farnborough Cl. HA9: Wemb ... 33Ra 67
Farnborough Comn. BR6: Farnb ... 76Pc 160
Farnborough Cres. BR2: Hayes ... 74Hc 159
CR2: Sels ... 81Ac 178
Farnborough Hill
BR6: Chels, Farnb ... 78Tc 160
Farnborough Ho. SW15 ... 60Wa 110
Farnborough Way
BR6: Chels, Farnb ... 78Sc 160
Farnburn Av. SL1: Slou ... 3F 80
Farncombe St. SE16 ... 47Wb 91
Farndale Av. N13 ... 19Rb 33
Farndale Ct. SE18 ... 52Nc 116
Farndale Cres. UB6: G'frd ... 41Ea 86
Farndale Ho. NW6 ... 39Db 69
(off Kilburn Vale)
Farne Ho. WD18: Wat ... 16V 26
(off Scammell Way)
Farnell M. KT13: Weyb ... 76R 150
SW5 ... 50Db 89
Farnell Pl. W3 ... 45Ra 87
Farnell Rd. TW7: Isle ... 55Fa 108
TW18: Staines ... 62J 127
Farnes Dr. RM2: Rom ... 26Ld 57
Farnham Cl. HP3: Bov ... 10C 2
N20 ... 17Eb 31
FARNHAM COMMON ... 7G 60
Farnham Ct. SM3: Cheam ... 79Ab 154
UB1: S'hall ... 45Ea 86
(off Redcroft Rd.)
Farnham Gdns. SW20 ... 68Xa 132
Farnham Ho. NW1 ... 6E 214
SE1 ... 7D 224
Farnham La. SL2: Slou ... 1C 80
Farnham Pk. Golf Course ... 9J 61
Farnham Pk. La. SL2: Farn R ... 8G 60
Farnham Pl. SE1 ... 7C 224 (46Rb 91)
Farnham Rd. DA16: Well ... 54Yc 117
IG3: Ilf ... 31Vc 75
RM3: Rom ... 22Md 57
SL1: Slou ... 1F 80
SL2: Farn R, Slou ... 1F 80
FARNHAM ROYAL ... 1G 80
Farnham Royal SE11 ... 50Pb 90
FARNINGHAM ... 73Pd 163
Farningham Ct. SW16 ... 66Mb 134
Farningham Cres. CR3: Cat'm ... 95Wb 197
Farningham Hill Rd. DA4: Farni ... 71Ld 163
Farningham Ho. N4 ... 31Tb 71
Farningham Rd. CR3: Cat'm ... 95Wb 197
N17 ... 24Wb 51
Farnley GU21: Wok ... 9K 167
Farnley Ho. SW8 ... 54Mb 112
Farnley Rd. E4 ... 17Gc 35
SE25 ... 70Tb 135
Farnol Rd. DA1: Dart ... 57Qd 119
Farnsworth Ct. SE10 ... 48Hc 93
(off West Parkside)
Farnworth Ho. E14 ... 49Fc 93
(off Manchester Rd.)
Faro Cl. BR1: Brom ... 68Qc 138
Faroe Rd. W14 ... 48Za 88
Farorna Wlk. EN2: Enf ... 11Qb 32
Farquhar Rd. SE19 ... 64Vb 135
SW19 ... 62Cb 133
Farquharson Rd. CR0: C'don ... 74Sb 157
Farraline Rd. WD18: Wat ... 14X 27
Farrance Rd. RM6: Chad H ... 30Ad 55
Farrance St. E14 ... 44Cc 92
Farrans Ct. HA3: Kenton ... 31Ka 66
Farrant Av. N22 ... 26Qb 50
Farrant Cl. BR6: Chels ... 80Wc 161
Farrant Way WD6: Bore ... 11Na 29
Farr Av. IG11: Bark ... 40Wc 75
Farrell Ct. DA2: Wilm ... 62Ld 141
Farrell Ho. E1 ... 44Yb 92
(off Ronald St.)
Farren Rd. SE23 ... 61Ac 136
Farrer Ct. TW1: Twick ... 59Ma 109
Farrer Ho. SE8 ... 52Cc 114
SL4: Eton ... 10G 80
(off Common La.)
Farrer M. N8 ... 28Lb 50
Farrer Rd. HA3: Kenton ... 29Na 47
N8 ... 28Lb 50
Farrer's Pl. CR0: C'don ... 77Zb 158
Farrier Cl. BR1: Brom ... 69Mc 137
TW16: Sun ... 70W 128
UB8: Hil ... 44Q 84
Farrier Pl. SM1: Sutt ... 76Db 155
Farrier Rd. UB5: N'olt ... 40Ca 65
Farriers Cl. DA12: Grav'nd ... 10H 123
HP3: Bov ... 10D 2
KT17: Eps ... 84Ua 174
Farriers Ct. WD25: Wat ... 4X 13
Farriers Ho. EC1 ... 6E 218
Farriers M. SE15 ... 55Yb 114
Farriers Rd. KT17: Eps ... 83Ua 174
Farrier St. NW1 ... 38Kb 70
Farriers Way WD6: Bore ... 15Ta 29
Farrier Wlk. SW10 ... 51Eb 111
Farringdon Ho. TW9: Kew ... 52Ra 109
UB7: W Dray ... 47P 83
Farringdon La. EC1 ... 6A 218 (42Qb 90)
Farringdon Rd. EC1 ... 5K 217 (42Qb 90)
Farringdon St. EC4 ... 1B 224 (43Rb 91)
Farringford Cl. AL2: Chis G ... 8N 5
Farrington Av. BR5: St P ... 69Xc 139
WD23: Bush ... 14Da 27
Farrington Pl. BR7: Chst ... 66Tc 138
HA6: Nwood ... 21V 44
Farrins Rents SE16 ... 46Ac 92
Farrow Gdns. RM16: Grays ... 46De 99
Farrow La. SE14 ... 52Yb 114
Farrow Pl. SE16 ... 48Ac 92
Farr Rd. EN2: Enf ... 11Tb 33
Farthingale Ct. EN9: Walt A ... 6Jc 21
Farthingale La. EN9: Walt A ... 6Jc 21
Farthingale Wlk. E15 ... 38Fc 73
Farthing All. SE1 ... 47Wb 91
Farthing Barn La. BR6: Downe ... 81Qc 180
Farthing Cl. DA1: Dart ... 56Pd 119
WD18: Wat ... 15Y 27
Farthing Ct. NW7 ... 24Ab 48
Farthingfield TN15: Wro ... 88Ce 185
Farthing Flds. E1 ... 46Xb 91
Farthing Grn. La. SL2: Stoke P ... 10L 61
Farthings GU21: Knap ... 8J 167
HP8: Chal G ... 13A 24
Farthings, The HP1: Hem H ... 2K 3
KT2: King T ... 67Qa 131
Farthings Cl. E4 ... 20Gc 35
HA5: Eastc ... 30X 45
FARTHING STREET ... 81Pc 180
Farthing St. BR6: Downe ... 80Pc 160
Farthing Way CR5: Coul ... 89Mb 176
Farwell Rd. DA14: Sidc ... 63Xc 139
Farwig La. BR1: Brom ... 67Hc 137
Fashion & Textile Mus. ... 1J 231 (47Ub 91)
Fashion St. E1 ... 1K 225 (43Vb 91)
Fashoda Rd. BR2: Brom ... 70Mc 137
Fassett Rd. E8 ... 37Wb 71
KT1: King T ... 70Na 131
Fassett Sq. E8 ... 37Wb 71
Fassnidge Vw. UB8: Uxb ... 38L 63
Fathom Ct. E16 ... 45Rc 94
(off Basin App.)
Fauconberg Ct. W4 ... 51Sa 109
(off Fauconberg Rd.)
Fauconberg Rd. W4 ... 51Sa 109
Faulkner Cl. RM8: Dag ... 31Zc 75
Faulkner Ct. AL1: St A ... 1C 6
(off Boundary Rd.)
Faulkners All. EC1 ... 7B 218 (43Rb 91)
Faulkners Rd. KT12: Hers ... 78Y 151
Faulkner St. SE14 ... 53Yb 114
Fauna Cl. HA7: Stan ... 21Ma 47
RM6: Chad H ... 30Yc 55
Faunce Ho. SE17 ... 51Rb 113
(off Doddington Gro.)
Faunce St. SE17 ... 50Rb 91
Favart Rd. SW6 ... 53Cb 111
Faversham Av. E4 ... 18Gc 35
EN1: Enf ... 16Tb 33
Faversham Cl. IG7: Chig ... 19Xc 37
Faversham Ho. NW1 ... 1C 216
SE17 ... 7H 231
Faversham Rd. BR3: Beck ... 68Bc 136
SE6 ... 59Bc 114
SM4: Mord ... 72Db 155
Fawcett Cl. SW11 ... 54Fb 111
SW16 ... 64Qb 134
Fawcett Ct. SW10 ... 51Eb 111
(off Fawcett St.)
Fawcett Est. E5 ... 32Wb 71
Fawcett Rd. CR0: C'don ... 76Sb 157
NW10 ... 38Va 68
SL4: Wind ... 3F 102
Fawcett St. SW10 ... 51Eb 111
Fawcus Cl. KT10: Clay ... 79Ga 152
Fawe Pk. M. SW15 ... 56Bb 111
Fawe Pk. Rd. SW15 ... 56Bb 111
Fawe St. E14 ... 43Dc 92
FAWKE COMMON ... 99Qd 203
Fawke Comn.
TN15: God G, Under ... 98Qd 203
Fawkes Av. DA1: Dart ... 61Pd 141
Fawke Wood Rd. TN15: Under ... 100Qd 203
FAWKHAM ... 73Xd 164
Fawkham Av. DA3: Lfield ... 69Ee 143
FAWKHAM GREEN ... 76Xd 164
Fawkham Grn. Rd. DA3: Fawk ... 76Xd 164
Fawkham Ho. SE1 ... 6K 231
Fawkham Rd. DA3: Fawk ... 77Vd 164
DA3: Fawk, Lfield ... 70Zd 143
TN15: W King ... 81Wd 184
Fawkham Valley Golf Course ... 72Zd 165
Fawley Lodge E14 ... 49Fc 93
(off Millennium Dr.)
Fawley Rd. NW6 ... 36Db 69
Fawnbrake Av. SE24 ... 57Rb 113
Fawn Rd. E13 ... 40Lc 73
IG7: Chig ... 22Vc 55
Fawns Mnr. Cl. TW14: Bedf ... 60S 106
Fawns Mnr. Rd. TW14: Bedf ... 60T 106
Fawood Av. NW10 ... 38Sa 67
Fawsley Cl. SL3: Poyle ... 52G 104
Fawters Cl. CM13: Hut ... 16Fe 41
Fayerfield EN6: Pot B ... 3Fb 17
Faygate Cres. DA6: Bex ... 57Cd 118
Faygate Rd. SW2 ... 61Pb 134
Fay Grn. WD5: Ab L ... 5T 12
Fayland Av. SW16 ... 64Lb 134
Faymore Gdns. RM15: S Ock ... 44Wd 98
Fazeley Ct. W9 ... 43Cb 89
(off Elmfield Way)
Feacey Down HP1: Hem H ... 1J 3
Fearn Cl. KT24: E Hor ... 100U 190
Fearney Mead WD3: Rick ... 18J 25
Fearnley Cres. TW12: Hamp ... 64Aa 129
Fearnley Ho. SE5 ... 54Ub 113
Fearnley St. WD18: Wat ... 14X 27
Fearns Mead CM14: W'ley ... 22Yd 58
Fearon St. SE10 ... 50Jc 93
Featherbed La. AL2: Pot C ... 7K 5
CR0: Sels ... 80Bc 158
CR6: W'ham ... 80Bc 158
HP3: Hem H ... 7J 3
(not continuous)
RM4: Abr ... 14Zc 37
(not continuous)
WD5: Bedm ... 8H 5
Feathers La. TW19: Wray ... 61C 126
Feathers Pl. SE10 ... 51Fc 115
Featherstone Av. SE23 ... 61Xb 135
Featherstone Gdns. WD6: Bore ... 14Ta 29
Featherstone Ho. UB4: Yead ... 43Y 85
Featherstone Ind. Est. UB2: S'hall ... 48Aa 85
(off Feather Rd.)
Featherstone Rd. NW7 ... 23Xa 48
UB2: S'hall ... 48Aa 85
Featherstone Sports Cen. ... 49Z 85
Featherstone St. EC1 ... 5F 219 (42Tb 91)
Featherstone Ter. UB2: S'hall ... 48Aa 85
Featley Rd. SW9 ... 55Rb 113
Federal Rd. UB6: G'frd ... 39La 66
Federal Way WD24: Wat ... 11Y 27
Federation Rd. SE2 ... 49Xc 95
Fee Farm Rd. KT10: Clay ... 80Ha 152
Feenan Highway RM18: Tilb ... 2D 122
Feeny Cl. NW10 ... 35Va 68
Felbridge Av. HA7: Stan ... 25Ja 46
Felbridge Cl. SM2: Sutt ... 81Db 175
SW16 ... 63Qb 134
Felbridge Ct. TW13: Felt ... 60X 107
(off High St.)
UB3: Harl ... 51T 106
Felbridge Ho. SE22 ... 55Ub 113
Felbrigge Rd. IG3: Ilf ... 33Vc 75
Felcott Cl. KT12: Hers ... 76Y 151
Felcott Rd. KT12: Hers ... 76Y 151
Felday Rd. SE13 ... 58Dc 114
FELDEN ... 6J 3
Felden Cl. HA5: Hat E ... 24Aa 45
WD25: Wat ... 6Z 13
Felden Dr. HP3: Hem H ... 6J 3
Felden La. HP3: Hem H ... 5H 3
Felden Lawns HP3: Hem H ... 6J 3
Felden St. SW6 ... 53Bb 111
Feldman Cl. N16 ... 32Wb 71
Feldspar Ct. EN3: Enf H ... 13Ac 34
(off Enstone Rd.)
Felgate M. W6 ... 49Xa 88
Felhampton Rd. SE9 ... 61Rc 138
Felhurst Cres. RM10: Dag ... 35Dd 76
Felicia Way RM16: Grays ... 9D 100
Feline Ct. EN4: E Barn ... 16Gb 31
Felipe Rd. RM16: Chaf H ... 48Yd 98
Felix Av. N8 ... 30Nb 50
Felix Ct. E17 ... 29Dc 52
Felix Dr. GU4: W Cla ... 100J 189
Felix Ho. E16 ... 45Qc 94
(off University Way)
Felix La. TW17: Shep ... 72U 150
Felix Mnr. BR7: Chst ... 65Uc 138
Felix Neubergh Ho. EN1: Enf ... 14Ub 33
Felix Pl. SW2 ... 57Qb 112
(off Talma Rd.)
Felix Rd. KT12: Walt T ... 72W 150
W13 ... 45Ja 86
Felixstowe Ct. E16 ... 46Rc 94
Felixstowe Rd. N9 ... 20Wb 33
N17 ... 27Vb 51
NW10 ... 41Xa 88
SE2 ... 48Xc 95
Felix St. E2 ... 40Xb 71
Felland Way RH2: Reig ... 10M 207
Fellbrigg Rd. SE22 ... 57Vb 113
Fellbrigg St. E1 ... 42Xb 91
Fellbrook TW10: Ham ... 62Ka 130
Fellmongers Path SE1 ... 2K 231
Fellmongers Yd. CR0: C'don ... 76Sb 157
Fellowes Cl. UB4: Yead ... 42Z 85
Fellowes La. AL4: Col H ... 5P 7
Fellowes Rd. SM5: Cars ... 76Gb 155
Fellow Grn. GU24: W End ... 5D 166
Fellow Grn. Rd. GU24: W End ... 5D 166
Fellows Ct. E2 ... 1K 219 (40Vb 71)
(not continuous)
Fellows Rd. NW3 ... 38Fb 69
Fell Path WD6: Bore ... 15Ta 29
(off Clydesdale Cl.)
Fell Rd. CR0: C'don ... 76Sb 157
(not continuous)
Felltram M. SE7 ... 50Jc 93
Felltram Way SE7 ... 50Jc 93
Fell Wlk. HA8: Edg ... 25Sa 47
Felmersham Cl. SW4 ... 56Nb 112
Felmingham Rd. SE20 ... 68Yb 136
Felnex Trad. Est. NW10 ... 40Ta 67
SM6: Wall ... 75Jb 156
Felsberg Rd. SW2 ... 58Nb 112
Fels Cl. RM10: Dag ... 34Dd 76
Fels Farm Av. RM10: Dag ... 34Ed 76
Felsham M. SW15 ... 55Za 110
(off Felsham Rd.)
Felsham Rd. SW15 ... 55Ya 110
Felspar Cl. SE18 ... 50Vc 95
Felstead Av. IG5: Ilf ... 25Qc 54
Felstead Cl. CM13: Hut ... 16Ee 41
N13 ... 22Qb 50
Felstead Gdns. E14 ... 50Ec 92
Felstead Rd. BR6: Chels ... 75Wc 161
E9 ... 37Bc 72
E11 ... 31Jc 73
EN8: Walt C ... 4Ac 20
IG10: Lough ... 17Nc 36
KT19: Eps ... 83Ta 173
RM5: Col R ... 24Ed 56
Felstead St. E9 ... 37Bc 72
Felstead Wharf E14 ... 50Ec 92
Felsted Rd. E16 ... 44Mc 93
FELTHAM ... 60X 107
Feltham Airparcs Leisure Cen. ... 61Z 129
Feltham Av. KT8: E Mos ... 70Ga 130
Felthambrook Ind. Est. TW13: Felt ... 62X 129
Felthambrook Way TW13: Felt ... 62X 129
Feltham Bus. Complex TW13: Felt ... 61X 129
Feltham Corporate Cen.
TW13: Felt ... 62X 129
FELTHAMHILL ... 64V 128
Feltham Hill Rd. TW15: Ashf ... 64Q 128
Feltham Rd. CR4: Mitc ... 68Hb 133
RH1: Redh ... 10P 207
TW15: Ashf ... 63Q 128
Feltham Wlk. RH1: Redh ... 10P 207
Felton Cl. BR5: Pet W ... 72Rc 160
WD6: Bore ... 10Na 15
Felton Gdns. IG11: Bark ... 39Uc 74
Felton Ho. N1 ... 39Tb 71
(off Branch Pl.)
SE3 ... 56Kc 115
Felton Lea DA14: Sidc ... 64Vc 139
Felton Rd. IG11: Bark ... 40Uc 74
W13 ... 47La 86
Felton St. N1 ... 39Tb 71
Fenbridge Ct. RH1: Redh ... 4B 208
Fencepiece Rd. IG6: Chig, Ilf ... 22Sc 54
IG7: Chig ... 22Sc 54
Fenchurch Av. EC3 ... 3H 225 (44Ub 91)
Fenchurch Bldgs.
EC3 ... 3J 225 (44Ub 91)
Fenchurch Ho. EC3 ... 3K 225
Fenchurch Pl. EC3 ... 4J 225 (44Ub 91)
Fenchurch St. EC3 ... 4H 225 (45Ub 91)
Fen Cl. CM15: Shenf ... 14Ee 41
Fen Ct. EC3 ... 3H 225 (44Ub 91)
Fendall Rd. KT19: Ewe ... 78Sa 153
Fendall St. SE1 ... 4J 231 (48Ub 91)
(not continuous)
Fendt Cl. E16 ... 44Hc 93
Fendyke Rd. DA17: Belv ... 49Zc 95
Fenelon Pl. W14 ... 49Bb 89
Fenemore Rd. CR8: Kenley ... 92Tb 197
Fengate Cl. KT9: Chess ... 79Ma 153
Fengates Rd. RH1: Redh ... 6N 207
Fen Gro. DA15: Sidc ... 57Vc 117
Fenham Rd. SE15 ... 52Wb 113
Fenland Ho. E5 ... 33Yb 72
Fen La. RM14: Bulp, N Ock ... 36Yd 78
RM16: Ors ... 1B 100
SW13 ... 53Xa 110
Fenman Ct. N17 ... 25Xb 51
Fenman Gdns. IG3: Ilf ... 32Xc 75
Fen Mdw. TN15: Igh ... 90Yd 184
Fenn Cl. BR1: Brom ... 65Jc 137
Fennel Apartments SE1 ... 1K 231
Fennel Cl. CR0: C'don ... 74Zb 158
E16 ... 42Gc 93
Fennells Mead KT17: Ewe ... 81Va 174
Fennell St. SE18 ... 51Qc 116
Fenner Cl. SE16 ... 49Xb 91
Fenner Ho. E1 ... 46Xb 91
(off Watts St.)
KT12: Hers ... 77W 150
Fenner Rd. RM16: Chaf H ... 49Yd 98
Fenners Marsh DA12: Grav'nd ... 10H 123
Fenner Sq. SW11 ... 55Fb 111
Fenn Ho. TW7: Isle ... 53Ka 108
Fennings Rd. SW4 ... 58Mb 112
Fenning St. SE1 ... 1H 231 (47Ub 91)
Fennscombe Ct. GU24: W End ... 5C 166
Fenns La. GU24: W End ... 5C 166
Fenn St. E9 ... 36Zb 72
Fenns Way GU21: Wok ... 87A 168
Fen Pond Cotts. TN15: Igh ... 90Yd 184
Fen Pond Rd. TN15: Igh, Wro ... 88Yd 184
Fensomes All. HP2: Hem H ... 1M 3
Fensomes Cl. HP2: Hem H ... 1M 3
Fenstanton N4 ... 32Pb 70
(off Marquis Rd.)
Fenstanton Av. N12 ... 23Fb 49
Fen St. E16 ... 45Hc 93
Fens Way BR8: Hext ... 65Jd 140
Fenswood Cl. DA5: Bexl ... 58Cd 118
Fentiman Rd. SW8 ... 51Nb 112
Fentiman Way HA2: Harr ... 33Da 65
RM11: Horn ... 32Nd 77
Fenton Av. TW18: Staines ... 65L 127
Fenton Cl. BR7: Chst ... 64Pc 138
E8 ... 37Vb 71
RH1: Redh ... 6A 208
SW9 ... 54Pb 112
Fenton House ... 35Eb 69
(off Windmill Hill)
Fenton Ho. SE14 ... 52Ac 114
TW5: Hest ... 51Ca 107
Fenton Rd. N17 ... 24Sb 51
RH1: Redh ... 6A 208
RM16: Chaf H ... 48Ae 99
Fentons Av. E13 ... 41Kc 93
Fenton St. E1 ... 44Xb 91
Fenwick Cl. GU21: Wok ... 10M 167
SE18 ... 51Qc 116
Fenwick Gro. SE15 ... 55Wb 113
Fenwick Path WD6: Bore ... 10Pa 15
Fenwick Pl. CR2: S Croy ... 80Rb 157
SW9 ... 55Nb 112
Fenwick Rd. SE15 ... 55Wb 113
Ferby Ct. DA14: Sidc ... 63Vc 139
(off Main Rd.)
Ferdinand Dr. SE15 ... 52Ub 113
Ferdinand Ho. NW1 ... 38Jb 70
(off Ferdinand Pl.)
Ferdinand Pl. NW1 ... 38Jb 70
Ferdinand St. NW1 ... 38Jb 70
Ferguson Av. DA12: Grav'nd ... 3E 144
KT5: Surb ... 71Pa 153
RM2: Rom ... 26Ld 57
Ferguson Centre, The E17 ... 30Ac 52
Ferguson Cl. BR2: Brom ... 69Fc 137
E14 ... 49Cc 92
Ferguson Ct. RM2: Rom ... 26Md 57
Ferguson Dr. W3 ... 44Ta 87
Ferguson Ho. SE10 ... 53Ec 114
(off Sparta St.)
Fergus Rd. N5 ... 36Rb 71
Ferial Ct. SE15 ... 52Wb 113
(off Fenham Rd.)
Fermain Ct. E. N1 ... 39Ub 71
(off De Beauvoir Est.)
Fermain Ct. Nth. N1 ... 39Ub 71
(off De Beauvoir Est.)
Fermain Ct. W. N1 ... 39Ub 71
(off De Beauvoir Est.)
Ferme Pk. Rd. N4 ... 29Nb 50
N8 ... 29Nb 50
Fermor Rd. SE23 ... 60Ac 114
Fermoy Ho. W9 ... 42Bb 89
(off Fermoy Rd.)
Fermoy Rd. UB6: G'frd ... 42Da 85
W9 ... 42Bb 89
(not continuous)
Fern Av. CR4: Mitc ... 70Mb 134
Fernbank DA4: Eyns ... 75Pd 163
IG9: Buck H ... 18Kc 35
Fernbank Av. HA0: Wemb ... 35Ha 66
KT12: Walt T ... 73Aa 151
RM12: Horn ... 35Ld 77
Fernbank M. SW12 ... 58Lb 112
Fernbank Rd. KT15: Add ... 78J 149
Fernbrook Av. DA15: Sidc ... 57Uc 116
Fernbrook Cres. SE13 ... 58Gc 115
(off Leahurst Rd.)
Fernbrook Dr. HA2: Harr ... 31Da 65
Fernbrook Rd. SE13 ... 57Gc 115
Ferncliff Rd. E8 ... 36Wb 71
Fern Cl. CR6: W'ham ... 90Ac 178
DA8: Erith ... 53Kd 119
N1 ... 1H 219 (40Ub 71)
Fern Ct. DA7: Bex ... 56Cd 118
RM5: Col R ... 24Cd 56
RM7: Rom ... 29Fd 56
SE14 ... 54Zb 114
SS17: Stan H ... 1M 101
Ferncroft Av. HA4: Ruis ... 33Y 65
N12 ... 23Hb 49
NW3 ... 34Cb 69
Ferndale BR1: Brom ... 68Lc 137
TN13: S'oaks ... 94Ld 203
Ferndale Av. E17 ... 29Fc 53
KT16: Chert ... 76G 148
TW4: Houn ... 55Aa 107
Ferndale Cl. DA7: Bex ... 53Ad 117
Ferndale Community Sports Cen.
... 55Pb 112
Ferndale Cres. UB8: Cowl ... 41L 83
Ferndale Rd. DA12: Grav'nd ... 1D 144
E7 ... 38Kc 73
E11 ... 33Gc 73
EN3: Enf W ... 9Ac 20
GU21: Wok ... 88B 168
N15 ... 30Vb 51
RM5: Col R ... 26Ed 56
SE25 ... 71Xb 157
SM7: Bans ... 88Bb 175
SW4 ... 56Nb 112
SW9 ... 56Nb 112
TW15: Ashf ... 64M 127
Ferndale St. E6 ... 45Rc 94
Ferndale Ter. HA1: Harr ... 28Ha 46
Ferndale Way BR6: Farnb ... 78Tc 160
Ferndell Av. DA5: Bexl ... 62Fd 140
Fern Dells AL10: Hat ... 1B 8
Fern Dene W13 ... 43Ka 86
Ferndene AL2: Brick W ... 3Ba 13
DA3: Lfield ... 69Fe 143
Ferndene Rd. SE24 ... 56Sb 113
Fernden Way RM7: Rom ... 30Dd 56
Ferndown HA6: Nwood ... 26W 44
NW1 ... 38Mb 70
(off Camley St.)
RM11: Horn ... 30Pd 57
Ferndown Av. BR6: Orp ... 74Tc 160
Ferndown Cl. HA5: Pinn ... 24Aa 45
SM2: Sutt ... 79Fb 155
Ferndown Ct. UB1: S'hall ... 44Ea 86
(off Haldane Rd.)
Ferndown Gdns. KT11: Cobh ... 85Y 171
Ferndown Lodge E14 ... 48Ec 92
(off Manchester Rd.)
Ferndown Rd. SE9 ... 59Mc 115
WD19: Wat ... 21Y 45
Fern Dr. HP3: Hem H ... 3N 3
SL6: Tap ... 4A 80
Fernecroft AL1: St A ... 5B 6
Fernery, The TW18: Staines ... 64G 126
Fernes Cl. UB8: Cowl ... 44L 83
Ferney Ct. KT14: Byfl ... 83M 169
Ferney Meade Way TW7: Isle ... 54Ja 108
Ferney Rd. EN4: E Barn ... 17Jb 32
KT14: Byfl ... 84M 169
Fern Gro. TW14: Felt ... 59X 107
Ferngrove Cl. KT22: Fet ... 95Ga 192
Fern Hall AL10: Hat ... 2B 8
(off Bishops Ri.)
Fernhall Dr. IG4: Ilf ... 29Mc 53
Fernhall La. EN9: Walt A ... 3Mc 21
Fernham Rd. CR7: Thor H ... 69Sb 135
Fernhead Rd. W9 ... 41Bb 89
Fernheath Way DA2: Wilm ... 64Fd 140
Fernhill KT22: Oxs ... 86Fa 172
Fernhill Cl. GU22: Wok ... 2N 187
Fernhill Ct. E17 ... 26Fc 53
Fernhill Gdns. KT2: King T ... 64Ma 131
Fernhill La. GU22: Wok ... 2N 187
Fernhill Pk. GU22: Wok ... 2N 187
Fern Hill Pl. BR6: Farnb ... 78Sc 160
Fernhills WD4: Hunt C ... 6T 12
Fernhill St. E16 ... 46Pc 94
Fernholme Rd. SE15 ... 57Zb 114
Fernhurst Gdns. HA8: Edg ... 23Qa 47
Fernhurst Rd. CR0: C'don ... 73Xb 157
SW6 ... 53Ab 110
TW15: Ashf ... 63S 128
Fernie Cl. IG7: Chig ... 22Wc 55
Fernie Way IG7: Chig ... 22Wc 55
Fernihough Cl. KT13: Weyb ... 82Q 170
Fernlands Cl. KT16: Chert ... 76G 148
Fern La. TW5: Hest ... 50Ba 85
Fernlea KT23: Bookh ... 96Da 191
Fernlea Pl. KT11: Cobh ... 83Z 171
Fernlea Rd. CR4: Mitc ... 68Jb 134
SW12 ... 60Kb 112
Fernleigh Cl. CR0: Wadd ... 77Qb 156
KT12: Walt T ... 76X 151
W9 ... 41Bb 89
Fernleigh Ct. HA2: Harr ... 26Da 45
HA9: Wemb ... 33Na 67
RM7: Rom ... 29Ed 56
Fernleigh Rd. N21 ... 19Qb 32
Fernley Cl. HA5: Eastc ... 28W 44
Ferns, The TN15: Plat ... 92Ee 205
Fernsbury St. WC1 ... 4K 217 (41Qb 90)
Ferns Cl. CR2: Sande ... 82Xb 177
EN3: Enf W ... 8Ac 20
Fernshaw Cl. SW10 ... 51Eb 111
Fernshaw Mans. SW10 ... 51Eb 111
(off Fernshaw Rd.)
Fernshaw Rd. SW10 ... 51Eb 111
Fernside IG9: Buck H ... 18Kc 35
KT7: T Ditt ... 74Ka 152
NW11 ... 33Cb 69
Fernside Av. NW7 ... 20Ta 29
TW13: Felt ... 63X 129
Fernside Ct. NW4 ... 26Za 48
(off Holders Hill Rd.)
Fernside Rd. SW12 ... 60Hb 111
Fernsleigh Cl. SL9: Chal P ... 23A 42
Ferns Rd. E15 ... 37Hc 73
Fern St. E3 ... 42Cc 92
Fernthorpe Rd. SW16 ... 65Lb 134
Ferntower Rd. N5 ... 36Tb 71
Fern Towers CR3: Cat'm ... 97Wb 197
Fernville La. HP2: Hem H ... 2M 3
Fern Wlk. SE16 ... 50Wb 91
TW15: Ashf ... 64M 127
Fern Way WD25: Wat ... 7X 13
Fernways IG1: Ilf ... 35Rc 74
Fernwood CR0: Sels ... 81Ac 178
SW19 ... 60Bb 111
Fernwood Av. HA0: Wemb ... 37La 66
SW16 ... 63Mb 134
Fernwood Cl. BR1: Brom ... 68Lc 137
Fernwood Ct. N14 ... 17Lb 32
Fernwood Cres. N20 ... 20Hb 31
Ferny Hill EN4: Had W ... 9Gb 17
Ferranti Cl. SE18 ... 48Mc 93
Ferraro Cl. TW5: Hest ... 51Ca 107
Ferrers Av. SM6: Bedd ... 77Mb 156
UB7: W Dray ... 47M 83
Ferrers Cl. SL1: Slou ... 6C 80
Ferrers Rd. SW16 ... 64Mb 134
Ferrestone Rd. N8 ... 28Pb 50
Ferrey M. SW9 ... 54Qb 112
Ferriby Cl. N1 ... 38Qb 70
Ferrier Ind. Est. SW18 ... 56Db 111
(off Ferrier St.)
Ferrier Point E16 ... 43Jc 93
(off Forty Acre La.)

Ferrier St. SW18 56Db 111
Ferriers Way KT18: Tatt C 90Ya 174
Ferring Cl. HA2: Harr 32Ea 66
Ferrings SE21 62Ub 135
Ferris Av. CR0: C'don 76Bc 158
Ferris Rd. SE22 56Wb 113
Ferron Rd. E5 34Xb 71
Ferro Rd. RM13: Rain 42Jd 96
Ferry App. SE18 48Qc 94
Ferry Av. TW18: Staines 66G 126
Ferrybridge Ho. SE11 4J 229
Ferrydale Lodge NW4 28Ya 48
(off Parson St.)
Ferryhills Cl. WD19: Wat 20Y 27
Ferry Ho. E5 32Xb 71
(off Harrington Hill)
Ferry Island Retail Pk. N17 27Wb 51
Ferry La. KT16: Chert 72J 149
N17 28Wb 51
RM13: Rain 45Gd 96
SW13 51Ua 110
TW8: Bford 51Na 109
TW9: Kew 51Pa 109
TW17: Shep 74Q 150
TW18: Lale 69L 127
TW19: Wray 61D 126
Ferry La. Ind. Est. E17 28Zb 52
RM13: Rain 43Hd 96
Ferryman's Quay SW6 54Eb 111
Ferrymead Av. UB6: G'frd 41Ca 85
Ferrymead Dr. UB6: G'frd 40Ca 65
Ferrymead Gdns.
UB6: G'frd 40Ea 66
Ferrymoor TW10: Ham 62Ka 130
Ferry Pl. SE18 48Qc 94
Ferry Quays TW8: Bford 51Na 109
(Ferry La.)
TW8: Bford 52Ma 109
(off Point Wharf La.)
Ferry Rd. KT7: T Ditt 72Ka 152
KT8: W Mole 69Ca 129
RM18: Tilb 5C 122
SW13 52Wa 110
TW1: Twick 60Ka 108
TW11: Tedd 64Ka 130
Ferry Sq. TW8: Bford 52Na 109
Ferry St. E14 50Ec 92
Ferry Wharf TW8: Bford 52Na 109
Feryby Rd. RM16: Grays 8D 100
Festing Rd. SW15 55Za 110
Festival Av. DA3: Lfield 69Fe 143
Festival Cl. DA5: Bexl 60Zc 117
DA8: Erith 52Hd 118
UB10: Hil 39R 64
Festival Ct. E8 38Vb 71
(off Holly St.)
SM1: Sutt 73Db 155
Festival Wlk. SM5: Cars 77Hb 155
Festoon Way E16 45Mc 93
FETCHAM 95Fa 192
Fetcham Comn. La.
KT22: Fet 93Da 191
FETCHAM DOWNS 98Fa 192
Fetcham Grove 94Ja 192
Fetcham Pk. Dr. KT22: Fet 95Ga 192
Fetherstone Cl. EN6: Pot B 4Fb 17
Fetherstone Cl. RM6: Chad H 30Bd 55
(off High Rd.)
Fetherston Rd. SS17: Stan H 1M 101
Fetherton Ct. IG11: Bark 40Sc 74
(off Spring Pl.)
Fetter La. EC4 3A 224 (44Qb 90)
(not continuous)
Fettes Ho. NW8 2C 214
Fews Lodge RM6: Chad H 28Zc 55
Ffinch St. SE8 52Cc 114
FICKLESHOLE 86Fc 179
Fiddicroft Av. SM7: Bans 86Db 175
Fiddler's Cl. DA9: Ghithe 56Xd 120
FIDDLERS HAMLET 4Yc 23
Fidelis Ho. E1 1K 225
Fidgeon Cl. BR1: Brom 69Qc 138
Fidler Pl. WD23: Bush 16Da 27
Field Cl. BR1: Brom 68Lc 137
CR2: Sande 86Xb 177
E4 23Dc 52
HA4: Ruis 32S 64
IG9: Buck H 20Lc 35
KT8: W Mole 71Da 151
KT9: Chess 78La 152
NW2 33Wa 68
RM4: Abr 13Xc 37
TW4: Cran 53X 107
UB3: Harl 52S 106
UB10: Ick 33R 64
FIELDCOMMON 73Ba 151
Fieldcommon La.
KT12: Walt T 74Aa 151
Field Ct. DA11: Nflt 1B 144
RH8: Oxt 99Gc 199
SW19 62Cb 133
WC1 1J 223 (43Pb 90)
Field End CR5: Coul 86Mb 176
EN5: Ark 14Xa 30
GU24: W End 5D 166
HA4: Ruis 37Y 65
UB5: N'olt 37Z 65
Fieldend TW1: Twick 63Ha 130
Field End Cl. WD19: Wat 17Aa 27
Field End M. WD19: Wat 17Aa 27
Field End Rd. HA4: Ruis 32Z 65
HA5: Eastc 29X 45
Fieldend Rd. SW16 67Lb 134
Fielden Ter. DA11: Nflt 60Ee 121
Fielders Cl. EN1: Enf 14Ub 33
HA2: Harr 32Ea 66
Fielders Way WD7: Shenl 5Na 15
Fieldfare La. DA9: Ghithe 59Wd 120
Fieldfare Rd. SE28 45Yc 95
Fieldfares AL2: Lon C 9H 7
Fieldgate Ct. KT11: Cobh 86W 170
Fieldgate La. CR4: Mitc 68Gb 133
Fieldgate Mans. E1 43Wb 91
(off Fieldgate St., not continuous)
Fieldgate St. E1 43Wb 91
Field Ho. NW6 41Za 88
(off Harvist Rd.)
Fieldhouse Cl. E18 25Jc 53
Fieldhouse Rd. SW12 60Lb 112
Fieldhouse Vs. SM7: Bans 87Gb 175
Fieldhurst SL3: L'ly 50B 82
Fieldhurst Cl. KT15: Add 78K 149
Fielding Av. RM18: Tilb 3D 122
TW2: Twick 62Ea 130
Fielding Ct. WC2 3F 223
Fielding Gdns. SL3: L'ly 7N 81
Fielding Ho. NW6 41Cb 89
NW8 39Eb 69
(off Ainsworth Way)
W4 51Ua 110
(off Devonshire Rd.)
Fielding La. BR2: Brom 70Lc 137
Fielding M. SW13 51Xa 110
Fielding Rd. W4 48Ta 87
W14 48Za 88
Fieldings, The GU21: Wok 8K 167
SE23 60Yb 114
SM7: Bans 89Bb 175
Fieldings Rd. EN8: Chesh 1Bc 20
Fielding St. SE17 51Sb 113
Fielding Ter. W5 45Pa 87
Fielding Wlk. W13 48Ka 86
Fielding Way CM13: Hut 16Ee 41
Field La. TW8: Bford 52La 108
TW11: Tedd 64Ja 130
Field Mead NW7 24Ua 48
NW9 24Va 48
Fieldoaks Way RH1: Mers 1C 208
Fieldpark Gdns. CR0: C'don 74Ac 158
Field Pl. KT3: N Mald 72Va 154
Field Point E7 35Jc 73
Field Rd. E7 35Hc 73
HP2: Hem H 3A 4
N17 27Tb 51
RM15: Avel 46Sd 98
TW14: Felt 58X 107
UB9: Den 35F 62
(not continuous)
W6 50Ab 88
WD19: Wat 16Aa 27
Fields, The SL1: Slou 7H 81
Fields Ct. EN6: Pot B 5Fb 17
FIELDS END 1F 2
Fields End La. HP1: Hem H 1F 2
Fieldsend Rd. SM3: Cheam 78Ab 154
Fields Est. E8 38Wb 71
Fieldside Cl. BR6: Farnb 77Sc 160
Fieldside Rd. BR1: Brom 64Fc 137
Fields Pk. Cres. RM6: Chad H 29Zc 55
Field St. WC1 3H 217 (41Pb 90)
Fieldsway Ho. N5 36Qb 70
Field Vw. TW13: Felt 63T 128
TW20: Egh 64E 126
Fieldview SW18 60Fb 111
Field Vw. Cl. RM7: Mawney 27Cd 56
Fieldview Cotts. N14 19Mb 32
(off Balaams La.)
Fieldview Ct. TW18: Staines 64J 127
Field Vw. Ri. AL2: Brick W 1Aa 13
Field Vw. Rd. EN6: Pot B 5Cb 17
Field Way GU23: Rip 97H 189
HA4: Ruis 32S 64
HP3: Bov 9C 2
NW10 38Sa 67
UB6: G'frd 39Da 65
UB8: Cowl 42M 83
WD3: Rick 18K 25
Fieldway BR5: Pet W 72Tc 160
CR0: New Ad 80Dc 158
HP4: Berk 3A 2
RM8: Dag 34Yc 75
RM16: Grays 46Ce 99
SL9: Chal P 24A 42
Fieldway Cres. N5 36Qb 70
Fiennes Cl. RM8: Dag 32Yc 75
Fiennes Way TN13: S'oaks 99Ld 203
Fifehead Cl. TW15: Ashf 65N 127
Fife Rd. E16 43Jc 93
KT1: King T 68Na 131
N22 24Rb 51
SW14 57Sa 109
Fife Ter. N1 1J 217 (40Pb 70)
Fife Way KT23: Bookh 97Ca 191
Fifield Path SE23 62Zb 136
Fifteenth Av. KT20: Lwr K 98Bb 195
Fifth Av. E12 35Pc 74
KT20: Lwr K 97Ab 194
RM20: W Thur 51Wd 120
UB3: Hayes 46V 84
W10 41Ab 88
WD25: Wat 7Z 13
Fifth Cross Rd. TW2: Twick 61Fa 130
Fifth Way HA9: Wemb 35Ra 67
Figges Rd. CR4: Mitc 66Jb 134
Figgswood CR5: Coul 94Lb 196
FIG STREET 100Jd 202
Fig St. TN14: S'oaks 100Hd 202
Fig Tree Cl. NW10 39Ua 68
Figtree Hill HP2: Hem H 1M 3
Figure Ct. SW3 50Hb 89
(off West Rd.)
Filanco Ct. W7 46Ha 86
Filbert Cl. AL10: Hat 3B 8
Filborough Way DA12: Grav'nd 1K 145
Filby Rd. KT9: Chess 79Pa 153
Filey Av. N16 32Wb 71
Filey Cl. SM2: Sutt 80Eb 155
TN16: Big H 91Kc 199
Filey Spur SL1: Slou 7F 80
Filey Waye HA4: Ruis 33W 64
Filigree Ct. SE16 46Bc 92
Fillebrook Av. EN1: Enf 12Ub 33
Fillebrook Rd. E11 32Fc 73
Filmer Chambers SW6 53Ab 110
(off Filmer Rd.)
Filmer Ho. SW6 53Bb 111
(off Filmer Rd.)
Filmer La. TN14: S'oaks 93Nd 203
Filmer M. SW6 53Bb 111
Filmer Rd. SL4: Wind 4B 102
SW6 53Ab 110
Filston La. TN13: Off, Dun G 88Fd 182
Filston Rd. DA8: Erith 50Ed 96
Filton Cl. NW9 25Ua 48
Filton Ct. SE14 52Yb 114
(off Farrow La.)
Filton Ho. WD19: Wat 20Z 27
Finborough Ho. SW10 51Eb 111
(off Finborough Rd.)
Finborough Rd. SW10 50Db 89
SW17 65Hb 133
Finborough Theatre, The 51Db 111
(off Finborough Rd.)
Finchale Rd. SE2 48Wc 95
Fincham Cl. UB10: Ick 34S 64
Finch Av. SE27 63Tb 135
Finch Cl. AL10: Hat 2C 8
EN5: Barn 15Cb 31
GU21: Knap 9G 166
NW10 37Ta 67
Finch Ct. DA14: Sidc 62Xc 139
Finchdale HP1: Hem H 2J 3
Finchdean Ho. SW15 59Va 110
Finch Dr. TW14: Felt 59Z 107
Finches, The UB9: Den 29H 43
Finches Av. WD3: Crox G 13P 25
Finch Gdns. E4 22Cc 52
Finch Grn. WD3: Chor 14H 25
Finch Ho. E3 39Bc 72
(off Jasmine Sq.)
SE8 52Dc 114
(off Bronze St.)
Finchingfield Av. IG8: Wfd G 24Lc 53
Finch La. EC3 3G 225 (44Tb 91)
WD23: Bush 13Ba 27
FINCHLEY 25Cb 49
Finchley Cl. DA1: Dart 58Qd 119
Finchley Ct. N3 23Db 49
Finchley Golf Course 23Bb 49
Finchley Ind. Est. N12 21Eb 49
Finchley La. NW4 28Ya 48
Finchley Lido 24Fb 49
Finchley Manor Club 25Bb 49
Finchley Pk. N12 21Eb 49
Finchley Pl. NW8 1B 214 (40Fb 69)
Finchley Rd. NW2 28Bb 49
NW3 35Cb 69
NW8 1B 214 (39Fb 69)
NW11 28Bb 49
RM17: Grays 51De 121
Finchley Way N3 24Cb 49
Finch Lodge W9 43Cb 89
(off Admiral Wlk.)
Finch M. SE15 53Vb 113
Finch's Ct. E14 45Dc 92
Finden Rd. E7 36Lc 73
Findhorn Av. UB4: Yead 43X 85
Findhorn St. E14 44Ec 92
Findon Cl. HA2: Harr 34Da 65
SW18 58Cb 111
Findon Ct. KT15: Add 78H 149
Findon Gdns. RM13: Rain 43Jd 96
Findon Rd. N9 18Xb 33
W12 47Wa 88
Fine Bush La. UB9: Hare 30R 44
Fingal St. SE10 50Hc 93
Fingest Ho. NW8 5D 214
Finglesham Cl. BR5: Orp 74Zc 161
Finians Cl. UB10: Uxb 38P 63
Finland Rd. SE4 55Ac 114
Finland St. SE16 48Ac 92
Finlay Gdns. KT15: Add 77L 149
Finlays Cl. KT9: Chess 78Qa 153
Finlay St. SW6 53Za 110
Finley Ct. SE5 52Sb 113
(off Redcar St.)
Finmere Ho. N4 31Sb 71
Finnart Cl. KT13: Weyb 77S 150
Finnart Ho. Dr. KT13: Weyb 77S 150
Finnemore Ho. N1 39Sb 71
(off Britannia Row)
Finney Dr. GU20: W'sham 9B 146
Finney La. TW7: Isle 53Ja 108
Finn Ho. N1 3G 219
Finnis St. E2 41Xb 91
Finnymore Rd. RM9: Dag 38Ad 76
FINSBURY 4A 218 (41Qb 90)
Finsbury Av. EC2 1G 225 (43Tb 91)
Finsbury Av. Sq. EC2 7H 219 (43Ub 91)
Finsbury Cir. EC2 1G 225 (43Tb 91)
Finsbury Cotts. N22 24Nb 50
Finsbury Ct. EN8: Walt C 6Ac 20
Finsbury Est. EC1 4B 218 (41Qb 90)
Finsbury Ho. N22 25Nb 50
Finsbury Leisure Cen. 5D 218 (41Sb 91)
Finsbury Mkt. EC2 6H 219 (42Ub 91)
(not continuous)
FINSBURY PARK 32Qb 70
Finsbury Pk. Av. N4 30Sb 51
Finsbury Pk. Rd. N4 33Rb 71
Finsbury Pavement EC2 7G 219 (43Tb 91)
Finsbury Rd. N22 24Pb 50
(not continuous)
Finsbury Sq. EC2 6G 219 (42Tb 91)
Finsbury St. EC2 7F 219 (43Tb 91)
Finsbury Way DA5: Bexl 58Bd 117
Finsen Rd. SE5 56Sb 113
Finstock Rd. W10 44Za 88
Finucane Ct. TW9: Rich 55Pa 109
(off Lwr. Mortlake Rd.)
Finucane Dr. BR5: Orp 73Yc 161
Finucane Gdns. RM13: Rain 37Jd 76
Finucane Ri. WD23: B Hea 19Ea 28
Finway Ct. WD18: Wat 15V 26
Finwhale Ho. E14 48Dc 92
(off Glengall Gro.)
Fiona Cl. KT23: Bookh 96Ca 191
Fiona Ct. EN2: Enf 13Rb 33
NW6 40Cb 69
Firbank Cl. E16 43Mc 93
EN2: Enf 14Sb 33
Firbank Dr. GU21: Wok 1M 187
WD19: Wat 17Aa 27
Firbank La. GU21: Wok 1M 187
Firbank Pl. TW20: Eng G 5M 125
Firbank Rd. RM5: Col R 22Dd 56
SE15 54Xb 113
Fir Cl. KT12: Walt T 73W 150
Fircroft Cl. GU22: Wok 90B 168
SL2: Stoke P 7L 61
Fircroft Ct. GU22: Wok 90B 168
Fircroft Gdns. HA1: Harr 34Ga 66
Fircroft Rd. KT9: Chess 77Pa 153
SW17 61Hb 133
TW20: Eng G 6N 125
Fir Dene BR6: Farnb 76Pc 160
Firdene KT5: Surb 74Sa 153
Fireball Hill SL5: S'dale 3B 146
Fire Bell All. KT6: Surb 72Na 153
Firecrest Cl. DA3: Lfield 69De 143
Firecrest Dr. NW3 34Db 69
Firefly Cl. UB3: Hayes 45V 84
Firefly Gdns. E6 42Nc 94
Firehorn Ho. E15 41Gc 93
(off Teasel Way)
Firemans Flats N22 24Nb 50
Firepower (The Royal Artillery Mus.)
48Rc 94
Fire Station All. EN5: Barn 13Ab 30
Firestation Cen. for Arts & Culture, The
4G 102
Fire Station M. BR3: Beck 67Cc 136
Firestone Ho. TW8: Bford 50Na 87
Firethorn Cl. HA8: Edg 21Sa 47
Firewatch Ct. E1 43Ac 92
(off Candle St.)
Firfield Rd. KT15: Add 77J 149
Firfields KT13: Weyb 79R 150
Fir Grange Av. KT13: Weyb 78R 150
Fir Gro. KT3: N Mald 72Va 154
Firgrove GU21: Wok 1M 187
Fir Gro. Rd. SW9 54Qb 112
Firham Pk. Av.
RM3: Hrld W 24Qd 57
Firhill Rd. SE6 63Cc 136
Fir Ho. W10 42Ab 88
(off Droop St.)
Firlands KT13: Weyb 79U 150
Firle Ct. KT17: Eps 84Va 174
Firle Ho. W10 43Ya 88
(off Sutton Way)
Firman Cl. KT3: N Mald 70Ua 132
Firmans Ct. E17 28Fc 53
Firmingers Rd. BR6: Well H 78Dd 162
Firmin Rd. DA1: Dart 57Ld 119
Fir Rd. SM3: Sutt 74Bb 155
TW13: Hanw 64Z 129
Firs, The AL1: St A 6F 6
CM15: Pil H 16Wd 40
CR3: Cat'm 94Tb 197
DA5: Bexl 60Fd 118
DA15: Sidc 61Vc 139
E6 38Nc 74
EN9: Walt A 7Lc 21
(in Woodbine Cl. Caravan Pk.)
GU24: Bisl 8E 166
HA8: Edg 21Ta 47
(off Stoneyfields La.)
IG8: Wfd G 24Lc 53
KT14: Byfl 84M 169
KT23: Bookh 96Ea 192
N20 18Fb 31
RM16: Grays 46Ee 99
SE26 64Xb 135
(Border Rd.)
SE26 64Yb 136
(Waverley Ct.)
W5 43Ma 87
Firs Av. N10 27Jb 50
N11 23Hb 49
SL4: Wind 5D 102
SW14 56Sa 109
Firsby Av. CR0: C'don 74Zb 158
Firsby Rd. N16 32Wb 71
Firs Cl. AL10: Hat 1D 8
CR4: Mitc 68Kb 134
KT10: Clay 79Ga 152
N10 28Jb 50
SE23 59Ac 114
SL0: Iver H 39E 62
Firscroft N13 20Sb 33
Firsdene Cl. KT16: Ott 79F 148
Firs Dr. IG10: Lough 11Qc 36
SL3: L'ly 46B 82
TW5: Cran 52X 107
Firs End SL9: Chal P 27A 42
Firsgrove Cres. CM14: W'ley 21Xd 58
Firsgrove Rd. CM14: W'ley 21Xd 58
Firs Ho. N22 25Qb 50
(off Acacia Rd.)
Firside Gro. DA15: Sidc 60Vc 117
Firs La. EN6: Pot B 5Db 17
N13 20Sb 33
N21 17Sb 33
Firs Pk., The AL9: Hat 5J 9
Firs Pk. Av. N21 18Tb 33
Firs Pk. Gdns. N21 18Sb 33
Firs Rd. CR8: Kenley 87Rb 177
First Av. DA7: Bex 52Yc 117
DA11: Nflt 10A 122
E12 35Nc 74
E13 41Jc 93
E17 29Cc 52
EN1: Enf 15Vb 33
EN9: Walt A 1Kc 21
HA9: Wemb 33Ma 67
KT8: W Mole 70Ba 129
KT12: Walt T 72X 151
KT19: Ewe 81Ua 174
KT20: Lwr K 97Ab 194
N18 21Yb 52
NW4 28Ya 48
RM6: Chad H 29Yc 55
RM10: Dag 40Dd 76
RM20: W Thur 51Wd 120
SS17: Stan H 1M 101
SW14 55Ua 110
UB3: Hayes 46V 84
W3 46Va 88
W10 42Bb 89
WD25: Wat 7Y 13
First Cl. KT8: W Mole 69Ea 130
First Cres. SL1: Slou 3G 80
First Cross Rd. TW2: Twick 61Ga 130
First Dr. NW10 38Sa 67
First Quarter KT19: Eps 83Ua 174
First Slip KT22: Lea 90Ja 172
First St. SW3 5E 226 (49Gb 89)
First Way HA9: Wemb 35Ra 67
Firstway SW20 68Ya 132
Firs Wlk. HA6: Nwood 23T 44
IG8: Wfd G 22Jc 53
Firswood Av. KT19: Ewe 78Ua 154
Firs Wood Cl. EN6: N'thaw 4Hb 17
Firth Gdns. SW6 53Ab 110
Firth Ho. E2 41Wb 91
(off Turin St.)
Fir Tree Av. SL2: Stoke P 2K 81
UB7: W Dray 48Q 84
Firtree Av. CR4: Mitc 68Jb 134
Fir Tree Cl. BR6: Chels 78Vc 161
HP3: Hem H 3A 4
KT10: Esh 78Ea 152
KT17: Eps D 87Ya 174
KT19: Ewe 77Va 154
KT22: Lea 95La 192
RM1: Rom 27Fd 56
RM17: Grays 51Fe 121
SW16 64Lb 134
W5 44Na 87
Fir Tree Ct. WD6: E'tree 14Pa 29
Fir Tree Gdns. CR0: C'don 77Cc 158
Fir Tree Gro. SM5: Cars 80Hb 155
Fir Tree Hill WD3: Chan C 10P 11
Firtree Ho. SE13 59Fc 115
(off Birdwood Av.)
Fir Tree Pl. TW15: Ashf 64Q 128
Fir Tree Rd. KT17: Eps D 88Xa 174
KT22: Lea 95La 192
SM7: Bans 86Ya 174
TW4: Houn 56Aa 107
Fir Trees CM16: Epp 1Xc 23
RM4: Abr 13Xc 37
Fir Trees Cl. SE16 46Ac 92
Fir Tree Wlk. EN1: Enf 13Tb 33
RH2: Reig 6M 207
RM10: Dag 34Ed 76
Fir Wlk. SM3: Cheam 79Za 154
Firwood Av. AL4: St A 2J 7
Firwood Cl. GU21: Wok 1J 187
Firwood Rd. GU25: Vir W 2J 147
Fisgard Ct. DA12: Grav'nd 8F 122
Fisher Cl. CR0: C'don 74Vb 157
E9 36Zb 72
EN3: Enf L 9Dc 20
KT12: Hers 77X 151
UB6: G'frd 41Ca 85
WD4: K Lan 1Q 12
Fisher Ho. E1 45Yb 92
(off Cable St.)
N1 1K 217
Fisherman KT16: Chert 74L 149
Fisherman Cl. TW10: Ham 63Ka 130
Fishermans Dr. SE16 47Zb 92
Fisherman's Pl. W4 51Va 110
Fishermans Wlk. E14 46Cc 92
SE28 47Uc 94
Fishermens Hill DA11: Nflt 57De 121
Fisher Rd. HA3: W'stone 26Ha 46
Fishers Cl. EN8: Walt C 6Cc 20
SW16 62Mb 134
WD23: Bush 13Aa 27
Fishers Ct. SE14 53Zb 114
Fishersdene KT10: Clay 80Ja 152
FISHERS GREEN 1Dc 20
Fishers Grn. La. EN9: Walt A 1Dc 20
Fisher's Ind. Est. WD18: Wat 15Y 27
Fishers La. CM16: Epp 4Uc 22
W4 49Ta 87
Fishers Oak TN14: S'oaks 93Ld 203
Fisher St. E16 43Jc 93
WC1 1H 223 (43Pb 90)
Fishers Way DA17: Belv 46Ed 96
Fishers Wood SL5: S'dale 4G 146
Fisherton St. NW8 6B 214 (42Fb 89)
Fishery Cotts. HP1: Hem H 4J 3
Fishery Pas. HP1: Hem H 4J 3
Fishery Rd. HP1: Hem H 4J 3
Fishguard Spur SL1: Slou 7M 81
Fishguard Way E16 46Rc 94
Fishing Temple Pk. Homes
TW18: Staines 67H 127
Fishmongers Hall Wharf EC4 5G 225
Fishponds Rd. BR2: Kes 78Mc 159
SW17 63Gb 133
Fishpool St. AL3: St A 2P 5
Fish St. Hill EC3 5G 225 (45Tb 91)
Fish Wharf EC3 5G 225 (45Tb 91)
Fisk Cl. TW16: Sun 65V 128
Fiske Ct. IG11: Bark 40Tc 74
N17 25Wb 51
SM2: Sutt 80Eb 155
Fitness4Less
Sutton 79Cb 155
Fitness First
Alperton 39Na 67
America Square 4K 225
Baker Street 1G 221 (43Hb 89)
Beckenham 64Bc 136
Bloomsbury 6F 217
Bow Wharf 40Zb 72
Brentwood 19Yd 40
(within The Baytree Cen.)
Brixton 55Qb 112
Camden 39Kb 70
Chancery Lane 2A 224
Clapham Junction 55Gb 111
(off Lavender Hill)
Covent Garden 5G 223
Crouch End 30Nb 50
Croydon 74Rb 157
Embankment 6G 223
(off Embankment Pl.)
Fetter Lane 2A 224
Gracechurch Street 4H 225
Great Marlborough Street 3B 222
Hammersmith 49Ya 88
Harrow 30Ga 46
(in St George's Shopping & Leisure Cen.)
High Holborn 2H 223
Holloway 34Pb 70
Ilford 33Sc 74
Islington 2B 218 (40Rb 71)
Kilburn 39Bb 69
Kingly Street 4B 222
Kingsbury 29Qa 47
Lewisham 55Ec 114
Leyton Mills 34Ec 72
London Bridge 7G 225
(off London Bri. St.)
London Victoria 4A 228
(off Victoria St.)
North Finchley 22Eb 49
Old Street 5F 219
Paternoster Square 2C 224
Pinner 27Z 45
Purley 84Pb 176
Queen Victoria Street 4D 224
Romford 30Gd 56
St Albans 2B 6
(off Verulam Rd.)
South Kensington 5B 226
Streatham 61Nb 134
Thomas More Square 45Wb 91
(off Thomas More Sq.)
Tooting Bec 62Jb 134
Tottenham 26Vb 51
Uxbridge 38L 63
Walworth Road 50Sb 91
Wembley 36Na 67
Fitness First for Women
Chalk Farm 38Jb 70
(off Chalk Farm Rd.)
Fitrooms 51Bb 111
FitSpace Gym 48Rc 94
Fitzalan Ho. KT17: Ewe 82Va 174
Fitzalan Rd. KT10: Clay 80Ga 152
N3 27Ab 48
Fitzalan St. SE11 5J 229 (49Pb 90)
Fitzclarence Ho. W11 47Ab 88
(off Holland Park Av.)
Fitzgeorge Av. KT3: N Mald 67Ta 131
W14 49Ab 88
Fitzgerald Av. SW14 55Ua 110
Fitzgerald Ct. E10 32Dc 72
(off Leyton Grange Est.)
Fitzgerald Ho. E14 44Dc 92
(off E. India Dock Rd.)
SW9 54Qb 112
UB3: Hayes 46X 85

Fitzgerald Rd. E11 .... 29Jc 53
KT7: T Ditt 72Ja 152
SW14 .... 55Ta 109
Fitzhardinge Ho. W1 .... 2H 221
Fitzhardinge St. W1 .... 2H 221 (44Jb 90)
Fitzherbert Wlk. UB1: S'hall 47Fa 86
Fitzhugh Gro. SW18 .... 58Fb 111
Fitzilian Av. RM3: Hrld W 25Pd 57
Fitzjames Av. CR0: C'don 75Wb 157
W14 .... 49Ab 88
Fitzjohn Av. EN5: Barn 15Ab 30
Fitzjohn's Av. NW3 .... 35Eb 69
Fitzmaurice Ho. SE16 .... 49Xb 91
(off Rennie Est.)
Fitzmaurice Pl. W1 .... 6A 222 (46Kb 90)
Fitzneal St. W12 .... 44Va 88
Fitzrobert Pl. TW20: Egh 65C 126
FITZROVIA 1A 222
Fitzrovia Apartments W1 .... 6A 216
Fitzroy Bri. NW1 .... 39Jb 70
Fitzroy Bus. Pk. BR5: St P 66Zc 139
Fitzroy Cl. N6 .... 32Hb 69
Fitzroy Ct. CR0: C'don 73Tb 157
DA1: Dart 60Rd 119
(off Churchill Cl.)
N6 .... 30Lb 50
W1 .... 6C 216
Fitzroy Cres. W4 .... 52Ta 109
Fitzroy Gdns. SE19 .... 66Ub 135
Fitzroy Ho. E14 .... 43Bc 92
(off Wallwood St.)
SE1 .... 50Vb 91
(off Cooper's Rd.)
Fitzroy House Mus. 6B 216 (42Lb 90)
Fitzroy M. W1 .... 6B 216
Fitzroy Pk. N6 .... 32Hb 69
Fitzroy Pl. RH2: Reig 6M 207
Fitzroy Rd. NW1 .... 39Jb 70
Fitzroy Sq. W1 .... 6B 216 (42Lb 90)
Fitzroy St. W1 .... 6B 216 (42Lb 90)
(not continuous)
Fitzroy Yd. NW1 .... 39Jb 70
Fitzstephen Rd. RM8: Dag 36Xc 75
Fitzwarren Gdns. N19 .... 32Lb 70
Fitzwilliam Av. TW9: Rich 54Pa 109
Fitzwilliam Cl. N20 .... 18Jb 32
Fitzwilliam Ct. AL1: St A 2C 6
(off St Peter's St.)
Fitzwilliam Hgts. SE23 .... 61Yb 136
Fitzwilliam Ho. TW9: Rich 56Ma 109
Fitzwilliam M. E16 .... 46Jc 93
Fitzwilliam Rd. SW4 .... 55Lb 112
Fitzwygram Cl. TW12: Hamp H 64Ea 130
Five Acre NW9 .... 25Va 48
Fiveacre Cl. CR7: Thor H 72Qb 156
Five Acres AL2: Lon C 7H 7
WD4: K Lan 1P 11
Five Acres Av. AL2: Brick W 1Ba 13
Five Arches Bus. Pk. DA14: Sidc 64Zc 139
Five Ash Rd. DA11: Grav'nd 9B 122
Five Bell All. E14 .... 44Bc 92
(off Three Colt St.)
Five Elms Rd. BR2: Hayes 76Kc 159
RM9: Dag 34Bd 75
Five Flds. Cl. WD19: Wat 19Ba 27
Five Oaks AL10: Hat 3D 8
(off Sandifield)
Five Oaks Cl. GU21: Wok 1H 187
Five Oaks La. IG7: Chig 23Ad 55
Five Oaks M. BR1: Brom 62Jc 137
Fives Ct. SE11 .... 4B 230 (48Rb 91)
FIVEWAYS 61Rc 138
Five Ways Bus. Cen. TW13: Felt 62X 129
FIVEWAYS CORNER
Croydon 77Qb 156
Hendon 25Wa 48
Fiveways Rd. SW9 .... 54Qb 112
Five Wents BR8: Swan 68Jd 140
Flack Ct. E10 .... 31Dc 72
Fladbury Rd. N15 .... 30Tb 51
Fladgate Rd. E11 .... 30Gc 53
Flag Cl. CR0: C'don 74Zb 158
Flagon Ct. CR0: C'don 77Sb 157
(off St Andrew's Rd.)
Flags, The HP2: Hem H 2B 4
Flagstaff Cl. EN9: Walt A 5Dc 20
Flagstaff Rd. EN9: Walt A 5Dc 20
Flag Wlk. HA5: Eastc 30W 44
Flambard Rd. HA1: Harr 30Ja 46
Flamborough Cl. TN16: Big H 91Kc 199
Flamborough Ho. SE15 .... 53Wb 113
(off Clayton Rd.)
Flamborough Rd. HA4: Ruis 34W 64
Flamborough Spur SL1: Slou 7E 80
Flamborough St. E14 .... 44Ac 92
Flamborough Wlk. E14 .... 44Ac 92
(off Flamborough St.)
Flamingo Ct. SE8 .... 52Cc 114
(off Hamilton St.)
SE17 .... 7D 230
Flamingo Gdns. UB5: N'olt 41Aa 85
Flamingo Wlk. RM12: Horn 37Jd 76
Flamstead End Rd. EN8: Chesh 1Xb 19
Flamstead Gdns. RM9: Dag 38Yc 75
Flamstead Ho. SW3 .... 7D 226
(off Cale St.)
Flamstead Rd. RM9: Dag 38Yc 75
Flamsted Av. HA9: Wemb 37Qa 67
Flamsteed Rd. SE7 .... 50Nc 94
Flanchford Ho. RH2: Reig 5J 207
(off Somers Cl.)
Flanchford Rd.
RH2: Leigh, Reig 10E 206
W12 .... 48Va 88
Flanders Ct. DA1: Dart 57Md 119
E17 .... 31Ac 72
TW20: Egh 64E 126
Flanders Cres. SW17 .... 66Hb 133
Flanders Mans. W4 .... 49Va 88
Flanders Rd. E6 .... 40Pc 74
W4 .... 49Ua 88
Flanders Way E9 .... 37Zb 72
Flandrian Cl. EN3: Enf L 10Dc 20
Flank St. E1 .... 45Wb 91
Flannery Ct. SE16 .... 48Xb 91
Flansham Ho. E14 .... 44Bc 92
(off Clemence St.)
Flash La. EN2: Enf 9Rb 19
Flask Wlk. NW3 .... 35Eb 69
Flatfield Rd. HP3: Hem H 4A 4
Flatford Ho. SE6 .... 63Ec 136
Flather Cl. SW16 .... 64Lb 134
Flat Iron Sq. SE1 .... 7E 224
Flatiron Yd. SE1 .... 7E 224
Flats, The DA9: Ghithe 57Yd 120
HP8: Chal G 15A 24
FLAUNDEN 4D 10
Flaunden Bottom HP5: Lat 9A 10
Flaunden Hill HP3: Flau 5B 10
Flaunden Ho. WD18: Wat 16U 26
Flaunden La.
HP3: Bov, Flau, Hem H 4D 10
WD3: Sarr 5G 10
Flaunden Pk. HP3: Flau 3C 10
Flavell M. SE10 .... 50Gc 93
Flavian Cl. AL3: St A 4M 5
Flaxen Cl. E4 .... 20Dc 34
Flaxen Rd. E4 .... 20Dc 34
Flaxley Ho. SW1 .... 7K 227
Flaxley Rd. SM4: Mord 73Db 155
Flaxman Ct. DA17: Belv 50Cd 96
(off Hoddesdon Rd.)
W1 .... 3D 222 (44Mb 90)
WC1 .... 4E 216
Flaxman Ho. SE1 .... 3B 230
W4 .... 50Ua 88
(off Devonshire St.)
Flaxman Rd. SE5 .... 55Rb 113
Flaxman Sports Cen. 54Sb 113
Flaxman Ter. WC1 .... 4E 216 (41Mb 90)
Flaxton Rd. SE18 .... 53Tc 116
Flecker Cl. HA7: Stan 22Ha 46
Flecker Ho. SE5 .... 52Tb 113
(off Lomond Gro.)
Fleece Dr. N9 .... 21Wb 51
Fleece Rd. KT6: Surb 74La 152
Fleece Wlk. N7 .... 37Nb 70
Fleeming Cl. E17 .... 26Bc 52
Fleeming Rd. E17 .... 26Bc 52
Fleet Av. DA2: Dart 60Sd 120
RM14: Upm 30Td 58
Fleetbank Ho. EC4 .... 3A 224
Fleetbrook Ho. SL3: Dat 3P 103
Fleet Bldg. EC4 .... 2B 224
Fleet Cl. HA4: Ruis 30S 44
KT8: W Mole 71Ba 151
RM14: Upm 30Td 58
Fleetdale Pde. DA2: Dart 60Sd 120
FLEET DOWNS 60Sd 120
Fleetfield WC1 .... 3G 217
Fleethall Gro. RM16: Grays 46Ce 99
Fleet Ho. E14 .... 45Ac 92
(off Victory Pl.)
Fleet Ho's. DA13: Sflt 65De 143
Fleet La. KT8: W Mole 73Ba 151
Fleet Pl. EC4 .... 2B 224 (44Rb 91)
(not continuous)
Fleet Rd. DA2: Dart 60Rd 119
DA11: Nflt 62Ee 143
NW3 .... 36Gb 69
Fleetside KT8: W Mole 71Ba 151
Fleet Sq. WC1 .... 4J 217 (41Pb 90)
Fleet St. EC4 .... 3K 223 (44Qb 90)
FLEETVILLE 2F 6
Fleetway TW20: Thorpe 69E 126
WC1 .... 3G 217
Fleetway W. UB6: G'frd 40Ka 66
Fleetwood Cl. CR0: C'don 76Vb 157
E16 .... 43Mc 93
KT9: Chess 80Ma 153
KT20: Tad 92Za 194
Fleetwood Ct. E6 .... 43Pc 94
(off Evelyn Dennington Rd.)
KT14: W Byf 85J 169
TW19: Stanw 58M 105
(off Douglas Rd.)
Fleetwood Rd. KT1: King T 69Ra 131
NW10 .... 36Wa 68
SL2: Slou 6K 81
Fleetwood Sq. KT1: King T 69Ra 131
Fleetwood St. N16 .... 33Ub 71
Fleetwood Way WD19: Wat 21Y 45
Fleming N8 .... 27Nb 50
(off Boyton Cl.)
Fleming Cl. SW10 .... 51Eb 111
(off Park Wlk.)
W9 .... 42Cb 89
Fleming Ct. CR0: Wadd 78Qb 156
DA11: Nflt 60Ee 121
W2 .... 7B 214
Fleming Dr. N21 .... 15Pb 32
Fleming Gdns. RM3: Hrld W 26Md 57
RM18: Tilb 3E 122
Fleming Ho. HA9: Wemb 34Sa 67
(off Barnhill Rd.)
N4 .... 32Sb 71
SE16 .... 47Wb 91
(off George Row)
SW17 .... 62Fb 133
Fleming Lodge W9 .... 43Cb 89
(off Admiral Wlk.)
Fleming Mead CR4: Mitc 66Gb 133
Fleming Rd. EN9: Walt A 7Dc 20
RM16: Chaf H 49Yd 98
SE17 .... 51Rb 113
UB1: S'hall 44Da 85
Flemings CM13: Gt War 23Yd 58
Fleming Wlk. NW9 .... 27Ua 48
Fleming Way SE28 .... 45Zc 95
TW7: Isle 56Ha 108
Flemish Flds. KT16: Chert 73J 149
Flemming Av. HA4: Ruis 32X 65
Flempton Rd. E10 .... 32Ac 72
Fletcher Bldgs. WC2 .... 3G 223
Fletcher Cl. E6 .... 44Rc 94
GU21: Wok 10K 167
(off Robin Hood Rd.)
KT16: Ott 79G 148
Fletcher Ho. N1 .... 1J 219
SE15 .... 52Yb 114
(off Clifton Way)
Fletcher La. E10 .... 31Ec 72
Fletcher Path SE8 .... 52Cc 114
Fletcher Rd. IG7: Chig 22Vc 55
KT16: Ott 79F 148
W4 .... 48Sa 87
Fletchers Cl. BR2: Brom 70Kc 137
Fletcher St. E1 .... 45Wb 91
Fletcher Way HP2: Hem H 1J 3
Fletching Rd. E5 .... 34Yb 72
SE7 .... 51Lc 115
Flete Ho. WD18: Wat 16U 26
Fletton Rd. N11 .... 24Nb 50
Fleur de Lis St. E1 .... 6J 219 (42Vb 91)
Fleur Gates SW19 .... 59Za 110
Flexlands La. GU24: Chob 2F 166
Flexmere Gdns. N17 .... 25Tb 51
Flexmere Rd. N17 .... 25Tb 51
Flight App. NW9 .... 26Va 48
Flight Ho. N1 .... 1H 219
Flimwell Cl. BR1: Brom 64Gc 137
Flinders Cl. AL1: St A 4E 6
Flinders Ho. E1 .... 46Xb 91
(off Green Bank)
Flint Cl. BR6: Chels 79Vc 161
CR0: C'don 72Pb 156
E15 .... 38Hc 73
KT23: Bookh 98Ea 192
RH1: Redh 5P 207
SM7: Bans 86Db 175
Flint Cotts. KT22: Lea 93Ka 192
(off Gravel Hill)
Flint Down Cl. BR5: St P 67Wc 139
Flintlock Cl. TW19: Stanw M 56J 105
Flintmill Cres. SE3 .... 54Nc 116
Flinton St. SE17 .... 7J 231 (50Ub 91)
Flint St. RM20: W Thur 51Xd 120
SE17 .... 6G 231 (49Tb 91)
Flitcroft St. WC2 .... 2E 222 (44Mb 90)
Flitton Ho. N1 .... 38Rb 71
(off The Sutton Est.)
Floathaven Cl. SE28 .... 46Wc 95
Floats, The TN13: Riv 93Gd 202
Flock Mill Pl. SW18 .... 60Db 111
Flockton Ho. KT13: Weyb 75Q 150
Flockton St. SE16 .... 47Wb 91
Flodden Rd. SE5 .... 53Sb 113
Flood La. TW1: Twick 60Ja 108
Flood Pas. SE18 .... 48Nc 94
Flood St. SW3 .... 7E 226 (50Gb 89)
Flood Wlk. SW3 .... 51Gb 111
Flora Cl. E14 .... 44Dc 92
HA7: Stan 20Na 29
Flora Gdns. CR0: New Ad 83Ec 178
RM6: Chad H 30Yc 55
W6 .... 49Xa 88
(off Albion Gdns.)
Flora Gro. AL1: St A 3D 6
Flora Ho. E3 .... 39Cc 72
(off Garrison Rd.)
Floral Ct. KT21: Asht 90La 172
Floral Dr. AL2: Lon C 8H 7
Floral Ho. KT16: Chert 74H 149
(off Fox La. Sth.)
Floral Pl. N1 .... 36Tb 71
Floral St. WC2 .... 4F 223 (45Nb 90)
Flora St. DA17: Belv 50Bd 95
Florence Av. EN2: Enf 13Sb 33
KT15: New H 83J 169
SM4: Mord 71Eb 155
Florence Cantwell Wlk. N19 .... 31Nb 70
(off Jessie Blythe La.)
Florence Cl. KT12: Walt T 73X 151
RM12: Horn 33Nd 77
RM20: Grays 51Ae 121
WD25: Wat 7W 12
Florence Ct. AL1: St A 2C 6
(off Alma Rd.)
E11 .... 28Kc 53
GU21: Knap 10G 166
N1 .... 38Rb 71
(off Florence St.)
SW19 .... 65Ab 132
W9 .... 4A 214
Florence Dr. EN2: Enf 13Sb 33
Florence Elson Cl. E12 .... 35Qc 74
Florence Farm Mobile Home Pk.
TN15: W King 79Td 164
Florence Gdns. RM6: Chad H 31Yc 75
TW18: Staines 66K 127
W4 .... 51Sa 109
Florence Ho. KT2: King T 66Pa 131
(off Florence Rd)
SE16 .... 50Xb 91
(off Rotherhithe New Rd.)
W11 .... 45Za 88
(off St Ann's Rd.)
WD18: Wat 14U 26
Florence Longman Ho. HP3: Hem H 6M 3
(off Weymouth St.)
Florence Mans. NW4 .... 29Xa 48
(off Vivian Av.)
SW6 .... 53Bb 111
(off Rostrevor Rd.)
Florence Nightingale Mus.
.... 2H 229 (47Pb 90)
Florence Rd. BR1: Brom 67Jc 137
BR3: Beck 68Ac 136
CR2: Sande 81Tb 177
E6 .... 39Lc 73
E13 .... 40Jc 73
KT2: King T 66Pa 131
KT12: Walt T 73X 151
N4 .... 31Pb 70
(not continuous)
SE2 .... 49Yc 95
SE14 .... 53Bc 114
SW19 .... 65Db 133
TW13: Felt 60X 107
UB2: S'hall 49Z 85
W4 .... 48Ta 87
W5 .... 45Na 87
Florence Root Ho. IG4: Ilf 29Nc 54
Florence Sq. E3 .... 42Dc 92
Florence St. E16 .... 42Hc 93
N1 .... 38Rb 71
NW4 .... 28Ya 48
Florence Ter. SE14 .... 53Bc 114
SW15 .... 62Ua 132
Florence Way GU21: Knap 10G 166
SW12 .... 60Hb 111
UB8: Uxb 38L 63
Florey Lodge W9 .... 43Cb 89
(off Admiral Wlk.)
Florey Sq. N21 .... 15Pb 32
Florfield Pas. E8 .... 37Xb 71
(off Reading La.)
Florfield Rd. E8 .... 37Xb 71
Florian SE5 .... 53Ub 113
Florian Av. SM1: Sutt 77Fb 155
Florian Rd. SW15 .... 56Ab 110
Florida Cl. WD23: B Hea 19Fa 28
Florida Ct. BR2: Brom 70Hc 137
(off Westmoreland Rd.)
TW18: Staines 63J 127
Florida Rd. CR7: Thor H 67Rb 135
Florida St. E2 .... 41Wb 91
Florin Ct. EC1 .... 7D 218
N18 .... 21Ub 51
SE1 .... 2K 231
Floris Pl. SW4 .... 55Lb 112
Floriston Av. UB10: Hil 38S 64
Floriston Cl. HA7: Stan 25Ka 46
Floriston Ct. UB5: N'olt 36Da 65
Floriston Gdns. HA7: Stan 25Ka 46
Florys Ct. SW19 .... 60Ab 110
Floss St. SW15 .... 54Ya 110
Flower & Dean Wlk. E1 .... 1K 225 (43Vb 91)
Flower Cres. KT16: Ott 79D 148
Flowerfield TN14: Otf 89Hd 182
Flowerhill Way DA13: Ist R 6A 144
Flower La. NW7 .... 22Va 48
RH9: G'stone 2B 210
Flower M. NW11 .... 30Ab 48
Flower Pot Cl. N15 .... 30Vb 51
Flowers Av. HA4: Ruis 30X 45
Flowers Cl. NW2 .... 34Wa 68
Flowersmead SW17 .... 61Jb 134
Flowers M. N19 .... 33Lb 70
Flower Walk, The SW7 .... 2A 226 (47Eb 89)
Floyd Rd. SE7 .... 50Lc 93
Floyd's La. GU22: Pyr 88J 169
Floyer Cl. TW10: Rich 57Pa 109
Fludyer St. SE13 .... 56Gc 115
Flux's La. CM16: Epp 5Wc 23
Flyers Way, The TN16: Westrm 98Tc 200
Flying Angel Ho. E16 .... 45Kc 93
(off Victoria Dock Rd.)
Flynn Ct. E14 .... 45Cc 92
(off Garford St.)
Fogerty Cl. EN3: Enf L 9Dc 20
Foley Ct. DA1: Dart 60Rd 119
(off Churchill Cl.)
Foley Ho. E1 .... 44Yb 92
(off Tarling St.)
Foley M. KT10: Clay 79Ga 152
Foley Rd. KT10: Clay 80Ga 152
TN16: Big H 90Mc 179
Foley St. W1 .... 1B 222 (43Lb 90)
Foley Wood KT10: Clay 80Ha 152
Folgate St. E1 .... 7J 219 (43Ub 91)
(not continuous)
Foliot Ho. N1 .... 1H 217
Foliot St. W12 .... 44Va 88
Folkes La. RM14: Upm 29Vd 58
Folkestone Ct. SL3: L'ly 50C 82
UB5: N'olt 36Da 65
(off Newmarket Av.)
Folkestone Ho. SE17 .... 7J 231
Folkestone Rd. E6 .... 40Qc 74
E17 .... 28Dc 52
N18 .... 21Wb 51
Folkingham La. NW9 .... 25Ta 47
Folkington Cnr. N12 .... 22Bb 49
Folland NW9 .... 26Va 48
(off Hundred Acre)
Follet Dr. WD5: Ab L 3V 12
Follett Cl. SL4: Old Win 8M 103
Follett Ho. SW10 .... 52Fb 111
(off Worlds End Est.)
Follett St. E14 .... 44Ec 92
Follingham Ct. N1 .... 3J 219
Folly, The GU18: Light 4A 166
Folly Av. AL3: St A 1A 6
Folly Brook & Darland's Lake Nature Reserve
.... 20Ab 30
Folly Cl. WD7: R'lett 8Ha 14
Folly Ct. AL3: St A 1B 6
(off Folly Av.)
Follyfield Rd. SM7: Bans 86Cb 175
Folly La. AL3: St A 1P 5
E4 .... 23Bc 52
E17 .... 25Ac 52
Folly M. W11 .... 44Bb 89
Folly Pathway WD7: R'lett 7Ha 14
Folly Wall E14 .... 47Ec 92
Fonda Ct. E14 .... 45Cc 92
(off Premiere Pl.)
Fondant Ct. E3 .... 40Dc 72
(off Taylor Pl.)
Fontaine Rd. SW16 .... 66Pb 134
Fontarabia Rd. SW11 .... 56Jb 112
Fontayne Av. IG7: Chig 21Sc 54
RM1: Rom 26Gd 56
RM13: Rain 38Gd 76
Fontenelle SE5 .... 53Ub 113
Fontenoy Ho. SE11 .... 6B 230
Fontenoy Rd. SW12 .... 61Kb 134
Fonteyne Gdns. IG8: Wfd G 26Mc 53
Fonthill Cl. SE20 .... 68Wb 135
Fonthill Ho. SW1 .... 7A 228
W14 .... 48Ab 88
(off Russell Rd.)
Fonthill M. N4 .... 33Pb 70
Fonthill Rd. N4 .... 32Pb 70
Font Hills N2 .... 26Eb 49
Fontley Way SW15 .... 59Wa 110
Fontmell Cl. TW15: Ashf 64Q 128
Fontmell Pk. TW15: Ashf 64P 127
Fontwell Cl. HA3: Hrw W 24Ga 46
UB5: N'olt 37Ca 65
Fontwell Dr. BR2: Brom 71Qc 160
Fontwell Pk. Gdns. RM12: Horn 35Nd 77
Foord Cl. DA2: Dart 61Ud 142
Football La. HA1: Harr 32Ha 66
Footbury Hill Rd. BR6: St M Cry 72Wc 161
Footpath, The SW15 .... 58Wa 110
FOOTS CRAY 65Yc 139
Foots Cray High St. DA14: Sidc 65Yc 139
Foots Cray La. DA14: Sidc 60Yc 117
Foots Cray Meadows (Nature Reserve)
.... 63Zc 139
Footscray Rd. SE9 .... 58Qc 116
Forbench Cl. GU23: Rip 94K 189
Forber Ho. E2 .... 41Yb 92
(off Cornwall Av.)
Forbes Av. EN6: Pot B 5Fb 17
Forbes Cl. NW2 .... 34Wa 68
RM11: Horn 32Kd 77
Forbes Ho. E7 .... 36Lc 73
(off Romford Rd.)
W4 .... 50Qa 87
(off Stonehill Rd.)
Forbes St. E1 .... 44Wb 91
Forbes Way HA4: Ruis 33X 65
Forburg Rd. N16 .... 32Wb 71
FORCE GREEN 96Tc 200
Force Grn. La. TN16: Westrm 96Tc 200
Fordbridge Cl. KT16: Chert 74K 149
Fordbridge Ct. TW15: Ashf 65N 127
Fordbridge Pk. TW16: Sun 72V 150
Fordbridge Rd. TW15: Ashf 65N 127
TW16: Sun 72U 150
TW17: Shep 72U 150
FORDBRIDGE RDBT. 65N 127
Ford Cl. CR7: Thor H 71Rb 157
E3 .... 40Ac 72
HA1: Harr 31Fa 66
RM13: Rain 38Hd 76
TW15: Ashf 65N 127
TW17: Shep 70Q 128
WD23: Bush 14Ea 28
Fordcroft Rd. BR5: St M Cry 71Xc 161
Forde Av. BR1: Brom 69Lc 137
Fordel Rd. SE6 .... 60Ec 114
Ford End IG8: Wfd G 23Kc 53
UB9: Den 33H 63
Fordgate Bus. Pk. DA17: Belv 47Ed 96
Fordham KT1: King T 68Qa 131
(off Excelsior Cl.)
Fordham Cl. EN4: Cockf 13Gb 31
KT4: Wor Pk 74Xa 154
RM11: Horn 31Qd 77
Fordham Ho. SE14 .... 52Ac 114
(off Angus St.)
Fordham Rd. EN4: Cockf 13Fb 31
Fordhams Row RM16: Ors 3D 100
Fordham St. E1 .... 44Wb 91
Fordhook Av. W5 .... 46Pa 87
Ford Ho. EN5: New Bar 15Db 31
Fordie Ho. SW1 .... 4G 227
Ford Ind. Pk. RM9: Dag 42Dd 96
Fordingley Rd. W9 .... 41Bb 89
Fordington Ho. SE26 .... 62Wb 135
Fordington Rd. N6 .... 29Hb 49
Ford La. RM13: Rain 38Hd 76
SL0: Iver 44J 83
Ford Lodge RM7: Rom 28Fd 56
Fordmill Rd. SE6 .... 61Cc 136
Ford Pl. RM15: S Ock 45Zd 99
Ford Rd. DA11: Nflt 57De 121
E3 .... 40Bc 72
GU22: Wok 92D 188
GU24: Bisl, W End 6C 166
GU24: Chob 2G 166
KT16: Chert 74K 149
RM9: Dag 38Bd 75
RM10: Dag 38Bd 75
TW15: Ashf 63P 127
Fords Gro. N21 .... 18Sb 33
Fords Pk. Rd. E16 .... 43Jc 93
Ford Sq. E1 .... 43Xb 91
Ford St. E3 .... 39Ac 72
E16 .... 44Hc 93
Fordview Ind. Est. RM13: Rain 41Fd 96
Fordwater Rd. KT16: Chert 74K 149
Fordwater Trad. Est. KT16: Chert 74L 149
Fordwich Cl. BR6: Orp 73Vc 161
Fordwych Rd. NW2 .... 35Ab 68
Fordyce Cl. RM11: Horn 31Pd 77
Fordyce Rd. SE13 .... 58Ec 114
Fordyke Rd. RM8: Dag 33Bd 75
Forefield AL2: Chis G 9N 5
Foreign St. SE5 .... 54Rb 113
Foreland Ct. NW4 .... 25Za 48
Foreland Ho. W11 .... 45Ab 88
(off Walmer Rd.)
Foreland St. SE18 .... 49Tc 94
Foreman Ct. TW1: Twick 60Ha 108
Foreman Ho. SE4 .... 56Zb 114
(off Billingford Cl.)
Foremark Cl. IG6: Ilf 22Vc 55
Foreshore SE8 .... 49Bc 92
Forest, The E11 .... 28Gc 53
Forest App. E4 .... 17Gc 35
IG8: Wfd G 24Jc 53
Forest Av. E4 .... 17Gc 35
HP3: Hem H 4M 3
IG7: Chig 22Qc 54
Forest Bus. Pk. E10 .... 31Zb 72
Forest Cl. BR7: Chst 67Qc 138
E11 .... 29Jc 53
EN9: Walt A 9Kc 21
GU22: Pyr 87F 168
IG8: Wfd G 20Kc 35
KT24: E Hor 97V 190
N10 .... 25Kb 50
NW6 .... 38Ab 68
SL2: Wex 3M 81
Forest Ct. E4 .... 18Hc 35
E11 .... 28Gc 53
N12 .... 22Db 49
Forest Cres. KT21: Asht 88Qa 173
Forest Cft. SE23 .... 61Xb 135
FORESTDALE 81Bc 178
Forestdale N14 .... 21Mb 50
Forestdale Centre, The CR0: Sels 80Bc 158
Forest Dene Ct. SM2: Sutt 79Eb 155
Forest Dr. BR2: Kes 77Nc 160
CM16: They B 8Uc 22
E12 .... 34Mc 73
IG8: Wfd G 24Fc 53
KT20: Kgswd 93Bb 195
TW16: Sun 66V 128
Forest Dr. E. E11 .... 31Fc 73
Forest Dr. W. E11 .... 31Ec 72
Forest Edge IG9: Buck H 21Lc 53
Forester Ho. E14 .... 45Ac 92
(off Victory Pl.)
Forester Rd. SE15 .... 55Xb 113
Foresters Cl. GU21: Wok 10K 167
SM6: Wall 80Mb 156
Foresters Ct. IG10: Lough 12Qc 36
Foresters Cres. DA7: Bex 56Dd 118
Foresters Dr. E17 .... 28Fc 53
SM6: Wall 80Mb 156
Forest Gdns. N17 .... 26Vb 51
FOREST GATE 36Jc 73
Forest Ga. NW9 .... 28Ua 48
Forest Ga. Retreat E7 .... 36Jc 73
(off Odessa Rd.)
Forest Glade E4 .... 21Gc 53
E11 .... 30Gc 53
Forest Gro. E8 .... 37Vb 71
Forest Hgts. IG9: Buck H 19Jc 35
FOREST HILL 61Yb 136
Forest Hill Bus. Cen. SE23 .... 61Yb 136
(off Clyde Va.)
Forest Hill Ind. Est. SE23 .... 61Yb 136
Forest Hill Pool 61Yb 136
Forest Hill Rd. SE22 .... 57Xb 113
SE23 .... 57Xb 113
Forestholme Cl. SE23 .... 61Yb 136
Forest Ind. Pk. IG6: Ilf 25Uc 54
Forest La. E7 .... 36Gc 73
E15 .... 36Gc 73
IG7: Chig 22Qc 54
KT24: E Hor 96V 190
WD7: Shenl 3La 14
Forest Lodge SE23 .... 62Yb 136
(off Dartmouth Rd.)
Forest Mt. Rd. IG8: Wfd G 24Fc 52
Forest Nature Reserve, The 96V 190
Forest Pk. Crematorium IG6: Ilf 23Yc 55
Forest Point E7 .... 36Kc 73
(off Windsor Rd.)
Fore St. EC2 .... 1E 224 (43Sb 91)
HA5: Eastc 28V 44
N9 .... 21Wb 51
N18 .... 23Vb 51

Fore St. Av. EC2 ....1F 225 (43Tb 91)
Forest Ridge BR2: Kes 77Nc 160
BR3: Beck 69Cc 136
Forest Ri. E17 ....27Fc 53
(not continuous)
Forest Rd. CM16: Epp 7Qc 22
DA8: Erith 53Jd 118
E7 ....35Jc 73
E8 ....37Vb 71
E11 ....31Fc 73
E17 ....28Yb 52
EN3: Enf W 8Ac 20
EN8: Chesh 1Zb 20
EN9: Epp, Walt A 8Nc 22
GU22: Pyr 87F 168
IG6: Chig, Ilf 26Tc 54
IG8: Wfd G 20Jc 35
IG10: Lough 13Mc 35
(Earl's Path)
IG10: Lough 9Qc 22
(The Ditches Ride)
KT24: E Hor, Eff J 99V 190
N9 ....18Xb 33
N17 ....28Yb 52
RM7: Mawney 27Dd 56
SL4: Wind 4B 102
(Ash La.)
SL4: Wind 10B 102
(Plain Ride)
SM3: Sutt 74Cb 155
TW9: Kew 52Qa 109
TW13: Felt 61Y 129
WD25: Wat 5W 12
Forest Side CM16: Epp 5Tc 22
E4 ....17Hc 35
E7 ....35Kc 73
EN9: Walt A 8Lc 21
IG9: Buck H 18Lc 35
KT4: Wor Pk 74Va 154
Forest St. E7 ....36Jc 73
Forest Ter. IG7: Chig 22Qc 54
Forest Trad. Est. E17 ....27Zb 52
Forest Vw. E4 ....17Fc 35
E11 ....31Hc 73
Forest Vw. Av. E10 ....29Fc 53
Forest Vw. Rd. E12 ....35Nc 74
E17 ....25Ec 52
IG10: Lough 14Mc 35
Forest Wlk. N10 ....25Kb 50
WD23: Bush 11Ba 27
Forest Way BR5: St M Cry 71Vc 161
DA15: Sidc 59Tc 116
IG8: Wfd G 21Kc 53
IG10: Lough 13Nc 36
KT21: Asht 89Pa 173
N19 ....33Lb 70
Forest Works Ind. Est. E17 ....27Zb 52
Forfar Ho. WD19: Wat 20Y 27
Forfar Rd. N22 ....25Rb 51
SW11 ....53Jb 112
Forge, The EN6: N'thaw 2Gb 17
UB3: Harl 51T 106
Forge Av. CR5: Coul 92Qb 196
Forge Bri. La. CR5: Coul 94Kb 196
Forge Cl. BR2: Hayes 74Jc 159
WD4: Chfd 3J 11
Forge Cotts. W5 ....46Ma 87
Forge Dr. KT10: Clay 80Ja 152
SL2: Farn C 7G 60
Forge End AL2: Chis G 8N 5
GU21: Wok 89A 168
Forgefield TN16: Big H 88Mc 179
Forge La. DA4: Hort K 70Sd 142
DA12: Grav'nd 1H 145
DA12: Shorne 4N 145
HA6: Nwood 24U 44
SM3: Cheam 80Ab 154
TN15: W King 82Wd 184
TW10: Ham 60Na 109
TW13: Hanw 64Aa 129
TW16: Sun 69W 128
Forge M. CR0: Addtn 78Cc 158
TW16: Sun 69W 128
(off Forge La.)
Forge Pl. DA12: Grav'nd 10H 123
NW1 ....37Jb 70
Forge Sq. E14 ....49Dc 92
Forge Steading SM7: Bans 87Db 175
Forge Way TN14: S'ham 83Hd 182
Forlong Path UB5: N'olt 37Aa 65
(off Cowings Mead)
Forman Pl. N16 ....35Vb 71
Formation, The E16 ....47Rc 94
(off Woolwich Mnr. Way)
Formby Av. HA7: Stan 27La 46
Formby Cl. SL3: L'ly 49E 82
Formby Ct. N7 ....36Qb 70
(off Morgan Rd.)
Formosa Ho. E1 ....42Ac 92
(off Ernest St.)
Formosa St. W9 ....42Db 89
Formunt Cl. E16 ....43Hc 93
Forres Gdns. NW11 ....30Cb 49
Forres Ho. CM14: W'ley 21Yd 58
Forrester Ho. AL1: St A 2B 6
(off St Peter's St.)
Forrester Path SE26 ....63Yb 136
Forrest Gdns. SW16 ....69Pb 134
Forris Av. UB3: Hayes 46V 84
Forset Ct. W2 ....2E 220
Forset St. W1 ....2E 220 (44Gb 89)
(not continuous)
Forstal Cl. BR2: Brom 69Jc 137
Forster Cl. IG8: Wfd G 24Fc 53
Forster Ho. BR1: Brom 63Fc 137
SW17 ....62Fb 133
(off Grosvenor Way)
Forster Rd. BR3: Beck 69Ac 136
E17 ....30Ac 52
N17 ....27Vb 51
SW2 ....59Nb 112
Forsters Cl. RM6: Chad H 30Bd 55
Forsters Way UB4: Yead 44X 85
Forston St. N1 ....1E 218 (40Sb 71)
Forsyte Cres. SE19 ....67Ub 135
Forsyte Ho. SW3 ....7E 226
Forsythe Shades Ct. BR3: Beck 67Ec 136
Forsyth Gdns. SE17 ....51Rb 113
Forsyth Ho. E9 ....38Yb 72
(off Frampton Pk. Rd.)
SW1 ....7C 228
Forsythia Cl. IG1: Ilf 36Rc 74
Forsythia Gdns. SL3: L'ly 48A 82
Forsyth Path GU21: Wok 85F 168
Forsyth Pl. EN1: Enf 15Ub 33
Forsyth Rd. GU21: Wok 87E 168
Forterie Gdns. IG3: Bark, Ilf 34Wc 75
Fortescue Av. E8 ....38Xb 71
TW2: Twick 62Ea 130
Fortescue Rd. HA8: Edg 25Ta 47
KT13: Weyb 77P 149
SW19 ....66Fb 133
Fortess Gro. NW5 ....36Lb 70
Fortess Rd. NW5 ....36Kb 70
Fortess Wlk. NW5 ....36Kb 70
Fortess Yd. NW5 ....35Kb 70
Forthbridge Rd. SW11 ....56Jb 112
Forth Ho. E3 ....40Bc 72
(off Tredegar Rd.)
Forth Rd. RM14: Upm 30Td 58
Fortin Cl. RM15: S Ock 45Wd 98
Fortin Path RM15: S Ock 45Wd 98
Fortin Way RM15: S Ock 45Wd 98
Fortis Cl. E16 ....44Lc 93
Fortis Ct. N10 ....27Jb 50
FORTIS GREEN 28Hb 49
Fortis Grn. N2 ....28Gb 49
N10 ....28Gb 49
Fortis Grn. Av. N2 ....27Hb 49
Fortis Grn. Rd. N10 ....27Jb 50
Fortismere Av. N10 ....27Jb 50
Fortius Apartments E3 ....40Cc 72
(off Tredegar La.)
Fort La. RH2: Reig 2K 207
Fortnam Rd. N19 ....33Mb 70
Fortnum's Acre HA7: Stan 23Ha 46
Fortress Distribution Pk.
RM18: Tilb 6C 122
Fort Rd. RM18: Tilb, W Til 6C 122
SE1 ....49Vb 91
TN14: Hals 87Ed 182
UB5: N'olt 38Ca 65
Fortrose Cl. E14 ....44Fc 93
Fortrose Gdns. SW2 ....60Nb 112
(not continuous)
Fortrye Cl. DA11: Nflt 1A 144
Fort St. E1 ....1J 225 (43Ub 91)
E16 ....46Kc 93
Fortuna Cl. DA3: Hartl 70Be 143
N7 ....37Pb 70
Fortune Av. HA8: Edg 25Ra 47
Fortune Ct. E8 ....38Vb 71
(off Queensbridge Rd.)
IG11: Bark 40Yc 75
Fortunegate Rd. NW10 ....39Ua 68
FORTUNE GREEN 36Cb 69
Fortune Grn. Rd. NW6 ....35Cb 69
Fortune Ho. EC1 ....6E 218
SE11 ....6K 229
Fortune La. WD6: E'tree 16Ma 29
Fortune Pl. SE1 ....50Vb 91
Fortunes Mead UB5: N'olt 37Aa 65
Fortune St. EC1 ....6E 218 (42Sb 91)
Fortune Theatre 3G 223
Fortune Wlk. SE28 ....48Tc 94
(off Broadwater Rd.)
Fortune Way NW10 ....41Wa 88
Forty Acre La. E16 ....43Jc 93
Forty Av. HA9: Wemb 34Pa 67
Forty Cl. HA9: Wemb 33Pa 67
Forty Footpath SW14 ....55Sa 109
Fortyfoot Rd. KT22: Lea 93La 192
Forty Foot Way SE9 ....59Sc 116
Forty Hall Mus. 9Vb 19
FORTY HILL 10Ub 19
Forty Hill EN2: Enf 10Ub 19
Forty La. HA9: Wemb 33Ra 67
Forum, The KT8: W Mole 70Da 129
Forum Cl. E3 ....39Cc 72
Forum Ho. HA9: Wemb 35Qa 67
(not continuous)
Forum Magnum Sq. SE1 ....1H 229
Forumside HA8: Edg 23Qa 47
Forum Way HA8: Edg 23Qa 47
Forval Cl. CR4: Mitc 71Hb 155
Forward Bus. Centre, The E16 ....42Fc 93
Forward Dr. HA3: W'stone 28Ha 46
Fosbrooke Ho. SW8 ....52Nb 112
(off Davidson Gdns.)
Fosbury M. W2 ....45Db 89
Foscote Ct. W9 ....42Cb 89
(off Foscote M.)
Foscote M. W9 ....42Cb 89
Foscote Rd. NW4 ....30Xa 48
Foskett Ho. N2 ....26Fb 49
(off The Grange)
Foskett M. E8 ....36Vb 71
Foskett Rd. SW6 ....54Bb 111
Foss Av. CR0: Wadd 78Qb 156
Fossdene Rd. SE7 ....50Kc 93
Fossdyke Cl. UB4: Yead 43Aa 85
Fosse Ho. AL3: St A 3N 5
Fosset Lodge DA7: Bex 53Ed 118
Fosse Way KT14: W Byf 85H 169
W13 ....43Ja 86
Foss Ho. NW8 ....40Db 69
(off Carlton Hill)
Fossil Ct. SE1 ....3H 231
(off Long La.)
Fossil Rd. SE13 ....55Cc 114
Fossington Rd. DA17: Belv 49Zc 95
Foss Rd. SW17 ....63Fb 133
Fossway RM8: Dag 33Yc 75
Foster Av. SL4: Wind 5C 102
Foster Ct. E16 ....45Hc 93
(off Tarling Rd.)
NW1 ....38Lb 70
(off Royal College St.)
NW4 ....28Ya 48
Fosterdown RH9: G'stone 1P 209
Foster Ho. SE14 ....53Bc 114
Foster La. EC2 ....2D 224 (44Sb 91)
Foster Rd. E13 ....42Jc 93
HP1: Hem H 4K 3
W3 ....45Ua 88
W4 ....50Ta 87
Fosters Cl. BR7: Chst 64Pc 138
E18 ....25Kc 53
EN8: Chesh 2Ac 20
Fosters Gro. GU20: W'sham 7A 146
Fosters La. GU21: Knap 9G 166
Fosters M. DA3: Lfield 68Ae 143
Fosters Path SL2: Slou 2D 80
Foster St. NW4 ....28Ya 48
Foster's Way SW18 ....60Db 111
Foster Wlk. NW4 ....28Ya 48
Fothergill Cl. E13 ....40Jc 73
Fothergill Dr. N21 ....15Nb 32
Fotheringay Gdns. SL1: Slou 5E 80
Fotheringham Rd. EN1: Enf 14Vb 33
(not continuous)
Fotherley Rd. WD3: Rick 19H 25
Foubert's Pl. W1 ....3B 222 (44Lb 90)
Foulden Rd. N16 ....35Vb 71
Foulden Ter. N16 ....35Vb 71
Foulis Ter. SW7 ....7C 226 (50Fb 89)
Foulser Rd. SW17 ....62Hb 133
Foulsham Rd. CR7: Thor H 69Sb 135
Foundation Pl. SE9 ....57Qc 116
(off Archery Rd.)
Founder Cl. E6 ....44Rc 94
Founders Cl. UB5: N'olt 41Ba 85
Founders Ct. EC2 ....2F 225
Founders Gdns. SE19 ....66Sb 135
Founders Ho. SW1 ....7D 228
Foundling Ct. WC1 ....5F 217
Foundling Museum, The 5G 217
Foundry, The EC2 ....4J 219
Foundry Cl. SE16 ....46Ac 92
Foundry Ct. KT16: Chert 73J 149
SL2: Slou 6K 81
Foundry Ga. EN8: Walt C 5Ac 20
Foundry Ho. E14 ....43Dc 92
(off Morris Rd.)
Foundry La. SL3: Hort 55D 104
Foundry M. KT16: Chert 73J 149
(off Gogmore La.)
NW1 ....5C 216 (42Lb 90)
TW3: Houn 56Da 107
Foundry Pl. E1 ....43Yb 92
(off Jubilee St.)
SW18 ....59Db 111
Founes Dr. RM16: Chaf H 48Ae 99
Fountain Cl. SE18 ....50Rc 94
UB8: Hil 43S 84
Fountain Ct. DA4: Eyns 75Nd 163
DA15: Sidc 58Xc 117
EC4 ....4K 223 (45Qb 90)
EN8: Chesh 2Zb 20
(off Westbury)
SE23 ....61Zb 136
SW1 ....6K 227
W11 ....47Za 88
(off Clearwater Ter.)
WD6: Bore 12Qa 29
Fountain Dr. SE19 ....63Vb 135
SM5: Cars 80Hb 155
Fountain Gdns. SL4: Wind 5H 103
Fountain Grn. Sq. SE16 ....47Wb 91
Fountain Ho. CR4: Mitc 68Hb 133
E2 ....5K 219
NW6 ....38Ab 68
SE16 ....47Wb 91
(off Bermondsey Wall E.)
SW6 ....54Eb 111
W1 ....5H 221
Fountain M. N5 ....35Sb 71
(off Highbury Grange)
NW3 ....37Hb 69
Fountain Pl. EN9: Walt A 6Ec 20
SW9 ....53Qb 112
Fountain Rd. CR7: Thor H 69Sb 135
RH1: Redh 8N 207
SW17 ....64Fb 133
Fountain Rdbt. KT3: N Mald 70Ua 132
Fountains, The IG10: Lough 17Mc 35
N3 ....24Db 49
(off Ballards La.)
Fountains Av. TW13: Hanw 62Ba 129
Fountains Cl. TW13: Hanw 61Ba 129
(not continuous)
Fountains Cres. N14 ....17Nb 32
Fountain Sq. SW1 ....5K 227 (49Kb 90)
Fountain Wlk. DA11: Nflt 8A 122
Fountayne Bus. Cen. N15 ....28Wb 51
Fountayne Rd. N15 ....28Wb 51
N16 ....33Wb 71
Fount St. SW8 ....52Mb 112
Fouracre Path SE25 ....72Ub 157
Four Acres KT11: Cobh 85Aa 171
N12 ....20Db 31
Fouracres EN3: Enf H 11Ac 34
Fouracres Dr. HP3: Hem H 4P 3
Fouracres Wlk. HP3: Hem H 4P 3
Four Dials E20 ....37Ec 72
(within Westfield Stratford City Shop. Cen.)
Fourdrinier Way HP3: Hem H 5M 3
Fourfield Cl. KT18: Head 94Sa 193
Fourland Wlk. HA8: Edg 23Sa 47
Fournier St. E1 ....7K 219 (43Vb 91)
Four Oaks CM15: B'wood 20Ae 41
Fourscore Mans. E8 ....38Wb 71
(off Shrubland Rd.)
Four Seasons Cl. E3 ....40Cc 72
Four Seasons Cres. SM3: Sutt 75Bb 155
Four Sq. Ct. TW3: Houn 58Ca 107
Fourteenth Av. KT20: Lwr K 98Ab 194
Fourth Av. DA11: Nflt 10A 122
E12 ....35Pc 74
KT20: Lwr K 97Ab 194
RM7: Rush G 32Fd 76
RM20: W Thur 51Wd 120
UB3: Hayes 46V 84
W10 ....42Ab 88
WD25: Wat 7Z 13
Fourth Cross Rd. TW2: Twick 61Fa 130
Fourth Dr. CR5: Coul 88Lb 176
Fourth Way HA9: Wemb 35Ra 67
Four Trees AL2: Chis G 7P 5
Four Tubs, The WD23: Bush 17Fa 28
Fourways Mkt. AL9: Wel G 6E 8
(off Dixons Hill Rd.)
Four Wents KT11: Cobh 86Y 171
Four Wents, The E4 ....18Fc 35
Four Wents Cl. TN15: Bor G 92Be 205
Fovant Ct. SW8 ....54Lb 112
Fowey Av. IG4: Ilf 29Mc 53
Fowey Cl. E1 ....46Xb 91
Fowey Ho. SE11 ....7A 230
Fowler Cl. SW11 ....55Fb 111
Fowler Ho. N15 ....29Tb 51
(off South Gro.)
Fowler Rd. CR4: Mitc 68Jb 134
E7 ....35Jc 73
IG6: Ilf 23Xc 55
N1 ....39Rb 71
Fowlers Cl. DA14: Sidc 64Ad 139
Fowlers Mead GU24: Chob 1J 167
Fowlers M. N19 ....33Lb 70
(off Holloway Rd.)
Fowler's Wlk. W5 ....42Ma 87
Fowley Cl. EN8: Walt C 6Bc 20
Fowley Mead Pk. EN8: Walt C 6Cc 20
Fownes St. SW11 ....55Gb 111
Foxacre CR3: Cat'm 94Ub 197
Fox All. WD18: Wat 15Y 27
Fox & Knot St. EC1 ....7C 218
Foxberry Rd. SE4 ....55Ac 114
Foxberry Wlk. DA11: Nflt 62Fe 143
Foxboro Rd. RH1: Redh 4B 208
Foxborough Cl. SL3: L'ly 50C 82
Foxborough Gdns. SE4 ....57Cc 114
Foxbourne Rd. SW17 ....61Jb 134
Foxburrow Rd. IG7: Chig 21Zc 55
Foxburrows Rare Breeds Farm & Zoo
..........21Zc 55
Foxbury DA3: New A 76Ae 165
TN15: Plat 92De 205
Foxbury Av. BR7: Chst 65Tc 138
Foxbury Cl. BR1: Brom 65Kc 137
BR6: Chels 78Wc 161
Foxbury Dr. BR6: Chels 79Wc 161
Foxbury Rd. BR1: Brom 65Jc 137
Fox Cl. BR6: Chels 78Wc 161
E1 ....42Yb 92
E16 ....43Jc 93
GU22: Pyr 87F 168
KT13: Weyb 78T 150
RM5: Col R 22Dd 56
WD6: E'tree 16Ma 29
WD23: Bush 15Da 27
Foxcombe CR0: New Ad 79Dc 158
(not continuous)
Foxcombe Cl. E6 ....40Mc 73
Foxcombe Rd. SW15 ....60Wa 110
FOX CORNER 7G 186
Fox Corner Community Wildlife Area
..........7G 186
Foxcote SE5 ....50Ub 91
Fox Covert KT22: Fet 96Fa 192
Fox Covert Cl. SL5: S'hill 1A 146
Foxcroft AL1: St A 4E 6
WC1 ....2J 217
Foxcroft Rd. SE18 ....53Rc 116
Foxdell HA6: Nwood 23T 44
Foxdell Way SL9: Chal P 22A 42
Foxdene Cl. E18 ....27Kc 53
Foxearth Cl. TN16: Big H 90Nc 180
Foxearth Rd. CR2: Sels 82Yb 178
Foxearth Spur CR2: Sels 81Yb 178
Foxes Dale BR2: Brom 69Fc 137
SE3 ....55Jc 115
Foxes Dr. EN7: Chesh 1Wb 19
Foxes Grn. RM16: Ors 7C 100
Foxes La. AL9: Wel G 5F 8
Foxes Pde. EN9: Walt A 6Ec 20
(off Stewardstone Rd.)
Foxes Path GU4: Sut G 98B 188
Foxfield NW1 ....1B 216
Foxfield Cl. HA6: Nwood 23V 44
Foxfield Rd. BR6: Orp 75Tc 160
Foxglove Cl. AL10: Hat 1D 8
DA15: Sidc 58Wc 117
N9 ....18Yb 34
TW19: Stanw 60M 105
UB1: S'hall 45Aa 85
Foxglove Ct. E3 ....40Cc 72
(off Four Seasons Cl.)
HA0: Wemb 40Na 67
Foxglove Gdns. CR8: Purl 83Nb 176
E11 ....28Lc 53
Foxglove La. KT9: Chess 77Qa 153
Foxglove Path SE28 ....46Uc 94
(off Martins Pl.)
Foxglove Rd. RM7: Rush G 33Gd 76
RM15: S Ock 43Yd 98
Foxgloves, The HP1: Hem H 3G 2
Foxglove St. W12 ....45Va 88
Foxglove Way SM6: Wall 74Kb 156
Fox Gro. KT12: Walt T 73X 151
Foxgrove N14 ....20Nb 32
Foxgrove Av. BR3: Beck 66Dc 136
Foxgrove Dr. GU21: Wok 87C 168
Foxgrove Path WD19: Wat 22Z 45
Foxgrove Rd. BR3: Beck 66Dc 136
Foxhall Rd. RM14: Upm 36Sd 78
Foxham Rd. N19 ....34Mb 70
Foxhanger Gdns. GU22: Wok 88C 168
FOX HATCH 11Ud 40
Foxherne SL3: L'ly 7N 81
Fox Hill BR2: Kes 78Lc 159
SE19 ....66Vb 135
Foxhill WD24: Wat 8W 12
Fox Hill Gdns. SE19 ....66Vb 135
Foxhills GU21: Wok 9N 167
Foxhills Cl. KT16: Ott 79D 148
Foxhills Golf Course 77B 148
Foxhills M. KT16: Ott 76D 148
Fox Hills Rd. RM16: Grays 46Fe 99
Foxhills Rd. KT16: Ott 77C 148
Foxhole Rd. SE9 ....57Nc 116
Foxholes KT13: Weyb 78T 150
Fox Hollow Cl. SE18 ....50Uc 94
Foxhollow Cl. KT12: Walt T 75Z 151
Fox Hollow Dr. DA7: Bex 55Zc 117
Foxhollow Dr. SL2: Farn C 6G 60
Foxhollows AL2: Lon C 9G 6
Foxholt Gdns. NW10 ....38Sa 67
Foxhome Cl. BR7: Chst 65Qc 138
Foxhounds La. DA13: Sflt 62Ce 143
Fox Ho. KT16: Chert 74H 149
(off Fox La. Nth.)
Fox Ho. Rd. DA17: Belv 50Dd 96
(not continuous)
Foxlake Rd. KT14: Byfl 84P 169
Foxlands Cl. WD25: Wat 6W 12
Foxlands Cres. RM10: Dag 36Ed 76
Foxlands La. RM10: Dag 36Fd 76
Foxlands Rd. RM10: Dag 36Ed 76
Fox La. BR2: Kes 78Kc 159
CR3: Cat'm 93Rb 197
KT23: Bookh 96Aa 191
N13 ....19Pb 32
RH2: Reig 3K 207
W5 ....42Na 87
Fox La. Nth. KT16: Chert 74H 149
Fox La. Sth. KT16: Chert 74H 149
Fox Lea TN15: Bor G 92Be 205
Foxlees HA0: Wemb 35Ja 66
Foxley Cl. E8 ....36Wb 71
IG10: Lough 12Rc 36
RH1: Redh 10A 208
Foxley Ct. SM2: Sutt 80Eb 155
Foxley Gdns. CR8: Purl 85Rb 177
Foxley Gro. SL1: Burn 1A 80
Foxley Hall CR8: Purl 85Qb 176
Foxley Hill Rd. CR8: Purl 84Qb 176
Foxley Ho. E3 ....41Dc 92
(off Bow Rd.)
Foxley La. CR8: Purl 83Lb 176
Foxley Rd. CR7: Thor H 70Rb 135
CR8: Kenley 86Qb 176
SW9 ....52Qb 112
Foxleys WD19: Wat 20Aa 27
Foxley Sq. SW9 ....53Rb 113
Foxley Wood (Local Nature Reserve)
..........85Qb 176
Fox Mnr. Way RM20: W Thur 51Xd 120
Foxmead Cl. EN2: Enf 13Pb 32
Foxmoor Ct. UB9: Den 30J 43
Foxmore St. SW11 ....53Hb 111
Foxon Cl. CR3: Cat'm 93Ub 197
Foxon La. CR3: Cat'm 93Tb 197
Foxon La. Gdns. CR3: Cat'm 93Ub 197
Fox Rd. E16 ....43Hc 93
SL3: L'ly 9P 81
Fox's Path CR4: Mitc 68Gb 133
Fox's Yd. E2 ....5K 219
Foxton Gro. CR4: Mitc 68Fb 133
Foxton Ho. E16 ....47Qc 94
(off Albert Rd.)
Foxton Rd. RM20: Grays 51Zd 121
Foxtree Ho. WD25: Wat 8Aa 13
Foxwarren KT10: Clay 81Ha 172
Foxwell M. SE4 ....55Ac 114
Foxwell St. SE4 ....55Ac 114
Fox Wood KT12: W Vill 80V 150
Foxwood Chase EN9: Walt A 7Ec 20
Foxwood Cl. NW7 ....21Ua 48
TW13: Felt 62X 129
Foxwood Grn. Cl. EN1: Enf 16Ub 33
Foxwood Gro. BR6: Prat B 82Yc 181
DA11: Nflt 10A 122
Fox Wood Nature Reserve 42Na 87
Foxwood Rd. DA2: Bean 62Xd 142
SE3 ....56Hc 115
Foxwood Way DA3: Lfield 68Fe 143
Foyle Dr. RM15: S Ock 43Wd 98
Foyle Rd. N17 ....25Wb 51
SE3 ....51Hc 115
Frailey Cl. GU22: Wok 88D 168
Frailey Hill GU22: Wok 88D 168
Framewood Rd. SL2: Stoke P, Wex 8N 61
SL3: Stoke P, Wex 8N 61
Framfield Cl. N12 ....20Cb 31
Framfield Ct. EN1: Enf 16Ub 33
(off Queen Anne's Gdns.)
Framfield Rd. CR4: Mitc 66Jb 134
N5 ....36Rb 71
W7 ....44Ga 86
Framlingham Cl. E5 ....33Yb 72
Framlingham Ct. RM6: Chad H 29Xc 55
(off Norwich Cres.)
Framlingham Cres. SE9 ....63Nc 138
Frampton NW1 ....38Mb 70
(off Wrotham Rd.)
Frampton Cl. SM2: Sutt 80Cb 155
Frampton Ct. UB9: Den 30H 43
W3 ....47Sa 87
(off Avenue Rd.)
Frampton Ho. NW8 ....6C 214
Frampton Pk. Est. E9 ....38Yb 72
Frampton Pk. Rd. E9 ....37Yb 72
Frampton Rd. CM16: Epp 1Wc 23
EN6: Pot B 2Eb 17
TW4: Houn 57Aa 107
Frampton St. NW8 ....6C 214 (42Fb 89)
Francemary Rd. SE4 ....57Cc 114
Frances Av. RM16: Chaf H 49Yd 98
Frances Ct. E17 ....30Cc 52
SE25 ....69Vb 135
Frances Gdns. RM15: S Ock 44Vd 98
Frances Ho. HP3: Hem H 4B 4
Frances Rd. E4 ....23Cc 52
SL4: Wind 5G 102
Frances St. SE18 ....48Pc 94
Frances Wharf E14 ....44Bc 92
Franche Ct. Rd. SW17 ....62Eb 133
Francis & Dick James Ct. NW7 ....24Ab 48
Francis Av. DA7: Bex 54Cd 118
IG1: Ilf 33Tc 74
TW13: Felt 62W 128
Francis Bacon Ct. SE16 ....49Xb 91
(off Galleywall Rd.)
Francis Barber Cl. SW16 ....64Pb 134
Francis Bentley M. SW4 ....55Lb 112
Franciscan Rd. SW17 ....64Hb 133
Francis Chichester Cl. SL5: Asc 10A 124
Francis Chichester Way SW11 ....53Jb 112
Francis Cl. E14 ....49Fc 93
KT19: Ewe 77Ta 153
SS17: Horn H 1H 101
TW17: Shep 70Q 128
Francisco Cl. RM16: Chaf H 48Yd 98
Francis Ct. AL1: St A 3C 6
DA8: Erith 50Gd 96
EC1 ....7B 218
KT5: Surb 70Na 131
(off Cranes Pk. Av.)
NW7 ....22Va 48
(off Watford Way)
SE14 ....51Zb 114
(off Myers La.)
Francis Greene Ho. EN9: Walt A 5Dc 20
(off Grove Ct.)
Francis Gro. SW19 ....65Bb 133
Francis Ho. E17 ....30Bc 52
N1 ....1H 219
SW10 ....52Db 111
(off Coleridge Gdns.)
Francis M. SE12 ....59Jc 115
Francis Pl. N6 ....31Kb 70
(off Shepherd's Cl.)
Francis Rd. BR5: St P 69Zc 139
CR0: C'don 73Rb 157
CR3: Cat'm 94Tb 197
DA1: Dart 57Md 119
E10 ....32Ec 72
HA1: Harr 29Ja 46
HA5: Eastc 29Y 45
IG1: Ilf 33Tc 74
N2 ....28Hb 49
SM6: Wall 79Lb 156
TW4: Houn 54Z 107
UB6: G'frd 40Ka 66
WD18: Wat 14X 27
Francis St. E15 ....36Gc 73
IG1: Ilf 33Tc 74
SW1 ....5B 228 (49Lb 90)
Francis Ter. N19 ....34Lb 70
Francis Ter. M. N19 ....34Lb 70
Francis Wlk. N1 ....39Pb 70
Francis Way SL1: Slou 5B 80
Francklyn Gdns. HA8: Edg 20Qa 29
Franconia Gdns. RM1: Rom 29Jd 56
Franconia Rd. SW4 ....57Mb 112
Frank Bailey Wlk. E12 ....37Qc 74
Frank Beswick Ho. SW6 ....51Bb 111
(off Clem Attlee Ct.)

Frank Burton Cl. SE7 50Kc 93
Frank Dixon Cl. SE21 59Ub 113
Frank Dixon Way SE21 60Ub 113
Frank Foster Ho. CM16: They B 9Uc 22
Frankfurt Rd. SE24 57Sb 113
Frank Godley Ct. DA14: Sidc 64Xc 139
Frankham Ho. *SE8* *52Cc 114*
(*off Frankham St.*)
Frankham St. SE8 52Cc 114
Frank Ho. *SW8* *52Nb 112*
(*off Wyvil Rd.*)
Frankland Cl. IG8: Wfd G 22Lc 53
SE16 48Xb 91
WD3: Crox G 17Q 26
Frankland Rd. E4 22Cc 52
SW7 4B 226 (48Fb 89)
WD3: Crox G 16R 26
Franklands Dr. KT15: Add 80H 149
Franklin Av. EN7: Chesh 2Wb 19
SL2: Slou 3F 80
WD18: Wat 16W 26
Franklin Bldg. E14 47Cc 92
Franklin Cl. AL4: Col H 4A 8
HP3: Hem H 5N 3
KT1: King T 69Qa 131
N20 17Eb 31
SE13 53Dc 114
SE27 62Rb 135
Franklin Cotts. HA7: Stan 21Ka 46
Franklin Cres. CR4: Mitc 70Lb 134
Franklin Ho. BR2: Brom 69Gc 137
E1 *46Xb 91*
(*off Watts St.*)
E14 *44Fc 93*
(*off E. India Dock Rd.*)
EN3: Enf L 9Bc 20
NW9 30Va 48
Franklin Ind. Est. *SE20* *67Yb 136*
(*off Franklin Rd.*)
Franklin Pas. SE9 55Nc 116
Franklin Pl. SE13 53Dc 114
Franklin Rd. DA2: Wilm 61Gd 140
DA7: Bex 53Ad 117
DA12: Grav'nd 4F 144
RM12: Horn 37Ld 77
SE20 66Yb 136
WD17: Wat 12X 27
Franklins WD3: Map C 21G 42
Franklins M. HA2: Harr 33Ea 66
Franklin Sq. W14 50Bb 89
Franklin's Row SW3 7G 227 (50Hb 89)
Franklin St. E3 41Dc 92
N15 30Ub 51
Franklin Way CR0: Wadd 73Nb 156
Franklyn Cres. SL4: Wind 5B 102
Franklyn Gdns. IG6: Ilf 23Tc 54
Franklyn Rd. KT12: Walt T 72W 150
NW10 37Va 68
Frank Martin Ct. EN7: Chesh 2Xb 19
Frank M. SE1 49Xb 91
Franks Av. KT3: N Mald 70Sa 131
Franks Cotts. RM14: Upm 32Wd 78
Franks La. DA4: Hort K 71Rd 163
Frank Soskice Ho. *SW6* *51Bb 111*
(*off Clem Attlee Ct.*)
Frank St. E13 42Jc 93
Frank Sutton Way SL1: Slou 5H 81
Franks Wood Av. BR5: Pet W 71Rc 160
Frankswood Av. UB7: Yiew 44P 83
Frank Towell Ct. TW14: Felt 59W 106
Frank Whymark Ho. *SE16* *47Yb 92*
(*off Rupack St.*)
Franlaw Cres. N13 21Sb 51
Franmil Rd. RM12: Horn 32Jd 76
Fransfield Gro. SE26 62Xb 135
Frans Hals Ct. E14 48Fc 93
Franshams *WD23: B Hea* *19Ga 28*
(*off Hartsbourne Rd.*)
Frant Cl. SE20 66Yb 136
Franthorne Way SE6 61Dc 136
Frant Rd. CR7: Thor H 71Rb 157
Fraserburgh Ho. *E3* *40Bc 72*
(*off Vernon Rd.*)
Fraser Cl. DA5: Bexl 60Ed 118
E6 44Nc 94
Fraser Ct. *E14* *50Ec 92*
(*off Ferry St.*)
SE1 3E 230
SW11 *53Gb 111*
(*off Surrey La. Est.*)
Fraser Ho. TW8: Bford 50Pa 87
Fraser Rd. DA8: Erith 50Fd 96
E17 29Dc 52
N9 20Xb 33
UB6: G'frd 39Ka 66
Fraser St. W4 50Ua 88
Frating Cres. IG8: Wfd G 23Kc 53
Frays Av. UB7: W Dray 47M 83
Frays Cl. UB7: W Dray 48M 83
Frays Island & Mabey's Meadow Nature Reserve 48L 83
Frayslea UB8: Uxb 40L 63
Frays Valley Local Nature Reserve 32M 63
Frays Waye UB8: Uxb 39L 63
Frazer Av. HA4: Ruis 36Y 65
Frazer Cl. RM1: Rom 31Hd 76
Frazier St. SE1 2K 229 (47Qb 90)
Frean St. SE16 48Wb 91
Frearson Ho. WC1 3J 217
Freda Corbett Cl. SE15 52Wb 113
Frederica Ct. SW2 60Rb 113
Frederica Rd. E4 17Fc 35
Frederica St. N7 38Pb 70
Frederick Andrews Ct. RM17: Grays 51Fe 121
Frederick Charrington Ho. *E1* *42Yb 92*
(*off Wickford St.*)
Frederick Cl. SM1: Sutt 77Bb 155
W2 4F 221 (45Hb 89)
Frederick Ct. SW3 6G 227
Frederick Cres. EN3: Enf H 12Yb 34
SW9 52Rb 113
Frederick Dobson Ho. *W11* *45Ab 88*
(*off Cowling Cl.*)
Frederick Gdns. CR0: C'don 72Rb 157
SM1: Sutt 78Bb 155
Frederick Ho. *SE18* *49Nc 94*
(*off Pett St.*)
Frederick Pl. AL2: F'mre 9C 6
N8 *30Mb 50*
(*off Crouch Hall Rd.*)
SE18 50Rc 94
Frederick Rd. RM13: Rain 40Fd 76
SE17 51Rb 113
SM1: Sutt 78Bb 155
Fredericks Pl. EC2 3F 225 (44Tb 91)
N12 21Eb 49
Frederick Sq. *SE16* *45Ac 92*
(*off Sovereign Cres.*)
Frederick's Row EC1 3B 218 (41Rb 91)
Frederick St. WC1 4H 217 (41Pb 90)
Frederick Ter. E8 38Vb 71
Frederick Vs. *W7* *46Ga 86*
(*off Lwr. Boston Rd.*)
Frederic M. SW1 2G 227
Frederic St. E17 29Ac 52
Fredora Av. UB4: Hayes 42V 84
Fred Styles Ho. SE7 51Lc 115
Fred Tibble Ct. RM9: Dag 35Ad 75
Fred White Wlk. N7 37Nb 70
Freeborne Gdns. RM13: Rain 37Jd 76
Freedom Cl. E17 28Ac 52
Freedom Rd. N17 26Tb 51
Freedom St. SW11 54Hb 111
Freedown La. SM2: Sutt 85Db 175
Freegrove Rd. N7 36Nb 70
(not continuous)
Freeland Ct. DA15: Sidc 62Wc 139
Freeland Pk. NW4 26Ab 48
Freeland Rd. W5 45Pa 87
Freelands Av. CR2: Sels 81Zb 178
Freelands Gro. BR1: Brom 67Kc 137
Freelands Rd. BR1: Brom 67Kc 137
KT11: Cobh 86X 171
Freeland Way DA8: Erith 53Jd 118
Freeling Ho. *NW8* *39Fb 69*
(*off Dorman Way*)
Freeling St. N1 38Pb 70
(Carnoustie Dr.)
N1 38Nb 70
(Pembroke St.)
Freeman Cl. TW17: Shep 70U 128
UB5: N'olt 38Aa 65
Freeman Ct. SW16 68Nb 134
Freeman Dr. KT8: W Mole 69Ba 129
Freeman Ho. SE11 5B 230
Freeman Rd. DA12: Grav'nd 2G 144
SM4: Mord 71Fb 155
Freemans Cl. SL2: Stoke P 7K 61
Freemans La. UB3: Hayes 45U 84
Freemantle Av. EN3: Pond E 15Zb 34
Freemantle St. SE17 7H 231 (50Ub 91)
Freeman Wlk. SE9 57Lc 115
Freeman Way RM11: Horn 30Pd 57
Freemasons' Hall 3G 223
Freemasons Pl. *CR0: C'don* *74Ub 157*
(*off Freemasons Rd.*)
Freemasons Rd. CR0: C'don 74Ub 157
E16 43Kc 93
Free Prae Rd. KT16: Chert 74J 149
Freesia Cl. BR6: Chels 78Vc 161
Freesia Dr. GU24: Bisl 8E 166
Freestone Yd. SL3: Coln 52F 104
Freethorpe Cl. SE19 66Tb 135
Free Trade Wharf E1 45Zb 92
Freezeland Way UB10: Hil 37R 64
FREEZY WATER 8Zb 20
Freight La. N1 38Mb 70
Freightliners City Farm 37Qb 70
Freightmaster Est. RM13: Rain 44Gd 96
Freke Rd. SW11 55Jb 112
Fremantle Ho. *E1* *42Xb 91*
(*off Somerford St.*)
RM18: Tilb 3B 122
Fremantle Rd. DA17: Belv 49Cd 96
IG6: Ilf 26Rc 54
Fremantle Way GU24: Brkwd 1B 186
UB3: Hayes 45V 84
Fremont St. E9 39Xb 71
(not continuous)
French Apartments, The CR8: Purl 84Qb 176
Frenchaye KT15: Add 78L 149
Frenches, The RH1: Redh 4A 208
Frenches Ct. RH1: Redh 4A 208
Frenches Rd. RH1: Redh 4A 208
French Gdns. KT11: Cobh 86Y 171
French Horn Yd. WC1 1H 223
Frenchlands Ga. KT24: E Hor 99U 190
French Ordinary Ct. EC3 4J 225
French Pl. E1 5J 219 (41Ub 91)
French Row AL3: St A 2B 6
FRENCH STREET 100Vc 201
French St. TN16: Westrm 100Uc 200
TW16: Sun 68Y 129
French's Wells GU21: Wok 9M 167
Frenchum Gdns. SL1: Slou 5C 80
Frendsbury Rd. SE4 56Ac 114
Frensham Cl. UB1: S'hall 42Ba 85
Frensham Ct. SW19 69Fb 133
Frensham Dr. CR0: New Ad 80Ec 158
SW15 62Va 132
Frensham Rd. CR8: Kenley 86Rb 177
SE9 61Tc 138
Frensham St. SE15 51Wb 113
Frensham Wlk. SL2: Farn C 6G 60
Frensham Way KT17: Eps D 88Ya 174
Frere St. SW11 54Gb 111
Fresham Ho. *BR2: Brom* *69Hc 137*
(*off Durham Rd.*)
Freshfield Av. E8 38Vb 71
Freshfield Cl. SE13 56Fc 115
Freshfield Ct. WD17: Wat 13Y 27
Freshfield Dr. N14 17Kb 32
Freshfield Flats KT20: Lwr K 99Bb 195
Freshfields CR0: C'don 74Bc 158
Freshfields Av. RM14: Upm 36Rd 77
Freshford St. SW18 62Eb 133
Freshill La. UB1: S'hall 42Ca 85
Freshmount Gdns. KT19: Eps 83Ra 173
Freshwater Cl. SW17 65Jb 134
Freshwater Ct. UB1: S'hall 41Ca 85
W1 *1E 220*
(*off Crawford St.*)
Freshwater Rd. RM8: Dag 32Zc 75
SW17 65Jb 134
Freshwell Av. RM6: Chad H 28Yc 55
Freshwell Gdns. CM13: W H'dn 30Fe 59
Fresh Wharf Est. IG11: Bark 40Rc 74
Fresh Wharf Rd. IG11: Bark 39Rc 74
Freshwood Cl. BR3: Beck 67Dc 136
Freshwood Way SM6: Wall 81Kb 176
Freston Gdns. EN4: Cockf 15Jb 32
Freston Pk. N3 26Bb 49
Freston Rd. W10 45Za 88
W11 45Za 88
Freswick Ho. *SE8* *49Ac 92*
(*off Chilton Gro.*)
Freta Rd. DA6: Bex 57Bd 117
Freud Mus. 37Eb 69
Frewell Ho. EC1 7K 217
Frewin Rd. SW18 60Fb 111
Friar M. SE27 62Rb 135
Friar Rd. BR5: St M Cry 71Wc 161
UB4: Yead 42Z 85
Friars, The IG7: Chig 21Uc 54
Friars Av. CM15: Shenf 18Ce 41
N20 20Gb 31
SW15 62Va 132
Friars Cl. CM15: Shenf 17Ce 41
E4 20Ec 34
IG1: Ilf 32Tc 74
SE1 6C 224
UB5: N'olt 41Z 85
Friars Ct. E17 25Bc 52
SM6: Wall 77Kb 156
Friars Gdns. W3 44Ta 87
Friarsgate NW10 40Ra 67
Friars Ga. Cl. IG8: Wfd G 21Jc 53
Friars La. TW9: Rich 57Ma 109
Friars Mead E14 48Ec 92
WD4: K Lan 2Q 12
Friars M. SE9 57Qc 116
Friars Orchard KT22: Fet 93Fa 192
Friars Pl. La. W3 45Ta 87
Friars Ri. GU22: Wok 90C 168
Friars Rd. E6 39Mc 73
GU25: Vir W 10P 125
Friars Stile Pl. TW10: Rich 58Na 109
Friars Stile Rd. TW10: Rich 58Na 109
Friar St. EC4 3C 224 (44Rb 91)
Friars Wlk. N14 17Kb 32
SE2 50Zc 95
Friars Way KT16: Chert 72J 149
W3 44Ta 87
WD4: K Lan 2Q 12
WD23: Bush 11Ba 27
Friars Wood CR0: Sels 81Ac 178
Friary, The EN8: Walt C 5Bc 20
SL4: Old Win 8N 103
Friary Cl. N12 22Gb 49
Friary Ct. GU21: Wok 10K 167
SW1 7C 222
Friary Est. SE15 51Wb 113
(not continuous)
FRIARY ISLAND 8N 103
Friary Island TW19: Wray 8N 103
Friary La. IG8: Wfd G 21Jc 53
Friary Pk. Ct. W3 44Sa 87
Friary Rd. N12 21Fb 49
N20 21Gb 49
SE15 52Wb 113
TW19: Wray 9N 103
W3 44Sa 87
Friary Way N12 21Gb 49
FRIDAY HILL 19Gc 35
Friday Hill E4 19Gc 35
Friday Hill E. E4 20Gc 35
(not continuous)
Friday Hill W. E4 19Gc 35
Friday Rd. CR4: Mitc 66Hb 133
DA8: Erith 50Fd 96
Friday St. EC4 4D 224 (45Sb 91)
Frideswide Pl. NW5 36Lb 70
Friendly Pl. SE13 53Dc 114
Friendly St. SE8 54Cc 114
Friendly St. M. SE8 54Cc 114
Friends Av. EN8: Chesh 4Zb 20
Friendship Ho. SE1 2C 230
Friendship Wlk. UB5: N'olt 41Z 85
Friendship Way E15 39Ec 72
Friends Rd. CR0: C'don 76Tb 157
CR8: Purl 84Rb 177
Friend St. EC1 3B 218 (41Rb 91)
Friends Wlk. TW18: Staines 64H 127
UB8: Uxb 38M 63
FRIERN BARNET 22Hb 49
Friern Barnet La. N11 19Fb 31
N20 19Fb 31
Friern Barnet Rd. N11 22Hb 49
Friern Barnet School Sports Cen. *22Hb 49*
(*off Hemington Av.*)
Friern Bri. Retail Pk. N11 23Kb 50
Friern Ct. N20 20Fb 31
Friern Mt. Dr. N20 17Eb 31
Friern Pk. N12 22Eb 49
Friern Rd. SE22 59Wb 113
(not continuous)
Friern Watch Av. N12 21Eb 49
Frigate Ho. *E14* *49Ec 92*
(*off Stebondale St.*)
Frigate M. SE8 51Cc 114
Frimley Av. RM11: Horn 32Qd 77
SM6: Wall 78Nb 156
Frimley Cl. CR0: New Ad 80Ec 158
SW19 61Ab 132
Frimley Ct. DA14: Sidc 64Yc 139
Frimley Cres. CR0: New Ad 80Ec 158
Frimley Dr. SL1: Slou 7D 80
Frimley Gdns. CR4: Mitc 69Gb 133
Frimley Rd. HP1: Hem H 1G 2
IG3: Ilf 34Uc 74
KT9: Chess 78Ma 153
Frimley St. *E1* *42Zb 92*
(*off Frimley Way*)
Frimley Way E1 42Zb 92
Fringewood Cl. HA6: Nwood 25R 44
Frinstead Gro. BR5: St M Cry 70Zc 139
Frinstead Ho. *W10* *45Za 88*
(*off Freston Rd.*)
Frinsted Rd. DA8: Erith 52Fd 118
Frinton Cl. WD19: Wat 19X 27
Frinton Ct. *W13* *43Ka 86*
(*off Hardwick Grn.*)
Frinton Dr. IG8: Wfd G 24Fc 53
Frinton M. IG2: Ilf 30Qc 54
Frinton Rd. DA14: Sidc 61Ad 139
E6 41Mc 93
N15 30Ub 51
RM5: Col R 24Bd 55
SW17 65Jb 134
Friston Path IG7: Chig 22Uc 54
Friston St. SW6 54Db 111
Friswell Pl. DA6: Bex 56Cd 118
Fritham Cl. KT3: N Mald 72Ua 154
Frith Ct. NW7 24Ab 48
Frithe, The SL2: Slou 4M 81
Frith Ho. NW8 6C 214
Frith Knowle KT12: Hers 78X 151
Frith La. NW7 24Ab 48
Frith Rd. CR0: C'don 75Sb 157
E11 35Ec 72
Friths Dr. RH2: Reig 3K 207
Frith St. W1 3D 222 (44Mb 90)
Frithville Ct. *W12* *46Ya 88*
(*off Frithville Gdns.*)
Frithville Gdns. W12 46Ya 88
Frithwald Rd. KT16: Chert 73H 149
Frithwood Av. HA6: Nwood 23U 44
Frizlands La. RM10: Dag 33Dd 76
Frobisher Cl. CR8: Kenley 89Sb 177
HA5: Pinn 31Z 65
WD23: Bush 16Ca 27
Frobisher Ct. NW9 26Ua 48
SE8 *50Ac 92*
(*off Evelyn St.*)
SE10 *51Fc 115*
(*off Old Woolwich Rd.*)
SE23 61Xb 135
SM3: Cheam 80Ab 154
W12 *47Ya 88*
(*off Lime Gro.*)
Frobisher Cres. EC2 7E 218
TW19: Stanw 59N 105
Frobisher Gdns. E10 31Dc 72
RM16: Chaf H 48Ae 99
TW19: Stanw 59N 105
Frobisher Ho. *E1* *46Xb 91*
(*off Watts St.*)
SW1 *51Mb 112*
(*off Dolphin Sq.*)
Frobisher M. EN2: Enf 14Tb 33
Frobisher Pas. E14 46Cc 92
Frobisher Pl. SE15 53Yb 114
Frobisher Rd. AL1: St A 4G 6
DA8: Erith 52Hd 118
E6 44Pc 94
N8 28Qb 50
Frobisher St. SE10 51Gc 115
Frobisher Way DA9: Ghithe 56Xd 120
DA12: Grav'nd 4G 144
Froggy La. UB9: Den 34F 62
Froghall La. IG7: Chig 21Tc 54
Frog La. GU4: Sut G 97A 188
RM13: Rain 44Fd 96
Frogley Rd. SE22 56Vb 113
Frogmoor Ct. WD3: Rick 19M 25
Frogmoor La. WD3: Rick 19M 25
FROGMORE
AL2 10C 6
SL4 4J 103
Frogmore AL2: F'mre 9B 6
SW18 57Cb 111
Frogmore Av. UB4: Hayes 42U 84
Frogmore Border SL4: Wind 5J 103
Frogmore Bus. Pk. AL2: F'mre 10C 6
Frogmore Cl. SL1: Slou 7E 80
SM3: Cheam 76Za 154
Frogmore Cotts. WD17: Wat 15Z 27
Frogmore Ct. UB2: S'hall 49Ba 85
Frogmore Dr. SL4: Wind 3J 103
FROGMORE END 5M 3
Frogmore Gdns. SM3: Cheam 77Ab 154
UB4: Hayes 42U 84
Frogmore Home Pk. AL2: F'mre 9B 6
Frogmore House 4K 103
Frogmore Ind. Est. N5 36Sb 71
NW10 41Sa 87
UB3: Hayes 47U 84
Frogmore Ind. Pk. RM20: W Thur 50Wd 98
Frogmore Paper Mill, The & Visitor Cen. 5M 3
Frogmore Rd. HP3: Hem H 5M 3
Frogmore Rd. Ind. Est. HP3: Hem H 6M 3
Frognal NW3 35Eb 69
Frognal Av. DA14: Sidc 65Wc 139
HA1: Harr 28Ha 46
Frognal Cl. NW3 36Eb 69
FROGNAL CORNER 65Vc 139
Frognal Ct. NW3 37Eb 69
Frognal Gdns. NW3 35Eb 69
Frognal La. NW3 36Db 69
Frognal Pde. NW3 37Eb 69
Frognal Pl. DA14: Sidc 65Wc 139
Frognal Ri. NW3 34Eb 69
Frognal Way NW3 35Eb 69
Frog St. CM15: Dodd, Kel H 11Ud 40
Frogwell Cl. N15 30Tb 51
Froissart Rd. SE9 57Mc 115
Frome RM18: E Til 9L 101
Frome Ho. SE15 56Xb 113
Frome Rd. N22 27Rb 51
Frome St. N1 1D 218 (40Sb 71)
Fromondes Rd. SM3: Cheam 78Ab 154
Fromow Gdns. GU20: W'sham 9B 146
Frontenac NW10 38Xa 68
Frontier Works N17 23Ub 51
Front La. RM14: Upm 33Ud 78
Frostic Wlk. E1 43Wb 91
Froude St. SW8 54Kb 112
Frowick Cl. AL9: Wel G 5D 8
Frowyke Cres. EN6: S Mim 4Wa 16
Fruen Rd. TW14: Felt 59V 106
Fruiterers Pas. *EC4* *5E 224*
(*off Queen St. Pl.*)
Fryatt Rd. N17 24Tb 51
(not continuous)
Fry Cl. RM5: Col R 22Cd 56
Fryday Gro. M. *SW12* *59Lb 112*
(*off Weir Rd.*)
Frye Ct. *E3* *41Bc 92*
(*off Benworth St.*)
Fryent Cl. NW9 30Qa 47
Fryent Country Pk. (Local Nature Reserve) 31Qa 67
Fryent Cres. NW9 30Ua 48
Fryent Flds. NW9 30Ua 48
Fryent Gro. NW9 30Ua 48
Fryent Way NW9 29Qa 47
Fryern Wood CR3: Cat'm 96Sb 197
Fryers Vw. *SE4* *56Zb 114*
(*off Frendsbury Rd.*)
Fry Ho. E6 38Lc 73
Frying Pan Alley E1 1K 225
Frylands Ct. CR0: New Ad 83Ec 178
Frymley Vw. SL4: Wind 3B 102
Fry Rd. E6 38Mc 73
NW10 39Va 68
Fryston Av. CR0: C'don 75Wb 157
CR5: Coul 86Kb 176
Fryth Mead AL3: St A 1P 5
Fuchsia Cl. RM7: Rush G 33Gd 76
Fuchsia St. SE2 50Xc 95
Fuchsia Way GU24: W End 5C 166
Fulbeck Dr. NW9 25Ua 48
Fulbeck Ho. *N7* *37Pb 70*
(*off Sutterton St.*)
Fulbeck Rd. N19 35Lb 70
Fulbeck Wlk. HA8: Edg 19Ra 29
Fulbeck Way HA2: Harr 26Ea 46
Fulbourn *KT1: King T* *68Qa 131*
(*off Eureka Rd.*)
Fulbourne Cl. RH1: Redh 4N 207
Fulbourne Rd. E17 25Ec 52
Fulbourne St. E1 43Xb 91
Fulbrook Av. KT15: New H 83J 169
Fulbrook La. RM15: S Ock 45Vd 98
Fulbrook M. N19 35Lb 70
Fulcher Ho. *N1* *39Ub 71*
(*off Colville Est.*)
SE8 50Bc 92
Fulford Gro. WD19: Wat 19X 27
Fulford Ho. KT19: Ewe 80Ta 153
Fulford Rd. CR3: Cat'm 93Tb 197
KT19: Ewe 80Ta 153
Fulford St. SE16 47Xb 91
FULHAM 54Ab 110
FULHAM BROADWAY 52Cb 111
Fulham B'way. SW6 52Cb 111
Fulham Broadway Shop. Cen. SW6 52Cb 111
Fulham Bus. Exchange *SW6* *53Eb 111*
(*off The Boulevard*)
Fulham Cl. UB10: Hil 42S 84
Fulham Ct. SW6 53Cb 111
Fulham FC 53Za 110
Fulham High St. SW6 54Ab 110
Fulham Island *SW6* *52Cb 111*
(*off Fulham Rd.*)
Fulham Palace 54Ab 110
Fulham Pal. Rd. SW6 50Ya 88
W6 50Ya 88
Fulham Pk. Gdns. SW6 54Bb 111
Fulham Pk. Rd. SW6 54Bb 111
Fulham Pools
Virgin Active 51Ab 110
Fulham Rd. SW3 7B 226 (52Db 111)
SW6 52Db 111
(Fulham B'way.)
SW6 54Ab 110
(Fulham High St.)
SW10 7B 226 (52Db 111)
Fullarton Cres. RM15: S Ock 44Vd 98
Fullbrooks Av. KT4: Wor Pk 74Va 154
Fullbrook School Sports Cen. 84J 169
Fuller Cl. BR6: Chels 78Vc 161
E2 *42Wb 91*
(*off Cheshire St.*)
WD23: Bush 17Fa 28
Fuller Ct. N8 29Mb 50
Fuller Gdns. WD24: Wat 9X 13
Fullerian Cres. WD18: Wat 14V 26
Fuller Rd. RM8: Dag 34Xc 75
WD24: Wat 9X 13
Fullers Av. IG8: Wfd G 24Hc 53
KT6: Surb 75Pa 153
Fullers Cl. EN9: Walt A 5Jc 21
RM5: Col R 24Ed 56
Fuller's Griffin Brewery & Visitors Cen. 51Va 110
Fullers Hill TN16: Westrm 98Tc 200
Fullers La. RM5: Col R 24Ed 56
Fullers Rd. E18 24Hc 53
Fuller St. NW4 28Ya 48
TN15: Seal 92Rd 203
Fullers Way Nth. KT6: Surb 76Pa 153
Fullers Way Sth. KT9: Chess 77Na 153
Fuller's Wood CR0: C'don 78Cc 158
Fullers Wood La. RH1: S Nut 7C 208
Fullerton Cl. KT14: Byfl 86P 169
Fullerton Ct. TW11: Tedd 65Ja 130
Fullerton Dr. KT14: Byfl 86N 169
Fullerton Rd. CR0: C'don 73Vb 157
KT14: Byfl 86N 169
SM5: Cars 81Gb 175
SW18 57Db 111
Fullerton Way KT14: Byfl 86N 169
Fuller Way UB3: Harl 50V 84
WD3: Crox G 15Q 26
Fullmer Way KT15: Wdhm 82H 169
Fullwell Av. IG5: Ilf 25Pc 54
IG6: Ilf 25Pc 54
FULLWELL CROSS 26Sc 54
Fullwell Cross IG6: Ilf 26Tc 54
Fullwell Cross Swimming Pool & Recreation Cen. 26Sc 54
Fullwell Pde. IG5: Ilf 25Qc 54
Fullwood's M. N1 3G 219 (41Tb 91)
Fulmar Cl. KT5: Surb 72Pa 153
Fulmar Cres. HP1: Hem H 2J 3
Fulmar Ho. *SE16* *49Zb 92*
(*off Tawny Way*)
Fulmar Rd. RM12: Horn 38Jd 76
Fulmead St. SW6 53Db 111
FULMER 5P 61
Fulmer Cl. TW12: Hamp 64Aa 129
Fulmer Comn. Rd. SL0: Iver H 6P 61
SL3: Ful 6P 61
Fulmer Cnr. SL9: Ger X 32D 62
Fulmer Dr. SL9: Ger X 3P 61
Fulmer Ho. NW8 6E 214
UB8: Uxb 37N 63
Fulmer La. SL3: Ful 34B 62
SL9: Ger X 34B 62
Fulmer Pl. SL3: Ful 35A 62
Fulmer Ri. SL3: Ful 37B 62
Fulmer Rd. E16 43Mc 93
SL3: Ful 5P 61
SL9: Ger X 31A 62
Fulmer Way SL9: Ger X 30A 42
W13 48Ka 86
Fulneck *E1* *43Yb 92*
(*off Mile End Rd.*)
Fulready Rd. E10 29Fc 53
Fulstone Cl. TW4: Houn 56Ba 107
Fulthorp Rd. SE3 54Hc 115
Fulton Ct. *WD6: Bore* *10Pa 15*
(*off Aycliffe Rd.*)
Fulton M. W2 45Eb 89
Fulton Rd. HA9: Wemb 34Qa 67
FULWELL 63Fa 130
Fulwell Ct. IG5: Ilf 25Qc 54
UB1: S'hall *45Ea 86*
(*off Baird Av.*)
Fulwell Golf Course 63Fa 130
Fulwell Pk. Av. TW2: Twick 61Da 129
Fulwell Rd. TW11: Tedd 63Fa 130
Fulwich Rd. DA1: Dart 58Pd 119
Fulwood Av. HA0: Wemb 40Pa 67
Fulwood Cl. UB3: Hayes 44V 84
Fulwood Ct. HA3: Kenton 30Ja 46
Fulwood Gdns. TW1: Twick 58Ha 108
Fulwood Pl. WC1 1J 223 (43Pb 90)
Fulwood Wlk. SW19 60Ab 110
Funky Footprints Nature Reserve 72Q 150
Funkykidz.Biz 13Aa 27
Funland *5D 222*
(*in Trocadero Cen.*)
Furber St. W6 48Xa 88

Furguson Gro. EN8: Chesh ... 1Zb 20
Furham Fld. HA5: Hat E ... 24Ca 45
Furley Ho. SE15 ... 52Wb 113
(off Peckham Pk. Rd.)
Furley Rd. SE15 ... 52Wb 113
Furlong Cl. SM6: Wall ... 74Kb 156
Furlong Rd. N7 ... 37Qb 70
Furlongs HP1: Hem H ... 1J 3
Furlongs, The KT10: Esh ... 76Da 151
Furlough, The GU22: Wok ... 88C 168
Furmage St. SW18 ... 59Db 111
Furneaux Av. SE27 ... 64Rb 135
Furner Cl. DA1: Cray ... 55Hd 118
Furness SL4: Wind ... 4A 102
Furness Cl. RM16: Grays ... 10D 100
(not continuous)
Furness Ho. SW1 ... 7A 228
Furness Pl. SL4: Wind ... 4A 102
(off Furness)
Furness Rd. HA2: Harr ... 31Da 65
NW10 ... 40Wa 68
SM4: Mord ... 72Db 155
SW6 ... 54Db 111
Furness Row SL4: Wind ... 4A 102
Furness Sq. SL4: Wind ... 4A 102
Furness Wlk. SL4: Wind ... 4A 102
Furness Way RM12: Horn ... 36Jd 76
SL4: Wind ... 4A 102
Furnival Av. SL2: Slou ... 3F 80
Furnival Cl. GU25: Vir W ... 2P 147
Furnival Ct. E3 ... 40Cc 72
(off Four Seasons Cl.)
Furnival Mans. W1 ... 1B 222
Furnival St. EC4 ... 2K 223 (44Qb 90)
Furrow La. E9 ... 36Yb 72
Furrows, The KT12: Walt T ... 75Y 151
UB9: Hare ... 29L 43
Furrows Pl. CR3: Cat'm ... 95Vb 197
Fursby Av. N3 ... 23Cb 49
Fursecroft W1 ... 2F 221
Further Acre NW9 ... 26Va 48
Furtherfield WD5: Ab L ... 4U 12
Furtherfield Cl. CR0: C'don ... 72Qb 156
Further Grn. Rd. SE6 ... 59Gc 115
Furtherground HP2: Hem H ... 3N 3
Furzebank SL5: S'hill ... 10B 124
Furzebushes La. AL2: Chis G ... 7L 5
Furze Cl. RH1: Redh ... 5P 207
WD19: Wat ... 22Y 45
FURZEDOWN ... 64Kb 134
Furzedown Cl. TW20: Egh ... 65A 126
Furzedown Dr. SW17 ... 64Kb 134
Furzedown Rd. SM2: Sutt ... 83Eb 175
SW17 ... 64Kb 134
Furze Farm Cl. RM6: Chad H ... 26Ad 55
Furze Fld. KT22: Oxs ... 85Fa 172
Furzefield EN8: Chesh ... 1Xb 19
Furzefield Cen. ... 3Za 16
Furzefield Cl. BR7: Chst ... 65Rc 138
Furze Fld. Ct. WD19: Wat ... 20W 26
Furzefield Ct. EN6: Pot B ... 3Ab 16
Furzefield Cres. RH2: Reig ... 8L 207
Furzefield Rd. RH2: Reig ... 8L 207
SE3 ... 51Kc 115
Furzeground Way
UB11: Stock P ... 46S 84
Furze Gro. KT20: Kgswd ... 93Bb 195
Furze Hall KT20: Kgswd ... 93Bb 195
Furzeham Rd. UB7: W Dray ... 47N 83
FURZE HILL ... 93Bb 195
Furze Hill CR8: Purl ... 83Nb 176
KT20: Kgswd ... 92Bb 195
RH1: Redh ... 5N 207
Furzehill Cotts. GU24: Pirb ... 4A 186
Furzehill Pde. WD6: Bore ... 13Qa 29
Furzehill Rd. WD6: Bore ... 14Qa 29
(not continuous)
Furzehill Sq. BR5: St M Cry ... 70Xc 139
Furze La. CR8: Purl ... 83Nb 176
Furzen Cl. SL2: Slou ... 1E 80
Furzen Cres. AL10: Hat ... 3B 8
Furze Pl. RH1: Redh ... 5P 207
Furze Rd. CR7: Thor H ... 69Sb 135
HP1: Hem H ... 3G 2
KT15: Add ... 79H 149
Furze St. E3 ... 43Cc 92
Furze Vw. WD3: Chor ... 16E 24
Furzewood TW16: Sun ... 67W 128
Fusedale Way RM15: S Ock ... 45Vd 98
Fusiliers Way TW4: Houn ... 55Y 107
Fuzzens Wlk. SL4: Wind ... 4C 102
Fydler's Cl. SL4: Wink ... 5A 124
Fye Foot La. EC4 ... 4D 224
Fyfe Apartments N8 ... 27Pb 50
Fyfe Way BR1: Brom ... 68Jc 137
Fyfield N4 ... 33Qb 70
(off Six Acres Est.)
Fyfield Cl. BR2: Brom ... 70Fc 137
CM13: W H'dn ... 30Fe 59
Fyfield Ct. E7 ... 37Jc 73
Fyfield Dr. RM15: S Ock ... 45Vd 98
Fyfield Ho. E6 ... 39Nc 74
(off Ron Leighton Way)
Fyfield Rd. E17 ... 27Fc 53
EN1: Enf ... 13Ub 33
IG8: Wfd G ... 24Lc 53
RM13: Rain ... 39Hd 76
SW9 ... 55Qb 112
Fynes St. SW1 ... 5D 228 (49Mb 90)

G

Gabion Av. RM19: Purf ... 49Td 98
Gable Cl. DA1: Cray ... 57Jd 118
HA5: Hat E ... 24Ca 45
WD5: Ab L ... 4U 12
Gable Ct. RH1: Redh ... 5A 208
(off St Annes Mt.)
SE26 ... 63Xb 135
Gables, The BR1: Brom ... 66Kc 137
CM13: Gt War ... 23Yd 58
DA3: Lfield ... 68Ee 143
HA9: Wemb ... 34Qa 67
HP2: Hem H ... 1M 3
IG11: Bark ... 37Sc 74
KT13: Weyb ... 78S 150
KT22: Oxs ... 84Ea 172
N10 ... 27Jb 50
(off Fortis Grn.)
RM17: Grays ... 49Be 99
SM7: Bans ... 89Bb 175
WD19: Wat ... 17Y 27
WD25: Wat ... 5Z 13
Gables Av. TW15: Ashf ... 64P 127
WD6: Bore ... 13Pa 29
Gables Cl. GU22: Wok ... 92B 188
SE5 ... 53Ub 113
SE12 ... 60Jc 115
SL3: Dat ... 1L 103
SL9: Chal P ... 21A 42
Gables Ct. CR8: Purl ... 84Rb 177
GU22: Wok ... 92B 188
Gables Lodge EN4: Had W ... 10Eb 17
Gables Way SM7: Bans ... 89Bb 175
Gabriel Cl. RM5: Col R ... 24Ed 56
RM16: Chaf H ... 48Yd 98
TW13: Hanw ... 63Aa 129
Gabriel Gdns. DA12: Grav'nd ... 4G 144
Gabriel Ho. N1 ... 1B 218
SE11 ... 5H 229 (49Pb 90)
SE16 ... 48Bc 92
(off Odessa St.)
Gabrielle Cl. HA9: Wemb ... 34Pa 67
Gabrielle Ct. NW3 ... 37Fb 69
Gabriel M. NW2 ... 33Bb 69
Gabriel's M. BR3: Beck ... 67Zb 136
Gabriel Spring Rd. DA3: Fawk ... 75Td 164
Gabriel Spring Rd. E.
DA3: Fawk, Hort K ... 75Ud 164
Gabriel St. SE23 ... 59Zb 114
Gabriels Wharf SE1 ... 6A 224 (46Qb 90)
Gadbrook Rd. RH3: Bet ... 10A 206
Gad Cl. E13 ... 41Kc 93
Gaddesden Av. HA9: Wemb ... 37Pa 67
Gaddesden Cres. WD25: Wat ... 6Z 13
Gaddesden Ho. EC1 ... 4G 219
Gade Av. WD18: Wat ... 14U 26
Gade Bank WD3: Crox G ... 14T 26
GADEBRIDGE ... 1K 3
Gadebridge Ct. HP1: Hem H ... 1L 3
Gadebridge Ho. SW3 ... 7D 226
(off Cale St.)
Gadebridge La. HP1: Hem H ... 1J 3
(not continuous)
Gadebridge Park (Park & Ride) ... 1L 3
Gadebridge Point HP1: Hem H ... 4L 3
(off Cotterells)
Gadebridge Rd. HP1: Hem H ... 1J 3
Gade Cl. UB3: Hayes ... 46X 85
WD18: Wat ... 14U 26
Gade Pl. HP1: Hem H ... 4L 3
(off Cotterells)
Gadesden Rd. KT19: Ewe ... 79Sa 153
(not continuous)
Gade Side WD25: Wat ... 7U 12
(not continuous)
Gade Twr. HP3: Hem H ... 7A 4
Gade Valley Cl. WD4: K Lan ... 10A 4
Gade Vw. Gdns. WD4: Hunt C ... 4S 12
Gadeview HP1: Hem H ... 2L 3
Gadeview Rd. HP3: Hem H ... 6L 3
Gadsbury Cl. NW9 ... 30Va 48
Gadsden Cl. RM14: Upm ... 30Ud 58
Gadsden Ho. W10 ... 42Ab 88
(off Hazlewood Cres.)
Gadswell Cl. WD25: Wat ... 8Z 13
Gadwall Cl. E16 ... 44Kc 93
Gadwall Way SE28 ... 47Tc 94
Gage Brown Ho. W10 ... 44Za 88
(off Bridge Cl.)
Gage M. CR2: S Croy ... 78Rb 157
Gage Rd. E16 ... 43Gc 93
Gage St. WC1 ... 7G 217 (43Nb 90)
Gainford Ho. E2 ... 41Xb 91
(off Ellsworth St.)
Gainford St. N1 ... 39Qb 70
Gainsboro Gdns. UB6: G'frd ... 36Ga 66
Gainsborough Av. AL1: St A ... 1D 6
DA1: Dart ... 57Ld 119
E12 ... 36Qc 74
(not continuous)
RM18: Tilb ... 3C 122
Gainsborough Cl. BR3: Beck ... 66Cc 136
KT10: Esh ... 74Ga 152
Gainsborough Ct. BR2: Brom ... 70Lc 137
CM14: W'ley ... 21Yd 58
(off Gt. Eastern Rd.)
KT12: Walt T ... 77W 150
KT19: Ewe ... 79Va 154
N12 ... 22Db 49
SE16 ... 50Xb 91
(off Stubbs Dr.)
SE21 ... 61Ub 135
W4 ... 50Ra 87
(off Chaseley Dr.)
W12 ... 47Ya 88
Gainsborough Dr. CR2: Sande ... 85Wb 177
DA11: Nflt ... 62Fe 143
Gainsborough Gdns. HA8: Edg ... 26Pa 47
NW3 ... 34Fb 69
NW11 ... 31Bb 69
TW7: Isle ... 57Fa 108
Gainsborough Ho. E14 ... 47Cc 92
(off Cassilis Rd.)
E14 ... 45Ac 92
(off Victory Pl.)
EN1: Enf ... 15Wb 33
RM8: Dag ... 35Xc 75
(off Longbridge Rd.)
SW1 ... 6E 228
Gainsborough Lodge HA1: Harr ... 29Ha 46
(off Hindes Rd.)
Gainsborough Mans. W14 ... 51Ab 110
(off Queen's Club Gdns.)
Gainsborough M. SE26 ... 62Xb 135
Gainsborough Pl. CM13: Hut ... 18Fe 41
IG7: Chig ... 20Vc 37
KT11: Cobh ... 87Aa 171
Gainsborough Rd. E11 ... 31Gc 73
E15 ... 41Gc 93
IG8: Wfd G ... 23Nc 54
KT3: N Mald ... 72Ta 153
KT19: Eps ... 82Sa 173
N12 ... 22Db 49
RM8: Dag ... 35Xc 75
RM13: Rain ... 39Jd 76
TW9: Rich ... 54Pa 109
UB4: Hayes ... 40S 64
W4 ... 49Va 88
Gainsborough Sq. DA6: Bex ... 55Zc 117
Gainsborough St. E9 ... 37Bc 72
Gainsborough Studios E. N1 ... 1F 219
Gainsborough Studios Nth. N1 ... 1F 219
Gainsborough Studios Sth. N1 ... 1F 219
Gainsborough Studios W. N1 ... 1F 219
Gainsborough Ter. SM2: Sutt ... 80Bb 155
(off Belmont Ri.)
Gainsborough Twr. UB5: N'olt ... 40Z 65
(off Academy Gdns.)
Gainsfield Ct. E11 ... 34Gc 73
Gainsford Rd. E17 ... 28Bc 52
Gainsford St. SE1 ... 7K 225 (47Vb 91)
Gairloch Ho. NW1 ... 38Mb 70
(off Stratford Vs.)
Gairloch Rd. SE5 ... 54Ub 113
Gaisford St. NW5 ... 37Lb 70
Gaist Av. CR3: Cat'm ... 94Xb 197
Gaitskell Ct. SW11 ... 54Gb 111
Gaitskell Ho. E6 ... 39Mc 73
E17 ... 27Dc 52
RM16: Grays ... 46De 99
(off Crammavill St.)
SE17 ... 51Ub 113
(off Villa St.)
WD6: Bore ... 14Ta 29
(off Howard Dr.)
Gaitskell Rd. SE9 ... 60Sc 116
Gaitskell Way SE1 ... 1D 230
Gala Bingo
Acton ... 46Ta 87
(off High St.)
Bexleyheath ... 56Dd 118
Borehamwood ... 13Qa 29
(within The Point)
Camberwell ... 52Sb 113
Dartford ... 58Md 119
Enfield ... 14Wb 33
Feltham ... 61X 129
Harrow ... 29Ha 46
Hounslow ... 56Ca 107
Ilford ... 26Sc 54
Kingston upon Thames ... 67Na 131
Leyton ... 32Bc 72
Slough ... 6J 81
Stratford ... 39Fc 73
Surrey Quays ... 48Zb 92
Tooting ... 64Gb 133
Upton Pk. ... 39Nc 74
Waltham Cross ... 6Ac 20
West Thurrock ... 49Wd 98
Woking ... 89B 168
(within The Big Apple)
Woolwich ... 48Qc 94
Gala Ct. CR7: Thor H ... 71Qb 156
Galahad Cl. SL1: Slou ... 7E 80
Galahad Rd. BR1: Brom ... 63Jc 137
N9 ... 20Wb 33
Galata Rd. SW13 ... 52Wa 110
Galatea Sq. SE15 ... 55Xb 113
Galaxy Bldg. E14 ... 49Cc 92
(off Crews St.)
Galaxy Ho. EC2 ... 5G 219
Galba Ct. TW8: Bford ... 52Ma 109
Galbraith St. E14 ... 48Ec 92
Galdana Av. EN5: New Bar ... 13Eb 31
Galeborough Av. IG8: Wfd G ... 24Fc 53
Gale Cl. CR4: Mitc ... 69Fb 133
TW12: Hamp ... 65Aa 129
Gale Cres. SM7: Bans ... 89Cb 175
Galena Arches W6 ... 49Xa 88
(off Galena Rd.)
Galena Ho. SE18 ... 50Vc 95
(off Grosmont Rd.)
Galena Rd. W6 ... 49Xa 88
Galen Cl. KT19: Eps ... 83Qa 173
Galen Pl. WC1 ... 1G 223 (43Nb 90)
Galesbury Rd. SW18 ... 58Eb 111
Gales Gdns. E2 ... 41Xb 91
Gale St. E3 ... 43Cc 92
RM9: Dag ... 36Yc 75
Gales Way IG8: Wfd G ... 24Nc 54
Galey Grn. RM15: S Ock ... 43Xd 98
Galgate Cl. SW19 ... 60Za 110
Gallants Farm Rd. EN4: E Barn ... 17Gb 31
Galleon Blvd. DA2: Dart ... 56Td 120
Galleon Cl. DA8: Erith ... 49Fd 96
SE16 ... 47Zb 92
Galleon Ho. E14 ... 49Ec 92
(off Glengarnock Av.)
Galleon M. DA11: Nflt ... 9A 122
Galleon Rd. RM16: Chaf H ... 49Yd 98
Galleons Dr. IG11: Bark ... 41Wc 95
Galleons La. SL3: Wex ... 2N 81
(not continuous)
Galleons Vw. E14 ... 47Ec 92
Galleria Ct. SE15 ... 51Vb 113
Galleria Shop. Mall, The E18 ... 26Jc 53
Galleries, The CM14: W'ley ... 22Xd 58
NW8 ... 2A 214
Gallery, The E20 ... 37Ec 72
(within Westfield Stratford City Shop. Cen.)
Gallery Apartments E1 ... 44Yb 92
(off Commercial Rd.)
Gallery Ct. SE1 ... 2F 231
SW10 ... 51Eb 111
(off Gunter Gro.)
Gallery Gdns. UB5: N'olt ... 40Z 65
Gallery Rd. SE21 ... 60Tb 113
Galley, The E16 ... 45Rc 94
Galley Hill HP1: Hem H ... 1H 3
Galley Hill Ind. Est. DA10: Swans ... 57Ae 121
Galley Hill Rd. DA10: Swans ... 57Be 121
DA11: Nflt ... 57Be 121
Galleyhill Rd. EN9: Walt A ... 5Gc 21
(not continuous)
Galley La. EN5: Barn ... 10Wa 16
Galleymead Rd. SL3: Poyle ... 53H 105
Galleywall Rd. SE16 ... 49Xb 91
Galleywall Rd. Trad. Est. SE16 ... 49Xb 91
Galleywood Cres. RM5: Col R ... 23Fd 56
Galleywood Ho. W10 ... 43Ya 88
(off Sutton Way)
Gallian Cl. SL0: Iver ... 44G 82
Galliard Cl. N9 ... 16Yb 34
Galliard Ct. N9 ... 16Wb 33
Galliard Rd. N9 ... 18Wb 33
Gallia Rd. N5 ... 36Rb 71
Gallica Ct. SM1: Sutt ... 74Db 155
Gallions Cl. IG11: Bark ... 41Wc 95
Gallions Entrance E16 ... 46Sc 94
Gallions Reach Shop. Pk. E6 ... 43Sc 94
Gallions Rd. E16 ... 45Rc 94
SE7 ... 49Kc 93
(not continuous)
Gallions Rdbt. E16 ... 45Rc 94
Gallions Vw. Rd. SE28 ... 47Uc 94
Gallon Cl. SE7 ... 49Lc 93
Gallop, The CR2: Sels ... 80Xb 157
SL4: Wind ... 9G 102
SM2: Sutt ... 81Fb 175
Gallops, The KT10: Esh ... 76Da 151
Gallosson Rd. SE18 ... 49Uc 94
Galloway Chase SL2: Slou ... 5L 81
Galloway Dr. DA1: Cray ... 59Gd 118
Galloway Path CR0: C'don ... 77Tb 157
Galloway Rd. W12 ... 46Wa 88
GALLOWS CORNER ... 26Ld 57
GALLOWS CORNER ... 25Ld 57
Gallows Hill WD4: Hunt C ... 4S 12
Gallows Hill La. WD5: Ab L ... 4S 12
Gallows Wood DA3: Fawk ... 77Wd 164
Gallus Cl. N21 ... 16Pb 32
Gallus Sq. SE3 ... 55Kc 115
Gallys Rd. SL4: Wind ... 4B 102
Galpins Rd. CR7: Thor H ... 71Nb 156
Galsworthy Av. E14 ... 44Ac 92
RM6: Chad H ... 31Xc 75
Galsworthy Cl. NW2 ... 35Ab 68
SE28 ... 46Xc 95
Galsworthy Ct. W3 ... 48Ra 87
(off Bollo Bri. Rd.)
Galsworthy Cres. SE3 ... 52Lc 115
Galsworthy Ho. W11 ... 44Ab 88
(off Elgin Cres.)
Galsworthy Rd. KT2: King T ... 66Ra 131
KT16: Chert ... 73J 149
NW2 ... 35Ab 68
RM18: Tilb ... 3E 122
Galsworthy Ter. N16 ... 34Ub 71
Galton Rd. SL5: S'dale ... 2D 146
Galton St. W10 ... 41Ab 88
Galva Cl. EN4: Cockf ... 14Jb 32
Galvani Way CR0: Wadd ... 74Pb 156
Galveston Ho. E1 ... 42Ac 92
(off Harford St.)
Galveston Rd. SW15 ... 57Bb 111
Galvin Rd. SL1: Slou ... 6G 80
Galway Cl. SE16 ... 50Xb 91
(off Masters Dr.)
Galway Ho. E1 ... 43Zb 92
(off White Horse La.)
EC1 ... 4E 218
Galway St. EC1 ... 4E 218 (41Sb 91)
Galy NW9 ... 26Va 48
Gambado
Beckenham ... 65Cc 136
Chelsea ... 53Eb 111
(off Station Ct.)
Gambetta St. SW8 ... 54Kb 112
Gambia St. SE1 ... 7C 224 (46Rb 91)
Gambier Ho. EC1 ... 4E 218
Gambles La. GU23: Rip ... 96L 189
Gambole Rd. SW17 ... 63Gb 133
Games Rd. EN4: Cockf ... 13Gb 31
Gamlen Rd. SW15 ... 56Za 110
Gamma Ct. CR0: C'don ... 74Tb 157
(off Sydenham Rd.)
Gammon Cl. HP3: Hem H ... 3A 4
Gammon Fld. RM16: Grays ... 5A 100
Gammons Farm Cl. WD24: Wat ... 8V 12
Gammons La. WD24: Wat ... 8U 12
(not continuous)
Gamuel Cl. E17 ... 30Cc 52
Gander Grn. Cres. TW12: Hamp ... 67Ca 129
Gander Grn. La. SM1: Sutt ... 76Bb 155
SM3: Cheam ... 75Ab 154
Ganders Ash WD25: Wat ... 5W 12
Gandhi Cl. E17 ... 30Cc 52
Gandhi Ct. WD24: Wat ... 12Z 27
Gandolfi St. SE15 ... 51Ub 113
Gangers Hill CR3: Wold ... 100Ac 198
RH9: G'stone ... 100Ac 198
Ganley Ct. SW11 ... 55Fb 111
(off Winstanley Est.)
Gant Ct. EN9: Walt A ... 6Hc 21
Ganton St. W1 ... 4B 222 (45Lb 90)
Ganton Wlk. WD19: Wat ... 21Z 45
GANTS HILL ... 30Qc 54
GANTS HILL ... 30Qc 54
Gants Hill IG2: Ilf ... 30Qc 54
Gantshill Cres. IG2: Ilf ... 29Qc 54
GANWICK ... 8Cb 17
GANWICK CORNER ... 7Cb 17
Gapemouth Rd. GU24: Pirb ... 4A 186
Gapp Cl. TN15: W King ... 80Ud 164
Gap Rd. SW19 ... 64Cb 133
Garage Rd. W3 ... 44Qa 87
Garand Ct. N7 ... 36Pb 70
Garbett Ho. SE17 ... 51Rb 113
(off Doddington Gro.)
Garbrand Wlk. KT17: Ewe ... 81Va 174
Garbutt Pl. W1 ... 7J 215 (43Jb 90)
Garbutt Rd. RM14: Upm ... 33Sd 78
Garden Av. AL10: Hat ... 4C 8
CR4: Mitc ... 66Kb 134
DA7: Bex ... 55Bd 117
Garden City HA8: Edg ... 23Qa 47
Garden Cl. AL1: St A ... 1F 6
E4 ... 22Cc 52
EN5: Ark ... 14Ya 30
HA4: Ruis ... 33U 64
KT3: N Mald ... 70Ua 132
KT15: Add ... 77M 149
KT22: Lea ... 96La 192
SE12 ... 62Kc 137
SM6: Wall ... 78Nb 156
SM7: Bans ... 87Cb 175
SW15 ... 59Ya 110
TW12: Hamp ... 64Ba 129
TW15: Ashf ... 65S 128
UB5: N'olt ... 39Aa 65
WD17: Wat ... 12V 26
Garden Cotts. AL2: F'mre ... 9B 6
BR5: St P ... 68Yc 139
Garden Ct. CR0: C'don ... 75Vb 157
EC4 ... 4K 223
HA7: Stan ... 22La 46
N12 ... 22Db 49
NW8 ... 3B 214
TN13: S'oaks ... 94Md 203
(off Garden Rd.)
TW9: Kew ... 53Pa 109
TW12: Hamp ... 64Ba 129
W4 ... 48Sa 87
W11 ... 45Ab 88
(off Clarendon Rd.)
Gardener Gro. TW13: Hanw ... 61Ba 129
Gardeners Cl. N11 ... 19Jb 32
SE9 ... 62Nc 138
Gardeners Cotts. TN14: Hals ... 83Ad 181
Gardeners Rd. CR0: C'don ... 74Rb 157
Gardener's Wlk. KT23: Bookh ... 98Da 191
Garden Fld. La. HP4: Berk ... 3B 2
Gardenfields KT20: Tad ... 91Ab 194
Garden Ho. N2 ... 26Fb 49
(off The Grange)
SW7 ... 48Db 89
(off Cornwall Gdns.)
Garden Houses, The W6 ... 51Za 110
(off Bothwell St.)
Gardenia Dr. GU24: W End ... 5D 166
Gardenia Rd. BR1: Brom ... 69Qc 138
EN1: Enf ... 16Ub 33
Gardenia Way IG8: Wfd G ... 23Jc 53
Garden La. BR1: Brom ... 65Kc 137
SW2 ... 60Pb 112
Garden M. SL1: Slou ... 6K 81
W2 ... 45Cb 89
Garden Museum, The ... 4H 229 (48Pb 90)
Garden Pl. DA2: Wilm ... 62Md 141
E8 ... 39Vb 71
Garden Reach HP8: Chal G ... 13A 24
Garden Rd. BR1: Brom ... 66Kc 137
KT12: Walt T ... 72X 151
NW8 ... 3A 214 (41Eb 89)
SE20 ... 67Yb 136
TN13: S'oaks ... 94Md 203
TW9: Rich ... 55Qa 109
WD5: Ab L ... 3U 12
Garden Row DA11: Nflt ... 2B 144
SE1 ... 4B 230 (48Rb 91)
Garden Royal SW15 ... 58Za 110
Gardens, The AL9: Brk P ... 9G 8
BR3: Beck ... 67Ec 136
E5 ... 31Vb 71
GU24: Pirb ... 4D 186
HA1: Harr ... 30Ea 46
HA5: Pinn ... 30Ba 45
KT10: Esh ... 77Ca 151
KT11: Cobh ... 91S 190
N8 ... 28Nb 50
(not continuous)
SE22 ... 56Wb 113
TW14: Felt ... 57T 106
WD17: Wat ... 12V 26
Gardens of the Rose ... 8M 5
Garden St. E1 ... 43Zb 92
Garden Ter. SW1 ... 7D 228 (50Mb 90)
SW7 ... 2E 226
TN15: Seal ... 93Qd 203
Garden Wlk. BR3: Beck ... 67Bc 136
CR5: Coul ... 95Kb 196
EC2 ... 5H 219 (41Ub 91)
Garden Way IG10: Lough ... 10Qc 22
NW10 ... 37Sa 67
Gardiner Av. NW2 ... 36Ya 68
Gardiner Cl. BR5: St P ... 68Yc 139
EN3: Pond E ... 16Zb 34
RM8: Dag ... 35Zc 75
Gardiner Ct. CR2: S Croy ... 79Tb 157
NW10 ... 39Ta 67
Gardiner Ho. SW11 ... 53Gb 111
Gardner Cl. E11 ... 30Kc 53
Gardner Ct. EC1 ... 5B 218
N5 ... 35Sb 71
WD25: Wat ... 7Y 13
Gardner Ho. TW13: Hanw ... 61Ba 129
UB1: S'hall ... 45Z 85
(off The Broadway)
Gardner Ind. Est. BR3 ... 64Bc 136
Gardner Pl. TW14: Felt ... 58X 107
Gardner Rd. E13 ... 42Kc 93
Gardners La. EC4 ... 4D 224 (45Sb 91)
Gardner's Way RM20: W Thur ... 52Wd 120
Gardnor Rd. NW3 ... 35Fb 69
Gard St. EC1 ... 3C 218 (41Rb 91)
Garendon Gdns. SM4: Mord ... 73Db 155
Garendon Rd. SM4: Mord ... 73Db 155
Garenne Ct. E4 ... 18Ec 34
Gareth Cl. KT4: Wor Pk ... 75Za 154
Gareth Ct. SW16 ... 62Mb 134
WD6: Bore ... 10Pa 15
(off Aycliffe Rd.)
Gareth Dr. N9 ... 19Wb 33
Gareth Gro. BR1: Brom ... 63Jc 137
Garfield EN2: Enf ... 15Tb 33
(off London Rd.)
Garfield Ct. NW6 ... 38Ab 68
(off Willesden La.)
Garfield M. SW11 ... 55Jb 112
Garfield Pl. SL4: Wind ... 4H 103
Garfield Rd. E4 ... 18Fc 35
E13 ... 42Hc 93
EN3: Pond E ... 14Yb 34
KT15: Add ... 78L 149
SW11 ... 55Jb 112
SW19 ... 64Eb 133
TW1: Twick ... 60Ja 108
Garfield St. WD24: Wat ... 10X 13
Garford St. E14 ... 45Cc 92
Garganey Ct. NW10 ... 37Ta 67
(off Elgar Av.)
Garganey Wlk. SE28 ... 45Yc 95
Gargery Cl. DA12: Grav'nd ... 10J 123
Garibaldi Rd. RH1: Redh ... 7P 207
Garibaldi St. SE18 ... 49Uc 94
Garland Cl. EN8: Chesh ... 3Ac 20
HP2: Hem H ... 1M 3
Garland Ct. AL1: St A ... 2C 6
(off Victoria St.)
E14 ... 45Cc 92
(off Premiere Pl.)
SE17 ... 6E 230
Garland Dr. TW3: Houn ... 54Ea 108
Garland Ho. KT2: King T ... 67Na 131
(off Seven Kings Way)
UB7: W Dray ... 47P 83
Garland Rd. HA7: Stan ... 25Na 47
SE18 ... 52Tc 116
Garlands Ct. CR0: C'don ... 77Tb 157
(off Chatsworth Rd.)
Garlands Ho. NW8 ... 40Eb 69
(off Carlton Hill)
Garlands La. HA1: Harr ... 32Ha 66
Garlands Rd. KT22: Lea ... 93Ka 192
RH1: Redh ... 7P 207
Garland Way CR3: Cat'm ... 94Tb 197
RM11: Horn ... 28Nd 57
Garlichill Rd. KT18: Tatt C ... 89Xa 174
Garlick Hill EC4 ... 4E 224 (45Sb 91)
Garlies Rd. SE23 ... 62Ac 136
Garlinge Ho. SW9 ... 53Qb 112
(off Gosling Way)
Garlinge Rd. NW2 ... 37Bb 69
Garman Cl. N18 ... 22Tb 51
Garman Rd. N17 ... 24Xb 51
(not continuous)
Garnault M. EC1 ... 4A 218
Garnault Pl. EC1 ... 4A 218 (41Qb 90)
Garnault Rd. EN1: Enf ... 10Vb 19
Garner Cl. RM8: Dag ... 32Zc 75
Garner Ct. TW19: Stanw ... 58M 105
(off Douglas Rd.)
Garner Rd. E17 ... 25Ec 52
Garners Cl. SL9: Chal P ... 23B 42
Garners End SL9: Chal P ... 23A 42
Garners Rd. SL9: Chal P ... 23A 42
Garner St. E2 ... 40Wb 71
Garnet Cl. SL1: Slou ... 7E 80

Garnet Ho. E1 46Yb 92
(off Garnet St.)
Garnet Rd. CR7: Thor H 70Sb 135
NW10 37Ua 68
Garnet St. E1 45Yb 92
Garnett Cl. SE9 55Pc 116
WD24: Wat 9Z 13
Garnett Dr. AL2: Brick W 1Ba 13
Garnett Rd. NW3 36Hb 69
Garnett Way E17 25Ac 52
(off McEntee Av.)
Garnet Wlk. E6 43Nc 94
Garnham Cl. N16 33Vb 71
Garnham St. N16 33Vb 71
Garnies Cl. SE15 52Vb 113
Garnon Mead CM16: Coop 1Zc 23
Garrad's Rd. SW16 62Mb 134
Garrard Cl. BR7: Chst 64Rc 138
DA7: Bex 55Cd 118
Garrard Rd. SL2: Slou 2C 80
SM7: Bans 88Cb 175
Garrard Wlk. NW10 37Ua 68
Garratt Cl. CR0: Bedd 77Nb 156
Garratt Ct. SW18 59Db 111
Garratt La. SW17 58Db 111
SW18 58Db 111
Garratt Rd. HA8: Edg 24Qa 47
Garratts La. SM7: Bans 88Bb 175
Garratts Rd. WD23: Bush 17Ea 28
Garratt Ter. SW17 63Gb 133
Garraway Ct. SW13 52Ya 110
(off Wyatt Dr.)
Garrett Cl. W3 43Ta 87
Garrett Ho. SE1 1B 230
Garrett St. EC1 5E 218 (42Sb 91)
Garrick Av. NW11 30Ab 48
Garrick Cl. KT12: Hers 77X 151
SW18 56Eb 111
TW9: Rich 57Ma 109
TW18: Staines 66J 127
W5 42Na 87
Garrick Ct. E8 38Vb 71
(off Jacaranda Gro.)
HA8: Edg 21Pa 47
Garrick Cres. CR0: C'don 75Ub 157
Garrick Dr. NW4 26Ya 48
SE28 48Tc 94
Garrick Gdns. KT8: W Mole 69Ca 129
Garrick Ho. KT1: King T 70Na 131
(off Surbiton Rd.)
W1 7K 221
W4 51Ua 110
Garrick Ind. Cen. NW9 29Va 48
Garrick Pk. NW4 26Za 48
Garrick Rd. NW9 30Va 48
TW9: Rich 54Qa 109
UB6: G'frd 42Da 85
Garricks Ho. KT1: King T 68Ma 131
(off Wadbrook St.)
Garrick St. DA11: Grav'nd 8D 122
WC2 4F 223 (45Nb 90)
Garrick Theatre 5F 223
Garrick Way NW4 28Za 48
Garrick Yd. WC2 4F 223
Garrison Cl. SE18 52Qc 116
TW4: Houn 57Ba 107
Garrison La. KT9: Chess 80Ma 153
Garrison Pde. RM19: Purf 49Qd 97
Garrison Rd. E3 39Cc 72
Garrolds Cl. BR8: Swan 68Fd 140
Garron La. RM15: S Ock 44Vd 98
Garrow DA3: Lfield 69De 143
Garrowsfield EN5: Barn 16Bb 31
Garry Cl. RM1: Rom 24Gd 56
Garry Way RM1: Rom 24Gd 56
Garsdale Cl. N11 23Jb 50
Garsdale Ter. W14 50Bb 89
(off Aisgill Av.)
Garside Cl. SE28 48Tc 94
TW12: Hamp 65Da 129
Garside Ct. TW11: Hamp W 67La 130
Garsington M. SE4 55Bc 114
Garsmouth Way WD25: Wat 8Z 13
Garson Cl. KT10: Esh 78Ba 151
Garson Ho. W2 4B 220
Garson La. TW19: Wray 9P 103
Garson Rd. KT10: Esh 79Ba 151
GARSTON 7Y 13
Garston Cres. WD25: Wat 6Y 13
Garston Dr. WD25: Wat 6Y 13
Garston Gdns. CR8: Kenley 87Tb 177
Garston Ho. N1 38Rb 71
(off The Sutton Est.)
Garston La. CR8: Kenley 86Tb 177
WD25: Wat 6Z 13
Garston Pk. Pde. WD25: Wat 6Z 13
Garstons, The KT23: Bookh 97Ca 191
Garter Way SE16 47Zb 92
Garth, The HA3: Kenton 30Pa 47
KT11: Cobh 85Aa 171
TW12: Hamp H 65Da 129
WD5: Ab L 5T 12
Garth Cl. HA4: Ruis 32Z 65
KT2: King T 64Pa 131
SM4: Mord 73Za 154
Garth Ct. HA1: Harr 30Ha 46
(off Northwick Pk. Rd.)
W4 50Ta 87
Garth Ho. NW2 33Bb 69
Garthland Dr. EN5: Barn 15Xa 30
Garth M. W5 42Na 87
Garthorne Rd. SE23 59Zb 114
Garthorne Road Nature Reserve 59Zb 114
Garth Rd. KT2: King T 64Pa 131
NW2 33Bb 69
RM15: S Ock 42Yd 98
SM4: Mord 72Ya 154
TN13: S'oaks 100Ld 203
W4 50Ta 87
Garth Rd. Ind. Cen., The
SM4: Mord 74Za 154
Garthside TW10: Ham 64Na 131
Garthway N12 23Gb 49
Gartlet Rd. WD17: Wat 13Y 27
Gartmoor Gdns. SW19 60Bb 111
Gartmore Rd. IG3: Ilf 33Vc 75
Garton Bank SM7: Bans 89Cb 175
Garton La. RM15: S Ock 44Vd 98
Garton Pl. SW18 58Eb 111
Gartons Cl. EN3: Pond E 14Yb 34
Gartons Way SW11 55Eb 111
Garvary Rd. E16 44Kc 93
Garvock Dr. TN13: S'oaks 98Jd 202
Garway Ct. E3 40Cc 72
(off Matilda Gdns.)
Garway Rd. W2 44Db 89
Garwood Cl. N17 25Xb 51
Gascoigne Cl. N17 25Vb 51
(off King's Rd.)
Gascoigne Gdns. IG8: Wfd G 24Gc 53
Gascoigne Pl. E2 3K 219 (41Vb 91)
(not continuous)
Gascoigne Rd. CR0: New Ad 82Ec 178
IG11: Bark 39Sc 74
KT13: Weyb 76R 150
Gascon's Gro. SL2: Slou 2E 80
Gascony Av. NW6 38Cb 69
Gascony Pl. W12 46Za 88
Gascoyne Cl. EN6: S Mim 4Wa 16
RM3: Rom 24Md 57
Gascoyne Dr. DA1: Cray 55Hd 118
Gascoyne Ho. E9 38Ac 72
Gascoyne Rd. E9 38Zb 72
Gaselee St. E14 46Ec 92
(off Baffin Way)
Gaskarth Rd. HA8: Edg 25Sa 47
SW12 58Kb 112
Gaskell Ct. SE20 66Zb 136
Gaskell Rd. N6 30Hb 49
Gaskell St. SW4 54Nb 112
Gaskin St. N1 39Rb 71
Gasoline All. TN15: Wro 89Fe 185
Gaspar Cl. SW5 49Db 89
Gaspar M. SW5 49Db 89
Gassiot Rd. SW17 63Hb 133
Gassiot Way SM1: Sutt 76Fb 155
Gasson Ho. SE14 51Zb 114
(off John Williams Cl.)
Gasson Rd. DA10: Swans 58Ae 121
Gastein Rd. W6 51Za 110
Gastigny Ho. EC1 4E 218
Gaston Bell Cl. TW9: Rich 55Pa 109
Gaston Bri. Rd. TW17: Shep 72T 150
Gaston Rd. CR4: Mitc 69Jb 134
Gaston Way TW17: Shep 71T 150
Gataker Ho. SE16 48Xb 91
(off Slippers Pl.)
Gataker St. SE16 48Xb 91
Gatcombe Ct. AL1: St A 3E 6
(off Dexter Cl.)
BR3: Beck 66Cc 136
Gatcombe Ho. SE22 55Ub 113
Gatcombe M. W5 45Pa 87
Gatcombe Rd. E16 46Jc 93
N19 34Mb 70
Gatcombe Way EN4: Cockf 13Hb 31
Gateacre Ct. DA14: Sidc 63Xc 139
Gate Cen., The TW8: Bford 52Ja 108
Gate Cinema 46Cb 89
(off Notting Hill Ga.)
Gate Cl. WD6: Bore 11Sa 29
Gate Cotts. WD3: Chor 14F 24
Gatecroft HP3: Hem H 4P 3
(not continuous)
Gate End HA6: Nwood 24W 44
Gateforth St. NW8 6D 214 (42Gb 89)
Gate Hill Ct. W11 46Bb 89
(off Ladbroke Ter.)
Gatehill Rd. HA6: Nwood 24V 44
Gatehope Dr. RM15: S Ock 44Vd 98
Gate Ho. E3 39Ac 72
(off Gunmakers La.)
N1 38Tb 71
(off Ufton Rd.)
Gatehouse Cl. KT2: King T 66Sa 131
SL4: Wind 6F 102
Gate Ho. Pl. WD18: Wat 13W 26
Gatehouse Sq. SE1 6E 224
Gatehouse Theatre 32Jb 70
(off Hopwood Rd.)
Gateley Ho. SE4 56Zb 114
(off Coston Wlk.)
Gateley Rd. SW9 55Pb 112
Gate Lodge W9 43Cb 89
(off Admiral Wlk.)
Gately Ct. SE15 52Vb 113
Gate M. SW7 2E 226
Gater Dr. EN2: Enf 11Tb 33
Gates NW9 25Ua 48
Gatesborough St. EC2 5H 219 (42Ub 91)
Gates Ct. SE17 7D 230 (50Sb 91)
Gatesden WC1 4G 217 (41Nb 90)
Gatesden Cl. KT22: Fet 95Ea 192
Gatesden Rd. KT22: Fet 94Ea 192
Gates Grn. Rd. BR2: Kes 76Hc 159
BR4: W W'ck 76Hc 159
Gateshead Rd. WD6: Bore 12Pa 29
Gateside Rd. SW17 62Hb 133
Gatestone Ct. SE19 65Ub 135
(off Central Hill)
Gatestone Rd. SE19 65Ub 135
Gate St. WC2 2H 223 (44Pb 90)
Gate Theatre, The 46Cb 89
(off Pembridge Rd.)
Gateway KT13: Weyb 76R 150
SE17 51Sb 113
Gateway, The GU21: Wok 86D 168
WD18: Wat 15U 26
Gateway Arc. N1 1B 218
Gateway Bus. Cen. BR3: Beck 65Ac 136
SE28 48Tc 94
Gateway Bus. Pk. CR5: Coul 87Mb 176
Gateway Cl. HA6: Nwood 23S 44
Gateway Ct. AL2: Brick W 2Aa 13
(off The Uplands)
IG2: Ilf 30Qc 54
(off Parham Dr.)
Gateway Ho. IG11: Bark 39Sc 74
Gateway Ind. Est. NW10 41Va 88
Gateway M. E8 36Vb 71
N11 23Lb 50
Gateway Pde. DA12: Grav'nd 3H 145
Gateway Retail Pk. E6 42Rc 94
Gateway Rd. E10 34Dc 72
Gateways KT6: Surb 71Na 153
(off Surbiton Hill Rd.)
Gateways, The EN7: G Oak 1Tb 19
SW3 6E 226 (49Gb 89)
TW9: Rich 56Ma 109
(off Park La.)
Gateways Ct. SM6: Wall 78Kb 156
Gatewick Cl. SL1: Slou 6J 81
Gatfield Gro. TW13: Hanw 61Ca 129
Gatfield Ho. TW13: Hanw 61Ba 129
Gathorne Rd. N22 26Qb 50
Gathorne St. E2 40Zb 72
Gatley Av. KT19: Ewe 78Ra 153
Gatliff Cl. SW1 7K 227
Gatliff Rd. SW1 7K 227 (50Kb 90)
Gatling Rd. SE2 50Wc 95
Gatonby St. SE15 53Vb 113
Gatting Cl. HA8: Edg 24Sa 47
Gatting Way UB8: Uxb 37N 63
Gattis Wharf N1 1G 217
GATTON 100Hb 195
GATTON BOTTOM 98Kb 196
Gatton Bottom RH1: Mers 1L 207
RH2: Reig 1L 207
Gatton Cl. RH2: Reig 3L 207
SM2: Sutt 81Db 175
Gatton Pk. Bus. Cen. RH1: Mers 1B 208
Gatton Pk. Ct. RH1: Redh 2P 207
Gatton Pk. Rd. RH1: Redh 4M 207
RH2: Reig 4M 207
Gatton Rd. RH2: Reig 4L 207
SW17 63Gb 133
Gattons Way DA14: Sidc 63Bd 139
Gatward Cl. N21 16Rb 33
Gatward Grn. N9 19Vb 33
Gatwick Ho. E14 44Bc 92
(off Clemence St.)
Gatwick Rd. DA12: Grav'nd 2D 144
SW18 59Bb 111
Gatwick Way RM12: Horn 34Pd 77
Gauden Cl. SW4 55Mb 112
Gauden Rd. SW4 54Mb 112
Gaudi Apartments N8 27Pb 50
(off Gt. Amwell La.)
Gaugin Ct. SE16 50Xb 91
(off Stubbs Dr.)
Gaumont App. WD17: Wat 13X 27
Gaumont Ter. W12 47Ya 88
(off Lime Gro.)
Gaumont Twr. E8 37Vb 71
(off Dalston Sq.)
Gauntlet NW9 26Va 48
(off Five Acre)
Gauntlet Cl. UB5: N'olt 38Aa 65
Gauntlett Ct. HA0: Wemb 36Ka 66
Gauntlett Rd. SM1: Sutt 78Fb 155
Gaunt St. SE1 3D 230 (48Sb 91)
Gautrey Rd. SE15 54Yb 114
Gautrey Sq. E6 44Pc 94
Gavell Rd. KT11: Cobh 85W 170
Gavel St. SE17 5G 231 (49Tb 91)
Gavenny Path RM15: S Ock 44Vd 98
Gaverick M. E14 49Cc 92
Gaveston Cl. KT14: Byfl 85P 169
Gavestone Cres. SE12 59Lc 115
Gavestone Rd. SE12 59Kc 115
Gaveston Rd. KT22: Lea 92Ja 192
SL2: Slou 1D 80
Gaviller Pl. E5 35Xb 71
Gavina Cl. SM4: Mord 71Gb 155
Gavin Ho. SE18 49Uc 94
Gaviots Cl. SL9: Ger X 32B 62
Gaviots Grn. SL9: Ger X 31A 62
(not continuous)
Gaviots Way SL9: Ger X 31A 62
Gawain Wlk. N9 20Wb 33
Gawber St. E2 41Yb 92
Gawsworth Cl. E15 36Hc 73
Gawthorne Ct. E3 40Cc 72
Gawton Cres. CR5: Coul 94Lb 196
Gay Cl. NW2 36Xa 68
Gaydon Ho. W2 43Db 89
(off Bourne Ter.)
Gaydon La. NW9 25Ua 48
Gayfere Rd. IG5: Ilf 27Pc 54
KT17: Ewe 78Wa 154
Gayfere St. SW1 4F 229 (48Nb 90)
Gayford Rd. W12 47Va 88
Gay Gdns. RM10: Dag 35Ed 76
Gay Ho. N16 36Ub 71
Gayhurst SE17 51Tb 113
(off Hopwood Rd.)
Gayhurst Ct. UB5: N'olt 41Y 85
Gayhurst Ho. NW8 5D 214
Gayhurst Rd. E8 38Wb 71
Gayler Cl. RH1: Blet 5M 209
Gaylor Rd. RM18: Tilb 3B 122
UB5: N'olt 36Ba 65
Gaymead NW8 39Db 69
(off Abbey Rd.)
Gaynes Ct. RM14: Upm 35Rd 77
Gaynesford Rd. SE23 61Zb 136
SM5: Cars 80Hb 155
Gaynes Hill Rd. IG8: Wfd G 23Nc 54
Gaynes Pk. Est. CM16: Coop 3Ad 23
Gaynes Pk. Rd. RM14: Upm 35Qd 77
Gaynes Rd. RM14: Upm 33Rd 77
Gay Rd. E15 40Fc 73
Gaysham Av. IG2: Ilf 29Qc 54
Gaysham Hall IG5: Ilf 27Rc 54
Gaysley Ho. SE11 6K 229
Gay St. SW15 55Za 110
Gayton HA1: Harr 31Ga 66
(off Grove Hill)
Gayton Cl. KT21: Asht 90Na 173
Gayton Ct. HA1: Harr 30Ha 46
RH2: Reig 5J 207
Gayton Cres. NW3 35Fb 69
Gayton Ho. E3 42Cc 92
(off Chiltern Rd.)
Gayton Rd. HA1: Harr 30Ha 46
NW3 35Fb 69
SE2 48Yc 95
Gayville Rd. SW11 58Hb 111
Gaywood Av. EN8: Chesh 2Zb 20
Gaywood Cl. SW2 60Pb 112
Gaywood Rd. E17 27Cc 52
KT21: Asht 90Pa 173
Gaywood St. SE1 4B 230 (48Rb 91)
Gaza St. SE17 7B 230 (50Rb 91)
Gaze Ho. E14 44Fc 93
(off Blair St.)
Gazelda Ind. Est. WD17: Wat 15Y 27
Gazelle Glade DA12: Grav'nd 4H 145
Gazelle Ho. E15 37Gc 73
Gean Ct. E11 35Fc 73
N11 23Lb 50
(off Cline Rd.)
Gean Wlk. AL10: Hat 3C 8
Geariesville Gdns. IG6: Ilf 28Rc 54
Gearing Cl. SW17 63Jb 134
Geary Ct. CM14: B'wood 18Yd 40
Geary Dr. CM14: B'wood 18Yd 40
CM15: B'wood 18Yd 40
Geary Rd. NW10 36Wa 68
Geary St. N7 36Pb 70
Geddes Pl. DA6: Bex 56Cd 118
(off Arnsberg Way)
Geddes Rd. WD23: Bush 14Ea 28
Geddington Ct. EN8: Walt C 6Cc 20
Geddy Ct. RM2: Rom 27Kd 57
Gedeney Rd. N17 25Sb 51
Gedling Ct. SE1 2K 231
Gedling Pl. SE1 3K 231 (48Vb 91)
Geere Rd. E15 39Hc 73
Geerings, The SS17: Stan H 1P 101
Gees Ct. W1 3J 221 (44Jb 90)
Gee St. EC1 5D 218 (42Sb 91)
Geffery's Ct. SE9 62Nc 138
Geffrye Ct. N1 2J 219 (40Ub 71)
Geffrye Est. N1 2J 219 (40Ub 71)
Geffrye Mus. 2K 219
Geffrye St. E2 1K 219 (40Vb 71)
Geisthorp Ct. EN9: Walt A 5Jc 21
Geldart Rd. SE15 52Xb 113
Geldeston Rd. E5 33Wb 71
Gellatly Rd. SE14 54Yb 114
Gell Cl. UB10: Ick 34P 63
Gelsthorpe Rd. RM5: Col R 24Dd 56
Gem Ct. SE10 52Dc 114
(off Merryweather Pl.)
Gemini Bus. Cen. E16 42Fc 93
Gemini Bus. Est. SE14 50Zb 92
Gemini Bus. Pk. E6 43Tc 94
Gemini Ct. E1 45Wb 91
(off Vaughan Way)
Gemini Gro. UB5: N'olt 41Aa 85
Gemini Ho. E3 39Cc 72
(off Garrison Rd.)
Gemini Pl. TW15: Ashf 65U 128
Gemmell Cl. CR8: Purl 86Pb 176
Genas Cl. IG6: Ilf 25Rc 54
General Gordon Pl. SE18 49Rc 94
General's Wlk., The EN3: Enf W 9Ac 20
General Wolfe Rd. SE10 53Fc 115
Genesis Bus. Pk. GU21: Wok 87E 168
NW10 40Ra 67
Genesis Cl. TW19: Stanw 60P 105
Genesta Glade DA12: Grav'nd 4J 145
Genesta Rd. SE18 51Rc 116
Geneva Cl. TW17: Shep 68U 128
Geneva Ct. NW9 29Va 48
Geneva Dr. SW9 56Qb 112
Geneva Gdns. RM6: Chad H 29Ad 55
Geneva Rd. CR7: Thor H 71Sb 157
KT1: King T 70Na 131
Genever Cl. E4 22Cc 52
Genista Rd. N18 22Xb 51
Genoa Av. SW15 57Ya 110
Genoa Ho. E1 42Zb 92
(off Ernest St.)
Genoa Rd. SE20 67Yb 136
Genotin M. RM12: Horn 36Ld 77
Genotin Rd. EN1: Enf 13Tb 33
Genotin Ter. EN1: Enf 13Tb 33
Gentlemans Row EN2: Enf 13Sb 33
Gentry Cl. SS17: Stan H 1L 101
Gentry Gdns. E13 42Jc 93
Geoffrey Av. RM3: Hrld W 23Qd 57
Geoffrey Bower Sports Cen. 26Pc 54
Geoffrey Chaucer Way E3 43Bc 92
Geoffrey Cl. SE5 54Sb 113
Geoffrey Ct. SE4 54Bc 114
Geoffrey Gdns. E6 40Nc 74
Geoffrey Ho. SE1 3G 231
Geoffrey Jones Ct. NW10 39Wa 68
Geoffrey Rd. SE4 55Bc 114
Geoffrey Whitworth Theatre 56Jd 118
Geographers' A-Z Map Company 91Be 205
George V Av. HA5: Pinn 26Ba 45
George V Cl. HA5: Pinn 27Ca 45
WD18: Wat 14V 26
George V Way UB6: G'frd 39Ka 66
WD3: Sarr 8K 11
George Beard Rd. SE8 49Bc 92
George Belt Ho. E2 41Zb 92
(off Smart St.)
George Comberton Wlk. E12 36Qc 74
George Ct. TW15: Ashf 63P 127
(off Church Rd.)
UB3: Hayes 43V 84
WC2 5G 223
George Cres. N10 24Jb 50
George Crooks Ho. RM17: Grays 51De 121
(off New Rd.)
George Davies Lodge IG6: Ilf 29Sc 54
(off Veronique Gdns.)
George Downing Est. N16 33Vb 71
George Eliot Ho. SW1 6C 228
George Elliot Ho. SE17 7D 230
George Elliston Ho. SE1 50Wb 91
(off Old Kent Rd.)
George Eyre Ho. NW8 2C 214
George Fld. Ho. WD3: Rick 17M 25
(off Northway)
George Furness Ho. NW10 37Xa 68
(off Grange Rd.)
George Gange Way HA3: W'stone 27Ga 46
George Gillett Ct. EC1 5E 218
GEORGE GREEN 44A 82
George Grn. Dr. SL3: G Grn 44A 82
George Grn. Rd. SL3: G Grn 4P 81
George Groves Rd. SE20 67Wb 135
George Hudson Twr. E15 40Dc 72
(off High St.)
George Inn Yd. SE1 7F 225 (46Tb 91)
Georgelands GU23: Rip 93K 189
George La. BR2: Hayes 74Kc 159
E18 26Jc 53
(not continuous)
SE13 58Dc 114
George Lansbury Ho. E3 41Bc 92
(off Bow Rd.)
N22 25Qb 50
(off Progress Way)
NW10 38Ua 68
George Leybourne Ho. E1 45Wb 91
(off Fletcher St.)
George Lindgren Ho. SW6 52Bb 111
(off Clem Attlee Ct.)
George Loveless Ho. E2 3K 219
George Lovell Dr. EN3: Enf L 9Cc 20
George Lowe Ct. W2 43Db 89
(off Bourne Ter.)
George Mathers Rd.
SE11 5B 230 (49Rb 91)
George M. EN2: Enf 13Tb 33
NW1 4B 216
SW9 54Qb 112
George Padmore Ho. E8 39Wb 71
(off Brougham Rd.)
George Peabody Ct. NW1 7D 214
George Pl. N17 27Ub 51
George Potter Ho. SW11 54Fb 111
(off George Potter Way)
George Potter Way SW11 54Fb 111
George Rd. E4 23Cc 52
KT2: King T 66Ra 131
KT3: N Mald 70Va 132
George Row SE16 47Wb 91
Georges Cl. BR5: St P 69Yc 139
George Scott Ho. E1 44Zb 92
(off W. Arbour St.)
Georges Dr. CM15: Pil H 15Vd 40
Georges Mead WD6: E'tree 16Na 29
Georges Pl. KT10: Esh 77Ea 152
George Sq. SW19 69Cb 133
George's Rd. N7 36Pb 70
TN16: Tats 92Mc 199
George's Sq. SW6 51Bb 111
(off North End Rd.)
George Ter. CR3: Cat'm 94Tb 197
George St. AL3: St A 2B 6
CR0: C'don 75Sb 157
E16 44Hc 93
HP2: Hem H 1M 3
HP4: Berk 1A 2
IG11: Bark 38Sc 74
RM1: Rom 30Hd 56
RM17: Grays 51Ce 121
TW3: Houn 54Ba 107
TW9: Rich 57Ma 109
TW18: Staines 63H 127
UB2: S'hall 49Aa 85
UB8: Uxb 38M 63
W1 2F 221 (44Hb 89)
W7 46Ga 86
WD18: Wat 14Y 27
Georges Wood Rd. AL9: Brk P 8J 9
George Tilbury Ho. RM16: Grays 7D 100
George Tingle Ho. SE1 3K 231
Georgetown Cl. SE19 64Ub 135
Georgette Pl. SE10 52Ec 114
George Vale Ho. E2 40Wb 71
(off Mansford St.)
Georgeville Gdns. IG6: Ilf 28Rc 54
George Walter Ct. SE16 49Yb 92
(off Millender Wlk.)
Georgewood Rd. HP3: Hem H 7P 3
George Wyver Cl. SW19 59Ab 110
George Yd. EC3 3G 225 (44Tb 91)
W1 4J 221 (45Jb 90)
Georgia Ct. SE16 48Wb 91
(off Priter Rd.)
Georgiana St. NW1 39Lb 70
Georgian Cl. BR2: Hayes 74Kc 159
HA7: Stan 24Ja 46
TW18: Staines 63K 127
UB10: Ick 35N 63
Georgian Ct. CR0: C'don 74Tb 157
(off Cross Rd.)
E9 39Yb 72
EN5: New Bar 14Eb 31
HA9: Wemb 37Qa 67
N3 25Bb 49
NW4 29Xa 48
SW16 63Nb 134
Georgian Ho. E16 46Jc 93
(off Capulet M.)
Georgian Way HA1: Harr 33Fa 66
Georgia Rd. CR7: Thor H 67Rb 135
KT3: N Mald 70Sa 131
Georgina Gdns. E2 3K 219 (41Vb 91)
Geraint Rd. BR1: Brom 63Jc 137
Geraldine Rd. SW18 57Eb 111
W4 51Qa 109
Geraldine St. SE11 4B 230 (48Rb 91)
Gerald M. SW1 5J 227
Gerald Rd. DA12: Grav'nd 9G 122
E16 42Hc 93
RM8: Dag 33Bd 75
SW1 5J 227 (49Jb 90)
Gerald's Gro. SM7: Bans 86Za 174
Gerard Av. TW4: Houn 59Ca 107
Gerard Gdns. RM13: Rain 40Gd 76
Gerard Pl. E9 38Zb 72
Gerard Rd. HA1: Harr 30Ja 46
SW13 53Va 110
Gerards Cl. SE16 50Yb 92
Gerda Rd. SE9 61Sc 138
Gerdview Dr. DA2: Wilm 63Ld 141
Germander Dr. GU24: Bisl 7E 166
Germander Way E15 41Gc 93
Gernigan Ho. SW18 58Fb 111
Gernon Bushes Nature Reserve 1Ad 23
Gernon Cl. RM13: Rain 40Md 77
Gernon Rd. E3 40Ac 72
Geron Way NW2 32Xa 68
Gerpins La. RM14: Upm 40Pd 77
Gerrard Cres. CM14: B'wood 20Yd 40
Gerrard Gdns. HA5: Eastc 29W 44
Gerrard Ho. SE14 52Yb 114
(off Briant St.)
Gerrard Pl. W1 4E 222 (45Mb 90)
Gerrard Rd. N1 1B 218 (40Rb 71)
Gerrards Cl. N14 15Lb 32
Gerrards Ct. W5 48Ma 87
GERRARDS CROSS 29A 42
Gerrards Cross Golf Course 27B 42
Gerrards Cross Rd.
SL2: Stoke P 7L 61
Gerrards Mead SM7: Bans 88Bb 175
Gerrards Pl. SW4 56Mb 112
Gerrard St. W1 4D 222 (45Mb 90)
Gerridge Ct. SE1 3A 230
(off Gerridge St.)
Gerridge St. SE1 3A 230 (48Qb 90)
Gerry Raffles Sq. E15 37Fc 73
Gertrude Rd. DA17: Belv 49Cd 96
Gertrude St. SW10 51Eb 111
Gervaise Cl. SL1: Slou 6D 80
Gervase Cl. HA9: Wemb 34Sa 67
Gervase Rd. HA8: Edg 25Sa 47
Gervase St. SE15 52Xb 113
Gervis Ct. TW7: Isle 52Ea 108
Gews Cnr. EN8: Chesh 1Zb 20
Ghent St. SE6 61Cc 136
Ghent Way E8 37Vb 71
Gherkin, The 2J 225
Giant Arches Rd. SE24 59Sb 113
Giant Tree Hill WD23: B Hea 18Fa 28
Gibbfield Cl. RM6: Chad H 27Ad 55
Gibbings Ho. SE1 2C 230
Gibbins Rd. E15 38Ec 72
Gibbon Ho. NW8 6C 214
Gibbon Rd. KT2: King T 67Na 131
SE15 54Yb 114
W3 45Ua 88
Gibbons Cl. WD6: Bore 11Na 29
Gibbons La. DA1: Dart 58Md 119
Gibbons M. NW11 29Bb 49
Gibbon's Rents SE1 7H 225
Gibbons Rd. NW10 37Ua 68
Gibbon Wlk. SW15 56Wa 110
Gibb's Acre GU24: Pirb 5D 186
Gibbs Av. SE19 64Tb 135
Gibbs Brook La. RH8: Oxt 8H 211

Gibbs Cl. EN8: Chesh 1Zb 20
SE19 65Tb 135
Gibbs Couch WD19: Wat 20Z 27
Gibbs Grn. HA8: Edg 21Sa 47
W14 50Bb 89
(not continuous)
Gibbs Ho. BR1: Brom 67Hc 137
(off Longfield)
Gibb's Rd. N18 21Yb 52
Gibbs Sq. SE19 64Tb 135
Gibney Ter. BR1: Brom 63Hc 137
Gibraltar Cl. CM13: Gt War 23Yd 58
Gibraltar Cres. KT19: Ewe 82Ua 174
Gibraltar Wlk. E2 41Vb 91
(off Shackwell St.)
Gibson Bus. Cen., The N17 24Vb 51
Gibson Cl. DA11: Nflt 2B 144
E1 42Yb 92
KT9: Chess 78La 152
N21 16Qb 32
TW7: Isle 55Ga 108
Gibson Ct. KT10: Hin W 75Ha 152
RM1: Rom 30Gd 56
SL3: L'ly 50B 82
Gibson Gdns. N16 33Vb 71
Gibson Ho. SM1: Sutt 77Cb 155
Gibson M. TW1: Twick 58La 108
Gibson Pl. TW19: Stanw 58L 105
Gibson Rd. RM8: Dag 32Yc 75
SE11 6J 229 (49Pb 90)
SM1: Sutt 78Db 155
UB10: Ick 35P 63
Gibsons Hill SW16 66Qb 134
(not continuous)
Gibsons Pl. DA4: Eyns 75Nd 163
Gibson Sq. N1 39Qb 70
Gibson Sq. Gdns. N1 39Qb 70
(off Gibson Sq.)
Gibson St. SE10 50Gc 93
Gidd Hill CR5: Coul 88Jb 176
Gidea Av. RM2: Rom 27Jd 56
Gidea Cl. RM2: Rom 27Jd 56
RM15: S Ock 41Yd 98
(off Benyon Path)
Gidea Lodge RM2: Rom 27Kd 57
GIDEA PARK 27Kd 57
Gideon Cl. DA17: Belv 49Dd 96
Gideon M. W5 47Ma 87
Gideon Rd. SW11 55Jb 112
Gidian Ct. AL2: Park 9B 6
Gielgud Theatre 4D 222
Giesbach Rd. N19 33Mb 70
Giffard Rd. N18 23Ub 51
Giffin Sq. Mkt. SE8 52Cc 114
(off Giffin St.)
Giffin St. SE8 52Cc 114
Gifford Gdns. W7 43Fa 86
Gifford Ho. SE10 50Fc 93
(off Eastney St.)
SW1 7B 228
Gifford Pl. CM14: W'ley 22Zd 59
Gifford Rd. NW10 38Ua 68
Giffords Cross Rd.
SS17: Corr 1P 101
Giffordside RM16: Grays 10D 100
Gifford St. N1 38Nb 70
Gift La. E15 39Gc 73
GIGGSHILL 73Ja 152
Giggs Hill BR5: St P 68Wc 139
Giggs Hill Gdns. KT7: T Ditt 74Ja 152
Giggs Hill Rd. KT7: T Ditt 73Ja 152
Gilbert Bri. EC2 1E 224
(off Wood St.)
Gilbert Burnet Ho. HP3: Hem H 4P 3
Gilbert Cl. DA10: Swans 58Zd 121
SE18 53Pc 116
SW19 67Db 133
(off High Path)
Gilbert Ct. W5 44Pa 87
(off Green Va.)
Gilbert Gro. HA8: Edg 25Ta 47
Gilbert Ho. E2 41Zb 92
(off Usk St.)
E17 27Dc 52
EC2 1E 224
SE8 51Cc 114
SW1 50Kb 90
(off Churchill Gdns.)
SW8 52Nb 112
(off Wyvil Rd.)
SW13 52Xa 110
(off Trinity Chu. Rd.)
Gilbert Pl. WC1 1F 223 (43Nb 90)
Gilbert Rd. BR1: Brom 66Jc 137
DA17: Belv 48Cd 96
HA5: Pinn 28Z 45
RM1: Rom 28Hd 56
RM16: Chaf H 48Yd 98
SE11 6A 230 (49Qb 90)
SW19 66Eb 133
UB9: Hare 26M 43
Gilbert Row DA11: Nflt 1B 144
Gilbert Scott Bldg. SW15 58Ab 110
Gilbert Sheldon Ho. W2 7C 214
Gilberts Lodge KT17: Eps 84Ua 174
Gilbertson Ho. E14 48Cc 92
(off Mellish St.)
Gilbert St. E15 35Gc 73
EN3: Enf W 9Xb 20
TW3: Houn 55Ea 108
W1 3J 221 (44Jb 90)
Gilbert Way CR0: Wadd 75Pb 156
SL3: L'ly 50B 82
Gilbert White Cl. UB6: G'frd 39Ja 66
Gilbey Cl. UB10: Ick 35R 64
Gilbey Ho. NW1 38Kb 70
Gilbey Rd. SW17 63Gb 133
Gilbeys Yd. NW1 38Jb 70
Gilbourne Rd. SE18 51Vc 117
Gilby Ho. E9 37Zb 72
Gilda Av. EN3: Pond E 15Ac 34
Gilda Ct. NW7 25Wa 48
Gilda Cres. N16 32Wb 71
Gildea Cl. HA5: Hat E 24Ca 45
Gildea St. W1 1A 222 (43Kb 90)
Gilden Cres. NW5 36Jb 70
Gildenhill Rd. BR8: Swan 66Ld 141
Gildersome St. SE18 51Qc 116
Gilders Rd. KT9: Chess 80Pa 153
Giles Cl. RM13: Rain 40Md 77
Giles Coppice SE19 63Vb 135
Giles Fld. DA12: Grav'nd 10H 123
Giles Ho. SL2: Stoke P 8L 61
(off Bells Hill Grn.)
W11 44Cb 89
(off Westbourne Gro.)
Gilesmead KT18: Eps 86Ua 174
(off Downside)
SE5 53Tb 113
Giles Travers Cl. TW20: Thorpe 69E 126
Gilford Ho. IG1: Ilf 33Rc 74
(off Clements Rd.)
Gilfrid Cl. UB8: Hil 44R 84
Gilhams Av. SM7: Bans 84Za 174
Gilkes Cres. SE21 58Ub 113
Gilkes Pl. SE21 58Ub 113
Gillam Ho. SE16 49Yb 92
(off Silwood St.)
Gillam Way RM13: Rain 37Jd 76
Gillan Ct. SE12 62Kc 137
Gillan Grn. WD23: B Hea 19Ea 28
Gillards M. E17 28Cc 52
Gillards Way E17 28Cc 52
Gill Av. E16 44Jc 93
Gill Cl. WD18: Wat 16S 26
Gill Cres. DA11: Nflt 2B 144
Gillender St. E3 42Ec 92
E14 42Ec 92
Gillespie Ho. GU25: Vir W 70A 126
(off Holloway Dr.)
Gillespie Pk. Nature Reserve 34Qb 70
Gillespie Rd. N5 34Qb 70
Gillett Av. E6 40Nc 74
GILLETTE CORNER 52Ja 108
Gillett Ho. N8 27Nb 50
(off Campsfield Rd.)
Gillett Pl. N16 36Ub 71
Gillett Rd. CR7: Thor H 70Tb 135
Gillett Sq. N16 36Ub 71
(off Gillett St.)
Gillett St. N16 36Ub 71
Gillfoot NW1 2B 216
Gillham Ter. N17 23Wb 51
Gilliam Gro. CR8: Purl 82Qb 176
Gillian Av. AL1: St A 6A 6
Gillian Cres. RM2: Rom 26Ld 57
Gillian Ho. HA3: Hrw W 23Ga 46
Gillian Pk. Rd. SM3: Sutt 74Bb 155
Gillian St. SE13 57Dc 114
Gilliat Rd. SL1: Slou 5J 81
Gilliats Grn. WD3: Chor 14F 24
Gillies Ct. DA14: Sidc 61Tc 139
Gillies Ho. NW6 38Fb 69
(off Hilgrove Rd.)
Gillies Rd. TN15: W King 78Ud 164
Gillies St. NW5 36Jb 70
Gilling Ct. NW3 37Gb 69
Gillingham Ho. RM3: Rom 22Nd 57
(off Lindfield Rd.)
Gillingham M. SW1 5B 228 (49Lb 90)
Gillingham Rd. NW2 34Ab 68
Gillingham Row SW1 5B 228 (49Lb 90)
Gillingham St. SW1 5A 228 (49Lb 90)
Gillings Ct. EN5: Barn 14Ab 30
(off Wood St.)
Gillison Wlk. SE16 48Xb 91
Gillis Sq. SW15 58Wa 110
Gillman Dr. E15 39Hc 73
Gillman Ho. E2 40Wb 71
(off Pritchard's Rd.)
Gillmans Rd. BR5: Orp 74Xc 161
Gillray Ho. SW10 51Fb 111
(off Ann La.)
Gills Hill WD7: R'lett 7Ha 14
Gills Hill La. WD7: R'lett 8Ha 14
Gills Hollow WD7: R'lett 8Ha 14
Gills Rd. DA2: Grn St 67Ud 142
DA4: S Dar 67Ud 142
Gill St. E14 44Bc 92
Gilmais KT23: Bookh 97Ea 192
Gilman Cres. SL4: Wind 5B 102
Gilman Ho. N1 38Qb 70
(off Drummond Way)
Gilmore Cl. SL3: L'ly 7N 81
UB10: Ick 34Q 64
Gilmore Ct. N11 22Hb 49
Gilmore Cres. TW15: Ashf 64Q 128
Gilmore Rd. SE13 56Fc 115
Gilmour Cl. EN2: Enf, Walt C 7Wb 19
Gilpin Av. SW14 56Ta 109
Gilpin Cl. CR4: Mitc 68Gb 133
W2 7B 214
Gilpin Cres. N18 22Vb 51
TW2: Whitt 59Da 107
Gilpin Rd. E5 35Ac 72
Gilpin's Ride HP4: Berk 1A 2
Gilpin Way UB3: Harl 52T 106
Gilray Ho. W2 4B 220
Gilroy Cl. RM13: Rain 37Hd 76
Gilroy Rd. HP2: Hem H 1M 3
Gilroy Way BR5: Orp 73Xc 161
Gilsland EN9: Walt A 7Gc 21
Gilsland Pl. CR7: Thor H 70Tb 135
Gilsland Rd. CR7: Thor H 70Tb 135
Gilson Pl. N10 24Hb 49
Gilstead Ho. IG11: Bark 40Xc 75
Gilstead Rd. SW6 54Db 111
Gilston Rd. SW10 7A 226 (50Eb 89)
Gilton Rd. SE6 62Gc 137
Giltspur St. EC1 2C 224 (44Rb 91)
Gilwell Cl. E4 14Dc 34
Gilwell La. E4 14Dc 34
(not continuous)
GILWELL PARK 14Fc 35
Gilwell Pk. E4 13Fc 35
Ginger Apartments SE1 1K 231
Ginsburg Yd. NW3 35Eb 69
Gippeswyck Cl. HA5: Pinn 25Z 45
Gipsy Hill SE19 63Ub 135
Gipsy La. RM17: Grays 51Ee 121
SW15 55Xa 110
Gipsy Rd. DA16: Well 52Zc 117
SE27 63Sb 135
Gipsy Rd. Gdns. SE27 63Sb 135
Giralda Cl. E16 43Mc 93
Giraud St. E14 44Dc 92
Girdler's Rd. W14 49Za 88
Girdlestone Wlk. N19 33Lb 70
Girdwood Rd. SW18 59Ab 110
Girling Ho. N1 39Ub 71
(off Colville Est.)
Girling Way TW14: Felt 55W 106
Girona Ct. RM16: Chaf H 48Yd 98
Gironde Rd. SW6 52Bb 111
Girtin Ho. UB5: N'olt 40Z 65
(off Academy Gdns.)
Girton Av. NW9 27Qa 47
Girton Cl. UB5: N'olt 37Ea 66
Girton Ct. EN8: Chesh 2Ac 20
Girton Gdns. CR0: C'don 76Cc 158
Girton Rd. SE26 64Zb 136
UB5: N'olt 37Ea 66
Girton Vs. W10 44Za 88
Girton Way WD3: Crox G 15S 26
Gisborne Gdns. RM13: Rain 41Hd 96
Gisbourne Cl. SM6: Bedd 76Mb 156
Gisbourne Way WD24: Wat 9W 12
Gisburn Ho. SE15 51Wb 113
(off Friary Est.)
Gisburn Rd. N8 28Pb 50
Gissing Wlk. N1 38Qb 70
Gittens Cl. BR1: Brom 63Hc 137
Given Wilson Wlk. E13 40Hc 73
Giverny Ho. SE16 47Zb 92
(off Water Gdns. Sq.)
GIVONS GROVE 98La 192
Givons Gro. KT22: Lea 97Ka 192
Givons Gro. Rdbt. KT22: Lea 96Ka 192
Glacier Way HA0: Wemb 40Ma 67
Gladbeck Way EN2: Enf 14Rb 33
Gladding Rd. E12 35Mc 73
Glade, The BR1: Brom 68Mc 137
BR4: W W'ck 76Dc 158
CM13: Hut 18Ce 41
CR0: C'don 71Zb 158
CR5: Coul 91Qb 196
E8 37Wb 71
EN2: Enf 13Qb 32
IG5: Ilf 25Pc 54
IG8: Wfd G 20Kc 35
KT14: W Byf 85G 168
KT17: Ewe 79Wa 154
KT20: Kgswd 93Cb 195
KT22: Fet 94Ca 191
N12 20Fb 31
N21 16Pb 32
RM14: Upm 36Sd 78
SE7 52Lc 115
SL5: S'hill 1A 146
SL9: Ger X 2P 61
SM2: Cheam 81Ab 174
TN13: S'oaks 95Kd 203
TW18: Staines 65K 127
W12 47Xa 88
(off Coningham Rd.)
Glade Bus. Cen., The
RM20: W Thur 50Vd 98
Glade Cl. KT6: Surb 75Ma 153
Glade Ct. IG5: Ilf 25Pc 54
UB8: Uxb 37L 63
Glade Gdns. CR0: C'don 73Ac 158
Glade La. UB2: S'hall 47Da 85
Glades, The DA12: Grav'nd 5F 144
HP1: Hem H 1G 2
KT6: Surb 73Na 153
Gladeside CR0: C'don 72Zb 158
N21 16Pb 32
Gladeside Cl. KT9: Chess 80Ma 153
Gladeside Ct. CR6: W'ham 92Xb 197
Gladesmere Ct. WD24: Wat 8X 13
Gladesmore Community School &
Sports Cen. 29Wb 51
Gladesmore Rd. N15 30Vb 51
Glades Pl. BR1: Brom 68Jc 137
Glade Spur KT20: Kgswd 93Db 195
Glades Shop. Cen., The
BR1: Brom 68Jc 137
Gladeswood Rd. DA17: Belv 49Dd 96
Gladeway, The EN9: Walt A 5Fc 21
Gladiator St. SE23 59Ac 114
Glading Ter. N16 34Vb 71
Gladioli Cl. TW12: Hamp 65Ca 129
Gladsdale Dr. HA5: Eastc 28W 44
Gladsmuir Cl. KT12: Walt T 75Y 151
Gladsmuir Rd. EN5: Barn 12Ab 30
N19 32Lb 70
Gladstone Av. E12 38Nc 74
N22 26Qb 50
TW2: Twick 60Fa 108
TW14: Felt 58W 106
Gladstone Ct. NW6 38Eb 69
(off Fairfax Rd.)
SW1 6E 228
Gladstone Ct. Bus. Cen. SW8 53Kb 112
(off Pagden St.)
Gladstone Gdns. TW3: Houn 53Ea 108
Gladstone Ho. CR4: Mitc 68Hb 133
E14 44Cc 92
(off E. India Dock Rd.)
Gladstone M. N22 26Qb 50
NW6 38Bb 69
SE20 66Yb 136
Gladstone Pde. NW2 33Ya 68
Gladstone Pk. Gdns. NW2 35Xa 68
Gladstone Pl. E3 40Bc 72
EN5: Barn 14Za 30
KT8: E Mos 71Ga 152
Gladstone Rd. BR6: Farnb 78Sc 160
CR0: C'don 73Tb 157
DA1: Dart 58Pd 119
IG9: Buck H 18Lc 35
KT1: King T 69Qa 131
KT6: Surb 75Ma 153
KT21: Asht 90Ma 173
SW19 66Cb 133
UB2: S'hall 47Aa 85
W4 48Ta 87
WD17: Wat 13Y 27
Gladstone St. SE1 4B 230 (48Rb 91)
Gladstone Ter. SE27 64Sb 135
(off Bentons La.)
SW8 53Kb 112
Gladstone Way HA3: W'stone 27Ga 46
SL1: Slou 6E 80
Gladwell Rd. BR1: Brom 65Jc 137
N8 30Pb 50
Gladwin Ho. NW1 2C 216
Gladwyn Rd. SW15 55Za 110
Gladys Dimson Ho. E7 36Hc 73
Gladys Rd. NW6 38Cb 69
Glaisher St. SE8 51Cc 114
Glaisyer Way SL0: Iver H 40E 62
Glamis Cl. EN7: Chesh 1Wb 19
Glamis Ct. W3 47Ra 87
Glamis Cres. UB3: Harl 48S 84
Glamis Dr. RM11: Horn 32Nd 77
Glamis Pl. E1 45Yb 92
HP2: Hem H 1N 3
Glamis Rd. E1 45Yb 92
Glamis Way UB5: N'olt 37Ea 66
Glamorgan Cl. CR4: Mitc 69Nb 134
Glamorgan Ct. W7 43Ha 86
(off Copley Cl.)
Glamorgan Rd. KT1: Hamp W 66La 130
Glandford Way RM6: Chad H 29Xc 55
Glanfield Rd. BR3: Beck 70Bc 136
Glanleam Rd. HA7: Stan 21Ma 47
Glanmead CM15: Shenf 18Ae 41
Glanmor Rd. SL2: Slou 5M 81
Glanthams Cl. CM15: Shenf 19Be 41
Glanthams Rd. CM15: Shenf 19Be 41
GLANTY 63E 126
Glanty, The TW20: Egh 63D 126
Glanville Dr. RM11: Horn 32Pd 77
Glanville M. HA7: Stan 22Ja 46
Glanville Rd. BR2: Brom 69Kc 137
SW2 57Nb 112
Glanville Way KT19: Eps 84Na 173
Glasbrook Av. TW2: Whitt 60Ba 107
Glasbrook Rd. SE9 59Mc 115
Glaserton Rd. N16 31Ub 71
Glasford St. SW17 65Hb 133
Glasfryn Ct. HA2: Harr 33Fa 66
(off Roxeth Hill)
Glasfryn Ho. HA2: Harr 33Fa 66
(off Roxeth Hill)
Glasgow Ho. W9 40Db 69
(off Maida Va.)
Glasgow Rd. E13 40Kc 73
N18 22Xb 51
Glasgow Ter. SW1 7B 228 (50Lb 90)
Glasier Ct. E15 38Gc 73
Glaskin M. E9 37Ac 72
Glass Art Gallery, The 1H 231
Glass Building, The NW1 39Kb 70
(off Jamestown Rd.)
Glasse Cl. W13 45Ja 86
Glass Foundry Yd. E13 43Kc 93
(off Denmark St.)
Glasshill St. SE1 1C 230 (47Rb 91)
Glass Ho. WC2 3F 223
Glass House, The SE1 2H 231
Glasshouse Cl. UB8: Hil 43R 84
Glasshouse Flds. E1 45Zb 92
(not continuous)
Glasshouse St. W1 5C 222 (45Lb 90)
Glasshouse Wlk. SE11 7G 229 (50Nb 90)
Glasshouse Yd. EC1 6D 218 (42Sb 91)
Glasslyn Rd. N8 29Mb 50
Glassmill Ho. HP4: Berk 1A 2
(off Robertson Rd.)
Glassmill La. BR2: Brom 68Hc 137
Glass St. E2 42Xb 91
Glassworks Studios E2 3J 219
Glass Yd. SE18 48Qc 94
Glastonbury Av. IG8: Wfd G 24Mc 53
Glastonbury Cl. BR5: Orp 74Yc 161
Glastonbury Ct. SE14 52Yb 114
(off Farrow La.)
W13 46Ja 86
(off Talbot Rd.)
Glastonbury Ho. SE12 57Hc 115
(off Wantage Rd.)
SW1 7K 227
Glastonbury Pl. E1 44Yb 92
Glastonbury Rd. N9 18Wb 33
SM4: Mord 73Cb 155
Glastonbury St. NW6 36Bb 69
Glaston Ct. W5 46Ma 87
(off Grange Rd.)
Glaucus St. E3 43Dc 92
Glazbury Rd. W14 49Ab 88
Glazebrook Cl. SE21 61Tb 135
Glazebrook Rd. TW11: Tedd 66Ha 130
Gleave Cl. AL1: St A 1F 6
Glebe, The BR7: Chst 67Sc 138
KT4: Wor Pk 74Va 154
SE3 55Gc 115
SW16 63Mb 134
UB7: W Dray 49P 83
WD4: K Lan 1Q 12
WD25: Wat 5Z 13
Glebe Av. CR4: Mitc 68Gb 133
EN2: Enf 13Rb 33
HA3: Kenton 28Na 47
HA4: Ruis 37X 65
IG8: Wfd G 23Jc 53
UB10: Ick 34S 64
Glebe Cl. CR2: Sande 83Vb 177
GU18: Light 2A 166
HP3: Hem H 5N 3
KT23: Bookh 98Ca 191
UB10: Ick 35S 64
W4 50Ua 88
Glebe Cotts. TW13: Hanw 62Ca 129
(off Twickenham Rd.)
Glebe Ct. CR4: Mitc 69Hb 133
E3 41Dc 92
(off Rainhill Way)
EN8: Chesh 1Zb 20
HA7: Stan 22La 46
N13 20Qb 32
SE3 55Gc 115
TN13: S'oaks 98Kd 203
W5 46Ma 87
W7 45Fa 86
WD25: Wat 5Z 13
Glebe Cres. HA3: Kenton 27Na 47
NW4 28Ya 48
Glebe Farm Bus. Pk. BR2: Kes 81Mc 179
Glebefield, The TN13: Riv 95Hd 202
Glebe Gdns. CM13: Heron 24Fe 59
KT3: N Mald 73Ua 154
KT14: Byfl 86M 169
Glebe Ho. SE16 48Xb 91
(off Slippers Pl.)
Glebe Ho. Dr. BR2: Hayes 74Kc 159
Glebe Hyrst CR2: Sande 84Vb 177
SE19 63Ub 135
Glebe Knoll BR2: Brom 68Hc 137
Glebeland Gdns. TW17: Shep 72S 150
Glebelands DA1: Cray 56Hd 118
E10 33Dc 72
IG7: Chig 20Xc 37
KT8: W Mole 71Da 151
KT10: Clay 81Ha 172
Glebelands Av. E18 26Jc 53
IG2: Ilf 31Tc 74
Glebelands Cl. N12 25Fb 49
SE5 55Ub 113
Glebelands Rd. TW14: Felt 60W 106
Glebe La. EN5: Ark 15Wa 30
HA3: Kenton 28Na 47
TN13: S'oaks 99Kd 203
Glebe M. DA15: Sidc 58Vc 117
Glebe Path CR4: Mitc 69Hb 133
Glebe Pl. DA4: Hort K 70Sd 142
SW3 51Gb 111
Glebe Rd. BR1: Brom 67Jc 137
CR6: W'ham 89Zb 178
DA11: Grav'nd 10B 122
E8 38Vb 71
HA7: Stan 22La 46
KT21: Asht 90Ma 173
Glebe Rd. N3 25Eb 49
N8 28Pb 50
NW10 37Wa 68
RH1: Mers 96Kb 196
RM10: Dag 37Dd 76
RM13: Rain 41Ld 97
SL4: Old Win 7M 103
SM2: Cheam 81Ab 174
SM5: Cars 79Hb 155
SW13 54Wa 110
TW18: Staines 64K 127
TW20: Egh 64E 126
UB3: Hayes 46V 84
UB8: Uxb 40L 63
Glebe Side TW1: Twick 58Ha 108
Glebe Sq. CR4: Mitc 69Hb 133
Glebe St. W4 50Ua 88
Glebe Ter. W4 50Ua 88
Glebe Way BR4: W W'ck 75Ec 158
CR2: Sande 83Vb 177
DA8: Erith 51Gd 118
IG8: Wfd G 22Lc 53
RM11: Horn 31Nd 77
TW13: Hanw 62Ca 129
Gledhow Gdns. SW5 6A 226 (49Eb 89)
Gledhow Wood KT20: Kgswd 93Db 195
Gledstanes Rd. W14 50Ab 88
Gledwood Av. UB4: Hayes 43V 84
Gledwood Cres. UB4: Hayes 43V 84
Gledwood Dr. UB4: Hayes 43V 84
Gledwood Gdns. UB4: Hayes 43V 84
Gleed Av. WD23: B Hea 19Fa 28
Gleeson Dr. BR6: Chels 78Vc 161
Gleeson M. KT15: Add 77L 149
Glegg Pl. SW15 56Za 110
Glen, The BR2: Brom 68Gc 137
BR6: Farnb 76Pc 160
CR0: C'don 76Zb 158
EN2: Enf 14Rb 33
HA5: Eastc 29X 45
HA5: Pinn 31Aa 65
HA6: Nwood 24T 44
HA9: Wemb 35Na 67
KT15: Add 78H 149
RH1: Redh 8P 207
RM13: Rain 42Ld 97
SL3: L'ly 9N 81
SL5: S'hill 10B 124
SS17: Stan H 1P 101
UB2: S'hall 50Ba 85
Glenaffric Av. E14 49Ec 92
Glen Albyn Rd. SW19 61Za 132
Glenallan Ho. W14 49Bb 89
(off North End Cres.)
Glenalla Rd. HA4: Ruis 31V 64
Glenalmond Ho. TW15: Ashf 62N 127
Glenalmond Rd. HA3: Kenton 28Na 47
Glenalvon Way SE18 49Nc 94
Glena Mt. SM1: Sutt 77Eb 155
Glenarm Rd. E5 35Yb 72
Glen Av. TW15: Ashf 63Q 128
Glenavon Cl. KT10: Clay 79Ja 152
Glenavon Ct. KT4: Wor Pk 75Xa 154
Glenavon Gdns. SL3: L'ly 9N 81
Glenavon Lodge BR3: Beck 66Cc 136
Glenavon Rd. E15 38Gc 73
Glenbarr Cl. SE9 55Rc 116
Glenbow Ct. AL4: St A 2H 7
Glenbow Rd. BR1: Brom 65Gc 137
Glenbrook Nth. EN2: Enf 14Pb 32
Glenbrook Rd. NW6 36Cb 69
Glenbrook Sth. EN2: Enf 14Pb 32
Glenbuck Ct. KT6: Surb 72Na 153
Glenbuck Rd. KT6: Surb 72Ma 153
Glenburnie Rd. SW17 62Hb 133
Glencairn Dr. W5 42La 86
Glencairne Cl. E16 43Mc 93
Glencairn Rd. SW16 67Nb 134
Glencar Ct. SE19 65Rb 135
Glen Chess WD3: Loud 14L 25
Glen Cl. KT20: Kgswd 95Ab 194
TW17: Shep 70Q 128
Glencoe Av. IG2: Ilf 31Tc 74
Glencoe Dr. RM10: Dag 35Cd 76
Glencoe Mans. SW9 52Qb 112
(off Mowll St.)
Glencoe Rd. KT13: Weyb 76Q 150
UB4: Yead 43Z 85
WD23: Bush 16Ca 27
Glencorse Grn. WD19: Wat 21Z 45
Glen Ct. DA15: Sidc 63Wc 139
GU21: Wok 1L 187
KT14: Byfl 83M 169
KT15: Add 78H 149
TW18: Staines 66H 127
(off Riverside Rd.)
Glen Cres. IG8: Wfd G 23Kc 53
Glendale BR8: Swan 70Hd 140
HP1: Hem H 2K 3
Glendale Av. HA8: Edg 21Pa 47
N22 24Qb 50
RM6: Chad H 31Yc 75
Glendale Cl. CM15: Shenf 18Ae 41
GU21: Wok 10N 167
SE9 55Qc 116
Glendale Dr. SW19 64Bb 133
Glendale Gdns. HA9: Wemb 32Ma 67
Glendale M. BR3: Beck 67Dc 136
Glendale Ri. CR8: Kenley 87Rb 177
Glendale Rd. DA8: Erith 49Ed 96
DA11: Nflt 3A 144
Glendale Wlk. EN8: Chesh 2Ac 20
Glendale Way SE28 45Yc 95
Glendall St. SW9 56Pb 112
Glendarvon St. SW15 55Za 110
Glendean Ct. EN3: Enf L 8Ac 20
Glendene Av. KT24: E Hor 98U 190
Glendevon Cl. HA8: Edg 20Ra 29
Glendish Rd. N17 25Xb 51
Glendor Gdns. NW7 21Ta 47
Glendower Cres. BR6: St M Cry 72Wc 161
Glendower Gdns. SW14 55Ta 109
Glendower Pl. SW7 5B 226 (49Fb 89)
Glendower Rd. E4 18Fc 35
SW14 55Ta 109
Glendown Ho. E8 36Wb 71
Glendown Rd. SE2 50Wc 95
Glendun Ct. W3 45Ua 88
Glen Dunlop Ho., The
TN13: S'oaks 94Kd 203
Glendun Rd. W3 45Ua 88
Gleneagle M. SW16 64Mb 134
Gleneagle Rd. SW16 64Mb 134
Gleneagles HA7: Stan 24Ka 46
W13 43Ka 86
(off Malvern Way)

Gleneagles Cl. BR6: Orp ... 74Tc 160
RM3: Hrld W ... 24Pd 57
SE16 ... 50Xb 91
TW19: Stanw ... 58L 105
WD19: Wat ... 21Z 45
Gleneagles Grn. BR6: Orp ... 74Tc 160
Gleneagles Twr. *UB1: S'hall* ... *44Ea 86*
(off Fleming Rd.)
Gleneldon M. SW16 ... 63Nb 134
Gleneldon Rd. SW16 ... 63Nb 134
Glenelg Rd. SW2 ... 57Nb 112
Glenesk Rd. SE9 ... 55Qc 116
Glenfarg Rd. SE6 ... 60Ec 114
Glenferrie Rd. AL1: St A ... 2E 6
Glenfield Cres. HA4: Ruis ... 31T 64
Glenfield Rd. SM7: Bans ... 87Db 175
SW12 ... 60Lb 112
TW15: Ashf ... 65R 128
W13 ... 47Ka 86
Glenfields SL2: Stoke P ... 9K 61
Glenfield Ter. W13 ... 47Ka 86
Glenfinlas Way SE5 ... 52Rb 113
Glenforth St. SE10 ... 50Hc 93
Glengall Bus. Cen. SE15 ... 51Vb 113
Glengall Gro. E14 ... 48Dc 92
Glengall Pas. *NW6* ... *39Cb 69*
(off Priory Pk. Rd.)
Glengall Pl. AL1: St A ... 5C 6
Glengall Rd. DA7: Bex ... 55Ad 117
HA8: Edg ... 20Ra 29
IG8: Wfd G ... 23Jc 53
NW6 ... 39Bb 69
SE15 ... 50Vb 91
Glengall Ter. SE15 ... 51Vb 113
Glen Gdns. CR0: Wadd ... 76Qb 156
Glengariff Mans. *SW9* ... *52Qb 112*
(off Sth. Island Pl.)
Glengarnock Av. E14 ... 49Ec 92
Glengarry Rd. SE22 ... 57Ub 113
Glenham Dr. IG2: Ilf ... 29Rc 54
Glenhaven Av. WD6: Bore ... 13Qa 29
Glenhaven Dr. TW19: Stanw M ... 57J 105
Glenhead Cl. SE9 ... 55Rc 116
Glenheadon Cl. KT22: Lea ... 95Ma 193
Glenheadon Ri. KT22: Lea ... 95Ma 193
Glenhill Cl. N3 ... 26Cb 49
Glen Ho. *E16* ... *46Qc 94*
(off Storey St.)
Glenhouse Rd. SE9 ... 57Qc 116
Glenhurst BR3: Beck ... 67Ec 136
Glenhurst Av. DA5: Bexl ... 60Bd 117
HA4: Ruis ... 31S 64
NW5 ... 35Jb 70
Glenhurst Ct. SE19 ... 64Vb 135
Glenhurst Ri. SE19 ... 66Sb 135
Glenhurst Rd. N12 ... 22Fb 49
TW8: Bford ... 51La 108
Glenilla Rd. NW3 ... 37Gb 69
Glenister Ho. *UB3: Hayes* ... *46X 85*
(off Avondale Dr.)
Glenister Pk. Rd. SW16 ... 66Mb 134
Glenister Rd. SE10 ... 50Hc 93
Glenister St. E16 ... 46Qc 94
Glenkerry Ho. *E14* ... *44Ec 92*
(off Burcham St.)
Glenlea Rd. SE9 ... 57Pc 116
Glenloch Rd. EN3: Enf H ... 12Yb 34
NW3 ... 37Gb 69
Glen Luce EN8: Chesh ... 3Zb 20
Glenluce Rd. SE3 ... 51Jc 115
Glenlyn Av. AL1: St A ... 3F 6
Glenlyon Rd. SE9 ... 57Qc 116
Glenmead IG9: Buck H ... 18Lc 35
Glenmere Av. NW7 ... 24Wa 48
Glenmere Row SE12 ... 58Jc 115
Glen M. E17 ... 29Bc 52
Glenmill TW12: Hamp ... 64Ba 129
Glenmore Cl. KT15: Add ... 76K 149
Glenmore Gdns. WD5: Ab L ... 4W 12
Glenmore Lawns W13 ... 44Ja 86
Glenmore Lodge BR3: Beck ... 67Dc 136
Glenmore Pde. HA0: Wemb ... 39Na 67
Glenmore Rd. DA16: Well ... 52Vc 117
NW3 ... 37Gb 69
Glenmore Way IG11: Bark ... 40Wc 75
Glenmount Path SE18 ... 50Sc 94
Glenn Av. CR8: Purl ... 83Rb 177
Glennie Ct. SE22 ... 60Wb 113
Glennie Ho. *SE10* ... *53Ec 114*
(off Blackheath Hill)
Glennie Rd. SE27 ... 62Qb 134
Glenny Rd. IG11: Bark ... 37Sc 74
Glenorchy Cl. UB4: Yead ... 43Aa 85
Glenpark Ct. W13 ... 45Ja 86
Glenparke Rd. E7 ... 37Kc 73
Glenridding NW1 ... 2C 216
Glen Ri. IG8: Wfd G ... 23Kc 53
Glen Rd. E13 ... 42Lc 93
E17 ... 29Bc 52
KT9: Chess ... 77Pa 153
Glen Rd. End SM6: Wall ... 81Kb 176
Glenrosa Gdns. DA12: Grav'nd ... 4H 145
Glenrosa St. SW6 ... 54Eb 111
Glenrose Ct. DA14: Sidc ... 64Xc 139
SE1 ... *3H 231*
(off Long La.)
Glenroy St. W12 ... 44Ya 88
Glensdale Rd. SE4 ... 55Bc 114
Glenshaw Mans. *SW9* ... *52Qb 112*
(off Brixton Rd.)
Glenshee Cl. HA6: Nwood ... 23S 44
Glenshiel Rd. SE9 ... 57Qc 116
Glenside IG7: Chig ... 23Rc 54
Glenside Cl. CR8: Kenley ... 87Tb 177
Glenston M. W1 ... 2F 221 (44Hb 89)
Glentanner Way SW17 ... 62Fb 133
Glen Ter. *E14* ... *47Ec 92*
(off Manchester Rd.)
Glentham Gdns. SW13 ... 51Xa 110
Glentham Rd. SW13 ... 51Wa 110
Glenthorne Av. CR0: C'don ... 74Xb 157
Glenthorne Cl. SM3: Sutt ... 74Cb 155
UB10: Hil ... 41Q 84
Glenthorne Gdns. IG6: Ilf ... 27Qc 54
SM3: Sutt ... 74Cb 155
Glenthorne M. W6 ... 49Xa 88
Glenthorne Rd. E17 ... 29Ac 52
KT1: King T ... 70Pa 131
N11 ... 22Hb 49
W6 ... 49Xa 88
Glenthorpe Av. SW15 ... 56Wa 110
Glenthorpe Rd. SM4: Mord ... 71Za 154
Glenton Cl. RM1: Rom ... 24Gd 56
Glenton Rd. SE13 ... 56Gc 115
Glenton Way RM1: Rom ... 24Gd 56
Glentrammon Av. BR6: Chels ... 79Vc 161
Glentrammon Cl. BR6: Chels ... 78Vc 161
Glentrammon Gdns. BR6: Chels ... 79Vc 161
Glentrammon Rd. BR6: Chels ... 79Vc 161
Glentworth Pl. SL1: Slou ... 6G 80
Glentworth St. NW1 ... 6G 215 (42Hb 89)
Glenure Rd. SE9 ... 57Qc 116
Glenvern Ct. *TW7: Isle* ... *54Ja 108*
(off White Lodge Cl.)
Glen Vw. DA12: Grav'nd ... 10E 122
Glenview SE2 ... 51Zc 117
Glenview Gdns. HP1: Hem H ... 2K 3
Glenview Rd. BR1: Brom ... 68Mc 137
HP1: Hem H ... 2K 3
Glenville Av. EN2: Enf ... 10Sb 19
Glenville Gro. SE8 ... 52Bc 114
Glenville M. SW18 ... 59Db 111
Glenville M. Ind. Est. SW18 ... 59Cb 111
Glenville Rd. KT2: King T ... 67Qa 131
Glen Wlk. TW7: Isle ... 57Fa 108
(not continuous)
Glen Way WD17: Wat ... 10U 12
Glenwood Av. NW9 ... 32Ua 68
RM13: Rain ... 42Jd 96
Glenwood Cl. HA1: Harr ... 29Ha 46
Glenwood Ct. DA14: Sidc ... 63Wc 139
E18 ... 27Jc 53
Glenwood Dr. RM2: Rom ... 29Jd 56
Glenwood Gdns. IG2: Ilf ... 29Qc 54
Glenwood Gro. NW9 ... 32Sa 67
Glenwood Rd. KT17: Ewe ... 79Wa 154
N15 ... 29Rb 51
NW7 ... 20Ua 30
SE6 ... 60Bc 114
TW3: Houn ... 55Fa 108
Glenwood Way CR0: C'don ... 72Zb 158
Glenworth Av. E14 ... 49Fc 93
Glevum Cl. AL3: St A ... 4M 5
Gliddon Dr. E5 ... 35Xb 71
Gliddon Rd. W14 ... 49Ab 88
Glimpsing Grn. DA18: Erith ... 48Ad 95
Glisson Rd. UB10: Hil ... 40Q 64
Gload Cres. BR5: Orp ... 75Zc 161
Global App. E3 ... 40Ec 72
Globe Ho. WD3: Chor ... 14E 24
Globe Ind. Est. RM17: Grays ... 50Ee 99
Globe Pond Rd. SE16 ... 46Ac 92
Globe Rd. E1 ... 41Yb 92
E2 ... 41Yb 92
E15 ... 36Hc 73
IG8: Wfd G ... 23Lc 53
RM11: Horn ... 30Jd 56
Globe Rope Wlk. *E14* ... *49Dc 92*
(off E. Ferry Rd.)
Globe St. SE1 ... 3F 231 (48Tb 91)
Globe Ter. E2 ... 41Yb 92
GLOBE TOWN ... 41Zb 92
Globe Town Mkt. E2 ... 41Zb 92
Globe Vw. EC4 ... 4D 224
Globe Wharf SE16 ... 45Zb 92
Globe Yd. W1 ... 3K 221
Glossop Ho. *RM3: Rom* ... *22Nd 57*
(off Lindfield Rd.)
Glossop Rd. CR2: Sande ... 81Tb 177
Gloster Ct. *GU21: Wok* ... *88B 168*
(off Walton Rd.)
Gloster Ridley Ct. *E14* ... *44Bc 92*
(off St Anne's Row)
Gloster Rd. GU22: Wok ... 92C 188
KT3: N Mald ... 70Ua 132
Gloucester *W14* ... *49Bb 89*
(off Mornington Av.)
Gloucester Arc. SW7 ... 5A 226 (49Eb 89)
Gloucester Av. DA15: Sidc ... 61Uc 138
DA16: Well ... 56Vc 117
EN8: Walt C ... 5Ac 20
NW1 ... 38Jb 70
RM11: Horn ... 28Qd 57
RM16: Grays ... 47Ee 99
RM18: E Til ... 10L 101
SL1: Slou ... 3G 80
Gloucester Cir. SE10 ... 52Ec 114
Gloucester Cl. KT7: T Ditt ... 74Ja 152
NW10 ... 38Ta 67
Gloucester Ct. CR4: Mitc ... 71Nb 156
EC3 ... 5J 225 (45Ub 91)
HA1: Harr ... 27Ga 46
NW11 ... *31Bb 69*
(off Golders Grn. Rd.)
RH1: Redh ... *5P 207*
(off Gloucester Rd.)
RM18: Tilb ... 4B 122
SE1 ... 7K 231
(Rolls Rd.)
SE1 ... 3E 230
(Swan St.)
SE22 ... 60Wb 113
TW9: Kew ... 52Qa 109
UB9: Den ... 31J 63
W7 ... *43Ha 86*
(off Copley Cl.)
WD18: Wat ... 14V 26
Gloucester Cres. NW1 ... 39Kb 70
TW18: Staines ... 65M 127
Gloucester Dr. N4 ... 33Rb 71
NW11 ... 28Cb 49
TW18: Staines ... 62E 126
Gloucester Gdns. EN4: Cockf ... 14Jb 32
IG1: Ilf ... 31Nc 74
NW11 ... 31Bb 69
SM1: Sutt ... 75Db 155
W2 ... 44Eb 89
Gloucester Ga. NW1 ... 1K 215 (40Kb 70)
(not continuous)
Gloucester Ga. Bri. NW1 ... 1K 215
Gloucester Ga. M.
NW1 ... 1K 215 (40Kb 70)
Gloucester Gro. HA8: Edg ... 25Ta 47
Gloucester Ho. *E16* ... *46Jc 93*
(off Gatcombe Rd.)
NW6 ... *40Cb 69*
(off Cambridge Rd.)
SW9 ... 52Qb 112
TW10: Rich ... 57Qa 109
WD6: Bore ... 12Qa 29
Gloucester M. E10 ... 31Cc 72
W2 ... 3A 220 (44Eb 89)
Gloucester M. W.
W2 ... 3A 220 (44Eb 89)
Gloucester Pde. DA15: Sidc ... 57Wc 117
UB3: Harl ... 48S 84
Gloucester Pk. Apartments
SW7 ... 5A 226 (49Eb 89)
Gloucester Pl. NW1 ... 5F 215 (42Hb 89)
SL4: Wind ... 4H 103
W1 ... 7G 215 (43Hb 89)
Gloucester Pl. M. W1 ... 1G 221 (43Hb 89)
Gloucester Rd. CM15: Pil H ... 15Xd 40
CR0: C'don ... 74Tb 157
DA1: Dart ... 59Kd 119
DA12: Grav'nd ... 3E 144
DA17: Belv ... 50Bd 95
E10 ... 31Cc 72
E11 ... 29Kc 53
E12 ... 34Pc 74
E17 ... 26Zb 52
EN2: Enf ... 10Sb 19
EN5: New Bar ... 15Db 31
HA1: Harr ... 29Da 45
KT1: King T ... 68Qa 131
N17 ... 26Tb 51
N18 ... 22Vb 51
RH1: Redh ... 5P 207
RM1: Rom ... 30Gd 56
SW7 ... 3A 226 (48Eb 89)
TW2: Twick ... 60Ea 108
TW4: Houn ... 56Aa 107
TW9: Kew ... 52Qa 109
TW11: Tedd ... 64Ga 130
TW12: Hamp ... 66Da 129
TW13: Felt ... 60Y 107
W3 ... 47Sa 87
W5 ... 47La 86
Gloucester Sq. E2 ... 39Wb 71
GU21: Wok ... 89A 168
W2 ... 3C 220 (44Fb 89)
(not continuous)
Gloucester St. SW1 ... 7B 228 (50Lb 90)
Gloucester Ter. *N14* ... *18Mb 32*
(off Crown La.)
W2 ... 2A 220 (44Db 89)
WD3: Crox G ... 13R 26
Gloucester Wlk. GU21: Wok ... 89A 168
W8 ... 47Cb 89
Gloucester Way EC1 ... 4A 218 (41Qb 90)
Glover Cl. SE2 ... 49Yc 95
Glover Dr. N18 ... 23Yb 52
Glover Ho. *NW6* ... *38Eb 69*
(off Harben Rd.)
SE15 ... 56Xb 113
Glover Rd. HA5: Pinn ... 30Z 45
Glovers Cl. TN16: Big H ... 88Kc 179
Glovers Gro. HA4: Ruis ... 31R 64
Glover's Rd. RH2: Reig ... 7K 207
Gloxinia Rd. DA13: Sflt ... 65De 143
Gloxinia Wlk. TW12: Hamp ... 65Ca 129
Glycena Rd. SW11 ... 55Hb 111
Glyn Av. EN4: E Barn ... 14Fb 31
Glyn Cl. KT17: Ewe ... 81Wa 174
SE25 ... 68Ub 135
Glyn Ct. HA7: Stan ... 23Ka 46
SW16 ... 62Qb 134
Glyndale Grange SM2: Sutt ... 79Db 155
Glyn Davies Cl. TN13: Dun G ... 92Gd 202
Glyndebourne Ct. *UB5: N'olt* ... *41Y 85*
(off Canberra Dr.)
Glyndebourne Pk. BR6: Farnb ... 75Rc 160
Glynde M. SW3 ... 4E 226
Glynde Reach WC1 ... 4G 217
Glynde Rd. DA7: Bex ... 55Zc 117
Glynde St. SE4 ... 58Bc 114
Glyndon Rd. SE18 ... 49Sc 94
(not continuous)
Glyn Dr. DA14: Sidc ... 63Xc 139
Glynfield Rd. NW10 ... 38Ua 68
Glyn Mans. *W14* ... *49Ab 88*
(off Hammersmith Rd.)
Glynne Rd. N22 ... 26Qb 50
Glyn Rd. E5 ... 34Zb 72
EN3: Pond E ... 14Yb 34
KT4: Wor Pk ... 75Za 154
Glyn St. SE11 ... 50Pb 90
Glynswood SL9: Chal P ... 24B 42
Glynswood Pl. HA6: Nwood ... 24R 44
Glynwood Ct. SE23 ... 61Yb 136
Goals Soccer Cen.
Bexleyheath ... 55Bd 117
Dartford ... 60Qd 119
Eltham ... 58Lc 115
Hayes ... 46Y 85
Heathrow ... 49S 84
Isleworth ... 51Ha 108
Ruislip ... 36Z 65
Sutton ... 76Za 154
Walthamstow ... 24Cc 52
Goater's All. *SW6* ... *52Bb 111*
(off Dawes Rd.)
Goat Ho. Bri. SE25 ... 69Wb 135
Goat La. EN1: Enf ... 10Vb 19
Goat Rd. CR4: Cars, Mitc ... 73Hb 155
Goatsfield Rd. TN16: Tats ... 92Lc 199
Goatswood La.
RM4: N'side, Noak H ... 17Kd 39
Goat Wharf TW8: Bford ... 51Na 109
Go Bananas Playbarn ... 75Zd 165
Gobions Av. RM5: Col R ... 24Fd 56
Gobions Way EN6: Pot B ... 10K 9
Godalming Av. SM6: Wall ... 78Nb 156
Godalming Rd. E14 ... 43Dc 92
Godbold Rd. E15 ... 42Gc 93
Goddard Cl. TW17: Shep ... 69P 127
Goddard Ct. HA3: Kenton ... 26Ja 46
Goddard Dr. WD23: Bush ... 15Ea 28
Goddard Ho. SE11 ... 6B 230
Goddard Pl. N19 ... 34Lb 70
Goddard Rd. BR3: Beck ... 70Zb 136
RM16: Grays ... 46Ce 99
Goddards Way IG1: Ilf ... 32Tc 74
Goddarts Ho. E17 ... 27Cc 52
GODDEN GREEN ... 96Qd 203
GODDINGTON ... 76Yc 161
Goddington Chase
BR6: Chels ... 77Xc 161
Goddington La. BR6: Chels ... 76Wc 161
Godfree Ct. SE1 ... 1F 231
Godfrey Av. TW2: Whitt ... 59Fa 108
UB5: N'olt ... 39Aa 65
Godfrey Hill SE18 ... 49Nc 94
Godfrey Ho. EC1 ... 4F 219
Godfrey Pl. E2 ... 4K 219
Godfrey Rd. SE18 ... 49Pc 94
Godfrey St. E15 ... 40Ec 72
SW3 ... 7E 226 (50Gb 89)
Godfrey Way TW4: Houn ... 59Aa 107
Goding St. SE11 ... 7G 229 (50Pb 90)
Godley Cl. SE14 ... 53Yb 114
Godley Rd. KT14: Byfl ... 86P 169
SW18 ... 60Fb 111
Godliman St. EC4 ... 3D 224 (44Rb 91)
Godman Rd. RM16: Grays ... 8C 100
SE15 ... 54Xb 113
Godolphin Cl. N13 ... 23Rb 51
SM2: Cheam ... 83Bb 175
Godolphin Ho. *NW3* ... *38Gb 69*
(off Fellows Rd.)
SL4: Eton ... *1H 103*
(off Common La.)
Godolphin Pl. W3 ... 45Ta 87
Godolphin Rd. KT13: Weyb ... 79T 150
SL1: Slou ... 5H 81
W12 ... 46Xa 88
(not continuous)
Godric Cres. CR0: New Ad ... 82Fc 179
Godson Rd. CR0: Wadd ... 76Qb 156
Godson St. N1 ... 1K 217 (40Qb 70)
Godson Yd. *W9* ... *41Cb 89*
(off Kilburn Pk. Rd.)
GODSTONE ... 3A 210
Godstone By-Pass RH9: G'stone ... 1A 210
Godstone Farm & Playbarn ... 4A 210
Godstone Golf Course ... 2C 210
Godstone Grn. RH9: G'stone ... 3P 209
Godstone Hill RH9: G'stone ... 99Xb 197
Godstone Ho. SE1 ... 3G 231
GODSTONE INTERCHANGE ... 1A 210
Godstone Mt. CR8: Purl ... 84Rb 177
Godstone Rd. CR3: Cat'm ... 96Wb 197
CR3: W'ham, Whyt ... 84Rb 177
CR8: Purl, Kenley ... 84Rb 177
RH1: Blet ... 5K 209
RH8: Oxt ... 3E 210
SM1: Sutt ... 77Eb 155
TW1: Twick ... 58Ka 108
Godstone Vineyards ... 100Yb 198
Godstow Rd. SE2 ... 47Xc 95
Godwin Cl. E4 ... 10Ec 20
KT19: Ewe ... 79Sa 153
N1 ... 1E 218 (40Sb 71)
Godwin Ct. NW1 ... 1C 216
Godwin Ho. E2 ... 1K 219
NW6 ... *40Db 69*
(off Tollgate Gdns., not continuous)
Godwin Rd. BR2: Brom ... 69Lc 137
E7 ... 35Kc 73
Goffers Rd. SE3 ... 53Gc 115
Goffs Cres. EN7: G Oak ... 1Sb 19
Goff's La. EN7: Chesh, G Oak ... 1Sb 19
GOFF'S OAK ... 1Sb 19
Goffs Oak Av. EN7: G Oak ... 1Rb 19
Goffs Rd. TW15: Ashf ... 65T 128
Goff's Sports & Arts Cen. ... 1Wb 19
Gogmore Farm Cl. KT16: Chert ... 73H 149
Gogmore La. KT16: Chert ... 73J 149
Goidel Cl. SM6: Bedd ... 77Mb 156
Golborne Gdns. W10 ... 42Bb 88
(not continuous)
Golborne M. W10 ... 43Ab 88
Golborne Rd. W10 ... 43Ab 88
Goldace RM17: Grays ... 51Be 121
Golda Cl. EN5: Barn ... 16Za 30
Golda Ct. N3 ... 26Bb 49
Goldbeaters Gro. HA8: Edg ... 23Ua 48
Goldbeaters Ho. *W1* ... *3E 222*
(off Manette St.)
Goldcliff Cl. SM4: Mord ... 73Cb 155
Goldcrest Cl. E16 ... 43Mc 93
SE28 ... 45Yc 95
Goldcrest M. W5 ... 43Ma 87
Goldcrest Way CR0: New Ad ... 81Fc 179
CR8: Purl ... 82Mb 176
WD23: Bush ... 18Ea 28
Goldcroft HP3: Hem H ... 4A 4
Golden Bus. Pk. E10 ... 32Ac 72
Golden Ct. EN4: E Barn ... 14Gb 31
TW7: Isle ... 54Fa 108
TW9: Rich ... 57Ma 109
Golden Cres. UB3: Hayes ... 46V 84
Golden Cross M. *W11* ... *44Bb 89*
(off Portobello Rd.)
Golden Hinde ... 6F 225 (46Tb 91)
Golden Hind Pl. *SE8* ... *49Bc 92*
(off Grove St.)
Golden Jubilee Bridges ... 7H 223
Golden La. EC1 ... 5D 218 (42Sb 91)
Golden La. Campus EC1 ... 6E 218
Golden La. Est. EC1 ... 6D 218 (42Sb 91)
Golden Lane Leisure Cen. ... 6D 218
Golden Mnr. W7 ... 45Ga 86
Golden M. SE20 ... 67Yb 136
Golden Oak Cl. SL2: Farn C ... 7G 60
Golden Pde. *E17* ... *27Ec 52*
(off Wood St.)
Golden Plover Cl. E16 ... 44Jc 93
Golden Sq. W1 ... 4C 222 (45Lb 90)
Golden Yd. *NW3* ... *35Eb 69*
(off Holly Mt.)
Golders Cl. HA8: Edg ... 22Ra 47
Golders Ct. NW11 ... 31Bb 69
Golders Gdns. NW11 ... 31Ab 68
GOLDERS GREEN ... 30Ab 48
Golders Grn. Crematorium
NW11 ... 31Cb 69
Golders Grn. Cres. NW11 ... 31Bb 69
Golders Grn. Rd. NW11 ... 30Ab 48
Golderslea NW11 ... 32Cb 69
Golders Mnr. Dr. NW11 ... 30Za 48
Golders Pk. Cl. NW11 ... 32Cb 69
Golders Ri. NW4 ... 29Za 48
Golders Way NW11 ... 31Bb 69
Golderton *NW4* ... *28Xa 48*
(off Prince of Wales Cl.)
Goldfinch Cl. BR6: Chels ... 78Wc 161
Goldfinch Ct. *E3* ... *40Cc 72*
(off Four Seasons Cl.)
Goldfinch Rd. CR2: Sels ... 82Ac 178
SE28 ... 48Tc 94
Goldfinch Way WD6: Bore ... 14Qa 29
Goldfort Wlk. GU21: Knap ... 8J 167
Goldhawk Ind. Est. W6 ... 48Xa 88
Goldhawk M. W12 ... 47Xa 88
Goldhawk Rd. W6 ... 49Va 88
W12 ... 48Wa 88
Goldhaze Cl. IG8: Wfd G ... 24Lc 53
Gold Hill HA8: Edg ... 23Ta 47
Gold Hill E. SL9: Chal P ... 25A 42
Goldhurst Mans. *NW6* ... *37Eb 69*
(off Goldhurst Ter.)
Goldhurst Ter. NW6 ... 38Db 69
Goldie Ho. N19 ... 31Mb 70
Goldie Leigh Hospital SE2 ... 52Xc 117
Golding Cl. KT9: Chess ... 79La 152
Golding Ct. IG1: Ilf ... 34Qc 74
Goldingham Av. IG10: Lough ... 12Sc 36
Golding Rd. TN13: S'oaks ... 94Ld 203
Goldings, The GU21: Wok ... 8K 167
Goldings Hill IG10: Lough ... 8Pc 22
Goldings Ri. IG10: Lough ... 11Qc 36
Goldings Rd. IG10: Lough ... 11Qc 36
Golding St. E1 ... 44Wb 91
Golding Ter. *E1* ... *44Wb 91*
(off Rope Wlk. Gdns.)
SW11 ... 54Jb 112
Goldington Bldgs. NW1 ... 1D 216
Goldington Cres. NW1 ... 1D 216 (40Mb 70)
Goldington St. NW1 ... 1D 216 (40Mb 70)
Gold La. HA8: Edg ... 23Ta 47
Goldman Cl. E2 ... 42Wb 91
Goldmark Ho. SE3 ... 55Kc 115
Goldney Rd. W9 ... 42Cb 89
Goldrill Dr. N11 ... 19Jb 32
Goldrings Rd. KT22: Oxs ... 85Da 171
Goldsboro' Rd. SW8 ... 53Mb 112
Goldsborough Cres. E4 ... 19Dc 34
Goldsborough Ho. *E14* ... *50Dc 92*
(off St Davids Sq.)
Goldsdown Cl. EN3: Enf H ... 12Ac 34
Goldsdown Rd. EN3: Enf H ... 12Zb 34
Goldsel Rd. BR8: Crock, Swan ... 71Fd 162
Goldsmere Ct. RM11: Horn ... 32Nd 77
Goldsmid St. SE18 ... 50Uc 94
Goldsmith Av. E12 ... 37Nc 74
NW9 ... 29Ua 48
RM7: Rush G ... 31Cd 76
W3 ... 45Ta 87
Goldsmith Cl. HA2: Harr ... 32Ca 65
TN16: Big H ... 89Nc 180
Goldsmith Ct. HA8: Edg ... 21Pa 47
WC2 ... 2G 223
Goldsmith Est. SE15 ... 53Wb 113
Goldsmith La. NW9 ... 28Ra 47
Goldsmith Rd. E10 ... 32Cc 72
E17 ... 26Zb 52
N11 ... 22Hb 49
SE15 ... 53Wb 113
W3 ... 46Ta 87
Goldsmiths RM17: Grays ... 51Be 121
Goldsmiths Av. SS17: Corr, Stan H ... 1P 101
Goldsmith's Bldgs. W3 ... 46Ta 87
Goldsmiths Cl. GU21: Wok ... 10N 167
W3 ... 46Ta 87
Goldsmiths College ... 53Ac 114
Goldsmith's Pl. *NW6* ... *39Db 69*
(off Springfield La.)
Goldsmith's Row E2 ... 40Wb 71
Goldsmith's Sq. E2 ... 40Wb 71
Goldsmith St. EC2 ... 2E 224 (44Sb 91)
Goldsmith Way AL3: St A ... 1A 6
Goldstone Farm Vw. KT23: Bookh ... 99Ca 191
GOLD STREET ... 10G 144
Gold St. DA12: Sole S ... 10F 144
GOLDSWORTH ... 10P 167
Goldsworth Orchard GU21: Wok ... 10L 167
GOLDSWORTH PARK ... 9L 167
Goldsworth Pk. Cen., The
GU21: Wok ... 9L 167
Goldsworth Pk. Trad. Est.
GU21: Wok ... 8L 167
Goldsworth Rd. GU21: Wok ... 10N 167
Goldsworth Rd. Ind. Est.
GU21: Wok ... 9P 167
Goldsworthy Gdns. SE16 ... 50Yb 92
Goldsworthy Way SL1: Slou ... 4A 80
Goldthorpe *NW1* ... *39Lb 70*
(off Camden St.)
Goldvale Ho. *GU21: Wok* ... *89A 168*
(off Church St. W.)
Goldwell Ho. *SE22* ... *55Ub 113*
(off Quorn Rd.)
Goldwell Rd. CR7: Thor H ... 70Pb 134
Goldwin Cl. SE14 ... 53Yb 114
Goldwing Cl. E16 ... 44Jc 93
Gole Rd. GU24: Pirb ... 3A 186
Golf Cl. CR7: Thor H ... 67Qb 134
GU22: Pyr ... 86G 168
HA7: Stan ... 24La 46
WD23: Bush ... 13Z 27
Golf Club Cotts. SL5: S'dale ... 4G 146
Golf Club Dr. KT2: King T ... 66Ta 131
Golf Club Rd. AL9: Brk P ... 8J 9
GU22: Wok ... 2L 187
KT13: Weyb ... 81R 170
Golfe Rd. IG1: Ilf ... 34Tc 74
Golf House Rd. RH8: Limp ... 1N 211
Golf Links Av. DA11: Grav'nd ... 4D 144
Golf Ride EN2: Crew H ... 7Qb 18
Golf Rd. BR1: Brom ... 69Qc 138
CR8: Kenley ... 90Tb 177
W5 ... 44Pa 87
Golf Side SM2: Cheam ... 83Ab 174
TW2: Twick ... 62Fa 130
Golfside Cl. KT3: N Mald ... 68Ua 132
N20 ... 20Gb 31
Gollogly Ter. SE7 ... 50Lc 93
Gombards AL3: St A ... 1B 6
Gombard's All. AL3: St A ... 2B 6
Gomer Gdns. TW11: Tedd ... 65Ja 130
Gomer Pl. TW11: Tedd ... 65Ja 130
Gomm Rd. SE16 ... 48Yb 92
Gomshall Av. SM6: Wall ... 78Nb 156
Gomshall Gdns. CR8: Kenley ... 87Ub 177
Gomshall Rd. SM2: Cheam ... 82Ya 174
Gondar Gdns. NW6 ... 36Bb 69
Gonnerston AL3: St A ... 1P 5
Gonson St. SE8 ... 51Dc 114
Gonston Cl. SW19 ... 61Ab 132
Gonville Av. WD3: Crox G ... 16R 26
Gonville Cres. UB5: N'olt ... 37Da 65
Gonville Rd. CR7: Thor H ... 71Pb 156
Gonville St. SW6 ... 55Ab 110
Gooch Ho. E5 ... 34Xb 71
EC1 ... 7K 217
KT13: Weyb ... 78S 150
Goodacre Cl. EN6: Pot B ... 4Db 17
Goodacre Ct. EN6: Pot B ... 4Db 17
Goodall Ho. SE4 ... 56Zb 114
Goodall Rd. E11 ... 34Ec 72
Goodbury Rd. TN15: Knat ... 85Rd 183
Gooden Ct. HA1: Harr ... 34Ga 66
Goodenough Cl. CR5: Coul ... 92Qb 196
Goodenough Rd. SW19 ... 66Bb 133
Goodenough Way CR5: Coul ... 92Pb 196
Gooderham Ho. RM16: Grays ... 7D 100
Goodey Rd. IG11: Bark ... 38Vc 75
Goodfaith Ho. *E14* ... *45Dc 92*
(off Simpson's Rd.)
Goodge Pl. W1 ... 1C 222 (43Lb 90)
Goodge St. W1 ... 1C 222 (43Lb 90)
Goodhall Cl. HA7: Stan ... 23Ja 46
Goodhall St. NW10 ... 41Va 88
(not continuous)
Goodhart Ho. SM7: Bans ... 90Eb 175
Goodhart Pl. E14 ... 45Ac 92
Goodhart Way BR4: W W'ck ... 73Gc 159
Goodhew Rd. CR0: C'don ... 72Wb 157

Goodhope Ho. *E14* 45Dc **92**
(off Poplar High St.)
Gooding Cl. KT3: N Mald 70Sa **131**
Goodinge Cl. N7 37Nb **70**
Gooding Ho. SE7 50Lc **93**
Goodison Cl. WD23: Bush 15Ea **28**
Goodlake Ct. UB9: Den 31H **63**
Goodley Stock Rd.
TN16: Westrm 100Rc **200**
Goodman Cres.
CR0: C'don 72Rb **157**
SW2 61Nb **134**
Goodman Pk. SL2: Slou 6N **81**
Goodman Pl. TW18: Staines 63H **127**
Goodman Rd. E10 31Ec **72**
Goodmans Ct. E1 4K **225** (45Vb **91**)
HA0: Wemb 35Ma **67**
Goodman's Stile E1 44Wb **91**
Goodmans Yd. E1 4K **225** (45Vb **91**)
GOODMAYES 33Wc **75**
Goodmayes Av. IG3: Ilf 32Wc **75**
Goodmayes La. IG3: Ilf 35Wc **75**
Goodmayes Lodge
RM8: Dag 35Wc **75**
Goodmayes Retail Pk.
RM6: Chad H 32Xc **75**
Goodmayes Rd. IG3: Ilf 32Wc **75**
Goodmead Rd.
BR6: Orp, St M Cry 73Wc **161**
Goodrich Cl. WD25: Wat 7W **12**
Goodrich Ct. W10 44Za **88**
Goodrich Ho. *E2* 40Yb **72**
(off Sewardstone Rd.)
Goodrich Rd. SE22 58Vb **113**
Goodson Ho. *SM4: Mord* 73Eb **155**
(off Green La.)
Goodson Rd. NW10 38Ua **68**
Goodspeed Ho. *E14* 45Dc **92**
(off Simpson's Rd.)
Goods Way N1 1F **217** (40Nb **70**)
Goodway Gdns. E14 44Fc **93**
Goodwill Dr. HA2: Harr 32Ca **65**
Goodwill Ho. *E14* 45Dc **92**
(off Simpson's Rd.)
Goodwin Cl. CR4: Mitc 69Fb **133**
SE16 48Vb **91**
Goodwin Ct. EN4: E Barn 16Gb **31**
N8 27Nb **50**
(off Campsbourne Rd.)
SW19 66Gb **133**
Goodwin Dr. DA14: Sidc 62Zc **139**
Goodwin Gdns. CR0: Wadd 79Rb **157**
Goodwin Ho. N9 18Yb **34**
WD18: Wat 16U **26**
Goodwin Rd. CR0: Wadd 78Rb **157**
N9 18Zb **34**
SL2: Slou 1D **80**
W12 47Wa **88**
Goodwins Ct. WC2 4F **223** (45Nb **90**)
Goodwin St. N4 33Ob **70**
Goodwood Av. EN3: Enf W 9Yb **20**
RM12: Horn 35Nd **77**
WD24: Wat 7U **12**
Goodwood Cl. HA7: Stan 22La **46**
SM4: Mord 70Cb **133**
Goodwood Ct. W1 7A **216**
Goodwood Cres.
DA12: Grav'nd 4E **144**
Goodwood Dr. UB5: N'olt 37Ca **65**
Goodwood Ho. *SE14* 52Ac **114**
(off Goodwood Rd.)
SL4: Wind 3D **102**
(off Paddock Cl.)
Goodwood Pde. BR3: Beck 70Ac **136**
WD24: Wat 8U **12**
Goodwood Path WD6: Bore 12Qa **29**
Goodwood Rd. RH1: Redh 4P **207**
SE14 52Ac **114**
Goodworth Rd. RH1: Redh 4B **208**
TN15: Wro 88Be **185**
Goodwyn Av. NW7 22Ua **48**
Goodwyns Va. N10 25Jb **50**
Goodyear Ho. *N2* 26Fb **49**
(off The Grange)
Goodyear Pl. SE5 51Sb **113**
Goodyer Ho. SW1 7D **228**
Goodyers Av. WD7: R'lett 5Ha **14**
Goodyers Gdns. NW4 29Za **48**
Goosander Way SE28 48Tc **94**
Gooseacre La. HA3: Kenton 29Ma **47**
Goosecroft HP1: Hem H 1H **3**
Goosefields WD3: Rick 16L **25**
Goose Grn. KT11: D'side 91W **190**
SL2: Farn R 1P **60**
Goose Grn. Cl. BR5: St P 68Wc **139**
Goose Grn. Trad. Est. SE22 56Vb **113**
Goose La. GU22: Wok 4M **187**
Gooseley La. E6 41Qc **94**
(Brighton Rd.)
E6 42Rc **94**
(Claps Ga. La.)
Goosens Cl. SM1: Sutt 78Eb **155**
Goosepool KT16: Chert 73H **149**
Goose Rye Rd. GU3: Worp 8H **187**
Goose Sq. E6 44Pc **94**
Gooshays Dr. RM3: Rom 22Nd **57**
Gooshays Gdns. RM3: Rom 23Nd **57**
Gophir La. EC4 4F **225** (45Tb **91**)
Gopsall St. N1 1G **219** (39Tb **71**)
Goral Mead WD3: Rick 18M **25**
Gordon Av. CR2: Sande 82Sb **177**
E4 23Gc **53**
HA7: Stan 24Ha **46**
RM12: Horn 33Hd **76**
SW14 56Ua **110**
TW1: Twick 57Ja **108**
Gordonbrock Rd. SE4 57Cc **114**
Gordon Cl. AL1: St A 3F **6**
E17 30Cc **52**
KT16: Chert 76G **148**
N19 32Lb **70**
RM18: E Til 2M **123**
TW18: Staines 64K **127**
Gordon Cotts. *W8* 47Db **89**
(off Dukes La.)
Gordon Ct. HA8: Edg 22Pa **47**
RH1: Redh 8P **207**
(off St John's Ter. Rd.)
Gordon Cres. CR0: C'don 74Ub **157**
UB3: Hayes 49W **84**
Gordondale Rd. SW19 61Cb **133**
Gordon Dr. KT16: Chert 76G **148**
TW17: Shep 73T **150**
Gordon Gdns. HA8: Edg 26Ra **47**
Gordon Gro. SE5 54Rb **113**
Gordon Hill EN2: Enf 11Sb **33**
Gordon Ho. AL1: St A 3F **6**
E1 45Yb **92**
(off Glamis Rd.)
SW1 4C **228**
W5 41Na **87**
Gordon Ho. Rd. NW5 35Jb **70**
Gordon Mans. *W14* 48Za **88**
(off Addison Gdns.)
WC1 6D **216**
Gordon Pl. DA12: Grav'nd 8E **122**
W8 47Cb **89**
Gordon Prom. DA12: Grav'nd 8E **122**
Gordon Prom. E. DA12: Grav'nd 8E **122**
Gordon Rd. BR3: Beck 69Bc **136**
CM15: Shenf 18Ce **41**
CR3: Cat'm 93Tb **197**
DA1: Dart 59Md **119**
DA11: Nflt 9A **122**
DA15: Sidc 57Uc **116**
DA17: Belv 49Ed **96**
E4 17Gc **35**
E11 30Jc **53**
E15 35Ec **72**
E18 25Kc **53**
EN2: Enf 11Sb **33**
EN9: Walt A 6Cc **20**
HA3: W'stone 27Ga **46**
IG1: Ilf 34Tc **74**
IG11: Bark 39Uc **74**
KT2: King T 67Pa **131**
KT5: Surb 73Pa **153**
KT10: Clay 80Ga **152**
N3 24Bb **49**
N9 19Xb **33**
N11 24Mb **50**
RH1: Redh 3A **208**
RM6: Chad H 30Bd **55**
RM16: Grays 7A **100**
SE15 54Xb **113**
SL4: Wind 4D **102**
SM5: Cars 79Hb **155**
SS17: Horn H 1H **101**
TN13: S'oaks 97Kd **203**
TW3: Houn 56Ea **108**
TW9: Rich 54Pa **109**
TW15: Ashf 62N **127**
TW17: Shep 72T **150**
TW18: Staines 63E **126**
UB2: S'hall 49Aa **85**
UB7: Yiew 45N **83**
W4 51Ra **109**
W5 45Ka **86**
W13 45Ka **86**
Gordon Sq. WC1 5D **216** (42Mb **90**)
Gordon St. E13 41Jc **93**
WC1 5D **216** (42Mb **90**)
Gordons Way RH8: Oxt 100Fc **199**
Gordon Way BR1: Brom 67Jc **137**
EN5: Barn 14Bb **31**
Gore Cl. UB9: Hare 28K **43**
Gore Cotts. DA2: Daren 62Sd **142**
Gore Ct. NW9 29Qa **47**
Gorefield Ho. *NW6* 40Cb **69**
(off Gorefield Pl.)
Gorefield Pl. NW6 40Cb **69**
Gore Ho. *N1* 38Qb **70**
(off Drummond Way)
Gorelands La. HP8: Chal G 18A **24**
Gore Rd. DA2: Dart 61Sd **142**
E9 39Yb **72**
SL1: Burn 1A **80**
SW20 68Ya **132**
GORESBROOK INTERCHANGE 40Bd **75**
Goresbrook Leisure Cen. 39Zc **75**
Goresbrook Rd. RM9: Dag 39Xc **75**
Gore St. SW7 3A **226** (48Eb **89**)
Gorhambury House 1J **5**
Gorham Dr. AL1: St A 5C **6**
Gorham Ho. *SE16* 47Zb **92**
(off Wolfe Cres.)
Gorham Pl. W11 45Ab **88**
Goring Cl. RM5: Col R 25Ed **56**
Goring Gdns. RM8: Dag 35Yc **75**
Goring Rd. N11 23Nb **50**
RM10: Dag 37Fd **76**
TW18: Staines 64F **126**
Gorings Sq. TW18: Staines 63G **126**
Goring St. EC3 2J **225**
Goring Way UB6: G'frd 40Ea **66**
Gorle Cl. WD25: Wat 7W **12**
Gorleston Rd. N15 29Tb **51**
Gorleston St. W14 49Ab **88**
(not continuous)
Gorman Rd. SE18 49Pc **94**
Gorringe Av. DA4: S Dar 68Td **142**
Gorringe Pk. Av. CR4: Mitc 66Hb **133**
Gorse Cl. AL10: Hat 3B **8**
E16 44Jc **93**
KT20: Tad 92Xa **194**
Gorsefield Ho. *E14* 45Cc **92**
(off E. India Dock Rd.)
Gorse Hill DA4: Farni 73Qd **163**
GU22: Wok 3K **187**
Gorse Hill La. GU25: Vir W 10P **125**
Gorse Hill Rd. GU25: Vir W 10P **125**
Gorselands Cl. KT14: W Byf 83L **169**
Gorse La. GU24: Chob 10J **147**
Gorse Meade SL1: Slou 6F **80**
Gorse Ri. SW17 64Jb **134**
Gorse Rd. BR5: St M Cry 75Cd **162**
CR0: C'don 77Cc **158**
Gorse Wlk. UB7: Yiew 44N **83**
Gorse Way DA3: Hartl 71Be **165**
Gorseway RM7: Rush G 32Gd **76**
Gorsewood Rd. DA3: Hartl 71Be **165**
(not continuous)
GU21: Wok 1H **187**
Gorst Rd. NW10 42Sa **87**
SW11 58Hb **111**
Gorsuch Pl. E2 3K **219** (41Vb **91**)
Gorsuch St. E2 3K **219** (40Vb **71**)
Gosberton Rd. SW12 60Hb **111**
Gosbury Hill KT9: Chess 77Na **153**
Gosden Rd. GU24: W End 5D **166**
Gosfield Rd. KT19: Eps 84Ta **173**
RM8: Dag 33Cd **76**
Gosfield St. W1 7B **216** (43Lb **90**)
Gosford Gdns. IG4: Ilf 29Pc **54**
Gosford Ho. *E3* 40Bc **72**
(off Tredegar Rd.)
WD18: Wat 16U **26**
Gosforth La. WD19: Wat 20W **26**
Gosforth Path WD19: Wat 20W **26**
Gosforth Pl. SL1: Slou 5D **80**
Goshawk Gdns. UB4: Hayes 41U **84**
Goslar Way SL4: Wind 4F **102**
Goslett Ct. WD23: Bush 15Ca **27**
Goslett Yd. WC2 3E **222** (44Mb **90**)
Gosling Cl. UB6: G'frd 41Ca **85**
Gosling Grn. SL3: L'ly 48A **82**
Gosling Ho. *E1* 45Yb **92**
(off Sutton St.)
Gosling Rd. SL3: L'ly 48A **82**
Gosling Way SW9 53Qb **112**
Gospatrick Rd. N17 24Sb **51**
GOSPEL OAK 35Jb **70**
Gosport Dr. RM12: Horn 37Ld **77**
Gosport Rd. E17 29Bc **52**
Gosport Wlk. N17 28Xb **51**
Gossage Rd. SE18 50Tc **94**
UB10: Uxb 38P **63**
Gossamers, The WD25: Wat 6Aa **13**
Gosset St. E2 3K **219** (41Vb **91**)
Goss Hill BR8: Swan 65Ld **141**
Gosshill Rd. BR7: Chst 68Qc **138**
Gossington Cl. BR7: Chst 63Rc **138**
Gosterwood St. SE8 51Ac **114**
Gostling Rd. TW2: Whitt 60Ca **107**
Goston Gdns. CR7: Thor H 69Qb **134**
Goston Ga. *SW8* 53Pb **112**
(off Hampson Way)
Goswell Hill SL4: Wind 3H **103**
Goswell Pl. EC1 4C **218**
Goswell Rd. EC1 2B **218** (40Rb **71**)
SL4: Wind 3H **103**
Gothic Cl. DA1: Dart 62Md **141**
Gothic Cotts. *EN2: Enf* 12Sb **33**
(off Chase Grn. Av.)
Gothic Ct. *SE5* 52Sb **113**
(off Wyndham Rd.)
UB3: Harl 51T **106**
Gothic Rd. TW2: Twick 61Fa **130**
Gottfried M. NW5 35Lb **70**
Goudhurst Rd. BR1: Brom 64Gc **137**
Gouge Av. DA11: Nflt 10A **122**
Gough Ho. *KT1: King T* 68Na **131**
(off Eden St.)
N1 39Rb **71**
(off Windsor St.)
Gough Rd. E15 35Hc **73**
EN1: Enf 12Xb **33**
Gough Sq. EC4 2A **224** (44Qb **90**)
Gough St. WC1 5J **217** (42Pb **90**)
Gough Wlk. E14 44Cc **92**
Gould Cl. AL9: Wel G 6D **8**
Goulden Ho. SW11 54Gb **111**
Goulden Ho. App. SW11 54Gb **111**
Goulding Gdns. CR7: Thor H 68Sb **135**
Gouldman Ho. *E1* 42Yb **92**
(off Wyllen Cl.)
Gould Rd. TW2: Twick 60Ga **108**
TW14: Felt 59U **106**
Goulds Cotts. RM4: Abr 13Xc **37**
GOULDS GREEN 43R **84**
Gould's Grn. UB8: Hil 45R **84**
Gould Ter. E8 36Xb **71**
Goulston St. E1 2K **225** (44Vb **91**)
Goulton Rd. E5 35Xb **71**
Gourley Pl. N15 29Ub **51**
Gourley St. N15 29Ub **51**
Gourney Gro. RM16: Grays 45De **99**
Gourock Rd. SE9 57Qc **116**
Govan St. E2 39Wb **71**
Gover Ct. SW4 54Nb **112**
GOVER HILL 100Fe **205**
Gover Hill TN11: Roug 100Fe **205**
Government Row EN3: Enf L 10Cc **20**
Govett Av. TW17: Shep 71S **150**
Govett Gro. GU20: W'sham 8B **146**
Govier Cl. E15 38Gc **73**
Gowan Av. SW6 53Ab **110**
Gowan Ho. E2 4K **219**
Gowan Rd. NW10 37Xa **68**
Gower Fld. EN6: S Mim 4Wa **16**
Gower, The TW20: Thorpe 69D **126**
Gower Cl. SW4 58Lb **112**
Gower Ct. WC1 5C **216** (42Mb **90**)
Gower Ho. E17 27Dc **52**
KT13: Weyb 79T **150**
SE17 7E **230**
Gower Lodge *KT13: Weyb* 79T **150**
(off St George's Rd.)
Gower M. WC1 1E **222** (43Mb **90**)
Gower M. Mans. WC1 7E **216**
Gower Pl. RM16: Chaf H 48Xd **98**
WC1 5C **216** (42Mb **90**)
Gower Rd. E7 37Jc **73**
KT13: Weyb 79T **150**
TW7: Isle 51Ha **108**
Gowers La. RM16: Ors 7B **100**
Gower St. WC1 5C **216** (42Lb **90**)
Gower's Wlk. E1 44Wb **91**
Gowings Grn. SL1: Slou 7C **80**
Gowland Pl. BR3: Beck 68Bc **136**
Gowlett Rd. SE15 55Wb **113**
Gowlland Cl. CR0: C'don 73Wb **157**
Gowrie Pl. CR3: Cat'm 94Sb **197**
Gowrie Rd. SW11 55Jb **112**
Graburn Way KT8: E Mos 69Fa **130**
Grace Av. DA7: Bex 54Bd **117**
WD7: Shenl 5Ma **15**
Grace Bus. Cen. CR4: Mitc 72Hb **155**
Gracechurch St. EC3 4G **225** (45Tb **91**)
Grace Cl. HA8: Edg 24Sa **47**
IG6: Ilf 23Vc **55**
SE9 62Mc **137**
WD6: Bore 11Ta **29**
Grace Ct. *CR0: C'don* 76Rb **157**
(off Waddon Rd.)
SL1: Slou 6G **80**
SM2: Sutt 81Db **175**
Gracedale Rd. SW16 64Kb **134**
Gracefield Gdns. SW16 62Nb **134**
Gracehill *E1* 43Yb **92**
(off Hannibal Rd.)
Grace Ho. *SE11* 51Pb **112**
(off Vauxhall St.)
Grace Jones Cl. E8 37Wb **71**
Grace M. BR3: Beck 65Cc **136**
SE20 68Yb **136**
(off Marlow Rd.)
Grace Path SE26 63Yb **136**
Grace Pl. E3 41Dc **92**
Grace Rd. CR0: C'don 72Sb **157**
Graces All. E1 1K **225** (45Wb **91**)
Graces M. NW8 2A **214** (40Eb **69**)
SE5 54Tb **113**
Grace's Rd. SE5 54Ub **113**
Grace St. E3 41Dc **92**
Gracious Pond Rd. GU24: Chob 10L **147**
Gradient, The SE26 63Wb **135**
Graduate Pl. SE1 3H **231**
Graeme Rd. EN1: Enf 12Tb **33**
Graemesdyke Av. SW14 55Ra **109**
Grafton Chambers NW1 4E **216**
Grafton Cl. AL4: St A 3H **7**
KT4: Wor Pk 76Ua **154**
KT14: W Byf 85H **169**
SL3: G Grn 44A **82**
TW4: Houn 60Aa **107**
W13 44Ja **86**
Grafton Ct. TW14: Bedf 60T **106**
Grafton Cres. NW1 37Kb **70**
Grafton Gdns. N4 30Sb **51**
RM8: Dag 33Ad **75**
Grafton Ho. *E3* 41Cc **92**
(off Wellington Way)
SE8 50Bc **92**
Grafton M. W1 6B **216** (42Lb **90**)
Grafton Pk. Rd. KT4: Wor Pk 75Ua **154**
Grafton Pl. NW1 4D **216** (41Mb **90**)
Grafton Rd. CR0: C'don 74Qb **156**
EN2: Enf 13Pb **32**
HA1: Harr 29Ea **46**
KT3: N Mald 69Ua **132**
KT4: Wor Pk 76Ta **153**
NW5 36Jb **70**
RM8: Dag 33Ad **75**
W3 45Sa **87**
Graftons, The NW2 34Cb **69**
Grafton Sq. SW4 55Lb **112**
Grafton St. W1 5A **222** (45Kb **90**)
Grafton Ter. NW5 36Hb **69**
Grafton Way KT8: W Mole 70Ba **129**
W1 6B **216** (42Lb **90**)
(not continuous)
WC1 6B **216** (42Lb **90**)
Grafton Yd. NW5 37Kb **70**
Graham Av. CR4: Mitc 67Jb **134**
W13 47Ka **86**
Graham Cl. AL1: St A 4B **6**
CM13: Hut 15Ee **41**
CR0: C'don 75Cc **158**
Graham Ct. *AL3: St A* 1B **6**
(off Grange St.)
SE14 51Zb **114**
(off Myers La.)
UB5: N'olt 36Aa **65**
Grahame Ho. RH1: Redh 4N **207**
GRAHAME PARK 25Ua **48**
Grahame Pk. Est. NW9 25Ua **48**
Grahame Pk. Way NW7 24Va **48**
NW9 26Va **48**
Grahame Twr. *W3* 48Ra **87**
(off Hanbury Rd.)
Grahame White Ho. HA3: Kenton 27Ma **47**
Graham Gdns. KT6: Surb 74Na **153**
Graham Ho. KT23: Bookh 96Ba **191**
N9 18Yb **34**
(off Cumberland Rd.)
Graham Lodge NW4 30Xa **48**
Graham Mans. *IG11: Bark* 38Wc **75**
(off Lansbury Av.)
Graham Rd. CR4: Mitc 67Jb **134**
CR8: Purl 85Qb **176**
DA6: Bex 56Bd **117**
E8 37Wb **71**
E13 42Jc **93**
GU20: W'sham 9A **146**
HA3: W'stone 27Ga **46**
N15 27Rb **51**
NW4 30Xa **48**
SW19 66Bb **133**
TW12: Hamp H 63Ca **129**
W4 48Ta **87**
Graham St. N1 2C **218** (40Rb **71**)
Graham Ter. *DA15: Sidc* 58Xc **117**
(off Westerham Dr.)
SW1 6H **227** (49Jb **90**)
Grainger Cl. UB5: N'olt 36Da **65**
Grainger Ct. SE5 52Sb **113**
Grainger Rd. N22 25Sb **51**
TW7: Isle 54Ha **108**
Grainges Yd. UB8: Uxb 38L **63**
Grainstore, The E16 45Jc **93**
Gramer Cl. E11 33Fc **73**
Gramophone La. UB3: Hayes 47U **84**
Grampian Cl. BR6: St M Cry 72Vc **161**
SM2: Sutt 80Eb **155**
UB3: Harl 52T **106**
Grampian Gdns. NW2 32Ab **68**
Grampians, The *W6* 47Za **88**
(off Shepherd's Bush Rd.)
Grampian Way SL3: L'ly 50C **82**
Gramsci Way SE6 62Dc **136**
Granada St. SW17 64Hb **133**
Granard Av. SW15 57Xa **110**
Granard Bus. Cen. NW7 23Ua **48**
Granard Ho. E9 37Zb **72**
Granard Rd. SW12 59Hb **111**
Granaries, The EN9: Walt A 6Gc **21**
Granary Cl. N9 17Yb **34**
Granary Ct. *E15* 37Fc **73**
(off Millstone Cl.)
Granary Mans. SE28 47Sc **94**
Granary Rd. E1 42Xb **91**
Granary Sq. N1 1F **217** (39Nb **70**)
Granary St. NW1 1E **216** (39Mb **70**)
Granby Pk. Rd. EN7: Chesh 1Vb **19**
Granby Pl. SE1 2K **229**
Granby Rd. DA11: Nflt 58Ee **121**
SE9 54Pc **116**
Granby St. E2 42Wb **91**
(not continuous)
Granby Ter. NW1 2B **216** (40Lb **70**)
Grand Arc. N12 22Eb **49**
Grand Av. EC1 7C **218** (43Rb **91**)
(not continuous)
HA9: Wemb 36Qa **67**
KT5: Surb 71Ra **153**
N10 28Jb **50**
Grand Av. E. HA9: Wemb 36Ra **67**
Grand Courts RM8: Dag 34Ad **75**
Grand Depot Rd. SE18 50Qc **94**
Grand Dr. SW20 68Ya **132**
UB2: S'hall 47Ea **86**
Granden Rd. SW16 68Nb **134**
Grandfield Av. WD17: Wat 11V **26**
Grandfield Ct. W4 51Ta **109**
Grandis Cotts. GU23: Rip 94K **189**
Grandison Rd. KT4: Wor Pk 75Ya **154**
SW11 57Hb **111**
Grand Junc. Wharf N1 2D **218** (40Sb **71**)
Grand Pde. HA9: Wemb 33Qa **67**
KT6: Surb 74Qa **153**
N4 29Rb **51**
SW14 56Sa **109**
(off Up. Richmond Rd. W.)
Grand Pde. M. SW15 57Ab **110**
Grandstand Rd. KT17: Eps D 89Va **174**
Grand Union Canal Wlk. *W10* 42Ya **88**
(off Canal Way)
Grand Union Cen. *W10* 42Za **88**
(off West Row)
Grand Union Cl. W9 43Cb **89**
Grand Union Cres. E8 39Wb **71**
Grand Union Ent. Pk. UB2: S'hall 48Ca **85**
Grand Union Hgts. HA0: Wemb 39Ma **67**
Grand Union Ind. Est. NW10 40Ra **67**
Grand Union Office Pk., The
UB8: Cowl 44L **83**
Grand Union Village UB5: N'olt 41Ba **85**
Grand Union Wlk. *NW1* 38Kb **70**
(off Kentish Town Rd.)
Grand Union Way UB2: S'hall 47Ca **85**
WD4: K Lan 1R **12**
Grand Vw. Av. TN16: Big H 89Lc **179**
Grand Vitesse Ind. Cen. SE1 7C **224**
Grand Wlk. E1 42Ac **92**
Granfield St. SW11 53Fb **111**
Grange, The AL4: Col H 5P **7**
CR0: C'don 75Bc **158**
DA4: S Dar 67Td **142**
E17 29Ac **52**
(off Lynmouth Rd.)
EN9: Walt A 9Fc **21**
GU24: Chob 2J **167**
GU25: Vir W 70A **126**
(off Holloway Dr.)
HA0: Wemb 38Qa **67**
KT3: N Mald 71Va **154**
KT4: Wor Pk 77Ta **153**
KT12: Walt T 75X **151**
N2 26Fb **49**
N20 18Eb **31**
(Grangeview Rd.)
N20 18Fb **31**
(Oxford Gdns.)
SE1 3K **231** (48Vb **91**)
SL1: Burn 1A **80**
(off Green La.)
SL4: Old Win 7M **103**
SW19 65Za **132**
TN15: W King 81Vd **184**
W3 47Ra **87**
W4 50Ra **87**
W13 43La **86**
W14 49Bb **89**
WD3: Rick 17M **25**
WD5: Ab L 3U **12**
Grange Av. EN4: E Barn 18Gb **31**
HA7: Stan 26Ka **46**
IG8: Wfd G 23Jc **53**
N12 22Eb **49**
N20 17Ab **30**
SE25 68Ub **135**
TW2: Twick 61Ga **130**
Grangecliffe Gdns. SE25 68Ub **135**
Grange Cl. CM13: Ingve 22Ee **59**
DA15: Sidc 62Wc **139**
HA8: Edg 22Sa **47**
HP2: Hem H 3A **4**
IG8: Wfd G 24Jc **53**
KT8: W Mole 70Da **129**
KT22: Lea 92Ma **193**
RH1: Blet 5K **209**
RH1: Mers 100Kb **196**
SL9: Chal P 25A **42**
TN16: Westrm 98Sc **200**
TW5: Hest 51Ba **107**
TW19: Wray 58A **104**
UB3: Hayes 43U **84**
WD17: Wat 11W **26**
Grange Ct. AL3: St A 1B **6**
(not continuous)
EN9: Walt A 6Ec **20**
HA1: Harr 35Ha **66**
HA5: Pinn 27Aa **45**
IG10: Lough 15Mc **35**
KT12: Walt T 75W **150**
NW10 34Ua **68**
(off Neasden La.)
RH1: Mers 100Kb **196**
RH9: S God 10C **210**
SM2: Sutt 80Db **155**
SM6: Wall 76Kb **156**
TW17: Shep 70Q **128**
TW18: Staines 64J **127**
TW20: Egh 64B **126**
UB5: N'olt 40Y **65**
WC2 3J **223** (44Pb **90**)
Grangecourt Rd. N16 32Ub **71**
Grange Cres. DA2: Dart 58Rd **119**
IG7: Chig 22Tc **54**
SE28 44Yc **95**
Grangedale Cl. HA6: Nwood 25U **44**
Grange Dr. BR6: Prat B 81Yc **181**
BR7: Chst 65Nc **138**
GU21: Wok 87A **168**
RH1: Mers 100Kb **196**
Grange Farm Cl. HA2: Harr 33Ea **66**
Grangefield *NW1* 38Mb **70**
(off Marquis Rd.)
Grange Flds. SL9: Chal P 25A **42**
Grangefields Rd. GU4: Jac W 10P **187**
Grange Gdns. HA5: Pinn 27Aa **45**
N14 18Mb **32**
NW3 34Db **69**
SE25 68Ub **135**
SL2: Farn C 6H **61**
SM7: Bans 85Db **175**
Grange Gro. N1 37Sb **71**
GRANGE HILL 23Tc **54**
Grange Hill HA8: Edg 22Sa **47**
SE25 68Ub **135**
TN15: Plax 99Ae **205**
Grangehill Pl. SE9 55Pc **116**
Grangehill Rd. SE9 56Pc **116**
Grange Ho. DA8: Erith 54Jd **118**
DA11: Grav'nd 9C **122**
IG11: Bark 39Tc **74**
NW10 38Xa **68**
SE1 4K **231** (48Vb **91**)
Grange La. DA3: Hartl 73Ce **165**
SE21 61Vb **135**
WD25: Let H 11Fa **28**
Grange Lodge SW19 65Za **132**
Grange Mans. KT17: Ewe 80Va **154**
Grange Mdw. SM7: Bans 85Db **175**
Grange M. N21 16Rb **33**
TW13: Felt 63W **128**
Grangemill Rd. SE6 62Cc **136**
Grangemill Way SE6 61Cc **136**
Grangemount KT22: Lea 92Ma **193**

GRANGE PARK . . . 16Rb 33
Grange Pk. GU21: Wok . . . 87A 168
W5 . . . 46Na 87
Grange Pk. Av. N21 . . . 16Sb 33
Grange Pk. Pl. SW20 . . . 66Xa 132
Grange Pk. Rd. CR7: Thor H . . . 70Tb 135
E10 . . . 32Dc 72
Grange Pl. KT12: Walt T . . . 75W 150
NW6 . . . 38Cb 69
TW18: Lale . . . 68L 127
Granger Ct. *WD6: Bore* . . . *14Qa 29*
(off Whitehall Cl.)
Grange Rd. BR6: Orp . . . 75Tc 160
CR2: S Croy . . . 82Sb 177
CR3: Cat'm . . . 97Wb 197
CR7: Thor H . . . 70Tb 135
DA11: Grav'nd . . . 9C 122
E10 . . . 32Cc 72
E13 . . . 41Hc 93
E17 . . . 29Ac 52
(not continuous)
GU2: Guild . . . 10M 187
GU21: Wok . . . 86A 168
GU24: Pirb . . . 4A 186
HA1: Harr . . . 29Ja 46
HA2: Harr . . . 33Fa 66
HA8: Edg . . . 23Ta 47
IG1: Ilf . . . 35Rc 74
KT1: King T . . . 69Na 131
KT8: W Mole . . . 70Da 129
KT9: Chess . . . 77Na 153
KT12: Hers . . . 77Aa 151
KT15: New H . . . 82J 169
KT22: Lea . . . 92Ma 193
N6 . . . 30Jb 50
N17 . . . 23Wb 51
N18 . . . 23Wb 51
NW10 . . . 37Xa 68
RM3: Rom . . . 23Kd 57
RM15: Avel . . . 46Sd 98
RM17: Grays . . . 51De 121
SE1 . . . 4J 231 (48Ub 91)
SE19 . . . 70Tb 135
SE25 . . . 70Tb 135
SL9: Chal P . . . 25A 42
SM2: Sutt . . . 80Cb 155
SW13 . . . 53Wa 110
TN13: S'oaks . . . 99Jd 202
TN15: Plat . . . 92Ee 205
TW20: Egh . . . 64B 126
UB1: S'hall . . . 47Aa 85
UB3: Hayes . . . 44U 84
W4 . . . 51Ra 109
W5 . . . 46Ma 87
WD6: E'tree . . . 15Pa 29
WD23: Bush . . . 15Aa 27
Granger Way RM1: Rom . . . 30Jd 56
Grange St. AL3: St A . . . 1B 6
N1 . . . 1G 219 (39Tb 71)
Grange St. M. AL3: St A . . . 1B 6
Grange Va. SM2: Sutt . . . 80Db 155
Grange Vw. Rd. N20 . . . 18Eb 31
Grange Wlk. SE1 . . . 3J 231 (48Ub 91)
Grange Wlk. M. SE1 . . . 4J 231
Grangewaters Outdoor Education Cen. . . . 43Be 99
Grange Way DA3: Hartl . . . 72Be 165
DA8: Erith . . . 52Kd 119
NW6 . . . 38Cb 69
SL0: Iver . . . 44H 83
Grangeway IG8: Wfd G . . . 21Lc 53
N12 . . . 21Db 49
Grangeway, The N21 . . . 16Rb 33
Grangeway Gdns. IG4: Ilf . . . 29Nc 54
Grangeways Cl. DA11: Nflt . . . 3B 144
Grangewood DA5: Bexl . . . 60Bd 117
EN6: Pot B . . . 2Db 17
SL3: Wex . . . 3N 81
Grangewood Av. RM13: Rain . . . 42Ld 97
RM16: Grays . . . 8A 100
Grangewood Cl.
CM13: B'wood . . . 20Be 41
HA5: Eastc . . . 29W 44
Grangewood Dr. TW16: Sun . . . 66V 128
Grangewood La. BR3: Beck . . . 65Bc 136
Grangewood St. E6 . . . 39Mc 73
Grangewood Ter. SE25 . . . 68Tb 135
Grange Yd. SE1 . . . 4K 231 (48Vb 91)
Granham Gdns. N9 . . . 19Vb 33
Granite Apartments E15 . . . 37Gc 73
Granite St. SE18 . . . 50Vc 95
Granleigh Rd. E11 . . . 33Gc 73
Gransden Av. E8 . . . 38Xb 71
Gransden Ho. SE8 . . . 50Bc 92
Gransden Rd. W12 . . . 47Va 88
Grant Av. SL1: Slou . . . 4J 81
Grantbridge St. N1 . . . 1C 218 (40Rb 71)
Grantchester *KT1: King T* . . . *68Qa 131*
(off St Peters Rd.)
Grantchester Cl. HA1: Harr . . . 34Ha 66
Grant Cl. DA17: Belv . . . 50Bd 95
N14 . . . 17Lb 32
N17 . . . 26Ub 51
TW17: Shep . . . 72R 150
Grant Ct. *E4* . . . *18Ec 34*
(off The Ridgeway)
NW9 . . . *26Va 48*
(off Hazel Cl.)
Grantham Cl. HA8: Edg . . . 20Na 29
Grantham Ct. KT2: King T . . . 64Ma 131
RM6: Chad H . . . 31Bd 75
SE16 . . . *47Zb 92*
(off Eleanor Cl.)
Grantham Gdns.
RM6: Chad H . . . 30Bd 55
Grantham Grn. WD6: Bore . . . 15Sa 29
Grantham Ho. *SE15* . . . *51Wb 113*
(off Friary Est.)
TW16: Sun . . . 66U 128
Grantham M. HP4: Berk . . . 1A 2
Grantham Pl. W1 . . . 7K 221 (46Kb 90)
Grantham Rd. E12 . . . 35Qc 74
SW9 . . . 54Nb 112
W4 . . . 52Ua 110
Grantham Way RM16: Grays . . . 46Ce 99
Grant Ho. *SW9* . . . *53Pb 112*
(off Liberty St.)
Grantley Ho. *SE14* . . . *51Zb 114*
(off Myers La.)
Grantley Pl. KT10: Esh . . . 78Ea 152
Grantley Rd. TW4: Cran . . . 54Y 107
Grantley St. E1 . . . 41Zb 92
Grant Mus. of Zoology . . . *6D 216*
(off Gower St.)
Grantock Rd. E17 . . . 25Fc 53
Granton Av. RM14: Upm . . . 34Pd 77
Granton Rd. DA14: Sidc . . . 65Yc 139
IG3: Ilf . . . 32Wc 75
SW16 . . . 67Lb 134
Grant Pl. CR0: C'don . . . 74Vb 157
Grant Rd. CR0: C'don . . . 74Vb 157
HA3: W'stone . . . 27Ha 46
SW11 . . . 56Fb 111
Grants Cl. NW7 . . . 24Ya 48
Grants La. RH8: Limp . . . 4N 211
TN8: Eden, Limp . . . 8N 211
Grants Quay Wharf EC3 . . . 5G 225 (45Tb 91)
Grant St. E13 . . . 41Jc 93
N1 . . . 1K 217 (40Qb 70)
Grant Ter. *N16* . . . *31Wb 71*
(off Castlewood Rd.)
Grantully Rd. W9 . . . 41Db 89
Grant Wlk. SL5: S'dale . . . 4C 146
Grant Way TW7: Isle . . . 51Ja 108
Grantwood Cl. RH1: Redh . . . 10A 208
Granville Arc. SW9 . . . 56Qb 112
Granville Av. N9 . . . 20Yb 34
SL2: Slou . . . 3H 81
TW3: Houn . . . 57Ca 107
TW13: Felt . . . 61W 128
Granville Cl. CR0: C'don . . . 75Ub 157
KT13: Weyb . . . 79S 150
KT14: Byfl . . . 85P 169
Granville Ct. *AL1: St A* . . . *2D 6*
(off Granville Rd.)
N1 . . . 39Ub 71
N4 . . . 30Pb 50
SE14 . . . *52Ac 114*
(off Nynehead St.)
Granville Dene HP3: Bov . . . 9C 2
Granville Gdns. SW16 . . . 67Pb 134
W5 . . . 46Pa 87
Granville Gro. SE13 . . . 55Ec 114
Granville Ho. *E14* . . . *44Cc 92*
(off E. India Dock Rd.)
Granville Mans. *W12* . . . *47Ya 88*
(off Shepherd's Bush Grn.)
Granville M. DA14: Sidc . . . 63Wc 139
Granville Pk. SE13 . . . 55Ec 114
Granville Pl. HA5: Pinn . . . 27Z 45
N12 . . . 24Eb 49
SW6 . . . 52Db 111
W1 . . . 3H 221 (44Jb 90)
Granville Point NW2 . . . 33Bb 69
Granville Rd. AL1: St A . . . 2D 6
CM16: Epp . . . 1Xc 23
DA11: Grav'nd . . . 9B 122
DA14: Sidc . . . 63Wc 139
DA16: Well . . . 55Yc 117
E17 . . . 30Dc 52
E18 . . . 26Kc 53
EN5: Barn . . . 14Ya 30
GU22: Wok . . . 92B 188
IG1: Ilf . . . 32Rc 74
KT13: Weyb . . . 80S 150
N4 . . . 30Pb 50
N12 . . . 24Eb 49
N13 . . . 23Pb 50
N22 . . . 25Rb 51
NW2 . . . 33Bb 69
NW6 . . . 40Cb 69
(not continuous)
RH8: Oxt . . . 1K 211
SW18 . . . 59Bb 111
SW19 . . . 66Cb 133
TN13: S'oaks . . . 96Jd 202
TN16: Westrm . . . 98Sc 200
UB3: Harl . . . 49V 84
UB10: Hil . . . 37R 64
WD18: Wat . . . 14Y 27
Granville Sq. SE15 . . . 52Ub 113
WC1 . . . 4J 217 (41Pb 70)
Granville St. WC1 . . . 4J 217 (41Pb 70)
Granwood Ct. TW7: Isle . . . 53Ga 108
Grape St. WC2 . . . 2F 223 (44Nb 90)
Graphite Apartments, The N1 . . . 2F 219
Graphite Sq. SE11 . . . 7H 229 (50Pb 90)
Grapsome Cl. KT9: Chess . . . 80La 152
Grasdene Rd. SE18 . . . 52Wc 117
Grasgarth Cl. W3 . . . 45Sa 87
Grasholm Way SL3: L'ly . . . 49E 82
Grasmere NW1 . . . 4A 216
SL4: Wind . . . 2C 102
Grasmere Av. BR6: Farnb . . . 76Rc 160
HA4: Ruis . . . 31S 64
HA9: Wemb . . . 31La 66
SL2: Slou . . . 5L 81
SW15 . . . 63Ta 131
SW19 . . . 69Cb 133
TW3: Houn . . . 58Da 107
W3 . . . 45Ta 87
Grasmere Cl. HP3: Hem H . . . 4B 4
IG10: Lough . . . 12Pc 36
TW14: Felt . . . 60V 106
TW20: Egh . . . 66D 126
WD25: Wat . . . 4X 13
Grasmere Ct. N22 . . . 23Pb 50
SE26 . . . 64Wb 135
SM2: Sutt . . . 79Eb 155
SW13 . . . *51Wa 110*
(off Verdun Rd.)
Grasmere Gdns. BR6: Farnb . . . 76Rc 160
HA3: W'stone . . . 26Ja 46
IG4: Ilf . . . 29Pc 54
Grasmere Pde. SL2: Slou . . . 5M 81
Grasmere Point *SE15* . . . *52Yb 114*
(off Old Kent Rd.)
Grasmere Rd. AL1: St A . . . 4F 6
BR1: Brom . . . 67Hc 137
BR6: Farnb . . . 76Rc 160
CR8: Purl . . . 83Rb 177
DA7: Bex . . . 54Ed 118
E13 . . . 40Jc 73
GU18: Light . . . 2A 166
N10 . . . 25Kb 50
N17 . . . 23Wb 51
SE25 . . . 72Xb 157
SW16 . . . 64Nb 134
Grasmere Way KT14: Byfl . . . 84P 169
Grassbanks DA1: Dart . . . 60Pd 119
Grassfield Cl. CR5: Coul . . . 91Kb 196
Grasshaven Way SE28 . . . 46Vc 95
(not continuous)
Grassingham End SL9: Chal P . . . 24A 42
Grassingham Rd. SL9: Chal P . . . 24A 42
Grassington Cl. AL2: Brick W . . . 2Ca 13
N11 . . . 23Jb 50
Grassington Rd. DA14: Sidc . . . 63Wc 139
Grassmere Rd. RM11: Horn . . . 28Pd 57
Grassmount CR8: Purl . . . 82Nb 176
SE23 . . . 61Xb 135
Grass Pk. N3 . . . 25Bb 49
Grass Rd. RM18: E Til . . . 1K 123
Grassway SM6: Wall . . . 77Lb 156
Grassy Cl. HP1: Hem H . . . 1J 3
Grassy La. TN13: S'oaks . . . 98Kd 203
Grasvenor Av. EN5: Barn . . . 15Cb 31
Gratton Dr. SL4: Wind . . . 6C 102
Gratton Rd. W14 . . . 48Ab 88
Gratton Ter. NW2 . . . 34Za 68
Gravel Cl. IG7: Chig . . . 19Wc 37
Graveley Av. WD6: Bore . . . 15Sa 29
GRAVEL HILL . . . 23B 42
Gravel Hill CR0: Addtn . . . 79Zb 158
DA6: Bex . . . 56Dd 118
HP1: Hem H . . . 2J 3
IG10: H Beech . . . 10Jc 21
KT22: Lea . . . 93Ka 192
N3 . . . 26Bb 49
SL9: Chal P . . . 23A 42
UB8: Uxb . . . 36M 63
Gravel Hill Cl. DA6: Bex . . . 57Dd 118
Gravelhill Ter. HP1: Hem H . . . 3J 3
Gravel La. E1 . . . 2K 225 (44Vb 91)
HP1: Hem H . . . 2J 3
IG7: Chig . . . 15Vc 37
Gravelly Hill CR3: Cat'm . . . 100Ub 197
Gravel Path HP1: Hem H . . . 2J 3
HP4: Berk . . . 1A 2
Gravel Pit La. SE9 . . . 57Rc 116
Gravel Pit Way BR6: Orp . . . 75Wc 161
Gravel Rd. BR2: Brom . . . 76Nc 160
DA4: Sut H . . . 66Rd 141
TW2: Twick . . . 60Ga 108
Gravelwood Cl. BR7: Chst . . . 62Sc 138
Gravely Ct. HP2: Hem H . . . 3C 4
Gravely Ho. *SE8* . . . *49Ac 92*
(off Chilton Gro.)
Gravenel Gdns. *SW17* . . . *64Gb 133*
(off Nutwell St.)
Graveney Gro. SE20 . . . 66Yb 136
Graveney Rd. SW17 . . . 63Gb 133
GRAVESEND . . . 8D 122
Gravesend Golf Centre . . . 3J 145
Gravesend Rd.
DA12: Shorne . . . 2M 145
ME3: High'm . . . 2M 145
TN15: Stans, Wro . . . 87De 185
W12 . . . 45Wa 88
Gravesend Sailing Club . . . 8F 122
Gravesham Ct. DA12: Grav'nd . . . 9D 122
Gray Av. RM8: Dag . . . 32Bd 75
Gray Cl. KT15: Add . . . 78K 149
Gray Ct. E1 . . . 43Ac 92
HA5: Pinn . . . 28Aa 45
SL4: Wind . . . 4E 102
Gray Gdns. RM13: Rain . . . 37Jd 76
Grayham Cres. KT3: N Mald . . . 70Ta 131
Grayham Rd. KT3: N Mald . . . 70Ta 131
Gray Ho. SE17 . . . 7E 230
SL2: Stoke P . . . *8L 61*
(off Bells Hill Grn.)
Grayland Cl. BR1: Brom . . . 67Mc 137
Graylands CM16: They B . . . 9Tc 22
GU21: Wok . . . 88A 168
RM17: Grays . . . 51Ae 121
Graylands Cl. GU21: Wok . . . 88A 168
SL1: Slou . . . 6D 80
Grayling KT16: Chert . . . 74L 149
Grayling Cl. E16 . . . 42Gc 93
Grayling Ct. *W5* . . . *46Ma 87*
(off Grange Rd.)
Grayling Rd. N16 . . . 33Tb 71
Graylings, The WD5: Ab L . . . 5T 12
Grayling Sq. *E2* . . . *41Wb 91*
(off Nelson Gdns.)
Gray Pl. KT16: Ott . . . 79F 148
GRAYS . . . 49De 99
Grays Ct. RM10: Dag . . . 38Dd 76
Grayscroft Rd. SW16 . . . 66Mb 134
Gray's End Cl. RM17: Grays . . . 48Ce 99
Grays Farm Production Village
BR5: St P . . . 67Xc 139
Grays Farm Rd. BR5: St P . . . 67Xc 139
Grayshott Rd. SW11 . . . 54Jb 112
Gray's Inn . . . 7J 217 (43Pb 90)
Gray's Inn Bldgs. *EC1* . . . *6K 217*
(off Rosebery Av.)
Gray's Inn Pl. WC1 . . . 1J 223 (43Pb 90)
Gray's Inn Rd. WC1 . . . 3G 217 (41Nb 90)
Gray's Inn Sq. WC1 . . . 7K 217 (43Pb 90)
Grays La. KT18: Eps D . . . 91Pa 193
KT21: Asht . . . 91Pa 193
TW15: Ashf . . . 63R 128
Grayson Ho. EC1 . . . 4E 218
Grays Pk. Rd. SL2: Stoke P . . . 10L 61
Grays Pl. SL2: Slou . . . 6K 81
Grays Rd. SL1: Slou . . . 6K 81
TN16: Westrm . . . 93Rc 200
UB10: Uxb . . . 40N 63
Grays Shop. Cen.
RM17: Grays . . . 51Ce 121
Grays Ter. E7 . . . 37Lc 73
Gray St. SE1 . . . 2A 230 (47Qb 90)
Grays Wlk. CM13: Hut . . . 17Fe 41
Grayswood Gdns. SW20 . . . 68Xa 132
Grayswood Point SW15 . . . 60Wa 110
Gray's Yd. W1 . . . 3J 221
Graywood Ct. N12 . . . 24Eb 49
Grazebrook Rd. N16 . . . 33Tb 71
Grazeley Cl. DA6: Bex . . . 57Ed 118
Grazeley Ct. SE19 . . . 64Ub 135
Grazings, The HP2: Hem H . . . 1P 3
Gt. Acre Ct. SW4 . . . 56Mb 112
Gt. Amwell La. N8 . . . 27Pb 50
Gt. Arthur Ho. EC1 . . . 6D 218
Gt. Bell All. EC2 . . . 2F 225 (44Tb 91)
Great Benty UB7: W Dray . . . 49N 83
GREAT BOOKHAM . . . 98Da 191
Great Bookham Common . . . 93Ba 191
Great Brownings SE21 . . . 63Vb 135
GREAT BURGH . . . 89Ya 174
Gt. Bushey Dr. N20 . . . 18Db 31
Gt. Cambridge Ind. Est.
EN1: Enf . . . 15Xb 33
GREAT CAMBRIDGE JUNC. . . . 21Tb 51
Gt. Cambridge Rd. EN1: Enf . . . 16Wb 33
EN8: Chesh, Walt C . . . 6Yb 20
N9 . . . 21Tb 51
N17 . . . 22Tb 51
N18 . . . 21Tb 51
Gt. Castle St. W1 . . . 2A 222 (44Kb 90)
Gt. Central Av. HA4: Ruis . . . 36Y 65
Gt. Central St. NW1 . . . 7F 215 (43Hb 89)
Gt. Central Way HA9: Wemb . . . 35Sa 67
NW10 . . . 36Ua 68
Gt. Chapel St. W1 . . . 2D 222 (44Mb 90)
Gt. Chart St. SW11 . . . 56Fb 111
Gt. Chertsey Rd. TW2: Twick . . . 62Ba 129
TW13: Hanw, Twick . . . 62Ba 129
W4 . . . 53Sa 109
(not continuous)
Gt. Church La. W6 . . . 49Za 88
Great Cockcrow Railway . . . 74F 148
Gt. College St. SW1 . . . 3F 229 (48Nb 90)
Great Comp Garden . . . 93Fe 205
Great Cft. WC1 . . . 4G 217
Gt. Cross Av. SE10 . . . 52Fc 115
(not continuous)
Great Cullings RM7: Rush G . . . 33Gd 76
Gt. Cumberland M. W1 . . . 3F 221 (44Hb 89)
Gt. Cumberland Pl. W1 . . . 2F 221 (44Hb 89)
Gt. Dover St. SE1 . . . 2E 230 (47Sb 91)
Greatdown Rd. W7 . . . 42Ha 86
Gt. Eastern Ent. Cen. E14 . . . 47Dc 92
Gt. Eastern Rd. CM14: W'ley . . . 21Yd 58
E15 . . . 38Fc 73
EN8: Walt C . . . 6Yb 20
Gt. Eastern St. EC2 . . . 4H 219 (41Ub 91)
Gt. Eastern Wlk. EC2 . . . 1J 225
Great Eastern Wharf SW11 . . . 52Gb 111
Great Ellshams SM7: Bans . . . 88Cb 175
Gt. Elms Rd. BR2: Brom . . . 70Lc 137
HP3: Hem H . . . 6P 3
Greater London Ho. NW1 . . . 1B 216
Great Fld. NW9 . . . 25Ua 48
Greatfield NW5 . . . 36Lb 70
Greatfield Av. E6 . . . 42Pc 94
Greatfield Cl. N19 . . . 35Lb 70
SE4 . . . 56Cc 114
Greatfields Dr. UB8: Hil . . . 43Q 84
Greatfields Rd. IG11: Bark . . . 39Tc 74
Gt. Fleete Way IG11: Bark . . . 40Yc 75
Gt. Galley Cl. IG11: Bark . . . 41Xc 95
Gt. Gdns. Rd. RM11: Horn . . . 30Kd 57
Gt. Gatton Cl. CR0: C'don . . . 73Ac 158
Gt. George St. SW1 . . . 2E 228 (47Mb 90)
Gt. Gregories La. CM16: Epp . . . 5Uc 22
Great Gro. WD23: Bush . . . 14Da 27
Gt. Guildford Bus. Sq.
SE1 . . . 7D 224 (46Sb 91)
Gt. Guildford St. SE1 . . . 6D 224 (46Sb 91)
Great Hall . . . 50Hb 89
Great Hall *SW11* . . . *53Jb 112*
(off Battersea Pk. Rd.)
Greatham Rd. WD23: Bush . . . 13Z 27
Greatham Rd. Ind. Est.
WD23: Bush . . . 13Z 27
Greatham Wlk. SW15 . . . 60Wa 110
Gt. Harry Dr. SE9 . . . 62Qc 138
Great Heart HP2: Hem H . . . 1N 3
Greathurst End KT23: Bookh . . . 96Ba 191
Gt. James St. WC1 . . . 7H 217 (43Pb 90)
Gt. Leys Ct. AL2: Lon C . . . 9E 6
Gt. Marlborough St. W1 . . . 3B 222 (44Lb 90)
Gt. Maze Pond SE1 . . . 1G 231 (47Tb 91)
Gt. Nelmes Chase RM11: Horn . . . 29Pd 57
GREATNESS . . . 92Ld 203
Greatness La. TN14: S'oaks . . . 93Ld 203
Greatness Rd. TN14: S'oaks . . . 93Ld 203
Gt. Newport St. WC2 . . . 4F 223 (45Nb 90)
Gt. New St. EC4 . . . 2A 224
Gt. Norman St. TN14: Ide H . . . 100Bd 201
Great Nth. Leisure Pk. N12 . . . 24Fb 49
Great Nth. Rd. AL9: Brk P, Hat, Wel G . . . 2D 8
EN5: Barn . . . 12Bb 31
EN5: New Bar . . . 15Cb 31
EN6: Pot B . . . 5G 8
N2 . . . 29Gb 49
N6 . . . 29Gb 49
Great Nth. Way NW4 . . . 26Xa 48
Great Oaks CM13: Hut . . . 16De 41
IG7: Chig . . . 21Sc 54
Greatorex Ho. *E1* . . . *43Wb 91*
(off Greatorex St.)
Greatorex St. E1 . . . 43Wb 91
Gt. Ormond St. WC1 . . . 7G 217 (43Nb 90)
Gt. Owl Rd. IG7: Chig . . . 20Qc 36
Great Pk. WD4: K Lan . . . 2P 11
Great Pk. Cl. UB10: Hil . . . 38Q 64
Gt. Percy St. WC1 . . . 3J 217 (41Pb 70)
Gt. Peter St. SW1 . . . 4D 228 (48Mb 90)
Gt. Portland St. W1 . . . 4A 216 (42Kb 90)
Gt. Pulteney St. W1 . . . 4C 222 (45Lb 90)
Gt. Queen St. DA1: Dart . . . 59Pd 119
WC2 . . . 3G 223 (44Nb 90)
Great Rd. HP2: Hem H . . . 1P 3
Gt. Ropers La. CM13: Gt War . . . 23Wd 58
Gt. Russell Mans. WC1 . . . 1F 223
Gt. Russell St. WC1 . . . 2E 222 (44Mb 90)
Gt. St Helen's EC3 . . . 2H 225 (44Ub 91)
Gt. St Thomas Apostle
EC4 . . . 4E 224 (45Sb 91)
Gt. Scotland Yd. SW1 . . . 7F 223 (46Nb 90)
Great Slades EN6: Pot B . . . 5Bb 17
Gt. Smith St. SW1 . . . 3E 228 (48Mb 90)
Great Sth. West Rd. TW4: Houn . . . 56V 106
TW14: Bedf, Felt . . . 59S 106
Great Spilmans SE22 . . . 57Ub 113
Great Strand NW9 . . . 25Va 48
Gt. Sturgess Rd. HP1: Hem H . . . 2H 3
Gt. Suffolk St. SE1 . . . 7C 224 (46Rb 91)
Gt. Sutton St. EC1 . . . 6C 218 (42Rb 91)
Gt. Swan All. EC2 . . . 2F 225 (44Tb 91)
Great Tattenhams KT18: Tatt C . . . 90Xa 174
Great Thrift BR5: Pet W . . . 70Sc 138
Great Till Cl. TN14: Otf . . . 88Gd 182
Gt. Titchfield St. W1 . . . 6A 216 (42Kb 90)
Gt. Tower St. EC3 . . . 4H 225 (45Ub 91)
Gt. Trinity La. EC4 . . . 4E 224 (45Sb 91)
Great Turnstile WC1 . . . 1J 223 (43Pb 90)
Gt. Turnstile Ho. WC1 . . . 1J 223
GREAT WARLEY . . . 25Wd 58
Gt. Warley St. CM13: Gt War . . . 25Wd 58
Gt. Western Ind. Pk. UB2: S'hall . . . 47Da 85
Gt. Western Rd. W9 . . . 43Bb 89
W11 . . . 43Bb 89
Gt. West Rd. TW5: Hest . . . 53Z 107
TW7: Bford, Isle . . . 52Ga 108
TW8: Bford . . . 52Ga 108
W4 . . . 50Va 88
(Gt. Chertsey Rd.)
W4 . . . 50Ra 87
(Harvard Rd.)
W6 . . . 50Va 88
Gt. West Trad. Est. TW8: Bford . . . 51Ka 108
Gt. Whites Rd. HP3: Hem H . . . 4P 3
Gt. Winchester St. EC2 . . . 2G 225 (44Tb 91)
Gt. Windmill St. W1 . . . 4D 222 (45Mb 90)
Greatwood BR7: Chst . . . 66Qc 138
Greatwood Cl. KT16: Ott . . . 81E 168
Gt. Woodcote Dr. CR8: Purl . . . 82Mb 176
Gt. Woodcote Pk. CR8: Purl . . . 82Mb 176
Great Wood Country Pk. . . . 8P 9
Great Wood Vis. Cen. . . . 8P 9
Great Yd. SE1 . . . 1J 231
Greaves Cl. IG11: Bark . . . 38Tc 74
Greaves Cotts. *E14* . . . *43Ac 92*
(off Maroon St.)
Greaves Pl. SW17 . . . 63Gb 133
Greaves Twr. *SW10* . . . *52Eb 111*
(off Worlds End Est.)
Grebe Av. UB4: Yead . . . 44Z 85
Grebe Cl. E7 . . . 36Hc 73
E17 . . . 24Ac 52
IG11: Bark . . . 42Wc 95
Grebe Ct. *E14* . . . *47Ec 92*
(off River Barge Cl.)
SE8 . . . *51Bc 114*
(off Dorking Cl.)
SM1: Sutt . . . 78Bb 155
Grebe Crest RM20: W Thur . . . 49Wd 98
Grebe Ter. KT1: King T . . . 69Na 131
Grecian Cres. SE19 . . . 65Rb 135
Greding Wlk.
CM13: Hut . . . 19De 41
Greek Ct. W1 . . . 3E 222 (44Mb 90)
Greek St. W1 . . . 3E 222 (44Mb 90)
Green, The AL2: Lon C . . . 9H 7
BR1: Brom . . . 62Jc 137
(not continuous)
BR2: Hayes . . . 73Jc 159
BR5: St P . . . 66Xc 139
CM16: They B . . . 8Uc 22
(not continuous)
CR0: Sels . . . 81Bc 178
CR3: Wold . . . 95Cc 198
CR6: W'ham . . . 89Zb 178
DA2: Dart . . . 61Td 142
DA7: Bex . . . 53Cd 118
DA14: Sidc . . . 63Wc 139
DA16: Well . . . 56Uc 116
E4 . . . 18Ec 34
E11 . . . 30Kc 53
E15 . . . 37Gc 73
EN8: Chesh . . . 1Yb 20
EN9: Walt A . . . 6Ec 20
GU23: Rip . . . 93L 189
HA0: Wemb . . . 33Ja 66
IG8: Wfd G . . . 22Jc 53
IG9: Buck H . . . 18Kc 35
KT3: N Mald . . . 69Ta 131
KT10: Clay . . . 79Ha 152
KT12: Hers . . . 78Z 151
KT12: W Vill . . . 82U 170
KT17: Ewe . . . 83Wa 174
KT20: Tad . . . 91Ab 194
(Oatlands Rd.)
KT20: Tad . . . 95Za 194
(Stokes Riding)
KT22: Fet . . . 96Fa 192
N9 . . . 19Wb 33
N14 . . . 19Mb 32
N17 . . . 23Sb 51
N21 . . . 17Qb 32
RH3: Bkld . . . 5C 206
RH9: G'stone . . . 4P 209
RM3: Rom . . . 19Ld 39
RM4: Have B . . . 20Gd 38
RM13: Wenn . . . 45Nd 97
RM15: S Ock . . . 41Zd 99
RM16: Ors . . . 3C 100
RM18: W Til . . . 1G 122
SL1: Burn . . . 3A 80
SL1: Slou . . . 7H 81
SL3: Dat . . . 2M 103
SM1: Sutt . . . 76Db 155
SM4: Mord . . . 70Ab 132
SM5: Cars . . . 77Jb 156
SM6: Wall . . . 75Jb 156
SS17: Stan H . . . 2M 101
SW19 . . . 64Za 132
TN13: S'oaks . . . 94Md 203
TN14: Otf . . . 88Kd 183
TN15: Seal . . . *93Pd 203*
(off Church Rd.)
TN16: Westrm . . . 98Tc 200
TW2: Twick . . . 60Ga 108
TW5: Hest . . . 51Ca 107
TW9: Rich . . . 57Ma 109
TW13: Felt . . . 61X 129
TW15: Ashf . . . 64M 127
TW17: Shep . . . 70U 128
TW19: Wray . . . 58A 104
TW20: Eng G . . . 3N 125
UB2: S'hall . . . 48Aa 85
UB7: W Dray . . . 48M 83
UB9: Hare . . . 25L 43
UB10: Ick . . . 33S 64
W3 . . . 44Ua 88
W5 . . . 46Ma 87
WD3: Crox G . . . 16P 25
WD3: Sarr . . . 7J 11
WD25: Let H . . . 11Ga 28
Greenacre DA1: Dart . . . 61Md 141
GU21: Knap . . . 8J 167
SL4: Wind . . . 4C 102
Greenacre Cl. BR8: Swan . . . 70Gd 140
EN5: Barn . . . 10Bb 17
UB5: N'olt . . . 36Ba 65
Greenacre Ct. TW20: Eng G . . . 5N 125
Greenacre Gdns. E17 . . . 28Ec 52
Greenacre Pl. SM6: Wall . . . 75Kb 156
Green Acres CR0: C'don . . . 76Vb 157
DA14: Sidc . . . 63Wc 139
Greenacres CM16: Epp . . . 1Vc 23
HP2: Hem H . . . 3D 4
KT20: Lwr K . . . 100Bb 195
KT23: Bookh . . . 96Da 191
N3 . . . 26Bb 49
RH8: Oxt . . . 99Gc 199
SE9 . . . 58Qc 116
WD23: B Hea . . . 19Fa 28
Greenacres Av. UB10: Ick . . . 34P 63
Greenacres Cl. BR6: Farnb . . . 77Sc 160
RM13: Rain . . . 41Nd 97
Greenacres Dr. HA7: Stan . . . 23Ka 46
Greenacre Sq. SE16 . . . 47Zb 92
Greenacre Wlk. N14 . . . 20Mb 32
Greenall Cl. EN8: Chesh . . . 2Ac 20
Greenan Ct. *E2* . . . *41Zb 92*
(off Meath Cres.)
Green Arbour Ct. EC1 . . . 2B 224
Green Av. NW7 . . . 21Ta 47
W13 . . . 48Ka 86
Greenaway Av. N18 . . . 23Zb 52
Greenaway Gdns. NW3 . . . 35Db 69
Greenaway Ho. *NW8* . . . *39Eb 69*
(off Boundary Rd.)
WC1 . . . 4K 217

Greenaway Ter. TW19: Stanw 60N 105
(off Victory Cl.)
Green Bank E1 ....46Xb 91
N12 ....21Db 49
Greenbank Av. HA0: Wemb 36Ja 66
Greenbank Cl. E4 ....19Ec 34
RM3: Rom 20Md 39
Greenbank Ct. TW7: Isle 54Ha 108
(off Lanadron Cl.)
Greenbank Cres. NW4 ....28Ab 48
Greenbank Lodge BR7: Chst 68Qc 138
(off Forest Cl.)
Greenbank Rd. WD17: Wat 8T 12
Greenbanks AL1: St A 4D 6
DA1: Dart 61Nd 141
HA1: Harr 35Ga 66
RM14: Upm 33Ud 78
Greenbay Rd. SE7 ....52Mc 115
Greenberry St. NW8 ....2D 214 (40Gb 69)
Greenbrook Av. EN4: Had W 11Eb 31
Greenbury Cl. WD3: Chor 14E 24
Green Bus. Cen., The
TW18: Staines 63E 126
Green Cl. AL9: Brk P 8G 8
BR2: Brom 69Gc 137
EN8: Chesh 3Ac 20
NW9 ....30Sa 47
NW11 ....31Eb 69
SM5: Cars 75Hb 155
TW13: Hanw 64Aa 129
Greencoat Mans. SW1 ....4C 228
Greencoat Pl. SW1 ....5C 228 (49Lb 90)
Greencoat Row SW1 ....4C 228 (48Lb 90)
Green Comn. La. HP10: Wbrn G 1A 60
Green Ct. TW16: Sun 65V 128
Greencourt Av. CR0: C'don 75Xb 157
HA8: Edg 25Ra 47
Greencourt Gdns. CR0: C'don 74Xb 157
Greencourt Ho. E1 ....42Zb 92
(off Mile End Rd.)
Green Ct. Rd. BR8: Crock 71Fd 162
Greencourt Rd. BR5: Pet W 71Tc 160
Greencrest Pl. NW2 ....34Wa 68
Greencroft HA8: Edg 22Sa 47
Greencroft Av. HA4: Ruis 33Y 65
Greencroft Cl. E6 ....43Mc 93
Greencroft Gdns. EN1: Enf 13Ub 33
NW6 ....38Db 69
Greencroft Rd. TW5: Hest 53Ba 107
Green Curve SM7: Bans 86Bb 175
Green Dale SE5 ....56Tb 113
SE22 ....57Ub 113
Greendale NW7 ....21Ua 48
Green Dale Cl. SE22 ....57Ub 113
Greendale M. SL2: Slou 5L 81
Greendale Wlk. DA11: Nflt 2A 144
Green Dell Way HP3: Hem H 3C 4
Green Dragon Ct. SE1 ....7F 225
Green Dragon Ho. WC2 ....2G 223
Green Dragon La. N21 ....16Qb 32
TW8: Bford 50Na 87
Green Dragons Airsports 92Dc 198
Green Dragon Yd. E1 ....43Wb 91
Green Dr. GU23: Rip 95H 189
SL3: L'ly 49A 82
(not continuous)
UB1: S'hall 46Ca 85
Greene Ct. SE14 ....51Zb 114
(off Samuel Cl.)
Green Edge WD25: Wat 7W 12
Greene Fielde End TW18: Staines 66M 127
Greene Ho. SE1 ....3F 231
SL9: Chal P 21A 42
GREEN END 3J 3
Green End KT9: Chess 77Na 153
N21 ....19Rb 33
Green End Bus. Cen. WD3: Sarr 9J 11
Green End Gdns. HP1: Hem H 3J 3
Green End La. HP1: Hem H 2H 3
Green End Rd. HP1: Hem H 2J 3
(not continuous)
Greenend Rd. W4 ....47Ua 88
Greener Ct. CR0: C'don 72Sb 157
(off Goodman Ct.)
Greener Ho. SW4 ....55Mb 112
Greene Wlk. HP4: Berk 2A 2
Green Farm Cl. BR6: Chels 78Vc 161
Green Farm La. DA12: Shorne 1N 145
Greenfell Mans. SE8 ....51Dc 114
Greenfern Av. SL1: Slou 4A 80
Green Ferry Way E17 ....27Zb 52
Greenfield Av. KT5: Surb 73Ra 153
WD19: Wat 19Z 27
Greenfield Dr. BR1: Brom 68Lc 137
N2 ....28Hb 49
Greenfield End SL9: Chal P 24B 42
Greenfield Gdns. BR5: Pet W 73Tc 160
NW2 ....33Ab 68
RM9: Dag 39Zc 75
Greenfield Ho. SW19 ....60Za 110
TW20: Eng G 5M 125
(off Kings La.)
Greenfield Link CR5: Coul 87Nb 176
Greenfield Rd. DA2: Wilm 64Fd 140
E1 ....43Wb 91
N15 ....29Ub 51
RM9: Dag 38Yc 75
Greenfields EN6: Cuff 2Nb 18
IG10: Lough 14Qc 36
UB1: S'hall 44Ca 85
Greenfields Cl. CM13: Gt War 23Yd 58
IG10: Lough 14Qc 36
Greenfield St. EN9: Walt A 6Ec 20
Greenfield Way HA2: Harr 27Da 45
Greenfinches DA3: Lfield 69De 143
GREENFORD 41Ca 85
Greenford Av. UB1: S'hall 45Ba 85
W7 ....42Ga 86
Greenford Bus. Cen. UB6: G'frd 38Fa 66
Greenford Gdns. UB6: G'frd 41Da 85
GREENFORD GREEN 37Ga 66
Greenford Ind. Est. UB6: G'frd 38Da 65
Greenford Pk. UB6: G'frd 38Fa 66
Greenford Rd. HA1: Harr 39Fa 66
SM1: Sutt 77Db 155
(not continuous)
UB1: S'hall 46Ea 86
UB6: G'frd 46Ea 86
GREENFORD RDBT. 40Fa 66
Greenford Sports Cen. 41Ca 85
Green Gdns. BR6: Farnb 78Sc 160
Greengate UB6: G'frd 37Ka 66
Greengate Lodge E13 ....40Kc 73
(off Hollybush St.)
Greengate Pde. IG2: Ilf 30Tc 54
Greengate St. E13 ....40Kc 73
Green Glade CM16: They B 9Uc 22
Green Glades RM11: Horn 30Pd 57
Greenhalgh Wlk. N2 ....28Eb 49
Greenham Cl. SE1 ....2K 229 (47Qb 90)
Greenham Cres. E4 ....23Bc 52
Greenham Ho. E9 ....39Yb 72
(off Templecombe Rd.)
TW7: Isle 55Fa 108
Greenham Rd. N10 ....26Jb 50
Greenham Wlk. GU21: Wok 10N 167
Greenhaven Dr. SE28 ....44Xc 95
Greenhayes Av. SM7: Bans 86Cb 175
Greenhayes Cl. RH2: Reig 6L 207
Greenhayes Gdns. SM7: Bans 87Cb 175
Greenheath Bus. Cen. E2 ....42Xb 91
(off Three Colts La.)
Green Hedges TW1: Twick 57La 108
Greenheys Cl. HA6: Nwood 25U 44
Greenheys Dr. E18 ....27Hc 53
Greenheys Pl. GU22: Wok 90B 168
GREENHILL 29Ga 46
Green Hill BR6: Downe 84Pc 180
SE18 ....50Pc 94
Greenhill HA9: Wemb 33Ra 67
IG9: Buck H 18Lc 35
NW3 ....35Fb 69
SM1: Sutt 75Eb 155
Greenhill Av. CR3: Cat'm 93Xb 197
Greenhill Ct. EN5: New Bar 15Db 31
HP1: Hem H 3K 3
SE18 ....50Pc 94
Greenhill Cres. WD18: Wat 16U 26
Greenhill Gdns. UB5: N'olt 40Ba 65
Greenhill Gro. E12 ....35Nc 74
Green Hill La. CR6: W'ham 89Ac 178
Greenhill Pde. EN5: New Bar 15Db 31
Greenhill Pk. EN5: New Bar 15Db 31
NW10 ....39Ua 68
Greenhill Rd. DA11: Nflt 1B 144
HA1: Harr 30Ga 46
NW10 ....39Ua 68
TN14: Otf 87Ld 183
Greenhills Cl. WD3: Rick 15K 25
Greenhill's Rents EC1 ....7B 218 (43Rb 91)
Greenhills Ter. N1 ....37Tb 71
Greenhill Ter. SE18 ....50Pc 94
UB5: N'olt 40Ba 65
Greenhill Way HA1: Harr 30Ga 46
HA9: Wemb 33Ra 67
GREENHITHE 56Xd 120
Greenhithe Cl. DA15: Sidc 59Uc 116
Greenholm Rd. SE9 ....57Rc 116
Green Hundred Rd. SE15 ....51Wb 113
Greenhurst La. RH8: Oxt 4K 211
Greenhurst Rd. SE27 ....64Qb 134
Greening St. SE2 ....49Yc 95
Greenlake Ter. TW18: Staines 66J 127
Greenland Cres. UB2: S'hall 48Y 85
Greenland Ho. E1 ....42Ac 92
(off Ernest St.)
Greenland M. SE8 ....50Zb 92
Greenland Pl. NW1 ....39Kb 70
Greenland Quay SE16 ....49Zb 92
Greenland Rd. EN5: Barn 16Ya 30
NW1 ....39Lb 70
Greenlands KT16: Chert 76E 148
KT19: Ewe 78Ra 153
TN15: Plat 92De 205
Greenlands La. NW4 ....25Xa 48
Greenlands Rd. KT13: Weyb 76R 150
TN15: Kems'g 91Rd 203
TW18: Staines 63J 127
Greenland St. NW1 ....39Kb 70
Greenland Way CR0: Bedd 73Mb 156
Green La. AL1: St A 6E 6
BR7: Chst 61Rc 138
CM14: B'wood 18Wd 40
CM14: Gt War 24Wd 58
CM14: Kel H 12Sd 40
CM15: Pil H 15Yd 40
CR3: Cat'm 94Sb 197
CR5: Coul 98Bb 195
CR6: W'ham 88Ac 178
CR7: Thor H 66Pb 134
CR8: Purl 83Lb 176
DA12: Shorne 5M 145
E4 ....11Gc 35
EN9: Walt A 6Lc 21
GU4: W Cla 99J 189
GU22: Wok 3M 187
GU23: Ock 96R 190
GU24: Chob 2K 167
HA1: Harr 34Ga 66
HA6: Nwood 23T 44
HA7: Stan 21Ka 46
HA8: Edg 21Pa 47
(not continuous)
HP2: Hem H 3C 4
HP3: Bov 10B 2
IG1: Ilf 33Tc 74
IG3: Ilf 32Xc 75
IG7: Chig 18Sc 36
KT3: N Mald 71Sa 153
KT4: Wor Pk 74Wa 154
KT8: W Mole 71Da 151
KT9: Chess 81Ma 173
KT11: Cobh 84Aa 171
KT12: Hers 79X 151
KT14: Byfl 84P 169
KT15: Add 75G 148
KT16: Chert 75G 148
KT20: Lwr K 98Bb 195
KT21: Asht 89La 172
KT22: Lea 93Ma 193
(not continuous)
NW4 ....28Za 48
RH1: Blet 3L 209
RH1: Redh 4N 207
RH2: Reig 6H 207
RM8: Dag 32Xc 75
RM14: Avel, Upm 39Td 78
RM16: N Stif, Ors 43De 99
SE9 ....60Rc 116
SE20 ....66Zb 136
SL1: Burn 1A 80
SL2: Farn C 7F 60
SL3: Dat 3M 103
SL4: Wind 4E 102
SL5: Asc 7C 124
SM4: Mord 72Cb 155
(Central Rd.)
SM4: Mord 73Ya 154
(Lwr. Morden La.)
SW16 ....66Pb 134
TW4: Houn 55X 107
TW13: Hanw 64Aa 129
Green La. TW16: Sun 66V 128
TW17: Shep 72S 150
TW18: Staines 67G 126
TW20: Egh 63D 126
(The Avenue)
TW20: Egh 64D 126
(Vicarage Cres.)
TW20: Thorpe 68E 126
UB8: Hil 43S 84
W7 ....47Ga 86
WD3: Crox G 15P 25
WD19: Wat 17Y 27
Green La. Av. KT12: Hers 78Y 151
Green La. Bus. Pk. SE9 ....61Qc 138
Green La. Cl. KT14: Byfl 84P 169
KT16: Chert 75G 148
Green La. Cotts. HA7: Stan 21Ka 46
Green La. Ct. SL1: Burn 1A 80
Green La. Gdns. CR7: Thor H 68Sb 135
Green Lanes KT19: Ewe 81Ua 174
(not continuous)
N4 ....27Rb 51
N8 ....27Rb 51
N13 ....23Pb 50
N15 ....27Rb 51
N16 ....27Rb 51
N21 ....20Qb 32
Green La. W. KT24: W Hor 97Q 190
Greenlaw Ct. W5 ....44Ma 87
(off Mount Pk. Rd.)
Greenlaw Gdns. KT3: N Mald 73Va 154
Greenlawn La. TW8: Bford 49Ma 87
Green Lawns HA4: Ruis 32Y 65
Greenlawns N12 ....23Db 49
Greenlawns, The SE18 ....49Rc 94
(off Vincent Rd.)
Greenlaw St. SE18 ....48Qc 94
Green Leaf Av. SM6: Bedd 77Mb 156
Greenleaf Cl. SW2 ....59Qb 112
Greenleafe Dr. IG6: Ilf 27Rc 54
Greenleaf Ho. Bus. Cen. EN6: Pot B 4Cb 17
Greenleaf Rd. E6 ....39Lc 73
E17 ....27Bc 52
Greenleaf Way HA3: W'stone 27Ha 46
Greenlea Pk. SW19 ....66Fb 133
Green Leas KT1: King T 69Na 131
(off Mill St.)
TW16: Sun 65V 128
Greenleas EN9: Walt A 6Gc 21
Green Leas Cl. TW16: Sun 65V 128
Greenleaves Ct. TW15: Ashf 65R 128
Greenleigh Av. BR5: St P 70Xc 139
Greenlink Wlk. TW9: Kew 53Ra 109
Green Man Gdns. W13 ....45Ja 86
Green Man La. TW14: Felt 56W 106
(not continuous)
W13 ....45Ja 86
Green Mnr. Way DA11: Nflt 56Be 121
Green Man Pas. W13 ....45Ka 86
(not continuous)
GREEN MAN RDBT. 31Hc 73
Greenman St. N1 ....38Sb 71
Green Mead KT10: Esh 79Ba 151
Greenmead DA18: Erith 48Ad 95
Greenmead Cl. SE25 ....71Wb 157
Green Mdw. EN6: Pot B 2Cb 17
Greenmeads GU22: Wok 94A 188
Green Moor Link N21 ....17Rb 33
Greenmoor Rd. EN3: Enf H 12Yb 34
Greenoak Pl. EN4: Cockf 12Hb 31
Greenoak Ri. TN16: Big H 90Lc 179
Green Oaks UB2: S'hall 49Z 85
Greenoak Way SW19 ....63Za 132
Greenock Rd. SL1: Slou 4E 80
SW16 ....67Mb 134
W3 ....48Ra 87
Greenock Way RM1: Rom 24Gd 56
Greeno Cres. TW17: Shep 71Q 150
Green Pde. TW3: Houn 57Da 107
Green Pk. 7A 222 (47Kb 90)
Green Pk. TW18: Staines 62G 126
Greenpark Ct. HA0: Wemb 38La 66
Green Pk. Way UB6: G'frd 38Ga 66
(not continuous)
Green Pl. DA1: Cray 57Gd 118
SE10 ....47Gc 93
Green Point E15 ....37Gc 73
Green Pond Cl. E17 ....27Bc 52
Green Pond Rd. E17 ....27Ac 52
Green Ride CM16: Epp 7Rc 22
IG10: Lough 14Lc 35
(not continuous)
Green Rd. GU23: Ock 96S 190
N14 ....16Kb 32
N20 ....20Eb 31
TW20: Thorpe 70C 126
Green Rd. Nth. EN3: Pond E 14Ac 34
Greenrod Pl. TW8: Bford 50Na 87
(off Clayponds La.)
Greenroof Way SE10 ....48Hc 93
Greensand Cl. RH1: Mers 100Mb 196
Green Sand Rd. RH1: Redh 5A 208
Greens Cl., The IG10: Lough 12Qc 36
Green's Ct. W1 ....4D 222
W11 ....46Bb 89
(off Lansdowne M.)
Green's End SE18 ....49Rc 94
Greenshank Cl. E17 ....24Ac 52
Greenshaw CM14: B'wood 18Xd 40
Greens Health & Fitness
Chingford 21Ec 52
Purley 79Qb 156
Greenshields Ind. Est. E16 ....47Jc 93
Greenside BR8: Swan 68Fd 140
DA5: Bexl 60Ad 117
RM8: Dag 32Yc 75
SL2: Slou 3E 80
WD6: Bore 10Qa 15
Greenside Cl. IG6: Ilf 23Sc 54
N20 ....19Fb 31
SE6 ....61Fc 137
Greenside Cotts. GU23: Rip 93L 189
Greenside Dr. KT21: Asht 90Ka 172
Greenside Rd. CR0: C'don 73Qb 156
W12 ....48Wa 88
Greenside Wlk. TN16: Big H 90Kc 179
Greenslade Av. KT21: Asht 91Ra 193
Greenslade Rd. IG11: Bark 38Tc 74
Greensleeves Cl. AL4: St A 3G 6
Greensleeves Dr. CM14: W'ley 22Xd 58
Greenstead Av. IG8: Wfd G 24Lc 53
Greenstead Cl. IG8: Wfd G 23Lc 53
Greenstead Gdns. IG8: Wfd G 23Lc 53
SW15 ....57Xa 110
Greensted Ct. CR3: Whyt 91Wb 197
(off Godstone Rd.)
Greensted Rd. IG10: Lough 17Nc 36
Greenstone M. E11 ....30Jc 53
Green St. AL9: Hat 2J 9
E7 ....37Kc 73
E13 ....37Kc 73
EN3: Brim, Enf H 12Yb 34
TW16: Sun 67W 128
W1 ....4G 221 (45Jb 90)
WD3: Chen, Chor 11E 24
WD6: Bore 7Qa 15
WD7: Shenl 7Qa 15
GREEN STREET GREEN
BR6 ....79Vc 161
DA2 ....65Wd 142
Green St. Grn. Rd. DA1: Dart 60Rd 119
DA2: Daren, Grn St 60Rd 119
Greenstreet Hill SE14 ....54Zb 114
Greensward WD23: Bush 16Da 27
Green Ter. EC1 ....4A 218 (41Qb 90)
Green Tiles UB9: Den 31H 63
Green Tiles La. UB9: Den 30H 43
Green Trees CM16: Epp 3Wc 23
Green Vale DA6: Bex 57Zc 117
W5 ....44Pa 87
Greenvale Rd. GU21: Knap 10H 167
SE9 ....56Pc 116
Green Verges HA7: Stan 24Ma 47
Green Vw. KT9: Chess 80Pa 153
RH9: G'stone 3P 209
Greenview Av. BR3: Beck 72Ac 158
CR0: C'don 72Ac 158
Green Vw. Cl. HP3: Bov 1C 10
Greenview Cl. W3 ....46Ua 88
Green Vw. Ct. WD5: Ab L 4T 12
Greenview Ct. TW15: Ashf 63P 127
Greenview Dr. SW20 ....69Ya 132
Green Wlk. DA1: Cray 57Hd 118
HA4: Ruis 32V 64
IG8: Wfd G 23Nc 54
IG10: Lough 17Nc 36
NW4 ....29Za 48
SE1 ....4H 231 (48Ub 91)
TW12: Hamp 65Ba 129
UB2: S'hall 50Ca 85
Green Wlk., The E4 ....18Fc 35
Greenwatt Way SL1: Slou 8H 81
Green Way BR2: Brom 72Nc 160
DA3: Hartl 71Ae 165
KT23: Bookh 95Da 191
RH1: Redh 4N 207
SE9 ....57Mc 115
TW16: Sun 70W 128
Greenway BR7: Chst 64Qc 138
CM13: Hut 17Ce 41
E6 ....42Qc 94
E15 ....40Fc 73
E20 ....39Dc 72
HA3: Kenton 29Na 47
HA5: Pinn 26X 45
HP2: Hem H 2B 4
IG8: Wfd G 22Lc 53
N14 ....19Nb 32
N20 ....19Cb 31
RM3: Hrld W 23Rd 57
RM8: Dag 33Yc 75
SL1: Burn 10A 60
SM6: Wall 77Lb 156
SW20 ....70Ya 132
TN16: Tats 92Lc 199
UB4: Yead 41W 84
Greenway, The BR5: St M Cry 72Xc 161
EN3: Enf W 7Zb 20
EN6: Pot B 5Cb 17
HA3: W'stone 25Ga 46
HA5: Pinn 30Ba 45
KT18: Eps 86Qa 173
NW9 ....26Ta 47
RH8: Oxt 5M 211
SL1: Slou 6N 80
SL9: Chal P 27A 42
TW4: Houn 56Ba 107
UB8: Uxb 40L 63
UB10: Ick 33R 64
WD3: Rick 17J 25
Greenway Av. E17 ....28Fc 53
Greenway Cl. KT14: W Byf 85J 169
N4 ....33Sb 71
N11 ....23Jb 50
N15 ....28Vb 51
N20 ....19Cb 31
NW9 ....26Ta 47
Greenway Ct. IG1: Ilf 32Qc 74
Greenway Dr. TW18: Staines 67M 127
Greenway Gdns. CR0: C'don 76Bc 158
HA3: W'stone 26Ga 46
NW9 ....26Ta 47
UB6: G'frd 41Ca 85
Greenways BR3: Beck 69Cc 136
DA3: Lfield 69Fe 143
EN7: G Oak 1Rb 19
KT10: Hin W 77Ga 152
KT20: Walt H 97Xa 194
TW20: Egh 64A 126
WD5: Ab L 5U 12
Greenways, The TW1: Twick 58Ja 108
Greenways Ct. RM11: Horn 30Md 57
Greenways Dr. SL5: S'dale 4C 146
Greenwell Cl. RH9: G'stone 2P 209
Greenwell St. W1 ....6A 216 (42Kb 90)
GREENWICH 52Ec 114
Greenwich Bus. Pk. SE10 ....52Dc 114
Greenwich Chu. St. SE10 ....51Ec 114
Greenwich Ct. AL1: St A 3E 6
E1 ....44Xb 91
(off Cavell St.)
EN8: Walt C 6Ac 20
Greenwich Cres. E6 ....43Nc 94
Greenwich Foot Tunnel SE10 ....50Ec 92
Greenwich Hgts. SE18 ....52Nc 116
Greenwich Heritage Cen. 48Rc 94
Greenwich High Rd. SE10 ....53Dc 114
Greenwich Ho. SE13 ....58Fc 115
Greenwich Mkt. SE10 ....51Ec 114
GREENWICH MILLENNIUM VILLAGE
....48Hc 93
Greenwich Pk. 52Fc 115
Greenwich Pk. St. SE10 ....51Fc 115
Greenwich Peninsula Ecology Pk. 48Jc 93
Greenwich Picturehouse 52Ec 114
Greenwich Quay SE8 ....51Dc 114
Greenwich Shop. Pk. SE7 ....49Kc 93
Greenwich Sth. St. SE10 ....53Dc 114
Greenwich Theatre 52Ec 114
Greenwich Vw. Pl. E14 ....48Dc 92
Greenwich Way EN9: Walt A 8Ec 20
Greenwich Yacht Club 48Jc 93
Greenwood NW5 ....36Lb 70
(off Osney Cres.)
Greenwood Av. EN3: Enf H 12Ac 34
EN7: Chesh 3Xb 19
RM10: Dag 35Dd 76
Greenwood Bus. Cen.
CR0: C'don 73Vb 157
Greenwood Cl. BR5: Pet W 72Uc 160
DA15: Sidc 61Wc 139
EN7: Chesh 3Xb 19
KT7: T Ditt 74Ja 152
KT15: Wdhm 83H 169
SM4: Mord 70Ab 132
UB3: Hayes 46W 84
WD23: B Hea 17Ga 28
Greenwood Cotts. SL5: S'dale 2G 146
Greenwood Dr. E4 ....22Fc 53
WD25: Wat 6X 13
Greenwood Gdns. CR3: Cat'm 97Wb 197
IG6: Ilf 24Sc 54
N13 ....20Rb 33
RH8: Oxt 6L 211
WD7: Shenl 5Na 15
Greenwood Ho. EC1 ....4K 217
N22 ....25Pb 50
RM17: Grays 51De 121
(off Argent St.)
SE4 ....56Zb 114
Greenwood La. TW12: Hamp H 64Da 129
Greenwood Mans. IG11: Bark 38Wc 75
(off Lansbury Av.)
Greenwood Pk. KT2: King T 66Ua 132
Greenwood Pk. Leisure Cen. 7P 5
Greenwood Pl. NW5 ....36Kb 70
TN15: Wro 89Ce 185
Greenwood Rd. CR0: C'don 73Rb 157
CR4: Mitc 69Mb 134
DA5: Bexl 63Fd 140
E8 ....37Wb 71
E13 ....40Hc 73
GU21: Wok 2J 187
GU24: Brkwd 3A 186
IG7: Chig 21Xc 55
KT7: T Ditt 74Ja 152
TW7: Isle 55Ha 108
Greenwoods, The HA2: Harr 34Ea 66
Greenwood Ter. NW10 ....39Ta 67
Greenwood Theatre 1G 231 (47Tb 91)
Greenwood Way TN13: S'oaks 97Hd 202
Green Wrythe Cres.
SM5: Cars 74Gb 155
Green Wrythe La. SM5: Cars 72Fb 155
Green Yd. WC1 ....5J 217 (42Pb 90)
Green Yard, The EC3 ....3H 225
Greenyard EN9: Walt A 5Ec 20
Greer Rd. HA3: Hrw W 25Ea 46
Greet Ho. SE1 ....2A 230
Greet St. SE1 ....7A 224 (46Qb 90)
Greg Cl. E10 ....30Ec 52
Gregor M. SE3 ....52Jc 115
Gregory Av. EN6: Pot B 5Eb 17
Gregory Cl. BR2: Brom 70Gc 137
GU21: Wok 9N 167
TN14: S'ham 83Hd 182
Gregory Cres. SE9 ....59Mc 115
Gregory Dr. SL4: Old Win 8M 103
Gregory M. EN9: Walt A 4Dc 20
Gregory Pl. W8 ....47Db 89
Gregory Rd. RM6: Chad H 28Zc 55
SL2: Hedg 3H 61
UB2: S'hall 48Ca 85
Gregson Cl. WD6: Bore 11Sa 29
Gregson's Ride IG10: Lough 10Qc 22
Greig Cl. N8 ....29Nb 50
Greig Ter. SE17 ....51Rb 113
Grenaby Av. CR0: C'don 73Tb 157
Grenaby Rd. CR0: C'don 73Tb 157
Grenada Ho. E14 ....45Bc 92
(off Limehouse C'way.)
Grenada Rd. SE7 ....52Lc 115
Grenade St. E14 ....45Bc 92
Grenadier Cl. AL4: St A 3G 6
Grenadier Pl. CR3: Cat'm 94Sb 197
Grenadier St. E16 ....46Qc 94
Grena Gdns. TW9: Rich 56Pa 109
Grenard Cl. SE15 ....52Wb 113
Grena Rd. TW9: Rich 56Pa 109
Grendon Gdns. HA9: Wemb 33Qa 67
Grendon Ho. E9 ....38Yb 72
(off Shore Pl.)
N1 ....2H 217
Grendon Lodge HA8: Edg 19Sa 29
Grendon St. NW8 ....5D 214 (42Gb 89)
Grenfell Av. RM12: Horn 32Hd 76
Grenfell Cl. WD6: Bore 11Sa 29
Grenfell Ct. NW7 ....23Xa 48
Grenfell Gdns. HA3: Kenton 31Na 67
IG3: Ilf 29Vc 55
Grenfell Ho. SE5 ....52Sb 113
Grenfell Rd. CR4: Mitc 65Hb 133
W11 ....45Za 88
Grenfell Twr. W11 ....45Za 88
Grenfell Wlk. W11 ....45Za 88
Grenier Apartments SE15 ....52Xb 113
Grennan Cl. CM13: Ingve 23Fe 59
Grennell Cl. SM1: Sutt 75Fb 155
Grennell Rd. SM1: Sutt 75Eb 155
Grenoble Gdns. N13 ....23Qb 50
Grenside Rd. KT13: Weyb 76R 150
Grenville Cl. EN8: Walt C 4Zb 20
KT5: Surb 74Sa 153
KT11: Cobh 85Z 171
N3 ....25Ab 48
SL1: Burn 10A 60
Grenville Ct. W13 ....43Ka 86
WD3: Chor 14E 24
Grenville Gdns. IG8: Wfd G 25Lc 53
Grenville Ho. E3 ....40Ac 72
(off Arbery Rd.)
SE8 ....51Cc 114
(off New King St.)
SW1 ....51Mb 112
(off Dolphin Sq.)
Grenville M. N19 ....32Nb 70
SW7 ....5A 226 (49Eb 89)
TW12: Hamp H 64Da 129
Grenville Pl. NW7 ....22Ta 47
SW7 ....4A 226 (48Eb 89)
Grenville Rd. CR0: New Ad 81Ec 178
N19 ....32Nb 70
RM16: Chaf H 49Xd 98
Grenville St. WC1 ....6G 217 (42Nb 90)
Gresford Cl. AL4: St A 2H 7
Gresham Av. CR6: W'ham 90Ac 178
DA3: Hartl 70Be 143
N20 ....21Hb 49

Gresham Cl. CM14: B'wood 20Yd 40
DA5: Bexl 58Ad 117
EN2: Enf 13Sb 33
RH8: Oxt 1K 211
Gresham Ct. CM14: B'wood 20Yd 40
CR8: Purl 83Qb 176
TW18: Staines 64J 127
Gresham Dr. RM6: Chad H 29Xc 55
Gresham Gdns. NW11 32Ab 68
Gresham Lodge E17 29Dc 52
Gresham Pl. N19 33Mb 70
RH8: Oxt 1K 211
Gresham Rd. BR3: Beck 68Ac 136
CM14: B'wood 20Yd 40
E6 40Pc 74
E16 44Kc 93
HA8: Edg 23Pa 47
NW10 36Ta 67
RH8: Oxt 100Hc 199
SE25 70Wb 135
SL1: Slou 4E 80
SW9 55Qb 112
TW3: Houn 53Ea 108
TW12: Hamp 65Ca 129
TW18: Staines 64H 127
UB10: Hil 40Q 64
Gresham St. EC2 2D 224 (44Sb 91)
Gresham Way SW19 62Db 133
Gresham Way Ind. Est. *SW19* 62Db 133
(off Gresham Way)
Gresley Cl. E17 30Ac 52
N15 28Tb 51
Gresley Ct. EN1: Enf 7Yb 20
EN6: Pot B 2Eb 17
Gresley Rd. N19 32Lb 70
Gressenhall Rd. SW18 58Bb 111
Gresse St. W1 1D 222 (44Mb 90)
Gresswell Cl. DA14: Sidc 62Wc 139
Greswell St. SW6 53Za 110
Greta Bank KT24: W Hor 98S 190
Gretton Ho. *E2* 41Yb 92
(off Globe Rd.)
Gretton Rd. N17 24Vb 51
Greville Av. CR2: Sels 82Zb 178
Greville Cl. AL9: Wel G 6E 8
KT21: Asht 91Na 193
TW1: Twick 59Ka 108
Greville Ct. *E5* 34Xb 71
(off Napoleon Rd.)
HA1: Harr 35Ga 66
KT21: Asht 90Na 173
(off Park Rd.)
KT23: Bookh 97Da 191
Greville Hall NW6 40Db 69
Greville Ho. SW1 3G 227
Greville Lodge E13 39Kc 73
HA8: Edg 21Ra 47
(off Broadhurst Av.)
N12 22Db 49
Greville M. *NW6* 39Db 69
(off Greville Rd.)
Greville Pk. Av. KT21: Asht 90Na 173
Greville Pk. Rd. KT21: Asht 90Na 173
Greville Pl. NW6 40Db 69
Greville Rd. E17 28Ec 52
NW6 40Db 69
TW10: Rich 58Pa 109
Greville St. EC1 1K 223 (43Qb 90)
(not continuous)
Grey Alders SM7: Bans 86Ya 174
Greycaine Rd. WD24: Wat 9Z 13
Greycaine Trad. Est. WD24: Wat 9Z 13
Grey Cl. NW11 30Eb 49
Greycoat Gdns. SW1 4D 228
Greycoat Pl. SW1 4D 228 (48Mb 90)
Greycoat St. SW1 4D 228 (48Mb 90)
Greycot Rd. BR3: Beck 64Cc 136
Grey Eagle St. E1 7K 219 (42Vb 91)
Greyfell Cl. HA7: Stan 22Ka 46
Greyfields Cl. CR8: Purl 85Rb 177
Greyfriars CM13: Hut 17De 41
SE26 62Wb 135
(off Wells Pk. Rd.)
Greyfriars Dr. GU24: Bisl 7E 166
SL5: Asc 1A 146
Greyfriars Ho. RM11: Horn 30Md 57
Greyfriars Pas. EC1 2C 224 (44Rb 91)
Greyfriars Rd. GU23: Rip 96J 189
Greyhound Commercial Cen., The
DA1: Cray 57Gd 118
Greyhound Ct. WC2 4J 223 (45Pb 90)
Greyhound Hill NW4 27Wa 48
Greyhound La. EN6: S Mim 5Wa 16
RM16: Ors 7C 100
SW16 65Mb 134
Greyhound Mans. *W6* 51Ab 110
(off Greyhound Rd.)
Greyhound Rd. N17 27Ub 51
NW10 41Xa 88
SM1: Sutt 78Eb 155
W6 51Za 110
W14 51Za 110
Greyhound Ter. SW16 67Lb 134
Greyhound Way DA1: Cray 57Gd 118
Grey Ho. *W12* 45Xa 88
(off White City Est.)
Grey Ho., The WD17: Wat 12W 26
Greyladies Gdns. SE10 54Ec 114
Greys Pk. Cl. BR2: Kes 78Mc 159
Greystead Rd. SE23 59Yb 114
Greystoke Av. HA5: Pinn 27Ca 45
Greystoke Ct. W5 42Na 87
Greystoke Dr. HA4: Ruis 30R 44
Greystoke Gdns. EN2: Enf 14Mb 32
W5 42Na 87
Greystoke Ho. *SE15* 51Wb 113
(off Peckham Pk. Rd.)
W5 42Na 87
Greystoke Lodge *W5* 42Pa 87
(off Hanger La.)
Greystoke Pk. Ter. W5 41Ma 87
Greystoke Pl. EC4 2K 223 (44Qb 90)
Greystoke Rd. SL2: Slou 3D 80
Greystone Cl. CR2: Sels 83Yb 178
Greystone Gdns. HA3: Kenton 30La 46
IG6: Ilf 26Sc 54
Greystone Pk. TN14: Sund 97Ad 201
Greystones Cl. RH1: Redh 8M 207
TN15: Kems'g 89Nd 183
Greystones Dr. RH2: Reig 4L 207
Greyswood Av. N18 23Zb 52
Greyswood St. SW16 65Kb 134
Greythorne Rd. GU21: Wok 10L 167
Grey Towers Av. RM11: Horn 31Md 77
Grey Towers Gdns. RM11: Horn 31Ld 77
Grey Turner Ho. W12 44Wa 88
Grice Av. TN16: Big H 85Kc 179
Gridiron Pl. RM14: Upm 34Rd 77
Grierson Ho. SW16 63Lb 134
Grierson Rd. SE23 59Zb 114
Grieves Rd. DA11: Nflt 2B 144
Griffen Ct. BR3: Beck 67Dc 136
Griffin Av. RM14: Upm 30Ud 58
Griffin Cen. TW14: Felt 55X 107
Griffin Cen., The *KT1: King T* 68Ma 131
(off Market Pl.)
Griffin Cl. NW10 36Xa 68
SL1: Slou 7G 80
Griffin Ct. DA11: Nflt 57Ce 121
KT21: Asht 91Pa 193
KT23: Bookh 98Da 191
TW8: Bford 51Na 109
W4 50Va 88
Griffin Ho. CR0: C'don 73Rb 157
E14 44Dc 92
(off Ricardo St.)
N1 1H 219
(off New Era Est.)
W6 49Za 88
(off Hammersmith Rd.)
Griffin Mnr. Way SE28 48Tc 94
Griffin Pk. 51Ma 109
Griffin Rd. N17 26Ub 51
SE18 50Tc 94
Griffins, The RM16: Grays 47De 99
Griffins Cl. N21 17Tb 33
Griffin's Wood Cotts.
CM16: Epp 4Tc 22
Griffin Wlk. DA9: Ghithe 57Vd 120
Griffin Way KT23: Bookh 98Ca 191
TW16: Sun 68W 128
Griffith Cl. RM8: Dag 31Yc 75
Griffiths Cl. KT4: Wor Pk 75Xa 154
Griffiths Rd. RM19: Purf 49Sd 98
SW19 66Cb 133
Griffiths Way AL1: St A 4A 6
Griffon Way WD25: Wat 6V 12
Grifon Cl. RM16: Chaf H 48Yd 98
Grifon Rd. RM16: Chaf H 49Yd 98
Griggs App. IG1: Ilf 33Sc 74
Griggs Cl. IG3: Ilf 35Uc 74
Griggs Ct. SE1 4J 231
Griggs Gdns. RM12: Horn 36Ld 77
Grigg's Pl. SE1 3J 231 (48Ub 91)
Griggs Rd. E10 30Ec 52
Griggs Way TN15: Bor G 92Ce 205
Grilse Cl. N9 21Xb 51
Grimaldi Ho. N1 1H 217
Grimsby Gro. E16 47Rc 94
Grimsby Rd. SL1: Slou 7D 80
Grimsby St. E2 6K 219 (42Vb 91)
Grimsdyke Cres. EN5: Barn 13Ya 30
Grim's Dyke Golf Course 22Ca 45
Grimsdyke Lodge AL1: St A 2E 6
Grimsdyke Rd. HA5: Hat E 24Aa 45
Grimsel Path SE5 52Rb 113
Grimshaw Cl. N6 31Jb 70
Grimshaw Way RM1: Rom 29Hd 56
Grimstone Cl. RM5: Col R 23Dd 56
Grimston Rd. AL1: St A 3D 6
SW6 54Bb 111
Grimthorpe Ho. EC1 5B 218
Grimwade Av. CR0: C'don 76Wb 157
Grimwade Cl. SE15 55Yb 114
Grimwood Rd. TW1: Twick 59Ha 108
Grindall Cl. CR0: Wadd 77Rb 157
Grindall Ho. *E1* 42Xb 91
(off Darling Row)
Grindal St. SE1 2K 229 (47Qb 90)
Grindcobbe AL1: St A 5B 6
Grindleford Av. N11 19Jb 32
Grindley Gdns. CR0: C'don 72Vb 157
Grindley Ho. *E3* 43Bc 92
(off Leopold St.)
Grindstone Cres. GU21: Knap 10F 166
GRINDSTONE HANDLE CORNER 10F 166
Grinling Pl. SE8 51Cc 114
Grinstead Rd. SE8 50Ac 92
Grisedale NW1 3B 216
Grisedale Cl. CR8: Purl 86Ub 177
Grisedale Gdns. CR8: Purl 86Ub 177
Grittleton Av. HA9: Wemb 37Ra 67
Grittleton Rd. W9 42Cb 89
Grizedale Ter. SE23 61Xb 135
Grobars Av. GU21: Wok 7N 167
Grocer's Hall Ct.
EC2 3F 225 (44Tb 91)
Grocer's Hall Gdns. EC2 3F 225
Grogan Cl. TW12: Hamp 65Ba 129
Groombridge Cl.
DA16: Well 57Wc 117
KT12: Hers 78X 151
Groombridge Ho. SE17 7J 231
Groombridge Rd. E9 38Zb 72
Groom Cl. BR2: Brom 70Kc 137
Groom Cres. SW18 59Fb 111
Groome Ho. SE11 6J 229 (49Pb 90)
Groomfield Cl. SW17 63Jb 134
Groom Pl. SW1 3J 227 (48Jb 90)
Grooms Dr. HA5: Eastc 29W 44
Grosmont Rd. SE18 50Vc 95
Grosse Way SW15 58Xa 110
Grosvenor Av. HA2: Harr 30Da 45
N5 36Sb 71
SM5: Cars 79Hb 155
SW14 55Ua 110
TW10: Rich 57Na 109
UB4: Hayes 40V 64
WD4: K Lan 10C 4
Grosvenor Cl. IG10: Lough 11Rc 36
SL0: Iver H 41F 82
Grosvenor Cotts. SW1 5H 227 (49Jb 90)
Grosvenor Ct. E10 32Dc 72
E14 44Bc 92
(off Wharf La.)
N14 17Lb 32
NW6 39Za 68
NW7 22Ta 47
(off Hale La.)
SE5 51Sb 113
SL1: Slou 4J 81
SL9: Ger X 28A 42
SM2: Sutt 79Db 155
SM4: Mord 70Cb 133
TW11: Tedd 65Ja 130
W3 46Qa 87
W5 45Na 87
(off The Grove)
W14 48Za 88
(off Irving Rd.)
WD3: Crox G 15T 26
Grosvenor Ct. Mans. W2 3F 221
Grosvenor Cres. DA1: Dart 57Md 119
NW9 28Qa 47
SW1 2J 227 (47Jb 90)
UB10: Hil 38R 64
Grosvenor Cres. M. SW1 2H 227 (47Jb 90)
Grosvenor Dr. IG10: Lough 12Rc 36
RM11: Horn 32Ld 77
Grosvenor Est. SW1 5E 228 (49Mb 90)
Grosvenor Gdns. E6 41Mc 93
IG8: Wfd G 23Jc 53
KT2: King T 65Ma 131
N10 27Lb 50
N14 14Mb 32
NW2 37Ya 68
NW11 30Bb 49
RM14: Upm 32Td 78
SM6: Wall 80Lb 156
SW1 3K 227 (48Kb 90)
SW14 55Ua 110
Grosvenor Gdns. M. E. SW1 3A 228
Grosvenor Gdns. M. Nth. SW1 4K 227
Grosvenor Gdns. M. Sth. SW1 4A 228
Grosvenor Ga. W1 5H 221 (45Jb 90)
Grosvenor Hgts. E4 17Gc 35
Grosvenor Hill SW19 65Ab 132
W1 4K 221 (45Kb 90)
Grosvenor Hill Ct. W1 4K 221
Grosvenor Ho. *SM1: Sutt* 78Db 155
(off West St.)
Grosvenor M. KT18: Eps D 91Ta 193
RH2: Reig 9K 207
Grosvenor Pde. *W5* 46Qa 87
(off Uxbridge Rd.)
Grosvenor Pk. SE5 52Sb 113
Grosvenor Pk. Rd. E17 29Cc 52
Grosvenor Path IG10: Lough 11Rc 36
Grosvenor Pl. *GU21: Wok* 89B 168
(off Stanley Rd.)
KT13: Weyb 76T 150
SW1 1J 227 (47Jb 90)
Grosvenor Ri. E. E17 29Dc 52
Grosvenor Rd. AL1: St A 3C 6
BR4: W W'ck 74Dc 158
BR5: St M Cry 72Uc 160
DA6: Bex 57Zc 117
DA17: Belv 51Cd 118
E6 39Mc 73
E7 37Kc 73
E10 32Ec 72
E11 29Kc 53
GU24: Chob 5H 167
HA6: Nwood 22V 44
IG1: Ilf 34Sc 74
KT18: Eps D 91Ta 193
N3 24Bb 49
N9 18Xb 33
N10 25Kb 50
RM7: Rush G 31Fd 76
RM8: Dag 32Bd 75
RM16: Ors 4F 100
SE25 70Vb 135
SM6: Wall 79Kb 156
SW1 7E 228 (51Kb 112)
TW1: Twick 60Ja 108
TW3: Houn 55Ba 107
TW8: Bford 51Ma 109
TW10: Rich 57Na 109
TW18: Staines 66J 127
UB2: S'hall 48Ba 85
W4 50Ra 87
W7 46Ja 86
WD6: Bore 13Qa 29
WD17: Wat 14Y 27
Grosvenor Sq. *DA3: Lfield* 69Ae 143
(off Park Dr.)
W1 4J 221 (45Jb 90)
WD4: K Lan 10C 4
Grosvenor St. W1 4K 221 (45Kb 90)
Grosvenor Studios SW1 5H 227
Grosvenor Ter. HP1: Hem H 3J 3
SE5 52Sb 113
Grosvenor Va. HA4: Ruis 33V 64
Grosvenor Way E5 33Yb 72
SW17 62Hb 133
Grosvenor Wharf Rd. E14 49Fc 93
Grotes Bldgs. SE3 54Gc 115
Grote's Pl. SE3 54Gc 115
Groton Rd. SW18 61Db 133
Grotto Ct. SE1 1D 230 (47Rb 91)
Grotto Pas. W1 7J 215 (43Jb 90)
Grotto Rd. KT13: Weyb 76R 150
TW1: Twick 61Ha 130
GROVE, THE 60Wb 113
Grove, The AL9: Brk P 8J 9
BR4: W W'ck 76Dc 158
BR8: Swan 69Hd 140
CM14: B'wood 21Vd 58
CR3: Cat'm 93Rb 197
CR5: Coul 87Mb 176
DA6: Bex 56Zc 117
DA10: Swans 57Be 121
DA12: Grav'nd 9D 122
DA14: Sidc 64Ad 139
E15 37Gc 73
EN2: Enf 12Qb 32
EN6: Pot B 4Eb 17
GU21: Wok 88B 168
HA1: Harr 31Ga 66
HA7: Stan 19Ja 28
HA8: Edg 21Ra 47
HP5: Lat 8A 10
KT12: Walt T 73X 151
KT15: Add 78K 149
KT17: Eps 85Ua 174
KT17: Ewe 82Va 174
KT24: Eff 100Z 191
N3 25Cb 49
N4 31Pb 70
N6 32Jb 70
N8 29Mb 50
N13 21Qb 50
(not continuous)
N14 15Lb 32
NW9 29Ta 47
NW11 31Ab 68
RM14: Upm 35Rd 77
SL1: Slou 7L 81
SS17: Stan H 3M 101
TN15: W King 82Vd 184
TN16: Big H 90Mc 179
TW1: Twick 58Ka 108
TW7: Isle 53Ga 108
TW11: Tedd 63Ja 130
TW20: Egh 64C 126
UB6: G'frd 44Ea 86
UB10: Ick 36Q 64
Grove, The W5 46Ma 87
WD3: Crox G 14Q 26
(off Dugdales)
WD4: K Lan 2L 11
WD7: R'lett 6Ja 14
Grove Av. HA5: Pinn 28Aa 45
KT17: Eps 85Ua 174
N3 24Cb 49
N10 26Lb 50
SM1: Sutt 79Cb 155
TW1: Twick 60Ha 108
W7 45Ga 86
Grove Bank WD19: Wat 18Z 27
Grovebarns TW18: Staines 65J 127
Grovebury Cl. DA8: Erith 51Fd 118
Grovebury Ct. DA6: Bex 57Dd 118
N14 17Mb 32
Grovebury Gdns. AL2: Park 9A 6
Grovebury Rd. SE2 47Xc 95
Grove Cl. BR2: Hayes 75Jc 159
KT1: King T 70Pa 131
KT19: Eps 82Qa 173
N14 17Lb 32
SE23 60Ac 114
SL1: Slou 8L 81
SL4: Old Win 9M 103
TW13: Hanw 63Aa 129
UB10: Ick 36Q 64
Grove Cnr. KT23: Bookh 98Da 191
Grove Cotts. *SW3* 51Gb 111
(off Chelsea Mnr. St.)
W4 51Ua 110
WD23: Bush 16Ca 27
(off Falconer Rd.)
Grove Ct. *EN5: Barn* 13Bb 31
(off Hadley Ridge)
EN9: Walt A 5Dc 20
KT1: King T 69Na 131
(off Grove Cres.)
KT8: E Mos 70Fa 130
NW8 3B 214
RH1: Redh 4B 208
(off Gumbrell M.)
RM14: Upm 35Qd 77
SE15 52Ub 113
(off Blake's Rd.)
SW10 7A 226
TW3: Houn 56Ca 107
TW20: Egh 64C 126
W5 46Na 87
Grove Craft Workshops, The
DA3: Fawk 73Wd 164
Grove Cres. E18 26Hc 53
KT1: King T 69Na 131
KT12: Walt T 73X 151
NW9 28Sa 47
TW13: Hanw 63Aa 129
WD3: Crox G 14Q 26
Grove Cres. Rd. E15 37Fc 73
Grovedale Cl. EN7: Chesh 2Vb 19
Grovedale Rd. N19 33Mb 70
Grove Dwellings E1 43Yb 92
Grove End E18 26Hc 53
NW5 35Kb 70
Grove End Gdns. NW8 2B 214 (40Fb 69)
Grove End Ho. NW8 4B 214
Grove End La. KT10: Esh 74Fa 152
Grove End Rd. NW8 2B 214 (40Fb 69)
Grove Farm Pk. HA6: Nwood 22T 44
Grove Farm Retail Pk.
RM6: Chad H 31Yc 75
Grovefield *N11* 21Kb 50
(off Coppies Gro.)
Grove Footpath KT5: Surb 70Na 131
Grove Gdns. EN3: Enf W 10Zb 20
NW4 29Wa 48
NW8 4E 214 (41Gb 89)
RM10: Dag 34Ed 76
TW10: Rich 58Pa 109
TW11: Tedd 63Ja 130
Grove Golf Course, The 9S 12
Grove Grn. HA6: Nwood 22T 44
Grove Grn. Rd. E11 34Ec 72
Grove Hall Ct. *E3* 40Cc 72
(off Jebb St.)
NW8 3A 214 (41Eb 89)
Grove Hall Rd. WD23: Bush 14Aa 27
GROVE HEATH 95K 189
Grove Heath Ct. GU23: Rip 96L 189
Grove Heath Nth. GU23: Rip 94K 189
Grove Heath Rd. GU23: Rip 95K 189
Groveherst Rd. DA1: Dart 55Pd 119
Grove Hill E18 26Hc 53
HA1: Harr 31Ga 66
Grovehill Ct. BR1: Brom 65Hc 137
Grove Hill Rd. HA1: Harr 31Ha 66
SE5 55Ub 113
Grovehill Rd. RH1: Redh 6P 207
Grove Ho. CM14: W'ley 21Xd 58
EN8: Chesh 2Xb 19
N3 27Za 48
RH1: Redh 6P 207
(off Huntingdon Rd.)
SW3 51Gb 111
(off Chelsea Mnr. St.)
WD23: Bush 16Ba 27
Grove Ho. Rd. N8 28Nb 50
Groveland Av. SW16 66Pb 134
Groveland Ct. EC4 3E 224
Groveland Rd. BR3: Beck 69Bc 136
Grovelands AL2: Park 9P 5
KT1: King T 70Ma 131
(off Palace Rd.)
KT8: W Mole 70Ca 129
Grovelands Cl. HA2: Harr 34Da 65
SE5 54Ub 113
Grovelands Ct. N14 17Mb 32
Grovelands Rd. BR5: St P 66Wc 139
CR8: Purl 84Nb 176
N13 21Pb 50
N15 30Wb 51
Grovelands Way RM17: Grays 50Be 99
Groveland Way KT3: N Mald 71Sa 153
Grove La. CM16: Epp 2Wc 23
CR5: Bans, Coul 84Hb 175
HP5: Whel 8A 2
IG7: Chig 20Vc 37
KT1: King T 70Na 131
SE5 53Tb 113
UB8: Hil 42P 83
Grove La. Ter. SE5 54Tb 113
Grove Lea AL10: Hat 3C 8
Groveley Rd. TW13: Felt 64V 128
TW16: Sun 64U 128
Grove Mans. *W6* 47Ya 88
(off Hammersmith Gro.)
Grove Mkt. Pl. SE9 58Pc 116
Grove Mead AL10: Hat 1B 8
Grove M. W6 48Ya 88
Grove Mill La. WD17: Wat 9R 12
Grove Mill Pl. SM5: Cars 76Jb 156
Grove Nature Reserve, The 42P 83
GROVE PARK
SE12 62Kc 137
W4 53Sa 109
Grove Pk. E11 30Kc 53
NW9 28Sa 47
SE5 54Ub 113
Grove Pk. Av. E4 24Dc 52
Grove Pk. Bri. W4 52Sa 109
Grove Pk. Gdns. W4 52Ra 109
Grove Pk. Ind. Est. NW9 27Ta 47
Grove Pk. M. W4 52Sa 109
Grove Pk. Nature Reserve 60Hc 115
Grove Pk. Rd. N15 28Ub 51
RM13: Rain 39Jd 76
SE9 62Lc 137
W4 52Ra 109
Grove Pk. Ter. W4 52Ra 109
Grove Pas. E2 40Xb 71
Grove Path EN7: Chesh 3Wb 19
Grove Pl. AL9: Wel G 6E 8
IG11: Bark 38Sc 74
KT13: Weyb 78S 150
NW3 34Fb 69
SW12 59Kb 112
W3 46Sa 87
WD25: A'ham 11Da 27
Grover Cl. HP2: Hem H 1M 3
Grover Ct. SE13 54Dc 114
Grover Ho. SE11 7J 229 (50Pb 90)
Grove Rd. AL1: St A 3B 6
CR4: Mitc 69Jb 134
(not continuous)
CR7: Thor H 70Qb 134
DA7: Bex 56Ed 118
DA11: Nflt 57De 121
DA17: Belv 51Bd 117
E3 39Zb 72
E4 21Ec 52
E11 31Hc 73
E17 30Dc 52
E18 26Hc 53
EN4: Cockf 13Gb 31
GU21: Wok 88B 168
HA5: Pinn 29Ba 45
HA6: Nwood 22T 44
HA8: Edg 23Qa 47
HP1: Hem H 4J 3
KT6: Surb 71Ma 153
KT8: E Mos 70Fa 130
KT16: Chert 72H 149
KT17: Eps 85Ua 174
KT21: Asht 90Pa 173
N11 22Kb 50
N12 22Fb 49
N15 29Ub 51
NW2 37Ya 68
RH1: Redh 6P 207
RH8: Tand 5G 210
RM6: Chad H 31Xc 75
RM17: Grays 51De 121
SL1: Burn 1B 80
SL4: Wind 4G 102
SM1: Sutt 79Cb 155
SS17: Stan H 3M 101
SW13 54Va 110
SW19 66Eb 133
TN14: S'oaks 93Ld 203
TN15: Seal 93Qd 203
TN16: Tats 92Lc 199
TW2: Twick 62Fa 130
TW3: Houn 56Ca 107
TW7: Isle 53Ga 108
TW8: Bford 50La 86
TW10: Rich 58Pa 109
TW17: Shep 72S 150
UB8: Uxb 38M 63
W3 46Sa 87
W5 45Ma 87
WD3: Rick 19J 25
WD6: Bore 11Qa 29
Grove Rd. W. EN3: Enf W 9Yb 20
Grover Rd. WD19: Wat 17Z 27
Grovers Farm Cotts. KT15: Wdhm 83G 168
Groves Cl. RM15: S Ock 45Vd 98
Grove Shaw KT20: Kgswd 96Ab 194
Groveside KT23: Bookh 98Ca 191
Groveside Cl. KT23: Bookh 99Ca 191
SM5: Cars 75Gb 155
W3 43Qa 87
Groveside Ct. SW11 54Fb 111
Groveside Rd. E4 19Gc 35
Grovestile Waye TW14: Bedf 59T 106
Grove St. N18 22Vb 51
SE8 49Bc 92
Grove Ter. NW5 34Kb 70
TW11: Tedd 63Ja 130
UB1: S'hall 45Ca 85
Grove Ter. M. NW5 34Kb 70
Grove Va. BR7: Chst 65Qc 138
SE22 56Vb 113
Grove Vs. E14 45Dc 92
Grove Way HA9: Wemb 36Ra 67
KT10: Esh 73Ea 152
UB8: Uxb 38M 63
WD3: Chor 15D 24
Groveway RM8: Dag 35Zc 75
SW9 53Pb 112
Grovewood TW9: Kew 53Qa 109
Grove Wood Cl. BR1: Brom 69Qc 138
Grovewood Cl. WD3: Chor 15D 24
Grove Wood Hill CR5: Coul 86Lb 176
Grovewood Pl. IG8: Wfd G 23Pc 54
Grubbs La. AL9: Hat 4J 9
GRUBB STREET 67Xd 142
Grub St. RH8: Limp 100Lc 199
Grummant Rd. SE15 53Vb 113
Grundy Pk. Leisure Cen. 22b 20
Grundy St. E14 44Dc 92
Gruneisen Rd. N3 24Db 49
Gtec Ho. *E15* 40Fc 73
(off Canning Rd.)
Guardian Av. RM16: N Stif 47Zd 99
Guardian Bus. Cen. RM3: Rom 24Md 57
Guardian Cl. RM11: Horn 33Kd 77
Guardian Ct. SE12 57Gc 115
Guards Av. CR3: Cat'm 94Sb 197
Guards Ct. SL5: S'dale 3F 146
Guardsman Cl. CM14: W'ley 22Yd 59
Guards Memorial 7E 222 (46Mb 90)
Guards' Mus. 2C 228 (47Lb 90)

Hawkhurst Way BR4: W W'ck ... 75Dc **158**
KT3: N Mald ... 71Ta **153**
Hawkinge *N17* ... *26Tb* ***51***
(off Gloucester Rd.)
Hawkinge Wlk. BR5: St P ... 69Xc **139**
Hawkinge Way RM12: Horn ... 37Ld **77**
Hawkins Av. DA12: Grav'nd ... 3E **144**
Hawkins Cl. HA1: Harr ... 31Fa **66**
NW7 ... 22Ta **47**
WD6: Bore ... 12Sa **29**
Hawkins Ct. SE18 ... 49Nc **94**
Hawkins Dr. RM16: Chaf H ... 47Zd **99**
Hawkins Ho. *SE8* ... *51Cc* ***114***
(off New King St.)
SW1 ... *51Lb* ***112***
(off Dolphin Sq.)
Hawkins Rd. NW10 ... 38Ua **68**
TW11: Tedd ... 65Ka **130**
Hawkins Ter. SE7 ... 50Nc **94**
Hawkins Way HP3: Bov ... 8C **2**
SE6 ... 64Cc **136**
Hawkley Gdns. SE27 ... 61Rb **135**
Hawkridge Cl. RM6: Chad H ... 30Yc **55**
Hawkridge Dr. RM17: Grays ... 50Fe **99**
Hawksbrook La. BR3: Beck ... 72Dc **158**
Hawkshaw Cl. SW2 ... 59Nb **112**
Hawkshead NW1 ... 3B **216**
Hawkshead Cl. BR1: Brom ... 66Gc **137**
Hawkshead Ct. *EN8: Walt C* ... *6Bc* ***20***
(off Eleanor Way)
Hawkshead La. AL9: Brk P, N Mym ... 10E **8**
Hawkshead Rd. EN6: Pot B ... 10H **9**
NW10 ... 38Va **68**
W4 ... 47Ua **88**
Hawk's Hill KT22: Fet ... 95Ha **192**
Hawkshill AL1: St A ... 3E **6**
Hawks Hill Cl. KT22: Fet ... 95Ha **192**
Hawkshill Cl. KT10: Esh ... 79Ca **151**
Hawk's Hill Ct. KT22: Fet ... 95Ha **192**
Hawkshill Dr. HP3: Hem H ... 5H **3**
Hawk's Hill Ho. KT22: Fet ... 96Ha **192**
Hawkshill Pl. KT10: Esh ... 79Ca **151**
Hawkshill Rd. SL2: Slou ... 1E **80**
Hawkshill Way KT10: Esh ... 79Ba **151**
Hawkslade Rd. SE15 ... 57Zb **114**
Hawksley Rd. N16 ... 34Ub **71**
Hawksmead Cl. EN3: Enf W ... 8Zb **20**
Hawks M. SE10 ... 52Ec **114**
Hawksmoor WD7: Shenl ... 5Qa **15**
Hawksmoor Cl. E6 ... 44Nc **94**
SE18 ... 50Uc **94**
Hawksmoor Grn. CM13: Hut ... 15Fe **41**
(not continuous)
Hawksmoor M. E1 ... 45Xb **91**
Hawksmoor Pl. *E2* ... *42Wb* ***91***
(off Cheshire St.)
Hawksmoor St. W6 ... 51Za **110**
Hawksmouth E4 ... 17Ec **34**
Hawks Pas. *KT1: King T* ... *68Pa* ***131***
(off Minerva Rd.)
Hawks Rd. KT1: King T ... 68Pa **131**
Hawkstone Rd. SE16 ... 49Yb **92**
Hawksview KT11: Cobh ... 85Ba **171**
Hawksway TW18: Staines ... 62H **127**
Hawkswell Cl. GU21: Wok ... 9K **167**
Hawkswell Wlk. GU21: Wok ... 9K **167**
Hawkswood Gro. SL3: Ful ... 37B **62**
Hawkswood La. SL3: Ful ... 36B **62**
SL9: Ger X ... 36B **62**
Hawksworth Ho. BR1: Brom ... 68Jc **137**
Hawkwell Ct. E4 ... 20Ec **34**
Hawkwell Ho. RM8: Dag ... 32Cd **76**
Hawkwell Wlk. *N1* ... *39Sb* ***71***
(off Maldon Cl.)
Hawkwood Cres. E4 ... 16Dc **34**
Hawkwood Dell KT23: Bookh ... 98Ca **191**
Hawkwood La. BR7: Chst ... 67Sc **138**
Hawkwood Mt. E5 ... 32Xb **71**
Hawkwood Ri. KT23: Bookh ... 98Ca **191**
Hawlands Dr. HA5: Pinn ... 31Aa **65**
HAWLEY ... 64Qd **141**
Hawley Cl. TW12: Hamp ... 65Ba **129**
Hawley Cres. NW1 ... 38Kb **70**
Hawley M. NW1 ... 38Kb **70**
Hawley Rd. DA1: Dart ... 61Nd **141**
DA2: Hawl ... 61Nd **141**
N18 ... 22Zb **52**
NW1 ... 38Kb **70**
(not continuous)
HAWLEY'S CORNER ... 93Rc **200**
Hawley St. NW1 ... 38Kb **70**
Hawley Ter. DA2: Hawl ... 64Qd **141**
Hawley Va. DA2: Hawl ... 64Qd **141**
Hawley Way TW15: Ashf ... 64Q **128**
Haws La. TW19: Stanw M ... 58J **105**
Hawstead La.
BR6: Chels, Well H ... 78Bd **161**
Hawstead Rd. SE6 ... 58Dc **114**
Hawsted IG9: Buck H ... 17Kc **35**
Hawthorn Av. CM13: B'wood ... 20Be **41**
CR7: Thor H ... 67Rb **135**
E3 ... 39Bc **72**
N13 ... 22Nb **50**
RM13: Rain ... 42Kd **97**
Hawthorn Cen., The HA1: Harr ... 29Ha **46**
Hawthorn Cl. BR5: Pet W ... 72Tc **160**
CR6: W'ham ... 90Ac **178**
GU22: Wok ... 92A **188**
RH1: Redh ... 10A **208**
SL0: Iver H ... 40E **62**
SM7: Bans ... 86Ab **174**
TW5: Cran ... 52X **107**
TW12: Hamp ... 64Ca **129**
WD5: Ab L ... 4W **12**
WD17: Wat ... 10V **12**
Hawthorn Cotts. *DA16: Well* ... *55Wc* ***117***
(off Hook La.)
Hawthorn Ct. *HA5: Pinn* ... *26Y* ***45***
(off Rickmansworth Rd.)
TW9: Kew ... 53Ra **109**
TW15: Ashf ... 66S **128**
Hawthorn Cres. CR2: Sels ... 83Yb **178**
SW17 ... 64Jb **134**
Hawthornden Cl. N12 ... 23Gb **49**
Hawthorndene Cl. BR2: Hayes ... 75Hc **159**
Hawthorndene Rd.
BR2: Hayes ... 75Hc **159**
Hawthorn Dr. BR4: W W'ck ... 77Gc **159**
HA2: Harr ... 30Ca **45**
UB9: Den ... 37L **63**
Hawthorne Av. CR4: Mitc ... 68Fb **133**
EN7: Chesh ... 3Xb **19**
HA3: Kenton ... 30Ja **46**
HA4: Ruis ... 30X **45**
SM5: Cars ... 80Jb **156**
TN16: Big H ... 87Mc **179**
Hawthorne Cl. BR1: Brom ... 69Pc **138**
DA12: Grav'nd ... 3D **144**
EN7: Chesh ... 3Xb **19**
N1 ... 37Ub **71**
SM1: Sutt ... 75Eb **155**
Hawthorne Ct. HA6: Nwood ... 26W **44**
KT12: Walt T ... 74Z **151**
TW19: Stanw ... *59M* ***105***
(off Hawthorne Way)
W5 ... 46Na **87**
Hawthorne Cres. SL1: Slou ... 4J **81**
UB7: W Dray ... 47P **83**
Hawthorne Dr. SL4: Wink ... 1A **124**
Hawthorne Gro. NW9 ... 31Sa **67**
Hawthorne Ho. N15 ... 29Wb **51**
SW1 ... *50Lb* ***90***
(off Churchill Gdns.)
Hawthorne La. HP1: Hem H ... 1H **3**
Hawthorne M. UB6: G'frd ... 44Ea **86**
Hawthorne Pl. KT17: Eps ... 84Ua **174**
UB3: Hayes ... 45V **84**
Hawthorne Rd. BR1: Brom ... 69Nc **138**
E17 ... 27Cc **52**
TW18: Staines ... 64E **126**
WD7: R'lett ... 6Ja **14**
Hawthornes AL10: Hat ... 2B **8**
Hawthorne Way N9 ... 19Vb **33**
TW19: Stanw ... 59M **105**
Hawthorn Farm Av.
UB5: N'olt ... 39Aa **65**
Hawthorn Gdns. W5 ... 48Ma **87**
Hawthorn Gro. EN2: Enf ... 10Tb **19**
EN5: Ark ... 16Va **30**
SE20 ... 66Xb **135**
Hawthorn Hatch TW8: Bford ... 52Ka **108**
Hawthorn La. SL2: Farn C ... 8D **60**
TN13: S'oaks ... 94Hd **202**
Hawthorn M. NW7 ... 25Ab **48**
Hawthorn Pk. BR8: Swan ... 68Jd **140**
Hawthorn Pl. DA8: Erith ... 50Ed **96**
Hawthorn Rd. DA1: Dart ... 61Md **141**
DA6: Bex ... 56Bd **117**
GU22: Wok ... 2P **187**
GU23: Rip ... 96J **189**
IG9: Buck H ... 21Mc **53**
N8 ... 27Mb **50**
N18 ... 23Vb **51**
NW10 ... 38Wa **68**
SM1: Sutt ... 79Gb **155**
SM6: Wall ... 80Kb **156**
TW8: Bford ... 52Ka **108**
TW13: Felt ... 60W **106**
Hawthorns *CR2: S Croy* ... *77Sb* ***157***
(off Bramley Hill)
DA3: Hartl ... 70Be **143**
IG8: Wfd G ... 20Jc **35**
Hawthorns, The EN6: Ridge ... 5Ua **16**
HP3: Hem H ... 6H **3**
IG10: Lough ... 14Qc **36**
KT17: Ewe ... 80Va **154**
RH8: Oxt ... 5L **211**
SL3: Poyle ... 53H **105**
WD3: Map C ... 22F **42**
Hawthorns School Sports Centre, The
... 3H **209**
Hawthorn Ter. DA15: Sidc ... 57Vc **117**
N19 ... *32Mb* ***70***
(off Calverley Gro.)
Hawthorn Wlk. W10 ... 42Ab **88**
Hawthorn Way AL2: Chis G ... 6N **5**
GU24: Bisl ... 8E **166**
KT15: New H ... 82L **169**
RH1: Redh ... 8B **208**
TW17: Shep ... 70T **128**
Hawtrees WD7: R'lett ... 7Ha **14**
Hawtrey Av. UB5: N'olt ... 40Z **65**
Hawtrey Cl. SL1: Slou ... 7M **81**
Hawtrey Dr. HA4: Ruis ... 31W **64**
Hawtrey Ho. *SL4: Eton* ... *1H* ***103***
(off Slough Rd.)
Hawtrey Rd. NW3 ... 38Gb **69**
SL4: Wind ... 4G **102**
Haxted Rd. BR1: Brom ... 67Kc **137**
Haybourn Mead HP1: Hem H ... 3K **3**
Hayburn Way RM12: Horn ... 32Hd **76**
Hay Cl. E15 ... 38Gc **73**
WD6: Bore ... 12Sa **29**
Haycroft Cl. CR5: Coul ... 90Rb **177**
Haycroft Gdns. NW10 ... 39Wa **68**
Haycroft Rd. KT6: Surb ... 75Ma **153**
SW2 ... 57Nb **112**
Hay Currie St. E14 ... 44Dc **92**
Hayday Rd. E16 ... 43Jc **93**
(not continuous)
Hayden Ct. KT15: New H ... 83K **169**
TW13: Felt ... 63U **128**
Hayden Piper Ho. *SW3* ... *51Hb* ***111***
(off Caversham St.)
Hayden Rd. EN9: Walt A ... 7Ec **20**
Haydens Cl. BR5: Orp ... 72Yc **161**
Haydens M. W3 ... 44Sa **87**
Hayden's Pl. W11 ... 44Bb **89**
Hayden Way RM5: Col R ... 26Ed **56**
Haydn Av. CR8: Purl ... 86Qb **176**
Haydock Av. UB5: N'olt ... 37Ca **65**
Haydock Cl. RM12: Horn ... 35Pd **77**
Haydock Grn. UB5: N'olt ... 37Ca **65**
Haydock Grn. Flats *UB5: N'olt* ... *37Ca* ***65***
(off Haydock Grn.)
Haydon Cl. EN1: Enf ... 16Ub **33**
NW9 ... 28Sa **47**
RM3: Rom ... 24Kd **57**
Haydon Ct. NW9 ... 28Sa **47**
Haydon Dell WD23: Bush ... 16Ba **27**
Haydon Dell Farm
WD23: Bush ... 17Ba **27**
Haydon Dr. HA5: Eastc ... 28W **44**
Haydon Pk. Rd. SW19 ... 64Cb **133**
Haydon Rd. RM8: Dag ... 33Yc **75**
WD19: Wat ... 16Aa **27**
Haydons Rd. SW19 ... 64Db **133**
Haydon St. E1 ... 4K **225** (44Vb **91**)
EC3 ... 4K **225**
Haydon Wlk. E1 ... 4K **225**
Haydon Way SW11 ... 56Fb **111**
HAYES
BR2 ... 74Jc **159**
UB3 ... 44U **84**
Hayes, The KT18: Eps D ... 91Ua **194**
Hayes & Yeading Utd. FC ... 46Y **85**
Hayes Barton GU22: Pyr ... 88F **168**
Hayes Botanical Gdns. ... 44V **84**
Hayes Bri. Retail Pk. UB4: Yead ... 45Y **85**
Hayes Chase BR4: W W'ck ... 72Fc **159**
Hayes Cl. BR2: Hayes ... 75Jc **159**
RM20: Grays ... 51Yd **120**
Hayes Ct. HA0: Wemb ... 39Na **67**
SE5 ... *52Sb* ***113***
(off Camberwell New Rd.)
SW2 ... 60Nb **112**
Hayes Cres. NW11 ... 29Bb **49**
SM3: Cheam ... 77Za **154**
Hayes Dr. RM13: Rain ... 38Kd **77**
HAYES END ... 42T **84**
Hayes End Cl. UB4: Hayes ... 42T **84**
Hayes End Dr. UB4: Hayes ... 42T **84**
Hayes End Rd. UB4: Hayes ... 42T **84**
Hayesens Ho. SW17 ... 63Eb **133**
Hayesford Pk. Dr. BR2: Brom ... 71Hc **159**
Hayes Gdn. BR2: Hayes ... 74Jc **159**
Hayes Gro. SE22 ... 55Vb **113**
Hayes Hill BR2: Hayes ... 74Gc **159**
Hayes Hill Rd. BR2: Hayes ... 74Hc **159**
Hayes La. BR2: Brom, Hayes ... 71Kc **159**
BR3: Beck ... 69Ec **136**
CR8: Kenley ... 88Rb **177**
Hayes Mead Rd. BR2: Hayes ... 74Gc **159**
Hayes Metro Cen. UB4: Yead ... 45Y **85**
Hayes Pl. NW1 ... 6E **214** (42Gb **89**)
Hayes Rd. BR2: Brom ... 70Jc **137**
DA9: Ghithe ... 59Ud **120**
UB2: S'hall ... 49X **85**
Hayes St. BR2: Hayes ... 74Kc **159**
Hayes Swimming Pool ... 46V **84**
Hayes Ter. DA12: Shorne ... 4N **145**
HAYES TOWN ... 47V **84**
Hayes Wlk. EN6: Pot B ... 5Db **17**
Hayes Way BR3: Beck ... 70Ec **136**
Hayes Wood Av. BR2: Hayes ... 74Kc **159**
Hayfield Cl. WD23: Bush ... 14Da **27**
Hayfield Pas. E1 ... 42Yb **92**
Hayfield Rd. BR5: St M Cry ... 71Wc **161**
Hayfield Yd. E1 ... 42Yb **92**
Haygarth Pl. SW19 ... 64Za **132**
Hay Green RM11: Horn ... 30Qd **57**
Haygreen Cl. KT2: King T ... 65Ra **131**
Hay Hill W1 ... 5A **222** (45Kb **90**)
Hayhurst Ct. *N1* ... *39Rb* ***71***
(off Dibden St.)
Hayland Cl. NW9 ... 28Ta **47**
Hay La. NW9 ... 28Sa **47**
SL3: Ful ... 5P **61**
Hayle RM18: E Til ... 8L **101**
Hayles Bldgs. SE11 ... 5C **230**
Hayles St. SE11 ... 5B **230** (49Rb **91**)
Haylett Gdns. KT1: King T ... 70Ma **131**
Hayley Cl. RM16: Chaf H ... 48Yd **98**
Hayling Av. TW13: Felt ... 62W **128**
Hayling Cl. N16 ... 36Ub **71**
SL1: Slou ... 6F **80**
Hayling Ct. SM3: Cheam ... 77Ya **154**
Hayling Rd. WD19: Wat ... 20W **26**
Haymaker Cl. UB10: Uxb ... 38P **63**
Hayman Cres. UB4: Hayes ... 40T **64**
Haymans Point SE11 ... 7H **229** (49Pb **90**)
Hayman St. N1 ... 38Rb **71**
Haymarket SW1 ... 5D **222** (45Mb **90**)
Haymarket Arc. SW1 ... 5D **222**
Haymarket Ct. *E8* ... *38Vb* ***71***
(off Jacaranda Gro.)
Haymarket Theatre Royal ... 5E **222**
Haymeads Dr. KT10: Esh ... 79Ea **152**
Haymer Gdns. KT4: Wor Pk ... 76Wa **154**
Haymerle Ho. *SE15* ... *51Wb* ***113***
(off Haymerle Rd.)
Haymerle Rd. SE15 ... 51Wb **113**
Hay M. NW3 ... 37Hb **69**
Haymill Cl. UB6: G'frd ... 41Ha **86**
Haymill Rd. SL1: Slou ... 2B **80**
SL2: Slou ... 2B **80**
Hayne Ho. *W11* ... *46Ab* ***88***
(off Penzance Pl.)
Hayne Rd. BR3: Beck ... 68Bc **136**
Haynes Cl. GU23: Rip ... 94K **189**
N11 ... 20Jb **32**
N17 ... 24Xb **51**
SE3 ... 55Gc **115**
SL3: L'ly ... 50B **82**
Haynes Dr. N9 ... 20Xb **33**
Haynes La. SE19 ... 65Ub **135**
Haynes Rd. DA11: Nflt ... 2B **144**
HA0: Wemb ... 38Na **67**
RM11: Horn ... 28Md **57**
Hayne St. EC1 ... 7C **218** (43Rb **91**)
Haynt Wlk. SW20 ... 69Ab **132**
Hay's Ct. *SE16* ... *47Yb* ***92***
(off Rotherhithe St.)
Hayse Hill SL4: Wind ... 3B **102**
Hay's Galleria SE1 ... 6H **225** (46Ub **91**)
Hays La. SE1 ... 6H **225** (46Ub **91**)
Haysleigh Gdns. SE20 ... 68Wb **135**
Hay's M. W1 ... 5K **221** (46Kb **90**)
Haysoms Cl. RM1: Rom ... 28Gd **56**
Haystall Cl. UB4: Hayes ... 40U **64**
Hay St. E2 ... 39Wb **71**
Hays Wlk. SM2: Cheam ... 82Za **174**
Hayter Ct. E11 ... 33Kc **73**
Hayter Rd. SW2 ... 57Nb **112**
Hayton Cl. E8 ... 37Vb **71**
Haywain RH8: Oxt ... 2H **211**
Hayward Cl. DA1: Cray ... 57Fd **118**
SW19 ... 66Db **133**
Hayward Copse WD3: Loud ... 14M **25**
Hayward Ct. *SW9* ... *54Nb* ***112***
(off Studley Rd.)
Hayward Dr. DA1: Dart ... 62Pd **141**
Hayward Gallery ... 6J **223** (46Pb **90**)
Hayward Gdns. SW15 ... 58Ya **110**
Hayward Ho. N1 ... 1K **217**
Hayward Rd. KT7: T Ditt ... 74Ha **152**
N20 ... 19Eb **31**
Haywards Cl. RM6: Chad H ... 29Xc **55**
Haywards Mead SL4: Eton W ... 10D **80**
Hayward's Pl. EC1 ... 6B **218** (42Rb **91**)
Haywards Yd. *SE4* ... *57Bc* ***114***
(off Lindal Rd.)
Haywood Cl. HA5: Pinn ... 26Z **45**
Haywood Ct. EN9: Walt A ... 6Hc **21**
Haywood Cres. WD17: Wat ... 10W **12**
Haywood Dr. HP3: Hem H ... 5H **3**
WD3: Chor ... 15H **25**
Haywood Lodge *N11* ... *23Nb* ***50***
(off York Rd.)
Haywood Pk. WD3: Chor ... 15H **25**
Haywood Pl. RM16: Grays ... 7E **100**
Haywood Ri. BR6: Orp ... 78Uc **160**
Haywood Rd. BR2: Brom ... 70Mc **137**
Hazel Av. UB7: W Dray ... 48Q **84**
Hazel Bank SE25 ... 68Ub **135**
Hazelbank KT5: Surb ... 74Sa **153**
WD3: Crox G ... 16S **26**
Hazelbank Ct. KT16: Chert ... 74L **149**
Hazelbank Rd. KT16: Chert ... 74L **149**
SE6 ... 61Fc **137**
Hazelbourne Rd. SW12 ... 58Kb **112**
Hazelbrouck Gdns. IG6: Ilf ... 24Tc **54**
Hazelbury Av. WD5: Ab L ... 4S **12**
Hazelbury Cl. SW19 ... 68Cb **133**
Hazelbury Grn. N9 ... 20Ub **33**
Hazelbury La. N9 ... 20Ub **33**
Hazel Cl. CR0: C'don ... 73Zb **158**
CR4: Mitc ... 70Mb **134**
KT19: Eps ... 82Ta **173**
N13 ... 20Tb **33**
N19 ... 33Lb **70**
NW9 ... 26Ua **48**
RH2: Reig ... 8L **207**
RM12: Horn ... 34Kd **77**
SE15 ... *54Wb* ***113***
(off Bournemouth Cl.)
TW2: Whitt ... 59Ea **108**
TW8: Bford ... 52Ka **108**
TW20: Eng G ... 5M **125**
Hazel Ct. CR6: W'ham ... 89Ac **178**
IG10: Lough ... 13Pc **36**
W5 ... 45Na **87**
WD7: Shenl ... 5Pa **15**
Hazelcroft HA5: Hat E ... 23Da **45**
Hazelcroft Cl. UB10: Hil ... 38P **63**
Hazeldean Rd. NW10 ... 38Ta **67**
Hazeldell Link HP1: Hem H ... 3G **2**
Hazeldell Rd. HP1: Hem H ... 3G **2**
Hazelden Cl. TN15: W King ... 81Wd **184**
Hazeldene EN8: Walt C ... 4Ac **20**
KT15: Add ... 78L **149**
Hazeldene Ct. CR8: Kenley ... 87Tb **177**
Hazeldene Dr. HA5: Pinn ... 27Y **45**
Hazeldene Gdns. UB10: Hil ... 39S **64**
Hazeldene Rd. DA16: Well ... 54Yc **117**
IG3: Ilf ... 33Xc **75**
Hazeldon Rd. SE4 ... 57Ac **114**
Hazel Dr. DA8: Erith ... 53Jd **118**
GU23: Rip ... 97H **189**
RM15: S Ock ... 41Zd **99**
Hazeleigh CM13: B'wood ... 20De **41**
Hazeleigh Gdns. IG8: Wfd G ... 22Nc **54**
Hazel End BR8: Swan ... 71Gd **162**
Hazel Gdns. HA8: Edg ... 21Ra **47**
RM16: Grays ... 8A **100**
Hazelgreen Cl. N21 ... 18Rb **33**
Hazel Gro. AL10: Hat ... 3B **8**
BR6: Farnb ... 75Rc **160**
EN1: Enf ... 16Wb **33**
HA0: Wemb ... 39Na **67**
RM6: Chad H ... 27Ad **55**
SE26 ... 63Zb **136**
TW13: Felt ... 60W **106**
TW18: Staines ... 65K **127**
WD25: Wat ... 7X **13**
Hazel Gro. Ho. AL10: Hat ... 2B **8**
Hazel Ho. *E3* ... *39Bc* ***72***
(off Barge La.)
Hazelhurst BR3: Beck ... 67Fc **137**
Hazelhurst Ct. *SE6* ... *64Ec* ***136***
(off Beckenham Hill Rd.)
Hazelhurst Rd. SL1: Burn ... 10A **60**
SW17 ... 63Eb **133**
Hazel La. IG6: Ilf ... 23Rc **54**
TW10: Ham ... 61Na **131**
Hazell Cres. RM5: Col R ... 25Dd **56**
Hazellville Rd. N19 ... 31Mb **70**
Hazell Way SL2: Stoke P ... 8K **61**
Hazel Mead EN5: Ark ... 15Xa **30**
KT17: Ewe ... 82Wa **174**
Hazelmere Cl. KT22: Lea ... 91Ka **192**
TW14: Felt ... 58U **106**
UB5: N'olt ... 40Ba **65**
Hazelmere Ct. SW2 ... 60Pb **112**
Hazelmere Dr. UB5: N'olt ... 40Ba **65**
Hazelmere Gdns. RM11: Horn ... 29Ld **57**
Hazelmere Rd. BR5: Pet W ... 70Sc **138**
NW6 ... 39Bb **69**
UB5: N'olt ... 40Ba **65**
Hazelmere Wlk. UB5: N'olt ... 40Ba **65**
(not continuous)
Hazelmere Way BR2: Hayes ... 72Jc **159**
Hazel M. *N22* ... *27Qb* ***50***
(off High Rd.)
Hazelnut Ho. *BR8: Swan* ... *69Hd* ***140***
(off Squirrels Cl.)
Hazel Pde. KT22: Fet ... 94Ea **192**
Hazel Ri. RM11: Horn ... 30Ld **57**
Hazel Rd. AL2: Park ... 10P **5**
DA1: Dart ... 61Md **141**
DA8: Erith ... 53Jd **118**
E15 ... 36Gc **73**
KT14: W Byf ... 86J **169**
NW10 ... 41Xa **88**
(not continuous)
RH2: Reig ... 8L **207**
Hazeltree La. UB5: N'olt ... 41Aa **85**
Hazel Tree Rd. WD24: Wat ... 9X **13**
Hazel Wlk. BR2: Brom ... 72Qc **160**
Hazel Way CR5: Chip ... 91Hb **195**
E4 ... 23Bc **52**
KT22: Fet ... 94Ea **192**
SE1 ... 5K **231** (49Vb **91**)
Hazelway Cl. KT22: Fet ... 95Ea **192**
HAZELWOOD ... 83Tc **180**
Hazelwood IG10: Lough ... 15Mc **35**
SS17: Linf ... 9J **101**
Hazelwood Av. SM4: Mord ... 70Db **133**
Hazelwood Cl. HA2: Harr ... 28Da **45**
W5 ... 47Na **87**
Hazelwood Ct. KT6: Surb ... 72Na **153**
N13 ... *21Pb* ***50***
(off Hazelwood La.)
NW10 ... 34Ua **68**
Hazelwood Cres. N13 ... 21Qb **50**
Hazelwood Dr. AL4: St A ... 1G **6**
HA5: Pinn ... 26X **45**
Hazelwood Gdns. CM15: Pil H ... 16Wd **40**
Hazelwood Golf Course ... 69V **128**
Hazelwood Gro. CR2: Sande ... 85Xb **177**
Hazelwood Hgts. RH8: Oxt ... 3L **211**
Hazelwood Ho. SE8 ... 49Ac **92**
Hazelwood Ho's. BR2: Brom ... 69Gc **137**
Hazelwood La. CR5: Chip ... 90Gb **175**
N13 ... 21Qb **50**
WD5: Ab L ... 4S **12**
Hazelwood Pk. Cl. IG7: Chig ... 22Uc **54**
Hazelwood Rd. E17 ... 29Ac **52**
EN1: Enf ... 16Vb **33**
GU21: Knap ... 10J **167**
RH8: Oxt ... 4M **211**
TN14: Cud ... 84Tc **180**
WD3: Crox G ... 16S **26**
Hazlebury Rd. SW6 ... 54Db **111**
Hazledean Rd. CR0: C'don ... 75Tb **157**
Hazledene Rd. W4 ... 51Sa **109**
Hazlemere Gdns. KT4: Wor Pk ... 74Wa **154**
Hazlemere Rd. SL2: Slou ... 6M **81**
Hazle's Pottery Barn ... 29Xd **58**
Hazlewell Rd. SW15 ... 57Ya **110**
Hazlewood Cl. E5 ... 34Ac **72**
Hazlewood Cres. W10 ... 42Ab **88**
Hazlewood M. SW9 ... 55Nb **112**
Hazlewood Twr. *W10* ... *42Ab* ***88***
(off Golborne Gdns.)
Hazlitt Cl. TW13: Hanw ... 63Aa **129**
Hazlitt M. W14 ... 48Ab **88**
Hazlitt Rd. W14 ... 48Ab **88**
Hazon Way KT19: Eps ... 84Sa **173**
Heacham Av. UB10: Ick ... 34S **64**
Headbourne Ho. SE1 ... 3G **231** (47Tb **91**)
Headcorn Pl. CR7: Thor H ... 70Pb **134**
Headcorn Rd. BR1: Brom ... 64Hc **137**
CR7: Thor H ... 70Pb **134**
N17 ... 24Vb **51**
Headfort Pl. SW1 ... 2J **227** (47Jb **90**)
Headingley Cl. IG6: Ilf ... 23Vc **55**
WD7: Shenl ... 4Na **15**
Headingley Dr. BR3: Beck ... 65Cc **136**
Headington Ct. *CR0: C'don* ... *77Sb* ***157***
(off Tanfield Rd.)
Headington Pl. *SL2: Slou* ... *6K* ***81***
(off Mill St.)
Headington Rd. SW18 ... 61Eb **133**
Headlam Rd. SW4 ... 58Mb **112**
(not continuous)
Headlam St. E1 ... 42Xb **91**
HEADLEY ... 98Ta **193**
Headley App. IG2: Ilf ... 29Rc **54**
Headley Av. SM6: Wall ... 78Pb **156**
Headley Chase CM14: W'ley ... 21Yd **58**
Headley Cl. KT19: Ewe ... 79Qa **153**
Headley Comn. Rd.
KT18: Head, Walt H ... 99Ta **193**
Headley Ct. KT18: Head ... 95Ra **193**
SE26 ... 64Yb **136**
Headley Dr. CR0: New Ad ... 80Dc **158**
IG2: Ilf ... 30Rc **54**
KT18: Tatt C ... 91Xa **194**
Headley Gro. KT20: Tad ... 92Ya **194**
Headley Heath ... 100Ra **193**
Headley La. RH5: Mick ... 100La **192**
Headley Rd. KT18: Eps D ... 92Sa **193**
KT18: Eps D, Head ... 94Qa **193**
KT18: Eps, Eps D ... 90Ra **173**
KT22: Lea ... 94La **192**
Head's M. W11 ... 44Cb **89**
HEADSTONE ... 27Fa **46**
Headstone Dr. HA1: Harr ... 27Fa **46**
HA3: W'stone ... 27Ga **46**
Headstone Gdns. HA2: Harr ... 28Ea **46**
Headstone La. HA2: Harr ... 28Ca **45**
HA3: Hrw W ... 24Da **45**
Headstone Manor ... 27Ea **46**
Headstone Pde. HA1: Harr ... 28Fa **46**
Headstone Rd. HA1: Harr ... 29Ga **46**
Head St. E1 ... 44Zb **92**
(not continuous)
Headway, The KT17: Ewe ... 81Va **174**
Headway Cl. TW10: Ham ... 63La **130**
Heald St. SE14 ... 53Cc **114**
Healey Ho. *E3* ... *42Cc* ***92***
(off Wellington Way)
SW9 ... 52Qb **112**
Healey Rd. WD18: Wat ... 16V **26**
Healey St. NW1 ... 37Kb **70**
Healy Dr. BR6: Orp ... 77Vc **161**
Heards La. CM15: Shenf ... 13Be **41**
Hearne Rd. W4 ... 51Qa **109**
Hearn Ri. UB5: N'olt ... 39Z **65**
Hearn Rd. RM1: Rom ... 30Hd **56**
Hearn's Bldgs. SE17 ... 6G **231** (49Tb **91**)
Hearnshaw St. E14 ... 44Ac **92**
Hearn's Rd. BR5: St P ... 70Yc **139**
Hearn St. EC2 ... 6J **219** (42Ub **91**)
Hearnville Rd. SW12 ... 60Jb **112**
Hearsall Av. SS17: Stan H ... 1N **101**
Heart, The KT12: Walt T ... 74W **150**
HEATH, THE ... 79R **150**
Heath, The CR3: Cat'm ... 96Sb **197**
W7 ... 46Ga **86**
WD7: R'lett ... 5Ja **14**
Heathacre SL3: Coln ... 53G **104**
Heatham Pk. TW2: Twick ... 59Ha **108**
Heath Av. AL3: St A ... 1B **6**
DA7: Bex ... 51Zc **117**
Heathbourne Rd. HA7: Stan ... 19Ga **28**
WD23: B Hea ... 18Ga **28**
Heathbridge KT13: Weyb ... 80Q **150**
Heathbridge App. KT13: Weyb ... 79Q **150**
Heath Brow HP1: Hem H ... 4L **3**
NW3 ... 34Eb **69**
Heath Bus. Cen. TW3: Houn ... 56Ea **108**
Heath Cl. BR5: Orp ... 73Yc **161**
BR8: Swan ... 68Gd **140**
CR2: S Croy ... 79Rb **157**
EN6: Pot B ... 2Db **17**
GU25: Vir W ... 10P **125**
HP1: Hem H ... 3L **3**
NW11 ... 31Db **69**
RM2: Rom ... 27Jd **56**
SM7: Bans ... 86Db **175**
TW19: Stanw ... 58L **105**
UB3: Harl ... 52T **106**
W5 ... 42Pa **87**
Heathclose Av. DA1: Dart ... 59Kd **119**
Heathclose Rd. DA1: Dart ... 60Jd **118**
Heathcock Ct. *WC2* ... *5G* ***223***
(off Exchange Ct.)
Heathcote KT20: Tad ... 93Za **194**
Heathcote Av. IG5: Ilf ... 26Pc **54**
Heathcote Ct. IG5: Ilf ... 25Pc **54**
(not continuous)
SL4: Wind ... *5H* ***103***
(off Osbourne Rd.)
Heathcote Gro. E4 ... 20Ec **34**
Heathcote Rd. KT18: Eps ... 86Ta **173**
TW1: Twick ... 58Ka **108**
Heathcote St. WC1 ... 5H **217** (42Pb **90**)
Heathcote Way UB7: Yiew ... 46M **83**
Heath Ct. *CR0: C'don* ... *77Tb* ***157***
(off Heathfield Rd.)
SE9 ... 60Sc **116**
TW4: Houn ... 56Ba **107**
UB8: Uxb ... 38M **63**
Heath Cft. NW11 ... 32Db **69**
Heathcroft W5 ... 42Pa **87**
Heathcroft Av. TW16: Sun ... 66V **128**
Heathcroft Gdns. E17 ... 25Fc **53**
Heathdale Av. TW4: Houn ... 55Aa **107**

Heathdene KT20: Tad 90Ab 174
Heathdene Dr. DA17: Belv 49Dd 96
Heathdene Mnr. WD17: Wat 11V 26
Heathdene Rd. SM6: Wall 80Kb 156
SW16 . . . . . 66Pb 134
Heathdown Rd. GU22: Pyr 87F 168
Heath Dr. CM16: They B 8Uc 22
EN6: Pot B 2Cb 17
GU23: Send 94D 188
GU24: Brkwd 2E 186
KT20: Walt H 97Wa 194
NW3 . . . . . 35Db 69
RM2: Rom 25Jd 56
SM2: Sutt 81Eb 175
SW20 . . . . . 70Ya 132
Heathedge SE26 . . . . . 61Xb 135
Heath End Rd. DA5: Bexl 60Gd 118
Heather Av. RM1: Rom 26Fd 56
Heatherbank BR7: Chst 68Qc 138
SE9 . . . . . 54Pc 116
Heatherbank Cl. DA1: Cray 58Gd 118
KT11: Cobh 83Z 171
Heather Cl. CM15: Pil H 15Xd 40
E6 . . . . . 44Qc 94
GU21: Wok 7N 167
KT15: New H 82K 169
KT20: Kgswd 94Ab 194
N7 . . . . . 34Pb 70
RH1: Redh 3B 208
RM1: Rom 25Fd 56
SE13 . . . . . 59Fc 115
SW8 . . . . . 55Kb 112
TW7: Isle 57Fa 108
TW12: Hamp 67Ba 129
UB8: Hil 43P 83
WD5: Ab L 4W 12
Heather Ct. AL2: Lon C 9H 7
DA14: Sidc 65Zc 139
Heatherdale Cl. KT2: King T 65Qa 131
Heatherdene KT24: W Hor 97T 190
Heatherdene Cl. CR4: Mitc 70Fb 133
N12 . . . . . 24Eb 49
Heatherden Grn. SL0: Iver H 39E 62
Heather Dr. DA1: Dart 59Jd 118
EN2: Enf 12Rb 33
RM1: Rom 26Fd 56
SL5: S'dale 3F 146
Heather End BR8: Swan 70Fd 140
Heatherfield La. KT13: Weyb 78U 150
Heatherfields KT15: New H 82K 169
Heatherfold Way HA5: Eastc 27V 44
Heather Gdns. EN9: Walt A 8Ec 20
NW11 . . . . . 30Ab 48
RM1: Rom 26Fd 56
SM2: Sutt 79Cb 155
Heather Glen RM1: Rom 26Fd 56
Heather Ho. E14 . . . . . 44Ec 92
(off Dee St.)
Heatherlands TW16: Sun 65W 128
Heather La. UB7: Yiew 44N 83
WD24: Wat 7V 12
Heatherlea Gro. KT4: Wor Pk 74Xa 154
Heatherley Ct. E5 . . . . . 34Wb 71
Heatherley Dr. IG5: Ilf 27Nc 54
Heather Pk. Dr. HA0: Wemb 38Qa 67
Heather Pk. Pde. HA0: Wemb 38Pa 67
(off Heather Pk. Dr.)
Heather Pl. KT10: Esh 77Da 151
Heather Ri. WD23: Bush 12Ba 27
Heather Rd. E4 . . . . . 23Bc 52
NW2 . . . . . 33Va 68
SE12 . . . . . 61Jc 137
Heathers, The TW19: Stanw 59P 105
Heatherset Cl. KT10: Esh 78Ea 152
Heatherset Gdns. SW16 . . . . . 66Pb 134
Heatherside Cl. KT23: Bookh 97Ba 191
Heatherside Dr. GU25: Vir W 2L 147
Heatherside Gdns. SL2: Farn C 4H 61
Heatherside Rd. DA14: Sidc 62Yc 139
KT19: Ewe 80Ta 153
Heatherton Ter. N3 . . . . . 26Db 49
Heathervale Caravan Pk.
KT15: New H 82L 169
Heathervale Rd. KT15: New H 82K 169
Heathervale Way KT15: New H 82L 169
Heather Wlk. GU24: Brkwd 3B 186
HA8: Edg 22Ra 47
KT12: W Vill 82U 170
TW2: Whitt 59Ca 107
(off Stephenson Rd.)
W10 . . . . . 42Ab 88
Heather Way CR2: Sels 81Zb 178
EN6: Pot B 4Bb 17
GU24: Chob 10J 147
HA7: Stan 23Ha 46
HP2: Hem H 1M 3
RM1: Rom 26Fd 56
Heatherwood Cl. E12 . . . . . 33Lc 73
Heatherwood Dr. UB4: Hayes 40T 64
Heath Farm Ct. WD17: Wat 9T 12
Heath Farm La. AL3: St A 1C 6
Heathfield BR7: Chst 65Sc 138
E4 . . . . . 20Ec 34
HA1: Harr 31Ha 66
KT11: Cobh 86Ca 171
Heathfield Av. SL5: S'dale 1C 146
SW18 . . . . . 59Fb 111
Heathfield Cl. BR2: Kes 78Lc 159
E16 . . . . . 43Mc 93
EN6: Pot B 2Db 17
GU22: Wok 90C 168
WD19: Wat 17Y 27
Heathfield Ct. AL1: St A 1C 6
(off Avenue Rd.)
E3 . . . . . 40Cc 72
(off Tredegar Rd.)
SE14 . . . . . 52Yb 114
SE20 . . . . . 66Yb 136
W4 . . . . . 50Ta 87
Heathfield Dr. CR4: Mitc 67Gb 133
RH1: Redh 10N 207
Heathfield Gdns. CR0: C'don 77Tb 157
NW11 . . . . . 30Za 48
SE3 . . . . . 54Gc 115
(off Baizdon Rd.)
SW18 . . . . . 58Fb 111
W4 . . . . . 50Sa 87
Heathfield Ho. SE3 . . . . . 54Gc 115
Heathfield La. BR7: Chst 65Sc 138
Heathfield Nth. TW2: Twick 59Ga 108
Heathfield Pk. NW2 . . . . . 37Ya 68
Heathfield Pk. Dr. RM6: Chad H 29Xc 55
Heathfield Ri. HA4: Ruis 31S 64
Heathfield Rd. BR1: Brom 66Hc 137
BR2: Kes 78Lc 159
CR0: C'don 77Tb 157
Heathfield Rd. DA6: Bex 56Bd 117
GU22: Wok 90C 168
KT12: Hers 77Aa 151
SL6: Tap 3A 60
SW18 . . . . . 58Eb 111
TN13: S'oaks 94Hd 202
W3 . . . . . 47Ra 87
WD23: Bush 14Aa 27
Heathfields Cl. KT21: Asht 90La 172
Heathfields Ct. TW4: Houn 57Aa 107
Heathfield Sth. TW2: Twick 59Ha 108
Heathfield Sq. SW18 . . . . . 59Fb 111
Heathfield Ter. BR8: Swan 68Fd 140
SE18 . . . . . 51Uc 116
W4 . . . . . 50Sa 87
Heathfield Va. CR2: Sels 81Zb 178
Heath Gdns. DA1: Dart 60Ld 119
TW1: Twick 60Ha 108
Heathgate NW11 . . . . . 30Db 49
Heathgate Pl. NW3 . . . . . 36Hb 69
Heath Gro. SE20 . . . . . 66Yb 136
TW16: Sun 66V 128
Heath Ho. DA15: Sidc 63Vc 139
Heath Ho. Rd. GU22: Wok 4G 186
Heath Hurst Rd. NW3 . . . . . 35Gb 69
Heathhurst Rd. CR2: Sande 81Tb 177
Heathland M. KT18: Tatt C 91Za 194
Heathland Rd. N16 . . . . . 32Ub 71
Heathlands KT20: Tad 94Za 194
Heathlands Cl. GU21: Wok 86A 168
TW1: Twick 61Ha 130
TW16: Sun 68W 128
Heathlands Ri. DA1: Dart 58Kd 119
Heathlands Way TW4: Houn 57Aa 107
Heath La. HP1: Hem H 4L 3
SE3 . . . . . 54Fc 115
(not continuous)
Heath La. (Lower) DA1: Dart 60Ld 119
Heath La. (Upper) DA1: Dart 61Jd 140
Heathlee Rd. DA1: Cray 58Gd 118
SE3 . . . . . 56Hc 115
Heathley End BR7: Chst 65Sc 138
Heath Lodge WD23: B Hea 18Ga 28
Heathmans Rd. SW6 . . . . . 53Bb 111
Heath Mead SW19 . . . . . 62Za 132
Heath M. GU23: Rip 95K 189
Heath Mill La. GU3: Worp 7F 186
HEATH PARK 30Jd 56
Heath Pk. Ct. RM2: Rom 29Jd 56
Heath Pk. Dr. BR1: Brom 69Nc 138
Heathpark Dr. GU20: W'sham 9C 146
Heathpark Golf Course 48Q 84
Heath Pk. Ho. HP1: Hem H 4L 3
Heath Pk. Rd. RM1: Rom 29Jd 56
RM2: Rom 29Jd 56
Heath Pas. NW3 . . . . . 33Db 69
Heathpool Ct. E1 . . . . . 42Xb 91
Heath Ridge Grn. KT11: Cobh 85Ca 171
Heath Ri. BR2: Hayes 72Hc 159
GU23: Rip 95K 189
GU25: Vir W 10P 125
SW15 . . . . . 58Za 110
Heath Rd. AL1: St A 1C 6
CR3: Cat'm 95Tb 197
CR7: Thor H 69Sb 135
DA1: Cray 58Hd 118
DA5: Bexl 60Ed 118
EN6: Pot B 2Cb 17
GU21: Wok 87B 168
HA1: Harr 31Ea 66
KT13: Weyb 77Q 150
KT22: Oxs 84Ea 172
RM6: Chad H 31Zc 75
RM16: Grays, Ors 6B 100
SW8 . . . . . 54Kb 112
TW1: Twick 60Ha 108
TW2: Twick 60Ha 108
TW3: Houn, Isle 56Da 107
TW7: Isle 56Da 107
UB10: Hil 42S 84
WD19: Wat 17Z 27
Heathrow Academy 53S 106
HEATHROW AIRPORT
Terminals 1, 2, 3 . . . . . 55Q 106
Terminal 4 . . . . . 57R 106
Terminal 5 . . . . . 55L 105
Heathrow Blvd. UB7: Sip 52P 105
(not continuous)
Heathrow Causeway Cen.
TW4: Houn 55X 107
Heathrow Cl. UB7: Lford 53K 105
Heathrow Est., The TW4: Cran 54X 107
Heathrow Gateway TW4: Houn 59Aa 107
Heathrow Interchange UB4: Yead 46Y 85
Heathrow Intl. Trad. Est.
TW4: Houn 55X 107
Heathrow Prologis Pk. UB3: Harl 48R 84
Heath Royal SW15 . . . . . 58Za 110
Heaths Cl. EN1: Enf 12Ub 33
HEATH SIDE 62Hd 140
Heath Side BR5: Pet W 74Sc 160
NW3 . . . . . 35Fb 69
Heathside AL4: Col H 5M 7
KT10: Hin W 76Ga 152
KT13: Weyb 78R 150
NW11 . . . . . 32Cb 69
SE13 . . . . . 54Ec 114
TW4: Houn 59Ba 107
Heathside Av. DA7: Bex 53Ad 117
Heathside Cl. HA6: Nwood 22T 44
IG2: Ilf 29Tc 54
KT10: Hin W 76Ga 152
Heathside Ct. KT20: Tad 95Xa 194
Heathside Cres. GU22: Wok 89B 168
Heathside Gdns. GU22: Wok 89C 168
Heathside Pk. Rd. GU22: Wok 90B 168
Heathside Pl. KT18: Tatt C 90Za 174
Heathside Rd. GU22: Wok 90B 168
HA6: Nwood 21T 44
Heathstan Rd. W12 . . . . . 44Wa 88
Heath St. DA1: Dart 59Md 119
NW3 . . . . . 34Eb 69
Heath Ter. RM6: Chad H 31Zc 75
Heath Vw. KT24: E Hor 97V 190
N2 . . . . . 28Eb 49
Heathview NW5 . . . . . 35Jb 70
Heathview Av. DA1: Cray 58Gd 118
Heath Vw. Cl. N2 . . . . . 28Eb 49
Heathview Cres. DA1: Dart 60Jd 118
Heathview Dr. SE2 . . . . . 51Zc 117
Heathview Gdns. RM16: Grays 48Ee 99
SW15 . . . . . 59Ya 110
Heathview Rd. CR7: Thor H 70Qb 134
RM16: Grays 47Ee 99
Heath Vs. NW3 . . . . . 34Fb 69
SE18 . . . . . 50Vc 95
Heathville Rd. N19 . . . . . 31Nb 70
Heathwall St. SW11 . . . . . 55Hb 111
HEATHWAY 39Cd 76
Heath Way DA8: Erith 53Ed 118
WD7: Shenl 2La 14
Heathway CR0: C'don 76Bc 158
CR3: Cat'm 97Sb 197
IG8: Wfd G 22Lc 53
KT24: E Hor 96V 190
RM9: Dag 34Bd 75
RM10: Dag 34Bd 75
SE3 . . . . . 52Jc 115
SL0: Iver H 40F 62
UB2: S'hall 49Z 85
Heathway Ct. NW3 . . . . . 33Cb 69
Heathway Ind. Est. RM10: Dag 35Dd 76
Heathwood Gdns. BR8: Swan 68Ed 140
SE7 . . . . . 49Nc 94
Heathwood Pde. BR8: Swan 68Ed 140
Heathwood Point SE23 . . . . . 62Zb 136
Heathwood Wlk. DA5: Bexl 60Gd 118
Heaton Av. RM3: Rom 24Kd 57
Heaton Cl. E4 . . . . . 20Ec 34
RM3: Rom 24Ld 57
Heaton Ct. EN8: Chesh 1Zb 20
Heaton Grange Rd. RM2: Rom 26Hd 56
Heaton Ho. SW10 . . . . . 51Eb 111
(off Seymour Wlk.)
Heaton Rd. CR4: Mitc 66Jb 134
SE15 . . . . . 54Xb 113
Heaton Way RM3: Rom 24Ld 57
Heaven Tree Cl. N1 . . . . . 37Sb 71
Heaver Cl. DA3: Lfield 69Ce 143
HEAVERHAM 89Ud 184
Heaverham Rd. TN15: Kems'g 89Rd 183
Heaver Rd. SW11 . . . . . 55Fb 111
Heavitree Cl. SE18 . . . . . 50Tc 94
Heavitree Rd. SE18 . . . . . 50Tc 94
(not continuous)
Hebden Ct. E2 . . . . . 1K 219 (39Vb 71)
Hebden Ter. N17 . . . . . 23Ub 51
Hebdon Rd. SW17 . . . . . 62Gb 133
Heberden Ct. RM19: Purf 50Rd 97
(off Wingrove Dr.)
Heber Mans. W14 . . . . . 51Ab 110
(off Queen's Club Gdns.)
Heber Rd. NW2 . . . . . 36Za 68
SE22 . . . . . 58Vb 113
Hebron Rd. W6 . . . . . 48Ya 88
Hecham Cl. E17 . . . . . 26Ac 52
Heckets Ct. KT10: Esh 82Ea 172
Heckfield Pl. SW6 . . . . . 52Cb 111
Heckford Cl. WD18: Wat 16S 26
Heckford Ho. E14 . . . . . 44Dc 92
(off Grundy St.)
Heckford St. E1 . . . . . 45Zb 92
Hector NW9 . . . . . 25Va 48
(off Five Acre)
Hector Cl. N9 . . . . . 19Wb 33
Hector Ct. SW9 . . . . . 52Qb 112
(off Caldwell St.)
Hector Ho. E2 . . . . . 40Xb 71
(off Old Bethnal Grn. Rd.)
Hector St. SE18 . . . . . 49Uc 94
Heddington Gro. N7 . . . . . 36Pb 70
Heddon Cl. TW7: Isle 56Ja 108
Heddon Ct. Av. EN4: Cockf 15Hb 31
Heddon Ct. Pde. EN4: Cockf 15Jb 32
Heddon Rd. EN4: Cockf 15Hb 31
Heddon St. W1 . . . . . 4B 222 (45Lb 90)
Hedgecroft Cotts. GU23: Rip 93K 189
Hedgegate Ct. W11 . . . . . 44Bb 89
(off Powis Ter.)
Hedge Hill EN2: Enf 11Rb 33
Hedge La. N13 . . . . . 20Rb 33
Hedgeley IG4: Ilf 28Pc 54
Hedgemans Rd. RM9: Dag 38Zc 75
Hedgemans Way RM9: Dag 37Ad 75
Hedge Pl. Rd. DA9: Ghithe 58Vd 120
HEDGERLEY 2H 61
Hedgerley Ct. GU21: Wok 9N 167
Hedgerley Gdns. UB6: G'frd 40Ea 66
HEDGERLEY GREEN 1J 61
HEDGERLEY HILL 3H 61
Hedgerley Hill SL2: Hedg 4H 61
Hedgerley La.
SL2: Ger X, Hedg 1J 61
SL9: Ger X 2N 61
Hedge Row HP1: Hem H 1J 3
Hedgerow SL9: Chal P 23A 42
Hedgerow Ct. E6 . . . . . 39Pc 74
(off Nelson St.)
Hedgerow La. EN5: Ark 15Xa 30
Hedgerows, The DA11: Nflt 1A 144
Hedgerow Wlk. EN8: Chesh 2Zb 20
Hedgers Cl. IG10: Lough 14Qc 36
Hedgers Gro. E9 . . . . . 37Ac 72
Hedger St. SE11 . . . . . 5B 230 (49Rb 91)
Hedgeside Rd. HA6: Nwood 22S 44
Hedges Way WD3: Crox G 17P 25
Hedge Wlk. SE6 . . . . . 64Dc 136
Hedgewood Gdns. IG5: Ilf 29Qc 54
Hedgley M. SE12 . . . . . 57Hc 115
Hedgley St. SE12 . . . . . 57Hc 115
Hedingham Cl. N1 . . . . . 38Sb 71
Hedingham Ho. KT2: King T 67Na 131
(off Royal Quarter)
Hedingham Rd. RM8: Dag 36Xc 75
RM11: Horn 32Qd 77
RM16: Chaf H 50Yd 98
Hedley Av. RM20: Grays 52Yd 120
Hedley Cl. RM1: Rom 29Gd 56
Hedley Ho. E14 . . . . . 48Ec 92
(off Stewart St.)
Hedley Rd. AL1: St A 2F 6
TW2: Whitt 59Ca 107
Hedley Row N5 . . . . . 36Tb 71
Hedley Vs. AL1: St A 2F 6
Hedsor Ho. E2 . . . . . 5K 219
Hedworth Av. EN8: Walt C 5Zb 20
Heenan Cl. IG11: Bark 37Sc 74
Heene Rd. EN2: Enf 11Tb 33
Hega Ho. E14 . . . . . 43Ec 92
(off Ullin St.)
Heideck Gdns. CM13: Hut 19De 41
Heidegger Cres. SW13 . . . . . 52Xa 110
Heigham Rd. E6 . . . . . 38Nc 74
Heighton Gdns. CR0: Wadd 78Rb 157
Heights, The BR3: Beck 66Ec 136
(not continuous)
IG10: Lough 12Pc 36
KT13: Weyb 82Q 170
SE7 . . . . . 50Lc 93
UB5: N'olt 36Ba 65
Heights Cl. SM7: Bans 88Ab 174
SW20 . . . . . 66Xa 132
Heiron St. SE17 . . . . . 51Rb 113
Helby Rd. SW4 . . . . . 58Mb 112
Heldar Ct. SE1 . . . . . 2G 231 (47Tb 91)
Helder Gro. SE12 . . . . . 59Hc 115
Helder St. CR2: S Croy 79Tb 157
Heldmann Cl. TW3: Houn 56Fa 108
Helegan Cl. BR6: Chels 77Vc 161
Helena Cl. EN4: Had W 10Fb 17
Helena Ct. W5 . . . . . 43Ma 87
Helena Pl. E9 . . . . . 39Xb 71
Helena Rd. E13 . . . . . 40Hc 73
E17 . . . . . 29Cc 52
NW10 . . . . . 36Xa 68
SL4: Wind 4H 103
W5 . . . . . 43Ma 87
Helena Sq. SE16 . . . . . 45Ac 92
(off Sovereign Cres.)
Helen Av. TW14: Felt 59X 107
Helen Cl. DA1: Dart 59Kd 119
KT8: W Mole 70Da 129
N2 . . . . . 27Eb 49
Helen Gladstone Ho. SE1 . . . . . 1B 230
Helen Ho. E2 . . . . . 40Xb 71
(off Old Bethnal Grn. Rd.)
Helen Mackay Ho. E14 . . . . . 44Fc 93
(off Blair St.)
Helen Peele Cotts. SE16 . . . . . 48Yb 92
(off Lower Rd.)
Helen Rd. RM11: Horn 27Md 57
Helenslea Av. NW11 . . . . . 32Cb 69
Helen's Pl. E2 . . . . . 41Yb 92
Helen St. SE18 . . . . . 49Rc 94
Helen Taylor Ho. SE16 . . . . . 48Wb 91
(off Evelyn Lowe Est.)
Helford Cl. HA4: Ruis 33U 64
Helford Ct. RM15: S Ock 45Xd 98
Helford Wlk. GU21: Wok 10L 167
Helford Way RM14: Upm 30Td 58
Helgiford Gdns. TW16: Sun 66U 128
Heligan Ho. SE16 . . . . . 47Zb 92
(off Water Gdns. Sq.)
Helios Rd. SM6: Wall 74Jb 156
Heliport Ind. Est. SW11 . . . . . 54Fb 111
Helix Ct. W11 . . . . . 46Za 88
(off Swanscombe Rd.)
Helix Gdns. SW2 . . . . . 58Pb 112
Helix Rd. SW2 . . . . . 58Pb 112
Helix Ter. SW19 . . . . . 61Za 132
Helleborine RM17: Grays 50Be 99
Hellen Way WD19: Wat 21Z 45
Hellings St. E1 . . . . . 46Wb 91
Helm, The E16 . . . . . 45Rc 94
Helm Cl. KT19: Eps 84Qa 173
Helme Cl. SW19 . . . . . 64Bb 133
Helmet Row EC1 . . . . . 4E 218 (42Sb 91)
Helmore Rd. IG11: Bark 38Vc 75
Helmsdale GU21: Wok 10M 167
Helmsdale Cl. RM1: Rom 24Gd 56
UB4: Yead 42Aa 85
Helmsdale Ho. NW6 . . . . . 40Db 69
(off Carlton Vale)
Helmsdale Rd. RM1: Rom 24Gd 56
SW16 . . . . . 67Mb 134
Helmsley Ho. RM3: Rom 24Nd 57
(off Leyburn Cres.)
Helmsley Pl. E8 . . . . . 38Xb 71
Helmsley St. E8 . . . . . 38Xb 71
Helperby Rd. NW10 . . . . . 38Ua 68
Helsby Ct. NW8 . . . . . 5B 214
Helsinki Sq. SE16 . . . . . 48Ac 92
Helston NW1 . . . . . 1C 216
Helston Cl. HA5: Hat E 24Ba 45
Helston Ct. N15 . . . . . 29Ub 51
(off Culvert Rd.)
Helston Ho. SE11 . . . . . 7A 230
Helston La. SL4: Wind 3F 102
Helston Pl. WD5: Ab L 4V 12
Helvellyn Cl. TW20: Egh 66D 126
Helvetia St. SE6 . . . . . 61Bc 136
Helwys Ct. E4 . . . . . 23Dc 52
Hemans St. SW8 . . . . . 52Mb 112
Hemans St. Est. SW8 . . . . . 52Mb 112
Hemberton Rd. SW9 . . . . . 55Nb 112
HEMEL HEMPSTEAD 1M 3
Hemel Hempstead Ind. Est.
HP2: Hem H 1B 4
Hemel Hempstead Rd.
AL3: St A 4D 4
HP3: Hem H 4D 4
Hemel Hempstead Town FC 2A 4
Hemel Indoor Tennis Cen. 7B 4
Hemery Rd. UB6: G'frd 36Fa 66
Hemingford Cl. N12 . . . . . 22Fb 49
Hemingford Rd. N1 . . . . . 39Pb 70
SM3: Cheam 77Ya 154
WD17: Wat 8U 12
Heming Rd. HA8: Edg 24Ra 47
Hemington Av. N11 . . . . . 22Hb 49
Hemingway Cl. NW5 . . . . . 35Jb 70
Hemley Rd. RM16: Ors 4F 100
Hemlock Cl. KT20: Kgswd 95Ab 194
SW16 . . . . . 68Lb 134
Hemlock Rd. W12 . . . . . 45Va 88
(not continuous)
Hemmen La. UB3: Hayes 44V 84
Hemming Cl. TW12: Hamp 67Ca 129
Hemmings Cl. DA14: Sidc 61Xc 139
Hemmings Mead KT19: Ewe 79Sa 153
Hemming St. E1 . . . . . 42Wb 91
Hemming Way SL2: Slou 1F 80
WD25: Wat 7W 12
Hemnall M. CM16: Epp 2Wc 23
(off Hemnall St.)
Hemnall St. CM16: Epp 3Vc 23
Hempshaw Av. SM7: Bans 88Hb 175
Hempson Av. SL3: L'ly 8N 81
Hempstead Cl. IG9: Buck H 19Jc 35
Hempstead Rd. E17 . . . . . 27Fc 53
HP3: Bov 9C 2
WD4: K Lan 8P 3
WD17: Wat 8T 12
(not continuous)
Hemp Wlk. SE17 . . . . . 5G 231 (49Tb 91)
Hemsby Rd. KT9: Chess 79Pa 153
Hemstal Rd. NW6 . . . . . 38Cb 69
Hemsted Rd. DA8: Erith 52Gd 118
Hemswell Dr. NW9 . . . . . 25Ua 48
Hemsworth Ct. N1 . . . . . 1H 219 (40Ub 71)
Hemsworth St. N1 . . . . . 1H 219 (40Ub 71)
Hemus Pl. SW3 . . . . . 7E 226 (50Gb 89)
Hemwood Rd. SL4: Wind 5B 102
Henage La. GU22: Wok 92E 188
Hen & Chicken Ct. EC4 . . . . . 3K 223
Hen & Chickens Theatre 37Rb 71
(off St Paul's Rd.)
Henbane Path RM3: Rom 24Md 57
Henbit Cl. KT20: Tad 91Xa 194
Henbury Way WD19: Wat 20Z 27
Henchman St. W12 . . . . . 44Va 88
Hencroft St. Nth. SL1: Slou 7K 81
Hencroft St. Sth. SL1: Slou 8K 81
Hendale Av. NW4 . . . . . 27Xa 48
Henderson Cl. NW10 . . . . . 37Sa 67
RM11: Horn 33Kd 77
Henderson Ct. N12 . . . . . 21Db 49
NW3 . . . . . 36Fb 69
(off Fitzjohn's Av.)
SE14 . . . . . 51Zb 114
(off Myers La.)
Henderson Dr. DA1: Dart 56Pd 119
NW8 . . . . . 5B 214 (42Fb 89)
Henderson Gro. TN16: Big H 84Lc 179
Henderson Ho. RM10: Dag 34Cd 76
(off Kershaw Rd.)
Henderson Pl. WD5: Bedm 9F 4
Henderson Rd. CR0: C'don 72Tb 157
E7 . . . . . 37Lc 73
N9 . . . . . 18Xb 33
SW18 . . . . . 59Gb 111
UB4: Yead 41W 84
Hendfield Ct. SM6: Wall 79Kb 156
Hendham Rd. SW17 . . . . . 61Gb 133
HENDON 28Ya 48
Hendon Av. N3 . . . . . 25Ab 48
Hendon Crematorium NW7 . . . . . 25Za 48
Hendon FC 32Za 68
Hendon Gdns. RM5: Col R 23Ed 56
Hendon Golf Course 24Ya 48
Hendon Gro. KT19: Eps 81Qa 173
Hendon Hall Ct. NW4 . . . . . 27Za 48
Hendon Ho. NW4 . . . . . 29Za 48
Hendon La. N3 . . . . . 27Ab 48
Hendon Leisure Cen. 31Za 68
Hendon Lodge NW4 . . . . . 27Xa 48
Hendon Pk. Mans. NW4 . . . . . 29Ya 48
Hendon Pk. Row NW11 . . . . . 30Bb 49
Hendon Rd. N9 . . . . . 19Wb 33
Hendon Way NW2 . . . . . 31Za 68
NW4 . . . . . 30Xa 48
TW19: Stanw 58M 105
Hendon Wood La. NW7 . . . . . 16Va 30
Hendre Ho. SE1 . . . . . 6J 231
Hendren Cl. UB6: G'frd 36Fa 66
Hendre Rd. SE1 . . . . . 6J 231 (49Ub 91)
Hendrick Av. SW12 . . . . . 59Hb 111
Heneage Cres. CR0: New Ad 82Ec 178
Heneage La. EC3 . . . . . 3J 225 (44Ub 91)
Heneage Pl. EC3 . . . . . 3J 225 (44Ub 91)
Heneage St. E1 . . . . . 1K 225 (43Vb 91)
Henera's Ct. BR1: Brom 69Qc 138
(off Brady Dr.)
Henfield Cl. DA5: Bexl 58Cd 118
N19 . . . . . 32Lb 70
Henfield Rd. SW19 . . . . . 67Bb 133
Hengelo Gdns. CR4: Mitc 70Fb 133
Hengest Av. KT10: Surb 76Ja 152
Hengist Rd. DA8: Erith 52Dd 118
SE12 . . . . . 59Kc 115
Hengist Way BR2: Brom 70Gc 137
SM6: Wall 80Mb 156
Hengrave Rd. SE23 . . . . . 58Yb 114
Hengrove Ct. DA5: Bexl 60Ad 117
Hengrove Cres. TW15: Ashf 62M 127
Henham Ct. RM5: Col R 25Ed 56
HENHURST 7G 144
Henhurst Rd. DA12: Cobh 6F 144
Henley Av. SM3: Cheam 76Ab 154
Henley Cl. SE16 . . . . . 47Yb 92
(off St Marychurch St.)
TW7: Isle 53Ha 108
UB6: G'frd 40Ea 66
Henley Ct. GU22: Wok 92D 188
N14 . . . . . 17Lb 32
NW2 . . . . . 37Za 68
TW20: Egh 63C 126
Henley Deane DA11: Nflt 3A 144
Henley Dr. KT2: King T 66Va 132
SE1 . . . . . 5K 231 (49Vb 91)
Henley Gdns. HA5: Eastc 27X 45
RM6: Chad H 29Ad 55
Henley Gate GU3: Norm 9A 186
GU24: Pirb 9A 186
Henley Ho. AL1: St A 3C 6
(off Lattimore Rd.)
E2 . . . . . 5K 219
Henley Pk. GU3: Norm 10A 186
Henley Prior N1 . . . . . 2H 217
Henley Rd. E16 . . . . . 47Pc 94
IG1: Ilf 35Sc 74
N18 . . . . . 21Ub 51
NW10 . . . . . 39Ya 68
SL1: Slou 4C 80
Henley St. SW11 . . . . . 54Jb 112
Henley Way TW13: Hanw 64Z 129
Henlow Pl. TW10: Ham 61Ma 131
HENLYS CORNER 28Bb 49
HENLYS RDBT. 54Y 107
Henneker Cl. RM5: Col R 23Ed 56
Hennel Cl. SE23 . . . . . 62Yb 136
Hennessy Ct. E10 . . . . . 30Ec 52
GU21: Wok 85E 168
Hennessy Rd. N9 . . . . . 19Yb 34
Henniker Gdns. E6 . . . . . 41Mc 93
Henniker M. SW3 . . . . . 51Fb 111
Henniker Point E15 . . . . . 36Gc 73
(off Leytonstone Rd.)
Henniker Rd. E15 . . . . . 36Fc 73
Henningham Rd. N17 . . . . . 25Tb 51
Henning St. SW11 . . . . . 53Gb 111
Henrietta Barnet Wlk. NW11 . . . . . 30Cb 49
Henrietta Cl. SE8 . . . . . 51Cc 114
Henrietta Ct. TW1: Twick 59La 108
(off Richmond Rd.)
Henrietta Ho. N15 . . . . . 30Ub 51
(off St Ann's Rd.)
W6 . . . . . 50Ya 88
(off Queen Caroline St.)
Henrietta M. WC1 . . . . . 5G 217 (42Nb 90)
Henrietta Pl. W1 . . . . . 3K 221 (44Kb 90)
Henrietta St. WC2 . . . . . 4G 223 (45Nb 90)
Henriques St. E1 . . . . . 44Wb 91
Henry Addlington Cl. E6 . . . . . 43Rc 94
Henry Cl. EN2: Enf 10Ub 19
Henry Cooper Way SE9 . . . . . 62Mc 137
Henry Darlot Dr. NW7 . . . . . 22Za 48
Henry De Grey Cl. RM17: Grays 49Be 99
Henry Dent Cl. SE5 . . . . . 55Tb 113
Henry Dickens Ct. W11 . . . . . 45Za 88
Henry Doulton Dr. SW17 . . . . . 63Jb 134
Henry Gdns. DA11: Nflt 1B 144
Henry Hatch Ct. SM2: Sutt 80Eb 155

Henry Ho. SE1 7A 224 (46Qb 90)
SW8 52Nb 112
(off Wyvil Rd.)
Henry Jackson Rd. SW15 55Za 110
Henry Lodge KT12: Hers 79Y 151
Henry Macaulay Av. KT2: King T 67Ma 131
Henry Moore Ct. SW3 7D 226 (50Gb 89)
Henry Peters Dr. TW11: Tedd 64Ga 130
(off Somerset Gdns.)
Henry Purcell Ho. E16 46Kc 93
(off Evelyn Rd.)
Henry Rd. E6 40Nc 74
EN4: E Barn 15Fb 31
N4 32Sb 71
SL1: Slou 7H 81
Henrys Av. IG8: Wfd G 22Hc 53
Henrys Grant AL1: St A 3C 6
Henryson Rd. SE4 57Cc 114
Henry St. BR1: Brom 67Kc 137
HP3: Hem H 6M 3
RM17: Grays 51Ee 121
Henry's Wlk. IG6: Ilf 24Tc 54
Henry Tate M. SW16 64Pb 134
Henry Tudor Ct. SE9 59Sc 116
Henry Wise Ho. SW1 6C 228
Hensby M. WD19: Wat 16Aa 27
Hensford Gdns. SE26 63Xb 135
Henshall Point E3 41Dc 92
(off Bromley High St.)
Henshall St. N1 37Tb 71
Henshawe Rd. RM8: Dag 34Zc 75
Henshaw St. SE17 5F 231 (49Tb 91)
Henslowe Rd. SE22 57Wb 113
Henslow Ho. SE15 52Wb 113
(off Peckham Pk. Rd.)
Henslow Way GU21: Wok 86F 168
Henson Av. NW2 36Ya 68
Henson Cl. BR6: Farnb 75Rc 160
Henson Path HA3: Kenton 27Ma 47
Henson Pl. UB5: N'olt 39Y 65
Henstridge Pl. NW8 1D 214 (39Gb 69)
Hensworth Rd.
TW15: Ashf 64M 127
Henty Cl. SW11 52Gb 111
Henty Wlk. SW15 57Xa 110
Henville Rd. BR1: Brom 67Kc 137
Henwick Rd. SE9 55Mc 115
Henwood Side IG8: Wfd G 23Pc 54
Hepburn Cl. RM16: Chaf H 49Zd 99
Hepburn Ct. EN6: S Mim 4Wa 16
WD6: Bore 14Qa 29
(off Whitehall Cl.)
Hepburn Gdns. BR2: Hayes 74Gc 159
Hepburn M. SW11 57Hb 111
Hepple Cl. TW7: Isle 54Ka 108
Hepplestone Cl. SW15 58Xa 110
Hepscott Rd. E9 37Cc 72
Hepworth Ct. N1 39Rb 71
(off Gaskin St.)
NW3 36Gb 69
SM3: Sutt 74Cb 155
SW1 7K 227 (50Kb 90)
Hepworth Gdns. IG11: Bark 36Wc 75
Hepworth Rd. SW16 66Nb 134
Hepworth Way KT12: Walt T 74V 150
Heracles NW9 25Va 48
(off Five Acre)
Heracles Cl. AL2: Park 10A 6
Hera Ct. E14 49Cc 92
(off Homer Dr.)
Herald Gdns. SM6: Wall 75Kb 156
Herald's Pl. SE11 5B 230 (49Rb 91)
Herald St. E2 42Xb 91
Herald Wlk. DA1: Dart 57Pd 119
Herbal Hill EC1 6A 218 (42Qb 90)
Herbal Hill Gdns. EC1 6A 218
Herbal Pl. EC1 6A 218
Herbert Cres. GU21: Knap 10J 167
SW1 3G 227 (48Hb 89)
Herbert Gdns. NW10 40Xa 68
RM6: Chad H 31Zc 75
W4 51Ra 109
Herbert Ho. E1 2K 225
Herbert M. SW2 58Qb 112
Herbert Morrison Ho. SW6 51Bb 111
(off Clem Attlee Ct.)
Herbert Pl. SE18 51Rc 116
TW7: Isle 54Fa 108
Herbert Rd. BR2: Brom 71Mc 159
BR8: Hext 65Kd 141
DA7: Bex 54Ad 117
DA10: Swans 58Be 121
E12 35Nc 74
E17 31Bc 72
IG3: Ilf 33Uc 74
KT1: King T 69Pa 131
N11 24Nb 50
N15 29Vb 51
NW9 30Wa 48
RM11: Horn 31Nd 77
SE18 52Qc 116
(not continuous)
SW19 66Bb 133
(not continuous)
UB1: S'hall 46Ba 85
Herbert St. E13 40Jc 73
HP2: Hem H 1M 3
NW5 37Jb 70
Herbrand Est. WC1 5F 217 (42Nb 90)
Herbrand St. WC1 5F 217 (42Nb 90)
Hercies Rd. UB10: Hil 38P 63
Hercules Ct. SE14 51Ac 114
Hercules Pl. N7 34Nb 70
(not continuous)
Hercules Rd. SE1 4J 229 (48Pb 90)
Hercules St. N7 34Nb 70
Hercules Way WD25: Wat 6V 12
Hercules Wharf E14 45Gc 93
(off Orchard Pl.)
Hercules Yd. N7 34Nb 70
Hereford Av. EN4: E Barn 18Hb 31
Hereford Bldgs. SW3 51Fb 111
(off Old Church St.)
Hereford Cl. KT18: Eps 85Ta 173
TW18: Staines 67K 127
Hereford Copse GU22: Wok 1M 187
Hereford Ct. HA1: Harr 28Ga 46
SM2: Sutt 80Cb 155
W7 43Ha 86
(off Copley Cl.)
Hereford Gdns. HA5: Pinn 29Aa 45
IG1: Ilf 31Nc 74
SE13 57Gc 115
TW2: Twick 60Ea 108
Hereford Ho. N18 22Xb 51
(off Cavendish Cl.)
Hereford Ho. NW6 40Cb 69
(off Carlton Vale)
SW3 3E 226
SW10 52Db 111
(off Fulham Rd.)
Hereford Mans. W2 44Cb 89
(off Hereford Rd.)
Hereford M. W2 44Cb 89
Hereford Pl. SE14 52Bc 114
Hereford Retreat SE15 52Wb 113
Hereford Rd. E3 40Bc 72
E11 29Kc 53
TW13: Felt 60Y 107
W2 44Cb 89
W3 45Ra 87
W5 48La 86
Hereford Sq. SW7 6A 226 (49Eb 89)
Hereford St. E2 42Wb 91
Hereford Way KT9: Chess 78La 152
Herent Dr. IG5: Ilf 28Nc 54
Herent Gdns. IG5: Ilf 28Pc 54
Hereward Av. CR8: Purl 83Qb 176
Hereward Cl. EN9: Walt A 4Fc 21
Hereward Gdns. N13 22Qb 50
Hereward Grn. IG10: Lough 11Sc 36
Hereward Lincoln Ho. DA11: Nflt 58Fe 121
(off London Rd.)
Hereward Rd. SW17 63Hb 133
Herga Ct. HA1: Harr 34Ga 66
WD17: Wat 12W 26
Herga Hyll RM16: Ors 3C 100
Herga Rd. HA3: W'stone 28Ha 46
Herington Gro. CM13: Hut 17Ce 41
Heriot Av. E4 19Cc 34
Heriot Cl. KT16: Chert 73H 149
Heriot Rd. KT16: Chert 73J 149
NW4 29Ya 48
Heriots Cl. HA7: Stan 21Ja 46
Heritage Av. NW9 27Va 48
Heritage Cl. AL3: St A 2B 6
SW9 55Rb 113
TW16: Sun 67W 128
UB8: Cowl 42L 83
Heritage Ct. SE8 50Zb 92
TW20: Egh 64C 126
(off Station Rd.)
Heritage Hill BR2: Kes 78Lc 159
Heritage Pl. SW18 60Eb 111
Heritage Quay DA12: Grav'nd 8E 122
Heritage Vw. HA1: Harr 34Ha 66
Heritage Wlk. WD3: Chor 13G 24
Herkomer Cl. WD23: Bush 16Da 27
Herkomer Rd. WD23: Bush 15Ca 27
Herlwyn Av. HA4: Ruis 34U 64
Herlwyn Gdns. SW17 63Hb 133
Her Majesty's Theatre 6D 222
Herm Cl. TW7: Isle 52Ea 108
Hermes Cl. W9 42Cb 89
Hermes Ct. SW2 58Pb 112
SW9 53Qb 112
(off Southey Rd.)
Hermes St. N1 2K 217 (40Qb 70)
Hermes Wlk. UB5: N'olt 40Ca 65
Herm Ho. EN3: Enf W 10Zb 20
N1 37Sb 71
(off Clifton Rd.)
Hermiston Av. N8 29Nb 50
Hermitage, The KT1: King T 70Ma 131
SE13 54Ec 114
SE23 60Yb 114
SW13 53Va 110
TW10: Rich 57Na 109
TW13: Felt 62V 128
UB8: Uxb 37M 63
Hermitage Bri. GU21: Wok 2H 187
Hermitage Bri. Cotts. GU21: Wok 1H 187
Hermitage Cl. E18 28Hc 53
EN2: Enf 12Rb 33
KT10: Clay 79Ja 152
SE2 48Yc 95
SL3: L'ly 8N 81
TW17: Shep 70Q 128
Hermitage Ct. E1 46Wb 91
(off Knighten St.)
E18 28Jc 53
EN6: Pot B 5Eb 17
NW2 34Cb 69
TW18: Staines 64H 127
Hermitage Gdns. NW2 34Cb 69
SE19 66Sb 135
Hermitage Grn. SW16 67Nb 134
Hermitage Ho. N1 1B 218
Hermitage La. CR0: C'don 73Wb 157
N18 22Tb 51
NW2 34Cb 69
SE25 72Wb 157
SL4: Wind 6E 102
SW16 66Pb 134
Hermitage Moorings E1 46Wb 91
Hermitage Path SW16 67Nb 134
Hermitage Rd. CR8: Kenley 87Sb 177
GU21: Wok 1H 187
N4 31Rb 71
N15 31Rb 71
SE19 66Sb 135
Hermitage Row E8 36Wb 71
Hermitage St. W2 1B 220 (43Fb 89)
Hermitage Vs. SW6 51Cb 111
(off Lillie Rd.)
Hermitage Wlk. E18 28Hc 53
Hermitage Wall E1 46Wb 91
Hermitage Waterside E1 46Wb 91
(off Thomas More St.)
Hermitage Way HA7: Stan 25Ja 46
Hermitage Woods Cres.
GU21: Wok 1J 187
Hermitage Woods Est. GU21: Wok 1J 187
Hermit Pl. NW6 39Db 69
Hermit Rd. E16 43Hc 93
Hermit St. EC1 3B 218 (41Rb 91)
Hermon Gro. UB3: Hayes 46W 84
Hermon Hill E11 29Jc 53
E18 29Jc 53
Hern, The TN15: Crou 94Ee 205
Herndon Cl. TW20: Egh 63C 126
Herndon Rd. SW18 57Eb 111
Herne Cl. NW10 36Ta 67
UB3: Hayes 44V 84
Herne Ct. WD23: Bush 17Ea 28
HERNE HILL 57Sb 113
Herne Hill SE24 58Sb 113
Herne Hill Ho. SE24 58Rb 113
(off Railton Rd.)
Herne Hill Rd. SE24 55Sb 113
Herne Hill Stadium 58Tb 113
Herne M. N18 21Wb 51
Herne Pl. SE24 57Rb 113
Herne Rd. KT6: Surb 75Ma 153
WD23: Bush 16Da 27
Hernes Cl. TW18: Staines 67K 127
Herneshaw AL10: Hat 2B 8
Hernshaw CM13: Heron 24Fe 59
Herold Ct. RM13: Rain 39Jd 76
Heron Chase CM13: Heron 24Fe 59
Heron Cl. E17 26Bc 52
HP3: Hem H 7P 3
IG9: Buck H 18Jc 35
NW10 37Ua 68
SM1: Sutt 78Bb 155
UB8: Uxb 37M 63
WD3: Rick 19M 25
Heron Ct. BR2: Brom 70Lc 137
CM13: Heron 25Fe 59
E14 45Ec 92
(off New Union Cl.)
HA4: Ruis 33T 64
KT1: King T 69Na 131
KT17: Eps 86Wa 174
NW9 26Ua 48
TW19: Stanw 60N 105
Heron Cres. DA14: Sidc 62Uc 138
Heron Dale KT15: Add 78M 149
Herondale CR2: Sels 81Zb 178
Herondale Av. SW18 60Fb 111
Heron Dr. N4 33Sb 71
SL3: L'ly 49D 82
Heronfield EN6: Pot B 2Eb 17
TW20: Eng G 5N 125
Heron Flight Av. RM12: Horn 38Jd 76
HERONGATE 24Fe 59
Herongate N1 39Sb 71
(off Ridgewell Cl.)
Herongate Cl. EN1: Enf 12Vb 33
Herongate Rd. BR8: Hext 65Gd 140
E12 33Lc 73
Heron Hill DA17: Belv 50Bd 95
Heron Ho. DA14: Sidc 62Xc 139
E3 39Bc 72
(off Sycamore Av.)
E6 38Nc 74
NW8 2D 214
SW11 52Gb 111
(off Searles Cl.)
W13 42Ja 86
Heron Mead EN3: Enf L 10Cc 20
Heron M. IG1: Ilf 33Rc 74
Heron Pl. E16 46Lc 93
(off Bramwell Way)
SE16 46Ac 92
UB9: Hare 23J 43
W1 2J 221
Heron Quay E14 46Cc 92
Heron Rd. CR0: C'don 75Ub 157
SE24 56Sb 113
TW1: Twick 56Ja 108
Heronry, The KT12: Hers 79W 150
Herons, The E11 30Hc 53
RM12: Horn 32Md 77
Heronsbrook SL5: Asc 8C 124
Heronscourt GU18: Light 3A 166
Herons Cft. KT13: Weyb 79S 150
Heronsforde W13 44La 86
HERONSGATE 17E 24
Heronsgate HA8: Edg 22Qa 47
Heronsgate Rd. WD3: Chor 16D 24
Heron's Lea N6 30Hb 49
Heronslea WD25: Wat 8Y 13
Heronslea Dr. HA7: Stan 22Na 47
Heron's Pl. TW7: Isle 55Ka 108
Heron Sq. TW9: Rich 57Ma 109
Herons Ri. EN4: E Barn 14Gb 31
Herons Way AL1: St A 6E 6
(not continuous)
GU24: Brkwd 3B 186
Heronswood EN9: Walt A 6Gc 21
Heron Tower 2H 225
Heron Trad. Est. W3 43Ra 87
Heron Vw. TW8: Bford 52La 108
(off Commerce Rd.)
Heron Wlk. GU21: Wok 86E 168
HA6: Nwood 21U 44
Heron Way AL10: Hat 2C 8
RM14: Upm 32Ud 78
RM20: W Thur 50Xd 98
SM6: Wall 80Mb 156
TW14: Felt 56W 106
Heronway CM13: Hut 18De 41
IG8: Wfd G 21Lc 53
Herrick Ho. N16 35Tb 71
(off Howard Rd.)
SE5 52Tb 113
(off Elmington Est.)
Herrick Rd. N5 34Sb 71
Herrick St. SW1 6E 228 (49Mb 90)
Herries St. W10 40Ab 68
Herringham Rd. SE7 48Lc 93
Herrings La. GU20: W'sham 3A 146
KT16: Chert 72J 149
Herron Ct. BR2: Brom 70Hc 137
Hersant Cl. NW10 39Wa 68
Herschell M. SE5 55Sb 113
Herschell Rd. SE23 59Ac 114
Herschel Pk. Dr. SL1: Slou 7K 81
Herschel Sports 5H 81
Herschel St. SL1: Slou 7K 81
HERSHAM 78Z 151
Hersham By-Pass KT12: Hers 78X 151
Hersham Cl. SW15 59Wa 110
Hersham Gdns. KT12: Hers 77Y 151
Hersham Golf Course 76Aa 151
HERSHAM GREEN 78Z 151
Hersham Grn. Shop. Cen.
KT12: Hers 78Z 151
Hersham Pl. KT12: Hers 78Z 151
Hersham Rd. KT12: Hers, Walt T 74W 150
Hersham Trad. Est. KT12: Walt T 75Aa 151
Hershell Ct. SW14 56Ra 109
Hertford Av. SW14 57Ta 109
Hertford Cl. EN4: Cockf 13Fb 31
Hertford Ct. E6 41Pc 94
N13 20Qb 32
WD3: Crox G 14R 26
Hertford Ho. UB5: N'olt 42Ba 85
Hertford Lock Ho. E3 39Bc 72
(off Parnell Rd.)
Hertford M. EN6: Pot B 3Eb 17
Hertford Pl. W1 6C 216 (42Lb 90)
WD3: Map C 21H 43
Hertford Rd. EN3: Enf H, Pond E 13Yb 34
EN4: Cockf 13Eb 31
EN8: Walt C 13Yb 34
IG2: Ilf 30Uc 54
Hertford Rd. IG11: Bark 38Qc 74
N1 39Ub 71
(not continuous)
N2 27Gb 49
N9 19Xb 33
Hertford St. W1 7K 221 (46Kb 90)
Hertford Wlk. DA17: Belv 50Cd 96
Hertford Way CR4: Mitc 70Nb 134
Hertsbourne Country Club & Golf Course
19Ea 28
Herts Bus. Cen. AL2: Lon C 8H 7
Hertslet Rd. N7 34Pb 70
Hertsmere Ho. E14 45Cc 92
(off Hertsmere Rd.)
Hertsmere Ind. Pk. WD6: Bore 13Ta 29
Hertsmere Rd. E14 46Cc 92
Hertswood Cen. 11Sa 29
Hertswood Ct. EN5: Barn 14Ab 30
Herts Young Mariners Base 2Bc 20
Hervey Cl. N3 25Cb 49
Hervey Pk. Rd. E17 28Ac 52
Hervey Rd. SE3 53Kc 115
Hervey Way N3 25Cb 49
Hesa Rd. UB3: Hayes 44W 84
Hesewall Cl. SW4 54Lb 112
Hesiers Hill CR6: W'ham 89Gc 179
Hesiers Rd. CR6: W'ham 88Gc 179
Hesketh Av. DA2: Dart 60Rd 119
Hesketh Pl. W11 45Ab 88
Hesketh Rd. E7 34Jc 73
Heslop Rd. SW12 60Hb 111
Hesper M. SW5 49Db 89
Hesperus Cres. E14 49Dc 92
Hessel Rd. W13 47Ja 86
Hessel St. E1 44Xb 91
Hesselyn Dr. RM13: Rain 38Kd 77
Hessle Gro. KT17: Ewe 83Va 174
Hestercombe Av. SW6 54Ab 110
Hesterman Way CR0: Wadd 74Pb 156
Hester Rd. N18 22Wb 51
SW11 52Gb 111
Hester Ter. TW9: Rich 55Qa 109
Hestia Ho. SE1 2H 231
HESTON 52Ca 107
Heston Av. TW5: Hest 51Aa 107
Heston Cen., The TW5: Cran 50Y 85
Heston Community Sports Hall 52Ca 107
Heston Grange TW5: Hest 51Ba 107
Heston Grange La. TW5: Hest 51Ba 107
Heston Ho. SE8 53Cc 114
Heston Ind. Mall TW5: Hest 52Ba 107
Heston Phoenix Distribution Pk.
TW5: Hest 51Y 107
Heston Pool 51Ba 107
Heston Rd. RH1: Redh 10P 207
TW5: Hest 51Ca 107
HESTON SERVICE AREA 51Z 107
Heston St. SE14 53Cc 114
Heston Wlk. RH1: Redh 10P 207
Heswell Grn. WD19: Wat 20W 26
Hetherington Cl. SL2: Slou 1D 80
Hetherington Rd. SW4 56Nb 112
TW17: Shep 68S 128
Hetherington Way UB10: Ick 35N 63
Hethersett Cl. RH2: Reig 3L 207
Hethpool Ho. W2 6B 214
Hetley Gdns. SE19 66Vb 135
Hetley Rd. W12 46Xa 88
Heton Gdns. NW4 28Xa 48
Heusden Way SL9: Ger X 32B 62
Hevelius Cl. SE10 50Hc 93
Hever Av. TN15: W King 78Ud 164
Hever Cotts. DA12: Sole S 10G 144
Hever Ct. DA12: Grav'nd 5E 144
Hever Cft. SE9 63Qc 138
Hever Gdns. BR1: Brom 68Qc 138
Heverham Rd. SE18 49Uc 94
Hever Ho. SE15 51Zb 114
(off Lovelinch Cl.)
Hever Rd. TN15: W King 79Ud 164
Heversham Ho. SE15 51Yb 114
Heversham Rd. DA7: Bex 54Cd 118
Hever Wood Rd. TN15: W King 80Ud 164
Hevingham Dr. RM6: Chad H 29Yc 55
Hewens Rd. UB4: Hil 42S 84
UB10: Hil 42S 84
Hewer St. W10 43Za 88
Hewers Way KT20: Tad 92Xa 194
Hewett Cl. HA7: Stan 21Ka 46
Hewett Pl. BR8: Swan 70Fd 140
Hewett Rd. RM8: Dag 36Zc 75
Hewetts Quay IG11: Bark 39Rc 74
Hewett St. EC2 6J 219 (42Ub 91)
Hewins Cl. EN9: Walt A 4Gc 21
Hewish Rd. N18 21Ub 51
Hewison St. E3 40Bc 72
Hewitt Av. N22 26Rb 51
Hewitt Cl. CR0: C'don 76Cc 158
Hewitt Rd. N8 29Qb 50
Hewitts Rd. BR6: Well H 80Bd 161
HEWITTS RDBT. 81Bd 181
Hewlett Ho. SW8 52Kb 112
(off Havelock Ter.)
Hewlett Rd. E3 40Ac 72
Hew Watt Cl. RM16: Ors 3C 100
Hexagon, The N6 32Hb 69
Hexagon Bus. Cen. UB4: Yead 45Y 85
Hexagon Ho. RM1: Rom 29Hd 56
(off Mercury Gdns.)
Hexal Rd. SE6 62Gc 137
Hexham Gdns. TW7: Isle 52Ja 108
UB5: N'olt 36Ba 65
Hexham Rd. EN5: New Bar 14Db 31
SE27 61Sb 135
SM4: Mord 74Db 155
HEXTABLE 66Hd 140
Hextable Heritage Cen. & Gardens
66Gd 140
Hextalls La. CR3: Blet, Cat'm 100Ub 197
RH1: Blet 100Tb 197
Heybourne Rd. N17 24Xb 51
Heybridge NW1 37Kb 70
(off Lewis St.)
Heybridge Av. SW16 66Nb 134
Heybridge Dr. IG6: Ilf 26Tc 54
Heybridge Way E10 31Ac 72
Heydon Ho. SE14 53Yb 114
(off Kender St.)
Heyford Av. SW8 52Nb 112
SW20 69Bb 133
Heyford End AL2: Park 10A 6
Heyford Rd. CR4: Mitc 68Gb 133
WD7: R'lett 9Ha 14
Heyford Ter. SW8 52Nb 112
Heygate St. SE17 6D 230 (49Sb 91)
Heylyn Sq. E3 41Bc 92
Heymede KT22: Lea 95La 192
Heynes Rd. RM8: Dag 35Yc 75
Heysham Dr. WD19: Wat 22Y 45
Heysham La. NW3 34Db 69
Heysham Rd. N15 30Tb 51
Heythorpe Cl. GU21: Wok 9K 167
Heythorp St. SW18 60Bb 111
Heythrop Dr. UB10: Ick 35P 63
Heywood Av. NW9 25Ua 48
Heywood Ct. HA7: Stan 22La 46
Heywood Ho. SE14 51Zb 114
(off Myers La.)
Heyworth Rd. E5 35Xb 71
E15 36Hc 73
Hibbert Av. WD24: Wat 10Z 13
Hibbert Ho. E14 48Cc 92
(off Tiller Rd.)
Hibbert Lodge SL9: Chal P 26A 42
Hibbert Rd. E17 31Bc 72
HA3: W'stone 26Ha 46
Hibbert's All. SL4: Wind 3H 103
Hibbert St. SW11 55Fb 111
Hibberts Way SL9: Ger X 27A 42
Hibbs Cl. BR8: Swan 68Fd 140
Hibernia Ct. DA9: Ghithe 56Wd 120
Hibernia Dr. DA12: Grav'nd 2H 145
Hibernia Gdns. TW3: Houn 56Ca 107
Hibernia Point SE2 47Zc 95
(off Wolvercote Rd.)
Hibernia Rd. TW3: Houn 56Ca 107
Hibiscus Cl. HA8: Edg 21Sa 47
Hibiscus Ho. TW13: Felt 60W 106
Hibiscus Lodge E15 38Gc 73
(off Gleavon Rd.)
Hichisson Rd. SE15 57Yb 114
Hicken Rd. SW2 57Pb 112
Hickes Ho. NW6 38Fb 69
Hickey's Almshouses TW9: Rich 56Pa 109
Hickin Cl. SE7 49Mc 93
Hickin St. E14 48Ec 92
Hickleton NW1 1C 216
Hickling Ho. SE16 48Xb 91
(off Slippers Pl.)
Hickling Rd. IG1: Ilf 36Rc 74
Hickman Av. E4 23Ec 52
Hickman Cl. E16 43Mc 93
Hickman Rd. RM6: Chad H 31Yc 75
Hickmans Cl. RH9: G'stone 4A 210
Hickmore Wlk. SW4 55Mb 112
Hickory Cl. N9 17Wb 33
Hicks Av. UB6: G'frd 41Fa 86
Hicks Bolton Ho. NW6 40Bb 69
(off Denmark Ho.)
Hicks Cl. SW11 55Gb 111
Hicks Ct. RM10: Dag 34Dd 76
Hicks Gallery 64Cb 133
Hicks Ho. SE16 48Wb 91
(off Spa Rd.)
Hicks St. SE8 50Ac 92
Hidcote Cl. GU22: Wok 88D 168
Hidcote Gdns. SW20 69Xa 132
Hidden Cl. KT8: W Mole 70Ea 130
Hide E6 44Qc 94
Hideaway, The WD5: Ab L 3V 12
Hide Pl. SW1 6D 228 (49Mb 90)
Hider Ct. SE3 52Lc 115
Hide Rd. HA1: Harr 28Ea 46
Hides St. N7 37Pb 70
Hide Twr. SW1 6D 228
Higgins Ho. N1 39Ub 71
(off Colville Est.)
Higginson Ho. NW3 38Hb 69
(off Fellows Rd.)
Higgins Wlk. TW12: Hamp 65Aa 129
(off Abbott Cl.)
Higgs Ind. Est. SE24 55Rb 113
High Acres EN2: Enf 13Rb 33
WD5: Ab L 4T 12
HIGHAM HILL 26Ac 52
Higham Hill Rd. E17 25Ac 52
Higham M. UB5: N'olt 42Ba 85
Higham Path E17 27Ac 52
Higham Pl. E17 27Ac 52
Higham Rd. IG8: Wfd G 23Jc 53
N17 27Tb 51
Highams, The E17 25Ec 52
Highams Ct. E4 20Fc 35
Highams Hill CR6: W'ham 84Jc 179
Highams La. GU24: Chob 9E 146
Highams Lodge Bus. Cen. E17 27Zb 52
HIGHAMS PARK 23Fc 53
Highams Sta. Av. E4 23Cc 52
Higham St. E17 27Ac 52
High Ash Cl. SS17: Linf 6J 101
High Ashton KT2: King T 66Ra 131
Highbanks Cl. DA16: Well 52Xc 117
Highbanks Rd. HA5: Hat E 23Da 45
Highbank Way N8 30Qb 50
HIGH BARNET 12Za 30
High Barn Rd. KT24: Eff, Ran C 100Z 191
Highbarns HP3: Hem H 7A 4
Highbarrow Cl. CR8: Purl 82Pb 176
Highbarrow Rd. CR0: C'don 74Wb 157
HIGH BEECH 10Kc 21
High Beech CR2: S Croy 80Ub 157
N21 16Pb 32
High Beeches BR6: Chels 79Wc 161
DA14: Sidc 64Ad 139
KT13: Weyb 79U 150
SL9: Ger X 2P 61
SM7: Bans 86Ya 174
High Beeches Cl. CR8: Purl 82Mb 176
High Beech Golf Course 9Kc 21
High Beech Rd. IG10: Lough 14Nc 36
High Birch Ct. EN4: E Barn 14Gb 31
(off Park Rd.)
High Bri. SE10 50Fc 93
Highbridge Cl. WD7: R'lett 5Ja 14
Highbridge Ct. SE14 52Yb 114
(off Farrow La.)
Highbridge Ind. Est. UB8: Uxb 38L 63
Highbridge Retail Pk. EN9: Walt A 6Dc 20
Highbridge Rd. IG11: Bark 39Rc 74
Highbridge St. EN9: Walt A 5Dc 20
(not continuous)
High Bri. Wharf SE10 50Fc 93
(off High Bri.)
Highbrook Rd. SE3 55Mc 115
High Broom Cres. BR4: W W'ck 73Dc 158
HIGHBURY 35Rb 71
Highbury Av. CR7: Thor H 68Qb 134
Highbury Cl. BR4: W W'ck 75Dc 158
KT3: N Mald 70Sa 131
HIGHBURY CORNER 37Rb 71
Highbury Cres. N5 36Rb 71
Highbury Dr. KT22: Lea 93Ja 192

Highbury Est. N5 . . . 36Sb 71
Highbury Gdns. IG3: Ilf . . . 33Uc 74
Highbury Grange N5 . . . 35Sb 71
Highbury Gro. N5 . . . 36Rb 71
Highbury Gro. Ct. N5 . . . 37Sb 71
Highbury Hill N5 . . . 34Qb 70
Highbury Mans. *N1* . . . *38Rb 71*
(off Upper St.)
Highbury New Pk. N5 . . . 36Sb 71
Highbury Pk. N5 . . . 34Rb 71
Highbury Pk. M. N5 . . . 35Sb 71
Highbury Pl. N5 . . . 37Rb 71
Highbury Pool . . . 37Rb 71
Highbury Quad. N5 . . . 34Sb 71
Highbury Rd. SW19 . . . 64Ab 132
Highbury Sq. N14 . . . 18Lb 32
Highbury Sta. Rd. N1 . . . 37Qb 70
Highbury Ter. N5 . . . 36Rb 71
Highbury Ter. M. N5 . . . 36Rb 71
High Canons WD6: Bore . . . 9Sa 15
High Cedar Dr. SW20 . . . 66Ya 132
Highclere SL5: S'hill . . . 1B 146
Highclere Cl. CR8: Kenley . . . 87Sb 177
Highclere Ct. *AL1: St A* . . . *1C 6*
(off Avenue Rd.)
GU21: Knap . . . 9G 166
Highclere Dr. HP3: Hem H . . . 6A 4
Highclere Gdns. GU21: Knap . . . 9G 166
Highclere Rd. GU21: Knap . . . 9G 166
KT3: N Mald . . . 69Ta 131
Highclere St. SE26 . . . 63Ac 136
Highcliffe *W13* . . . *43Ka 86*
(off Clivedon Ct.)
Highcliffe Dr. SW15 . . . 58Va 110
Highcliffe Gdns. IG4: Ilf . . . 29Nc 54
High Cl. WD3: Rick . . . 15L 25
Highcombe SE7 . . . 51Kc 115
Highcombe Cl. SE9 . . . 60Mc 115
High Coombe Pl. KT2: King T . . . 65Ta 131
Highcotts La. GU4: W Cla . . . 98H 189
Highcroft NW9 . . . 29Ua 48
Highcroft Av. HA0: Wemb . . . 38Qa 67
High Cft. Cotts. BR8: Swan . . . 70Jd 140
Highcroft Ct. KT23: Bookh . . . 95Ca 191
Highcroft Est. N19 . . . 31Nb 70
Highcroft Gdns. NW11 . . . 30Bb 49
Highcroft Rd. HP3: Hem H . . . 6J 3
N19 . . . 31Nb 70
Highcroft Trailer Gdns. HP3: Bov . . . 8D 2
HIGH CROSS . . . 9Fa 14
High Cross WD25: A'ham . . . 9Fa 14
High Cross Centre, The N15 . . . 28Wb 51
High Cross Rd. N17 . . . 27Wb 51
TN15: Ivy H . . . 98Xd 204
Highcross Rd. DA13: Sflt . . . 64Zd 143
Highcross Way SW15 . . . 60Wa 110
Highdaun Dr. SW16 . . . 70Pb 134
High Dells AL10: Hat . . . 1B 8
Highdene *GU22: Wok* . . . *90B 168*
(off Constitution Hill)
Highdown KT4: Wor Pk . . . 75Ua 154
Highdown Cl. SM7: Bans . . . 88Bb 175
Highdown La. SM2: Sutt . . . 83Db 175
Highdown Rd. SW15 . . . 58Xa 110
High Dr. CR3: Wold . . . 94Bc 198
KT3: N Mald . . . 67Sa 131
KT22: Oxs . . . 86Fa 172
High Elms IG7: Chig . . . 21Uc 54
IG8: Wfd G . . . 22Jc 53
RM14: Upm . . . 32Ud 78
High Elms Cl. HA6: Nwood . . . 23S 44
High Elms Country Pk.
(Local Nature Reserve) . . . 80Tc 160
High Elms Golf Course . . . 80Sc 160
High Elms La. WD25: Wat . . . 3X 13
High Elms Rd. BR6: Downe . . . 83Qc 180
HIGHER DENHAM . . . 31E 62
Higher Dr. CR8: Purl . . . 85Qb 176
KT24: E Hor . . . 99U 190
SM7: Bans . . . 84Za 174
Higher Grn. KT17: Eps . . . 85Wa 174
HIGHFIELD . . . 1N 3
Highfield HP8: Chal G . . . 18A 24
SM7: Bans . . . 89Gb 175
WD4: K Lan . . . 10N 3
WD19: Wat . . . 20Ba 27
WD23: B Hea . . . 19Ga 28
WD25: Wat . . . 6V 12
Highfield Av. BR6: Chels . . . 78Vc 161
DA8: Erith . . . 51Dd 118
HA5: Pinn . . . 29Ba 45
HA9: Wemb . . . 34Pa 67
NW9 . . . 29Sa 47
NW11 . . . 31Za 68
UB6: G'frd . . . 36Ga 66
Highfield Cl. HA6: Nwood . . . 25U 44
KT6: Surb . . . 74La 152
KT14: W Byf . . . 85J 169
KT22: Oxs . . . 83Fa 172
N22 . . . 25Qb 50
NW9 . . . 29Sa 47
RM5: Col R . . . 23Ed 56
SE13 . . . 58Fc 115
TW20: Eng G . . . 5N 125
Highfield Cotts. DA2: Wilm . . . 65Kd 141
Highfield Ct. N14 . . . 16Lb 32
NW11 . . . 30Ab 48
SL2: Farn R . . . 9F 60
SL9: Chal P . . . 22B 42
TW20: Eng G . . . *5P 125*
(off Highfield Rd.)
Highfield Cres. HA6: Nwood . . . 25U 44
RM12: Horn . . . 33Pd 77
Highfield Dr. BR2: Brom . . . 70Gc 137
BR4: W W'ck . . . 75Dc 158
CR3: Cat'm . . . 94Wb 197
KT19: Ewe . . . 79Va 154
UB10: Ick . . . 35N 63
Highfield Gdns. NW11 . . . 30Ab 48
RM16: Grays . . . 47Fe 99
Highfield Grn. CM16: Epp . . . 3Uc 22
Highfield Hall AL4: St A . . . 6J 7
Highfield Hill SE19 . . . 66Tb 135
Highfield La. AL4: St A . . . 4G 6
HP2: Hem H . . . 1P 3
Highfield Link RM5: Col R . . . 23Ed 56
Highfield Mnr. AL4: St A . . . 6J 7
Highfield M. *NW6* . . . *38Db 69*
(off Compayne Gdns.)
Highfield Pk. Cen. . . . 3G 6
Highfield Pk. Dr. AL4: St A . . . 5F 6
Highfield Pl. CM16: Epp . . . 3Uc 22
Highfield Rd. BR1: Brom . . . 70Pc 138
BR7: Chst . . . 69Vc 139
CR3: Cat'm . . . 94Wb 197
CR8: Purl . . . 82Pb 176
Highfield Rd. DA1: Dart . . . 59Md 119
DA6: Bex . . . 57Bd 117
HA6: Nwood . . . 25U 44
IG8: Wfd G . . . 24Nc 54
KT5: Surb . . . 73Sa 153
KT12: Walt T . . . 74W 150
KT14: W Byf . . . 85J 169
KT16: Chert . . . 74J 149
N21 . . . 19Rb 33
NW11 . . . 30Ab 48
RM5: Col R . . . 24Ed 56
RM12: Horn . . . 33Pd 77
SL4: Wind . . . 5D 102
SM1: Sutt . . . 78Gb 155
TN15: Kems'g . . . 88Nd 183
TN16: Big H . . . 89Lc 179
TW7: Isle . . . 53Ha 108
TW13: Felt . . . 61W 128
TW16: Sun . . . 71V 150
TW20: Eng G . . . 5N 125
W3 . . . 43Ra 87
WD23: Bush . . . 15Aa 27
Highfield Rd. Nth. DA1: Dart . . . 58Md 119
Highfield Rd. Sth. DA1: Dart . . . 59Md 119
High Flds. SL5: S'dale . . . 1D 146
Highfields KT21: Asht . . . 91Ma 193
KT22: Fet . . . 96Fa 192
KT24: E Hor . . . 100V 190
SM1: Sutt . . . 75Cb 155
WD7: R'lett . . . 7Ha 14
Highfields Gro. N6 . . . 32Hb 69
Highfield Towers RM5: Col R . . . 22Fd 56
Highfield Way EN6: Pot B . . . 4Db 17
RM12: Horn . . . 33Pd 77
WD3: Rick . . . 16J 25
High Firs BR8: Swan . . . 70Gd 140
WD7: R'lett . . . 7Ja 14
High Foleys KT10: Clay . . . 80Ka 152
High Gables BR2: Brom . . . 68Gc 137
IG10: Lough . . . 15Mc 35
High Gdns. GU22: Wok . . . 1M 187
High Garth KT10: Esh . . . 79Ea 152
HIGHGATE . . . 30Jb 50
Highgate Av. N6 . . . 31Kb 70
Highgate Cemetery N6 . . . 32Jb 70
Highgate Cl. N6 . . . 31Jb 70
Highgate Edge N2 . . . 29Gb 49
Highgate Golf Course . . . 30Gb 49
Highgate Hgts. N6 . . . 30Lb 50
Highgate High St. N6 . . . 32Kb 70
Highgate Hill N6 . . . 32Kb 70
N19 . . . 32Kb 70
Highgate Ho. SE26 . . . 62Wb 135
Highgate Rd. NW5 . . . 34Jb 70
Highgate Spinney N8 . . . 30Mb 50
Highgate Wlk. SE23 . . . 61Yb 136
Highgate W. Hill N6 . . . 32Jb 70
Highgate Wood School Sports Cen.
. . . 29Lb 50
High Gro. BR1: Brom . . . 67Mc 137
SE18 . . . 52Tc 116
Highgrove CM15: Pil H . . . 16Xd 40
Highgrove Cl. BR7: Chst . . . 67Nc 138
N11 . . . 22Jb 50
Highgrove Ct. BR3: Beck . . . 66Cc 136
EN8: Walt C . . . 6Yb 20
SM1: Sutt . . . 79Cb 155
Highgrove Ho.
CM14: B'wood . . . *19Yd 40*
(off Regency Ct.)
Highgrove M. RM17: Grays . . . 50Ee 99
SM5: Cars . . . 76Hb 155
Highgrove Rd. RM8: Dag . . . 36Yc 75
Highgrove Swimming Pool . . . 30W 44
Highgrove Ter. E4 . . . 19Fc 35
Highgrove Way HA4: Ruis . . . 30W 44
High Hill Est. E5 . . . 32Xb 71
High Hill Ferry E5 . . . 32Xb 71
High Hill Rd. CR6: W'ham . . . 87Ec 178
High Holborn WC1 . . . 2F 223 (44Nb 90)
High Ho. La. RM18: W Til . . . 8F 100
Highland Av. CM15: B'wood . . . 18Yd 40
IG10: Lough . . . 16Nc 36
RM10: Dag . . . 34Ed 76
(not continuous)
W7 . . . 44Ga 86
Highland Cotts. SM6: Wall . . . 77Lb 156
Highland Ct. BR1: Brom . . . 67Hc 137
E18 . . . 25Kc 53
Highland Cft. BR3: Beck . . . 64Dc 136
Highland Dr. HP3: Hem H . . . 2B 4
WD23: Bush . . . 17Da 27
Highland Pk. TW13: Felt . . . 63V 128
Highland Rd. BR1: Brom . . . 67Hc 137
BR2: Brom . . . 67Hc 137
CR8: Purl . . . 86Qb 176
DA6: Bex . . . 57Cd 118
HA6: Nwood . . . 26V 44
SE19 . . . 65Ub 135
TN14: Bad M . . . 82Dd 182
Highlands KT21: Asht . . . 91La 192
N20 . . . 19Fb 31
SL2: Farn C . . . 6G 60
WD19: Wat . . . 18Y 27
Highlands, The EN5: New Bar . . . 14Cb 31
EN6: Pot B . . . 2Eb 17
HA8: Edg . . . 26Ra 47
KT24: E Hor . . . 97U 190
WD3: Rick . . . 17K 25
Highlands Av. KT22: Lea . . . 94La 192
N21 . . . 15Pb 32
W3 . . . 45Sa 87
Highlands Cl. KT22: Lea . . . 94Ka 192
N4 . . . 31Nb 70
SL9: Chal P . . . 24B 42
TW3: Houn . . . 53Da 107
Highlands Ct. SE19 . . . 65Ub 135
Highlands End SL9: Chal P . . . 24B 42
Highlands Farm Bus. Pk.
BR8: Swan . . . 67Jd 140
Highlands Gdns. IG1: Ilf . . . 32Pc 74
Highlands Heath SW15 . . . 59Ya 110
Highlands Hill BR8: Swan . . . 67Jd 140
Highlands La. GU22: Wok . . . 93A 188
SL9: Chal P . . . 24B 42
Highlands Pk. KT22: Lea . . . 95Ma 193
TN15: Seal . . . 93Nd 203
Highlands Rd. BR5: Orp . . . 73Xc 161
EN5: New Bar . . . 15Cb 31
KT22: Lea . . . 94Ka 192
RH2: Reig . . . 5M 207
HIGHLANDS VILLAGE . . . 15Pb 32
Highland Ter. *SE13* . . . *55Dc 114*
(off Algernon Rd.)
Highland Vw. Pk. Homes
UB7: W Dray . . . 49L 83
High La. CR3: Wold . . . 91Bc 198
CR6: W'ham, Wold . . . 90Bc 178
W7 . . . 43Fa 86
Highlawn Hall HA1: Harr . . . 34Ga 66
Highlea Cl. NW9 . . . 24Ua 48
High Level Dr. SE26 . . . 63Wb 135
Highlever Rd. W10 . . . 43Ya 88
High Mead BR4: W W'ck . . . 75Fc 159
HA1: Harr . . . 29Ga 46
IG7: Chig . . . 19Sc 36
Highmead *N18* . . . *22Wb 51*
(off Fore St.)
SE18 . . . 52Vc 117
Highmead Ct. CM15: B'wood . . . 18Zd 41
Highmead Cres. HA0: Wemb . . . 38Pa 67
High Mdw. Cl. HA5: Eastc . . . 28Y 45
Highmeadow Cres.
NW9 . . . 29Ta 47
High Mdw. Pl. KT16: Chert . . . 72H 149
High Mdws. IG7: Chig . . . 22Tc 54
High Meads Rd. E16 . . . 44Mc 93
Highmore Rd. SE3 . . . 52Gc 115
High Mt. NW4 . . . 30Wa 48
High Oaks EN2: Enf . . . 10Pb 18
HA6: Nwood . . . 22V 44
High Oaks Cl. CR5: Coul . . . 91Kb 196
High Parade, The SW16 . . . 62Nb 134
High Pk. Av. KT24: E Hor . . . 98V 190
TW9: Kew . . . 53Qa 109
High Pk. Rd. TW9: Kew . . . 53Qa 109
High Path SW19 . . . 67Db 133
High Pine Cl.
KT13: Weyb . . . 78S 150
High Pines CR6: W'ham . . . 91Yb 198
High Point N6 . . . 31Jb 70
SE9 . . . 62Rc 138
Highpoint KT13: Weyb . . . 78Q 150
High Ridge N10 . . . 25Kb 50
High Ridge Cl.
HP3: Hem H . . . 7M 3
Highridge Cl. KT18: Eps . . . 86Ua 174
Highridge Pl. *EN2: Enf* . . . *10Pb 18*
(off Oak Av.)
High Ridge Rd. HP3: Hem H . . . 7M 3
High Rd. AL9: Ess . . . 3N 9
CM16: Epp . . . 5Rc 22
CR5: Chip, Coul . . . 97Gb 195
DA2: Wilm . . . 62Ld 141
E18 . . . 25Jc 53
HA0: Wemb . . . 36Ma 67
HA3: Hrw W . . . 24Ga 46
HA5: Eastc . . . 30W 44
HA9: Wemb . . . 36Ma 67
IG1: Ilf . . . 34Rc 74
(not continuous)
IG3: Chad H, Ilf . . . 32Vc 75
IG7: Chig . . . 22Qc 54
IG8: Wfd G . . . 24Hc 53
IG9: Buck H . . . 19Kc 35
IG10: Lough . . . 16Lc 35
KT14: Byfl . . . 84M 169
N11 . . . 22Kb 50
N15 . . . 28Vb 51
N17 . . . 26Vb 51
N22 . . . 25Pb 50
NW10 . . . 37Ua 68
RH2: Reig . . . 99Eb 195
RM6: Chad H . . . 31Zc 75
RM16: N Stif . . . 46Zd 99
RM16: Ors . . . 4A 100
SS17: Corr, Stan H . . . 2P 101
UB4: Hayes . . . 43U 84
UB8: Cowl . . . 43L 83
UB10: Ick . . . 34R 64
WD23: B Hea . . . 18Fa 28
WD25: Wat . . . 7V 12
High Rd. E. Finchley N2 . . . 25Fb 49
High Rd. Leyton E10 . . . 30Dc 52
E15 . . . 33Dc 72
High Rd. Leytonstone E11 . . . 35Gc 73
E15 . . . 35Gc 73
High Rd. Nth. Finchley N12 . . . 20Eb 31
High Rd. Whetstone N20 . . . 17Eb 31
High Rd. Woodford Grn.
IG8: Wfd G . . . 23Hc 53
High Sheldon N6 . . . 30Hb 49
Highshore Rd. SE15 . . . 54Vb 113
(not continuous)
High Silver IG10: Lough . . . 14Mc 35
High Standing CR3: Cat'm . . . 97Sb 197
Highstead Cres. DA8: Erith . . . 53Gd 118
Highstone Av. E11 . . . 30Jc 53
Highstone Ct. *E11* . . . *30Hc 53*
(off New Wanstead)
Highstone Mans. *NW1* . . . *38Lb 70*
(off Camden Rd.)
High St. AL2: Lon C . . . 7G 6
AL3: St A . . . 2B 6
AL4: Col H . . . 4M 7
BR1: Brom . . . 68Jc 137
(not continuous)
BR3: Beck . . . 68Cc 136
BR4: W W'ck . . . 74Dc 158
BR5: St M Cry . . . 72Yc 161
(not continuous)
BR6: Chels . . . 80Vc 161
BR6: Downe . . . 83Qc 180
BR6: Farnb . . . 78Rc 160
BR6: Orp . . . 75Wc 161
BR7: Chst . . . 65Rc 138
BR8: Swan . . . 69Hd 140
CM14: B'wood . . . 19Yd 40
CM16: Epp . . . 3Vc 23
CR0: C'don . . . 76Sb 157
CR3: Cat'm . . . 95Ub 197
CR7: Thor H . . . 70Sb 135
CR8: Purl . . . 83Qb 176
DA1: Dart . . . 58Nd 119
DA2: Bean . . . 62Xd 142
DA4: Eyns . . . 75Nd 163
DA4: Farni . . . 72Pd 163
DA9: Ghithe . . . 56Xd 120
DA10: Swans . . . 57Be 121
DA11: Grav'nd . . . 8D 122
DA11: Nflt . . . 58De 121
E11 . . . 29Jc 53
E13 . . . 40Jc 73
E15 . . . 40Ec 72
E17 . . . 29Ac 52
EN3: Pond E . . . 16Yb 34
EN5: Barn . . . 13Ab 30
EN6: Pot B . . . 5Db 17
EN8: Chesh . . . 1Zb 20
EN8: Walt C . . . 5Ac 20
(not continuous)
GU21: Knap . . . 9G 166
High St. GU21: Wok . . . 89B 168
(Commercial Way)
GU21: Wok . . . 7M 167
(Horsell Birch)
GU22: Wok . . . 93C 188
GU23: Rip . . . 93L 189
GU24: Chob . . . 3J 167
GU24: W End . . . 4D 166
HA1: Harr . . . 32Ga 66
HA3: Hrw W, W'stone . . . 26Ga 46
(not continuous)
HA4: Ruis . . . 31U 64
HA5: Pinn . . . 27Aa 45
HA6: Nwood . . . 25V 44
HA8: Edg . . . 23Qa 47
HA9: Wemb . . . 35Pa 67
HP1: Hem H . . . 1L 3
HP3: Bov . . . 9C 2
HP4: Berk . . . 1A 2
IG6: Ilf . . . 27Sc 54
KT1: Hamp W . . . 67La 130
KT1: King T . . . 69Ma 131
KT3: N Mald . . . 70Ua 132
KT7: T Ditt . . . 72Ja 152
KT8: W Mole . . . 70Ca 129
KT10: Clay . . . 79Ha 152
KT10: Esh . . . 77Da 151
KT11: Cobh . . . 86X 171
KT12: Walt T . . . 74W 150
KT13: Weyb . . . 77Q 150
KT15: Add . . . 77K 149
KT17: Eps . . . 85Ta 173
KT17: Ewe . . . 81Va 174
KT19: Eps . . . 85Ta 173
KT20: Tad . . . 95Ya 194
KT22: Lea . . . 94Ka 192
KT22: Oxs . . . 85Fa 172
KT23: Bookh . . . 97Da 191
N8 . . . 28Nb 50
N14 . . . 18Mb 32
NW7 . . . 22Xa 48
RH1: Blet . . . 5J 209
RH1: Mers . . . 100Kb 196
RH1: Nutf . . . 6M 209
RH1: Redh . . . 6P 207
RH2: Reig . . . 6J 207
RH8: Limp . . . 100Jc 199
RH8: Oxt . . . 2H 211
RH9: G'stone . . . 2A 210
RM1: Rom . . . 29Gd 56
RM11: Horn . . . 32Md 77
RM12: Horn . . . 32Md 77
RM15: Avel . . . 46Sd 98
RM17: Grays . . . 51Ce 121
(not continuous)
RM19: Purf . . . 50Qd 97
SE20 . . . 65Yb 136
SE25 . . . 70Vb 135
SL0: Iver . . . 44G 82
SL1: Burn . . . 1A 80
SL1: Slou . . . 8G 80
(Brammas Cl.)
SL1: Slou . . . 6J 81
(Wellington St.)
SL1: Slou . . . 7K 81
(William St., not continuous)
SL3: Coln . . . 52E 104
SL3: Dat . . . 3M 103
SL3: L'ly . . . 50B 82
SL4: Eton . . . 1H 103
SL4: Wind . . . 3H 103
SL5: S'dale . . . 1E 146
SL5: S'hill . . . 1B 146
SL9: Chal P . . . 25A 42
SM1: Sutt . . . 77Db 155
SM3: Cheam . . . 79Ab 154
SM5: Cars . . . 78Jb 156
SM7: Bans . . . 87Cb 175
SS17: Stan H . . . 2L 101
SW19 . . . 64Za 132
TN13: Chip . . . 94Ed 202
TN13: S'oaks . . . 97Ld 203
TN14: Otf . . . 88Jd 182
TN14: S'ham . . . 82Hd 182
TN15: Bor G . . . 92Be 205
TN15: Kems'g . . . 89Rd 183
TN15: Seal . . . 93Pd 203
TN15: Wro . . . 88Ce 185
TN16: Bras . . . 96Xc 201
TN16: Westrm . . . 99Sc 200
TW2: Whitt . . . 59Ea 108
TW3: Houn . . . 55Da 107
TW5: Cran . . . 53W 106
TW8: Bford . . . 52La 108
TW11: Tedd . . . 64Ha 130
TW12: Hamp, Hamp H . . . 67Ea 130
TW13: Felt . . . 62V 128
TW17: Shep . . . 72R 150
TW18: Staines . . . 63G 126
(not continuous)
TW19: Stanw . . . 58M 105
TW19: Wray . . . 58A 104
TW20: Egh . . . 64B 126
UB1: S'hall . . . 46Ba 85
UB3: Harl . . . 51T 106
UB7: Harm . . . 51M 105
UB7: Yiew . . . 45M 83
UB8: Cowl . . . 42L 83
UB8: Uxb . . . 38L 63
UB9: Hare . . . 26L 43
W3 . . . 46Ra 87
W5 . . . 46Ma 87
WD3: Rick . . . 18M 25
WD4: K Lan . . . 1Q 12
WD5: Ab L . . . 3U 12
WD5: Bedm . . . 9F 4
WD6: E'tree . . . 16Ma 29
WD17: Wat . . . 13X 27
WD23: Bush . . . 16Ca 27
High St. Colliers Wood SW19 . . . 66Fb 133
High St. Grn. HP2: Hem H . . . 1A 4
High St. Harlesden NW10 . . . 40Va 68
High St. Mews SW19 . . . 64Ab 132
High St. Nth. E6 . . . 36Nc 74
E12 . . . 36Nc 74
High St. Sth. E6 . . . 40Pc 74
High St. West SL1: Slou . . . 7J 81
High Timber St.
EC4 . . . 4D 224 (45Sb 91)
High Tor Cl. BR1: Brom . . . 66Kc 137
High Tor Vw. SE28 . . . 46Uc 94
High Tree Cl. KT15: Add . . . 78J 149
High Trees CR0: C'don . . . 74Ac 158
DA2: Dart . . . 58Rd 119
EN4: E Barn . . . 15Gb 31
HP2: Hem H . . . 2M 3
High Trees N20 . . . 20Eb 31
SW2 . . . 60Qb 112
High Trees Cl. CR3: Cat'm . . . 94Vb 197
High Trees Ct. CR3: Cat'm . . . 95Vb 197
Hightrees Ct. CM14: W'ley . . . 21Yd 58
W7 . . . 45Ga 86
Hightrees Ho. SW12 . . . 58Jb 112
High Trees Rd. RH2: Reig . . . 7L 207
High Vw. AL10: Hat . . . 2B 8
HA5: Pinn . . . 28Y 45
HP8: Chal G . . . 19A 24
WD3: Chor . . . 14J 25
WD18: Wat . . . 16V 26
Highview CR3: Cat'm . . . 96Ub 197
GU21: Knap . . . 9J 167
N6 . . . 30Lb 50
NW7 . . . 20Ta 29
SM2: Cheam . . . 83Bb 175
UB5: N'olt . . . 41Aa 85
High Vw. Av. RM17: Grays . . . 50Ee 99
Highview Av. HA8: Edg . . . 21Sa 47
SM6: Wall . . . 78Pb 156
High Vw. Cl. IG10: Lough . . . 15Lc 35
SE19 . . . 68Vb 135
Highview Cl. EN6: Pot B . . . 5Eb 17
KT20: Tad . . . 93Wa 194
High Vw. Ct. HA3: Hrw W . . . 24Ga 46
Highview Ct. *IG10: Lough* . . . *15Mc 35*
(off High Rd.)
RH2: Reig . . . *6M 207*
(off Wray Comn. Rd.)
Highview Cres. CM13: Hut . . . 16Ee 41
High Vw. Gdns. RM17: Grays . . . 50Ee 99
Highview Gdns. EN6: Pot B . . . 5Eb 17
HA8: Edg . . . 21Sa 47
N3 . . . 27Ab 48
N11 . . . 22Lb 50
RM14: Upm . . . 33Rd 77
Highview Ho. RM6: Chad H . . . 28Ad 55
Highview Lodge *EN2: Enf* . . . *13Rb 33*
(off The Ridgeway)
High Vw. Pde. IG4: Ilf . . . 29Pc 54
High Vw. Pk. WD4: K Lan . . . 10D 4
Highview Path SM7: Bans . . . 87Cb 175
High Vw. Rd. BR6: Downe . . . 82Qc 180
E18 . . . 26Hc 53
SE19 . . . 65Tb 135
Highview Rd. DA14: Sidc . . . 63Xc 139
W13 . . . 43Ja 86
Highway, The BR6: Chels . . . 78Xc 161
E1 . . . 45Wb 91
HA7: Stan . . . 25Ha 46
SM2: Sutt . . . 81Eb 175
Highway Bus. Park, The *E1* . . . *45Zb 92*
(off Heckford St.)
Highwayman's Ridge
GU20: W'sham . . . 7A 146
Highway Trad. Centre, The *E1* . . . *45Zb 92*
(off Heckford St.)
Highwold CR5: Chip . . . 90Jb 176
Highwood BR2: Brom . . . 69Fc 137
Highwood Av. N12 . . . 21Eb 49
WD23: Bush . . . 11Ba 27
Highwood Cl. BR6: Farnb . . . 75Sc 160
CM14: B'wood . . . 17Xd 40
CR8: Kenley . . . 89Sb 177
SE22 . . . 60Wb 113
Highwood Ct. EN5: New Bar . . . 15Cb 31
N12 . . . 20Eb 31
Highwood Dr. BR6: Farnb . . . 75Sc 160
Highwood Gdns. IG5: Ilf . . . 29Pc 54
Highwood Gro. NW7 . . . 22Ta 47
Highwoodhall La. HP3: Hem H . . . 7A 4
HIGHWOOD HILL . . . 20Va 30
Highwood Hill NW7 . . . 19Va 30
Highwood La. IG10: Lough . . . 15Qc 36
Highwood Rd. N19 . . . 34Nb 70
Highwoods CR3: Cat'm . . . 97Ub 197
KT22: Lea . . . 93La 192
High Worple HA2: Harr . . . 31Ba 65
Highworth Rd. N11 . . . 23Mb 50
Highworth St. NW1 . . . 7E 214
Hi-Gloss Cen. SE8 . . . 50Ac 92
Hilary Av. CR4: Mitc . . . 69Jb 134
Hilary Cl. DA8: Erith . . . 53Dd 118
RM12: Horn . . . 36Md 77
SW6 . . . 52Db 111
Hilary Dennis Ct. E11 . . . 28Jc 53
Hilary Rd. W12 . . . 44Va 88
(not continuous)
Hilberry Ct. WD23: Bush . . . 17Da 27
Hilbert Rd. SM3: Cheam . . . 76Za 154
Hilborough Ct. E8 . . . 38Vb 71
Hilborough Way BR6: Farnb . . . 78Tc 160
Hilbury AL10: Hat . . . 1B 8
Hilda Ct. KT6: Surb . . . 73Ma 153
Hilda Lockert Wlk. *SW9* . . . *54Rb 113*
(off Loughborough Rd.)
Hilda May Av. BR8: Swan . . . 68Gd 140
Hilda Rd. E6 . . . 38Mc 73
E16 . . . 42Gc 93
Hilda Ter. SW9 . . . 54Qb 112
Hilda Va. Cl. BR6: Farnb . . . 77Rc 160
Hilda Va. Rd. BR6: Farnb . . . 77Qc 160
Hildenborough Gdns. BR1: Brom . . . 65Gc 137
Hildenborough Ho. *BR3: Beck* . . . *66Bc 136*
(off Bethersden Cl.)
Hilden Dr. DA8: Erith . . . 52Kd 119
Hildenlea Pl. BR2: Brom . . . 68Fc 137
Hildenley Cl. RH1: Mers . . . 100Mb 196
Hilderley Ho. *KT1: King T* . . . *69Pa 131*
(off Winery La.)
Hilders, The KT21: Asht . . . 89Ra 173
Hildreth St. SW12 . . . 60Kb 112
Hildreth St. M. SW12 . . . 60Kb 112
Hildyard Rd. SW6 . . . 51Cb 111
Hiley Rd. NW10 . . . 41Ya 88
Hilfield La. WD25: A'ham . . . 11Da 27
Hilfield La. Sth.
WD23: Bush . . . 16Ha 28
Hilgrove Rd. NW6 . . . 38Eb 69
Hiliary Gdns. HA7: Stan . . . 26La 46
Hiljon Cres. SL9: Chal P . . . 25A 42
Hill, The CR3: Cat'm . . . 96Vb 197
DA11: Nflt . . . 58Ee 121
Hillacre CR3: Cat'm . . . 97Ub 197
Hillars Heath Rd. CR5: Coul . . . 87Nb 176
Hillary *N8* . . . *27Nb 50*
(off Boyton Cl.)
Hillary Av. DA11: Nflt . . . 2A 144
Hillary Ct. *TW19: Stanw* . . . *60N 105*
(off Explorer Av.)
W12 . . . *47Ya 88*
(off Titmuss St.)
Hillary Cres. KT12: Walt T . . . 74Y 151
Hillary Dr. TW7: Isle . . . 57Ha 108

Hillary Ho. *WD6: Bore* *13Ra 29*
(off Eldon Av.)
Hillary Ri. EN5: New Bar 14Cb 31
Hillary Rd. HP2: Hem H 1A 4
SL3: L'ly 47A 82
UB2: S'hall 48Ca 85
Hill Barn CR2: Sande 83Ub 177
Hillbeck Cl. SE15 .... 52Yb 114
(not continuous)
Hillbeck Way UB6: G'frd 39Fa 66
Hillborne Cl. UB3: Harl 50W 84
Hillboro Ct. E11 .... 31Fc 73
Hillborough Av. TN13: S'oaks 94Md 203
Hillborough Cl. SW19 .... 66Eb 133
Hillbrook Gdns. KT13: Weyb 80Q 150
Hillbrook Rd. SW17 .... 62Hb 133
Hill Brow BR1: Brom 67Mc 137
DA1: Cray 58Hd 118
Hillbrow KT3: N Mald 69Va 132
RH2: Reig 6L 207
Hillbrow Cl. DA5: Bexl 63Fd 140
Hillbrow Cotts. RH9: G'stone 4A 210
Hillbrow Ct. RH9: G'stone 4A 210
Hillbrow Rd. BR1: Brom 66Gc 137
KT10: Esh 77Ea 152
Hillbury Av. HA3: Kenton 29Ka 46
Hillbury Cl. CR6: W'ham 90Yb 178
Hillbury Cres. CR6: W'ham 90Yb 178
Hillbury Gdns. CR6: W'ham 90Yb 178
Hillbury Rd. CR3: Whyt 89Wb 177
CR6: W'ham 89Wb 177
SW17 .... 62Kb 134
Hill Cl. BR7: Chst 64Rc 138
CR8: Purl 85Sb 177
DA13: Ist R 6A 144
EN5: Barn 15Ya 30
GU21: Wok 8P 167
HA1: Harr 34Ga 66
HA7: Stan 21Ka 46
KT11: Cobh 84Ca 171
NW2 .... 34Xa 68
NW11 .... 30Cb 49
Hill Comn. HP3: Hem H 6A 4
Hillcote Av. SW16 .... 66Qb 134
Hill Ct. EN4: E Barn 14Gb 31
EN6: Pot B 6Eb 17
RM1: Rom 28Hd 56
UB5: N'olt 36Ca 65
W5 .... 42Pa 87
Hillcourt Av. N12 .... 23Db 49
Hillcourt Est. N16 .... 32Tb 71
Hillcourt Rd. SE22 .... 58Xb 113
Hill Cres. DA5: Bexl 60Ed 118
HA1: Harr 29Ja 46
KT4: Wor Pk 75Ya 154
KT5: Surb 71Pa 153
N20 .... 19Db 31
RM11: Horn 30Ld 57
Hill Crest DA15: Sidc 59Wc 117
EN6: Pot B 6Eb 17
KT6: Surb 73Na 153
TN13: S'oaks 94Jd 202
Hillcrest AL3: St A 4P 5
AL10: Hat 1C 8
KT13: Weyb 77R 150
N6 .... 31Jb 70
N21 .... 17Qb 32
SE24 .... 56Tb 113
W11 .... *45Bb 89*
(off St John's Gdns.)
Hillcrest Av. HA5: Pinn 28Z 45
HA8: Edg 21Ra 47
KT16: Chert 76G 148
NW11 .... 29Bb 49
RM20: W Thur 51Wd 120
Hillcrest Cl. BR3: Beck 72Bc 158
EN7: G Oak 1Sb 19
KT18: Eps 87Va 174
SE26 .... 63Wb 135
Hillcrest Ct. KT13: Weyb 77R 150
RM5: Col R 25Fd 56
SM2: Sutt *79Fb 155*
(off Eaton Rd.)
Hillcrest Dr. DA9: Ghithe 57Wd 120
Hillcrest Gdns. KT10: Hin W 76Ha 152
N3 .... 28Ab 48
NW2 .... 34Wa 68
Hillcrest Pde. CR5: Coul 86Kb 176
Hillcrest Rd. BR1: Brom 64Jc 137
BR6: Chels 75Wc 161
CR3: Whyt 89Vb 177
CR8: Purl 82Pb 176
DA1: Dart 59Gd 118
E17 .... 26Fc 53
E18 .... 26Hc 53
IG10: Lough 16Mc 35
RM11: Horn 31Jd 76
TN16: Big H 88Mc 179
W3 .... 46Ra 87
W5 .... 43Na 87
WD7: Shenl 5Qa 15
Hillcrest Vw. BR3: Beck 72Bc 158
Hillcrest Way CM16: Epp 3Wc 23
Hillcrest Waye SL9: Ger X 31B 62
Hill Cft. WD7: R'lett 5Ja 14
Hillcroft IG10: Lough 12Qc 36
Hillcroft Av. CR8: Purl 85Lb 176
HA5: Pinn 30Ba 45
Hillcroft Ct. CR3: Cat'm 95Ub 197
Hillcroft Cres. HA4: Ruis 34Z 65
HA9: Wemb 35Pa 67
W5 .... 44Ma 87
WD19: Wat 18X 27
Hillcroft Rd. E6 .... 43Rc 94
Hillcroome Rd. SM2: Sutt 79Fb 155
Hillcross Av. SM4: Mord 72Za 154
Hilldale Rd. SM1: Sutt 77Bb 155
Hilldeane Rd. CR8: Purl 81Qb 176
Hilldene Av. RM3: Rom 23Ld 57
Hilldene Cl. RM3: Rom 22Md 57
Hilldown Ct. SW16 .... 66Nb 134
Hilldown Rd. BR2: Hayes 74Gc 159
SW16 .... 66Nb 134
Hill Dr. NW9 .... 32Sa 67
SW16 .... 69Pb 134
Hilldrop Cres. N7 .... 36Mb 70
Hilldrop Est. N7 .... 36Mb 70
(not continuous)
Hilldrop La. N7 .... 36Mb 70
Hilldrop Rd. BR1: Brom 65Kc 137
N7 .... 36Mb 70
Hille Bus. Cen. WD24: Wat 11X 27
HILL END 23K 43
Hill End BR6: Orp 75Vc 161
Hillend SE18 .... 53Qc 116
Hill End La. AL4: St A 5F 6
Hill End Rd. UB9: Hare 24L 43
Hillersden Ho. SW1 .... 7K 227
Hillersdon SL2: Slou 3M 81
Hillersdon Av. HA8: Edg 22Pa 47
SW13 .... 54Wa 110
Hillery Cl. SE17 .... 6G 231 (49Tb 91)
Hilley Fld. La. KT22: Fet 94Ea 192
Hill Farm Av. WD25: Wat 5W 12
(not continuous)
Hill Farm Cl. WD25: Wat 5W 12
Hill Farm Cotts. HA4: Ruis 31S 64
Hill Farm Ind. Est. WD25: Wat 5W 12
Hill Farm Rd. SL9: Chal P 24A 42
UB10: Ick 35T 64
W10 .... 43Ya 88
Hillfield Av. HA0: Wemb 38Na 67
N8 .... 29Nb 50
NW9 .... 29Ua 48
SM4: Mord 72Gb 155
Hillfield Cl. HA2: Harr 28Ea 46
RH1: Redh 6A 208
Hillfield Ct. HP2: Hem H 2N 3
KT10: Esh 78Da 151
NW3 .... 36Gb 69
Hillfield Ho. N5 .... 36Sb 71
Hillfield M. N8 .... 28Pb 50
Hillfield Pk. N10 .... 28Kb 50
N21 .... 19Qb 32
Hillfield Pk. M. N10 .... 28Kb 50
Hillfield Pl. TN13: Dun G 92Fd 202
Hill Fld. Rd. TW12: Hamp 66Ba 129
Hillfield Rd. HP2: Hem H 2M 3
NW6 .... 36Bb 69
RH1: Redh 6A 208
SL9: Chal P 24A 42
TN13: Dun G 92Gd 202
Hillfield Sq. SL9: Chal P 24A 42
Hillfoot Av. RM5: Col R 25Ed 56
Hillfoot Rd. RM5: Col R 25Ed 56
Hillgate Pl. SW12 .... 59Kb 112
W8 .... 46Cb 89
Hillgate St. W8 .... 46Cb 89
Hill Ga. Wlk. N6 .... 30Lb 50
Hillground Gdns. CR2: S Croy 82Rb 177
Hill Gro. RM1: Rom 27Gd 56
TW13: Hanw 61Ba 129
Hillgrove SL9: Chal P 25A 42
Hill Hall 8Bd 23
Hillhampton Pl. SL5: S'dale 3D 146
Hill Ho. BR2: Brom 68Hc 137
E5 .... *32Xb 71*
(off Harrington Hill)
SE28 .... 46Tc 94
Hillhouse EN9: Walt A 5Hc 21
Hill Ho. Apartments N1 .... 2J 217
Hill Ho. Av. HA7: Stan 24Ha 46
Hill Ho. Cl. N21 .... 17Qb 32
SL9: Chal P 24A 42
Hill Ho. Dr. KT13: Weyb 83Q 170
RH2: Reig 8K 207
RM16: Grays 10D 100
TW12: Hamp 67Ca 129
Hill Ho. M. BR2: Brom 68Hc 137
Hill Ho. Rd. DA2: Dart 59Sd 120
SW16 .... 64Pb 134
Hillhurst Gdns. CR3: Cat'm 92Ub 197
Hilliard Ho. *E1* *46Xb 91*
(off Prusom St.)
Hilliard Rd. HA6: Nwood 25V 44
Hilliards Ct. E1 .... 46Yb 92
Hilliards Rd. UB8: Cowl 44M 83
Hillier Cl. EN5: New Bar 16Db 31
Hillier Gdns. CR0: Wadd 78Qb 156
Hillier Ho. *NW1* *38Mb 70*
(off Camden Sq.)
Hillier Lodge TW11: Tedd 64Fa 130
Hillier Pl. KT9: Chess 79Ma 153
Hillier Rd. SW11 .... 58Hb 111
Hilliers Av. UB8: Hil 41Q 84
Hilliers La. CR0: Bedd 76Nb 156
Hillingdale TN16: Big H 90Kc 179
HILLINGDON 41Q 84
Hillingdon Athletic Club 29T 44
Hillingdon Athletics Stadium 37N 63
Hillingdon Av. TN13: S'oaks 93Ld 203
TW19: Stanw 60N 105
HILLINGDON CIRCUS 37R 64
Hillingdon Ct. HA3: Kenton 28Ma 47
Hillingdon Cycling Circuit 46Y 85
Hillingdon Golf Course 40P 63
HILLINGDON HEATH 42R 84
Hillingdon Hill UB10: Hil 40N 63
Hillingdon Outdoor Activities Cen. 31L 63
Hillingdon Ri. TN13: S'oaks 94Md 203
Hillingdon Rd. DA7: Bex 54Ed 118
DA11: Grav'nd 1D 144
UB8: Uxb 39M 63
UB10: Uxb 39N 63
WD25: Wat 6W 12
Hillingdon Sports & Leisure Complex
.... 37N 63
Hillingdon St. SE17 .... 51Rb 113
Hillington Gdns. IG8: Wfd G 26Mc 53
Hill La. HA4: Ruis 32S 64
KT20: Kgswd 93Ab 194
Hill Ley AL10: Hat 1B 8
Hillman Cl. RM11: Horn 27Md 57
UB8: Uxb 36N 63
Hillman Dr. W10 .... 42Ya 88
Hillman St. E8 .... 37Xb 71
Hillmarton Rd. N7 .... 36Nb 70
Hillmarton Ter. *N7* *36Nb 70*
(off Hillmarton Rd.)
Hillmead Dr. SW9 .... 56Rb 113
Hillmont Rd. KT10: Hin W 76Ga 152
Hillmore Ct. *SE13* *55Fc 115*
(off Belmont Hill)
Hillmore Gro. SE26 .... 64Ac 136
Hillmount *GU22: Wok* *90A 168*
(off Constitution Hill)
HILL PARK 95Rc 200
Hill Pk. Ct. KT22: Lea 91Ha 192
Hill Pk. Dr. KT22: Lea 91Ha 192
Hill Pk. (Local Nature Reserve) 94Nc 200
Hill Pk. Sth. KT22: Lea 92Ha 192
Hill Path SW16 .... 64Pb 134
Hill Pl. SL2: Farn C 8F 60
Hillpoint WD3: Loud 15L 25
Hillreach SE18 .... 50Pc 94
Hill Ri. DA2: Daren 64Td 142
EN6: Cuff 1Nb 18
EN6: Pot B 6Eb 17
HA4: Ruis 32S 64
KT10: Hin W 75Ka 152
N9 .... 16Xb 33
NW11 .... 28Db 49
Hill Ri. RM14: Upm 33Qd 77
SE23 .... 60Xb 113
SL9: Chal P 26A 42
TW10: Rich 57Ma 109
UB6: G'frd 38Ea 66
WD3: Rick 16K 25
Hillrise KT12: Walt T 73V 150
SL3: L'ly 51C 104
Hillrise Av. WD24: Wat 10Z 13
Hill Ri. Ct. *KT22: Lea* *93Ka 192*
(off Park Ri.)
Hill Ri. Cres. SL9: Chal P 26A 42
Hillrise Mans. *N19* *31Nb 70*
(off Warltersville Rd.)
Hillrise Rd. N19 .... 31Nb 70
RM5: Col R 23Ed 56
Hill Rd. CM14: B'wood 20Wd 40
CM16: They B 10Uc 22
CR4: Mitc 67Kb 134
CR8: Purl 84Pb 176
DA2: Wilm 61Nd 141
HA0: Wemb 34Ka 66
HA1: Harr 29Ja 46
HA5: Pinn 29Aa 45
HA6: Nwood 23T 44
KT22: Fet 94Da 191
N10 .... 25Hb 49
NW8 .... 3A 214 (40Eb 69)
SM1: Sutt 78Db 155
SM5: Cars 79Gb 155
Hillsboro' Rd. SE22 .... 57Ub 113
Hillsborough Ct. *NW6* *39Db 69*
(off Mortimer Cres.)
Hillsborough Grn. WD19: Wat 20W 26
Hill's Chace CM14: W'ley 21Yd 58
Hillsgrove Cl. DA16: Well 52Yc 117
HILLSIDE 49Ed 96
Hillside AL10: Hat 1C 8
DA2: Daren 64Ud 142
DA4: Farni 73Pd 163
DA8: Erith 49Ed 96
EN5: New Bar 15Eb 31
GU22: Wok 2P 187
GU25: Vir W 7N 147
KT10: Esh 78Da 151
N8 .... 30Mb 50
NW5 .... 34Jb 70
NW9 .... 28Ta 47
NW10 .... 38Sa 67
RM3: Rom 21Md 57
RM17: Grays 49Fe 99
SE10 .... *52Fc 115*
(off Croom's Hill)
SL1: Slou 7J 81
SL5: S'hill 1A 146
SM7: Bans 87Ab 174
SW19 .... 65Za 132
UB9: Hare 29L 43
Hillside, The BR6: Prat B 81Xc 181
Hillside Av. CR8: Purl 85Rb 177
DA12: Grav'nd 1F 144
EN8: Chesh 3Zb 20
HA9: Wemb 35Pa 67
IG8: Wfd G 23Lc 53
N11 .... 23Hb 49
WD6: Bore 14Ra 29
Hillside Cl. GU21: Knap 9H 167
IG8: Wfd G 22Lc 53
NW8 .... 40Db 69
SL9: Chal P 23A 42
SM4: Mord 70Ab 132
SM7: Bans 88Ab 174
WD5: Ab L 4U 12
Hillside Cotts. HP3: Hem H 3C 4
Hillside Ct. *AL1: St A* *1C 6*
(off Hillside Rd.)
BR8: Swan 70Jd 140
EN8: Chesh 3Zb 20
Hillside Cres. EN2: Enf 10Tb 19
EN8: Chesh 3Zb 20
HA2: Harr 32Ea 66
HA6: Nwood 25W 44
WD19: Wat 16Aa 27
Hillside Dr. DA12: Grav'nd 1F 144
HA8: Edg 23Qa 47
Hillside Gdns. E17 .... 27Fc 53
EN5: Barn 14Ab 30
HA3: Kenton 31Na 67
HA6: Nwood 24W 44
HA8: Edg 21Pa 47
HP4: Berk 2A 2
KT15: Add 78H 149
N6 .... 30Kb 50
N11 .... 23Lb 50
SM6: Wall 80Lb 156
SW2 .... 61Qb 134
Hillside Ga. *AL1: St A* *1C 6*
(off Hillside Rd.)
Hillside Gro. N14 .... 17Mb 32
NW7 .... 24Wa 48
Hillside Ho. *CR0: Wadd* *77Rb 157*
(off Duppas Av.)
Hillside La. BR2: Hayes 75Hc 159
(not continuous)
Hillside Mans. EN5: Barn 14Bb 31
Hillside Pk. SL5: S'dale 4D 146
Hillside Pas. SW16 .... 61Pb 134
Hillside Path CR5: Coul 90Nb 176
Hillside Ri. HA6: Nwood 24W 44
Hillside Rd. AL1: St A 1C 6
BR2: Brom 69Hc 137
CR0: Wadd 78Rb 157
CR3: Whyt 90Wb 177
CR5: Coul 90Nb 176
DA1: Cray 58Jd 118
HA5: Pinn 24X 45
HA6: Nwood 24W 44
KT5: Surb 70Pa 131
KT17: Ewe 82Ya 174
KT21: Asht 89Pa 173
N15 .... 31Ub 71
SM2: Sutt 80Bb 155
SW2 .... 61Pb 134
TN13: S'oaks 95Md 203
TN15: Kems'g 89Pd 183
TN16: Tats 91Nc 200
UB1: S'hall 42Ca 85
W5 .... 43Na 87
WD3: Chor 15E 24
WD7: R'lett 7Ka 14
WD23: Bush 15Aa 27
Hillside Wlk. CM14: B'wood 20Vd 40
Hills La. HA6: Nwood 25U 44
TN15: Knat 85Rd 183
Hillsleigh Rd. W8 .... 46Bb 89
Hillsmead Way CR2: Sande 85Wb 177
Hills M. W5 .... 45Na 87
Hills Pl. W1 .... 3B 222 (44Lb 90)
Hills Rd. IG9: Buck H 18Kc 35
Hillstone Ct. *E3* *42Dc 92*
(off Empson St.)
Hillstowe St. E5 .... 34Yb 72
Hill St. AL3: St A 2A 6
TW9: Rich 57Ma 109
W1 .... 6J 221 (46Jb 90)
Hillswood Dr. KT16: Chert 77D 148
Hillthorpe Cl. CR8: Purl 82Pb 176
Hill Top IG10: Lough 12Qc 36
NW11 .... 28Db 49
SM3: Sutt 73Bb 155
SM4: Mord 72Cb 155
Hilltop E17 .... 27Dc 52
Hilltop Av. NW10 .... 38Sa 67
Hill Top Cl. IG10: Lough 13Qc 36
Hilltop Cl. KT22: Lea 95La 192
SL5: Asc 8C 124
Hill Top Ct. IG8: Wfd G 23Pc 54
Hilltop Ct. *NW8* *38Eb 69*
(off Alexandra Rd.)
Hilltop Gdns. BR6: Orp 75Uc 160
DA1: Dart 57Pd 119
NW4 .... 26Xa 48
Hilltop Ho. N6 .... 31Mb 70
Hilltop La. CR3: Cat'm 98Qb 196
RH1: Mers 98Qb 196
Hill Top Pl. IG10: Lough 13Qc 36
Hilltop Ri. KT23: Bookh 98Ea 192
Hilltop Rd. CR3: Whyt 89Ub 177
NW6 .... 38Cb 69
RH2: Reig 8K 207
RM20: W Thur 51Xd 120
WD4: K Lan 9D 4
Hill Top Vw. IG8: Wfd G 23Pc 54
Hilltop Wlk. CR3: Wold 92Ac 198
Hilltop Way HA7: Stan 20Ja 28
Hill Vw. CR3: Whyt 89Vb 177
NW3 .... *39Hb 69*
(off Ainger Rd.)
TN15: Bor G 92Ce 205
Hillview SW20 .... 66Xa 132
TN15: Bor G 95Be 205
Hillview Av. HA3: Kenton 29Na 47
RM11: Horn 30Ld 57
Hill Vw. Cl. KT20: Tad 93Ya 194
TN15: Bor G 92Ce 205
Hillview Cl. CR8: Purl 83Rb 177
HA5: Hat E 23Ba 45
HA9: Wemb 33Pa 67
Hillview Ct. GU22: Wok 90B 168
Hill Vw. Cres. IG1: Ilf 30Pc 54
Hillview Cres. BR6: Orp 74Uc 160
Hill Vw. Dr. DA16: Well 54Uc 116
SE28 .... 46Uc 94
Hillview Dr. RH1: Redh 7A 208
Hill Vw. Gdns. NW9 .... 29Ta 47
Hillview Gdns. HA2: Harr 27Ca 45
NW4 .... 28Za 48
Hillview Ho. DA12: Grav'nd 10E 122
Hill Vw. Pl. KT11: Cobh 85Ba 171
Hill Vw. Rd. DA3: Lfield 69De 143
GU22: Wok 90B 168
KT10: Clay 80Ja 152
TW1: Twick 58Ja 108
TW19: Wray 8P 103
Hillview Rd. BR6: Orp 74Vc 161
BR7: Chst 64Qc 138
HA5: Hat E 24Ba 45
NW7 .... 21Za 48
SM1: Sutt 76Eb 155
Hillway N6 .... 33Jb 70
NW9 .... 32Ua 68
Hillway, The CM15: Mount 11Fe 41
Hill Waye SL9: Ger X 30B 42
Hillwood Cl. CM13: Hut 18De 41
Hillwood Gro. CM13: Hut 18De 41
Hill-Wood Ho. NW1 .... 2C 216
Hillworth BR3: Beck 68Dc 136
Hillworth Rd. SW2 .... 59Qb 112
Hillyard Ho. SW9 .... 53Qb 112
Hillyard Rd. W7 .... 43Ga 86
Hillyard St. SW9 .... 53Qb 112
Hillydeal Rd. TN14: Otf 87Ld 183
Hillyfield E17 .... 26Ac 52
Hillyfield Cl. E9 .... 36Ac 72
Hillyfields IG10: Lough 12Qc 36
Hilly Flds. Cres. SE4 .... 55Cc 114
SE13 .... 55Cc 114
Hilmay Dr. HP1: Hem H 3K 3
Hilperton Rd. SL1: Slou 7J 81
Hilsea Point SW15 .... 60Xa 110
Hilsea St. E5 .... 35Yb 72
Hilton Av. N12 .... 22Fb 49
Hilton Cl. UB8: Uxb 40K 63
Hilton Ho. SE4 .... 56Zb 114
Hilton's Wharf *SE10* *51Dc 114*
(off Norman Rd.)
Hilton Way CR2: Sande 87Xb 177
Hilversum Cres. SE22 .... 57Ub 113
Himalayan Way WD18: Wat 16V 26
Himalaya Palace Cinema 46Ba 85
Himley Rd. SW17 .... 64Gb 133
Hinchinbrook Ho. *NW6* *39Db 69*
(off Mortimer Cres.)
Hinchley Cl. KT10: Hin W 77Ha 152
Hinchley Dr. KT10: Hin W 76Ha 152
Hinchley Mnr. KT10: Hin W 76Ha 152
Hinchley Way KT10: Hin W 76Ja 152
HINCHLEY WOOD 76Ha 152
Hinckley Rd. SE15 .... 56Wb 113
Hind Cl. IG7: Chig 22Vc 55
Hind Ct. EC4 .... 3A 224 (44Qb 90)
Hind Cres. DA8: Erith 51Fd 118
Hinde Ho. W1 .... 2J 221
Hinde M. W1 .... 2J 221
Hindes Rd. HA1: Harr 29Fa 46
Hinde St. W1 .... 2J 221 (44Jb 90)
Hind Gro. E14 .... 44Cc 92
Hindhead Cl. N16 .... 32Ub 71
UB8: Hil 43R 84
Hindhead Gdns. UB5: N'olt 39Aa 65
Hindhead Grn. WD19: Wat 22Y 45
Hindhead Point SW15 .... 60Xa 110
Hindhead Way SM6: Wall 78Nb 156
Hind Ho. N7 .... 35Qb 70
SE14 .... *51Zb 114*
(off Myers La.)
Hindle Ho. E8 .... 36Vb 71
Hindlip Ho. SW8 .... 53Mb 112
Hindmans Rd. SE22 .... 57Wb 113
Hindmans Way RM9: Dag 42Bd 95
Hindmarsh Cl. E1 .... 45Wb 91
Hindon Ct. SW1 .... 5B 228
Hindrey Rd. E5 .... 36Xb 71
Hindsley's Pl. SE23 .... 61Yb 136
Hind Ter. RM20: Grays 51Zd 121
Hine Cl. CR5: Coul 94Lb 196
KT19: Eps 83Ra 173
Hine Ho. AL4: St A 3H 7
Hinkler Rd. HA3: Kenton 27Ma 47
Hinkley Cl. UB9: Hare 28L 43
Hinksey Cl. SL3: L'ly 48D 82
Hinksey Path SE2 .... 47Zc 95
Hinstock *NW6* *39Db 69*
(off Belsize Rd.)
Hinstock Rd. SE18 .... 51Sc 116
Hinton Av. TW4: Houn 56Z 107
Hinton Cl. SE9 .... 60Nc 116
Hinton Ct. *E10* *32Dc 72*
(off Leyton Grange Est.)
Hinton Ho. W5 .... 44La 86
Hinton Rd. N18 .... 21Ub 51
SE24 .... 55Rb 113
SL1: Slou 5C 80
SM6: Wall 79Lb 156
SW9 .... 55Rb 113
UB8: Uxb 39L 63
Hipley St. GU22: Wok 92D 188
Hippisley Ct. TW7: Isle 55Ha 108
Hippodrome M. W11 .... 45Ab 88
Hippodrome Pl. W11 .... 45Ab 88
Hiroshima Prom. SE7 .... 48Lc 93
Hirst Ct. SW1 .... 51Kb 112
Hirst Cres. HA9: Wemb 34Na 67
Hispano M. EN3: Enf L 9Cc 20
Hitcham Rd. E17 .... 31Bc 72
Hitchcock Cl. TW17: Shep 69P 127
Hitchcock La. E20 .... 37Ec 72
Hitchen Hatch La. TN13: S'oaks 96Jd 202
Hitchen Hatch Pl. TN13: S'oaks 95Kd 203
Hitchens Cl. HP1: Hem H 1H 3
Hitchin Cl. RM3: Rom 21Ld 57
Hitchings Way RH2: Reig 10J 207
Hitchin La. HA7: Stan 24Ma 47
Hitchin Rd. HA7: Stan 24Ma 47
Hitchin Sq. E3 .... 40Ac 72
Hithe Gro. SE16 .... 48Yb 92
Hitherbroom Rd. UB3: Hayes 46W 84
Hither Farm Rd. SE3 .... 55Lc 115
Hitherfield Rd. RM8: Dag 33Ad 75
SW16 .... 61Pb 134
HITHER GREEN 58Fc 115
Hither Green Crematorium SE6 .... 61Hc 137
Hither Grn. La. SE13 .... 57Ec 114
Hither Mdw. SL9: Chal P 25A 42
Hithermoor Rd. TW19: Stanw M 58H 105
Hitherwell Dr. HA3: Hrw W 25Fa 46
Hitherwood Cl. RH2: Reig 4M 207
RM12: Horn 35Md 77
Hitherwood Dr. SE19 .... 63Vb 135
Hive, The DA11: Nflt 58De 121
Hive Cl. CM14: B'wood 19Wd 40
WD23: B Hea 19Fa 28
Hive La. DA11: Nflt 58De 121
Hive Rd. WD23: B Hea 19Fa 28
(not continuous)
Hixberry La. AL4: St A 3H 7
HMP Belmarsh SE28 .... 47Uc 94
HMP Brixton SW2 .... 58Nb 112
HMP Bronzefield TW15: Ashf 63L 127
HMP Coldingley GU24: Bisl 9D 166
HMP Downview SM2: Sutt 84Eb 175
HMP High Down SM2: Sutt 84Eb 175
HMP Holloway N7 .... 35Nb 70
HMP Latchmere House
TW10: Ham 64Na 131
HMP Pentonville N7 .... 37Pb 70
HMP Send GU23: Send 99L 189
HMP The Mount HP3: Bov 8C 2
HMP Wandsworth SW18 .... 59Fb 111
HMP Wormwood Scrubs W12 .... 44Wa 88
HMS Belfast 6J 225 (46Ub 91)
HMYOI Feltham TW13: Felt 62T 128
Hoadly Ho. SE1 .... 7D 224
Hoadly Rd. SW16 .... 62Mb 134
Hobart Cl. N20 .... 19Gb 31
UB4: Yead 42Z 85
Hobart Ct. *CR2: S Croy* *78Tb 157*
(off South Pk. Hill Rd.)
Hobart Dr. UB4: Yead 42Z 85
Hobart Gdns. CR7: Thor H 69Tb 135
Hobart La. UB4: Yead 42Z 85
Hobart Pl. SW1 .... 3K 227 (48Kb 90)
TW10: Rich 59Pa 109
Hobart Rd. IG6: Ilf 26Sc 54
KT4: Wor Pk 76Xa 154
RM9: Dag 35Zc 75
RM18: Tilb 3C 122
UB4: Yead 42Z 85
Hobbayne Rd. W7 .... 44Fa 86
Hobbes Wlk. SW15 .... 57Xa 110
Hobbs Cl. AL4: St A 3J 7
EN8: Chesh 1Zb 20
KT14: W Byf 85K 169
Hobbs Ct. *SE1* *47Vb 91*
(off Mill St.)
HOBBS CROSS 8Zc 23
Hobbs Cross Golf Course 8Zc 23
Hobbs Cross Open Farm 8Zc 23
Hobbs Cross Rd.
CM16: Abr, Epp, Fidd H, They G
.... 6Yc 23
Hobbs Grn. N2 .... 27Eb 49
Hobbs Hill Rd. HP3: Hem H 6N 3
Hobbs La. EN8: Chesh 1Zb 20
Hobbs M. IG3: Ilf 33Vc 75
Hobbs Pl. N1 .... 1H 219 (39Ub 71)
Hobbs Pl. Est. N1 .... 1H 219
Hobbs Rd. SE27 .... 63Sb 135
Hobby Ho. SE1 .... 49Xb 91
Hobby St. EN3: Pond E 15Zb 34
Hobday St. E14 .... 44Dc 92
Hobhouse Ct. *WC2* *5E 222*
(off Whitcomb St.)
Hobill Wlk. KT5: Surb 72Pa 153
Hoblands End BR7: Chst 65Uc 138
Hobletts Rd. HP2: Hem H 1P 3
Hobson's Pl. E1 .... 43Wb 91
Hobury St. SW10 .... 51Eb 111
HOCKENDEN 69Cd 140
Hockenden La. BR8: Swan 69Cd 140
Hockering Gdns. GU22: Wok 90D 168
Hockering Gdns. GU22: Wok 90C 168
Hockering Rd. GU22: Wok 90C 168
Hocker St. E2 .... 4K 219 (41Vb 91)
Hockett Cl. SE8 .... 49Ac 92
Hockford Cl. GU24: Pirb 8F 186
Hockington Ct. EN5: New Bar 14Db 31
Hockley Av. E6 .... 40Nc 74

Hockley Ct. E18 ... 25Jc 53
Hockley Dr. RM2: Rom ... 26Kd 57
HOCKLEY HOLE ... 9M 61
Hockley La. SL2: Stoke P ... 8M 61
Hockley M. IG11: Bark ... 41Uc 94
Hockliffe Ho. W10 ... 43Ya 88
(off Sutton Way)
Hockney Ct. SE16 ... 50Xb 91
(off Rossetti Rd.)
Hocroft Av. NW2 ... 34Bb 69
Hocroft Ct. NW2 ... 34Bb 69
Hocroft Rd. NW2 ... 34Bb 69
Hocroft Wlk. NW2 ... 34Bb 69
Hodder Dr. UB6: G'frd ... 40Ha 66
Hoddesdon Rd. DA17: Belv ... 50Cd 96
Hodes Row NW3 ... 35Jb 70
Hodford Rd. NW11 ... 32Bb 69
Hodges Cl. RM16: Chaf H ... 50Zd 99
Hodges Way WD18: Wat ... 16W 26
Hodgkin Cl. SE28 ... 45Zc 95
Hodgkins M. HA7: Stan ... 22Ka 46
Hodister Cl. SE5 ... 52Sb 113
Hodnet Gro. SE16 ... 49Zb 92
Hodsoll Ct. BR5: St M Cry ... 71Zc 161
HODSOLL STREET ... 81Fe 185
Hodsoll St. TN15: Hod S ... 81Fe 185
Hodson Cl. HA2: Harr ... 34Ba 65
Hodson Cres. BR5: St M Cry ... 71Zc 161
Hodson Pl. EN3: Enf L ... 10Cc 20
Hoe, The WD19: Wat ... 19Z 27
Hoebridge Golf Course ... 91E 188
Hoebrook Cl. GU22: Wok ... 3P 187
Hoe Ct. GU22: Wok ... 91A 188
Hoecroft Ct. EN3: Enf W ... 10Yb 20
(off Hoe La.)
Hoe La. EN1: Enf ... 10Wb 19
EN3: Enf W ... 10Xb 19
RM4: Abr ... 13Xc 37
Hoe St. E17 ... 28Cc 52
Hoever Ho. SE6 ... 63Ec 136
Hoffmann Gdns. CR2: Sels ... 80Xb 157
Hoffman Sq. N1 ... 3G 219
Hofland Rd. W14 ... 48Ab 88
Hoford Rd. RM18: Linf, W Til ... 9F 100
SS17: Linf ... 6H 101
Hogan Bus. Cen. GU21: Wok ... 89A 168
Hogan M. W2 ... 7B 214 (43Eb 89)
Hogan Way E5 ... 33Wb 71
Hogarth Av. CM15: B'wood ... 20Ae 41
TW15: Ashf ... 65S 128
Hogarth Bus. Pk. W4 ... 51Ua 110
Hogarth Cl. E16 ... 43Mc 93
SL1: Slou ... 5C 80
UB8: Uxb ... 41L 83
W5 ... 43Na 87
Hogarth Ct. E1 ... 44Wb 91
(off Batty St.)
EC3 ... 3J 225 (44Ub 91)
NW1 ... 38Lb 70
(off St Pancras Way)
SE19 ... 63Vb 135
TW5: Hest ... 52Aa 107
WD23: Bush ... 17Da 27
Hogarth Cres. CR0: C'don ... 73Sb 157
SW19 ... 67Fb 133
Hogarth Gdns. TW5: Hest ... 52Ca 107
Hogarth Health Club, The ... 49Va 88
Hogarth Hill NW11 ... 28Bb 49
Hogarth Ho. SW1 ... 6E 228
UB5: N'olt ... 40Z 65
(off Gallery Gdns.)
Hogarth Ind. Est. NW10 ... 42Wa 88
Hogarth La. W4 ... 51Ua 110
Hogarth Pl. SW5 ... 49Db 89
(off Hogarth Rd.)
Hogarth Reach IG10: Lough ... 15Pc 36
Hogarth Rd. HA8: Edg ... 26Qa 47
RM8: Dag ... 36Xc 75
RM16: Grays ... 46Ce 99
SW5 ... 49Db 89
HOGARTH RDBT. ... 51Ua 110
Hogarth's House ... 51Ua 110
(off Hogarth La.)
Hogarth Ter. W4 ... 51Ua 110
Hogarth Way TW12: Hamp ... 67Ea 130
Hogden Cl. KT20: Kgswd ... 97Bb 195
Hogfair La. SL1: Burn ... 1A 80
Hogg La. RM16: Grays ... 48Ce 99
RM17: Grays ... 47Ce 99
(Lodge La.)
RM17: Grays ... 50Ce 99
(London Rd.)
WD6: E'tree ... 14Ja 28
Hog Hill Rd. RM5: Col R ... 24Bd 55
Hognore La. TN15: Wro ... 86Fe 185
HOGPITS BOTTOM ... 4D 10
Hogscross La. CR5: Coul ... 95Hb 195
Hogshead Pas. E1 ... 45Xb 91
(off Tobacco Dock)
Hogshill La. KT11: Cobh ... 86X 171
Hogs La. DA11: Nflt ... 62Fe 143
Hogsmill Ho. KT1: King T ... 69Pa 131
(off Vineyard Cl.)
Hogsmill La. KT1: King T ... 69Pa 131
Hogsmill Local Nature Reserve ... 78Ra 153
Hogsmill Wlk. KT1: King T ... 69Na 131
(off Penrhyn Rd.)
Hogsmill Way KT19: Ewe ... 78Sa 153
Hogs Orchard BR8: Swan ... 67Kd 141
Hogtrough Hill
TN16: Bras, S'oaks ... 92Vc 201
Hogtrough La. RH1: S Nut ... 7C 208
RH8: Oxt ... 100Dc 198
RH9: G'stone ... 99Cc 198
Holbeach Cl. NW9 ... 25Ua 48
Holbeach Gdns. DA15: Sidc ... 58Uc 116
Holbeach M. SW12 ... 60Kb 112
Holbeach Rd. SE6 ... 59Cc 114
Holbeck Row SE15 ... 52Wb 113
Holbein Ga. HA6: Nwood ... 22U 44
Holbein Ho. SW1 ... 7H 227
Holbein M. SW1 ... 7H 227 (50Jb 90)
Holbein Pl. SW1 ... 6H 227 (49Jb 90)
Holbein Ter. RM8: Dag ... 35Yc 75
(off Marlborough Rd.)
Holberton Gdns. NW10 ... 41Xa 88
HOLBORN ... 1H 223 (43Pb 90)
Holborn EC1 ... 1K 223 (43Qb 90)
Holborn Bars EC1 ... 1K 223
Holborn Cir. EC1 ... 1A 224 (43Qb 90)
Holborn Ho. W12 ... 44Xa 88
Holborn Pl. WC1 ... 1H 223 (43Pb 90)
Holborn Rd. E13 ... 42Kc 93
Holborn Viaduct EC1 ... 1A 224 (43Rb 91)
Holborn Way CR4: Mitc ... 68Hb 133
Holbreck Pl. GU22: Wok ... 90B 168
Holbrook Cl. EN1: Enf ... 11Vb 33
N19 ... 32Kb 70
Holbrook Ct. TW20: Egh ... 64E 126
Holbrooke Ct. N7 ... 35Nb 70
Holbrooke Pl. TW10: Rich ... 57Ma 109
Holbrook Gdns. WD25: A'ham ... 8Da 13
Holbrook Ho. BR7: Chst ... 67Tc 138
Holbrook La. BR7: Chst ... 66Tc 138
Holbrook Mdw. TW20: Egh ... 65E 126
Holbrook Rd. E15 ... 40Hc 73
Holbrook Way BR2: Brom ... 72Pc 160
Holburne Cl. SE3 ... 53Lc 115
Holburne Gdns. SE3 ... 53Mc 115
Holburne Rd. SE3 ... 53Lc 115
Holcombe Cl. TN16: Westrm ... 98Tc 200
Holcombe Hill NW7 ... 20Wa 30
Holcombe Ho. SW9 ... 55Nb 112
(off Landor Rd.)
Holcombe Pl. SE4 ... 55Ac 114
(off St Asaph Rd.)
Holcombe Rd. IG1: Ilf ... 31Qc 74
N17 ... 27Vb 51
(not continuous)
Holcombe St. W6 ... 49Xa 88
Holcon Ct. RH1: Redh ... 3A 208
Holcote Cl. DA17: Belv ... 48Ad 95
Holcroft Ct. W1 ... 7B 216
Holcroft Ho. SW11 ... 55Fb 111
Holcroft Rd. E9 ... 38Yb 72
HOLDBROOK ... 6Bc 20
Holdbrook Nth. EN8: Walt C ... 5Bc 20
Holdbrook Sth. EN8: Walt C ... 6Bc 20
Holdbrook Way RM3: Hrld W ... 26Pd 57
Holden Av. N12 ... 22Db 49
NW9 ... 32Sa 67
Holdenby Rd. SE4 ... 57Ac 114
Holden Cl. RM8: Dag ... 34Xc 75
Holden Gdns. CM14: W'ley ... 22Zd 59
Holden Ho. N1 ... 39Sb 71
(off Prebend St.)
SE8 ... 52Cc 114
Holdenhurst Av. N12 ... 24Eb 49
Holden Pl. KT11: Cobh ... 86X 171
Holden Point E15 ... 37Fc 73
(off Waddington St.)
Holden Rd. N12 ... 22Db 49
Holden St. SW11 ... 54Jb 112
Holden Way RM14: Upm ... 32Td 78
Holder Cl. N3 ... 24Db 49
Holdernesse Cl. TW7: Isle ... 53Ja 108
Holdernesse Rd. SW17 ... 62Hb 133
Holderness Ho. SE5 ... 55Ub 113
Holderness Way SE27 ... 64Rb 135
HOLDERS HILL ... 26Za 48
Holder's Hill Av. NW4 ... 26Za 48
Holders Hill Cir. NW7 ... 24Ab 48
Holders Hill Cres. NW4 ... 26Za 48
Holders Hill Dr. NW4 ... 27Za 48
Holder's Hill Gdns. NW4 ... 26Ab 48
Holders Hill Pde. NW7 ... 25Ab 48
Holders Hill Rd. NW4 ... 26Za 48
NW7 ... 26Za 48
Holecroft EN9: Walt A ... 6Gc 21
Hole Farm La. CM13: Gt War ... 27Xd 58
Holford Ho. SE16 ... 49Xb 91
(off Camilla Rd.)
WC1 ... 3J 217
Holford M. WC1 ... 3K 217
Holford Pl. WC1 ... 3J 217 (41Pb 90)
Holford Rd. NW3 ... 34Eb 69
Holford St. WC1 ... 3K 217 (41Pb 90)
Holford Way SW15 ... 58Wa 110
Holford Yd. WC1 ... 2J 217
Holgate Av. SW11 ... 55Fb 111
Holgate Ct. RM1: Rom ... 29Gd 56
(off Western Rd.)
Holgate Gdns. RM10: Dag ... 37Cd 76
Holgate Rd. RM10: Dag ... 36Cd 76
Holgate St. SE7 ... 48Mc 93
Holgrave Ho. N8 ... 28Pb 50
HOLLAND ... 5L 211
Holland Av. SM2: Sutt ... 81Cb 175
SW20 ... 67Va 132
Holland Cl. BR2: Hayes ... 75Hc 159
EN5: New Bar ... 17Fb 31
HA7: Stan ... 22Ka 46
KT19: Eps ... 83Sa 173
RH1: Redh ... 6P 207
RM7: Rom ... 29Ed 56
Holland Ct. E17 ... 28Ec 52
(off Evelyn Rd.)
KT6: Surb ... 73Ma 153
NW7 ... 23Wa 48
Holland Cres. RH8: Oxt ... 5L 211
Holland Dr. SE23 ... 62Ac 136
Holland Dwellings WC2 ... 2G 223
Holland Gdns. TW8: Bford ... 51Pa 109
TW20: Thorpe ... 68H 127
W14 ... 48Ab 88
WD25: Wat ... 7Y 13
Holland Gro. SW9 ... 52Qb 112
Holland Ho. E4 ... 21Ec 52
NW10 ... 40Xa 68
(off Holland Rd.)
SL4: Eton ... 1G 102
(off Common La.)
Holland La. RH8: Oxt ... 5L 211
HOLLAND PARK ... 46Bb 89
Holland Pk. ... 47Bb 89
Holland Pk. W11 ... 46Ab 88
Holland Pk. Av. IG3: Ilf ... 30Uc 54
W11 ... 47Ab 88
Holland Pk. Ct. W14 ... 47Ab 88
(off Holland Pk. Gdns.)
Holland Pk. Gdns. W14 ... 47Ab 88
Holland Pk. Mans. W14 ... 46Ab 88
(off Holland Pk. Gdns.)
Holland Pk. M. W11 ... 46Ab 88
Holland Pk. Rd. W14 ... 48Bb 89
HOLLAND PARK RDBT. ... 47Za 88
Holland Pk. Ter. W11 ... 46Ab 88
(off Portland Rd.)
Holland Pk. Theatre (Open Air) ... 47Bb 89
Holland Pas. N1 ... 39Sb 71
(off Basire St.)
Holland Pl. W8 ... 47Db 89
(off Kensington Chu. St.)
Holland Pl. Chambers W8 ... 47Db 89
(off Holland Pl.)
Holland Ri. Ho. SW9 ... 52Pb 112
(off Clapham Rd.)
Holland Rd. E6 ... 39Pc 74
E15 ... 41Gc 93
HA0: Wemb ... 37Ma 67
NW10 ... 39Wa 68
RH8: Oxt ... 5L 211
Holland Rd. SE25 ... 71Wb 157
W14 ... 47Za 88
Hollands, The GU22: Wok ... 90A 168
KT4: Wor Pk ... 74Va 154
TW13: Hanw ... 63Z 129
Hollands Cl. DA12: Shorne ... 4N 145
Holland St. SE1 ... 6C 224 (46Rb 91)
W8 ... 47Cb 89
Holland Vs. Rd. W14 ... 47Ab 88
Holland Wlk. HA7: Stan ... 22Ja 46
N19 ... 32Mb 70
W8 ... 46Bb 89
Holland Way BR2: Hayes ... 75Hc 159
Hollar Rd. N16 ... 34Vb 71
Hollen St. W1 ... 2D 222 (44Mb 90)
Holles Cl. TW12: Hamp ... 65Ca 129
Holles Ho. SW9 ... 54Qb 112
Holles St. W1 ... 2A 222 (44Kb 90)
Holley Rd. W3 ... 47Ua 88
Hollickwood Av. N12 ... 23Hb 49
Holliday Sq. SW11 ... 55Fb 111
(off Fowler Cl.)
Holliday St. HP4: Berk ... 1A 2
Hollidge Way RM10: Dag ... 38Dd 76
Holliers Way AL10: Hat ... 1C 8
Hollies, The AL3: St A ... 1C 6
(off Carlisle Av.)
DA3: Lfield ... 69Ee 143
DA12: Grav'nd ... 5F 144
E11 ... 29Jc 53
(off New Wanstead)
EN9: Walt A ... 7Lc 21
(in Woodbine Cl. Caravan Pk.)
HA3: W'stone ... 28Ja 46
HP3: Bov ... 1C 10
KT15: Add ... 78L 149
(off Bourne Way)
N20 ... 18Fb 31
RH8: Oxt ... 5M 211
SS17: Stan H ... 2L 101
WD18: Wat ... 14V 26
Hollies Av. DA15: Sidc ... 61Vc 139
KT14: W Byf ... 85H 169
Hollies Cl. SW16 ... 65Qb 134
TW1: Twick ... 61Ha 130
Hollies Ct. KT15: Add ... 78L 149
Hollies End NW7 ... 22Xa 48
Hollies Rd. W5 ... 49La 86
Hollies Way EN6: Pot B ... 3Eb 17
SW12 ... 59Jb 112
Holligrave Rd. BR1: Brom ... 67Jc 137
Hollingbourne Av. DA7: Bex ... 53Bd 117
Hollingbourne Gdns. W13 ... 43Ka 86
Hollingbourne Rd. SE24 ... 57Sb 113
Hollingsworth Ct. KT6: Surb ... 73Ma 153
Hollingsworth M. WD25: Wat ... 6W 12
Hollingsworth Rd. CR0: C'don ... 79Xb 157
Hollington Ct. BR7: Chst ... 65Rc 138
Hollington Cres. KT3: N Mald ... 72Va 154
Hollington Rd. E6 ... 41Pc 94
N17 ... 26Wb 51
Hollingworth Cl. KT8: W Mole ... 70Ba 129
Hollingworth Rd. BR5: Pet W ... 72Rc 160
Hollingworth Way TN16: Westrm ... 98Tc 200
Hollins Ho. N7 ... 35Nb 70
Hollisfield WC1 ... 4G 217
Hollis Pl. RM17: Grays ... 49Ce 99
Hollis Row RH1: Redh ... 8P 207
Hollman Gdns. SW16 ... 65Rb 135
Hollow, The IG8: Wfd G ... 21Hc 53
HOLLOWAY ... 34Nb 70
Holloway Cl. UB7: Harm ... 50N 83
Holloway Dr. GU25: Vir W ... 70A 126
Holloway Hill KT16: Chert, Lyne ... 76E 148
Holloway Ho. NW2 ... 34Ya 68
(off Stoll Cl.)
TW20: Egh ... 64B 126
Holloway La. UB7: Harm, W Dray ... 51M 105
WD3: Chen, Sarr ... 10D 10
Holloway Rd. E6 ... 41Pc 94
E11 ... 34Fc 73
N7 ... 35Pb 70
N19 ... 33Mb 70
Holloways La. AL9: Wel G ... 5F 8
Holloway St. TW3: Houn ... 55Da 107
Hollow Cotts. RM19: Purf ... 50Qd 97
Hollowfield Av. RM17: Grays ... 49Fe 99
Hollowfield Wlk. UB5: N'olt ... 37Aa 65
Hollow Hill La. SL0: Iver ... 45D 82
Hollow La. GU25: Vir W ... 9N 125
Hollows, The TW8: Bford ... 51Pa 109
Holly Av. HA7: Stan ... 26Na 47
KT12: Walt T ... 74Z 151
KT15: New H ... 82J 169
Hollybank GU24: W End ... 5D 166
HP3: Hem H ... 1H 5
Hollybank Cl. TW12: Hamp ... 64Ca 129
Holly Bank Rd. GU22: Wok ... 3M 187
Hollybank Rd. KT14: W Byf ... 86J 169
Hollyberry La. NW3 ... 35Eb 69
Hollybrake Cl. BR7: Chst ... 66Tc 138
Hollybush Av. AL2: Chis G ... 6N 5
Hollybush Cl. E11 ... 29Jc 53
HA3: Hrw W ... 25Ga 46
TN13: S'oaks ... 96Ld 203
WD19: Wat ... 17Y 27
Hollybush Ct. TN13: S'oaks ... 96Ld 203
Hollybush Gdns. E2 ... 41Xb 91
Holly Bush Hill NW3 ... 35Eb 69
Hollybush Hill E11 ... 30Hc 53
SL2: Stoke P ... 8L 61
Hollybush Ho. E2 ... 41Xb 91
Holly Bush La. TN13: S'oaks ... 96Ld 203
TW12: Hamp ... 66Ba 129
Hollybush La. BR6: Well H ... 79Cd 162
GU23: Rip ... 91M 189
HP1: Hem H ... 1H 3
SL0: Iver ... 44D 82
UB9: Den ... 33E 62
Hollybush Pl. E2 ... 41Xb 91
Hollybush Rd. DA12: Grav'nd ... 1E 144
KT2: King T ... 64Na 131
Hollybush Sports Complex ... 95Md 203
Holly Bush Steps NW3 ... 35Eb 69
(off Holly Mt.)
Hollybush St. E13 ... 41Kc 93
Holly Bush Va. NW3 ... 35Eb 69
Hollybush Wlk. SW9 ... 56Rb 113
Hollybush Way EN7: Chesh ... 1Wb 19
Holly Cl. AL10: Hat ... 1B 8
BR3: Beck ... 70Ec 136
GU21: Wok ... 1M 187
IG9: Buck H ... 20Mc 35
KT16: Longc ... 6L 147
SL2: Farn C ... 5G 60
SM6: Wall ... 80Kb 156
Holly Cl. TW13: Hanw ... 64Aa 129
TW16: Sun ... 69X 129
TW20: Eng G ... 5M 125
Hollycombe TW20: Eng G ... 3N 125
Holly Cott. M. UB8: Hil ... 43Q 84
Holly Ct. DA11: Nflt ... 57De 121
DA14: Sidc ... 63Xc 139
(off Sidcup Hill)
KT16: Chert ... 74H 149
(off King St.)
KT22: Lea ... 94Ja 192
(off Belmont Rd.)
N15 ... 28Ub 51
RM1: Rom ... 28Hd 56
(off Dolphin App.)
SE10 ... 48Hc 93
SM2: Sutt ... 80Cb 155
Holly Cres. BR3: Beck ... 71Bc 158
IG8: Wfd G ... 24Fc 53
SL4: Wind ... 4B 102
Hollycroft Av. HA9: Wemb ... 33Pa 67
NW3 ... 34Cb 69
Hollycroft Cl. CR2: S Croy ... 78Ub 157
UB7: Sip ... 51Q 106
Hollycroft Gdns. UB7: Sip ... 51Q 106
Hollydale Cl. UB5: N'olt ... 35Da 65
Hollydale Dr. BR2: Brom ... 76Pc 160
Hollydale Rd. SE15 ... 53Yb 114
Hollydene BR2: Brom ... 67Hc 137
(off Beckenham La.)
SE13 ... 58Fc 115
SE15 ... 53Xb 113
Hollydown Way E11 ... 34Fc 73
Holly Dr. E4 ... 17Dc 34
EN6: Pot B ... 5Db 17
HP4: Berk ... 2A 2
RM15: S Ock ... 42Zd 99
SL4: Old Win ... 8J 103
Holly Farm Rd. UB2: S'hall ... 50Aa 85
Hollyfield AL10: Hat ... 3C 8
Hollyfield Av. N11 ... 22Hb 49
Hollyfield Rd. KT5: Surb ... 73Pa 153
Holly Gdns. DA7: Bex ... 56Ed 118
UB7: W Dray ... 47P 83
Holly Ga. KT15: Add ... 77K 149
Holly Grn. KT13: Weyb ... 77T 150
Holly Gro. HA5: Pinn ... 25Aa 45
NW9 ... 31Sa 67
SE15 ... 54Vb 113
Hollygrove WD23: Bush ... 17Fa 28
Hollygrove Cl. TW3: Houn ... 56Ba 107
Hollyhedge Rd. KT11: Cobh ... 86X 171
Holly Hedges La. HP3: Bov ... 2E 10
Holly Hedge Ter. SE13 ... 57Fc 115
Holly Hill N21 ... 16Pb 32
NW3 ... 35Eb 69
Holly Hill Dr. SM7: Bans ... 88Cb 175
Holly Hill Pk. SM7: Bans ... 89Cb 175
Holly Hill Rd. DA8: Erith ... 50Dd 96
DA17: Belv, Erith ... 50Dd 96
Hollyhock Cl. HP1: Hem H ... 1G 2
Hollyhock Dr. GU24: Bisl ... 7E 166
Holly Ho. CM15: B'wood ... 18Zd 41
TW8: Bford ... 51La 108
W10 ... 42Ab 88
(off Hawthorn Wlk.)
Holly Ind. Pk. WD24: Wat ... 11Y 27
Holly La. GU3: Worp ... 10G 186
SM7: Bans ... 88Cb 175
Holly La. E. SM7: Bans ... 88Cb 175
Holly La. W. SM7: Bans ... 89Cb 175
Holly Lea GU4: Jac W ... 10P 187
Holly Lodge GU22: Wok ... 89B 168
(off Heathside Cres.)
HA1: Harr ... 29Fa 46
KT20: Lwr K ... 98Ab 194
W8 ... 47Cb 89
(off Thornwood Gdns.)
Holly Lodge Gdns. N6 ... 33Jb 70
Holly Lodge Mans. N6 ... 33Jb 70
Hollymead SM5: Cars ... 76Hb 155
Hollymead Rd. CR5: Chip ... 90Jb 176
Hollymeoak Rd. CR5: Coul ... 91Kb 196
Holly M. SW10 ... 7A 226 (50Eb 89)
Hollymoor La. KT19: Ewe ... 82Ta 173
Holly Mt. NW3 ... 35Eb 69
Hollymount Cl. SE10 ... 53Ec 114
Holly Pde. KT11: Cobh ... 86X 171
(off High St.)
TW13: Felt ... 62Y 128
(off High St.)
Holly Pk. N3 ... 27Bb 49
N4 ... 31Nb 70
(not continuous)
Holly Pk. Est. N4 ... 31Pb 70
Holly Pk. Gdns. N3 ... 27Cb 49
Holly Pk. Rd. N11 ... 22Jb 50
W7 ... 46Ha 86
Holly Pl. NW3 ... 35Eb 69
(off Holly Berry La.)
Holly Rd. BR6: Chels ... 80Wc 161
DA1: Dart ... 60Md 119
E11 ... 31Hc 73
EN3: Enf W ... 8Zb 20
RH2: Reig ... 8K 207
TW1: Twick ... 60Ha 108
TW3: Houn ... 56Da 107
TW12: Hamp H ... 65Ea 130
W4 ... 49Ta 87
Holly St. E8 ... 38Vb 71
Holly Ter. N6 ... 32Jb 70
N20 ... 19Eb 31
Hollytree Av. BR8: Swan ... 68Gd 140
Holly Tree Cl. SW19 ... 60Za 110
Hollytree Cl. SL9: Chal P ... 22A 42
Holly Tree Ct. HP2: Hem H ... 2B 4
Holly Tree Ho. SE4 ... 55Bc 114
(off Brockley Rd.)
Hollytree Ho. WD24: Wat ... 8U 12
Hollytree Pde. DA14: Sidc ... 65Yc 139
(off Sidcup Hill)
Holly Tree Rd. CR3: Cat'm ... 94Ub 197
Hollyview Cl. NW4 ... 30Wa 48
Holly Village N6 ... 33Kb 70
Holly Vs. W6 ... 48Xa 88
(off Wellesley Av.)
Holly Wlk. EN2: Enf ... 13Sb 33
NW3 ... 35Eb 69
SL4: Wind ... 3C 124
Holly Way CR4: Mitc ... 70Mb 134
Hollywell Gro. RM12: Horn ... 32Hd 76
Hollywood Bowl
Barking ... 41Sc 94
Finchley ... 24Fb 49
Surrey Quays ... 48Zb 92
Watford ... 5Y 13
Hollywood Ct. SW10 ... 51Eb 111
(off Hollywood Rd.)
W5 ... 45Pa 87
WD6: E'tree ... 14Qa 29
Hollywood Gdns. UB4: Yead ... 44X 85
Hollywood La. TN15: W King ... 83Vd 184
Hollywood M. SW10 ... 51Eb 111
Hollywood Rd. E4 ... 22Ac 52
SW10 ... 51Eb 111
Hollywoods CR0: Sels ... 81Bc 178
Hollywood Way DA8: Erith ... 52Kd 119
IG8: Wfd G ... 24Fc 53
Holman Ct. KT17: Ewe ... 81Wa 174
Holman Ho. E2 ... 41Zb 92
(off Roman Rd.)
Holman Hunt Ho. W6 ... 50Ab 88
(off Field Rd.)
Holman Rd. KT19: Ewe ... 78Sa 153
SW11 ... 54Fb 111
Holmbank Dr. TW17: Shep ... 70U 128
Holmbridge Gdns. EN3: Pond E ... 14Zb 34
Holmbrook NW1 ... 2C 216
Holmbrook Dr. NW4 ... 29Za 48
Holmbury Ct. CR2: S Croy ... 78Ub 157
SW17 ... 62Hb 133
SW19 ... 66Gb 133
Holmbury Gdns. UB3: Hayes ... 46V 84
Holmbury Gro. CR0: Sels ... 80Bc 158
Holmbury Ho. SE24 ... 57Rb 113
Holmbury Mnr. DA14: Sidc ... 63Wc 139
Holmbury Pk. BR1: Brom ... 66Nc 138
Holmbury Vw. E5 ... 32Xb 71
Holmbush Rd. SW15 ... 58Ab 110
Holm Cl. KT15: Wdhm ... 84G 168
Holmcote Gdns. N5 ... 36Sb 71
Holm Ct. SE12 ... 62Kc 137
Holmcroft KT20: Walt H ... 97Xa 194
Holmcroft Ho. E17 ... 28Dc 52
Holmcroft Way BR2: Brom ... 71Pc 160
Holmdale Cl. WD6: Bore ... 12Pa 29
Holmdale Gdns. NW4 ... 29Za 48
Holmdale Rd. BR7: Chst ... 64Sc 138
NW6 ... 36Cb 69
Holmdale Ter. N15 ... 31Ub 71
Holmdene N12 ... 22Db 49
Holmdene Av. HA2: Harr ... 27Da 45
NW7 ... 23Wa 48
SE24 ... 57Sb 113
Holmdene Cl. BR3: Beck ... 68Ec 136
Holmdene Ct. BR1: Brom ... 69Nc 138
Holmead Rd. SW6 ... 52Db 111
Holmebury Cl. WD23: B Hea ... 19Ga 28
Holme Chase KT13: Weyb ... 79S 150
Holme Cl. EN8: Chesh ... 3Ac 20
Holme Ct. TW7: Isle ... 55Ja 108
Holmedale SL2: Slou ... 5N 81
Holmefield Ho. W10 ... 42Ab 88
(off Hazlewood Cres.)
Holmefield Pl. KT15: New H ... 82K 169
Holme Ho. SE15 ... 52Xb 113
(off Studholme St.)
Holme Lacey Rd. SE12 ... 58Hc 115
Holme Lea WD25: Wat ... 6Y 13
Holme Pk. WD6: Bore ... 12Pa 29
Holme Pl. HP2: Hem H ... 1C 4
Holme Rd. E6 ... 39Nc 74
RM11: Horn ... 32Qd 77
Holmes Av. E17 ... 27Bc 52
NW7 ... 22Ab 48
Holmes Cl. CR8: Purl ... 85Pb 176
GU22: Wok ... 93B 188
SE22 ... 56Wb 113
SL5: S'hill ... 2A 146
Holmes Ct. AL3: St A ... 1C 6
(off Carlisle Av.)
DA12: Grav'nd ... 10H 123
Holmesdale EN8: Walt C ... 7Yb 20
KT13: Weyb ... 79T 150
(off Bridgewater Rd.)
Holmesdale Av. RH1: Mers ... 3C 208
SW14 ... 55Ra 109
Holmesdale Cl. SE25 ... 69Vb 135
Holmesdale Hill DA4: S Dar ... 67Sd 142
Holmesdale Ho. NW6 ... 39Cb 69
(off Kilburn Vale)
Holmesdale Mnr. RH1: Redh ... 4A 208
Holmesdale Natural History Mus. ... 6K 207
Holmesdale Pk. RH1: Nutf ... 6F 208
Holmesdale Rd. CR0: C'don ... 71Tb 157
DA4: S Dar ... 67Sd 142
DA7: Bex ... 54Zc 117
N6 ... 31Kb 70
RH1: S Nut ... 8F 208
RH2: Reig ... 5J 207
SE25 ... 71Tb 157
TN13: S'oaks ... 95Ld 203
TW9: Kew ... 53Pa 109
TW11: Tedd ... 66La 130
Holmesdale Tunnel EN8: Walt C ... 6Zb 20
Holmesley Rd. SE23 ... 58Ac 114
Holmes Pl. SW10 ... 51Eb 111
Holmes Rd. NW5 ... 36Kb 70
SW19 ... 66Eb 133
TW1: Twick ... 61Ha 130
Holmes Ter. SE1 ... 1K 229
Holmeswood SM2: Sutt ... 79Db 155
Holmeswood Ct. N22 ... 26Qb 50
HOLMETHORPE ... 3B 208
Holmethorpe Av. RH1: Redh ... 3B 208
Holmethorpe Ind. Est.
RH1: Redh ... 3B 208
Holme Way HA7: Stan ... 23Ha 46
Holmewood Gdns. SW2 ... 59Pb 112
Holmewood Rd. SE25 ... 69Ub 135
SW2 ... 59Pb 112
Holmfield Av. NW4 ... 29Za 48
Holmfield Ct. NW3 ... 36Gb 69
Holm Gro. UB10: Hil ... 38Q 64
Holmgrove Ho. CR8: Purl ... 84Qb 176
Holmhurst SE13 ... 58Fc 115
Holmhurst Rd. DA17: Belv ... 50Dd 96
Holmlea Ct. CR0: C'don ... 77Tb 157
(off Chatsworth Rd.)
Holmlea Rd. SL3: Dat ... 3P 103
Holmlea Wlk. SL3: Dat ... 3N 103
Holmleigh Av. DA1: Dart ... 57Md 119
Holmleigh Ct. EN3: Pond E ... 14Yb 34
Holmleigh Rd. N16 ... 32Ub 71
Holmleigh Rd. Est. N16 ... 32Ub 71
Holm Oak Cl. SW15 ... 58Bb 111
Holmoak Cl. CR8: Purl ... 82Pb 176
Holm Oak M. SW4 ... 57Nb 112
Holm Oak Pk. WD18: Wat ... 15V 26
Holmoaks Ho. BR3: Beck ... 68Ec 136
Holmsdale Cl. SL0: Iver ... 44H 83
Holmsdale Gro. DA7: Bex ... 54Gd 118

Kenilworth Dr. KT12: Walt T 76Z 151
WD3: Crox G 14R 26
WD6: Bore 13Sa 29
Kenilworth Gdns. IG3: Ilf 33Vc 75
IG10: Lough 16Pc 36
RM12: Horn 34Ld 77
SE18 54Rc 116
TW18: Staines 64L 127
UB1: S'hall 41Ba 85
UB4: Hayes 43V 84
WD19: Wat 22Y 45
Kenilworth Rd. BR5: Pet W 72Sc 160
E3 40Ac 72
HA8: Edg 20Sa 29
KT17: Ewe 78Wa 154
NW6 39Bb 69
SE20 67Zb 136
TW15: Ashf 62M 127
W5 46Na 87
KENLEY 86Sb 177
Kenley N17 26Tb 51
(off Gloucester Rd.)
KENLEY AERODROME 91Tb 197
Kenley Av. NW9 25Ua 48
Kenley Cl. BR7: Chst 69Uc 138
DA5: Bexl 59Cd 118
EN4: E Barn 14Gb 31
Kenley Gdns. CR7: Thor H 70Rb 135
RM12: Horn 33Pd 77
Kenley La. CR8: Kenley 86Sb 177
Kenley Rd. KT1: King T 68Ra 131
SW19 68Cb 133
TW1: Twick 58Ka 108
Kenley Wlk. SM3: Cheam 77Za 154
W11 45Ab 88
Kenlor Rd. SW17 64Fb 133
Kenmare Dr. CR4: Mitc 66Hb 133
N17 26Vb 51
Kenmare Gdns. N13 21Sb 51
Kenmare Rd. CR7: Thor H 72Qb 156
Kenmere Gdns. HA0: Wemb 39Qa 67
Kenmere Rd. DA16: Well 54Yc 117
Kenmont Gdns. NW10 41Xa 88
Kenmore Av. HA3: Kenton, W'stone 28Ja 46
Kenmore Cl. TW9: Kew 52Qa 109
Kenmore Ct. NW6 38Db 69
(off Acol Rd.)
Kenmore Cres. UB4: Hayes 41V 84
Kenmore Gdns. HA8: Edg 26Ra 47
Kenmore Rd. CR8: Kenley 86Rb 177
HA3: Kenton 27Ma 47
Kenmure Rd. E8 36Xb 71
Kenmure Yd. E8 36Xb 71
Kennacraig Cl. E16 46Jc 93
Kennard Ho. SW11 54Jb 112
Kennard Rd. E15 38Fc 73
N11 22Hb 49
Kennard St. E16 46Pc 94
SW11 53Jb 112
Kenneally SL4: Wind 4A 102
Kenneally Cl. SL4: Wind 4A 102
(off Kenneally)
Kenneally Pl. SL4: Wind 4A 102
(off Kenneally)
Kenneally Row SL4: Wind 4A 102
(off Kenneally)
Kenneally Wlk. SL4: Wind 4A 102
Kennedy Av. EN3: Pond E 16Yb 34
Kennedy Cl. AL2: Lon C 8H 7
BR5: Pet W 74Tc 160
CR4: Mitc 67Jb 134
E13 40Jc 73
HA5: Hat E 23Ba 45
SL2: Farn C 7G 60
Kennedy Ct. TW15: Ashf 64S 128
WD23: B Hea 19Fa 28
Kennedy Cox Ho. E16 43Hc 93
(off Burke St.)
Kennedy Gdns. TN13: S'oaks 95Ld 203
Kennedy Ho. DA11: Nflt 2A 144
SE11 7H 229
SL1: Slou 6B 80
(off Harrison Way)
Kennedy Path W7 42Ha 86
Kennedy Rd. IG11: Bark 39Uc 74
W7 43Ga 86
Kennedy Wlk. SE17 6G 231
Kennel Cl. KT22: Fet 96Ea 192
Kennel Cotts. HP3: Hem H 7M 3
Kennel La. CM15: Dodd, Kel H 11Ud 40
GU20: W'sham 8A 146
KT22: Fet 94Da 191
Kennelwood Cres. CR0: New Ad 83Fc 179
Kennet Cl. RM14: Upm 30Ud 58
SW11 56Fb 111
Kennet Ct. W9 43Cb 89
(off Elmfield Way)
Kennet Grn. RM15: S Ock 45Xd 98
Kenneth Av. IG1: Ilf 35Rc 74
Kenneth Campbell Ho. NW8 5C 214
Kenneth Chambers Ct. IG8: Wfd G 23Nc 54
Kenneth Ct. SE11 5A 230 (49Qb 90)
Kenneth Cres. NW2 36Xa 68
Kenneth Gdns. HA7: Stan 23Ja 46
Kenneth Moore Rd. IG1: Ilf 34Rc 74
Kenneth More Theatre 34Rc 74
Kennet Ho. NW8 6C 214
Kenneth Rd. RM6: Chad H 31Zc 75
SM7: Bans 87Fb 175
Kenneth Robbins Ho. N17 24Xb 51
Kenneth Younger Ho. SW6 51Bb 111
(off Clem Attlee Ct.)
Kennet Rd. DA1: Cray 55Jd 118
TW7: Isle 55Ha 108
W9 42Bb 89
Kennet Sq. CR4: Mitc 67Gb 133
Kennet St. E1 46Wb 91
Kennett Ct. BR8: Swan 69Gd 140
(off Oakleigh Cl.)
W4 52Ra 109
WD18: Wat 14X 27
(off Whippendell Rd.)
Kennett Dr. UB4: Yead 43Aa 85
Kennett Rd. SL3: L'ly 48D 82
Kennett Wharf La. EC4 4E 224 (45Sb 91)
KENNINGHALL JUNC. 22Yb 52
Kenninghall Rd. E5 34Wb 71
N18 22Yb 52
Kenning Ho. N1 39Ub 71
(off Colville Est.)
Kenning St. SE16 47Yb 92
Kennings Way SE11 7A 230 (50Qb 90)
KENNINGTON 7A 230 (51Qb 112)
Kennington Grn. SE11 50Qb 90
Kennington La. SE11 7J 229 (50Pb 90)
KENNINGTON OVAL 51Qb 112
Kennington Oval SE11 51Pb 112
Kennington Pal. Ct. SE11 7K 229
Kennington Pk. (Belhus Woods Country Pk.) 44Rd 97
Kennington Pk. Gdns. SE11 51Rb 113
Kennington Pk. Ho. SE11 50Qb 90
(off Kennington Pk. Pl.)
Kennington Pk. Pl. SE11 51Qb 112
Kennington Pk. Rd.
SE11 7B 230 (51Qb 112)
Kennington Rd. SE1 3K 229 (48Qb 90)
SE11 7K 229 (48Qb 90)
Kennistoun Ho. NW5 36Lb 70
Kennoldes SE21 61Tb 135
(off Croxted Rd.)
Kenny Dr. SM5: Cars 81Jb 176
Kennyland Ct. NW4 30Xa 48
(off Hendon Way)
Kennylands Rd. IG6: Ilf 24Wc 55
Kenrick Pl. W1 7H 215 (43Jb 90)
Kenrick Sq. RH1: Blet 5L 209
KENSAL GREEN 41Ya 88
Kensal Ho. W10 42Za 88
(off Ladbroke Gro.)
KENSAL RISE 40Za 68
Kensal Rd. W10 42Ab 88
KENSAL TOWN 42Ab 88
Kensal Wharf W10 42Za 88
KENSINGTON 48Cb 89
Kensington Arc. W8 47Db 89
(off Kensington High St.)
Kensington Av. CR7: Thor H 67Qb 134
E12 37Nc 74
WD18: Wat 14V 26
Kensington Cen. W14 49Ab 88
(not continuous)
Kensington Chu. Ct. W8 47Db 89
Kensington Chu. St. W8 46Cb 89
Kensington Chu. Wlk. W8 47Db 89
(not continuous)
Kensington Cl. AL1: St A 4E 6
N11 23Jb 50
Kensington Ct. RM17: Grays 51Ee 121
SE16 46Zb 92
(off King & Queen Wharf)
W8 47Db 89
Kensington Ct. Gdns. W8 48Db 89
(off Kensington Ct. Pl.)
Kensington Ct. Mans. W8 47Db 89
(off Kensington Ct.)
Kensington Ct. M. W8 48Db 89
(off Kensington Ct. Pl.)
Kensington Ct. Pl. W8 48Db 89
Kensington Dr. IG8: Wfd G 26Mc 53
Kensington Gdns. 6A 220 (46Eb 89)
Kensington Gdns. IG1: Ilf 32Pc 74
KT1: King T 69Ma 131
RM18: E Til 9L 101
(off Queen Mary Av.)
Kensington Gdns. Sq. W2 44Db 89
Kensington Ga. W8 3A 226 (48Eb 89)
Kensington Gore SW7 2A 226 (47Eb 89)
Kensington Hall Gdns. W14 50Bb 89
Kensington Hgts. HA1: Harr 30Ha 46
(off Sheepcote Rd.)
W8 46Cb 89
Kensington High St. W8 48Bb 89
W14 48Bb 89
Kensington Ho. IG8: Wfd G 24Qc 54
UB7: W Dray 47P 83
W8 47Db 89
(off Kensington Ct.)
W14 47Za 88
Kensington Mall W8 46Cb 89
Kensington Mans. SW5 50Cb 89
(off Trebovir Rd., not continuous)
Kensington Palace 46Db 89
Kensington Pal. Gdns. W8 46Db 89
Kensington Pk. RM4: Stap A 17Gd 38
Kensington Pk. Gdns. W11 45Bb 89
Kensington Pk. M. W11 44Bb 89
Kensington Pk. Rd. W11 44Bb 89
Kensington Path E10 33Dc 72
(off Osborne Rd.)
Kensington Pl. W8 46Cb 89
Kensington Rd. CM15: Pil H 16Wd 40
RM7: Rom 30Ed 56
SW7 2C 226
UB5: N'olt 41Ca 85
W8 2A 226 (47Db 89)
Kensington Sports Cen. 45Ab 88
Kensington Sq. W8 48Db 89
Kensington Ter. CR2: S Croy 80Tb 157
Kensington Village W14 49Bb 89
Kensington Way WD6: Bore 13Ta 29
Kensington W. W14 49Ab 88
Kensworth Ho. EC1 4G 219
Kent Av. DA16: Well 57Vc 117
RM9: Dag 42Cd 96
SL1: Slou 3G 80
W13 43Ka 86
Kent Cl. BR6: Chels 79Uc 160
CR4: Mitc 70Nb 134
TN15: W King 80Ud 164
TW18: Staines 65M 127
UB8: Uxb 37L 63
WD6: Bore 10Ta 15
Kent Ct. E2 40Vb 71
NW9 26Ua 48
Kent Dr. EN4: Cockf 14Jb 32
RM12: Horn 35Md 77
TW11: Tedd 64Ga 130
Kentford Way UB5: N'olt 39Aa 65
Kent Gdns. HA4: Ruis 30W 44
W13 43Ka 86
Kent Ga. Way CR0: Addtn 79Bc 158
Kent Hatch Rd. RH8: Limp 101Jc 211
Kent Ho. SE1 7K 231 (50Vb 91)
SL9: Chal P 22A 42
SW1 7D 228
W4 50Ua 88
(off Devonshire St.)
W8 47Db 89
(off Kensington Ct.)
W11 46Bb 89
(off Boyne Ter. M.)
Kent Ho. App. Rd. BR3: Beck 67Ac 136
Kent Ho. La. BR3: Beck 65Ac 136
Kent Ho. Rd. BR3: Beck 67Zb 136
SE26 64Ac 136
Kent Bldgs. SE1 7F 225 (47Tb 91)
Kentish La. AL9: Brk P, Hat 8L 9
Kentish Rd. DA17: Belv 49Cd 96
KENTISH TOWN 36Kb 70
Kentish Town Forum 36Kb 70
Kentish Town Ind. Est. NW5 36Kb 70
Kentish Town Rd. NW1 38Kb 70
NW5 38Kb 70
Kentish Town Sports Cen. 37Kb 70
Kentish Way BR1: Brom 68Kc 137
BR2: Brom 68Kc 137
Kent Kraft Ind. Est. DA11: Nflt 57Be 121
Kentlea Rd. SE28 47Uc 94
Kentmere Ho. SE15 51Yb 114
Kentmere Mans. W5 42Ka 86
Kentmere Rd. SE18 49Uc 94
KENTON 29La 46
Kenton Av. HA1: Harr 31Ha 66
TW16: Sun 68Z 129
UB1: S'hall 45Ca 85
Kenton Ct. HA3: Kenton 30Ka 46
SE26 63Ac 136
(off Adamsrill Rd.)
TW1: Twick 58Ma 109
W14 48Bb 89
Kenton Ct. SE25 70Xb 135
Kenton Gdns. AL1: St A 3D 6
HA3: Kenton 29La 46
Kenton Ho. E1 42Yb 92
(off Mantus Cl.)
Kenton La.
HA3: Hrw W, Kenton, W'stone 23Ha 46
Kenton Pk. Av. HA3: Kenton 29Ma 47
Kenton Pk. Cl. HA3: Kenton 28La 46
Kenton Pk. Cres. HA3: Kenton 28Ma 47
Kenton Pk. Mans. HA3: Kenton 29La 46
(off Kenton Rd.)
Kenton Pk. Pde. HA3: Kenton 29La 46
Kenton Pk. Rd. HA3: Kenton 28La 46
Kenton Rd. E9 37Zb 72
HA1: Harr 31Ha 66
HA3: Kenton 30Ja 46
Kentons La. SL4: Wind 4C 102
Kenton St. WC1 5F 217 (42Nb 90)
Kenton Way GU21: Wok 9K 167
UB4: Hayes 41U 84
Kent Pk. Ind. Est. SE15 51Xb 113
Kent Pas. NW1 5F 215 (42Hb 89)
Kent Rd. BR4: W W'ck 74Dc 158
BR5: St M Cry 72Xc 161
DA1: Dart 58Md 119
DA3: Lfield 68Zd 143
DA11: Grav'nd 10C 122
GU20: W'sham 8B 146
GU22: Wok 88D 168
KT1: King T 69Ma 131
KT8: E Mos 70Ea 130
N21 18Tb 33
RM10: Dag 36Dd 76
RM17: Grays 51Ee 121
TW9: Kew 52Qa 109
W4 48Sa 87
Kents Av. HP3: Hem H 6M 3
Kent's Pas. TW12: Hamp 67Ba 129
Kent St. E2 1K 219 (40Vb 71)
E13 41Lc 93
Kent Ter. NW1 4E 214 (41Gb 89)
Kent Vw. RM13: Wenn 45Md 97
RM15: Avel 47Sd 98
Kent Vw. Gdns. IG3: Ilf 33Uc 74
Kent Wlk. SW9 56Rb 113
Kent Way KT6: Surb 76Na 153
Kentwell Cl. SE4 56Ac 114
Kent Wharf SE8 52Dc 114
(off Creekside)
Kentwode Grn. SW13 52Wa 110
Kentwyns Ri. RH1: S Nut 7F 208
Kent Yd. SW7 2E 226 (47Gb 89)
Kenver Av. N12 23Fb 49
Kenward Rd. SE9 57Lc 115
Kenward Way SW11 54Jb 112
Ken Way HA9: Wemb 34Sa 67
Kenway RM5: Col R 26Ed 56
RM13: Rain 41Md 97
Kenway Cl. RM13: Rain 41Ld 97
Kenway Rd. SW5 49Db 89
Kenway Wlk. RM13: Rain 41Md 97
Ken Wilson Ho. E2 40Wb 71
(off Pritchards Rd.)
Kenwood Av. DA3: Lfield 69Ee 143
N14 15Mb 32
Kenwood Cl. NW3 32Fb 69
UB7: Sip 51Q 106
Kenwood Ct. NW9 28Sa 47
(off Elmwood Cres.)
Kenwood Dr. BR3: Beck 69Ec 136
KT12: Hers 79X 151
WD3: Rick 19H 25
Kenwood Gdns. E18 27Kc 53
IG2: Ilf 29Qc 54
IG5: Ilf 28Qc 54
Kenwood House 32Gb 69
Kenwood Ho. SW9 56Rb 113
WD18: Wat 17T 26
Kenwood Pk. KT13: Weyb 79T 150
Kenwood Pl. N6 32Hb 69
Kenwood Ridge CR8: Kenley 89Rb 177
Kenwood Rd. N6 30Hb 49
N9 18Wb 33
Kenworth Cl. EN8: Walt C 5Zb 20
Kenworthy Rd. E9 36Ac 72
Kenwrick Ho. N1 1J 217
Kenwyn Dr. NW2 33Ua 68
Kenwyn Lodge N2 28Hb 49
Kenwyn Rd. DA1: Dart 57Md 119
SW4 56Mb 112
SW20 67Ya 132
Kenya Rd. SE7 52Mc 115
Kenyngton Ct. TW16: Sun 64W 128
Kenyngton Dr. TW16: Sun 64W 128
Kenyngton Pl. HA3: Kenton 29La 46
Kenyon Ho. SE5 52Sb 113
(off Camberwell Rd.)
Kenyon Mans. W14 51Ab 110
(off Queen's Club Gdns.)
Kenyons KT24: W Hor 100R 190
Kenyon St. SW6 53Za 110
Keogh Rd. E15 37Gc 73
Kepler Ho. SE10 50Hc 93
(off Armitage Rd.)
Kepler Rd. SW4 56Nb 112
Keppel Cl. DA9: Ghithe 56Xd 120
Keppel Ho. SE8 50Bc 92
SW3 6D 226
Keppel Rd. E6 38Pc 74
RM9: Dag 35Ad 75
Keppel Row SE1 7D 224 (46Sb 91)
Keppel Spur SL4: Old Win 9M 103
Keppel St. WC1 7E 216 (43Mb 90)
Kepplestone M. BR3: Beck 68Ec 136
Kepple St. SL4: Wind 4H 103
Kerbela St. E2 42Wb 91
Kerbey St. E14 44Dc 92
Kerdistone Cl. EN6: Pot B 2Db 17
Kerfield Cres. SE5 53Tb 113
Kerfield Pl. SE5 53Tb 113
Kernow Cl. RM12: Horn 33Nd 77
Kerria Way GU24: W End 5C 166
Kerri Cl. EN5: Ark 14Ya 30
Kerridge Ct. N1 37Ub 71
(off Balls Pond Rd.)
Kerrier Ho. SW10 52Eb 111
(off Stadium St.)
Kerrill Av. CR5: Coul 91Qb 196
Kerrington Ct. W10 42Ab 88
(off Wornington Rd.)
W12 47Ya 88
(off Uxbridge Rd.)
Kerris Ho. SE11 7A 230
Kerrison Pl. W5 46Ma 87
Kerrison Rd. E15 39Fc 73
SW11 55Gb 111
W5 46Ma 87
Kerrison Vs. W5 46Ma 87
Kerry Av. HA7: Stan 21La 46
RM15: Avel 47Pd 97
Kerry Cl. E16 44Kc 93
N13 19Pb 32
RM14: Upm 31Vd 78
Kerry Ct. HA7: Stan 21Ma 47
Kerry Dr. RM14: Upm 31Vd 78
Kerry Ho. E1 44Yb 92
(off Sidney St.)
Kerry Path SE14 51Bc 114
Kerry Rd. RM16: Grays 46Fe 99
SE14 51Bc 114
Kerry Ter. GU21: Wok 88D 168
Kerscott Ho. E3 41Dc 92
(off Rainhill Way)
Kersey Dr. CR2: Sels 84Yb 178
Kersey Gdns. RM3: Hrld W 24Nd 57
SE9 63Nc 138
Kersfield Ho. SW15 58Za 110
Kersfield Rd. SW15 58Za 110
Kershaw Cl. RM11: Horn 31Nd 77
RM16: Chaf H 49Yd 98
SW18 58Fb 111
Kershaw Rd. RM10: Dag 34Cd 76
Kerslake Ho. SL9: Chal P 22A 42
Kersley M. SW11 53Hb 111
Kersley Rd. N16 33Ub 71
Kersley St. SW11 54Hb 111
Kerstin Cl. UB3: Hayes 45V 84
Kerswell Cl. N15 29Ub 51
Kerwick Cl. N7 38Nb 70
Keslake Mans. NW10 40Za 68
(off Station Ter.)
Keslake Rd. NW6 40Za 68
Kessock Cl. N17 29Xb 51
Kesteven Cl. IG6: Ilf 23Vc 55
Kestlake Rd. DA5: Bexl 58Yc 117
KESTON 78Lc 159
Keston Av. BR2: Kes 78Lc 159
CR5: Coul 91Qb 196
KT15: New H 83J 169
Keston Cl. DA16: Well 52Yc 117
N18 20Tb 33
Keston Ct. DA5: Bexl 59Bd 117
KT5: Surb 71Pa 153
(off Cranes Pk.)
Keston Gdns. BR2: Kes 77Lc 159
Keston Ho. SE17 7J 231
KESTON MARK 77Nc 160
KESTON MARK 76Nc 160
Keston M. WD17: Wat 12X 27
Keston Pk. Cl. BR2: Kes 76Pc 160
Keston Rd. CR7: Thor H 72Qb 156
N17 27Tb 51
SE15 55Wb 113
Kestrel Av. E6 43Nc 94
SE24 57Rb 113
TW18: Staines 62H 127
Kestrel Cl. IG6: Ilf 21Xc 55
KT2: King T 63Ma 131
KT19: Eps 84Qa 173
NW9 26Ua 48
NW10 36Ta 67
RM12: Horn 38Kd 77
WD25: Wat 6Aa 13
Kestrel Ct. CR2: S Croy 79Sb 157
E3 40Cc 72
(off Four Seasons Cl.)
E17 26Zb 52
HA4: Ruis 33U 64
SM6: Wall 78Lb 156
Kestrel Grn. AL10: Hat 1C 8
Kestrel Ho. EC1 3D 218
EN3: Pond E 15Ac 34
Kestrel Pk. CM13: Hut 15Fe 41
Kestrel Path SL2: Slou 2C 80
Kestrel Pl. DA9: Ghithe 58Wd 120
(off Woodpecker Dr.)
SE14 51Ac 114
Kestrel Rd. EN9: Walt A 6Jc 21
Kestrels, The AL2: Brick W 3Ba 13
UB9: Den 29H 43
(off Patrons Way E.)
Kestrel Way CR0: New Ad 81Fc 179
GU21: Wok 7M 167
UB3: Hayes 47T 84
Keswick Av. RM11: Horn 32Md 77
SW15 64Ua 132
SW19 68Cb 133
TW17: Shep 69U 128
Keswick B'way. SW15 57Bb 111
(off Up. Richmond Rd.)
Keswick Cl. AL1: St A 3F 6
SM1: Sutt 77Eb 155
Keswick Ct. BR2: Brom 70Hc 137
SE6 60Hc 115
SE13 57Dc 114
SL2: Slou 5K 81
Keswick Dr. EN3: Enf W 8Yb 20
GU18: Light 3A 166
Keswick Gdns. HA4: Ruis 30T 44
HA9: Wemb 35Na 67
IG4: Ilf 28Nc 54
RM19: Purf 51Sd 120
Keswick Ho. RM3: Rom 23Md 57
(off Dartfields)
SE5 54Sb 113
Keswick M. W5 46Na 87
Keswick Rd.
BR4: W W'ck 75Gc 159
BR6: Orp 74Vc 161
DA7: Bex 53Cd 118
KT22: Fet 96Ea 192
KT23: Bookh 97Da 191
Keswick Rd. SW15 57Ab 110
TW2: Whitt 58Ea 108
TW20: Egh 66D 126
Kettering Ct. CR7: Thor H 70Sb 135
Kettering Rd. EN3: Enf W 9Zb 20
RM3: Rom 24Nd 57
Kettering St. SW16 65Lb 134
Kett Gdns. SW2 57Pb 112
Kettlebaston Rd. E10 32Bc 72
Kettleby Ho. SW9 55Rb 113
(off Barrington Rd.)
Kettlewell Cl. GU21: Wok 6P 167
N11 23Jb 50
Kettlewell Ct. BR8: Swan 68Hd 140
Kettlewell Dr. GU21: Wok 86A 168
Kettlewell Hill GU21: Wok 86A 168
Ketton Grn. RH1: Mers 100Mb 196
Ketton Ho. W10 42Ya 88
(off Sutton Way)
Kevan Ct. E17 28Cc 52
Kevan Dr. GU23: Send 96G 188
Kevan Ho. SE5 52Sb 113
Kevelioc Rd. N17 25Sb 51
Kevere Ct. HA6: Nwood 22R 44
Kevin Cl. TW4: Houn 54Z 107
KEVINGTON 72Ad 161
Kevington Cl. BR5: St P 70Vc 139
Kevington Dr. BR5: St P 70Vc 139
BR7: Chst 70Vc 139
KEW 53Qa 109
KEW BRIDGE 50Pa 87
Kew Bri. TW8: Bford 51Qa 109
Kew Bri. Arches TW9: Kew 51Qa 109
Kew Bri. Ct. W4 50Qa 87
Kew Bri. Distribution Cen.
TW8: Bford 50Pa 87
Kew Bri. Rd. TW8: Bford 51Pa 109
Kew Bridge Steam Mus. 50Pa 87
Kew Cl. RM1: Rom 23Gd 56
UB8: Uxb 40M 63
Kew Ct. KT2: King T 67Na 131
Kew Cres. SM3: Cheam 76Ab 154
Kewferry Dr. HA6: Nwood 22R 44
Kewferry Rd. HA6: Nwood 23S 44
Kew Foot Rd. TW9: Rich 56Na 109
Kew Gdns. 52Na 109
Kew Gdns. Rd. TW9: Kew 52Pa 109
KEW GREEN 52Qa 109
Kew Grn. TW9: Kew 51Pa 109
Kew Mdw. Path TW9: Kew 54Sa 109
(Clifford Av.)
TW9: Kew 53Ra 109
(Magnolia Ct.)
Kew Retail Pk. TW9: Kew 53Ra 109
Kew Riverside Pk. TW9: Kew 52Ra 109
Kew Rd. TW9: Kew 51Qa 109
TW9: Rich, Kew 56Na 109
Keybridge Ho. SW8 51Nb 112
(off Miles St.)
Key Cl. E1 42Yb 92
Keyes Ho. SW1 7D 228
Keyes Rd. DA1: Dart 56Pd 119
NW2 36Za 68
Keyfield Ter. AL1: St A 3B 6
(not continuous)
Keyham Ho. W2 43Cb 89
(off Westbourne Pk. Rd.)
Key Ho. SE11 51Qb 112
Keymer Cl. TN16: Big H 88Lc 179
Keymer Rd. SW2 61Pb 134
Keynes Cl. N2 28Hb 49
Keynes Ct. SE28 45Xc 95
(off Attlee Rd.)
Keynsham Av. IG8: Wfd G 21Gc 53
Keynsham Gdns. SE9 57Nc 116
Keynsham Rd. SE9 57Mc 115
SM4: Mord 74Db 155
Keynsham Wlk. SM4: Mord 74Db 155
Keys Ct. CR0: C'don 76Tb 157
(off Beech Ho. Rd.)
Keyse Rd. SE1 4K 231 (48Vb 91)
Keysham Av. TW5: Cran 53W 106
Keystone Cres. N1 2G 217 (40Nb 70)
Keywood Dr. TW16: Sun 65W 128
Keyworth Cl. E5 35Ac 72
Keyworth Pl. SE1 3C 230
Keyworth St. SE1 3C 230 (48Rb 91)
Kezia M. SE8 50Ac 92
Kezia St. SE8 50Ac 92
Khalsa Av. DA12: Grav'nd 9E 122
Khalsa Ct. N22 25Rb 51
Khama Rd. SW17 63Gb 133
Khartoum Pl. DA12: Grav'nd 8E 122
Khartoum Rd. E13 41Kc 93
IG1: Ilf 35Rc 74
SW17 63Fb 133
Khyber Rd. SW11 54Gb 111
Kia Oval 51Pb 112
Kibworth St. SW8 52Pb 112
Kidborough Down KT23: Bookh 99Ca 191
KIDBROOKE 54Kc 115
Kidbrooke Est. SE3 55Lc 115
Kidbrooke Gdns. SE3 54Jc 115
Kidbrooke Green Nature Reserve 55Lc 115
Kidbrooke Gro. SE3 53Jc 115
Kidbrooke La. SE9 56Nc 116
Kidbrooke Pk. Cl. SE3 53Kc 115
Kidbrooke Pk. Rd. SE3 53Kc 115
Kidbrooke Way SE3 54Kc 115
Kidderminster Pl. CR0: C'don 74Rb 157
Kidderminster Rd. CR0: C'don 74Rb 157
SL2: Slou 2E 80
Kidderpore Av. NW3 35Cb 69
Kidderpore Gdns. NW3 35Cb 69
Kidd Pl. SE7 50Nc 94
Kidman Cl. RM2: Rom 27Ld 57
Kidspace 79Qb 156
Kielder Cl. IG6: Ilf 23Vc 55
Kierbeck Bus. Complex E16 47Kc 93
(not continuous)
Kier Hardie Ho. RM16: Grays 6A 100
Kier Pk. SL5: Asc 9A 124
Kiffen St. EC2 5G 219 (42Tb 91)
Kilberry Cl. TW7: Isle 53Fa 108
Kilbrennan Ho. E14 44Ec 92
(off Findhorn St.)
KILBURN 40Bb 69
Kilburn Bri. NW6 39Cb 69
Kilburn Ga. NW6 40Db 69
Kilburn High Rd. NW6 38Bb 69
Kilburn Ho. NW6 40Bb 69
(off Malvern Pl.)
Kilburn La. W9 41Za 88
W10 41Za 88
Kilburn Pk. Rd. NW6 41Cb 69
Kilburn Pl. NW6 39Cb 69

Kilburn Priory NW6 39Db 69
Kilburn Sq. NW6 39Cb 69
Kilburn Vale NW6 39Db 69
Kilburn Vale Est. NW6 39Db 69
(off Kilburn Vale)
Kilby Cl. WD25: Wat 7Z 13
Kilby Ct. SE10 48Hc 93
(off Greenroof Way)
Kilcorral Cl. KT17: Eps 86Wa 174
Kildare Cl. HA4: Ruis 32Y 65
Kildare Ct. W2 44Cb 89
(off Kildare Ter.)
Kildare Gdns. W2 44Cb 89
Kildare Rd. E16 43Jc 93
Kildare Ter. W2 44Cb 89
Kildare Wlk. E14 44Cc 92
Kildonan Cl. WD17: Wat 11V 26
Kildoran Rd. SW2 57Nb 112
Kildowan Rd. IG3: Ilf 32Wc 75
Kilgour Rd. SE23 58Ac 114
Kilkie St. SW6 54Eb 111
Killarney Rd. SW18 58Eb 111
Killasser Ct. KT20: Tad 95Ya 194
Killburns Mill Cl. SM6: Wall 75Kb 156
Killearn Rd. SE6 60Fc 115
Killester Gdns. KT4: Wor Pk 77Xa 154
Killewarren Way BR5: Orp 72Yc 161
Killick Cl. TN13: Dun G 93Gd 202
Killick Ho. SM1: Sutt 77Db 155
Killick M. SM3: Cheam 79Ab 154
Killick St. N1 1H 217 (40Pb 70)
Killieser Av. SW2 61Nb 134
Killigarth Ct. DA14: Sidc 63Wc 139
Killigrew Ho. TW16: Sun 66U 128
Killip Cl. E16 44Hc 93
Killoran Ho. E14 48Ec 92
(off Galbraith St.)
Killowen Av. UB5: N'olt 36Ea 66
Killowen Cl. KT20: Tad 94Za 194
Killowen Rd. E9 37Zb 72
Killy Hill GU24: Chob 10J 147
Killyon Rd. SW8 54Lb 112
Killyon Ter. SW8 54Lb 112
Kilmaine Rd. SW6 52Ab 110
Kilmarnock Gdns. RM8: Dag 34Yc 75
Kilmarnock Pk. RH2: Reig 5K 207
Kilmarnock Rd. WD19: Wat 21Z 45
Kilmarsh Rd. W6 49Ya 88
Kilmartin Av. SW16 69Qb 134
Kilmartin Rd. IG3: Ilf 33Wc 75
Kilmartin Way RM12: Horn 36Kd 77
Kilmington Cl. CM13: Hut 19De 41
Kilmington Rd. SW13 51Wa 110
Kilmiston Av. TW17: Shep 72S 150
Kilmiston Ho. TW17: Shep 72S 150
Kilmore Ho. E14 44Dc 92
(off Vesey Path)
Kilmorey Gdns. TW1: Twick 57Ka 108
Kilmorey Rd. TW1: Twick 56Ka 108
Kilmorie Rd. SE23 60Ac 114
Kilmuir Ho. KT17: Eps 85Ua 174
(off Depot Rd.)
SW1 6J 227
Kiln Cl. UB3: Harl 51T 106
Kiln Cotts. HP2: Hem H 1B 4
Kiln Ct. E14 45Bc 92
(off Newell St.)
Kilncroft HP3: Hem H 4B 4
Kilndown DA12: Grav'nd 5F 144
Kilner Ho. E16 43Kc 93
(off Freemasons Rd.)
SE11 51Qb 112
(off Clayton St.)
Kilner St. E14 43Cc 92
Kilnfields BR6: Well H 79Cd 162
Kiln Ground HP3: Hem H 4A 4
Kiln La. GU23: Rip 96J 189
GU24: Bisl 9F 166
KT17: Eps 83Ua 174
SL2: Hedg 2G 60
SL4: Wink 5A 124
SL5: S'dale 1E 146
Kiln M. SW17 64Fb 133
Kiln Pl. NW5 36Jb 70
Kilns, The RH1: Mers, Redh 3B 208
Kilnside KT10: Clay 80Ja 152
Kiln Wlk. RH1: Redh 10A 208
Kiln Way HA6: Nwood 23U 44
RM17: Grays 50Be 99
Kilnwood TN14: Hals 85Bd 181
Kiln Wood La. RM4: Have B 22Fd 56
Kilpatrick Way UB4: Yead 43Aa 85
Kilravock St. W10 41Ab 88
Kilronan W3 44Ta 87
Kilross Rd. TW14: Bedf 60T 106
Kilrue La. KT12: Hers 77V 150
Kilrush Ter. GU21: Wok 88C 168
Kilsby Wlk. RM9: Dag 37Xc 75
Kilsha Rd. KT12: Walt T 72Y 151
Kilsmore La. EN8: Chesh 1Zb 20
Kilvinton Dr. EN2: Enf 10Tb 19
Kilworth Av. CM15: Shenf 16Ce 41
Kimbell Gdns. SW6 53Ab 110
Kimbell Pl. SE3 56Lc 115
Kimber Cl. SL4: Wind 5E 102
Kimber Ct. SE1 3H 231
(off Long La.)
Kimberley Av. E6 40Nc 74
IG2: Ilf 31Tc 74
RM7: Rom 30Ed 56
SE15 54Xb 113
Kimberley Cl. SL3: L'ly 49B 82
Kimberley Ct. NW6 39Ab 68
(off Kimberley Rd.)
Kimberley Dr. DA14: Sidc 61Zc 139
Kimberley Gdns. EN1: Enf 13Vb 33
N4 29Rb 51
Kimberley Ga. BR1: Brom 66Gc 137
Kimberley Ho. E14 48Ec 92
(off Galbraith St.)
Kimberley Ind. Est. E17 25Bc 52
Kimberley Pl. CR8: Purl 83Qb 176
Kimberley Ride KT11: Cobh 85Da 171
Kimberley Rd. AL3: St A 1A 6
BR3: Beck 68Zb 136
CR0: C'don 72Rb 157
E4 18Gc 35
E11 33Fc 73
E16 42Hc 93
E17 25Ac 52
N17 26Wb 51
N18 23Xb 51
NW6 39Ab 68
SW9 54Nb 112
Kimberley Wlk. KT12: Walt T 73X 151
Kimberley Way E4 18Gc 35
Kimber Pl. TW4: Houn 59Ba 107
(Conway Rd.)
TW4: Houn 56Ba 107
(Marryat Cl.)
Kimber Rd. SW18 59Cb 111
Kimbers Dr. SL1: Burn 1B 80
Kimble Cl. WD18: Wat 17U 26
Kimble Cres. WD23: Bush 17Ea 28
Kimble Ho. NW8 5E 214
Kimble Rd. SW19 65Fb 133
Kimblewick WD19: Wat 18Aa 27
Kimbolton Cl. SE12 58Hc 115
Kimbolton Ct. SW3 6D 226
Kimbolton Grn. WD6: Bore 14Sa 29
Kimbolton Row SW3 6D 226
Kimmeridge Gdns. SE9 63Nc 138
Kimmeridge Rd. SE9 63Nc 138
Kimps Way HP3: Hem H 5A 4
Kimpton Av. CM15: B'wood 17Xd 40
Kimpton Ho. SW15 59Wa 110
Kimpton Ind. Est. SM3: Sutt 75Bb 155
Kimpton Link Bus. Cen.
SM3: Sutt 75Bb 155
Kimpton Pk. Way SM1: Sutt 75Ab 154
SM3: Sutt 75Ab 154
Kimpton Pl. WD25: Wat 6Z 13
Kimpton Rd. SE5 53Tb 113
SM3: Sutt 75Bb 155
Kimptons Cl. EN6: Pot B 4Za 16
Kimptons Mead EN6: Pot B 5Za 16
Kimpton Trade & Business Cen.
SM3: Sutt 75Bb 155
Kinburn Dr. TW20: Egh 64A 126
Kinburn St. SE16 47Zb 92
Kincaid Rd. SE15 52Xb 113
Kincardine Gdns. W9 42Cb 89
(off Harrow Rd.)
Kincha Lodge KT2: King T 67Pa 131
(off Elm Rd.)
Kinch Gro. HA9: Wemb 31Pa 67
Kincraig Dr. TN13: S'oaks 96Jd 202
Kinder Cl. SE28 45Zc 95
Kinder Ho. N1 1G 219
Kinderscout HP3: Hem H 4A 4
Kindersley Ho. E1 44Wb 91
(off Pinchin St.)
Kindersley Way WD5: Ab L 3S 12
Kinder St. E1 44Xb 91
(not continuous)
Kinderton Cl. N14 18Lb 32
Kinefold Ho. N7 37Nb 70
(off York Way Est.)
Kinetic Bus. Cen. WD6: Bore 13Qa 29
Kinetic Cres. EN3: Enf L 8Bc 20
Kinfauns Av. RM11: Horn 30Ld 57
Kinfauns Rd. IG3: Ilf 32Wc 75
SW2 61Qb 134
Kingaby Gdns. RM13: Rain 38Jd 76
King Acre Ct. TW18: Staines 62G 126
King Alfred Av. SE6 63Cc 136
(not continuous)
King Alfred Rd. RM3: Hrld W 26Pd 57
King & Queen Cl. SE9 63Nc 138
King & Queen St. SE17 6E 230 (50Sb 91)
King & Queen Wharf SE16 45Zb 92
King Arthur Cl. SE15 52Yb 114
King Arthur Ct. EN8: Chesh 3Ac 20
King Charles I Island WC2 6F 223
King Charles Ct. SE17 51Rb 113
(off Royal Rd.)
King Charles Cres. KT5: Surb 73Pa 153
King Charles Ho. SW6 52Db 111
(off Wandon Rd.)
King Charles Rd. KT5: Surb 71Pa 153
WD7: Shenl 4Na 15
King Charles's Ct. SE10 51Ec 114
(off Park Row)
King Charles St. SW1 1E 228 (47Mb 90)
King Charles Ter. E1 45Xb 91
(off Sovereign Cl.)
King Charles Wlk. SW19 60Ab 110
King Ct. E10 31Dc 72
Kingcup Cl. CR0: C'don 73Zb 158
Kingcup Dr. GU24: Bisl 7E 166
King David La. E1 45Yb 92
Kingdom St. W2 1A 220 (43Eb 89)
Kingdom Way UB8: Cowl 43M 83
Kingdon Ho. E14 48Ec 92
(off Galbraith St.)
Kingdon Rd. NW6 37Cb 69
King Edward III M. SE16 47Xb 91
King Edward VII Av. SL4: Wind 2J 103
King Edward Av. DA1: Dart 58Md 119
RM13: Rain 40Md 77
King Edward Bldg. EC1 2C 224
King Edward Ct. HA9: Wemb 36Na 67
(off Elm Rd.)
King Edward Ct. Shop. Cen.
SL4: Wind 3H 103
King Edward Dr. KT9: Chess 76Na 153
RM16: Grays 7A 100
King Edward Ho. WD23: Bush 14Ba 27
King Edward Mans. E8 39Xb 71
(off Mare St.)
King Edward M. SW13 53Wa 110
King Edward Pl. WD23: Bush 14Ba 27
King Edward Rd. CM14: B'wood 20Yd 40
DA9: Ghithe 57Wd 120
(not continuous)
E10 32Ec 72
E17 27Ac 52
EN5: New Bar 14Cb 31
EN8: Walt C 5Ac 20
RM1: Rom 30Hd 56
SS17: Stan H 3M 101
WD7: Shenl 5Pa 15
WD19: Wat 16Aa 27
King Edward's Gdns. W3 46Qa 87
King Edwards Gro. TW11: Tedd 65Ka 130
King Edwards Mans. SW6 52Cb 111
(off Fulham Rd.)
King Edward's Pl. W3 46Qa 87
King Edwards Rd. E9 39Xb 71
EN3: Pond E 14Zb 34
HA4: Ruis 32T 64
IG11: Bark 39Tc 74
N9 17Xb 33
King Edward St. EC1 2D 224 (44Sb 91)
HP3: Hem H 6L 3
SL1: Slou 7H 81
King Edward Wlk.
SE1 3A 230 (48Qb 90)
KINGFIELD 92C 188
Kingfield Cl. GU22: Wok 92B 188
Kingfield Dr. GU22: Wok 92B 188
Kingfield Gdns. GU22: Wok 92B 188
KINGFIELD GREEN 92B 188
Kingfield Grn. GU22: Wok 92B 188
Kingfield Rd. GU22: Wok 92A 188
W5 42Ma 87
Kingfield Stadium 92B 188
Kingfield St. E14 49Ec 92
Kingfisher Av. E11 30Kc 53
Kingfisher Cl. BR5: St P 70Zc 139
CM13: Hut 17Ce 41
HA3: Hrw W 24Ha 46
HA6: Nwood 25R 44
KT12: Hers 78Aa 151
KT22: Lea 92La 192
SE28 45Yc 95
Kingfisher Ct. CR0: C'don 76Sb 157
(off Wandle Rd.)
E14 47Ec 92
(off River Barge Cl.)
EN2: Enf 10Pb 18
GU21: Wok 89A 168
(off Vale Farm Rd.)
GU21: Wok 86E 168
(Woodlands Ho.)
KT8: E Mos 70Ga 130
SE1 2E 230
SL2: Slou 2F 80
SM1: Sutt 78Bb 155
SW19 61Za 132
TN15: W King 80Ud 164
TW3: Houn 57Da 107
TW7: Isle 54Fa 108
Kingfisher Dr. DA9: Ghithe 57Wd 120
HP3: Hem H 7P 3
RH1: Redh 3A 208
TW10: Ham 63Ka 130
TW18: Staines 63H 127
Kingfisher Gdns. CR2: Sels 83Zb 178
Kingfisher Hgts. E16 46Lc 93
(off Branwell Way)
RM17: Grays 50Ce 99
Kingfisher Ho. SW18 55Eb 111
W14 48Bb 89
(off Melbury Rd.)
Kingfisher Leisure Cen. 68Na 131
Kingfisher Lure WD3: Loud 14K 25
WD4: K Lan 1R 12
Kingfisher M. SE13 56Cc 114
Kingfisher Pl. DA4: S Dar 68Sd 142
N22 26Pb 50
Kingfisher Rd. RM14: Upm 32Vd 78
Kingfishers, The UB9: Den 30J 43
(off Patrons Way E.)
Kingfisher Sq. SE8 51Bc 114
(off Clyde St.)
Kingfisher St. E6 43Nc 94
Kingfisher Wlk. NW9 26Ua 48
Kingfisher Way BR3: Beck 71Zb 158
NW10 37Ta 67
King Frederick IX Twr. SE16 48Bc 92
King Gdns. CR0: Wadd 78Rb 157
King George IV Ct. SE17 7F 231
(off Dawes St.)
King George VI Av. CR4: Mitc 70Hb 133
RM18: E Til 9K 101
TN16: Big H 88Mc 179
King George VI Memorial 7D 222
King George Av. E16 44Lc 93
IG2: Ilf 29Tc 54
KT12: Walt T 74Z 151
WD23: Bush 16Da 27
King George Cl. RM7: Mawney 27Ed 56
TW16: Sun 64U 128
King George Cres. HA0: Wemb 36Ma 67
King George M. SW17 64Hb 133
King George Rd. EN9: Walt A 6Ec 20
King George's Av. WD18: Wat 15U 26
King George's Dr. KT15: New H 82J 169
UB1: S'hall 43Ba 85
King George Sq. TW10: Rich 58Pa 109
King Georges Rd. CM15: Pil H 16Xd 40
King George's Sailing Club 16Cc 34
King George's Trad. Est.
KT9: Chess 77Qa 153
King George St. SE10 52Ec 114
Kingham Cl. SW18 59Eb 111
W11 47Ab 88
King Harold Ct. EN9: Walt A 5Ec 20
(off Sun St.)
King Harolds Way DA7: Belv, Bex 52Zc 117
DA17: Belv 52Zc 117
King Harry La. AL3: St A 3N 5
King Harry St. HP2: Hem H 3M 3
King Henry Ct. EN9: Walt A 8Ec 20
King Henry M. BR6: Chels 78Vc 161
HA2: Harr 32Ga 66
King Henry's Dr. CR0: New Ad 81Dc 178
King Henry's M. EN3: Enf L 9Cc 20
(off Shepley M.)
King Henry's Reach W6 51Ya 110
King Henry's Rd. KT1: King T 69Ra 131
NW3 38Gb 69
King Henry's Stairs E1 46Xb 91
King Henry St. N16 36Ub 71
King Henrys Wlk. CM16: Epp 1Xc 23
(off Boleyn Row)
N1 37Ub 71
King Henry Ter. E1 45Xb 91
(off Sovereign Cl.)
Kinghorn St. EC1 7C 218 (43Sb 91)
King Ho. W12 44Xa 88
Kingisholt Ct. NW10 41Za 88
(off Wellington Rd.)
King James' Av. EN6: Cuff 1Nb 18
King James Ct. SE1 2C 230
King James St. SE1 2C 230 (47Rb 91)
King John Ct. EC2 5J 219 (42Ub 91)
King John La. TW19: Wray 7P 103
King John's Cl. TW19: Wray 7P 103
King Johns Pl. TW20: Egh 64A 126
King John St. E1 43Zb 92
King John's Wlk. SE9 59Nc 116
Kinglake Ct. GU21: Wok 10J 167
Kinglake Est. SE17 7J 231 (50Ub 91)
Kinglake St. SE17 7H 231 (50Ub 91)
(not continuous)
Kinglet Cl. E7 37Jc 73
Kingley Pk. WD4: K Lan 1R 12
Kingly Ct. W1 4C 222
Kingly St. W1 3B 222 (44Lb 90)
Kings Acre RH1: S Nut 9F 208
Kingsand Rd. SE12 61Jc 137
Kings Arbour UB2: S'hall 50Aa 85
King's Arms All. TW8: Bford 51Ma 109
Kings Arms Ct. E1 43Wb 91
Kings Arms Yd. EC2 2F 225 (44Tb 91)
RM1: Rom 29Gd 56
Kingsash Dr. UB4: Yead 42Aa 85
Kings Av. BR1: Brom 65Hc 137
GU24: Brkwd 1B 186
HP3: Hem H 6P 3
IG8: Wfd G 23Kc 53
IG9: Buck H 19Mc 35
(Langfords)
IG9: Buck H 23Kc 53
(The Broadway)
KT3: N Mald 70Ua 132
KT14: Byfl 84M 169
N10 27Jb 50
N21 18Rb 33
RH1: Redh 8N 207
RM6: Chad H 30Bd 55
SM5: Cars 80Gb 155
SW4 60Mb 112
SW12 60Mb 112
TW3: Houn 53Da 107
TW16: Sun 64V 128
UB6: G'frd 43Da 85
W5 44Ma 87
WD18: Wat 14V 26
King's Bench St. SE1 1C 230 (47Rb 91)
King's Bench Wlk. EC4 3A 224 (44Qb 90)
King's Blvd. N1 2F 217 (40Nb 70)
Kingsbridge Av. W3 47Pa 87
Kingsbridge Cir. RM3: Rom 23Nd 57
Kingsbridge Cl. RM3: Rom 23Nd 57
Kingsbridge Ct. E14 48Cc 92
(off Dockers Tanner Rd.)
NW1 38Kb 70
(off Castlehaven Rd.)
Kingsbridge Cres. UB1: S'hall 43Ba 85
Kingsbridge Dr. NW7 24Za 48
Kingsbridge Rd. IG11: Bark 40Tc 74
KT12: Walt T 73X 151
RM3: Rom 23Nd 57
SM4: Mord 72Za 154
UB2: S'hall 49Ba 85
W10 44Ya 88
Kingsbridge Way UB4: Hayes 41U 84
Kingsbridge Wharf IG11: Bark 41Uc 94
Kingsbrook KT22: Lea 90Ja 172
KINGSBURY 29Ra 47
Kingsbury Av. AL3: St A 1A 6
Kingsbury Circ. NW9 29Qa 47
Kingsbury Cres. TW18: Staines 63F 126
Kingsbury Dr. SL4: Old Win 9L 103
KINGSBURY GREEN 30Ta 47
Kingsbury M. AL3: St A 1P 5
Kingsbury Rd. N1 37Ub 71
NW9 29Qa 47
Kingsbury Ter. N1 37Ub 71
Kingsbury Trad. Est. NW9 30Ta 47
Kingsbury Watermill Mus. 1P 5
Kings Chase CM14: B'wood 20Yd 40
KT8: E Mos 69Ea 130
Kings Chase Vw. EN2: Enf 12Qb 32
Kingsclere Cl. SW15 59Wa 110
Kingsclere Ct. N12 22Gb 49
Kingsclere Pl. EN2: Enf 12Sb 33
Kingscliffe Gdns. SW19 60Bb 111
Kings Cl. DA1: Cray 56Gd 118
E10 31Dc 72
HA6: Nwood 23V 44
HP8: Chal G 19A 24
KT7: T Ditt 72Ja 152
KT12: Walt T 74X 151
NW4 28Za 48
TW18: Staines 66M 127
WD4: Chfd 3K 11
WD18: Wat 14X 27
King's Club, The 65Ya 132
Kings Coll. Ct. NW3 38Gb 69
King's College London
Denmark Hill Campus 54Tb 113
Guy's Campus 1F 231
(within Guy's Hospital)
St Thomas' Campus -
Lambeth Pal. Rd. 4G 229
St Thomas' House 3H 229
Strand Campus 4J 223 (45Pb 90)
Waterloo Campus 7K 223 (46Qb 90)
Kings Coll. Rd. HA4: Ruis 30V 44
NW3 38Gb 69
King's College School of Medicine & Dentistry
54Sb 113
Kingscote Rd. CR0: C'don 73Xb 157
KT3: N Mald 69Ta 131
W4 48Ta 87
Kingscote St. EC4 4B 224 (45Rb 91)
Kings Ct. E13 39Kc 73
HA9: Wemb 33Ra 67
IG9: Buck H 19Mc 35
KT12: Walt T 76X 151
KT14: Byfl 83M 169
KT20: Tad 94Xa 194
N7 38Pb 70
(off Caledonian Rd.)
NW8 1F 215
SE1 1D 230 (47Rb 91)
W6 49Wa 88
Kings Ct. Mans. SW6 53Bb 111
(off Fulham Rd.)
Kings Ct. M. KT8: E Mos 71Fa 152
Kings Ct. Nth. SW3 50Gb 89
Kingscourt Rd. SW16 62Mb 134
Kings Ct. Sth. SW3 50Gb 89
(off Chelsea Mnr. Gdns.)
King's Cres. N4 34Sb 71
Kings Cres. Est. N4 33Sb 71
Kingscroft SW4 58Nb 112
Kingscroft Rd. KT22: Lea 92Ka 192
NW2 37Bb 69
SM7: Bans 87Fb 175
KING'S CROSS 1F 217 (40Nb 70)
King's Cross Bri. N1 3G 217
Kings Cross La. RH1: S Nut 8D 208
King's Cross Rd. WC1 3H 217 (41Pb 90)
Kingsdale Ct. DA10: Swans 58Ae 121
EN9: Walt A 6Jc 21
(off Lamplighters Cl.)
Kingsdale Gdns. W11 46Za 88
Kingsdale Rd. SE18 52Vc 117
SE20 66Zb 136
Kingsdene KT20: Tad 93Xa 194
Kingsdown Av. CR2: S Croy 82Rb 177
W3 45Ua 88
W13 47Ka 86
Kingsdown Cl. DA12: Grav'nd 10H 123
SE16 50Xb 91
(off Masters Dr.)
W10 44Za 88
Kingsdowne Rd. KT6: Surb 73Na 153
Kingsdown Ho. E8 36Wb 71
Kingsdown Point SW2 61Qb 134
Kingsdown Rd. E11 34Gc 73
KT17: Eps 85Wa 174
N19 33Nb 70
SM3: Cheam 78Ab 154
Kingsdown Way BR2: Hayes 73Jc 159
Kings Dr. DA12: Grav'nd 2D 144
HA8: Edg 21Pa 47
HA9: Wemb 33Ra 67
KT5: Surb 73Qa 153
KT7: T Ditt 73Ka 152
KT12: W Vill 81V 170
TW11: Tedd 64Fa 130
Kingsend HA4: Ruis 32T 64
Kingsend Ct. HA4: Ruis 32U 64
KINGS FARM 2E 144
Kings Farm E17 25Dc 52
Kings Farm Av. TW10: Rich 56Qa 109
Kings Farm Rd. WD3: Chor 16F 24
Kingsfield SL4: Wind 3B 102
Kingsfield Av. HA2: Harr 28Da 45
Kingsfield Bus. Cen. RH1: Redh 7A 208
Kingsfield Ct. WD19: Wat 17Z 27
Kingsfield Dr. EN3: Enf W 7Zb 20
Kingsfield Ho. SE9 62Mc 137
Kingsfield Rd. HA1: Harr 31Fa 66
WD19: Wat 17Z 27
Kingsfield Ter. DA1: Dart 57Md 119
HA1: Harr 32Fa 66
Kingsfield Way EN3: Enf W 7Zb 20
RH1: Redh 7A 208
Kingsford St. NW5 36Hb 69
Kingsford Way E6 43Pc 94
Kings Gdns. IG1: Ilf 32Tc 74
NW6 38Cb 69
RM14: Upm 31Ud 78
Kings Gth. M. SE23 61Yb 136
Kings Ga. KT15: Add 77K 149
Kingsgate AL3: St A 4P 5
HA9: Wemb 34Sa 67
Kingsgate Av. N3 27Cb 49
Kingsgate Bus. Cen. KT2: King T 67Na 131
(off Kingsgate Rd.)
Kingsgate Cl. BR5: St P 68Yc 139
DA7: Bex 53Ad 117
Kingsgate Est. N1 37Ub 71
Kingsgate Ho. SW9 53Qb 112
Kingsgate Mans. WC1 7H 217
Kings Ga. M. N8 29Pb 50
(off Spencer Rd.)
Kingsgate Pde. SW1 4C 228
Kingsgate Pl. NW6 38Cb 69
Kingsgate Rd. KT1: King T 67Na 131
KT2: King T 67Na 131
NW6 38Cb 69
Kings Grange HA4: Ruis 32V 64
Kings Grn. IG10: Lough 13Nc 36
Kingsground SE9 59Mc 115
Kings Gro. RM1: Rom 29Jd 56
SE15 52Xb 113
(not continuous)
Kings Hall Leisure Cen. 36Yb 72
Kingshall M. SE13 55Ec 114
Kings Hall Rd. BR3: Beck 66Ac 136
Kings Head Hill E4 17Dc 34
Kingshead Ho. NW7 21Xa 48
Kingshead La. KT14: Byfl 83M 169
Kings Head Pas. SW4 56Mb 112
(off Clapham Pk. Rd.)
Kings Head Theatre 39Rb 71
(off Upper St.)
King's Head Yd. SE1 7F 225 (46Tb 91)
King's Highway SE18 51Uc 116
King's Hill IG10: Lough 12Nc 36
Kingshill SE17 6D 230
Kingshill Av. HA3: Kenton 28Ka 46
KT4: Wor Pk 73Wa 154
RM5: Col R 23Ed 56
UB4: Hayes, Yead 41U 84
UB5: N'olt 41U 84
Kingshill Cl. UB4: Hayes 41W 84
Kingshill Ct. EN5: Barn 14Ab 30
Kingshill Dr. HA3: Kenton 26Ka 46
Kingshold Rd. E9 38Yb 72
Kingsholm Gdns. SE9 56Mc 115
Kings Ho. SW8 52Nb 112
(off Sth. Lambeth Rd.)
SW10 51Fb 111
(off King's Rd.)
King's Ho. Studios SW10 51Fb 111
(off Lamont Rd. Pas.)
Kingshurst Rd. SE12 59Jc 115
Kingside SE18 48Nc 94
Kingsingfield Cl. TN15: W King 80Ud 164
Kingsingfield Rd. TN15: W King 81Ud 184
Kings Keep BR2: Brom 68Gc 137
KT1: King T 70Na 131
SW15 57Za 110
KINGSLAND 37Ub 71
Kingsland EN6: Pot B 5Bb 17
NW8 1E 214 (39Gb 69)
Kingsland Grn. E8 37Ub 71
Kingsland High St. E8 37Vb 71
Kingsland Pas. E8 37Ub 71
Kingsland Rd. E2 3J 219 (41Ub 91)
E8 41Ub 91
E13 41Lc 93
HP1: Hem H 4J 3
Kingsland Shop. Cen. E8 37Vb 71
Kings La. GU20: W'sham 8C 146
SM1: Sutt 79Fb 155
TW20: Eng G 4L 125
WD4: Chfd 3J 11
KINGS LANGLEY 1Q 12
Kings Langley By-Pass
HP1: Hem H 4G 2
HP3: Hem H 4G 2
WD4: K Lan 7L 3
Kingslawn Cl. SW15 57Xa 110
Kingslea KT22: Lea 92Ja 192
Kingslee Ct. SM2: Sutt 80Db 155
Kingsleigh Cl. TW8: Bford 51Ma 109
Kingsleigh Pl. CR4: Mitc 69Hb 133
Kingsleigh Wlk. BR2: Brom 70Hc 137
(off Stamford Dr.)
Kingsley Av. DA1: Dart 57Qd 119
EN8: Chesh 1Xb 19
SM1: Sutt 77Fb 155
SM7: Bans 87Cb 175
TW3: Houn 54Ea 108
TW20: Eng G 5M 125
UB1: S'hall 45Ca 85
W13 43Ja 86
WD6: Bore 12Pa 29
Kingsley Cl. N2 29Eb 49
RM10: Dag 35Dd 76

Kingsley Ct. DA6: Bex ... 56Cd 118
HA8: Edg ... 20Ra 29
KT4: Wor Pk ... 75Va 154
(off The Avenue)
KT12: Walt T ... 76W 150
(off Ashley Pk. Rd.)
NW2 ... 37Xa 68
RM2: Rom ... 30Kd 57
Kingsley Dr. KT4: Wor Pk ... 75Va 154
Kingsley Flats SE1 ... 5H 231
Kingsley Gdns. E4 ... 22Cc 52
KT16: Ott ... 79F 148
RM11: Horn ... 28Md 57
Kingsley Gro. RH2: Reig ... 9J 207
Kingsley Ho. SW3 ... 51Fb 111
(off Beaufort St.)
W14 ... 49Ab 88
(off Avonmore Pl.)
Kingsley Mans. W14 ... 51Ab 110
(off Greyhound Rd.)
Kingsley M. BR7: Chst ... 65Rc 138
E1 ... 45Xb 91
W8 ... 48Db 89
Kingsley Path SL2: Slou ... 2B 80
Kingsley Pl. N6 ... 31Jb 70
Kingsley Rd. BR6: Chels ... 80Vc 161
CM13: Hut ... 17Fe 41
CR0: C'don ... 74Qb 156
E7 ... 38Jc 73
E17 ... 26Ec 52
HA2: Harr ... 35Ea 66
HA5: Pinn ... 28Ba 45
IG6: Ilf ... 25Sc 54
IG10: Lough ... 13Tc 36
N13 ... 21Qb 50
NW6 ... 39Bb 69
SW19 ... 64Db 133
TW3: Houn ... 53Da 107
Kingsley St. SW11 ... 55Hb 111
Kingsley Wlk. RM16: Grays ... 9C 100
Kingsley Way N2 ... 29Eb 49
Kingsley Wood Dr. SE9 ... 62Pc 138
Kings Lodge HA4: Ruis ... 32U 64
(off Pembroke Rd.)
N12 ... 23Eb 49
Kingslyn Cres. SE19 ... 67Ub 135
Kings Lynn Cl. RM3: Rom ... 23Md 57
Kings Lynn Dr. RM3: Rom ... 23Md 57
Kings Lynn Path RM3: Rom ... 23Md 57
Kings Mall W6 ... 49Ya 88
(not continuous)
Kingsman Dr. RM16: Grays ... 45De 99
Kingsman Pde. SE18 ... 48Pc 94
Kingsman Rd. SS17: Stan H ... 2K 101
Kings Mans. SW3 ... 51Gb 111
(off Lawrence St.)
Kingsman St. SE18 ... 48Pc 94
Kings Mead RH1: S Nut ... 8E 208
Kingsmead EN5: New Bar ... 14Cb 31
EN6: Cuff ... 1Nb 18
EN8: Chesh ... 1Zb 20
GU21: Wok ... 88C 168
KT13: Weyb ... 79T 150
TN16: Big H ... 88Mc 179
TW10: Rich ... 58Pa 109
Kingsmead Av. CR4: Mitc ... 69Lb 134
KT4: Wor Pk ... 75Xa 154
KT6: Surb ... 75Qa 153
N9 ... 18Xb 33
NW9 ... 31Ta 67
RM1: Rom ... 30Gd 56
TW16: Sun ... 68Y 129
Kingsmead Cl. DA15: Sidc ... 61Wc 139
KT19: Ewe ... 80Ta 153
TW11: Tedd ... 65Ka 130
Kingsmead Cotts. BR2: Brom ... 74Nc 160
Kingsmead Ct. N6 ... 31Mb 70
Kingsmead Dr. UB5: N'olt ... 38Ba 65
Kingsmead Ho. E9 ... 35Ac 72
SL1: Slou ... 6G 80
Kingsmead Lodge SM2: Sutt ... 79Fb 155
Kingsmead Mans. RM1: Rom ... 30Hd 56
(off Kingsmead Av.)
Kingsmeadow ... 69Qa 131
Kings Mdw. WD4: K Lan ... 10A 4
Kingsmeadow Athletics Cen. ... 69Qa 131
Kings Mdw. Ct. EN9: Walt A ... 6Jc 21
(off Horseshoe Cl.)
Kings Mead Pk. KT10: Clay ... 80Ga 152
Kingsmead Rd. SW2 ... 61Qb 134
Kingsmead Way E9 ... 35Ac 72
Kingsmere Cl. SW15 ... 55Za 110
Kingsmere Pk. NW9 ... 32Ra 67
Kingsmere Pl. N16 ... 32Tb 71
Kingsmere Rd. SW19 ... 61Za 132
Kings M. HP2: Hem H ... 1M 3
(off George St.)
IG7: Chig ... 19Sc 36
SW4 ... 57Nb 112
WC1 ... 6J 217 (42Pb 90)
Kingsmill NW8 ... 1C 214
Kingsmill Bus. Pk. KT1: King T ... 69Pa 131
Kingsmill Ct. AL10: Hat ... 2D 8
Kingsmill Gdns. RM9: Dag ... 36Bd 75
Kingsmill Ho. SW3 ... 7E 226
(off Cale St.)
Kings Mill La. RH1: Redh, S Nut ... 10C 208
Kingsmill Rd. RM9: Dag ... 36Bd 75
Kingsmill Ter. NW8 ... 1C 214 (40Fb 69)
Kingsnorth Ho. W10 ... 44Za 88
Kingsnympton Pk. KT2: King T ... 66Ra 131
Kings Oak RM7: Mawney ... 27Cd 56
WD3: Crox G ... 14Q 26
Kingsoak Ho. GU21: Wok ... 88C 168
King's Orchard SE9 ... 58Nc 116
King's Paddock TW12: Hamp ... 67Ea 130
Kings Pde. HA8: Edg ... 22Qa 47
(off Edgwarebury La.)
N17 ... 27Vb 51
NW10 ... 39Ya 68
SM5: Cars ... 76Hb 155
(off Wrythe La.)
SS17: Stan H ... 2L 101
(off King St.)
W12 ... 48Wa 88
WD18: Wat ... 15X 27
(off Vicarage Rd.)
Kings Pk. SL3: Coln ... 52F 104
Kingspark Bus. Cen.
KT3: N Mald ... 70Sa 131
Kingspark Ct. E18 ... 27Jc 53
Kings Pk. Ind. Est. WD4: K Lan ... 1R 12
Kings Pas. E11 ... 31Gc 73
KT1: King T ... 68Ma 131
KT2: King T ... 67Ma 131
Kings Place ... 1G 217 (40Nb 70)
Kings Pl. IG9: Buck H ... 19Lc 35
IG10: Lough ... 17Mc 35
SE1 ... 2D 230 (47Sb 91)
W4 ... 50Sa 87
King Sq. EC1 ... 4D 218 (41Sb 91)
Kings Quarter Apartments N1 ... 39Pb 70
(off Copenhagen St.)
King's Quay SW10 ... 53Eb 111
(off Chelsea Harbour Dr.)
Kings Reach Twr. SE1 ... 6A 224
Kings Ride Ga. TW10: Rich ... 56Qa 109
Kingsridge SW19 ... 61Ab 132
Kingsridge Gdns. DA1: Dart ... 58Md 119
Kings Rd. AL2: Lon C ... 8G 6
AL3: St A ... 2P 5
BR6: Orp ... 77Vc 161
CM14: B'wood ... 19Yd 40
CR4: Mitc ... 69Jb 134
E4 ... 18Fc 35
E6 ... 39Lc 73
E11 ... 31Gc 73
EN5: Barn ... 13Ya 30
EN8: Walt C ... 5Ac 20
GU21: Wok ... 88C 168
GU24: W End ... 6E 166
HA2: Harr ... 33Ba 65
HP8: Chal G ... 19A 24
IG11: Bark ... 38Sc 74
KT2: King T ... 66Na 131
KT6: Surb ... 74La 152
KT12: Walt T ... 75X 151
KT15: New H ... 82K 169
N17 ... 25Vb 51
N18 ... 22Wb 51
N22 ... 25Pb 50
NW10 ... 38Xa 68
RM1: Rom ... 29Jd 56
SE25 ... 69Wb 135
SL1: Slou ... 8J 81
SL4: Wind ... 4H 103
SL5: S'dale, S'hill ... 1B 146
SM2: Sutt ... 82Cb 175
SW3 ... 7E 226 (52Db 111)
SW6 ... 52Db 111
SW10 ... 52Db 111
SW14 ... 55Ta 109
SW19 ... 65Cb 133
TN16: Big H ... 88Lc 179
TW1: Twick ... 58Ka 108
TW10: Rich ... 58Pa 109
TW11: Tedd ... 64Fa 130
TW13: Felt ... 60Y 107
TW20: Egh ... 63C 126
UB7: W Dray ... 47P 83
UB8: Uxb ... 40M 63
W5 ... 43Ma 87
King's Scholars' Pas. SW1 ... 4B 228
King's Shade Wlk. KT19: Eps ... 85Ta 173
King Stable St. SL4: Eton ... 2H 103
King Stairs Cl. SE16 ... 47Xb 91
Kings Ter. NW1 ... 1B 216 (39Lb 70)
SL3: L'ly ... 51D 104
TW7: Isle ... 56Ja 108
Kingsthorpe Rd. SE26 ... 63Zb 136
Kingston Av. KT22: Lea ... 93Ka 192
KT24: E Hor ... 98U 190
SM3: Cheam ... 76Ab 154
TW14: Felt ... 58U 106
UB7: Yiew ... 45P 83
(Ash Gro.)
UB7: Yiew ... 46P 83
(Whitethorn Av.)
Kingston Bri. KT1: King T ... 68Ma 131
Kingston Bus. Cen. KT9: Chess ... 76Na 153
Kingston By-Pass KT3: N Mald ... 71Ua 154
KT6: Surb ... 76Ma 153
SW15 ... 63Ua 132
SW20 ... 68Wa 132
Kingston By-Pass Rd. KT6: Surb ... 75Ga 152
KT10: Hin W, Surb ... 75Ga 152
Kingston Cl. RM6: Chad H ... 27Ad 55
(not continuous)
TW11: Tedd ... 65Ka 130
UB5: N'olt ... 39Ba 65
Kingston Ct. DA11: Nflt ... 57De 121
Kingston Crematorium
KT1: King T ... 69Qa 131
Kingston Cres. BR3: Beck ... 67Bc 136
TW15: Ashf ... 64L 127
Kingston Gdns. CR0: Bedd ... 76Nb 156
Kingston Hall Rd. KT1: King T ... 69Ma 131
Kingston Hill KT2: King T ... 67Qa 131
Kingston Hill Av. RM6: Chad H ... 27Ad 55
Kingston Hill Pl. KT2: King T ... 63Sa 131
Kingston Ho. KT1: King T ... 70Ma 131
(off Surbiton Rd.)
NW1 ... 1C 216
(off Camden St.)
NW6 ... 38Ab 68
Kingston Ho. E. SW7 ... 2D 226
Kingston Ho. Est. KT6: Surb ... 72Ka 152
Kingston Ho. Gdns. KT22: Lea ... 93Ka 192
Kingston Ho. Nth. SW7 ... 2D 226
Kingston Ho. Sth. SW7 ... 2D 226
Kingstonian FC ... 69Qa 131
Kingston La. KT24: W Hor ... 99Q 190
TW11: Tedd ... 64Ja 130
UB7: W Dray ... 47P 83
UB8: Hil ... 41N 83
Kingston Lodge KT3: N Mald ... 70Ua 132
Kingston Mans. SW9 ... 53Pb 112
(off Clapham Rd.)
Kingston Pl. HA3: Hrw W ... 24Ha 46
Kingston Ri. KT15: New H ... 82J 169
Kingston Rd. EN4: E Barn ... 15Fb 31
IG1: Ilf ... 35Rc 74
KT1: King T ... 69Ra 131
KT3: N Mald ... 69Ra 131
KT4: Wor Pk ... 75Ra 153
KT5: Surb ... 75Ra 153
KT17: Ewe ... 81Va 174
KT19: Ewe ... 75Ra 153
KT22: Lea ... 90Ja 172
(not continuous)
N9 ... 19Wb 33
RM1: Rom ... 28Hd 56
SW15 ... 61Wa 132
SW19 ... 61Wa 132
(Roehampton Va.)
SW19 ... 48Bb 89
(Rothesay Av.)
SW20 ... 68Za 132
TW11: Tedd ... 64Ka 130
TW15: Ashf ... 65N 127
TW18: Staines ... 63H 127
UB2: S'hall ... 47Ba 85
Kingston Sq. KT22: Lea ... 91Ja 192
(off Buffers La.)
SE19 ... 64Tb 135
Kingston University
Kingston Hill Campus ... 64Ta 131
Knights Pk. Campus ... 69Na 131
Penrhyn Road Campus -
Penrhyn Rd. ... 70Na 131
Reg Bailey Building ... 69Ma 131
Roehampton Vale Cen. ... 62Va 132
KINGSTON UPON THAMES ... 68Ma 131
Kingston upon Thames (Park & Ride) ... 81La 172
Kingston upon Thames Art Gallery and Mus. ... 68Na 131
KINGSTON VALE ... 63Ua 132
Kingston Va. SW15 ... 63Ta 131
Kingstown St. NW1 ... 39Jb 70
(not continuous)
King St. DA12: Grav'nd ... 8D 122
E13 ... 42Jc 93
EC2 ... 3E 224 (44Sb 91)
KT16: Chert ... 74J 149
N2 ... 27Fb 49
N17 ... 25Vb 51
SS17: Stan H ... 2L 101
SW1 ... 7C 222 (46Lb 90)
TW1: Twick ... 60Ja 108
TW9: Rich ... 57Ma 109
UB2: S'hall ... 48Aa 85
W3 ... 46Sa 87
W6 ... 49Wa 88
WC2 ... 4F 223 (45Nb 90)
WD18: Wat ... 14Y 27
King St. Cloisters W6 ... 49Xa 88
(off King St.)
King St. Pde. TW1: Twick ... 60Ja 108
(off King St.)
Kingsville Ct. UB7: Yiew ... 45M 83
Kings Wlk. CR2: Sande ... 86Xb 177
RM17: Grays ... 51Ce 121
Kings Wlk. Shop. Cen.
SW3 ... 7F 227 (50Hb 89)
Kings Warren KT22: Oxs ... 83Ea 172
Kingswater Pl. SW11 ... 52Gb 111
Kings Way CR0: Wadd ... 78Pb 156
HA1: Harr ... 28Ga 46
Kingsway BR4: W W'ck ... 76Gc 159
BR5: Pet W ... 71Tc 160
EN3: Pond E ... 15Xb 33
EN6: Cuff ... 2Nb 18
GU21: Wok ... 10P 167
HA9: Wemb ... 35Na 67
IG8: Wfd G ... 22Lc 53
KT3: N Mald ... 70Ya 132
N12 ... 23Eb 49
SL0: Iver ... 44G 82
SL2: Farn C ... 7F 60
SL9: Chal P ... 27A 42
SW14 ... 55Ra 109
TW19: Stanw ... 60M 105
UB3: Hayes ... 43S 84
WC2 ... 2H 223 (44Pb 90)
Kingsway, The KT17: Ewe ... 83Ua 174
Kingsway Av. CR2: Sels ... 81Yb 178
GU21: Wok ... 10P 167
Kingsway Bus. Pk. TW12: Hamp ... 67Ba 129
Kingsway Cres. HA2: Harr ... 28Ea 46
Kingsway Est. N18 ... 23Zb 52
Kingsway Mans. WC1 ... 7H 217
Kingsway M. SL2: Farn C ... 7F 60
Kingsway Nth. Orbital Rd.
WD25: Wat ... 7V 12
Kingsway Pde. N16 ... 34Tb 71
(off Albion Rd.)
Kingsway Pl. EC1 ... 5A 218
Kingsway Rd. SM3: Cheam ... 80Ab 154
Kingsway Ter. KT13: Weyb ... 81Q 170
Kingswear Rd. HA4: Ruis ... 33W 64
NW5 ... 34Kb 70
Kingswell Ride EN6: Cuff ... 2Nb 18
Kingswey Bus. Pk. GU21: Wok ... 86E 168
Kings Wharf E8 ... 39Ub 71
(off Kingsland Rd.)
Kingswick Cl. SL5: S'hill ... 10C 124
Kingswick Dr. SL5: S'hill ... 10C 124
KINGSWOOD
KT20 ... 96Ab 194
WD25 ... 6X 13
Kingswood E2 ... 40Yb 72
(off Cyprus St.)
Kingswood Av. BR2: Brom ... 69Gc 137
BR8: Swan ... 70Hd 140
CR2: Sande ... 87Xb 177
CR7: Thor H ... 71Qb 156
DA17: Belv ... 49Bd 95
NW6 ... 39Ab 68
TW3: Houn ... 53Ba 107
TW12: Hamp ... 65Da 129
Kingswood Cl. BR6: Orp ... 73Uc 160
DA1: Dart ... 58Ld 119
EN1: Enf ... 15Ub 33
KT3: N Mald ... 72Va 154
KT6: Surb ... 73Na 153
KT13: Weyb ... 80R 150
N20 ... 17Eb 31
SW8 ... 52Nb 112
TW15: Ashf ... 64T 128
TW20: Eng G ... 3P 125
Kingswood Ct. E4 ... 22Cc 52
GU21: Wok ... 88A 168
KT20: Kgswd ... 96Ab 194
NW6 ... 38Cb 69
(off West End La.)
SE13 ... 58Fc 115
TN15: W King ... 80Ud 164
Kingswood Creek TW19: Wray ... 7P 103
Kingswood Dr. SE19 ... 63Ub 135
SM2: Sutt ... 81Db 175
SM5: Cars ... 74Hb 155
Kingswood Est. SE21 ... 63Ub 135
Kingswood Flds. Bus. Pk.
KT20: Kgswd ... 97Cb 195
Kingswood Golf Course ... 96Cb 195
Kingswood Grange
KT20: Lwr K ... 100Cb 195
Kingswood Hgts. E18 ... 25Jc 53
(off Queen Mary Av.)
Kingswood Ho. KT20: Kgswd ... 92Bb 195
SL2: Slou ... 3G 80
Kingswood La. CR6: W'ham ... 87Yb 178
Kingswood M. N15 ... 28Rb 51
Kings Wood Pk. CM16: Epp ... 1Xc 23
Kingswood Pk. CM16: Epp ... 1Xc 23
KT20: Kgswd ... 93Ab 194
N3 ... 26Bb 49
Kingswood Pl. CR3: Cat'm ... 95Vb 197
SE13 ... 56Gc 115
Kingswood Ri. TW20: Eng G ... 4P 125
Kingswood Rd. BR2: Brom ... 70Fc 137
E11 ... 31Gc 73
HA9: Wemb ... 34Qa 67
IG3: Ilf ... 32Wc 75
KT20: Tad ... 93Xa 194
SE20 ... 65Yb 136
SW2 ... 58Nb 112
SW19 ... 66Bb 133
TN13: Dun G ... 92Gd 202
W4 ... 48Sa 87
WD25: Wat ... 6X 13
Kingswood Ter. W4 ... 48Sa 87
Kingswood Way
CR2: Sande, Sels ... 85Yb 178
(not continuous)
SM6: Wall ... 78Nb 156
Kingsworth Cl. BR3: Beck ... 71Ac 158
Kingsworthy Cl. KT1: King T ... 69Pa 131
Kings Yd. SW15 ... 55Ya 110
(off Lwr. Richmond Rd.)
Kingthorpe Rd. NW10 ... 38Ta 67
Kingthorpe Ter. NW10 ... 37Ta 67
Kington Ho. NW6 ... 39Db 69
(off Mortimer Cres.)
Kingward Ho. E1 ... 43Wb 91
(off Hanbury St.)
King Wardrobe Apartments EC4 ... 3C 224
(off Carter La.)
Kingwell Rd. EN4: Had W ... 10Fb 17
Kingweston Cl. NW2 ... 34Ab 68
King William IV Gdns. SE20 ... 65Yb 136
King William Ct. EN9: Walt A ... 7Ec 20
(off Kendal Rd.)
King William La. SE10 ... 50Gc 93
King William's Ct. SE10 ... 51Fc 115
(off Park Row)
King William St. EC4 ... 3G 225 (44Tb 91)
King William Wlk. SE10 ... 51Ec 114
(not continuous)
Kingwood Rd. SW6 ... 53Ab 110
Kinlet Rd. SE18 ... 53Sc 116
Kinloch Dr. NW9 ... 31Ta 67
Kinloch St. N7 ... 34Pb 70
Kinloss Ct. N3 ... 28Bb 49
Kinloss Gdns. N3 ... 27Bb 49
Kinloss Rd. SM5: Cars ... 73Eb 155
Kinnaird Av. BR1: Brom ... 65Hc 137
W4 ... 52Ra 109
Kinnaird Cl. BR1: Brom ... 65Hc 137
SL1: Slou ... 4A 80
Kinnaird Way IG8: Wfd G ... 23Pc 54
Kinnear Apartments N8 ... 27Pb 50
Kinnear Rd. W12 ... 47Va 88
Kinnersley Wlk. RH2: Reig ... 10J 207
Kinnerton Pl. Nth. SW1 ... 2G 227
Kinnerton Pl. Sth. SW1 ... 2G 227
Kinnerton St. SW1 ... 2H 227 (47Jb 90)
Kinnerton Yd. SW1 ... 2G 227
Kinnoul Rd. W6 ... 51Ab 110
Kinross Av. KT4: Wor Pk ... 75Wa 154
Kinross Cl. HA3: Kenton ... 29Pa 47
HA8: Edg ... 19Ra 29
TW16: Sun ... 64V 128
Kinross Ct. BR1: Brom ... 67Hc 137
(off Highland Rd.)
SE6 ... 60Hc 115
Kinross Dr. TW16: Sun ... 64V 128
Kinross Ho. N1 ... 39Pb 70
(off Bemerton Est.)
Kinross Ter. E17 ... 26Bc 52
Kinsale Rd. SE15 ... 55Wb 113
Kinsella Gdns. SW19 ... 64Xa 132
Kinsham Ho. E2 ... 42Wb 91
(off Ramsey St.)
Kintore Way SE1 ... 5K 231 (49Vb 91)
Kintyre Cl. SW16 ... 68Pb 134
Kintyre Ct. SW2 ... 59Nb 112
Kintyre Ho. E14 ... 46Ec 92
(off Coldharbour)
Kintyre Pl. WD18: Wat ... 16V 26
(off Explorer Dr.)
Kinveachy Gdns. SE7 ... 50Nc 94
Kinver Ho. N19 ... 33Mb 70
Kinver Rd. SE26 ... 63Yb 136
Kipings KT20: Tad ... 93Za 194
Kipling Av. RM18: Tilb ... 3D 122
Kipling Cl. CM14: W'ley ... 22Xd 58
Kipling Ct. SL4: Wind ... 4F 102
W7 ... 45Ha 86
Kipling Dr. SW19 ... 65Fb 133
Kipling Est. SE1 ... 2G 231 (47Tb 91)
Kipling Ho. SE5 ... 52Tb 113
(off Elmington Est.)
Kipling Pl. HA7: Stan ... 23Ha 46
Kipling Rd. DA1: Dart ... 57Rd 119
DA7: Bex ... 53Ad 117
Kipling St. SE1 ... 2G 231 (47Tb 91)
Kipling Ter. N9 ... 20Tb 33
Kipling Twr. W3 ... 48Sa 87
(off Palmerston Rd.)
Kipling Towers RM3: Rom ... 24Kd 57
KIPPINGTON ... 98Jd 202
Kippington Cl.
TN13: S'oaks ... 96Hd 202
Kippington Dr. SE9 ... 60Mc 115
Kippington Rd.
TN13: S'oaks ... 96Jd 202
Kira Bldg. E3 ... 41Bc 92
Kiran Apartments E1 ... 43Vb 91
(off Chicksand St.)
Kirby Cl. HA6: Nwood ... 23V 44
IG6: Ilf ... 23Uc 54
IG10: Lough ... 17Nc 36
KT19: Ewe ... 78Va 154
RM3: Rom ... 22Qd 57
Kirby Est. SE16 ... 48Xb 91
Kirby Gro. SE1 ... 1H 231 (47Ub 91)
Kirby Ind. Est. UB7: Yiew ... 45M 83
Kirby Rd. DA2: Dart ... 59Td 120
GU21: Wok ... 9N 167
Kirby St. EC1 ... 7A 218 (43Qb 90)
Kirby Way KT12: Walt T ... 72Y 151
UB8: Hil ... 42P 83
Kirchen Rd. W13 ... 45Ka 86
Kirkby Cl. N11 ... 23Jb 50
Kirkcaldy Grn. WD19: Wat ... 20Y 27
Kirkcourt TN13: S'oaks ... 95Jd 202
Kirkdale SE26 ... 61Xb 135
Kirkdale Cnr. SE26 ... 63Yb 136
Kirkdale Rd. E11 ... 32Gc 73
Kirkeby Ho. EC1 ... 7K 217
Kirkfield Cl. W13 ... 46Ka 86
Kirkgate, The KT17: Eps ... 85Ua 174
Kirkham Ho. RM3: Rom ... 22Md 57
(off Montgomery Cres.)
Kirkham Rd. E6 ... 44Nc 94
Kirkham St. SE18 ... 51Uc 116
Kirk Ho. HA9: Wemb ... 34Na 67
Kirkland Av. GU21: Wok ... 8J 167
IG5: Ilf ... 26Qc 54
Kirkland Cl. DA15: Sidc ... 58Uc 116
Kirkland Dr. EN2: Enf ... 11Sb 33
Kirkland Ho. E14 ... 50Dc 92
(off St Davids Sq.)
E14 ... 50Dc 92
(off Westferry Rd.)
Kirkland Ter. BR3: Beck ... 65Cc 136
Kirkland Wlk. E8 ... 37Vb 71
Kirk La. SE18 ... 51Sc 116
Kirkleas Rd. KT6: Surb ... 74Na 153
Kirklees Rd. CR7: Thor H ... 71Qb 156
RM8: Dag ... 36Yc 75
Kirkley Rd. SW19 ... 67Cb 133
Kirkly Cl. CR2: Sande ... 81Ub 177
Kirkman Pl. W1 ... 1D 222
Kirkmichael Rd. E14 ... 44Ec 92
Kirk Ri. SM1: Sutt ... 76Db 155
Kirk Rd. E17 ... 30Bc 52
Kirkside Rd. SE3 ... 51Jc 115
Kirk's Place ... 43Bc 92
Kirkstall Av. N17 ... 28Tb 51
Kirkstall Gdns. SW2 ... 60Nb 112
Kirkstall Ho. SW1 ... 7K 227
Kirkstall Rd. SW2 ... 60Mb 112
Kirkstead Ct. E5 ... 35Zb 72
Kirksted Rd. SM4: Mord ... 74Db 155
Kirkstone NW1 ... 3B 216
Kirkstone Way BR1: Brom ... 66Gc 137
Kirk St. WC1 ... 6J 217
Kirkton Rd. N15 ... 28Ub 51
Kirkwall Pl. E2 ... 41Yb 92
Kirkwall Spur SL1: Slou ... 3J 81
Kirkwood Pl. NW1 ... 38Jb 70
Kirkwood Rd. SE15 ... 54Xb 113
Kirn Rd. W13 ... 45Ka 86
Kirrane Cl. KT3: N Mald ... 71Va 154
Kirtley Ho. SW8 ... 53Lb 112
Kirtley Rd. SE26 ... 63Ac 136
Kirtling St. SW8 ... 52Lb 112
Kirton Cl. RM12: Horn ... 37Ld 77
W4 ... 49Ta 87
Kirton Gdns. E2 ... 4K 219 (41Vb 91)
(not continuous)
Kirton Lodge SW18 ... 58Db 111
Kirton Rd. E13 ... 40Lc 73
Kirton Wlk. HA8: Edg ... 24Sa 47
Kirwyn Way SE5 ... 52Rb 113
Kitcat Ter. E3 ... 41Cc 92
Kitchen Ct. E10 ... 33Dc 72
Kitchener Av. DA12: Grav'nd ... 3E 144
Kitchener Cl. AL1: St A ... 3F 6
Kitchener Ho. SE18 ... 52Qc 116
SL9: Chal P ... 21A 42
Kitchener Rd. CR7: Thor H ... 69Tb 135
E7 ... 37Kc 73
E17 ... 25Dc 52
N2 ... 27Gb 49
N17 ... 27Ub 51
RM10: Dag ... 37Dd 76
Kite Ho. SE1 ... 49Xb 91
Kite Pl. E2 ... 41Wb 91
(off Warner Pl.)
Kite Yd. SW11 ... 53Hb 111
(off Cambridge Rd.)
Kitley Gdns. SE19 ... 67Vb 135
Kitsmead La.
KT16: Longc, Vir W ... 4N 147
Kitson Rd. SE5 ... 52Tb 113
SW13 ... 53Wa 110
Kitswell Way WD7: R'lett ... 5Ha 14
Kitters Grn. WD5: Ab L ... 3U 12
Kittiwake Cl. CR2: Sels ... 82Ac 178
Kittiwake Ct. SE1 ... 2E 230
(off Gt. Dover St.)
SE8 ... 51Bc 114
(off Abinger Gro.)
Kittiwake Pl. SM1: Sutt ... 78Bb 155
Kittiwake Rd. UB5: N'olt ... 41Z 85
Kittiwake Way UB4: Yead ... 43Z 85
Kitto Rd. SE14 ... 54Zb 114
KITT'S END ... 9Ab 16
Kitts End Rd. EN5: Barn ... 8Za 16
Kiver Rd. N19 ... 33Mb 70
Klea Av. SW4 ... 58Lb 112
Kleine Wharf N1 ... 39Ub 71
Klein's Wharf E14 ... 48Cc 92
(off Westferry Rd.)
Knapdale Cl. SE23 ... 61Xb 135
KNAPHILL ... 9H 167
Knapmill Rd. SE6 ... 61Cc 136
Knapmill Way SE6 ... 61Dc 136
Knapp Cl. NW10 ... 37Ua 68
Knapp Rd. E3 ... 42Cc 92
TW15: Ashf ... 63P 127
Knapton M. SW17 ... 65Jb 134
Knaresborough Dr. SW18 ... 60Db 111
Knaresborough Pl. SW5 ... 49Db 89
Knatchbull Rd. NW10 ... 39Ta 67
SE5 ... 54Rb 113
Knatts La. TN15: Knat, W King ... 83Td 184
KNATTS VALLEY ... 83Td 184
Knatts Valley Rd. TN15: Knat ... 79Sd 164
Knave Wood Rd.
TN15: Kems'g ... 89Nd 183
Knebworth Av. E17 ... 25Cc 52
Knebworth Cl. EN5: New Bar ... 14Db 31
Knebworth Ho. SW8 ... 54Mb 112
Knebworth Path WD6: Bore ... 14Ta 29
Knebworth Rd. N16 ... 35Ub 71
Knee Hill SE2 ... 49Xc 95
Knee Hill Cres. SE2 ... 49Xc 95
Kneller Gdns. TW7: Isle ... 58Fa 108
Kneller Ho. UB5: N'olt ... 40Z 65
(off Academy Gdns.)
Kneller Rd. KT3: N Mald ... 73Ua 154
SE4 ... 56Ac 114
TW2: Whitt ... 58Ea 108
Knevett Ter. TW3: Houn ... 56Ca 107
Knight Cl. RM8: Dag ... 33Yc 75
Knight Ct. E4 ... 18Ec 34
(off The Ridgeway)
N15 ... 29Ub 51
Knighten St. E1 ... 46Xb 91
Knighthead Point E14 ... 47Cc 92
Knight Ho. SE17 ... 6H 231
Knightland Rd. E5 ... 33Xb 71
Knightleas Ct. NW2 ... 37Ya 68
Knightleys Ct. E10 ... 32Ac 72
(off Wellington Rd.)

Knighton Cl. CR2: S Croy 81Rb 177
IG8: Wfd G 21Kc 53
RM7: Rom 30Fd 56
Knighton Dr. IG8: Wfd G 21Kc 53
Knighton Grn. IG9: Buck H 19Kc 35
Knighton La. IG9: Buck H 19Kc 35
Knighton Pk. Rd. SE26 64Zb 136
Knighton Pl. KT11: Cobh 88Aa 171
Knighton Rd. E7 34Jc 73
RH1: Redh 8A 208
RM7: Rom 30Ed 56
TN14: Otf 88Hd 182
Knighton Way La. UB9: Den 37K 63
Knightrider Ct. EC4 4D 224
Knightrider St. EC4 4C 224 (44Rb 91)
Knights Arc. SW1 2F 227
Knights Av. W5 47Na 87
KNIGHTSBRIDGE 2E 226 (47Gb 89)
Knightsbridge SW1 2E 226 (47Hb 89)
SW7 2E 226 (47Hb 89)
Knightsbridge Apartments, The
SW7 2F 227
Knightsbridge Ct. SL3: L'ly 49C 82
(off High St.)
SW1 2G 227
WD18: Wat 14U 26
Knightsbridge Cres.
TW18: Staines 65K 127
Knightsbridge Gdns. RM7: Rom 29Fd 56
Knightsbridge Grn. SW1 2F 227 (47Hb 89)
(not continuous)
Knightsbridge Way HP2: Hem H 1N 3
Knights Cl. E9 36Yb 72
KT8: W Mole 71Ba 151
SL4: Wind 3B 102
TW20: Egh 65F 126
Knightscote Cl. UB9: Hare 26M 43
Knights Ct. BR1: Brom 62Hc 137
KT1: King T 69Na 131
RM6: Chad H 30Ad 55
(off High Rd.)
WD23: B Hea 18Fa 28
Knights Cft. DA3: New A 76Be 165
(not continuous)
Knights Fld. DA4: Eyns 76Nd 163
Knights Grn. WD3: Chor 13G 24
Knights Hill SE27 64Rb 135
Knight's Hill Sq. SE27 63Rb 135
Knights Ho. SW8 52Nb 112
(off Sth. Lambeth Rd.)
SW10 52Eb 111
(off Hortensia Rd.)
W14 50Bb 89
(off Baron's Ct. Rd.)
Knights Mnr. Way DA1: Dart 57Pd 119
Knights Mead KT16: Chert 73K 149
Knights Orchard AL3: St A 2A 6
Knight's Pk. KT1: King T 69Na 131
Knights Pl. RH1: Redh 5A 208
SL4: Wind 4G 102
TW2: Twick 60Ga 108
Knights Ridge BR6: Chels 78Xc 161
Knights Rd. E16 47Jc 93
HA7: Stan 21La 46
Knights Wlk. RM4: Abr 13Xc 37
SE11 6B 230 (49Rb 91)
(not continuous)
Knights Way CM13: B'wood 20Ce 41
IG6: Ilf 23Sc 54
Knightswood GU21: Wok 10K 167
Knightswood Cl. HA8: Edg 19Sa 29
Knightswood Ct. N6 31Mb 70
Knightswood Ho. N12 23Eb 49
Knightswood Rd. RM13: Rain 40Jd 76
Knightwood Cl. RH2: Reig 8J 207
Knightwood Cres. KT3: N Mald 72Ua 154
Knipp Hill KT11: Cobh 85Ba 171
Knivet Rd. SW6 51Cb 111
KNOCKHALL 57Yd 120
Knockhall Chase DA9: Ghithe 57Xd 120
Knockhall Rd. DA9: Ghithe 58Yd 120
KNOCKHOLT 89Xc 181
Knockholt Cl. SM2: Sutt 82Db 175
Knockholt Main Rd. TN14: Knock 91Vc 201
KNOCKHOLT POUND 87Ad 181
Knockholt Rd. SE9 57Mc 115
TN14: Hals 86Bd 181
KNOCKMILL 84Vd 184
Knock Mill La. TN15: W King 85Wd 184
Knole 98Nd 203
Knole, The DA13: Ist R 6A 144
SE9 63Qc 138
Knole Cl. CR0: C'don 72Yb 158
Knole Ct. UB5: N'olt 41Y 85
(off Broomcroft Av.)
Knole Ga. DA15: Sidc 62Uc 138
Knole La. TN13: S'oaks 98Ld 203
Knole Park 97Md 203
Knole Pk. Golf Course 96Md 203
Knole Rd. DA1: Dart 59Jd 118
TN13: S'oaks 95Md 203
Knole Way TN13: S'oaks 97Ld 203
Knole Wood SL5: S'dale 4C 146
Knoll, The BR2: Hayes 75Jc 159
BR3: Beck 67Dc 136
HA1: Harr 32Ha 66
KT11: Cobh 85Ca 171
KT16: Chert 74H 149
KT22: Lea 93La 192
W13 43La 86
Knoll Ct. SE19 64Vb 135
(off Farquhar Rd.)
Knoll Cres. HA6: Nwood 26U 44
(not continuous)
Knoll Dr. N14 17Jb 32
Knolles Cres. AL9: Wel G 5D 8
Knoll Ho. NW8 40Eb 69
(off Carlton Hill)
Knollmead KT5: Surb 74Sa 153
Knoll Pk. Rd. KT16: Chert 74H 149
Knoll Ri. BR6: Orp 74Vc 161
Knoll Rd. DA5: Bexl 59Cd 118
DA14: Sidc 64Xc 139
SW18 57Eb 111
KNOLL RDBT. 93La 192
Knoll Rdbt. KT22: Lea 93La 192
Knolls, The KT17: Eps D 88Ya 174
Knolls Cl. KT4: Wor Pk 76Xa 154
Knollys Cl. SW16 62Qb 134
Knolly's Ho. WC1 5F 217
Knollys Rd. SW16 62Pb 134
Knolton Way SL2: Slou 4M 81
Knot Ho. SE1 7K 225
Knotley Way BR4: W W'ck 75Dc 158
Knottisford St. E2 41Yb 92
Knotts Grn. M. E10 30Dc 52
Knotts Grn. Rd. E10 30Dc 52
Knotts Pl. TN13: S'oaks 96Jd 202
Knowlden Ho. E1 45Yb 92
(off Cable St.)
Knowle, The KT20: Tad 93Ya 194
Knowle Academy Sports Cen. 93Nd 203
Knowle Av. DA7: Bex 52Ad 117
Knowle Cl. SW9 55Qb 112
Knowledge Ct. SW16 69Pb 134
Knowle Gdns. KT14: W Byf 85H 169
KNOWLE GREEN 64K 127
Knowle Grn. TW18: Staines 64J 127
Knowle Gro. GU25: Vir W 3N 147
Knowle Gro. Cl. GU25: Vir W 3N 147
KNOWLE HILL 3N 147
Knowle Hill GU25: Vir W 3M 147
Knowle Lodge CR3: Cat'm 95Wb 197
Knowle Pk. KT11: Cobh 88Aa 171
Knowle Pk. Av. TW18: Staines 65K 127
Knowle Rd. BR2: Brom 75Pc 160
TW2: Twick 60Ga 108
Knowles Cl. UB7: Yiew 46N 83
Knowles Ct. HA1: Harr 30Ha 46
(off Gayton Rd.)
Knowles Hill Cres. SE13 57Fc 115
Knowles Ho. SW18 58Db 111
(off Neville Gill Cl.)
Knowles Wlk. SW4 55Lb 112
Knowles Wharf NW1 39Lb 70
(off St Pancras Way)
Knowl Hill GU22: Wok 91D 188
Knowl Pk. WD6: E'tree 15Na 29
Knowlton Cotts.
RM15: S Ock 43Yd 98
Knowlton Grn. BR2: Brom 71Hc 159
Knowlton Ho. SW9 53Qb 112
(off Cowley Rd.)
Knowl Way WD6: E'tree 15Pa 29
Knowsley Av. UB1: S'hall 46Da 85
Knowsley Rd. SW11 54Hb 111
Knox Ct. SW4 54Nb 112
Knox Rd. E7 37Hc 73
Knox St. W1 7F 215 (43Hb 89)
Knoyle Ho. W14 48Ab 88
(off Russell Rd.)
Knoyle St. SE14 51Ac 114
Knutsford Av. WD24: Wat 10Z 13
Koblenz Ho. N8 27Nb 50
(off Newland Rd.)
Kohat Rd. SW19 64Db 133
Koh-I-Noor Av. WD23: Bush 16Ca 27
Kola Ct. SL2: Slou 4M 81
Koonowla Cl. TN16: Big H 87Mc 179
Kooringa CR6: W'ham 91Xb 197
Korda Cl. TW17: Shep 69P 127
Korea Cotts. KT11: Cobh 88Z 171
Kossuth St. SE10 50Gc 93
Kotan Dr. TW18: Staines 63E 126
Kotree Way SE1 49Wb 91
Kramer M. SW5 50Cb 89
Kreedman Wlk. E8 36Wb 71
Kreisel Wlk. TW9: Kew 51Pa 109
Kristina Ct. SM2: Sutt 79Cb 155
(off Overton Rd.)
Krupnik Pl. EC2 5J 219
Kuala Gdns. SW16 67Pb 134
Kubrick Bus. Est. E7 35Kc 73
(off Station App.)
Kuhn Way E7 36Jc 73
Kurdish Mus. 49Wa 88
Kwame Ho. E16 45Rc 94
(off University Way)
Kwesi M. SE27 64Qb 134
Kydbrook Cl. BR5: Pet W 73Sc 160
Kyle Ho. NW6 39Cb 69
Kylemore Cl. E6 40Mc 73
Kylemore Rd. NW6 38Cb 69
Kylestrome Ho. SW1 6J 227
Kymberley Rd. HA1: Harr 30Ga 46
Kyme Rd. RM11: Horn 30Hd 56
Kynes Ct. HA2: Harr 33Fa 66
Kynance Cl. RM3: Rom 21Ld 57
Kynance Gdns. HA7: Stan 25La 46
Kynance M. SW7 4A 226 (48Db 89)
Kynance Pl. SW7 4A 226 (48Eb 89)
Kynaston Av. CR7: Thor H 71Sb 157
N16 34Vb 71
Kynaston Cl. HA3: Hrw W 24Fa 46
Kynaston Ct. CR3: Cat'm 97Ub 197
Kynaston Cres. CR7: Thor H 71Sb 157
Kynaston Rd. BR1: Brom 64Jc 137
BR5: Orp 73Xc 161
CR7: Thor H 71Sb 157
EN2: Enf 11Tb 33
N16 34Ub 71
Kynaston Wood HA3: Hrw W 24Fa 46
Kynersley Cl. SM5: Cars 76Hb 155
Kynoch Ct. SS17: Stan H 2N 101
Kynoch Rd. N18 21Yb 52
Kyrkly Ct. RM19: Purf 50Rd 97
(off Linnet Way)
Kyrle Rd. SW11 58Jb 112
Kytes Dr. WD25: Wat 5Z 13
Kytes Est. WD25: Wat 5Z 13
Kyverdale Rd. N16 31Vb 71

L

Laban Cen. 51Dc 114
(off Creekside)
Laban Wlk. SE8 51Dc 114
(off Copperas St.)
Laboratory Spa and Health Club, The
27Lb 50
Labour in Vain Rd.
TN15: Stans, Wro 85Zd 185
Laburnham Cl. EN5: Barn 13Bb 31
RM14: Upm 31Wd 78
Laburnham Gdns.
RM14: Upm 31Vd 78
Laburnum Av. BR8: Swan 69Ed 140
DA1: Dart 60Ld 119
N9 19Vb 33
N17 24Tb 51
RM12: Horn 33Jd 76
SM1: Sutt 76Gb 155
UB7: Yiew 45P 83
Laburnum Cl. E4 23Bc 52
EN8: Chesh 3Zb 20
HA0: Wemb 39Qa 67
N11 23Jb 50
SE15 52Yb 114
Laburnum Ct. E2 1K 219 (39Tb 71)
HA1: Harr 30Da 45
HA7: Stan 21La 46
Laburnum Ct. SE16 47Yb 92
(off Albion St.)
UB8: Uxb 37L 63
(off Harefield Rd.)
Laburnum Cres. TW16: Sun 67X 129
Laburnum Gdns. CR0: C'don 73Zb 158
N21 19Sb 33
Laburnum Gro. AL2: Chis G 7P 5
DA11: Nflt 59Fe 121
HA4: Ruis 30T 44
KT3: N Mald 68Ta 131
N21 19Sb 33
NW9 31Sa 67
RM15: S Ock 41Yd 98
SL3: L'ly 51D 104
TW3: Houn 56Ba 107
UB1: S'hall 42Ba 85
Laburnum Ho. BR2: Brom 67Fc 137
RM10: Dag 33Cd 76
Laburnum Lodge N3 26Bb 49
Laburnum Pl. SE9 57Qc 116
TW20: Eng G 5M 125
Laburnum Rd. CM16: Coop 1Yc 23
CR4: Mitc 68Jb 134
GU22: Wok 2P 187
KT16: Chert 74J 149
KT18: Eps 85Ua 174
SW19 66Eb 133
UB3: Harl 49V 84
Laburnums, The E6 42Nc 94
Laburnum St. E2 1K 219 (39Vb 71)
Laburnum Wlk. RM12: Horn 36Ld 77
Laburnum Way BR2: Brom 73Qc 160
TW19: Stanw 60P 105
Labyrinth Twr. E8 37Vb 71
(off Dalston Sq.)
Lacebark Cl. DA15: Sidc 59Vc 117
Lacewing Cl. E13 41Jc 93
Lacey Av. CR5: Coul 92Qb 196
Lacey Cl. N9 19Wb 33
TW20: Egh 66F 126
Lacey Dr. CR5: Coul 92Rb 197
HA8: Edg 21Pa 47
RM8: Dag 34Yc 75
TW12: Hamp 67Ba 129
Lacey Grn. CR5: Coul 92Qb 196
Lacey M. E3 40Cc 72
Lacine Ct. SE16 47Zb 92
(off Christopher Cl.)
Lackford Rd. CR5: Chip 90Hb 175
Lackington St. EC2 7G 219 (43Tb 91)
Lackland Ho. SE1 7K 231
Lackmore Rd. EN1: Enf 7Yb 20
Lacland Ho. SW10 52Fb 111
(off Worlds End Est.)
Lacock Cl. SW19 65Eb 133
Lacock Ct. W13 46Ja 86
Lacon Ho. WC1 7H 217
Lacon Rd. SE22 56Wb 113
Lacrosse Way SW16 67Mb 134
Lacy Rd. SW15 56Za 110
Ladas Rd. SE27 63Sb 135
Ladbroke Cotts. RH1: Redh 5A 208
(off Ladbroke Rd.)
Ladbroke Ct. RH1: Redh 4A 208
Ladbroke Cres. W11 44Ab 88
Ladbroke Gdns. W11 45Bb 89
Ladbroke Gro. RH1: Redh 5A 208
W10 42Za 88
W11 42Za 88
Ladbroke Gro. Ho. W11 45Bb 89
(off Ladbroke Gro.)
Ladbroke Grove Memorial 42Za 88
(off Canal Way)
Ladbroke M. W11 46Ab 88
Ladbroke Rd. EN1: Enf 16Vb 33
KT18: Eps 86Ta 173
RH1: Redh 5A 208
W11 46Bb 89
Ladbroke Sq. W11 45Bb 89
Ladbroke Ter. W11 45Bb 89
Ladbroke Wlk. W11 46Bb 89
Ladbrook Cl. BR1: Brom 65Gc 137
HA5: Pinn 29Ba 45
Ladbrooke Cl. EN6: Pot B 4Cb 17
Ladbrooke Cres. DA14: Sidc 62Zc 139
Ladbrooke Dr. EN6: Pot B 4Cb 17
Ladbrook Rd. SL1: Slou 8G 80
Ladbrook Rd. SE25 70Tb 135
Ladderstile Ride KT2: King T 64Ra 131
Ladderswood Way N11 22Lb 50
Ladds Way BR8: Swan 70Fd 140
Ladies Gro. AL3: St A 1P 5
(not continuous)
Ladlands SE22 59Wb 113
Lady Anne Ct. E18 25Jc 53
(off Queen Mary Av.)
Lady Astor Ct. SL1: Slou 7J 81
Lady Aylesford Av. HA7: Stan 22Ja 46
Lady Booth Rd. KT1: King T 68Na 131
Ladycroft Gdns. BR6: Farnb 78Sc 160
Ladycroft Rd. SE13 55Dc 114
Ladycroft Wlk. HA7: Stan 25Ma 47
Ladycroft Way BR6: Farnb 78Sc 160
Ladyday Pl. SL1: Slou 6G 80
Lady Dock Path SE16 47Ac 92
Lady Elizabeth Ho. SW14 55Sa 109
Ladyfern Ho. E3 43Cc 92
(off Gail St.)
Ladyfields DA11: Nflt 3B 144
IG10: Lough 14Sc 36
Ladyfields Cl. IG10: Lough 14Sc 36
Lady Florence Courtyard SE8 52Cc 114
(off Reginald Sq.)
Lady Forsdyke Way KT19: Eps 81Qa 173
Ladygate La. HA4: Ruis 30R 44
Ladygrove CR0: Sels 81Ac 178
Lady Harewood Way KT19: Eps 81Qa 173
Lady Hay KT4: Wor Pk 75Va 154
Lady Jane Ct. KT2: King T 68Pa 131
(off London Rd.)
Lady Margaret Ho. SE17 51Tb 113
(off Queen's Row)
Lady Margaret Rd. N19 35Lb 70
NW5 36Lb 70
SL5: S'dale 4D 146
UB1: S'hall 45Ba 85
Lady May Ho. SE5 52Sb 113
(off Pitman St.)
Lady Mdw. WD4: K Lan 9M 3
Lady Micos Almshouses E1 44Yb 92
(off Aylward St.)
Lady Sarah Cohen Ho. N11 23Hb 49
(off Asher Loftus Way)
Lady's Cl. WD18: Wat 14Y 27
Lady Shaw Ct. N13 19Pb 32
Ladyship Ter. SE22 59Wb 113
Ladysmith Av. E6 40Nc 74
IG2: Ilf 31Tc 74
Ladysmith Cl. NW7 24Wa 48
Ladysmith Rd. AL3: St A 1B 6
E16 41Hc 93
EN1: Enf 13Ub 33
(not continuous)
HA3: W'stone 26Ga 46
N17 26Wb 51
N18 22Xb 51
SE9 58Qc 116
Lady Somerset Rd. NW5 35Kb 70
Lady Spencer's Gro. AL1: St A 3A 6
Lady's Wlk. TN15: Igh, Ivy H 96Wd 204
Ladythorpe Cl. KT15: Add 77K 149
Ladywalk WD3: Map C 22G 42
LADYWELL 57Dc 114
Ladywell Arena (Running Track) 58Cc 114
Ladywell Cl. SE4 57Cc 114
Ladywell Hgts. SE4 58Bc 114
Ladywell Leisure Cen. 57Ec 114
Ladywell Rd. SE13 57Cc 114
Ladywell St. E15 39Hc 73
Ladywood Av. BR5: Pet W 71Uc 160
Ladywood Cl. WD3: Loud 13K 25
Ladywood Rd. DA2: Daren 64Ud 142
KT6: Surb 75Qa 153
Lady Yorke Pk. SL0: Iver H 37F 62
Laelia Ho's. AL1: St A 3E 6
LA Fitness
Aldgate 4K 225
Bayswater 45Db 89
(off Moscow Pl.)
Bloomsbury 7H 217
Burnham 4C 80
Croydon 80Qb 156
Edgware 23Qa 47
Epsom 77Ta 153
Ewell 84Ya 174
Finchley 27Db 49
Golders Green 31Bb 69
Goldsworth 9P 167
Gospel Oak 35Kb 70
Isleworth 55Ka 108
(off Swan St.)
Leadenhall 3J 225
London Wall 1F 225
Marylebone 7F 215 (43Hb 89)
Muswell Hill 28Kb 50
(off Hillfield Pk.)
New Barnet 14Fb 31
Northwood 26V 44
Novello 3H 223
Orpington 67Zc 139
Piccadilly 6D 222
Purley 82Sb 177
St Pauls 1D 224
Southgate 18Mb 32
South Kensington 5D 226 (49Gb 89)
Sydenham 63Yb 136
Victoria 3B 228
West India Quay 45Cc 92
Lafone Av. TW13: Felt 61Y 129
Lafone St. SE1 1K 231 (47Vb 91)
Lagado M. SE16 46Zb 92
Lagare Apartments SE1 1C 230
Lagham Pk. RH9: S God 9C 210
Lagham Rd. RH9: S God 10C 210
Laglands Cl. RH2: Reig 4L 207
Lagonda Av. IG6: Ilf 23Vc 55
Lagonda Ho. E3 42Cc 92
(off Tidworth Rd.)
Lagonda Way DA1: Dart 56Ld 119
Lagonier Ho. EC1 4E 218
Lagoon Rd. BR5: St M Cry 71Yc 161
Laguna Ct. AL1: St A 2C 6
(off Beaconsfield Rd.)
Laharna Trad. Est. WD24: Wat 10Y 13
Laidlaw Dr. N21 15Pb 32
Laing Cl. IG6: Ilf 23Tc 54
Laing Dean UB5: N'olt 39Y 65
Laing Ho. SE5 52Sb 113
Laings Av. CR4: Mitc 68Hb 133
Lainlock Pl. TW3: Houn 53Da 107
Lainson St. SW18 59Cb 111
Lairdale Cl. SE21 60Sb 113
Laird Av. RM16: Grays 47Fe 99
Laird Ho. SE5 52Sb 113
(off Redcar St.)
Lairs Cl. N7 36Nb 70
Lait Ho. BR3: Beck 67Dc 136
Laitwood Rd. SW12 60Kb 112
Lakanal SE5 53Ub 113
(off Sceaux Gdns.)
Lake, The WD23: B Hea 18Fa 28
Lake Av. BR1: Brom 65Jc 137
RM13: Rain 40Md 77
SL1: Slou 5H 81
Lake Bus. Cen. N17 24Wb 51
Lake Cl. KT14: Byfl 84M 169
RM8: Dag 34Zc 75
SW19 64Bb 133
Lakedale Ct. IG11: Bark 42Xc 95
Lakedale Rd. SE18 51Uc 116
Lake Dr. WD23: B Hea 19Fa 28
LAKE END 7A 80
Lake End Rd. SL4: Dor 5A 80
SL6: Dor R, Tap 5A 80
Lake Farm Country Pk. 46U 84
Lakefield Cl. SE20 66Xb 135
Lakefield Rd. N22 26Rb 51
Lakefields Cl. RM13: Rain 40Md 77
Lake Gdns. RM10: Dag 36Cd 76
SM6: Wall 76Kb 156
TW10: Ham 61Ka 130
Lakehall Gdns. CR7: Thor H 71Rb 157
Lakehall Rd. CR7: Thor H 71Rb 157
Lake Ho. SE1 2D 230
Lake Ho. Rd. E11 34Jc 73
Lakehurst Rd. KT19: Ewe 78Ua 154
Lakeland Cl. HA3: Hrw W 23Fa 46
IG7: Chig 21Xc 55
Lakeman Ho. SL9: Chal P 22B 42
Lakenheath N14 15Lb 32
Laker Ct. SW4 53Nb 112
Laker Ind. Est. BR3: Beck 64Ac 136
Lake Ri. RM1: Rom 26Hd 56
RM20: W Thur 49Wd 98
Lake Rd. CR0: C'don 75Bc 158
E10 31Dc 72
GU25: Vir W 1M 147
RM6: Chad H 28Zc 55
RM9: Dag 41Dd 96
SW19 64Bb 133
Laker Pl. SW15 58Ab 110
Lakers Ri. SM7: Bans 88Gb 175
Lakeside BR3: Beck 69Dc 136
EN2: Enf 14Mb 32
GU21: Wok 1J 187
KT2: King T 66Ra 131
KT13: Weyb 75U 150
KT19: Ewe 79Ua 154
N3 26Db 49
RH1: Redh 4A 208
RM13: Rain 40Nd 77
SM6: Wall 77Kb 156
W13 44La 86
Lakeside Av. IG4: Ilf 28Mc 53
SE28 46Wc 95
Lakeside Bus. Village
RM16: Chaf H 49Xd 98
(off Fleming Rd.)
Lakeside Cl. DA15: Sidc 57Yc 117
GU21: Wok 1J 187
HA4: Ruis 28T 44
IG7: Chig 21Vc 55
SE25 68Wb 135
Lakeside Ct. N4 33Sb 71
WD6: E'tree 15Qa 29
Lakeside Cres. CM14: B'wood 20Zd 41
EN4: E Barn 15Hb 31
Lakeside Dr. BR2: Brom 76Nc 160
GU24: Chob 5J 167
KT10: Esh 79Ea 152
NW10 41Pa 87
SL2: Stoke P 9J 61
Lakeside Grange KT13: Weyb 76S 150
Lakeside Ind. Est. SL3: Coln 51J 105
Lakeside Karting Cen. 47Xd 98
Lakeside Leisure Pk.
RM20: W Thur 49Wd 98
Lakeside Pk. KT16: Chert 74L 149
Lakeside Pl. AL2: Lon C 9H 7
Lakeside Retail Pk.
RM20: W Thur 49Wd 98
Lakeside Rd. N13 21Pb 50
SL0: Rich P 51J 105
SL3: Coln, Rich P 52H 105
W14 48Za 88
Lakeside Ter. EC2 7E 218
Lakeside Way HA9: Wemb 35Qa 67
Lakes Rd. BR2: Kes 78Lc 159
Lakestreet Grn. RH8: Limp 1J 211
Lakeswood Rd. BR5: Pet W 72Rc 160
Lake Vw. EN6: Pot B 5Eb 17
(not continuous)
HA8: Edg 22Pa 47
WD4: K Lan 10B 4
Lake Vw. Ct. SW1 3A 228
Lakeview Ct. SE28 45Xc 95
Lake Vw. Est. E3 40Ac 72
Lakeview Pk. RM3: Rom 20Ld 39
Lakeview Rd. TN13: S'oaks 95Jd 202
Lakeview Rd. DA16: Well 56Xc 117
SE27 64Qb 134
Lake Vw. Ter. N18 21Vb 51
(off Sweet Briar Wlk.)
Lakewood KT10: Esh 83Ba 171
Lakis Cl. NW3 35Eb 69
LALEHAM 69L 127
Laleham Abbey TW18: Lale 70L 127
Laleham Av. NW7 20Ta 29
Laleham Camping Site TW18: Lale 71L 149
Laleham Cl. TW18: Staines 67K 127
Laleham Ct. GU21: Wok 88A 168
SM1: Sutt 78Eb 155
Laleham Golf Course 70K 127
Laleham Ho. E2 5K 219
Laleham Pk. 70L 127
LALEHAM REACH 69J 127
Laleham Reach KT16: Chert 69J 127
Laleham Rd. SE6 59Ec 114
TW17: Shep 70P 127
TW18: Staines 64H 127
Lalor St. SW6 54Ab 110
Lalsham Ho. WD19: Wat 20Y 27
Lambarde Av. SE9 63Qc 138
Lambarde Dr. TN13: S'oaks 95Jd 202
Lambarde Rd. TN13: S'oaks 94Jd 202
Lambardes DA3: New A 76Be 165
Lambardes Cl. BR6: Prat B 83Yc 181
Lambard Ho. SE10 52Ec 114
(off Langdale Rd.)
Lamb Cl. AL10: Hat 1D 8
RM18: Tilb 4E 122
UB5: N'olt 41Aa 85
WD25: Wat 6Y 13
Lamb Ct. E14 45Ac 92
(off Narrow St.)
Lamberhurst Cl. BR5: Orp 74Zc 161
Lamberhurst Ho. SE15 51Yb 114
Lamberhurst Rd. RM8: Dag 32Bd 75
SE27 63Qb 134
Lambert Av. SL3: L'ly 48A 82
TW9: Rich 55Qa 109
Lambert Cl. TN16: Big H 88Mc 179
Lambert Cotts. RH1: Blet 5L 209
Lambert Ct. DA8: Erith 51Ed 118
(off Park Cres.)
WD23: Bush 14Z 27
Lambert Jones M. EC2 7D 218
Lambert Lodge TW8: Bford 50Ma 87
(off Layton Rd.)
Lamberton Ct. WD6: Bore 11Qa 29
(off Gateshead Rd.)
Lambert Rd. E16 44Kc 93
N12 22Fb 49
SM7: Bans 86Cb 175
SW2 57Nb 112
Lambert's Pl. CR0: C'don 74Tb 157
Lamberts Rd. KT5: Surb 71Na 153
Lambert St. N1 38Qb 70
Lambert Wlk. HA9: Wemb 34Na 67
Lambert Way N12 22Eb 49
LAMBETH 4H 229 (48Pb 90)
Lambeth Bri. SW1 5G 229 (49Nb 90)
Lambeth Crematorium
SW17 63Eb 133
Lambeth High St. SE1 6H 229 (49Pb 90)
Lambeth Hill EC4 4D 224 (45Sb 91)
Lambeth Palace 4H 229 (48Pb 90)
Lambeth Pal. Rd. SE1 4H 229 (48Pb 90)
Lambeth Rd. CR0: C'don 73Qb 156
SE1 5H 229 (49Pb 90)
SE11 5H 229 (49Pb 90)
Lambeth Towers SE11 4K 229
Lambeth Wlk. SE11 4K 229 (49Pb 90)
(not continuous)
Lambfold Ho. N7 37Nb 70
(off North Rd.)

Lamb Ho. *SE5* . . . *52Sb* ***113***
(off Elmington Est.)
SE10 . . . *51Ec* ***114***
(off Haddo St.)
Lambkins M. E17 . . . 28Ec **52**
Lamb La. E8 . . . 38Xb **71**
Lamble St. NW5 . . . 36Jb **70**
Lambley Rd. RM9: Dag . . . 37Xc **75**
Lambly Hill GU25: Vir W . . . 69A **126**
Lambolle Pl. NW3 . . . 37Gb **69**
Lambolle Rd. NW3 . . . 37Gb **69**
Lambourn Chase WD7: R'lett . . . 8Ha **14**
Lambourn Cl. CR2: S Croy . . . 81Rb **177**
NW5 . . . 35Lb **70**
W7 . . . 47Ha **86**
LAMBOURNE . . . 14Zc **37**
Lambourne RM18: E Til . . . 9L **101**
Lambourne Av. SW19 . . . 63Bb **133**
Lambourne Cl. IG7: Chig . . . 20Xc **37**
SL1: Burn . . . 10A **60**
Lambourne Ct. IG8: Wfd G . . . 24Lc **53**
UB8: Uxb . . . 39K **63**
Lambourne Cres. GU21: Wok . . . 85F **168**
IG7: Chig . . . 19Xc **37**
Lambourne Dr. CM13: Hut . . . 17Fe **41**
KT11: Cobh . . . 87Z **171**
LAMBOURNE END . . . 17Ad **37**
Lambourne Gdns. E4 . . . 19Cc **34**
EN1: Enf . . . 12Vb **33**
IG11: Bark . . . 38Vc **75**
RM12: Horn . . . 33Md **77**
Lambourne Golf Course . . . 7A **60**
Lambourne Gro. SE16 . . . 50Zb **92**
Lambourne Ho. NW8 . . . 7C **214**
Lambourne Pl. SE3 . . . 53Kc **115**
Lambourne Rd. E11 . . . 31Ec **72**
IG3: Ilf . . . 33Uc **74**
IG7: Chig . . . 21Vc **55**
IG11: Bark . . . 38Uc **74**
Lambourne Sq. RM4: Abr . . . 18Yc **37**
Lambourn Gro. KT1: King T . . . 68Ra **131**
Lambourn Rd. SW4 . . . 55Kb **112**
Lambrook Ho. SE15 . . . 53Wb **113**
Lambrook Ter. SW6 . . . 53Ab **110**
Lamb's Bldgs. EC1 . . . 6F **219** (42Tb **91**)
Lambs Bus. Pk. RH9: S God . . . 10P **209**
Lambs Cl. EN6: Cuff . . . 1Pb **18**
N9 . . . 19Wb **33**
Lamb's Conduit Pas.
WC1 . . . 7H **217** (43Pb **90**)
Lamb's Conduit St. WC1 . . . 6H **217** (42Pb **90**)
(not continuous)
Lambscroft Av. SE9 . . . 62Lc **137**
Lambscroft Way SL9: Chal P . . . 26A **42**
Lambs La. Ind. Est. RM13: Rain . . . 42Ld **97**
Lamb's La. Nth. RM13: Rain . . . 42Md **97**
Lamb's La. Sth. RM13: Rain . . . 43Kd **97**
Lambs Mdw. IG8: Wfd G . . . 26Mc **53**
Lamb's M. N1 . . . 1B **218** (39Rb **71**)
Lamb's Pas. EC1 . . . 7F **219** (42Tb **91**)
Lambs Ter. N9 . . . 19Tb **33**
Lamb St. E1 . . . 7K **219** (43Vb **91**)
Lamb's Wlk. EN2: Enf . . . 12Sb **33**
Lambton Av. EN8: Walt C . . . 5Zb **20**
Lambton Ho. SL4: Wind . . . 5E **102**
Lambton M. *N19* . . . *32Nb* ***70***
(off Lambton Rd.)
Lambton Pl. W11 . . . 45Bb **89**
Lambton Rd. N19 . . . 32Nb **70**
SW20 . . . 67Ya **132**
Lamb Wlk. SE1 . . . 2H **231** (47Ub **91**)
LAMDA . . . *50Za* ***88***
(off Talgarth Rd.)
LAMDA Theatre . . . *49Cb* ***89***
(off Logan Pl.)
Lamerock Rd. BR1: Brom . . . 63Hc **137**
Lamerton Rd. IG6: Ilf . . . 26Rc **54**
Lamerton St. SE8 . . . 51Cc **114**
Lamford Cl. N17 . . . 24Tb **51**
Lamington St. W6 . . . 49Xa **88**
Lamlash St. SE11 . . . 5B **230** (49Rb **91**)
Lamley Ho. *SE10* . . . *52Dc* ***114***
(off Ashburnham Pl.)
Lammas Av. CR4: Mitc . . . 68Jb **134**
SL4: Wind . . . 4G **102**
Lammas Cl. TW18: Staines . . . 62G **126**
Lammas Ct. SL4: Wind . . . 4G **102**
TW19: Staines . . . 61F **126**
Lammas Dr. TW18: Staines . . . 63F **126**
Lammas Grn. SE26 . . . 62Xb **135**
Lammas Hill KT10: Esh . . . 77Da **151**
Lammas La. KT10: Esh, Hers . . . 77Ba **151**
Lammas Pk. Gdns. W5 . . . 46La **86**
Lammas Pk. Rd. W5 . . . 47Ma **87**
Lammas Rd. E9 . . . 38Zb **72**
E10 . . . 33Ac **72**
SL1: Slou . . . 3B **80**
TW10: Ham . . . 63La **130**
WD18: Wat . . . 15Y **27**
Lammermoor Rd. SW12 . . . 59Kb **112**
Lamont Rd. SW10 . . . 51Fb **111**
Lamont Rd. Pas. *SW10* . . . *51Fb* ***111***
(off Lamont Rd.)
LAMORBEY . . . 60Vc **117**
Lamorbey Cl. DA15: Sidc . . . 60Vc **117**
Lamorna Av. DA12: Grav'nd . . . 1F **144**
Lamorna Cl. BR6: Orp . . . 73Wc **161**
E17 . . . 26Ec **52**
WD7: R'lett . . . 6Ka **14**
Lamorna Gro. HA7: Stan . . . 25Ma **47**
Lampard Gro. N16 . . . 32Vb **71**
Lampern Sq. E2 . . . 41Wb **91**
Lampeter Cl. GU22: Wok . . . 90A **168**
NW9 . . . 30Ua **48**
Lampeter Ho. *RM3: Rom* . . . *24Nd* ***57***
(off Kingsbridge Cir.)
Lampeter Sq. W6 . . . 51Ab **110**
Lamplighter Cl. E1 . . . 42Yb **92**
Lamplighters Cl. DA1: Dart . . . 58Pd **119**
EN9: Walt A . . . 6Jc **21**
Lampmead Rd. SE12 . . . 57Hc **115**
Lamp Office Ct. WC1 . . . 6H **217**
Lamport Cl. SE18 . . . 49Pc **94**
LAMPTON . . . 53Da **107**
Lampton Av. TW3: Houn . . . 53Da **107**
Lampton Ct. TW3: Houn . . . 53Da **107**
Lampton Ho. Cl. SW19 . . . 63Za **132**
Lampton Pk. Rd. TW3: Houn . . . 54Da **107**
Lampton Rd. TW3: Houn . . . 54Ca **107**
Lampton Sports Cen. . . . 54Ca **107**
Lamsey Rd. HP3: Hem H . . . 4M **3**
Lamson Rd. RM13: Rain . . . 42Hd **96**
Lanacre Av. NW9 . . . 25Ta **47**
Lanadron Cl. TW7: Isle . . . 54Ha **108**
Lanain Ct. SE12 . . . 59Hc **115**
Lanark Cl. W5 . . . 43La **86**
Lanark Ct. *UB5: N'olt* . . . *36Ca* ***65***
(off Newmarket Av.)
Lanark Ho. *SE1* . . . *50Wb* ***91***
(off Old Kent Rd.)
Lanark Mans. W9 . . . 5A **214**
W12 . . . *47Ya* ***88***
(off Pennard Rd.)
Lanark M. W9 . . . 4A **214** (41Eb **89**)
Lanark Pl. W9 . . . 5A **214** (42Eb **89**)
Lanark Rd. W9 . . . 4A **214** (40Db **69**)
Lanark Sq. E14 . . . 48Dc **92**
Lanata Wlk. *UB4: Yead* . . . *42Z* ***85***
(off Alba Cl.)
Lanbury Rd. SE15 . . . 56Zb **114**
Lancashire Ct. W1 . . . 4K **221**
Lancaster Av. CR4: Mitc . . . 71Nb **156**
E18 . . . 28Kc **53**
EN4: Had W . . . 10Eb **17**
IG11: Bark . . . 38Uc **74**
SE27 . . . 61Rb **135**
SL2: Slou . . . 2G **80**
SW19 . . . 64Za **132**
Lancaster Cl. BR2: Brom . . . 70Hc **137**
CM15: Pil H . . . 15Wd **40**
GU21: Wok . . . 88C **168**
KT2: King T . . . 64Ma **131**
N1 . . . 38Ub **71**
N17 . . . 24Wb **51**
NW9 . . . 24Va **48**
TW15: Ashf . . . 63N **127**
TW19: Stanw . . . 58N **105**
TW20: Eng G . . . 4P **125**
W2 . . . *45Db* ***89***
(off St Petersburgh Pl.)
Lancaster Cotts. TW10: Rich . . . 58Na **109**
Lancaster Ct. DA12: Grav'nd . . . 2E **144**
KT12: Walt T . . . 73W **150**
KT19: Ewe . . . 82Ta **173**
SE27 . . . 61Rb **135**
SM2: Sutt . . . *80Cb* ***155***
(off Mulgrave Rd.)
SM7: Bans . . . 86Bb **175**
SW6 . . . 52Bb **111**
TW19: Stanw . . . 60N **105**
W2 . . . 4A **220**
Lancaster Dr. E14 . . . 46Ec **92**
HP3: Bov . . . 9B **2**
IG10: Lough . . . 16Nc **36**
NW3 . . . 37Gb **69**
RM12: Horn . . . 36Kd **77**
Lancaster Gdns. BR1: Brom . . . 71Nc **160**
KT2: King T . . . 64Ma **131**
SW19 . . . 64Ab **132**
W13 . . . 47Ka **86**
Lancaster Ga. W2 . . . 5A **220** (45Eb **89**)
Lancaster Gro. NW3 . . . 37Fb **69**
Lancaster Hall *E16* . . . *46Jc* ***93***
(off Wesley Av.)
Lancaster House . . . 1C **228**
Lancaster Ho. E11 . . . 33Hc **73**
EN2: Enf . . . 11Tb **33**
RH1: Redh . . . 9N **207**
TW7: Isle . . . 52Ha **108**
Lancaster Lodge *W11* . . . *44Ab* ***88***
(off Lancaster Rd.)
Lancaster M. SW18 . . . 57Db **111**
TW10: Rich . . . 58Na **109**
W2 . . . 4A **220** (45Eb **89**)
Lancaster Pk. TW10: Rich . . . 57Na **109**
Lancaster Pl. IG1: Ilf . . . 36Sc **74**
SW19 . . . 64Za **132**
TW1: Twick . . . 58Ja **108**
TW4: Houn . . . 54Y **107**
WC2 . . . 4H **223** (45Pb **90**)
Lancaster Rd. AL1: St A . . . 1D **6**
E7 . . . 38Jc **73**
E11 . . . 33Gc **73**
E17 . . . 26Zb **52**
EN2: Enf . . . 11Tb **33**
EN4: E Barn . . . 15Fb **31**
HA2: Harr . . . 29Ca **45**
N4 . . . 31Pb **70**
N11 . . . 23Mb **50**
N18 . . . 22Vb **51**
NW10 . . . 36Wa **68**
RM16: Chaf H . . . 50Zd **99**
SE25 . . . 68Vb **135**
SW19 . . . 64Za **132**
UB1: S'hall . . . 45Aa **85**
UB5: N'olt . . . 37Ea **66**
UB8: Uxb . . . 37M **63**
W11 . . . 44Ab **88**
Lancaster Rd. Ind. Est.
EN4: E Barn . . . 15Fb **31**
Lancaster Stables NW3 . . . 37Gb **69**
Lancaster St. SE1 . . . 2B **230** (47Rb **91**)
Lancaster Ter. W2 . . . 4B **220** (45Fb **89**)
Lancaster Wlk. UB3: Hayes . . . 44S **84**
W2 . . . 5A **220** (46Eb **89**)
Lancaster Way KT4: Wor Pk . . . 73Xa **154**
WD5: Ab L . . . 3V **12**
Lancastrian Rd. SM6: Wall . . . 80Nb **156**
Lance Cft. DA3: New A . . . 75Be **165**
Lancefield Ho. SE15 . . . 56Xb **113**
Lancefield St. W10 . . . 41Bb **89**
Lancell St. N16 . . . 33Vb **71**
Lancelot Av. HA0: Wemb . . . 35Ma **67**
Lancelot Cl. SL1: Slou . . . 7E **80**
Lancelot Ct. BR6: Orp . . . 75Xc **161**
Lancelot Cres. HA0: Wemb . . . 35Ma **67**
Lancelot Gdns. EN4: E Barn . . . 17Jb **32**
Lancelot Pl. SW7 . . . 2F **227** (47Hb **89**)
Lancelot Rd. DA16: Well . . . 56Wc **117**
HA0: Wemb . . . 35Ma **67**
IG6: Ilf . . . 23Uc **54**
Lance Rd. HA1: Harr . . . 31Ea **66**
Lancer Sq. *W8* . . . *47Db* ***89***
(off Kensington Chu. St.)
Lancey Cl. SE7 . . . 49Nc **94**
Lanchester Ct. W2 . . . 3F **221**
Lanchester Rd. N6 . . . 29Hb **49**
Lanchester Way SE14 . . . 53Yb **114**
Lancing Gdns. N9 . . . 18Vb **33**
Lancing Ho. *CR0: C'don* . . . *77Tb* ***157***
(off Coombe Rd.)
WD24: Wat . . . *12Y* ***27***
(off Hallam Cl.)
Lancing Rd. BR6: Orp . . . 75Wc **161**
CR0: C'don . . . 73Pb **156**
IG2: Ilf . . . 30Tc **54**
RM3: Rom . . . 24Nd **57**
TW13: Felt . . . 61V **128**
W13 . . . 45Ka **86**
Lancing St. NW1 . . . 4D **216** (41Mb **90**)
Lancing Way WD3: Crox G . . . 15R **26**
Lancresse Cl. UB8: Uxb . . . 37M **63**
Lancresse Ct. *N1* . . . *39Ub* ***71***
(off De Beauvoir Est.)
Landale Gdns. DA1: Dart . . . 59Ld **119**
Landale Ho. *SE16* . . . *48Yb* ***92***
(off Lower Rd.)
Landau Ct. *CR2: S Croy* . . . *78Sb* ***157***
(off Warham Rd.)
Landau Way DA8: Erith . . . 50Md **97**
Landcroft Rd. SE22 . . . 57Vb **113**
Landells Rd. SE22 . . . 58Vb **113**
Lander Cl. DA12: Grav'nd . . . 3F **144**
Lander Rd. RM17: Grays . . . 50Fe **99**
Landford Cl. WD3: Rick . . . 19N **25**
Landford Rd. SW15 . . . 55Ya **110**
Landgrove Rd. SW19 . . . 64Cb **133**
Landin Ho. *E14* . . . *44Cc* ***92***
(off Thomas Rd.)
Landleys Fld. *N7* . . . *36Mb* ***70***
(off Long Mdw.)
Landmann Ho. *SE16* . . . *49Xb* ***91***
(off Rennie Est.)
Landmann Way SE14 . . . 50Zb **92**
Landmark Arts Cen. . . . 64Ka **130**
Landmark Commercial Cen. N18 . . . 23Ub **51**
Landmark East Twr. *E14* . . . *47Cc* ***92***
(off Marsh Wall)
Landmark Hgts. E5 . . . 35Ac **72**
Landmark Ho. *W6* . . . *50Ya* ***88***
(off Hammersmith Bri. Rd.)
Landmark Sq. E14 . . . 47Cc **92**
Landmark West Twr. *E14* . . . *47Cc* ***92***
(off Marsh Wall)
Landmead Rd. EN8: Chesh . . . 1Ac **20**
Landon Pl. SW1 . . . 3F **227** (48Hb **89**)
Landon's Cl. E14 . . . 46Ec **92**
Landon Wlk. E14 . . . 45Dc **92**
Landon Way TW15: Ashf . . . 65R **128**
Landor Ho. *SE5* . . . *52Tb* ***113***
(off Elmington Est.)
W2 . . . *43Cb* ***89***
(off Westbourne Pk. Rd.)
Landor Rd. SW9 . . . 55Nb **112**
Landor Theatre . . . 55Nb **112**
Landor Wlk. W12 . . . 47Wa **88**
Landra Gdns. N21 . . . 16Rb **33**
Landrake NW1 . . . 1C **216**
Landridge Dr. EN1: Enf . . . 10Xb **19**
Landridge Rd. SW6 . . . 54Bb **111**
Landrock Rd. N8 . . . 30Nb **50**
Landscape Rd. CR6: W'ham . . . 91Xb **197**
IG8: Wfd G . . . 24Kc **53**
Landsdown Cl. EN5: New Bar . . . 14Eb **31**
Landseer Av. DA11: Nflt . . . 62Fe **143**
E12 . . . 36Qc **74**
Landseer Cl. HA8: Edg . . . 26Qa **47**
RM11: Horn . . . 32Kd **77**
SW19 . . . 67Eb **133**
Landseer Ct. UB4: Hayes . . . 40T **64**
Landseer Ho. NW8 . . . 5C **214**
SW1 . . . 6E **228**
SW11 . . . 53Jb **112**
UB5: N'olt . . . *40Z* ***65***
(off Parkfield Dr.)
Landseer Rd. EN1: Enf . . . 15Wb **33**
KT3: N Mald . . . 73Ta **153**
N19 . . . 34Nb **70**
(not continuous)
SM1: Sutt . . . 79Cb **155**
Lands End WD6: E'tree . . . 16Ma **29**
Landstead Rd. SE18 . . . 52Tc **116**
Landulph Ho. SE11 . . . 7A **230**
Landward Ct. W1 . . . 2E **220**
Landway TN15: Seal . . . 92Pd **203**
Landway, The BR5: St P . . . 69Yc **139**
TN15: Bor G . . . 92Be **205**
TN15: Kems'g . . . 89Qd **183**
Lane, The GU25: Vir W . . . 69A **126**
KT16: Chert . . . 69J **127**
NW8 . . . 2A **214** (40Eb **69**)
SE3 . . . 55Jc **115**
Lane Av. DA9: Ghithe . . . 58Yd **120**
Lane Cl. KT15: Add . . . 78K **149**
NW2 . . . 34Xa **68**
LANE END . . . 63Td **142**
Lane End AL10: Hat . . . 3B **8**
DA7: Bex . . . 55Dd **118**
KT18: Eps . . . 86Ra **173**
SW15 . . . 58Za **110**
Lane End Dr. GU21: Knap . . . 9G **166**
Lane Gdns. KT10: Clay . . . 80Ha **152**
WD23: B Hea . . . 17Ga **28**
Lane M. E12 . . . 34Pc **74**
Lanercost Cl. SW2 . . . 61Qb **134**
Lanercost Gdns. N14 . . . 17Nb **32**
Lanercost Rd. SW2 . . . 61Qb **134**
Lanes Av. DA11: Nflt . . . 2B **144**
Lanesborough Ct. N1 . . . 3H **219**
Lanesborough Pl. SW1 . . . 1J **227**
Lanesborough Way SW17 . . . 62Fb **133**
Lanes Golf Course . . . 3K **81**
Laneside BR7: Chst . . . 64Rc **138**
HA8: Edg . . . 22Sa **47**
Laneside Av. RM8: Dag . . . 32Ad **75**
Laneway SW15 . . . 57Xa **110**
Laney Ho. EC1 . . . 7K **217**
Lanfranc Ct. HA1: Harr . . . 34Ha **66**
Lanfranc Rd. E3 . . . 40Ac **72**
Lanfrey Pl. W14 . . . 50Bb **89**
Langafel Cl. DA3: Lfield . . . 68Ae **143**
Langaller La. KT22: Fet . . . 94Da **191**
Langbourne Av. N6 . . . 33Jb **70**
Langbourne Ct. E17 . . . 30Ac **52**
Langbourne Mans. N6 . . . 33Jb **70**
Langbourne Pl. E14 . . . 50Dc **92**
Langbourne Way
KT10: Clay . . . 79Ja **152**
Langbrook Rd. SE3 . . . 55Mc **115**
Lang Cl. KT22: Fet . . . 95Da **191**
Langcroft Cl. SM5: Cars . . . 76Hb **155**
Langdale NW1 . . . 3B **216**
Langdale Av. CR4: Mitc . . . 69Hb **133**
Langdale Cl. BR6: Farnb . . . 76Rc **160**
GU21: Wok . . . 8N **167**
RM8: Dag . . . 32Yc **75**
SE17 . . . 51Sb **113**
SW14 . . . 56Ra **109**
Langdale Cres. DA7: Bex . . . 52Cd **118**
Langdale Dr. UB4: Hayes . . . 40U **64**
Langdale Gdns. EN8: Walt C . . . 7Zb **20**
RM12: Horn . . . 36Jd **76**
UB6: G'frd . . . 41Ka **86**
Langdale Ho. *SW1* . . . *50Lb* ***90***
(off Churchill Gdns.)
Langdale Lodge *WD3: Rick* . . . *17M* ***25***
(off Parsonage Rd.)
Langdale Pde. CR4: Mitc . . . 69Hb **133**
Langdale Rd. CR7: Thor H . . . 70Qb **134**
SE10 . . . 52Ec **114**
Langdale St. E1 . . . 44Xb **91**
Langdale Ter. WD6: Bore . . . 13Sa **29**
Langdale Wlk. *DA11: Nflt* . . . *2A* ***144***
(off Landseer Av.)
Langdon Ct. EC1 . . . 2C **218**
NW10 . . . 39Ua **68**
Langdon Cres. E6 . . . 40Qc **74**
Langdon Dr. NW9 . . . 32Sa **67**
Langdon Ho. *E14* . . . *44Ec* ***92***
(off Ida St.)
Langdon Pk. TW11: Tedd . . . 66La **130**
Langdon Pk. Leisure Cen. . . . 44Ec **92**
Langdon Pk. Rd. N6 . . . 31Lb **70**
Langdon Pl. SW14 . . . 55Sa **109**
Langdon Rd. BR2: Brom . . . 69Kc **137**
E6 . . . 39Qc **74**
SM4: Mord . . . 71Eb **155**
Langdons Ct. UB2: S'hall . . . 48Ca **85**
Langdon Shaw DA14: Sidc . . . 64Vc **139**
Langdon Wlk. SM4: Mord . . . 71Eb **155**
Langdon Way SE1 . . . 49Wb **91**
Langford Cl. AL4: St A . . . 1G **6**
E8 . . . 36Wb **71**
NW8 . . . 1A **214** (40Eb **69**)
W3 . . . 47Ra **87**
Langford Ct. NW8 . . . 2A **214**
Langford Cres. EN4: Cockf . . . 14Hb **31**
Langford Grn. CM13: Hut . . . 15Ee **41**
SE5 . . . 55Ub **113**
Langford Ho. SE8 . . . 51Cc **114**
Langford M. N1 . . . 38Qb **70**
SW11 . . . *56Fb* ***111***
(off St John's Hill)
Langford Pl. DA14: Sidc . . . 62Wc **139**
NW8 . . . 1A **214** (40Eb **69**)
Langford Rd. EN4: Cockf . . . 14Hb **31**
IG8: Wfd G . . . 23Lc **53**
SW6 . . . 54Db **111**
Langfords IG9: Buck H . . . 19Mc **35**
Langham Cl. BR2: Brom . . . 75Nc **160**
N15 . . . *27Rb* ***51***
(off Langham Rd.)
Langham Ct. HA4: Ruis . . . 36X **65**
NW4 . . . 29Za **48**
RM11: Horn . . . 31Md **77**
SW20 . . . 68Ya **132**
Langham Dene CR8: Kenley . . . 87Rb **177**
Langham Dr. RM6: Chad H . . . 30Xc **55**
Langham Gdns. HA0: Wemb . . . 33La **66**
HA8: Edg . . . 24Sa **47**
N21 . . . 15Qb **32**
TW10: Ham . . . 63La **130**
W13 . . . 45Ka **86**
Langham Ho. Cl. TW10: Ham . . . 63Ma **131**
Langham Mans. *SW5* . . . *50Db* ***89***
(off Earl's Ct. Sq.)
Langham Pk. Pl. BR2: Brom . . . 70Hc **137**
Langham Pl. N15 . . . 27Rb **51**
TW20: Egh . . . 64B **126**
W1 . . . 1A **222** (43Kb **90**)
W4 . . . 51Ua **110**
Langham Rd. HA8: Edg . . . 23Sa **47**
N15 . . . 27Rb **51**
SW20 . . . 67Ya **132**
TW11: Tedd . . . 64Ka **130**
Langham St. W1 . . . 1A **222** (43Kb **90**)
(not continuous)
Langhedge Cl. N18 . . . 23Vb **51**
Langhedge La. N18 . . . 23Vb **51**
Langhedge La. Ind. Est. N18 . . . 23Wb **51**
Langholm Cl. SW12 . . . 59Mb **112**
Langholme WD23: Bush . . . 18Ea **28**
Langhorn Dr. TW2: Twick . . . 59Ga **108**
Langhorne Ct. *NW8* . . . *38Fb* ***69***
(off Dorman Way)
Langhorne Rd. RM10: Dag . . . 38Cd **76**
Langhorne St. SE18 . . . 52Pc **116**
Lang Ho. *SW8* . . . *52Nb* ***112***
(off Hartington Rd.)
TW19: Stanw . . . 60N **105**
Langland Ct. HA6: Nwood . . . 24S **44**
Langland Cres. HA7: Stan . . . 26Ma **47**
Langland Dr. HA5: Pinn . . . 24Aa **45**
Langland Gdns. CR0: C'don . . . 75Bc **158**
NW3 . . . 36Db **69**
Langland Ho. *SE5* . . . *52Tb* ***113***
(off Edmund St.)
Langlands Dr. DA2: Daren . . . 64Ud **142**
Langlands Ri. KT19: Eps . . . 85Sa **173**
Langler Rd. NW10 . . . 40Ya **68**
LANGLEY . . . 48C **82**
Langley Av. HA4: Ruis . . . 33X **65**
HP3: Hem H . . . 5N **3**
KT4: Wor Pk . . . 74Za **154**
KT6: Surb . . . 74Ma **153**
LANGLEY BOTTOM . . . 91Ta **193**
Langley Broom SL3: L'ly . . . 50B **82**
LANGLEYBURY . . . 6R **12**
Langleybury Flds. WD4: Lang . . . 6P **11**
Langleybury La. WD4: Lang . . . 9R **12**
WD17: Wat . . . 9R **12**
Langley Bus. Cen. SL3: L'ly . . . 47C **82**
Langley Bus. Pk. SL3: L'ly . . . 47C **82**
Langley Cl. KT18: Eps D . . . 91Ta **193**
RM3: Rom . . . 24Md **57**
Langley Ct. EN7: G Oak . . . 1Sb **19**
RH2: Reig . . . 5K **207**
WC2 . . . 4F **223** (45Nb **90**)
Langley Cres. E11 . . . 31Lc **73**
HA8: Edg . . . 20Sa **29**
RM9: Dag . . . 38Yc **75**
UB3: Harl . . . 52V **106**
WD4: K Lan . . . 2Q **12**
Langley Dr. CM14: B'wood . . . 20Wd **40**
E11 . . . 31Kc **73**
W3 . . . 47Ra **87**
Langley Gdns. BR2: Brom . . . 70Lc **137**
BR5: Pet W . . . 72Rc **160**
RM9: Dag . . . 38Zc **75**
Langley Gro. KT3: N Mald . . . 68Ua **132**
Langley Hill WD4: K Lan . . . 1P **11**
Langley Hill Cl. WD4: K Lan . . . 1Q **12**
Langley Ho. *W2* . . . *43Cb* ***89***
(off Alfred Rd.)
Langley La. KT18: Head . . . 97Ra **193**
SW8 . . . 51Pb **112**
WD5: Ab L . . . 3V **12**
WD25: Wat . . . 3V **12**
Langley Leisure Cen. . . . 49D **82**
Langley Lodge La. WD4: K Lan . . . 3N **11**
Langley Mans. *SW8* . . . *51Pb* ***112***
(off Langley La.)
Langley Mdw. IG10: Lough . . . 12Tc **36**
Langley M. RM9: Dag . . . 38Zc **75**
Langley Oaks Av. CR2: Sande . . . 82Wb **177**
Langley Pk. NW7 . . . 23Ua **48**
SL3: L'ly . . . 47B **82**
Langley Pk. Country Pk. . . . 42B **82**
Langley Pk. Golf Course . . . 72Fc **159**
Langley Pk. La. SL0: Iver . . . 45D **82**
Langley Pk. Rd. SL0: Iver . . . 47C **82**
SL3: L'ly . . . 47C **82**
SM1: Sutt . . . 78Eb **155**
SM2: Sutt . . . 78Eb **155**
Langley Pk. Sports Cen. . . . 72Ec **158**
Langley Quay SL3: L'ly . . . 47C **82**
Langley Rd. BR3: Beck . . . 70Ac **136**
CR2: Sels . . . 81Zb **178**
DA16: Well . . . 51Yc **117**
KT6: Surb . . . 73Na **153**
SL3: L'ly . . . 7N **81**
SW19 . . . 67Bb **133**
TW7: Isle . . . 54Ha **108**
TW18: Staines . . . 65H **127**
WD4: Chfd . . . 2K **11**
WD5: Ab L . . . 3U **12**
WD17: Wat . . . 11V **26**
LANGLEY RDBT. . . . 50C **82**
Langley Row EN5: Barn . . . 11Bb **31**
Langley St. WC2 . . . 3F **223** (44Nb **90**)
LANGLEY VALE . . . 91Ua **194**
Langley Va. Rd. KT18: Eps D . . . 92Sa **193**
Langley Wlk. GU22: Wok . . . 91A **188**
Langley Way BR4: W W'ck . . . 74Fc **159**
WD17: Wat . . . 12U **26**
Langley Wharf WD4: K Lan . . . 9A **4**
Langmans La. GU21: Wok . . . 10M **167**
Langmans Way GU21: Wok . . . 8J **167**
Langmead Dr. WD23: B Hea . . . 18Ga **28**
Langmead Ho. *E3* . . . *41Dc* ***92***
(off Bruce Rd.)
Langmead St. SE27 . . . 63Rb **135**
Langmore Ct. DA6: Bex . . . 55Zc **117**
Langmore Ho. *E1* . . . *44Wb* ***91***
(off Stutfield St.)
Langport Ct. KT12: Walt T . . . 74Y **151**
Langport Ho. *RM3: Rom* . . . *24Nd* ***57***
(off Leyburn Rd.)
SW9 . . . 54Rb **113**
Langridge M. TW12: Hamp . . . 65Ba **129**
Langroyd Rd. SW17 . . . 61Hb **133**
Langshott Cl. KT15: Wdhm . . . 83G **168**
Langside Av. SW15 . . . 56Wa **110**
Langside Cres. N14 . . . 20Mb **32**
Langstone Way NW7 . . . 24Za **48**
Langston Hughes Cl. SE24 . . . 56Rb **113**
Langston Rd. IG10: Lough . . . 15Sc **36**
Lang St. E1 . . . 42Yb **92**
Langthorn Ct. EC2 . . . 2G **225** (44Tb **91**)
Langthorne Ct. BR1: Brom . . . 63Ec **136**
Langthorne Cres. RM17: Grays . . . 49Ee **99**
Langthorne Ho. *E3* . . . *41Bc* ***92***
(off Merchant St.)
UB3: Harl . . . 49U **84**
Langthorne Rd. E11 . . . 34Ec **72**
(not continuous)
Langthorne St. SW6 . . . 52Za **110**
Langton Av. E6 . . . 41Qc **94**
KT17: Ewe . . . 83Va **174**
N20 . . . 17Eb **31**
Langton Cl. GU21: Wok . . . 9K **167**
KT15: Add . . . 76K **149**
SL1: Slou . . . 6B **80**
WC1 . . . 5J **217** (42Pb **90**)
Langton Gro. HA6: Nwood . . . 22S **44**
Langton Ho. SE11 . . . 5J **229**
Langton Pl. SW18 . . . 60Cb **111**
Langton Ri. SE23 . . . 59Xb **113**
Langton Rd. HA3: Hrw W . . . 24Ea **46**
KT8: W Mole . . . 70Ea **130**
NW2 . . . 34Ya **68**
SW9 . . . 52Rb **113**
Langton's Mdw. SL2: Farn C . . . 7G **60**
Langton St. SW10 . . . 51Eb **111**
Langton Way CR0: C'don . . . 76Ub **157**
RM16: Grays . . . 9E **100**
SE3 . . . 53Hc **115**
TW20: Egh . . . 65E **126**
Langtree Av. SL1: Slou . . . 7D **80**
Langtry Ct. TW7: Isle . . . 54Ha **108**
Langtry Ho. *KT2: King T* . . . *67Qa* ***131***
(off London Rd.)
Langtry Pl. SW6 . . . 51Cb **111**
Langtry Rd. NW8 . . . 39Db **69**
UB5: N'olt . . . 40Z **65**
Langtry Wlk. NW8 . . . 39Db **69**
Langwood WD17: Wat . . . 11W **26**
Langwood Chase
TW11: Tedd . . . 65La **130**
Langwood Cl. KT21: Asht . . . 89Qa **173**
Langwood Gdns. WD17: Wat . . . 11W **26**
Langworth Cl. DA2: Wilm . . . 62Md **141**
Langworth Dr. UB4: Yead . . . 44X **85**
Langworthy HA5: Hat E . . . 23Ca **45**
Lanhill Rd. W9 . . . 42Cb **89**
Lanier Rd. SE13 . . . 58Fc **115**
Lanigan Dr. TW3: Houn . . . 57Da **107**
Lankaster Gdns. N2 . . . 25Fb **49**
Lankers Dr. HA2: Harr . . . 30Ba **45**
Lankester Sq. RH8: Oxt . . . 100Fc **199**
Lankton Cl. BR3: Beck . . . 67Ec **136**
Lannock Rd. UB3: Hayes . . . 46V **84**
Lannoy Point *SW6* . . . *52Ab* ***110***
(off Pellant Rd.)
Lannoy Rd. SE9 . . . 60Sc **116**
Lanrick Rd. E14 . . . 44Fc **93**
Lanridge Rd. SE2 . . . 48Zc **95**
Lansbury Av. IG11: Bark . . . 38Wc **75**
N18 . . . 22Tb **51**
RM6: Chad H . . . 29Ad **55**
TW14: Felt . . . 58X **107**
Lansbury Cl. NW10 . . . 36Sa **67**
Lansbury Ct. *SE28* . . . *45Xc* ***95***
(off Saunders Way)
Lansbury Cres. DA1: Dart . . . 57Qd **119**
Lansbury Dr. UB4: Hayes . . . 40U **64**
Lansbury Est. E14 . . . 44Dc **92**
GU21: Knap . . . 10H **167**
Lansbury Gdns. E14 . . . 44Fc **93**
RM18: Tilb . . . 3C **122**
Lansbury Rd. EN3: Enf H . . . 11Zb **34**
Lansbury Way N18 . . . 22Ub **51**
Lanscombe Wlk. SW8 . . . 53Nb **112**
Lansdell Ho. SW2 . . . 58Qb **112**
Lansdell Rd. CR4: Mitc . . . 68Jb **134**
Lansdown Cl. GU21: Wok . . . 1K **187**
KT12: Walt T . . . 74Y **151**
Lansdowne Av. BR6: Farnb . . . 74Rc **160**
DA7: Bex . . . 52Zc **117**
SL1: Slou . . . 6J **81**

Lansdowne Cl. KT6: Surb 75Ra 153
SW20 66Za 132
TW1: Twick 60Ha 108
WD25: Wat 7Z 13
Lansdowne Ct. CR8: Purl 82Rb 177
IG5: Ilf 27Nc 54
KT4: Wor Pk 75Wa 154
SL1: Slou 6J 81
W11 45Ab 88
(off Lansdowne Ri.)
Lansdowne Cres. W11 45Ab 88
Lansdowne Dr. E8 37Wb 71
Lansdowne Gdns. SW8 53Nb 112
Lansdowne Grn. SW8 53Nb 112
Lansdowne Gro. NW10 35Ua 68
Lansdowne Hill SE27 62Rb 135
Lansdowne Ho. KT18: Eps 86Sa 173
(off Dalmeny Way)
W11 46Bb 89
(off Ladbroke Rd.)
Lansdowne La. SE7 51Mc 115
Lansdowne M. SE7 50Mc 93
W11 46Bb 89
Lansdowne Pl. AL1: St A 2B 6
SE1 3G 231 (48Tb 91)
SE19 66Vb 135
Lansdowne Ri. W11 45Ab 88
Lansdowne Rd. BR1: Brom 66Jc 137
CR0: C'don 75Tb 157
CR8: Purl 84Qb 176
E4 19Cc 34
E11 33Hc 73
E17 30Cc 52
E18 27Jc 53
HA1: Harr 31Ga 66
HA7: Stan 23La 46
IG3: Ilf 32Vc 75
KT19: Ewe 80Sa 153
N3 24Cb 49
N10 26Lb 50
N17 25Vb 51
RM18: Tilb 4B 122
SW20 66Ya 132
TN13: S'oaks 94Md 203
TW3: Houn 55Da 107
TW18: Staines 66K 127
UB8: Hil 44S 84
W11 45Ab 88
Lansdowne Row W1 6A 222 (46Kb 90)
Lansdowne Sq. DA11: Nflt 8B 122
Lansdowne Ter. WC1 6G 217 (42Nb 90)
Lansdowne Wlk. W11 46Bb 89
Lansdowne Way SW8 53Mb 112
Lansdowne Wood Cl. SE27 62Rb 135
Lansdowne Workshops SE7 50Lc 93
Lansdown Pl. DA11: Nflt 10B 122
Lansdown Rd. DA11: Nflt 10B 122
DA14: Sidc 62Xc 139
E7 38Lc 73
Lansfield Av. N18 21Wb 51
Lanson Apartments SW8 52Kb 112
Lantern SE1 1D 230
Lantern Cl. BR6: Farnb 77Rc 160
HA0: Wemb 36Ma 67
SW15 56Wa 110
Lantern Ho. UB3: Harl 48S 84
(off Nine Acres Cl.)
Lanterns Way E14 47Cc 92
Lantern Way UB7: W Dray 47N 83
Lant Ho. SE1 2D 230
Lantry Ct. W3 46Ra 87
Lant St. SE1 1D 230 (47Sb 91)
Lanvanor Rd. SE15 54Yb 114
Lanyard Ho. SE8 49Bc 92
Lapford Cl. W9 42Bb 89
Lapis Cl. DA12: Grav'nd 10K 123
NW10 41Qa 87
Lapis M. E15 39Ec 72
La Plata Gro. CM14: B'wood 20Xd 40
Lapponum Wlk. UB4: Yead 42Z 85
Lapse Wood Wlk. SE23 60Xb 113
Lapstone Gdns. HA3: Kenton 30La 46
Lapwing Cl. CR2: Sels 82Ac 178
DA8: Erith 52Kd 119
Lapwing Ct. KT6: Surb 76Qa 153
SE1 2E 230
(off Swan St.)
Lapwing Pl. WD25: Wat 4Y 13
Lapwings DA3: Lfield 69De 143
Lapwings, The DA12: Grav'nd 1F 144
Lapwing Ter. E7 36Mc 73
Lapwing Twr. SE8 51Bc 114
(off Taylor Cl.)
Lapwing Way UB4: Yead 44Z 85
WD5: Ab L 3W 12
Lapworth N11 21Kb 50
(off Coppies Gro.)
Lapworth Cl. BR6: Chels 75Yc 161
Lapworth Ct. W2 43Db 89
(off Delamere Ter.)
Lara Cl. KT9: Chess 80Na 153
SE13 58Ec 114
Larbert Rd. SW16 66Lb 134
Larby Pl. KT17: Ewe 82Ua 174
Larch Av. AL2: Brick W 2Aa 13
SL5: S'dale 1C 146
W3 46Ua 88
Larch Cl. CR6: W'ham 91Ac 198
E13 42Kc 93
KT20: Kgswd 93Eb 195
N11 24Jb 50
N19 33Lb 70
RH1: Redh 8L 207
SE8 51Bc 114
SL2: Slou 3F 80
SW12 61Kb 134
Larch Ct. SE1 2H 231
W9 43Cb 89
(off Admiral Wlk.)
Larch Cres. KT19: Ewe 79Ra 153
UB4: Yead 42Y 85
Larch Dene BR6: Farnb 75Qc 160
Larch Dr. W4 50Qa 87
Larches, The GU21: Wok 88A 168
HA6: Nwood 23S 44
N13 20Sb 33
UB10: Hil 41R 84
WD23: Bush 15Z 27
Larches Av. EN1: Enf 7Yb 20
SW14 56Ta 109
Larchfield Cl. KT13: Weyb 76V 150
Larch Grn. NW9 25Ua 48
Larch Gro. DA15: Sidc 60Vc 117
Larch Ho. BR2: Brom 67Gc 137
SE16 47Yb 92
(off Ainsty Est.)
Larch Ho. UB4: Yead 43Y 85
W10 42Ab 88
(off Rowan Wlk.)
Larchmoor Pk. SL2: Stoke P 6L 61
Larch Rd. DA1: Dart 59Md 119
E10 33Cc 72
NW2 35Ya 68
Larch Tree Way CR0: C'don 76Cc 158
Larchvale Ct. SM2: Sutt 80Db 155
Larch Vw. HP1: Hem H 3K 3
Larch Wlk. BR8: Swan 68Fd 140
Larch Way BR2: Brom 73Qc 160
Larchwood Av. RM5: Col R 23Dd 56
Larchwood Cl. RM5: Col R 23Ed 56
SM7: Bans 87Ab 174
Larchwood Dr. TW20: Eng G 5M 125
Larchwood Gdns.
CM15: Pil H 16Wd 40
Larchwood Ho. UB7: W Dray 47P 83
(off Park Lodge Av.)
Larchwood Rd. GU21: Wok 2H 187
SE9 61Rc 138
Larcombe Cl. CR0: C'don 77Vb 157
Larcombe Ct. SM2: Sutt 80Db 155
(off Worcester Rd.)
Larcom St. SE17 6D 230 (49Sb 91)
Larden Rd. W3 46Ua 88
Largewood Av. KT6: Surb 75Qa 153
Largo Wlk. DA8: Erith 53Gd 118
Larissa St. SE17 7G 231 (50Tb 91)
Lark Av. TW18: Staines 62H 127
Larkbere Rd. SE26 63Ac 136
Lark Cl. CM14: W'ley 21Xd 58
Larken Cl. WD23: Bush 18Ea 28
Larken Dr. WD23: Bush 18Ea 28
Larkfield KT11: Cobh 85W 170
Larkfield Av. HA3: Kenton 27Ka 46
Larkfield Cl. BR2: Hayes 75Hc 159
Larkfield Rd. DA14: Sidc 62Vc 139
TN13: Bes G 95Ed 202
TW9: Rich 56Na 109
Larkfields DA11: Nflt 2A 144
Larkhall Cl. KT12: Hers 79Y 151
Larkhall La. SW4 54Mb 112
Larkhall Ri. SW4 55Lb 112
(not continuous)
Larkham Cl. TW13: Felt 62U 128
Lark Hill Ter. SE18 52Qc 116
(off Prince Imperial Rd.)
Larkin Cl. CM13: Hut 17Ee 41
CR5: Coul 89Pb 176
Larkings La. SL2: Stoke P 9M 61
Lark Ri. AL10: Hat 2C 8
Lark Row E2 39Yb 72
Larks Fld. DA3: Hartl 70Be 143
Larksfield TW20: Eng G 6M 125
Larksfield Gro. EN1: Enf 11Xb 33
Larks Gro. IG11: Bark 38Uc 74
Larkshall Ct. RM7: Mawney 26Ed 56
Larkshall Cres. E4 21Ec 52
Larkshall Rd. E4 22Ec 52
Larkspur Cl. BR6: Chels 75Yc 161
E6 43Nc 94
HA4: Ruis 31S 64
HP1: Hem H 1G 2
N17 24Tb 51
NW9 29Ra 47
RM15: S Ock 41Yd 98
Larkspur Gro. HA8: Edg 21Sa 47
Larkspur Lodge DA14: Sidc 62Xc 139
Larkspur Way KT19: Ewe 78Sa 153
Larks Ridge AL2: Chis G 9N 5
Larks Way GU21: Knap 8G 166
Larkswood Cl. DA8: Erith 53Jd 118
Larkswood Ct. E4 22Fc 53
Larkswood Leisure Cen. 21Ec 52
Larkswood Ri. HA5: Eastc 28Y 45
Larkswood Rd. E4 21Cc 52
Lark Way SM5: Cars 73Gb 155
Larkway Cl. NW9 28Ta 47
Larkwell La. DA3: Hartl 70Be 143
Larmans Rd. EN3: Enf W 8Yb 20
Larnaca Ho. SE1 3K 231
Larnach Rd. W6 51Za 110
Larne Rd. HA4: Ruis 31V 64
Larner Rd. DA8: Erith 52Gd 118
La Roche Cl. SL3: L'ly 8N 81
Larpent Av. SW15 57Ya 110
Larsen Dr. EN9: Walt A 6Fc 21
Larwood Cl. UB6: G'frd 36Fa 66
Lascar Wharf Bldg. E14 44Ac 92
(off Parnham St.)
Lascelles Av. HA1: Harr 31Fa 66
Lascelles Cl. CM15: Pil H 15Wd 40
E11 33Fc 73
Lascelles Ho. NW1 6E 214
Lascelles Rd. SL3: Slou 8M 81
Lascotts Rd. N22 23Pb 50
Laseron Ho. N15 28Vb 51
(off Tottenham Grn. E.)
Laser Quest
Sutton 78Db 155
Woking 89B 168
(within The Big Apple)
Las Palmas Est. TW17: Shep 73S 150
Lassa Rd. SE9 57Nc 116
Lassell St. SE10 50Fc 93
Lasseter Pl. SE3 51Hc 115
Lasswade Ct. KT16: Chert 73G 148
Lasswade Rd. KT16: Chert 73G 148
Lastingham Ct. TW18: Staines 65J 127
Latchett Rd. E18 25Kc 53
Latchford Pl. HP1: Hem H 3J 3
IG7: Chig 21Xc 55
Latching Cl. RM3: Rom 21Md 57
Latchingdon Ct. E17 28Zb 52
Latchingdon Gdns. IG8: Wfd G 23Nc 54
Latchmere Cl. TW10: Ham 64Na 131
Latchmere La. KT2: King T 65Pa 131
TW10: Ham 65Pa 131
Latchmere Leisure Cen. 54Hb 111
Latchmere Pas. SW11 54Gb 111
Latchmere Pl. TW15: Ashf 61N 127
Latchmere Rd. KT2: King T 66Na 131
SW11 54Hb 111
Latchmere St. SW11 54Hb 111
Latchmoor Av. SL9: Chal P 28A 42
Latchmoor Gro. SL9: Chal P 28A 42
Latchmoor Way SL9: Chal P 28A 42
Lateward Rd. TW8: Bford 51Ma 109
Latham Cl. DA2: Dart 61Ud 142
E6 43Nc 94
TN16: Big H 88Lc 179
TW1: Twick 59Ja 108
Latham Ct. N11 23Nb 50
(off Brownlow Rd.)
Latham Ct. SW5 49Cb 89
(off W. Cromwell Rd.)
UB5: N'olt 41Z 85
(off Delta Gro.)
Latham Ho. E1 44Zb 92
(off Chudleigh St.)
Latham Pl. RM14: Upm 32Sd 78
Latham Rd. DA6: Bex 57Cd 118
TW1: Twick 59Ha 108
Latham's Way CR0: Wadd 74Pb 156
Lathkill Cl. EN1: Enf 17Wb 33
Lathkill Ct. BR3: Beck 67Bc 136
Lathom Rd. E6 38Nc 74
LATIMER 9A 10
Latimer Av. E6 39Pc 74
Latimer Cl. GU22: Wok 88D 168
HA5: Pinn 25Y 45
KT4: Wor Pk 77Xa 154
WD18: Wat 17U 26
Latimer Ct. BR2: Brom 70Hc 137
(off Durham Rd.)
EN8: Walt C 6Bc 20
RH1: Redh 8P 207
Latimer Dr. RM12: Horn 34Md 77
Latimer Gdns. HA5: Pinn 25Y 45
Latimer Ho. E9 37Zb 72
W11 45Bb 89
(off Kensington Pk. Rd.)
Latimer Ind. Est. W10 44Ya 88
Latimer Pl. W10 44Ya 88
Latimer Rd. CR0: C'don 76Rb 157
E7 35Kc 73
EN5: New Bar 13Db 31
HP5: Lat 9A 10
N15 30Ub 51
SW19 65Db 133
TW11: Tedd 64Ha 130
W10 43Ya 88
(not continuous)
WD3: Chen 9A 10
Latitude KT16: Chert 74L 149
(off Bridge Wharf)
Latitude Apartments CR0: C'don 76Tb 157
(off Addiscombe Gro.)
Latitude Ct. E16 45Sc 94
Latitude Ho. NW1 39Kb 70
(off Oval Rd.)
Latium Cl. AL1: St A 3B 6
Latona Ct. SW9 52Qb 112
(off Caldwell St.)
Latona Dr. DA12: Grav'nd 4H 145
Latona Rd. SE15 51Wb 113
La Tourne Gdns. BR6: Farnb 76Sc 160
Lattimer Pl. W4 52Ua 110
Lattimore Ho. AL1: St A 2C 6
(off Lattimore Rd.)
Lattimore Rd. AL1: St A 3C 6
Lattitude Apartments CR0: C'don 76Tb 157
(off Addiscombe Gro.)
Latton Cl. KT10: Esh 77Da 151
KT12: Walt T 73Aa 151
Latvia Ct. SE17 50Sb 91
(off Sutherland Sq.)
Latymer Cl. KT13: Weyb 77S 150
Latymer Ct. W6 49Za 88
Latymer Gdns. N3 26Ab 48
Latymer Rd. N9 18Vb 33
Latymer Way N9 19Ub 33
Laubin Cl. TW1: Twick 56Ka 108
Lauder Cl. UB5: N'olt 40Z 65
Lauder Ct. N14 17Nb 32
Lauderdale Community Arts Cen. 32Kb 70
(within Lauderdale House)
Lauderdale Dr. TW10: Ham 62Ma 131
Lauderdale House 32Kb 70
Lauderdale Ho. SW9 53Qb 112
(off Gosling Way)
TW18: Staines 64H 127
(off Gresham Rd.)
Lauderdale Mans. W9 41Db 89
(off Lauderdale Rd.)
Lauderdale Pde. W9 42Db 89
Lauderdale Pl. EC2 7D 218
Lauderdale Rd. W9 41Db 89
WD4: Hunt C 5S 12
Lauderdale Twr. EC2 7D 218
Laud St. CR0: C'don 76Sb 157
SE11 7H 229 (50Pb 90)
Laugan Wlk. SE17 7E 230 (50Sb 91)
Laughton Ct. WD6: Bore 12Sa 29
Laughton Rd. UB5: N'olt 39Z 65
Launcelot Rd. BR1: Brom 63Jc 137
Launcelot St. SE1 2K 229 (47Qb 90)
Launceston WD3: Chor 16D 24
Launceston Cl. RM3: Rom 25Ld 57
Launceston Gdns.
UB6: G'frd 39La 66
Launceston Pl. W8 4A 226 (48Eb 89)
Launceston Rd. UB6: G'frd 39La 66
Launch St. E14 48Ec 92
Launders Ga. W3 47Ra 87
Launder's La.
RM13: Rain, Wenn 41Pd 97
Laundress La. N16 34Wb 71
Laundry La. CM15: Mount 11Fe 41
N1 39Sb 71
Laundry M. SE23 59Ac 114
Laundry Rd. W6 51Ab 110
Launton Dr. DA6: Bex 56Zc 117
Laura Cl. E11 29Lc 53
EN1: Enf 15Ub 33
Lauradale Rd. N2 28Hb 49
Laura Dr. BR8: Hext 66Jd 140
Laura Pl. E5 35Yb 72
Laura Ter. N4 33Rb 71
Laureate Way HP1: Hem H 1K 3
Laurel Apartments SE17 5H 231
Laurel Av. DA12: Grav'nd 1E 144
EN6: Pot B 4Bb 17
SL3: L'ly 47A 82
TW1: Twick 60Ha 108
TW20: Eng G 4M 125
Laurel Bank GU24: Chob 3J 167
(off Bagshot Rd.)
HP3: Hem H 5H 3
N12 21Eb 49
Laurel Bank Gdns. SW6 54Bb 111
Laurel Bank Rd. EN2: Enf 11Sb 33
Laurel Bank Vs. W7 47Ga 86
(off Lwr. Boston Rd.)
Laurel Cl. CM13: Hut 15De 41
DA1: Dart 60Ld 119
DA14: Sidc 62Wc 139
HP2: Hem H 1P 3
IG6: Ilf 23Sc 54
N19 33Lb 70
Laurel Cl. SL3: Poyle 52G 104
SW17 64Gb 133
WD19: Wat 17Z 27
Laurel Ct. CM13: Hut 16Ee 41
(off The Spinney)
CM16: Epp 3Wc 23
CR2: S Croy 77Ub 157
(off South Pk. Hill Rd.)
EN6: Cuff 1Pb 18
HA0: Wemb 40Na 67
RM13: Rain 42Ld 97
SL0: Iver H 38F 62
Laurel Cres. CR0: C'don 76Cc 158
GU21: Wok 85E 168
RM7: Rush G 32Gd 76
Laurel Dr. N21 17Qb 32
RH8: Oxt 3K 211
RM15: S Ock 42Zd 99
Laurel Edge AL1: St A 1D 6
(off Avenue Rd.)
Laurel Flds. EN6: Pot B 3Bb 17
Laurel Gdns. BR1: Brom 70Nc 138
E4 17Dc 34
KT15: New H 82K 169
NW7 20Ta 29
TW4: Houn 56Aa 107
TW15: Ashf 64S 128
W7 46Ga 86
Laurel Gro. SE20 66Yb 136
SE26 63Zb 136
Laurel Ho. BR2: Brom 67Gc 137
E3 39Bc 72
(off Hornbeam Sq.)
SE8 51Bc 114
Laurel La. RM12: Horn 33Nd 77
UB7: W Dray 49N 83
Laurel Lodge La. EN5: Barn 8Ya 16
Laurel Mnr. SM2: Sutt 80Eb 155
Laurel Pk. HA3: Hrw W 24Ha 46
Laurel Rd. AL1: St A 2D 6
SL9: Chal P 25A 42
SW13 54Wa 110
SW20 67Xa 132
TW12: Hamp H 64Fa 130
Laurels, The AL2: Brick W 10N 5
BR1: Brom 67Kc 137
BR2: Brom 70Jc 137
DA2: Wilm 62Ld 141
DA3: Lfield 69Ee 143
IG9: Buck H 18Lc 35
KT11: Cobh 87Aa 171
KT13: Weyb 76T 150
NW10 39Xa 68
SM7: Bans 89Bb 175
SW9 52Rb 113
(off Langton Rd.)
WD6: Bore 11Qa 29
WD23: B Hea 19Ga 28
Laurelsfield AL3: St A 5P 5
Laurels Rd. SL0: Iver H 40F 62
Laurel St. E8 37Vb 71
Laurel Vw. N12 20Db 31
Laurel Way E18 28Hc 53
N20 20Cb 31
Laurence Ct. E10 31Dc 72
W11 45Ab 88
(off Lansdowne Rd.)
Laurence M. W12 47Wa 88
Laurence Pountney Hill
EC4 4F 225 (45Tb 91)
Laurence Pountney La.
EC4 4F 225 (45Tb 91)
Laurence Rd. TW3: Houn 55Ea 108
Laurie Gro. SE14 53Ac 114
Laurie Ho. SE1 4C 230
W8 46Cb 89
(off Airlie Gdns.)
Laurie Rd. W7 43Ga 86
Laurier Rd. CR0: C'don 73Vb 157
NW5 34Kb 70
Lauries Cl. HP1: Hem H 4E 2
Laurie Wlk. RM1: Rom 29Gd 56
Laurimel Cl. HA7: Stan 23Ka 46
Laurino Pl. WD23: B Hea 19Ea 28
Lauriston Cl. GU21: Knap 9H 167
Lauriston Ho. E9 38Yb 72
(off Lauriston Rd.)
Lauriston Rd. E9 38Yb 72
SW19 65Za 132
Lausanne Rd. N8 28Qb 50
SE15 53Yb 114
Lauser Rd. TW19: Stanw 59L 105
Lavell St. N16 35Tb 71
Lavender Av. CM15: Pil H 15Xd 40
CR4: Mitc 67Gb 133
KT4: Wor Pk 76Ya 154
NW9 32Sa 67
Lavender Cl. BR2: Brom 72Nc 160
CR3: Cat'm 97Sb 197
CR5: Coul 91Lb 196
E4 21Cc 52
KT22: Lea 94La 192
RM3: Rom 24Md 57
RM15: S Ock 42Ae 99
SM5: Cars 77Kb 156
SW3 51Fb 111
Lavender Ct. KT8: W Mole 69Da 129
KT22: Lea 94La 192
SM2: Sutt 80Eb 155
TW14: Felt 58X 107
Lavender Gdns. EN2: Enf 11Rb 33
HA3: Hrw W 23Ga 46
SW11 56Hb 111
Lavender Ga. KT22: Oxs 86Da 171
Lavender Gro. CR4: Mitc 67Gb 133
E8 38Wb 71
Lavender Hill BR8: Swan 69Fd 140
EN2: Enf 11Qb 32
SW11 56Gb 111
Lavender Ho. SE16 46Zb 92
(off Rotherhithe St.)
TW9: Kew 53Ra 109
Lavender M. SS17: Stan H 1N 101
Lavender Pk. Rd. KT14: W Byf 84J 169
Lavender Pl. IG1: Ilf 36Rc 74
Lavender Pond Nature Pk. 46Ac 92
Lavender Ri. UB7: W Dray 47Q 84
Lavender Rd. CR0: C'don 72Pb 156
EN2: Enf 11Tb 33
GU22: Wok 88D 168
KT19: Ewe 78Ra 153
SE16 46Ac 92
SM1: Sutt 77Fb 155
SM5: Cars 77Jb 156
SW11 55Fb 111
UB8: Hil 43P 83
Lavender St. E15 37Gc 73
Lavender Sweep SW11 56Hb 111
Lavender Ter. SW11 55Gb 111
Lavender Va. SM6: Wall 79Mb 156
Lavender Wlk. CR4: Mitc 69Jb 134
HP2: Hem H 1M 3
SW11 56Hb 111
Lavender Way CR0: C'don 72Zb 158
Lavendon Ho. NW8 5E 214
Lavengro Rd. SE27 61Sb 135
Lavenha Ct. CM15: B'wood 18Zd 41
Lavenham Rd. SW18 61Bb 133
Lavernock Rd. DA7: Bex 54Cd 118
Lavers Rd. N16 34Ub 71
Laverstoke Gdns. SW15 59Va 110
Laverton M. SW5 49Db 89
Laverton Pl. SW5 49Db 89
Lavette Ho. E3 41Cc 92
(off Rainhill Way)
Lavidge Rd. SE9 61Nc 138
Lavina Gro. N1 1H 217 (40Pb 70)
Lavington Cl. E9 37Bc 72
Lavington Rd. CR0: Bedd 76Pb 156
W13 46Ka 86
Lavington St. SE1 7C 224 (46Rb 91)
Lavinia Av. WD25: Wat 6Z 13
Lavinia Rd. DA1: Dart 58Pd 119
Lavisham Ho. BR1: Brom 64Kc 137
Lavrock La. WD3: Crox G 17P 25
Lawdons Gdns. CR0: Wadd 77Rb 157
Lawes Ho. W10 41Bb 89
(off Lancefield St.)
Lawford Av. WD3: Chor 16E 24
Lawford Cl. RM12: Horn 35Ld 77
WD3: Chor 16E 24
Lawford Gdns. CR8: Kenley 88Sb 177
DA1: Dart 57Ld 119
Lawford Rd. N1 38Ub 71
NW5 37Lb 70
W4 52Sa 109
Lawford's Hill Cl. GU3: Worp 6G 186
Lawford's Hill Rd. GU3: Worp 6G 186
Lawfords Wharf NW1 38Lb 70
(off Lyme St.)
Law Ho. IG11: Bark 40Wc 75
Lawkland SL2: Farn R 1G 80
Lawless Ho. E14 45Ec 92
(off Bazely St.)
Lawless St. E14 45Dc 92
Lawley Ho. TW1: Twick 58Ma 109
Lawley Rd. N14 17Kb 32
Lawley St. E5 35Yb 72
Lawn, The SL3: Dat 3N 103
UB2: S'hall 50Ca 85
Lawn Av. UB7: W Dray 47L 83
Lawn Cl. BR1: Brom 65Kc 137
BR8: Swan 68Ed 140
HA4: Ruis 34V 64
KT3: N Mald 68Ua 132
N9 17Vb 33
SL3: Dat 2N 103
Lawn Cres. TW9: Kew 54Qa 109
Lawn Farm Gro. RM6: Chad H 28Ad 55
Lawnfield Ct. NW6 38Za 68
(off Coverdale Rd.)
Lawn Gdns. W7 46Ga 86
Lawn Ho. Cl. E14 47Ec 92
Lawn La. HP3: Hem H 4M 3
SW8 51Pb 112
Lawn Pk. TN13: S'oaks 99Kd 203
Lawn Rd. BR3: Beck 66Bc 136
DA11: Nflt 57Ee 121
(not continuous)
NW3 36Hb 69
UB8: Uxb 38L 63
Lawns, The AL3: St A 1A 6
CM14: W'ley 22Ae 59
(off Uplands Rd.)
DA14: Sidc 63Xc 139
E4 22Cc 52
HA5: Hat E 24Da 45
HP1: Hem H 1G 2
SE3 55Hc 115
SE19 67Tb 135
SL3: Poyle 53G 104
SM2: Cheam 80Ab 154
SW19 64Bb 133
WD7: Shenl 5Na 15
Lawns Ct. HA9: Wemb 33Pa 67
Lawns Cres. RM17: Grays 51Fe 121
Lawnside SE3 56Hc 115
Lawns Pl. RM17: Grays 51Fe 121
Lawns Way RM5: Col R 24Ed 56
Lawnswood EN5: Barn 15Ab 30
Lawn Ter. SE3 55Gc 115
Lawn Va. HA5: Pinn 26Aa 45
Lawrance Gdns. EN8: Chesh 1Zb 20
Lawrance Sq. DA11: Nflt 2B 144
Lawrence Av. E12 35Qc 74
E17 25Zb 52
KT3: N Mald 72Ta 153
N13 21Rb 51
NW7 21Ua 48
NW10 39Ta 67
Lawrence Bldgs. N16 34Vb 71
Lawrence Campe Cl. N20 20Fb 31
Lawrence Cl. E3 41Cc 92
N15 28Ub 51
W12 45Xa 88
Lawrence Ct. N10 27Lb 50
N16 34Vb 71
(off Smalley Rd. Est.)
NW7 22Ua 48
SL4: Wind 4G 102
W3 48Sa 87
(off Stanley Rd.)
WD19: Wat 20Z 27
Lawrence Cres. GU20: W'sham 9B 146
HA8: Edg 26Qa 47
RM10: Dag 34Dd 76
Lawrence Dr. DA12: Cobh 10J 145
UB10: Ick 35S 64
Lawrence Est. TW4: Houn 56Y 107
Lawrence Gdns. NW7 20Va 30
RM18: Tilb 2D 122
Lawrence Hill E4 19Cc 34
Lawrence Hill Gdns.
DA1: Dart 58Ld 119
Lawrence Hill Rd. DA1: Dart 58Ld 119
Lawrence Ho. NW1 38Kb 70
(off Hawley Cres.)
SW1 6E 228
Lawrence La. EC2 3E 224 (44Sb 91)
RH3: Bkld 4D 206
Lawrence Mans. SW3 51Gb 111
(off Lordship Pl.)

Lawrence Pde. TW7: Isle 55Ka 108
(off Lower Sq.)
Lawrence Pl. N1 39Nb 70
(off Brydon Wlk.)
Lawrence Rd. BR4: W W'ck 77Jc 159
DA8: Erith 52Dd 118
E6 39Nc 74
E13 39Kc 73
HA5: Pinn 30Z 45
N15 28Ub 51
N18 21Xb 51
(not continuous)
RM2: Rom 29Kd 57
SE25 70Vb 135
TW4: Houn 56Y 107
TW10: Ham 63La 130
TW12: Hamp 66Ba 129
UB4: Hayes 40S 64
W5 49Ma 87
Lawrence St. E16 43Hc 93
NW7 22Va 48
SW3 51Gb 111
Lawrence Trad. Est. RM17: Grays 50Ae 99
SE10 49Gc 93
Lawrence Way NW10 34Sa 67
SL1: Slou 3A 80
Lawrence Weaver Cl. SM4: Mord 72Cb 155
Lawrence Yd. N15 28Ub 51
Lawrie Ho. SW19 64Db 133
(off Dunsford Rd.)
Lawrie Pk. Av. SE26 64Xb 135
Lawrie Pk. Cres. SE26 64Xb 135
Lawrie Pk. Gdns. SE26 63Xb 135
Lawrie Pk. Rd. SE26 65Xb 135
Laws Cl. SE25 70Tb 135
Lawson Cl. E16 43Lc 93
IG1: Ilf 36Tc 74
SW19 62Za 132
Lawson Ct. KT6: Surb 73Ma 153
N4 32Pb 70
(off Lorne Rd.)
N11 23Lb 50
(off Ring Way)
Lawson Gdns. DA1: Dart 57Md 119
HA5: Eastc 27X 45
Lawson Ho. SE18 51Qc 116
(off Nightingale Pl.)
W12 45Xa 88
(off White City Est.)
Lawson Rd. DA1: Dart 56Md 119
EN3: Enf H 11Yb 34
UB1: S'hall 42Ca 85
Lawson Wlk. SM5: Cars 81Jb 176
Lawson Way SL5: S'dale 2F 146
Law St. SE1 3G 231 (48Tb 91)
Lawton Rd. E3 41Ac 92
(not continuous)
E10 32Ec 72
EN4: Cockf 13Fb 31
IG10: Lough 12Rc 36
Laxcon Cl. NW10 36Ta 67
Laxey Rd. BR6: Chels 79Vc 161
Laxfield Ct. E8 39Wb 71
(off Pownall Rd.)
Laxford Ho. SW1 6J 227
Laxley Cl. SE5 52Rb 113
Laxton Ct. CR7: Thor H 70Sb 135
Laxton Gdns. RH1: Mers 100Mb 196
WD7: Shenl 4Na 15
Laxton Pl. NW1 5A 216 (42Kb 90)
Layard Rd. CR7: Thor H 68Tb 135
EN1: Enf 11Vb 33
SE16 49Xb 91
Layard Sq. SE16 49Xb 91
Layborne Av. RM3: Rom 19Ld 39
Layburne Ho. E14 47Cc 92
(off Admirals Way)
Laybrook Lodge E18 28Hc 53
Layburn Cres. SL3: L'ly 51D 104
Laycock St. N1 37Qb 70
Layer Gdns. W3 45Qa 87
Layfield Cl. NW4 31Xa 68
Layfield Cres. NW4 31Xa 68
Layfield Ho. SE10 50Jc 93
(off Kemsing Rd.)
Layfield Rd. NW4 31Xa 68
Layhams Rd. BR2: Kes 77Gc 159
BR4: W W'ck 77Gc 159
CR6: Kes, W'ham 84Hc 179
Laymarsh Cl. DA17: Belv 48Bd 95
Laymead Cl. UB5: N'olt 37Aa 65
Laystall Ct. WC1 6K 217
Laystall St. EC1 6K 217 (42Qb 90)
Layters Way SL9: Ger X 29A 42
Layton Ct. KT13: Weyb 77R 150
TW8: Bford 50Ma 87
Layton Cres. CR0: Wadd 78Qb 156
Layton Pl. TW9: Kew 53Qa 109
Layton Rd. TW3: Houn 56Da 107
TW8: Bford 50Ma 87
Layton's La. TW16: Sun 68V 128
Layzell Wlk. SE9 60Mc 115
Lazare Ct. TW18: Staines 64H 127
(off Gresham Rd.)
Lazar Wlk. N7 33Pb 70
Lazenby Ct. WC2 4F 223
Lea, The TW20: Egh 66E 126
Leabank Cl. HA1: Harr 34Ga 66
Leabank Sq. E9 37Cc 72
Leabank Vw. N15 30Wb 51
Lea Bon Ct. E15 39Hc 73
(off Plaistow Gro.)
Leabourne Rd. N16 31Wb 71
LEA BRIDGE 34Zb 72
Lea Bri. Ind. Cen. E10 32Ac 72
Lea Bri. Rd. E5 34Yb 72
E10 34Yb 72
E17 29Fc 53
Lea Bushes WD25: Wat 7Aa 13
Leach Gro. KT22: Lea 94La 192
Lea Cl. TW2: Whitt 59Ba 107
WD23: Bush 15Da 27
Lea Ct. E4 19Ec 34
E13 41Jc 93
N15 28Wb 51
Lea Cres. HA4: Ruis 35V 64
Leacroft SL1: Slou 7D 80
SL5: S'dale 1E 146
TW18: Staines 64J 127
Leacroft Av. SW12 59Hb 111
Leacroft Cl. CR8: Kenley 88Sb 177
N21 19Rb 33
TW18: Staines 63K 127
UB7: Yiew 44N 83
Leacroft Rd. SL0: Iver 44G 82
Leadale Av. E4 19Cc 34
Leadale Rd. N15 30Wb 51
N16 30Wb 51
Leadbeaters Cl. N11 22Hb 49
Leadbetter Ct. NW10 38Ta 67
(off Melville Rd.)
Leaden Cl. IG10: Lough 13Rc 36
Leadenhall Mkt. EC3 3H 225 (44Ub 91)
Leadenhall Pl. EC3 3H 225 (44Ub 91)
Leadenhall St. EC3 3H 225 (44Ub 91)
Leadenham Ct. E3 42Cc 92
Leader Av. E12 36Qc 74
Leadings, The HA9: Wemb 34Sa 67
Leaf Cl. HA6: Nwood 24T 44
KT7: T Ditt 71Ga 152
Leaf Gro. SE27 64Qb 134
Leaf Ho. HA1: Harr 29Ha 46
(off Catherine Pl.)
Leafield Cl. GU21: Wok 10N 167
SW16 65Rb 135
Leafield La. DA14: Sidc 62Bd 139
Leafield Rd. SM1: Sutt 75Cb 155
SW20 69Bb 133
Leaford Ct. WD24: Wat 8V 12
Leaford Cres. WD24: Wat 9V 12
Leaf Way AL1: St A 5B 6
Leafy Gro. BR2: Kes 78Lc 159
Leafy Oak Rd. SE12 63Lc 137
Leafy Way CM13: Hut 18Fe 41
CR0: C'don 75Vb 157
Lea Gdns. HA9: Wemb 35Pa 67
Leagrave St. E5 34Yb 72
Lea Hall Gdns. E10 32Cc 72
Lea Hall Rd. E10 32Cc 72
Leaholme Gdns. SL1: Slou 3A 80
Leaholme Way HA4: Ruis 30S 44
Lea Ho. NW8 6D 214
Leahurst Rd. SE13 57Fc 115
LEA INTERCHANGE 36Cc 72
Leake Ct. SE1 2J 229 (47Pb 90)
Leake St. SE1 1J 229 (47Pb 90)
(not continuous)
Lealand Rd. N15 30Vb 51
Leamington Av. BR1: Brom 64Lc 137
BR6: Orp 77Uc 160
E17 29Cc 52
SM4: Mord 70Ab 132
Leamington Cl. BR1: Brom 63Lc 137
E12 36Nc 74
RM3: Rom 23Qd 57
TW3: Houn 57Ea 108
Leamington Ct. SE3 51Gc 115
Leamington Cres. HA2: Harr 34Aa 65
Leamington Gdns. IG3: Ilf 33Vc 75
Leamington Ho. HA8: Edg 22Pa 47
W11 43Bb 89
(off Leamington Rd. Vs.)
Leamington Pk. W3 43Ta 87
Leamington Pl. UB4: Hayes 42V 84
Leamington Rd. RM3: Rom 22Qd 57
UB2: S'hall 49Z 85
Leamington Rd. Vs. W11 43Bb 89
Leamore Ct. E2 41Zb 92
Leamore St. W6 49Ya 88
Lea Mt. EN7: G Oak 1Ub 19
LEAMOUTH 45Gc 93
Leamouth Rd. E6 43Nc 94
E14 44Fc 93
Leander Ct. E9 38Zb 72
(off Lauriston Rd.)
KT6: Surb 73Ma 153
NW9 25Ua 48
SE8 53Cc 114
Leander Dr. DA12: Grav'nd 3H 145
Leander Gdns. WD25: Wat 9Aa 13
Leander Rd. CR7: Thor H 70Pb 134
SW2 58Pb 112
UB5: N'olt 40Ca 65
Lea Pk. Trad. Est. E10 31Bc 72
Learner Dr. HA2: Harr 33Ca 65
Lea Rd. BR3: Beck 68Cc 136
EN2: Enf 11Tb 33
EN9: Walt A 6Cc 20
RM16: Grays 10C 100
TN13: S'oaks 99Ld 203
UB2: S'hall 49Aa 85
WD24: Wat 10X 13
Lea Rd. Ind. Pk. EN9: Walt A 6Cc 20
Lea Rd. Trad. Est.
EN9: Walt A 6Cc 20
Learoyd Gdns. E6 45Qc 94
Leary Ho. SE11 7J 229 (50Pb 90)
Leas, The HP3: Hem H 6A 4
RM14: Upm 31Td 78
WD23: Bush 11Ba 27
Leas Cl. KT9: Chess 80Pa 153
Leas Dale SE9 62Qc 138
Leas Dr. SL0: Iver 44G 82
Leas Grn. BR7: Chst 65Vc 139
Leaside HP2: Hem H 3C 4
KT23: Bookh 95Ca 191
Leaside Av. N10 27Jb 50
Leaside Bus. Cen. EN3: Brim 12Bc 34
Leaside Ct. UB10: Hil 41R 84
Leaside Mans. N10 27Jb 50
(off Fortis Grn.)
Leaside Rd. E5 32Yb 72
Leas La. CR6: W'ham 90Zb 178
Leasowes Rd. E10 32Cc 72
Lea Sq. E3 39Bc 72
Leas Rd. CR6: W'ham 90Zb 178
Leasway CM14: B'wood 20Zd 41
RM14: Upm 35Sd 78
RM16: Grays 46Ee 99
Leathart Cl. RM12: Horn 38Kd 77
Leatherbottle Grn.
DA18: Erith 48Bd 95
Leather Bottle La. DA17: Belv 49Ad 95
Leather Cl. CR4: Mitc 68Jb 134
Leatherdale St. E1 42Yb 92
(Harpley Sq.)
E1 41Zb 92
(Portelet Rd.)
Leather Gdns. E15 39Gc 73
LEATHERHEAD 94Ka 192
Leatherhead Bus. Pk.
KT22: Lea 91Ha 192
Leatherhead Cl. N16 32Vb 71
LEATHERHEAD COMMON 91Ja 192
Leatherhead FC 94Ja 192
Leatherhead Fitness & Wellbeing Cen.
94Ka 192
(off The Crescent)
Leatherhead Golf Course 88Ja 172
Leatherhead Leisure Cen. 95Ja 192
Leatherhead Mus. of Local History
94Ka 192
Leatherhead Rd. KT9: Chess 86Ka 172
KT21: Asht 93Ma 193
KT22: Lea 93Ma 193
KT22: Oxs 86Fa 172
KT23: Bookh 98Da 191
Leatherhead Theatre 94Ka 192
Leatherhead Trade Pk. KT22: Lea 93Ja 192
Leather La. EC1 7K 217 (43Qb 90)
(not continuous)
RM11: Horn 32Md 77
Leathermarket, The SE1 2H 231
Leathermarket Ct. SE1 2H 231 (47Ub 91)
Leathermarket St. SE1 2H 231 (47Ub 91)
Leather Rd. SE16 49Zb 92
Leathersellers Cl. EN5: Barn 13Ab 30
(off The Avenue)
Leather St. E1 45Zb 92
Leathsail Rd. HA2: Harr 34Da 65
Leathwaite Rd. SW11 56Hb 111
Leathwell Rd. SE8 54Dc 114
Lea Va. DA1: Cray 56Fd 118
Lea Valley Bus. Pk. E10 33Ac 72
Lea Valley Rd. E4 15Ac 34
EN3: Pond E 15Ac 34
Lea Valley Sports Cen. 7Yb 20
Lea Valley Trad. Est. N18 23Zb 52
Lea Valley Viaduct E4 22Zb 52
N18 22Zb 52
Leaveland Cl. BR3: Beck 70Cc 136
Leaver Gdns. UB6: G'frd 40Fa 66
LEAVESDEN 4V 12
Leavesden Country Pk. 4W 12
Leavesden Ct. WD5: Ab L 3W 12
LEAVESDEN GREEN 5W 12
LEAVESDEN GREEN 7U 12
Leavesden Pk. WD25: Wat 5V 12
Leavesden Rd. HA7: Stan 23Ja 46
KT13: Weyb 78R 150
WD24: Wat 10X 13
Leavesden Studios WD4: Hunt C 5U 12
LEAVES GREEN 83Mc 179
Leaves Grn. Cres. BR2: Kes 83Lc 179
Leaves Grn. Rd. BR2: Kes 83Mc 179
Lea Vw. EN9: Walt A 5Dc 20
Lea Vw. Ho. E5 32Xb 71
Leaway E10 32Zb 72
Leazes Av. CR3: Cat'm 95Qb 196
Leazes La. CR3: Cat'm 95Qb 196
Lebanon Av. TW13: Hanw 64Z 129
Lebanon Cl. WD17: Wat 8T 12
Lebanon Ct. TW1: Twick 59Ka 108
Lebanon Dr. KT11: Cobh 85Ca 171
Lebanon Gdns. SW18 58Cb 111
TN16: Big H 89Mc 179
Lebanon Pk. TW1: Twick 59Ka 108
Lebanon Rd. CR0: C'don 74Ub 157
SW18 57Cb 111
Lebrun Sq. SE3 56Kc 115
Lebus Ho. NW8 2D 214
Lebus St. N17 27Xb 51
Le Chateau CR0: C'don 76Tb 157
(off Chatsworth Rd.)
Lechmere App. IG8: Wfd G 26Lc 53
Lechmere Av. IG7: Chig 21Sc 54
IG8: Wfd G 26Mc 53
Lechmere Rd. NW2 37Xa 68
Leckford Rd. SW18 61Eb 133
Leckhampton Pl. SW2 59Qb 112
Leckwith Av. DA7: Bex 51Ad 117
Lecky St. SW7 7B 226 (50Fb 89)
Leclair Ho. SE3 55Kc 115
Leconfield Av. SW13 55Va 110
Leconfield Ho. SE5 56Ub 113
Leconfield Rd. N5 35Tb 71
Leconfield Wlk. RM12: Horn 37Ld 77
Le Cordon Bleu London Culinary Arts Institute
1J 221
(off Marylebone La.)
Le Corte Cl. WD4: K Lan 1P 11
Lectern La. AL1: St A 6C 6
Leda Av. EN3: Enf W 10Zb 20
Leda Ct. SW9 52Qb 112
(off Caldwell St.)
Ledam Ho. EC1 7K 217
Leda Rd. SE18 48Pc 94
Ledbury Ho. SE22 55Ub 113
W11 44Bb 89
(off Colville Rd.)
Ledbury M. Nth. W11 45Cb 89
Ledbury M. W. W11 45Cb 89
Ledbury Pl. CR0: C'don 77Sb 157
Ledbury Rd. CR0: C'don 77Tb 157
RH2: Reig 6J 207
W11 44Bb 89
Ledbury St. SE15 52Wb 113
Ledger Dr. KT15: Add 78H 149
Ledgers La. CR6: W'ham 89Dc 178
Ledgers Rd. CR6: W'ham 88Cc 178
SL1: Slou 7H 81
Ledrington Rd. SE19 65Wb 135
Ledway Dr. HA9: Wemb 30Pa 47
LEE 58Jc 115
Lee, The HA6: Nwood 22V 44
Lee Av. RM6: Chad H 30Ad 55
Lee Bri. SE13 55Ec 114
Leechcroft Av. BR8: Swan 69Hd 140
DA15: Sidc 57Vc 117
Leechcroft Rd. SM6: Wall 76Jb 156
Leech La. KT18: Head 98Ra 193
Lee Chu. St. SE13 56Gc 115
Lee Cl. E17 25Zb 52
EN5: New Bar 14Eb 31
Lee Conservancy Rd. E9 36Ac 72
Lee Ct. SE13 56Fc 115
(off Lee High Rd.)
Leecroft Rd. EN5: Barn 15Ab 30
Leeds Cl. BR6: Chels 75Zc 161
Leeds Ct. EC1 5B 218
Leeds Pl. N4 32Pb 70
Leeds Rd. IG1: Ilf 32Tc 74
SL1: Slou 5J 81
Leeds St. N18 22Wb 51
Leefern Rd. W12 47Wa 88
Leefe Way EN6: Cuff 1Mb 18
Lee Gdns. Av. RM11: Horn 30Qd 77
Leegate SE12 57Hc 115
Leegate Cl. GU21: Wok 8M 167
LEE GREEN 57Hc 115
Lee Grn. BR5: St M Cry 71Wc 161
Lee Grn. La. KT18: Head 96Ra 193
Lee Gro. IG7: Chig 19Rc 36
Lee High Rd. SE12 55Ec 114
SE13 55Ec 114
Leeke St. WC1 3H 217 (41Pb 90)
Leeland Rd. W13 46Ja 86
Leeland Ter. W13 46Ja 86
Leeland Way NW10 35Va 68
Lee M. BR3: Beck 69Ac 136
Leeming Rd. WD6: Bore 11Pa 29
Leemount Ho. NW4 28Za 48
Lee Pk. SE3 56Hc 115
Lee Pk. Way N9 21Zb 52
N18 21Zb 52
Leerdam Dr. E14 48Ec 92
Lee Rd. EN1: Enf 16Wb 33
NW7 24Za 48
SE3 55Hc 115
SW19 67Db 133
UB6: G'frd 39La 66
Lees, The CR0: C'don 75Bc 158
Lees Av. HA6: Nwood 25V 44
Lees Ct. W1 4H 221
Lees Ho. SE17 7G 231
Leeside EN5: Barn 15Ab 30
EN6: Pot B 4Fb 17
Leeside Ct. SE16 46Zb 92
(off Rotherhithe St.)
Leeside Cres. NW11 30Ab 48
Leeside Ind. Est. N17 24Yb 52
Leeside Rd. N17 23Xb 51
Leeside Works N17 24Yb 52
Leeson Gdns. SL4: Eton W 9C 80
Leeson Ho. TW1: Twick 59Ka 108
Leeson Rd. SE24 56Qb 112
Leesons Hill BR5: St P 69Uc 138
BR7: Chst 69Uc 138
Leeson's Way BR5: St P 68Vc 139
Lees Pde. UB10: Hil 42R 84
Lees Pl. W1 4H 221 (45Jb 90)
Lees Rd. UB8: Hil 42R 84
Lee St. E8 39Vb 71
Lee Ter. SE3 55Gc 115
SE13 55Gc 115
Lee Valley Athletics Cen. 18Ac 34
Lee Valley Golf Course 17Ac 34
Lee Valley Ice Cen. 33Zb 72
Lee Valley Pk. 24Zb 52
Lee Valley Pk. Info. Cen. 8Vb 19
Lee Valley Regional Pk. 3Cc 20
Lee Valley Technopark N17 27Wb 51
Lee Valley White Water Cen. 5Cc 20
Leeve Ho. W10 41Bb 89
(off Lancefield St.)
Lee Vw. EN2: Enf 11Rb 33
Leeward Ct. E1 45Wb 91
Leeward Gdns. SW19 64Ab 132
Leeward Ho. N1 39Ub 71
(off New Era Est.)
Leeway SE8 50Bc 92
Leeway Cl. HA5: Hat E 24Ba 45
Leeways, The SM3: Cheam 79Ab 154
Leewood Cl. SE12 58Jc 115
Leewood Pl. BR8: Swan 70Fd 140
Leewood Way KT24: Eff 99Y 191
Lefa Business & Industrial Pk.
DA14: Sidc 65Zc 139
Lefevre Wlk. E3 40Cc 72
Leff Ho. NW6 39Ab 68
Lefroy Ho. SE1 2D 230
Lefroy Rd. W12 47Va 88
Left Side N14 18Mb 32
(off Statione Pde.)
Legard Rd. N5 34Rb 71
Legatt Rd. SE9 57Mc 115
Leggatt Rd. E15 40Ec 72
Leggatts Cl. WD24: Wat 8V 12
Leggatts Ri. WD25: Wat 7W 12
Leggatts Way WD24: Wat 8V 12
Leggatts Wood Av. WD24: Wat 8X 13
Legge St. SE13 57Ec 114
Leggfield Ter. HP1: Hem H 2H 3
Leghorn Rd. NW10 40Va 68
SE18 50Tc 94
Legion Ct. N1 38Qb 70
Legion Ct. SM4: Mord 72Cb 155
Legion Rd. UB6: G'frd 39Ea 66
Legion Ter. E3 39Bc 72
Legion Way N12 24Gb 49
Legoland 7B 102
Legon Av. RM7: Rush G 32Ed 76
Legrace Av. TW4: Houn 54Z 107
Leicester Av. CR4: Mitc 70Nb 134
Leicester Cl. KT4: Wor Pk 77Ya 154
Leicester Ct. TW1: Twick 58Ma 109
(off Clevedon Rd.)
W9 43Cb 89
(off Elmfield Way)
WC2 4E 222
Leicester Flds. WC2 5E 222
Leicester Gdns. IG3: Ilf 31Uc 74
Leicester Ho. N18 22Xb 51
(off Cavendish Cl.)
SW9 55Rb 113
(off Loughborough Rd.)
Leicester M. N2 27Gb 49
Leicester Pl. WC2 4E 222 (45Mb 90)
Leicester Rd. CR0: C'don 73Ub 157
E11 29Kc 53
EN5: New Bar 15Db 31
N2 27Gb 49
NW10 38Ta 67
RM18: Tilb 3B 122
Leicester Sq. WC2 5E 222 (45Mb 90)
Leicester Square Theatre 4E 222
Leicester St. WC2 4E 222 (45Mb 90)
Leigh, The KT2: King T 66Ua 132
Leigham Av. SW16 62Nb 134
Leigham Cl. SW16 62Pb 134
Leigham Ct. SM6: Wall 79Lb 156
Leigham Ct. Rd. SW16 61Nb 134
Leigham Dr. TW7: Isle 52Ga 108
Leigham Hall Pde. SW16 62Nb 134
(off Streatham High Rd.)
Leigham Va. SW2 62Pb 134
SW16 62Pb 134
Leigh Av. IG4: Ilf 28Mc 53
Leigh Cl. KT3: N Mald 70Sa 131
KT15: Add 80H 149
Leigh Cl. Ind. Est. KT3: N Mald 70Ta 131
Leigh Cnr. KT11: Cobh 87Y 171
Leigh Ct. HA2: Harr 32Ga 66
KT11: Cobh 86Z 171
W14 49Bb 89
(off Avonmore Pl.)
WD6: Bore 12Ta 29
Leigh Ct. Cl. KT11: Cobh 86Y 171
Leigh Cres. CR0: New Ad 80Dc 158
Leigh Dr. RM3: Rom 21Md 57
Leigh Gdns. NW10 40Ya 68
Leigh Hill Rd. KT11: Cobh 87Y 171
Leigh Hunt Dr. N14 18Mb 32
Leigh Orchard Cl. SW16 62Pb 134
Leigh Pk. SL3: Dat 2M 103
Leigh Pl. DA2: Hawl 63Qd 141
DA16: Well 54Wc 117
EC1 7K 217 (43Qb 90)
KT11: Cobh 87Y 171
TW13: Felt 60Y 107
Leigh Pl. La. RH9: G'stone 4B 210
Leigh Rd. DA11: Grav'nd 1D 144
E6 37Qc 74
E10 31Ec 72
KT11: Cobh 86X 171
N5 35Rb 71
SL1: Slou 5F 80
TW3: Houn 56Fa 108
Leigh Rodd WD19: Wat 20Ba 27
Leigh Sq. SL4: Wind 4B 102
Leigh St. WC1 5F 217 (41Nb 90)
Leigh Ter. BR5: St P 69Xc 139
Leighton Av. E12 36Qc 74
HA5: Pinn 27Aa 45
Leighton Buzzard Rd. HP1: Hem H 1L 3
(not continuous)
Leighton Cl. HA8: Edg 26Qa 47
Leighton Ct. EN8: Chesh 1Zb 20
Leighton Cres. NW5 36Lb 70
Leighton Gdns. CR0: C'don 74Rb 157
CR2: Sande 85Xb 177
NW10 40Xa 68
RM18: Tilb 2C 122
Leighton Gro. NW5 36Lb 70
Leighton Ho. SW1 6E 228
Leighton House Mus. 48Bb 89
Leighton Mans. W14 51Ab 110
(off Greyhound Rd.)
Leighton Pl. NW5 36Lb 70
Leighton Rd. EN1: Enf 15Vb 33
HA3: Hrw W 26Fa 46
NW5 36Lb 70
W13 47Ja 86
Leighton St. CR0: C'don 74Rb 157
Leighton Way KT18: Eps 86Ta 173
Leila Parnell Pl. SE7 51Lc 115
Leinster Av. SW14 55Sa 109
Leinster Gdns.
W2 3A 220 (44Eb 89)
Leinster M. EN5: Barn 13Ab 30
W2 4A 220 (45Eb 89)
Leinster Pl. W2 3A 220 (44Eb 89)
Leinster Rd. N10 28Kb 50
Leinster Sq. W2 44Cb 89
(not continuous)
Leinster Ter. W2 4A 220 (45Eb 89)
Leiston Spur SL1: Slou 4J 81
Leisure La. KT14: W Byf 84K 169
Leisure Way N12 24Fb 49
Leisure W. TW13: Felt 61X 129
Leisure World
Hemel Hempstead 3P 3
Leitch Ho. NW8 38Fb 69
(off Hilgrove Rd.)
Leith Cl. NW9 32Ta 67
SL1: Slou 6L 81
Leithcote Gdns. SW16 63Pb 134
Leithcote Path SW16 62Pb 134
Leith Hill BR5: St P 67Wc 139
Leith Hill Grn. BR5: St P 67Wc 139
Leith Mans. W9 41Db 89
(off Grantully Rd.)
Leith Pk. Rd. DA12: Grav'nd 10D 122
Leith Rd. KT17: Eps 84Ua 174
N22 25Rb 51
Leith Towers SM2: Sutt 80Db 155
Leith Yd. NW6 39Cb 69
(off Quex Rd.)
Lela Av. TW4: Houn 54Y 107
Lelitia Cl. E8 39Wb 71
Lely Ho. UB5: N'olt 40Z 65
(off Academy Gdns.)
Leman Pas. E1 44Wb 91
(off Leman St.)
Leman St. E1 2K 225 (44Vb 91)
Lemark Cl. HA7: Stan 23La 46
Le May Av. SE12 62Kc 137
Lemna Ho. SE10 51Gc 115
Lemna Rd. E11 31Hc 73
Le Moal Ho. E1 43Yb 92
(off Stepney Way)
Lemonade Bldg. IG11: Bark 38Sc 74
(off Ripple Rd.)
Lemonfield Dr. WD25: Wat 4Aa 13
Lemon Gro. TW13: Felt 60W 106
Lemon Tree Ho. E3 41Bc 92
(off Bow Rd.)
Lemonwell Dr. SE9 57Sc 116
Lemsford Cl. N15 30Wb 51
Lemsford Ct. N4 33Sb 71
WD6: Bore 14Sa 29
Lemsford Rd. AL1: St A 2D 6
Lemuel St. SW18 58Eb 111
Lena Cres. N9 19Yb 34
Lena Gdns. W6 48Ya 88
Lena Kennedy Cl. E4 23Ec 52
Lenanton Steps E14 47Cc 92
(off Manilla St.)
Len Bishop Ct. E1 45Zb 92
(off Schoolhouse La.)
Len Clifton Ho. SE18 49Pc 94
(off Cambridge Barracks Rd.)
Lendal Ter. SW4 55Mb 112
Lenderyou Ct. DA1: Dart 59Md 119
(off Phoenix Pl.)
Lendon Rd. TN15: Bor G 93Be 205
Lenelby Rd. KT6: Surb 74Qa 153
Len Freeman Pl. SW6 51Bb 111
W6 49Va 88
(off Goldhawk Rd.)
Lenham Ho. SE1 3G 231
Lenham Rd. CR7: Thor H 68Tb 135
DA7: Bex 51Bd 117
SE12 56Hc 115
SM1: Sutt 77Db 155
Lenmore Av. RM17: Grays 48Ee 99
Lennard Av. BR4: W W'ck 75Gc 159
Lennard Cl. BR4: W W'ck 75Gc 159
Lennard Rd. BR2: Brom 74Pc 160
BR3: Beck 65Zb 136
CR0: C'don 74Sb 157
SE20 65Zb 136
TN13: Dun G 92Gd 202
Lennard Row RM15: Avel 46Td 98
Lennon Rd. NW2 36Ya 68
Lennox Av. DA11: Grav'nd 8B 122
Lennox Cl. RM1: Rom 30Hd 56
RM16: Chaf H 49Yd 98
Lennox Ct. RH1: Redh 5A 208
(off St Anne's Ri.)

Lennox Gdns. CR0: Wadd 77Rb 157
IG1: Ilf 32Pc 74
NW10 35Va 68
SW1 4F 227 (48Hb 89)
Lennox Gdns. M. SW1 4F 227 (48Hb 89)
Lennox Ho. *DA17: Belv* 48Cd 96
(off Picardy St.)
TW1: Twick 58Ma 109
(off Clevedon Rd.)
Lennox Rd. DA11: Grav'nd 8B 122
E17 30Bc 52
N4 33Pb 70
Lennox Rd. E. DA11: Grav'nd 9C 122
Lenor Cl. DA6: Bex 56Ad 117
Lensbury Av. SW6 54Eb 111
Lensbury Cl. EN8: Chesh 1Ac 20
Lensbury Way SE2 48Yc 95
Lens Rd. E7 38Lc 73
LENT 2A 80
Len Taylor Cl. UB4: Hayes 42U 84
Lent Grn. La. SL1: Burn 2A 80
Lenthall Av. RM17: Grays 47Ce 99
Lenthall Ho. *SW1* 50Lb 90
(off Churchill Gdns.)
Lenthall Rd. E8 38Wb 71
IG10: Lough 14Tc 36
Lenthorp Rd. SE10 49Hc 93
Lentmead Rd. BR1: Brom 62Hc 137
Lenton Path SE18 51Tc 116
Lenton Ri. TW9: Rich 55Na 109
Lenton St. SE18 49Tc 94
Lenton Ter. N4 33Qb 70
LENT RISE 4A 80
Len Williams Ct. NW6 40Cb 69
Leo Ct. TW8: Bford 52Ma 109
Leof Cres. SE6 64Dc 136
Leominster Rd. SM4: Mord 72Eb 155
Leominster Wlk. SM4: Mord 72Eb 155
Leonard Av. DA10: Swans 59Ae 121
RM7: Rush G 32Fd 76
SM4: Mord 71Eb 155
TN14: Otf 88Kd 183
Leonard Ct. HA3: Hrw W 25Ga 46
W8 48Cb 89
WC1 5E 216 (42Mb 90)
Leonard Pl. N16 35Ub 71
Leonard Rd. E4 23Cc 52
E7 35Jc 73
N9 20Vb 33
SW16 67Lb 134
UB2: S'hall 48Z 85
Leonard Robbins Path *SE28* 45Xc 95
(off Tawney Rd.)
Leonard St. E16 46Nc 94
EC2 5G 219 (42Tb 91)
Leonard Way CM14: B'wood 21Ud 58
Leonora Ho. W9 5A 214
Leonora Tyson M. SE21 61Tb 135
Leontine Cl. SE15 52Wb 113
Leopards Ct. EC1 7K 217
Leopold Av. SW19 64Bb 133
Leopold Bldgs. E2 3K 219
Leopold Ct. *KT10: Esh* 79Ea 152
(off Princess Sq.)
Leopold M. E9 39Yb 72
Leopold Rd. E17 29Cc 52
N2 27Fb 49
N18 22Xb 51
NW10 38Ua 68
SW19 63Bb 133
W5 46Pa 87
Leopold St. E3 43Bc 92
Leopold Ter. SW19 64Bb 133
Leopold Wlk. SE11 7H 229
Leo St. SE15 52Xb 113
Leo Yd. EC1 6C 218
Le Personne Homes *CR3: Cat'm* 94Tb 197
(off Banstead Rd.)
Le Personne Rd. CR3: Cat'm 94Tb 197
Leppoc Rd. SW4 57Mb 112
Leret Way KT22: Lea 93Ka 192
Leroy St. SE1 4H 231 (49Ub 91)
Lerry Cl. W14 51Bb 111
Lerwick Ct. EN1: Enf 15Ub 33
Lerwick Dr. SL1: Slou 3J 81
Lesbourne Rd. RH2: Reig 7K 207
Lescombe Cl. SE23 62Ac 136
Lescombe Rd. SE23 62Ac 136
Lesley Cl. BR8: Swan 69Fd 140
DA5: Bexl 59Dd 118
DA13: Ist R 7B 144
Lesley Ct. SW1 4D 228
Leslie Dunne Ho. SL4: Wind 4C 102
Leslie Gdns. SM2: Sutt 79Cb 155
Leslie Gro. CR0: C'don 74Ub 157
Leslie Gro. Pl. CR0: C'don 74Ub 157
Leslie Ho. *SW8* 52Nb 112
(off Wheatsheaf La.)
Leslie Pk. Rd. CR0: C'don 74Ub 157
Leslie Prince Ct. SE5 52Tb 113
Leslie Rd. E11 35Ec 72
E16 44Kc 93
GU24: Chob 2J 167
N2 27Fb 49
Leslie Smith Sq. SE18 51Qc 116
Lesnes Abbey 49Zc 95
Lesney Farm Est. DA8: Erith 52Fd 118
Lesney Pk. DA8: Erith 51Fd 118
Lesney Pk. Rd. DA8: Erith 51Fd 118
Lessar Av. SW4 58Lb 112
Lessingham Av. IG5: Ilf 27Qc 54
SW17 63Hb 133
Lessing St. SE23 59Ac 114
Lessington Av. RM7: Rom 30Ed 56
Lessness Av. DA7: Bex 52Zc 117
LESSNESS HEATH 50Dd 96
Lessness Pk. DA17: Belv 50Bd 95
Lessness Rd. DA17: Belv 51Cd 118
SM4: Mord 72Eb 155
Lester Av. E15 42Gc 93
Lester Ct. *E3* 41Dc 92
(off Bruce Rd.)
WD24: Wat 9Y 13
Lestock Cl. *SE25* 69Wb 135
(off Manor Rd.)
Leston Cl. RM13: Rain 41Kd 97
Leswin Pl. N16 34Vb 71
Leswin Rd. N16 34Vb 71
Letchford Gdns. NW10 41Wa 88
Letchford Ho. *E3* 40Cc 72
(off Thomas Fyre Dr.)
Letchford M. NW10 41Wa 88
Letchford Ter. HA3: Hrw W 25Da 45
LETCHMORE HEATH 11Ga 28
Letchmore Ho. *W10* 42Ya 88
(off Sutton Way)
Letchmore Rd. WD7: R'lett 8Ja 14
Letchworth Av. TW14: Felt 59V 106
Letchworth Cl. BR2: Brom 71Jc 159
WD19: Wat 22Z 45
Letchworth Dr. BR2: Brom 71Jc 159
Letchworth Rd. HA7: Stan 24Na 47
Letchworth St. SW17 63Hb 133
Lethbridge Cl. SE13 53Ec 114
Letter Box La. TN13: S'oaks 100Ld 203
Letterstone Rd. SW6 52Bb 111
Lettice St. SW6 53Bb 111
Lett Rd. E15 38Fc 73
SW9 53Pb 112
LETT'S GREEN 88Vc 181
Lettsom St. SE5 54Ub 113
Lettsom Wlk. E13 40Jc 73
Leucha Rd. E17 29Ac 52
Levana Cl. SW19 60Ab 110
Levant Ho. *E1* 42Zb 92
(off Ernest St.)
Levehurst Ho. SE27 64Sb 135
Leven Cl. EN8: Walt C 5Zb 20
WD19: Wat 22Z 45
Levendale Rd. SE23 61Ac 136
Leven Dr. EN8: Walt C 5Zb 20
Levenhurst Way SW4 54Nb 112
Leven Rd. E14 43Ec 92
Leven Way UB3: Hayes 44U 84
Leveret Cl. CR0: New Ad 83Fc 179
WD25: Wat 6W 12
Leverett St. SW3 5E 226 (49Gb 89)
Leverholme Gdns. SE9 63Qc 138
Leverington Pl. N1 4H 219 (41Tb 91)
Leverson St. SW16 65Lb 134
Lever Sq. RM16: Grays 9B 100
LEVERSTOCK GREEN 3C 4
Leverstock Grn. Rd. HP2: Hem H 1A 4
HP3: Hem H 2B 4
(not continuous)
Leverstock Grn. Way HP3: Hem H 2C 4
Leverstock Ho. SW3 7E 226
Lever St. EC1 4C 218 (41Rb 91)
Leverton Pl. NW5 36Lb 70
Leverton St. NW5 36Lb 70
Leverton Way EN9: Walt A 5Ec 20
Leveson Rd. RM16: Grays 8D 100
Levett Gdns. IG3: Ilf 35Vc 75
Levett Rd. IG11: Bark 37Uc 74
KT22: Lea 92Ka 192
SS17: Stan H 1N 101
Levine Gdns. IG11: Bark 40Zc 75
Levison Way N19 32Mb 70
Levita Ho. NW1 3E 216
(not continuous)
Levyne Ct. EC1 5K 217
Lewes Cl. RM17: Grays 51Ce 121
UB5: N'olt 37Ca 65
Lewes Ct. *CR4: Mitc* 69Hb 133
(off Chatsworth Pl.)
SL1: Slou 8G 80
Lewesdon Cl. SW19 60Za 110
Lewes Ho. SE1 1J 231
SE15 51Wb 113
(off Friary Est.)
Lewes Rd. BR1: Brom 68Mc 137
N12 22Gb 49
RM3: Rom 21Md 57
Leweston Pl. N16 31Vb 71
Lewes Way WD3: Crox G 14S 26
Lew Evans Ho. SE22 57Wb 113
Lewey Ho. *E3* 42Bc 92
(off Joseph St.)
Lewgars Av. NW9 30Sa 47
Lewing Cl. BR6: Orp 74Uc 160
Lewington Apartments *SE16* 49Yb 92
(off Alpine Rd.)
Lewington Cen. *SE16* 49Yb 92
(off Alpine Rd.)
Lewington Ct. EN3: Enf W 9Zb 20
Lewin Rd. DA6: Bex 56Ad 117
SW14 55Ta 109
SW16 65Mb 134
Lewins Farm Ct. SL1: Slou 5D 80
Lewins Rd. KT18: Eps 86Ra 173
SL9: Chal P 27A 42
Lewins Way SL1: Slou 5D 80
Lewin Ter. TW14: Bedf 59T 106
Lewis Av. E17 25Cc 52
Lewis Cl. CM15: Shenf 17Be 41
KT15: Add 77L 149
N14 17Lb 32
UB9: Hare 26L 43
Lewis Ct. DA11: Nflt 1B 144
KT22: Lea 93Ja 192
(off Highbury Dr.)
SE16 50Xb 91
(off Stubbs Dr.)
Lewis Cres. NW10 36Ta 67
Lewis Gdns. N2 26Fb 49
N16 30Vb 51
Lewis Gro. SE13 56Ec 114
LEWISHAM 55Ec 114
Lewisham Cen. SE13 56Ec 114
Lewisham Hgts. SE23 60Yb 114
Lewisham High St. SE13 58Dc 114
(not continuous)
Lewisham Hill SE13 54Ec 114
Lewisham Indoor Bowls Cen. 64Bc 136
Lewisham Lions Cen. 50Yb 92
Lewisham Model Mkt. *SE13* 56Ec 114
(off Lewisham High St.)
Lewisham Pk. SE13 57Ec 114
Lewisham Rd. SE13 53Dc 114
Lewisham St. SW1 2E 228 (47Mb 90)
Lewisham Way SE4 53Bc 114
SE14 53Bc 114
Lewis Ho. *E14* 46Ec 92
(off Coldharbour)
WD18: Wat 16V 26
Lewis La. SL9: Chal P 25A 42
Lewis M. BR7: Chst 64Pc 138
Lewis Pl. E8 36Wb 71
Lewis Rd. CR4: Mitc 68Fb 133
DA10: Swans 58Ae 121
DA13: Ist R 7B 144
DA14: Sidc 62Yc 139
DA16: Well 55Yc 117
RM11: Horn 30Ld 57
SM1: Sutt 77Db 155
TW10: Rich 57Ma 109
UB1: S'hall 47Aa 85
Lewis Silkin Ho. *SE15* 51Yb 114
(off Lovelinch Cl.)
Lewis Sports and Leisure Cen. 67Vb 135
Lewis St. NW1 37Kb 70
(not continuous)
Lewiston Cl. KT4: Wor Pk 73Xa 154
Lewis Way RM10: Dag 37Dd 76
Leworth Pl. SL4: Wind 3H 103
Lexden Dr. RM6: Chad H 30Xc 55
Lexden Rd. CR4: Mitc 70Mb 134
W3 45Ra 87
Lexden Ter. *EN9: Walt A* 6Ec 20
(off Sewardstone Rd.)
Lexham Gdns. W8 49Cb 89
Lexham Gdns. M. W8 48Db 89
Lexham Ho. *IG11: Bark* 39Tc 74
(off St Margarets)
W8 49Db 89
(off Lexham Gdns.)
Lexham M. W8 49Cb 89
Lexham Wlk. W8 48Db 89
Lexicon Apartments
RM1: Rom 28Hd 56
(off Mercury Gdns.)
Lexington Apartments
EC1 5F 219 (42Tb 91)
Lexington Bldg. E3 40Cc 72
Lexington Cl. WD6: Bore 13Pa 29
Lexington Ct. CR8: Purl 82Sb 177
EN6: Pot B 3Za 16
(off Mimms Hall Rd.)
Lexington Ho. UB7: W Dray 47P 83
Lexington Pl. KT1: Hamp W 66Ma 131
Lexington St. W1 3C 222 (45Lb 90)
Lexington Way EN5: Barn 14Za 30
RM14: Upm 30Vd 58
Lexton Gdns. SW12 60Mb 112
Leyborne Av. W13 47Ka 86
Leyborne Pk. TW9: Kew 53Qa 109
Leybourne Av. KT14: Byfl 85P 169
Leybourne Cl. BR2: Brom 72Jc 159
KT14: Byfl 85P 169
Leybourne Ho. *E14* 44Bc 92
(off Dod St.)
SE15 51Yb 114
Leybourne Rd. E11 32Hc 73
NW1 38Kb 70
NW9 29Qa 47
UB10: Hil 39S 64
Leybourne St. NW1 38Kb 70
Leybridge Ct. SE12 57Jc 115
Leyburn Cl. E17 28Dc 52
Leyburn Cres. RM3: Rom 24Nd 57
Leyburn Gdns. CR0: C'don 75Ub 157
Leyburn Gro. N18 23Wb 51
Leyburn Rd. N18 23Wb 51
RM3: Rom 24Nd 57
Leycester Cl. GU20: W'sham 7A 146
Leycroft Cl. IG10: Lough 15Qc 36
Leycroft Gdns. DA8: Erith 53Kd 119
Leydenhatch La. BR8: Swan 67Ed 140
Leyden Mans. N19 31Nb 70
Leyden St. E1 1K 225 (43Vb 91)
Leydon Cl. SE16 46Zb 92
Leyes Rd. E16 44Mc 93
Leyfield KT4: Wor Pk 74Ua 154
Leyhill Cl. BR8: Swan 70Gd 140
Ley Hill Rd. HP3: Bov 1A 10
Ley Ho. SE1 2D 230
Leyland Av. AL1: St A 4B 6
EN3: Enf H 12Ac 34
Leyland Cl. EN8: Chesh 1Yb 20
Leyland Gdns. IG8: Wfd G 22Lc 53
Leyland Ho. *E14* 45Dc 92
(off Hale St.)
Leyland Rd. SE12 57Jc 115
Leylands SW18 58Bb 111
Leylands La. TW19: Stanw M 56H 105
(not continuous)
Leylang Rd. SE14 52Zb 114
Leys, The HA3: Kenton 30Pa 47
KT12: Hers 77Ba 151
N2 28Eb 49
WD7: R'lett 9Ja 14
Leys Av. RM10: Dag 39Ed 76
Leys Cl. HA1: Harr 29Fa 46
RM10: Dag 38Ed 76
UB9: Hare 25M 43
Leys Ct. SW9 54Qb 112
Leysdown Av. DA7: Bex 56Ed 118
Leysdown Ho. SE17 7J 231
Leysdown Rd. SE9 61Nc 138
Leysfield Rd. W12 48Wa 88
Leys Gdns. EN4: Cockf 15Jb 32
Leyspring Rd. E11 32Hc 73
Leys Rd. HP3: Hem H 4N 3
KT22: Oxs 84Fa 172
Leys Rd. E. EN3: Enf H 11Ac 34
Leys Rd. W. EN3: Enf H 11Ac 34
Leys Sq. N3 25Db 49
Ley St. IG1: Ilf 33Rc 74
IG2: Ilf 33Sc 74
Leyswood Dr. IG2: Ilf 29Uc 54
Leythe Rd. W3 47Sa 87
LEYTON 33Ec 72
Leyton Bus. Cen. E10 33Cc 72
Leyton Ct. SE23 60Yb 114
LEYTON CROSS 61Jd 140
Leyton Cross Rd. DA2: Wilm 62Hd 140
Leyton Grange Est. E10 32Cc 72
Leyton Grn. Rd. E10 30Ec 52
Leyton Grn. Twr. *E10* 30Ec 52
(off Leyton Grn. Rd.)
Leyton Ho. *E2* 4K 219
(off Calvert Av.)
Leyton Ind. Village E10 31Zb 72
Leyton Leisure Lagoon 31Dc 72
Leyton Link Est. E10 31Ac 72
Leyton Mills E10 35Ec 72
Leyton Orient FC 34Dc 72
Leyton Pk. Rd. E10 34Ec 72
Leyton Rd. E15 36Ec 72
SW19 66Eb 133
LEYTONSTONE 32Gc 73
Leytonstone Ho. *E11* 31Hc 73
(off Hanbury Dr.)
Leytonstone Rd. E15 37Gc 73
Leyton Way E11 31Gc 73
Leywick St. E15 40Gc 73
Lezayre Rd. BR6: Chels 79Vc 161
Lianne Gro. SE9 62Lc 137
Liardet St. SE14 51Ac 114
Liberia Rd. N5 37Rb 71
Liberty, The RM1: Rom 29Gd 56
Liberty Av. SW19 67Fb 133
Liberty Cen. HA0: Wemb 39Pa 67
Liberty Cl. KT4: Wor Pk 74Ya 154
N18 21Vb 51
Liberty Ct. CR8: Purl 84Qb 176
IG11: Bark 40Xc 75
Liberty Hall Rd. KT15: Add 78J 149
Liberty Ho. *E1* 45Wb 91
(off Ensign St.)
E13 40Jc 73
KT16: Chert 74H 149
(off Guildford St.)
Liberty La. KT15: Add 78J 149
Liberty M. N22 25Rb 51
SW12 58Kb 112
Liberty Point *CR0: C'don* 73Wb 157
(off Blackhorse La.)
Liberty Ri. KT15: Add 79J 149
Liberty St. SW9 53Pb 112
Liberty Wlk. AL1: St A 3G 6
Libra Mans. *E3* 40Bc 72
(off Libra Rd.)
Libra Rd. E3 39Bc 72
E13 40Jc 73
Library Ct. N17 27Vb 51
Library Hill CM14: B'wood 19Zd 41
Library Mans. *W12* 47Ya 88
(off Pennard Rd.)
Library Pde. *NW10* 39Ua 68
(off Craven Pk. Rd.)
Library Pl. E1 45Xb 91
Library St. SE1 3B 230 (47Rb 91)
Library Way TW2: Whitt 59Ea 108
Libro Ct. E4 21Cc 52
Lichfield Cl. EN4: Cockf 13Hb 31
Lichfield Ct. *KT6: Surb* 71Na 153
(off Claremont Rd.)
TW9: Rich 57Na 109
Lichfield Gdns. TW9: Rich 56Na 109
Lichfield Gro. N3 25Cb 49
Lichfield Ho. *WD6: Bore* 12Qa 29
(off Stratfield Rd.)
Lichfield Pl. AL1: St A 1D 6
Lichfield Rd. E3 41Ac 92
E6 41Mc 93
HA6: Nwood 27W 44
IG8: Wfd G 21Gc 53
N9 19Wb 33
NW2 35Ab 68
RM8: Dag 35Xc 75
TW4: Houn 55Y 107
TW9: Kew 53Pa 109
Lichfield Ter. RM14: Upm 33Ud 78
TW9: Rich 57Na 109
(off Sheen Rd.)
Lichfield Way CR2: Sels 82Zb 178
Lichlade Cl. BR6: Orp 77Vc 161
Lickey Ho. *W14* 51Bb 111
(off North End Rd.)
Lidbury Rd. NW7 23Ab 48
Lidcote Gdns. SW9 54Pb 112
Liddall Way UB7: Yiew 46P 83
Liddell SL4: Wind 5A 102
Liddell Cl. HA3: Kenton 27Ma 47
Liddell Gdns. NW10 40Ya 68
Liddell Pl. SL4: Wind 4A 102
Liddell Rd. NW6 37Cb 69
Liddell Sq. SL4: Wind 4A 102
Liddell Way SL4: Wind 5A 102
Liddiard Ho. *W11* 45Ab 88
(off Lansdowne Rd.)
Lidding Rd. HA3: Kenton 29Ma 47
Liddington Rd. E15 39Hc 73
Liddon Rd. BR1: Brom 69Lc 137
E13 41Kc 93
Liden Cl. E17 31Bc 72
Lidfield Rd. N16 35Tb 71
Lidgate Rd. SE15 52Vb 113
Lidgould Gro. HA4: Ruis 30W 44
Lidiard Rd. SW18 61Eb 133
Lidlington Pl. NW1 2C 216 (40Lb 70)
Lido Sq. N17 26Tb 51
Lidstone Cl. GU21: Wok 9M 167
Lidstone Ct. SL3: G Grn 4P 81
Lidyard Rd. N19 32Lb 70
Lieutenant Ellis Way
EN7: Chesh, G Oak 2Vb 19
EN8: Chesh, Walt C 3Vb 19
Liffler Rd. SE18 50Uc 94
Liffords Pl. SW13 54Va 110
Lifford St. SW15 56Za 110
Lightbox Museum, The 88A 168
Lightcliffe Rd. N13 21Qb 50
Lighter Cl. SE16 49Ac 92
Lighterman Ho. E14 45Ec 92
Lighterman M. E1 44Zb 92
Lighterman's M. DA11: Nflt 9A 122
Lightermans Rd. E14 47Cc 92
Lightermans Wlk. SW18 56Cb 111
Lightermans Way DA9: Ghithe 56Yd 120
Lightfoot Rd. N8 29Nb 50
Lightfoot Vs. *N1* 38Qb 70
(off Augustas La.)
Light Horse Ct. SW3 7H 227
Lighthouse Apartments *E1* 44Yb 92
(off Commercial Rd.)
Lightley Cl. HA0: Wemb 39Na 67
LIGHTWATER 2A 166
Lightwater By-Pass GU18: Light 2A 166
Lightwater Mdw. GU18: Light 3A 166
Lightwater Rd. GU18: Light 3A 166
Ligonier St. E2 5K 219 (42Vb 91)
Lilac Av. EN1: Enf 8Yb 20
GU22: Wok 2P 187
Lilac Cl. CM15: Pil H 15Xd 40
E4 23Bc 52
EN7: Chesh 3Xb 19
Lilac Ct. E13 39Lc 73
SL2: Slou 1D 80
TW11: Tedd 63Ha 130
Lilac Gdns. BR8: Swan 70Ed 140
CR0: C'don 76Cc 158
RM7: Rush G 32Gd 76
UB3: Hayes 44U 84
W5 48Ma 87
Lilac Ho. SE4 55Cc 114
Lilac M. *N22* 27Qb 50
(off High Rd.)
Lilac Pl. SE11 6H 229 (49Pb 90)
UB7: Yiew 45P 83
Lilac St. W12 45Wa 88
Lilah M. BR2: Brom 68Hc 137
Lila Pl. BR8: Swan 70Gd 140
Lilburne Gdns. SE9 57Nc 116
Lilburne Rd. SE9 57Nc 116
Lilburne Wlk. NW10 37Sa 67
Lile Cres. W7 43Ga 86
Lilestone Ho. NW8 5C 214
Lilestone St. NW8 5D 214 (42Gb 89)
Lilford Ho. SE5 54Sb 113
Lilford Rd. SE5 54Rb 113
Lilian Barker Cl. SE12 57Jc 115
Lilian Board Way UB6: G'frd 36Fa 66
Lilian Cl. N16 34Ub 71
Lilian Cres. CM13: Hut 19Ee 41
Lilian Gdns. IG8: Wfd G 25Kc 53
Lilian Knowles Ho. E1 1K 225
Lilian Rd. SW16 67Lb 134
Lillechurch Rd.
RM8: Dag 37Xc 75
Lilleshall Rd. SM4: Mord 72Fb 155
Lilley Cl. CM14: B'wood 21Vd 58
E1 46Wb 91
Lilley Dr. KT20: Kgswd 94Db 195
Lilley La. NW7 22Ta 47
Lilley Mead RH1: Mers 3C 208
Lilley Way SL1: Slou 6C 80
Lillian Av. W3 47Qa 87
Lillian Rd. SW13 51Wa 110
Lillie Bri. Dpt. W14 50Bb 89
Lillie Mans. *SW6* 51Ab 110
(off Lillie Rd.)
Lillie Rd. SW6 51Ab 110
TN16: Big H 90Mc 179
Lillie Road Fitness Cen. 52Za 110
Lillieshall Rd. SW4 55Kb 112
Lillie Yd. SW6 51Cb 111
Lillingston Ho. N7 35Qb 70
Lillington Gdns. Est. SW1 6C 228
Lilliot's La. KT22: Lea 91Ja 192
Lilliput Av. UB5: N'olt 39Aa 65
Lilliput Ct. SE12 57Kc 115
Lilliput Rd. RM7: Rush G 31Fd 76
Lily Cl. RM13: Rain 42Ld 97
W14 49Za 88
Lily Dr. UB7: W Dray 49M 83
Lily Gdns. HA0: Wemb 40La 66
Lily Nichols Ho. *E16* 46Mc 93
(off Connaught Br.)
Lily Pl. EC1 7A 218 (43Qb 90)
Lily Rd. E17 30Cc 52
Lilyville Rd. SW6 53Bb 111
Limborough Ho. *E14* 43Cc 92
(off Thomas Rd.)
Limbourne Av. RM8: Dag 31Bd 75
Limburg Rd. SW11 56Gb 111
Lime Av. CM13: B'wood 20Be 41
DA11: Nflt 59Fe 121
RM14: Upm 35Qd 77
SL4: Wind 3K 103
(Adelaide Rd.)
SL4: Wind 2D 124
(Holly Wlk.)
UB7: Yiew 45P 83
Limeburner La. EC4 3B 224 (44Rb 91)
Limebush Cl. KT15: New H 81L 169
Lime Cl. BR1: Brom 70Nc 138
E1 46Wb 91
GU4: W Cla 100K 189
HA3: W'stone 26Ja 46
HA5: Eastc 27V 44
IG9: Buck H 19Mc 35
RH2: Reig 9K 207
RM7: Rom 28Ed 56
RM15: S Ock 41Yd 98
SM5: Cars 75Hb 155
WD19: Wat 17Z 27
Lime Ct. CR4: Mitc 68Fb 133
E11 33Gc 73
(off Trinity Cl.)
E17 29Ec 52
HA1: Harr 30Ha 46
HA4: Ruis 31X 65
SE9 61Rc 138
Lime Cres. TW16: Sun 68Y 129
Limecroft Cl. KT19: Ewe 80Ta 153
Limerston Rd. GU21: Knap 9F 166
Limedene Cl. HA5: Pinn 25Z 45
Lime Gro. BR6: Farnb 75Rc 160
CR6: W'ham 90Ac 178
DA15: Sidc 58Vc 117
E4 23Bc 52
GU4: W Cla 100J 189
GU22: Wok 93A 188
HA4: Ruis 30X 45
IG6: Ilf 23Vc 55
KT3: N Mald 69Ta 131
KT15: Add 77J 149
N20 18Bb 31
TW1: Twick 58Ha 108
UB3: Hayes 45T 84
W12 47Ya 88
Limeharbour E14 48Dc 92
LIMEHOUSE 44Bc 92
Lime Ho. TW9: Kew 53Ra 109
Limehouse C'way. E14 45Bc 92
Lime Ho. Ct. *E14* 44Bc 92
(off Wharf La.)
Limehouse Ct. E14 44Cc 92
Limehouse Cut *E14* 43Dc 92
(off Morris Rd.)
Limehouse Flds. Est. E14 43Ac 92
Limehouse Link E14 44Ac 92
Lime Kiln Dr. SE7 51Kc 115
Limekiln Pl. SE19 66Vb 135
Limekiln Wharf E14 45Bc 92
Limelight Ho. SE11 6B 230
Lime Lodge *TW16: Sun* 66V 128
(off Forest Dr.)
Lime Mdw. Av.
CR2: Sande 85Wb 177
Lime Pit La. TN13: Dun G 89Ed 182
Limerick Cl. SW12 59Lb 112
Limerick Gdns. RM14: Upm 31Vd 78
Limerick M. *N2* 27Gb 49
(off Bedford Rd.)
Lime Rd. BR8: Swan 69Fd 140
TW9: Rich 56Pa 109
Lime Row DA18: Erith 48Bd 95
Limerston St. SW10 51Eb 111
Limes, The AL1: St A 1C 6
BR2: Brom 75Nc 160
CM13: B'wood 20Be 41
DA1: Dart 59Pd 119
GU21: Wok 88C 168
(off Maybury Rd.)
GU21: Wok 7P 167
(Ridgeway)
HP3: Hem H 5M 3
KT8: W Mole 70Da 129
KT19: Eps 82Ra 173
KT22: Lea 95Ka 192
RM11: Horn 27Md 57
RM19: Purf 50Qd 97
SL4: Wind 4A 102
SW18 58Cb 111
W2 45Cb 89
WD4: Hunt C 5S 12
(off Bridge Rd.)

Limes Av. CR0: Wadd 76Qb **156**
E11 28Kc **53**
IG7: Chig 22Sc **54**
N12 21Eb **49**
NW7 23Ua **48**
NW11 31Ab **68**
SE20 66Xb **135**
SM5: Cars 74Hb **155**
SW13 54Va **110**
Limes Av., The N11 22Kb **50**
Limes Cl. KT22: Lea 93La **192**
N11 22Lb **50**
TW15: Ashf 64Q **128**
Limes Ct. CM15: B'wood 18Zd **41**
NW6 *38Ab* ***68***
(off Brondesbury Pk.)
Limesdale Gdns. HA8: Edg 26Sa **47**
Limes Fld. Rd. SW14 55Ua **110**
Limesford Rd. SE15 56Zb **114**
Limes Gdns. SW18 58Cb **111**
Limes Gro. SE13 56Ec **114**
Limes M. TW20: Egh 64B **126**
Limes Pl. CR0: C'don 73Tb **157**
Limes Rd. BR3: Beck 68Dc **136**
CR0: C'don 73Tb **157**
EN8: Chesh 4Ac **20**
KT13: Weyb 77Q **150**
TW20: Egh 64B **126**
Limes Row BR6: Farnb 78Rc **160**
Limestone Wlk.
DA18: Erith 47Zc **95**
Lime St. E17 28Ac **52**
EC3 4H **225** (45Ub **91**)
Lime St. Pas. EC3 3H **225** (44Ub **91**)
Limes Wlk. SE15 56Yb **114**
W5 47Ma **87**
Lime Ter. W7 45Ga **86**
Lime Tree Av. DA9: Bluew 59Wd **120**
KT7: T Ditt 74Fa **152**
KT10: Esh 74Fa **152**
Lime Tree Cl. E18 28Lc **53**
KT23: Bookh 96Ca **191**
Limetree Cl. SW2 60Pb **112**
Lime Tree Ct. AL2: Lon C 8F **6**
CR2: S Croy 79Sb **157**
E3 43Cc **92**
HA5: Hat E *24Ca* ***45***
(off The Avenue)
KT21: Asht 90Na **173**
Lime Tree Gro. CR0: C'don 76Bc **158**
Lime Tree Ho. DA4: Farni 72Nd **163**
Lime Tree Pl. AL1: St A 3D **6**
BR5: St M Cry 73Ad **161**
CR4: Mitc 67Kb **134**
Lime Tree Rd. TW5: Hest 53Da **107**
Lime Trees Pk. Golf Course 39Y **65**
Limetree Ter. DA16: Well 55Wc **117**
SE6 60Bc **114**
Lime Tree Wlk. BR4: W W'ck 77Hc **159**
EN2: Enf 10Sb **19**
GU21: Wok 8P **167**
GU25: Vir W 70A **126**
TN13: S'oaks 97Kd **203**
WD3: Rick 15K **25**
WD23: B Hea 18Ga **28**
Limetree Wlk. SW17 64Jb **134**
Lime Wlk. E15 39Gc **73**
HP3: Hem H 4P **3**
KT8: E Mos 70Ha **130**
UB9: Den 36L **63**
Lime Way WD7: Shenl 3La **14**
Limewood Cl. BR3: Beck 71Ec **158**
E17 28Bc **52**
GU21: Wok 2H **187**
W13 44Ka **86**
Limewood Ct. IG4: Ilf 29Pc **54**
Limewood Ho. KT19: Eps 81Ta **173**
Limewood Rd. DA8: Erith 52Ed **118**
Lime Works Rd. RH1: Mers 98Lb **196**
LIMPSFIELD 1M **211**
Limpsfield Av. CR7: Thor H 71Pb **156**
SW19 61Za **132**
LIMPSFIELD CHART 2P **211**
Limpsfield Chart Golf Course 1N **211**
Limpsfield Rd. CR2: Sande 84Wb **177**
CR6: W'ham 84Wb **177**
Limscott Ho. *E3* *41Dc* ***92***
(off Bruce Rd.)
Linacre Cl. SE15 55Xb **113**
Linacre Ct. W6 50Za **88**
Linacre Rd. NW2 37Xa **68**
Linale Ho. N1 2F **219**
Linberry Wlk. SE8 49Bc **92**
Linchfield Rd. SL3: Dat 3N **103**
Linchmere Rd. SE12 59Hc **115**
Lincoln Av. N14 20Lb **32**
RM7: Rush G 33Fd **76**
SW19 62Za **132**
TW2: Twick 61Ea **130**
Lincoln Cl. DA8: Erith 54Hd **118**
HA2: Harr 29Ba **45**
RM11: Horn 29Qd **57**
SE25 72Wb **157**
UB6: G'frd 39Ea **66**
Lincoln Ct. *CR2: S Croy* *78Sb* ***157***
(off Warham Rd.)
IG2: Ilf 30Sc **54**
KT13: Weyb *79T* ***150***
(off Old Av.)
N16 31Tb **71**
SE12 62Kc **137**
SL1: Slou 8J **81**
UB9: Den 30H **43**
WD6: Bore 15Ta **29**
WD25: Wat 5X **13**
Lincoln Cres. EN1: Enf 15Ub **33**
Lincoln Dr. GU22: Pyr 87G **168**
WD3: Crox G 14R **26**
WD19: Wat 20Y **27**
Lincoln Fld. WD23: Bush 13Ba **27**
Lincoln Gdns. IG1: Ilf 31Nc **74**
Lincoln Grn. Rd.
BR5: St M Cry 71Vc **161**
Lincoln Gro. KT13: Weyb 76R **150**
Lincoln Hatch La. SL1: Burn 2A **80**
Lincoln Ho. SE5 52Qb **112**
SW3 2F **227** (47Hb **89**)
TW8: Bford *50Na* ***87***
(off Ealing Rd.)
Lincoln M. AL3: St A 3A **6**
N15 28Sb **51**
NW6 39Bb **69**
SE21 61Tb **135**
Lincoln Pde. HA9: Wemb 32Na **67**
N2 *27Gb* ***49***
(off Lincoln Rd.)
Lincoln Rd. CR4: Mitc 71Nb **156**
DA8: Erith 54Hd **118**
DA14: Sidc 64Xc **139**
E7 37Mc **73**
E13 42Kc **93**
E18 25Jc **53**
EN1: Enf 14Ub **33**
EN3: Pond E 15Wb **33**
HA0: Wemb 37Ma **67**
HA2: Harr 29Ba **45**
HA6: Nwood 27V **44**
KT3: N Mald 69Sa **131**
KT4: Wor Pk 74Xa **154**
N2 27Gb **49**
SE25 69Xb **135**
SL9: Chal P 25A **42**
TW13: Hanw 62Ba **129**
Lincolns, The NW7 20Va **30**
Lincolns Fld. CM16: Epp 2Vc **23**
Lincolnshire Ter. DA2: Daren 63Td **142**
Lincolns Inn Flds. WC2 2H **223** (44Pb **90**)
Lincoln's Inn Hall 2J **223** (44Pb **90**)
Lincolns La. CM14: Pil H, S Weald 15Sd **40**
Lincoln St. E11 33Gc **73**
SW3 6F **227** (49Hb **89**)
Lincoln Wlk. KT19: Ewe 82Ta **173**
Lincoln Way EN1: Enf 15Xb **33**
SL1: Slou 5B **80**
TW16: Sun 67U **128**
WD3: Crox G 14R **26**
Lincombe Ct. KT15: Add 78K **149**
Lincombe Rd. BR1: Brom 62Hc **137**
Lindal Ct. E18 25Hc **53**
Lindal Cres. EN2: Enf 14Nb **32**
Lindale Cl. GU25: Vir W 10K **125**
Lindales, The *N17* *23Wb* ***51***
(off Grasmere Rd.)
Lindal Rd. SE4 57Bc **114**
Lindbergh Rd. SM6: Wall 80Nb **156**
Linden SL3: L'ly 50D **82**
Linden Av. CR5: Coul 88Kb **176**
CR7: Thor H 70Rb **135**
DA1: Dart 60Ld **119**
EN1: Enf 11Wb **33**
HA4: Ruis 32W **64**
HA9: Wemb 36Pa **67**
NW10 40Za **68**
TW3: Houn 57Da **107**
WD18: Wat 14U **26**
Linden Chase TN13: S'oaks 94Kd **203**
Linden Cl. BR6: Chels 78Wc **161**
EN7: Chesh 2Xb **19**
HA4: Ruis 32W **64**
HA7: Stan 22Ka **46**
KT7: T Ditt 73Ha **152**
KT15: New H 83J **169**
KT20: Tad 92Za **194**
N14 16Lb **32**
RM19: Purf 51Sd **120**
SL0: Iver H 40F **62**
Linden Ct. DA14: Sidc 63Uc **138**
KT22: Lea 93Ka **192**
SE20 *66Xb* ***135***
(off Anerley Pk.)
TW20: Eng G 5M **125**
W12 46Ya **88**
Linden Cres. AL1: St A 2G **6**
IG8: Wfd G 23Kc **53**
KT1: King T 68Pa **131**
UB6: G'frd 37Ha **66**
Linden Dr. CR3: Cat'm 96Sb **197**
SL2: Farn R 9G **60**
SL9: Chal P 25A **42**
Lindenfield BR7: Chst 68Rc **138**
Linden Gdns. EN1: Enf 11Wb **33**
KT22: Lea 93La **192**
W2 45Cb **89**
W4 50Ua **88**
Linden Glade HP1: Hem H 3K **3**
Linden Gro. CR6: W'ham 90Ac **178**
KT3: N Mald 69Ua **132**
KT12: Walt T 75V **150**
SE15 55Xb **113**
SE26 65Yb **136**
TW11: Tedd 64Ha **130**
Linden Ho. *SE8* *51Bc* ***114***
(off Abinger Gro.)
TW12: Hamp 65Ca **129**
Linden Lawns HA9: Wemb 35Pa **67**
Linden Lea HA5: Hat E 24Ba **45**
N2 29Eb **49**
WD25: Wat 5W **12**
Linden Leas BR4: W W'ck 75Fc **159**
Linden Mans. *N6* *32Kb* ***70***
(off Hornsey La.)
Linden M. N1 36Tb **71**
W2 45Cb **89**
Linden Pit Path KT22: Lea 92La **192**
(Kingfisher Cl.)
KT22: Lea 93Ka **192**
(Linden Rd.)
Linden Pl. CR4: Mitc 70Gb **133**
KT17: Eps 84Ua **174**
KT24: E Hor 98U **190**
TW18: Staines 63J **127**
Linden Ri. CM14: W'ley 22Yd **59**
Linden Rd. KT13: Weyb 81S **170**
KT22: Lea 93Ka **192**
N10 28Kb **50**
N11 19Hb **31**
N15 28Sb **51**
TW12: Hamp 66Ca **129**
Lindens, The CR0: New Ad 79Ec **158**
E17 *28Dc* ***52***
(off Prospect Hill)
EN9: Walt A *7Lc* ***21***
(in Woodbine Cl. Caravan Pk.)
HP3: Hem H 5H **3**
IG10: Lough 15Pc **36**
N12 22Fb **49**
W4 53Sa **109**
Lindens Cl. KT24: Eff 100Aa **191**
Linden Sq. TN13: Riv 94Gd **202**
UB9: Hare 23J **43**
Linden St. RM7: Rom 28Fd **56**
Linden Wlk. N19 33Lb **70**
Linden Way CR8: Purl 82Lb **176**
GU22: Wok 93B **188**
GU23: Rip 97H **189**
N14 16Lb **32**
TW17: Shep 71S **150**
Lindeth Cl. HA7: Stan 23Ka **46**
Lindfield Gdns. NW3 36Db **69**
Lindfield Rd. CR0: C'don 72Vb **157**
RM3: Rom 22Nd **57**
W5 42La **86**
Lindfield St. E14 44Cc **92**
Lindhill Cl. EN3: Enf H 12Zb **34**
Lindholme Ct. *NW9* *25Ua* ***48***
(off Pageant Av.)
Lindie Gdns. UB8: Uxb 38N **63**
Lindisfarne Cl. DA12: Grav'nd 1G **144**
Lindisfarne Rd. RM8: Dag 34Yc **75**
SW20 66Wa **132**
Lindisfarne Way E9 35Ac **72**
Lindiswara Ct. WD3: Crox G 16Q **26**
Lindley Ct. KT1: Hamp W 67La **130**
Lindley Est. SE15 52Wb **113**
Lindley Ho. *E1* *43Yb* ***92***
(off Lindley St.)
SE15 *52Wb* ***113***
(off Peckham Pk. Rd.)
Lindley Pl. TW9: Kew 53Qa **109**
Lindley Rd. E10 33Ec **72**
KT12: Walt T 76Z **151**
RH9: G'stone 2A **210**
Lindley St. E1 43Yb **92**
Lindlings HP1: Hem H 3G **2**
Lindop Ho. *E1* *42Ac* ***92***
(off Mile End Rd.)
Lindore Rd. SW11 56Hb **111**
Lindores Rd. SM5: Cars 73Eb **155**
Lindo St. SE15 54Yb **114**
Lindrick Ho. WD19: Wat 20Y **27**
Lind Rd. SM1: Sutt 78Eb **155**
Lindrop St. SW6 54Eb **111**
Lindsay Cl. KT9: Chess 80Na **153**
KT19: Eps 85Sa **173**
TW19: Stanw 57M **105**
Lindsay Ct. *AL3: St A* *2A* ***6***
(off Verulam Rd.)
CR0: C'don *77Tb* ***157***
(off Eden Rd.)
SW11 *53Fb* ***111***
(off Battersea High St.)
Lindsay Dr. HA3: Kenton 30Na **47**
TW17: Shep 72T **150**
Lindsay Ho. SW7 3A **226**
Lindsay Pl. EN7: Chesh 2Xb **19**
Lindsay Rd. KT4: Wor Pk 75Xa **154**
KT15: New H 82J **169**
TW12: Hamp H 63Da **129**
Lindsay Sq. SW1 7E **228** (50Mb **90**)
Lindsell St. SE10 53Ec **114**
Lindsey Cl. BR1: Brom 69Mc **137**
CM14: B'wood 21Wd **58**
CR4: Mitc 70Nb **134**
Lindsey Ct. *N13* *20Qb* ***32***
(off Green Lanes)
Lindsey Gdns. TW14: Bedf 59T **106**
Lindsey Ho. W5 49Ma **87**
Lindsey M. N1 38Sb **71**
Lindsey Rd. RM8: Dag 35Yc **75**
UB9: Den 34J **63**
Lindsey St. CM16: Epp 1Vc **23**
EC1 7C **218** (43Rb **91**)
Lindsey Way RM11: Horn 29Ld **57**
Lind St. SE8 54Cc **114**
Lindum Pl. AL3: St A 4M **5**
Lindum Rd. TW11: Tedd 66La **130**
Lindvale GU21: Wok 87A **168**
Lindway SE27 64Rb **135**
Lindwood Cl. E6 44Pc **94**
Linen House, The W10 40Ab **68**
Linfield WC1 4H **217**
Linfield Cl. KT12: Hers 78X **151**
NW4 27Ya **48**
LINFORD 1J **101**
Linford Christie Stadium 43Wa **88**
Linford Ho. *E2* *39Wb* ***71***
(off Whiston Rd.)
Linford Rd. E17 27Ec **52**
RM16: Grays, W Til 9D **100**
Linford St. SW8 53Lb **112**
Linford St. Bus. Est. *SW8* *53Lb* ***112***
(off Linford St.)
Linford Woods Local Nature Reserve
7J **101**
Lingard Ho. *E14* *48Ec* ***92***
(off Marshfield St.)
Lingards Rd. SE13 56Ec **114**
Lingey Cl. DA15: Sidc 61Vc **139**
Lingfield Av. DA2: Dart 59Rd **119**
KT1: King T 70Na **131**
RM14: Upm 34Pd **77**
Lingfield Cl. EN1: Enf 16Ub **33**
HA6: Nwood 24U **44**
Lingfield Ct. UB5: N'olt 40Ca **65**
Lingfield Cres. SE9 56Tc **116**
Lingfield Gdns. CR5: Coul 91Rb **197**
N9 17Xb **33**
Lingfield Ho. SE1 2C **230**
Lingfield Rd. DA12: Grav'nd 1D **144**
KT4: Wor Pk 76Ya **154**
SW19 64Za **132**
TN15: Bor G 92De **205**
Lingfield Way WD17: Wat 10V **12**
Lingham Ct. SW9 54Nb **112**
Lingham St. SW9 54Nb **112**
Lingholm Way EN5: Barn 15Za **30**
Lingmere Cl. IG7: Chig 19Sc **36**
Lingmoor Dr. WD25: Wat 5Y **13**
Ling Rd. DA8: Erith 51Ed **118**
E16 43Jc **93**
Lingrove Gdns. IG9: Buck H 19Kc **35**
Lings Coppice SE21 61Tb **135**
Lingwell Rd. SW17 62Gb **133**
Lingwood DA7: Bex 54Dd **118**
Lingwood Ct. *N2* *27Gb* ***49***
(off Norfolk Cl.)
Lingwood Gdns. TW7: Isle 52Ga **108**
Lingwood Rd. E5 31Wb **71**
Linhope St. NW1 5F **215** (42Hb **89**)
Link, The DA3: New A 75Be **165**
EN3: Enf H 11Ac **34**
HA0: Wemb 32La **66**
HA5: Eastc 31Y **65**
NW2 32Wa **68**
SE9 *62Qc* ***138***
(off William Barefoot Dr.)
SL2: Slou 4M **81**
TW11: Tedd 65Ha **130**
UB5: N'olt 36Ba **65**
W3 44Ra **87**
Link Av. GU22: Pyr 87F **168**
Linkenholt Mans. *W6* *49Va* ***88***
(off Stamford Brook Av.)
Linkfield BR2: Hayes 72Jc **159**
KT8: W Mole 69Da **129**
Linkfield Cnr. RH1: Redh 5N **207**
Linkfield Gdns. RH1: Redh 6N **207**
Linkfield La. RH1: Redh 5N **207**
Linkfield Lodge RH1: Redh 5N **207**
Linkfield Rd. TW7: Isle 54Ha **108**
Linkfield St. RH1: Redh 6N **207**
Link Ho. E3 40Dc **72**
W10 *44Za* ***88***
(off Kingsdown Cl.)
Link La. SM6: Wall 79Mb **156**
Linklea Cl. NW9 24Ua **48**
Link Pl. IG6: Ilf 23Vc **55**
Link Rd. E1 45Wb **91**
KT15: Add 77N **149**
N11 21Jb **50**
RM9: Dag 40Dd **76**
SL3: Dat 3N **103**
SM6: Wall 74Jb **156**
TW14: Felt 59V **106**
WD23: Bush 12Z **27**
WD24: Bush, Wat 12Z **27**
Links, The E17 28Ac **52**
KT12: Walt T 75W **150**
Links Av. RM2: Rom 26Kd **57**
SM4: Mord 70Cb **133**
Links Brow KT22: Fet 96Ga **192**
Links Bus. Cen. GU22: Wok 91E **188**
Links Cl. KT21: Asht 89La **172**
Linkscroft Av. TW15: Ashf 65R **128**
Links Dr. N20 18Cb **31**
WD6: E'tree 13Pa **29**
WD7: R'lett 5Ha **14**
Links Gdns. SW16 66Qb **134**
Links Grn. Way
KT11: Cobh 86Ca **171**
Linkside IG7: Chig 22Sc **54**
KT3: N Mald 68Ua **132**
N12 23Cb **49**
Linkside Cl. EN2: Enf 13Pb **32**
Linkside Gdns. EN2: Enf 13Pb **32**
Links Pl. KT21: Asht 89Ma **173**
Links Rd. BR4: W W'ck 74Ec **158**
IG8: Wfd G 22Jc **53**
KT17: Eps 85Wa **174**
KT21: Asht 90La **172**
NW2 33Va **68**
SW17 65Jb **134**
TW15: Ashf 64N **127**
W3 44Qa **87**
Links Side EN2: Enf 13Pb **32**
Link St. E9 37Yb **72**
Links Vw. AL3: St A 1P **5**
DA1: Dart 60Kd **119**
N3 24Bb **49**
Linksview *N2* *29Hb* ***49***
(off Great Nth. Rd.)
Links Vw. Cl. HA7: Stan 24Ja **46**
Links Vw. Ct. TW12: Hamp H 63Fa **130**
Links Vw. Rd. CR0: C'don 76Cc **158**
TW12: Hamp H 64Ea **130**
Links Way BR3: Beck 72Cc **158**
KT23: Bookh 100Aa **191**
WD3: Crox G 13S **26**
Linksway HA6: Nwood 24S **44**
NW4 26Za **48**
Linkswood Rd. SL1: Burn 10A **60**
Links Yd. *E1* *43Wb* ***91***
(off Spelman St.)
Link Way BR2: Brom 73Nc **160**
HA5: Pinn 25Z **45**
RM11: Horn 32Nd **77**
TW18: Staines 65K **127**
UB9: Den 30J **43**
Linkway GU22: Wok 89E **168**
N4 31Sb **71**
RM8: Dag 35Yc **75**
SW20 69Xa **132**
TW10: Ham 61Ka **130**
Linkway, The EN5: Barn 16Db **31**
SM2: Sutt 81Eb **175**
Linkway Rd. CM14: B'wood 20Vd **40**
Linkwood Wlk. NW1 38Mb **70**
Linley Cl. RM18: E Til 2M **123**
Linley Ct. SM1: Sutt 77Eb **155**
Linley Cres. RM7: Mawney 27Dd **56**
Linley Rd. N17 26Ub **51**
Linley Sambourne House *48Cb* ***89***
(off Stafford Ter.)
Linnell Cl. NW11 30Db **49**
Linnell Dr. NW11 30Db **49**
Linnell Ho. E1 7K **219**
NW8 *39Eb* ***69***
(off Ainsworth Way)
Linnell Rd. N18 22Wb **51**
RH1: Redh 7A **208**
SE5 54Ub **113**
Linnet Cl. CR2: Sels 82Zb **178**
N9 18Zb **34**
SE28 45Yc **95**
WD23: Bush 17Ea **28**
Linnet Ho. *DA9: Ghithe* *58Wd* ***120***
(off Waterstone Way)
Linnet M. SW12 59Jb **112**
Linnett Rd. WD5: Ab L 3W **12**
Linnett Cl. E4 21Ec **52**
Linnet Wlk. AL10: Hat 2C **8**
Linnet Way RM19: Purf 50Rd **97**
Linom Rd. SW4 56Nb **112**
Linscott Rd. E5 35Yb **72**
Linsdell Rd. IG11: Bark 39Sc **74**
Linsey Cl. HP3: Hem H 6A **4**
Linsey Ct. *E10* *32Cc* ***72***
(off Grange Rd.)
Linsey St. SE16 49Wb **91**
(not continuous)
Linslade Cl. HA5: Eastc 27X **45**
TW4: Houn 57Aa **107**
Linslade Ho. E2 39Wb **71**
NW8 5E **214**
Linslade Rd. BR6: Chels 79Wc **161**
Linstead St. NW6 38Cb **69**
Linstead Way SW18 59Ab **110**
Linsted Ct. SE9 58Uc **116**
Linster Gro. WD6: Bore 15Sa **29**
Lintaine Cl. W6 51Ab **110**
Linters Ct. RH1: Redh 4P **207**
Linthorpe Av. HA0: Wemb 37La **66**
Linthorpe Rd. EN4: Cockf 13Gb **31**
N16 31Ub **71**
Linton Av. WD6: Bore 11Pa **29**
Linton Cl. CR4: Mitc 73Hb **155**
DA16: Well 53Xc **117**
SE7 50Lc **93**
Linton Ct. *NW1* *38Lb* ***70***
(off Agar Gro.)
RM1: Rom 26Gd **56**
Linton Gdns. E6 44Nc **94**
Linton Glade CR0: Sels 81Ac **178**
Linton Gro. SE27 64Rb **135**
Linton Ho. *E3* *43Cc* ***92***
(off St Paul's Way)
Linton Rd. IG11: Bark 38Sc **74**
Lintons, The IG11: Bark 38Sc **74**
Lintons La. KT17: Eps 84Ua **174**
Linton St. N1 1E **218** (39Sb **71**)
(not continuous)
Lintott Ct. TW19: Stanw 58M **105**
Linver Rd. SW6 54Cb **111**
Linwood Cl. SE5 54Vb **113**
Linwood Cres. EN1: Enf 11Wb **33**
Linzee Rd. N8 28Nb **50**
Lion & Lamb Ct. *CM14: B'wood* *19Yd* ***40***
(off High St.)
Lion Apartments *SE16* *50Xb* ***91***
(off Rotherhithe New Rd.)
Lion Av. TW1: Twick 60Ha **108**
Lion Bus. Pk. DA12: Grav'nd 9H **123**
Lion Cl. SE4 58Cc **114**
TW17: Shep 69N **127**
Lion Ct. *E1* *45Zb* ***92***
(off The Highway)
N1 *39Pb* ***70***
(off Copenhagen St.)
SE1 7J **225**
WD6: Bore 11Sa **29**
Lionel Gdns. SE9 57Mc **115**
Lionel Ho. *W10* *43Ab* ***88***
(off Portobello Rd.)
Lionel Mans. *W14* *48Za* ***88***
(off Haarlem Rd.)
Lionel M. W10 43Ab **88**
Lionel Oxley Ho. *RM17: Grays* *51De* ***121***
(off New Rd.)
Lionel Rd. SE9 57Mc **115**
Lionel Rd. Nth. TW8: Bford 48Na **87**
Lionel Rd. Sth. TW8: Bford 50Pa **87**
Liongate Ent. Pk. CR4: Mitc 70Fb **133**
Lion Ga. Gdns. TW9: Rich 55Pa **109**
Lion Ga. M. SW18 59Cb **111**
Liongate M. KT8: E Mos 69Ha **130**
Lion Grn. Rd. CR5: Coul 88Mb **176**
Lion Head Ct. *CR0: C'don* *77Sb* ***157***
(off Southbridge Rd.)
Lion La. RH1: Redh 5P **207**
Lion Mills E2 40Wb **71**
Lion Pk. Av. KT9: Chess 77Qa **153**
Lion Retail Pk. GU22: Wok 88D **168**
Lion Rd. CR0: C'don 71Sb **157**
DA6: Bex 56Ad **117**
E6 43Pc **94**
N9 19Wb **33**
TW1: Twick 60Ha **108**
Lions Cl. SE9 62Lc **137**
Lions Row CM14: W'ley 21Yd **58**
Lion Way TW8: Bford 52Ma **109**
Lion Wharf Rd. TW7: Isle 55Ka **108**
Lion Yd. SW4 56Mb **112**
Liphook Cl. RM12: Horn 35Hd **76**
Liphook Cres. SE23 59Yb **114**
Liphook Rd. WD19: Wat 21Z **45**
Lippitts Hill IG10: Lough 11Gc **35**
Lipsham Cl. SM7: Bans 85Fb **175**
Lipton Cl. SE28 45Yc **95**
Lipton Rd. E1 44Zb **92**
Lisbon Av. TW2: Twick 61Ea **130**
Lisbon Cl. E17 26Bc **52**
Lisburne Rd. NW3 35Hb **69**
Lisford St. SE15 53Vb **113**
Lisgar Ter. W14 49Bb **89**
Liskeard Cl. BR7: Chst 65Sc **138**
Liskeard Gdns. SE3 53Jc **115**
Liskeard Ho. SE11 7A **230**
Liskeard Lodge CR3: Cat'm 98Wb **197**
Lisle Cl. DA12: Grav'nd 1K **145**
SW17 63Kb **134**
Lisle Ct. NW2 34Ab **68**
Lisle Pl. RM17: Grays 48Ce **99**
Lisle St. WC2 4E **222** (45Mb **90**)
Lismirrane Ind. Pk. WD6: E'tree 16Ka **28**
Lismore HP3: Hem H 4C **4**
SW19 *64Bb* ***133***
(off Woodside)
Lismore Cir. NW5 36Jb **70**
Lismore Cl. TW7: Isle 54Ja **108**
Lismore Pk. SL2: Slou 4K **81**
Lismore Rd. CR2: S Croy 79Ub **157**
N17 27Tb **51**
Lismore Wlk. *N1* *37Sb* ***71***
(off Clephane Rd. Nth.)
Lissant Cl. KT6: Surb 73Ma **153**
Lisselton Ho. *NW4* *28Za* ***48***
(off Belle Vue Est.)
Lissenden Gdns. NW5 35Jb **70**
(not continuous)
Lissenden Mans. NW5 35Jb **70**
Lissoms Rd. CR5: Chip 90Jb **176**
Lisson Grn. Est. NW8 5D **214**
LISSON GROVE 7D **214** (43Gb **89**)
Lisson Gro. NW1 6D **214** (43Gb **89**)
NW8 4C **214** (42Fb **89**)
Lisson Ho. NW1 7D **214**
Lisson St. NW1 7D **214** (43Gb **89**)
Lister Av. RM3: Hrld W 26Md **57**
Lister Cl. CR4: Mitc 67Gb **133**
W3 43Ta **87**
Lister Cotts. WD6: E'tree 15Ja **28**
Lister Ct. HA1: Harr 31Ka **66**
N16 33Ub **71**
NW9 26Ua **48**
Lister Dr. DA11: Nflt 60Ee **121**
Lister Gdns. N18 22Sb **51**
Listergate Ct. SW15 56Ya **110**
Lister Ho. E1 43Wb **91**
HA9: Wemb *34Sa* ***67***
(off Barnhill Rd.)
UB3: Harl 49U **84**
Lister Lodge *W9* *43Cb* ***89***
(off Admiral Wlk.)
Lister Rd. E11 32Gc **73**
RM18: Tilb 4C **122**
Lister Wlk. SE28 45Zc **95**
Liston Rd. N17 25Wb **51**
SW4 55Lb **112**
Liston Way IG8: Wfd G 24Lc **53**
Listowel Cl. SW9 52Qb **112**
Listowel Rd. RM10: Dag 34Cd **76**
Listria Pk. N16 33Ub **71**
Litcham Ho. *E1* *41Zb* ***92***
(off Longnor Rd.)
Litcham Spur SL1: Slou 4H **81**
Litchfield Av. E15 37Gc **73**
SM4: Mord 73Bb **155**
Litchfield Ct. E17 30Cc **52**
Litchfield Gdns. KT11: Cobh 86X **171**
NW10 37Wa **68**

Litchfield Rd. SM1: Sutt 77Eb 155
Litchfield St. WC2 .... 4E 222 (45Mb 90)
Litchfield Way NW11 .... 29Db 49
Lithgow's Rd. TW6: H'row A 5U 106
Lithos Rd. NW3 .... 37Db 69
Litten Cl. RM5: Col R 23Cd 56
Litten Nature Reserve 41Ea 86
Little Acre BR3: Beck 69Cc 136
Lit. Albany St. NW1 .... 5A 216
Little Angel Theatre 39Rb 71
(off Dagmar Pl.)
Lit. Argyll St. W1 .... 3B 222 (44Lb 90)
Lit. Aston Rd. RM3: Hrld W 24Qd 57
Lit. Belhus Cl. RM15: S Ock 42Xd 98
Little Benty UB7: W Dray 50M 83
Lit. Birch Cl. KT15: New H 81M 169
Little Birches DA15: Sidc 61Uc 138
Little Boltons, The SW5 .... 50Db 89
SW10 .... 50Db 89
LITTLE BOOKHAM 96Ba 191
LITTLE BOOKHAM COMMON 94Aa 191
Lit. Bookham St. KT23: Bookh 95Ba 191
Little Bornes SE21 .... 63Ub 135
Littlebourne SE13 .... 59Gc 115
Littlebourne Ho. SE17 .... 7J 231
Little Bri. Rd. HP4: Berk 1A 2
LITTLE BRITAIN 44L 83
Little Britain EC1 .... 1C 224 (43Rb 91)
Littlebrook Av. SL2: Slou 2C 80
Littlebrook Bus. Cen. DA1: Dart 54Rd 119
Littlebrook Cl. CR0: C'don 72Zb 158
Littlebrook Gdns. EN8: Chesh 2Zb 20
LITTLEBROOK INTERCHANGE 56Rd 119
Littlebrook Mnr. Way DA1: Dart 55Rd 119
(Rennie Dr.)
DA1: Dart 57Qd 119
(St Vincents Av.)
Little Brownings SE23 .... 61Xb 135
Little Buntings SL4: Wind 5D 102
Littlebury Ct. WD18: Wat 14W 26
Littlebury Rd. SW4 .... 55Mb 112
Lit. Bury St. N9 .... 18Tb 33
Lit. Bushey La. WD23: Bush 12Ca 27
Little Cedars N12 .... 21Eb 49
LITTLE CHALFONT 11A 24
Lit. Chapels Way SL1: Slou 7E 80
Lit. Chelsea Ho. SW10 .... 51Eb 111
(off Netherton Gro.)
Little Chesters KT20: Walt H 97Wa 194
Lit. Chester St. SW1 .... 3K 227 (48Kb 90)
Little Cloisters SW1 .... 3F 229 (48Nb 90)
Lit. College La. EC4 .... 4F 225
Lit. College St. SW1 .... 3F 229 (48Nb 90)
Littlecombe SE7 .... 51Kc 115
Littlecombe Cl. SW15 .... 58Za 110
Little Comn. HA7: Stan 20Ja 28
Little Comn. La. RH1: Blet 4H 209
Littlecote Cl. SW19 .... 59Ab 110
Littlecote Pl. HA5: Hat E 25Aa 45
Lit. Cottage Pl. SE10 .... 52Dc 114
Little Ct. BR4: W W'ck 75Gc 159
Littlecourt Rd. TN13: S'oaks 96Jd 202
Lit. Cranmore La. KT24: W Hor 100R 190
Little Cft. DA13: Ist R 6A 144
Littlecroft SE9 .... 55Qc 116
Little Cft. Cl. AL2: Lon C 9E 6
Littlecroft Rd. TW20: Egh 64B 126
Littledale DA2: Daren 62Sd 142
SE2 .... 51Wc 117
Lit. Dean's Yd. SW1 .... 3F 229
Little Dimocks SW12 .... 61Kb 134
Lit. Dorrit Ct. SE1 .... 1E 230 (47Sb 91)
Littledown Rd. SL1: Slou 6K 81
Little Dragons IG10: Lough 14Mc 35
LITTLE EALING 48Ma 87
Lit. Ealing La. W5 .... 49La 86
Lit. East Fld. CR5: Coul 93Mb 196
Lit. Edward St. NW1 .... 3A 216 (41Kb 90)
Little Elms UB3: Harl 52T 106
Lit. Essex St. WC2 .... 4K 223
Lit. Ferry Rd. TW1: Twick 60Ka 108
Littlefield Cl. KT1: King T 68Na 131
N19 .... 35Lb 70
LITTLEFIELD COMMON 10F 186
Littlefield Ho. KT1: King T 68Na 131
(off Littlefield Cl.)
Littlefield Rd. HA8: Edg 24Sa 47
Lit. Friday Rd. E4 .... 19Gc 35
Lit. Gaynes Gdns. RM14: Upm 35Rd 77
Lit. Gaynes La. RM14: Upm 35Pd 77
Little Gearies IG6: Ilf 28Rc 54
Lit. George St. SW1 .... 2F 229 (47Nb 90)
Lit. Gerpins La. RM14: Upm 39Pd 77
Lit. Goldings Est. IG10: Lough 11Qc 36
Little Grange UB6: G'frd 41Ja 86
Little Graylings WD5: Ab L 5U 12
Little Green TW9: Rich 56Ma 109
Lit. Green La. KT16: Chert 76G 148
WD3: Crox G 13P 25
Lit. Green St. NW5 .... 35Kb 70
Lit. Gregories La. CM16: They B 7Tc 22
Little Gro. WD23: Bush 14Da 27
Littlegrove EN4: E Barn 16Gb 31
Little Halliards KT12: Walt T 72W 150
Littlehayes WD4: K Lan 1Q 12
Little Hay Golf Course 6E 2
LITTLE HEATH
EN6 .... 2Eb 17
HP4 .... 1C 2
RM6 .... 29Xc 55
Little Heath RM6: Chad H 28Xc 55
SE7 .... 51Nc 116
Lit. Heath La. HP4: Berk, Pott E 3D 2
Littleheath La.
KT11: Cobh, Stoke D 86Ca 171
Lit. Heath Rd. DA7: Bex 53Bd 117
GU24: Chob 1J 167
Littleheath Rd. CR2: Sels 80Xb 157
Little Hill WD3: Herons 17E 24
Lit. Holland Bungs. CR3: Cat'm 95Tb 197
Little Holland House 80Hb 155
Little Holt E11 .... 29Jc 53
Lit. How Cft. WD5: Ab L 3S 12
LITTLE ILFORD 36Pc 74
Lit. Ilford La. E12 .... 35Pc 74
Littlejohn Rd. BR5: St M Cry 72Wc 161
W7 .... 44Ha 86
Lit. Julians Hill TN13: S'oaks 99Jd 202
Little Larkins EN5: Barn 16Ab 30
Lit. London Cl. UB8: Hil 43R 84
Lit. London Ct. SE1 .... 47Vb 91
(off Wolseley St.)
Lit. Marlborough St. W1 .... 3B 222
Little Martins WD23: Bush 15Da 27
Littlemead GU21: Wok 8K 167
KT10: Esh 77Fa 152
Littlemede SE9 .... 62Pc 138
Little Mimms HP2: Hem H 1M 3
Littlemoor Rd. IG1: Ilf 34Tc 74
Littlemore Rd. SE2 .... 47Wc 95
Lit. Moreton Cl. KT14: W Byf 84K 169
Lit. Moss La. HA5: Pinn 26Aa 45
Lit. Newport St. WC2 .... 4E 222 (45Mb 90)
Lit. New St. EC4 .... 2A 224 (44Qb 90)
Lit. Norman St. TN14: Ide H 100Ad 201
Lit. Oaks Cl. TW17: Shep 70P 127
Little Orchard GU21: Wok 86C 168
HP2: Hem H 1A 4
KT15: Wdhm 83J 169
Lit. Orchard Cl. HA5: Pinn 26Aa 45
WD5: Ab L 4T 12
Lit. Orchard Pl. KT10: Esh 76Fa 152
Little Orchards KT18: Eps 86Ua 174
(off Worple Rd.)
Lit. Oxhey La. WD19: Wat 22Z 45
Little Park HP3: Bov 10C 2
Lit. Park Dr. TW13: Felt 61Aa 129
Lit. Park Gdns. EN2: Enf 13Sb 33
Little Pastures CM14: B'wood 21Vd 58
Lit. Pipers Cl. EN7: G Oak 1Rb 19
Lit. Pluckett's Way IG9: Buck H 18Mc 35
Lit. Portland St. W1 .... 2A 222 (44Lb 90)
Littleport Spur SL1: Slou 4J 81
Little Potters WD23: Bush 17Fa 28
Lit. Queen's Rd. TW11: Tedd 65Ha 130
Lit. Queen St. DA1: Dart 59Pd 119
Little Redlands BR1: Brom 68Nc 138
Little Riding GU22: Wok 88D 168
Little Rd. HP2: Hem H 1N 3
UB3: Hayes 47V 84
Lit. Roke Av. CR8: Kenley 86Rb 177
Lit. Roke Rd. CR8: Kenley 86Sb 177
Littlers Cl. SW19 .... 67Fb 133
Lit. Russell St. WC1 .... 1F 223 (43Nb 90)
Lit. St James's St. SW1 .... 7B 222 (46Lb 90)
Lit. St Leonard's SW14 .... 55Sa 109
Little Sanctuary SW1 .... 2F 229 (47Mb 90)
Lit. Smith St. SW1 .... 3E 228 (48Mb 90)
Lit. Somerset St. E1 .... 3K 225 (44Vb 91)
Lit. South St. SE5 .... 53Ub 113
LITTLE STANMORE 24Pa 47
Littlestone Cl. BR3: Beck 65Cc 136
Little Strand NW9 .... 26Va 48
Lit. Stream Cl. HA6: Nwood 22U 44
Little St. EN9: Walt A 8Ec 20
Lit. Sutton La. SL3: L'ly 50E 82
(Hurricane Way)
SL3: L'ly 51D 104
(Kings Ter.)
Little Thrift BR5: Pet W 70Sc 138
LITTLE THURROCK 48Fe 99
Lit. Titchfield St. W1 .... 1B 222 (43Lb 90)
LITTLETON 69Q 128
Littleton Av. E4 .... 18Hc 35
LITTLETON COMMON 66S 128
Littleton Cres. HA1: Harr 33Ha 66
Littleton Ho. RH2: Reig 5J 207
(off Somers Cl.)
SW1 .... 7B 228
Littleton La. RH2: Reig 8F 206
TW17: Shep 73M 149
Littleton Rd. HA1: Harr 33Ha 66
TW15: Ashf 66S 128
Littleton St. SW18 .... 61Eb 133
Lit. Trinity La. EC4 .... 4E 224 (45Sb 91)
Little Turnstile WC1 .... 1H 223 (43Pb 90)
Little Venice 7A 214
Little Venice Sports Cen.
.... 7B 214 (43Eb 89)
LITTLE WARLEY 26Ae 59
Lit. Warley Hall La. CM13: L War 26Ae 59
LITTLEWICK 8J 167
LITTLEWICK COMMON 7J 167
Littlewick Rd. GU21: Knap, Wok 8J 167
Lit. Windmill Hill WD4: Chfd 4H 11
Littlewold Dr. CR6: W'ham 91Zb 198
Little Wood TN13: S'oaks 94Ld 203
Littlewood SE13 .... 58Ec 114
Lit. Wood Cl. BR5: St P 67Wc 139
Littlewood Cl. W13 .... 48Ka 86
LITTLE WOODCOTE 83Kb 176
Lit. Woodcote Est. SM6: Wall 83Kb 176
Lit. Woodcote La. CR8: Purl 84Kb 176
SM5: Cars 84Kb 176
Little Woodlands SL4: Wind 6C 102
Lit. Wood St. KT1: King T 68Ma 131
Littleworth Av. KT10: Esh 78Fa 152
LITTLEWORTH COMMON 4B 60
Littleworth Comn. Rd. KT10: Esh 76Fa 152
Littleworth La. KT10: Esh 77Fa 152
Littleworth Pl. KT10: Esh 77Fa 152
Littleworth Rd. KT10: Esh 78Fa 152
SL1: Burn 4A 60
Livermere Ct. E8 .... 39Vb 71
(off Queensbridge Rd.)
Livermere Rd. E8 .... 39Vb 71
Liverpool Gro. SE17 .... 7F 231 (50Sb 91)
Liverpool Rd. AL1: St A 2C 6
CR7: Thor H 69Sb 135
E10 .... 30Ec 52
E16 .... 43Gc 93
KT2: King T 66Qa 131
N1 .... 1A 218 (38Qb 70)
N7 .... 36Qb 70
SL1: Slou 4F 80
W5 .... 47Ma 87
WD18: Wat 15X 27
Liverpool St. EC2 .... 1H 225 (43Ub 91)
Liverymen Wlk. DA9: Ghithe 56Yd 120
Livesey Cl. KT1: King T 69Pa 131
SE28 .... 48Sc 94
Livesey Pl. SE15 .... 51Wb 113
Livingstone Ct. E10 .... 30Ec 52
EN5: Barn 12Ab 30
(off Church La.)
HA3: W'stone 27Ha 46
TW19: Stanw 60N 105
(off Explorer Av.)
Livingstone Gdns. DA12: Grav'nd 4F 144
Livingstone Ho. NW10 .... 38Ua 68
SE5 .... 52Sb 113
(off Wyndham Rd.)
Livingstone Lodge W9 .... 43Cb 89
(off Admiral Wlk.)
Livingstone Mans. W14 .... 51Ab 110
(off Queen's Club Gdns.)
Livingstone Pl. E14 .... 50Ec 92
Livingstone Rd. CR3: Cat'm 94Tb 197
CR7: Thor H 68Sb 135
DA12: Grav'nd 4F 144
E17 .... 30Dc 52
N13 .... 23Nb 50
Livingstone Rd. SW11 .... 55Fb 111
TW3: Houn 56Ea 108
UB1: S'hall 45Z 85
Livingstone Ter. RM13: Rain 39Gd 76
LivingWell Health Club
London Heathrow Hilton 58S 106
Regents Plaza 40Db 69
(off Greville Rd.)
Wembley 36Pa 67
Livonia St. W1 .... 3C 222 (44Lb 90)
Lizard St. EC1 .... 4E 218 (41Sb 91)
Lizban St. SE3 .... 52Kc 115
Lizmans Ter. W8 .... 48Cb 89
(off Earl's Ct. Rd.)
Llanbury Cl. SL9: Chal P 24A 42
Llandovery Ho. E14 .... 47Ec 92
(off Chipka St.)
Llanelly Rd. NW2 .... 33Bb 69
Llanover Rd. HA9: Wemb 34Ma 67
SE18 .... 51Qc 116
Llanthony Rd. SM4: Mord 71Fb 155
Llanvanor Rd. NW2 .... 33Bb 69
Llewellyn Ct. SE20 .... 67Yb 136
Llewellyn Mans. W14 .... 49Ab 88
(off Hammersmith Rd.)
Llewellyn St. SE16 .... 47Wb 91
Lloyd Av. CR5: Coul 86Jb 176
SW16 .... 67Nb 134
Lloyd Baker St. WC1 .... 4J 217 (41Pb 90)
(not continuous)
Lloyd Ct. HA5: Pinn 29Z 45
Lloyd Ho. BR3: Beck 65Dc 136
CR0: C'don 74Tb 157
(off Tavistock Rd.)
Lloyd M. EN3: Enf L 10Cc 20
Lloyd Pk. Av. CR0: C'don 77Vb 157
Lloyd Pk. Ho. E17 .... 27Cc 52
Lloyd Rd. E6 .... 39Pc 74
E17 .... 28Zb 52
KT4: Wor Pk 76Ya 154
RM9: Dag 37Bd 75
Lloyd's Av. EC3 .... 3J 225 (44Ub 91)
Lloyd's Building 3H 225 (44Ub 91)
Lloyds Lanes Raynes Pk. 69Za 132
Lloyd's Pl. SE3 .... 54Gc 115
Lloyd Sq. WC1 .... 3K 217 (41Qb 90)
Lloyd's Row EC1 .... 4A 218 (41Qb 90)
Lloyd St. WC1 .... 3K 217 (41Qb 90)
Lloyds Way BR3: Beck 71Ac 158
Lloyds Wharf SE1 .... 1K 231
Lloyd Thomas Ct. N22 .... 24Pb 50
Lloyd Vs. E6 .... 42Nc 94
SE4 .... 54Cc 114
Loam Ct. DA1: Dart 60Nd 119
Loampit Hill SE13 .... 54Cc 114
LOAMPIT VALE 55Ec 114
Loampit Va. SE13 .... 55Dc 114
Loanda Cl. E8 .... 39Vb 71
Loates La. WD17: Wat 13Y 27
Loats Rd. SW2 .... 58Nb 112
Lobelia Cl. E6 .... 43Nc 94
Lobelia Rd. GU24: Bisl 7E 166
Local Board Rd. WD17: Wat 15Z 27
Locarno Cl. SW16 .... 64Lb 134
Locarno Rd. UB6: G'frd 42Fa 86
W3 .... 46Sa 87
Lochaber Rd. SE13 .... 56Gc 115
Lochaline St. W6 .... 51Ya 110
Lochan Cl. UB4: Yead 42Aa 85
Lochinvar Cl. SL1: Slou 7F 80
Lochinvar St. SW12 .... 59Kb 112
Lochleven Ho. N2 .... 26Fb 49
(off The Grange)
Lochmere Cl. DA8: Erith 51Dd 118
Lochmore Ho. SW1 .... 6J 227
Lochnagar St. E14 .... 43Ec 92
Lockbridge Ct. W9 .... 43Cb 89
(off Woodfield Rd.)
Lock Building, The E15 .... 40Ec 72
Lock Chase SE3 .... 55Gc 115
Lock Cl. KT15: Wdhm 84G 168
UB2: S'hall 47Ea 86
Locke Cl. RM13: Rain 37Hd 76
Locke Gdns. SL3: L'ly 8A 82
Locke Ho. SW8 .... 53Lb 112
(off Wadhurst Rd.)
Locke King Cl. KT13: Weyb 80Q 150
Locke King Rd. KT13: Weyb 80Q 150
Lockers, The HP1: Hem H 1L 3
Lockers Pk. La. HP1: Hem H 2K 3
Lockesfield Pl. E14 .... 50Dc 92
Lockesley Dr. BR5: St M Cry 72Vc 161
Lockesley Sq. KT6: Surb 72Ma 153
Lockestone KT13: Weyb 79P 149
Lockestone Cl. KT13: Weyb 79P 149
Locket Rd. HA3: W'stone 27Ga 46
Locket Rd. M. HA3: W'stone 26Ga 46
Lockets Cl. SL4: Wind 3B 102
Locke Way GU21: Wok 89B 168
Lockfield Av. EN3: Brim 12Ac 34
Lockfield Dr. GU21: Wok 8J 167
Lockgate Cl. E9 .... 36Bc 72
Lockhart Cl. EN3: Pond E 15Xb 33
N7 .... 37Pb 70
Lockhart Rd. KT11: Cobh 85Y 171
WD17: Wat 11W 26
Lockhart St. E3 .... 42Bc 92
Lock Ho. HP3: Hem H 6N 3
Lockhouse, The NW1 .... 39Jb 70
Lockhurst St. E5 .... 35Zb 72
Lockie Pl. SE25 .... 69Wb 135
Lockier Wlk. HA9: Wemb 34Ma 67
Lockington Rd. SW8 .... 53Kb 112
Lock Keepers Hgts. SE16 .... 48Zb 92
(off Brunswick Quay)
Lock La. GU22: Pyr 88K 169
Lockmead Rd. N15 .... 30Wb 51
SE13 .... 55Ec 114
Lock M. NW1 .... 37Mb 70
(off Northpoint Sq.)
Lock Path SL4: Dor, Eton W 1B 102
Lock Rd. TW10: Ham 63La 130
LOCKSBOTTOM 76Qc 160
Locksfields SE17 .... 6G 231
Lockside E14 .... 45Ac 92
(off Narrow St.)
Locks La. CR4: Mitc 67Jb 134
Locksley Dr. GU21: Wok 9K 167
Locksley Est. E14 .... 44Bc 92
Locksley St. E14 .... 43Bc 92
Locksmeade Rd. TW10: Ham 63La 130
Locksons Cl. E14 .... 43Dc 92
Lockswood GU24: Brkwd 2F 186
Lockwood Cl. EN4: Cockf 14Hb 31
Locks Yd. TN13: S'oaks 97Ld 203
(off High St.)
Lockton St. W10 .... 45Za 88
(off Bramley Rd.)
Lock Vw. Ct. E14 .... 45Ac 92
(off Narrow St.)
Lockwell Rd. RM10: Dag 34Cd 76
Lockwood Cl. SE26 .... 63Zb 136
Lockwood Ho. E5 .... 33Yb 72
SE11 .... 51Qb 112
Lockwood Ind. Pk. N17 .... 27Xb 51
Lockwood Path GU21: Wok 85F 168
Lockwood Pl. E4 .... 23Cc 52
Lockwood Sq. SE16 .... 48Xb 91
Lockwood Wlk. RM1: Rom 29Gd 56
Lockwood Way E17 .... 26Zb 52
KT9: Chess 78Qa 153
Lockyer Est. SE1 .... 1G 231
(not continuous)
Lockyer Ho. SE10 .... 50Hc 93
(off Armitage Rd.)
SW8 .... 52Mb 112
(off Wandsworth Rd.)
SW15 .... 55Za 110
Lockyer M. EN3: Enf L 10Dc 20
Lockyer Rd. RM19: Purf 51Sd 120
Lockyer St. SE1 .... 2G 231 (47Tb 91)
Locomotive Dr.
TW14: Felt 60W 106
Locton Grn. E3 .... 39Bc 72
Loddiges Ho. E9 .... 38Yb 72
Loddiges Rd. E9 .... 38Yb 72
Loddon Ho. NW8 .... 6C 214
Loddon Spur SL1: Slou 5J 81
Loder Cl. GU21: Wok 85F 168
Loder St. SE15 .... 52Yb 114
Lodge, The CM16: Epp 1Yc 23
SM7: Bans 89Eb 175
W12 .... 47Za 88
(off Richmond Way)
WD24: Wat 12Y 27
Lodge Av. CR0: Wadd 76Qb 156
DA1: Dart 58Ld 119
HA3: Kenton 28Na 47
RM2: Rom 28Jd 56
RM8: Dag 37Xc 75
RM9: Dag 39Wc 75
SW14 .... 55Ua 110
WD6: E'tree 15Pa 29
LODGE AVENUE FLYOVER JUNC. 39Wc 75
Lodgebottom Rd. KT18: Head 99Qa 193
RH5: Mick 99Qa 193
Lodge Cl. BR6: Orp 74Xc 161
HA8: Edg 23Pa 47
IG7: Chig 20Wc 37
KT11: Stoke D 88Ba 171
KT17: Ewe 82Ya 174
KT22: Fet 94Fa 192
N18 .... 22Sb 51
SL1: Slou 7G 80
SL5: Asc 8A 124
SM6: Wall 74Jb 156
TW7: Isle 53Ka 108
TW20: Eng G 4P 125
UB8: Cowl 42L 83
WD25: Wat 4Aa 13
Lodge Ct. HA0: Wemb 36Na 67
(off Station Gro.)
RM12: Horn 33Nd 77
Lodge Cres. BR6: Orp 74Xc 161
EN8: Walt C 6Zb 20
Lodge Dr. N13 .... 21Qb 50
WD3: Loud 14L 25
Lodge End WD3: Crox G 14T 26
WD7: R'lett 6Ka 14
Lodge Gdns. BR3: Beck 71Bc 158
Lodge Hill CR8: Purl 87Qb 176
DA16: Well 52Xc 117
IG4: Ilf 28Nc 54
SE2 .... 52Xc 117
Lodgehill Pk. Cl. HA2: Harr 33Da 65
Lodge La. CR0: New Ad 79Cc 158
DA5: Bexl 58Zc 117
DA12: Cobh 10J 145
EN9: Walt A 7Fc 21
HP8: Chal G 11A 24
N12 .... 22Eb 49
RM5: Col R 24Cd 56
RM16: Grays 47Ce 99
RM17: Grays 47Ce 99
TN16: Westrm 99Sc 200
Lodge Pl. SM1: Sutt 78Db 155
Lodge Rd. BR1: Brom 66Lc 137
CM16: Epp, Walt A 6Qc 22
CR0: C'don 72Rb 157
KT22: Fet 94Ea 192
NW4 .... 28Ya 48
NW8 .... 4C 214 (41Fb 89)
SM6: Wall 78Kb 156
Lodge Vs. IG8: Wfd G 23Hc 53
Lodge Wlk. CR6: W'ham 88Cc 178
Lodge Way SL4: Wind 5C 102
TW15: Ashf 61N 127
TW17: Shep 68S 128
Lodore Gdns. NW9 .... 29Ua 48
Lodore Grn. UB10: Ick 34N 63
Lodore St. E14 .... 44Ec 92
Lodysons Cl. RM16: Ors 3C 100
Loewen Rd. RM16: Grays 8C 100
Lofthouse Pl. KT9: Chess 79La 152
Loftie St. SE16 .... 47Wb 91
Lofting Ho. N1 .... 38Qb 70
(off Liverpool Rd.)
Lofting Rd. N1 .... 38Pb 70
Lofts on the Pk. E9 .... 37Zb 72
(off Cassland Rd.)
Loftus Road 46Xa 88
Loftus Rd. IG11: Bark 37Sc 74
W12 .... 46Xa 88
Loftus Vs. W12 .... 46Xa 88
(off Loftus Rd.)
Logan Cl. EN3: Enf H 11Zb 34
TW4: Houn 55Ba 107
Logan Ct. AL2: Lon C 9F 6
RM1: Rom 29Gd 56
Logan M. RM1: Rom 29Gd 56
W8 .... 49Cb 89
Logan Pl. W8 .... 49Cb 89
Logan Rd. HA9: Wemb 33Ma 67
N9 .... 19Xb 33
Loggetts SE21 .... 61Ub 135
Logs Hill BR1: Brom 66Nc 138
BR7: Chst 66Nc 138
Logs Hill Cl. BR7: Chst 67Nc 138
Lohmann Ho. SE11 .... 51Qb 112
(off Kennington Oval)
Lois Dr. TW17: Shep 71R 150
Lolesworth Cl. E1 .... 1K 225 (43Vb 91)
Lolland Ho. SE7 .... 49Nc 94
Lollard St. SE11 .... 5J 229 (49Pb 90)
(not continuous)
Lollesworth La. KT24: W Hor 98S 190
Loman Path RM15: S Ock 44Vd 98
Loman St. SE1 .... 1C 230 (47Rb 91)
Lomas Cl. CR0: New Ad 80Ec 158
Lomas Dr. E8 .... 38Vb 71
Lomas St. E1 .... 43Wb 91
Lombard Av. EN3: Enf H 11Yb 34
IG3: Ilf 32Uc 74
Lombard Bus. Pk.
CR0: C'don 73Pb 156
SW19 .... 68Db 133
Lombard Ct. EC3 .... 4G 225 (45Tb 91)
RM7: Rom 28Ed 56
W3 .... 46Ra 87
Lombard La. EC4 .... 3A 224 (44Qb 90)
Lombard Rd. N11 .... 22Kb 50
SW11 .... 54Fb 111
SW19 .... 68Db 133
LOMBARD RDBT. 73Pb 156
Lombards, The RM11: Horn 31Pd 77
Lombards Chase
CM13: W H'dn 30Fe 59
Lombard St. DA4: Hort K 71Sd 164
EC3 .... 3G 225 (44Tb 91)
Lombard Trad. Est. SE7 .... 49Kc 93
Lombard Wall SE7 .... 48Kc 93
Lombardy Cl. GU21: Wok 9K 167
HP2: Hem H 3D 4
IG6: Ilf 24Rc 54
Lombardy Dr. HP4: Berk 2A 2
Lombardy Pl. W2 .... 45Db 89
Lombardy Retail Pk. UB3: Hayes 45X 85
Lombardy Way WD6: Bore 11Na 29
Lomond Cl. HA0: Wemb 38Pa 67
N15 .... 29Ub 51
Lomond Gdns. CR2: Sels 80Ac 158
Lomond Gro. SE5 .... 52Tb 113
Lomond Ho. SE5 .... 52Tb 113
Loncin Mead Av. KT15: New H 81L 169
Loncroft Rd. SE5 .... 51Ub 113
Londesborough Rd. N16 .... 35Ub 71
Londinium Twr. E1 .... 4K 225
London 2012 Games Venue 1A 102
London Ambulance Service Mus. 29Vc 55
LONDON BIGGIN HILL AIRPORT 84Mc 179
London Bombing Memorial
.... 7J 221 (46Jb 90)
London Bri. SE1 .... 6G 225 (46Tb 91)
London Bridge Experience 6G 225
(off Tooley St.)
London Bri. St. SE1 .... 7G 225 (46Tb 91)
London Bri. Wlk. SE1 .... 6G 225
London Business School 5F 215 (42Hb 89)
London Bus Museum, The 81Q 170
London Canal Mus. 1G 217 (40Nb 70)
LONDON CITY AIRPORT 46Nc 94
London City College 7K 223
London Coliseum 5F 223
(off St Martin's La.)
London College of Fashion, The
Hackney 38Xb 71
LONDON COLNEY 8H 7
London Colney By-Pass AL2: Lon C 7H 7
London Ct. CM14: W'ley 22Xd 58
Londonderry Pde. DA8: Erith 52Fd 118
London Dungeon 7G 225
London Eye 1H 229 (47Pb 90)
London Flds. E. Side E8 .... 38Xb 71
London Fields Lido 38Xb 71
London Flds. W. Side E8 .... 38Wb 71
London Film Mus. 1H 229 (47Pb 90)
London Fire Brigade Mus.
.... 1D 230 (47Sb 91)
London Fruit Exchange E1 .... 1K 225
London Ga. UB3: Hayes 47U 84
LONDON GATEWAY SERVICE AREA
.... 19Sa 29
London Golf Course, The 80Yd 164
London Group Bus. Pk. NW2 .... 32Va 68
LONDON HEATHROW AIRPORT
Terminals 1, 2, 3 .... 55Q 106
Terminal 4 .... 57R 106
Terminal 5 .... 55L 105
London Heliport, The 54Eb 111
London Ho. EC1 .... 1D 224
NW8 .... 1E 214
WC1 .... 5H 217 (42Pb 90)
London Ind. Pk., The E6 .... 43Rc 94
(not continuous)
London Intl. Cruise Terminal
RM18: Tilb 6C 122
London International Gallery of Children's Art
.... 32Kb 70
(off Dartmouth Pk. Hill)
London La. BR1: Brom 66Hc 137
E8 .... 38Xb 71
London Master Bakers Almshouses
E10 .... 30Dc 52
London Metropolitan Archives
.... 5A 218 (42Qb 90)
London Metropolitan University
London City Campus -
Calcutta House & Goulston St.
.... 2K 225
Central House 44Wb 91
(off Whitechapel High St.)
Commercial Rd. 44Wb 91
Jewry St. 3K 225
Moorgate 1G 225
Tower Hill 4K 225
North London Campus -
Eden Grove 36Pb 70
Stapleton House 36Pb 70
Tower Building & Graduate Cen.
.... 36Qb 70
Old Castle St. 44Vb 91
London M. W2 .... 3C 220 (44Fb 89)
London Motorcycle Mus. 41Ea 86
London Motor Mus. 48V 84
London Palladium 3B 222
London Pavilion 5D 222
London Plane Ho. E15 .... 41Gc 93
(off Teasel Way)
London Regatta Cen. 45Mc 93
London Rd. AL1: St A 3C 6
BR1: Brom 66Hc 137
BR8: Swan 67Ed 140
(Birchwood Rd., not continuous)
BR8: Swan 70Hd 140
(Pine Cl.)
CM14: B'wood 21Vd 58
CR0: C'don 73Rb 157
CR3: Cat'm 95Tb 197

London Rd. CR4: Mitc 73Jb 156
(Mill Grn. Rd.)
CR4: Mitc 71Gb 155
(Mitcham Pk.)
CR7: Thor H 71Qb 156
DA1: Bexl, Cray 57Fd 118
DA2: Dart, Ghithe, Swans 59Rd 119
DA4: Farni 72Nd 163
DA9: Ghithe, Swans 57Xd 120
DA10: Swans 57Xd 120
DA11: Nflt 58Fe 121
E13 ....40Jc 73
EN2: Enf 13Tb 33
GU4: Burp 100E 188
(not continuous)
GU20: W'sham 6A 146
GU23: Send 100E 188
GU25: Vir W 10J 125
HA1: Harr 33Ga 66
HA7: Stan 22La 46
HA9: Wemb 36Na 67
HP1: Hem H 4G 2
HP3: Hem H 5K 3
HP4: Berk 2A 2
IG11: Bark 38Rc 74
KT2: King T 68Pa 131
KT17: Ewe 81Va 174
RH1: Redh 5P 207
RH2: Reig 6J 207
RM4: Abr 14Vc 37
RM4: Stap T 11Ed 38
RM6: Chad H 30Cd 56
RM7: Chad H, Rom 30Cd 56
RM15: Avel, Purf 46Pd 97
RM17: Grays 51Yd 120
RM18: Tilb 4D 122
RM19: Purf 46Pd 97
RM19: Purf, W Thur 50Qd 97
(not continuous)
RM20: Grays, W Thur 51Ud 120
SE1 ....3B 230 (48Rb 91)
SE23 ....60Xb 113
SL3: Dat 2M 103
(not continuous)
SL3: L'ly 8N 81
SL5: Asc, S'hill 9A 124
SL5: S'dale 3E 146
SM3: Cheam 76Za 154
SM4: Mord 71Db 155
SM6: Wall 77Kb 156
SS17: Stan H 2K 101
SW16 ....67Pb 134
SW17 ....66Hb 133
TN13: Dun G, Riv 89Fd 182
TN13: S'oaks 95Hd 202
TN14: Hals 84Dd 182
(Shacklands Rd.)
TN14: Hals 81Bd 181
(Wheatsheaf Hill)
TN15: Bor G, W King, Wro, Wro H 78Td 164
TN16: Westrm 95Sc 200
TW1: Twick 59Ja 108
TW3: Houn, Isle 55Ea 108
TW7: Bford, Isle 54Ha 108
TW7: Isle, Twick 57Ja 108
TW8: Bford 57Ha 108
TW14: Bedf 62K 127
TW15: Ashf 62K 127
TW18: Staines 63J 127
TW20: Eng G 10J 125
WD3: Rick 19N 25
WD6: Bore 6Qa 15
WD7: Shenl 5Pa 15
WD23: Bush 16Aa 27
London Rd. Moor La. Rdbt.
WD3: Rick 19N 25
London Rd. Nth. RH1: Mers 98Kb 196
London Rd. Retail Pk. HP3: Hem H 5L 3
LONDON ROAD RDBT. 58Ja 108
London Rd. Sth. RH1: Mers, Redh 2A 208
London School of Economics & Political Science, The 3J 223 (44Pb 90)
Londons Cl. RM14: Upm 36Sd 78
London Scottish Golf Course 62Xa 132
London Scottish RUFC 55Ma 109
London's Death Trap 2H 229
London South Bank University
Keyworth St. 3C 230 (48Rb 91)
Southwark Campus 3C 230 (48Rb 91)
London South Bank University (Havering) 25Nd 57
London South Bank University Sports Cen. 3C 230
London South Bank University Technopark 3C 230
London's Pleasure Gdns. 46Lc 93
London Stile W4 ....50Qa 87
London Stock Exchange 2C 224
London St. EC3 ....4J 225 (45Ub 91)
KT16: Chert 73J 149
W2 ....2B 220 (44Fb 89)
London Telecom Tower, The 7B 216
London Television Centre, The 6K 223 (45Qb 90)
London Ter. E2 ....40Wb 71
London Transport Mus. 4G 223 (45Nb 90)
London Transport Mus. Depot 47Qa 87
London Trocadero 5D 222 (45Mb 90)
London Underwriting Cen. 4J 225
London Wall EC2 ....1E 224 (43Sb 91)
London Wall Bldgs. EC2 ....1G 225
London Welsh RUFC 55Na 109
London Wetland Cen. 53Xa 110
London Wetland Cen. Vis. Cen. 53Xa 110
London Wharf *E2* *39Xb 71*
(off Wharf Pl.)
London Zoo 1H 215 (40Jb 70)
Londrina Ct. *HP4: Berk* *1A 2*
(off Londrina Ter.)
Londrina Ter. HP4: Berk 1A 2
Loneacre GU20: W'sham 9C 146
LONESOME 67Lb 134
Lonesome Caravan Site SW16 ....67Kb 134
Lonesome La. RH2: Reig 10K 207
Lonesome Way SW16 ....67Kb 134
Long Acre BR6: Orp 75Zc 161
WC2 ....4F 223 (45Nb 90)
Long Acre Ct. W13 ....43Ja 86
Longacre Pl. SM5: Cars 79Jb 156
Longacre Rd. E17 ....25Fc 53
Longacres AL4: St A 2H 7
(not continuous)
Longaford Way CM13: Hut 18Ee 41
Long Arrotts HP1: Hem H 1K 3
Long Barn Cl. WD25: Wat 4W 12
Longbeach Rd. SW11 ....55Hb 111
Longberrys NW2 ....34Bb 69
Longboat Row UB1: S'hall 44Ba 85
Longbourn SL4: Wind 5E 102
Longbourne Way KT16: Chert 72H 149
Longbow Ho. EC1 ....7F 219
Longboyds KT11: Cobh 87X 171
Longbridge Ho. *E16* *45Rc 94*
(off University Way)
RM8: Dag *35Xc 75*
(off Longbridge Rd.)
Longbridge Rd. IG11: Bark 37Tc 74
RM8: Dag 35Wc 75
Longbridge Way SE13 ....57Ec 114
UB8: Uxb 40K 63
Longbury Cl. BR5: St P 69Xc 139
Longbury Dr. BR5: St P 69Xc 139
Long Chaulden HP1: Hem H 2G 2
Longcliffe Path WD19: Wat 20W 26
Long Cl. SL2: Farn C 8F 60
Long Copse Cl. KT23: Bookh 95Da 191
Long Ct. RM19: Purf 49Qd 97
Longcourt M. *E11* *28Lc 53*
(off Elmcroft Av.)
Longcroft SE9 ....62Pc 138
WD19: Wat 17X 27
Longcroft Av. SM7: Bans 86Eb 175
Longcroft Dr. EN8: Walt C 6Bc 20
Longcrofte Rd. HA8: Edg 24Ma 47
Longcroft La. HP3: Bov, Hem H 10E 2
Longcroft Ri. IG10: Lough 15Qc 36
Longcroft Rd. WD3: Map C 22F 42
Longcrofts EN9: Walt A 6Gc 21
LONGCROSS 6L 147
Longcross Rd. KT16: Longc 6K 147
Long Deacon Rd. E4 ....18Gc 35
Longdean Pk. HP3: Hem H 6A 4
Long Deans Nature Reserve 7B 4
Longden Av. KT15: Add 80J 149
LONG DITTON 74La 152
Longdon Ct. RM1: Rom 29Hd 56
Longdon Wood BR2: Kes 76Nc 160
Longdown La. Nth. KT17: Eps 86Wa 174
Longdown La. Sth.
KT17: Eps, Eps D 86Wa 174
Longdown Rd. KT17: Eps 86Wa 174
SE6 ....63Cc 136
Long Dr. HA4: Ruis 36Y 65
SL1: Burn 1A 80
UB6: G'frd 39Da 65
UB7: W Dray 47N 83
W3 ....44Ua 88
Long Elmes HA3: Hrw W 25Da 45
Long Elms WD5: Ab L 5T 12
Long Elms Cl. WD5: Ab L 5T 12
Long Fallow AL2: Chis G 9N 5
Longfellow Dr. CM13: Hut 17Ee 41
Longfellow Rd. E17 ....30Bc 52
KT4: Wor Pk 75Wa 154
Longfellow Way SE1 ....6K 231 (49Vb 91)
LONGFIELD 68Ae 143
Long Fld. NW9 ....24Ua 48
Longfield BR1: Brom 67Hc 137
HP3: Hem H 4B 4
IG10: Lough 15Mc 35
SL2: Hedg 4H 61
Longfield Av. DA3: Lfield 68Ee 143
DA13: Meop 68Ee 143
E17 ....28Ac 52
EN3: Enf W 9Yb 20
HA9: Wemb 32Na 67
NW7 ....24Wa 48
RM11: Horn 31Hd 76
SM6: Wall 74Jb 156
W5 ....45La 86
Longfield Chalk Bank Local Nature Reserve 68Yd 142
Longfield Cres. KT20: Tad 92Ya 194
SE26 ....62Yb 136
Longfield Dr. CR4: Mitc 67Gb 133
SW14 ....57Ra 109
Longfield Est. SE1 ....5K 231 (49Vb 91)
LONGFIELD HILL 70Fe 143
Longfield Ho. W5 ....45La 86
Longfield Rd. DA3: Long H 71Fe 165
W5 ....44La 86
Longfield St. SW18 ....59Cb 111
Longfield Wlk. W5 ....44La 86
LONGFORD
TN13 ....92Gd 202
UB7 ....53K 105
Longford Av. TW14: Felt 58U 106
TW19: Stanw 60N 105
UB1: S'hall 45Da 85
Longford Cir. UB7: Lford 53K 105
Longford Cl. TW12: Hamp H 63Ca 129
TW13: Hanw 62Aa 129
UB4: Yead 45Z 85
Longford Ct. *E5* *35Zb 72*
(off Pedro St.)
KT19: Ewe 77Sa 153
NW4 ....28Za 48
TN13: Dun G 92Gd 202
TW12: Hamp H 65Da 129
UB1: S'hall *46Ca 85*
(off Uxbridge Rd.)
Longford Gdns. SM1: Sutt 76Eb 155
UB4: Yead 45Z 85
Longford Ho. *BR1: Brom* *64Fc 137*
(off Brangbourne Rd.)
E1 ....*44Yb 92*
(off Jubilee St.)
TW12: Hamp H 63Ca 129
Longford Ind. Est. TW12: Hamp 65Da 129
LONGFORDMOOR 53J 105
Longford Rd. TW2: Whitt 60Ca 107
Longford St. NW1 ....5A 216 (42Kb 90)
Longford Wlk. SW2 ....59Qb 112
Longford Way TW19: Stanw 60N 105
Long Furlong Dr. SL2: Slou 2B 80
Long Gables SL9: Ger X 29B 42
Long Grn. IG7: Chig 21Uc 54
Long Gro. RM3: Hrld W 26Nd 57
Long Gro. Rd. KT19: Eps 83Sa 173
Longhayes Av. RM6: Chad H 28Zc 55
Longhayes Ct. RM6: Chad H 28Zc 55
Long Heath Dr. KT23: Bookh 96Aa 191
Longheath Gdns. CR0: C'don 71Yb 158
Longhedge Ho. *SE26* *63Wb 135*
(off High Level Dr.)
Long Hedges TW3: Houn 54Ca 107
Longhedge St. SW11 ....54Jb 112
Long Hill CR3: Wold 93Zb 198
Longhill Rd. SE6 ....61Fc 137
Longhook Gdns. UB5: N'olt 40W 64
Longhope Cl. SE15 ....51Ub 113
Longhouse Rd. RM16: Grays 8D 100
Long Houses GU24: Pirb 6B 186
Longhurst Ho. *W10* *41Bb 89*
(off Lancefield St.)
Longhurst Rd. CR0: C'don 72Xb 157
SE13 ....57Fc 115
Longitude Apartments *CR0: C'don* *75Tb 157*
(off Addiscombe Gro.)
Long John HP3: Hem H 4P 3
Longland Ct. *E9* *36Ac 72*
(off Mabley St.)
SE1 ....50Wb 91
Longland Dr. N20 ....20Db 31
Longland Pl. KT19: Eps 84Na 173
LONGLANDS 62Sc 138
Longlands HP2: Hem H 2P 3
Longlands Av. CR5: Coul 86Jb 176
Longlands Cl. EN8: Chesh 4Zb 20
Longlands Ct. CR4: Mitc 67Jb 134
DA15: Sidc 61Vc 139
W11 ....45Bb 89
Longlands Pk. Cres. DA15: Sidc 62Uc 138
Longlands Rd. DA15: Sidc 62Uc 138
Long La. CR0: C'don 72Xb 157
DA7: Bex 52Zc 117
EC1 ....1C 224 (43Rb 91)
HP3: Bov, Flau 3B 10
N2 ....25Db 49
N3 ....25Db 49
(not continuous)
RM16: Grays 47Ce 99
SE1 ....2F 231 (47Tb 91)
TW19: Stanw 61P 127
UB10: Hil, Ick 40Q 64
WD3: Herons 16E 24
WD3: Rick 18G 24
Longleat Ho. SW1 ....7D 228
Longleat M. BR5: St M Cry 70Yc 139
Longleat Rd. EN1: Enf 15Ub 33
Longleat Way TW14: Bedf 59T 106
Longlees WD3: Map C 22F 42
Longleigh Ho. *SE5* *53Ub 113*
(off Peckham Rd.)
Longleigh La. DA7: Bex 51Yc 117
SE2 ....51Yc 117
Long Lents Ho. *NW10* *39Ta 67*
(off Shrewsbury Cres.)
Longley Av. HA0: Wemb 39Pa 67
Longley Ct. SW8 ....53Nb 112
Longley M. RM16: Ors 7B 100
Longley Rd. CR0: C'don 73Rb 157
HA1: Harr 29Ea 46
SW17 ....65Gb 133
Long Leys E4 ....23Dc 52
Longley St. SE1 ....49Wb 91
Longley Way NW2 ....34Ya 68
Long Lodge Dr. KT12: Walt T 76Y 151
Longman Ct. HP3: Hem H 7N 3
Longman Ho. *E2* *40Zb 72*
(off Mace St.)
E8 ....*39Vb 71*
(off Haggerston Rd.)
Longmans Cl. WD18: Wat 16S 26
Long Mark Rd. E16 ....43Mc 93
Longmarsh La. SE28 ....46Uc 94
Longmarsh Vw. DA4: Sut H 67Rd 141
Long Mead NW9 ....25Va 48
Longmead BR7: Chst 68Qc 138
SL4: Wind 3C 102
Longmead Bus. Pk. KT19: Eps 83Ta 173
Longmead Cl. CM15: Shenf 18Ae 41
CR3: Cat'm 94Ub 197
Longmead Dr. DA14: Sidc 61Zc 139
Longmeade DA12: Grav'nd 10H 123
Longmead Ho. SE27 ....64Sb 135
Longmead La. SL1: Burn 8B 60
Long Meadow CM13: Hut 19Ee 41
NW5 ....36Mb 70
RM3: Rom 19Ld 39
TN13: Riv 93Fd 202
Longmeadow KT23: Bookh 97Ba 191
Long Mdw. Cl. BR4: W W'ck 73Ec 158
Longmeadow Rd. DA15: Sidc 60Uc 116
Longmead Rd. KT7: T Ditt 73Ga 152
KT19: Eps, Ewe 83Ta 173
SW17 ....64Hb 133
UB3: Hayes 45V 84
Longmere Gdns. KT20: Tad 91Ya 194
Long Mill *SE10* *53Dc 114*
(off Greenwich High Rd.)
Long Mill La. TN11: D Grn 99Ce 205
TN15: Crou, Plat 92De 205
Long Mill La. Crouch TN15: Crou 94Ee 205
Long Mimms HP2: Hem H 1N 3
Long Moor EN8: Chesh 1Ac 20
Longmoore St. SW1 ....6B 228 (49Lb 90)
Longmoor Point *SW15* *60Xa 110*
(off Norley Va.)
Longmore Av. EN4: E Barn 16Eb 31
EN5: New Bar 16Eb 31
Longmore Cl. WD3: Map C 21H 43
Longmore Gdns. Est. SW1 ....6C 228
Longmore Rd. KT12: Hers 77Aa 151
Longnor Est. E1 ....41Zb 92
Longnor Rd. E1 ....41Zb 92
Long Orchards KT20: Kgswd 92Ab 194
Long Pond Rd. SE3 ....53Gc 115
Longport Cl. IG6: Ilf 23Wc 55
Long Reach GU23: Ock 95Q 190
KT24: W Hor 95Q 190
Longreach *DA1: Dart* *55Qd 119*
(off Vickers La.)
Longreach Ct. IG11: Bark 40Tc 74
Long Reach Rd. IG11: Bark 42Vc 95
Longreach Rd. DA8: Erith 52Kd 119
Long Readings La. SL2: Slou 1F 80
Longridge WD7: R'lett 6Ka 14
Longridge Gro. GU22: Pyr 86H 169
Longridge Ho. SE1 ....4E 230 (48Sb 91)
Longridge La. UB1: S'hall 44Da 85
Longridge Rd. IG11: Bark 38Sc 74
SW5 ....49Cb 89
Long Ridges *N2* *27Jb 50*
(off Fortis Grn.)
Longridge Vw. CR5: Chip 92Hb 195
Long Ridings Av. CM13: Hut 15De 41
Long Rd. SW4 ....56Kb 112
Long Room, The UB9: Hare 24J 43
Longroyd *KT24: E Hor* *98U 190*
(off Cobham Way)
Longs Cl. GU22: Pyr 88J 169
Longs Ct. TW9: Rich 56Pa 109
WC2 ....5E 222
Longsdon Way CR3: Cat'm 96Wb 197
Longshaw KT22: Lea 92Ja 192
Longshaw Rd. E4 ....20Fc 35
Longshore SE8 ....49Bc 92
Longshott Ct. *SW5* *49Cb 89*
(off W. Cromwell Rd.)
Longside Cl. TW20: Egh 67E 126
Longspring WD24: Wat 9X 13
Longspring Wood Nature Reserve 10E 4
Longstaff Cres. SW18 ....58Cb 111
Longstaff Rd. SW18 ....58Cb 111
Longstone Av. NW10 ....38Va 68
Longstone Ct. SE1 ....2F 231
Longstone Rd. SL0: Iver H 40E 62
SW17 ....64Kb 134
Long St. E2 ....3K 219 (41Vb 91)
EN9: Walt A 2Mc 21
Longthornton Rd. SW16 ....68Lb 134
Longthorpe Ct. W6 ....49Wa 88
Longton Av. SE26 ....63Wb 135
Longton Gro. SE26 ....63Xb 135
Longtown Cl. RM3: Rom 22Ld 57
Longtown Ct. *DA2: Dart* *58Rd 119*
(off Osbourne Rd.)
Longtown Rd. RM3: Rom 22Ld 57
Longview Vs. RM5: Col R 25Bd 55
Longview Way RM5: Col R 25Fd 56
Longville Rd. SE11 ....5B 230 (49Rb 91)
Long Wlk. DA13: Ist R 7A 144
EN9: Walt A 2Cc 20
GU4: E Clan 100P 189
HP8: Chal G 13A 24
KT3: N Mald 69Sa 131
KT14: W Byf 86L 169
KT18: Tatt C 91Ya 194
SE1 ....3J 231 (48Ub 91)
SE18 ....51Rc 116
SL4: Wind 6H 103
SW13 ....54Ua 110
Long Wlk., The SL4: Wind 10H 103
Longwalk Rd. UB11: Stock P 46Ra 84
Long Wall E15 ....41Fc 93
Longwater Ho. *KT1: King T* *69Ma 131*
(off Portsmouth Rd.)
Longwood Av. SL3: L'ly 50D 82
Longwood Bus. Pk. TW16: Sun 71V 150
Longwood Cl. RM14: Upm 36Sd 78
Longwood Ct. *RM14: Upm* *36Sd 78*
(off Corbets Tey Rd.)
Longwood Dr. SW15 ....58Wa 110
Longwood Gdns. IG5: Ilf 28Pc 54
IG6: Ilf 28Pc 54
Longwood Rd. CR8: Kenley 88Tb 177
Longworth Cl. SE28 ....44Zc 95
Long Yd. WC1 ....6H 217 (42Pb 90)
Loning, The EN3: Enf W 10Yb 20
NW9 ....28Ua 48
Lonsdale Av. CM13: Hut 16Fe 41
E6 ....42Mc 93
HA9: Wemb 36Na 67
RM7: Rom 30Ed 56
Lonsdale Cl. E6 ....42Nc 94
HA5: Hat E 24Aa 45
HA8: Edg 22Pa 47
SE9 ....62Mc 137
UB8: Hil 43S 84
Lonsdale Ct. KT6: Surb 73Ma 153
Lonsdale Cres. DA2: Dart 60Sd 120
IG2: Ilf 30Rc 54
Lonsdale Dr. EN2: Enf 14Mb 32
Lonsdale Dr. Nth. EN2: Enf 15Nb 32
Lonsdale Gdns. CR7: Thor H 70Pb 134
Lonsdale Ho. *W11* *44Bb 89*
(off Lonsdale Rd.)
Lonsdale M. TW9: Kew 53Qa 109
W11 ....*44Bb 89*
(off Colville M.)
Lonsdale Pl. N1 ....38Qb 70
Lonsdale Rd. DA7: Bex 54Bd 117
E11 ....30Hc 53
KT13: Weyb 80Q 150
NW6 ....40Bb 69
SE25 ....70Xb 135
SW13 ....53Va 110
UB2: S'hall 48Z 85
W4 ....49Va 88
W11 ....44Bb 89
Lonsdale Road Reservoir Local Nature Reserve 52Va 110
Lonsdale Sq. N1 ....38Qb 70
Lonsdale Yd. W11 ....45Cb 89
Loobert Rd. N15 ....27Ub 51
Looe Gdns. IG6: Ilf 27Rc 54
Look Ahead SL1: Slou 7J 81
Lookout Education Centre, The 6F 221 (46Hb 89)
Loom La. WD7: R'lett 9Ha 14
Loom Pl. WD7: R'lett 8Ja 14
Loop Rd. BR7: Chst 65Sc 138
GU22: Wok 92B 188
KT18: Eps 88Sa 173
Lopen Rd. N18 ....21Ub 51
Lopez Ho. SW9 ....55Nb 112
Lorac Ct. SM2: Sutt 80Cb 155
Loraine Cl. EN3: Pond E 15Yb 34
Loraine Cotts. N7 ....35Pb 70
Loraine Ct. BR7: Chst 64Rc 138
Loraine Gdns. KT21: Asht 89Na 173
Loraine Ho. SM6: Wall 77Kb 156
Loraine Rd. N7 ....35Pb 70
W4 ....51Ra 109
Lorane Ct. WD17: Wat 12W 26
Lord Admiral's Vw. *SE18* *49Pc 94*
(off Frances St.)
Lord Alexander Ho. HP1: Hem H 3L 3
Lord Amory Way E14 ....47Ec 92
Lord Av. IG5: Ilf 28Pc 54
Lord Chancellor Wlk. KT2: King T 67Sa 131
Lord Ct. IG5: Ilf 28Pc 54
Lord Darby M. TN14: Cud 87Tc 180
Lordell Pl. SW19 ....65Ya 132
Lorden Wlk. E2 ....41Wb 91
Lord Gdns. IG5: Ilf 28Pc 54
Lord Hills Bri. W2 ....43Db 89
Lord Hills Rd. W2 ....43Db 89
Lord Holland La. SW9 ....54Qb 112
Lord Knyvett Cl. TW19: Stanw 58M 105
Lord Knyvetts Ct. TW19: Stanw 58M 105
Lord Mayor's Dr. SL2: Farn C 7D 60
Lord Napier Pl. W6 ....50Wa 88
Lord Nth. St. SW1 ....4F 229 (48Nb 90)
Lord Raglan Ho. SL4: Wind 5G 102
Lord Roberts M. SW6 ....52Db 111
Lord Robert's Ter. SE18 ....50Qc 94
Lord Rosebery Lodge
KT18: Eps 86Sa 173
Lord's 4C 214 (41Fb 89)
Lordsbury Fld. SM6: Wall 82Lb 176
Lords Cl. SE21 ....61Sb 135
TW13: Hanw 61Aa 129
WD7: Shenl 4Na 15
Lordsgrove Cl. KT20: Tad 92Xa 194
Lordship Cl. CM13: Hut 17Fe 41
Lordship Gro. N16 ....33Tb 71
Lordship La. N17 ....25Tb 51
N22 ....26Qb 50
SE22 ....56Vb 113
Lordship La. Est. SE21 ....59Wb 113
Lordship Pk. N16 ....33Sb 71
Lordship Pk. M. N16 ....33Sb 71
Lordship Pl. SW3 ....51Gb 111
Lordship Rd. EN7: Chesh 2Xb 19
N16 ....32Tb 71
UB5: N'olt 38Aa 65
Lordship Ter. N16 ....33Tb 71
Lordsmead Rd. N17 ....25Ub 51
Lord St. DA12: Grav'nd 9D 122
E16 ....46Nc 94
WD17: Wat 13Y 27
Lords Vw. NW8 ....4D 214 (41Fb 89)
(not continuous)
Lordswood Cl. DA2: Daren 63Ud 142
DA6: Bex 57Ad 117
Lords Wood Ho. CR5: Coul 94Mb 196
Lord Warwick St. SE18 ....48Pc 94
Loreburn Ho. N7 ....35Pb 70
Lorenzo Ho. IG3: Ilf 30Vc 55
Lorenzo St. WC1 ....3H 217 (41Pb 90)
Loretto Gdns. HA3: Kenton 28Na 47
Lorian Cl. N12 ....21Db 49
Lorian Dr. RH2: Reig 5L 207
Lorimer Row BR2: Brom 72Mc 159
Loriners Cl. KT11: Cobh 86W 170
Loriners Link HP2: Hem H 1N 3
Loring Rd. N20 ....19Gb 31
SE14 ....53Ac 114
SL4: Wind 3D 102
TW7: Isle 54Ha 108
Loris Rd. W6 ....48Ya 88
Lorn Ct. SW9 ....54Qb 112
Lorne, The KT23: Bookh 98Ca 191
Lorne Av. CR0: C'don 73Zb 158
Lorne Cl. NW8 ....4E 214 (41Gb 89)
SL1: Slou 8F 80
Lorne Ct. SL1: Slou 8G 80
Lorne Gdns. CR0: C'don 73Zb 158
E11 ....28Lc 53
GU21: Knap 1H 187
W11 ....47Za 88
Lorne Ho. *E1* *43Ac 92*
(off Ben Jonson Rd.)
Lorne Rd. CM14: W'ley 21Yd 58
E7 ....35Kc 73
E17 ....29Cc 52
HA3: W'stone 26Ha 46
N4 ....32Pb 70
TW10: Rich 57Pa 109
Lorne Ter. N3 ....26Bb 49
Lorn Rd. SW9 ....54Pb 112
Lorraine Ct. NW1 ....38Kb 70
Lorraine Pk. HA3: Hrw W 24Ga 46
Lorrimore Rd. SE17 ....51Rb 113
Lorrimore Sq. SE17 ....51Rb 113
Lorton Cl. DA12: Grav'nd 1G 144
Lorton Ho. *NW6* *39Cb 69*
(off Kilburn Vale)
Loseberry Rd. KT10: Clay 78Fa 152
Losfield Rd. SL4: Wind 3C 102
Lossie Dr. SL0: Iver 45D 82
Lothair Rd. W5 ....47Ma 87
Lothair Rd. Nth. N4 ....30Rb 51
Lothair Rd. Sth. N4 ....31Qb 70
Lothair St. SW11 ....55Gb 111
Lothbury EC2 ....2F 225 (44Tb 91)
Lothian Av. UB4: Yead 43X 85
Lothian Cl. HA0: Wemb 34Ja 66
Lothian Rd. SW9 ....53Rb 113
Lothian Wood KT20: Tad 94Xa 194
Lothrop St. W10 ....41Ab 88
Lots Rd. SW10 ....52Eb 111
Lotus Cl. SE21 ....62Tb 135
Lotus Pk. TW18: Staines 63F 126
Lotus Rd. TN16: Big H 90Pc 180
Loubet St. SW17 ....65Hb 133
Loudhams Wood La. HP8: Chal G 12A 24
Loudoun Av. IG6: Ilf 29Rc 54
Loudoun Rd. NW8 ....1A 214 (39Eb 69)
LOUDWATER 13L 25
Loudwater Cl. TW16: Sun 70W 128
Loudwater Dr. WD3: Loud 14L 25
Loudwater Hgts. WD3: Loud 13K 25
Loudwater Ho. WD3: Loud 14L 25
Loudwater La. WD3: Crox G, Loud 15L 25
Loudwater Ridge WD3: Loud 14L 25
Loudwater Rd. TW16: Sun 70W 128
Loughborough Est. SW9 ....55Rb 113
Loughborough Ho. RM8: Dag 35Wc 75
Loughborough Pk. SW9 ....56Rb 113
Loughborough Rd. SW9 ....54Qb 112
Loughborough St. SE11 ....7J 229 (50Pb 90)
Lough Rd. N7 ....36Pb 70
LOUGHTON 14Nc 36
Loughton Bus. Cen. IG10: Lough 14Tc 36
Loughton Ct. EN9: Walt A 5Kc 21
Loughton Golf Course 11Rc 36
Loughton La. CM16: They B 10Tc 22
Loughton Leisure Cen. 14Nc 36
Loughton Seedbed Cen.
IG10: Lough 14Tc 36
Loughton Way IG9: Buck H 18Mc 35
Louisa Cl. E9 ....39Zb 72
Louisa Ct. TW2: Twick 61Ga 130
Louisa Gdns. E1 ....42Zb 92
Louisa Ho. IG3: Ilf 30Wc 55
Louisa Oakes Cl. E4 ....21Dc 52
Louisa St. E1 ....42Zb 92
Louise Aumonier Wlk. *N19* *31Nb 70*
(off Jessie Blythe La.)
Louise Bennett Cl. SE24 ....56Rb 113
Louise Ct. N22 ....25Qb 50
Louise De Marillac Ho. *E1* *43Yb 92*
(off Smithy St.)
Louise Gdns. RM13: Rain 41Gd 96
Louise Rd. E15 ....37Gc 73
Louise Wlk. HP3: Bov 10C 2
Louise White Ho. N19 ....32Mb 70
Louis Gdns. BR7: Chst 63Pc 138
Louis M. N10 ....25Kb 50
Louisville Rd. SW17 ....62Jb 134
Lousada Lodge *N14* *16Lb 32*
(off Avenue Rd.)
Louvaine Rd. SW11 ....56Fb 111
Louvain Rd. DA9: Ghithe 59Ud 120
Louvain Way WD25: Wat 4X 13

Lovage App. E6 43Nc 94
Lovat Cl. NW2 34Va 68
Lovat La. EC3 4H 225 (45Ub 91)
(not continuous)
Lovats Cotts. AL2: Park 9B 6
Lovatt Cl. HA8: Edg 23Ra 47
Lovatt Ct. SW12 60Kb 112
Lovatt Dr. HA4: Ruis 29W 44
Lovatts WD3: Crox G 14Q 26
Lovat Wlk. TW5: Hest 52Aa 107
Loveday Rd. W13 47Ka 86
Love Grn. La. SL0: Iver 43F 82
Lovegrove Cl. CR2: Sande 82Tb 177
Lovegrove Dr. SL2: Slou 2D 80
Lovegrove St. SE1 50Wb 91
Lovegrove Wlk. E14 46Ec 92
Love Hill La. SL3: L'ly 45C 82
Lovejoy La. SL4: Wind 4B 102
Lovekyn Cl. KT2: King T 68Na 131
Lovelace Av. BR2: Brom 72Qc 160
Lovelace Cl. KT24: Eff J 95W 190
TN15: W King 79Ud 164
Lovelace Dr. GU22: Pyr 88G 168
Lovelace Gdns. IG11: Bark 35Wc 75
KT6: Surb 73Ma 153
KT12: Hers 78Y 151
Lovelace Grn. SE9 55Pc 116
Lovelace Ho. W13 45Ka 86
Lovelace Rd. EN4: E Barn 17Gb 31
KT6: Surb 73La 152
SE21 61Sb 135
Lovelace Vs. *KT7: T Ditt* *73Ka 152*
(off Portsmouth Rd.)
Loveland Mans. *IG11: Bark* *38Vc 75*
(off Upney La.)
Lovelands La. GU24: Chob 5G 166
KT20: Lwr K 99Db 195
Love La. AL9: N Mym 10D 8
BR1: Brom 69Kc 137
CR4: Mitc 69Gb 133
(not continuous)
DA5: Bexl 58Bd 117
DA12: Grav'nd 9E 122
EC2 2E 224 (44Sb 91)
HA5: Pinn 26Z 45
IG8: Wfd G 23Pc 54
KT6: Surb 75La 152
KT20: Walt H 99Va 194
N17 24Vb 51
RH9: G'stone 4A 210
RM15: Avel 47Sd 98
RM18: E Til 1K 123
SE18 49Qc 94
SE25 69Xb 135
SL0: Iver 44F 82
SM1: Sutt 79Bb 155
SM3: Cheam, Sutt 79Ab 154
SM4: Mord 73Cb 155
WD4: K Lan 10N 3
WD5: Ab L 2V 12
Lovel Av. DA16: Well 54Wc 117
Lovel Cl. HP1: Hem H 2J 3
Lovelinch Cl. SE15 51Yb 114
Lovel La. SL4: Wink 4A 124
Lovell Ho. *E8* *39Wb 71*
(off Shrubland Rd.)
Lovell Pl. SE16 48Ac 92
Lovell Rd. EN1: Enf 7Xb 19
TW10: Ham 62La 130
UB1: S'hall 44Da 85
Lovells Cl. GU18: Light 2A 166
Lovell Wlk. RM13: Rain 37Jd 76
Lovelock Cl. CR8: Kenley 89Sb 177
Loveridge M. NW6 37Bb 69
Loveridge Rd. NW6 37Bb 69
Lovers La. DA9: Ghithe 56Zd 121
Lovers Wlk. N3 24Cb 49
(not continuous)
NW7 23Bb 49
RM5: Col R 22Fd 56
SE10 51Fc 115
W1 6H 221 (46Jb 90)
Lovett Dr. SM5: Cars 73Eb 155
Lovett Rd. AL2: Lon C 8E 6
TW18: Staines 63D 126
UB9: Hare 27L 43
Lovett's Pl. SW18 56Db 111
Lovett Way NW10 36Sa 67
Love Wlk. SE5 54Tb 113
Lovibonds Av. BR6: Farnb 77Rc 160
UB7: Yiew 44P 83
Lowbell La. AL2: Lon C 9J 7
Lowbrook Rd. IG1: Ilf 35Rc 74
Low Cl. DA9: Ghithe 57Wd 120
Low Cross Wood La. SE21 62Vb 135
Lowdell Cl. UB7: Yiew 44N 83
Lowden Rd. N9 18Xb 33
SE24 56Rb 113
UB1: S'hall 45Aa 85
Lowder Ho. *E1* *46Xb 91*
(off Wapping La.)
Lowe, The IG7: Chig 21Wc 55
Lowe Av. E16 43Jc 93
Lowe Cl. IG7: Chig 22Wc 55
Lowell Ho. *SE5* *52Sb 113*
(off Wyndham Est.)
Lowell St. E14 44Ac 92
Lowen Rd. RM13: Rain 40Fd 76
Lwr. Addiscombe Rd. CR0: C'don 74Ub 157
Lwr. Addison Gdns. W14 47Ab 88
Lwr. Adeyfield Rd. HP2: Hem H 1M 3
Lwr. Alderton Hall La.
IG10: Lough 15Qc 36
Lwr. Ash Est. TW17: Shep 72V 150
LOWER ASHTEAD 91Ma 193
Lower Barn HP3: Hem H 5P 3
Lwr. Barn Rd. CR8: Purl 84Sb 177
Lwr. Bedfords Rd.
RM1: Have B, Rom 23Gd 56
Lwr. Belgrave St. SW1 4K 227 (48Kb 90)
LOWER BITCHET 98Sd 204
Lwr. Boston Rd. W7 46Ga 86
Lwr. Bridge Rd. RH1: Redh 6P 207
Lwr. Britwell Rd. SL2: Slou 2B 80
(not continuous)
Lwr. Broad St. RM10: Dag 39Cd 76
Lwr. Bury La. CM16: Epp 3Uc 22
Lower Camden BR7: Chst 66Pc 138
Lwr. Church Hill DA9: Ghithe 57Ud 120
Lwr. Church St. CR0: C'don 75Rb 157
Lwr. Cippenham La. SL1: Slou 6C 80
LOWER CLAPTON 35Xb 71
Lwr. Clapton Rd. E5 34Xb 71
Lwr. Clarendon Wlk. *W11* *44Ab 88*
(off Clarendon Rd.)
Lwr. Common Sth. SW15 55Xa 110
Lwr. Coombe St. CR0: C'don 77Sb 157
Lower Ct. Rd. KT19: Eps 83Sa 173
Lower Cres. SS17: Linf 8J 101
Lower Cft. BR8: Swan 70Hd 140
Lwr. Dagnall St. AL3: St A 2A 6
Lwr. Derby Rd. WD17: Wat 14Y 27
Lwr. Downs Rd. SW20 67Za 132
Lwr. Drayton Pl. CR0: C'don 75Rb 157
Lower Dunnymans SM7: Bans 86Bb 175
LOWER EDMONTON 19Wb 33
Lwr. Farm Rd. KT24: Eff 96X 191
LOWER FELTHAM 62W 128
Lower Fosters *NW4* *29Ya 48*
(off New Brent St.)
Lwr. George St. TW9: Rich 57Ma 109
Lwr. Gravel Rd. BR2: Brom 74Nc 160
LOWER GREEN 75Da 151
Lower Grn. Gdns. KT4: Wor Pk 74Wa 154
Lower Grn. Rd. KT10: Esh 75Da 151
Lower Grn. W. CR4: Mitc 69Gb 133
Lwr. Grosvenor Pl. SW1 3A 228 (48Kb 90)
Lower Gro. Rd. TW10: Rich 58Pa 109
Lwr. Guildford Rd. GU21: Knap 9H 167
Lwr. Guild Hall DA9: Bluew 59Vd 120
LOWER HALLIFORD 73T 150
Lwr. Hall La. E4 22Ac 52
(not continuous)
Lwr. Hampton Rd. TW16: Sun 69Y 129
Lwr. Ham Rd. KT2: King T 64Ma 131
Lwr. Higham Rd.
DA12: Grav'nd, Shorne 10H 123
Lwr. High St. WD17: Wat 14Y 27
Lwr. Hill Rd. KT19: Eps 84Ra 173
LOWER HOLLOWAY 36Pb 70
Lwr. Hook Bus. Pk. BR6: Downe 80Pc 160
Lwr. James St. W1 4C 222 (45Lb 90)
Lwr. John St. W1 4C 222 (45Lb 90)
Lwr. Kenwood Av. EN2: Enf 15Nb 32
Lwr. King's Rd. KT2: King T 67Na 131
LOWER KINGSWOOD 99Bb 195
Lwr. Lea Crossing E14 45Gc 93
E16 45Gc 93
Lwr. Lees Rd. SL2: Slou 1E 80
Lwr. Maidstone Rd. N11 23Lb 50
Lower Mall W6 50Xa 88
Lwr. Mardyke Av. RM13: Rain 40Ed 76
Lower Marsh SE1 2K 229 (47Qb 90)
Lwr. Marsh La. KT1: King T 70Pa 131
Lower Mead RH1: Redh 4P 207
SL0: Iver H 41F 82
Lwr. Merton Ri. NW3 38Gb 69
Lower Mill KT17: Ewe 80Va 154
Lwr. Morden La. SM4: Mord 72Ya 154
Lwr. Mortlake Rd. TW9: Rich 56Na 109
Lwr. New Change Pas. *EC4* *3E 224*
(off One New Change)
Lwr. Noke Cl.
CM14: Rom, S Weald 19Nd 39
Lower Northfield SM7: Bans 86Bb 175
Lower Nursery SL5: S'dale 1E 146
Lwr. Paddock Rd. WD19: Wat 16Aa 27
Lwr. Park Rd. CR5: Chip 90Gb 175
DA17: Belv 49Cd 96
IG10: Lough 15Mc 35
N11 22Lb 50
Lwr. Park Trad. Est. NW10 42Sa 87
Lwr. Paxton Rd. AL1: St A 3C 6
Lower Peryers KT24: E Hor 100U 190
Lwr. Pillory Down CR5: Coul 85Kb 176
SM6: Wall 85Kb 176
LOWER PLACE 40Sa 67
Lower Pl. Bus. Cen. *NW10* *40Ta 67*
(off Steele Rd.)
Lower Plantation WD3: Loud 13L 25
Lwr. Pyrford Rd. GU22: Pyr 88K 169
Lwr. Queen's Rd. IG9: Buck H 19Mc 35
Lwr. Range Rd. DA12: Grav'nd 9G 122
Lwr. Richmond Rd. SW14 55Qa 109
SW15 55Xa 110
TW9: Rich 55Qa 109
Lower Rd. BR5: St M Cry 72Xc 161
BR8: Hext, Swan 66Jd 140
CM15: Mount 12Fe 41
CR8: Kenley 85Rb 177
DA8: Erith 48Dd 96
DA11: Nflt 56Ae 121
DA12: High'm, Shorne 1N 145
DA17: Belv 48Dd 96
HA2: Harr 32Fa 66
HP3: Hem H 8A 4
IG10: Lough 11Qc 36
KT22: Fet 96Fa 192
KT23: Bookh 97Ca 191
KT24: Eff 99Z 191
RH1: Redh 8M 207
SE1 1K 229 (47Qb 90)
SE8 48Yb 92
SE16 47Yb 92
(not continuous)
SL9: Chal P, Ger X 25A 42
(not continuous)
SL9: Ger X 29B 42
SM1: Sutt 77Eb 155
UB9: Den 31E 62
WD3: Chor 14E 24
Lwr. Robert St. WC2 5G 223
Lwr. Rose Gallery DA9: Bluew 59Vd 120
Lower Sales HP1: Hem H 3H 3
Lower Sandfields GU23: Send 96F 188
Lwr. Sand Hills KT6: Surb 73La 152
Lwr. Sawley Wood SM7: Bans 86Bb 175
LOWER SHORNE 3N 145
Lower Shott KT23: Bookh 98Ca 191
Lwr. Sloane St. SW1 6H 227 (49Jb 90)
Lower Sq. TW7: Isle 55Ka 108
Lower Square, The *SM1: Sutt* *78Db 155*
(off St Nicholas Way)
Lwr. Station Rd. DA1: Cray 58Gd 118
Lower Strand NW9 26Va 48
Lwr. Sunbury Rd. TW12: Hamp 68Ba 129
Lower Swaines CM16: Epp 2Uc 22
LOWER SYDENHAM 63Zb 136
Lwr. Sydenham Ind. Est. SE26 64Bc 136
Lower Tail WD19: Wat 20Aa 27
Lwr. Teddington Rd.
KT1: Hamp W 67Ma 131
Lower Ter. NW3 34Eb 69
SE27 *64Rb 135*
(off Woodcote Pl.)
Lwr. Thames St. EC3 5G 225 (45Tb 91)
Lwr. Thames Wlk. DA9: Bluew 60Vd 120
Lower Tub WD23: Bush 17Fa 28
Lwr. Village Rd. SL5: S'hill 1A 146
Lowerwood Ct. *W11* *44Ab 88*
(off Westbourne Pk. Rd.)
Lwr. Wood Rd. KT10: Clay 79Ka 152
LOWER WOODSIDE 4H 9
Lower Yott HP2: Hem H 3P 3
Lowestoft Cl. *E5* *33Yb 72*
(off Theydon Rd.)
Lowestoft Dr. SL1: Slou 4B 80
Lowestoft M. E16 47Rc 94
Lowestoft Rd. WD24: Wat 11X 27
Loweswater Cl. HA9: Wemb 33Ma 67
WD25: Wat 5Y 13
Loweswater Ho. E3 42Bc 92
Lowfield Rd. NW6 38Cb 69
W3 44Ra 87
Lowfield St. DA1: Dart 59Nd 119
Low Hall Cl. E4 17Dc 34
Low Hall La. E17 30Ac 52
Low Hall Mnr. Bus. Cen. E17 30Ac 52
Lowick Rd. HA1: Harr 28Ga 46
Lowlands Dr. TW19: Stanw 57M 105
Lowlands Gdns. RM7: Rom 30Dd 56
Lowlands Rd. HA1: Harr 30Ga 46
HA5: Eastc 31Y 65
RM15: Avel 46Sd 98
Lowman Rd. N7 35Pb 70
Lownde M. SW16 61Nb 134
Lowndes Cl. SW1 4J 227 (48Jb 90)
Lowndes Ct. SW1 3G 227 (48Hb 89)
W1 3B 222
Lowndes Lodge SW1 3G 227
Lowndes M. SW16 61Nb 134
Lowndes Pl. SW1 4H 227 (48Jb 90)
Lowndes Sq. SW1 2G 227 (47Hb 89)
Lowndes St. SW1 3G 227 (48Jb 90)
Lownds Ct. BR1: Brom 68Jc 137
Lowood Ct. *SE19* *64Vb 135*
(off Farquhar Rd.)
Lowood Ho. *E1* *45Yb 92*
(off Bewley St.)
Lowood St. E1 45Xb 91
Lowry Cl. DA8: Erith 49Fd 96
Lowry Ct. *SE16* *50Xb 91*
(off Stubbs Dr.)
Lowry Cres. CR4: Mitc 68Gb 133
Lowry Ho. *E14* *47Cc 92*
(off Cassilis Rd.)
N17 *25Vb 51*
(off Pembury Rd.)
Lowry Rd. RM8: Dag 36Xc 75
Lowshoe La. RM5: Col R 25Cd 56
Lowson Gro. WD19: Wat 17Aa 27
LOW STREET 1H 123
Low St. La. RM18: W Til 9H 101
Lowswood Cl. HA6: Nwood 25S 44
Lowther Cl. WD6: E'tree 15Pa 29
Lowther Dr. EN2: Enf 14Nb 32
Lowther Hill SE23 59Ac 114
Lowther Ho. *SW1* *50Lb 90*
(off Churchill Gdns.)
Lowther Rd. E17 26Ac 52
HA7: Stan 27Pa 47
KT2: King T 67Pa 131
N7 36Qb 70
SW13 53Va 110
Lowthorpe GU21: Wok 10L 167
Lowth Rd. SE5 53Sb 113
LOXFORD 36Sc 74
Loxford Av. E6 40Mc 73
Loxford Cl. CR3: Cat'm 97Vb 197
Loxford Ho. KT17: Eps 84Ua 174
Loxford La. IG1: Ilf 36Sc 74
IG3: Ilf 36Sc 74
Loxford Rd. CR3: Cat'm 97Vb 197
IG11: Bark 37Rc 74
Loxford Ter. IG11: Bark 37Sc 74
Loxford Way CR3: Cat'm 97Vb 197
Loxham Rd. E4 24Dc 52
Loxham St. WC1 4G 217 (41Nb 90)
Loxley Cl. KT14: Byfl 86N 169
SE26 64Zb 136
Loxley Ho. HA9: Wemb 34Na 67
Loxley Rd. SW18 60Fb 111
TW12: Hamp 63Ba 129
Loxton Rd. SE23 60Zb 114
Loxwood KT13: Weyb 76U 150
Loxwood Cl. BR5: Orp 75Zc 161
HP3: Hem H 5H 3
TW14: Bedf 60T 106
Loxwood Rd. N17 27Ub 51
Loyd Ct. AL4: St A 4G 6
LSO St Lukes 5E 218
Lubbock Ho. *E14* *45Dc 92*
(off Poplar High St.)
Lubbock Rd. BR7: Chst 66Pc 138
Lubbock St. SE14 52Yb 114
Lucan Dr. TW18: Staines 66M 127
Lucan Ho. *N1* *39Tb 71*
(off Colville Est.)
Lucan Pl. SW3 6D 226 (49Gb 89)
Lucan Rd. EN5: Barn 13Ab 30
Lucas Av. E13 39Kc 73
HA2: Harr 33Ca 65
Lucas Cl. NW10 38Wa 68
Lucas Ct. EN9: Walt A 5Hc 21
SE26 64Ac 136
SW11 53Jb 112
Lucas Cres. *DA9: Ghithe* *56Yd 120*
(off Ingress Pk. Av.)
Lucas Gdns. N2 26Eb 49
LUCAS GREEN 7B 166
Lucas Grn. Rd. GU24: W End 7B 166
Lucas Ho. *SW10* *52Db 111*
(off Coleridge Gdns.)
WC1 4G 217
Lucas Rd. RM17: Grays 48Ce 99
SE20 65Yb 136
Lucas Sq. NW11 30Cb 49
Lucas St. SE8 53Cc 114
Lucerne Cl. GU22: Wok 91A 188
N13 20Nb 32
Lucerne Ct. DA18: Erith 48Ad 95
Lucerne Gro. E17 28Fc 53
Lucerne M. W8 46Cb 89
Lucerne Rd. BR6: Orp 74Vc 161
CR7: Thor H 71Rb 157
N5 35Rb 71
Lucerne Way RM3: Rom 23Md 57
Lucey Rd. SE16 48Wb 91
Lucey Way SE16 48Wb 91
Lucida Ct. *WD18: Wat* *15U 26*
(off Whippendell Rd.)
Lucie Av. TW15: Ashf 65R 128
Lucien Rd. SW17 63Jb 134
SW19 61Db 133
Lucinda Ct. E17 26Ac 52
EN1: Enf 14Ub 33
Lucknow St. SE18 52Uc 116
Lucks Hill HP1: Hem H 2G 2
Lucorn Cl. SE12 58Hc 115
Lucton M. IG10: Lough 14Rc 36
Luctons Av. IG9: Buck H 18Lc 35
Lucy Brown Ho. SE1 7E 224
Lucy Cres. W3 43Sa 87
Lucy Gdns. RM8: Dag 34Bd 75
Luddesdon Rd. DA8: Erith 52Cd 118
Luddington Av. GU25: Vir W 68B 126
Ludford Cl. CR0: Wadd 76Rb 157
Ludgate B'way. EC4 3B 224 (44Rb 91)
Ludgate Cir. EC4 3B 224 (44Rb 91)
Ludgate Hill EC4 3B 224 (44Rb 91)
Ludgate Sq. EC4 3C 224 (44Rb 91)
Ludham NW5 36Hb 69
Ludham Cl. IG6: Ilf 25Sc 54
SE28 44Yc 95
Ludlow Cl. BR2: Brom 69Jc 137
HA2: Harr 35Ba 65
Ludlow Ct. W3 47Sa 87
Ludlow Mead WD19: Wat 20X 27
Ludlow Pl. RM17: Grays 48De 99
Ludlow Rd. TW13: Felt 63W 128
W5 42La 86
Ludlow St. EC1 5D 218 (42Sb 91)
Ludlow Way N2 28Eb 49
WD3: Crox G 14S 26
Ludovick Wlk. SW15 56Ua 110
Ludwell Ho. *W14* *48Ab 88*
(off Russell Rd.)
Ludwick M. SE14 52Ac 114
Luff Cl. SL4: Wind 5C 102
Luffenham Ho. WD19: Wat 20Z 27
Luffield Rd. SE2 48Xc 95
Luffman Rd. SE12 62Kc 137
Lugard Ho. *W12* *46Xa 88*
(off Bloemfontein Rd.)
Lugard Rd. SE15 54Xb 113
Lugg App. E12 34Qc 74
Luke Ho. *E1* *44Xb 91*
(off Tillman St.)
Luke St. EC2 5H 219 (42Ub 91)
Lukin Cres. E4 20Fc 35
Lukin St. E1 44Yb 92
Lukintone Cl. IG10: Lough 16Nc 36
Luli Ct. SE14 51Bc 114
Lullarook Cl. TN16: Big H 88Lc 179
LULLINGSTONE 78Ld 163
Lullingstone Av. BR8: Swan 69Hd 140
Lullingstone Castle 78Ld 163
Lullingstone Cl. BR5: St P 66Xc 139
Lullingstone Country Pk. 78Gd 162
Lullingstone Country Pk. Vis. Cen.
79Kd 163
Lullingstone Cres. BR5: St P 66Wc 139
Lullingstone Ho. *SE15* *51Yb 114*
(off Lovelinch Cl.)
Lullingstone La. DA4: Eyns 76Ld 163
SE13 58Fc 115
Lullingstone Pk. Golf Course 77Fd 162
Lullingstone Rd. DA17: Belv 51Bd 117
Lullingstone Roman Villa 76Kd 163
Lullington Gth. BR1: Brom 66Gc 137
N12 22Bb 49
WD6: Bore 15Ra 29
Lullington Rd. RM9: Dag 38Ad 75
SE20 66Wb 135
Lulot Gdns. N19 33Kb 70
Lulworth *NW1* *38Mb 70*
(off Wrotham Rd.)
SE17 7F 231
Lulworth Av. EN7: G Oak 1Rb 19
HA9: Wemb 31La 66
TW5: Hest 53Da 107
Lulworth Cl. HA2: Harr 34Ba 65
SS17: Stan H 3K 101
Lulworth Ct. *N1* *38Ub 71*
(off St Peter's Way)
Lulworth Cres. CR4: Mitc 68Gb 133
Lulworth Dr. HA5: Pinn 30Z 45
RM5: Col R 22Dd 56
Lulworth Gdns. HA2: Harr 33Aa 65
Lulworth Ho. SW8 52Pb 112
Lulworth Pl. KT19: Eps 84Na 173
Lulworth Rd. DA16: Well 54Vc 117
SE9 61Nc 138
SE15 54Xb 113
Lulworth Waye UB4: Yead 44X 85
Lumen Rd. HA9: Wemb 33Ma 67
Lumiere Apartments SW11 56Fb 111
Lumiere Building, The *E7* *36Mc 73*
(off Romford Rd.)
Lumiere Ct. SW17 61Jb 134
Lumina Bldgs. *E14* *46Ec 92*
(off Prestons Rd.)
Lumina Loft Apartments SE1 2J 231
Luminosity Ct. W13 45Ka 86
Lumley Cl. DA17: Belv 50Cd 96
Lumley Ct. WC2 5G 223 (45Nb 90)
Lumley Flats SW1 7H 227
Lumley Gdns. SM3: Cheam 78Ab 154
Lumley Rd. SM3: Cheam 78Ab 154
Lumley St. W1 3J 221 (44Jb 90)
Lumsdon *NW8* *39Db 69*
(off Abbey Rd.)
Luna Ho. SE16 47Wb 91
Lunan Ho. *E3* *40Bc 72*
(off Shetland Rd.)
Luna Pl. AL1: St A 2E 6
Lunar Cl. TN16: Big H 88Mc 179
Luna Rd. CR7: Thor H 69Sb 135
Lundin Wlk. WD19: Wat 21Z 45
Lund Point E15 39Ec 72
Lundy Ct. SL1: Slou 5C 80
Lundy Dr. UB3: Harl 49U 84
Lundy Ho. WD18: Wat 15V 26
Lundy Wlk. N1 37Sb 71
Lunedale Rd. DA2: Dart 60Sd 120
Lunghurst Rd. CR3: Wold 92Bc 198
Lunham Rd. SE19 65Ub 135
Luntley Pl. *E1* *43Wb 91*
(off Chicksand St.)
Lupin Cl. CR0: C'don 74Zb 158
RM7: Rush G 33Fd 76
SW2 61Rb 135
UB7: W Dray 50M 83
Lupin Cres. IG1: Ilf 37Rc 74
Lupino Ct. SE11 5J 229 (49Pb 90)
Lupin Point *SE1* *47Vb 91*
(off Abbey St.)
Luppits Cl. CM13: Hut 18Ce 41
Lupton Cl. SE12 62Kc 137
Lupton St. NW5 35Lb 70
(not continuous)
Lupus St. SW1 7A 228 (50Kb 90)
Luralda Wharf E14 50Fc 93
Lurgan Av. W6 51Za 110
Lurline Gdns. SW11 53Jb 112
Luscombe Ct. BR2: Brom 68Gc 137
Luscombe Way SW8 52Nb 112
Lushes Ct. IG10: Lough 15Rc 36
Lushes Rd. IG10: Lough 15Rc 36
Lushington Dr. KT11: Cobh 86X 171
Lushington Ho. KT12: Walt T 72Y 151
Lushington Rd. NW10 40Xa 68
SE6 63Dc 136
Lushington Ter. E8 36Wb 71
Lusted Hall La. TN16: Big H, Tats 92Lc 199
TN16: Tats 92Kc 199
Lusted Rd. TN13: Dun G 92Gd 202
Lutea Ho. *SM2: Sutt* *80Eb 155*
(off Walnut M.)
Luther Cl. HA8: Edg 19Sa 29
Luther King Cl. E17 30Bc 52
Luther M. TW11: Tedd 64Ha 130
Luther Rd. TW11: Tedd 64Ha 130
Luton Ho. *E13* *42Jc 93*
(off Luton Rd.)
RM3: Rom *22Nd 57*
(off Lindfield Rd.)
Luton Pl. SE10 52Ec 114
Luton Rd. DA14: Sidc 62Yc 139
E13 42Jc 93
E17 27Bc 52
Luton St. NW8 6C 214 (42Fb 89)
Lutton Ter. *NW3* *35Eb 69*
(off Lakis Cl.)
Luttrell Av. SW15 57Xa 110
Lutwyche Rd. SE6 61Bc 136
Lutyens Cl. KT24: Eff 99Z 191
Lutyens Ho. *SW1* *50Lb 90*
(off Churchill Gdns.)
Luxborough Ho. W1 7H 215
Luxborough La. IG7: Chig 20Nc 36
Luxborough St. W1 6H 215 (43Jb 90)
Luxborough Twr. W1 7H 215
Luxembourg M. E15 36Gc 73
Luxemburg Gdns. W6 49Za 88
Luxfield Rd. SE9 60Nc 116
Luxford St. SE16 49Zb 92
Luxmore St. SE4 53Bc 114
Luxor St. SE5 55Sb 113
LUXTED 86Qc 180
Luxted Rd. BR6: Downe 84Qc 180
Lyall Av. SE21 63Ub 135
Lyall M. SW1 4H 227 (48Jb 90)
Lyall M. W. SW1 4H 227 (48Jb 90)
Lyall St. SW1 4H 227 (48Jb 90)
Lyal Rd. E3 40Ac 72
Lycaste Cl. AL1: St A 3D 6
Lycett Pl. W12 47Wa 88
Lyceum Theatre
Covent Garden 4H 223
Lych Ga. WD25: Wat 5Z 13
Lychgate Mnr. HA1: Harr 31Ga 66
Lych Ga. Rd. BR6: Orp 74Wc 161
Lych Ga. Wlk. UB3: Hayes 45V 84
(not continuous)
Lych Way GU21: Wok 8P 167
Lyconby Gdns. CR0: C'don 73Ac 158
Lydd Cl. DA14: Sidc 62Uc 138
Lydden Ct. SE9 58Uc 116
Lydden Gro. SW18 59Db 111
Lydden Rd. SW18 59Db 111
Lydd Rd. DA7: Bex 52Bd 117
Lydeard Rd. E6 38Pc 74
Lydele Cl. GU21: Wok 87B 168
Lydford NW1 1C 216
Lydford Av. SL2: Slou 3H 81
Lydford Cl. *N16* *36Ub 71*
(off Pellerin Rd.)
Lydford Ct. *DA2: Dart* *58Rd 119*
(off Osbourne Rd.)
Lydford Rd. N15 29Tb 51
NW2 37Ya 68
W9 42Bb 89
Lydger Cl. GU22: Wok 92D 188
Lydhurst Av. SW2 61Pb 134
Lydia Cotts. DA11: Grav'nd 9D 122
Lydia Ct. AL9: Wel G 6E 8
KT1: King T *69Na 131*
(off Grove Cres., not continuous)
N12 23Eb 49
Lydia M. AL9: Wel G 6E 8
Lydia Rd. DA8: Erith 51Hd 118
Lydney Cl. SW19 61Ab 132
Lydon Rd. SW4 55Lb 112
Lydsey Cl. SL2: Slou 1E 80
Lydstep Rd. BR7: Chst 63Qc 138
Lye, The KT20: Tad 94Ya 194
Lye La. AL2: Brick W 10N 5
Lyell Pl. E. SL4: Wind 5A 102
Lyell Pl. W. SL4: Wind 5A 102
Lyell Rd. SL4: Wind 5A 102
Lyell Wlk. E. SL4: Wind 5A 102
Lyell Wlk. W. SL4: Wind 5A 102
Lyfield KT22: Oxs 86Da 171
Lyford Rd. SW18 59Fb 111
Lyford St. SE7 49Nc 94
Lygon Ho. *E2* *41Vb 91*
(off Gosset St.)
SW6 *53Ab 110*
(off Fulham Pal. Rd.)
Lygon Pl. SW1 4K 227 (48Kb 90)
Lyham Cl. SW2 58Nb 112
Lyham Rd. SW2 57Nb 112
Lyle Cl. CR4: Mitc 73Jb 156
Lyle Ct. SM4: Mord 72Fb 155
Lyle Pk. TN13: S'oaks 95Kd 203
Lyly House SE1 4G 231
Lymbourne Cl. SM2: Sutt 82Cb 175
Lymden Gdns. RH2: Reig 7K 207
Lyme Farm Rd. SE12 56Jc 115
Lyme Gro. E9 38Yb 72
Lyme Gro. Ho. *E9* *38Yb 72*
(off Lyme Gro.)
Lymer Av. SE19 64Vb 135
Lyme Regis Rd. SM7: Bans 89Bb 175
Lyme Rd. DA16: Well 53Xc 117
Lymescote Gdns. SM1: Sutt 75Cb 155
Lyme St. NW1 38Lb 70
Lyme Ter. NW1 38Lb 70
Lyminge Cl. DA14: Sidc 63Vc 139
Lyminge Gdns. SW18 60Gb 111
Lymington Av. N22 26Qb 50
Lymington Cl. E6 43Pc 94
SW16 68Mb 134
Lymington Ct. SM1: Sutt 76Db 155
WD25: Wat 6W 12
Lymington Dr. HA4: Ruis 33T 64
Lymington Gdns. KT19: Ewe 78Va 154
Lymington Lodge *E14* *48Fc 93*
(off Schooner Cl.)

Lymington Rd. NW6 .... 37Db 69
RM8: Dag 32Zc 75
Lyminster Cl. UB4: Yead 43Aa 85
Lympne *N17* *26Tb 51*
(off Gloucester Rd.)
Lympstone Gdns. SE15 .... 52Wb 113
Lynbridge Gdns. N13 .... 21Rb 51
Lynbrook Cl. RM13: Rain 40Fd 76
Lynbrook Gro. SE15 .... 52Ub 113
Lynbury Ct. WD18: Wat 13W 26
Lynceley Grange CM16: Epp 1Wc 23
Lynch, The UB8: Uxb 38L 63
Lynch Cl. SE3 .... 54Hc 115
UB8: Uxb 38L 63
Lynch Ct. AL4: St A 3G 6
Lynchen Cl. TW5: Cran 53X 107
LYNCH HILL 1C 80
Lynch Hill La. SL2: Slou 2C 80
Lynch Wlk. *SE8* *51Bc 114*
(off Prince St.)
Lyncott Cres. SW4 .... 56Kb 112
Lyncourt SE3 .... 54Fc 115
Lyncroft Av. HA5: Pinn 29Aa 45
Lyncroft Gdns. KT17: Ewe 81Va 174
NW6 .... 36Cb 69
TW3: Houn 57Ea 108
W13 .... 47La 86
Lyncroft Mans. NW6 .... 36Cb 69
Lyndale KT7: T Ditt 73Ga 152
NW2 .... 35Bb 69
Lyndale Av. NW2 .... 34Bb 69
Lyndale Cl. SE3 .... 51Hc 115
Lyndale Ct. KT14: W Byf 85J 169
RH1: Redh 3A 208
Lyndale Est. RM20: W Thur 51Xd 120
Lyndean Ind. Est. SE2 .... 48Yc 95
Lynde Ho. KT12: Walt T 72Y 151
SW4 .... 55Mb 112
Lynden Ho. *E1* *41Zb 92*
(off Westfield Way)
Lynden Hyrst CR0: C'don 75Vb 157
Lynden Way BR8: Swan 69Ed 140
Lyndhurst Av. HA5: Pinn 25X 45
KT5: Surb 74Ra 153
N12 .... 23Hb 49
NW7 .... 23Ua 48
SW16 .... 68Mb 134
TW2: Whitt 60Ba 107
TW16: Sun 69W 128
UB1: S'hall 46Da 85
Lyndhurst Cl. BR6: Farnb 77Rc 160
CR0: C'don 76Vb 157
DA7: Bex 55Dd 118
GU21: Wok 7P 167
NW10 .... 34Ta 67
Lyndhurst Ct. E18 .... 25Jc 53
NW8 .... 1B 214
SM2: Sutt *80Cb 155*
(off Grange Rd.)
Lyndhurst Dr. E10 .... 31Ec 72
KT3: N Mald 73Ua 154
RM11: Horn 32Ld 77
TN13: S'oaks 96Gd 202
Lyndhurst Gdns. EN1: Enf 14Ub 33
HA5: Pinn 25X 45
IG2: Ilf 30Tc 54
IG11: Bark 37Uc 74
N3 .... 25Ab 48
NW3 .... 36Fb 69
Lyndhurst Gro. SE15 .... 54Ub 113
Lyndhurst Lodge *E14* *49Fc 93*
(off Millennium Dr.)
Lyndhurst Ri. IG7: Chig 21Qc 54
Lyndhurst Rd. CR5: Coul 88Jb 176
CR7: Thor H 70Qb 134
DA7: Bex 55Dd 118
E4 .... 24Ec 52
N18 .... 21Wb 51
N22 .... 23Qb 50
NW3 .... 36Fb 69
RH2: Reig 9J 207
UB6: G'frd 42Da 85
Lyndhurst Sq. SE15 .... 53Vb 113
Lyndhurst Ter. NW3 .... 36Fb 69
Lyndhurst Vs. RH1: Redh 3P 207
Lyndhurst Wlk. WD6: Bore 11Pa 29
Lyndhurst Way CM13: Hut 17Ee 41
DA13: Ist R 7A 144
KT16: Chert 76G 148
SE15 .... 53Vb 113
SM2: Sutt 81Cb 175
Lyndon Av. DA15: Sidc 57Vc 117
HA5: Hat E 23Aa 45
SM6: Wall 76Jb 156
Lyndon Ho. *E18* *25Jc 53*
(off Queen Mary Av.)
Lyndon Rd. DA17: Belv 49Cd 96
Lyndon Yd. SW17 .... 63Eb 133
Lyndwood Dr. SL4: Old Win 8L 103
Lyndwood Pde. *SL4: Old Win* *8L 103*
(off St Luke's Rd.)
LYNE 74C 148
Lyne Cl. GU25: Vir W 72B 148
Lyne Cres. E17 .... 25Bc 52
Lyne Crossing Rd.
KT16: Lyne 72C 148
Lyne Gdns. TN16: Big H 90Nc 180
Lynegrove Av. TW15: Ashf 64S 128
Lyneham Dr. NW9 .... 25Ua 48
Lyneham Wlk. E5 .... 36Ac 72
HA5: Eastc 27V 44
Lyne La. GU25: Vir W 72C 148
KT16: Lyne 72C 148
TW20: Thorpe 72C 148
Lyne Rd. GU25: Vir W 2P 147
Lynette Av. SW4 .... 58Kb 112
Lyne Way HP1: Hem H 1H 3
Lynford Cl. EN5: Ark 15Va 30
HA8: Edg 25Sa 47
Lynford Ct. *CR2: S Croy* *77Ub 157*
(off Coombe Rd.)
Lynford French Ho. SE17 .... 7D 230
Lynford Gdns. HA8: Edg 20Ra 29
IG3: Ilf 33Vc 75
Lynford Ter. N9 .... 18Vb 33
Lyngarth Cl. KT23: Fet 97Fa 192
Lynhurst KT13: Weyb 79R 150
Lynhurst Cres. UB10: Hil 38S 64
Lynhurst Rd. UB10: Hil 38S 64
Lynmere Rd. DA16: Well 54Xc 117
Lyn M. E3 .... 41Bc 92
N16 .... 35Ub 71
Lynmouth Av. EN1: Enf 16Vb 33
SM4: Mord 72Za 154
Lynmouth Dr. HA4: Ruis 33X 65
Lynmouth Gdns. TW5: Hest 52Z 107
UB6: G'frd 39Ka 66
Lynmouth Ho. *RM3: Rom* *22Nd 57*
(off Dagnam Pk. Dr.)
Lynmouth Ri. BR5: St M Cry 70Xc 139
Lynmouth Rd. E17 .... 30Ac 52
N2 .... 27Hb 49
N16 .... 32Vb 71
UB6: G'frd 39Ka 66
Lynn Cl. HA3: Hrw W 26Fa 46
TW15: Ashf 64T 128
Lynn Ct. CR3: Whyt 90Vb 177
Lynne Cl. BR6: Chels 79Vc 161
CR2: Sels 83Yb 178
SE23 .... 59Bc 114
Lynne Ct. *CR2: S Croy* *77Ub 157*
(off Birdhurst Rd.)
NW6 .... *38Db 69*
(off Priory Rd.)
Lynnett Ct. *E9* *37Ac 72*
(off Annis Rd.)
Lynnett Rd. RM8: Dag 33Zc 75
Lynne Wlk. KT10: Esh 78Ea 152
Lynne Way UB5: N'olt 40Z 65
Lynn Ho. *SE15* *51Xb 113*
(off Friary Est.)
Lynn M. E11 .... 33Gc 73
Lynn Rd. E11 .... 33Gc 73
IG2: Ilf 31Tc 74
SW12 .... 59Kb 112
Lynn St. EN2: Enf 11Tb 33
Lynn Wlk. RH2: Reig 9K 207
Lynross Cl. RM3: Hrld W 26Pd 57
Lynscott Way CR2: S Croy 81Rb 177
Lynstead Ct. BR3: Beck 68Ac 136
Lynsted Cl. BR1: Brom 68Lc 137
DA6: Bex 57Dd 118
Lynsted Gdns. SE9 .... 56Mc 115
Lynton Av. AL1: St A 3G 6
BR5: St M Cry 70Xc 139
N12 .... 21Fb 49
NW9 .... 28Va 48
RM7: Mawney 25Cd 56
W13 .... 44Ja 86
Lynton Cl. KT9: Chess 77Na 153
NW10 .... 36Ua 68
TW7: Isle 56Ha 108
Lynton Ct. KT17: Ewe 83Va 174
Lynton Cres. IG2: Ilf 30Rc 54
Lynton Crest EN6: Pot B 4Cb 17
Lynton Est. SE1 .... 49Wb 91
Lynton Gdns. EN1: Enf 17Ub 33
N11 .... 23Mb 50
Lynton Grange N2 .... 27Hb 49
Lynton Ho. *IG1: Ilf* *33Sc 74*
(off High Rd.)
W2 .... *44Eb 89*
(off Hallfield Est.)
Lynton Mans. SE1 .... 3K 229
Lynton Mead N20 .... 20Cb 31
Lynton Pde. EN8: Chesh 2Ac 20
Lynton Rd. CR0: C'don 72Qb 156
DA11: Grav'nd 10C 122
E4 .... 22Dc 52
HA2: Harr 33Aa 65
KT3: N Mald 71Ta 153
N8 .... 29Mb 50
(not continuous)
NW6 .... 40Bb 69
SE1 .... 6K 231 (49Vb 91)
W3 .... 45Qa 87
Lynton Rd. Sth. DA11: Grav'nd 10C 122
Lynton Ter. W3 .... 44Sa 87
Lynton Wlk. UB4: Hayes 41U 84
Lynwood SL5: S'dale 2C 146
Lynwood Av. CR5: Coul 87Kb 176
KT17: Eps 86Va 174
SL3: L'ly 8P 81
TW20: Egh 65A 126
Lynwood Cl. E18 .... 25Lc 53
GU21: Wok 85F 168
HA2: Harr 34Aa 65
RM5: Col R 23Dd 56
Lynwood Ct. KT1: King T 68Ra 131
KT17: Eps 85Va 174
Lynwood Cres. SL5: S'dale 2C 146
Lynwood Dr. HA6: Nwood 25V 44
KT4: Wor Pk 75Wa 154
RM5: Col R 23Dd 56
Lynwood Gdns. CR0: Wadd 77Pb 156
UB1: S'hall 44Ba 85
Lynwood Gro. BR6: Orp 73Uc 160
N21 .... 18Qb 32
Lynwood Hgts. WD3: Rick 15K 25
Lynwood Rd. KT7: T Ditt 75Ha 152
KT17: Eps 86Va 174
RH1: Redh 4A 208
SW17 .... 62Hb 133
W5 .... 41Ma 87
Lynx Hill KT24: E Hor 100V 190
Lynx Way E16 .... 45Mc 93
Lyon Bus. Pk. IG11: Bark 40Uc 74
Lyon Ct. HA4: Ruis 32V 64
Lyon Ho. NW8 .... 6D 214
(off Broadley St.)
Lyon Ind. Est. NW2 .... 33Xa 68
Lyon Meade HA7: Stan 25La 46
Lyon Pk. Av. HA0: Wemb 37Na 67
(not continuous)
Lyon Rd. HA1: Harr 30Ha 46
KT12: Walt T 75Aa 151
RM1: Rom 31Hd 76
SW19 .... 67Eb 133
Lyonsdene KT20: Lwr K 99Bb 195
LYONSDOWN 15Eb 31
Lyonsdown Av. EN5: New Bar 16Eb 31
Lyonsdown Rd. EN5: New Bar 16Eb 31
Lyons Dr. GU2: Guild 10L 187
Lyons Ind. Est. UB8: Cowl 45M 83
Lyons Pl. NW8 .... 6B 214 (42Fb 89)
Lyon St. N1 .... 38Pb 70
Lyons Wlk. W14 .... 49Ab 88
Lyon Way AL4: St A 2L 7
UB6: G'frd 39Ga 66
Lyoth Rd. BR5: Farnb 75Sc 160
Lyrical Way HP1: Hem H 1K 3
Lyric Ct. *E8* *38Vb 71*
(off Holly St.)
Lyric Dr. UB6: G'frd 42Da 85
Lyric M. SE26 .... 63Yb 136
Lyric Rd. SW13 .... 53Va 110
Lyric Sq. *W6* *49Ya 88*
(off King St.)
Lyric Theatre
Hammersmith 49Ya 88
Westminster 4D 222
(off Shaftesbury Av.)
Lysander NW9 .... 25Va 48
Lysander Cl. HP3: Bov 9B 2
Lysander Gdns. KT6: Surb 72Pa 153
Lysander Gro. N19 .... 32Mb 70
Lysander Ho. *E2* *40Xb 71*
(off Temple St.)
Lysander M. N19 .... 32Lb 70
Lysander Rd. CR0: Wadd 79Pb 156
HA4: Ruis 33T 64
Lysander Way BR6: Farnb 76Sc 160
WD5: Ab L 4W 12
Lysia Ct. *SW6* *52Za 110*
(off Lysia St.)
Lysias Rd. SW12 .... 58Kb 112
Lysia St. SW6 .... 52Za 110
Lysley Pl. AL9: Brk P 9L 9
Lysons Wlk. SW15 .... 56Wa 110
Lyster M. KT11: Cobh 85Y 171
Lytchet Rd. BR1: Brom 66Jc 137
Lytchet Way EN3: Enf H 11Yb 34
Lytchgate Cl. CR2: S Croy 80Ub 157
Lytcott Dr. KT8: W Mole 69Ba 129
Lytcott Gro. SE22 .... 57Ub 113
Lytham Av. WD19: Wat 22Z 45
Lytham Cl. SE28 .... 44Ad 95
Lytham Ct. SL5: S'hill 1A 146
UB1: S'hall *44Da 85*
(off Whitecote Rd.)
Lytham Gro. W5 .... 41Pa 87
Lytham St. SE17 .... 50Tb 91
Lyttelton Cl. NW3 .... 38Gb 69
Lyttelton Ct. N2 .... 29Eb 49
Lyttelton Ho. *E9* *38Yb 72*
(off Well St.)
Lyttelton Rd. E10 .... 34Dc 72
N2 .... 29Eb 49
Lyttelton Theatre *6K 223*
(in National Theatre)
Lyttleton Ct. *UB4: Yead* *42Y 85*
(off Dunedin Way)
Lyttleton Rd. N8 .... 27Qb 50
Lytton Av. EN3: Enf L 10Ac 20
N13 .... 19Qb 32
Lytton Cl. IG10: Lough 13Tc 36
N2 .... 30Fb 49
UB5: N'olt 38Ba 65
Lytton Ct. WC1 .... 1G 223
Lytton Gdns. SM6: Bedd 77Mb 156
Lytton Gro. SW15 .... 57Za 110
Lytton Pk. KT11: Cobh 84Ba 171
Lytton Rd. E11 .... 31Gc 73
EN5: New Bar 14Eb 31
GU22: Wok 88D 168
HA5: Pinn 24Aa 45
RM2: Rom 29Kd 57
RM16: Grays 9C 100
Lytton Strachey Path SE28 .... 45Xc 95
Lytton Ter. E12 .... 37Pc 74
Lyveden Rd. SE3 .... 52Kc 115
SW17 .... 65Hb 133
Lywood Cl. KT20: Tad 94Ya 194

M

Mabbett Ho. *SE18* *51Qc 116*
(off Nightingale Pl.)
Mabbots KT20: Tad 93Za 194
Mabbutt Cl. AL2: Brick W 2Aa 13
Mabel Evetts Ct. UB3: Hayes 45X 85
Mabel Rd. BR8: Hext 65Jd 140
Mabel St. GU21: Wok 10P 167
Maberley Cres. SE19 .... 66Wb 135
Maberley Rd. BR3: Beck 69Zb 136
SE19 .... 67Vb 135
Mabledon Pl. WC1 .... 4E 216 (41Mb 90)
Mablethorpe Rd. SW6 .... 52Ab 110
Mabley St. E9 .... 36Ac 72
Mablin Lodge IG9: Buck H 18Lc 35
McAdam Dr. EN2: Enf 12Rb 33
McArdle Way SL3: Coln 52F 104
Macaret Cl. N20 .... 17Db 31
Macarthur Cl. DA8: Erith 50Gd 96
E7 .... 37Jc 73
HA9: Wemb 37Ra 67
Macarthur Ter. SE7 .... 51Mc 115
Macartney Ho. *SE10* *52Fc 115*
(off Chesterfield Wlk.)
SW9 .... *53Qb 112*
(off Gosling Way)
Macaulay Av. KT10: Hin W 75Ha 152
Macaulay Ct. SW4 .... 55Kb 112
Macaulay Rd. CR3: Cat'm 94Ub 197
E6 .... 40Mc 73
SW4 .... 55Kb 112
Macaulay Sq. SW4 .... 56Kb 112
Macaulay Way SE28 .... 46Xc 95
McAuley Cl. SE1 .... 3K 229 (48Qb 90)
SE9 .... 57Rc 116
Macauley Ho. *W10* *43Ab 88*
(off Portobello Rd.)
Macauley M. SE13 .... 54Ec 114
McAuliffe Dr. SL2: Farn C 5D 60
McAusland Ho. *E3* *40Bc 72*
(off Wright's Rd.)
Macbean St. SE18 .... 48Rc 94
Macbeth Ho. N1 .... 1H 219 (40Ub 71)
Macbeth St. W6 .... 50Xa 88
McBride Ho. *E3* *40Bc 72*
(off Libra Rd.)
McCabe Ct. *E16* *43Hc 93*
(off Barking Rd.)
McCall Cl. SW4 .... 54Nb 112
McCall Cres. SE7 .... 50Nc 94
McCall Ho. N7 .... 35Nb 70
McCarthy Rd. TW13: Hanw 64Z 129
McClaren Technology Cen.
GU21: Wok 83C 168
Macclesfield Ho. EC1 .... 4D 218
(off Central St.)
RM3: Rom *22Nd 57*
(off Dagnam Pk. Dr.)
Macclesfield Rd. EC1 .... 3D 218 (41Sb 91)
SE25 .... 71Yb 158
Macclesfield St. W1 .... 4E 222 (45Mb 90)
McCoid Way SE1 .... 2D 230 (47Sb 91)
McCrone M. NW3 .... 37Fb 69
McCudden Rd. DA1: Dart 55Pd 119
McCullum Rd. E3 .... 39Bc 72
McDermott Cl. SW11 .... 55Gb 111
McDermott Rd. SE15 .... 55Wb 113
TN15: Bor G 92Be 205
Macdonald Av. RM10: Dag 34Dd 76
RM11: Horn 27Nd 57
McDonald Ct. AL10: Hat 2C 8
(not continuous)
Macdonald Ho. *SW11* *54Jb 112*
(off Dagnall St.)
Macdonald Rd. E7 .... 35Jc 73
E17 .... 26Ec 52
(not continuous)
N11 .... 22Hb 49
N19 .... 33Lb 70
Macdonald Way RM11: Horn 28Nd 57
Macdonnell Gdns. WD25: Wat 7V 12
McDonough Cl. KT9: Chess 77Na 153
McDougall Ct. TW9: Rich 54Qa 109
McDougall Rd. HP4: Berk 1A 2
McDowall Cl. E16 .... 43Hc 93
McDowall Rd. SE5 .... 53Sb 113
Macduff Rd. SW11 .... 53Jb 112
Mace Cl. E1 .... 46Xb 91
Mace Ct. RM17: Grays 1A 122
Mace Ho. TW7: Isle 53Ka 108
Mace La. TN14: Cud 85Tc 180
McEntee Av. E17 .... 25Ac 52
Mace St. E2 .... 40Zb 72
McEwan Ho. *E3* *40Bc 72*
(off Roman Rd.)
McEwen Way *E15* *39Fc 73*
(off Rokeby St.)
Macey Ho. SW11 .... 53Gb 111
Macey St. *SE10* *51Ec 114*
(off Thames St.)
McFadden Ct. *E10* *34Dc 72*
(off Buckingham Rd.)
Macfarland Gro. SE15 .... 52Ub 113
Macfarlane La. TW7: Isle 51Ha 108
Macfarlane Rd. W12 .... 46Ya 88
Macfarren Pl. NW1 .... 6J 215 (42Jb 90)
Macfarron Ho. *W10* *41Ab 88*
(off Parry Rd.)
McGlashon Ho. *E1* *42Wb 91*
(off Hunton St.)
McGrath Rd. E15 .... 36Hc 73
McGredy EN7: Chesh 1Xb 19
McGregor Ct. N1 .... 3J 219
Macgregor Rd. E16 .... 43Lc 93
McGregor Rd. W11 .... 44Bb 89
Machell Rd. SE15 .... 55Yb 114
McIndoe Ct. *N1* *39Tb 71*
(off Sherborne St.)
McIntosh Cl. RM1: Rom 27Gd 56
SM6: Wall 80Nb 156
Macintosh Ho. W1 .... 7J 215
McIntosh Ho. *SE16* *49Yb 92*
(off Millender Wlk.)
McIntosh Rd. RM1: Rom 27Gd 56
McIntyre Ct. *SE18* *49Nc 94*
(off Prospect Va.)
Mackay Ho. *W12* *45Xa 88*
(off White City Est.)
Mackay Rd. SW4 .... 55Kb 112
McKay Rd. SW20 .... 66Xa 132
McKay Trad. Est. SL3: Poyle 54G 104
McKellar Cl. WD23: B Hea 19Ea 28
McKenna Ho. *E3* *40Bc 72*
(off Wright's Rd.)
Mackennal St. NW8 .... 2E 214 (40Gb 69)
Mackenzie Cl. W12 .... 45Xa 88
Mackenzie Ho. *N8* *28Nb 50*
(off Pembroke Rd.)
NW2 .... 34Wa 68
Mackenzie Mall *SL1: Slou* *7K 81*
(within Queensmere Shop. Cen.)
Mackenzie Rd. BR3: Beck 68Yb 136
N7 .... 37Pb 70
Mackenzie St. SL1: Slou 7K 81
Mackenzie Wlk. E14 .... 46Cc 92
Mackenzie Way DA12: Grav'nd 5F 144
McKenzie Way KT19: Eps 81Qa 173
McKerrell Rd. SE15 .... 53Wb 113
Mackeson Rd. NW3 .... 35Hb 69
Mackie Rd. SW2 .... 59Qb 112
McKillop Way DA14: Sidc 66Yc 139
Mackintosh Ct. SL9: Ger X 28A 42
Mackintosh La. E9 .... 36Zb 72
Mackintosh St. BR2: Brom 72Mc 159
Macklin St. WC2 .... 2G 223 (44Nb 90)
Mackonochie Ho. EC1 .... 7K 217
Mackrells RH1: Redh 9L 207
Mackrow Wlk. E14 .... 45Ec 92
Mack's Rd. SE16 .... 49Wb 91
Mackworth Ho. NW1 .... 3B 216
Mackworth St. NW1 .... 3B 216 (41Lb 90)
McLaren Ho. SE1 .... 2B 230
Maclaren M. SW15 .... 56Ya 110
Maclean Rd. SE23 .... 58Ac 114
Maclean Ter. DA12: Grav'nd 1H 145
Maclennan Av. RM13: Rain 41Md 97
Macleod Cl. RM17: Grays 49Fe 99
McLeod Ct. SE22 .... 60Wb 113
Macleod Rd. N21 .... 15Nb 32
McLeod Rd. SE2 .... 49Xc 95
McLeod's M. SW7 .... 49Db 89
Macleod St. SE17 .... 50Sb 91
Maclise Ho. SW1 .... 6F 229
Maclise Rd. W14 .... 48Ab 88
Macmahon Cl. GU24: Chob 2J 167
Macmillan Cl. DA12: Grav'nd 3E 144
Macmillan Ct. HA2: Harr 32Ca 65
UB6: G'frd 42Fa 86
Macmillan Gdns. DA1: Dart 56Qd 119
Macmillan Ho. NW8 .... 4E 214
SM7: Bans *86Bb 175*
(off Basing Rd.)
McMillan Ho. *SE4* *55Ac 114*
(off Arica Rd.)
SE14 .... 53Ac 114
McMillan St. SE8 .... 51Cc 114
McMillan Student Village SE8 .... 51Cc 114
Macmillan Way SW17 .... 63Kb 134
McNair Rd. UB2: S'hall 48Da 85
Macnamara Ho. *SW10* *52Fb 111*
(off Worlds End Est.)
McNeil Rd. SE5 .... 54Ub 113
McNicol Dr. NW10 .... 40Sa 67
Macoma Rd. SE18 .... 51Tc 116
Macoma Ter. SE18 .... 51Tc 116
Maconochies Rd. E14 .... 50Dc 92
Macon Way RM14: Upm 31Ud 78
Macquarie Way E14 .... 49Dc 92
McRae La. CR4: Mitc 73Hb 155
Macready Ho. W1 .... 1E 220
Macready Pl. N7 .... 35Nb 70
(not continuous)
Macrea Ho. *E3* *41Bc 92*
(off Bow Rd.)
Macroom Ho. *W9* *41Bb 89*
(off Macroom Rd.)
Macroom Rd. W9 .... 41Bb 89
Macs Ho. E17 .... 27Dc 52
Mac's Pl. EC4 .... 2A 224
Madame Tussaud's 6H 215 (42Jb 90)
Madan Cl. TN16: Westrm 97Uc 200
Madan Rd. TN16: Westrm 97Tc 200
Madans Wlk. KT18: Eps 87Ta 173
(not continuous)
Mada Rd. BR6: Farnb 76Rc 160
Maddams St. E3 .... 42Dc 92
Madden Cl. DA10: Swans 58Zd 121
Madderfields Ct. N11 .... 25Mb 50
Maddison Cl. N2 .... 26Eb 49
TW11: Tedd 65Ha 130
Maddison Hgts. *WD18: Wat* *14V 26*
(off Chiltern Cl.)
Maddocks Cl. DA14: Sidc 64Ad 139
Maddocks Ho. *E1* *45Xb 91*
(off Cornwall St.)
Maddock Way SE17 .... 51Rb 113
Maddox La. KT23: Bookh 94Aa 191
Maddox Pk. KT23: Bookh 95Aa 191
Maddox Rd. HP2: Hem H 2B 4
Maddox St. W1 .... 4A 222 (45Kb 90)
Madeira Av. BR1: Brom 66Gc 137
Madeira Cl. KT14: W Byf 85J 169
Madeira Cres. KT14: W Byf 85H 169
Madeira Gro. IG8: Wfd G 23Lc 53
Madeira Rd. CR4: Mitc 70Hb 133
E11 .... 32Fc 73
KT14: W Byf 85H 169
N13 .... 21Rb 51
SW16 .... 64Nb 134
Madeira Wlk. CM15: B'wood 20Ae 41
RH2: Reig 5M 207
SL4: Wind 3H 103
Madeleine Cl. RM6: Chad H 30Yc 55
Madeley Rd. W5 .... 44Ma 87
Madeline Gro. IG1: Ilf 36Tc 74
Madeline Rd. SE20 .... 66Wb 135
Madells CM16: Epp 3Vc 23
Madge Gill Way *E6* *39Nc 74*
(off High St. Nth.)
Madge Hill W7 .... 45Ga 86
Madinah Rd. E8 .... 37Wb 71
Madison, The SE1 .... 1F 231
Madison Bldg. *SE10* *53Dc 114*
(off Blackheath Rd.)
Madison Cl. SM2: Sutt 80Fb 155
Madison Ct. RM10: Dag 37Dd 76
Madison Cres. DA7: Bex 52Yc 117
Madison Gdns. BR2: Brom 69Hc 137
DA7: Bex 52Yc 117
Madison Ho. *E14* *45Bc 92*
(off Victory Pl.)
Madison Wlk. RM16: Chaf H 47Be 99
Madison Way TN13: S'oaks 95Hd 202
Madoc Cl. NW2 .... 33Cb 69
Madras Pl. N7 .... 37Qb 70
Madras Rd. IG1: Ilf 35Rc 74
Madresfield Ct. WD7: Shenl 4Ma 15
Madrid Rd. SW13 .... 53Wa 110
Madrigal La. SE5 .... 52Rb 113
Madron St. SE17 .... 7J 231 (50Ub 91)
Maesmaur Rd. TN16: Tats 93Mc 199
Mafeking Av. E6 .... 40Nc 74
IG2: Ilf 31Tc 74
TW8: Bford 51Na 109
Mafeking Rd. E16 .... 42Hc 93
EN1: Enf 13Vb 33
N17 .... 26Wb 51
TW19: Wray 61D 126
Magazine Ga. W2 .... 6E 220 (46Gb 89)
Magazine Pl. KT22: Lea 94Ka 192
Magazine Rd. CR3: Cat'm 94Rb 197
Magdala Av. N19 .... 33Lb 70
Magdala Rd. CR2: S Croy 80Tb 157
TW7: Isle 55Ja 108
Magdalen Cl. KT14: Byfl 86N 169
Magdalen Ct. *AL1: St A* *1C 6*
(off Newsom Pl.)
Magdalen Cres. KT14: Byfl 86N 169
Magdalene Cl. SE15 .... 54Xb 113
Magdalene Gdns. E6 .... 42Qc 94
N20 .... 18Hb 31
Magdalene Rd. TW17: Shep 70P 127
Magdalen Gro. BR6: Chels 77Xc 161
Magdalen Ho. *E16* *46Kc 93*
(off Keats Av.)
Magdalen M. *NW3* *37Eb 69*
(off Frognal)
Magdalen Pas. E1 .... 45Vb 91
Magdalen Rd. SW18 .... 60Eb 111
Magdalen St. SE1 .... 7H 225 (46Ub 91)
Magee St. SE11 .... 51Qb 112
Magellan Blvd. E16 .... 45Sc 94
Magellan Ct. *NW10* *38Ta 67*
(off Brentfield Rd.)
Magellan Ho. *E1* *42Zb 92*
(off Ernest St.)
Magellan Pl. E14 .... 49Cc 92
Magisters Lodge WD3: Crox G 16Q 26
Magistrates' Court
Belmarsh 47Uc 94
Bexley 56Cd 118
Bromley 67Hc 137
Camberwell Green 53Tb 113
Cheshunt 3Ac 20
City of London 3F 225
City of Westminster
.... 4E 228 (49Nb 90)
Clerkenwell 3J 217
Croydon 76Tb 157
Dartford 58Md 119
Ealing *46Ja 86*
(off Green Man La.)
East Berkshire, Slough 7J 81
Enfield 25Vb 51
Feltham 60X 107
Greenwich 53Dc 114
Havering 28Hd 56
Hendon 30Va 48
Highbury Corner 37Qb 70
Inner London Family Proceedings Court
.... 2B 222 (43Lb 90)
Redbridge 27Sc 54
Redhill 6M 207
Richmond-upon-Thames 56Ma 109
St Albans 2B 6
Sevenoaks 95Hd 202
South Western 55Hb 111
Staines 64J 127
Stratford 38Fc 73
Thames 41Cc 92
Uxbridge 38L 63
Waltham Forest 27Dc 52
Watford 12X 27
West London 50Za 88
Wimbledon 65Cb 133
Magna Carta La. TW19: Wray 10P 103

Magna Carta Memorial 1P 125
Magna Ct. TW18: Staines 64G 126
Magna Rd. TW20: Eng G 5M 125
Magnaville Rd. WD23: B Hea 17Ga 28
Magnetic Cres. EN3: Enf L 9Bc 20
Magnet Point Est. RM20: Grays 51Yd 120
Magnet Rd. HA9: Wemb 33Ma 67
RM20: Grays 51Yd 120
Magnin Cl. E8 39Wb 71
Magnolia Av. WD5: Ab L 4W 12
Magnolia Cl. AL2: Park 8B 6
E10 33Cc 72
KT2: King T 65Ra 131
RM15: S Ock 42Ae 99
Magnolia Ct. HA3: Kenton 31Pa 67
SM2: Sutt 80Cb 155
(off Grange Rd.)
SM6: Wall 78Kb 156
TW9: Kew 53Ra 109
TW13: Felt 60W 106
(off Plum Cl.)
UB5: N'olt 42Aa 85
UB10: Hil 37R 64
Magnolia Dr. SM7: Bans 88Bb 175
TN16: Big H 88Mc 179
Magnolia Gdns. E10 33Cc 72
HA8: Edg 21Sa 47
SL3: L'ly 8N 81
Magnolia Ho. *SE8 51Bc 114*
(off Evelyn St.)
Magnolia Lodge E4 20Dc 34
W8 48Db 89
(off St Mary's Ga.)
Magnolia Pl. SW4 57Nb 112
W5 43Ma 87
Magnolia Rd. W4 51Ra 109
Magnolia St. UB7: W Dray 50M 83
Magnolia Vs. TW18: Staines 66K 127
Magnolia Way CM15: Pil H 15Xd 40
KT19: Ewe 78Sa 153
Magnolia Wharf W4 51Qa 109
Magnum Cl. RM13: Rain 42Kd 97
Magpie All. EC4 3A 224 (44Qb 90)
Magpie Bottom TN15: Knat 85Md 183
Magpie Cl. CR5: Coul 90Lb 176
E7 36Hc 73
EN1: Enf 10Wb 19
NW9 26Ua 48
Magpie Hall Cl. BR2: Brom 72Nc 160
Magpie Hall La. BR2: Brom 71Pc 160
Magpie Hall Rd. WD23: B Hea 19Ga 28
Magpie Ho. *E3 39Bc 72*
(off Sycamore Av.)
Magpie La. CM13: L War 26Zd 59
Magpie Pl. SE14 51Ac 114
WD25: Wat 4Y 13
Magpie Wlk. AL10: Hat 2C 8
Magpie Way SL2: Slou 2D 80
Magri Wlk. E1 43Yb 92
Maguire Dr. TW10: Ham 63La 130
Maguire St. SE1 1K 231 (47Vb 91)
Maha Bldg. *E3 41Cc 92*
(off Merchant St.)
Mahatma Gandhi Ind. Est. SE24 56Rb 113
Mahlon Av. HA4: Ruis 36X 65
(not continuous)
Mahogany Cl. SE16 46Ac 92
Mahon Cl. EN1: Enf 11Vb 33
Mahoney Ho. *SE14 53Bc 114*
(off Heald St.)
Mahonia Cl. GU24: W End 5D 166
Maibeth Gdns. BR3: Beck 70Ac 136
Maida Av. E4 17Dc 34
W2 7A 214 (43Eb 89)
MAIDA HILL 42Bb 89
Maida Rd. DA17: Belv 48Cd 96
MAIDA VALE 3A 214 (42Db 89)
Maida Va. W9 3A 214 (40Db 69)
Maida Vale Rd. DA1: Dart 57Jd 118
Maida Way E4 17Dc 34
Maiden Erlegh Av. DA5: Bexl 60Ad 117
Maidenhead Rd. SL4: Wind 2A 102
Maiden La. DA1: Cray 55Jd 118
NW1 38Mb 70
SE1 7E 224 (46Sb 91)
WC2 5G 223 (45Nb 90)
Maiden Pl. NW5 34Lb 70
Maiden Rd. E15 38Gc 73
Maidenshaw Rd. KT19: Eps 84Ta 173
Maidenstone Hill SE10 53Ec 114
Maids of Honour Row TW9: Rich 57Ma 109
Maidstone Av. RM5: Col R 26Ed 56
Maidstone Bldgs. M. SE1 7E 224 (46Sb 91)
Maidstone Ho. *E14 44Dc 92*
(off Carmen St.)
Maidstone Rd. DA14: Sidc, Swan 65Zc 139
N11 23Lb 50
RM17: Grays 51Ce 121
TN13: Riv 94Gd 202
TN15: Bor G, Plat, Wro H 92Ce 205
TN15: Seal 93Od 203
Mail Coach Yd. E2 3J 219 (41Ub 91)
Main Av. EN1: Enf 15Vb 33
HA6: Nwood 20S 26
Main Dr. HA9: Wemb 34Ma 67
SL0: Rich P 49G 82
Main Mill *SE10 52Dc 114*
(off Greenwich High St.)
Main Pde. WD3: Chor 14E 24
Main Pde. Flats WD3: Chor 14E 24
Mainridge Rd. BR7: Chst 63Qc 138
Main Rd. BR2: Kes 85Lc 179
BR5: St P 67Yc 139
BR8: Crock 72Fd 162
BR8: Hext 66Hd 140
DA3: Lfield, Long H 68Zd 143
DA4: Farni 75Sd 164
(Donkey La.)
DA4: Farni 72Nd 163
(London Rd.)
DA4: Sut H 65Rd 141
DA14: Sidc 62Tc 138
RM1: Rom 28Hd 56
RM2: Rom 28Hd 56
SL4: Wind 2A 102
TN14: Sund 96Zc 201
TN16: Big H, Westrm 85Lc 179
Main Rd. Cotts. BR6: Prat B 81Yc 181
Mainstone Cres. GU24: Brkwd 3B 186
Mainstone Rd. GU24: Bisl 8D 166
Main St. KT15: Add 76N 149
TW13: Hanw 64Z 129
Mainwaring Ct. CR4: Mitc 68Jb 134
Mais Ho. SE26 61Xb 135
Maisie Webster Cl. TW19: Stanw 59M 105
Maismore St. SE15 51Wb 113
Maisonettes, The SM1: Sutt 78Bb 155
Maitland Cl. KT12: Walt T 75Aa 151
KT14: W Byf 85J 169
SE10 52Dc 114
TW4: Houn 55Ba 107
Maitland Ct. W2 4B 220
Maitland Ho. *E2 40Yb 72*
(off Waterloo Gdns.)
SW1 51Lb 112
(off Churchill Gdns.)
Maitland Pk. Est. NW3 37Hb 69
Maitland Pk. Rd. NW3 37Hb 69
Maitland Pk. Vs. NW3 37Hb 69
Maitland Pl. E5 35Xb 71
Maitland Rd. E15 37Hc 73
SE26 65Zb 136
Maitlands IG10: Lough 13Pc 36
Maitland Yd. W13 46Ja 86
Maize Row E14 45Bc 92
Maizey Ct. CM15: Pil H 15Wd 40
Majendie Rd. SE18 50Tc 94
Majestic Way CR4: Mitc 68Hb 133
Major Cl. SW9 55Rb 113
Major Draper St. SE18 48Rc 94
Major Rd. E15 36Fc 73
SE16 48Wb 91
Majors Farm Rd. SL3: Dat 2P 103
Makepeace Av. N6 33Jb 70
Makepeace Mans. N6 33Jb 70
Makepeace Rd. E11 28Jc 53
UB5: N'olt 40Aa 65
Makinen Ho. IG9: Buck H 18Lc 35
Makins St. SW3 6E 226 (49Gb 89)
Malabar Ct. *W12 45Xa 88*
(off India Way)
Malabar St. E14 47Cc 92
Malacca Farm GU4: W Cla 99K 189
Malam Ct. SE11 6K 229 (49Qb 90)
Malam Gdns. E14 45Dc 92
Malan Cl. TN16: Big H 89Nc 180
Malan Sq. RM13: Rain 37Kd 77
Malbrook Rd. SW15 56Xa 110
Malcolm Cl. SE20 66Yb 136
Malcolm Ct. E7 37Hc 73
HA7: Stan 22La 46
NW4 30Wa 48
Malcolm Cres. NW4 30Wa 48
Malcolm Dr. KT6: Surb 74Na 153
Malcolm Ho. N1 2H 219
Malcolm Pl. E2 42Yb 92
Malcolm Rd. CR5: Coul 87Mb 176
E1 42Yb 92
SE20 66Yb 136
SE25 72Wb 157
SW19 65Ab 132
UB10: Ick 35P 63
Malcolm Sargent Ho. *E16 46Kc 93*
(off Evelyn Rd.)
Malcolmson Ho. SW1 7D 228
Malcolms Way N14 15Lb 32
Malcolm Way E11 29Jc 53
Malden Av. SE25 70Xb 135
UB6: G'frd 36Ga 66
Malden Centre, The 70Va 132
Malden Ct. KT3: N Mald 69Xa 132
N4 30Sb 51
Malden Cres. NW1 37Jb 70
Malden Flds. WD23: Bush 15Z 27
Malden Golf Course 68Ua 132
MALDEN GREEN 74Wa 154
Malden Grn. Av.
KT4: Wor Pk 74Va 154
Malden Grn. M. KT4: Wor Pk 74Wa 154
Malden Hill KT3: N Mald 69Ua 132
Malden Hill Gdns.
KT3: N Mald 69Ua 132
Malden Ho. WD19: Wat 20Y 27
MALDEN JUNC. 71Va 154
Malden Lodge WD17: Wat 12X 27
Malden Pk. KT3: N Mald 72Va 154
Malden Pl. NW5 36Jb 70
Malden Rd. KT3: N Mald 71Ua 154
KT4: Wor Pk 72Va 154
NW5 36Hb 69
SM3: Cheam 78Za 155
WD6: Bore 13Qa 29
WD17: Wat 12X 27
MALDEN RUSHETT 83La 172
Malden Way KT3: N Mald 72Ta 153
Maldon Cl. E15 36Gc 73
N1 39Sb 71
SE5 55Ub 113
Maldon Ct. E6 39Qc 74
SM6: Wall 78Lb 156
Maldon Rd. N9 20Vb 33
RM7: Rush G 31Ed 76
SM6: Wall 78Kb 156
W3 45Sa 87
Maldon Wlk. IG8: Wfd G 23Lc 53
Malet Cl. TW20: Egh 65F 126
Malet Pl. WC1 6D 216 (42Mb 90)
Malet St. WC1 6D 216 (42Mb 90)
Maley Av. SE27 61Rb 135
Malford Ct. E18 26Jc 53
Malford Gro. E18 28Hc 53
Malfort Rd. SE5 55Ub 113
Malham Cl. N11 23Jb 50
Malham Rd. SE23 60Zb 114
Malham Rd. Ind. Est.
SE23 60Zb 114
Malham Ter. N18 22Xb 51
Malibu Ct. SE26 62Xb 135
Malin Ct. HP3: Hem H 5L 3
Malins Cl. EN5: Barn 15Xa 30
Malkin Way WD18: Wat 14U 26
Mall, The AL2: Park 9A 6
BR1: Brom 69Jc 137
BR8: Swan 69Gd 140
CR0: C'don 75Sb 157
DA6: Bex 56Cd 118
E15 38Fc 73
HA3: Kenton 31Pa 67
KT6: Surb 71Ma 153
KT12: Hers 78Z 151
(off Hersham Grn. Shop. Cen.)
N14 20Nb 32
RM10: Dag 37Cd 76
RM11: Horn 32Kd 77
(not continuous)
RM17: Grays 51Ce 121
(off Grays Shop. Cen.)
SW1 1C 228 (47Lb 90)
SW14 57Sa 109
TW8: Bford 51Ma 109
W5 45Na 87
Mallams M. SW9 55Rb 113
Mallard Cl. DA1: Dart 57Pd 119
E9 37Bc 72
EN5: New Bar 16Fb 31
NW6 40Cb 69
RH1: Redh 3A 208
RM14: Upm 31Vd 78
TW2: Whitt 59Ca 107
W7 47Ga 86
Mallard Ct. E17 27Fc 53
WD3: Rick 17M 25
(off Swan Cl.)
Mallard Dr. SL1: Slou 5D 80
Mallard Ho. NW8 2D 214
SW6 53Eb 111
(off Station Ct.)
Mallard Path SE28 48Tc 94
Mallard Pl. N22 26Pb 50
TW1: Twick 62Ja 130
Mallard Point *E3 41Dc 92*
(off Rainhill Way)
Mallard Rd. CR2: Sels 82Zb 178
WD5: Ab L 3W 12
Mallards *E11 31Jc 73*
(off Blake Hall Rd.)
Mallards, The HP3: Hem H 7P 3
TW18: Lale 68K 127
Mallards Ct. *WD19: Wat 20Ba 27*
(off Hangar Ruding)
Mallards Reach KT13: Weyb 75T 150
Mallards Rd. IG8: Wfd G 24Kc 53
IG11: Bark 41Wc 95
Mallard Wlk. BR3: Beck 71Zb 158
DA14: Sidc 65Yc 139
Mallard Way CM13: Hut 17De 41
HA6: Nwood 24S 44
NW9 32Sa 67
SM6: Wall 81Lb 176
WD25: Wat 9Aa 13
Mall Chambers *W8 46Cb 89*
(off Kensington Mall)
Mallet Dr. UB5: N'olt 36Ba 65
Mallet Rd. SE13 58Fc 115
Mall Galleries 6E 222
Malling SE13 57Dc 114
Malling Cl. CR0: C'don 72Yb 158
Malling Gdns. SM4: Mord 72Eb 155
Malling Way BR2: Hayes 73Hc 159
Mallinson Cl. RM12: Horn 36Ld 77
Mallinson Rd. CR0: Bedd 76Mb 156
SW11 57Gb 111
Mallinson Sports Cen. 31Hb 69
Mallion Ct. EN9: Walt A 5Hc 21
Mallon Gdns. E1 1K 225
Mallord St. SW3 51Fb 111
Mallory Bldgs. EC1 6B 218
Mallory Cl. E14 43Dc 92
SE4 56Ac 114
Mallory Ct. SE12 59Kc 115
Mallory Gdns. EN4: E Barn 17Jb 32
Mallory St. NW8 5E 214 (42Gb 89)
Mallow Cl. CR0: C'don 74Zb 158
DA11: Nflt 3A 144
KT20: Tad 92Xa 194
Mallow Ct. RM17: Grays 51Fe 121
Mallow Mead NW7 24Ab 48
Mallows, The UB10: Ick 34R 64
Mallow St. EC1 5F 219 (42Tb 91)
Mall Rd. W6 50Xa 88
Mall Shopping Centre, The
RM1: Rom 29Hd 56
Mall Vs. *W6 50Xa 88*
(off Mall Rd.)
Mallys Pl. DA4: S Dar 67Sd 142
Malmains Cl. BR3: Beck 70Fc 137
Malmains Way BR3: Beck 70Ec 136
Malm Cl. WD3: Rick 19M 25
Malmesbury *E2 40Yb 72*
(off Cyprus St.)
Malmesbury Cl. HA5: Eastc 28V 44
Malmesbury Rd. E3 41Bc 92
E16 43Gc 93
E18 25Hc 53
SM4: Mord 73Eb 155
Malmesbury Ter. E16 43Hc 93
Malmes Cft. HP3: Hem H 4C 4
Malmsey Ho. SE11 7J 229 (50Pb 90)
Malmsmead Ho. *E9 36Bc 72*
(off King's Mead Way)
Malmstone Av. RH1: Mers 100Lb 196
Malory Cl. BR3: Beck 68Ac 136
Malpas Dr. HA5: Pinn 29Z 45
Malpas Rd. E8 36Xb 71
RM9: Dag 37Zc 75
RM16: Grays 8E 100
SE4 54Bc 114
SL2: Slou 5M 81
Malswick Ct. *SE15 52Ub 113*
(off Tower Mill Rd.)
Malta Rd. E10 32Cc 72
RM18: Tilb 4B 122
Malta St. EC1 5C 218 (42Rb 91)
Maltby Cl. BR6: Orp 74Wc 161
Maltby Dr. EN1: Enf 10Xb 19
Maltby Ho. SE1 3K 231
Maltby Rd. KT9: Chess 79Qa 153
Maltby St. SE1 2K 231 (47Vb 91)
Malt Hill TW20: Egh 64A 126
Malt Ho. Cl. SL4: Old Win 9M 103
Malthouse Ct. *AL1: St A 3B 6*
(off Sopwell La.)
GU24: W End 4D 166
Malthouse Dr. TW13: Hanw 64Z 129
W4 51Va 110
Malthouse La. DA12: Shorne 4N 145
GU3: Worp 6G 186
GU24: Pirb 5F 186
GU24: W End 5D 166
TW20: Egh 64C 126
Malthouse Pas. *SW13 54Va 110*
(off Clevelands Gdns.)
Malt Ho. Pl. RM1: Rom 29Gd 56
Malthouse Pl. WD7: R'lett 6Ja 14
Malthouse Rd. TN15: Stans, Ash 81Be 185
Malthus Path SE28 46Yc 95
Malting Ho. *E14 45Bc 92*
(off Oak La.)
Malting La. RM16: Ors 2C 100
Maltings, The AL1: St A 2B 6
BR6: Orp 74Vc 161
DA11: Grav'nd 8C 122
(off West St.)
HP2: Hem H 1M 3
KT14: Byfl 85P 169
RH8: Oxt 3K 211
RM1: Rom 31Hd 76
TW18: Staines 63G 126
Maltings, The *W4 50Qa 87*
(off Spring Gro.)
WD4: Hunt C 6S 12
Maltings Arts Theatre 2B 6
Maltings Cl. E3 41Ec 92
SW13 54Va 110
Maltings Dr. CM16: Epp 1Wc 23
Maltings Ent. Cen., The
DA12: Grav'nd 10H 123
Maltings La. CM16: Epp 1Wc 23
Maltings Lodge *W4 51Ua 110*
(off Corney Reach Way)
Maltings M. DA15: Sidc 62Wc 139
Maltings Pl. SE1 2J 231
SW6 53Db 111
Malting Way TW7: Isle 55Ha 108
Malt La. WD7: R'lett 7Ja 14
Malton Av. SL1: Slou 4F 80
Malton M. SE18 51Uc 116
W10 44Ab 88
Malton Rd. W10 44Ab 88
Malton St. SE18 51Uc 116
Maltravers St. WC2 4J 223 (45Pb 90)
Malt Shovel Cotts.
DA4: Eyns 76Md 163
Malt St. SE1 51Wb 113
Malus Cl. HP2: Hem H 1A 4
KT15: Add 80H 149
Malus Dr. KT15: Add 80H 149
Malva Cl. SW18 57Db 111
Malvern Av. DA7: Bex 52Ad 117
E4 24Fc 53
HA2: Harr 34Aa 65
Malvern Cl. CR4: Mitc 69Lb 134
KT6: Surb 74Na 153
KT16: Ott 79E 148
SE20 68Wb 135
UB10: Ick 33Q 64
W10 43Bb 89
WD23: Bush 16Ea 28
Malvern Ct. KT18: Eps 86Ta 173
SL3: L'ly 51C 104
SM2: Sutt 80Cb 155
SW7 5C 226
W12 47Wa 88
(off Hadyn Pk. Rd.)
Malvern Dr. IG3: Bark, Ilf 35Vc 75
IG8: Wfd G 22Lc 53
TW13: Hanw 64Z 129
Malvern Gdns. HA3: Kenton 28Na 47
IG10: Lough 16Pc 36
NW2 33Ab 68
Malvern Ho. *DA11: Nflt 58Fe 121*
(off Laburnum Gro.)
N16 32Vb 71
SE17 7E 230
WD18: Wat 16T 26
Malvern M. NW6 41Cb 89
Malvern Pl. NW6 41Bb 89
Malvern Rd. BR6: Chels 77Xc 161
CR7: Thor H 70Qb 134
E6 39Nc 74
E8 38Wb 71
E11 33Gc 73
EN3: Enf W 9Ac 20
KT6: Surb 75Na 153
N8 27Qb 50
N17 27Wb 51
NW6 40Bb 69
(not continuous)
RM11: Horn 30Jd 56
RM17: Grays 9A 100
TW12: Hamp 66Ca 129
UB3: Harl 52U 106
Malvern Ter. N1 39Qb 70
N9 18Vb 33
Malvern Way W13 43Ka 86
WD3: Crox G 15R 26
Malvina Av. DA12: Grav'nd 1D 144
Malwood Rd. SW12 58Kb 112
Malyons, The TW17: Shep 72T 150
Malyons Rd. BR8: Hext 66Hd 140
SE13 58Dc 114
Malyons Ter. SE13 57Dc 114
Managers St. E14 46Ec 92
Manan Cl. HP3: Hem H 4C 4
Manatee Pl. SM6: Bedd 76Mb 156
Manaton Cl. SE15 55Xb 113
Manaton Cres. UB1: S'hall 44Ca 85
Manbey Gro. E15 37Gc 73
Manbey Pk. Rd. E15 37Gc 73
Manbey Rd. E15 37Gc 73
Manbey St. E15 37Gc 73
Manbre Rd. W6 51Ya 110
Manbrough Av. E6 41Pc 94
Manchester Ct. *E16 44Kc 93*
(off Garvary Rd.)
Manchester Dr. W10 42Ab 88
Manchester Gro. E14 50Ec 92
Manchester Ho. SE17 7E 230
Manchester M. W1 1H 221
Manchester Rd. CR7: Thor H 69Sb 135
E14 50Ec 92
N15 30Tb 51
Manchester Sq. W1 2J 221 (44Jb 90)
Manchester St. W1 1H 221 (43Jb 90)
Manchester Way RM10: Dag 35Dd 76
Manchuria Rd. SW11 58Jb 112
Manciple St. SE1 2F 231 (47Tb 91)
Mancroft Ct. *NW8 39Fb 69*
(off St John's Wood Pk.)
Mandalay Rd. SW4 57Lb 112
Mandarin Ct. *NW10 37Ta 67*
(off Mitchellbrook Way)
SE8 51Bc 114
Mandarin St. E14 45Cc 92
Mandarin Way UB4: Yead 44Aa 85
Mandarin Wharf *N1 39Ub 71*
(off De Beauvoir Cres.)
Mandela Cl. NW10 38Sa 67
W12 45Xa 88
Mandela Ct. UB8: Cowl 43L 83
Mandela Ho. E2 3K 219
SE5 54Rb 113
Mandela Pl. WD24: Wat 12Z 27
Mandela Rd. E16 44Jc 93
Mandela St. NW1 39Lb 70
SW9 52Qb 112
(not continuous)
Mandela Way SE1 5H 231 (49Ub 91)
Mandel Ho. SW18 56Cb 111
Manderley *W14 48Bb 89*
(off Oakwood La.)
Mandeville Cl. SE3 52Hc 115
SW20 66Ab 132
WD17: Wat 10V 12
Mandeville Ct. E4 22Ac 52
TW20: Egh 63C 126
Mandeville Dr. AL1: St A 5B 6
KT6: Surb 74Ma 153
Mandeville Ho. SE1 7K 231
SW4 57Lb 112
Mandeville M. SW4 56Nb 112
Mandeville Pl. W1 2J 221 (44Jb 90)
Mandeville Rd. EN3: Enf W 8Ac 20
EN6: Pot B 4Eb 17
N14 19Kb 32
TW7: Isle 54Ja 108
TW17: Shep 71Q 150
UB5: N'olt 38Ca 65
Mandeville St. E5 34Ac 72
Mandeville Wlk. CM13: Hut 17Fe 41
Mandrake Rd. SW17 62Hb 133
Mandrake Way E15 38Gc 73
Mandrell Rd. SW2 57Nb 112
Manesty Ct. *N14 17Mb 32*
(off Ivy Rd.)
Manette St. W1 3E 222 (44Mb 90)
Manfield Cl. SL2: Slou 1E 80
Manford Cl. IG7: Chig 21Wc 55
Manford Ct. *IG7: Chig 22Vc 55*
(off Manford Way)
Manford Cross IG7: Chig 22Wc 55
Manford Ind. Est. DA8: Erith 51Jd 118
Manford Way IG7: Chig 22Uc 54
Manfred Rd. SW15 57Bb 111
Manger Rd. N7 37Nb 70
Mangold Way DA18: Erith 48Zc 95
Manhattan Av. WD18: Wat 14V 26
Manhattan Bldg. E3 40Cc 72
Manhattan Bus. Pk. W5 41Na 87
Manilla Ct. *RM6: Chad H 30Xc 55*
(off Quarles Pk. Rd.)
Manilla St. E14 47Cc 92
Manister Rd. SE2 48Wc 95
Manitoba Ct. *SE16 47Yb 92*
(off Canada Est.)
Manitoba Gdns. BR6: Chels 79Vc 161
Manley Ct. N16 34Vb 71
Manley Ho. SE11 7K 229 (49Qb 90)
Manley Rd. HP2: Hem H 1N 3
Manley St. NW1 39Jb 70
Manly Dixon Dr. EN3: Enf W 9Ac 20
Mannamead KT18: Eps D 91Ua 194
Mannamead Cl. KT18: Eps D 91Ua 194
Mannan Ho. *E3 40Bc 72*
(off Roman Rd.)
Mann Cl. CR0: C'don 76Sb 157
Manneby Prior N1 2J 217
Manning Ct. *SE28 46Xc 95*
(off Titmuss Av.)
WD19: Wat 16Z 27
Manningford Cl. EC1 3B 218 (41Rb 91)
Manning Gdns. CR0: C'don 73Xb 157
HA3: Kenton 31Ma 67
Manning Ho. *W11 44Ab 88*
(off Westbourne Pk. Rd.)
Manning Pl. TW10: Rich 58Pa 109
Manning Rd. BR5: St M Cry 71Zc 161
E17 29Ac 52
RM10: Dag 37Cd 76
Manning St. RM15: Avel 46Sd 98
Manningtree Cl. SW19 60Ab 110
Manningtree Rd. HA4: Ruis 35X 65
Manningtree St. E1 44Wb 91
Mannin Rd. RM6: Chad H 31Xc 75
Mannock Cl. NW9 27Ta 47
Mannock Dr. IG10: Lough 12Sc 36
Mannock M. E18 25Lc 53
Mannock Rd. DA1: Dart 55Pd 119
N22 27Rb 51
Mann's Cl. TW7: Isle 57Ha 108
Manns Rd. HA8: Edg 23Qa 47
Manny Shinwell Ho. *SW6 51Bb 111*
(off Clem Attlee Ct.)
Manoel Rd. TW2: Twick 61Ea 130
Manor, The IG8: Wfd G 24Qc 54
Manor Av. CR3: Cat'm 96Ub 197
HP3: Hem H 5M 3
RM11: Horn 29Ld 57
SE4 54Bc 114
TW4: Houn 55Z 107
UB5: N'olt 38Ba 65
Manorbrook SE3 56Jc 115
Manor Chase KT13: Weyb 78R 150
MANOR CIRCUS 55Qa 109
Manor Cl. CR6: W'ham 89Ac 178
DA1: Cray 56Fd 118
DA2: Wilm 62Jd 140
DA12: Grav'nd 1K 145
E17 25Ac 52
EN5: Barn 14Ab 30
GU22: Pyr 89H 169
HA4: Ruis 32V 64
KT4: Wor Pk 74Ua 154
KT24: E Hor 100U 190
NW7 22Ta 47
NW9 29Ra 47
RH9: S God 10D 210
RM1: Rom 29Jd 56
RM10: Dag 37Fd 76
RM15: Avel 46Sd 98
SE28 45Yc 95
Manor Cl. Sth. RM15: Avel 46Sd 98
Manor Cotts. HA6: Nwood 25V 44
N2 26Eb 49
(off Manor Cotts. App.)
WD3: Chor 16D 24
Manor Cotts. App. N2 26Eb 49
Manor Ct. BR4: W W'ck 74Dc 158
DA7: Bex 56Dd 118
DA13: Sole S 10F 144
E4 18Gc 35
E10 32Dc 72
EN1: Enf 8Xb 19
EN6: Pot B 4Bb 17
EN8: Chesh 3Zb 20
HA1: Harr 30Ha 46
HA9: Wemb 36Na 67
IG11: Bark 38Vc 75
KT2: King T 67Qa 131
KT8: W Mole 70Ca 129
KT13: Weyb 77R 150
N2 29Hb 49
N14 19Mb 32
N20 20Hb 31
(off York Way)
SL1: Slou 6D 80
SM5: Cars 76Jb 156
SW2 57Pb 112
SW3 7E 226
SW6 53Db 111

Manor Ct. SW16 62Nb 134
TW2: Twick 61Ea 130
TW18: Staines 64F 126
UB9: Hare 26L 43
W3 49Qa 87
WD7: R'lett 10Ha 14
Manor Ct. Rd. W7 45Ga 86
Manor Cres. GU24: Brkwd 2B 186
KT5: Surb 72Qa 153
KT14: Byfl 85P 169
KT19: Eps 84Qa 173
RM11: Horn 29Ld 57
Manorcroft Pde. EN8: Chesh 2Zb 20
Manorcrofts Rd. TW20: Egh 65C 126
Manor Dene SE28 44Yc 95
Manordene Cl. KT7: T Ditt 74Ja 152
Manordene Rd. SE28 44Yc 95
Manor Dr. AL2: Chis G 9N 5
DA3: Hartl 72Ce 165
HA9: Wemb 35Pa 67
KT5: Surb 72Pa 153
KT10: Hin W 75Ha 152
KT15: New H 82J 169
KT19: Ewe 79Ua 154
N14 18Kb 32
N20 21Hb 49
NW7 22Ta 47
TW13: Hanw 64Z 129
TW16: Sun 68W 128
Manor Dr., The KT4: Wor Pk 74Ua 154
Manor Dr. Nth. KT3: N Mald 73Ta 153
KT4: Wor Pk 73Ta 153
Manor Est. SE16 49Xb 91
Manor Farm 31U 64
Manor Farm TW20: Egh 64C 126
Mnr. Farm Av. TW17: Shep 72R 150
Mnr. Farm Cl. KT4: Wor Pk 74Ua 154
SL4: Wind 5D 102
Mnr. Farm Cotts. SL4: Old Win 7L 103
TN15: Igh 93Wd 204
Mnr. Farm Ct. E6 41Pc 94
TW20: Egh 64C 126
Mnr. Farm Dr. E4 20Gc 35
MANOR FARM ESTATE 9N 103
Mnr. Farm Ho. SL4: Wind 5D 102
Mnr. Farm La. TW20: Egh 64C 126
Mnr. Farm Rd. EN1: Enf 7Xb 19
HA0: Wemb 40Ma 67
SW16 68Qb 134
Manor Fld. DA12: Shorne 4N 145
Manorfield Cl. *N19* *35Lb 70*
(off Fulbrook M.)
Manor Flds. SW15 58Za 110
Manorfields Cl. BR7: Chst 69Vc 139
Manor Forstal DA3: New A 76Be 165
Manor Gdns. CR2: S Croy 79Vb 157
HA4: Ruis 36Y 65
KT24: Eff 100Z 191
N7 34Nb 70
SW4 *54Lb 112*
(off Larkhall Ri.)
SW20 68Bb 133
TW9: Rich 56Pa 109
TW12: Hamp 66Da 129
TW16: Sun 67W 128
W3 49Qa 87
W4 50Ua 88
Manor Ga. UB5: N'olt 38Aa 65
Manor Ga. La. DA2: Wilm 62Jd 140
Manorgate Rd. KT2: King T 67Qa 131
Manor Grn. Rd. KT19: Eps 85Ra 173
Manor Gro. BR3: Beck 68Dc 136
SE15 51Yb 114
TW9: Rich 56Qa 109
Manor Hall IG7: Chig 22Sc 54
Mnr. Hall Av. NW4 26Za 48
Mnr. Hall Dr. NW4 26Za 48
Manorhall Gdns. E10 32Cc 72
Manor Hill SM7: Bans 87Hb 175
MANOR HOUSE 31Tb 71
MANOR HOUSE 31Sb 71
Manor Ho. DA3: New A 76Be 165
NW1 7E 214
SL4: Eton *1H 103*
(off Common La.)
UB2: S'hall 48Aa 85
Manor Ho., The KT20: Kgswd 95Eb 195
Manor Ho. Ct. KT18: Eps 85Sa 173
TW17: Shep 73R 150
W9 *42Eb 89*
(off Warrington Gdns.)
Manor Ho. Dr. HA6: Nwood 24R 44
KT12: Hers 78V 150
NW6 38Za 68
Manor Ho. Est. HA7: Stan 23Ka 46
Manor Ho. Gdn. E11 30Kc 53
Manor Ho. Gdns. WD5: Ab L 3T 12
Manor Ho. La. KT23: Bookh 98Aa 191
SL3: Dat 3M 103
Manor Ho. Way TW7: Isle 55Ka 108
Manor La. DA3: Fawk 73Yd 164
DA3: Hartl 72Ce 165
KT20: Lwr K 1J 207
SE12 57Gc 115
SE13 57Gc 115
SL9: Ger X 1P 61
SM1: Sutt 78Eb 155
TN15: Ash 73Yd 164
TW13: Felt 61W 128
TW16: Sun 68W 128
UB3: Harl 51T 106
Manor La. Ter. SE13 56Gc 115
Manor Leaze TW20: Egh 64D 126
Manor Lodge *NW6* *38Za 68*
(off Willesden La.)
Manor M. *NW6* *40Cb 69*
(off Cambridge Av.)
SE4 54Bc 114
Manor Mt. SE23 60Yb 114
Manor Pde. HA1: Harr 30Ha 46
N16 33Vb 71
NW10 *40Va 68*
(off High St. Harlesden)
MANOR PARK
E12 35Mc 73
SL2 3H 81
Manor Pk. BR7: Chst 68Tc 138
DA8: Erith 51Jd 118
SE13 56Fc 115
TW9: Rich 56Pa 109
TW13: Felt 61W 128
TW18: Staines 62F 126
Manor Pk. Cl. BR4: W W'ck 74Dc 158
Manor Pk. Crematorium E7 35Lc 73
Manor Pk. Cres. HA8: Edg 23Qa 47
Manor Pk. Dr. HA2: Harr 27Da 45
Manor Pk. Gdns. HA8: Edg 22Qa 47
Manor Pk. Pde. *SE13* *56Fc 115*
(off Lee High Rd.)
Manor Pk. Rd. BR4: W W'ck 74Dc 158
BR7: Chst 67Sc 138
E12 35Mc 73
(not continuous)
N2 27Eb 49
NW10 39Va 68
SM1: Sutt 78Eb 155
Manor Pl. BR7: Chst 68Tc 138
CR4: Mitc 69Lb 134
DA1: Dart 60Nd 119
KT12: Walt T 73V 150
(not continuous)
KT23: Bookh 98Ca 191
SE17 7C 230 (50Rb 91)
SM1: Sutt 77Db 155
TW14: Felt 60W 106
TW18: Staines 64K 127
Manor Pl. Ind. Est. WD6: Bore 13Sa 29
Manor Rd. AL1: St A 1C 6
AL2: Lon C 8G 6
BR3: Beck 68Dc 136
BR4: W W'ck 75Dc 158
CR4: Mitc 70Lb 134
DA1: Cray 56Gd 118
DA3: Lfield, Long H 71Ee 165
DA5: Bexl 60Dd 118
DA8: Erith 51Hd 118
DA10: Swans 58Zd 121
DA12: Grav'nd 8D 122
DA13: Sole S 10E 144
DA15: Sidc 62Vc 139
E10 31Cc 72
E15 40Gc 73
E16 41Gc 93
E17 26Ac 52
EN2: Enf 12Sb 33
EN5: Barn 14Ab 30
EN6: Pot B 3Bb 17
EN9: Walt A 5Fc 21
GU21: Wok 8N 167
GU23: Rip 95H 189
HA1: Harr 30Ja 46
HA4: Ruis 32T 64
IG7: Chig 22Sc 54
IG8: Wfd G 23Pc 54
IG10: H Beech 11Kc 35
IG10: Lough 16Kc 35
IG11: Bark 37Vc 75
KT8: E Mos 70Fa 130
KT12: Walt T 73V 150
N16 33Tb 71
N17 25Wb 51
N22 23Nb 50
RH1: Mers 1C 208
RH2: Reig 4H 207
RM1: Rom 29Jd 56
RM4: Abr, Stap A 19Yc 37
RM6: Chad H 30Zc 55
RM10: Dag 37Ed 76
RM17: Grays 51Ee 121
RM18: Tilb 4C 122
RM20: W Thur 51Yd 120
SE25 70Wb 135
SL4: Wind 4C 102
SM2: Cheam 80Bb 155
SM6: Wall 77Kb 156
SS17: Stan H 1M 101
SW20 68Bb 133
TN14: Sund 96Zc 201
TN15: W King 83Vd 184
TN16: Tats 92Nc 200
TW2: Twick 61Ea 130
TW9: Rich 56Qa 109
TW11: Tedd 64Ja 130
(not continuous)
TW15: Ashf 64P 127
UB3: Hayes 44W 84
W13 45Ja 86
WD17: Wat 11X 27
Manor Rd. Ho. HA1: Harr 30Ja 46
Manor Rd. Nth. KT7: T Ditt 76Ha 152
KT10: Hin W, T Ditt 76Ha 152
SM6: Wall 77Kb 156
Manor Rd. Sth. KT10: Hin W 77Ga 152
Manorside EN5: Barn 14Ab 30
Manorside Cl. SE2 49Yc 95
Manor Sq. RM8: Dag 33Yc 75
Manor Va. TW8: Bford 51Ka 86
Manor Vw. DA3: Hartl 72Ce 165
N3 26Db 49
Manorville Rd. HP3: Hem H 6L 3
Manor Wlk. KT13: Weyb 78R 150
Manor Way BR2: Brom 72Nc 160
BR3: Beck 68Cc 136
BR5: Pet W 70Sc 138
CM14: B'wood 20Wd 40
CR2: S Croy 79Ub 157
CR4: Mitc 69Lb 134
CR8: Purl 84Nb 176
DA5: Bexl 60Cd 118
DA7: Bex 55Fd 118
DA10: Nflt, Swans 56Zd 121
DA11: Nflt 55Zd 121
(Botany Rd.)
DA11: Nflt 56Zd 121
(Lovers La.)
E4 21Fc 53
EN6: Pot B 2Cb 17
EN8: Chesh 3Ac 20
GU22: Wok 93D 188
HA2: Harr 28Da 45
HA4: Ruis 31U 64
KT4: Wor Pk 74Ua 154
KT22: Oxs 87Ea 172
NW9 28Ua 48
RM13: Rain 42Gd 96
RM17: Grays 52De 121
SE3 56Hc 115
SE23 59Yb 114
SM7: Bans 88Hb 175
SS17: Stan H 1P 101
TW20: Egh 65B 126
UB2: S'hall 49Z 85
WD3: Crox G 14Q 26
WD6: Bore 13Sa 29
Manor Way, The SM6: Wall 77Kb 156
Manorway EN1: Enf 17Ub 33
IG8: Wfd G 22Lc 53
SE7 49Mc 93
Manorway, The
SS17: Corr, Stan H 1L 101
Manor Way Bus. Cen.
RM13: Rain 43Fd 96
Manor Way Bus. Pk. DA10: Nflt 57Be 121
Manor Waye UB8: Uxb 39M 63
Mnr. Wood Rd. CR8: Purl 85Nb 176
Manpreet Ct. E12 36Pc 74
Manresa Rd. SW3 7D 226 (50Gb 89)
Mansard Beeches SW17 64Jb 134
Mansard Cl. HA5: Pinn 27Z 45
RM12: Horn 33Jd 76
Mansards, The AL1: St A 1C 6
Manse Cl. UB3: Harl 51T 106
Mansel Cl. GU2: Guild 10M 187
SL2: Slou 3M 81
Mansel Gro. E17 25Cc 52
Mansell Cl. SL4: Wind 3C 102
Mansell Rd. UB6: G'frd 43Da 85
W3 47Ta 87
Mansell St. E1 3K 225 (44Vb 91)
EC3 5K 225 (44Vb 91)
Mansell Way CR3: Cat'm 94Tb 197
Mansel Rd. SW19 65Ab 132
Manse Pde. BR8: Swan 70Jd 140
Manser Ct. RM13: Rain 41Gd 96
Mansergh Cl. SE18 52Nc 116
Manse Rd. N16 34Vb 71
Manser Rd. RM13: Rain 41Gd 96
Manse Way BR8: Swan 70Jd 140
Mansfield Av. EN4: E Barn 16Hb 31
HA4: Ruis 32X 65
N15 28Tb 51
Mansfield Cl. BR5: St M Cry 73Zc 161
N9 16Wb 33
Mansfield Ct. E2 1K 219
SE15 *52Vb 113*
(off Sumner Rd.)
Mansfield Dr. RH1: Mers 100Mb 196
UB4: Hayes 42U 84
Mansfield Gdns. RM12: Horn 33Md 77
Mansfield Hgts. N2 29Gb 49
Mansfield Hill E4 17Dc 34
Mansfield Ho. *N1* *39Ub 71*
(off New Era Est.)
Mansfield M. W1 1K 221 (43Kb 90)
Mansfield Outdoor Cen. 17Ad 37
Mansfield Pl. CR2: S Croy 79Tb 157
NW3 35Eb 69
Mansfield Rd. BR8: Hext 65Gd 140
CR2: S Croy 79Tb 157
E11 30Kc 53
E17 28Bc 52
IG1: Ilf 33Qc 74
KT9: Chess 78La 152
NW3 36Hb 69
W3 42Ra 87
Mansfield St. W1 1K 221 (43Kb 90)
Mansford St. E2 40Wb 71
Manship Rd. CR4: Mitc 66Jb 134
Mansion Caravan Site SL0: Iver 46E 82
Mansion Cl. SW9 53Qb 112
(not continuous)
Mansion Gdns. NW3 34Db 69
Mansion House 3F 225 (44Tb 91)
Mansion Ho. Pl. EC4 3F 225 (44Tb 91)
Mansion Ho. St. EC4 3F 225
Mansion La. SL0: Iver 46E 82
Mansions, The SW5 50Db 89
Manson Ho. *N1* *38Qb 70*
(off Drummond Way)
Manson M. SW7 6A 226 (49Fb 89)
Manson Pl. SW7 6B 226 (49Fb 89)
Manstead Gdns. RM13: Rain 44Kd 97
Mansted Gdns. RM6: Chad H 31Yc 75
Manston *N17* *26Tb 51*
(off Adams Rd.)
NW1 *38Lb 70*
(off Agar Gro.)
Manston Av. UB2: S'hall 49Ca 85
Manston Cl. EN8: Chesh 1Zb 20
SE20 67Yb 136
Manstone Rd. NW2 36Ab 68
Manston Gro. KT2: King T 64Ma 131
Manston Ho. *W14* *48Ab 88*
(off Russell Rd.)
Manston Way AL4: St A 3H 7
RM12: Horn 37Kd 77
Manthorp Rd. SE18 50Sc 94
Mantilla Rd. SW17 63Jb 134
Mantle Ct. *SW18* *58Db 111*
(off Mapleton Rd.)
Mantle Rd. SE4 55Ac 114
Mantlet Cl. SW16 66Lb 134
Mantle Way E15 38Gc 73
Manton Av. W7 47Ha 86
Manton Cl. UB3: Hayes 45U 84
Manton Rd. EN3: Enf L 9Cc 20
SE2 49Wc 95
Manton Way EN3: Enf L 10Cc 20
Mantua St. SW11 55Fb 111
Mantus Cl. E1 42Yb 92
Mantus Rd. E1 42Yb 92
Manuka Cl. W7 46Ja 86
Manus Way N20 19Eb 31
Manville Gdns. SW17 62Kb 134
Manville Rd. SW17 61Jb 134
Manwood Rd. SE4 57Bc 114
Manwood St. E16 46Pc 94
Manygate La. TW17: Shep 73S 150
Manygate Pk. Caravan Site
TW17: Shep *72T 150*
(off Mitre Cl.)
Manygates SW12 61Kb 134
Mapesbury Ct. NW2 36Ab 68
Mapesbury M. NW4 30Wa 48
Mapesbury Rd. NW2 38Ab 68
Mapeshill Pl. NW2 37Ya 68
Mapes Ho. NW6 38Ab 68
Mape St. E2 42Xb 91
(not continuous)
Maple Av. E4 22Bc 52
HA2: Harr 33Da 65
RM14: Upm 34Rd 77
UB7: Yiew 45N 83
W3 46Ua 88
Maple Cl. AL10: Hat 1C 8
BR5: Pet W 71Tc 160
BR8: Swan 68Gd 140
CM13: B'wood 20Be 41
CM16: They B 7Uc 22
CR3: Whyt 89Vb 177
CR4: Mitc 67Kb 134
HA4: Ruis 30X 45
IG6: Ilf 22Uc 54
IG9: Buck H 20Mc 35
KT19: Eps 81Ta 173
N3 23Cb 49
N16 30Wb 51
RM12: Horn 34Kd 77
Maple Cl. SW4 58Mb 112
TW12: Hamp 65Ba 129
UB4: Yead 41Z 85
WD23: Bush 12Aa 27
Maple Ct. *CR0: C'don* *77Sb 157*
(off Lwr. Coombe St.)
CR0: C'don *77Sb 157*
(off The Waldrons)
DA8: Erith 52Hd 118
DA9: Ghithe 59Ud 120
E3 *40Cc 72*
(off Four Seasons Cl.)
E6 43Qc 94
GU21: Wok 8N 167
KT3: N Mald 69Ta 131
KT22: Lea 92Ha 192
SE6 60Dc 114
SL4: Wind 5G 102
SL9: Ger X 29B 42
TW15: Ashf 66T 128
TW20: Eng G 5M 125
WD6: Bore *14Qa 29*
(off Drayton Rd.)
WD25: Wat 8Z 13
Maple Cres. DA15: Sidc 58Wc 117
SL2: Slou 5M 81
Maplecroft Cl. E6 44Mc 93
MAPLE CROSS 22F 42
Maple Cross Ind. Est. WD3: Map C 21H 43
Mapledale Av. CR0: C'don 75Wb 157
Mapledene BR7: Chst 65Sc 138
Mapledene Est. E8 38Wb 71
Mapledene Rd. E8 38Vb 71
Maple Dr. KT23: Bookh 97Da 191
RM15: S Ock 42Zd 99
Maplefield AL2: Park 1Da 13
Maple Gdns. HA8: Edg 24Ua 48
KT17: Eps *85Ua 174*
(off Up. High St.)
TW19: Stanw 61N 127
Maple Ga. IG10: Lough 12Qc 36
Maple Grn. HP1: Hem H 1G 2
Maple Gro. GU22: Wok 93A 188
KT23: Bookh 99Ca 191
NW9 31Sa 67
TW8: Bford 52Ka 108
UB1: S'hall 43Ba 85
W5 48Ma 87
WD17: Wat 11W 26
Maple Gro. Bus. Cen. TW4: Houn 56Y 107
MAPLE HILL 2A 10
Maple Ho. E17 27Dc 52
EN6: Pot B 5Db 17
KT1: King T *71Na 153*
(off Maple Rd.)
N19 34Lb 70
RH1: Redh *6P 207*
(off Chapel Rd.)
SE8 *52Bc 114*
(off Idonia St.)
TW9: Kew 53Ra 109
Maplehurst BR2: Brom 68Gc 137
KT22: Fet 95Fa 192
Maplehurst Cl. DA2: Wilm 61Gd 140
KT1: King T 70Na 131
Maple Ind. Est. TW13: Felt 62W 128
Maple Leaf Cl. TN16: Big H 88Mc 179
WD5: Ab L 4W 12
Mapleleaf Cl. CR2: Sels 83Zb 178
Maple Leaf Dr. DA15: Sidc 60Vc 117
Mapleleafe Gdns. IG6: Ilf 27Rc 54
Maple Leaf Sq. SE16 47Zb 92
Maple Lodge *W8* *48Db 89*
(off Abbots Wlk.)
Maple Lodge Cl. WD3: Map C 21G 42
Maple Lodge Nature Reserve 22H 43
Maple M. NW6 40Db 69
SE16 47Zb 92
SW16 64Pb 134
Maple Pl. N17 24Wb 51
SM7: Bans 86Za 174
UB7: Yiew 46N 83
W1 6C 216 (42Lb 90)
Maple Rd. CR3: Whyt 89Vb 177
DA1: Dart 60Ld 119
DA12: Grav'nd 3E 144
E11 30Gc 53
GU23: Rip 96J 189
KT6: Surb 72Ma 153
KT21: Asht 91Ma 193
RH1: Redh 10P 207
RM17: Grays 51Ee 121
SE20 67Xb 135
UB4: Yead 41Y 85
Maples SS17: Stan H 1N 101
Maples, The DA3: Lfield 68De 143
EN7: G Oak 1Ub 19
EN9: Walt A 7Lc 21
KT10: Clay 80Ja 152
KT16: Ott 79D 148
SM7: Bans 86Db 175
WD6: Bore 11Qa 29
MAPLESCOMBE 78Sd 164
Maplescombe La. DA4: Farni 76Qd 163
Maples Pl. E1 43Xb 91
Maple Springs EN9: Walt A 5Jc 21
Maplestead Rd. RM9: Dag 39Xc 75
SW2 59Pb 112
Maple St. E2 40Xb 71
RM7: Rom 28Ed 56
W1 7B 216 (43Lb 90)
Maplethorpe Rd. CR7: Thor H 70Qb 134
Mapleton Cl. BR2: Brom 72Jc 159
Mapleton Cres. EN3: Enf W 10Yb 20
SW18 58Db 111
Mapleton Rd. E4 20Ec 34
EN1: Enf 12Xb 33
SW18 58Cb 111
(not continuous)
Maple Tree Pl. SE3 53Nc 116
Maple Wlk. SM2: Sutt 82Db 175
W10 41Za 88
Maple Way CR5: Coul 93Kb 196
EN9: Walt A 1Kc 21
TW13: Felt 62W 128
Maplewood Ct. *HA6: Nwood* *22V 44*
(off Eastbury Av.)
Maplin Cl. N21 16Pb 32
Maplin Ho. *SE2* *47Zc 95*
(off Wolvercote Rd.)
Maplin Pk. SL3: L'ly 47D 82
Maplin Rd. E16 44Jc 93
Maplin St. E3 41Bc 92
Mapperley Cl. E11 30Hc 53
Mapperley Dr. IG8: Wfd G 24Gc 53
Marabou Cl. E12 36Nc 74
Maran Way DA18: Erith 47Zc 95
Marathon Ho. NW1 7F 215
Marathon Way SE28 47Vc 95
Marban Rd. W9 41Bb 89
Marbeck Cl. SL4: Wind 3B 102
Marble Arch 4G 221
MARBLE ARCH 4F 221 (45Hb 89)
Marble Arch W1 4F 221 (45Hb 89)
Marble Arch Apartments W1 2F 221
Marble Cl. W3 46Ra 87
Marble Dr. NW2 32Za 68
Marble Hill Cl. TW1: Twick 59Ka 108
Marble Hill Gdns. TW1: Twick 59Ka 108
Marble Hill House 59La 108
Marble Ho. SE18 50Vc 95
W9 42Bb 89
Marble Quay E1 46Wb 91
Marbles Ho. *SE5* *51Sb 113*
(off Grosvenor Ter.)
Marbles Way KT20: Tad 91Za 194
Marbrook Ct. SE12 62Lc 137
Marcella Rd. SW9 54Qb 112
Marcellina Way BR6: Orp 76Uc 160
Marcet Rd. DA1: Dart 57Ld 119
March *NW9* *25Va 48*
(off The Concourse)
Marchant Cl. NW7 23Ua 48
Marchant Ho. *N1* *1H 219*
(off New Era Est.)
Marchant Rd. E11 33Fc 73
Marchant St. SE14 51Ac 114
Marchbank Rd. W14 51Bb 111
March Ct. SW15 56Xa 110
Marchmant Cl. RM12: Horn 34Ld 77
Marchmont Gdns. TW10: Rich 57Pa 109
Marchmont Rd. SM6: Wall 80Lb 156
TW10: Rich 57Pa 109
Marchmont St. WC1 5F 217 (42Nb 90)
March Rd. KT13: Weyb 78Q 150
TW1: Twick 59Ja 108
Marchside Cl. TW5: Hest 53Z 107
Marchwood Cl. SE5 52Ub 113
Marchwood Cres. W5 44La 86
Marcia Ct. SE1 6J 231
SL1: Slou 6D 80
Marcia Rd. SE1 6J 231 (49Ub 91)
Marcilly Rd. SW18 57Fb 111
Marco Dr. HA5: Hat E 24Ba 45
Marcon Ct. *E8* *36Xb 71*
(off Amhurst Rd.)
Marconi Gdns. CM15: Pil H 15Yd 40
Marconi Pl. N11 21Kb 50
Marconi Rd. DA11: Nflt 62Fe 143
E10 32Cc 72
Marconi Way AL4: St A 2H 7
UB1: S'hall 44Da 85
Marcon Pl. E8 37Xb 71
Marco Polo Ho. SW8 52Kb 112
Marco Rd. W6 48Ya 88
Marcourt Lawns W5 42Na 87
Marcus Ct. E15 39Gc 73
GU22: Wok 90B 168
Marcuse Rd. CR3: Cat'm 95Tb 197
Marcus Garvey M. SE22 58Xb 113
Marcus Garvey Way SE24 56Qb 112
Marcus Rd. DA1: Dart 59Jd 118
Marcus St. E15 39Hc 73
SW18 58Db 111
Marcus Ter. SW18 58Db 111
Mardale Ct. NW7 24Wa 48
Mardale Dr. NW9 29Ta 47
Mardell Rd. CR0: C'don 71Zb 158
Marden Av. BR2: Hayes 72Jc 159
Marden Cl. IG7: Chig 19Xc 37
Marden Cres. CR0: C'don 72Pb 156
DA5: Bexl 57Ed 118
Marden Ho. E8 36Xb 71
MARDEN PARK 95Ac 198
Marden Rd. CR0: C'don 72Pb 156
N17 26Ub 51
RM1: Rom 30Gd 56
Marden Sq. SE16 48Xb 91
Marder Rd. W13 47Ja 86
Mardon HA5: Hat E 24Ba 45
Mardyke Cl. RM13: Rain 40Ed 76
Mardyke Ho. RM13: Rain 40Fd 76
SE17 5G 231
Mardyke Valley Golf Course 45Zd 99
Mardyke Vw. RM19: Purf 48Ud 98
Mardyke Wlk. RM16: Grays 46Ce 99
Marechal Niel Av. DA15: Sidc 62Tc 138
Marechal Niel Pde. *DA14: Sidc* *62Tc 138*
(off Main Rd.)
Maresby Ho. E4 19Dc 34
Marescroft Rd. SL2: Slou 2C 80
Maresfield CR0: C'don 76Ub 157
Maresfield Gdns. NW3 36Eb 69
Mare St. E8 36Xb 71
Marfleet Cl. SM5: Cars 75Gb 155
Margaret Av. CM15: Shenf 17Be 41
E4 16Dc 34
Margaret Barr Row DA10: Swans 59Ae 121
Margaret Bondfield Av.
IG11: Bark 38Wc 75
Margaret Bondfield Ho. *E3* *40Ac 72*
(off Driffield Rd.)
Margaret Bldgs. N16 32Vb 71
Margaret Cl. CM16: Epp 1Vc 23
E11 30Gc 53
EN6: Pot B 5Eb 17
EN9: Walt A 5Fc 21
RM2: Rom 29Kd 57
TW18: Staines 65M 127
WD5: Ab L 4V 12
Margaret Ct. EN4: E Barn 14Fb 31
W1 2B 222
Margaret Dr. RM11: Horn 32Pd 77
Margaret Gardner Dr. SE9 61Pc 138
Margaret Harvey Gallery 1C 6
(within University of Hertfordshire)
Margaret Herbison Ho. *SW6* *51Bb 111*
(off Clem Attlee Ct.)
Margaret Ho. *W6* *50Ya 88*
(off Queen Caroline St.)
WD5: Ab L 2U 12
Margaret Ingram Cl. SW6 51Bb 111
Margaret Lockwood Cl.
KT1: King T 70Pa 131
Margaret McMillan Ho. E16 44Lc 93
Margaret Rd. CM16: Epp 1Wc 23
DA5: Bexl 58Zc 117
EN4: E Barn 14Fb 31
N16 32Vb 71
RM2: Rom 29Kd 57
Margaret Rutherford Pl. SW12 60Lb 112
Margaret St. W1 2A 222 (44Kb 90)

Margaretta Ter. SW3 51Gb 111
Margaretting Rd. E12 32Lc 73
Margaret Way CR5: Coul 91Rb 197
IG4: Ilf 30Nc 54
Margaret White Ho. NW1 3D 216
Margate Rd. SW2 57Nb 112
Margeholes WD19: Wat 19Aa 27
MARGERY 1J 207
Margery Fry Ct. N7 34Nb 70
Margery Gro. KT20: Lwr K 1G 206
Margery La. KT20: Lwr K 1H 207
Margery Pk. Rd. E7 37Jc 73
Margery Rd. RM8: Dag 34Zc 75
Margery St. WC1 4K 217 (41Qb 90)
Margery Ter. E7 37Jc 73
(off Margery Pk. Rd.)
Margery Wood La.
KT20: Lwr K, Reig 1H 207
Margherita Pl. EN9: Walt A 6Hc 21
Margherita Rd. EN9: Walt A 6Jc 21
Margin Dr. SW19 64Za 132
Margravine Gdns. W6 50Za 88
Margravine Rd. W6 50Za 88
Marham Dr. NW9 25Ua 48
Marham Gdns. SM4: Mord 72Eb 155
SW18 60Gb 111
Maria Cl. SE1 49Xb 91
Maria Ct. SE25 68Ub 135
Mariam Gdns. RM12: Horn 33Pd 77
Marian Cl. RM16: N Stif 46Ae 99
UB4: Yead 42Z 85
Marian Ct. E9 36Yb 72
SM1: Sutt 78Db 155
Marian Gdns. WD25: Wat 5X 13
Marian Lawson Ct. IG7: Chig 22Wc 55
Marian Pl. E2 40Xb 71
Marian Rd. SW16 67Lb 134
Marian St. E2 40Xb 71
Marian Way NW10 38Va 68
Maria Ter. E1 43Zb 92
Maria Theresa Cl. KT3: N Mald 71Ta 153
Maribor SE10 52Ec 114
(off Burney St.)
Maricas Av. HA3: Hrw W 25Fa 46
Marie Curie SE5 53Ub 113
Marie Lloyd Gdns. N19 31Nb 70
Marie Lloyd Ho. N1 2F 219
Marie Lloyd Wlk. E8 37Vb 71
Marie Mnr. Way DA2: Dart 56Ud 120
Mariette Way SM6: Wall 81Nb 176
Marigold All. SE1 5B 224 (45Rb 91)
Marigold Ct. UB1: S'hall 45Aa 85
Marigold Dr. GU24: Bisl 7E 166
Marigold Rd. N17 24Yb 52
Marigold St. SE16 47Xb 91
Marigold Way CR0: C'don 74Zb 158
Marina App. UB4: Yead 43Aa 85
Marina Av. KT3: N Mald 71Xa 154
Marina Cl. BR2: Brom 69Jc 137
KT16: Chert 74L 149
Marina Ct. E3 41Bc 92
(off Alfred St.)
SW6 54Eb 111
Marina Dr. DA1: Dart 60Qd 119
DA11: Nflt 9B 122
DA16: Well 54Uc 116
Marina Gdns. EN8: Chesh 2Yb 20
RM7: Rom 29Ed 56
Marina One N1 1G 217
Marina Pl. KT1: Hamp W 67Ma 131
Marina Point E14 48Dc 92
(off Goulston St.)
Marina Way SL0: Iver 45J 83
SL1: Slou 5B 80
TW11: Tedd 66Ma 131
Marine Ct. DA8: Erith 52Hd 118
E11 33Gc 73
RM19: Purf 49Pd 97
Marine Dr. IG11: Bark 42Wc 95
SE18 49Pc 94
Marinefield Rd. SW6 54Db 111
Marinel Ho. SE5 52Sb 113
Mariner Bus. Cen. CR0: Wadd 78Qb 156
Mariner Gdns. TW10: Ham 62La 130
Mariner Rd. E12 35Qc 74
Mariners Cl. EN4: E Barn 15Fb 31
Mariners Ct. DA9: Ghithe 56Xd 120
(off High St.)
Mariners M. E14 49Fc 93
Mariners Wlk. DA8: Erith 51Hd 118
Mariners Way DA11: Nflt 9A 122
Mariner Way HP2: Hem H 3A 4
Marine St. SE16 48Wb 91
Marine Twr. SE8 51Bc 114
(off Abinger Gro.)
Marion Av. TW17: Shep 71R 150
Marion Cl. IG6: Ilf 24Tc 54
WD23: Bush 11Ba 27
Marion Cres. BR5: St M Cry 71Wc 161
Marion Gro. IG8: Wfd G 22Gc 53
Marion Ho. NW1 39Hb 69
(off Regent's Pk. Rd.)
Marion M. SE21 62Tb 135
Marion Rd. CR7: Thor H 71Sb 157
NW7 22Wa 48
Marischal Rd. SE13 55Fc 115
Marisco Cl. RM16: Grays 9D 100
Marish Ct. SL3: L'ly 48C 82
Marish La. UB9: Den 29E 42
(not continuous)
Marish Wharf SL3: L'ly 47A 82
Maritime Cl. DA9: Ghithe 57Xd 120
Maritime Ga. DA11: Nflt 9A 122
Maritime Ho. SE18 49Rc 94
Maritime Ind. Est. SE7 49Kc 93
Maritime Quay E14 50Cc 92
Maritime St. E3 42Bc 92
Marius Mans. SW17 61Jb 134
Marius Rd. SW17 61Jb 134
Marjoram Cl. SS17: Stan H 1M 101
Marjorams Av. IG10: Lough 12Qc 36
Marjorie Fosters Way GU24: Brkwd 1B 186
Marjorie Gro. SW11 56Hb 111
Marjorie M. E1 44Zb 92
Markab Rd. HA6: Nwood 22V 44
Mark Av. E4 16Dc 34
Mark Cl. DA7: Bex 53Ad 117
UB1: S'hall 45Da 85
Mark Dr. SL9: Chal P 21A 42
Marke Cl. BR2: Kes 77Nc 160
Markedge La. CR5: Coul 96Hb 195
RH1: Mers 96Hb 195
Markeston Grn. WD19: Wat 21Z 45
Market, The SM5: Sutt 74Eb 155
Market All. DA12: Grav'nd 8D 122
Market App. W12 47Ya 88
Market Centre, The UB2: S'hall 49X 85
Market Chambers EN2: Enf 13Tb 33
(off Church St.)
Market Ct. W1 2B 222
Market Dr. W4 52Ua 110
Market Entrance SW8 52Lb 112
Market Est. N7 37Nb 70
Marketfield Rd. RH1: Redh 6P 207
Marketfield Way RH1: Redh 6P 207
Market Hall N22 26Qb 50
Market Hill SE18 48Qc 94
Market Ho. SL9: Chal P 25A 42
Market La. HA8: Edg 25Sa 47
SL0: Iver 48E 82
SL3: L'ly 48E 82
W12 47Ya 88
Market Link RM1: Rom 28Gd 56
Market Mdw. BR5: St M Cry 70Yc 139
Market M. W1 7K 221 (46Kb 90)
Market Oak La. HP3: Hem H 6A 4
Market Pde. BR1: Brom 67Jc 137
(off East St.)
DA14: Sidc 63Xc 139
E10 30Ec 52
(off High Rd. Leyton)
E17 27Bc 52
(off Higham Hill Rd.)
KT17: Ewe 81Va 174
(off High St.)
N9 19Wb 33
(off Winchester Rd.)
N16 32Wb 71
(off Oldhill St.)
SE25 70Wb 135
TW13: Hanw 62Aa 129
Market Pav. E10 34Cc 72
Market Pl. AL3: St A 2B 6
DA1: Dart 59Nd 119
DA6: Bex 56Cd 118
EN2: Enf 13Tb 33
KT1: King T 68Ma 131
N2 27Gb 49
RM1: Rom 29Gd 56
RM4: Abr 13Xc 37
RM18: Tilb 4C 122
SE16 49Wb 91
(not continuous)
SL3: Coln 52E 104
SL9: Chal P 25A 42
TW8: Bford 52La 108
UB1: S'hall 46Ba 85
W1 2B 222 (44Lb 90)
W3 46Sa 87
Market Pl., The NW11 28Eb 49
Market Rd. N7 37Nb 70
TW9: Rich 55Qa 109
Market Row SW9 56Qb 112
Market Sq. BR1: Brom 68Jc 137
(not continuous)
E14 44Dc 92
EN9: Walt A 5Ec 20
GU21: Wok 89A 168
KT1: King T 68Ma 131
(off Market Pl.)
TN16: Westrm 98Tc 200
TW18: Staines 64G 126
UB8: Uxb 38L 63
Market Sq., The N9 19Xb 33
(within Edmonton Grn. Shop. Cen.)
Market St. DA1: Dart 59Nd 119
E1 7K 219 (43Vb 91)
E6 40Pc 74
SE18 49Qc 94
SL4: Wind 3H 103
WD18: Wat 14X 27
Market Ter. TW8: Bford 51Na 109
(off Albany Rd.)
Market Trad. Est. UB2: S'hall 49X 85
Market Way E14 44Dc 92
HA0: Wemb 36Na 67
TN16: Westrm 98Tc 200
Market Yd. M. SE1 3H 231 (47Ub 91)
Markfield CR0: Sels 82Bc 178
(not continuous)
Markfield Beam Engine & Museum
29Wb 51
Markfield Gdns. E4 17Dc 34
Markfield Rd. CR3: Cat'm 98Xb 197
N15 28Wb 51
Markham Cl. WD6: Bore 12Pa 29
Markham Ho. RM10: Dag 34Cd 76
(off Uvedale Rd.)
Markham Pl. SW3 7F 227 (50Hb 89)
Markhams SS17: Stan H 1P 101
Markham Sq.
SW3 7F 227 (50Hb 89)
Markham St. SW3 7E 226 (50Gb 89)
Markhole Cl. TW12: Hamp 66Ba 129
Mark Ho. E2 40Zb 72
(off Sewardstone Rd.)
Markhouse Av. E17 30Ac 52
Markhouse Pas. E17 30Bc 52
(off Downsfield Rd.)
Markhouse Rd. E17 30Bc 52
Markland Ho. W10 45Za 88
(off Darfield Way)
Mark La. DA12: Grav'nd 9G 122
(not continuous)
EC3 4J 225 (45Ub 91)
Mark Lodge EN4: Cockf 14Gb 31
(off Edgeworth Rd.)
Markmanor Av. E17 31Ac 72
Mark Oak La. KT22: Fet 94Ca 191
Mark Rd. HP2: Hem H 1B 4
N22 26Rb 51
Marksbury Av. TW9: Rich 55Qa 109
MARKS GATE 25Ad 55
Mark Sq. EC2 5H 219 (42Ub 91)
Marks Rd. CR6: W'ham 90Ac 178
RM7: Rom 29Ed 56
(not continuous)
Marks Sq. DA11: Nflt 3B 144
Markstone Ho. SE1 2B 230
Mark St. E15 38Gc 73
EC2 5H 219 (42Ub 91)
RH2: Reig 5K 207
Markville Gdns. CR3: Cat'm 97Wb 197
Mark Wade Cl. E12 32Mc 73
Mark Way BR8: Swan 71Jd 162
Markway TW16: Sun 68Y 129
Markwell Cl. SE26 63Xb 135
Markyate Ho. W10 42Ya 88
(off Sutton Way)
Markyate Rd. RM8: Dag 36Xc 75
Marland Ho. SW1 3G 227
Marlands Rd. IG5: Ilf 27Nc 54
Marlborough SW19 60Za 110
(off Inner Pk. Rd.)
W9 3A 214
Marlborough Av. E8 39Wb 71
(not continuous)
HA4: Ruis 30S 44
HA8: Edg 20Ra 29
N14 20Lb 32
Marlborough Bldgs. AL1: St A 2C 6
Marlborough Bus. Cen.
KT16: Chert 75H 149
Marlborough Cl. BR6: Orp 72Vc 161
KT12: Hers 76Z 151
N20 20Hb 31
RM14: Upm 32Ud 78
RM16: Grays 47Ee 99
SE17 6C 230 (49Sb 91)
SW19 65Gb 133
Marlborough Ct. CR2: S Croy 77Ub 157
(off Birdhurst Rd.)
EN1: Enf 15Ub 33
HA1: Harr 28Fa 46
HA6: Nwood 24V 44
IG9: Buck H 19Lc 35
N17 25Wb 51
(off Kemble Rd.)
SM6: Wall 80Lb 156
TN16: Westrm 98Sc 200
(off Croydon Rd.)
W1 3B 222
W8 49Cb 89
(off Pembroke Rd.)
Marlborough Cres. TN13: S'oaks 96Gd 202
UB3: Harl 52T 106
W4 48Ta 87
Marlborough Dr. IG5: Ilf 27Nc 54
KT13: Weyb 76S 150
WD23: Bush 14Ba 27
Marlborough Flats SW3 5E 226
Marlborough Gdns. KT6: Surb 73Ma 153
N20 20Hb 31
RM14: Upm 32Td 78
Marlborough Ga. AL1: St A 2C 6
Marlborough Ga. Ho. W2 4B 220
Marlborough Gro. SE1 50Wb 91
Marlborough Hill HA1: Harr 28Fa 46
NW8 1A 214 (40Eb 69)
Marlborough House 7C 222 (46Lb 90)
Marlborough Ho. E16 46Jc 93
(off Hardy Av.)
UB7: W Dray 47P 83
Marlborough La. SE7 51Lc 115
Marlborough Lodge NW8 2A 214
Marlborough Mans. NW6 36Db 69
(off Canon Hill)
Marlborough M. SM7: Bans 87Cb 175
SW2 56Pb 112
Marlborough Pde. HA8: Edg 20Ra 29
(off Marlborough Av.)
UB10: Hil 42R 84
Marlborough Pk. Av. DA15: Sidc 59Wc 117
Marlborough Pl. NW8 2A 214 (40Eb 69)
Marlborough Rd. AL1: St A 2C 6
BR2: Brom 70Lc 137
CM15: Pil H 16Wd 40
CR2: S Croy 80Sb 157
DA1: Dart 58Ld 119
DA7: Bex 55Zc 117
E4 23Dc 52
E7 38Lc 73
E15 35Gc 73
E18 26Jc 53
GU21: Wok 88C 168
N9 18Wb 33
N19 33Mb 70
N22 24Nb 50
RM7: Mawney 28Cd 56
RM8: Dag 35Xc 75
SE18 48Rc 94
SE28 48Sc 94
SL3: L'ly 9P 81
SM1: Sutt 76Cb 155
SW1 7C 222 (46Lb 90)
SW19 65Gb 133
TW7: Isle 53Ka 108
TW10: Rich 58Pa 109
TW12: Hamp 65Ca 129
TW13: Felt 61Z 129
TW15: Ashf 64M 127
UB2: S'hall 48Y 85
UB10: Hil 42R 84
W4 50Sa 87
W5 47Ma 87
WD18: Wat 14X 27
Marlborough St. SW3 6D 226 (49Gb 89)
Marlborough Yd. N19 33Mb 70
Marlbury NW8 39Db 69
(off Abbey Rd.)
Marld, The KT21: Asht 90Pa 173
Marle Gdns. EN9: Walt A 4Ec 20
Marler Ho. DA8: Erith 54Hd 118
Marler Rd. SE23 60Ac 114
Marlescroft Way IG10: Lough 15Rc 36
Marley Av. DA7: Bex 51Zc 117
Marley Cl. KT15: Add 79H 149
N15 28Rb 51
UB6: G'frd 41Ca 85
Marley Ho. E16 45Rc 94
(off University Way)
W11 45Za 88
(off St Ann's Rd.)
Marley St. SE16 49Zb 92
Marley Wlk. NW2 36Ya 68
Marlfield Cl. KT4: Wor Pk 74Wa 154
Marlin Cl. TW16: Sun 65U 128
Marling Ct. TW12: Hamp 65Ba 129
Marlingdene Cl. TW12: Hamp 65Ca 129
MARLING PARK 66Ba 129
Marlings Cl. BR7: Chst 70Uc 138
CR3: Whyt 89Ub 177
Marlings Pk. Av. BR7: Chst 70Uc 138
Marling Way DA12: Grav'nd 5G 144
Marlin Ho. WD18: Wat 16T 26
Marlins, The HA6: Nwood 22V 44
Marlins Cl. SM1: Sutt 78Eb 155
WD3: Chor 12G 24
Marlins Mdw. WD18: Wat 16T 26
Marlin Sq. WD5: Ab L 3V 12
Marloes Cl. HA0: Wemb 35Ma 67
Marloes Rd. W8 48Db 89
Marlow Av. RM19: Purf 49Qd 97
Marlow Cl. SE20 69Xb 135
Marlow Ct. N14 17Lb 32
NW6 38Za 68
NW9 27Va 48
Marlow Cres. TW1: Twick 58Ha 108
Marlow Dr. SM3: Cheam 75Za 154
Marlowe Bus. Cen. SE14 52Ac 114
(off Batavia Rd.)
Marlowe Cl. BR7: Chst 65Tc 138
IG6: Ilf 25Sc 54
Marlowe Ct. SE19 64Vb 135
SW3 6E 226
Marlowe Gdns. RM3: Rom 25Ld 57
SE9 58Qc 116
Marlowe Ho. IG8: Wfd G 24Qc 54
KT1: King T 70Ma 131
(off Portsmouth Rd.)
Marlowe Path SE8 51Cc 114
Marlowe Rd. E17 28Ec 52
Marlowes HP1: Hem H 2M 3
Marlowes, The DA1: Cray 56Fd 118
NW8 39Fb 69
Marlowes Cen., The HP1: Hem H 3L 3
Marlowe Sq. CR4: Mitc 70Lb 134
Marlowe Way CR0: Bedd 75Nb 156
Marlow Gdns. UB3: Harl 48T 84
Marlow Ho. E2 4K 219
KT5: Surb 71Na 153
(off Cranes Pk.)
SE1 3K 231
TW11: Tedd 63Ja 130
W2 44Db 89
(off Hallfield Est.)
Marlow Rd. E6 41Pc 94
SE20 69Xb 135
UB2: S'hall 48Ba 85
Marlow Way SE16 47Zb 92
Marlow Workshops E2 4K 219
Marlpit Av. CR5: Coul 89Nb 176
Marlpit La. CR5: Coul 88Mb 176
Marl Rd. SW18 56Eb 111
Marlton St. SE10 50Hc 93
Marlwood Cl. DA15: Sidc 61Uc 138
Marlyon Rd. IG6: Ilf 22Xc 55
Marmadon Rd. SE18 49Vc 95
Marmara Apartments E16 45Jc 93
(off Western Gateway)
Marmion App. E4 21Cc 52
Marmion Av. E4 21Bc 52
Marmion Cl. E4 21Bc 52
Marmion M. SW11 55Jb 112
Marmion Rd. SW11 56Jb 112
Marmont Rd. SE15 53Wb 113
Marmora Rd. SE22 58Yb 114
Marmot Rd. TW4: Houn 55Z 107
Marncrest Cl. KT12: Hers 78X 151
Marne Av. DA16: Well 55Wc 117
N11 21Kb 50
Marnell Way TW4: Houn 55Z 107
Marne St. W10 41Ab 88
Marney Rd. SW11 56Jb 112
Marneys Cl. KT18: Eps 87Qa 173
Marnfield Cres. SW2 60Qb 112
Marnham Av. NW2 35Ab 68
Marnham Ct. HA0: Wemb 36La 66
Marnham Cres. UB6: G'frd 41Da 85
Marnham Pl. KT15: Add 77L 149
Marnham Ri. HP1: Hem H 1J 3
Marnock Ho. SE17 7F 231
Marnock Rd. SE4 57Bc 114
Maroon St. E14 43Ac 92
Maroons Way SE6 64Cc 136
Marqueen Ct. W8 47Db 89
(off Kensington Chu. St.)
Marqueen Towers SW16 66Pb 134
Marquess Hgts. E18 25Kc 53
Marquess Rd. N1 37Tb 71
Marquis Cl. HA0: Wemb 38Pa 67
Marquis Ct. IG11: Bark 36Uc 74
KT1: King T 70Ma 131
(off Anglesea Rd.)
KT19: Eps 85Ta 173
N4 32Pb 70
(off Marquis Rd.)
TW19: Stanw 60N 105
Marquis Rd. N4 32Pb 70
N22 23Pb 50
NW1 37Mb 70
Marrabon Cl. DA15: Sidc 60Wc 117
Marram Ct. RM17: Grays 1A 122
Marrick Cl. SW15 56Wa 110
Marrick Ho. NW6 39Db 69
(off Mortimer Cres.)
Marriett Ho. SE6 63Ec 136
Marrilyne Av. EN3: Enf L 10Bc 20
Marriner Ct. UB3: Hayes 45U 84
(off Barra Hall Rd.)
Marriott Cl. TW14: Felt 58T 106
Marriot Ter. WD3: Chor 14H 25
Marriott Lodge Cl. KT15: Add 77L 149
Marriott Rd. DA1: Dart 59Pd 119
E15 39Gc 73
EN5: Barn 13Za 30
N4 32Pb 70
N10 25Hb 49
Marriotts Cl. NW9 30Va 48
Marriotts Way HP3: Hem H 4M 3
Marriotts Wharf DA11: Grav'nd 7D 122
Mar Rd. RM15: S Ock 42Yd 98
Marrowells KT13: Weyb 76V 150
Marryat Cl. TW4: Houn 56Ba 107
Marryat Ho. SW1 7B 228
Marryat Pl. SW19 63Ab 132
Marryat Rd. EN1: Enf 7Xb 19
SW19 64Za 132
Marryat Sq. SW6 53Ab 110
Marsala Rd. SE13 56Dc 114
Marsalis Ho. E3 41Cc 92
(off Rainhill Way)
Marsden Gdns. DA1: Dart 54Pd 119
Marsden Rd. N9 19Xb 33
SE15 55Vb 113
Marsden St. NW5 37Jb 70
Marsden Way BR6: Orp 77Vc 161
Marshall Bldg. W2 1B 220
Marshall Cl. CR2: Sande 85Wb 177
HA1: Harr 31Fa 66
SW18 58Eb 111
TW4: Houn 57Ba 107
Marshall Ct. NW6 38Za 68
(off Coverdale Rd.)
SE20 66Xb 135
(off Anerley Pk.)
Marshall Dr. UB4: Hayes 43V 84
Marshall Est. NW7 21Wa 48
Marshall Ho. N1 1G 219
NW6 40Bb 69
(off Albert Rd.)
SE1 4J 231
SE17 7F 231
Marshall Pde. GU22: Pyr 87H 169
Marshall Path SE28 45Xc 95
Marshall Pl. KT15: New H 81L 169
Marshall Rd. E10 34Dc 72
(not continuous)
N17 25Tb 51
Marshalls Cl. KT19: Eps 85Sa 173
N11 21Kb 50
Marshalls Ct. AL1: St A 1F 6
Marshalls Dr. RM1: Rom 27Gd 56
Marshalls Gro. SE18 49Nc 94
Marshall's Pl. SE16 4K 231 (48Vb 91)
Marshalls Rd. RM7: Rom 28Fd 56
SM1: Sutt 77Db 155
Marshall St. NW10 38Ta 67
W1 3C 222 (44Lb 90)
Marshall Street Leisure Cen.
3C 222 (44Lb 90)
Marshalsea Rd. SE1 1E 230 (47Sb 91)
Marshalswick La. AL1: St A 1F 6
Marsham Cl. BR7: Chst 64Rc 138
Marsham Ct. SW1 5E 228 (49Mb 90)
Marsham La. SL9: Ger X 30A 42
Marsham Lodge SL9: Ger X 30A 42
Marsham St. SW1 4E 228 (48Mb 90)
Marsham Way SL9: Ger X 29A 42
Marsh Av. CR4: Mitc 68Hb 133
KT19: Ewe 82Ua 174
Marshbrook Cl. SE3 55Mc 115
Marsh Centre, The E1 2K 225
Marsh Cl. EN8: Walt C 5Ac 20
NW7 20Va 30
Marsh Ct. E8 37Wb 71
SW19 67Eb 133
Marshcroft Dr. EN8: Chesh 2Ac 20
Marsh Dr. NW9 30Va 48
Marshe Cl. EN6: Pot B 4Fb 17
Marsh Farm Rd. TW2: Twick 60Ha 108
Marshfield SL3: Dat 3N 103
Marshfield St. E14 48Ec 92
Marshfoot Rd. RM16: Grays 10B 100
RM17: Grays 10A 100
Marshgate La. E15 40Ec 72
Marshgate Path SE28 48Sc 94
Marsh Grn. Rd. RM10: Dag 39Cd 76
Marsh Hall HA9: Wemb 34Pa 67
Marsh Hill E9 36Ac 72
Marsh Ho. SW1 50Mb 90
(off Aylesford St.)
SW8 53Lb 112
Marsh La. E10 33Bc 72
HA7: Stan 22La 46
KT15: Add 77K 149
N17 24Xb 51
NW7 20Ua 30
MARSHMOOR 4E 8
Marshmoor Cres. AL9: Wel G 4F 8
Marshmoor La. AL9: Wel G 4E 8
Marsh Rd. HA0: Wemb 41Ma 87
HA5: Pinn 28Aa 45
Marshside Cl. N9 18Yb 34
Marsh St. DA1: Dart 55Qd 119
(Halcrow Av., not continuous)
DA1: Dart 57Pd 119
(Hilltop Gdns.)
E14 49Dc 92
Marsh St. Nth. DA1: Dart 54Qd 119
Marsh Vw. DA12: Grav'nd 10H 123
Marsh Wall E14 46Cc 92
Marsh Way RM13: Dag, Rain 41Fd 96
Marshwood Ho. NW6 39Cb 69
(off Kilburn Vale)
Marshwood Rd. GU18: Light 3B 166
Marsland Cl. SE17 7C 230 (50Rb 91)
Marsom Ho. N1 2F 219
Marston KT19: Eps 83Sa 173
Marston Av. KT9: Chess 79Na 153
RM10: Dag 33Cd 76
Marston Cl. HP3: Hem H 3A 4
NW6 38Eb 69
RM10: Dag 34Cd 76
Marston Ct. DA9: Ghithe 56Wd 120
KT12: Walt T 74Y 151
Marston Dr. CR6: W'ham 90Ac 178
Marston Ho. RM17: Grays 51Ce 121
SW9 54Qb 112
Marston Rd. GU21: Wok 9M 167
IG5: Ilf 25Nc 54
TW11: Tedd 64Ka 130
Marston Way SE19 66Rb 135
Marsworth Av. HA5: Pinn 25Z 45
Marsworth Cl. UB4: Yead 43Aa 85
WD18: Wat 16U 26
Marsworth Ho. E2 39Wb 71
(off Whiston Rd.)
Martaban Rd. N16 33Vb 71
Martara M. SE17 7D 230 (50Sb 91)
Marta Rose Ct. SE20 68Xb 135
(off Wadhurst Cl.)
Martello Ct. RM17: Grays 51Fe 121
Martello St. E8 38Xb 71
Martello Ter. E8 38Xb 71
Martell Rd. SE21 62Tb 135
Martel Pl. E8 37Vb 71
Marten Rd. E17 26Cc 52
Martens Av. DA7: Bex 56Dd 118
Martens Cl. DA7: Bex 56Ed 118
Martham Cl. IG6: Ilf 25Rc 54
SE28 45Zc 95
Martha Rd. E15 37Gc 73
Martha's Bldgs. EC1 5F 219 (42Tb 91)
Martha St. E1 44Yb 92
Marthorne Cres. HA3: Hrw W 26Fa 46
Martina Ter. IG7: Chig 22Uc 54
Martin Bowes Rd. SE9 55Pc 116
Martinbridge Trad. Est.
EN1: Enf 15Wb 33
Martin Cl. AL10: Hat 2C 8
CR2: Sels 83Zb 178
CR6: W'ham 88Xb 177
N9 18Zb 34
SL4: Wind 3A 102
UB10: Uxb 40N 63
Martin Ct. AL1: St A 2C 6
(off St Peter's St.)
CR2: S Croy 78Ub 157
(off Birdhurst Rd.)
E14 47Ec 92
(off River Barge Cl.)
Martin Cres. CR0: C'don 74Qb 156
Martindale SL0: Iver 42F 82
SW14 57Sa 109
Martindale Av. BR6: Chels 78Wc 161
E16 45Jc 93
Martindale Ho. E14 45Dc 92
(off Poplar High St.)
Martin Dale Ind. Est. EN1: Enf 13Xb 33

Martindale Rd. GU21: Wok ... 10L 167
HP1: Hem H ... 1H 3
SW12 ... 59Kb 112
TW4: Houn ... 55Aa 107
Martin Dene DA6: Bex ... 57Bd 117
Martin Dr. DA2: Dart ... 59Sd 120
RM13: Rain ... 42Kd 97
UB5: N'olt ... 36Ba 65
Martineau Cl. KT10: Esh ... 77Fa 152
Martineau Dr. TW1: Twick ... 56Ka 108
Martineau Est. E1 ... 45Yb 92
Martineau Ho. SL9: Chal P ... 22A 42
SW1 ... 7B 228
Martineau M. N5 ... 35Rb 71
Martineau Rd. N5 ... 35Rb 71
Martingale Cl. TW16: Sun ... 70W 128
Martingales Cl. TW10: Ham ... 62Ma 131
Martin Gdns. RM8: Dag ... 35Yc 75
Martin Gro. SM4: Mord ... 69Cb 133
Martin Ho. DA11: Nflt ... 2C 144
E3 ... 39Bc 72
(off Old Ford Rd.)
SE1 ... 4E 230 (48Sb 91)
SW8 ... 52Nb 112
(off Wyvil Rd.)
Martini Dr. EN3: Enf L ... 9Cc 20
Martin La. EC4 ... 4G 225 (45Tb 91)
(not continuous)
Martin Ri. DA6: Bex ... 57Bd 117
Martin Rd. DA2: Wilm ... 62Ld 141
RM8: Dag ... 35Yc 75
RM15: Avel ... 46Td 98
SL1: Slou ... 8J 81
Martins, The HA9: Wemb ... 34Pa 67
SE26 ... 64Xb 135
Martins Cl. BR4: W W'ck ... 74Fc 159
BR5: St P ... 69Zc 139
SS17: Stan H ... 1M 101
WD7: R'lett ... 8Ga 14
Martins Ct. AL1: St A ... 5F 6
Martins Dr. EN8: Chesh ... 1Ac 20
Martinsfield Cl. IG7: Chig ... 21Uc 54
Martin's Mt. EN5: New Bar ... 14Cb 31
Martins Pl. SE28 ... 46Uc 94
Martin's Plain SL2: Stoke P ... 1K 81
Martin's Rd. BR2: Brom ... 68Gc 137
Martins Shaw TN13: Chip ... 94Ed 202
Martinstown Cl. RM11: Horn ... 30Qd 57
Martin St. SE28 ... 46Uc 94
Martins Wlk. N10 ... 25Jb 50
N22 ... 27Qb 50
SE28 ... 46Uc 94
WD6: Bore ... 14Qa 29
Martinsyde GU22: Wok ... 89E 168
Martin Way GU21: Wok ... 10L 167
SM4: Mord ... 68Za 132
SW20 ... 68Za 132
Martlands Ind. Est. GU22: Wok ... 5L 187
Martlesham *N17* ... 26Ub 51
(off Adams Rd.)
Martlesham Cl. RM12: Horn ... 36Ld 77
Martlesham Wlk. NW9 ... 26Ua 48
(not continuous)
Martlet Gro. UB5: N'olt ... 41Z 85
Martlett Ct. WC2 ... 3G 223 (44Nb 90)
Martley Dr. IG2: Ilf ... 29Rc 54
Martock Cl. HA3: W'stone ... 28Ja 46
Martock Gdns. N11 ... 22Hb 49
Marton Cl. SE6 ... 62Cc 136
Marton Rd. N16 ... 33Ub 71
Martynside NW9 ... 25Va 48
Martyr Cl. AL1: St A ... 6B 6
MARTYR'S GREEN ... 92T 190
Martyr's La. GU21: Wok ... 84D 168
Martys Yd. NW3 ... 35Fb 69
Marunden Grn. SL2: Slou ... 1D 80
Marvell Av. UB4: Hayes ... 43W 84
Marvell Ct. *RM6: Chad H* ... 30Xc 55
(off Quarles Pk. Rd.)
Marvell Ho. *SE5* ... 52Tb 113
(off Camberwell Rd.)
Marvels Cl. SE12 ... 61Kc 137
Marvels La. SE12 ... 61Kc 137
Marville Rd. SW6 ... 52Bb 111
Marvin St. E8 ... 37Xb 71
Marwell TN16: Westrm ... 98Rc 200
Marwell Cl. BR4: W W'ck ... 75Hc 159
RM1: Rom ... 29Jd 56
Marwood Cl. DA16: Well ... 55Xc 117
WD4: K Lan ... 1P 11
Marwood Dr. NW7 ... 24Za 48
Mary Adelaide Cl. SW15 ... 63Ua 132
Mary Ann Gdns. SE8 ... 51Cc 114
Maryatt Av. HA2: Harr ... 33Da 65
Marybank SE18 ... 49Pc 94
Mary Bayly Ho. *W11* ... 46Ab 88
(off Wilsham St.)
Mary Boast Wlk. SE5 ... 54Tb 113
Mary Burrows Gdns.
TN15: Kems'g ... 89Rd 183
Mary Cl. HA7: Stan ... 28Pa 47
Mary Datchelor Cl. SE5 ... 53Tb 113
Mary Datchelor Ho. *SE5* ... 53Tb 113
(off Grove La.)
Mary Drew Almshouses
TW20: Eng G ... 5P 125
Maryfield Cl. DA5: Bexl ... 62Gd 140
Mary Flux Ct. *SW5* ... 50Db 89
(off Bramham Gdns.)
Mary Grn. NW8 ... 39Db 69
Maryhill Cl. CR8: Kenley ... 89Sb 177
Mary Holben Ho. SW16 ... 64Lb 134
Mary Ho. *W6* ... 50Ya 88
(off Queen Caroline St.)
Mary Jones Ct. *E14* ... 45Cc 92
(off Garford St.)
Maryland AL10: Hat ... 1B 8
Maryland Ind. Est. E15 ... 36Gc 73
Maryland Pk. E15 ... 36Gc 73
(not continuous)
Maryland Point *E15* ... 37Gc 73
(off The Grove)
Maryland Rd. CR7: Thor H ... 67Rb 135
E15 ... 36Fc 73
N22 ... 23Pb 50
MARYLANDS INTERCHANGE ... 13Ee 41
Maryland Sq. E15 ... 36Gc 73
Marylands Rd. W9 ... 42Cb 89
(not continuous)
Maryland St. E15 ... 36Fc 73
Maryland Wlk. *N1* ... 39Sb 71
(off Popham St.)
Maryland Way TW16: Sun ... 68W 128
Mary Lawrenson Pl. SE3 ... 52Jc 115
MARYLEBONE ... 7J 215 (43Jb 90)
Marylebone Cricket Club ... 3C 214
MARYLEBONE FLYOVER ... 1D 220 (43Gb 89)
Marylebone Fly-Over
NW1 ... 1C 220 (43Fb 89)
W2 ... 1C 220 (43Fb 89)
Marylebone Gdns. TW9: Rich ... 56Qa 109
Marylebone High St. W1 ... 7J 215 (43Jb 90)
Marylebone La. W1 ... 1J 221 (43Jb 90)
Marylebone M. W1 ... 1K 221 (43Kb 90)
Marylebone Pas. W1 ... 2C 222 (44Lb 90)
Marylebone Rd. NW1 ... 7E 214 (43Gb 89)
Marylebone St. W1 ... 1J 221 (43Jb 90)
Marylee Way SE11 ... 6J 229 (49Pb 90)
Mary Macarthur Ho. *E2* ... 41Zb 92
(off Warley St.)
RM10: Dag ... 34Cd 76
(off Wythenshawe Rd.)
W6 ... 51Ab 110
Mary Morgan Ct. SL2: Slou ... 3H 81
Mary Neuner Rd. N8 ... 27Pb 50
N22 ... 27Pb 50
Maryon Gro. SE7 ... 49Nc 94
Maryon Ho. *NW6* ... 38Eb 69
(off Goldhurst Ter.)
Maryon M. NW3 ... 35Gb 69
Maryon Rd. SE7 ... 49Nc 94
SE18 ... 49Nc 94
Mary Peters Dr. UB6: G'frd ... 36Fa 66
Mary Pl. W11 ... 45Ab 88
Mary Rose Cl. RM16: Chaf H ... 49Yd 98
TW12: Hamp ... 67Ca 129
Mary Rose Mall E6 ... 43Pc 94
Maryrose Way N20 ... 18Fb 31
Marys Ct. NW1 ... 5E 214
Mary Seacole Cl. E8 ... 39Vb 71
Mary Seacole Ho. *W6* ... 48Wa 88
(off Invermead Cl.)
Maryside SL3: L'ly ... 47A 82
Mary Smith Ct. *SW5* ... 49Cb 89
(off Trebovir Rd.)
Marysmith Ho. SW1 ... 7E 228
Mary's Ter. TW1: Twick ... 59Ja 108
Mary St. E16 ... 43Hc 93
N1 ... 1E 218 (39Sb 71)
Mary Ter. NW1 ... 1A 216 (39Kb 70)
Maryville DA16: Well ... 54Vc 117
Mary Wallace Theatre ... 60Ja 108
Mary Way WD19: Wat ... 21Y 45
Mary Wharrie Ho. *NW3* ... 38Hb 69
(off Fellows Rd.)
Marzell Ho. *W14* ... 50Bb 89
(off North End Rd.)
Marzena Ct. TW3: Houn ... 58Ea 108
Masault Ct. *TW9: Rich* ... 56Na 109
(off Kew Foot Rd.)
Masbro' Rd. W14 ... 48Za 88
Mascalls Ct. SE7 ... 51Lc 115
Mascalls Gdns. CM14: B'wood ... 21Vd 58
Mascalls La. CM13: Gt War ... 21Vd 58
CM14: B'wood, Gt War ... 21Vd 58
Mascalls Rd. SE7 ... 51Lc 115
Mascoll Path SL2: Slou ... 1D 80
Mascotte Rd. SW15 ... 56Za 110
Mascotts Cl. NW2 ... 34Xa 68
Masefield Av. HA7: Stan ... 22Ha 46
UB1: S'hall ... 45Ca 85
WD6: Bore ... 15Ra 29
Masefield Cl. DA8: Erith ... 53Hd 118
RM3: Rom ... 24Kd 57
Masefield Ct. CM14: W'ley ... 21Yd 58
EN5: New Bar ... 14Eb 31
KT6: Surb ... 73Ma 153
Masefield Cres. N14 ... 15Lb 32
RM3: Rom ... 25Ld 57
Masefield Dr. RM14: Upm ... 31Sd 78
Masefield Gdns. E6 ... 42Qc 94
Masefield Ho. *NW6* ... 41Cb 89
(off Stafford Rd.)
Masefield La. UB4: Yead ... 42X 85
Masefield Rd. DA1: Dart ... 57Rd 119
DA11: Nflt ... 62Fe 143
RM16: Grays ... 7A 100
TW12: Hamp ... 63Ba 129
Masefield Vw. BR6: Farnb ... 76Sc 160
Masefield Way TW19: Stanw ... 60P 105
Masham Ho. *DA18: Erith* ... 47Zc 95
(off Kale Rd.)
Mashie Rd. W3 ... 44Ua 88
Mashiters Hill RM1: Rom ... 25Fd 56
Mashiters Wlk. RM1: Rom ... 27Gd 56
Maskall Cl. SW2 ... 60Qb 112
Maskani Wlk. SW16 ... 66Lb 134
Maskell Rd. SW17 ... 62Eb 133
Maskelyne Cl. SW11 ... 53Gb 111
Maslen Rd. AL4: St A ... 5G 6
Mason Cl. DA7: Bex ... 55Dd 118
E16 ... 45Jc 93
EN9: Walt A ... 6Hc 21
SE16 ... 50Wb 91
SW20 ... 67Za 132
TW12: Hamp ... 67Ba 129
WD6: Bore ... 12Ta 29
Mason Dr. RM3: Hrld W ... 26Nd 57
Mason Ho. *E9* ... 38Yb 72
(off Frampton Pk. Rd.)
SE1 ... 49Wb 91
(off Simms Rd.)
Masonic Hall Rd. KT16: Chert ... 72H 149
Mason Rd. IG8: Wfd G ... 21Gc 53
SM1: Sutt ... 78Db 155
Mason's Arms M. W1 ... 3A 222 (44Kb 90)
Masons Av. CR0: C'don ... 76Sb 157
EC2 ... 2F 225 (44Tb 91)
HA3: W'stone ... 28Ha 46
Mason's Bri. Rd. RH1: Redh ... 10B 208
Masons Ct. SL1: Slou ... 5C 80
Masons Grn. La. W3 ... 42Qa 87
W5 ... 42Qa 87
Masons Hill BR1: Brom ... 69Jc 137
BR2: Brom ... 69Kc 137
SE18 ... 49Rc 94
Mason's Pde. EN7: G Oak ... 1Sb 19
Masons Pl. CR4: Mitc ... 66Hb 133
EC1 ... 3C 218 (41Sb 91)
Masons Rd. EN1: Enf ... 8Xb 19
HP2: Hem H ... 1B 4
SL1: Slou ... 5C 80
Mason St. SE17 ... 6G 231 (49Tb 91)
Masons Yd. EC1 ... 3C 218 (41Rb 91)
SW1 ... 6C 222 (46Lb 90)
SW19 ... 64Za 132
Mason Way EN9: Walt A ... 5Gc 21
Massey Cl. N11 ... 22Kb 50
Massey Ct. *E6* ... 39Lc 73
(off Florence Rd.)
Massie Rd. E8 ... 37Wb 71
Massingberd Way SW17 ... 63Kb 134
Massinger St. SE17 ... 6H 231 (49Ub 91)
Massingham St. E1 ... 42Zb 92
Masson Av. HA4: Ruis ... 37Y 65
Mast, The E16 ... 45Sc 94
Mast Ct. *SE16* ... 49Ac 92
(off Boat Lifter Way)
Master Cl. RH8: Oxt ... 1J 211
Master Gunner Pl. SE18 ... 52Nc 116
Masterman Ho. *SE5* ... 52Tb 113
(off Elmington Est.)
Masterman Rd. E6 ... 41Nc 94
Masters Cl. SW16 ... 65Lb 134
Masters Ct. *RM2: Rom* ... 29Kd 57
(off Academy Flds. Rd.)
Masters Dr. SE16 ... 50Xb 91
Masters Lodge *E1* ... 44Yb 92
(off Johnson St.)
Masters St. E1 ... 43Zb 92
Masthead Cl. DA2: Dart ... 56Sd 120
Mast Ho. Ter. E14 ... 49Cc 92
(not continuous)
Mastmaker Ct. E14 ... 47Cc 92
Mastmaker Rd. E14 ... 47Cc 92
Mast Quay SE18 ... 48Pc 94
MASWELL PARK ... 57Ea 108
Maswell Pk. Cres. TW3: Houn ... 57Ea 108
Maswell Pk. Rd. TW3: Houn ... 57Da 107
Matcham Ct. *TW1: Twick* ... 58Ma 109
(off Clevedon Rd.)
Matcham Rd. E11 ... 34Gc 73
Match Ct. *E3* ... 40Cc 72
(off Blondin St.)
Matching Ct. *E3* ... 41Bc 92
(off Merchant St.)
Matchless Dr. SE18 ... 52Qc 116
Matfield Cl. BR2: Brom ... 71Jc 159
Matfield Rd. DA17: Belv ... 51Cd 118
Matham Gro. SE22 ... 56Vb 113
Matham Rd. KT8: E Mos ... 71Fa 152
Mathecombe Rd. SL1: Slou ... 7D 80
Matheson Lang Ho. SE1 ... 2K 229
Matheson Rd. W14 ... 49Bb 89
Mathews Av. E6 ... 40Qc 74
Mathews Pk. Av. E15 ... 37Hc 73
Mathews Yd. WC2 ... 3F 223 (44Nb 90)
Mathias Cl. KT18: Eps ... 85Sa 173
Mathieson Ct. SE1 ... 2C 230
Mathisen Way SL3: Poyle ... 53G 104
Mathison Ho. *SW10* ... 52Eb 111
(off Coleridge Gdns.)
Matilda Cl. SE19 ... 66Tb 135
Matilda Gdns. E3 ... 40Cc 72
Matilda Ho. *E1* ... 46Wb 91
(off St Katherine's Way)
Matilda St. N1 ... 39Pb 70
Matisse Ct. EC1 ... 5F 219 (42Tb 91)
Matisse Rd. TW3: Houn ... 55Da 107
Matlock Cl. EN5: Barn ... 15Za 30
SE24 ... 56Sb 113
Matlock Ct. NW8 ... 1A 214
SE5 ... 56Tb 113
W11 ... 45Cb 89
(off Kensington Pk. Rd.)
Matlock Cres. SM3: Cheam ... 77Ab 154
WD19: Wat ... 20Y 27
Matlock Gdns. RM12: Horn ... 34Nd 77
SM3: Cheam ... 77Ab 154
Matlock Pl. SM3: Cheam ... 77Ab 154
Matlock Rd. CR3: Cat'm ... 93Ub 197
E10 ... 30Ec 52
Matlock St. E14 ... 44Ac 92
Matlock Way KT3: N Mald ... 67Ta 131
Maton Ho. *SW6* ... 52Bb 111
(off Estcourt Rd.)
Matrimony Pl. SW8 ... 54Lb 112
Matson Ct. IG8: Wfd G ... 24Gc 53
Matson Ho. SE16 ... 48Xb 91
Matthew Arnold Cl. KT11: Cobh ... 86W 170
TW18: Staines ... 65L 127
Matthew Arnold Sports Cen. ... 65L 127
Matthew Cl. W10 ... 42Za 88
Matthew Ct. CR4: Mitc ... 71Mb 156
E17 ... 27Ec 52
Matthew Parker St. SW1 ... 2E 228 (47Mb 90)
Matthews Cl. RM3: Hrld W ... 25Pd 57
Matthews Ct. *E17* ... 25Cc 52
(off Chingford Rd.)
SL5: S'hill ... 10B 124
Matthews Gdns. CR0: New Ad ... 83Fc 179
Matthews Ho. *E14* ... 43Cc 92
(off Burgess St.)
Matthews La. TW18: Staines ... 63H 127
Matthews Lodge KT15: Add ... 77M 149
Matthews Rd. UB6: G'frd ... 36Fa 66
Matthews St. RH2: Reig ... 10J 207
SW11 ... 54Hb 111
Matthews Yd. *CR0: C'don* ... 76Sb 157
(off Surrey St.)
Matthias Apartments *N1* ... 38Tb 71
(off Northchurch Rd.)
Matthias Ct. TW10: Rich ... 57Na 109
Matthias Rd. N16 ... 36Ub 71
Mattison Rd. N4 ... 30Qb 50
Mattock La. W5 ... 46Ka 86
W13 ... 46Ka 86
Maud Cashmore Way SE18 ... 48Pc 94
Maud Chadburn Pl. SW4 ... 58Kb 112
Maude Cres. WD24: Wat ... 9X 13
Maude Ho. *E2* ... 40Wb 71
(off Ropley St.)
Maude Rd. BR8: Hext ... 65Jd 140
E17 ... 29Ac 52
SE5 ... 53Ub 113
Maude Ter. E17 ... 28Ac 52
Maud Gdns. E13 ... 39Hc 73
IG11: Bark ... 40Vc 75
Maudlins Grn. E1 ... 46Wb 91
Maud Rd. E10 ... 34Ec 72
E13 ... 40Hc 73
Maudslay Rd. SE9 ... 55Pc 116
Maudsley Ho. TW8: Bford ... 50Na 87
Maud St. E16 ... 43Hc 93
Maudsville Cotts. W7 ... 46Ga 86
Maud Wilkes Cl. NW5 ... 36Lb 70
Maugham Ct. *W3* ... 48Sa 87
(off Palmerston Rd.)
Maugham Way W3 ... 48Sa 87
Mauleverer Rd. SW2 ... 57Nb 112
Maundeby Wlk. NW10 ... 37Ua 68
Maunder Cl. RM16: Chaf H ... 49Zd 99
Maunder Rd. W7 ... 46Ha 86
Maunsel St. SW1 ... 5D 228 (49Mb 90)
Maureen Campbell Ct.
TW17: Shep ... 71R 150
(off Harrison Way)
Maureen Ct. BR3: Beck ... 68Yb 136
Maurer Ct. SE10 ... 48Hc 93
Mauretania Bldg. *E1* ... 45Zb 92
(off Jardine Rd.)
Maurice Av. CR3: Cat'm ... 94Tb 197
N22 ... 26Rb 51
Maurice Brown Cl. NW7 ... 22Za 48
Maurice Ct. E1 ... 41Zb 92
N22 ... 25Pb 50
TW8: Bford ... 52Ma 109
Maurice Drummond Ho. *SE10* ... 53Dc 114
(off Catherine Gro.)
Maurice St. W12 ... 44Xa 88
Maurice Wlk. NW11 ... 28Eb 49
Maurier Cl. UB5: N'olt ... 39Y 65
Mauritius Rd. SE10 ... 49Gc 93
Maury Rd. N16 ... 33Wb 71
Mausoleum ... 5K 103
Mauveine Gdns. TW3: Houn ... 56Ca 107
Mavelstone Cl. BR1: Brom ... 67Nc 138
Mavelstone Rd. BR1: Brom ... 67Mc 137
Maverton Rd. E3 ... 39Cc 72
Mavis Av. KT19: Ewe ... 78Ua 154
Mavis Cl. KT19: Ewe ... 78Ua 154
Mavis Gro. RM12: Horn ... 33Nd 77
Mavis Wlk. *E6* ... 43Nc 94
(off Greenwich Cres.)
Mavor Ho. N1 ... 1J 217
Mawbey Ho. SE1 ... 50Wb 91
Mawbey Pl. SE1 ... 7K 231 (50Vb 91)
Mawbey Rd. KT16: Ott ... 79F 148
SE1 ... 50Vb 91
Mawbey St. SW8 ... 52Nb 112
Mawdley Ho. SE1 ... 2A 230
MAWNEY ... 28Ed 56
Mawney Cl. RM7: Mawney ... 26Dd 56
Mawney Rd. RM7: Mawney, Rom ... 26Dd 56
Mawson Cl. SW20 ... 68Ab 132
Mawson Ct. N1 ... 1G 219
Mawson Ho. EC1 ... 7K 217
Mawson La. W4 ... 51Va 110
Maxden Ct. SE15 ... 55Vb 113
Maxey Gdns. RM9: Dag ... 35Ad 75
Maxey Rd. RM9: Dag ... 35Ad 75
SE18 ... 49Sc 94
Maxfield Cl. N20 ... 17Eb 31
Maxilla Wlk. W10 ... 44Za 88
Maxim Apartments *BR2: Brom* ... 70Kc 137
(off Tiger La.)
Maximfeldt Rd. DA8: Erith ... 50Gd 96
Maxim Rd. DA1: Cray ... 57Gd 118
DA8: Erith ... 49Gd 96
N21 ... 16Qb 32
Maxin Tower *RM1: Rom* ... 28Hd 56
(off Mercury Gdns.)
Maxted Cl. HP2: Hem H ... 1C 4
Maxted Pk. HA1: Harr ... 31Ga 66
Maxted Rd. SE15 ... 55Vb 113
Maxwell Cl. CR0: Wadd ... 74Nb 156
UB3: Hayes ... 45W 84
WD3: Rick ... 19J 25
Maxwell Ct. IG7: Chig ... 20Xc 37
SE22 ... 60Wb 113
SW4 ... 57Mb 112
Maxwell Dr. KT14: W Byf ... 83L 169
Maxwell Gdns. BR6: Orp ... 76Vc 161
Maxwell Ri. WD19: Wat ... 17Aa 27
Maxwell Rd. AL1: St A ... 3F 6
DA16: Well ... 55Vc 117
HA6: Nwood ... 24T 44
SW6 ... 52Db 111
TW15: Ashf ... 65S 128
UB7: W Dray ... 49P 83
WD6: Bore ... 13Ra 29
Maxwelton Av. NW7 ... 22Ta 47
Maxwelton Cl. NW7 ... 22Ta 47
Maya Angelou Ct. E4 ... 21Ec 52
Maya Cl. SE15 ... 54Xb 113
Mayall Cl. EN3: Enf L ... 10Cc 20
Mayall Rd. SE24 ... 57Rb 113
Maya Pl. N11 ... 24Mb 50
Maya Rd. N2 ... 28Eb 49
May Av. BR5: St M Cry ... 71Xc 161
DA11: Nflt ... 10B 122
May Av. Ind. Est. *DA11: Nflt* ... 10B 122
(off May Av.)
Maybank Av. E18 ... 26Kc 53
HA0: Wemb ... 36Ha 66
RM12: Horn ... 36Kd 77
Maybank Gdns. HA5: Eastc ... 29W 44
Maybank Lodge RM12: Horn ... 36Ld 77
Maybank Rd. E18 ... 25Kc 53
May Bate Av. KT2: King T ... 67Ma 131
Maybells Commercial Est.
IG11: Bark ... 40Zc 75
Mayberry Ct. *BR3: Beck* ... 66Bc 136
(off Copers Cope Rd.)
Mayberry Pl. KT5: Surb ... 73Pa 153
Maybourne Cl. SE26 ... 65Xb 135
Maybourne Ri. GU22: Wok ... 6P 187
Maybrick Rd. RM11: Horn ... 30Ld 57
MAYBURY ... 88E 168
Maybury Av. DA2: Dart ... 60Sd 120
EN8: Chesh ... 1Xb 19
Maybury Cl. BR5: Pet W ... 71Rc 160
EN1: Enf ... 10Xb 19
IG10: Lough ... 14Rc 36
KT20: Tad ... 91Ab 194
SL1: Slou ... 4B 80
Maybury Ct. *CR2: S Croy* ... 78Rb 157
(off Haling Pk. Rd.)
HA1: Harr ... 30Fa 46
W1 ... 1J 221
Maybury Est. GU22: Wok ... 88E 168
Maybury Gdns. NW10 ... 37Xa 68
Maybury Hill GU22: Wok ... 88D 168
Maybury M. N6 ... 31Lb 70
Maybury Rd. E13 ... 42Lc 93
GU21: Wok ... 89B 168
IG11: Bark ... 40Vc 75
Maybury Rough GU22: Wok ... 89D 168
Maybury St. SW17 ... 64Gb 133
Maybush Rd. RM11: Horn ... 31Nd 77
Maychurch Cl. HA7: Stan ... 24Ma 47
May Cl. AL3: St A ... 1B 6
KT9: Chess ... 79Pa 153
Maycock Gro. HA6: Nwood ... 23V 44
May Cotts. *WD18: Wat* ... 15Y 27
(off Lammas Rd.)
May Ct. RM17: Grays ... 1A 122
SW19 ... 67Eb 133
(off Pincott Rd.)
Maycroft HA5: Pinn ... 26X 45
Maycroft Av. RM17: Grays ... 50Fe 99
Maycroft Gdns. RM17: Grays ... 50Fe 99
Maycross Av. SM4: Mord ... 70Bb 133
Mayday Gdns. SE3 ... 54Nc 116
Mayday Rd. CR7: Thor H ... 72Rb 157
Maydeb Ct. RM6: Chad H ... 30Bd 55
Maydew Ho. *SE16* ... 49Yb 92
(off Abbeyfield Est.)
Maydwell Ho. *E14* ... 43Cc 92
(off Thomas Rd.)
Maydwell Lodge WD6: Bore ... 12Pa 29
Mayell Cl. KT22: Lea ... 95La 192
Mayerne Rd. SE9 ... 57Mc 115
Mayer Rd. EN9: Walt A ... 6Dc 20
Mayesbrook Pk. Arena ... 36Wc 75
Mayesbrook Rd. IG3: Ilf ... 34Wc 75
IG11: Bark ... 39Vc 75
RM8: Dag ... 34Wc 75
Mayes Cl. BR8: Swan ... 70Jd 140
CR0: New Ad ... 80Fc 159
CR6: W'ham ... 90Zb 178
Mayesford Rd. RM6: Chad H ... 31Yc 75
Mayes Rd. N22 ... 26Pb 50
Mayeswood Rd. SE12 ... 63Lc 137
MAYFAIR ... 5K 221 (45Kb 90)
Mayfair Av. DA7: Bex ... 53Zc 117
IG1: Ilf ... 33Pc 74
KT4: Wor Pk ... 74Wa 154
RM6: Chad H ... 30Zc 55
TW2: Whitt ... 59Ea 108
Mayfair Cl. BR3: Beck ... 67Dc 136
KT6: Surb ... 74Na 153
Mayfair Ct. HA8: Edg ... 22Pa 47
WD18: Wat ... 14U 26
Mayfair Gdns. IG8: Wfd G ... 24Jc 53
N17 ... 23Sb 51
Mayfair M. *NW1* ... 38Hb 69
(off Regents Pk. Rd.)
Mayfair Pl. W1 ... 6A 222 (46Kb 90)
Mayfair Rd. DA1: Dart ... 57Md 119
Mayfair Ter. N14 ... 17Mb 32
Mayfare WD3: Crox G ... 15T 26
Mayfield DA7: Bex ... 55Bd 117
EN9: Walt A ... 6Fc 21
KT22: Lea ... 93La 192
Mayfield Av. BR6: Orp ... 74Vc 161
HA3: Kenton ... 29Ka 46
IG8: Wfd G ... 23Jc 53
KT15: New H ... 82K 169
N12 ... 21Eb 49
N14 ... 19Mb 32
W4 ... 49Ua 88
W13 ... 48Ka 86
Mayfield Caravan Pk. UB7: W Dray ... 48L 83
Mayfield Cl. E8 ... 37Vb 71
KT7: T Ditt ... 74Ka 152
KT12: Hers ... 77W 150
KT15: New H ... 82L 169
SE20 ... 67Xb 135
SW4 ... 57Mb 112
TW15: Ashf ... 65R 128
UB10: Hil ... 41R 84
Mayfield Ct. *EN9: Walt A* ... 6Jc 21
(off Lamplighters Cl.)
RH1: Redh ... 10P 207
Mayfield Cres. CR7: Thor H ... 70Pb 134
N9 ... 16Xb 33
Mayfield Dr. HA5: Pinn ... 28Ba 45
SL4: Wind ... 5E 102
Mayfield Gdns. CM14: B'wood ... 18Xd 40
KT12: Hers ... 77W 150
KT15: New H ... 82K 169
NW4 ... 30Za 48
TW18: Staines ... 65H 127
W7 ... 44Ga 86
Mayfield Grn. KT23: Bookh ... 99Ca 191
Mayfield Gro. RM13: Rain ... 41Ld 97
Mayfield Ho. *E2* ... 40Xb 71
(off Cambridge Heath Rd.)
Mayfield Light Ind. Est. SL4: Wink ... 2A 124
Mayfield Mans. SW15 ... 57Bb 111
Mayfield Rd. BR1: Brom ... 71Nc 160
CR2: Sande ... 81Tb 177
CR7: Thor H ... 70Pb 134
DA11: Grav'nd ... 9B 122
DA17: Belv ... 49Ed 96
E4 ... 19Ec 34
E8 ... 38Vb 71
E13 ... 42Hc 93
E17 ... 26Ac 52
EN3: Enf H ... 12Zb 34
KT12: Hers ... 77W 150
KT13: Weyb ... 78P 149
N8 ... 29Pb 50
RM8: Dag ... 32Yc 75
SM2: Sutt ... 79Fb 155
SW19 ... 67Bb 133
W3 ... 45Ra 87
W12 ... 47Ua 88
Mayfield Rd. Flats N8 ... 30Pb 50
Mayfields DA10: Swans ... 58Ae 121
HA9: Wemb ... 33Qa 67
RM16: Grays ... 47Ee 99
Mayfields Cl. HA9: Wemb ... 33Qa 67
Mayfield Vs. DA14: Sidc ... 65Yc 139
Mayflower Av. HP2: Hem H ... 2M 3
Mayflower Cl. HA4: Ruis ... 30S 44
RM15: S Ock ... 42Yd 98
SE16 ... 49Zb 92
Mayflower Ho. CM13: Gt War ... 23Yd 58
E14 ... 47Cc 92
(off Westferry Rd.)
IG11: Bark ... 39Tc 74
(off Westbury Rd.)
Mayflower Path CM13: Gt War ... 23Yd 58
Mayflower Rd. AL2: Park ... 9P 5
RM16: Chaf H ... 50Yd 98
SW9 ... 55Nb 112
Mayflower St. SE16 ... 47Yb 92
Mayflower Way SL2: Farn C ... 6G 60
Mayfly Cl. BR5: St P ... 70Zc 139
HA5: Eastc ... 31Y 65
Mayfly Gdns. UB5: N'olt ... 41Z 85
MAYFORD ... 4N 187
Mayford NW1 ... 1C 216 (40Lb 70)
(not continuous)
Mayford Cl. BR3: Beck ... 69Zb 136
GU22: Wok ... 4P 187
SW12 ... 59Hb 111
Mayford Grn. GU22: Wok ... 4N 187
Mayford Meadows Local Nature Reserve
... 4P 187
Mayford Rd. SW12 ... 59Hb 111
May Gdns. HA0: Wemb ... 41La 86
WD6: E'tree ... 16Ma 29
Maygood Ho. N1 ... 1K 217
Maygoods Cl. UB8: Cowl ... 43M 83
Maygoods Grn. UB8: Cowl ... 43M 83
Maygoods La. UB8: Cowl ... 43M 83
Maygood St. N1 ... 1K 217 (40Qb 70)

Maygoods Vw. UB8: Cowl .43L 83
Maygreen Cres. RM11: Horn .31Jd 76
Maygrove Rd. NW6 .37Bb 69
Mayhew Cl. E4 .20Cc 34
Mayhew Ct. SE5 .56Tb 113
Mayhill Ct. *SE15* .*52Ub 113*
(off Newent Cl.)
Mayhill Rd. EN5: Barn .16Ab 30
SE7 .51Kc 115
May Ho. *E3* .*40Cc 72*
(off Thomas Fyre Dr.)
Mayhurst Av. GU22: Wok .88E 168
Mayhurst Cl. GU22: Wok .88E 168
Mayhurst Cres. GU22: Wok .88E 168
Mayhurst M. GU22: Wok .88E 168
Mayland Mans. *IG11: Bark* .*38Rc 74*
(off Whiting Av.)
Maylands Av. HP2: Hem H .1B 4
RM12: Horn .35Kd 77
Maylands Ct. HP2: Hem H .1B 4
Maylands Dr. DA14: Sidc .62Zc 139
UB8: Uxb .37M 63
Maylands Golf Course .22Rd 57
Maylands Ho. SW3 .6E 226
Maylands Rd. WD19: Wat .21Y 45
Maylands Way RM3: Hrld W .23Sd 58
Maylie Ho. *SE16* .*47Xb 91*
(off Marigold St.)
Maynard Cl. DA8: Erith .52Hd 118
N15 .29Ub 51
SW6 .52Db 111
Maynard Ct. EN3: Enf L .10Cc 20
EN9: Walt A .6Hc 21
SL4: Wind .3E 102
TW18: Staines .63J 127
Maynard Dr. AL1: St A .5B 6
Maynard Path E17 .29Ec 52
Maynard Pl. EN6: Cuff .1Pb 18
Maynard Rd. E17 .29Ec 52
HP2: Hem H .3M 3
Maynards RM11: Horn .31Nd 77
Maynards Quay E1 .45Yb 92
Mayne Av. AL3: St A .4M 5
Mayne Ct. SE26 .64Xb 135
Maynooth Gdns.
SM5: Cars .73Hb 155
Mayo Ct. W13 .48Ka 86
Mayo Gdns. HP1: Hem H .3K 3
Mayo Ho. *E1* .*43Yb 92*
(off Lindley St.)
Mayola Rd. E5 .35Yb 72
Mayo Rd. CR0: C'don .71Tb 157
KT12: Walt T .73W 150
NW10 .37Ua 68
Mayor's and City of London Court, The
.2F 225
Mayor's La. DA2: Wilm .63Ld 141
Mayow Rd. SE23 .63Zb 136
SE26 .63Zb 136
Mayplace Av. DA1: Cray .56Jd 118
Mayplace Cl. DA7: Bex .55Dd 118
Mayplace La. SE18 .51Rc 116
(not continuous)
Mayplace Rd. E. DA1: Cray .55Ed 118
DA7: Bex .55Dd 118
Mayplace Rd. W. DA7: Bex .56Cd 118
MAYPOLE
BR6 .79Cd 162
DA2 .61Gd 140
Maypole Ct. *UB2: S'hall* .*47Ba 85*
(off Merrick Rd.)
Maypole Cres. DA8: Erith .51Md 119
IG6: Ilf .24Tc 54
Maypole Dr. IG7: Chig .20Wc 37
Maypole Rd.
BR6: Chels, Well H .78Bd 161
DA12: Grav'nd .10H 123
May Rd. DA2: Hawl .63Pd 141
E4 .23Cc 52
E13 .40Jc 73
TW2: Twick .60Ga 108
Mayroyd Av. KT6: Surb .75Qa 153
May's Bldgs. M. SE10 .52Ec 114
Mays Cl. KT13: Weyb .82P 169
Mays Ct. SE10 .52Fc 115
WC2 .5F 223 (45Nb 90)
Maysfield Rd. GU23: Send .95F 188
MAY'S GREEN .92U 190
Mays Gro. GU23: Send .95F 188
Mays Hill Rd. BR2: Brom .68Gc 137
Mays La. EN5: Ark, Barn .17Xa 30
Maysoule Rd. SW11 .56Fb 111
Mays Rd. TW11: Tedd .64Fa 130
Mayston M. *SE10* .*50Jc 93*
(off Ormiston Rd.)
May St. W14 .50Bb 89
(Kelway Ho.)
W14 .50Bb 89
(Orchard Sq.)
Mayswood Gdns. RM10: Dag .37Ed 76
Maythorne Cl. WD18: Wat .14U 26
Maythorne Cotts. SE13 .57Fc 115
Mayton St. N7 .34Pb 70
Maytree Cl. HA8: Edg .20Sa 29
RM13: Rain .40Gd 76
Maytree Ct. CR4: Mitc .69Jb 134
UB5: N'olt .41Aa 85
Maytree Cres. WD24: Wat .7V 12
Maytree Gdns. W5 .47Ma 87
May Tree Ho. *SE4* .*55Bc 114*
(off Wickham Rd.)
Maytree La. HA7: Stan .24Ja 46
Maytrees GU21: Knap .9G 166
WD7: R'lett .9Ja 14
Maytree Wlk. SW2 .61Qb 134
Mayville Est. N16 .36Ub 71
Mayville Rd. E11 .33Gc 73
(not continuous)
IG1: Ilf .36Rc 74
May Wlk. E13 .40Kc 73
Mayward Ho. *SE5* .*53Ub 113*
(off Peckham Rd.)
Maywater Cl. CR2: Sande .83Tb 177
Maywin Dr. RM11: Horn .32Pd 77
Maywood Cl. BR3: Beck .66Dc 136
May Wynne Ho. *E16* .*45Kc 93*
(off Murray Sq.)
Maze Hill SE3 .52Hc 115
SE10 .51Gc 115
Maze Hill Lodge *SE10* .*51Fc 115*
(off Park Vista)
Mazenod Av. NW6 .38Cb 69
Maze Rd. TW9: Kew .52Qa 109
MCC Cricket Mus. & Tours
.4B 214 (41Fb 89)
MC Clintock Pl. EN3: Enf L .10Dc 20

Mead, The BR3: Beck .67Ec 136
BR4: W W'ck .74Fc 159
DA3: New A .75Ae 165
EN8: Chesh .1Yb 20
KT21: Asht .91Na 193
N2 .26Eb 49
SM6: Wall .79Mb 156
UB10: Ick .33Q 64
W13 .43Ka 86
WD19: Wat .20Aa 27
Mead Av. SL3: L'ly .47D 82
Meadbank Studios *SW11* .*52Gb 111*
(off Parkgate Rd.)
Mead Cl. BR8: Swan .71Jd 162
HA3: Hrw W .25Fa 46
IG10: Lough .12Rc 36
NW1 .37Jb 70
RH1: Redh .3A 208
RM2: Rom .26Jd 56
RM16: Grays .47De 99
SL3: L'ly .47D 82
TW20: Egh .65D 126
UB9: Den .33J 63
Mead Ct. EN9: Walt A .6Dc 20
GU21: Knap .8J 167
NW9 .29Sa 47
TW20: Egh .65E 126
Mead Cres. DA1: Dart .60Md 119
E4 .21Ec 52
KT23: Bookh .97Ca 191
SM1: Sutt .76Gb 155
Meadcroft Rd. SE11 .51Rb 113
(not continuous)
SE17 .51Rb 113
Meade Cl. W4 .51Qa 109
Meade Ct. KT20: Walt H .96Wa 194
Mead End KT21: Asht .89Pa 173
Meader Ct. SE14 .52Zb 114
Meades, The KT13: Weyb .79S 150
Mead Fld. HA2: Harr .34Ba 65
Meadfield HA8: Edg .19Ra 29
(not continuous)
Meadfield Av. SL3: L'ly .47C 82
Meadfield Grn. HA8: Edg .19Ra 29
Meadfield Rd. SL3: L'ly .48C 82
Meadfoot Rd. SW16 .66Lb 134
Meadgate Av. IG8: Wfd G .22Nc 54
Mead Gro. RM6: Chad H .27Zc 55
Mead Ho. SL0: Iver H .41F 82
W11 .*46Bb 89*
(off Ladbroke Rd.)
Mead Ho. La. UB4: Hayes .42T 84
Meadhurst Club .64V 128
Meadhurst Pk. TW16: Sun .65U 128
Meadhurst Rd. KT16: Chert .74K 149
Meadlands Dr. TW10: Ham .61Ma 131
Mead La. KT16: Chert .73K 149
Mead Lodge W4 .47Ta 87
Meadow, The BR7: Chst .65Sc 138
N10 .27Jb 50
Meadow Av. CR0: C'don .72Zb 158
WD7: Shenl .3La 14
Meadow Bank KT24: E Hor .99V 190
N21 .16Pb 32
Meadowbank KT5: Surb .72Pa 153
NW3 .38Hb 69
SE3 .55Hc 115
WD4: K Lan .2Q 12
WD19: Wat .17Y 27
Meadow Bank Cl. TN15: W King .81Vd 184
Meadowbank Cl. HP3: Bov .10D 2
SW6 .52Ya 110
TW7: Isle .53Ga 108
Meadowbank Gdns. TW5: Cran .53W 106
Meadowbank Rd. GU18: Light .2A 166
NW9 .31Ta 67
Meadowbanks EN5: Ark .15Wa 30
Meadowbridge Ct. *CR0: C'don* .*71Tb 157*
(off Princess Rd.)
Meadowbrook RH8: Oxt .2G 210
Meadowbrook Cl. SL3: Poyle .53H 105
Meadowbrook Ct. TW7: Isle .55Ga 108
Meadow Cl. AL2: Brick W .1Ca 13
AL2: Lon C .9H 7
AL9: Wel G .6F 8
BR7: Chst .64Rc 138
CR8: Purl .85Mb 176
DA6: Bex .57Bd 117
E4 .18Dc 34
E9 .37Bc 72
EN3: Enf W .10Ac 20
EN5: Barn .16Bb 31
HA4: Ruis .30V 44
IG11: Bark .38Wc 75
KT10: Hin W .76Ha 152
KT12: Hers .77Ba 151
RM3: Rom .20Ld 39
SE6 .64Cc 136
SL4: Old Win .7M 103
SM1: Sutt .75Eb 155
SS17: Linf .8J 101
SW20 .70Ya 132
TN13: S'oaks .95Jd 202
TW4: Houn .58Ca 107
TW10: Ham .60Na 109
UB5: N'olt .40Ca 65
WD7: Shenl .2La 14
Meadow Cotts. GU24: W End .4D 166
Meadow Ct. *E16* .*46Lc 93*
(off Booth Rd.)
KT18: Eps .85Sa 173
N1 .1H 219 (40Ub 71)
RH1: Mers .2C 208
TW3: Houn .58Da 107
TW18: Staines .62G 126
Meadowcourt Rd. SE3 .56Hc 115
Meadow Cft. *TW18: Staines* .*65G 126*
(off Bowes Rd.)
Meadowcroft AL1: St A .5E 6
BR1: Brom .69Pc 138
SL9: Chal P .26A 42
W4 .*50Qa 87*
(off Brooks Rd.)
WD23: Bush .16Da 27
Meadowcroft Cl. N13 .19Qb 32
Meadowcroft Rd. N13 .19Qb 32
Meadowcross EN9: Walt A .6Gc 21
Meadow Dr. GU23: Rip .95H 189
N10 .27Kb 50
NW4 .26Ya 48
Meadowford Cl. SE28 .45Wc 95
Meadow Gdns. HA8: Edg .23Ra 47
TW18: Staines .64F 126
Meadow Gth. NW10 .37Sa 67
(not continuous)
Meadow Ga. KT21: Asht .89Na 173

Meadowgate Cl. NW7 .22Va 48
Meadow Hill CR5: Coul .86Lb 176
CR8: Purl .86Lb 176
KT3: N Mald .72Ua 154
Meadowlands KT11: Cobh .85W 170
RH8: Oxt .6L 211
RM11: Horn .31Nd 77
TN15: Seal .92Pd 203
Meadowlands Pk. KT15: Add .76N 149
Meadow La. DA3: New A .75Be 165
KT22: Fet .94Ea 192
SE12 .62Kc 137
SL4: Eton, Eton W .1F 102
Meadowlea Cl. UB7: Harm .51M 105
Meadow M. SW8 .51Pb 112
Meadow Pl. SW8 .52Nb 112
W4 .52Ua 110
Meadow Ri. CR5: Coul .85Mb 176
GU21: Knap .9G 166
Meadow Rd. BR2: Brom .68Gc 137
CM16: Epp .1Vc 23
DA11: Grav'nd .1C 144
GU25: Vir W .1J 147
HA5: Pinn .28Z 45
HP3: Hem H .6A 4
IG10: Lough .15Nc 36
IG11: Bark .38Vc 75
KT10: Clay .79Ga 152
KT21: Asht .89Na 173
RM7: Rush G .32Ed 76
RM9: Dag .37Bd 75
RM16: Grays .46Ee 99
SL3: L'ly .48A 82
SM1: Sutt .77Gb 155
SW8 .52Pb 112
SW19 .66Eb 133
TW13: Felt .61Aa 129
TW15: Ashf .64T 128
UB1: S'hall .45Ba 85
WD6: Bore .12Ra 29
WD23: Bush .15Da 27
WD25: Wat .6W 12
Meadow Row SE1 .4D 230 (48Sb 91)
Meadows, The BR6: Chels .79Yc 161
CM13: Ingve .23Ee 59
CR6: W'ham .89Zb 178
E4 .21Fc 53
E6: S Mim .5Wa 16
HP1: Hem H .1G 2
TN14: Hals .85Bd 181
WD25: Wat .8Z 13
Meadows Cl. CM13: Ingve .23Ee 59
E10 .33Cc 72
Meadows Ct. DA14: Sidc .65Xc 139
Meadows End TW16: Sun .67W 128
Meadowside DA1: Dart .60Md 119
KT12: Walt T .75Y 151
KT23: Bookh .95Ca 191
SE9 .56Lc 115
TW1: Twick .59Ma 109
TW18: Staines .64J 127
WD25: Wat .3X 13
Meadowside Rd. RM14: Upm .36Sd 78
SM2: Cheam .81Ab 174
Meadows Leigh Cl. KT13: Weyb .76R 150
Meadow Stile CR0: C'don .76Sb 157
Meadowsweet Cl. E16 .43Mc 93
SW20 .70Ya 132
Meadow Vw. BR5: St P .69Yc 139
CM16: Epp .1Wc 23
DA15: Sidc .59Xc 117
GU22: Wok .93B 188
(not continuous)
HA1: Harr .32Ga 66
KT16: Chert .74L 149
SL3: L'ly .46B 82
TN13: Dun G .90Fd 182
UB8: Cowl .43L 83
Meadowview TW19: Stanw M .57H 105
Meadow Vw. Rd.
CR7: Thor H .71Rb 157
UB4: Hayes .42T 84
Meadowview Rd. DA5: Bexl .58Ad 117
KT19: Ewe .81Ua 174
SE6 .64Bc 136
Meadow Wlk. DA2: Wilm .63Ld 141
(not continuous)
E18 .28Jc 53
KT17: Ewe .79Ua 154
KT19: Ewe .79Ua 154
KT20: Walt H .96Xa 194
RM9: Dag .37Bd 75
SM6: Wall .76Kb 156
Meadow Walks EN5: New Bar .16Db 31
Meadow Way BR6: Farnb .76Qc 160
DA2: Dart .59Sd 120
EN6: Pot B .6Cb 17
GU24: W End .4D 166
HA4: Ruis .30X 45
HA9: Wemb .35Ma 67
HP3: Hem H .5H 3
IG7: Chig .20Sc 36
KT9: Chess .78Na 153
KT15: Add .77K 149
KT20: Tad .89Ab 174
KT23: Bookh .95Da 191
KT24: W Hor .97T 190
NW9 .29Ta 47
RH2: Reig .10K 207
RM14: Upm .34Sd 78
SL4: Old Win .8M 103
WD3: Rick .17L 25
WD4: K Lan .2Q 12
WD5: Bedm .9F 4
Meadow Way, The
HA3: Hrw W .25Ga 46
Meadow Waye TW5: Hest .51Aa 107
Mead Path SW17 .63Eb 133
Mead Pl. CR0: C'don .74Sb 157
E9 .37Yb 72
WD3: Rick .18K 25
Mead Plat NW10 .37Sa 67
Mead Rd. BR7: Chst .65Sc 138
CR3: Cat'm .95Vb 197
DA1: Dart .60Md 119
DA11: Grav'nd .1D 144
HA8: Edg .23Qa 47
KT12: Hers .77Aa 151
TW10: Ham .62La 130
UB8: Uxb .38M 63
WD7: Shenl .5Qa 15
Mead Row SE1 .3K 229 (48Qb 90)
Meads, The AL2: Brick W .1Ba 13
HA8: Edg .23Ta 47
RM14: Upm .33Ud 78
SL4: Wind .4E 102

Meads, The SM3: Cheam .76Ab 154
SM4: Mord .71Gb 155
UB8: Cowl .42N 83
Meads Ct. E15 .37Hc 73
Meadside *GU22: Wok* .*90B 168*
(off Park Dr.)
KT18: Eps .*86Ta 173*
(off South St.)
Meadside Cl. BR3: Beck .67Ac 136
Meads La. IG3: Ilf .31Uc 74
Meads Rd. EN3: Enf H .11Ac 34
N22 .26Rb 51
Meadsway CM13: Gt War .23Xd 58
Mead Ter. HA9: Wemb .35Ma 67
MEAD VALE .8M 207
Meadvale Rd. CR0: C'don .73Vb 157
W5 .42Ka 86
Mead Wlk. SL3: L'ly .47D 82
Mead Way BR2: Hayes .72Hc 159
CR0: C'don .75Ac 158
CR5: Coul .90Nb 176
HA4: Ruis .30T 44
SL1: Slou .3B 80
WD23: Bush .12Aa 27
Meadway AL4: Col H .5P 7
BR3: Beck .67Ec 136
CR6: W'ham .88Yb 178
EN3: Enf W .8Yb 20
EN5: Barn, New Bar .14Cb 31
HP4: Berk .1A 2
IG3: Bark, Ilf .35Uc 74
IG8: Wfd G .22Lc 53
KT5: Surb .74Sa 153
KT10: Esh .81Da 171
KT19: Eps .84Sa 173
KT22: Oxs .86Ga 172
KT24: Eff .100Aa 191
N14 .19Mb 32
NW11 .30Cb 49
RM2: Rom .26Jd 56
RM17: Grays .49Fe 99
SW20 .70Ya 132
TN14: Hals .85Bd 181
TW2: Twick .60Fa 108
TW15: Ashf .63Q 128
TW18: Staines .66J 127
Meadway, The BR6: Chels .78Xc 161
EN6: Cuff .1Pb 18
IG9: Buck H .18Mc 35
IG10: Lough .16Pc 36
(not continuous)
SE3 .54Fc 115
TN13: S'oaks .94Hd 202
Meadway Cl. EN5: Barn .14Cb 31
HA5: Hat E .23Da 45
NW11 .30Db 49
TW18: Staines .66H 127
Meadway Ct. RM8: Dag .33Bd 75
TW11: Tedd .64La 130
W5 .42Pa 87
Meadway Dr. GU21: Wok .8N 167
KT15: Add .80L 149
Meadway Gdns. HA4: Ruis .30T 44
Meadway Ga. NW11 .30Cb 49
Meadway Pk. SL9: Ger X .2P 61
Mead Way Path CR5: Coul .90Pb 176
Meaford Way SE20 .66Xb 135
Meakin Est. SE1 .3H 231 (48Ub 91)
Meanley Rd. E12 .35Nc 74
Meard St. W1 .3D 222 (44Mb 90)
(not continuous)
Meare Cl. KT20: Tad .95Ya 194
Mears Cl. *E1* .*43Wb 91*
(off Settles St.)
Meath Cl. BR5: St M Cry .71Xc 161
Meath Cres. E2 .41Zb 92
Meath Ho. *SE24* .*58Rb 113*
(off Dulwich Rd.)
Meath Rd. E15 .40Hc 73
IG1: Ilf .34Sc 74
Meath St. SW11 .53Kb 112
Meautys AL3: St A .4M 5
Mecca Bingo
Camden .*39Kb 70*
(off Arlington Rd.)
Catford .59Dc 114
Chadwell Heath .31Zc 75
Croydon .*75Sb 157*
(off Tamworth Rd.)
Dagenham Leisure Pk. .39Ad 75
Edgware .26Sa 47
Grays .*50Ce 99*
(off Quarry Hill)
Hackney .2K 219
Hayes .44X 85
Hornchurch .32Md 77
Morden .73Eb 155
Romford .*29Hd 56*
(off The Mall Shopping Centre)
Wandsworth .60Db 111
Watford .14Y 27
Wood Green .*26Qb 50*
(off Lordship La.)
Mecklenburgh Pl. WC1 .5H 217 (42Pb 90)
Mecklenburgh Sq. WC1 .5H 217 (42Pb 90)
Mecklenburgh St. WC1 .5H 217 (42Pb 90)
Medbree Ct. RM16: Ors .3C 100
Medburn St. NW1 .1D 216 (40Mb 70)
Medbury Rd. DA12: Grav'nd .10H 123
Medcalf Rd. EN3: Enf L .9Bc 20
Medcroft Gdns. SW14 .56Sa 109
Medd Ct. *AL1: St A* .*2C 6*
(off St Peter's St.)
Medebourne Cl. SE3 .55Jc 115
Medebridge Rd.
RM16: N Stif, S Ock .45Be 99
Mede Cl. TW19: Wray .10P 103
Mede Ct. TW18: Staines .62G 126
Medefield KT22: Fet .96Fa 192
Mede Ho. *BR1: Brom* .*64Kc 137*
(off Pike Cl.)
Medesenge Way N13 .23Rb 51
Medfield St. SW15 .59Wa 110
Medhurst Cl. E3 .40Ac 72
(not continuous)
GU24: Chob .1K 167
Medhurst Cres. DA12: Grav'nd .2G 144
Medhurst Dr. BR1: Brom .64Gc 137
Medhurst Gdns. DA12: Grav'nd .2H 145
Median Rd. E5 .36Yb 72
Medici Cl. IG3: Ilf .30Wc 55
(not continuous)
Medick Ct. RM17: Grays .1A 122
Medina Av. KT10: Hin W .76Ga 152
Medina Gro. N7 .34Qb 70
Medina Ho. DA8: Erith .52Gd 118

Medina Rd. N7 .34Qb 70
RM17: Grays .50Fe 99
Medina Sq. KT19: Eps .81Qa 173
Medlake Pl. TW20: Egh .66E 126
Medlake Rd. TW20: Egh .65E 126
Medland Cl. SM6: Wall .74Jb 156
Medland Ho. E14 .45Ac 92
Medlar Cl. UB5: N'olt .40Z 65
Medlar Ct. SL2: Slou .6N 81
Medlar Dr. RM15: S Ock .42Ae 99
Medlar Ho. DA15: Sidc .62Wc 139
Medlar Rd. RM17: Grays .51Fe 121
Medlar St. SE5 .53Sb 113
Medley Rd. NW6 .37Cb 69
Medman Cl. UB8: Uxb .40L 63
Medora Rd. RM7: Rom .28Fd 56
SW2 .59Pb 112
Medow Mead WD7: R'lett .5Ha 14
Medusa Ct. *DA12: Grav'nd* .*8F 122*
(off Admirals Way)
Medusa Rd. SE6 .58Dc 114
Medway Bldgs. *E3* .*40Ac 72*
(off Medway Rd.)
Medway Cl. CR0: C'don .72Yb 158
IG1: Ilf .36Sc 74
WD25: Wat .6Y 13
Medway Ct. NW11 .30Db 49
WC1 .4F 217
Medway Dr. UB6: G'frd .41Ha 66
Medway Gdns. HA0: Wemb .35Ja 66
Medway Ho. KT2: King T .67Ma 131
NW8 .6D 214
SE1 .2G 231
Medway M. E3 .40Ac 72
Medway Pde. UB6: G'frd .40Ha 66
Medway Rd. DA1: Cray .55Jd 118
E3 .40Ac 72
Medway St. SW1 .4D 228 (48Mb 90)
Medwin St. SW4 .56Pb 112
Meerbrook Rd. SE3 .55Lc 115
Meeson Rd. E15 .38Hc 73
Meesons La. RM17: Grays .49Be 99
Meeson St. E5 .35Ac 72
Meeson's Wharf E15 .40Ec 72
Meeting All. WD17: Wat .13X 27
Meeting Fld. Path E9 .37Yb 72
Meeting Ho. All. E1 .46Xb 91
Meeting Ho. La. SE15 .53Xb 113
Megelish M. UB1: S'hall .41Ca 85
Megg La. WD4: Chfd .1K 11
Mehetabel Rd. E9 .36Yb 72
Meister Cl. IG1: Ilf .32Tc 74
Melancholy Wlk. TW10: Ham .61La 130
Melanda Cl. BR7: Chst .64Pc 138
Melanie Cl. DA7: Bex .53Ad 117
Melba Gdns. RM18: Tilb .2C 122
Melba Way SE13 .53Dc 114
Melbourne Av. HA5: Pinn .27Da 45
N13 .23Pb 50
SL1: Slou .4G 80
W13 .46Ja 86
Melbourne Cl. BR6: Orp .73Uc 160
SE20 .66Wb 135
SM6: Wall .78Lb 156
UB10: Ick .35Q 64
Melbourne Ct. *E5* .*35Ac 72*
(off Daubeney Rd.)
EN8: Walt C .*6Bc 20*
(off Holdbrook Sth.)
N10 .24Kb 50
W9 .5A 214
Melbourne Gdns. RM6: Chad H .29Ad 55
Melbourne Gro. SE22 .56Ub 113
Melbourne Ho. UB4: Yead .42Y 85
W8 .*46Cb 89*
(off Kensington Pl.)
Melbourne Mans. *W14* .*51Ab 110*
(off Musard Rd.)
Melbourne M. SE6 .59Ec 114
SW9 .53Qb 112
Melbourne Pl. WC2 .4J 223 (45Pb 90)
Melbourne Quay DA11: Grav'nd .8D 122
Melbourne Rd. E6 .40Pc 74
E10 .31Dc 72
E17 .28Ac 52
IG1: Ilf .32Rc 74
RM18: Tilb .3A 122
SM6: Wall .78Kb 156
SW19 .67Cb 133
TW11: Tedd .65La 130
WD23: Bush .15Da 27
Melbourne Sq. SW9 .53Qb 112
Melbourne Ter. *SW6* .*52Db 111*
(off Moore Pk. Rd.)
Melbourne Way EN1: Enf .16Vb 33
Melbourne Yd. SE19 .65Ub 135
Melbray M. SW6 .54Bb 111
Melbreak Ho. SE22 .55Ub 113
Melbury Av. UB2: S'hall .48Da 85
Melbury Cl. BR7: Chst .65Nc 138
KT10: Clay .79Ka 152
KT14: W Byf .86J 169
KT16: Chert .73J 149
Melbury Ct. W8 .48Bb 89
Melbury Dr. SE5 .52Ub 113
Melbury Gdns. CR2: Sande .83Ub 177
SW20 .67Xa 132
Melbury Ho. *SW8* .*52Pb 112*
(off Richborne Ter.)
Melbury Rd. HA3: Kenton .29Pa 47
W14 .48Bb 89
Melchester *W11* .*44Bb 89*
(off Ledbury Rd.)
Melchester Ho. *N19* .*34Mb 70*
(off Wedmore St.)
Melcombe Ct. NW1 .7F 215
Melcombe Gdns. HA3: Kenton .30Pa 47
Melcombe Ho. *SW8* .*52Pb 112*
(off Dorset Rd.)
Melcombe Pl. NW1 .7F 215 (43Hb 89)
Melcombe Regis Ct. *W1* .*1J 221*
(off Weymouth St.)
Melcombe St. NW1 .6G 215 (42Hb 89)
Meldex Cl. NW7 .23Ya 48
Meldon Cl. SW6 .53Db 111
Meldone Cl. KT5: Surb .73Ra 153
Meldrum Cl. BR5: Orp .72Yc 161
RH8: Oxt .4K 211
Meldrum Rd. IG3: Ilf .33Wc 75
Melfield Gdns. SE6 .63Ec 136
Melford Av. IG11: Bark .37Uc 74
Melford Cl. KT9: Chess .78Pa 153
Melford Ct. SE1 .3J 231
SE22 .60Wb 113
(not continuous)
Melford Pas. SE22 .59Wb 113

Melford Pl. CM15: B'wood 18Yd 40
Melford Rd. E6 42Pc 94
E11 33Gc 73
E17 28Ac 52
IG1: Ilf 33Tc 74
SE22 59Wb 113
Melfort Av. CR7: Thor H 69Rb 135
Melfort Rd. CR7: Thor H 69Rb 135
Melgund Rd. N5 36Qb 70
Melia Cl. WD25: Wat 7Y 13
Melina Cl. UB3: Hayes 43T 84
Melina Ct. NW8 4B 214
SW15 55Wa 110
Melina Pl. NW8 4B 214 (41Fb 89)
Melina Rd. W12 47Xa 88
Melior Ct. N6 30Lb 50
Melior Pl. SE1 1H 231 (47Ub 91)
Melior St. SE1 1H 231 (47Ub 91)
Meliot Rd. SE6 61Fc 137
Melksham Cl. RM3: Rom 24Pd 57
Melksham Dr. RM3: Rom 24Pd 57
Melksham Gdns.
RM3: Rom 24Nd 57
Melksham Grn. RM3: Rom 24Pd 57
Meller Cl. CR0: Bedd 76Nb 156
Mellifont Cl. SM5: Cars 73Fb 155
Melling Dr. EN1: Enf 11Wb 33
Melling St. SE18 51Uc 116
Mellish Cl. IG11: Bark 39Vc 75
Mellish Flats E10 31Cc 72
Mellish Gdns. IG8: Wfd G 22Jc 53
Mellish Ho. *E1 44Xb 91*
(off Varden St.)
Mellish Ind. Est. SE18 48Mc 93
Mellish St. E14 48Cc 92
Mellish Way RM11: Horn 29Ld 57
Mellison Rd. SW17 64Gb 133
Melliss Av. TW9: Kew 53Ra 109
Mellitus St. W12 43Va 88
Mellor Cl. KT12: Walt T 73Ba 151
Mellor Wlk. *SL4: Wind 3H 103*
(off Batchelors Acre)
Mellow Cl. SM7: Bans 86Eb 175
Mellow La. E. UB4: Hayes 41S 84
Mellow La. W. UB10: Hil 41S 84
Mellows Rd. IG5: Ilf 27Pc 54
SM6: Wall 78Mb 156
Mells Cres. SE9 63Pc 138
Mell St. SE10 50Gc 93
Melody La. N5 36Sb 71
Melody Rd. SW18 57Eb 111
TN16: Big H 90Lc 179
Melon Pl. W8 47Cb 89
Melon Rd. E11 34Gc 73
SE15 53Wb 113
Melrose Av. CR4: Mitc 66Kb 134
DA1: Cray 59Gd 118
EN6: Pot B 4Cb 17
N22 25Rb 51
NW2 36Xa 68
SW16 69Pb 134
SW19 61Bb 133
TW2: Whitt 59Da 107
UB6: G'frd 40Da 65
WD6: Bore 15Ra 29
Melrose Cl. SE12 60Jc 115
UB4: Hayes 43W 84
UB6: G'frd 40Da 65
Melrose Ct. EN8: Chesh 1Zb 20
W13 46Ja 86
(off Williams Rd.)
Melrose Cres. BR6: Orp 77Tc 160
Melrose Dr. UB1: S'hall 46Ca 85
Melrose Gdns. HA8: Edg 27Ra 47
KT3: N Mald 69Ta 131
KT12: Hers 78Y 151
W6 48Ya 88
Melrose Ho. *NW6 41Cb 89*
(off Carlton Vale)
SW1 7K 227
Melrose Pl. WD17: Wat 10V 12
Melrose Rd. CR5: Coul 87Kb 176
HA5: Pinn 28Ba 45
KT13: Weyb 78Q 150
SW13 54Va 110
SW18 58Bb 111
SW19 68Cb 133
TN16: Big H 88Lc 179
W3 48Sa 87
Melrose Ter. W6 48Ya 88
Melrose Tudor *SM6: Wall 78Nb 156*
(off Plough La.)
Melsa Rd. SM4: Mord 72Eb 155
Melsted Rd. HP1: Hem H 2K 3
Melstock Av. RM14: Upm 35Sd 78
Melthorne Dr. HA4: Ruis 34Y 65
Melthorpe Gdns. SE3 53Nc 116
Melton Cl. HA4: Ruis 32Y 65
Melton Ct. SM2: Sutt 80Eb 155
SW7 6C 226 (49Fb 89)
Melton Flds. KT19: Ewe 81Ta 173
Melton Gdns. RM1: Rom 31Hd 76
Melton Pl. KT19: Ewe 81Ta 173
Melton Rd. RH1: Mers 2C 208
Melton St. NW1 4C 216 (41Lb 90)
Melville Av. CR2: S Croy 78Vb 157
SW20 66Wa 132
UB6: G'frd 36Ha 66
Melville Cl. UB10: Ick 33T 64
Melville Ct. RM3: Rom 24Nd 57
SE8 49Ac 92
W4 50Qa 87
(off Haining Cl.)
W12 48Xa 88
(off Goldhawk Rd.)
Melville Gdns. N13 22Rb 51
Melville Ho. EN5: New Bar 15Fb 31
SE10 53Ec 114
(off Sparta St.)
Melville Pl. N1 38Sb 71
Melville Rd. DA14: Sidc 61Yc 139
E17 27Bc 52
NW10 38Ta 67
RM5: Col R 24Dd 56
RM13: Rain 42Jd 96
SW13 53Wa 110
Melville Vs. Rd. W3 46Sa 87
Melvin Rd. SE20 67Yb 136
Melvinshaw KT22: Lea 93La 192
Melwood Ho. *E1 44Xb 91*
(off Watney Mkt.)
Melyn Cl. N7 35Lb 70
Memel Ct. EC1 6D 218
Memel St. EC1 6D 218 (42Sb 91)
Memess Path SE18 51Qc 116
Memorial Av. E15 41Gc 93
Memorial Cl. RH8: Oxt 99Fc 199
TW5: Hest 51Ba 107
Menai Pl. *E3 40Cc 72*
(off Blondin St.)
Menard Ct. EC1 4E 218
Mendez Way SW15 58Wa 110
Mendham Ho. SE1 3H 231
Mendip Cl. KT4: Wor Pk 74Ya 154
SE26 63Yb 136
SL3: L'ly 50C 82
UB3: Harl 52T 106
Mendip Ct. *SE14 51Yb 114*
(off Avonley Rd.)
SW11 55Eb 111
Mendip Dr. NW2 33Ab 68
Mendip Ho. *N9 19Wb 33*
(within Edmonton Grn. Shop. Cen.)
Mendip Ho's. *E2 41Yb 92*
(off Welwyn St.)
Mendip Rd. DA7: Bex 53Gd 118
IG2: Ilf 29Uc 54
RM11: Horn 31Jd 76
SW11 55Eb 111
WD23: Bush 16Ea 28
Mendora Rd. SW6 52Ab 110
Mendoza Cl. RM11: Horn 29Nd 57
Menelik Rd. NW2 35Ab 68
Menier Chocolate Factory
(Theatre and Art Gallery) 7E 224
Menlo Gdns. SE19 66Tb 135
Menlo Lodge *N13 20Pb 32*
(off Crothall Cl.)
Menon Dr. N9 20Xb 33
Menotti St. E2 42Wb 91
Menteath Ho. *E14 44Cc 92*
(off Dod St.)
Menthone Pl. RM11: Horn 31Md 77
Mentmore Cl. HA3: Kenton 30La 46
Mentmore Ho. *KT18: Eps 86Sa 173*
(off Dalmeny Way)
Mentmore Rd. AL1: St A 4B 6
Mentmore Ter. E8 38Xb 71
Mentone Mans. *SW10 52Db 111*
(off Fulham Rd.)
Meon Cl. KT20: Tad 94Xa 194
Meon Ct. TW7: Isle 54Ga 108
Meon Rd. W3 47Sa 87
Mepham Rd. CR4: Mitc 67Lb 134
Mepham Cres. HA3: Hrw W 24Ea 46
Mepham Gdns.
HA3: Hrw W 24Ea 46
Mepham St. SE1 7J 223 (46Qb 90)
Mera Dr. DA7: Bex 56Cd 118
Merantun Way SW19 67Db 133
Merbury Cl. SE13 57Ec 114
SE28 46Tc 94
Merbury Rd. SE28 46Tc 94
Mercator Pl. E14 50Cc 92
Mercator Rd. SE13 56Fc 115
Mercedes-Benz World 81P 169
Mercer Bldg. EC2 5J 219
Mercer Cl. KT7: T Ditt 73Ha 152
Mercer Ct. E1 43Ac 92
Mercer Ho. SW1 7K 227
Merceron Ho's. *E2 41Yb 92*
(off Globe Rd.)
Merceron St. E1 42Xb 91
Mercer Pl. HA5: Pinn 26Y 45
Mercers HP2: Hem H 1N 3
Mercers Cl. SE10 49Hc 93
Mercer's Cotts. *E1 44Ac 92*
(off White Horse Rd.)
Mercers Country Pk. 3D 208
Mercers M. N19 34Mb 70
Mercers Pl. W6 49Za 88
Mercers Rd. N19 34Mb 70
(not continuous)
Mercers Row AL1: St A 4A 6
Mercer St. WC2 3F 223 (44Nb 90)
Mercer Wlk. UB8: Uxb 38L 63
Merchant Ct. *E1 46Yb 92*
(off Wapping Wall)
Merchant Ho. *E14 48Dc 92*
(off Goulston St.)
Merchant Ind. Ter. NW10 42Sa 87
Merchants Cl. GU21: Knap 9G 166
SE25 70Wb 135
Merchants Ho. *SE10 50Fc 93*
(off Collington St.)
Merchants Lodge *E17 28Cc 52*
(off Westbury Rd.)
Merchant Sq. W2 1C 220
Merchants Row *SE10 50Fc 93*
(off Hoskins St.)
Merchant St. E3 41Bc 92
Merchiston Rd. SE6 61Fc 137
Merchland Rd. SE9 60Sc 116
Mercia Gro. SE13 56Ec 114
Mercia Ho. *SE5 54Sb 113*
(off Denmark Rd.)
TW15: Ashf 67S 128
Mercian Way SL1: Slou 6D 80
Mercia Wlk. GU21: Wok 89B 168
Mercier Rd. SW15 57Ab 110
Mercury *NW9 25Wa 48*
(off The Concourse)
Mercury Cen. TW14: Felt 57W 106
Mercury Ct. *E14 49Cc 92*
(off Homer Dr.)
RM1: Rom 29Hd 56
SW9 53Qb 112
(off Southey Rd.)
Mercury Gdns. RM1: Rom 29Gd 56
Mercury Hgts. IG2: Ilf 30Tc 54
Mercury Ho. *E3 39Cc 72*
(off Garrison Rd.)
E16 44Hc 93
(off Jude St.)
KT17: Ewe 82Wa 174
(off Cheam Rd.)
TW8: Bford 51La 108
(off Glenhurst Rd.)
W5 42Pa 87
Mercury Rd. TW8: Bford 51La 108
Mercury Way SE14 51Zb 114
Mercy Ter. SE13 57Dc 114
Merebank La. CR0: Wadd 78Pb 156
Mere Cl. BR6: Farnb 75Qc 160
SW15 59Za 110
Mereden Ct. *AL1: St A 5A 6*
(off Tavistock Av.)
Meredith Av. NW2 36Ya 68
Meredith Cl. HA5: Pinn 24Z 45
Meredith Ho. N16 36Ub 71
Meredith M. SE4 56Bc 114
Meredith Rd. RM16: Grays 9C 100
Meredith St. E13 41Jc 93
EC1 4B 218 (41Rb 91)
Meredith Twr. *W3 48Ra 87*
(off Hanbury Rd.)
Meredyth Rd. SW13 54Wa 110
Mere End CR0: C'don 73Zb 158
Merefield Gdns. KT20: Tad 91Za 194
Mere Rd. KT13: Weyb 76T 150
KT20: Tad 96Xa 194
SE2 47Zc 95
SL1: Slou 8K 81
TW17: Shep 72R 150
Mereside BR6: Farnb 75Qc 160
Mereside Pk. TW15: Ashf 63S 128
Mereside Pl. GU25: Vir W 4L 147
Meretone Cl. SE4 56Ac 114
Mereton Mans. *SE8 53Cc 114*
(off Brookmill Rd.)
Merevale Cres. SM4: Mord 72Eb 155
Mereway Rd. TW2: Twick 60Fa 108
Merewood Cl. BR1: Brom 68Qc 138
Merewood Gdns. CR0: C'don 73Zb 158
Merewood Rd. DA7: Bex 54Ed 118
Mereworth Cl. BR2: Brom 71Hc 159
Mereworth Dr. SE18 52Rc 116
Mereworth Ho. SE15 51Yb 114
Merganser Ct. *E1 45Wb 91*
(off Star Pl.)
SE8 51Bc 114
(off Edward St.)
Merganser Gdns. SE28 48Tc 94
MERIDEN 8Aa 13
Meriden Cl. BR1: Brom 66Mc 137
IG6: Ilf 25Sc 54
Meriden Ct. SW3 7D 226
Meriden Ho. N1 1J 219
Meriden Way WD25: Wat 8Aa 13
Merideth Ct. KT1: King T 68Pa 131
Meridia Ct. *E15 39Ec 72*
(off Biggerstaff Rd.)
Meridiam Ct. UB4: Yead 42Y 85
Meridian Bus. Pk. EN9: Walt A 7Dc 20
Meridian Cen. CR0: New Ad 82Gc 179
Meridian Cl. NW7 21Ta 47
Meridian Ct. RM17: Grays 52De 121
SE15 52Xb 113
(off Gervase St.)
SE16 47Wb 91
(off East La.)
SL5: Asc 4A 146
Meridian Ga. E14 47Dc 92
Meridian Ho. *NW1 38Lb 70*
(off Baynes St.)
SE10 49Gc 93
(off Azof St.)
SE10 52Ec 114
(off Royal Hill)
MERIDIAN PARK 8Ec 20
Meridian Pl. E14 47Dc 92
Meridian Point SE8 51Dc 114
Meridian Rd. SE7 52Mc 115
Meridian Sq. E15 38Fc 73
Meridian Trad. Est. SE7 49Kc 93
Meridian Wlk. N17 23Ub 51
Meridian Way EN3: Pond E 21Yb 52
EN9: Walt A 6Dc 20
N9 21Yb 52
N18 22Yb 52
Meriel Wlk. DA9: Ghithe 56Xd 120
Merifield Rd. SE9 56Lc 115
Merileys Cl. DA3: Lfield 69Ee 143
Merino Cl. E11 28Lc 53
Merino Ct. EC1 4E 218
Merino Pl. DA15: Sidc 58Wc 117
Merioneth Ct. *W7 43Ha 86*
(off Copley Cl.)
Merita Ho. *E1 46Wb 91*
(off Nesham St.)
Merivale Rd. HA1: Harr 31Ea 66
SW15 56Ab 110
Merland Cl. KT20: Tad 92Ya 194
Merland Grn. KT20: Tad 92Ya 194
Merland Ri. KT18: Tatt C 91Ya 194
KT20: Tad 91Ya 194
Merle Av. UB9: Hare 26K 43
MERLE COMMON 8M 211
Merle Comn. Rd. RH8: Oxt 7L 211
Merlewood TN13: S'oaks 95Kd 203
Merlewood Cl. CR3: Cat'm 92Tb 197
Merlewood Dr. BR7: Chst 67Pc 138
Merley Ct. NW9 32Sa 67
Merlin *NW9 25Wa 48*
(off The Concourse)
Merlin Cen., The AL4: St A 2K 7
Merlin Cl. CR0: C'don 77Ub 157
CR4: Mitc 69Gb 133
EN9: Walt A 6Jc 21
IG6: Ilf 22Yc 55
RM5: Col R 23Fd 56
RM16: Chaf H 48Ae 99
SL3: L'ly 51D 104
SM6: Wall 79Pb 156
UB5: N'olt 41Y 85
Merlin Ct. BR2: Brom 69Hc 137
DA9: Ghithe 58Wd 120
(off Waterstone Way)
GU21: Wok 86E 168
HA4: Ruis 33T 64
HA7: Stan 22Ka 46
(off William Dr.)
Merlin Cres. HA8: Edg 25Pa 47
Merlin Gdns. BR1: Brom 62Jc 137
RM5: Col R 23Fd 56
Merling Cl. KT9: Chess 78La 152
Merlin Gro. BR3: Beck 70Bc 136
IG6: Ilf 24Rc 54
Merlin Ho. EN3: Pond E 15Zb 34
Merlin Rd. DA16: Well 56Wc 117
E12 33Mc 73
RM5: Col R 23Fd 56
Merlin Rd. Nth. DA16: Well 56Wc 117
Merlins Av. HA2: Harr 34Ba 65
Merlins Ct. WC1 4K 217
Merlin St. WC1 4K 217 (41Qb 90)
Merlin Way WD25: Wat 6V 12
Mermagen Dr. RM13: Rain 38Kd 77
Mermaid Cl. DA11: Nflt 59Fe 121
Mermaid Ct. *E8 38Vb 71*
(off Celandine Dr.)
SE1 1F 231 (47Tb 91)
SE16 46Bc 92
Mermaid Ho. *E14 45Ec 92*
(off Bazely St.)
Mermaid Twr. *SE8 51Bc 114*
(off Abinger Gro.)
Mermerus Gdns. DA12: Grav'nd 3H 145
Meroe Ct. N16 33Ub 71
Merredene St. SW2 58Pb 112
Merriam Av. E9 37Bc 72
Merriam Cl. E4 22Ec 52
Merrick Rd. UB2: S'hall 47Ba 85
Merrick Sq. SE1 3F 231 (48Tb 91)
Merridene N21 16Rb 33
Merrielands Cres. RM9: Dag 40Bd 75
Merrielands Retail Pk. RM9: Dag 39Bd 75
Merrilands Rd. KT4: Wor Pk 74Ya 154
Merrilees Rd. DA15: Sidc 59Uc 116
Merrilyn Cl. KT10: Clay 79Ja 152
Merriman Rd. SE3 53Lc 115
Merrington Rd. SW6 51Cb 111
Merrin Hill CR2: Sande 83Ub 177
Merrion Av. HA7: Stan 22Ma 47
Merrion Ct. *HA4: Ruis 32V 64*
(off Pembroke Rd.)
Merrist Wood Golf Course 10F 186
Merritt Gdns. KT9: Chess 79La 152
Merritt Ho. *RM1: Rom 31Hd 76*
(off South St.)
Merritt Rd. SE4 57Bc 114
Merritt Wlk. AL9: Wel G 5D 8
Merrivale N14 16Mb 32
NW1 1C 216
Merrivale Av. IG4: Ilf 28Mc 53
Merrivale Gdns. GU21: Wok 9N 167
Merrivale M. UB7: Yiew 46M 83
Merrow Bldgs. SE1 1C 230
Merrow Ct. CR4: Mitc 68Fb 133
Merrow Dr. HP1: Hem H 1G 2
Merrow La. GU4: Burp, Guild 100E 188
Merrow Rd. SM2: Cheam 81Za 174
Merrows Cl. HA6: Nwood 23S 44
Merrow St. SE17 7G 231 (50Tb 91)
Merrow Wlk. SE17 7G 231 (50Tb 91)
Merrow Way CR0: New Ad 79Ec 158
Merrydown Way BR7: Chst 67Nc 138
Merryfield SE3 54Hc 115
Merryfield Gdns. HA7: Stan 22La 46
Merryfield Ho. *SE9 62Lc 137*
(off Grove Pk. Rd.)
Merryfields AL4: St A 2J 7
UB8: Uxb 40M 63
UB10: Uxb 40N 63
WD24: Wat 10W 12
Merryfields Cl. DA3: Hartl 70Be 143
Merryfields Way SE6 59Dc 114
MERRY HILL 18Da 27
Merryhill Cl. E4 17Dc 34
Merry Hill Mt. WD23: Bush 18Da 27
Merry Hill Rd. WD23: Bush 16Ba 27
Merryhills Cl. TN16: Big H 88Mc 179
Merryhills Ct. N14 15Lb 32
Merryhills Dr. EN2: Enf 14Mb 32
Merrylands KT16: Chert 76G 148
Merrylands Rd. KT23: Bookh 95Ba 191
Merrymeade Chase CM15: B'wood 18Zd 41
Merrymeet SM7: Bans 86Hb 175
Merryweather Cl. DA1: Dart 58Pd 119
Merryweather Ct. KT3: N Mald 71Ua 154
N19 34Lb 70
Merryweather Pl. SE10 52Dc 114
Merrywood Gro. KT20: Lwr K 2G 206
Merrywood Pk. RH2: Reig 4K 207
Mersea Ho. IG11: Bark 37Rc 74
Mersey Av. RM14: Upm 30Td 58
Mersey Ct. *KT2: King T 67Ma 131*
(off Samuel Gray Gdns.)
Mersey Rd. E17 27Bc 52
Mersey Wlk. UB5: N'olt 40Ca 65
Mersham Dr. NW9 29Qa 47
Mersham Pl. *CR7: Thor H 68Tb 135*
(off Livingstone Rd.)
SE20 67Xb 135
Mersham Rd. CR7: Thor H 69Tb 135
MERSTHAM 100Lb 196
Merstham Rd. RH1: Blet 1G 208
Merten Rd. RM6: Chad H 31Ad 75
Merthyr Ter. SW13 51Xa 110
MERTON 66Eb 133
Merton Abbey Mills SW19 67Eb 133
Merton Av. DA3: Hartl 70Ae 143
(not continuous)
UB5: N'olt 36Ea 66
UB10: Hil 38R 64
W4 49Va 88
Merton Ct. DA16: Well 54Xc 117
IG1: Ilf 30Nc 54
WD6: Bore 11Pa 29
Merton Gdns. BR5: Pet W 71Rc 160
KT20: Tad 91Za 194
Merton Hall Gdns. SW20 67Ab 132
Merton Hall Rd. SW19 66Ab 132
Merton High St. SW19 66Db 133
Merton Ind. Pk. SW19 67Db 133
Merton La. N6 33Hb 69
Merton Lodge EN5: New Bar 15Eb 31
Merton Mans. SW20 68Za 132
MERTON PARK 68Cb 133
Merton Pk. Pde. SW19 67Bb 133
Merton Pl. RM16: Grays 9C 100
SW19 67Eb 133
(off Nelson Gro. Rd.)
Merton Ri. NW3 38Gb 69
Merton Rd. E17 29Ec 52
EN2: Enf 10Tb 19
HA2: Harr 32Ea 66
IG3: Ilf 31Vc 75
IG11: Bark 38Vc 75
SE25 71Vb 157
SL1: Slou 8L 81
SW18 58Cb 111
SW19 66Db 133
WD18: Wat 14X 27
Merton's Intergenerational Cen. 68Kb 134
Merton Wlk. KT22: Lea 90Ja 172
Merton Way KT8: W Mole 70Da 129
KT22: Lea 91Ja 192
UB10: Hil 38R 64
Mertoun Ter. W1 1F 221
Merttins Rd. SE15 57Zb 114
Meru Cl. NW5 35Jb 70
Mervan Rd. SW2 56Qb 112
Mervyn Av. SE9 62Sc 138
Mervyn Rd. TW17: Shep 73S 150
W13 48Ja 86
Merwin Way SL4: Wind 4B 102
Meryfield Cl. WD6: Bore 12Pa 29
Meryon Ho. SL4: Wind 5E 102
Mesne Way TN14: S'ham 84Hd 182
Messaline Av. W3 43Sa 87
Messant Cl. RM3: Hrld W 26Md 57
Messenger Ct. *SE16 48Wb 91*
(off Spa Rd.)
Messent Rd. SE9 57Lc 115
Messeter Pl. SE9 58Qc 116
Messina Av. NW6 38Cb 69
Messiter Ho. N1 1J 217
Metcalfe Ct. SE10 48Hc 93
Metcalf Rd. TW15: Ashf 64R 128
Metcalf Wlk. TW13: Hanw 63Aa 129
Meteor St. SW11 56Jb 112
Meteor Way SM6: Wall 80Nb 156
Metford Cres. EN3: Enf L 10Cc 20
Methley St. SE11 7A 230 (50Qb 90)
Methuen Cl. HA8: Edg 24Qa 47
Methuen Pk. N10 27Kb 50
Methuen Rd. DA6: Bex 56Bd 117
DA17: Belv 49Dd 96
HA8: Edg 24Qa 47
Methven Ct. *N9 20Wb 33*
(off The Broadway)
Methwold Rd. W10 43Za 88
Metro Bus. Cen. SE26 65Bc 136
Metro Central Hgts. SE1 4D 230
Metro Cen. BR5: St M Cry 72Xc 161
Metro Ind. Cen. TW7: Isle 54Ga 108
Metro Playgolf Driving Range 24Ya 48
Metropolis SE11 4C 230
Metropolitan Bus. Cen. *N1 38Ub 71*
(off Enfield Rd.)
Metropolitan Cen., The UB6: G'frd 39Da 65
Metropolitan Cl. E14 43Cc 92
Metropolitan M. WD18: Wat 14U 26
Metropolitan Pl. WD18: Wat 14V 26
Metropolitan Sta. App. WD18: Wat 13V 26
Metropolitan Sta. Bldgs. *W6 49Ya 88*
(off Beadon Rd.)
Metropolitan Wharf E1 46Yb 92
Metro Trad. Est. HA9: Wemb 35Ra 67
Meux Cl. EN7: Chesh 3Wb 19
Mews, The AL1: St A 1C 6
DA3: Lfield 69Ae 143
(off Bramblefield Cl.)
DA14: Sidc 63Wc 139
IG4: Ilf 29Mc 53
N1 39Sb 71
N8 27Qb 50
RH2: Reig 5K 207
RM1: Rom 28Gd 56
RM17: Grays 49Ee 99
TN13: S'oaks 95Jd 202
(Burlington Pl.)
TN13: S'oaks 95Ld 203
(Hartslands Rd.)
TW1: Twick 58Ka 108
WD18: Wat 14Y 27
(off Smith St.)
Mews End TN16: Big H 90Mc 179
Mews Pl. IG8: Wfd G 21Jc 53
Mews St. E1 46Wb 91
Mexborough NW1 39Lb 70
Mexfield Rd. SW15 57Bb 111
Meyer Grn. EN1: Enf 10Wb 19
Meyer Rd. DA8: Erith 51Fd 118
Meymott St. SE1 7B 224 (46Rb 91)
Meynell Cres. E9 38Zb 72
Meynell Gdns. E9 38Zb 72
Meynell Rd. E9 38Zb 72
RM3: Rom 24Kd 57
Meyrick Cl. GU21: Knap 8J 167
Meyrick Ct. AL1: St A 2F 6
Meyrick Ho. *E14 43Cc 92*
(off Burgess St.)
Meyrick Rd. NW10 37Wa 68
SW11 55Fb 111
Mezen Cl. HA6: Nwood 22T 44
Miah Ter. E1 46Wb 91
Miall Wlk. SE26 63Ac 136
Micawber Av. UB8: Hil 42Q 84
Micawber Ct. N1 3E 218
Micawber Ho. *SE16 47Wb 91*
(off Llewellyn St.)
Micawber St. N1 3E 218 (41Sb 91)
Michael Cliffe Ho. EC1 4A 218
Michael Faraday Ho. SE17 7H 231
Michael Gdns. DA12: Grav'nd 4G 144
RM11: Horn 28Md 57
Michael Gaynor Cl. W7 46Ha 86
Michael Haines Ho. *SW9 52Qb 112*
(off Sth. Island Pl.)
Michael Manley Ind. Est. SW8 53Lb 112
Michaelmas Cl. SW20 69Ya 132
Michael Rd. E11 32Gc 73
SE25 69Ub 135
SW6 53Db 111
Michaels Cl. SE13 56Gc 115
Michaels La. DA3: Fawk 75Xd 164
TN15: Ash 75Xd 164
Michael Stewart Ho. *SW6 51Bb 111*
(off Clem Attlee Ct.)
Michelangelo Ct. *SE16 50Xb 91*
(off Stubbs Dr.)
Micheldever Rd. SE12 58Gc 115
Michelet Cl. GU18: Light 2A 166
Michelham Gdns. KT20: Tad 92Ya 194
TW1: Twick 62Ha 130
Michelle Ct. *BR1: Brom 67Hc 137*
(off Blyth Rd.)
N12 22Eb 49
W3 45Ta 87
Michelsdale Dr. TW9: Rich 56Na 109
Michelson Ho. SE11 6J 229
Michel's Row *TW9: Rich 56Na 109*
(off Michelsdale Dr.)
Michel Wlk. SE18 50Rc 94
Michigan Av. E12 35Pc 74
Michigan Bldg. *E14 46Fc 93*
(off Biscayne Av.)
Michigan Ho. E14 48Cc 92
Michleham Down N12 21Bb 49
Micholls Av. SL9: Chal P 21A 42
Micholls Cotts. *SL9: Chal P 22B 42*
(off Micholls Av.)
Mick Jagger Centre, The *58Ld 119*
(off Shepherd's La.)
Mickledore NW1 2C 216
MICKLEFIELD GREEN 10K 11
Micklefield Rd. HP2: Hem H 2C 4
Micklefield Way WD6: Bore 10Na 15
MICKLEHAM 100La 192
Mickleham By-Pass RH5: Mick 99Ka 192
Mickleham Cl. BR5: St P 68Vc 139
MICKLEHAM DOWNS 98Ma 193
Mickleham Dr. RH5: Mick 98La 192
Mickleham Gdns. SM3: Cheam 79Ab 154
Mickleham Rd. BR5: St P 67Vc 139
Mickleham Way CR0: New Ad 79Ec 159
Micklem Dr. HP1: Hem H 1H 3
Micklethwaite Rd. SW6 51Cb 111

Mickleton Ho. W2 .... 43Cb 89
(off Westbourne Pk. Rd.)
Midas Bus. Cen. RM10: Dag 35Dd 76
Midas Ind. Est. UB8: Uxb 40K 63
Midas Metropolitan Ind. Est.
SM4: Mord 73Ya 154
MID BECKTON 44Pc 94
Midcroft HA4: Ruis 32U 64
SL2: Slou 2F 80
Mid Cross La. SL9: Chal P 22B 42
Middle Boy RM4: Abr 13Yc 37
Middle Cl. CR5: Coul 92Qb 196
KT17: Eps 84Ua 174
Middle Cres. UB9: Den 31F 62
Middle Dartrey Wlk. SW10 .... 52Eb 111
(off Dartrey Wlk.)
Middle Dene NW7 .... 20Ta 29
Middle Down WD25: A'ham 8Da 13
Middle Farm Cl. KT24: Eff 99Z 191
Middle Farm Pl. KT24: Eff 99Y 191
Middlefield NW8 .... 39Fb 69
Middlefielde W13 .... 43Ka 86
Middlefield Gdns. IG2: Ilf 30Rc 54
Middlefields CR0: Sels 81Ac 178
Middle Furlong WD23: Bush 14Da 27
MIDDLE GREEN 46A 82
Middle Grn. SL3: L'ly 46A 82
TW18: Staines 66M 127
Middle Grn. Cl. KT5: Surb 72Pa 153
Middlegreen Rd. SL3: L'ly 7P 81
Middlegreen Trad. Est. SL3: L'ly 7P 81
Middleham Ct. DA2: Dart 58Rd 119
(off Osbourne Rd.)
Middleham Gdns. N18 .... 23Wb 51
Middleham Rd. N18 .... 23Wb 51
Middle Hill HP1: Hem H 2G 2
TW20: Egh, Eng G 3N 125
Middle La. HP3: Bov 1C 10
KT17: Eps 84Ua 174
N8 .... 29Nb 50
TN15: Seal 93Pd 203
TW11: Tedd 65Ha 130
Middle La. M. N8 .... 29Nb 50
Middlemarch Lodge WD3: Rick 17N 25
Middlemead Cl. KT23: Bookh 97Ca 191
Middlemead Rd. KT23: Bookh 97Ba 191
Middle Mill Halls of Residence
KT1: King T 69Pa 131
Middle New St. EC4 .... 2A 224
Middle Ope WD24: Wat 9X 13
Middle Pk. Av. SE9 .... 58Mc 115
Middle Path HA2: Harr 32Fa 66
Middle Rd. CM13: Ingve 22Ee 59
E13 .... 40Jc 73
EN4: E Barn 16Gb 31
HA2: Harr 33Fa 66
KT22: Lea 93Ka 192
SW16 .... 68Mb 134
UB9: Den 31E 62
Middle Row W10 .... 42Ab 88
Middlesborough Ho. RM3: Rom 24Nd 57
(off Kingsbridge Cir.)
Middlesborough Rd. N18 .... 23Wb 51
Middlesex Building, The E1 .... 1J 225
(off Artillery La.)
Middlesex Bus. Cen. UB2: S'hall 47Ca 85
Middlesex CCC 3C 214 (41Fb 89)
Middlesex Cl. UB1: S'hall 42Da 85
Middlesex County Cricket School 26Db 49
Middlesex Ct. HA1: Harr 29Ha 46
KT15: Add 78L 149
(off Bush Cl.)
TW8: Bford 50La 86
(off Glenhurst Rd.)
W4 .... 49Va 88
Middlesex Filter Beds Nature Reserve
.... 34Zb 72
Middlesex Ho. HA0: Wemb 39Ma 67
UB8: Uxb 38L 63
(off Mercer Wlk.)
Middlesex Pas. EC1 .... 1C 224
Middlesex Pl. E9 .... 37Yb 72
(off Elsdale St.)
Middlesex Rd. CR4: Mitc 71Nb 156
Middlesex St. E1 .... 1J 225 (43Ub 91)
Middlesex University
Cat Hill Campus 15Jb 32
Hendon Campus 28Xa 48
The Archway Campus 32Lb 70
Trent Pk. Campus 12Lb 32
Middlesex Wharf E5 .... 33Yb 72
Middle St. CR0: C'don 75Sb 157
(not continuous)
EC1 .... 7D 218 (43Sb 91)
Middle Temple La. EC4 .... 3K 223 (44Qb 90)
Middleton Av. DA14: Sidc 65Xc 139
E4 .... 21Bc 52
UB6: G'frd 40Fa 66
Middleton Cl. E4 .... 20Bc 34
Middleton Dr. HA5: Eastc 27W 44
SE16 .... 47Zb 92
Middleton Gdns. IG2: Ilf 30Rc 54
Middleton Gro. N7 .... 36Nb 70
Middleton Hall La. CM15: B'wood 19Ae 41
Middleton Ho. E8 .... 38Wb 71
SE1 .... 4F 231
SW1 .... 6E 228
Middleton M. N7 .... 36Nb 70
Middleton Pl. W1 .... 1B 222
Middleton Rd. CM15: Shenf 18Ae 41
E8 .... 38Vb 71
KT11: D'side 91X 191
KT19: Ewe 82Ta 173
NW11 .... 31Cb 69
SM4: Mord 72Db 155
SM5: Cars 72Db 155
UB3: Hayes 43T 84
WD3: Rick 18J 25
Middleton St. E2 .... 41Xb 91
Middleton Way SE13 .... 56Fc 115
Middle Wlk. GU21: Wok 89A 168
SL1: Burn 1A 80
Middle Way DA18: Erith 48Bd 95
SW16 .... 68Mb 134
UB4: Yead 42Y 85
WD24: Wat 9W 12
Middle Way, The HA3: W'stone 26Ha 46
Middleway NW11 .... 29Db 49
Middle Yd. SE1 .... 6H 225 (46Ub 91)
Middlings, The TN13: S'oaks 98Hd 202
Middlings Ri. TN13: S'oaks 97Hd 202
Middlings Wood TN13: S'oaks 97Jd 202
Midfield Av. BR8: Hext 65Jd 140
DA7: Bex 55Ed 118
Midfield Pde. DA7: Bex 55Ed 118
Midfield Way BR5: St P 67Wc 139
Midford Ho. NW4 .... 28Ya 48
(off Stratford Rd.)
Midford Pl. W1 .... 6C 216 (42Lb 90)
Midgarth Cl. KT22: Oxs 86Ea 172
Midholm HA9: Wemb 32Qa 67
NW11 .... 28Db 49
Midholm Cl. NW11 .... 28Db 49
Midholm Rd. CR0: C'don 75Ac 158
Midhope Cl. GU22: Wok 91A 188
Midhope Gdns. GU22: Wok 91A 188
Midhope Ho. WC1 .... 4G 217
Midhope Rd. GU22: Wok 91A 188
Midhope St. WC1 .... 4G 217 (41Nb 90)
Midhurst SE26 .... 65Yb 136
Midhurst Av. CR0: C'don 73Qb 156
N10 .... 27Jb 50
Midhurst Cl. RM12: Horn 35Jd 76
Midhurst Gdns. UB10: Hil 39S 64
Midhurst Hill DA6: Bex 58Cd 118
Midhurst Ho. E14 .... 44Bc 92
(off Salmon La.)
Midhurst Pde. N10 .... 27Jb 50
(off Fortis Grn.)
Midhurst Rd. W13 .... 47Ja 86
Midhurst Way E5 .... 35Wb 71
Mid Kent Golf Course 2D 144
Midland Ho. AL1: St A 2C 6
(off Alma Rd.)
Midland Pde. NW6 .... 37Db 69
Midland Pl. E14 .... 50Ec 92
Midland Rd. E10 .... 31Ec 72
HP2: Hem H 2M 3
NW1 .... 2E 216 (40Mb 70)
Midland Ter. NW2 .... 34Za 68
NW10 .... 42Ua 88
Midleton Rd. KT3: N Mald 69Sa 131
Midlothian Rd. E3 .... 42Bc 92
(off Burdett Rd.)
Midmoor Rd. SW12 .... 60Lb 112
SW19 .... 67Za 132
Midnight Av. SE5 .... 51Rb 113
Midship Cl. SE16 .... 46Zb 92
Midship Point E14 .... 47Cc 92
(off The Quarterdeck)
Midstrath Rd. NW10 .... 35Ua 68
Mid St. RH1: S Nut 9F 208
Midsummer Av. TW4: Houn 56Ba 107
Midsummer Wlk. GU21: Wok 8P 167
Midway AL3: St A 5P 5
KT12: Walt T 75X 151
SM3: Sutt 73Bb 155
Midway Av. KT16: Chert 69J 127
TW20: Thorpe 69D 126
Midway Cl. TW18: Staines 62K 127
(not continuous)
Midway Ho. EC1 .... 3C 218
Midwinter Cl. DA16: Well 55Wc 117
Midwood Cl. NW2 .... 34Xa 68
Miena Way KT21: Asht 89Ma 173
Miers Cl. E6 .... 39Qc 74
Mighell Av. IG4: Ilf 29Mc 53
Mikado Cl. UB9: Hare 26M 43
Mikardo Ct. E14 .... 45Ec 92
(off Poplar High St.)
Mike Spring Ct.
DA12: Grav'nd 3F 144
Milan Ct. N11 .... 25Mb 50
Milan Rd. UB1: S'hall 47Ba 85
Milan Wlk. CM14: B'wood 18Xd 40
Milborne Gro. SW10 .... 50Eb 89
Milborne St. E9 .... 37Yb 72
Milborough Cres. SE12 .... 58Gc 115
Milbourne Ct. WD17: Wat 12W 26
Milbourne La. KT10: Esh 79Ea 152
Milbourne Pl. KT19: Ewe 77Ta 153
Milbrook KT10: Esh 79Ea 152
Milburn Dr. UB7: Yiew 45N 83
Milburn Wlk. KT18: Eps 87Ua 174
Milbury Grn. CR6: W'ham 90Fc 179
Milby Ct. WD6: Bore 11Pa 29
Milcombe Cl. GU21: Wok 10N 167
Milcote St. SE1 .... 2B 230 (47Rb 91)
Mildenhall Ho. RM3: Rom 22Qd 57
(off Redcar Rd.)
Mildenhall Rd. E5 .... 35Yb 72
SL1: Slou 4J 81
Mildmay Av. N1 .... 37Tb 71
Mildmay Gro. Nth. N1 .... 36Tb 71
Mildmay Gro. Sth. N1 .... 36Tb 71
Mildmay Pk. N1 .... 36Tb 71
Mildmay Pl. N16 .... 36Ub 71
TN14: S'ham 83Hd 182
Mildmay Rd. IG1: Ilf 34Rc 74
N1 .... 36Tb 71
RM7: Rom 29Ed 56
Mildmay St. N1 .... 37Tb 71
Mildred Av. UB3: Harl 49T 84
UB5: N'olt 36Da 65
WD6: Bore 14Qa 29
(not continuous)
WD18: Wat 14V 26
Mildred Cl. DA1: Dart 58Qd 119
Mildred Ct. CR0: C'don 74Wb 157
Mildred Rd. DA8: Erith 50Gd 96
Mildrose Ct. NW6 .... 41Cb 89
(off Malvern M.)
Mildura Ct. N8 .... 28Pb 50
Mile Cl. EN9: Walt A 5Ec 20
MILE END 42Bc 92
Mile End, The E17 .... 25Zb 52
Mile End Climbing Wall 41Ac 92
MILE END GREEN 68Zd 143
Mile End Pk. 40Ac 72
Mile End Pk. Leisure Cen. 43Ac 92
Mile End Pl. E1 .... 42Zb 92
Mile End Rd. E1 .... 43Yb 92
E3 .... 43Yb 92
Mile End Stadium 43Bc 92
Milehams Ind. Est.
RM19: Purf 48Qd 97
Mile Ho. Cl. AL1: St A 5E 6
Mile Ho. La. AL1: St A 5E 6
Mile Path GU22: Wok 3K 187
Mile Rd. SM6: Bedd, Wall 74Kb 156
(not continuous)
Miles Bldg. NW1 .... 7D 214
Miles Bldgs. NW1 .... 7D 214
Miles Cl. SE28 .... 46Tc 94
Miles Ct. CR0: C'don 75Rb 157
(off Cuthbert Rd.)
E1 .... 44Xb 91
(off Tillman St.)
Miles Dr. SE28 .... 46Uc 94
MILES GREEN 9D 166
Miles Ho. SE10 .... 50Gc 93
(off Tuskar St.)
Miles La. KT11: Cobh 85Aa 171
RH8: Tand 8D 210
RH9: S God 8D 210
Miles Lodge E15 .... 36Fc 73
(off Colegrave Rd.)
HA1: Harr 29Fa 46
Milespit Hill NW7 .... 22Xa 48
Miles Pl. KT5: Surb 70Pa 131
NW8 .... 7C 214
Miles Rd. CR4: Mitc 69Gb 133
KT19: Eps 84Ta 173
N8 .... 27Nb 50
Miles St. SW8 .... 51Nb 112
(not continuous)
Milestone Cl. GU23: Rip 94J 189
N9 .... 19Wb 33
SM2: Sutt 79Fb 155
Milestone Ct. E10 .... 31Dc 72
Milestone Dr. CR8: Purl 86Pb 176
MILESTONE GREEN 56Sa 109
Milestone Ho.
KT1: King T 69Ma 131
(off Surbiton Rd.)
Milestone Rd. DA2: Dart 58Rd 119
SE19 .... 65Vb 135
Miles Way N20 .... 19Gb 31
Milfoil St. W12 .... 45Wa 88
Milford Cl. SE2 .... 51Ad 117
Milford Ct. SL1: Slou 7L 81
UB1: S'hall 46Ca 85
Milford Gdns. CR0: C'don 71Yb 158
HA0: Wemb 35Ma 67
HA8: Edg 24Qa 47
Milford Gro. SM1: Sutt 77Eb 155
Milford La. WC2 .... 4K 223 (45Qb 90)
Milford M. SW16 .... 62Pb 134
Milford Rd. RM16: Grays 46Fe 99
UB1: S'hall 45Ca 85
W13 .... 46Ka 86
Milford Towers SE6 .... 59Dc 114
Milking La. BR2: Kes 83Mc 179
BR6: Downe 84Nc 180
Milk St. BR1: Brom 65Kc 137
E16 .... 46Rc 94
EC2 .... 3E 224 (44Sb 91)
Milkwell Gdns. IG8: Wfd G 24Kc 53
Milkwell Yd. SE5 .... 53Sb 113
Milkwood Rd. SE24 .... 57Rb 113
Milk Yd. E1 .... 45Yb 92
Mill, The KT13: Weyb 75Q 150
Millais Av. E12 .... 36Qc 74
Millais Ct. UB5: N'olt 40Z 65
(off Academy Gdns.)
Millais Cres. KT19: Ewe 78Ua 154
Millais Gdns. HA8: Edg 26Qa 47
Millais Ho. SW1 .... 6F 229
Millais Pl. RM18: Tilb 2C 122
Millais Rd. E11 .... 35Ec 72
EN1: Enf 15Vb 33
KT3: N Mald 73Ua 154
Millais Way KT19: Ewe 77Sa 153
Millan Cl. KT15: New H 82K 169
Milland Ct. WD6: Bore 11Ta 29
Millard Cl. N16 .... 36Ub 71
Millard Rd. SE8 .... 50Bc 92
Millard Ter. RM10: Dag 37Cd 76
Mill Av. UB8: Uxb 40L 63
Millbank HP3: Hem H 6M 3
SM6: Wall 78Mb 156
SW1 .... 4F 229 (48Nb 90)
Millbank Ct. SW1 .... 5F 229
Millbank Twr. SW1 .... 6F 229 (49Nb 90)
Millbank Way SE12 .... 57Jc 115
Millbourne Rd. TW13: Hanw 63Aa 129
Mill Bri. EN5: Barn 16Bb 31
Mill Bri. Pl. UB8: Uxb 40L 63
Millbro BR8: Hext 67Jd 140
Millbrook KT13: Weyb 77U 150
Millbrook Av. DA16: Well 56Tc 116
Millbrook Gdns. RM2: Rom 26Gd 56
RM6: Chad H 30Bd 55
Millbrook Ho. SE15 .... 51Wb 113
(off Peckham Pk. Rd.)
Millbrook Pas. SW9 .... 55Rb 113
Millbrook Pl. NW1 .... 1B 216
(off Hampstead Rd.)
Mill Brook Rd. BR5: St M Cry 70Yc 139
Millbrook Rd. N9 .... 18Xb 33
SW9 .... 55Rb 113
WD23: Bush 11Ba 27
Millbrook Way SL3: Poyle 54G 104
Mill Cleave KT14: W Byf 84J 169
(off Claremont Rd.)
Mill Cl. HP3: Hem H 7A 4
KT23: Bookh 96Ca 191
SM5: Cars 75Jb 156
UB7: W Dray 48M 83
Mill Cnr. EN5: Barn 11Bb 31
Mill Ct. DA4: S Dar 68Sd 142
E10 .... 34Ec 72
SE28 .... 45Xc 95
(off Titmuss Av.)
SL2: Slou 6K 81
Millcrest Rd. EN7: G Oak 1Rb 19
Millcroft Ho. SE6 .... 63Ec 136
(off Melfield Gdns.)
Millen Ct. DA4: Hort K 70Sd 142
MILL END 18H 25
Millender Wlk. SE16 .... 49Yb 92
(off New Rotherhithe Rd.)
Millennium Arena 52Jb 112
Millennium Bridge 5C 224 (45Rb 91)
Millennium Bri. Ho. EC4 .... 4D 224
Millennium Bus. Cen. NW2 .... 33Xa 68
Millennium Centre, The 35Fd 76
Millennium Cl. E16 .... 44Kc 93
UB8: Uxb 40L 63
Millennium Ct. EN8: Chesh 1Xb 19
Millennium Dome
(The O2) 46Gc 93
Millennium Dr. E14 .... 49Fc 93
Millennium Ho. E17 .... 29Zb 52
Millennium Pl. E2 .... 40Xb 71
Millennium Sq. SE1 .... 1K 231 (47Vb 91)
Millennium Wlk. CM14: B'wood 19Zd 41
(off High St.)
Millennium Way SE10 .... 47Gc 93
Millennium Wharf WD3: Rick 17N 25
Miller Av. EN3: Enf L 10Cc 20
Miller Centre, The 96Wb 197
(off Godstone Rd.)
Miller Cl. BR1: Brom 64Kc 137
CR4: Mitc 73Hb 155
HA5: Pinn 26Y 45
RM5: Col R 24Cd 56
Miller Ct. DA7: Bex 55Ed 118
Miller Ho. W10 .... 42Bb 89
(off Harrow Rd.)
Miller Pl. SL9: Ger X 29A 42
Miller Rd. CR0: C'don 74Pb 156
DA12: Grav'nd 1J 145
SW19 .... 65Fb 133
Miller's Av. E8 .... 36Vb 71
Millers Cl. DA1: Dart 59Md 119
IG7: Chig 19Xc 37
KT12: Hers 77Y 151
NW7 .... 21Wa 48
TW18: Staines 64K 127
WD3: Chor 13H 25
Millers Copse KT18: Eps D 91Ta 193
Millers Ct. HA0: Wemb 40Na 67
(off Vicars Bri. Cl.)
TW20: Egh 65F 126
Millers Grn. Cl. EN2: Enf 13Rb 33
Miller's La. IG7: Chig 18Xc 37
SL4: Old Win 8K 103
Millers Mdw. Cl. SE3 .... 56Hc 115
Millers Ri. AL1: St A 3C 6
Miller's Ter. E8 .... 36Vb 71
Miller St. NW1 .... 1B 216 (40Lb 70)
(not continuous)
Millers Way W6 .... 47Ya 88
Millers Wharf Ho. E1 .... 46Wb 91
(off St Katherine's Way)
Millers Yd. N3 .... 25Db 49
Miller Wlk. SE1 .... 7A 224 (46Qb 90)
Millet Rd. UB6: G'frd 40Da 65
Mill Farm Av. TW16: Sun 66U 128
Mill Farm Bus. Pk. TW4: Houn 59Aa 107
Mill Farm Cl. HA5: Pinn 26Y 45
Mill Farm Cres. TW4: Houn 60Aa 107
Mill Field, The 45Sd 98
Millfield DA3: New A 75Ae 165
HP4: Berk 1A 2
KT1: King T 69Pa 131
N4 .... 33Qb 70
TW16: Sun 67T 128
Millfield Av. E17 .... 25Ac 52
Millfield Cl. AL2: Lon C 8H 7
Millfield Dr. DA11: Nflt 1A 144
Millfield Ho. WD18: Wat 16T 26
Millfield La. DA3: New A 75Ae 165
KT20: Kgswd 97Bb 195
N6 .... 32Gb 69
Millfield Pl. N6 .... 33Jb 70
Millfield Rd. HA8: Edg 26Sa 47
TN15: W King 79Td 164
TW4: Houn 60Aa 107
Millfields Cl. BR5: St P 70Xc 139
Millfields Cotts. BR5: St M Cry 70Yc 139
Millfields Rd. E5 .... 35Yb 72
Millfield Theatre 21Tb 51
Millfield Wlk. HP3: Hem H 5A 4
Mill Footpath RM1: Rom 30Hd 56
(off Thurloe Gdns.)
Millford GU21: Wok 9M 167
Mill Gdns. SE26 .... 62Xb 135
Mill Grn. CR4: Mitc 73Jb 156
Mill Grn. Bus. Pk. CR4: Mitc 73Jb 156
Mill Grn. Rd. CR4: Mitc 73Hb 155
Millgrove St. SW11 .... 53Jb 112
Millharbour E14 .... 47Dc 92
Millhaven Cl. RM6: Chad H 30Xc 55
Millhedge Cl. KT11: Cobh 88Aa 171
MILL HILL 22Ua 48
Mill Hill CM15: Shenf 17Ae 41
SW13 .... 54Wa 110
MILL HILL CIRCUS 22Va 48
Mill Hill Cir. NW7 .... 22Va 48
Mill Hill Golf Course 19Ua 30
Mill Hill Gro. W3 .... 46Sa 87
Mill Hill Ind. Est. NW7 .... 23Va 48
Mill Hill La. DA12: Shorne 4M 145
Mill Hill Old Railway Nature Reserve
.... 23Sa 47
Mill Hill Rd. SW13 .... 54Wa 110
W3 .... 47Ra 87
Mill Hill School Leisure Cen. 21Wa 48
Mill Hill Ter. W3 .... 46Ra 87
Millhoo Ct. EN9: Walt A 6Hc 21
Mill Ho. IG8: Wfd G 22Hc 53
Mill Ho. Cl. DA4: Eyns 74Nd 163
Mill Ho. La. TW20: Thorpe 70D 126
Millhouse La. WD5: Bedm 9F 4
Millhouse Pl. SE27 .... 63Rb 135
Millicent Fawcett Ct. N17 .... 25Vb 51
Millicent Gro. N13 .... 22Rb 51
Millicent Preston Ho. IG11: Bark 39Tc 74
(off Ripple Rd.)
Millicent Rd. E10 .... 32Bc 72
Milligan St. E14 .... 45Bc 92
Milliner Ho. SW10 .... 52Eb 111
(off Hortensia Rd.)
Milliners Ct. AL1: St A 2C 6
IG10: Lough 12Qc 36
Milliners Ho. SE1 .... 2J 231
SW18 .... 56Cb 111
Milling Rd. HA8: Edg 24Ta 47
Millington Ho. N16 .... 34Tb 71
Millington Rd. UB3: Harl 48U 84
Mill La. BR6: Downe 82Qc 180
CR0: Wadd 76Pb 156
DA4: Eyns 74Nd 163
E4 .... 13Dc 34
GU23: Rip 91M 189
GU24: Pirb 6B 186
IG8: Wfd G 22Hc 53
KT14: Byfl 85P 169
KT17: Ewe 81Va 174
KT22: Fet 94Ja 192
NW6 .... 36Bb 69
RH1: Mers 3C 208
RH8: Oxt 4K 211
RM4: Nave 11Kd 39
RM6: Chad H 30Ad 55
RM16: Chaf H 49Zd 99
RM16: Ors 3C 100
(not continuous)
RM20: Chaf H, Grays 50Zd 99
SE18 .... 50Qc 94
SL3: Hort 55D 104
SL4: Wind 2E 102
SL5: S'hill 8D 124
SL9: Ger X 30B 42
SM5: Cars 77Hb 155
TN14: S'ham 82Hd 182
TN14: S'oaks 93Ld 203
TN15: Bor G, Igh 94Zd 205
TN16: Westrm 99Sc 200
TW20: Thorpe 70E 126
WD3: Crox G 16S 26
WD4: K Lan 1Q 12
Mill La. Trad. Est. CR0: Wadd 76Pb 156
Mill Link Rd. WD4: K Lan 2R 12
Millman Ct. WC1 .... 6H 217
Millman M. WC1 .... 6H 217 (42Pb 90)
Millman Pl. WC1 .... 6H 217
Millman Rd. E16 .... 45Pc 94
Millman St. WC1 .... 6H 217 (42Pb 90)
Millmark Gro. SE14 .... 54Ac 114
Millmarsh La. EN3: Brim 12Ac 34
Mill Mead TW18: Staines 63H 127
Millmead KT10: Esh 75Ca 151
KT14: Byfl 84P 169
Millmead Ind. Cen. N17 .... 26Xb 51
Mill Mead Rd. N17 .... 27Xb 51
MILL MEADS 40Fc 73
Mill Pk. Av. RM12: Horn 33Nd 77
Mill Pl. BR7: Chst 67Qc 138
DA1: Cray 56Jd 118
E14 .... 44Ac 92
KT1: King T 69Pa 131
SL3: Dat 4P 103
Mill Pl. Caravan Pk. SL3: Dat 4N 103
Mill Plat TW7: Isle 54Ja 108
(not continuous)
Mill Plat Av. TW7: Isle 54Ja 108
Mill Pond Cl. SW8 .... 52Mb 112
TN14: S'oaks 93Md 203
Millpond Ct. KT15: Add 78N 149
Millpond Est. SE16 .... 47Xb 91
Millpond Pl. SM5: Cars 76Jb 156
Mill Pond Rd. DA1: Dart 58Nd 119
GU20: W'sham 7A 146
Mill Ridge HA8: Edg 22Pa 47
Mill River Trad. Est. EN3: Pond E 13Ac 34
Mill Rd. DA2: Hawl 63Pd 141
DA8: Erith 52Ed 118
DA11: Nflt 9A 122
E16 .... 46Kc 93
IG1: Ilf 34Qc 74
KT10: Esh 75Ca 151
KT11: Cobh 87Y 171
KT17: Eps 84Va 174
KT20: Tad 95Za 194
RM15: Avel 45Sd 98
RM19: Purf 51Rd 119
SW19 .... 66Eb 133
TN13: Dun G 92Gd 202
TW2: Twick 61Ea 130
UB7: W Dray 48L 83
Mill Row DA5: Bexl 60Dd 118
N1 .... 1J 219 (39Ub 71)
Mills Cl. UB10: Hil 40Q 64
Mills Ct. EC2 .... 5H 219
Mills Cres. TN15: Seal 91Pd 203
Mills Gro. E14 .... 44Ec 92
NW4 .... 27Za 48
Mill Shaw RH8: Oxt 4K 211
Millshott Cl. SW6 .... 53Ya 110
Mills Ho. SW8 .... 53Lb 112
(off Thessaly Rd.)
Millside SM5: Cars 75Hb 155
Millside Ct. KT23: Bookh 97Ca 191
SL0: Thorn 47K 83
Millside Ind. Est. DA1: Dart 56Md 119
Millside Pl. TW7: Isle 54Ka 108
Millsmead Way IG10: Lough 12Pc 36
Millson Cl. N20 .... 19Fb 31
Mills Rd. KT12: Hers 78Y 151
Mills Row W4 .... 49Ta 87
Mills Spur SL4: Old Win 9M 103
Millstead Cl. KT20: Tad 94Xa 194
Millstone Cl. DA4: S Dar 68Sd 142
E15 .... 37Fc 73
Millstone M. DA4: S Dar 67Sd 142
Millstream Cl. N13 .... 22Qb 50
Millstream Ho. SE16 .... 47Xb 91
(off Jamaica Rd.)
Millstream La. SL1: Slou 6C 80
Mill Stream Lodge WD3: Rick 19J 25
Millstream Rd. SE1 .... 2K 231 (47Vb 91)
Mill St. HP3: Hem H 5M 3
(off Durrants Hill Rd.)
KT1: King T 69Na 131
RH1: Redh 7N 207
SE1 .... 2K 231 (47Vb 91)
SL2: Slou 6K 81
SL3: Coln 52F 104
TN16: Westrm 99Tc 200
W1 .... 4A 222 (45Kb 90)
Mills Way CM13: Hut 18Ee 41
Mills Yd. SW6 .... 55Db 111
Mill Trad. Estate, The
NW10 .... 41Sa 87
Mill Va. BR2: Brom 68Hc 137
Mill Vw. AL2: Park 9B 6
Mill Vw. Cl. KT17: Ewe 80Va 154
Millview Ct. RH2: Reig 4M 207
Mill Vw. Gdns. CR0: C'don 76Zb 158
MILLWALL 49Dc 92
Millwall Dock Rd. E14 .... 48Cc 92
Millwall FC 50Yb 92
Millwall Pk. 49Ec 92
Millwards AL10: Hat 3D 8
Millward's Pk. 3F 8
Mill Way KT18: Head, Lea 96Pa 193
KT22: Lea 96Pa 193
TW14: Felt 57X 107
WD3: Rick 18H 25
WD23: Bush 12Aa 27
Millway NW7 .... 21Ua 48
RH2: Reig 6M 207
Millway Gdns. UB5: N'olt 37Ba 65
Millwell Cres. IG7: Chig 22Tc 54
Mill West SL2: Slou 6J 81
Millwood Rd. BR5: St P 69Yc 139
TW3: Houn 57Ea 108
Millwood St. W10 .... 43Ab 88
Millwrights Wlk. HP3: Hem H 7P 3
(off Belswains La.)
Mill Yd. E1 .... 45Wb 91
Mill Yd. Ind. Est. HA8: Edg 25Ra 47
Milman Cl. HA5: Pinn 27Z 45
Milman Rd. NW6 .... 40Za 68
Milman's Ho. SW10 .... 51Fb 111
(off Milman's St.)
Milman's St. SW10 .... 51Fb 111
Milne Ct. E18 .... 25Jc 53
Milne Feild HA5: Hat E 24Ca 45
Milne Gdns. SE9 .... 57Nc 116
Milne Ho. SE18 .... 49Pc 94
(off Ogilby St.)
Milne Pk. E. CR0: New Ad 83Fc 179
Milne Pk. W. CR0: New Ad 83Fc 179
Milner App. CR3: Cat'm 93Wb 197
Milner Cl. CR3: Cat'm 94Vb 197
WD25: Wat 6X 13

Milner Ct. *SE15* .52Vb **113**
(off Colegrove Rd.)
WD23: Bush .16Da **27**
Milner Dr. KT11: Cobh .84Ba **171**
TW2: Whitt .59Fa **108**
Milner Pl. N1 .39Qb **70**
SM5: Cars .77Jb **156**
Milner Rd. CR3: Cat'm .94Wb **197**
CR7: Thor H .69Tb **135**
E15 .41Gc **93**
KT1: King T .69Ma **131**
RM8: Dag .33Yc **75**
SM4: Mord .71Fb **155**
SW19 .67Db **133**
Milner Sq. N1 .38Rb **71**
Milner St. SW3 .5F **227** (49Hb **89**)
Milner Wlk. SE9 .61Tc **138**
Milne Way UB9: Hare .25K **43**
Milnthorpe Rd. W4 .51Ta **109**
Milo Gdns. SE22 .58Vb **113**
Milo Rd. SE22 .58Vb **113**
Milrood Ho. *E1* .43Zb **92**
(off Stepney Grn.)
Milroy Av. DA11: Nflt .1A **144**
Milroy Wlk. SE1 .6B **224** (46Rb **91**)
Milson Rd. W14 .48Za **88**
Milstead Ho. E5 .36Xb **71**
Milthorne Cl. WD3: Crox G .15P **25**
MILTON .8E **122**
Milton Av. CR0: C'don .73Tb **157**
DA12: Grav'nd .10E **122**
E6 .38Mc **73**
EN5: Barn .15Bb **31**
N6 .31Lb **70**
NW9 .27Sa **47**
NW10 .39Sa **67**
RM12: Horn .33Hd **76**
SL9: Chal P .28A **42**
SM1: Sutt .76Fb **155**
TN14: Bad M .82Dd **182**
Milton Cl. N2 .29Eb **49**
SE1 .6K **231** (49Vb **91**)
SL3: Hort .55C **104**
SM1: Sutt .76Fb **155**
UB4: Hayes .44W **84**
Milton Ct. DA12: Grav'nd .10E **122**
E17 .28Cc **52**
EC2 .7F **219** (43Tb **91**)
EN9: Walt A .6Ec **20**
RM6: Chad H .31Yc **75**
SE14 .51Bc **114**
(not continuous)
SW18 .57Cb **111**
TW2: Twick .62Ga **130**
UB10: Ick .34R **64**
Milton Ct. Rd. SE14 .51Ac **114**
Milton Cres. IG2: Ilf .31Rc **74**
Milton Dr. TW17: Shep .70N **127**
WD6: Bore .15Ra **29**
Milton Gdn. Est. N16 .35Tb **71**
Milton Gdns. KT18: Eps .86Ua **174**
RM18: Tilb .3D **122**
TW19: Stanw .60P **105**
Milton Gro. N11 .22Lb **50**
N16 .35Tb **71**
Milton Hall Rd. DA12: Grav'nd .10F **122**
Milton Ho. *E2* .41Yb **92**
(off Roman Rd.)
E17 .28Cc **52**
SE5 .52Tb **113**
(off Elmington Est.)
SL9: Chal P .21A **42**
SM1: Sutt .76Cb **155**
Milton Lodge DA14: Sidc .63Wc **139**
TW2: Twick .59Ha **108**
Milton Mans. *W14* .51Ab **110**
(off Queen's Club Gdns.)
Milton Pk. N6 .31Lb **70**
Milton Pl. DA12: Grav'nd .9E **122**
N7 .36Ob **70**
(off Eastwood Cl.)
Milton Rd. CM14: W'ley .21Yd **58**
CR0: C'don .73Tb **157**
CR3: Cat'm .93Tb **197**
CR4: Mitc .66Jb **134**
DA10: Swans .58Ae **121**
DA12: Grav'nd .8D **122**
DA16: Well .53Vc **117**
DA17: Belv .49Cd **96**
E17 .28Cc **52**
HA1: Harr .28Ga **46**
KT12: Walt T .76Z **151**
KT15: Add .79J **149**
N6 .31Lb **70**
N15 .28Rb **51**
NW7 .22Wa **48**
NW9 .31Wa **68**
RM1: Rom .30Jd **56**
RM17: Grays .49De **99**
SE24 .57Rb **113**
SL2: Slou .2H **81**
SM1: Sutt .76Cb **155**
SM6: Wall .79Lb **156**
SW14 .55Ta **109**
SW19 .65Eb **133**
TN13: Dun G .93Gd **202**
TW12: Hamp .66Ca **129**
TW20: Egh .64B **126**
UB10: Ick .35R **64**
W3 .46Ta **87**
W7 .45Ha **86**
Milton Rd. Bus. Pk. DA12: Grav'nd .9E **122**
Milton St. DA10: Swans .58Zd **121**
EC2 .7F **219** (43Tb **91**)
EN9: Walt A .6Ec **20**
WD24: Wat .10X **13**
Milton Way KT22: Fet .97Ea **192**
UB7: W Dray .49P **83**
Milverton Dr. UB10: Ick .35S **64**
Milverton Gdns. IG3: Ilf .33Vc **75**
Milverton Ho. SE6 .62Ac **136**
Milverton Rd. NW6 .38Ya **68**
Milverton St. SE11 .7A **230** (50Qb **90**)
Milverton Way SE9 .63Qc **138**
Milward St. E1 .43Xb **91**
Milward Wlk. SE18 .51Qc **116**
MIMBRIDGE .5L **167**
Mimms Hall Rd. EN6: Pot B .3Za **16**
Mimms La. EN6: Ridge .5Qa **15**
WD7: Shenl .5Qa **15**
Mimosa Cl. BR6: Chels .75Yc **161**
CM15: Pil H .15Xd **40**
RM3: Rom .24Ld **57**
Mimosa Ho. UB4: Yead .43Y **85**
Mimosa Lodge NW10 .36Va **68**
Mimosa Rd. UB4: Yead .43Y **85**
Mimosa St. SW6 .53Bb **111**
Mina Av. SL3: L'ly .7P **81**
Minard Rd. SE6 .59Gc **115**
Mina Rd. SE17 .7J **231** (50Ub **91**)
SW19 .67Cb **133**
Minchenden Ct. N14 .19Mb **32**
Minchenden Cres. N14 .20Lb **32**
Minchin Cl. KT22: Lea .94Ja **192**
Minchin Ho. *E14* .44Cc **92**
(off Dod St.)
Mincing La. EC3 .4H **225** (45Ub **91**)
GU24: Chob .10K **147**
Minden Rd. SE20 .67Xb **135**
SM3: Sutt .75Ab **154**
Minehead Ho. *RM3: Rom* .22Nd **57**
(off Dagnam Pk. Dr.)
Minehead Rd. HA2: Harr .34Ca **65**
SW16 .64Pb **134**
Mineral Cl. EN5: Barn .16Ya **30**
Mineral St. SE18 .49Uc **94**
Minera M. SW1 .5J **227** (49Jb **90**)
Minerva Cl. DA14: Sidc .62Uc **138**
SW9 .52Qb **112**
TW19: Stanw M .57J **105**
Minerva Ct. EC1 .6A **218**
Minerva Dr. WD24: Wat .8U **12**
Minerva Lodge N7 .37Pb **70**
Minerva Rd. E4 .24Dc **52**
KT1: King T .68Pa **131**
NW10 .42Sa **87**
Minerva St. E2 .40Xb **71**
Minerva Wlk. EC1 .2C **224** (44Rb **91**)
Minet Av. NW10 .40Ua **68**
Minet Country Pk. .47Y **85**
Minet Dr. UB3: Hayes .46W **84**
Minet Gdns. NW10 .40Ua **68**
UB3: Hayes .46X **85**
Minet Rd. SW9 .54Rb **113**
Minford Gdns. W14 .47Za **88**
Minford Ho. *W14* .47Za **88**
(off Minford Gdns.)
Mingard Wlk. N7 .33Pb **70**
Ming St. E14 .45Cc **92**
Minimax Cl. TW14: Felt .58W **106**
Minister Ct. AL2: F'mre .10C **6**
Ministry Way SE9 .61Pc **138**
Miniver Pl. EC4 .4E **224**
Mink Ct. TW4: Houn .54Y **107**
Minley Ct. RH2: Reig .5J **207**
Minniecroft Rd. SL1: Burn .1A **80**
Minniedale KT5: Surb .71Pa **153**
Minnow St. SE17 .6J **231** (49Ub **91**)
Minnow Wlk. SE17 .6J **231** (49Ub **91**)
Minoan Dr. HP3: Hem H .6N **3**
Minorca Rd. KT13: Weyb .77Q **150**
Minories EC3 .3K **225** (44Vb **91**)
Minshaw Ct. DA14: Sidc .63Vc **139**
Minshill St. SW8 .53Mb **112**
Minshull Pl. BR3: Beck .66Cc **136**
Minson Rd. E9 .39Zb **72**
Minstead Gdns. SW15 .59Va **110**
Minstead Way KT3: N Mald .72Ua **154**
Minster Av. SM1: Sutt .75Cb **155**
Minster Cl. AL10: Hat .2C **8**
Minster Ct. EC3 .4J **225**
RM11: Horn .33Qd **77**
W5 .42Na **87**
(not continuous)
Minster Dr. CR0: C'don .77Ub **157**
Minster Gdns. KT8: W Mole .70Ba **129**
Minster Ho. AL10: Hat .2C **8**
Minsterley Av. TW17: Shep .70U **128**
Minster Pavement EC3 .4J **225**
Minster Rd. BR1: Brom .66Kc **137**
NW2 .36Ab **68**
Minster Wlk. N8 .28Nb **50**
Minster Way RM11: Horn .32Pd **77**
SL3: L'ly .47B **82**
Minstrel Cl. HP1: Hem H .1K **3**
Minstrel Gdns. KT5: Surb .70Pa **131**
Mint Bus. Pk. E16 .43Kc **93**
Mint Cl. UB10: Hil .41R **84**
Mintern Cl. N13 .20Rb **33**
Minterne Av. UB2: S'hall .49Ca **85**
Minterne Rd. HA3: Kenton .29Pa **47**
Minterne Waye UB4: Yead .44Y **85**
Mintern St. N1 .1G **219** (40Tb **71**)
Minters Orchard TN15: Plat .92De **205**
Mint La. KT20: Lwr K .1J **207**
Minton Ho. SE11 .5K **229**
Minton M. NW6 .37Db **69**
Minton Ri. SL6: Tap .4G **80**
Mint Rd. SM6: Wall .77Kb **156**
SM7: Bans .88Eb **175**
Mint St. SE1 .1D **230** (47Sb **91**)
Mint Wlk. CR0: C'don .76Sb **157**
CR6: W'ham .89Zb **178**
GU21: Knap .9J **167**
Mintwater Cl. KT17: Ewe .82Wa **174**
Mirabel Rd. SW6 .52Bb **111**
Mirador Cres. SL2: Slou .5M **81**
Miramar Way RM12: Horn .36Md **77**
Miranda Cl. E1 .43Yb **92**
Miranda Ct. W3 .44Pa **87**
Miranda Ho. N1 .2H **219**
Miranda Rd. N19 .32Lb **70**
Mirfield St. SE7 .49Mc **93**
Miriam La. AL2: Chis G .8M **5**
Miriam Rd. SE18 .50Uc **94**
Mirravale Trad. Est. RM8: Dag .31Ad **75**
Mirren Cl. HA2: Harr .35Ba **65**
Mirrie La. UB9: Den .29E **42**
Mirror Path SE9 .62Lc **137**
Misbourne Av. SL9: Chal P .22A **42**
Misbourne Cl. SL9: Chal P .22A **42**
Misbourne Ct. SL3: L'ly .49C **82**
Misbourne Mdws. UB9: Den .32E **62**
Misbourne Rd. UB10: Hil .39Q **64**
Misbourne Va. SL9: Chal P .22A **42**
Miskin Rd. DA1: Dart .59Ld **119**
(not continuous)
Miskin Theatre .61Ld **141**
Miskin Way DA12: Grav'nd .5F **144**
Missden Dr. HP3: Hem H .4C **4**
Missenden SE17 .7G **231**
Missenden Cl. TW14: Felt .60V **106**
Missenden Gdns. SL1: Burn .4A **80**
SM4: Mord .72Eb **155**
Missenden Ho. NW8 .5D **214**
WD18: Wat .17U **26**
(off Chenies Way)
Mission, The *E14* .44Bc **92**
(off Commercial Rd.)
Mission Gro. E17 .29Ac **52**
Mission Pl. SE15 .53Wb **113**
Mission Sq. TW8: Bford .51Na **109**
Missouri Ct. HA5: Eastc .30Y **45**
Mistletoe Cl. CR0: C'don .74Zb **158**
Mistley Ct. *KT18: Eps* .85Ta **173**
(off Ashley Rd.)
Mistral SE5 .53Ub **113**
Mistral Ct. *AL1: St A* .3E **6**
(off Bakers Ct.)
Misty's Fld. KT12: Walt T .74Y **151**
Mitali Pas. E1 .44Wb **91**
MITCHAM .69Hb **133**
Mitcham Gdn. Village CR4: Mitc .71Jb **156**
Mitcham Golf Course .71Jb **156**
Mitcham Ho. SE5 .53Sb **113**
Mitcham Ind. Est. CR4: Mitc .67Jb **134**
Mitcham La. SW16 .65Lb **134**
Mitcham Pk. CR4: Mitc .70Gb **133**
Mitcham Rd. CR0: C'don .72Nb **156**
E6 .41Nc **94**
IG3: Ilf .31Vc **75**
SW17 .64Hb **133**
Mitchell *NW9* .25Va **48**
(off The Concourse)
Mitchell Av. DA11: Nflt .61Fe **143**
Mitchellbrook Way NW10 .37Ta **67**
Mitchell Cl. AL1: St A .6B **6**
DA1: Dart .61Nd **141**
DA17: Belv .48Ed **96**
HP3: Bov .9B **2**
RM13: Rain .40Ld **77**
SE2 .49Yc **95**
SL1: Slou .8E **80**
WD5: Ab L .4W **12**
Mitchell Ho. *N1* .38Rb **71**
(off College Cross)
W12 .45Xa **88**
(off White City Est.)
Mitchell Rd. BR6: Orp .77Vc **161**
N13 .22Sb **51**
Mitchell's Pl. *SE21* .58Ub **113**
(off Aysgarth Rd.)
Mitchell St. EC1 .5D **218** (42Sb **91**)
(not continuous)
Mitchell Wlk. DA10: Swans .59Ae **121**
E6 .43Nc **94**
(off Allhallows Rd.)
E6 .43Pc **94**
(Elmley Cl.)
Mitchell Way BR1: Brom .67Jc **137**
NW10 .37Sa **67**
Mitchem Cl. TN15: W King .80Ud **164**
Mitchener's La. RH1: Blet .6K **209**
Mitchison Cl. *TW16: Sun* .67W **128**
(off Downside)
Mitchison Rd. N1 .37Tb **71**
Mitchley Av. CR2: Sande .85Sb **177**
CR8: Purl .85Sb **177**
Mitchley Gro. CR2: Sande .85Wb **177**
Mitchley Hill CR2: Sande .85Vb **177**
Mitchley Rd. N17 .27Wb **51**
Mitchley Vw. CR2: Sande .85Wb **177**
Mitford Bldgs. *SW6* .52Cb **111**
(off Dawes Rd.)
Mitford Cl. KT9: Chess .79La **152**
Mitford Rd. N19 .33Nb **70**
Mitre, The E14 .45Bc **92**
Mitre Av. E17 .27Cc **52**
Mitre Bri. Ind. Pk. W10 .42Xa **88**
(not continuous)
Mitre Cl. BR2: Brom .68Hc **137**
SM2: Sutt .80Eb **155**
TW17: Shep .72T **150**
Mitre Ho. SW3 .7F **227**
Mitre Pas. SE10 .47Gc **93**
Mitre Rd. E15 .40Gc **73**
SE1 .1A **230** (47Qb **90**)
Mitre Sq. EC3 .3J **225** (44Ub **91**)
Mitre St. EC3 .3J **225** (44Ub **91**)
Mitre Way W10 .42Xa **88**
Mitre Yd. SW3 .5E **226** (49Gb **89**)
Mixbury Gro. KT13: Weyb .79T **150**
Mixnams La. KT16: Chert .69J **127**
Mizen Cl. KT11: Cobh .86Z **171**
Mizen Ct. *E14* .47Cc **92**
(off Alpha Gro.)
Mizens Railway .8H **167**
Mizen Way KT11: Cobh .87Y **171**
Mizzen Mast Ho. SE18 .48Pc **94**
Moat, The KT3: N Mald .67Ua **132**
Moat Cl. BR6: Chels .79Vc **161**
TN13: Chip .94Ed **202**
WD23: Bush .15Da **27**
Moat Ct. DA15: Sidc .62Vc **139**
KT16: Ott .79E **148**
KT21: Asht .89Na **173**
SE9 .58Pc **116**
Moat Cres. N3 .27Db **49**
Moat Cft. DA16: Well .55Yc **117**
Moat Dr. E13 .40Lc **73**
HA1: Harr .28Ea **46**
HA4: Ruis .31U **64**
SL2: Slou .3N **81**
Moated Farm Dr.
KT15: Add, New H .80L **149**
Moat Farm Rd. UB5: N'olt .37Ba **65**
Moatfield NW6 .38Ab **68**
Moatfield Rd. WD23: Bush .15Da **27**
Moatlands Ho. WC1 .4G **217**
Moat La. DA8: Erith .53Jd **118**
KT8: E Mos .69Ha **130**
Moat Lodge, The HA2: Harr .33Ga **66**
Moat Pl. SW9 .55Pb **112**
UB9: Den .35K **63**
W3 .44Ra **87**
Moat Side EN3: Pond E .14Zb **34**
TW13: Hanw .63Y **129**
Moat Vw. Ct. WD23: Bush .15Da **27**
Moberly Rd. SW4 .59Mb **112**
Moberly Sports & Education Cen. .42Za **88**
(off Chamberlayne Rd.)
Moberly Way CR8: Kenley .92Tb **197**
Mobil Ct. *WC2* .3J **223**
(off Clement's Inn)
MOBY DICK .28Ad **55**
Mocatta Ho. *E1* .42Xb **91**
(off Brady St.)
Mocatta M. RH1: Mers .3C **208**
Mocha Ct. *E3* .40Dc **72**
(off Taylor Pl.)
Mockford M. RH1: Mers .3C **208**
Modbury Gdns. NW5 .37Jb **70**
Modder Pl. SW15 .56Za **110**
Model Cotts. GU24: Pirb .3B **186**
SW14 .56Sa **109**
W13 .47Ka **86**
Model Farm Cl. SE9 .62Nc **138**
Modena M. WD18: Wat .14U **26**
Modern Ct. EC4 .2B **224**
Modling Ho. *E2* .40Zb **72**
(off Mace St.)
Moelwyn N7 .36Mb **70**
Moelyn M. HA1: Harr .29Ja **46**
Moffat Ct. SW19 .64Cb **133**
Moffat Ho. SE5 .52Sb **113**
Moffat Rd. CR7: Thor H .68Sb **135**
N13 .23Nb **50**
SW17 .63Hb **133**
Moffats Cl. AL9: Brk P .8J **9**
Moffats La. AL9: Brk P .9G **8**
MOGADOR .100Ab **194**
Mogador Rd. KT20: Lwr K .100Ab **194**
Mogden La. TW7: Isle .57Ha **108**
Mohammedi Pk. UB5: N'olt .39Ca **65**
Mohawk Ho. *E3* .40Ac **72**
(off Gernon Rd.)
Mohmmad Khan Rd. E11 .32Hc **73**
Moineau *NW9* .25Va **48**
(off The Concourse)
Moira Cl. N17 .26Ub **51**
Moira Ho. *SW9* .53Qb **112**
(off Gosling Way)
Moira Rd. SE9 .56Pc **116**
Moir Cl. CR2: Sande .81Wb **177**
Mokswell Ct. N10 .25Jb **50**
Molash Rd. BR5: St M Cry .70Zc **139**
Molasses Ho. *SW11* .55Eb **111**
(off Clove Hitch Quay)
Molasses Row SW11 .55Eb **111**
Mole Abbey Gdns. KT8: W Mole .69Da **129**
Mole Bus. Pk. KT22: Lea .93Ja **192**
Mole Ct. KT19: Ewe .77Sa **153**
Mole Ho. NW8 .6C **214**
Molember Ct. KT8: E Mos .70Ga **130**
Molember Rd. KT8: E Mos .71Ga **152**
Mole Rd. KT12: Hers .78Z **151**
KT22: Fet .93Fa **192**
Molescroft SE9 .62Sc **138**
Molesey Av. KT8: W Mole .71Ba **151**
Molesey Cl. KT12: Hers .77Aa **151**
Molesey Dr. SM3: Cheam .75Ab **154**
Molesey Heath Local Nature Reserve .72Ca **151**
Molesey Pk. Av. KT8: W Mole .71Da **151**
Molesey Pk. Cl. KT8: E Mos .71Ea **152**
Molesey Pk. Rd.
KT8: W Mole, E Mos .71Da **151**
Molesey Road .75Aa **151**
Molesey Rd. KT8: W Mole .73Aa **151**
KT12: Hers, Walt T .77Aa **151**
Molesford Rd. SW6 .53Cb **111**
Molesham Cl. KT8: W Mole .69Da **129**
Molesham Way KT8: W Mole .69Da **129**
Moles Hill KT22: Oxs .83Fa **172**
Molesworth Ho. *SE17* .51Rb **113**
(off Brandon Est.)
Molesworth Rd. KT11: Cobh .85W **170**
Molesworth St. SE13 .56Ec **114**
Mole Valley Pl. KT21: Asht .91Ma **193**
Moliner Ct. BR3: Beck .66Cc **136**
Mollands Ct. RM15: S Ock .42Ae **99**
Mollands La. RM15: S Ock .42Yd **98**
Mollis Ho. *E3* .43Cc **92**
(off Gale St.)
Mollison Av.
EN3: Brim, Enf L, Enf W, Pond E .7Ac **20**
Mollison Dr. SM6: Wall .80Mb **156**
Mollison Ri. DA12: Grav'nd .4G **144**
Mollison Sq. *SM6: Wall* .80Mb **156**
(off Mollison Dr.)
Mollison Way HA8: Edg .26Pa **47**
Molloy Ct. GU21: Wok .88C **168**
Molly Huggins Cl. SW12 .59Lb **112**
Molteno Rd. WD17: Wat .10W **12**
Molton Ho. N1 .1J **217**
Molyneaux Av. HP3: Bov .9B **2**
Molyneux Dr. SW17 .63Kb **134**
Molyneux Rd. GU20: W'sham .9B **146**
KT13: Weyb .79S **150**
Molyneux St. W1 .1E **220** (43Gb **89**)
Molyns M. SL1: Slou .6C **80**
Monahan Av. CR8: Purl .84Pb **176**
Monarch Cl. BR4: W W'ck .77Hc **159**
RM13: Rain .40Jd **76**
RM18: Tilb .4D **122**
TW14: Felt .59U **106**
Monarch Ct. N2 .29Fb **49**
Monarch Dr. E16 .43Mc **93**
UB3: Hayes .45V **84**
Monarch Ho. *W8* .48Cb **89**
(off Earl's Ct. Rd.)
Monarch M. E17 .30Dc **52**
SW16 .64Qb **134**
Monarch Pde. CR4: Mitc .68Hb **133**
Monarch Pl. IG9: Buck H .19Lc **35**
Monarch Point SW6 .54Eb **111**
Monarch Rd. DA17: Belv .48Cd **96**
Monarchs Way EN8: Walt C .5Ac **20**
HA4: Ruis .32T **64**
Monarch Wlk. WD7: Shenl .5Pa **15**
Monarch Way IG2: Ilf .30Tc **54**
Mona Rd. SE15 .54Yb **114**
Monastery Cl. AL3: St A .2A **6**
Monastery Gdns. EN2: Enf .12Tb **33**
SL3: Dat .5M **103**
Mona St. E16 .43Hc **93**
Monaveen Gdns. KT8: W Mole .69Da **129**
Moncks Row SW18 .58Bb **111**
Monck St. SW1 .4E **228** (48Mb **90**)
Monckton Ct. *W14* .48Bb **89**
(off Strangways Ter.)
Monckton Rd. TN15: Bor G .92Be **205**
Monclar Rd. SE5 .56Tb **113**
Moncorvo Cl. SW7 .2D **226** (47Gb **89**)
Moncrieff Cl. E6 .44Nc **94**
Moncrieff Pl. SE15 .54Wb **113**
Moncrieff St. SE15 .54Wb **113**
Monday All. *N16* .33Vb **71**
(off High St.)
Mondial Way UB3: Harl .52S **106**
Mondragon Ho. *SW8* .53Nb **112**
(off Guildford Rd.)
Monds Cotts. TN14: Sund .96Ad **201**
Monega Rd. E7 .37Lc **73**
E12 .37Lc **73**
Monet Ct. *SE16* .50Xb **91**
(off Stubbs Dr.)
Money Av. CR3: Cat'm .94Ub **197**
Moneyer Ho. N1 .3F **219**
MONEYHILL .18L **25**
Moneyhill Ct. WD3: Rick .18K **25**
Moneyhill Pde. WD3: Rick .18K **25**
Money Hill Rd. WD3: Rick .18L **25**
Money La. UB7: W Dray .48M **83**
Money Rd. CR3: Cat'm .94Tb **197**
Mongers Almshouses *E9* .38Zb **72**
(off Church Cres.)
Mongers La. KT17: Ewe .82Va **174**
(not continuous)
Monica Cl. WD24: Wat .12Y **27**
Monica Ct. EN1: Enf .15Ub **33**
Monica James Ho. DA14: Sidc .62Wc **139**
Monica Shaw Ct. NW1 .2E **216**
(not continuous)
Monier Rd. E3 .38Cc **72**
Monivea Rd. BR3: Beck .66Bc **136**
Monkchester Cl. IG10: Lough .11Pc **36**
Monk Ct. W12 .46Wa **88**
Monk Dr. E16 .45Jc **93**
MONKEN HADLEY .12Bb **31**
Monkfrith Av. N14 .16Kb **32**
Monkfrith Cl. N14 .17Kb **32**
Monkfrith Way N14 .17Jb **32**
Monkhams EN9: Walt A .2Ec **20**
Monkham's Av. IG8: Wfd G .22Kc **53**
Monkham's Dr. IG8: Wfd G .22Kc **53**
Monkham's La. IG8: Wfd G .22Jc **53**
IG9: Buck H .20Kc **35**
Monkleigh Rd. SM4: Mord .69Ab **132**
Monk Pas. *E16* .45Jc **93**
(off Monk Dr.)
Monks Av. EN5: New Bar .16Eb **31**
KT8: W Mole .71Ba **151**
Monks Chase CM13: Ingve .22Ee **59**
Monks Cl. AL1: St A .4C **6**
EN2: Enf .12Sb **33**
HA2: Harr .33Ca **65**
HA4: Ruis .35Z **65**
SE2 .49Zc **95**
SL5: Asc .2A **146**
Monks Ct. RH2: Reig .6K **207**
Monks Cres. KT12: Walt T .74X **151**
KT15: Add .78K **149**
Monksdene Gdns. SM1: Sutt .76Db **155**
Monks Dr. SL5: Asc .2A **146**
W3 .43Qa **87**
Monksfield Way SL2: Slou .2E **80**
Monks Ga. AL1: St A .4C **6**
Monks Grn. KT22: Fet .93Ea **192**
Monksgrove IG10: Lough .15Qc **36**
Monks Haven SS17: Stan H .1N **101**
Monks Hill Sports Cen. .80Zb **158**
Monks Horton Way AL1: St A .1E **6**
Monks La. TN8: Eden .9P **211**
Monksmead WD6: Bore .14Sa **29**
MONKS ORCHARD .73Ac **158**
Monks Orchard Rd.
BR3: Beck .74Cc **158**
Monks Pk. HA9: Wemb .37Ra **67**
Monks Pk. Gdns.
HA9: Wemb .38Ra **67**
Monks Pl. CR3: Cat'm .94Xb **197**
Monks Rd. EN2: Enf .12Rb **33**
GU25: Vir W .10P **125**
SL4: Wind .4B **102**
SM7: Bans .89Cb **175**
Monk St. SE18 .49Qc **94**
Monks Wlk. DA13: Sflt .65Ce **143**
KT16: Chert .70G **126**
RH2: Reig .6K **207**
SL5: Asc .2A **146**
TW20: Thorpe .69F **126**
Monks Way BR3: Beck .72Cc **158**
BR5: Farnb .74Sc **160**
NW11 .28Bb **49**
TW18: Staines .66M **127**
UB7: Harm .51N **105**
Monks Well *DA9: Ghithe* .56Yd **120**
(off Watermans Way)
Monkswell La. CR5: Coul .96Db **195**
Monkswood Av. EN9: Walt A .5Fc **21**
Monkswood Gdns. IG5: Ilf .27Qc **54**
WD6: Bore .15Ta **29**
Monkton Ho. E5 .36Xb **71**
SE16 .47Zb **92**
(off Wolfe Cres.)
Monkton Rd. DA16: Well .54Vc **117**
Monkton St. SE11 .5A **230** (49Qb **90**)
Monkville Av. NW11 .28Bb **49**
Monkville Pde. NW11 .28Bb **49**
Monkwell Sq. EC2 .1E **224** (43Sb **91**)
Monkwood Cl. RM1: Rom .29Jd **56**
Monmouth Av. E18 .27Kc **53**
KT1: Hamp W .66La **130**
Monmouth Cl. CR4: Mitc .70Nb **134**
DA16: Well .56Wc **117**
W4 .48Sa **87**
Monmouth Ct. *DA12: Grav'nd* .8F **122**
(off Romulus Rd.)
W7 .43Ha **86**
(off Copley Cl.)
Monmouth Gro. TW8: Bford .49Na **87**
Monmouth Pl. *W2* .44Db **89**
(off Monmouth Rd.)
Monmouth Rd. E6 .41Pc **94**
N9 .19Xb **33**
RM9: Dag .36Bd **75**
UB3: Harl .49U **84**
W2 .44Cb **89**
WD17: Wat .13X **27**
Monmouth St. WC2 .3F **223** (44Nb **90**)
Monnery Rd. N19 .34Lb **70**
Monnow Grn. RM15: Avel .45Sd **98**
Monnow Rd. RM15: Avel .45Sd **98**
SE1 .50Wb **91**
Mono La. TW13: Felt .61X **129**
Monoux Almshouses E17 .28Dc **52**
Monoux Gro. E17 .25Cc **52**
Monroe Cres. EN1: Enf .11Xb **33**
Monroe Dr. SW14 .57Ra **109**
Monroe Ho. NW8 .4E **214**
Monro Gdns. HA3: Hrw W .24Ga **46**
Monro Ind. Est. EN8: Walt C .6Ac **20**
Monro Pl. KT19: Eps .81Qa **173**
Monro Way E5 .35Wb **71**
Monsell Ct. N4 .34Rb **71**
Monsell Gdns. TW18: Staines .64G **126**
Monsell Rd. N4 .34Qb **70**
Monson Rd. NW10 .40Wa **68**
RH1: Redh .3P **207**
SE14 .52Zb **114**
Mons Wlk. TW20: Egh .64E **126**
Mons Way BR2: Brom .72Nc **160**
Montacute Rd. CR0: New Ad .81Ec **178**
SE6 .59Bc **114**
SM4: Mord .72Fb **155**
WD23: B Hea .17Ga **28**
Montagu Ct. W1 .1G **221**
Montagu Cres. N18 .21Xb **51**

Montague Av. CR2: Sande 84Ub 177
SE4 56Bc 114
W7 46Ha 86
Montague Cl. EN5: Barn 14Bb 31
KT12: Walt T 73X 151
SE1 6F 225 (46Tb 91)
SL2: Farn R 10F 60
Montague Ct. DA15: Sidc 62Wc 139
N7 38Qb 70
(off St Clements St.)
Montague Dr. CR3: Cat'm 94Sb 197
Montague Gdns. W3 45Qa 87
Montague Hall Pl. WD23: Bush 16Ca 27
Montague Ho. E16 46Kc 93
(off Wesley Av.)
IG3: Ilf 32Wc 75
N1 39Ub 71
(off New Era Est.)
Montague M. E3 41Bc 92
(off Tredegar Ter.)
Montague Pas. UB8: Uxb 38M 63
Montague Pl. BR8: Swan 70Hd 140
WC1 7E 216 (43Mb 90)
Montague Rd. CR0: C'don 74Rb 157
E8 36Wb 71
E11 33Hc 73
N8 29Pb 50
N15 28Wb 51
SL1: Slou 5K 81
SW19 66Db 133
TW3: Houn 55Da 107
TW10: Rich 58Na 109
UB2: S'hall 49Aa 85
UB8: Uxb 38M 63
W7 46Ha 86
W13 44Ka 86
Montague Sq. SE15 52Yb 114
Montague St. EC1 1D 224 (43Sb 91)
WC1 7F 217 (43Nb 90)
Montague Ter. BR2: Brom 70Hc 137
Montague Walks HA0: Wemb 39Pa 67
Montague Waye UB2: S'hall 48Aa 85
Montagu Gdns. N18 21Xb 51
SM6: Wall 77Lb 156
Montagu Ind. Est. N18 21Yb 52
Montagu Mans. W1 7G 215 (43Hb 89)
Montagu M. Nth. W1 1G 221 (43Hb 89)
Montagu M. Sth. W1 2G 221 (44Hb 89)
Montagu M. W. W1 2G 221 (44Hb 89)
Montagu Pl. W1 1F 221 (43Hb 89)
Montagu Rd. N9 22Xb 51
N18 22Xb 51
NW4 30Wa 48
SL3: Dat 3M 103
Montagu Row W1 1G 221 (43Hb 89)
Montagu Sq. W1 1G 221 (43Hb 89)
Montagu St. W1 2G 221 (44Hb 89)
Montaigne Cl. SW1 6E 228 (49Mb 90)
Montalt Rd. IG8: Wfd G 21Hc 53
Montana Bldg. SE10 53Dc 114
(off Deal's Gateway)
Montana Cl. CR2: Sande 82Tb 177
Montana Gdns. SE26 64Bc 136
SM1: Sutt 78Eb 155
Montana Rd. SW17 62Jb 134
SW20 67Ya 132
Montayne Rd. EN8: Chesh 4Zb 20
Montbazon Ct. CM15: B'wood 18Xd 40
Montbelle Rd. SE9 62Rc 138
Montbretia Cl. BR5: St M Cry 70Yc 139
Montcalm Cl. BR2: Hayes 72Jc 159
UB4: Yead 41X 85
Montcalm Ho. E14 49Bc 92
Montcalm Rd. SE7 52Mc 115
Montclare St. E2 4K 219 (42Vb 91)
Monteagle Av. IG11: Bark 37Sc 74
Monteagle Ct. N1 1J 219 (40Ub 71)
Monteagle Way E5 34Wb 71
SE15 55Xb 113
Montefiore Ct. N16 32Vb 71
Montefiore St. SW8 54Kb 112
Montego Cl. SE24 56Qb 112
Montem La. SL1: Slou 6H 81
Montem Leisure Cen. 7H 81
Montem Rd. KT3: N Mald 70Ua 132
SE23 59Bc 114
Montem St. N4 32Pb 70
Montenotte Rd. N8 29Lb 50
Monterey Apartments N15 29Tb 51
Monterey Cl. DA5: Bexl 61Ed 140
NW7 22Ua 48
UB10: Hil 38Q 64
Monterey Studios W10 40Ab 68
Montesole Ct. HA5: Pinn 26Y 45
Montevetro SW11 53Fb 111
Montfichet Rd. E20 38Ec 72
Montford Pl. SE11 50Qb 90
Montford Rd. TW16: Sun 70W 128
Montfort Gdns. IG6: Ilf 23Sc 54
Montfort Ho. E2 41Yb 92
(off Victoria Pk. Sq.)
E14 48Ec 92
(off Galbraith St.)
Montfort Pl. SW19 60Za 110
Montfort Rd. TN15: Kems'g 89Nd 183
Montgolfier Wlk. UB5: N'olt 41Aa 85
Montgomerie M. SE23 59Yb 114
Montgomery Av. HP2: Hem H 1A 4
KT10: Hin W 75Ga 152
Montgomery Cl. CR4: Mitc 70Nb 134
DA12: Grav'nd 3F 144
DA15: Sidc 58Vc 117
RM16: Grays 47Ee 99
Montgomery Ct. CR2: S Croy 78Tb 157
(off Birdhurst Rd.)
KT22: Lea 92Ka 192
(off Levett Rd.)
W4 52Sa 109
Montgomery Cres. RM3: Rom 22Ld 57
Montgomery Gdns. SM2: Sutt 80Fb 155
Montgomery Ho. W2 1B 220
Montgomery Lodge E1 42Yb 92
(off Cleveland Gro.)
Montgomery Pl. SL2: Slou 4N 81
Montgomery Rd. DA4: S Dar 67Td 142
GU22: Wok 90A 168
HA8: Edg 23Pa 47
W4 49Sa 87
Montgomery St. E14 46Dc 92
Montgomery Way CR8: Kenley 92Tb 197
Montholme Rd. SW11 58Hb 111
Monthope Rd. E1 43Wb 91
Montolieu Gdns. SW15 57Xa 110
Montpelier Av. DA5: Bexl 59Zc 117
W5 43La 86
Montpelier Cl. UB10: Hil 39Q 64
Montpelier Ct. BR2: Brom 70Hc 137
(off Westmoreland Rd.)
SL4: Wind 4G 102
W5 43Ma 87
Montpelier Gdns. E6 41Mc 93
RM6: Chad H 31Yc 75
Montpelier Gro. NW5 36Lb 70
Montpelier M. SW7 3E 226 (48Gb 89)
Montpelier Pl. E1 44Yb 92
SW7 3E 226 (48Gb 89)
Montpelier Ri. HA9: Wemb 32Ma 67
NW11 31Ab 68
Montpelier Rd. CR8: Purl 82Rb 177
N3 25Eb 49
SE15 53Xb 113
SM1: Sutt 77Eb 155
W5 43Ma 87
Montpelier Row SE3 54Hc 115
TW1: Twick 59La 108
Montpelier Sq. SW7 2E 226 (47Gb 89)
Montpelier St. SW7 3E 226 (48Gb 89)
Montpelier Ter. SW7 2E 226 (47Gb 89)
Montpelier Va. SE3 54Hc 115
Montpelier Wlk. SW7 2E 226 (48Gb 89)
Montpelier Way NW11 31Ab 68
Montpellier Ct. KT12: Walt T 72W 150
Montpellier Ho. IG7: Chig 22Sc 54
Montrave Rd. SE20 65Yb 136
Montreal Ho. SE16 47Zb 92
(off Maple M.)
Montreal Pl. WC2 4H 223 (45Pb 90)
Montreal Rd. IG1: Ilf 31Sc 74
RM18: Tilb 5C 122
TN13: Riv 95Gd 202
Montrell Rd. SW2 60Nb 112
Montrose SL1: Slou 4F 80
Montrose Av. DA15: Sidc 59Wc 117
DA16: Well 55Tc 116
HA8: Edg 26Sa 47
NW6 40Ab 68
RM2: Rom 26Ld 57
SL1: Slou 4F 80
(not continuous)
SL3: Dat 2N 103
TW2: Whitt 59Da 107
Montrose Cl. DA16: Well 55Vc 117
IG8: Wfd G 21Jc 53
TW15: Ashf 65S 128
Montrose Ct. HA1: Harr 29Da 45
NW9 26Sa 47
NW11 28Bb 49
SE6 61Hc 137
SW7 2C 226 (47Fb 89)
Montrose Cres. HA0: Wemb 37Na 67
N12 23Eb 49
Montrose Gdns. CR4: Mitc 68Hb 133
KT22: Oxs 84Fa 172
SM1: Sutt 75Db 155
Montrose Ho. E14 48Cc 92
SW1 2J 227
Montrose Pl. SW1 2J 227 (47Jb 90)
Montrose Rd. HA3: W'stone 26Ga 46
TW14: Bedf 58T 106
Montrose Wlk. HA7: Stan 23Ka 46
KT13: Weyb 76R 150
Montrose Way SE23 60Zb 114
SL3: Dat 3P 103
Montrouge Cres. KT17: Eps D 88Ya 174
Montserrat Av. IG8: Wfd G 24Fc 53
Montserrat Cl. SE19 64Tb 135
Montserrat Rd. SW15 56Ab 110
Monument, The 4G 225 (45Tb 91)
Monument Bri. Ind. Est. E.
GU21: Wok 87D 168
Monument Bri. Ind. Est. W.
GU21: Wok 87C 168
Monument Bus. Cen.
GU21: Wok 87D 168
Monument Gdns. SE13 57Ec 114
Monument Grn. KT13: Weyb 76R 150
Monument Hill KT13: Weyb 77R 150
Monument La. SL9: Chal P 23A 42
Monument Pl. AL3: St A 1B 6
(off Ashwell St.)
Monument Rd. GU21: Wok 86C 168
KT13: Weyb 77R 150
Monument St. EC3 4G 225 (45Tb 91)
Monument Way N17 27Vb 51
Monument Way E. GU21: Wok 87D 168
Monument Way W.
GU21: Wok 87C 168
Monza St. E1 45Yb 92
Moodkee St. SE16 48Yb 92
Moodys Rd. SE15 53Vb 113
Moody St. E1 41Zb 92
Moon Ct. SE12 56Jc 115
Moon Ho. HA1: Harr 28Ga 46
Moon La. EN5: Barn 13Bb 31
Moon St. N1 39Rb 71
MOOR, THE 61F 126
Moorcroft HA8: Edg 25Ra 47
Moorcroft Gdns. BR2: Brom 71Nc 160
Moorcroft La. UB8: Hil 43Q 84
Moorcroft Rd. SW16 62Nb 134
Moorcroft Way HA5: Pinn 29Aa 45
Moordown SE18 52Rc 116
Moore Av. RM18: Tilb 4D 122
RM20: Grays 50Ae 99
Moore Cl. CR4: Mitc 68Kb 134
DA2: Dart 61Td 142
KT15: Add 78K 149
SL1: Slou 7D 80
SW14 55Sa 109
Moore Ct. HA0: Wemb 37Na 67
N1 39Rb 71
(off Gaskin St.)
Moore Cres. RM9: Dag 39Xc 75
Moorefield Rd. N17 26Vb 51
Moore Gro. Cres. TW20: Egh 65B 126
Moorehead Way SE3 55Jc 115
Moore Ho. E1 45Yb 92
(off Cable St.)
E2 41Yb 92
(off Roman Rd.)
E14 47Cc 92
N8 28Nb 50
(off Pembroke Rd.)
RM11: Horn 30Jd 56
(off Benjamin Cl.)
SE10 50Hc 93
(off Armitage Rd.)
SW1 7K 227
Mooreland Rd. BR1: Brom 66Hc 137
Moor End Rd. HP1: Hem H 3L 3
Moore Pk. Rd. SW6 52Cb 111
Moore Place Golf Course 78Ca 151
Moore Rd. DA10: Swans 58Ae 121
GU24: Brkwd 3A 186
SE19 65Sb 135
Moores La. SL4: Eton W 9D 80
Moores Pl. CM14: B'wood 19Zd 41
Moore St. SW3 5F 227 (49Hb 89)
Moore Wlk. E7 35Jc 73
Moore Way SM2: Sutt 81Cb 175
Moorey Cl. E15 39Hc 73
Moorfield Av. W5 42Ma 87
Moorfield Rd. BR6: Orp 73Wc 161
EN3: Enf H 11Yb 34
KT9: Chess 78Na 153
UB8: Cowl 44M 83
UB9: Den 31J 63
Moorfields EC2 1F 225 (43Tb 91)
Moorfields Cl. TW18: Staines 67G 126
Moorfields Highwalk EC2 1F 225
(not continuous)
Moor Furlong SL1: Slou 6B 80
Moorgate EC2 2F 225 (44Tb 91)
Moorgate Pl. EC2 2F 225
Moorgreen Ho. EC1 3B 218
Moorhall Rd. UB9: Hare 30K 43
Moorhayes Dr. TW18: Lale 69L 127
Moorhen Cl. DA8: Erith 51Kd 119
Moorhen Ho. E3 39Bc 72
(off Old Ford Rd.)
Moorhen Wlk. DA9: Ghithe 58Wd 120
(off Sanderling Way)
Moorholme GU22: Wok 91A 188
MOORHOUSE 99Pc 200
Moorhouse NW9 25Va 48
MOORHOUSE BANK 100Qc 200
Moorhouse Rd. HA3: Kenton 27Ma 47
RH8: Limp, Westrm 100Qc 200
TN16: Westrm 100Qc 200
W2 44Cb 89
Moorhurst Av. EN7: G Oak 1Qb 18
Moorings, The AL1: St A 1D 6
(off Althorp Rd.)
E16 43Lc 93
(off Prince Regent La.)
KT14: W Byf 84L 169
KT23: Bookh 97Ca 191
SL4: Wind 2A 102
WD23: Bush 14Aa 27
Moorings Ho. TW8: Bford 52La 108
MOOR JUNC. 52K 105
Moorland Cl. RM5: Col R 24Dd 56
TW2: Whitt 59Ca 107
Moorland Rd. HP1: Hem H 4J 3
SW9 56Rb 113
UB7: Harm 51L 105
Moorlands AL2: F'mre 10C 6
KT12: Walt T 76W 150
(off Ashley Pk. Rd.)
UB5: N'olt 39Aa 65
Moorlands, The GU22: Wok 93B 188
Moorlands Av. NW7 23Xa 48
Moor La. EC2 1F 225 (43Tb 91)
(not continuous)
GU22: Wok 94A 188
KT9: Chess 77Na 153
RM14: Upm 32Ud 78
TW18: Staines 62G 126
TW19: Staines 60F 104
UB7: Harm 51L 105
WD3: Rick 18P 25
WD3: Sarr 8G 10
Moor La. Crossing WD18: Wat 18S 26
Moormead Dr. KT19: Ewe 78Ua 154
Moor Mead Rd. TW1: Twick 58Ja 108
Moormede Cres. TW18: Staines 63H 127
Moor Mill La. AL2: Col S 1Ga 14
(not continuous)
MOOR PARK 20S 26
Moor Pk. 20Q 26
Moor Pk. Gdns. KT2: King T 66Ua 132
Moor Pk. Golf Course 20Q 26
Moor Pk. Ind. Cen. WD18: Wat 17S 26
Moor Pk. Rd. HA6: Nwood 22T 44
Moor Pl. EC2 1F 225 (43Tb 91)
GU20: W'sham 8A 146
Moor Rd. TN14: S'oaks 92Kd 203
Moors, The RH1: Mers 3C 208
Moorside HP3: Hem H 5K 3
Moorside Rd. BR1: Brom 62Gc 137
Moorsom Way CR5: Coul 89Mb 176
Moorstown Ct. SL1: Slou 7J 81
Moor St. W1 3E 222 (44Mb 90)
Moortown Rd. WD19: Wat 21Y 45
Moor Vw. WD18: Wat 17W 26
Moot Ct. NW9 29Qa 47
Moran Cl. AL2: Brick W 3Ba 13
Moran Ho. E1 46Xb 91
(off Wapping La.)
Morant Gdns. RM5: Col R 22Dd 56
Morant Pl. N22 25Pb 50
Morant Rd. RM16: Grays 8D 100
Morants Ct. Rd. TN13: Dun G 90Ed 182
TN14: Dun G 90Ed 182
Morant St. E14 45Cc 92
Mora Rd. NW2 35Ya 68
Mora St. EC1 4E 218 (41Sb 91)
Morat St. SW9 53Pb 112
Moravian Cl. SW10 51Fb 111
Moravian Pl. SW10 51Fb 111
Moravian St. E2 40Yb 72
Moray Av. UB3: Hayes 46V 84
Moray Cl. HA8: Edg 19Ra 29
RM1: Rom 24Gd 56
Moray Ct. CR2: S Croy 78Sb 157
(off Warham Rd.)
Moray Dr. SL2: Slou 4L 81
Moray Ho. E1 42Ac 92
(off Harford St.)
Moray M. N7 33Pb 70
Moray Rd. N4 33Pb 70
Moray Way RM1: Rom 24Fd 56
Mordaunt Gdns. RM9: Dag 38Ad 75
Mordaunt Ho. NW10 39Ta 67
(off Stracey Rd.)
Mordaunt Rd. NW10 39Ta 67
Mordaunt St. SW9 55Pb 112
MORDEN 69Db 133
Morden Cl. KT20: Tad 92Za 194
Morden Ct. SM4: Mord 70Db 133
Morden Ct. Pde. SM4: Mord 70Db 133
Morden Gdns. CR4: Mitc 70Fb 133
UB6: G'frd 36Ha 66
Morden Hall Pk. 69Eb 133
Morden Hall Rd. SM4: Mord 69Db 133
Morden Hill SE13 54Ec 114
(not continuous)
Morden Ho. SM4: Mord 70Cb 133
Morden La. SE13 54Ec 114
MORDEN PARK 72Ab 154
Morden Pk. Pool 72Bb 155
Morden Rd. CR4: Mitc 70Eb 133
RM6: Chad H 31Ad 75
SE3 54Jc 115
SM4: Mord 70Eb 133
SW19 67Db 133
Morden Rd. M. SE3 54Jc 115
Morden St. SE13 53Dc 114
Morden Way SM3: Sutt 73Cb 155
Morden Wharf SE10 48Gc 93
(off Morden Wharf Rd.)
Morden Wharf Rd. SE10 48Gc 93
Mordern Ho. NW1 6E 214
Mordon Rd. IG3: Ilf 31Vc 75
Mordred Rd. SE6 61Gc 137
Moreau Wlk. SL3: G Grn 44A 82
Morecambe Cl. E1 43Zb 92
RM12: Horn 36Kd 77
Morecambe Gdns. HA7: Stan 21Ma 47
Morecambe Ho. RM3: Rom 22Nd 57
(off Chudleigh Rd.)
Morecambe St. SE17 6E 230 (49Sb 91)
Morecambe Ter. N18 21Tb 51
(off Gt. Cambridge Rd.)
More Cl. CR8: Purl 83Qb 176
E16 44Hc 93
W14 49Za 88
Morecoombe Cl. KT2: King T 66Ra 131
More Copper Ho. SE1 7H 225
(off Magdalen St.)
Moree Way N18 21Wb 51
Moreing Rd. DA9: Ghithe 56Yd 120
Moreland Av. RM16: Grays 47Ee 99
SL3: Coln 52E 104
Moreland Cl. SL3: Coln 52E 104
Moreland Cotts. E3 40Cc 72
(off Fairfield Rd.)
Moreland Ct. NW2 34Cb 69
Moreland Dr. SL9: Ger X 31B 62
Moreland St. EC1 3C 218 (41Rb 91)
Moreland Way E4 20Dc 34
More La. KT10: Esh 75Da 151
Morel Ct. TN13: S'oaks 94Kd 203
Morella Cl. GU25: Vir W 10P 125
Morella Rd. SW12 59Hb 111
Morell Cl. EN5: New Bar 13Eb 31
Morello Av. UB8: Hil 43R 84
Morello Cl. BR8: Swan 70Fd 140
Morello Dr. SL3: L'ly 46B 82
More London Pl. SE1 7H 225 (46Ub 91)
(not continuous)
More London Riverside
SE1 7J 225 (46Ub 91)
(not continuous)
Moremead EN9: Walt A 5Fc 21
Moremead Rd. SE6 63Bc 136
Morena St. SE6 59Dc 114
Moresby Av. KT5: Surb 73Ra 153
Moresby Rd. E5 32Xb 71
Moresby Wlk. SW8 54Lb 112
More's Gdn. SW3 51Fb 111
(off Cheyne Wlk.)
Mores La. CM14: Pil H 14Sd 40
Moretaine Rd. TW15: Ashf 62M 127
Moreton Almshouses
TN16: Westrm 98Tc 200
Moreton Av. TW7: Isle 53Ga 108
Moreton Bay Ind. Est. RM2: Rom 26Md 57
Moreton Cl. BR8: Swan 68Gd 140
E5 33Xb 71
N15 30Tb 51
NW7 23Ya 48
SW1 7C 228
Moreton Ct. DA1: Cray 55Hd 118
Moreton Gdns. IG8: Wfd G 22Nc 54
Moreton Ho. SE16 48Xb 91
Moreton Ind. Est. BR8: Swan 70Kd 141
Moreton Pl. SW1 7C 228 (50Lb 90)
Moreton Rd. CR2: S Croy 78Tb 157
KT4: Wor Pk 75Wa 154
N15 30Tb 51
Moretons HA1: Harr 32Ga 66
Moreton St. SW1 7C 228 (50Lb 90)
Moreton Ter. SW1 7C 228
Moreton Ter. M. Nth. SW1 7C 228
Moreton Ter. M. Sth. SW1 7C 228
Moreton Twr. W3 46Ra 87
Moreton Way SL1: Slou 6B 80
Morewood Cl. TN13: S'oaks 95Hd 202
Morewood Cl. Ind. Est.
TN13: S'oaks 95Hd 202
Morford Cl. HA4: Ruis 31X 65
Morford Way HA4: Ruis 31X 65
Morgan Av. E17 28Fc 53
Morgan Cl. HA6: Nwood 23V 44
RM10: Dag 38Cd 76
Morgan Ct. SM5: Cars 77Hb 155
TW15: Ashf 64R 128
Morgan Cres. CM16: They B 8Tc 22
Morgan Dr. DA9: Ghithe 59Ud 120
Morgan Gdns. WD25: A'ham 10Da 13
Morgan Ho. SW1 6C 228
SW8 53Lb 112
(off Wadhurst Rd.)
Morgan Mans. N7 36Qb 70
(off Morgan Rd.)
Morgan Rd. BR1: Brom 66Jc 137
N7 36Qb 70
W10 43Bb 89
Morgans La. SE1 7H 225
(off Tooley St.)
UB3: Hayes 43T 84
Morgan St. E3 41Ac 92
(not continuous)
E16 43Hc 93
Morgan Wlk. BR3: Beck 70Dc 136
Morgan Way IG8: Wfd G 23Nc 54
RM13: Rain 41Ld 97
Moriarty Cl. BR1: Brom 70Qc 138
Moriatry Cl. N7 35Nb 70
Morie St. SW18 57Db 111
Morieux Rd. E10 32Bc 72
Moring Rd. SW17 63Jb 134
Morkyns Wlk. SE21 62Ub 135
Morland Av. CR0: C'don 74Ub 157
DA1: Dart 57Kd 119
Morland Cl. CR4: Mitc 69Gb 133
NW11 32Db 69
TW12: Hamp 64Ba 129
Morland Ct. W12 47Xa 88
(off Coningham Rd.)
Morland Est. E8 38Wb 71
Morland Gdns. NW10 38Ta 67
UB1: S'hall 46Da 85
Morland Ho. NW1 2C 216
NW6 39Cb 69
SW1 5F 229
W11 44Ab 88
(off Lancaster Rd.)
Morland M. N1 38Qb 70
Morland Pl. N15 28Ub 51
Morland Rd. CR0: C'don 74Ub 157
E17 29Zb 52
HA3: Kenton 29Na 47
IG1: Ilf 33Rc 74
RM10: Dag 38Cd 76
SE20 65Zb 136
SM1: Sutt 78Eb 155
Morland Way EN8: Chesh 1Ac 20
Morley Av. E4 24Fc 53
N18 21Wb 51
N22 26Qb 50
Morley Cl. BR6: Farnb 75Rc 160
SL3: L'ly 47B 82
Morley Ct. BR2: Brom 70Hc 137
E4 22Bc 52
KT22: Fet 93Fa 192
Morley Cres. HA4: Ruis 33Y 65
HA8: Edg 19Sa 29
Morley Cres. E. HA7: Stan 26La 46
Morley Cres. W. HA7: Stan 27La 46
Morley Hill EN2: Enf 10Tb 19
Morley Ho. SE15 52Vb 113
(off Commercial Way)
Morley Rd. BR7: Chst 67Sc 138
CR2: Sande 82Vb 177
E10 32Ec 72
E15 40Hc 73
IG11: Bark 39Tc 74
RM6: Chad H 29Ad 55
SE13 56Ec 114
SM3: Sutt 74Bb 155
TW1: Twick 58Ma 109
Morley Sq. RM16: Grays 9C 100
Morley St. SE1 3A 230 (48Qb 90)
Morna Rd. SE5 54Sb 113
Morning La. E9 37Yb 72
Morningside WD3: Rick 18L 25
Morningside Rd. KT4: Wor Pk 75Ya 154
Mornington Av. BR1: Brom 69Lc 137
IG1: Ilf 31Qc 74
W14 49Bb 89
Mornington Av. Mans. W14 49Bb 89
(off Mornington Av.)
Mornington Cl. IG8: Wfd G 21Jc 53
TN16: Big H 89Mc 179
Mornington Ct. DA5: Bexl 60Fd 118
NW1 1B 216
Mornington Cres. NW1 1B 216 (40Lb 70)
TW5: Cran 53X 107
Mornington Gro. E3 41Cc 92
Mornington M. SE5 53Sb 113
Mornington Pl. NW1 1A 216 (40Lb 70)
SE8 52Bc 114
(off Mornington Rd.)
Mornington Rd. E4 17Fc 35
E11 31Hc 73
(not continuous)
IG8: Wfd G 21Hc 53
IG10: Lough 13Sc 36
SE8 52Bc 114
TW15: Ashf 64S 128
UB6: G'frd 43Da 85
WD7: R'lett 6Ja 14
Mornington Sports & Leisure Cen.
39Kb 70
(off Arlington Rd.)
Mornington St. NW1 1A 216 (40Kb 70)
Mornington Ter. NW1 1A 216 (39Kb 70)
Mornington Wlk. TW10: Ham 63La 130
Morocco St. SE1 2H 231 (47Ub 91)
Morocco Wharf E1 46Xb 91
(off Wapping High St.)
Morpeth Av. WD6: Bore 10Pa 15
Morpeth Cl. HP2: Hem H 3N 3
Morpeth Gro. E9 39Zb 72
Morpeth Mans. SW1 4B 228
Morpeth Rd. E9 39Zb 72
Morpeth St. E2 41Yb 92
Morpeth Ter. SW1 4B 228 (48Lb 90)
Morpeth Wlk. N17 24Xb 51
Morphou Rd. NW7 23Ab 48
Morrab Gdns. IG3: Ilf 34Vc 75
Morrel Ct. E2 40Wb 71
(off Goldsmiths Row)
Morrells Yd. SE11 7A 230
Morrice Cl. SL3: L'ly 49B 82
Morris Av. E12 36Pc 74
UB8: Uxb 37N 63
Morris Blitz Ct. N16 35Vb 71
Morris Cl. BR6: Orp 76Uc 160
CR0: C'don 71Ac 158
SL9: Chal P 25B 42
Morris Ct. E4 20Dc 34
EN9: Walt A 6Hc 21
SL4: Wind 3C 102
Morris Gdns. DA1: Dart 57Qd 119
SW18 59Cb 111
Morris Ho. E2 41Yb 92
(off Roman Rd.)
NW8 6D 214
W3 47Va 88
Morrish Rd. SW2 59Nb 112
Morrison Av. E4 23Cc 52
N17 27Ub 51
Morrison Bldgs. Nth. E1 44Wb 91
(off Commercial Rd.)
Morrison Ct. EN5: Barn 14Ab 30
(off Manor Way)
N12 24Gb 49
SW1 3E 228
Morrison Ho. RM16: Grays 47Fe 99
SW2 60Qb 112
(off High Trees)
Morrison Rd. IG11: Bark 40Ad 75
RM9: Bark, Dag 40Ad 75
SW9 54Qb 112
UB4: Yead 41X 85
Morrison St. SW11 55Jb 112
Morris Pl. N4 33Qb 70
Morris Rd. E14 43Dc 92
E15 35Gc 73
RH1: S Nut 8E 208
RM3: Rom 24Kd 57
RM8: Dag 33Bd 75
TW7: Isle 55Ha 108
Morriss Ho. SE16 47Xb 91
(off Cherry Gdn. St.)
Morris St. E1 44Xb 91
Morriston Cl. WD19: Wat 22Y 45

Morris Wlk. DA1: Dart 54Qd 119
Morris Way AL2: Lon C 8H 7
Morritt Ho. HA0: Wemb 36Ma 67
(off Talbot Rd.)
Morse Cl. E13 41Jc 93
UB9: Hare 26L 43
Morshead Mans. W9 41Cb 89
(off Morshead Rd.)
Morshead Rd. W9 41Cb 89
Morson Rd. EN3: Pond E 16Ac 34
Morston Cl. KT20: Tad 92Xa 194
Morston Gdns. SE9 63Pc 138
Mortain Ho. SE16 49Xb 91
(off Roseberry St.)
Morten Cl. SW4 58Mb 112
Morten Gdns. UB9: Den 31J 63
Morteyne Rd. N17 25Tb 51
Mortgramit Sq. SE18 48Qc 94
Mortham St. E15 39Gc 73
Mortimer Cl. NW2 33Bb 69
SW16 61Mb 134
WD23: Bush 16Da 27
Mortimer Ct. NW8 2A 214
Mortimer Cres.
KT4: Wor Pk 76Ta 153
NW6 39Db 69
Mortimer Dr. EN1: Enf 15Ub 33
TN16: Big H 84Lc 179
Mortimer Est. NW6 39Db 69
(off Mortimer Pl.)
Mortimer Ho. W11 46Za 88
W14 49Ab 88
(off North End Rd.)
Mortimer Mkt. WC1 6C 216 (42Lb 90)
Mortimer Pl. NW6 39Db 69
Mortimer Rd. BR6: Orp 74Wc 161
CR4: Mitc 67Hb 133
DA8: Erith 51Fd 118
E6 41Pc 94
N1 38Ub 71
(not continuous)
NW10 41Ya 88
SL3: L'ly 8P 81
W13 44La 86
Mortimer Sq. W11 45Za 88
Mortimer St. W1 2A 222 (44Lb 90)
Mortimer Ter. NW5 35Kb 70
MORTLAKE 55Ta 109
Mortlake Cl. CR0: Bedd 76Nb 156
Mortlake Crematorium
TW9: Kew 54Ra 109
Mortlake Dr. CR4: Mitc 67Gb 133
Mortlake High St. SW14 55Ta 109
Mortlake Rd. E16 44Kc 93
IG1: Ilf 35Sc 74
TW9: Kew, Rich 52Qa 109
Mortlake Ter. TW9: Kew 52Qa 109
(off Mortlake Rd.)
Mortlock Cl. SE15 53Xb 113
Mortlock Ct. E7 35Mc 73
Morton KT20: Tad 93Za 194
Morton Cl. E1 44Yb 92
GU21: Wok 7N 167
SM6: Wall 80Pb 156
UB8: Hil 42P 83
Morton Ct. UB5: N'olt 36Ea 66
Morton Cres. N14 21Mb 50
Morton Dr. SL2: Farn C 5C 60
Morton Gdns. SM6: Wall 78Lb 156
Morton Ho. SE17 51Rb 113
Morton M. SW5 49Db 89
Morton Pl. SE1 4K 229 (48Qb 90)
Morton Rd. E15 38Hc 73
GU21: Wok 7P 167
N1 38Sb 71
SM4: Mord 71Fb 155
Morton Way N14 20Lb 32
Morvale Cl. DA17: Belv 49Bd 95
Morval Rd. SW2 57Qb 112
Morven Cl. EN6: Pot B 3Eb 17
Morven Rd. SW17 62Hb 133
Morville Ho. SW18 58Fb 111
(off Fitzhugh Gro.)
Morville St. E3 40Cc 72
Morwell St. WC1 1D 222 (43Mb 90)
Mosbach Gdns. CM13: Hut 19De 41
Moscow Mans. SW5 49Cb 89
(off Cromwell Rd.)
Moscow Pl. W2 45Db 89
Moscow Rd. W2 45Db 89
Mosedale NW1 4B 216
Moseley Row SE10 49Hc 93
Moselle Av. N22 26Qb 50
Moselle Cl. N8 27Pb 50
Moselle Ho. N17 24Vb 51
(off William St.)
Moselle Pl. N17 24Vb 51
Moselle Rd. TN16: Big H 90Nc 180
Moselle St. N17 24Vb 51
Mospey Cres. KT17: Eps 87Va 174
Mosque Ter. E1 43Wb 91
(off Whitechapel Rd.)
Mosque Twr. E1 43Wb 91
(off Fieldgate St.)
E3 40Ac 72
(off Ford St.)
Mosquito Cl. SM6: Wall 80Nb 156
Moss Bank RM17: Grays 49Be 99
(not continuous)
Mossborough Cl. N12 23Db 49
Mossbury Rd. SW11 55Gb 111
Moss Cl. E1 43Wb 91
HA5: Pinn 26Ba 45
N9 18Wb 33
WD3: Rick 19M 25
Mossdown Cl. DA17: Belv 49Cd 96
Mossendew Cl. UB9: Hare 25M 43
Mossfield KT11: Cobh 85W 170
Mossford Ct. IG6: Ilf 27Rc 54
Mossford Grn. IG6: Ilf 27Rc 54
Mossford La. IG6: Ilf 26Rc 54
Mossford St. E3 42Bc 92
Moss Gdns. CR2: Sels 80Zb 158
TW13: Felt 61W 128
Moss Hall Ct. N12 23Db 49
Moss Hall Cres. N12 23Db 49
Moss Hall Gro. N12 23Db 49
Mossington Gdns. SE16 49Yb 92
Moss La. HA5: Pinn 25Aa 45
RM1: Rom 30Hd 56
Mosslea Rd. BR2: Brom 71Mc 159
BR6: Farnb 76Sc 160
CR3: Whyt 88Vb 177
SE20 65Yb 136
(not continuous)
Mossop St. SW3 5E 226 (49Gb 89)
Moss Rd. RM10: Dag 38Cd 76
RM15: S Ock 43Yd 98
WD25: Wat 6X 13
Moss Side AL2: Brick W 2Ba 13
Mossville Gdns. SM4: Mord 69Bb 133
Moss Way DA2: Daren 63Td 142
Mosswell Ho. N10 25Jb 50
Moston Cl. UB3: Harl 50V 84
Mostyn Av. HA9: Wemb 36Pa 67
Mostyn Gdns. NW10 41Za 88
Mostyn Gro. E3 40Cc 72
Mostyn Rd. HA8: Edg 24Ua 48
SW9 53Qb 112
SW19 67Bb 133
WD23: Bush 15Ea 28
Mostyn Ter. RH1: Redh 7A 208
Mosul Way BR2: Brom 72Nc 160
Mosyer Dr. BR5: Orp 75Zc 161
Motcomb St. SW1 3H 227 (48Jb 90)
Mote, The DA3: New A 75Be 165
Mote Rd. TN11: S'brne 100Wd 204
TN15: S'brne, Ivy H 100Wd 204
Moth Cl. SM6: Wall 80Nb 156
Mothers Sq. E5 35Xb 71
Motherwell Way
RM20: W Thur 50Wd 98
Motley Av. EC2 5H 219
Motley St. SW8 54Lb 112
MOTSPUR PARK 72Wa 154
Motspur Pk. KT3: N Mald 72Va 154
MOTTINGHAM 61Nc 138
Mottingham Gdns. SE9 60Mc 115
Mottingham La. SE9 60Lc 115
SE12 60Lc 115
Mottingham Rd. N9 16Zb 34
SE9 61Nc 138
Mottisfont Rd. SE2 48Wc 95
Motts Hill La. KT20: Tad, Walt H 95Wa 194
Motts La. RM8: Dag 33Bd 75
Mott St. E4: Lough 10Fc 21
IG10: H Beech, Lough 11Gc 35
Mouchotte Cl. TN16: Big H 84Kc 179
Moules Ct. SE5 52Sb 113
Moulins Rd. E9 38Yb 72
Moulsford Ho. N7 36Mb 70
W2 43Cb 89
(off Westbourne Pk. Rd.)
Moultain Hill BR8: Swan 70Jd 140
Moulton Av. TW3: Houn 54Aa 107
Moultrie Way RM14: Upm 30Ud 58
Mound, The SE9 62Qc 138
Moundfield Rd. N16 30Wb 51
Moundsfield Way SL1: Slou 7C 80
Mounsey Ho. W10 41Ab 88
(off Third Av.)
Mount, The CR2: S Croy 78Sb 157
(off Warham Rd.)
CR5: Coul 87Jb 176
CR6: W'ham 91Wb 197
DA6: Bex 57Dd 118
E5 33Xb 71
(not continuous)
EN6: Pot B 2Db 17
GU21: Knap 1G 186
GU21: Wok 10P 167
(Elm Rd.)
GU21: Wok 1L 187
(St Johns Ct.)
GU25: Vir W 2P 147
HA9: Wemb 33Ra 67
KT3: N Mald 69Va 132
KT4: Wor Pk 77Xa 154
KT10: Esh 79Ca 151
KT13: Weyb 75U 150
KT17: Ewe 82Va 174
KT20: Lwr K 98Bb 195
KT22: Fet 95Ga 192
N20 19Eb 31
NW3 34Eb 69
RM3: Rom 20Ld 39
SS17: Stan H 1P 101
UB5: N'olt 36Da 65
W3 46Sa 87
W8 46Cb 89
(off Bedford Gdns.)
WD3: Rick 16L 25
Mountacre Cl. SE26 63Vb 135
Mt. Adon Pk. SE22 59Wb 113
Mountague Pl. E14 45Ec 92
Mountain Ct. TN15: Wro 88Be 185
Mountain Ho.
SE11 7J 229 (49Pb 90)
Mt. Angelus Rd. SW15 59Va 110
Mt. Ararat Rd. TW10: Rich 57Na 109
Mt. Arlington BR2: Brom 68Gc 137
(off Park Hill Rd.)
Mt. Ash Rd. SE26 62Xb 135
Mount Av. CM13: Hut 17De 41
CR3: Cat'm 96Sb 197
E4 20Cc 34
RM3: Hrld W 23Sd 58
UB1: S'hall 44Ca 85
W5 43La 86
Mountbatten Cl. AL1: St A 5F 6
SE18 51Uc 116
SE19 64Ub 135
SL1: Slou 8L 81
Mountbatten Ct. IG9: Buck H 19Mc 35
SE16 46Yb 92
(off Rotherhithe St.)
Mountbatten Gdns.
BR3: Beck 70Ac 136
Mountbatten Ho. N6 31Jb 70
(off Hillcrest)
RM2: Rom 28Ld 57
Mountbatten M. SW18 59Eb 111
Mountbatten Sq. SL4: Wind 3G 102
Mountbel Rd. HA7: Stan 25Ja 46
Mt. Carmel Chambers W8 47Cb 89
(off Dukes La.)
Mount Cl. BR1: Brom 67Nc 138
CR8: Kenley 88Tb 177
EN4: Cockf 14Jb 32
GU22: Wok 3N 187
HP1: Hem H 2H 3
KT22: Fet 95Ga 192
SL2: Farn C 5G 60
SM5: Cars 81Jb 176
TN13: S'oaks 95Hd 202
W5 43La 86
Mount Cl., The GU25: Vir W 2P 147
Mountcombe Cl. KT6: Surb 73Na 153
Mount Ct. BR4: W W'ck 75Gc 159
SW15 55Ab 110
Mount Cres. CM14: W'ley 21Zd 59
Mt. Culver Av. DA14: Sidc 65Zc 139
Mount Dr. AL2: Park 7B 6
DA6: Bex 57Ad 117
HA2: Harr 29Ba 45
HA9: Wemb 33Sa 67
Mount Dr., The RH2: Reig 4M 207
Mountearl Gdns. SW16 62Pb 134
Mt. Eaton Ct. W5 43La 86
(off Mount Av.)
Mt. Echo Av. E4 19Dc 34
Mt. Echo Dr. E4 18Dc 34
MOUNT END 4Bd 23
Mt. Ephraim La. SW16 62Mb 134
Mt. Ephraim Rd. SW16 62Mb 134
Mount Felix KT12: Walt T 74V 150
Mountfield TN15: Bor G 92Ce 205
Mountfield Cl. SE6 59Fc 115
SS17: Stan H 1N 101
Mountfield Rd. E6 40Qc 74
HP2: Hem H 2N 3
N3 27Bb 49
W5 44Ma 87
Mountfield Ter. SE6 59Fc 115
Mountfield Way BR5: St M Cry 70Yc 139
Mountford Mans. SW11 53Jb 112
(off Battersea Pk. Rd.)
Mountford Rd. E8 36Wb 71
Mountfort Cres. N1 38Qb 70
Mountfort Ter. N1 38Qb 70
Mount Gdns. SE26 62Xb 135
Mt. Grace Rd. EN6: Pot B 3Cb 17
Mount Gro. HA8: Edg 20Sa 29
Mountgrove Rd. N5 34Rb 71
Mt. Harry Rd. TN13: S'oaks 95Jd 202
MOUNT HERMON 1N 187
Mt. Hermon Cl. GU22: Wok 1P 187
Mt. Hermon Rd. GU22: Wok 1P 187
Mount Hill TN14: Knock 89Wc 181
Mount Hill La. SL9: Ger X 2M 61
Mount Holme KT7: T Ditt 73Ka 152
Mounthurst Rd. BR2: Hayes 73Hc 159
Mountington Pk. Cl. HA3: Kenton 30Ma 47
Mountjoy Cl. EC2 1E 224
(off Monkwell Sq.)
SE2 47Xc 95
Mountjoy Ho. EC2 1D 224
Mount La. UB9: Den 33F 62
Mount Lee TW20: Egh 64B 126
Mount Lodge N6 30Lb 50
Mount M. TW12: Hamp 67Ca 129
Mount Mills EC1 4C 218 (41Rb 91)
MOUNTNESSING 11Fe 41
Mountnessing By-Pass
CM15: Mount, Shenf 13Fe 41
Mountnessing La. CM15: Dodd 11Zd 41
Mountnessing Windmill 11Fe 41
Mount Nod DA9: Ghithe 57Yd 120
Mt. Nod Rd. SW16 62Pb 134
Mt. Olive Ct. W7 47Ga 86
Mount Pde. EN4: Cockf 14Gb 31
Mount Pk. SM5: Cars 80Jb 156
Mount Pk. Av. CR2: S Croy 81Rb 177
HA1: Harr 33Fa 66
Mount Pk. Cres. W5 44Ma 87
Mount Pk. Rd. HA1: Harr 34Fa 66
HA5: Eastc 29W 44
W5 43Ma 87
Mount Pl. W3 46Ra 87
MOUNT PLEASANT 25J 43
Mt. Pleasant AL3: St A 1P 5
EN4: Cockf 14Gb 31
HA0: Wemb 39Na 67
HA4: Ruis 33Y 65
IG1: Ilf 36Sc 74
KT13: Weyb 76Q 150
KT17: Ewe 82Va 174
KT24: Eff 100Aa 191
KT24: W Hor 100R 190
SE27 63Sb 135
SL9: Chal P 22A 42
TN16: Big H 89Mc 179
UB9: Hare 25J 43
WC1 6K 217 (42Qb 90)
Mt. Pleasant Av. CM13: Hut 16Fe 41
Mt. Pleasant Cotts. N14 17Mb 32
(off The Wells)
Mt. Pleasant Cres. N4 32Pb 70
Mt. Pleasant Hill E5 33Xb 71
Mt. Pleasant La. AL2: Brick W 2Aa 13
E5 32Xb 71
Mt. Pleasant M. N4 32Pb 70
(off Mt. Pleasant Cres.)
Mt. Pleasant Pl. SE18 49Tc 94
Mt. Pleasant Rd. CR3: Cat'm 95Wb 197
DA1: Dart 58Pd 119
E17 26Ac 52
IG7: Chig 21Tc 54
KT3: N Mald 69Sa 131
N17 26Ub 51
NW10 38Ya 68
RM5: Col R 23Fd 56
SE13 58Dc 114
W5 42La 86
Mt. Pleasant Vs. N4 31Pb 70
Mt. Pleasant Wlk. DA5: Bexl 57Ed 118
Mount Ri. RH1: Redh 8M 207
Mount Rd.
CM16: Fidd H, Stap T, They M 4Zc 23
CR4: Mitc 68Fb 133
DA1: Cray 58Hd 118
DA6: Bex 57Zc 117
EN4: E Barn 15Gb 31
GU22: Wok 3M 187
GU24: Chob 4M 167
KT3: N Mald 69Ta 131
KT9: Chess 78Pa 153
NW2 34Xa 68
NW4 30Wa 48
RM4: Stap T 6Bd 23 & 11Cd 38
RM8: Dag 32Bd 75
SE19 65Tb 135
SW19 61Cb 133
TW13: Hanw 62Aa 129
UB3: Hayes 47W 84
Mount Row W1 5K 221 (45Kb 90)
Mountsfield Cl. TW19: Stanw M 58J 105
Mountsfield Ct. SE13 58Fc 115
Mounts Hill SL4: Wink 1A 124
Mountside CR3: Cat'm 96Vb 197
HA7: Stan 25Ja 46
Mount Side Pl. GU22: Wok 90B 168
Mounts Pond Rd. SE3 54Fc 115
(not continuous)
Mount Square, The NW3 34Eb 69
Mounts Rd. DA9: Ghithe 57Xd 120
Mt. Stewart Av. HA3: Kenton 31Ma 67
Mount St. W1 5H 221 (45Jb 90)
Mount St. M. W1 5K 221 (45Kb 90)
Mountstuart Ct. TW11: Hamp W 67Ka 130
Mount Ter. E1 43Xb 91
Mount Vernon NW3 35Eb 69
Mount Vw. AL2: Lon C 9J 7
EN2: Enf 10Pb 18
HA6: Nwood 23V 44
NW7 20Ta 29
UB2: S'hall 49Z 85
W5 42Ma 87
WD3: Rick 18K 25
Mountview Cl. NW11 32Db 69
Mountview Ct. N8 28Rb 51
Mountview Dr. RH1: Redh 8N 207
Mount Vw. Rd. E4 17Fc 35
KT10: Clay 80Ka 152
N4 31Nb 70
NW9 29Ta 47
Mountview Rd.
BR6: Orp, St M Cry 73Wc 161
(not continuous)
Mount Vs. SE27 62Rb 135
Mount Way SM5: Cars 81Jb 176
Mountway EN6: Pot B 2Cb 17
Mountwood KT8: W Mole 69Da 129
Mountwood Cl. CR2: Sande 82Xb 177
MOVERS LANE 40Uc 74
Movers La. IG11: Bark 39Tc 74
Mowat Ct. KT4: Wor Pk 75Va 154
(off The Avenue)
Mowat Ind. Est. WD24: Wat 10Y 13
Mowatt Cl. N19 32Mb 70
Mowbray Av. KT14: Byfl 85N 169
Mowbray Ct. N22 25Qb 50
SE19 66Vb 135
Mowbray Cres. TW20: Egh 64C 126
Mowbray Gdns. UB5: N'olt 39Ca 65
Mowbray Ho. N2 26Fb 49
(off The Grange)
Mowbray Pde. HA8: Edg 21Qa 47
Mowbray Rd. EN5: New Bar 15Eb 31
HA8: Edg 21Qa 47
NW6 38Ab 68
SE19 67Vb 135
TW10: Ham 62La 130
Mowbrays Cl. RM5: Col R 25Ed 56
Mowbrays Rd. RM5: Col R 26Ed 56
Mowbrey Gdns. IG10: Lough 11Sc 36
(not continuous)
Mowlem St. E2 40Xb 71
Mowlem Trad. Est. N17 24Yb 52
Mowll St. SW9 52Qb 112
Moxey Cl. TN16: Big H 85Lc 179
Moxom Av. EN8: Chesh 2Ac 20
Moxon Cl. E13 40Hc 73
Moxon St. EN5: Barn 13Bb 31
W1 1H 221 (43Jb 90)
Moye Cl. E2 40Wb 71
Moyers Rd. E10 31Ec 72
Moylan Rd. W6 51Ab 110
Moyle Ho. SW1 50Lb 90
(off Churchill Gdns.)
Moyne Ct. GU21: Wok 10K 167
Moyne Ho. SW9 57Rb 113
Moyne Pl. NW10 40Qa 67
Moynihan Dr. N21 15Nb 32
Moys Cl. CR0: C'don 72Nb 156
Moyser Rd. SW16 64Kb 134
Mozart St. W10 41Bb 89
Mozart Ter. SW1 6J 227 (49Jb 90)
MTV Europe 38Kb 70
Muchelney Rd. SM4: Mord 72Eb 155
Muckhatch La. TW20: Thorpe 69D 126
MUCKING 4M 101
MUCKINGFORD 8J 101
Muckingford Rd. RM18: W Til 9F 100
SS17: Linf 9F 100
Mucking Wharf Rd. SS17: Stan H 4L 101
Mudchute Farm 49Ec 92
Muddy La. SL2: Slou 3J 81
Mudlands Ind. Est. RM13: Rain 41Gd 96
Mudlarks Blvd. SE10 48Hc 93
Mudlarks Way SE10 48Jc 93
Muggeridge Cl. CR2: S Croy 78Tb 157
Muggeridge Rd. RM10: Dag 35Dd 76
Muggins La. DA12: Shorne 3L 145
MUGSWELL 97Db 195
Muirdown Av. SW14 56Ta 109
Muir Dr. SW18 58Gb 111
Muirfield W3 44Ua 88
Muirfield Cl. SE16 50Xb 91
WD19: Wat 22Y 45
Muirfield Cres. E14 48Dc 92
Muirfield Grn. WD19: Wat 21X 45
Muirfield Rd. GU21: Wok 10L 167
WD19: Wat 21X 45
Muirhead Quay IG11: Bark 40Sc 74
Muirkirk Rd. SE6 60Ec 114
Muir Rd. E5 34Wb 71
Muir St. E16 46Nc 94
(not continuous)
Mulberry Av. SL4: Wind 5K 103
TW19: Stanw 60N 105
Mulberry Bus. Cen. SE16 47Zb 92
Mulberry Cl. AL2: Park 10P 5
E4 19Cc 34
EN4: E Barn 14Fb 31
GU21: Wok 86A 168
KT13: Weyb 76R 150
KT19: Eps 81Sa 173
N8 29Nb 50
NW3 35Fb 69
NW4 27Ya 48
RM2: Rom 28Ld 57
SE7 51Mc 115
SE22 57Wb 113
SW3 51Fb 111
(off Beaufort St.)
SW16 63Lb 134
UB5: N'olt 40Aa 65
WD17: Wat 8U 12
Mulberry Ct. E11 35Fc 73
(off Langthorne Rd.)
EC1 4C 218
HP1: Hem H 1M 3
IG11: Bark 37Vc 75
KT6: Surb 73Ma 153
N2 27Gb 49
(off Bedford Rd.)
SW3 51Fb 111
(not continuous)
TW1: Twick 62Ha 130
W9 41Bb 89
(off Ashmore Rd.)
Mulberry Cres. TW8: Bford 52Ka 108
UB7: W Dray 47Q 84
Mulberry Dr. RM19: Purf 49Pd 97
SL3: L'ly 50A 82
Mulberry Gdns. WD7: Shenl 5Na 15
Mulberry Ga. SM7: Bans 88Bb 175
Mulberry Hill CM15: Shenf 17Be 41
Mulberry Ho. BR2: Brom 67Gc 137
E2 41Yb 92
(off Victoria Pk. Sq.)
SE8 51Bc 114
Mulberry Housing Co-operative
SE1 6A 224
Mulberry La. CR0: C'don 74Vb 157
Mulberry Lodge WD19: Wat 16Z 27
(off Eastbury Rd.)
Mulberry M. SE14 53Bc 114
SM6: Wall 79Lb 156
Mulberry Pde. UB7: W Dray 48Q 84
Mulberry Pl. E14 45Ec 92
(off Clove Cres.)
HA2: Harr 26Ea 46
SE9 56Mc 115
TN16: Bras 96Yc 201
W6 50Wa 88
Mulberry Rd. DA11: Nflt 2A 144
E8 38Vb 71
Mulberry St. E1 44Wb 91
Mulberry Tree M. W4 47Sa 87
Mulberry Trees TW17: Shep 73T 150
Mulberry Wlk. SW3 51Fb 111
Mulberry Way DA17: Belv 47Ed 96
E18 26Kc 53
IG6: Ilf 28Sc 54
KT21: Asht 91Na 193
Mulgrave Ct. SM2: Sutt 79Db 155
(off Mulgrave Rd.)
Mulgrave Rd. CR0: C'don 76Tb 157
HA1: Harr 33Ja 66
NW10 35Va 68
SE18 49Pc 94
SM2: Sutt 80Bb 155
SW6 51Bb 111
W5 41Ma 87
Mulgrave Way GU21: Knap 10J 167
Mulholland Cl. CR4: Mitc 68Kb 134
Mulkern Rd. N19 32Mb 70
(not continuous)
Mullards Cl. CR4: Mitc 74Hb 155
Mullein Ct. RM17: Grays 51Fe 121
Mullender Ct. DA12: Grav'nd 10J 123
Mullens Rd. TW20: Egh 64D 126
Mullen Twr. WC1 6K 217
Muller Ho. SE18 50Qc 94
Muller Rd. SW4 58Mb 112
Mullet Gdns. E2 41Wb 91
Mulletsfield WC1 4G 217
Mull Ho. E3 40Bc 72
(off Stafford Rd.)
WD18: Wat 15V 26
Mulligans Apartments NW6 38Cb 69
(off Kilburn High Rd.)
Mullins Path SW14 55Ta 109
Mullion Cl. HA3: Hrw W 25Da 45
Mullion Wlk. WD19: Wat 21Z 45
Mull Wlk. N1 37Sb 71
(off Clephane Rd.)
Mulready Ho. SW1 6F 229
Mulready St. NW8 6D 214 (42Gb 89)
Mulready Wlk. HP3: Hem H 6N 3
Multimedia Ho. NW10 42Sa 87
Multon Ho. E9 38Yb 72
Multon Rd. SW18 59Fb 111
TN15: W King 79Ud 164
Mulvaney Way SE1 2G 231 (47Tb 91)
(not continuous)
Mumford Mills SE10 53Dc 114
(off Greenwich High Rd.)
Mumford Rd. SE24 57Rb 113
Muncaster Cl. TW15: Ashf 63Q 128
Muncaster Rd. SW11 57Hb 111
TW15: Ashf 64R 128
Muncies M. SE6 61Ec 136
Mundania Ct. SE22 58Xb 113
Mundania Rd. SE22 58Xb 113
Munday Ho. SE1 4F 231
Munday Rd. E16 45Jc 93
MUNDEN 6Da 13
Munden Dr. WD25: Wat 9Aa 13
Munden Gro. WD24: Wat 10Y 13
Munden Ho. E3 41Dc 92
(off Bromley High St.)
Munden St. W14 49Ab 88
Munden Vw. WD25: Wat 8Z 13
Mundesley Cl. WD19: Wat 21Y 45
Mundesley Spur SL1: Slou 4J 81
Mundford Rd. E5 33Yb 72
Mundon Gdns. IG1: Ilf 33Tc 74
Mund St. W14 50Bb 89
Mundy Ct. SL4: Eton 1H 103
Mundy Ho. W10 41Ab 88
(off Dart St.)
Mundy St. N1 3H 219 (41Ub 91)
Munford Dr. DA10: Swans 59Ae 121
Mungo Pk. Cl. WD23: B Hea 19Ea 28
Mungo Pk. Rd. DA12: Grav'nd 4F 144
RM13: Rain 37Jd 76
Mungo Pk. Way BR5: Orp 73Yc 161
Munkenbeck Bldg. W2 1B 220
Munnery Way BR6: Farnb 76Qc 160
Munnings Gdns. TW7: Isle 57Fa 108
Munnings Ho. E16 46Kc 93
(off Portsmouth M.)
Munro Dr. N11 23Lb 50
Munro Ho. KT11: Cobh 84Z 171
SE1 2K 229 (47Qb 90)
Munro M. W10 43Ab 88
(not continuous)
Munro Ter. SW10 52Fb 111
Munslow Gdns. SM1: Sutt 77Fb 155
Munster Av. TW4: Houn 57Aa 107
Munster Ct. SW6 54Bb 111
TW11: Tedd 65La 130
Munster Gdns. N13 21Rb 51
Munster M. SW6 52Ab 110
Munster Rd. SW6 52Ab 110
TW11: Tedd 65Ka 130
Munster Sq. NW1 4A 216 (41Kb 90)
Munton Rd. SE17 5E 230 (49Sb 91)
Murchison Av. DA5: Bexl 60Zc 117
Murchison Ho. W10 43Ab 88
(off Ladbroke Gro.)
Murchison Rd. E10 33Ec 72
Murdoch Cl. TW18: Staines 64J 127
Murdoch Ho. SE16 48Yb 92
(off Moodkee St.)
Murdock Cl. E16 44Hc 93
Murdock St. SE15 51Xb 113

Murfett Cl. SW19 61Ab 132
Murfitt Way RM14: Upm 35Qd 77
Muriel Av. WD18: Wat 15Y 27
Muriel St. N1 1J 217 (40Pb 70)
(not continuous)
Murillo Rd. SE13 56Fc 115
Muro Ct. SE1 2C 230
Murphy Ho. SE1 3C 230
Murphy St. SE1 2K 229 (47Qb 90)
Murray Av. BR1: Brom 69Kc 137
TW3: Houn 57Da 107
Murray Bus. Cen. BR5: St P 69Xc 139
Murray Cl. SE28 46Uc 94
Murray Ct. HA1: Harr 30Ha 46
SL5: S'hill 2A 146
TW2: Twick 61Fa 130
W7 47Ga 86
Murray Cres. HA5: Pinn 25Z 45
Murray Grn. GU21: Wok 86E 168
Murray Gro. N1 2E 218 (40Sb 71)
Murray Ho. KT16: Ott 79E 148
SE18 49Pc 94
(off Rideout St.)
Murray M. NW1 38Mb 70
Murray Rd. BR5: St P 69Xc 139
HA6: Nwood 25U 44
KT16: Ott 79E 148
SW19 65Za 132
TW10: Ham 61Ka 130
W5 49La 86
Murray's La. KT14: W Byf, Byfl 86M 169
Murray Sq. E16 44Jc 93
Murray St. NW1 38Lb 70
Murrays Yd. SE18 49Rc 94
Murray Ter. NW3 35Eb 69
W5 49Ma 87
Murrell's Wlk. KT23: Bookh 95Ca 191
Murreys, The KT21: Asht 90La 172
Murreys Ct. KT21: Asht 90Ma 173
Mursell Est. SW8 53Pb 112
Murthering La. RM4: Nave, Stap A 17Hd 38
Murton Ct. AL1: St A 1C 6
Murtwell Dr. IG7: Chig 23Sc 54
Musard Rd. W6 51Ab 110
Musbury St. E1 44Yb 92
Muscal W6 51Ab 110
(off Field Rd.)
Muscatel Pl. SE5 53Ub 113
Muschamp Rd. SE15 55Vb 113
SM5: Cars 75Gb 155
Muscott Ho. E2 39Wb 71
(off Whiston Rd.)
Muscovy Ho. DA18: Erith 47Ad 95
(off Kale Rd.)
Muscovy St. EC3 4J 225 (45Ub 91)
Museum Chambers WC1 1F 223
Museum Ho. E2 41Yb 92
(off Burnham St.)
Museum La. SW7 4C 226 (48Fb 89)
Museum Mans. WC1 1F 223
Mus. of Brands, Packaging and Advertising 44Bb 89
(off Colville M.)
Mus. of Childhood 41Yb 92
Mus. of Classical Archaeology 5D 216
(off Gower Pl.)
Mus. of Croydon 76Sb 157
(off High St.)
Mus. of Domestic Design & Architecture 15Jb 32
Mus. of Eton Life 1H 103
Mus. of Freemasonry 3G 223
(within Freemasons' Hall)
Mus. of London 1D 224 (43Sb 91)
Mus. of London Docklands, The 45Cc 92
Mus. of Richmond 57Ma 109
Mus. of St Albans 1C 6
Mus. of The Order of St John 6B 218
Museum Pas. E2 41Yb 92
Museum St. WC1 1F 223 (43Nb 90)
Museum Way W3 47Qa 87
Musgrave Cl. EN4: Had W 11Eb 31
Musgrave Ct. SW11 53Gb 111
Musgrave Cres. SW6 52Cb 111
Musgrave Rd. TW7: Isle 53Ha 108
Musgrove Cl. CR8: Purl 85Pb 176
Musgrove Rd. SE14 53Zb 114
Musical Museum, The 51Pa 109
Musjid Rd. SW11 54Fb 111
Musket Cl. EN4: E Barn 16Fb 31
Musk Hill HP1: Hem H 3G 2
Musquash Way TW4: Houn 55Y 107
Mussenden La. DA3: Fawk 71Sd 164
DA4: Hort K 71Sd 164
Mustard Mill Rd. TW18: Staines 63H 127
Mustians SL4: Eton 1G 102
(off Eton Wick Rd.)
Muston Rd. E5 33Xb 71
Mustow Pl. SW6 54Bb 111
Muswell Av. N10 25Kb 50
MUSWELL HILL 27Kb 50
Muswell Hill N10 27Kb 50
Muswell Hill B'way. N10 27Kb 50
Muswell Hill Golf Course 25Lb 50
Muswell Hill Pl. N10 28Kb 50
Muswell Hill Rd. N6 30Jb 50
N10 30Jb 50
Muswell M. N10 27Kb 50
Muswell Rd. N10 27Kb 50
Mutchetts Cl. WD25: Wat 5Aa 13
Mutrix Rd. NW6 39Cb 69
Mutton La. EN6: Pot B, S Mim 3Ya 16
Mutton Pl. NW1 37Jb 70
Muybridge Rd. KT3: N Mald 68Sa 131
Muybridge Yd. KT5: Surb 73Pa 153
Myatt Rd. SW9 53Rb 113
Myatts Fld. Sth. SW9 54Qb 112
Mycenae Rd. SE3 52Jc 115
Myddelton Av. EN1: Enf 10Ub 19
Myddelton Cl. EN1: Enf 11Vb 33
Myddelton Gdns. N21 17Sb 33
Myddelton House Gdns. 8Vb 19
Myddelton Pk. N20 20Fb 31
Myddelton Pas. EC1 3A 218 (41Qb 90)
Myddelton Rd. N8 28Nb 50
(not continuous)
Myddelton Sq. EC1 3A 218 (41Qb 90)
Myddelton St. EC1 4A 218 (41Qb 90)
Myddleton Av. N4 33Sb 71
Myddleton Cl. HA7: Stan 19Ja 28
Myddleton Ct. RM11: Horn 31Hd 76
Myddleton Ho. N1 2K 217
Myddleton M. N22 24Nb 50
Myddleton Path EN7: Chesh 3Xb 19
Myddleton Rd. N22 24Nb 50
UB8: Uxb 39L 63
Myers Cl. WD7: Shenl 4Na 15
Myers Ct. CM14: W'ley 22Yd 58
Myers Dr. SL2: Farn C 6F 60
Myers Ho. SE5 52Sb 113
(off Bethwin Rd.)
Myers La. SE14 51Zb 114
Mygrove Cl. RM13: Rain 40Md 77
Mygrove Gdns. RM13: Rain 40Md 77
Mygrove Rd. RM13: Rain 40Md 77
Myles Ct. EN7: G Oak 1Sb 19
SE16 48Yb 92
(off Neptune St.)
Mylis Cl. SE26 63Xb 135
Mylius Cl. SE14 52Yb 114
Mylne Cl. W6 50Wa 88
Mylne St. EC1 3K 217 (41Qb 90)
Mylor Cl. GU21: Wok 86A 168
Mymms Dr. AL9: Brk P 8J 9
Mymms Ho. AL9: Wel G 5E 8
Mynn's Cl. KT18: Eps 86Ra 173
Myra St. SE2 49Wc 95
Myrdle Ct. E1 44Wb 91
(off Myrdle St.)
Myrdle St. E1 43Wb 91
MYRKE 10K 81
Myrke, The SL3: Dat 9K 81
Myrna Cl. SW19 66Gb 133
Myron Pl. SE13 55Ec 114
Myrtle Av. HA4: Ruis 31W 64
TW14: Felt 57U 106
Myrtleberry Cl. E8 37Vb 71
(off Beechwood Rd.)
Myrtle Cl. DA8: Erith 52Gd 118
EN4: E Barn 18Hb 31
GU18: Light 3A 166
SL3: Poyle 53G 104
UB7: W Dray 48P 83
UB8: Hil 43P 83
Myrtle Cres. SL2: Slou 5K 81
Myrtledene Rd. SE2 50Wc 95
Myrtle Gdns. W7 46Ga 86
Myrtle Grn. HP1: Hem H 1G 2
Myrtle Gro. EN2: Enf 10Tb 19
KT3: N Mald 68Sa 131
RM15: Avel 47Sd 98
Myrtle Pl. DA2: Dart 59Td 120
Myrtle Rd. CM14: W'ley 21Yd 58
CR0: C'don 76Cc 158
DA1: Dart 60Md 119
E6 39Pc 74
E17 30Ac 52
IG1: Ilf 33Rc 74
N13 20Sb 33
RM3: Rom 23Ld 57
SM1: Sutt 78Eb 155
TW3: Houn 54Ea 108
TW12: Hamp H 65Ea 130
W3 46Sa 87
Myrtleside Cl. HA6: Nwood 24T 44
Myrtle Wlk. N1 2H 219 (40Ub 71)
Mysore Rd. SW11 55Hb 111
Myton Rd. SE21 62Tb 135
Mytton Ho. SW8 52Pb 112
(off St Stephens Ter.)

N

N1 Shop. Cen. N1 1A 218 (40Qb 70)
N16 Fitness Cen. 35Tb 71
Nacton Ct. RM6: Chad H 29Yc 55
(off Hevingham Dr.)
Nadine Ct. SM6: Wall 81Lb 176
Nadine St. SE7 50Lc 93
Nafferton Ri. IG10: Lough 15Mc 35
Nagasaki Wlk. SE7 48Kc 93
Nagle Cl. E17 26Fc 53
NAG'S HEAD 34Nb 70
Nags Head Ct. EC1 6E 218
Nags Head La.
CM14: B'wood, Upm 25Sd 58
DA16: Well 55Xc 117
RM14: Upm 25Sd 58
Nags Head Rd. EN3: Pond E 14Yb 34
Nags Head Shop. Cen. N7 35Pb 70
Nailsworth Cres. RH1: Mers 1D 208
Nailzee Cl. SL9: Ger X 31A 62
Nainby Ho. SE11 6K 229
Nairn Ct. RM18: Tilb 4B 122
Nairne Gro. SE24 57Tb 113
Nairn Grn. WD19: Wat 20W 26
Nairn Ho. CM14: W'ley 21Yd 58
(off Cameron Cl.)
Nairn Rd. HA4: Ruis 37Y 65
Nairn St. E14 43Ec 92
Naldera Gdns. SE3 51Jc 115
Nallhead Rd. TW13: Hanw 64Y 129
Nalton Ho. NW6 38Eb 69
(off Belsize Rd.)
Namba Roy Cl. SW16 63Pb 134
Namton Dr. CR7: Thor H 70Pb 134
Nan Clark's La. NW7 19Ua 30
Nancy Downs WD19: Wat 17Y 27
Nankin St. E14 44Cc 92
Nanscott Ho. WD19: Wat 20Z 27
Nansen Ho. NW10 37Ta 67
(off Stonebridge Pk.)
Nansen Rd. DA12: Grav'nd 3F 144
SW11 55Jb 112
Nansen Village N12 21Db 49
Nant Ct. NW2 33Bb 69
Nanterre Ct. WD17: Wat 12W 26
Nantes Cl. SW18 56Eb 111
Nantes Pas. E1 7K 219 (43Vb 91)
Nant Rd. NW2 33Bb 69
Nant St. E2 41Xb 91
Nantwich Ho. RM3: Rom 22Nd 57
(off Lindfield Rd.)
Naoroji St. WC1 4K 217 (41Qb 90)
Nap, The WD4: K Lan 1Q 12
Napier NW9 25Va 48
Napier Av. E14 50Cc 92
SW6 55Bb 111
Napier Cl. AL2: Lon C 7H 7
RM11: Horn 32Kd 77
SE8 52Bc 114
UB7: W Dray 48P 83
W14 48Ab 88
Napier Ct. CR3: Cat'm 94Ub 197
GU21: Wok 88A 168
N1 1F 219
SE12 62Kc 137
SW6 55Bb 111
(off Ranelagh Gdns.)
UB4: Yead 42Y 85
(off Dunedin Way)
Napier Dr. WD23: Bush 14Aa 27
Napier Gro. N1 2E 218 (40Sb 71)
Napier Ho. RM13: Rain 41Hd 96
(off Dunedin Rd.)
SE17 51Rb 113
(off Cooks Rd.)
Napier Lodge TW15: Ashf 65T 128
Napier Pl. W14 48Bb 89
Napier Rd. BR2: Brom 70Kc 137
CR2: S Croy 80Tb 157
DA11: Nflt 10B 122
DA17: Belv 49Bd 95
E6 39Qc 74
E11 35Gc 73
E15 40Gc 73
(not continuous)
EN3: Pond E 15Zb 34
HA0: Wemb 37Ma 67
N17 27Ub 51
NW10 41Xa 88
SE25 70Xb 135
TW7: Isle 56Ja 108
TW15: Ashf 66T 128
W14 48Bb 89
Napier St. SE8 52Bc 114
(off Napier Cl.)
Napier Ter. N1 38Rb 71
Napier Wlk. TW15: Ashf 66T 128
Napoleon Rd. E5 34Xb 71
TW1: Twick 59Ka 108
NAPSBURY 9G 6
Napsbury Av. AL2: Lon C 8G 6
Napsbury La. AL1: St A 5E 6
Napton Cl. UB4: Yead 42Aa 85
Nara SE13 54Dc 114
Narbonne Av. SW4 57Lb 112
Narboro Ct. RM1: Rom 29Jd 56
Narborough Cl. UB10: Ick 33S 64
Narborough St. SW6 54Db 111
Narcissus Rd. NW6 36Cb 69
Nardini NW9 25Va 48
(off The Concourse)
Nare Rd. RM15: Avel 45Sd 98
Naresby Fold HA7: Stan 23La 46
Narford Rd. E5 34Wb 71
Narrow Boat Cl. SE28 47Tc 94
Narrow La. CR6: W'ham 91Xb 197
Narrow St. E14 45Ac 92
W3 46Ra 87
Narrow Way BR2: Brom 72Nc 160
Narvic Ho. SE5 54Sb 113
Narwhal Inuit Art Gallery 49Ta 87
Nascot Pl. WD17: Wat 12X 27
Nascot Rd. WD17: Wat 12X 27
Nascot St. W12 44Ya 88
WD17: Wat 12X 27
Nascot Wood Rd. WD17: Wat 9V 12
Naseby Cl. NW6 38Eb 69
TW7: Isle 53Ga 108
Naseby Ct. DA14: Sidc 63Vc 139
KT12: Walt T 75Y 151
Naseby Rd. IG5: Ilf 25Pc 54
RM10: Dag 34Cd 76
SE19 65Tb 135
NASH 79Jc 159
Nash Bank DA13: Meop, Ist R 8B 144
Nash Cl. AL9: Wel G 5F 8
SM1: Sutt 76Fb 155
WD6: E'tree 14Pa 29
Nash Ct. HA3: Kenton 30Ka 46
Nash Cft. DA11: Nflt 3A 144
Nashdom La. SL1: Burn 7A 60
Nash Dr. RH1: Redh 4P 207
Nashe Ho. SE1 4F 231
Nash Gdns. RH1: Redh 4P 207
Nash Grn. BR1: Brom 65Jc 137
HP3: Hem H 7P 3
Nash Ho. E14 47Cc 92
(off Alpha Gro.)
E17 27Dc 52
NW1 1K 215
SW1 7A 228
Nash La. BR2: Kes 80Jc 159
NASH MILLS 8P 3
Nash Mills La. HP3: Hem H 8P 3
Nash Pl. E14 46Dc 92
Nash Rd. N9 19Yb 34
RM6: Chad H 28Zc 55
SE4 56Ac 114
SL3: L'ly 49B 82
NASH STREET 8B 144
Nash St. DA13: Meop 8B 144
NW1 3A 216 (41Kb 90)
Nash's Yd. UB8: Uxb 38M 63
Nash Way HA3: Kenton 30Ka 46
Nasmyth St. W6 48Xa 88
Nassau Path SE28 46Yc 95
Nassau Rd. SW13 53Va 110
Nassau St. W1 1B 222 (43Lb 90)
Nassington Rd. NW3 35Hb 69
NAST HYDE 6B 8
Nasturtium Dr. GU24: Bisl 7E 166
Natalie Cl. TW14: Bedf 59T 106
Natalie M. TW2: Twick 62Fa 130
Natal Rd. CR7: Thor H 69Tb 135
IG1: Ilf 35Rc 74
N11 23Nb 50
SW16 65Mb 134
Natasha Ct. RM3: Rom 24Ld 57
Nathan Cl. RM14: Upm 32Ud 78
Nathan Ct. N9 17Yb 34
(off Causeyware Rd.)
Nathan Ho. SE11 6A 230
Nathaniel Cl. E1 1K 225 (43Vb 91)
Nathaniel Ct. E17 31Ac 72
Nathans Rd. HA0: Wemb 32La 66
Nathan Way SE28 49Uc 94
National Archives, The 52Ra 109
National Army Mus. 51Hb 111
National Gallery 5E 222 (45Mb 90)
National Maritime Mus. 51Fc 115
National Portrait Gallery 5E 222
National Rifle Association & National Shooting Centre Headquarters 1B 186
(off Queen's Way)
National Rifle Association Mus. 1B 186
National Tennis Cen. 57Ua 110
National Ter. SE16 47Xb 91
(off Bermondsey Wall E.)
National Theatre 6J 223 (46Qb 90)
National Works TW4: Houn 55Ba 107
Nation Way E4 18Ec 34
Natural History Mus.
Eton 1H 103
Knightsbridge 4B 226 (48Fb 89)
Naunton Way RM12: Horn 34Md 77
Nautilus Building, The EC1 3A 218
Naval Ho. E14 45Fc 93
(off Quixley St.)
Naval Row E14 45Ec 92
Naval Wlk. BR1: Brom 68Jc 137
(off Mitre Cl.)
Navarino Gro. E8 37Wb 71
Navarino Mans. E8 37Wb 71
Navarino Rd. E8 37Wb 71
Navarre Ct. WD4: K Lan 10B 4
Navarre Gdns. RM5: Col R 22Dd 56
Navarre Rd. E6 40Nc 74
Navarre St. E2 5K 219 (42Vb 91)
Navenby Wlk. E3 42Cc 92
NAVESTOCK 12Md 39
Navestock Cl. E4 20Ec 34
Navestock Cres. IG8: Wfd G 24Lc 53
Navestock Ho. IG11: Bark 40Xc 75
NAVESTOCK SIDE 12Sd 40
Navestockside CM14: Kel C, N'side 12Sd 40
Navigation Ct. E16 45Sc 94
Navigation Dr. EN3: Enf L 10Cc 20
Navigation Ho. KT15: Add 77N 149
Navigator Dr. UB2: S'hall 47Ea 86
Navigator Pk. UB2: S'hall 49Y 85
Navy St. SW4 55Mb 112
Naxos Bldg. E14 47Bc 92
Nayim Pl. E8 36Xb 71
Nayland Ho. SE6 63Ec 136
Naylor Bldg. E. E1 44Wb 91
(off Assam St.)
Naylor Bldg. W. E1 44Wb 91
(off Adler St.)
Naylor Gro. EN3: Pond E 15Zb 34
Naylor Ho. SE17 6G 231
W10 41Ab 88
(off Dart St.)
Naylor Rd. N20 19Eb 31
SE15 52Xb 113
Nazareth Gdns. SE15 54Xb 113
Nazeing Wlk. RM13: Rain 38Hd 76
Nazrul St. E2 3K 219 (41Vb 91)
NCR Bus. Cen. NW10 36Ua 68
Neagle Cl. WD6: Bore 11Sa 29
Neagle Ho. NW2 34Ya 68
(off Stoll Cl.)
Neal Av. UB1: S'hall 42Ba 85
Neal Cl. HA6: Nwood 25W 44
SL9: Ger X 32D 62
Neal Ct. EN9: Walt A 5Hc 21
Nealden St. SW9 55Pb 112
Neale Cl. N2 27Eb 49
Neale Ct. RM9: Dag 37Xc 75
Neal Rd. TN15: W King 79Ud 164
Neal St. WC2 3F 223 (44Nb 90)
WD18: Wat 15Y 27
Neal's Yd. WC2 3F 223 (44Nb 90)
Near Acre NW9 25Va 48
NEASDEN 34Ua 68
Neasden Cl. NW10 36Ua 68
NEASDEN JUNC. 35Ua 68
Neasden La. NW10 34Ua 68
Neasden La. Nth. NW10 34Ta 67
Neasham Rd. RM8: Dag 36Xc 75
Neate Ho. SW1 7C 228
Neate St. SE5 51Ub 113
Neath Gdns. SM4: Mord 72Eb 155
Neathouse Pl. SW1 5B 228 (49Lb 90)
Neats Acre HA4: Ruis 31T 64
Neatscourt Rd. E6 43Mc 93
Neave Cres. RM3: Rom 25Ld 57
Neb La. RH8: Oxt 3G 210
Nebraska Bldg. SE10 53Dc 114
(off Deal's Gateway)
Nebraska St. SE1 2F 231 (47Tb 91)
Nebula SW11 54Hb 111
Nebula Ct. E13 40Jc 73
(off Umbriel Pl.)
Neckinger SE16 3K 231 (48Vb 91)
Neckinger Est. SE16 3K 231 (48Vb 91)
Neckinger St. SE1 2K 231 (47Vb 91)
Nectarine Way SE13 54Dc 114
Needham Cl. SL4: Wind 3C 102
Needham Ho. SE11 6K 229
Needham Rd. W11 44Cb 89
Needham Ter. NW2 34Za 68
Needleman St. SE16 47Zb 92
Needles Bank RH9: G'stone 3P 209
(not continuous)
Needwood Ho. N4 32Sb 71
Neela Cl. UB10: Ick 35R 64
Neeld Cres. HA9: Wemb 36Qa 67
NW4 29Xa 48
Neeld Pde. HA9: Wemb 36Pa 67
Neil Cl. TW15: Ashf 64S 128
Neild Way WD3: Rick 17H 25
Neil Wates Cres. SW2 60Qb 112
Nelgarde Rd. SE6 59Cc 114
Nella Rd. W6 51Za 110
Nelldale Rd. SE16 49Yb 92
Nellgrove Rd. UB10: Hil 42R 84
Nell Gwynn Cl. WD7: Shenl 4Na 15
Nell Gwynne Av. SL5: S'hill 10B 124
TW17: Shep 72T 150
Nell Gwynne Cl. KT19: Eps 83Qa 173
SL5: S'hill 10B 124
Nell Gwynn Ho. SW3 6E 226 (49Gb 89)
Nello James Gdns. SE27 63Tb 135
Nelmes Cl. RM11: Horn 29Pd 57
Nelmes Cres. RM11: Horn 29Nd 57
Nelmes Rd. RM11: Horn 31Nd 77
Nelmes Way RM11: Horn 28Md 57
Nelson Av. AL1: St A 5F 6
Nelson Cl. CM14: W'ley 22Zd 59
CR0: C'don 74Rb 157
KT12: Walt T 74X 151
NW6 41Cb 89
RM7: Mawney 25Dd 56
SL3: L'ly 9P 81
TN16: Big H 89Nc 180
TW14: Felt 60V 106
UB10: Hil 41R 84
Nelson Ct. DA8: Erith 52Hd 118
(off Frobisher Rd.)
KT16: Chert 74J 149
SE16 46Yb 92
(off Brunel Rd.)
Nelson Gdns. E2 41Wb 91
TW3: Houn 58Ca 107
Nelson Gro. Rd. SW19 67Db 133
Nelson Ho. DA9: Ghithe 57Zd 121
RM3: Rom 22Nd 57
(off Lindfield Rd.)
SW1 51Lb 112
(off Dolphin Sq.)
Nelson La. UB10: Hil 41R 84
Nelson Mandela Cl. N10 26Jb 50
Nelson Mandela Ho. N16 33Wb 71
Nelson Mandela Rd. SE3 55Lc 115
Nelson Pas. EC1 3E 218 (41Sb 91)
Nelson Pl. DA14: Sidc 63Wc 139
N1 2C 218 (40Rb 71)
Nelson Rd. BR2: Brom 70Lc 137
CR3: Cat'm 95Tb 197
DA1: Dart 58Ld 119
DA11: Nflt 1B 144
DA14: Sidc 63Wc 139
DA17: Belv 50Bd 95
E4 23Dc 52
E11 28Jc 53
EN3: Pond E 16Zb 34
HA1: Harr 32Fa 66
HA7: Stan 23La 46
KT3: N Mald 71Ta 153
N8 29Pb 50
N9 19Xb 33
N15 28Ub 51
RM13: Rain 40Hd 76
RM15: S Ock 40Yd 78
RM16: Ors 4F 100
SE10 51Ec 114
SL4: Wind 5D 102
SW19 66Db 133
TW2: Whitt 59Da 107
TW4: Houn 58Ca 107
TW6: H'row A 53P 105
TW15: Ashf 64N 127
UB10: Hil 41R 84
Nelson Rd. M. SW19 66Db 133
(off Nelson Rd.)
Nelson's Column 6F 223 (46Mb 90)
Nelson Sq. SE1 1B 230 (47Rb 91)
Nelson's Row SW4 56Mb 112
Nelson St. E1 44Xb 91
E6 40Pc 74
(not continuous)
E16 44Hc 93
Nelsons Yd. NW1 1B 216
Nelson Ter. N1 2C 218 (40Rb 71)
Nelson Trad. Est. SW19 67Db 133
Nelson Wlk. E3 42Dc 92
KT19: Eps 81Qa 173
SE16 46Ac 92
Nelwyn Av. RM11: Horn 29Pd 57
Nemoure Rd. W3 45Sa 87
Nene Gdns. TW13: Hanw 62Ba 129
Nene Rd. TW6: H'row A 53R 106
Nene Rd. Rdbt. TW6: H'row A 53R 106
Nepaul Rd. SW11 54Gb 111
Nepean St. SW15 58Wa 110
Nepicar Farm 90Fe 185
Nepicar La. TN15: Wro 87Ee 185
Neptune Bus. Pk. RM19: Purf 50Ud 98
Neptune Cl. RM13: Rain 40Hd 76
Neptune Ct. DA8: Erith 52Hd 118
(off Frobisher Rd.)
E14 49Cc 92
(off Homer Dr.)
E16 43Jc 93
(off Hammersley Rd.)
WD6: Bore 13Qa 29
Neptune Dr. HP2: Hem H 1N 3
Neptune Ho. E3 39Cc 72
(off Garrison Rd.)
SE16 48Yb 92
(off Moodkee St.)
Neptune Rd. HA1: Harr 30Fa 46
TW6: H'row A 53T 106
Neptune St. SE16 48Yb 92
Neptune Wlk. DA8: Erith 49Fd 96
Neptune Way SL1: Slou 7C 80
Nero Ct. TW8: Bford 52Ma 109
Nero Ho. AL1: St A 3D 6
Nesbit Rd. SE9 56Mc 115
Nesbitt Cl. SE3 55Gc 115
Nesbitts All. EN5: Barn 13Bb 31
Nesbitt Sq. SE19 66Ub 135
Nescot Sports Cen. 83Wa 174
Nesham Ho. N1 1H 219
Nesham St. E1 45Wb 91
Ness Rd. DA8: Erith 51Md 119
Ness St. SE16 48Wb 91
Nesta Rd. IG8: Wfd G 23Gc 53
Nestles Av. UB3: Hayes 48V 84
Neston Rd. WD24: Wat 9Y 13
Nestor Av. N21 16Rb 33
Nestor Ho. E2 40Xb 71
(off Old Bethnal Grn. Rd.)
Nethan Dr. RM15: Avel 45Sd 98
Netheravon Rd. W4 49Va 88
W7 46Ha 86
Netheravon Rd. Sth. W4 50Va 88
Netherbury Rd. W5 48Ma 87
Netherby Gdns. EN2: Enf 14Nb 32
Netherby Pk. KT13: Weyb 78U 150
Netherby Rd. SE23 59Yb 114
Nether Cl. N3 24Cb 49
Nethercote Av. GU21: Wok 9K 167
Nethercourt Ho. E3 41Dc 92
(off Bruce Rd.)
Nethercourt Av. N3 23Cb 49
Netherene La. CR5: Coul 95Lb 196
Netherfield Gdns. IG11: Bark 37Tc 74
Netherfield Rd. N12 22Db 49
SW17 62Jb 134
Netherford Rd. SW4 54Lb 112
Netherhall Gdns. NW3 37Eb 69
Netherhall Way NW3 36Eb 69
Netherheys Dr. CR2: S Croy 80Rb 157
Netherlands, The CR5: Coul 91Lb 196
Netherlands Rd. EN5: New Bar 16Fb 31
Netherleigh Cl. N6 32Kb 70
Netherleigh Pk. RH1: S Nut 9E 208
Nethern Ct. Rd. CR3: Wold 95Cc 198
Netherne Dr. CR5: Coul 93Kb 196
Netherne La. CR5: Coul 93Lb 196
RH1: Coul 95Lb 196
NETHERNE-ON-THE-HILL 94Mb 196
Netherpark Dr. RM2: Rom 26Hd 56
Nether St. N3 24Cb 49
N12 24Cb 49
(not continuous)
Netherton Gro. SW10 51Eb 111
Netherton Rd. N15 30Tb 51
TW1: Twick 57Ja 108
Netherway AL3: St A 5N 5
Netherwood N2 26Fb 49
Netherwood Pl. W14 48Za 88
(off Netherwood Rd.)
Netherwood Rd. W14 48Za 88
Netherwood St. NW6 38Bb 69

Nethewode Ct. DA17: Belv 48Dd 96
(off Lower Pk. Rd.)
Netley SE5 53Ub 113
(off Redbridge Gdns.)
Netley Cl. CR0: New Ad 80Ec 158
SM3: Cheam 78Za 154
Netley Dr. KT12: Walt T 73Ba 151
Netley Gdns. SM4: Mord 73Eb 155
Netley Rd. E17 29Bc 52
IG2: Ilf 29Tc 54
SM4: Mord 73Eb 155
TW8: Bford 51Na 109
Netley St. NW1 4B 216 (41Lb 90)
Nettlecombe NW1 38Mb 70
(off Agar Gro.)
Nettlecombe Cl. SM2: Sutt 81Db 175
Nettlecroft HP1: Hem H 3K 3
Nettleden Av. HA9: Wemb 37Qa 67
Nettleden Ho. SW3 6E 226
Nettlefold Pl. SE27 62Rb 135
Nettlefold Wlk. KT12: Walt T 74V 150
Nettlestead Cl. BR3: Beck 66Bc 136
Nettleton Ct. EC2 1D 224
Nettleton Rd. SE14 53Zb 114
TW6: H'row A 53R 106
UB10: Ick 35P 63
Nettlewood Rd. SW16 66Mb 134
Neuchatel Rd. SE6 61Bc 136
Neutron Twr. E14 45Fc 93
Nevada Bldg. SE10 53Dc 114
(off Blackheath Rd.)
Nevada Cl. KT3: N Mald 70Sa 131
Nevada St. SE10 51Ec 114
Nevell Rd. RM16: Grays 8D 100
Nevern Mans. SW5 50Cb 89
(off Warwick Rd.)
Nevern Pl. SW5 49Cb 89
Nevern Rd. SW5 49Cb 89
Nevern Sq. SW5 49Cb 89
Nevil Cl. HA6: Nwood 22T 44
Nevil Ho. SW9 54Rb 113
(off Loughborough Est.)
Nevill Ct. SW10 52Eb 111
(off Edith Ter.)
Neville Av. KT3: N Mald 67Ta 131
Neville Cl. DA15: Sidc 63Vc 139
E11 34Hc 73
EN6: Pot B 3Bb 17
KT10: Esh 79Ba 151
NW1 2E 216 (40Mb 70)
NW6 40Bb 69
SE15 53Wb 113
SL2: Stoke P 7K 61
SM7: Bans 86Db 175
TW3: Houn 54Da 107
W3 47Sa 87
Neville Ct. NW8 2B 214
SL1: Burn 1A 80
Neville Dr. N2 30Eb 49
Neville Gdns. RM8: Dag 34Zc 75
Neville Gill Cl. SW18 58Cb 111
Neville Ho. N11 21Jb 50
N22 25Pb 50
(off Neville Pl.)
NW6 40Bb 69
(off Denmark Rd.)
Neville Ho. Yd. KT1: King T 68Na 131
Neville Pl. N22 25Pb 50
Neville Rd. CR0: C'don 73Tb 157
E7 38Jc 73
IG6: Ilf 25Sc 54
KT1: King T 68Qa 131
NW6 40Bb 69
RM8: Dag 33Zc 75
TW10: Ham 62La 130
W5 42Ma 87
Nevilles Ct. NW2 34Wa 68
Neville St. SW7 7B 226 (50Fb 89)
Neville Ter. SW7 7B 226 (50Fb 89)
Neville Wlk. SM5: Cars 73Gb 155
Nevill Gro. WD24: Wat 11X 27
Nevill La. EC4 2A 224
Nevill Rd. N16 35Ub 71
Nevill Way IG10: Lough 16Nc 36
Nevin Dr. E4 18Dc 34
Nevin Ho. UB3: Harl 48S 84
Nevinson Cl. SW18 58Fb 111
Nevis Cl. E13 40Kc 73
RM1: Rom 23Gd 56
Nevis Rd. SW17 61Jb 134
Nevitt Ho. N1 2G 219
New Acres Rd. SE28 47Uc 94
(not continuous)
NEW ADDINGTON 82Ec 178
New Addington Leisure Cen. 82Ec 178
Newall Ho. SE1 3E 230
Newall Rd. TW6: H'row A 53S 106
New Arc. UB8: Uxb 39M 63
Newark Cl. GU23: Rip 93J 189
Newark Cotts. GU23: Rip 93J 189
Newark Ct. KT12: Walt T 74Y 151
Newark Cres. NW10 41Ta 87
Newark Grn. WD6: Bore 13Ta 29
Newark Ho. SW9 54Rb 113
Newark Knok E6 44Qc 94
Newark La. GU22: Pyr 91H 189
GU23: Rip 91H 189
Newark Rd. CR2: S Croy 79Tb 157
GU20: W'sham 7A 146
Newark St. E1 43Xb 91
(not continuous)
Newark Way NW4 28Wa 48
New Ash Cl. N2 27Fb 49
NEW ASH GREEN 75Be 165
New Atlas Wharf E14 48Cc 92
(off Arnhem Pl.)
New Baltic Wharf SE8 50Ac 92
(off Evelyn St.)
NEW BARN 69Ee 143
New Barn Cl. SM6: Wall 79Pb 156
New Barnes Av. AL1: St A 5E 6
NEW BARNET 14Fb 31
New Barn La. CR3: Whyt 88Ub 177
TN14: Cud 90Sc 180
TN16: Cud, Westrm 90Sc 180
New Barn Rd. BR8: Swan 67Gd 140
DA3: Ist R, Lfield 69De 143
DA13: Ist R, Lfield, Nflt G, Sflt
62Ee 143
New Barns Av. CR4: Mitc 70Mb 134
New Barn St. E13 42Jc 93
New Barns Way IG7: Chig 20Rc 36
New Battlebridge La. RH1: Mers 2B 208
Newbeach Ho. SL2: Slou 1F 80
NEW BECKENHAM 65Bc 136
New Bell Yd. EC4 3C 224
New Bentham Ct. N1 38Sb 71
(off Ecclesbourne Rd.)
Newberries Av. WD7: R'lett 7Ka 14
Newberry Cres. SL4: Wind 4B 102
New Berry La. KT12: Hers 78Z 151
Newbery Cl. CR3: Cat'm 97Ub 197
Newbery Ho. N1 38Sb 71
(off Northampton St.)
Newbery Rd. DA8: Erith 53Hd 118
Newbery Way SL1: Slou 7H 81
Newbiggin Path WD19: Wat 21Y 45
Newbold Cotts. E1 44Yb 92
Newbolt Av. SM3: Cheam 78Ya 154
Newbolt Ho. SE17 7F 231
Newbolt Rd. HA7: Stan 22Ha 46
New Bond St. W1 3K 221 (44Kb 90)
Newborough Grn. KT3: N Mald 70Ta 131
New Brent St. NW4 29Ya 48
Newbridge Point SE23 62Zb 136
(off Windrush La.)
New Bri. St. EC4 3B 224 (44Rb 91)
New Broad St. EC2 1G 225 (43Ub 91)
New Broadway TW12: Hamp H 64Fa 130
UB10: Hil 41R 84
W5 45Ma 87
New Broadway Bldgs. W5 45Ma 87
New Bldgs. SL4: Eton 1H 103
(off Westons Yd.)
Newburgh Rd. RM17: Grays 50Fe 99
W3 46Sa 87
Newburgh St. W1 3B 222 (44Lb 90)
New Burlington M. W1 4B 222 (45Lb 90)
New Burlington Pl. W1 4B 222 (45Lb 90)
New Burlington St. W1 4B 222 (45Lb 90)
Newburn Ho. SE11 7J 229
Newburn St. SE11 7J 229 (50Pb 90)
Newbury Av. EN3: Enf L 10Bc 20
Newbury Cl. DA2: Dart 59Rd 119
RM3: Rom 23Ld 57
UB5: N'olt 37Ba 65
Newbury Ct. DA14: Sidc 63Vc 139
E5 36Ac 72
(off Daubeney Rd.)
Newbury Gdns. KT19: Ewe 77Va 154
RM3: Rom 23Md 57
RM14: Upm 34Pd 77
Newbury Ho. N22 25Nb 50
SW9 54Rb 113
W2 44Db 89
(off Hallfield Est.)
Newbury M. NW5 37Jb 70
NEWBURY PARK 29Tc 54
Newbury Rd. BR2: Brom 69Jc 137
E4 23Ec 52
IG2: Ilf 30Uc 54
RM3: Rom 22Md 57
TW6: H'row A 53P 105
Newbury St. EC1 7D 218 (43Sb 91)
Newbury Wlk. RM3: Rom 22Md 57
Newbury Way UB5: N'olt 37Aa 65
New Bus. Centre, The NW10 41Va 88
New Butt La. SE8 52Cc 114
New Butt La. Nth. SE8 52Cc 114
(off Hales St.)
Newby NW1 4B 216
Newby Cl. EN1: Enf 12Ub 33
Newby Ho. E14 45Ec 92
(off Newby Pl.)
Newby Pl. E14 45Ec 92
Newby St. SW8 55Kb 112
New Caledonian Mkt. SE1 3J 231
New Caledonian Wharf SE16 48Bc 92
Newcastle Av. IG6: Ilf 23Wc 55
Newcastle Cl. EC4 2B 224 (44Rb 91)
Newcastle Ct. EC4 4E 224
Newcastle Ho. W1 7H 215
Newcastle Pl. W2 7C 214 (43Fb 89)
Newcastle Row EC1 6A 218 (42Qb 90)
New Causeway RH2: Reig 9K 207
New Cavendish St. W1 1J 221 (43Jb 90)
New Century Ho. E16 44Hc 93
(off Jude St.)
New Change EC4 3D 224 (44Sb 91)
New Change Pas. EC4 3D 224
New Chapel Sq. TW13: Felt 60X 107
New Charles St. EC1 3C 218 (41Rb 91)
NEW CHARLTON 49Lc 93
New Chiswick Pool 52Ua 110
New Church Rd. SE5 52Sb 113
(not continuous)
Newchurch Rd. SL2: Slou 3D 80
New City Rd. E13 41Lc 93
New Clocktower Pl. N7 37Nb 70
New Cl. SW19 69Eb 133
TW13: Hanw 64Aa 129
New Colebrooke Ct. SM5: Cars 80Hb 155
(off Stanley Rd.)
New College Ct. NW3 37Eb 69
(off College Cres.)
New College M. N1 38Qb 70
New College Pde. NW3 37Fb 69
(off Finchley Rd.)
Newcombe Gdns. SW16 63Nb 134
TW4: Houn 56Ba 107
Newcombe Ho. E5 34Xb 71
Newcombe Pk. HA0: Wemb 39Pa 67
NW7 22Ua 48
Newcombe Ri. UB7: Yiew 44N 83
Newcombe St. W8 46Cb 89
Newcomen Rd. E11 34Hc 73
SW11 55Fb 111
Newcomen St. SE1 1F 231 (47Tb 91)
Newcome Path WD7: Shenl 6Qa 15
Newcome Rd. WD7: Shenl 6Qa 15
New Compton St. WC2 3E 222 (44Mb 90)
New Concordia Wharf SE1 47Wb 91
New Coppice GU21: Wok 1J 187
New Cotts. GU24: Pirb 4B 186
RM13: Wenn 44Ld 97
New Ct. EC4 3K 223
KT15: Add 76L 149
UB5: N'olt 36Da 65
Newcourt UB8: Cowl 43L 83
Newcourt Ho. E2 41Xb 91
(off Pott St.)
Newcourt St. NW8 2D 214 (40Gb 69)
New Covent Garden Market 52Mb 112
New Crane Pl. E1 46Yb 92
New Crane Wharf E1 46Yb 92
(off New Crane Pl.)
New Cres. Yd. NW10 40Va 68
Newcroft Cl. UB8: Hil 43P 83
Newcroft Ho. CR0: C'don 75Vb 157
(off Homefield Pl.)
NEW CROSS 52Bc 114
NEW CROSS 53Bc 114
NEW CROSS GATE 53Zb 114
NEW CROSS GATE 53Zb 114
New Cross Rd. SE14 52Yb 114
New Curzon Cinema 28Rb 51
Newdales Cl. N9 19Wb 33
Newdene Av. UB5: N'olt 40Z 65
NEW DENHAM 37K 63
Newdigate Grn. UB9: Hare 25M 43
Newdigate Ho. E14 44Bc 92
(off Norbiton Rd.)
Newdigate Rd. UB9: Hare 25L 43
Newdigate Rd. E. UB9: Hare 25M 43
New Diorama Theatre 5A 216 (42Kb 90)
Newell Ri. HP3: Hem H 5N 3
Newell Rd. HP3: Hem H 5N 3
Newell St. E14 44Bc 92
NEW ELTHAM 61Sc 138
New End NW3 34Eb 69
New End Sq. NW3 35Fb 69
New End Theatre 34Eb 69
(off New End)
New England Hill GU24: W End 4B 166
New England Ind. Est. IG11: Bark 40Sc 74
New England St. AL3: St A 2A 6
Newenham Rd. KT23: Bookh 98Ca 191
Newent Cl. SE15 52Ub 113
SM5: Cars 74Hb 155
New Era Est. N1 1H 219
New Era Ho. N1 39Ub 71
(off New Era Est.)
New Farm Av. BR2: Brom 70Jc 137
New Farm Cl. TW18: Staines 67L 127
New Farm Dr. RM4: Abr 13Yc 37
New Farm La. HA6: Nwood 25U 44
New Fetter La. EC4 2A 224 (44Qb 90)
Newfield Cl. TW12: Hamp 67Ca 129
Newfield La. HP2: Hem H 2N 3
Newfield Ri. NW2 34Wa 68
Newfield Way AL4: St A 4G 6
Newford Cl. HP2: Hem H 1B 4
New Ford Rd. EN8: Walt C 6Bc 20
New Forest La. IG7: Chig 23Qc 54
Newgale Gdns. HA8: Edg 25Pa 47
New Garden Dr. UB7: W Dray 47N 83
Newgate CR0: C'don 74Sb 157
Newgate Cl. TW13: Hanw 61Aa 129
Newgate St. E4 20Gc 35
(not continuous)
EC1 2C 224 (44Rb 91)
Newgatestreet Rd. EN7: G Oak 1Sb 19
New Globe Wlk. SE1 6D 224 (46Sb 91)
New Goulston St. E1 2K 225 (44Vb 91)
New Grn. Pl. SE19 65Ub 135
New Hall Cl. HP3: Bov 9C 2
Newhall Ct. EN9: Walt A 5Hc 21
N1 39Sb 71
(off Popham Rd.)
New Hall Dr. RM3: Hrld W 25Nd 57
Newhall Gdns. KT12: Walt T 75Y 151
Newham City Farm 44Mc 93
Newham Leisure Cen. 42Lc 93
Newham's Row SE1 2J 231 (48Ub 91)
Newham Way E6 43Hc 93
E16 43Hc 93
Newhaven Cl. UB3: Harl 49V 84
Newhaven Cres. TW15: Ashf 64T 128
Newhaven Gdns. SE9 56Mc 115
Newhaven La. E16 42Hc 93
Newhaven Rd. SE25 71Tb 157
Newhaven Spur SL2: Slou 2F 80
NEW HAW 81K 169
New Haw Rd. KT15: Add 78L 149
New Heston Rd. TW5: Hest 52Ba 107
Newholme Ct. KT13: Weyb 76U 150
New Hope Ct. NW10 41Xa 88
New Horizons Ct. TW8: Bford 51Ja 108
NEW HOUSE 2B 144
Newhouse Av. RM6: Chad H 27Zc 55
Newhouse Cl. KT3: N Mald 73Ua 154
Newhouse Cres. WD25: Wat 4X 13
New Ho. La.
DA11: Nflt, Grav'nd 2B 144
TN15: Wro 88Ae 185
New Ho. Pk. AL1: St A 5E 6
Newhouse Rd. HP3: Bov 8C 2
Newhouse Wlk. SM4: Mord 73Eb 155
Newick Cl. DA5: Bexl 58Dd 118
Newick Rd. E5 35Xb 71
Newing Grn. BR1: Brom 66Mc 137
NEWINGTON 4D 230 (48Sb 91)
Newington Barrow Way N7 34Pb 70
Newington Butts SE1 6C 230 (49Rb 91)
SE11 6C 230 (49Rb 91)
Newington C'way. SE1 4C 230 (48Rb 91)
Newington Ct. N16 35Sb 71
(off Green Lanes)
Newington Ct. Bus. Cen. SE1 3D 230
Newington Grn. N1 36Tb 71
N16 36Tb 71
Newington Grn. Community Gdns.
N16 36Tb 71
Newington Grn. Mans. N16 36Tb 71
Newington Grn. Rd. N1 37Tb 71
Newington Ind. Est.
SE17 6D 230 (49Rb 91)
New Inn B'way. EC2 5J 219 (42Ub 91)
New Inn Pas. WC2 3J 223
New Inn Sq. EC2 5J 219
New Inn St. EC2 5J 219 (42Ub 91)
New Inn Yd. EC2 5J 219 (42Ub 91)
New Jubilee Ct. IG8: Wfd G 24Jc 53
New Jubilee Wharf E1 46Yb 92
(off Wapping Wall)
New Kelvin Av. TW11: Tedd 65Ga 130
New Kent Rd. AL1: St A 2B 6
SE1 4D 230 (48Sb 91)
New Kings Rd. SW6 54Bb 111
New King St. SE8 51Cc 114
Newland Cl. AL1: St A 5E 6
HA5: Hat E 23Aa 45
Newland Ct. EC1 5F 219
HA9: Wemb 33Qa 67
Newland Dr. EN1: Enf 11Xb 33
Newland Gdns. W13 47Ja 86
Newland Ho. N8 27Nb 50
(off Newland Rd.)
SE14 51Zb 114
(off John Williams Cl.)
Newland Rd. N8 27Nb 50
NEWLANDS
HA8 20Na 29
SE23 57Zb 114
Newlands HA1: Harr 32Ga 66
NW1 3B 216
Newlands, The KT7: T Ditt 74Ga 152
SM6: Wall 80Lb 156
Newlands Av. GU22: Wok 93B 188
KT7: T Ditt 74Ga 152
WD7: R'lett 6Ha 14
Newlands Cl. CM13: Hut 17Fe 41
HA0: Wemb 37La 66
HA8: Edg 20Na 29
KT12: Hers 77Aa 151
UB2: S'hall 50Aa 85
Newlands Ct. CR3: Cat'm 93Sb 197
(off Coulsdon Rd.)
KT15: Add 78K 149
(off Church Rd.)
SE9 58Qc 116
Newlands Dr. SL3: Poyle 55G 104
Newlands Pk. SE26 65Yb 136
Newlands Pk. Caravan Site
WD5: Bedm 8F 4
Newlands Pl. EN5: Barn 15Za 30
Newlands Quay E1 45Yb 92
Newlands Rd. HP1: Hem H 1G 2
IG8: Wfd G 19Hc 35
SW16 68Nb 134
Newland St. E16 46Nc 94
Newlands Wlk. WD25: Wat 5Z 13
Newlands Way EN6: Pot B 2Db 17
KT9: Chess 78La 152
Newlands Woods CR0: Sels 81Bc 178
Newling Cl. E6 44Pc 94
New Lodge Dr. RH8: Oxt 100Hc 199
New London St. EC3 4J 225
New London Theatre 2G 223
New Lydenburg Commercial Est.
SE7 48Lc 93
New Lydenburg St. SE7 48Lc 93
Newlyn KT13: Weyb 77V 150
NW1 1C 216
Newlyn Cl. AL2: Brick W 2Aa 13
BR6: Chels 77Wc 161
UB8: Hil 43Q 84
Newlyn Gdns. HA2: Harr 31Ba 65
Newlyn Ho. HA5: Hat E 24Ba 45
Newlyn Rd. DA16: Well 54Vc 117
EN5: Barn 14Bb 31
N17 25Vb 51
NEW MALDEN 70Ua 132
New Maltings RM15: Avel 46Td 98
Newman Cl. RM11: Horn 29Nd 57
Newman Ct. BR1: Brom 67Jc 137
(off North St.)
TW15: Ashf 65R 128
Newman Ho. SE1 4B 230 (48Rb 91)
Newman Pas. W1 1C 222 (43Lb 90)
Newman Rd. BR1: Brom 67Jc 137
CR0: C'don 74Pb 156
E13 41Kc 93
E17 29Zb 52
UB3: Hayes 45X 85
Newman Rd. Ind. Est. CR0: C'don 73Pb 156
Newmans Cl. IG10: Lough 13Qc 36
Newman's Ct. EC3 3G 225
Newmans Dr. CM13: Hut 17Ee 41
Newmans Ga. CM13: Hut 17Ee 41
Newmans La. IG10: Lough 13Qc 36
KT6: Surb 72Ma 153
Newmans Pl. SL5: S'dale 3F 146
Newmans Rd. DA11: Nflt 1B 144
Newman's Row WC2 1J 223 (43Pb 90)
Newman St. W1 1C 222 (43Lb 90)
Newman's Way EN4: Had W 11Eb 31
Newman Yd. W1 2D 222 (44Lb 90)
Newmarket Av. UB5: N'olt 36Ca 65
Newmarket Ct. AL3: St A 1A 6
Newmarket Grn. SE9 59Mc 115
Newmarket Ho. RM3: Rom 22Nd 57
(off Lindfield Rd.)
Newmarket Way RM12: Horn 35Nd 77
Newmarsh Rd. SE28 46Vc 95
New Mile Rd. SL5: Asc 8A 124
Newmill Ho. E3 42Ec 92
New Mill Rd. BR5: St P 67Yc 139
Newminster Rd. SM4: Mord 72Eb 155
New Mount St. E15 38Fc 73
Newnes Path SW15 56Xa 110
Newnham Av. HA4: Ruis 32Y 65
Newnham Cl. CR7: Thor H 68Sb 135
IG10: Lough 16Mc 35
SL2: Slou 6K 81
UB5: N'olt 37Ea 66
Newnham Gdns. UB5: N'olt 37Ea 66
Newnham Grn. N22 25Qb 50
(off Highfield Cl.)
Newnham Ho. IG10: Lough 16Mc 35
Newnham Lodge DA17: Belv 50Cd 96
(off Erith Rd.)
Newnham M. N22 24Qb 50
Newnham Pde. EN8: Chesh 2Zb 20
Newnham Pl. RM16: Grays 9C 100
Newnham Rd. N22 25Pb 50
Newnhams Cl. BR1: Brom 69Pc 138
Newnham Ter. SE1 3K 229 (48Qb 90)
Newnham Way HA3: Kenton 29Ma 47
New North Pl. EC2 5H 219 (42Ub 91)
New North Rd. IG6: Ilf 24Tc 54
N1 1F 219 (38Sb 71)
RH2: Reig 9H 207
New North St. WC1 7H 217 (43Pb 90)
Newnton Cl. N4 31Tb 71
(not continuous)
New Oak Rd. N2 26Eb 49
New Orleans Wlk. N19 31Mb 70
New Oxford St. WC1 2E 222 (44Mb 90)
New Pde. KT23: Bookh 97Ea 192
TW15: Ashf 63P 127
UB7: Yiew 46N 83
WD3: Chor 14E 24
New Pde. Flats WD3: Chor 14E 24
New Pk. Av. N13 20Sb 33
New Pk. Cl. UB5: N'olt 37Aa 65
New Pk. Dr. HP2: Hem H 1B 4
New Pk. Est. N18 22Yb 52
New Pk. Ho. N13 21Pb 50
New Pk. Pde. SW2 59Nb 112
(off New Pk. Rd.)
New Pk. Rd. SW2 60Mb 112
TW15: Ashf 64S 128
UB9: Hare 25L 43
New Peachey La. UB8: Cowl 44M 83
Newpiece IG10: Lough 13Rc 36
New Pl. CR0: Addtn 79Cc 158
New Pl. Gdns. RM14: Upm 33Td 78
New Pl. Sq. SE16 48Xb 91
New Plaistow Rd. E15 39Gc 73
New Players Theatre 6G 223
New Plymouth Ho. RM13: Rain 41Hd 96
(off Dunedin Rd.)
New Pond Pde. HA4: Ruis 34W 64
Newport Av. E13 42Kc 93
E14 45Fc 93
Newport Cl. EN3: Enf W 9Ac 20
Newport Ct. WC2 4E 222 (45Mb 90)
Newport Ho. E3 41Ac 92
(off Strahan Rd.)
Newport Lodge EN1: Enf 15Ub 33
(off Village Rd.)
Newport Mead WD19: Wat 21Z 45
Newport Pl. WC2 4E 222 (45Mb 90)
Newport Rd. E10 33Ec 72
E17 28Ac 52
SL2: Slou 2C 80
SW13 53Wa 110
TW6: H'row A 53Q 106
UB4: Hayes 43T 84
W3 47Sa 87
Newports BR8: Crock 73Fd 162
Newport St. SE11 6H 229 (49Pb 90)
New Priory Ct. NW6 38Cb 69
(off Mazenod Av.)
New Providence Wharf E14 46Fc 93
New Provident Pl. HP4: Berk 1A 2
Newquay Cres. HA2: Harr 33Aa 65
Newquay Gdns. WD19: Wat 19X 27
Newquay Ho. SE11 7K 229 (50Qb 90)
Newquay Rd. SE6 61Dc 136
New Quebec St. W1 3G 221 (44Hb 89)
New Ride SW1 2C 226 (47Gb 89)
SW7 2C 226 (47Gb 89)
New River Av. N8 27Pb 50
New River Ct. EN7: Chesh 3Xb 19
N5 35Sb 71
New River Cres. N13 21Rb 51
New River Head EC1 3A 218 (41Qb 90)
New River Stadium 24Rb 51
New River Wlk. N1 37Sb 71
(not continuous)
New River Way N4 31Tb 71
New Rd. BR6: Orp 73Wc 161
BR8: Hext 66Hd 140
BR8: Swan 69Hd 140
CM14: B'wood 19Zd 41
CR4: Mitc 74Hb 155
DA4: S Dar 68Sd 142
DA11: Grav'nd 8C 122
DA16: Well 54Xc 117
E1 43Xb 91
E4 21Dc 52
EN6: S Mim 5Wa 16
GU19: W'sham 9A 146
HA1: Harr 35Ha 66
HP4: Berk 1A 2
HP8: Chal G 13A 24
IG3: Ilf 33Uc 74
KT2: King T 66Qa 131
KT8: W Mole 70Ca 129
KT10: Esh 76Ea 152
KT13: Weyb 78S 150
KT20: Tad 95Ya 194
KT22: Oxs 83Ha 172
N8 29Nb 50
N9 19Xb 33
N17 25Vb 51
N22 25Sb 51
NW7 24Ab 48
(Bittacy Ct.)
NW7 17Va 30
(Hendon Wood La.)
RH8: Limp 2M 211
RH8: Tand 8E 210
RM4: Abr 16Zc 37
RM9: Dag 40Cd 76
RM10: Dag 40Cd 76
RM13: Avel, Rain, Wenn 41Jd 96
RM17: Grays 51Ce 121
(not continuous)
SE2 49Zc 95
SL3: Dat 3P 103
SL3: L'ly 48C 82
TN14: Sund 96Zc 201
TW3: Houn 56Da 107
TW8: Bford 51Ma 109
TW10: Ham 63La 130
TW13: Hanw 64Aa 129
TW14: Bedf 58T 106
TW14: Felt 60X 107
TW17: Shep 69Q 128
TW18: Staines 64E 126
UB3: Harl 52S 106
UB8: Hil 42S 84
WD3: Crox G 15Q 26
WD3: Sarr 11H 25
WD4: Chfd 2H 11
WD6: E'tree 16Ma 29
WD7: R'lett 8Ga 14
WD7: Shenl 6Qa 15
WD17: Wat 14Y 27
WD25: Let H 11Ga 28
New Rd. Hill BR2: Kes 81Nc 180
BR6: Downe 81Nc 180
New Rochford St. NW5 36Hb 69
New Row NW2 34Ya 68
WC2 4F 223 (45Nb 90)
Newry Rd. TW1: Twick 57Ja 108
Newsam Av. N15 29Tb 51
Newsham Rd. GU21: Wok 9K 167
Newsholme Dr. N21 15Pb 32
New Site KT15: Add 76N 149
Newsom Pl. AL1: St A 1C 6
NEW SOUTHGATE 22Kb 50
New Southgate Crematorium
N11 20Kb 32
New Southgate Ind. Est. N11 22Lb 50
New Spitalfields Mkt. E10 34Cc 72
New Spring Gdns. Wlk.
SE11 7G 229 (50Nb 90)
New Sq. SL1: Slou 7J 81
TW14: Bedf 60S 106
WC2 2K 223 (44Qb 90)
New Sq. Pk. TW14: Bedf 60S 106
New Sq. Pas. WC2 2K 223
Newstead AL10: Hat 3B 8
Newstead Av. BR6: Orp 76Tc 160
Newstead Cl. N12 23Gb 49
Newstead Ct. UB5: N'olt 41Aa 85
Newstead Ho. CR3: Cat'm 98Xb 197
N1 1A 218
RM3: Rom 21Md 57
(off Troopers Dr.)
Newstead Ri. CR3: Cat'm 98Xb 197
Newstead Rd. SE12 59Hc 115
Newstead Wlk. SM5: Cars 73Eb 155
Newstead Way SW19 63Za 132
NEW STREET 78Fe 165

New St. EC2 . . . . . 1J 225 (43Ub 91)
HP4: Berk 1A 2
TN16: Westrm 99Sc 200
TW18: Staines 63J 127
WD18: Wat 14Y 27
New St. Hill BR1: Brom 64Kc 137
New St. Rd. DA13: Meop 76Ee 165
TN15: Ash, New A 77Ee 165
New St. Sq. EC4 . . . . . 2A 224 (44Qb 90)
(not continuous)
New Swan Yd. DA12: Grav'nd 8D 122
New Tank Hill Rd. RM15: Avel 48Qd 97
RM19: Avel, Purf 48Qd 97
New Tavern Fort 8E 122
(off Commercial Pl.)
Newteswell Dr. EN9: Walt A 4Fc 21
Newton Abbot Rd. DA11: Nflt 1B 144
Newton Av. N10 . . . . . 25Jb 50
W3 . . . . . 47Sa 87
Newton Cl. E17 . . . . . 30Ac 52
HA2: Harr 33Ca 65
SL3: L'ly 47B 82
Newton Ct. NW6 . . . . . 38Eb 69
(off Fairfax Rd.)
SL4: Old Win 8L 103
SW17 . . . . . 62Fb 133
(off Grosvenor Way)
W8 . . . . . 47Cb 89
(off Kensington Chu. St.)
Newton Cres. WD6: Bore 14Sa 29
Newton Gro. W4 . . . . . 49Ua 88
Newton Ho. E1 . . . . . 45Xb 91
(off Cornwall St.)
E17 . . . . . 27Dc 52
(off Prospect Hill)
EN3: Enf H 13Zb 34
NW8 . . . . . 39Db 69
(off Abbey Rd.)
SE20 . . . . . 66Zb 136
Newton Ind. Est. RM6: Chad H 28Zc 55
Newton La. SL4: Old Win 8M 103
Newton Lodge SE10 . . . . . 48Hc 93
(off Teal St.)
Newton Mans. W14 . . . . . 51Ab 110
(off Queen's Club Gdns.)
Newton Pk. Pl. BR7: Chst 66Pc 138
Newton Pl. E14 . . . . . 49Cc 92
Newton Rd. CR8: Purl 84Lb 176
DA16: Well 55Wc 117
E15 . . . . . 36Fc 73
HA0: Wemb 38Pa 67
HA3: Hrw W 26Ga 46
IG7: Chig, Ilf 22Xc 55
N15 . . . . . 29Wb 51
NW2 . . . . . 35Ya 68
RM18: Tilb 5C 122
SW19 . . . . . 66Ab 132
TW7: Isle 54Ha 108
W2 . . . . . 44Db 89
Newtons Cl. RM13: Rain 38Hd 76
Newtons Ct. DA2: Dart 56Td 120
Newtonside Orchard SL4: Old Win 8L 103
Newton St. WC2 . . . . . 2G 223 (44Nb 90)
Newton's Yd. SW18 . . . . . 57Cb 111
Newton Ter. BR2: Brom 72Mc 159
Newton Wlk. HA8: Edg 25Ra 47
Newton Way N18 . . . . . 22Sb 51
Newton Wood Rd. KT21: Asht 88Pa 173
New Tower Bldgs. E1 . . . . . 46Xb 91
NEW TOWN 58Pd 119
Newtown Rd. UB9: Den 36H 63
Newtown St. SW11 . . . . . 53Kb 112
New Trinity Rd. N2 . . . . . 27Fb 49
New Turnstile WC1 . . . . . 1H 223
New Union Cl. E14 . . . . . 48Ec 92
New Union St. EC2 . . . . . 1F 225 (43Tb 91)
New Victoria Theatre 89A 168
New Wlk. TN15: Wro 88Be 185
New Wanstead E11 . . . . . 30Hc 53
New Way Rd. NW9 . . . . . 28Ua 48
New Wharf Rd. N1 . . . . . 1G 217 (40Nb 70)
New Wickham La. TW20: Egh 66C 126
NEW WINDSOR 5H 103
New Windsor St. UB8: Uxb 39L 63
NEWYEARS GREEN 31P 63
New Years Grn. La. UB9: Hare 30N 43
New Years La. TN14: Knock 88Vc 181
New Zealand Av. KT12: Walt T 74V 150
New Zealand Golf Course 84F 168
New Zealand War Memorial 1J 227
New Zealand Way RM13: Rain 41Hd 96
W12 . . . . . 45Xa 88
Nexus Ct. AL1: St A 3B 6
E11 . . . . . 32Gc 73
NW6 . . . . . 41Cb 89
Niagara Av. W5 . . . . . 49La 86
Niagara Cl. EN8: Chesh 1Zb 20
N1 . . . . . 1E 218 (40Sb 71)
Niagra Ct. SE16 . . . . . 48Yb 92
(off Canada Est.)
Nibthwaite Rd. HA1: Harr 29Ga 46
Nice Bus. Pk. SE15 . . . . . 51Xb 113
Nicholas Cl. RM15: S Ock 41Yd 98
UB6: G'frd 40Da 65
WD24: Wat 9X 13
Nicholas Ct. E13 . . . . . 41Kc 93
SE12 . . . . . 60Jc 115
W4 . . . . . 51Ua 110
(off Corney Reach Way)
Nicholas Gdns. GU22: Pyr 88H 169
SL1: Slou 6C 80
W5 . . . . . 47Ma 87
Nicholas Ho. AL4: St A 3H 7
Nicholas La. EC4 . . . . . 4G 225 (45Tb 91)
(not continuous)
Nicholas Lodge KT10: Esh 75Ca 151
Nicholas M. W4 . . . . . 51Ua 110
Nicholas Pas. EC4 . . . . . 4G 225
Nicholas Rd. CR0: Bedd 77Nb 156
E1 . . . . . 42Yb 92
RM8: Dag 33Bd 75
W11 . . . . . 45Za 88
WD6: E'tree 16Pa 29
Nicholas Stacey Ho. SE7 . . . . . 50Kc 93
(off Frank Burton Cl.)
Nicholas Way HA6: Nwood 25S 44
HP2: Hem H 1P 3
Nicholay Rd. N19 . . . . . 32Mb 70
(not continuous)
Nichol Cl. N14 . . . . . 18Mb 32
Nicholes Rd. TW3: Houn 56Ca 107
Nichol La. BR1: Brom 66Jc 137
Nicholl Ho. N4 . . . . . 32Sb 71
Nicholl Rd. CM16: Epp 3Vc 23
Nicholls SL4: Wind 5A 102
Nicholls Av. UB8: Hil 42Q 84
Nicholls Cl. CR3: Cat'm 94Sb 197
Nichollsfield Wlk. N7 . . . . . 36Pb 70
Nicholls M. SW16 . . . . . 63Nb 134
Nicholls Point E15 . . . . . 39Jc 73
(off Park Gro.)
Nicholl St. E2 . . . . . 39Wb 71
Nichols Wlk. SL4: Wind 5A 102
Nichols Cl. KT9: Chess 79La 152
N4 . . . . . 32Qb 70
(off Osborne Rd.)
Nichols Ct. E2 . . . . . 2K 219 (40Vb 71)
Nichols Grn. W5 . . . . . 43Na 87
Nicholson Ct. E17 . . . . . 28Ac 52
N17 . . . . . 27Vb 51
Nicholson Ho. SE17 . . . . . 7F 231 (50Tb 91)
Nicholson M. KT1: King T 70Na 131
TW20: Egh 64C 126
(off Station Rd.)
Nicholson Rd. CR0: C'don 74Vb 157
Nicholson St. SE1 . . . . . 7B 224 (46Rb 91)
Nicholson Wlk. TW20: Egh 64C 126
Nickelby Apartments E15 . . . . . 37Fc 73
(off Grove Cres. Rd.)
Nickelby Cl. SE28 . . . . . 44Yc 95
Nickleby Cl. UB8: Hil 44R 84
Nickleby Ho. SE16 . . . . . 47Wb 91
(off Parkers Row)
W11 . . . . . 46Za 88
(off St Ann's Rd.)
Nickleby Rd. DA12: Grav'nd 10J 123
Nickols Wlk. SW18 . . . . . 56Db 111
Nicky La. HP2: Hem H 1N 3
Nicola Cl. CR2: S Croy 79Sb 157
HA3: Hrw W 26Fa 46
Nicola M. IG6: Ilf 23Rc 54
Nicolas Wlk. RM16: Grays 7D 100
Nicola Ter. DA7: Bex 53Ad 117
Nicol Cl. TW1: Twick 58Ka 108
Nicoll Ct. N10 . . . . . 24Kb 50
NW10 . . . . . 39Ua 68
Nicoll Pl. NW4 . . . . . 30Xa 48
Nicoll Rd. NW10 . . . . . 39Ua 68
Nicoll Way WD6: Bore 15Ta 29
Nicolson NW9 . . . . . 25Ua 48
Nicolson Dr. WD23: B Hea 18Ea 28
Nicolson Rd. BR5: Orp 73Zc 161
Nicolson Way TN13: S'oaks 94Md 203
Nicosia Rd. SW18 . . . . . 59Gb 111
Niederwald Rd. SE26 . . . . . 63Ac 136
Nield Rd. UB3: Hayes 47V 84
Nigel Cl. UB5: N'olt 39Aa 65
Nigel Ct. N3 . . . . . 24Db 49
Nigel Fisher Way KT9: Chess 80La 152
Nigel Ho. EC1 . . . . . 7K 217
Nigel M. IG1: Ilf 35Rc 74
Nigel Playfair Av. W6 . . . . . 49Xa 88
Nigel Rd. E7 . . . . . 36Lc 73
SE15 . . . . . 55Wb 113
Nigeria Rd. SE7 . . . . . 52Lc 115
Nighthawk NW9 . . . . . 25Va 48
Nightingale Av. E4 . . . . . 22Gc 53
HA1: Harr 31Ka 66
KT24: W Hor 96T 190
RM14: Upm 32Vd 78
Nightingale Cl. DA11: Nflt 2A 144
E4 . . . . . 21Fc 53
HA5: Eastc 29Y 45
KT11: Cobh 83Z 171
KT19: Eps 84Qa 173
SM5: Cars 75Jb 156
TN16: Big H 87Lc 179
W4 . . . . . 51Sa 109
WD5: Ab L 3W 12
WD7: R'lett 8Ha 14
Nightingale Cnr. BR5: St M Cry 70Zc 139
Nightingale Ct. BR2: Brom 68Gc 137
E14 . . . . . 47Ec 92
(off Ovex Cl.)
GU21: Wok 10J 167
HA1: Harr 30Ha 46
N4 . . . . . 33Pb 70
(off Tollington Pk.)
RH1: Redh 5A 208
(off St Anne's Mt.)
SL1: Slou 8L 81
SM1: Sutt 78Eb 155
SW6 . . . . . 53Db 111
(off Maltings Pl.)
WD3: Rick 17L 25
WD7: R'lett 7Ja 14
Nightingale Cres. KT24: W Hor 97S 190
RM3: Hrld W 26Nd 57
Nightingale Dr. KT19: Ewe 79Ra 153
Nightingale Gro. DA1: Dart 56Qd 119
SE13 . . . . . 57Fc 115
Nightingale Hgts. SE18 . . . . . 51Rc 116
Nightingale Ho. BR8: Swan 69Gd 140
(off London Rd.)
E1 . . . . . 46Wb 91
(off Thomas More St.)
E2 . . . . . 1J 219
KT17: Eps 84Ua 174
NW8 . . . . . 6D 214
SE18 . . . . . 50Qc 94
(off Connaught M.)
UB7: W Dray 47P 83
W12 . . . . . 44Ya 88
(off Du Cane Rd.)
Nightingale La. AL1: St A 5G 6
AL4: St A 6G 6
BR1: Brom 68Lc 137
E11 . . . . . 28Kc 53
N8 . . . . . 28Nb 50
SW4 . . . . . 58Kb 112
SW12 . . . . . 59Hb 111
TW10: Rich 59Na 109
Nightingale Lodge W9 . . . . . 43Cb 89
(off Admiral Wlk.)
Nightingale M. E3 . . . . . 40Zb 72
E11 . . . . . 29Jc 53
KT1: King T 69Ma 131
(off South La.)
SE11 . . . . . 5B 230 (49Rb 91)
Nightingale Pk. SL2: Farn C 8D 60
Nightingale Pl. SE18 . . . . . 51Qc 116
SW10 . . . . . 51Eb 111
WD3: Rick 17M 25
Nightingale Rd. BR5: Pet W 72Sc 160
CR2: Sels 83Zb 178
E5 . . . . . 34Xb 71
KT8: W Mole 71Da 151
KT10: Esh 78Ba 151
KT12: Walt T 73Y 151
KT24: E Hor 97V 190
N1 . . . . . 37Sb 71
N9 . . . . . 16Yb 34
Nightingale Rd. N22 . . . . . 25Nb 50
NW10 . . . . . 40Va 68
SM5: Cars 76Hb 155
TN15: Kems'g 89Md 183
TW12: Hamp 64Ca 129
W7 . . . . . 46Ha 86
WD3: Rick 17L 25
WD23: Bush 15Ca 27
Nightingales EN9: Walt A 6Gc 21
Nightingales, The TW19: Stanw 60P 105
Nightingale Shott TW20: Egh 65B 126
Nightingales La. HP8: Chal G 14A 24
Nightingale Sq. SW12 . . . . . 59Jb 112
Nightingale Va. SE18 . . . . . 51Qc 116
Nightingale Wlk. N1 . . . . . 37Sb 71
SL4: Wind 5G 102
SW4 . . . . . 58Kb 112
Nightingale Way BR8: Swan 69Gd 140
E6 . . . . . 43Nc 94
RH1: Blet 6L 209
UB9: Den 31H 63
Nile Cl. N16 . . . . . 34Vb 71
Nile Dr. N9 . . . . . 19Yb 34
Nile Ho. N1 . . . . . 3F 219
Nile Path SE18 . . . . . 51Qc 116
Nile Rd. E13 . . . . . 40Lc 73
Nile St. N1 . . . . . 3E 218 (41Sb 91)
Nile Ter. SE15 . . . . . 7K 231 (50Vb 91)
Nimbus Rd. KT19: Eps 82Ta 173
Nimegen Way SE22 . . . . . 57Ub 113
Nimmo Dr. WD23: B Hea 17Fa 28
Nimrod NW9 . . . . . 25Ua 48
Nimrod Cl. UB5: N'olt 41Z 85
Nimrod Ho. E16 . . . . . 43Kc 93
(off Vanguard Cl.)
Nimrod Pas. N1 . . . . . 37Ub 71
Nimrod Rd. SW16 . . . . . 65Kb 134
Nina Mackay Cl. E15 . . . . . 39Gc 73
Nine Acre La. AL10: Hat 1B 8
Nine Acres SL1: Slou 6D 80
Nine Acres Cl. E12 . . . . . 36Nc 74
UB3: Harl 48S 84
Nineacres Way CR5: Coul 88Nb 176
NINE ELMS 52Lb 112
Nine Elms Av. UB8: Cowl 43M 83
Nine Elms Cl. TW14: Felt 60V 106
UB8: Cowl 44M 83
Nine Elms Gro. DA11: Grav'nd 9C 122
Nine Elms La. SW8 . . . . . 52Lb 112
Ninefields EN9: Walt A 5Hc 21
Ninehams Cl. CR3: Cat'm 92Tb 197
Ninehams Gdns. CR3: Cat'm 92Tb 197
Ninehams Rd. CR3: Cat'm 93Tb 197
TN16: Tats 93Lc 199
Nine Stiles Cl. UB9: Den 37K 63
Nineteenth Rd. CR4: Mitc 70Nb 134
Ninhams Wood BR6: Farnb 77Qc 160
Ninnings Rd. SL9: Chal P 24B 42
Ninnings Way SL9: Chal P 24B 42
Ninth Av. KT20: Lwr K 97Bb 195
UB3: Hayes 45W 84
Nipper All. KT1: King T 68Na 131
(off Clarence St.)
Nipponzan Myohoji Peace Pagoda
. . . . . 51Hb 111
Nisbet Ho. E9 . . . . . 36Zb 72
Nisbett Wlk. DA14: Sidc 63Wc 139
(off Sidcup High St.)
Nita Ct. SE12 . . . . . 60Jc 115
Nita Rd. CM14: W'ley 22Yd 58
Nithdale Rd. SE18 . . . . . 52Rc 116
Nithsdale Gro. UB10: Ick 34S 64
Niton Cl. EN5: Barn 16Za 30
Niton Ct. SS17: Stan H 3L 101
Niton Rd. TW9: Rich 55Qa 109
Niton St. SW6 . . . . . 52Za 110
Niven Cl. WD6: Bore 11Sa 29
Nixey Cl. SL1: Slou 7L 81
No 1 St. SE18 . . . . . 48Rc 94
NOAH'S ARK 91Rd 203
Noah's Ark TN15: Kems'g 90Rd 183
Noakes Ind. Site RM13: Wenn 45Pd 97
NOAK HILL 19Nd 39
Noak Hill Rd. RM3: Rom 22Kd 57
Nobel Dr. UB3: Harl 53T 106
Nobel Ho. RH1: Redh 5P 207
SE5 . . . . . 54Sb 113
Nobel Rd. N18 . . . . . 21Yb 52
Nobel Vs. EN9: Walt A 6Fc 21
Noble Cnr. TW5: Hest 53Ca 107
Noble Ct. CR4: Mitc 68Fb 133
E1 . . . . . 45Xb 91
SL2: Slou 6K 81
(off Mill St.)
Noblefield Hgts. N2 . . . . . 29Gb 49
Noble M. N16 . . . . . 34Tb 71
(off Albion Rd.)
Noble St. EC2 . . . . . 2D 224 (44Sb 91)
KT12: Walt T 76Y 151
Nobles Way TW20: Egh 65A 126
Noble Yd. N1 . . . . . 1B 218
Nocavia Ho. SW6 . . . . . 54Eb 111
(off Townmead Rd.)
Noel NW9 . . . . . 25Ua 48
Noel Ct. TW4: Houn 55Ba 107
Noel Coward Ho. SW1 . . . . . 6C 228
Noel Coward Theatre 4F 223
Noel Ho. NW6 . . . . . 38Fb 69
(off Harben Rd.)
NOEL PARK 26Rb 51
Noel Pk. Rd. N22 . . . . . 26Qb 50
Noel Rd. E6 . . . . . 42Nc 94
N1 . . . . . 1B 218 (40Rb 71)
W3 . . . . . 44Ra 87
Noel Sq. RM8: Dag 35Yc 75
Noel St. W1 . . . . . 3C 222 (44Lb 90)
Noel Ter. DA14: Sidc 63Xc 139
SE23 . . . . . 61Yb 136
Noke Dr. RH1: Redh 5A 208
Noke La. AL2: Chis G 8L 5
Noke La. Bus. Cen. AL2: Chis G 9M 5
Noke Side AL2: Chis G 9N 5
Noko W10 . . . . . 41Za 88
Nolan Path WD6: Bore 11Pa 29
(off Bennington Dr.)
Nolan Way E5 . . . . . 35Wb 71
Noll Ho. N7 . . . . . 33Pb 70
(off Tomlins Wlk.)
Nolton Pl. HA8: Edg 25Pa 47
Nomad Theatre 100V 190
Nonsuch Cl. IG6: Ilf 23Rc 54
Nonsuch Ct. Av. KT17: Ewe 82Xa 174
Nonsuch Ho. SW19 . . . . . 67Fb 133
Nonsuch Ind. Est. KT17: Eps 83Ua 174
Nonsuch Pl. SM3: Cheam 80Za 154
(off Ewell Rd.)
Nonsuch Wlk. SM2: Cheam 82Ya 174
Nora Gdns. NW4 . . . . . 28Za 48
Nora Leverton Ct. NW1 . . . . . 38Lb 70
(off Randolph St.)
NORBITON 68Qa 131
Norbiton Av. KT1: King T 67Qa 131
Norbiton Comn. Rd.
KT1: King T 69Ra 131
Norbiton Hall KT2: King T 68Pa 131
Norbiton Ho. NW1 . . . . . 1C 216
(off Camden St.)
Norbiton Rd. E14 . . . . . 44Bc 92
Norbreck Gdns. NW10 . . . . . 41Pa 87
Norbreck Pde. NW10 . . . . . 41Na 87
Norbroke St. W12 . . . . . 45Va 88
Norburn St. W10 . . . . . 43Ab 88
NORBURY 67Pb 134
Norbury Av. CR7: Thor H 67Pb 134
SW16 . . . . . 67Pb 134
TW3: Houn 56Fa 108
WD24: Wat 11Y 27
Norbury Cl. SW16 . . . . . 67Qb 134
Norbury Ct. Rd. SW16 . . . . . 69Nb 134
Norbury Cres. SW16 . . . . . 67Pb 134
Norbury Cross SW16 . . . . . 69Nb 134
Norbury Gdns.
RM6: Chad H 29Zc 55
Norbury Gro. NW7 . . . . . 20Ua 30
Norbury Hill SW16 . . . . . 66Qb 134
NORBURY PARK 98Ka 192
Norbury Ri. SW16 . . . . . 69Nb 134
Norbury Rd. CR7: Thor H 68Sb 135
E4 . . . . . 22Cc 52
RH2: Reig 6H 207
TW13: Felt 62V 128
Norbury Trad. Est. SW16 . . . . . 68Pb 134
Norbury Way KT23: Bookh 97Ea 192
Norcombe Gdns.
HA3: Kenton 30La 46
Norcombe Ho. N19 . . . . . 34Mb 70
(off Wedmore St.)
Norcott Cl. UB4: Yead 42Y 85
Norcott Rd. N16 . . . . . 33Wb 71
Norcroft Gdns. SE22 . . . . . 59Wb 113
Norcutt Rd. TW2: Twick 60Ga 108
Nordenfeldt Rd. DA8: Erith 50Fd 96
Norden Ho. E2 . . . . . 41Xb 91
(off Pott St.)
Nordmann Pl. RM15: S Ock 42Zd 99
Nore Hill Pinnacle (Local Nature Reserve)
. . . . . 91Dc 198
Norelands Dr. SL1: Burn 10A 60
Norfield Rd. DA2: Wilm 63Ed 140
Norfolk Av. CR2: Sande 82Vb 177
N13 . . . . . 23Rb 51
N15 . . . . . 30Vb 51
SL1: Slou 3G 80
WD24: Wat 10Y 13
Norfolk Cl. DA1: Dart 58Qd 119
EN4: Cockf 14Jb 32
N2 . . . . . 27Gb 49
N13 . . . . . 23Rb 51
TW1: Twick 58Ka 108
Norfolk Ct. EN5: Barn 14Ab 30
RM6: Chad H 29Xc 55
(off Norwich Cres.)
Norfolk Cres. DA15: Sidc 59Uc 116
W2 . . . . . 2D 220 (44Gb 89)
Norfolk Farm Cl. GU22: Pyr 88F 168
Norfolk Farm Rd. GU22: Pyr 87F 168
Norfolk Gdns. DA7: Bex 53Bd 117
WD6: Bore 14Ta 29
Norfolk Ho. BR2: Brom 70Hc 137
(off Westmoreland Rd.)
EC4 . . . . . 4D 224
SE20 . . . . . 67Yb 136
SW1 . . . . . 5E 228
Norfolk Ho. Rd. SW16 . . . . . 62Mb 134
Norfolk Mans. SW11 . . . . . 53Hb 111
(off Prince of Wales Dr.)
Norfolk M. W10 . . . . . 43Ab 88
(off Blagrove Rd.)
Norfolk Pl. DA16: Well 54Wc 117
RM16: Chaf H 50Yd 98
W2 . . . . . 2C 220 (44Fb 89)
(not continuous)
Norfolk Rd. CR7: Thor H 69Sb 135
DA12: Grav'nd 8F 122
(not continuous)
E6 . . . . . 39Pc 74
E17 . . . . . 26Zb 52
EN3: Pond E 16Xb 33
EN5: New Bar 13Cb 31
HA1: Harr 29Da 45
IG3: Ilf 32Uc 74
IG11: Bark 38Uc 74
KT10: Clay 78Ga 152
NW8 . . . . . 1C 214 (39Fb 69)
NW10 . . . . . 38Ua 68
RM7: Rom 30Ed 56
RM10: Dag 36Dd 76
RM14: Upm 34Qd 77
SW19 . . . . . 66Gb 133
TW13: Felt 60Y 107
UB8: Uxb 37M 63
WD3: Rick 18N 25
Norfolk Row SE1 . . . . . 5H 229 (49Pb 90)
(not continuous)
Norfolk Sq. W2 . . . . . 3C 220 (44Fb 89)
Norfolk Sq. M. W2 . . . . . 3C 220
Norfolk St. E7 . . . . . 36Jc 73
Norfolk Ter. W6 . . . . . 50Ab 88
Norgrove Pk. SL9: Ger X 28A 42
Norgrove St. SW12 . . . . . 59Jb 112
Norham Ct. DA2: Dart 58Rd 119
(off Osbourne Rd.)
Norheads La. CR6: W'ham 91Jc 199
TN16: Big H 91Jc 199
Norhyrst Av. SE25 . . . . . 69Vb 135
NORK 87Za 174
Nork Gdns. SM7: Bans 86Ab 174
Nork Ri. SM7: Bans 88Za 174
Nork Way SM7: Bans 88Ya 174
Norland Ho. W11 . . . . . 46Za 88
(off Queensdale Cres.)
Norland Pl. W11 . . . . . 46Ab 88
Norland Rd. W11 . . . . . 46Za 88
Norlands Cres.
BR7: Chst 67Rc 138
Norlands La. TW20: Thorpe 69G 126
Norland Sq. W11 . . . . . 46Ab 88
Norland Sq. Mans. W11 . . . . . 46Ab 88
(off Norland Sq.)
Norley Va. SW15 . . . . . 60Wa 110
Norlington Rd. E10 . . . . . 32Ec 72
E11 . . . . . 32Ec 72
Norman Av. CR2: Sande 82Sb 177
KT17: Eps 84Va 174
N22 . . . . . 25Rb 51
TW1: Twick 59La 108
TW13: Hanw 61Aa 129
UB1: S'hall 45Aa 85
Norman Butler Ho. W10 . . . . . 42Ab 88
(off Ladbroke Gro.)
Normanby Cl. SW15 . . . . . 57Bb 111
Normanby Rd. NW10 . . . . . 35Va 68
Norman Cl. AL1: St A 5C 6
BR6: Farnb 76Sc 160
EN9: Walt A 5Fc 21
KT18: Tatt C 91Xa 194
N22 . . . . . 25Sb 51
RM5: Col R 25Dd 56
TN15: Kems'g 89Md 183
Norman Colyer Ct. KT19: Eps 82Ta 173
Norman Ct. EN6: Pot B 2Eb 17
IG2: Ilf 31Tc 74
N3 . . . . . 25Cb 49
(off Nether St.)
N4 . . . . . 31Qb 70
NW10 . . . . . 38Wa 68
W13 . . . . . 46Ka 86
(off Kirkfield Cl.)
Norman Cres. CM13: B'wood 20Ce 41
HA5: Pinn 25Y 45
TW5: Hest 52Z 107
Normand Gdns. W14 . . . . . 51Ab 110
(off Greyhound Rd.)
Normand Mans. W14 . . . . . 51Ab 110
(off Normand M.)
Normand M. W14 . . . . . 51Ab 110
Normand Rd. W14 . . . . . 51Bb 111
Normandy Av. EN5: Barn 15Bb 31
Normandy Cl. SE26 . . . . . 62Ac 136
Normandy Ct. HP2: Hem H 1M 3
Normandy Dr. UB3: Hayes 44S 84
Normandy Ho. E14 . . . . . 47Ec 92
(off Plevna St.)
EN2: Enf 10Sb 19
Normandy Pl. W12 . . . . . 46Za 88
Normandy Rd. AL3: St A 1B 6
SW9 . . . . . 53Qb 112
Normandy Ter. E16 . . . . . 44Kc 93
Normandy Wlk. TW20: Egh 64E 126
Normandy Way DA8: Erith 53Gd 118
Norman Gro. E3 . . . . . 40Ac 72
Norman Hay Trad. Estate, The
UB7: Sip 52P 105
Norman Ho. SE1 . . . . . 3J 231
SW8 . . . . . 52Nb 112
(off Wyvil Rd.)
TW13: Hanw 61Ba 129
(off Watermill Way)
Normanhurst CM13: Hut 16Ee 41
TW15: Ashf 64Q 128
Normanhurst Av. DA7: Bex 53Zc 117
DA16: Well 53Zc 117
Normanhurst Dr. TW1: Twick 57Ja 108
Normanhurst Rd. BR5: St P 68Xc 139
KT12: Walt T 75Z 151
SW2 . . . . . 61Pb 134
TN15: Bor G 92Ce 205
Norman Pde. DA14: Sidc 61Zc 139
Norman Pk. Athletics Track 72Kc 159
Norman Rd. CR7: Thor H 71Rb 157
DA1: Dart 60Nd 119
DA17: Belv 48Dd 96
(not continuous)
E6 . . . . . 42Pc 94
E11 . . . . . 33Fc 73
IG1: Ilf 36Rc 74
N15 . . . . . 29Vb 51
RM11: Horn 31Jd 76
SE10 . . . . . 52Dc 114
SM1: Sutt 78Cb 155
SW19 . . . . . 66Eb 133
TW15: Ashf 65T 128
Normans, The SL2: Slou 4M 81
Normans Cl. DA11: Grav'nd 9C 122
NW10 . . . . . 37Ta 67
UB8: Hil 43P 83
Normansfield Av. TW11: Tedd 66La 130
Normansfield Cl. WD23: Bush 17Da 27
Normanshire Dr. E4 . . . . . 21Cc 52
Norman's Mead NW10 . . . . . 37Ta 67
Norman St. EC1 . . . . . 4D 218 (41Sb 91)
Norman Ter. NW6 . . . . . 36Bb 69
Normanton Av. SW19 . . . . . 61Cb 133
Normanton Ct. CR2: S Croy 78Ub 157
(off Croham Rd.)
Normanton Pk. E4 . . . . . 19Gc 35
Normanton Rd. CR2: S Croy 78Ub 157
Normanton St. SE23 . . . . . 61Zb 136
Norman Way N14 . . . . . 19Nb 32
W3 . . . . . 43Ra 87
Normington Cl. SW16 . . . . . 64Qb 134
Norrels Dr. KT24: E Hor 98V 190
Norrels Ride KT24: E Hor 97V 190
Norrice Lea N2 . . . . . 29Fb 49
Norris NW9 . . . . . 25Va 48
(off The Concourse)
Norris Cl. AL2: Lon C 8F 6
KT19: Eps 83Ra 173
Norris Ho. E9 . . . . . 39Yb 72
(off Handley Rd.)
N1 . . . . . 1H 219
SE8 . . . . . 50Bc 92
(off Grove St.)
TW7: Isle 54Ja 108
Norris Rd. TW18: Staines 63H 127
Norris St. SW1 . . . . . 5D 222 (45Mb 90)
Norris Way DA1: Cray 55Hd 118
Norroy Rd. SW15 . . . . . 56Za 110
Norry's Cl. EN4: Cockf 14Hb 31
Norry's Rd. EN4: Cockf 14Hb 31
Norseman Cl. IG3: Ilf 32Xc 75
Norseman Way UB6: G'frd 39Da 65
Norstead Pl. SW15 . . . . . 61Wa 132
Norsted La. BR6: Prat B 84Wc 181
Nth. Access Rd. E17 . . . . . 30Zb 52
North Acre NW9 . . . . . 25Ua 48
SM7: Bans 88Bb 175
NORTH ACTON 42Ta 87
Nth. Acton Bus. Pk. W3 . . . . . 43Ta 87
Nth. Acton Rd. NW10 . . . . . 40Ta 67
Northallerton Way
RM3: Rom 22Md 57
Northall Rd. DA7: Bex 54Ed 118
Northampton Av. SL1: Slou 4G 80
Northampton Gro. N1 . . . . . 36Tb 71
Northampton Ho. RM3: Rom 21Nd 57
(off Broseley Rd.)
Northampton Pk. N1 . . . . . 37Sb 71

Northampton Rd. CR0: C'don 75Wb 157
EC1 ......5A 218 (42Qb 90)
EN3: Pond E 14Ac 34
Northampton Row EC1 ......4A 218
Northampton Sq. EC1 ......4B 218 (41Rb 91)
Northampton St. N1 ......38Sb 71
Northanger Rd. SW16 ......65Nb 134
North App. HA6: Nwood 19S 26
WD25: Wat 7V 12
North Ash Rd. DA3: New A 76Ae 165
Nth. Audley St. W1 ......3H 221 (45Jb 90)
North Av. HA2: Harr 30Da 45
KT12: W Vill 81U 170
N18 ......21Wb 51
SM5: Cars 80Jb 156
TW9: Kew 53Qa 109
UB1: S'hall 45Ba 85
UB3: Hayes 44V 84
W13 ......43Ka 86
WD7: Shenl 4Na 15
NORTHAW 2Hb 17
Northaw Ho. W10 ......42Ya 88
(off Sutton Way)
NORTHAW PARK 4Hb 17
Northaw Pl. EN6: N'thaw 2Fb 17
Northaw Rd. E. EN6: Cuff 3Mb 18
Northaw Rd. W. EN6: N'thaw 2Hb 17
North Bank NW8 ......4D 214 (41Gb 89)
Northbank Rd. E17 ......26Ec 52
NORTH BECKTON 43Nc 94
Nth. Birkbeck Rd. E11 ......34Fc 73
North Block RM2: Rom 27Md 57
SE1 ......1J 229
Northborough Rd. SL2: Slou 2E 80
SW16 ......69Mb 134
Northbourne BR2: Hayes 73Jc 159
Northbourne Rd. SW4 ......57Mb 112
Northbrook Dr. HA6: Nwood 25U 44
Northbrook Rd. CR0: C'don 71Tb 157
EN5: Barn 16Ab 30
IG1: Ilf 33Qc 74
N22 ......24Nb 50
SE13 ......57Gc 115
Northburgh St. EC1 ......6C 218 (42Rb 91)
Nth. Burnham Cl. SL1: Burn 10A 60
Nth. Carriage Dr. W2 ......4D 220
NORTH CHEAM 76Ya 154
North Cheam Sports Club 76Za 154
Northchurch SE17 ......7G 231 (50Tb 91)
(not continuous)
Northchurch Ho. E2 ......39Wb 71
(off Whiston Rd.)
Northchurch Rd. HA9: Wemb 37Qa 67
N1 ......38Tb 71
(not continuous)
Northchurch Ter. N1 ......38Ub 71
Nth. Circular Rd. E4 ......23Bc 52
E18 ......26Lc 53
IG1: Ilf 31Nc 74
IG11: Bark 38Qc 74
N3 ......27Cb 49
N12 ......27Cb 49
N13 ......22Qb 50
NW2 ......36Ua 68
NW4 ......36Ua 68
NW10 ......40Pa 67
NW11 ......36Ua 68
Northcliffe Cl. KT4: Wor Pk 76Ua 154
Northcliffe Dr. N20 ......18Bb 31
North Cl. AL2: Chis G 7P 5
DA6: Bex 56Zc 117
EN5: Barn 15Ya 30
IG7: Chig 22Wc 55
RM10: Dag 39Cd 76
SL4: Wind 3D 102
SM4: Mord 70Ab 132
TW14: Bedf 58T 106
Nth. Colonnade, The E14 ......46Cc 92
(not continuous)
North Comn. KT13: Weyb 77S 150
North Comn. Rd. UB8: Uxb 36M 63
W5 ......45Na 87
Northcote HA5: Pinn 26Y 45
KT15: Add 77M 149
Northcote Av. KT5: Surb 73Ra 153
TW7: Isle 57Ja 108
UB1: S'hall 45Aa 85
W5 ......45Na 87
Northcote Cl. KT24: W Hor 97S 190
Northcote Cres. KT24: W Hor 97S 190
Northcote M. SW11 ......56Gb 111
Northcote Pk. KT22: Oxs 86Ea 172
Northcote Rd. CR0: C'don 72Tb 157
DA11: Grav'nd 10B 122
DA14: Sidc 63Uc 138
E17 ......28Ac 52
KT3: N Mald 69Sa 131
KT24: W Hor 97S 190
NW10 ......38Ua 68
SW11 ......57Gb 111
TW1: Twick 57Ja 108
North Cotts. AL2: Lon C 7E 6
Northcott Av. N22 ......25Nb 50
Northcotts Long Elms Cl. WD5: Ab L 5T 12
(off Long Elms Cl.)
Nth. Countess Rd. E17 ......26Bc 52
North Ct. BR1: Brom 67Kc 137
(off Palace Gro.)
SE24 ......55Rb 113
SW1 ......4F 229
W1 ......7C 216 (43Lb 90)
Northcourt WD3: Rick 18J 25
NORTH CRAY 64Ad 139
Nth. Cray Rd. DA5: Bexl 60Dd 118
DA14: Sidc 65Ad 139
North Cray Woods 63Zc 139
North Cres. E16 ......42Fc 93
N3 ......26Bb 49
WC1 ......7D 216 (43Mb 90)
Northcroft SL2: Slou 2F 80
Northcroft Cl. TW20: Eng G 4M 125
Northcroft Ct. W12 ......47Wa 88
Northcroft Gdns. TW20: Eng G 4M 125
Northcroft Rd. KT19: Ewe 80Ua 154
TW20: Eng G 4M 125
W13 ......47Ka 86
North Crofts SE23 ......60Xb 113
Northcroft Ter. W13 ......47Ka 86
Northcroft Vs. TW20: Eng G 4M 125
Nth. Cross Rd. IG6: Ilf 28Sc 54
SE22 ......57Vb 113
Northdale Ct. SE25 ......69Vb 135
North Dene NW7 ......20Ta 29
TW3: Houn 53Db 107
Northdene IG7: Chig 22Tc 54
Northdene Gdns. N15 ......30Vb 51
North Down CR2: Sande 83Ub 177
Northdown Cl. HA4: Ruis 34V 64
Northdown Gdns. IG2: Ilf 29Uc 54
Northdown Rd. AL10: Hat 3C 8
CR3: Wold 96Cc 198
DA3: Lfield 68Zd 143
DA16: Well 54Xc 117
RM11: Horn 31Kd 77
SL9: Chal P 23A 42
SM2: Sutt 82Cb 175
TN15: Kems'g 89Nd 183
Nth. Downs Bus. Pk.
TN13: Dun G 88Ed 182
Nth. Downs Cres. CR0: New Ad 81Dc 178
North Downs Golf Course 97Cc 198
Nth. Downs Rd. CR0: New Ad 82Dc 178
Northdown St. N1 ......1G 217 (40Nb 70)
North Dr. AL4: St A 1J 7
BR3: Beck 70Dc 136
BR6: Orp 77Uc 160
GU24: Brkwd 3A 186
GU25: Vir W 2J 147
HA4: Ruis 31U 64
RM2: Rom 27Ld 57
SL2: Stoke P 1J 81
SW16 ......63Lb 134
TW3: Houn 54Ea 108
North E. Surrey Crematorium
SM4: Mord 72Ya 154
NORTH END
DA8 ......53Hd 118
NW3 ......33Eb 69
North End CR0: C'don 75Sb 157
IG9: Buck H 17Lc 35
NW3 ......33Eb 69
RM3: Rom 19Ld 39
Northend CM14: W'ley 22Yd 58
HP3: Hem H 4B 4
North End Av. NW3 ......33Eb 69
North End Cres. W14 ......49Bb 89
North End Ho. W14 ......49Ab 88
North End La. BR6: Downe 83Qc 180
SL5: S'dale 3F 146
North End Pde. W14 ......49Ab 88
(off North End Rd.)
North End Rd. HA9: Wemb 34Qa 67
NW11 ......32Cb 69
SW6 ......51Bb 111
W14 ......49Ab 88
Northend Rd. DA1: Erith 52Hd 118
DA8: Erith 52Hd 118
Northend Trad. Est. DA8: Erith 53Gd 118
North End Way NW3 ......33Eb 69
Northern Av. N9 ......19Ub 33
Northernhay Wlk. SM4: Mord 70Ab 132
Northern Hgts. N8 ......31Mb 70
(off Crescent Rd.)
Northern Perimeter Rd.
TW6: H'row A 53R 106
Northern Perimeter Rd. (West)
TW6: H'row A 53M 105
Northern Pct. RM20: W Thur 49Vd 98
Northern Rd. E13 ......40Kc 73
SL2: Slou 2H 81
Northesk Ho. E1 ......42Xb 91
(off Tent St.)
Northey Av. SM2: Cheam 82Za 174
Nth. Eyot Gdns. W6 ......50Va 88
Northey St. E14 ......45Ac 92
NORTH FELTHAM 58X 107
Nth. Feltham Trad. Est. TW14: Felt 57X 107
Northfield DA3: Hartl 69Be 143
GU18: Light 3A 166
IG10: Lough 14Mc 35
Northfield Av. BR5: Orp 72Yc 161
HA5: Pinn 28Z 45
W5 ......46Ka 86
W13 ......46Ka 86
Northfield Cl. BR1: Brom 67Nc 138
UB3: Harl 48V 84
Northfield Ct. TW18: Staines 67K 127
Northfield Cres. SM3: Cheam 77Ab 154
Northfield Farm M. KT11: Cobh 85W 170
Northfield Gdns. RM9: Dag 35Bd 75
WD24: Wat 9Y 13
Northfield Ho. SE15 ......51Wb 113
Northfield Pde. UB3: Harl 48U 84
Northfield Pk. UB3: Harl 48V 84
Northfield Path RM9: Dag 35Bd 75
Northfield Pl. KT13: Weyb 80R 150
Northfield Rd. E6 ......38Pc 74
EN3: Pond E 15Xb 33
EN4: Cockf 13Gb 31
EN8: Walt C 4Ac 20
KT11: Cobh 85W 170
N16 ......31Ub 71
RM9: Dag 35Bd 75
SL4: Eton W 9D 80
TW5: Hest 51Z 107
TW18: Staines 67K 127
W13 ......47Ka 86
WD6: Bore 11Ra 29
NORTHFIELDS 48Ka 86
Northfields KT17: Eps 83Ua 174
KT21: Asht 90Na 173
(not continuous)
RM17: Grays 49Ee 99
SW18 ......56Cb 111
Northfields Ind. Est. HA0: Wemb 39Qa 67
Northfields Prospect Bus. Cen.
SW18 ......56Cb 111
Northfields Rd. W3 ......43Ra 87
NORTH FINCHLEY 22Eb 49
NORTHFLEET 58De 121
NORTHFLEET GREEN 64Ee 143
Northfleet Grn. Rd. DA13: Nflt G 65Ee 143
Northfleet Ho. SE1 ......1F 231
Northfleet Ind. Est.
DA11: Nflt 56Be 121
Northfleet Lodge GU22: Wok 91A 188
Northfleet Urban Country Pk. 60Fe 121
Northflock St. SE16 ......47Wb 91
Nth. Flower Wlk. W2 ......5A 220
North Gdn. E14 ......46Bc 92
North Gdns. SW19 ......66Fb 133
North Gate NW8 ......2D 214
Northgate HA6: Nwood 24S 44
Northgate Bus. Cen. EN1: Enf 13Xb 33
Northgate Ct. SW9 ......55Qb 112
Northgate Dr. NW9 ......30Ua 48
Northgate Ho. E14 ......45Cc 92
(off E. India Dock Rd.)
EN8: Chesh 1Ac 20
(off Turners Hill)
Northgate Ind. Pk. RM5: Col R 25Bd 55
Northgate Path WD6: Bore 10Pa 15
North Gates N12 ......25Eb 49
(off Bow La.)
Nth. Glade, The DA5: Bexl 59Bd 117
Nth. Gower St. NW1 ......4B 216 (41Lb 90)
North Grn. NW9 ......24Ua 48
SL1: Slou 5J 81
North Gro. KT16: Chert 72H 149
N6 ......31Jb 70
N15 ......29Tb 51
NORTH HARROW 29Da 45
Nth. Hatton Rd. TW6: H'row A 53T 106
North Hill N6 ......30Hb 49
WD3: Chor 12G 24
North Hill Av. N6 ......30Jb 50
North Hill Dr. RM3: Rom 20Md 39
North Hill Grn. RM3: Rom 21Md 57
NORTH HILLINGDON 38S 64
North Ho. SE8 ......50Bc 92
Nth. Hyde Gdns. UB3: Harl, Hayes 48W 84
Nth. Hyde La. TW5: Hest 50Aa 85
UB2: S'hall 50Z 85
Nth. Hyde Rd. UB3: Harl 48U 84
Northiam N12 ......21Cb 49
(not continuous)
WC1 ......4G 217
Northiam St. E9 ......39Xb 71
Northington St. WC1 ......6J 217 (42Pb 90)
NORTH KENSINGTON 43Ya 88
Nth. Kent Av. DA11: Nflt 58Ee 121
North Kent Indoor Bowls Club 48Dd 96
Northlands EN6: Pot B 3Fb 17
Northlands Av. BR6: Orp 77Uc 160
Northlands St. SE5 ......54Sb 113
North La. DA11: Grav'nd 4E 144
TW11: Tedd 65Ha 130
North Lawns DA11: Nflt 58Ee 121
(off Lawn Rd.)
Northleigh Ho. E3 ......41Dc 92
(off Powis Rd.)
North Lodge E16 ......46Kc 93
(off Wesley Av.)
EN5: New Bar 15Eb 31
Nth. Lodge Cl. SW15 ......57Za 110
Nth. London Bus. Pk. N11 ......19Jb 32
NORTH LOOE 85Ya 174
North Mall N9 ......19Xb 33
(within Edmonton Grn. Shop. Cen.)
RM17: Grays 51De 121
(off Grays Shop. Cen.)
SW18 ......57Db 111
(off Southside Shop. Cen.)
TW18: Staines 63H 127
(in The Elmsleigh Cen.)
Northmead RH1: Redh 3P 207
Northmead Rd. SL2: Slou 2D 80
North M. WC1 ......6J 217 (42Pb 90)
North Middlesex Golf Course 20Fb 31
Northmoor Hill Wood Local Nature Reserve
......28H 43
North Mt. N20 ......19Eb 31
(off High Rd.)
NORTH MYMMS 7C 8
North Mymms Pk. 7A 8
NORTH OCKENDON 37Xd 78
Northolm HA8: Edg 21Ta 47
Northolme Cl. RM16: Grays 48Ee 99
Northolme Gdns. HA8: Edg 25Qa 47
Northolme Ri. BR6: Orp 75Uc 160
Northolme Rd. N5 ......35Sb 71
NORTHOLT 38Ca 65
Northolt N17 ......26Ub 51
(off Griffin Rd.)
Northolt Av. HA4: Ruis 36X 65
Northolt Gdns. UB6: G'frd 36Ha 66
Northolt Golf Course 40Aa 65
Northolt Leisure Cen. 37Ca 65
Northolt Rd. HA2: Harr 35Da 65
TW6: H'row A 53N 105
(not continuous)
Northolt Trad. Est. UB5: N'olt 38Da 65
Northolt Way RM12: Horn 37Ld 77
Nth. Orbital Commercial Pk. AL1: St A 6E 6
Nth. Orbital Rd. AL1: St A 6B 6
AL2: Chis G 2Z 13
AL2: St A 6B 6
AL4: S'ford, St A 6H 7
UB9: Den 29J 43
WD3: Map C 22G 42
WD3: W Hyd 25G 42
WD25: Wat 6W 12
Northover BR1: Brom 62Hc 137
North Pde. HA8: Edg 26Qa 47
KT9: Chess 78Pa 153
UB1: S'hall 44Ca 85
(off North Rd.)
North Pk. SE9 ......58Pc 116
SL0: Rich P 48E 82
SL9: Chal P 27A 42
North Pk. La. RH9: G'stone 1N 209
North Pas. SW18 ......57Cb 111
North Pl. CR4: Mitc 66Hb 133
EN9: Walt A 5Dc 20
TW11: Tedd 65Ha 130
North Point N8 ......29Pb 50
Northpoint Cl. SM1: Sutt 76Eb 155
Northpoint Ho. N1 ......37Tb 71
(off Essex Rd.)
Northpoint Sq. NW1 ......37Mb 70
Nth. Pole La. BR2: Kes 79Hc 159
Nth. Pole Rd. W10 ......43Ya 88
Northport St. N1 ......1G 219 (39Tb 71)
Nth. Quay Pl. E14 ......45Dc 92
North Ride W2 ......4D 220 (45Gb 89)
Northridge Rd. DA12: Grav'nd 2E 144
Northridge Way HP1: Hem H 3H 3
North Riding AL2: Brick W 2Ca 13
North Ri. W2 ......3E 220 (44Gb 89)
North Rd. BR1: Brom 67Kc 137
BR4: W W'ck 74Dc 158
CM14: B'wood 18Yd 40
DA1: Dart 58Hd 118
DA17: Belv 48Dd 96
EN8: Walt C 5Ac 20
GU21: Wok 88C 168
HA1: Harr 31Ja 66
HA8: Edg 22Ra 47
IG3: Ilf 33Uc 74
KT6: Surb 72Ma 153
KT12: Hers 78Y 151
N6 ......31Jb 70
N7 ......37Nb 70
N9 ......18Xb 33
RH2: Reig 9H 207
RM4: Have B 20Gd 38
RM6: Chad H 29Ad 55
North Rd. RM15: N Ock, S Ock 38Zd 79
RM19: Purf 49Sd 98
SE18 ......49Uc 94
SW19 ......65Eb 133
TW5: Hest 51Y 107
TW8: Bford 51Na 109
TW9: Kew 53Qa 109
TW9: Rich 55Qa 109
TW14: Bedf 58T 106
UB1: S'hall 44Ca 85
UB3: Hayes 43T 84
UB7: W Dray 48P 83
W5 ......48Ma 87
WD3: Chor 15F 24
North Rd. Av. CM14: B'wood 18Yd 40
Northrop Rd. TW6: H'row A 53U 106
North Row SL3: Ful 35A 62
W1 ......4G 221 (45Hb 89)
Nth. Row Bldgs. W1 ......4H 221
Nth. Service Rd. CM14: B'wood 19Yd 40
North Several SE3 ......54Fc 115
NORTH SHEEN 55Qa 109
North Side EN9: Walt A 2Kc 21
Northside Rd. BR1: Brom 67Jc 137
Northside Studios E8 ......39Xb 71
(off Andrew's Rd.)
Nth. Side Wandsworth Comn.
SW18 ......57Fb 111
Northspur Rd. SM1: Sutt 76Cb 155
North Sq. DA3: New A 75Be 165
N9 ......19Xb 33
(off New Rd.)
NW11 ......29Cb 49
North Stand N5 ......34Rb 71
Nth. Star Blvd. DA9: Ghithe 56Wd 120
(off Evelyn Wlk.)
Nth. Station App. RH1: S Nut 8F 208
Northstead Rd. SW2 ......61Qb 134
NORTH STIFFORD 46Ae 99
North St. BR1: Brom 67Jc 137
DA1: Dart 59Md 119
DA7: Bex 56Cd 118
DA12: Grav'nd 9D 122
E13 ......40Kc 73
IG11: Bark 37Rc 74
KT22: Lea 93Ja 192
NW4 ......29Ya 48
RH1: Redh 5P 207
RM1: Rom 27Fd 56
(not continuous)
RM11: Horn 31Md 77
SL4: Wink ......10A 102 & 1A 124
SM5: Cars 76Hb 155
SW4 ......55Lb 112
TW7: Isle 55Ja 108
TW20: Egh 64B 126
North St. Pas. E13 ......40Kc 73
Nth. Tenter St. E1 ......3K 225 (44Vb 91)
North Ter. SL4: Wind 2H 103
SW3 ......4D 226 (48Gb 89)
WC2 ......6E 222
Northumberland All. EC3 ......3J 225 (44Ub 91)
(not continuous)
Northumberland Av. DA16: Well 56Tc 116
E12 ......32Lc 73
EN1: Enf 11Xb 33
RM11: Horn 29Ld 57
TW7: Isle 53Ha 108
WC2 ......6F 223 (46Nb 90)
Northumberland Cl. DA8: Erith 52Ed 118
TW19: Stanw 58N 105
Northumberland Cres. TW14: Felt 58U 106
Northumberland Gdns.
BR1: Brom 70Qc 138
CR4: Mitc 71Mb 156
N9 ......20Vb 33
TW7: Isle 52Ja 108
Northumberland Gro. N17 ......24Xb 51
Northumberland Hall AL9: N Mym 10F 8
NORTHUMBERLAND HEATH 52Ed 118
Northumberland Ho. IG8: Wfd G 24Qc 54
SW1 ......6F 223
Northumberland Pk. DA8: Erith 52Ed 118
N17 ......24Vb 51
Northumberland Pk. Ind. Est. N17 ......24Xb 51
Northumberland Pk. Sports Cen. 24Wb 51
Northumberland Pl. TW10: Rich 57Ma 109
W2 ......44Cb 89
Northumberland Rd. DA13: Ist R 6B 144
E6 ......44Nc 94
E17 ......31Cc 72
EN5: New Bar 16Eb 31
HA2: Harr 29Ba 45
SS17: Linf 7J 101
Northumberland St. WC2 ......6F 223 (46Nb 90)
Northumberland Wlk. SL0: Rich P 47G 82
Northumberland Way DA8: Erith 53Ed 118
Northumbria St. E14 ......44Cc 92
Nth. Verbena Gdns. W6 ......50Wa 88
North Vw. HA5: Eastc 31Y 65
SW19 ......64Ya 132
W5 ......42La 86
Northview BR8: Swan 68Gd 140
HP1: Hem H 4F 2
Northview Av. RM18: Tilb 3C 122
North Vw. Caravan Site IG6: Ilf 24Wc 55
North Vw. Cres. KT18: Tatt C 89Ya 174
Northview Cres. NW10 ......35Va 68
North Vw. Dr. IG8: Wfd G 26Mc 53
Northview Pde. N7 ......34Nb 70
North Vw. Rd. N8 ......28Mb 50
TN14: S'oaks 93Ld 203
North Vs. NW1 ......37Mb 70
North Wlk. CR0: New Ad 79Dc 158
(not continuous)
W2 ......5A 220 (45Db 89)
W8 ......45Db 89
(off The Broad Wlk.)
NORTH WATFORD 9X 13
North Way HA5: Pinn 28Z 45
N9 ......19Zb 34
N11 ......23Lb 50
NW9 ......27Ra 47
UB10: Uxb 38N 63
Northway NW11 ......29Db 49
SM4: Mord 69Ab 132
SM6: Wall 77Lb 156
WD3: Rick 17M 25
Northway Cir. NW7 ......21Ta 47
Northway Ct. NW7 ......21Ua 48
Northway Cres. NW7 ......21Ta 47
Northway Gdns. NW11 ......29Db 49
Northway Rd. CR0: C'don 72Vb 157
SE5 ......55Sb 113
Northways NW3 ......38Fb 69
(off College Cres.)
Northways Pde. NW3 ......38Fb 69
(off College Cres., not continuous)
Nth. Weald Cl. RM12: Horn 38Kd 77
Northweald La. KT2: King T 64Ma 131
NORTH WEMBLEY 34Ma 67
Nth. Western Av. WD24: Wat 7V 12
WD25: A'ham 12Da 27
(Elton Way)
WD25: A'ham 15Ga 28
(Tylers Way)
WD25: A'ham, Wat 9Aa 13
WD25: Wat 7T 12
(not continuous)
Nth. Western Commercial Cen.
NW1 ......38Nb 70
Northwest Pl. N1 ......1A 218 (40Qb 70)
Nth. Weylands Ind. Est.
KT12: Walt T 75Aa 151
North Wharf E14 ......46Ec 92
(off Coldharbour)
Nth. Wharf Rd. W2 ......1B 220 (43Fb 89)
Northwick Av. HA3: Kenton 30Ja 46
Northwick Circ. HA3: Kenton 30La 46
Northwick Cl. HA1: Harr 32Ka 66
NW8 ......5B 214 (42Fb 89)
Northwick Ho. NW8 ......5A 214
Northwick Pk. Playgolf 32Ja 66
Northwick Pk. Rd. HA1: Harr 30Ha 46
Northwick Pk. Rdbt. HA1: Harr 31Ja 66
Northwick Rd. HA0: Wemb 39Ma 67
WD19: Wat 21Y 45
Northwick Ter. NW8 ......5B 214 (42Fb 89)
Northwick Wlk. HA1: Harr 31Ha 66
Northwold Dr. HA5: Pinn 26Y 45
Northwold Rd. E5 ......33Vb 71
N16 ......33Vb 71
NORTHWOOD 23U 44
Northwood RM16: Grays 7D 100
Northwood Av. CR8: Purl 84Qb 176
GU21: Knap 10H 167
RM12: Horn 35Jd 76
Nth. Wood Ct. SE25 ......69Wb 135
Northwood Dr. DA9: Ghithe 58Wd 120
Northwood Est. E5 ......33Wb 71
Northwood Gdns. IG5: Ilf 28Qc 54
N12 ......22Fb 49
UB6: G'frd 36Ha 66
Northwood Golf Course 24T 44
Northwood Hall N6 ......31Lb 70
NORTHWOOD HILLS 26W 44
Northwood Hills Cir. HA6: Nwood 25W 44
Northwood Ho. KT2: King T 68Qa 131
(off Coombe Rd.)
SE27 ......63Tb 135
Northwood Pl. DA18: Erith 48Bd 95
Northwood Rd. CR7: Thor H 68Rb 135
N6 ......31Kb 70
SE23 ......60Bc 114
SM5: Cars 79Jb 156
TW6: H'row A 53M 105
UB9: Hare 25L 43
Northwood Sports Cen. 25X 45
Northwood Way HA6: Nwood 24V 44
SE19 ......65Tb 135
UB9: Hare 25M 43
NORTH WOOLWICH 47Qc 94
Nth. Woolwich Rd. E16 ......46Hc 93
Nth. Worple Way SW14 ......55Ta 109
Nortoft Rd. SL9: Chal P 23B 42
Norton Almshouses EN8: Chesh 2Zb 20
(off Turner's Hill)
Norton Av. KT5: Surb 73Ra 153
Norton Cl. E4 ......22Cc 52
EN1: Enf 12Xb 33
GU3: Worp 9H 187
WD6: Bore 11Qa 29
Norton Ct. BR3: Beck 68Bc 136
Norton Folgate E1 ......7J 219 (43Ub 91)
Norton Folgate Ho. E1 ......7K 219
Norton Gdns. SW16 ......68Nb 134
Norton Ho. E1 ......44Xb 91
(off Bigland St.)
E2 ......40Zb 72
(off Mace St.)
SW1 ......4E 228
SW9 ......54Pb 112
(off Aytoun Rd.)
Norton La. KT11: Cobh 91V 190
Norton Pk. SL5: S'hill 1A 146
Norton Rd. E10 ......32Bc 72
HA0: Wemb 37Ma 67
RM10: Dag 37Fd 76
UB8: Uxb 41M 83
Norval Rd. HA0: Wemb 33Ka 66
Norvic Ho. DA8: Erith 52Hd 118
Norway Dr. SL2: Slou 3M 81
Norway Ga. SE16 ......48Ac 92
Norway Pl. E14 ......44Bc 92
Norway St. SE10 ......51Dc 114
Norway Wlk. RM13: Rain 42Ld 97
Norway Wharf E14 ......44Bc 92
Norwich Cres. RM6: Chad H 29Xc 55
Norwich Ho. E14 ......44Dc 92
(off Cordelia St.)
WD6: Bore 12Qa 29
(off Stratfield Rd.)
Norwich M. IG3: Ilf 32Wc 75
Norwich Pl. DA6: Bex 56Cd 118
Norwich Rd. CR7: Thor H 69Sb 135
E7 ......36Jc 73
HA6: Nwood 27V 44
RM9: Dag 40Cd 76
UB6: G'frd 39Da 65
Norwich St. EC4 ......2K 223 (44Qb 90)
Norwich Wlk. HA8: Edg 24Sa 47
Norwich Way WD3: Crox G 13R 26
NORWOOD 65Ub 135
Norwood Av. HA0: Wemb 39Pa 67
RM7: Rush G 31Gd 76
Norwood Cl. KT24: Eff 100Aa 191
NW2 ......34Bb 69
TW2: Twick 61Fa 130
UB2: S'hall 49Ca 85
Norwood Ct. DA1: Dart 57Qd 119
(off Farnol Rd.)
Norwood Dr. HA2: Harr 30Ba 45
Norwood Farm La. KT11: Cobh 83W 170
KT12: Cobh 83W 170
Norwood Gdns. UB2: S'hall 49Ba 85
UB4: Yead 42Y 85
NORWOOD GREEN 49Ba 85
Norwood Grn. Rd. UB2: S'hall 49Ca 85
Norwood High St. SE27 ......62Rb 135
Norwood Ho. E14 ......45Dc 92
(off Poplar High St.)
Norwood La. SL0: Iver 42F 82

NORWOOD NEW TOWN .65Sb 135
Norwood Pk. Rd. SE27 .64Sb 135
Norwood Rd. EN8: Chesh .2Ac 20
KT24: Eff .100Aa 191
SE24 .60Rb 113
SE27 .61Rb 135
UB2: S'hall .48Aa 85
Norwood Ter. UB2: S'hall .49Da 85
Nota M. N3 .25Cb 49
Notley End TW20: Eng G .6N 125
Notley St. SE5 .52Tb 113
Notson Rd. SE25 .70Xb 135
Notting Barn Rd. W10 .42Za 88
Nottingdale Sq. W11 .46Ab 88
Nottingham Av. E16 .43Lc 93
Nottingham Cl. GU21: Wok .10K 167
WD25: Wat .5W 12
Nottingham Ct. GU21: Wok .10K 167
(off Nottingham Cl.)
WC2 .3F 223 (44Nb 90)
Nottingham Ho. WC2 .3F 223
Nottingham Pl. W1 .6H 215 (43Jb 90)
Nottingham Rd. CR2: S Croy .77Sb 157
E10 .30Ec 52
SW17 .60Hb 111
TW7: Isle .54Ha 108
WD3: Herons .17E 24
Nottingham St. W1 .7H 215 (43Jb 90)
Nottingham Ter. NW1 .6H 215
NOTTING HILL .45Bb 89
Notting Hill Ga. W11 .46Cb 89
Nottingwood Ho. W11 .45Ab 88
(off Clarendon Rd.)
Nova Bldg. E14 .49Cc 92
Nova Ct. E. E14 .46Ec 92
(off Yabsley St.)
Nova Ct. W. E14 .46Ec 92
(off Yabsley St.)
Nova M. SM3: Sutt .74Ab 154
Novar Cl. BR6: Orp .73Vc 161
Nova Rd. CR0: C'don .74Rb 157
Novar Rd. SE9 .60Sc 116
Novello Ct. N1 .39Sb 71
(off Popham Rd.)
Novello St. SW6 .53Cb 111
Novello Theatre
Covent Garden .4H 223
Sunninghill .1B 146
Novello Way WD6: Bore .11Ta 29
Novem Ho. E1 .43Wb 91
(off Chicksand St.)
Nowell Rd. SW13 .51Wa 110
Nower, The TN14: Knock .91Vc 201
Nower Ct. HA5: Pinn .28Ba 45
Nower Hill HA5: Pinn .28Ba 45
Noyna Rd. SW17 .62Hb 133
Nubia Way BR1: Brom .62Gc 137
Nucleus Bus. & Innovation Cen., The
DA1: Dart .55Qd 119
Nuding Cl. SE13 .55Cc 114
Nuffield Ct. TW5: Hest .52Ba 107
Nuffield Health Club
Battersea .54Hb 111
(within Latchmere Leisure Cen.)
Bloomsbury .5H 217
Bromley .71Kc 159
Cannon Street .4F 225
Cheam .80Ab 154
Fulham .53Za 110
Norbury .68Pb 134
Paddington .1A 220
St Albans .5F 6
Southfields .59Cb 111
Stoke Poges .10M 61
Surbiton .72La 152
Twickenham .59Ga 108
West Byfleet .86K 169
Westminster .43Eb 89
Willesden Green .38Ya 68
Nuffield Lodge N6 .30Lb 50
W9 .43Cb 89
(off Admiral Wlk.)
Nuffield Rd. BR8: Hext .65Jd 140
Nugent Rd. N19 .32Nb 70
SE25 .69Vb 135
Nugents Ct. HA5: Pinn .25Aa 45
Nugent Shop. Pk. BR5: St M Cry .70Yc 139
Nugent's Pk. HA5: Hat E .25Aa 45
Nugent Ter. NW8 .2A 214 (40Eb 69)
Numa Ct. TW8: Bford .52Ma 109
No. 10 Bowling Alley .30Gd 56
Number One EC1 .6F 219 (42Sb 91)
Numbers Farm WD4: K Lan .1S 12
Nunappleton Way RH8: Oxt .4L 211
Nun Ct. EC2 .2F 225
Nuneaton Rd. RM9: Dag .38Ad 75
Nunfield WD4: Chfd .3K 11
NUNHEAD .55Xb 113
Nunhead Cemetery Nature Reserve
.56Yb 114
Nunhead Cres. SE15 .55Xb 113
Nunhead Est. SE15 .56Xb 113
Nunhead Grn. SE15 .55Xb 113
Nunhead Gro. SE15 .55Xb 113
Nunhead La. SE15 .55Xb 113
Nunhead Pas. SE15 .55Wb 113
Nunnery Cl. AL1: St A .4C 6
Nunnery Stables AL1: St A .4B 6
Nunnington Cl. SE9 .62Nc 138
Nunns Rd. EN2: Enf .12Sb 33
Nunns Way RM17: Grays .49Fe 99
Nuns La. AL1: St A .6C 6
Nuns Wlk. GU25: Vir W .1P 147
NUPER'S HATCH .17Gd 38
Nupton Dr. EN5: Barn .16Ya 30
Nuralite Ind. Cen. ME3: High'm .9P 123
Nurse Cl. HA8: Edg .25Sa 47
Nursery, The DA8: Erith .52Hd 118
Nursery App. N12 .23Gb 49
Nursery Av. CR0: C'don .75Zb 158
DA7: Bex .55Bd 117
N3 .26Eb 49
Nursery Cl. BR6: Orp .73Wc 161
BR8: Swan .68Ed 140
CR0: C'don .75Zb 158
DA2: Dart .59Sd 120
EN3: Enf H .11Zb 34
GU21: Wok .8N 167
IG8: Wfd G .22Kc 53
KT15: Wdhm .82H 169
KT17: Ewe .82Ua 174
KT20: Walt H .97Xa 194
RM6: Chad H .30Zc 55
RM15: S Ock .42Yd 98
SE4 .54Bc 114
SW15 .56Za 110
Nursery Cl. TN13: S'oaks .94Ld 203
TW14: Felt .59X 107
(not continuous)
WD19: Wat .18X 27
Nursery Cotts. AL3: St A .5P 5
Nursery Ct. N17 .24Vb 51
W13 .43Ja 86
Nursery Gdns. BR7: Chst .65Rc 138
EN3: Enf H .11Zb 34
TW4: Houn .57Ba 107
TW12: Hamp .63Ba 129
TW16: Sun .68V 128
TW18: Staines .65K 127
Nursery Gro. DA11: Grav'nd .4D 144
Nursery La. E2 .1K 219 (39Vb 71)
E7 .37Jc 73
SL3: L'ly .6P 81
UB8: Cowl .42M 83
W10 .43Ya 88
Nurserymans Rd. N11 .19Jb 32
Nursery M. DA11: Grav'nd .4E 144
Nursery Pl. SL4: Old Win .8M 103
TN13: Chip .94Fd 202
Nursery Rd. CR4: Mitc .69Gb 133
CR7: Thor H .70Tb 135
DA13: Meop .10C 144
E9 .37Yb 72
EN9: Walt A .3Ec 20
GU21: Knap .9H 167
HA5: Pinn .27Y 45
IG10: Lough .15Lc 35
KT20: Walt H .97Wa 194
N2 .25Fb 49
N14 .17Lb 32
SL6: Tap .6B 60
SM1: Sutt .77Eb 155
SS17: Stan H .1N 101
SW9 .56Pb 112
SW19 .66Ab 132
(Elm Gro.)
SW19 .68Db 133
(Parkleigh Rd.)
TW16: Sun .68U 128
Nursery Row EN5: Barn .13Ab 30
SE17 .6F 231 (49Tb 91)
Nursery St. N17 .24Vb 51
Nursery Wlk. NW4 .27Ya 48
RM7: Rush G .31Fd 76
Nursery Way RH8: Oxt .1J 211
TW19: Wray .8P 103
Nursery Waye UB8: Uxb .39M 63
NURSTEAD .9B 144
Nurstead Av. DA3: Lfield .70Fe 143
Nurstead Chu. La.
DA13: Meop, Sole S .10B 144
Nurstead La.
DA3: Lfield, Long H, Meop .70Fe 143
DA13: Meop .70Fe 143
Nurstead Rd. DA8: Erith .52Cd 118
Nutberry Av. RM16: Grays .47Ce 99
Nutberry Cl. RM16: Grays .47Ce 99
Nutbourne Ct. TW18: Staines .66H 127
(off Riverside Rd.)
Nutbourne St. W10 .41Ab 88
Nutbrook St. SE15 .55Wb 113
Nutbrowne Rd. RM9: Dag .39Bd 75
Nutcroft Gro. KT22: Fet .93Ga 192
Nutcroft Rd. SE15 .52Xb 113
NUTFIELD .5F 208
Nutfield Cl. N18 .23Wb 51
SM5: Cars .76Gb 155
Nutfield Ct. BR1: Brom .69Jc 137
RH1: Nutf .4F 208
RH1: Redh .4B 208
(off Goodworth Rd.)
Nutfield Gdns. IG3: Ilf .33Vc 75
UB5: N'olt .40Y 65
Nutfield Marsh Rd. RH1: Nutf .3D 208
NUTFIELD PARK .9G 208
Nutfield Pas. CR7: Thor H .70Rb 135
(off Nutfield Rd.)
Nutfield Rd. CR5: Coul .88Jb 176
CR7: Thor H .70Rb 135
E15 .35Ec 72
NW2 .34Wa 68
RH1: Mers .1C 208
RH1: Redh, Nutf .6B 208
SE22 .56Vb 113
Nutfields TN15: Igh .95Xd 204
Nutfield Way BR6: Farnb .75Rc 160
Nutford Pl. W1 .2E 220 (44Hb 89)
Nuthatch DA3: Lfield .69De 143
Nuthatch Cl. TW19: Stanw .60P 105
Nuthatch Gdns. RH2: Reig .10L 207
SE28 .47Tc 94
(not continuous)
Nuthurst Av. SW2 .61Pb 134
Nutkin Wlk. UB8: Uxb .38N 63
Nutley Cl. BR8: Hext .67Hd 140
Nutley Ct. RH2: Reig .6H 207
(off Nutley La.)
Nutley Gro. RH2: Reig .6J 207
Nutley La. RH2: Reig .5H 207
Nutley Ter. NW3 .37Eb 69
Nutmead Cl. DA5: Bexl .60Ed 118
Nutmeg Cl. E16 .42Gc 93
Nutmeg La. E14 .44Fc 93
Nuttall St. N1 .1J 219 (40Ub 71)
Nutter La. E11 .30Lc 53
Nuttfield Cl. WD3: Crox G .16S 26
Nut Gro. HA8: Edg .19Ma 29
Nut Tree Cl. BR6: Chels .76Zc 161
Nutt St. SE15 .52Vb 113
Nutty La. TW17: Shep .69S 128
Nutwell St. SW17 .64Gb 133
Nuxley Rd. DA17: Belv .51Bd 117
Nyall Ct. RM2: Rom .27Ld 57
Nyanza St. SE18 .51Tc 116
Nye Bevan Est. E5 .34Zb 72
Nye Bevan Ho. SW6 .52Bb 111
(off St Thomas's Way)
Nyefield Pk. KT20: Walt H .98Wa 194
Nye Way HP3: Bov .10C 2
Nylands Av. TW9: Kew .53Qa 109
Nymans Gdns. SW20 .69Xa 132
Nynehead St. SE14 .52Ac 114
Nyon Gro. SE6 .61Bc 136
Nyssa Cl. IG8: Wfd G .23Pc 54
Nyth Cl. RM14: Upm .30Td 58
Nyton Cl. N19 .32Nb 70

O

O2, The .46Gc 93
O2 Brixton Academy .55Qb 112
O2 Cen. NW3 .37Eb 69
Oakapple Cl. CR2: Sande .86Xb 177
Oak Apple Ct. SE12 .60Jc 115
Oak Av. AL2: Brick W .2Ca 13
CR0: C'don .74Cc 158
EN2: Enf .10Pb 18
N8 .28Nb 50
N10 .24Kb 50
N17 .24Tb 51
RM14: Upm .34Rd 77
TN13: S'oaks .100Kd 203
TW5: Hest .52Z 107
TW12: Hamp .64Aa 129
TW20: Egh .66E 126
UB7: W Dray .48Q 84
UB10: Ick .33R 64
Oak Avenue Local Nature Reserve
.64Aa 129
Oak Bank CR0: New Ad .79Ec 158
Oakbank CM13: Hut .15Fe 41
GU22: Wok .91A 188
KT22: Fet .95Ea 192
WD7: R'lett .8Ka 14
Oakbank Av. KT12: Walt T .73Ba 151
Oakbank Gro. SE24 .56Sb 113
Oakbark Ho. TW8: Bford .52La 108
(off High St.)
Oakbrook Cl. BR1: Brom .63Kc 137
Oakbury Rd. SW6 .54Db 111
Oak Cl. DA1: Cray .56Hd 118
EN9: Walt A .6Fc 21
HP3: Hem H .6P 3
N14 .17Kb 32
RH8: Oxt .4L 211
SM1: Sutt .75Eb 155
Oakcombe Cl. KT3: N Mald .67Ua 132
Oak Cott. Cl. SE6 .60Hc 115
Oak Cotts. W7 .47Ga 86
Oak Ct. HA6: Nwood .23T 44
RM15: S Ock .40Yd 78
SE15 .52Vb 113
(off Sumner Rd.)
Oak Cres. E16 .43Gc 93
Oakcroft Bus. Cen. KT9: Chess .77Pa 153
Oakcroft Cl. HA5: Pinn .26X 45
KT14: W Byf .86H 169
Oakcroft Rd. KT9: Chess .77Pa 153
KT14: W Byf .86H 169
SE13 .54Fc 115
Oakcroft Vs. KT9: Chess .77Pa 153
Oakdale N14 .18Kb 32
Oakdale Av. HA3: Kenton .29Na 47
HA6: Nwood .26W 44
Oakdale Cl. WD19: Wat .21Y 45
Oakdale Ct. E4 .22Ec 52
Oakdale Gdns. E4 .22Ec 52
Oakdale Rd. E7 .38Kc 73
E11 .33Fc 73
E18 .26Kc 53
KT13: Weyb .76Q 150
KT19: Ewe .81Ta 173
N4 .30Sb 51
SE15 .55Yb 114
SW16 .64Nb 134
WD19: Wat .20Y 27
Oakdale Way CR4: Mitc .73Jb 156
Oak Dene W13 .43Ka 86
Oakdene EN8: Chesh .2Ac 20
GU24: Chob .2K 167
KT20: Tad .92Ab 194
RM3: Hrld W .26Pd 57
SE15 .53Xb 113
SL5: S'dale .2D 146
Oakdene Av. BR7: Chst .64Qc 138
DA8: Erith .51Ed 118
KT7: T Ditt .74Ja 152
Oakdene Cl. HA5: Hat E .24Ba 45
KT23: Bookh .99Ea 192
RM11: Horn .30Kd 57
Oakdene Ct. KT11: Cobh .86X 171
(off Between Streets)
KT12: Walt T .76X 151
KT13: Weyb .77Q 150
Oakdene Dr. KT5: Surb .73Sa 153
Oakdene M. SM3: Sutt .74Bb 155
Oakdene Pde. KT11: Cobh .86X 171
Oakdene Pk. N3 .24Bb 49
Oakdene Rd. BR5: St M Cry .71Vc 161
HP3: Hem H .6P 3
KT11: Cobh .86X 171
KT23: Bookh .96Ba 191
RH1: Redh .6P 207
TN13: S'oaks .94Jd 202
UB10: Hil .40R 64
WD24: Wat .8X 13
Oakdene Way AL1: St A .2G 6
Oakden St. SE11 .5A 230 (49Qb 90)
Oak Dr. HP4: Berk .2A 2
Oake Ct. SW15 .57Ab 110
Oakeford Ho. W14 .48Ab 88
(off Russell Rd.)
Oaken Coppice KT21: Asht .91Qa 193
Oak End Dr. SL0: Iver H .40E 62
Oakend Ho. N4 .31Tb 71
Oaken Dr. KT10: Clay .79Ha 152
Oak End Way KT15: Wdhm .84G 168
SL9: Ger X .29B 42
Oakenholt Ho. SE2 .46Zc 95
(off Sycamore Wlk.)
Oaken La. KT10: Clay .77Ga 152
Oakenshaw Cl.
CR6: W'ham .87Yb 178
KT6: Surb .73Na 153
Oakes Cl. E6 .44Pc 94
Oakeshott Av. N6 .33Jb 70
Oakey La. SE1 .3K 229 (48Qb 90)
Oak Farm WD6: Bore .15Sa 29
Oak Farm La. TN15: Fair .82Fe 185
Oakfield E4 .22Dc 52
GU21: Wok .9J 167
WD3: Rick .17H 25
Oakfield Av. HA3: Kenton .27Ka 46
SL1: Slou .6F 80
Oakfield Cen. SE20 .66Xb 135
Oakfield Cl. EN6: Pot B .3Bb 17
HA4: Ruis .30V 44
KT3: N Mald .71Va 154
KT13: Weyb .77S 150
Oakfield Ct. KT13: Weyb .77S 150
N8 .31Nb 70
NW2 .31Za 68
WD6: Bore .13Ra 29
Oakfield Dr. RH2: Reig .4J 207
Oakfield Gdns. BR3: Beck .71Dc 158
N18 .21Ub 51
SE19 .64Ub 135
(not continuous)
Oakfield Gdns. SM5: Cars .74Gb 155
UB6: G'frd .42Fa 86
Oakfield Glade KT13: Weyb .77S 150
Oakfield Ho. E3 .43Cc 92
(off Gale St.)
Oakfield La. BR2: Kes .77Lc 159
DA1: Dart .61Kd 141
(Hulsewood Cl.)
DA1: Dart .61Gd 140
(Pinewood Pl.)
DA2: Wilm .61Kd 141
Oakfield Lodge IG1: Ilf .34Rc 74
(off Albert Rd.)
Oakfield Pk. Rd. DA1: Dart .61Md 141
Oakfield Pl. DA1: Dart .61Md 141
Oakfield Rd. BR6: Orp .73Wc 161
CR0: C'don .74Sb 157
E6 .39Nc 74
E17 .26Ac 52
IG1: Ilf .34Rc 74
KT11: Cobh .86X 171
KT21: Asht .89Ma 173
N3 .25Db 49
N4 .30Qb 50
N14 .19Nb 32
SE20 .66Xb 135
SW19 .62Za 132
TW15: Ashf .64R 128
Oakfield Rd. Ind. Est. SE20 .66Xb 135
Oakfields IG10: Lough .15Qc 36
KT12: Walt T .74W 150
KT14: W Byf .86K 169
TN13: S'oaks .98Kd 203
Oakfields Rd. NW11 .30Ab 48
Oakfield St. SW10 .51Eb 111
Oakford Rd. NW5 .35Lb 70
Oak Gdns. CR0: C'don .75Cc 158
HA8: Edg .26Sa 47
Oak Glade CM16: Coop .1Zc 23
HA6: Nwood .25R 44
KT19: Eps .84Qa 173
Oak Glen RM11: Horn .27Nd 57
Oak Grange Rd. GU4: W Cla .100K 189
Oak Grn. WD5: Ab L .4U 12
Oak Grn. Way WD5: Ab L .4U 12
Oak Gro. AL10: Hat .1B 8
BR4: W W'ck .74Ec 158
HA4: Ruis .31X 65
NW2 .35Ab 68
TW16: Sun .66X 129
Oak Gro. Rd. SE20 .67Yb 136
Oakhall Ct. E11 .30Kc 53
TW16: Sun .64V 128
Oakhall Dr. TW16: Sun .64V 128
Oak Hall Rd. E11 .30Kc 53
Oakham Cl. EN4: Cockf .13Hb 31
SE6 .61Bc 136
Oakham Dr. BR2: Brom .70Hc 137
Oakham Ho. W10 .42Ya 88
(off Sutton Way)
Oakhampton Rd. NW7 .24Za 48
Oak Hill IG8: Wfd G .24Fc 53
KT6: Surb .73Na 153
KT18: Eps .88Ta 173
TN13: S'oaks .96Jd 202
Oakhill KT10: Clay .79Ja 152
Oakhill Av. HA5: Pinn .26Aa 45
NW3 .35Db 69
Oak Hill Cl. IG8: Wfd G .24Fc 53
Oakhill Cl. KT21: Asht .90La 172
WD3: Map C .21G 42
Oak Hill Ct. IG8: Wfd G .24Fc 53
Oakhill Ct. SE23 .58Yb 114
SW19 .66Za 132
Oak Hill Cres. IG8: Wfd G .24Fc 53
KT6: Surb .73Na 153
Oakhill Dr. KT6: Surb .73Na 153
Oak Hill Gdns. IG8: Wfd G .25Gc 53
Oakhill Gdns. KT13: Weyb .75U 150
Oak Hill Gro. KT6: Surb .72Na 153
Oak Hill Pk. NW3 .35Db 69
Oak Hill Pk. M. NW3 .35Eb 69
Oak Hill Path KT6: Surb .72Na 153
Oakhill Pl. SW15 .57Cb 111
Oak Hill Rd. KT6: Surb .72Na 153
RM4: Stap A .17Fd 38
Oakhill Rd. BR3: Beck .68Ec 136
BR6: Orp .74Vc 161
KT15: Add .79H 149
KT21: Asht .90La 172
RH2: Reig .7K 207
RH19: Purf .50Rd 97
SM1: Sutt .76Db 155
SW15 .57Bb 111
SW16 .67Pb 134
TN13: S'oaks .96Jd 202
WD3: Map C .21F 42
Oak Hill Way NW3 .35Db 69
(not continuous)
Oak Hill Woods Nature Reserve .16Hb 31
Oak Ho. KT19: Eps .82Sa 173
KT22: Lea .92Ha 192
N2 .26Fb 49
RM7: Rom .29Fd 56
TN13: S'oaks .96Kd 203
TW9: Kew .53Ra 109
W10 .42Ab 88
(off Sycamore Wlk.)
Oakhouse Rd. DA6: Bex .57Cd 118
Oakhurst GU21: Wok .8P 167
GU24: Chob .1J 167
Oakhurst Av. DA7: Bex .52Ad 117
EN4: E Barn .17Gb 31
Oakhurst Cl. BR7: Chst .67Pc 138
E17 .28Gc 53
IG6: Ilf .25Sc 54
KT2: King T .65Ta 131
TW11: Tedd .64Ga 130
Oakhurst Ct. E17 .28Gc 53
(off Woodford New Rd.)
Oakhurst Gdns. DA7: Bex .52Ad 117
E4 .18Hc 35
E17 .28Gc 53
Oakhurst Gro. SE22 .56Wb 113
Oakhurst Pl. WD18: Wat .14V 26
Oakhurst Ri. SM5: Cars .82Gb 175
Oakhurst Rd. EN3: Enf W .8Zb 20
KT19: Ewe .79Sa 153
Oakington Av. HA2: Harr .31Ca 65
HA9: Wemb .34Pa 67
HP6: L Chal .11A 24
UB3: Harl .49T 84
Oakington Cl. TW16: Sun .68Y 129
Oakington Ct. EN2: Enf .12Rb 33
Oakington Dr. TW16: Sun .68Y 129
Oakington Mnr. Dr. HA9: Wemb .36Qa 67
Oakington Rd. W9 .42Cb 89
Oakington Way N8 .31Nb 70
Oakland Ct. KT15: Add .76K 149
Oakland Gdns. CM13: Hut .15Ee 41
Oakland Pl. IG9: Buck H .19Jc 35
Oakland Quay E14 .48Dc 92
Oakland Rd. E15 .35Fc 73
Oaklands BR3: Beck .67Dc 136
CR8: Kenley .86Sb 177
KT22: Fet .96Fa 192
N21 .19Pb 32
RH9: S God .9C 210
W13 .43Ja 86
Oaklands, The WD5: Bedm .1V 12
Oaklands Av. AL9: Brk P .9G 8
BR4: W W'ck .76Dc 158
CR7: Thor H .70Qb 134
DA15: Sidc .59Vc 117
KT10: Esh .74Fa 152
N9 .16Xb 33
RM1: Rom .27Gd 56
TW7: Isle .51Ha 108
WD19: Wat .18X 27
Oaklands Cl. BR5: Pet W .72Uc 160
DA6: Bex .57Bd 117
HA0: Wemb .36Ma 67
KT9: Chess .77La 152
TN15: W King .79Ud 164
Oaklands College
St Albans City Campus .2C 6
(off Hatfield Rd.)
Smallford Campus .1J 7
Oaklands Ct. HA0: Wemb .36Ma 67
NW10 .39Ua 68
(off Nicoll Rd.)
SE20 .66Yb 136
(off Chestnut Gro.)
WD17: Wat .11W 26
Oaklands Dr. RH1: Redh .8B 208
RM15: S Ock .43Yd 98
TW2: Whitt .59Ea 108
Oaklands Est. SW4 .58Lb 112
Oaklands Gdns. CR8: Kenley .86Sb 177
Oaklands Ga. HA6: Nwood .23U 44
Oaklands Gro. W12 .46Wa 88
Oaklands La. AL4: S'ford .1K 7
EN5: Ark .14Xa 30
TN16: Big H .85Kc 179
Oaklands M. NW2 .35Za 68
(off Oaklands Rd.)
Oaklands Pk. CM13: Hut .18De 41
Oaklands Pk. Av. IG1: Ilf .33Sc 74
Oaklands Pas. NW2 .35Za 68
(off Oaklands Rd.)
Oaklands Pl. SW4 .56Lb 112
Oaklands Rd. BR1: Brom .66Gc 137
DA2: Dart .60Rd 119
DA6: Bex .56Bd 117
DA11: Nflt .3B 144
N20 .17Bb 31
NW2 .35Za 68
SW14 .55Ta 109
W7 .47Ha 86
(not continuous)
Oaklands Way KT20: Tad .94Ya 194
SM6: Wall .80Mb 156
Oakland Way KT19: Ewe .79Ua 154
Oak La. E14 .45Bc 92
EN6: Cuff .1Pb 18
GU22: Wok .88D 168
IG8: Wfd G .21Hc 53
N2 .26Fb 49
N11 .23Mb 50
SL4: Wind .3E 102
TN13: S'oaks .100Hd 202
TW1: Twick .59Ja 108
TW7: Isle .56Ga 108
TW20: Eng G .2N 125
Oaklawn Rd. KT22: Lea .90Ga 172
Oak Leaf Cl. KT19: Eps .84Sa 173
Oakleafe Gdns. IG6: Ilf .27Rc 54
Oaklea Lodge IG3: Ilf .34Wc 75
Oaklea Pas. KT1: King T .69Ma 131
Oakleigh GU18: Light .3A 166
KT18: Eps .86Ua 174
RH9: G'stone .2A 210
Oakleigh Av. HA8: Edg .26Ra 47
KT6: Surb .74Qa 153
N20 .19Fb 31
Oakleigh Cl. BR8: Swan .69Gd 140
N20 .20Hb 31
Oakleigh Ct. EN4: E Barn .16Gb 31
HA8: Edg .26Sa 47
N1 .3F 219
RH8: Oxt .1J 211
(not continuous)
UB1: S'hall .46Ba 85
Oakleigh Cres. N20 .19Gb 31
Oakleigh Dr. WD3: Crox G .16S 26
Oakleigh Gdns. BR6: Orp .77Uc 160
HA8: Edg .22Pa 47
N20 .18Eb 31
Oakleigh M. N20 .18Eb 31
OAKLEIGH PARK .18Eb 31
Oakleigh Pk. Av. BR7: Chst .67Qc 138
Oakleigh Pk. Nth. N20 .18Fb 31
Oakleigh Pk. Sth. N20 .17Gb 31
Oakleigh Ri. CM16: Epp .4Wc 23
Oakleigh Rd. HA5: Hat E .23Ba 45
UB10: Hil .38S 64
Oakleigh Rd. Nth. N20 .19Fb 31
Oakleigh Rd. Sth. N11 .20Jb 32
Oakleigh Way CR4: Mitc .67Kb 134
KT6: Surb .74Qa 153
Oakley Av. CR0: Bedd .77Pb 156
IG11: Bark .38Vc 75
W5 .45Qa 87
Oakley Cl. E4 .20Ec 34
E6 .44Nc 94
KT15: Add .77M 149
RM20: Grays .51Yd 120
TW7: Isle .53Fa 108
W7 .45Ga 86
Oakley Ct. CR4: Mitc .73Jb 156
IG10: Lough .12Qc 36
RH1: Redh .5A 208
(off St Anne's Ri.)
Oakley Cres. EC1 .2C 218 (40Rb 71)
SL1: Slou .5J 81
Oakley Dr. BR2: Brom .76Nc 160
RM3: Rom .22Qd 57
SE9 .60Tc 116
SE13 .58Fc 115
Oakley Gdns. N8 .29Pb 50
SM7: Bans .87Db 175
SW3 .51Gb 111

Oakley Grange HA1: Harr . . . 33Fa 66
OAKLEY GREEN . . . 4A 102
Oakley Grn. Rd. SL4: Oak G, Wind . . . 4A 102
(not continuous)
Oakley Ho. SE11 . . . 6K 229
SW1 . . . 5G 227 (49Hb 89)
W5 . . . 45Qa 87
Oakley Pk. DA5: Bexl . . . 59Yc 117
Oakley Pl. SE1 . . . 7K 231 (50Vb 91)
Oakley Rd. BR2: Brom . . . 76Nc 160
CR6: W'ham . . . 90Wb 177
HA1: Harr . . . 30Ga 46
N1 . . . 38Tb 71
SE25 . . . 71Xb 157
Oakley Sq. NW1 . . . 1C 216 (40Lb 70)
Oakley St. SW3 . . . 51Gb 111
Oakley Studios SW3 . . . 51Gb 111
(off Up. Cheyne Row)
Oakley Wlk. W6 . . . 51Za 110
Oakley Yd. E2 . . . 42Vb 91
Oak Lock M. W4 . . . 50Ua 88
Oak Lodge E11 . . . 30Jc 53
KT11: Cobh . . . 87Y 171
(off Leigh Cnr.)
SM1: Sutt . . . 77Eb 155
TN13: S'oaks . . . 96Jd 202
TW16: Sun . . . 66V 128
(off Forest Dr.)
W8 . . . 48Db 89
(off Chantry Sq.)
Oak Lodge Av. IG7: Chig . . . 22Tc 54
Oak Lodge Cl. HA7: Stan . . . 22La 46
KT12: Hers . . . 78Y 151
Oak Lodge Dr. BR4: W W'ck . . . 73Dc 158
Oak Lodge La. TN16: Westrm . . . 97Tc 200
Oaklodge Way NW7 . . . 22Va 48
Oakman Ho. SW19 . . . 60Za 110
Oakmead Av. BR2: Hayes . . . 72Jc 159
Oakmead Ct. HA7: Stan . . . 21La 46
Oakmeade HA5: Hat E . . . 23Ca 45
Oakmead Gdns. HA8: Edg . . . 21Ta 47
Oakmead Grn. KT18: Eps . . . 87Sa 173
Oakmead Pl. CR4: Mitc . . . 67Gb 133
Oakmead Rd. CR0: C'don . . . 72Mb 156
SW12 . . . 60Jb 112
Oakmede EN5: Barn . . . 14Za 30
OAKMERE . . . 4Eb 17
Oakmere Av. EN6: Pot B . . . 5Eb 17
Oakmere Cl. EN6: Pot B . . . 3Fb 17
Oakmere La. EN6: Pot B . . . 4Eb 17
Oakmere M. EN6: Pot B . . . 4Eb 17
Oakmere Rd. SE2 . . . 51Wc 117
Oakmont Pl. BR6: Orp . . . 74Tc 160
Oakmoor Way IG7: Chig . . . 22Uc 54
Oak Pk. KT14: W Byf . . . 85G 168
Oak Pk. Gdns. SW19 . . . 60Za 110
Oak Pk. M. N16 . . . 34Vb 71
Oak Path WD23: Bush . . . 16Da 27
(off Mortimer Cl.)
Oak Pavilion M. SE19 . . . 64Ub 135
Oak Pl. SW18 . . . 57Db 111
Oakridge AL2: Brick W . . . 1Ba 13
GU24: W End . . . 5D 166
Oakridge Av. WD7: R'lett . . . 6Ha 14
Oakridge Dr. N2 . . . 27Fb 49
Oakridge La. BR1: Brom . . . 64Fc 137
WD7: R'lett . . . 5Ha 14
WD25: A'ham, R'lett . . . 6Fa 14
Oakridge Pl. SL2: Farn C . . . 5G 60
Oakridge Rd. BR1: Brom . . . 63Fc 137
Oak Ri. IG9: Buck H . . . 20Mc 35
Oak Rd. BR6: Chels . . . 80Wc 161
CM16: Epp . . . 2Vc 23
CR3: Cat'm . . . 94Ub 197
DA8: Erith . . . 52Ed 118
(Mill Rd.)
DA8: Erith . . . 54Jd 118
(Moat La.)
DA9: Ghithe . . . 58Ud 120
DA12: Grav'nd . . . 2E 144
KT3: N Mald . . . 68Ta 131
KT11: Cobh . . . 87Z 171
KT22: Lea . . . 90Ja 172
RH2: Reig . . . 5K 207
RM3: Hrld W . . . 25Pd 57
RM17: Grays . . . 51Ee 121
TN16: Westrm . . . 97Tc 200
W5 . . . 45Ma 87
Oak Row SW16 . . . 68Lb 134
Oakroyd Av. EN6: Pot B . . . 5Bb 17
Oakroyd Cl. EN6: Pot B . . . 5Bb 17
Oaks, The BR2: Brom . . . 72Qc 160
BR8: Swan . . . 68Gd 140
DA2: Dart . . . 58Rd 119
EN2: Enf . . . 13Rb 33
EN9: Walt A . . . 7Lc 21
(in Woodbine Cl. Caravan Pk.)
HA4: Ruis . . . 31T 64
IG8: Wfd G . . . 24Gc 53
KT14: W Byf . . . 86J 169
KT18: Eps . . . 86Va 174
KT20: Tad . . . 95Ya 194
KT22: Fet . . . 95Ea 192
N12 . . . 21Db 49
NW6 . . . 38Za 68
(off Brondesbury Pk.)
NW10 . . . 38Xa 68
SE18 . . . 50Sc 94
SM4: Mord . . . 70Ab 132
TW13: Felt . . . 61Z 129
TW18: Staines . . . 63H 127
UB4: Hayes . . . 40S 64
WD6: Bore . . . 11Qa 29
WD19: Wat . . . 18Y 27
Oaks Av. KT4: Wor Pk . . . 76Xa 154
RM5: Col R . . . 26Ed 56
SE19 . . . 64Ub 135
TW13: Felt . . . 61Aa 129
Oaks Caravan Park, The
KT9: Chess . . . 76La 152
Oaks Cl. KT22: Lea . . . 93Ja 192
WD7: R'lett . . . 7Ha 14
Oaksend Cl. KT22: Oxs . . . 83Ea 172
Oaksford Av. SE26 . . . 62Xb 135
Oaks Gro. E4 . . . 19Gc 35
Oakshade Rd. BR1: Brom . . . 63Fc 137
KT22: Oxs . . . 86Ea 172
Oakshaw RH8: Oxt . . . 99Fc 199
Oakshaw Rd. SW18 . . . 59Db 111
Oakshott Ct. NW1 . . . 2D 216 (40Mb 70)
(not continuous)
Oakside UB9: Den . . . 36K 63
Oakside Ct. IG6: Ilf . . . 26Tc 54
Oakside Stadium . . . 28Tc 54
Oaks La. CR0: C'don . . . 76Xb 157
IG2: Ilf . . . 29Uc 54
Oak Sq. SW9 . . . 54Pb 112
TN13: S'oaks . . . 98Ld 203
Oaks Rd. CR0: C'don . . . 78Xb 157
CR8: Kenley . . . 86Rb 177
GU21: Wok . . . 89A 168
RH2: Reig . . . 5M 207
TW19: Stanw . . . 58M 105
Oaks Shop. Centre, The W3 . . . 46Sa 87
Oaks Sports Cen. . . . 83Gb 175
Oaks Sports Cen. Golf Course . . . 83Hb 175
Oaks Sq., The KT19: Eps . . . 85Ta 173
(off High St.)
Oaks Track SM5: Cars . . . 83Hb 175
SM6: Wall . . . 83Hb 175
Oak St. E14 . . . 47Ec 92
(off Stewart St.)
HP3: Hem H . . . 6P 3
RM7: Rom . . . 29Ed 56
Oaks Way CR8: Kenley . . . 86Sb 177
GU23: Rip . . . 96J 189
KT6: Surb . . . 74Ma 153
KT18: Tatt C . . . 91Xa 194
SM5: Cars . . . 80Hb 155
Oakthorpe Ct. N13 . . . 22Sb 51
Oakthorpe Est. N13 . . . 22Sb 51
Oakthorpe Rd. N13 . . . 22Qb 50
Oak Tree Av. DA9: Bluew . . . 59Vd 120
Oaktree Av. N13 . . . 20Rb 33
Oak Tree Cl. GU4: Jac W . . . 10P 187
GU21: Knap . . . 10F 166
GU25: Vir W . . . 2P 147
HA7: Stan . . . 24La 46
IG10: Lough . . . 11Sc 36
TN13: S'oaks . . . 98Ld 203
W5 . . . 44La 86
WD5: Ab L . . . 4T 12
Oaktree Cl. CM13: B'wood . . . 20Be 41
Oak Tree Ct. UB5: N'olt . . . 40Y 65
W3 . . . 45Ra 87
Oaktree Ct. KT15: Add . . . 78K 149
WD6: E'tree . . . 16Na 29
Oak Tree Dell NW9 . . . 29Sa 47
Oak Tree Dr. N20 . . . 18Db 31
SL3: L'ly . . . 50D 82
TW20: Eng G . . . 4N 125
Oak Tree Gdns. BR1: Brom . . . 64Kc 137
Oaktree Gro. IG1: Ilf . . . 36Tc 74
Oak Tree Ho. W9 . . . 42Cb 89
(off Shirland Rd.)
Oak Tree M. NW2 . . . 37Wa 68
Oak Tree Pl. KT10: Esh . . . 75Da 151
Oak Tree Rd. GU21: Knap . . . 10F 166
NW8 . . . 4C 214 (41Gb 89)
Oaktree Wlk. CR3: Cat'm . . . 94Ub 197
Oak Vw. HP3: Bov . . . 10D 2
WD18: Wat . . . 13U 26
Oakview Apartments SM1: Sutt . . . 77Fb 155
Oakview Cl. EN7: Chesh . . . 1Xb 19
WD19: Wat . . . 16Y 27
Oak Vw. Gdns. SL3: L'ly . . . 49B 82
Oakview Gdns. N2 . . . 28Fb 49
Oakview Gro. CR0: C'don . . . 74Ac 158
Oakview Lodge NW11 . . . 31Bb 69
(off Beechcroft Av.)
Oakview Rd. SE6 . . . 64Dc 136
Oak Village NW5 . . . 35Jb 70
Oak Vs. NW11 . . . 30Bb 49
(off Hendon Pk. Row)
Oak Wlk. SM6: Wall . . . 74Jb 156
(off Helios Rd.)
Oak Way CR0: C'don . . . 72Zb 158
KT21: Asht . . . 88Qa 173
N14 . . . 17Kb 32
RH2: Reig . . . 7M 207
TW14: Felt . . . 60U 106
W3 . . . 46Ua 88
Oakway BR2: Brom . . . 68Fc 137
GU21: Wok . . . 1J 187
RM16: Grays . . . 46De 99
SW20 . . . 70Ya 132
Oakway Cl. DA5: Bexl . . . 58Ad 117
Oakway Pl. WD7: R'lett . . . 6Ja 14
Oakways SE9 . . . 58Rc 116
Oakwell Dr. EN6: N'thaw . . . 4Kb 18
OAKWOOD . . . 14Mb 32
Oakwood EN9: Walt A . . . 7Gc 21
KT18: Eps . . . 86Ua 174
(off Worple Rd.)
SM6: Wall . . . 81Kb 176
Oakwood Av. BR2: Brom . . . 69Kc 137
BR3: Beck . . . 68Ec 136
CR4: Mitc . . . 68Fb 133
CR8: Purl . . . 84Rb 177
KT19: Eps . . . 81Qa 173
N14 . . . 17Mb 32
UB1: S'hall . . . 45Ca 85
WD6: Bore . . . 14Ra 29
Oakwood Bus. Pk. NW10 . . . 42Ta 87
Oakwood Chase RM11: Horn . . . 30Pd 57
Oakwood Cl. BR7: Chst . . . 65Pc 138
DA1: Dart . . . 60Rd 119
IG8: Wfd G . . . 23Nc 54
KT24: E Hor . . . 99U 190
N14 . . . 16Lb 32
RH1: Redh . . . 6A 208
RH1: S Nut . . . 8F 208
RM3: Rom . . . 23Nd 57
SE13 . . . 58Fc 115
Oakwood Ct. BR8: Swan . . . 68Ed 140
(off Lawn Cl.)
E6 . . . 39Nc 74
GU24: Bisl . . . 8E 166
HA1: Harr . . . 30Fa 46
SL1: Slou . . . 4J 81
(off Mildenhall Rd.)
W14 . . . 48Bb 89
Oakwood Cres. N21 . . . 16Nb 32
UB6: G'frd . . . 37Ja 66
Oakwood Dr. AL4: St A . . . 1G 6
DA7: Bex . . . 56Ed 118
HA8: Edg . . . 23Sa 47
KT24: E Hor . . . 99U 190
SE19 . . . 65Tb 135
TN13: S'oaks . . . 95Kd 203
Oakwood Gdns. BR6: Farnb . . . 75Sc 160
GU21: Knap . . . 10E 166
IG3: Ilf . . . 33Vc 75
SM1: Sutt . . . 75Cb 155
Oakwood Grange KT13: Weyb . . . 76U 150
Oakwood Hall KT20: Kgswd . . . 95Eb 195
Oakwood Hill IG10: Lough . . . 16Pc 36
Oakwood Hill Ind. Est.
IG10: Lough . . . 15Sc 36
Oakwood Ho. E9 . . . 37Yb 72
(off Frampton Pk. Rd.)
Oakwood Ind. Est. DA11: Nflt . . . 57Ce 121
Oakwood La. W14 . . . 48Bb 89
Oakwood Lodge N14 . . . 16Lb 32
(off Avenue Rd.)
Oakwood Mans. W14 . . . 48Bb 89
(off Oakwood Ct.)
Oakwood Pde. N14: Cockf . . . 15Lb 32
Oakwood Pk. Rd. N14 . . . 17Mb 32
Oakwood Pl. CR0: C'don . . . 72Qb 156
Oakwood Ri. CR3: Cat'm . . . 97Ub 197
DA3: Lfield . . . 69Ae 143
Oakwood Rd. AL2: Brick W . . . 1Ba 13
BR6: Farnb . . . 75Sc 160
CR0: C'don . . . 72Qb 156
GU20: W'sham . . . 9C 146
GU21: Wok . . . 1J 187
GU25: Vir W . . . 1N 147
HA5: Pinn . . . 26X 45
NW11 . . . 28Cb 49
RH1: Mers . . . 1G 208
SW20 . . . 67Wa 132
Oakwood Vw. N14 . . . 16Mb 32
Oakworth Rd. W10 . . . 43Ya 88
Oarsman Pl. KT8: E Mos . . . 70Ga 130
Oasis, The BR1: Brom . . . 68Lc 137
Oasis Sports Cen. . . . 2F 223 (44Nb 90)
Oast Cotts. TN13: S'oaks . . . 94Jd 202
Oast Ct. E14 . . . 45Bc 92
(off Newell St.)
Oast Ho. Cl. TW19: Wray . . . 59A 104
Oasthouse Way BR5: St M Cry . . . 70Xc 139
Oast Lodge W4 . . . 52Ua 110
(off Corney Reach Way)
Oast Rd. RH8: Oxt . . . 3K 211
Oast Way DA3: Hartl . . . 72Ae 165
Oates Cl. BR2: Brom . . . 69Fc 137
Oates Rd. RM5: Col R . . . 22Dd 56
Oatfield Ho. N15 . . . 30Ub 51
(off Perry Ct.)
Oatfield Rd. BR6: Orp . . . 74Vc 161
KT20: Tad . . . 92Xa 194
Oatland Ri. E17 . . . 26Ac 52
Oatlands Av. KT13: Weyb . . . 78T 150
Oatlands Chase KT13: Weyb . . . 76U 150
Oatlands Cl. KT13: Weyb . . . 77S 150
Oatlands Dr. KT13: Weyb . . . 77S 150
SL1: Slou . . . 4H 81
Oatlands Grn. KT13: Weyb . . . 76T 150
Oatlands Mere KT13: Weyb . . . 76T 150
OATLANDS PARK . . . 76T 150
Oatlands Rd. EN3: Enf H . . . 11Yb 34
KT20: Tad . . . 91Ab 194
Oat La. EC2 . . . 2D 224 (44Sb 91)
Oatridge Gdns. HP2: Hem H . . . 1B 4
Oatwell Ho. SW3 . . . 7E 226
Oavendish Ct. HP3: Hem H . . . 7N 3
Oban Cl. E13 . . . 42Lc 93
Oban Ct. SL1: Slou . . . 7H 81
Oban Ho. E14 . . . 44Fc 93
(off Oban St.)
IG11: Bark . . . 40Tc 74
Oban Rd. E13 . . . 41Lc 93
SE25 . . . 70Tb 135
Oban St. E14 . . . 44Fc 93
Obelisk Ride TW20: Eng G . . . 5J 125
Oberon Cl. WD6: Bore . . . 11Sa 29
Oberon Ct. UB9: Den . . . 30H 43
Oberon Ho. N1 . . . 1H 219
Oberon Way TW17: Shep . . . 69N 127
Oberstein Rd. SW11 . . . 56Fb 111
Oborne Cl. SE24 . . . 57Rb 113
O'Brien Ho. E2 . . . 41Zb 92
(off Roman Rd.)
Observatory Gdns. W8 . . . 47Cb 89
Observatory M. E14 . . . 49Fc 93
Observatory Rd. SW7 . . . 4B 226 (48Fb 89)
SW14 . . . 56Sa 109
Observatory Shop. Cen., The
SL1: Slou . . . 7L 81
Observatory Wlk. RH1: Redh . . . 6P 207
Observer Dr. WD18: Wat . . . 14U 26
Occupation La. SE18 . . . 53Rc 116
W5 . . . 49Ma 87
Occupation Rd. KT19: Ewe . . . 80Ta 153
SE17 . . . 7D 230 (50Sb 91)
W13 . . . 47Ka 86
WD18: Wat . . . 15X 27
Ocean Est. E1 . . . 42Ac 92
(Ben Jonson Rd.)
E1 . . . 42Zb 92
(Ernest St.)
Oceanis Apartments E16 . . . 45Jc 93
(off Seagull La.)
Ocean Music Venue . . . 37Xb 71
(off Mare St.)
Ocean St. E1 . . . 43Zb 92
Ocean Wharf E14 . . . 47Bc 92
Ockbrook E1 . . . 43Yb 92
(off Hannibal Rd.)
Ockenden GU22: Wok . . . 91A 188
(off Constitution Hill)
Ockenden Cl. GU22: Wok . . . 90B 168
Ockenden Gdns. GU22: Wok . . . 90B 168
Ockenden Leisure Cen. . . . 43Wd 98
Ockenden Rd. GU22: Wok . . . 90B 168
Ockendon M. N1 . . . 37Tb 71
Ockendon Rd. N1 . . . 37Tb 71
RM14: N Ock, Upm . . . 36Sd 78
OCKHAM . . . 93R 190
Ockham Dr. BR5: St P . . . 66Wc 139
KT24: W Hor . . . 96T 190
UB6: G'frd . . . 38Ea 66
Ockham La. GU23: Ock . . . 93Q 190
KT11: Cobh . . . 92U 190
Ockham Rd. Nth. GU23: Ock . . . 92N 189
KT24: E Hor, W Hor . . . 92N 189
Ockham Rd. Sth. KT24: E Hor . . . 98U 190
Ockley Ct. DA14: Sidc . . . 62Uc 138
SM1: Sutt . . . 77Eb 155
Ockley Rd. CR0: C'don . . . 73Pb 156
SW16 . . . 63Nb 134
Ockleys Mead RH9: G'stone . . . 1A 210
Octagon, The SW10 . . . 52Db 111
(off Coleridge Gdns.)
Octagon Arc. EC2 . . . 1H 225 (43Ub 91)
Octagon Ct. SE16 . . . 46Zb 92
(off Rotherhithe St.)
Octagon Rd. KT12: W Vill . . . 81U 170
Octavia Cl. CR4: Mitc . . . 71Gb 155
Octavia Ct. WD24: Wat . . . 12Y 27
Octavia Ho. SW1 . . . 4D 228
W10 . . . 42Ab 88
Octavia M. W9 . . . 42Bb 89
Octavia Rd. TW7: Isle . . . 55Ga 108
Octavia St. SW11 . . . 53Gb 111
Octavia Way SE28 . . . 45Xc 95
TW18: Staines . . . 65J 127
Octavius St. SE8 . . . 52Cc 114
October Pl. NW4 . . . 27Za 48
Odard Rd. KT8: W Mole . . . 70Ca 129
Oddesey Rd. WD6: Bore . . . 11Ra 29
Oddmark Ho. IG11: Bark . . . 40Tc 74
Odelia Ct. E15 . . . 39Ec 72
(off Biggerstaff Rd.)
Odell Cl. IG11: Bark . . . 38Vc 75
Odell Wlk. SE13 . . . 55Ec 114
Odencroft Rd. SL2: Slou . . . 1E 80
Odeon, The IG11: Bark . . . 38Tc 74
Odeon Cinema
Barnet . . . 15Cb 31
Beckenham . . . 68Bc 136
Camden Town . . . 39Kb 70
(off Parkway)
Covent Garden . . . 3E 222
Edmonton . . . 17Zb 34
Eltham . . . 56Nc 116
(off Well Hall Rd.)
Epsom . . . 85Ua 174
Esher . . . 77Da 151
Gerrards Cross . . . 29A 42
Greenwich . . . 49Hc 93
Holloway . . . 34Nb 70
Kensington . . . 48Cb 89
Kingston upon Thames . . . 68Na 131
(in The Rotunda Cen.)
Leicester Square . . . 5E 222
Marble Arch . . . 3G 221
Muswell Hill . . . 28Kb 50
Panton Street . . . 5E 222
Putney . . . 55Ab 110
Richmond, Hill Street . . . 57Ma 109
Richmond, Red Lion Street
. . . 57Ma 109
South Woodford . . . 26Jc 53
Streatham . . . 62Nb 134
Surrey Quays . . . 48Zb 92
Swiss Cottage . . . 38Fb 69
Tottenham Court Road . . . 1D 222
Uxbridge . . . 39M 63
West End . . . 5E 222
West Thurrock . . . 49Vd 98
Whiteleys . . . 44Db 89
Wimbledon . . . 65Bb 133
Odeon Ct. E16 . . . 43Jc 93
NW10 . . . 39Ua 68
(off St Albans Rd.)
Odeon Pde. SE9 . . . 56Nc 116
(off Well Hall Rd.)
UB6: G'frd . . . 37Ka 66
(off Allendale Rd.)
W3 . . . 47Qa 87
(off Allendale Rd.)
Odessa Rd. E7 . . . 34Hc 73
NW10 . . . 40Wa 68
Odessa St. SE16 . . . 47Bc 92
Odessa Wharf SE16 . . . 48Bc 92
(off Odessa St.)
Odette Ct. WD6: Bore . . . 14Qa 29
(off Whitehall Cl.)
Odette Duval Ho. E1 . . . 43Yb 92
(off Stepney Way)
Odger St. SW11 . . . 54Hb 111
Odhams Trad. Est. WD24: Wat . . . 9Y 13
Odhams Wlk. WC2 . . . 3F 223 (44Nb 90)
Odiam Hall AL9: N Mym . . . 10F 8
Odin Ho. SE5 . . . 54Sb 113
O'Donaghue Ho's. SS17: Stan H . . . 1N 101
O'Donnell Ct. WC1 . . . 5G 217 (42Nb 90)
Odontological Museum, The . . . 2J 223
(within Royal College of Surgeons)
O'Driscoll Ho. W12 . . . 44Xa 88
Odyssey Bus. Pk. HA4: Ruis . . . 36X 65
Offa Rd. AL3: St A . . . 2A 6
Offa's Mead E9 . . . 35Bc 72
Offenbach Ho. E2 . . . 40Zb 72
(off Mace St.)
Offenham Rd. SE9 . . . 63Pc 138
Offers Ct. KT1: King T . . . 69Pa 131
Offerton Ho. WD19: Wat . . . 20Y 27
Offerton Rd. SW4 . . . 55Lb 112
Offham Ho. SE17 . . . 6H 231
Offham Slope N12 . . . 22Bb 49
Office Pk., The KT22: Lea . . . 91Ha 192
Offley Pl. TW7: Isle . . . 54Fa 108
Offley Rd. SW9 . . . 52Qb 112
Offord Cl. N17 . . . 23Wb 51
Offord Rd. N1 . . . 38Pb 70
Offord St. N1 . . . 38Pb 70
Ogden Ho. TW13: Hanw . . . 62Aa 129
Ogilby St. SE18 . . . 49Pc 94
Ogilvie Ho. E1 . . . 44Zb 92
(off Stepney C'way.)
Oglander Rd. SE15 . . . 56Vb 113
Ogle St. W1 . . . 7B 216 (43Lb 90)
Oglethorpe Rd. RM10: Dag . . . 34Bd 75
O'Gorman Ho. SW10 . . . 52Eb 111
(off King's Rd.)
O'Grady Ho. E17 . . . 27Dc 52
Ohio Bldg. SE10 . . . 53Dc 114
(off Deal's Gateway)
Ohio Cotts. HA5: Pinn . . . 26Y 45
Ohio Rd. E13 . . . 42Hc 93
Oil Mill La. W6 . . . 50Wa 88
Okeburn Rd. SW17 . . . 64Jb 134
Okehampton Cl. N12 . . . 22Fb 49
Okehampton Cres. DA16: Well . . . 53Xc 117
Okehampton Rd. NW10 . . . 39Ya 68
RM3: Rom . . . 23Ld 57
Okehampton Sq. RM3: Rom . . . 23Ld 57
Okemore Gdns. BR5: St M Cry . . . 70Yc 139
Olaf Ct. W8 . . . 47Cb 89
(off Kensington Chu. St.)
Olaf St. W11 . . . 45Za 88
Old Acre GU22: Pyr . . . 86J 169
Oldacre GU24: W End . . . 4D 166
Oldacre M. SW12 . . . 59Jb 112
Old Aeroworks, The NW8 . . . 6C 214
Old Amersham Rd. SL9: Ger X . . . 32D 62
Old Av. KT13: Weyb . . . 80S 150
KT14: W Byf . . . 85G 168
Old Av. Cl. KT14: W Byf . . . 85G 168
Old Bailey
Central Criminal Court
. . . 2C 224 (44Rb 91)
Old Bailey EC4 . . . 3C 224 (44Rb 91)
Old Bakery Ct. SL0: Iver . . . 44H 83
Old Barge Ho. All. SE1 . . . 5A 224
Old Barn Cl. SM2: Cheam . . . 80Ab 154
TN15: Kems'g . . . 89Qd 183
Old Barn La. CR8: Kenley . . . 88Vb 177
WD3: Crox G . . . 15P 25
Old Barn M. WD3: Crox G . . . 15P 25
Old Barn Rd. KT18: Eps . . . 89Sa 173
Old Barn Way DA7: Bex . . . 55Fd 118
Old Barracks W8 . . . 47Db 89
Old Barrack Yd. SW1 . . . 2H 227 (47Jb 90)
(not continuous)
Old Barrowfield E15 . . . 39Gc 73
Old Beaconsfield Rd. SL2: Farn C . . . 7G 60
Old Bell Ct. HP2: Hem H . . . 1M 3
Old Bellgate Pl. E14 . . . 48Cc 92
Oldberry Rd. HA8: Edg . . . 23Ta 47
Old Bethnal Grn. Rd. E2 . . . 41Wb 91
OLD BEXLEY . . . 59Dd 118
Old Bexley Bus. Pk. DA5: Bexl . . . 59Dd 118
Old Bexley La. DA1: Dart . . . 60Hd 118
DA5: Bexl, Dart . . . 61Fd 140
Old Billingsgate Mkt. EC3 . . . 5H 225
Old Billingsgate Wlk.
EC3 . . . 5H 225 (45Ub 91)
Old Bond St. W1 . . . 5B 222 (45Lb 90)
Oldborough Rd. HA0: Wemb . . . 34La 66
OLD BRENTFORD . . . 52Ma 109
Old Brewer's Yd. WC2 . . . 3F 223 (44Nb 90)
Old Brewery M. NW3 . . . 35Fb 69
Old Brickworks Ind. Est., The
RM3: Hrld W . . . 25Qd 57
Old Bridge Cl. UB5: N'olt . . . 40Ca 65
Old Bri. La. KT17: Eps . . . 84Va 174
Old Bridge St. KT1: Hamp W . . . 68Ma 131
Old Broad St. EC2 . . . 3G 225 (44Tb 91)
Old Bromley Rd. BR1: Brom . . . 64Fc 137
Old Brompton Rd. SW5 . . . 7A 226 (50Cb 89)
SW7 . . . 7A 226 (50Cb 89)
Old Buildings WC2 . . . 2K 223
Old Burlington St. W1 . . . 4B 222 (45Lb 90)
OLDBURY . . . 94Xd 204
Oldbury Cl. BR5: St M Cry . . . 70Zc 139
TN15: Igh . . . 94Xd 204
Oldbury Cotts. TN15: Igh . . . 93Xd 204
Oldbury Ct. E9 . . . 36Ac 72
(off Mabley St.)
Oldbury Hill . . . 93Wd 204
Oldbury Hill Camping &
Caravanning Club Site
TN15: Seal . . . 94Vd 204
Oldbury Hillfort . . . 94Wd 204
Oldbury Ho. W2 . . . 43Db 89
(off Harrow Rd.)
Oldbury La. TN15: Igh . . . 93Xd 204
Oldbury Pl. W1 . . . 6J 215 (43Jb 90)
Oldbury Rd. EN1: Enf . . . 12Wb 33
KT16: Chert . . . 73G 148
Oldbury Vs. TN15: Igh . . . 94Xd 204
Old Canal M. SE15 . . . 7K 231
Old Carriageway, The TN13: Chip . . . 94Ed 202
Old Castle St. E1 . . . 1K 225 (44Vb 91)
Old Cavendish St. W1 . . . 2K 221 (44Kb 90)
Old Change Ct. EC4 . . . 3D 224
Old Chapel Pl. SW9 . . . 54Qb 112
Old Chapel Rd. BR8: Crock . . . 73Ed 162
Old Charlton Rd. TW17: Shep . . . 71S 150
Old Chelsea M. SW3 . . . 51Gb 111
Old Chertsey Rd. GU24: Chob . . . 2M 167
Old Chestnut Av. KT10: Esh . . . 79Ca 151
Old Chiswick Yd. W4 . . . 51Ua 110
(off Pumping Sta. Rd.)
Old Chorleywood Rd. WD3: Rick . . . 16M 25
Old Church Cl. BR6: Orp . . . 74Xc 161
Old Church Ct. N11 . . . 22Kb 50
Oldchurch Gdns. RM7: Rush G . . . 31Fd 76
Old Church La. HA7: Stan . . . 22Ka 46
NW9 . . . 33Ta 67
UB6: G'frd . . . 41Ja 86
Old Church Path KT10: Esh . . . 77Ea 152
Oldchurch Ri. RM7: Rush G . . . 31Gd 76
Old Church Rd. E1 . . . 44Zb 92
E4 . . . 21Cc 52
Oldchurch Rd. RM7: Rush G . . . 31Fd 76
Old Church St. SW3 . . . 7C 226 (50Fb 89)
Old Claygate La. KT10: Clay . . . 79Ja 152
Old Clem Sq. SE18 . . . 51Qc 116
(off Woolwich Comn.)
Old Coach Rd. KT16: Chert . . . 71F 148
TN15: Wro . . . 86Ae 185
Old Coal Yd. SE28 . . . 49Tc 94
Old Coalyard, The TW20: Egh . . . 65B 126
Old College Ct. DA17: Belv . . . 50Dd 96
OLD COMMON . . . 85X 171
Old Common (Local Nature Reserve)
. . . 84X 171
Old Common Rd. KT11: Cobh . . . 84X 171
WD3: Chor . . . 14F 24
Old Compton St. W1 . . . 4D 222 (45Mb 90)
Old Cople La. SE19 . . . 64Vb 135
Old Cote Dr. TW5: Hest . . . 51Ca 107
Old Cotts. AL2: Lon C . . . 1Na 15
TN15: Igh . . . 94Xd 204
OLD COULSDON . . . 91Qb 196
Old Ct. KT21: Asht . . . 91Na 193
Old Court Ho. W8 . . . 47Db 89
(off Old Court Pl.)
Old Court Pl. W8 . . . 47Db 89
Old Courtyard, The BR1: Brom . . . 67Kc 137
Old Crabtree La. HP2: Hem H . . . 3N 3
Old Crown SL1: Slou . . . 7K 81
Old Crown La. CM14: Kel H . . . 12Td 40
Old Curiosity Shop . . . 2J 223
Old Dairy M. NW5 . . . 37Kb 70
SW12 . . . 60Jb 112
Old Dairy Pl. N15 . . . 30Ub 51
Old Dairy Sq. N21 . . . 17Qb 32
(off Wade Hill)
Old Dartford Rd. DA4: Farni . . . 72Pd 163
Old Dean HP3: Bov . . . 10C 2
Old Deer Pk. . . . 54La 108
Old Deer Pk. Gdns. TW9: Rich . . . 55Na 109
Old Devonshire Rd. SW12 . . . 59Kb 112
Old Dock Cl. TW9: Kew . . . 51Qa 109
Old Dover Rd. SE3 . . . 52Jc 115
Old Downs DA3: Hartl . . . 71Ae 165
Oldegate Ho. E6 . . . 38Mc 73
Olden La. CR8: Purl . . . 84Qb 176
Old Esher Cl. KT12: Hers . . . 78Z 151
Old Esher Rd. KT12: Hers . . . 78Z 151
Old Farleigh Rd. CR2: Sels . . . 82Yb 178
CR6: W'ham . . . 82Yb 178
Old Farm Av. DA15: Sidc . . . 60Tc 116
N14 . . . 17Lb 32
Old Farm Cl. SW17 . . . 61Gb 133
TW4: Houn . . . 56Ba 107
Old Farm Gdns. BR8: Swan . . . 69Hd 140
Old Farmhouse Dr. KT22: Oxs . . . 87Fa 172
Old Farm Pas. TW12: Hamp . . . 67Ea 130
Old Farm Rd. N2 . . . 25Fb 49
TW12: Hamp . . . 65Ba 129
UB7: W Dray . . . 47M 83
Old Farm Rd. E. DA15: Sidc . . . 61Wc 139
Old Farm Rd. W. DA15: Sidc . . . 61Vc 139

Old Ferry Dr. TW19: Wray 8N 103
Old Field Cl. HP6: L Chal 11A 24
Oldfield Cl. BR1: Brom 70Pc 138
HA7: Stan 22Ja 46
UB6: G'frd 36Ga 66
Oldfield Ct. AL1: St A 3C 6
KT5: Surb 70Pa 131
(off Cranes Pk. Cres.)
Oldfield Farm Gdns. UB6: G'frd 39Fa 66
Oldfield Gdns. KT21: Asht 91Ma 193
Oldfield Gro. SE16 49Zb 92
Oldfield Ho. W4 50Ua 88
(off Devonshire Rd.)
Oldfield La. Nth. UB6: G'frd 40Fa 66
Oldfield La. Sth. UB6: G'frd 42Ea 86
Oldfield M. N6 31Lb 70
Oldfield Rd. AL2: Lon C 7H 7
BR1: Brom 70Pc 138
DA7: Bex 54Ad 117
HP1: Hem H 3G 2
N16 34Ub 71
NW10 38Va 68
SW19 65Ab 132
TW12: Hamp 67Ba 129
W3 47Va 88
Oldfields CM14: W'ley 21Yd 58
Oldfields Cir. UB5: N'olt 37Ea 66
Oldfields Rd. SM1: Sutt 76Bb 155
Oldfields Trad. Est.
SM1: Sutt 76Cb 155
Oldfield Wood GU22: Wok 89D 168
Old Fire Station, The SE18 52Rc 116
Old Fishery La. HP1: Hem H 5H 3
(not continuous)
Old Fish St. Hill EC4 4D 224
Old Fives Ct. SL1: Burn 1A 80
Old Fleet La. EC4 2B 224 (44Rb 91)
Old Fold Cl. EN5: Barn 11Bb 31
Old Fold La. EN5: Barn 11Bb 31
Old Fold Manor Golf Course 11Ab 30
Old Fold Vw. EN5: Barn 13Ya 30
OLD FORD 39Bc 72
OLD FORD 39Cc 72
Old Ford Rd. E2 41Yb 92
E3 40Ac 72
Old Ford Trading Cen. E3 39Cc 72
(off Maverton Rd.)
Old Forge Cl. HA7: Stan 21Ja 46
WD25: Wat 5W 12
Old Forge Ct. EN9: Walt A 6Jc 21
(off Lamplighters Cl.)
Old Forge Cres. TW17: Shep 72R 150
Old Forge M. W12 47Xa 88
Old Forge Rd. EN1: Enf 10Vb 19
N19 33Mb 70
Old Forge Way DA14: Sidc 63Xc 139
Old Fox Cl. CR3: Cat'm 93Rb 197
Old Gannon Cl. HA6: Nwood 21S 44
Old Garden, The TN13: Chip 95Ed 202
Old Garden Ct. AL3: St A 2A 6
Old Gloucester St. WC1 7G 217 (43Nb 90)
Old Goods Yard, The W2 1A 220 (43Eb 89)
Old Gorhambury House (remains of) 1H 5
Old Hall Cl. HA5: Pinn 25Aa 45
Old Hall Dr. HA5: Pinn 25Aa 45
Oldham Ter. W3 46Sa 87
(not continuous)
Old Harrow La. TN16: Westrm 91Sc 200
Old Hatch Mnr. HA4: Ruis 31V 64
Old Hat Factory, The AL1: St A 3C 6
(off Inkerman Rd.)
Old Heath Rd. KT13: Weyb 79Q 150
Old Hill BR6: Downe 79Tc 160
BR7: Chst 67Qc 138
GU22: Wok 2P 187
Old Hill Est. GU22: Wok 2P 187
Oldhill St. N16 32Wb 71
Old Homesdale Rd. BR2: Brom 70Lc 137
Old Hospital Cl. SW12 60Hb 111
Old House Cl. KT17: Ewe 82Va 174
SW19 64Ab 132
Old House Ct. HP2: Hem H 2P 3
SL3: Wex 3P 81
Old House Gdns. TW1: Twick 58La 108
Old House La. WD4: Bucks, Lang 7N 11
Oldhouse La.
GU20: W'sham 10A 146 & 1A 166
GU24: Bisl 6E 166
Old House Rd. HP2: Hem H 2P 3
Old Howlett's La. HA4: Ruis 30T 44
OLD ISLEWORTH 55Ka 108
Old Jamaica Bus. Est. SE16 48Vb 91
Old Jamaica Rd. SE16 48Wb 91
Old James St. SE15 55Xb 113
Old Jenkins Cl. SS17: Stan H 2K 101
Old Jewry EC2 3F 225 (44Tb 91)
Old Kenton La. NW9 29Ra 47
Old Kent Rd. SE1 5H 231 (49Ub 91)
SE15 49Ub 91
Old Kingston Rd. KT4: Wor Pk 75Sa 153
Old La. KT11: Cobh 89R 170
RH8: Oxt 1K 211
(not continuous)
TN15: Igh 95Xd 204
TN16: Tats 92Mc 199
Old La. Gdns. KT11: Cobh 94W 190
Old Laundry, The BR7: Chst 67Sc 138
Old Leys AL10: Hat 3C 8
Old Library Ct. HA4: Ruis 33W 64
Old Library Ho. E3 40Ac 72
(off Roman Rd.)
Old Lodge La. CR8: Kenley, Purl 89Rb 177
CR8: Purl 85Pb 176
Old Lodge Pl. TW1: Twick 58Ka 108
Old Lodge Way HA7: Stan 22Ja 46
Old London Rd. AL1: St A 3B 6
DA14: Sidc, Swan 66Cd 140
KT2: King T 68Na 131
KT18: Eps D 91Wa 194
(not continuous)
KT24: E Hor 98W 190
RH5: Mick 99La 192
TN14: Bad M, Hals 81Bd 181
TN14: Knock 87Ad 181
TN15: Wro 87Be 185
Old Lyonian Sports Club 29Ea 46
Old Macdonald's Farm
Educational & Leisure Pk. 18Pd 39
Old Maidstone Rd. DA14: Sidc 66Bd 139
OLD MALDEN 74Ua 154
Old Malden La. KT4: Wor Pk 75Ta 153
Old Malt Way GU21: Wok 9P 167
Old Manor Ct. NW8 1A 214 (40Eb 69)
Old Manor Dr. DA12: Grav'nd 10E 122
TW7: Isle 58Ea 108
Old Manor Ho. M. TW17: Shep 69Q 128
Old Manor Rd. UB2: S'hall 49Z 85
Old Manor Way BR7: Chst 64Pc 138
DA7: Bex 54Fd 118
Old Manor Yd. SW5 49Db 89
Old Market Ct. SM1: Sutt 77Db 155
Old Market Sq. E2 3K 219 (41Vb 91)
Old Marylebone Rd.
NW1 1E 220 (43Gb 89)
Old Mead SL9: Chal P 23A 42
Oldmead Ho. RM10: Dag 37Dd 76
Old Mews HA1: Harr 29Ga 46
Old Mile Ho. Ct. AL1: St A 5E 6
Old Mill Cl. DA4: Eyns 74Nd 163
UB8: Cowl 43K 83
Old Mill Ct. E18 27Lc 53
Old Mill Gdns. HP4: Berk 1A 2
Old Mill La. RH1: Mers 100Kb 196
UB8: Cowl 44K 83
Old Mill Pde. RM1: Rom 29Hd 56
Old Mill Pl. RM7: Rom 30Fd 56
TW19: Wray 58D 104
Old Mill Rd. SE18 51Tc 116
UB9: Den 34J 63
WD4: Hunt C 5S 12
Old Mitre Ct. EC4 3A 224 (44Qb 90)
Old Montague St. E1 43Wb 91
Old Nichol St. E2 5K 219 (42Vb 91)
Old North St. WC1 7H 217
Old Nurseries La. KT11: Cobh 85X 171
Old Nursery Ct. E2 2K 219
SL2: Hedg 3G 60
Old Nursery Pl. TW15: Ashf 64R 128
Old Oak AL1: St A 5C 6
Old Oak Av. CR5: Chip 91Gb 195
Old Oak Cl. KT9: Chess 77Pa 153
KT11: Cobh 85X 171
OLD OAK COMMON 43Ua 88
Old Oak Comn. La. NW10 43Ua 88
W3 43Ua 88
Old Oak Gdns. GU21: Wok 7P 167
Old Oak La. NW10 41Ua 88
Old Oak Rd. W3 45Va 88
Old Oaks EN9: Walt A 4Gc 21
Old Operating Theatre Mus. & Herb Garret
7G 225
Old Orchard AL2: Park 8A 6
KT14: Byfl 84P 169
SL0: Iver 44H 83
(off Bangors Rd. Sth.)
TW16: Sun 68Y 129
Old Orchard, The NW3 35Hb 69
SL0: Iver 44H 83
Old Orchard Cl. EN4: Had W 10Fb 17
UB8: Hil 44Q 84
Old Otford Rd. TN14: Otf, S'oaks 89Kd 183
(not continuous)
OLD OXTED 2H 211
Old Palace La. TW9: Rich 57La 108
Old Palace Rd. CR0: C'don 76Rb 157
KT13: Weyb 76R 150
Old Palace Ter. TW9: Rich 57Ma 109
Old Palace Yd. SW1 3F 229 (48Nb 90)
TW9: Rich 57La 108
Old Paradise St. SE11 5H 229 (49Pb 90)
Old Park Av. EN2: Enf 15Sb 33
SW12 58Jb 112
Old Parkbury La. AL2: Col S 1Ha 14
Old Park Gro. EN2: Enf 14Sb 33
Old Park La. W1 7J 221 (46Kb 90)
Old Park M. TW5: Hest 52Ba 107
Old Park Ride EN7: Walt C 3Rb 19
Old Park Ridings N21 16Rb 33
Old Park Rd. EN2: Enf 13Rb 33
N13 21Pb 50
SE2 50Wc 95
Old Park Rd. Sth. EN2: Enf 14Rb 33
Old Park Vw. EN2: Enf 13Qb 32
Old Parsonage Yd., The
DA4: Hort K 69Sd 142
Old Parvis Rd. KT14: W Byf 84L 169
Old Pearson St. SE10 52Dc 114
Old Perry St. BR7: Chst 65Uc 138
DA11: Nflt 1A 144
Old Polhill TN14: Hals, Otf 86Ed 182
Old Police House, The 46Hb 89
Old Post Office La. SE3 55Kc 115
Old Post Office Wlk. KT6: Surb 72Ma 153
(off Victoria Rd.)
Old Pottery Cl. RH2: Reig 8K 207
Old Pound Cl. TW7: Isle 53Ja 108
Old Priory UB9: Hare 31R 64
Old Priory Pk. AL1: St A 3C 6
(off Old London Rd.)
Old Pye St. SW1 3D 228 (48Mb 90)
Old Pye St. Est. SW1 4D 228
Old Quebec St. W1 3G 221 (44Hb 89)
(not continuous)
Old Queen St. SW1 2E 228 (47Mb 90)
Old Rectory, The KT23: Bookh 99Ba 191
Old Rectory Cl. KT20: Walt H 96Wa 194
Old Rectory Dr. AL10: Hat 1D 8
Old Rectory Gdns. HA8: Edg 23Qa 47
Old Rectory La. KT24: E Hor 98U 190
UB9: Den 31G 62
Old Redding HA3: Hrw W 22Da 45
Old Red Lion Theatre 2A 218
Old Redstone Dr. RH1: Redh 7A 208
Old Reigate Rd. RH3: Bet 6A 206
Oldridge Rd. SW12 59Jb 112
Old Rd. CM14: Nave, N'side 14Nd 39
DA1: Cray 57Fd 118
EN3: Enf H 11Yb 34
KT15: Add 80H 149
RH3: Bkld 6A 206
RM4: Nave 12Md 39
SE13 56Gc 115
Old Rd. E. DA12: Grav'nd 10D 122
Old Rd. W. DA11: Grav'nd 10B 122
Old Rope Wlk. TW16: Sun 69X 129
Old Royal Free Pl. N1 39Qb 70
Old Royal Free Sq. N1 39Qb 70
Old Royal Naval College 50Fc 93
Old Ruislip Rd. UB5: N'olt 40Y 65
Old's App. WD18: Wat 18R 26
Old Saw Mill, The TN15: Plat 94Fe 205
Old School, The WC1 7J 217
Old School Cl. BR3: Beck 68Zb 136
SE10 48Gc 93
SW19 68Cb 133
Old School Cotts. HP5: Whel 8A 2
Old School Ct. BR8: Swan 68Gd 140
(off Bonney Way)
KT22: Lea 94Ka 192
N17 27Vb 51
TN13: S'oaks 94Ld 203
TW19: Wray 59A 104
Old School Cres. E7 37Jc 73
Old School Houses
TN15: God G 96Qd 203
Old School M. KT13: Weyb 77T 150
TW18: Staines 64F 126
Old School Pl. CR0: Wadd 77Qb 156
GU22: Wok 93A 188
Old School Rd. UB8: Hil 42P 83
Old Schools La. KT17: Ewe 81Va 174
Old School Sq. E14 44Cc 92
(off Pelling St.)
KT7: T Ditt 72Ha 152
Old School Ter. SM3: Cheam 80Za 154
Old School Wlk. TN13: S'oaks 97Kd 203
(off London Rd.)
Old School Yd. RH1: Nutf 5F 208
Old's Cl. WD18: Wat 18R 26
Old Seacoal La. EC4 3B 224 (44Rb 91)
Old Shire La. EN9: Walt A 7Jc 21
WD3: Chor 16C 24
Old Slade La. SL0: Rich P 48G 82
SL3: Coln 50H 83
Old Soar Manor 98De 205
Old Soar Rd. TN15: Plax 99De 205
Old Solesbridge La. WD3: Chor 13J 25
Old Sopwell Gdns. AL1: St A 4C 6
Old South Cl. HA5: Pinn 25Z 45
Old Sth. Lambeth Rd. SW8 52Nb 112
Old Speech Room Gallery 32Ga 66
Old Spitalfields Market 7K 219 (43Vb 91)
Old Square WC2 2K 223 (44Pb 90)
Old Stable M. N5 34Sb 71
Old Stables Ct. SE5 53Sb 113
(off Camberwell New Rd.)
Old Stable Yd., The BR8: Swan 67Ld 141
Old Station App. KT22: Lea 93Ja 192
Old Station Bus. Cen., The AL1: St A 4D 6
Old Station Gdns. TW11: Tedd 65Ja 130
(off Victoria Rd.)
Old Station Ho. SE17 7E 230 (50Sb 91)
Old Station Pas. TW9: Rich 56Ma 109
(off Little Green)
Old Station Rd. IG10: Lough 15Nc 36
UB3: Harl 48V 84
Old Station Way SW4 55Mb 112
(off Voltaire Rd.)
Old Station Yard, The E17 28Ec 52
Oldstead Rd. BR1: Brom 63Ec 136
Old Stede Cl. KT21: Asht 89Pa 173
Old Stockley Rd. UB7: W Dray 47R 84
OLD STREET 4F 219 (42Tb 91)
Old St. E13 40Kc 73
EC1 6D 218 (42Sb 91)
Old St., The KT22: Fet 95Fa 192
Old Studio Cl. CR0: C'don 73Tb 157
Old Sungate Cotts. RM5: Col R 25Bd 55
Old Sun Wharf E14 45Ac 92
(off Narrow St.)
Old Swan Wharf SW11 53Fb 111
Old Swan Yd. SM5: Cars 77Hb 155
Old Terry's Lodge Rd.
TN15: Kems'g 88Vd 184
Old Theatre Ct. SE1 6E 224
Old Tilburstow Rd.
RH9: S God 6A 210
Old Town CR0: C'don 76Rb 157
SW4 55Lb 112
Old Town Hall Arts Centre, The 1L 3
Old Tramyard SE18 49Uc 94
Old Trowley WD5: Ab L 3V 12
Old Twelve Cl. W7 42Ga 86
Old Tye Av. TN16: Big H 88Nc 180
Old Uxbridge Rd.
WD3: Map C, W Hyd 22G 42
Old Vic Theatre, The 1A 230
Old Vic Tunnels, The 2J 229
Old Walk, The TN14: Otf 89Ld 183
Old Watford Rd. AL2: Brick W 2Aa 13
Old Watling St. DA11: Grav'nd 4C 144
Oldway La. SL1: Slou 5B 80
(not continuous)
Old Westhall Cl. CR6: W'ham 91Yb 198
Old Wharf Way KT13: Weyb 77P 149
OLD WINDSOR 8L 103
Old Windsor Lock SL4: Old Win 7N 103
OLD WOKING 93D 188
Old Woking Rd.
GU22: Wok, Pyr 91D 188
KT14: W Byf 85H 169
Old Woolwich Rd. SE10 51Fc 115
Old Works, The AL1: St A 3C 6
(off Black Cut)
Old Yard, The RH1: Blet 5J 209
TN16: Bras 96Yc 201
Old Yews, The DA3: Lfield 69De 143
Old York Rd. SW18 57Db 111
Oleander Cl. BR6: Farnb 78Tc 160
O'Leary Sq. E1 43Yb 92
Olga St. E3 40Ac 72
Olinda Rd. N16 30Vb 51
Oliphant St. W10 41Za 88
Olive Blythe Ho. W10 42Ab 88
(off Ladbroke Gro.)
Olive Cl. AL1: St A 3F 6
Olive Ct. E5 33Yb 72
(off Woodmill Rd.)
N1 1A 218
Olive Gro. N15 28Sb 51
Olive Haines Lodge SW15 57Bb 111
Olive Ho. EC1 5A 218
Oliver Av. SE25 69Ub 135
Oliver Bus. Pk. NW10 40Sa 67
Oliver Cl. AL2: Park 9B 6
HP3: Hem H 6N 3
KT15: Add 77J 149
RM20: W Thur 52Vd 120
W4 51Ra 109
Oliver Cl. Ind. Est.
RM20: W Thur 52Vd 120
Oliver Ct. SE18 49Sc 94
Oliver Cres. DA4: Farni 73Pd 163
Oliver Gdns. E6 43Nc 94
Oliver Goldsmith Est. SE15 53Wb 113
Oliver Gro. SE25 70Vb 135
Oliver Ho. SE14 52Bc 114
(off New Cross Rd.)
SE16 47Wb 91
(off George Row)
SW8 52Nb 112
(off Wyvil Rd.)
Oliver M. SE15 54Wb 113
Olive Rd. DA1: Dart 60Md 119
E13 41Lc 93
NW2 35Xa 68
SW19 66Eb 133
W5 48Ma 87
Oliver Ri. HP3: Hem H 6N 3
Oliver Rd. BR8: Swan 69Fd 140
CM15: Shenf 15Ce 41
E10 33Dc 72
E17 29Ec 52
HP3: Hem H 6N 3
KT3: N Mald 68Sa 131
NW10 40Sa 67
RM13: Rain 39Hd 76
RM20: W Thur 53Vd 120
SM1: Sutt 77Fb 155
Olivers Mill DA3: New A 75Ae 165
Olivers Wharf E1 46Xb 91
(off Wapping High St.)
Olivers Yd. EC1 5G 219 (42Tb 91)
Olive St. RM7: Rom 29Fd 56
Olive Tree Ho. SE15 51Yb 114
(off Sharratt St.)
Olivette St. SW15 55Za 110
Olive Waite Ho. NW6 38Cb 69
Olivia Ct. EN2: Enf 11Sb 33
(off Chase Side)
Olivia Dr. SL3: L'ly 50B 82
Olivia Gdns. UB9: Hare 25L 43
Olivia M. HA3: Hrw W 24Ga 46
Olivier Ct. UB9: Den 30H 43
(off Patrons Way E.)
Olivier Theatre 6K 223
(in National Theatre)
Ollard's Ct. IG10: Lough 15Mc 35
Ollard's Gro. IG10: Lough 14Mc 35
Olleberrie La. WD3: Sarr 3F 10
Ollerton Grn. E3 39Bc 72
Ollerton Rd. N11 22Mb 50
Olley Cl. SM6: Wall 80Nb 156
Ollgar Cl. W12 46Va 88
Olliffe St. E14 48Ec 92
Olmar St. SE1 51Wb 113
Olney Ho. NW8 5E 214
Olney Rd. SE17 51Rb 113
(not continuous)
Olron Cres. DA6: Bex 57Zc 117
Olven Rd. SE18 51Sc 116
Olveston Wlk. SM5: Cars 72Fb 155
Olwen M. HA5: Pinn 26Z 45
Olyffe Av. DA16: Well 53Wc 117
Olyffe Dr. BR3: Beck 67Ec 136
Olympia 48Ab 88
Olympia Ind. Est. N22 27Pb 50
Olympia M. W2 45Db 89
Olympian Ct. E3 40Cc 72
(off Wick La.)
E14 49Cc 92
(off Homer Dr.)
Olympia Way W14 48Ab 88
Olympic, The 70Kd 141
Olympic Ho. N16 35Vb 71
Olympic Pk. 38Dc 72
Olympic Pk. Avenue E20 37Dc 72
Olympic Sq. HA9: Wemb 34Qa 67
Olympic Way HA9: Wemb 34Qa 67
UB6: G'frd 39Ea 66
Olympus Gro. N22 25Qb 50
Olympus Sq. E5 34Wb 71
O'Mahoney Ct. SW17 62Eb 133
Oman Av. NW2 35Ya 68
O'Meara St. SE1 7E 224 (46Sb 91)
Omega Cl. E14 48Dc 92
Omega Ct. RM7: Rom 29Fd 56
WD18: Wat 15U 26
Omega Ho. SW10 52Eb 111
(off King's Rd.)
Omega Pl. N1 2G 217
Omega Rd. GU21: Wok 88C 168
Omega St. SE14 53Cc 114
Omega Way TW20: Thorpe 67E 126
Omega Works E3 38Cc 72
Ommaney Rd. SE14 53Zb 114
Omnibus Bldg. RH2: Reig 7K 207
Omnibus Ho. N22 26Qb 50
(off Lordship La.)
Omnibus Way E17 26Cc 52
Omnium Ct. WC1 7H 217
(off Princeton St.)
Ondine Rd. SE15 56Vb 113
Onedin Ct. E1 45Wb 91
(off Ensign St.)
Onega Ga. SE16 48Ac 92
One Hyde Pk. SW1 1F 227 (47Hb 89)
O'Neill Ho. NW8 2D 214
O'Neill Path SE18 51Qc 116
One New Change EC4 3E 224 (44Sb 91)
One Owen St. EC1 2B 218
One Pin La. SL2: Farn C 5G 60
One Pin Pl. SL2: Farn C 4H 61
One Tree Cl. SE23 58Yb 114
One Tree Hill Local Nature Reserve
58Yb 114
Ongar Cl. KT15: Add 79H 149
RM6: Chad H 29Yc 55
Ongar Hill KT15: Add 79J 149
Ongar Pde. KT15: Add 79J 149
Ongar Pl. CM14: B'wood 19Zd 41
KT15: Add 79J 149
Ongar Rd.
CM15: B'wood, Kel H, Pil H 13Td 40
CM15: Kel H, Pil H 13Td 40
KT15: Add 78J 149
RM4: Abr, Stap T 13Xc 37
SW6 51Cb 111
Ongar Way RM13: Rain 39Gd 76
Onra Rd. E17 31Cc 72
Onslow Av. SM2: Cheam 82Bb 175
TW10: Rich 57Na 109
Onslow Cl. E4 19Ec 34
GU22: Wok 89C 168
KT7: T Ditt 74Ga 152
W10 41Bb 89
Onslow Ct. SW10 7A 226
Onslow Cres. BR7: Chst 67Rc 138
GU22: Wok 89C 168
SW7 6C 226 (49Fb 89)
Onslow Dr. DA14: Sidc 61Zc 139
Onslow Gdns. CR2: Sande 84Wb 177
E18 27Kc 53
KT7: T Ditt 74Ga 152
N10 29Kb 50
N21 15Qb 32
SM6: Wall 79Lb 156
SW7 6B 226 (49Fb 89)
Onslow Ho. KT2: King T 67Pa 131
(off Acre Rd.)
Onslow M. KT16: Chert 72H 149
Onslow M. E. SW7 6B 226 (49Fb 89)
Onslow M. W. SW7 6B 226 (49Fb 89)
Onslow Pde. N14 18Kb 32
Onslow Rd. CR0: C'don 73Pb 156
KT3: N Mald 70Wa 132
KT12: Hers 77V 150
SL5: S'dale 3F 146
TW10: Rich 57Na 109
Onslow Sq. SW7 5C 226 (49Fb 89)
Onslow St. EC1 6A 218 (42Qb 90)
Onslow Way GU22: Pyr 87H 169
KT7: T Ditt 74Ga 152
Ontario St. SE1 4C 230 (48Rb 91)
Ontario Twr. E14 45Fc 93
Ontario Way E14 45Cc 92
(not continuous)
On the Hill WD19: Wat 19Aa 27
Onyx M. E15 37Hc 73
Opal Apartments W2 44Cb 89
(off Hereford Rd.)
Opal Cl. E16 44Mc 93
Opal Ct. E15 39Ec 72
SL3: Wex 2N 81
Opal M. IG1: Ilf 33Rc 74
NW6 39Bb 69
Opal St. SE11 6B 230 (50Rb 91)
Opeck's Cl. SL2: Stoke P 2M 81
SL2: Wex 2M 81
Open Air Stage 32Gb 69
Opendale Rd. SL1: Burn 3A 80
Openshaw Rd. SE2 49Xc 95
Openview SW18 60Eb 111
Opera Ct. N19 34Mb 70
(off Wedmore St.)
Ophelia Gdns. NW2 34Ab 68
Ophelia Ho. W6 50Za 88
(off Fulham Pal. Rd.)
Ophir Ter. SE15 53Wb 113
Opie Ho. NW8 1D 214
Opossum Way TW4: Houn 55Y 107
Oppenheim Rd. SE13 54Ec 114
Oppidan Apartments NW6 38Cb 69
(off Netherwood St.)
Oppidans Rd. NW3 38Hb 69
Optima Pk. DA1: Cray 54Jd 118
Opulens Pl. HA6: Nwood 24R 44
Opus Ct. WD6: Bore 13Qa 29
Oram Pl. HP3: Hem H 5M 3
Orange Ct. La. BR6: Downe 81Qc 180
Orange Gro. E11 34Gc 73
IG7: Chig 23Sc 54
Orange Hill Rd. HA8: Edg 24Sa 47
Orange Pl. SE16 48Yb 92
Orangery, The TW10: Ham 61La 130
Orangery Gallery, The 47Bb 89
Orangery La. SE9 57Pc 116
Orange St. WC2 5E 222 (45Mb 90)
Orange Tree Ct. SE5 52Ub 113
(off Havil St.)
Orange Tree Hill RM4: Have B 22Fd 56
Orange Tree Theatre 56Na 109
Orange Yd. W1 3E 222
Oransay Rd. N1 37Sb 71
Oratory La. SW3 7D 226 (50Fb 89)
Orbain Rd. SW6 52Ab 110
Orbel St. SW11 53Gb 111
Orbis Wharf SW11 55Fb 111
Orbital 25 Bus. Pk. WD18: Wat 17T 26
Orbital Bus. Cen. EN9: Walt A 6Ec 20
Orbital Centre, The IG8: Wfd G 26Mc 53
Orbital Cres. WD25: Wat 7V 12
Orbital One DA1: Dart 61Rd 141
Orbital One Ind. Est. DA1: Dart 61Qd 141
Orb St. SE17 6F 231 (49Tb 91)
Orchard, The BR8: Swan 68Fd 140
GU21: Wok 8M 167
GU22: Wok 94A 188
GU25: Vir W 71A 148
KT13: Weyb 77R 150
KT17: Ewe 80Va 154
(Meadow Wlk.)
KT17: Ewe 82Va 174
(Tayles Hill Dr.)
N14 15Kb 32
N20 18Db 31
N21 16Tb 33
NW11 29Cb 49
SE3 54Fc 115
SM7: Bans 87Cb 175
TN13: Dun G 93Gd 202
TW3: Houn 54Ea 108
W4 49Ta 87
W5 43Ma 87
(off Montpelier Rd.)
WD4: K Lan 1Q 12
WD17: Wat 9U 12
Orchard Av. CM13: B'wood 20Be 41
CR0: C'don 75Ac 158
CR4: Mitc 74Jb 156
DA1: Dart 59Kd 119
DA11: Grav'nd 4D 144
DA17: Belv 51Ad 117
KT3: N Mald 68Ua 132
KT7: T Ditt 74Ja 152
KT15: Wdhm 83H 169
N3 27Cb 49
N14 16Lb 32
N20 19Fb 31
RM13: Rain 42Ld 97
SL1: Slou 3B 80
SL4: Wind 3E 102
TW5: Hest 52Aa 107
TW14: Felt 57T 106
TW15: Ashf 65S 128
UB1: S'hall 46Ba 85
WD25: Wat 4X 13
Orchard Bungs. SL2: Farn C 8D 60
Orchard Bus. Cen. SE26 64Bc 136
Orchard Cl. AL1: St A 3D 6
DA3: Lfield 68De 143
DA7: Bex 53Ad 117
E4 21Cc 52
E11 28Kc 53
GU22: Wok 88D 168
GU24: W End 5B 166
HA0: Wemb 39Na 67
HA4: Ruis 31S 64
HA8: Edg 23Na 47
HP2: Hem H 1P 3
KT6: Surb 74Ka 152
KT12: Walt T 73X 151
KT19: Ewe 79Ra 153
KT21: Fet 94Fa 192
KT22: Lea 91Ha 192
KT24: E Hor 96V 190
N1 38Sb 71
NW2 34Wa 68
RM15: S Ock 42Yd 98
SE23 58Yb 114

Orchard Cl. SL1: Burn 2A **80**
SM7: Bans 86Db **175**
SW20 70Ya **132**
TN14: S'oaks 92Ld **203**
TW15: Ashf 65S **128**
TW20: Egh 64D **126**
UB5: N'olt 37Ea **66**
UB9: Den 37K **63**
W10 43Bb **89**
WD3: Chor 14F **24**
WD6: E'tree 14Pa **29**
WD7: R'lett 9Ga **14**
WD17: Wat 12V **26**
WD23: B Hea 18Fa **28**
Orchard Cotts. KT2: King T 67Pa **131**
UB3: Hayes 47U **84**
Orchard Ct. CR3: Cat'm 96Vb **197**
E10 32Dc **72**
EN5: New Bar 13Db **31**
EN6: Pot B 3Cb **17**
HA8: Edg 22Pa **47**
HP3: Bov 9C **2**
KT4: Wor Pk 74Wa **154**
KT12: Walt T 74V ***150***
(off Bridge St.)
N14 16Lb **32**
SM6: Wall 78Kb **156**
TW2: Twick 61Fa **130**
TW7: Isle 53Fa **108**
UB7: Lford 52L **105**
UB8: Uxb 40N ***63***
(off The Greenway)
W1 2H **221**
Orchard Cres. EN1: Enf 11Vb **33**
HA8: Edg 22Sa **47**
Orchard Dene *KT14: W Byf 85J* ***169***
(off Madeira Rd.)
Orchard Dr. AL2: Park 9P **5**
CM16: They B 8Uc **22**
DA13: Meop 10B **144**
GU21: Wok 87A **168**
HA8: Edg 22Pa **47**
KT21: Asht 92Ma **193**
RM17: Grays 47Ce **99**
SE3 54Fc **115**
TW17: Shep 69U **128**
UB8: Cowl 42M **83**
WD3: Chor 13E **24**
WD17: Wat 11V **26**
Orchard End CR3: Cat'm 94Ub **197**
KT13: Weyb 75U **150**
KT22: Fet 96Ea **192**
Orchard Gdns. EN9: Walt A 6Ec **20**
KT9: Chess 77Na **153**
KT18: Eps 86Sa **173**
KT24: Eff 100Aa **191**
SM1: Sutt 78Cb **155**
Orchard Ga. KT10: Esh 74Fa **152**
NW9 28Ua **48**
SL2: Farn C 6G **60**
UB6: G'frd 37Ka **66**
Orchard Grn. BR6: Orp 75Uc **160**
Orchard Gro. BR6: Orp 75Vc **161**
CR0: C'don 73Ac **158**
HA3: Kenton 29Pa **47**
HA8: Edg 25Qa **47**
SE20 66Wb **135**
Orchard Hill DA1: Cray 57Gd **118**
GU20: W'sham 10B **146**
SE13 54Dc **114**
SM5: Cars 78Hb **155**
Orchard Ho. DA8: Erith 53Hd **118**
SE5 53Sb ***113***
(off County Gro.)
SE16 48Yb **92**
SW6 52Bb ***111***
(off Varna Rd.)
W12 46Wa **88**
Orchard Ho. La. AL1: St A 3B **6**
Orchard La. CM15: Pil H 15Vd **40**
IG8: Wfd G 21Lc **53**
KT8: E Mos 72Fa **152**
RH9: G'stone 2P **209**
SW20 67Xa **132**
Orchard Lea DA13: Sflt 64Be **143**
Orchard Lea Cl. GU22: Pyr 87G **168**
Orchardleigh KT22: Lea 94Ka **192**
Orchardleigh Av. EN3: Enf H 12Yb **34**
Orchard Lodge *SL1: Slou 6C* ***80***
(off Streamside)
Orchard Mains GU22: Wok 1N **187**
Orchard Mead Ho. NW2 33Cb **69**
Orchardmede N21 16Tb **33**
Orchard M. GU21: Knap 10F **166**
N1 38Tb **71**
N6 31Kb **70**
SW17 62Eb **133**
Orchard on the Green, The
WD3: Crox G 15P **25**
Orchard Pde. EN6: Pot B 3Za **16**
Orchard Pl. BR2: Kes 81Lc **179**
BR5: St P 69Yc **139**
E5 36Xb **71**
E14 45Gc **93**
(not continuous)
EN8: Chesh 2Zb **20**
N17 24Vb **51**
TN14: Sund 96Ad **201**
UB8: Uxb 38M **63**
Orchard Ri. CR0: C'don 74Ac **158**
HA5: Eastc 27V **44**
KT2: King T 67Sa **131**
TW10: Rich 56Ra **109**
Orchard Ri. E. DA15: Sidc 57Vc **117**
Orchard Ri. W. DA15: Sidc 57Uc **116**
Orchard Rd. BR1: Brom 67Lc **137**
BR6: Farnb 78Rc **160**
BR6: Prat B 82Yc **181**
CR2: Sande 86Xb **177**
CR4: Mitc 74Jb **156**
DA10: Swans 57Ae **121**
DA11: Nflt 61Ee **143**
DA14: Sidc 63Uc **138**
DA16: Well 55Xc **117**
DA17: Belv 49Cd **96**
EN3: Pond E 15Yb **34**
EN5: Barn 14Bb **31**
KT1: King T 68Na **131**
KT9: Chess 77Na **153**
N6 31Kb **70**
RH2: Reig 6K **207**
RM7: Mawney 25Dd **56**
RM10: Dag 39Cd **76**
RM15: S Ock 42Yd **98**
SE3 54Gc **115**
SE18 49Tc **94**
Orchard Rd. SL4: Old Win 8M **103**
SM1: Sutt 78Cb **155**
TN13: Riv 94Gd **202**
TN14: Otf 88Hd **182**
TW1: Twick 57Ja **108**
TW4: Houn 57Ba **107**
TW8: Bford 51La **108**
TW9: Rich 55Qa **109**
TW12: Hamp 66Ba **129**
TW13: Felt 60W **106**
TW16: Sun 66X **129**
UB3: Hayes 45W **84**
Orchards, The CM16: Epp 4Wc **23**
Orchards Cl. KT14: W Byf 86J **169**
Orchardson Ho. NW8 5B **214**
Orchardson St. NW8 6B **214** (42Fb **89**)
Orchard Sq. W14 50Bb **89**
Orchards Res. Pk. SL3: L'ly 46B **82**
Orchards Shop. Cen. DA1: Dart 58Nd **119**
Orchard St. AL3: St A 3A **6**
DA1: Dart 58Nd **119**
E17 28Ac **52**
HP3: Hem H 5M **3**
W1 3H **221** (44Jb **90**)
Orchard Studios *W6 49Za* ***88***
(off Brook Grn.)
Orchard Ter. DA9: Ghithe 57Ud **120**
EN1: Enf 16Wb **33**
NW10 35Va **68**
Orchard Theatre, The 58Nd **119**
Orchard Vw. KT16: Chert 72J **149**
UB8: Cowl 42M **83**
Orchard Vs. DA14: Sidc 65Yc **139**
Orchardville SL1: Burn 2A **80**
Orchard Wlk. *KT2: King T 67Qa* ***131***
(off Gordon Rd.)
Orchard Way BR3: Beck 73Ac **158**
CR0: C'don 73Ac **158**
DA2: Wilm 62Md **141**
EN1: Enf 13Ub **33**
EN6: Pot B 10K **9**
GU3: Worp 6H **187**
GU23: Send 97E **188**
HP3: Bov 10C **2**
IG7: Chig 20Wc **37**
KT10: Esh 79Ea **152**
KT15: Add 78K **149**
KT20: Lwr K 98Bb **195**
RH2: Reig 9K **207**
RH8: Oxt 5L **211**
SL3: L'ly 46A **82**
SM1: Sutt 77Fb **155**
TN15: Kems'g 89Qd **183**
TW15: Ashf 61P **127**
WD3: Rick 17J **25**
Orchard Waye UB8: Uxb 40M **63**
Orchard Wharf *E14 45Gc* ***93***
(off Orchard Pl.)
Orchehill Av. SL9: Ger X 28A **42**
Orchehill Ri. SL9: Ger X 29A **42**
Orchestra Ct. HA8: Edg 24Ra **47**
Orchid Cl. E6 43Nc **94**
EN7: G Oak 2Sb **19**
KT9: Chess 80La **152**
RM4: Abr 13Xc **37**
SE13 57Fc **115**
UB1: S'hall 45Aa **85**
Orchid Ct. HA9: Wemb 33Na **67**
TW20: Egh 63D **126**
Orchid Dr. GU24: Bisl 7E **166**
Orchid Gdns. TW3: Houn 56Ba **107**
Orchid Grange N14 17Lb **32**
Orchid Mead SM7: Bans 86Db **175**
Orchid Rd. N14 17Lb **32**
Orchid St. W12 45Wa **88**
Orchis Gro. RM17: Grays 50Be **99**
Orchis Way RM3: Rom 23Pd **57**
Orde NW9 25Va **48**
Orde Hall St. WC1 6H **217** (42Pb **90**)
Ordell Ct. *E3 40Bc* ***72***
(off Ordell Rd.)
Ordell Rd. E3 40Bc **72**
Ordnance Cl. TW13: Felt 61W **128**
Ordnance Cres. SE10 47Gc **93**
Ordnance Hill NW8 1C **214** (39Fb **69**)
Ordnance M. NW8 1C **214** (40Fb **69**)
Ordnance Rd. DA12: Grav'nd 8E **122**
E16 43Hc **93**
EN3: Enf L, Enf W 9Zb **20**
SE18 51Qc **116**
Oregano Cl. UB7: Yiew 44N **83**
Oregano Dr. E14 44Fc **93**
Oregon Av. E12 35Pc **74**
Oregon Bldg. *SE10 53Dc* ***114***
(off Deal's Gateway)
Oregon Cl. KT3: N Mald 70Sa **131**
Oregon Sq. BR6: Orp 74Tc **160**
Orestan La. KT24: Eff 99X **191**
Orestes M. NW6 36Cb **69**
Oreston Rd. RM13: Rain 41Md **97**
Orewell Gdns. RH2: Reig 8K **207**
Orford Ct. *DA2: Dart 58Rd* ***119***
(off Osbourne Rd.)
HA7: Stan 23La **46**
SE27 61Rb **135**
Orford Gdns. TW1: Twick 61Ha **130**
Orford Rd. E17 29Cc **52**
E18 27Kc **53**
SE6 62Dc **136**
ORGAN CROSSROADS 80Wa **154**
Organ Hall Rd. WD6: Bore 11Na **29**
Organ La. E4 19Ec **34**
Oriana Ho. *E14 45Bc* ***92***
(off Victory Pl.)
Oriel Cl. CR4: Mitc 70Mb **134**
Oriel Ct. AL1: St A 1C **6**
CR0: C'don 74Tb **157**
NW3 35Eb **69**
Oriel Dr. SW13 51Ya **110**
Oriel Gdns. IG5: Ilf 27Pc **54**
Oriel Ho. *NW6 39Cb* ***69***
(off Priory Pk. Rd.)
RM7: Rom 30Fd **56**
Oriel M. E18 26Jc **53**
Oriel Pl. *NW3 35Eb* ***69***
(off Heath St.)
Oriel Rd. E9 37Zb **72**
Oriel Way UB5: N'olt 38Da **65**
Oriental City NW9 27Ta **47**
Oriental Cl. GU22: Wok 89B **168**
Oriental Rd. E16 46Mc **93**
GU22: Wok 89B **168**
SL5: S'hill 10B **124**
Oriental St. *E14 45Cc* ***92***
(off Pennyfields)
Orient Cl. AL1: St A 4C **6**
Orient Ho. *SW6 53Eb* ***111***
(off Station Ct.)
Orient Ind. Pk. E10 33Cc **72**
Orient St. SE11 5B **230** (49Rb **91**)
Orient Way E5 34Zb **72**
E10 32Ac **72**
Orient Wharf *E1 46Xb* ***91***
(off Wapping High St.)
Oriole Cl. WD5: Ab L 3W **12**
Oriole Way SE28 45Xc **95**
Orion *E14 49Cc* ***92***
(off Crews St.)
Orion Bus. Cen. SE14 50Zb **92**
Orion Cen., The CR0: Bedd 75Nb **156**
Orion Ho. *E1 42Xb* ***91***
(off Coventry Rd.)
Orion M. SM4: Mord 70Cb **133**
Orion Rd. N11 24Jb **50**
Orion Way HA6: Nwood 21V **44**
Orissa Rd. SE18 50Uc **94**
Orkney Ho. *N1 39Pb* ***70***
(off Bemerton Est.)
WD18: Wat 15V ***26***
(off Himalayan Way)
Orkney St. SW11 54Jb **112**
Orlando Gdns. KT19: Ewe 82Ta **173**
Orlando Rd. SW4 55Lb **112**
Orleans Cl. KT10: Esh 75Fa **152**
Orleans Ct. KT12: Walt T 75Y **151**
TW1: Twick 59Ka **108**
Orleans House Gallery 60Ka **108**
Orleans Pk. School Sports Cen. *59Ka* ***108***
(off Richmond Rd.)
Orleans Rd. SE19 65Tb **135**
TW1: Twick 59Ka **108**
Orlestone Gdns. BR6: Chels 78Ad **161**
Orleston M. N7 37Qb **70**
Orleston Rd. N7 37Qb **70**
Orley Ct. HA1: Harr 35Ha **66**
Orley Farm Rd. HA1: Harr 34Ga **66**
Orlick Rd. DA12: Grav'nd 10K **123**
Orlop St. SE10 50Gc **93**
Ormanton Rd. SE26 63Wb **135**
Orme Ct. W2 45Db **89**
Orme Ct. M. *W2 45Db* ***89***
(off Orme La.)
Orme Ho. E8 39Vb **71**
Orme La. W2 45Db **89**
Ormeley Rd. SW12 60Kb **112**
Orme Rd. KT1: King T 68Ra **131**
SM1: Sutt 79Db **155**
Ormerod Gdns. CR4: Mitc 68Jb **134**
Ormesby Cl. SE28 45Zc **95**
Ormesby Dr. EN6: Pot B 4Za **16**
Ormesby Way HA3: Kenton 30Pa **47**
Orme Sq. W2 45Db **89**
Ormiston Gro. W12 46Xa **88**
Ormiston Rd. SE10 50Jc **93**
Ormond Av. TW10: Rich 57Ma **109**
TW12: Hamp 67Da **129**
Ormond Cl. RM3: Hrld W 26Md **57**
WC1 7G **217** (43Nb **90**)
Ormond Cres. TW12: Hamp 67Da **129**
Ormond Dr. TW12: Hamp 66Da **129**
Ormonde Av. BR6: Farnb 75Sc **160**
KT19: Ewe 82Ta **173**
Ormonde Ct. NW8 1F **215**
RM11: Horn 31Hd ***76***
(off Clydesdale Rd.)
SW15 56Ya **110**
Ormonde Ga. SW3 50Hb **89**
(not continuous)
Ormonde Mans. WC1 7G **217**
Ormonde Pl. KT13: Weyb 79T **150**
SW1 6J **227** (49Jb **90**)
Ormonde Ri. IG9: Buck H 18Lc **35**
Ormonde Rd. GU21: Wok 8N **167**
HA6: Nwood 21T **44**
SW14 55Sa **109**
Ormonde Ter. NW8 1F **215** (39Hb **69**)
Ormond Ho. N16 33Tb **71**
Ormond M. WC1 6G **217** (42Nb **90**)
Ormond Rd. N19 32Nb **70**
TW10: Rich 57Ma **109**
Ormond Yd. SW1 6C **222** (46Lb **90**)
Ormrod Ct. *W11 44Ab* ***88***
(off Westbourne Pk. Rd.)
Ormsby SM2: Sutt 80Db **155**
Ormsby Gdns. UB6: G'frd 40Ea **66**
Ormsby Lodge W4 48Ua **88**
Ormsby Pl. N16 34Vb **71**
Ormsby Point *SE18 49Rc* ***94***
(off Vincent Rd.)
Ormsby St. E2 1K **219** (40Vb **71**)
Ormside St. SE15 51Yb **114**
Ormside Way RH1: Redh 2B **208**
Ormskirk Rd. WD19: Wat 21Z **45**
Ornan Rd. NW3 36Gb **69**
Oronsay HP3: Hem H 4B **4**
Orpen Ho. *SW5 49Cb* ***89***
(off Trebovir Rd.)
Orpen Wlk. N16 34Ub **71**
Orphanage Rd. WD17: Wat 12Y **27**
WD24: Wat 12Y **27**
Orpheus Centre, The 2N **209**
Orpheus Ho. *W10 42Bb* ***89***
(off Harrow Rd.)
Orpheus St. SE5 53Tb **113**
ORPINGTON 74Wc **161**
Orpington By-Pass
BR6: Chels, Orp 75Xc **161**
Orpington By-Pass Rd.
TN14: Bad M 81Cd **182**
Orpington Gdns. N18 20Ub **33**
Orpington Mans. N21 18Rb **33**
Orpington Retail Pk.
BR5: St M Cry 70Yc **139**
Orpington Rd. BR7: Chst 69Uc **138**
N21 18Rb **33**
Orpington Superbowl 74Wc **161**
Orpington Trade Cen.
BR5: St P 69Xc **139**
Orpin Rd. RH1: Mers 2B **208**
Orpwood Cl. TW12: Hamp 65Ba **129**
ORSETT 3C **100**
Orsett Golf Course 5G **100**
ORSETT HEATH 7B **100**
Orsett Heath Cres.
RM16: Grays 8C **100**
Orsett Ind. Pk. RM16: Ors 3H **101**
Orsett M. W2 44Db **89**
(not continuous)
Orsett Rd. RM16: Horn H, Ors 2E **100**
RM17: Grays 50De **99**
SS17: Horn H 2E **100**
Orsett St. SE11 7J **229** (50Pb **90**)
Orsett Ter. IG8: Wfd G 24Lc **53**
W2 2A **220** (44Db **89**)
Orsman Rd. N1 39Ub **71**
Ortman Cl. SL9: Ger X 31A **62**
Orton Gro. EN1: Enf 11Wb **33**
Orton Ho. *RM3: Rom 24Nd* ***57***
(off Leyburn Rd.)
Orton St. E1 46Wb **91**
Orville Rd. SW11 54Fb **111**
Orwell RM18: E Til 9L **101**
Orwell Cl. RM13: Rain 43Fd **96**
SL4: Wind 5H **103**
UB3: Hayes 45U **84**
Orwell Ct. *E8 39Wb* ***71***
(off Pownall Rd.)
N5 35Sb **71**
SW17 62Fb ***133***
(off Grosvenor Way)
WD24: Wat 13Z **27**
Orwell Rd. E13 40Lc **73**
Osbaldeston Rd. N16 33Wb **71**
Osberton Rd. SE12 57Jc **115**
Osbert St. SW1 6D **228** (49Mb **90**)
Osborn Cl. E8 39Wb **71**
Osborne Av. TW19: Stanw 60N **105**
Osborne Cl. BR3: Beck 70Ac **136**
EN4: Cockf 13Hb **31**
RM11: Horn 30Kd **57**
TW13: Hanw 64Z **129**
Osborne Ct. E10 31Dc **72**
EN6: Pot B 1Db **17**
SL4: Wind 4G **102**
W5 43Na **87**
Osborne Gdns. CR7: Thor H 68Sb **135**
EN6: Pot B 2Db **17**
Osborne Gro. E17 28Bc **52**
N4 32Qb **70**
Osborne Hgts. CM14: W'ley 21Xd **58**
Osborne Ho. *E16 46Jc* ***93***
(off Wesley Av.)
Osborne M. E17 28Bc **52**
SL4: Wind 4G **102**
Osborne Pl. SM1: Sutt 78Fb **155**
Osborne Rd. CM15: Pil H 16Wd **40**
CR7: Thor H 68Sb **135**
DA17: Belv 50Bd **95**
E7 36Kc **73**
E9 37Bc **72**
E10 33Dc **72**
EN3: Enf H 12Ac **34**
EN6: Pot B 2Db **17**
IG9: Buck H 18Kc **35**
KT2: King T 66Na **131**
KT12: Walt T 74W **150**
N4 32Qb **70**
N13 20Qb **32**
NW2 37Xa **68**
RH1: Redh 3A **208**
RM9: Dag 36Bd **75**
RM11: Horn 30Kd **57**
SL4: Wind 4G **102**
TW3: Houn 55Ba **107**
TW20: Egh 65B **126**
UB1: S'hall 44Ea **86**
UB8: Uxb 38L **63**
W3 48Ra **87**
WD24: Wat 10Y **13**
Osborne Sq. RM9: Dag 35Bd **75**
Osborne St. SL1: Slou 7K **81**
Osborne Ter. *SW17 64Hb* ***133***
(off Church La.)
Osborne Way KT9: Chess 78Pa **153**
KT19: Eps 84Na **173**
Osborn Gdns. NW7 24Za **48**
Osborn La. SE23 59Ac **114**
Osborn St. E1 43Vb **91**
Osborn Ter. SE3 56Hc **115**
Osbourne Av. WD4: K Lan 10P **3**
Osbourne Ct. HA2: Harr 28Da **45**
Osbourne Ho. IG8: Wfd G 24Qc **54**
TW2: Twick 61Ea **130**
Osbourne Rd. DA2: Dart 58Rd **119**
Oscar Cl. CR8: Purl 82Qb **176**
Oscar Faber Pl. N1 38Ub **71**
Oscar St. SE8 54Cc **114**
(not continuous)
Oseney Cres. NW5 36Lb **70**
Osgood Av. BR6: Chels 78Vc **161**
Osgood Gdns. BR6: Chels 78Vc **161**
OSIDGE 18Kb **32**
Osidge La. N14 18Jb **32**
Osier Ct. *E1 42Zb* ***92***
(off Osier St.)
RM7: Rom 30Fd **56**
TW8: Bford 51Na ***109***
(off Ealing Rd.)
Osier Cres. N10 25Hb **49**
Osier La. SE10 48Hc **93**
Osier M. W4 51Ua **110**
Osier Pl. TW20: Egh 65E **126**
Osiers, The WD3: Crox G 16S **26**
Osiers Ct. *KT1: King T 67Ma* ***131***
(off Steadfast Rd.)
Osiers Estate, The SW18 56Cb **111**
Osiers Rd. SW18 56Cb **111**
Osier St. E1 42Yb **92**
Osier Way CR4: Mitc 71Hb **155**
E10 34Dc **72**
SM7: Bans 86Ab **174**
Oslac Rd. SE6 64Dc **136**
Oslo Ct. NW8 2D **214**
Oslo Ho. *E9 37Bc* ***72***
(off Felstead St.)
SE5 54Sb ***113***
(off Carew St.)
Oslo Sq. SE16 48Ac **92**
Osman Cl. N15 30Tb **51**
Osmani School Sports Cen. 42Wb **91**
Osman Rd. N9 20Wb **33**
W6 48Ya **88**
Osmington Ho. *SW8 52Pb* ***112***
(off Dorset Rd.)
Osmond Cl. HA2: Harr 33Ea **66**
Osmond Gdns. SM6: Wall 78Lb **156**
Osmunda Ct. *E1 44Wb* ***91***
(off Myrdle St.)
Osmund St. W12 43Va **88**
Osnaburgh St. NW1 6A **216** (42Kb **90**)
(Euston Rd.)
NW1 4A **216**
(Robert St.)
Osnaburgh Ter. NW1 5A **216** (42Kb **90**)
Osney Ho. SE2 47Zc **95**
Osney Wlk. SM5: Cars 72Fb **155**
Osney Way DA12: Grav'nd 1H **145**
Osprey NW9 25Va **48**
Osprey Cl. BR2: Brom 74Nc **160**
E6 43Nc **94**
E11 28Jc **53**
E17 24Ac **52**
KT22: Fet 94Ea **192**
SM1: Sutt 78Bb **155**
UB7: W Dray 47N **83**
WD25: Wat 6Aa **13**
Osprey Ct. BR3: Beck 66Cc **136**
CM14: B'wood 20Xd **40**
CR0: C'don 76Sb ***157***
(off Innes Yd.)
E1 45Wb ***91***
(off Star Pl.)
EN9: Walt A 6Jc **21**
Osprey Dr. KT18: Tatt C 89Xa **174**
Osprey Est. SE16 49Zb **92**
Osprey Gdns. CR2: Sels 82Ac **178**
Osprey Ho. *E14 45Ac* ***92***
(off Victory Pl.)
SE1 50Xb ***91***
(off Lynton Rd.)
Osprey M. EN3: Pond E 15Yb **34**
Osprey Rd. EN9: Walt A 6Jc **21**
Ospringe Cl. SE20 66Yb **136**
Ospringe Ct. SE9 58Tc **116**
Ospringe Ho. SE1 1A **230**
Ospringe Rd. NW5 35Lb **70**
Osram Ct. W6 48Ya **88**
Osram Rd. HA9: Wemb 34Ma **67**
Osric Path N1 2H **219** (40Ub **71**)
Ossian M. N4 31Pb **70**
Ossian Rd. N4 31Pb **70**
Ossie Garvin Rdbt.
UB4: Yead 45X **85**
Ossington Bldgs. W1 7H **215** (43Jb **90**)
Ossington Cl. W2 45Cb **89**
Ossington St. W2 45Cb **89**
Ossory Rd. SE1 51Wb **113**
Ossulston St. NW1 2D **216** (40Mb **70**)
Ossulton Pl. N2 27Eb **49**
Ossulton Way N2 28Eb **49**
Ostade Rd. SW2 59Pb **112**
Ostell Cres. EN3: Enf L 10Cc **20**
Ostend Pl. SE1 5D **230** (49Sb **91**)
Osten M. SW7 48Db **89**
Osterberg Rd. DA1: Dart 56Pd **119**
OSTERLEY 52Fa **108**
Osterley Av. TW7: Isle 52Fa **108**
Osterley Cl. BR5: St P 67Wc **139**
Osterley Ct. TW7: Isle 53Fa **108**
UB5: N'olt 41Y ***85***
(off Canberra Dr.)
Osterley Cres. TW7: Isle 53Ga **108**
Osterley Gdns. CR7: Thor H 68Sb **135**
UB2: S'hall 47Ea **86**
Osterley Ho. *E14 44Dc* ***92***
(off Giraud St.)
Osterley La. TW7: Isle 49Ea **86**
UB2: S'hall 50Ca **85**
(not continuous)
Osterley Lodge *TW7: Isle 52Ga* ***108***
(off Church Rd.)
Osterley Pk. 51Ea **108**
Osterley Pk. House 51Ea **108**
Osterley Pk. Rd. UB2: S'hall 48Ba **85**
Osterley Pk. Vw. Rd. W7 47Ga **86**
Osterley Rd. N16 35Ub **71**
TW7: Isle 52Ga **108**
Osterley Sports & Athletics Cen. 52Ga **108**
Osterley Sports Club 48Ea **86**
Osterley Views UB2: S'hall 46Ea **86**
Oster St. AL3: St A 1A **6**
Oster Ter. E17 29Zb **52**
Ostlers Dr. TW15: Ashf 64S **128**
Ostliffe Rd. N13 22Sb **51**
Oswald Bldg. SW8 51Kb **112**
Oswald Cl. KT22: Fet 94Ea **192**
Oswald Rd. AL1: St A 3C **6**
KT22: Fet 94Ea **192**
UB1: S'hall 46Aa **85**
Oswald's Mead E9 35Ac **72**
Oswald St. E5 34Zb **72**
Oswald Ter. NW2 34Ya **68**
Osward CR0: Sels 81Bc **178**
(not continuous)
Osward Pl. N9 19Xb **33**
Osward Rd. SW17 61Hb **133**
Oswell Ho. *E1 46Xb* ***91***
(off Farthing Flds.)
Oswin St. SE11 5C **230** (49Rb **91**)
Oswyth Rd. SE5 54Ub **113**
OTFORD 88Kd **183**
Otford Cl. BR1: Brom 69Qc **138**
DA5: Bexl 58Dd **118**
SE20 67Yb **136**
Otford Cres. SE4 58Bc **114**
Otford Heritage Cen. 88Kd **183**
Otford Ho. SE1 2G **231**
SE15 51Yb ***114***
(off Lovelinch Cl.)
Otford La. TN14: Hals 84Bd **181**
Otford Rd. TN14: S'oaks 91Kd **203**
Othello Cl. SE11 7B **230** (50Rb **91**)
Otho Ct. TW8: Bford 52Ma **109**
Otis St. E3 41Ec **92**
Otium Leisure Cen. 9M **5**
Otley App. IG2: Ilf 30Rc **54**
Otley Dr. IG2: Ilf 29Rc **54**
Otley Ho. N5 34Qb **70**
Otley Rd. E16 44Lc **93**
Otley Ter. E5 34Zb **72**
Otley Way WD19: Wat 20Y **27**
Otlinge Rd. BR5: St M Cry 70Zc **139**
Ottawa Gdns. RM10: Dag 38Fd **76**
Ottawa Rd. RM18: Tilb 4C **122**
Ottaway Ct. E5 34Wb **71**
Ottaway St. E5 34Wb **71**
Otterbourne Rd. CR0: C'don 75Sb **157**
E4 20Fc **35**
Otterburn Gdns. TW7: Isle 52Ja **108**
Otterburn Ho. *SE5 52Sb* ***113***
(off Sultan St.)
Otterburn St. SW17 65Hb **133**
Otter Cl. E15 39Ec **72**
KT16: Ott 79D **148**
Otterden Cl. BR6: Orp 76Uc **160**
Otterden St. SE6 63Cc **136**
Otterden Ter. SE1 6K **231**
Otterfield Rd. UB7: Yiew 45N **83**
Otter Gdns. AL10: Hat 1D **8**
Ottermead La. KT16: Ott 79E **148**
Otter Mdw. KT22: Lea 91Ha **192**
Otter Rd. UB6: G'frd 42Ea **86**
Otters Cl. BR5: St P 70Zc **139**
OTTERSHAW 79E **148**

Ottershaw Pk. KT16: Ott ...80C 148
(not continuous)
Otterspool La. WD25: A'ham ...10Aa 13
(not continuous)
Otterspool Way WD25: A'ham ...10Ba 13
(not continuous)
Otto Cl. SE26 ...62Xb 135
Ottoman Ter. WD17: Wat ...13Y 27
Otto St. SE17 ...51Rb 113
Ottway's Av. KT21: Asht ...91Ma 193
Ottways La. KT21: Asht ...92Ma 193
Otway Gdns. WD23: Bush ...17Ga 28
Otways Cl. EN6: Pot B ...4Db 17
Oulton Cl. E5 ...33Yb 72
SE28 ...44Yc 95
Oulton Cres. EN6: Pot B ...3Za 16
IG11: Bark ...36Vc 75
Oulton Rd. N15 ...29Tb 51
Oulton Way WD19: Wat ...21Ba 45
Oundle Av. WD23: Bush ...16Ea 28
Oundle Ho. *RM3: Rom* ...*22Md 57*
(off Montgomery Cres.)
Ousden Cl. EN8: Chesh ...2Ac 20
Ousden Dr. EN8: Chesh ...2Ac 20
Ouseley Lodge SL4: Old Win ...9N 103
Ouseley Rd. SL4: Old Win ...9N 103
SW12 ...60Hb 111
TW19: Wray ...9N 103
Outer Circ. NW1 ...2E 214 (41Gb 89)
Outgate Rd. NW10 ...38Va 68
Outlook Pl. WD17: Wat ...11W 26
Outram Pl. KT13: Weyb ...78S 150
N1 ...39Nb 70
Outram Rd. CR0: C'don ...75Vb 157
E6 ...39Nc 74
N22 ...25Mb 50
Outwich St. EC3 ...2J 225
Outwood Ho. *SW2* ...*59Pb 112*
(off Deepdene Gdns.)
Outwood La.
CR5: Chip, Kgswd ...92Gb 195
KT20: Kgswd ...94Db 195
RH1: Blet, S Nut ...10K 209
Oval, The ...51Pb 112
Oval, The DA3: Lfield ...69Ee 143
DA15: Sidc ...59Wc 117
E2 ...40Xb 71
SM7: Bans ...86Cb 175
Oval Ct. HA8: Edg ...24Sa 47
Oval Gdns. RM17: Grays ...48Ee 99
Oval Ho. *CR0: C'don* ...*74Ub 157*
(off Oval Rd.)
Oval House Theatre ...51Qb 112
Oval Mans. SE11 ...51Pb 112
Oval Pl. SW8 ...52Pb 112
Oval Rd. CR0: C'don ...75Tb 157
NW1 ...39Kb 70
Oval Rd. Nth. RM10: Dag ...39Dd 76
Oval Rd. Sth. RM10: Dag ...40Dd 76
Ovaltine Ct. WD4: K Lan ...1R 12
Ovaltine Dr. WD4: K Lan ...1R 12
Oval Way SE11 ...50Pb 90
SL9: Ger X ...28A 42
Ovanna M. N1 ...37Ub 71
Ovenden Rd.
TN14: Chev, Sund ...92Zc 201
Overbrae BR3: Beck ...65Cc 136
Overbrook KT24: W Hor ...100R 190
Overbrook Wlk. HA8: Edg ...24Qa 47
(not continuous)
Overbury Av. BR3: Beck ...69Dc 136
Overbury Cres. CR0: New Ad ...82Ec 178
Overbury Rd. N15 ...30Tb 51
Overbury St. E5 ...35Zb 72
Overchess Ridge WD3: Chor ...13H 25
Overcliffe DA11: Grav'nd ...8C 122
Overcliff Rd. RM17: Grays ...50Fe 99
(not continuous)
SE13 ...55Cc 114
Overcourt Cl. DA15: Sidc ...58Xc 117
Overdale KT21: Asht ...87Na 173
RH1: Blet ...5J 209
Overdale Av. KT3: N Mald ...68Sa 131
Overdale Rd. W5 ...48La 86
Overdown Rd. SE6 ...63Cc 136
Overhill CR6: W'ham ...91Yb 198
Overhill Rd. CR8: Purl ...81Qb 176
SE22 ...59Wb 113
Overhill Way BR3: Beck ...71Fc 159
Overlea Rd. E5 ...31Wb 71
Overlord Ct. KT22: Fet ...93Fa 192
Overmead BR8: Swan ...71Gd 162
DA15: Sidc ...59Tc 116
Over Minnis DA3: New A ...76Be 165
Oversley Ho. *W2* ...*43Cb 89*
(off Alfred Rd.)
Overstand Cl. BR3: Beck ...71Cc 158
Overstone Gdns. CR0: C'don ...73Bc 158
Overstone Ho. *E14* ...*44Cc 92*
(off E. India Dock Rd.)
Overstone Rd. W6 ...48Ya 88
Overstrand Ho. RM12: Horn ...34Kd 77
Overstrand Mans. SW11 ...53Hb 111
Overstream WD3: Loud ...14K 25
Over The Misbourne Rd. SL9: Ger X ...30C 42
UB9: Den ...30D 42
Overthorpe Cl. GU21: Knap ...9J 167
Overton Cl. NW10 ...37Sa 67
TW7: Isle ...53Ha 108
Overton Ct. E11 ...31Jc 73
SM2: Sutt ...80Cb 155
Overton Dr. E11 ...31Jc 73
RM6: Chad H ...31Yc 75
Overton Ho. *SW15* ...*59Va 110*
(off Tangley Gro.)
Overton Rd. E10 ...32Ac 72
N14 ...15Nb 32
SE2 ...48Yc 95
SM2: Sutt ...79Cb 155
SW9 ...54Qb 112
Overton Rd. E. SE2 ...48Zc 95
Overton's Yd. CR0: C'don ...76Sb 157
Overy Ho. SE1 ...2B 230 (47Rb 91)
Overy Liberty DA1: Dart ...59Nd 119
Overy St. DA1: Dart ...58Nd 119
Ovesdon Av. HA2: Harr ...32Ba 65
Oveton Way KT23: Bookh ...98Ca 191
Ovett Cl. SE19 ...65Ub 135
Ovex Cl. E14 ...47Ec 92
Ovington Ct. GU21: Wok ...8K 167
SW3 ...4E 226
Ovington Gdns.
SW3 ...4E 226 (48Gb 89)
Ovington M. SW3 ...4E 226
Ovington Sq. SW3 ...4E 226 (48Gb 89)
Ovington St. SW3 ...4E 226 (49Gb 89)
Owen Cl. CR0: C'don ...72Tb 157
RM5: Col R ...23Dd 56
SE28 ...46Yc 95
SL3: L'ly ...50B 82
TW16: Sun ...67U 128
UB5: N'olt ...37Aa 65
(Arnold Rd.)
UB5: N'olt ...41X 85
(Attlee Rd.)
Owen Gdns. IG8: Wfd G ...23Nc 54
Owen Ho. TW1: Twick ...59Ka 108
TW14: Felt ...59W 106
Owenite St. SE2 ...49Xc 95
Owen Mans. *W14* ...*51Ab 110*
(off Queen's Club Gdns.)
Owen Pl. KT22: Lea ...94Ka 192
Owen Rd. GU20: W'sham ...8B 146
N13 ...22Sb 51
UB4: Yead ...41X 85
Owens M. E11 ...33Gc 73
Owen's Row EC1 ...3B 218 (41Rb 91)
Owen St. EC1 ...2B 218 (40Rb 71)
Owens Way SE23 ...59Ac 114
WD3: Crox G ...15Q 26
Owen Wlk. SE20 ...67Wb 135
Owen Way NW10 ...37Sa 67
Owgan Cl. SE5 ...52Tb 113
Owl Caravan Site, The
IG10: Lough ...13Hc 35
Owl Cl. CR2: Sels ...82Zb 178
Owlets Hall Cl.
RM11: Horn, Hrld W ...27Pd 57
Owletts ...9H 145
Ownstead Gdns. CR2: Sande ...83Vb 177
Ownsted Hill CR0: New Ad ...82Ec 178
Oxberry Av. SW6 ...54Ab 110
Oxdowne Cl. KT11: Stoke D ...86Da 171
Oxenden Wood Rd. BR6: Chels ...79Xc 161
Oxendon St. SW1 ...5D 222 (45Mb 90)
Oxenford St. SE15 ...55Vb 113
Oxenham Ho. *SE8* ...*51Cc 114*
(off Benbow St.)
Oxenhill Rd. TN15: Kems'g ...89Nd 183
Oxenhoath Rd. TN11: S'brne ...100Fe 205
Oxenholme NW1 ...2C 216
Oxenpark Av. HA9: Wemb ...31Na 67
Oxestall's Rd. SE8 ...50Ac 92
Oxford & Cambridge Mans. NW1 ...1E 220
Oxford Av. AL1: St A ...3G 6
N14 ...18Lb 32
RM11: Horn ...28Qd 57
RM16: Grays ...9C 100
SL1: Burn ...10A 60
SL1: Slou ...3D 80
SW20 ...68Ab 132
TW5: Hest ...50Ca 85
UB3: Harl ...52V 106
Oxford Cir. W1 ...3B 222
Oxford Cir. Av. W1 ...3B 222 (44Lb 90)
Oxford Cl. CR4: Mitc ...69Lb 134
DA12: Grav'nd ...1H 145
EN8: Chesh ...1Zb 20
HA6: Nwood ...21T 44
N9 ...19Xb 33
RM2: Rom ...29Jd 56
TW15: Ashf ...66S 128
Oxford Ct. CM14: W'ley ...21Zd 59
EC4 ...4F 225
KT18: Eps ...86Ua 174
TW13: Hanw ...63Z 129
W3 ...44Qa 87
W4 ...50Ra 87
W7 ...*43Ha 86*
(off Copley Cl.)
W9 ...*43Cb 89*
(off Elmfield Way)
Oxford Cres. KT3: N Mald ...72Ta 153
Oxford Dr. HA4: Ruis ...33Y 65
SE1 ...7H 225 (46Ub 91)
Oxford Gdns. N20 ...18Fb 31
N21 ...17Sb 33
UB9: Den ...34H 63
W4 ...50Qa 87
W10 ...44Ya 88
Oxford Ga. W6 ...49Za 88
Oxford Ho. *E3* ...*43Bc 92*
(off William Whiffin Sq.)
WD6: Bore ...*12Qa 29*
(off Stratfield Rd.)
Oxford M. DA5: Bexl ...59Cd 118
Oxford Pl. *NW10* ...*34Ta 67*
(off Press Rd.)
Oxford Rd. DA14: Sidc ...64Xc 139
E15 ...37Fc 73
(not continuous)
EN3: Pond E ...15Xb 33
HA1: Harr ...30Ea 46
HA3: W'stone ...27Ha 46
IG1: Ilf ...36Sc 74
IG8: Wfd G ...22Mc 53
N4 ...32Qb 70
N9 ...19Xb 33
NW6 ...40Cb 69
RH1: Redh ...5N 207
RM3: Rom ...23Pd 57
SE19 ...65Tb 135
SL4: Wind ...3G 102
SL9: Ger X ...30A 42
SM5: Cars ...79Gb 155
SM6: Wall ...78Lb 156
SS17: Stan H ...2K 101
SW15 ...56Ab 110
TW11: Tedd ...64Fa 130
UB8: Uxb ...36K 63
UB9: Den ...33F 62
W5 ...45Ma 87
Oxford Rd. E. SL4: Wind ...3G 102
Oxford Rd. Nth. W4 ...50Ra 87
Oxford Rd. Sth. W4 ...50Qa 87
Oxford Sq. W2 ...3E 220 (44Gb 89)
Oxford St. W1 ...3G 221 (44Jb 90)
WD18: Wat ...15X 27
Oxford Wlk. UB1: S'hall ...46Ba 85
Oxford Way TW13: Hanw ...63Z 129
Oxgate Cen. NW2 ...33Xa 68
Oxgate Ct. NW2 ...33Wa 68
Oxgate Ct. Pde. NW2 ...33Wa 68
Oxgate Gdns. NW2 ...34Xa 68
Oxgate La. NW2 ...33Wa 68
Oxgate Pde. NW2 ...33Wa 68
Oxhawth Cres. BR2: Brom ...71Qc 160
OXHEY ...16Y 27
Oxhey Av. WD19: Wat ...17Z 27
Oxhey Dr. HA6: Nwood ...21X 45
WD19: Wat ...21X 45
Oxhey Dr. Sth. HA6: Nwood ...22X 45
Oxhey La. HA3: Hrw W ...18Aa 27
HA5: Hat E ...18Aa 27
WD19: Wat ...18Aa 27
Oxhey Pk. ...16Y 27
Oxhey Pk. Golf Course ...19Z 27
Oxhey Ridge Cl. HA6: Nwood ...21X 45
Oxhey Rd. WD19: Wat ...17Y 27
Oxhey Woods Local Nature Reserve
...21W 44
Ox La. KT17: Ewe ...81Wa 174
Oxleas E6 ...44Rc 94
Oxleas Cl. DA16: Well ...54Tc 116
OXLEASE ...1C 8
Oxlease Dr. AL10: Hat ...1D 8
Oxleay Rd. HA2: Harr ...32Ca 65
Oxleigh Cl. KT3: N Mald ...71Ua 154
Oxley Cl. RM2: Rom ...26Ld 57
SE1 ...7K 231 (50Vb 91)
Oxleys Rd. EN9: Walt A ...4Jc 21
NW2 ...34Xa 68
Oxlip Cl. CR0: C'don ...74Zb 158
Oxlow La. RM9: Dag ...35Bd 75
RM10: Dag ...35Bd 75
Oxonian St. SE22 ...56Vb 113
Oxo Tower Wharf SE1 ...5A 224 (45Qb 90)
OXSHOTT ...85Fa 172
Oxshott Ri. KT11: Cobh ...85Z 171
Oxshott Rd. KT22: Lea ...88Ga 172
Oxshott Village Sports Club ...86Ea 172
Oxshott Way KT11: Cobh ...87Aa 171
OXTED ...1J 211
Oxted Cl. CR4: Mitc ...69Fb 133
Oxted Ct. *RH1: Redh* ...*4B 208*
(off Reynolds Av.)
Oxted Ho. *RM3: Rom* ...*22Pd 57*
(off Redcar Rd.)
Oxted Rd. RH9: G'stone ...2A 210
Oxtoby Way SW16 ...67Mb 134
Oxygen, The E16 ...45Jc 93
Oystercatcher Cl. E16 ...44Kc 93
Oyster Ct. SE17 ...6D 230
Oysterfields AL3: St A ...1P 5
Oystergate Wlk. EC4 ...5F 225
Oyster La. KT14: Byfl ...82M 169
Oyster Row E1 ...44Yb 92
Oyster Wharf SW11 ...54Fb 111
Ozolins Way E16 ...44Jc 93

P

Pablo Neruda Cl. SE24 ...56Rb 113
Paceheath Cl. RM5: Col R ...23Fd 56
Pace Pl. E1 ...44Xb 91
Pachesham Dr. KT22: Lea ...88Ha 172
PACHESHAM PARK ...88Ja 172
Pachesham Pk. KT22: Lea ...88Ja 172
Pachesham Pk. Golf Course ...90Ga 172
Pacific Cl. DA10: Swans ...57Ae 121
TW14: Felt ...60V 106
Pacific Ct. E1 ...43Yb 92
Pacific Ho. *E1* ...*42Zb 92*
(off Ernest St.)
Pacific M. SW2 ...56Qb 112
Pacific Rd. E16 ...44Jc 93
Pacific Wharf SE16 ...46Zb 92
Packenham Ho. *E2* ...*41Vb 91*
(off Wellington Row)
Packet Boat La. UB8: Cowl ...44K 83
Packham Cl. BR6: Chels ...75Xc 161
Packham Ct. KT4: Wor Pk ...76Ya 154
Packham Rd. DA11: Nflt ...2B 144
Packhorse La. EN6: Ridge ...2Ta 15
WD6: Bore ...9Ua 16
Packhorse Rd. SL9: Ger X ...28A 42
TN13: Bes G ...95Ed 202
Packington Rd. W3 ...48Sa 87
Packington Sq. N1 ...1D 218 (39Sb 71)
(not continuous)
Packington St. N1 ...39Rb 71
Packmores Rd. SE9 ...57Tc 116
Padbrook RH8: Limp ...1L 211
(not continuous)
Padbrook Cl. RH8: Limp ...1L 211
Padbury SE17 ...7H 231
Padbury Cl. TW14: Bedf ...60T 106
Padbury Ct. E2 ...4K 219 (41Vb 91)
Padbury Ho. NW8 ...5E 214
Padbury Oaks UB7: Lford ...53K 105
Padcroft Rd. UB7: Yiew ...46M 83
Paddenswick Rd. W6 ...48Wa 88
PADDINGTON ...3B 220 (44Fb 89)
Paddington Bowling & Sports Club
...42Db 89
Paddington Cl. UB4: Yead ...42Z 85
Paddington Ct. *W7* ...*43Ha 86*
(off Copley Cl.)
Paddington Grn. W2 ...7C 214 (43Fb 89)
Paddington St. W1 ...7H 215 (43Jb 90)
Paddock, The DA2: Dart ...61Ud 142
GU18: Light ...3A 166
N10 ...27Jb 50
NW9 ...29Qa 47
SL3: Dat ...3M 103
SL4: Wink ...10A 102
SL9: Chal P ...22A 42
TN16: Westrm ...98Sc 200
UB10: Ick ...35R 64
Paddock Cl. BR6: Farnb ...77Rc 160
DA4: S Dar ...67Sd 142
KT4: Wor Pk ...74Ua 154
RH8: Oxt ...3K 211
RM16: Ors ...3C 100
SE3 ...54Jc 115
SE26 ...63Zb 136
SL4: Wind ...3D 102
TN15: Plat ...93Ee 205
UB5: N'olt ...40Ca 65
WD19: Wat ...16Aa 27
Paddock Gdns. SE19 ...65Ub 135
Paddock Ho. DA11: Grav'nd ...4E 144
Paddock La. EN5: Ark ...15Ua 30
Paddock Lodge *EN1: Enf* ...*15Ub 33*
(off Village Rd.)
Paddock Mobile Home Pk.
BR2: Kes ...81Nc 180
Paddock Pas. *SE19* ...*65Ub 135*
(off Paddock Gdns.)
Paddock Rd. DA6: Bex ...56Ad 117
HA4: Ruis ...34Z 65
NW2 ...34Wa 68
Paddocks, The AL4: St A ...4L 7
BR8: Swan ...67Ld 141
CR0: Addtn ...79Cc 158
EN4: Cockf ...13Hb 31
GU25: Vir W ...72A 148
Paddocks, The HA9: Wemb ...33Ra 67
KT13: Weyb ...76U 150
KT15: New H ...82K 169
KT23: Bookh ...98Da 191
RM4: Stap A ...16Hd 38
RM16: Ors ...3C 100
TN13: S'oaks ...96Md 203
W5 ...*48Ma 87*
(off Popes La.)
WD3: Chor ...14H 25
Paddocks Cl. BR5: Orp ...75Zc 161
HA2: Harr ...35Da 65
KT11: Cobh ...86Y 171
KT21: Asht ...90Na 173
Paddocks Grn. NW9 ...32Ra 67
Paddocks Mead GU21: Wok ...8J 167
Paddocks Way KT16: Chert ...74K 149
KT21: Asht ...90Na 173
Paddock Wlk. CR6: W'ham ...91Xb 197
Paddock Way BR7: Chst ...66Tc 138
GU21: Wok ...86D 168
HP1: Hem H ...2G 2
RH8: Oxt ...3K 211
SW15 ...59Ya 110
Padelford La. HA7: Stan ...19Ja 28
Padfield Ct. HA9: Wemb ...34Pa 67
Padfield Rd. SE5 ...55Sb 113
Padgate Ho. WD19: Wat ...20Y 27
Padgets, The EN9: Walt A ...6Gc 21
Padley Cl. KT9: Chess ...78Pa 153
Padnall Ct. RM6: Chad H ...27Zc 55
Padnall Rd. RM6: Chad H ...27Zc 55
Padstone Ho. *E3* ...*41Dc 92*
(off Talwin St.)
Padstow Cl. BR6: Chels ...77Vc 161
SL3: L'ly ...47A 82
Padstow Ho. *E14* ...*45Bc 92*
(off Three Colt St.)
Padstow Rd. EN2: Enf ...11Rb 33
Padstow Wlk. TW14: Felt ...60V 106
Padua Rd. SE20 ...67Yb 136
Pagden St. SW8 ...53Kb 112
Pageant Av. NW9 ...25Ta 47
Pageant Cl. RM18: Tilb ...3E 122
Pageant Cres. SE16 ...46Ac 92
Pageantmaster Ct. EC4 ...3B 224
Pageant Rd. AL1: St A ...3B 6
Pageant Wlk. CR0: C'don ...76Ub 157
Page Av. HA9: Wemb ...34Sa 67
Page Cl. DA2: Bean ...62Yd 142
HA3: Kenton ...30Pa 47
RM9: Dag ...36Ad 75
TW12: Hamp ...65Aa 129
Page Ct. NW7 ...24Xa 48
Page Cres. CR0: Wadd ...78Rb 157
DA8: Erith ...52Hd 118
Page Cft. KT15: Add ...75K 149
Page Grn. Rd. N15 ...29Wb 51
Page Grn. Ter. N15 ...29Vb 51
Page Heath La. BR1: Brom ...69Mc 137
Page Heath Vs. BR1: Brom ...69Mc 137
Page High *N22* ...*26Qb 50*
(off Lymington Av.)
Page Ho. *SE10* ...*51Ec 114*
(off Welland St.)
Pagehurst Rd. CR0: C'don ...73Xb 157
Page Mdw. NW7 ...24Xa 48
Page Pl. AL2: F'mre ...10C 6
Page Rd. TW14: Bedf ...58T 106
Pages Hill N10 ...26Jb 50
Pages La. N10 ...26Jb 50
RM3: Hrld W ...26Rd 57
UB8: Uxb ...37L 63
Page St. NW7 ...25Wa 48
SW1 ...5E 228 (49Mb 90)
Page's Wlk. SE1 ...5H 231 (49Ub 91)
Pages Yd. W4 ...51Va 110
Paget Av. SM1: Sutt ...76Fb 155
Paget Cl. TW12: Hamp H ...63Fa 130
Paget Gdns. BR7: Chst ...67Rc 138
Paget Ho. *E2* ...*40Yb 72*
(off Bishop's Way)
SL9: Chal P ...*21A 42*
(off Micholls Av.)
Paget La. TW7: Isle ...55Fa 108
Paget Pl. KT2: King T ...65Ta 131
KT7: T Ditt ...74Ha 152
Paget Ri. SE18 ...51Qc 116
Paget Rd. IG1: Ilf ...35Rc 74
N16 ...32Tb 71
SL3: L'ly ...49B 82
UB10: Hil ...42S 84
Paget St. EC1 ...3B 218 (41Rb 91)
Paget Ter. SE18 ...51Rc 116
Pagette Way RM17: Grays ...50Ce 99
Pagham Ho. *W10* ...*42Ya 88*
(off Sutton Way)
Pagin Ho. *N15* ...*29Ub 51*
(off Braemar Rd.)
Pagitts Gro. EN4: Had W ...11Db 31
Paglesfield CM13: Hut ...16Ee 41
Pagnell St. SE14 ...52Bc 114
Pagoda Av. TW9: Rich ...55Pa 109
Pagoda Gdns. SE3 ...54Fc 115
Pagoda Gro. SE27 ...61Sb 135
Paignton Cl. RM3: Rom ...25Md 57
Paignton Rd. HA4: Ruis ...34W 64
N15 ...30Ub 51
Paines Brook Ct. RM3: Rom ...23Pd 57
Paines Brook Rd. RM3: Rom ...23Pd 57
Paines Brook Way RM3: Rom ...23Pd 57
Paines Cl. HA5: Pinn ...27Aa 45
Painesfield Dr. KT16: Chert ...74J 149
Paines La. HA5: Pinn ...25Aa 45
Pain's Cl. CR4: Mitc ...68Kb 134
PAINS HILL
KT11 ...86V 170
RH8 ...3N 211
PAINSHILL ...85V 170
Pains Hill RH8: Limp ...4N 211
Pains Hill Ho. KT11: Cobh ...86V 170
Painshill Pk. ...86V 170
Painsthorpe Rd. N16 ...34Ub 71
Painted Hall
Greenwich ...51Ec 114
Painters Ash La. DA11: Nflt ...62Fe 143
Painters La. EN3: Enf W ...7Ac 20
Painters M. SE16 ...49Wb 91
Painters Rd. IG2: Ilf ...27Vc 55
Paisley Rd. N22 ...25Rb 51
SM5: Cars ...74Fb 155
Paisley Ter. SM5: Cars ...73Fb 155
Pakeman Ho. SE1 ...1C 230
Pakeman St. N7 ...34Pb 70
Pakenham Cl. SW12 ...60Jb 112
Pakenham St. WC1 ...4J 217 (41Pb 90)
Pakes Way CM16: They B ...9Uc 22
Pakington Ho. *SW9* ...*54Nb 112*
(off Stockwell Gdns. Est.)
Palace Av. W8 ...47Db 89
Palace Bingo Club ...5D 230
Palace Cl. E9 ...37Bc 72
SL1: Slou ...6D 80
WD4: K Lan ...2P 11
Palace Ct. *BR1: Brom* ...*67Kc 137*
(off Palace Gro.)
GU21: Wok ...*88C 168*
(off Maybury Rd.)
HA3: Kenton ...30Na 47
NW3 ...36Db 69
W2 ...45Db 89
(not continuous)
Palace Ct. Gdns. N10 ...27Lb 50
Palace Dr. KT13: Weyb ...76R 150
Palace Exchange EN2: Enf ...14Tb 33
Palace Gdns. IG9: Buck H ...18Mc 35
Palace Gdns. M. W8 ...46Db 89
Palace Gdns. Shop. Cen. EN2: Enf ...14Tb 33
Palace Gdns. Ter. W8 ...46Cb 89
Palace Ga. W8 ...2A 226 (47Eb 89)
Palace Gates M. *N8* ...*28Nb 50*
(off The Campsbourne)
Palace Gates Rd. N22 ...25Mb 50
Palace Grn. CR0: Sels ...80Bc 158
W8 ...46Db 89
Palace Gro. BR1: Brom ...67Kc 137
SE19 ...66Vb 135
Palace Ice Rink, The ...26Mb 50
Palace Mans. *KT1: King T* ...*70Ma 131*
(off Palace Rd.)
W14 ...*49Ab 88*
(off Hammersmith Rd.)
Palace M. E17 ...28Bc 52
EN2: Enf ...13Tb 33
SW1 ...6J 227
SW6 ...52Bb 111
Palace Pde. E17 ...28Bc 52
Palace Pl. SW1 ...3B 228 (48Lb 90)
Palace Pl. Mans. *W8* ...*47Db 89*
(off Kensington Ct.)
Palace Rd. BR1: Brom ...67Kc 137
HA4: Ruis ...35Aa 65
KT1: King T ...70Ma 131
KT8: E Mos ...69Ea 130
N8 ...29Mb 50
(not continuous)
N11 ...24Nb 50
SE19 ...66Vb 135
SW2 ...60Pb 112
TN16: Westrm ...93Qc 200
Palace Sq. SE19 ...66Vb 135
Palace St. SW1 ...3B 228 (48Lb 90)
Palace Superbowl ...5C 230
Palace Theatre
Soho ...3E 222
Palace Vw. BR1: Brom ...69Kc 137
(not continuous)
CR0: C'don ...77Bc 158
SE12 ...61Jc 137
Palace Vw. Rd. E4 ...22Dc 52
Palace Way GU22: Wok ...92D 188
KT13: Weyb ...76R 150
Palace Wharf *W6* ...*52Ya 110*
(off Rainville Rd.)
Palamos Rd. E10 ...32Cc 72
Palatine Av. N16 ...35Ub 71
Palatine Rd. N16 ...35Ub 71
Palazzo Apartments *N1* ...*38Ub 71*
(off Ardleigh Rd.)
Palemead Cl. SW6 ...53Za 110
Palermo Rd. NW10 ...40Wa 68
Palestine Gro. SW19 ...67Fb 133
Palestra Ho. SE1 ...7B 224
Palewell Cl. BR5: St P ...68Xc 139
Palewell Comn. Dr. SW14 ...57Ta 109
Palewell Pk. SW14 ...57Ta 109
Paley Gdns. IG10: Lough ...13Rc 36
Palfrey Cl. AL3: St A ...1B 6
Palfrey Pl. SW8 ...52Pb 112
Palgrave Av. UB1: S'hall ...45Ca 85
Palgrave Gdns. NW1 ...5E 214 (42Gb 89)
Palgrave Ho. *SE5* ...*52Sb 113*
(off Wyndham Est.)
TW2: Whitt ...59Ea 108
Palgrave Rd. W12 ...48Va 88
Palins Way RM16: Grays ...46Ce 99
Palissy St. E2 ...4K 219 (41Vb 91)
(not continuous)
Palladian Cir. DA9: Ghithe ...56Yd 120
Palladino Ho. *SW17* ...*64Gb 133*
(off Laurel Cl.)
Palladio Ct. *SW18* ...*58Db 111*
(off Mapleton Cres.)
Palladium Ct. *E8* ...*38Vb 71*
(off Queensbridge Rd.)
Pallant Ho. SE1 ...4G 231
Pallant Way BR6: Farnb ...76Qc 160
Pallet Way SE18 ...53Nc 116
Palliser Ct. *W14* ...*50Ab 88*
(off Palliser Rd.)
Palliser Dr. RM13: Rain ...43Jd 96
Palliser Ho. *E1* ...*42Zb 92*
(off Ernest St.)
SE10 ...*51Fc 115*
(off Trafalgar Rd.)
Palliser Rd. W14 ...50Ab 88
Pallister Ter. SW15 ...62Va 132
Pall Mall SW1 ...7C 222 (46Lb 90)
Pall Mall E. SW1 ...6E 222 (46Mb 90)
Pall Mall Pl. SW1 ...7C 222
Palmar Cres. DA7: Bex ...55Cd 118
Palmar Rd. DA7: Bex ...54Cd 118
Palmarsh Rd. BR5: St M Cry ...70Zc 139
Palm Av. DA14: Sidc ...65Zc 139
Palm Cl. E10 ...34Dc 72
Palm Ct. *SE15* ...*52Vb 113*
(off Garnies Cl.)
Palmeira Rd. DA7: Bex ...55Zc 117
Palmer Av. DA12: Grav'nd ...3F 144
SM3: Cheam ...77Ya 154
WD23: Bush ...15Da 27
Palmer Cl. BR4: W W'ck ...76Fc 159
RH1: Redh ...7A 208
TW5: Hest ...53Ca 107
UB5: N'olt ...37Aa 65
Palmer Cres. KT1: King T ...69Na 131
KT16: Ott ...79F 148
Palmer Dr. BR1: Brom ...70Rc 138
Palmer Gdns. EN5: Barn ...15Za 30
Palmer Ho. *SE14* ...*52Zb 114*
(off Lubbock St.)
Palmer Pl. N7 ...36Qb 70

Petworth Cl. CR5: Coul 91Lb 196
UB5: N'olt 38Ba 65
Petworth Ct. SL4: Wind 3E 102
Petworth Gdns. SW20 69Xa 132
UB10: Hil 39S 64
Petworth Rd. DA6: Bex 57Cd 118
N12 22Gb 49
Petworth St. SW11 53Gb 111
Petworth Way RM12: Horn 35Hd 76
Petyt Pl. SW3 51Gb 111
Petyward SW3 6E 226 (49Gb 89)
Pevensey Av. EN1: Enf 12Ub 33
N11 22Mb 50
Pevensey Cl. TW7: Isle 52Ea 108
Pevensey Ct. SW16 62Qb 134
W3 47Ra 87
Pevensey Ho. *E1* *43Zb 92*
(off Ben Jonson Rd.)
Pevensey Rd. E7 35Hc 73
SL2: Slou 3E 80
SW17 63Fb 133
TW13: Felt 60Aa 107
Pevensey Way WD3: Crox G 14R 26
Peverel E6 44Qc 94
Peverel Ho. RM10: Dag 33Cd 76
Peveret Cl. N11 22Kb 50
Peveril Ct. *DA2: Dart* *58Rd 119*
(off Osbourne Rd.)
Peveril Dr. TW11: Tedd 64Fa 130
Peveril Ho. SE1 4G 231
Pewsey Cl. E4 22Cc 52
Peyton Pl. SE10 52Ec 114
Peyton's Cotts. RH1: Nutf 4F 208
Pharamond NW2 37Za 68
Pharaoh Cl. CR4: Mitc 73Hb 155
Pharaoh's Island TW17: Shep 75P 149
Pheasant Cl. CR8: Purl 85Rb 177
E16 44Kc 93
Pheasant Ct. WD25: Wat 7Y 13
Pheasantry Ho. SW3 7E 226
Pheasantry Welcome Centre, The 67Ha 130
Pheasants Way WD3: Rick 17K 25
Pheasant Wlk. SL9: Chal P 23A 42
Phelps Cl. TN15: W King 79Ud 164
Phelp St. SE17 51Tb 113
Phelps Way UB3: Harl 49T 84
Phene St. SW3 51Gb 111
Philadelphia Ct. *SW10* *52Eb 111*
(off Uverdale Rd.)
Philanthropic Rd. RH1: Redh 7A 208
Philan Way RM5: Col R 23Fd 56
Philbeach Gdns. SW5 50Cb 89
Phil Brown Pl. *SW8* *55Kb 112*
(off Daley Thompson Way)
Philbye M. SL1: Slou 7D 80
Philchurch Pl. E1 44Wb 91
Philia Ho. *NW1* *38Lb 70*
(off Farrier St.)
Philimore Cl. SE18 50Uc 94
Philip Av. BR8: Swan 70Fd 140
RM7: Rush G 32Fd 76
Philip Cl. CM15: Pil H 16Xd 40
RM7: Rush G 32Fd 76
Philip Ct. W2 7B 214
Philip Gdns. CR0: C'don 75Bc 158
Philip Ho. *NW6* *39Db 69*
(off Mortimer Pl.)
Philip Jones Ct. N4 32Pb 70
Philip La. N15 28Tb 51
Philip Mole Ho. *W9* *42Cb 89*
(off Chippenham Rd.)
Philipot Path SE9 58Pc 116
Philippa Gdns. SE9 57Mc 115
Philippa Way RM16: Grays 9D 100
Philip Rd. RM13: Rain 41Gd 96
TW18: Staines 65M 127
Philips Cl. SM5: Cars 74Jb 156
Philip Sidney Ct. *RM16: Chaf H* *50Zd 99*
(off Philip Sidney Rd.)
Philip Sq. SW8 54Kb 112
Philip St. E13 42Jc 93
Philip Sydney Rd. RM16: Chaf H 50Zd 99
Philip Wlk. SE15 55Wb 113
(not continuous)
Phillida Rd. RM3: Hrld W 26Qd 57
Phillimore Ct. *W8* *47Cb 89*
(off Kensington High St.)
WD7: R'lett 8Ga 14
Phillimore Gdns. NW10 39Ya 68
W8 47Cb 89
Phillimore Gdns. Cl. W8 48Cb 89
Phillimore Pl. W8 47Cb 89
WD7: R'lett 8Ga 14
Phillimore Ter. *W8* *48Cb 89*
(off Allen St.)
Phillimore Wlk. W8 48Cb 89
Phillipers WD25: Wat 8Z 13
Phillip Ho. *E1* *43Vb 91*
(off Heneage St.)
Phillippines Shaw TN14: Ide H 100Yc 201
Phillipp St. N1 1H 219 (39Ub 71)
Phillips Cl. DA1: Dart 58Kd 119
Phillips Ct. HA8: Edg 23Qa 47
Phillip's Quad. GU22: Wok 90A 168
Philpot La. EC3 4H 225 (45Ub 91)
GU24: Chob 5M 167
Philpot Path IG1: Ilf 34Sc 74
Philpots Cl. UB7: Yiew 45M 83
Philpot Sq. SW6 55Db 111
Philpot St. E1 44Xb 91
Phineas Pett Rd. SE9 55Nc 116
Phipps Bri. Rd. CR4: Mitc 69Fb 133
SW19 68Eb 133
Phipps Hatch La. EN2: Enf 10Sb 19
Phipps Ho. *SE7* *50Kc 93*
(off Woolwich Rd.)
W12 *45Xa 88*
(off White City Est.)
Phipp's M. SW1 4A 228
Phipps Rd. SL1: Slou 3B 80
(not continuous)
Phipp St. EC2 5H 219 (42Ub 91)
Phoebeth Rd. SE4 57Cc 114
Phoebe Wlk. E16 44Kc 93
Phoenix Apartments *WD17: Wat* *15Z 27*
(off Lwr. High St.)
Phoenix Av. SE10 47Gc 93
Phoenix Cen. 80Nb 156
Phoenix Cinema 28Gb 49
Phoenix Cl. BR4: W W'ck 75Fc 159
E8 39Vb 71
E17 26Bc 52
HA6: Nwood 21V 44
KT19: Eps 84Qa 173
W12 45Xa 88
Phoenix Ct. CR2: S Croy 78Vb 157
DA11: Nflt 57Ce 121
E1 *42Xb 91*
(off Buckhurst St.)
E4 20Dc 34
E14 49Cc 92
KT3: N Mald 69Va 132
KT17: Eps *85Ua 174*
(off Church St.)
NW1 2E 216
SE14 *51Ac 114*
(off Chipley St.)
TW3: Houn 55Ca 107
TW4: Houn 57Z 107
TW8: Bford 50Na 87
TW13: Felt 63U 128
Phoenix Dr. BR2: Kes 77Mc 159
Phoenix Hgts. E. *E14* *47Cc 92*
(off Byng St.)
Phoenix Hgts. W. *E14* *47Cc 92*
(off Mastmaker Ct.)
Phoenix Ho. *AL1: St A* *3E 6*
(off Campfield Rd.)
SM1: Sutt 77Db 155
Phoenix Ind. Est. HA1: Harr 28Ha 46
Phoenix Lodge Mans. *W6* *49Za 88*
(off Brook Grn.)
Phoenix Pk. NW2 33Wa 68
Phoenix Pl. DA1: Dart 59Md 119
WC1 5J 217 (42Pb 90)
Phoenix Point SE28 46Yc 95
Phoenix Rd. NW1 3D 216 (41Mb 90)
SE20 65Yb 136
Phoenix Sports & Fitness Cen. 45Wa 88
Phoenix St. WC2 3E 222 (44Mb 90)
Phoenix Theatre 3E 222
Phoenix Trad. Est. UB6: G'frd 39La 66
Phoenix Trad. Pk. TW8: Bford 50Ma 87
Phoenix Way SW18 57Eb 111
TW5: Hest 51Z 107
Phoenix Wharf *E1* *46Xb 91*
(off Wapping High St.)
Phoenix Wharf Rd. SE1 2K 231
Phoenix Yd. WC1 4J 217
Photographers Gallery 3B 222
Phygtle, The SL9: Chal P 23A 42
Phyllis Av. KT3: N Mald 71Xa 154
Phyllis Hodges Ho. *NW1* *2D 216*
(off Aldenham St.)
Phyllis Ho. *CR0: Wadd* *77Rb 157*
(off Ashley La.)
Physic Pl. SW3 51Hb 111
Piano La. N16 34Tb 71
Piano Works *IG11: Bark* *38Sc 74*
(off Ripple Rd.)
Piazza, The UB8: Uxb 38M 63
WC2 4G 223
(not continuous)
Picardy Ho. EN2: Enf 10Sb 19
Picardy Manorway DA17: Belv 48Dd 96
Picardy Rd. DA17: Belv 50Cd 96
Picardy St. DA17: Belv 48Cd 96
Piccadilly W1 1K 227 (46Kb 90)
Piccadilly Arc. SW1 6B 222
Piccadilly Circus 5D 222 (45Mb 90)
Piccadilly Cir. W1 5D 222 (45Mb 90)
Piccadilly Ct. *N7* *37Pb 70*
(off Caledonian Rd.)
Piccadilly Pl. W1 5C 222
Piccadilly Theatre 4C 222
Piccotts End HP1: Hem H 1L 3
Pickard Cl. N14 18Mb 32
Pickard Gdns. E3 43Bc 92
Pickard St. EC1 3C 218 (41Rb 91)
Pickering Av. E6 40Qc 74
Pickering Cl. E9 38Zb 72
Pickering Ct. *DA2: Dart* *58Rd 119*
(off Osbourne Rd.)
Pickering Gdns. CR0: C'don 72Vb 157
N11 23Jb 50
Pickering Ho. *W2* *44Eb 89*
(off Hallfield Est.)
W5 *49La 86*
(off Windmill Rd.)
Pickering M. W2 44Db 89
Pickering Pl. SW1 7C 222
Pickering Rd. IG11: Bark 37Sc 74
Pickering St. N1 39Rb 71
Pickets Cl. WD23: B Hea 18Fa 28
Pickets St. SW12 59Kb 112
Pickett Cft. HA7: Stan 25Ma 47
Picketts Lock La. N9 19Xb 34
Picketts Lock La. Ind. Est.
N9 19Ac 34
Picketts Ter. SE22 57Wb 113
Pickford Cl. DA7: Bex 54Ad 117
Pickford Dr. SL3: L'ly 46A 82
Pickford La. DA7: Bex 54Ad 117
Pickford Rd. AL1: St A 2F 6
DA7: Bex 55Ad 117
Pickfords Gdns. SL1: Slou 6J 81
Pickfords Wharf N1 2D 218 (40Sb 71)
SE1 6F 225 (46Tb 91)
Pick Hill EN9: Walt A 4Hc 21
Pickhurst Grn. BR2: Hayes 73Hc 159
Pickhurst La. BR2: Hayes 71Gc 159
BR4: W W'ck 71Gc 159
Pickhurst Mead BR2: Hayes 73Hc 159
Pickhurst Pk. BR2: Brom 71Gc 159
Pickhurst Ri. BR4: W W'ck 73Ec 158
Pickins Piece SL3: Hort 54C 104
Pickmoss La. TN14: Otf 88Jd 182
Pickwick Cl. TW4: Houn 57Aa 107
Pickwick Ct. SE9 60Nc 116
Pickwick Gdns. DA11: Nflt 62Fe 143
Pickwick Ho. DA11: Nflt 62Fe 143
SE16 *47Wb 91*
(off George Row)
W11 *46Za 88*
(off St Ann's Rd.)
Pickwick M. N18 21Ub 51
Pickwick Pl. HA1: Harr 31Ga 66
Pickwick Rd. SE21 59Tb 113
Pickwick St. SE1 2D 230 (47Sb 91)
Pickwick Way BR7: Chst 65Sc 138
Pickworth Cl. SW8 52Nb 112
Picquets Way SM7: Bans 88Ab 174
Picton M. CR6: W'ham 91Wb 197
Picton Pl. KT6: Surb 74Qa 153
W1 3J 221 (44Jb 90)
Picton St. SE5 52Tb 113
Picture Ho. SW16 61Nb 134
Pied Bull Ct. WC1 1G 223
Pied Bull Yd. *N1* *39Rb 71*
(off Theberton St.)
WC1 1F 223
Piedmont Rd. SE18 50Tc 94
(not continuous)
PIELD HEATH 42P 83
Pield Heath Av. UB8: Hil 42Q 84
Pield Heath Rd.
UB8: Cowl, Hil 42N 83
Pierce Campion Ct. E17 27Bc 52
Piercing Hill CM16: They B 7Tc 22
Pier Head E1 46Xb 91
(not continuous)
Pierhead Wharf *E1* *46Xb 91*
(off Wapping High St.)
Pier Ho. SW3 51Gb 111
Pierian Spring HP1: Hem H 1K 3
Pieris Ho. *TW13: Felt* *61W 128*
(off High St.)
Piermont Grn. SE22 57Xb 113
Piermont Pl. BR1: Brom 68Nc 138
Piermont Rd. SE22 57Xb 113
Pier Pde. *E16* *46Qc 94*
(off Pier Rd.)
Pierpoint Bldg. E14 47Bc 92
Pierrepoint Rd. W3 45Ra 87
Pierrepont Arc. N1 1B 218
Pierrepont Row N1 1B 218
Pier Rd. DA8: Erith 51Gd 118
(not continuous)
DA9: Ghithe 56Xd 120
DA11: Nflt 8B 122
E16 46Qc 94
TW14: Felt 57X 107
Pierson Rd. SL4: Wind 3B 102
Pier St. E14 49Ec 92
(not continuous)
Pier Ter. SW18 56Db 111
Pier Wlk. SE10 47Gc 93
Pier Way SE28 47Sc 94
Pier Wharf RM17: Grays 52Ce 121
Pietra Lara Bldg. EC1 5D 218
Pigeon Ho. La. CR5: Coul 97Eb 195
Pigeon La. TW12: Hamp 63Ca 129
Piggott Ho. *E2* *40Zb 72*
(off Sewardstone Rd.)
Piggs Cnr. RM17: Grays 48Ee 99
Piggy La. WD3: Chor 16D 24
Pigott St. E14 44Cc 92
Pike Cl. BR1: Brom 64Kc 137
UB10: Uxb 39P 63
Pike La. RM14: Upm 36Vd 78
Pikemans Ct. *SW5* *49Cb 89*
(off W. Cromwell Rd.)
Pike Rd. NW7 21Ta 47
Pikes Cotts. EN5: Ark 14Ya 30
Pike's End HA5: Eastc 28X 45
Pikes Hill KT17: Eps 85Ua 174
Pikestone Cl. UB4: Yead 42Aa 85
Pikethorne SE23 61Zb 136
Pilgrimage St. SE1 2F 231 (47Tb 91)
Pilgrim Cl. AL2: Park 9A 6
SM4: Mord 73Db 155
Pilgrim Hill SE27 63Sb 135
Pilgrim Ho. SE1 4G 231
SE16 *47Yb 92*
(off Brunel Rd.)
Pilgrim M. RH2: Reig 6J 207
Pilgrims Cloisters *SE5* *52Ub 113*
(off Sedgmoor Pl.)
Pilgrims Cl. CM15: Pil H 15Vd 40
N13 21Pb 50
UB5: N'olt 36Ea 66
WD25: Wat 5Z 13
Pilgrims Cnr. *NW6* *40Cb 69*
(off Chichester Rd.)
Pilgrims Ct. DA1: Dart 57Qd 119
EN1: Enf 12Tb 33
PILGRIMS HATCH 16Xd 40
Pilgrims La. CM14: Pil H 14Td 40
CR3: Cat'm 98Pb 196
NW3 35Fb 69
RH8: T'sey 97Kc 199
RM16: Chaf H 48Zd 99
RM16: N Stif 46Yd 98
TN16: Westrm 97Kc 199
Pilgrims M. E14 45Gc 93
Pilgrims Pl. NW3 35Fb 69
RH2: Reig 4J 207
Pilgrims Ri. EN4: E Barn 15Gb 31
Pilgrims Rd. DA10: Nflt, Swans 56Ae 121
Pilgrims Rdbt.
RM16: Chaf H, N Stif 47Yd 98
Pilgrim St. EC4 3B 224 (44Rb 91)
Pilgrims Vw. DA9: Ghithe 58Yd 120
Pilgrims Way CR2: S Croy 79Vb 157
DA1: Dart 60Qd 119
E6 39Nc 74
GU24: Bisl 8E 166
HA9: Wemb 32Ra 67
ME19: Tros 86Fe 185
N19 32Mb 70
RH2: Reig 4H 207
TN13: Dun G 89Ed 182
(not continuous)
TN14: Otf 88Md 183
TN14: Sund 94Wc 201
TN15: Kems'g 88Md 183
TN15: Wro 88Be 185
(Battlefields Rd.)
TN15: Wro 88De 185
(Gravesend Rd.)
TN16: Westrm, Bras 95Pc 200
Pilgrims Way Cotts.
TN15: Kems'g 89Qd 183
Pilgrims Way E. TN14: Otf 87Ld 183
Pilgrims Way W. TN14: Otf 89Fd 182
Pilkington Rd. BR6: Farnb 76Sc 160
SE15 54Xb 113
Pillar Box La. TN15: Seal 94Qd 204
Pillfold Ho. SE11 5H 229
Pillions La. UB4: Hayes 42T 84
Pilot Cl. SE8 51Bc 114
Pilot Ind. Cen. NW10 42Ta 87
Pilots Pl. DA12: Grav'nd 8E 122
Pilsdon Cl. SW19 60Za 110
Piltdown Rd. WD19: Wat 21Z 45
Pilton Est., The CR0: C'don 75Rb 157
Pilton Pl. SE17 7E 230 (50Sb 91)
Pimento Ct. W5 48Ma 87
PIMLICO
HP3 6E 4
SW1 7B 228 (50Lb 90)
Pimlico Ho. SW1 7K 227
Pimlico Rd. SW1 7H 227 (50Jb 90)
Pimlico Wlk. N1 3H 219
Pimpernel Way RM3: Rom 23Md 57
Pinchbeck Rd. BR6: Chels 79Vc 161
Pinchfield WD3: Map C 22F 42
Pinchin & Johnsons Yd. *E1* *45Wb 91*
(off Pinchin St.)
Pinchin St. E1 45Wb 91
Pincombe Ho. SE17 7F 231
Pincott La. KT24: W Hor 100R 190
Pincott Pl. SE4 55Zb 114
Pincott Rd. DA6: Bex 57Cd 118
SW19 66Eb 133
Pincroft Wood DA3: Lfield 69Ee 143
Pindar St. EC2 7H 219 (43Ub 91)
PINDEN 68Yd 142
Pindock M. W9 42Db 89
Pineapple Ct. SW1 3B 228
Pine Av. BR4: W W'ck 74Dc 158
DA12: Grav'nd 10F 122
E15 36Fc 73
Pine Cl. BR8: Swan 70Hd 140
CR8: Kenley 89Tb 177
E10 33Dc 72
EN8: Chesh 1Zb 20
GU21: Wok 8N 167
HA7: Stan 21Ka 46
KT15: New H 83K 169
N14 17Lb 32
N19 33Lb 70
SE20 67Yb 136
Pine Coombe CR0: C'don 77Zb 158
Pinecote Dr. SL5: S'dale 3D 146
Pine Ct. KT13: Weyb 78S 150
KT15: Add *77K 149*
(off Church Rd.)
N21 15Pb 32
RM14: Upm 35Rd 77
UB5: N'olt 42Aa 85
Pine Cres. CM13: Hut 14Fe 41
SM5: Cars 83Fb 175
Pinecrest Gdns. BR6: Farnb 77Rc 160
Pine Cft. *KT13: Weyb* *79T 150*
(off St George's Rd.)
Pinecroft CM13: Hut 17De 41
HP3: Hem H 6P 3
RM2: Rom 28Ld 57
Pinecroft Ct. DA16: Well 52Wc 117
HP3: Hem H 6P 3
Pinecroft Cres. EN5: Barn 14Ab 30
Pine Dean KT23: Bookh 97Da 191
Pinedene SE15 53Xb 113
Pinefield Cl. E14 45Cc 92
Pinefields *KT15: Add* *77K 149*
(off Church Rd.)
Pine Gdns. HA4: Ruis 32X 65
KT5: Surb 72Qa 153
Pine Glade BR6: Farnb 77Pc 160
Pine Gro. AL2: Brick W 2Ba 13
AL9: Brk P 7K 9
GU20: W'sham 9B 146
KT13: Weyb 78R 150
N4 33Nb 70
N20 18Bb 31
SW19 64Bb 133
WD23: Bush 12Ba 27
Pine Gro. M. KT13: Weyb 78S 150
Pine Hill KT18: Eps 87Ta 173
Pine Ho. *E3* *39Ac 72*
(off Barge La.)
SE16 *47Yb 92*
(off Ainsty Est.)
W10 *42Ab 88*
(off Droop St.)
Pinehurst *GU22: Wok* *90B 168*
(off Park Dr.)
SL5: S'hill 1B 146
TN14: S'oaks 93Nd 203
TW20: Eng G 6N 125
Pinehurst Cl. KT20: Kgswd 94Cb 195
WD5: Ab L 4U 12
Pinehurst Ct. *W11* *44Bb 89*
(off Colville Gdns.)
Pinehurst Gdns. KT14: W Byf 84L 169
Pinehurst Wlk. BR6: Orp 74Tc 160
Pinel Cl. GU25: Vir W 70A 126
Pine Lodge *KT11: Cobh* *87Y 171*
(off Leigh Cnr.)
Pinemartin Cl. NW2 34Ya 68
Pine M. *NW10* *40Za 68*
(off Clifford Gdns.)
Pineneedle La. TN13: S'oaks 95Kd 203
Pine Pl. SM7: Bans 86Za 174
UB4: Hayes 42V 84
Piner Cotts. SL4: Wind 5C 102
Pine Ridge AL1: St A 2H 7
SM5: Cars 80Jb 156
Pineridge Cl. KT13: Weyb 77U 150
Pineridge Ct. EN5: Barn 14Za 30
Pine Rd. GU22: Wok 2N 187
N11 19Jb 32
NW2 35Ya 68
Pines, The CR5: Coul 89Mb 176
CR8: Purl 85Sb 177
GU21: Wok 86B 168
HP3: Hem H 6H 3
IG8: Wfd G 20Hc 35
KT9: Chess 76Na 153
N14 15Lb 32
RM16: Grays 46De 99
SE19 65Rb 135
SL2: Wex 3M 81
SL3: L'ly 46B 82
TN14: S'oaks 93Md 203
TW16: Sun 69W 128
WD6: Bore 12Pa 29
Pines Av. EN1: Enf 8Yb 20
Pines Cl. HA6: Nwood 23U 44
Pines Rd. BR1: Brom 68Nc 138
Pine St. EC1 5K 217 (42Qb 90)
Pine Tree Cl. HP2: Hem H 1M 3
TW5: Cran 53X 107
Pinetree Gdns. HP3: Hem H 4N 3
Pine Tree Hill GU22: Pyr 88F 168
Pinetree Ho. WD25: Wat 8Aa 13
Pine Tree La. TN15: Ivy H 97Wd 204
Pine Tree Lodge BR2: Brom 70Hc 137
Pine Trees Bus. Pk. TW18: Staines 64G 126
Pine Trees Dr. UB10: Ick 35N 63
Pine Tree Way SE13 55Dc 114
Pine Vw. TN15: Plat 92Ee 205
Pineview Ct. E4 18Ec 34
Pine Vw. Mnr. CM16: Epp 2Wc 23
Pine Wlk. CR3: Cat'm 94Ub 197
KT5: Surb 72Qa 153
KT11: Cobh 86Z 171
KT23: Bookh 97Da 191
KT24: E Hor 100V 190
SM5: Cars 82Fb 175
SM7: Bans 89Hb 175
Pine Wlk. E. SM5: Cars 83Fb 175
Pine Wlk. W. SM5: Cars 82Fb 175
Pine Way TW20: Eng G 5M 125
Pine Wood TW16: Sun 67W 128
Pinewood Av. DA15: Sidc 60Uc 116
HA5: Hat E 23Da 45
KT15: New H 81L 169
RM13: Rain 42Kd 97
TN14: S'oaks 93Md 203
UB8: Hil 44P 83
Pinewood Cl. AL4: St A 2G 6
BR6: Orp 74Tc 160
CR0: C'don 76Ac 158
GU21: Wok 87C 168
HA5: Hat E 23Da 45
HA6: Nwood 22W 44
SL0: Iver H 38E 62
SL9: Ger X 31A 62
SS17: Linf 8K 101
WD6: Bore 11Ta 29
WD17: Wat 11W 26
Pinewood Ct. EN2: Enf 13Rb 33
KT15: Add 77M 149
SW4 58Mb 112
Pinewood Dr. BR6: Orp 78Uc 160
EN6: Pot B 3Bb 17
KT15: New H 82L 169
TW18: Staines 64J 127
Pinewood Film Studios 38D 62
Pinewood Gdns. HP1: Hem H 2K 3
Pinewood Grn. SL0: Iver H 38E 62
Pinewood Gro. KT15: New H 82K 169
W5 44La 86
Pinewood Lodge WD23: B Hea 18Fa 28
Pinewood M. TW19: Stanw 58M 105
Pinewood Pk. KT15: New H 83K 169
Pinewood Pl. DA2: Wilm 61Gd 140
(not continuous)
KT19: Ewe 77Ta 153
Pinewood Rd. BR2: Brom 70Jc 137
GU25: Vir W 10L 125
RM4: Have B 21Ed 56
SE2 51Zc 117
SL0: Iver H 37D 62
TW13: Felt 62X 129
Pinewood Way CM13: Hut 15Fe 41
Pinfold Rd. SW16 63Nb 134
WD23: Bush 12Ba 27
Pinglestone Cl. UB7: Harm 52N 105
Pinkcoat Cl. TW13: Felt 62X 129
Pinkerton Pl. SW16 63Mb 134
Pinkham Mans. W4 50Qa 87
Pinkham Way N11 24Jb 50
Pink La. SL1: Burn 10A 60
Pinks Farm WD7: Shenl 3Sa 15
Pink's Hill BR8: Swan 71Gd 162
Pinkwell Av. UB3: Harl 49T 84
Pinkwell La. UB3: Harl 49S 84
Pinley Gdns. RM9: Dag 39Xc 75
Pinnace Ho. *E14* *48Ec 92*
(off Manchester Rd.)
Pinnacle, The TN13: S'oaks 96Jd 202
Pinnacle Hill DA7: Bex 56Dd 118
Pinnacle Hill Nth. DA7: Bex 56Dd 118
Pinnacle Ho. *NW9* *26Va 48*
(off Heritage Av.)
Pinnacle Pl. HA7: Stan 21Ka 46
Pinnacles EN9: Walt A 6Gc 21
Pinnacle Way *E14* *44Ac 92*
(off Commercial Rd.)
Pinnata Cl. EN2: Enf 11Sb 33
Pinn Cl. UB8: Cowl 44M 83
Pinnell Rd. SE9 56Mc 115
PINNER 28Aa 45
Pinner Ct. HA5: Pinn 28Ca 45
NW8 5B 214
PINNER GREEN 26Y 45
Pinner Grn. HA5: Pinn 26Y 45
Pinner Gro. HA5: Pinn 28Aa 45
Pinner Hill HA5: Pinn 24X 45
Pinner Hill Farm HA5: Pinn 25X 45
Pinner Hill Golf Course 23X 45
Pinner Hill Rd. HA5: Pinn 24X 45
Pinner Pk. 25Ca 45
Pinner Pk. HA5: Pinn 26Ca 45
Pinner Pk. Av. HA2: Harr 27Da 45
Pinner Pk. Gdns. HA2: Harr 26Ea 46
Pinner Rd. HA1: Harr 28Ca 45
HA2: Harr 28Ca 45
HA5: Pinn 25V 44
(High St.)
HA5: Pinn 28Ba 45
(Nower Hill)
HA6: Nwood, Pinn 25V 44
WD19: Wat 16Z 27
Pinners Cl. SM5: Cars 75Gb 155
Pinners Pas. EC2 2G 225
Pinner Vw. HA1: Harr 30Ea 46
HA2: Harr 28Ea 46
PINNERWOOD PARK 25Y 45
Pinnocks Av. DA11: Grav'nd 10D 122
Pinn Way HA4: Ruis 31T 64
Pinson Way BR5: Orp 74Zc 161
Pinstone Way SL9: Ger X 33D 62
Pintail Cl. E6 43Nc 94
Pintail Ct. *SE8* *51Bc 114*
(off Pilot Cl.)
Pintail Rd. IG8: Wfd G 24Kc 53
Pintail Way UB4: Yead 43Z 85
Pinter Ho. *SW9* *54Nb 112*
(off Grantham Rd.)
Pinto Cl. WD6: Bore 16Ta 29
Pinto Way SE3 56Kc 115
Pioneer Centre, The SE15 53Yb 114
Pioneer Cl. E14 43Dc 92
Pioneer Ho. WC1 3H 217
Pioneer Pl. CR0: Sels 81Cc 178
Pioneer Point IG1: Ilf 34Rc 74
Pioneers Ind. Pk. CR0: Bedd 74Nb 156
Pioneer St. SE15 53Wb 113
Pioneer Way BR8: Swan 69Gd 140
W12 44Xa 88
WD18: Wat 16V 26
Piper Building, The SW6 55Db 111
Piper Cl. N7 36Pb 70
Piper Rd. KT1: King T 69Qa 131
Pipers Cl. KT11: Cobh 87Z 171
SL1: Burn 1A 80
Piper's End GU25: Vir W 9P 125
Piper's Gdns. CR0: C'don 73Ac 158
Pipers Grn. NW9 29Sa 47
Pipers Grn. La. HA8: Edg 20Na 29
(not continuous)
Piper's Grn. Rd. TN16: B Char 100Wc 201
Pipers Ho. *SE10* *50Fc 93*
(off Collington St.)
Pipers La. TN16: B Char 99Wc 201

Pipers Rd. CR5: Coul 88Mb 176
Piper Way IG1: Ilf 32Tc 74
Pipewell Rd. SM5: Cars 72Gb 155
Pippenhall SE9 58Rc 116
Pippin Cl. CR0: C'don 74Bc 158
NW2 34Wa 68
SL1: Slou 3H 81
WD7: Shenl 5Na 15
Pippin Ct. *SW8* 51Pb 112
(off Vauxhall Gro.)
Pippin Ho. *W10* 45Za 88
(off Freston Rd.)
Pippins, The SL3: L'ly 46B 82
WD25: Wat 6Y 13
Pippins Cl. UB7: W Dray 48M 83
Pippins Ct. TW15: Ashf 65R 128
Piquet Rd. SE20 68Yb 136
PIRBRIGHT 5D 186
PIRBRIGHT CAMP 3A 186
Pirbright Cres. CR0: New Ad 79Ec 158
Pirbright Golf Course 3B 186
Pirbright Grn. GU24: Pirb 5D 186
Pirbright Rd. GU3: Norm 10A 186
SW18 60Bb 111
Pirbright Ter. GU24: Pirb 5D 186
Pirie Cl. SE5 55Tb 113
Pirie St. E16 46Kc 93
Pirin Ct. E4 21Cc 52
Pirrip Cl. DA12: Grav'nd 10H 123
Pirton Cl. HP2: Hem H 1P 3
Pisa Pl. WD18: Wat 13U 26
Pissaro Ho. *N1* 38Qb 70
(off Augustas La.)
Pitcairn Cl. RM7: Mawney 28Cd 56
Pitcairn Ho. E9 38Yb 72
Pitcairn Rd. CR4: Mitc 66Hb 133
Pitcairn's Path HA2: Harr 34Ea 66
Pitchfont La. RH8: Limp, T'sey 97Hc 199
Pitchford St. E15 38Fc 73
PITCH PLACE 10L 187
Pitfield DA3: Hartl 70Be 143
Pitfield Cres. SE28 46Wc 95
Pitfield Est. N1 3H 219 (41Ub 91)
Pitfield St. N1 4H 219 (41Ub 91)
Pitfield Way EN3: Enf H 11Yb 34
NW10 37Sa 67
Pitfold Cl. SE12 58Kc 115
Pitfold Rd. SE12 58Jc 115
Pitlake CR0: C'don 75Rb 157
Pitlochry Ho. *SE27* 61Rb 135
(off Elmcourt Rd.)
Pitman Ho. SE8 53Cc 114
Pitman St. SE5 52Sb 113
Pitmaston Ho. *SE13* 54Ec 114
(off Lewisham Rd.)
Pitsea Pl. E1 44Zb 92
Pitsea St. E1 44Zb 92
Pitshanger La. W5 42Ka 86
Pitson Cl. KT15: Add 77M 149
Pitt Cres. SW19 63Db 133
Pitt Dr. AL4: St A 5G 6
Pittman Cl. CM13: Ingve 22Ee 59
Pittman Gdns. IG1: Ilf 36Sc 74
Pitt Pl. KT17: Eps 86Ua 174
Pitt Rd. BR6: Farnb 77Sc 160
CR0: C'don 71Sb 157
CR7: Thor H 71Sb 157
HA2: Harr 33Ea 66
KT17: Eps 86Ua 174
Pitt's Head M. W1 7J 221 (46Jb 90)
Pittsmead Av. BR2: Hayes 73Jc 159
Pitts Rd. SL1: Slou 6G 80
Pitt St. W8 47Cb 89
Pittville Gdns. SE25 69Wb 135
Pitwood CM15: Shenf 18Ce 41
Pitwood Grn. KT20: Tad 92Ya 194
Pitwood Pk. Ind. Est. KT20: Tad 92Xa 194
Pix Farm La. HP1: Hem H 3D 2
Pixfield Ct. *BR2: Brom* 68Hc 137
(off Beckenham La.)
Pixies Hill Cres. HP1: Hem H 4H 3
(not continuous)
Pixies Hill Rd. HP1: Hem H 3H 3
Pixley St. E14 44Bc 92
Pixton Way CR0: Sels 81Ac 178
Place, The 4E 216 (41Mb 90)
Place Farm Av. BR6: Orp 74Tc 160
Place Farm Rd. RH1: Blet 2K 209
Placehouse La. CR5: Coul 91Pb 196
Plackett Way SL1: Slou 6B 80
Plain, The CM16: Epp 1Xc 23
Plaines Cl. SL1: Slou 6D 80
Plain Ride SL4: Wind 10A 102
Plaisterers Highwalk EC2 1D 224
PLAISTOW
BR1 66Jc 137
E13 40Jc 73
Plaistow Cl. SS17: Stan H 1M 101
Plaistow Gro. BR1: Brom 66Kc 137
E15 39Hc 73
Plaistow La. BR1: Brom 66Jc 137
Plaistow Pk. Rd. E13 40Kc 73
(not continuous)
Plaistow Rd. E13 39Hc 73
E15 39Hc 73
Plaistow Wharf E16 47Jc 93
Plaitford Cl. WD3: Rick 19N 25
Plane Av. DA11: Nflt 59Fe 121
Plane Ho. BR2: Brom 68Gc 137
Planes, The KT16: Chert 73L 149
Plane St. SE26 62Xb 135
Planetarium
Greenwich 52Fc 115
Planetree Ct. *W6* 49Za 88
(off Brook Grn.)
Plane Tree Cres. TW13: Felt 62X 129
Plane Tree Ho. *SE8* 51Ac 114
(off Etta St.)
W8 47Bb 89
(off Duchess of Bedford's Wlk.)
Plane Tree Wlk. N2 27Gb 49
SE19 65Ub 135
Plantaganet Pl. EN9: Walt A 5Dc 20
Plantagenet Cl. KT4: Wor Pk 77Ta 153
Plantagenet Gdns. RM6: Chad H 31Zc 75
Plantagenet Ho. *SE18* 48Pc 94
(off Leda Rd.)
Plantagenet Pl. RM6: Chad H 31Zc 75
Plantagenet Rd. EN5: New Bar 14Eb 31
Plantain Gdns. *E11* 34Fc 73
(off Hollydown Way)
Plantain Pl. SE1 1F 231 (47Tb 91)
Plantation, The SE3 54Jc 115
Plantation Cl. DA9: Ghithe 58Vd 120
SW4 57Nb 112
Plantation Dr. BR5: Orp 74Zc 161
Plantation La. CR3: W'ham, Wold 91Ac 198
CR6: W'ham 91Ac 198
EC3 4H 225
Plantation Pl. EC3 4H 225
Plantation Rd. BR8: Hext 66Jd 140
DA8: Erith 53Jd 118
Plantation Wharf SW11 55Eb 111
Plantree Path *E17* 28Cc 52
(off Selborne Rd.)
Plasel Ct. *E13* 39Kc 73
(off Pawsey Cl.)
PLASHET 37Nc 74
Plashet Cl. SS17: Stan H 1M 101
Plashet Gdns. CM13: B'wood 21Ce 59
Plashet Gro. E6 39Lc 73
Plashet Rd. E13 39Jc 73
Plassy Rd. SE6 59Dc 114
Plate Ho. *E14* 50Dc 92
(off Burrells Wharf Sq.)
Platford Grn. RM11: Horn 28Nd 57
Platina St. EC2 5G 219
Platinum Ct. *E1* 42Yb 92
(off Cephas Av.)
Platinum M. N15 29Vb 51
Plato Rd. SW2 56Nb 112
Platt, The SW15 55Za 110
Platt Comn. TN15: Plat 92Ee 205
Platt Ct. *AL1: St A* 2C 6
(off Hatfield Rd.)
Platt Halls NW9 26Va 48
Platt Ho. La. TN15: Stans, Wro 85Ee 185
Platt Ind. Est. TN15: Plat 91De 205
Platt Mill Cl. TN15: Plat 92De 205
Platt Mill Ter. TN15: Plat 92De 205
Platt's Eyot TW12: Hamp 68Ca 129
Platt's La. NW3 35Cb 69
Platts Rd. EN3: Enf H 11Yb 34
Platt St. NW1 1D 216 (40Mb 70)
Plawsfield Rd. BR3: Beck 67Zb 136
Plaxdale Grn. Rd. TN15: Stans 85Zd 185
Plaxdale Ho. SE17 6H 231
PLAXTOL 99Ae 205
Plaxtol Cl. BR1: Brom 67Lc 137
Plaxtol La. TN15: Plax 99Yd 204
Plaxtol Rd. DA8: Erith 52Gd 118
PLAXTOL SPOUTE 99Ce 205
Plaxton Ct. E11 34Hc 73
Playfair Ho. *E14* 44Cc 92
(off Saracen St.)
Playfair Mans. *W14* 51Ab 110
(off Queen's Club Gdns.)
Playfair St. W6 50Ya 88
Playfield Av. RM5: Col R 25Ed 56
Playfield Cres. SE22 57Vb 113
Playfield Rd. HA8: Edg 26Sa 47
Playford Rd. N4 33Pb 70
(not continuous)
Playgreen Way SE6 62Cc 136
Playground Cl. BR3: Beck 68Zb 136
Playhouse, The 74V 150
(off Hepworth Way)
Playhouse Ct. SE1 7D 224
Playhouse Theatre 6G 223
Playhouse Yd.
EC4 3B 224 (44Rb 91)
Plaza Bus. Cen. EN3: Brim 12Bc 34
Plaza Hgts. E10 34Ec 72
Plaza Pde. *HA0: Wemb* 37Na 67
(off Ealing Rd.)
NW6 40Db 69
Plaza Shop. Centre, The
W1 2C 222 (44Lb 90)
Plaza Wlk. NW9 27Sa 47
Pleasance, The SW15 56Xa 110
Pleasance Rd. BR5: St P 68Xc 139
SW15 57Xa 110
Pleasance Theatre 37Nb 70
(off Carpenters M.)
Pleasant Gro. CR0: C'don 76Bc 158
Pleasant Pl. HA2: Harr 33Fa 66
KT12: Hers 79Y 151
N1 38Rb 71
WD3: W Hyd 24G 42
Pleasant Row NW1 39Kb 70
Pleasant Vw. DA8: Erith 50Gd 96
Pleasant Vw. Pl. BR6: Farnb 78Rc 160
Pleasant Way HA0: Wemb 40La 66
Pleasaunce Mans. *SE10* 50Jc 93
(off Halstow Rd.)
Pleasure Pit Rd. KT21: Asht 90Ra 173
Plender Ct. *NW1* 39Lb 70
(off College Pl.)
Plender St. NW1 1B 216 (39Lb 70)
Pleshey Rd. N7 35Mb 70
Plesman Way SM6: Wall 81Nb 176
Plessey Bldg. *E14* 44Cc 92
(off Dod St.)
Plevna Cres. N15 30Ub 51
Plevna Rd. N9 20Wb 33
TW12: Hamp 67Da 129
Plevna St. E14 48Ec 92
Pleydell Av. SE19 66Vb 135
W6 49Va 88
Pleydell Ct. EC4 3A 224
Pleydell Est. EC1 4E 218
Pleydell Gdns. *SE19* 65Vb 135
(off Anerley Hill)
Pleydell Ho. *EC4* 3A 224
(off Pleydell St.)
Pleydell St. EC4 3A 224
Plimley Pl. *W12* 47Za 88
(off Shepherd's Bush Pl.)
Plimsoll Cl. E14 44Dc 92
Plimsoll Rd. N4 34Qb 70
Plough Cl. NW10 41Xa 88
Plough Ct. EC3 4G 225 (45Tb 91)
Plough Farm Cl. HA4: Ruis 30T 44
Plough Hill EN6: Cuff 1Nb 18
TN15: Bor G 95Be 205
Plough Ind. Est. KT22: Lea 92Ja 192
Plough La. CR8: Purl 81Nb 176
KT11: Cobh 89W 170
SE22 58Vb 113
SL2: Stoke P 9M 61
SM6: Bedd, Wall 77Nb 156
SW17 64Db 133
SW19 64Db 133
TW11: Tedd 64Ja 130
UB9: Hare 23L 43
WD3: Sarr 5H 11
Plough La. Cl. SM6: Bedd 78Nb 156
Ploughlees La. SL1: Slou 5J 81
Ploughmans Cl. NW1 39Mb 70
Ploughmans End TW7: Isle 57Fa 108
Ploughmans Wlk. *N2* 26Eb 49
(off Long La.)
Plough M. SW11 56Fb 111
Plough Pl. EC4 2A 224 (44Qb 90)
Plough Ri. RM14: Upm 31Ud 78
Plough Rd. KT19: Ewe 81Ta 173
SW11 55Fb 111
Plough St. E1 44Vb 91
Plough Ter. SW11 56Fb 111
Plough Way SE16 49Zb 92
Plough Yd. EC2 6J 219 (42Ub 91)
Plover Cl. TW18: Staines 62H 127
Plover Gdns. RM14: Upm 32Vd 78
Plover Ho. *SW9* 52Qb 112
(off Brixton Rd.)
Plovers Ri. GU24: Brkwd 2C 186
Plover Way SE16 48Ac 92
UB4: Yead 44Z 85
Plowden Bldgs. *EC4* 4K 223
(off Middle Temple La.)
Plowman Cl. N18 22Tb 51
Plowman Way RM8: Dag 32Yc 75
Plumber's Row E1 43Wb 91
Plumbridge St. SE10 53Ec 114
Plum Cl. TW13: Felt 60W 106
Plume Ho. *SE10* 51Dc 114
(off Creek Rd.)
Plum Gth. TW8: Bford 49Ma 87
Plum La. SE18 52Rc 116
Plummer La. CR4: Mitc 68Hb 133
Plummer Rd. SW4 59Mb 112
Plummers Cft. TN13: Dun G 93Gd 202
Plumpton Av. RM12: Horn 35Nd 77
Plumpton Cl. UB5: N'olt 37Ca 65
Plumpton Way SM5: Cars 76Gb 155
PLUMSTEAD 49Uc 94
PLUMSTEAD COMMON 51Rc 116
Plumstead Comn. Rd. SE18 51Rc 116
Plumstead High St. SE18 49Tc 94
Plumstead Leisure Cen. 50Vc 95
Plumstead Rd. SE18 49Rc 94
(not continuous)
Plumtree Cl. RM10: Dag 37Dd 76
SM6: Wall 80Mb 156
Plum Tree Ct. RM3: Rom 21Nd 57
Plumtree Ct. EC4 2B 224 (44Rb 91)
Plumtree Mead IG10: Lough 13Qc 36
Pluto Cl. SL1: Slou 7C 80
Pluto Ri. HP2: Hem H 1N 3
Plymen Ho. KT8: W Mole 71Ca 151
Plymouth Ct. *KT5: Surb* 70Pa 131
(off Cranes Pk. Av.)
Plymouth Dr. TN13: S'oaks 96Ld 203
Plymouth Ho. *IG11: Bark* 38Wc 75
(off Margaret Bondfield Av.)
SE10 53Dc 114
(off Devonshire Dr.)
Plymouth Pk. TN13: S'oaks 96Ld 203
Plymouth Rd. BR1: Brom 67Kc 137
E16 43Jc 93
RM16: Chaf H 49Yd 98
SL1: Slou 3C 80
Plymouth Ter. *NW2* 37Ya 68
(off Glengall Rd.)
Plymouth Wharf E14 49Fc 93
Plympton Av. NW6 38Bb 69
Plympton Cl. DA17: Belv 48Ad 95
Plympton Pl. NW8 6D 214 (42Gb 89)
Plympton Rd. NW6 38Bb 69
Plympton St. NW8 6D 214 (42Gb 89)
Plymstock Rd. DA16: Well 52Yc 117
PM Gallery & House 46Ma 87
Pocahontas Memorial 8D 122
(off Church St.)
Pocket Hill TN13: S'oaks 100Jd 202
Pocketsdell La. HP3: Bov 10A 2
Pocklington Cl. NW9 26Ua 48
W12 48Wa 88
(off Ashchurch Pk. Vs.)
Pocklington Ct. SW15 60Wa 110
Pocklington Lodge W12 48Wa 88
Pocock Av. UB7: W Dray 48P 83
Pococks La. SL4: Eton 10J 81
Pocock St. SE1 1B 230 (47Rb 91)
Podmore Rd. SW18 56Eb 111
Poets Chase HP1: Hem H 1K 3
Poets Ct. SE25 70Wb 135
W3 46Sa 87
Poet's Rd. N5 36Tb 71
Poets Way HA1: Harr 28Ga 46
Point, The 13Qa 29
Point, The *E17* 28Cc 52
(off Tower M.)
GU21: Wok 88B 168
(off Chertsey Rd.)
HA4: Ruis 35W 64
W2 1B 220
Pointalls Cl. N3 26Eb 49
Point Cl. SE10 53Ec 114
Pointer Cl. SE28 44Zc 95
Pointers, The KT21: Asht 92Na 193
Pointers Cl. E14 50Dc 92
Pointers Cotts. TW10: Ham 61La 130
POINTERS GREEN 90W 170
Pointers Rd. KT11: Cobh 88S 170
Point Hill SE10 52Ec 114
Point Pl. HA9: Wemb 38Ra 67
Point Pleasant SW18 56Cb 111
Point Ter. *E7* 36Kc 73
(off Claremont Rd.)
Point West SW7 49Db 89
Point Wharf TW8: Bford 52Na 109
Point Wharf La. TW8: Bford 52Ma 109
Poland Ho. *E15* 39Fc 73
(off High St.)
Poland St. W1 2C 222 (44Lb 90)
Polar Pk. UB7: Harm 52P 105
Polebrook Rd. SE3 55Lc 115
Pole Cat All. BR2: Hayes 75Hc 159
Polecroft La. SE6 61Bc 136
Polehamptons, The TW12: Hamp 66Ea 130
Pole Hill Rd. E4 17Ec 34
UB4: Hayes 40S 64
UB10: Hil 42R 84
Polesden Gdns. SW20 68Xa 132
Polesden La. GU23: Rip 95H 189
Polesden Rd. KT23: Bookh 100Da 191
Polesden Vw. KT23: Bookh 99Da 191
Poles Hill WD3: Sarr 5G 10
Polesteeple Hill TN16: Big H 89Mc 179
Polesworth Ho. *W2* 43Cb 89
(off Alfred Rd.)
Polesworth Rd. RM9: Dag 38Zc 75
Poley Rd. SS17: Stan H 2L 101
Polhill TN14: Hals 87Ed 182
Police Sta. La. WD23: Bush 17Da 27
Police Sta. Rd. KT12: Hers 79Y 151
POLISH WAR MEMORIAL 38Y 65
Polka Theatre for Children 65Db 133
Pollard Av. UB9: Den 30H 43
Pollard Cl. E16 45Jc 93
IG7: Chig 22Wc 55
N7 35Pb 70
SL4: Old Win 7M 103
Pollard Ho. KT4: Wor Pk 77Ya 154
N1 2H 217
SE16 48Yb 91
(off Spa Rd.)
Pollard Rd. GU22: Wok 88D 168
N20 19Gb 31
SM4: Mord 71Fb 155
Pollard Row E2 41Wb 91
Pollards WD3: Map C 22F 42
Pollards Cl. EN7: G Oak 1Sb 19
IG10: Lough 15Lc 35
Pollards Cres. SW16 69Nb 134
Pollards Hill E. SW16 69Pb 134
Pollards Hill Nth. SW16 69Nb 134
Pollards Hill Sth. SW16 69Nb 134
Pollards Hill W. SW16 69Pb 134
Pollards Oak Cres. RH8: Oxt 4L 211
Pollards Oak Rd. RH8: Oxt 4L 211
Pollard St. E2 41Wb 91
Pollardswood Grange HP8: Chal G 14A 24
Pollards Wood Hill RH8: Oxt 2M 211
Pollards Wood Rd. RH8: Oxt 3M 211
SW16 69Nb 134
Pollard Wlk. DA14: Sidc 65Yc 139
Pollen St. W1 3B 222 (44Lb 90)
Pollitt Dr. NW8 5B 214 (42Fb 89)
Pollock Ho. *W10* 42Ab 88
(off Kensal Rd.)
Pollock's Toy Mus. 7C 216 (43Lb 90)
Pollyhaugh DA4: Eyns 76Nd 163
Polo Centre, The SL5: S'hill 9G 124
Polperro Cl. BR6: St M Cry 72Vc 161
Polperro Ho. *W2* 43Cb 89
(off Westbourne Pk. Rd.)
Polperro M. SE11 5A 230 (49Rb 91)
Polsted Rd. SE6 59Bc 114
Polsten M. EN3: Enf L 9Cc 20
Polthorne Est. *SE18* 49Tc 94
(off Polthorne Gro.)
Polthorne Gro. SE18 49Sc 94
Polworth Rd. SW16 64Nb 134
Polychrome Ct. SE1 2B 230
Polygon, The *NW8* 39Fb 69
(off Avenue Rd.)
SW4 56Lb 112
Polygon Bus. Cen. SL3: Poyle 54H 105
Polygon Rd. NW1 2D 216 (40Mb 70)
(not continuous)
Polytechnic St. SE18 49Qc 94
Pomell Way E1 2K 225 (44Vb 91)
Pomeroy Cl. TW1: Twick 56Ka 108
Pomeroy Cres. WD24: Wat 8X 13
Pomeroy Ho. *E2* 40Zb 72
(off St James's Av.)
W11 44Ab 88
(off Lancaster Rd.)
Pomeroy St. SE14 52Yb 114
Pomfret Rd. SE5 55Rb 113
Pomoja La. N19 33Nb 70
Pomona Ho. *SE8* 49Ac 92
(off Evelyn St.)
Pompadour Cl. CM14: W'ley 22Yd 58
Pond Cl. KT12: Hers 79V 150
(not continuous)
N12 23Gb 49
SE3 54Jc 115
UB9: Hare 26L 43
Pond Cott. La. BR4: W W'ck 74Cc 158
Pond Cotts. SE21 60Ub 113
PONDERS END 15Yb 34
Ponders End Ind. Est. EN3: Pond E 15Ac 34
Ponder St. N7 38Pb 70
Pond Farm Cl. KT20: Walt H 96Xa 194
Pond Farm Est. E5 34Yb 72
Pond Fld. End IG10: Lough 16Lc 35
Pondfield Ho. SE27 64Sb 135
Pondfield La. CM13: B'wood 21Ce 59
DA12: Shorne 6N 145
Pondfield Rd. BR2: Hayes 74Gc 159
BR6: Farnb 76Rc 160
CR8: Kenley 88Rb 177
RM10: Dag 36Dd 76
Pond Grn. HA4: Ruis 33U 64
Pond Hill Gdns. SM3: Cheam 79Ab 154
Pond Ho. HA7: Stan 23Ka 46
KT16: Chert 73K 149
SW3 6D 226 (49Gb 89)
Pond La. TN15: Ivy H 97Ud 204
Pond Lees Cl. RM10: Dag 38Fd 76
Pond Mead SE21 58Tb 113
Pond Path BR7: Chst 65Rc 138
Pond Piece KT22: Oxs 85Da 171
Pond Pl. KT21: Asht 89Na 173
SW3 6D 226 (49Gb 89)
Pond Rd. E15 40Gc 73
GU22: Wok 2L 187
HP3: Hem H 7A 4
SE3 54Hc 115
TW20: Egh 65E 126
Ponds, The KT13: Weyb 79T 150
Pondside Av. KT4: Wor Pk 74Ya 154
Pondside Cl. UB3: Harl 51T 106
Pond Sq. N6 32Jb 70
Pond St. NW3 36Gb 69
Pond Wlk. RM14: Upm 33Ud 78
Pond Way TW11: Tedd 65La 130
Pondwicks Cl. AL1: St A 3A 6
Pondwood Ri. BR6: Orp 73Uc 160
Ponler St. E1 44Xb 91
Ponsard Rd. NW10 41Xa 88
Ponsford St. E9 37Yb 72
Ponsonby Ho. *E2* 40Yb 72
(off Bishop's Way, not continuous)
Ponsonby Pl. SW1 7E 228 (50Mb 90)
Ponsonby Rd. SW15 59Xa 110
Ponsonby Ter. SW1 7E 228 (50Mb 90)
Pontefract Ct. *UB5: N'olt* 36Da 65
(off Newmarket Av.)
Pontefract Rd. BR1: Brom 64Hc 137
Pontoise Cl. TN13: S'oaks 94Hd 202
Ponton Rd. SW8 52Mb 112
Pont St. SW1 4F 227 (48Hb 89)
Pont St. M. SW1 4F 227 (48Hb 89)
Pontypool Pl. SE1 1B 230 (47Rb 91)
Pontypool Wlk. RM3: Rom 23Ld 57
Pony Chase KT11: Cobh 85Ba 171
Pooja Ct. *NW1* 38Lb 70
(off Agar Gro.)
Pool Cl. BR3: Beck 64Cc 136
KT8: W Mole 71Ba 151
Pool Ct. SE6 61Cc 136
Poole Cl. HA4: Ruis 33U 64
Poole Ct. *N1* 38Ub 71
(off St Peter's Way)
TW4: Houn 54Aa 107
Poole Ct. Rd. TW4: Houn 54Aa 107
Poole Ho. RM16: Grays 7E 100
SE11 5J 229
POOL END 71Q 150
Pool End Cl. TW17: Shep 71Q 150
Poole Rd. E9 37Zb 72
GU21: Wok 90A 168
KT19: Ewe 79Ta 153
RM11: Horn 31Pd 77
Pooles Bldgs. WC1 6K 217
Pooles Cotts. TW10: Ham 61Ma 131
Pooles La. RM9: Dag 40Ad 75
SW10 52Eb 111
Pooles Pk. N4 33Qb 70
Poole St. N1 1F 219 (39Tb 71)
Poole Way UB4: Hayes 41U 84
Pooley Av. TW20: Egh 64D 126
Pooley Dr. SW14 55Sa 109
POOLEY GREEN 64E 126
Pooley Grn. Cl. TW20: Egh 64D 126
Pooley Grn. Rd. TW20: Egh 64D 126
Pooley Ho. E1 41Zb 92
E18 25Jc 53
Pooleys La. AL9: Wel G 5D 8
Pool Ho. NW8 7C 214
Pool in the Park 91B 188
Pool La. SL1: Slou 5J 81
Poolmans Rd. SL4: Wind 5B 102
Poolmans St. SE16 47Zb 92
Pool Rd. HA1: Harr 31Fa 66
KT8: W Mole 71Ba 151
Poolsford Rd. NW9 28Ua 48
Pools on the Park 56Ma 109
Poonah St. E1 44Yb 92
Pope Cl. SW19 65Fb 133
TW14: Felt 60V 106
Pope Ct. CM14: W'ley 22Xd 58
Pope Ho. *SE5* 52Tb 113
(off Elmington Est.)
SE16 49Xb 91
(off Manor Est.)
Pope Rd. BR2: Brom 71Mc 159
Popes Av. TW2: Twick 61Ga 130
Popes Cl. SL3: Coln 52D 104
Popes Ct. TW2: Twick 61Ga 130
WD5: Ab L 3U 12
Popes Dr. N3 25Cb 49
Popes Gro. CR0: C'don 76Bc 158
TW1: Twick 61Ha 130
TW2: Twick 61Ha 130
Pope's Head All. EC3 3G 225 (44Tb 91)
Popes La. RH8: Oxt 6J 211
W5 48Ma 87
WD24: Wat 9X 13
Pope's Rd. SW9 55Qb 112
WD5: Ab L 3U 12
Pope St. SE1 2J 231 (47Ub 91)
Popham Cl. TW13: Hanw 62Ba 129
Popham Gdns. TW9: Rich 55Qa 109
Popham Rd. N1 39Sb 71
Popham St. N1 39Rb 71
(not continuous)
Pop in Commercial Cen.
HA9: Wemb 36Ra 67
Popinjays Row *SM3: Cheam* 78Za 154
(off Netley Cl.)
POPLAR 45Dc 92
Poplar Av. AL10: Hat 1P 7
BR6: Farnb 75Rc 160
CR4: Mitc 67Hb 133
DA12: Grav'nd 3E 144
KT22: Lea 94Ka 192
UB2: S'hall 48Da 85
UB7: Yiew 45P 83
Poplar Bath St. E14 44Dc 92
Poplar Bus. Pk. E14 45Ec 92
Poplar Cl. E9 36Bc 72
HA5: Pinn 25Z 45
KT17: Eps D 87Xa 174
RM15: S Ock 42Zd 99
SL3: Poyle 53G 104
Poplar Ct. SW19 64Cb 133
TW1: Twick 58La 108
UB5: N'olt 40Y 65
Poplar Cres. KT19: Ewe 79Sa 153
Poplar Dr. CM13: Hut 16Ee 41
SM7: Bans 86Za 174
Poplar Farm Cl. KT19: Ewe 79Sa 153
Poplar Gdns. KT3: N Mald 68Ta 131
SE28 45Yc 95
Poplar Gro. GU22: Wok 91A 188
HA9: Wemb 34Sa 67
KT3: N Mald 68Ta 131
N11 23Jb 50
W6 47Ya 88
Poplar High St. E14 45Dc 92
Poplar Ho. KT19: Eps 81Ta 173
SE4 56Bc 114
(off Wickham Rd.)
SE16 47Zb 92
(off Woodland Cres.)
SL3: L'ly 50B 82
Poplar M. W12 46Ya 88
Poplar Mt. DA17: Belv 49Dd 96
Poplar Pl. SE28 45Yc 95
UB3: Hayes 45W 84
W2 45Db 89
Poplar Rd. KT10: Surb 76Ka 152
KT22: Lea 94Ka 192
SE24 56Sb 113
SM3: Sutt 74Bb 155
SW19 68Cb 133
TW15: Ashf 64S 128
UB9: Den 36L 63
Poplar Rd. Sth. SW19 69Cb 133
Poplar Row CM16: They B 9Uc 22
Poplars, The AL1: St A 6F 6
DA12: Grav'nd 9G 122
EN9: Walt A 7Lc 21
HP1: Hem H 3K 3
N14 15Kb 32
RM4: Abr 13Xc 37
UB9: Hare 25L 43
WD6: Bore 11Qa 29
Poplars Av. NW2 37Ya 68
Poplars Cl. AL10: Hat 1P 7
DA3: Lfield 69Ee 143
HA4: Ruis 32U 64
WD25: Wat 4X 13
Poplar Shaw EN9: Walt A 5Hc 21
Poplars Rd. E17 30Dc 52

Poplar St. RM7: Rom 28Ed 56
Poplar Vw. HA9: Wemb 33Ma 67
Poplar Wlk. CR0: C'don 75Sb 157
CR3: Cat'm 95Ub 197
SE24 55Sb 113
(not continuous)
Poplar Way IG6: Ilf 28Sc 54
TW13: Felt 62W 128
Poppins Ct. EC4 3B 224 (44Rb 91)
Poppleton Rd. E11 30Gc 53
Poppy Cl. CM15: Pil H 15Xd 40
DA17: Belv 48Dd 96
EN5: New Bar 16Eb 31
HP1: Hem H 1G 2
SM6: Wall 74Jb 156
UB5: N'olt 37Ba 65
Poppy Dr. EN3: Pond E 14Xb 33
Poppy La. CR0: C'don 73Yb 158
Porchester Cl. DA3: Hartl 70Be 143
RM11: Horn 30Nd 57
SE5 56Sb 113
Porchester Ct. *W2* *45Db 89*
(off Porchester Gdns.)
Porchester Gdns. W2 45Db 89
Porchester Gdns. M. W2 44Db 89
Porchester Ga. W2 5A 220
(not continuous)
Porchester Ho. *E1* *44Xb 91*
(off Philpot St.)
Porchester Leisure Cen. 44Db 89
Porchester Mead BR3: Beck 65Dc 136
Porchester Pl. W2 3E 220 (44Gb 89)
Porchester Rd. KT1: King T 68Ra 131
W2 44Db 89
Porchester Sq. W2 44Db 89
Porchester Sq. M. W2 44Db 89
Porchester Ter. W2 4A 220 (45Eb 89)
Porchester Ter. Nth. W2 44Db 89
Porchester Wlk. *W2* *44Db 89*
(off Porchester Ter. Nth.)
Porchfield Cl. DA12: Grav'nd 1E 144
SM2: Sutt 82Db 175
Porch Way N20 20Hb 31
Porcupine Cl. SE9 61Nc 138
Porden Rd. SW2 56Pb 112
Porlock Av. HA2: Harr 32Ea 66
Porlock Ho. SE26 62Wb 135
Porlock Rd. EN1: Enf 17Vb 33
Porlock St. SE1 1G 231 (47Tb 91)
Porrington Cl. BR7: Chst 67Pc 138
Porson Ct. SE13 55Dc 114
Portal Cl. HA4: Ruis 35W 64
SE27 62Qb 134
UB10: Uxb 38N 63
Portal Way W3 43Ta 87
Port Av. DA9: Ghithe 58Xd 120
Portbury Cl. SE15 53Wb 113
Port Cres. E13 42Kc 93
Portcullis Ho. SW1 2F 229
Portcullis Lodge Rd. EN1: Enf 13Tb 33
Port E. Apartments *E14* *45Cc 92*
(off Hertsmere Rd.)
Portelet Ct. *N1* *39Ub 71*
(off De Beauvoir Est.)
Portelet Rd. E1 41Zb 92
Porten Ho's. *W14* *48Ab 88*
(off Porten Rd.)
Porten Rd. W14 48Ab 88
Porter Cl. RM20: Grays 51Yd 120
Porter Rd. E6 44Pc 94
Porters & Walters Almshouses
N22 *24Pb 50*
(off Nightingale Rd.)
Porters Av. RM8: Dag 37Xc 75
RM9: Dag 37Xc 75
Porters Cl. CM14: B'wood 18Wd 40
Porters Lodge, The *SW10* *52Eb 111*
(off Coleridge Gdns.)
Porters Pk. Dr. WD7: Shenl 5Ma 15
Porters Pk. Golf Course 6La 14
Porter Sq. N19 32Nb 70
Porter St. SE1 6E 224 (46Sb 91)
W1 7G 215 (43Hb 89)
Porters Wlk. *E1* *45Xb 91*
(off Tobacco Dock)
Porters Way N12 23Gb 49
UB7: W Dray 48P 83
Porteus Rd. W2 7A 214 (43Eb 89)
Portgate Cl. W9 42Bb 89
Porthallow Cl. BR6: Chels 77Vc 161
Porthcawe Rd. SE26 63Ac 136
Port Hill BR6: Prat B 84Xc 181
Porthkerry Av. DA16: Well 56Wc 117
Port Ho. *E14* *50Dc 92*
(off Burrells Wharf Sq.)
Portia Ct. IG11: Bark 38Wc 75
SE11 7B 230
Portia Way E3 42Bc 92
Porticos, The *SW3* *51Fb 111*
(off King's Rd.)
Portinscale Rd. SW15 57Ab 110
Portishead Ho. *W2* *43Cb 89*
(off Westbourne Pk. Rd.)
Portland Av. DA12: Grav'nd 1D 144
DA15: Sidc 58Wc 117
KT3: N Mald 73Va 154
N16 31Vb 71
Portland Bus. Cen. SL3: Dat 3M 103
Portland Cl. KT4: Wor Pk 73Xa 154
RM6: Chad H 29Ad 55
SL2: Slou 2B 80
Portland Commercial Est.
IG11: Bark 40Yc 75
Portland Cotts. CR0: Bedd 73Mb 156
Portland Ct. *N1* *38Ub 71*
(off St Peter's Way)
SE1 3F 231
SE14 *51Ac 114*
(off Whitcher Cl.)
Portland Cres. HA7: Stan 26Ma 47
SE9 61Nc 138
TW13: Felt 63T 128
UB6: G'frd 42Da 85
Portland Dr. EN2: Enf 10Ub 19
EN7: Chesh 3Wb 19
RH1: Mers 1D 208
Portland Gdns. N4 30Rb 51
RM6: Chad H 29Zc 55
Portland Gro. SW8 53Pb 112
Portland Hgts. HA6: Nwood 21V 44
Portland Ho. RH1: Mers 1D 208
SW1 4B 228
SW15 57Za 110
Portland Mans. *W14* *49Bb 89*
(off Addison Bri. Pl.)
Portland M. W1 3C 222 (44Lb 90)
Portland Pk. SL9: Ger X 30A 42
Portland Pl. *DA3: Lfield* *69Ae 143*
(off Park Dr.)
DA9: Ghithe 56Yd 120
KT17: Eps 84Ua 174
SE25 *70Wb 135*
(off Sth. Norwood Hill)
W1 6K 215 (43Kb 90)
Portland Ri. N4 32Rb 71
(not continuous)
Portland Rd. BR1: Brom 63Lc 137
CR4: Mitc 68Gb 133
DA11: Nflt 58Fe 121
DA12: Grav'nd 10D 122
KT1: King T 69Na 131
N15 28Vb 51
SE9 61Nc 138
SE25 70Wb 135
TW15: Ashf 62N 127
UB2: S'hall 48Ba 85
UB4: Hayes 41U 84
W11 45Ab 88
Portlands SL9: Ger X 30A 42
Portland Sq. E1 46Xb 91
Portland St. AL3: St A 2A 6
SE17 7F 231 (50Tb 91)
Portland Ter. HA8: Edg 24Qa 47
TW9: Rich 56Ma 109
Portland Wlk. SE17 51Tb 113
Portley La. CR3: Cat'm 93Ub 197
Portley Wood Rd. CR3: Whyt 92Vb 197
Portmadoc Ho. *RM3: Rom* *21Nd 57*
(off Broseley Rd.)
Portman Av. SW14 55Ta 109
Portman Cl. DA5: Bexl 60Gd 118
DA7: Bex 55Ad 117
W1 2G 221 (44Hb 89)
Portman Dr. IG8: Wfd G 26Mc 53
Portman Gdns. NW9 26Ta 47
UB10: Hil 38Q 64
Portman Ga. NW1 6E 214 (42Gb 89)
Portman Mans. W1 7G 215
Portman M. Sth. W1 3H 221 (44Jb 90)
Portman Pl. E2 41Yb 92
Portman Rd. KT1: King T 68Pa 131
Portman Sq. W1 2H 221 (44Jb 90)
Portman St. W1 3H 221 (44Jb 90)
Portman Towers W1 2G 221 (44Hb 89)
Portmeadow Wlk. SE2 47Zc 95
Portmeers Cl. E17 30Bc 52
Portmore Gdns. RM5: Col R 22Cd 56
Portmore Pk. Rd. KT13: Weyb 77Q 150
Portmore Pl. *KT13: Weyb* *76T 150*
(off Oatlands Dr.)
Portmore Quays KT13: Weyb 77P 149
Portmore Way KT13: Weyb 76Q 150
Portnall Dr. GU25: Vir W 10K 125
Portnall Ho. *W9* *41Bb 89*
(off Portnall Rd.)
Portnall Ri. GU25: Vir W 1K 147
Portnall Rd. GU25: Vir W 1K 147
W9 40Bb 69
Portnalls Cl. CR5: Coul 88Kb 176
Portnalls Ri. CR5: Coul 88Lb 176
Portnalls Rd. CR5: Coul 90Kb 176
Portnoi Cl. RM1: Rom 26Fd 56
Portobello Ct. Est. W11 44Bb 89
Portobello Grn. *W10* *43Ab 88*
(off Portobello Rd.)
Portobello M. W11 45Cb 89
Portobello Pde. TN15: W King 81Wd 184
Portobello Rd. W10 43Ab 88
W11 44Bb 89
Portobello Road Market *45Bb 89*
(off Portobello Rd.)
Port of London Authority Bldg. EC3 4J 225
Porton Ct. KT6: Surb 72La 152
Portpool La. EC1 7K 217 (43Qb 90)
Portree Cl. N22 24Pb 50
Portree St. E14 44Fc 93
Portrush Ct. *UB1: S'hall* *44Ea 86*
(off Whitecote Rd.)
Portsdown HA8: Edg 22Qa 47
Portsdown Av. NW11 30Bb 49
Portsdown M. NW11 30Bb 49
Portsea Hall W2 3E 220
Portsea M. W2 3E 220
Portsea Pl. W2 3E 220 (44Gb 89)
Portsea Rd. RM18: Tilb 3E 122
Portslade Rd. SW8 54Lb 112
Portsmouth Av. KT7: T Ditt 73Ja 152
Portsmouth Ct. SL1: Slou 5J 81
Portsmouth M. E16 46Kc 93
Portsmouth Rd. GU23: Rip, Wis 93M 189
GU23: Send, Rip 97H 189
KT1: King T 73Ja 152
KT6: Surb 73Ja 152
KT7: T Ditt 73Ja 152
KT10: Esh 79Ca 151
(Hawkshill Cl.)
KT10: Esh 77Ea 152
(Sandown Rd.)
KT10: Esh 85V 170
(Seven Hills Rd. Sth.)
KT11: Cobh 85V 170
SW15 59Xa 110
Portsmouth St. WC2 2H 223 (44Pb 90)
Portsoken St. E1 4K 225 (45Vb 91)
Portswood Pl. SW15 58Va 110
Portugal Gdns. TW2: Twick 61Ea 130
Portugal Rd. GU21: Wok 88B 168
Portugal St. WC2 3H 223 (44Pb 90)
Port Way GU24: Bisl 8E 166
Portway E15 39Hc 73
KT17: Ewe 81Wa 174
RM13: Rain 39Jd 76
Portway Cres. KT17: Ewe 81Wa 174
Portway Gdns. SE18 52Mc 115
Pory Ho. SE11 6J 229 (49Pb 90)
Poseidon Ct. *E14* *49Cc 92*
(off Homer Dr.)
POSK *49Wa 88*
(off King St.)
Post Boys Row KT11: Cobh 86W 170
Postern, The EC2 1E 224
Postern Grn. EN2: Enf 12Qb 32
Post Ho. La. KT23: Bookh 97Ca 191
Post La. TW2: Twick 60Fa 108
Postmasters Lodge HA5: Pinn 31Aa 65
Post Mdw. SL0: Iver H 41F 82
Postmill Cl. CR0: C'don 76Yb 158
Post Office All. *W4* *51Ra 109*
(off Thames Rd.)
Post Office App. E7 36Kc 73
Post Office Ct. EC3 3G 225
Post Office La. SL3: G Grn 4P 81
Post Office Way SW8 52Mb 112
Post Rd. UB2: S'hall 48Da 85
Postway M. IG1: Ilf 34Rc 74
(not continuous)
Potash La. TN15: Plat 93Ee 205
Potbury Cl. SL4: Wink 5A 124
Potier St. SE1 4G 231 (48Tb 91)
Potiphar Pl. CM14: W'ley 21Xd 58
Potter Cl. CR4: Mitc 68Kb 134
SE15 52Ub 113
Potterells AL9: N Mym 7F 8
Potteries, The EN5: Barn 15Cb 31
KT16: Ott 79G 148
Potterne Cl. SW19 59Za 110
POTTERS BAR 4Bb 17
Potters Bar Golf Course 3Cb 17
Potters Bar Mus. 4Bb 17
Potters Cl. CR0: C'don 74Ac 158
IG10: Lough 12Nc 36
Potters Ct. EN6: Pot B 4Cb 17
SM1: Sutt *79Bb 155*
(off Rosebery Rd.)
Potters Cross SL0: Iver H 41G 82
POTTERS CROUCH 6K 5
Potterscrouch La. AL2: Pot C 6K 5
AL3: St A 6K 5
Potters End HA5: Pinn 23X 45
Potters Fld. *EN1: Enf* *14Ub 33*
(off Lincoln Rd.)
Potters Flds. SE1 7J 225 (46Ub 91)
Potters Gro. KT3: N Mald 70Sa 131
Potters Hgts. Cl. HA5: Pinn 24X 45
Potters La. EN5: New Bar 14Cb 31
GU23: Send 95D 188
SW16 65Mb 134
WD6: Bore 11Sa 29
Potters Lodge *E14* *50Ec 92*
(off Manchester Rd.)
Potters M. WD6: E'tree 16Ma 29
Potters Rd. EN5: New Bar 14Db 31
SW6 54Eb 111
Potter St. HA5: Pinn 25X 45
HA6: Nwood 25W 44
Potter St. Hill HA5: Pinn 23X 45
Potters Way RH2: Reig 10L 207
Pottery Cl. SE25 69Wb 135
Pottery La. W11 46Ab 88
Pottery Rd. DA5: Bexl 61Ed 140
TW8: Bford 51Na 109
Pottery St. SE16 47Xb 91
Pott St. E2 41Xb 91
POUCHEN END 3F 2
Pouchen End La. HP1: Hem H 1F 2
Poulcott TW19: Wray 58A 104
Poulett Gdns. TW1: Twick 60Ja 108
Poulett Rd. E6 40Pc 74
Poulters Wood BR2: Kes 78Mc 159
Poultney Cl. WD7: Shenl 4Pa 15
Poulton Av. SM1: Sutt 76Fb 155
Poulton Cl. E8 37Xb 71
Poulton Ho. *W3* *43Ta 87*
(off Victoria Rd.)
Poultry EC2 3F 225 (44Tb 91)
Pound, The SL1: Burn 2B 80
Pound Bank Cl.
TN15: W King 81Vd 184
Pound Cl. BR6: Orp 75Tc 160
KT6: Surb 74La 152
KT19: Eps 83Ta 173
Pound Ct. KT21: Asht 90Pa 173
Pound Ct. Dr. BR6: Orp 75Tc 160
Pound Cres. KT22: Fet 93Fa 192
Pound Farm Cl. KT10: Esh 74Fa 152
Poundfield WD25: Wat 7V 12
Poundfield Ct. GU22: Wok 93E 188
Poundfield Gdns.
GU22: Wok 92E 188
(not continuous)
Poundfield Rd. IG10: Lough 15Qc 36
Pound Grn. DA5: Bexl 59Cd 118
Pound La. GU20: W'sham 9A 146
KT19: Eps 84Sa 173
NW10 37Wa 68
RM16: Ors 2C 100
TN13: S'oaks 96Ld 203
TN14: Knock 87Zc 181
WD7: Shenl 5Pa 15
Pound Pk. Rd. SE7 49Mc 93
Pound Pl. SE9 58Qc 116
Pound Rd. KT16: Chert 73K 149
SM7: Bans 89Bb 175
Pound St. SM5: Cars 78Hb 155
Pound Way BR7: Chst 66Sc 138
Pounsley Rd.
TN13: Dun G 93Gd 202
Pountney Rd. SW11 55Jb 112
POVEREST 70Wc 139
Poverest Rd. BR5: St M Cry 71Vc 161
Povey Ho. SE17 6H 231
Powderham Ct. GU21: Knap 10H 167
Powder Mill La. DA1: Dart 61Nd 141
TW2: Whitt 59Ba 107
Powdermill La. EN9: Walt A 5Dc 20
Powdermill M. *EN9: Walt A* *5Dc 20*
(off Powdermill La.)
Powell Av. DA2: Dart 61Ud 142
Powell Cl. HA8: Edg 23Pa 47
KT9: Chess 78Ma 153
Powell Ct. *CR2: S Croy* *77Rb 157*
(off Bramley Hill)
E17 27Dc 52
Powell Gdns. RH1: Redh 4B 208
RM10: Dag 35Cd 76
Powell Ho. W2 4B 220
Powell Rd. E5 34Xb 71
IG9: Buck H 17Lc 35
Powell's Wlk. W4 51Ua 110
Power Dr. EN3: Enf L 8Bc 20
Powergate Bus. Pk. NW10 41Ta 87
Powerleague
Barking 41Sc 94
Bushey 13Ca 27
Catford 60Cc 114
Colney Hatch 24Jb 50
Croydon 79Pb 156
Ilford 24Vc 55
Mill Hill 24Xa 48
Norbury 67Nb 134
Slough 8H 81
Tottenham 23Xb 51
Power Rd. W4 49Qa 87
Powers Ct. TW1: Twick 59Ma 109
Powerscroft Rd. DA14: Sidc 65Yc 139
(not continuous)
E5 35Yb 72
Power Works DA8: Erith 53Jd 118
Powis Ct. EN6: Pot B 6Eb 17
W11 *44Bb 89*
(off Powis Gdns.)
WD23: B Hea *18Fa 28*
(off Rutherford Way)
Powis Gdns. NW11 31Bb 69
W11 44Bb 89
Powis Ho. WC2 2G 223
Powis M. W11 44Bb 89
Powis Pl. WC1 6G 217 (42Nb 90)
Powis Rd. E3 41Dc 92
Powis Sq. W11 44Bb 89
(not continuous)
Powis St. SE18 48Qc 94
Powis Ter. W11 44Bb 89
Powlesland Ct. *E1* *44Ac 92*
(off White Horse Rd.)
Powlett Ho. *NW1* *37Kb 70*
(off Powlett Pl.)
Powlett Pl. NW1 38Jb 70
Pownall Gdns. TW3: Houn 56Da 107
Pownall Rd. E8 39Vb 71
TW3: Houn 56Da 107
Pownsett Ter. IG1: Ilf 36Sc 74
Powster Rd. BR1: Brom 64Jc 137
Powys Cl. DA7: Bex 51Zc 117
Powys Ct. N11 22Nb 50
WD6: Bore 13Ta 29
Powys La. N13 21Nb 50
N14 21Nb 50
POYLE 54G 104
Poyle Ind. Est. SL3: Poyle 55H 105
Poyle La. SL1: Burn 10A 60
Poyle New Cotts. SL3: Poyle 54H 105
Poyle Pk. SL3: Poyle 55G 104
Poyle Rd. SL3: Poyle 55G 104
Poyle Technical Cen. SL3: Poyle 54G 104
Poyle Trad. Est. SL3: Poyle 55G 104
Poynder Rd. RM18: Tilb 3D 122
Poynders Ct. SW4 58Lb 112
Poynders Gdns. SW4 59Lb 112
Poynders Hill HP2: Hem H 3C 4
Poynders Rd. SW4 58Lb 112
Poynings, The SL0: Rich P 49H 83
Poynings Cl. BR6: Chels 75Yc 161
Poynings Rd. N19 34Lb 70
Poynings Way N12 22Cb 49
RM3: Hrld W 25Nd 57
Poyntell Cres. BR7: Chst 67Tc 138
Poynter Ct. *UB5: N'olt* *40Z 65*
(off Gallery Gdns.)
Poynter Ho. NW8 5B 214
W11 *46Za 88*
(off Queensdale Cres.)
Poynter Rd. EN1: Enf 15Wb 33
Poynton Rd. N17 26Wb 51
Poyntz Rd. SW11 54Hb 111
Poyser St. E2 40Xb 71
Prado Path *TW1: Twick* *60Ha 108*
(off Laurel Av.)
Prae Cl. AL3: St A 1P 5
Praed M. W2 2C 220 (44Fb 89)
Praed St. W2 3B 220 (44Fb 89)
Praetorian Ct. AL1: St A 5A 6
Pragel St. E13 40Lc 73
Pragnell Rd. SE12 61Kc 137
Prague Pl. SW2 57Nb 112
Prah Rd. N4 33Qb 70
Prairie Cl. KT15: Add 76K 149
Prairie Rd. KT15: Add 76K 149
Prairie St. SW8 54Jb 112
Praline Ct. *E3* *40Dc 72*
(off Taylor Pl.)
Pratt M. NW1 39Lb 70
PRATT'S BOTTOM 82Yc 181
PRATT'S BOTTOM 81Yc 181
Pratts La. KT12: Hers 77Z 151
Pratts Pas. KT1: King T 68Na 131
Pratt St. NW1 39Lb 70
Pratt Wlk. SE11 5J 229 (49Pb 90)
Prayle Gro. NW2 32Za 68
Preachers Ct. EC1 6C 218
Prebend Gdns. W4 49Va 88
W6 49Va 88
(not continuous)
Prebend Mans. *W4* *49Va 88*
(off Chiswick High Rd.)
Prebend St. N1 1D 218 (39Sb 71)
Precinct, The N1 1D 218 (39Sb 71)
(not continuous)
SS17: Stan H 2M 101
TW20: Egh 64C 126
Precinct Rd. UB3: Hayes 45W 84
Precincts, The SL1: Burn 2A 80
SM4: Mord 72Cb 155
Precista Ct. BR6: Orp 73Xc 161
Premier Av. RM16: Grays 47Ee 99
Premier Cinema 54Wb 113
Premier Cnr. W9 40Bb 69
Premier Ct. EN3: Enf W 10Zb 20
Premiere Pl. E14 45Cc 92
Premier Ho. *N1* *38Rb 71*
(off Waterloo Ter.)
Premier Pk. NW10 39Ra 67
(not continuous)
Premier Pk. Rd. NW10 40Ra 67
Premier Pl. SW15 56Ab 110
WD18: Wat 15V 26
Prendergast Rd. SE3 55Gc 115
Prentice Ct. SW19 64Bb 133
Prentis Rd. SW16 63Mb 134
Prentiss Ct. SE7 49Mc 93
Presburg Rd. KT3: N Mald 71Ua 154
Presburg St. E5 34Zb 72
Presbury Ct. GU21: Wok 10L 167
Prescelly Pl. HA8: Edg 25Pa 47
Prescot St. E1 4K 225 (45Vb 91)
Prescott Av. BR5: Pet W 72Rc 160
Prescott Cl. SW16 66Nb 134
Prescott Grn. IG10: Lough 13Sc 36
Prescott Ho. *SE17* *51Rb 113*
(off Hillingdon St.)
Prescott Pl. SW4 55Mb 112
Prescott Rd. SL3: Poyle 54G 104
Presentation M. SW2 61Pb 134
Preshaw Cres. CR4: Mitc 69Gb 133
President Dr. E1 46Xb 91
President Ho. EC1 4C 218 (41Rb 91)
President Quay *E1* *46Vb 91*
(off St Katherine's Way)
President St. EC1 3D 218
Prespa Cl. N9 19Yb 34
Press Ct. SE1 50Wb 91
Press Ho. NW10 34Ta 67
Press Rd. NW10 34Ta 67
UB8: Uxb 37M 63
Prestage Way E14 45Ec 92
Prestbury Cres. SM7: Bans 88Hb 175
Prestbury Rd. E7 38Lc 73
Prestbury Sq. SE9 63Pc 138
Prested Rd. SW11 56Gb 111
Prestige Way NW4 29Ya 48
PRESTON 32Na 67
Preston Av. E4 23Fc 53
Preston Cl. SE1 5H 231 (49Ub 91)
TW2: Twick 62Ga 130
Preston Ct. *DA14: Sidc* *63Vc 139*
(off The Crescent)
EN5: New Bar 14Eb 31
KT12: Walt T 74Y 151
Preston Dr. DA7: Bex 53Zc 117
E11 29Lc 53
KT19: Ewe 79Ua 154
Preston Gdns. EN3: Enf L 9Ac 20
IG1: Ilf 30Nc 54
NW10 37Va 68
Preston Gro. KT21: Asht 89La 172
Preston Hill HA3: Kenton 31Na 67
Preston Ho. *RM10: Dag* *34Cd 76*
(off Uvedale Rd.)
SE1 5H 231
(Preston Cl.)
SE1 3K 231
(St Saviour's Est.)
Preston La. KT20: Tad 93Xa 194
Preston Pl. NW2 37Wa 68
TW10: Rich 57Na 109
Preston Rd. DA11: Nflt 10A 122
E11 30Gc 53
HA3: Kenton 32Na 67
HA9: Wemb 32Na 67
RM3: Rom 21Md 57
SE19 65Rb 135
SL2: Slou 5N 81
SW20 66Va 132
TW17: Shep 71Q 150
Prestons Rd. BR2: Hayes 76Jc 159
E14 45Ec 92
Preston St. E2 40Zb 72
Preston Waye HA3: Kenton 32Na 67
Prestwich Ter. SW4 57Lb 112
Prestwick Cl. UB2: S'hall 50Aa 85
Prestwick Ct. *UB1: S'hall* *45Ea 86*
(off Baird Av.)
Prestwick Rd. WD19: Wat 18Y 27
Prestwick Road Meadows
Local Nature Reserve 22Z 45
Prestwood SL2: Slou 4M 81
WD19: Wat 19Aa 27
Prestwood Av. HA3: Kenton 28Ka 46
Prestwood Cl. HA3: Kenton 28Ka 46
SE18 51Wc 117
Prestwood Dr. RM5: Col R 22Ed 56
Prestwood Gdns. CR0: C'don 73Sb 157
Prestwood Ga. AL1: St A 1C 6
Prestwood Ho. *SE16* *48Xb 91*
(off Drummond Rd.)
Prestwood St. N1 2E 218 (40Sb 71)
Pretoria Av. E17 28Ac 52
Pretoria Cres. E4 18Ec 34
Pretoria Ho. DA8: Erith 52Gd 118
Pretoria Rd. E4 18Ec 34
E11 32Fc 73
E16 42Hc 93
IG1: Ilf 36Rc 74
KT16: Chert 74H 149
N17 24Vb 51
RM7: Rom 28Ed 56
SW16 65Kb 134
WD18: Wat 14W 26
Pretoria Rd. Nth. N18 23Vb 51
Pretty La. CR5: Coul 93Lb 196
Prevost Rd. N11 19Jb 32
PREY HEATH 5N 187
Prey Heath Cl. GU22: Wok 6N 187
Prey Heath Rd. GU22: Wok 6M 187
Priam Ho. *E2* *40Xb 71*
(off Old Bethnal Grn. Rd.)
Price Cl. NW7 23Ab 48
SW17 62Hb 133
Price Ho. *N1* *39Sb 71*
(off Britannia Row)
Price Rd. CR0: Wadd 78Rb 157
Price's Ct. SW11 55Fb 111
Prices La. RH2: Reig 9J 207
Price's M. N1 39Pb 70
Price's St. SE1 6C 224 (46Rb 91)
Price Way TW12: Hamp 65Aa 129
Prichard Ct. N7 37Pb 70
Prichard Ho. SE11 6K 229
Pricklers Hill EN5: New Bar 16Db 31
Prickley Wood BR2: Hayes 74Hc 159
Priddy Pl. RH1: Mers 3C 208
Priddy's Yd. CR0: C'don 75Sb 157
Prideaux Ho. WC1 3J 217
Prideaux Pl. W3 45Ta 87
WC1 3J 217 (41Pb 90)
Prideaux Rd. SW9 55Nb 112
Pridham Rd. CR7: Thor H 70Tb 135
Priestfield Rd. SE23 62Ac 136
Priest Hill RH8: Limp 1M 211
SL4: Old Win 2N 125
TW20: Eng G, Old Win 2N 125
Priestlands Pk. Rd. DA15: Sidc 62Vc 139
Priest La. GU24: W End 5A 166
Priestley Cl. N16 31Vb 71
Priestley Ct. RM17: Grays 49Ee 99
Priestley Gdns. GU22: Wok 92C 188
RM6: Chad H 30Xc 55
Priestley Ho. EC1 5D 218
HA9: Wemb *34Sa 67*
(off Barnhill Rd.)
Priestley Rd. CR4: Mitc 68Jb 134
Priestley Way E17 27Zb 52
NW2 32Wa 68
Priestman Point *E3* *41Dc 92*
(off Rainhill Way)
Priest Pk. Av. HA2: Harr 33Ca 65
Priests Av. RM1: Rom 26Fd 56
Priests Bri. SW14 55Ua 110
SW15 55Ua 110
Priest's Ct. EC2 2D 224
Priest's Fld. CM13: Ingve 22Ee 59
Priest's La. CM15: B'wood, Shenf 17Be 41
Priest's Wlk. DA12: Grav'nd 1J 145
Prima Rd. SW9 52Qb 112
Primary Rd. SL1: Slou 8H 81
Prime Meridian Line 52Fc 115
Prime Meridian Wlk. E14 45Fc 93
Primeplace M. CR7: Thor H 68Sb 135
Primezone M. N8 30Nb 50
Primmett Cl. TN15: W King 79Ud 164

Primrose Av. EN2: Enf 11Tb 33
RM6: Chad H 31Xc 75
Primrose Cl. AL10: Hat 1D 8
E3 40Cc 72
HA2: Harr 34Ba 65
HP1: Hem H 3G 2
N3 26Db 49
SE6 64Ec 136
SM6: Wall 73Kb 156
Primrose Ct. CM14: B'wood 20Yd 40
NW8 1F 215
SW12 59Mb 112
Primrose Dr. GU24: Bisl 7E 166
UB7: W Dray 49M 83
Primrose Gdns. HA4: Ruis 36Y 65
NW3 37Gb 69
WD7: R'lett 7Ja 14
WD23: Bush 17Da 27
Primrose Glen RM11: Horn 28Nd 57
PRIMROSE HILL 39Jb 70
Primrose Hill CM14: B'wood 20Yd 40
EC4 3A 224 (44Qb 90)
WD4: K Lan 10B 4
Primrose Hill Ct. NW3 38Hb 69
Primrose Hill Rd. NW3 38Hb 69
Primrose Hill Studios NW1 39Jb 70
Primrose Ho. KT18: Eps 85Sa 173
(off Dalmeny Way)
SE15 53Wb 113
(off Peckham Hill St.)
Primrose La. CR0: C'don 74Yb 158
WD25: A'ham 10Fa 14
Primrose Mans. SW11 53Jb 112
Primrose M. NW1 38Hb 69
(off Sharpleshall St.)
SE3 52Jc 115
Primrose Path EN7: Chesh 3Wb 19
Primrose Pl. TW7: Isle 54Ha 108
Primrose Rd. E10 32Dc 72
E18 26Kc 53
KT12: Hers 78Y 151
Primrose Sq. E9 38Yb 72
Primrose St. EC2 7H 219 (43Ub 91)
Primrose Ter. DA12: Grav'nd 10E 122
Primrose Wlk. KT17: Ewe 80Va 154
SE14 52Ac 114
Primrose Way HA0: Wemb 40Ma 67
Primula St. W12 44Wa 88
Prince Albert Ct. NW8 1F 215
TW16: Sun 66V 128
Prince Albert Rd.
NW1 3D 214 (41Gb 89) & 1J 215
NW8 3D 214 (41Gb 89)
Prince Albert's Wlk. SL4: Wind 3L 103
Prince Arthur M. NW3 35Eb 69
Prince Arthur Rd. NW3 36Eb 69
Prince Charles Av. DA4: S Dar 68Td 142
RM16: Ors 2D 100
Prince Charles Cinema 4E 222
Prince Charles Dr. NW4 31Ya 68
Prince Charles Rd. SE3 54Hc 115
Prince Charles Way SM6: Wall 76Kb 156
Prince Consort Cotts. SL4: Wind 4H 103
Prince Consort Dr. BR7: Chst 67Tc 138
Prince Consort Rd. SW7 3A 226 (48Eb 89)
Prince Consort's Dr. SL4: Wind 8D 102
Princedale Rd. W11 46Ab 88
Prince Edward Mans. W2 45Cb 89
(off Moscow Rd.)
Prince Edward Rd. E9 37Bc 72
Prince Edward Theatre 3E 222
Prince Eugene Pl. AL1: St A 5A 6
Prince George Av. N14 15Mb 32
Prince George Rd. N16 35Ub 71
Prince George's Av. SW20 68Ya 132
Prince George's Rd. SW19 67Fb 133
Prince Henry Rd. SE7 52Mc 115
Prince Imperial Rd. BR7: Chst 67Rc 138
SE18 53Pc 116
Prince John Rd. SE9 57Nc 116
Princelet St. E1 7K 219 (43Vb 91)
Prince Michael of Kent Ct.
DA1: Cray 54Jd 118
Prince of Orange Ct. SE16 48Yb 92
(off Lower Rd.)
Prince of Orange La. SE10 52Ec 114
Prince of Wales Cl. NW4 28Xa 48
Prince of Wales Dr. SW8 52Kb 112
SW11 53Gb 111
Prince of Wales Footpath
EN3: Enf W 10Zb 20
Prince of Wales Mans. SW11 53Jb 112
Prince of Wales Pas. NW1 4B 216
Prince of Wales Rd. E16 44Lc 93
NW5 37Jb 70
SE3 54Hc 115
SM1: Sutt 75Fb 155
Prince of Wales Ter. W4 50Ua 88
W8 47Db 89
Prince of Wales Theatre 5D 222
Prince Pk. HP1: Hem H 3J 3
Prince Philip Av. RM16: Grays 46Ce 99
Prince Regent Ct. NW8 1E 214
SE16 45Ac 92
(off Edward Sq.)
Prince Regent La. E13 41Kc 93
E16 41Kc 93
Prince Regent M. NW1 4B 216
Prince Regent Rd. TW3: Houn 55Da 107
Prince Rd. SE25 71Ub 157
Prince Rupert Rd. SE9 56Pc 116
Princes Arc. SW1 6C 222
Princes Av. BR5: Pet W 71Uc 160
CR2: Sande 87Xb 177
DA2: Dart 60Rd 119
EN3: Enf W 8Ac 20
IG8: Wfd G 21Kc 53
KT6: Surb 74Qa 153
N3 25Cb 49
N10 27Kb 50
N13 22Qb 50
N22 25Mb 50
NW9 28Qa 47
SM5: Cars 80Hb 155
UB6: G'frd 44Da 85
W3 48Qa 87
WD18: Wat 15V 26
Princes Cir. WC2 2F 223 (44Nb 90)
Princes Cl. CR2: Sande 87Xb 177
DA14: Sidc 62Zc 139
HA8: Edg 22Qa 47
N4 32Rb 71
NW9 28Qa 47
SL4: Eton W 10D 80
SW4 55Lb 112
TW11: Tedd 63Fa 130
Princes Club 61R 128
Princes Ct. HA9: Wemb 36Na 67
HP3: Hem H 5K 3
KT13: Weyb 78R 150
(off Princes Rd.)
SE16 48Bc 92
SW3 3F 227
Princes Ct. Bus. Cen. E1 45Xb 91
Princes Dr. HA1: Harr 27Ga 46
KT22: Oxs 84Ga 172
Princesfield Rd. EN9: Walt A 5Kc 21
Princes Gdns. SW7 3C 226 (48Fb 89)
W3 43Qa 87
W5 42La 86
Prince's Ga. SW7 2C 226 (47Fb 89)
(not continuous)
Prince's Ga. Ct. SW7 2C 226 (47Fb 89)
Prince's Ga. M. SW7 3C 226 (48Fb 89)
Princes Ho. W11 45Bb 89
Princes La. HA4: Ruis 32U 64
N10 27Kb 50
Princes M. TW3: Houn 56Ca 107
W2 45Db 89
W6 50Xa 88
(off Down Pl.)
Princes Pde. EN6: Pot B 4Db 17
NW11 30Ab 48
(off Golders Grn. Rd.)
Princes Pk. 60Qd 119
Princes Pk. RM13: Rain 38Jd 76
Princes Pk. Av. NW11 30Ab 48
UB3: Hayes 45T 84
Princes Pk. Circ. UB3: Hayes 45T 84
Princes Pk. Cl. UB3: Hayes 45T 84
Princes Pk. Golf Course 60Qd 119
Princes Pk. La. UB3: Hayes 45T 84
Princes Pk. Pde. UB3: Hayes 45T 84
Princes Pl. SW1 6C 222
W11 46Ab 88
Prince's Plain BR2: Brom 73Nc 160
Prince's Ri. SE13 54Ec 114
Princes Riverside Rd. SE16 46Zb 92
Princes Rd. BR8: Hext 65Jd 140
CM14: Kel C, N'side 11Nd 39
DA1: Dart 58Jd 118
DA2: Dart 60Rd 119
(not continuous)
DA12: Grav'nd 3E 144
IG6: Ilf 28Tc 54
IG9: Buck H 19Lc 35
KT2: King T 66Qa 131
KT13: Weyb 78R 150
N18 21Yb 52
RH1: Redh 8P 207
RM1: Rom 29Jd 56
SE20 65Zb 136
SW14 55Ta 109
SW19 65Cb 133
TW9: Kew 53Pa 109
TW10: Rich 57Pa 109
TW11: Tedd 63Fa 130
TW13: Felt 61V 128
TW15: Ashf 64P 127
TW20: Egh 65B 126
W13 46Ka 86
PRINCES ROAD INTERCHANGE 60Rd 119
Princessa Ct. EN2: Enf 15Tb 33
Princess Alice Ho. W10 42Ya 88
Princess Alice Way SE28 47Tc 94
Princess Av. HA9: Wemb 33Na 67
RM18: E Til 9L 101
SL4: Wind 5F 102
Princess Cl. SE28 44Zc 95
Princess Ct. KT1: King T 69Pa 131
(off Horace Rd.)
N6 31Lb 70
NW6 37Db 69
(off Compayne Gdns.)
W1 1F 221
W2 45Db 89
(off Queensway)
Princess Cres. N4 33Rb 71
Princess Diana Dr. AL4: St A 3H 7
Princesses Pde. DA1: Cray 57Gd 118
(off Waterside)
Princess Gdns. GU22: Wok 88D 168
Princess Ho. RH1: Redh 5A 208
Princess Louise Bldg. SE8 52Cc 114
(off Hales St.)
Princess Louise Cl. W2 7C 214 (43Fb 89)
Princess Margaret Rd. RM18: E Til 8K 101
SS17: E Til, Linf 8K 101
Princess Mary Ho. SW1 5E 228
Princess Marys Rd. KT15: Add 77L 149
Princess May Rd. N16 35Ub 71
Princess M. KT1: King T 69Pa 131
NW3 36Fb 69
Princess of Wales Ho.
SL9: Chal P 21B 42
Princess of Wales Memorial Fountain
1C 226 (47Fb 89)
Princess Pde. BR6: Farnb 76Qc 160
RM10: Dag 40Cd 76
Princess Pk. KT15: Add 77J 149
Princess Pk. Mnr. N11 22Jb 50
Princes Sq. W2 45Db 89
(not continuous)
Princess Rd. CR0: C'don 72Sb 157
GU22: Wok 88D 168
NW1 39Jb 70
NW6 40Cb 69
Princess Sq. KT10: Esh 79Ea 152
Princess St. SE1 4C 230 (48Rb 91)
Princes St. DA7: Bex 55Bd 117
DA11: Grav'nd 8D 122
EC2 3F 225 (44Tb 91)
N17 23Ub 51
SL1: Slou 7M 81
SM1: Sutt 77Fb 155
TW9: Rich 56Na 109
W1 3A 222 (44Kb 90)
Princess Way RH1: Redh 5A 208
Princes Ter. E13 39Kc 73
Prince's Twr. SE16 47Yb 92
(off Elephant La.)
Prince St. SE8 51Bc 114
WD17: Wat 13Y 27
Princes Vw. DA1: Dart 60Qd 119
Princes Way BR4: W W'ck 77Hc 159
CM13: Hut 19Ce 41
CR0: Wadd 78Pb 156
HA4: Ruis 35Aa 65
IG9: Buck H 19Lc 35
SW19 59Za 110
W3 48Qa 87
Prince's Yd. W11 46Ab 88
Princethorpe Ho. W2 43Db 89
(off Woodchester Sq.)
Princethorpe Rd. SE26 63Zb 136
Princeton Ct. SW15 55Za 110
Princeton M. KT2: King T 67Qa 131
Princeton St. WC1 1H 223 (43Pb 90)
Prince William Ct.
TW15: Ashf 64P 127
(off Clarendon Rd.)
Principal Cl. N14 18Lb 32
Principal Sq. E9 36Zb 72
Pringle Gdns. CR8: Purl 82Pb 176
SW16 63Lb 134
(not continuous)
Printers Av. WD18: Wat 15U 26
Printers Ct. AL1: St A 3B 6
(off Thorpe Rd.)
Printers Inn Ct. EC4 2K 223 (44Qb 90)
Printers M. E3 39Ac 72
Printers Rd. SW9 53Pb 112
Printer St. EC4 2A 224 (44Qb 90)
Printing Ho. La. UB3: Hayes 47U 84
Printing Ho. Yd. E2 4J 219 (41Ub 91)
Printon Ho. E14 43Bc 92
(off Wallwood St.)
Print Room, The 44Cb 89
(off Hereford Rd.)
Print Village SE15 54Vb 113
Printwork Apartments
SE1 3H 231
SE5 54Sb 113
(off Coldharbour La.)
Priolo Rd. SE7 50Lc 93
Prior Av. SM2: Sutt 80Gb 155
Prior Bolton St. N1 37Rb 71
Prior Chase RM17: Grays 49Ce 99
Prioress Cres. DA9: Ghithe 56Yd 120
Prioress Ho. E3 41Dc 92
(off Bromley High St.)
Prioress Rd. SE27 62Rb 135
Prioress St. SE1 4G 231 (48Ub 91)
Prior Rd. IG1: Ilf 34Qc 74
Priors, The KT21: Asht 91Ma 193
Priors Cl. SL1: Slou 8L 81
Priors Ct. GU21: Wok 10L 167
Priors Cft. E17 26Ac 52
GU22: Wok 92C 188
Priors Farm La. UB5: N'olt 37Aa 65
Priors Fld. UB5: N'olt 37Aa 65
Priorsford Av. BR5: St M Cry 70Wc 139
Priors Gdns. HA4: Ruis 36Y 65
Priors Golf Course, The 16Ld 39
Priors Mead EN1: Enf 11Ub 33
KT23: Bookh 97Ea 192
Priors Pk. RM12: Horn 34Ld 77
Priors Rd. SL4: Wind 5B 102
Prior St. SE10 52Ec 114
Priors Wood KT10: Hin W 75Ha 152
Priory, The CR0: Wadd 77Qb 156
KT22: Lea 94Ka 192
N8 28Mb 50
RH9: G'stone 3P 209
SE3 56Hc 115
Priory Apartments, The SE6 60Dc 114
Priory Av. BR5: Pet W 72Tc 160
E4 20Bc 34
E17 29Cc 52
HA0: Wemb 35Ha 66
N8 28Mb 50
SM3: Cheam 77Za 154
UB9: Hare 28L 43
W4 49Ua 88
Priory Cl. BR3: Beck 69Ac 136
BR7: Chst 67Pc 138
CM15: Pil H 15Wd 40
DA1: Dart 57Ld 119
E4 20Bc 34
E18 25Jc 53
GU21: Wok 85F 168
HA0: Wemb 35Ha 66
HA4: Ruis 32V 64
HA7: Stan 20Ha 28
KT12: Walt T 76W 150
N3 25Bb 49
N14 15Kb 32
N20 18Bb 31
SL5: S'dale 3E 146
SW19 67Db 133
TW12: Hamp 67Ba 129
TW16: Sun 66W 128
UB3: Hayes 45X 85
UB9: Den 34J 63
UB9: Hare 28K 43
Priory Ct. AL1: St A 3C 6
DA1: Dart 58Md 119
E6 39Lc 73
E9 36Zb 72
E17 26Bc 52
EC4 3C 224
HA0: Wemb 40Na 67
KT1: King T 69Na 131
(off Denmark Rd.)
KT17: Ewe 81Va 174
SM3: Cheam 77Ab 154
SW8 53Mb 112
TW3: Houn 55Da 107
TW20: Egh 65E 126
WD23: Bush 18Ea 28
(off Sparrows Herne)
Priory Ct. Est. E17 26Bc 52
Priory Cres. HA0: Wemb 34Ja 66
SE19 66Sb 135
SM3: Cheam 77Za 154
Priory Dr. HA7: Stan 20Ha 28
RH2: Reig 8J 207
SE2 50Zc 95
Priory Fld. Dr. HA8: Edg 21Ra 47
Priory Flds. DA4: Eyns 75Pd 163
WD17: Wat 11W 26
Priory Gdns. 73Xc 161
Priory Gdns. DA1: Dart 57Md 119
HA0: Wemb 35Ja 66
N6 30Kb 50
NW10 41Na 87
SE25 70Vb 135
SW13 55Va 110
TW12: Hamp 66Ba 129
TW15: Ashf 64T 128
UB9: Hare 28L 43
W4 49Ua 88
W5 41Na 87
Priory Grange N2 27Hb 49
(off Fortis Grn.)
Priory Grn. N1 1H 217 (40Pb 70)
(not continuous)
TW18: Staines 64K 127
Priory Grn. Est. N1 1J 217 (40Pb 70)
Priory Gro. EN5: Barn 15Cb 31
RM3: Rom 20Nd 39
SW8 53Nb 112
Priory Hgts. N1 1J 217
Priory Hill DA1: Dart 57Md 119
HA0: Wemb 35Ja 66
Priory Ho. E1 7K 219
EC1 5B 218
SW1 7D 228
Priory La. DA4: Eyns 74Pd 163
KT8: W Mole 70Da 129
SW15 58Ua 110
Priory Leas SE9 60Nc 116
Priory Lodge W4 50Qa 87
(off Kew Bri. Ct.)
WD3: Rick 17M 25
(off Nightingale Pl.)
Priory Mans. SW10 7A 226
Priory Mkt. Pl. DA1: Dart 59Nd 119
Priory M. RM11: Horn 32Kd 77
SW8 53Nb 112
TW18: Staines 64K 127
Priory Pk. SE3 55Hc 115
Priory Pk. Rd. HA0: Wemb 35Ja 66
NW6 39Bb 69
Priory Path RM3: Rom 20Nd 39
Priory Pl. DA1: Dart 58Md 119
KT12: Walt T 76W 150
Priory Retail Pk. SW19 66Fb 133
Priory Rd. CR0: C'don 73Qb 156
E6 39Mc 73
IG10: Lough 14Nc 36
IG11: Bark 38Tc 74
KT9: Chess 76Na 153
N8 28Lb 50
NW6 39Db 69
RH2: Reig 8J 207
RM3: Rom 20Nd 39
SL1: Slou 3A 80
SL5: S'dale 3E 146
SL9: Chal P 26A 42
SM3: Cheam 77Za 154
SS17: Stan H 1N 101
SW19 66Fb 133
TW3: Houn 57Ea 108
TW9: Kew 51Qa 109
TW12: Hamp 66Ba 129
W4 48Ta 87
Priory Rd. Nth. DA1: Dart 56Md 119
Priory Rd. Sth. DA1: Dart 58Md 119
Priory Shop. Cen. DA1: Dart 58Nd 119
Priory Sports Cen. 74Xc 161
Priory St. E3 41Dc 92
Priory Ter. NW6 39Db 69
TW16: Sun 66W 128
Priory Vw. WD23: B Hea 17Ga 28
Priory Vs. N11 23Hb 49
(off Colney Hatch La.)
Priory Wlk. AL1: St A 5C 6
SW10 7A 226 (50Eb 89)
Priory Way HA2: Harr 28Da 45
SL3: Dat 2M 103
UB2: S'hall 48Z 85
UB7: Harm 51N 105
Priscilla Cl. N15 29Sb 51
Pritchard Ho. E2 40Xb 71
(off Ada Pl.)
Pritchard's Rd. E2 39Wb 71
Pritchett Cl. EN3: Enf L 9Cc 20
Priter Rd. SE16 48Wb 91
Priter Rd. Hostel SE16 48Wb 91
(off Dockley Rd.)
Priter Way SE16 48Wb 91
Private Rd. EN1: Enf 15Tb 33
Privet M. CR8: Purl 84Lb 176
Probert Rd. SW2 57Qb 112
Probyn Ho. SW1 5E 228
Probyn Rd. SW2 61Rb 135
Procter Ho. SE1 50Wb 91
(off Avondale Sq.)
SE5 52Tb 113
(off Picton St.)
Procter St. WC1 1H 223 (43Pb 90)
Proctor Cl. CR4: Mitc 67Jb 134
Proctor Gdns. KT23: Bookh 97Da 191
Proctors Cl. TW14: Felt 60W 106
Proffits Cotts. KT20: Tad 94Za 194
Profumo Rd. KT12: Hers 78Z 151
Progress Bus. Cen. SL1: Slou 4B 80
Progress Bus. Pk. CR0: Wadd 75Pb 156
Progress Cen., The EN3: Pond E 13Zb 34
Progress Way CR0: Wadd 75Pb 156
EN1: Enf 15Wb 33
N22 25Qb 50
Project Pk. E16 42Fc 93
Prologis Pk. CR0: Bedd 73Mb 156
E3 42Ec 92
TW4: Houn 56Y 107
Promenade, The HA8: Edg 22Qa 47
W4 54Ua 110
Promenade App. Rd. W4 52Ua 110
Promenade de Verdun CR8: Purl 83Mb 176
Pronto Trad. Est. UB3: Hayes 43U 84
Propeller Cres. CR0: Wadd 78Qb 156
Prospect Av. SS17: Stan H 3K 101
Prospect Bus. Pk. IG10: Lough 14Tc 36
Prospect Cl. DA17: Belv 49Cd 96
HA4: Ruis 31Z 65
SE26 63Xb 135
TW3: Houn 53Ba 107
WD23: Bush 17Fa 28
Prospect Cotts. SW18 56Cb 111
Prospect Cres. TW2: Whitt 58Ea 108
Prospect Gro. DA12: Grav'nd 9F 122
Prospect Hill E17 28Dc 52
Prospect Ho. E17 27Ec 52
(off Prospect Hill)
KT19: Eps 81Ra 173
N1 2K 217
SE1 4B 230
SE16 48Wb 91
(off Frean St.)
SW19 67Fb 133
(off Chapter Way)
W10 44Za 88
(off Bridge Cl.)
Prospect La. TW20: Eng G 4L 125
Prospect Pl. BR2: Brom 69Kc 137
CR2: S Croy 79Sb 157
DA1: Dart 58Nd 119
DA12: Grav'nd 9F 122
(not continuous)
E1 46Yb 92
(not continuous)
KT17: Eps 84Ua 174
N2 28Fb 49
Prospect Pl. N7 35Nb 70
N17 24Ub 51
NW2 34Bb 69
NW3 35Eb 69
RM5: Col R 26Ed 56
RM17: Grays 51De 121
SE8 51Bc 114
(off Evelyn St.)
SL4: Wind 5H 103
(off Osbourne Rd.)
SW20 66Xa 132
TW18: Staines 64H 127
W4 50Ta 87
Prospect Quay SW18 56Cb 111
(off Lightermans Wlk.)
Prospect Ring N2 27Fb 49
Prospect Rd. AL1: St A 4B 6
EN5: New Bar 14Cb 31
EN8: Chesh 1Yb 20
IG8: Wfd G 23Lc 53
KT6: Surb 72La 152
NW2 34Bb 69
RM11: Horn 27Pd 57
TN13: S'oaks 95Ld 203
Prospect St. SE16 48Xb 91
Prospect Va. SE18 49Nc 94
Prospect Way CM13: Hut 14Fe 41
Prospect Wharf E1 45Yb 92
Prospero Ho. E1 4K 225
Prospero Rd. N19 32Mb 70
Prossers KT20: Tad 93Za 194
Protea Cl. E16 42Hc 93
Protheroe Ho. N17 27Vb 51
Prothero Gdns. NW4 29Xa 48
Prothero Ho. NW10 38Ta 67
(off Ayres Cres.)
Prothero Rd. SW6 52Ab 110
Proton Twr. E14 45Fc 93
Proud Ho. E1 44Xb 91
(off Amazon St.)
Prout Gro. NW10 35Ua 68
Prout Rd. E5 34Xb 71
Provence St. N1 1D 218 (40Sb 71)
Providence Av. HA2: Harr 32Ca 65
Providence Cl. E9 39Zb 72
Providence Ct. W1 4J 221 (45Jb 90)
Providence Ho. E14 44Bc 92
(off Three Colt St.)
Providence La. UB3: Harl 52T 106
Providence Pl. GU22: Pyr 86J 169
KT17: Eps 84Ua 174
N1 39Rb 71
RM5: Col R 25Bd 55
Providence Rd. UB7: Yiew 46N 83
Providence Row N1 2H 217
Providence Row Cl. E2 41Xb 91
Providence Sq. SE1 47Wb 91
Providence St. DA9: Ghithe 57Wd 120
Providence Twr. SE16 47Wb 91
(off Bermondsey Wall W.)
Providence Yd. E2 41Wb 91
(off Ezra St.)
Provident Ind. Est. UB3: Hayes 47W 84
Provost Ct. NW3 37Hb 69
(off Eton Rd.)
Provost Est. N1 3F 219
Provost Rd. NW3 38Hb 69
Provost St. N1 2F 219 (40Tb 71)
Prowse Av. WD23: B Hea 18Ea 28
Prowse Pl. NW1 38Lb 70
Pryors Path HA1: Harr 31Ka 66
Prudence La. BR6: Farnb 77Qc 160
Pruden Cl. N14 19Lb 32
Prudent Pas. EC2 3E 224
Prudhoe Ct. DA2: Dart 58Rd 119
(off Osbourne Rd.)
Prune Hill TW20: Egh, Eng G 6P 125
Prunus Cl. GU24: W End 5C 166
Prusom's Island E1 46Yb 92
(off Wapping High St.)
Prusom St. E1 46Xb 91
Pryor Cl. WD5: Ab L 4V 12
Pryors, The NW3 34Fb 69
Puccinia Ct. TW19: Stanw 60N 105
(off Yeoman Dr.)
Puck La. EN9: Walt A 1Fc 21
Pucknells Cl. BR8: Swan 67Ed 140
Pucks Hill GU21: Knap 9H 167
Pudding La. AL1: St A 2B 6
(off Chequer St.)
EC3 5G 225 (45Tb 91)
HP1: Hem H 1J 3
IG7: Chig 16Uc 36
TN15: Seal 93Pd 203
Pudding Mill La. E15 39Dc 72
Puddingstone Dr.
AL4: St A 4G 6
PUDDLEDOCK 65Gd 140
Puddle Dock EC4 4C 224 (45Rb 91)
(not continuous)
Puddledock La. DA2: Wilm 64Gd 140
PUDDS CROSS 1A 10
Puffin Cl. BR3: Beck 71Zb 158
IG11: Bark 41Xc 95
Pugin Ct. N1 38Qb 70
(off Liverpool Rd.)
Pulborough Ho. RM3: Rom 24Nd 57
(off Kingsbridge Cir.)
Pulborough Rd. SW18 59Bb 111
Pulborough Way TW4: Houn 56Y 107
Pulford Rd. N15 30Tb 51
Pulham Av. N2 28Eb 49
Pulham Ho. SW8 52Pb 112
(off Dorset Rd.)
Puller's Bldgs. SE17 7C 230
Puller Rd. EN5: Barn 12Ab 30
HP1: Hem H 3J 3
Pulleyns Av. E6 41Nc 94
Pulleys Cl. HP1: Hem H 1H 3
Pulleys La. HP1: Hem H 1G 2
(not continuous)
Pullman Cl. AL1: St A 4C 6
Pullman Ct. SW2 60Nb 112
Pullman Gdns. SW15 58Ya 110
Pullman M. SE12 62Kc 137
Pullman Pl. RH1: Mers 100Lb 196
(off Station Rd.)
SE9 57Nc 116
Pullmans Pl. TW18: Staines 64J 127
Pulross Rd. SW9 55Pb 112
Pulse Apartments NW6 36Db 69
(off Lymington Rd.)
Pulteney Cl. E3 39Bc 72
TW7: Isle 55Ja 108
Pulteney Gdns. E18 27Jc 53
Pulteney Rd. E18 27Kc 53

Pulteney Ter. N1 ... 39Pb 70
(not continuous)
Pulton Ho. SE4 ... 56Ac 114
(off Turnham Rd.)
Pulton Pl. SW6 ... 52Cb 111
Puma Ct. E1 ... 7K 219 (43Vb 91)
Pump All. TW8: Bford ... 52Ma 109
Pump Cl. UB5: N'olt ... 40Ca 65
Pump Ct. EC4 ... 3K 223 (44Qb 90)
Pumphandle Path N2 ... 26Fb 49
(off Oak La.)
Pump Hill IG10: Lough ... 12Pc 36
Pumphouse, The N8 ... 28Pb 50
Pump Ho. Cl. BR2: Brom ... 68Gc 137
SE16 ... 47Yb 92
Pumphouse Cres. WD17: Wat ... 15Y 27
Pumphouse Educational Museum, The ... 46Ac 92
Pump House Gallery ... 52Jb 112
Pump Ho. M. E1 ... 45Wb 91
(off Hooper St.)
Pump House Steam & Transport Mus. ... 30Ac 52
Pump House Theatre & Arts Cen. ... 15Z 27
Pumping Ho. E14 ... 45Fc 93
(off Naval Row)
Pumping Sta. Rd. W4 ... 52Ua 110
Pumpkin Hill SL1: Burn ... 7C 60
Pump La. BR6: Well H ... 78Dd 162
SE14 ... 52Yb 114
SL5: Asc ... 7C 124
UB3: Hayes ... 47W 84
Pump Pail Nth. CR0: C'don ... 76Sb 157
Pump Pail Sth. CR0: C'don ... 76Sb 157
Pump St. SS17: Horn H ... 1J 101
Punchard Cres. EN3: Enf L ... 10Dc 20
Punch Cft. DA3: New A ... 76Ae 165
Punderson's Gdns. E2 ... 41Xb 91
Purbeck Av. KT3: N Mald ... 72Va 154
Purbeck Cl. RH1: Mers ... 100Lb 196
(not continuous)
Purbeck Dr. GU21: Wok ... 86B 168
NW2 ... 33Za 68
Purbeck Ho. SW8 ... 52Pb 112
(off Bolney St.)
WD18: Wat ... 16V 26
(off Scammell Way)
Purbeck Rd. RM11: Horn ... 31Jd 76
Purberry Gro. KT17: Ewe ... 82Va 174
Purberry Shot KT17: Ewe ... 82Va 174
Purbrock Av. WD25: Wat ... 8Y 13
Purbrook Est. SE1 ... 3J 231 (47Ub 91)
Purbrook St. SE1 ... 3J 231 (48Ub 91)
Purcell Cl. CR8: Kenley ... 86Sb 177
SS17: Stan H ... 1L 101
WD6: Bore ... 11Ma 29
Purcell Cres. SW6 ... 52Za 110
Purcell Ho. EN1: Enf ... 10Wb 19
SW10 ... 51Fb 111
(off Milman's St.)
Purcell Mans. W14 ... 51Ab 110
(off Queen's Club Gdns.)
Purcell M. NW10 ... 38Ua 68
Purcell Rd. UB6: G'frd ... 43Da 85
Purcell Room ... 6J 223
Purcells Av. HA8: Edg ... 22Qa 47
Purcell's Cl. KT21: Asht ... 90Pa 173
Purcell St. N1 ... 1H 219 (40Ub 71)
Purcell Way SS17: Stan H ... 1L 101
Purchese St. NW1 ... 1D 216 (40Mb 70)
Purday Ho. W10 ... 41Ab 88
(off Bruckner St.)
Purdon Ho. SE15 ... 53Wb 113
(off Oliver Goldsmith Est.)
Purdy Ct. KT4: Wor Pk ... 75Wa 154
Purdy St. E3 ... 42Dc 92
Purelake M. SE13 ... 55Fc 115
(off Marischal Rd.)
PURFLEET ... 49Qd 97
Purfleet By-Pass RM19: Purf ... 49Rd 97
Purfleet Deep Wharf RM19: Purf ... 51Sd 120
Purfleet Heritage & Military Cen. ... 49Pd 97
Purfleet Ind. Access Rd.
RM15: Avel ... 48Qd 97
Purfleet Ind. Pk. RM15: Avel ... 46Pd 97
(not continuous)
Purfleet Rd. RM15: Avel ... 47Qd 97
Purfleet Thames Terminal
RM19: Purf ... 52Sd 120
Purkis Cl. UB8: Hil ... 45S 84
Purland Cl. RM8: Dag ... 32Bd 75
Purland Rd. SE28 ... 47Vc 95
(not continuous)
Purleigh Av. IG8: Wfd G ... 23Nc 54
PURLEY ... 83Qb 176
Purley Av. NW2 ... 33Ab 68
Purley Bury Av. CR8: Purl ... 83Sb 177
Purley Bury Cl. CR8: Purl ... 83Sb 177
Purley Cl. IG5: Ilf ... 26Qc 54
PURLEY CROSS ... 83Qb 176
Purley Downs Golf Course ... 83Tb 177
Purley Downs Rd. CR2: Sande ... 82Sb 177
CR8: Purl ... 82Sb 177
Purley Hill CR8: Purl ... 84Rb 177
Purley Knoll CR8: Purl ... 83Pb 176
Purley Leisure Cen. ... 83Qb 176
Purley Oaks Rd. CR2: Sande ... 81Tb 177
Purley Pde. CR8: Purl ... 83Qb 176
Purley Pk. Rd. CR8: Purl ... 82Rb 177
Purley Pl. N1 ... 38Rb 71
Purley Ri. CR8: Purl ... 84Pb 176
Purley Rd. CR2: S Croy ... 80Tb 157
CR8: Purl ... 83Qb 176
N9 ... 20Ub 33
Purley Va. CR8: Purl ... 85Rb 177
Purley Vw. Ter. CR2: S Croy ... 80Tb 157
(off Sanderstead Rd.)
Purley Way CR0: C'don, Wadd ... 73Pb 156
CR8: Purl ... 82Qb 176
Purley Way Centre, The
CR0: Wadd ... 75Qb 156
Purley Way Cres. CR0: C'don ... 73Pb 156
Purlieu Way CM16: They B ... 7Uc 22
Purlings Rd. WD23: Bush ... 15Da 27
Purneys Rd. SE9 ... 56Mc 115
Purrett Rd. SE18 ... 50Vc 95
Purser Ho. SW2 ... 58Qb 112
Pursers Ct. SL2: Slou ... 4J 81
Pursers Cross Rd. SW6 ... 53Bb 111
Pursewardens Cl. W13 ... 46La 86
Pursey Cl. TN15: W King ... 79Ud 164
Pursley Gdns. WD6: Bore ... 10Qa 15
Pursley Rd. NW7 ... 24Xa 48
Purton Ct. SL2: Farn R ... 8G 60
Purton La. SL2: Farn C, Farn R ... 8G 60
Purves Rd. NW10 ... 41Xa 88
Purvis Ho. CR0: C'don ... 73Tb 157
Pusey Ho. E14 ... 44Cc 92
(off Saracen St.)
Puteaux Ho. E2 ... 40Zb 72
(off Mace St.)
PUTNEY ... 56Za 110
Putney Arts Theatre ... 56Za 110
Putney Bri. SW15 ... 55Ab 110
Putney Bri. App. SW6 ... 55Ab 110
Putney Bri. Rd. SW15 ... 56Ab 110
SW18 ... 56Ab 110
Putney Comn. SW15 ... 55Ya 110
Putney Exchange (Shopping Centre)
SW15 ... 56Za 110
Putney Gdns. RM6: Chad H ... 29Xc 55
PUTNEY HEATH ... 58Ya 110
Putney Heath SW15 ... 59Xa 110
Putney Heath La. SW15 ... 58Za 110
Putney High St. SW15 ... 56Za 110
Putney Hill SW15 ... 59Za 110
(not continuous)
Putney Leisure Cen. ... 56Ya 110
Putney Pk. Av. SW15 ... 56Wa 110
Putney Pk. La. SW15 ... 56Xa 110
(not continuous)
Putney Rd. EN3: Enf W ... 8Zb 20
PUTNEY VALE ... 62Wa 132
Putney Va. Crematorium SW19 ... 61Xa 132
Putney Wharf SW15 ... 55Ab 110
Puttenham Cl. WD19: Wat ... 19Y 27
Puttocks Cl. AL9: Wel G ... 5E 8
Puttocks Dr. AL9: Wel G ... 5E 8
Pycroft Way N9 ... 21Vb 51
Pye Cl. CR3: Cat'm ... 95Tb 197
Pyecombe Cnr. N12 ... 21Bb 49
Pyghtle, The UB9: Den ... 31J 63
Pyghtle Footpath UB9: Den ... 32J 63
Pylbrook Rd. SM1: Sutt ... 76Cb 155
PYLE HILL ... 6P 187
Pyle Hill GU22: Wok ... 6P 187
Pylon Way CR0: Bedd ... 74Nb 156
Pym Cl. EN4: E Barn ... 15Fb 31
Pymers Mead SE21 ... 60Sb 113
Pymmes Brook Dr. EN4: E Barn ... 14Gb 31
Pymmes Brook Ho. N10 ... 24Jb 50
Pymmes Cl. N13 ... 22Pb 50
N17 ... 25Xb 51
Pymmes Gdns. Nth. N9 ... 20Vb 33
Pymmes Gdns. Sth. N9 ... 20Vb 33
Pymmes Grn. Rd. N11 ... 21Kb 50
Pymmes Rd. N13 ... 22Nb 50
Pym Orchard TN16: Bras ... 96Yc 201
Pym Pl. RM17: Grays ... 49Ce 99
Pynchester Cl. UB10: Ick ... 33Q 64
Pynefield Ho. WD3: Rick ... 17H 25
Pyne Rd. KT6: Surb ... 74Qa 153
Pynest Grn. La. EN9: Lough, Walt A ... 10Jc 21
Pynfolds SE16 ... 47Xb 91
Pynham Cl. SE2 ... 48Xc 95
Pynnacles Cl. HA7: Stan ... 22Ka 46
Pynnersmead SE24 ... 57Sb 113
Pyramid Ct. KT1: King T ... 68Pa 131
(off Cambridge Rd.)
Pyramid Ho. TW4: Houn ... 54Aa 107
Pyrcroft La. KT13: Weyb ... 78R 150
Pyrcroft Rd. KT16: Chert ... 73G 148
PYRFORD ... 88J 169
Pyrford Comn. Rd. GU22: Pyr ... 88F 168
Pyrford Ct. GU22: Pyr ... 89G 168
Pyrford Golf Course ... 89K 169
PYRFORD GREEN ... 89K 169
Pyrford Heath GU22: Pyr ... 88H 169
Pyrford Ho. SW9 ... 56Rb 113
Pyrford Lock GU23: Wis ... 88L 169
Pyrford Rd. GU22: Pyr ... 85J 169
KT14: W Byf ... 85J 169
PYRFORD VILLAGE ... 90J 169
Pyrford Wood Est. GU22: Pyr ... 88H 169
Pyrford Woods GU22: Pyr ... 87G 168
Pyrford Woods Cl. GU22: Pyr ... 87H 169
Pyrian Cl. GU22: Wok ... 88F 168
Pyrland Rd. N5 ... 36Tb 71
TW10: Rich ... 58Pa 109
Pyrles Grn. IG10: Lough ... 11Rc 36
Pyrles La. IG10: Lough ... 12Rc 36
Pyrmont Gro. SE27 ... 62Rb 135
Pyrmont Rd. W4 ... 51Qa 109
Pytchley Cres. SE19 ... 65Sb 135
Pytchley Rd. SE22 ... 55Ub 113

Q

Q Building, The E15 ... 37Gc 73
(off The Grove)
QED - Queen Elizabeth Distribution Pk.
RM19: Purf ... 50Td 98
Quad Ct. SE1 ... 3J 231
Quadrangle, The E15 ... 37Gc 73
SE24 ... 57Sb 113
SW6 ... 52Ab 110
SW10 ... 53Eb 111
W2 ... 2D 220 (44Gb 89)
Quadrangle Cl. SE1 ... 5H 231 (49Ub 91)
Quadrangle M. HA7: Stan ... 24La 46
Quadrant, The DA7: Bex ... 52Zc 117
HA2: Harr ... 27Fa 46
HA8: Edg ... 23Qa 47
KT17: Eps ... 85Ua 174
NW4 ... 28Ya 48
RM19: Purf ... 49Sd 98
SM2: Sutt ... 79Eb 155
SW20 ... 67Ab 132
TW9: Rich ... 56Ma 109
W10 ... 41Za 88
WD3: Rick ... 17N 25
Quadrant Arc. RM1: Rom ... 29Gd 56
W1 ... 5C 222
Quadrant Bus. Cen. NW6 ... 39Ab 68
Quadrant Cl. NW4 ... 29Xa 48
Quadrant Ct. DA9: Ghithe ... 56Vd 120
HA9: Wemb ... 35Qa 67
Quadrant Courtyard, The
KT13: Weyb ... 77Q 150
(off Quadrant Way)
Quadrant Gro. NW5 ... 36Hb 69
Quadrant Ho. E15 ... 41Gc 93
(off Durban Rd.)
SE1 ... 7B 224
Quadrant Rd. CR7: Thor H ... 70Rb 135
TW9: Rich ... 56Ma 109
Quadrant Way KT13: Weyb ... 77Q 150
Quadrivium Point SL1: Slou ... 6G 80
Quad Rd. HA9: Wemb ... 34Ma 67
Quaggy Wlk. SE3 ... 56Jc 115
Quail Gdns. CR2: Sels ... 82Ac 178
Quain Mans. W14 ... 51Ab 110
(off Queen's Club Gdns.)
Quainton St. NW10 ... 34Ta 67
Quaker Cl. TN13: S'oaks ... 95Md 203
Quaker Ct. E1 ... 6K 219
EC1 ... 5E 218
Quaker La. EN9: Walt A ... 6Ec 20
UB2: S'hall ... 48Ca 85
Quakers Cl. DA3: Hartl ... 69Ae 143
Quakers Course NW9 ... 25Va 48
Quakers Hall La. TN13: S'oaks ... 94Ld 203
Quakers La. EN6: Pot B ... 2Db 17
TW7: Isle ... 52Ja 108
Quakers Pl. E7 ... 36Mc 73
Quaker St. E1 ... 6K 219 (42Vb 91)
Quakers Wlk. N21 ... 15Tb 33
Quality Ct. WC2 ... 2K 223
Quality Hotel Leisure Club ... 4D 6
Quality St. RH1: Mers ... 100Kb 196
Quantock Cl. SL3: L'ly ... 50C 82
UB3: Harl ... 52T 106
Quantock Dr. KT4: Wor Pk ... 75Ya 154
Quantock Gdns. NW2 ... 33Za 68
Quantock Ho. N16 ... 32Vb 71
Quantock M. SE15 ... 54Wb 113
Quantock Rd. DA7: Bex ... 54Gd 118
Quantum Ct. E1 ... 45Yb 92
(off King David La.)
Quarles Cl. RM5: Col R ... 24Cd 56
Quarles Pk. Rd. RM6: Chad H ... 30Xc 55
Quarrendon St. SW6 ... 54Cb 111
Quarr Rd. SM5: Cars ... 72Fb 155
Quarry, The RH3: Bet ... 4A 206
Quarry Cl. DA11: Grav'nd ... 9B 122
KT22: Lea ... 93Ma 193
RH8: Oxt ... 2J 211
Quarry Cotts. RH2: Reig ... 3K 207
TN13: S'oaks ... 95Jd 202
Quarry Gdns. KT22: Lea ... 93Ma 193
Quarry Hill RM17: Grays ... 50Ce 99
TN15: S'oaks ... 95Md 203
Quarry Hill Pk. RH2: Reig ... 3L 207
Quarry Hill Rd. TN15: Bor G ... 93Be 205
Quarry M. RM19: Purf ... 49Qd 97
Quarry Pk. Rd. SM1: Sutt ... 79Bb 155
Quarry Path RH8: Oxt ... 3J 211
Quarry Ri. SM1: Sutt ... 79Bb 155
Quarry Rd. RH8: Oxt ... 2J 211
RH9: G'stone ... 100Yb 198
SW18 ... 58Eb 111
Quarryside Bus. Pk. RH1: Redh ... 3B 208
Quarry Vw. DA9: Ghithe ... 58Wd 120
(off Woodpecker Dr.)
Quarterdeck, The E14 ... 47Cc 92
Quartermaine Av. GU22: Wok ... 94B 188
Quartermass Cl. HP1: Hem H ... 1J 3
Quartermass Rd. HP1: Hem H ... 1J 3
Quartz Ho. HA2: Harr ... 32Ca 65
Quastel Ho. SE1 ... 2F 231
Quatre Ports E4 ... 22Fc 53
Quaves Rd. SL3: Slou ... 8M 81
Quay Ho. E14 ... 47Cc 92
(off Admirals Way)
Quay La. DA9: Ghithe ... 56Xd 120
Quayside Cotts. E1 ... 46Wb 91
(off Mews St.)
Quayside Ct. SE16 ... 46Zb 92
(off Abbotshade Rd.)
Quayside Ho. E14 ... 46Bc 92
W10 ... 42Ab 88
Quayside Wlk. KT1: King T ... 68Ma 131
(off Wadbrook St.)
Quay Sth. Ct. UB9: Hare ... 25J 43
Quay Vw. Apartments E14 ... 48Cc 92
(off Arden Cres.)
Quay W. Ct. WD3: W Hyd ... 24H 43
Quebec Av. TN16: Westrm ... 98Tc 200
Quebec Cotts. TN16: Westrm ... 99Tc 200
Quebec House ... 98Tc 200
Quebec M. W1 ... 3G 221 (44Hb 89)
Quebec Rd. IG1: Ilf ... 31Rc 74
IG2: Ilf ... 31Rc 74
RM18: Tilb ... 4C 122
UB4: Yead ... 44Y 85
Quebec Sq. TN16: Westrm ... 98Tc 200
Quebec Way SE16 ... 47Zb 92
Quebec Way Ind. Est. SE16 ... 47Ac 92
(not continuous)
Quebec Wharf E8 ... 39Ub 71
(off Kingsland Rd.)
E14 ... 44Cc 92
Quedgeley Ct. SE15 ... 51Vb 113
(off Ebley Cl.)
Queen Adelaide Ct. SE20 ... 65Yb 136
Queen Adelaide Rd. SE20 ... 65Yb 136
Queen Adelaide's Ride SL4: Wink ... 8B 102
Queen Alexandra Mans. WC1 ... 3F 217
Queen Alexandra's Ct. SW19 ... 64Bb 133
Queen Alexandra's Way
KT19: Eps ... 83Qa 173
Queen Anne Av. BR2: Brom ... 69Hc 137
Queen Anne Dr. KT10: Clay ... 80Ga 152
Queen Anne Ho. E16 ... 46Jc 93
(off Hardy Av.)
Queen Anne M. W1 ... 1A 222 (43Kb 90)
Queen Anne Rd. E9 ... 37Zb 72
Queen Anne's Cl. SL4: Wind ... 2F 124
TW2: Twick ... 62Fa 130
Queen Anne's Ct. SE10 ... 50Fc 93
(off Park Row)
Queen Anne's Gdns. CR4: Mitc ... 69Hb 133
EN1: Enf ... 16Ub 33
KT22: Lea ... 93Ka 192
W4 ... 48Ua 88
W5 ... 47Na 87
Queen Anne's Ga. DA7: Bex ... 55Zc 117
SW1 ... 2D 228 (47Mb 90)
Queen Anne's Gro. EN1: Enf ... 17Tb 33
W4 ... 48Ua 88
W5 ... 47Na 87
Queen Anne's Pl. EN1: Enf ... 16Ub 33
Queen Anne's Ride SL4: Wind ... 6G 102
Queen Anne's Rd. SL4: Wind ... 6G 102
Queen Annes Sq. SE1 ... 49Wb 91
(off Monnow Rd.)
Queen Anne's Ter. KT22: Lea ... 93Ka 192
Queen Anne St. W1 ... 2K 221 (44Kb 90)
Queen Anne's Wlk. WC1 ... 6G 217
Queen Anne Ter. E1 ... 45Xb 91
(off Sovereign Cl.)
Queen Ann's Ct. SL4: Wind ... 3H 103
(off Peascod St.)
Queenborough Gdns. BR7: Chst ... 65Tc 138
IG2: Ilf ... 28Qc 54
Queenbridge Ind. Pk.
RM20: W Thur ... 51Wd 120
Queen Caroline St. W6 ... 50Ya 88
Queen Catherine Ho. SW6 ... 52Db 111
(off Wandon Rd.)
Queen Charlotte St. SL4: Wind ... 3H 103
(off Market St.)
Queen Ct. WC1 ... 6G 217
(off Queen Sq.)
Queendale Ct. GU21: Wok ... 8K 167
Queen Elizabeth II Bri. DA1: Dart ... 55Td 120
RM20: Dart, W Thur ... 55Td 120
Queen Elizabeth Av. RM18: E Til ... 9K 101
Queen Elizabeth Bldgs. EC4 ... 4K 223
Queen Elizabeth Ct. EN5: Barn ... 13Cb 31
EN9: Walt A ... 8Ec 20
(off Greenwich Way)
Queen Elizabeth Gdns.
SM4: Mord ... 70Cb 133
Queen Elizabeth Hall ... 6H 223 (46Pb 90)
Queen Elizabeth Ho. SW12 ... 59Jb 112
Queen Elizabeth II Conference Cen.
... 2E 228 (47Mb 90)
Queen Elizabeth Rd. E17 ... 27Ac 52
KT2: King T ... 68Pa 131
Queen Elizabeth's Cl. N16 ... 33Tb 71
Queen Elizabeth's Coll. SE10 ... 52Ec 114
Queen Elizabeth's Dr.
CR0: New Ad ... 81Fc 179
N14 ... 18Nb 32
Queen Elizabeth's Gdns.
CR0: New Ad ... 82Fc 179
Queen Elizabeth's Hunting Lodge ... 17Hc 35
Queen Elizabeth Sports Cen. ... 14Bb 31
Queen Elizabeth Stadium ... 12Vb 33
Queen Elizabeth St. SE1 ... 1K 231 (47Ub 91)
Queen Elizabeth's Wlk. N16 ... 32Tb 71
SL4: Wind ... 4J 103
SM6: Bedd ... 77Mb 156
Queen Elizabeth Wlk. SW13 ... 53Wa 110
Queen Elizabeth Way GU22: Wok ... 91B 188
Queenhill Rd. CR2: Sels ... 82Xb 177
Queenhithe EC4 ... 4E 224 (45Sb 91)
Queenhythe Cres. GU4: Jac W ... 10P 187
Queenhythe Rd. GU4: Jac W ... 10P 187
Queen Isabella Way EC1 ... 2C 224
Queen Margaret Flats E2 ... 41Xb 91
(off St Jude's Rd.)
Queen Margaret's Gro. N1 ... 36Ub 71
Queen Mary Av. E18 ... 25Jc 53
RM18: E Til ... 9L 101
SM4: Mord ... 71Za 154
Queen Mary Cl. GU22: Wok ... 88E 168
KT6: Surb ... 76Qa 153
RM1: Rom ... 30Hd 56
Queen Mary Ct. RM18: E Til ... 9L 101
TW19: Stanw ... 60N 105
Queen Mary Ho. E16 ... 46Kc 93
(off Wesley Av.)
E18 ... 25Kc 53
Queen Mary Rd. SE19 ... 65Rb 135
TW17: Shep ... 68S 128
Queen Mary's Av. SM5: Cars ... 80Hb 155
WD18: Wat ... 14U 26
Queen Marys Bldgs. SW1 ... 5C 228
Queen Marys Ct. EN9: Walt A ... 7Ec 20
(off Harrison Rd.)
SE10 ... 51Fc 115
(off Park Row)
Queen Mary's Dr. KT15: New H ... 82H 169
Queen Mary's Ho. SW15 ... 58Wa 110
Queen Mary University of London
Charterhouse Square
... 6C 218 (42Rb 91)
Lincoln's Inn Fields Campus ... 2H 223
Mile End Campus ... 42Ac 92
West Smithfield Campus ... 1C 224
Queen Mary Works WD18: Wat ... 14U 26
Queen Mothers Dr. UB9: Den ... 30H 43
Queen Mother Sports Centre, The ... 5B 228
Queen of Denmark Ct. SE16 ... 48Bc 92
Queens Acre SL4: Wind ... 6H 103
SM3: Cheam ... 80Za 154
Queens Acre Ho. SL4: Wind ... 5H 103
Queens All. CM16: Epp ... 3Vc 23
Queens Av. HA7: Stan ... 27La 46
IG8: Wfd G ... 22Kc 53
KT14: Byfl ... 84M 169
N3 ... 24Eb 49
N10 ... 27Jb 50
N20 ... 19Fb 31
N21 ... 18Rb 33
TW13: Hanw ... 63Y 129
UB6: G'frd ... 44Da 85
WD18: Wat ... 14V 26
Queensberry Ho. TW9: Rich ... 57La 108
Queensberry Mews W.
SW7 ... 5B 226 (49Fb 89)
Queensberry Pl. E12 ... 36Mc 73
SW7 ... 5B 226 (49Fb 89)
TW9: Rich ... 57Ma 109
(off Friars La.)
Queensberry Way SW7 ... 5B 226 (49Fb 89)
Queensborough Ct. N3 ... 28Bb 49
(off Tillingbourne Gdns.)
Queensborough M. W2 ... 45Eb 89
Queensborough Pas. W2 ... 45Eb 89
(off Queensborough M.)
Queensborough Studios W2 ... 45Eb 89
(off Queensborough M.)
Queensborough Ter. W2 ... 45Db 89
Queensbridge Ct. E2 ... 1K 219
Queensbridge Pk. TW7: Isle ... 57Ga 108
Queensbridge Rd. E2 ... 37Vb 71
E8 ... 37Vb 71
Queensbridge Sports & Community Cen.
... 38Vb 71
QUEENSBURY ... 27Na 47
Queensbury Circ. Pde.
HA3: Kenton ... 27Na 47
HA7: Kenton ... 27Na 47
Queensbury Rd. HA0: Wemb ... 40Pa 67
NW9 ... 31Ta 67
Queensbury Sta. Pde. HA8: Edg ... 27Pa 47
Queensbury St. N1 ... 38Sb 71
Queen's Chapel of the Savoy, The ... 5H 223
Queen's Cir. SW8 ... 52Kb 112
Queens Cl. GU24: Bisl ... 8E 166
HA8: Edg ... 22Qa 47
KT10: Esh ... 77Da 151
KT20: Walt H ... 96Wa 194
SL4: Old Win ... 7L 103
SM6: Wall ... 78Kb 156
Queen's Club Gdns. W14 ... 51Ab 110
Queen's Club, The (Tennis Courts)
... 50Ab 88
Queens Club Ter. W14 ... 51Bb 111
(off Normand Rd.)
Queens Ct. AL1: St A ... 2F 6
CR2: S Croy ... 78Sb 157
(off Warham Rd.)
CR7: Thor H ... 71Qb 156
E11 ... 31Gc 73
GU22: Wok ... 90B 168
HA3: Kenton ... 26Ka 46
IG9: Buck H ... 19Mc 35
KT13: Weyb ... 78T 150
KT19: Ewe ... 82Ua 174
NW6 ... 36Db 69
NW8 ... 1B 214
NW11 ... 29Bb 49
RH1: Redh ... 5A 208
(off St Anne's Mt.)
RM11: Horn ... 32Md 77
SE23 ... 61Yb 136
SL1: Slou ... 5K 81
SM2: Sutt ... 83Cb 175
TW10: Rich ... 58Pa 109
TW18: Staines ... 65M 127
W2 ... 45Db 89
(off Queensway)
WD17: Wat ... 13Y 27
(off Queen's Rd.)
Queenscourt HA9: Wemb ... 35Na 67
Queens Ct. Ride KT11: Cobh ... 85W 170
Queen's Cres. NW5 ... 37Jb 70
TW10: Rich ... 57Pa 109
Queenscroft Rd. SE9 ... 57Mc 115
Queensdale Cres. W11 ... 46Za 88
(not continuous)
Queensdale Pl. W11 ... 46Ab 88
Queensdale Rd. W11 ... 46Za 88
Queensdale Wlk. W11 ... 46Ab 88
Queensdown Rd. E5 ... 35Xb 71
Queens Dr. E10 ... 31Cc 72
EN8: Walt C ... 6Cc 20
KT5: Surb ... 73Qa 153
KT7: T Ditt ... 72Ja 152
KT22: Oxs ... 83Ea 172
N4 ... 33Rb 71
SL3: Ful, Wex ... 38B 62
TN14: S'oaks ... 92Ld 203
W3 ... 44Pa 87
W5 ... 44Pa 87
WD5: Ab L ... 4V 12
Queens Dr., The WD3: Rick ... 17H 25
Queen's Elm Pde. SW3 ... 7C 226
(off Old Church St.)
Queen's Elm Sq. SW3 ... 7C 226 (50Fb 89)
Queen's Farm Rd.
DA12: Shorne, Grav'nd ... 1N 145
Queensferry Wlk. N17 ... 28Xb 51
Queensfield Ct. SM3: Cheam ... 77Ya 154
Queen's Gallery ... 2A 228 (47Kb 90)
Queens Gdns. DA2: Dart ... 60Rd 119
NW4 ... 29Ya 48
RM13: Rain ... 40Fd 76
RM14: Upm ... 30Vd 58
TW5: Hest ... 53Aa 107
W2 ... 4A 220 (45Eb 89)
W5 ... 42La 86
Queens Ga. SW7 ... 2A 226 (47Eb 89)
WD17: Wat ... 13Y 27
(off Lord St.)
Queensgate EN8: Walt C ... 6Bc 20
KT11: Cobh ... 84Z 171
Queensgate Cen. RM17: Grays ... 50Ce 99
Queens Ga. Cotts. SL4: Wind ... 6H 103
Queensgate Ct. N12 ... 22Db 49
Queens Ga. Gdns. BR7: Chst ... 67Tc 138
SW7 ... 4A 226 (48Eb 89)
SW15 ... 56Xa 110
Queensgate Ho. E3 ... 40Bc 72
(off Hereford Rd.)
Queen's Ga. M. SW7 ... 2A 226 (48Eb 89)
Queensgate M. BR3: Beck ... 67Ac 136
Queen's Ga. Pl. SW7 ... 4A 226 (48Eb 89)
Queensgate Pl. NW6 ... 38Cb 69
Queen's Ga. Pl. M. SW7 ... 4A 226 (48Eb 89)
Queen's Ga. Ter. SW7 ... 3A 226 (48Eb 89)
Queens Ga. Vs. E9 ... 38Ac 72
Queen's Gro. NW8 ... 1B 214 (39Fb 69)
Queens Gro. Rd. E4 ... 18Fc 35
Queen's Gro. Studios
NW8 1B 214 (39Fb 69)
Queen's Head Pas. EC4 ... 2D 224 (44Sb 91)
Queen's Head St. N1 ... 39Rb 71
Queen's Head Yd. SE1 ... 7F 225
Queens Hill Ri. SL5: Asc ... 9A 124
Queen's House, The ... 51Fc 115
(within National Maritime Mus.)
Queens Ho. SE17 ... 51Tb 113
(off Merrow St.)
SW8 ... 52Nb 112
(off Sth. Lambeth Rd.)
TW11: Tedd ... 65Ha 130
W2 ... 45Db 89
(off Queensway)
Queen's Ice Bowl ... 45Db 89
Queenside M. RM12: Horn ... 33Nd 77
Queen's Keep TW1: Twick ... 58La 108
Queensland Av. N18 ... 23Sb 51
SW19 ... 67Db 133
Queensland Cl. E17 ... 26Bc 52
Queensland Ho. E16 ... 46Qc 94
(off Rymill St.)
Queensland Rd. N7 ... 35Qb 70
Queens La. N10 ... 27Kb 50
Queen's Mans. W6 ... 49Za 88
(off Brook Grn.)
Queen's Mkt. E13 ... 39Lc 73
Queens Mead HA8: Edg ... 23Pa 47
Queensmead KT22: Oxs ... 83Ea 172
NW8 ... 39Fb 69
SL3: Dat ... 2M 103
Queensmead Av. KT17: Ewe ... 82Xa 174
Queens Mead Rd. BR2: Brom ... 68Hc 137
Queensmead Sports Cen. ... 35Z 65
Queensmere Cl. SW19 ... 61Za 132
Queensmere Ct. SW13 ... 52Va 110
Queensmere Rd. SL1: Slou ... 7K 81
SW19 ... 61Za 132
Queensmere Shop. Cen. SL1: Slou ... 7K 81
Queen's M. W2 ... 45Db 89
Queensmill Rd. SW6 ... 52Za 110
Queens Pde. N8 ... 28Rb 51
N11 ... 22Hb 49
(off Friern Barnet Rd.)
NW2 ... 37Ya 68
(off Willesden La.)
NW4 ... 29Ya 48
(off Queens Rd.)
W5 ... 44Pa 87
Queen's Pde. Cl. N11 ... 22Hb 49

Queens Pk. Ct. W10 . . . . . 41Za 88
Queen's Pk. Gdns. TW13: Felt 62V 128
Queen's Pk. Rangers FC 46Xa 88
Queen's Pk. Rd. CR3: Cat'm 95Ub 197
RM3: Hrld W 25Qd 57
Queens Pas. BR7: Chst 65Rc 138
Queens Pl. SM4: Mord 70Cb 133
WD17: Wat 13Y 27
Queen's Prom. KT1: King T, Surb . . . 70Ma 131
Queen Sq. WC1 . . . . . 6G 217 (42Nb 90)
Queen Sq. Pl. WC1 . . . . . 6G 217
Queen's Quay EC4 . . . . . 4E 224
Queens Reach KT1: King T 68Ma 131
KT8: E Mos 70Ga 130
Queens Ride SW13 . . . . . 55Wa 110
SW15 . . . . . 55Wa 110
Queens Ri. TW10: Rich 58Pa 109
Queens Rd. BR1: Brom 68Jc 137
BR3: Beck 68Ac 136
BR7: Chst 65Rc 138
CM14: B'wood 20Yd 40
CR0: C'don 72Rb 157
CR4: Mitc 69Fb 133
DA8: Erith 51Gd 118
DA12: Grav'nd 2E 144
DA16: Well 54Xc 117
E11 . . . . . 31Fc 73
E13 . . . . . 39Kc 73
E17 . . . . . 30Bc 52
EN1: Enf 14Ub 33
EN5: Barn 13Za 30
EN8: Walt C 5Ac 20
GU21: Knap 10G 166
GU24: Bisl, Brkwd 2C 186
IG9: Buck H 19Kc 35
IG10: Lough 13Nc 36
IG11: Bark 37Sc 74
KT2: King T 66Qa 131
KT3: N Mald 70Va 132
KT7: T Ditt 71Ha 152
KT12: Hers 77V 150
KT13: Weyb 77S 150
N3 . . . . . 25Eb 49
N9 . . . . . 20Xb 33
N11 . . . . . 24Nb 50
NW4 . . . . . 29Ya 48
SE14 . . . . . 53Xb 113
SE15 . . . . . 53Xb 113
SL1: Slou 5K 81
SL3: Dat 2M 103
SL4: Eton W 10D 80
SL4: Wind 4G 102
SL5: S'hill 1B 146
SM2: Sutt 82Cb 175
SM4: Mord 70Cb 133
SM6: Wall 78Kb 156
SW14 . . . . . 55Ta 109
SW19 . . . . . 65Bb 133
TW1: Twick 60Ja 108
TW3: Houn 55Da 107
TW10: Rich 59Pa 109
TW11: Tedd 65Ha 130
TW12: Hamp H 63Da 129
TW13: Felt 60X 107
TW20: Egh 64B 126
UB2: S'hall 47Z 85
UB3: Hayes 44U 84
UB7: W Dray 47P 83
UB8: Uxb 41L 83
W5 . . . . . 44Na 87
WD17: Wat 14Y 27
(Carey Pl., not continuous)
WD17: Wat 12Y 27
(Orphanage Rd.)
Queens Rd. Est. EN5: Barn 13Za 30
Queens Rd. W. E13 . . . . . 40Jc 73
Queen's Row SE17 . . . . . 51Tb 113
Queen's Sq., The HP2: Hem H 2P 3
Queens St. TW15: Ashf 63P 127
Queens Ter. E1 . . . . . 42Yb 92
(off Cephas St.)
E13 . . . . . 39Kc 73
KT7: T Ditt 72Ja 152
(off Queens Dr.)
NW8 . . . . . 1B 214 (39Fb 69)
SL4: Wind 5H 103
TW7: Isle 56Ja 108
Queen's Ter. Cotts. W7 . . . . . 47Ga 86
Queens Theatre
Hornchurch 31Md 77
Westminster 4D 222
Queensthorpe M. SE26 . . . . . 63Zb 136
Queensthorpe Rd. SE26 . . . . . 63Zb 136
Queens Tower 3B 226
Queenstown Gdns. RM13: Rain 41Hd 96
Queenstown M. SW8 . . . . . 54Kb 112
Queenstown Rd. SW8 . . . . . 51Kb 112
Queen St. AL3: St A 2A 6
CM14: W'ley 22Yd 58
CR0: C'don 77Sb 157
DA7: Bex 55Bd 117
DA8: Erith 51Gd 118
DA12: Grav'nd 8D 122
EC4 . . . . . 4E 224 (45Sb 91)
(not continuous)
KT16: Chert 74J 149
N17 . . . . . 23Ub 51
RM7: Rom 30Fd 56
W1 . . . . . 6K 221 (46Kb 90)
WD4: Chfd 4J 11
Queen St. Pl. EC4 . . . . . 5E 224 (45Sb 91)
Queensville Rd. SW12 . . . . . 59Mb 112
Queens Wlk. E4 . . . . . 18Fc 35
HA1: Harr 28Ga 46
HA4: Ruis 33Y 65
N5 . . . . . 36Rb 71
NW9 . . . . . 33Sa 67
SW1 . . . . . 6B 222 (46Lb 90)
TW15: Ashf 63M 127
W5 . . . . . 42La 86
Queen's Walk, The SE1 . . . 5A 224 (45Qb 90)
(Oxo Tower Wharf)
SE1 . . . . . 6G 225 (46Ub 91)
(Tooley St.)
SE1 . . . . . 6J 223 (46Pb 90)
(Waterloo Rd.)
Queens Wlk. Ter. HA4: Ruis 34Y 65
Queens Way EN8: Walt C 6Bc 20
GU24: Brkwd 1B 186
NW4 . . . . . 29Ya 48
TW13: Hanw 63Y 129
WD7: Shenl 4Na 15
Queensway BR4: W W'ck 76Gc 159
BR5: Pet W 71Sc 160
CR0: Wadd 79Pb 156
EN3: Pond E 14Xb 33
Queensway HP1: Hem H 1L 3
HP2: Hem H 1N 3
RH1: Redh 5P 207
TW16: Sun 68X 129
W2 . . . . . 44Db 89
Queensway, The SL9: Chal P 28A 42
Queensway Bus. Cen.
EN3: Pond E 14Xb 33
Queensway Ind. Est. EN3: Pond E . . . 14Yb 34
Queensway Nth. KT12: Hers 77Y 151
Queensway Sth. KT12: Hers 78Y 151
Queenswell Av. N20 . . . . . 20Gb 31
Queens Wharf W6 . . . . . 50Ya 88
Queenswood Av. CM13: Hut 14Fe 41
CR7: Thor H 71Qb 156
E17 . . . . . 25Ec 52
SM6: Bedd 77Mb 156
TW3: Houn 54Ba 107
TW12: Hamp 65Da 129
Queenswood Ct. SE27 . . . . . 63Tb 135
SW4 . . . . . 57Nb 112
Queenswood Cres. WD25: Wat 5W 12
Queenswood Gdns. E11 . . . . . 32Kc 73
Queenswood Ho. CM14: B'wood 19Zd 41
(off Eastfield Rd.)
Queenswood Lodge RM2: Rom 27Jd 56
Queenswood Pk. N3 . . . . . 26Ab 48
Queens Wood Rd. N10 . . . . . 30Kb 50
Queenswood Rd. DA15: Sidc 57Vc 117
GU21: Wok 1H 187
SE23 . . . . . 62Zb 136
Queens Yd. E9 . . . . . 37Cc 72
WC1 . . . . . 6C 216 (43Lb 90)
QUEEN VICTORIA 76Ya 154
Queen Victoria Av. HA0: Wemb 38Ma 67
Queen Victoria Memorial
. . . . . 2B 228 (47Lb 90)
Queen Victoria Rd. GU24: Brkwd 1B 186
Queen Victoria Seaman's Rest
E14 . . . . . 44Dc 92
(off E. India Dock Rd.)
Queen Victoria St. EC4 . . . 4B 224 (45Rb 91)
Queen Victoria Ter. E1 . . . . . 45Xb 91
(off Sovereign Cl.)
Queen Victoria Wlk. SL4: Wind 3J 103
Queenwood Golf Course 79B 148
Quelmans Head Ride SL4: Wind 1B 124
Quemerford Rd. N7 . . . . . 36Pb 70
Quendell Wlk. HP2: Hem H 2N 3
Quendon Dr. EN9: Walt A 5Fc 21
Quendon Ho. W10 . . . . . 42Ya 88
(off Sutton Way)
Quenington Ct. SE15 . . . . . 51Vb 113
Quennell Cl. KT21: Asht 91Pa 193
Quennell Way CM13: Hut 17Ee 41
Quentin Ho. SE1 . . . . . 1B 230
(not continuous)
Quentin Pl. SE13 . . . . . 55Gc 115
Quentin Rd. SE13 . . . . . 55Gc 115
Quentins Dr. TN16: Big H 88Rc 180
Quentins Wlk. TN16: Big H 88Rc 180
(off St Anns Way)
Quentin Way GU25: Vir W 10M 125
Quernmore Cl. BR1: Brom 65Jc 137
Quernmore Rd. BR1: Brom 65Jc 137
N4 . . . . . 30Qb 50
Querrin St. SW6 . . . . . 54Eb 111
Quest, The W11 . . . . . 45Ab 88
(off Clarendon Rd.)
Quested Ct. E8 . . . . . 36Xb 71
(off Brett Rd.)
Questor DA1: Dart 61Nd 141
Questors Theatre, The 45La 86
Quex Ct. NW6 . . . . . 39Db 69
(off West End La.)
Quex M. NW6 . . . . . 39Cb 69
Quex Rd. NW6 . . . . . 39Cb 69
Quiberon Ct. TW16: Sun 69W 128
Quickley Brow WD3: Chor 16D 24
Quickley La. WD3: Chor 16D 24
Quickley Ri. WD3: Chor 16E 24
Quickmoor La. WD4: Bucks 5K 11
Quick Rd. W4 . . . . . 50Ua 88
Quicks Rd. SW19 . . . . . 66Db 133
Quick St. N1 . . . . . 2C 218 (40Rb 71)
Quick St. M. N1 . . . . . 2B 218 (40Rb 71)
Quickswood NW3 . . . . . 38Gb 69
Quickwood Cl. WD3: Rick 16J 25
Quiet Cl. KT15: Add 77J 149
Quiet Nook BR2: Hayes 76Mc 159
Quill Ho. E2 . . . . . 42Wb 91
(off Cheshire St.)
Quill La. SW15 . . . . . 56Za 110
Quillot, The KT12: Hers 78V 150
Quill St. N4 . . . . . 34Qb 70
W5 . . . . . 41Na 87
Quilp St. SE1 . . . . . 1D 230 (47Sb 91)
(not continuous)
Quilter Gdns. BR5: Orp 74Yc 161
Quilter Rd. BR5: Orp 74Yc 161
Quilters Pl. SE9 . . . . . 60Sc 116
Quilter St. E2 . . . . . 41Wb 91
SE18 . . . . . 50Vc 95
Quilting Ct. SE16 . . . . . 47Zb 92
(off Garter Way)
Quinbrookes SL2: Slou 4N 81
Quince Cl. SL5: S'hill 10A 124
Quince Dr. GU24: Bisl 7F 166
Quince Ho. SE13 . . . . . 54Dc 114
(off Quince Rd.)
Quince Rd. SE13 . . . . . 54Dc 114
Quince Tree Cl. RM15: S Ock 41Yd 98
Quincy Rd. TW20: Egh 64C 126
Quinnell Cl. SE18 . . . . . 50Vc 95
Quinta Dr. EN5: Barn 15Xa 30
Quintain Ho. KT1: King T 68Ma 131
(off Wood St.)
Quintet, The KT12: Walt T 74W 150
Quintin Av. SW20 . . . . . 67Bb 133
Quintin Cl. HA5: Eastc 29X 45
Quinton Cl. BR3: Beck 69Ec 136
SM6: Wall 77Kb 156
TW5: Cran 52X 107
Quinton Ho. SW8 . . . . . 52Nb 112
(off Wyvil Rd.)
Quinton Rd. KT7: T Ditt 74Ja 152
Quinton St. SW18 . . . . . 61Eb 133
Quintrell Cl. GU21: Wok 9M 167
Quixley St. E14 . . . . . 45Fc 93
Quorn Rd. SE22 . . . . . 56Ub 113

R

Rabbit La. KT12: Hers 80W 150
Rabbit Row W8 . . . . . 46Cb 89
Rabbits Rd. DA4: S Dar 68Td 142
E12 . . . . . 35Nc 74
Rabbs Mill Ho. UB8: Uxb 40M 63
Rabies Heath Rd. RH1: Blet 5L 209
RABLEY 4Ta 15
Rabournmead Dr. UB5: N'olt 36Aa 65
Raby Rd. KT3: N Mald 70Ta 132
Raby St. E14 . . . . . 44Ac 92
Raccoon Way TW4: Houn 54Y 107
Racefield Cl. DA12: Shorne 6N 145
RAC Golf Course 89Sa 173
Rachel Cl. IG6: Ilf 27Tc 54
Racine SE5 . . . . . 53Ub 113
(off Sceaux Gdns.)
Rackham Cl. DA16: Well 54Xc 117
Rackham M. SW16 . . . . . 65Lb 134
Rackstraw Ho. NW3 . . . . . 38Hb 69
Racton Rd. SW6 . . . . . 51Cb 111
RADA
Chenies St. 7D 216
Gower St. 7D 216
Radbourne Av. W5 . . . . . 49La 86
Radbourne Cl. E5 . . . . . 35Zb 72
Radbourne Ct. HA3: Kenton 30Ka 46
Radbourne Cres. E17 . . . . . 26Fc 53
Radbourne Rd. SW12 . . . . . 59Lb 112
Radburn Pl. DA10: Swans 57Ae 121
Radcliffe Av. EN2: Enf 11Sb 33
NW10 . . . . . 40Wa 68
Radcliffe Gdns. SM5: Cars 81Gb 175
Radcliffe Ho. CM14: B'wood 20Xd 40
SE16 . . . . . 49Xb 91
(off Anchor St.)
Radcliffe M. TW12: Hamp H 64Ea 130
Radcliffe Path SW8 . . . . . 54Kb 112
Radcliffe Rd. CR0: C'don 75Vb 157
HA3: W'stone 26Ja 46
N21 . . . . . 18Rb 33
SE1 . . . . . 3J 231 (48Ub 91)
Radcliffe Sq. SW15 . . . . . 58Za 110
Radcliffe Way UB5: N'olt 41Z 85
Radcot Av. SL3: L'ly 48D 82
Radcot Point SE23 . . . . . 62Zb 136
Radcot St. SE11 . . . . . 7A 230 (50Qb 90)
Raddington Rd. W10 . . . . . 43Ab 88
Raddon Twr. E8 . . . . . 37Vb 71
(off Dalston Sq.)
Radfield Dr. DA2: Dart 60Sd 120
Radfield Way DA15: Sidc 59Tc 116
Radford Ct. SE15 . . . . . 52Xb 113
(off Old Kent Rd.)
Radford Est. NW10 . . . . . 41Ua 88
Radford Ho. E14 . . . . . 43Dc 92
(off St Leonard's Rd.)
N7 . . . . . 36Pb 70
Radford Rd. SE13 . . . . . 58Ec 114
Radford Way IG11: Bark 41Vc 95
Radipole Rd. SW6 . . . . . 53Bb 111
Radisson Ct. SE1 . . . . . 3H 231
(off Long La.)
Radius Apartments N1 . . . . . 2G 217
Radius Pk. TW14: Felt 56V 106
Radland Rd. E16 . . . . . 44Hc 93
Radlet Av. SE26 . . . . . 62Xb 135
RADLETT 7Ja 14
Radlett Cl. E7 . . . . . 37Hc 73
Radlett Golf Cen. 4Ja 14
Radlett La. WD7: R'lett, Shenl 6Ma 15
Radlett Pk. Golf Course 13Ma 29
Radlett Pk. Rd. WD7: R'lett 6Ja 14
Radlett Pl. NW8 . . . . . 39Gb 69
Radlett Rd. AL2: Col S, F'mre 10C 6
WD17: Wat 13Y 27
WD24: Wat 13Y 27
WD25: A'ham 11Da 27
Radley Av. IG3: Bark, Ilf 35Wc 75
Radley Cl. TW14: Felt 60V 106
Radley Ct. AL1: St A 2C 6
(off Newsome Pl.)
SE16 . . . . . 47Zb 92
Radley Gdns. HA3: Kenton 28Na 47
Radley Ho. NW1 . . . . . 5F 215
SE2 . . . . . 47Zc 95
(off Wolvercote Rd.)
Radley M. W8 . . . . . 48Cb 89
Radley Rd. N17 . . . . . 26Ub 51
Radley's La. E18 . . . . . 26Jc 53
Radleys Mead RM10: Dag 37Dd 76
Radley Sq. E5 . . . . . 33Yb 72
Radley Ter. E16 . . . . . 43Hc 93
(off Hermit Rd.)
Radlix Rd. E10 . . . . . 32Cc 72
Radnor Av. DA16: Well 57Xc 117
HA1: Harr 29Ga 46
Radnor Cl. BR7: Chst 65Uc 138
CR4: Mitc 70Nb 134
Radnor Ct. HA3: Hrw W 25Ha 46
RH1: Redh 6N 207
W7 . . . . . 44Ha 86
(off Copley Cl.)
Radnor Cres. IG4: Ilf 29Pc 54
SE18 . . . . . 52Wc 117
Radnor Gdns. EN1: Enf 11Ub 33
TW1: Twick 61Ha 130
Radnor Gro. UB10: Hil 40Q 64
Radnor Ho. EC1 . . . . . 4E 218
SW16 . . . . . 68Pb 134
Radnor Lodge W2 . . . . . 3C 220
Radnor M. W2 . . . . . 3C 220 (44Fb 89)
Radnor Pl. W2 . . . . . 3D 220 (44Gb 89)
Radnor Rd. HA1: Harr 29Fa 46
KT13: Weyb 76Q 150
NW6 . . . . . 39Ab 68
SE15 . . . . . 52Wb 113
TW1: Twick 60Ha 108
Radnor St. EC1 . . . . . 4E 218 (41Sb 91)
Radnor Ter. SM2: Sutt 80Cb 155
W14 . . . . . 49Bb 89
Radnor Wlk. CR0: C'don 72Ac 158
E14 . . . . . 49Cc 92
(off Barnsdale Av.)
SW3 . . . . . 7E 226 (50Gb 89)
Radnor Way NW10 . . . . . 42Ra 87
SL3: L'ly 49A 82
Radolphs KT20: Tad 94Za 194
Radstock Av. HA3: Kenton 27Ja 46
Radstock Cl. N11 . . . . . 23Jb 50
Radstock Ho. RM3: Rom 22Md 57
(off Darlington Gdns.)
Radstock St. SW11 . . . . . 52Gb 111
(not continuous)
Radstock Way RH1: Mers 100Mb 196
Radstone Ct. GU22: Wok 90B 168
Radway Ho. W2 . . . . . 43Cb 89
(off Alfred Rd.)
Radzan Cl. DA2: Wilm 61Gd 140
Raebarn Gdns. EN5: Barn 15Xa 30
Raeburn Av. DA1: Dart 57Kd 119
KT5: Surb 74Ra 153
Raeburn Cl. KT1: Hamp W 66Ma 131
NW11 . . . . . 30Eb 49
Raeburn Ct. GU21: Wok 1L 187
Raeburn Gro. GU21: Wok 10L 167
Raeburn Ho. UB5: N'olt 40Z 65
(off Academy Gdns.)
Raeburn Rd. DA15: Sidc 58Uc 116
HA8: Edg 25Qa 47
UB4: Hayes 40T 64
Raeburn St. SW2 . . . . . 56Nb 112
Rafdene Copse GU22: Wok 1N 187
Raffles Ct. HA8: Edg 21Pa 47
Raffles Ho. NW4 . . . . . 28Xa 48
Rafford Way BR1: Brom 68Kc 137
RAF Mus. London 26Wa 48
RAF Northolt Aerodrome 37V 64
Ragged Hall La.
AL2: Chis G, Pot C 6K 5
Ragged School Mus. 43Ac 92
Ragge Way TN15: Seal 92Pd 203
Raggleswood BR7: Chst 67Qc 138
Rag Hill Cl. TN16: Tats 93Nc 200
Rag Hill Rd. TN16: Tats 93Mc 199
Raglan Av. EN8: Walt C 6Zb 20
Raglan Cl. RH2: Reig 4M 207
TW4: Houn 57Ba 107
Raglan Ct. CR2: S Croy 78Rb 157
HA9: Wemb 35Pa 67
SE12 . . . . . 57Jc 115
Raglan Gdns. WD19: Wat 18X 27
Raglan Pct. CR3: Cat'm 94Ub 197
Raglan Rd. BR2: Brom 70Lc 137
DA17: Belv 49Bd 95
E17 . . . . . 29Ec 52
EN1: Enf 17Vb 33
GU21: Knap, Wok 10J 167
RH2: Reig 3K 207
SE18 . . . . . 50Sc 94
Raglan St. NW5 . . . . . 37Kb 70
Raglan Ter. HA2: Harr 35Da 65
Raglan Way UB5: N'olt 37Ea 66
Ragley Cl. W3 . . . . . 47Sa 87
Ragstone Rd. SL1: Slou 8J 81
Ragwort Ct. SE26 . . . . . 64Xb 135
Rahere Ct. E1 . . . . . 42Ac 92
(off Toby La.)
Rahn Rd. CM16: Epp 3Wc 23
Raider Cl. RM7: Mawney 25Cd 56
Railey M. NW5 . . . . . 36Lb 70
Railpit La. CR6: W'ham 87Gc 179
Railshead Rd. TW1: Isle 56Ka 108
TW7: Isle 56Ka 108
Rails La. GU24: Pirb 7A 186
Railton Rd. SE24 . . . . . 56Qb 112
Railway App. HA1: Harr 28Ha 46
HA3: Harr 28Ha 46
N4 . . . . . 30Qb 50
RM7: Rush G 30Fd 56
SE1 . . . . . 6G 225 (46Tb 91)
SM6: Wall 78Kb 156
TW1: Twick 59Ja 108
Railway Arches E1 . . . . . 44Zb 92
(off Barnardo St.)
E1 . . . . . 45Xb 91
(off Chapman St.)
E2 . . . . . 2K 219
(off Cremer St.)
E2 . . . . . 1K 219
(Geffrye St.)
E2 . . . . . 1K 219
(Laburnum St.)
E3 . . . . . 42Bc 92
(off Cantrell Rd.)
E8 . . . . . 38Xb 71
(off Mentmore Ter.)
E16 . . . . . 46Jc 93
W6 . . . . . 48Ya 88
W12 . . . . . 47Ya 88
(off Shepherd's Bush Mkt.)
Railway Av. SE16 . . . . . 47Yb 92
(not continuous)
Railway Children Wlk.
BR1: Brom 61Jc 137
SE12 . . . . . 61Jc 137
Railway Cotts. E15 . . . . . 40Gc 73
(off Baker's Row)
SW19 . . . . . 63Db 133
W6 . . . . . 47Ya 88
(off Sulgrave Rd.)
WD4: K Lan 2R 12
WD7: R'lett 7Ka 14
WD24: Wat 11X 27
Railway Fields Local Nature Reserve
. . . . . 30Rb 51
Railway Gro. SE14 . . . . . 52Bc 114
Railway M. W10 . . . . . 44Ab 88
Railway Pde. CM15: Shenf 17Ce 41
(off Hutton Rd.)
Railway Pas. TW11: Tedd 65Ja 130
Railway Pl. DA12: Grav'nd 8D 122
DA17: Belv 48Cd 96
Railway Ri. SE22 . . . . . 56Ub 113
Railway Rd. EN8: Walt C 5Bc 20
TW11: Tedd 63Ga 130
Railway Side SW13 . . . . . 55Ua 110
Railway Sidings DA13: Meop 10C 144
Railway Sidings Ind. Est.
DA13: Meop 10C 144
Railway Sq. CM14: B'wood 20Yd 40
Railway St. DA11: Nflt 57Ce 121
N1 . . . . . 2G 217 (40Nb 70)
RM6: Chad H 31Yc 75
Railway Ter. CR5: Coul 87Mb 176
(off Station App.)
E17 . . . . . 25Ec 52
SE13 . . . . . 57Dc 114
SL2: Slou 6K 81
TN16: Westrm 97Tc 200
TW13: Felt 60W 106
TW18: Staines 64F 126
WD4: K Lan 9A 4
Railway Vw. SL3: Hort 55B 104
Rainborough Cl. NW10 . . . . . 37Sa 67
Rainbow Av. E14 . . . . . 50Dc 92
Rainbow Ct. GU21: Wok 8J 167
SE14 . . . . . 51Ac 114
(off Chipley St.)
WD19: Wat 16Y 27
Rainbow Ind. Est. SW20 . . . . . 68Xa 132
UB7: Yiew 45M 83
Rainbow La. RM18: W Til 9F 100
SS17: Stan H 1P 101
Rainbow Leisure Cen. 84Ua 174
Rainbow Quay SE16 . . . . . 48Ac 92
(not continuous)
Rainbow Rd. RM16: Chaf H 49Yd 98
Rainbow St. SE5 . . . . . 52Ub 113
Rainbow Theatre 33Qb 70
Raine Gdns. IG8: Wfd G 21Jc 53
Rainer Cl. EN8: Chesh 1Zb 20
Raines Est. Ct. N16 . . . . . 33Vb 71
Raine St. E1 . . . . . 46Xb 91
RAINHAM 42Jd 96
Rainham Cl. SE9 . . . . . 58Uc 116
SW11 . . . . . 58Gb 111
Rainham Hall 42Jd 96
Rainham Ho. NW1 . . . . . 1C 216
Rainham Marshes 45Jd 96
Rainham Marshes Nature Reserve
. . . . . 48Nd 97
Rainham Marshes Nature Reserve Vis. Cen.
. . . . . 49Pd 97
Rainham Rd. NW10 . . . . . 41Ya 88
RM12: Horn, Rain 36Hd 76
RM13: Rain 38Gd 76
Rainham Rd. Nth. RM10: Dag 33Cd 76
Rainham Rd. Sth. RM10: Dag 35Dd 76
Rainham Trad. Est. RM13: Rain 42Hd 96
Rainhill Way E3 . . . . . 41Cc 92
(not continuous)
Rainsborough Av. SE8 . . . . . 49Ac 92
Rainsford Cl. HA7: Stan 22La 46
Rainsford Rd. NW10 . . . . . 41Qa 87
Rainsford St. W2 . . . . . 2D 220 (44Gb 89)
Rainsford Way RM12: Horn 32Jd 76
Rainton Rd. SE7 . . . . . 50Jc 93
Rainville Rd. W6 . . . . . 51Ya 110
Raisins Hill HA5: Eastc 27Y 45
Raith Av. N14 . . . . . 20Mb 32
Rajsee Apartments E2 . . . . . 41Wb 91
(off Bethnal Grn. Rd.)
Raleana Rd. E14 . . . . . 46Ec 92
Raleigh Av. SM6: Bedd 77Mb 156
UB4: Yead 43X 85
Raleigh Cl. DA8: Erith 51Hd 118
HA4: Ruis 33V 64
HA5: Pinn 31Z 65
NW4 . . . . . 29Ya 48
SL1: Slou 6E 80
Raleigh Ct. BR3: Beck 67Dc 136
DA8: Erith 52Hd 118
SE8 . . . . . 50Ac 92
(off Evelyn St.)
SE16 . . . . . 46Zb 92
(off Clarence M.)
SM6: Wall 79Kb 156
TW18: Staines 63J 127
W12 . . . . . 47Ya 88
(off Scott's Rd.)
W13 . . . . . 43Ka 86
Raleigh Dr. KT5: Surb 74Sa 153
KT10: Clay 78Fa 152
N20 . . . . . 20Gb 31
Raleigh Gdns. CR4: Mitc 69Hb 133
(not continuous)
SW2 . . . . . 58Pb 112
Raleigh Ho. BR1: Brom 67Jc 137
(off Hammelton Rd.)
E14 . . . . . 47Dc 92
(off Admirals Way)
SW1 . . . . . 51Mb 112
(off Dolphin Sq.)
Raleigh M. BR6: Chels 78Vc 161
N1 . . . . . 39Rb 71
(off Packington St.)
Raleigh Rd. EN2: Enf 14Tb 33
N8 . . . . . 28Qb 50
SE20 . . . . . 66Zb 136
TW9: Rich 55Pa 109
TW13: Felt 62V 128
UB2: S'hall 50Aa 85
Raleigh St. N1 . . . . . 1C 218 (39Rb 71)
Raleigh Way N14 . . . . . 18Mb 32
TW13: Hanw 64Y 129
Rale La. E4 . . . . . 17Fc 35
Ralliwood Rd. KT21: Asht 91Qa 193
Ralph Brook Ct. N1 . . . . . 3G 219
Ralph Ct. W2 . . . . . 44Db 89
(off Queensway)
Ralph Perring Ct. BR3: Beck 70Cc 136
Ralston Ct. SL4: Wind 3H 103
(off Russell St.)
Ralston St. SW3 . . . . . 50Hb 89
Ralston Way WD19: Wat 19Z 27
Ramac Ind. Est. SE7 . . . . . 49Kc 93
Rama Cl. SW16 . . . . . 66Nb 134
Rama Ct. HA1: Harr 33Ga 66
Ramac Way SE7 . . . . . 49Kc 93
Rama La. SE19 . . . . . 66Vb 135
Ramar Ho. E1 . . . . . 43Wb 91
(off Hanbury St.)
Rambler Cl. SL6: Tap 2A 80
SW16 . . . . . 63Lb 134
Rambler La. SL3: L'ly 8N 81
Rame Cl. SW17 . . . . . 64Jb 134
Ramilles Cl. SW2 . . . . . 58Nb 112
Ramillies Pl. W1 . . . . . 3B 222 (44Lb 90)
Ramillies Rd. DA15: Sidc 58Xc 117
NW7 . . . . . 19Ua 30
W4 . . . . . 49Ta 87
Ramillies St. W1 . . . . . 3B 222 (44Lb 90)
Ramney Dr. EN3: Enf L 8Ac 20
Ramones Ter. CR4: Mitc 70Nb 134
(off Yorkshire Rd.)
Ramornie Cl. KT12: Hers 77Ba 151
Ramparts, The AL3: St A 3P 5
Rampart St. E1 . . . . . 44Xb 91
Ram Pas. KT1: King T 68Ma 131
Rampayne St. SW1 . . . . . 7D 228 (50Mb 90)
Ram Pl. E9 . . . . . 37Yb 72
Rampton Cl. E4 . . . . . 20Cc 34
Ramryge Ct. AL1: St A 4B 6
Ramsay Gdns. RM3: Rom 25Ld 57
Ramsay Ho. NW8 . . . . . 1D 214
Ramsay M. SW3 . . . . . 51Gb 111
Ramsay Pl. HA1: Harr 33Ga 66
Ramsay Rd. E7 . . . . . 35Gc 73
GU20: W'sham 8C 146
W3 . . . . . 48Sa 87
Ramsbury Rd. AL1: St A 3C 6
Ramscroft Cl. N9 . . . . . 17Ub 33
Ramsdale Rd. SW17 . . . . . 64Jb 134
RAMSDEN 74Yc 161
Ramsden Cl. BR5: Orp 74Yc 161
Ramsden Dr. RM5: Col R 24Cd 56
Ramsden Rd. BR5: Orp 73Xc 161
BR6: Orp 73Xc 161
DA8: Erith 52Fd 118
N11 . . . . . 21Hb 49
SW12 . . . . . 58Jb 112

Ramsey Cl. AL1: St A . . . 4E 6
AL9: Brk P . . . 9M 9
NW9 . . . 30Va 48
UB6: G'frd . . . 36Fa 66
Ramsey Ct. CR0: C'don . . . 75Rb 157
(off Church St.)
SL2: Slou . . . 2B 80
Ramsey Ho. SW9 . . . 52Qb 112
Ramsey Lodge Ct. AL1: St A . . . 1C 6
Ramsey Pl. CR3: Cat'm . . . 94Sb 197
Ramsey Rd. CR7: Thor H . . . 72Pb 156
Ramsey St. E2 . . . 42Wb 91
Ramsey Wlk. N1 . . . 37Tb 71
Ramsey Way N14 . . . 17Lb 32
Ramsfort Ho. SE16 . . . 49Xb 91
(off Camilla Rd.)
Ramsgate Cl. E16 . . . 46Kc 93
Ramsgate St. E8 . . . 37Vb 71
Ramsgill App. IG2: Ilf . . . 28Vc 55
Ramsgill Dr. IG2: Ilf . . . 29Vc 55
Rams Gro. RM6: Chad H . . . 28Ad 55
Ramson Ri. HP1: Hem H . . . 3G 2
Ram St. SW18 . . . 57Db 111
Ramulis Dr. UB4: Yead . . . 42Z 85
Ramuswood Av. BR6: Chels . . . 78Uc 160
Rancliffe Gdns. SE9 . . . 56Nc 116
Rancliffe Rd. E6 . . . 40Nc 74
Randal Cres. RH2: Reig . . . 8J 207
Randall Av. NW2 . . . 33Ua 68
Randall Cl. DA8: Erith . . . 51Ed 118
SL3: L'ly . . . 50B 82
SW11 . . . 53Gb 111
Randall Ct. NW7 . . . 24Wa 48
RM13: Rain . . . 42Kd 97
SL4: Old Win . . . 8L 103
(off Lyndwood Dr.)
Randall Dr. RM12: Horn . . . 35Ld 77
RM16: Ors . . . 3C 100
Randall Hill Rd. TN15: Wro . . . 88Be 185
Randall Pl. SE10 . . . 52Ec 114
Randall Rd. SE11 . . . 6H 229 (50Pb 90)
Randall Row SE11 . . . 6H 229 (49Pb 90)
Randalls Cres. KT22: Lea . . . 92Ja 192
Randalls Dr. CM13: Hut . . . 16Fe 41
Randalls Pk. Av. KT22: Lea . . . 92Ja 192
Randalls Pk. Crematorium (Leatherhead)
KT22: Lea . . . 92Ga 192
Randalls Pk. Dr. KT22: Lea . . . 93Ja 192
Randalls Rents SE16 . . . 48Bc 92
(off Gulliver St.)
Randalls Ride HP2: Hem H . . . 1M 3
Randalls Rd. KT22: Lea . . . 91Ga 192
Randalls Wlk. AL2: Brick W . . . 2Ba 13
Randalls Way KT22: Lea . . . 93Ja 192
Randell's Rd. N1 . . . 39Nb 70
Randisbourne Gdns. SE6 . . . 62Dc 136
Randle Rd. TW10: Ham . . . 63La 130
Randlesdown Rd. SE6 . . . 63Cc 136
(not continuous)
Randles La. TN14: Knock . . . 87Zc 181
Randolph App. E16 . . . 44Lc 93
Randolph Av. W9 . . . 4A 214 (40Db 69)
Randolph Cl. DA7: Bex . . . 55Ed 118
GU21: Knap . . . 9J 167
KT2: King T . . . 64Sa 131
KT11: Stoke D . . . 87Ca 171
Randolph Ct. HA5: Hat E . . . 24Ca 45
(off The Avenue)
NW8 . . . 39Eb 69
Randolph Cres. W9 . . . 6A 214 (42Eb 89)
Randolph Gdns. NW6 . . . 40Db 69
Randolph Gro. RM6: Chad H . . . 29Yc 55
Randolph Ho. KT18: Eps . . . 86Sa 173
(off Dalmeny Way)
Randolph M. W9 . . . 6A 214 (42Eb 89)
Randolph Rd. BR2: Brom . . . 74Pc 160
E17 . . . 29Dc 52
KT17: Eps . . . 86Va 174
SL3: L'ly . . . 48A 82
UB1: S'hall . . . 47Ba 85
W9 . . . 6A 214 (42Eb 89)
Randolph's La. TN16: Westrm . . . 98Rc 200
Randolph St. NW1 . . . 38Lb 70
Randon Cl. HA2: Harr . . . 26Da 45
Ranelagh SL4: Wink . . . 1A 124
Ranelagh Av. SW6 . . . 55Bb 111
SW13 . . . 54Wa 110
Ranelagh Bri. W2 . . . 43Db 89
Ranelagh Cl. HA8: Edg . . . 21Qa 47
Ranelagh Cotts. SW1 . . . 7J 227
Ranelagh Dr. HA8: Edg . . . 21Qa 47
TW1: Twick . . . 56Ka 108
Ranelagh Gdns. DA11: Nflt . . . 9B 122
E11 . . . 29Lc 53
IG1: Ilf . . . 32Pc 74
SW6 . . . 55Ab 110
(not continuous)
W4 . . . 52Sa 109
W6 . . . 49Va 88
Ranelagh Gdns. Mans. SW6 . . . 55Ab 110
(off Ranelagh Gdns.)
Ranelagh Gro. SW1 . . . 7J 227 (50Jb 90)
Ranelagh Ho. SW3 . . . 7F 227
Ranelagh M. W5 . . . 47Ma 87
Ranelagh Pl. KT3: N Mald . . . 71Ua 154
Ranelagh Rd. E6 . . . 39Qc 74
E11 . . . 35Gc 73
E15 . . . 40Gc 73
HA0: Wemb . . . 37Ma 67
HP2: Hem H . . . 27Ub 51
N17 . . . 27Ub 51
N22 . . . 25Pb 50
NW10 . . . 40Va 68
RH1: Redh . . . 6N 207
SW1 . . . 7C 228 (50Lb 90)
UB1: S'hall . . . 46Z 85
W5 . . . 47Ma 87
Ranfurly Rd. SM1: Sutt . . . 75Cb 155
Rangbourne Ho. N7 . . . 36Nb 70
Rangefield Rd. BR1: Brom . . . 64Gc 137
Rangemoor Rd. N15 . . . 29Vb 51
Range Rd. DA12: Grav'nd . . . 9G 122
Ranger's House . . . 53Fc 115
Ranger's Rd. E4 . . . 17Gc 35
IG10: Lough . . . 17Gc 35
Rangers Sq. SE10 . . . 53Fc 115
Ranger Wlk. KT15: Add . . . 78K 149
Range Way TW17: Shep . . . 73Q 150
Rangeworth Pl. DA15: Sidc . . . 62Vc 139
Rangoon St. EC3 . . . 3K 225
Rankin Cl. NW9 . . . 27Ua 48
Rankine Ho. SE1 . . . 4D 230
Ranleigh Gdns. DA7: Bex . . . 52Bd 117
Ranmere St. SW12 . . . 60Kb 112
Ranmoor Cl. HA1: Harr . . . 28Fa 46
Ranmoor Gdns. HA1: Harr . . . 28Fa 46
Ranmore Av. CR0: C'don . . . 76Vb 157
Ranmore Cl. RH1: Redh . . . 3A 208
Ranmore Path BR5: St M Cry . . . 70Wc 139
Ranmore Pl. KT13: Weyb . . . 78S 150
Ranmore Rd. SM2: Cheam . . . 81Za 174
Rannoch Cl. HA8: Edg . . . 19Ra 29
Rannoch Rd. W6 . . . 51Ya 110
Rannock Av. NW9 . . . 31Ta 67
Ranskill Cl. WD6: Bore . . . 11Qa 29
Ranskill Rd. WD6: Bore . . . 11Qa 29
Ransom Cl. WD19: Wat . . . 17Y 27
Ransome's Dock Bus. Cen.
SW11 . . . 52Gb 111
Ransom Rd. SE7 . . . 49Lc 93
Ranston Cl. UB9: Den . . . 30H 43
Ranston St. NW1 . . . 7D 214 (43Gb 89)
Rant Mdw. HP3: Hem H . . . 4A 4
(not continuous)
Ranulf Rd. NW2 . . . 35Bb 69
Ranwell Cl. E3 . . . 39Bc 72
Ranwell Ho. E3 . . . 39Bc 72
(off Ranwell Cl.)
Ranworth Cl. DA8: Erith . . . 54Gd 118
HP3: Hem H . . . 4M 3
Ranworth Gdns. EN6: Pot B . . . 3Za 16
Ranworth Rd. N9 . . . 19Yb 34
Ranyard Cl. KT9: Chess . . . 76Pa 153
Raphael Av. RM1: Rom . . . 27Hd 56
RM18: Tilb . . . 2C 122
Raphael Cl. KT1: King T . . . 70Ma 131
WD7: Shenl . . . 4Na 15
Raphael Ct. SE16 . . . 50Xb 91
(off Stubbs Dr.)
Raphael Dr. IG10: Lough . . . 12Rc 36
KT7: T Ditt . . . 73Ha 152
WD24: Wat . . . 12Z 27
Raphael Rd. DA12: Grav'nd . . . 9F 122
Raphael St. SW7 . . . 2F 227 (47Hb 89)
Raphen Apartments E3 . . . 40Ac 72
(off Medway Rd.)
Rapier Cl. RM19: Purf . . . 49Pd 97
Rapley Ho. E2 . . . 41Wb 91
(off Turin St.)
Rapley's Fld. GU24: Pirb . . . 5C 186
Rapsley La. GU21: Knap . . . 10F 166
Raquel Ct. SE1 . . . 1H 231
Rasehill Cl. WD3: Rick . . . 15L 25
Rashleigh Ct. SW8 . . . 54Kb 112
Rashleigh Ho. WC1 . . . 4F 217
Rashleigh St. SW8 . . . 54Kb 112
(off Peardon St.)
Rashleigh Way DA4: Hort K . . . 70Sd 142
Rasper Rd. N20 . . . 19Eb 31
Rastell Av. SW2 . . . 61Mb 134
RATCLIFF . . . 43Ac 92
Ratcliffe Cl. SE12 . . . 59Jc 115
UB8: Cowl . . . 41M 83
Ratcliffe Ct. SE1 . . . 2E 230
Ratcliffe Cross St. E1 . . . 44Zb 92
Ratcliffe Ho. E14 . . . 44Ac 92
(off Barnes St.)
Ratcliffe La. E14 . . . 44Ac 92
Ratcliffe Orchard E1 . . . 45Zb 92
Ratcliff Rd. E7 . . . 36Lc 73
Rathbone Ho. E16 . . . 44Hc 93
(off Rathbone St.)
NW6 . . . 39Cb 69
Rathbone Mkt. E16 . . . 43Hc 93
Rathbone Pl. W1 . . . 1D 222 (43Mb 90)
Rathbone Sq. CR0: C'don . . . 77Sb 157
Rathbone St. E16 . . . 44Hc 93
W1 . . . 1C 222 (43Lb 90)
Rathcoole Av. N8 . . . 29Pb 50
Rathcoole Gdns. N8 . . . 29Pb 50
Rathfern Rd. SE6 . . . 60Bc 114
Rathgar Av. W13 . . . 46Ka 86
Rathgar Cl. N3 . . . 26Bb 49
RH1: Redh . . . 10A 208
Rathgar Rd. SW9 . . . 55Rb 113
Rathlin HP3: Hem H . . . 5B 4
Rathmell Dr. SW4 . . . 58Mb 112
Rathmore Rd. DA11: Grav'nd . . . 9D 122
SE7 . . . 50Kc 93
Rathnew Ct. E2 . . . 41Zb 92
(off Meath Cres.)
Rats La. IG10: H Beech, Lough . . . 10Kc 21
Rattray Ct. SE6 . . . 61Hc 137
Rattray Rd. SW2 . . . 56Qb 112
Raul Rd. SE15 . . . 54Wb 113
Raveley St. NW5 . . . 35Lb 70
(not continuous)
Ravel Gdns. RM15: Avel . . . 44Sd 98
Ravel Rd. RM15: Avel . . . 44Sd 98
Raven Cl. NW9 . . . 26Ua 48
WD3: Rick . . . 17L 25
Raven Ct. AL10: Hat . . . 1G 8
DA12: Grav'nd . . . 8F 122
(off Admirals Way)
Ravencroft RM16: Grays . . . 7D 100
Ravendale Rd. TW16: Sun . . . 68V 128
Ravenet St. SW11 . . . 53Kb 112
(not continuous)
Ravenfield TW20: Eng G . . . 5N 125
Ravenfield Rd. SW17 . . . 62Hb 133
Ravenhill Rd. E13 . . . 40Lc 73
Raven Ho. SE16 . . . 49Zb 92
(off Tawny Way)
Ravenings Pde. IG3: Ilf . . . 32Wc 75
Ravenna Rd. SW15 . . . 57Za 110
Ravenoak Way IG7: Chig . . . 22Uc 54
Ravenor Ct. UB6: G'frd . . . 42Da 85
Ravenor Pk. Rd. UB6: G'frd . . . 41Da 85
Raven Rd. E18 . . . 26Lc 53
Raven Row E1 . . . 43Xb 91
Raven Row Contemporary Art Cen. . . . 1K 225
Raven's Ait . . . 71Ma 153
Ravensbourne Av. BR2: Brom . . . 66Fc 137
BR3: Brom . . . 66Fc 137
TW19: Stanw . . . 60N 105
Ravensbourne Ct. SE6 . . . 59Cc 114
Ravensbourne Cres. RM3: Hrld W . . . 27Pd 57
Ravensbourne Gdns. IG5: Ilf . . . 25Qc 54
W13 . . . 43Ka 86
Ravensbourne Ho. BR1: Brom . . . 64Fc 137
NW8 . . . 7D 214
Ravensbourne Mans. SE8 . . . 51Cc 114
(off Berthon St.)
Ravensbourne Pk. SE6 . . . 59Cc 114
Ravensbourne Pk. Cres. SE6 . . . 59Bc 114
Ravensbourne Pl. SE13 . . . 54Dc 114
Ravensbourne Rd. BR1: Brom . . . 69Jc 137
DA1: Cray . . . 55Jd 118
SE6 . . . 59Bc 114
TW1: Twick . . . 58La 108
Ravensbourne Ter. TW19: Stanw . . . 60N 105
Ravensbury Av. SM4: Mord . . . 71Eb 155
Ravensbury Ct. CR4: Mitc . . . 70Fb 133
(off Ravensbury Gro.)
Ravensbury Gro. CR4: Mitc . . . 70Fb 133
Ravensbury La. CR4: Mitc . . . 70Fb 133
Ravensbury Path CR4: Mitc . . . 70Fb 133
Ravensbury Rd. BR5: St P . . . 69Vc 139
SW18 . . . 61Db 133
Ravensbury Ter. SW18 . . . 61Db 133
Ravenscar NW1 . . . 1B 216
Ravenscar Rd. BR1: Brom . . . 63Gc 137
KT6: Surb . . . 75Pa 153
Ravens Cl. BR2: Brom . . . 68Hc 137
EN1: Enf . . . 12Ub 33
GU21: Knap . . . 8G 166
KT6: Surb . . . 72Ma 153
RH1: Redh . . . 5P 207
Ravens Ct. KT1: King T . . . 71Ma 153
(off Uxbridge Rd.)
Ravenscourt CM15: B'wood . . . 17Yd 40
TW16: Sun . . . 67V 128
Ravenscourt Av. W6 . . . 49Wa 88
Ravenscourt Cl. HA4: Ruis . . . 31S 64
RM12: Horn . . . 34Nd 77
Ravenscourt Dr. RM12: Horn . . . 34Nd 77
Ravenscourt Gdns. W6 . . . 49Wa 88
Ravenscourt Gro. RM12: Horn . . . 33Nd 77
Ravenscourt Pk. EN5: Barn . . . 14Za 30
W6 . . . 48Wa 88
Ravenscourt Pk. Mans. W6 . . . 48Xa 88
(off Paddenswick Rd.)
Ravenscourt Pl. W6 . . . 49Xa 88
Ravenscourt Rd. BR5: St P . . . 69Wc 139
W6 . . . 49Xa 88
Ravenscourt Sq. W6 . . . 48Wa 88
Ravenscraig Rd. N11 . . . 21Lb 50
Ravenscroft WD25: Wat . . . 7Aa 13
Ravenscroft Av. HA9: Wemb . . . 32Na 67
NW11 . . . 31Bb 69
(not continuous)
Ravenscroft Cl. E16 . . . 43Jc 93
Ravenscroft Cotts. EN5: New Bar . . . 14Cb 31
Ravenscroft Cres. SE9 . . . 62Pc 138
Ravenscroft Pk. E2 . . . 3K 219
EN5: Barn . . . 13Za 30
Ravenscroft Rd. BR3: Beck . . . 68Yb 136
E16 . . . 43Jc 93
KT13: Weyb . . . 83S 170
W4 . . . 49Sa 87
Ravenscroft School Sports Cen. . . . 16Bb 31
Ravenscroft St. E2 . . . 2K 219 (40Vb 71)
Ravensdale Av. N12 . . . 21Eb 49
Ravensdale Gdns. SE19 . . . 66Tb 135
TW4: Houn . . . 55Aa 107
Ravensdale Ind. Est. N16 . . . 30Wb 51
Ravensdale Mans. N8 . . . 30Nb 50
(off Haringey Pk.)
Ravensdale M. TW18: Staines . . . 65K 127
Ravensdale Rd. N16 . . . 31Vb 51
TW4: Houn . . . 55Aa 107
Ravensdell HP1: Hem H . . . 1H 3
Ravensdon St. SE11 . . . 7A 230 (50Qb 90)
Ravens Dr. BR7: Chst . . . 64Pc 138
Ravens Fld. SL3: L'ly . . . 7P 81
Ravensfield Cl. RM9: Dag . . . 35Zc 75
Ravensfield Gdns. KT19: Ewe . . . 78Ua 154
Ravens Ga. M. BR2: Brom . . . 68Gc 137
Ravenshaw St. NW6 . . . 36Bb 69
Ravenshead Cl. CR2: Sels . . . 83Yb 178
Ravenshill BR7: Chst . . . 67Rc 138
Ravenshurst Av. NW4 . . . 28Ya 48
Ravenside KT1: King T . . . 71Ma 153
(off Portsmouth Rd.)
Ravenside Cl. N18 . . . 22Zb 52
Ravenside Retail Pk. N18 . . . 22Zb 52
Ravens La. HP4: Berk . . . 1A 2
Ravenslea Rd. SW12 . . . 59Hb 111
Ravensleigh Gdns. BR1: Brom . . . 64Kc 137
Ravensmead SL9: Chal P . . . 22B 42
Ravensmead Rd. BR2: Brom . . . 66Fc 137
Ravensmede Way W4 . . . 49Va 88
Ravensmere CM16: Epp . . . 3Wc 23
Ravens M. SE12 . . . 57Jc 115
Ravensquay Bus. Cen.
BR5: St M Cry . . . 71Xc 161
Ravenstone SE17 . . . 7J 231 (50Ub 91)
Ravenstone Rd. N8 . . . 27Qb 50
NW9 . . . 30Va 48
Ravenstone St. SW12 . . . 60Jb 112
Ravens Way SE12 . . . 57Jc 115
Ravens Wharf HP4: Berk . . . 1A 2
Ravenswold CR8: Kenley . . . 87Sb 177
Ravenswood DA5: Bexl . . . 60Ad 117
Ravenswood Av. BR4: W W'ck . . . 74Ec 158
KT6: Surb . . . 75Pa 153
Ravenswood Cl. KT11: Cobh . . . 87Z 171
RM5: Col R . . . 22Dd 56
Ravenswood Ct. GU22: Wok . . . 90B 168
KT2: King T . . . 65Ra 131
Ravenswood Cres. BR4: W W'ck . . . 74Ec 158
HA2: Harr . . . 33Ba 65
Ravenswood Gdns. TW7: Isle . . . 53Ga 108
Ravenswood Ind. Est. E17 . . . 28Ec 52
Ravenswood Pk. HA6: Nwood . . . 23W 44
Ravenswood Rd. CR0: Wadd . . . 76Rb 157
E17 . . . 28Ec 52
SW12 . . . 59Kb 112
Ravensworth Ct. SW6 . . . 52Cb 111
(off Fulham Rd.)
Ravensworth Rd. NW10 . . . 41Xa 88
SE9 . . . 62Pc 138
SL2: Slou . . . 1E 80
Raven Wharf SE1 . . . 1K 231
Ravey St. EC2 . . . 5H 219 (42Ub 91)
Ravine Gro. SE18 . . . 51Uc 116
Rav Pinter Cl. N16 . . . 31Ub 71
Rawalpindi Ho. E16 . . . 42Hc 93
Rawchester Cl. SW18 . . . 60Bb 111
Rawlings Cl. BR3: Beck . . . 71Ec 158
BR6: Chels . . . 78Vc 161
Rawlings Cres. HA9: Wemb . . . 34Ra 67
Rawlings St. SW3 . . . 5F 227 (49Hb 89)
Rawlins Cl. CR2: Sels . . . 80Bc 158
N3 . . . 27Ab 48
Rawlinson Ct. NW2 . . . 31Ya 68
Rawlinson Ho. SE13 . . . 56Fc 115
(off Mercator Rd.)
Rawlyn Cl. RM16: Chaf H . . . 50Yd 98
Rawnsley Av. CR4: Mitc . . . 71Fb 155
Rawreth Wlk. N1 . . . 39Sb 71
(off Basire St.)
Rawson St. SW11 . . . 53Jb 112
(not continuous)
Rawsthorne Cl. E16 . . . 46Pc 94
Rawsthorne Ct. TW4: Houn . . . 56Ba 107
Rawstone Wlk. E13 . . . 40Jc 73
Rawstorne Pl. EC1 . . . 3B 218 (41Rb 91)
Rawstorne St. EC1 . . . 3B 218 (41Rb 91)
(not continuous)
Raybell Ct. TW7: Isle . . . 54Ha 108
Rayburne Ct. IG9: Buck H . . . 18Lc 35
W14 . . . 48Ab 88
Rayburn Rd. RM11: Horn . . . 31Qd 77
Ray Cl. KT9: Chess . . . 79La 152
Raydean Rd. EN5: New Bar . . . 15Db 31
Raydon Rd. EN8: Chesh . . . 4Zb 20
Raydons Gdns. RM9: Dag . . . 35Ad 75
Raydons Rd. RM9: Dag . . . 36Ad 75
Raydon St. N19 . . . 33Kb 70
Rayfield CM16: Epp . . . 2Wc 23
Rayfield Cl. BR2: Brom . . . 72Nc 160
Rayford Av. SE12 . . . 59Hc 115
Rayford Cl. DA1: Dart . . . 57Ld 119
Ray Gdns. HA7: Stan . . . 22Ka 46
IG11: Bark . . . 40Wc 75
Ray Gunter Ho. SE17 . . . 7C 230
Ray Ho. N1 . . . 39Ub 71
(off Colville Est.)
W10 . . . 44Za 88
(off Cambridge Gdns.)
Ray Lamb Way DA8: Erith . . . 51Kd 119
Rayleas Cl. SE18 . . . 53Rc 116
Rayleigh Av. TW11: Tedd . . . 65Ga 130
Rayleigh Cl. CM13: Hut . . . 16Ee 41
N13 . . . 20Tb 33
Rayleigh Ct. KT1: King T . . . 68Qa 131
N22 . . . 25Sb 51
Rayleigh Ho. WD5: Ab L . . . 4V 12
Rayleigh Pde. CM13: Hut . . . 16Ee 41
Rayleigh Ri. CR2: S Croy . . . 79Ub 157
Rayleigh Rd. CM13: Hut . . . 16De 41
E16 . . . 46Kc 93
IG8: Wfd G . . . 23Lc 53
N13 . . . 20Sb 33
SS17: Stan H . . . 2K 101
SW19 . . . 67Bb 133
Ray Lodge Rd. IG8: Wfd G . . . 23Lc 53
Ray Massey Way E6 . . . 39Nc 74
(off High St. Nth.)
Raymead Av. CR7: Thor H . . . 71Qb 156
Raymead Cl. KT22: Fet . . . 94Ga 192
Raymead Pas.
CR7: Thor H . . . 71Qb 156
(off Raymead Av.)
Raymead Way KT22: Fet . . . 94Ga 192
Raymede Towers W10 . . . 43Za 88
(off Treverton St.)
Raymer Cl. AL1: St A . . . 1C 6
Raymere Gdns. SE18 . . . 52Tc 116
Raymond Av. E18 . . . 27Hc 53
W13 . . . 48Ja 86
Raymond Bldgs.
WC1 . . . 7J 217 (43Pb 90)
Raymond Chadburn Ho. E7 . . . 35Kc 73
Raymond Cl. SE26 . . . 64Yb 136
SL3: Poyle . . . 53G 104
WD5: Ab L . . . 4T 12
Raymond Ct. EN6: Pot B . . . 6Eb 17
N10 . . . 24Kb 50
Raymond Gdns. IG7: Chig . . . 20Xc 37
Raymond Postgate Ct.
SE28 . . . 45Xc 95
Raymond Rd. BR3: Beck . . . 70Ac 136
E13 . . . 39Lc 73
IG2: Ilf . . . 31Tc 74
SL3: L'ly . . . 48C 82
SW19 . . . 65Ab 132
Raymond Way KT10: Clay . . . 79Ja 152
Raymouth Rd. SE16 . . . 49Xb 91
Raynald Ho. SW16 . . . 62Nb 134
Rayne Ct. E18 . . . 28Hc 53
Rayne Ho. SW12 . . . 58Jb 112
W9 . . . 42Db 89
(off Delaware Rd.)
Rayner Ct. W12 . . . 47Ya 88
(off Bamborough Gdns.)
Rayners Cl. HA0: Wemb . . . 36Ma 67
SL3: Coln . . . 52E 104
Rayner's Ct. DA11: Nflt . . . 57De 121
Rayners Cres. UB5: N'olt . . . 41X 85
Rayners Gdns.
UB5: N'olt . . . 40X 65
RAYNERS LANE . . . 32Ba 65
Rayners La. HA2: Harr . . . 29Ba 45
HA5: Pinn . . . 29Ba 45
Rayners Rd. SW15 . . . 57Ab 110
Rayners Ter. E14 . . . 44Ac 92
(off Carr St.)
Rayner Towers E10 . . . 31Cc 72
(off Albany Rd.)
Raynes Av. E11 . . . 31Lc 73
Raynes Cl. GU21: Knap . . . 1F 186
RAYNES PARK . . . 70Ya 132
Raynes Pk. Bri. SW20 . . . 68Ya 132
Raynes Pk. School Sports Cen. . . . 69Xa 132
Raynham W2 . . . 2E 220
Raynham Av. N18 . . . 23Wb 51
Raynham Ho. E1 . . . 42Zb 92
(off Harpley Sq.)
Raynham Rd. N18 . . . 22Wb 51
W6 . . . 49Xa 88
Raynham Ter. N18 . . . 22Wb 51
Raynor Cl. UB1: S'hall . . . 46Ba 85
Raynor Pl. N1 . . . 38Sb 71
Raynton Cl. HA2: Harr . . . 32Aa 65
UB4: Hayes . . . 42Y 84
Raynton Dr. UB4: Hayes . . . 42Y 84
Raynton Rd. EN3: Enf W . . . 9Zb 20
Ray Rd. KT8: W Mole . . . 71Da 151
RM5: Col R . . . 22Dd 56
Rays Av. N18 . . . 21Yb 52
SL4: Wind . . . 2D 102
Rays Hill DA4: Hort K . . . 70Sd 142
Rays Rd. BR4: W W'ck . . . 73Ec 158
N18 . . . 21Yb 52
Ray St. EC1 . . . 6A 218 (42Qb 90)
Ray St. Bri. EC1 . . . 6A 218
Ray Wlk. N7 . . . 33Pb 70
Raywood Cl. UB3: Harl . . . 52S 106
Razia M. E12 . . . 36Pc 74
Reachview Cl. NW1 . . . 38Lb 70
Read Cl. KT7: T Ditt . . . 73Ja 152
Read Ct. E17 . . . 30Cc 52
EN9: Walt A . . . 5Jc 21
Reade Ct. W3 . . . 48Sa 87
(off Stanley Rd.)
Readens, The SM7: Bans . . . 88Gb 175
Reader Ho. SE5 . . . 53Sb 113
(off Badsworth Rd.)
Read Ho. SE11 . . . 51Qb 112
(off Clayton St.)
Reading Arch Rd. RH1: Redh . . . 6P 207
Reading Cl. SE22 . . . 58Wb 113
Reading Ho. SE15 . . . 51Wb 113
(off Friary Est.)
W2 . . . 44Eb 89
(off Hallfield Est.)
Reading La. E8 . . . 37Xb 71
Reading Rd. SM1: Sutt . . . 78Eb 155
UB5: N'olt . . . 36Da 65
Readings, The WD3: Chor . . . 13H 25
Reading Way NW7 . . . 22Za 48
Readman Ct. SE20 . . . 67Xb 135
Read Rd. KT21: Asht . . . 89Ma 173
Reads Cl. IG1: Ilf . . . 34Rc 74
Reads Rest La. KT20: Tad . . . 91Bb 195
Read Way DA12: Grav'nd . . . 4F 144
Ream Apartments SE23 . . . 61Yb 136
(off Clyde Ter.)
Reapers Cl. NW1 . . . 39Mb 70
Reapers Way TW7: Isle . . . 57Fa 108
Reardon Ct. N21 . . . 19Rb 33
Reardon Ho. E1 . . . 46Xb 91
(off Reardon St.)
Reardon Path E1 . . . 46Xb 91
(not continuous)
Reardon St. E1 . . . 46Xb 91
Reaston St. SE14 . . . 52Zb 114
Rebecca Ct. DA14: Sidc . . . 63Xc 139
Rebecca Ho. E3 . . . 42Bc 92
(off Brokesley St.)
Reckitt Rd. W4 . . . 50Ua 88
Recognition Ho. SL4: Wind . . . 4E 102
Record St. SE15 . . . 51Yb 114
Recovery St. SW17 . . . 64Gb 133
Recreation Av. RM3: Hrld W . . . 26Pd 57
RM7: Rom . . . 29Ed 56
Recreation Rd. BR2: Brom . . . 68Hc 137
DA15: Sidc . . . 62Uc 138
SE26 . . . 63Zb 136
UB2: S'hall . . . 49Aa 85
Recreation Way CR4: Mitc . . . 69Mb 134
Rector St. N1 . . . 39Sb 71
Rectory Bus. Cen. DA14: Sidc . . . 63Xc 139
Rectory Chambers SW3 . . . 51Gb 111
(off Old Church St.)
Rectory Chase CM13: L War . . . 28Zd 59
Rectory Cl. DA1: Cray . . . 56Gd 118
DA14: Sidc . . . 63Xc 139
E4 . . . 20Cc 34
HA7: Stan . . . 22Ka 46
KT6: Surb . . . 74La 152
KT14: Byfl . . . 85M 169
KT21: Asht . . . 91Pa 193
N3 . . . 25Bb 49
SL2: Farn R . . . 1G 80
SL4: Wind . . . 3E 102
SW20 . . . 69Ya 132
TW17: Shep . . . 69Q 128
Rectory Ct. E18 . . . 25Hc 53
SM6: Wall . . . 77Lb 156
TW13: Felt . . . 63Y 129
Rectory Cres. E11 . . . 30Lc 53
(not continuous)
Rectory Farm Rd. EN2: Enf . . . 10Pb 18
(not continuous)
Rectory Field . . . 52Kc 115
Rectory Fld. Cres. SE7 . . . 52Lc 115
Rectory Flds. RM16: Ors . . . 3D 100
Rectory Gdns. BR3: Beck . . . 67Cc 136
(off Rectory Rd.)
N8 . . . 28Nb 50
RM14: Upm . . . 33Td 78
SW4 . . . 55Lb 112
UB5: N'olt . . . 39Ba 65
Rectory Grn. BR3: Beck . . . 67Bc 136
Rectory Gro. CR0: C'don . . . 75Rb 157
SW4 . . . 55Lb 112
TW12: Hamp . . . 63Ba 129
Rectory La. CM13: Heron . . . 24Fe 59
DA14: Sidc . . . 63Xc 139
GU20: W'sham . . . 9A 146
HA7: Stan . . . 22Ka 46
HA8: Edg . . . 23Qa 47
IG10: Lough . . . 12Qc 36
KT6: Surb . . . 74Ka 152
KT14: Byfl . . . 85N 169
KT21: Asht . . . 91Pa 193
KT23: Bookh . . . 98Ba 191
RH3: Bkld . . . 3B 206
SM6: Wall . . . 77Lb 156
SM7: Bans . . . 86Hb 175
SW17 . . . 65Jb 134
TN13: S'oaks . . . 98Ld 203
TN15: Igh . . . 94Yd 204
TN16: Bras . . . 96Yc 201
TN16: Westrm . . . 95Nc 200
WD3: Rick . . . 18M 25
WD4: K Lan . . . 10A 4
WD7: Shenl . . . 5Pa 15
Rectory Mdw. DA13: Sflt . . . 65Ce 143
Rectory Orchard SW19 . . . 63Ab 132
Rectory Pk. CR2: Sande . . . 85Ub 177
Rectory Pk. Av. UB5: N'olt . . . 41Ba 85
Rectory Pl. SE18 . . . 49Qc 94
Rectory Rd. BR2: Kes . . . 80Mc 159
BR3: Beck . . . 67Cc 136
CR5: Coul . . . 97Eb 195
DA10: Swans . . . 59Ae 121
E12 . . . 36Pc 74
E17 . . . 28Dc 52
N16 . . . 33Vb 71
RM10: Dag . . . 37Dd 76
RM16: Ors . . . 2C 100
RM17: Grays . . . 48Fe 99
RM18: W Til . . . 1F 122
SM1: Sutt . . . 76Cb 155
SS17: Stan H . . . 2L 101
SW13 . . . 54Wa 110
TN15: Ash . . . 78De 165
TW4: Cran . . . 54Y 107
UB2: S'hall . . . 48Ba 85
UB3: Hayes . . . 44W 84
W3 . . . 46Ra 87
WD3: Rick . . . 18M 25
Rectory Sq. E1 . . . 43Zb 92
Rectory Ter. SS17: Stan H . . . 2L 101
Rectory Way UB10: Ick . . . 33R 64
Reculver Ho. SE15 . . . 51Yb 114
(off Lovelinch Cl.)
Reculver M. N18 . . . 21Wb 51
Reculver Rd. SE16 . . . 50Zb 92
Red Anchor Cl. SW3 . . . 51Fb 111
Redan Pl. W2 . . . 44Db 89
Redan St. W14 . . . 48Za 88
Redan Ter. SE5 . . . 54Rb 113
Redbarn Cl. CR8: Purl . . . 83Rb 177
Red Barracks Rd. SE18 . . . 49Pc 94
Redberry Gro. SE26 . . . 62Yb 136

Redbourne Av. N3 25Cb 49
Redbourne Dr. SE28 44Zc 95
(not continuous)
Redbourne Ho. E14 44Bc 92
(off Norbiton Rd.)
Redbourn Ho. W10 42Ya 88
(off Sutton Way)
Redbourn Rd. AL3: St A 1N 5
REDBRIDGE 30Nc 54
Redbridge Cycling Cen. 23Yc 55
Redbridge Ent. Cen. IG1: Ilf 33Sc 74
Redbridge FC 28Tc 54
Redbridge Foyer IG1: Ilf 33Sc 74
(off Hainault St.)
Redbridge Gdns. SE5 52Ub 113
Redbridge Ho. E16 45Rc 94
(off University Way)
Redbridge La. E. IG4: Ilf 30Mc 53
Redbridge La. W. E11 30Kc 53
REDBRIDGE RDBT. 30Mc 53
Redbridge Sports & Leisure Cen. 25Tc 54
Redbrooke Ct. SS17: Linf 8J 101
Redburn Ind. Est. EN3: Pond E 16Zb 34
Redburn St. SW3 51Hb 111
Redbury Cl. RM13: Rain 42Ld 97
Redcar Cl. UB5: N'olt 36Da 65
Redcar Rd. RM3: Rom 22Pd 57
Redcar St. SE5 52Sb 113
Redcastle Cl. E1 45Yb 92
Red Cedars Rd. BR6: Orp 73Uc 160
Redchurch St. E2 5K 219 (42Vb 91)
Redcliffe Cl. SW5 50Db 89
(off Old Brompton Rd.)
Redcliffe Ct. E5 34Xb 71
(off Napoleon Rd.)
Redcliffe Gdns. IG1: Ilf 32Qc 74
SW10 50Db 89
W4 52Ra 109
Redcliffe M. SW10 50Db 89
Redcliffe Pl. SW10 51Eb 111
Redcliffe Rd. SW10 50Eb 89
Redcliffe Sq. SW10 50Db 89
Redcliffe St. SW10 51Db 111
Redclose Av. SM4: Mord 71Cb 155
Redclyffe Rd. E6 39Lc 73
Redclyf Ho. E1 42Yb 92
(off Cephas St.)
Red Cottage M. SL3: L'ly 8N 81
Red Ct. SL1: Slou 6J 81
Redcourt CR0: C'don 76Ub 157
GU22: Pyr 87F 168
Red Cow La. EC1 5D 218 (42Sb 91)
Redcroft Rd. UB1: S'hall 45Ea 86
Red Cross Cotts. SE1 1E 230
Redcross Way SE1 1E 230 (47Sb 91)
Redden Ct. Rd.
RM3: Hrld W 27Nd 57
Redding Cl. DA2: Dart 61Ud 142
Redding Ho. SE18 48Nc 94
WD18: Wat 16U 26
Reddings HP3: Hem H 4A 4
Reddings, The NW7 20Va 30
WD6: Bore 13Pa 29
Reddings Av. WD23: Bush 15Da 27
Reddings Cl. NW7 21Va 48
Reddington Cl. CR2: Sande 81Tb 177
Reddington Dr. SL3: L'ly 48A 82
Redding Way GU21: Knap 1F 186
Reddins Rd. SE15 51Wb 113
Reddons Rd. BR3: Beck 66Ac 136
Reddown Rd. CR5: Coul 90Mb 176
Reddy Rd. DA8: Erith 51Hd 118
Rede Ct. KT13: Weyb 76R 150
(off Old Palace Rd.)
Redenham Ho. SW15 59Wa 110
(off Ellisfield Dr.)
Rede Pl. W2 44Cb 89
Redesdale Gdns. TW7: Isle 52Ja 108
Redesdale St. SW3 51Gb 111
Redfern Av. TW4: Houn 59Ca 107
Redfern Cl. UB8: Uxb 39L 63
Redfern Ct. WD18: Wat 15U 26
Redfern Gdns. RM2: Rom 26Md 57
Redfern Ho. E13 39Hc 73
(off Redriffe Rd.)
NW8 39Fb 69
(off Dorman Way)
Redfern Rd. NW10 38Ua 68
SE6 59Ec 114
Redfield La. SW5 49Cb 89
Redfield M. SW5 49Db 89
Redford Av. CR5: Coul 87Kb 176
CR7: Thor H 70Pb 134
SM6: Wall 79Nb 156
Redford Cl. TW13: Felt 61V 128
Redford Rd. SL4: Wind 4B 102
Redford Wlk. N1 39Sb 71
(off Popham St.)
Redford Way UB8: Uxb 38M 63
Redgate Dr. BR2: Hayes 75Kc 159
Redgate Ter. SW15 58Za 110
Redgrave Cl. CR0: C'don 72Vb 157
Redgrave Ct. UB9: Den 29H 43
Redgrave Rd. SW15 55Za 110
Redgrave Ter. E2 41Wb 91
(off Derbyshire St.)
Redgrove Ho. CM16: Epp 1Wc 23
(off Stonards Hill)
Redhall Cl. AL10: Hat 3B 8
Redhall Ct. CR3: Cat'm 95Tb 197
Redhall Dr. AL10: Hat 4B 8
Redhall End AL4: Col H 4A 8
Redhall La. AL4: Col H 4A 8
WD3: Chan C 11N 25
Redheath Cl. WD25: Wat 7V 12
REDHILL 5P 207
Red Hill BR7: Chst 64Rc 138
UB9: Den 33F 62
Redhill Aerodrome and Heliport 10D 208
Redhill & Reigate Golf Course 9M 207
Redhill Comn. RH1: Redh 7N 207
Redhill Ct. SW2 61Qb 134
Redhill Dr. HA8: Edg 26Ra 47
Redhill Golf Course 10A 208
Redhill Ho. RH1: Redh 4P 207
Redhill Rd. DA3: New A 76Ae 165
KT11: Cobh 84R 170
Redhill St. NW1 2A 216 (40Kb 70)
Redhill Wood DA3: New A 76Ce 165
(not continuous)
Red House 56Ad 117
Red Ho. SE20 66Xb 135
(off Anerley Pk.)
Red Ho. Cotts. TN13: S'oaks 97Ld 203
Red Ho. La. DA6: Bex 56Zc 117
KT12: Walt T 75W 150
Redhouse Rd. CR0: C'don 72Mb 156
TN16: Tats 92Lc 199
Red Ho. Sq. N1 38Sb 71
Redif Ho. RM10: Dag 35Dd 76
Redington Gdns. NW3 35Db 69
Redington Ho. N1 1J 217
Redington Rd. NW3 34Db 69
Redknap Ho. TW10: Ham 62La 130
Redland Gdns. KT8: W Mole 70Ba 129
Redlands CR5: Coul 88Nb 176
N15 28Tb 51
TW11: Tedd 65Ja 130
Redlands, The BR3: Beck 68Dc 136
Redlands Ct. BR1: Brom 66Hc 137
Redlands Rd. EN3: Enf H 11Ac 34
TN13: S'oaks 96Hd 202
Redlands Way SW2 59Pb 112
Red La. KT10: Clay 79Ja 152
RH8: Oxt 6M 211
Red Leaf Cl. SL3: L'ly 46B 82
Redleaf Cl. DA17: Belv 51Cd 118
KT22: Fet 96Fa 192
Redleaves Av. TW15: Ashf 65R 128
Redlees Cl. TW7: Isle 56Ja 108
Red Leys UB8: Uxb 38N 63
Redlibbets Golf Course 74Zd 165
Redlin Ct. RH1: Redh 4P 207
Red Lion Bus. Pk. KT6: Surb 76Pa 153
Red Lion Cl. BR5: St M Cry 72Yc 161
SE17 51Tb 113
(off Red Lion Row)
WD25: A'ham 9Ea 14
Red Lion Ct. EC4 3A 224 (44Qb 90)
SE1 6E 224 (46Sb 91)
TW3: Houn 55Da 107
(off Alexandra Rd.)
Red Lion Hill N2 26Fb 49
(not continuous)
Red Lion La. GU24: Chob 1J 167
HP3: Hem H 8A 4
SE18 52Qc 116
WD3: Sarr 7J 11
Red Lion Pde. HA5: Pinn 27Aa 45
Red Lion Pl. SE18 53Qc 116
Red Lion Rd. GU24: Chob 1J 167
KT6: Surb 75Pa 153
Red Lion Row SE17 51Sb 113
Red Lion Sq. SW18 57Cb 111
WC1 1H 223 (43Pb 90)
Red Lion St. TW9: Rich 57Ma 109
WC1 7H 217 (43Pb 90)
Red Lion Yd. W1 6K 221
WD17: Wat 13Y 27
Red Lodge BR4: W W'ck 74Ec 158
WD6: Bore 13Pa 29
Red Lodge Cres. DA5: Bexl 62Fd 140
Red Lodge Rd. BR4: W W'ck 74Ec 158
DA5: Bexl 62Fd 140
Redlynch Ct. W14 47Ab 88
(off Addison Cres.)
Redlynch Ho. SW9 53Qb 112
(off Gosling Way)
Redman Cl. UB5: N'olt 40Y 65
Redman Ho. EC1 7K 217
SE1 2E 230
Redmans La. TN14: S'ham 79Ed 162
Redmans Pl. TN13: S'oaks 97Jd 203
(off Akehurst La.)
Redman's Rd. E1 43Yb 92
Redmead La. E1 46Wb 91
Redmead Rd. UB3: Harl 49U 84
Redmill Ho. E1 42Xb 91
(off Headlam St.)
Redmond Ho. N1 1J 217
Redmore Rd. W6 49Xa 88
Red Oak Cl. BR6: Farnb 76Rc 160
CR0: C'don 75Cc 158
Red Oaks Mead CM16: They B 9Tc 22
Redo Ho. E12 36Qc 74
(off Dore Av.)
Red Path E9 37Ac 72
Red Pl. W1 4H 221 (45Jb 90)
Redpoll Way DA18: Erith 48Zc 95
Red Post Hill SE21 56Tb 113
SE24 56Tb 113
Red Post Ho. E6 38Mc 73
Redriffe Rd. E13 39Hc 73
Redriff Est. SE16 48Bc 92
Redriff Rd. RM7: Mawney 26Dd 56
SE16 49Zb 92
Red Rd. CM14: W'ley 21Xd 58
GU18: Light 4A 166
WD6: Bore 13Pa 29
Redroofs Cl. BR3: Beck 67Dc 136
Redrose Trad. Cen.
EN4: E Barn 15Fb 31
RED ROVER 56Wa 110
Redrup Ho. SE14 51Zb 114
(off John Williams Cl.)
Redruth Cl. N22 24Pb 50
Redruth Gdns. KT10: Clay 80Ha 152
RM3: Rom 22Pd 57
Redruth Ho. SM2: Sutt 80Db 155
Redruth Rd. E9 39Yb 72
RM3: Rom 22Pd 57
Redruth Wlk. RM3: Rom 22Pd 57
Redsan Cl. CR2: S Croy 80Tb 157
Redshank Ho. SE1 50Vb 91
(off Avocet Cl.)
Red Sq. N16 34Tb 71
(off Wheeler Pl.)
Redstart Cl. CR0: New Ad 82Fc 179
E6 43Nc 94
SE14 52Ac 114
Redstart Mans. IG1: Ilf 34Qc 74
(off Mill Rd.)
Redstone Hill RH1: Redh 6A 208
Redstone Hollow RH1: Redh 7A 208
Redstone Mnr. RH1: Redh 6A 208
Redstone Pk. RH1: Redh 6A 208
Redstone Rd. RH1: Redh 7A 208
Redston Rd. N8 28Mb 50
REDSTREET 65De 143
Red St. DA13: Sflt 64Ce 143
Redtiles Gdns.
CR8: Kenley 87Rb 177
Redvers Ct. CR6: W'ham 90Zb 178
(off Redvers Rd.)
Redvers Rd. CR6: W'ham 90Zb 178
N22 26Qb 50
Redvers St. N1 3J 219 (41Ub 91)
Redwald Rd. E5 35Zb 72
Redway Dr. TW2: Whitt 59Ea 108
Redwell Cotts. TN15: Igh 95Yd 204
Redwell Ct. EN8: Walt C 6Bc 20
Redwell La. TN15: Igh 95Xd 204
Redwing Cl. CR2: Sels 83Zb 178
Redwing Ct. BR6: Orp 73Wc 161
(off High St.)
RM3: Rom 25Md 57
SE1 2E 230
Redwing Cres. DA9: Ghithe 58Wd 120
Redwing Gdns. KT14: W Byf 84K 169
Redwing Gro. WD5: Ab L 3W 12
Redwing M. SE5 54Sb 113
Redwing Path SE28 47Tc 94
Redwing Rd. SM6: Wall 80Nb 156
Redwood TW20: Thorpe 68G 126
Redwood Chase
RM15: S Ock 42Yd 98
Redwood Cl. AL1: St A 2G 6
CR8: Kenley 86Sb 177
DA15: Sidc 60Wc 117
E3 40Cc 72
N14 17Mb 32
SE16 46Ac 92
UB10: Hil 40R 64
WD19: Wat 21Y 45
Redwood Ct. DA1: Dart 58Qd 119
KT6: Surb 73Ma 153
KT17: Ewe 83Va 174
KT22: Lea 92Ha 192
(off Park Vw. Rd.)
N19 31Mb 70
NW6 38Ab 68
UB5: N'olt 41Aa 85
Redwood Dr. HP3: Hem H 4N 3
KT19: Eps 82Sa 173
SL5: S'dale 2F 146
Redwood Est. TW5: Cran 51X 107
Redwood Gdns. E4 16Dc 34
IG7: Chig 22Wc 55
SL1: Slou 5H 81
Redwood Gro. W5 48Ka 86
Redwood Ho. TN16: Westrm 95Rc 200
Redwood Mans. W8 48Db 89
(off Chantry Sq.)
Redwood M. SW4 55Kb 112
TW15: Ashf 66T 128
(off Staines Rd. W.)
Redwood Mt. RH2: Reig 3J 207
Redwood Ri. WD6: Bore 9Ra 15
Redwoods KT15: Add 79J 149
SW15 60Wa 110
Redwoods, The SL4: Wind 5H 103
Redwoods Cl. IG9: Buck H 19Kc 35
Redwood Wlk. KT6: Surb 74Ma 153
Redwood Way EN5: Barn 15Za 30
Reece M. SW7 6B 226 (49Fb 89)
Reed Av. BR6: Orp 76Uc 160
Reed Cl. AL2: Lon C 9J 7
E16 43Jc 93
SE12 57Jc 115
Reed Ct. DA9: Ghithe 56Yd 120
Reed Dr. RH1: Redh 9A 208
Reede Gdns. RM10: Dag 36Dd 76
Reede Rd. RM10: Dag 37Cd 76
Reede Way RM10: Dag 37Dd 76
Reedham Cl. AL2: Brick W 1Ca 13
N17 28Xb 51
Reedham Dr. CR8: Purl 85Pb 176
Reedham Pk. Av. CR8: Purl 88Qb 176
Reedham Rd. SL1: Burn 1A 80
Reedham St. SE15 54Wb 113
Reedholm Vs. N16 35Tb 71
Reed Ho. SW19 63Db 133
Reed Pl. KT14: W Byf 85G 168
SW4 56Mb 112
TW17: Shep 74P 149
Reed Pond Wlk. RM2: Rom 26Hd 56
Reed Rd. N17 26Vb 51
Reeds Chapel WD24: Wat 12Y 27
(off Keele Cl.)
Reeds Cres. WD24: Wat 12Y 27
Reedsfield Cl. TW15: Ashf 62R 128
Reedsfield Rd. TW15: Ashf 63R 128
Reeds Mdw. RH1: Mers 2C 208
Reed's Pl. NW1 38Lb 70
Reeds Wlk. WD24: Wat 12Y 27
(not continuous)
Reedworth St. SE11 6A 230 (49Qb 90)
Reef Ho. E14 48Ec 92
(off Manchester St.)
Reel Cinema, The
Borehamwood 13Qa 29
(within The Point)
Reenglass Rd. HA7: Stan 21Ma 47
Rees Dr. HA7: Stan 21Na 47
Rees Gdns. CR0: C'don 72Vb 157
Reesland Cl. E12 37Qc 74
Rees St. N1 1E 218 (39Sb 71)
Reets Farm Cl. NW9 30Ua 48
Reeve Rd. RH2: Reig 10L 207
Reeves Av. NW9 31Ta 67
Reeves Cnr. CR0: C'don 75Rb 157
Reeves Cres. BR8: Swan 69Fd 140
Reeves Ho. SE1 2K 229
Reeves M. W1 5H 221 (45Jb 90)
Reeves Rd. E3 42Dc 92
SE18 51Rc 116
Reflection, The E16 47Rc 94
(off Woolwich Mnr. Way)
Reflection Ho. E2 42Wb 91
(off Cheshire St.)
Reflex Apartments
BR2: Brom 70Kc 137
(off Wheeler Pl.)
Reform Row N17 26Vb 51
Reform St. SW11 54Hb 111
Regal Bldg. W10 41Za 88
Regal Cl. E1 43Wb 91
W5 43Ma 87
Regal Ct. CR4: Mitc 69Hb 133
N18 22Vb 51
NW6 40Bb 69
(off Malvern Rd.)
SW6 52Cb 111
(off Dawes Rd.)
Regal Cres. SM6: Wall 76Kb 156
Regal Dr. N11 22Kb 50
Regal Ho. IG2: Ilf 30Tc 54
Regal House, The SW6 54Eb 111
Regal La. NW1 1K 215 (39Jb 70)
Regal Pl. E3 41Bc 92
SW6 52Db 111
Regal Row SE15 53Yb 114
Regal Way HA3: Kenton 30Na 47
WD24: Wat 10Y 13
Regan Ho. N18 23Vb 51
Regan Way N1 1H 219 (40Ub 71)
Regarder Rd. IG7: Chig, Ilf 22Wc 55
Regarth Av. RM1: Rom 30Gd 56
Regatta Ho. TW11: Tedd 63Ja 130
Regatta Point E14 47Cc 92
(off Westferry Rd.)
TW8: Bford 51Pa 109
Regency Cl. IG7: Chig 22Sc 55
TN15: W King 79Ud 164
TW12: Hamp 64Ba 129
W5 44Na 87
Regency Ct. AL1: St A 2F 6
BR2: Brom 72Mc 159
CM14: B'wood 19Yd 40
E3 40Bc 72
(off Norman Gro.)
E9 39Yb 72
(off Park Cl.)
E18 26Jc 53
EN1: Enf 15Tb 33
HP2: Hem H 2M 3
KT15: Add 76M 149
(off Albert Rd.)
SE8 52Bc 114
(off Glenville Gro.)
SM1: Sutt 77Eb 155
TW11: Tedd 65Ka 130
WD17: Wat 11W 26
(off Langley Rd.)
Regency Cres. NW4 26Za 48
Regency Dr. HA4: Ruis 32U 64
KT14: W Byf 85H 169
Regency Gdns. KT12: Walt T 74Y 151
KT13: Weyb 79S 150
RM11: Horn 31Ld 77
Regency Ho. E16 46Jc 93
(off Pepys Cres.)
N3 26Bb 49
SW1 5E 228
SW6 53Eb 111
Regency Lawn NW5 34Kb 70
Regency Lodge IG9: Buck H 19Mc 35
KT13: Weyb 76U 150
(off Oatlands Chase)
NW3 38Fb 69
(off Adelaide Rd.)
Regency M. BR3: Beck 67Ec 136
NW10 37Wa 68
SW9 52Rb 113
TW7: Isle 57Ga 108
Regency Pde. NW3 38Fb 69
(off Finchley Rd.)
Regency Pl. SW1 5E 228 (49Mb 90)
Regency St. NW10 42Ua 88
SW1 5D 228 (49Mb 90)
Regency Ter. SW7 7B 226
Regency Wlk. CR0: C'don 72Bc 158
TW10: Rich 57Na 109
(off Grosvenor Av.)
Regency Way DA6: Bex 55Zc 117
Regeneration Rd. SE16 49Zb 92
Regent Av. UB10: Hil 38R 64
Regent Bus. Cen. UB3: Hayes 47X 85
Regent Cl. HA3: Kenton 30Na 47
KT15: New H 81M 169
N12 22Eb 49
RH1: Mers 1C 208
RM16: Grays 47Ee 99
TW4: Cran 53X 107
WD4: K Lan 1Q 12
Regent Ct. N3 24Db 49
N20 19Fb 31
NW6 38Bb 69
(off Cavendish Rd.)
NW8 4D 214
RM15: Avel 46Td 98
SL1: Slou 4J 81
SL4: Wind 3H 103
W8 48Db 89
(off Wright's La.)
Regent Cres. RH1: Redh 4P 207
Regent Gdns. IG3: Ilf 31Wc 75
Regent Gate EN8: Walt C 6Zb 20
Regent Ho. CM14: B'wood 20Xd 40
KT17: Eps 83Ua 174
RH1: Redh 5P 207
W14 49Ab 88
(off Windsor Way)
Regent Pde. SM2: Sutt 79Eb 155
Regent Pk. KT22: Lea 90Ja 172
Regent Pl. CR0: C'don 74Vb 157
SW19 64Eb 133
W1 4C 222 (45Lb 90)
Regent Rd. CM16: Epp 2Vc 23
KT5: Surb 71Pa 153
SE24 58Rb 113
Regents Av. N13 22Qb 50
Regent's Bri. Gdns. SW8 52Nb 112
Regents Canal Ho. E14 44Ac 92
(off Commercial Rd.)
Regents Cl. CR2: S Croy 79Ub 157
CR3: Whyt 90Ub 177
HA8: Edg 21Na 47
UB4: Hayes 43V 84
WD7: R'lett 6Ja 14
Regent's College 5H 215
Regents Ct. BR1: Brom 66Hc 137
DA11: Grav'nd 7D 122
E8 39Vb 71
(off Pownall Rd.)
HA5: Pinn 26Z 45
KT2: King T 67Na 131
(off Sopwith Way)
KT13: Weyb 79R 150
Regents Dr. BR2: Kes 78Mc 159
IG8: Wfd G 23Qc 54
Regents Ga. Ho. E14 45Ac 92
(off Horseferry Rd.)
Regents M. NW8 1A 214 (40Eb 69)
REGENT'S PARK 4A 216 (41Hb 90)
Regent's Pk. 2G 215 (41Hb 89)
Regent's Pk. Barracks 2A 216
Regents Pk. Est. NW1 3B 216
Regent's Pk. Gdns. M. NW1 3A 214
Regent's Pk. Ho. NW8 4E 214
Regent's Pk. Open Air Theatre
4H 215 (41Jb 90)
Regents Pk. Rd. N3 27Bb 49
NW1 38Hb 69
(not continuous)
Regent's Pk. Ter. NW1 39Kb 70
Regents Pl. IG10: Lough 17Mc 35
NW1 5A 216 (42Kb 90)
SE3 54Jc 115
Regents Plaza NW6 40Db 69
(off Kilburn High Rd.)
Regent Sq. DA17: Belv 49Dd 96
E3 41Dc 92
WC1 4G 217 (41Nb 90)
Regent's Row E8 39Wb 71
Regent St. NW10 41Za 88
SW1 5D 222 (45Mb 90)
W1 2A 222 (44Kb 90)
W4 50Qa 87
WD24: Wat 10X 13
Regents Wlk. SL5: Asc 2A 146
Regents Wharf E2 39Xb 71
(off Wharf Pl.)
N1 1H 217 (40Pb 70)
Regent Ter. SW8 51Nb 112
Regina Cl. EN5: Barn 13Za 30
Regina Ho. SE20 67Zb 136
Reginald Pl. SE8 52Cc 114
(off Deptford High St.)
Reginald Rd. E7 38Jc 73
HA6: Nwood 25V 44
RM3: Hrld W 25Qd 57
SE8 52Cc 114
Reginald Sorenson Ho. E11 31Fc 73
Reginald Sq. SE8 52Cc 114
Regina Point SE16 48Yb 92
Regina Rd. N4 32Pb 70
SE25 69Wb 135
UB2: S'hall 49Aa 85
W13 46Ja 86
Regina Ter. W13 46Ka 86
Regis Ct. CR4: Mitc 67Gb 133
N8 28Pb 50
NW1 7F 215
Regis Ho. W1 7J 215
Regis Pl. SW2 56Pb 112
Regis Rd. NW5 36Kb 70
Regnart Bldgs. NW1 4C 216
Regnas Ho. E15 37Hc 73
(off Carnarvon Rd.)
Regnolruf Ct. KT12: Walt T 73W 150
Reid Av. CR3: Cat'm 93Tb 197
Reid Cl. CR5: Coul 88Kb 176
HA5: Eastc 28W 44
UB3: Hayes 44U 84
Reidhaven Rd. SE18 49Uc 94
Reidonhill Cotts. GU21: Knap 10F 166
REIGATE 6J 207
Reigate Av. SM1: Sutt 74Cb 155
Reigate Bus. M. RH2: Reig 5H 207
REIGATE HEATH 6F 206
Reigate Heath Golf Course 6E 206
Reigate Heath (Local Nature Reserve)
6F 206
Reigate Hill RH2: Reig 2L 207
Reigate Hill Cl. RH2: Reig 3J 207
Reigate Hill Golf Course 100Jb 196
REIGATE HILL INTERCHANGE 1K 207
Reigate Priory Mus. 7J 207
Reigate Rd. BR1: Brom 62Hc 137
IG3: Ilf 33Vc 75
KT17: Eps D 86Ya 174
KT17: Eps, Ewe 82Va 174
KT18: Tatt C 89Za 174
KT20: Tad 89Za 174
KT22: Lea 94La 192
RH1: Redh 6K 207
RH2: Reig 6K 207
(Chart La.)
RH2: Reig 5A 206
(Station Rd.)
RH3: Bet, Bkld 5A 206
Reigate Way SM6: Wall 78Nb 156
Reighton Rd. E5 34Wb 71
Reindeer Cl. E13 39Jc 73
Reinickendorf Av. SE9 58Sc 116
Reis Pl. N15 28Vb 51
(off Blenheim Ri.)
Reizel Cl. N16 32Vb 71
Relay Rd. W12 46Ya 88
Relf Rd. SE15 55Wb 113
Reliance Arc. SW9 56Qb 112
Reliance Sq. EC2 5J 219 (42Ub 91)
Relko Ct. KT19: Eps 83Ta 173
Relko Gdns. SM1: Sutt 78Fb 155
Relton M. SW7 3E 226 (48Gb 89)
Rembrandt Cl. E14 48Fc 93
SW1 7H 227
Rembrandt Ct. KT19: Ewe 79Va 154
SE16 50Xb 91
(off Stubbs Dr.)
Rembrandt Dr. DA11: Nflt 62Fe 143
Rembrandt Rd. HA8: Edg 26Qa 47
SE13 56Gc 115
Rembrandt Way KT12: Walt T 75X 151
Remington Rd. E6 44Nc 94
N15 30Tb 51
Remington St. N1 2C 218 (40Rb 71)
Remnant St. WC2 2H 223 (44Pb 90)
Remsted Ho. NW6 39Db 69
(off Mortimer Cres.)
Remus Building, The EC1 4A 218
Remus Cl. AL1: St A 6B 6
Remus Rd. E3 38Cc 72
Renaissance KT15: Add 77L 149
(off High St.)
Renaissance Ct. SM1: Sutt 74Eb 155
TW3: Houn 55Ea 108
Renaissance Ho. KT17: Eps 85Ua 174
(off Up. High St.)
Renaissance Wlk. SE10 48Hc 93
(off Teal St.)
Renbold Ho. SE10 53Ec 114
(off Blissett St.)
Rendalls HA1: Harr 32Ga 66
(off Grove Hill)
Rendel Ho. SM7: Bans 90Eb 175
Rendle Cl. CR0: C'don 71Vb 157
Rendle Ho. W10 42Ab 88
(off Wornington Rd.)
Rendlesham Av. WD7: R'lett 9Ha 14
Rendlesham Rd. E5 35Wb 71
EN2: Enf 11Rb 33
Rendlesham Way WD3: Chor 16E 24
Renforth St. SE16 48Yb 92
Renfree Way TW17: Shep 73Q 150
Renfrew Cl. E6 45Qc 94
Renfrew Ct. TW4: Houn 54Aa 107
Renfrew Ho. E17 26Bc 52
NW6 40Db 69
(off Carlton Vale)
Renfrew Rd. KT2: King T 66Ra 131
SE11 5B 230 (49Rb 90)
TW4: Houn 54Z 107
Renmans, The KT21: Asht 88Pa 173
Renmuir St. SW17 65Hb 133
Rennell St. SE13 55Ec 114
Rennels Way TW7: Isle 54Ga 108
Renness Rd. E17 27Ac 52
Rennets Cl. SE9 57Uc 116
Rennets Wood Rd. SE9 57Tc 116

St Andrews Cl. KT7: T Ditt . . . 74Ka 152
N12 . . . 21Eb 49
NW2 . . . 34Xa 68
RH2: Reig . . . 7K 207
SE16 . . . 50Xb 91
SE28 . . . 44Zc 95
SL4: Old Win . . . 8L 103
SW19 . . . 65Db 133
TW7: Isle . . . 53Ga 108
TW17: Shep . . . 70T 128
TW19: Wray . . . 58A 104
St Andrews Cotts. SL4: Wind . . . 4E 102
(off Cross Oak)
St Andrews Ct. BR8: Swan . . . 69Gd 140
DA12: Grav'nd . . . 8D 122
(off Queen St.)
E17 . . . 26Ac 52
RM18: Tilb . . . 4C 122
SL1: Slou . . . 8J 81
(off Upton Pk.)
SM1: Sutt . . . 76Gb 155
SW18 . . . 61Eb 133
WD17: Wat . . . 11X 27
St Andrew's Cres. SL4: Wind . . . 4D 102
St Andrews Dr. AL1: St A . . . 5F 6
BR5: St M Cry . . . 72Xc 161
HA7: Stan . . . 25La 46
St Andrews Gdns.
KT11: Cobh . . . 85Y 171
St Andrew's Ga. GU22: Wok . . . 90B 168
St Andrew's Gro. N16 . . . 32Tb 71
St Andrew's Hill EC4 . . . 4C 224 (45Rb 91)
(not continuous)
St Andrews Ho. KT17: Eps . . . 85Ta 173
(off High St.)
SE16 . . . 48Xb 91
(off Southwark Pk. Rd.)
St Andrews Mans. W1 . . . 1H 221
W14 . . . 51Ab 110
(off St Andrews Rd.)
St Andrews M. N16 . . . 32Ub 71
SE3 . . . 52Jc 115
SW12 . . . 60Mb 112
St Andrew's Pl. CM15: Shenf . . . 19Be 41
NW1 . . . 5A 216 (42Kb 90)
St Andrews Rd. CR0: C'don . . . 77Sb 157
CR5: Coul . . . 88Jb 176
DA12: Grav'nd . . . 9D 122
DA14: Sidc . . . 62Zc 139
E11 . . . 30Gc 53
E13 . . . 41Kc 93
E17 . . . 26Zb 52
EN1: Enf . . . 13Tb 33
HP3: Hem H . . . 6M 3
IG1: Ilf . . . 31Pc 74
KT6: Surb . . . 72Ma 153
N9 . . . 17Yb 34
NW9 . . . 32Ta 67
NW10 . . . 37Xa 68
NW11 . . . 30Bb 49
RM7: Rom . . . 30Fd 56
RM18: Tilb . . . 3A 122
SM5: Cars . . . 76Gb 155
UB10: Uxb . . . 39N 63
W3 . . . 45Ua 88
W7 . . . 47Ga 86
W14 . . . 51Ab 110
WD19: Wat . . . 20Z 27
St Andrews Sq. KT6: Surb . . . 72Ma 153
W11 . . . 44Ab 88
St Andrews Ter. WD19: Wat . . . 22Y 45
St Andrew's Twr. UB1: S'hall . . . 45Ea 86
(off Baird Av.)
St Andrew St. EC4 . . . 1A 224 (43Qb 90)
St Andrew's Wlk. KT11: Cobh . . . 87X 171
St Andrews Way E3 . . . 42Dc 92
SL1: Slou . . . 5B 80
St Andrew's Wharf SE1 . . . 1K 231 (47Vb 91)
St Anna Rd. EN5: Barn . . . 15Za 30
St Anne's Av. TW19: Stanw . . . 59M 105
St Annes Blvd. RH1: Redh . . . 4B 208
St Annes Cl. N6 . . . 34Jb 70
RM16: Grays . . . 46De 99
WD19: Wat . . . 21Y 45
St Anne's Ct. BR4: W W'ck . . . 77Gc 159
NW6 . . . 39Ab 68
W1 . . . 3D 222 (44Mb 90)
St Anne's Dr. RH1: Redh . . . 5A 208
St Annes Dr. Nth. RH1: Redh . . . 4A 208
St Anne's Flats NW1 . . . 3D 216
St Anne's Gdns. NW10 . . . 41Pa 87
St Anne's Mt. RH1: Redh . . . 5A 208
St Anne's Pas. E14 . . . 44Bc 92
St Anne's Ri. RH1: Redh . . . 5A 208
St Anne's Rd. AL2: Lon C . . . 9H 7
CM15: Mount, Shenf . . . 11Ee 41
E11 . . . 33Fc 73
HA0: Wemb . . . 36Ma 67
UB9: Hare . . . 27L 43
St Anne's Row E14 . . . 44Bc 92
St Annes Ter. IG6: Ilf . . . 22Uc 54
St Anne's Trad. Est. E14 . . . 44Bc 92
(off St Anne's Row)
St Anne St. E14 . . . 44Bc 92
St Annes Way RH1: Redh . . . 5A 208
(off St Annes Mt.)
St Anns GU22: Wok . . . 90A 168
IG11: Bark . . . 39Sc 74
St Ann's Cl. KT16: Chert . . . 72H 149
St Ann's Ct. NW4 . . . 27Xa 48
St Ann's Cres. SW18 . . . 58Db 111
St Ann's Gdns. NW5 . . . 37Jb 70
St Ann's Hill SW18 . . . 57Db 111
St Ann's Hill Rd. KT16: Chert . . . 72E 148
St Ann's Ho. WC1 . . . 4K 217
St Ann's La. SW1 . . . 4E 228 (48Mb 90)
St Ann's M. KT16: Chert . . . 73G 148
ST ANN'S PARK . . . 70B 126
St Ann's Pk. Rd. SW18 . . . 58Eb 111
St Ann's Pas. SW13 . . . 55Ua 110
St Ann's Rd. HA1: Harr . . . 30Ga 46
IG11: Bark . . . 39Sc 74
KT16: Chert . . . 72G 148
(Chilsey Grn. Rd.)
KT16: Chert . . . 72H 149
(Twynersh Av.)
N9 . . . 19Vb 33
N15 . . . 29Rb 51
SW13 . . . 54Va 110
W11 . . . 45Za 88
St Ann's Shop. Cen. HA1: Harr . . . 30Ga 46
St Ann's St. SW1 . . . 3E 228 (48Mb 90)
St Ann's Ter. NW8 . . . 1C 214 (40Fb 69)
St Ann's Vs. W11 . . . 46Za 88
St Anns Way CR2: S Croy . . . 79Rb 157
TN16: Big H . . . 88Rc 180
St Anselms Ct. SW16 . . . 64Nb 134
St Anselm's Pl. W1 . . . 4K 221 (45Kb 90)
St Anselm's Rd. UB3: Hayes . . . 47V 84
St Anthonys Av. HP3: Hem H . . . 4B 4
IG8: Wfd G . . . 23Lc 53
St Anthony's Cl. E1 . . . 46Wb 91
E9 . . . 37Bc 72
(off Wallis Rd.)
SW17 . . . 61Gb 133
St Anthony's Ct. BR6: Farnb . . . 75Rc 160
SW17 . . . 61Jb 134
St Anthony's Flats NW1 . . . 2D 216
St Anthony's Way TW14: Felt . . . 56V 106
St Antony's Rd. E7 . . . 38Kc 73
St Arvan's Cl. CR0: C'don . . . 76Ub 157
St Asaph Rd. SE4 . . . 55Zb 114
St Aubins Ct. N1 . . . 39Tb 71
St Aubyn's Av. SW19 . . . 64Bb 133
TW3: Houn . . . 57Ca 107
St Aubyn's Cl. BR6: Orp . . . 76Vc 161
St Aubyn's Gdns. BR6: Orp . . . 75Vc 161
St Aubyn's Rd. SE19 . . . 65Vb 135
St Audrey Av. DA7: Bex . . . 54Cd 118
St Audreys Cl. AL10: Hat . . . 3D 8
St Augustine Rd. RM16: Grays . . . 9D 100
St Augustine's Av. BR2: Brom . . . 71Nc 160
CR2: S Croy . . . 79Sb 157
HA9: Wemb . . . 34Na 67
W5 . . . 40Na 67
St Augustine's Ct. SE1 . . . 50Xb 91
(off Lynton Rd.)
St Augustine's Ho. NW1 . . . 3D 216
St Augustines Mans. SW1 . . . 6C 228
St Augustine's Path N5 . . . 35Sb 71
St Augustine's Rd. DA17: Belv . . . 49Bd 95
NW1 . . . 38Mb 70
St Austell Cl. HA8: Edg . . . 26Pa 47
St Austell Rd. SE13 . . . 54Ec 114
St Awdry's Rd. IG11: Bark . . . 38Tc 74
St Awdry's Wlk. IG11: Bark . . . 38Sc 74
St Barnabas Cl. BR3: Beck . . . 68Ec 136
SE22 . . . 57Ub 113
St Barnabas Ct. HA3: Hrw W . . . 25Ea 46
HP2: Hem H . . . 2A 4
St Barnabas Gdns.
KT8: W Mole . . . 71Ca 151
St Barnabas M. SW1 . . . 7J 227
St Barnabas Rd. CR4: Mitc . . . 66Jb 134
E17 . . . 30Cc 52
IG8: Wfd G . . . 25Kc 53
SM1: Sutt . . . 78Fb 155
St Barnabas St. SW1 . . . 7J 227 (50Jb 90)
St Barnabas Ter. E9 . . . 36Zb 72
St Barnabas Vs. SW8 . . . 53Nb 112
St Bartholomew's Cl. SE26 . . . 63Xb 135
St Bartholomew's Ct. E6 . . . 40Nc 74
(off St Bartholomew's Rd.)
St Bartholomew's Hospital Mus. . . . 1C 224
St Bartholomew's Rd. E6 . . . 40Pc 74
St Bart's Cl. AL4: St A . . . 3H 7
St Benedict's Av. DA12: Grav'nd . . . 1F 144
St Benedict's Cl. SW17 . . . 64Jb 134
St Benet's Cl. SW17 . . . 61Gb 133
St Benet's Gro. SM5: Cars . . . 73Eb 155
St Benet's Pl. EC3 . . . 4G 225 (45Tb 91)
St Benjamins Dr. BR6: Prat B . . . 81Yc 181
St Bernards CR0: C'don . . . 76Ub 157
St Bernard's Cl. SE27 . . . 63Tb 135
St Bernards Ho. E14 . . . 48Ec 92
(off Galbraith St.)
St Bernards Rd. AL3: St A . . . 1C 6
E6 . . . 39Mc 73
SL3: L'ly . . . 8N 81
St Blaise Av. BR1: Brom . . . 68Kc 137
St Botolph Row EC3 . . . 3K 225 (44Vb 91)
St Botolphs E1 . . . 2K 225
St Botolph's Av. TN13: S'oaks . . . 96Jd 202
St Botolphs Rd. DA11: Nflt . . . 62Fe 143
TN13: S'oaks . . . 96Kd 203
St Botolph St. EC3 . . . 2K 225 (44Vb 91)
St Brelades Ct. N1 . . . 39Ub 71
St Bride's Av. EC4 . . . 3B 224
HA8: Edg . . . 25Pa 47
St Brides Cl. DA18: Erith . . . 47Zc 95
St Bride's Crypt Mus. . . . 3B 224
St Bride's Ho. E3 . . . 40Cc 72
(off Ordell Rd.)
St Bride's Pas. EC4 . . . 3B 224
St Bride St. EC4 . . . 2B 224 (44Rb 91)
St Catherines GU22: Wok . . . 1N 187
KT13: Weyb . . . 76R 150
(off Thames St.)
St Catherine's Apartments E3 . . . 41Dc 92
(off Bow Rd.)
St Catherines Cl. KT9: Chess . . . 79Ma 153
SW17 . . . 61Gb 133
St Catherines Ct. TW13: Felt . . . 60W 106
TW18: Staines . . . 63J 127
W4 . . . 48Ua 88
St Catherine's Cross RH1: Blet . . . 6L 209
St Catherine's Dr. SE14 . . . 54Zb 114
St Catherine's Farm Ct. HA4: Ruis . . . 30T 44
St Catherines M. SW3 . . . 5F 227 (49Hb 89)
St Catherines Pl. TW20: Egh . . . 64C 126
St Catherine's Rd. E4 . . . 19Cc 34
HA4: Ruis . . . 30T 44
St Cecelia's Pl. SE3 . . . 50Jc 93
St Cecilia Rd. RM16: Grays . . . 9D 100
St Cecilia's Cl. SM3: Sutt . . . 74Ab 154
St Cedd's Ct. RM16: Grays . . . 46De 99
St Chads Cl. KT6: Surb . . . 73La 152
St Chad's Dr. DA12: Grav'nd . . . 2G 144
St Chad's Gdns. RM6: Chad H . . . 31Ad 75
St Chad's Pl. WC1 . . . 3G 217 (41Nb 90)
St Chads Rd. RM6: Chad H . . . 31Ad 75
RM16: Grays . . . 4C 122
RM18: Grays, Tilb . . . 4C 122
St Chad's St. WC1 . . . 3G 217 (41Nb 90)
(not continuous)
St Charles Ct. KT13: Weyb . . . 78Q 150
St Charles Pl. KT13: Weyb . . . 78Q 150
W10 . . . 43Ab 88
St Charles Rd. CM14: B'wood . . . 18Xd 40
St Charles Sq. W10 . . . 43Za 88
St Chloe's Ho. E3 . . . 40Cc 72
(off Ordell Rd.)
St Christopher Rd. UB8: Cowl . . . 44M 83
St Christopher's Cl. TW7: Isle . . . 53Ga 108
St Christophers Ct. KT12: Walt T . . . 75Y 151
(off Rydens Av.)
WD3: Chor . . . 15F 24
St Christophers Dr. UB3: Hayes . . . 45X 85
St Christopher's Gdns.
CR7: Thor H . . . 69Qb 134
St Christopher's Ho. NW1 . . . 2C 216
St Christopher's M. SM6: Wall . . . 78Lb 156
St Christopher's Pl. W1 . . . 2J 221 (44Jb 90)
St Clair Cl. IG5: Ilf . . . 26Pc 54
RH2: Reig . . . 6L 207
RH8: Oxt . . . 2G 210
St Clair Dr. KT4: Wor Pk . . . 76Xa 154
St Clair Ho. E3 . . . 41Bc 92
(off British St.)
St Clair Rd. E13 . . . 40Kc 73
St Clair's Rd. CR0: C'don . . . 75Ub 157
St Clare Bus. Pk.
TW12: Hamp H . . . 65Ea 130
St Clare St. EC3 . . . 3K 225 (44Vb 91)
St Clement Cl. UB8: Cowl . . . 44M 83
St Clement's Av. RM20: W Thur . . . 51Wd 120
St Clement's Cl. DA11: Nflt . . . 2B 144
St Clements Ct. EC4 . . . 4G 225
EN9: Walt A . . . 5Ec 20
N7 . . . 37Qb 70
RM17: Grays . . . 51Be 121
RM19: Purf . . . 49Qd 97
SE14 . . . 51Zb 114
(off Myers La.)
W11 . . . 45Za 88
(off Stoneleigh St.)
St Clement's Hgts. SE26 . . . 62Wb 135
St Clements Ho. E1 . . . 1K 225
St Clement's La.
WC2 . . . 3H 223 (44Pb 90)
St Clements Mans. SW6 . . . 51Za 110
(off Lillie Rd.)
St Clements Rd. DA9: Ghithe . . . 56Yd 120
RM20: Grays . . . 52Yd 120
St Clements St. N7 . . . 37Qb 70
St Clements Way
DA2: Bean, Bluew . . . 57Wd 120
DA9: Bluew, Ghithe . . . 57Wd 120
RM20: W Thur . . . 51Vd 120
St Clements Yd. SE22 . . . 56Vb 113
St Clere TN15: Kems'g . . . 88Vd 184
St Clere Hill Rd. TN15: W King . . . 84Vd 184
St Clere's Hall Golf Course . . . 3K 101
St Cloud Rd. SE27 . . . 63Sb 135
St Columba's Cl. DA12: Grav'nd . . . 2F 144
(not continuous)
St Columba's Ct. E15 . . . 35Gc 73
(off Janson Rd.)
St Columbas Ho. E17 . . . 28Dc 52
St Columb's Ho. W10 . . . 43Ab 88
(off Blagrove Rd.)
St Crispin's Cl. NW3 . . . 35Gb 69
UB1: S'hall . . . 44Ba 85
St Crispins Way KT16: Ott . . . 81E 168
St Cross St. EC1 . . . 7A 218 (43Qb 90)
St Cuthbert La. UB8: Cowl . . . 44M 83
St Cuthberts Cl. TW20: Eng G . . . 5P 125
St Cuthberts Gdns. HA5: Hat E . . . 24Ba 45
St Cuthberts Rd. N13 . . . 23Qb 50
NW2 . . . 37Bb 69
St Cyprian's St. SW17 . . . 63Hb 133
St Daniel Ct. BR3: Beck . . . 66Cc 136
(off Brackley Rd.)
St David Cl. UB8: Cowl . . . 43M 83
St David's CR5: Coul . . . 89Pb 176
St Davids Cl. BR4: W W'ck . . . 73Dc 158
HA9: Wemb . . . 34Sa 67
HP3: Hem H . . . 3D 4
RH2: Reig . . . 5L 207
SE16 . . . 50Xb 91
(off Masters Dr.)
SL0: Iver H . . . 39F 62
St Davids Ct. BR1: Brom . . . 69Rc 138
E17 . . . 27Ec 52
TW15: Ashf . . . 61P 127
St David's Cres. DA12: Grav'nd . . . 3F 144
St Davids Dr. HA8: Edg . . . 25Pa 47
TW20: Eng G . . . 6N 125
St Davids M. E3 . . . 41Ac 92
(off Morgan St.)
E18 . . . 25Jc 53
St David's Pl. NW4 . . . 31Xa 68
St Davids Rd. BR8: Hext . . . 65Hd 140
St Davids Sq. E14 . . . 50Dc 92
St Denis Rd. SE27 . . . 63Tb 135
St Denys Cl. CR8: Purl . . . 82Rb 177
GU21: Knap . . . 10H 167
St Dionis Rd. SW6 . . . 54Bb 111
St Domingo Ho. SE18 . . . 48Pc 94
(off Leda Rd.)
St Donatt's Rd. SE14 . . . 53Bc 114
ST DUNSTAN'S . . . 79Bb 155
St Dunstans All. EC3 . . . 5H 225
St Dunstans Av. W3 . . . 45Ta 87
St Dunstan's Cl. UB3: Harl . . . 50V 84
St Dunstan's Ct. EC4 . . . 3A 224 (44Qb 90)
St Dunstan's Dr. DA12: Grav'nd . . . 3G 144
St Dunstan's Gdns. W3 . . . 45Ta 87
St Dunstans Hill EC3 . . . 5H 225 (45Ub 91)
SM1: Sutt . . . 78Ab 154
St Dunstan's La. BR3: Beck . . . 72Ec 158
EC3 . . . 5H 225 (45Ub 91)
St Dunstans M. E1 . . . 43Ac 92
(off White Horse Rd.)
St Dunstan's Rd. E7 . . . 37Kc 73
SE25 . . . 70Vb 135
TW4: Cran . . . 54X 107
(not continuous)
TW13: Felt . . . 62V 128
W6 . . . 50Za 88
W7 . . . 47Ga 86
St Edith Cl. KT18: Eps . . . 86Sa 173
St Edith Cotts. TN15: Kems'g . . . 88Xd 184
St Edith's Farm Ct.
TN15: Kems'g . . . 90Rd 183
St Edith's Rd. TN15: Kems'g . . . 90Qd 183
St Edmund's Av. HA4: Ruis . . . 30T 44
St Edmunds Cl. DA18: Erith . . . 47Zc 95
NW8 . . . 1F 215 (39Hb 69)
SW17 . . . 61Gb 133
St Edmund's Ct. NW8 . . . 1F 215
TN15: W King . . . 81Vd 184
St Edmunds Dr. HA7: Stan . . . 25Ja 46
St Edmund's La. TW2: Whitt . . . 59Da 107
St Edmund's Rd. DA1: Dart . . . 56Qd 119
IG1: Ilf . . . 30Pc 54
N9 . . . 17Wb 33
St Edmunds Sq. SW13 . . . 51Ya 110
St Edmund's Ter. NW8 . . . 1E 214 (39Gb 69)
St Edmunds Wlk. AL4: St A . . . 3H 7
St Edward's Cl. CR0: New Ad . . . 83Fc 179
NW11 . . . 30Cb 49
St Edwards Ct. NW11 . . . 30Cb 49
St Edwards Way RM1: Rom . . . 29Fd 56
St Egberts Way E4 . . . 18Ec 34
St Elizabeth Dr. KT18: Eps . . . 86Sa 173
St Elmo Cl. SL2: Slou . . . 2H 81
St Elmo Cres. SL2: Slou . . . 2H 81
St Elmo Rd. W12 . . . 46Va 88
(not continuous)
St Elmos Rd. SE16 . . . 47Ac 92
St Erkenwald M. IG11: Bark . . . 39Tc 74
St Erkenwald Rd. IG11: Bark . . . 39Tc 74
St Ermin's Hill SW1 . . . 3D 228
St Ervan's Rd. W10 . . . 43Bb 89
St Ethelburga Ct. RM3: Hrld W . . . 26Qd 57
St Eugene Ct. NW6 . . . 39Ab 68
(off Salusbury Rd.)
St Faith's Cl. EN2: Enf . . . 11Sb 33
St Faith's Rd. SE21 . . . 60Rb 113
St Fidelis Rd. DA8: Erith . . . 49Fd 96
St Fillans GU22: Wok . . . 88D 168
St Fillans Rd. SE6 . . . 60Ec 114
St Francis Av. DA12: Grav'nd . . . 3G 144
St Francis Cl. BR5: Pet W . . . 72Uc 160
EN6: Pot B . . . 6Eb 17
WD19: Wat . . . 18X 27
St Francis' Ho. NW1 . . . 2D 216
St Francis Pl. SW12 . . . 58Kb 112
St Francis Rd. DA8: Erith . . . 49Fd 96
SE22 . . . 56Ub 113
UB9: Den . . . 30H 43
St Francis Way IG1: Ilf . . . 35Tc 74
RM16: Grays . . . 8E 100
St Frideswide's M. E14 . . . 44Ec 92
St Gabriel's Cl. E11 . . . 33Kc 73
E14 . . . 43Dc 92
St Gabriels Ct. N11 . . . 24Mb 50
St Gabriels Mnr. SE5 . . . 53Rb 113
(off Cormont Rd.)
St Gabriels Rd. NW2 . . . 36Za 68
St George Ga. KT15: Add . . . 76M 149
St George's Av. E7 . . . 38Kc 73
KT13: Weyb . . . 79R 150
N7 . . . 35Mb 70
NW9 . . . 28Ta 47
RM11: Horn . . . 31Pd 77
RM17: Grays . . . 49Ee 99
UB1: S'hall . . . 45Ba 85
W5 . . . 47Ma 87
St George's Bldgs. SE1 . . . 4B 230
St Georges Bus. Pk. KT13: Weyb . . . 81Q 170
St George's Cathedral . . . 3A 216
St Georges Chapel . . . 2H 103
St George's Cir. SE1 . . . 3B 230 (48Rb 91)
St Georges Cl. HA0: Wemb . . . 34Ja 66
KT13: Weyb . . . 78S 150
NW11 . . . 30Bb 49
SE28 . . . 44Zc 95
SL4: Wind . . . 3C 102
SW8 . . . 53Lb 112
St Georges Ct. AL1: St A . . . 2C 6
(off Lemsford Rd.)
CM13: Hut . . . 17Ee 41
CM14: B'wood . . . 17Xd 40
E6 . . . 42Pc 94
E17 . . . 29Fc 53
EC4 . . . 2B 224 (44Rb 91)
HA3: Kenton . . . 30Ja 46
(off Kenton Rd.)
KT13: Weyb . . . 79S 150
KT15: Add . . . 77L 149
SE1 . . . 4B 230
SW1 . . . 7B 228
SW3 . . . 5D 226
SW7 . . . 3A 226 (48Eb 89)
SW15 . . . 56Bb 111
TN15: Wro . . . 88Be 185
St George's Cres. DA12: Grav'nd . . . 3F 144
SL1: Slou . . . 5B 80
St George's Dr. SW1 . . . 6A 228 (49Kb 90)
UB10: Ick . . . 34P 63
WD19: Wat . . . 20Aa 27
ST GEORGE'S FIELD . . . 45Gb 89
St George's Flds. W2 . . . 3E 220 (44Gb 89)
St George's Gdns. KT6: Surb . . . 75Ra 153
KT17: Eps . . . 86Va 174
St George's Gro. SW17 . . . 62Fb 133
ST GEORGE'S HILL . . . 82R 170
St George's Hill Golf Course . . . 83S 170
St Georges Ho. NW1 . . . 2D 216
SW11 . . . 53Jb 112
(off Charlotte Despard Av.)
St Georges Ind. Est. KT2: King T . . . 64Ma 131
N22 . . . 24Rb 51
St George's La. EC3 . . . 4G 225
SL5: Asc . . . 9A 124 & 1A 146
St George's Mans. SW1 . . . 7E 228
St George's M. NW1 . . . 38Hb 69
SE1 . . . 3A 230
SE8 . . . 49Bc 92
St Georges Pde. SE6 . . . 61Bc 136
(off Perry Hill)
St George's Path SE4 . . . 56Cc 114
(off Adelaide Av.)
St George's Pl. TW1: Twick . . . 60Ja 108
St George's Pools . . . 45Xb 91
St George's RC Cathedral
. . . 3A 230 (48Qb 90)
St Georges Rd. BR1: Brom . . . 68Pc 138
BR3: Beck . . . 67Dc 136
BR5: Pet W . . . 72Tc 160
BR8: Swan . . . 70Hd 140
(not continuous)
CR4: Mitc . . . 69Kb 134
DA14: Sidc . . . 65Zc 139
E7 . . . 38Kc 73
E10 . . . 34Ec 72
EN1: Enf . . . 10Vb 19
HP3: Hem H . . . 6L 3
IG1: Ilf . . . 31Pc 74
KT2: King T . . . 66Qa 131
KT13: Weyb . . . 79T 150
KT15: Add . . . 77L 149
N13 . . . 20Pb 32
NW11 . . . 30Bb 49
RM9: Dag . . . 36Ad 75
SE1 . . . 3A 230 (48Qb 90)
SM6: Wall . . . 78Kb 156
SW19 . . . 66Bb 133
(not continuous)
TN13: S'oaks . . . 94Kd 203
TW1: Twick . . . 57Ka 108
TW9: Rich . . . 55Pa 109
TW13: Hanw . . . 63Z 129
W4 . . . 47Ta 87
St Georges Rd. W7 . . . 46Ha 86
WD24: Wat . . . 10X 13
St George's Rd. W. BR1: Brom . . . 67Nc 138
St George's Shopping & Leisure Cen.
HA1: Harr . . . 30Ga 46
St George's Shopping Cen.
DA11: Grav'nd . . . 8D 122
St Georges Sq. DA3: Lfield . . . 69Ae 143
DA11: Grav'nd . . . 8D 122
E7 . . . 38Kc 73
E14 . . . 45Ac 92
KT3: N Mald . . . 69Ua 132
SE8 . . . 49Bc 92
(not continuous)
SW1 . . . 7D 228 (50Mb 90)
St George's Sq. M. SW1 . . . 7D 228 (50Mb 90)
St George's Stadium . . . 33V 64
St George's Ter. E6 . . . 41Nc 94
(off Masterman Rd.)
NW1 . . . 38Hb 69
SE15 . . . 52Wb 113
(off Peckham Hill St.)
St George St. W1 . . . 3A 222 (45Kb 90)
St George's Wlk. CR0: C'don . . . 76Sb 157
St George's Way SE15 . . . 51Ub 113
St George's Wharf SE1 . . . 1K 231
St George Wharf SW8 . . . 51Nb 112
St Gerards Cl. SW4 . . . 57Lb 112
St German's Pl. SE3 . . . 53Jc 115
St German's Rd. SE23 . . . 60Ac 114
St Giles Av. EN6: S Mim . . . 4Xa 16
RM10: Dag . . . 38Dd 76
UB10: Ick . . . 35S 64
St Giles Cir. W1 . . . 2E 222
St Giles Cl. BR6: Farnb . . . 78Tc 160
RM10: Dag . . . 38Dd 76
RM16: Ors . . . 2C 100
TW5: Hest . . . 52Aa 107
St Giles Ct. EN1: Enf . . . 7Yb 20
HP8: Chal G . . . 19C 24
St Giles High St. WC2 . . . 2E 222 (44Mb 90)
St Giles Ho. EN5: New Bar . . . 14Eb 31
SE5 . . . 53Ub 113
St Giles Pas. WC2 . . . 3E 222
St Giles Quad. HP8: Chal G . . . 19C 24
St Giles Rd. SE5 . . . 52Ub 113
St Giles Ter. EC2 . . . 1E 224
St Giles Twr. SE5 . . . 53Ub 113
(off Gables Cl.)
St Gilles Ho. E2 . . . 40Zb 72
(off Mace St.)
St Gothard Rd. SE27 . . . 63Tb 135
(not continuous)
St Gregory Cl. HA4: Ruis . . . 35Y 65
St Gregory's Ct. DA12: Grav'nd . . . 1G 144
St Gregory's Cres. DA12: Grav'nd . . . 1G 144
St Helena Ho. WC1 . . . 4K 217
St Helena Rd. SE16 . . . 49Zb 92
St Helena St. WC1 . . . 4K 217 (41Qb 90)
St Helens KT7: T Ditt . . . 73Ha 152
St Helens Cl. UB8: Cowl . . . 43M 83
St Helens Ct. CM16: Epp . . . 2Wc 23
RM13: Rain . . . 42Jd 96
St Helen's Cres. SW16 . . . 67Pb 134
St Helen's Gdns. W10 . . . 43Za 88
St Helen's M. CM14: B'wood . . . 19Zd 41
St Helens Pl. E10 . . . 31Ac 72
EC3 . . . 2H 225 (44Ub 91)
St Helen's Rd. DA18: Erith . . . 47Zc 95
IG1: Ilf . . . 30Pc 54
SW16 . . . 67Pb 134
W13 . . . 46Ka 86
ST HELIER . . . 73Gb 155
St Helier Av. SM4: Mord . . . 73Eb 155
St Helier Ct. N1 . . . 39Ub 71
(off De Beauvoir Est.)
SE16 . . . 47Zb 92
(off Poolmans St.)
St Helier's Av. TW3: Houn . . . 57Ca 107
St Helier's Rd. E10 . . . 30Ec 52
St Hilary's Ct. BR1: Brom . . . 69Rc 138
St Hildas TN15: Plax . . . 99Be 205
St Hilda's Av. TW15: Ashf . . . 64N 127
St Hilda's Cl. GU21: Knap . . . 9H 167
NW6 . . . 38Za 68
SW17 . . . 61Gb 133
St Hilda's Rd. SW13 . . . 51Xa 110
St Hilda's Way DA12: Grav'nd . . . 3F 144
St Hilda's Wharf E1 . . . 46Yb 92
(off Wapping High St.)
St Huberts Cl. SL9: Ger X . . . 32A 62
St Hubert's Ho. E14 . . . 48Cc 92
(off Janet St.)
St Hubert's La. SL9: Ger X . . . 33B 62
St Hughes Cl. SW17 . . . 61Gb 133
St Hugh's Rd. SE20 . . . 67Xb 135
St Ignatius College Sports Cen. . . . 9Xb 19
St Ives Cl. RM3: Rom . . . 24Pd 57
St Ivian Ct. N10 . . . 26Jb 50
St Ivian's Dr. RM2: Rom . . . 27Jd 56
St James SE14 . . . 53Ac 114
St James Apartments E17 . . . 29Ac 52
(off Pretoria Av.)
St James Av. KT17: Ewe . . . 83Va 174
N20 . . . 20Gb 31
SM1: Sutt . . . 78Cb 155
W13 . . . 46Ja 86
St James Cl. EN4: E Barn . . . 14Fb 31
GU21: Wok . . . 10L 167
HA4: Ruis . . . 33Y 65
KT3: N Mald . . . 71Va 154
KT18: Eps . . . 86Ua 174
N20 . . . 20Gb 31
SE18 . . . 50Sc 94
St James Ct. AL1: St A . . . 3E 6
CR0: C'don . . . 73Rb 157
DA9: Ghithe . . . 58Vd 120
E2 . . . 41Wb 91
(off Bethnal Grn. Rd.)
E12 . . . 33Lc 73
KT21: Asht . . . 89Ma 173
RM1: Rom . . . 28Hd 56
SE3 . . . 53Kc 115
SW1 . . . 3C 228 (48Lb 90)
St James Dr. RM3: Rom . . . 23Nd 57
St James Gdns. HA0: Wemb . . . 38Ma 67
RM6: Chad H . . . 28Xc 55
St James Ga. IG9: Buck H . . . 18Lc 35
SL5: S'dale . . . 3D 146
St James Gro. SW11 . . . 54Hb 111
St James Hall N1 . . . 39Sb 71
(off Prebend St.)
St James Ho. RM1: Rom . . . 29Hd 56
(off Eastern Rd.)

St James Ind. M. SE1 50Wb 91
St James La. DA9: Dart, Ghithe 60Ud 120
St James Mans. NW6 38Cb 69
(off West End La.)
SE1 3K 229
St James M. E14 48Ec 92
E17 29Ac 52
(off St James's St.)
KT13: Weyb 77R 150
St James Oaks DA11: Grav'nd 9C 122
St James Path E17 29Ac 52
St James Pl. DA1: Dart 58Md 119
SL1: Slou 4A 80
St James Residences W1 4D 222
St James Rd. CM14: B'wood 20Yd 40
CR4: Mitc 66Jb 134
CR8: Purl 85Rb 177
E15 36Hc 73
KT6: Surb 72Ma 153
N9 19Xb 33
SM1: Sutt 78Cb 155
SM5: Cars 76Gb 155
WD18: Wat 15X 27
ST JAMES'S 7C 222 (46Mb 90)
St James's App. EC2 6H 219 (42Ub 91)
St James's Av. BR3: Beck 69Ac 136
DA11: Grav'nd 9C 122
E2 40Yb 72
TW12: Hamp H 64Ea 130
St James's Chambers SW1 6C 222
St James's Cl. NW8 1F 215
SW17 61Hb 133
St James's Cotts. TW9: Rich 57Ma 109
St James's Ct. HA1: Harr 30Ja 46
KT1: King T 69Na 131
N18 22Wb 51
(off Fore St.)
St James's Cres. SW9 55Qb 112
St James's Dr. SW12 60Hb 111
SW17 60Hb 111
St James's Gdns. W11 46Ab 88
(not continuous)
St James's Ho. SE1 49Wb 91
(off Strathnairn St.)
St James's La. N10 28Kb 50
St James's Mkt. SW1 5D 222 (45Mb 90)
St James's Palace 1C 228 (47Lb 90)
St James's Pk. 1D 228 (47Mb 90)
St James's Pk. CR0: C'don 73Sb 157
St James's Pas. EC3 3J 225
St James's Pl. SW1 7B 222 (46Lb 90)
St James Sq. DA3: Lfield 69Ae 143
(off Park Dr.)
St James's Rd. CR0: C'don 73Rb 157
DA11: Grav'nd 8C 122
KT1: King T 68Ma 131
SE1 51Wb 113
SE16 48Wb 91
TN13: S'oaks 94Kd 203
TW12: Hamp H 64Da 129
St James's Sq. SW1 6C 222 (46Lb 90)
St James's St. DA11: Grav'nd 8C 122
E17 29Ac 52
SW1 6B 222 (46Lb 90)
St James's Ter. NW8 1F 215
St James's Ter. M. NW8 1F 215 (39Hb 69)
St James St. W6 50Ya 88
St James's Wlk. EC1 5B 218 (42Rb 91)
St James Ter. BR6: Prat B 81Yc 181
(off St Benjamins Dr.)
SW12 60Jb 112
St James Wlk. SL0: Rich P 47G 82
St James Way DA14: Sidc 64Ad 139
St Jeromes Gro. UB3: Hayes 44S 84
St Joan's Ho. NW1 3D 216
St Joan's Rd. N9 19Vb 33
St John Fisher Rd. DA18: Erith 48Zc 95
ST JOHNS
GU21 10K 167
RH1 8N 207
SE8 54Cc 114
TN13 94Ld 203
St Johns RH1: Redh 8N 207
St John's Av. CM14: W'ley 21Zd 59
KT17: Eps 84Wa 174
KT22: Lea 93Ka 192
N11 22Hb 49
NW10 39Va 68
SW15 57Za 110
St Johns Caravan Pk. EN2: Enf 9Rb 19
St Johns Chu. Rd. E9 36Yb 72
St Johns Cl. EN6: Pot B 5Eb 17
HA9: Wemb 36Na 67
HP1: Hem H 4K 3
KT22: Lea 93La 192
N14 16Lb 32
N20 20Eb 31
(off Rasper Rd.)
RM13: Rain 38Jd 76
SW6 52Cb 111
TN16: Big H 88Rc 180
UB8: Uxb 39K 63
St John's Cnr. RH1: Redh 8P 207
(off St John's Rd.)
St John's Cotts. SE20 66Yb 136
St Johns Ct. AL1: St A 1F 6
DA8: Erith 49Fd 96
E1 46Xb 91
(off Scandrett St.)
GU21: Wok 1L 187
GU24: Brkwd 2D 186
HA1: Harr 30Ha 46
HA6: Nwood 24U 44
(off Murray Rd.)
IG9: Buck H 18Kc 35
KT1: King T 70Na 131
(off Beaufort Rd.)
N4 33Rb 71
N5 35Rb 71
RH9: S God 10D 210
SE13 54Ec 114
SW10 52Eb 111
(off Ashburnham Rd.)
TN13: S'oaks 94Ld 203
TW7: Isle 54Ha 108
TW20: Egh 64C 126
W6 49Xa 88
(off Glenthorne Rd.)
St John's Cres. SW9 55Qb 112
St Johns Dr. KT12: Walt T 74Y 151
SL4: Wind 4E 102
SW18 60Db 111
St John's Est. N1 2G 219 (40Tb 71)
SE1 1K 231
St John's Gdns. GU21: Wok 10L 167
(off St John's Rd.)
W11 45Ab 88
St John's Gate 6B 218
St John's Gro. N19 33Lb 70
SW13 54Va 110
TW9: Rich 56Na 109
St John's Hill CR5: Coul 89Qb 176
SW11 57Fb 111
TN13: S'oaks 93Ld 203
St John's Hill Gro. SW11 56Fb 111
St John's Hill Rd. GU21: Wok 1L 187
St Johns Ho. E14 49Ec 92
(off Pier St.)
SE17 51Tb 113
(off Lytham St.)
St John's Jerusalem 66Rd 141
St John's La. DA3: Hartl 72Be 165
EC1 6B 218 (42Rb 91)
St Johns Lodge GU21: Wok 1L 187
NW3 38Gb 69
(off King Henry's Rd.)
St John's Lye GU21: Wok 1K 187
St John's Mans. EC1 3B 218
St John's M. GU21: Wok 1L 187
KT1: Hamp W 68La 130
W11 44Cb 89
St Johns Pde. DA14: Sidc 63Wc 139
(off Sidcup High St.)
W13 46Ka 86
St John's Pk. SE3 52Hc 115
St John's Pk. Mans. N19 34Lb 70
St John's Pas. SW19 65Ab 132
St John's Path EC1 6B 218
St Johns Pathway SE23 60Yb 114
St John's Pl. EC1 6B 218 (42Rb 91)
St Johns Ri. GU21: Wok 1L 187
TN16: Big H 88Rc 180
St Johns Rd. BR5: Pet W 72Tc 160
CM16: Epp 2Vc 23
CR0: C'don 76Rb 157
DA2: Dart 59Sd 120
DA8: Erith 50Fd 96
DA12: Grav'nd 9F 122
DA14: Sidc 63Xc 139
(not continuous)
DA16: Well 55Xc 117
E4 21Dc 52
E6 39Nc 74
E16 44Jc 93
E17 26Dc 52
GU21: Wok 1K 187
HA1: Harr 30Ha 46
HA9: Wemb 35Ma 67
HP1: Hem H 4J 3
IG2: Ilf 31Tc 74
IG10: Lough 12Pc 36
IG11: Bark 39Uc 74
KT1: Hamp W 68La 130
KT3: N Mald 69Sa 131
KT8: E Mos 70Fa 130
KT22: Lea 93La 192
N15 30Ub 51
NW11 30Bb 49
RH1: Redh 8P 207
RM5: Col R 22Ed 56
RM16: Grays 10D 100
SE20 65Yb 136
SL2: Slou 5L 81
SL4: Wind 4E 102
SM1: Sutt 75Db 155
SM5: Cars 76Gb 155
SW11 56Gb 111
SW19 66Ab 132
TN13: S'oaks 93Kd 203
TW7: Isle 54Ha 108
TW9: Rich 56Na 109
TW13: Hanw 63Aa 129
UB2: S'hall 48Aa 85
UB8: Uxb 39K 63
WD17: Wat 12X 27
St Johns Sq. EC1 6B 218 (42Rb 91)
SL4: Eton 1H 103
St John's Ter. E7 37Kc 73
EN2: Enf 9Tb 19
SE18 51Sc 116
SW15 62Ua 132
(off Kingston Va.)
W10 42Za 88
St John's Ter. Rd. RH1: Redh 8P 207
St John St. EC1 2A 218 (40Qb 70)
St John's Va. SE8 54Cc 114
St John's Vs. N11 22Hb 49
(off Friern Barnet Rd.)
N19 33Mb 70
W8 48Db 89
(off St Mary's Pl.)
St Johns Waterside GU21: Wok 10K 167
(off Copse Rd.)
St John's Way KT16: Chert 74J 149
N19 33Lb 70
ST JOHN'S WOOD 2C 214 (40Fb 69)
St John's Wood Ct. NW8 4C 214
St John's Wood High St.
NW8 2C 214 (40Fb 69)
St John's Wood Pk. NW8 39Fb 69
St John's Wood Rd. NW8 5B 214 (42Fb 89)
St John's Wood Ter. NW8 1C 214 (40Fb 69)
St John's Yd. N17 24Vb 51
St Josephs Almshouses W6 49Za 88
(off Brook Grn.)
St Joseph's Cl. BR6: Orp 77Vc 161
W10 43Ab 88
St Joseph's College Sports Cen. 65Rb 135
St Joseph's Cotts. SW3 6F 227
St Josephs Ct. E4 17Ec 34
SE7 51Kc 115
St Joseph's Dr. UB1: S'hall 46Aa 85
St Joseph's Flats NW1 3D 216
St Joseph's Gro. NW4 28Xa 48
St Josephs Ho. W6 49Za 88
(off Brook Grn.)
St Joseph's Rd. EN8: Walt C 5Ac 20
N9 17Xb 33
St Joseph's St. SW8 53Kb 112
St Joseph's Va. SE3 55Fc 115
St Jude's Cl. TW20: Eng G 4N 125
St Jude's Cotts. TW20: Eng G 4N 125
St Judes Ct. IG8: Wfd G 24Nc 54
St Judes Rd. E2 40Xb 71
TW20: Eng G 2N 125
St Jude St. N16 36Ub 71
St Julian Rd.
TN15: S'oaks, Under 100Nd 203
ST JULIANS 5B 6
St Julian's Cl. SW16 63Qb 134
St Julian's Farm Rd. SE27 63Qb 134
St Julian's Rd. AL1: St A 4B 6
NW6 39Cb 69
St Justin Cl. BR5: St P 69Zc 139
St Katharine Docks 5K 225
St Katharine's Pct. NW1 1K 215 (40Kb 70)
St Katharine's Way E1 6K 225 (46Vb 91)
(not continuous)
St Katharine's Yacht Haven 46Vb 91
(off St Katharine's Way)
St Katherines Rd. CR3: Cat'm 97Wb 197
DA18: Erith 47Zc 95
St Katherine's Row EC3 3J 225
St Katherines Wlk. W11 46Za 88
(off St Ann's Rd.)
St Kathryn's Pl. RM14: Upm 33Sd 78
St Keverne Rd. SE9 63Nc 138
St Kilda Rd. BR6: Orp 74Vc 161
W13 46Ja 86
St Kilda's Rd. CM15: B'wood 17Xd 40
HA1: Harr 30Ga 46
N16 32Tb 71
St Kitts Ter. SE19 64Ub 135
St Laurence Cl. BR5: St P 69Zc 139
NW6 39Za 68
UB8: Cowl 43L 83
St Laurence Way SL1: Slou 8L 81
St Lawrence Bus. Cen. TW13: Felt 61X 129
St Lawrence Cl. HA8: Edg 24Pa 47
HP3: Bov 9C 2
WD5: Ab L 2U 12
St Lawrence Cotts. E14 46Ec 92
(off St Lawrence St.)
St Lawrence Ct. GU24: Chob 3J 167
N1 38Tb 71
WD5: Ab L 2U 12
St Lawrence Dr. HA5: Eastc 29X 45
St Lawrence Ho. GU24: Chob 3J 167
(off Bagshot Rd.)
SE1 3J 231
St Lawrence Rd. RM14: Upm 33Sd 78
St Lawrence St. E14 46Ec 92
St Lawrence's Way RH2: Reig 6J 207
St Lawrence Ter. W10 43Ab 88
St Lawrence Way AL2: Brick W 2Ba 13
CR3: Cat'm 95Sb 197
SW9 53Qb 112
St Leger Ct. NW6 38Za 68
(off Coverdale Rd.)
St Leonard M. N1 1H 219
St Leonard's Av. E4 23Fc 53
HA3: Kenton 29La 46
SL4: Wind 4G 102
St Leonards Cl. DA16: Well 55Wc 117
RM17: Grays 51Be 121
WD23: Bush 14Aa 27
St Leonards Ct. N1 3G 219
SW14 55Sa 109
St Leonard's Gdns. IG1: Ilf 36Sc 74
TW5: Hest 52Aa 107
ST LEONARDS HAMLET 32Kd 77
St Leonard's Hill SL4: Wind 6B 102
St Leonard's Ri. BR6: Orp 77Uc 160
St Leonard's Rd. CR0: Wadd 76Rb 157
E14 43Dc 92
(not continuous)
KT6: Surb 71Ma 153
KT7: T Ditt 72Ja 152
KT10: Clay 79Ha 152
KT18: Tatt C 91Ya 194
NW10 42Ta 87
SL4: Wind 5E 102
(Imperial Rd.)
SL4: Wind 4G 102
(Osborne M.)
SL4: Wink 8A 102
SW14 55Ra 109
W13 45La 86
(not continuous)
St Leonards Sq. KT6: Surb 71Ma 153
NW5 37Jb 70
St Leonard's St. E3 41Dc 92
St Leonard's Ter. SW3 7F 227 (50Hb 89)
St Leonards Wlk. SL0: Rich P 48H 83
SW16 66Pb 134
St Leonards Way RM11: Horn 33Kd 77
St Loo Av. SW3 51Gb 111
St Loo Ct. SW3 51Gb 111
(off St Loo Av.)
St Louis Cl. EN6: Pot B 5Eb 17
St Louis Rd. SE27 63Tb 135
St Loy's Rd. N17 26Ub 51
St Lucia Dr. E15 39Hc 73
St Luke Cl. UB8: Cowl 44M 83
ST LUKE'S 5E 218 (42Sb 91)
St Luke's Av. EN2: Enf 10Tb 19
IG1: Ilf 36Rc 74
SW4 56Mb 112
St Luke's Cl. BR8: Swan 68Fd 140
DA2: Daren 64Ud 142
EC1 5E 218 (42Sb 91)
SE25 72Xb 157
St Lukes Ct. E10 31Dc 72
(off Capworth St.)
GU21: Wok 86E 168
W11 44Bb 89
(off St Luke's Rd.)
St Luke's Est. EC1 4F 219 (41Tb 91)
St Luke's M. W11 44Bb 89
St Luke's Pas. KT2: King T 67Pa 131
St Luke's Path IG1: Ilf 36Rc 74
St Luke's Rd. CR3: Whyt 90Vb 177
SL4: Old Win 8L 103
UB10: Uxb 38N 63
W11 43Bb 89
St Luke's Sq. E16 44Hc 93
St Luke's St. SW3 7E 226 (50Gb 89)
St Luke's Yd. W9 40Bb 69
(not continuous)
St Magnus Ct. HP3: Hem H 4B 4
St Malo Av. N9 20Yb 34
St Margaret Dr. KT18: Eps 86Sa 173
ST MARGARETS
DA4 66Ud 142
TW1 58Ka 108
St Margarets IG11: Bark 39Tc 74
KT2: King T 64Sa 131
St Margarets Av. DA15: Sidc 62Tc 138
HA2: Harr 34Ea 66
N15 28Rb 51
N20 18Eb 31
SM3: Cheam 76Ab 154
St Margarets Av. SS17: Stan H 3L 101
TN16: Big H 88Rc 180
TW15: Ashf 64R 128
UB8: Hil 42Q 84
St Margarets Bus. Cen.
TW1: Twick 58Ka 108
St Margarets Cl. BR6: Chels 77Xc 161
DA2: Dart 61Td 142
EC2 2F 225 (44Tb 91)
HP4: Berk 2A 2
SL0: Iver H 40F 62
St Margarets Ct. HA8: Edg 22Ra 47
N11 21Jb 50
SE1 7F 225 (46Sb 91)
SL0: Iver H 40F 62
SW15 56Xa 110
St Margaret's Cres. DA12: Grav'nd 2G 144
SW15 57Xa 110
St Margaret's Dr. TW1: Twick 57Ka 108
St Margarets Ga. SL0: Iver H 40F 62
St Margaret's Gro. E11 34Hc 73
SE18 51Sc 116
TW1: Twick 58Ja 108
St Margaret's Ho. NW1 2D 216
(off Polygon Rd.)
St Margaret's La. W8 48Db 89
St Margarets M. KT2: King T 64Sa 131
St Margaret's Pas. SE13 55Gc 115
(not continuous)
St Margarets Path SE18 50Sc 94
St Margarets Rd. CR5: Coul 93Kb 196
DA2: Grn St 66Ud 142
DA4: S Dar 66Ud 142
DA11: Nflt 10A 122
E12 33Lc 73
HA4: Ruis 30T 44
HA8: Edg 22Ra 47
N17 27Ub 51
NW10 41Ya 88
SE4 56Bc 114
(not continuous)
TW1: Twick 58Ka 108
TW7: Isle 56Ka 108
W7 47Ga 86
ST MARGARETS RDBT. 58Ka 108
St Margaret's Sports Cen. 18Da 27
St Margaret's Ter. SE18 50Sc 94
St Margaret St. SW1 2F 229 (47Nb 90)
St Margarets Way HP2: Hem H 2C 4
St Margaret Way SL1: Slou 7D 80
St Mark's Av. DA11: Nflt 9A 122
St Marks Cl. AL4: Col H 4M 7
EN5: New Bar 13Db 31
HA1: Harr 31Ka 66
SE10 52Ec 114
SW6 53Cb 111
St Marks Ct. GU22: Wok 91A 188
(off Brooklyn Rd.)
NW8 2A 214
W7 47Ga 86
(off Lwr. Boston Rd.)
St Mark's Cres. NW1 39Jb 70
St Mark's Ga. E9 38Bc 72
St Mark's Gro. SW10 52Db 111
St Mark's Hill KT6: Surb 72Ma 153
St Marks Ho. SE17 51Tb 113
(off Lytham St.)
St Marks Ind. Est. E16 46Mc 93
St Marks Pl. RM10: Dag 37Cd 76
SL4: Wind 4G 102
SW19 65Bb 133
W11 44Ab 88
St Mark's Ri. E8 36Vb 71
St Marks Rd. BR2: Brom 69Jc 137
CR4: Mitc 68Hb 133
EN1: Enf 16Vb 33
KT18: Tatt C 90Ya 174
SE25 70Wb 135
SL4: Wind 4G 102
TW11: Tedd 66Ka 130
W5 46Na 87
W7 47Ga 86
W10 43Za 88
W11 44Ab 88
St Mark's Sq. NW1 39Jb 70
St Mark St. E1 44Vb 91
St Mark's Vs. N4 33Pb 70
(off Moray Rd.)
St Martha's Av. GU22: Wok 93B 188
St Martin Cl. UB8: Cowl 44M 83
St Martin-in-the-Fields Church 5F 223
St Martins HA6: Nwood 22T 44
St Martin's Almshouses NW1 39Lb 70
St Martin's App. HA4: Ruis 31U 64
St Martin's Av. E6 40Mc 73
KT18: Eps 86Ua 174
St Martins Cl. CM13: Hut 19Ee 41
DA18: Erith 47Zc 95
EN1: Enf 11Xb 33
KT17: Eps 85Va 174
KT24: E Hor 100U 190
NW1 39Lb 70
UB7: W Dray 48M 83
WD19: Wat 21Y 45
St Martins Ct. EC4 2D 224
KT24: E Hor 100U 190
N1 39Ub 71
(off De Beauvoir Est.)
TW15: Ashf 64L 127
WC2 4F 223 (45Nb 90)
St Martin's Courtyard WC2 4F 223
St Martins Dr. DA4: Eyns 77Md 163
KT12: Walt T 76Y 151
St Martins Est. SW2 60Qb 112
St Martin's Ho. NW1 3D 216
(off Polygon Rd.)
St Martin's La. BR3: Beck 71Dc 158
WC2 4F 223 (45Nb 90)
St Martin's Le-Grand
EC1 2D 224 (44Sb 91)
St Martins Mdw. TN16: Bras 95Yc 201
St Martins M. GU22: Pyr 88J 169
St Martin's Pl. WC2 5F 223 (45Nb 90)
St Martin's Rd. DA1: Dart 58Pd 119
N9 19Xb 33
SW9 54Pb 112
UB7: W Dray 48L 83
St Martin's St. WC2 5E 222 (45Mb 90)
(not continuous)
St Martin's Theatre 4F 223
St Martins Way SW17 62Eb 133
St Mary Abbot's Ct. W14 48Bb 89
(off Warwick Gdns.)
St Mary Abbot's Pl. W8 48Bb 89
St Mary Abbot's Ter. W14 48Bb 89
St Mary at Hill EC3 5H 225 (45Ub 91)
St Mary Av. SM6: Wall 76Jb 156
St Mary Axe EC3 3H 225 (44Ub 91)
St Marychurch St. SE16 47Yb 92
ST MARY CRAY 70Yc 139
St Mary Graces Ct. E1 45Vb 91
St Marylebone Cl. NW10 39Ua 68
St Marylebone Crematorium
N2 27Db 49
St Mary le-Park Ct. SW11 52Gb 111
(off Parkgate Rd.)
St Mary Newington Cl. SE17 7J 231
St Mary Rd. E17 28Cc 52
St Marys IG11: Bark 39Tc 74
KT13: Weyb 76T 150
St Mary's App. E12 36Pc 74
St Mary's Av. BR2: Brom 69Gc 137
CM15: Shenf 15Ce 41
E11 31Kc 73
HA6: Nwood 22U 44
N3 26Ab 48
TW11: Tedd 65Ha 130
TW19: Stanw 59M 105
St Mary's Av. Central UB2: S'hall 49Da 85
St Mary's Av. Nth. UB2: S'hall 49Da 85
St Mary's Av. Sth. UB2: S'hall 49Da 85
St Mary's Chu. Rd. TN14: Sund 97Bd 201
St Marys Cl. BR5: St P 68Xc 139
DA12: Grav'nd 1E 144
HP1: Hem H 1L 3
IG10: Lough 14Nc 36
KT9: Chess 80Pa 153
KT17: Ewe 80Va 154
KT22: Fet 95Fa 192
N17 25Wb 51
RH8: Oxt 1J 211
RM17: Grays 51Fe 121
TN15: Plat 92Ee 205
TW16: Sun 70W 128
TW19: Stanw 59M 105
UB9: Hare 27K 43
WD18: Wat 14Y 27
(off George St.)
St Mary's Copse KT4: Wor Pk 75Ua 154
St Marys Ct. E3 41Dc 92
(off Bow Rd.)
E6 42Pc 94
EN6: Pot B 4Db 17
HP2: Hem H 1M 3
SE7 52Mc 115
SM6: Wall 77Lb 156
TN16: Westrm 98Tc 200
W5 47Ma 87
W6 48Va 88
WD3: Rick 18N 25
St Mary's Cres. NW4 27Xa 48
TW7: Isle 52Fa 108
TW19: Stanw 59M 105
UB3: Hayes 45V 84
St Mary's Dr. TN13: Riv 95Gd 202
TW14: Bedf 59S 106
St Mary's Est. SE16 47Yb 92
(off Elephant La.)
St Mary's Flats NW1 3D 216
St Marys Gdn. GU21: Worp 9J 187
St Mary's Gdns. SE11 5A 230 (49Qb 90)
St Mary's Ga. W8 48Db 89
St Mary's Grn. N2 26Eb 49
TN16: Big H 90Lc 179
St Mary's Gro. N1 37Rb 71
SW13 55Xa 110
TN16: Big H 90Lc 179
TW9: Rich 56Pa 109
W4 51Ra 109
St Mary's Hill SL5: S'hill 2A 146
St Mary's Ho. N1 39Rb 71
(off St Mary's Path)
St Mary's La. CM13: W H'dn 31De 79
RM14: Upm 33Qd 77
St Mary's Mans. W2 7B 214 (43Fb 89)
St Marys M. NW6 38Db 69
TW10: Ham 61La 130
St Mary's Mt. CR3: Cat'm 96Vb 197
St Mary's Path E1 44Wb 91
(off White Church La.)
N1 39Rb 71
St Mary's Pl. SE9 58Pc 116
W5 47Ma 87
W8 48Db 89
ST MARYS PLATT 92Ee 205
St Marys Rd. BR8: Swan 82Td 184
CR2: Sande 82Tb 177
DA5: Bexl 60Ed 118
DA9: Ghithe 57Ud 120
E10 34Ec 72
E13 40Kc 73
EN4: E Barn 17Hb 31
EN8: Chesh 1Yb 20
GU21: Wok 9N 167
HP2: Hem H 1M 3
IG1: Ilf 33Sc 74
KT4: Wor Pk 75Ua 154
KT6: Surb 73La 152
(St Chads Cl.)
KT6: Surb 72Ma 153
(Victoria Rd.)
KT8: E Mos 71Fa 152
KT13: Weyb 77T 150
KT22: Lea 94Ka 192
N8 28Nb 50
N9 18Xb 33
(not continuous)
NW10 39Ua 68
NW11 31Ab 68
RH2: Reig 7K 207
RM16: Grays 8D 100
SE15 53Yb 114
SE25 69Ub 135
SL3: L'ly 46A 82
SL5: Asc 3A 146
SW19 64Ab 132
TN15: Wro 89Ce 185
UB3: Hayes 45V 84
UB9: Den 30H 43
UB9: Hare 27K 43
W5 47Ma 87
WD18: Wat 14X 27
St Mary's Sq. W2 7B 214 (43Fb 89)
W5 47Ma 87
St Mary's Ter. W2 7A 214 (43Fb 89)
St Mary's Twr. EC1 6E 218
St Mary St. SE18 49Pc 94
St Mary's University College 62Ha 130

St Mary's University College Sports Cen. 63Ha 130
St Mary's Vw. HA3: Kenton 29La 46
WD18: Wat 14Y 27
(off King St.)
St Mary's Wlk. RH1: Blet 5K 209
SE11 5A 230 (49Qb 90)
UB3: Hayes 45V 84
St Mary's Way DA3: Lfield 69Ae 143
IG7: Chig 22Qc 54
SL9: Chal P 26A 42
St Matthew Cl. UB8: Cowl 44M 83
St Matthew's Av. KT6: Surb 74Na 153
St Matthews Cl. RM13: Rain 38Jd 76
WD19: Wat 16Z 27
St Matthews Ct. E10 31Dc 72
N10 26Jb 50
SE1 4D 230
TW15: Ashf 63Q 128
(off Feltham Rd.)
St Matthews Dr. BR1: Brom 69Pc 138
St Matthews Ho. *SE17* 51Tb 113
(off Phelp St.)
St Matthew's Lodge NW1 1C 216
St Matthew's Rd. RH1: Redh 5P 207
SW2 56Pb 112
W5 46Na 87
St Matthew's Row E2 41Wb 91
St Matthew St. SW1 4D 228 (48Mb 90)
St Matthias Cl. NW9 29Va 48
St Maur Rd. SW6 53Bb 111
St Mawes Cl. WD3: Crox G 14R 26
St Mellion Cl. SE28 44Zc 95
St Merryn Cl. SE18 52Tc 116
St Merryn Ct. BR3: Beck 66Cc 136
St Michaels AL3: St A 2P 5
RH8: Limp 2L 211
St Michael's All. EC3 3G 225 (44Tb 91)
St Michaels Av. HA9: Wemb 37Qa 67
HP3: Hem H 4B 4
N9 17Yb 34
St Michaels Cl. BR1: Brom 69Nc 138
DA18: Erith 47Zc 95
E16 43Mc 93
KT4: Wor Pk 75Va 154
KT12: Walt T 75Y 151
N3 26Bb 49
N12 22Gb 49
RM15: Avel 45Sd 98
St Michaels Ct. *CR0: C'don* 74Sb 157
(off Station Rd.)
E14 43Ec 92
(off St Leonard's Rd.)
KT13: Weyb 78S 150
(off Pine Gro.)
SE1 2E 230
SL2: Slou 2B 80
St Michael's Cres. HA5: Pinn 30Aa 45
St Michaels Dr. TN14: Otf 88Md 183
WD25: Wat 5X 13
St Michael's Flats NW1 2D 216
St Michael's Gdns. W10 43Ab 88
St Michael's M. SW1 6H 227 (49Jb 90)
St Michael's Pde.
WD24: Wat 10X 13
St Michael's Ri. DA16: Well 53Xc 117
St Michael's Rd. CR0: C'don 74Sb 157
CR3: Cat'm 94Tb 197
DA16: Well 55Xc 117
GU21: Wok 86F 168
NW2 35Ya 68
RM16: Grays 10D 100
SM6: Wall 79Lb 156
SW9 54Pb 112
TW15: Ashf 64Q 128
St Michael's St. AL3: St A 2P 5
W2 2C 220 (44Fb 89)
St Michaels Ter. *N6* 32Jb 70
(off South Gro.)
N22 25Nb 50
St Michaels Way EN6: Pot B 2Db 17
St Mildred's Ct. EC2 3F 225 (44Tb 91)
St Mildreds Rd. SE6 59Gc 115
SE12 59Gc 115
St Mirren Ct. EN5: New Bar 15Eb 31
St Monica's Rd.
KT20: Kgswd 93Bb 195
St Nazaire Cl. TW20: Egh 64E 126
St Neots Cl. WD6: Bore 10Qa 15
St Neot's Rd. RM3: Rom 24Pd 57
St Nicholas Av. KT23: Bookh 97Da 191
RM12: Horn 34Jd 76
St Nicholas Cen. SM1: Sutt 78Db 155
St Nicholas Cl. UB8: Cowl 44M 83
WD6: E'tree 16Ma 29
St Nicholas Ct. *KT1: King T* 70Na 131
(off Surbiton Rd.)
TN13: S'oaks 97Kd 203
(off Lime Tree Wlk.)
St Nicholas Cres. GU22: Pyr 88J 169
St Nicholas Dr. TN13: S'oaks 98Kd 203
TW17: Shep 73Q 150
St Nicholas' Flats NW1 2D 216
St Nicholas Glebe SW17 64Jb 134
St Nicholas Gro. CM13: Ingve 22Ee 59
St Nicholas Hill KT22: Lea 94Ka 192
St Nicholas Ho. *SE8* 51Cc 114
(off Deptford Grn.)
St Nicholas Ho's. EN2: Enf 7Jb 18
St Nicholas M. KT7: T Ditt 72Ha 152
St Nicholas Mt. HP1: Hem H 2H 3
St Nicholas Pl. IG10: Lough 14Qc 36
St Nicholas Rd. KT7: T Ditt 72Ha 152
SE18 50Vc 95
SM1: Sutt 78Db 155
St Nicholas St. SE8 53Bc 114
St Nicholas Way SM1: Sutt 77Db 155
St Nicolas La. BR7: Chst 67Nc 138
St Ninian's Ct. N20 20Hb 31
St Norbert Grn. SE4 56Ac 114
St Norbert Rd. SE4 57Zb 114
St Normans Way KT17: Ewe 82Wa 174
St Olaf Ho. SE1 6G 225
St Olaf's Rd. SW6 52Ab 110
St Olaf Stairs SE1 6G 225
St Olaves Cl. TW18: Staines 66H 127
St Olave's Ct. EC2 3F 225 (44Tb 91)
St Olave's Est. SE1 1J 231 (47Ub 91)
St Olave's Gdns. SE11 5K 229 (49Qb 90)
St Olaves Ho. SE11 5K 229
St Olave's Mans. SE11 5K 229
St Olave's Rd. E6 39Qc 74
St Olaves Wlk. SW16 68Lb 134
St Olav's Sq. SE16 47Yb 92
St Onge Pde. *EN1: Enf* 13Tb 33
(off Southbury Rd.)
St Oswald's Pl. SE11 7H 229 (50Pb 90)
St Oswald's Rd. SW16 67Rb 135
St Oswalds Studios *SW6* 51Cb 111
(off Sedlescombe Rd.)
St Oswulf St. SW1 6E 228 (49Mb 90)
St Owen Ho. SE1 3J 231
ST PANCRAS 4F 217 (41Nb 90)
St Pancras Commercial Cen. *NW1* 39Lb 70
(off Pratt St.)
St Pancras Ct. N2 26Fb 49
St Pancras Way NW1 1D 216 (38Lb 70)
St Patrick's Ct. IG8: Wfd G 24Gc 53
St Patrick's Gdns. DA12: Grav'nd 2F 144
St Patrick's Pl. RM16: Grays 9D 100
St Paul Cl. UB8: Cowl 43M 83
St Paulinus Ct. *DA1: Cray* 56Gd 118
(off Manor Rd.)
St Paul's All. *EC4* 3C 224
(off St Paul's Chyd.)
St Pauls Av. HA3: Kenton 28Pa 47
NW2 37Xa 68
SE16 46Zb 92
SL2: Slou 5K 81
St Paul's Bldgs. EC1 5C 218
St Paul's Cathedral 3D 224 (44Sb 91)
St Paul's Chyd. EC4 3C 224 (44Rb 91)
St Pauls Cl. DA10: Swans 59Ae 121
KT9: Chess 77Ma 153
KT15: Add 78J 149
RM15: Avel 45Sd 98
SE7 50Mc 93
SM5: Cars 74Gb 155
TW3: Houn 54Aa 107
TW15: Ashf 64S 128
UB3: Harl 50T 84
W5 47Pa 87
WD6: Bore 15Sa 29
St Pauls Ct. SW4 57Mb 112
TW4: Houn 55Aa 107
WD4: Bucks 5M 11
WD4: Chfd 5M 11
St Pauls Courtyard *SE8* 52Cc 114
(off Crossfield St.)
ST PAUL'S CRAY 68Xc 139
St Paul's Cray Rd. BR7: Chst 67Tc 138
St Paul's Cres. NW1 38Mb 70
(not continuous)
St Paul's Dr. E15 36Fc 73
St Paul's M. NW1 38Mb 70
St Pauls Pl. AL1: St A 2E 6
N1 37Tb 71
RM15: Avel 45Sd 98
St Paul's Ri. N13 23Rb 51
St Paul's Rd. CR7: Thor H 69Sb 135
DA8: Erith 52Ed 118
GU22: Wok 89C 168
HP2: Hem H 1M 3
IG11: Bark 39Sc 74
N1 37Rb 71
N17 24Wb 51
TW8: Bford 51Ma 109
TW9: Rich 55Pa 109
TW18: Staines 64F 126
St Paul's Shrubbery N1 37Tb 71
St Paul's Sq. BR2: Brom 68Hc 137
St Paul's Studios *W14* 50Ab 88
(off Talgarth Rd.)
St Pauls Ter. SE17 51Rb 113
St Paul St. N1 1D 218 (39Sb 71)
(not continuous)
St Pauls Vw. Apartments EC1 4K 217
St Paul's Wlk. KT2: King T 66Qa 131
St Pauls Way E3 43Bc 92
EN9: Walt A 5Fc 21
N3 24Db 49
WD24: Wat 12Y 27
St Paul's Wood Hill BR5: St P 68Uc 138
St Peter Claver Ct. *BR3: Beck* 67Dc 136
(off Albemarle Rd.)
St Peters HP8: Chal G 19C 24
KT16: Chert 76E 148
St Peter's All. EC3 3G 225
St Peters Av. E2 40Wb 71
E17 28Gc 53
N18 21Wb 51
TN16: Big H 88Rc 180
St Petersburgh M. W2 45Db 89
St Petersburgh Pl. W2 45Db 89
St Peter's Cen. *E1* 46Xb 91
(off Reardon St.)
St Peter's Chu. Ct. N1 1C 218
St Peters Cl. AL1: St A 1B 6
BR7: Chst 66Tc 138
DA10: Swans 59Be 121
E2 40Wb 71
EN5: Barn 15Xa 30
GU22: Wok 92E 188
HA4: Ruis 33Z 65
IG2: Ilf 28Uc 54
SL1: Burn 2A 80
SL4: Old Win 7L 103
SL9: Chal P 25A 42
SW17 61Gb 133
TW18: Staines 65H 127
WD3: Rick 18K 25
WD23: B Hea 18Fa 28
St Peters Ct. *E1* 42Yb 92
(off Cephas St.)
KT8: W Mole 70Ca 129
NW4 29Ya 48
SE12 57Hc 115
SL9: Chal P 25A 42
WC1 4G 217
St Peter's Gdns. SE27 62Qb 134
St Peter's Gro. W6 49Wa 88
St Peters Ho. SE17 51Tb 113
WC1 4G 217
St Peter's La. BR5: St P 68Wc 139
St Peters M. AL1: St A 1B 6
N4 29Rb 51
N8 29Qb 50
St Peter's Path E17 27Gc 53
St Peters Pl. W9 42Db 89
St Peters Rd. AL1: St A 2C 6
CM14: W'ley 21Xd 58
CR0: C'don 77Tb 157
GU22: Wok 93D 188
KT1: King T 68Qa 131
KT8: W Mole 70Ca 129
N9 18Xb 33
RM16: Grays 9D 100
SL4: Old Win 7L 103
St Peters Rd. TW1: Twick 57Ka 108
UB1: S'hall 43Ca 85
UB8: Cowl 43M 83
W6 50Wa 88
St Peter's Sq. E2 40Wb 71
W6 49Va 88
St Peter's St. AL1: St A 2B 6
(not continuous)
CR2: S Croy 78Tb 157
N1 1C 218 (39Rb 71)
St Peter's St. M. N1 1C 218
St Peter's Ter. SW6 52Bb 111
St Peter's Vs. W6 49Wa 88
St Peters Way KT15: Add 77F 148
KT16: Chert 77F 148
N1 38Ub 71
UB3: Harl 50T 84
W5 43Ma 87
WD3: Chor 14D 24
St Peter's Wharf W4 50Wa 88
St Philip Ho. WC1 4K 217
St Philip's Av. KT4: Wor Pk 75Xa 154
St Philip's Ga. KT4: Wor Pk 75Xa 154
St Philip Sq. SW8 54Kb 112
St Philips Rd. E8 37Wb 71
KT6: Surb 72Ma 153
St Philip St. SW8 54Kb 112
St Philip's Way N1 39Sb 71
St Pinnock Av.
TW18: Staines 67J 127
St Quentin Ho. SW18 58Fb 111
St Quentin Rd. DA16: Well 55Vc 117
St Quintin Av. W10 43Ya 88
St Quintin Ct. W10 43Ya 88
St Quintin Gdns. W10 43Ya 88
St Quintin Rd. E13 41Kc 93
St Raphaels Ct. *AL1: St A* 1C 6
(off Avenue Rd.)
St Raphael's Way NW10 36Sa 67
St Regis Cl. N10 26Kb 50
St Regis Hgts. NW3 34Db 69
St Richard's Ho. NW1 3D 216
St Ronan's Cl. EN4: Had W 10Fb 17
St Ronan's Cres. IG8: Wfd G 24Jc 53
St Ronans Vw. DA1: Dart 59Pd 119
St Rule St. SW8 54Lb 112
St Saviours Ct. *CR8: Purl* 85Pb 176
(off OLd Lodge La.)
HA1: Harr 29Ga 46
N22 26Mb 50
St Saviour's Est. SE1 3K 231 (47Vb 91)
St Saviour's Rd. CR0: C'don 72Rb 157
SW2 57Pb 112
St Saviours Vw. *AL1: St A* 1D 6
(off Lemsford Rd.)
St Saviours Wlk. *DA1: Dart* 58Nd 119
(off Bullace La.)
St Saviour's Wharf *SE1* 47Vb 91
(off Mill St.)
SE1 1K 231
(off Shad Thames)
Saints Cl. SE27 63Rb 135
Saints Dr. E7 36Mc 73
St Silas Pl. NW5 37Jb 70
St Simon's Av. SW15 57Ya 110
Saints M. CR4: Mitc 69Gb 133
ST STEPHENS 4A 6
St Stephen's Av. AL3: St A 4P 5
E17 29Ec 52
KT21: Asht 88Na 173
W12 46Xa 88
(not continuous)
W13 44Ka 86
St Stephens Cl. AL3: St A 5P 5
E17 29Dc 52
NW5 36Hb 69
(off Malden Rd.)
NW8 1E 214 (39Gb 69)
UB1: S'hall 43Ca 85
St Stephens Ct. *EN1: Enf* 16Ub 33
(off Park Av.)
N8 30Pb 50
RH9: S God 10C 210
(off Oaklands)
W13 44Ka 86
St Stephen's Cres. CM13: B'wood 21Ce 59
CR7: Thor H 69Qb 134
W2 44Cb 89
St Stephen's Gdns. SW15 57Bb 111
TW1: Twick 58La 108
W2 44Cb 89
(not continuous)
St Stephens Gro. SE13 55Ec 114
St Stephen's Hill AL1: St A 4A 6
St Stephens Ho. *SE17* 51Tb 113
(off Lytham St.)
St Stephen's M. W2 43Cb 89
St Stephens Pde. E7 38Lc 73
St Stephen's Pas. TW1: Twick 58La 108
St Stephens Rd. E3 39Ac 72
E6 38Lc 73
E17 29Dc 52
EN3: Enf W 9Zb 20
EN5: Barn 15Za 30
TW3: Houn 58Ca 107
UB7: Yiew 46M 83
W13 44Ka 86
St Stephen's Row EC4 3F 225
St Stephen's Ter. SW8 52Pb 112
St Stephen's Wlk. SW7 5A 226
Saint's Wlk. RM16: Grays 9E 100
St Swithins La. EC4 4F 225 (45Tb 91)
St Swithun's Rd. SE13 58Fc 115
St Teresa Wlk. RM16: Grays 9D 100
St Theresa Cl. KT18: Eps 86Sa 173
St Theresa Ct. E4 17Fc 35
St Theresa's Cl. E9 35Cc 72
St Theresa's Rd. TW14: Felt 56V 106
St Thomas' Almshouses
DA11: Grav'nd 10C 122
St Thomas Cl. GU21: Wok 9N 167
KT6: Surb 74Pa 153
St Thomas Ct. DA5: Bexl 59Cd 118
E10 31Dc 72
(off Lake Rd.)
HA5: Pinn 25Aa 45
NW1 38Lb 70
(off Wrotham Rd.)
St Thomas Dr. BR5: Farnb 74Sc 160
HA5: Pinn 25Aa 45
St Thomas Gdns. IG1: Ilf 37Sc 74
St Thomas Ho. *E1* 44Zb 92
(off W. Arbour St.)
St Thomas M. SW18 57Cb 111
St Thomas Rd. CM14: B'wood 19Zd 41
DA11: Nflt 1A 144
DA17: Belv 47Ed 96
E16 44Jc 93
N14 17Mb 32
W4 51Sa 109
St Thomas's Av. DA11: Grav'nd 10D 122
St Thomas's Cl. EN9: Walt A 5Kc 21
St Thomas's Gdns. NW5 37Jb 70
St Thomas's Pl. E9 38Yb 72
RM17: Grays 51De 121
St Thomas's Rd. N4 33Qb 70
NW10 39Ua 68
St Thomas's Sq. E9 38Yb 72
St Thomas St. SE1 7F 225 (46Tb 91)
St Thomas's Way SW6 52Bb 111
St Thomas Wlk. SL3: Coln 52F 104
St Timothys M. BR1: Brom 67Kc 137
St Ursula Gro. HA5: Pinn 29Z 45
St Ursula Rd. UB1: S'hall 44Ca 85
St Vincent Cl. SE27 64Rb 135
St Vincent De Paul Ho. *E1* 43Yb 92
(off Jubilee St.)
St Vincent Dr. AL1: St A 5E 6
St Vincent Ho. SE1 3K 231
St Vincent Rd. KT12: Walt T 76X 151
TW2: Whitt 58Ea 108
St Vincents Av. DA1: Dart 57Qd 119
St Vincent's Cotts. *WD18: Wat* 14X 27
(off Marlborough Rd.)
ST VINCENT'S HAMLET 18Rd 39
St Vincent's La. NW7 21Ya 48
St Vincents Rd. DA1: Dart 58Qd 119
St Vincent St. W1 1J 221 (43Jb 90)
St Vincents Vs. DA1: Dart 58Pd 119
St Vincents Way EN6: Pot B 6Eb 17
St Wilfrid's Cl. EN4: E Barn 15Gb 31
St Wilfrid's Rd. EN4: E Barn 15Fb 31
St Williams Ct. N1 38Nb 70
St Winefride's Av. E12 36Pc 74
St Winifreds CR8: Kenley 87Sb 177
St Winifred's Cl. IG7: Chig 22Sc 54
St Winifred's Rd. TN16: Big H 90Pc 180
TW11: Tedd 65Ka 130
St Yon Ct. AL4: St A 2J 7
Sakura Dr. N22 25Mb 50
Saladin Dr. RM19: Purf 49Qd 97
Sala Ho. SE3 56Kc 115
Salamanca Pl. SE1 6H 229 (49Pb 90)
Salamanca Sq. SE1 6H 229
Salamanca St. SE1 6H 229 (49Pb 90)
SE11 6H 229 (49Pb 90)
Salamander Cl. KT2: King T 64La 130
Salamander Quay KT1: Hamp W 67Ma 131
UB9: Hare 24J 43
Salamons Way RM13: Rain 44Gd 96
Salcombe Dr. RM6: Chad H 30Bd 55
SM4: Mord 74Za 154
Salcombe Gdns. NW7 23Ya 48
Salcombe Pk. IG10: Lough 15Mc 35
Salcombe Rd. E17 31Bc 72
N16 36Ub 71
TW15: Ashf 62N 127
Salcombe Vs. TW10: Rich 57Na 109
Salcombe Way HA4: Ruis 33W 64
UB4: Hayes 41T 84
Salcot Cres. CR0: New Ad 82Ec 178
Salcote Rd. DA12: Grav'nd 4G 144
Salcott Rd. CR0: Bedd 76Nb 156
SW11 57Gb 111
Salehurst Cl. HA3: Kenton 29Na 47
Salehurst Rd. SE4 58Bc 114
Salem Pl. CR0: C'don 76Sb 157
DA11: Nflt 59Fe 121
Salem Rd. W2 45Db 89
Salento Cl. N3 24Cb 49
Sale Pl. W2 1D 220 (43Gb 89)
Salesian Gdns. KT16: Chert 74J 149
Sale St. E2 42Wb 91
Salford Ho. *E14* 49Ec 92
(off Seyssel St.)
Salford Rd. SW2 60Mb 112
Salhouse Cl. SE28 44Yc 95
Salisbury Av. AL1: St A 1F 6
BR8: Swan 70Jd 140
IG11: Bark 38Tc 74
N3 27Bb 49
SL2: Slou 2G 80
SM1: Sutt 79Bb 155
SS17: Stan H 2M 101
Salisbury Cl. EN6: Pot B 4Eb 17
KT4: Wor Pk 76Va 154
RM14: Upm 33Ud 78
SE17 5F 231 (49Tb 91)
Salisbury Ct. *E9* 36Ac 72
(off Mabley St.)
EC4 3B 224 (44Rb 91)
EN2: Enf 14Tb 33
(off London Rd.)
HA8: Edg 21Pa 47
SE16 48Wb 91
(off Stork's Rd.)
SM5: Cars 78Hb 155
UB5: N'olt 36Da 65
(off Newmarket Av.)
Salisbury Cres. EN8: Chesh 4Zb 20
Salisbury Gdns. IG9: Buck H 19Mc 35
SW19 66Ab 132
Salisbury Hall Gdns. E4 23Cc 52
Salisbury Ho. AL3: St A 1A 6
E14 44Dc 92
(off Hobday St.)
EC2 1G 225
HA7: Stan 23Ja 46
N1 39Rb 71
(off St Mary's Path)
SM6: Wall 78Kb 156
SW1 7E 228
SW9 52Qb 112
(off Cranmer Rd.)
Salisbury Mans. N15 29Rb 51
Salisbury M. SW6 52Bb 111
Salisbury Pas. *SW6* 52Bb 111
(off Dawes Rd.)
Salisbury Pavement *SW6* 52Bb 111
(off Dawes Rd.)
Salisbury Pl. KT14: W Byf 83L 169
SW9 52Rb 113
W1 7F 215 (43Hb 89)
Salisbury Prom. N8 29Rb 51
Salisbury Rd. BR2: Brom 71Nc 160
DA2: Dart 60Sd 120
DA5: Bexl 60Cd 118
DA11: Grav'nd 10B 122
Salisbury Rd. E4 20Cc 34
E7 37Jc 73
E10 33Ec 72
E12 36Mc 73
E17 29Ec 52
EN3: Enf L 9Bc 20
EN5: Barn 13Ab 30
GU22: Wok 91A 188
HA1: Harr 29Fa 46
HA5: Eastc 28W 44
IG3: Ilf 33Uc 74
KT3: N Mald 69Ta 131
KT4: Wor Pk 77Ta 153
N4 29Rb 51
N22 25Rb 51
RH9: G'stone 3A 210
RM2: Rom 29Kd 57
RM10: Dag 37Dd 76
RM17: Grays 51Ee 121
SE25 72Wb 157
SM5: Cars 79Hb 155
SM7: Bans 86Db 175
SW19 66Ab 132
TW4: Houn 55Y 107
TW6: H'row A 58S 106
(not continuous)
TW9: Rich 56Na 109
TW13: Felt 60Y 107
UB2: S'hall 49Aa 85
UB8: Uxb 40K 63
W13 47Ka 86
WD24: Wat 10X 13
Salisbury Sq. EC4 3A 224 (44Qb 90)
Salisbury St. NW8 6C 214 (42Gb 89)
W3 47Sa 87
Salisbury Ter. SE15 55Yb 114
Salisbury Wlk. N19 33Lb 70
Salix Cl. KT22: Fet 95Da 191
TW16: Sun 66X 129
Salix Ct. N3 23Cb 49
Salix La. IG8: Wfd G 25Nc 54
Salix Rd. RM17: Grays 51Fe 121
Salliesfield TW2: Whitt 58Fa 108
Sallows Shaw DA13: Sole S 10E 144
Sally Murray Cl. E12 35Qc 74
Salmen Rd. E13 40Hc 73
Salmond Cl. HA7: Stan 23Ja 46
Salmonds Gro. CM13: Ingve 22Ee 59
Salmon La. E14 44Ac 92
Salmon Mdw. HP3: Hem H 6M 3
Salmon M. NW6 36Cb 69
Salmon Rd. DA1: Dart 55Pd 119
DA17: Belv 50Cd 96
Salmons La.
CR3: Whyt, Cat'm 92Ub 197
Salmons La. W. CR3: Cat'm 92Ub 197
Salmons Rd. KT9: Chess 79Na 153
KT24: Eff 100X 191
N9 18Wb 33
Salmon St. E14 44Bc 92
NW9 32Ra 67
Salomons Rd. E13 43Lc 93
Salop Rd. E17 30Zb 52
Saltash Cl. SM1: Sutt 77Bb 155
Saltash Rd. DA16: Well 53Yc 117
IG6: Ilf 24Tc 54
Salt Box Cotts. GU2: Guild 10L 187
Saltbox Hill TN16: Big H 85Kc 179
Saltbox Hill Nature Reserve 84Kc 179
Salt Box Rd. GU3: Guild 10K 187
GU4: Guild 10K 187
Saltcoats Rd. W4 47Ua 88
Saltcote Cl. DA1: Cray 58Gd 118
Saltcroft Cl. HA9: Wemb 32Ra 67
Saltdene N4 32Pb 70
Salter Cl. HA2: Harr 35Ba 65
Salterford Rd. SW17 65Jb 134
Saltern Ct. *IG11: Bark* 41Xc 95
(off Galleons Dr.)
Salter Rd. SE16 46Zb 92
Salters Cl. WD3: Rick 18N 25
Salters Ct. EC4 3E 224
Salters Gdns. WD17: Wat 11W 26
Salter's Hall Ct. EC4 4F 225
Salter's Hill SE19 64Tb 135
Salters Rd. E17 28Fc 53
W10 42Za 88
Salters Row *N1* 37Tb 71
(off Tilney Gdns.)
Salter St. E14 45Bc 92
NW10 41Wa 88
Salterton Rd. N7 34Pb 70
Saltford Cl. DA8: Erith 50Gd 96
SALT HILL 6G 80
Salt Hill Av. SL1: Slou 6G 80
Salt Hill Cl. UB8: Uxb 36N 63
Salt Hill Dr. SL1: Slou 6G 80
Salt Hill Mans. SL1: Slou 6G 80
Salt Hill Way SL1: Slou 6G 80
Saltings, The DA9: Ghithe 56Yd 120
Saltley Cl. E6 44Nc 94
Salton Cl. N3 26Cb 49
Saltoun Rd. SW2 56Qb 112
Saltram Cl. N15 28Vb 51
Saltram Cres. W9 41Bb 89
Saltwell St. E14 45Cc 92
Saltwood Cl. BR6: Chels 77Yc 161
Saltwood Gro. SE17 7F 231 (50Tb 91)
Saltwood Ho. *SE15* 51Yb 114
(off Lovelinch Cl.)
Salusbury Rd. NW6 39Ab 68
Salutation Rd. SE10 49Gc 93
Salvador SW17 64Hb 133
Salvation Pl. KT22: Fet 96Ja 192
Salvia Ct. GU24: Bisl 8E 166
Salvia Gdns. UB6: G'frd 40Ja 66
Salvin Rd. SW15 55Za 110
Salway Cl. IG8: Wfd G 24Jc 53
Salway Pl. E15 37Fc 73
Salway Rd. E15 37Fc 73
Samantha Cl. E17 31Bc 72
Samantha M. RM4: Have B 20Gd 38
Sam Bartram Cl. SE7 50Lc 93
Sambrook Ho. *E1* 43Yb 92
(off Jubilee St.)
SE11 6K 229
Sambruck M. SE6 60Dc 114
Samels Ct. W6 50Wa 88
Samford Ho. N1 1K 217
Samford St. NW8 6D 214 (42Fb 89)
Samian Ga. AL3: St A 4M 5
Samira Cl. E17 30Cc 52
Sam Manners Ho. *SE10* 50Gc 93
(off Tuskar St.)

Sam March Ho. E14 44Fc 93
(off Blair St.)
Sammi Ct. CR7: Thor H 70Sb 135
Samos Rd. SE20 68Xb 135
Samphire Ct. RM17: Grays 1A 122
Sampson Av. EN5: Barn 15Za 30
Sampson Cl. DA17: Belv 48Zc 95
Sampson Ct. TW17: Shep 71S 150
Sampson Ho. SE1 6C 224 (46Rb 91)
Sampson's Grn. SL2: Slou 1D 80
Sampson St. E1 46Wb 91
Samsbrooke Ct. EN1: Enf 16Ub 33
Samson St. E13 40Lc 73
Samuda Est. E14 48Ec 92
Samuel Cl. E8 39Vb 71
HA7: Stan 19Ja 28
SE14 51Zb 114
SE18 49Nc 94
Samuel Ct. N1 4H 219
Samuel Gray Gdns. KT2: King T 67Ma 131
Samuel Johnson Cl. SW16 63Pb 134
Samuel Jones Ct. SE15 52Ub 113
Samuel Lewis Bldgs. N1 37Qb 70
Samuel Lewis Trust Dwellings E8 36Wb 71
(off Amhurst Rd.)
N16 30Ub 51
SW3 6D 226 (49Gb 89)
SW6 52Cb 111
(off Vanston Pl.)
W14 49Bb 89
(off Lisgar Ter.)
Samuel Lewis Trust Est. SE5 53Sb 113
(off Warner Rd.)
Samuel Palmer Ct. BR6: Orp 73Wc 161
(off Chislehurst Rd.)
Samuel Richardson Ho. W14 49Bb 89
(off North End Cres.)
Samuel's Cl. W6 49Ya 88
Samuel Sq. AL1: St A 3B 6
(off Pageant Rd.)
Samuel St. SE15 52Vb 113
SE18 49Pc 94
Samuel Wallis Lodge SE10 49Gc 93
(off Banning St.)
Sanchia Ct. E2 41Wb 91
(off Wellington Row)
Sancroft Cl. NW2 34Xa 68
Sancroft Ho. SE11 7J 229
Sancroft Rd. HA3: W'stone 26Ha 46
Sancroft St. SE11 7J 229 (50Pb 90)
Sanctuary, The DA5: Bexl 58Zc 117
SM4: Mord 72Cb 155
SW1 3E 228
Sanctuary Cl. DA1: Dart 58Ld 119
UB9: Hare 24L 43
Sanctuary Gdns. SS17: Stan H 1N 101
Sanctuary M. E8 37Vb 71
Sanctuary Rd. TW6: H'row A 58Q 106
Sanctuary St. SE1 1E 230 (47Sb 91)
Sandale Cl. N16 34Tb 71
Sandall Cl. W5 42Na 87
Sandall Ho. E3 40Ac 72
Sandall Rd. NW5 37Lb 70
W5 42Na 87
Sandal Rd. KT3: N Mald 71Ta 153
N18 22Wb 51
Sandal St. E15 39Gc 73
Sandalwood Av. KT16: Chert 76G 148
Sandalwood Cl. E1 42Ac 92
EN5: Ark 15Va 30
Sandalwood Dr. HA4: Ruis 31S 64
Sandalwood Ho. DA15: Sidc 61Vc 139
Sandalwood Mans. W8 48Db 89
(off Stone Hall Gdns.)
Sandalwood Rd. TW13: Felt 62X 129
Sanday Cl. HP3: Hem H 4B 4
Sandbach Pl. SE18 49Sc 94
Sandbanks TW14: Felt 60U 106
Sandbanks Hill DA2: Grn St 65Xd 142
Sandbourne NW8 39Db 69
(off Abbey Rd.)
W11 44Cb 89
(off Dartmouth Cl.)
Sandbourne Av. SW19 68Db 133
Sandbourne Rd. SE4 54Ac 114
Sandbrook Cl. NW7 23Ta 47
Sandbrook Rd. N16 34Ub 71
Sandby Ct. NW10 41Xa 88
(off Plough Cl.)
Sandby Grn. SE9 55Nc 116
Sandby Ho. NW6 39Cb 69
Sandcliff Rd. DA8: Erith 49Fd 96
Sandcroft Cl. N13 23Rb 51
Sandcross La. RH2: Reig 9H 207
Sandell's Av. TW15: Ashf 63S 128
Sandell St. SE1 1K 229 (47Qb 90)
Sanderling Ct. SE8 51Bc 114
(off Abinger Gro.)
SE28 45Yc 95
Sanderling Lodge E1 45Vb 91
(off Star Pl.)
Sanderling Way DA9: Ghithe 58Wd 120
Sanders Cl. AL2: Lon C 9H 7
HP3: Hem H 6P 3
TW12: Hamp H 64Ea 130
Sandersfield Gdns. SM7: Bans 87Cb 175
Sandersfield Rd. SM7: Bans 87Db 175
Sanders Ho. WC1 3K 217
Sanders La. NW7 24Ya 48
(Bittacy Ri.)
NW7 24Za 48
(Grants Cl.)
Sanderson Cl. CM13: W H'dn 30Ee 59
NW5 35Kb 70
Sanderson Ho. SE8 50Bc 92
(off Grove St.)
Sanderson Rd. UB8: Uxb 37L 63
Sandersons Av. TN14: Bad M 82Cd 182
Sanderson Sq. BR1: Brom 69Qc 138
Sanders Rd. HP3: Hem H 6A 4
SANDERSTEAD 84Wb 177
Sanderstead Av. NW2 33Ab 68
Sanderstead Cl. SW12 59Lb 112
Sanderstead Ct. Av. CR2: Sande 85Wb 177
Sanderstead Hill CR2: Sande 83Ub 177
Sanderstead Rd. BR5: St M Cry 72Xc 161
CR2: Sande, S Croy 80Tb 157
E10 32Ac 72
Sanders Way N19 32Mb 70
Sandes Pl. KT22: Lea 90Ja 172
Sandfield WC1 4G 217
Sandfield Gdns. CR7: Thor H 69Rb 135
Sandfield Pas. CR7: Thor H 69Sb 135
Sandfield Pl. CR7: Thor H 69Sb 135
Sandfield Rd. AL1: St A 2E 6
CR7: Thor H 69Rb 135
Sandfields GU23: Send 96F 188
Sandford Av. IG10: Lough 13Sc 36
N22 25Sb 51
Sandford Cl. E6 42Pc 94
Sandford Ct. EN5: New Bar 13Db 31
N16 32Ub 71
Sandford Rd. BR2: Brom 69Jc 137
DA7: Bex 56Ad 117
E6 41Nc 94
Sandford Row SE17 7F 231 (50Tb 91)
Sandford St. SW6 52Db 111
Sandgate Cl. RM7: Rush G 31Ed 76
Sandgate Ho. E5 36Xb 71
W5 43La 86
Sandgate La. SW18 60Gb 111
Sandgate Rd. DA16: Well 52Yc 117
Sandgates KT16: Chert 75G 148
Sandgate St. SE15 51Xb 113
Sandgate Trad. Est. SE15 51Xb 113
(off Sandgate St.)
Sandham Ct. SW4 53Nb 112
Sandham Point SE18 49Rc 94
(off Vincent Rd.)
Sandhills SM6: Bedd 77Mb 156
Sandhills, The SW10 51Eb 111
(off Limerston St.)
Sandhills Ct. GU25: Vir W 71A 148
Sandhills La. GU25: Vir W 71A 148
Sandhills Mdw. TW17: Shep 73S 150
Sandhills Rd. RH2: Reig 7J 207
Sandhurst Av. HA2: Harr 30Da 45
KT5: Surb 73Ra 153
Sandhurst Cl. CR2: Sande 81Ub 177
NW9 27Qa 47
Sandhurst Ct. SW2 56Nb 112
Sandhurst Dr. IG3: Bark, Ilf 35Vc 75
Sandhurst Ho. E1 43Yb 92
(off Wolsy St.)
Sandhurst Mkt. SE6 60Ec 114
(off Sandhurst Rd.)
Sandhurst Rd. BR6: Chels 76Wc 161
DA5: Bexl 57Zc 117
DA15: Sidc 62Vc 139
N9 16Yb 34
NW9 27Qa 47
RM18: Tilb 4E 122
SE6 60Fc 115
Sandhurst Way CR2: Sande 80Ub 157
Sandifer Dr. NW2 34Za 68
Sandifield AL10: Hat 3D 8
Sandiford Rd. SM3: Sutt 75Bb 155
Sandiland Cres. BR2: Hayes 75Hc 159
Sandilands CR0: C'don 75Wb 157
TN13: Chip 94Fd 202
Sandilands Rd. SW6 53Db 111
Sandison St. SE15 55Wb 113
Sandlands Gro. KT20: Walt H 95Wa 194
Sandlands Rd. KT20: Walt H 95Wa 194
Sandland St. WC1 1J 223 (43Pb 90)
Sandlers End SL2: Slou 2F 80
Sandling Ri. SE9 62Qc 138
Sandlings, The N22 26Qb 50
Sandlings Cl. SE15 54Xb 113
Sandmartin Way SM6: Wall 74Jb 156
Sandmere Cl. HP2: Hem H 3A 4
Sandmere Rd. SW4 56Nb 112
Sandon Cl. KT10: Esh 73Fa 152
Sandon Rd. EN8: Chesh 2Yb 20
Sandover Ho. SE16 48Wb 91
(off Spa Rd.)
Sandow Cres. UB3: Hayes 48V 84
Sandown Av. KT10: Esh 78Ea 152
RM10: Dag 37Ed 76
RM12: Horn 33Md 77
Sandown Cl. RM16: Ors 3G 100
TW5: Cran 53W 106
Sandown Ct. HA7: Stan 22La 46
RH1: Redh 5N 207
(off Station Rd.)
RM10: Dag 37Ed 76
(off Sandown Av.)
SE26 62Xb 135
SM2: Sutt 80Db 155
Sandown Dr. SM5: Cars 81Jb 176
Sandown Ga. KT10: Esh 76Fa 152
Sandown Ind. Pk. KT10: Esh 75Ca 151
Sandown Lodge KT18: Eps 86Ta 173
Sandown Pk. Golf Course 76Da 151
Sandown Pk. Racecourse 75Ea 152
Sandown Rd. CR5: Coul 88Jb 176
DA12: Grav'nd 5E 144
KT10: Esh 77Ea 152
RM16: Ors 3G 100
SE25 71Xb 157
SL2: Slou 3D 80
WD24: Wat 10Y 13
Sandown Rd. Ind. Est. WD24: Wat 9Y 13
Sandown Sports Club 76Da 151
Sandown Way UB5: N'olt 37Aa 65
Sandpiper Cl. DA9: Ghithe 58Wd 120
E17 24Zb 52
SE16 47Bc 92
Sandpiper Ct. E1 45Wb 91
(off Thomas More St.)
E14 48Ec 92
(off New Union Cl.)
SE8 51Cc 114
(off Edward Pl.)
Sandpiper Dr. DA8: Erith 52Kd 119
Sandpiper Rd. CR2: Sels 83Zb 178
SM1: Sutt 78Bb 155
Sandpipers, The
DA12: Grav'nd 1F 144
Sandpiper Ter. IG5: Ilf 27Rc 54
Sandpiper Way BR5: St P 70Zc 139
Sandpit Cotts. GU24: Pirb 4C 186
Sandpit Hall Rd. GU24: Chob 4L 167
Sandpit La. AL1: St A 1C 6
AL4: St A 1C 6
CM14: Pil H, S Weald 18Vd 40
CM15: Pil H 18Vd 40
GU21: Knap 6F 166
(not continuous)
Sandpit Pl. SE7 50Nc 94
Sandpit Rd. BR1: Brom 64Gc 137
DA1: Dart 56Ld 119
RH1: Redh 7N 207
Sandpits Rd. CR0: C'don 77Zb 158
TW10: Ham 61Ma 131
Sandra Cl. N22 25Sb 51
TW3: Houn 57Da 107
Sandra Ct. CR4: Mitc 65Hb 133
Sandra Ho. KT8: E Mos 71Fa 152
Sandridge Cl. EN4: Had W 9Gb 17
HA1: Harr 28Ga 46
Sandridge Ct. AL1: St A 1C 6
Sandridge St. N19 33Lb 70
Sandringham Av. SW20 67Ab 132
Sandringham Bldgs. SE17 5F 231
Sandringham Cl. EN1: Enf 12Ub 33
GU22: Pyr 88J 169
IG6: Ilf 27Sc 54
SW19 60Za 110
Sandringham Ct. DA15: Sidc 58Vc 117
KT2: King T 67Na 131
(off Skerne Wlk.)
SE16 46Zb 92
(off King & Queen Wharf)
SL1: Slou 4B 80
SM2: Sutt 81Cb 175
UB10: Hil 42S 84
W1 3C 222
W9 4A 214
Sandringham Cres. HA2: Harr 33Ca 65
Sandringham Dr. DA2: Wilm 61Gd 140
DA16: Well 54Uc 116
TW15: Ashf 63M 127
Sandringham Flats WC2 4E 222
Sandringham Gdns. IG6: Ilf 27Sc 54
KT8: W Mole 70Ca 129
N8 30Nb 50
N12 23Fb 49
TW5: Cran 53W 106
Sandringham Ho. W14 49Ab 88
(off Windsor Way)
Sandringham M. TW12: Hamp 67Ba 129
W5 45Ma 87
Sandringham Pk. KT11: Cobh 84Ca 171
Sandringham Rd. BR1: Brom 64Jc 137
CM15: Pil H 16Xd 40
CR7: Thor H 71Sb 157
E7 36Lc 73
E8 36Vb 71
E10 30Fc 53
EN6: Pot B 2Db 17
IG11: Bark 36Vc 75
KT4: Wor Pk 76Wa 154
N22 27Sb 51
NW2 37Xa 68
NW11 31Ab 68
TW6: H'row A 57N 105
UB5: N'olt 38Ca 65
WD24: Wat 9Y 13
Sandringham Way
EN8: Walt C 6Yb 20
Sandrock Pl. CR0: C'don 77Zb 158
Sandrock Rd. SE13 55Cc 114
Sandroyd Way KT11: Cobh 85Ca 171
SANDS END 53Eb 111
Sand's End La. SW6 53Db 111
Sands Farm Dr. SL1: Burn 2A 80
Sandstone La. E16 45Kc 93
Sandstone Pl. N19 33Kb 70
Sandstone Rd. SE12 61Kc 137
Sands Way IG8: Wfd G 23Pc 54
Sandtoft Rd. SE7 51Kc 115
Sandway Path BR5: St M Cry 70Yc 139
(off Okemore Gdns.)
Sandway Rd. BR5: St M Cry 70Yc 139
Sandwell Cres. NW6 37Cb 69
Sandwich Ho. SE16 47Yb 92
(off Swan Rd.)
WC1 4F 217
Sandwich St. WC1 4F 217 (41Nb 90)
Sandwick Cl. NW7 24Wa 48
Sandy Bank Rd. DA12: Grav'nd 10D 122
Sandy Bury BR6: Orp 76Tc 160
Sandy Cl. GU22: Wok 89E 168
Sandycombe Rd. TW9: Kew, Rich 55Pa 109
TW14: Felt 60W 106
Sandycoombe Rd. TW1: Twick 58La 108
Sandy Ct. KT11: Cobh 85Ba 171
Sandy Cft. KT17: Ewe 82Ya 174
Sandycroft SE2 51Wc 117
Sandy Dr. KT11: Cobh 83Ca 171
TW14: Felt 60U 106
Sandy Gro. WD6: Bore 12Pa 29
Sandy Hill Av. SE18 50Rc 94
Sandy Hill Rd. SE18 50Rc 94
SM6: Wall 81Lb 176
Sandyhill Rd. IG1: Ilf 35Rc 74
Sandy Holt KT11: Cobh 85Ba 171
Sandy La. BR5: St P 68Zc 139
BR6: Orp 73Wc 161
CR4: Mitc 67Jb 134
DA2: Bean, Sflt 61Yd 142
DA14: Sidc 68Zc 139
GU22: Pyr 89J 169
(not continuous)
GU22: Wok 89D 168
GU23: Send 95E 188
GU24: Chob 1J 167
GU25: Vir W 70A 126
(not continuous)
HA3: Kenton 30Pa 47
HA6: Nwood 19V 26
KT1: Hamp W 66Ja 130
KT11: Cobh 84Ba 171
KT12: Walt T 72X 151
KT20: Kgswd 96Bb 195
KT22: Oxs 84Ca 171
RH1: Blet 4H 209
RH1: S Nut 7D 208
RH2: Reig 7D 206
RH3: Bet 7A 206
RH8: Limp 99Kc 199
RH8: Oxt 1G 210
RM15: Avel, Wenn 45Pd 97
RM16: Grays 1D 122
RM20: W Thur 50Xd 98
SL5: S'dale 1E 146
SM2: Cheam 80Ab 154
SM6: Wall 79Mb 156
TN13: S'oaks 95Ld 203
TN15: Ivy H, Igh 97Xd 204
TN16: Westrm 97Tc 200
TW10: Ham 61La 130
TW11: Hamp W, Tedd 66Ja 130
WD23: Bush 13Ea 28
WD25: A'ham 13Ea 28
Sandy La. Caravan Site
WD25: A'ham 13Ea 28
Sandy La. Nth. SM6: Wall 79Mb 156
Sandy La. Sth. SM6: Wall 81Lb 176
Sandy Lodge HA5: Hat E 23Ca 45
HA6: Nwood 19U 26
Sandy Lodge Ct. HA6: Nwood 22U 44
Sandy Lodge Golf Course 19T 26
Sandy Lodge La. HA6: Nwood 19T 26
Sandy Lodge Rd. WD3: Rick 19R 26
Sandy Lodge Way HA6: Nwood 22T 44
Sandy Mead KT19: Eps 82Qa 173
Sandymount Av. HA7: Stan 22La 46
Sandy Ride SL5: S'hill 10C 124
Sandy Ridge BR7: Chst 65Qc 138
TN15: Bor G 92Ce 205
Sandy Ri. SL9: Chal P 25A 42
Sandy Rd. KT15: Add 79J 149
NW3 33Db 69
NW11 33Db 69
Sandys Row E1 1J 225 (43Ub 91)
Sandy Way CR0: C'don 76Bc 158
GU22: Wok 89E 168
KT11: Cobh 84Ca 171
KT12: Walt T 74V 150
Sanford La. N16 34Vb 71
Sanford St. SE14 51Ac 114
Sanford Ter. N16 34Vb 71
Sanford Wlk. N16 33Vb 71
SE14 51Ac 114
Sangam Cl. UB2: S'hall 48Aa 85
Sanger Av. KT9: Chess 78Na 153
Sanger Dr. GU23: Send 95E 188
Sangley Rd. SE6 59Dc 114
SE25 70Ub 135
Sangora Rd. SW11 56Fb 111
San Juan Dr. RM16: Chaf H 49Yd 98
Sankey Ho. E2 40Yb 72
(off St James's Av.)
San Luis Dr. RM16: Chaf H 49Yd 98
San Marcos Dr.
RM16: Chaf H 49Yd 98
Sansom Cl. WD3: Crox G 15T 26
Sansom Rd. E11 33Hc 73
Sansom St. SE5 53Tb 113
Sans Wlk. EC1 5A 218 (42Qb 90)
Santers La. EN6: Pot B 5Ab 16
Sant Ho. SE17 6E 230
Santiago Way RM16: Chaf H 50Zd 99
Santley Ho. SE1 2A 230 (47Qb 90)
Santley St. SW4 56Pb 112
Santos Rd. SW18 57Cb 111
Santway, The HA7: Stan 22Ga 46
SANWAY 86N 169
Sanway Cl. KT14: Byfl 86N 169
Sanway Rd. KT14: Byfl 86N 169
Sapcote Trad. Cen. NW10 37Va 68
Saperton Wlk. SE11 5J 229
Saphire Ct. E15 39Ec 72
(off Warton Rd.)
Sapho Pk. DA12: Grav'nd 3H 145
Saphora Cl. BR6: Farnb 78Tc 160
Sapperton Ct. EC1 5D 218
Sapperton Ho. W2 43Cb 89
(off Westbourne Pk. Rd.)
Sapphire Cl. E6 44Qc 94
RM8: Dag 32Yc 75
Sapphire Ct. E1 45Wb 91
(off Cable St.)
Sapphire Rd. NW10 38Sa 67
SE8 49Ac 92
Sappho Ct. GU21: Wok 8J 167
Saracen Cl. CR0: C'don 72Tb 157
Saracen Est. HP2: Hem H 1B 4
Saracen Ind. Area HP2: Hem H 1A 4
Saracens Head HP2: Hem H 1A 4
Saracens Head Yd. AL1: St A 3B 6
(off Pageant Rd.)
EC3 3K 225
Saracens RUFC 24Ya 48
Saracen St. E14 44Cc 92
Sara Cres. DA9: Ghithe 56Xd 120
Sarah Ct. UB5: N'olt 39Ba 65
Sarah Ho. E1 44Xb 91
(off Commercial Rd.)
Sara Ho. DA8: Erith 52Gd 118
Sarah Swift Ho. SE1 1G 231
Sara La. Ct. N1 1J 219
Sara Pk. DA12: Grav'nd 3G 144
Saratoga Rd. E5 35Yb 72
Sara Turnbull Ho. SE18 49Pc 94
Sarcus Dean SL9: Chal P 22B 42
Sardinia St. WC2 3H 223 (44Pb 90)
Sargeant Cl. UB8: Cowl 41M 83
Sarita Cl. HA3: Hrw W 26Fa 46
Sarjant Path SW19 61Za 132
(off Blincoe Cl.)
Sarjeant Ct. BR4: W W'ck 75Fc 159
(off Bencurtis Pk.)
Sark Cl. TW5: Hest 52Ca 107
Sark Ho. EN3: Enf W 10Zb 20
WD18: Wat 16V 26
(off Scammell Way)
Sark Twr. SE28 47Sc 94
Sark Wlk. E16 44Kc 93
Sarnes Ct. N11 21Kb 50
(off Oakleigh Rd. Sth.)
Sarnesfield Ho. SE15 51Xb 113
(off Pencraig Way)
Sarnesfield Rd. EN2: Enf 14Tb 33
SARRATT 8J 11
SARRATT BOTTOM 9G 10
SARRATT HALL 7J 11
Sarratt Ho. W10 43Ya 88
(off Sutton Way)
Sarratt La. WD3: Chor, Loud, Sarr 12K 25
Sarratt Rd.
WD3: Sarr, Chan C, Crox G 9K 11
Sarre Av. RM12: Horn 37Ld 77
Sarre Rd. BR5: St M Cry 71Yc 161
NW2 36Bb 69
Sarsby Dr. TW19: Wray 61C 126
Sarsen Av. TW3: Houn 54Ca 107
Sarsens Cl. DA12: Cobh 9H 145
Sarsfeld Rd. SW12 61Hb 133
Sarsfield Rd. UB6: G'frd 40Ka 66
Sartor Rd. SE15 56Zb 114
Sarum Complex UB8: Uxb 41K 83
Sarum Grn. KT13: Weyb 76U 150
Sarum Ho. W11 45Bb 89
(off Portobello Rd.)
Sarum Ter. E3 42Bc 92
Sassoon NW9 25Va 48
Satanita Cl. E16 44Mc 93
Satchell Mead NW9 25Va 48
Satchwell Rd. E2 41Wb 91
Satchwell St. E2 41Wb 91
Satinwood Ct. HP3: Hem H 4N 3
Satis Ct. KT17: Ewe 83Va 174
Satis Ho. SL3: Dat 2N 103
Sattar M. N16 34Tb 71
Saturn Ho. E3 39Cc 72
(off Garrison Rd.)
E15 39Fc 73
(off High St.)
Sauls Grn. E11 34Gc 73
Saunders Cl. DA11: Nflt 1A 144
E14 45Bc 92
(off Limehouse C'way.)
IG1: Ilf 32Tc 74
Saunders Copse GU22: Wok 4M 187
Saunders Ho. SE16 47Zb 92
(off Quebec Way)
Saunders La. GU22: Wok 4J 187
Saunders Ness Rd. E14 50Ec 92
Saunders Rd. SE18 50Vc 95
UB10: Uxb 39M 63
Saunders St. SE11 5K 229 (49Qb 90)
Saunders Way DA1: Dart 61Pd 141
SE28 45Xc 95
Saunderton Rd. HA0: Wemb 36Ka 66
Saunton Av. UB3: Harl 52V 106
Saunton Ct. UB1: S'hall 45Ea 86
(off Haldane Rd.)
Saunton Rd. RM12: Horn 33Jd 76
Savage Gdns. E6 44Pc 94
EC3 4J 225 (45Ub 91)
(not continuous)
Savanna Ct. WD18: Wat 14V 26
(off Rickmansworth Rd.)
Savannah Cl. SE15 52Vb 113
Savay Cl. UB9: Den 31J 63
Savay La. UB9: Den 30J 43
Savera Cl. UB2: S'hall 48Y 85
Savernake Ct. HA7: Stan 23Ka 46
Savernake Ho. N4 31Sb 71
Savernake Rd. N9 16Wb 33
NW3 35Hb 69
Savery Dr. KT6: Surb 73Ka 152
Savile Cl. KT3: N Mald 71Ua 154
KT7: T Ditt 74Ha 152
Savile Gdns. CR0: C'don 75Vb 157
Savile Row W1 4B 222 (45Lb 90)
Savill Building, The 5K 125
Saville Ct. KT19: Eps 83Ra 173
Saville Cres. TW15: Ashf 65T 128
Saville Pl. TW20: Eng G 4P 125
Saville Rd. E16 46Nc 94
RM6: Chad H 30Bd 55
TW1: Twick 60Ha 108
W4 48Ta 87
Saville Row BR2: Hayes 74Hc 159
EN3: Enf H 12Zb 34
Savill Garden, The 5J 125
Savill Gdns. SW20 69Wa 132
Savill Ho. E16 46Rc 94
(off Robert St.)
SW4 58Mb 112
Savill M. TW20: Eng G 5P 125
Savill Row IG8: Wfd G 23Hc 53
Savin Lodge SM2: Sutt 80Eb 155
(off Walnut M.)
Savona Cl. SW19 66Za 132
Savona Ho. SW8 52Lb 112
(off Savona St.)
Savona St. SW8 52Lb 112
Savoy Av. UB3: Harl 50U 84
Savoy Bldgs. WC2 5H 223
SAVOY CIRCUS 45Va 88
Savoy Cl. E15 39Gc 73
HA8: Edg 22Qa 47
UB9: Hare 26M 43
Savoy Ct. HA2: Harr 29Da 45
NW3 34Eb 69
SW5 49Cb 89
(off Cromwell Rd.)
WC2 5G 223 (45Nb 90)
Savoy Hill WC2 5H 223 (45Pb 90)
Savoy M. AL1: St A 5P 5
SW9 55Nb 112
Savoy Pde. EN1: Enf 13Ub 33
Savoy Pl. W12 46Za 88
WC2 5G 223 (45Nb 90)
Savoy Rd. DA1: Dart 57Md 119
Savoy Row WC2 4H 223
Savoy Steps WC2 5H 223
Savoy St. WC2 4H 223 (45Pb 90)
Savoy Theatre 5H 223
Savoy Way WC2 5H 223
Sawbill Cl. UB4: Yead 43Z 85
Sawbridgeworth Ct. WD23: Bush 15Ea 28
(off Goddard Dr.)
Sawkins Cl. SW19 61Ab 132
Sawley Rd. W12 46Wa 88
Saw Mill Way N16 30Wb 51
Sawmill Yd. E3 39Ac 72
Sawston Ct. RM19: Purf 50Rd 97
(off Linnet Way)
Sawtry Cl. SM5: Cars 73Gb 155
Sawtry Way WD6: Bore 10Qa 15
Sawyer Cl. N9 19Wb 33
Sawyer Ct. NW10 38Ta 67
Sawyers Chase RM4: Abr 13Xc 37
Sawyers Cl. RM10: Dag 37Ed 76
SL4: Wind 2C 102
Sawyers Ct. CM15: Shenf 17Be 41
EN8: Walt C 5Zb 20
Sawyers Gro. CM15: B'wood 18Zd 41
Sawyers Hall La.
CM15: B'wood 17Yd 40
Sawyer's Hill TW10: Rich 59Pa 109
Sawyers La. EN6: Pot B 5Za 16
Sawyers Lawn W13 44Ja 86
Sawyer St. SE1 1D 230 (47Sb 91)
Sawyers Way HP2: Hem H 2P 3
Saxby Rd. SW2 59Nb 112
Saxbys Rd. TN15: Seal 94Td 204
Saxham Rd. IG11: Bark 40Uc 74
Saxlingham Rd. E4 20Fc 35
Saxon Av. TW13: Hanw 61Aa 129
Saxonbury Av. TW16: Sun 69X 129
Saxonbury Cl. CR4: Mitc 69Fb 133
Saxonbury Ct. N7 36Nb 70
Saxonbury Gdns. KT6: Surb 74La 152
Saxon Bus. Cen. SW19 68Eb 133
Saxon Chase N8 30Pb 50
Saxon Cl. CM13: B'wood 20Ce 41
DA11: Nflt 62Ee 143
E17 31Cc 72
KT6: Surb 72Ma 153
RM3: Hrld W 26Pd 57
SL3: L'ly 47B 82
TN14: Otf 89Hd 182
UB8: Hil 43P 83

Saxon Ct. HA6: Nwood 24V 44
SL0: Iver 44G 82
WD6: Bore 11Na 29
Saxon Dr. W3 44Qa 87
Saxonfield Cl. SW2 59Pb 112
Saxon Gdns. UB1: S'hall 45Aa 85
Saxon Hall *W2* 45Db 89
(off Palace Ct.)
Saxon Ho. E1 1K 225
KT1: King T 70Pa 131
TN14: S'oaks 93Md 203
TW13: Hanw 61Ba 129
Saxon Lea Ct. *E3* 40Bc 72
(off Saxon Rd.)
Saxon Lodge *CR0: C'don* 74Sb 157
(off Tavistock Rd.)
Saxon Pl. DA4: Hort K 71Sd 164
Saxon Rd. BR1: Brom 66Hc 137
DA2: Hawl 63Nd 141
E3 40Bc 72
E6 42Pc 94
HA9: Wemb 34Sa 67
IG1: Ilf 37Rc 74
KT2: King T 67Na 131
KT12: Walt T 76Z 151
N22 25Rb 51
SE25 71Tb 157
TW15: Ashf 65T 128
UB1: S'hall 45Aa 85
Saxons KT20: Tad 93Za 194
Saxon Ter. SE6 61Bc 136
Saxon Wlk. DA14: Sidc 65Yc 139
Saxon Way EN9: Walt A 5Ec 20
N14 16Mb 32
RH2: Reig 5H 207
SL4: Old Win 8M 103
UB7: Harm 51L 105
Saxon Way Ind. Est. UB7: Harm 51L 105
Saxony Pde. UB3: Hayes 43S 84
Saxton Cl. SE13 55Fc 115
Saxton M. WD17: Wat 12W 26
Saxville Rd. BR5: St P 69Xc 139
Sayer Cl. DA9: Ghithe 57Wd 120
Sayers Cl. KT22: Fet 95Ea 192
Sayers Ho. *N2* 26Fb 49
(off The Grange)
Sayer's Wlk. TW10: Rich 59Pa 109
Sayesbury La. N18 22Wb 51
Sayes Ct. KT15: Add 78L 149
SE8 51Bc 114
Sayes Ct. Farm Dr. KT15: Add 78K 149
Sayes Ct. Rd. BR5: St P 70Wc 139
Sayes Ct. St. SE8 51Bc 114
Scadbury Gdns. BR5: St P 68Wc 139
Scadbury Pk. (Nature Reserve) 66Vc 139
Scads Hill Cl. BR6: Pet W 72Vc 161
Scafell NW1 3B 216
Scafell Rd. SL2: Slou 2D 80
Scala 3G 217
(off Pentonville Rd.)
Scala St. W1 7C 216 (43Lb 90)
Scales Rd. N17 27Vb 51
Scammell Way WD18: Wat 16V 26
Scampston M. W10 44Za 88
Scandrett St. E1 46Xb 91
Scarab Cl. E16 45Hc 93
Scarba Wlk. *N1* 37Tb 71
(off Essex Rd.)
Scarborough Cl. SM2: Cheam 83Bb 175
TN16: Big H 90Lc 179
Scarborough Dr. WD3: Crox G 14R 26
Scarborough Rd. E11 32Fc 73
N4 31Qb 70
N9 17Yb 34
TW6: H'row A 58S 106
Scarborough St. E1 3K 225 (44Vb 91)
Scarborough Way SL1: Slou 8F 80
Scarbrook Rd. CR0: C'don 76Sb 157
Scarle Rd. HA0: Wemb 37Ma 67
Scarlet Cl. BR5: St P 70Xc 139
Scarlet Rd. SE6 62Gc 137
Scarlett Cl. GU21: Wok 10K 167
Scarlette Mnr. Way SW2 59Qb 112
Scarsbrook Rd. SE3 55Mc 115
Scarsdale Pl. W8 48Db 89
Scarsdale Rd. HA2: Harr 34Ea 66
Scarsdale Studios *W8* 48Cb 89
(off Stratford Rd.)
Scarsdale Vs. W8 48Cb 89
Scarth Rd. SW13 55Va 110
Scatterdells La. WD4: Chfd 2H 11
Scatterdells Pk. WD4: Chfd 2J 11
Scawen Cl. SM5: Cars 77Jb 156
Scawen Rd. SE8 50Ac 92
Scawfell St. E2 40Vb 71
SCC Smallholdings Rd. KT17: Eps 86Ya 174
(not continuous)
Sceaux Gdns. SE5 53Ub 113
Sceptre Ct. EC3 4K 225
Sceptre Ho. *E1* 42Yb 92
(off Malcolm Rd.)
Sceptre Rd. E2 41Yb 92
Sceynes Link N12 21Cb 49
Schafer Ho. NW1 5B 216 (41Lb 90)
Schiller International University 7K 223
Schofield Wlk. SE3 52Jc 115
Scholars, The *WD18: Wat* 15Y 27
(off Lady's Cl.)
Scholars Cl. EN5: Barn 14Ab 30
Scholars Ct. *AL1: St A* 2C 6
(off Newsom Pl.)
AL4: Col H 5N 7
RM2: Rom 29Jd 56
(off Academy Flds. Rd.)
Scholars Ho. *NW6* 39Cb 69
(off Glengall Rd.)
Scholars Pl. KT12: Walt T 74Y 151
N16 34Ub 71
Scholars Rd. E4 18Fc 35
SW12 60Lb 112
Scholars Wlk. AL10: Hat 3C 8
(not continuous)
SL3: L'ly 47C 82
SL9: Chal P 23A 42
Scholars Way RM2: Rom 29Kd 57
Scholefield Rd. N19 33Mb 70
Scholey Ho. SW11 55Gb 111
Schomberg Ho. SW1 5E 228
Schonfeld Sq. N16 33Tb 71
School All. TW1: Twick 60Ja 108
School Allotment Ride SL4: Wink 9A 102
School App. E2 3J 219
TN15: Bor G 92Ce 205
Schoolbank Rd. SE10 48Hc 93
Schoolbell M. E3 40Ac 72
School Cl. GU24: Bisl 7D 166
School Cotts. GU22: Wok 4N 187
School Cres. DA1: Cray 56Hd 118
Schoolfield Rd. RM20: W Thur 51Wd 120
Schoolfield Way RM20: W Thur 51Wd 120
Schoolgate Dr. SM4: Mord 71Db 155
School Hill RH1: Mers 100Lb 196
School Ho. SE1 5H 231
Schoolhouse Gdns. IG10: Lough 14Rc 36
School Ho. La. TW11: Tedd 66Ka 130
Schoolhouse La. E1 45Zb 92
Schoolhouse Yd. SE18 50Rc 94
School La. AL2: Brick W 6Ba 13
BR8: Swan 67Kd 141
CM13: Ingve 23Ee 59
CR3: Cat'm 98Vb 197
DA2: Bean 63Yd 142
DA3: Fawk 70Sd 142
DA4: Hort K 70Sd 142
DA16: Well 55Xc 117
GU20: W'sham 8B 146
GU23: Ock 94R 190
GU24: Pirb 4C 186
HA5: Pinn 28Aa 45
IG7: Chig 21Vc 55
KT1: Hamp W 67La 130
KT6: Surb 74Pa 153
KT15: Add 78J 149
KT20: Walt H 97Wa 194
KT22: Fet 94Fa 192
KT24: W Hor 100R 190
RH5: Mick 99La 192
RM16: Ors 3C 100
SE23 61Xb 135
SL2: Slou 5K 81
SL2: Stoke P 8M 61
SL9: Chal P 26A 42
TN11: Plax, S'brne 100Ae 205
TN15: Plax 100Ae 205
TN15: Seal 93Pd 203
TN15: W King 84Ud 184
TW17: Shep 72R 150
TW20: Egh 64C 126
WD23: Bush 17Da 27
WD25: Wat 6Ba 13
School Mead WD5: Ab L 4U 12
School Pas. KT1: King T 68Pa 131
UB1: S'hall 45Ba 85
School Rd. BR7: Chst 67Sc 138
DA12: Grav'nd 2E 144
E12 35Pc 74
EN6: Pot B 2Eb 17
GU20: W'sham 8A 146
KT1: Hamp W 67La 130
KT8: E Mos 70Fa 130
NW10 42Ta 87
RM10: Dag 39Cd 76
SL5: S'hill 1B 146
TW3: Houn 55Ea 108
TW12: Hamp H 65Ea 130
TW15: Ashf 65R 128
UB7: Harm 51M 105
School Rd. Av. TW12: Hamp H 65Ea 130
SCHOOL ROAD JUNC. 66R 128
School Row HP1: Hem H 3H 3
School Sq. SE10 48Hc 93
School Wlk. SL2: Slou 5M 81
TW16: Sun 70V 128
School Way N12 23Fb 49
RM8: Dag 34Yc 75
(not continuous)
Schooner Cl. E14 48Fc 93
IG11: Bark 41Xc 95
SE16 47Zb 92
Schooner Ct. DA2: Dart 56Sd 120
Schooner Ho. DA8: Erith 50Gd 96
Schroder Ct. TW20: Eng G 4M 125
Schroders Av. RH1: Redh 4B 208
Schubert Rd. SW15 57Bb 111
WD6: E'tree 16Ma 29
Science Mus.
Knightsbridge 4B 226 (48Fb 89)
Scilla Ct. RM17: Grays 51Fe 121
SCILLY ISLES 75Ga 152
Sclater St. E1 5K 219 (42Vb 91)
Scoble Pl. N16 35Vb 71
Scoles Cres. SW2 60Rb 113
Scoop, The 7J 225 (46Ub 91)
Scope Way KT1: King T 70Na 131
Score Complex, The 34Dc 72
Scoresby St. SE1 7B 224 (46Rb 91)
Scorton Av. UB6: G'frd 40Ja 66
Scorton Ho. N1 1J 219
Scotch Comn. W13 43Ja 86
SCOTCH HOUSE 2F 227 (47Hb 89)
Scoter Cl. IG8: Wfd G 24Kc 53
Scoter Ct. *SE8* 51Bc 114
(off Abinger Gro.)
Scot Gro. HA5: Pinn 24Z 45
Scotia Bldg. *E1* 45Zb 92
(off Jardine Rd.)
Scotia Ct. *SE16* 47Yb 92
(off Canada Est.)
Scotia Rd. SW2 59Qb 112
Scotland Bri. Lock KT15: New H 83J 169
Scotland Bri. Rd. KT15: New H 83J 169
Scotland Grn. N17 26Vb 51
Scotland Grn. Rd. EN3: Pond E 15Zb 34
Scotland Grn. Rd. Nth.
EN3: Pond E 14Zb 34
Scotland La. DA12: Cobh 9H 145
(not continuous)
Scotland Pl. SW1 6F 223 (46Nb 90)
Scotland Rd. IG9: Buck H 18Lc 35
Scotlands Dr. SL2: Farn C 7F 60
Scotney Cl. BR6: Farnb 77Qc 160
WD3: Crox G 14R 26
Scotney Ho. E9 37Yb 72
Scotney Wlk. RM12: Horn 36Ld 77
Scots Cl. TW19: Stanw 60M 105
Scotscraig WD7: R'lett 7Ha 14
Scotsdale Cl. BR5: Pet W 70Uc 138
SM3: Cheam 80Ab 154
Scotsdale Rd. SE12 57Kc 115
Scotshall La. CR6: W'ham 87Ec 178
Scots Hill WD3: Crox G 16P 25
Scots Hill Cl. WD3: Crox G 16P 25
Scotsmill La. WD3: Crox G 16P 25
Scotson Ho. SE11 6K 229
Scotswood Pk. GU21: Wok 86F 168
Scotswood St. EC1 5A 218 (42Qb 90)
Scotswood Wlk. N17 24Wb 51
Scott Av. SW15 58Ab 110
Scott Cl. KT19: Ewe 78Sa 153
SL2: Farn C 6G 60
SW16 67Pb 134
UB7: W Dray 49P 83
Scott Ct. W3 47Ta 87
Scott Cres. DA8: Erith 53Hd 118
HA2: Harr 32Da 65
Scott Ellis Gdns. NW8 4B 214 (41Fb 89)
Scottes La. RM8: Dag 32Zc 75
Scott Farm Cl. KT7: T Ditt 74Ka 152
Scott Gdns. TW5: Hest 52Z 107
Scott Ho. DA17: Belv 50Bd 95
E13 40Jc 73
(off Queens Rd. W.)
E14 47Cc 92
(off Admirals Way)
N7 37Pb 70
(off Caledonian Rd.)
N18 22Wb 51
(off Woolmer Rd.)
NW8 6D 214
NW10 38Ta 67
(off Stonebridge Pk.)
RM11: Horn 30Jd 56
(off Benjamin Cl.)
SE8 50Bc 92
(off Grove St.)
Scott Lidgett Cres. SE16 47Wb 91
Scott Rd. DA12: Grav'nd 4F 144
HA8: Edg 26Ra 47
RM16: Grays 9C 100
Scott Russell Pl. E14 50Dc 92
Scotts Av. BR2: Brom 68Fc 137
TW16: Sun 66U 128
Scotts Cl. RM12: Horn 36Ld 77
Scotts Ct. *W12* 47Ya 88
(off Scott's Rd.)
Scotts Dr. TW12: Hamp 66Da 129
Scotts Farm Rd. KT19: Ewe 79Sa 153
Scott's Gro. Cl. GU24: Chob 5H 167
Scott's Gro. Rd. GU24: Chob 5H 167
Scotts La. BR2: Brom 69Fc 137
KT12: Hers 77Z 151
Scotts Pas. SE18 49Rc 94
Scotts Rd. BR1: Brom 66Jc 137
E10 32Ec 72
UB2: S'hall 48Y 85
W12 47Xa 88
Scott's Sufferance Wharf SE1 2K 231
Scotts Ter. SE9 61Nc 138
Scott St. E1 42Xb 91
Scotts Way TN13: Riv 94Gd 202
TW16: Sun 66U 128
Scottswood Cl. WD23: Bush 12Aa 27
Scottswood Rd. WD23: Bush 12Aa 27
Scott's Yd. EC4 4F 225 (45Tb 91)
Scott Trimmer Way TW3: Houn 54Aa 107
Scottwell Dr. NW9 29Va 48
Scoulding Ho. *E14* 48Cc 92
(off Mellish St.)
Scoulding Rd. E16 44Jc 93
Scouler St. E14 45Ec 92
Scout App. NW10 35Ua 68
Scout La. SW4 55Lb 112
Scout Pk. 24Mb 50
Scout Way NW7 21Ta 47
Scovell Cres. SE1 2D 230
Scovell Rd. SE1 2D 230 (47Sb 91)
Scratchers La. DA3: Fawk 75Td 164
Scratton Flds. DA12: Sole S 10F 144
Scratton Rd. SS17: Stan H 1M 101
Scrattons Ter. IG11: Bark 40Zc 75
Screen at Walton, The 74W 150
Screen on Baker Street (Cinema) 7G 215
Screen on the Green Cinema 39Rb 71
(off Upper St.)
Screen on the Hill (Cinema)
Belsize Pk. 36Gb 69
Scriven Ct. E8 39Vb 71
Scriveners Cl. HP2: Hem H 2N 3
Scriven St. E8 39Vb 71
Scrooby St. SE6 58Dc 114
Scrope Ho. EC1 7K 217
Scrubbitts Pk. Rd. WD7: R'lett 7Ja 14
Scrubbitts Sq. WD7: R'lett 7Ja 14
Scrubs La. NW10 41Wa 88
W10 41Wa 88
Scrutton Cl. SW12 59Mb 112
Scrutton St. EC2 6H 219 (42Ub 91)
Scudamore La. NW9 28Sa 47
Scudders Hill DA3: Fawk 72Xd 164
Scutari Rd. SE22 57Yb 114
Scutley La. GU18: Light 1C 166
GU20: W'sham 1C 166
Scylla Cres. TW6: H'row A 59R 106
(not continuous)
Scylla Pl. GU21: Wok 1L 187
Scylla Rd. SE15 55Wb 113
(not continuous)
TW6: H'row A 58R 106
Seaborough Rd. RM16: Grays 8E 100
Seabright St. E2 41Xb 91
Seabrook Dr. BR4: W W'ck 75Gc 159
Seabrooke Ri. RM17: Grays 51De 121
Seabrook Gdns. RM7: Rush G 31Cd 76
Seabrook Rd. RM8: Dag 34Zc 75
WD4: K Lan 9D 4
Seaburn Cl. RM13: Rain 40Gd 76
Seacole Cl. W3 44Ta 87
Seacole Ct. *N21* 15Pb 32
(off Pennington Dr.)
Sea Containers Ho. SE1 5A 224
Seacon Twr. E14 47Bc 92
Seacourt Rd. SE2 47Zc 95
SL3: L'ly 49D 82
Seacroft Gdns. WD19: Wat 20Z 27
Seafield Rd. N11 21Mb 50
Seaford Cl. HA4: Ruis 32T 64
Seaford Ho. *SE16* 47Yb 92
(off Swan Rd.)
Seaford Rd. E17 27Dc 52
EN1: Enf 14Ub 33
N15 29Tb 51
TW6: H'row A 57M 105
W13 46Ka 86
Seaford St. WC1 4G 217 (41Nb 90)
Seaforth Av. KT3: N Mald 71Xa 154
Seaforth Cl. RM1: Rom 24Gd 56
Seaforth Cres. N5 36Sb 71
Seaforth Dr. EN8: Walt C 6Zb 20
Seaforth Gdns. IG8: Wfd G 22Lc 53
KT19: Ewe 77Va 154
N21 17Pb 32
Seaforth Pl. SW1 3C 228
Seagrave Cl. E1 43Zb 92
Seagrave Lodge *SW6* 51Cb 111
(off Seagrave Rd.)
Seagrave Rd. SW6 51Cb 111
Seagry Rd. E11 31Jc 73
Seagull Cl. IG11: Bark 41Wc 95
Seagull La. E16 45Jc 93
Seahorse Sailing Club 33Ta 67
SEAL 93Pd 203
Sealand Rd. TW6: H'row A 58Q 106
Sealand Wlk. UB5: N'olt 41Z 85
SEAL CHART 95Sd 204
Sealcroft Cotts. TN15: Seal 91Pd 203
Seal Dr. TN15: Seal 93Pd 203
Seale Hill RH2: Reig 8J 207
Seal Hollow Rd.
TN13: S'oaks 96Ld 203
TN15: S'oaks 96Ld 203
Seal Ho. SE1 3G 231
Sea Life London Aquarium
1H 229 (47Pb 90)
Seally Rd. RM17: Grays 50Ce 99
Seal Rd. TN14: S'oaks 93Ld 203
TN15: S'oaks 93Ld 203
Seal St. E8 35Vb 71
Seaman Cl. AL2: Park 7B 6
Searches La. WD5: Bedm 9J 5
Searchwood Hgts.
CR6: W'ham 90Xb 177
Searchwood Rd. CR6: W'ham 90Xb 177
Searle Ho. *SW11* 53Jb 112
(off Macduff Rd.)
Searle Pl. N4 32Pb 70
Searles Cl. SW11 52Gb 111
Searles Ct. BR8: Swan 71Jd 162
Searles Dr. E6 43Rc 94
Searles Rd. SE1 5G 231 (49Tb 91)
Searson Ho. SE17 6C 230
Sears St. SE5 52Tb 113
Seasalter Ho. *SW9* 53Qb 112
(off Gosling Way)
Seasons Cl. W7 46Ha 86
Seasprite Cl. UB5: N'olt 41Z 85
Seaton Av. IG3: Ilf 36Vc 75
Seaton Cl. E13 42Jc 93
SE11 7A 230 (50Qb 90)
SW15 60Xa 110
TW2: Whitt 58Fa 108
Seaton Dr. TW15: Ashf 61N 127
Seaton Gdns. HA4: Ruis 34V 64
Seaton Point E5 35Wb 71
Seaton Rd. AL2: Lon C 8H 7
CR4: Mitc 68Gb 133
DA1: Dart 59Jd 118
DA16: Well 52Yc 117
HA0: Wemb 40Na 67
HP3: Hem H 5M 3
TW2: Whitt 58Ea 108
UB3: Harl 49T 84
Seaton Sq. NW7 24Za 48
Seaton St. N18 22Wb 51
Seawell Ct. *IG11: Bark* 40Sc 74
(off Dock Rd.)
Sebastian Av. CM15: Shenf 16Ce 41
Sebastian Ct. IG11: Bark 39Vc 75
Sebastian Ho. N1 2H 219
Sebastian St. EC1 4C 218 (41Rb 91)
Sebastopol Rd. N9 21Wb 51
Sebbon St. N1 38Rb 71
Sebergham Gro. NW7 24Wa 48
Sebert Rd. E7 36Kc 73
Sebright Ho. *E2* 40Wb 71
(off Coate St.)
Sebright Pas. E2 40Wb 71
Sebright Rd. EN5: Barn 12Za 30
HP1: Hem H 4J 3
Secker Cres. HA3: Hrw W 25Ea 46
Secker Ho. *SW9* 54Rb 113
(off Loughborough Est.)
Secker St. SE1 7K 223 (46Qb 90)
Secombe Theatre 78Db 155
Second Av. E12 35Nc 74
E13 41Jc 93
E17 29Cc 52
EN1: Enf 15Vb 33
EN9: Walt A 2Kc 21
HA9: Wemb 33Ma 67
KT12: Walt T 72X 151
KT20: Lwr K 97Ab 194
N18 21Yb 52
NW4 28Za 48
RM6: Chad H 29Yc 55
RM10: Dag 39Dd 76
RM20: W Thur 51Wd 120
SS17: Stan H 1M 101
SW14 55Ua 110
UB3: Hayes 46V 84
W3 46Va 88
W10 42Ab 88
WD25: Wat 7Z 13
Second Cl. KT8: W Mole 70Ea 130
Second Cres. SL1: Slou 3G 80
Second Cross Rd. TW2: Twick 61Ga 130
Second Way HA9: Wemb 35Ra 67
Sedan Way SE17 7H 231 (50Ub 91)
Sedcombe Cl. DA14: Sidc 63Xc 139
Sedcote Rd. EN3: Pond E 15Yb 34
Sedding St. SW1 5H 227 (49Jb 90)
Sedding Studios SW1 5H 227
Seddon Highwalk *EC2* 7D 218
(off Aldersgate St.)
Seddon Ho. EC2 7D 218
Seddon Rd. SM4: Mord 71Fb 155
Seddon St. WC1 4J 217 (41Pb 90)
Sedgebrook Rd. SE3 54Mc 115
Sedgecombe Av. HA3: Kenton 29La 46
Sedge Ct. RM17: Grays 2A 122
Sedgefield Cl. RM3: Rom 21Pd 57
Sedgefield Ct. *UB5: N'olt* 36Da 65
(off Newmarket Av.)
Sedgefield Cres. RM3: Rom 22Pd 57
Sedgeford Rd. W12 46Va 88
Sedgehill Rd. SE6 63Cc 136
Sedgemere Av. N2 27Eb 49
Sedgemere Rd. SE2 48Yc 95
Sedgemoor Dr. RM10: Dag 35Cd 76
Sedgeway SE6 60Hc 115
Sedgewood Cl. BR2: Hayes 73Hc 159
Sedgmoor Pl. SE5 52Ub 113
Sedgwick Av. UB10: Hil 38R 64
Sedgwick Ho. *E3* 43Cc 92
(off Gale St.)
Sedgwick Pl. WD17: Wat 15Y 27
Sedgwick Rd. E10 33Ec 72
Sedgwick St. E9 36Zb 72
Sedleigh Rd. SW18 58Bb 111
Sedlescombe Rd. SW6 51Cb 111
Sedley DA13: Sflt 65Ce 143
Sedley Cl. EN1: Enf 10Xb 19
Sedley Ct. SE26 61Xb 135
Sedley Gro. UB9: Hare 28L 43
Sedley Ho. SE11 7K 229
Sedley Pl. W1 3K 221 (44Kb 90)
Sedley Ri. IG10: Lough 12Pc 36
Sedum Cl. NW9 29Ra 47
Seedbed Cen., The RM7: Rush G 31Gd 76
Seeley Dr. SE21 63Ub 135
Seelig Av. NW9 31Wa 68
Seely Rd. SW17 65Jb 134
Seetha Ho. *IG1: Ilf* 33Tc 74
(off High Rd.)
Seething La. EC3 4J 225 (45Ub 91)
SEETHING WELLS 72La 152
Seething Wells La. KT6: Surb 72La 152
Sefton Av. HA3: Hrw W 26Fa 46
NW7 22Ta 47
Sefton Cl. AL1: St A 1D 6
BR5: St M Cry 70Vc 139
GU24: W End 5D 166
SL2: Stoke P 9K 61
Sefton Ct. EN2: Enf 12Rb 33
TW3: Houn 53Da 107
Sefton Paddock SL2: Stoke P 8L 61
Sefton Pk. SL2: Stoke P 8L 61
Sefton Rd. BR5: St M Cry 70Vc 139
CR0: C'don 74Wb 157
KT19: Ewe 82Ta 173
Sefton St. SW15 55Ya 110
Sefton Way UB8: Cowl 44L 83
Segal Cl. SE23 59Ac 114
Segrave Cl. KT13: Weyb 80Q 150
Sejant Ho. *RM17: Grays* 51De 121
(off Bridge Rd.)
Sekforde St. EC1 6B 218 (42Rb 91)
Sekhon Ter. TW13: Hanw 62Ca 129
Selah Dr. BR8: Swan 67Ed 140
Selan Gdns. UB4: Yead 43X 85
Selbie Av. NW10 36Va 68
Selborne Av. DA5: Bexl 60Ad 117
E12 35Qc 74
Selborne Gdns. NW4 28Wa 48
UB6: G'frd 39Ja 66
Selborne Pl. KT13: Weyb 79T 150
Selborne Rd. CR0: C'don 76Ub 157
DA14: Sidc 63Xc 139
E17 29Bc 52
IG1: Ilf 33Qc 74
KT3: N Mald 68Ua 132
N14 20Nb 32
N22 25Pb 50
SE5 54Tb 113
Selborne Wlk. E17 29Bc 52
Selborne Wlk. Shop. Cen. E17 28Bc 52
Selbourne Av. KT6: Surb 75Pa 153
KT15: New H 81K 169
Selbourne Cl. DA3: Lfield 69Fe 143
KT15: New H 81K 169
Selbourne Ho. SE1 3F 231
Selbourne Sq. RH9: G'stone 2A 210
Selby Av. AL3: St A 2B 6
Selby Centre, The 23Ub 51
Selby Chase HA4: Ruis 33X 65
Selby Cl. BR7: Chst 65Qc 138
E6 43Nc 94
KT9: Chess 80Na 153
Selby Gdns. UB1: S'hall 42Ca 85
Selby Grn. SM5: Cars 73Gb 155
Selby Rd. E11 34Gc 73
E13 43Kc 93
N17 24Ub 51
SE20 68Wb 135
SM5: Cars 73Gb 155
TW15: Ashf 65S 128
W5 42Ka 86
Selby Sq. *W10* 41Ab 88
(off Dowland St.)
Selby St. E1 42Wb 91
Selby Wlk. GU21: Wok 10M 167
Selcroft Ho. *SE10* 50Hc 93
(off Glenister Rd.)
Selcroft Rd. CR8: Purl 84Rb 177
Selden Hill HP2: Hem H 3M 3
Selden Ho. *SE15* 54Yb 114
(off Selden Rd.)
Selden Rd. SE15 54Yb 114
Selden Wlk. N7 33Pb 70
Seldon Ho. *SW1* 50Lb 90
(off Churchill Gdns.)
SW8 52Lb 112
(off Stewart's Rd.)
Selfridges 3J 221
SELHURST 72Ub 157
Selhurst Cl. GU21: Wok 87B 168
SW19 60Za 110
Selhurst New Rd. SE25 72Ub 157
Selhurst Pk. 70Ub 135
Selhurst Pl. SE25: C'don 72Ub 157
Selhurst Rd. N9 20Tb 33
SE25 72Ub 157
Selig Ct. NW11 31Ab 68
Selim Ct. *SL1: Slou* 7M 81
(off Clifton Rd.)
Selina Ho. NW8 5C 214
Selinas La. RM8: Dag 31Ad 75
Selkirk Dr. DA8: Erith 53Gd 118
Selkirk Ho. *N1* 39Pb 70
(off Bingfield St.)
Selkirk Rd. SW17 63Gb 133
TW2: Twick 61Ea 130
Sellers Cl. WD6: Bore 11Sa 29
Sellers Hall Cl. N3 24Cb 49
Sellincourt Rd. SW17 64Gb 133
Sellindge Cl. BR3: Beck 66Bc 136
Sellons Av. NW10 39Va 68
Sellwood Dr. EN5: Barn 15Za 30
Selman Ho. E9 37Ac 72
SELSDON 82Yb 178
Selsdon Av. CR2: S Croy 79Tb 157
Selsdon Cl. KT6: Surb 71Na 153
RM5: Col R 24Ed 56
Selsdon Cres. CR2: Sels 81Yb 178
Selsdon Pk. Hotel Golf Course 83Yb 178
Selsdon Pk. Rd. CR0: Sels 81Zb 178
CR2: Sels 81Zb 178
Selsdon Rd. CR2: S Croy 78Tb 157
E11 31Jc 73
E13 39Lc 73

Selsdon Rd. KT15: New H . . . 83J 169
NW2 . . . 33Va 68
SE27 . . . 62Qb 134
Selsdon Way E14 . . . 48Dc 92
Selsdon Wood Nature Reserve . . . 83Ac 178
Selsea Pl. N16 . . . 36Ub 71
Selsey WC1 . . . 4G 217
Selsey Cres. DA16: Well . . . 53Zc 117
Selsey St. E14 . . . 43Cc 92
Selvage La. NW7 . . . 22Ta 47
Selway Cl. HA5: Eastc . . . 28X 45
Selway Ho. SW8 . . . 53Nb 112
(off Sth. Lambeth Rd.)
Selwin Ct. KT12: Walt T . . . 74Y 151
Selwood Cl. TW19: Stanw . . . 58L 105
Selwood Gdns. TW19: Stanw . . . 58L 105
Selwood Pl. SW7 . . . 7B 226 (50Fb 89)
Selwood Rd. CM14: B'wood . . . 20Vd 40
CR0: C'don . . . 75Xb 157
GU22: Wok . . . 92D 188
KT9: Chess . . . 77Ma 153
SM3: Sutt . . . 74Bb 155
Selwoods SW2 . . . 59Qb 112
Selwood Ter. SW7 . . . 7B 226 (50Fb 89)
Selworthy Cl. E11 . . . 29Jc 53
Selworthy Ho. SW11 . . . 53Fb 111
(off Battersea Church Rd.)
Selworthy Rd. SE6 . . . 62Bc 136
Selwyn Av. AL10: Hat . . . 1P 7
E4 . . . 23Ec 52
IG3: Ilf . . . 30Vc 55
TW9: Rich . . . 55Na 109
Selwyn Cl. SL4: Wind . . . 4B 102
TW4: Houn . . . 56Aa 107
Selwyn Ct. E17 . . . 29Cc 52
(off Yunus Khan Cl.)
HA8: Edg . . . 24Ra 47
HA9: Wemb . . . 34Sa 67
SE3 . . . 55Hc 115
TW10: Rich . . . 57Pa 109
(off Church Rd.)
Selwyn Cres. AL10: Hat . . . 1A 8
DA16: Well . . . 55Xc 117
Selwyn Dr. AL10: Hat . . . 1P 7
Selwyn Pl. BR5: St P . . . 69Xc 139
SL1: Slou . . . 5D 80
Selwyn Rd. E3 . . . 40Bc 72
E13 . . . 39Kc 73
KT3: N Mald . . . 71Ta 153
NW10 . . . 38Ua 68
RM18: Tilb . . . 4B 122
Semley Ga. E9 . . . 37Bc 72
(not continuous)
Semley Ho. SW1 . . . 6K 227
Semley Pl. SW1 . . . 6J 227 (49Jb 90)
Semley Rd. SW16 . . . 68Nb 134
Semper Cl. GU21: Knap . . . 9J 167
Semper Rd. RM16: Grays . . . 7E 100
Sempill Rd. HP3: Hem H . . . 5N 3
Semples SS17: Stan H . . . 1P 101
Senate St. SE15 . . . 54Yb 114
Senators Lodge E3 . . . 40Ac 72
(off Roman Rd.)
Senator Wlk. SE28 . . . 48Tc 94
SEND . . . 95F 188
Sendall Ct. SW11 . . . 55Fb 111
(off Winstanley Rd.)
Send & Ripley Local History Mus.
. . . 93K 189
Send Barns La. GU23: Send . . . 96F 188
Send Cl. GU23: Send . . . 95E 188
Send Hill GU23: Send . . . 97E 188
SEND MARSH . . . 95H 189
Send Marsh Grn. GU23: Rip . . . 95H 189
Send Marsh Rd. GU23: Rip, Send . . . 96F 188
Send Pde. Cl. GU23: Send . . . 95E 188
Send Rd. GU23: Send . . . 95D 188
Seneca Rd. CR7: Thor H . . . 70Sb 135
Sener Ct. CR2: S Croy . . . 79Sb 157
Senga Rd. SM6: Wall . . . 74Jb 156
Senhouse Rd. SM3: Cheam . . . 76Za 154
Senior St. W2 . . . 43Db 89
Senlac Rd. SE12 . . . 60Kc 115
Sennen Rd. EN1: Enf . . . 17Vb 33
Sennen Wlk. SE9 . . . 62Nc 138
Sennocke Ct. TN13: S'oaks . . . 97Kd 203
Senrab St. E1 . . . 44Zb 92
Sentamu Cl. SE24 . . . 60Rb 113
Sentinel WD17: Wat . . . 12X 27
Sentinel Cl. UB5: N'olt . . . 42Aa 85
Sentinel Sq. NW4 . . . 28Ya 48
Sentis Ct. HA6: Nwood . . . 23V 44
September Ct. UB1: S'hall . . . 46Da 85
(off Dormer's Wells La.)
UB8: Uxb . . . 40M 63
September Way HA7: Stan . . . 23Ka 46
Septimus Pl. EN1: Enf . . . 15Wb 33
Sequoia Cl. WD23: B Hea . . . 18Fa 28
Sequoia Gdns. BR6: Orp . . . 73Vc 161
Sequoia Pk. HA5: Hat E . . . 23Da 45
Seraph Ct. EC1 . . . 3D 218
Serbin Cl. E10 . . . 31Ec 72
Serenaders Rd. SW9 . . . 54Qb 112
Serenity Apartments E17 . . . 29Dc 52
Serenity Ct. DA9: Ghithe . . . 56Wd 120
(off Evelyn Wlk.)
Seren Pk. Gdns. SE3 . . . 51Gc 115
Sergeant Ind. Est. SW18 . . . 58Db 111
Sergeants Grn. La. EN9: Walt A . . . 5Lc 21
Sergeants Pl. CR3: Cat'm . . . 94Sb 197
Sergehill La. WD5: Bedm . . . 9F 4
Serica Ct. SE10 . . . 52Ec 114
Serjeants Inn EC4 . . . 3A 224 (44Qb 90)
Serlby Ct. W14 . . . 48Bb 89
(off Somerset Sq.)
Serle St. WC2 . . . 2J 223 (44Pb 90)
Sermed Ct. SL2: Slou . . . 6N 81
Sermon Dr. BR8: Swan . . . 69Ed 140
Sermon La. EC4 . . . 3D 224
Serpentine, The . . . 7D 220 (46Gb 89)
Serpentine Ct. SE16 . . . 47Zb 92
(off Christopher Cl.)
TN13: S'oaks . . . 94Md 203
Serpentine Gallery . . . 7B 220 (47Fb 89)
Serpentine Grn. RH1: Mers . . . 1D 208
Serpentine Rd.
TN13: S'oaks . . . 95Ld 203
W2 . . . 7D 220 (46Gb 89)
Service Rd., The EN6: Pot B . . . 4Cb 17
Serviden Dr. BR1: Brom . . . 67Mc 137
Servite Ho. BR3: Beck . . . 67Bc 136
GU21: Knap . . . 9H 167
KT4: Wor Pk . . . 75Va 154
(off The Avenue)
Servite Ho. N14 . . . 15Kb 32
(off Bramley Rd.)
Servius Ct. TW8: Bford . . . 52Ma 109
Setchell Rd. SE1 . . . 5K 231 (49Vb 91)
Setchell Way SE1 . . . 5K 231 (49Vb 91)
Seth St. SE16 . . . 47Yb 92
Seton Gdns. RM9: Dag . . . 38Yc 75
Settle Point E13 . . . 40Jc 73
Settle Rd. RM3: Rom . . . 21Qd 57
Settlers Ct. E14 . . . 45Fc 93
Settles St. E1 . . . 43Wb 91
Settrington Rd. SW6 . . . 54Db 111
Seven Acres BR8: Crock . . . 72Fd 162
DA3: New A . . . 76Ae 165
HA6: Nwood . . . 23X 45
SM5: Cars . . . 75Gb 155
Seven Arches App. KT13: Weyb . . . 80P 149
Seven Arches Rd. CM14: B'wood . . . 20Zd 41
Seven Dials WC2 . . . 3F 223 (44Nb 90)
Seven Dials Ct. WC2 . . . 3F 223
Sevenex Pde. HA9: Wemb . . . 36Na 67
Seven Hills Cl. KT12: W Vill . . . 81U 170
Seven Hills Rd. KT11: Cobh . . . 82U 170
KT12: Hers, W Vill . . . 81U 170
SL0: Iver H . . . 36D 62
Seven Hills Rd. Sth.
KT11: Cobh . . . 85U 170
Seven Islands Leisure Cen. . . . 48Yb 92
SEVEN KINGS . . . 32Uc 74
Seven Kings Rd. IG3: Ilf . . . 32Uc 74
Seven Kings Way KT2: King T . . . 67Na 131
SEVENOAKS . . . 97Ld 203
Sevenoaks Bus. Cen.
TN14: S'oaks . . . 93Ld 203
Sevenoaks By-Pass
TN14: Ide H, S'oaks, Sund . . . 95Ed 202
Sevenoaks Cl. DA7: Bex . . . 56Dd 118
RM3: Rom . . . 21Ld 57
SM2: Sutt . . . 82Cb 175
SEVENOAKS COMMON . . . 100Kd 203
Sevenoaks Ct. HA6: Nwood . . . 24S 44
Sevenoaks Leisure Cen. . . . 97Ld 203
Sevenoaks Mus. & Art Gallery . . . 97Ld 203
Sevenoaks Rd.
BR6: Chels, Orp . . . 78Vc 161
BR6: Prat B . . . 80Vc 161
SE4 . . . 58Ac 114
TN14: Hals . . . 81Ad 181
TN14: Otf, S'oaks . . . 88Kd 183
TN15: Bor G . . . 92Ae 205
TN15: Igh, Seal . . . 95Vd 204
Sevenoaks Way BR5: St P . . . 66Yc 139
DA14: Sidc . . . 66Yc 139
Sevenoaks Wildlife Reserve . . . 93Hd 202
Sevenseas Rd.
TW6: H'row A . . . 58S 106
SEVEN SISTERS . . . 29Vb 51
Seven Sisters Rd. N4 . . . 33Qb 70
N7 . . . 34Pb 70
N15 . . . 33Qb 70
Seven Stars Cnr. W12 . . . 48Wa 88
Seven Stars Yd. E1 . . . 7K 219
Seventh Av. E12 . . . 35Pc 74
KT20: Lwr K . . . 97Ab 194
UB3: Hayes . . . 46W 84
Seven Ways Pde. IG2: Ilf . . . 29Qc 54
Severn RM18: E Til . . . 8K 101
Severnake Cl. E14 . . . 49Cc 92
Severn Av. RM2: Rom . . . 27Kd 57
W10 . . . 41Ab 88
Severn Ct. KT2: King T . . . 67Ma 131
(off John Williams Cl.)
Severn Cres. SL3: L'ly . . . 50D 82
Severn Dr. EN1: Enf . . . 10Wb 19
KT10: Hin W . . . 75Ja 152
KT12: Walt T . . . 75Z 151
RM14: Upm . . . 30Td 58
Severn Rd. RM15: Avel . . . 44Sd 98
Severns Fld. CM16: Epp . . . 1Wc 23
Severnvale AL2: Lon C . . . 9K 7
Severn Way NW10 . . . 36Va 68
WD25: Wat . . . 6Y 13
Severus Ho. UB3: Hayes . . . 44T 84
Severus Rd. SW11 . . . 56Gb 111
Seville Ho. E1 . . . 46Wb 91
(off Hellings St.)
Seville M. N1 . . . 38Ub 71
Seville St. SW1 . . . 2G 227 (47Hb 89)
Sevington Rd. NW4 . . . 30Xa 48
Sevington St. W9 . . . 42Db 89
Seward Rd. BR3: Beck . . . 68Zb 136
W7 . . . 47Ja 86
SEWARDSTONE . . . 12Ec 34
SEWARDSTONEBURY . . . 15Gc 35
Sewardstone Cl. E4 . . . 11Ec 34
Sewardstone Gdns. E4 . . . 15Dc 34
Sewardstone Rd. E2 . . . 40Yb 72
E4 . . . 17Dc 34
EN9: Enf, Walt A . . . 6Ec 20
Sewardstone St. EN9: Walt A . . . 6Ec 20
Seward St. EC1 . . . 5C 218 (41Rb 91)
Sewdley St. E5 . . . 34Zb 72
Sewell Cl. AL4: St A . . . 2J 7
RM16: Chaf H . . . 50Yd 98
Sewell Rd. SE2 . . . 48Wc 95
Sewell St. E13 . . . 41Jc 93
Sextant Av. E14 . . . 49Fc 93
Sexton Cl. RM13: Rain . . . 39Hd 76
Sexton Ct. E14 . . . 45Fc 93
(off Newport Av.)
Sexton Rd. RM18: Tilb . . . 3B 122
Sextons Ho. SE10 . . . 51Ec 114
(off Bardsley La.)
Seymer Rd. RM1: Rom . . . 27Fd 56
Seymore M. SE14 . . . 52Bc 114
(off New Cross Rd.)
Seymour Av. CR3: Cat'm . . . 95Sb 197
KT17: Ewe . . . 81Xa 174
N17 . . . 26Wb 51
SM4: Mord . . . 73Za 154
Seymour Chase CM16: Epp . . . 1Xc 23
Seymour Cl. HA5: Hat E . . . 25Ba 45
IG10: Lough . . . 16Nc 36
KT8: E Mos . . . 71Ea 152
Seymour Ct. E4 . . . 19Hc 35
KT1: Hamp W . . . 67Ma 131
(off Seymour Rd.)
KT11: Cobh . . . 85V 170
KT19: Ewe . . . 81Ua 174
N10 . . . 26Jb 50
N21 . . . 16Pb 32
NW2 . . . 33Xa 68
Seymour Cres. HP2: Hem H . . . 2N 3
Seymour Dr. BR2: Brom . . . 74Pc 160
Seymour Gdns. HA4: Ruis . . . 32Z 65
IG1: Ilf . . . 32Pc 74
KT5: Surb . . . 71Pa 153
SE4 . . . 55Ac 114
TW1: Twick . . . 59Ka 108
TW13: Hanw . . . 63Y 129
Seymour Gro. WD19: Wat . . . 17Y 27
Seymour Ho. E16 . . . 46Jc 93
(off De Quincey M.)
NW1 . . . 3E 216
SL3: L'ly . . . 47A 82
SM2: Sutt . . . 79Db 155
(off Mulgrave Rd.)
WC1 . . . 5F 217
Seymour Leisure Cen. . . . 1F 221 (43Hb 89)
Seymour M. KT17: Ewe . . . 82Wa 174
W1 . . . 2H 221 (44Jb 90)
Seymour Pl. GU22: Wok . . . 2M 187
KT13: Weyb . . . 76R 150
RM11: Horn . . . 31Md 77
SE25 . . . 70Xb 135
W1 . . . 7E 214 (43Hb 89)
Seymour Rd. CR4: Mitc . . . 73Jb 156
DA11: Nflt . . . 10B 122
E4 . . . 18Dc 34
E6 . . . 40Mc 73
E10 . . . 32Bc 72
KT1: Hamp W . . . 67Ma 131
KT8: W Mole, E Mos . . . 71Ea 152
N3 . . . 24Db 49
N8 . . . 29Qb 50
N9 . . . 19Xb 33
RM18: Tilb . . . 3B 122
SL1: Slou . . . 7G 80
SM5: Cars . . . 78Jb 156
SW18 . . . 59Bb 111
SW19 . . . 62Za 132
TW12: Hamp H . . . 64Ea 130
W4 . . . 49Sa 87
Seymours, The IG10: Lough . . . 11Qc 36
Seymour St. SE18 . . . 48Sc 94
W1 . . . 3F 221 (44Hb 89)
W2 . . . 3F 221 (44Hb 89)
Seymour Ter. SE20 . . . 67Xb 135
Seymour Vs. SE20 . . . 67Xb 135
Seymour Wlk. DA10: Swans . . . 59Ae 121
SW10 . . . 51Eb 111
Seymour Way TW16: Sun . . . 66V 128
Seyssel St. E14 . . . 49Ec 92
Shaa Rd. W3 . . . 45Ta 87
Shabana Rd. W12 . . . 46Xa 88
Shabden Cotts. CR5: Chip . . . 93Hb 195
Shab Hall Cotts. TN13: Dun G . . . 90Ed 182
Shacklands Rd.
TN14: Bad M, S'ham . . . 83Dd 182
Shackleford Rd. GU22: Wok . . . 92C 188
Shacklegate La. TW11: Tedd . . . 63Ga 130
Shackleton Cl. SE23 . . . 61Xb 135
Shackleton Ct. E14 . . . 50Cc 92
(off Maritime Quay)
TW19: Stanw . . . 58N 105
(off Whitley Cl.)
W12 . . . 47Xa 88
(off Scott's Rd.)
Shackleton Ho. E1 . . . 46Yb 92
(off Prusom St.)
NW10 . . . 38Ta 67
Shackleton Rd. SL1: Slou . . . 5K 81
UB1: S'hall . . . 45Ba 85
Shackleton Way WD5: Ab L . . . 4W 12
(off Lysander Way)
SHACKLEWELL . . . 35Vb 71
Shacklewell Grn. E8 . . . 35Vb 71
Shacklewell Ho. E8 . . . 35Vb 71
Shacklewell La. E8 . . . 36Vb 71
Shacklewell Rd. N16 . . . 35Vb 71
Shacklewell Row E8 . . . 35Vb 71
Shacklewell St. E2 . . . 5K 219 (41Vb 91)
Shadbolt Av. E4 . . . 22Ac 52
Shadbolt Cl. KT4: Wor Pk . . . 75Va 154
Shad Thames SE1 . . . 7K 225 (46Vb 91)
(Anchor Brewhouse)
SE1 . . . 2K 231 (47Vb 91)
(Jamaica Rd.)
SHADWELL . . . 45Xb 91
Shadwell Ct. UB5: N'olt . . . 40Ba 65
Shadwell Dr. UB5: N'olt . . . 41Ba 85
Shadwell Gdns. E1 . . . 45Yb 92
Shadwell Pierhead E1 . . . 45Yb 92
Shadwell Pl. E1 . . . 45Yb 92
(off Sutton St.)
Shady Bush Cl. WD23: Bush . . . 17Ea 28
Shady La. WD17: Wat . . . 12X 27
Shaef Way TW11: Tedd . . . 66Ja 130
Shafter Rd. RM10: Dag . . . 37Ed 76
Shaftesbury IG10: Lough . . . 13Mc 35
Shaftesbury Av. EN3: Enf H . . . 12Zb 34
EN5: New Bar . . . 14Eb 31
HA2: Harr . . . 32Da 65
HA3: Kenton . . . 29Ma 47
TW14: Felt . . . 58W 106
UB2: S'hall . . . 49Ca 85
W1 . . . 4D 222 (45Mb 90)
WC1 . . . 2F 223 (44Nb 90)
WC2 . . . 2F 223 (44Nb 90)
Shaftesbury Barnet Harriers . . . 24Ya 48
Shaftesbury Cen. W10 . . . 42Za 88
(off Barlby Rd.)
Shaftesbury Circ. HA2: Harr . . . 32Ea 66
Shaftesbury Ct. E6 . . . 44Qc 94
(off Sapphire Cl.)
N1 . . . 2F 219
SE1 . . . 3J 231
SE5 . . . 56Tb 113
SL1: Slou . . . 7J 81
SW6 . . . 53Db 111
(off Maltings Pl.)
SW16 . . . 62Mb 134
WD3: Crox G . . . 14R 26
Shaftesbury Cres. TW18: Staines . . . 66M 127
Shaftesbury Gdns. NW10 . . . 42Ua 88
Shaftesbury Ho. CR5: Coul . . . 94Mb 196
E16 . . . 44Hc 93
(off Tarling Rd.)
Shaftesbury La. DA1: Dart . . . 56Rd 119
Shaftesbury Lodge E14 . . . 44Dc 92
(off Upper Nth. St.)
Shaftesbury M. SW4 . . . 57Lb 112
W8 . . . 48Cb 89
Shaftesbury Pde. HA2: Harr . . . 32Ea 66
Shaftesbury Pl. EC2 . . . 1D 224
(off Aldersgate St.)
W14 . . . 49Bb 89
(off Warwick Rd.)
Shaftesbury Point E13 . . . 40Jc 73
(off High St.)
Shaftesbury Rd. BR3: Beck . . . 68Bc 136
CM16: Epp . . . 1Vc 23
E4 . . . 18Fc 35
E7 . . . 38Lc 73
E10 . . . 32Cc 72
E17 . . . 30Dc 52
GU22: Wok . . . 89D 168
GU24: Bisl . . . 8D 166
N18 . . . 23Ub 51
N19 . . . 32Nb 70
RM1: Rom . . . 30Hd 56
SM5: Cars . . . 73Fb 155
TW9: Rich . . . 55Na 109
WD17: Wat . . . 13Y 27
Shaftesbury Row SE8 . . . 52Cc 114
(off Speedwell St.)
Shaftesburys, The IG11: Bark . . . 40Sc 74
Shaftesbury St. N1 . . . 2E 218 (40Sb 71)
(not continuous)
Shaftesbury Theatre . . . 2F 223
Shaftesbury Vs. W8 . . . 48Cb 89
(off Allen St.)
Shaftesbury Way TW2: Twick . . . 62Fa 130
WD4: K Lan . . . 10C 4
Shaftesbury Waye UB4: Yead . . . 43Y 85
Shafto M. SW1 . . . 4G 227 (48Hb 89)
Shafton M. E9 . . . 39Zb 72
Shafton Rd. E9 . . . 39Zb 72
Shaftsbury Ct. DA8: Erith . . . 53Hd 118
(off Selkirk Dr.)
Shafts Ct. EC3 . . . 3H 225 (44Ub 91)
Shaggy Calf La. SL2: Slou . . . 5L 81
Shahjalal Ho. E2 . . . 40Wb 71
(off Pritchards Rd.)
Shakespeare Av. N11 . . . 22Lb 50
NW10 . . . 39Ta 67
RM18: Tilb . . . 4D 122
TW14: Felt . . . 58W 106
UB4: Hayes, Yead . . . 44W 84
(not continuous)
Shakespeare Cl. HA3: Kenton . . . 31Qa 67
Shakespeare Ct. EN5: New Bar . . . 13Db 31
HA3: Kenton . . . 30Pa 47
NW6 . . . 38Eb 69
(off Fairfax Rd.)
Shakespeare Cres. E12 . . . 37Pc 74
Shakespeare Dr. HA3: Kenton . . . 30Pa 47
WD6: Bore . . . 14Qa 29
Shakespeare Gdns. N2 . . . 28Hb 49
Shakespeare Ho. E9 . . . 38Yb 72
(off Lyme Gro.)
N14 . . . 19Mb 32
Shakespeare Ind. Est. WD24: Wat . . . 10W 12
Shakespeare Rd. DA1: Dart . . . 56Qd 119
DA7: Bex . . . 53Ad 117
E17 . . . 26Zb 52
KT15: Add . . . 77M 149
N3 . . . 25Cb 49
NW7 . . . 21Va 48
NW10 . . . 39Ta 67
RM1: Rom . . . 30Hd 56
SE24 . . . 57Rb 113
W3 . . . 46Sa 87
W7 . . . 45Ha 86
Shakespeare's Globe & Exhibition
. . . 5D 224 (46Sb 91)
Shakespeare Sq. IG6: Ilf . . . 23Sc 54
Shakespeare St. WD24: Wat . . . 10X 13
Shakespeare Twr. EC2 . . . 7E 218
Shakespeare Way TW13: Hanw . . . 63Y 129
Shakspeare M. N16 . . . 35Ub 71
Shakspeare Wlk. N16 . . . 35Ub 71
Shalbourne Sq. E9 . . . 37Bc 72
Shalcomb St. SW10 . . . 51Eb 111
Shalcross Dr. EN8: Chesh . . . 2Bc 20
Shalden Ho. SW15 . . . 58Va 110
Shaldon Dr. HA4: Ruis . . . 35Y 65
SM4: Mord . . . 71Ab 154
Shaldon Rd. HA8: Edg . . . 26Pa 47
Shaldon Way KT12: Walt T . . . 76Y 151
Shale Grn. RH1: Mers . . . 1D 208
Shalfleet Dr. W10 . . . 45Za 88
Shalford Cl. BR6: Farnb . . . 77Sc 160
Shalford Ct. N1 . . . 1B 218 (40Rb 71)
Shalford Ho. SE1 . . . 3G 231 (48Tb 91)
Shalimar Gdns. W3 . . . 45Sa 87
Shalimar Rd. W3 . . . 45Sa 87
Shallcross Cres. AL10: Hat . . . 3C 8
Shallons Rd. SE9 . . . 63Rc 138
Shalstone Rd. SW14 . . . 55Ra 109
Shalston Vs. KT6: Surb . . . 72Pa 153
Shambles, The TN13: S'oaks . . . 97Ld 203
Shamrock Cl. KT22: Fet . . . 93Fa 192
Shamrock Cotts. GU23: Worp . . . 10M 187
Shamrock Ho. SE26 . . . 63Wb 135
(off Talisman Sq.)
Shamrock Rd. CR0: C'don . . . 72Pb 156
DA12: Grav'nd . . . 9G 122
Shamrock St. SW4 . . . 55Mb 112
Shamrock Way N14 . . . 18Kb 32
Shandon Rd. SW4 . . . 58Lb 112
Shand St. SE1 . . . 1H 231 (47Ub 91)
Shandy St. E1 . . . 43Zb 92
Shan Ho. WC1 . . . 6H 217
Shanklin Cl. EN7: Chesh . . . 1Vb 19
Shanklin Gdns. WD19: Wat . . . 21Y 45
Shanklin Ho. E17 . . . 26Bc 52
Shanklin Rd. N8 . . . 29Mb 50
N15 . . . 28Wb 51
Shannon Cl. NW2 . . . 34Za 68
UB2: S'hall . . . 50Z 85
Shannon Commercial Cen.
KT3: N Mald . . . 70Wa 132
SHANNON CORNER . . . 70Wa 132
Shannon Cnr. Retail Pk.
KT3: N Mald . . . 70Wa 132
Shannon Ct. CR0: C'don . . . 74Sb 157
(off Tavistock Rd.)
N16 . . . 34Ub 71
SE15 . . . 52Vb 113
(off Garnies Cl.)
Shannon Gro. SW9 . . . 56Pb 112
Shannon M. SE3 . . . 56Hc 115
Shannon Pl. NW8 . . . 1E 214 (40Gb 69)
Shannon Way BR3: Beck . . . 65Dc 136
RM15: Avel . . . 45Sd 98
Shanti Ct. SW18 . . . 60Cb 111
Shantock Hall La. HP3: Bov . . . 1A 10
Shantock La. HP3: Bov . . . 2A 10
Shap Cres. SM5: Cars . . . 74Hb 155
Shapland Way N13 . . . 22Pb 50
Shapwick Cl. N11 . . . 22Hb 49
Shard, The SE1 . . . 7G 225
Shardcroft Av. SE24 . . . 57Rb 113
Shardeloes Rd. SE14 . . . 54Bc 114
Shard's Sq. SE15 . . . 51Wb 113
Sharland Cl. CR7: Thor H . . . 72Qb 156
Sharland Rd. DA12: Grav'nd . . . 1E 144
Sharman Ct. DA14: Sidc . . . 63Wc 139
Sharman Row SL3: L'ly . . . 50B 82
Sharnbrooke Cl. DA16: Well . . . 55Yc 117
Sharnbrook Ho. W14 . . . 51Cb 111
Sharney Av. SL3: L'ly . . . 48D 82
Sharon Cl. KT6: Surb . . . 74La 152
KT19: Eps . . . 85Sa 173
KT23: Bookh . . . 96Ca 191
Sharon Ct. CR2: S Croy . . . 78Sb 157
(off Warham Rd.)
Sharon Gdns. E9 . . . 39Yb 72
Sharon Rd. EN3: Enf H . . . 12Ac 34
W4 . . . 50Ta 87
Sharpe Cl. W7 . . . 43Ha 86
Sharpes La. HP1: Hem H . . . 4D 2
Sharp Ho. SW8 . . . 55Kb 112
TW1: Twick . . . 58Ma 109
Sharpleshall St. NW1 . . . 38Hb 69
Sharpley Ct. SE1 . . . 1B 230
Sharpness Cl. UB4: Yead . . . 43Aa 85
Sharp's La. HA4: Ruis . . . 31T 64
Sharp Way DA1: Dart . . . 55Pd 119
Sharratt St. SE15 . . . 51Yb 114
Sharsted St. SE17 . . . 7B 230 (50Rb 91)
Sharvel La. UB5: N'olt . . . 39W 64
Sharwood WC1 . . . 2J 217
Shaver's Pl. SW1 . . . 5D 222
Shaw, The BR7: Chst . . . 66Sc 138
Shaw Av. IG11: Bark . . . 40Ad 75
Shawbrooke Rd. SE9 . . . 57Lc 115
Shawbury Cl. NW9 . . . 25Ua 48
Shawbury Rd. SE22 . . . 57Vb 113
Shaw Cl. CR2: Sande . . . 84Vb 177
EN8: Chesh . . . 1Yb 20
KT16: Ott . . . 79E 148
KT17: Ewe . . . 83Va 174
RM11: Horn . . . 32Kd 77
SE28 . . . 46Xc 95
TW19: Stanw . . . 60N 105
WD23: B Hea . . . 19Ga 28
Shaw Ct. CR3: Cat'm . . . 93Tb 197
SL4: Old Win . . . 7L 103
SM4: Mord . . . 73Eb 155
W3 . . . 48Sa 87
(off All Saints Rd.)
Shaw Cres. CM13: Hut . . . 14Fe 41
CR2: Sande . . . 84Vb 177
E14 . . . 43Ac 92
RM18: Tilb . . . 3D 122
Shaw Dr. KT12: Walt T . . . 73Y 151
SHAW FARM . . . 6J 103
Shawfield Ct. UB7: W Dray . . . 48N 83
Shawfield Pk. BR1: Brom . . . 68Mc 137
Shawfield St. SW3 . . . 7E 226 (50Gb 89)
Shawford Ct. SW15 . . . 59Wa 110
Shawford Rd. KT19: Ewe . . . 79Ta 153
Shaw Gdns. IG11: Bark . . . 40Ad 75
SL3: L'ly . . . 50B 82
Shaw Gro. CR5: Coul . . . 92Sb 197
Shaw Ho. DA17: Belv . . . 50Bd 95
E16 . . . 46Qc 94
(off Claremont St.)
SM7: Bans . . . 91Eb 195
Shawley Cres. KT18: Tatt C . . . 90Ya 174
Shawley Way KT18: Tatt C . . . 90Xa 174
Shaw Path BR1: Brom . . . 62Hc 137
Shaw Pl. N2 . . . 27Jb 50
Shaw Rd. BR1: Brom . . . 62Hc 137
EN3: Enf H . . . 11Zb 34
SE22 . . . 56Ub 113
TN16: Tats . . . 92Lc 199
Shaw's Cnr. RH1: Redh . . . 6N 207
Shaws Cotts. SE23 . . . 62Ac 136
Shaws Path KT1: Hamp W . . . 67La 130
(off Bennett Cl.)
Shaw Sq. E17 . . . 25Ac 52
Shaw Theatre . . . 4E 216 (41Mb 90)
Shaw Way SM6: Wall . . . 80Nb 156
Shaxton Cres. CR0: New Ad . . . 81Ec 178
Shead Ct. E1 . . . 44Xb 91
(off James Voller Way)
Sheaf Cotts. KT7: T Ditt . . . 74Ga 152
(off Weston Grn.)
Shearing Dr. SM5: Cars . . . 73Eb 155
Shearling Way N7 . . . 37Nb 70
Shearman Rd. SE3 . . . 56Hc 115
SHEARS, THE . . . 66U 128
Shears Ct. DA1: Dart . . . 61Ld 141
Shears Ct. TW16: Sun . . . 66U 128
Shears Grn. Ct. DA11: Nflt . . . 1C 144
Shearsmith Ho. E1 . . . 45Wb 91
(off Hindmarsh Cl.)
Shears Way TW16: Sun . . . 67U 128
Shearwater DA3: Lfield . . . 69De 143
Shearwater Cl. IG11: Bark . . . 41Wc 95
Shearwater Ct. DA9: Ghithe . . . 58Wd 120
(off Waterstone Way)
E1 . . . 45Wb 91
(off Star Pl.)
SE8 . . . 51Bc 114
(off Abinger Gro.)
Shearwater Rd. SM1: Sutt . . . 78Bb 155
Shearwater Way UB4: Yead . . . 44Z 85
Shearwood Cres. DA1: Cray . . . 55Hd 118
Sheath Cotts. KT7: T Ditt . . . 72Ka 152
(off Ferry Rd.)
Sheath La. KT22: Oxs . . . 85Da 171
Sheaveshill Av. NW9 . . . 28Ua 48
Sheaveshill Ct. NW9 . . . 28Ta 47
Sheaveshill Pde. NW9 . . . 28Ua 48
(off Sheaveshill Av.)
Sheba Ct. N17 . . . 23Wb 51
(off Altair Cl.)
Sheba Pl. E1 . . . 6K 219 (42Vb 91)
Sheehy Way SL2: Slou . . . 5M 81
Sheen Comn. Dr. TW10: Rich . . . 56Qa 109
Sheen Ct. TW10: Rich . . . 56Qa 109
Sheen Ct. Rd. TW10: Rich . . . 56Qa 109
Sheendale Rd. TW9: Rich . . . 56Pa 109
Sheenewood SE26 . . . 63Xb 135
Sheen Ga. Gdns. SW14 . . . 56Sa 109
Sheengate Mans. SW14 . . . 56Ta 109
Sheen Gro. N1 . . . 39Qb 70
Sheen La. SW14 . . . 57Sa 109
Sheen Pk. TW9: Rich . . . 56Pa 109
Sheen Rd. BR5: St M Cry . . . 70Vc 139
TW9: Rich . . . 57Na 109
TW10: Rich . . . 57Na 109

Sheen Way SM6: Wall 78Pb **156**
Sheen Wood SW14 . . . . .57Sa **109**
Sheepbarn La. CR6: W'ham 84Hc **179**
Sheepcot Dr. WD25: Wat 6Y **13**
Sheepcote Cl. TW5: Cran 52W **106**
Sheepcote Gdns. UB9: Den 30J **43**
Sheepcote La. BR5: St M Cry 71Bd **161**
BR8: Swan 71Bd **161**
SW11 . . . . .54Hb **111**
Sheepcote Rd. HA1: Harr 30Ha **46**
HP2: Hem H 2P **3**
SL4: Eton W 10E **80**
SL4: Wind 4C **102**
Sheepcotes Rd. RM6: Chad H 28Ad **55**
Sheepcot La. WD25: Wat 5W **12**
(not continuous)
Sheephouse Rd. HP3: Hem H 4P **3**
Sheephouse Way KT3: N Mald 74Ta **153**
Sheep La. E8 . . . . .39Xb **71**
Sheep Wlk. KT18: Eps D 93Ta **193**
RH2: Reig 3H **207**
TW17: Shep 73P **149**
Sheep Wlk., The GU22: Wok 90F **168**
Sheep Wlk. M. SW19 . . . . .65Za **132**
Sheerness M. E16 . . . . .47Rc **94**
SHEERWATER 86F **168**
Sheerwater Av. KT15: Wdhm 84G **168**
Sheerwater Bus. Cen. GU21: Wok . . .87E **168**
Sheerwater Rd. E16 . . . . .43Mc **93**
GU21: Wok 84G **168**
KT14: W Byf 84G **168**
KT15: Wdhm 84G **168**
Sheethanger La. HP3: Hem H 5J **3**
SHEET HILL 97Be **205**
Sheet Hill TN15: Plax 97Zd **205**
SHEET'S BRIDGE 1D **186**
Sheet's Heath La. GU24: Brkwd 1E **186**
Sheet St. SL4: Wind 4H **103**
Sheet St. Rd. SL4: Wind 3B **124**
Sheffield Dr. RM3: Rom 22Qd **57**
Sheffield Gdns. RM3: Rom 22Qd **57**
Sheffield Rd. SL1: Slou 4G **80**
TW6: H'row A 58S **106**
Sheffield Sq. E3 . . . . .41Bc **92**
Sheffield St. WC2 . . . . .3H **223** (44Pb **90**)
Sheffield Ter. W8 . . . . .46Cb **89**
Sheffield Way TW6: H'row A 57T **106**
Shefton Ri. HA6: Nwood 24W **44**
Sheila Cl. RM5: Col R 24Dd **56**
Sheila Rd. RM5: Col R 24Dd **56**
Sheilings, The RM11: Horn 29Pd **57**
TN15: Seal 92Pd **203**
Shelbourne Cl. HA5: Pinn 27Ba **45**
Shelbourne Pl. BR3: Beck 66Bc **136**
Shelbourne Rd. N17 . . . . .26Xb **51**
Shelburne Dr. TW4: Houn 58Ca **107**
Shelburne Rd. N7 . . . . .35Pb **70**
Shelbury Cl. DA14: Sidc 62Wc **139**
Shelbury Rd. SE22 . . . . .57Xb **113**
Sheldon Av. IG5: Ilf 26Rc **54**
N6 . . . . .31Gb **69**
Sheldon Cl. RH2: Reig 7K **207**
SE12 . . . . .57Kc **115**
SE20 . . . . .67Xb **135**
Sheldon Ct. EN5: New Bar 14Db **31**
RM7: Rush G 30Fd **56**
(off Union Rd.)
SW8 . . . . .52Nb **112**
(off Lansdowne Grn.)
Sheldon Ho. *N1 . . . . .39Ub* **71**
(off Kingsland Rd.)
Sheldon Pl. E2 . . . . .40Wb **71**
(not continuous)
Sheldon Rd. DA7: Bex 53Bd **117**
N18 . . . . .21Ub **51**
NW2 . . . . .35Za **68**
RM9: Dag 38Ad **75**
Sheldon Sq. W2 . . . . .1A **220** (43Eb **89**)
Sheldon St. CR0: C'don 76Sb **157**
Sheldrake Cl. E16 . . . . .46Pc **94**
Sheldrake Ct. *E6 . . . . .40Nc* **74**
(off St Bartholomew's Rd.)
Sheldrake Ho. *SE16 . . . . .49Zb* **92**
(off Tawny Way)
Sheldrake Pl. W8 . . . . .47Cb **89**
Sheldrick Cl. SW19 . . . . .68Fb **133**
Shelduck Cl. E15 . . . . .36Hc **73**
Shelduck Ct. *SE8 . . . . .51Bc* **114**
(off Pilot Cl.)
Sheldwich Ter. BR2: Brom 72Nc **160**
Shelford KT1: King T 68Qa **131**
Shelford Cl. RM16: Ors 3C **100**
Shelford Pl. N16 . . . . .34Tb **71**
Shelford Ri. SE19 . . . . .66Vb **135**
Shelford Rd. EN5: Barn 16Ya **30**
Shelgate Rd. SW11 . . . . .57Gb **111**
Shellbank La.
DA2: Bean, Grn St 65Wd **142**
Shell Cen. SE1 . . . . .7J **223** (47Pb **90**)
Shell Cl. BR2: Brom 72Nc **160**
Shellduck Cl. NW9 . . . . .26Ua **48**
Shelley *N8 .27Nb* **50**
(off Boyton Rd.)
Shelley Av. E12 . . . . .37Nc **74**
RM12: Horn 33Hd **76**
UB6: G'frd 41Fa **86**
Shelley Cl. BR6: Orp 76Uc **160**
CR5: Coul 89Pb **176**
HA6: Nwood 22V **44**
HA8: Edg 21Qa **47**
SE15 . . . . .54Xb **113**
SL3: L'ly .50B **82**
SM7: Bans 87Za **174**
UB4: Hayes 43W **84**
UB6: G'frd 41Fa **86**
WD6: Bore 14Qa **29**
Shelley Ct. *E10 . . . . .31Dc* **72**
(off Skelton's La.)
E11 . . . . .28Kc **53**
(off Makepeace Rd.)
EN9: Walt A 5Hc **21**
(off Ninefields)
N19 . . . . .32Pb **70**
SW3 . . . . .51Hb **111**
(off Tite St.)
Shelley Cres. TW5: Hest 53Z **107**
UB1: S'hall 44Ba **85**
Shelley Dr. DA16: Well 53Uc **116**
Shelley Gdns. HA0: Wemb 33La **66**
Shelley Gro. IG10: Lough 14Pc **36**
Shelley Ho. *E2 . . . . .41Yb* **92**
(off Cornwall Av.)
N16 . . . . .35Ub **71**
SE17 . . . . .7E **230**
Shelley Ho. *SW1 . . . . .51Lb* **112**
(off Churchill Gdns.)
Shelley La. UB9: Hare 25J **43**
Shelley Lodge EN2: Enf 11Tb **33**
Shelley M. HP3: Hem H 5K **3**
Shelley Pl. RM18: Tilb 3D **122**
Shelley Rd. CM13: Hut 17Fe **41**
NW10 . . . . .39Ta **67**
Shelleys La. TN14: Knock 88Vc **181**
Shelley Way SW19 . . . . .64Fb **133**
Shellfield Cl. TW19: Stanw M 57J **105**
Shellness Rd. E5 . . . . .36Xb **71**
Shell Rd. SE13 . . . . .55Dc **114**
Shellwood Rd. SW11 . . . . .54Hb **111**
Shelmerdine Cl. E3 . . . . .43Cc **92**
Shelson Av. TW13: Felt 62V **128**
Shelson Pde. TW13: Felt 62V **128**
Shelton Av. CR6: W'ham 89Yb **178**
Shelton Cl. CR6: W'ham 89Yb **178**
Shelton Ct. SL3: L'ly 8N **81**
Shelton Rd. SW19 . . . . .67Db **133**
Shelton St. WC2 . . . . .3F **223** (44Nb **90**)
(not continuous)
Shelvers Grn. KT20: Tad 93Ya **194**
Shelvers Hill KT20: Tad 93Xa **194**
Shelvers Spur KT20: Tad 93Ya **194**
Shelvers Way KT20: Tad 93Ya **194**
Shenden Cl. TN13: S'oaks 99Ld **203**
Shenden Way TN13: S'oaks 100Ld **203**
Shendish Edge HP3: Hem H 7P **3**
Shendish Manor Golf Course 8M **3**
Shene Ho. EC1 . . . . .7K **217**
Shene Sports & Fitness Cen. 56Ta **109**
SHENFIELD 16Ce **41**
Shenfield Cl. CR5: Coul 91Lb **196**
Shenfield Cres. CM15: B'wood 19Ae **41**
Shenfield Gdns. CM13: Hut 16De **41**
Shenfield Grn. CM15: Shenf 17Ce **41**
Shenfield Ho. *SE18 . . . . .53Mc* **115**
(off Portway Gdns.)
Shenfield Pl. CM15: Shenf 17Ae **41**
Shenfield Rd.
CM15: B'wood, Shenf 19Zd **41**
IG8: Wfd G 24Kc **53**
Shenfield St. N1 . . . . .2J **219** (40Ub **71**)
(not continuous)
SHENLEY 6Qa **15**
Shenley Av. HA4: Ruis 33V **64**
SHENLEYBURY 3Na **15**
Shenleybury WD7: Shenl 2Na **15**
Shenleybury Cotts. WD7: Shenl 3Na **15**
Shenleybury Vs. WD7: Shenl 3Na **15**
Shenley Cl. CR2: Sande 82Vb **177**
Shenley Hill WD7: R'lett 7Ka **14**
Shenley La. AL2: Lon C 7F **6**
Shenley Pk. .5Na **15**
Shenley Rd. DA1: Dart 58Qd **119**
SE5 . . . . .53Ub **113**
TW5: Hest 53Aa **107**
WD6: Bore 14Qa **29**
WD7: R'lett 6Ka **14**
Shen Pl. Almshouses
CM15: B'wood 19Zd **41**
Shenston Ct. *SL4: Wind 3H* **103**
(off James St.)
Shenstone W13 . . . . .46La **86**
Shenstone Cl. DA1: Cray 56Fd **118**
Shenstone Dr. SL1: Burn 2B **80**
Shenstone Gdns. RM3: Rom 25Ld **57**
Shenstone Ho. SW16 . . . . .64Lb **134**
Shenstone Pk. SL5: S'hill 10C **124**
Shenwood Ct. WD6: Bore 9Qa **15**
Shepherd Cl. TW13: Hanw 63Aa **129**
WD5: Ab L 2V **12**
Shepherdess Pl. N1 . . . . .3E **218** (41Sb **91**)
Shepherdess Wlk.
N1 . . . . .1E **218** (40Sb **71**)
Shepherd Ho. *E14 . . . . .44Dc* **92**
(off Annabel Cl.)
E16 . . . . .45Rc **94**
(off University Way)
Shepherd Mkt. W1 . . . . .7K **221** (46Kb **90**)
SHEPHERD'S BUSH 47Ya **88**
Shepherd's Bush Empire Theatre . . .47Ya **88**
Shepherd's Bush Grn. W12 . . . . .47Ya **88**
Shepherd's Bush Mkt. W12 . . . . .47Ya **88**
(not continuous)
Shepherd's Bush Pl. W12 . . . . .47Za **88**
Shepherd's Bush Rd. W6 . . . . .49Ya **88**
Shepherds Cl. BR6: Orp 76Vc **161**
HA7: Stan 22Ja **46**
(not continuous)
N6 . . . . .30Kb **50**
RM6: Chad H 29Zc **55**
TW17: Shep 72R **150**
UB8: Cowl 42L **83**
W1 . . . . .4H **221**
Shepherds Ct. SL4: Wind 4C **102**
W12 . . . . .47Za **88**
(off Shepherd's Bush Grn.)
Shepherds Farm WD3: Rick 18J **25**
Shepherds Grn. BR7: Chst 66Tc **138**
HP1: Hem H 3G **2**
(not continuous)
Shepherds Hill N6 . . . . .30Kb **50**
RH1: Mers 98Lb **196**
RM3: Hrld W 26Qd **57**
RM14: Upm 26Qd **57**
Shepherds La. DA1: Dart 60Jd **118**
E9 . . . . .37Zb **72**
GU20: W'sham 8D **146**
SE28 . . . . .46Uc **94**
WD3: Chor, Rick 16F **24**
Shepherds Leas SE9 . . . . .56Sc **116**
Shepherds Path CM14: S Weald 17Ud **40**
NW3 . . . . .36Fb **69**
(off Lyndhurst Rd.)
UB5: N'olt 37Aa **65**
(off Arnold Rd.)
Shepherds Pl. W1 . . . . .4H **221** (45Jb **90**)
Shepherd's Rd. WD18: Wat 13V **26**
Shepherd St. DA11: Nflt 59Fe **121**
W1 . . . . .7K **221** (46Kb **90**)
Shepherds Wlk. KT18: Eps D 93Ra **193**
NW2 . . . . .33Wa **68**
NW3 . . . . .36Fb **69**
WD23: B Hea 19Fa **28**
Shepherds Way AL9: Brk P 9L **9**
CR2: Sels 80Zb **158**
WD3: Rick 17K **25**
Shepiston La. UB3: Harl 49R **84**
Shepley Cl. SM5: Cars 76Jb **156**
Shepley Dr. SL5: S'dale 2G **146**
Shepley End SL5: S'dale 1G **146**
Shepley M. EN3: Enf L 9Cc **20**
Sheppard Cl. EN1: Enf 11Xb **33**
KT1: King T 70Na **131**
Sheppard Dr. SE16 . . . . .50Xb **91**
Sheppard Ho. *E2 . . . . .40Wb* **71**
(off Warner Pl.)
SW2 . . . . .60Qb **112**
Sheppards Coll. *BR1: Brom 67Jc* **137**
(off London Rd.)
Sheppard St. E16 . . . . .42Hc **93**
Sheppards Yd. *HP2: Hem H 1M* **3**
(off Figtree Hill)
SHEPPERTON 72R **150**
Shepperton Bus. Pk. TW17: Shep 71S **150**
Shepperton Cl. WD6: Bore 11Ta **29**
Shepperton Ct. TW17: Shep 72R **150**
Shepperton Ct. Dr. TW17: Shep 71R **150**
Shepperton Film Studios 69P **127**
SHEPPERTON GREEN 70Q **128**
Shepperton Marina TW17: Shep 72U **150**
Shepperton Rd. BR5: Pet W 72Sc **160**
N1 . . . . .39Sb **71**
TW18: Lale, Shep 69L **127**
Sheppey Cl. DA8: Erith 52Kd **119**
Sheppey Gdns. RM9: Dag 38Yc **75**
Sheppey Rd. RM9: Dag 38Xc **75**
Sheppey's La. WD4: K Lan 1S **12**
WD5: Bedm 1S **12**
Sheppy Pl. DA12: Grav'nd 9D **122**
Shepton Ho's. *E2 . . . . .41Yb* **92**
(off Welwyn St.)
Sherard Ct. N7 . . . . .34Nb **70**
Sherard Ho. *E9 . . . . .38Yb* **72**
(off Frampton Pk. Rd.)
Sherard Rd. SE9 . . . . .57Nc **116**
Sheraton Bus. Cen. UB6: G'frd 40Ka **66**
Sheraton Cl. WD6: E'tree 15Pa **29**
Sheraton Dr. KT19: Eps 85Sa **173**
Sheraton Ho. *SW1 . . . . .51Kb* **112**
(off Churchill Gdns.)
WD3: Chor 14E **24**
Sheraton M. WD18: Wat 14U **26**
Sheraton St. W1 . . . . .3D **222** (44Mb **90**)
Sherborne *NW1 . . . . .38Mb* **70**
(off Agar Gro.)
Sherborne Av. EN3: Enf H 12Yb **34**
UB2: S'hall 49Ca **85**
Sherborne Cl. KT18: Tatt C 89Ya **174**
SL3: Poyle 53G **104**
UB4: Yead 44Y **85**
Sherborne Cotts. *WD18: Wat 15Y* **27**
(off Muriel Av.)
Sherborne Cres. SM5: Cars 73Gb **155**
Sherborne Gdns. NW9 . . . . .27Qa **47**
RM5: Col R 22Cd **56**
W13 . . . . .43Ka **86**
Sherborne Gro. TN15: Kems'g 89Qd **183**
Sherborne Ho. SW1 . . . . . . .7A **228** (50Kb **90**)
SW8 . . . . .52Pb **112**
(off Bolney St.)
Sherborne La. EC4 . . . . . . .4F **225** (45Tb **91**)
Sherborne Pl. HA6: Nwood 23T **44**
Sherborne Rd. BR5: St M Cry 70Vc **139**
KT9: Chess 78Na **153**
SM3: Sutt 75Cb **155**
TW14: Bedf 60T **106**
(not continuous)
Sherborne St. N1 . . . . .39Tb **71**
Sherborne Wlk. KT22: Lea 93La **192**
Sherborne Way WD3: Crox G 14R **26**
Sherboro Rd. N15 . . . . .30Vb **51**
Sherbourne Cl. HP2: Hem H 3N **3**
TN15: W King 79Ud **164**
Sherbourne Ct. *AL1: St A 2D* **6**
(off Beaconsfield Rd.)
SM2: Sutt 79Eb **155**
SW5 . . . . .49Db **89**
(off Cromwell Rd.)
Sherbourne Dr. SL4: Wind 6D **102**
SL5: S'dale 1H **147**
Sherbourne Gdns. TW17: Shep 73U **150**
Sherbourne Ho. WD18: Wat 16T **26**
Sherbourne Pl. HA7: Stan 23Ja **46**
Sherbourne Wlk. SL2: Farn C 5G **60**
Sherbrooke Cl. DA6: Bex 56Cd **118**
Sherbrooke Ho. *E2 . . . . .40Yb* **72**
(off Bonner Rd.)
SW1 . . . . .4E **228**
Sherbrooke Rd. SW6 . . . . .52Ab **110**
Sherbrooke Ter. *SW6 . . . . .52Ab* **110**
(off Sherbrook Rd.)
Sherbrooke Way KT4: Wor Pk 73Xa **154**
Sherbrook Gdns. N21 . . . . .17Rb **33**
Shere Av. SM2: Cheam 82Ya **174**
Shere Cl. KT9: Chess 78Ma **153**
Sheredan Rd. E4 . . . . .22Fc **53**
Shere Ho. SE1 . . . . .3F **231**
Shere Rd. IG2: Ilf 29Qc **54**
Sherfield Av. WD3: Rick 20M **25**
Sherfield Cl. KT3: N Mald 70Ra **131**
Sherfield Gdns. SW15 . . . . .58Va **110**
Sherfield M. UB3: Hayes 44U **84**
Sherfield Rd. RM17: Grays 51De **121**
Sheridan Bldgs. WC2 . . . . .3G **223**
Sheridan Cl. BR8: Swan 70Hd **140**
HP1: Hem H 3K **3**
RM3: Rom 24Ld **57**
UB10: Hil .42S **84**
Sheridan Ct. *CR0: C'don 77Ub* **157**
(off Coombe Rd.)
DA1: Dart 56Qd **119**
HA1: Harr 30Fa **46**
NW6 . . . . .38Eb **69**
(off Belsize Rd.)
SL1: Slou .5C **80**
SW5 . . . . .49Db **89**
(off Barkston Gdns.)
TW4: Houn 57Aa **107**
UB5: N'olt 36Da **65**
W7 . . . . .45Ha **86**
(off Milton Rd.)
Sheridan Cres. BR7: Chst 68Rc **138**
Sheridan Dr. RH2: Reig 4K **207**
Sheridan Gdns. HA3: Kenton 30Ma **47**
Sheridan Grange SL5: S'dale 2E **146**
Sheridan Hgts. *E1 . . . . .44Xb* **91**
(off Watney St.)
Sheridan Ho. KT22: Lea 93Ja **192**
SE11 . . . . .6A **230**
Sheridan Lodge *BR2: Brom 70Lc* **137**
(off Homesdale Rd.)
Sheridan M. E11 . . . . .30Kc **53**
Sheridan Pl. BR1: Brom 68Mc **137**
SW13 . . . . .55Va **110**
Sheridan Rd. DA7: Bex 55Ad **117**
DA17: Belv 49Cd **96**
E7 . . . . .34Hc **73**
E12 . . . . .36Nc **74**
SW19 . . . . .67Bb **133**
TW10: Ham 62La **130**
WD19: Wat 17Z **27**
Sheridans Rd. KT23: Bookh 98Ea **192**
Sheridan Ter. UB5: N'olt 36Da **65**
Sheridan Wlk. NW11 . . . . .30Cb **49**
SM5: Cars 78Hb **155**
Sheridan Way BR3: Beck 67Bc **136**
Sheriden Pl. HA1: Harr 31Ga **66**
TW12: Hamp 67Da **129**
Sheriff Way WD25: Wat 5W **12**
Sheringham NW8 . . . . .39Fb **69**
Sheringham Av. E12 . . . . .35Pc **74**
N14 . . . . .15Mb **32**
RM7: Rom 30Ed **56**
TW2: Whitt 60Ba **107**
TW13: Felt 62W **128**
Sheringham Ct. *TW13: Felt 62W* **128**
(off Sheringham Av.)
UB3: Hayes 47V **84**
Sheringham Dr. IG11: Bark 36Vc **75**
Sheringham Ho. NW1 . . . . .7D **214**
Sheringham Rd. N7 . . . . .37Pb **70**
SE20 . . . . .69Yb **136**
Sheringham Twr. UB1: S'hall 45Da **85**
Sherington Av. HA5: Hat E 24Ca **45**
Sherington Rd. SE7 . . . . .51Kc **115**
Sherland Ct. *WD7: R'lett 8Ja* **14**
(off The Dell)
Sherland Rd. TW1: Twick 60Ha **108**
Sherleys Ct. HA4: Ruis 33U **64**
Sherlies Av. BR6: Orp 75Uc **160**
Sherlock Cl. SW16 . . . . .68Pb **134**
Sherlock Ct. *NW8 . . . . .39Fb* **69**
(off Dorman Way)
Sherlock Holmes Mus. 6G **215**
Sherlock M. W1 . . . . .7H **215** (43Jb **90**)
Shermanbury Cl. DA8: Erith 52Hd **118**
Shermanbury Pl. DA8: Erith 52Hd **118**
Sherman Gdns. RM6: Chad H 30Yc **55**
Sherman Ho. *E14 . . . . .44Ec* **92**
(off Dee St.)
UB3: Harl .48S **84**
(off Nine Acres Cl.)
Sherman Rd. BR1: Brom 67Jc **137**
SL1: Slou 3J **81**
Shernbroke Rd. EN9: Walt A 6Hc **21**
Shernhall St. E17 . . . . .27Ec **52**
Sherrard Rd. E7 . . . . .37Lc **73**
E12 . . . . .37Lc **73**
Sherrards Way EN5: Barn 15Cb **31**
Sherren Ho. E1 . . . . .42Yb **92**
Sherrick Grn. Rd. NW10 . . . . .36Xa **68**
Sherriff Cl. KT10: Esh 75Da **151**
Sherriff Ct. *NW6 . . . . .37Cb* **69**
(off Sherriff Rd.)
Sherriff Rd. NW6 . . . . .37Cb **69**
Sherringham Av. N17 . . . . .26Wb **51**
Sherrin Rd. E10 . . . . .35Dc **72**
Sherrock Gdns. NW4 . . . . .28Xa **48**
Sherry M. IG11: Bark 38Tc **74**
Sherston Ct. SE1 . . . . .5C **230**
WC1 . . . . .4K **217**
Sherwin Ho. *SE11 . . . . .51Qb* **112**
(off Kennington Rd.)
Sherwin Rd. SE14 . . . . .53Zb **114**
Sherwood KT6: Surb 75Ma **153**
NW6 . . . . .38Ab **68**
RM16: N Stif 46Ae **99**
Sherwood Av. E18 . . . . .27Kc **53**
EN6: Pot B 4Ab **16**
HA4: Ruis .30U **44**
SW16 . . . . .66Mb **134**
UB4: Yead 42X **85**
UB6: G'frd 37Ga **66**
Sherwood Cl. DA5: Bexl 58Yc **117**
E17 . . . . .26Bc **52**
KT22: Fet 95Ea **192**
SL3: L'ly .48A **82**
SW13 . . . . .55Xa **110**
W13 . . . . .46Ka **86**
Sherwood Ct. *CR2: S Croy 78Sb* **157**
(off Nottingham Rd.)
HA2: Harr 33Da **65**
SL3: L'ly .50B **82**
SW11 . . . . .55Eb **111**
W1 . . . . .1F **221**
WD25: Wat .6V **12**
Sherwood Cres. RH2: Reig 10K **207**
Sherwood Gdns. E14 . . . . .49Cc **92**
IG11: Bark 38Tc **74**
SE16 . . . . .50Wb **91**
Sherwood Ho. *WD5: Ab L 3V* **12**
(off College Rd.)
Sherwood Pk. Av. DA15: Sidc 59Wc **117**
Sherwood Pk. Rd. CR4: Mitc 70Lb **134**
SM1: Sutt 78Cb **155**
Sherwood Rd. CR0: C'don 73Xb **157**
CR5: Coul 88Lb **176**
DA16: Well 54Uc **116**
GU21: Knap 9J **167**
Sherwood Rd. HA2: Harr 33Ea **66**
IG6: Ilf 28Tc **54**
NW4 . . . . .27Ya **48**
SW19 . . . . .66Bb **133**
TW12: Hamp H 64Ea **130**
Sherwoods Rd. WD19: Wat 17Aa **27**
Sherwood St. N20 . . . . .20Fb **31**
W1 . . . . .4C **222** (45Lb **90**)
Sherwood Ter. *E16 . . . . .44Lc* **93**
(off Bingley Rd.)
N20 . . . . .20Fb **31**
Sherwood Way BR4: W W'ck 75Ec **158**
KT19: Eps 84Pa **173**
Shetland Cl. WD6: Bore 16Ta **29**
Shetland Ho. *WD18: Wat 16V* **26**
(off Pioneer Way)
Shetland Rd. E3 . . . . .40Bc **72**
TW6: H'row A 58S **106**
Shevon Way CM14: B'wood 21Vd **58**
Shewens Rd. KT13: Weyb 77T **150**
Shey Copse GU22: Wok 89E **168**
Shield Dr. TW8: Bford 51Ja **108**
Shieldhall St. SE2 . . . . .49Yc **95**
Shield Rd. TW15: Ashf 63S **128**
Shields Ct. *RM18: E Til 9L* **101**
(off Coronation Av.)
Shifford Path SE23 . . . . .62Zb **136**
Shilburn Way GU21: Wok 10L **167**
Shillaker Ct. W3 . . . . .46Va **88**
Shillibeer Pl. W1 . . . . .1E **220**
Shillibeer Wlk. IG7: Chig 20Vc **37**
Shillingford Cl. NW7 . . . . .24Za **48**
Shillingford Ho. *E3 . . . . .41Dc* **92**
(off Talwin St.)
Shillingford St. N1 . . . . .38Rb **71**
Shilling Pl. W7 . . . . .47Ja **86**
Shillingshaw Lodge *E16 . . . . .44Jc* **93**
(off Butchers Rd.)
Shillingstone Ho. *W14 . . . . .48Ab* **88**
(off Russell Rd.)
Shillington Gro. WD17: Wat 11W **26**
Shillitoe Av. EN6: Pot B 4Za **16**
Shinecroft TN14: Otf 88Jd **182**
Shinfield St. W12 . . . . .44Ya **88**
Shingle Ct. EN9: Walt A 5Jc **21**
Shinglewell Rd. DA8: Erith 52Cd **118**
Shinners Cl. SE25 . . . . .71Wb **157**
Ship All. W4 . . . . .51Qa **109**
Ship & Mermaid Row
SE1 . . . . .1G **231** (47Tb **91**)
Shipfield Cl. TN16: Tats 93Lc **199**
Ship Hill SL1: Burn 2C **60**
TN16: Tats 93Lc **199**
Shipka Rd. SW12 . . . . .60Kb **112**
Shiplake Ho. E2 . . . . .4K **219**
Ship La. BR8: Swan 67Md **141**
DA4: Sut H 67Md **141**
RM15: Avel, Purf 46Td **98**
RM19: Purf 46Td **98**
SW14 . . . . .55Sa **109**
Shipley Hills Rd. DA13: Meop 75Fe **165**
Shipman Rd. E16 . . . . .44Kc **93**
SE23 . . . . .61Zb **136**
Ship St. SE8 . . . . .53Cc **114**
Ship Tavern Pas. EC3 . . . . .4H **225** (45Ub **91**)
Shipton Cl. RM8: Dag 34Zc **75**
Shipton Ho. *E2 . . . . .40Vb* **71**
(off Shipton St.)
Shipton Rd. UB10: Ick 35P **63**
Shipton St. E2 . . . . .3K **219** (40Vb **71**)
Shipwright Rd. SE16 . . . . .47Ac **92**
Shipwright Yd. SE1 . . . . . . .7H **225** (46Ub **91**)
Ship Yd. E14 . . . . .50Dc **92**
KT13: Weyb 76R **150**
Shirburn Cl. SE23 . . . . .59Yb **114**
Shirebrook Rd. SE3 . . . . .55Mc **115**
Shire Ct. DA18: Erith 48Zc **95**
HP2: Hem H 1A **4**
KT17: Ewe 80Va **154**
Shirehall Cl. NW4 . . . . .30Za **48**
Shirehall Gdns. NW4 . . . . .30Za **48**
Shirehall La. NW4 . . . . .30Za **48**
Shirehall Pk. NW4 . . . . .29Za **48**
Shirehall Rd. DA2: Dart, Wilm 64Ld **141**
Shire Horse Way TW7: Isle 55Ha **108**
Shire Ho. *E3 . . . . .41Dc* **92**
(off Talwin St.)
EC1 . . . . .6F **219**
Shire La. BR2: Kes 81Nc **180**
BR6: Chels, Downe 80Rc **160**
(not continuous)
SL9: Chal P 20D **24**
(not continuous)
WD3: Chor 18C **24**
(Bullsland La.)
WD3: Chor 15D **24**
(Chalfont La.)
Shiremeade WD6: E'tree 15Pa **29**
Shire M. TW2: Whitt 58Ea **108**
Shire Pl. RH1: Redh 8P **207**
SW18 . . . . .59Eb **111**
TW8: Bford 52Ma **109**
Shires, The TW10: Ham 63Na **131**
TW18: Staines 64G **126**
(off Wapshott Rd.)
WD25: Wat .3X **13**
Shires Cl. KT21: Asht 91Ma **193**
Shires Ho. KT14: Byfl 85N **169**
Shirland M. W9 . . . . .41Bb **89**
Shirland Rd. W9 . . . . .41Bb **89**
Shirlbutt St. E14 . . . . .45Dc **92**
SHIRLEY 75Zb **158**
Shirley Av. CR0: C'don 74Yb **158**
CR5: Coul 91Rb **197**
DA5: Bexl 59Zc **117**
RH1: Redh 10P **207**
SL4: Wind .3D **102**
SM1: Sutt 77Fb **155**
SM2: Cheam 81Bb **175**
Shirley Chu. Rd. CR0: C'don 76Zb **158**
Shirley Cl. DA1: Dart 56Ld **119**
DA12: Grav'nd 1K **145**
E17 . . . . .29Dc **52**
EN8: Chesh 1Yb **20**
TW3: Houn 57Ea **108**
Shirley Ct. IG10: Lough 12Pc **36**
SW16 . . . . .66Nb **134**
Shirley Cres. BR3: Beck 70Ac **136**
Shirley Dr. TW3: Houn 57Ea **108**
Shirley Gdns. IG11: Bark 37Uc **74**
RM12: Horn 33Ld **77**
W7 . . . . .46Ha **86**
Shirley Gro. N9 . . . . .17Yb **34**
SW11 . . . . .55Jb **112**
Shirley Hgts. SM6: Wall 81Lb **176**
Shirley Hills Rd. CR0: C'don 78Yb **158**
Shirley Ho. *SE5 . . . . .52Tb* **113**
(off Picton St.)
Shirley Ho. Dr. SE7 . . . . .52Lc **115**
Shirleyhyrst KT13: Weyb 79T **150**
SHIRLEY OAKS 74Zb **158**
Shirley Oaks Rd. CR0: C'don 74Zb **158**
Shirley Pk. CR0: C'don 75Yb **158**
Shirley Pk. Golf Course 75Xb **157**
Shirley Pk. Rd. CR0: C'don 74Xb **157**
Shirley Pl. GU21: Knap 9G **166**
Shirley Rd. AL1: St A 3D **6**
CR0: C'don 73Xb **157**
DA15: Sidc 62Uc **138**
E15 . . . . .38Gc **73**
EN2: Enf .13Sb **33**
SM6: Wall 81Lb **176**
W4 . . . . .47Ta **87**
WD5: Ab L .4V **12**
Shirley St. E16 . . . . .44Hc **93**
Shirley Way CR0: C'don 76Ac **158**
Shirley Windmill 76Yb **158**
Shirlock Rd. NW3 . . . . .35Hb **69**
Shirwell Cl. NW7 . . . . .24Za **48**
Shobden Rd. N17 . . . . .25Tb **51**
Shobroke Cl. NW2 . . . . .34Ya **68**
Shoebury Rd. E6 . . . . .38Pc **74**
Shoelands Ct. NW9 . . . . .27Ta **47**

Shoe La. EC4 . . . . 2A 224 (44Qb 90)
Sholden Gdns. BR5: St M Cry 71Yc 161
Sholto Rd. TW6: H'row A 57P 105
Shona Ho. E13 . . . . 43Lc 93
Shonks Mill Rd. RM4: Nave 11Kd 39
Shooters Av. HA3: Kenton 28La 46
SHOOTERS HILL 53Qc 116
Shooters Hill DA16: Well 53Pc 116
SE18 . . . . 53Pc 116
Shooters Hill Golf Course 53Sc 116
Shooters Hill Rd. SE3 . . . . 52Lc 115
SE10 . . . . 53Fc 115
SE18 . . . . 52Lc 115
Shooters Rd. EN2: Enf 11Rb 33
Shoot Up Hill NW2 . . . . 36Ab 68
Shopping Hall, The E6 . . . . 39Nc 74
Shop Rd. SL4: Wind 2A 102
Shopwick Pl. WD6: E'tree 16Ma 29
Shord Hill CR8: Kenley 88Tb 177
Shore, The DA11: Nflt 8B 122
(Clifton Marine Pde.)
DA11: Nflt 57Ee 121
(Lawn Rd.)
Shore Bus. Cen. E9 . . . . 38Yb 72
Shore Cl. TW12: Hamp 65Aa 129
TW14: Felt 59W 106
Shorediche Cl. UB10: Ick 34P 63
SHOREDITCH 3H 219 (41Ub 91)
Shoreditch Ct. E8 . . . . 38Vb 71
(off Queensbridge Rd.)
Shoreditch High St. E1 . . . . 4J 219 (42Ub 91)
Shoreditch Ho. N1 . . . . 4G 219
Shore Gro. TW13: Hanw 61Ca 129
SHOREHAM 83Hd 182
Shoreham Aircraft Museum, The
. . . . 83Hd 182
Shoreham Cl. CR0: C'don 72Yb 158
DA5: Bexl 60Zc 117
SW18 . . . . 57Db 111
Shoreham La. BR6: Well H 79Cd 162
TN13: Riv, S'oaks 94Hd 202
TN14: Hals 84Bd 181
Shoreham Pl. TN14: S'ham 84Jd 182
Shoreham Ri. SL2: Slou 2B 80
Shoreham Rd. BR5: St P 67Xc 139
DA4: Eyns 79Ld 163
TN14: Otf, S'ham 83Kd 183
Shoreham Rd. E. TW6: H'row A 57N 105
Shoreham Rd. W. TW6: H'row A 57N 105
Shoreham Way BR2: Hayes 72Jc 159
Shorehill Ct. TN15: Kems'g 89Pd 183
Shorehill La. TN15: Kems'g, Knat . . . 87Pd 183
Shore Ho. SW8 . . . . 55Kb 112
Shore M. E9 . . . . 38Yb 72
(off Shore Rd.)
Shore Pl. E9 . . . . 38Yb 72
Shore Point IG9: Buck H 19Kc 35
Shore Rd. E9 . . . . 38Yb 72
Shores Rd. GU21: Wok 86A 168
Shore Way SW9 . . . . 54Qb 112
(off Crowhurst Cl.)
Shorncliffe Rd. SE1 . . . . . . 7K 231 (50Vb 91)
Shorndean St. SE6 . . . . 60Ec 114
SHORNE 4N 145
Shorne Cl. BR5: St M Cry 70Zc 139
DA15: Sidc 58Xc 117
Shornefield Cl. BR1: Brom 69Qc 138
Shorne Ifield Rd. DA12: Shorne 5J 145
Shornells Way SE2 . . . . 49Yc 95
SHORNE RIDGEWAY 6N 145
Shorne Woods Country Pk. 6K 145
Shorne Woods Country Pk. Vis. Cen.
. . . . 6L 145
Shorrold's Rd. SW6 . . . . 52Bb 111
Shortacres RH1: Nutf 5F 208
Shortcroft Rd. KT17: Ewe 80Va 154
Shortcrofts Rd. RM9: Dag 37Bd 75
Shorter Av. CM15: Shenf 17Be 41
Shorter St. E1 . . . . 4K 225 (45Vb 91)
Shortfern SL2: Slou 4N 81
Shortgate N12 . . . . 21Bb 49
Short Hedges TW3: Houn 53Ca 107
Short Hill HA1: Harr 32Ga 66
SHORTLANDS 68Gc 137
Shortlands UB3: Harl 51T 106
W6 . . . . 49Za 88
Shortlands Cl. DA17: Belv 48Bd 95
N18 . . . . 20Tb 33
Shortlands Gdns. BR2: Brom 68Gc 137
Shortlands Golf Course 67Gc 137
Shortlands Gro. BR2: Brom 69Fc 137
Shortlands Rd. BR2: Brom 69Fc 137
E10 . . . . 31Dc 72
KT2: King T 66Pa 131
Short La. AL2: Brick W 1Aa 13
RH8: Limp 4M 211
TN15: Igh 95Xd 204
TW19: Stanw 59P 105
Shortmead Dr. EN8: Chesh 3Ac 20
Short Path SE18 . . . . 51Rc 116
Short Rd. E11 . . . . 33Gc 73
TW6: H'row A 58N 105
W4 . . . . 51Ua 110
Shorts Cft. NW9 . . . . 28Ra 47
Shorts Gdns. WC2 . . . . 3F 223 (44Nb 90)
Shorts Rd. SM5: Cars 77Gb 155
Short St. NW4 . . . . 28Ya 48
(off Foster St.)
SE1 . . . . 1A 230 (47Qb 90)
Short Wall E15 . . . . 41Ec 92
Shortwave Cinema 3J 231
Short Way N12 . . . . 23Gb 49
SE9 . . . . 55Nc 116
TW2: Whitt 59Ea 108
Shortwood GU22: Wok 1P 187
(off Mt. Hermon Rd.)
Shortwood Av. TW18: Staines 62K 127
Shortwood Comn. TW18: Staines 63K 127
Shorwell Ct. RM19: Purf 50Rd 97
Shotfield SM6: Wall 79Kb 156
Shothanger Way HP3: Bov 7F 2
Shott Cl. SM1: Sutt 78Eb 155
Shottendane Rd. SW6 . . . . 53Cb 111
Shottery Cl. SE9 . . . . 62Nc 138
Shottfield Av. SW14 . . . . 56Ua 110
Shottsford W2 . . . . 44Cb 89
(off Talbot Rd.)
Shoulder of Mutton All. E14 . . . . 45Ac 92
Shouldham St. W1 . . . . 1E 220 (43Gb 89)
Showcase Cinema
Barking 41Tc 94
Bluewater 60Vd 120
Wood Green 26Qb 50
Showers Way UB3: Hayes 46W 84
Shrapnel Cl. SE18 . . . . 52Nc 116
Shrapnel Rd. SE9 . . . . 55Pc 116
SHREDING GREEN 44E 82
Shrewsbury Av. HA3: Kenton 28Na 47
SW14 . . . . 56Sa 109
Shrewsbury Cl. KT6: Surb 75Na 153
Shrewsbury Ct. EC1 . . . . 6E 218
Shrewsbury Ho. SW3 . . . . 51Gb 111
(off Cheyne Wlk.)
SW8 . . . . 51Pb 112
(off Kennington Oval)
Shrewsbury La. SE18 . . . . 53Rc 116
Shrewsbury M. W2 . . . . 43Cb 89
(off Chepstow Rd.)
Shrewsbury Rd. BR3: Beck 69Ac 136
E7 . . . . 36Mc 73
N11 . . . . 23Lb 50
NW10 . . . . 39Ta 67
RH1: Redh 6N 207
SM5: Cars 72Gb 155
TW6: H'row A 58S 106
(not continuous)
W2 . . . . 44Cb 89
Shrewsbury St. W10 . . . . 42Ya 88
Shrewsbury Wlk. TW7: Isle 55Ja 108
Shrewton Rd. SW17 . . . . 66Hb 133
Shri Swaminarayan Mandir
London 37Ta 67
Shroffold Rd. BR1: Brom 63Gc 137
Shropshire Cl. CR4: Mitc 70Nb 134
Shropshire Ct. W7 . . . . 44Ha 86
(off Copley Cl.)
Shropshire Ho. N18 . . . . 22Xb 51
(off Cavendish Cl.)
Shropshire Pl. WC1 . . . . . . 6D 216 (42Lb 90)
Shropshire Rd. N22 . . . . 24Pb 50
Shroton St. NW1 . . . . 7D 214 (43Gb 89)
Shrubberies, The E18 . . . . 26Jc 53
IG7: Chig 22Sc 54
Shrubbery, The E11 . . . . 29Kc 53
HP1: Hem H 1G 2
KT6: Surb 74Na 153
RM14: Upm 34Sd 78
Shrubbery Cl. N1 . . . . 39Sb 71
Shrubbery Gdns. N21 . . . . 17Rb 33
Shrubbery Rd. DA4: S Dar 67Td 142
DA12: Grav'nd 10D 122
N9 . . . . 20Wb 33
SW16 . . . . 63Nb 134
UB1: S'hall 46Ba 85
Shrubbs Hill GU24: Chob 1G 166
Shrubbs Hill La. SL5: S'dale 2G 146
Shrubhill Rd. HP1: Hem H 3H 3
Shrubland Ct. SM7: Bans 88Bb 175
(off Garratts La.)
Shrubland Gro. KT4: Wor Pk 76Ya 154
Shrubland Rd. E8 . . . . 39Vb 71
E10 . . . . 31Cc 72
E17 . . . . 29Cc 52
SM7: Bans 88Bb 175
Shrublands AL9: Brk P 8K 9
Shrublands, The EN6: Pot B 5Ab 16
Shrublands Av. CR0: C'don 76Cc 158
Shrublands Cl. IG7: Chig 23Sc 54
N20 . . . . 18Fb 31
SE26 . . . . 62Yb 136
Shrubsall Cl. SE9 . . . . 60Nc 116
Shrubshall Mdw.
TN15: Plax 99Ce 205
SHRUBS HILL 2G 146
Shrubs Rd. UB9: Rick 23P 43
Shuna Wlk. N1 . . . . 37Tb 71
Shurland Av. EN4: E Barn 16Fb 31
Shurland Gdns. SE15 . . . . 52Vb 113
Shurlock Av. BR8: Swan 68Fd 140
Shurlock Dr. BR6: Farnb 77Sc 160
Shuters Sq. W14 . . . . 50Bb 89
Shuttle Cl. DA15: Sidc 59Vc 117
Shuttlemead DA5: Bexl 59Bd 117
Shuttle Rd. DA1: Cray 55Jd 118
Shuttle St. E1 . . . . 42Wb 91
Shuttleworth Rd. SW11 . . . . 54Gb 111
Siamese M. N3 . . . . 25Cb 49
Siani M. N8 . . . . 28Rb 51
Sibella Rd. SW4 . . . . 54Mb 112
Sibley Cl. BR1: Brom 71Nc 160
DA6: Bex 57Ad 117
Sibley Ct. BR2: Brom 68Fc 137
UB8: Hil 43S 84
Sibley Gro. E12 . . . . 38Nc 74
Sibthorpe Rd. AL9: Wel G 6F 8
SE12 . . . . 58Kc 115
Sibthorp Rd. CR4: Mitc 68Hb 133
Sibton Rd. SM5: Cars 73Gb 155
Sicilian Av. WC1 . . . . 1G 223
Sickle Cnr. RM9: Dag 42Dd 96
Sidbury Cl. SL5: S'dale 1E 146
Sidbury St. SW6 . . . . 53Ab 110
SIDCUP 63Wc 139
Sidcup By-Pass
BR5: Sidc, St P, Swan 65Wc 139
BR7: Chst, Sidc 62Tc 138
DA14: Sidc 65Wc 139
Sidcup Golf Course 60Xc 117
Sidcup High St. DA14: Sidc 63Wc 139
Sidcup Hill DA14: Sidc 63Xc 139
Sidcup Hill Gdns. DA14: Sidc 64Yc 139
Sidcup Leisure Cen. 61Wc 139
Sidcup Place 64Wc 139
Sidcup Pl. DA14: Sidc 64Wc 139
Sidcup Rd. SE9 . . . . 58Lc 115
SE12 . . . . 58Lc 115
Sidcup Technical Cen.
DA14: Sidc 64Zc 139
Siddeley Dr. TW4: Houn 55Aa 107
Siddeley Rd. E17 . . . . 26Ec 52
Siddons Cl. SS17: Linf 8J 101
Siddons La. NW1 . . . . 6G 215 (42Hb 89)
Siddons Rd. CR0: Wadd 76Qb 156
N17 . . . . 25Wb 51
SE23 . . . . 61Ac 136
Side Rd. E17 . . . . 29Bc 52
UB9: Den 31F 62
Sidewood Rd. SE9 . . . . 60Tc 116
Sidford Cl. HP1: Hem H 2H 3
Sidford Ho. SE1 . . . . 4K 229
Sidford Pl. SE1 . . . . 4J 229 (48Qb 90)
Sidgwick Ho. SW9 . . . . 54Pb 112
(off Stockwell Rd.)
Sidi Ct. N15 . . . . 27Rb 51
Sidings, The AL10: Hat 1A 8
E11 . . . . 32Ec 72
HP2: Hem H 2M 3
IG10: Lough 16Nc 36
Sidings, The TN13: Dun G 92Gd 202
TW18: Staines 63K 127
Sidings Apartments, The E16 . . . . . . 47Qc 94
Sidings M. N7 . . . . 34Qb 70
Siding Way AL2: Lon C 8E 6
Sidlaw Ho. N16 . . . . 32Vb 71
Sidmouth Av. TW7: Isle 54Ga 108
Sidmouth Cl. WD19: Wat 19X 27
Sidmouth Ct. DA1: Dart 60Rd 119
(off Churchill Cl.)
Sidmouth Dr. HA4: Ruis 34W 64
Sidmouth Ho. SE15 . . . . 52Wb 113
(off Lindsey Est.)
W1 . . . . 2E 220
Sidmouth M. WC1 . . . . 4H 217
Sidmouth Pde. NW2 . . . . 38Ya 68
Sidmouth Rd. BR5: St M Cry 71Xc 161
(not continuous)
DA16: Well 52Yc 117
E10 . . . . 34Ec 72
NW2 . . . . 38Ya 68
Sidmouth St. WC1 . . . . 4G 217 (41Pb 90)
Sidney Av. N13 . . . . 22Pb 50
Sidney Boyd Ct. NW6 . . . . 38Db 69
Sidney Cl. UB8: Uxb 38L 63
Sidney Elson Way E6 . . . . 40Qc 74
Sidney Est. E1 . . . . 44Yb 92
(Bromhead St.)
E1 . . . . 43Yb 92
(Lindley St.)
Sidney Gdns. TN14: Otf 88Ld 183
TW8: Bford 51Ma 109
Sidney Godley (VC) Ho. E2 . . . . 41Yb 92
(off Digby St.)
Sidney Gro. EC1 . . . . 2B 218 (40Rb 71)
Sidney Ho. E2 . . . . 40Zb 72
(off Old Ford Rd.)
Sidney Miller Ct. W3 . . . . 46Ra 87
(off Crown St.)
Sidney Rd. BR3: Beck 68Ac 136
CM16: They B 8Tc 22
E7 . . . . 34Jc 73
HA2: Harr 27Ea 46
KT12: Walt T 73W 150
N22 . . . . 24Pb 50
SE25 . . . . 71Wb 157
SL4: Wind 5A 102
SW9 . . . . 54Pb 112
TW1: Twick 58Ja 108
TW18: Staines 63J 127
Sidney Sq. E1 . . . . 43Yb 92
Sidney St. E1 . . . . 43Xb 91
(not continuous)
Sidney Webb Ho. SE1 . . . . 3G 231
Sidworth St. E8 . . . . 38Xb 71
Siebel Ct. TW20: Egh 63D 126
Siebert Rd. SE3 . . . . 51Jc 115
Siege Ho. E1 . . . . 44Xb 91
(off Sidney St.)
Siemens Rd. SE18 . . . . 48Mc 93
Sienna SE28 . . . . 48Wc 95
Sienna Cl. KT9: Chess 79Ma 153
Sienna Ter. NW2 . . . . 33Wa 68
Sierra Dr. RM9: Dag 40Dd 76
Sigdon Pas. E8 . . . . 36Wb 71
Sigdon Rd. E8 . . . . 36Wb 71
Sigers, The HA5: Eastc 30X 45
Sigmund Freud Statue 37Fb 69
Signal Ho. E8 . . . . 38Xb 71
(off Martello Ter.)
SE1 . . . . 2D 230
Signmakers Yd. NW1 . . . . 39Kb 70
(off Delancey St.)
Sigrist Sq. KT2: King T 67Na 131
Sikorski Mus. 2C 226 (47Fb 89)
Silas Ct. WD17: Wat 11W 26
(off Lockhart Rd.)
Silbury Av. CR4: Mitc 67Gb 133
Silbury Ho. SE26 . . . . 62Wb 135
Silbury St. N1 . . . . 3F 219 (41Tb 91)
Silchester Ct. CR7: Thor H 70Qb 134
TW15: Ashf 61N 127
Silchester Rd. W10 . . . . 44Za 88
Silecroft Rd. DA7: Bex 53Cd 118
Silesia Bldgs. E8 . . . . 38Xb 71
Silex St. SE1 . . . . 2C 230 (47Rb 91)
Silistria Cl. GU21: Knap 10G 166
Silk Cl. SE12 . . . . 57Jc 115
Silk Ct. E2 . . . . 41Wb 91
(off Squirries St.)
Silkfield Rd. NW9 . . . . 29Ua 48
Silkham Rd. RH8: Oxt 99Fc 199
Silk Ho. NW9 . . . . 27Ta 47
Silkin M. SE15 . . . . 52Wb 113
Silk M. SE11 . . . . 7A 230
Silk Mill Ct. WD19: Wat 16X 27
Silk Mill Rd. WD19: Wat 17X 27
Silk Mills Cl. TN14: S'oaks 93Ld 203
Silk Mills Pas. SE13 . . . . 54Dc 114
Silk Mills Path SE13 . . . . 54Ec 114
(not continuous)
Silk Mills Sq. E9 . . . . 37Bc 72
Silkmore La. KT24: W Hor 97Q 190
Silks Ct. E11 . . . . 32Hc 73
Silkstream Pde. HA8: Edg 25Sa 47
Silkstream Rd. HA8: Edg 25Sa 47
Silk St. EC2 . . . . 7E 218 (43Sb 91)
Silk Weaver Way E2 . . . . 40Xb 71
Sillitoe Ho. N1 . . . . 39Tb 71
(off Colville Est.)
Silsoe Ho. NW1 . . . . 2A 216 (40Kb 70)
Silsoe Rd. N22 . . . . 26Pb 50
Silverbeck Way TW19: Stanw M 57J 105
Silver Birch Av. E4 . . . . 22Bc 52
Silver Birch Cl. DA2: Wilm 63Gd 140
KT15: Wdhm 84G 168
N11 . . . . 23Jb 50
SE6 . . . . 62Bc 136
SE28 . . . . 46Wc 95
UB10: Ick 35N 63
Silver Birch Ct. EN8: Chesh 3Zb 20
Silver Birches CM13: Hut 18Ce 41
Silver Birch Gdns. E6 . . . . 42Pc 94
Silver Birch M. IG6: Ilf 23Sc 54
Silverbirch Wlk. NW5 . . . . 37Jb 70
Silver Blades Ice Rink 3P 3
Silverburn Ho. SW9 . . . . 53Rb 113
(off Lothian Rd.)
Silvercliffe Gdns. EN4: E Barn 14Gb 31
Silver Cl. HA3: Hrw W 24Fa 46
KT20: Kgswd 96Ab 194
SE14 . . . . 52Ac 114
Silver Ct. KT22: Lea 92Ka 192
Silver Cres. W4 . . . . 49Ra 87
Silverdale DA3: Hartl 70Be 143
EN2: Enf 14Nb 32
NW1 . . . . 3B 216
SE26 . . . . 63Yb 136
Silverdale Av. IG2: Ilf 29Uc 54
KT12: Walt T 75V 150
KT22: Oxs 86Ea 172
Silverdale Centre, The
HA0: Wemb 39Pa 67
Silverdale Cl. SM1: Sutt 77Bb 155
UB5: N'olt 36Ba 65
W7 . . . . 46Ga 86
Silverdale Ct. EC1 . . . . 5C 218
TW18: Staines 63K 127
Silverdale Dr. RM12: Horn 36Kd 77
SE9 . . . . 61Nc 138
TW16: Sun 68X 129
Silverdale Factory Cen.
UB3: Hayes 48W 84
Silverdale Gdns. UB3: Hayes 47W 84
Silverdale Ind. Est. UB3: Hayes 47W 84
Silverdale Rd. BR5: Pet W 70Sc 138
BR5: St P 69Wc 139
DA7: Bex 54Dd 118
E4 . . . . 23Fc 53
UB3: Hayes 47W 84
WD23: Bush 15Aa 27
Silver Dell WD24: Wat 7V 12
Silverdene N12 . . . . 23Db 49
(off Thyra Gro.)
Silvergate KT19: Ewe 78Sa 153
Silverglade Bus. Pk. KT9: Chess 84La 172
Silverhall St. TW7: Isle 55Ja 108
Silver Hill WD6: Bore 8Sa 15
Silverholme Cl. HA3: Kenton 31Na 67
Silver Jubilee Way TW4: Cran 54X 107
Silverlands Cl. KT16: Chert 76F 148
Silverland St. E16 . . . . 46Pc 94
Silver La. BR4: W W'ck 75Fc 159
CR8: Purl 84Mb 176
Silverleigh Rd. CR7: Thor H 70Pb 134
Silverlocke Rd. RM17: Grays 51Fe 121
Silver Mead E18 . . . . 25Jc 53
Silvermere Av. RM5: Col R 23Dd 56
Silvermere Ct. CR3: Cat'm 96Vb 197
CR8: Purl 84Qb 176
Silvermere Dr. N18 . . . . 23Zb 52
Silvermere Golf Course 85S 170
Silvermere Rd. SE6 . . . . 59Dc 114
Silver Pl. W1 . . . . 4C 222 (44Lb 90)
WD18: Wat 14U 26
Silver Rd. DA12: Grav'nd 1G 144
SE13 . . . . 55Dc 114
W12 . . . . 45Za 88
Silvers IG9: Buck H 18Lc 35
(off Palmerston Rd.)
Silversmiths Way GU21: Wok 10N 167
Silver Spring Cl. DA8: Erith 51Dd 118
Silverstead La. TN16: Westrm 93Tc 200
Silverstone Ct. RH1: Redh 4P 207
Silverston Way HA7: Stan 23La 46
Silver St. EN1: Enf 13Tb 33
EN7: Walt C, G Oak 2Rb 19
EN9: Walt A 6Ec 20
N18 . . . . 21Tb 51
RM4: Abr 13Xc 37
Silverthorn NW8 . . . . 39Db 69
(off Abbey Rd.)
Silverthorn Dr. HP3: Hem H 6B 4
Silverthorne Loft Apartments SE5 . . . 51Tb 113
(off Albany Rd.)
Silverthorne Rd. SW8 . . . . 54Kb 112
Silverthorn Gdns. E4 . . . . 19Cc 34
Silverton Rd. W6 . . . . 51Za 110
SILVERTOWN 46Lc 93
Silvertown Av. SS17: Stan H 1M 101
Silvertown Viaduct E16 . . . . 44Hc 93
Silvertown Way E16 . . . . 44Gc 93
(Clarkson Rd.)
E16 . . . . 46Jc 93
(Hanover Av.)
Silver Tree Cl. KT12: Walt T 76W 150
Silvertree La. UB6: G'frd 41Fa 86
Silver Trees AL2: Brick W 2Ba 13
Silver Wlk. SE16 . . . . 46Ac 92
Silver Way RM7: Mawney 27Dd 56
UB10: Hil 40R 64
Silver Wing Ind. Est.
CR0: Wadd 79Pb 156
Silverwood Cl. BR3: Beck 66Cc 136
CR0: Sels 81Bc 178
HA6: Nwood 25S 44
RM16: Grays 45Ce 99
Silvester Ho. E1 . . . . 44Xb 91
(off Varden St.)
E2 . . . . 41Yb 92
(off Sceptre Rd.)
W11 . . . . 44Bb 89
(off Basing St.)
Silvester Rd. SE22 . . . . 57Vb 113
Silvester St. SE1 . . . . 2F 231 (47Tb 91)
Silvocea Way E14 . . . . 44Fc 93
Silwood Cl. SL5: Asc 8B 124
Silwood Est. SE16 . . . . 49Yb 92
Silwood Pk. 9C 124
Silwood Rd. SL5: S'dale, S'hill 10D 124
Silwood St. SE16 . . . . 49Yb 92
(off Rotherhithe New Rd.)
Simla Ct. N7 . . . . 38Nb 70
(off Brewery Rd.)
Simla Ho. SE1 . . . . 2G 231
Simmil Rd. KT10: Clay 78Ga 152
Simmonds Ct. SW5 . . . . 49Db 89
(off Earl's Ct. Gdns.)
Simmonds Dr. DA3: Hartl 71Ce 165
Simmonds Ri. HP3: Hem H 4M 3
Simmons Cl. KT9: Chess 79La 152
N20 . . . . 19Gb 31
SL3: L'ly 49C 82
Simmons Dr. RM8: Dag 34Ad 75
Simmons Ga. KT10: Esh 78Ea 152
Simmons La. E4 . . . . 19Fc 35
Simmons Pl. RM16: Grays 46Ce 99
TW18: Staines 64G 126
Simmons Rd. SE18 . . . . 50Rc 94
Simmons Way N20 . . . . 19Gb 31
Simms Cl. SM5: Cars 75Gb 155
Simms Gdns. N2 . . . . 26Eb 49
Simms Rd. SE1 . . . . 49Wb 91
Simnel Rd. SE12 . . . . 59Kc 115
Simon Cl. W11 . . . . 45Bb 89
Simon Ct. W9 . . . . 41Cb 89
(off Saltram Cres.)
WD23: Bush 16Ca 27
Simon Dean HP3: Bov 9C 2
Simonds Rd. E10 . . . . 33Cc 72
Simone Cl. BR1: Brom 67Mc 137
Simone Ct. SE26 . . . . 62Yb 136
Simone Dr. CR8: Kenley 88Sb 177
Simon Peter Ct. EN2: Enf 12Rb 33
Simons Cl. KT16: Ott 79E 148
Simons Ct. N16 . . . . 33Vb 71
Simons Wlk. E15 . . . . 36Fc 73
TW20: Eng G 6N 125
Simplemarsh Ct. KT15: Add 77K 149
Simplemarsh Rd. KT15: Add 77J 149
Simpson Cl. CR0: C'don 71Sb 157
N21 . . . . 15Nb 32
Simpson Dr. W3 . . . . 44Ta 87
Simpson Ho. NW8 . . . . 4D 214 (42Gb 89)
SE11 . . . . 7J 229 (50Pb 90)
Simpson Rd. RM13: Rain 37Hd 76
TW4: Houn 58Ba 107
TW10: Ham 63La 130
Simpsons Rd. BR2: Brom 69Jc 137
E14 . . . . 45Dc 92
Simpson St. SW11 . . . . 54Gb 111
Simpsons Way SL1: Slou 6H 81
Simpson Way KT6: Surb 72La 152
Simrose Ct. SW18 . . . . 57Cb 111
Sims Cl. RM1: Rom 28Hd 56
Sims Wlk. SE3 . . . . 56Hc 115
Sinclair Ct. CR0: C'don 75Ub 157
Sinclair Dr. SM2: Sutt 81Db 175
Sinclair Gdns. W14 . . . . 47Za 88
Sinclair Gro. NW11 . . . . 30Za 48
Sinclair Ho. WC1 . . . . 4F 217
Sinclair Mans. W12 . . . . 47Za 88
(off Richmond Way)
Sinclair Pl. SE4 . . . . 58Cc 114
Sinclair Rd. E4 . . . . 22Bc 52
SL4: Wind 5G 102
W14 . . . . 47Za 88
Sinclairs Ho. E3 . . . . 40Bc 72
(off St Stephen's Rd.)
Sinclair Way DA2: Daren 63Td 142
Sinclare Cl. EN1: Enf 11Vb 33
Sincots Rd. RH1: Redh 6P 207
Sinderby Cl. WD6: Bore 11Pa 29
Singapore Rd. W13 . . . . 46Ja 86
Singer M. SW4 . . . . 54Nb 112
(off Union Rd.)
Singer St. EC2 . . . . 4G 219 (41Tb 91)
Singles Cross La. TN14: Knock 86Yc 181
SINGLE STREET 87Rc 180
Single St. TN16: Big H 87Rc 180
Singleton Cl. CR0: C'don 73Sb 157
RM12: Horn 35Hd 76
SW17 . . . . 66Hb 133
Singleton Rd. RM9: Dag 36Bd 75
Singleton Scarp N12 . . . . 22Cb 49
SINGLEWELL 4F 144
Singlewell La. DA11: Grav'nd 2D 144
Singlewell Rd. DA11: Grav'nd 2D 144
Singret Pl. UB8: Cowl 42L 83
Sinnott Rd. E17 . . . . 25Zb 52
Siobhan Davis Dance Studios 4B 230
Sion Ct. TW1: Twick 60Ka 108
Sion Rd. TW1: Twick 60Ka 108
Sippets Ct. IG1: Ilf 32Tc 74
SIPSON 51Q 106
Sipson Cl. UB7: Sip 51Q 106
Sipson La. UB3: Harl 51Q 106
UB7: Sip 51Q 106
Sipson Rd. UB7: Sip, W Dray 48P 83
(not continuous)
Sipson Way UB7: Sip 52Q 106
Sir Abraham Dawes Cotts. SW15 . . . 56Ab 110
Sir Alexander Cl. W3 . . . . 46Va 88
Sir Alexander Rd. W3 . . . . 46Va 88
Sir Christopher France Ho. E1 . . . . . 41Ac 92
Sir Cyril Black Way SW19 . . . . 66Cb 133
Sirdar Rd. CR4: Mitc 65Jb 134
N22 . . . . 27Rb 51
W11 . . . . 45Za 88
Sirdar Strand DA12: Grav'nd 4H 145
Sir Francis Drake Ct. SE10 . . . . 50Fc 93
Sir Francis Way CM14: B'wood 19Xd 40
Sir Henry Peakes Dr. SL2: Farn C 7E 60
Siri Guru Nanak Sports Cen. & Arts Studio
. . . . 9E 122
Sirinham Point SW8 . . . . 51Pb 112
(off Meadow Rd.)
Sirius SW11 . . . . 54Hb 111
Sirius Bldg. E1 . . . . 45Zb 92
(off Jardine Rd.)
Sirius Rd. HA6: Nwood 22V 44
Sir James Altham Pool 22Z 45
Sir James Black Ho. SE5 . . . . 54Tb 113
(off Coldharbour La.)
Sir John Kirk Cl. SE5 . . . . 52Sb 113
Sir John Lyon Ho. EC4 . . . . 4D 224
Sir John Morden Wlk. SE3 . . . . 54Jc 115
Sir John Soane's Mus. 2H 223 (44Pb 90)
Sir Nicholas Garrow Ho. W10 . . . . . . 42Ab 88
(off Kensal Rd.)
Sir Oswald Stoll Foundation, The
SW6 . . . . 52Db 111
(off Fulham Rd.)
Sir Oswald Stoll Mans. SW6 . . . . . . 52Db 111
(off Fulham Rd.)
Sir Robert M. SL3: L'ly 50C 82
Sir Sydney Camm Ho.
SL4: Wind 3F 102
Sir Walter Raleigh Ct. SE10 . . . . 50Gc 93
Sir William Atkins Ho.
KT18: Eps 85Ta 173
Sir William Powell's Almshouses
SW6 . . . . 54Ab 110
Sise La. EC4 . . . . 3F 225 (44Tb 91)
Siskin Cl. WD6: Bore 14Qa 29
WD23: Bush 14Aa 27
Siskin Ho. SE16 . . . . 49Zb 92
(off Tawny Way)
WD18: Wat 16T 26
Sisley Rd. IG11: Bark 39Uc 74
Sispara Gdns. SW18 . . . . 58Bb 111
Sissinghurst Cl.
BR1: Brom 64Gc 137
Sissinghurst Ho. SE15 . . . . 51Yb 114
(off Sharratt St.)
Sissinghurst Rd. CR0: C'don 73Wb 157
Sissulu Ct. E6 . . . . 39Lc 73
Sister Mabel's Way SE15 . . . . 52Wb 113
Sisters Av. SW11 . . . . 55Hb 111
Sistova Rd. SW12 . . . . 60Kb 112
Sisulu Pl. SW9 . . . . 55Qb 112
Sitarey Ct. W12 . . . . 46Xa 88

Sittingbourne Av. EN1: Enf 16Tb 33
Sitwell Gro. HA7: Stan 22Ha 46
Siverst Cl. UB5: N'olt 37Da 65
Sivill Ho. E2 .....3K 219
Siviter Way RM10: Dag 38Dd 76
Siward Rd. BR2: Brom 69Kc 137
N17 .....25Tb 51
SW17 .....62Eb 133
Six Acres HP3: Hem H 5A 4
Six Acres Est. N4 .....33Pb 70
Six Bells La. TN13: S'oaks 98Ld 203
Six Bridges Ind. Est. SE1 .....50Wb 91
(not continuous)
Sixpenny Ct. IG11: Bark 37Sc 74
Sixteenth Av. KT20: Lwr K 98Ab 194
Sixth Av. E12 .....35Pc 74
KT20: Lwr K 97Ab 194
UB3: Hayes 46V 84
W10 .....41Ab 88
WD25: Wat 7Z 13
Sixth Cross Rd. TW2: Twick 62Ea 130
Skardu Rd. NW2 .....36Ab 68
Skarnings Ct. EN9: Walt A 5Jc 21
Skeena Hill SW18 .....59Ab 110
Skeet Hill La. BR5: Orp 76Cd 162
BR6: Orp 74Ad 161
Skeffington Rd. E6 .....39Pc 74
Skeffington St. SE18 .....48Sc 94
Skeggs Ho. E14 .....48Ec 92
(off Glengall St.)
Skegness Ho. N7 .....38Pb 70
(off Sutterton St.)
Skelbrook St. SW18 .....61Eb 133
Skelgill Rd. SW15 .....56Bb 111
Skelley Rd. E15 .....38Hc 73
Skelton Cl. E8 .....37Vb 71
Skelton Rd. E7 .....37Jc 73
Skelton's La. E10 .....31Dc 72
Skelwith Rd. W6 .....51Ya 110
Skenfrith Ho. SE15 .....51Xb 113
(off Commercial Way)
Skerne Rd. KT2: King T 67Ma 131
Skerne Wlk. KT2: King T 67Ma 131
Skerries Ct. SL3: L'ly 49C 82
Sketchley Gdns. SE16 .....50Zb 92
Sketty Rd. EN1: Enf 13Vb 33
Skibbs La. BR5: Orp, St M Cry 75Bd 161
BR6: Chels, Orp 78Ad 161
Skid Hill La. CR6: W'ham 84Hc 179
Skidmore Way WD3: Rick 18N 25
Skiers St. E15 .....39Gc 73
Skiffington Cl. SW2 .....60Qb 112
Skillen Lodge HA5: Pinn 25Z 45
Skimmington Cotts. RH2: Reig 7F 206
Skimpans Cl. AL9: Wel G 6F 8
Skinner Pl. SW1 .....6H 227
Skinners La. EC4 .....4E 224 (45Sb 91)
KT21: Asht 90Ma 173
TW5: Hest 53Da 107
Skinner's Row SE10 .....53Dc 114
Skinner St. EC1 .....4A 218 (41Qb 90)
Skinney La. DA4: Hort K, S Dar 69Td 142
Skip La. UB9: Hare 32M 63
Skipper Ct. IG11: Bark 39Sc 74
Skippers Cl. DA9: Ghithe 57Xd 120
Skipsea Ho. SW18 .....58Gb 111
Skipsey Av. E6 .....41Pc 94
Skipton Cl. N11 .....23Jb 50
Skipton Dr. UB3: Harl 48S 84
Skipton Ho. SE4 .....56Ac 114
Skipwith Ho. EC1 .....7K 217
Skipworth Rd. E9 .....39Yb 72
Skua Ct. SE8 .....51Bc 114
(off Dorking Cl.)
Sky Bus. Pk. TW20: Thorpe 68E 126
Skydmore Path SL2: Slou 1D 80
Skye Ho. WD18: Wat 16V 26
Skye Lodge SL1: Slou 6J 81
(off Lansdowne Av.)
Skylark Av. DA9: Ghithe 58Wd 120
Skylark Ct. SE1 .....2E 230
Skylark Rd. UB9: Den 32E 62
Skyline Ct. CR0: C'don 76Tb 157
(off Park La.)
SE1 .....4K 231 (48Vb 91)
Skyline Plaza Bldg. E1 .....44Wb 91
(off Commercial Rd.)
Skylines E14 .....47Ec 92
Skylines Village E14 .....47Ec 92
Sky Peals Rd. IG8: Wfd G 24Fc 53
Skyport Dr. UB7: Harm 52M 105
Sky Studios E16 .....47Qc 94
Skyvan Cl. TW6: H'row A 57S 106
Skyview Apartments CR0: C'don 75Sb 157
(off Park St.)
Skyway 14 SL3: Poyle 55H 105
Slade, The SE18 .....51Uc 116
Sladebrook Rd. SE3 .....55Mc 115
Slade Ct. EN5: New Bar 13Db 31
KT16: Ott 79F 148
WD7: R'lett 7Ja 14
Sladedale Rd. SE18 .....50Uc 94
Slade End CM16: They B 8Uc 22
Slade Gdns. DA8: Erith 53Hd 118
SLADE GREEN 53Jd 118
Slade Grn. Rd. DA8: Erith 52Kd 119
Slade Ho. TW4: Houn 58Ba 107
Sladen Pl. E5 .....35Xb 71
Slade Oak La. SL9: Ger X, Den 27D 42
UB9: Den 29E 42
Slade Rd. GU24: Brkwd 2B 186
KT16: Ott 79F 148
Slades Cl. EN2: Enf 13Qb 32
Slades Dr. BR7: Chst 62Sc 138
Slades Gdns. EN2: Enf 12Qb 32
Slades Hill EN2: Enf 13Qb 32
Slades Ri. EN2: Enf 13Qb 32
Slade Twr. E10 .....33Cc 72
(off Leyton Grange Est.)
Slade Wlk. SE17 .....51Rb 113
Slade Way CR4: Mitc 67Jb 134
Slagrove Pl. SE13 .....57Cc 114
Slaidburn St. SW10 .....51Eb 111
Slaithwaite Rd. SE13 .....56Ec 114
Slaney Ct. NW10 .....38Ya 68
Slaney Pl. N7 .....36Qb 70
Slaney Rd. RM1: Rom 29Gd 56
Slapleys GU22: Wok 92A 188
Slater Cl. SE18 .....50Qc 94
Slatter NW9 .....24Va 48
Slattery Rd. TW13: Felt 60Z 107
Sleaford Grn. WD19: Wat 20Z 27
Sleaford Ho. E3 .....42Cc 92
(off Fern St.)
Sleaford Ind. Est. SW8 .....52Lb 112
Sleaford St. SW8 .....52Lb 112
Sleapcross Gdns. AL4: S'ford 3M 7
SLEAPSHYDE 3M 7
Sleapshyde La. AL4: S'ford 3M 7
Sleat Ho. E3 .....40Bc 72
(off Saxon Rd.)
Sledmere Ct. TW14: Bedf 60U 106
Sleepers Farm Rd. RM16: Grays 7D 100
Sleigh Ho. E2 .....41Yb 92
(off Bacton St.)
Slewins Cl. RM11: Horn 29Ld 57
Slewins La. RM11: Horn 29Ld 57
Slievemore Cl. SW4 .....55Mb 112
Sligo Ho. E1 .....42Zb 92
(off Beaumont Gro.)
Slindon Ct. N16 .....34Vb 71
Slines Oak Rd.
CR3: W'ham, Wold 95Cc 198
CR6: W'ham 95Cc 198
Slingsby Pl. WC2 .....4F 223 (45Nb 90)
Slip, The TN16: Westrm 98Sc 200
Slippers Hill HP2: Hem H 1M 3
Slippers Pl. SE16 .....48Xb 91
Slipshatch Rd. RH2: Reig 10F 206
Slipshoe St. RH2: Reig 6H 207
Slipway Ho. E14 .....50Dc 92
(off Burrells Wharf Sq.)
Sloane Av. SW3 .....6E 226 (49Gb 89)
Sloane Av. Mans.
SW3 .....6F 227 (49Hb 89)
Sloane Ct. TW7: Isle 53Ga 108
Sloane Ct. E. SW3 .....7H 227 (50Jb 90)
Sloane Ct. W.
SW3 .....7H 227 (50Jb 90)
Sloane Gdns. BR6: Farnb 76Sc 160
SW1 .....6H 227 (49Jb 90)
Sloane Ga. Mans. SW1 .....5H 227
Sloane Ho. E9 .....38Yb 72
(off Loddiges Rd.)
Sloane M. N8 .....29Nb 50
Sloane Sq. DA3: Lfield 69Ae 143
SW1 .....6G 227 (49Jb 90)
Sloane St. SW1 .....2G 227 (47Hb 89)
Sloane Ter. SW1 .....5G 227 (49Jb 90)
Sloane Ter. Mans. SW1 .....5H 227
Sloane Wlk. CR0: C'don 72Bc 158
Slocock Hill GU21: Wok 9N 167
Slocum Cl. SE28 .....45Yc 95
SLOUGH 7K 81
Slough Crematorium SL2: Slou 3K 81
Slough Ice Arena 6H 81
Slough Ind. Est. SL1: Slou 3E 80
(not continuous)
Slough Interchange Ind. Est.
SL1: Slou 6L 81
Slough La. KT18: Head 97Sa 193
NW9 .....29Sa 47
RH3: Bkld 4C 206
Slough Mus. 7L 81
Slough Retail Pk. SL1: Slou 6F 80
Slough Rd. SL0: Iver H 41E 82
SL1: Slou 9J 81
SL3: Dat 10L 81
SL4: Eton 1H 103
Slough Trad. Est. SL1: Slou 5D 80
(Ajax Av.)
SL1: Slou 4F 80
(Liverpool Rd.)
SL1: Slou 3D 80
(Oxford Av.)
Slowmans Cl. AL2: Park 10A 6
Sly St. E1 .....44Xb 91
Smaldon Cl. UB7: W Dray 48Q 84
Small Acre HP1: Hem H 2H 3
Smallberry Av. TW7: Isle 54Ha 108
Smallbrook M. W2 .....3B 220 (44Fb 89)
Smalley Cl. N16 .....34Vb 71
Smalley Rd. Est. N16 .....34Vb 71
(off Smalley Cl.)
SMALLFORD 2M 7
Smallford La. AL4: S'ford 3M 7
Smallford Works AL4: S'ford 3M 7
Small Grains DA3: Fawk 76Xd 164
Smallwood Rd. SW17 .....63Fb 133
Smarden Cl. DA17: Belv 50Cd 96
Smarden Gro. SE9 .....63Pc 138
Smart Cl. RM3: Rom 25Kd 57
Smart's Heath La. GU22: Wok 5L 187
Smart's Heath Rd. GU22: Wok 5K 187
Smart's La. IG10: Lough 14Mc 35
Smart's Pl. N18 .....22Wb 51
WC2 .....2G 223 (44Nb 90)
Smarts Rd. DA12: Grav'nd 2D 144
Smart St. E2 .....41Zb 92
Smead Way SE13 .....55Dc 114
Smeathman Ct. HP1: Hem H 3L 3
Smeaton Cl. EN9: Walt A 4Gc 21
KT9: Chess 79Ma 153
Smeaton Ct. SE1 .....4D 230 (48Sb 91)
Smeaton Dr. GU22: Wok 92D 188
Smeaton Rd. EN3: Enf L 9Cc 20
IG8: Wfd G 22Pc 54
SW18 .....59Cb 111
Smeaton St. E1 .....46Xb 91
Smedley St. SW4 .....54Mb 112
Smeed Rd. E3 .....38Cc 72
Smikle Ct. SE14 .....53Zb 114
(off Hatcham Pk. M.)
Smiles Pl. GU22: Wok 88D 168
SE13 .....54Ec 114
Smitham Bottom La. CR8: Purl 83Lb 176
Smitham Downs Rd.
CR8: Purl 85Mb 176
Smith Cl. SE16 .....46Zb 92
Smith Ct. GU21: Wok 85F 168
Smithfield HP2: Hem H 1M 3
Smithfield (Central Markets) 1B 224
Smithfield St. EC1 .....1B 224 (43Rb 91)
Smith Hill TW8: Bford 51Na 109
Smithies Rd. SE2 .....49Xc 95
Smith Rd. RH2: Reig 9H 207
Smith's Ct. W1 .....4D 222
Smiths Cres. AL4: S'ford 3M 7
Smith's La. SL4: Wind 4C 102
Smith's Lawn (Polo & Equestrian Grounds) 6J 125
Smithson Rd. N17 .....25Tb 51
Smiths Point E13 .....39Jc 73
(off Brooks Rd.)
Smith Sq. SW1 .....4F 229 (48Nb 90)
Smith St. KT5: Surb 72Pa 153
SW3 .....7F 227 (50Hb 89)
WD18: Wat 14Y 27
Smiths Yd. CR0: C'don 76Sb 157
(off St George's Wlk.)
SW18 .....61Eb 133
Smith Ter. SW3 .....7F 227 (50Hb 89)
Smithwood Cl. SW19 .....60Ab 110
Smithy Cl. KT20: Lwr K 98Bb 195
Smithy La. KT20: Lwr K 99Bb 195
Smithy's Grn. GU20: W'sham 9B 146
Smithy St. E1 .....43Yb 92
Smock Wlk. CR0: C'don 72Sb 157
Smokehouse Yd. EC1 .....7C 218
Smoke La. RH2: Reig 8K 207
Smoothfield Ct. TW3: Houn 56Ca 107
Smugglers Wlk. DA9: Ghithe 57Xd 120
Smugglers Way SW18 .....56Db 111
SMUG OAK 2Da 13
Smug Oak Grn. Bus. Cen.
AL2: Brick W 1Da 13
Smug Oak La. AL2: Brick W, Col S 2Da 13
Smyrk's Rd. SE17 .....7J 231 (50Ub 91)
Smyrna Mans. NW6 .....38Cb 69
(off Smyrna Rd.)
Smyrna Rd. NW6 .....38Cb 69
Smythe Cl. N9 .....20Wb 33
Smythe Rd. DA4: Sut H 67Qd 141
Smythe St. E14 .....45Dc 92
Snag La. BR6: Prat B 83Uc 180
TN14: Cud 84Tc 180
Snakes Hill CM14: N'side, Pil H 12Sd 40
Snakes La. N14 .....13Kb 32
Snakes La. E. IG8: Buck H, Wfd G 23Lc 53
Snakes La. W. IG8: Wfd G 22Jc 53
Snakey La. TW13: Felt 63W 128
Snape Spur SL1: Slou 4J 81
SNARESBROOK 29Jc 53
Snaresbrook Dr. HA7: Stan 21Ma 47
Snaresbrook Hall E18 .....28Jc 53
Snaresbrook Ho. E18 .....28Hc 53
Snaresbrook Rd. E11 .....28Gc 53
Snarsgate St. W10 .....43Ya 88
Snatts Hill RH8: Oxt 1K 211
Sneath Av. NW11 .....31Bb 69
Snelling Av. DA11: Nflt 1A 144
Snellings Rd. KT12: Hers 78Y 151
Snells Pk. N18 .....23Vb 51
Sneyd Rd. NW2 .....35Ya 68
Snipe Cl. DA8: Erith 52Kd 119
Snodland Cl. BR6: Downe 82Qc 180
Snowberry Cl. E15 .....35Fc 73
EN5: Barn 13Bb 31
Snowbury Rd. SW6 .....54Db 111
Snow Centre, The 4P 3
Snowcrete SL3: Wex 10N 61
Snowden Av. UB10: Hil 40R 64
Snowden Cl. SL4: Wind 6B 102
Snowden Hill DA11: Nflt 57Ce 121
Snowden St. EC2 .....6H 219 (42Ub 91)
Snowdon Aviary 1G 215
Snowdon Ct. RM2: Rom 28Ld 57
Snowdon Cres. UB3: Harl 48S 84
Snowdon Dr. NW9 .....30Ua 48
Snowdon Rd. TW6: H'row A 58S 106
Snowdown Cl. SE20 .....67Zb 136
Snowdrop Cl. TW12: Hamp 65Ca 129
Snowdrop Path RM3: Rom 24Md 57
Snowdrop Way GU24: Bisl 9E 166
Snowerhill Rd. RH3: Bet 8A 206
Snow Hill EC1 .....1B 224 (43Rb 91)
Snow Hill Ct. EC1 .....2C 224 (44Rb 91)
Snowman Ho. NW6 .....39Db 69
Snowsfields SE1 .....1G 231 (47Tb 91)
Snowshill Rd. E12 .....36Nc 74
Snows Paddock
GU20: W'sham 6A 146
Snow's Ride GU20: W'sham 8A 146
Snowy Fielder Waye TW7: Isle 54Ka 108
Soames Pl. EN4: Had W 12Db 31
Soames St. SE15 .....55Vb 113
Soames Wlk. KT3: N Mald 67Ua 132
Soane Cl. W5 .....47Ma 87
Soane Ct. NW1 .....38Lb 70
(off St Pancras Way)
Soane Ho. SE17 .....50Tb 91
(off Roland Way)
Soap Ho. La. TW8: Bford 52Na 109
Sobell Leisure Cen. 34Pb 70
Sobraon Ho. KT2: King T 66Pa 131
(off Elm Rd.)
Socket La. BR2: Hayes 72Kc 159
Soda Studios E8 .....39Vb 71
(off Kingsland Rd.)
Soham Rd. EN3: Enf L 9Bc 20
SOHO 3D 222 (44Lb 90)
Soho Sq. W1 .....2D 222 (44Mb 90)
Soho St. W1 .....2D 222 (44Mb 90)
Soho Theatre & Writers Cen. 3D 222
Sojourner Truth Cl. E8 .....37Xb 71
Sola Ct. CR0: C'don 74Tb 157
(off Sydenham Rd.)
Solander Gdns. E1 .....45Xb 91
(off Cable St.)
E1 .....45Yb 92
(The Highway)
Solar Ct. N3 .....24Db 49
SE16 .....47Wb 91
(off Chambers St.)
WD18: Wat 15V 26
Solar Ho. E6 .....43Qc 94
E15 .....37Gc 73
(off Romford Rd.)
Solarium Ct. SE1 .....5K 231
Solar Way EN3: Enf L 8Bc 20
Soldene Ct. N7 .....36Pb 70
(off George's Rd.)
Solebay St. E1 .....42Ac 92
Solecote KT23: Bookh 97Ca 191
Sole Farm Av. KT23: Bookh 97Ba 191
Sole Farm Cl. KT23: Bookh 96Ba 191
Sole Farm Rd. KT23: Bookh 97Ba 191
Solefields Rd. TN13: S'oaks 100Kd 203
Solent Ct. SW16 .....68Pb 134
Solent Ho. E1 .....43Ac 92
(off Ben Jonson Rd.)
Solent Ri. E13 .....41Jc 93
Solent Rd. NW6 .....36Cb 69
Soleoak Dr. TN13: S'oaks 99Kd 203
Solesbridge Cl. WD3: Chor 13H 25
Solesbridge La. WD3: Chor, Sarr 13H 25
SOLE STREET 10F 144
Sole St. DA12: Cobh, Sole S 10F 144
Soley M. WC1 .....3K 217 (41Qb 90)
Solid La. CM15: Dodd, Pil H 11Vd 40
Solna Av. SW15 .....57Ya 110
Solna Rd. N21 .....18Tb 33
Solomon Av. N9 .....21Wb 51
Solomons Ct. N12 .....24Eb 49
Solomon's Hill WD3: Rick 17M 25
Solomon's Pas. SE15 .....56Xb 113
Soloms Ct. Rd. SM7: Bans 89Fb 175
Solon New Rd. SW4 .....56Nb 112
Solon New Rd. Est. SW4 .....56Nb 112
Solon Rd. SW2 .....56Nb 112
Solway RM18: E Til 8L 101
Solway Cl. E8 .....37Vb 71
(off Queensbridge Rd.)
TW4: Houn 55Aa 107
Solway Ho. E1 .....42Zb 92
(off Ernest St.)
Solway Rd. N22 .....25Rb 51
SE22 .....56Wb 113
Somaford Gro. EN4: E Barn 16Fb 31
Somali Rd. NW2 .....36Bb 69
Sombourne Ho. SW15 .....59Wa 110
(off Fontley Way)
Somerby Rd. IG11: Bark 38Tc 74
Somercoates Cl. EN4: Cockf 13Gb 31
Somer Ct. SW6 .....51Cb 111
(off Anselm Rd.)
Somerden Rd. BR5: St M Cry 73Zc 161
Somerfield Cl. KT20: Tad 91Ab 194
Somerfield Rd. N4 .....33Rb 71
(not continuous)
Somerfield St. SE16 .....50Zb 92
Somerford Cl. HA5: Eastc 28W 44
Somerford Gro. N16 .....35Vb 71
N17 .....24Wb 51
(not continuous)
Somerford Gro. Est. N16 .....35Vb 71
Somerford St. E1 .....42Xb 91
Somerford Way SE16 .....47Ac 92
Somerhill Av. DA15: Sidc 59Xc 117
Somerhill Rd. DA16: Well 54Xc 117
Someries Rd. HP1: Hem H 1H 3
Somerleyton Pas. SW9 .....56Rb 113
Somerleyton Rd. SW9 .....56Qb 112
Somersby Gdns. IG4: Ilf 29Pc 54
Somers Cl. NW1 .....1D 216 (40Mb 70)
RH2: Reig 5J 207
Somers Cres. W2 .....3D 220 (44Gb 89)
Somerset Av. DA16: Well 57Vc 117
KT9: Chess 77Ma 153
SW20 .....68Xa 132
Somerset Cl. IG8: Wfd G 25Jc 53
KT3: N Mald 72Ua 154
KT12: Hers 78X 151
KT19: Ewe 81Ta 173
N17 .....26Tb 51
SM3: Wor Pk 77Ya 154
Somerset Ct. IG9: Buck H 19Lc 35
NW1 .....2D 216 (40Mb 70)
W7 .....44Ha 86
(off Copley Cl.)
Somerset Est. SW11 .....53Fb 111
Somerset Gdns. HA0: Wemb 36La 66
N6 .....31Jb 70
N17 .....24Ub 51
RM11: Horn 32Qd 77
SE13 .....54Dc 114
SW16 .....69Pb 134
TW11: Tedd 64Ga 130
Somerset Hall N17 .....24Ub 51
Somerset House 4H 223 (45Pb 90)
Somerset Ho. RH1: Redh 5P 207
SW19 .....62Za 132
Somerset Lodge TW8: Bford 51Ma 109
Somerset Rd. BR6: Orp 73Wc 161
DA1: Dart 58Kd 119
E17 .....29Cc 52
EN3: Enf L 10Ac 20
EN5: New Bar 15Db 31
HA1: Harr 29Ea 46
KT1: King T 68Pa 131
N17 .....27Vb 51
N18 .....22Vb 51
NW4 .....28Ya 48
RH1: Redh 8M 207
SS17: Linf 7J 101
SW19 .....62Za 132
TW8: Bford 51La 108
TW11: Tedd 64Ga 130
UB1: S'hall 43Ba 85
W4 .....48Ta 87
W13 .....46Ka 86
Somerset Sq. W14 .....47Ab 88
Somerset Way SL0: Rich P 47H 83
Somerset Waye TW5: Hest 51Aa 107
Somersham Rd. DA7: Bex 54Ad 117
Somers Pl. RH2: Reig 5J 207
SW2 .....59Pb 112
Somers Rd. AL9: Wel G 6E 8
E17 .....28Bc 52
RH2: Reig 5J 207
SW2 .....58Pb 112
Somers Sq. AL9: Wel G 5E 8
Somerston Ho. NW1 .....39Lb 70
(off St Pancras Way)
SOMERS TOWN 2D 216 (40Mb 70)
Somers Town Community Sports Cen. 2D 216 (40Mb 70)
Somers Way WD23: Bush 17Ea 28
Somerton Av. TW9: Rich 55Ra 109
Somerton Cl. CR8: Purl 87Qb 176
Somerton Ho. WC1 .....4E 216
Somerton Rd. NW2 .....34Za 68
SE15 .....56Xb 113
Somertrees Av. SE12 .....61Kc 137
Somervell Rd. HA2: Harr 36Ba 65
Somerville Av. SW13 .....51Xa 110
Somerville Cl. SW9 .....53Pb 112
Somerville Ct. RH1: Redh 5N 207
(off Oxford Rd.)
Somerville Point SE16 .....47Bc 92
Somerville Rd. DA1: Dart 58Pd 119
KT11: Cobh 86Ca 171
RM6: Chad H 30Yc 55
SE20 .....66Zb 136
SL4: Eton 10G 80
Somery Wlk. WD25: A'ham 8Da 13
Sommerville Ct.
WD6: Bore 11Pa 29
(off Alconbury Cl.)
Sonderburg Rd. N7 .....33Pb 70
Sondes St. SE17 .....51Tb 113
Sonesta Apartments SE15 .....53Xb 113
Songhurst Cl. CR0: C'don 72Pb 156
Sonia Ct. HA1: Harr 30Ha 46
HA8: Edg 24Pa 47
Sonia Gdns. N12 .....21Eb 49
NW10 .....35Va 68
TW5: Hest 52Ca 107
Sonnets, The HP1: Hem H 1K 3
Sonnet Wlk. TN16: Big H 90Kc 179
Sonning Gdns. TW12: Hamp 65Aa 129
Sonning Ho. E2 .....4K 219
Sonning Rd. SE25 .....72Wb 157
Sontan Ct. TW2: Twick 60Fa 108
Soper Cl. E4 .....22Bc 52
SE23 .....60Zb 114
Soper Dr. CR3: Cat'm 95Tb 197
Soper M. EN3: Enf L 10Cc 20
Sopers Rd. EN6: Cuff 1Pb 18
Sophia Cl. N7 .....37Pb 70
Sophia Ho. W6 .....50Ya 88
(off Queen Caroline St.)
Sophia Rd. E10 .....32Dc 72
E16 .....44Kc 93
Sophia Sq. SE16 .....45Ac 92
(off Sovereign Cres.)
Sophie Gdns. SL3: L'ly 7P 81
Soprano Ct. E15 .....39Hc 73
(off Plaistow Rd.)
Soprano Way KT10: Surb 76Ka 152
SOPWELL 5C 6
Sopwell La. AL1: St A 3B 6
Sopwell Nunnery (remains) 4C 6
Sopwith NW9 .....24Va 48
Sopwith Av. KT9: Chess 78Na 153
Sopwith Cl. KT2: King T 64Pa 131
TN16: Big H 88Mc 179
Sopwith Dr. KT13: Weyb 83N 169
Sopwith Rd. TW5: Hest 52Y 107
Sopwith Way KT2: King T 67Na 131
SW8 .....52Kb 112
Sorbie Cl. KT13: Weyb 79T 150
Sorbus Ct. EN2: Enf 12Rb 33
Sorensen Ct. E10 .....33Dc 72
(off Leyton Grange Est.)
Sorrel Bank CR0: Sels 82Ac 178
(not continuous)
Sorrel Cl. SE28 .....46Wc 95
Sorrel Ct. RM17: Grays 51Fe 121
Sorrel Gdns. E6 .....43Nc 94
Sorrel La. E14 .....44Fc 93
Sorrell Cl. SE14 .....52Ac 114
SW9 .....54Qb 112
Sorrells, The SS17: Stan H 1P 101
Sorrel Wlk. RM1: Rom 27Hd 56
Sorrel Way DA11: Nflt 3A 144
Sorrento Rd. SM1: Sutt 76Db 155
Sospel Ct. SL2: Farn R 10G 60
Sotheby Rd. N5 .....34Rb 71
Sotheran Cl. E8 .....39Wb 71
Sotherby Lodge E2 .....40Yb 72
(off Sewardstone Rd.)
Sotheron Rd. SW6 .....52Db 111
WD17: Wat 13Y 27
Soudan Rd. SW11 .....53Hb 111
Souldern Rd. W14 .....48Za 88
Souldern St. WD18: Wat 15X 27
Sounding All. E3 .....39Cc 72
Sounds Lodge BR8: Crock 72Ed 162
Sth. Access Rd. E17 .....31Ac 72
Southacre W2 .....3D 220
Southacre Way HA5: Pinn 25Y 45
SOUTH ACTON 47Sa 87
Sth. Africa Rd. W12 .....46Xa 88
Sth. Albert Rd. RH2: Reig 5H 207
SOUTHALL 46Ba 85
Southall Ct. UB1: S'hall 45Ba 85
Southall Ent. Cen. UB2: S'hall 47Ca 85
SOUTHALL GREEN 48Aa 85
Southall Ho. RM3: Rom 23Nd 57
(off Kingsbridge Cir.)
Southall La. TW5: Cran 51X 107
UB2: S'hall 51X 107
Southall Pl. SE1 .....2F 231 (47Tb 91)
Southall Sports Cen. 46Aa 85
Southall Way CM14: B'wood 21Vd 58
Southam Ho. KT15: Add 78K 149
(off Addlestone Pk.)
W10 .....42Ab 88
(off Southam St.)
Southam M. WD3: Crox G 16R 26
Southampton Bldgs.
WC2 .....1K 223 (43Qb 90)
Southampton Gdns. CR4: Mitc 71Nb 156
Southampton M. E16 .....46Kc 93
Southampton Pl. WC1 .....1G 223 (43Nb 90)
Southampton Rd. NW5 .....36Hb 69
Southampton Rd. E. TW6: H'row A 58P 105
Southampton Rd. W.
TW6: H'row A 58N 105
Southampton Row WC1 .....7G 217 (43Nb 90)
Southampton St. WC2 .....4G 223 (45Nb 90)
Southampton Way SE5 .....52Tb 113
Southam St. W10 .....42Ab 88
South App. HA6: Nwood 20T 26
SOUTH ASCOT 2A 146
South Ash Rd. TN15: Ash 82Yd 184
Sth. Audley St. W1 .....5J 221 (45Jb 90)
South Av. E4 .....17Dc 34
KT12: W Vill 82U 170
KT13: Weyb 82Q 170
SM5: Cars 80Jb 156
TW9: Kew 54Qa 109
TW20: Egh 65E 126
UB1: S'hall 45Ba 85
South Av. Gdns. UB1: S'hall 45Ba 85
South Bank KT6: Surb 72Na 153
TN16: Westrm 99Sc 200
Southbank BR8: Hext 66Hd 140
(not continuous)
KT7: T Ditt 73Ka 152
Southbank Bus. Cen. SW8 .....51Mb 112
SW11 .....53Hb 111
Southbank Cen. 6J 223 (46Pb 90)
Sth. Bank Ter. KT6: Surb 72Na 153
SOUTH BARNET 18Jb 32
SOUTH BEDDINGTON 79Mb 156
Sth. Birkbeck Rd. E11 .....34Fc 73
Sth. Black Lion La. W6 .....50Wa 88
South Block RM2: Rom 27Md 57
SE1 .....2H 229
Sth. Bolton Gdns. SW5 .....50Db 89
Sth. Border, The CR8: Purl 83Mb 176
SOUTHBOROUGH
BR2 .....71Pc 160
KT6 .....74Na 153
Southborough Cl. KT6: Surb 74Ma 153
Southborough Ho. SE17 .....7H 231
Southborough La. BR2: Brom 71Nc 160

Southborough Rd. BR1: Brom ... 69Nc 138
E9 ... 39Zb 72
KT6: Surb ... 74Na 153
Southbourne BR2: Hayes ... 73Jc 159
Southbourne Av. NW9 ... 26Sa 47
Southbourne Cl. HA5: Pinn ... 31Aa 65
Southbourne Ct. NW9 ... 26Sa 47
Southbourne Cres. NW4 ... 28Ab 48
Southbourne Gdns. HA4: Ruis ... 32X 65
IG1: Ilf ... 36Sc 74
SE12 ... 57Kc 115
Southbridge Pl. CR0: C'don ... 77Sb 157
Southbridge Rd. CR0: C'don ... 77Sb 157
Southbridge Way UB2: S'hall ... 47Aa 85
SOUTH BROMLEY ... 45Ec 92
Southbrook M. SE12 ... 58Hc 115
Southbrook Rd. SE12 ... 58Hc 115
SW16 ... 67Nb 134
Southbury *NW8* ... *39Eb 69*
(off Loudoun Rd.)
Southbury Av. EN1: Enf ... 14Wb 33
Southbury Cl. RM12: Horn ... 36Md 77
Southbury Ho. *EN8: Walt C* ... *4Zb 20*
(off High St.)
Southbury Leisure Cen. ... 13Wb 33
Southbury Rd. EN1: Enf ... 13Ub 33
EN3: Pond E ... 13Ub 33
Sth. Carriage Dr. SW1 ... 2C 226 (47Fb 89)
SW7 ... 2C 226 (47Fb 89)
SOUTH CHINGFORD ... 22Bc 52
Southchurch Ct. *E6* ... *40Pc 74*
(off High St. Sth.)
Southchurch Rd. E6 ... 40Pc 74
South City Ct. SE15 ... 52Ub 113
Southcliffe Dr. SL9: Chal P ... 22A 42
South Cl. AL2: Chis G ... 7P 5
DA6: Bex ... 56Zc 117
EN5: Barn ... 13Bb 31
GU21: Wok ... 8N 167
HA5: Pinn ... 31Ba 65
N6 ... 30Kb 50
RM10: Dag ... 39Cd 76
SL1: Slou ... 5B 80
SM4: Mord ... 72Cb 155
TW2: Twick ... 62Ca 129
UB7: W Dray ... 48P 83
South Cl. Grn. RH1: Mers ... 1B 208
Sth. Colonnade, The E14 ... 46Cc 92
(not continuous)
Southcombe St. W14 ... 49Ab 88
South Comn. Rd. UB8: Uxb ... 37N 63
Southcote GU21: Wok ... 7P 167
Southcote Av. KT5: Surb ... 73Ra 153
TW13: Felt ... 61V 128
Southcote Ho. KT15: Add ... 75M 149
Southcote Ri. HA4: Ruis ... 31T 64
Southcote Rd. CR2: Sande ... 82Ub 177
E17 ... 29Zb 52
N19 ... 35Lb 70
RH1: Mers ... 2C 208
SE25 ... 71Xb 157
Sth. Cottage Dr. WD3: Chor ... 15H 25
Sth. Cottage Gdns. WD3: Chor ... 15H 25
Southcott Ho. *E3* ... *41Dc 92*
(off Devons Rd.)
W9 ... 6A 214
Southcott M. NW8 ... 2D 214 (40Gb 69)
Southcott Rd. TW11: Hamp W ... 67Ka 130
Sth. Countess Rd. E17 ... 27Bc 52
South Cres. E16 ... 42Fc 93
WC1 ... 1D 222 (43Mb 90)
Sth. Crescent M. WC1 ... 5F 217 (42Nb 90)
Southcroft SL2: Slou ... 2F 80
TW20: Eng G ... 4M 125
Southcroft Av. BR4: W W'ck ... 75Ec 158
DA16: Well ... 55Uc 116
Southcroft Rd. BR6: Orp ... 76Uc 160
SW16 ... 65Jb 134
SW17 ... 65Jb 134
Sth. Cross Rd. IG6: Ilf ... 29Sc 54
Sth. Croxted Rd. SE21 ... 62Tb 135
SOUTH CROYDON ... 78Tb 157
South Croydon Sports Club ... 78Ub 157
Southdale IG7: Chig ... 22Tc 54
SOUTH DARENTH ... 67Sd 142
Southdean Gdns. SW19 ... 61Bb 133
South Dene NW7 ... 20Ta 29
Southdene TN14: Hals ... 85Bd 181
(not continuous)
Southdene Ct. N11 ... 20Kb 32
Southdown Av. W7 ... 48Ja 86
Southdown Ct. AL10: Hat ... 3C 8
Southdown Cres. HA2: Harr ... 32Ea 66
IG2: Ilf ... 29Uc 54
Southdown Dr. SW20 ... 66Za 132
Southdown Rd. AL10: Hat ... 3C 8
CR3: Wold ... 94Bc 198
KT12: Hers ... 77Aa 151
RM11: Horn ... 31Kd 77
SM5: Cars ... 81Jb 176
SW20 ... 67Za 132
Southdowns DA4: S Dar ... 68Td 142
South Dr. AL4: St A ... 2H 7
BR6: Orp ... 78Uc 160
CM14: W'ley ... 21Zd 59
CR5: Coul ... 87Mb 176
EN6: Cuff ... 2Nb 18
GU24: Brkwd ... 3A 186
GU25: Vir W ... 4L 147
HA4: Ruis ... 32U 64
RM2: Rom ... 27Ld 57
SM2: Cheam ... 82Ab 174
SM7: Bans ... 85Gb 175
Sth. Ealing Rd. W5 ... 47Ma 87
South East Dance Studios ... 67Gd 140
Sth. Eastern Av. N9 ... 20Vb 33
Sth. Eaton Pl. SW1 ... 5J 227 (49Jb 90)
Sth. Eden Pk. Rd.
BR3: Beck ... 72Dc 158
Sth. Edwardes Sq. W8 ... 48Bb 89
SOUTHEND ... 63Fc 137
South End CR0: C'don ... 77Sb 157
CR2: S Croy ... 77Sb 157
KT23: Bookh ... 98Da 191
W8 ... 48Db 89
Southend Arterial Rd.
CM13: Gt War, L War, W H'dn
... 29Zd 59
RM2: Rom ... 26Md 57
RM3: Hrld W ... 26Md 57
RM11: Horn, Upm ... 26Md 57
RM14: Gt War, Upm ... 26Md 57
South End Cl. NW3 ... 35Gb 69
Southend Cl. SE9 ... 58Rc 116
Southend Cres. SE9 ... 58Rc 116
South End Grn. NW3 ... 35Gb 69
Southend Ho. SS17: Stan H ... 1N 101
Southend La. EN9: Walt A ... 6Kc 21
SE6 ... 63Bc 136
SE26 ... 63Bc 136
South End Rd. NW3 ... 35Gb 69
RM12: Horn ... 37Kd 77
RM13: Horn, Rain ... 40Jd 76
Southend Rd. BR3: Beck ... 67Cc 136
E4 ... 22Ac 52
E6 ... 38Pc 74
E17 ... 25Dc 52
E18 ... 25Jc 53
IG8: Wfd G ... 26Lc 53
RM17: Grays ... 49Ee 99
SS17: Corr, Stan H ... 1M 101
South End Row W8 ... 48Db 89
Southerland Cl. KT13: Weyb ... 77S 150
Southern Av. SE25 ... 69Vb 135
TW14: Felt ... 60W 106
Southern Cotts.
TW19: Stanw M ... 57J 105
Southern Dr. IG10: Lough ... 16Pc 36
Southerngate Way SE14 ... 52Ac 114
Southern Gro. E3 ... 41Bc 92
Southernhay IG10: Lough ... 14Mc 35
Southern Perimeter Rd.
TW6: H'row A, Stanw ... 57K 105
(not continuous)
Southern Pl. BR8: Swan ... 70Fd 140
HA1: Harr ... 35Ha 66
Southern Rd. E13 ... 40Kc 73
N2 ... 28Hb 49
Southern Row W10 ... 42Ab 88
Southerns La. CR5: Coul ... 97Eb 195
Southern St. N1 ... 1H 217 (40Pb 70)
Southern Valley Golf Course ... 3J 145
Southern Way RM7: Rom ... 30Cd 56
SE10 ... 49Hc 93
Southernwood Cl. HP2: Hem H ... 1A 4
Southernwood Retail Pk.
SE1 ... 7K 231 (50Vb 91)
Southerton Rd. W6 ... 49Ya 88
Southerton Way WD7: Shenl ... 5Na 15
South Esk Rd. E7 ... 37Lc 73
Sth. Essex Crematorium
RM14: Upm ... 36Td 78
Southey Ct. KT23: Bookh ... 96Da 191
Southey Ho. SE17 ... 7E 230
Southey M. E16 ... 46Jc 93
Southey Rd. N15 ... 29Ub 51
SW9 ... 53Qb 112
SW19 ... 66Cb 133
Southey St. SE20 ... 66Zb 136
Southey Wlk. RM18: Tilb ... 3D 122
Southfield EN5: Barn ... 16Za 30
Southfield Av. WD24: Wat ... 10Y 13
Southfield Cl. SL4: Dor ... 8A 80
UB8: Hil ... 42Q 84
Southfield Cotts. W7 ... 47Ha 86
Southfield Ct. E11 ... 34Hc 73
Southfield Gdns. SL1: Burn ... 3A 80
TW1: Twick ... 63Ha 130
Southfield Pk. HA2: Harr ... 28Da 45
Southfield Pl. KT13: Weyb ... 80R 150
Southfield Rd. BR7: Chst ... 69Wc 139
EN3: Pond E ... 16Xb 33
EN8: Walt C ... 4Ac 20
N17 ... 26Ub 51
W4 ... 47Ta 87
SOUTHFIELDS
RM16 ... 4F 100
SW18 ... 60Bb 111
Southfields BR8: Hext ... 66Gd 140
KT8: E Mos ... 72Ga 152
NW4 ... 27Xa 48
Southfields Av. TW15: Ashf ... 65R 128
Southfields Ct. SM1: Sutt ... 75Cb 155
Southfields Grn.
DA11: Grav'nd ... 4D 144
Southfields M. SW18 ... 58Cb 111
Southfields Pas. SW18 ... 58Cb 111
Southfields Rd. CR3: Wold ... 94Dc 198
SW18 ... 58Cb 111
TN15: W King ... 80Vd 164
SOUTHFLEET ... 64Ce 143
Southfleet NW5 ... 37Jb 70
Southfleet Av. DA3: Lfield ... 68De 143
Southfleet Rd. BR6: Orp ... 76Uc 160
DA2: Bean ... 63Yd 142
DA10: Swans ... 59Be 121
DA11: Nflt ... 10B 122
South Gdns. HA9: Wemb ... 33Qa 67
SW19 ... 66Fb 133
SOUTHGATE ... 18Mb 32
Southgate RM19: Purf ... 49Sd 98
Southgate Av. TW13: Felt ... 63T 128
Southgate Cir. N14 ... 18Mb 32
Southgate Cotts. WD3: Rick ... 17M 25
Southgate Ct. *N1* ... *38Tb 71*
(off Downham Rd.)
Southgate Gro. N1 ... 38Tb 71
Southgate Ho. *EN8: Chesh* ... *2Ac 20*
(off Turner's Hill)
Southgate Leisure Cen. ... 17Mb 32
Southgate Rd. EN6: Pot B ... 5Eb 17
N1 ... 39Tb 71
Sth. Gipsy Rd. DA16: Well ... 55Zc 117
Sth. Glade, The DA5: Bexl ... 60Bd 117
SOUTH GODSTONE ... 10C 210
South Grn. NW9 ... 25Ua 48
SL1: Slou ... 5J 81
South Gro. E17 ... 29Bc 52
KT16: Chert ... 72H 149
N6 ... 32Jb 70
N15 ... 29Tb 51
South Gro. Ho. N6 ... 32Jb 70
Sth. Guildford St. KT16: Chert ... 74H 149
SOUTH HACKNEY ... 39Zb 72
South Hall Cl. DA4: Farni ... 73Pd 163
South Hall Dr. RM13: Rain ... 43Kd 97
SOUTH HAMPSTEAD ... 38Eb 69
SOUTH HAREFIELD ... 29L 43
SOUTH HARROW ... 34Ea 66
Sth. Harrow Ind. Est. HA2: Harr ... 33Ea 66
SOUTH HATFIELD ... 2B 8
South Herts Golf Course ... 18Cb 31
South Hill BR7: Chst ... 65Pc 138
HA6: Nwood ... 25U 44
SS17: Horn H ... 1J 101
South Hill Av. HA1: Harr ... 34Ea 66
HA2: Harr ... 34Ea 66
South Hill Cres. SS17: Horn H ... 1J 101
South Hill Gro. HA1: Harr ... 35Ga 66
South Hill Pk. NW3 ... 35Gb 69
South Hill Pk. Gdns. NW3 ... 34Gb 69
South Hill Rd. BR2: Brom ... 69Gc 137
DA12: Grav'nd ... 10E 122
HP1: Hem H ... 2L 3
Southholme Cl. SE19 ... 67Ub 135
SOUTH HORNCHURCH ... 40Hd 76
Southill Ct. BR2: Brom ... 71Hc 159
Southill La. HA5: Eastc ... 28X 45
Southill Rd. BR7: Chst ... 66Nc 138
Southill St. E14 ... 44Dc 92
Sth. Island Pl. SW9 ... 52Pb 112
SOUTH KENSINGTON ... 5C 226 (49Fb 89)
Sth. Kensington Sta. Arc.
SW7 ... 5C 226
Sth. Kent Av. DA11: Nflt ... 58Ee 121
SOUTH LAMBETH ... 52Nb 112
Sth. Lambeth Pl. SW8 ... 51Nb 112
Sth. Lambeth Rd. SW8 ... 51Nb 112
Southland Rd. SE18 ... 52Vc 117
Southlands Av. BR6: Orp ... 77Tc 160
Southlands Cl. CR5: Coul ... 89Pb 176
Southlands Dr. SW19 ... 61Za 132
Southlands Gro. BR1: Brom ... 69Nc 138
Southlands La. RH8: Oxt, Tand ... 6F 210
Southlands Rd. BR1: Brom ... 70Mc 137
BR2: Brom ... 70Mc 137
SL0: Den, Iver H ... 37G 62
UB9: Den ... 35H 63
Southland Way TW3: Houn ... 57Fa 108
South La. KT1: King T ... 69Ma 131
KT3: N Mald ... 70Ta 131
South La. W. KT3: N Mald ... 70Ta 131
South Lawn *SL4: Eton* ... *1G 102*
(off South Mdw. La.)
South Lawns *DA11: Nflt* ... *58Ee 121*
(off Lawn Rd.)
SOUTHLEA ... 4M 103
Southlea Rd. SL3: Dat ... 3M 103
SL4: Wind ... 6L 103
South Lodge *E16* ... *46Kc 93*
(off Audley Dr.)
NW8 ... 3B 214 (40Fb 69)
SW7 ... 2E 226
TW2: Whitt ... 58Ea 108
Sth. Lodge Av. CR4: Mitc ... 70Nb 134
Sth. Lodge Cres. EN2: Enf ... 14Mb 32
(not continuous)
Sth. Lodge Dr. N14 ... 14Mb 32
Sth. Lodge Rd. KT12: Hers ... 81W 170
Sth. London Crematorium
CR4: Mitc ... 68Lb 134
South London Gallery ... 53Ub 113
South London Theatre ... *62Rb 135*
(off Norwood High St.)
South Mall *N9* ... *20Wb 33*
(off Plevna Rd.)
RM17: Grays ... *51Ce 121*
(off Grays Shop. Cen.)
SW18 ... 58Db 111
TW18: Staines ... *63H 127*
(in The Elmsleigh Cen.)
South Mead KT19: Ewe ... 80Va 154
NW9 ... 25Va 48
RH1: Redh ... 3P 207
Southmead Cres.
EN8: Chesh ... 2Ac 20
Southmead Gdns.
TW11: Tedd ... 65Ja 130
South Mdw. La. SL4: Eton ... 1G 102
Southmead Rd. SW19 ... 60Ab 110
Southmere Dr. SE2 ... 47Zc 95
SOUTH MERSTHAM ... 2C 208
SOUTH MIMMS ... 4Wa 16
SOUTH MIMMS SERVICE AREA ... 6Xa 16
Sth. Molton La.
W1 ... 3K 221 (44Kb 90)
Sth. Molton Rd. E16 ... 44Jc 93
Sth. Molton St. W1 ... 3K 221 (44Kb 90)
Southmont Rd. KT10: Hin W ... 75Ga 152
Southmoor Way E9 ... 37Bc 72
South Mt. *N20* ... *19Eb 31*
(off High Rd.)
SOUTH NORWOOD ... 70Vb 135
South Norwood Country Pk. ... 70Yb 136
South Norwood Country Pk. Vis. Cen.
... 70Xb 135
Sth. Norwood Hill SE25 ... 67Ub 135
South Norwood Leisure Cen. ... 71Xb 157
SOUTH NUTFIELD ... 8F 208
South Oak Rd. SW16 ... 63Pb 134
SOUTH OCKENDON ... 44Wd 98
Southold Ri. SE9 ... 62Pc 138
Southolm St. SW11 ... 53Kb 112
Sth. Ordnance Rd.
EN3: Enf L ... 10Cc 20
Southover BR1: Brom ... 64Jc 137
N12 ... 20Cb 31
SOUTH OXHEY ... 21Y 45
South Pde. HA8: Edg ... 26Qa 47
RH1: Mers ... 100Lb 196
SM6: Wall ... 79Lb 156
SW3 ... 7C 226 (50Fb 89)
W4 ... 49Ta 87
SOUTH PARK
RH1 ... 9N 209
RH2 ... 9J 207
South Pk. SL9: Ger X ... 29B 42
TN13: S'oaks ... 97Kd 203
South Pk. Av. WD3: Chor ... 15H 25
South Pk. Ct. BR3: Beck ... 66Cc 136
SL9: Ger X ... *29B 42*
(off South Pk.)
South Pk. Cres. IG1: Ilf ... 34Tc 74
SE6 ... 60Gc 115
SL9: Ger X ... 28A 42
South Pk. Dr. IG3: Ilf ... 33Uc 74
IG11: Bark ... 36Uc 74
SL9: Ger X ... 28A 42
South Pk. Gro. KT3: N Mald ... 70Sa 131
South Pk. Hill Rd.
CR2: S Croy ... 78Tb 157
South Pk. La. RH1: Blet ... 8N 209
South Pk. M. SW6 ... 55Db 111
South Pk. Rd. IG1: Ilf ... 34Tc 74
SW19 ... 65Cb 133
South Pk. Ter. IG1: Ilf ... 34Uc 74
South Pk. Vw. SL9: Ger X ... 28B 42
South Pk. Vs. IG3: Ilf ... 35Uc 74
South Pk. Way HA4: Ruis ... 37Y 65
South Path SL4: Wind ... 3G 102
South Pl. EC2 ... 7G 219 (43Tb 91)
EN3: Pond E ... 15Yb 34
South Pl. EN9: Walt A ... 5Ec 20
KT5: Surb ... 73Pa 153
South Pl. M. EC2 ... 1G 225 (43Tb 91)
Southport Rd. SE18 ... 49Tc 94
Sth. Quay Plaza E14 ... 47Dc 92
Sth. Quay Sq. E14 ... 47Dc 92
South Ridge KT13: Weyb ... 82R 170
Southridge Pl. SW20 ... 66Za 132
South Riding AL2: Brick W ... 2Ba 13
South Ri. SM5: Cars ... 81Gb 175
W2 ... 4E 220
South Ri. Way SE18 ... 50Tc 94
South Rd. DA8: Erith ... 52Hd 118
GU21: Wok ... 7N 167
GU24: Bisl ... 8D 166
HA1: Harr ... 32Ja 66
HA8: Edg ... 25Ra 47
KT13: Weyb ... 78S 150
(Birchwood Ct.)
KT13: Weyb ... 81R 170
(West Rd.)
N9 ... 18Wb 33
RH2: Reig ... 7K 207
RM6: Chad H ... 29Yc 55
(Dunmow Cl.)
RM6: Chad H ... 30Ad 55
(Mill La.)
RM15: S Ock ... 43Yd 98
(not continuous)
SE23 ... 61Zb 136
SW19 ... 65Eb 133
TW2: Twick ... 62Fa 130
TW5: Hest ... 51Y 107
TW12: Hamp ... 65Aa 129
TW13: Hanw ... 64Z 129
TW20: Eng G ... 5N 125
UB1: S'hall ... 47Ba 85
UB7: W Dray ... 48Q 84
W5 ... 49Ma 87
WD3: Chor ... 15E 24
South Row SE3 ... 54Hc 115
SL3: Ful ... 35A 62
SOUTH RUISLIP ... 35Y 65
Southsea Av. WD18: Wat ... 14W 26
Southsea Ho. *RM3: Rom* ... *22Md 57*
(off Darlington Gdns.)
Southsea Rd. KT1: King T ... 70Na 131
South Sea St. SE16 ... 48Bc 92
South Side EN9: Walt A ... 2Kc 21
KT16: Chert ... 69J 127
N15 ... 28Vb 51
SL9: Chal P ... 27A 42
W6 ... 48Va 88
Southside N7 ... 35Mb 70
Southside Comn. SW19 ... 65Ya 132
Southside Halls SW7 ... 3C 226
Southside House ... 65Ya 132
Southside Ind. Est. *SW8* ... *53Lb 112*
(off Havelock Ter.)
Southside Shop. Cen. SW18 ... 58Db 111
Southspring DA15: Sidc ... 59Tc 116
South Sq. NW11 ... 30Db 49
WC1 ... 1K 223 (43Qb 90)
South Stand N5 ... 35Rb 71
Sth. Station App. RH1: S Nut ... 8E 208
SOUTH STIFFORD ... 51Zd 121
SOUTH STREET ... 91Qc 200
South St. BR1: Brom ... 68Jc 137
CM14: B'wood ... 19Yd 40
DA12: Grav'nd ... 9D 122
EN3: Pond E ... 15Yb 34
KT18: Eps ... 85Ta 173
RM1: Rom ... 29Gd 56
RM13: Rain ... 40Ed 76
TW7: Isle ... 55Ja 108
TW18: Staines ... 64H 127
W1 ... 6J 221 (46Jb 90)
Sth. Tenter St. E1 ... 4K 225 (45Vb 91)
South Ter. DA4: Farni ... 73Pd 163
KT6: Surb ... 72Na 153
SL4: Wind ... 3J 103
SW7 ... 5D 226 (49Gb 89)
SOUTH TOTTENHAM ... 29Vb 51
South Vale HA1: Harr ... 35Ga 66
SE19 ... 65Ub 135
Southvale Rd. SE3 ... 54Gc 115
South Vw. BR1: Brom ... 68Lc 137
KT19: Eps ... 82Qa 173
RM16: Ors ... 3D 100
SL4: Eton, Eton W ... 10F 80
SW19 ... 65Za 132
Southview Av. NW10 ... 36Va 68
RM18: Tilb ... 3C 122
South Vw. Cl. DA5: Bexl ... 58Bd 117
Southview Cl. BR8: Swan ... 70Jd 140
SW17 ... 64Jb 134
South Vw. Ct. GU22: Wok ... 90A 168
SE19 ... 66Sb 135
Southview Cres. IG2: Ilf ... 30Rc 54
South Vw. Dr. E18 ... 27Kc 53
RM14: Upm ... 34Qd 77
Southview Gdns. SM6: Wall ... 80Lb 156
South Vw. Hgts. RM20: Grays ... 51Yd 120
Southview Pde. RM13: Rain ... 41Fd 96
South Vw. Rd. DA2: Wilm ... 62Md 141
HA5: Pinn ... 23X 45
IG10: Lough ... 16Pc 36
KT21: Asht ... 91Ma 193
N8 ... 27Mb 50
RM20: Grays ... 51Yd 120
Southview Rd. BR1: Brom ... 63Fc 137
CR3: Wold ... 96Dc 198
CR6: W'ham ... 91Wb 197
Southviews CR2: Sels ... 82Zb 178
South Vw. Vs. HP4: Berk ... 2A 2
South Vs. NW1 ... 37Mb 70
Southville SW8 ... 53Mb 112
Southville Cl. KT19: Ewe ... 81Ta 173
TW14: Bedf, Felt ... 60U 106
(not continuous)
Southville Cres. TW14: Felt ... 60U 106
Southville Rd. KT7: T Ditt ... 73Ja 152
TW14: Felt ... 60U 106
South Wlk. BR4: W W'ck ... 76Gc 159
RH2: Reig ... 6K 207
UB3: Hayes ... 43T 84
SOUTHWARK ... 7C 224 (46Rb 91)
Southwark Bri. SE1 ... 5E 224 (45Sb 91)
Southwark Bri. Bus. Cen. *SE1* ... *7E 224*
(off Southwark Bri. Rd.)
Southwark Bri. Rd. SE1 ... 3C 230 (48Rb 91)
Southwark Cathedral ... 6F 225 (46Tb 91)
Southwark Ho. *WD6: Bore* ... *12Qa 29*
(off Stratfield Rd.)
Southwark Pk. Est. SE16 ... 49Xb 91
Southwark Pk. Rd. SE16 ... 5K 231 (49Vb 91)
Southwark Pk. Sports Complex ... 49Yb 92
Southwark Pl. BR1: Brom ... 69Pc 138
Southwark Playhouse ... 7H 225
Southwark St. SE1 ... 6B 224 (46Rb 91)
Southwater Cl. BR3: Beck ... 66Dc 136
E14 ... 44Bc 92
South Way AL9: Hat ... 3D 8
AL10: Hat ... 4B 8
CR0: C'don ... 76Ac 158
EN9: Walt A ... 8Ec 20
HA2: Harr ... 28Ca 45
HA9: Wemb ... 36Qa 67
N9 ... 19Yb 34
N11 ... 23Lb 50
RM19: Purf ... 48Ud 98
WD5: Ab L ... 5T 12
Southway BR2: Hayes ... 73Jc 159
N20 ... 19Cb 31
NW11 ... 30Db 49
SM5: Cars ... 82Fb 175
SM6: Wall ... 77Lb 156
SW20 ... 71Ya 154
Southway Cl. W12 ... 47Xa 88
SOUTH WEALD ... 19Ud 40
Sth. Weald Dr. EN9: Walt A ... 5Fc 21
Sth. Weald Rd. CM14: B'wood ... 20Wd 40
Southwell Av. UB5: N'olt ... 37Ca 65
Southwell Cl. RM16: Chaf H ... 50Yd 98
Southwell Gdns. SW7 ... 5A 226 (49Eb 89)
Southwell Gro. Rd. E11 ... 33Gc 73
Southwell Ho. *SE16* ... *49Xb 91*
(off Anchor St.)
Southwell Rd. CR0: C'don ... 72Qb 156
HA3: Kenton ... 30Ma 47
SE5 ... 55Sb 113
Sth. Western Rd. TW1: Twick ... 58Ja 108
South W. India Dock Entrance
E14 ... 47Ec 92
South W. Middlesex Crematorium
TW13: Felt ... 60Aa 107
Southwest Rd. E11 ... 32Fc 73
Sth. Wharf Rd. W2 ... 2B 220 (44Fb 89)
Southwick M. W2 ... 2C 220 (44Fb 89)
Southwick Pl. W2 ... 3D 220 (44Gb 89)
Southwick St. W2 ... 2D 220 (44Gb 89)
Southwick Yd. W2 ... 3D 220
SOUTH WIMBLEDON ... 65Db 133
Southwold Dr. IG11: Bark ... 36Wc 75
Southwold Mans. *W9* ... *41Cb 89*
(off Widley Rd.)
Southwold Rd. DA5: Bexl ... 58Dd 118
E5 ... 33Xb 71
WD24: Wat ... 9Y 13
Southwold Spur SL3: L'ly ... 47E 82
Southwood Av. CR5: Coul ... 87Lb 176
GU21: Knap ... 10H 167
KT2: King T ... 67Sa 131
KT16: Ott ... 80E 148
N6 ... 31Kb 70
Southwood Cl. BR1: Brom ... 70Pc 138
KT4: Wor Pk ... 74Za 154
Southwood Ct. EC1 ... 3B 218
KT13: Weyb ... 78R 150
NW11 ... 29Db 49
Southwood Dr. KT5: Surb ... 73Sa 153
SOUTH WOODFORD ... 26Jc 53
South Woodford to Barking Relief Rd.
E11 ... 29Mc 53
E12 ... 32Nc 74
IG1: Ilf ... 29Mc 53
IG4: Ilf ... 29Mc 53
Southwood Gdns. IG2: Ilf ... 28Rc 54
KT10: Hin W ... 76Ja 152
Southwood Hall N6 ... 30Kb 50
Southwood Hgts. N6 ... 31Kb 70
Southwood Ho. *W11* ... *45Ab 88*
(off Avondale Pk. Rd.)
Southwood La. N6 ... 31Jb 70
Southwood Lawn Rd. N6 ... 31Jb 70
Southwood Mans. *N6* ... *30Jb 50*
(off Southwood La.)
Southwood Pk. N6 ... 31Jb 70
Southwood Rd. SE9 ... 61Rc 138
SE28 ... 46Xc 95
Southwood Smith Ho. *E2* ... *41Xb 91*
(off Florida St.)
Southwood Smith St. N1 ... 39Rb 71
Sth. Worple Av. SW14 ... 55Ua 110
Sth. Worple Way SW14 ... 55Ta 109
Southwyck Ho. SW9 ... 56Rb 113
Soval Ct. HA6: Nwood ... 24T 44
Sovereign Beeches SL2: Farn C ... 7F 60
Sovereign Bus. Cen.
EN3: Brim ... 13Bc 34
Sovereign Cl. CR8: Purl ... 82Pb 176
E1 ... 45Xb 91
HA4: Ruis ... 32U 64
W5 ... 43La 86
Sovereign Ct. *CR2: S Croy* ... *78Sb 157*
(off Warham Rd.)
DA4: Sut H ... *67Rd 141*
(off Ship La.)
HA6: Nwood ... 25W 44
KT8: W Mole ... 70Ba 129
SL5: S'dale ... 3F 146
TW3: Houn ... 55Ca 107
W8 ... *48Db 89*
(off Wright's La.)
WD18: Wat ... 14W 26
Sovereign Cres. SE16 ... 45Ac 92
Sovereign Gro. HA0: Wemb ... 34Ma 67
Sovereign Hgts. SL3: Dat ... 51C 104
Sovereign Ho. *E1* ... *42Xb 91*
(off Cambridge Heath Rd.)
SE18 ... *48Pc 94*
(off Leda Rd.)
TW15: Ashf ... 63N 127
Sovereign M. E2 ... 1K 219 (40Vb 71)
EN4: Cockf ... 13Hb 31
Sovereign Pk. AL4: St A ... 3H 7
HP2: Hem H ... 1B 4
NW10 ... 42Ra 87
Sovereign Pk. Trad. Est. NW10 ... 42Ra 87
Sovereign Pl. HA1: Harr ... 29Ha 46
Sovereign Rd. IG11: Bark ... 41Yc 95
Sowerby Cl. SE9 ... 57Pc 116
Sowrey Av. RM13: Rain ... 37Hd 76
Soyer Ct. GU21: Wok ... 10J 167
Spa at Beckenham, The ... 67Bc 136
Space Arts Centre, The ... *49Cc 92*
(off Westferry Rd.)
Space Bus. Pk. NW10 ... 41Ra 87

Space Waye TW14: Felt .57W 106
Spackmans Way SL1: Slou .8G 80
Spa Cl. SE25 .67Ub 135
Spa Ct. SE16 .48Wb 91
SW16 .63Pb 134
Spa Dr. KT18: Eps .86Qa 173
Spafield St. EC1 .5K 217 (42Qb 90)
Spa Grn. Est. EC1 .3B 218 (41Rb 91)
Spa Hill SE19 .67Tb 135
Spalding Cl. HA8: Edg .24Ua 48
Spalding Ho. SE4 .56Ac 114
Spalding Rd. NW4 .31Ya 68
SW17 .64Kb 134
Spalt Cl. CM13: Hut .19De 41
Spanbrook IG7: Chig .20Rc 36
Spanby Rd. E3 .42Cc 92
Spaniards Cl. NW11 .32Fb 69
Spaniards End NW3 .32Eb 69
Spaniards Rd. NW3 .33Eb 69
Spanish Pl. W1 .2J 221 (44Jb 90)
Spanish Rd. SW18 .57Eb 111
Spanswick Lodge N15 .28Rb 51
Spareleaze Hill IG10: Lough .14Pc 36
Sparepenny La.
DA4: Eyns, Farni .75Md 163
Sparkbridge Rd. HA1: Harr .28Ga 46
Sparkes Cl. BR2: Brom .70Kc 137
Sparkes Cotts. SW1 .6H 227
Sparkford Gdns. N11 .22Jb 50
Sparkford Ho. *SW11* .*53Fb 111*
(off Battersea Church Rd.)
Sparks Cl. RM8: Dag .33Zc 75
TW12: Hamp .65Aa 129
W3 .44Ta 87
Spa Rd. SE16 .4K 231 (48Vb 91)
Sparrick's Row SE1 .1G 231 (47Tb 91)
Sparrow Cl. TW12: Hamp .65Aa 129
Sparrow Dr. BR5: Farnb .74Sc 160
Sparrow Farm Dr. TW14: Felt .59Y 107
Sparrow Farm Rd. KT17: Ewe .77Wa 154
Sparrow Grn. RM10: Dag .34Dd 76
Sparrow Ho. *E1* .*42Yb 92*
(off Cephas Av.)
SPARROW ROW .9F 146
Sparrow Row GU24: Chob .9F 146
Sparrow's Farm Leisure Cen. .59Sc 116
Sparrows Herne WD23: Bush .17Da 27
Sparrows La. SE9 .59Sc 116
Sparrows Mead RH1: Redh .3A 208
Sparrows Way WD23: Bush .17Ea 28
Sparrow Wlk. WD25: Wat .7W 12
Sparsholt Cl. *IG11: Bark* .*39Uc 74*
(off St John's Rd.)
Sparsholt Rd. IG11: Bark .39Uc 74
N19 .32Pb 70
Spartan Cl. SM6: Wall .80Nb 156
Sparta St. SE10 .53Ec 114
Sparvell Rd. GU21: Knap .1F 186
Spa SPC .1H 81
Speakers' Corner .4G 221 (45Hb 89)
Speakers Ct. CR0: C'don .74Tb 157
Speakman Ho. *SE4* .*55Ac 114*
(off Arica Rd.)
Spearman Ho. *E14* .*44Cc 92*
(off Upper Nth. St.)
Spearman St. SE18 .51Qc 116
Spear M. SW5 .49Cb 89
Spearpoint Gdns. IG2: Ilf .29Vc 55
Spears Rd. N19 .32Nb 70
Speart La. TW5: Hest .52Aa 107
Spectacle Works E13 .41Lc 93
Spectrum Pl. *SE17* .*51Tb 113*
(off Lytham St.)
Spectrum Twr. *IG1: Ilf* .*33Sc 74*
(off Hainault St.)
Spedan Cl. NW3 .34Eb 69
Speechly M. E8 .36Vb 71
Speedbird Way UB7: Harm .52K 105
SPEEDGATE .75Vd 164
Speedgate Hill DA3: Fawk .75Wd 164
Speed Highwalk EC2 .7E 218
Speed Ho. EC2 .7E 218
Speedway Ind. Est. UB3: Hayes .47T 84
Speedwell Cl. HP1: Hem H .3G 2
Speedwell Ct. RM17: Grays .2A 122
Speedwell Ho. N12 .21Db 49
Speedwell St. SE8 .52Cc 114
Speedy Pl. WC1 .4F 217
Speer Rd. KT7: T Ditt .72Ha 152
Speirs Cl. KT3: N Mald .72Va 154
Spekehill SE9 .62Pc 138
Speke Rd. CR7: Thor H .68Tb 135
Speke's Monument .6A 220 (46Fb 89)
Speldhurst Cl. BR2: Brom .71Hc 159
Speldhurst Rd. E9 .38Zb 72
W4 .48Ta 87
Spellbrook Wlk. N1 .39Sb 71
Spelman Ho. *E1* .*43Wb 91*
(off Spelman St.)
Spelman St. E1 .43Wb 91
(not continuous)
Spelthorne Gro. TW16: Sun .66V 128
Spelthorne La. TW15: Ashf .67S 128
Spelthorne Leisure Cen. .64J 127
Spelthorne Mus. .64H 127
Spence Av. KT14: Byfl .86N 169
Spence Cl. SE16 .47Bc 92
Spencer Av. N13 .23Pb 50
UB4: Hayes .43W 84
Spencer Cl. BR6: Orp .75Uc 160
CM16: Epp .1Xc 23
GU21: Wok .85E 168
IG8: Wfd G .22Lc 53
KT18: Eps D .91Ua 194
N3 .26Cb 49
NW10 .41Pa 87
UB8: Cowl .41L 83
Spencer Ct. BR6: Farnb .78Sc 160
DA12: Grav'nd .8F 122
KT22: Lea .95La 192
NW8 .*40Eb 69*
(off Marlborough Pl.)
SW20 .67Xa 132
Spencer Courtyard *N3* .*26Bb 49*
(off Regents Pk. Rd.)
Spencer Dr. N2 .30Eb 49
Spencer Gdns. SE9 .57Pc 116
SW14 .57Sa 109
TW20: Eng G .4P 125
Spencer Ga. AL1: St A .1C 6
Spencer Hill SW19 .65Ab 132
Spencer Hill Rd. SW19 .66Ab 132
Spencer House .7B 222
Spencer Ho. NW4 .29Xa 48
Spencer Mans. *W14* .*51Ab 110*
(off Queen's Club Gdns.)
Spencer M. *SW9* .*53Pb 112*
(off Lansdowne Way)
W6 .51Ab 110
SPENCER PARK .57Fb 111
Spencer Pk. KT8: E Mos .71Ea 152
SW18 .57Fb 111
Spencer Pl. CR0: C'don .73Tb 157
N1 .38Rb 71
Spencer Ri. NW5 .35Kb 70
Spencer Rd. BR1: Brom .66Hc 137
CR2: S Croy .78Ub 157
CR3: Cat'm .93Tb 197
CR4: Mitc .69Jb 134
(Commonside E.)
CR4: Mitc .73Jb 156
(Wood St.)
E6 .39Mc 73
E17 .26Ec 52
HA0: Wemb .33La 66
HA3: W'stone .26Ga 46
IG3: Ilf .32Vc 75
KT8: E Mos .70Ea 130
KT11: Cobh .87X 171
N8 .29Pb 50
(not continuous)
N11 .21Kb 50
N17 .25Wb 51
RM13: Rain .41Fd 96
SL3: L'ly .48B 82
SW18 .56Fb 111
SW20 .67Xa 132
TW2: Twick .62Ga 130
TW7: Isle .53Ea 108
W3 .46Sa 87
W4 .52Sa 109
Spencers Cotts.
TN15: Bor G .92Ce 205
Spencer St. AL3: St A .2B 6
DA11: Grav'nd .9C 122
EC1 .4B 218 (41Rb 91)
UB2: S'hall .47Z 85
Spencer Wlk. NW3 .35Fb 69
RM18: Tilb .4D 122
SW15 .56Za 110
WD3: Rick .15L 25
Spencer Way E1 .44Xb 91
RH1: Redh .10B 208
Spencer Yd. *SE3* .*54Hc 115*
(off Tranquil Va.)
Spenlow Ho. *SE16* .*48Wb 91*
(off Jamaica Rd.)
Spenser Av. KT13: Weyb .81Q 170
Spenser Cres. RM14: Upm .31Sd 78
Spenser Gro. N16 .36Ub 71
Spenser M. SE21 .61Tb 135
Spenser Rd. SE24 .57Rb 113
Spenser St. SW1 .3C 228 (48Lb 90)
Spens Ho. WC1 .6H 217
Spensley Wlk. N16 .34Tb 71
Speranza St. SE18 .50Vc 95
Sperling Rd. N17 .26Ub 51
Spert St. E14 .45Ac 92
Speyhawk Pl. EN6: Pot B .1Eb 17
Speyside N14 .16Lb 32
Spey St. E14 .43Ec 92
Spey Way RM1: Rom .24Gd 56
Spezia Rd. NW10 .40Wa 68
Sphere, The *E16* .*44Hc 93*
(off Hallsville Rd.)
Sphere Ind. Est., The AL1: St A .2E 6
Spice Ct. E1 .45Wb 91
Spice Quay Hgts. SE1 .7K 225 (46Vb 91)
Spicer Cl. KT12: Walt T .72Y 151
SW9 .54Rb 113
Spicer Ct. EN1: Enf .13Ub 33
Spicers Fld. KT22: Oxs .85Fa 172
Spicer St. AL3: St A .2A 6
Spice's Yd. CR0: C'don .77Sb 157
Spielman Rd. DA1: Dart .56Pd 119
Spigurnell Rd. N17 .25Tb 51
Spikes Bri. Rd. UB1: S'hall .44Aa 85
Spilsby Rd. RM3: Rom .24Md 57
Spindle Cl. SE18 .48Nc 94
Spindles RM18: Tilb .2C 122
Spindlewood Gdns. CR0: C'don .77Ub 157
Spindlewoods KT20: Tad .94Xa 194
Spindrift Av. E14 .49Cc 92
Spinel Cl. SE18 .50Vc 95
Spingate Cl. RM12: Horn .36Ld 77
Spinnaker Cl. IG11: Bark .41Xc 95
KT11: Cobh .86Z 171
Spinnaker Ct. *KT1: Hamp W* .*67Ma 131*
(off Becketts Pl.)
Spinnaker Ho. *E14* .*47Cc 92*
(off Byng St.)
Spinnells Rd. HA2: Harr .32Ba 65
Spinners Wlk. SL4: Wind .3G 102
Spinney SL1: Slou .6F 80
Spinney, The BR8: Swan .68Gd 140
CM13: Hut .16Ee 41
CR8: Purl .83Rb 177
DA14: Sidc .64Ad 139
EN5: New Bar .12Db 31
EN6: Pot B .3Fb 17
EN7: Chesh .2Xb 19
GU23: Send .99L 189
HA0: Wemb .34Ja 66
HA7: Stan .21Na 47
IG10: Lough .14Rc 36
KT18: Head .98Sa 193
KT18: Tatt C .91Xa 194
KT22: Oxs .84Ea 172
KT23: Bookh .96Da 191
N21 .17Qb 32
RM16: Ors .2C 100
SL5: S'dale .1C 146
SL9: Ger X .2P 61
SM3: Cheam .77Ya 154
SW13 .52Xa 110
SW16 .62Lb 134
TW16: Sun .67W 128
WD17: Wat .11W 26
WD25: A'ham .10Fa 14
Spinney Cl. BR3: Beck .70Dc 136
KT3: N Mald .71Ua 154
KT4: Wor Pk .75Va 154
KT11: Cobh .83Ca 171
RM13: Rain .40Gd 76
SL5: Asc .8A 124
UB7: Yiew .45N 83
Spinneycroft KT22: Oxs .87Fa 172
Spinney Dr. TW14: Bedf .59S 106
Spinney Gdns. KT10: Esh .76Ca 151
RM9: Dag .36Ad 75
SE19 .64Vb 135
Spinney Hill KT15: Add .78G 148
Spinney Oak BR1: Brom .68Nc 138
KT16: Ott .79F 148
Spinney Row AL2: Lon C .8F 6
Spinneys, The BR1: Brom .68Pc 138
Spinneys Dr. AL3: St A .4P 5
Spinney Way TN14: Cud .83Tc 180
Spire Cl. DA12: Grav'nd .10D 122
Spire Ct. *BR3: Beck* .*68Dc 136*
(off Crescent Rd.)
Spire Ho. W2 .4A 220
Spire Pl. CR6: W'ham .90Ac 178
Spires, The CM14: B'wood .19Zd 41
DA1: Dart .61Md 141
HP2: Hem H .3M 3
Spires Shop. Cen., The
EN5: Barn .13Ab 30
Spirit Quay E1 .46Wb 91
SPITAL .6F 102
SPITALFIELDS .7K 219 (43Vb 91)
Spitalfields City Farm .42Wb 91
Spital La. CM14: B'wood .20Vd 40
Spital Sq. E1 .7J 219 (43Ub 91)
Spital St. DA1: Dart .58Md 119
E1 .43Wb 91
Spital Yd. E1 .7J 219 (43Ub 91)
Spitfire Bus. Pk. CR0: Wadd .79Qb 156
Spitfire Cl. SL3: L'ly .49C 82
Spitfire Est., The TW5: Cran .50Y 85
Spitfire Rd. SM6: Wall .80Nb 156
TW6: H'row A .58S 106
Spitfire Way TW5: Cran .50Y 85
Splendour Wlk. *SE16* .*50Yb 92*
(off Verney Rd.)
Spode Ho. SE11 .4K 229
Spode Wlk. NW6 .36Db 69
Spondon Rd. N15 .28Wb 51
Spoonbill Way UB4: Yead .43Z 85
Spooner Ho. TW5: Hest .51Ca 107
Spooners Dr. AL2: Park .9A 6
Spooners M. W3 .46Ta 87
Spooner Wlk. SM6: Wall .78Nb 156
Sporle Rd. Ct. SW11 .55Fb 111
Sportsbank St. SE6 .59Ec 114
Sportsman Pl. E2 .39Wb 71
Sportz Academy Health Club
Potters Bar .3Cb 17
Spottiswood Ct. *CR0: C'don* .*72Sb 157*
(off Harry Cl.)
Spottons Gro. N17 .25Sb 51
Spout Hill CR0: Addtn .78Cc 158
Spout La. TW19: Stanw M .57J 105
Spout La. Nth. TW19: Stanw M .56K 105
Spratt Hall Rd. E11 .30Jc 53
Spratts All. KT16: Ott .79G 148
Spratts La. KT16: Ott .79G 148
Spray La. TW2: Whitt .58Ga 108
Spray St. SE18 .49Rc 94
Spread Eagle Wlk.
KT19: Eps .85Ta 173
Spreighton Rd. KT8: W Mole .70Da 129
Spriggs Ct. *CM16: Epp* .*1Wc 23*
(off Palmers Hill)
Spriggs Ho. *N1* .*38Rb 71*
(off Canonbury Rd.)
Spriggs Oak *CM16: Epp* .*1Wc 23*
(off Palmers Hill)
Sprimont Pl. SW3 .7F 227 (50Hb 89)
Springall St. SE15 .52Xb 113
Springalls Wharf *SE16* .*47Wb 91*
(off Bermondsey Wall W.)
Springate Fld. SL3: L'ly .47A 82
Spring Av. TW20: Egh .65A 126
Springbank N21 .16Pb 32
Springbank Av. RM12: Horn .36Ld 77
Springbank Rd. SE13 .58Fc 115
Springbank Wlk. NW1 .38Mb 70
Springbottom La.
RH1: Blet .99Qb 196
Springbourne Ct. BR3: Beck .67Ec 136
Spring Bri. M. W5 .45Ma 87
Spring Bri. Rd. W5 .45Ma 87
Spring Cl. EN5: Barn .15Za 30
HP5: Lat .8A 10
RM8: Dag .32Zc 75
UB9: Hare .25M 43
WD6: Bore .11Qa 29
Springclose La.
SM3: Cheam .79Ab 154
Springcopse Rd. RH2: Reig .8L 207
Spring Cnr. TW13: Felt .62W 128
Spring Cotts. KT6: Surb .71Ma 153
Spring Ct. KT17: Ewe .81Va 174
NW6 .37Bb 69
W7 .45Fa 86
Spring Ct. Rd. EN2: Enf .10Qb 18
Springcroft DA3: Hartl .72Ce 165
Springcroft Av. N2 .28Hb 49
Spring Crofts WD23: Bush .15Ca 27
Spring Cross DA3: New A .76Ce 165
(not continuous)
Springdale M. N16 .35Tb 71
Springdale Rd. N16 .35Tb 71
Spring Dr. HA5: Eastc .30W 44
Springett Ho. *SW2* .*57Qb 112*
(off St Matthews Rd.)
Springfarm Cl. RM13: Rain .41Md 97
Springfield CM16: Epp .4Vc 23
E5 .32Xb 71
GU18: Light .3B 166
RH8: Oxt .2H 211
SE25 .69Wb 135
SL1: Slou .8M 81
WD23: B Hea .18Fa 28
Springfield Av. BR8: Swan .70Hd 140
CM13: Hut .17Fe 41
N10 .27Lb 50
SW20 .69Bb 133
TW12: Hamp .65Da 129
Springfield Cl. EN6: Pot B .3Gb 17
GU21: Knap .10J 167
HA7: Stan .20Ja 28
N12 .22Db 49
SL4: Wind .4F 102
WD3: Crox G .15R 26
Springfield Ct. IG1: Ilf .36Rc 74
KT1: King T .*69Na 131*
(off Springfield Rd.)
NW3 .*38Gb 69*
(off Eton Av.)
RM14: Upm .34Sd 78
Springfield Ct. SM6: Wall .78Kb 156
WD3: Rick .18K 25
Springfield Dr. IG2: Ilf .29Sc 54
KT22: Lea .91Ga 192
Springfield Gdns. BR1: Brom .70Pc 138
BR4: W W'ck .75Dc 158
E5 .32Xb 71
HA4: Ruis .32X 65
IG8: Wfd G .24Lc 53
NW9 .29Ta 47
RM14: Upm .34Rd 77
Springfield Gro. SE7 .51Lc 115
TW16: Sun .67V 128
Springfield La. KT13: Weyb .77R 150
NW6 .39Db 69
Springfield Mdws. KT13: Weyb .77R 150
Springfield Mt. NW9 .29Ua 48
Springfield Pde. M. N13 .21Qb 50
Springfield Pl. KT3: N Mald .70Sa 131
SL9: Ger X .29A 42
Springfield Ri. SE26 .62Xb 135
Springfield Rd. AL1: St A .3E 6
AL4: S'ford .2M 7
BR1: Brom .70Pc 138
CR7: Thor H .67Sb 135
DA7: Bex .56Dd 118
DA16: Well .55Xc 117
E4 .18Gc 35
E6 .38Pc 74
E15 .41Gc 93
E17 .30Bc 52
EN8: Chesh .4Ac 20
HA1: Harr .30Ga 46
HP2: Hem H .1P 3
KT1: King T .69Na 131
KT17: Ewe .82Ya 174
KT22: Lea .91Ha 192
N11 .22Kb 50
N15 .28Wb 51
NW8 .39Eb 69
RM16: Grays .47Fe 99
SE26 .64Xb 135
SL3: L'ly .52D 104
SL4: Wind .4F 102
SM6: Wall .78Kb 156
SW19 .64Bb 133
TW2: Whitt .60Ca 107
TW11: Tedd .64Ja 130
TW15: Ashf .64P 127
UB4: Yead .46Y 85
W7 .46Ga 86
WD25: Wat .5X 13
Springfields *EN5: New Bar* .*15Db 31*
(off Somerset Rd.)
EN9: Walt A .6Gc 21
Springfields Cl. KT16: Chert .74K 149
Springfield Wlk. *BR6: Orp* .*74Tc 160*
(off Place Farm Av.)
NW6 .39Db 69
Spring Gdns. BR6: Chels .79Xc 161
IG8: Wfd G .24Lc 53
KT8: W Mole .71Da 151
N5 .36Sb 71
RM7: Rom .29Ed 56
RM12: Horn .35Kd 77
SM6: Wall .78Lb 156
SW1 .6E 222 (46Mb 90)
(not continuous)
TN16: Big H .90Lc 179
WD25: Wat .7Y 13
Spring Gdns. Bus. Pk. RM7: Rom .30Ed 56
Spring Glen AL10: Hat .1B 8
SPRING GROVE .53Ga 108
Spring Gro. CR4: Mitc .67Jb 134
DA12: Grav'nd .10D 122
IG10: Lough .16Mc 35
KT22: Fet .95Da 191
SE19 .66Vb 135
TW12: Hamp .67Da 129
W4 .50Qa 87
W7 .45Ga 86
Spring Gro. Cres. TW3: Houn .53Ea 108
Spring Gro. Rd. TW3: Houn, Isle .53Da 107
TW7: Isle .53Da 107
TW10: Rich .57Pa 109
Springhead Ent. Pk. DA11: Nflt .60De 121
Springhead Parkway DA11: Nflt .60De 121
Spring Head Rd. TN15: Kems'g .89Pd 183
Springhead Rd. DA8: Erith .51Hd 118
DA11: Nflt .61Ee 143
SpringHealth Leisure Club
Brentwood .24Yd 58
Richmond .*56Ma 109*
(in Pools on the Park)
Spring Hill E5 .31Wb 71
SE26 .63Yb 136
Springhill Cl. SE5 .55Tb 113
Springholm Cl. TN16: Big H .90Lc 179
Spring Ho. WC1 .4K 217
Springhouse La. SS17: Corr .1P 101
Springhouse Rd. SS17: Corr .1P 101
Springhurst Cl. CR0: C'don .77Bc 158
Spring Lake HA7: Stan .21Ka 46
Spring La. E5 .31Xb 71
HP1: Hem H .1H 3
N10 .27Jb 50
RH8: Oxt .3H 211
SE25 .72Xb 157
SL1: Slou .6D 80
SL2: Farn R .8F 60
TN15: Igh .94Xd 204
Spring M. KT17: Ewe .81Va 174
TW9: Rich .*56Na 109*
(off Rosedale Rd.)
W1 .7G 215 (43Hb 89)
SPRING PARK .76Cc 158
Spring Pk. Av. CR0: C'don .75Zb 158
Spring Pk. Dr. N4 .32Sb 71
Springpark Dr. BR3: Beck .69Ec 136
Spring Pk. Rd. CR0: C'don .75Zb 158
Spring Pas. SW15 .55Za 110
Spring Path NW3 .36Fb 69
Spring Pl. IG11: Bark .40Sc 74
KT11: Cobh .85Aa 171
N3 .27Cb 49
NW5 .36Kb 70
Springpond Rd. RM9: Dag .36Ad 75
Springrice Rd. SE13 .58Fc 115
Spring Ri. TW20: Egh .65A 126
Spring Rd. TW13: Felt .62V 128
Springshaw Cl. TN13: Bes G .95Fd 202
Spring Shaw Rd. BR5: St P .67Wc 139
Spring St. KT17: Ewe .81Va 174
W2 .3B 220 (44Fb 89)
Spring Ter. TW9: Rich .57Na 109
Spring Tide Cl. SE15 .53Xb 113
Spring Vale DA7: Bex .56Dd 118
DA9: Ghithe .58Yd 120
Springvale Av. TW8: Bford .50Ma 87
Spring Vale Cl. BR8: Hext .67Hd 140
Springvale Cl. KT23: Bookh .97Da 191
Springvale Ct. DA11: Nflt .61Ee 143
Spring Vale Nth. DA1: Dart .59Md 119
Springvale Retail Pk. BR5: St P .69Yc 139
(not continuous)
Spring Vale Sth. DA1: Dart .59Md 119
Springvale Ter. W14 .48Za 88
Springvale Way BR5: St P .69Yc 139
Spring Villa Pk. HA8: Edg .24Qa 47
Spring Villa Rd. HA8: Edg .24Qa 47
Spring Wlk. E1 .43Wb 91
Springwater WC1 .7H 217
Springwater Cl. SE18 .53Qc 116
Spring Way HP2: Hem H .1B 4
Springway HA1: Harr .31Fa 66
Springwell Av. NW10 .39Va 68
WD3: Rick .19J 25
Springwell Cl. SW16 .63Pb 134
Springwell Ct. WD3: Rick .19J 25
Springwell La. UB9: Hare .20J 25
WD3: Rick .20J 25
Springwell Rd. SW16 .63Qb 134
TW4: Houn .54Z 107
TW5: Hest .54Z 107
Springwood Cl. E3 .40Cc 72
UB9: Hare .25M 43
Springwood Ct. *CR2: S Croy* .*77Ub 157*
(off Birdhurst Rd.)
Springwood Cres. HA8: Edg .19Ra 29
Springwood Pl. KT13: Weyb .80R 150
Spring Woods GU25: Vir W .10M 125
Springwood Way RM1: Rom .29Jd 56
Sprint Ind. Est. KT14: Byfl .83M 169
Sproggit Ind. Est. TW19: Stanw .58P 105
Sprowston M. E7 .37Jc 73
Sprowston Rd. E7 .36Jc 73
Spruce Cl. RH1: Redh .5P 207
Spruce Ct. SL1: Slou .8K 81
W5 .48Na 87
Sprucedale Cl. BR8: Swan .68Gd 140
Sprucedale Gdns. CR0: C'don .77Zb 158
SM6: Wall .81Nb 176
Spruce Hills Rd. E17 .26Ec 52
Spruce Ho. *SE16* .*47Zb 92*
(off Woodland Cres.)
Spruce Pk. BR2: Brom .70Hc 137
Spruce Rd. TN16: Big H .88Mc 179
Spruce Way AL2: Park .9P 5
Sprules Rd. SE4 .54Ac 114
Spur, The GU21: Knap .10F 166
KT12: Walt T .75Y 151
SL1: Slou .3B 80
Spur Cl. RM4: Abr .13Xc 37
WD5: Ab L .5T 12
Spur Dr. SL1: Slou .3J 81
Spurfield KT8: W Mole .69Da 129
Spurgate CM13: Hut .19Ce 41
Spurgeon Av. SE19 .67Tb 135
Spurgeon Cl. RM17: Grays .51Ee 121
Spurgeon Rd. SE19 .67Tb 135
Spurgeon St. SE1 .3F 231 (48Tb 91)
Spurling Rd. RM9: Dag .37Bd 75
SE22 .56Vb 113
Spurrell Av. DA5: Bexl .63Fd 140
Spur Rd. BR6: Orp .75Wc 161
HA8: Edg .21Na 47
N15 .28Tb 51
SE1 .1K 229 (47Qb 90)
SW1 .2B 228 (47Lb 90)
TW7: Isle .52Ka 108
TW14: Felt .56X 107
Spurstowe Rd. E8 .37Xb 71
Spurstowe Ter. E8 .36Wb 71
Spurway Pde. *IG2: Ilf* .*29Pc 54*
(off Woodford Av.)
Squadrons App. RM12: Horn .37Ld 77
Square, The BR8: Swan .69Fd 140
CM14: B'wood .19Yd 40
CR3: Cat'm .96Wb 197
E10 .34Ec 72
GU18: Light .2A 166
GU23: Wis .88N 169
HP1: Hem H .2M 3
IG1: Ilf .31Qc 74
IG8: Wfd G .22Jc 53
IG10: Lough .13Rc 36
KT13: Weyb .77S 150
SM5: Cars .78Jb 156
TN13: Riv .94Gd 202
TN16: Tats .92Lc 199
TW9: Rich .57Ma 109
UB7: Lford .53K 105
UB11: Stock P .46T 84
W6 .50Ya 88
WD24: Wat .9X 13
Square of Fame .*35Qa 67*
(off Arena Sq.)
Square Rigger Row SW11 .55Eb 111
Squarey St. SW17 .62Eb 133
Squerryes .100Sc 200
Squerryes TN16: Westrm .100Sc 200
Squerryes, The CR3: Cat'm .93Ub 197
Squerryes Mede TN16: Westrm .99Sc 200
Squerryes Pk. Cotts.
TN16: Westrm .99Sc 200
Squire Gdns. NW8 .4B 214
Squires, The RM7: Rom .30Ed 56
Squire's Bri. Rd. TW17: Shep .70P 127
Squires Ct. KT16: Chert .74K 149
SW4 .53Nb 112
SW19 .63Cb 133
Squires Fld. BR8: Hext .67Jd 140
Squires La. N3 .26Db 49
Squires Mt. NW3 .34Fb 69
Squire's Rd. TW17: Shep .70Q 128
Squires Wlk. TW15: Ashf .66T 128
(not continuous)
Squires Way DA2: Wilm .63Fd 140
Squires Wood Dr. BR7: Chst .66Nc 138
Squirrel Chase HP1: Hem H .1G 2
Squirrel Cl. TW4: Houn .55Y 107
Squirrel Dr. SL4: Wink .10A 102
Squirrel Keep KT14: W Byf .84K 169
Squirrel La. SL4: Wink .10A 102
Squirrel M. W13 .45Ha 86
Squirrels, The HA5: Pinn .27Ba 45
SE13 .55Fc 115
WD23: Bush .16Fa 28

Squirrels Chase RM16: Ors 7C 100
Squirrels Cl. BR6: Orp 74Uc 160
BR8: Swan 69Hd 140
N12 .... 21Eb 49
UB10: Hil 38Q 64
Squirrels Ct. KT4: Wor Pk 75Va 154
(off The Avenue)
Squirrels Drey BR2: Brom 68Gc 137
(off Park Hill Rd.)
Squirrels Grn. KT4: Wor Pk 75Va 154
KT23: Bookh 95Ca 191
RH1: Redh 5P 207
SQUIRREL'S HEATH 27Md 57
Squirrels Heath Av. RM2: Rom 27Kd 57
Squirrels Heath La.
RM2: Horn, Rom 28Ld 57
RM11: Horn, Rom 28Ld 57
Squirrels Heath Rd.
RM3: Hrld W 27Nd 57
Squirrel's La. IG9: Buck H 20Mc 35
Squirrels Trad. Est., The
UB3: Hayes 48V 84
Squirrels Way KT18: Eps 86Ta 173
Squirrel Wood KT14: W Byf 84K 169
Squirries St. E2 .... 41Wb 91
SS Robin 45Cc 92
Stable Cl. KT2: King T 65Pa 131
KT18: Eps D 91Ua 194
UB5: N'olt 40Ca 65
Stable Ct. AL1: St A 1C 6
CR3: Cat'm 94Wb 197
EC1 .... 6C 218
SM6: Wall 76Jb 156
TN13: S'oaks 98Ld 203
Stable M. AL1: St A 1C 6
(off Hillside Rd.)
NW5 .... 37Kb 70
RH2: Reig 6J 207
SE6 .... 60Gc 115
TW1: Twick 60Ha 108
Stables, The IG9: Buck H 17Lc 35
KT11: Cobh 86Ba 171
WD25: A'ham 8Da 13
Stables End BR6: Farnb 76Sc 160
Stables Gallery & Arts Cen. 34Wa 68
Stables Lodge E8 .... 38Xb 71
(off Mare St.)
Stables Market, The NW1 .... 38Kb 70
Stables M. AL9: Brk P 10M 9
SE27 .... 64Sb 135
Stables Way SE11 .... 7K 229 (50Qb 90)
Stables Yd. SW18 .... 58Cb 111
Stable Wlk. N2 .... 25Fb 49
Stable Way W10 .... 44Ya 88
Stable Yd. SW1 .... 1B 228
SW15 .... 55Ya 110
TN15: Kems'g 89Qd 183
Stableyard, The SW9 .... 54Pb 112
Stableyard M. TW11: Tedd 65Ha 130
Stable Yd. Rd. SW1 .... 7C 222 (47Lb 90)
(not continuous)
Staburn Ct. HA8: Edg 26Sa 47
Stacey Av. N18 .... 21Yb 52
Stacey Cl. DA12: Grav'nd 4G 144
E10 .... 29Ec 53
Stacey Ct. RH1: Mers 1C 208
Stacey St. N7 .... 34Qb 70
WC2 .... 3E 222 (44Mb 90)
Stack Ho. RH8: Oxt 2J 211
SW1 .... 6J 227
Stackhouse St. SW3 .... 3F 227
Stacklands Cl. TN15: W King 79Ud 164
Stack La. DA3: Hartl 71Be 165
Stack Rd. DA4: Hort K 70Td 142
Stacy Path SE5 .... 52Ub 113
Staddleswood Pl. TN15: Plat 92De 205
Staddon Cl. BR3: Beck 70Ac 136
Stadium, The
AFC Hornchurch 33Qd 77
Cheshunt FC 4Yb 20
Stadium Bus. Cen. HA9: Wemb 34Ra 67
Stadium M. N5 .... 34Qb 70
Stadium Retail Pk. HA9: Wemb 34Qa 67
Stadium Rd. SE18 .... 52Nc 116
Stadium Rd. E. NW4 .... 31Xa 68
Stadium St. SW10 .... 52Eb 111
Stadium Way DA1: Cray 57Gd 118
HA9: Wemb 35Pa 67
Staffa Rd. E10 .... 32Ac 72
Staffhurst Wood Nature Reserve 9N 211
Staffhurst Wood Rd. TN8: Eden 9N 211
Stafford Av. RM11: Horn 27Md 57
SL2: Slou 2G 80
Stafford Cl. CR3: Cat'm 95Vb 197
DA9: Ghithe 57Vd 120
E17 .... 30Bc 52
(not continuous)
EN8: Chesh 1Xb 19
N14 .... 15Lb 32
NW6 .... 41Cb 89
RM16: Chaf H 49Yd 98
SL6: Tap 4A 80
SM3: Cheam 79Ab 154
SS17: Linf 8J 101
Stafford Ct. DA5: Bexl 59Bd 117
SW8 .... 52Nb 112
W7 .... 44Ha 86
(off Copley Cl.)
W8 .... 48Cb 89
Stafford Cripps Ho. E2 .... 41Yb 92
(off Globe Rd.)
SW6 .... 51Bb 111
(off Clem Attlee Ct.)
Stafford Cross Bus. Pk.
CR0: Wadd 78Pb 156
Stafford Gdns. CR0: Wadd 78Pb 156
Stafford Ho. SE1 .... 7K 231
Stafford Ind. Est. RM11: Horn 27Md 57
STAFFORDLAKE 10D 166
Stafford Lake GU21: Knap 10D 166
Stafford Mans. SW1 .... 3B 228
SW4 .... 56Nb 112
SW11 .... 52Hb 111
(off Albert Bri. Rd.)
W14 .... 48Za 88
(off Haarlem Rd.)
Stafford Pl. SW1 .... 3B 228 (48Lb 90)
TW10: Rich 59Pa 109
Stafford Ri. CR3: Cat'm 94Wb 197
Stafford Rd. CR0: Wadd 77Qb 156
CR3: Cat'm 95Vb 197
DA14: Sidc 63Uc 138
E3 .... 40Bc 72
E7 .... 38Lc 73
Stafford Rd. HA3: Hrw W 24Ea 46
HA4: Ruis 35V 64
KT3: N Mald 69Sa 131
NW6 .... 41Cb 89
SM6: Wall 79Lb 156
Staffordshire St. SE15 .... 53Wb 113
Stafford Sq. KT13: Weyb 77T 150
Stafford St. W1 .... 6B 222 (46Lb 90)
Stafford Ter. W8 .... 48Cb 89
Stafford Way TN13: S'oaks 99Ld 203
Staff St. EC1 .... 4G 219 (41Tb 91)
Stagbury Av. CR5: Chip 90Gb 175
Stagbury Cl. CR5: Chip 91Gb 195
Stagbury Ho. CR5: Chip 91Gb 195
Stag Cl. HA8: Edg 26Ra 47
Stag Community Arts Cen. 97Kd 203
Stag Ct. KT2: King T 67Qa 131
(off Coombe Rd.)
Staggart Grn. IG7: Chig, Ilf 22Vc 55
Stagg Hill EN4: Had W 7Fb 17
EN6: Pot B 7Fb 17
STAG LANE 61Va 132
Stag La. HA8: Edg 26Ra 47
IG9: Buck H 19Kc 35
NW9 .... 26Ra 47
SW15 .... 62Va 132
WD3: Chor 16E 24
Stag Leys KT21: Asht 92Na 193
Stag Leys Cl. SM7: Bans 87Gb 175
Stags Way TW7: Isle 51Ha 108
Stainash Cres. TW18: Staines 64K 127
Stainash Pde. TW18: Staines 64K 127
(off Kingston Rd.)
Stainbank Rd. CR4: Mitc 69Kb 134
Stainby Cl. UB7: W Dray 48N 83
Stainby Rd. N15 .... 28Vb 51
Stainer Ho. SE3 .... 56Lc 115
Stainer Rd. WD6: Bore 11Ma 29
Stainer St. SE1 .... 7G 225 (46Tb 91)
STAINES 63H 127
Staines Av. SM3: Cheam 75Za 154
Staines Boat Club 64G 126
Staines Bri. TW18: Staines 64G 126
Staines By-Pass TW15: Ashf 63K 127
TW18: Staines 63K 127
TW19: Staines 61E 126
Staines La. KT16: Chert 72H 149
Staines La. Cl. KT16: Chert 72H 149
Staines Rd. IG1: Ilf 36Sc 74
KT16: Chert 68H 127
TW2: Twick 62Ca 129
TW3: Houn 58X 107
TW4: Houn 58X 107
TW14: Bedf, Felt 60Q 106
TW18: Lale, Staines 67K 127
TW19: Wray 59A 104
Staines Rd. E. TW16: Sun 66W 128
Staines Rd. W. TW15: Ashf 65R 128
TW16: Sun 65R 128
Staines Town FC 66J 127
Staines Wlk. DA14: Sidc 65Yc 139
Stainford Cl. TW15: Ashf 64T 128
Stainforth Rd. E17 .... 28Cc 52
IG2: Ilf 31Tc 74
Staining La. EC2 .... 2E 224 (44Sb 91)
Stainmore Cl. BR7: Chst 67Tc 138
Stainsbury St. E2 .... 40Yb 72
Stainsby Rd. E14 .... 44Cc 92
Stains Cl. EN8: Chesh 1Ac 20
Stainton Ct. WD23: Bush 15Da 27
(off Farrington Av.)
Stainton Rd. EN3: Enf H 11Yb 34
SE6 .... 58Fc 115
Stainton Wlk. GU21: Wok 10N 167
Stairfoot La. TN13: Chip 94Ed 202
Staiths Way KT20: Tad 92Xa 194
Stalbridge Flats W1 .... 3J 221
Stalbridge Ho. NW1 .... 2B 216
Stalbridge St. NW1 .... 7E 214 (43Gb 89)
Staleys Acre TN15: Bor G 92Be 205
Staleys Rd. TN15: Bor G 92Ae 205
Stalham St. SE16 .... 48Xb 91
Stalham Way IG6: Ilf 25Rc 54
Stalisfield Pl. BR6: Downe 82Qc 180
Stambourne Way
BR4: W W'ck 75Ec 158
SE19 .... 66Ub 135
Stambourne Woodland Wlk.
SE19 .... 66Ub 135
Stamford Bridge 52Db 111
Stamford Bri. Studios SW6 .... 52Db 111
(off Wandon Rd.)
Stamford Brook Arches W6 .... 49Wa 88
Stamford Brook Av. W6 .... 48Va 88
Stamford Brook Gdns. W6 .... 48Va 88
Stamford Brook Mans. W6 .... 49Va 88
(off Goldhawk Rd.)
Stamford Brook Rd. W6 .... 48Va 88
Stamford Bldgs. SW8 .... 52Nb 112
(off Meadow Pl.)
Stamford Cl. EN6: Pot B 4Fb 17
HA3: Hrw W 24Ga 46
N15 .... 28Wb 51
NW3 .... 34Eb 69
(off Heath St.)
UB1: S'hall 45Ca 85
Stamford Cotts. SW10 .... 52Db 111
(off Billing St.)
Stamford Ct. HA8: Edg 21Pa 47
W6 .... 49Wa 88
Stamford Dr. BR2: Brom 70Hc 137
Stamford Gdns. RM9: Dag 38Yc 75
Stamford Ga. SW6 .... 52Db 111
STAMFORD GREEN 85Ra 173
Stamford Grn. Rd.
KT18: Eps 85Ra 173
Stamford Gro. E. N16 .... 32Wb 71
Stamford Gro. W. N16 .... 32Wb 71
STAMFORD HILL 32Vb 71
Stamford Hill N16 .... 33Vb 71
Stamford Ho. GU24: Chob 3J 167
(off Bagshot Rd.)
Stamford Lodge N16 .... 31Vb 71
Stamford Rd. E6 .... 39Nc 74
KT12: Walt T 76Z 151
N1 .... 38Ub 71
N15 .... 29Wb 51
RM9: Dag 39Xc 75
WD17: Wat 12X 27
Stamford St. SE1 .... 7K 223 (46Qb 90)
Stamp Pl. E2 .... 3K 219 (40Vb 71)
Stanacre Ct. KT20: Kgswd 93Bb 195
Stanard Cl. N16 .... 31Ub 71
Stanborough Av. WD6: Bore 9Qa 15
Stanborough Cl. TW12: Hamp 65Ba 129
WD6: Bore 10Qa 15
Stanborough Ho. E3 .... 42Dc 92
(off Empson St.)
Stanborough Pk. WD25: Wat 7Y 13
Stanborough Pas. E8 .... 37Vb 71
Stanborough Rd. TW3: Houn 55Fa 108
Stanbridge Pl. N21 .... 19Rb 33
Stanbridge Rd. SW15 .... 55Ya 110
Stanbrook Rd. DA11: Grav'nd 10B 122
SE2 .... 47Xc 95
Stanbury Av. WD17: Wat 9U 12
Stanbury Ct. NW3 .... 37Hb 69
Stanbury Rd. SE15 .... 54Xb 113
(not continuous)
Stancroft NW9 .... 29Ua 48
Standale Gro. HA4: Ruis 29S 44
Standard Ind. Est. E16 .... 47Pc 94
Standard Pl. EC2 .... 4J 219
Standard Rd. BR6: Downe 82Qc 180
DA6: Bex 56Ad 117
DA17: Belv 50Cd 96
EN3: Enf W 10Ac 20
NW10 .... 42Sa 87
TW4: Houn 55Aa 107
Standen Av. RM12: Horn 34Nd 77
Standen Rd. SW18 .... 59Bb 111
Standfield WD5: Ab L 3U 12
Standfield Gdns. RM10: Dag 37Cd 76
Standfield Rd. RM10: Dag 36Cd 76
Standish Ho. SE3 .... 56Kc 115
(off Elford Cl.)
W6 .... 49Wa 88
(off St Peter's Gro.)
Standish Rd. W6 .... 49Wa 88
Standlake Point SE23 .... 62Zb 136
Standring Ri. HP3: Hem H 5K 3
Stane Cl. SW19 .... 66Db 133
Stane Gro. SW9 .... 54Nb 112
Stanesgate Ho. SE15 .... 52Wb 113
(off Friary Est.)
Stane Way KT17: Ewe 82Wa 174
SE18 .... 52Mc 115
Stanfield Ho. NW8 .... 5C 214
UB5: N'olt 40Z 65
(off Academy Gdns.)
Stanfield Rd. E3 .... 40Ac 72
Stanford Cl. HA4: Ruis 30S 44
IG8: Wfd G 22Nc 54
RM7: Rom 30Dd 56
TW12: Hamp 65Ba 129
STANFORD COMMON 8C 186
Stanford Cotts. GU24: Pirb 8C 186
Stanford Ct. EN9: Walt A 5Jc 21
SW6 .... 53Db 111
W8 .... 48Db 89
(off Cornwall Gdns.)
Stanford Gdns. RM15: Avel 46Ud 98
Stanford Ho. IG11: Bark 40Xc 75
Stanford Ind. Est.
SS17: Stan H 2L 101
STANFORD-LE-HOPE 2M 101
Stanford M. E8 .... 36Wb 71
Stanford Pl. SE17 .... 6H 231 (49Ub 91)
Stanford Rd. N11 .... 22Hb 49
RM16: Grays, Ors 7A 100
SW16 .... 68Mb 134
W8 .... 48Db 89
Stanfords, The KT17: Eps 84Va 174
(off East St.)
Stanford St. SW1 .... 6D 228 (49Mb 90)
Stanford Warren Nature Reserve 4M 101
Stanford Way SW16 .... 68Mb 134
Stangate SE1 .... 3J 229
Stangate Cres. WD6: Bore 15Ta 29
Stangate Gdns. HA7: Stan 21Ka 46
Stangate Lodge N21 .... 16Pb 32
Stanger Rd. SE25 .... 70Wb 135
Stanham Pl. DA1: Cray 56Jd 118
Stanham Rd. DA1: Dart 57Ld 119
Stanhill Cotts. DA2: Wilm 66Fd 140
Stanhope Av. BR2: Hayes 74Hc 159
HA3: Hrw W 25Fa 46
N3 .... 27Bb 49
Stanhope Cl. SE16 .... 47Zb 92
Stanhope Gdns. IG1: Ilf 32Pc 74
N4 .... 30Rb 51
N6 .... 30Kb 50
NW7 .... 22Va 48
RM8: Dag 34Bd 75
SW7 .... 5A 226 (49Eb 89)
Stanhope Ga. W1 .... 7J 221 (46Jb 90)
Stanhope Gro. BR3: Beck 71Bc 158
Stanhope Heath TW19: Stanw 58L 105
Stanhope Ho. N11 .... 21Kb 50
(off Coppies Gro.)
SE8 .... 52Bc 114
(off Adolphus St.)
Stanhope Ind. Pk. SS17: Stan H 4P 101
Stanhope M. E.
SW7 .... 5A 226 (49Eb 89)
Stanhope M. Sth.
SW7 .... 6A 226 (49Eb 89)
Stanhope M. W. SW7 .... 5A 226 (49Eb 89)
Stanhope Pde. NW1 .... 3B 216 (41Lb 90)
Stanhope Pk. Rd. UB6: G'frd 42Ea 86
Stanhope Pl. W2 .... 3F 221 (45Hb 89)
Stanhope Rd. AL1: St A 2D 6
CR0: C'don 76Ub 157
DA7: Bex 54Ad 117
DA10: Swans 58Be 121
DA15: Sidc 63Wc 139
E17 .... 29Dc 52
EN5: Barn 16Ya 30
EN8: Walt C 5Ac 20
N6 .... 30Lb 50
N12 .... 22Eb 49
RM8: Dag 33Bd 75
RM13: Rain 40Jd 76
SL1: Slou 4B 80
SM5: Cars 80Jb 156
UB6: G'frd 43Ea 86
Stanhope Row W1 .... 7K 221 (46Kb 90)
Stanhopes RH8: Limp 100Kc 199
Stanhope St. NW1 .... 2B 216 (40Lb 70)
Stanhope Ter. TW2: Twick 59Ha 108
W2 .... 4C 220 (45Fb 89)
Stanhope Way TN13: Riv 94Fd 202
TW19: Stanw 58L 105
Stanier Cl. W14 .... 50Bb 89
Stanier Ho. SW6 .... 53Eb 111
(off Station Ct.)
Staniland Dr. KT13: Weyb 83P 169
Stanlake M. W12 .... 46Ya 88
Stanlake Rd. W12 .... 46Ya 88
Stanlake Vs. W12 .... 46Ya 88
Stanley Av. AL2: Chis G 7N 5
BR3: Beck 68Ec 136
HA0: Wemb 38Na 67
IG11: Bark 40Vc 75
KT3: N Mald 71Wa 154
RM2: Rom 28Jd 56
RM8: Dag 32Bd 75
UB6: G'frd 39Ea 66
Stanley Bri. Studios SW6 .... 52Db 111
(off King's Rd.)
Stanley Cl. CR5: Coul 89Pb 176
DA9: Ghithe 57Ud 120
HA0: Wemb 38Na 67
RM2: Rom 28Jd 56
RM12: Horn 33Ld 77
SE9 .... 60Sc 116
SW8 .... 51Pb 112
UB8: Uxb 40M 63
Stanley Cohen Ho. EC1 .... 6D 218
Stanley Cotts. DA2: Daren 64Ud 142
SL2: Slou 6K 81
Stanley Ct. SM2: Sutt 80Db 155
SM5: Cars 80Jb 156
W5 .... 43La 86
Stanley Cres. DA12: Grav'nd 4F 144
W11 .... 45Bb 89
Stanleycroft Cl. TW7: Isle 53Ga 108
Stanley Dr. AL10: Hat 2D 8
Stanley Gdns. CR2: Sande 84Wb 177
CR4: Mitc 65Jb 134
KT12: Hers 79Y 151
NW2 .... 36Ya 68
SM6: Wall 79Lb 156
W3 .... 47Ua 88
W11 .... 45Bb 89
WD6: Bore 11Na 29
Stanley Gdns. M. W11 .... 45Bb 89
(off Kensington Pk. Rd.)
Stanley Gdns. Rd.
TW11: Tedd 64Ga 130
Stanley Grn. E. SL3: L'ly 49B 82
Stanley Grn. W. SL3: L'ly 49B 82
Stanley Gro. CR0: C'don 72Qb 156
SW8 .... 54Jb 112
Stanley Hill GU24: Pirb 4A 186
Stanley Holloway Ct. E16 .... 44Jc 93
(off Coolfin Rd.)
Stanley Ho. E14 .... 44Cc 92
(off Saracen St.)
SW10 .... 52Eb 111
(off Coleridge Gdns.)
Stanley Mans. SW10 .... 51Eb 111
(off Park Wlk.)
Stanley Maude Ho. SL9: Chal P 21A 42
(off Micholls Av.)
Stanley M. SW10 .... 52Eb 111
(off Coleridge Gdns.)
Stanley Pk. Dr. HA0: Wemb 39Pa 67
Stanley Pk. Rd. SM5: Cars 80Gb 155
SM6: Wall 79Kb 156
Stanley Picker Gallery 69Na 131
(off Springfield Rd.)
Stanley Rd. BR2: Brom 70Kc 137
BR6: Orp 74Wc 161
CR0: C'don 73Qb 156
CR4: Mitc 66Jb 134
DA10: Swans 58Be 121
DA11: Nflt 1A 144
DA14: Sidc 62Wc 139
E4 .... 18Fc 35
E10 .... 30Dc 52
E12 .... 36Nc 74
E18 .... 25Hc 53
EN1: Enf 13Ub 33
GU21: Wok 88B 168
HA2: Harr 33Ea 66
HA6: Nwood 25W 44
HA9: Wemb 37Pa 67
IG1: Ilf 33Tc 74
N2 .... 27Fb 49
N9 .... 18Vb 33
N10 .... 24Kb 50
N11 .... 23Mb 50
N15 .... 28Rb 51
NW9 .... 31Wa 68
RM12: Horn 33Ld 77
RM17: Grays 50De 99
SM2: Sutt 79Db 155
SM4: Mord 70Cb 133
SM5: Cars 80Jb 156
SW14 .... 56Ra 109
SW19 .... 65Cb 133
TW2: Twick 62Fa 130
TW3: Houn 56Ea 108
TW11: Tedd 63Ga 130
TW15: Ashf 64N 127
UB1: S'hall 45Aa 85
W3 .... 48Sa 87
WD17: Wat 14Y 27
Stanley Rd. Nth. RM13: Rain 39Gd 76
Stanley Rd. Sth. RM13: Rain 40Hd 76
Stanley Sq. SM5: Cars 81Hb 175
Stanley St. CR3: Cat'm 94Sb 197
SE8 .... 52Bc 114
Stanley Studios SW10 .... 51Eb 111
(off Fulham Rd.)
Stanley Ter. DA6: Bex 56Cd 118
N19 .... 33Nb 70
Stanley Way BR5: St M Cry 71Xc 161
Stanliff Ho. E14 .... 48Cc 92
Stanmer St. SW11 .... 53Gb 111
STANMORE 22Ka 46
Stanmore & Edgware Golf Cen. 20Ma 29
Stanmore Chase AL4: St A 3H 7
Stanmore Common Local Nature Reserve
.... 19Ha 28
Stanmore Country Pk. &
Local Nature Reserve 20La 28
Stanmore Gdns. SM1: Sutt 76Eb 155
TW9: Rich 55Pa 109
Stanmore Golf Course 24Ka 46
Stanmore Hill HA7: Stan 20Ja 28
Stanmore Lodge HA7: Stan 21Ka 46
Stanmore Pl. NW1 .... 39Kb 70
Stanmore Rd. DA17: Belv 49Ed 96
E11 .... 32Hc 73
N15 .... 28Rb 51
TW9: Rich 55Pa 109
WD24: Wat 11X 27
Stanmore St. N1 .... 39Pb 70
Stanmore Ter. BR3: Beck 68Cc 136
Stanmore Way IG10: Lough 11Qc 36
Stanmount Rd. AL2: Chis G 7N 5
Stannard Cotts. E1 .... 42Yb 92
(off Fox Cl.)
Stannard Ct. SE6 .... 60Dc 114
Stannard Ho. SW19 .... 63Eb 133
Stannard M. E8 .... 37Wb 71
(off Stannard Rd.)
Stannard Rd. E8 .... 37Wb 71
Stannary Pl. SE11 .... 50Qb 90
Stannary St. SE11 .... 51Qb 112
STANNERS HILL 10P 147
Stannet Way SM6: Wall 77Lb 156
Stannington Path WD6: Bore 11Qa 29
Stansborough Ho. E3 .... 42Dc 92
(off Empson St.)
Stansbury Sq. W10 .... 41Ab 88
Stansfeld Ho. SE1 .... 6K 231
Stansfeld Rd. E6 .... 43Mc 93
E16 .... 43Mc 93
Stansfield Rd. SW9 .... 55Pb 112
TW4: Cran 54X 107
Stansgate Rd. RM10: Dag 33Cd 76
Stanstead WC1 .... 4G 217
Stanstead Cl. BR2: Brom 71Hc 159
CR3: Cat'm 96Ub 197
Stanstead Gro. SE6 .... 60Bc 114
Stanstead Ho. E3 .... 42Ec 92
(off Devas St.)
Stanstead Mnr. SM1: Sutt 79Cb 155
Stanstead Rd. CR3: Cat'm 99Tb 197
E11 .... 29Kc 53
SE6 .... 60Zb 114
SE23 .... 60Zb 114
STANSTED 82Be 185
Stansted Cl. RM12: Horn 37Kd 77
Stansted Cres. DA5: Bexl 60Zc 117
Stansted Hill TN15: Stans 82Be 185
Stansted La. TN15: Ash 82Xd 184
Stansted Rd. TW6: H'row A 58P 105
Stanswood Gdns. SE5 .... 52Ub 113
Stanthorpe Cl. SW16 .... 64Nb 134
Stanthorpe Rd. SW16 .... 64Nb 134
Stanton Av. TW11: Tedd 65Ga 130
Stanton Cl. BR5: Orp 73Yc 161
KT4: Wor Pk 74Za 154
KT19: Ewe 78Ra 153
Stanton Ct. CR2: S Croy 78Tb 157
(off Birdhurst Ri.)
Stanton Ho. SE10 .... 51Ec 114
(off Thames St.)
SE16 .... 47Bc 92
(off Rotherhithe St.)
Stanton Rd. CR0: C'don 73Sb 157
SE26 .... 63Bc 136
SW13 .... 54Va 110
SW20 .... 67Za 132
Stanton Sq. SE26 .... 63Bc 136
Stanton Way SE26 .... 63Bc 136
SL3: L'ly 49A 82
Stanway Cl. IG7: Chig 22Uc 54
Stanway Cotts. KT16: Chert 74J 149
Stanway Ct. N1 .... 2J 219 (40Ub 71)
(not continuous)
Stanway Gdns. HA8: Edg 22Sa 47
W3 .... 46Qa 87
Stanway Rd. EN9: Walt A 5Jc 21
Stanway St. N1 .... 1J 219 (40Ub 71)
STANWELL 58M 105
Stanwell Cl. TW19: Stanw 58M 105
Stanwell Gdns. TW19: Stanw 58M 105
STANWELL MOOR 57J 105
Stanwell Moor Rd. TW18: Staines 62J 127
TW19: Staines, Stanw M 62J 127
UB7: Lford 56K 105
Stanwell New Rd. TW18: Staines 62J 127
Stanwell Rd. SL3: Hort 55C 104
TW14: Bedf 59R 106
TW15: Ashf 61N 127
Stanwick Rd. W14 .... 49Bb 89
Stanworth Ct. TW5: Hest 52Ba 107
Stanworth St. SE1 .... 2K 231 (48Vb 91)
Stanwyck Dr. IG7: Chig 22Sc 54
Stanwyck Gdns. RM3: Rom 22Kd 57
Stanyhurst SE23 .... 60Ac 114
Stapenhill Rd. HA0: Wemb 34Ka 66
Staple Cl. DA5: Bexl 62Fd 140
Staplefield Cl. HA5: Pinn 24Aa 45
SW2 .... 60Nb 112
Stapleford N17 .... 26Ub 51
(off Willan Rd.)
Stapleford Abbots Golf Course 17Jd 38
STAPLEFORD ABBOTTS 15Ed 38
Stapleford Abbotts Golf Course 17Jd 38
Stapleford Av. IG2: Ilf 29Uc 54
Stapleford Cl. E4 .... 20Ec 34
KT1: King T 68Qa 131
SW19 .... 59Ab 110
Stapleford Ct. TN13: S'oaks 96Hd 202
Stapleford Gdns. RM5: Col R 23Cd 56
Stapleford Rd. HA0: Wemb 38Ma 67
RM4: Stap A, Stap T 14Ed 38
Stapleford Way IG11: Bark 41Xc 95
Staple Hill Rd. GU24: Chob 9H 147
Staplehurst Ct. RH2: Reig 10L 207
Staplehurst Rd. RH2: Reig 10L 207
SE13 .... 57Fc 115
SM5: Cars 80Gb 155
Staple Inn WC1 .... 1K 223
Staple Inn Bldgs. WC1 .... 1K 223 (43Qb 90)
Staples, The BR8: Swan 67Kd 141
Staples Cl. SE16 .... 46Ac 92
STAPLES CORNER 32Xa 68
Staples Cnr. Bus. Pk. NW2 .... 32Xa 68
Staples Cnr. Retail Pk. NW2 .... 32Xa 68
Staples Ho. E6 .... 44Qc 94
(off Savage Gdns.)
Staple's Rd. IG10: Lough 13Mc 35
Staple St. SE1 .... 2G 231 (47Tb 91)
Stapleton Cl. EN6: Pot B 3Fb 17
Stapleton Cres. RM13: Rain 37Jd 76
Stapleton Gdns. CR0: Wadd 78Qb 156
Stapleton Hall Rd. N4 .... 32Pb 70
Stapleton Ho. E2 .... 41Xb 91
(off Ellsworth St.)
Stapleton Rd. BR6: Orp 77Vc 161
DA7: Bex 52Bd 117
SW17 .... 62Jb 134
WD6: Bore 10Qa 14
Stapleton Vs. N16 .... 35Ub 71
(off Wordsworth Rd.)
Stapley Rd. AL3: St A 1B 6
DA17: Belv 50Cd 96
Stapylton Rd. EN5: Barn 13Ab 30
Star All. EC3 .... 4J 225

Star & Garter Hill
TW10: Rich 60Na 109
Star Apartments KT12: Hers 79Y 151
Starboard Av. DA9: Ghithe 58Xd 120
Starboard Way E14 48Cc 92
Starbuck Cl. SE9 59Qc 116
Star Bus. Cen. RM13: Rain 43Fd 96
Starch Ho. La. IG6: Ilf 26Tc 54
Star Cl. EN3: Pond E 16Yb 34
Starcross St. NW1 4C 216 (41Lb 90)
Starfield Rd. W12 47Wa 88
Star Hill DA1: Cray 57Gd 118
Star Hill Rd. TN14: Dun G 88Bd 181
Star La.
BR5: St M Cry, St P 70Yc 139
CM16: Epp 2Wc 23
CR5: Coul 93Jb 196
E16 42Gc 93
Starlight Way AL4: St A 4G 6
TW6: H'row A 57S 106
Starling Cl. CR0: C'don 72Ac 158
DA3: Lfield 69De 143
HA5: Pinn 27Y 45
IG9: Buck H 18Jc 35
Starling Ho. NW8 1D 214
Starling La. EN6: Cuff 1Pb 18
Starling Pl. WD25: Wat 4Y 13
Starlings, The KT22: Oxs 85Ea 172
Starling Wlk. TW12: Hamp 64Aa 129
Starmans Cl. RM9: Dag 39Ad 75
Star Path *UB5: N'olt* 40Ca 65
(off Brabazon Rd.)
Star Pl. E1 45Vb 91
Star Rd. TW7: Isle 54Fa 108
UB10: Hil 42S 84
W14 51Bb 111
Starrock La. CR5: Chip 92Hb 195
Starrock Rd. CR5: Coul 91Kb 196
Star St. W2 2C 220 (44Gb 89)
Starts Cl. BR6: Farnb 76Qc 160
Starts Hill Av. BR6: Farnb 77Rc 160
Starts Hill Rd. BR6: Farnb 76Qc 160
Starveall Cl. UB7: W Dray 48P 83
Star Wharf *NW1* 39Lb 70
(off St Pancras Way)
Starwood Cl. KT14: W Byf 83L 169
Starwood Ct. SL3: L'ly 8N 81
Star Yd. WC2 2K 223 (44Qb 90)
State Farm Av.
BR6: Farnb 77Rc 160
Staten Bldg. *E3* 40Cc 72
(off Fairfield Rd.)
Staten Gdns. TW1: Twick 60Ha 108
Statham Gro. N16 35Tb 71
N18 22Ub 51
Statham Ho. *SW8* 53Lb 112
(off Wadhurst Rd.)
Station App. *BR1: Brom* 69Jc 137
(off High St.)
BR2: Hayes 74Jc 159
BR3: Beck 67Cc 136
BR4: W W'ck 73Ec 158
BR5: St M Cry 70Xc 139
BR6: Chels 78Xc 161
BR6: Orp 75Vc 161
BR7: Chst 65Nc 138
(Bennetts Copse)
BR7: Chst 67Qc 138
(Vale Rd.)
BR8: Swan 70Gd 140
CM13: W H'dn 31Ee 79
CM16: They B 8Uc 22
CR0: C'don 75Tb 157
(off Dingwall Rd.)
CR2: Sande 81Tb 177
CR3: Whyt 89Wb 177
CR5: Chip 90Hb 175
CR5: Coul 88Mb 176
CR8: Purl 83Qb 176
DA1: Cray 58Hd 118
DA1: Dart 58Nd 119
DA5: Bexl 60Cd 118
DA7: Bex 54Ed 118
(Barnehurst Rd.)
DA7: Bex 54Ad 117
(Percy Rd.)
DA13: Meop 10C 144
DA16: Well 54Wc 117
E4 23Fc 53
E7 35Kc 73
E11 29Jc 53
E17 29Cc 52
(not continuous)
E18 26Kc 53
EN5: New Bar 14Eb 31
EN8: Walt C 6Ac 20
GU22: Wok 90B 168
GU25: Vir W 10P 125
HA0: Wemb 37Ka 66
HA1: Harr 31Ga 66
HA4: Ruis 36X 65
(Mahlon Av.)
HA4: Ruis 32U 64
(Pembroke Rd.)
HA5: Pinn 27Aa 45
HA6: Nwood 24U 44
HP3: Hem H 5J 3
IG8: Wfd G 23Kc 53
IG9: Buck H 21Mc 53
IG10: Lough 15Nc 36
(Alderton Hill)
IG10: Lough 14Sc 36
(Torrington Dr.)
KT1: King T 67Qa 131
KT4: Wor Pk 74Wa 154
KT10: Hin W 76Ha 152
KT13: Weyb 79Q 150
KT14: W Byf 84J 169
KT17: Ewe 81Va 174
(Fennells Mead)
KT17: Ewe 82Xa 174
(Nonsuch Ct. Av.)
KT19: Eps 85Ta 173
KT19: Ewe 78Wa 154
KT20: Tad 94Ya 194
KT22: Lea 93Ja 192
KT22: Oxs 84Ea 172
KT24: E Hor 98U 190
N11 22Kb 50
N12 21Db 49
N16 33Vb 71
(off Stamford Hill)
NW1 6G 215 (42Hb 89)
NW10 41Va 88
Station App. NW11 31Za 68
RH1: Redh 5A 208
(off Redstone Hill)
RH8: Oxt 1J 211
RM14: Upm 33Sd 78
RM15: S Ock 41Yd 98
RM17: Grays 51Ce 121
RM18: Tilb 60Ge 122
SE3 55Kc 115
SE9 61Sc 138
(Bercta Rd.)
SE9 60Pc 116
(Crossmead)
SE12 58Jc 115
(off Burnt Ash Hill)
SE26 63Yb 136
SL9: Ger X 29A 42
SM2: Cheam 80Ab 154
SM2: Sutt 82Db 175
SM5: Cars 77Hb 155
SW6 55Ab 110
SW14 55Sa 109
SW16 65Mb 134
(Estreham Rd.)
SW16 64Mb 134
(Gleneagle Rd.)
SW20 68Xa 132
TN13: Dun G 92Gd 202
TN15: Bor G 92Be 205
TW8: Bford 51La 108
(off Sidney Gdns.)
TW9: Kew 53Qa 109
TW12: Hamp 67Ca 129
TW15: Ashf 63P 127
TW16: Sun 66W 128
TW17: Shep 71S 150
TW18: Staines 64J 127
UB3: Hayes 48V 84
UB6: G'frd 38Ea 66
UB7: Yiew 46N 83
UB9: Den 31F 62
W7 46Ga 86
WD3: Chor 14F 24
WD4: K Lan 2R 12
WD7: R'lett 7Ja 14
WD19: Wat 20Z 27
Station App. E. RH1: Redh 8P 207
Station App. Nth.
DA15: Sidc 61Wc 139
Station App. Rd.
CR5: Coul 87Mb 176
SE1 2K 229 (47Qb 90)
W4 52Sa 109
Station App. Sth. *DA15: Sidc* 61Wc 139
(off Jubilee Way)
Station App. W. RH1: Redh 8P 207
Station Arc. W1 6A 216
Station Av. CR3: Cat'm 96Wb 197
KT3: N Mald 69Ua 132
KT12: Walt T 77W 150
KT19: Ewe 81Ua 174
SW9 55Rb 113
TW9: Kew 53Qa 109
Station Bldgs. *KT1: King T* 68Na 131
(off Fife Rd.)
Station Chambers *E6* 38Nc 74
(off High St. Nth.)
Station Cl. AL9: Brk P 8G 8
EN6: Pot B 3Bb 17
N3 25Cb 49
N12 21Db 49
TW12: Hamp 67Da 129
Station Cotts. BR6: Orp 75Vc 161
Station Ct. N15 29Vb 51
SW6 53Eb 111
TN15: Bor G 91Be 205
Station Cres. HA0: Wemb 37Ka 66
N15 28Tb 51
SE3 50Jc 93
TW15: Ashf 62M 127
Stationer's Hall Ct.
EC4 3C 224 (44Rb 91)
Stationers Pl. HP3: Hem H 7N 3
Station Est. BR3: Beck 69Zb 136
E18 26Kc 53
Station Est. Rd. TW14: Felt 60X 107
Station Footpath WD4: K Lan 2R 12
(not continuous)
Station Forecourt *WD3: Rick* 17M 25
(off Homestead Rd.)
Station Garage M. SW16 65Mb 134
Station Gdns. W4 52Sa 109
Station Gro. HA0: Wemb 37Na 67
Station Hill BR2: Hayes 75Jc 159
Station Ho. M. N9 21Wb 51
Station La. RM12: Horn 34Md 77
Station M. EN6: Pot B 3Cb 17
Station Pde. *BR1: Brom* 67Jc 137
(off Tweedy Rd.)
DA7: Bex 54Ad 117
(off Pickford La.)
DA8: Erith 50Gd 96
DA15: Sidc 61Wc 139
E6 38Nc 74
E11 29Jc 53
E13 39Lc 73
(off Green St.)
EN4: Cockf 14Jb 32
GU25: Vir W 10P 125
HA2: Harr 35Da 65
HA3: Kenton 26Ja 46
HA4: Ruis 33W 64
HA8: Edg 24Na 47
IG9: Buck H 21Mc 53
IG11: Bark 38Sc 74
KT24: E Hor 98U 190
N14 18Mb 32
NW2 37Ya 68
RM1: Rom 30Gd 56
RM9: Dag 37Cd 76
Station Pde. RM12: Horn 35Kd 77
SL5: S'dale 3E 146
SM2: Sutt 79Eb 155
(off High St.)
SW12 60Jb 112
TN13: S'oaks 96Jd 202
TW9: Kew 53Qa 109
TW14: Felt 60X 107
TW15: Ashf 63P 127
UB5: N'olt 35Da 65
(Dorchester Rd.)
UB5: N'olt 36Ca 65
(Ealing Rd.)
UB9: Den 31J 63
Station Pde. W3 44Qa 87
W4 52Sa 109
W5 46Pa 87
Station Pas. E18 26Kc 53
SE15 53Yb 114
Station Path *E8* 37Xb 71
(off Graham Rd.)
SW6 55Bb 111
TW18: Staines 63H 127
Station Pl. N4 33Qb 70
Station Ri. SE27 61Rb 135
Station Rd. AL2: Brick W 3Ca 13
AL4: S'ford 1M 7
AL9: Brk P, N Mym, Wel G 6E 8
BR1: Brom 67Jc 137
BR2: Brom 68Gc 137
BR4: W W'ck 74Ec 158
BR5: St P 70Yc 139
BR6: Orp 75Vc 161
BR8: Swan 70Gd 140
CM13: W H'dn 30Ee 59
CM16: Epp 3Vc 23
CR0: C'don 74Sb 157
CR3: Whyt 90Vb 177
CR3: Wold 94Ac 198
CR8: Kenley 86Sb 177
DA1: Cray 59Hd 118
DA3: Lfield 69Ae 143
DA4: Eyns 76Md 163
DA4: S Dar 68Rd 141
DA7: Bex 55Ad 117
DA9: Ghithe 57Wd 120
(not continuous)
DA11: Nflt 58De 121
DA13: Meop 10C 144
DA13: Sflt 63Be 143
DA15: Sidc 61Wc 139
DA17: Belv 48Cd 96
E4 18Fc 35
E7 35Jc 73
E12 35Nc 74
E17 30Ac 52
EN5: New Bar 15Db 31
EN6: Cuff 1Pb 18
EN9: Walt C, Walt A 6Cc 20
GU24: Chob 3K 167
HA1: Harr 28Ha 46
HA2: Harr 29Da 45
HA8: Edg 23Qa 47
HP1: Hem H 4K 3
HP4: Berk 1A 2
IG1: Ilf 34Rc 74
IG6: Ilf 27Tc 54
IG7: Chig 20Rc 36
IG10: Lough 14Nc 36
KT1: Hamp W 67La 130
KT2: King T 67Qa 131
KT3: N Mald 71Xa 154
KT7: T Ditt 73Ha 152
KT9: Chess 78Na 153
KT10: Clay 79Ga 152
KT10: Esh 75Fa 152
KT11: Stoke D 89Aa 171
KT14: W Byf 84J 169
KT15: Add 77L 149
KT16: Chert 74H 149
KT22: Lea 93Ja 192
N3 25Cb 49
N11 22Kb 50
N17 27Wb 51
N19 34Lb 70
N21 18Rb 33
N22 26Nb 50
NW4 30Wa 48
NW7 23Ua 48
NW10 40Va 68
RH1: Mers 100Lb 196
RH1: Redh 5N 207
RH3: Bet 3A 206
RH9: S God 10C 210
RM2: Rom 28Kd 57
RM3: Hrld W 25Pd 57
RM6: Chad H, Dag 31Zc 75
RM14: Upm 33Sd 78
RM18: E Til, W Til 1H 123
SE13 55Ec 114
SE20 65Yb 136
SE25 70Vb 135
SL1: Slou 4C 80
SL3: L'ly 48C 82
SL5: S'dale 2E 146
SL9: Ger X 29A 42
SM2: Sutt 82Cb 175
SM5: Cars 77Hb 155
SW13 54Va 110
SW19 67Eb 133
TN13: Dun G 92Gd 202
TN14: Hals 82Bd 181
TN14: Otf 88Kd 183
TN14: S'ham 83Jd 182
TN15: Bor G 92Be 205
TN16: Bras 95Xc 201
TW1: Twick 60Ha 108
TW3: Houn 56Da 107
TW11: Tedd 65Ja 130
TW12: Hamp 67Ca 129
TW15: Ashf 63P 127
TW16: Sun 66W 128
TW17: Shep 71S 150
TW19: Wray 58B 104
TW20: Egh 64C 126
UB3: Harl, Hayes 49U 84
(not continuous)
UB7: W Dray 47N 83
UB8: Cowl 42L 83
W5 44Pa 87
W7 46Ga 86
WD3: Rick 17M 25
WD4: K Lan 1R 12
WD6: Bore 14Qa 29
WD7: R'lett 7Ja 14
WD17: Wat 12X 27
Station Rd. E. RH8: Oxt 1J 211
Station Rd. Nth. DA17: Belv 48Dd 96
RH1: Mers 100Lb 196
TW20: Egh 64C 126
Station Rd. Sth. RH1: Mers 100Lb 196
Station Rd. W. RH8: Oxt 1J 211
Station Sq. BR5: Pet W 71Sc 160
RM2: Rom 28Kd 57
Station St. E15 38Fc 73
E16 46Rc 94
Station Ter. AL2: Park 8B 6
NW10 40Za 68
Station Ter. RM19: Purf 50Qd 97
SE5 53Sb 113
Station Ter. M. SE3 50Jc 93
Station Vw. UB6: G'frd 39Fa 66
Station Wlk. *IG1: Ilf* 33Rc 74
(in The Exchange)
Station Way AL1: St A 2D 6
IG9: Buck H 21Lc 53
KT10: Clay 79Ga 152
KT19: Eps 85Ta 173
SE15 54Wb 113
SM3: Cheam 79Ab 154
Station Yd. AL4: S'ford 2M 7
CR8: Purl 84Rb 177
KT20: Kgswd 93Bb 195
TW1: Twick 59Ja 108
UB9: Den 31J 63
Staton Ct. *E10* 31Dc 72
(off Kings Cl.)
Staunton Ho. SE17 6H 231
Staunton Rd. KT2: King T 65Na 131
SL2: Slou 3H 81
Staunton St. SE8 51Bc 114
Stave Hill Ecological Pk. 47Ac 92
Staveley NW1 3B 216
Staveley Cl. E9 36Yb 72
N7 35Nb 70
SE15 53Xb 113
Staveley Ct. E11 29Jc 53
Staveley Gdns. W4 53Ta 109
Staveley Rd. TW15: Ashf 65T 128
W4 51Sa 109
Staveley Way GU21: Knap 9J 167
Stavers Ho. *E3* 40Bc 72
(off Tredegar Rd.)
Staverton Rd. NW2 38Ya 68
RM11: Horn 30Md 57
Stave Yd. Rd. SE16 46Ac 92
Stavordale Lodge *W14* 48Bb 89
(off Melbury Rd.)
Stavordale Rd. N5 35Rb 71
SM5: Cars 73Eb 155
Stayne End GU25: Vir W 10L 125
Stayner's Rd. E1 42Zb 92
Stayton Rd. SM1: Sutt 76Cb 155
Steadfast Rd. KT1: King T 67Ma 131
Steadman Ct. EC1 5E 218
Steadman Ho. *RM10: Dag* 34Cd 76
(off Uvedale Rd.)
Stead St. SE17 6F 231 (49Tb 91)
Steam Farm La.
TW14: Felt 56V 106
Stean St. E8 39Vb 71
Stebbing Ho. *W11* 46Za 88
(off Queensdale Cres.)
Stebbing Way IG11: Bark 40Wc 75
Stebondale St. E14 49Ec 92
Stedham Pl. WC1 2F 223
Stedman Cl. DA5: Bexl 62Gd 140
UB10: Ick 34Q 64
Steed Cl. RM11: Horn 33Kd 77
Steedman St. SE17 6D 230 (49Sb 91)
Steeds Rd. N10 25Hb 49
Steeds Way IG10: Lough 13Nc 36
Steele Av. DA9: Ghithe 57Vd 120
Steele Ct. TW11: Tedd 66La 130
Steele Ho. *E15* 40Gc 73
(off Eve Rd.)
Steele Rd. E11 35Gc 73
N17 27Ub 51
NW10 40Sa 67
TW7: Isle 56Ja 108
W4 48Sa 87
Steele's M. Nth. NW3 37Hb 69
Steele's M. Sth. NW3 37Hb 69
Steele's Rd. NW3 37Hb 69
Steele's Studios NW3 37Hb 69
Steele Wlk. DA8: Erith 52Dd 118
Steel's La. E1 44Yb 92
KT22: Oxs 86Da 171
Steelyard Pas. EC4 5F 225
Steen Way SE22 57Ub 113
Steep Cl. BR6: Chels 79Vc 161
Steep Hill CR0: C'don 77Ub 157
GU24: Chob 10G 146
SW16 62Mb 134
Steeplands WD23: Bush 17Da 27
Steeple Cl. SW6 54Ab 110
SW19 64Ab 132
Steeple Ct. E1 42Xb 91
TW20: Egh 64D 126
Steeple Gdns. KT15: Add 78K 149
Steeple Hgts. Dr.
TN16: Big H 89Mc 179
Steeple Point SL5: Asc 9A 124
Steeplestone Cl. N18 22Sb 51
Steeple Wlk. *N1* 39Sb 71
(off New Nth. Rd.)
Steerforth St. SW18 61Eb 133
Steering Cl. N9 18Yb 34
Steers Mead CR4: Mitc 67Hb 133
Steers Way SE16 47Ac 92
Stelfox Ho. WC1 3J 217
Stella Cl. UB8: Hil 43R 84
Stellar Ho. N17 23Vb 51
Stella Rd. SW17 65Hb 133
Stelling Rd. DA8: Erith 52Fd 118
Stellman Cl. E5 34Wb 71
Stembridge Rd. SE20 68Xb 135
Stem Ct. KT16: Chert 74L 149
Sten Cl. EN3: Enf L 9Cc 20
Stenning Av. SS17: Linf 9K 101
Stents La. KT11: Stoke D 92Ba 191
Stepbridge Path GU21: Wok 9P 167
Stepgates KT16: Chert 73K 149
Stepgates Cl. KT16: Chert 73K 149
Stephan Cl. E8 39Wb 71
Stephen Av. RM13: Rain 37Jd 76
Stephen Cl. BR6: Orp 76Uc 160
TW20: Egh 65E 126
Stephendale Rd. SW6 55Db 111
Stephen Fox Ho. *W4* 50Ua 88
(off Chiswick La.)
Stephen M. W1 1D 222 (43Mb 90)
Stephen Pl. SW4 55Lb 112
Stephen Rd. DA7: Bex 55Ed 118
Stephens Cl. RM3: Rom 22Ld 57
Stephens Ct. E16 42Hc 93
SE4 55Ac 114
Stephens Lodge *N12* 20Eb 31
(off Woodside La.)
Stephenson Av. RM18: Tilb 3C 122
Stephenson Cl. DA16: Well 54Wc 117
E3 41Dc 92
Stephenson Ct. *SL1: Slou* 7K 81
(off Osborne St.)
SM2: Cheam 80Ab 154
(off Station App.)
Stephenson Dr. SL4: Wind 2F 102
Stephenson Ho. SE1 3D 230 (48Sb 91)
Stephenson Pl. *RH1: Mers* 100Lb 196
(off Station Rd. Nth.)
Stephenson Rd. E17 29Ac 52
TW2: Whitt 59Ca 107
W7 44Ha 86
Stephenson St. E16 42Gc 93
NW10 41Ua 88
Stephenson Way NW1 5C 216 (42Lb 90)
WD23: Bush 13Z 27
Stephenson Wharf HP3: Hem H 7P 3
Stephen's Rd. E15 39Gc 73
Stephen St. W1 1D 222 (43Mb 90)
Stephyns Chambers HP1: Hem H 3M 3
STEPNEY 43Zb 92
Stepney C'way. E1 44Zb 92
Stepney City Apartments E1 43Yb 92
Stepney Cl. CR4: Mitc 67Jb 134
Stepney Grn. E1 43Yb 92
Stepney Grn. Ct. *E1* 43Zb 92
(off Stepney Grn.)
Stepney High St. E1 43Zb 92
Stepney Way E1 43Xb 91
Stepping Stones Farm 43Zb 92
Sterling Av. EN8: Walt C 6Zb 20
HA8: Edg 21Pa 47
Sterling Cl. NW10 38Wa 68
Sterling Ct. KT16: Chert 73J 149
Sterling Gdns. SE14 51Ac 114
Sterling Ho. SE3 56Kc 115
Sterling Ind. Est.
RM10: Dag 35Dd 76
Sterling Pl. KT13: Weyb 77U 150
W5 49Na 87
Sterling Rd. EN2: Enf 11Tb 33
Sterling St. SW7 3E 226 (48Gb 89)
Sterling Way N18 21Tb 51
Sternberg Centre, The 27Cb 49
Stern Cl. IG11: Bark 40Yc 75
Sterndale Rd. DA1: Dart 59Pd 119
W14 48Za 88
Sterne St. W12 47Za 88
Sternhall La. SE15 55Wb 113
Sternhold Av. SW2 61Mb 134
Sterry Cres. RM10: Dag 36Cd 76
Sterry Dr. KT7: T Ditt 72Ga 152
KT19: Ewe 77Ua 154
Sterry Gdns. RM10: Dag 37Cd 76
Sterry Rd. IG11: Bark 39Vc 75
RM10: Dag 35Cd 76
Sterry St. SE1 2F 231 (47Tb 91)
Steucers La. SE23 60Ac 114
Stevannie Ct. DA17: Belv 50Bd 95
Steve Biko Ct. *W10* 42Za 88
(off St John's Ter.)
Steve Biko La. SE6 63Cc 136
Steve Biko Lodge *E13* 40Jc 73
(off London Rd.)
Steve Biko Rd. N7 34Qb 70
Steve Biko Way TW3: Houn 55Ca 107
Stevedale Rd. DA16: Well 54Yc 117
Stevedore St. E1 46Xb 91
Stevenage Cres. WD6: Bore 11Na 29
Stevenage Rd. E6 37Qc 74
SW6 52Za 110
Stevens Av. E9 37Yb 72
Stevens Cl. BR3: Beck 65Cc 136
DA2: Daren 64Ud 142
DA5: Bexl 63Fd 140
EN6: Pot B 5Za 16
HA5: Eastc 29Y 45
KT17: Eps 84Ua 174
TW12: Hamp 65Ba 129
Stevens Grn. WD23: B Hea 18Ea 28
Stevens La. KT10: Clay 80Ja 152
Stevenson Cl. DA8: Erith 52Kd 119
EN5: New Bar 17Fb 31
Stevenson Ct. SE6 61Hc 137
Stevenson Cres. SE16 50Wb 91
Stevenson Ho. *NW8* 39Eb 69
(off Boundary Rd.)
Stevenson Rd. SL2: Hedg 3H 61
Stevens Pl. CR8: Purl 85Rb 177
Stevens Rd. RM8: Dag 33Yc 75
Stevens St. SE1 3J 231 (48Ub 91)
Stevens Way IG7: Chig 21Uc 54
Steventon Rd. W12 45Va 88
Steward Cl. EN8: Chesh 2Ac 20
Stewards Cl. CM16: Epp 4Wc 23
STEWARD'S GREEN 4Xc 23
Stewards Grn. La. CM16: Epp 4Xc 23
Stewards Grn. Rd.
CM16: Epp, Fidd H 5Wc 23
Stewards Holte Wlk. N11 21Kb 50
Steward St. E1 1J 225 (43Ub 91)
Stewards Wlk. RM1: Rom 29Gd 56
Stewart KT20: Tad 93Za 194
Stewart Av. RM14: Upm 34Rd 77
SL1: Slou 3K 81
TW17: Shep 70Q 128
Stewart Cl. BR7: Chst 64Rc 138
GU21: Wok 9K 167
NW9 30Sa 47
TW12: Hamp 65Aa 129
WD5: Ab L 4V 12
Stewart Ct. CM16: Epp 3Uc 22
UB9: Den 30H 43
Stewart Ho. KT1: King T 69Pa 131
Stewart Quay UB3: Hayes 47U 84
Stewart Rainbird Ho. *E12* 36Qc 74
(off Parkhurst Rd.)
Stewart Rd. E15 35Fc 73
Stewartsby Cl. N18 22Sb 51
Stewart's Dr. SL2: Farn C 5F 60
Stewart's Gro. SW3 7C 226 (50Fb 89)
Stewarts Lodge WD5: Ab L 3V 12
Stewart's Pl. SW2 58Pb 112
Stewart's Rd. SW8 52Lb 112
Stewart St. E14 47Ec 92
Stew La. EC4 4D 224 (45Sb 91)
Steyne Ho. *W3* 46Sa 87
(off Narrow St.)
Steyne Rd. W3 46Ra 87
Steyning Cl. CR8: Kenley 88Rb 177
Steyning Gro. SE9 63Pc 138
Steyning Way TW4: Houn 56Y 107
Steynings Way N12 22Cb 49
Steynton Av. DA5: Bexl 61Zc 139
Stibbington Ho. NW1 1C 216

STICKING HILL 1E 100
Stickland Rd. DA17: Belv 49Cd 96
Stickleton Cl. UB6: G'frd 41Da 85
Stifford Clays Rd.
RM16: Grays, N Stif, Ors 46Be 99
(not continuous)
Stifford Hill RM15: N Stif, S Ock 45Yd 98
RM16: N Stif 45Yd 98
Stifford Ho. *E1* *43Yb 92*
(off Stepney Way)
Stifford Rd. RM15: Avel, S Ock 46Ud 98
Stilecroft Gdns. HA0: Wemb 34Ka 66
Stile Footpath RH1: Redh 6P 207
Stile Hall Gdns. W4 50Qa 87
Stile Hall Mans. *W4* *50Qa 87*
(off Wellesley Rd.)
Stile Hall Pde. W4 50Qa 87
Stileman Ho. *E3* *43Bc 92*
(off Ackroyd Dr.)
Stile Path TW16: Sun 69W 128
Stile Rd. SL3: L'ly 8P 81
Stiles Cl. BR2: Brom 72Pc 160
DA8: Erith 50Dd 96
Stillingfleet Rd. SW13 51Wa 110
Stillington St. SW1 5C 228 (49Lb 90)
Stillness Rd. SE23 58Ac 114
Stilton Path WD6: Bore 10Qa 15
Stilwell Dr. UB8: Hil 42P 83
Stilwell Rdbt. UB8: Hil 45Q 84
Stipularis Dr. UB4: Yead 42Z 85
Stirling Av. HA5: Pinn 32Z 65
SM6: Wall 80Nb 156
TW17: Shep 69U 128
Stirling Bus. Pk. EN8: Walt C 6Bc 20
Stirling Cl. DA14: Sidc 63Uc 138
RM13: Rain 41Kd 97
SL4: Wind 4B 102
SM7: Bans 89Bb 175
SW16 67Mb 134
UB8: Cowl 41L 83
STIRLING CORNER 16Ta 29
Stirling Cnr. EN5: Ark 16Ta 29
Stirling Ct. EC1 5B 218
W13 45Ka 86
Stirling Dr. BR6: Chels 78Xc 161
CR3: Cat'm 93Sb 197
Stirling Gro. TW3: Houn 54Ea 108
Stirling Ho. RH1: Redh 6P 207
SE18 50Rc 94
WD6: Bore 14Sa 29
Stirling Retail Pk. WD6: Bore 16Ta 29
Stirling Rd. E13 40Kc 73
E17 27Ac 52
HA3: W'stone 27Ha 46
N17 25Wb 51
N22 25Rb 51
SL1: Slou 3E 80
SW9 54Nb 112
TW2: Whitt 59Ca 107
TW6: H'row A 58P 105
UB3: Hayes 45X 85
W3 48Ra 87
Stirling Rd. Path E17 27Ac 52
Stirling Wlk. KT5: Surb 72Ra 153
Stirling Way CR0: Bedd 73Nb 156
WD5: Ab L 4W 12
WD6: Bore 16Ta 29
Stites Hill Rd. CR5: Coul 92Rb 197
Stiven Cres. HA2: Harr 34Ba 65
Stoats Nest Rd. CR5: Coul 86Nb 176
Stoats Nest Village CR5: Coul 87Nb 176
Stockbeck NW1 2C 216
Stockbury Rd. CR0: C'don 72Yb 158
Stockdale Rd. RM8: Dag 33Bd 75
Stockdales Rd. SL4: Eton W 9D 80
Stockdove Way UB6: G'frd 41Ha 86
Stocker Gdns. RM9: Dag 38Yc 75
Stockers Farm Rd. WD3: Rick 20M 25
Stocker's Lake (Nature Reserve) 20K 25
Stockers La. GU22: Wok 92B 188
(not continuous)
Stockfield Rd. KT10: Clay 78Ga 152
SW16 62Pb 134
Stockford Av. NW7 24Za 48
Stockham's Cl. CR2: Sande 82Tb 177
Stock Hill TN16: Big H 88Mc 179
Stockholm Apartments *NW1* *38Jb 70*
(off Chalk Farm Rd.)
Stockholm Ho. *E1* *45Wb 91*
(off Swedenborg Gdns.)
Stockholm Rd. SE16 50Yb 92
Stockholm Way E1 46Wb 91
Stockhurst Cl. SW15 54Ya 110
Stockingswater La.
EN3: Brim 12Bc 34
Stockland Rd. RM7: Rom 30Fd 56
Stock La. DA2: Wilm 62Ld 141
Stockleigh Hall NW8 1E 214
Stockley Cl. UB7: W Dray 47R 84
Stockley Country Pk. 45Q 84
Stockley Farm Rd.
UB7: W Dray 48R 84
STOCKLEY PARK 46R 84
Stockley Pk. Golf Course 45S 84
Stockley Rd. UB7: W Dray 49R 84
UB8: Hil 44Q 84
UB11: Stock P 44Q 84
Stock Orchard Cres. N7 36Pb 70
Stock Orchard St. N7 36Pb 70
Stockport Rd. SW16 67Mb 134
WD3: Herons 17E 24
Stocksfield Rd. E17 27Ec 52
Stocks Mdw. HP2: Hem H 1A 4
Stocks Pl. E14 45Bc 92
UB10: Hil 39Q 64
Stock St. E13 40Jc 73
Stockton Cl. EN5: New Bar 14Eb 31
Stockton Ct. SW1 4D 228
Stockton Gdns. N17 24Sb 51
NW7 20Ua 30
Stockton Ho. *E2* *41Xb 91*
(off Ellsworth St.)
HA2: Harr 32Ca 65
Stockton Rd. N17 24Sb 51
N18 23Wb 51
RH2: Reig 9J 207
STOCKWELL 54Pb 112
Stockwell Av. SW9 55Pb 112
Stockwell Cl. BR1: Brom 68Kc 137
HA8: Edg 26Sa 47
Stockwell Gdns. SW9 53Pb 112
Stockwell Gdns. Est. SW9 54Nb 112
Stockwell Grn. SW9 54Pb 112
Stockwell Grn. Ct. SW9 54Pb 112
Stockwell La. EN7: Chesh 1Wb 19
(not continuous)
SW9 54Pb 112
Stockwell M. SW9 54Pb 112
Stockwell Pk. Cres. SW9 54Pb 112
Stockwell Pk. Est. SW9 55Pb 112
Stockwell Pk. Rd. SW9 53Pb 112
Stockwell Pk. Wlk. SW9 55Qb 112
Stockwell Rd. SW9 54Pb 112
Stockwell St. SE10 51Ec 114
Stockwell Ter. SW9 53Pb 112
Stodart Rd. SE20 67Yb 136
Stoddart Ho. SW8 51Pb 112
Stodmarsh Ho. *SW9* *53Qb 112*
(off Cowley Rd.)
Stofield Gdns. SE9 62Mc 137
Stoford Cl. SW19 59Ab 110
Stoke Av. IG6: Ilf 23Wc 55
Stoke Cl. KT11: Stoke D 88Ba 171
STOKE COMMON 5L 61
Stoke Comn. Rd. SL3: Ful 5L 61
Stoke Cotts. KT22: Fet 93Fa 192
Stoke Ct. Dr. SL2: Stoke P 9J 61
STOKE D'ABERNON 89Aa 171
Stoke Gdns. SL1: Slou 6J 81
STOKE GREEN 2L 81
Stoke Grn. SL2: Stoke P 2L 81
Stokenchurch St. SW6 53Db 111
STOKE NEWINGTON 34Vb 71
Stoke Newington Chu. St. N16 34Tb 71
Stoke Newington Comn. N16 33Vb 71
Stoke Newington High St. N16 34Vb 71
Stoke Newington Rd. N16 36Vb 71
Stoke Pk. 8J 61
Stoke Pk. Av. SL2: Farn R 1G 80
Stoke Pl. NW10 41Va 88
STOKE POGES 8L 61
Stoke Poges Golf Course 1H 81
Stoke Poges La. SL1: Slou 6J 81
SL2: Slou, Stoke P 4J 81
Stoke Rd. KT2: King T 66Sa 131
KT11: Cobh, Stoke D 87Y 171
KT12: Walt T 76Y 151
RM13: Rain 40Md 77
SL2: Slou, Stoke P 6K 81
Stokesay SL2: Slou 5K 81
Stokesay Ct. *DA2: Dart* *58Rd 119*
(off Osbourne Rd.)
Stokesby Rd. KT9: Chess 79Pa 153
Stokes Cotts. IG6: Ilf 25Sc 54
Stokes Ct. N2 28Gb 49
Stokes Field (Local Nature Reserve)
75Ka 152
Stokesheath Rd. KT22: Oxs 83Ea 172
Stokesley St. W12 44Va 88
Stokes M. TW11: Tedd 64Ja 130
Stokes Ridings KT20: Tad 95Za 194
Stokes Rd. CR0: C'don 72Zb 158
E6 42Nc 94
Stoke Vw. SL1: Slou 6K 81
Stoke Wood SL2: Stoke P 5K 61
Stokley Ct. N8 28Nb 50
Stoll Cl. NW2 34Ya 68
Stompond La. KT12: Walt T 75W 150
Stomp Rd. SL1: Burn 3A 80
Stoms Path *SE6* *64Cc 136*
(off Maroons Way)
Stonard Rd. N13 20Qb 32
RM8: Dag 36Xc 75
Stonards Hill CM16: Coop, Epp 1Wc 23
IG10: Lough 16Pc 36
Stondon Pk. SE23 58Ac 114
Stondon Wlk. E6 40Mc 73
STONE 57Ud 120
Stonebanks KT12: Walt T 73W 150
STONEBRIDGE 39Ta 67
Stonebridge Cen. N15 29Vb 51
Stonebridge Fld. SL4: Eton 10F 80
Stonebridge M. SE19 66Tb 135
Stonebridge Pk. NW10 38Ta 67
Stonebridge Rd. DA11: Nflt 57Ce 121
N15 29Vb 51
Stonebridge Way HA9: Wemb 37Ra 67
Stone Bldgs. WC2 1J 223
Stone Castle Dr. DA9: Ghithe 58Wd 120
Stonechat M. DA9: Ghithe 58Wd 120
Stonechat Sq. E6 43Nc 94
Stone Cl. RM8: Dag 33Bd 75
SW4 54Lb 112
UB7: Yiew 46P 83
Stonecot Cl. SM3: Sutt 74Ab 154
Stonecot Hill SM3: Sutt 74Ab 154
Stone Ct. CR3: Cat'm 97Ub 197
DA8: Erith 50Hd 96
TN15: Bor G 91Ce 205
Stone Cres. TW14: Felt 59V 106
Stonecroft Av. SL0: Iver 44G 82
Stonecroft Cl. EN5: Ark 14Xa 30
Stonecroft Rd. DA8: Erith 52Ed 118
Stonecroft Way CR0: C'don 73Nb 156
Stonecrop Cl. NW9 27Ta 47
Stonecross AL1: St A 1C 6
Stonecross Cl. AL1: St A 1C 6
Stonecutter St. EC4 2B 224 (44Rb 91)
Stonefield N4 33Pb 70
Stonefield Cl. DA7: Bex 55Cd 118
HA4: Ruis 36Aa 65
Stonefield Mans. *N1* *39Qb 70*
(off Cloudesley St.)
Stonefield St. N1 39Qb 70
Stonefield Way HA4: Ruis 35Aa 65
SE7 52Mc 115
Stonegate Cl. BR5: St P 69Yc 139
STONEGROVE 21Pa 47
Stonegrove HA8: Edg 21Na 47
Stone Gro. Ct. HA8: Edg 22Pa 47
Stonegrove Gdns. HA8: Edg 22Na 47
Stone Hall *W8* *48Db 89*
(off Stone Hall Gdns.)
Stonehall Av. IG1: Ilf 30Nc 54
Stone Hall Gdns. W8 48Db 89
Stone Hall Pl. W8 48Db 89
Stone Hall Rd. N21 17Pb 32
Stoneham Rd. N11 22Lb 50
STONEHILL 79A 148
Stonehill Bus. Pk. N18 23Ac 52
Stonehill Cl. KT23: Bookh 97Ca 191
SW14 57Ta 109
Stonehill Ct. E4 17Dc 34
Stonehill Cres. KT16: Ott 79A 148
Stonehill Ga. SL5: S'hill 2B 146
STONEHILL GREEN 66Ed 140
Stonehill Rd. GU24: Chob 2N 167
KT16: Ott 10N 147
Stonehill Rd. SW14 57Sa 109
W4 50Qa 87
Stonehills Ct. SE21 62Ub 135
Stonehill Woods Pk. DA14: Sidc 65Dd 140
Stonehorse Rd. EN3: Pond E 15Yb 34
Stonehouse NW1 1C 216
Stone Ho. Ct. EC3 2J 225
Stone Ho. Fld. TN15: Plat 92Pe 205
Stone Ho. Gdns. CR3: Cat'm 97Ub 197
Stonehouse Ho. *W2* *43Cb 89*
(off Westbourne Pk. Rd.)
Stonehouse La. RM19: Purf 50Ud 98
TN14: Hals 81Zc 181
Stonehouse Rd. TN14: Hals 82Yc 181
Stoneings La. TN14: Knock 90Vc 181
Stone Lake Ind. Pk. SE7 49Lc 93
Stone Lake Retail Pk. SE7 49Lc 93
Stonelea Rd. HP3: Hem H 4P 3
STONELEIGH 78Wa 154
Stoneleigh Av. EN1: Enf 10Xb 19
KT4: Wor Pk 77Wa 154
Stoneleigh B'way. KT17: Ewe 78Wa 154
Stoneleigh Cl. EN8: Walt C 5Zb 20
Stoneleigh Ct. IG5: Ilf 27Nc 54
KT11: Stoke D 89Aa 171
Stoneleigh Cres. KT19: Ewe 78Va 154
Stoneleigh M. E3 40Ac 72
Stoneleigh Pk. KT13: Weyb 78S 150
Stoneleigh Pk. Av. CR0: C'don 72Zb 158
Stoneleigh Pk. Rd. KT19: Ewe 79Va 154
Stoneleigh Pl. W11 45Za 88
Stoneleigh Rd. BR1: Brom 69Rc 138
IG5: Ilf 27Nc 54
N17 27Vb 51
RH8: Limp 2P 211
SM5: Cars 73Gb 155
Stoneleigh St. W11 45Za 88
Stoneleigh Ter. N19 33Kb 70
Stonell's Rd. SW11 58Hb 111
Stonely Cres. DA9: Ghithe 56Yd 120
Stonemason Ct. SE1 2D 230
Stonemasons Cl. N15 28Tb 51
Stonemasons Yd. SW18 59Fb 111
Stoneness Rd. RM20: W Thur 51Xd 120
Stonenest St. N4 32Pb 70
Stone Pk. Av. BR3: Beck 70Cc 136
Stone Pl. KT4: Wor Pk 75Wa 154
Stone Pl. Rd. DA9: Ghithe 57Ud 120
Stone Rd. BR2: Brom 71Hc 159
Stones All. WD18: Wat 14X 27
Stones Cross Rd. BR8: Crock 71Ed 162
Stones End St. SE1 2D 230 (47Sb 91)
Stone's Rd. KT17: Eps 84Ua 174
STONE STREET 97Vd 204
Stone St. DA11: Grav'nd 9D 122
Stone St. TN15: Ivy H, Seal 95Sd 204
Stoneswood Rd. RH8: Limp 2M 211
Stonewall E6 43Qc 94
Stonewold Ct. W5 44Ma 87
STONEWOOD 62Zd 143
Stonewood DA2: Bean 62Yd 142
Stonewood Rd. DA8: Erith 50Gd 96
Stoney All. SE18 54Qc 116
Stoneyard La. E14 45Dc 92
Stoney Bri. Dr. EN9: Walt A 6Jc 21
Stoney Cft. CR5: Coul 94Lb 196
Stoneycroft HP1: Hem H 2J 3
Stoneycroft Cl. SE12 59Hc 115
Stoneycroft Rd. IG8: Wfd G 23Nc 54
Stoneydeep TW11: Tedd 63Ja 130
Stoneydown E17 28Ac 52
Stoneydown Av. E17 28Ac 52
Stoneydown Ho. *E17* *28Ac 52*
(off Blackhorse Rd.)
Stoneyfield SL9: Ger X 2N 61
Stoneyfield Rd. CR5: Coul 89Pb 176
Stoneyfields Gdns. HA8: Edg 21Ta 47
Stoneyfields La. HA8: Edg 22Sa 47
Stoneylands Ct. TW20: Egh 64B 126
Stoneylands Rd. TW20: Egh 64B 126
Stoney La. E1 2J 225 (44Vb 91)
HP1: Hem H 5C 2
HP3: Bov 9D 2
SE19 65Vb 135
SL2: Farn R 9E 60
WD4: Chfd 10E 10
Stoney Meade SL1: Slou 6F 80
Stoney St. SE1 6F 225 (46Tb 91)
Stonhouse St. SW4 56Mb 112
Stonny Cft. KT21: Asht 89Pa 173
Stonor Rd. W14 49Bb 89
Stony Cnr. DA13: Lfield, Meop 10A 144
Stonycroft Cl. EN3: Enf H 12Ac 34
Stony Hill KT10: Esh 80Ba 151
Stony La. HP6: L Chal 10A 10
Stony Path IG10: Lough 11Pc 36
Stonyshotts EN9: Walt A 6Gc 21
Stoop Ct. KT14: W Byf 84K 169
Stopes St. SE15 52Vb 113
Stopford Rd. E13 39Jc 73
SE17 7C 230 (50Rb 91)
Stopher Ho. SE1 2C 230
Storas Ct. *RM19: Purf* *50Rd 97*
(off Linnet Way)
Storehouse M. E14 45Cc 92
Store Rd. E16 47Qc 94
Storers Quay E14 49Fc 93
Store St. E15 36Fc 73
WC1 1D 222 (43Mb 90)
Storey Cl. UB10: Ick 34S 64
Storey Ct. NW8 4B 214
WD23: Bush 15Da 27
Storey Ho. *E14* *45Dc 92*
(off Cottage St.)
Storey Rd. E17 28Bc 52
N6 30Hb 49
Storey's Ga. SW1 2E 228 (47Mb 90)
Storey St. E16 46Qc 94
HP3: Hem H 6M 3
Stories M. SE5 54Ub 113
Stories Rd. SE5 55Ub 113
Stork Rd. E7 37Hc 73
Storksmead Rd. HA8: Edg 24Ua 48
Stork's Rd. SE16 48Wb 91
Stormont Rd. N6 31Hb 69
SW11 55Jb 112
Stormont Way KT9: Chess 78La 152
Stormount Dr. UB3: Harl 47S 84
Stornaway Rd. SL3: L'ly 49E 82
Stornaway Strand DA12: Grav'nd 2H 145
Stornoway HP3: Hem H 4B 4
Storr Gdns. CM13: Hut 15Fe 41
Storrington WC1 4G 217
Storrington Rd. CR0: C'don 74Vb 157
Storr's La. GU3: Worp 6G 186
Storth Oak Mead BR7: Chst 64Pc 138
Story St. N1 38Pb 70
Stothard Ho. *E1* *42Yb 92*
(off Amiel St.)
Stothard Pl. E1 7J 219 (43Ub 91)
Stothard St. E1 42Yb 92
Stott Cl. SW18 58Fb 111
Stoughton Av. SM3: Cheam 78Za 154
Stoughton Cl. SE11 6J 229 (49Pb 90)
SW15 60Wa 110
Stour Av. UB2: S'hall 48Ca 85
Stourcliffe Cl. W1 2F 221 (44Hb 89)
Stourcliffe St. W1 3F 221 (44Hb 89)
Stour Cl. BR2: Kes 77Lc 159
SL1: Slou 8F 80
Stourhead Cl. SW19 59Za 110
Stourhead Gdns. SW20 69Wa 132
Stourhead Ho. SW1 7D 228
Stour Rd. DA1: Cray 55Jd 118
E3 38Cc 72
RM10: Dag 33Cd 76
RM16: Grays 10C 100
Stourton Av. TW13: Hanw 63Ba 129
Stour Way RM14: Upm 30Ud 58
Stovell Rd. SL4: Wind 2F 102
Stowage SE8 51Cc 114
Stow Ct. DA2: Dart 59Sd 120
Stow Cres. E17 24Ac 52
Stowe Cres. HA4: Ruis 30R 44
Stowe Gdns. N9 18Vb 33
Stowe Ho. NW11 30Eb 49
Stowell Av. CR0: New Ad 82Fc 179
Stowell Ho. *N8* *28Nb 50*
(off Pembroke Rd.)
Stowe Pl. N15 27Ub 51
Stowe Rd. BR6: Chels 77Xc 161
SL1: Slou 5C 80
W12 47Xa 88
Stowting Rd. BR6: Orp 77Uc 160
Stox Mead HA3: Hrw W 25Fa 46
Stracey Rd. E7 35Jc 73
NW10 39Ta 67
Strachan Pl. SW19 65Ya 132
Stradbroke Dr. IG7: Chig 23Qc 54
Stradbroke Gro. IG5: Ilf 27Nc 54
IG9: Buck H 18Mc 35
Stradbroke Pk. IG7: Chig 23Rc 54
Stradbroke Rd. N5 35Sb 71
Stradbrook Cl. HA2: Harr 34Ba 65
Stradella Rd. SE24 58Sb 113
Strafford Av. IG5: Ilf 26Qc 54
Strafford Cl. EN6: Pot B 4Cb 17
Strafford Ga. EN6: Pot B 4Cb 17
Strafford Ho. *SE8* *50Bc 92*
(off Grove St.)
Strafford Rd. EN5: Barn 13Ab 30
TW1: Twick 59Ja 108
TW3: Houn 55Ba 107
W3 47Sa 87
Strafford St. E14 47Cc 92
Strahan Rd. E3 41Ac 92
Straight, The UB1: S'hall 47Z 85
Straight Rd. RM3: Rom 22Ld 57
SL4: Old Win 7L 103
Straightsmouth SE10 52Ec 114
Strait Rd. E6 45Nc 94
Strakers Rd. SE15 56Xb 113
Strale Ho. N1 1H 219
Strand WC2 6F 223 (45Nb 90)
Strandburgh Pl. HP3: Hem H 4B 4
Strand Cl. KT18: Eps D 91Ta 193
Strand Ct. SE18 50Vc 95
Strand Dr. TW9: Kew 52Ra 109
Strandfield Cl. SE18 50Uc 94
Strand Ho. SE28 46Tc 94
SW18 56Eb 111
Strand La. WC2 4J 223 (45Pb 90)
STRAND ON THE GREEN 51Qa 109
Strand on the Grn. W4 51Qa 109
Strand Pl. N18 21Ub 51
Strand School App. W4 51Qa 109
Strand Theatre 4H 223
Strangeways WD17: Wat 8U 12
Strang Ho. N1 39Sb 71
Strangways Ter. W14 48Bb 89
Stranraer Gdns. SL1: Slou 6J 81
Stranraer Way N1 38Nb 70
Strasburg Rd. SW11 53Jb 112
Strata Ct. KT12: Walt T 74V 150
Strata Twr. SE1 5D 230
Stratfield Pk. Cl. N21 17Rb 33
Stratfield Rd. SL1: Slou 7L 81
WD6: Bore 13Qa 29
STRATFORD 38Fc 73
Stratford Av. UB10: Hil 40P 63
Stratford Centre, The E15 38Fc 73
Stratford Circus (Performing Arts Cen.)
37Fc 73
Stratford Cl. IG11: Bark 38Wc 75
RM10: Dag 38Ed 76
SL2: Slou 2B 80
Stratford Ct. KT3: N Mald 70Ta 131
WD17: Wat 11X 27
Stratford Eye E15 37Fc 73
Stratford Gdns. SS17: Stan H 1M 101
Stratford Gro. SW15 56Za 110
Stratford Ho. *RM3: Rom* *23Md 57*
(off Dartfields)
Stratford Ho. Av. BR1: Brom 69Nc 138
STRATFORD NEW TOWN 37Fc 73
Stratford Office Village, The
E15 *38Gc 73*
(off Romford Rd.)
Stratford Picture House 37Fc 73
Stratford Pl. *E20* *37Ec 72*
(within Westfield Stratford City Shop. Cen.)
W1 3K 221 (44Kb 90)
Stratford Rd. CR7: Thor H 70Qb 134
E13 39Hc 73
(not continuous)
NW4 28Za 48
TW6: H'row A 58R 106
UB2: S'hall 49Aa 85
UB4: Yead 42X 85
W8 48Cb 89
WD17: Wat 12W 26
Stratford Studios W8 48Cb 89
Stratford Vs. NW1 38Lb 70
Stratford Way AL2: Brick W 1Ba 13
HP3: Hem H 5K 3
WD17: Wat 12V 26
Stratford Workshops *E15* *39Fc 73*
(off Burford Rd.)
Stratham Ct. *N19* *34Nb 70*
(off Alexander Rd.)
Strathan Cl. SW18 58Ab 110
Strathaven Rd. SE12 58Kc 115
Strathblaine Rd. SW11 57Fb 111
Strathbrook Rd. SW16 66Pb 134
Strathcona Av. KT23: Bookh 100Aa 191
Strathcona Gdns. GU21: Knap 10H 167
(not continuous)
Strathcona Rd. HA9: Wemb 33Ma 67
Strathdale SW16 64Pb 134
Strathdon Dr. SW17 62Fb 133
Strathearn Av. TW2: Whitt 60Da 107
UB3: Harl 52V 106
Strathearn Ho. W2 4D 220
Strathearn Pl. W2 4D 220 (44Gb 89)
Strathearn Rd. SM1: Sutt 78Cb 155
SW19 64Cb 133
Stratheden Pde. SE3 52Jc 115
Stratheden Rd. SE3 53Jc 115
Strathfield Gdns. IG11: Bark 37Tc 74
Strathleven Rd. SW2 57Nb 112
Strathmore RM18: E Til 9L 101
Strathmore Cl. CR3: Cat'm 93Ub 197
Strathmore Ct. NW8 3D 214
Strathmore Gdns. HA8: Edg 26Ra 47
N3 25Db 49
RM12: Horn 32Hd 76
W8 46Cb 89
Strathmore Rd. CR0: C'don 73Tb 157
SW19 62Cb 133
TW11: Tedd 63Ga 130
Strathnairn St. SE1 49Wb 91
Strathray Gdns. NW3 37Gb 69
Strath Ter. SW11 56Gb 111
Strathville Rd. SW18 61Cb 133
(not continuous)
Strathyre Av. SW16 69Qb 134
STRATTON 4A 210
Stratton Av. EN2: Enf 9Tb 19
SM6: Wall 81Mb 176
Stratton Cl. DA7: Bex 55Ad 117
HA8: Edg 23Pa 47
KT12: Walt T 74Y 151
SW19 68Cb 133
TW3: Houn 53Ca 107
Stratton Ct. *HA5: Hat E* *24Ba 45*
(off Devonshire Rd.)
N1 *38Ub 71*
(off Hertford Rd.)
Strattondale St. E14 48Ec 92
Stratton Dr. IG11: Bark 36Uc 74
Stratton Gdns. UB1: S'hall 44Ba 85
Stratton Ho. *HA8: Edg* *21Pa 47*
(off Lacey Dr.)
Stratton Rd. DA7: Bex 55Ad 117
RM3: Rom 22Qd 57
SW19 68Cb 133
TW16: Sun 68V 128
Stratton St. W1 6A 222 (46Kb 90)
Stratton Ter. TN16: Westrm 99Sc 200
Stratton Wlk. RM3: Rom 22Qd 57
Strauss Rd. W4 47Ta 87
Strawberry Cl. GU24: Brkwd 3B 186
Strawberry Cres. AL2: Lon C 8F 6
Strawberry Fld. AL10: Hat 3C 8
Strawberry Flds. BR6: Farnb 78Rc 160
BR8: Swan 67Gd 140
GU24: Bisl 7E 166
STRAWBERRY HILL 62Ha 130
Strawberry Hill 62Ha 130
Strawberry Hill KT9: Chess 79Ma 153
TW1: Twick 62Ha 130
Strawberry Hill Cl. TW1: Twick 62Ha 130
Strawberry Hill Golf Course 62Ga 130
Strawberry Hill Rd. TW1: Twick 62Ha 130
Strawberry La. SM5: Cars 76Jb 156
Strawberry Ri. GU24: Bisl 7E 166
Strawberry Ter. N10 25Hb 49
Strawberry Va. N2 25Fb 49
TW1: Twick 62Ja 130
(not continuous)
Strawbery Flds. KT15: Add 80H 149
Straw Cl. CR3: Cat'm 95Sb 197
Strayfield Rd. EN2: Enf 8Qb 18
Streakes Fld. Rd. NW2 33Wa 68
Stream Cl. KT14: Byfl 84M 169
Streamdale SE2 51Xc 117
Stream La. HA8: Edg 22Ra 47
Streamline Ct. *SE22* *60Wb 113*
(off Streamline M.)
Streamline M. SE22 60Wb 113
Streamside SL1: Slou 6D 80
Streamside Cl. BR2: Brom 70Jc 137
N9 18Vb 33
Streamway DA17: Belv 51Cd 118
Streatfeild Av. E6 39Pc 74
Streatfield Rd. HA3: Kenton 27La 46
STREATHAM 62Nb 134
Streatham Cl. SW16 61Nb 134
STREATHAM COMMON 65Mb 134
Streatham Comn. Nth. SW16 64Nb 134
Streatham Comn. Sth. SW16 65Nb 134
Streatham Ct. SW16 62Nb 134
Streatham High Rd. SW16 63Nb 134
STREATHAM HILL 61Nb 134
Streatham Hill SW2 61Nb 134
Streatham Hub 64Mb 134
Streatham Kart Raceway 64Mb 134
STREATHAM PARK 64Lb 134
Streatham Pl. SW2 59Nb 112
Streatham Rd. CR4: Mitc 67Jb 134
SW16 67Jb 134
Streatham St. WC1 2F 223 (44Nb 90)
STREATHAM VALE 66Lb 134
Streatham Va. SW16 67Lb 134
Streathbourne Rd. SW17 61Jb 134
Streatley Pl. NW3 35Eb 69
Streatley Rd. NW6 38Bb 69
Street, The DA4: Hort K 70Rd 141
DA12: Cobh 9H 145
DA12: Shorne 4N 145
E20 *37Ec 72*
(within Westfield Stratford City Shop. Cen.)
GU4: W Cla 100J 189
KT21: Asht 91Na 193
KT22: Fet 94Fa 192
KT24: Eff 99Z 191
KT24: W Hor 100R 190
RH3: Bet 7A 206
TN15: Ash 78Zd 165
TN15: Igh 93Zd 205
TN15: Plax 99Ae 205
WD4: Chfd 3J 11

Streeters La. SM6: Bedd 76Mb 156
Streetfield M. SE3 . . . . . 55Jc 115
Streets Heath GU24: W End 4D 166
Streimer Rd. E15 . . . . . 40Ec 72
Strelley Way W3 . . . . . 45Ua 88
Stretton Mans. SE8 . . . . . 50Cc 92
Stretton Rd. CR0: C'don 73Ub 157
TW10: Ham 61La 130
Stretton Way WD6: Bore 10Na 15
Strickland Av. DA1: Dart 55Pd 119
(not continuous)
Strickland Ct. SE15 . . . . . 55Wb 113
Strickland Ho. E2 . . . . . 4K 219
Strickland Row SW18 . . . . . 59Fb 111
Strickland St. SE8 . . . . . 54Cc 114
Strickland Way BR6: Orp 77Vc 161
Stride Rd. E13 . . . . . 40Hc 73
Strides Ct. *KT16: Ott* *79E 148*
(off Brox Rd.)
Strimon Cl. N9 . . . . . 19Yb 34
Stringer Ho. N1 . . . . . 1J 219
Stringer's Av. GU4: Jac W 10P 187
STRINGERS COMMON 10N 187
Stringers Cotts. *SL9: Chal P* *25A 42*
(off The Vale)
Stringhams Copse GU23: Rip 96H 189
Stripling Way WD18: Wat 16W 26
Strode Cl. N10 . . . . . 24Jb 50
Strode Rd. E7 . . . . . 35Jc 73
N17 . . . . . 26Ub 51
NW10 . . . . . 37Wa 68
SW6 . . . . . 52Ab 110
Strode's Coll. La. TW20: Egh 64B 126
Strode's Cres.
TW18: Staines 64L 127
Strode St. TW20: Egh 63C 126
Stroma Cl. HP3: Hem H 4C 4
Stroma Ct. SL1: Slou 5B 80
Strome Ho. *NW6* *40Db 69*
(off Carlton Vale)
Strone Rd. E7 . . . . . 37Lc 73
E12 . . . . . 37Lc 73
Strone Way UB4: Yead 42Aa 85
Strongbow Cres. SE9 . . . . . 57Pc 116
Strongbow Rd. SE9 . . . . . 57Pc 116
Strongbridge Cl. HA2: Harr 32Ca 65
Stronsa Rd. W12 . . . . . 47Va 88
Stronsay Cl. HP3: Hem H 4C 4
Strood Av. RM7: Rush G 32Fd 76
Strood Ho. SE1 . . . . . 2G 231
Strood La. SL4: Wink 5A 124
Stroud Cl. SL4: Wind 5B 102
Stroud Cres. SW15 . . . . . 62Wa 132
STROUDE 68B 126
Stroude Rd. GU25: Vir W 71A 148
TW20: Egh 65C 126
Stroudes Cl. KT4: Wor Pk 73Ua 154
Stroud Fld. UB5: N'olt 37Aa 65
Stroud Ga. HA2: Harr 35Da 65
STROUD GREEN 31Pb 70
Stroud Grn. Gdns.
CR0: C'don 73Yb 158
Stroud Grn. Rd. N4 . . . . . 32Pb 70
Stroud Grn. Way CR0: C'don 73Xb 157
Stroud Ho. *RM3: Rom* *22Md 57*
(off Montgomery Cres.)
Stroudley Ho. SW8 . . . . . 53Lb 112
Stroudley Wlk. E3 . . . . . 41Dc 92
Stroud Rd. SE25 . . . . . 72Wb 157
SW19 . . . . . 62Cb 133
Stroud's Cl. RM6: Chad H 29Xc 55
Stroudwater Pk. KT13: Weyb 79R 150
Stroud Way TW15: Ashf 65R 128
Stroud Wood Bus. Cen.
AL2: F'mre 9C 6
Strouts Pl. E2 . . . . . 3K 219 (41Vb 91)
Struan Gdns. GU21: Wok 87A 168
Strudwick Ct. *SW4* *53Nb 112*
(off Binfield Rd.)
Strutton Ct. SW1 . . . . . 4D 228
Strutton Ground SW1 . . . . . 3D 228 (48Mb 90)
Struttons Av. DA11: Nflt 1B 144
Strype St. E1 . . . . . 1K 225 (43Vb 91)
Stuart Av. BR2: Hayes 74Jc 159
HA2: Harr 34Ba 65
KT12: Walt T 74X 151
NW9 . . . . . 31Wa 68
W5 . . . . . 47Pa 87
Stuart Cl. BR8: Hext 66Hd 140
CM15: Pil H 15Xd 40
SL4: Wind 4D 102
UB10: Hil 37Q 64
Stuart Ct. *CR0: C'don* *76Rb 157*
(off St John's Rd.)
RH1: Redh *5A 208*
(off St Anne's Ri.)
WD6: E'tree 16Ma 29
Stuart Cres. CR0: C'don 76Bc 158
N22 . . . . . 25Pb 50
RH2: Reig 9J 207
UB3: Hayes 44S 84
Stuart Evans Cl. DA16: Well 55Yc 117
Stuart Gro. TW11: Tedd 64Ga 130
Stuart Ho. *E9* *37Zb 72*
(off Queen Anne Rd.)
E16 . . . . . *46Kc 93*
(off Beaulieu Av.)
W14 . . . . . *49Ab 88*
(off Windsor Way)
Stuart Lodge *KT18: Eps* *85Ta 173*
(off Ashley Rd.)
Stuart Mantle Way DA8: Erith 52Fd 118
Stuart Mill Ho. N1 . . . . . 2H 217
Stuart Pl. CR4: Mitc 67Hb 133
Stuart Rd. CR6: W'ham 92Xb 197
CR7: Thor H 70Sb 135
DA11: Grav'nd 8C 122
DA16: Well 53Xc 117
EN4: E Barn 17Gb 31
HA3: W'stone 27Ha 46
IG11: Bark 38Vc 75
NW6 . . . . . 41Cb 89
RH2: Reig 9J 207
RM17: Grays 50De 99
SE15 . . . . . 56Yb 114
SW19 . . . . . 62Cb 133
TW10: Ham 61Ka 130
W3 . . . . . 46Sa 87
Stuarts *RM11: Horn* *32Pd 77*
(off High St.)
Stuarts Cl. HP3: Hem H 4M 3
Stuart Twr. W9 . . . . . 4A 214
Stuart Way EN7: Chesh 3Xb 19
GU25: Vir W 10L 125
Stuart Way SL4: Wind 4C 102
TW18: Staines 65K 127
Stubbers Adventure Cen. 37Ud 78
Stubbers La. RM14: Upm 37Td 78
Stubbings Hall La. EN9: Walt A 1Ec 20
Stubbs Cl. NW9 . . . . . 29Sa 47
Stubbs Ct. *W4* *50Ra 87*
(off Chaseley Dr.)
Stubbs Dr. SE16 . . . . . 50Xb 91
Stubbs Hill BR6: Prat B 85Yc 181
Stubbs Ho. *E2* *41Zb 92*
(off Bonner St.)
SW1 . . . . . 6E 228
Stubbs La. KT20: Lwr K 100Bb 195
Stubbs M. *RM8: Dag* *35Xc 75*
(off Marlborough Rd.)
Stubbs Point E13 . . . . . 42Jc 93
Stubbs Way SW19 . . . . . 67Fb 133
Stucley Pl. NW1 . . . . . 38Kb 70
Stucley Rd. TW5: Hest 52Ea 108
Studdridge St. SW6 . . . . . 54Cb 111
Studd St. N1 . . . . . 39Rb 71
Stud Grn. WD25: Wat 4W 12
Studholme Ct. NW3 . . . . . 35Cb 69
Studholme St. SE15 . . . . . 52Xb 113
Studio Ct. N15 . . . . . 28Ub 51
Studio La. W5 . . . . . 46Ma 87
Studio M. NW4 . . . . . 28Ya 48
Studio Pl. SW1 . . . . . 2G 227
Studio Plaza KT12: Walt T 74W 150
Studios, The *DA3: New A* *75Be 165*
(off The Row)
SW4 . . . . . *56Lb 112*
(off Crescent La.)
W8 . . . . . *46Cb 89*
(off Edge St.)
WD23: Bush 16Ca 27
Studios Rd. TW17: Shep 69P 127
Studio Theatre
Carshalton 77Jb 156
Studio Way WD6: Bore 12Sa 29
Studland SE17 . . . . . 7F 231
Studland Cl. DA15: Sidc 62Vc 139
Studland Ho. *E14* *44Ac 92*
(off Aston St.)
Studland Rd. KT2: King T 65Na 131
KT14: Byfl 85P 169
SE26 . . . . . 64Zb 136
W7 . . . . . 44Fa 86
Studland St. W6 . . . . . 49Xa 88
Studley Av. E4 . . . . . 24Fc 53
Studley Cl. E5 . . . . . 36Ac 72
Studley Ct. DA14: Sidc 64Xc 139
E14 . . . . . *45Fc 93*
(off Jamestown Way)
Studley Cres. DA3: Lfield 68Ee 143
Studley Dr. IG4: Ilf 30Mc 53
Studley Est. SW4 . . . . . 53Nb 112
Studley Grange Rd. W7 . . . . . 47Ga 86
Studley Rd. E7 . . . . . 37Kc 73
RM9: Dag 38Zc 75
SW4 . . . . . 53Nb 112
Stukeley Rd. E7 . . . . . 38Kc 73
Stukeley St. WC2 . . . . . 2G 223 (44Nb 90)
Stumble Hill TN11: S'brne 100Yd 204
Stumps Hill La. BR3: Beck 65Cc 136
Stumps La. CR3: Whyt 89Vb 177
(not continuous)
Stunell Ho. *SE14* *51Zb 114*
(off John Williams Cl.)
Sturdee Ho. *E2* *40Wb 71*
(off Horatio St.)
Sturdy Ho. *E3* *40Ac 72*
(off Gernon Rd.)
Sturdy Rd. SE15 . . . . . 54Xb 113
Sturge Av. E17 . . . . . 26Dc 52
Sturgeon Rd. SE17 . . . . . 7D 230 (50Sb 91)
Sturges Fld. BR7: Chst 65Tc 138
Sturgess Av. NW4 . . . . . 31Xa 68
Sturge St. SE1 . . . . . 1D 230 (47Sb 91)
Sturlas Way EN8: Walt C 5Zb 20
Sturmer Cl. AL4: St A 3G 6
Sturmer Way N7 . . . . . 36Pb 70
Sturminster *NW1* *38Mb 70*
(off Agar Gro.)
Sturminster Cl. UB4: Yead 44Y 85
Sturminster Ho. *SW8* *52Pb 112*
(off Dorset Rd.)
Sturrock Cl. N15 . . . . . 28Tb 51
Sturry St. E14 . . . . . 44Dc 92
Sturt's La. KT20: Walt H 99Va 194
Sturt St. N1 . . . . . 2E 218 (40Sb 71)
Stutfield St. E1 . . . . . 44Wb 91
Stuttle Ho. *E1* *42Wb 91*
(off Buxton St.)
STYANTS BOTTOM 94Vd 204
Styants Bottom Rd. TN15: Seal 93Vd 204
Stychens Cl. RH1: Blet 5J 209
Stychens La. RH1: Blet 3J 209
Stylecroft Rd. HP8: Chal G 20A 24
Styles End KT23: Bookh 99Da 191
Styles Gdns. SW9 . . . . . 55Rb 113
Styles Ho. SE1 . . . . . 7B 224
Styles Way BR3: Beck 70Ec 136
Stylus Ho. E1 . . . . . 44Yb 92
Styventon Pl. KT16: Chert 73H 149
Subrosa Dr. RH1: Mers 2B 208
Subrosa Pk. RH1: Mers 2B 208
Success Ho. SE1 . . . . . 7K 231
Succombs Hill CR3: W'ham 92Xb 197
CR6: W'ham 92Xb 197
Succombs Pl. CR6: W'ham 91Xb 197
Sudbourne Rd. SW2 . . . . . 57Nb 112
Sudbrooke Rd. SW12 . . . . . 58Hb 111
Sudbrook Gdns. TW10: Ham 62Ma 131
Sudbrook La. TW10: Ham 60Na 109
SUDBURY 36Ka 66
Sudbury E6 . . . . . 43Qc 94
Sudbury Av. HA0: Wemb 34La 66
Sudbury Cl. RM6: Chad H 29Xc 55
Sudbury Ct. AL1: St A 3C 6
SW8 . . . . . *53Mb 112*
(off Allen Edwards Dr.)
Sudbury Ct. Dr. HA1: Harr 34Ha 66
Sudbury Ct. Rd. HA1: Harr 34Ha 66
Sudbury Cres. BR1: Brom 65Jc 137
HA0: Wemb 36Ka 66
Sudbury Cft. HA0: Wemb 35Ha 66
Sudbury Gdns. CR0: C'don 77Ub 157
Sudbury Golf Course 38La 66
Sudbury Hgts. Av. UB6: G'frd 36Ha 66
Sudbury Hill HA1: Harr 33Ga 66
Sudbury Hill Cl. HA0: Wemb 35Ha 66
Sudbury Ho. SW18 . . . . . 57Db 111
Sudbury Rd. IG11: Bark 36Vc 75
Sudeley St. N1 . . . . . 2C 218 (40Rb 71)
Sudicamps Ct. EN9: Walt A 5Jc 21
Sudlow Rd. SW18 . . . . . 57Cb 111
Sudrey St. SE1 . . . . . 2D 230 (47Sb 91)
Suez Av. UB6: G'frd 40Ha 66
Suez Rd. EN3: Brim 14Ac 34
Suffield Cl. CR2: Sels 84Zb 178
SUFFIELD HATCH 21Ec 52
Suffield Ho. SE17 . . . . . 7C 230
Suffield Rd. E4 . . . . . 20Dc 34
N15 . . . . . 29Vb 51
SE20 . . . . . 68Yb 136
Suffolk Cl. AL2: Lon C 7G 6
SL1: Slou 4C 80
WD6: Bore 15Ta 29
Suffolk Ct. E10 . . . . . 31Cc 72
IG3: Ilf 30Uc 54
RM6: Chad H 30Yc 55
Suffolk Ho. *CR0: C'don* *75Tb 157*
(off George St.)
KT13: Weyb *78S 150*
(off Princes Rd.)
SE20 . . . . . *67Zb 136*
(off Croydon Rd.)
Suffolk La. EC4 . . . . . 4F 225 (45Tb 91)
Suffolk Pk. Rd. E17 . . . . . 28Ac 52
Suffolk Pl. SW1 . . . . . 6E 222 (46Mb 90)
Suffolk Rd. DA1: Dart 58Nd 119
DA12: Grav'nd 8F 122
DA14: Sidc 65Yc 139
E13 . . . . . 41Jc 93
EN3: Pond E 15Xb 33
EN6: Pot B 4Ab 16
HA2: Harr 30Ba 45
IG3: Ilf 30Uc 54
IG11: Bark 38Tc 74
KT4: Wor Pk 75Va 154
N15 . . . . . 29Tb 51
NW10 . . . . . 38Ua 68
RM10: Dag 36Ed 76
SE25 . . . . . 70Vb 135
SW13 . . . . . 52Va 110
Suffolk St. E7 . . . . . 35Jc 73
SW1 . . . . . 5E 222 (45Mb 90)
Suffolk Way RM11: Horn 28Qd 57
TN13: S'oaks 97Ld 203
Sugar Bakers Ct. EC3 . . . . . 3J 225
Sugar Ho. *E1* *44Wb 91*
(off Leman St.)
Sugar Ho. La. E15 . . . . . 40Ec 72
Sugar La. HP1: Hem H 4D 2
Sugar Loaf Wlk. E2 . . . . . 41Yb 92
Sugar Quay EC3 . . . . . 5J 225
Sugar Quay Wlk. EC3 . . . . . 5J 225 (45Ub 91)
Sugden Rd. KT7: T Ditt 74Ka 152
SW11 . . . . . 55Jb 112
Sugden Way IG11: Bark 40Vc 75
Sulby Ho. *SE4* *56Ac 114*
(off Turnham Rd.)
Sulgrave Gdns. W6 . . . . . 47Ya 88
Sulgrave Rd. W6 . . . . . 48Ya 88
Sulina Rd. SW2 . . . . . 59Nb 112
Sulivan Ct. SW6 . . . . . 54Cb 111
Sulivan Ent. Cen. SW6 . . . . . 55Db 111
Sulivan Rd. SW6 . . . . . 55Cb 111
Sulkin Ho. *E2* *41Zb 92*
(off Knottisford St.)
Sullivan Av. E16 . . . . . 43Mc 93
Sullivan Cl. DA1: Dart 58Kd 119
KT8: W Mole 69Da 129
SW11 . . . . . 55Gb 111
UB4: Yead 43Y 85
Sullivan Ct. N16 . . . . . 31Vb 71
SW5 . . . . . *49Cb 89*
(off Earls Ct. Rd.)
Sullivan Cres. UB9: Hare 26M 43
Sullivan Ho. SE11 . . . . . 6J 229
SW1 . . . . . *51Kb 112*
(off Churchill Gdns.)
Sullivan Rd. RM18: Tilb 3C 122
SE11 . . . . . 5A 230 (49Qb 90)
Sullivans Reach KT12: Walt T 73V 150
Sullivan Way WD6: E'tree 16La 28
Sultan Ho. *SE1* *50Wb 91*
(off St James's Rd.)
Sultan Rd. E11 . . . . . 28Kc 53
Sultan St. BR3: Beck 68Zb 136
SE5 . . . . . 52Sb 113
Sultan Ter. N22 . . . . . 26Qb 50
Sumatra Rd. NW6 . . . . . 36Cb 69
Sumburgh Rd. SW12 . . . . . 58Jb 112
Sumburgh Way SL1: Slou 3J 81
Sumeria Ct. *SE16* *49Yb 92*
(off Rotherhithe New Rd.)
Summer Av. KT8: E Mos 71Ga 152
Summer Cl. KT14: Byfl 86P 169
Summer Ct. HP2: Hem H 1M 3
Summercourt Rd. E1 . . . . . 44Yb 92
Summer Crossing KT7: T Ditt 71Ga 152
Summerene Cl. SW16 . . . . . 66Lb 134
Summerfield AL10: Hat 3C 8
BR1: Brom *67Kc 137*
(off Freelands Rd.)
KT21: Asht 91Ma 193
Summerfield Av. NW6 . . . . . 40Ab 68
Summerfield Cl. AL2: Lon C 8G 6
KT15: Add 78H 149
Summerfield La. KT6: Surb 75Ma 153
Summerfield Pl. KT16: Ott 79F 148
Summerfield Rd.
IG10: Lough 16Mc 35
W5 . . . . . 42Ka 86
WD25: Wat 7W 12
Summerfields Av. N12 . . . . . 23Gb 49
Summerfield St. SE12 . . . . . 59Hc 115
Summer Gdns. KT8: E Mos 71Ga 152
Summer Gro. BR4: W W'ck 75Gc 159
WD6: E'tree 16Ma 29
Summerhayes Cl.
GU21: Wok 86A 168
Summerhays KT11: Cobh 85Z 171
Summer Hill BR7: Chst 68Qc 138
WD6: E'tree 15Qa 29
Summerhill Cl. BR6: Orp 76Uc 160
Summerhill Ct. *AL1: St A* *1D 6*
(off Avenue Rd)
Summerhill Gro. EN1: Enf 16Ub 33
Summerhill Rd. DA1: Dart 59Md 119
N15 . . . . . 28Tb 51
Summerhill Vs. *BR7: Chst* *67Qc 138*
(off Susan Wood)
Summerhill Way CR4: Mitc 67Jb 134
Summerhouse Av. TW5: Hest 53Aa 107
Summerhouse Dr. DA2: Wilm 63Fd 140
DA5: Bexl, Dart 63Fd 140
Summerhouse La. UB7: Harm 51M 105
UB9: Hare 24J 43
WD25: A'ham 12Ea 28
Summerhouse Rd. N16 . . . . . 33Ub 71
Summerhouse Way WD5: Ab L 2V 12
Summerland Gdns. N10 . . . . . 27Kb 50
Summerland Grange N10 . . . . . 27Kb 50
Summerlands Av. W3 . . . . . 45Sa 87
Summerlands Lodge BR6: Farnb 77Qc 160
Summerlay Cl. KT20: Tad 92Ab 194
Summerlea SL1: Slou 6F 80
Summerleas HP2: Hem H 2N 3
Summerlee Av. N2 . . . . . 28Hb 49
Summerlee Gdns. N2 . . . . . 28Hb 49
Summerleigh *KT13: Weyb* *79T 150*
(off Gower Rd.)
Summerley St. SW18 . . . . . 61Db 133
Summerly Av. RH2: Reig 5J 207
Summer Pl. WD18: Wat 16V 26
Summer Rd. KT7: T Ditt 71Ga 152
KT8: E Mos 71Fa 152
(not continuous)
Summersby Rd. N6 . . . . . 30Kb 50
Summers Cl. HA9: Wemb 32Ra 67
KT13: Weyb 83Q 170
SM2: Sutt 80Cb 155
Summerskill Cl. SE15 . . . . . 55Xb 113
Summerskille Cl. N9 . . . . . 20Xb 33
Summers La. N12 . . . . . 24Fb 49
Summerstown Pl. SL1: Burn 1A 80
Summers Row N12 . . . . . 23Gb 49
Summers St. EC1 . . . . . 6K 217 (42Qb 90)
SUMMERSTOWN 62Eb 133
Summerstown SW17 . . . . . 62Eb 133
Summers Way AL2: Lon C 9J 7
Summerswood Cl. CR8: Kenley 88Tb 177
Summerswood La. WD6: Bore 6Ua 16
Summerton Way SE28 . . . . . 44Zc 95
Summer Trees TW16: Sun 67X 129
Summerville Gdns. SM1: Sutt 79Bb 155
Summerwood Rd. TW7: Isle 57Ha 108
Summit, The IG10: Lough 11Pc 36
Summit Av. NW9 . . . . . 29Ta 47
Summit Bus. Pk. TW16: Sun 66W 128
Summit Cen. EN6: Pot B 2Ab 16
Summit Cl. HA8: Edg 24Qa 47
N14 . . . . . 19Lb 32
NW9 . . . . . 28Ta 47
Summit Ct. NW2 . . . . . 36Ab 68
Summit Dr. IG8: Wfd G 26Mc 53
Summit Est. N16 . . . . . 31Wb 71
Summit Pl. KT13: Weyb 80Q 150
Summit Rd. E17 . . . . . 28Dc 52
EN6: Pot B 2Ab 16
UB5: N'olt 38Ca 65
Summit Way N14 . . . . . 19Kb 32
SE19 . . . . . 66Ub 135
Sumner Av. SE15 . . . . . 53Vb 113
Sumner Bldgs. SE1 . . . . . 6D 224
Sumner Cl. BR6: Farnb 77Sc 160
KT22: Fet 96Fa 192
Sumner Ct. SW8 . . . . . 52Nb 112
Sumner Est. SE15 . . . . . 52Vb 113
Sumner Gdns. CR0: C'don 74Qb 156
Sumner Ho. *E3* *43Dc 92*
(off Watts Gro.)
Sumner Pl. KT15: Add 78J 149
SW7 . . . . . 6B 226 (49Fb 89)
Sumner Pl. M. SW7 . . . . . 6C 226 (49Fb 89)
Sumner Rd. CR0: C'don 74Qb 156
HA1: Harr 31Ea 66
SE15 . . . . . 51Vb 113
Sumner Rd. Sth. CR0: C'don 74Qb 156
Sumner St. SE1 . . . . . 6C 224 (46Rb 91)
Sumpter Cl. NW3 . . . . . 37Eb 69
Sumpter Yd. AL1: St A 3B 6
Sun All. TW9: Rich 56Na 109
Sunbeam Cres. W10 . . . . . 42Ya 88
Sunbeam Rd. NW10 . . . . . 42Sa 87
SUNBURY 69Y 129
Sunbury Av. NW7 . . . . . 22Ta 47
SW14 . . . . . 56Ta 109
Sunbury Av. Pas. SW14 . . . . . 56Ua 110
Sunbury Bus. Cen. TW16: Sun 67V 128
Sunbury Cl. KT12: Walt T 72W 150
SUNBURY COMMON 66V 128
Sunbury Ct. EN5: Barn 14Ab 30
SL4: Eton 1H 103
Sunbury Ct. Island
TW16: Sun 69Z 129
Sunbury Ct. M. TW16: Sun 68Z 129
Sunbury Ct. Rd. TW16: Sun 68Y 129
Sunbury Cres. TW13: Felt 63V 128
SUNBURY CROSS 66W 128
Sunbury Cross Cen.
TW16: Sun 66V 128
Sunbury Embroidery Gallery, The 69X 129
Sunbury Gdns. NW7 . . . . . 22Ta 47
Sunbury Golf Course 70T 128
Sunbury Ho. E2 . . . . . 4K 219
SE14 . . . . . *51Zb 114*
(off Myers La.)
TW16: Sun *67U 128*
(off Brooklands Cl.)
Sunbury La. KT12: Walt T 72W 150
SW11 . . . . . 53Fb 111
(not continuous)
Sunbury Leisure Cen. 67V 128
Sunburylock Ait
KT12: Walt T 70X 129
Sunbury Pk. Walled Garden 69X 129
Sunbury Rd. SL4: Eton 1H 103
SM3: Cheam 76Za 154
TW13: Felt 62V 128
Sunbury St. SE18 . . . . . 48Pc 94
Sunbury Way TW13: Hanw 64Y 129
Sunbury Workshops E2 . . . . . 4K 219
Sun Cl. SL4: Eton 1H 103
Sun Ct. DA8: Erith 54Hd 118
EC3 . . . . . 3G 225
Suncroft Pl. SE26 . . . . . 62Yb 136
Sundale *AL1: St A* *1D 6*
(off Althorp Rd.)
Sundale Av. CR2: Sels 82Yb 178
Sundeala Cl. *TW16: Sun* *66W 128*
(off Hanworth Rd.)
Sunderland Av. AL1: St A 1E 6
Sunderland Ct. SE22 . . . . . 59Wb 113
TW19: Stanw *58N 105*
(off Whitley Cl.)
Sunderland Est. WD4: K Lan 1R 12
Sunderland Gro. WD25: Wat 6V 12
Sunderland Ho. *W2* *43Cb 89*
(off Westbourne Pk. Rd.)
Sunderland Mt. SE23 . . . . . 61Zb 136
Sunderland Point E16 . . . . . 46Sc 94
Sunderland Rd. SE23 . . . . . 60Zb 114
W5 . . . . . 48Ma 87
Sunderland Ter. W2 . . . . . 44Db 89
Sunderland Way E12 . . . . . 33Mc 73
Sundew Av. W12 . . . . . 45Wa 88
Sundew Cl. GU18: Light 3B 166
W12 . . . . . 45Wa 88
Sundew Ct. *HA0: Wemb* *40Na 67*
(off Elmore Cl.)
RM17: Grays 51Fe 121
Sundew Rd. HP1: Hem H 3G 2
Sundial Av. SE25 . . . . . 69Vb 135
Sundial Ct. EC1 . . . . . 7E 218
Sundon Cres. GU25: Vir W 1M 147
Sundorne Rd. SE7 . . . . . 50Lc 93
Sundown Av. CR2: Sande 83Vb 177
Sundown Rd. TW15: Ashf 64S 128
Sundra Wlk. E1 . . . . . 42Zb 92
SUNDRIDGE
BR1 . . . . . 65Kc 137
TN14 . . . . . 96Ad 201
Sundridge Av. BR1: Brom 67Mc 137
BR7: Chst 67Mc 137
DA16: Well 54Tc 116
Sundridge Cl. DA1: Dart 58Qd 119
Sundridge Hill
TN14: Knock, Sund 90Yc 181
Sundridge Ho. *E9* *38Zb 72*
(off Church Cres.)
Sundridge La. TN14: Knock 89Xc 181
Sundridge Pde. BR1: Brom 66Kc 137
SUNDRIDGE PARK 66Kc 137
Sundridge Pk. Golf Course 65Kc 137
Sundridge Pl. CR0: C'don 74Wb 157
Sundridge Rd. CR0: C'don 73Vb 157
GU22: Wok 91C 188
TN14: Dun G 92Cd 202
Sunfields Pl. SE3 . . . . . 52Kc 115
Sunflower Ct. NW2 . . . . . 33Bb 69
Sunflower Way RM3: Hrld W 25Md 57
Sungate Cotts. RM5: Col R 25Bd 55
Sun Hill DA3: Fawk 76Wd 164
GU22: Wok 3L 187
SUN-IN-THE-SANDS 52Kc 115
Sunken Rd. CR0: C'don 78Yb 158
Sunkist Way SM6: Wall 81Nb 176
Sunland Av. DA6: Bex 56Ad 117
Sun La. DA12: Grav'nd 1E 144
SE3 . . . . . 52Kc 115
Sunleigh Rd. HA0: Wemb 39Na 67
Sunley Gdns. UB6: G'frd 39Ja 66
Sun Life Trad. Est. TW14: Felt 55W 106
Sunlight Cl. SW19 . . . . . 65Eb 133
Sunlight Sq. E2 . . . . . 41Xb 91
Sunmead Cl. KT22: Fet 94Ha 192
Sunmead Rd. HP2: Hem H 1M 3
TW16: Sun 69W 128
Sunna Gdns. TW16: Sun 68X 129
Sunna Lodge TW16: Sun 66V 128
Sunniholme Ct. *CR2: S Croy* *78Sb 157*
(off Warham Rd.)
Sunning Av. SL5: S'dale 3C 146
SUNNINGDALE 1E 146
Sunningdale N14 . . . . . 22Mb 50
W13 . . . . . *43Ka 86*
(off Hardwick Grn.)
Sunningdale Av. HA4: Ruis 32Y 65
IG11: Bark 39Tc 74
RM13: Rain 42Kd 97
TW13: Hanw 61Aa 129
W3 . . . . . 45Ua 88
Sunningdale Cl. E6 . . . . . 41Pc 94
HA7: Stan 23Ja 46
KT6: Surb 75Na 153
SE16 . . . . . 50Xb 91
SE28 . . . . . 44Ad 95
Sunningdale Ct. *TW7: Isle* *58Fa 108*
(off Whitton Dene)
UB1: S'hall *44Ea 86*
(off Fleming Rd.)
Sunningdale Gdns. NW9 . . . . . 29Sa 47
W8 . . . . . *48Cb 89*
(off Stratford Rd.)
Sunningdale Golf Course 4E 146
Sunningdale Ladies Golf Course 4E 146
Sunningdale Lodge *HA8: Edg* *22Pa 47*
(off Stonegrove)
Sunningdale Rd. BR1: Brom 70Nc 138
RM13: Rain 38Jd 76
SM1: Sutt 76Bb 155
Sunningfields Cres. NW4 . . . . . 26Xa 48
Sunningfields Rd. NW4 . . . . . 26Xa 48
SUNNINGHILL 1B 146
Sunninghill DA11: Nflt 1A 144
Sunninghill Cl. SL5: S'hill 10B 124
Sunninghill Ct. SL5: S'hill 10B 124
W3 . . . . . 47Sa 87
SUNNINGHILL PARK 7A 124
Sunninghill Rd. SE13 . . . . . 54Dc 114
SL4: Wink 4B 124
SL5: Asc 4B 124
SL5: S'hill 1B 146
Sunnings La. RM14: Upm 36Sd 78
Sunningvale Av. TN16: Big H 87Lc 179
Sunningvale Cl. TN16: Big H 88Mc 179
Sunny Bank SE25 . . . . . 69Wb 135
Sunnybank CR6: W'ham 89Ac 178
KT18: Eps 88Sa 173
Sunnybank Rd. EN6: Pot B 5Cb 17
Sunnybank Vs. RH1: Blet 4M 209
Sunny Cres. NW10 . . . . . 38Sa 67
Sunnycroft Gdns. RM14: Upm 31Vd 78
Sunnycroft Rd. SE25 . . . . . 69Wb 135
TW3: Houn 54Da 107
UB1: S'hall 43Ca 85
Sunnydale BR6: Farnb 75Qc 160
Sunnydale Gdns. NW7 . . . . . 23Ta 47
Sunnydale Rd. SE12 . . . . . 57Kc 115
Sunnydell AL2: Chis G 8P 5
Sunnydene Av. E4 . . . . . 22Fc 53
HA4: Ruis 32W 64
Sunnydene Cl. RM3: Hrld W 24Pd 57
Sunnydene Gdns. HA0: Wemb 37Ka 66
Sunnydene Rd. CR8: Purl 85Rb 177
Sunnydene St. SE26 . . . . . 63Ac 136
Sunnyfield NW7 . . . . . 21Va 48
Sunnyfield Rd. BR7: Chst 69Wc 139
Sunny Gdns. Pde. NW4 . . . . . 26Xa 48
Sunny Gdns. Rd. NW4 . . . . . 26Xa 48
Sunny Hill NW4 . . . . . 27Xa 48

Sunnyhill Cl. E5 35Ac 72
Sunnyhill Rd. HP1: Hem H 2K 3
SW16 63Nb 134
WD3: W Hyd 23F 42
Sunnyhurst Cl. SM1: Sutt 76Cb 155
Sunnymead Av. CR4: Mitc 69Mb 134
Sunnymead Rd. NW9 31Ta 67
SW15 57Xa 110
SUNNYMEADS 56A 104
Sunnymede IG7: Chig 20Xc 37
Sunnymede Av. KT19: Ewe 81Ua 174
SM5: Cars 83Fb 175
Sunnymede Dr. IG2: Ilf 29Rc 54
IG6: Ilf 29Rc 54
Sunny M. NW1 38Jb 70
RM5: Col R 24Ed 56
Sunny Nook Gdns. CR2: S Croy 79Tb 157
Sunny Pl. NW4 28Ya 48
Sunny Ri. CR3: Cat'm 96Tb 197
Sunny Rd., The EN3: Enf H 11Zb 34
Sunnyside GU21: Knap 1F 186
KT12: Walt T 71Y 151
NW2 34Bb 69
SE6 59Bc 114
(off Blythe Hill)
SW19 65Ab 132
Sunnyside Dr. E4 17Ec 34
Sunnyside Gdns. RM14: Upm 34Sd 78
Sunnyside Ho's. NW2 34Bb 69
(off Sunnyside)
Sunnyside Pas. SW19 65Ab 132
Sunnyside Pl. SW19 65Ab 132
Sunnyside Rd. CM16: Epp 5Vc 23
E10 32Cc 72
IG1: Ilf 34Sc 74
N19 31Mb 70
TW11: Tedd 63Fa 130
W5 46Ma 87
Sunnyside Rd. E. N9 20Wb 33
Sunnyside Rd. Nth. N9 20Vb 33
Sunnyside Rd. Sth. N9 20Vb 33
Sunnyside Ter. NW9 27Ta 47
Sunny Vw. NW9 29Ta 47
Sunny Way N12 24Gb 49
Sun Pas. SE16 48Wb 91
(off Old Jamaica Rd.)
SL4: Wind 3H 103
Sunray Av. BR2: Brom 72Nc 160
CM13: Hut 16Fe 41
KT5: Surb 75Ra 153
SE24 56Tb 113
UB7: W Dray 47M 83
Sunrise Av. RM12: Horn 34Ld 77
Sunrise Cl. TW13: Hanw 62Ba 129
Sunrise Cotts. TN13: S'oaks 94Hd 202
Sunrise Cres. HP3: Hem H 5N 3
Sunrise Vw. NW7 23Va 48
Sun Rd. DA10: Swans 58Be 121
W14 50Bb 89
Sunset Av. E4 18Dc 34
IG8: Wfd G 21Hc 53
Sunset Cl. DA8: Erith 52Kd 119
Sunset Ct. IG8: Wfd G 24Lc 53
Sunset Dr. RM4: Have B 22Kd 57
Sunset Gdns. SE25 68Vb 135
Sunset Lodge NW10 38Ya 68
(off Hanover Rd.)
Sunset Rd. SE5 56Sb 113
SE28 46Wc 95
SW19 64Xa 132
Sunset Vw. EN5: Barn 12Ab 30
Sunshine Way CR4: Mitc 68Hb 133
Sun Sq. HP1: Hem H 1M 3
(off Chapel St.)
Sunstone Gro. RH1: Mers 1D 208
Sun St. EC2 7G 219 (43Tb 91)
(Finsbury Sq.)
EC2 7H 219 (43Ub 91)
(Primrose St.)
EN9: Walt A 5Ec 20
Sun St. Pas. EC2 1H 225 (43Ub 91)
Sun Wlk. E1 45Vb 91
Sunwell Cl. SE15 53Xb 113
Sun Wharf SE8 52Dc 114
(off Creekside)
Superior Dr. BR6: Chels 79Vc 161
Supreme Court
Westminster 2F 229 (47Nb 90)
SURBITON 72Ma 153
Surbiton Ct. KT6: Surb 72La 152
Surbiton Cres. KT1: King T 70Na 131
Surbiton Golf Course 77Ka 152
Surbiton Hall Cl. KT1: King T 70Na 131
Surbiton Hill Pk. KT5: Surb 71Pa 153
Surbiton Hill Rd. KT6: Surb 70Na 131
Surbiton Pde. KT6: Surb 72Na 153
Surbiton Raceway 76Ta 153
Surbiton Rd. KT1: King T 70Ma 131
Surlingham Cl. SE28 45Zc 95
Surly Hall Wlk. SL4: Wind 3D 102
Surma Cl. E1 42Xb 91
Surman Cres. CM13: Hut 17Ee 41
Surmans Cl. RM9: Dag 39Yc 75
Surrendale Pl. W9 42Cb 89
Surrey Av. SL2: Slou 3G 80
Surrey Canal Rd. SE14 51Yb 114
SE15 51Yb 114
Surrey Cl. N3 27Ab 48
TN15: W King 80Ud 164
Surrey County Cricket Club 51Pb 112
Surrey Cres. W4 50Qa 87
Surrey Docks Farm 47Bc 92
Surrey Docks Watersports Cen. 48Ac 92
Surrey Downs Golf Course 94Eb 195
Surrey Dr. RM11: Horn 28Qd 57
Surrey Gdns. KT24: Eff J 94W 190
N4 30Sb 51
Surrey Gro. SE17 7H 231 (50Ub 91)
SM1: Sutt 76Fb 155
Surrey History Cen. 10P 167
Surrey Ho. SE16 46Zb 92
(off Rotherhithe St.)
Surrey La. SW11 53Gb 111
Surrey La. Est. SW11 53Gb 111
Surrey Lodge KT12: Hers 78X 151
(off Queens Rd.)
Surrey M. SE27 63Ub 135
Surrey Mt. SE23 60Xb 113
Surrey National Golf Course 95Rb 197
Surrey Quays Rd. SE16 48Yb 92
Surrey Quays Shop. Cen. SE16 48Zb 92
Surrey Rd. BR4: W W'ck 74Dc 158
HA1: Harr 29Ea 46
IG11: Bark 38Uc 74
Surrey Rd. RM10: Dag 36Dd 76
SE15 57Zb 114
Surrey Row SE1 1B 230 (47Rb 91)
Surrey Sq. SE17 7H 231 (50Ub 91)
Surrey Steps WC2 4J 223
Surrey St. CR0: C'don 75Sb 157
E13 41Kc 93
WC2 4J 223 (45Pb 90)
Surrey Ter. SE17 7J 231 (50Ub 91)
Surrey Towers KT15: Add 78L 149
(off Bush Cl.)
Surrey Water Rd. SE16 46Zb 92
Surridge Cl. RM13: Rain 41Ld 97
Surridge Ct. SW9 54Nb 112
(off Clapham Rd.)
Surridge Gdns. SE19 65Tb 135
Surr St. N7 36Nb 70
Sury Basin KT2: King T 67Na 131
Susan Cl. RM7: Mawney 27Ed 56
Susan Constant Ct. E14 45Fc 93
(off Newport Av.)
Susan Edwards Ho. SL9: Chal P 21A 42
(off Micholls Av.)
Susan Lawrence Ho. E3 40Ac 72
(off Zealand Rd.)
E12 35Qc 74
(off Walton Rd.)
Susannah St. E14 44Dc 92
Susan Rd. SE3 54Kc 115
Susan Wood BR7: Chst 67Qc 138
Sussex Av. RM3: Hrld W 24Pd 57
TW7: Isle 55Ga 108
Sussex Cl. GU21: Knap 10G 166
IG4: Ilf 29Pc 54
KT3: N Mald 70Ua 132
N19 33Nb 70
RH2: Reig 7M 207
SL1: Slou 7M 81
TN15: W King 80Ud 164
TW1: Twick 58Ka 108
Sussex Ct. GU21: Knap 9G 166
KT15: Add 78L 149
SE10 51Ec 114
(off Roan St.)
W2 3B 220
Sussex Cres. UB5: N'olt 37Ca 65
Sussex Gdns. KT9: Chess 79Ma 153
N4 29Sb 51
N6 29Hb 49
W2 4B 220 (45Fb 89)
Sussex Ga. N6 29Hb 49
Sussex Ho. NW1 1D 216
SL2: Farn C 7G 60
Sussex Keep SL1: Slou 7M 81
Sussex Lodge W2 3C 220
Sussex Mans. SW7 6B 226
WC2 4G 223
Sussex M. SE6 59Cc 114
Sussex M. E. W2 3C 220
Sussex M. W. W2 4C 220 (45Fb 89)
Sussex Pl. GU21: Knap 10G 166
KT3: N Mald 70Ua 132
NW1 5F 215 (42Hb 89)
SL1: Slou 7L 81
W2 3C 220 (44Fb 89)
W6 50Ya 88
Sussex Ring N12 22Cb 49
Sussex Rd. BR4: W W'ck 74Dc 158
BR5: Orp 72Yc 161
CM14: W'ley 21Xd 58
CR2: S Croy 79Tb 157
CR4: Mitc 71Nb 156
DA1: Dart 59Od 119
DA8: Erith 52Dd 118
DA14: Sidc 64Xc 139
E6 39Qc 74
GU21: Knap 10G 166
HA1: Harr 29Ea 46
KT3: N Mald 70Ua 132
SM5: Cars 79Hb 155
UB2: S'hall 48Z 85
UB10: Ick 35S 64
WD24: Wat 9W 12
Sussex Sq. W2 4C 220 (45Fb 89)
Sussex St. E13 41Kc 93
SW1 7A 228 (50Kb 90)
Sussex Ter. RM19: Purf 50Rd 97
SE20 66Yb 136
(off Graveney Gro.)
Sussex Way EN4: Cockf 15Kb 32
N7 33Nb 70
N19 32Mb 70
(not continuous)
Sutcliffe Cl. NW11 29Db 49
WD23: Bush 14Ea 28
Sutcliffe Ho. UB3: Hayes 44W 84
Sutcliffe Pk. Athletics Track 57Lc 115
Sutcliffe Rd. DA16: Well 54Yc 117
SE18 51Uc 116
Sutherland Av. BR5: St M Cry 72Vc 161
DA16: Well 56Uc 116
EN6: Cuff 1Mb 18
GU4: Jac W 100A 188
TN16: Big H 89Mc 179
TW16: Sun 68V 128
UB3: Hayes 49W 84
W9 4A 214 (42Cb 89)
W13 44Ka 86
Sutherland Cl. DA9: Ghithe 57Vd 120
DA12: Grav'nd 1K 145
EN5: Barn 14Ab 30
Sutherland Ct. N16 34Tb 71
NW9 29Ra 47
W9 42Cb 89
(off Marylands Rd.)
WD18: Wat 17S 26
Sutherland Dr. SW19 67Fb 133
Sutherland Gdns. KT4: Wor Pk 74Xa 154
SW14 55Ua 110
TW16: Sun 68V 128
Sutherland Grange SL4: Wind 2B 102
Sutherland Gro. SW18 58Ab 110
TW11: Tedd 64Ga 130
Sutherland Ho. IG8: Wfd G 24Qc 54
W8 48Db 89
Sutherland Pl. W2 44Cb 89
Sutherland Rd. CR0: C'don 73Qb 156
DA17: Belv 48Cd 96
E3 40Bc 72
E17 26Zb 52
EN3: Pond E 16Zb 34
N9 18Xb 33
N17 24Wb 51
UB1: S'hall 44Ba 85
Sutherland Rd. W4 51Ua 110
W13 44Ja 86
Sutherland Rd. Path E17 26Zb 52
Sutherland Row SW1 7A 228 (50Kb 90)
Sutherland Sq. SE17 50Sb 91
Sutherland St. SW1 7K 227 (50Kb 90)
Sutherland Wlk.
SE17 7E 230 (50Sb 91)
Sutherland Way EN6: Cuff 1Mb 18
Sutlej Rd. SE7 52Lc 115
Sutterton St. N7 37Pb 70
SUTTON
SL3 50E 82
SM1 78Db 155
Sutton Arena Leisure Cen. 73Eb 155
SUTTON AT HONE 66Rd 141
Sutton Av. GU21: Wok 1J 187
SL3: L'ly 7N 81
Sutton Cl. BR3: Beck 67Dc 136
HA5: Eastc 29W 44
IG10: Lough 17Nc 36
W4 51Sa 109
(off Sutton La. Sth.)
Sutton Comn. Rd. SM1: Sutt 73Bb 155
SM3: Sutt 73Bb 155
Sutton Ct. KT8: W Mole 71Ba 151
SE19 66Vb 135
SM2: Sutt 79Eb 155
W4 51Sa 109
W5 46Na 87
Sutton Ct. Rd. E13 41Lc 93
SM1: Sutt 79Eb 155
UB10: Hil 39R 64
W4 52Sa 109
Sutton Cres. EN5: Barn 15Za 30
Sutton Dene TW3: Houn 53Da 107
Sutton Ecology Cen. 77Hb 155
Sutton Est. EC1 4G 219
W10 43Ya 88
Sutton Estate, The N1 38Rb 71
SW3 7E 226 (50Gb 89)
Sutton Gdns. CR0: C'don 71Vb 157
IG11: Bark 39Uc 74
RH1: Mers 1D 208
SUTTON GREEN 98B 188
Sutton Grn. IG11: Bark 39Uc 74
(off Sutton Rd.)
Sutton Green Golf Course 95A 188
Sutton Grn. Rd.
GU4: Sut G 98A 188
Sutton Gro. SM1: Sutt 77Fb 155
Sutton Hall Rd. TW5: Hest 52Ca 107
Sutton Hgts. SM2: Sutt 80Fb 155
Sutton La. EC1 6C 218
SL3: L'ly 51D 104
SM2: Sutt 83Db 175
SM7: Bans 83Db 175
TW3: Houn 55Ba 107
Sutton La. Nth. W4 50Sa 87
Sutton La. Sth. W4 51Sa 109
Sutton Pde. NW4 28Ya 48
(off Church Rd.)
SUTTON PARK 98B 188
Sutton Pk. Rd. SM1: Sutt 79Db 155
Sutton Path WD6: Bore 13Qa 29
Sutton Pl. E9 36Yb 72
SL3: L'ly 51D 104
Sutton Rd. AL1: St A 3F 6
E13 42Hc 93
E17 25Zb 52
IG11: Bark 40Uc 74
N10 25Jb 50
TW5: Hest 53Ca 107
WD17: Wat 13Y 27
(not continuous)
Sutton Row W1 2E 222 (44Mb 90)
Suttons Av. RM12: Horn 34Ld 77
Suttons Bus. Pk.
RM13: Rain 41Fd 96
Suttons Gdns. RM12: Horn 34Md 77
Suttons La. RM12: Horn 36Md 77
Sutton Sq. E9 36Yb 72
TW5: Hest 53Ba 107
Sutton St. E1 45Yb 92
Sutton Superbowl 78Db 155
Sutton's Way EC1 6E 218
Sutton Tennis Academy 74Db 155
Sutton United FC 77Cb 155
Sutton Wlk. SE1 7J 223 (46Pb 90)
Sutton Way TW5: Hest 53Ba 107
W10 42Ya 88
SW1 Gallery 3B 228 (48Lb 90)
Swabey Rd. SL3: L'ly 49C 82
Swaby Rd. SW18 60Eb 111
Swaffam Ct. RM6: Chad H 30Yc 55
Swaffham Way N22 24Rb 51
Swaffield Rd. SW18 59Db 111
TN13: S'oaks 94Ld 203
Swail Ho. KT18: Eps 85Ta 173
Swain Cl. SW16 65Kb 134
Swain Rd. CR7: Thor H 71Sb 157
Swains Cl. UB7: W Dray 47N 83
Swains La. N6 32Jb 70
Swainson Rd. W3 47Va 88
Swains Rd. SW17 66Hb 133
Swain St. NW8 5D 214 (42Gb 89)
Swaisland Dr. DA1: Cray 57Hd 118
Swaisland Rd. DA1: Dart 57Kd 119
Swakeleys Dr. UB10: Ick 35Q 64
Swakeleys Rd. UB10: Ick 35N 63
SWAKELEYS RDBT. 35N 63
Swakeleys Rd. DA17: Belv 50Dd 96
Swale Cl. RM15: Avel 44Sd 98
Swaledale Cl. N11 23Jb 50
Swaledale Rd. DA2: Dart 60Sd 120
Swale Rd. DA1: Cray 56Jd 118
Swaley's Way
RM15: S Ock 44Zd 99
Swallands Rd. SE6 62Cc 136
(not continuous)
Swallow Cl. DA8: Erith 53Gd 118
DA9: Ghithe 57Vd 120
RM16: Chaf H 49Yd 98
SE14 53Zb 114
TW18: Staines 63H 127
WD3: Rick 17L 25
WD23: Bush 18Ea 28
Swallow Ct. EN3: Enf W 9Yb 20
HA4: Ruis 32Y 65
IG2: Ilf 29Rc 54
SE1 2E 230
SE12 59Jc 115
W9 43Cb 89
(off Admiral Wlk.)
Swallowdale CR2: Sels 81Zb 178
SL0: Iver H 41F 82
Swallow Dr. NW10 37Ta 67
UB5: N'olt 40Ca 65
Swallowfield NW1 4A 216
TW20: Eng G 5M 125
Swallowfield Rd. SE7 50Kc 93
Swallow Flds. SL0: Iver 42F 82
Swallowfields DA11: Nflt 2A 144
Swallowfield Way
UB3: Hayes 47T 84
Swallow Gdns. AL10: Hat 2C 8
SW16 64Mb 134
Swallow Ho. NW8 1D 214
Swallow La. AL1: St A 5F 6
Swallow Pk. KT6: Surb 76Pa 153
Swallow Pas. W1 3B 222
Swallow Pl. E14 44Bc 92
(off Newell St.)
W1 3A 222 (44Kb 90)
Swallow Ri. GU21: Knap 9G 166
Swallows, The UB9: Den 29H 43
(off Patrons Way W.)
Swallows Ct. DA1: Dart 55Pd 119
Swallows Oak WD5: Ab L 3V 12
Swallow St. E6 43Nc 94
SL0: Iver, Iver H 41F 82
W1 5C 222 (45Lb 90)
Swallowtail Cl. BR5: St P 70Zc 139
Swallow Wlk. RM12: Horn 37Kd 77
SWAN, THE 75Ec 158
Swanage Ct. N1 38Ub 71
(off Hertford Rd.)
Swanage Ho. SW8 52Pb 112
(off Dorset Rd.)
Swanage Rd. E4 24Ec 52
SW18 58Eb 111
Swanage Waye UB4: Yead 44Y 85
Swan & Pike Rd. EN3: Enf L 10Cc 20
Swan App. E6 43Nc 94
Swan Av. RM14: Upm 32Vd 78
Swanbourne SE17 6D 230
Swanbourne Dr. RM12: Horn 36Ld 77
Swanbourne Ho. NW8 5D 214
Swanbridge Rd. DA7: Bex 53Cd 118
Swan Bus. Pk. DA1: Dart 56Md 119
Swan Centre, The KT22: Lea 93Ka 192
Swan Cen., The SW17 62Db 133
Swan Cl. BR5: St P 69Wc 139
CR0: C'don 73Ub 157
E17 25Ac 52
TW13: Hanw 63Aa 129
WD3: Rick 17M 25
Swan Ct. E1 45Wb 91
(off Star Pl.)
E14 44Bc 92
(off Agnes St.)
HA4: Ruis 31T 64
HP1: Hem H 3L 3
KT22: Lea 94Ka 192
SW3 50Gb 89
SW6 52Cb 111
(off Fulham Rd.)
TW7: Isle 55Ka 108
(off Swan St.)
Swandon Way SW18 56Db 111
Swandrift TW18: Staines 66H 127
Swan Dr. NW9 26Ua 48
Swan Fld. Ho. WD3: Rick 17M 25
Swanfield Rd. EN8: Walt C 5Ac 20
Swanfield St. E2 4K 219 (41Vb 91)
Swan Ho. E15 38Fc 73
(off Broadway)
EN3: Pond E 15Yb 34
N1 38Tb 71
(off Oakley Rd.)
Swan Island TW1: Twick 62Ja 130
Swanland Rd. AL9: N Mym 7D 8
EN6: S Mim 6Xa 16
Swan La. CM14: B'wood 19Yd 40
DA1: Dart 59Hd 118
EC4 5F 225 (45Tb 91)
IG10: Lough 17Lc 35
N20 20Eb 31
SWANLEY 69Gd 140
SWANLEY BAR 10K 9
Swanley Bar La. EN6: Pot B 10K 9
Swanley By-Pass BR8: Swan 67Dd 140
DA14: Sidc 67Dd 140
Swanley Cen. BR8: Swan 69Gd 140
Swanley Ct. WD24: Wat 9Y 13
Swanley Cres. EN6: Pot B 1Db 17
Swanley Ho. SE17 7J 231
SWANLEY INTERCHANGE 71Kd 163
Swanley La. BR8: Swan 69Hd 140
Swanley Rd. DA16: Well 53Yc 117
SWANLEY VILLAGE 67Kd 141
Swanley Village Rd. BR8: Swan 67Kd 141
Swan Mead HP3: Hem H 7P 3
SE1 4H 231 (48Ub 91)
Swan M. CR4: Mitc 67Hb 133
RM7: Mawney 28Dd 56
SW6 53Bb 111
SW9 54Pb 112
Swann Ct. SL1: Slou 8J 81
TW7: Isle 55Ja 108
(off South St.)
Swanne Ho. SE10 52Ec 114
(off Gloucester Cir.)
Swanns Mdw. KT23: Bookh 98Ca 191
Swan Paddock CM14: B'wood 19Yd 40
Swan Pas. E1 45Vb 91
(off Cartwright St.)
Swan Path KT1: King T 69Pa 131
Swan Pl. SW13 54Va 110
TN16: Westrm 99Tc 200
Swan Rd. EN8: Walt C 6Ac 20
SE16 47Yb 92
SE18 48Mc 93
SL0: Iver 44H 83
TW13: Hanw 64Aa 129
UB1: S'hall 44Da 85
UB7: W Dray 47M 83
Swans, The UB9: Den 29H 43
Swans Cl. AL4: St A 3J 7
SWANSCOMBE 57Be 121
Swanscombe Bus. Cen.
DA10: Swans 56Ae 121
Swanscombe Cen. 58Zd 121
Swanscombe Heritage Pk. 58Zd 121
Swanscombe Ho. W11 46Za 88
(off St Ann's Rd.)
Swanscombe Rd. W4 50Ua 88
W11 46Za 88
Swanscombe Skull Site
National Nature Reserve 58Zd 121
Swanscombe St. DA10: Swans 59Ae 121
Swans Ct. EN8: Walt C 6Ac 20
Swansea Cl. RM5: Col R 24Fd 56
Swansea Ct. E16 46Rc 94
(off Fishguard Way)
Swansea Rd. EN3: Pond E 14Yb 34
TW14: Felt 58S 106
Swanshope IG10: Lough 12Rc 36
Swansland Gdns. E17 25Ac 52
Swansmere Cl. KT12: Walt T 74Y 151
Swanston Ho. WD18: Wat 14W 26
(off Whippendell Rd.)
Swanston Path WD19: Wat 20Y 27
Swan St. SE1 3E 230 (48Sb 91)
TW7: Isle 55Ka 108
Swansway, The KT13: Weyb 76Q 150
Swan Ter. SL4: Wind 2F 102
Swanton Gdns. SW19 60Za 110
Swanton La. TN11: Roug 100Fe 205
Swanton Rd. DA8: Erith 52Dd 118
Swan Wlk. RM1: Rom 29Gd 56
SW3 51Hb 111
TW17: Shep 73U 150
Swan Way EN3: Enf H 12Zb 34
Swan Wharf Bus. Cen. UB8: Uxb 40K 63
Swanwick Cl. SW15 59Va 110
Swanworth La. RH5: Mick 100Ja 192
Swan Yd. N1 37Rb 71
Swanzy Rd. TN14: S'oaks 92Ld 203
Sward Rd. BR5: St M Cry 72Wc 161
Swathling Ho. SW15 58Va 110
(off Tunworth Cres.)
Swaton Rd. E3 42Cc 92
Swaylands Rd. DA17: Belv 51Cd 118
Swaythling Cl. N18 21Xb 51
Swedeland Ct. E1 1J 225
Swedenborg Gdns. E1 45Xb 91
Sweden Ga. SE16 48Ac 92
Swedish Quays SE16 48Ac 92
(not continuous)
Sweeney Cres. SE1 2K 231 (47Vb 91)
Sweeps Ditch Cl. TW18: Staines 66J 127
Sweeps La. BR5: St M Cry 71Zc 161
TW20: Egh 64B 126
Sweet Briar Grn. N9 20Vb 33
Sweet Briar Gro. N9 20Vb 33
Sweet Briar La. KT18: Eps 86Ta 173
Sweet Briar Wlk. N18 21Vb 51
Sweetcroft La. UB10: Hil 38P 63
Sweetland Ct. RM8: Dag 37Xc 75
Sweetmans Av. HA5: Pinn 27Z 45
Sweets Way N20 19Fb 31
Swell Ct. E17 30Cc 52
Swetenham Wlk. SE18 50Sc 94
Swete St. E13 40Jc 73
Sweyne Rd. DA10: Swans 58Ae 121
Sweyn Pl. SE3 54Jc 115
Swievelands Rd. TN16: Big H 91Kc 199
Swift Cen. CR0: Wadd 80Pb 156
Swift Cl. E17 24Ac 52
HA2: Harr 33Da 65
RM14: Upm 32Ud 78
SE28 45Xc 95
SL1: Slou 5D 80
UB3: Hayes 44V 84
Swift Ct. SM2: Sutt 80Db 155
TN15: Seal 93Qd 203
Swift Ho. E3 39Bc 72
(off Old Ford Rd.)
Swift Lodge W9 43Cb 89
(off Admiral Wlk.)
Swift Rd. TW13: Hanw 62Aa 129
UB2: S'hall 48Ca 85
Swiftsden Way BR1: Brom 65Gc 137
Swift St. SW6 53Bb 111
Swiftsure Rd. RM16: Chaf H 49Yd 98
Swiller's La. DA12: Shorne 4N 145
SWILLET, THE 16D 24
Swinbrook Rd. W10 43Ab 88
Swinburne Ct. SE5 56Tb 113
(off Basingdon Way)
Swinburne Cres. CR0: C'don 72Yb 158
Swinburne Gdns. RM18: Tilb 4D 122
Swinburne Ho. E2 41Yb 92
(off Roman Rd.)
Swinburne Rd. SW15 56Wa 110
Swinderby Rd. HA0: Wemb 37Na 67
Swindon Cl. IG3: Ilf 33Uc 74
RM3: Rom 22Pd 57
Swindon Gdns. RM3: Rom 22Pd 57
Swindon La. RM3: Rom 22Pd 57
Swindon Rd. TW6: H'row A 57S 106
Swindon St. W12 46Xa 88
Swinfield Cl. TW13: Hanw 62Aa 129
Swinford Gdns. SW9 55Rb 113
Swingate La. SE18 51Uc 116
Swingfield Ho. E9 39Yb 72
(off Templecombe Rd.)
Swing Ga. La. HP4: Berk 3A 2
Swinley Ho. NW1 3A 216
Swinnerton St. E9 36Ac 72
Swinson Ho. N11 22Lb 50
Swinton Cl. HA9: Wemb 32Ra 67
Swinton Pl. WC1 3H 217 (41Pb 90)
Swinton St. WC1 3H 217 (41Pb 90)
Swires Shaw BR2: Kes 77Mc 159
Swiss Av. WD18: Wat 14U 26
Swiss Cl. WD18: Wat 13U 26
SWISS COTTAGE 38Fb 69
Swiss Cottage Sports Cen. 38Fb 69
Swiss Ct. WC2 5E 222
Swiss Ter. NW6 38Fb 69
Switch Ho. E14 45Fc 93
Swithland Gdns. SE9 63Qc 138
Swyncombe Av. W5 49Ka 86
Swynford Gdns. NW4 28Wa 48
Sybil M. N4 30Rb 51
Sybil Phoenix Cl. SE8 50Zb 92
Sybil Thorndike Casson Ho.
SW5 50Cb 89
(off Kramer M.)
Sybourn St. E17 31Bc 72
Sycamore App. WD3: Crox G 15S 26
Sycamore Av. AL10: Hat 1C 8
DA15: Sidc 58Vc 117
E3 39Bc 72
RM14: Upm 34Qd 77
UB3: Hayes 45U 84
W5 48Ma 87
Sycamore Cl. CR2: S Croy 78Ub 157
DA12: Grav'nd 9F 122
E16 42Gc 93

Vanguard Ct. SE5 ... 53Ub 113
Vanguard Ho. E8 ... 38Xb 71
Vanguard St. SE8 ... 53Cc 114
Vanguard Way SM6: Wall ... 80Nb 156
TW6: H'row A ... 54U 106
Vanilla & Sesame Ct. SE1 ... 1K 231
Vanneck Sq. SW15 ... 57Wa 110
Vanners Pde. KT14: Byfl ... 85N 169
Vanoc Gdns. BR1: Brom ... 63Jc 137
Vanquish Cl. TW2: Whitt ... 59Ca 107
Vanquisher Wlk.
DA12: Grav'nd ... 2H 145
Vanryne Ho. IG10: Lough ... 13Nc 36
Vansittart Est. SL4: Wind ... 2G 102
Vansittart Rd. E7 ... 35Hc 73
SL4: Wind ... 3F 102
Vansittart St. SE14 ... 52Ac 114
Vanstone Ct. *N7* ... *37Qb 70*
(off Blackthorn Av.)
Vanston Pl. SW6 ... 52Cb 111
Vantage Bldg. *UB3: Hayes* ... *48V 84*
(off Station App.)
Vantage Ct. GU21: Wok ... 9P 167
UB3: Harl ... 52U 106
Vantage M. *E14* ... *46Ec 92*
(off Coldharbour)
HA6: Nwood ... 23T 44
Vantage Pl. TW14: Felt ... 58W 106
W8 ... 48Cb 89
Vantage Point CR2: Sande ... 81Tb 177
DA9: Ghithe ... 59Wd 120
EN5: Barn ... *14Bb 31*
(off Victors Way)
Vantage Rd. SL1: Slou ... 6F 80
Vantage W. TW8: Bford ... 49Pa 87
Vantrey Ho. SE11 ... 6K 229
Vant Rd. SW17 ... 64Hb 133
Vapery La. GU24: Pirb ... 3B 186
Varcoe Gdns. UB3: Hayes ... 44T 84
Varcoe Rd. SE16 ... 50Xb 91
Vardens Rd. SW11 ... 56Fb 111
Varden St. E1 ... 44Xb 91
Vardon Cl. W3 ... 44Ta 87
Vardon Ho. SE10 ... 53Ec 114
Varley Dr. TW1: Isle ... 56Ka 108
Varley Ho. NW6 ... 39Cb 69
SE1 ... 4E 230
Varley Pde. NW9 ... 28Ua 48
Varley Rd. E16 ... 44Kc 93
Varley Way CR4: Mitc ... 68Fb 133
Varna Rd. SW6 ... 52Ab 110
TW12: Hamp ... 67Da 129
Varndell St. NW1 ... 3B 216 (41Lb 90)
Varney Cl. HP1: Hem H ... 2H 3
Varney Rd. HP1: Hem H ... 2H 3
Varnishers Yd. N1 ... 2G 217
Varsity Dr. TW1: Twick ... 57Ga 108
Varsity Row SW14 ... 54Sa 109
Vartry Rd. N15 ... 30Tb 51
Vascroft Est. NW10 ... 42Ra 87
Vassall Ho. *E3* ... *41Ac 92*
(off Antill Rd.)
Vassall Rd. SW9 ... 52Qb 112
Vat Ho. *SW8* ... *52Nb 112*
(off Rita Rd.)
Vauban Est. SE16 ... 4K 231 (48Vb 91)
Vauban St. SE16 ... 4K 231 (48Vb 91)
Vaudeville Ct. N4 ... 33Qb 70
Vaudeville Theatre ... 5G 223
Vaughan Almshouses
TW15: Ashf ... *64R 128*
(off Feltham Hill Rd.)
Vaughan Av. DA9: Ghithe ... 56Yd 120
NW4 ... 29Wa 48
RM12: Horn ... 35Md 77
W6 ... 49Va 88
Vaughan Cl. DA1: Dart ... 59Md 119
TW12: Hamp ... 65Aa 129
Vaughan Copse SL4: Eton ... 9H 81
Vaughan Est. E2 ... 3K 219
Vaughan Gdns. IG1: Ilf ... 31Pc 74
SL4: Eton W ... 9D 80
Vaughan Ho. SE1 ... 1B 230
SW4 ... 59Lb 112
Vaughan Rd. DA16: Well ... 54Vc 117
E15 ... 37Hc 73
HA1: Harr ... 30Ea 46
KT7: T Ditt ... 73Ka 152
SE5 ... 54Sb 113
Vaughan St. SE16 ... 47Bc 92
Vaughan Way E1 ... 45Wb 91
SL2: Slou ... 2C 80
Vaughan Williams Cl. SE8 ... 52Cc 114
Vaughan Williams Way
CM14: Gt War, W'ley ... 23Wd 58
Vaux Cres. KT12: Hers ... 79X 151
VAUXHALL ... 7G 229 (51Nb 112)
Vauxhall Bri. SW1 ... 7E 228 (50Nb 90)
Vauxhall Bri. Rd. SW1 ... 4B 228 (48Lb 90)
Vauxhall City Farm ... 7H 229
Vauxhall Cl. DA11: Nflt ... 9B 122
VAUXHALL CROSS ... 50Nb 90
Vauxhall Distribution Pk. SW8 ... 51Mb 112
Vauxhall Gdns. CR2: S Croy ... 79Sb 157
Vauxhall Gro. SW8 ... 51Pb 112
Vauxhall Pl. DA1: Dart ... 59Nd 119
Vauxhall Rd. HP2: Hem H ... 2A 4
Vauxhall St. SE11 ... 7J 229 (50Pb 90)
Vauxhall Wlk. SE11 ... 7H 229 (50Pb 90)
Vawdrey Cl. E1 ... 42Yb 92
Veals Mead CR4: Mitc ... 67Gb 133
Vectis Gdns. SW17 ... 65Kb 134
Vectis Rd. SW17 ... 65Kb 134
Veda Rd. SE13 ... 56Cc 114
Vega Cres. HA6: Nwood ... 22V 44
Vegal Cres. TW20: Eng G ... 4M 125
Vega Rd. WD23: Bush ... 17Ea 28
Veitch Cl. TW14: Felt ... 59V 106
Veldene Way HA2: Harr ... 34Ba 65
Velde Way SE22 ... 57Ub 113
Vellacott Cl. RM19: Purf ... 50Td 98
Velletri Ho. *E2* ... *40Zb 72*
(off Mace St.)
Vellum Ct. E17 ... 27Ac 52
Vellum Dr. SM5: Cars ... 76Jb 156
Velocity Way EN3: Enf L ... 9Bc 20
(not continuous)
Venables Cl. RM10: Dag ... 35Dd 76
Venables St. NW8 ... 6C 214 (42Fb 89)
Vencourt Pl. W6 ... 49Wa 88
Venetian Rd. SE5 ... 54Sb 113
Venetia Rd. N4 ... 30Rb 51
W5 ... 47Ma 87
Venette Cl. RM13: Rain ... 43Kd 97
Venice Av. WD18: Wat ... 14U 26
Venice Ct. *SE5* ... *52Sb 113*
(off Bowyer St.)
Venice Wlk. W2 ... 1A 220 (43Eb 89)
(not continuous)
Venner Cl. RH1: Redh ... 5A 208
Venner Rd. SE26 ... 65Yb 136
(not continuous)
Venners Cl. DA7: Bex ... 54Gd 118
Venn Ho. N1 ... 1J 217
Venn St. SW4 ... 56Lb 112
Ventnor Av. HA7: Stan ... 25Ka 46
Ventnor Dr. N20 ... 20Db 31
Ventnor Gdns. IG11: Bark ... 37Uc 74
Ventnor Rd. SE14 ... 52Zb 114
SM2: Sutt ... 80Db 155
Venton Cl. GU21: Wok ... 9M 167
Ventura Pk. AL2: Col S ... 1Ha 14
Venture Cl. DA5: Bexl ... 59Ad 117
Venture Ct. DA12: Grav'nd ... 8F 122
SE1 ... 3J 231
SE12 ... 59Jc 115
Venture Ho. *W10* ... *44Za 88*
(off Bridge Cl.)
Venue, The (Leisure Cen.) ... 12Sa 29
Venue St. E14 ... 43Ec 92
Venus Cl. SL2: Slou ... 2D 80
VENUS HILL ... 3C 10
Venus Hill HP3: Bov ... 3C 10
Venus Ho. *E3* ... *39Cc 72*
(off Garrison Rd.)
E14 ... *49Cc 92*
(off Westferry Rd.)
Venus M. CR4: Mitc ... 69Gb 133
Venus Rd. SE18 ... 48Pc 94
Veny Cres. RM12: Horn ... 36Md 77
Vera Av. N21 ... 15Qb 32
Vera Ct. *E3* ... *41Dc 92*
(off Grace Pl.)
WD19: Wat ... 17Z 27
Vera Lynn Cl. E7 ... 35Jc 73
Vera Rd. SW6 ... 53Ab 110
Verbena Cl. E16 ... 42Hc 93
RM15: S Ock ... 44Yd 98
UB7: W Dray ... 50M 83
Verbena Gdns. W6 ... 50Wa 88
Verdana Ct. *WD18: Wat* ... *15U 26*
(off Whippendell Rd.)
Verdant Ct. *SE6* ... *59Gc 115*
(off Verdant La.)
Verdant La. SE6 ... 59Gc 115
Verdayne Av. CR0: C'don ... 75Zb 158
Verdayne Gdns. CR6: W'ham ... 88Yb 178
Verderers Rd. IG7: Chig ... 22Wc 55
Verdi Cres. W10 ... 40Ab 68
Verdon Ct. SL2: Farn R ... 1F 80
Verdun Rd. SE18 ... 51Wc 117
SW13 ... 51Wa 110
Verdure Cl. WD25: Wat ... 4Aa 13
Vere Ct. *W2* ... *44Db 89*
(off Westbourne Gdns.)
Vereker Dr. TW16: Sun ... 69W 128
Vereker Rd. W14 ... 50Ab 88
Vere Rd. IG10: Lough ... 13Sc 36
Vere St. W1 ... 3K 221 (44Kb 90)
Veridion Way DA18: Erith ... 47Bd 95
Veritas Ho. *DA15: Sidc* ... *61Wc 139*
(off Station Rd.)
Verity Cl. W11 ... 45Ab 88
Verity Ho. *E3* ... *41Bc 92*
(off Merchant St.)
Veritys AL10: Hat ... 1C 8
Vermeer Ct. E14 ... 48Fc 93
Vermeer Gdns. SE15 ... 56Yb 114
Vermont Cl. EN2: Enf ... 14Rb 33
Vermont Ho. E17 ... 26Bc 52
Vermont Rd. SE19 ... 65Tb 135
SL2: Slou ... 2D 80
SM1: Sutt ... 76Db 155
SW18 ... 58Db 111
Verne Ct. *W3* ... *48Sa 87*
(off Vincent Rd.)
Verney Gdns. RM9: Dag ... 35Ad 75
Verney Ho. NW8 ... 5D 214
Verney Rd. RM9: Dag ... 35Ad 75
(not continuous)
SE16 ... 51Wb 113
SL3: L'ly ... 49C 82
Verney St. NW10 ... 34Ta 67
Verney Way SE16 ... 50Xb 91
Vernham Rd. SE18 ... 51Sc 116
Vernon Av. E12 ... 35Pc 74
EN3: Enf W ... 8Ac 20
IG8: Wfd G ... 24Kc 53
SW20 ... 68Za 132
Vernon Cl. AL1: St A ... 3B 6
BR5: St P ... 69Xc 139
KT16: Ott ... 79F 148
KT19: Ewe ... 79Sa 153
TN15: W King ... 81Vd 184
TW19: Stanw ... 60N 105
Vernon Ct. HA7: Stan ... 25Ka 46
NW2 ... 34Bb 69
W5 ... 45La 86
Vernon Cres. CM13: B'wood ... 20Ce 41
EN4: E Barn ... 16Jb 32
Vernon Dr. CR3: Cat'm ... 94Sb 197
HA7: Stan ... 25Ja 46
UB9: Hare ... 25L 43
Vernon Ho. SE11 ... 7J 229
WC1 ... 1G 223
Vernon Mans. *W14* ... *51Bb 111*
(off Queen's Club Mans.)
Vernon M. E17 ... 29Bc 52
W14 ... 49Ab 88
Vernon Pl. WC1 ... 1G 223 (43Nb 90)
Vernon Ri. UB6: G'frd ... 36Ka 66
WC1 ... 3J 217 (41Pb 90)
Vernon Rd. DA10: Swans ... 58Be 121
E3 ... 40Bc 72
E11 ... 32Gc 73
E15 ... 38Gc 73
E17 ... 29Bc 52
IG3: Ilf ... 32Vc 75
N8 ... 27Qb 50
RM5: Col R ... 22Ed 56
SM1: Sutt ... 78Eb 155
SW14 ... 55Ta 109
TW13: Felt ... 61V 128
WD23: Bush ... 15Aa 27
Vernon Sq. WC1 ... 3J 217 (41Pb 90)
Vernon St. W14 ... 49Ab 88
Vernon Wlk. KT20: Tad ... 92Za 194
Vernon Yd. W11 ... 45Bb 89
Vern Pl. TN16: Tats ... 93Lc 199
Veroan Rd. DA7: Bex ... 54Ad 117
Verona Cl. UB8: Cowl ... 44L 83
Verona Ct. *SE14* ... *51Zb 114*
(off Myers La.)
TW15: Ashf ... 63R 128
W4 ... 50Ua 88
Verona Dr. KT6: Surb ... 75Na 153
Verona Gdns.
DA12: Grav'nd ... 3G 144
Verona Ho. DA8: Erith ... 52Gd 118
Verona Rd. E7 ... 38Jc 73
Veronica Cl. RM3: Rom ... 24Ld 57
Veronica Gdns. SW16 ... 67Lb 134
Veronica Ho. *E3* ... *41Dc 92*
(off Talwin St.)
SE4 ... 55Bc 114
Veronica Rd. SW17 ... 61Kb 134
Veronique Gdns.
IG6: Ilf ... 29Sc 54
Verralls GU22: Wok ... 89D 168
(not continuous)
Verran Rd. SW12 ... 59Kb 112
Ver Rd. AL3: St A ... 2A 6
Versailles Rd. SE20 ... 66Wb 135
Vert Ho. RM17: Grays ... 52Ee 121
Verulam Av. CR8: Purl ... 84Lb 176
E17 ... 30Bc 52
Verulam Bldgs. WC1 ... 7J 217
Verulam Ct. NW9 ... 31Wa 68
UB1: S'hall ... *44Ea 86*
(off Haldane Rd.)
Verulam Golf Course ... 4D 6
Verulam Ho. *W6* ... *47Ya 88*
(off Hammersmith Gro.)
Verulam Ind. Est. AL1: St A ... 4D 6
Verulamium Mus. ... 2P 5
Verulamium Pk. ... 3P 5
Verulamium Roman Town ... 2N 5
Verulam Pas. WD17: Wat ... 12X 27
Verulam Rd. AL3: St A ... 1A 6
UB6: G'frd ... 42Ca 85
Verulam St. WC1 ... 7K 217 (43Qb 90)
Vervian Ho. *SE15* ... *52Wb 113*
(off Reddins Rd.)
Verwood Dr. EN4: Cockf ... 13Hb 31
Verwood Ho. *SW8* ... *52Pb 112*
(off Cobbett St.)
Verwood Lodge *E14* ... *48Fc 93*
(off Manchester Rd.)
Verwood Rd. HA2: Harr ... 26Ea 46
Veryan GU21: Wok ... 6N 167
Veryan Ct. BR5: St P ... 70Yc 139
Veryan Ct. N8 ... 29Mb 50
Vesage Ct. EC1 ... 1A 224
Vesey Path E14 ... 44Dc 92
Vespan Rd. W12 ... 47Wa 88
Vesta Av. AL1: St A ... 5A 6
Vesta Ct. SE1 ... 2H 231
Vesta Ho. *E3* ... *39Cc 72*
(off Garrison Rd.)
Vesta Rd. SE4 ... 54Ac 114
Vestris Rd. SE23 ... 61Zb 136
Vestry Cotts. DA3: Lfield ... 70Ee 143
TN14: S'oaks ... 91Ld 203
Vestry Ct. SW1 ... 4E 228
Vestry House Mus. ... 28Dc 52
Vestry Ind. Est. TN14: S'oaks ... 91Ld 203
Vestry M. SE5 ... 53Ub 113
SW18 ... 57Fb 111
Vestry Rd. E17 ... 28Dc 52
SE5 ... 53Ub 113
TN14: S'oaks ... 91Kd 203
Vestry St. N1 ... 3F 219 (41Tb 91)
Vesuvius Apartments *E3* ... *40Bc 72*
(off Centurion La.)
Vevers Rd. RH2: Reig ... 9L 207
Vevey St. SE6 ... 61Bc 136
Vexil Cl. RM19: Purf ... 49Td 98
Veysey Cl. HP1: Hem H ... 4K 3
Veysey Gdns. RM10: Dag ... 34Cd 76
Viaduct, The E18 ... 26Jc 53
HA0: Wemb ... 39Na 67
N10 ... 28Kb 50
Viaduct Bldgs. EC1 ... 1A 224 (43Qb 90)
Viaduct Pl. E2 ... 41Xb 91
Viaduct Rd. N2 ... 26Fb 49
Viaduct St. E2 ... 41Xb 91
Viaduct Ter. DA4: S Dar ... 68Sd 142
Vian Av. EN3: Enf W ... 7Ac 20
Vian St. SE13 ... 55Dc 114
Viant Ho. *NW10* ... *38Ta 67*
(off Fawood Av.)
Via Romana DA12: Grav'nd ... 10K 123
Vibart Gdns. SW2 ... 59Pb 112
Vibart Wlk. *N1* ... *39Nb 70*
(off Outram Pl.)
Vibeca Apartments *E1* ... *43Vb 91*
(off Chicksands St.)
Vibia Cl. TW19: Stanw ... 59M 105
Viburnum Ct. GU24: W End ... 5C 166
Vicarage Av. SE3 ... 52Jc 115
TW20: Egh ... 64D 126
Vicarage Cl. AL1: St A ... 5A 6
CM14: B'wood ... 21Ud 58
DA8: Erith ... 51Ed 118
EN6: N'thaw ... 2Hb 17
EN6: Pot B ... 4Ab 16
HA4: Ruis ... 31T 64
HP1: Hem H ... 4L 3
KT4: Wor Pk ... 74Ua 154
KT20: Kgswd ... 96Ab 194
KT23: Bookh ... 97Ca 191
UB5: N'olt ... 38Ba 65
Vicarage Ct. BR3: Beck ... 69Ac 136
DA12: Grav'nd ... 10J 123
EN9: Walt A ... *6Jc 21*
(off Horseshoe La.)
IG1: Ilf ... 36Rc 74
TW14: Bedf ... 59S 106
TW20: Egh ... 65D 126
W8 ... 47Db 89
Vicarage Cres. SW11 ... 53Fb 111
TW20: Egh ... 64D 126
Vicarage Dr. BR3: Beck ... 67Cc 136
DA11: Nflt ... 58Ee 121
IG11: Bark ... 38Sc 74
SW14 ... 57Ta 109
Vicarage Farm Ct. TW5: Hest ... 52Ba 107
Vicarage Farm Rd. TW3: Houn ... 54Aa 107
TW5: Hest ... 53Aa 107
Vicarage Flds. KT12: Walt T ... 72Y 151
Vicarage Fld. Shop. Cen.
IG11: Bark ... 38Sc 74
Vicarage Gdns. CR4: Mitc ... 69Gb 133
SW14 ... 57Sa 109
W8 ... 46Cb 89
Vicarage Ga. W8 ... 46Db 89
Vicarage Ga. M. KT20: Kgswd ... 96Ab 194
Vicarage Gro. SE5 ... 53Tb 113
Vicarage Hill TN16: Westrm ... 98Tc 200
Vicarage Ho. *KT1: King T* ... *68Pa 131*
(off Cambridge Rd.)
Vicarage La. DA12: Grav'nd ... 1J 145
E6 ... 41Pc 94
E15 ... 38Gc 73
GU23: Send ... 98E 188
HP3: Bov ... 8D 2
IG1: Ilf ... 32Tc 74
IG7: Chig ... 19Sc 36
KT17: Ewe ... 81Wa 174
(not continuous)
KT20: Kgswd ... 95Ab 194
KT22: Lea ... 94Ka 192
TN13: Dun G ... 91Fd 202
TW18: Lale ... 69L 127
TW19: Wray ... 60A 104
WD4: K Lan ... 1P 11
Vicarage M. NW9 ... 33Ta 67
Vicarage Pde. N15 ... 28Sb 51
Vicarage Pk. SE18 ... 50Sc 94
Vicarage Path N8 ... 31Nb 70
Vicarage Rd. CM16: Coop ... 1Yc 23
CR0: Wadd ... 76Qb 156
DA5: Bexl ... 60Dd 118
E10 ... 31Cc 72
E15 ... 38Hc 73
GU22: Wok ... 93B 188
GU24: Chob ... 3H 167
IG8: Wfd G ... 23Nc 54
KT1: Hamp W ... 67La 130
KT1: King T ... 68Ma 131
N17 ... 25Wb 51
NW4 ... 30Wa 48
RM10: Dag ... 38Dd 76
RM12: Horn ... 32Jd 76
SE18 ... 50Sc 94
(not continuous)
SM1: Sutt ... 76Db 155
SW14 ... 57Sa 109
TW2: Twick ... 61Ga 130
TW2: Whitt ... 58Ea 108
TW11: Tedd ... 64Ja 130
TW16: Sun ... 64V 128
TW18: Staines ... 62G 126
TW20: Egh ... 64C 126
WD18: Wat ... 17W 26
Vicarage Rd. Pct. *WD18: Wat* ... *14X 27*
(off Vicarage Rd.)
Vicarage Road Stadium ... 15X 27
Vicarage Sq. RM17: Grays ... 51Ce 121
Vicarage Wlk. KT12: Walt T ... 73W 150
SW11 ... 53Fb 111
Vicarage Way HA2: Harr ... 31Ca 65
NW10 ... 34Ta 67
SL3: Coln ... 52E 104
SL9: Ger X ... 30B 42
Vicars Bri. Cl. HA0: Wemb ... 40Na 67
Vicars Cl. E9 ... 39Yb 72
E15 ... 39Jc 73
EN1: Enf ... 12Ub 33
Vicar's Hill SE13 ... 56Dc 114
Vicars Moor La. N21 ... 17Qb 32
Vicars Oak Rd. SE19 ... 65Ub 135
Vicar's Rd. NW5 ... 36Jb 70
Vicars Wlk. RM8: Dag ... 34Xc 75
Vicentia Ct. SW11 ... 55Eb 111
Viceroy Cl. *N2* ... *28Gb 49*
(off East End Rd.)
Viceroy Ct. CR0: C'don ... 74Tb 157
HA6: Nwood ... 23U 44
NW8 ... 1E 214
Viceroy Pde. *N2* ... *28Gb 49*
(off High Rd.)
Viceroy Rd. SW8 ... 53Nb 112
Vicinity Ho. *E14* ... *45Cc 92*
(off Storehouse M.)
Vic Johnson Ho. *E3* ... *39Bc 72*
(off Armagh Rd.)
Vickers Cl. SM6: Wall ... 80Pb 156
Vickers Ct. SE20 ... 66Zb 136
TW19: Stanw ... *58N 105*
(off Whitley Cl.)
Vickers Dr. Nth. KT13: Weyb ... 82N 169
Vickers Dr. Sth. KT13: Weyb ... 85N 169
Vickers La. DA1: Dart ... 55Qd 119
Vickers Rd. DA8: Erith ... 50Fd 96
Vickers Way TW4: Houn ... 57Aa 107
Vickery Ct. EC1 ... 5E 218
Vickery's Wharf E14 ... 44Cc 92
Victor App. RM12: Horn ... 32Md 77
Victor Cazalet Ho. *N1* ... *39Rb 71*
(off Gaskin St.)
Victor Cl. RM12: Horn ... 32Md 77
Victor Ct. *RM12: Horn* ... *32Md 77*
(off Victor App.)
Victor Gdns. RM12: Horn ... 32Md 77
Victor Gro. HA0: Wemb ... 38Na 67
Victor Ho. SE7 ... 51Lc 115
Victoria Almshouses RH1: Redh ... 3A 208
RH2: Reig ... 6L 207
Victoria & Albert Mus. ... 4C 226 (48Fb 89)
Victoria Arc. SW1 ... 4A 228
Victoria Av. CR2: Sande ... 82Sb 177
DA12: Grav'nd ... 9D 122
E6 ... 39Mc 73
EC2 ... 1J 225 (43Ub 91)
EN4: E Barn ... 14Fb 31
HA9: Wemb ... 37Ra 67
KT6: Surb ... 72Ma 153
KT8: W Mole ... 69Da 129
N3 ... 25Bb 49
RM5: Col R ... 23Dd 56
RM16: Grays ... 47Ee 99
SM6: Wall ... 76Jb 156
TW3: Houn ... 57Ca 107
UB10: Hil ... 37R 64
Victoria Beamish Av. CR3: Cat'm ... 92Ub 197
Victoria Bldgs. *E8* ... *39Xb 71*
(off Mare St.)
Victoria Chambers EC2 ... 5H 219
Victoria Cl. EN4: E Barn ... 14Fb 31
EN8: Chesh ... 2Zb 20
HA1: Harr ... 30Ha 46
KT8: W Mole ... 69Ca 129
KT13: Weyb ... 76T 150
RM16: Grays ... 47Ee 99
SE22 ... 57Wb 113
Victoria Cl. UB3: Hayes ... 44T 84
WD3: Rick ... 17M 25
Victoria Colonnade WC1 ... 1G 223
Victoria Cotts. *E1* ... *43Wb 91*
(off Deal St.)
N10 ... 26Jb 50
TW9: Kew ... 53Pa 109
Victoria Ct. CM14: W'ley ... 21Yd 58
E18 ... 27Kc 53
HA9: Wemb ... 37Qa 67
RH1: Redh ... 9A 208
RM1: Rom ... 29Jd 56
SE1 ... 6J 231
SE26 ... 65Yb 136
SL1: Slou ... *6J 81*
(off Blair Rd.)
SS17: Stan H ... 1L 101
W3 ... 47Qa 87
WD17: Wat ... 13Y 27
Victoria Cres. N15 ... 29Ub 51
SE19 ... 65Ub 135
SL0: Iver ... 45H 83
SW19 ... 66Bb 133
Victoria Dock Rd. E16 ... 45Hc 93
Victoria Dr. DA4: S Dar ... 68Td 142
SL1: Burn, Farn C ... 7C 60
SL2: Farn C ... 7C 60
SW19 ... 59Za 110
Victoria Emb. EC4 ... 2G 229 (47Nb 90)
SW1 ... 2G 229 (47Nb 90)
WC2 ... 2G 229 (47Nb 90)
Victoria Gdns. TN16: Big H ... 87Lc 179
TW5: Hest ... 53Aa 107
W11 ... 46Cb 89
Victoria Gro. N12 ... 22Fb 49
W8 ... 3A 226 (48Eb 89)
Victoria Gro. M. W2 ... 45Cb 89
Victoria Hall *E16* ... *46Jc 93*
(off Wesley Av., not continuous)
Victoria Hill Rd. BR8: Hext ... 67Hd 140
Victoria Ho. E6 ... 44Qc 94
HA8: Edg ... 23Ra 47
KT22: Lea ... 93La 192
RM2: Rom ... 28Ld 57
SL9: Chal P ... *21A 42*
(off Micholls Av.)
SW1 ... 7K 227
(Ebury Bri. Rd.)
SW1 ... 5C 228
(Francis St.)
SW8 ... *52Nb 112*
(off Sth. Lambeth Rd.)
Victoria Ind. Est. W3 ... 43Ua 88
Victoria La. EN5: Barn ... 14Bb 31
UB3: Harl ... 50T 84
Victoria Mans. NW10 ... 38Xa 68
SW8 ... *52Nb 112*
(off Sth. Lambeth Rd.)
W14 ... *51Bb 111*
(off Queen's Club Mans.)
Victoria M. E8 ... 37Wb 71
KT13: Weyb ... *77Q 150*
(off Balfour Rd.)
NW6 ... 39Cb 69
SW4 ... 56Kb 112
SW18 ... 60Eb 111
TW20: Eng G ... 5N 125
Victoria Mills Studios E15 ... 39Fc 73
Victorian Gro. N16 ... 35Ub 71
Victorian Hgts. *SW8* ... *54Kb 112*
(off Thackeray Rd.)
Victorian Rd. N16 ... 34Ub 71
Victoria Palace Theatre ... 4B 228
Victoria Pde. *TW9: Kew* ... *53Qa 109*
(off Sandycombe Rd.)
Victoria Pk. ... 39Zb 72
Victoria Pk. Ct. *E9* ... *38Yb 72*
(off Well St.)
Victoria Pk. Ind. Cen. *E9* ... *38Cc 72*
(off Rothbury Rd.)
Victoria Pk. Ind. Est. DA1: Dart ... 57Nd 119
Victoria Pk. Rd. E9 ... 39Yb 72
Victoria Pk. Sq. E2 ... 41Yb 92
Victoria Pk. Studios *E9* ... *37Yb 72*
(off Milborne St.)
Victoria Pas. NW8 ... 5B 214
WD18: Wat ... 14X 27
Victoria Pl. *GU21: Wok* ... *88C 168*
(off North Rd.)
HP2: Hem H ... 2M 3
KT10: Esh ... *77Da 151*
(off Esher Pk. Av.)
KT11: Cobh ... 86X 171
KT17: Eps ... 84Ua 174
TW9: Rich ... 57Ma 109
Victoria Pl. Shop. Cen. SW1 ... 5A 228
Victoria Point *E13* ... *40Jc 73*
(off Victoria Rd.)
Victoria Retail Pk. HA4: Ruis ... 36Z 65
Victoria Ri. *NW6* ... *38Eb 69*
(off Hilgrove Rd.)
SW4 ... 55Kb 112
Victoria Rd. BR2: Brom ... 71Mc 159
BR7: Chst ... 64Qc 138
CM14: W'ley ... 17Yd 58
CR4: Mitc ... 66Gb 133
CR5: Coul ... 87Mb 176
DA1: Dart ... 57Md 119
DA6: Bex ... 56Cd 118
DA8: Erith ... 51Gd 118
(not continuous)
DA11: Nflt ... 10B 122
DA15: Sidc ... 62Vc 139
E4 ... 18Gc 35
E11 ... 35Gc 73
E13 ... 40Jc 73
E17 ... 26Ec 52
E18 ... 26Kc 53
EN4: E Barn ... 14Fb 31
EN9: Walt A ... 6Ec 20
GU21: Knap ... 9H 167
GU22: Wok ... 89A 168
HA4: Ruis ... 32W 64
IG9: Buck H ... 19Mc 35
IG11: Bark ... 37Rc 74
KT1: King T ... 68Pa 131
KT6: Surb ... 72Ma 153
KT13: Weyb ... 76T 150
KT15: Add ... 77M 149
N4 ... 31Pb 70
N9 ... 21Vb 51
N15 ... 28Wb 51
N18 ... 21Vb 51
N22 ... 25Lb 50

Victoria Rd. NW4 . . . 28Ya 48
NW6 . . . 40Bb 69
NW7 . . . 22Va 48
NW10 . . . 43Ta 87
RH1: Redh . . . 7A 208
RM1: Rom . . . 30Hd 56
RM10: Dag . . . 36Dd 76
SL2: Farn C . . . 7G 60
SL2: Slou . . . 6M 81
SL4: Eton W . . . 9C 80
SL5: Asc . . . 1A 146
SM1: Sutt . . . 78Fb 155
SS17: Horn H . . . 1H 101
SS17: Stan H . . . 2L 101
SW14 . . . 55Ta 109
TN13: S'oaks . . . 97Kd 203
TW1: Twick . . . 59Ka 108
TW11: Tedd . . . 65Ja 130
TW13: Felt . . . 60X 107
TW18: Staines . . . 62G 126
UB2: S'hall . . . 48Ba 85
UB8: Uxb . . . 38L 63
W3 . . . 43Ta 87
W5 . . . 43Ka 86
W8 . . . 48Eb 89
WD23: Bush . . . 18Da 27
WD24: Wat . . . 10X 13
Victoria Scott Ct. DA1: Cray . . . 55Gd 118
Victoria Sq. AL1: St A . . . 3D 6
SW1 . . . 3A 228 (48Kb 90)
Victoria St. AL1: St A . . . 2B 6
DA17: Belv . . . 50Bd 95
E15 . . . 38Gc 73
SL1: Slou . . . 7K 81
SL4: Wind . . . 3H 103
SW1 . . . 4A 228 (48Lb 90)
TW20: Eng G . . . 5N 125
Victoria's Way RM15: S Ock . . . 44Yd 98
Victoria Ter. HA1: Harr . . . 32Ga 66
N4 . . . 32Qb 70
NW10 . . . 42Va 88
W5 . . . 46Ma 87
Victoria Vs. TW9: Rich . . . 55Pa 109
Victoria Way GU21: Wok . . . 89A 168
HA4: Ruis . . . 36Z 65
KT13: Weyb . . . 76T 150
SE7 . . . 50Kc 93
Victoria Wharf E2 . . . 40Zb 72
(off Palmers Rd.)
E14 . . . 45Ac 92
SE8 . . . 50Bc 92
(off Dragoon Rd.)
Victoria Works NW2 . . . 33Xa 68
Victoria Yd. E1 . . . 44Wb 91
Victor Rd. HA2: Harr . . . 27Ea 46
NW10 . . . 41Xa 88
SE20 . . . 66Zb 136
SL4: Wind . . . 5G 102
TW11: Tedd . . . 63Ga 130
Victor's Cres. CM13: Hut . . . 19De 41
Victors Dr. TW12: Hamp . . . 65Aa 129
Victor Smith Ct.
AL2: Brick W . . . 3Ca 13
Victors Way EN5: Barn . . . 13Bb 31
Victor Vs. N9 . . . 20Tb 33
Victor Wlk. NW9 . . . 26Ua 48
RM12: Horn . . . 32Md 77
Victor Way AL2: Col S . . . 3Ha 14
Victor Wharf SE1 . . . 6F 225
(off Clink St.)
Victory Av. SM4: Mord . . . 71Eb 155
Victory Bus. Cen. TW7: Isle . . . 56Ha 108
Victory Cl. RM16: Chaf H . . . 49Yd 98
TW19: Stanw . . . 60N 105
Victory Cotts. KT24: Eff . . . 100Aa 191
Victory Ct. DA8: Erith . . . 52Hd 118
(off Frobisher Rd.)
IG11: Bark . . . 42Xc 95
W9 . . . 42Cb 89
(off Hermes Cl.)
Victory M. UB2: S'hall . . . 48Aa 85
Victory Pk. HA9: Wemb . . . 34Ma 67
Victory Pk. M. KT15: Add . . . 77L 149
(off Victory Pk. Rd.)
Victory Pk. Rd. KT15: Add . . . 76L 149
(not continuous)
Victory Pl. E14 . . . 45Ac 92
SE17 . . . 5E 230 (49Tb 91)
SE19 . . . 66Ub 135
Victory Rd. E11 . . . 28Jc 53
KT16: Chert . . . 74J 149
RM13: Rain . . . 40Jd 76
SW19 . . . 66Eb 133
Victory Rd. M. SW19 . . . 66Eb 133
(off Victory Rd.)
Victory Wlk. SE8 . . . 53Cc 114
Victory Way DA2: Dart . . . 56Sd 120
RM7: Mawney . . . 26Dd 56
SE16 . . . 47Ac 92
TW5: Cran . . . 50Y 85
Video Ct. N4 . . . 31Pb 70
Vidler Cl. KT9: Chess . . . 79La 152
Vienna Cl. IG5: Ilf . . . 26Mc 53
View, The SE2 . . . 50Ad 95
View Cl. HA1: Harr . . . 28Fa 46
IG7: Chig . . . 22Tc 54
N6 . . . 31Hb 69
TN16: Big H . . . 88Lc 179
View Cres. N8 . . . 29Mb 50
Viewfield Cl. HA3: Kenton . . . 31Na 67
Viewfield Rd. DA5: Bexl . . . 60Yc 117
SW18 . . . 58Bb 111
Viewland Rd. SE18 . . . 50Vc 95
Viewlands Av. TN16: Westrm . . . 92Uc 200
View Rd. EN6: Pot B . . . 4Eb 17
N6 . . . 31Hb 69
Viga Rd. N21 . . . 16Qb 32
Vigerons Way RM16: Grays . . . 9D 100
Vigers Ct. NW10 . . . 41Xa 88
(off Harrow Rd.)
Viggory La. GU21: Wok . . . 7N 167
Vigilant Cl. SE26 . . . 63Wb 135
Vigilant Way DA12: Grav'nd . . . 4H 145
Vignoles Rd. RM7: Rush G . . . 31Cd 76
Vigo Hill ME19: Tros . . . 85Fe 185
Vigo Rd. TN15: Fair . . . 83De 185
Vigors Cft. AL10: Hat . . . 1B 8
Vigo St. W1 . . . 5B 222 (45Lb 90)
Viking Bus. Cen.RM7: Rush G . . . 31Ed 76
Viking Cl. E3 . . . 40Ac 72
Viking Ct. SW6 . . . 51Cb 111
Viking Gdns. E6 . . . 42Nc 94
Viking Ho. SE5 . . . 54Sb 113
(off Denmark Rd.)
Viking Ho. SE18 . . . 49Nc 94
(off Pett St.)
Viking Pl. E10 . . . 32Bc 72
Viking Rd. DA11: Nflt . . . 62Ee 143
UB1: S'hall . . . 45Aa 85
Viking Way CM15: Pil H . . . 16Xd 40
DA8: Erith . . . 48Ed 96
RM13: Rain . . . 42Jd 96
TN15: W King . . . 78Ud 164
Villa Cl. DA12: Grav'nd . . . 1K 145
Villa Ct. DA1: Dart . . . 61Nd 141
Villacourt Rd. SE18 . . . 52Wc 117
VILLAGE, THE . . . 2E 124
Village, The DA9: Bluew . . . 59Vd 120
NW3 . . . 33Eb 69
SE7 . . . 51Lc 115
Village Arc. AL3: St A . . . 2B 6
(off High St.)
E4 . . . 18Fc 35
Village Cen. HP3: Hem H . . . 3C 4
Village Cl. E4 . . . 22Ec 52
KT13: Weyb . . . 76T 150
NW3 . . . 36Fb 69
(off Belsize La.)
Village Ct. E17 . . . 29Dc 52
(off Eden Rd.)
KT13: Weyb . . . 77T 150
(off Oatlands Dr.)
SE3 . . . 55Gc 115
(off Hurren Cl.)
Village Cres., The DA9: Bluew . . . 59Vd 120
Village Gdns. KT17: Ewe . . . 82Va 174
Village Ga. TW17: Shep . . . 71R 150
Village Grn. Av. TN16: Big H . . . 89Nc 180
Village Grn. Rd. DA1: Cray . . . 56Jd 118
Village Grn. Way
TN16: Big H . . . 89Nc 180
Village Health Club, The . . . 94Sb 197
Village Hgts. IG8: Wfd G . . . 22Hc 53
Village La. SL2: Hedg . . . 2H 61
Village M. HP3: Bov . . . 9C 2
NW9 . . . 33Ta 67
Village Mt. NW3 . . . 35Eb 69
(off Perrins Ct.)
Village Pk. Cl. EN1: Enf . . . 16Ub 33
Village Rd. EN1: Enf . . . 15Ub 33
N3 . . . 26Ab 48
SL4: Dor . . . 8A 80
TW20: Thorpe . . . 69E 126
UB9: Den . . . 33H 63
Village Row SM2: Sutt . . . 80Cb 155
Village Shop. Cen.
SL1: Slou . . . 7K 81
Village Sq., The CR5: Coul . . . 94Mb 196
Village Way BR3: Beck . . . 68Cc 136
CR2: Sande . . . 85Wb 177
HA5: Pinn . . . 31Aa 65
HP7: L Chal . . . 12A 24
IG6: Ilf . . . 28Sc 54
NW10 . . . 35Ta 67
SE21 . . . 58Tb 113
TW15: Ashf . . . 63P 127
Village Way E. HA2: Harr . . . 31Ca 65
Villa Rd. SW9 . . . 55Qb 112
Villas on the Heath NW3 . . . 34Eb 69
Villas Rd. SE18 . . . 50Sc 94
Villa St. SE17 . . . 7G 231 (50Tb 91)
Villa Wlk SE17 . . . 50Tb 91
(off Villa St.)
Villiers, The KT13: Weyb . . . 79T 150
Villiers Av. KT5: Surb . . . 71Pa 153
TW2: Whitt . . . 60Ba 107
Villiers Cl. E10 . . . 33Cc 72
KT5: Surb . . . 70Pa 131
Villiers Ct. SL4: Wind . . . 2E 102
SW11 . . . 53Gb 111
(off Battersea Bri. Rd.)
Villiers Gro. SM2: Cheam . . . 81Za 174
Villiers Ho. SL4: Eton . . . 10G 80
(off Common La.)
Villiers M. NW2 . . . 37Wa 68
Villiers Path KT6: Surb . . . 71Na 153
Villiers Rd. BR3: Beck . . . 68Zb 136
KT1: King T . . . 70Pa 131
NW2 . . . 37Wa 68
SL2: Slou . . . 3H 81
TW7: Isle . . . 54Ga 108
UB1: S'hall . . . 46Ba 85
WD19: Wat . . . 16Aa 27
Villiers St. WC2 . . . 5F 223 (46Nb 90)
Villier St. UB8: Uxb . . . 41M 83
Vimy Cl. TW4: Houn . . . 57Ba 107
Vimy Dr. DA1: Dart . . . 55Pd 119
Vincam Cl. TW2: Whitt . . . 59Ca 107
Vince Ct. N1 . . . 4G 219 (41Tb 91)
Vincennes Est. SE27 . . . 63Tb 135
Vincent Av. KT5: Surb . . . 75Sa 153
SM5: Cars . . . 83Fb 175
Vincent Cl. BR2: Brom . . . 70Kc 137
CR5: Chip . . . 92Hb 195
DA15: Sidc . . . 60Uc 116
EN5: New Bar . . . 13Db 31
EN8: Chesh . . . 1Ac 20
IG6: Ilf . . . 23Sc 54
KT10: Esh . . . 76Da 151
KT16: Chert . . . 73G 148
KT22: Fet . . . 95Da 191
SE16 . . . 47Ac 92
UB7: Sip . . . 51Q 106
Vincent Ct. HA6: Nwood . . . 25V 44
N4 . . . 32Nb 70
NW4 . . . 28Za 48
SW9 . . . 53Pb 112
W1 . . . 2F 221
Vincent Dr. TW17: Shep . . . 69U 128
UB10: Uxb . . . 39P 63
Vincent Gdns. NW2 . . . 34Va 68
Vincent Ho. SW1 . . . 5E 228
(Regency St.)
SW1 . . . 6D 228
(Vincent Sq.)
Vincent M. E3 . . . 40Cc 72
Vincent Rd. CR0: C'don . . . 73Ub 157
CR5: Coul . . . 88Lb 176
E4 . . . 23Fc 53
HA0: Wemb . . . 38Pa 67
KT1: King T . . . 69Qa 131
KT11: Stoke D . . . 88Aa 171
KT16: Chert . . . 73G 148
N15 . . . 28Sb 51
N22 . . . 26Qb 50
RM9: Dag . . . 38Ad 75
RM13: Rain . . . 42Ld 97
SE18 . . . 49Rc 94
Vincent Rd. TW4: Houn . . . 54Z 107
TW7: Isle . . . 53Fa 108
W3 . . . 48Sa 87
Vincent Row TW12: Hamp H . . . 65Ea 130
Vincents Path UB5: N'olt . . . 37Aa 65
(off Arnold Rd.)
Vincent Sq. N22 . . . 26Qb 50
SW1 . . . 5C 228 (49Mb 90)
TN16: Big H . . . 85Lc 179
Vincent Sq. Mans. SW1 . . . 5C 228
(off Walcott St.)
Vincent St. E16 . . . 43Hc 93
SW1 . . . 5D 228 (49Mb 90)
Vincent Ter. N1 . . . 1B 218 (40Rb 71)
Vincenzo Cl. AL9: Wel G . . . 5E 8
Vince St. EC1 . . . 4G 219 (41Tb 91)
Vine, The TN13: S'oaks . . . 96Kd 203
Vine Av. TN13: S'oaks . . . 96Kd 203
Vine Cl. E5 . . . 35Wb 71
GU3: Worp . . . 8H 187
KT5: Surb . . . 72Pa 153
SM1: Sutt . . . 76Eb 155
TW19: Stanw M . . . 57J 105
UB7: W Dray . . . 49Q 84
Vine Cotts. E1 . . . 44Yb 92
(off Sidney Sq.)
W7 . . . 46Ga 86
Vine Ct. E1 . . . 43Wb 91
HA3: Kenton . . . 30Na 47
KT12: Hers . . . 79Y 151
Vine Ct. Rd. TN13: S'oaks . . . 96Ld 203
Vine Gdns. IG1: Ilf . . . 36Sc 74
Vinegar All. E17 . . . 28Dc 52
Vinegar St. E1 . . . 46Xb 91
Vinegar Yd. SE1 . . . 1H 231 (47Ub 91)
Vine Gro. UB10: Hil . . . 38Q 64
Vine Hill EC1 . . . 6K 217 (42Qb 90)
Vine La. SE1 . . . 7J 225 (46Ub 91)
UB10: Hil . . . 39P 63
Vine Lodge TN13: S'oaks . . . 96Ld 203
Vine Lodge Ct. TN13: S'oaks . . . 96Ld 203
Vine Pl. TW3: Houn . . . 56Da 107
W5 . . . 46Na 87
(off St Mark's Rd.)
Viner Cl. KT12: Walt T . . . 72Y 151
Vineries, The EN1: Enf . . . 13Ub 33
N14 . . . 16Lb 32
SE6 . . . 60Cc 114
Vineries Bank NW7 . . . 22Xa 48
Vineries Cl. RM9: Dag . . . 37Bd 75
UB7: Sip . . . 51Q 106
Vine Rd. BR6: Chels . . . 79Vc 161
E15 . . . 38Hc 73
KT8: E Mos . . . 70Ea 130
SL2: Stoke P . . . 7K 61
SW13 . . . 55Va 110
Vinery, The SW8 . . . 52Nb 112
(off Regent's Bri. Gdns.)
Vinery Row W6 . . . 48Xa 88
Vines Av. N3 . . . 25Db 49
Vine Sq. W14 . . . 50Bb 89
(off Star Rd.)
Vine St. EC3 . . . 3K 225 (44Vb 91)
RM7: Rom . . . 28Ed 56
UB8: Uxb . . . 39M 63
W1 . . . 5C 222 (45Lb 90)
Vine St. Bri. EC1 . . . 6A 218 (42Qb 90)
Vine Tree Ct. WD3: Rick . . . 19K 25
Vine Way CM14: B'wood . . . 18Yd 40
Vine Yd. SE1 . . . 1E 230
Vineyard, The TW10: Rich . . . 57Na 109
Vineyard Av. NW7 . . . 24Ab 48
Vineyard Cl. KT1: King T . . . 69Pa 131
SE6 . . . 60Cc 114
Vineyard Gro. N3 . . . 25Db 49
Vineyard Hill EN6: N'thaw . . . 1Jb 18
Vineyard Hill Rd. SW19 . . . 63Bb 133
Vineyard M. TW10: Rich . . . 57Na 109
Vineyard Pas. TW10: Rich . . . 57Na 109
Vineyard Path SW14 . . . 55Ta 109
Vineyard Rd. TW13: Felt . . . 62W 128
Vineyard Row KT1: Hamp W . . . 67La 130
Vineyards, The TW13: Felt . . . 62W 128
(off High St.)
TW16: Sun . . . 69W 128
Vineyards Rd. EN6: N'thaw . . . 2Hb 17
Vineyard Wlk. EC1 . . . 5K 217 (42Qb 90)
Viney Bank CR0: Sels . . . 81Bc 178
Viney Rd. SE13 . . . 55Dc 114
Vining St. SW9 . . . 56Qb 112
Vinlake Av. UB10: Ick . . . 34P 63
Vinopolis . . . 6E 224 (46Sb 91)
Vinson Cl. BR6: Orp . . . 74Wc 161
Vinson Ho. N1 . . . 2G 219
Vintage M. E4 . . . 21Cc 52
Vinter Ct. TW17: Shep . . . 71Q 150
Vintner's Ct. EC4 . . . 4E 224 (45Sb 91)
Vintry M. E17 . . . 28Cc 52
Viola Av. SE2 . . . 49Xc 95
TW14: Felt . . . 58Y 107
TW19: Stanw . . . 60M 105
Viola Cl. RM15: S Ock . . . 41Yd 98
Viola Sq. W12 . . . 45Va 88
Violet Av. EN2: Enf . . . 10Tb 19
UB8: Hil . . . 43P 83
Violet Cl. E16 . . . 42Gc 93
SE8 . . . 51Bc 114
SM3: Sutt . . . 74Ab 154
SM6: Wall . . . 74Jb 156
Violet Ct. E15 . . . 38Gc 73
(off Victoria St.)
Violet Gdns. CR0: Wadd . . . 78Rb 157
Violet Hill NW8 . . . 2A 214 (40Eb 69)
Violet Hill Ho. NW8 . . . 2A 214
Violet La. CR0: Wadd . . . 79Rb 157
Violet Rd. E3 . . . 42Dc 92
E17 . . . 30Cc 52
E18 . . . 26Kc 53
Violet St. E2 . . . 42Xb 91
Violet Way WD3: Loud . . . 14L 25
VIP Trading Est. SE7 . . . 49Lc 93
Virgil Pl. W1 . . . 1F 221 (43Hb 89)
Virgil St. SE1 . . . 3J 229 (48Pb 90)
Virgin Active
Barbican . . . 7D 218
(off Aldersgate St.)
Borehamwood . . . 13Qa 29
(within The Point)
Bromley . . . 70Mc 137
Cricklewood . . . 34Ab 68
Crouch End . . . 29Nb 50
(off Topsfield Pde.)
Croydon . . . 76Sb 157
(off Surrey St.)
Virgin Active
Ealing . . . 45Ma 87
(within Ealing Broadway Cen.)
Epsom . . . 85Ta 173
(off The Ebbisham Cen.)
Fulham . . . 51Ab 110
(within Fulham Pools)
Hammersmith . . . 49Za 88
(off Hammersmith Rd.)
Hendon . . . 29Ya 48
Holloway . . . 34Nb 70
Islington . . . 2B 218
Kensington . . . 47Db 89
(off Old Court Pl.)
Mayfair . . . 4H 221 (44Jb 90)
Merton . . . 67Fb 133
(off Merantum Way)
Mill Hill East . . . 24Ab 48
Moorgate . . . 6F 219 (42Tb 91)
Notting Hill . . . 44Ab 88
Putney . . . 56Ab 110
Slough . . . 7L 81
South Wimbledon . . . 65Eb 133
Stockley Park . . . 45S 84
Sunbury . . . 67W 128
Uxbridge . . . 38M 63
(off Vine St.)
Wandsworth . . . 57Db 111
West London . . . 46Ua 88
Virginia Av. GU25: Vir W . . . 1N 147
Virginia Beeches GU25: Vir W . . . 9M 125
Virginia Cl. BR2: Brom . . . 69Gc 137
KT3: N Mald . . . 70Sa 131
KT13: Weyb . . . 79S 150
KT21: Asht . . . 90Ma 173
RM5: Col R . . . 24Ed 56
TW18: Lale . . . 69L 127
Virginia Ct. GU25: Vir W . . . 10P 125
SE16 . . . 47Zb 92
(off Eleanor Cl.)
WC1 . . . 5E 216
Virginia Dr. GU25: Vir W . . . 1N 147
Virginia Gdns. IG6: Ilf . . . 26Sc 54
Virginia Ho. E14 . . . 45Ec 92
(off Newby Pl.)
TW11: Tedd . . . 64Ka 130
Virginia Pk. GU25: Vir W . . . 70A 126
Virginia Pl. KT11: Cobh . . . 86W 170
Virginia Rd. CR7: Thor H . . . 67Rb 135
E2 . . . 4K 219 (41Vb 91)
Virginia St. E1 . . . 45Wb 91
Virginia Wlk. DA12: Grav'nd . . . 5F 144
SW2 . . . 58Pb 112
VIRGINIA WATER . . . 10P 125
Virginia Water . . . 9J 125
Viridian Apartments SW8 . . . 52Lb 112
Visage NW3 . . . 38Fb 69
(off Winchester Rd.)
Viscount Cl. N11 . . . 23Kb 50
Viscount Ct. SL4: Wind . . . 3G 102
W2 . . . 44Cb 89
(off Pembridge Vs.)
Viscount Dr. E6 . . . 43Pc 94
Viscount Gdns. KT14: Byfl . . . 84N 169
Viscount Gro. UB5: N'olt . . . 41Z 85
Viscount Ind. Est.
SL3: Poyle . . . 55G 104
Viscount Rd. TW19: Stanw . . . 60N 105
Viscount St. EC1 . . . 6D 218 (42Sb 91)
Viscount Way TW6: H'row A . . . 56U 106
Vision 20 IG1: Ilf . . . 33Sc 74
Vision Ind. Pk. W3 . . . 43Ra 87
Vista, The DA14: Sidc . . . 64Vc 139
SE9 . . . 58Mc 115
Vista Av. EN3: Enf H . . . 12Zb 34
Vista Bldg. E3 . . . 41Bc 92
(off Bow Rd.)
SE18 . . . 49Qc 94
Vista Dr. IG4: Ilf . . . 29Mc 53
Vista Ho. N4 . . . 33Qb 70
SW19 . . . 67Eb 133
(off Chapter Way)
Vista Way HA3: Kenton . . . 30Na 47
Vitae Apartments W6 . . . 48Wa 88
Vitali Cl. SW15 . . . 58Wa 110
Vittoria Ho. N1 . . . 1J 217
Viveash Cl. UB3: Hayes . . . 48V 84
Vivenne Ho. TW18: Staines . . . 64J 127
Vivian Av. HA9: Wemb . . . 36Qa 67
NW4 . . . 29Xa 48
Vivian Cl. WD19: Wat . . . 18W 26
Vivian Comma Cl. N4 . . . 34Rb 71
Vivian Ct. N12 . . . 22Db 49
NW6 . . . 40Db 69
Vivian Gdns. HA9: Wemb . . . 36Qa 67
WD19: Wat . . . 18W 26
Vivian Mans. NW4 . . . 29Xa 48
(off Vivian Av.)
Vivian Rd. E3 . . . 40Ac 72
Vivian Sq. SE15 . . . 55Xb 113
Vivian Way N2 . . . 29Fb 49
Vivien Cl. KT9: Chess . . . 80Na 153
Vivienne Cl. TW1: Twick . . . 58Ma 109
Vixen M. E8 . . . 38Vb 71
(off Haggerston Rd.)
Voce Rd. SE18 . . . 52Tc 116
Voewood Cl. KT3: N Mald . . . 72Va 154
Vogan Cl. RH2: Reig . . . 9K 207
Vogans Mill SE1 . . . 1K 231 (47Vb 91)
Vogler Ho. E1 . . . 45Yb 92
(off Cable St.)
Vogue Ct. BR1: Brom . . . 67Kc 137
Vollasky Ho. E1 . . . 43Wb 91
(off Daplyn St.)
Volta Cl. N9 . . . 20Yb 34
Voltaire Rd. SW4 . . . 55Mb 112
Voltaire Way UB3: Hayes . . . 45U 84
Volt Av. NW10 . . . 41Ua 88
Volta Way CR0: Wadd . . . 74Pb 156
Voluntary Pl. E11 . . . 30Jc 53
Vorley Rd. N19 . . . 33Lb 70
Voss Ct. SW16 . . . 65Nb 134
Voss St. E2 . . . 41Wb 91
Voyager Bus. Est. SE16 . . . 48Wb 91
(off Spa Rd.)
Voyager Ct. E16 . . . 43Jc 93
(off Hammersley Rd.)
Voyagers Cl. SE28 . . . 44Yc 95
Voysey Cl. N3 . . . 27Ab 48
Vue Cinema
Acton . . . 42Qa 87
Croydon, High St. . . . 76Sb 157
Croydon, Purley Way . . . 74Pb 156
Dagenham . . . 39Ad 75
Vue Cinema
Fallow Corner . . . 24Fb 49
Finchley Rd. . . . 37Eb 69
(in O2 Cen.)
Fulham Broadway . . . 52Cb 111
Harrow . . . 30Ga 46
(in St George's Shopping & Leisure Cen.)
Islington . . . 1A 218 (40Qb 70)
Leicester Sq. . . . 4E 222
Romford . . . 30Gd 56
Shepherds Bush . . . 47Za 88
Staines . . . 63G 126
The O2 . . . 46Gc 93
(in The O2)
Watford . . . 5Y 13
West Thurrock . . . 48Wd 98
Westfield . . . 46Ya 88
Vulcan Bus. Cen. CR0: New Ad . . . 81Gc 179
Vulcan Cl. E6 . . . 44Qc 94
Vulcan Ga. EN2: Enf . . . 12Qb 32
Vulcan Rd. SE4 . . . 54Bc 114
Vulcan Sq. E14 . . . 49Dc 92
Vulcan Ter. SE4 . . . 54Bc 114
Vulcan Way CR0: New Ad . . . 82Gc 179
N7 . . . 37Pb 70
SM6: Wall . . . 81Nb 176
Vulcan Wharf E15 . . . 40Dc 72
(off Cook's Rd.)
Vyne, The DA7: Bex . . . 55Dd 118
Vyner Rd. W3 . . . 45Ta 87
Vyner St. E2 . . . 39Xb 71
Vyners Way UB10: Ick . . . 36Q 64
Vyse Cl. EN5: Barn . . . 14Ya 30

W

Wadard Ter. BR8: Swan . . . 71Ld 163
Wadbrook St. KT1: King T . . . 68Ma 131
Wadding St. SE17 . . . 6F 231 (49Tb 91)
Waddington Av. CR5: Coul . . . 92Qb 196
Waddington Cl. CR5: Coul . . . 91Rb 197
EN1: Enf . . . 14Ub 33
Waddington Rd. AL3: St A . . . 2B 6
E15 . . . 36Fc 73
Waddington St. E15 . . . 37Fc 73
Waddington Way SE19 . . . 66Sb 135
WADDON . . . 76Qb 156
Waddon Cl. CR0: Wadd . . . 76Qb 156
Waddon Ct. Rd. CR0: Wadd . . . 76Qb 156
Waddon Marsh Way CR0: Wadd . . . 74Pb 156
Waddon New Rd. CR0: C'don . . . 76Rb 157
Waddon Pk. Av. CR0: Wadd . . . 77Qb 156
Waddon Rd. CR0: C'don, Wadd . . . 76Qb 156
Waddon Way CR0: Wadd . . . 79Qb 156
Wade Av. BR5: Orp . . . 73Zc 161
Wade Ct. N10 . . . 24Kb 50
Wade Dr. SL1: Slou . . . 6E 80
Wade Ho. EN1: Enf . . . 15Tb 33
SE1 . . . 47Wb 91
(off Parkers Row)
Wades, The AL10: Hat . . . 3C 8
Wades Gro. N21 . . . 17Qb 32
Wades Hill N21 . . . 16Qb 32
Wades La. TW11: Tedd . . . 64Ja 130
Wades M. N21 . . . 17Qb 32
Wadeson St. E2 . . . 40Xb 71
Wade's Pl. E14 . . . 45Dc 92
Wadeville Av. RM6: Chad H . . . 30Ad 55
Wadeville Cl. DA17: Belv . . . 50Cd 96
Wadham Av. E17 . . . 24Dc 52
Wadham Cl. TW17: Shep . . . 73S 150
Wadham Gdns. NW3 . . . 39Gb 69
UB6: G'frd . . . 37Fa 66
Wadham Ho. N18 . . . 22Vb 51
Wadham Rd. E17 . . . 24Dc 52
SW15 . . . 56Ab 110
WD5: Ab L . . . 3V 12
Wadhurst Cl. SE20 . . . 68Xb 135
Wadhurst Rd. SW8 . . . 53Lb 112
W4 . . . 48Ta 87
Wadley Cl. HP2: Hem H . . . 3P 3
Wadley Rd. E11 . . . 31Gc 73
Wadsworth Bus. Cen.
UB6: G'frd . . . 40La 66
Wadsworth Cl. EN3: Pond E . . . 15Zb 34
UB6: G'frd . . . 40La 66
Wadsworth Rd. UB6: G'frd . . . 40Ka 66
Wager St. E3 . . . 42Bc 92
WAGGONERS RDBT. . . . 53X 107
Waggon La. N17 . . . 23Wb 51
Waggon M. N14 . . . 18Lb 32
Waggon Rd. EN4: Barn . . . 7Cb 17
EN5: Barn . . . 7Cb 17
Waghorn Rd. E13 . . . 39Lc 73
HA3: Kenton . . . 27Ma 47
Waghorn St. SE15 . . . 55Wb 113
Wagner M. KT6: Surb . . . 71Na 153
(off Avenue Elmers)
Wagner St. SE15 . . . 52Yb 114
Wagon Rd. EN4: Had W . . . 9Eb 17
Wagon Way WD3: Loud . . . 13L 25
Wagstaff Gdns. RM9: Dag . . . 38Yc 75
Wagtail Cl. EN1: Enf . . . 11Xb 33
NW9 . . . 26Ua 48
Wagtail Gdns. CR2: Sels . . . 82Ac 178
Wagtail Rd. TW6: H'row A . . . 54K 105
Wagtail Wlk. BR3: Beck . . . 71Ec 158
Wagtail Way BR5: St P . . . 70Zc 139
Waid Cl. DA1: Dart . . . 58Pd 119
Waight's Ct. KT2: King T . . . 67Na 131
Wain Cl. EN6: Pot B . . . 1Db 17
Wainfleet Av. RM5: Col R . . . 26Ed 56
Wainford Cl. SW19 . . . 60Za 110
Wainscot SL5: S'dale . . . 2D 146
Wainwright Av. CM13: Hut . . . 16Fe 41
DA9: Ghithe . . . 56Yd 120
Wainwright Gro. TW7: Isle . . . 56Fa 108
Wainwright Ho. E1 . . . 46Yb 92
(off Garnet St.)
Waite Davies Rd. SE12 . . . 59Hc 115
Waite St. SE15 . . . 51Vb 113
Waithman St. EC4 . . . 3B 224
Wakefield Ct. KT14: Byfl . . . 84N 169
Wakefield Ct. SE26 . . . 65Yb 136
Wakefield Cres. SL2: Stoke P . . . 7K 61
Wakefield Gdns. IG1: Ilf . . . 30Nc 54
SE19 . . . 66Ub 135
Wakefield Ho. SE15 . . . 53Wb 113
Wakefield M. WC1 . . . 4G 217 (41Nb 90)
Wakefield Rd. DA9: Ghithe . . . 57Yd 120
N11 . . . 22Mb 50
N15 . . . 29Vb 51
TW10: Rich . . . 57Ma 109

Wakefield St. DA11: Grav'nd 8D 122
E6 39Mc 73
N18 22Wb 51
WC1 4G 217 (41Nb 90)
Wakefields Wlk. EN8: Chesh 3Ac 20
Wakeford Cl. DA5: Bexl 60Zc 117
SW4 57Lb 112
Wakehams Hill HA5: Pinn 27Ba 45
Wakeham St. N1 37Tb 71
Wakehurst Path GU21: Wok 86E 168
Wakehurst Rd. SW11 57Gb 111
Wakeling Ct. CR8: Purl 82Nb 176
Wakeling La. HA0: Wemb 34Ka 66
Wakeling Rd. W7 43Ha 86
Wakeling St. E14 44Ac 92
Wakelin Ho. N1 38Rb 71
(off Sebbon St.)
Wakelin Rd. E15 40Gc 73
Wakely Cl. TN16: Big H 90Lc 179
Wakely Ct. AL1: St A 2C 6
(off Hatfield Rd.)
Wakeman Ho. NW10 41Za 88
(off Wakeman Rd.)
Wakeman Rd. NW10 41Ya 88
Wakemans Hill Av. NW9 29Ta 47
Wakerfield Cl. RM11: Horn 29Pd 57
Wakering Rd. IG11: Bark 38Sc 74
Wakerley Cl. E6 44Pc 94
Wake Rd. IG10: H Beech 10Lc 21
Wakley St. EC1 3B 218 (41Rb 91)
Walberswick St. SW8 52Nb 112
Walbrook EC4 4F 225 (45Tb 91)
(not continuous)
Walbrook Ct. N1 1H 219
Walbrook Ho. N9 19Yb 34
(off Huntingdon Rd.)
Walbrook Wharf EC4 5E 224
Walburgh St. E1 44Xb 91
Walburton Rd. CR8: Purl 85Lb 176
Walcorde Av. SE17 6E 230 (49Sb 91)
Walcot Gdns. SE11 5K 229
Walcot Rd. EN3: Brim 12Bc 34
Walcot Sq. SE11 5A 230 (49Qb 90)
Walcott St. SW1 5C 228 (49Lb 90)
Waldair Ct. E16 47Rc 94
Waldeck Gro. SE27 62Rb 135
Waldeck Rd. DA1: Dart 59Pd 119
N15 28Rb 51
SW14 55Sa 109
W4 51Qa 109
W13 44Ka 86
Waldeck Ter. SW14 55Sa 109
(off Waldeck Rd.)
Waldegrave Ct. IG11: Bark 39Tc 74
RM14: Upm 32Rd 77
Waldegrave Gdns. RM14: Upm 32Rd 77
TW1: Twick 61Ha 130
Waldegrave Pk. TW1: Twick 63Ha 130
Waldegrave Rd. BR1: Brom 70Nc 138
N8 27Qb 50
RM8: Dag 33Yc 75
SE19 66Vb 135
TW1: Twick 63Ha 130
TW11: Tedd 63Ha 130
W5 45Pa 87
Waldegrove CR0: C'don 76Vb 157
Waldemar Av. SW6 53Ab 110
W13 46La 86
Waldemar Rd. SW19 64Cb 133
Walden Av. BR7: Chst 63Pc 138
N13 21Sb 51
RM13: Rain 40Fd 76
Walden Cl. DA17: Belv 50Bd 95
Walden Ct. SW8 53Mb 112
Walden Gdns. CR7: Thor H 69Pb 134
Walden Ho. SW1 6J 227
SW11 53Jb 112
(off Dagnall St.)
Waldenhurst Rd. BR5: St M Cry 73Zc 161
Walden Pde. BR7: Chst 65Pc 138
(not continuous)
Walden Rd. BR7: Chst 65Pc 138
N17 25Tb 51
RM11: Horn 30Md 57
Waldens Cl. BR5: St M Cry 73Zc 161
Waldenshaw Rd. SE23 60Yb 114
Waldens Pk. Rd. GU21: Wok 8N 167
Waldens Rd. BR5: St M Cry 73Ad 161
GU21: Wok 9P 167
Walden St. E1 44Xb 91
(not continuous)
Walden Way IG6: Ilf 24Uc 54
NW7 23Za 48
RM11: Horn 30Md 57
Waldo Cl. SW4 57Lb 112
Waldo Ho. NW10 41Xa 88
(off Waldo Rd.)
Waldo Ind. Est. BR1: Brom 69Mc 137
Waldon RM18: E Til 8K 101
Waldo Pl. CR4: Mitc 66Gb 133
Waldorf Cl. CR2: S Croy 81Rb 177
Waldo Rd. BR1: Brom 69Mc 137
NW10 41Wa 88
(not continuous)
Waldram Cres. SE23 60Yb 114
Waldram Pk. Rd. SE23 60Zb 114
Waldram Pl. SE23 60Yb 114
Waldrist Way DA18: Erith 48Bd 95
Waldron Gdns. BR2: Brom 69Fc 137
Waldronhyrst CR2: S Croy 77Rb 157
Waldron M. SW3 51Fb 111
Waldron Rd. HA1: Harr 32Ga 66
HA2: Harr 32Ga 66
SW18 62Eb 133
Waldrons, The CR0: C'don 77Rb 157
RH8: Oxt 3K 211
Waldron's Path CR2: S Croy 77Sb 157
Waldrons Yd. HA2: Harr 33Fa 66
Waldstock Rd. SE28 45Wc 95
Waleran Cl. HA7: Stan 22Ha 46
Walerand Rd. SE13 54Ec 114
Waleran Flats
SE1 5H 231 (49Ub 91)
Wales Av. SM5: Cars 78Gb 155
Wales Cl. SE15 51Xb 113
Wales Farm Rd. W3 43Ta 87
Waleton Acres SM6: Wall 79Lb 156
Waley St. E1 43Ac 92
Walfield Av. N20 17Db 31
Walford Ho. E1 44Wb 91
Walford Rd. N16 35Ub 71
UB8: Uxb 40L 63
Walfrey Gdns. RM9: Dag 38Ad 75
WALHAM GREEN 53Cb 111
Walham Grn. Ct. SW6 52Db 111
(off Waterford Rd.)
Walham Gro. SW6 52Cb 111
Walham Ri. SW19 65Ab 132
Walham Yd. SW6 52Cb 111
Walk, The EN6: Pot B 4Cb 17
N13 20Qb 32
(off Fox La.)
RH8: Tand 5E 210
RM11: Horn 33Pd 77
SL4: Eton W 10E 80
TW16: Sun 66V 128
Walkato Lodge IG9: Buck H 18Lc 35
Walkden Rd. BR7: Chst 64Qc 138
Walker Cl. CR0: New Ad 80Ec 158
DA1: Cray 55Hd 118
N11 21Lb 50
SE18 49Sc 94
TW12: Hamp 65Ba 129
TW14: Felt 59V 106
W7 46Ga 86
Walker Cres. SL3: L'ly 50B 82
Walker Ho. NW1 2D 216 (40Mb 70)
SE16 48Bc 92
(off Redriff Est.)
Walker M. SW2 57Qb 112
Walker Pl. TN15: Igh 93Zd 205
Walker's Ct. W1 4D 222
Walkerscroft Mead SE21 60Sb 113
Walkers Lodge E14 47Ec 92
(off Manchester Rd.)
Walkers Pl. SW15 56Ab 110
Walkers Sq. SS17: Stan H 2M 101
Walkfield Dr. KT18: Tatt C 89Xa 174
Walkinshaw Ct. N1 38Sb 71
(off Rotherfield St.)
Walkley Rd. DA1: Dart 57Kd 119
Walks, The N2 27Fb 49
Walkynscroft SE15 54Xb 113
(off Caulfield Rd.)
Wallace Bldg. NW8 6C 214
Wallace Cl. SE28 45Zc 95
TW17: Shep 70T 128
UB10: Uxb 40N 63
Wallace Collection 2H 221 (44Jb 90)
Wallace Ct. NW1 1E 220
Wallace Cres. SM5: Cars 78Hb 155
Wallace Flds. KT17: Eps 84Va 174
Wallace Gdns. DA10: Swans 58Ae 121
Wallace Ho. N7 37Pb 70
(off Caledonian Rd.)
Wallace Rd. N1 37Sb 71
RM17: Grays 48Ce 99
Wallace Sq. CR5: Coul 94Mb 196
Wallace Wlk. KT15: Add 77L 149
SL4: Eton 10K 81
Wallace Way N19 33Mb 70
(off St John's Way)
RM1: Rom 25Fd 56
Wallasey Cres. UB10: Ick 33Q 64
Wallbrook Bus. Cen. TW4: Houn 55X 107
Wallbutton Rd. SE4 54Ac 114
Wallcote Av. NW2 32Za 68
Wall Ct. N4 32Pb 70
(off Stroud Grn. Rd.)
Walled Garden, The KT20: Tad 94Za 194
RH3: Bet 7A 206
Walled Gdn. Cl. BR3: Beck 70Dc 136
WALLEND 39Qc 74
Wall End Ct. E6 39Qc 74
(off Wall End Rd.)
Wall End Rd. E6 38Qc 74
Wallenger Av. RM2: Rom 27Kd 57
Waller Dr. HA6: Nwood 26W 44
Waller La. CR3: Cat'm 95Vb 197
Waller Rd. SE14 53Zb 114
Wallers Cl. IG8: Wfd G 23Pc 54
RM9: Dag 39Ad 75
Waller's Hoppet IG10: Lough 12Pc 36
Waller Way SE10 52Dc 114
Wallfield Pk. RH2: Reig 6H 207
Wallflower St. W12 45Va 88
Wallgrave Rd. SW5 49Db 89
Wall Hall WD25: A'ham 9Da 13
Wall Hall Dr. WD25: A'ham 8Da 13
Wallhouse Rd. DA8: Erith 52Kd 119
Wallingford Av. W10 43Za 88
Wallingford Ho. RM3: Rom 23Nd 57
(off Kingsbridge Rd.)
Wallingford Rd. UB8: Uxb 40K 63
Wallingford Wlk. AL1: St A 5B 6
WALLINGTON 79Kb 156
Wallington Cl. HA4: Ruis 30S 44
Wallington Cnr. SM6: Wall 77Kb 156
(off Manor Rd. Nth.)
Wallington Ct. SM6: Wall 79Kb 156
(off Stanley Pk. Rd.)
WALLINGTON GREEN 77Kb 156
Wallington Rd. IG3: Ilf 31Vc 75
Wallington Sq. SM6: Wall 79Kb 156
Wallis All. SE1 1E 230
Wallis Cl. DA2: Wilm 62Hd 140
RM11: Horn 32Kd 77
SW11 55Fb 111
Wallis Ct. SL1: Slou 7L 81
Wallis Ho. HA4: Ruis 32T 64
SE14 53Ac 114
TW8: Bford 50Na 87
Wallis M. KT22: Lea 94Ja 192
N8 27Qb 50
(off Courcy Rd.)
Wallis Pk. DA11: Nflt 57De 121
Wallis Rd. E9 37Bc 72
TW6: H'row A 54K 105
UB1: S'hall 44Da 85
Wallis's Cotts. SW2 59Nb 112
Wallman Pl. N22 25Pb 50
Wallorton Gdns. SW14 56Ta 109
Wallpaper Apartments, The
N1 38Qb 70
(off Offord Rd.)
Wallside EC2 1E 224
Wall St. N1 37Tb 71
Wallwood Rd. E11 31Fc 73
Wallwood St. E14 43Bc 92
Walmar Cl. EN4: Had W 11Fb 31
Walmer Cl. BR6: Farnb 77Tc 160
E4 19Dc 34
RM7: Mawney 26Dd 56
Walmer Ct. KT5: Surb 71Na 153
(off Cranes Pk.)
Walmer Gdns. W13 47Ja 86
Walmer Ho. W10 44Za 88
(off Bramley Rd.)
Walmer Pl. W1 7F 215
Walmer Rd. W10 44Ya 88
W11 45Ab 88
Walmers Av. ME3: High'm 3P 145
Walmer St. W1 7F 215 (43Hb 89)
Walmer Ter. SE18 49Sc 94
Walmgate Rd. UB6: G'frd 39Ka 66
Walmington Fold N12 23Cb 49
Walm La. NW2 37Ya 68
Walney Wlk. N1 37Sb 71
Walnut Av. UB7: W Dray 48Q 84
Walnut Cl. AL2: Park 9P 5
DA4: Eyns 76Md 163
IG6: Ilf 28Sc 54
KT18: Eps 87Va 174
SE8 51Bc 114
SM5: Cars 78Hb 155
UB3: Hayes 45U 84
Walnut Ct. E17 28Ec 52
W5 47Na 87
W8 48Db 89
(off St Mary's Ga.)
Walnut Dr. KT20: Kgswd 96Ab 194
Walnut Flds. KT17: Ewe 81Va 174
Walnut Gdns. E15 36Gc 73
Walnut Grn. WD23: Bush 12Ba 27
Walnut Gro. EN1: Enf 15Tb 33
HP2: Hem H 2M 3
RM12: Horn 32Md 77
SM7: Bans 86Za 174
Walnut Hill Rd. DA13: Meop, Ist R 9A 144
Walnut Ho. E3 39Bc 72
(off Barge La.)
RH2: Reig 8L 207
Walnut Lodge SL1: Slou 8H 81
Walnut M. N22 27Qb 50
(off High Rd.)
SM2: Sutt 80Eb 155
Walnut Rd. E10 33Cc 72
Walnuts, The BR6: Orp 74Wc 161
Walnuts Leisure Cen. 74Wc 161
Walnuts Rd. BR6: Orp 74Xc 161
Walnut Tree Av. CR4: Mitc 69Gb 133
(off De'Arn Gdns.)
DA1: Dart 61Nd 141
Walnut Tree Cl. BR7: Chst 67Tc 138
EN8: Chesh 3Zb 20
KT23: Fet 97Fa 192
SM7: Bans 84Ab 174
SW13 53Va 110
TN16: Westrm 98Tc 200
TW17: Shep 69S 128
UB10: Ick 35N 63
Walnut Tree Cotts. SW19 64Ab 132
Walnut Tree Ho. SW10 51Db 111
(off Tregunter Rd.)
Walnut Tree La. KT14: Byfl 84M 169
Walnut Tree Pl. GU23: Send 95F 188
Walnut Tree Rd. DA8: Erith 50Gd 96
RM8: Dag 33Ad 75
SE10 50Gc 93
(not continuous)
TW5: Hest 51Ba 107
TW8: Bford 51Na 109
TW17: Shep 68S 128
Walnut Tree Wlk. SE11 5K 229 (49Qb 90)
Walnut Way BR8: Swan 68Fd 140
HA4: Ruis 37Y 65
IG9: Buck H 20Mc 35
Walpole Av. CR5: Chip 91Hb 195
TW9: Kew 54Pa 109
Walpole Cl. HA5: Hat E 23Ca 45
RM17: Grays 49Ee 99
W13 47La 86
Walpole Ct. NW6 38Eb 69
(off Fairfax Rd.)
TW2: Twick 61Ga 130
W14 48Za 88
(off Blythe Rd.)
Walpole Cres. TW11: Tedd 64Ha 130
Walpole Gdns. TW2: Twick 61Ga 130
W4 50Sa 87
Walpole Ho. KT8: W Mole 71Ca 151
(off Approach Rd.)
SE1 2K 229
SL4: Eton 1G 102
(off Eton Wick Rd.)
Walpole Lodge W13 46La 86
Walpole M. NW8 1B 214 (39Fb 69)
SW19 65Fb 133
Walpole Pk. KT13: Weyb 80Q 150
Walpole Pl. SE18 49Rc 94
TW11: Tedd 64Ha 130
Walpole Rd. BR2: Brom 71Mc 159
CR0: C'don 75Tb 157
E6 38Lc 73
E17 28Ac 52
E18 25Hc 53
KT6: Surb 73Na 153
N17 26Sb 51
(not continuous)
SL1: Slou 4B 80
SL4: Old Win 9M 103
SW19 65Fb 133
TW2: Twick 61Ga 130
TW11: Tedd 64Ha 130
Walpole St. SW3 7F 227 (50Hb 89)
Walrond Av. HA9: Wemb 36Na 67
Walsham Cl. N16 32Wb 71
SE28 45Zc 95
Walsham Ent. Cen.
RM17: Grays 50Ee 99
Walsham Ho. SE14 54Zb 114
SE17 7F 231
Walsham Rd. SE14 54Zb 114
TW14: Felt 59X 107
Walsh Cres. CR0: New Ad 84Gc 179
Walshford Way WD6: Bore 10Qa 15
Walsingham NW8 39Fb 69
Walsingham Gdns. KT19: Ewe 77Ua 154
Walsingham Ho. E4 17Fc 35
Walsingham Lodge SW13 53Wa 110
Walsingham Mans. SW6 52Db 111
(off Fulham Rd.)
Walsingham Pk. BR7: Chst 68Tc 138
Walsingham Pl. SW4 58Jb 112
Walsingham Rd. BR5: St P 67Xc 139
CR0: New Ad 82Ec 178
CR4: Mitc 71Hb 155
E5 34Wb 71
EN2: Enf 14Tb 33
W13 46Ja 86
Walsingham Wlk.
DA17: Belv 51Cd 118
Walsingham Way AL2: Lon C 9G 6
Walston Ho. SW1 7D 228
Walter Besant Ho. E1 41Zb 92
(off Bancroft Rd.)
Walter Ct. W3 44Sa 87
(off Lynton Ter.)
Walter Grn. Ho. SE15 53Yb 114
(off Lausanne Rd.)
Walter Ho. SW10 52Fb 111
(off Riley St.)
Walter Hurford Pde. E12 35Qc 74
(off Grantham Rd.)
Walter Langley Ct. SE16 47Yb 92
(off Brunel Rd.)
Walter Rodney Cl. E6 37Pc 74
Walter Savil Twr. E17 30Cc 52
(off Colchester Rd.)
Walters Cl. SE17 6E 230
UB3: Hayes 47V 84
Walters Ho. SE17 51Rb 113
(off Otto St.)
Walter Sickert Hall N1 2D 218
Walters Mead KT21: Asht 89Na 173
Walters Rd. EN3: Pond E 14Yb 34
SE25 70Ub 135
Walter St. E2 41Zb 92
KT2: King T 67Na 131
Walters Way SE23 58Zb 114
Walters Yd. BR1: Brom 68Jc 137
Walter Ter. E1 44Zb 92
Walterton Rd. W9 42Bb 89
Walter Wlk. HA8: Edg 23Sa 47
WALTHAM ABBEY 5Ec 20
Waltham Abbey Church & Gatehouse
5Ec 20
Waltham Abbey Sports Cen. 5Gc 21
Waltham Abbey Swimming Pool 6Fc 21
Waltham Av. NW9 30Qa 47
UB3: Harl 48S 84
Waltham Cl. BR5: Orp 74Zc 161
CM13: Hut 16Ee 41
DA1: Dart 58Jd 118
WALTHAM CROSS 5Ac 20
Waltham Dr. HA8: Edg 26Qa 47
Waltham Forest Pool & Track 26Dc 52
Waltham Forest Theatre 27Cc 52
Waltham Gdns. EN3: Enf W 8Yb 20
Waltham Ho. NW8 39Eb 69
Waltham Pk. Way E17 25Cc 52
Waltham Rd. CR3: Cat'm 94Xb 197
IG8: Wfd G 23Nc 54
SM5: Cars 73Fb 155
UB2: S'hall 48Aa 85
WALTHAMSTOW 27Cc 52
Walthamstow Av. E4 23Bc 52
Walthamstow Bus. Cen. E17 26Ec 52
Walthamstow Marsh Nature Reserve
31Xb 71
Waltham Way E4 21Bc 52
Waltheof Av. N17 25Tb 51
Waltheof Gdns. N17 25Tb 51
Walton & Hersham FC 75W 150
Walton Av. HA2: Harr 36Ba 65
HA9: Wemb 34Ra 67
KT3: N Mald 70Va 132
SM3: Cheam 76Bb 155
Walton Bri. TW17: Shep 73U 150
Walton Bri. Rd. TW17: Shep 73U 150
Walton Cl. E5 34Zb 72
(off Orient Way)
HA1: Harr 28Fa 46
NW2 33Xa 68
SW8 52Nb 112
Walton Ct. CR2: S Croy 78Sb 157
(off Warham Rd.)
EN5: New Bar 15Eb 31
GU21: Wok 88C 168
NW6 38Eb 69
(off Fairfax Rd.)
Walton Cft. HA1: Harr 35Ga 66
Walton Dr. HA1: Harr 28Fa 46
NW10 37Ta 67
Walton Gdns. CM13: Hut 15Ee 41
EN9: Walt A 5Dc 20
HA9: Wemb 33Na 67
TW13: Felt 63V 128
W3 43Ra 87
Walton Grn. CR0: New Ad 81Dc 178
Walton Hall Campsite
SS17: Stan H 6J 101
WALTON HEATH 99Va 194
Walton Heath Golf Course 97Xa 194
Walton Ho. E2 5K 219
E17 27Dc 52
NW1 5A 216
SW1 4F 227
Walton La. KT12: Walt T 75R 150
KT13: Weyb 75R 150
SL2: Farn R 10D 60
TW17: Shep 73T 150
WALTON-ON-THAMES 74W 150
Walton on Thames Camping & Caravan Site
KT12: Walt T 73Ca 151
WALTON ON THE HILL 96Wa 194
Walton Pk. KT12: Walt T 75Z 151
Walton Pk. La. KT12: Walt T 75Z 151
Walton Pl. SW3 3F 227 (48Hb 89)
Walton Rd. DA14: Sidc 61Yc 139
E12 35Qc 74
(not continuous)
E13 40Lc 73
GU21: Wok 88B 168
HA1: Harr 28Fa 46
KT8: W Mole, E Mos 71Y 151
KT12: Walt T 71Y 151
KT18: Eps D 89Va 174
KT18: Eps D, Head 93Sa 193
N15 28Vb 51
RM5: Col R 24Bd 55
WD23: Bush 14Z 27
Walton's Hall Rd.
SS17: Stan H 7J 101
Walton St. AL1: St A 1D 6
EN2: Enf 11Tb 33
KT20: Walt H 96Wa 194
SW3 5E 226 (49Gb 89)
Walton Ter. GU21: Wok 87D 168
WD6: E'tree 16Ma 29
(off Watford Rd.)
Walton Vs. N1 38Ub 71
(off Downham Rd.)
Walton Way CR4: Mitc 70Lb 134
W3 43Ra 87
Walt Whitman Cl. SE24 56Rb 113
Walverns Cl. WD19: Wat 16Y 27
WALWORTH 7E 230 (50Sb 91)
Walworth Pl. SE17 7E 230 (50Sb 91)
Walworth Rd. SE1 5D 230 (49Sb 91)
SE17 5D 230 (49Sb 91)
Walwyn Av. BR1: Brom 69Mc 137
Wambrook Cl. CM13: Hut 18Ee 41
Wanborough Dr. SW15 60Xa 110
Wanderer Dr. IG11: Bark 41Yc 95
Wander Wharf WD4: K Lan 1R 12
Wandle Bank CR0: Bedd 76Nb 156
SW19 66Fb 133
Wandle Ct. CR0: Bedd 76Nb 156
KT19: Ewe 77Sa 153
Wandle Ct. Gdns. CR0: Bedd 76Nb 156
Wandle Ho. BR1: Brom 64Fc 137
NW8 7D 214
Wandle Industrial Mus. 69Hb 133
Wandle Meadow Nature Pk. 64Eb 133
Wandle Pk. Trad. Estate, The
CR0: C'don 74Rb 157
Wandle Recreation Cen. 58Db 111
Wandle Rd. CR0: Bedd 76Nb 156
CR0: C'don 76Sb 157
SM4: Mord 70Eb 133
SM6: Wall 76Kb 156
SW17 61Gb 133
Wandle Side CR0: Wadd 76Pb 156
SM6: Wall 76Kb 156
Wandle Technology Pk.
CR4: Mitc 73Hb 155
Wandle Trad. Est. CR4: Mitc 71Hb 155
Wandle Way CR4: Mitc 71Hb 155
SW18 60Db 111
Wandon Rd. SW6 52Db 111
WANDSWORTH 57Db 111
Wandsworth Bri. SW6 55Db 111
Wandsworth Bri. Rd. SW6 53Db 111
WANDSWORTH COMMON 60Hb 111
Wandsworth Comn. W. Side
SW18 57Eb 111
WANDSWORTH GYRATORY 57Db 111
Wandsworth High St. SW18 57Cb 111
Wandsworth Mus. 57Cb 111
Wandsworth Plain SW18 57Db 111
Wandsworth Rd. SW8 55Kb 112
Wangey Rd. RM6: Chad H 31Zc 75
Wangford Ho. SW9 56Rb 113
(off Loughborough Pk.)
Wanless Rd. SE24 55Sb 113
Wanley Rd. SE5 56Tb 113
Wanlip Rd. E13 42Kc 93
Wanmer Ct. RH2: Reig 5J 207
(off Birkheads Rd.)
Wannock Gdns. IG6: Ilf 24Rc 54
Wansbeck Ct. EN2: Enf 13Rb 33
(off Waverley Rd.)
Wansbeck Rd. E9 38Bc 72
Wansbury Way BR8: Swan 71Jd 162
Wansdown Pl. SW6 52Db 111
Wansey St. SE17 6D 230 (49Sb 91)
Wansford Cl. CM14: B'wood 20Vd 40
Wansford Grn. GU21: Wok 9K 167
Wansford Pk. WD6: Bore 14Ta 29
Wansford Rd. IG8: Wfd G 25Lc 53
WANSTEAD 30Kc 53
Wanstead Cl. BR1: Brom 68Lc 137
Wanstead Gdns. IG4: Ilf 30Mc 53
Wanstead Golf Course 31Lc 73
Wanstead La. IG1: Ilf 30Mc 53
Wanstead Leisure Cen. 30Lc 53
Wanstead Pk. Av. E12 32Mc 73
Wanstead Pk. Rd. IG1: Ilf 30Mc 53
Wanstead Pl. E11 30Jc 53
Wanstead Rd. BR1: Brom 68Lc 137
Wansunt Rd. DA5: Bexl 60Ed 118
Wantage Rd. SE12 57Hc 115
Wantz La. RM13: Rain 42Kd 97
(not continuous)
Wantz Rd. RM10: Dag 35Dd 76
Waplings, The KT20: Walt H 96Xa 194
WAPPING 46Xb 91
Wapping Dock St. E1 46Xb 91
Wapping High St. E1 46Wb 91
Wapping La. E1 45Xb 91
Wapping Wall E1 46Yb 92
Wapses Lodge CR3: Wold 92Xb 197
WAPSES LODGE RDBT. 92Xb 197
Wapseys La. SL2: Hedg 1J 61
Wapshott Rd. TW18: Staines 65G 126
Waratah Dr. BR7: Chst 64Pc 138
Warbank Cl. CR0: New Ad 82Gc 179
Warbank Cres. CR0: New Ad 82Gc 179
Warbank La. KT2: King T 66Va 132
Warbeck Ho. KT13: Weyb 78T 150
(off Queens Rd.)
Warbeck Rd. W12 47Xa 88
Warberry Rd. N22 25Pb 50
Warbler's Grn. KT11: Cobh 86Ba 171
Warboys App. KT2: King T 65Ra 131
Warboys Cres. E4 22Ec 52
Warboys Rd. KT2: King T 65Ra 131
Warburton Cl. HA3: Hrw W 23Fa 46
N1 37Ub 71
(off Culford Rd.)
Warburton Ct. HA4: Ruis 33W 64
Warburton Ho. E8 39Xb 71
(off Warburton St.)
Warburton Rd. E8 39Xb 71
TW2: Whitt 60Da 107
Warburtons SS17: Stan H 1P 101
Warburton St. E8 39Xb 71
Warburton Ter. E17 26Dc 52
Warbury La. GU21: Knap 7F 166
War Coppice Rd.
CR3: Cat'm 99Tb 197
Wardalls Ho. SE8 51Bc 114
(off Staunton St.)
Ward Av. RM17: Grays 49Ce 99
Ward Cl. CR2: S Croy 79Ub 157
DA8: Erith 51Fd 118
SL0: Iver 45H 83
Wardell Cl. NW7 24Ua 48
Wardell Fld. NW9 25Ua 48
Wardell Ho. SE10 51Ec 114
(off Welland St.)
Warden Av. HA2: Harr 32Ba 65
RM5: Col R 22Ed 56
Warden Rd. NW5 37Jb 70
Wardens Fld. Cl. BR6: Chels 79Uc 160
Wardens Gro. SE1 7D 224 (46Sb 91)
Ward Gdns. RM3: Hrld W 25Md 57
SL1: Slou 5C 80
Ward La. CR6: W'ham 88Yb 178

Wardle St. E9 ... 36Zb 72
Wardley St. SW18 ... 59Db 111
Wardo Av. SW6 ... 53Ab 110
Wardona Ct. DA10: Swans ... 58Be 121
Wardona Ho. DA10: Swans ... 58Be 121
Wardour Ct. *DA2: Dart* ... *58Rd 119*
(off Bow Arrow La.)
Wardour M. W1 ... 3C 222
Wardour St. W1 ... 2C 222 (44Lb 90)
Ward Point SE11 ... 6K 229 (49Qb 90)
Ward Rd. E15 ... 39Fc 73
N19 ... 34Lb 70
SW19 ... 67Eb 133
Wardrobe, The *TW9: Rich* ... *57Ma 109*
(off Old Palace Yd.)
Wardrobe Pl. EC4 ... 3C 224
Wardrobe Ter. EC4 ... 4C 224
Wardroper Ho. SE1 ... 4C 230
Ward Royal SL4: Wind ... 3G 102
Ward Royal Pde. *SL4: Wind* ... *3G 102*
(off Alma Rd.)
Wards Dr. WD3: Sarr ... 8H 11
Wards La. WD6: E'tree ... 12Ha 28
Ward's Pl. TW20: Egh ... 65E 126
Wards Rd. IG2: Ilf ... 31Tc 74
Wards Wharf App. E16 ... 46Mc 93
Wardur Ho. KT12: Walt T ... 76W 150
Ware Ct. HA8: Edg ... 21Na 47
SM1: Sutt ... 77Bb 155
Wareham Cl. TW3: Houn ... 56Da 107
Wareham Ct. *N1* ... *38Ub 71*
(off Hertford Rd.)
Wareham Ho. SW8 ... 52Pb 112
Warehouse Theatre ... 75Tb 157
Warehouse Way E16 ... 45Kc 93
Waremead Rd. IG2: Ilf ... 29Rc 54
Warenford Way WD6: Bore ... 11Qa 29
Warenne Hgts. RH1: Redh ... 8M 207
Warenne Rd. KT22: Fet ... 94Ea 192
Warepoint Dr. SE28 ... 47Tc 94
Warescot Cl. CM15: B'wood ... 17Xd 40
Warescot Rd. CM15: B'wood ... 17Xd 40
Warfield Rd. NW10 ... 41Za 88
TW12: Hamp ... 67Da 129
TW14: Felt ... 59U 106
Warfield Yd. *NW10* ... *41Za 88*
(off Warfield Rd.)
Wargrave Av. N15 ... 30Vb 51
Wargrave Ho. E2 ... 4K 219
Wargrave Rd. HA2: Harr ... 34Ea 66
Warham Rd. CR2: S Croy ... 78Rb 157
HA3: W'stone ... 26Ha 46
N4 ... 29Qb 50
TN14: Otf ... 88Kd 183
Warham St. SE5 ... 52Rb 113
Waring & Gillow Est. W3 ... 42Qa 87
Waring Cl. BR6: Chels ... 79Vc 161
Waring Dr. BR6: Chels ... 79Vc 161
Waring Rd. DA14: Sidc ... 65Yc 139
Waring St. SE27 ... 63Sb 135
Warkworth Gdns. TW7: Isle ... 52Ja 108
Warkworth Rd. N17 ... 24Tb 51
Warland Rd. SE18 ... 52Tc 116
TN15: W King ... 81Vd 184
WARLEY ... 22Yd 58
Warley Av. RM8: Dag ... 31Bd 75
UB4: Hayes ... 44W 84
Warley Cl. E10 ... 32Bc 72
Warley Country Pk. ... 21Wd 58
Warley Gap CM13: Gt War, L War ... 24Xd 58
Warley Hall La. RM14: Upm ... 31Be 79
Warley Hill CM13: Gt War, W'ley ... 23Xd 58
CM14: W'ley ... 23Xd 58
Warley Hill Bus. Pk., The
CM13: Gt War ... 23Yd 58
Warley Mt. CM14: W'ley ... 21Yd 58
Warley Pk. Golf Course ... 26Zd 59
Warley Place Nature Reserve ... 24Wd 58
Warley Rd. CM13: Gt War ... 25Wd 58
IG5: Ilf ... 25Qc 54
IG8: Wfd G ... 24Kc 53
N9 ... 19Yb 34
RM14: Gt War, Upm ... 26Sd 58
UB4: Hayes ... 44W 84
Warley St. CM13: Gt War, Upm ... 28Yd 58
E2 ... 41Zb 92
RM14: Upm ... 28Yd 58
Warleywoods Cres.
CM14: W'ley ... 21Xd 58
WARLINGHAM ... 90Zb 178
Warlingham Ct. SE13 ... 58Ec 114
Warlingham Rd. CR7: Thor H ... 70Rb 135
Warlock Rd. W9 ... 42Bb 89
Warlow Cl. EN3: Enf L ... 9Cc 20
Warlters Cl. N7 ... 35Nb 70
Warlters Rd. N7 ... 35Nb 70
Warltersville Mans. N19 ... 31Nb 70
Warltersville Rd. N19 ... 31Nb 70
Warmark Rd. HP1: Hem H ... 1G 2
Warmington Cl. E5 ... 34Zb 72
Warmington Rd. SE24 ... 58Sb 113
Warmington St. E13 ... 42Jc 93
Warminster Gdns. SE25 ... 68Wb 135
Warminster Ho. *RM3: Rom* ... *22Pd 57*
(off Redcar Rd.)
Warminster Rd. SE25 ... 68Vb 135
Warminster Sq. SE25 ... 68Wb 135
Warminster Way CR4: Mitc ... 67Kb 134
Warmsworth *NW1* ... *39Lb 70*
(off Pratt St.)
Warmwell Av. NW9 ... 25Ua 48
Warndon St. SE16 ... 49Zb 92
Warneford Pl. WD19: Wat ... 16Aa 27
Warneford Rd. HA3: Kenton ... 27Ma 47
TW6: H'row A ... 54K 105
Warneford St. E9 ... 39Xb 71
Warne Pl. DA15: Sidc ... 58Xc 117
Warner Av. SM3: Cheam ... 75Ab 154
Warner Bros. Studios Leavesden ... 6U 12
Warner Cl. E15 ... 36Gc 73
EN4: Had W ... 9Gb 17
NW9 ... 31Va 68
SL1: Slou ... 6C 80
TW12: Hamp ... 64Ba 129
UB3: Harl ... 52T 106
Warner Ho. BR3: Beck ... 65Dc 136
NW8 ... 3A 214 (41Eb 89)
SE13 ... *54Dc 114*
(off Russett Way)
Warner Pl. E2 ... 40Wb 71
Warner Rd. BR1: Brom ... 66Hc 137
E17 ... 28Ac 52
N8 ... 28Mb 50
SE5 ... 53Sb 113
Warners Cl. IG8: Wfd G ... 22Jc 53
WARNERS END ... 1G 2
Warners End Rd. HP1: Hem H ... 2J 3
Warners La. KT2: King T ... 63Ma 131
Warners Path IG8: Wfd G ... 22Jc 53
Warner St. EC1 ... 6K 217 (42Qb 90)
Warner Ter. *E14* ... *43Dc 92*
(off Broomfield St.)
Warner Yd. EC1 ... 6K 217
Warnford Ct. EC2 ... 2G 225
Warnford Ho. *SW15* ... *58Ua 110*
(off Tunworth Cres.)
Warnford Ind. Est. UB3: Hayes ... 47U 84
Warnford Rd. BR6: Chels ... 78Vc 161
Warnham WC1 ... 4H 217
Warnham Ct. Rd. SM5: Cars ... 80Hb 155
Warnham Ho. *SW2* ... *59Pb 112*
(off Up. Tulse Hill)
Warnham Rd. N12 ... 22Gb 49
Warple M. W3 ... 47Ua 88
Warple Way W3 ... 47Ua 88
(not continuous)
Warre Ho. *SL4: Eton* ... *10G 80*
(off Common La.)
Warren, The ... 47Y 85
Warren, The AL2: Park ... 10A 6
DA12: Grav'nd ... 3F 144
E12 ... 35Nc 74
KT4: Wor Pk ... 77Ta 153
KT20: Kgswd ... 95Ab 194
KT21: Asht ... 91Na 193
KT22: Oxs ... 84Ea 172
SE7 ... 51Lc 115
SL9: Chal P ... 24B 42
SM5: Cars ... 81Fb 175
SS17: Stan H ... 4N 101
TW5: Hest ... 52Ba 107
UB4: Hayes ... 44W 84
WD4: K Lan ... 1P 11
WD7: R'lett ... 5Ja 14
Warren Av. BR1: Brom ... 66Gc 137
BR6: Chels ... 78Vc 161
CR2: Sels ... 80Zb 158
E10 ... 34Ec 72
SM2: Cheam ... 82Bb 175
TW10: Rich ... 56Ra 109
Warren Cl. DA6: Bex ... 57Cd 118
HA9: Wemb ... 33Ma 67
KT10: Esh ... 77Da 151
N9 ... 17Zb 34
SE21 ... 59Sb 113
SL3: L'ly ... 48A 82
UB4: Yead ... 43Y 85
Warren Ct. BR3: Beck ... 66Cc 136
CR0: C'don ... 74Ub 157
IG7: Chig ... 21Tc 54
KT13: Weyb ... 78Q 150
KT21: Asht ... 91Na 193
N17 ... *27Wb 51*
(off High Cross Rd.)
NW1 ... 5B 216
SL2: Farn C ... 6G 60
TN13: S'oaks ... 96Ld 203
W5 ... 43La 86
WD25: Wat ... 2X 13
Warren Ct. Farm TN14: Hals ... 85Ad 181
Warren Cres. N9 ... 17Vb 33
Warren Cutting KT2: King T ... 66Ta 131
Warrender Rd. N19 ... 34Lb 70
Warrender Way HA4: Ruis ... 31W 64
Warren Dr. BR6: Chels ... 78Xc 161
HA4: Ruis ... 31Z 65
KT20: Kgswd ... 94Bb 195
RM12: Horn ... 35Jd 76
UB6: G'frd ... 42Da 85
Warren Dr., The E11 ... 31Lc 73
Warren Dr. Nth. KT5: Surb ... 74Ra 153
Warren Dr. Sth. KT5: Surb ... 74Sa 153
Warrene Cl. SS17: Stan H ... 2M 101
Warreners La. KT13: Weyb ... 80T 150
Warren Farm Cl. KT17: Bans ... 87Ya 174
Warren Farm Cotts. RM6: Chad H ... 28Bd 55
Warren Farm Mobile Home Pk.
GU22: Pyr ... 91K 189
Warren Farm Sports Cen. ... 48Fa 86
Warren Fld. CM16: Epp ... 4Wc 23
SL0: Iver H ... 40E 62
Warrenfield Cl. EN7: Chesh ... 3Wb 19
Warren Flds. HA7: Stan ... 21La 46
Warren Footpath TW1: Twick ... 60La 108
Warren Gdns. BR6: Chels ... 78Wc 161
E15 ... 36Fc 73
Warrengate La. EN6: S Mim ... 3Ya 16
Warrengate Rd. AL9: N Mym ... 8D 8
Warren Gro. WD6: Bore ... 14Ta 29
Warren Hastings Ct. DA11: Nflt ... 8B 122
Warren Hgts. IG10: Lough ... 15Lc 35
RM16: Chaf H ... 49Ae 99
Warren Hill IG10: Lough ... 15Lc 35
KT18: Eps ... 88Ta 173
Warren Ho. *E3* ... *41Dc 92*
(off Bromley High St.)
N17 ... *27Wb 51*
(off High Cross Rd.)
W14 ... 49Bb 89
Warrenhurst Gdns. KT13: Weyb ... 79T 150
Warren La. CM15: Dodd, Kel H ... 11Vd 40
GU22: Pyr ... 90J 169
HA7: Stan ... 19Ja 28
KT22: Oxs ... 83Ea 172
RH8: Oxt ... 6L 211
RM16: Chaf H ... 49Zd 99
SE18 ... 48Rc 94
Warren La. Ga. SE18 ... 48Rc 94
Warren Lodge KT20: Kgswd ... 96Ab 194
Warren Lodge Dr. KT20: Kgswd ... 96Ab 194
Warren Mead SM7: Bans ... 87Ya 174
Warren M. KT13: Weyb ... 76V 150
W1 ... 6B 216 (42Lb 90)
Warrenne Way RH2: Reig ... 6J 207
Warren Pde. SL2: Slou ... 6N 81
Warren Pk. CR6: W'ham ... 90Zb 178
KT2: King T ... 65Sa 131
Warren Pk. Golf Cen. ... 29Bd 55
Warren Pk. Rd. SM1: Sutt ... 79Fb 155
Warren Pl. *E1* ... *44Zb 92*
(off Pitsea St.)
Warren Pond Rd. E4 ... 18Hc 35
Warren Ri. KT3: N Mald ... 67Ta 131
Warren Rd. AL1: St A ... 6A 6
BR2: Hayes ... 75Jc 159
BR6: Chels ... 78Vc 161
CR0: C'don ... 74Ub 157
CR8: Purl ... 84Rb 177
Warren Rd. DA1: Dart ... 62Nd 141
DA6: Bex ... 57Cd 118
DA13: Sflt ... 64De 143
DA14: Sidc ... 62Yc 139
E4 ... 19Ec 34
E10 ... 34Ec 72
E11 ... 30Lc 53
IG6: Ilf ... 29Tc 54
KT2: King T ... 65Sa 131
KT15: New H ... 82J 169
NW2 ... 33Va 68
RH2: Reig ... 5K 207
SM7: Bans ... 86Ya 174
SW19 ... 65Gb 133
TW2: Whitt ... 58Ea 108
TW15: Ashf ... 66U 128
UB10: Ick ... 35N 63
WD23: B Hea ... 18Ea 28
Warrens, The DA3: Hartl ... 72Be 165
Warren Sports Cen. ... 29Bd 55
Warrens Shawe La. HA8: Edg ... 19Ra 29
Warren St. W1 ... 6B 216 (42Lb 90)
Warren Ter. RM6: Chad H ... 28Zc 55
RM16: N Stif ... 47Zd 99
Warren Vw. DA12: Shorne ... 4N 145
Warren Wlk. SE7 ... 51Lc 115
Warren Way HA8: Edg ... 26Ra 47
KT13: Weyb ... 78S 150
WARREN WOOD ... 4M 9
Warren Wood Cl. BR2: Hayes ... 75Hc 159
Warrenwood M. AL9: Hat ... 4M 9
Warriner Av. RM12: Horn ... 33Md 77
Warriner Dr. N9 ... 20Wb 33
Warriner Gdns. SW11 ... 53Hb 111
Warrington Av. SL1: Slou ... 4G 80
Warrington Ct. *CR0: Wadd* ... *76Rb 157*
(off Warrington Rd.)
Warrington Cres. W9 ... 5A 214 (42Eb 89)
Warrington Gdns. RM11: Horn ... 30Ld 57
W9 ... 42Eb 89
(not continuous)
Warrington Rd. CR0: Wadd ... 76Rb 157
HA1: Harr ... 29Ga 46
RM8: Dag ... 33Zc 75
TW10: Rich ... 57Ma 109
Warrington Spur SL4: Old Win ... 9M 103
Warrington Sq. RM8: Dag ... 33Zc 75
Warrior Av. DA12: Grav'nd ... 3E 144
Warrior Cl. SE28 ... 46Tc 94
Warrior Ct. *SW9* ... *55Rb 113*
(off Coldharbour Rd.)
Warrior Sq. E12 ... 35Qc 74
Warsaw Cl. HA4: Ruis ... 37X 65
Warspite Ho. *E14* ... *49Dc 92*
(off Cahir St.)
Warspite Rd. SE18 ... 48Nc 94
Warton Ct. *E1* ... *45Zb 92*
(off Cable St.)
Warton Ho. *E15* ... *39Ec 72*
(off High St.)
Warton Rd. E15 ... 39Ec 72
Warwall E6 ... 44Rc 94
Warwark Ct. KT6: Surb ... 75Na 153
Warwick *W14* ... *49Bb 89*
(off Kensington Village)
Warwick Av. HA2: Harr ... 35Ba 65
HA8: Edg ... 20Ra 29
SL2: Slou ... 2G 80
TW18: Staines ... 65L 127
TW20: Egh ... 67E 126
W2 ... 6A 214 (42Eb 89)
W9 ... 6A 214 (42Db 89)
Warwick Bldg. SW8 ... 51Kb 112
Warwick Chambers *W8* ... *48Cb 89*
(off Pater St.)
Warwick Cl. BR6: Chels ... 76Wc 161
DA5: Bexl ... 59Bd 117
EN4: E Barn ... 15Fb 31
RM11: Horn ... 30Pd 57
TW12: Hamp ... 66Ea 130
W8 ... *48Bb 89*
(off Kensington High St.)
WD23: B Hea ... 17Ga 28
Warwick Ct. BR2: Brom ... 68Gc 137
DA8: Erith ... 52Hd 118
EC4 ... 3C 224
EN5: New Bar ... *15Db 31*
(off Station Rd.)
HA1: Harr ... 27Ga 46
KT13: Weyb ... 78Q 150
N11 ... 23Mb 50
SL4: Wind ... *4G 102*
(off Queen's Rd.)
TN13: S'oaks ... 97Kd 203
UB5: N'olt ... *36Ca 65*
(off Newmarket Av.)
W7 ... *44Ha 86*
(off Copley Cl.)
WC1 ... 1J 223 (43Pb 90)
WD3: Chor ... 13H 25
Warwick Cres. UB4: Hayes ... 42V 84
W2 ... 7A 214 (43Eb 89)
Warwick Deeping KT16: Ott ... 78E 148
Warwick Dene W5 ... 46Na 87
Warwick Dr. EN8: Chesh ... 1Zb 20
SW15 ... 55Xa 110
Warwick Est. W2 ... 43Db 89
Warwick Gdns. CR7: Thor H ... 69Qb 134
EN5: Barn ... 10Bb 17
IG1: Ilf ... 32Rc 74
KT7: T Ditt ... 71Ha 152
KT21: Asht ... 89La 172
N4 ... 29Sb 51
RM2: Rom ... 27Ld 57
W14 ... 48Bb 89
Warwick Gro. E5 ... 32Xb 71
KT5: Surb ... 73Pa 153
Warwick Ho. *AL1: St A* ... *2B 6*
(off London Rd.)
BR8: Swan ... 70Gd 140
E16 ... *46Jc 93*
(off Wesley Av.)
KT2: King T ... *67Na 131*
(off Acre Rd.)
SW9 ... 54Qb 112
Warwick Ho. St. SW1 ... 6E 222 (46Mb 90)
Warwick La. EC4 ... 2C 224 (44Rb 91)
GU21: Wok ... 1L 187
RM13: Rain ... 41Pd 97
RM14: Avel, Upm ... 40Pd 77
Warwick Lodge TW2: Twick ... 62Da 129
Warwick Mans. *SW5* ... *49Cb 89*
(off Cromwell Cres.)
Warwick M. WD3: Crox G ... 16Q 26
Warwick Pde. HA3: Kenton ... 26Ka 46
Warwick Pas. EC4 ... 2C 224
Warwick Pl. CM14: Pil H ... 14Sd 40
DA11: Nflt ... 57De 121
KT7: T Ditt ... 72Ja 152
RH2: Reig ... 6M 207
UB8: Uxb ... 38L 63
W5 ... 47Ma 87
W9 ... 7A 214 (43Eb 89)
WD6: Bore ... 13Ta 29
Warwick Pl. Nth. SW1 ... 6B 228 (49Lb 90)
Warwick Quad. RH1: Redh ... 5A 208
Warwick Rd. AL1: St A ... 1D 6
CR5: Coul ... 86Lb 176
CR7: Thor H ... 69Qb 134
DA14: Sidc ... 64Xc 139
DA16: Well ... 55Yc 117
E4 ... 22Cc 52
E11 ... 29Kc 53
E12 ... 36Nc 74
E15 ... 37Hc 73
E17 ... 25Bc 52
EN3: Enf L ... 9Bc 20
EN5: New Bar ... 14Db 31
KT1: Hamp W ... 67La 130
KT3: N Mald ... 69Sa 131
KT7: T Ditt ... 71Ha 152
N11 ... 23Mb 50
N18 ... 21Ub 51
RH1: Redh ... 5P 207
RM13: Rain ... 42Ld 97
SE20 ... 69Xb 135
SM1: Sutt ... 77Eb 155
SW5 ... 49Bb 89
TN15: Ash ... 60Ga 108
TW2: Twick ... 60Ga 108
TW4: Houn ... 55X 107
TW15: Ashf ... 64N 127
UB2: S'hall ... 48Ba 85
UB7: W Dray ... 47N 83
W5 ... 47Ma 87
W14 ... 49Bb 89
WD6: Bore ... 13Ta 29
Warwick Row SW1 ... 3A 228 (48Kb 90)
Warwickshire Path SE8 ... 52Bc 114
Warwickshire Rd. N16 ... 35Ub 71
Warwick Sq. EC4 ... 2C 224 (44Rb 91)
SW1 ... 7B 228 (50Lb 90)
(not continuous)
Warwick Sq. M. SW1 ... 6B 228 (49Lb 90)
Warwick St. W1 ... 4C 222 (45Lb 90)
Warwick Ter. *E17* ... *29Fc 53*
(off Lea Bri. Rd.)
SE18 ... 51Tc 116
Warwick Vs. TW20: Egh ... 67E 126
Warwick Way DA1: Dart ... 61Nd 141
SW1 ... 7K 227 (50Kb 90)
WD3: Crox G ... 14S 26
WARWICK WOLD ... 1G 208
Warwick Wold Rd. RH1: Mers ... 1G 208
Warwick Yd. EC1 ... 6E 218 (42Sb 91)
Wasdale NW1 ... 4A 216
Washbourne Ct. *N9* ... *19Wb 33*
(off Acton Cl.)
Washbourne Rd. NW10 ... 39Ta 67
Washington Av. E12 ... 35Pc 74
Washington Bldg. *SE10* ... *53Dc 114*
(off Deal's Gateway)
Washington Cl. E3 ... 41Dc 92
RH2: Reig ... 4J 207
Washington Dr. SL1: Slou ... 5B 80
SL4: Wind ... 5C 102
Washington Ho. E17 ... 26Bc 52
SW3 ... 2F 227
Washington Rd. E6 ... 38Lc 73
E18 ... 26Hc 53
KT1: King T ... 68Qa 131
KT4: Wor Pk ... 75Xa 154
SW13 ... 52Wa 110
TW6: H'row A ... 55L 105
Wash La. EN6: S Mim ... 5Xa 16
WASHMILLS ... 60Yd 120
Washneys Rd. BR6: Prat B ... 86Wc 181
Washpond La. CR6: W'ham ... 90Ec 178
Wash Rd. CM13: Hut, Mount ... 16Fe 41
Wasp Rd. *TW6: H'row A* ... *54K 105*
(off Welland Rd.)
Wastdale Rd. SE23 ... 60Zb 114
Watch, The N12 ... 21Eb 49
Watchfield Ct. W4 ... 50Sa 87
Watchgate DA2: Daren ... 64Td 142
(not continuous)
Watcombe Cotts. TW9: Kew ... 51Qa 109
Watcombe Pl. SE25 ... 71Xb 157
Watcombe Rd. SE25 ... 71Xb 157
Waterbank Rd. SE6 ... 62Dc 136
Waterbeach Cl. SL1: Slou ... 4H 81
Waterbeach Rd. RM9: Dag ... 37Yc 75
SL1: Slou ... 4H 81
Waterbourne Way CR8: Kenley ... 86Tb 177
Water Brook La. NW4 ... 29Ya 48
Water Cir. DA9: Bluew ... 60Vd 120
Watercress Cl. TN14: S'oaks ... 92Ld 203
Watercress Dr. TN14: S'oaks ... 92Ld 203
Watercress Pl. N1 ... 38Ub 71
Watercress Way GU21: Wok ... 9M 167
Watercroft Rd. TN14: Hals ... 82Bd 181
WATERDALE ... 2Y 13
WATERDALE ... 2Z 13
Waterdale AL2: Brick W ... 2Aa 13
Waterdale Rd. SE2 ... 51Wc 117
Waterdales DA11: Nflt ... 61Ee 143
Waterden Ct. W11 ... 46Ab 88
Water Dr. WD3: Rick ... 18N 25
WATER END ... 8D 8
Water End Cl. WD6: Bore ... 12Pa 29
Waterer Gdns. KT20: Tad ... 90Za 174
Waterer Ho. SE6 ... 63Ec 136
Waterer Ri. SM6: Wall ... 79Mb 156
Waterers Ri. GU21: Knap ... 9H 167
Waterfall Cl. GU25: Vir W ... 9L 125
N14 ... 20Lb 32
Waterfall Cotts. SW19 ... 65Fb 133
Waterfall Rd. N11 ... 21Kb 50
N14 ... 21Kb 50
SW19 ... 65Fb 133
Waterfall Ter. SW17 ... 65Gb 133
Waterfall Wlk. N14 ... 19Lb 32
Waterfield KT20: Tad ... 92Xa 194
WD3: Herons ... 17E 24
Waterfield Cl. DA17: Belv ... 48Cd 96
SE28 ... 46Xc 95
Waterfield Dr. CR6: W'ham ... 91Yb 198
KT18: Tatt C ... 91Xa 194
KT20: Tad ... 91Xa 194
Waterfield Gdns. SE25 ... 70Tb 135
Waterfield Grn. KT20: Tad ... 92Xa 194
Waterfields KT22: Lea ... 91Ka 192
Waterfields Shop. Pk. WD17: Wat ... 14Z 27
Waterfields Way WD17: Wat ... 14Z 27
Waterford Cl. KT11: Cobh ... 83Aa 171
Waterford Ho. UB7: W Dray ... 48L 83
W11 ... *45Bb 89*
(off Kensington Pk. Rd.)
Waterford Rd. SW6 ... 52Db 111
(not continuous)
Waterford Way NW10 ... 36Xa 68
Waterfront W6 ... 51Ya 110
Waterfront, The WD6: E'tree ... 16Ka 28
Waterfront Ho. *E5* ... *33Yb 72*
(off Harry Zeital Way)
Waterfront Leisure Cen.
Woolwich ... 48Qc 94
Waterfront M. N1 ... 1E 218 (40Sb 71)
Waterfront Studios Bus. Cen. *E16* ... *46Hc 93*
(off Dock Rd.)
Water Gdns. HA7: Stan ... 23Ka 46
Water Gdns., The W2 ... 2E 220 (44Gb 89)
Watergardens, The KT2: King T ... 65Sa 131
Water Gdns. Sq. SE16 ... 47Zb 92
Watergate EC4 ... 4B 224 (45Rb 91)
Watergate, The WD19: Wat ... 19Z 27
Watergate St. SE8 ... 51Cc 114
Watergate Wlk. WC2 ... 6G 223 (46Nb 90)
Waterglade Ind. Pk.
RM20: W Thur ... 51Vd 120
WATERHALES ... 15Md 39
Waterhall Av. E4 ... 21Gc 53
Waterhall Cl. E17 ... 25Zb 52
Waterhead NW1 ... 3B 216
Waterhead Cl. DA8: Erith ... 52Gd 118
Waterhouse, The HP1: Hem H ... 3L 3
Waterhouse Cl. E16 ... 43Mc 93
NW3 ... 36Fb 69
W6 ... 49Za 88
Waterhouse La. CR8: Kenley ... 91Sb 197
KT20: Kgswd ... 93Ab 194
RH1: Blet ... 4M 209
Waterhouse Sq. EC1 ... 1K 223 (43Qb 90)
Waterhouse St. HP1: Hem H ... 2L 3
Wateridge Cl. E14 ... 48Cc 92
Wateringbury Cl. BR5: St P ... 69Xc 139
Water La. AL2: Lon C ... 10H 7
DA14: Sidc ... 61Bd 139
E15 ... 37Gc 73
EC3 ... 5J 225 (45Ub 91)
GU24: Bisl ... 1C 186
GU24: Chob ... 1F 166
HP3: Bov ... 1C 10
IG3: Ilf ... 34Uc 74
KT1: King T ... 67Ma 131
KT11: Cobh ... 87Aa 171
KT23: Bookh ... 97Z 191
N9 ... 18Xb 33
NW1 ... 38Kb 70
RH1: Blet ... 2H 209
RH8: Limp ... 98Jc 199
RH9: S God ... 10B 210
RM19: Purf ... 49Qd 97
SE14 ... 52Yb 114
TN14: S'ham ... 84Hd 182
TN16: Westrm ... 99Tc 200
TW1: Twick ... 60Ja 108
TW9: Rich ... 57Ma 109
WD4: K Lan ... 1R 12
WD17: Wat ... 14Y 27
Water Lily Cl. UB2: S'hall ... 47Ea 86
Waterline Ho. W2 ... 1C 220
Waterloo Bri. WC2 ... 5H 223 (45Pb 90)
Waterloo Cl. E9 ... 36Yb 72
TW14: Felt ... 60V 106
Waterloo East Theatre ... 7A 224
Waterloo Gdns. E2 ... 40Yb 72
N1 ... 38Rb 71
RM7: Rom ... 30Fd 56
Waterloo Pas. NW6 ... 38Bb 69
Waterloo Pl. *SM5: Cars* ... *76Hb 155*
(off Wrythe La.)
SW1 ... 6D 222 (46Mb 90)
TW9: Rich ... 56Na 109
Waterloo Rd. CM14: B'wood ... 18Yd 40
E6 ... 38Lc 73
E7 ... 36Hc 73
E10 ... 31Cc 72
IG6: Ilf ... 26Sc 54
KT19: Eps ... 84Ta 173
NW2 ... 32Wa 68
RM7: Rom, Rush G ... 30Gd 56
SE1 ... 6J 223 (46Pb 90)
SM1: Sutt ... 78Fb 155
UB8: Uxb ... 39L 63
Waterloo St. DA12: Grav'nd ... 9E 122
Waterloo Ter. *KT13: Weyb* ... *77R 150*
(off Baker St.)
N1 ... 38Rb 71
Waterlow Ct. NW11 ... 31Db 69
Waterlow Pk. Cen. ... 32Kb 70
Waterlow Rd. N19 ... 32Lb 70
RH2: Reig ... 7L 207
Waterman Bldg. E14 ... 47Bc 92
Waterman Cl. WD19: Wat ... 16X 27
Waterman Ct. SL1: Slou ... 6C 80
Watermans RM1: Rom ... 29Hd 56
Watermans Art Centre, Cinema & Theatre
... 51Na 109
Watermans Bus. Pk.
TW18: Staines ... 63G 126
Watermans Cl. KT2: King T ... 66Na 131
Watermans Ct. *TW8: Bford* ... *51Ma 109*
(off High St.)
Watermans M. W5 ... 45Na 87
Waterman's Quay SW6 ... 54Eb 111
Watermans St. SW15 ... 55Za 110
Watermans Wlk. SE16 ... 47Ac 92
Watermans Way
DA9: Ghithe ... 56Xd 120
Waterman Way E1 ... 46Xb 91
Watermark Ct. *RM6: Chad H* ... *30Xc 55*
(off Quarles Pk. Rd.)
Water Mead CR5: Chip ... 89Hb 175
Watermead GU21: Wok ... 8K 167
KT20: Tad ... 93Xa 194
TW14: Felt ... 60U 106
Watermead Ho. E9 ... 36Ac 72
Watermead La. SM5: Cars ... 73Hb 155
Watermead Lodge *SE16* ... *46Zb 92*
(off Princes Riverside Rd.)
Watermeadow Cl. DA8: Erith ... 52Kd 119
Watermeadow La. SW6 ... 54Eb 111

Water Mdws. AL2: F'mre 10B 6
Watermead Rd. SE6 63Ec 136
Watermead Way N17 27Xb 51
Watermen's Sq. SE20 66Yb 136
Water M. SE15 56Yb 114
Watermill Bus. Cen. EN3: Brim 12Bc 34
Watermill Cl. TN16: Bras 96Yc 201
TW10: Ham 62La 130
Water Mill Ho. TW13: Hanw 61Ca 129
Watermill La. N18 22Ub 51
Water Mill Way DA4: S Dar 68Rd 141
Watermill Way SW19 67Eb 133
TW13: Hanw 61Ba 129
Watermint Cl. BR5: St P 70Zc 139
Watermint Quay N16 31Wb 71
Waterperry La. GU24: Chob 2K 167
Water Rd. HA0: Wemb 39Pa 67
Waters Dr. TW18: Staines 62H 127
Water's Edge *SW6* *53Ya 110*
(off Palemead Cl.)
Watersedge KT19: Ewe 77Sa 153
Waters Edge Ct. DA8: Erith 50Hd 96
Watersfield Way HA8: Edg 24Ma 47
Waters Gdns. RM10: Dag 36Cd 76
Waterside AL2: Lon C 9J 7
(not continuous)
BR3: Beck 67Bc 136
DA1: Cray 57Gd 118
DA11: Nflt 8A 122
E17 30Yb 52
HP4: Berk 1A 2
N1 2D 218 (40Sb 71)
UB7: Harm 52L 105
UB8: Cowl 43L 83
W2 1B 220
WD4: K Lan 1Q 12
WD7: R'lett 6Ka 14
Waterside Av. *BR3: Beck* *71Ec 158*
(off Adamson Way)
Waterside Bus. Cen. TW7: Isle 56Ka 108
Waterside Cl. E3 39Bc 72
IG11: Bark 35Wc 75
KT6: Surb 75Na 153
RM3: Hrld W 24Qd 57
SE16 47Wb 91
SE28 46Vc 95
TW17: Shep 67S 128
UB5: N'olt 41Ba 85
WD4: K Lan 1R 12
Waterside Ct. *SM5: Cars* *76Jb 156*
(off Millpond Pl.)
Waterside Dr. KT12: Walt T 71W 150
SL3: L'ly 47B 82
Waterside Hgts. *E16* *47Lc 93*
(off Booth Rd.)
Waterside M. UB9: Hare 23J 43
Waterside Pl. NW1 39Jb 70
Waterside Point SW11 52Gb 111
Waterside Rd. UB2: S'hall 48Ca 85
Waterside Twr. *SW6* *54Eb 111*
(off The Boulevard)
Waterside Trad. Cen. W7 48Ga 86
Waterside Trad. Est. KT15: Add 77N 149
Waterside Way GU21: Wok 10M 167
SW17 63Eb 133
Waterslade RH1: Redh 6N 207
Watersmeet Theatre 18N 25
Watersmeet Way SE28 44Yc 95
Waterson Rd. RM16: Grays 9D 100
Waterson St. E2 3J 219 (41Ub 91)
Waters Pl. SW15 54Ya 110
Watersplash Cl. KT1: King T 69Na 131
Watersplash Ct. AL2: Lon C 9K 7
Watersplash La. SL5: Asc 7B 124
TW5: Cran 50X 85
UB3: Harl 49W 84
Watersplash Rd. TW17: Shep 71Q 150
Waters Rd. KT1: King T 68Ra 131
SE6 62Gc 137
Waters Sq. KT1: King T 69Ra 131
Waterstone Way DA9: Ghithe 58Wd 120
Water St. WC2 4K 223
Waterton BR8: Swan 70Fd 140
Waterton Av. DA12: Grav'nd 9G 122
Water Twr. CM14: W'ley 22Xd 58
Water Twr. Cl. UB8: Uxb 36N 63
Water Twr. Hill CR0: C'don 77Tb 157
Water Twr. Pl. N1 39Qb 70
Water Twr. Rd. CM14: Gt War 22Yd 58
Waterview Cl. DA6: Bex 57Zc 117
Waterview Ho. *E14* *43Ac 92*
(off Carr St.)
Waterway Av. SE13 55Dc 114
Waterway Pk. UB3: Hayes 47S 84
Waterway Rd. KT22: Lea 94Ja 192
Waterways Bus. Cen. EN3: Enf L 10Bc 20
Waterweave W2 1C 220
WATERWORKS CORNER 25Gc 53
Waterworks Golf Course 33Ac 72
Waterworks La. E5 33Zb 72
Waterworks Nature Reserve 33Ac 72
Waterworks Rd. SW2 58Pb 112
Waterworks Vs. TN13: S'oaks 98Kd 203
Waterworks Vis. Cen. 33Ac 72
Waterworks Yd. *CR0: C'don* *76Sb 157*
(off Charles St.)
Watery La. AL10: Hat 1A 8
DA14: Sidc 65Xc 139
GU24: Chob 2H 167
KT16: Lyne 73F 148
SW20 68Bb 133
TN15: Kems'g, Seal 93Sd 204
UB3: Harl 50T 84
UB5: N'olt 40Y 65
Wates Way CM15: B'wood 18Zd 41
CR4: Mitc 72Hb 155
Wateville Rd. N17 25Sb 51
WATFORD 14Y 27
Watford Arches Retail Pk.
WD17: Wat 15Z 27
Watford By-Pass HA8: Edg 19Ma 29
WD6: E'tree 16Ja 28
Watford Cl. SW11 53Gb 111
Watford Ent. Cen. WD18: Wat 16U 26
Watford FC 15X 27
Watford Fld. Rd. WD18: Wat 15Y 27
WATFORD HEATH 17Z 27
Watford Heath WD19: Wat 17Z 27
Watford Heath Farm
WD19: Wat 17Aa 27
Watford Ho. *RM3: Rom* *22Pd 57*
(off Redruth Rd.)
Watford Ho. La. WD17: Wat 13X 27
Watford Indoor Bowls Club 5Y 13
Watford Leisure Cen.
CENTRAL 13W 26
WOODSIDE 5Y 13
Watford Metro Cen. WD18: Wat 17S 26
Watford Mus. 14Y 27
Watford Palace Theatre 13X 27
Watford Rd. AL1: St A 9N 5
AL2: Chis G 9N 5
E16 43Jc 93
HA0: Wemb 31Ja 66
HA1: Harr 31Ja 66
HA6: Nwood 24V 44
WD3: Crox G 16Q 26
WD4: Hunt C, K Lan 2Q 12
WD6: E'tree 16Ka 28
WD7: R'lett 8Ga 14
Watford Way NW4 28Wa 48
NW7 21Ua 48
Watkin M. EN3: Enf L 9Cc 20
Watkin Rd. HA9: Wemb 34Ra 67
Watkins Cl. HA6: Nwood 25V 44
Watkins Ho. *E14* *47Ec 92*
(off Manchester Rd.)
Watkinson Rd. N7 37Pb 70
Watkins Ri. EN6: Pot B 4Db 17
WATLING 24Ta 47
Watling Av. HA8: Edg 25Sa 47
Watling Ct. EC4 3E 224
WD6: E'tree 16Ma 29
Watling Farm Cl. HA7: Stan 18La 28
Watling Gdns. NW2 37Ab 68
Watling Ga. NW9 28Ua 48
Watling Ho. *AL3: St A* *4P 5*
(off King Harry La.)
SE17 5E 230
Watling Knoll WD7: R'lett 5Ha 14
Watling Mans. WD7: R'lett 6Ka 14
Watlings Cl. CR0: C'don 72Ac 158
Watling St. AL1: St A 4A 6
AL2: Park 7B 6
DA1: Cray 57Fd 118
DA1: Dart 58Kd 119
(Broomhill Rd.)
DA1: Dart 59Pd 119
(East Hill)
DA1: Dart 59Qd 119
(Lingfield Av.)
DA2: Bean, Bluew, Dart, Ghithe, Sflt
60Td 120
DA6: Bex 56Dd 118
DA11: Nflt 61De 143
DA12: Cobh, Grav'nd 7J 145
EC4 3D 224 (44Sb 91)
SE15 51Ub 113
WD6: E'tree 3Ha 14
WD7: R'lett 3Ha 14
Watling St. Caravan Pk.
AL2: Park 7A 6
Watlington Gro. SE26 64Ac 136
Watling Vw. AL1: St A 5A 6
Watney Cl. CR8: Purl 85Pb 176
Watney Cotts. SW14 55Sa 109
Watney Mkt. E1 44Xb 91
Watney Rd. SW14 55Sa 109
Watney's Rd. CR4: Mitc 71Mb 156
Watney St. E1 44Xb 91
Watson Av. E6 38Qc 74
SM3: Cheam 75Ab 154
Watson Cl. N16 36Tb 71
RM20: W Thur 53Wd 120
SW19 65Gb 133
Watson Gdns. RM3: Hrld W 26Md 57
Watson Ho. RH2: Reig 5J 207
Watsons Ho. N1 1J 219
Watson's M. W1 1E 220 (43Gb 89)
Watsons Rd. N22 25Pb 50
Watsons St. SE8 52Cc 114
Watson St. E13 40Kc 73
Watson's Wlk. AL1: St A 3C 6
Watsons Yd. BR6: Orp 73Xc 161
Watt Ct. W3 47Ua 88
Wattendon Rd. CR8: Kenley 88Rb 177
Wattisfield Rd. E5 34Yb 72
WATTON'S GREEN 16Kd 39
Watts Bri. Rd. DA8: Erith 51Hd 118
Watts Cl. KT20: Tad 94Za 194
N15 29Ub 51
Watt's Cres. RM19: Purf 49Sd 98
Wattsdown Cl. E13 39Jc 73
Watts Farm Pde. *GU24: Chob* *2K 167*
(off Barnmead)
Watts Gro. E3 43Cc 92
Watts Ho. *W10* *43Ab 88*
(off Wornington Rd.)
Watts La. BR7: Chst 67Rc 138
KT20: Tad 94Za 194
TW11: Tedd 64Ja 130
Watts Lea GU21: Wok 7L 167
Watt's Mead KT20: Tad 94Za 194
Watts Point *E13* *39Jc 73*
(off Brooks Rd.)
Watts Rd. KT7: T Ditt 73Ja 152
Watts St. E1 46Xb 91
SE15 53Vb 113
Wat Tyler Ho. *N8* *27Nb 50*
(off Boyton Rd.)
Wat Tyler Rd. SE3 54Fc 115
SE10 54Ec 114
Wauthier Cl. N13 22Rb 51
Wavel Ct. *CR0: C'don* *78Tb 157*
(off Hurst Rd.)
E1 *46Yb 92*
(off Garnet St.)
Wavelengths Leisure Cen. 52Cc 114
Wavell Dr. DA15: Sidc 58Uc 116
Wavell Gdns. SL2: Slou 1D 80
Wavell Ho. AL1: St A 4F 6
Wavel M. N8 28Mb 50
NW6 38Db 69
Wavel Pl. SE26 63Vb 135
Wavendene Av. TW20: Egh 66D 126
Wavendon Av. W4 50Ta 87
Waveney Av. SE15 56Xb 113
Waveney Cl. E1 46Wb 91
Waveney Ho. SE15 56Xb 113
Waverley Av. CR8: Kenley 88Ub 177
E4 21Bc 52
E17 27Fc 53
HA9: Wemb 36Pa 67
KT5: Surb 72Ra 153
SM1: Sutt 75Db 155
TW2: Whitt 60Ba 107
Waverley Cl. BR2: Brom 71Mc 159
E18 25Lc 53
Waverley Cl. KT8: W Mole 71Ca 151
UB3: Harl 49T 84
Waverley Ct. EN2: Enf 13Rb 33
GU22: Wok 90A 168
NW3 37Hb 69
NW6 38Ab 68
SE26 64Yb 136
Waverley Cres. RM3: Rom 24Ld 57
SE18 50Tc 94
Waverley Dr. GU25: Vir W 9L 125
KT16: Chert 76F 148
Waverley Gdns. E6 43Nc 94
HA6: Nwood 25W 44
IG6: Ilf 26Sc 54
IG11: Bark 40Uc 74
NW10 40Pa 67
RM16: Grays 47Ce 99
Waverley Gro. N3 27Za 48
Waverley Ind. Est. HA1: Harr 27Fa 46
Waverley Lodge *AL3: St A* *1B 6*
(off Falmouth Ct.)
E15 *37Gc 73*
(off Litchfield Av.)
Waverley Pl. KT22: Lea 94Ka 192
N4 33Rb 71
NW8 1B 214 (40Fb 69)
Waverley Rd. AL3: St A 1B 6
E17 27Ec 52
E18 25Lc 53
EN2: Enf 13Rb 33
HA2: Harr 33Aa 65
KT11: Stoke D, Oxs 86Da 171
KT13: Weyb 78Q 150
KT17: Ewe 78Xa 154
KT22: Oxs 86Da 171
N8 30Nb 50
N17 25Xb 51
RM13: Rain 42Kd 97
SE18 50Sc 94
SE25 70Xb 135
SL1: Slou 3G 80
UB1: S'hall 45Ca 85
Waverley Vs. N17 26Vb 51
Waverley Way SM5: Cars 79Gb 155
Waverton Ho. E3 39Bc 72
Waverton Rd. SW18 59Eb 111
Waverton St. W1 6J 221 (46Jb 90)
Wavertree Ct. SW2 60Nb 112
Wavertree Rd. E18 26Jc 53
SW2 60Pb 112
Waxham NW3 36Hb 69
Waxhouse Ga. AL3: St A 2B 6
Waxlow Cres. UB1: S'hall 44Ca 85
Waxlow Ho. UB4: Yead 43Z 85
Waxlow Rd. NW10 40Sa 67
Waxlow Way UB5: N'olt 42Ba 85
Waxwell Cl. HA5: Pinn 26Z 45
Waxwell Farm Ho. HA5: Pinn 26Z 45
Waxwell La. HA5: Pinn 26Z 45
Way, The RH2: Reig 5M 207
Wayborne Gro. HA4: Ruis 30S 44
Waycross Rd. RM14: Upm 31Ud 78
Waye Av. TW5: Cran 53W 106
Wayfarer Rd. TW6: H'row A 54K 105
UB5: N'olt 41Z 85
Wayfaring Grn. RM17: Grays 50Be 99
Wayfield Link SE9 58Tc 116
Wayford St. SW11 54Gb 111
Wayland Av. E8 36Wb 71
Wayland Ho. *SW9* *54Qb 112*
(off Robsart St.)
Waylands BR8: Swan 70Hd 140
TW19: Wray 58A 104
UB3: Hayes 43T 84
Waylands Cl. TN14: Knock 87Ad 181
Waylands Mead BR3: Beck 67Dc 136
Waylen Gdns. DA1: Dart 54Pd 119
Waylett Ho. SE11 7K 229
Waylett Pl. HA0: Wemb 35Ma 67
SE27 62Rb 135
Wayman Ct. E8 37Xb 71
Wayne Cl. BR6: Orp 76Vc 161
Wayneflete Ho. KT10: Esh 76Da 151
Wayneflete Twr. Av. KT10: Esh 76Ca 151
Wayne Kirkum Way NW6 36Bb 69
Waynflete *SL4: Eton* *1G 102*
(off Common La.)
Waynflete Av. CR0: Wadd 76Rb 157
Waynflete Ho. *KT10: Esh* *77Da 151*
(off High St.)
SE1 7D 224
Waynflete Sq. W10 45Za 88
(not continuous)
Waynflete St. SW18 61Eb 133
Wayside CR0: New Ad 79Dc 158
EN6: Pot B 5Fb 17
NW11 32Ab 68
SW14 57Sa 109
WD4: Chfd 2K 11
WD7: Shenl 5Ma 15
Wayside, The HP3: Hem H 3C 4
Wayside Av. RM12: Horn 33Md 77
WD23: Bush 16Fa 28
Wayside Cl. N14 16Lb 32
RM1: Rom 27Hd 56
Wayside Commercial Est.
IG11: Bark 39Vc 75
Wayside Ct. AL2: Brick W 2Ba 13
GU21: Wok 8J 167
HA9: Wemb 34Qa 67
TW1: Twick 58La 108
Wayside Gdns. RM10: Dag 36Cd 76
SL9: Ger X 1P 61
Wayside Gro. SE9 63Pc 138
Wayside M. IG2: Ilf 29Qc 54
Wayville Rd. DA1: Dart 59Rd 119
Way Volante DA12: Grav'nd 3G 144
Weald, The BR7: Chst 65Pc 138
Weald Cl. BR2: Brom 75Nc 160
CM14: B'wood 20Wd 40
DA13: Ist R 6A 144
SE16 50Xb 91
Weald Country Pk. 17Td 40
Weald Country Pk. Vis. Cen. 18Td 40
Wealden Ho. *E3* *41Dc 92*
(off Talwin St.)
Wealden Pl. TN13: S'oaks 93Ld 203
Weald La. HA3: Hrw W 26Fa 46
Weald Pk. Golf Course 15Qd 39
Weald Pk. Way CM14: S Weald 20Ud 40
Weald Ri. HA3: Hrw W 24Ha 46
Weald Rd. CM14: B'wood, S Weald 18Qd 39
TN13: S'oaks 100Kd 203
UB10: Hil 40Q 64
Weald Sq. E5 33Wb 71
WEALDSTONE 27Ga 46
Wealdstone Centre, The *27Ga 46*
(off Canning Rd.)
Wealdstone FC 33V 64
Wealdstone Rd. SM3: Sutt 75Bb 155
Weald Way CR3: Cat'm 100Ub 197
RH2: Reig 10L 207
RM7: Rom 30Dd 56
UB4: Hayes 41U 84
Wealdwood Gdns.
HA5: Hat E 23Da 45
Weale Rd. E4 20Fc 35
Weall Cl. CR8: Purl 84Pb 176
Weall Ct. HA5: Pinn 28Aa 45
Weall Grn. WD25: Wat 4X 13
Weardale Av. DA2: Dart 61Sd 142
Weardale Gdns. EN2: Enf 11Tb 33
Weardale Rd. SE13 56Fc 115
Wearmouth Ho. *E3* *43Bc 92*
(off Joseph St.)
Wear Pl. E2 41Xb 91
(not continuous)
Wearside Rd. SE13 56Dc 114
Weasdale Ct. GU21: Wok 8K 167
Weatherall Cl. KT15: Add 78K 149
Weatherbury *W2* *44Cb 89*
(off Talbot Rd.)
Weatherbury Ho. *N19* *34Mb 70*
(off Wedmore St.)
Weatherley Cl. E3 43Bc 92
Weaver Cl. CR0: C'don 77Vb 157
E6 45Rc 94
Weaver Ho. *E1* *42Wb 91*
(off Pedley St.)
Weavers Almshouses *E11* *30Hc 53*
(off Cambridge Rd.)
Weavers Cl. DA11: Grav'nd 10C 122
TW7: Isle 56Ga 108
Weavers Ho. *E11* *30Jc 53*
(off New Wanstead)
Weavers La. SE1 7J 225 (46Ub 91)
TN14: S'oaks 93Ld 203
Weavers Orchard DA13: Sflt 65Ce 143
Weavers Ter. *SW6* *51Cb 111*
(off Micklethwaite Rd.)
Weaver St. E1 42Wb 91
(not continuous)
Weavers Way NW1 39Mb 70
Weaver Wlk. SE27 63Sb 135
Webb Cl. SL3: L'ly 9P 81
W10 42Ya 88
Webb Ct. *SE28* *45Xc 95*
(off Attlee Rd.)
Webber Cl. DA8: Erith 52Kd 119
WD6: E'tree 16Ma 29
Webber Ho. *IG11: Bark* *38Sc 74*
(off North St.)
Webber Row SE1 2A 230 (47Rb 91)
Webber St. SE1 1A 230 (47Qb 90)
Webb Est. E5 31Wb 71
Webb Gdns. E13 42Jc 93
Webb Ho. *RM10: Dag* *34Cd 76*
(off Kershaw Rd.)
SW8 52Mb 112
TW13: Hanw 62Aa 129
Webb Pl. NW10 41Va 88
Webb Rd. SE3 51Hc 115
Webb's All. TN13: S'oaks 97Ld 203
(not continuous)
Webbscroft Rd. RM10: Dag 35Dd 76
Webbs Mdw. TN13: S'oaks 97Ld 203
Webbs Rd. SW11 56Hb 111
UB4: Yead 41X 85
Webb St. SE1 4H 231 (48Ub 91)
Webheath NW6 38Bb 69
(not continuous)
Webley Ct. *EN3: Enf L* *9Cc 20*
(off Sten Cl.)
Webster Cl. EN9: Walt A 5Hc 21
KT22: Oxs 86Da 171
RM12: Horn 34Md 77
Webster Ct. WD3: Rick 18N 25
Webster Gdns. W5 46Ma 87
Webster Rd. E11 34Ec 72
SE16 48Wb 91
SS17: Stan H 1N 101
Websters Cl. GU22: Wok 2M 187
Weddell Ho. *E1* *42Zb 92*
(off Duckett St.)
Wedderburn Ho. SW1 7H 227
Wedderburn Rd. IG11: Bark 39Uc 74
NW3 36Fb 69
Wedgewood Cl. CM16: Epp 2Wc 23
HA6: Nwood 24S 44
Wedgewood Ct. *BR2: Brom* *69Hc 137*
(off Cumberland Rd.)
DA5: Bexl 59Cd 118
Wedgewood Ho. *SW1* *50Kb 90*
(off Churchill Gdns.)
Wedgwood Ct. N7 35Pb 70
Wedgwood Ho. *E2* *41Zb 92*
(off Warley St.)
SE11 4K 229
Wedgwood M. W1 3E 222 (44Mb 90)
Wedgwood Pl. KT11: Cobh 85W 170
Wedgwoods TN16: Tats 93Lc 199
Wedgwood Wlk. *NW6* *36Db 69*
(off Dresden Cl.)
Wedgwood Way SE19 66Sb 135
Wedlake Cl. RM11: Horn 32Nd 77
Wedlake St. W10 42Ab 88
Wedmore Av. IG5: Ilf 25Qc 54
Wedmore Gdns. N19 33Mb 70
Wedmore M. N19 34Mb 70
Wedmore Rd. UB6: G'frd 41Fa 86
Wedmore St. N19 34Mb 70
Wednesbury Gdns.
RM3: Rom 24Pd 57
Wednesbury Grn. RM3: Rom 24Pd 57
Wednesbury Rd. RM3: Rom 24Pd 57
Weech Rd. NW6 35Cb 69
Weedington Rd. NW5 36Jb 70
Weedon Ho. W12 44Wa 88
Weekes Dr. SL1: Slou 6F 80
Weekley Sq. SW11 55Fb 111
Weelkes Cl. SS17: Stan H 1L 101
Weigall Rd. SE12 57Jc 115
Weighhouse St. W1 4J 221 (44Jb 90)
Weightman Ho. SE16 48Wb 91
Weighton M. SE20 68Xb 135
Weighton Rd. HA3: Hrw W 25Fa 46
SE20 68Xb 135
Weihurst Ct. SM1: Sutt 78Gb 155
Weihurst Gdns. SM1: Sutt 78Fb 155
Weimar St. SW15 55Ab 110
Weind, The CM16: They B 8Uc 22
Weint, The SL3: Coln 52E 104
Weir Ct. KT13: Weyb 75R 150
Weirdale Av. N20 19Hb 31
Weird Wood DA3: Lfield 69Ee 143
Weir Hall Av. N18 23Tb 51
Weir Hall Gdns. N18 22Tb 51
Weir Hall Rd. N17 22Tb 51
N18 22Tb 51
Weir Pl. TW18: Staines 67G 126
Weir Rd. DA5: Bexl 59Dd 118
KT12: Walt T 72W 150
KT16: Chert 73K 149
SW12 59Lb 112
SW19 62Db 133
Weirside Gdns.
UB7: W Dray 46M 83
Weir's Pas. NW1 3E 216 (41Mb 70)
Weiss Rd. SW15 55Za 110
Welbeck Av. BR1: Brom 63Jc 137
DA15: Sidc 60Wc 117
UB4: Yead 42X 85
Welbeck Cl. KT3: N Mald 71Va 154
KT17: Ewe 80Wa 154
N12 22Fb 49
WD6: Bore 13Qa 29
Welbeck Ct. *W14* *49Bb 89*
(off Addison Bri. Pl.)
Welbeck Ho. W1 2K 221
Welbeck Rd. E6 41Mc 93
EN4: E Barn 16Gb 31
HA2: Harr 32Da 65
SM1: Sutt 75Fb 155
SM5: Cars 75Fb 155
Welbeck St. W1 1J 221 (43Jb 90)
Welbeck Vs. N21 19Sb 33
Welbeck Wlk. SM5: Cars 74Fb 155
Welbeck Way W1 2K 221 (44Kb 90)
Welbury Ct. *E8* *38Ub 71*
(off Kingsland Rd.)
Welby Ho. N19 31Mb 70
Welby St. SE5 53Rb 113
Welch Pl. HA5: Pinn 25Y 45
Welclose St. AL3: St A 2A 6
Welcome Ct. *E17* *31Cc 72*
(off Saxon Cl.)
SS17: Stan H 2L 101
Welcomes Cotts.
CR3: Wold 95Cc 198
Welcomes Rd. CR8: Kenley 89Tb 177
Welcomes Ter. CR3: Whyt 88Vb 177
Welcote Dr. HA6: Nwood 23T 44
Welden SL2: Slou 4N 81
WELDON 60Be 121
Weldon Cl. HA4: Ruis 37X 65
Weldon Ct. N21 15Pb 32
Weldon Dr. KT8: W Mole 70Ba 129
Weldon Way DA9: Ghithe 57Xd 120
RH1: Mers 1D 208
Weld Pl. N11 22Kb 50
(not continuous)
Weld Works M. SW2 58Pb 112
Welfare Rd. E15 38Gc 73
Welford Cl. E5 34Zb 72
Welford Ct. *NW1* *38Kb 70*
(off Castlehaven Rd.)
SW8 54Lb 112
W9 *43Cb 89*
(off Elmfield Way)
Welford Ho. UB5: N'olt 42Ba 85
Welford Pl. SW19 63Ab 132
Welham Cl. AL9: Wel G 6E 8
WD6: Bore 11Qa 29
Welham Ct. *AL9: Wel G* *6E 8*
(off Dixons Hill Rd.)
WELHAM GREEN 6E 8
Welham Mnr. AL9: Wel G 6E 8
Welham Rd. SW16 65Kb 134
SW17 64Jb 134
Welhouse Rd. SM5: Cars 74Gb 155
Welkin Grn. HP2: Hem H 1C 4
Wellacre Rd. HA3: Kenton 30Ka 46
Wellan Cl. DA15: Sidc 57Xc 117
Welland RM18: E Til 9L 101
Welland Cl. SL3: L'ly 51D 104
Welland Ct. *SE6* *61Bc 136*
(off Oakham Cl.)
Welland Gdns. UB6: G'frd 40Ha 66
Welland Ho. SE15 56Yb 114
Welland M. E1 46Wb 91
Welland Rd. TW6: H'row A 54K 105
Wellands Cl. BR1: Brom 68Pc 138
Welland St. SE10 51Ec 114
Well App. EN5: Barn 15Ya 30
Wellbrook Rd. BR6: Farnb 77Qc 160
Wellbury Ter. HP2: Hem H 2C 4
Wellby Cl. N9 18Wb 33
Wellby Ct. E13 39Lc 73
Well Cl. GU21: Wok 9N 167
HA4: Ruis 34Aa 65
SW16 63Pb 134
Wellclose Sq. E1 45Wb 91
(not continuous)
Wellclose St. E1 45Wb 91
Wellcome Av. DA1: Dart 56Nd 119
Wellcome Collection 5D 216
Wellcome Museum, The *2J 223*
(within Royal College of Surgeons)
Well Cott. Cl. E11 30Lc 53
Well Ct. EC4 3E 224 (44Sb 91)
(not continuous)
Wellcroft HP1: Hem H 1K 3
Wellcroft Rd. SL1: Slou 6F 80
Wellday Ho. *E9* *37Ac 72*
(off Hedger's Gro.)
Welldon Ct. HA1: Harr 29Ga 46
Welldon Cres. HA1: Harr 29Ga 46
WELL END 10Ta 15
Well End Rd. WD6: Bore 9Sa 15
Wellen Ri. HP3: Hem H 5N 3
Weller Ct. *W11* *46Bb 89*
(off Ladbroke Rd.)
Weller Ho. *SE16* *47Wb 91*
(off George Row)
Weller M. BR2: Brom 70Kc 137
EN2: Enf 11Qb 32
Weller Pl. BR6: Downe 83Qc 180
Wellers Cl. TN16: Westrm 99Sc 200
Weller St. SE1 1D 230 (47Sb 91)
Welles Ct. *E14* *45Cc 92*
(off Premiere Pl.)
Wellesford Cl. SM7: Bans 89Bb 175

Wellesley Av. HA6: Nwood ... 22V 44
SL0: Rich P ... 48H 83
W6 ... 48Xa 88
Wellesley Cl. SE7 ... 50Lc 93
Wellesley Cnr. DA11: Nflt ... 60De 121
Wellesley Ct. NW2 ... 33Wa 68
SE1 ... 4D 230 (48Sb 91)
SL0: Rich P ... 47H 83
SM3: Sutt ... 74Ab 154
W9 ... 3A 214 (41Eb 89)
Wellesley Ct. Rd. CR0: C'don ... 75Tb 157
Wellesley Cres. EN6: Pot B ... 5Ab 16
TW2: Twick ... 61Ga 130
Wellesley Gro. CR0: C'don ... 75Tb 157
Wellesley Ho. NW1 ... 4D 216
SL4: Wind ... 3F 102
(off Vansittart Rd.)
SW1 ... 7K 227
Wellesley Mans. *W14 ... 50Bb 89*
(off Edith Vs.)
Wellesley Pde. TW2: Twick ... 62Ga 130
Wellesley Pk. M. EN2: Enf ... 12Rb 33
Wellesley Pas. CR0: C'don ... 75Sb 157
Wellesley Path SL1: Slou ... 7L 81
Wellesley Pl. NW1 ... 4D 216 (41Mb 90)
NW5 ... 36Jb 70
Wellesley Rd. CM14: B'wood ... 17Yd 40
CR0: C'don ... 74Sb 157
E11 ... 29Jc 53
E17 ... 30Cc 52
HA1: Harr ... 29Ga 46
IG1: Ilf ... 33Rc 74
N22 ... 26Qb 50
NW5 ... 36Jb 70
SE18 ... 52Qc 116
SL1: Slou ... 6L 81
SM2: Sutt ... 79Eb 155
(not continuous)
TW2: Twick ... 62Fa 130
W4 ... 50Qa 87
Wellesley St. E1 ... 43Zb 92
Wellesley Ter. N1 ... 3E 218 (41Sb 91)
Welley Av. TW19: Wray ... 56A 104
Welley Rd. SL3: Hort ... 58A 104
TW19: Wray ... 58A 104
Well Farm Hgts. CR3: Whyt ... 91Wb 197
Well Farm Rd. CR6: W'ham ... 91Wb 197
Wellfield DA3: Hartl ... 70Be 143
Wellfield Av. N10 ... 27Kb 50
Wellfield Gdns. SM5: Cars ... 81Gb 175
Wellfield Rd. SW16 ... 63Nb 134
Wellfields IG10: Lough ... 13Qc 36
Wellfield Wlk. SW16 ... 63Pb 134
Wellfit St. SE24 ... 55Rb 113
Wellgarth UB6: G'frd ... 37Ka 66
Wellgarth Rd. NW11 ... 32Db 69
Well Gro. N20 ... 18Eb 31
Well Hall Pde. SE9 ... 56Pc 116
Well Hall Rd. SE9 ... 55Nc 116
WELL HALL RDBT. ... 56Nc 116
WELL HILL ... 79Dd 162
Well Hill BR6: Well H ... 79Dd 162
Well Hill La. BR6: Well H ... 79Dd 162
Well House SM7: Bans ... 87Db 175
Wellhouse La. EN5: Barn ... 14Ya 30
RH3: Bet ... 10A 206
Wellhouse Rd. BR3: Beck ... 70Cc 136
Wellhurst Cl. BR6: Chels ... 80Vc 161
WELLING ... 55Xc 117
Wellingborough Ho.
RM3: Rom ... 22Pd 57
(off Redruth Rd.)
Welling High St. DA16: Well ... 55Xc 117
Welling Rd. RM16: Ors ... 4E 100
Wellings Ho. UB3: Hayes ... 46X 85
Wellington N8 ... 28Nb 50
(not continuous)
Wellington Arch ... 1J 227 (47Jb 90)
Wellington Av. DA15: Sidc ... 58Wc 117
E4 ... 19Cc 34
GU25: Vir W ... 1M 147
HA5: Hat E ... 25Ba 45
KT4: Wor Pk ... 76Ya 154
N9 ... 20Xb 33
N15 ... 30Vb 51
TW3: Houn ... 57Ca 107
Wellington Bldgs. *E3 ... 41Cc 92*
(off Wellington Way)
SW1 ... 50Jb 90
Wellington Cl. KT12: Walt T ... 74V 150
RM10: Dag ... 38Ed 76
SE14 ... 53Zb 114
W11 ... 44Cb 89
WD19: Wat ... 20Ba 27
Wellington Ct. NW8 ... 2B 214
RM16: Grays ... 46De 99
SW1 ... 2F 227
SW6 ... 53Db 111
(off Maltings Pl.)
TW12: Hamp H ... 64Fa 130
TW15: Ashf ... 64N 127
TW19: Stanw ... 59N 105
Wellington Cres.
KT3: N Mald ... 69Sa 131
Wellington Dr. CR8: Purl ... 82Pb 176
RM10: Dag ... 38Ed 76
Wellington Gdns. SE7 ... 51Lc 115
TW2: Twick ... 63Fa 130
Wellington Gro. SE10 ... 52Fc 115
Wellington Hill
IG10: H Beech, Lough ... 9Jc 21
Wellington Ho. *E16 ... 46Jc 93*
(off Pepys Cres.)
NW3 ... 37Hb 69
(off Eton Rd.)
RM2: Rom ... 28Ld 57
SE17 ... 51Sb 113
(off Arnside St.)
UB5: N'olt ... 38Ca 65
(off The Farmlands)
W5 ... 41Na 87
WD24: Wat ... 12Y 27
(off Exeter Cl.)
Wellingtonia Av. RM4: Have B ... 21Ed 56
Wellingtonia Ho. KT15: Add ... 78J 149
Wellingtonia Pl. RH2: Reig ... 5J 207
Wellington Lodge SL4: Wink ... 1A 124
Wellington Mans. E10 ... 32Cc 72
SE7 ... 50Lc 93
(off Wellington Gdns.)
W14 ... 51Bb 111
(off Queen's Club Mans.)
Wellington M. *N7 ... 37Pb 70*
(off Roman Way)
Wellington M. SE7 ... 51Lc 115
SE22 ... 56Wb 113
SW16 ... 62Mb 134
Wellington Monument ... 1J 227
Wellington Mus. ... 1J 227 (47Jb 90)
Wellington Pde. DA15: Sidc ... 57Wc 117
Wellington Pk. Est. NW2 ... 33Wa 68
Wellington Pas. E11 ... 29Jc 53
Wellington Pl. CM14: W'ley ... 22Yd 58
KT11: Cobh ... 84Ca 171
N2 ... 29Gb 49
NW8 ... 3C 214 (41Fb 89)
Wellington Rd. AL1: St A ... 3F 6
AL2: Lon C ... 8H 7
BR2: Brom ... 70Lc 137
BR5: St M Cry ... 72Xc 161
CR0: C'don ... 73Rb 157
CR3: Cat'm ... 94Sb 197
DA1: Dart ... 58Ld 119
DA5: Bexl ... 57Zc 117
DA17: Belv ... 50Bd 95
E6 ... 39Pc 74
E7 ... 35Hc 73
E10 ... 32Ac 72
E11 ... 29Jc 53
E17 ... 28Ac 52
EN1: Enf ... 15Ub 33
HA3: W'stone ... 27Ga 46
HA5: Hat E ... 25Ba 45
NW8 ... 1C 214 (40Fb 69)
NW10 ... 41Za 88
RM18: Tilb ... 4C 122
SW19 ... 61Cb 133
TW2: Twick ... 64Fa 130
TW6: H'row A ... 55L 105
(off Whittle Rd.)
TW12: Hamp H ... 64Fa 130
TW14: Felt ... 57U 106
TW15: Ashf ... 64N 127
UB8: Uxb ... 39L 63
W5 ... 48La 86
WD17: Wat ... 12X 27
Wellington Rd. Nth. TW4: Houn ... 55Ba 107
Wellington Rd. Sth. TW4: Houn ... 56Ba 107
Wellington Row E2 ... 41Vb 91
Wellington Sq. N1 ... 39Nb 70
SW3 ... 7F 227 (50Hb 89)
Wellington St. DA12: Grav'nd ... 9E 122
IG11: Bark ... 39Sc 74
SE18 ... 49Qc 94
SL1: Slou ... 6J 81
WC2 ... 4G 223 (45Pb 90)
Wellington Ter. E1 ... 46Xb 91
GU21: Knap ... 10J 167
HA1: Harr ... 32Fa 66
N8 ... 27Qb 50
(off Turnpike La.)
W2 ... 45Cb 89
Wellington Way E3 ... 41Cc 92
KT13: Weyb ... 82P 169
Welling United FC ... 55Yc 117
Welling Way DA16: Well ... 55Sc 116
SE9 ... 55Sc 116
Well La. CM15: Pil H ... 13Vd 40
GU21: Wok ... 9N 167
RM16: N Stif ... 46Ae 99
SW14 ... 57Sa 109
Wellmeade Dr. TN13: S'oaks ... 99Kd 203
Wellmeadow Rd. SE6 ... 59Gc 115
SE13 ... 58Gc 115
(not continuous)
W7 ... 49Ja 86
Wellow Wlk. SM5: Cars ... 74Fb 155
Well Path GU21: Wok ... 9N 167
Well Pl. NW3 ... 34Fb 69
Well Rd. EN5: Barn ... 15Ya 30
EN6: N'thaw ... 10N 9
NW3 ... 34Fb 69
TN14: Otf ... 88Ld 183
WELLS, THE ... 86Qa 173
Wells, The N14 ... 17Mb 32
Wells Cl. AL3: St A ... 1A 6
CR2: S Croy ... 78Ub 157
KT23: Bookh ... 96Ea 192
SL4: Wind ... 3E 102
UB5: N'olt ... 41Y 85
Wells Ct. BR2: Brom ... 68Fc 137
NW6 ... 40Cb 69
(off Cambridge Av.)
WD17: Wat ... 15Y 27
Wells Dr. NW9 ... 32Ta 67
Wellsfield WD23: Bush ... 15Z 27
Wells Gdns. IG1: Ilf ... 31Nc 74
RM10: Dag ... 36Dd 76
RM13: Rain ... 37Hd 76
Wells Ho. *BR1: Brom ... 64Kc 137*
(off Pike Cl.)
EC1 ... 3A 218
IG11: Bark ... 38Wc 75
(off Margaret Bondfield Av.)
KT18: Eps ... 86Qa 173
SE16 ... 48Yb 92
(off Howland Est.)
W5 ... 46Ma 87
(off Grove Rd.)
W10 ... 42Ab 88
(off Wornington Rd.)
Wells Ho. Rd. NW10 ... 43Ua 88
Wellside Cl. EN5: Barn ... 14Ya 30
Wellside Gdns. SW14 ... 56Sa 109
Wells La. SL5: Asc ... 9A 124
Wells M. W1 ... 1C 222 (43Lb 90)
Wellsmoor Gdns.
BR1: Brom ... 69Qc 138
Wells Pk. Rd. SE26 ... 62Wb 135
Wells Path UB4: Hayes ... 41U 84
Wells Pl. RH1: Mers ... 2B 208
SW18 ... 59Eb 111
TN16: Westrm ... 99Sc 200
Wells Pl. Ind. Est. RH1: Mers ... 1B 208
Wellspring Cres. HA9: Wemb ... 34Ra 67
Wellspring M. SE26 ... 62Xb 135
Wells Ri. NW8 ... 1F 215 (39Hb 69)
Wells Rd. BR1: Brom ... 68Pc 138
KT18: Eps ... 86Qa 173
W12 ... 47Ya 88
Wells Sq. WC1 ... 4H 217 (41Pb 90)
Wells St. W1 ... 1B 222 (43Lb 90)
Wellstead Av. N9 ... 17Zb 34
Wellstead Rd. E6 ... 40Qc 74
Wells Ter. N4 ... 33Qb 70
Wellstones WD17: Wat ... 14X 27
Well St. E9 ... 38Yb 72
E15 ... 37Gc 73
Wells Way SE5 ... 51Tb 113
SW7 ... 3B 226 (48Fb 89)
Wellswood SL5: Asc ... 9A 124
Wellswood Cl. HP2: Hem H ... 1B 4
Wells Yd. N7 ... 36Qb 70
WD17: Wat ... 13X 27
Well Wlk. NW3 ... 35Fb 69
Well Way KT18: Eps ... 87Qa 173
Wellwood Cl. CR5: Coul ... 86Nb 176
Wellwood Rd. IG3: Ilf ... 32Wc 75
Welmar M. *SW4 ... 57Mb 112*
(off Clapham Pk. Rd.)
Welsby Ct. W5 ... 43La 86
Welsford St. SE1 ... 49Wb 91
(not continuous)
Welsh Cl. E13 ... 41Jc 93
Welsh Harp (Brent Reservoir) Nature Reserve
... 32Va 68
Welsh Ho. *E1 ... 46Xb 91*
(off Wapping La.)
Welshpool Ho. *E8 ... 39Wb 71*
(off Welshpool St.)
Welshpool St. E8 ... 39Wb 71
(not continuous)
Welshside *NW9 ... 30Ua 48*
(off Ruthin Cl.)
Welshside Wlk. NW9 ... 30Ua 48
Welstead Ho. *E1 ... 44Xb 91*
(off Cannon St. Rd.)
Welstead Way W4 ... 49Va 88
Weltje Rd. W6 ... 49Wa 88
Welton Ct. SE5 ... 53Ub 113
Welton Ho. *E1 ... 43Zb 92*
(off Stepney Way)
Welton Rd. SE18 ... 52Uc 116
Welwyn Av. TW14: Felt ... 58V 106
Welwyn St. E2 ... 41Yb 92
Welwyn Way UB4: Hayes ... 42U 84
WEMBLEY ... 36Na 67
Wembley Arena ... 35Qa 67
Wembley Commercial Cen.
HA9: Wemb ... 33Ma 67
Wembley Hill Rd. HA9: Wemb ... 34Pa 67
WEMBLEY PARK ... 35Qa 67
Wembley Pk. Blvd. HA9: Wemb ... 35Qa 67
Wembley Pk. Bus. Cen.
HA9: Wemb ... 35Ra 67
Wembley Pk. Dr. HA9: Wemb ... 35Pa 67
Wembley Retail Pk. HA9: Wemb ... 35Ra 67
Wembley Rd. TW12: Hamp ... 67Ca 129
Wembley Sailing Club ... 33Ta 67
Wembley Stadium ... 35Qa 67
Wembley Stadium Ind. Est.
HA9: Wemb ... 35Ra 67
Wembley Way HA9: Wemb ... 37Ra 67
Wemborough Rd. HA7: Stan ... 25Ka 46
Wembury M. N6 ... 31Lb 70
Wembury Rd. N6 ... 31Kb 70
Wemyss Rd. SE3 ... 54Hc 115
Wend, The CR5: Coul ... 86Mb 176
Wendela Cl. GU22: Wok ... 90B 168
Wendela Ct. HA1: Harr ... 33Ga 66
Wendell Rd. W12 ... 48Va 88
Wenderholme *CR2: S Croy ... 78Tb 157*
(off South Pk. Hill Rd.)
Wendle Ct. SW8 ... 51Nb 112
Wendle Sq. SW11 ... 53Gb 111
Wendley Dr. KT15: New H ... 82H 169
Wendling NW5 ... 36Hb 69
Wendling Rd. SM1: Sutt ... 74Fb 155
Wendon St. E3 ... 39Bc 72
Wendover SE17 ... 7H 231 (50Ub 91)
(not continuous)
Wendover Cl. UB4: Yead ... 42Aa 85
Wendover Ct. *BR2: Brom ... 69Kc 137*
(off Wendover Rd.)
NW2 ... 34Cb 69
NW10 ... 42Ra 87
W1 ... 1H 221
Wendover Dr. KT3: N Mald ... 72Va 154
Wendover Gdns. CM13: B'wood ... 19De 41
Wendover Ho. W1 ... 1H 221
WD18: Wat ... 17U 26
(off Chenies Way)
Wendover Pl. TW18: Staines ... 64F 126
Wendover Rd. BR2: Brom ... 70Kc 137
NW10 ... 40Va 68
SE9 ... 55Mc 115
SL1: Burn ... 3A 80
TW18: Staines ... 64E 126
Wendover Way BR6: St M Cry ... 72Wc 161
DA16: Well ... 57Wc 117
RM12: Horn ... 36Ld 77
WD23: Bush ... 16Ea 28
Wendron Cl. GU21: Wok ... 10L 167
Wendy Cl. EN1: Enf ... 16Vb 33
Wendy Way HA0: Wemb ... 39Na 67
Wenham Gdns. CM13: Hut ... 16Ee 41
Wenham Ho. SW8 ... 52Lb 112
Wenlack Cl. UB9: Den ... 34K 63
Wenlake Ho. EC1 ... 5D 218
Wenlock Barn Est. N1 ... 2F 219
Wenlock Ct. N1 ... 2G 219 (40Tb 71)
Wenlock Gdns. NW4 ... 28Xa 48
Wenlock Rd. HA8: Edg ... 24Ra 47
N1 ... 2D 218 (40Sb 71)
Wenlock St. N1 ... 2E 218 (40Sb 71)
WENNINGTON ... 45Nd 97
Wennington Rd. E3 ... 40Zb 72
RM13: Rain, Wenn ... 42Jd 96
Wensdale Ho. E5 ... 33Wb 71
Wensley Av. IG8: Wfd G ... 24Hc 53
Wensley Cl. N11 ... 23Jb 50
RM5: Col R ... 22Cd 56
SE9 ... 58Pc 116
Wensleydale Av. IG5: Ilf ... 26Nc 54
Wensleydale Gdns. TW12: Hamp ... 66Da 129
Wensleydale Pas. TW12: Hamp ... 67Ca 129
Wensleydale Rd. TW12: Hamp ... 65Ca 129
Wensley Rd. N18 ... 23Xb 51
Wensum Ct. WD3: Rick ... 18M 25
Wensum Way WD3: Rick ... 18M 25
Wenta Bus. Cen., The WD24: Wat ... 9Z 13
Wentbridge Path WD6: Bore ... 10Qa 15
Wentland Cl. SE6 ... 61Fc 137
Wentland Rd. SE6 ... 61Fc 137
Wentway Ct. *W13 ... 42Ha 86*
(off Ruislip Rd. E.)
WENTWORTH ... 1K 147
Wentworth Av. N3 ... 24Cb 49
SL2: Slou ... 1E 80
WD6: E'tree ... 15Pa 29
Wentworth Cl. BR2: Hayes ... 75Jc 159
BR6: Farnb ... 78Uc 160
Wentworth Cl. DA11: Grav'nd ... 4C 144
EN6: Pot B ... 3Cb 17
GU23: Rip ... 93K 189
KT6: Surb ... 75Ma 153
N3 ... 24Db 49
SE28 ... 44Zc 95
SM4: Mord ... 73Cb 155
TW15: Ashf ... 63R 128
WD17: Wat ... 10V 12
Wentworth Ct. SW1 ... 7K 227 (50Kb 90)
SW18 ... 58Db 111
(off Garratt La.)
TW2: Twick ... 62Ga 130
W6 ... 51Ab 110
(off Paynes Wlk.)
Wentworth Cres. SE15 ... 52Wb 113
UB3: Harl ... 48T 84
Wentworth Dene
KT13: Weyb ... 78R 150
Wentworth Dr. DA1: Dart ... 58Jd 118
GU25: Vir W ... 10K 125
HA5: Eastc ... 29W 44
WD19: Pinn, Wat ... 22Z 45
Wentworth Dwellings E1 ... 2K 225
Wentworth Flds.
UB4: Hayes ... 40T 64
Wentworth Gdns. N13 ... 20Rb 33
Wentworth Golf Course (East Course)
... 2M 147
Wentworth Golf Course (Edinburgh Course)
... 4K 147
Wentworth Golf Course (West Course)
... 1K 147
Wentworth Hill HA9: Wemb ... 32Pa 67
Wentworth Ho. KT15: Add ... 77K 149
Wentworth Ind. Ct. SL2: Slou ... 1D 80
Wentworth M. E3 ... 42Ac 92
W3 ... 44Ua 88
Wentworth Pk. N3 ... 24Cb 49
Wentworth Pl. HA7: Stan ... 23Ka 46
RM16: Grays ... 48Fe 99
Wentworth Rd. CR0: C'don ... 73Qb 156
E12 ... 35Mc 73
EN5: Barn ... 13Za 30
NW11 ... 30Bb 49
UB2: S'hall ... 49Y 85
Wentworth St. E1 ... 2K 225 (44Vb 91)
Wentworth Tennis & Health Club, The
... 1L 147
Wentworth Way CR2: Sande ... 86Wb 177
HA5: Pinn ... 28Aa 45
RM13: Rain ... 41Kd 97
Wenvoe Av. DA7: Bex ... 54Dd 118
Wepham Cl. UB4: Yead ... 43Z 85
Wernbrook St. SE18 ... 51Sc 116
Werndee Rd. SE25 ... 70Wb 135
Werneth Hall Rd. IG5: Ilf ... 27Pc 54
Werrington St. NW1 ... 2C 216 (40Lb 70)
Werter Rd. SW15 ... 56Ab 110
Wesco Ct. GU21: Wok ... 88C 168
Wescott Way UB8: Uxb ... 40L 63
Wesleyan Pl. NW5 ... 35Kb 70
Wesley Apartments SW8 ... 53Mb 112
Wesley Av. E16 ... 46Jc 93
NW10 ... 41Ta 87
TW3: Houn ... 54Aa 107
Wesley Cl. BR5: St P ... 69Yc 139
EN7: G Oak ... 1Sb 19
HA2: Harr ... 33Ea 66
N7 ... 33Pb 70
RH2: Reig ... 7H 207
SE17 ... 6C 230 (49Rb 91)
Wesley Ct. SE16 ... 48Xb 91
Wesley Dr. TW20: Egh ... 65C 126
Wesley Ho. *AL1: St A ... 2B 6*
(off Marlborough Rd.)
Wesley Pl. KT18: Tatt C ... 90Za 174
SL4: Wink ... 1A 124
Wesley Rd. E10 ... 31Ec 72
KT22: Lea ... 95La 192
NW10 ... 39Sa 67
UB3: Hayes ... 45W 84
Wesley's Chapel & Mus. of Methodism
... 5G 219 (42Tb 91)
Wesley's House ... 5G 219 (42Tb 91)
Wesley Sq. W11 ... 44Ab 88
Wesley St. W1 ... 1J 221 (43Jb 90)
Wessels KT20: Tad ... 93Za 194
Wessex Av. SW19 ... 69Cb 133
Wessex Cl. IG3: Ilf ... 30Uc 54
KT1: King T ... 67Ra 131
KT7: T Ditt ... 75Ha 152
Wessex Ct. BR3: Beck ... 67Ac 136
EN5: Barn ... 14Za 30
HA9: Wemb ... 33Pa 67
TW19: Stanw ... 58N 105
Wessex Dr. DA8: Erith ... 54Gd 118
HA5: Hat E ... 24Aa 45
Wessex Gdns. NW11 ... 32Ab 68
Wessex Ho. SE1 ... 7K 231 (50Vb 91)
WD23: Bush ... 14Ba 27
Wessex La. UB6: G'frd ... 41Fa 86
Wessex St. E2 ... 41Yb 92
Wessex Wlk. DA2: Wilm ... 61Gd 140
Wessex Way NW11 ... 32Ab 68
Wesson Mead *SE5 ... 52Sb 113*
(off Camberwell Rd.)
West 12 Shop. Cen. W12 ... 47Za 88
Westacott UB4: Hayes ... 43U 84
Westacott Cl. N19 ... 32Mb 70
West Acre HA2: Harr ... 33Ga 66
West Acres KT10: Esh ... 80Ba 151
WEST ACTON ... 44Qa 87
Westall Rd. IG10: Lough ... 13Rc 36
West App. BR5: Pet W ... 71Sc 160
W. Arbour St. E1 ... 44Zb 92
West Av. AL2: Chis G ... 7P 5
E17 ... 28Dc 52
HA5: Pinn ... 30Ba 45
KT12: W Vill ... 82U 170
N3 ... 23Cb 49
NW4 ... 29Za 48
SM6: Wall ... 78Nb 156
UB1: S'hall ... 45Ba 85
UB3: Hayes ... 45V 84
West Av. Rd. E17 ... 28Cc 52
West Bank EN2: Enf ... 12Sb 33
IG11: Bark ... 39Rc 74
N16 ... 31Ub 71
Westbank Rd. TW12: Hamp H ... 65Ea 130
WEST BARNES ... 71Xa 154
W. Barnes La. KT3: N Mald ... 69Xa 132
SW20 ... 69Xa 132
WEST BECKTON ... 44Mc 93
WEST BEDFONT ... 58P 105
Westbeech Rd. N22 ... 27Qb 50
Westbere Dr. HA7: Stan ... 22Ma 47
Westbere Rd. NW2 ... 35Ab 68
West Block SE1 ... 2H 229
Westbourne Av. SM3: Cheam ... 75Ab 154
W3 ... 44Ta 87
Westbourne Bri. W2 ... 1A 220 (43Eb 89)
Westbourne Cl. UB4: Yead ... 42Y 85
Westbourne Ct. W2 ... 2A 220 (43Eb 89)
Westbourne Cres. W2 ... 4B 220 (45Fb 89)
Westbourne Cres. M. W2 ... 4B 220
Westbourne Dr. CM14: B'wood ... 21Vd 58
SE23 ... 61Zb 136
Westbourne Gdns. W2 ... 44Db 89
WESTBOURNE GREEN ... 43Cb 89
Westbourne Gro. W2 ... 44Cb 89
W11 ... 45Bb 89
Westbourne Gro. M. W11 ... 44Cb 89
Westbourne Gro. Ter. W2 ... 44Db 89
Westbourne Ho. SW1 ... 7K 227
TW5: Hest ... 51Ca 107
Westbourne M. AL1: St A ... 2B 6
Westbourne Pde. UB10: Hil ... 42R 84
Westbourne Pk. Pas. W2 ... 43Cb 89
(not continuous)
Westbourne Pk. Rd. W2 ... 43Cb 89
W11 ... 44Ab 88
Westbourne Pk. Vs. W2 ... 43Cb 89
Westbourne Pl. N9 ... 20Xb 33
Westbourne Rd. CR0: C'don ... 72Vb 157
DA7: Bex ... 52Zc 117
N7 ... 37Pb 70
SE26 ... 65Zb 136
TW13: Felt ... 62V 128
TW18: Staines ... 66K 127
UB8: Hil ... 42R 84
Westbourne St. W2 ... 4B 220 (45Fb 89)
Westbourne Ter. *SE23 ... 61Zb 136*
(off Westbourne Dr.)
W2 ... 2A 220 (44Eb 89)
Westbourne Ter. M. W2 ... 2A 220 (44Eb 89)
Westbourne Ter. Rd. W2 ... 7A 214 (43Db 89)
Westbourne Ter. Rd. Bri. W2 ... 7A 214
Westbridge Cl. W12 ... 47Wa 88
Westbridge Ho. *SW11 ... 53Gb 111*
(off Westbridge Rd.)
Westbridge Rd. SW11 ... 53Fb 111
WEST BROMPTON ... 51Eb 111
Westbrook Av. TW12: Hamp ... 66Ba 129
Westbrook Cl. EN4: Cockf ... 13Fb 31
Westbrook Cres. EN4: Cockf ... 13Fb 31
Westbrook Dr. BR5: Orp ... 74Zc 161
Westbrooke Cres. DA16: Well ... 55Yc 117
Westbrooke Rd. DA15: Sidc ... 61Tc 138
DA16: Well ... 55Xc 117
Westbrook Ho. *E2 ... 41Yb 92*
(off Victoria Pk. Sq.)
Westbrook Rd. CR7: Thor H ... 67Tb 135
SE3 ... 53Kc 115
TW5: Hest ... 52Ba 107
TW18: Staines ... 64H 127
Westbrook Sq. EN4: Cockf ... 13Fb 31
Westbury EN8: Chesh ... 2Zb 20
SL4: Eton ... 1G 102
(off Eton Wick Rd.)
Westbury Av. HA0: Wemb ... 38Na 67
KT10: Clay ... 79Ha 152
N22 ... 27Rb 51
UB1: S'hall ... 42Ca 85
Westbury Cl. CR3: Whyt ... 90Vb 177
HA4: Ruis ... 31W 64
TW17: Shep ... 72R 150
Westbury Ct. *IG11: Bark ... 39Tc 74*
(off Ripple Rd.)
Westbury Dr. CM14: B'wood ... 19Yd 40
Westbury Gro. N12 ... 23Cb 49
Westbury Ho. E17 ... 28Bc 52
W11 ... 43Cb 89
(off Aldridge Rd. Vs.)
Westbury La. IG9: Buck H ... 19Kc 35
Westbury Lodge Cl.
HA5: Pinn ... 27Z 45
Westbury Pde. *SW12 ... 58Kb 112*
(off Balham Hill)
Westbury Pl. TW8: Bford ... 51Ma 109
Westbury Rd. BR1: Brom ... 67Mc 137
BR3: Beck ... 69Ac 136
CM14: B'wood ... 19Yd 40
CR0: C'don ... 72Tb 157
E7 ... 37Kc 73
E17 ... 28Bc 52
HA0: Wemb ... 38Na 67
HA6: Nwood ... 21U 44
IG1: Ilf ... 33Qc 74
IG9: Buck H ... 19Lc 35
IG11: Bark ... 39Tc 74
KT3: N Mald ... 70Ta 131
N11 ... 23Nb 50
N12 ... 23Cb 49
SE20 ... 67Zb 136
TW13: Felt ... 60Z 107
W5 ... 44Na 87
WD18: Wat ... 15X 27
Westbury Ter. E7 ... 37Kc 73
RM14: Upm ... 33Ud 78
TN16: Westrm ... 99Sc 200
Westbush Ct. *W12 ... 47Xa 88*
(off Goldhawk M.)
WEST BYFLEET ... 85J 169
West Byfleet Golf Courses ... 85H 169
W. Cadet Apartments SE18 ... 52Qc 116
Westcar La. KT12: Hers ... 79X 151
W. Carriage Dr.
W2 ... 5D 220 (45Gb 89)
(North Ride)
W2 ... 1C 226 (47Fb 89)
(Rotten Row)
W. Carriage Ho. SE18 ... 48Rc 94
W. Central St.
WC1 ... 2F 223 (44Nb 90)
West Chantry HA3: Hrw W ... 25Da 45
Westchester Dr. NW4 ... 27Za 48
WEST CLANDON ... 100J 189
Westcliffe Apartments
W2 ... 1C 220 (43Fb 89)
West Cl. EN4: Cockf ... 14Jb 32
EN5: Barn ... 15Xa 30
HA9: Wemb ... 32Pa 67
N9 ... 20Vb 33
RM13: Rain ... 42Kd 97
TW12: Hamp ... 65Aa 129
TW15: Ashf ... 63N 127
UB6: G'frd ... 40Ea 66

Westcombe Av. CR0: C'don 73Nb 156
Westcombe Ct. SE3 52Hc 115
Westcombe Dr. EN5: Barn 15Cb 31
Westcombe Hill SE3 52Jc 115
SE10 50Jc 93
Westcombe Lodge Dr. UB4: Hayes 43U 84
Westcombe Pk. Rd. SE3 51Gc 115
West Comn. SL9: Ger X 29A 42
(not continuous)
West Comn. Cl. SL9: Ger X 29A 42
West Comn. Rd. BR2: Hayes, Kes 74Jc 159
UB8: Uxb 36M 63
Westcoombe Av. SW20 67Va 132
Westcote Ri. HA4: Ruis 31S 64
Westcote Rd. KT19: Eps 83Ra 173
SW16 64Lb 134
West Cotts. NW6 36Cb 69
Westcott Av. DA11: Nflt 2B 144
Westcott Cl. BR1: Brom 71Pc 160
CR0: New Ad 81Dc 178
N15 30Vb 51
Westcott Cres. W7 44Ga 86
Westcott Ho. E14 45Cc 92
Westcott Rd. SE17 51Rb 113
Westcott Way SM2: Cheam 82Ya 174
WESTCOURT 1F 144
West Ct. E17 28Cc 52
HA0: Wemb 33La 66
TW7: Isle 52Ea 108
Westcourt La. DA12: Grav'nd 10H 123
Westcourt Pde. DA12: Grav'nd 2G 144
West Cres. SL4: Wind 3D 102
West Cres. Rd. DA12: Grav'nd 8D 122
Westcroft SL2: Slou 2F 80
Westcroft Cl. EN3: Enf W 10Yb 20
NW2 35Ab 68
Westcroft Est. NW2 35Ab 68
Westcroft Gdns. SM4: Mord 69Bb 133
Westcroft Leisure Cen. 77Jb 156
Westcroft Rd. SM5: Cars 77Jb 156
SM6: Wall 77Jb 156
Westcroft Sq. W6 49Wa 88
Westcroft Way NW2 35Ab 68
W. Cromwell Rd. SW5 50Bb 89
W14 50Bb 89
W. Cross Cen. TW8: Bford 51Ja 108
W. Cross Route W10 45Za 88
W11 45Za 88
W12 45Za 88
W. Cross Way TW8: Bford 51Ka 108
Westdale Pas. SE18 51Rc 116
Westdale Rd. SE18 51Rc 116
Westdean Av. SE12 60Kc 115
Westdean Cl. SW18 58Db 111
West Dene SM3: Cheam 79Ab 154
Westdene KT12: Hers 77X 151
W. Dene Dr. RM3: Rom 22Md 57
Westdene Way KT13: Weyb 76U 150
West Down KT23: Bookh 99Da 191
Westdown Rd. E15 35Ec 72
SE6 59Cc 114
WEST DRAYTON 47N 83
W. Drayton Pk. Av. UB7: W Dray 48N 83
W. Drayton Rd. UB8: Hil 44R 84
West Dr. GU25: Vir W 3J 147
(not continuous)
HA3: Hrw W 23Fa 46
KT15: New H 82K 169
KT20: Tad 90Za 174
SL5: S'dale, Vir W 1H 147
SM2: Cheam 81Za 174
SM5: Cars 82Fb 175
SW16 63Lb 134
WD25: Wat 8X 13
West Dr. Gdns. HA3: Hrw W 23Fa 46
WEST DULWICH 61Tb 135
WEST EALING 46Ka 86
W. Ealing Bus. Cen. W13 45Ja 86
W. Eaton Pl. SW1 5H 227 (49Jb 90)
W. Eaton Pl. M. SW1 5H 227
Wested La. BR8: Crock, Swan 73Jd 162
(not continuous)
W. Ella Rd. NW10 38Ua 68
WEST END
GU24 4D 166
KT10 79Ba 151
UB5 40Z 65
West End TN15: Kems'g 89Pd 183
TN16: Bras 97Xc 201
West End Av. E10 29Fc 53
HA5: Pinn 28Z 45
West End Cl. NW10 38Sa 67
West End Common (Local Nature Reserve)
80Aa 151
West End Ct. HA5: Pinn 28Z 45
NW6 38Db 69
SL2: Stoke P 9K 61
West End Gdns. KT10: Esh 78Ba 151
UB5: N'olt 40Y 65
West End La. AL9: Ess, Hat 1L 9
EN5: Barn 14Za 30
HA5: Pinn 27Z 45
KT10: Esh 80Ba 151
NW6 36Cb 69
(not continuous)
SL2: Stoke P 9J 61
UB3: Harl 52S 106
West End Quay W2 1C 220
West End Rd. HA4: Ruis 33U 64
UB1: S'hall 46Aa 85
UB5: N'olt 38Y 65
Westerdale Rd. SE10 50Jc 93
Westerfield Rd. N15 29Vb 51
Westerfolds Cl. GU22: Wok 89E 168
Westergate W5 43Na 87
Westergate Ho. KT1: King T 70Ma 131
(off Portsmouth Rd.)
Westergate Rd. SE2: Belv 51Ad 117
WESTERHAM 98Tc 200
Westerham NW1 1C 216
Westerham Av. N9 20Tb 33
Westerham Cl. KT15: Add 79L 149
SM2: Sutt 82Cb 175
Westerham Dr. DA15: Sidc 58Xc 117
Westerham Golf Course 98Wc 201
WESTERHAM HILL 92Qc 200
Westerham Hill TN16: Westrm 93Rc 200
Westerham Ho. SE1 3G 231
Westerham Lodge BR3: Beck 66Cc 136
(off Park Rd.)
Westerham Rd. BR2: Kes 79Mc 159
E10 31Dc 72
RH8: Limp, Oxt 1K 211
TN13: Bes G 95Ed 202
Westerham Rd. TN14: Sund 95Dd 202
TN16: Westrm 100Nc 200
TN16: Westrm, Bras 97Vc 201
Westerham Trade Cen.
TN16: Westrm 97Tc 200
Westerley Cres. SE26 64Bc 136
Westerley Ware TW9: Kew 51Qa 109
(off Kew Grn.)
Westermain KT15: New H 82L 169
Western Av. CM14: B'wood 18Yd 40
CM16: Epp 4Vc 23
HA4: Ruis 36Q 64
KT16: Chert 69J 127
NW11 30Za 48
RM2: Rom 26Ld 57
RM10: Dag 37Ed 76
TW20: Thorpe 69D 126
UB5: N'olt 38Z 65
UB6: G'frd 40Fa 66
UB9: Den, Uxb 35L 63
UB10: Hil, Uxb 35L 63
W3 42Pa 87
W5 42Pa 87
Western Av. Bus. Pk. W3 42Ra 87
Western Beach Apartments E16 45Jc 93
Western Cl. KT16: Chert 69J 127
Western Ct. N3 23Cb 49
NW6 40Bb 69
RM1: Rom 29Gd 56
(off Chandlers Way)
W3 44Ta 87
Western Courtyard EC2 1J 225
WESTERN CROSS 60Xd 120
Western Cross Cl. DA9: Ghithe 58Yd 120
Western Dr. TW17: Shep 72T 150
Western Gdns.
CM14: B'wood 19Yd 40
W5 45Qa 87
Western Gateway E16 45Jc 93
Western Intl. Mkt. UB2: S'hall 49X 85
Western La. SW12 59Jb 112
Western Mans. EN5: New Bar 15Db 31
(off Great Nth. Rd.)
Western M. W9 42Bb 89
Western Pde. EN5: New Bar 15Cb 31
RH2: Reig 9K 207
Western Pathway RM12: Horn 38Kd 77
RM13: Rain 38Kd 77
Western Perimeter Rd.
TW6: H'row A, Lford 54K 105
Western Pl. SE16 47Yb 92
Western Rd. CM14: B'wood 19Yd 40
CM16: Epp 4Vc 23
CR4: Mitc 67Fb 133
E13 40Lc 73
E17 29Ec 52
N2 28Hb 49
N22 26Pb 50
NW10 42Sa 87
RM1: Rom 29Gd 56
SM1: Sutt 78Cb 155
SW9 55Qb 112
SW19 67Fb 133
TN15: Bor G 92Be 205
UB2: S'hall 49Y 85
W5 45Ma 87
Western Ter. DA1: Dart 58Kd 119
W6 50Wa 88
Western Vw. UB3: Hayes 47V 84
Westernville Gdns. IG2: Ilf 31Sc 74
Western Way EN5: Barn 16Cb 31
SE28 48Tc 94
West Essex Golf Course 14Gc 35
WEST EWELL 81Ta 173
W. Farm Av. KT21: Asht 90La 172
W. Farm Cl. KT21: Asht 91La 192
W. Farm Dr. KT21: Asht 91Ma 193
Westferry Cir. E14 46Bc 92
Westferry Rd. E14 45Bc 92
WESTFIELD 93A 188
Westfield AL9: Hat 5H 9
DA3: New A 77Be 165
IG10: Lough 15Mc 35
KT21: Asht 90Pa 173
RH2: Reig 3K 207
TN13: S'oaks 94Ld 203
Westfield Av. CR2: Sande 85Tb 177
E20 37Dc 72
GU22: Wok 93A 188
WD24: Wat 9Y 13
Westfield Cl. DA12: Grav'nd 5E 144
EN3: Enf H 13Ac 34
EN8: Walt C 3Bc 20
GU22: Wok 93B 188
NW9 27Sa 47
SM1: Sutt 77Bb 155
SW10 52Eb 111
Westfield Comn. GU22: Wok 94A 188
Westfield Community Sports Cen. 15V 26
Westfield Ct. KT6: Surb 71Ma 153
(off Portsmouth Rd)
NW10 41Za 88
(off Chamberlayne Rd.)
Westfield Dr. HA3: Kenton 28Ma 47
KT23: Bookh 94Ca 191
Westfield Gdns. HA3: Kenton 28Ma 47
RM6: Chad H 30Yc 55
Westfield Gro. GU22: Wok 92A 188
Westfield Ho. SE16 49Zb 92
(off Rotherhithe New Rd.)
SW10 52Fb 111
(off Cremorne Est.)
SW18 60Db 111
Westfield La. HA3: Kenton 29Ma 47
SL3: G Grn 4P 81
Westfield London Shop. Cen. W12 46Ya 88
Westfield Pde. KT15: New H 82M 169
Westfield Pk. HA5: Hat E 24Ba 45
Westfield Pk. Dr. IG8: Wfd G 23Nc 54
Westfield Rd. BR3: Beck 68Bc 136
CR0: C'don 75Rb 157
CR4: Mitc 68Gb 133
DA7: Bex 55Ed 118
GU22: Wok 4P 187
KT6: Surb 71Ma 153
KT12: Walt T 73Aa 151
NW7 20Ta 29
RM9: Dag 35Ad 75
SL2: Slou 2F 80
SM1: Sutt 77Bb 155
W13 46Ja 86
Westfields AL3: St A 4N 5
SW13 55Va 110
Westfields Av. SW13 55Ua 110
Westfield Sq. GU22: Wok 94A 188
Westfields Rd. W3 43Ra 87
Westfield Stratford City Shop. Cen.
E20 37Ec 72
Westfield St. SE18 48Mc 93
Westfield Wlk. EN8: Walt C 3Bc 20
Westfield Way E1 41Ac 92
GU22: Wok 94A 188
HA4: Ruis 34U 64
West Gdn. Pl. W2 3E 220 (44Gb 89)
West Gdns. E1 45Xb 91
KT17: Ewe 82Ua 174
SW17 65Gb 133
Westgate W5 41Na 87
Westgate Apartments E16 45Jc 93
(off Western Gateway)
Westgate Centre, The E8 39Xb 71
(off Bocking St.)
Westgate Cl. KT18: Eps 87Ta 173
Westgate Ct. EN8: Walt C 7Zb 20
SE12 60Jc 115
(off Burnt Ash Hill)
SW9 55Qb 112
(off Canterbury Cres.)
Westgate Cres. SL1: Slou 5D 80
Westgate Est. TW14: Bedf 60R 106
Westgate Ho. KT18: Eps 87Ta 173
(off Chalk La.)
TW7: Isle 54Fa 108
Westgate M. W10 42Ab 88
(off West Row)
Westgate Retail Pk. SL1: Slou 5E 80
Westgate Rd. BR3: Beck 67Ec 136
DA1: Dart 58Md 119
SE25 70Xb 135
Westgate St. E8 39Xb 71
Westgate Ter. SW10 51Db 111
Westglade Ct. HA3: Kenton 29Ma 47
WEST GREEN 28Rb 51
West Grn. Pl. UB6: G'frd 39Fa 66
West Grn. Rd. N15 28Rb 51
West Gro. IG8: Wfd G 23Lc 53
KT12: Hers 78X 151
SE10 53Ec 114
Westgrove La. SE10 53Ec 114
W. Halkin St. SW1 3H 227 (48Jb 90)
West Hall KT14: W Byf 85L 169
West Hallowes SE9 60Mc 115
Westhall Pk. CR6: W'ham 91Yb 198
West Hall Rd. TW9: Kew 53Ra 109
Westhall Rd. CR6: W'ham 90Wb 177
WEST HAM 39Hc 73
West Ham La. E15 38Fc 73
(not continuous)
WEST HAMPSTEAD 37Db 69
W. Hampstead M. NW6 37Db 69
West Ham United FC 40Lc 73
W. Harding St. EC4 2A 224 (44Qb 90)
West Harold BR8: Swan 69Fd 140
WEST HARROW 31Ea 66
W. Hatch Mnr. HA4: Ruis 32V 64
Westhay Gdns. SW14 57Ra 109
WEST HEATH
RH8 2L 211
SE2 51Zc 117
West Heath GU24: Pirb 5B 186
W. Heath Av. NW11 32Cb 69
W. Heath Cl. DA1: Cray 58Hd 118
NW3 34Cb 69
W. Heath Cotts. TN13: S'oaks 100Kd 203
W. Heath Ct. NW11 32Cb 69
W. Heath Dr. NW11 32Cb 69
W. Heath Gdns. NW3 34Cb 69
W. Heath La. TN13: S'oaks 100Kd 203
W. Heath Rd. DA1: Cray 58Hd 118
NW3 33Cb 69
SE2 51Yc 117
WEST HENDON 31Wa 68
W. Hendon B'way. NW9 30Va 48
W. Hertfordshire Crematorium
WD25: Wat 3Z 13
W. Herts Bus. Cen. WD6: Bore 13Ra 29
(off Eldon Av.)
West Herts Golf Course 13T 26
WEST HILL 58Bb 111
West Hill BR6: Downe 84Pc 180
CR2: Sande 82Ub 177
DA1: Dart 58Md 119
HA2: Harr 33Ga 66
HA9: Wemb 32Pa 67
KT19: Eps 85Ra 173
RH8: Oxt 2H 211
SW15 59Za 110
SW18 59Za 110
West Hill Av. KT19: Eps 85Ra 173
West Hill Bank RH8: Oxt 2H 211
West Hill Cl. GU24: Brkwd 2F 186
Westhill Cl. DA12: Grav'nd 10D 122
West Hill Ct. KT19: Eps 85Sa 173
(off Court La.)
N6 34Jb 70
Westhill Ct. W11 45Bb 89
(off Denbigh Rd.)
West Hill Dr. DA1: Dart 58Ld 119
West Hill Golf Course 2F 186
West Hill Pk. N6 33Hb 69
(not continuous)
West Hill Pl. RH8: Oxt 1J 211
Westhill Ri. DA1: Dart 58Md 119
West Hill Rd. GU22: Wok 1P 187
SW18 58Bb 111
West Hill Way N20 18Db 31
Westholm NW11 28Db 49
West Holme DA8: Erith 53Ed 118
Westholme BR6: Orp 73Uc 160
Westholme Gdns. HA4: Ruis 32W 64
Westhope Ho. E2 42Wb 91
(off Derbyshire St.)
WEST HORNDON 30Fe 59
Westhorne Av. SE9 59Jc 115
SE12 59Jc 115
Westhorpe Gdns. NW4 27Ya 48
Westhorpe Rd. SW15 55Ya 110
WEST HORSLEY 100R 190
West Ho. IG11: Bark 37Rc 74
West Ho. Cl. SW19 60Ab 110
West Ho. Cotts. HA5: Pinn 28Z 45
Westhurst Dr. BR7: Chst 64Rc 138
WEST HYDE 24G 42
W. Hyde La. SL9: Chal P 24B 42
W. India Av. E14 46Cc 92
W. India Dock Rd. E14 45Bc 92
W. India Ho. E14 45Cc 92
(off W. India Dock Rd.)
WEST KENSINGTON 49Ab 88
W. Kensington Ct. W14 50Bb 89
(off Edith Vs.)
W. Kensington Mans. W14 50Bb 89
(off Beaumont Cres.)
W. Kent Av. DA11: Nflt 58Ee 121
West Kent Golf Course 84Nc 180
WEST KILBURN 41Bb 69
WEST KINGSDOWN 79Ud 164
W. Kingsdown Ind. Est.
TN15: W King 81Ud 184
Westlake SE16 49Yb 92
(off Rotherhithe New Rd.)
Westlake Cl. N13 20Qb 32
UB4: Yead 42Aa 85
Westlake Rd. HA9: Wemb 33Ma 67
Westland Av. RM11: Horn 32Nd 77
Westland Cl. TW19: Stanw 58N 105
WD25: Wat 6V 12
Westland Ct. UB5: N'olt 41Z 85
(off Seasprite Cl.)
Westland Dr. AL9: Brk P 9G 8
BR2: Hayes 75Hc 159
Westland Ho. E16 46Qc 94
(off Rymill St.)
Westland Pl. N1 3F 219 (41Tb 91)
Westland Rd. WD17: Wat 12X 27
Westlands Av. SL1: Slou 4A 80
Westlands Cl. SL1: Slou 4A 80
UB3: Harl 52V 106
Westlands Ct. KT8: E Mos 70Fa 130
KT18: Eps 87Sa 173
Westlands Ter. SW12 58Lb 112
Westlands Way RH8: Oxt 99Fc 199
Westland Vw. RM16: Grays 46Ce 99
West La. SE16 47Xb 91
West Lawn WD25: A'ham 8Da 13
Westlea Av. WD25: Wat 8Aa 13
Westlea Rd. W7 48Ja 86
Westleigh Av. CR5: Coul 88Jb 176
SW15 57Xa 110
Westleigh Ct. CR2: S Croy 77Ub 157
(off Birdhurst Rd.)
E11 29Jc 53
Westleigh Dr. BR1: Brom 67Nc 138
Westleigh Gdns. HA8: Edg 25Qa 47
West Links HA0: Wemb 41Ma 87
Westlinton Cl. NW7 23Bb 49
West Lodge E16 46Jc 93
(off Britannia Ga.)
W. Lodge Av. W3 46Qa 87
W. Lodge Ct. W3 46Qa 87
W. London Crematorium
NW10 42Xa 88
W. London Studios SW6 52Db 111
(off Fulham Rd.)
Westlyn Cl. RM13: Rain 42Ld 97
Westmacott Dr. TW14: Felt 60V 106
Westmacott Ho. NW8 6C 214
West Mall N9 20Wb 33
RM17: Grays 51Ce 121
(off Grays Shop. Cen.)
W8 46Cb 89
(off Kensington Mall)
W. Malling Way RM12: Horn 36Ld 77
Westmark Point SW15 60Xa 110
(off Norley Va.)
West Mead HA4: Ruis 35Y 65
KT19: Ewe 79Ua 154
Westmead GU21: Wok 9M 167
SL4: Wind 5F 102
SW15 58Xa 110
Westmead Cnr. SM5: Cars 77Gb 155
Westmeade Cl. EN7: Chesh 1Xb 19
Westmead Ho. SM1: Sutt 77Fb 155
Westmead Rd. SM1: Sutt 77Fb 155
Westmede IG7: Chig 23Sc 54
Westmere Dr. NW7 20Ta 29
W. Mersea Cl. E16 46Kc 93
West M. N17 24Xb 51
SW1 6B 228
West Middlesex Golf Course 45Ea 86
West Mill DA11: Grav'nd 8B 122
WESTMINSTER 2F 229 (47Nb 90)
Westminster Abbey 3F 229 (48Mb 90)
Westminster Abbey Chapter House 3F 229
Westminster Abbey Mus. 3F 229
Westminster Abbey Pyx Chamber 3F 229
Westminster Av. CR7: Thor H 68Rb 135
Westminster Boating Base & Pier
51Mb 112
Westminster Bri. SW1 2G 229 (47Nb 90)
Westminster Bri. Ho. SE1 3B 230
Westminster Bri. Rd.
SE1 2H 229 (47Pb 90)
Westminster Bus. Sq. SE11 51Pb 112
(off Durham St.)
Westminster Cl. IG6: Ilf 26Tc 54
TW11: Tedd 64Ja 130
TW14: Felt 60W 106
Westminster Ct. AL1: St A 4A 6
E11 30Kc 53
(off Cambridge Pk.)
EN8: Walt C 5Cc 20
GU22: Wok 93D 188
NW8 6B 214
SE16 46Zb 92
(off King & Queen Wharf)
Westminster Dr. N13 22Nb 50
Westminster Gdns. E4 18Gc 35
IG6: Ilf 26Sc 54
IG11: Bark 40Uc 74
SW1 5F 229
Westminster Hall 2F 229
Westminster Ho. HA3: Hrw W 24Ha 46
WD24: Wat 12Y 27
(off Hallam Cl.)
Westminster Ind. Est. SE18 48Mc 93
Westminster Lodge Leisure Cen. 4A 6
Westminster Mans. SW1 3E 228
Westminster Pal. Gdns. SW1 4D 228
Westminster RC Cathedral
4B 228 (48Lb 90)
Westminster Rd. N9 18Xb 33
SM1: Sutt 75Fb 155
W7 46Ga 86
Westmoat Cl. BR3: Beck 66Ec 136
WEST MOLESEY 70Ca 129
Westmont Rd. KT10: Hin W 75Ga 152
Westmoor Gdns. EN3: Enf H 12Zb 34
Westmoor Rd. EN3: Enf H 12Zb 34
Westmoor St. SE7 48Lc 93
Westmore Ct. SW15 57Ab 110
Westmore Grn. TN16: Tats 92Lc 199
Westmoreland Av. DA16: Well 55Uc 116
RM11: Horn 29Ld 57
Westmoreland Dr. SM2: Sutt 80Db 155
Westmoreland Ho. E16 46Jc 93
(off Gatcombe Rd.)
Westmoreland Pl. BR1: Brom 69Jc 137
SW1 7A 228 (50Kb 90)
W5 43Ma 87
Westmoreland Rd. BR1: Brom 71Gc 159
BR2: Brom 71Gc 159
NW9 27Pa 47
SE17 51Tb 113
(not continuous)
SW13 53Va 110
Westmoreland St. W1 1J 221 (43Jb 90)
Westmoreland Ter. SE20 66Xb 135
SW1 7A 228 (50Kb 90)
Westmoreland Wlk. SE17 51Tb 113
(not continuous)
Westmore Rd. TN16: Tats 93Lc 199
Westmorland Cl. E12 33Mc 73
KT19: Ewe 82Ua 174
TW1: Twick 58Ka 108
Westmorland Ct. KT6: Surb 73Ma 153
Westmorland Rd. E17 30Cc 52
HA1: Harr 29Da 45
Westmorland Sq. CR4: Mitc 71Nb 156
Westmorland Way CR4: Mitc 70Mb 134
Westmount Apartments WD18: Wat 14V 26
(off Metropolitan Sta. App.)
Westmount Ct. W5 44Pa 87
Westmount Rd. SE9 54Pc 116
Westmouth Cl. KT4: Wor Pk 74Ya 154
WEST NORWOOD 63Sb 135
West Norwood Crematorium
SE27 62Sb 135
West Oak BR3: Beck 67Fc 137
Westoe Rd. N9 19Xb 33
Weston Av. KT7: T Ditt 73Ga 152
KT8: W Mole 69Aa 129
KT15: Add 77K 149
RM20: W Thur 51Vd 120
Westonbirt Ct. SE15 51Vb 113
(off Ebley Cl.)
Weston Cl. CM13: Hut 17Ee 41
CR5: Coul 92Pb 196
EN6: Pot B 4Bb 17
Weston Ct. KT1: King T 69Na 131
(off Grove Cres.)
N4 34Sb 71
N20 17Eb 31
(off Farnham Cl.)
Weston Dr. CR3: Cat'm 94Sb 197
HA7: Stan 25Ka 46
West One Ho. W1 1B 222
Westone Mans. IG11: Bark 38Vc 75
(off Upney La.)
West One Shop. Cen. W1 3J 221
Weston Gdns. GU22: Pyr 88G 168
TW7: Isle 53Ga 108
WESTON GREEN 74Ga 152
Weston Grn. KT7: T Ditt 74Ga 152
(Weston Grn. Rd.)
KT7: T Ditt 75Ga 152
(Weston Rd.)
RM9: Dag 35Bd 75
Weston Grn. Rd. KT7: T Ditt 74Ga 152
KT10: Esh 74Fa 152
Weston Gro. BR1: Brom 67Hc 137
Weston Ho. E9 39Yb 72
(off King Edward's Rd.)
NW6 38Ab 68
Westonia Ct. EN3: Enf W 8Zb 20
Weston Lea KT24: W Hor 97T 190
Weston Pk. KT1: King T 68Na 131
KT7: T Ditt 74Ga 152
N8 30Nb 50
Weston Pk. Cl. KT7: T Ditt 74Ga 152
Weston Ri. WC1 2J 217 (41Pb 90)
Weston Rd. BR1: Brom 66Hc 137
EN2: Enf 12Tb 33
KT7: T Ditt 74Ga 152
KT17: Eps 83Ua 174
RM9: Dag 35Ad 75
SL1: Slou 3D 80
W4 48Sa 87
Weston St. SE1 7G 225 (47Ub 91)
(not continuous)
Westons Yd. SL4: Eton 1H 103
Weston Wlk. E8 38Xb 71
Weston Way GU22: Pyr 88G 168
Westover Cl. SM2: Sutt 81Db 175
Westover Hill NW3 33Cb 69
Westover Rd. SW18 59Eb 111
Westow Hill SE19 65Ub 135
Westow St. SE19 65Ub 135
West Pal. Gdns. KT13: Weyb 76R 150
West Pk. SE9 61Nc 138
West Pk. Av. TW9: Kew 53Qa 109
West Pk. Cl. RM6: Chad H 29Zc 55
TW5: Hest 51Ba 107
West Pk. Hill CM14: B'wood 20Wd 40
West Pk. Rd. KT19: Eps 83Pa 173
TW9: Kew 53Qa 109
UB2: S'hall 46Ea 86
West Parkside CR6: W'ham 87Cc 178
SE10 47Gc 93
West Pl. SW19 64Ya 132
West Point E14 45Bc 92
(off Grenade St.)
KT19: Ewe 81Ua 174
SE1 50Wb 91
SL1: Slou 5K 79
Westpoint Apartments N8 27Pb 50
W. Point Cl. TW4: Houn 55Ba 107
(off Grosvenor Rd.)
Westpoint Trad. Est. W3 43Ra 87
West Pole Av. EN4: Cockf 14Jb 32
Westport Ct. UB4: Yead 42Y 85
Westport Rd. E13 42Kc 93
Westport St. E1 44Zb 92
W. Poultry Av. EC1 1B 224 (43Rb 91)
West Quarters W12 44Wa 88
West Quay SW10 53Eb 111
W. Quay Dr. UB4: Yead 43Aa 85
West Quay Wlk. E14 48Dc 92
West Ramp TW6: H'row A 53Q 106
Westray HP3: Hem H 4C 4
West Reservoir Cen. 32Sb 71
Westridge Cl. HP1: Hem H 2H 3
W. Ridge Gdns.
UB6: G'frd 40Ea 66
West Riding AL2: Brick W 2Ba 13
West Ri. W2 4E 220

West Rd. E15 39Hc 73
EN4: E Barn 18Jb 32
KT2: King T 67Sa 131
KT9: Chess 84La 172
KT13: Weyb 81R 170
N17 23Xb 51
RH2: Reig 7K 207
RM6: Chad H 30Zc 55
RM7: Rush G 31Fd 76
RM15: S Ock 41Wd 98
SE1 1J 229 (47Pb 90)
SW3 50Hb 89
SW4 57Mb 112
TW14: Bedf 58T 106
UB7: W Dray 48P 83
W5 43Na 87
Westrovia Ct. SW1 6D 228
West Row W10 42Ab 88
Westrow SW15 58Ya 110
Westrow Dr. IG11: Bark 36Wc 75
Westrow Gdns. IG3: Ilf 33Vc 75
WEST RUISLIP 33S 64
W. Ruislip Ct. HA4: Ruis 33T 64
(off Ickenham Rd.)
West Shaw DA3: Lfield 68Zd 143
W. Sheen Va. TW9: Rich 56Pa 109
West Side HP3: Hem H 7P 3
Westside N2 27Hb 49
NW4 26Xa 48
Westside Apartments IG1: Ilf 34Qc 74
(off Roden St.)
West Side Comn. SW19 64Ya 132
West Side Ct. TW16: Sun 66U 128
(off Scotts Av.)
Westside Ct. GU24: W End 5C 166
W9 42Cb 89
(off Elgin Av.)
West Smithfield EC1 1B 224 (43Rb 91)
W. Spur Rd. UB8: Cowl 41M 83
West Sq. E10 31Dc 72
SE11 4B 230 (48Rb 91)
SL0: Iver 44H 83
West Stand N5 34Rb 71
West St. BR1: Brom 67Jc 137
CR0: C'don 77Sb 157
DA7: Bex 55Bd 117
DA8: Erith 49Fd 96
DA11: Grav'nd 8C 122
E2 40Xb 71
E11 34Gc 73
E17 29Dc 52
GU21: Wok 89B 168
HA1: Harr 32Fa 66
KT17: Ewe 82Ua 174
KT18: Eps 85Sa 173
RH2: Reig 6G 206
RM17: Grays 51Ce 121
SM1: Sutt 78Db 155
SM5: Cars 76Hb 155
TN15: Wro 88Be 185
TW8: Bford 51La 108
WC2 3E 222 (44Mb 90)
WD17: Wat 12X 27
West St. La. SM5: Cars 77Hb 155
West St. Pl. CR0: C'don 77Sb 157
(off West St.)
W. Temple Sheen SW14 57Ra 109
W. Tenter St. E1 3K 225 (44Vb 91)
West Ter. DA15: Sidc 60Uc 116
W. Thamesmead Bus. Pk.
SE28 48Uc 94
(not continuous)
WEST THURROCK 51Wd 120
W. Thurrock Way
RM20: Chaf H, Grays, W Thur
48Vd 98
WEST TILBURY 1G 122
West Twr. E14 47Dc 92
(off Pan Peninsula Sq.)
West Towers HA5: Pinn 29Z 45
Westvale M. W3 47Ua 88
W. Valley Rd. HP3: Hem H 7L 3
West Vw. IG10: Lough 13Pc 36
KT21: Asht 91La 192
NW4 28Ya 48
TW14: Bedf 59S 106
Westview GU22: Wok 90B 168
(off Park Dr.)
W7 44Ga 86
Westview Av. CR3: Whyt 90Vb 177
Westview Cl. NW10 36Va 68
RH1: Redh 8N 207
RM13: Rain 41Ld 97
W10 44Ya 88
West Vw. Ct. WD6: E'tree 16Ma 29
Westview Ct. N20 18Eb 31
Westview Cres. N9 17Ub 33
Westview Dr. IG8: Wfd G 26Mc 53
West Vw. Gdns. WD6: E'tree 16Ma 29
Westview Ri. HP2: Hem H 1M 3
West Vw. Rd. AL3: St A 1B 6
BR8: Crock 72Fd 162
BR8: Swan 70Jd 140
DA1: Dart 58Pd 119
Westview Rd. CR6: W'ham 91Xb 197
Westville Rd. KT7: T Ditt 74Ja 152
W12 47Wa 88
West Wlk. EN4: E Barn 17Jb 32
NW9 25Ua 48
UB3: Hayes 46W 84
W5 43Na 87
Westward Rd. E4 22Bc 52
(not continuous)
Westward Way HA3: Kenton 30Na 47
W. Warwick Pl. SW1 6B 228 (49Lb 90)
WEST WATFORD 14W 26
Westway BR4: W W'ck 72Fc 159
BR5: Pet W 71Tc 160
CM14: B'wood 20Wd 40
CR0: C'don 75Ac 158
HA4: Ruis 32V 64
HA5: Pinn 28Z 45
HA8: Edg 23Ra 47
NW10 34Ta 67
SM5: Cars 82Fb 175
TW5: Hest 53Ba 107
TW17: Shep 72T 150
WD3: Rick 16M 25
Westway CR3: Cat'm 94Tb 197
N18 21Tb 51
SW20 69Xa 132
UB6: G'frd 39Ga 66
W2 1A 220 (43Bb 89)
W9 43Bb 89
Westway W10 43Bb 89
W12 45Va 88
Westway Cl. SW20 69Xa 132
Westway Ct. CR3: Cat'm 95Tb 197
UB5: N'olt 39Ca 65
Westway Est. W3 43Ua 88
West Way Gdns. CR0: C'don 75Zb 158
Westway Gdns. RH1: Redh 3A 208
Westway Lodge W9 43Cb 89
(off Amberley Rd.)
West Ways HA6: Nwood 26W 44
Westways KT19: Ewe 77Va 154
TN16: Westrm 98Sc 200
Westway Sports Cen. 44Za 88
Westway Travellers Site
W12 45Za 88
(off Stable Way)
Westwell Cl. BR5: Orp 74Zc 161
Westwell M. SW16 65Nb 134
Westwell Rd. SW16 65Nb 134
Westwell Rd. App. SW16 65Nb 134
Westwick KT1: King T 68Qa 131
(off Chesterton Ter.)
Westwick Cl. HP2: Hem H 3D 4
Westwick Gdns. TW4: Cran 54X 107
W14 47Za 88
WEST WICKHAM 74Ec 158
West Wickham Leisure Cen. 74Ec 158
Westwick Pl. WD25: Wat 6Y 13
Westwick Row HP2: Hem H 2D 4
West Wing Arts Cen. 4L 81
West Wintergarden 46Dc 92
(off Bank St.)
WESTWOOD 66Zd 143
Westwood Av. CM14: B'wood 21Wd 58
HA2: Harr 35Da 65
KT15: Wdhm 84H 169
SE19 67Sb 135
Westwood Bus. Cen. NW10 42Ua 88
Westwood Cl. BR1: Brom 68Mc 137
EN6: Pot B 2Cb 17
HA4: Ruis 30R 44
HP6: L Chal 11A 24
KT10: Esh 76Fa 152
Westwood Ct. EN1: Enf 16Ub 33
(off Village Rd.)
HA0: Wemb 35Ka 66
UB6: G'frd 36Fa 66
Westwood Dr. HP6: L Chal 11A 24
Westwood Gdns. SW13 55Va 110
Westwood Hill SE26 64Wb 135
Westwood Ho. W12 46Ya 88
(off Wood La.)
Westwood La. DA15: Sidc 57Wc 117
DA16: Well 55Vc 117
Westwood M. E3 41Cc 92
(off Addington Rd.)
Westwood Pk. SE23 59Xb 113
Westwood Pk. Trad. Est. W3 43Ra 87
Westwood Pl. SE26 63Wb 135
Westwood Rd. CR5: Coul 90Mb 176
DA13: Sflt 66Ae 143
E16 46Kc 93
GU20: W'sham 5C 146
IG3: Ilf 32Vc 75
SW13 55Va 110
West Woodside DA5: Bexl 59Ad 117
Westwood Way TN13: S'oaks 94Hd 202
WEST YOKE 76Ae 165
West Yoke TN15: Ash 75Zd 165
W. Yoke Rd. DA3: New A 76Ae 165
Wetheral Dr. HA7: Stan 25Ka 46
Wetherall M. AL1: St A 3C 6
Wetherby Cl. UB5: N'olt 37Da 65
Wetherby Gdns. SW5 6A 226 (49Eb 89)
Wetherby Mans. SW5 50Db 89
(off Earls Ct. Sq.)
Wetherby M. SW5 50Db 89
Wetherby Pl. SW7 6A 226 (49Eb 89)
Wetherby Rd. EN2: Enf 11Sb 33
WD6: Bore 11Na 29
Wetherby Way KT9: Chess 80Na 153
Wetherden St. E17 31Bc 72
Wethered Dr. SL1: Burn 3A 80
Wetherell Rd. E9 39Zb 72
Wetherill Rd. N10 25Jb 50
Wettern Cl. CR2: Sande 82Ub 177
Wetton Ct. TW20: Egh 64B 126
(off Wetton Pl.)
Wetton Pl. TW20: Egh 64B 126
Wevco Wharf SE15 51Xb 113
Wevell Ho. N6 31Jb 70
(off Hillcrest)
Wexfenne Gdns. GU22: Pyr 88K 169
Wexford Ho. E1 43Yb 92
(off Sidney St.)
Wexford Rd. SW12 59Hb 111
WEXHAM 2N 81
WEXHAM COURT 4N 81
Wexham Lodge SL2: Wex 2N 81
Wexham Pk. Golf Course 10N 61
Wexham Pk. La. SL3: Wex 2N 81
Wexham Pl. SL2: Wex 7P 61
Wexham Rd. SL1: Slou 7L 81
SL2: Slou 4M 81
Wexham Springs SL3: Wex 8P 61
WEXHAM STREET 10N 61
Wexham St.
SL2: Stoke P, Wex, Slou 2M 81
SL3: Stoke P, Wex 2M 81
Wexham Woods SL3: Wex 3N 81
Wexner Bldg. E1 1K 225
Wey Av. KT16: Chert 69J 127
Weybank GU23: Wis 88N 169
Wey Barton KT14: Byfl 85P 169
Weybourne Pl. CR2: Sande 82Tb 177
Weybourne St. SW18 61Eb 133
Weybourne Way KT15: New H 81L 169
WEYBRIDGE 77Q 150
Weybridge Bus. Pk.
KT15: Add 77N 149
Weybridge Ct. SE16 50Xb 91
Weybridge Ho. KT13: Weyb 78T 150
Weybridge Pk. KT13: Weyb 78Q 150
Weybridge Point SW11 54Hb 111
Weybridge Rd. CR7: Thor H 70Qb 134
KT13: Weyb 77N 149
KT15: Add 77N 149
Weybrook Dr. GU4: Burp 100E 188
Wey Cl. KT14: W Byf 85K 169
Wey Ct. GU22: Wok 91A 188
(off Claremont Av.)
KT15: New H 81M 169
KT19: Ewe 77Sa 153
Weydown Cl. SW19 60Ab 110
Weyhill Rd. E1 44Wb 91
Wey Ho. NW8 6C 214
Weylands Cl. KT12: Walt T 74Ba 151
Weylands Ct. KT15: Add 77M 149
(off Corrie Rd.)
Weylands Pk. KT13: Weyb 79T 150
Weylond Rd. RM8: Dag 34Bd 75
Wey Mnr. Rd. KT15: New H 81M 169
Weyman Rd. SE3 53Lc 115
Weymarks, The N17 23Tb 51
Weymead Cl. KT16: Chert 74L 149
Wey Mdws. KT13: Weyb 78N 149
Weymede KT14: Byfl 84P 169
Weymouth Av. NW7 22Ua 48
W5 48La 86
Weymouth Cl. E6 44Rc 94
Weymouth Ct. E2 1K 219
SM2: Sutt 80Cb 155
Weymouth Dr. RM16: Chaf H 50Zd 99
Weymouth Ho. BR2: Brom 68Hc 137
(off Beckenham La.)
SW8 52Pb 112
(off Bolney St.)
Weymouth M. W1 7K 215 (43Kb 90)
Weymouth Rd. UB4: Hayes 41U 84
Weymouth St. HP3: Hem H 6M 3
W1 1J 221 (43Jb 90)
Weymouth Ter. E2 1K 219 (40Vb 71)
Weymouth Vs. N4 33Pb 70
(off Moray Rd.)
Weymouth Wlk. HA7: Stan 23Ja 46
Wey Retail Pk. KT14: Byfl 84N 169
Wey Rd. KT13: Weyb 76P 149
Weyside Cl. KT14: Byfl 84P 169
Weystone Rd. KT13: Weyb 77P 149
Weyver Ct. AL1: St A 1C 6
(off Avenue Rd.)
Whadcoat St. N4 33Qb 70
Whalebone Av. RM6: Chad H 30Bd 55
Whalebone Ct. EC2 2F 225
Whalebone Gro. RM6: Chad H 30Bd 55
Whalebone La. E15 38Gc 73
Whalebone La. Nth.
RM6: Chad H, Col R 24Ad 55
Whalebone La. Sth.
RM6: Chad H, Dag 30Bd 55
RM8: Dag 30Bd 55
Whales Yd. E15 38Gc 73
(off West Ham La.)
Whaley Rd. EN6: Pot B 5Eb 17
Wharf, The DA9: Ghithe 56Wd 120
(off Evelyn Wlk.)
EC3 6J 225 (46Vb 91)
KT13: Weyb 75Q 150
Wharf Cl. SS17: Stan H 2M 101
Wharfdale Cl. N11 23Jb 50
Wharfdale Rd. N1 1G 217 (40Nb 70)
Wharfedale Ct. E5 35Zb 72
Wharfedale Gdns. CR7: Thor H 70Pb 134
Wharfedale Ho. NW6 39Db 69
(off Kilburn Vale)
Wharfedale Rd. DA2: Dart 60Sd 120
Wharfedale St. SW10 50Db 89
Wharfedale Yd. N1 1G 217
Wharf Ho. DA8: Erith 50Gd 96
(off West St.)
Wharf La. E14 44Bc 92
GU23: Rip 90M 169
GU23: Send 95E 188
TW1: Twick 60Ja 108
WD3: Rick 18N 25
Wharf Pl. E2 39Xb 71
Wharf Rd. CM14: B'wood 20Yd 40
DA12: Grav'nd 8G 122
EN3: Pond E 16Ac 34
HP1: Hem H 4K 3
N1 2D 218 (40Sb 71)
RM17: Grays 51Be 121
SS17: Stan H 2M 101
(not continuous)
TW19: Wray 9N 103
Wharf Rd. Ind. Est.
EN3: Pond E 16Ac 34
Wharf Rd. Sth. RM17: Grays 51Be 121
Wharfside Cl. DA8: Erith 50Hd 96
Wharfside Point Nth. E14 45Ec 92
(off Poplar High St.)
Wharfside Point Sth. E14 45Ec 92
Wharfside Rd. E16 43Gc 93
Wharf St. E16 43Gc 93
Wharf Vw. Ct. E14 44Ec 92
(off Blair St.)
Wharf Vs. HP1: Hem H 4K 3
Wharf Way WD4: Hunt C 5S 12
Wharncliffe Dr. UB1: S'hall 46Fa 86
Wharncliffe Gdns. SE25 68Ub 135
Wharncliffe Rd. SE25 68Ub 135
Wharnecliffe DA9: Ghithe 58Xd 120
Wharton Cl. NW10 37Ua 68
Wharton Cotts. WC1 4K 217 (41Qb 90)
Wharton Ho. SE1 3K 231
Wharton Rd. BR1: Brom 67Kc 137
Wharton St. WC1 4J 217 (41Pb 90)
Whatcote Cotts. TN15: Plat 92Ee 205
Whatcott's Yd. N16 35Ub 71
Whateley Rd. SE20 66Zb 136
SE22 57Vb 113
Whatley Av. SW20 69Za 132
Whatman Ho. E14 44Bc 92
(off Wallwood St.)
Whatman Rd. SE23 59Zb 114
Whatmore Cl. TW19: Stanw M 58J 105
Wheatash Rd. KT15: Add 75K 149
Wheatbutts, The SL4: Eton W 9D 80
Wheatcroft EN7: Chesh 1Xb 19
Wheatcroft Ct. SM1: Sutt 74Db 155
(off Cleeve Way)
Wheatfield Ho. NW6 41Cb 89
(off Kilburn Pk. Rd.)
Wheatfields CM14: W'ley 21Yd 58
E6 44Rc 94
EN3: Enf H 11Ac 34
Wheatfields Ct. EN9: Walt A 6Jc 21
(off Farthingale La.)
Wheatfield Way KT1: King T 68Na 131
Wheathill Ho. SE20 68Xb 135
(off Croydon Rd.)
Wheathill Rd. SE20 69Xb 135
Wheat Knoll CR8: Kenley 88Sb 177
Wheatland Ho. SE22 55Ub 113
Wheatlands TW5: Hest 51Ca 107
Wheatlands Rd. SL3: Slou 8M 81
SW17 62Jb 134
Wheatley Cl. DA9: Ghithe 57Wd 120
NW4 26Wa 48
RM11: Horn 29Md 57
Wheatley Ct. E3 41Dc 92
(off Bruce Rd.)
Wheatley Cres. UB3: Hayes 45W 84
Wheatley Dr. WD25: Wat 6Y 13
Wheatley Gdns. N9 19Ub 33
Wheatley Ho. SW15 59Wa 110
(off Ellisfield Dr)
Wheatley Mans. IG11: Bark 38Wc 75
(off Lansbury Av.)
Wheatley Rd. TW7: Isle 55Ha 108
Wheatley's Eyot TW16: Sun 71W 150
Wheatley St. W1 1J 221 (43Jb 90)
Wheatley Ter. Rd. DA8: Erith 51Hd 118
Wheatley Way SL9: Chal P 23A 42
Wheat Sheaf Cl. E14 49Dc 92
Wheatsheaf Cl. GU21: Wok 88A 168
KT16: Ott 79F 148
UB5: N'olt 36Aa 65
Wheatsheaf Hill TN14: Hals 81Bd 181
Wheatsheaf La. SW6 52Ya 110
SW8 52Nb 112
TW18: Staines 66H 127
Wheatsheaf Pde. SL4: Old Win 7L 103
(off St Luke's Rd.)
Wheatsheaf Pk. 67J 127
Wheatsheaf Rd. RM1: Rom 30Hd 56
Wheatsheaf Ter. SW6 52Bb 111
Wheatstone Cl. CR4: Mitc 67Gb 133
SL3: Slou 8L 81
Wheatstone Ho. SE1 4E 230
W10 43Ab 88
(off Telford Rd.)
Wheatstone Rd. DA8: Erith 50Fd 96
W10 43Ab 88
Wheeler Av. RH8: Oxt 1H 211
Wheeler Cl. IG8: Wfd G 23Pc 54
Wheeler Gdns. N1 39Nb 70
(off Outram Pl.)
Wheeler Pl. BR2: Brom 70Kc 137
Wheelers CM16: Epp 1Vc 23
Wheelers Cross IG11: Bark 40Tc 74
Wheelers Dr. HA4: Ruis 30S 44
Wheelers La. CM14: N'side, Pil H 14Rd 39
HP3: Hem H 4N 3
KT18: Eps 86Ra 173
Wheelers Orchard SL9: Chal P 23A 42
Wheeler's St. SM1: Sutt 76Cb 155
Wheel Farm Dr. RM10: Dag 34Ed 76
Wheel Ho. E14 50Dc 92
(off Burrells Wharf Sq.)
Wheelock Cl. DA8: Erith 52Dd 118
Wheelwright Cl. WD23: Bush 16Da 27
Wheelwrights TN15: Plax 100Ae 205
Wheelwrights Pl. SL3: Coln 52E 104
Wheelwright St. N7 38Pb 70
Whelan Way SM6: Bedd 76Mb 156
Wheler Ho. E1 6K 219
Wheler St. E1 6K 219 (42Vb 91)
Whellock Rd. W4 48Ua 88
WHELPLEY HILL 8A 2
Whelpley Hill Pk. HP5: Whel 8A 2
Whenman Av. DA5: Bexl 61Ed 140
Whernside Cl. SE28 45Yc 95
WHETSTONE 19Eb 31
Whetstone Cl. N20 19Fb 31
Whetstone Pk. WC2 2H 223 (44Pb 90)
Whetstone Rd. SE3 54Lc 115
Whewell Rd. N19 33Nb 70
Whidborne Bldgs. WC1 4G 217
Whidborne Cl. SE8 54Cc 114
Whidborne St. WC1 4G 217 (41Nb 90)
(not continuous)
Whidbourne M. SW8 53Mb 112
Whiffins Orchard CM16: Coop 1Zc 23
Whimbrel Cl. CR2: Sande 83Tb 177
SE28 45Yc 95
Whimbrel Way UB4: Yead 43Z 85
Whinchat Rd. SE28 48Tc 94
Whinfell Cl. SW16 64Mb 134
Whinfell Way DA12: Grav'nd 3H 145
Whinshill Ct. SL5: S'dale 4E 146
Whinyates Rd. SE9 55Nc 116
Whippendell Cl. BR5: St P 67Xc 139
Whippendell Hill WD4: Chfd 2L 11
Whippendell Rd. WD18: Wat 15U 26
Whippendell Way BR5: St P 67Xc 139
Whippingham Ho. E3 41Bc 92
(off Merchant St.)
Whipps Cross E17 29Fc 53
Whipps Cross Ho. E17 29Fc 53
(off Wood St.)
Whipps Cross Rd. E11 29Fc 53
(not continuous)
Whiskin St. EC1 4B 218 (41Rb 91)
Whisper Wood WD3: Loud 13K 25
Whisperwood Cl.
HA3: Hrw W 25Ga 46
Whistler Ct. WD25: Wat 8Z 13
Whistler Gdns. HA8: Edg 26Pa 47
Whistler M. RM8: Dag 36Xc 75
(off Fitzstephen Rd.)
SE15 52Vb 113
Whistlers Av. SW11 52Fb 111
Whistler St. N5 36Rb 71
Whistler Twr. SW10 52Eb 111
(off Worlds End Est.)
Whistler Wlk. SW10 52Fb 111
Whiston Ho. N1 38Rb 71
(off Richmond Gro.)
Whiston Rd. E2 1K 219 (40Vb 71)
Whitacre M. SE11 50Qb 90
Whitakers Lodge EN2: Enf 11Tb 33
Whitakers Way IG10: Lough 11Pc 36
Whitbread Cl. N17 25Wb 51
Whitbread Pl. CM14: B'wood 20Yd 40
(off Rollason Way)
Whitbread Rd. SE4 56Ac 114
Whitburn Rd. SE13 56Dc 114
Whitby Av. CM13: Ingve 23Fe 59
NW10 41Ra 87
Whitby Cl. DA9: Ghithe 57Wd 120
TN16: Big H 91Kc 199
Whitby Ct. N7 35Nb 70
Whitby Gdns. NW9 27Qa 47
SM1: Sutt 75Fb 155
Whitby Ho. NW8 39Eb 69
(off Boundary Rd.)
Whitby Pde. HA4: Ruis 33Y 65
Whitby Rd. HA2: Harr 34Ea 66
HA4: Ruis 34X 65
SE18 49Pc 94
Whitby Rd. SL1: Slou 5G 80
SM1: Sutt 75Fb 155
Whitby Rd. Bus. Cen. SL1: Slou 5G 80
Whitby St. E1 5K 219 (42Vb 91)
(not continuous)
Whitcher Cl. SE14 51Ac 114
Whitcher Pl. NW1 37Lb 70
Whitchurch Av. HA8: Edg 24Pa 47
Whitchurch Cl. HA8: Edg 23Pa 47
Whitchurch Gdns. HA8: Edg 23Pa 47
Whitchurch Ho. W10 44Za 88
(off Kingsdown Cl.)
Whitchurch La. HA8: Edg 24Ma 47
Whitchurch Pde. HA8: Edg 24Qa 47
Whitchurch Rd. RM3: Rom 21Md 57
W11 45Za 88
Whitcomb Ct. WC2 5E 222
Whitcombe M. TW9: Kew 53Ra 109
Whitcomb St. WC2 5E 222 (45Mb 90)
Whitcome M. TW9: Kew 53Ra 109
Whiteadder Way E14 49Dc 92
Whitear Wlk. E15 37Fc 73
White Av. DA11: Nflt 2B 144
Whitebarn La. RM10: Dag 39Cd 76
Whitebeam Av. BR2: Brom 73Qc 160
Whitebeam Cl. SW9 52Pb 112
TN15: Kems'g 89Qd 183
WD7: Shenl 5Pa 15
Whitebeam Dr. RH2: Reig 9K 207
RM15: S Ock 41Yd 98
Whitebeam Ho. E15 41Gc 93
(off Teasel Way)
White Beams AL2: Park 10A 6
Whitebeams AL10: Hat 3C 8
White Beam Way KT20: Tad 93Wa 194
White Bear Pl. NW3 35Fb 69
White Bear Yd. EC1 6K 217
White Bri. Av. CR4: Mitc 69Fb 133
Whitebridge Cl. TW14: Felt 58V 106
Whitebroom Rd. HP1: Hem H 1G 2
WHITE BUSHES 10A 208
Whitebushes RH1: Redh 10A 208
White Butts Rd. HA4: Ruis 34Z 65
WHITECHAPEL 43Wb 91
Whitechapel Art Gallery 44Vb 91
Whitechapel High St.
E1 2K 225 (44Vb 91)
Whitechapel Rd. E1 43Wb 91
Whitechapel Sports Cen. 43Xb 91
White Church La. E1 44Wb 91
White Church Pas. E1 44Wb 91
(off White Church La.)
WHITE CITY 45Xa 88
WHITE CITY 44Ya 88
White City Cl. W12 45Ya 88
White City Est. W12 45Xa 88
(off Australia Rd.)
W12 45Xa 88
(Havelock Cl.)
White City Rd. W12 45Ya 88
White Cl. SL1: Slou 6H 81
White Conduit St. N1 1A 218 (40Qb 70)
Whitecote Rd. UB1: S'hall 44Ea 86
White Craig Cl. HA5: Hat E 22Ca 45
White Cft. BR8: Swan 68Gd 140
Whitecroft AL1: St A 5F 6
Whitecroft Cl. BR3: Beck 70Fc 137
Whitecroft Way BR3: Beck 71Ec 158
Whitecross Pl. EC2 7G 219 (43Tb 91)
Whitecross St. EC1 5E 218 (42Sb 91)
Whitefield Av. CR8: Purl 88Qb 176
NW2 32Ya 68
Whitefield Cl. BR5: St P 69Yc 139
SW15 58Ab 110
Whitefields Rd. EN8: Chesh 1Yb 20
Whitefoot La. BR1: Brom 63Ec 136
(not continuous)
Whitefoot Ter. BR1: Brom 62Hc 137
Whiteford Rd. SL2: Slou 3J 81
White Friars TN13: S'oaks 99Jd 202
Whitefriars Av. HA3: W'stone 26Ga 46
Whitefriars Ct. N12 22Fb 49
Whitefriars Dr. HA3: Hrw W 26Fa 46
Whitefriars St. EC4 3A 224 (44Qb 90)
Whitefriars Trad. Est.
HA3: W'stone 27Fa 46
White Gables Ct. CR2: S Croy 78Ub 157
White Gdns. RM10: Dag 37Cd 76
White Ga. GU22: Wok 92B 188
Whitegate Gdns. HA3: Hrw W 24Ha 46
White Gates KT7: T Ditt 73Ja 152
RM12: Horn 33Ld 77
Whitegates CR3: W'ham 91Wb 197
Whitegates Av. TN15: W King 79Ud 164
Whitegates Cl. WD3: Crox G 14Q 26
Whitegate Way KT20: Tad 92Xa 194
Whitehall 79Ab 154
White Hall RM4: Abr 13Xc 37
Whitehall SW1 6F 223 (46Nb 90)
Whitehall Cl. IG7: Chig 20Wc 37
UB8: Uxb 39L 63
WD6: Bore 14Qa 29
Whitehall Ct. SW1 7F 223 (46Nb 90)
(not continuous)
Whitehall Cres. KT9: Chess 78Ma 153
Whitehall Farm La. GU25: Vir W 68A 126
Whitehall Gdns. E4 18Gc 35
SW1 7F 223
W3 46Qa 87
W4 51Ra 109
Whitehall La. DA8: Erith 54Hd 118
IG9: Buck H 19Jc 35
RH2: Reig 10H 207
RM17: Grays 50Ee 99
TW19: Wray 58C 104
TW20: Egh 66B 126
Whitehall Lodge N10 26Jb 50
Whitehall Pde. DA12: Grav'nd 2E 144
Whitehall Pk. N19 32Lb 70
Whitehall Pk. Rd. W4 51Ra 109
Whitehall Pl. E7 36Jc 73
SM6: Wall 77Kb 156
SW1 7F 223 (46Nb 90)
Whitehall Rd. BR2: Brom 71Mc 159
CR7: Thor H 71Qb 156
E4 19Gc 35
HA1: Harr 31Ga 66
IG8: Wfd G 19Gc 35
RM17: Grays 49Ee 99
UB8: Uxb 39M 63
W7 47Ja 86
Whitehall St. N17 24Vb 51
White Hart Av. SE18 49Vc 95
SE28 49Vc 95

White Hart Cl. TN13: S'oaks 100Ld 203
UB3: Harl 51T 106
White Hart Ct. EC2 ......1H 225
EN8: Walt C 5Ac 20
GU23: Rip 93L 189
White Hart Dr. HP2: Hem H 3P 3
White Hart Lane 24Wb 51
White Hart La. N17 ......24Sb 51
N22 ......25Pb 50
NW10 ......37Va 68
RM7: Col R, Mawney 25Cd 56
SW13 ......55Ua 110
White Hart Lane Community Sports Cen. 24Rb 51
White Hart Mdws. GU23: Rip 93L 189
White Hart Pde. TN13: Riv 94Gd 202
White Hart Rd. BR6: Orp 73Wc 161
HP2: Hem H 3A 4
SE18 ......49Uc 94
SL1: Slou 8H 81
White Hart Rdbt. UB5: N'olt 40Z 65
White Hart Row KT16: Chert 73J 149
White Hart School Sports Cen. 24Rb 51
White Hart Slip BR1: Brom 68Jc 137
White Hart St. EC4 ......2C 224 (44Rb 91)
SE11 ......7A 230 (50Qb 90)
White Hart Triangle SE28 ......47Vc 95
White Hart Triangle Bus. Pk.
SE28 ......47Wc 95
White Hart Wood TN13: S'oaks 100Ld 203
White Hart Yd. DA11: Grav'nd 8D 122
(off High St.)
SE1 ......7F 225 (46Tb 91)
Whitehaven SL1: Slou 5K 81
Whitehaven Cl. BR2: Brom 70Jc 137
EN7: G Oak 1Ub 19
Whitehaven St.
NW8 ......6D 214 (42Gb 89)
Whitehead Cl. DA2: Wilm 62Ld 141
N18 ......22Tb 51
SW18 ......59Eb 111
Whiteheads Gro. SW3 ......7E 226 (49Gb 89)
White Heart Av. UB8: Hil 43S 84
Whiteheath Av. HA4: Ruis 31S 64
White Heather Ho. WC1 ......4G 217
(off Cromer St.)
White Hedge Dr. AL3: St A 1A 6
White Hermitage SL4: Old Win 7N 103
White Heron M. TW11: Tedd 65Ha 130
White Hill CR2: Sande 82Tb 177
CR5: Chip 95Gb 195
GU20: W'sham 7A 146
HP1: Hem H 3H 3
HP4: Berk 1A 2
TN15: Wro 88De 185
WD3: Rick 23P 43
White Hill La. RH1: Blet 99Tb 197
Whitehill La. DA12: Grav'nd 2E 144
GU23: Ock 95S 190
Whitehill Pl. GU25: Vir W 71A 148
Whitehill Rd. DA1: Cray 57Jd 118
DA3: Dart, Lfield 68Zd 143
DA12: Grav'nd 1E 144
DA13: Sflt 68Zd 143
Whitehills Rd. IG10: Lough 13Qc 36
White Horse All. EC1 ......7B 218
White Horse Dr. KT18: Eps 86Sa 173
White Horse Hill BR7: Chst 63Qc 138
White Horse La. AL2: Lon C 8H 7
E1 ......43Zb 92
GU23: Rip 93L 189
Whitehorse La. SE25 ......70Tb 135
White Horse M. EN3: Enf H 12Zb 34
Whitehorse M. SE1 ......3A 230 (48Qb 90)
White Horse Rd. E1 ......44Ac 92
(not continuous)
E6 ......41Pc 94
SL4: Wind 5B 102
Whitehorse Rd. CR0: C'don 73Sb 157
CR7: Thor H 73Sb 157
White Horse St. W1 ......7A 222 (46Kb 90)
White Horse Yd. EC2 ......2F 225 (44Tb 91)
White Ho. SW4 ......59Mb 112
(off Clapham Pk. Est.)
SW11 ......53Fb 111
White House, The NW1 ......5A 216
Whitehouse Apartments
SE1 ......7J 223 (46Pb 90)
Whitehouse Av. WD6: Bore 13Ra 29
White Ho. Cl. SL9: Chal P 24A 42
White Ho. Ct. N14 ......19Nb 32
White Ho. Dr. HA7: Stan 21La 46
IG8: Wfd G 23Hc 53
Whitehouse Est. E10 ......30Ec 52
White Ho. La. EN2: Enf 11Sb 33
GU4: Jac W 10P 187
Whitehouse La. WD5: Bedm 8H 5
Whitehouse Way N14 ......19Kb 32
SL0: Iver H 41F 82
SL3: L'ly 8P 81
Whitehurst Dr. N18 ......22Zb 52
White Kennett St. E1 ......2J 225 (44Vb 91)
White Knights Rd. KT13: Weyb 80S 150
White Knobs Way CR3: Cat'm 97Wb 197
Whitelands Av. WD3: Chor 13D 24
Whitelands Cres. SW18 ......59Ab 110
Whitelands Ho. SW3 ......7F 227
Whitelands Way RM3: Hrld W 25Md 57
White La. RH8: T'sey 95Kc 199
TN16: Tats, T'sey 95Kc 199
Whiteleaf Rd. HP3: Hem H 5L 3
Whiteledges W13 ......44La 86
Whitelegg Rd. E13 ......40Hc 73
Whiteley SL4: Wind 2C 102
Whiteley Rd. SE19 ......64Tb 135
Whiteleys Cen. (Shopping Cen.)
W2 ......44Db 89
Whiteleys Pde. UB10: Hil 42R 84
Whiteley's Way TW13: Hanw 62Ca 129
WHITELEY VILLAGE 81U 170
White Lillies Island SL4: Wind 2E 102
White Lion Ct. EC3 ......3H 225
SE15 ......51Yb 114
TW7: Isle 55Ka 108
White Lion Gdns. KT11: Cobh 86W 170
White Lion Hill EC4 ......4C 224 (45Rb 91)
White Lion St. HP3: Hem H 6M 3
N1 ......2K 217 (40Qb 70)
White Lodge KT21: Asht 92Na 193
SE19 ......66Rb 135
TN13: S'oaks 100Jd 202
W5 ......43La 86
White Lodge Cl. N2 ......30Fb 49
SM2: Sutt 80Eb 155
White Lodge Cl. TN13: S'oaks 95Kd 203
TW7: Isle 54Ja 108
White Lodge Ct. TW16: Sun 67Y 129
White Lodge Mus. 60Ta 109
White Lyon Ct. EC2 ......7D 218
White Lyons Rd. CM14: B'wood 19Yd 40
White Oak Ct. BR8: Swan 69Gd 140
Whiteoak Ct. BR7: Chst 65Qc 138
White Oak Dr. BR3: Beck 68Ec 136
White Oak Gdns. DA15: Sidc 59Vc 117
White Oak Leisure Cen. 68Fd 140
Whiteoaks SM7: Bans 85Db 175
Whiteoaks La. UB6: G'frd 41Fa 86
White Oak Sq. BR8: Swan 69Gd 140
(off London Rd.)
White Orchards HA7: Stan 22Ja 46
N20 ......18Bb 31
White Pillars GU22: Wok 2M 187
WHITE POST 5L 209
White Post Hill DA4: Farni 73Qd 163
Whitepost Hill RH1: Redh 6N 207
(not continuous)
White Post La. DA13: Sole S 10D 144
E9 ......38Bc 72
White Post St. SE15 ......52Yb 114
White Rd. E15 ......38Gc 73
White Rose La. GU22: Wok 90B 168
White Rose Lane Local Nature Reserve 91D 188
Whiterose Trad. Est. EN4: E Barn 15Fb 31
(off Margaret Rd.)
Whites Av. IG2: Ilf 30Uc 54
Whites Cl. DA9: Ghithe 58Yd 120
White's Grounds SE1 ......2J 231 (47Ub 91)
White's Grounds Est. SE1 ......1J 231
White Shack La. WD3: Chan C 9P 11
Whites La. GU24: Pirb 6E 186
SL3: Dat 1M 103
White's Mdw. BR1: Brom 70Qc 138
White's Row E1 ......1K 225 (43Vb 91)
Whites Sq. SW4 ......56Mb 112
Whitestile Rd. TW8: Bford 50La 86
Whitestone Cl. EN4: Had W 10Gb 17
Whitestone La. NW3 ......34Eb 69
Whitestone Wlk. NW3 ......34Eb 69
Whitestone Way CR0: Wadd 75Qb 156
White St. UB1: S'hall 47Z 85
White Swan M. W4 ......50Ua 88
Whitethorn Av. CR5: Coul 87Jb 176
UB7: Yiew 45N 83
Whitethorn Gdns. CR0: C'don 75Xb 157
EN2: Enf 15Tb 33
RM11: Horn 30Ld 57
Whitethorn Ho. E1 ......46Yb 92
(off Prusom St.)
Whitethorn Pas. E3 ......42Cc 92
(off Whitethorn St.)
Whitethorn Pl. UB7: Yiew 46P 83
Whitethorn St. E3 ......43Cc 92
White Twr. Way E1 ......43Ac 92
Whiteway KT23: Bookh 98Da 191
Whiteways Ct. TW18: Staines 66K 127
Whitewebbs Golf Course 9Tb 19
Whitewebbs La. EN2: Enf 7Ub 19
Whitewebbs Mus. of Transport 7Rb 19
Whitewebbs Pk. 8Sb 19
Whitewebbs Rd. EN2: Crew H, Enf 7Rb 19
Whitewebbs Way BR5: St P 67Vc 139
Whitewood Cotts. TN16: Tats 92Lc 199
Whitfield Ct. IG1: Ilf 31Pc 74
Whitfield Cres. DA2: Dart 59Sd 120
Whitfield Ho. NW8 ......6D 214
Whitfield Pl. W1 ......6B 216
Whitfield Rd. DA7: Bex 52Bd 117
E6 ......38Lc 73
SE3 ......53Fc 115
Whitfields SS17: Stan H 1P 101
Whitfield St. W1 ......6B 216 (42Lb 90)
Whitfield Way WD3: Rick 18H 25
Whitford Gdns. CR4: Mitc 69Hb 133
Whitgift Av. CR2: S Croy 78Rb 157
Whitgift Cen. CR0: C'don 75Sb 157
Whitgift Ct. CR2: S Croy 78Sb 157
(off Nottingham Rd.)
Whitgift Ho. SE11 ......5H 229 (49Pb 90)
SW11 ......53Gb 111
Whitgift Sq. CR0: C'don 75Sb 157
Whitgift St. CR0: C'don 76Sb 157
SE11 ......5H 229 (49Pb 90)
Whit Hern Ct. EN8: Chesh 2Yb 20
Whiting Av. IG11: Bark 38Rc 74
Whitings IG2: Ilf 29Uc 54
Whitings Rd. EN5: Barn 15Ya 30
Whitings Way E6 ......43Qc 94
Whitland Rd. SM5: Cars 74Fb 155
Whitlars Dr. WD4: K Lan 10P 3
Whitley Cl. TW19: Stanw 58N 105
WD5: Ab L 4W 12
Whitley Ct. AL1: St A 2C 6
(off Hatfield Rd.)
Whitley Ho. SW1 ......51Lb 112
(off Churchill Gdns.)
Whitley Rd. N17 ......26Ub 51
WHITLEY ROW 100Dd 202
Whitlock Dr. SW19 ......59Ab 110
Whitman Ho. E2 ......41Yb 92
(off Cornwall Av.)
Whitman Rd. E3 ......42Ac 92
Whitmead Cl. CR2: S Croy 79Ub 157
Whitmoor & Rickford Commons
Local Nature Reserve 9L 187
WHITMOOR COMMON 8L 187
Whitmoor La. GU4: Sut G 8P 187
Whitmore Av. RM3: Hrld W 26Nd 57
RM16: Grays 46De 99
Whitmore Cl. N11 ......22Kb 50
RM16: Ors 4G 100
Whitmore Est. N1 ......1J 219 (39Ub 71)
Whitmore Gdns. NW10 ......40Ya 68
Whitmore Ho. N1 ......1J 219
Whitmore La. SL5: S'dale, S'hill 1E 146
Whitmore Rd. BR3: Beck 69Bc 136
HA1: Harr 31Ea 66
N1 ......1H 219 (39Ub 71)
Whitmores Cl. KT18: Eps 87Sa 173
Whitmore Sports Cen. 31Ea 66
Whitmores Wood HP2: Hem H 1C 4
Whitnell Way SW15 ......57Ya 110
(not continuous)
Whitney Av. IG4: Ilf 28Mc 53
Whitney Rd. E10 ......31Dc 72
Whitney Wlk. DA14: Sidc 65Ad 139
Whitstable Cl. BR3: Beck 67Bc 136
HA4: Ruis 33U 64
Whitstable Ho. W10 ......44Za 88
(off Silchester Rd.)
Whitstable Pl. CR0: C'don 77Sb 157
Whitstone La. BR3: Beck 71Dc 158
Whittaker Av. TW9: Rich 57Ma 109
Whittaker Ct. KT21: Asht 89Ma 173
Whittaker Pl. TW9: Rich 57Ma 109
(off Whittaker Av.)
Whittaker Rd. E6 ......38Lc 73
SL2: Slou 2B 80
SM3: Sutt 76Bb 155
Whittaker St. SW1 ......6H 227 (49Jb 90)
Whittaker Way SE1 ......49Wb 91
Whitta Rd. E12 ......35Mc 73
Whittell Gdns. SE26 ......62Yb 136
Whittenham Cl. SL2: Slou 6L 81
Whittingham N17 ......24Xb 51
Whittingham Ct. W4 ......52Ua 110
Whittingstall Rd. SW6 ......53Bb 111
Whittington Apartments E1 ......44Zb 92
(off E. Arbour St.)
Whittington Av. EC3 ......3H 225 (44Ub 91)
UB4: Hayes 43V 84
Whittington Ct. N2 ......29Hb 49
Whittington M. N12 ......21Eb 49
Whittington Rd. CM13: Hut 16Ee 41
N22 ......24Nb 50
Whittington Way HA5: Pinn 29Aa 45
Whittlebury Cl. SM5: Cars 80Hb 155
Whittle Cl. E17 ......30Ac 52
UB1: S'hall 44Da 85
WD25: Wat 6V 12
Whittle Parkway SL1: Slou 4B 80
Whittle Rd. TW5: Hest 52Y 107
TW6: H'row A 55K 105
UB2: S'hall 47Da 85
Whittlesea Cl. HA3: Hrw W 24Ea 46
Whittlesea Path HA3: Hrw W 25Ea 46
Whittlesea Rd. HA3: Hrw W 24Ea 46
Whittlesey St. SE1 ......7K 223 (46Qb 90)
WHITTON 59Ea 108
Whitton NW3 ......38Hb 69
Whitton Av. E. UB6: G'frd 36Ga 66
Whitton Av. W. UB5: N'olt 36Da 65
UB6: G'frd 36Da 65
Whitton Cl. UB6: G'frd 37Ka 66
Whitton Dene TW3: Houn, Isle 57Ea 108
TW7: Isle 58Fa 108
Whitton Dr. UB6: G'frd 37Ja 66
Whitton Mnr. Rd. TW7: Isle 58Ea 108
Whitton Rd. TW1: Twick 58Ha 108
TW2: Twick 58Ga 108
TW3: Houn 56Da 107
WHITTON ROAD RDBT. 58Ha 108
Whitton Sports & Fitness Cen. 61Da 129
Whitton Wlk. E3 ......41Cc 92
(not continuous)
Whitton Waye TW3: Houn 58Ca 107
Whitwell Rd. E13 ......41Jc 93
WD25: Wat 7Z 13
Whitworth Cen., The
RM3: Rom 22Ld 57
Whitworth Cres. EN3: Enf L 9Cc 20
Whitworth Ho. SE1 ......4E 230 (48Sb 91)
Whitworth Rd. SE18 ......52Qc 116
SE25 ......69Ub 135
Whitworth St. SE10 ......50Gc 93
Whopshott Av. GU21: Wok 8N 167
Whopshott Cl. GU21: Wok 8N 167
Whopshott Dr. GU21: Wok 8N 167
Whorlton Rd. SE15 ......55Xb 113
Whybrews SS17: Stan H 1P 101
Whybridge Cl. RM13: Rain 39Hd 76
Whychcote Point NW2 ......32Ya 68
(off Whitefield Av.)
Whymark Av. N22 ......27Qb 50
Whyteacre CR3: W'ham 92Xb 197
Whytebeam Vw. CR3: Whyt 90Vb 177
Whytecliffe Rd. Nth. CR8: Purl 83Rb 177
Whytecliffe Rd. Sth. CR8: Purl 83Qb 176
Whytecroft TW5: Hest 52Z 107
WHYTELEAFE 90Vb 177
Whyteleafe Bus. Village
CR3: Whyt 89Vb 177
Whyteleafe Hill CR3: Whyt 92Ub 197
Whyteleafe Rd. CR3: Cat'm 92Ub 197
Whyte M. SM3: Cheam 80Ab 154
Whyteville Rd. E7 ......37Kc 73
Whytlaw Ho. E3 ......43Bc 92
(off Baythorne St.)
Wichling Cl. BR5: Orp 74Zc 161
Wickenden Rd. TN13: S'oaks 94Ld 203
Wickens Caravan Site
TN14: Dun G 91Jd 202
Wickens Mdw. TN14: Dun G 91Hd 202
Wickersley Rd. SW11 ......54Jb 112
Wickers Oake SE19 ......63Vb 135
Wicker St. E1 ......44Xb 91
Wicket, The CR0: Addtn 78Cc 158
Wicket Rd. UB6: G'frd 41Ja 86
Wickets, The TW15: Ashf 63N 127
Wickets Cl. BR5: St M Cry 71Yc 161
Wickets End WD7: Shenl 5Na 15
Wickets Way IG6: Ilf 23Vc 55
Wickfield Apartments E15 ......37Fc 73
(off Grove Cres. Rd.)
Wickfield Ho. SE16 ......47Xb 91
(off Wilson Gro.)
Wickfields IG7: Chig 23Tc 54
Wickford Cl. RM3: Rom 22Pd 57
Wickford Dr. RM3: Rom 22Pd 57
Wickford Ho. E1 ......42Yb 92
(off Wickford St.)
Wickford St. E1 ......42Yb 92
Wickford Way E17 ......28Zb 52
Wickham Av. CR0: C'don 75Ac 158
SM3: Cheam 78Ya 154
Wickham Chase BR4: W W'ck 74Fc 159
Wickham Cl. E1 ......43Yb 92
EN3: Enf H 13Xb 33
KT3: N Mald 72Va 154
UB9: Hare 25M 43
Wickham Ct. KT5: Surb 71Pa 153
(off Cranes Pk.)
Wickham Ct. Rd. BR4: W W'ck 75Ec 158
Wickham Cres. BR4: W W'ck 75Ec 158
Wickham Fld. TN14: Off 88Hd 182
Wickham Gdns. SE4 ......55Bc 114
Wickham Ho. N1 ......39Ub 71
(off New Era Est.)
Wickham La. DA16: Well 50Wc 95
SE2 ......50Wc 95
TW20: Egh 66C 126
Wickham M. SE4 ......54Bc 114
Wickham Rd. BR3: Beck 68Dc 136
CR0: C'don 75Zb 158
E4 ......24Ec 52
HA3: Hrw W 26Fa 46
RM16: Grays 7E 100
SE4 ......56Bc 114
Wickham St. DA16: Well 54Uc 116
SE11 ......7H 229 (50Pb 90)
Wickhams Way DA3: Hartl 71Be 165
Wickham Theatre Cen. 75Fc 159
Wickham Way BR3: Beck 70Ec 136
Wick Ho. KT1: Hamp W 67Ma 131
(off Station Rd.)
Wick La. E3 ......39Cc 72
TW20: Eng G 5K 125
Wickliffe Av. N3 ......26Ab 48
Wickliffe Gdns.
HA9: Wemb 33Ra 67
Wicklow Ho. N16 ......32Vb 71
Wicklow St. WC1 ......3H 217 (41Pb 90)
Wick M. E9 ......37Ac 72
Wick Rd. E9 ......37Zb 72
TW11: Tedd 66Ka 130
TW20: Eng G 7L 125
Wicks Cl. SE9 ......63Mc 137
Wick Sq. E9 ......37Bc 72
Wicksteed Cl. DA5: Bexl 62Fd 140
Wicksteed Ho. SE1 ......4E 230 (48Sb 91)
TW8: Bford 50Pa 87
Wickway Ct. SE15 ......51Vb 113
(off Cator St.)
Wickwood Ct. AL1: St A 1F 6
Wickwood St. SE5 ......54Rb 113
Wid Cl. CM13: Hut 15Fe 41
Widdecombe Av. HA2: Harr 33Aa 65
Widdenham Rd. N7 ......35Pb 70
Widdin St. E15 ......38Gc 73
Widecombe Cl. RM3: Rom 25Md 57
Widecombe Gdns. IG4: Ilf 28Nc 54
Widecombe Rd. SE9 ......62Nc 138
Widecombe Way N2 ......29Fb 49
Widecroft Rd. SL0: Iver 44G 82
Widegate St. E1 ......1J 225 (43Ub 91)
Widenham Cl. HA5: Eastc 29Y 45
Widewater Pl. UB9: Hare 29L 43
Wide Way CR4: Mitc 69Mb 134
Widewing Cl. TW11: Tedd 66Ka 130
Widford NW1 ......37Kb 70
(off Lewis St.)
Widford Ho. N1 ......2B 218
Widgeon Cl. E16 ......44Kc 93
Widgeon Rd. DA8: Erith 52Kd 119
TW6: H'row A 54K 105
Widgeon Way WD25: Wat 9Aa 13
Widley Rd. W9 ......41Cb 89
Widmer Ct. TW3: Houn 54Aa 107
WIDMORE 69Lc 137
Widmore Dr. HP2: Hem H 1A 4
WIDMORE GREEN 68Mc 137
Widmore Lodge Rd. BR1: Brom 68Mc 137
Widmore Rd. BR1: Brom 68Jc 137
UB8: Hil 42R 84
Widvale Rd. CM13: Mount 13Fe 41
CM15: Shenf, Mount 13Ee 41
Widworthy Hayes CM13: Hut 18De 41
Wieland Rd. HA6: Nwood 24W 44
Wigan Ho. E5 ......32Xb 71
Wigeon Path SE28 ......48Tc 94
Wigeon Way UB4: Yead 44Aa 85
Wiggenhall Rd. WD18: Wat 15X 27
Wiggenhall Rd. Goods Yd.
WD18: Wat 16X 27
Wiggie La. RH1: Redh 4A 208
Wiggington Ho. SL4: Eton 2H 103
(off High St.)
Wiggins La. TW10: Ham 61La 130
Wiggins Mead NW9 ......24Va 48
Wigginton Av. HA9: Wemb 37Ra 67
Wight Ho. KT1: King T 69Ma 131
(off Portsmouth Rd.)
WD18: Wat 15V 26
Wightman Rd. N4 ......28Qb 50
N8 ......28Qb 50
Wighton M. TW7: Isle 54Ga 108
Wigley Bush La.
CM14: B'wood, S Weald 19Ud 40
Wigley Rd. TW13: Felt 61Z 129
Wigmore Ct. W13 ......46Ja 86
(off Singapore Rd.)
Wigmore Hall 2K 221
Wigmore Pl. E17 ......27Ac 52
W1 ......2K 221 (44Kb 90)
Wigmore Rd. SM5: Cars 75Fb 155
Wigmore St. W1 ......3H 221 (44Jb 90)
Wigmore Wlk. SM5: Cars 75Fb 155
Wigram Ho. E14 ......45Dc 92
(off Wade's Pl.)
Wigram Rd. E11 ......30Lc 53
Wigram Sq. E17 ......27Ec 52
Wigston Cl. N18 ......22Ub 51
Wigston Rd. E13 ......42Kc 93
Wigton Gdns. HA7: Stan 25Na 47
Wigton Pl. SE11 ......7A 230 (50Qb 90)
Wigton Rd. E17 ......25Bc 52
RM3: Rom 21Nd 57
Wigton Way RM3: Rom 21Nd 57
Wilberforce Ct. BR2: Kes 80Mc 159
HA8: Edg 21Pa 47
(off King's Dr.)
KT18: Eps 87Ta 173
(off Heathcote Rd.)
Wilberforce M. SW4 ......56Mb 112
Wilberforce Rd. N4 ......33Rb 71
NW9 ......30Wa 48
Wilberforce Wlk. E15 ......36Gc 73
Wilberforce Way DA12: Grav'nd 4F 144
SW19 ......65Za 132
Wilbraham Ho. SW8 ......52Nb 112
(off Wandsworth Rd.)
Wilbraham Mans. SW1 ......5H 227
(off Wilbraham Pl.)
Wilbraham Pl. SW1 ......5G 227 (49Hb 89)
Wilbrahams Almshouses
EN5: Barn 12Bb 31
Wilbrooke Pl. SE3 ......53Kc 115
Wilbury Av. SM2: Cheam 82Bb 175
Wilbury Rd. GU21: Wok 9P 167
Wilbury Way N18 ......22Tb 51
Wilby M. W11 ......46Bb 89
Wilcon Way WD25: Wat 6Z 13
Wilcot Av. WD19: Wat 17Aa 27
Wilcot Cl. GU24: Bisl 8E 166
WD19: Wat 17Aa 27
Wilcot Gdns. GU24: Bisl 8E 166
Wilcox Cl. SW8 ......52Nb 112
(not continuous)
WD6: Bore 11Sa 29
Wilcox Gdns. TW17: Shep 69N 127
Wilcox Ho. E3 ......43Bc 92
(off Ackroyd Dr.)
Wilcox Pl. SW1 ......4C 228 (48Lb 90)
Wilcox Rd. SM1: Sutt 77Db 155
SW8 ......52Nb 112
TW11: Tedd 63Fa 130
Wild Acres KT14: W Byf 83L 169
Wildacres HA6: Nwood 21V 44
Wildbank Ct. GU22: Wok 90B 168
Wildberry Cl. W7 ......49Ja 86
Wildcat Rd. TW6: H'row A 55K 105
(off Wayfarer Rd.)
Wild Ct. WC2 ......3H 223 (44Pb 90)
(not continuous)
Wildcroft Gdns. HA8: Edg 23Ma 47
Wildcroft Mnr. SW15 ......59Ya 110
Wildcroft Rd. SW15 ......59Ya 110
Wilde Cl. E8 ......39Wb 71
RM18: Tilb 4E 122
Wilde Ct. AL2: Lon C 9F 6
Wilde Ho. W2 ......4B 220
(off Gloucester Ter.)
Wilde Pl. N13 ......23Rb 51
SW18 ......59Fb 111
Wilder Cl. HA4: Ruis 32X 65
Wilderness, The
KT8: W Mole, E Mos 71Ea 152
TW12: Hamp H 63Da 129
WILDERNESSE 94Nd 203
Wildernesse Av.
TN15: Seal, S'oaks 94Nd 203
Wildernesse Golf Course 94Qd 203
Wildernesse Mt.
TN13: S'oaks 94Md 203
Wilderness Island Nature Reserve 75Jb 156
Wilderness Local Nature Reserve, The 51Jb 112
Wilderness M. SW4 ......56Kb 112
Wilderness Rd. BR7: Chst 66Rc 138
RH8: Oxt 2H 211
Wilde Rd. DA8: Erith 52Dd 118
Wilders Cl. GU21: Wok 10N 167
Wilderton Rd. N16 ......31Ub 71
Wildfell Rd. SE6 ......59Dc 114
Wild Goose Dr. SE14 ......53Yb 114
Wild Grn. Nth. SL3: L'ly 49C 82
Wild Grn. Sth. SL3: L'ly 49C 82
Wild Hatch NW11 ......30Cb 49
WILDHILL 3M 9
Wildhill Rd. AL9: Hat 5G 8
Wilding Ct. WD6: Bore 14Qa 29
(off Whitehall Cl.)
Wildmarsh Ct. EN3: Enf W 9Ac 20
(off Manly Dixon Dr.)
Wild Oaks Cl. HA6: Nwood 23V 44
Wild's Rents
SE1 ......3H 231 (48Ub 91)
Wild St. WC2 ......3G 223 (44Nb 90)
Wildwood HA6: Nwood 23T 44
Wildwood Av. AL2: Brick W 2Ba 13
Wildwood Cl. GU22: Pyr 87H 169
KT24: E Hor 97V 190
SE12 ......59Hc 115
Wildwood Ct. CR8: Kenley 87Tb 177
WD3: Chor 14H 25
Wildwood Gro. NW3 ......32Eb 69
Wildwood Ri. NW11 ......32Eb 69
Wildwood Rd. NW11 ......30Db 49
Wildwood Ter. NW3 ......32Eb 69
Wilford Cl. EN2: Enf 13Tb 33
HA6: Nwood 24T 44
Wilford Rd. CR0: C'don 72Sb 157
SL3: L'ly 49A 82
Wilfred Av. RM13: Rain 43Jd 96
Wilfred Ct. N15 ......29Tb 51
(off South Gro.)
Wilfred Owen Cl. SW19 ......65Eb 133
Wilfred St. DA12: Grav'nd 8D 122
GU21: Wok 10P 167
SW1 ......3B 228 (48Lb 90)
Wilfred Wood Ct. W6 ......49Ya 88
(off Samuel's Cl)
Wilfrid Gdns. W3 ......43Sa 87
Wilhelmina Av. CR5: Coul 91Lb 196
Wilkes Rd. CM13: Hut 15Fe 41
TW8: Bford 51Na 109
Wilkes St. E1 ......7K 219 (43Vb 91)
Wilkie Ho. SW1 ......7E 228
Wilkin Cl. CR4: Mitc 67Gb 133
UB3: Harl 50V 84
WILKINS GREEN 1N 7
Wilkin's Grn. La. AL4: S'ford 1N 7
AL10: Hat 2M 7
Wilkins Grn. Ter. AL4: S'ford 2M 7
Wilkins Ho. SW1 ......51Kb 112
(off Churchill Gdns.)
Wilkinson Cl. DA1: Dart 56Pd 119
UB10: Hil 39R 64
Wilkinson Ct. SW17 ......63Fb 133
Wilkinson Gdns. SE25 ......67Ub 135
Wilkinson Ho. N1 ......2G 219
Wilkinson Rd. E16 ......44Lc 93
Wilkinson St. SW8 ......52Pb 112
Wilkinson Way HP3: Hem H 6P 3
W4 ......47Ta 87
Wilkin St. NW5 ......37Jb 70
Wilkin St. M. NW5 ......37Kb 70
Wilkins Way TN16: Bras 96Xc 201
Wilks Av. DA1: Dart 61Pd 141
Wilks Gdns. CR0: C'don 74Ac 158
Wilks Pl. N1 ......2J 219 (40Ub 71)
Willan Rd. N17 ......26Tb 51
Willard St. SW8 ......55Kb 112
Willats Cl. KT16: Chert 72H 149
Willcocks Cl. KT9: Chess 76Na 153
Willcott Rd. W3 ......46Ra 87
Will Crooks Gdns. SE9 ......56Lc 115
Willen Fld. Rd. NW10 ......40Sa 67
Willenhall Av. EN5: New Bar 16Eb 31
Willenhall Ct. EN5: New Bar 16Eb 31
Willenhall Dr. UB3: Hayes 45U 84
Willenhall Rd. SE18 ......50Rc 94
Willersley Av. BR6: Orp 76Tc 160
DA15: Sidc 60Vc 117
Willersley Cl. DA15: Sidc 60Vc 117
Willerton Lodge KT13: Weyb 79T 150
WILLESDEN 37Wa 68
Willesden Belle Vue Cinema 37Xa 68
(off High Rd.)

WILLESDEN GREEN .37Ya 68
Willesden La. NW2 .37Ya 68
NW6 .37Ya 68
Willesden Section Ho. *NW6* .37Za 68
(off Willesden La.)
Willesden Sports Cen. .39Xa 68
Willesden Sports Stadium .39Xa 68
Willes Rd. NW5 .37Kb 70
Willett Cl. BR5: Pet W .72Uc 160
UB5: N'olt .41Y 85
Willett Ho. *E13* .40Kc 73
(off Queens Rd. W.)
Willett Pl. CR7: Thor H .71Qb 156
Willett Rd. CR7: Thor H .71Qb 156
Willetts La. UB9: Den .36H 63
Willett Way BR5: Pet W .71Tc 160
Willey Broom La. CR3: Cat'm .97Qb 196
Willey Farm La. CR3: Cat'm .98Sb 197
Willey La. CR3: Cat'm .97Tb 197
William IV St. WC2 .5F 223 (45Nb 90)
William Allen Ho.
HA8: Edg .24Pa 47
William Ash Cl. RM9: Dag .37Xc 75
William Banfield Ho. *SW6* .54Bb 111
(off Munster Rd.)
William Barefoot Dr. SE9 .63Qc 138
William Blake Ho. SW11 .53Gb 111
William Bonney Est. SW4 .56Mb 112
William Booth Ho. *E14* .44Cc 92
(off Hind Gro.)
William Booth Rd. SE20 .67Wb 135
William Carey Way HA1: Harr .30Ga 46
William Caslon Ho. *E2* .40Xb 91
(off Patriot Sq.)
William Channing Ho. *E2* .41Xb 91
(off Canrobert St.)
William Cl. N2 .27Fb 49
RM5: Col R .25Ed 56
SE13 .55Ec 114
UB2: S'hall .47Ea 86
William Cobbett Ho. *W8* .48Db 89
(off Scarsdale Pl.)
William Cory Prom. DA8: Erith .50Gd 96
William Ct. HP3: Hem H .6M 3
NW8 .3A 214 (41Eb 89)
SE25 .69Vb 135
(off Chalfont Rd.)
SW16 .66Pb 134
(off Streatham High Rd.)
W5 .43La 86
William Covell Cl. EN2: Enf .10Pb 18
William Crook Ho. HP1: Hem H .2H 3
William Dr. HA7: Stan .23Ja 46
William Dromey Ct. NW6 .38Bb 69
William Dunbar Ho. *NW6* .40Bb 69
(off Albert Rd.)
William Dyce M. SW16 .63Mb 134
William Ellis Cl. SL4: Old Win .7L 103
William Ellis Way *SE16* .49Wb 91
(off St James's Rd.)
William Evans Ho. *SE8* .49Zb 92
(off Haddonfield)
William Evans Rd. KT19: Eps .83Qa 173
William Farm La. SW15 .55Xa 110
William Fenn Ho. *E2* .41Wb 91
(off Shipton Rd.)
William Foster La. DA16: Well .54Wc 117
William Fry Ho. *E1* .44Zb 92
(off W. Arbour St.)
William Gdns. SW15 .57Xa 110
William Gibbs Ct. SW1 .4D 228
William Gunn Ho. NW3 .36Gb 69
William Guy Gdns. E3 .41Dc 92
William Harvey Ho. *SW19* .60Ab 110
(off Whitlock Dr.)
William Henry Wlk. SW8 .51Mb 112
William Ho. DA12: Grav'nd .9D 122
William Hunter Way
CM14: B'wood .19Yd 40
William Hunt Mans. SW13 .51Ya 110
William Margrie Cl. SE15 .54Wb 113
William M. SW1 .2G 227 (47Hb 89)
William Morley Cl. E6 .39Mc 73
William Morris Cl. E17 .27Bc 52
William Morris Gallery .27Cc 52
William Morris Ho. W6 .51Za 110
William Morris Way SW6 .55Eb 111
William Nash Ct. BR5: St P .69Yc 139
William Owston Ct. *E16* .46Nc 94
(off Connaught Rd.)
William Penn Leisure Cen. .18H 25
William Perkin Ct. UB6: G'frd .37Ga 66
William Petty Way BR5: Orp .74Yc 161
William Pike Ho. *RM7: Rom* .30Fd 56
(off Waterloo Gdns.)
William Pl. E3 .40Bc 72
William Rathbone Ho. *E2* .41Xb 91
(off Florida St.)
William Rd. CR3: Cat'm .94Tb 197
NW1 .4B 216 (41Lb 90)
SM1: Sutt .78Eb 155
SW19 .66Ab 132
William Rushbrooke Ho. *SE16* .49Wb 91
(off Rouel Rd.)
William Russell Ct. GU21: Wok .10J 167
Williams Av. E17 .25Bc 52
William Saville Ho. *NW6* .40Bb 69
(off Denmark Rd.)
William's Bldgs. E2 .42Yb 92
Williams Cl. KT15: Add .78K 149
N8 .30Mb 50
SW6 .52Ab 110
Williams Ct. EN8: Chesh .1Zb 20
Williams Dr. TW3: Houn .56Ca 107
William Sellars Cl.
CR3: Cat'm .93Ub 197
Williams Gro. KT6: Surb .72La 152
N22 .25Qb 50
Williams Ho. *E3* .41Cc 92
(off Alfred St.)
E9 .39Xb 71
(off King Edward's Rd.)
NW2 .34Ya 68
(off Stoll Cl.)
SW1 .6E 228
Williams La. SM4: Mord .71Eb 155
SW14 .55Sa 109
William Smith Ho. *DA17: Belv* .48Cd 96
(off Ambrooke Rd.)
E3 .41Cc 92
(off Ireton St.)
Williamson Cl. SE10 .50Hc 93
Williamson Ct. SE17 .7D 230 (50Sb 91)
Williamson Rd. N4 .30Rb 51
Williamson St. N7 .35Nb 70
Williamson Way WD3: Rick .18J 25
William Sq. *SE16* .45Ac 92
(off Sovereign Cres.)
Williams Rd. UB2: S'hall .49Aa 85
W13 .46Ja 86
Williams Ter. CR0: Wadd .79Qb 156
William St. DA12: Grav'nd .9D 122
E10 .30Dc 52
HP4: Berk .1A 2
IG11: Bark .38Sc 74
N17 .24Vb 51
RM17: Grays .51De 121
(not continuous)
SL1: Slou .7K 81
SL4: Wind .3H 103
SM5: Cars .76Gb 155
SW1 .2G 227 (47Hb 89)
WD23: Bush .13Z 27
Williams Way DA2: Wilm .61Fd 140
WD7: R'lett .7Ka 14
William Whiffin Sq. E3 .42Bc 92
William White Ct. *E13* .39Lc 73
(off Green St.)
William Wood Ho. *SE26* .62Yb 136
(off Shrublands Cl.)
Willifield Way NW11 .28Bb 49
Willingale Cl. CM13: Hut .16Fe 41
IG8: Wfd G .23Lc 53
IG10: Lough .12Sc 36
Willingale Ct. CM16: They B .8Uc 22
Willingale Rd. IG10: Lough .11Sc 36
Willingdon Rd. N22 .26Rb 51
Willinghall Cl. EN9: Walt A .4Fc 21
Willingham Cl. NW5 .36Lb 70
Willingham Ter. NW5 .36Lb 70
Willingham Way KT1: King T .69Qa 131
Willington Ct. E5 .34Ac 72
Willington Rd. SW9 .55Nb 112
Willis Av. SM2: Sutt .79Gb 155
Willis Cl. KT18: Eps .86Ra 173
Willis Ct. BR4: W W'ck .75Fc 159
CR7: Thor H .72Qb 156
Willis Ho. *E14* .45Dc 92
(off Hale St.)
Willis Rd. CR0: C'don .73Sb 157
DA8: Erith .49Ed 96
E15 .40Hc 73
Willis St. E14 .44Dc 92
Willis Yd. N14 .17Mb 32
Will Miles Ct. SW19 .66Eb 133
Willmore End SW19 .67Db 133
Willoners SL2: Slou .3E 80
Willoughby Av. CR0: Bedd .77Pb 156
Willoughby Ct. AL2: Lon C .8H 7
Willoughby Dr. RM13: Rain .38Gd 76
Willoughby Gro. N17 .24Xb 51
Willoughby Highwalk EC2 .1F 225
Willoughby Ho. *E1* .46Xb 91
(off Reardon Path)
EC2 .1F 225
Willoughby La. BR1: Brom .66Kc 137
N17 .23Xb 51
Willoughby M. N17 .24Xb 51
SW4 .56Kb 112
(off Cedars M.)
Willoughby Pk. Rd. N17 .24Xb 51
Willoughby Pas. *E14* .46Cc 92
(off W. India Av.)
Willoughby Rd. KT2: King T .67Pa 131
N8 .27Qb 50
NW3 .35Fb 69
SL3: L'ly .48C 82
TW1: Twick .57La 108
(not continuous)
Willoughbys, The SW14 .55Ua 110
Willoughby St. WC1 .1F 223
Willoughby Way SE7 .49Kc 93
Willow Av. BR8: Swan .69Hd 140
DA15: Sidc .58Wc 117
SW13 .54Va 110
UB7: Yiew .45P 83
UB9: Den .37L 63
WILLOWBANK .36L 63
Willow Bank GU22: Wok .94A 188
SW6 .55Ab 110
TW10: Ham .62Ka 130
Willowbank CR5: Coul .86Nb 176
KT7: T Ditt .74Ja 152
Willowbank Gdns.
KT20: Tad .94Xa 194
Willowbank Pl. CR8: Purl .81Rb 177
Willowbay Cl. EN5: Barn .16Za 30
Willow Bri. Rd. N1 .37Sb 71
(not continuous)
Willowbrook SL4: Eton .9H 81
TW12: Hamp H .64Da 129
Willowbrook Est. SE15 .52Wb 113
Willow Brook Rd. SE15 .52Vb 113
Willowbrook Rd.
TW19: Stanw .61N 127
UB2: S'hall .48Ca 85
Willow Bus. Pk. SE26 .62Yb 136
Willow Cl. BR2: Brom .71Pc 160
BR5: St M Cry .73Xc 161
CM13: Hut .16De 41
DA5: Bexl .58Bd 117
IG9: Buck H .20Mc 35
KT15: Wdhm .83H 169
KT16: Chert .75G 148
RM12: Horn .34Kd 77
SE6 .60Hc 115
SL3: Coln .52E 104
SL9: Chal P .26A 42
SM7: Bans .86Ab 174
TW8: Bford .51La 108
Willow Cotts. TW9: Kew .51Qa 109
TW13: Hanw .62Aa 129
Willow Ct. *E11* .33Gc 73
(off Trinity Cl.)
EC2 .5H 219 (42Ub 91)
HA3: Hrw W .25Ha 46
HA8: Edg .21Na 47
N12 .21Db 49
NW6 .38Ab 68
SM6: Wall .80Kb 156
(off Willow Rd.)
TW16: Sun .66U 128
(off Staines Rd. W.)
W4 .52Ua 110
(off Corney Reach Way)
W9 .43Cb 89
(off Admiral Wlk.)
Willowcourt Av. HA3: Kenton .29Ka 46
Willow Cres. AL1: St A .2G 6
Willow Cres. E. UB9: Den .36L 63
Willow Cres. W. UB9: Den .36L 63
Willow Dene HA5: Pinn .26Z 45
WD23: B Hea .17Ga 28
Willowdene CM15: Pil H .15Vd 40
N6 .31Hb 69
SE15 .52Xb 113
Willowdene Cl. TW2: Whitt .59Ea 108
Willowdene Ct.
CM14: W'ley .21Yd 58
N20 .17Eb 31
(off High Rd.)
Willow Dr. EN5: Barn .14Ab 30
GU23: Rip .96J 189
Willow Edge WD4: K Lan .1Q 12
Willow End HA6: Nwood .23W 44
KT6: Surb .74Na 153
N20 .19Db 31
Willowfields Cl. SE18 .50Uc 94
Willow Gdns. HA4: Ruis .33V 64
TW3: Houn .53Ca 107
Willow Glade RH2: Reig .9L 207
Willow Grange DA14: Sidc .62Xc 139
WD17: Wat .11W 26
Willow Grn. GU24: W End .5D 166
NW9 .25Ua 48
WD6: Bore .15Ta 29
Willow Gro. BR7: Chst .65Qc 138
E13 .40Jc 73
HA4: Ruis .33V 64
Willowhayne Ct. *KT12: Walt T* .73X 151
(off Willowhayne Dr.)
Willowhayne Dr. KT12: Walt T .73X 151
Willowhayne Gdns. KT4: Wor Pk .76Ya 154
Willowherb Wlk. RM3: Rom .24Ld 57
Willow Ho. BR2: Brom .68Gc 137
CR6: W'ham .87Dc 178
SE1 .5K 231
W10 .42Za 88
(off Maple Wlk.)
Willow La. CR4: Mitc .71Hb 155
SE18 .49Pc 94
WD18: Wat .15W 26
Willow La. Bus. Pk.
CR4: Mitc .72Hb 155
Willow La. Ind. Est.
CR4: Mitc .72Hb 155
Willow Lodge RM7: Rom .29Fd 56
SW6 .53Za 110
TW16: Sun .66V 128
(off Forest Dr.)
Willowmead IG7: Chig .20Wc 37
TW18: Staines .67K 127
Willowmead Cl. GU21: Wok .8L 167
W5 .42Ma 87
Willowmere KT10: Esh .77Ea 152
Willow Mt. CR0: C'don .76Ub 157
Willow Pde. RM14: Upm .32Ud 78
SL3: L'ly .48C 82
Willow Pk. SL2: Stoke P .8L 61
TN14: Otf .89Hd 182
Willow Path EN9: Walt A .6Gc 21
Willow Pl. SL4: Eton .1G 103
SW1 .5C 228 (49Lb 90)
Willow Rd. DA1: Dart .60Ld 119
DA8: Erith .53Jd 118
EN1: Enf .13Ub 33
KT3: N Mald .70Sa 131
NW3 .35Fb 69
RH1: Redh .9L 207
RM6: Chad H .30Ad 55
SL3: Poyle .54G 104
SM6: Wall .80Kb 156
W5 .47Na 87
Willows, The AL1: St A .6F 6
BR3: Beck .67Cc 136
E6 .38Pc 74
GU18: Light .3A 166
HP2: Hem H .1B 4
IG10: Lough .15Mc 35
KT10: Clay .79Ga 152
KT13: Weyb .76Q 150
KT14: Byfl .85N 169
RH1: Redh .7P 207
RM17: Grays .51Fe 121
SE1 .5J 231
SL4: Wind .2B 102
TN15: Igh .93Zd 205
WD3: Rick .19J 25
WD6: Bore .11Qa 29
WD19: Wat .17X 27
Willows Av. SM4: Mord .71Db 155
Willows Cl. HA5: Pinn .26Y 45
Willows Farm Village .8K 7
Willowside AL2: Lon C .9J 7
Willowside Ct. EN2: Enf .13Rb 33
Willows Lodge SL4: Wind .2B 102
Willows Path KT18: Eps .86Ra 173
SL4: Wind .3A 102
Willows Riverside Pk. SL4: Wind .2A 102
Willows Ter. *NW10* .40Va 68
(off Rucklidge Av.)
Willow St. E4 .17Fc 35
EC2 .5H 219 (42Ub 91)
RM7: Rom .28Ed 56
Willow Ter. DA4: Eyns .75Nd 163
Willow Tree Cl. E3 .39Bc 72
RM4: Abr .13Xc 37
SW18 .60Db 111
UB4: Yead .42Y 85
UB5: N'olt .37Ba 65
Willowtree Cl. UB10: Ick .34S 64
Willow Tree Ct.
DA14: Sidc .64Wc 139
HA0: Wemb .36Ma 67
Willow Tree La. UB4: Yead .42Y 85
Willow Tree Lodge
HA6: Nwood .22V 44
Willow Tree Rdbt. UB4: Yead .43Z 85
Willow Tree Wlk. BR1: Brom .67Kc 137
Willowtree Way CR7: Thor H .67Qb 134
Willow Va. BR7: Chst .65Rc 138
KT22: Fet .95Da 191
(not continuous)
W12 .46Wa 88
Willow Vw. SW19 .67Fb 133
Willow Wlk. BR6: Farnb .76Rc 160
DA1: Cray, Dart .56Ld 119
(not continuous)
E17 .29Bc 52
IG1: Ilf .33Rc 74
KT16: Chert .73J 149
KT23: Bookh .97Ea 192
Willow Wlk. N1 .1C 218 (40Rb 71)
N2 .26Fb 49
N15 .28Rb 51
N21 .16Pb 32
RH1: Redh .8B 208
RM14: Upm .32Ud 78
SE1 .5J 231 (48Ub 91)
SM3: Sutt .76Bb 155
TW20: Eng G .4N 125
Willow Way AL2: Chis G .9N 5
AL10: Hat .3B 8
EN6: Pot B .5Db 17
GU22: Wok .93A 188
HA0: Wemb .34Ja 66
HP1: Hem H .1K 3
KT14: W Byf .83L 169
KT19: Ewe .79Ta 153
N3 .24Db 49
RH9: G'stone .4P 209
RM3: Hrld W .23Rd 57
SE26 .62Yb 136
TW2: Twick .61Da 129
TW16: Sun .70W 128
W11 .45Za 88
WD7: R'lett .8Ga 14
Willow Wood Cres. SE25 .72Ub 157
Willow Wren Wharf UB2: S'hall .49X 85
Will Perrin Ct. RM13: Rain .39Jd 76
Willrose Cres. SE2 .50Xc 95
Willsbridge Ct. SE15 .51Vb 113
Wills Cres. TW3: Houn .58Da 107
Wills Gro. NW7 .22Wa 48
Wills Hill SS17: Stan H .1M 101
Willson Rd. TW20: Eng G .4M 125
Will Wyatt Ct. N1 .2H 219
Wilman Gro. E8 .38Wb 71
Wilmar Cl. UB4: Hayes .42T 84
UB8: Uxb .38M 63
Wilmar Gdns. BR4: W W'ck .74Dc 158
Wilmar Way TN15: Seal .92Pd 203
Wilmcote Ho. *W2* .43Db 89
(off Woodchester Sq.)
Wilment Ct. NW2 .34Ya 68
Wilmer Cl. KT2: King T .64Pa 131
Wilmer Cres. KT2: King T .64Pa 131
Wilmer Gdns. N1 .1H 219 (39Ub 71)
(not continuous)
Wilmerhatch La. KT18: Eps .90Ra 173
Wilmer Ho. *E3* .40Ac 72
(off Daling Way)
Wilmer Lea Cl. E15 .38Ec 72
Wilmer Pl. N16 .33Vb 71
Wilmers Ct. *NW10* .39Ta 67
(off Lawrence Av.)
Wilmer Way N14 .22Mb 50
WILMINGTON .62Ld 141
Wilmington Av. BR6: Orp .75Yc 161
W4 .52Ta 109
Wilmington Cl. WD18: Wat .13X 27
Wilmington Ct. SW16 .66Nb 134
Wilmington Ct. Rd. DA2: Wilm .62Jd 140
Wilmington Gdns. IG11: Bark .37Tc 74
Wilmington Sq. WC1 .4K 217 (41Qb 90)
(not continuous)
Wilmington St. WC1 .4K 217 (41Qb 90)
Wilmot Cl. N2 .26Eb 49
SE15 .52Wb 113
Wilmot Cotts. SM7: Bans .87Db 175
Wilmot Grn. CM13: Gt War .23Yd 58
Wilmot Ho. SE11 .6B 230
Wilmot Pl. NW1 .38Lb 70
(not continuous)
W7 .46Ga 86
Wilmot Rd. CR8: Purl .84Qb 176
DA1: Dart .57Jd 118
E10 .33Dc 72
N17 .27Tb 51
SL1: Burn .1A 80
SM5: Cars .78Hb 155
Wilmots Cl. RH2: Reig .5L 207
Wilmot St. E2 .42Xb 91
Wilmot Way SM7: Bans .86Cb 175
Wilmount St. SE18 .49Rc 94
Wilmslow Ho. *RM3: Rom* .22Nd 57
(off Chudleigh Rd.)
Wilna Rd. SW18 .59Eb 111
Wilsham St. W11 .46Za 88
Wilshaw Cl. NW4 .27Wa 48
Wilshaw Ho. SE8 .52Cc 114
Wilshaw St. SE14 .53Cc 114
Wilshere Av. AL1: St A .4A 6
Wilsman Rd. RM15: S Ock .40Yd 78
Wilsmere Dr. HA3: Hrw W .24Ga 46
UB5: N'olt .37Aa 65
Wilson Av. CR4: Mitc .66Gb 133
Wilson Cl. CR2: S Croy .78Tb 157
HA9: Wemb .31Pa 67
SS17: Stan H .3L 101
Wilson Ct. *RM7: Rush G* .30Fd 56
(off Union Rd.)
SE28 .48Sc 94
Wilson Dr. HA9: Wemb .31Pa 67
KT16: Ott .78D 148
Wilson Gdns. HA1: Harr .31Ea 66
Wilson Gro. SE16 .47Xb 91
Wilson Ho. *NW6* .38Eb 69
(off Goldhurst Ter.)
Wilson La. DA4: S Dar .68Vd 142
Wilson Rd. E6 .41Mc 93
IG1: Ilf .31Pc 74
KT9: Chess .79Pa 153
SE5 .53Ub 113
Wilsons KT20: Tad .93Za 194
Wilson's Av. N17 .26Vb 51
Wilsons Cnr. *CM14: B'wood* .19Zd 41
(off High St.)
Wilson's Pl. E14 .44Bc 92
Wilson's Rd. W6 .50Za 88
Wilson St. E17 .29Ec 52
EC2 .7G 219 (43Tb 91)
N21 .17Qb 32
Wilson Wlk. *W4* .49Va 88
(off Prebend Gdns.)
W6 .49Va 88
(off Prebend Gdns.)
Wilson Way GU21: Wok .8P 167
Wilstone Cl. UB4: Yead .42Aa 85
Wiltern Ct. NW2 .37Ab 68
Wilthorne Gdns. RM10: Dag .38Dd 76
Wilton Av. W4 .50Ua 88
Wilton Cl. UB7: Harm .51M 105
Wilton Ct. *E1* .44Xb 91
(off Cavell St.)
WD17: Wat .13Y 27
Wilton Cres. SL4: Wind .6B 102
SW1 .2H 227 (47Jb 90)
SW19 .66Bb 133
Wilton Dr. RM5: Col R .24Ed 56
Wilton Est. E8 .37Wb 71
Wilton Gdns. KT8: W Mole .69Ca 129
KT12: Walt T .74Z 151
Wilton Gro. KT3: N Mald .72Va 154
SW19 .67Bb 133
Wilton Ho. *CR2: S Croy* .78Sb 157
(off Nottingham Rd.)
Wilton M. E8 .37Xb 71
SW1 .3J 227 (48Jb 90)
Wilton Pde. TW13: Felt .61W 128
Wilton Pl. E4 .23Fc 53
HA1: Harr .30Ha 46
KT15: New H .81M 169
SW1 .2H 227 (47Jb 90)
Wilton Plaza SW1 .5B 228
Wilton Rd. EN4: Cockf .14Hb 31
N10 .26Jb 50
RH1: Redh .7P 207
SE2 .49Yc 95
SW1 .4A 228 (48Kb 90)
SW19 .66Gb 133
TW4: Houn .55Z 107
Wilton Row SW1 .2H 227 (47Jb 90)
Wiltons Music Hall .45Wb 91
(off Graces All.)
Wilton Sq. N1 .39Tb 71
Wilton St. SW1 .3K 227 (48Kb 90)
Wilton Ter. SW1 .3H 227 (48Jb 90)
Wilton Vs. *N1* .39Tb 71
(off Wilton Sq.)
Wilton Way E8 .37Wb 71
Wiltshire Av. RM11: Horn .28Pd 57
SL2: Slou .2G 80
Wiltshire Cl. DA2: Dart .59Td 120
NW7 .22Va 48
SW3 .6F 227 (49Hb 89)
Wiltshire Ct. CR2: S Croy .78Sb 157
IG1: Ilf .37Sc 74
N4 .32Pb 70
(off Marquis Rd.)
Wiltshire Gdns. N4 .30Sb 51
TW2: Twick .60Ea 108
Wiltshire La. HA5: Eastc .27V 44
Wiltshire Rd. BR6: Orp .73Wc 161
CR7: Thor H .69Qb 134
SW9 .55Qb 112
Wiltshire Row N1 .39Tb 71
Wilverley Cres. KT3: N Mald .72Ua 154
Wimbart Rd. SW2 .59Pb 112
WIMBLEDON .65Ab 132
Wimbledon
All England Lawn Tennis & Croquet Club
.63Ab 132
Wimbledon Bri. SW19 .65Bb 133
Wimbledon Cl. SW20 .66Za 132
Wimbledon Common .63Wa 132
Wimbledon Common Golf Course
.64Xa 132
Wimbledon Hill Rd. SW19 .65Ab 132
Wimbledon Lawn Tennis Mus. .62Ab 132
Wimbledon Leisure Cen. .65Db 133
Wimbledon Mus. of Local History
.65Ab 132
WIMBLEDON PARK .62Cb 133
Wimbledon Pk. Athletics Track .61Bb 133
Wimbledon Pk. Ct. SW19 .60Bb 111
Wimbledon Pk. Golf Course .62Bb 133
Wimbledon Pk. Rd. SW18 .61Ab 132
SW19 .61Ab 132
Wimbledon Pk. Side SW19 .62Za 132
Wimbledon Pk. Watersports Cen.
.61Bb 133
Wimbledon Pk. Women's Fitness Suite
.62Bb 133
Wimbledon Rd. SW17 .63Eb 133
Wimbledon Stadium Bus. Cen.
SW17 .62Db 133
Wimbledon Stadium (Greyhound)
.63Eb 133
Wimbledon Theatre .66Cb 133
Wimbledon Windmill Mus. .61Xa 132
Wimbolt St. E2 .41Wb 91
Wimborne Av. BR5: St P .70Vc 139
BR7: Chst .70Vc 139
RH1: Redh .10P 207
UB2: S'hall .49Ca 85
UB4: Yead .44X 85
Wimborne Cl. IG9: Buck H .19Kc 35
KT4: Wor Pk .74Ya 154
KT17: Eps .85Ua 174
SE12 .57Hc 115
Wimborne Ct. SW12 .62Lb 134
UB5: N'olt .37Ca 65
Wimborne Dr. HA5: Pinn .31Z 65
NW9 .27Qa 47
Wimborne Gdns. W13 .43Ka 86
Wimborne Gro. WD17: Wat .9U 12
Wimborne Ho. *E16* .45Hc 93
(off Victoria Dock Rd.)
NW1 .6E 214
SW8 .52Pb 112
(off Dorset Rd.)
SW12 .62Lb 134
Wimborne Rd. N9 .19Wb 33
N17 .26Ub 51
Wimborne Way BR3: Beck .69Zb 136
Wimbourne Ct. N1 .1F 219
Wimbourne St.
N1 .1F 219 (40Tb 71)
Wimpole Cl. BR2: Brom .70Lc 137
KT1: King T .68Pa 131
Wimpole M. W1 .7K 215 (43Kb 90)
Wimpole Rd. UB7: Yiew .46M 83
Wimpole St. W1 .7K 215 (43Kb 90)
Wimshurst Cl.
CR0: Wadd .74Nb 156
Winans Wlk. SW9 .54Qb 112
Winant Ho. *E14* .45Dc 92
(off Simpson's Rd.)
Wincanton Ct. *N11* .23Jb 50
(off Martock Gdns.)
Wincanton Cres. UB5: N'olt .36Ca 65
Wincanton Gdns. IG6: Ilf .27Rc 54
Wincanton Rd. RM3: Rom .20Md 39
SW18 .59Bb 111
Winchcombe Rd.
SM5: Cars .73Fb 155
Winchcomb Gdns. SE9 .55Mc 115
Winchdells HP3: Hem H .5A 4
Winchelsea Av. DA7: Bex .52Bd 117

Winchelsea Cl. SW15 . . . . .57Za 110
Winchelsea Ho. SE16 . . . . .47Yb 92
(off Swan Rd.)
Winchelsea Rd. E7 . . . . .34Jc 73
N17 . . . . .27Ub 51
NW10 . . . . .39Ta 67
Winchelsey Ri. CR2: S Croy 79Vb 157
Winchendon Rd. SW6 . . . . .53Bb 111
TW11: Tedd 63Fa 130
Winchester Av. NW6 . . . . .39Ab 68
NW9 . . . . .27Qa 47
RM14: Upm 32Vd 78
TW5: Hest 51Ba 107
Winchester Bldgs. SE1 . . . . .1D 230
Winchester Cl. BR2: Brom 69Hc 137
E6 . . . . .44Pc 94
EN1: Enf 15Ub 33
EN9: Walt A 5Dc 20
KT2: King T 66Ra 131
KT10: Esh 77Ca 151
SE17 . . . . .6C 230 (49Rb 91)
SL3: Poyle 53G 104
Winchester Ct. AL1: St A 2D 6
(off Lemsford Rd.)
W8 . . . . .47Cb 89
(off Vicarage Ga.)
Winchester Cres.
DA12: Grav'nd 2F 144
Winchester Dr. HA5: Pinn 29Z 45
Winchester Gro. TN13: S'oaks 95Kd 203
Winchester Ho. AL3: St A 3A 6
E3 . . . . .41Bc 92
(off Hamlets Way)
IG11: Bark 38Wc 75
(off Margaret Bondfield Av.)
KT19: Eps 84Qa 173
(off Phoenix Cl.)
SE18 . . . . .52Mc 115
(off Portway Gdns.)
SW3 . . . . .51Fb 111
(off Beaufort St.)
SW9 . . . . .52Qb 112
W2 . . . . .3A 220
Winchester M. KT4: Wor Pk 75Za 154
NW3 . . . . .38Fb 69
(off Winchester Rd.)
Winchester Pk. BR2: Brom 69Hc 137
Winchester Pl. E8 . . . . .36Vb 71
N6 . . . . .32Kb 70
Winchester Rd. BR2: Brom 69Hc 137
BR6: Chels 77Yc 161
DA7: Bex 54Zc 117
E4 . . . . .24Ec 52
HA3: Kenton 28Na 47
HA6: Nwood 26V 44
IG1: Ilf .34Tc 74
KT12: Walt T 74W 150
N6 . . . . .31Kb 70
N9 . . . . .18Vb 33
NW3 . . . . .38Fb 69
TW1: Twick 58Ka 108
TW13: Hanw 62Ba 129
UB3: Harl 52U 106
Winchester Sq. SE1 . . . . .6F 225
Winchester St. SW1 . . . . . .7A 228 (50Kb 90)
W3 . . . . .46Sa 87
Winchester Wlk. SE1 . . . . . .6F 225 (46Tb 91)
Winchester Way WD3: Crox G 15R 26
Winchester Wharf SE1 . . . . .6F 225
Winchet Wlk. CR0: C'don 72Yb 158
Winchfield Cl. HA3: Kenton 30La 46
Winchfield Ho. SW15 . . . . .58Va 110
Winchfield Rd. SE26 . . . . .64Ac 136
Winchfield Way WD3: Rick 17L 25
Winch Ho. E14 . . . . .48Dc 92
(off Tiller Rd.)
SW10 . . . . .52Eb 111
(off King's Rd.)
Winchilsea Cres. KT8: W Mole 68Ea 130
Winchilsea Ho. NW8 . . . . .4B 214
WINCHMORE HILL 17Qb 32
Winchmore Hill Rd. N14 . . . . .18Mb 32
N21 . . . . .18Mb 32
Winchmore Vs. N21 . . . . .17Pb 32
(off Winchmore Hill Rd.)
Winch's Mdw. SL1: Burn 1A 80
Winchstone Cl. TW17: Shep 70P 127
Winckley Cl. HA3: Kenton 29Pa 47
Winckworth Ct. N1 . . . . .4G 219
Wincott Pde. SE11 . . . . .5A 230
Wincott St. SE11 . . . . .5A 230 (49Qb 90)
Wincrofts Dr. SE9 . . . . .56Tc 116
Windall Cl. SE19 . . . . .67Wb 135
Windborough Rd. SM5: Cars 80Jb 156
Windermere NW1 . . . . .4A 216
Windermere Av. AL1: St A 4F 6
(not continuous)
HA4: Ruis 31Y 65
HA9: Kenton, Wemb 31La 66
N3 . . . . .27Cb 49
NW6 . . . . .39Ab 68
RM12: Horn 36Jd 78
RM19: Purf 50Sd 98
SW19 . . . . .69Db 133
Windermere Cl. BR6: Farnb 76Rc 160
DA1: Dart 60Kd 119
HP3: Hem H 3C 4
TW14: Felt 60V 106
TW19: Stanw 60N 105
TW20: Egh 66D 126
WD3: Chor 15F 24
Windermere Ct. CR8: Kenley 87Rb 177
GU21: Wok 10L 167
(off St John's Rd.)
HA9: Wemb 31La 66
SM5: Cars 76Jb 156
SW13 . . . . .51Va 110
WD17: Wat 12W 26
Windermere Gdns. IG4: Ilf 29Nc 54
Windermere Gro.
HA9: Wemb 32La 66
Windermere Hall HA8: Edg 22Pa 47
Windermere Ho. E3 . . . . .42Bc 92
EN5: New Bar 14Db 31
TW7: Isle 57Ha 108
Windermere Point SE15 . . . . .52Yb 114
(off Old Kent Rd.)
Windermere Rd. BR4: W W'ck 75Gc 159
CR0: C'don 74Vb 157
CR5: Coul 87Nb 176
DA7: Bex 54Ed 118
GU18: Light 2A 166
N10 . . . . .25Kb 50
N19 . . . . .33Lb 70
Windermere Rd. SW15 . . . . .63Ua 132
SW16 . . . . .67Lb 134
UB1: S'hall 43Ba 85
W5 . . . . .48La 86
Windermere Way RH2: Reig 5N 207
SL1: Slou .3A 80
UB7: Yiew 46N 83
Winders Rd. SW11 . . . . .54Gb 111
(not continuous)
Windfield KT22: Lea 93Ka 192
Windfield Cl. SE26 . . . . .63Zb 136
Windham Av. CR0: New Ad 82Fc 179
Windham Rd. TW9: Rich 55Pa 109
Windhover Way DA12: Grav'nd 3G 144
Windings, The CR2: Sande 83Vb 177
Winding Shot HP1: Hem H 1J 3
Winding Way RM8: Dag 34Yc 75
Windlass Pl. SE8 . . . . .49Ac 92
Windle Cl. GU20: W'sham 9B 146
Windlemere Golf Course 3C 166
WINDLESHAM 9B 146
Windlesham Ct. GU20: W'sham 6A 146
Windlesham Ct. Dr. GU20: W'sham . . .7A 146
Windlesham Gro. SW19 . . . . .60Za 110
Windlesham Rd. GU24: Chob 10E 146
GU24: W End 3C 166
Windley Cl. SE23 . . . . .61Yb 136
Windmill WC1 . . . . .7H 217
Windmill Av. KT17: Ewe 83Va 174
UB2: S'hall 46Ea 86
Windmill Bri. Ho. CR0: C'don 74Ub 157
(off Freemasons Rd.)
Windmill Bus. Village TW16: Sun . . .67U 128
Windmill Cl. CR3: Cat'm 93Sb 197
EN9: Walt A 6Gc 21
KT6: Surb 74La 152
KT17: Eps 84Va 174
RM14: Upm 33Qd 77
SE1 . . . . .49Wb 91
(off Beatrice Rd.)
SE13 . . . . .54Ec 114
SL4: Wind 4F 102
TW16: Sun 66U 128
Windmill Ct. HA4: Ruis 32W 64
NW2 . . . . .37Ab 68
W5 . . . . .49La 86
(off Windmill Rd.)
Windmill Dr. BR2: Kes 77Lc 159
KT22: Lea 95La 192
NW2 . . . . .34Ab 68
RH2: Reig 4M 207
SW4 . . . . .57Kb 112
WD3: Crox G 16P 25
Windmill End KT17: Eps 84Va 174
Windmill Fld. GU20: W'sham 9A 146
Windmill Gdns. EN2: Enf 13Qb 32
Windmill Grange TN15: W King 80Ud 164
Windmill Grn. TW17: Shep 73U 150
(off Walton La.)
Windmill Gro. CR0: C'don 72Sb 157
Windmill Hill EN2: Enf 13Rb 33
HA4: Ruis 31V 64
NW3 . . . . .34Eb 69
TN15: Wro H 93Fe 205
WD4: Chfd .4H 11
(not continuous)
Windmill Ho. E14 . . . . .49Cc 92
SE1 . . . . .7A 224
Windmill La. E15 . . . . .37Fc 73
EN5: Ark .16Va 30
EN8: Chesh 2Ac 20
KT6: Surb 72Ka 152
KT17: Eps 84Va 174
TW7: Isle 48Ea 86
UB2: S'hall 46Ea 86
UB6: G'frd 44Ea 86
WD23: B Hea 18Ga 28
Windmill M. W4 . . . . .49Ua 88
Windmill Pk. TN15: Wro H 92Fe 205
Windmill Pas. W4 . . . . .49Ua 88
Windmill Pl. UB2: S'hall 46Ea 86
Windmill Ri. KT2: King T 66Ra 131
Windmill Rd. CR0: C'don 73Sb 157
CR4: Mitc 71Lb 156
HP2: Hem H 2N 3
N18 . . . . .21Tb 51
SL1: Slou .6H 81
SL3: Ful 6P 61
SW18 . . . . .58Fb 111
SW19 . . . . .61Xa 132
TW8: Bford 49La 86
TW12: Hamp H 64Da 129
TW16: Sun 67U 128
W4 . . . . .49Ua 88
W5 . . . . .49La 86
Windmill Rd. W. TW16: Sun 68U 128
Windmill Row
SE11 . . . . .7K 229 (50Qb 90)
Windmill Shott TW20: Egh 65B 126
Windmill St. DA12: Grav'nd 8D 122
(not continuous)
W1 . . . . .1D 222 (43Mb 90)
(not continuous)
WD23: B Hea 18Ga 28
Windmill Ter. TW17: Shep 73U 150
Windmill Wlk.
SE1 . . . . .7A 224 (46Qb 90)
Windmill Way HA4: Ruis 32V 64
RH2: Reig 4M 207
Windmore Av. EN6: Pot B 3Ya 16
Windmore Cl. HA0: Wemb 36Ja 66
Windridge Cl. AL3: St A 3N 5
Windrose Cl. SE16 . . . . .47Zb 92
Windrush KT3: N Mald 70Ra 131
SE28 . . . . .46Xc 95
Windrush Av. SL3: L'ly 48D 82
Windrush Cl. E8 . . . . .38Wb 71
N17 . . . . .25Ub 51
SW11 . . . . .56Fb 111
UB10: Ick .35P 63
W4 . . . . .53Sa 109
Windrush Ct. DA8: Erith 50Gd 96
Windrushes CR3: Cat'm 97Wb 197
Windrush Ho. NW8 . . . . .6C 214
Windrush La. SE23 . . . . .62Zb 136
Windrush Rd. NW10 . . . . .39Ta 67
Winds End Cl. HP2: Hem H 1A 4
Windsock Cl. SE16 . . . . .49Bc 92
Windsock Way TW6: H'row A 54K 105
WINDSOR 3H 103
Windsor (Home Park) (Park & Ride)
. . . . .1J 103
Windsor (Legoland) (Park & Ride)
. . . . .7C 102
Windsor & Eton Relief Rd.
SL4: Eton, Wind 3F 102
Windsor & Royal Borough Mus. 3H 103
(off Bachelors Acre)
Windsor Av. E17 . . . . .26Ac 52
HA8: Edg 21Ra 47
KT3: N Mald 71Sa 153
KT8: W Mole 69Ca 129
RM16: Grays 47De 99
SM3: Cheam 76Ab 154
SW19 . . . . .67Eb 133
UB10: Hil 39R 64
Windsor Boys' School Sports Cen.
. . . . .3F 102
Windsor Bus. Cen. SL4: Wind 2G 102
Windsor Castle 2J 103
Windsor Centre, The N1 . . . . .39Rb 71
(off Windsor St.)
Windsor Cl. BR7: Chst 64Rc 138
EN7: Chesh 2Wb 19
HA2: Harr 34Ca 65
HA6: Nwood 26W 44
HP2: Hem H 4N 3
HP3: Bov .10C 2
N3 . . . . .26Ab 48
SE27 . . . . .63Sb 135
SL1: Burn .2A 80
TW6: H'row A 55L 105
(off Whittle Rd.)
TW8: Bford 51Ka 108
WD6: Bore 11Qa 29
Windsor Cotts. SE14 . . . . .52Bc 114
(off Amersham Gro.)
Windsor Ct. AL1: St A 3E 6
CR3: Whyt 90Vb 177
E3 . . . . .40Cc 72
(off Mostyn Gro.)
GU24: Chob 1J 167
HA5: Pinn .27Z 45
KT1: King T 70Ma 131
(off Palace Rd.)
N11 . . . . .22Hb 49
N14 . . . . .17Lb 32
NW3 . . . . .35Cb 69
NW11 . . . . .30Ab 48
(off Golders Grn. Rd.)
SE16 . . . . .45Zb 92
(off King & Queen Wharf)
SW3 . . . . .7E 226
SW11 . . . . .54Fb 111
TW16: Sun 66W 128
W2 . . . . .45Db 89
(off Moscow Rd.)
W10 . . . . .44Za 88
(off Bramley Rd.)
WD4: K Lan 1Q 12
WD6: Bore 12Sa 29
WD23: Bush 17Ea 28
(off Catsey La.)
Windsor Ct. Rd. GU24: Chob 1J 167
Windsor Cres. HA2: Harr 34Ca 65
HA9: Wemb 34Ra 67
Windsor Dr. BR6: Chels 79Wc 161
DA1: Dart 58Jd 118
EN4: E Barn 16Hb 31
TW15: Ashf 63M 127
Windsor Fitness Club, The 3F 102
Windsor Gdns. CR0: Bedd 76Nb 156
UB3: Harl .48T 84
W9 . . . . .43Cb 89
Windsor Great Pk. 2F 124
Windsor Gro. SE27 . . . . .63Sb 135
Windsor Hall E16 . . . . .46Kc 93
(off Wesley Av.)
Windsor Ho. E2 . . . . .41Zb 92
(off Knottisford St.)
N1 . . . . .1E 218 (40Sb 71)
NW1 . . . . .3A 216
NW2 . . . . .37Ab 68
(off Chatsworth Rd.)
UB5: N'olt 37Ca 65
(off The Farmlands)
WD23: Bush 14Ba 27
Windsor La. SL1: Burn 2A 80
Windsor Leisure Cen. 2F 102
Windsor M. SE6 . . . . .60Ec 114
SE23 . . . . .60Ac 114
Windsor Pk. Rd. UB3: Harl 52V 106
Windsor Pl.
KT16: Chert 72J 149
SW1 . . . . .5C 228 (48Lb 90)
Windsor Rd.
CM15: Pil H 16Xd 40
CR7: Thor H 68Rb 135
DA6: Bex .56Ad 117
DA12: Grav'nd 2D 144
E4 . . . . .21Dc 52
E7 . . . . .36Kc 73
E10 . . . . .33Dc 72
E11 . . . . .32Jc 73
EN3: Enf W 8Zb 20
EN5: Barn 16Za 30
GU24: Chob 7G 146
HA3: Hrw W 25Ea 46
HP9: Beac .1E 60
IG1: Ilf 35Rc 74
KT2: King T 66Na 131
KT4: Wor Pk 75Wa 154
N3 . . . . .26Ab 48
N7 . . . . .34Nb 70
N13 . . . . .20Qb 32
N17 . . . . .26Wb 51
NW2 . . . . .37Xa 68
RM8: Dag 34Ad 75
RM11: Horn 31Ld 77
SL1: Slou 8J 81
SL2: Ger X, Stoke P 5L 61
SL3: Dat .2L 103
SL4: Old Win 10N 103
SL4: Wat O, Wind 2A 102
(not continuous)
SL4: Wink .5A 124
SL9: Ger X .2M 61
TW4: Cran 54X 107
TW9: Kew 54Pa 109
TW11: Tedd 64Fa 130
TW16: Sun 65W 128
TW19: Wray 58A 104
TW20: Egh 10N 103
UB2: S'hall 48Ba 85
W5 . . . . .45Na 87
(not continuous)
WD24: Wat 10Y 13
Windsors, The IG9: Buck H 19Nc 36
Windsor St. KT16: Chert 72J 149
N1 . . . . .39Rb 71
UB8: Uxb .39L 63
Windsor Ter. N1 . . . . .3E 218 (41Sb 91)
Windsor Wlk. KT12: Walt T 74Z 151
KT13: Weyb 78R 150
SE5 . . . . .54Tb 113
Windsor Way GU22: Wok 88E 168
W14 . . . . .49Za 88
WD3: Rick .18J 25
Windsor Wharf E9 . . . . .36Bc 72
Windsor Wood EN9: Walt A 5Gc 21
Windspoint Dr. SE15 . . . . .51Xb 113
Winds Ridge GU23: Send 97E 188
Windus Rd. N16 . . . . .32Vb 71
Windus Wlk. N16 . . . . .32Vb 71
Windward Cl. EN3: Enf W 7Zb 20
Windward Ct. E16 . . . . .45Rc 94
(off Gallions Rd.)
Windycroft Cl. CR8: Purl 85Mb 176
Windy Hill CM13: Hut 18Ee 41
Windy Ridge BR1: Brom 67Nc 138
Windy Ridge Cl. SW19 . . . . .64Za 132
Wine Cl. E1 .46Yb 92
(not continuous)
Wine Office Ct. EC4 . . . . . . .2A 224 (44Qb 90)
Winern Glebe KT14: Byfl 85M 169
Winery La. KT1: King T 69Pa 131
Winey Cl. KT9: Chess 80La 152
Winfield La. TN15: Bor G 97Ae 205
Winfield Mobile Home Pk.
WD25: A'ham 11Da 27
Winford Ct. SE15 . . . . .53Xb 113
Winford Ho. E3 . . . . .38Bc 72
Winford Pde. UB1: S'hall 44Da 85
(off Marconi Way)
Winforton St. SE10 . . . . .53Ec 114
Winfrith Rd. SW18 . . . . .59Eb 111
Wingate Bus. Cen. AL9: Wel G 5E 8
Wingate Cres. CR0: C'don 72Nb 156
Wingate Ho. E3 . . . . .41Dc 92
(off Bruce Rd.)
Wingate Rd. DA14: Sidc 65Yc 139
IG1: Ilf 36Rc 74
W6 . . . . .48Xa 88
Wingate Sq. SW4 . . . . .55Lb 112
Wingate Trad. Est. N17 . . . . .24Vb 51
Wingate Way AL1: St A 3E 6
Wingfield RM17: Grays 50Be 99
Wingfield Bank DA11: Nflt 61Ee 143
Wingfield Cl. CM13: B'wood 20Ce 41
KT15: New H 82K 169
Wingfield Ct. DA15: Sidc 61Vc 139
E14 . . . . .45Fc 93
(off Newport Av.)
SM7: Bans 87Cb 175
WD18: Wat 16S 26
Wingfield Dr. RM16: Ors 3C 100
Wingfield Gdns. RM14: Upm 30Ud 58
Wingfield Ho. E2 . . . . .4K 219
NW6 . . . . .40Db 69
(off Tollgate Gdns.)
Wingfield M. SE15 . . . . .55Wb 113
Wingfield Rd. DA12: Grav'nd 9D 122
E15 . . . . .35Gc 73
E17 . . . . .29Dc 52
KT2: King T 65Pa 131
Wingfield St. SE15 . . . . .55Wb 113
Wingfield Way HA4: Ruis 36X 65
Wingford Rd. SW2 . . . . .58Nb 112
Wingletye La. RM11: Horn 28Pd 57
Wingmore Rd. SE24 . . . . .55Sb 113
Wingrad Ho. E1 . . . . .43Yb 92
(off Jubilee St.)
Wingrave SE17 . . . . .5F 231 (49Tb 91)
Wingrave Cres.
CM14: B'wood 21Ud 58
Wingrave Rd. W6 . . . . .51Ya 110
Wingreen NW8 . . . . .39Db 69
(off Abbey Rd.)
Wingrove E4 . . . . .17Cc 34
Wingrove Ct. RM7: Rom 29Ed 56
Wingrove Dr. RM19: Purf 50Rd 97
Wingrove Rd. SE6 . . . . .61Gc 137
Wings Cl. SM1: Sutt 77Cb 155
Wings Rd. TW6: H'row A 55K 105
(off Whittle Rd.)
Wingway CM14: B'wood 18Yd 40
Wing Yip Bus. Cen. NW2 . . . . .33Xa 68
Winicotte Ho. W2 . . . . .7C 214
Winifred Av. RM12: Horn 35Md 77
Winifred Cl. EN5: Ark 16Va 30
Winifred Dell Ho. CM13: Gt War 23Yd 58
Winifred Pl. N12 . . . . .22Eb 49
Winifred Rd. CR5: Coul 88Jb 176
DA1: Dart 57Kd 119
DA8: Erith 50Gd 96
HP3: Hem H 6M 3
RM8: Dag .33Ad 75
SW19 . . . . .67Cb 133
TW12: Hamp H 63Ca 129
Winifred St. E16 . . . . .46Pc 94
Winifred Ter. E13 . . . . .40Jc 73
(off Upper Rd.)
EN1: Enf .17Vb 33
Winifred Whittington Ho.
RM13: Rain 43Kd 97
Winkers Cl. SL9: Chal P 25B 42
Winkers La. SL9: Chal P 25B 42
Winkfield Rd. E13 . . . . .40Kc 73
N22 . . . . .25Qb 50
SL4: Wind, Wink 10A 102
SL5: Asc .9A 124
Winkley Ct. HA2: Harr 34Ca 65
N10 . . . . .28Kb 50
(off St James's La.)
Winkley St. E2 . . . . .40Xb 71
WINKWELL 4F 2
Winkwell HP1: Hem H 4F 2
Winkworth Cotts. E1 . . . . .42Yb 92
(off Cephas St.)
Winkworth Pl. SM7: Bans 86Bb 175
Winkworth Rd. SM7: Bans 86Cb 175
Winlaton Rd. BR1: Brom 63Fc 137
Winmill Rd. RM8: Dag 34Bd 75
Winnards GU21: Wok 10L 167
Winnett St. W1 . . . . .4D 222 (45Mb 90)
Winningales Ct. IG5: Ilf 26Nc 54
Winnings Wlk. UB5: N'olt 37Aa 65
Winnington Cl. N2 . . . . .30Fb 49
Winnington Ho. SE5 . . . . .52Sb 113
(off Wyndham Est.)
W10 . . . . .42Ab 88
(off Southern Row)
Winnington Rd. EN3: Enf W 10Yb 20
N2 . . . . .30Fb 49
Winnington Way GU21: Wok 10M 167
Winnipeg Dr. BR6: Chels 79Vc 161
Winnock Rd. UB7: Yiew 46M 83
Winn Rd. SE12 . . . . .60Jc 115
Winns Av. E17 . . . . .27Bc 52
Winns Comn. Rd. SE18 . . . . .51Uc 116
Winns M. N15 . . . . .28Ub 51
Winns Ter. E17 . . . . .27Cc 52
Winsbeach E17 . . . . .26Fc 53
Winscombe Cres. W5 . . . . .42Ma 87
Winscombe St. N19 . . . . .33Kb 70
Winscombe Way HA7: Stan 22Ja 46
Winsford Rd. SE6 . . . . .62Bc 136
Winsford Ter. N18 . . . . .22Tb 51
Winsham Gro. SW11 . . . . .57Jb 112
Winsham Ho. NW1 . . . . .3E 216
Winslade Rd. SW2 . . . . .57Nb 112
Winslade Way SE6 . . . . .59Dc 114
Winsland M. W2 . . . . .2B 220 (44Fb 89)
Winsland St. W2 . . . . .2B 220 (44Fb 89)
Winsley St. W1 . . . . .2B 222 (44Lb 90)
Winslow SE17 . . . . .7H 231 (50Ub 91)
Winslow Cl. HA5: Eastc 30X 45
NW10 . . . . .34Ua 68
Winslow Gro. E4 . . . . .19Gc 35
Winslow Rd. W6 . . . . .51Ya 110
Winslow Way KT12: Walt T 76Y 151
TW13: Hanw 62Z 129
Winsmoor Ct. EN2: Enf 13Rb 33
WINSOR PARK 43Rc 94
Winsor Ter. E6 . . . . .43Qc 94
Winstanley Cl. KT11: Cobh 86X 171
Winstanley Est. SW11 . . . . .55Fb 111
Winstanley Rd. SW11 . . . . .55Fb 111
(not continuous)
Winstanley Wlk. KT11: Cobh 86X 171
(off Winstanley Cl.)
Winstead Gdns. RM10: Dag 36Ed 76
Winston Av. NW9 . . . . .31Ua 68
Winston Churchill's Britain at War Experience
. . . . .7H 225
Winston Churchill School Sports Cen.
. . . . .10J 167
Winston Churchill Way EN8: Walt C . . .5Yb 20
Winston Cl. DA9: Ghithe 58Vd 120
HA3: Hrw W 23Ha 46
RM7: Mawney 28Dd 56
Winston Ct. BR1: Brom 67Kc 137
(off Widmore Rd.)
HA3: Hrw W 24Da 45
Winston Dr. KT11: Stoke D 88Aa 171
TN16: Big H 89Mc 179
Winston Ho. W13 . . . . .47Ja 86
(off Balfour Rd.)
WC1 . . . . .5E 216
Winston Rd. N16 . . . . .35Tb 71
Winston Wlk. W4 . . . . .48Ta 87
Winston Way EN6: Pot B 5Cb 17
GU22: Wok 92D 188
IG1: Ilf 34Rc 74
Winstre Rd. WD6: Bore 11Qa 29
Winter Av. E6 . . . . .39Nc 74
Winterborne Av. BR6: Orp 76Tc 160
Winterbourne Gro. KT13: Weyb 79S 150
Winterbourne Ho. W11 . . . . .45Ab 88
(off Portland Rd.)
Winterbourne M. RH8: Oxt 2G 210
Winterbourne Rd. CR7: Thor H 70Qb 134
RM8: Dag 33Yc 75
SE6 . . . . .60Bc 114
Winter Box Wlk. TW10: Rich 57Pa 109
Winterbrook Rd. SE24 . . . . .58Sb 113
Winterburn Cl. N11 . . . . .23Jb 50
Winterdown Gdns. KT10: Esh 79Ba 151
Winterdown Rd. KT10: Esh 79Ba 151
Winterfold Cl. SW19 . . . . .61Ab 132
Wintergarden Cres. DA9: Bluew 59Wd 120
Winter Gdns. TW11: Tedd 63Ja 130
Wintergreen Cl. E6 . . . . .43Nc 94
Winterleys NW6 . . . . .40Bb 69
(off Denmark Rd.)
Winter Lodge SE16 . . . . .50Wb 91
(off Fern Wlk.)
Winter's Ct. E4 . . . . .20Dc 34
Winters Cft. DA12: Grav'nd 5F 144
Wintersells Ind. Est. KT14: Byfl 82N 169
Wintersells Rd. KT14: Byfl 82M 169
Winterslow Ho. SE5 . . . . .54Sb 113
(off Flaxman Rd.)
Winters Rd. KT7: T Ditt 73Ka 152
Winterstoke Gdns. NW7 . . . . .22Wa 48
Winterstoke Rd. SE6 . . . . .60Bc 114
Winters Way EN9: Walt A 5Jc 21
Winterton Ct. KT1: Hamp W 67Ma 131
(off Lwr. Teddington Rd.)
SE20 . . . . .68Wb 135
TN16: Westrm 99Tc 200
(off Market Sq.)
Winterton Ho. E1 . . . . .44Yb 92
(off Deancross St.)
Winterton Pl. SW10 . . . . .51Eb 111
Winterwell Rd. SW2 . . . . .57Nb 112
Winthorpe Gdns. WD6: Bore 11Pa 29
Winthorpe Rd. SW15 . . . . .56Ab 110
Winthrop Ho. W12 . . . . .45Xa 88
(off White City Est.)
Winthrop St. E1 . . . . .43Xb 91
Winthrop Wlk. HA9: Wemb 34Na 67
(off Everard Way)
Winton App. WD3: Crox G 15S 26
Winton Av. N11 . . . . .24Lb 50
Winton Cl. N9 . . . . .17Zb 34
Winton Ct. BR8: Swan 70Gd 140
N1 . . . . .1H 217
Winton Cres. WD3: Crox G 15R 26
Winton Dr. EN8: Chesh 1Ac 20
WD3: Crox G 16R 26
Winton Gdns. HA8: Edg 24Pa 47
Winton Rd. BR6: Farnb 77Rc 160
Winton Ter. AL1: St A 3C 6
(off Old London Rd.)
Winton Way SW16 . . . . .64Qb 134
Wintoun Path SL2: Slou 2C 80
Winvale SL1: Slou 8J 81
Winwood SL2: Slou 4N 81
SL4: Wind .3C 102
Wireless Rd. TN16: Big H 87Mc 179
Wireworks Ct. SE1 . . . . .2C 230
Wirrall Ho. SE26 . . . . .62Wb 135
Wirral Wood Cl. BR7: Chst 65Qc 138
Wirra Rd. TW6: H'row A 54K 105
(off Wayfarer Rd.)

Wisbeach Rd. CR0: C'don .71Tb 157
Wisbech N4 .32Pb 70
(off Lorne Rd.)
Wisborough Rd. CR2: Sande .81Vb 177
Wisden Ho. SW8 .51Pb 112
Wisdom Ct. TW7: Isle .55Ja 108
(off South St.)
Wisdons Cl. RM10: Dag .32Dd 76
Wise La. NW7 .22Wa 48
UB7: W Dray .48M 83
Wiseman Rd. E10 .33Cc 72
Wise Rd. E15 .39Fc 73
Wise's La. AL9: N Mym .9E 8
TN15: Ash, Stans .81Zd 185
Wiseton Rd. SW17 .60Gb 111
Wishart Rd. SE3 .54Mc 115
Wishaw Wlk. N13 .23Nb 50
Wishbone Way GU21: Wok .8K 167
Wishford Ct. KT21: Asht .90Pa 173
WISLEY .88N 169
WISLEY COMMON .88Q 170
Wisley Common, Ockham & Chatley Heath Nature Reserve .90S 170
Wisley Ct. CR2: Sande .82Tb 177
RH1: Redh .5P 207
(off Clarendon Rd.)
Wisley Golf Course .89M 169
Wisley Ho. SW1 .7D 228
WISLEY INTERCHANGE .88S 170
Wisley La. GU23: Wis .88L 169
Wisley Rd. BR5: St P .66Wc 139
SW11 .57Jb 112
Wistaria Cl. BR6: Farnb .75Rc 160
CM15: Pil H .15Yd 40
Wistaria Dr. AL2: Lon C .8F 6
Wisteria Apartments E9 .37Yb 72
(off Chatham Pl.)
Wisteria Cl. IG1: Ilf .36Rc 74
NW7 .23Va 48
Wisteria Gdns. BR8: Swan .68Fd 140
IG8: Wfd G .22Jc 53
Wisteria Rd. SE13 .56Fc 115
Wistlea Cres. AL4: Col H .4M 7
Wistow Ho. E2 .39Wb 71
(off Whiston Rd.)
Witanhurst La. N6 .32Jb 70
Witan St. E2 .41Xb 91
Witches La. TN13: Riv .94Fd 202
Witchwood Ho. SW9 .55Qb 112
(off Gresham Rd.)
Witham Cl. IG10: Lough .16Nc 36
Witham Ct. E10 .34Dc 72
SW17 .62Hb 133
Witham Gdns. CM13: W H'dn .30Fe 59
Witham Rd. RM2: Rom .29Kd 57
RM10: Dag .36Cd 76
SE20 .69Yb 136
TW7: Isle .53Fa 108
W13 .46Ja 86
Withens Cl. BR5: St M Cry .70Yc 139
Witherby Cl. CR0: C'don .78Ub 157
Witherings, The RM11: Horn .29Nd 57
Witherington Rd. N5 .36Qb 70
Withers Cl. KT9: Chess .79La 152
Withers Mead NW9 .25Va 48
Withers Pl. EC1 .5E 218 (42Sb 91)
Witherston Way SE9 .61Qc 138
Withey Beds Local Nature Reserve, The .19R 26
Withey Cl. SL4: Wind .3C 102
Witheygate Av. TW18: Staines .65K 127
Withies, The GU21: Knap .9J 167
KT22: Lea .92Ka 192
Withybed Cnr. KT20: Walt H .95Xa 194
Withy Cl. GU18: Light .2A 166
Withycombe Rd. SW19 .59Za 110
Withycroft SL3: G Grn .44A 82
Withy Ho. E1 .42Zb 92
(off Globe Rd.)
Withy La. HA4: Ruis .29S 44
Withy Mead E4 .20Fc 35
Withy Pl. AL2: Park .10A 6
Witley Ct. WC1 .6F 217
Witley Cres. CR0: New Ad .79Ec 158
Witley Gdns. UB2: S'hall .49Ba 85
Witley Ho. SW2 .59Nb 112
Witley Ind. Est. UB2: S'hall .49Ba 85
Witley Point SW15 .60Xa 110
(off Wanborough Dr.)
Witley Rd. N19 .33Lb 70
Witney Cl. HA5: Hat E .23Ba 45
UB10: Ick .35P 63
Witney Path SE23 .62Zb 136
Wittenham Way E4 .20Fc 35
Wittering Cl. KT2: King T .64Ma 131
Wittering Wlk. RM12: Horn .37Ld 77
Wittersham Rd. BR1: Brom .64Hc 137
Witts Ho. KT1: King T .69Pa 131
(off Winery La.)
Wivenhoe Cl. SE15 .55Xb 113
Wivenhoe Ct. TW3: Houn .56Ba 107
Wivenhoe Rd. IG11: Bark .40Wc 75
Wiverton Rd. SE26 .65Yb 136
Wixom Ho. SE3 .56Lc 115
Wix Rd. RM9: Dag .39Zc 75
Wix's La. SW4 .55Kb 112
WLA Community Sports Cen. .39Aa 65
Woburn W13 .43Ka 86
(off Clivedon Ct.)
Woburn Av. CM16: They B .9Uc 22
CR8: Purl .83Qb 176
RM12: Horn .35Jd 76
Woburn Cl. SE28 .44Zc 95
SW19 .65Eb 133
WD23: Bush .16Ea 28
Woburn Ct. CR0: C'don .74Sb 157
E18 .26Jc 53
SE16 .50Xb 91
(off Masters Dr.)
WC1 .6F 217
(off Bernard St.)
Woburn Hill KT15: Add .75L 149
Woburn Mans. WC1 .7D 216
Woburn M. WC1 .5E 216 (42Mb 90)
WOBURN PARK .75L 149
Woburn Pl. WC1 .5E 216 (42Nb 90)
Woburn Rd. CR0: C'don .74Sb 157
SM5: Cars .74Gb 155
Woburn Sq. WC1 .6E 216 (42Mb 90)
(not continuous)
Woburn Twr. UB5: N'olt .41Z 85
(off Broomcroft Av.)
Woburn Wlk. WC1 .4E 216 (41Mb 90)
Wodeham Gdns. E1 .43Wb 91
Wodehouse Av. SE5 .53Vb 113
Wodehouse Ct. W3 .48Sa 87
(off Vincent Rd.)
Wodehouse Rd. DA1: Dart .56Qd 119
Woffington Cl. KT1: Hamp W .67La 130
Wokindon Rd. RM16: Grays .8D 100
WOKING .89B 168
Woking Bus. Pk. GU21: Wok .87D 168
Woking Cl. SW15 .56Va 110
Woking Crematorium GU21: Wok .1J 187
Woking FC .92B 188
Woking Golf Course .2L 187
Woking Leisure Cen. .91B 188
Woking Rd. GU4: Jac W .9N 187
Wolcot Ho. NW1 .2C 216
Wold, The CR3: Wold .94Cc 198
Woldham Pl. BR2: Brom .70Lc 137
Woldham Rd. BR2: Brom .70Lc 137
WOLDINGHAM .95Cc 198
WOLDINGHAM GARDEN VILLAGE .92Ac 198
Woldingham Golf Course .92Zb 198
Woldingham Rd. CR3: Wold .92Xb 197
Wolds Dr. BR6: Farnb .77Qc 160
Wolesley Ct. GU21: Knap .10G 166
(off Tudor Way)
Wolfe Cl. BR2: Hayes .72Jc 159
UB4: Yead .41X 85
Wolfe Cotts. TN16: Westrm .99Tc 200
Wolfe Cres. SE7 .50Mc 93
SE16 .47Zb 92
Wolfe Ho. W12 .45Xa 88
(off White City Est.)
Wolfendale Cl. RH1: Mers .2C 208
Wolferton Rd. E12 .35Pc 74
Wolffe Gdns. E15 .37Hc 73
Wolfington Rd. SE27 .63Rb 135
Wolf La. SL4: Wind .5B 102
Wolfram Cl. SE13 .57Gc 115
Wolf's Hill RH8: Oxt .3L 211
Wolf's Rd. RH8: Limp .2M 211
Wolf's Row RH8: Limp .1M 211
Wolfs Wood RH8: Oxt .4L 211
Wolftencroft Cl. SW11 .55Gb 111
Wollaston Cl. SE1 .5D 230 (49Sb 91)
Wollaton Ho. N1 .1A 218
Wollett Ct. NW1 .38Lb 70
(off St Pancras Way)
Wolmer Cl. HA8: Edg .21Qa 47
Wolmer Gdns. HA8: Edg .20Qa 29
Wolseley Av. SW19 .61Cb 133
Wolseley Gdns. W4 .51Ra 109
Wolseley Rd. CR4: Mitc .73Jb 156
E7 .38Kc 73
HA3: W'stone .27Ga 46
N8 .30Mb 50
N22 .25Pb 50
RM7: Rush G .31Fd 76
W4 .49Sa 87
Wolseley St. SE1 .47Wb 91
Wolsey Av. E6 .41Qc 94
E17 .27Bc 52
EN7: Chesh .1Vb 19
KT7: T Ditt .71Ha 152
Wolsey Bus. Pk. WD18: Wat .17T 26
Wolsey Cl. KT2: King T .67Ra 131
KT4: Wor Pk .77Wa 154
SE2 .47Yc 95
SW20 .66Xa 132
TW3: Houn .56Ea 108
UB2: S'hall .48Ea 86
Wolsey Ct. NW6 .38Eb 69
SW11 .53Gb 111
(off Westbridge Rd.)
Wolsey Cres. CR0: New Ad .81Ec 178
DA9: Ghithe .58Wd 120
SM4: Mord .73Ab 154
Wolsey Dr. KT2: King T .64Na 131
KT12: Walt T .74Z 151
Wolsey Gdns. IG6: Ilf .23Rc 54
Wolsey Gro. HA8: Edg .24Ta 47
KT10: Esh .77Da 151
Wolsey M. BR6: Chels .78Vc 161
NW5 .37Lb 70
Wolsey Pl. Shop. Cen. GU21: Wok .89A 168
Wolsey Rd. EN1: Enf .12Xb 33
HA6: Nwood .19S 26
HP2: Hem H .3M 3
KT8: E Mos .70Fa 130
KT10: Esh .77Da 151
N1 .36Tb 71
TW12: Hamp H .65Da 129
TW15: Ashf .63N 127
TW16: Sun .66V 128
Wolsey St. E1 .43Yb 92
Wolsey Wlk. GU21: Wok .89A 168
Wolsey Way KT9: Chess .78Qa 153
Wolsley Cl. DA1: Cray .57Gd 118
Wolstan Cl. UB9: Den .34J 63
Wolsternholme HA7: Stan .22Ka 46
Wolstonbury N12 .22Cb 49
Wolvercote Rd. SE2 .47Zc 95
Wolverley St. E2 .41Xb 91
Wolverton SE17 .7G 231
(not continuous)
Wolverton Av. KT2: King T .67Qa 131
Wolverton Gdns. W5 .45Pa 87
W6 .49Za 88
Wolverton Ho. RM3: Rom .22Nd 57
(off Chudleigh Rd.)
Wolverton Rd. HA7: Stan .23Ka 46
Wolverton Way N14 .15Lb 32
Wolves La. N13 .24Qb 50
N22 .24Qb 50
Wombwell Gdns. DA11: Nflt .1A 144
WOMBWELL PARK .61Fe 143
Womersley Rd. N8 .30Pb 50
Wonersh Way SM2: Cheam .81Za 174
Wonford Cl. KT2: King T .67Ua 132
KT20: Walt H .98Wa 194
Wonham La. RH3: Bet .7A 206
Wonham Pl. RH9: S God .7D 210
Wonnacott Pl. EN3: Enf W .3Zb 20
Wontford Rd. CR8: Purl .87Qb 176
Wontner Cl. N1 .38Sb 71
Wontner Rd. SW17 .61Hb 133
Wooburn Cl. UB8: Hil .42R 84
Wooburn Comn. Rd. HP10: Wbrn G .3A 60
SL1: Burn .3A 60
Wood, The WD19: Wat .19Aa 27
Woodall Av. EN3: Pond E .16Zb 34
Woodall Cl. E14 .45Dc 92
KT9: Chess .80La 152
Woodall Rd. EN3: Pond E .16Zb 34
Wood Av. RM19: Purf .49Sd 98
Woodbank WD3: Rick .16L 25
Woodbank Rd. BR1: Brom .62Hc 137
Woodbastwick Rd. SE26 .64Zb 136
Woodberry Av. HA2: Harr .28Da 45
N21 .19Qb 32
Woodberry Cl. NW7 .24Za 48
TW16: Sun .65W 128
Woodberry Cres. N10 .27Kb 50
Woodberry Down CM16: Epp .1Wc 23
N4 .31Sb 71
Woodberry Down Est. N4 .32Sb 71
(Spring Pk. Dr.)
N4 .31Sb 71
(Woodberry Gro.)
Woodberry Gdns. N12 .23Eb 49
Woodberry Gro. DA5: Bexl .62Fd 140
N4 .31Sb 71
N12 .23Eb 49
Woodberry Way E4 .17Ec 34
N12 .23Eb 49
Woodbine Cl. EN9: Walt A .7Lc 21
TW2: Twick .61Fa 130
Woodbine Cl. Caravan Pk. EN9: Walt A .7Lc 21
Woodbine Gro. EN2: Enf .10Tb 19
SE20 .66Xb 135
Woodbine La. KT4: Wor Pk .76Xa 154
Woodbine Pl. E11 .30Jc 53
Woodbine Rd. DA15: Sidc .63Uc 138
Woodbines Av. KT1: King T .69Ma 131
Woodbine Ter. E9 .37Yb 72
Woodborough Rd. SW15 .56Xa 110
Woodbourne Av. SW16 .62Mb 134
Woodbourne Cl. SW16 .62Nb 134
Woodbourne Dr. KT10: Clay .79Ha 152
Woodbourne Gdns. SM6: Wall .80Kb 156
Woodbridge Av. KT22: Lea .90Ja 172
Woodbridge Cl. N7 .33Pb 70
NW2 .34Wa 68
RM3: Rom .21Md 57
Woodbridge Cnr. KT22: Lea .90Ja 172
Woodbridge Ct. IG8: Wfd G .24Nc 54
Woodbridge Gro. KT22: Lea .90Ja 172
Woodbridge Ho. E11 .32Hc 73
Woodbridge La. RM3: Rom .20Md 39
Woodbridge Rd. IG11: Bark .36Vc 75
Woodbridge St. EC1 .5B 218 (42Rb 91)
(not continuous)
Woodbridge Ter. RM6: Chad H .30Xc 55
Woodbrook Gdns. EN9: Walt A .5Gc 21
Woodbrook Rd. SE2 .51Wc 117
Woodburn Cl. NW4 .29Za 48
Woodbury Cl. CR0: C'don .75Vb 157
E11 .28Kc 53
TN16: Big H .92Pc 180
Woodbury Dr. SM2: Sutt .82Eb 175
Woodbury Gdns. SE12: Brom .62Kc 137
Woodbury Hill IG10: Lough .13Nc 36
Woodbury Hollow IG10: Lough .12Nc 36
Woodbury Ho. SE26 .62Wb 135
Woodbury Pk. Rd. W13 .42Ka 86
Woodbury Rd. E17 .28Dc 52
Woodbury St. SW17 .64Gb 133
Woodby Dr. SL5: S'dale .3D 146
Woodchester Ho. E14 .48Dc 92
(off Selsdon Way)
Woodchester Sq. W2 .43Db 89
Woodchurch Cl. DA14: Sidc .62Tc 138
Woodchurch Dr. BR1: Brom .66Mc 137
Woodchurch Rd. NW6 .38Cb 69
Wood Cl. DA5: Bexl .62Gd 140
E2 .42Wb 91
HA1: Harr .31Fa 66
NW9 .31Ta 67
SL4: Wind .6G 102
Woodclyffe Dr. BR7: Chst .68Qc 138
Woodcock Ct. HA3: Kenton .31Na 67
Woodcock Dell Av. HA3: Kenton .31Ma 67
Woodcock Dr. GU24: Chob .10G 146
WOODCOCK HILL .22N 43
Woodcock Hill HA3: Kenton .29La 46
WD3: Rick .22N 43
WD6: E'tree .16Ra 29
Woodcock Hill Est. WD3: Rick .21N 43
Woodcock Ho. E14 .43Cc 92
(off Burgess St.)
Woodcock La. GU24: Chob .10F 146
Woodcock Rd. TW6: H'row A .56K 105
Woodcocks E16 .43Lc 93
Woodcombe Cres. SE23 .60Yb 114
WOODCOTE
CR8 .84Mb 176
KT18 .87Sa 173
Woodcote Av. CR7: Thor H .70Rb 135
NW7 .23Ya 48
RM12: Horn .35Jd 76
SM6: Wall .81Kb 176
Woodcote Cl. EN3: Pond E .16Yb 34
EN8: Chesh .2Yb 20
KT2: King T .64Pa 131
KT18: Eps .86Ta 173
Woodcote Dr. BR6: Orp .74Tc 160
CR8: Purl .82Mb 176
Woodcote End KT18: Eps .87Ta 173
WOODCOTE GREEN .81Lb 176
Woodcote Grn. SM6: Wall .81Lb 176
Woodcote Grn. Rd. KT18: Eps .87Sa 173
WOODCOTE GROVE .85Kb 176
Woodcote Gro. Rd. CR5: Coul .87Mb 176
Woodcote Hall KT18: Eps .86Ta 173
Woodcote Ho. KT18: Eps .87Sa 173
SE8 .51Bc 114
(off Prince St.)
Woodcote Ho. Ct. KT18: Eps .87Ta 173
Woodcote Hurst KT18: Eps .88Sa 173
Woodcote La. CR8: Purl .83Mb 176
Woodcote Lodge KT18: Eps .87Sa 173
Woodcote M. IG10: Lough .17Mc 35
SM6: Wall .79Kb 156
WOODCOTE PARK .89Sa 173
Woodcote Pk. Av. CR8: Purl .84Lb 176
Woodcote Pk. Golf Course .86Kb 176
Woodcote Pk. Rd. KT18: Eps .88Sa 173
Woodcote Pl. SE27 .64Rb 135
Woodcote Rd. CR8: Purl .79Kb 156
E11 .31Jc 73
KT18: Eps .86Ta 173
SM6: Wall .79Kb 156
Woodcote Side KT18: Eps .87Ra 173
Woodcote Valley Rd. CR8: Purl .85Mb 176
Woodcote Vs. SE27 .64Sb 135
(off Woodcote Pl.)
Wood Cres. HP3: Hem H .3M 3
Wood Crest SM2: Sutt .80Eb 155
(off Christchurch Pk.)
Woodcrest Rd. CR8: Purl .85Nb 176
Woodcrest Wlk. RH2: Reig .4N 207
Woodcroft N21 .18Qb 32
SE9 .62Pc 138
UB6: G'frd .37Ja 66
Woodcroft Av. HA7: Stan .25Ja 46
NW7 .23Ua 48
Woodcroft Cres. UB10: Hil .39R 64
Woodcroft M. SE8 .49Ac 92
Woodcroft Rd. CR7: Thor H .71Rb 157
Woodcutter Pl. AL2: Park .9A 6
Woodcutters Av. RM16: Grays .47Ee 99
Woodcutters Cl. RM11: Horn .28Md 57
Wood Dr. BR7: Chst .65Nc 138
TN13: S'oaks .98Hd 202
Woodedge Cl. E4 .18Hc 35
WOOD END
SL4 .5A 124
UB4 .43V 84
UB5 .36Ea 66
Wood End AL2: Park .10A 6
BR8: Swan .70Ed 140
UB3: Hayes .44U 84
Wood End, The SM6: Wall .81Kb 176
Woodend KT10: Esh .75Ea 152
KT22: Lea .97La 192
SE19 .65Sb 135
SM1: Sutt .75Eb 155
Wood End Av. HA2: Harr .35Da 65
UB5: N'olt .35Ea 66
Wood End Cl. HP2: Hem H .1C 4
SL2: Farn C .4H 61
UB5: N'olt .36Fa 66
Woodend Cl. GU21: Wok .1L 187
Woodend Dr. SL5: S'hill .1A 146
Wood End Gdns. UB5: N'olt .36Ea 66
Woodend Gdns. EN2: Enf .14Nb 32
WOOD END GREEN .43T 84
Wood End Grn. Rd. UB3: Hayes .43T 84
Wood End La. UB5: N'olt .37Da 65
(not continuous)
Woodend Pk. KT11: Cobh .87Z 171
Woodend Ride SL4: Wink .5A 124
SL5: Asc .5A 124
Wood End Rd. HA1: Harr .35Fa 66
Woodend Rd. E17 .26Ec 52
Wood End Way UB5: N'olt .36Ea 66
Wooder Gdns. E7 .35Jc 73
Wooderson Cl. SE25 .70Ub 135
Woodfall Av. EN5: Barn .15Bb 31
Woodfall Dr. DA1: Cray .56Gd 118
Woodfall Rd. N4 .33Qb 70
Woodfall St. SW3 .7F 227 (50Hb 89)
Woodfarm Rd. HP2: Hem H .2N 3
Woodfarrs SE5 .56Tb 113
Wood Fld. NW3 .36Hb 69
Woodfield KT21: Asht .89Ma 173
Woodfield Av. DA11: Grav'nd .10D 122
HA0: Wemb .34La 66
HA6: Nwood .21U 44
NW9 .28Ua 48
SM5: Cars .79Jb 156
SW16 .62Mb 134
W5 .42La 86
Woodfield Cl. CR5: Coul .91Lb 196
EN1: Enf .14Ub 33
KT21: Asht .89Ma 173
RH1: Redh .4N 207
SE19 .66Sb 135
Woodfield Cres. W5 .42La 86
Woodfield Dr. EN4: E Barn .18Jb 32
HP3: Hem H .4D 4
RM2: Rom .28Jd 56
Woodfield Gdns. HP3: Hem H .4D 4
KT3: N Mald .71Va 154
Woodfield Gro. SW16 .62Mb 134
Woodfield Hill CR5: Coul .91Kb 196
Woodfield Ho. KT7: T Ditt .75Ha 152
(off Woodfield Rd.)
SE23 .62Zb 136
(off Dacres Rd.)
Woodfield La. AL9: Hat .5M 9
KT21: Asht .89Na 173
SG13: New S .5M 9
SW16 .62Mb 134
Woodfield Pl. W9 .42Bb 89
Woodfield Ri. WD23: Bush .17Fa 28
Woodfield Rd. KT7: T Ditt .75Ha 152
KT21: Asht .89Ma 173
TW4: Cran .54X 107
W5 .42La 86
W9 .43Bb 89
WD7: R'lett .8Ja 14
Woodfields TN13: Chip .95Fd 202
WD18: Wat .14Y 27
(off George St.)
Woodfields, The CR2: Sande .83Vb 177
Woodfield Ter. UB9: Hare .26K 43
Woodfield Way N11 .24Mb 50
RH1: Redh .4N 207
RM12: Horn .32Md 77
Woodfines, The RM11: Horn .30Md 57
WOODFORD .23Lc 53
Woodford Av. IG2: Ilf .29Pc 54
IG4: Ilf, Wfd G .27Mc 53
WOODFORD BRIDGE .23Nc 54
Woodford Bri. Rd. IG4: Ilf .27Mc 53
Woodford Ct. EN9: Walt A .5Jc 21
W12 .47Za 88
(off Shepherd's Bush Grn.)
Woodford Cres. HA5: Pinn .26X 45
Woodforde Ct. UB3: Harl .50T 84
Woodford Golf Course .22Jc 53
WOODFORD GREEN .23Jc 53
Woodford Grn. IG8: Wfd G .24Hc 53
Woodford Green Athletics Club .23Nc 54
Woodford Hall Path E18 .25Hc 53
Woodford Ho. E18 .28Jc 53
Woodford New Rd. E17 .28Gc 53
E18 .25Gc 53
IG8: Wfd G .25Gc 53
Woodford Pl. HA9: Wemb .32Na 67
Woodford Rd. E7 .34Kc 73
E18 .28Jc 53
WD17: Wat .12Y 27
WOODFORD SIDE .22Hc 53
Woodford Trad. Est. IG8: Wfd G .26Mc 53
Woodford Way SL2: Slou .1E 80
WOODFORD WELLS .20Kc 35
Woodgate WD25: Wat .5X 13
Woodgate Av. EN6: N'thaw .5Kb 18
KT9: Chess .78Ma 153
Woodgate Cl. KT11: Cobh .85X 171
Woodgate Ct. RM11: Horn .27Md 57
Woodgate Cres. HA6: Nwood .23W 44
Woodgate Dr. SW16 .66Mb 134
Woodgate M. WD17: Wat .11W 26
Woodgates Ho. DA12: Grav'nd .4E 144
(off Nursery M.)
Woodgavil SM7: Bans .88Bb 175
Woodger Rd. W12 .47Ya 88
Woodgers Gro. BR8: Swan .68Hd 140
Woodget Cl. E6 .44Nc 94
Woodgrange Av. EN1: Enf .16Wb 33
HA3: Kenton .29La 46
N12 .23Fb 49
W5 .46Qa 87
Woodgrange Cl. HA3: Kenton .29Ma 47
Woodgrange Gdns. EN1: Enf .16Wb 33
Woodgrange Ho. W5 .46Pa 87
(off Woodgrange Av.)
Woodgrange Mans. HA3: Kenton .29Ma 47
Woodgrange Rd. E7 .36Kc 73
Woodgrange Ter. EN1: Enf .16Wb 33
WOOD GREEN
EN9 .7Lc 21
N22 .26Pb 50
Wood Grn. Hall N22 .26Pb 50
(off Station Rd.)
Woodgreen Rd. EN9: Walt A .5Kc 21
Wood Green Shop. City N22 .26Qb 50
Wood Grn. Way EN8: Chesh .3Ac 20
Woodhall NW1 .4B 216
Woodhall Av. HA5: Pinn .25Aa 45
SE21 .62Vb 135
Woodhall Cl. UB8: Uxb .36M 63
Woodhall Cres. RM11: Horn .31Pd 77
Woodhall Dr. HA5: Pinn .25Z 45
SE21 .62Vb 135
Woodhall Ga. HA5: Pinn .24Z 45
Woodhall Ho. SW18 .58Fb 111
Woodhall La. HP2: Hem H .1N 3
SL5: S'dale .5C 146
WD7: Shenl .7Na 15
WD19: Wat .20Z 27
Woodhall Rd. HA5: Pinn .24Z 45
WOODHAM .83H 169
Woodham Ct. E18 .28Hc 53
Woodham Ga. GU21: Wok .85E 168
Woodham Hall Est. GU21: Wok .86D 168
Woodham La. GU21: Wok .86D 168
KT15: Wdhm, New H .84G 168
Woodham Lock KT14: W Byf .84H 169
Woodham Pk. Rd. KT15: Wdhm .81H 169
Woodham Pk. Way KT15: Wdhm .83H 169
Woodham Pl. GU21: Wok .86B 168
Woodham Ri. GU21: Wok .86B 168
Woodham Rd. GU21: Wok .87A 168
SE6 .62Ec 136
Woodham Waye GU21: Wok .85D 168
WOODHATCH .9K 207
Woodhatch Cl. E6 .43Nc 94
Woodhatch Rd. RH1: Redh .9K 207
RH2: Reig .9K 207
Woodhatch Spinney CR5: Coul .88Nb 176
Woodhaven Gdns. IG6: Ilf .28Sc 54
Woodhaven M. KT12: Walt T .77W 150
Woodhaw TW20: Egh .63D 126
Woodhayes Rd. SW19 .66Ya 132
Woodhead Dr. BR6: Orp .76Uc 160
Woodheyes Rd. NW10 .36Ta 67
WOODHILL .5M 9
Woodhill GU23: Send .98F 188
SE18 .49Nc 94
Woodhill Av. SL9: Ger X .30C 42
Woodhill Ct. GU23: Send .97F 188
SL9: Ger X .31A 62
Woodhill Cres. HA3: Kenton .30Ma 47
Wood Ho. NW6 .40Bb 69
(off Albert Rd.)
Woodhouse Av. UB6: G'frd .40Ha 66
Woodhouse Cl. SE22 .56Wb 113
UB3: Harl .48U 84
UB6: G'frd .39Ha 66
Woodhouse Eaves HA6: Nwood .22W 44
Woodhouse Gro. E12 .37Nc 74
Woodhouse Rd. E11 .34Hc 73
N12 .23Fb 49
Woodhurst Av. BR5: Pet W .72Sc 160
WD25: Wat .6Z 13
Woodhurst Dr. UB9: Den .29H 43
Woodhurst La. RH8: Oxt .2J 211
Woodhurst Pk. RH8: Oxt .2J 211
Woodhurst Rd. SE2 .50Wc 95
W3 .45Sa 87
Woodhyrst Gdns. CR8: Kenley .87Rb 177
Woodies La. KT3: N Mald .72Ta 153
Woodin Cl. DA1: Dart .58Md 119
Woodington Cl. SE9 .58Qc 116
Woodknoll Dr. BR7: Chst .67Pc 138
Woodland App. UB6: G'frd .37Ja 66
Woodland Av. CM13: Hut .15Ee 41
DA3: Hartl .71Be 165
HP1: Hem H .3K 3
SL1: Slou .5H 81
SL4: Wind .6D 102
Woodland Cen. (YMCA) .3W 12
Woodland Cl. CM13: Hut .15Ee 41
DA3: Lfield .69Ee 143
HP1: Hem H .3K 3
IG8: Wfd G .20Kc 35
KT13: Weyb .77T 150
KT19: Ewe .79Ua 154
KT24: E Hor .99V 190
NW9 .30Sa 47
SE19 .65Ub 135
UB10: Ick .33R 64
Woodland Ct. E11 .30Jc 53
(off New Wanstead)
KT17: Eps .84Va 174
N7 .37Nb 70
RH8: Oxt .100Fc 199
Woodland Cres. SE10 .51Gc 115
SE16 .47Zb 92
Woodland Dr. AL4: St A .1G 6
KT11: Cobh .83Ba 171
KT24: E Hor .99V 190
WD17: Wat .11V 26
(not continuous)

ELLENOR LIONS HOSPICE 3B 144
Coldharbour Road
Northfleet
GRAVESEND
DA11 7HQ
Tel: 01474 320007

EPSOM DAY SURGERY CENTRE 85Va 174
Alexandra Road, The Old Cottage Hospital
EPSOM
KT17 4BL
Tel: 01372 739002

EPSOM GENERAL HOSPITAL 87Sa 173
Dorking Road
EPSOM
KT18 7EG
Tel: 01372 735735

ERITH & DISTRICT HOSPITAL 51Fd 118
Park Crescent
ERITH
DA8 3EE
Tel: 020 8308 3131

EVELINA CHILDREN'S HOSPITAL 3H 229 (48Pb 90)
St Thomas' Hospital
Westminster Bridge Road
LONDON
SE1 7EH
Tel: 020 7188 7188

FAWKHAM MANOR BMI HOSPITAL 74Yd 164
Manor Lane
Fawkham
LONGFIELD
DA3 8ND
Tel: 01474 879900

FINCHLEY MEMORIAL HOSPITAL 24Eb 49
Granville Road
LONDON
N12 0JE
Tel: 020 8349 7500

FITZROY SQUARE BMI HOSPITAL 6B 216 (42Lb 90)
14 Fitzroy Square
LONDON
W1T 6AH
Tel: 020 7388 4954

GARDEN BMI HOSPITAL 27Ya 48
46-50 Sunny Gardens Road
LONDON
NW4 1RP
Tel: 020 8457 4500

GATEWAY SURGICAL CENTRE 42Mc 93
Cherry Tree Way, Glen Road
LONDON
E13 8SL
Tel: 020 7476 4000

GENERAL MEDICAL WALK-IN CENTRE (LIVERPOOL STREET) 7J 219 (43Ub 91)
Exchange Arcade
Bishopsgate
LONDON
EC2M 3WA
Tel: 0845 880 1242

GODDEN GREEN CYGNET HOSPITAL 97Rd 203
Godden Green
SEVENOAKS
TN15 0JR
Tel: 01732 763491

GOODMAYES HOSPITAL 29Wc 55
Barley Lane
ILFORD
IG3 8XJ
Tel: 0844 600 1200

GORDON HOSPITAL 6D 228 (49Mb 90)
Bloomburg Street
LONDON
SW1V 2RH
Tel: 020 8746 8733

GRAVESHAM COMMUNITY HOSPITAL 8C 122
Bath Street
GRAVESEND
DA11 0DG
Tel: 01474 360500

GREAT ORMOND STREET HOSPITAL FOR CHILDREN 6H 217 (42Nb 90)
Great Ormond Street
LONDON
WC1N 3JH
Tel: 020 7405 9200

GREENACRES 58Rd 119
Bow Arrow Lane
DARTFORD
DA2 6PB
Tel: 01322 622222

GREENWICH & BEXLEY COMMUNITY HOSPICE 50Yc 95
185 Bostall Hill
LONDON
SE2 0GB
Tel: 020 8312 2244

GROVE HOUSE (HOSPICE) 1A 6
Waverley Road
ST. ALBANS
AL3 5QX
Tel: 01727 731000

GUY'S HOSPITAL 7G 225 (47Tb 91)
Great Maze Pond
LONDON
SE1 9RT
Tel: 020 7188 7188

GUY'S NUFFIELD HOUSE 1F 231
Guy's Hospital
Newcomen Street
LONDON
SE1 1YR
Tel: 020 7188 5292

HAMMERSMITH HOSPITAL 44Wa 88
Du Cane Road
LONDON
W12 0HS
Tel: 020 3313 1111

HAND CLINIC 3A 102
Dedworth Road
Oakley Green
WINDSOR
SL4 4LH
Tel: 01753 831333

HAREFIELD HOSPITAL 25L 43
Hill End Road
Harefield
UXBRIDGE
UB9 6JH
Tel: 01895 823737

HARLEY STREET CLINIC 7K 215 (43Kb 90)
35 Weymouth Street
LONDON
W1G 8BJ
Tel: 020 7935 7700

HARLINGTON HOSPICE (REG HOPKINS DAY CARE HOSPICE) 50T 84
St Peters Way
HAYES
UB3 5AB
Tel: 020 8759 0453

HARRIS HOSPISCARE 77Vc 161
Tregony Road
ORPINGTON
BR6 9XA
Tel: 01689 825755

HARROW CYGNET HARROW 33Ga 66
London Road
HARROW
HA1 3JL
Tel: 020 8966 7000

HARTSWOOD SPIRE HOSPITAL 23Xd 58
Eagle Way
Great Warley
BRENTWOOD
CM13 3LE
Tel: 01277 232 525

HAVEN HOUSE FOUNDATION (HOSPICE) 23Hc 53
High Road
WOODFORD GREEN
IG8 9LB
Tel: 020 8505 9944

HAYES GROVE PRIORY HOSPITAL 75Jc 159
Prestons Road
Hayes
BROMLEY
BR2 7AS
Tel: 020 8462 7722

HEART HOSPITAL 1K 221 (43Jb 90)
16-18 Westmoreland St.
LONDON
W1G 8PH
Tel: 020 7573 8888

HEMEL HEMPSTEAD GENERAL HOSPITAL 3M 3
Hillfield Road
HEMEL HEMPSTEAD
HP2 4AD
Tel: 01442 213141

HEMEL HEMPSTEAD PRIORY GRANGE 7H 3
Longcroft Lane
Felden
HEMEL HEMPSTEAD
HP3 0BN
Tel: 01442 255371

HIGHGATE HOSPITAL 30Hb 49
17- 19 View Road
LONDON
N6 4DJ
Tel: 020 8341 4182

HIGHGATE MENTAL HEALTH CENTRE 33Kb 70
Dartmouth Park Hill
LONDON
N19 5NX
Tel: 020 7561 4000

HILLINGDON HOSPITAL 43P 83
Pield Heath Road
UXBRIDGE
UB8 3NN
Tel: 01895 238282

HOLLY HOUSE HOSPITAL 19Kc 35
High Road
BUCKHURST HILL
IG9 5HX
Tel: 020 8505 3311

HOMERTON UNIVERSITY HOSPITAL 36Zb 72
Homerton Row
LONDON
E9 6SR
Tel: 020 8510 5555

HOSPITAL FOR TROPICAL DISEASES 6C 216 (42Lb 90)
Mortimer Market,
Capper Street
LONDON
WC1E 6JB
Tel: 0845 155 5000

HOSPITAL OF ST JOHN & ST ELIZABETH 2B 214 (40Fb 69)
60 Grove End Road
LONDON
NW8 9NH
Tel: 020 7806 4000

JOHN HOWARD CENTRE 36Ac 72
12 Kenworthy Road
LONDON
E9 5TD
Tel: 0208 9198447

KING EDWARD VII HOSPITAL 5G 102
St Leonard's Road
WINDSOR
SL4 3DP
Tel: 01753 860 441

KING EDWARD VII'S HOSPITAL SISTER AGNES 7J 215 (43Jb 90)
5-10 Beaumont Street
LONDON
W1G 6AA
Tel: 020 7486 4411

KING GEORGE HOSPITAL 28Wc 55
Barley Lane
ILFORD
IG3 8YB
Tel: 0845 130 4204

KING'S COLLEGE HOSPITAL 55Sb 113
Denmark Hill
LONDON
SE5 9RS
Tel: 0203 299 9000

KINGSLEY GREEN 3La 14
Harper Lane
Shenley
RADLETT
WD7 9HQ
Tel: 01923 854861

KING'S OAK BMI HOSPITAL 10Qb 18
The Ridgeway
ENFIELD
EN2 8SD
Tel: 020 8370 9500

KINGSTON HOSPITAL 67Ra 131
Galsworthy Road
KINGSTON UPON THAMES
KT2 7QB
Tel: 020 8546 7711

LAMBETH HOSPITAL 55Pb 112
108 Landor Road
LONDON
SW9 9NT
Tel: 020 32286000

LEATHERHEAD COMMUNITY HOSPITAL 94La 192
Poplar Road
LEATHERHEAD
KT22 8SD
Tel: 01372 384384

LEWISHAM UNIVERSITY HOSPITAL 57Dc 114
Lewisham High Street
LONDON
SE13 6LH
Tel: 020 8333 3000

LISTER HOSPITAL 50Kb 90
Chelsea Bridge Road
LONDON
SW1W 8RH
Tel: 020 7730 7733

LITTLE BROOK HOSPITAL 58Sd 120
Bow Arrow Lane
DARTFORD
DA2 6PH
Tel: 01322 622222

LIVINGSTONE HOSPITAL 59Pd **119**
East Hill
DARTFORD
DA1 1SA
Tel: 01322 622222

LONDON BRIDGE HOSPITAL 6G **225** (46Tb **91**)
27 Tooley Street
LONDON
SE1 2PR
Tel: 020 7407 3100

LONDON CHEST HOSPITAL 40Yb **72**
Bonner Road
LONDON
E2 9JX
Tel: 020 7377 7000

LONDON CLINIC 6J **215** (42Jb **90**)
20 Devonshire Place
LONDON
W1G 6BW
Tel: 020 7935 4444

LONDON INDEPENDENT BMI HOSPITAL 43Zb **92**
1 Beaumont Square
LONDON
E1 4NL
Tel: 020 7780 2400

LONDON WELBECK HOSPITAL 1K **221** (43Kb **90**)
27 Welbeck St.
LONDON
W1G 8EN
Tel: 020 7224 2242

MAIDENHEAD HUNTERCOMBE HOSPITAL 5A **80**
Huntercombe Lane South
Taplow
MAIDENHEAD
SL6 0PQ
Tel: 01628 667881

MARGARET CENTRE (HOSPICE) 30Gc **53**
Whipps Cross University Hospital
Whipps Cross Road
LONDON
E11 1NR
Tel: 020 8535 6604

MARIE CURIE HOSPICE, HAMPSTEAD 36Fb **69**
11 Lyndhurst Gardens
LONDON
NW3 5NS
Tel: 020 7853 3400

MAUDSLEY HOSPITAL 54Tb **113**
Denmark Hill
LONDON
SE5 8AZ
Tel: 020 32286000

MEADOW HOUSE HOSPICE 47Fa **86**
Ealing Hospital
Uxbridge Road
SOUTHALL
UB1 3HW
Tel: 020 8967 5179

MEMORIAL HOSPITAL 54Qc **116**
Shooters Hill
LONDON
SE18 3RZ
Tel: 020 8836 8500

MICHAEL SOBELL HOUSE (HOSPICE) 23R **44**
Mount Vernon Hospital
Rickmansworth Road
NORTHWOOD
HA6 2RN
Tel: 01923 844531

MILDMAY HOSPITAL 4K **219** (41Vb **91**)
Austin Street
LONDON
E2 7NA
Tel: 020 7613 6300

MILE END HOSPITAL 41Zb **92**
Bancroft Road
LONDON
E1 4DG
Tel: 020 8223 8211

MOLESEY HOSPITAL 71Ca **151**
High Street
WEST MOLESEY
KT8 2LU
Tel: 020 8941 4481

MOORFIELDS EYE HOSPITAL 4F **219** (41Tb **91**)
162 City Road
LONDON
EC1V 2PD
Tel: 020 7253 3411

MOUNT VERNON HOSPITAL 23R **44**
Rickmansworth Road
NORTHWOOD
HA6 2RN
Tel: 01923 826111

NATIONAL HOSPITAL FOR NEUROLOGY & NEUROSURGERY
....6G **217** (42Nb **90**)
Queen Square
LONDON
WC1N 3BG
Tel: 0845 155 5000

NATIONAL SOCIETY FOR EPILEPSY 21B **42**
Chesham Lane
Chalfont St Peter
GERRARDS CROSS
SL9 0RJ
Tel: 01494 601300

NELSON HOSPITAL 68Bb **133**
Kingston Road
LONDON
SW20 8DB
Tel: 020 8251 1111

NEW EPSOM & EWELL COMMUNITY HOSPITAL 83Na **173**
West Park
Horton Lane
EPSOM
KT19 8PB
Tel: 01372 734834

NEWHAM CENTRE FOR MENTAL HEALTH 42Mc **93**
Cherry Tree Way
Glen Road
LONDON
E13 8S
Tel: 0207 5404380

NEWHAM UNIVERSITY HOSPITAL 42Lc **93**
Glen Road
LONDON
E13 8SL
Tel: 020 7476 4000

NEW VICTORIA HOSPITAL 67Ua **132**
184 Coombe Lane West
KINGSTON UPON THAMES
KT2 7EG
Tel: 020 8949 9000

NHS WALK-IN CENTRE (ANGEL MEDICAL PRACTICE)
....1A **218** (40Qb **70**)
Ritchie Street Group Practice
34 Ritchie Street
LONDON
N1 0DG
Tel: 020 7527 1000

NHS WALK-IN CENTRE (ASHFORD) 61N **127**
Ashford Hospital
London Road
ASHFORD
TW15 3AA
Tel: 01784 884000

NHS WALK-IN CENTRE (BROAD STREET) 39Cd **76**
Broad Street Centre
Morland Road
DAGENHAM
RM10 9HU
Tel: 020 8596 4400

NHS WALK-IN CENTRE (CHARING CROSS) 50Za **88**
Charing Cross Hospital
Fulham Palace Road
LONDON
W6 8RF
Tel: 020 8383 0904

NHS WALK-IN CENTRE (EDGWARE) 24Ra **47**
Edgware Community Hospital
Burnt Oak Broadway
EDGWARE
HA8 0AD
Tel: 020 8732 6459

NHS WALK-IN CENTRE (FINCHLEY) 24Eb **49**
Finchley Memorial Hospital
Granville Road
LONDON
N12 0JE
Tel: 020 8349 7470

NHS WALK-IN CENTRE (HAROLD WOOD) 25Nd **57**
The Drive
ROMFORD
RM3 0FE

NHS WALK-IN CENTRE (HEART OF HOUNSLOW) 55Ca **107**
92 Bath Road
HOUNSLOW
TW3 3LN
Tel: 020 8104 0810

NHS WALK-IN CENTRE (LISTER HEALTH CENTRE) 53Vb **113**
101 Peckham Road
LONDON
SE15 5LJ
Tel: 020 3049 8430

NHS WALK-IN CENTRE (NEWHAM) 42Lc **93**
Newham University Hospital
Glen Road
LONDON
E13 8SH
Tel: 020 7363 9200

NHS WALK-IN CENTRE (NORTH MIDDLESEX UNIVERSITY HOSPITAL)
....22Ub **51**
North Middlesex University Hospital
Sterling Way
LONDON
N18 1QX
Tel: 020 8887 2680

NHS WALK-IN CENTRE (PARSONS GREEN) 53Cb **111**
5-7 Parsons Green
LONDON
SW6 4UL
Tel: 020 8846 6758

NHS WALK-IN CENTRE (QUEEN'S HOSPITAL) 31Gd **76**
Oldchurch Park Hospital
Rom Valley Way
ROMFORD
RM7 0BE

NHS WALK-IN CENTRE (REDHILL) 10B **208**
East Surrey Hospital
Canada Avenue
REDHILL
RH1 5RH

NHS WALK-IN CENTRE (ST ANDREWS) 41Dc **92**
1-3 Birchdown House
Devons Road
LONDON
E3 3NS
Tel: 020 8980 1888

NHS WALK-IN CENTRE (SLOUGH) 8K **81**
Upton Hospital
Albert Street
SLOUGH
SL1 2BJ
Tel: 01753 635505

NHS WALK-IN CENTRE (SOHO) 3D **222**
1 Frith Street
LONDON
W1D 3HZ
Tel: 020 7534 6500

NHS WALK-IN CENTRE (TEDDINGTON) 65Ga **130**
Teddington Memorial Hospital
Hampton Road
TEDDINGTON
TW11 0JL
Tel: 020 8714 4004

NHS WALK-IN CENTRE (TOLLGATE LODGE PRIMARY CARE CENTRE)
....32Vb **71**
57 Stamford Hill
LONDON
N16 5SR
Tel: 020 7689 3140

NHS WALK-IN CENTRE (TOOTING) 64Gb **133**
St George's Hospital
Blackshaw Road
LONDON
SW17 0QT
Tel: 020 8700 0505

NHS WALK-IN CENTRE (UPNEY LANE) 37Vc **75**
132 Upney Lane
BARKING
IG11 9YD
Tel: 020 8924 6262

NHS WALK-IN CENTRE (VICTORIA) 3D **228**
63 Buckingham Gate
LONDON
SW1E 6AS
Tel: 020 7340 1190

NHS WALK-IN CENTRE (WALDRON HEALTH CENTRE) 52Bc **114**
off Amersham Vale
LONDON
SE14 6LD
Tel: 020 3049 2370

NHS WALK-IN CENTRE (WEMBLEY) 37Ma **67**
116 Chaplin Road
WEMBLEY
HA0 4UZ
Tel: 0208 795 6000

NHS WALK-IN CENTRE (WEYBRIDGE) 77Q **150**
Weybridge Community Hospital
22 Church Street
WEYBRIDGE
KT13 8DY
Tel: 01932 826013

NHS WALK-IN CENTRE (WHITECHAPEL) 43Xb **91**
Royal London Hospital
174 Whitechapel Road
LONDON
E1 1BZ
Tel: 020 7943 1333

NHS WALK-IN CENTRE (WOKING) 90B **168**
Woking Community Hospital
Heathside Road
WOKING
GU22 7HS
Tel: 01483 846209

RAIL, LONDON TRAMLINK, DOCKLANDS LIGHT RAILWAY, RIVERBUS, CABLE CAR, UNDERGROUND AND OVERGROUND STATIONS

with their map square reference

A

Abbey Road (DLR) 40Gc 73
Abbey Wood (Rail) 48Yc 95
Acton Central (Overground) 46Ta 87
Acton Main Line (Rail) 44Sa 87
Acton Town (Underground) 47Qa 87
Addington Village Stop (Tramlink) 79Cc 158
Addiscombe Stop (Tramlink) 74Wb 157
Addlestone (Rail) 77M 149
Albany Park (Rail) 61Zc 139
Aldgate (Underground) 3K 225 (44Vb 91)
Aldgate East (Underground) 2K 225 (44Vb 91)
Alexandra Palace (Rail) 26Nb 50
All Saints (DLR) 45Dc 92
Alperton (Underground) 39Ma 67
Ampere Way Stop (Tramlink) 74Pb 156
Anerley (Rail & Overground) 67Xb 135
Angel (Underground) 1A 218 (40Qb 70)
Angel Road (Rail) 22Yb 52
Apsley (Rail) 7N 3
Archway (Underground) 33Lb 70
Arena Stop (Tramlink) 71Yb 158
Arnos Grove (Underground) 22Lb 50
Arsenal (Underground) 34Qb 70
Ashford (Rail) 63P 127
Ashtead (Rail) 89Na 173
Avenue Road Stop (Tramlink) 68Zb 136

B

Baker Street (Underground) 6G 215 (42Hb 89)
Balham (Rail & Underground) 60Kb 112
Bank (Underground & DLR) 3F 225 (44Tb 91)
Bankside Pier (Riverbus) 5D 224 (45Sb 91)
Banstead (Rail) 86Bb 175
Barbican (Underground) 7D 218 (43Sb 91)
Barking (Rail, Underground & Overground) 38Sc 74
Barkingside (Underground) 27Tc 54
Barnehurst (Rail) 54Ed 118
Barnes (Rail) 55Wa 110
Barnes Bridge (Rail) 54Va 110
Barons Court (Underground) 50Ab 88
Bat & Ball (Rail) 93Ld 203
Battersea Park (Rail) 52Kb 112
Bayswater (Underground) 45Db 89
Beckenham Hill (Rail) 64Ec 136
Beckenham Junction (Rail & Tramlink) 67Cc 136
Beckenham Road Stop (Tramlink) 67Ac 136
Beckton (DLR) 43Qc 94
Beckton Park (DLR) 45Pc 94
Becontree (Underground) 37Zc 75
Beddington Lane Stop (Tramlink) 72Lb 156
Belgrave Walk Stop (Tramlink) 70Fb 133
Bellingham (Rail) 62Dc 136
Belmont (Rail) 82Db 175
Belsize Park (Underground) 36Gb 69
Belvedere (Rail) 48Dd 96
Bermondsey (Underground) 48Wb 91
Berrylands (Rail) 70Ra 131
Betchworth (Rail) 4A 206
Bethnal Green (Rail) 42Xb 91
Bethnal Green (Underground) 41Yb 92
Bexley (Rail) 60Cd 118
Bexleyheath (Rail) 54Ad 117
Bickley (Rail) 69Nc 138
Birkbeck (Rail & Tramlink) 69Yb 136
Blackfriars (Rail & Underground) 4B 224 (45Rb 91)
Blackfriars Millennium Pier (Riverbus) 4A 224 (45Rb 91)
Blackheath (Rail) 55Hc 115
Blackhorse Lane Stop (Tramlink) 73Wb 157
Blackhorse Road (Underground & Overground) 28Zb 52
Blackwall (DLR) 45Ec 92
Bond Street (Underground) 3K 221 (44Kb 90)
Bookham (Rail) 95Ba 191
Borough (Underground) 2E 230 (47Sb 91)
Borough Green & Wrotham (Rail) 92Be 205
Boston Manor (Underground) 49Ja 86
Bounds Green (Underground) 23Mb 50
Bow Church (DLR) 41Cc 92
Bowes Park (Rail) 24Nb 50
Bow Road (Underground) 41Cc 92
Brent Cross (Underground) 31Za 68
Brentford (Rail) 51La 108
Brentwood (Rail) 20Yd 40
Bricket Wood (Rail) 2Ca 13
Brimsdown (Rail) 13Ac 34
Brixton (Rail & Underground) 56Qb 112
Brockley (Rail & Overground) 55Ac 114
Bromley-by-Bow (Underground) 41Dc 92
Bromley North (Rail) 67Jc 137
Bromley South (Rail) 69Jc 137
Brondesbury (Overground) 38Bb 69
Brondesbury Park (Overground) 39Ab 68
Brookmans Park (Rail) 9G 8
Brookwood (Rail) 3E 186
Bruce Grove (Rail) 26Vb 51
Buckhurst Hill (Underground) 19Mc 35
Burnham (Rail) 4B 80
Burnt Oak (Underground) 25Sa 47
Bushey (Rail & Overground) 16Z 27
Bush Hill Park (Rail) 16Vb 33
Byfleet & New Haw (Rail) 82M 169

C

Caledonian Road (Underground) 37Pb 70
Caledonian Road & Barnsbury (Overground) 38Pb 70
Cambridge Heath (Rail) 40Xb 71
Camden Road (Overground) 38Lb 70
Camden Town (Underground) 39Kb 70
Canada Water (Underground & Overground) 47Yb 92
Canary Wharf (Underground & DLR) 46Cc 92
Canary Wharf Pier (Riverbus) 46Bc 92
Canning Town (Underground & DLR) 44Gc 93
Cannon Street (Rail & Underground) 4F 225 (45Tb 91)
Canonbury (Overground) 36Sb 71
Canons Park (Underground) 24Na 47
Carpenders Park (Overground) 20Z 27
Carshalton (Rail) 77Hb 155
Carshalton Beeches (Rail) 79Hb 155
Castle Bar Park (Rail) 43Ha 86
Caterham (Rail) 96Wb 197
Catford (Rail) 59Cc 114
Catford Bridge (Rail) 59Cc 114
Centrale Stop (Tramlink) 75Sb 157
Chadwell Heath (Rail) 31Zc 75
Chafford Hundred (Rail) 49Xd 98
Chalk Farm (Underground) 38Jb 70
Chancery Lane (Underground) 1K 223 (43Qb 90)
Charing Cross (Rail & Underground) 6F 223 (46Nb 90)
Charlton (Rail) 50Lc 93
Cheam (Rail) 80Ab 154
Chelsea Harbour Pier (Riverbus) 53Fb 111
Chelsfield (Rail) 78Xc 161
Chertsey (Rail) 74H 149
Cheshunt (Rail) 2Bc 20
Chessington North (Rail) 78Na 153
Chessington South (Rail) 80Ma 153
Chigwell (Underground) 20Rc 36
Chingford (Rail) 17Gc 35
Chipstead (Rail) 90Hb 175
Chislehurst (Rail) 68Qc 138
Chiswick (Rail) 52Sa 109
Chiswick Park (Underground) 49Sa 87
Chorleywood (Rail & Underground) 14F 24
Church Street Stop (Tramlink) 75Sb 157
City Thameslink (Rail) 2B 224 (44Rb 91)
Clandon (Rail) 100K 189
Clapham Common (Underground) 56Lb 112
Clapham High Street (Rail) 55Mb 112
Clapham Junction (Rail & Overground) 55Gb 111
Clapham North (Underground) 55Nb 112
Clapham South (Underground) 58Kb 112
Clapton (Rail) 33Xb 71
Claygate (Rail) 79Ga 152
Clock House (Rail) 67Ac 136
Cobham & Stoke D'Abernon (Rail) 89Aa 171
Cockfosters (Underground) 14Jb 32
Colindale (Underground) 27Ua 48
Colliers Wood (Underground) 66Fb 133
Coombe Lane Stop (Tramlink) 78Yb 158
Coulsdon South (Rail) 88Mb 176
Coulsdon Town (Rail) 87Nb 176
Covent Garden (Underground) 3G 223 (45Nb 90)
Crayford (Rail) 58Gd 118
Crews Hill (Rail) 6Pb 18
Cricklewood (Rail) 35Za 68
Crofton Park (Rail) 57Bc 114
Crossharbour (Underground & DLR) 48Dc 92
Crouch Hill (Overground) 31Pb 70
Croxley (Underground) 16R 26
Crystal Palace (Rail & Overground) 65Wb 135
Cuffley (Rail) 1Pb 18
Custom House for ExCeL (DLR) 45Kc 93
Cutty Sark for Maritime Greenwich (DLR) 51Ec 114
Cyprus (DLR) 45Qc 94

D

Dagenham Dock (Rail) 40Bd 75
Dagenham East (Underground) 36Ed 76
Dagenham Heathway (Underground) 37Bd 75
Dalston Junction (Overground) 37Vb 71
Dalston Kingsland (Overground) 36Ub 71
Dartford (Rail) 58Nd 119
Datchet (Rail) 3M 103
Debden (Underground) 14Sc 36
Denham (Rail) 31J 63
Denham Golf Club (Rail) 31F 62
Denmark Hill (Rail) 54Tb 113
Deptford (Rail) 52Cc 114
Deptford Bridge (DLR) 53Cc 114
Devons Road (DLR) 42Dc 92
Dollis Hill (Underground) 36Wa 68
Drayton Green (Rail) 44Ha 86
Drayton Park (Rail) 35Qb 70
Dundonald Road Stop (Tramlink) 66Bb 133
Dunton Green (Rail) 91Gd 202

E

Ealing Broadway (Rail & Underground) 45Ma 87
Ealing Common (Underground) 46Pa 87
Earl's Court (Underground) 49Cb 89
Earlsfield (Rail) 60Eb 111
Earlswood (Rail) 8P 207
East Acton (Underground) 44Va 88
Eastcote (Underground) 31Y 65
East Croydon (Rail & Tramlink) 75Tb 157
East Dulwich (Rail) 56Ub 113
East Finchley (Underground) 28Gb 49
East Ham (Underground) 38Nc 74
East India (DLR) 45Fc 93
East Putney (Underground) 57Ab 110
East Tilbury (Rail) 9K 101
Ebbsfleet International (Rail) 58Ce 121
Eden Park (Rail) 71Cc 158
Edgware (Underground) 23Ra 47
Edgware Road (Underground) 1D 220 (43Gb 89)
Edmonton Green (Rail) 19Wb 33
Effingham Junction (Rail) 95W 190
Egham (Rail) 64C 126
Elephant & Castle (Rail & Underground) 5D 230 (49Sb 91)
Elmers End (Rail & Tramlink) 70Zb 136
Elm Park (Underground) 35Kd 77
Elmstead Woods (Rail) 65Nc 138
Elstree & Borehamwood (Rail) 14Qa 29
Eltham (Rail) 57Pc 116
Elverson Road (DLR) 54Dc 114
Embankment (Underground) 6G 223 (46Nb 90)
Embankment Pier (Riverbus) 6G 223 (46Nb 90)
Emerson Park (Rail) 31Nd 77
Emirates Greenwich Peninsula (Emirates Air Line) 47Hc 93
Emirates Royal Docks (Emirates Air Line) 45Jc 93
Enfield Chase (Rail) 13Sb 33
Enfield Lock (Rail) 9Ac 20
Enfield Town (Rail) 13Ub 33
Epping (Underground) 3Wc 23
Epsom (Rail) 85Ta 173
Epsom Downs (Rail) 87Xa 174
Erith (Rail) 50Gd 96
Esher (Rail) 75Fa 152
Essex Road (Rail) 38Sb 71
Euston (Rail, Underground & Overground) 4D 216 (41Lb 90)
Euston Square (Underground) 5C 216 (42Lb 90)
Ewell East (Rail) 82Xa 174
Ewell West (Rail) 81Ua 174
Eynsford (Rail) 77Md 163

F

Fairlop (Underground) 25Tc 54
Falconwood (Rail) 56Tc 116
Farningham Road (Rail) 68Rd 141
Farringdon (Rail & Underground) 7B 218 (43Rb 91)
Feltham (Rail) 60X 107
Fenchurch Street (Rail) 4J 225 (45Vb 91)
Festival Pier (Riverbus) 6H 223
Fieldway Stop (Tramlink) 80Dc 158
Finchley Central (Underground) 25Cb 49
Finchley Road (Underground) 37Eb 69
Finchley Road & Frognal (Overground) 36Eb 69
Finsbury Park (Rail & Underground) 33Qb 70
Forest Gate (Rail) 36Jc 73
Forest Hill (Rail & Overground) 61Yb 136
Fulham Broadway (Underground) 52Cb 111
Fulwell (Rail) 63Fa 130

G

Gallions Reach (DLR) 45Rc 94
Gants Hill (Underground) 30Qc 54
Garston (Rail) 7Z 13
George Street Stop (Tramlink) 75Sb 157
Gerrards Cross (Rail) 29A 42
Gidea Park (Rail) 28Kd 57
Gipsy Hill (Rail) 64Ub 135
Gloucester Road (Underground) 5A 226 (49Eb 89)
Godstone (Rail) 10C 210
Golders Green (Underground) 32Cb 69
Goldhawk Road (Underground) 47Ya 88
Goodge Street (Underground) 7D 216 (43Mb 90)
Goodmayes (Rail) 32Wc 75
Gordon Hill (Rail) 11Rb 33
Gospel Oak (Overground) 35Jb 70
Grange Hill (Underground) 21Tc 54
Grange Park (Rail) 15Rb 33
Gravel Hill Stop (Tramlink) 79Ac 158
Gravesend (Rail) 8D 122
Grays (Rail) 51Ce 121
Great Portland Street (Underground) 6A 216 (42Kb 90)
Greenford (Rail & Underground) 39Fa 66
Greenhithe for Bluewater (Rail) 57Wd 120
Greenland Pier (Riverbus) 48Bc 92
Green Park (Underground) 6A 222 (46Lb 90)
Greenwich (Rail & DLR) 52Dc 114
Greenwich Pier (Riverbus) 50Ec 92
Grove Park (Rail) 62Kc 137
Gunnersbury (Underground & Overground) 50Ra 87

H

Hackbridge (Rail) 75Kb 156
Hackney Central (Overground) 37Xb 71
Hackney Downs (Rail) 36Xb 71
Hackney Wick (Overground) 37Cc 72
Hadley Wood (Rail) 10Eb 17
Haggerston (Overground) 39Vb 71
Hainault (Underground) 24Uc 54
Hammersmith (Underground) 49Ya 88
Hampstead (Underground) 35Eb 69
Hampstead Heath (Overground) 35Gb 69
Hampton (Rail) 67Ca 129
Hampton Court (Rail) 70Ga 130
Hampton Wick (Rail) 67La 130
Hanger Lane (Underground) 41Na 87
Hanwell (Rail) 45Ga 86
Harlesden (Underground & Overground) 40Ta 67
Harold Wood (Rail) 25Pd 57
Harringay (Rail) 30Qb 50
Harringay Green Lanes (Overground) 30Rb 51
Harrington Road Stop (Tramlink) 69Yb 136
Harrow-on-the-Hill (Rail & Underground) 30Ga 46
Harrow & Wealdstone (Rail, Underground & Overground) 28Ga 46
Hatch End (Overground) 24Ca 45
Hatton Cross (Underground) 56V 106

Rail, London Tramlink, DLR, Riverbus, Cable Car, Underground and Overground Stations

Haydons Road (Rail) 64Eb 133
Hayes (Rail) 74Jc 159
Hayes & Harlington (Rail) 48V 84
Headstone Lane (Overground) 25Da 45
Heathrow Central (Rail) 55Q 106
Heathrow Terminals 1, 2, 3 (Underground) 55R 106
Heathrow Terminal 4 (Rail) 58S 106
Heathrow Terminal 4 (Underground) 57S 106
Heathrow Terminal 5 (Rail & Underground) 55L 105
Hemel Hempstead (Rail) 5J 3
Hendon (Rail) 30Wa 48
Hendon Central (Underground) 29Xa 48
Herne Hill (Rail) 58Rb 113
Heron Quays (DLR) 46Cc 92
Hersham (Rail) 76Aa 151
Highams Park (Rail) 23Fc 53
High Barnet (Underground) 14Cb 31
Highbury & Islington (Rail, Underground & Overground) 37Rb 71
Highgate (Underground) 30Kb 50
High Street Kensington (Underground) 47Db 89
Hillingdon (Underground) 36R 64
Hilton Docklands Pier (Riverbus) 46Bc 92
Hinchley Wood (Rail) 76Ha 152
Hither Green (Rail) 58Gc 115
Holborn (Underground) 1H 223 (44Pb 90)
Holland Park (Underground) 46Bb 89
Holloway Road (Underground) 36Pb 70
Homerton (Overground) 37Zb 72
Honor Oak Park (Rail & Overground) 58Zb 114
Hornchurch (Underground) 34Md 77
Hornsey (Rail) 28Pb 50
Horsley (Rail) 97U 190
Hounslow (Rail) 57Da 107
Hounslow Central (Underground) 55Da 107
Hounslow East (Underground) 54Ea 108
Hounslow West (Underground) 54Aa 107
How Wood (Rail) 10A 6
Hoxton (Overground) 2K 219 (40Vb 71)
Hurst Green (Rail) 4K 211
Hyde Park Corner (Underground) 1J 227 (47Jb 90)

I

Ickenham (Underground) 35S 64
Ilford (Rail) 34Qc 74
Imperial Wharf (Rail & Overground) 53Eb 111
Island Gardens (DLR) 50Ec 92
Isleworth (Rail) 54Ha 108
Iver (Rail) 47H 83

K

Kempton Park (Rail) 66X 129
Kemsing (Rail) 91Td 204
Kenley (Rail) 86Sb 177
Kennington (Underground) 7B 230 (50Rb 91)
Kensal Green (Underground & Overground) 41Ya 88
Kensal Rise (Overground) 40Za 68
Kensington Olympia (Rail, Underground & Overground) 48Ab 88
Kent House (Rail) 67Ac 136
Kentish Town (Rail & Underground) 36Lb 70
Kentish Town West (Overground) 37Kb 70
Kenton (Underground & Overground) 30Ka 46
Kew Bridge (Rail) 50Pa 87
Kew Gardens (Underground & Overground) 53Qa 109
Kidbrooke (Rail) 55Kc 115
Kilburn (Underground) 37Bb 69
Kilburn High Road (Overground) 39Db 69
Kilburn Park (Underground) 40Cb 69
King George V (DLR) 46Qc 94
King Henry's Drive Stop (Tramlink) 81Dc 178
Kingsbury (Underground) 29Qa 47
King's Cross (Rail & Underground) 2F 217 (40Nb 70)
King's Cross St Pancras (Underground) 3F 217 (41Nb 90)
Kings Langley (Rail) 2S 12
Kingston (Rail) 67Na 131
Kingswood (Rail) 93Bb 195
Knightsbridge (Underground) 2G 227 (47Hb 89)
Knockholt (Rail) 81Ad 181

L

Ladbroke Grove (Underground) 44Ab 88
Ladywell (Rail) 57Dc 114
Lambeth North (Underground) 3K 229 (48Qb 90)
Lancaster Gate (Underground) 4B 220 (45Fb 89)
Langdon Park (DLR) 44Dc 92
Langley (Rail) 47C 82
Latimer Road (Underground) 45Za 88
Leatherhead (Rail) 93Ja 192
Lebanon Road Stop (Tramlink) 75Ub 157
Lee (Rail) 58Jc 115
Leicester Square (Underground) 4E 222 (45Nb 90)
Lewisham (Rail & DLR) 55Ec 114
Leyton (Underground) 34Ec 72
Leyton Midland Road (Overground) 31Ec 72
Leytonstone (Underground) 32Gc 73
Leytonstone High Road (Overground) 33Gc 73
Limehouse (Rail & DLR) 44Ac 92
Liverpool Street (Rail & Underground) 1H 225 (43Ub 91)
Lloyd Park Stop (Tramlink) 77Vb 157
London Bridge (Rail & Underground) 7G 225 (46Tb 91)
London Bridge City Pier (Riverbus) 6H 225 (46Ub 91)
London City Airport (DLR) 46Nc 94
London Eye Millennium Pier (Riverbus) 1H 229 (47Pb 90)
London Fields (Rail) 38Xb 71
Longcross (Rail) 4K 147
Longfield (Rail) 69Ae 143
Loughborough Junction (Rail) 55Rb 113
Loughton (Underground) 15Nc 36
Lower Sydenham (Rail) 64Bc 136

M

Maida Vale (Underground) 41Db 89
Malden Manor (Rail) 73Ua 154
Manor House (Underground) 31Sb 71
Manor Park (Rail) 35Mc 73
Mansion House (Underground) 3E 224 (45Sb 91)
Marble Arch (Underground) 3G 221 (44Hb 89)
Maryland (Rail) 37Gc 73
Marylebone (Rail & Underground) 6F 215 (42Hb 89)
Masthouse Terrace Pier (Riverbus) 50Cc 92
Maze Hill (Rail) 51Gc 115
Meopham (Rail) 10C 144
Merstham (Rail) 100Lb 196
Merton Park Stop (Tramlink) 67Cb 133
Mile End (Underground) 42Bc 92
Millbank Millennium Pier (Riverbus) 6G 229 (49Nb 90)
Mill Hill Broadway (Rail) 23Ua 48
Mill Hill East (Underground) 24Ab 48
Mitcham Eastfields (Rail) 68Jb 134
Mitcham Junction (Rail & Tramlink) 71Jb 156
Mitcham Stop (Tramlink) 70Gb 133
Monument (Underground) 4G 225 (45Tb 91)
Moorgate (Rail & Underground) 1F 225 (43Tb 91)
Moor Park (Underground) 20T 26
Morden (Underground) 69Db 133
Morden Road Stop (Tramlink) 68Db 133
Morden South (Rail) 71Cb 155
Mornington Crescent (Underground) 1B 216 (40Lb 70)
Mortlake (Rail) 55Sa 109
Motspur Park (Rail) 71Xa 154
Mottingham (Rail) 60Pc 116
Mudchute (DLR) 49Dc 92

N

Neasden (Underground) 36Ua 68
New Addington Stop (Tramlink) 82Ec 178
New Barnet (Rail) 15Fb 31
New Beckenham (Rail) 66Bc 136
Newbury Park (Underground) 30Tc 54
New Cross (Rail & Overground) 52Bc 114
New Cross Gate (Rail & Overground) 53Ac 114
New Eltham (Rail) 60Rc 116
New Malden (Rail) 69Ua 132
New Southgate (Rail) 22Kb 50
Norbiton (Rail) 67Qa 131
Norbury (Rail) 67Pb 134
North Acton (Underground) 43Ta 87
North Dulwich (Rail) 57Tb 113
North Ealing (Underground) 44Pa 87
Northfields (Underground) 48La 86
Northfleet (Rail) 58De 121
North Greenwich (Underground) 47Gc 93
North Greenwich Pier (Riverbus) 46Hc 93
North Harrow (Underground) 29Da 45
Northolt (Underground) 37Ca 65
Northolt Park (Rail) 35Da 65
North Sheen (Rail) 56Qa 109
Northumberland Park (Rail) 24Xb 51
North Wembley (Underground & Overground) 34Ma 67
Northwick Park (Underground) 31Ka 66
Northwood (Underground) 24U 44
Northwood Hills (Underground) 26W 44
Norwood Junction (Rail & Overground) 70Wb 135
Notting Hill Gate (Underground) 46Cb 89
Nunhead (Rail) 54Yb 114
Nutfield (Rail) 8E 208

O

Oakleigh Park (Rail) 17Fb 31
Oakwood (Underground) 15Lb 32
Ockendon (Rail) 41Xd 98
Old Street (Rail & Underground) 5G 219 (42Tb 91)
Orpington (Rail) 75Uc 160
Osterley (Underground) 52Fa 108
Otford (Rail) 88Ld 183
Oval (Underground) 51Qb 112
Oxford Circus (Underground) 2B 222 (44Lb 90)
Oxshott (Rail) 85Ea 172
Oxted (Rail) 1J 211

P

Paddington (Rail & Underground) 2B 220 (44Fb 89)
Palmers Green (Rail) 21Pb 50
Park Royal (Underground) 42Qa 87
Park Street (Rail) 8B 6
Parsons Green (Underground) 53Cb 111
Peckham Rye (Rail) 54Wb 113
Penge East (Rail) 65Yb 136
Penge West (Rail & Overground) 65Xb 135
Perivale (Underground) 40Ja 66
Petts Wood (Rail) 71Sc 160
Phipps Bridge Stop (Tramlink) 69Fb 133
Piccadilly Circus (Underground) 5D 222 (45Mb 90)
Pimlico (Underground) 7D 228 (50Mb 90)
Pinner (Underground) 28Aa 45
Plaistow (Underground) 40Hc 73
Plumstead (Rail) 49Tc 94
Ponders End (Rail) 15Ac 34
Pontoon Dock (DLR) 46Lc 93
Poplar (DLR) 45Dc 92
Potters Bar (Rail) 4Bb 17
Preston Road (Underground) 32Na 67
Prince Regent (DLR) 45Lc 93
Pudding Mill Lane (DLR) 39Dc 72
Purfleet (Rail) 50Qd 97
Purley (Rail) 83Qb 176
Purley Oaks (Rail) 81Tb 177
Putney (Rail) 56Ab 110
Putney Bridge (Underground) 55Bb 111
Putney Pier (Riverbus) 55Ab 110

Q

Queensbury (Underground) 27Pa 47
Queen's Park (Underground & Overground) 40Bb 69
Queens Road, Peckham (Rail) 53Yb 114
Queenstown Road, Battersea (Rail) 53Kb 112
Queensway (Underground) 45Db 89

R

Radlett (Rail) 7Ja 14
Rainham (Rail) 42Jd 96
Ravensbourne (Rail) 66Fc 137
Ravenscourt Park (Underground) 49Xa 88
Rayners Lane (Underground) 31Ba 65
Raynes Park (Rail) 68Ya 132
Rectory Road (Rail) 34Vb 71
Redbridge (Underground) 30Mc 53
Redhill (Rail) 5A 208
Reedham (Rail) 85Pb 176
Reeves Corner Stop (Tramlink) 75Rb 157
Regent's Park (Underground) 6K 215 (42Kb 90)
Reigate (Rail) 5J 207
Richmond (Rail, Underground & Overground) 56Na 109
Rickmansworth (Rail & Underground) 17M 25
Riddlesdown (Rail) 85Sb 177
Roding Valley (Underground) 21Mc 53
Romford (Rail) 30Gd 56
Rotherhithe (Overground) 47Yb 92
Royal Albert (DLR) 45Nc 94
Royal Oak (Underground) 43Db 89
Royal Victoria (DLR) 45Jc 93
Ruislip (Underground) 32U 64
Ruislip Gardens (Underground) 35W 64
Ruislip Manor (Underground) 32W 64
Russell Square (Underground) 6F 217 (42Nb 90)

S

St Albans Abbey (Rail) 4B 6
St Albans (Rail) 2D 6
St George Wharf Pier (Riverbus) 51Nb 112
St Helier (Rail) 72Cb 155
St James's Park (Underground) 3D 228 (47Mb 90)
St James Street (Rail) 29Ac 52
St Johns (Rail) 54Cc 114
St John's Wood (Underground) 1B 214 (40Fb 69)
St Katharine's Pier (Riverbus) 6K 225
St Margarets (Rail) 58Ka 108
St Mary Cray (Rail) 70Xc 139
St Pancras International (Rail) 2F 217 (41Nb 90)
St Paul's (Underground) 2D 224 (44Sb 91)
Sanderstead (Rail) 81Tb 177
Sandilands Stop (Tramlink) 75Vb 157
Selhurst (Rail) 71Ub 157
Seven Kings (Rail) 32Uc 74
Sevenoaks (Rail) 96Jd 202
Seven Sisters (Rail & Underground) 29Ub 51
Shadwell (Overground & DLR) 45Xb 91
Shenfield (Rail) 17Ce 41
Shepherd's Bush (Rail, Underground & Overground) 47Za 88
Shepherd's Bush Market (Underground) 46Ya 88
Shepperton (Rail) 71S 150
Shoreditch High Street (Overground) 5K 219 (42Vb 91)
Shoreham (Rail) 83Kd 183
Shortlands (Rail) 68Gc 137
Sidcup (Rail) 61Wc 139
Silver Street (Rail) 21Vb 51
Slade Green (Rail) 53Jd 118
Sloane Square (Underground) 6H 227 (49Jb 90)
Slough (Rail) 6K 81
Snaresbrook (Underground) 29Jc 53
South Acton (Overground) 48Sa 87
Southall (Rail) 47Ba 85
South Bermondsey (Rail) 50Yb 92
Southbury (Rail) 14Xb 33
South Croydon (Rail) 78Tb 157
South Ealing (Underground) 48Ma 87
Southfields (Underground) 60Bb 111
Southgate (Underground) 18Mb 32
South Greenford (Rail) 41Ga 86
South Hampstead (Overground) 38Eb 69
South Harrow (Underground) 34Ea 66
South Kensington (Underground) 5C 226 (49Fb 89)
South Kenton (Underground & Overground) 32La 66
South Merton (Rail) 69Bb 133
South Quay (DLR) 47Dc 92
South Ruislip (Rail & Underground) 36Y 65
South Tottenham (Overground) 29Vb 51
Southwark (Underground) 7B 224 (46Rb 91)
South Wimbledon (Underground) 66Db 133
South Woodford (Underground) 26Kc 53
Staines (Rail) 64J 127
Stamford Brook (Underground) 49Va 88
Stamford Hill (Rail) 31Ub 71
Stanford-le-Hope (Rail) 2L 101
Stanmore (Underground) 21Ma 47
Star Lane (DLR) 42Gc 93
Stepney Green (Underground) 42Zb 92
Stockwell (Underground) 53Nb 112
Stoke Newington (Rail) 33Vb 71
Stonebridge Park (Underground & Overground) 38Ra 67
Stone Crossing (Rail) 57Ud 120
Stoneleigh (Rail) 78Wa 154
Stratford (Rail, Underground, Overground & DLR) 38Ec 72
Stratford High Street (DLR) 39Fc 73
Stratford International (Rail & DLR) 37Ec 72
Strawberry Hill (Rail) 62Ha 130
Streatham (Rail) 64Mb 134
Streatham Common (Rail) 65Mb 134
Streatham Hill (Rail) 61Nb 134
Sudbury & Harrow Road (Rail) 36Ka 66
Sudbury Hill (Underground) 35Ga 66
Sudbury Hill Harrow (Rail) 35Ga 66
Sudbury Town (Underground) 37Ka 66
Sunbury (Rail) 67W 128
Sundridge Park (Rail) 66Kc 137
Sunningdale (Rail) 3E 146
Sunnymeads (Rail) 55A 104
Surbiton (Rail) 72Na 153
Surrey Quays (Overground) 49Zb 92
Sutton (Rail) 79Eb 155

Sutton Common (Rail) 75Db 155
Swanley (Rail) 70Fd 140
Swanscombe (Rail) 57Be 121
Swiss Cottage (Underground) 38Fb 69
Sydenham (Rail & Overground) 63Yb 136
Sydenham Hill (Rail) 62Vb 135
Syon Lane (Rail) 52Ja 108

T

Tadworth (Rail) 94Ya 194
Tattenham Corner (Rail) 90Xa 174
Teddington (Rail) 65Ja 130
Temple (Underground) 4J 223 (45Pb 90)
Thames Ditton (Rail) 73Ha 152
Theobalds Grove (Rail) 4Zb 20
Therapia Lane Stop (Tramlink) 73Nb 156
Theydon Bois (Underground) 8Vc 23
Thornton Heath (Rail) 70Sb 135
Tilbury Town (Rail) 4B 122
Tolworth (Rail) 75Ra 153
Tooting (Rail) 65Hb 133
Tooting Bec (Underground) 62Jb 134
Tooting Broadway (Underground) 64Gb 133
Tottenham Court Road (Underground) 2E 222 (44Mb 90)
Tottenham Hale (Rail & Underground) 27Xb 51
Totteridge & Whetstone (Underground) 19Eb 31
Tower Gateway (DLR) 4K 225 (45Vb 91)
Tower Hill (Underground) 4K 225 (45Vb 91)
Tower Millennium Pier (Riverbus) 6J 225 (46Ub 91)
Tufnell Park (Underground) 35Lb 70
Tulse Hill (Rail) 61Rb 135
Turkey Street (Rail) 9Yb 20
Turnham Green (Underground) 49Ua 88
Turnpike Lane (Underground) 27Rb 51
Twickenham (Rail) 59Ja 108

U

Upminster (Rail & Underground) 33Sd 78
Upminster Bridge (Underground) 33Qd 77
Upney (Underground) 38Vc 75
Upper Halliford (Rail) 68U 128
Upper Holloway (Overground) 33Mb 70
Upper Warlingham (Rail) 90Wb 177
Upton Park (Underground) 39Lc 73
Uxbridge (Underground) 38M 63

V

Vauxhall (Rail & Underground) 50Nb 90
Victoria (Coach) 6A 228 (49Kb 90)
Victoria (Rail & Underground) 4A 228 (49Kb 90)
Virginia Water (Rail) 71A 148

W

Waddon Marsh Stop (Tramlink) 75Qb 156
Waddon (Rail) 77Qb 156
Wallington (Rail) 79Kb 156
Waltham Cross (Rail) 6Bc 20
Walthamstow Central (Rail & Underground) 29Cc 52
Walthamstow Queens Road (Overground) 29Cc 52
Walton-on-Thames (Rail) 77W 150
Wandle Park Stop (Tramlink) 75Qb 156
Wandsworth Common (Rail) 60Hb 111
Wandsworth Riverside Quarter Pier (Riverbus) 56Cb 111
Wandsworth Road (Rail) 54Lb 112
Wandsworth Town (Rail) 56Db 111
Wanstead (Underground) 30Kc 53
Wanstead Park (Overground) 35Kc 73
Wapping (Overground) 46Yb 92
Warren Street (Underground) 5C 216 (42Lb 90)
Warwick Avenue (Underground) 6A 214 (42Eb 89)
Waterloo (Rail & Underground) 1K 229 (47Qb 90)
Waterloo East (Rail) 7K 223 (46Qb 90)
Watford (Underground) 13V 26
Watford High Street (Overground) 14Y 27
Watford Junction (Rail & Overground) 12Y 27
Watford North (Rail) 9Y 13
Welham Green (Rail) 5F 8
Wellesley Road Stop (Tramlink) 75Tb 157
Welling (Rail) 54Wc 117
Wembley Central (Rail, Underground & Overground) 36Na 67
Wembley Park (Underground) 34Qa 67
Wembley Stadium (Rail) 36Pa 67
West Acton (Underground) 44Qa 87
Westbourne Park (Underground) 43Bb 89
West Brompton (Rail, Underground & Overground) 51Cb 111
West Byfleet (Rail) 84J 169
Westcombe Park (Rail) 50Jc 93
West Croydon (Rail, Overground & Tramlink) 74Sb 157
West Drayton (Rail) 46N 83
West Dulwich (Rail) 61Tb 135
West Ealing (Rail) 45Ka 86
Westferry (DLR) 45Cc 92
West Finchley (Underground) 23Db 49
West Hampstead (Underground & Overground) 37Cb 69
West Hampstead Thameslink (Rail) 37Cb 69
West Ham (DLR) 41Gc 93
West Ham (Rail & Underground) 41Gc 93
West Harrow (Underground) 30Ea 46
West Horndon (Rail) 30Ee 59
West India Quay (DLR) 45Cc 92
West Kensington (Underground) 50Bb 89
Westminster (Underground) 2G 229 (47Nb 90)
Westminster Millennium Pier (Riverbus) 1G 229
West Norwood (Rail) 63Rb 135
West Ruislip (Rail & Underground) 33S 64
West Silvertown (DLR) 46Jc 93
West Sutton (Rail) 77Cb 155
West Wickham (Rail) 73Ec 158
Weybridge (Rail) 79Q 150
Whitechapel (Underground & Overground) 43Xb 91
White City (Underground) 45Ya 88
White Hart Lane (Rail) 24Vb 51
Whitton (Rail) 59Ea 108
Whyteleafe (Rail) 89Vb 177
Whyteleafe South (Rail) 91Wb 197
Willesden Green (Underground) 37Ya 68
Willesden Junction (Underground & Overground) 41Va 88
Wimbledon (Rail, Underground & Tramlink) 65Bb 133
Wimbledon Chase (Rail) 68Ab 132
Wimbledon Park (Underground) 62Cb 133
Winchmore Hill (Rail) 17Rb 33
Windsor & Eton Central (Rail) 3H 103
Windsor & Eton Riverside (Rail) 2H 103
Woking (Rail) 89B 168
Woldingham (Rail) 94Zb 198
Woodford (Underground) 23Kc 53
Woodgrange Park (Overground) 36Mc 73
Wood Green (Underground) 26Qb 50
Wood Lane (Underground) 45Ya 88
Woodmansterne (Rail) 88Kb 176
Woodside Park (Underground) 21Db 49
Woodside Stop (Tramlink) 72Xb 157
Wood Street Walthamstow (Rail) 28Fc 53
Woolwich Arsenal Pier (Riverbus) 48Rc 94
Woolwich Arsenal (Rail & DLR) 49Rc 94
Woolwich Dockyard (Rail) 49Pc 94
Worcester Park (Rail) 74Wa 154
Worplesdon (Rail) 6M 187
Wraysbury (Rail) 58C 104

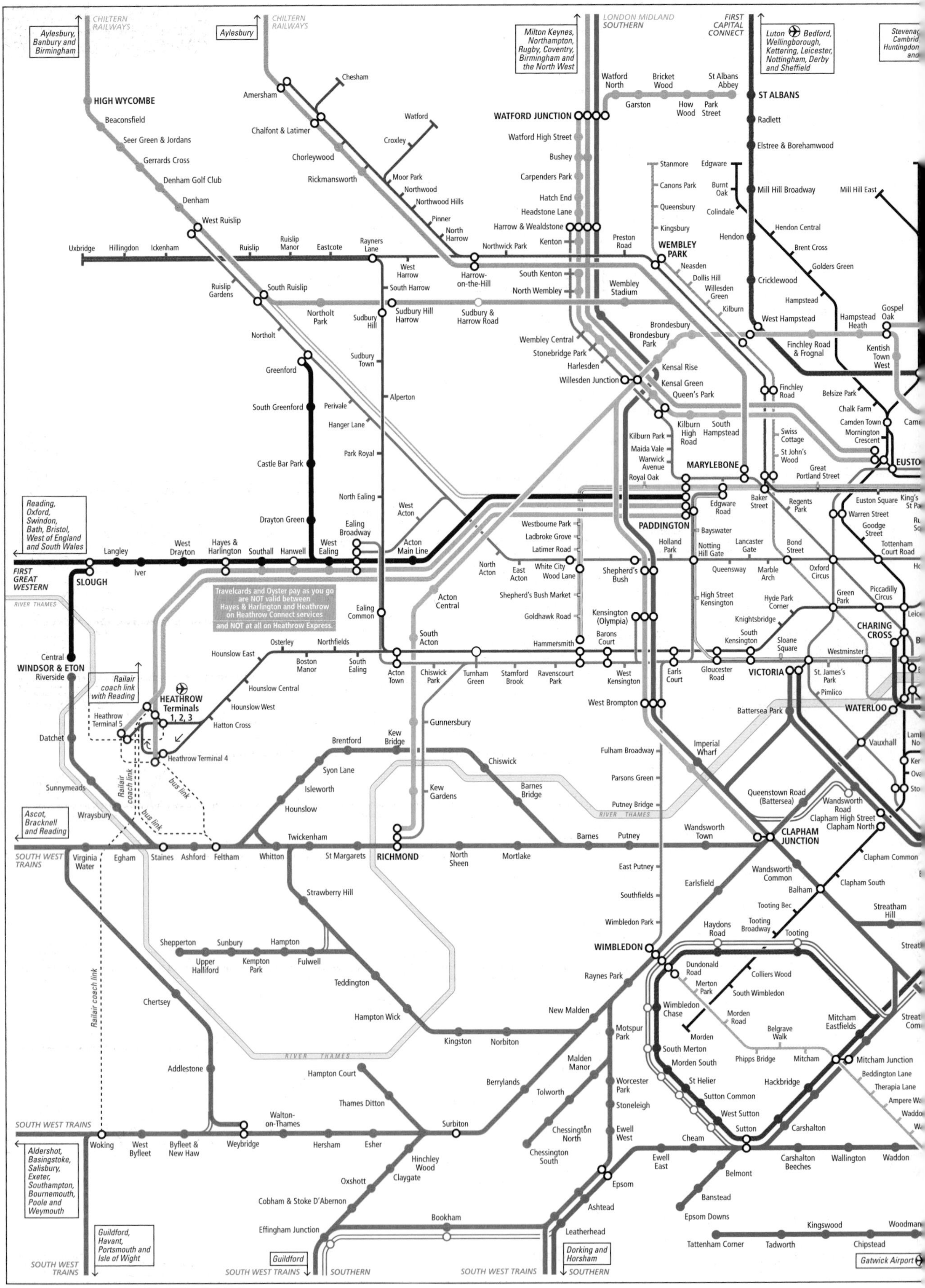

Aylesbury, Banbury and Birmingham
CHILTERN RAILWAYS
Aylesbury
CHILTERN RAILWAYS
Milton Keynes, Northampton, Rugby, Coventry, Birmingham and the North West
LONDON MIDLAND SOUTHERN
FIRST CAPITAL CONNECT
Luton Bedford, Wellingborough, Kettering, Leicester, Nottingham, Derby and Sheffield
HIGH WYCOMBE
Beaconsfield
Seer Green & Jordans
Gerrards Cross
Denham Golf Club
Denham
West Ruislip
Amersham
Chesham
Chalfont & Latimer
Chorleywood
Rickmansworth
Watford
Croxley
Moor Park
Northwood
Northwood Hills
Pinner
North Harrow
Watford North
Garston
Bricket Wood
How Wood
Park Street
St Albans Abbey
WATFORD JUNCTION
Watford High Street
Bushey
Carpenders Park
Hatch End
Headstone Lane
Harrow & Wealdstone
Kenton
ST ALBANS
Radlett
Elstree & Borehamwood
Mill Hill Broadway
Mill Hill East
Stanmore
Canons Park
Queensbury
Kingsbury
Edgware
Burnt Oak
Colindale
Hendon
Hendon Central
Brent Cross
Golders Green
Uxbridge
Hillingdon
Ickenham
Ruislip
Ruislip Manor
Eastcote
Rayners Lane
West Harrow
South Harrow
Northwick Park
Preston Road
WEMBLEY PARK
Neasden
Dollis Hill
Willesden Green
Kilburn
Cricklewood
Hampstead
West Hampstead
Hampstead Heath
Gospel Oak
Ruislip Gardens
South Ruislip
Northolt Park
Northolt
Sudbury Hill
Sudbury Hill Harrow
Harrow-on-the-Hill
South Kenton
North Wembley
Sudbury & Harrow Road
Wembley Stadium
Brondesbury
Brondesbury Park
Finchley Road & Frognal
Kentish Town West
Greenford
Sudbury Town
Wembley Central
Stonebridge Park
Harlesden
Willesden Junction
Kensal Rise
Kensal Green
Queen's Park
Finchley Road
Belsize Park
Chalk Farm
Camden Town
Mornington Crescent
South Greenford
Perivale
Alperton
Hanger Lane
Kilburn Park
Kilburn High Road
South Hampstead
Swiss Cottage
St John's Wood
Park Royal
Maida Vale
Warwick Avenue
Royal Oak
MARYLEBONE
Great Portland Street
EUSTON
Castle Bar Park
North Ealing
West Acton
Edgware Road
Baker Street
Regents Park
Euston Square
Warren Street
Goodge Street
Tottenham Court Road
King's St Pancras
Reading, Oxford, Swindon, Bath, Bristol, West of England and South Wales
Drayton Green
Ealing Broadway
Acton Main Line
PADDINGTON
Westbourne Park
Ladbroke Grove
Latimer Road
Bayswater
Holland Park
Notting Hill Gate
Lancaster Gate
Bond Street
Langley
West Drayton
Hayes & Harlington
Southall
Hanwell
West Ealing
FIRST GREAT WESTERN
SLOUGH
Iver
North Acton
East Acton
White City
Wood Lane
Shepherd's Bush
Queensway
Marble Arch
Oxford Circus
Travelcards and Oyster pay as you go are NOT valid between Hayes & Harlington and Heathrow on Heathrow Connect services and NOT at all on Heathrow Express.
Ealing Common
Acton Central
Shepherd's Bush Market
High Street Kensington
Hyde Park Corner
Green Park
Piccadilly Circus
RIVER THAMES
Goldhawk Road
Kensington (Olympia)
Knightsbridge
CHARING CROSS
Central
WINDSOR & ETON
Riverside
Hounslow East
Osterley
Northfields
South Acton
Barons Court
South Kensington
Sloane Square
Westminster
Hammersmith
Boston Manor
South Ealing
Acton Town
Chiswick Park
Turnham Green
Stamford Brook
Ravenscourt Park
West Kensington
Earls Court
Gloucester Road
VICTORIA
St. James's Park
Railair coach link with Reading
HEATHROW Terminals 1, 2, 3
Hounslow Central
Hounslow West
Pimlico
Heathrow Terminal 5
Hatton Cross
West Brompton
Battersea Park
WATERLOO
Datchet
Heathrow Terminal 4
Brentford
Kew Bridge
Gunnersbury
Fulham Broadway
Imperial Wharf
Vauxhall
Chiswick
Syon Lane
Isleworth
Parsons Green
Sunnymeads
Railair coach link
bus link
bus link
Kew Gardens
Barnes Bridge
Queenstown Road (Battersea)
Wandsworth Road
Ascot, Bracknell and Reading
Wraysbury
Hounslow
Putney Bridge
RIVER THAMES
Clapham High Street
Clapham North
Wandsworth Town
CLAPHAM JUNCTION
SOUTH WEST TRAINS
Virginia Water
Egham
Staines
Ashford
Feltham
Whitton
Twickenham
St Margarets
RICHMOND
North Sheen
Mortlake
Barnes
Putney
Clapham Common
East Putney
Wandsworth Common
Earlsfield
Balham
Clapham South
Strawberry Hill
Southfields
Tooting Bec
Streatham Hill
Wimbledon Park
Haydons Road
Tooting Broadway
Tooting
Shepperton
Sunbury
Hampton
WIMBLEDON
Upper Halliford
Kempton Park
Fulwell
Dundonald Road
Colliers Wood
Raynes Park
Merton Park
South Wimbledon
Teddington
Chertsey
Wimbledon Chase
Morden Road
Mitcham Eastfields
Hampton Wick
New Malden
Motspur Park
Morden
Belgrave Walk
Railair coach link
Kingston
Norbiton
South Merton
RIVER THAMES
Malden Manor
Morden South
Phipps Bridge
Mitcham
Mitcham Junction
Beddington Lane
Addlestone
Hampton Court
Berrylands
Worcester Park
St Helier
Hackbridge
Therapia Lane
Tolworth
Sutton Common
Thames Ditton
Stoneleigh
West Sutton
SOUTH WEST TRAINS
Walton-on-Thames
Surbiton
Chessington North
Ewell West
Sutton
Carshalton
Woking
West Byfleet
Byfleet & New Haw
Weybridge
Hersham
Esher
Chessington South
Cheam
Ewell East
Carshalton Beeches
Wallington
Waddon
Aldershot, Basingstoke, Salisbury, Exeter, Southampton, Bournemouth, Poole and Weymouth
Hinchley Wood
Claygate
Belmont
Oxshott
Epsom
Banstead
Cobham & Stoke D'Abernon
Ashtead
Epsom Downs
Bookham
Kingswood
Effingham Junction
Leatherhead
Tattenham Corner
Tadworth
Chipstead
Guildford, Havant, Portsmouth and Isle of Wight
Guildford
Dorking and Horsham
Gatwick Airport
SOUTH WEST TRAINS
SOUTH WEST TRAINS
SOUTHERN
SOUTH WEST TRAINS
SOUTHERN

National Rail Train Operating Companies

- Chiltern Railways
- c2c
- First Capital Connect
- First Great Western
- Heathrow Connect
- Heathrow Express
- London Midland
- London Overground
- National Express East Anglia
- Southern
- Southeastern
- Southeastern high speed
- South West Trains

Peak hour or limited service routes and/or stations (in Train Company colours)

Interchange stations

Bus and coach links

Stations with Airport links

NOTES: This map is a guide to services provided by the train operators on weekdays but does not guarantee direct trains between the stations shown; some peak period services are omitted. A few services do not operate and some stations are not served in the early mornings and late evenings, or at weekends and on public holidays.

Improvement work to track and signalling can affect services and may apply for extended periods in some instances. It is recommended that journey details are checked prior to travel.

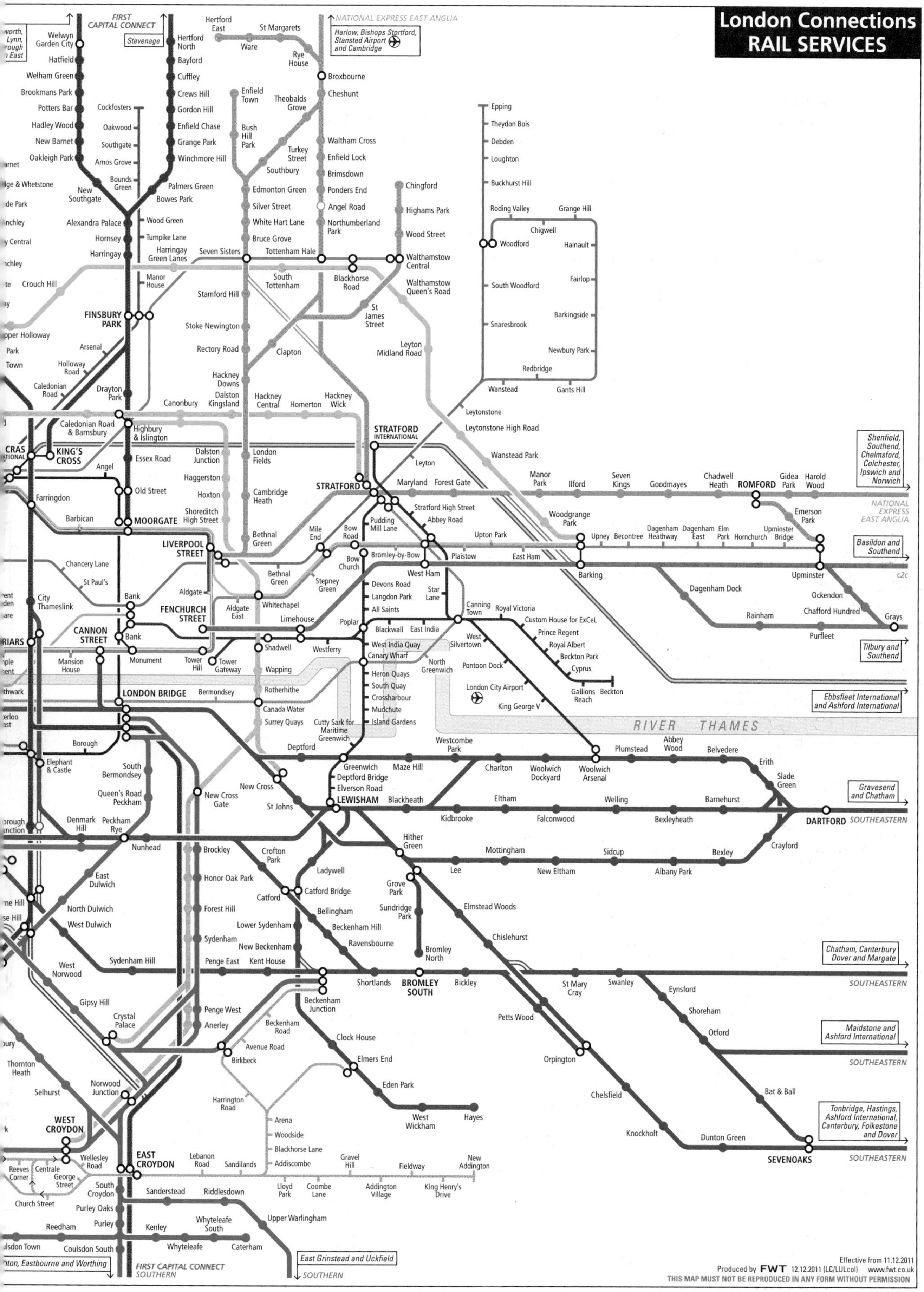
London Connections
RAIL SERVICES
FIRST CAPITAL CONNECT
Stevenage
Welwyn Garden City
Hatfield
Welham Green
Brookmans Park
Potters Bar
Hadley Wood
New Barnet
Oakleigh Park
Cockfosters
Oakwood
Southgate
Arnos Grove
Bounds Green
New Southgate
Alexandra Palace
Hornsey
Harringay
Crouch Hill
Hertford North
Bayford
Cuffley
Crews Hill
Gordon Hill
Enfield Chase
Grange Park
Winchmore Hill
Palmers Green
Bowes Park
Wood Green
Turnpike Lane
Harringay Green Lanes
Manor House
Hertford East
Ware
St Margarets
Rye House
Broxbourne
Cheshunt
Enfield Town
Bush Hill Park
Theobalds Grove
Turkey Street
Southbury
Waltham Cross
Enfield Lock
Brimsdown
Ponders End
Angel Road
Northumberland Park
Edmonton Green
Silver Street
White Hart Lane
Bruce Grove
Tottenham Hale
Seven Sisters
South Tottenham
Stamford Hill
Blackhorse Road
NATIONAL EXPRESS EAST ANGLIA
Harlow, Bishops Stortford, Stansted Airport and Cambridge
Chingford
Highams Park
Wood Street
Walthamstow Central
Walthamstow Queen's Road
St James Street
Leyton Midland Road
Epping
Theydon Bois
Debden
Loughton
Buckhurst Hill
Roding Valley
Grange Hill
Chigwell
Woodford
Hainault
Fairlop
South Woodford
Barkingside
Snaresbrook
Newbury Park
Redbridge
Wanstead
Gants Hill
FINSBURY PARK
Arsenal
Holloway Road
Caledonian Road
Drayton Park
Stoke Newington
Rectory Road
Clapton
Hackney Downs
Dalston Kingsland
Canonbury
Hackney Central
Homerton
Hackney Wick
Caledonian Road & Barnsbury
Highbury & Islington
KING'S CROSS
Essex Road
Angel
Dalston Junction
Haggerston
Hoxton
Shoreditch High Street
London Fields
Cambridge Heath
Bethnal Green
Old Street
Farringdon
Barbican
MOORGATE
LIVERPOOL STREET
Chancery Lane
St Paul's
City Thameslink
Bank
Aldgate
FENCHURCH STREET
Aldgate East
Whitechapel
CANNON STREET
Mansion House
Monument
Tower Hill
Tower Gateway
Shadwell
Limehouse
Westferry
Wapping
Rotherhithe
Canada Water
Surrey Quays
Bermondsey
LONDON BRIDGE
Borough
Elephant & Castle
South Bermondsey
Queen's Road Peckham
Denmark Hill
Peckham Rye
Nunhead
STRATFORD INTERNATIONAL
STRATFORD
Leyton
Leytonstone
Leytonstone High Road
Wanstead Park
Maryland
Forest Gate
Manor Park
Ilford
Seven Kings
Goodmayes
Chadwell Heath
ROMFORD
Gidea Park
Harold Wood
Shenfield, Southend, Chelmsford, Colchester, Ipswich and Norwich
NATIONAL EXPRESS EAST ANGLIA
Emerson Park
Stratford High Street
Abbey Road
Pudding Mill Lane
Mile End
Bow Road
Bow Church
Bromley-by-Bow
Stepney Green
Upton Park
Plaistow
East Ham
West Ham
Woodgrange Park
Upney
Becontree
Dagenham Heathway
Dagenham East
Elm Park
Hornchurch
Upminster Bridge
Upminster
Barking
Basildon and Southend
c2c
Dagenham Dock
Rainham
Ockendon
Chafford Hundred
Grays
Purfleet
Tilbury and Southend
Devons Road
Langdon Park
All Saints
Star Lane
Canning Town
Royal Victoria
Custom House for ExCeL
Prince Regent
Royal Albert
Beckton Park
Cyprus
Gallions Reach
Beckton
Poplar
Blackwall
East India
West India Quay
Canary Wharf
West Silvertown
North Greenwich
Pontoon Dock
London City Airport
King George V
Heron Quays
South Quay
Crossharbour
Mudchute
Island Gardens
Cutty Sark for Maritime Greenwich
Ebbsfleet International and Ashford International
RIVER THAMES
Westcombe Park
Plumstead
Abbey Wood
Belvedere
Erith
Slade Green
Gravesend and Chatham
Deptford
Greenwich
Maze Hill
Charlton
Woolwich Dockyard
Woolwich Arsenal
Deptford Bridge
Elverson Road
LEWISHAM
Blackheath
New Cross
New Cross Gate
St Johns
Kidbrooke
Eltham
Falconwood
Welling
Bexleyheath
Barnehurst
DARTFORD
SOUTHEASTERN
Brockley
Crofton Park
Honor Oak Park
Forest Hill
Catford
Catford Bridge
Ladywell
Hither Green
Lee
Mottingham
New Eltham
Sidcup
Albany Park
Bexley
Crayford
Grove Park
Sundridge Park
Bellingham
Beckenham Hill
Ravensbourne
Elmstead Woods
Chislehurst
Bromley North
Lower Sydenham
Sydenham
New Beckenham
Penge East
Kent House
East Dulwich
North Dulwich
West Dulwich
Sydenham Hill
West Norwood
Gipsy Hill
Crystal Palace
Shortlands
BROMLEY SOUTH
Bickley
St Mary Cray
Swanley
Eynsford
Shoreham
Otford
Chatham, Canterbury Dover and Margate
SOUTHEASTERN
Beckenham Junction
Penge West
Anerley
Beckenham Road
Avenue Road
Birkbeck
Clock House
Elmers End
Eden Park
West Wickham
Hayes
Petts Wood
Orpington
Chelsfield
Knockholt
Dunton Green
Bat & Ball
SEVENOAKS
Maidstone and Ashford International
SOUTHEASTERN
Tonbridge, Hastings, Ashford International, Canterbury, Folkestone and Dover
SOUTHEASTERN
Thornton Heath
Selhurst
Norwood Junction
WEST CROYDON
Harrington Road
Arena
Woodside
Blackhorse Lane
Addiscombe
Wellesley Road
EAST CROYDON
Lebanon Road
Sandilands
Gravel Hill
Fieldway
New Addington
Reeves Corner
Centrale
George Street
Church Street
South Croydon
Sanderstead
Riddlesdown
Lloyd Park
Coombe Lane
Addington Village
King Henry's Drive
Purley Oaks
Reedham
Purley
Kenley
Whyteleafe South
Whyteleafe
Upper Warlingham
Caterham
Coulsdon South
East Grinstead and Uckfield
SOUTHERN
FIRST CAPITAL CONNECT
SOUTHERN
Eastbourne and Worthing
Effective from 11.12.2011
Produced by FWT 12.12.2011 (LC/LULcol) www.fwt.co.uk
THIS MAP MUST NOT BE REPRODUCED IN ANY FORM WITHOUT PERMISSION

Rail franchises or Train Company trading names may change during the currency of this publication. Every effort has been made to ensure the information shown is correct at the time of going to press: December 2011.

For further information and prices of Travelcards, train times and fares, contact your local station, telephone National Rail Enquiries on 08457 48 49 50 or visit: www.nationalrail.co.uk

Underground and other services (thinner lines)

- Bakerloo Line
- Central Line
- Circle Line
- District Line
- Hammersmith & City Line
- Jubilee Line
- Metropolitan Line
- Northern Line
- Piccadilly Line
- Victoria Line
- Waterloo & City Line
- Docklands Light Railway
- London Tramlink

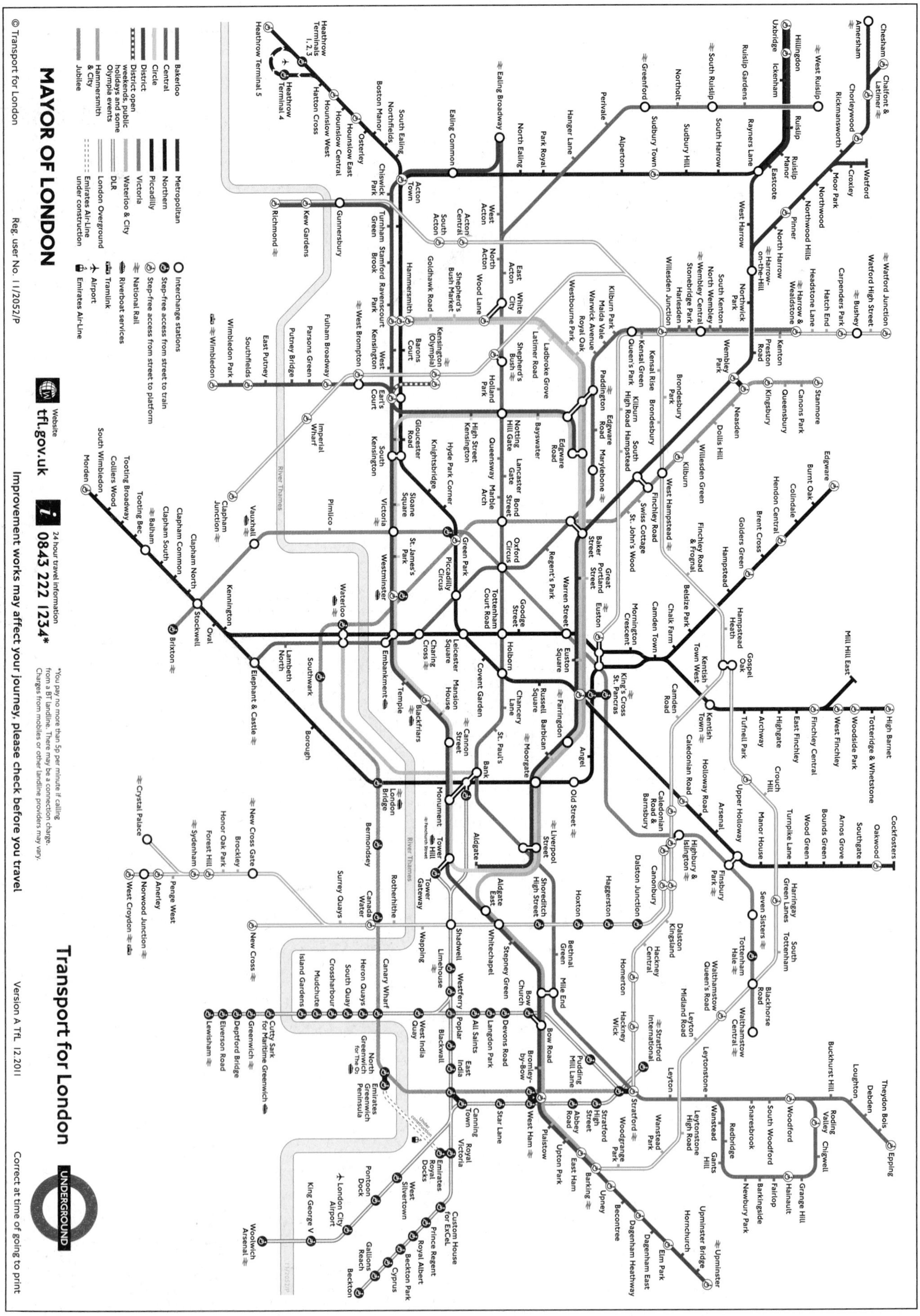

Transport for London
UNDERGROUND
MAYOR OF LONDON
Bakerloo
Central
Circle
District
District open weekends, public holidays and some Olympia events
Hammersmith & City
Jubilee
Metropolitan
Northern
Piccadilly
Victoria
Waterloo & City
DLR
London Overground
Emirates Air Line under construction
Interchange stations
Step-free access from street to train
Step-free access from street to platform
National Rail
Riverboat services
Tramlink
Airport
Emirates Air Line
Website
tfl.gov.uk
24 hour travel information
0843 222 1234*
*You pay no more than 5p per minute if calling from a BT landline. There may be a connection charge. Charges from mobiles or other landline providers may vary.
Improvement works may affect your journey, please check before you travel
© Transport for London
Reg. user No. 11/2052/P
Version A TfL 12.2011
Correct at time of going to print
River Thames
Chesham
Amersham
Chalfont & Latimer
Chorleywood
Rickmansworth
Croxley
Watford
Moor Park
Northwood
Northwood Hills
Pinner
North Harrow
Harrow-on-the-Hill
West Harrow
Rayners Lane
Eastcote
Ruislip Manor
Ruislip
Ickenham
Hillingdon
Uxbridge
West Ruislip
Ruislip Gardens
South Ruislip
Northolt
Greenford
Perivale
Hanger Lane
Sudbury Hill
Sudbury Town
South Harrow
Alperton
Park Royal
North Ealing
Ealing Broadway
Ealing Common
Acton Town
West Acton
North Acton
East Acton
White City
Wood Lane
Acton Central
South Acton
Chiswick Park
Turnham Green
Stamford Brook
Ravenscourt Park
Hammersmith
Goldhawk Road
Shepherd's Bush Market
Shepherd's Bush
Gunnersbury
Kew Gardens
Richmond
South Ealing
Northfields
Boston Manor
Osterley
Hounslow East
Hounslow Central
Hounslow West
Hatton Cross
Heathrow Terminals 1, 2, 3
Heathrow Terminal 4
Heathrow Terminal 5
Watford Junction
Watford High Street
Bushey
Carpenders Park
Hatch End
Headstone Lane
Harrow & Wealdstone
Kenton
South Kenton
North Wembley
Wembley Central
Stonebridge Park
Harlesden
Willesden Junction
Kensal Green
Queen's Park
Kilburn Park
Maida Vale
Warwick Avenue
Royal Oak
Westbourne Park
Ladbroke Grove
Latimer Road
Wembley Park
Preston Road
Northwick Park
Kingsbury
Queensbury
Canons Park
Stanmore
Neasden
Dollis Hill
Willesden Green
Kilburn
West Hampstead
Finchley Road
Swiss Cottage
St. John's Wood
Kensal Rise
Brondesbury Park
Brondesbury
Kilburn High Road
South Hampstead
Finchley Road & Frognal
Hampstead Heath
Gospel Oak
Edgware
Burnt Oak
Colindale
Hendon Central
Brent Cross
Golders Green
Hampstead
Belsize Park
Chalk Farm
Camden Town
Kentish Town West
Camden Road
Mill Hill East
High Barnet
Totteridge & Whetstone
Woodside Park
West Finchley
Finchley Central
East Finchley
Highgate
Archway
Tufnell Park
Kentish Town
Crouch Hill
Upper Holloway
Caledonian Road & Barnsbury
Caledonian Road
Holloway Road
Arsenal
Cockfosters
Oakwood
Southgate
Arnos Grove
Bounds Green
Wood Green
Turnpike Lane
Manor House
Finsbury Park
Harringay Green Lanes
Seven Sisters
South Tottenham
Tottenham Hale
Blackhorse Road
Walthamstow Central
Walthamstow Queen's Road
Leyton Midland Road
Paddington
Edgware Road
Marylebone
Baker Street
Great Portland Street
Regent's Park
Euston
Warren Street
Mornington Crescent
Euston Square
King's Cross St. Pancras
Goodge Street
Tottenham Court Road
Oxford Circus
Bond Street
Marble Arch
Lancaster Gate
Queensway
Notting Hill Gate
Holland Park
Bayswater
High Street Kensington
Kensington (Olympia)
West Kensington
Barons Court
Earl's Court
West Brompton
Gloucester Road
South Kensington
Knightsbridge
Hyde Park Corner
Green Park
Piccadilly Circus
Sloane Square
Victoria
St. James's Park
Westminster
Fulham Broadway
Parsons Green
Putney Bridge
East Putney
Southfields
Wimbledon Park
Wimbledon
Imperial Wharf
Clapham Junction
Pimlico
Vauxhall
Stockwell
Brixton
Oval
Kennington
Clapham North
Clapham Common
Clapham South
Balham
Tooting Bec
Tooting Broadway
Colliers Wood
South Wimbledon
Morden
Waterloo
Lambeth North
Elephant & Castle
Southwark
Borough
Embankment
Charing Cross
Leicester Square
Covent Garden
Holborn
Russell Square
Chancery Lane
Temple
Blackfriars
Mansion House
Cannon Street
St. Paul's
Barbican
Farringdon
Angel
Old Street
Moorgate
Bank
Monument
London Bridge
Tower Hill
Fenchurch Street
Tower Gateway
Aldgate
Aldgate East
Liverpool Street
Shoreditch High Street
Hoxton
Haggerston
Dalston Junction
Dalston Kingsland
Canonbury
Highbury & Islington
Hackney Central
Homerton
Hackney Wick
Bethnal Green
Mile End
Whitechapel
Stepney Green
Bow Church
Bow Road
Bromley-by-Bow
Pudding Mill Lane
Stratford
Stratford International
Stratford High Street
Abbey Road
West Ham
Plaistow
Upton Park
East Ham
Barking
Upney
Becontree
Dagenham Heathway
Dagenham East
Elm Park
Hornchurch
Upminster Bridge
Upminster
Leyton
Leytonstone
Leytonstone High Road
Wanstead Park
Woodgrange Park
Wanstead
Redbridge
Gants Hill
Newbury Park
Barkingside
Fairlop
Hainault
Grange Hill
Chigwell
Roding Valley
Woodford
South Woodford
Snaresbrook
Buckhurst Hill
Loughton
Debden
Theydon Bois
Epping
Bermondsey
Canada Water
Rotherhithe
Surrey Quays
Wapping
Shadwell
Limehouse
Westferry
Poplar
All Saints
Langdon Park
Devons Road
Blackwall
East India
Canning Town
Star Lane
Royal Victoria
Custom House for ExCeL
Prince Regent
Royal Albert
Beckton Park
Cyprus
Gallions Reach
Beckton
West Silvertown
Pontoon Dock
London City Airport
King George V
Woolwich Arsenal
Emirates Royal Docks
Emirates Greenwich Peninsula
North Greenwich
Canary Wharf
West India Quay
Heron Quays
South Quay
Crossharbour
Mudchute
Island Gardens
Cutty Sark for Maritime Greenwich
Greenwich
Deptford Bridge
Elverson Road
Lewisham
New Cross
New Cross Gate
Brockley
Honor Oak Park
Forest Hill
Sydenham
Crystal Palace
Penge West
Anerley
Norwood Junction
West Croydon

SCOTLAND VISITORS' ATLAS & GUIDE
SCOTLAND NORTH & SOUTH
INVERNESS
ABERDEEN
DUNDEE
GLASGOW EDINBURGH & CENTRAL SCOTLAND ROAD MAP
BIG GLASGOW
PERTH
EDINBURGH
GLASGOW
LIVINGSTON
50 MILES AROUND NEWCASTLE upon TYNE ROAD MAP
NORTHERN ENGLAND
PREMIER MAP NEWCASTLE upon TYNE
NEWCASTLE upon TYNE SUNDERLAND DURHAM
LAKE DISTRICT VISITORS' ATLAS & GUIDE
LANCASTER HEYSHAM MORECAMBE
CITY OF DURHAM
MIDDLESBROUGH STOCKTON-ON-TEES
YORK
BLACKPOOL
PRESTON
LEEDS
LIVERPOOL
MANCHESTER
HULL
SHEFFIELD
WARRINGTON RUNCORN WIDNES
CHESTERFIELD
GRIMSBY
WIRRAL
MACCLESFIELD
NOTTINGHAM
LINCOLN
CREWE
DERBY
BANGOR CONWY RHYL COLWYN BAY LLANDUDNO
STOKE-ON-TRENT
LOUGHBOROUGH
WREXHAM OSWESTRY
BIRMINGHAM
LEICESTER
NORWICH
SHREWSBURY TELFORD
PETERBOROUGH
CAMBRIDGE
GREAT YARMOUTH LOWESTOFT
SOUTH WALES VALLEYS
WOLVERHAMPTON
COVENTRY RUGBY
IPSWICH FELIXSTOWE
WORCESTER
NORTHAMPTON
BURY ST. EDMUNDS
WALES
CARDIFF NEWPORT
STRATFORD-UPON-AVON
BEDFORD
SWANSEA
HIGH WYCOMBE
CHELMSFORD
CHELTENHAM GLOUCESTER
SWINDON
LONDON
READING
BRISTOL BATH
CANTERBURY MARGATE RAMSGATE
NEWBURY
HASTINGS
WESTON-SUPER-MARE
PORTSMOUTH
BRIGHTON
TAUNTON
BOURNEMOUTH POOLE CHRISTCHURCH
SOUTHAMPTON
EXETER
BARNSTAPLE BIDEFORD ILFRACOMBE
PLYMOUTH
CORNWALL VISITORS' MAP
A-Z Direct
Customer Service
If you experience difficulty obtaining any of our 300 titles, please contact us direct for help and advice.
www.az.co.uk
Tel: 01732 783422 Fax: 01732 780677

ADMINISTRATIVE BOUNDARIES
County or Unitary Authority Boundary
Local Authoritory Boundary
SCALE
0 1 2 3 4 Miles
0 1 2 3 4 5 Kilometres
AYLESBURY VALE
Wendover
BERKHAMSTED
DACORUM
HEMEL HEMPSTEAD
ST. ALBANS
ST. ALBANS
HATFIELD
WELWYN HATFIELD
Welham Green
Brookmans Park
HERTFORDSHIRE
Cuffley
Ashley Green
Bovingdon
Kings Langley
Chiswell Green
London Colney
Colney Heath
Frogmore
Colney Street
Chipperfield
Abbots Langley
Bricket Wood
Shenleybury
South Mimms
POTTERS BAR
SOUTH MIMMS
Ridge
HERTSMERE
Great Missenden
CHESHAM
CHILTERN
Latimer
Sarratt
Chenies
Chandler's Cross
RADLETT
Aldenham
Shenley
Green Street
Patchetts Green
Bentley Heath
Hadley Wood
Botany Bay
Monken Hadley
AMERSHAM
Little Chalfont
THREE RIVERS
WATFORD
WATFORD
BOREHAMWOOD
EAST BARNET
Cockfosters
CHORLEYWOOD
Elstree
Arkley
BARNET
Totteridge
BUCKINGHAMSHIRE
WYCOMBE
Heronsgate
Chalfont St. Giles
RICKMANSWORTH
Batchworth
BUSHEY
Oxhey
Bushey Heath
LONDON GATEWAY
M1
Whetstone
FRIERN BARNET
HIGH WYCOMBE
Chalfont Common
Maple Cross
Eastbury
South Oxhey
Hatch End
STANMORE
EDGWARE
BARNET
BEACONSFIELD
Chalfont St. Peter
West Hyde
Harefield
NORTHWOOD
HARROW
Mill Hill
FINCHLEY
Wooburn Green
Wooburn
M40
BEACONSFIELD
Gerrards Cross
Hedgerley
M25
Denham Green
HILLINGDON
Ruislip Common
PINNER
HARROW
KENTON
Kingsbury
HENDON
Golders Green
Muswell Hill
Bourne End
SOUTH BUCKS
Tatling End
Denham
Ickenham
Eastcote
RUISLIP
Rayners Lane
Harrow on the Hill
Neasden
Cricklewood
Highgate
HAMPSTEAD
BRENT
CAMDEN
Cookham
Egypt
New Denham
UXBRIDGE
NORTHOLT
WEMBLEY
WILLESDEN
CAMDEN TOWN
Kilburn
Farnham Common
Farnham Royal
Stoke Poges
Hillingdon
Burnham
Iver Heath
Cowley
GREENFORD
Yeading
EALING
MARYLEBONE
PADDINGTON
CITY OF WESTMINSTER
Taplow
SLOUGH
SLOUGH
George Green
EALING
MAIDENHEAD
A404(M)
Bray
Cippenham
Richings Park
Langley
Yiewsley
HAYES
SOUTHALL
Hanwell
ACTON
Shepherd's Bush
KENSINGTON & CHELSEA
KENSINGTON
WESTMINSTER
CHELSEA
HAMMERSMITH & FULHAM
West Drayton
Eton Wick
Upton
Eton
Datchet
Colnbrook
Horton
Poyle
Harmondsworth
Sipson
LONDON HEATHROW AIRPORT
Harlington
Cranford
HESTON
Heston
Brentford
Osterley
CHISWICK
Kew
North Sheen
HAMMERSMITH
BARNES
FULHAM
BATTERSEA
ISLEWORTH
HOUNSLOW
WINDSOR & MAIDENHEAD
WINDSOR
M4
Old Windsor
Wraysbury
Stanwell Moor
Stanwell
Hatton
HOUNSLOW
RICHMOND
PUTNEY
Roehampton
WANDSWORTH
WANDSWORTH
CLAPHAM
BRACKNELL FOREST
Cranbourne
Winkfield
Winkfield Row
Windsor Great Park
Woodside
Hythe End
STAINES
SPELTHORNE
ASHFORD
East Bedfont
FELTHAM
RICHMOND UPON THAMES
TWICKENHAM
Ham
Richmond Park
WIMBLEDON
STREATHAM
BRACKNELL
North Ascot
Ascot
Englefield Green
EGHAM
Egham Hythe
Feltham hill
Hanworth
Hampton
TEDDINGTON
Hampton Wick
KINGSTON UPON THAMES
KINGSTON UPON THAMES
NEW MALDEN
MERTON
MERTON
MORDEN
MITCHAM
Sunningdale
South Ascot
Sunninghill
Virginia Water
RUNNYMEDE
Thorpe
Laleham
Littleton
SUNBURY
Upper Halliford
West Molesey
East Molesey
Thames Ditton
SURBITON
Long Ditton
Broomhall
Lyne
CHERTSEY
Shepperton
WALTON-ON-THAMES
Beddington
Windlesham
M3
Addlestone
WEYBRIDGE
Hersham
ESHER
Claygate
Worcester Park
SUTTON
Cheam
CARSHALTON
SUTTON
WALLINGTON
Bagshot
Ottershaw
New Haw
ELMBRIDGE
Hook
Chessington
EPSOM & EWELL
SURREY HEATH
CAMBERLEY
Lightwater
Chobham
Row Town
Woodham
Whiteley Village
Fairmile
Malden Rushett
EPSOM
EWELL
PURLEY
West Byfleet
Byfleet
Cobham
Stoke D'Abernon
Oxshott
Pachesham
Ashtead
Woodmansterne
BANSTEAD
COULSDON
Horsell
Sheerwater
Bisley
Knaphill
WOKING
WOKING
Pyrford
Wisley
COBHAM (Open Late 2012)
Frimley
Brookwood
Old Woking
Ripley
Ockham
Effingham Common
M25
LEATHERHEAD
Burgh Heath
Chipstead
Hooley
Tadworth
Kingswood
Mayford
Send Marsh
Send
Fetcham
REIGATE
Lower Kingswood
Chaldon
Pirbright
FARNBOROUGH
Worplesdon
Sutton Green
SURREY
East Horsley
Little Bookham
Effingham
Great Bookham
Headley
Mickleham
Walton on the Hill
REIGATE & BANSTEAD
Gatton
Merstham
ALDERSHOT
West Clandon
East Clandon
West Horsley
MOLE VALLEY
Buckland
REDHILL
Normandy
GUILDFORD
Ranmore Common
Betchworth
Ash
Westcott
Brockham
REIGATE
South Nutfield
Tongham
GUILDFORD
Gomshall
DORKING
Puttenham
Compton
Shalford
Shere
FARNHAM